The Wiersbe Bible Commentary

The Wiersbe Bible Commentary

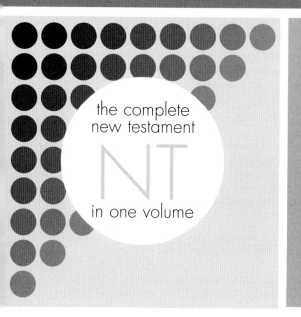

the complete
new testament

NT

in one volume

Warren W. Wiersbe

DAVID **C** COOK

transforming lives together

THE WIERSBE BIBLE COMMENTARY: NEW TESTAMENT
Published by David C Cook
4050 Lee Vance Drive
Colorado Springs, CO 80918 U.S.A.

Integrity Music Limited, a Division of David C Cook
Brighton, East Sussex BN1 2RE, England

DAVID C COOK® and related marks are registered trademarks of David C Cook.

Bible permissions information appears on page 1085 of the commentary.

Library of Congress Control Number 2007934009
ISBN 978-0-7814-4539-9
eISBN 978-1-4347-6665-6

Cover Photo: © Jamie Grill/Corbis
Cover Design: Morris & Winrow

Printed in China
Second Edition 2007

21 22 23 24 25 26 27 28 29 30

022124

CONTENTS

FOREWORD

The *Wiersbe Bible Commentary* had a modest beginning in 1972 when Victor Books published my commentary on 1 John and called it *Be Real.* Nobody remembers who named the book, but for me it was the beginning of three decades of intensive Bible study as I wrote additional commentaries, all of them falling under the new "BE" series. It took twenty-three books to cover the New Testament, and they were published in two bound volumes in 1989. Then I started the Old Testament "BE" series; and *Be Obedient*, on the life of Abraham, was published in 1991. There are now forty-two books available in the entire series, and compiled together to create the *Wiersbe Bible Commentary,* this publication represents the culmination of over thirty years of joyful work. During this time I was writing books for several publishers, but writing the next "BE" book was always at the top of my agenda.

I owe a great debt of gratitude to the editorial staff for their encouragement and cooperation these many years, including Mark Sweeney, Jim Adair, Lloyd Cory, and Greg Clouse. Greg was always faithful to "shepherd" me through book after book, and I appreciate his friendship and ministry more and more with each passing year. Every author should be as fortunate as I've been to work with such dedicated, skillful people who always take a personal interest in their authors. To the best of my knowledge, during these years we've ministered together, we've never had a cross word or a serious misunderstanding.

I especially want to thank the Lord for His kindness and mercy in allowing me to minister in this way through the printed page. I can think of many of my friends who could have done a far better job than I in this series, but the Lord graciously gave the privilege to me. He also gave me the wisdom and strength to get each book written on time—and sometimes ahead of time—in the midst of a very busy life as a husband and father, a pastor, a radio Bible teacher, a seminary instructor, and a conference speaker.

This leads me to say that I couldn't have done it without the loving care of my wife, Betty. She manages our household affairs so well and takes such good care of me that I've always had the time needed for studying and writing. When I started this series, our four children were all at home. Now they're all married, and my wife and I have many wonderful grandchildren! Time flies when you're checking proofs!

The numerous readers of the "BE" series have been a great source of encouragement to me, even when they have written to disagree with me! I have received letters from many parts of the world, written by people in various walks of life, and they have gladdened my heart. Unless a writer hears from readers, the writing becomes a one-way street; and he or she never knows if that writing did anybody any good. I want to thank the pastors, missionaries, Sunday school teachers, and other students of the Word, who have been kind enough to write. We could compile a book of letters telling what God has done in the lives of people who have studied the "BE" series. To God be the glory!

As I close, there are some other people whom ought to be thanked: Dr. Donald Burdick taught me New Testament at Northern Baptist Seminary and showed me how to study the Word of God. Dr. Lloyd Perry and the late Dr. Charles W. Koller both taught me how to "unlock" a Scripture passage and organize an exposition that was understandable and practical. I recommend their books on preaching to any preacher or teacher who wants to organize material better.

For ten happy years, I was privileged to pastor the Calvary Baptist Church in Covington, Kentucky, just across the river from Cincinnati. One of my happy duties was writing Bible study notes for "The Whole Bible Study Course," which was developed by the late Dr. D. B. Eastep, who pastored the church for thirty-five fruitful years. I can't think of a church that has a greater love for the Bible or a deeper hunger for spiritual truth than the dear people of Calvary Baptist. The "BE" series is, in many respects, a by-product of Dr. Eastep's kindness in sharing his ministry with me, and the church's love and encouragement while I was their pastor. I honor his memory and thank God for their continued friendship and prayer support.

Now, to you who study God's Word with me, "I commend you to God, and to the word of His grace, which is able to build you up, and to give you an inheritance among all them who are sanctified" (Acts 20:32).

—Warren W. Wiersbe

MATTHEW

OUTLINE

Key theme: The King and His kingdom
Key verses: Matthew 2:2; 4:17

I. THE REVELATION OF THE KING (1—10)
    A. His person—1—4
    B. His principles—5—7
    C. His power—8—10
(Note: The message during this period of His ministry was, "The kingdom of heaven is at hand" [3:2; 4:17; 10:7].)

II. THE REBELLION AGAINST THE KING (11—13)
    A. His messenger rejected—11:1–19
    B. His works denied—11:20–30
    C. His principles refused—12:1–21
    D. His person attacked—12:22–50
    E. Result: the "mysteries of the kingdom"—13

III. THE RETIREMENT OF THE KING (14—20)
(The Lord seeks to leave the multitudes to be alone with His disciples.)
    A. Before Peter's confession—14:1—16:12
    B. Peter's confession—16:13–28 (First mention of the cross—16:21)
    C. After Peter's confession—17:1—20:34
        (Second mention of the cross—17:22)
(Third mention of the cross—20:17–19)

IV. THE REJECTION OF THE KING (21—27)
("The kingdom of God shall be taken from you," 21:43.)
    A. His public presentation as King—21:1–16
    B. His conflict with the rulers—21:17—23:39
    C. His prophetic message—24—25
    D. His suffering and death—26—27

V. THE RESURRECTION OF THE KING (28)

CONTENTS
Here's Good News!

CHAPTER ONE
HERE'S GOOD NEWS!

Twenty or thirty years after Jesus had gone back to heaven, a Jewish disciple named Matthew was inspired by the Spirit of God to write a book. The finished product is what we know today as "The Gospel According to Matthew."

Nowhere in the four gospels do we find a single recorded word that Matthew spoke. Yet in his gospel, he gives us the words and works of Jesus Christ, "the Son of David, the Son of Abraham" (Matt. 1:1). Matthew did not write to tell us about himself. But let's get acquainted with him and the book he wrote. Then we can learn all that he wanted us to know about Jesus Christ.

The Holy Spirit used Matthew to accomplish three important tasks in the writing of his gospel.

The Bridge-Builder: He Introduced a New Book

That book was the New Testament. If a Bible reader were to jump from Malachi into Mark, or Acts, or Romans, he would be bewildered. Matthew's gospel is the bridge that leads us out of the Old Testament and into the New Testament.

The theme of the Old Testament is given in Genesis 5:1: "This is the book of the generations of Adam." The Old Testament gives the history of "the Adam family," and it is a sad history indeed. God created man in His own image, but man sinned—thus defiling and deforming that image. Then man brought forth children "in his own likeness, after his image" (Gen. 5:3). These children proved themselves to be sinners like their parents. No matter where you read in the Old Testament, you meet sin and sinners.

But the New Testament is "The book of the generation of Jesus Christ" (Matt. 1:1). Jesus is the last Adam (1 Cor. 15:45), and He came to earth to save the "generations of Adam." (This includes you and me, by the way.) Through no choice of our own, we were born into the generations of Adam, and this made us

sinners. But by a choice of faith, we can be born into the generation of Jesus Christ and become the children of God!

When you read the genealogy in Genesis 5, the repeated phrase *and he died* sounds like the tolling of a funeral bell. The Old Testament illustrates the truth that "the wages of sin is death" (Rom. 6:23). But when you turn to the New Testament, that first genealogy emphasizes *birth* and not death! The message of the New Testament is that "the gift of God is eternal life through Jesus Christ our Lord" (Rom. 6:23).

The Old Testament is a book of promise, while the New Testament is a book of fulfillment. (To be sure, there are many precious promises in the New Testament, but I am referring to the emphasis of each half of the Bible.) Beginning with Genesis 3:15, God promised a Redeemer; and Jesus Christ fulfilled that promise. *Fulfilled* is one of the key words in the gospel of Matthew, used about fifteen times.

One purpose of this gospel is to show that Jesus Christ fulfilled the Old Testament promises concerning the Messiah. His birth at Bethlehem fulfilled Isaiah 7:14 (Matt. 1:22–23). Jesus was taken to Egypt for safety, and this fulfilled Hosea 11:1 (Matt. 2:14–15). When Joseph and the family returned and decided to settle in Nazareth, this fulfilled several Old Testament prophecies (Matt. 2:22–23). Matthew used at least 129 quotations or allusions to the Old Testament in this gospel. He wrote primarily for Jewish readers to show them that Jesus Christ was indeed their promised Messiah.

The Biographer: He Introduced a New King

None of the four gospels is a biography in the modern sense of the word. In fact, the apostle John doubted that a complete biography of Jesus could ever be written (John 21:25). There are many details about the earthly life of Jesus that are not given in any of the Gospels.

Each of the four gospels has its own emphasis. Matthew's book is called, "the gospel of the King." It was written primarily for Jewish readers. Mark's book, the gospel of the Servant, was written to instruct Roman readers. Luke wrote mainly to the Greeks and presented Christ as the perfect "Son of Man." John's appeal is universal, and his message was "This is the Son of God." No one gospel is able to tell the whole story as God wants us to see it. But when we put these four gospel accounts together, we have a composite picture of the person and work of our Lord.

Being accustomed to keeping systematic records, Matthew gave us a beautifully organized account of our Lord's life and ministry. The book can be divided into ten sections in which "doing" and "teaching" alternate. Each teaching section ends with "When Jesus had ended these sayings" or a similar transitional statement. The chapters can be divided like this:

Narrative	Teaching	Transition
1—4	5—7	7:28
8:1—9:34	9:35—10:42	11:1
11:2—12:50	13:1–52	13:53
13:53—17:27	18:1–35	19:1
19:1—23:39	24:1—25:46	26:1
26:1—28:20 (the Passion narrative)		

Matthew described Jesus as the *Doer* and the *Teacher.* He recorded at least twenty specific miracles and six major messages: the Sermon on the Mount (chaps. 5—7), the charge to the apostles (chap. 10), the parables of the kingdom (chap. 13), the lesson on forgiveness (chap. 18), the denunciation of the Pharisees (chap. 23), and the prophetic discourse on the Mount of Olives (chaps. 24—25). At least 60 percent of this book focuses on the teachings of Jesus.

Remember, Matthew focuses on the *kingdom.* In the Old Testament, the Jewish nation was God's kingdom on earth: "And you shall be unto me a kingdom of priests, and an holy nation" (Ex. 19:6). Many people in Jesus' day were looking for the God-sent Deliverer who would release them from Roman bondage and reestablish the glorious kingdom of Israel.

The message of the kingdom of heaven was first preached by John the Baptist (Matt. 3:1–2). The Lord Jesus also preached this message from the very beginning of His ministry (Matt. 4:23). He sent out the twelve apostles with the same proclamation (Matt. 10:1–7).

However, the good news of the kingdom required a moral and spiritual response from the people, and not simply the acceptance of a ruler. John the Baptist called for repentance. Likewise, Jesus made it clear that He had not come to overcome Rome, but to transform the hearts and lives of those who trusted Him. Before He could enter into the glory of the kingdom, Jesus endured the suffering of the cross.

One further word about this gospel. Matthew arranged his material in a topical order, rather than chronological. He grouped ten miracles together in chapters 8—9 instead of putting them into their historical sequence in the gospel's narrative. Certain other events are totally omitted. By consulting a good harmony of the Gospels, you will see that, while Matthew does not contradict the other three gospel writers, he does follow his own pattern.

Matthew was not only a bridge-builder who introduced a new book, the New Testament; and a biographer who introduced a new King, Jesus Christ; but he also accomplished a third task when he wrote his book.

The Believer: He Introduced a New People

This new people, of course, was the church. Matthew is the only gospel writer to use the word *church* (Matt. 16:18; 18:17). The Greek word translated *church* means "a called-out assembly." In the New Testament, for the most part, this word refers to a local assembly of believers. In the Old Testament, Israel was God's called-out people, beginning with the call of Abraham (Gen. 12:1ff.; Deut. 7:6–8). In fact, Stephen called the nation of Israel "the church [assembly] in the wilderness" (Acts 7:38), for they were God's called-out people.

But the New Testament church is a different people, for it is composed of *both* Jews and Gentiles. In this church there were no racial distinctions (Gal. 3:28). Even though Matthew wrote primarily for the Jews, he has a "universal" element in his book that includes the Gentiles. For example, Gentile leaders came to worship the Infant Jesus (Matt. 2:1–12). Jesus performed miracles for Gentiles and even commended them for their faith (Matt. 8:5–13; 15:21–28). The Gentile Queen of Sheba was praised for her willingness to make a long journey to hear God's wisdom (Matt. 12:42). At a crisis hour in Jesus' ministry He turned to a prophecy about the Gentiles (Matt. 12:14–21). Even in the parables, Jesus indicated that the blessings which Israel refused would be shared with the Gentiles (Matt. 22:8–10; 21:40–46). The Olivet Discourse stated that the message would go "unto all nations" (Matt. 24:14); and the Lord's commission involves all nations (Matt. 28:19–20).

There were only believing Jews and believing Jewish proselytes in the church at the beginning (Acts 2—7). When the gospel went to Samaria (Acts 8), people who were part Jewish and part Gentile came into the church. When Peter went to the household of Cornelius (Acts 10), the Gentiles became fully accepted in the church. The Conference at Jerusalem (Acts 15) settled the decision that a Gentile did not have to become a Jew before he could become a Christian.

But Matthew anticipated all of this. And when his book was read by members of the early church, both Jews and Gentiles, it helped to settle differences and create unity. Matthew made it clear that this new people, the church, must not maintain a racial or social exclusiveness. Faith in Jesus Christ makes believers "all one" in the body of Christ, the church.

Matthew's own experience with the Lord is recorded in Matthew 9:9–17, and it is a beautiful example of the grace of God. His old name was Levi, the son of Alphaeus (Mark 2:14). "Matthew" means "the gift of God." Apparently, the name was given to commemorate his conversion and his call to be a disciple.

Remember that tax collectors were among the most hated people in Jewish society. To begin with, they were traitors to their own nation because they "sold themselves" to the Romans to work for the government. Each tax collector purchased from Rome the right to gather taxes, and the more he gathered, the more he could keep. They were considered thieves as well as traitors, and their constant contacts with Gentiles made them religiously suspect, if not unclean. Jesus reflected the popular view of the publicans when He classified them with harlots and other sinners (Matt. 5:46–47; 18:17); but it was obvious that He was the "friend of publicans and sinners" (Matt. 11:19; 21:31–32).

Matthew opened his heart to Jesus Christ and became a new person. This was not an easy decision for him to make. He was a native of Capernaum, and Capernaum had rejected the Lord (Matt. 11:23). Matthew was a well-known businessman in the city, and his old friends probably persecuted him. Certainly Matthew lost a good deal of income when he left all to follow Christ.

Matthew not only opened his heart, but he also opened his home. He knew that most, if not all, of his old friends would drop him when he began to follow Jesus Christ, so Matthew took advantage of the situation and invited them to meet Jesus. He gave a great feast and invited all the other tax collectors (some of whom could have been Gentiles), and the Jewish people who were not keeping the law ("sinners").

Of course, the Pharisees criticized Jesus for daring to eat with such a defiled group of people. They even tried to get the disciples of John the Baptist to create a disagreement (Luke 5:33). The Lord explained why He was fellowshipping with "publicans and sinners": They were spiritually sick and needed a physician. He had not come to call the righteous *because there were no righteous people.* He came to call sinners, and that included the Pharisees. Of course, His critics did not consider themselves "spiritually sick," but they *were* just the same.

Matthew not only opened his heart and home, but he also opened his hands and worked for Christ. Alexander Whyte of Edinburgh once said that when Matthew left his job to follow Christ, he brought his pen with him! Little did this ex-publican realize that the Holy Spirit would one day use him to write the first of the four gospels in the New Testament

According to tradition, Matthew ministered in Palestine for several years after the Lord's return to heaven, and then made missionary journeys to the Jews who were dispersed among the Gentiles. His work is associated with Persia, Ethiopia, and Syria, and some traditions associate him with Greece. The New Testament is silent on his life, but this we do know:

Wherever the Scriptures travel in this world, the gospel written by Matthew continues to minister to hearts.

CHAPTER TWO
Matthew 1—2
THE KING'S BIRTH

If a man suddenly appears and claims to be a king, the public immediately asks for proof. What is his background? Who pays homage to him? What credentials can he present? Anticipating these important questions, Matthew opened his book with a careful account of the birth of Jesus Christ and the events that accompanied it. He presented four facts about the King.

The Heredity of the King (1:1–25)
Since royalty depends on heredity, it was important for Jesus to establish His rights to David's throne. Matthew gave His human heredity (Matt. 1:1–17) as well as His divine heredity (Matt. 1:18–25).

His human heredity (vv. 1–17). Genealogies were very important to the Jews, for without them they could not prove their tribal memberships or their rights to inheritances. Anyone claiming to be "the Son of David" had to be able to prove it. It is generally concluded that Matthew gave our Lord's family tree through His foster father, Joseph, while Luke gave Mary's lineage (Luke 3:23ff.).

Many Bible readers skip over this list of ancient (and, in some cases, unpronounceable) names. But this "list of names" is a vital part of the gospel record. It shows that Jesus Christ is a part of history, that all of Jewish history prepared the way for His birth. God in His providence ruled and overruled to accomplish His great purpose in bringing His Son into the world.

This genealogy also illustrates God's wonderful grace. It is most unusual to find the names of women in Jewish genealogies, since names and inheritances came through the fathers. But in this list we find references to four women from Old Testament history: Tamar (Matt. 1:3), Rahab and Ruth (Matt. 1:5), and Bathsheba "the wife of Uriah" (Matt. 1:6).

Matthew clearly omitted some names from this genealogy. Probably, he did this to give a systematic summary of three periods in Israel's history, each with fourteen generations. The numerical value of the Hebrew letters for "David" equals fourteen. Matthew probably used this approach as a memory aid to help his readers remember this difficult list

But there were many Jewish men who could trace their family back to King David. It would take more than human pedigree to make Jesus Christ "the Son of David" and heir to David's throne. This is why the divine heredity was so important.

His divine heredity (vv. 18–25). Matthew 1:16 and 18 make it clear that Jesus Christ's birth was different from that of any other Jewish boy named in the genealogy. Matthew pointed out that Joseph did not "beget" Jesus Christ. Rather, Joseph was the "husband of Mary, of whom was born Jesus, who is called Christ." Jesus was born of an earthly mother without the need of an earthly father. This is known as the doctrine of the virgin birth.

Every child born into the world is a totally new creature. But Jesus Christ, being eternal God (John 1:1, 14), existed before Mary and Joseph or any of His earthly ancestors. If Jesus Christ were conceived and born just as any other baby, then He could not be God. It was necessary for Him to enter this world through an earthly mother, but not to be begotten by an earthly father. By a miracle of the Holy Spirit, Jesus was conceived in the womb of Mary, a virgin (Luke 1:26–38).

Some have raised the question that perhaps Mary was not a virgin. They say that Matthew 1:23 should be translated "young woman." But the word translated *virgin* in this verse always means virgin and cannot be translated "young woman."

Both Mary and Joseph belonged to the house of David. The Old Testament prophecies indicated that the Messiah would be born of a woman (Gen. 3:15), of the seed of Abraham (Gen. 22:18), through the tribe of Judah (Gen. 49:10), and of the family of David (2 Sam. 7:12–13). Matthew's genealogy traced the line through Solomon, while Luke's traced it through Nathan, another one of David's sons. It is worth noting that Jesus Christ is the only Jew alive who can actually prove His claims to the throne of David! All of the other records were destroyed when the Romans took Jerusalem in AD 70.

To the Jewish people in that day, betrothal (engagement) was equivalent to marriage—except that the man and woman did not live together. They were called "husband and wife," and, at the end of the engagement period, the marriage was consummated. If a betrothed woman became pregnant, it was considered adultery (see Deut. 22:13–21). But Joseph did not punish or divorce Mary when he discovered she was with child, for the Lord had revealed the truth to him. All of this fulfilled Isaiah 7:14.

Before we leave this important section, we must consider the three names assigned to God's Son. The name *Jesus* means "Savior" and comes from the Hebrew name Joshua ("Jehovah is salvation"). There were many Jewish boys with the name Joshua (or, in the Greek, Jesus), but Mary's Boy was called "Jesus the Christ." The word *Christ* means "anointed"; it is the Greek equivalent of *Messiah*. He is "Jesus the Messiah." Jesus is His human name; Christ is His official title; and Emmanuel describes who He is—"God with us." Jesus Christ is God! We find this name "Emmanuel" in Isaiah 7:14 and 8:8.

The King, then, was a Jewish male who is also the divine Son of God. But, did anybody acknowledge His kingship? Yes, the magi from the East came and worshipped Him.

The Homage to the King (2:1–12)

We must confess that we know little about these men. The word translated "wise men" (magi) refers to a group of scholars who studied the stars. Their title connects them with magic, but they were probably more like astrologers. However, their presence in the biblical record is not a divine endorsement of astrology.

God gave them a special sign, a miraculous star that announced the birth of the King. The star led them to Jerusalem, where God's prophets told them that the King would be born in Bethlehem. They went to Bethlehem, and there they worshipped the Christ Child.

We do not know how many magi there were. From the three gifts listed in Matthew 2:11, some people have assumed there were three kings from the Orient, though this is not certain. But when their caravan arrived in Jerusalem, there were enough of them to trouble the whole city.

Keep in mind that these men were *Gentiles.* From the very beginning, Jesus came to be "the Savior of the world" (John 4:42). These men were also wealthy, and they were scholars—scientists in their own right. No scholarly person who follows the light God gives him can miss worshipping at the feet of Jesus. In Jesus Christ "are hid all the treasures of wisdom and knowledge" (Col. 2:3). In Him dwells "all the fullness of the Godhead bodily" (Col. 2:9).

The magi were seeking the King, but Herod was afraid of the King and wanted to destroy Him. This was Herod the Great, called *king* by the Roman senate because of the influence of Mark Antony. Herod was a cruel and crafty man who permitted no one, not even his own family, to interfere with his rule or prevent the satisfying of his evil desires. A ruthless murderer, he had his own wife and her two brothers slain because he suspected them of treason. He was married at least nine times in order to fulfill his lusts and strengthen his political ties.

It is no surprise that Herod tried to kill Jesus, for Herod alone wanted to bear the title "King of the Jews." But there was another reason. Herod was not a full-blooded Jew; he was actually an Idumaean, a descendant of Esau. This is a picture of the old struggle between Esau and Jacob that began even before the boys were born (Gen. 25:19–34). It is the spiritual versus the carnal, the godly versus the worldly.

The magi were seeking the King; Herod was opposing the King; and the Jewish priests were ignoring the King. These priests knew the Scriptures and pointed others to the Savior, *but they would not go to worship Him themselves!* They quoted Micah 5:2 but did not obey it. They were *five miles* from the very Son of God, yet they did not go to see Him! The Gentiles sought and found Him, but the Jews did not.

Matthew 2:9 indicates that the miraculous star was not always visible to the magi. As they started toward Bethlehem, they saw the star again; and it led them to the house where Jesus was. By now, Joseph had moved Mary and the baby from the temporary dwelling where the Lord Jesus had been born (Luke 2:7). The traditional manger scenes that assemble together the shepherds and wise men are not true to Scripture, since the magi arrived much later.

Matthew cites a second fulfilled prophecy to prove that Jesus Christ is the King (Matt. 2:5). *How* He was born was a fulfillment of prophecy, and *where* He was born was a fulfillment of prophecy. Bethlehem means "house of bread," and this was where the "Bread of Life" came to earth (John 6:48ff.). Bethlehem in the Old Testament was associated with David, who was a type of Jesus Christ in His suffering and glory.

Hostility against the King (2:13–18)

A person is identified not only by his friends, but also by his enemies. Herod pretended that he wanted to worship the newborn King (Matt. 2:8), when in reality he wanted to destroy Him. God warned Joseph to take the child and Mary and flee to Egypt. Egypt was close. There were many Jews there, and the treasures received from the magi would more than pay the expenses for traveling and living there. But there was also another prophecy to fulfill, Hosea 11:1: "I called my Son out of Egypt."

Herod's anger was evidence of his pride; he could not permit anyone to get the best of him, particularly some Gentile scholars! This led him to kill the boy babies two years of age and under who were still in Bethlehem. We must not envision hundreds of little boys being killed, for there were not that many male children of that age in a small village like Bethlehem. Even today only about twenty thousand people live there. It is likely that not more than twenty children were slain. But, of course, *one* is too many!

Matthew introduced here the theme of hostility, which he focused on throughout his book. Satan is a liar and a murderer (John 8:44), as was King Herod. He lied to the magi and he murdered the babies. But even this horrendous crime of murder was the fulfillment of prophecy found in Jeremiah 31:15. In order to understand this fulfillment, we must review Jewish history.

The first mention of Bethlehem in Scripture is in connection with the death of Jacob's favorite wife, Rachel (Gen. 35:16–20). Rachel died giving birth to a son whom she named Benoni, "son of my sorrow." Jacob renamed his son Benjamin, "son of my right hand." Both of these names relate to Jesus Christ, for He was a "man of sorrows, and acquainted with grief" (Isa. 53:3), and He is now the Son of God's right hand (Acts 5:31; Heb. 1:3). Jacob put up a pillar to mark Rachel's grave, which is near Bethlehem.

Jeremiah's prophecy was given about six hundred years before Christ was born. It grew out of the captivity of Jerusalem. Some of the captives were taken to Ramah in Benjamin, near Jerusalem, and this reminded Jeremiah of Jacob's sorrow when Rachel died. However, now it was *Rachel* who was weeping. She represented the mothers of Israel weeping as they saw their sons going into captivity. It was as though

Rachel said, "I gave my life to bear a son, and now his descendants are no more."

Jacob saw Bethlehem as a place of death, but the birth of Jesus made it a place of life! Because of His coming, there would be spiritual deliverance for Israel and, in the future, the establishment of David's throne and kingdom. Israel, "the son of my sorrow," would one day become "the son of my right hand." Jeremiah gave a promise to the nation that they would be restored to their land again (Jer. 31:16–17), and this promise was fulfilled. But he gave an even greater promise that the nation would be regathered in the future, and the kingdom established (Jer. 31:27ff.). This promise shall also be fulfilled.

Very few people today think of Bethlehem as a burial place; they think of it as the birthplace of Jesus Christ. And because He died for us and rose again, we have a bright future before us. We shall live forever with Him in that glorious city where death is no more and where tears never fall.

The Humility of the King (2:19–23)

Herod died in 4 BC, which means that Jesus was born sometime between 6 and 5 BC. It is impossible not to notice the parallel between Matthew 2:20 and Exodus 4:19, the call of Moses. As God's Son, Jesus was in Egypt and was called out to go to Israel. Moses was outside Egypt, hiding for his life, and he was called to return to Egypt. But in both cases, God's program of redemption was involved. It took courage for Joseph and his family to leave Egypt, and it took courage for Moses to return to Egypt.

Archelaus was one of Herod's sons, and to him Herod had willed the title of king. However, the Jews discovered that, in spite of his promises of kindness, Archelaus was as wicked as his father. So they sent a delegation to Rome to protest his crowning. Augustus Caesar agreed with the Jews and made Archelaus an ethnarch over half of his father's kingdom. (Jesus may have had this bit of Jewish history in mind when He told the parable of the pounds in Luke 19:11–27.)

The whole episode is a good example of how God leads His children. Joseph knew that he and his family were no safer under the rule of Archelaus than they had been under Herod the Great. It is likely they were heading back to Bethlehem when they discovered that Archelaus was on the throne. Certainly, Joseph and Mary prayed, waited, and sought God's will. Common sense told them to be careful; faith told them to wait. In due time, God spoke to Joseph in a dream, and he took his wife and her Son to Nazareth, which had been their home earlier (Matt. 2:19–20).

But even this fulfilled prophecy! Once again, Matthew points out that every detail in the life of Jesus was foretold in the Scriptures. It is important to note that Matthew did not refer to only one prophet in Matthew 2:23, but instead says "that it might be fulfilled which was spoken by the prophets" (plural). We will not find any specific prophecy that called

Jesus a "Nazarene." The term *Nazarene* was one of reproach: "Can there any good thing come out of Nazareth?" (John 1:46). In many Old Testament prophecies, the Messiah's lowly life of rejection is mentioned, and this may be what Matthew had in mind (see Ps. 22; Isa. 53:2–3, 8). The term *Nazarene* was applied both to Jesus and His followers (Acts 24:5), and He was often called "Jesus of Nazareth" (Matt. 21:11; Mark 14:67; John 18:5, 7).

But perhaps Matthew, led by the Spirit, saw a spiritual connection between the name "Nazarene" and the Hebrew word *netzer,* which means "a branch or shoot." Several prophets apply this title to Jesus (see Isa. 4:2; 11:1; Jer. 23:5; 33:15; Zech. 3:8; 6:12–13).

Our Lord grew up in Nazareth and was identified with that city. In fact, His enemies thought He had been born there, for they said that He came from Galilee (John 7:50–52). Had they investigated the temple records, they would have discovered that He had been born in Bethlehem.

Who ever heard of a king being born in a humble village and growing up in a despised city? The humility of the King is certainly something to admire and imitate (Phil. 2:1–13).

CHAPTER THREE
Matthew 3—4
THE KING'S CREDENTIALS

Some thirty years passed between chapters 2 and 3 of Matthew, during which Jesus lived in Nazareth and worked as a carpenter (Matt. 13:55; Mark 6:3). But the time came for Him to begin His public ministry, which would culminate at the cross. Was He still qualified to be King? Had anything taken place that would disqualify Him? In chapters 2 and 3, Matthew assembled the testimonies of five witnesses to the person of Jesus Christ, that He is the Son of God and the King.

John the Baptist (3:1–15)
For over four hundred years, the nation had not heard the voice of a prophet. Then John appeared and a great revival took place. Consider four facts about John.

His message (vv. 1–2, 7–10). John's preaching centered on repentance and the kingdom of heaven. The word *repent* means "to change one's mind and act on that change." John was not satisfied with regret or remorse; he wanted "fruits meet for repentance" (Matt. 3:8). There had to be evidence of a changed mind and a changed life.

All kinds of people came to hear John preach and to watch the great baptismal services he conducted. Many publicans and sinners came in sincere humility (Matt. 21:31–32), but the religious leaders refused to submit. They thought that they were good enough to please God, yet John called them a "generation of vipers."

Jesus used the same language when He dealt with this self-righteous crowd (Matt. 12:34; 23:33; John 8:44).

The Pharisees were the traditionalists of their day, while the Sadducees were more liberal (see Acts 23:6–9). The wealthy Sadducees controlled the "temple business" that Jesus cleaned out. These two groups usually fought each other for control of the nation, but when it came to opposing Jesus Christ, the Pharisees and Sadducees united forces.

John's message was one of judgment. Israel had sinned and needed to repent, and the religious leaders ought to lead the way. The ax was lying at the root of the tree, and if the tree (Israel) did not bear good fruit, it would be cut down (see Luke 13:6–10). If the nation repented, the way would be prepared for the coming of the Messiah.

His authority (vv. 3–4). John fulfilled the prophecy given in Isaiah 40:3. In a spiritual sense, John was "Elijah who was to come" for he came in the "spirit and power of Elijah" (Luke 1:16–17). He even dressed as Elijah did and preached the same message of judgment (2 Kings 1:8). John was the last of the Old Testament prophets (Luke 16:16) and the greatest of them (Matt. 11:7–15; see 17:9–13).

His baptism (vv. 5–6, 11–12). The Jews baptized Gentile converts, but John was baptizing Jews! His baptism was authorized from heaven (Matt. 21:23–27); it was not something John devised or borrowed. It was a baptism of repentance, *looking forward* to the Messiah's coming (Acts 19:1–7). His baptism fulfilled two purposes: it prepared the nation for Christ, and it presented Christ to the nation (John 1:31).

But John mentioned two other baptisms: a baptism of the Spirit and a baptism of fire (Matt. 3:11). The baptism of the Spirit came at Pentecost (Acts 1:5, and note that Jesus said *nothing* about fire). Today, whenever a sinner trusts Christ, he is born again and immediately baptized by the Spirit into the body of Christ, the church (1 Cor. 12:12–13). In contrast, the baptism of fire refers to the future judgment, as Matthew explains (Matt. 3:12).

His obedience (vv. 13–15). Jesus was not baptized because He was a repentant sinner. Even John tried to stop Jesus, but the Lord knew it was His Father's will. Why was Jesus baptized? First, His baptism gave approval to John's ministry. Second, He identified Himself with publicans and sinners, the very people He came to save. But mainly, His baptism pictured His future baptism on the cross (Matt. 20:22; Luke 12:50) when all the "waves and billows" of God's judgment would go over Him (Ps. 42:7; Jonah 2:3).

Thus, John the Baptist bore witness to Jesus Christ as the Son of God and also as the Lamb of God (John 1:29). Because of John's witness, many sinners trusted Jesus Christ (John 10:39–42).

The Holy Spirit (3:16)
The coming of the Holy Spirit like a dove identified Jesus to John (John 1:31–34), and also assured Jesus as

He began His ministry that the Spirit's ministry would always be His (John 3:34). The dove is a beautiful symbol of the Spirit of God in its purity and in its ministry of peace. The first time we see a dove in Scripture is in Genesis 8:6–11. Noah sent out two birds, a raven and a dove, but only the dove came back. The raven represented the flesh; there was plenty for the raven to eat outside the ark! But the dove would not defile itself on the carcasses, so it came back to the ark. The second time the dove was released, it returned with an olive leaf, a symbol of peace. The third time, the dove did not return.

There may be another picture here. The name Jonah means "dove," and he too experienced a baptism! Jesus used Jonah as a type of Himself in death, burial, and resurrection (Matt. 12:38–40). Jonah was sent to the Gentiles, and Jesus would minister to the Gentiles.

The Father (3:17)

On three special occasions, the Father spoke from heaven: at Christ's baptism, at the Transfiguration (Matt. 17:3), and as Christ approached the cross (John 12:27–30). In the past, God spoke to His Son; today He is speaking *through* His Son (Heb. 1:1–2).

The Father's statement from heaven seems to be an echo of Psalm 2:7—"The Lord hath said unto me, 'Thou art my Son; this day have I begotten thee.'" Acts 13:33 informs us that this "begetting" refers to His resurrection from the dead and not to His birth at Bethlehem. This statement ties in perfectly with the Lord's baptismal experience of death, burial, and resurrection.

But the Father's statement also relates Jesus Christ to the "Suffering Servant" prophesied in Isaiah 40—53. In Matthew 12:18, Matthew quoted from Isaiah 42:1–3, where the Messiah-Servant is called "My beloved, in whom my soul is well pleased." The Servant described in Isaiah is humble, rejected, made to suffer and die, but is also seen to come forth in victory. While the nation of Israel is seen dimly in some of these "Servant Songs," it is the Messiah, Jesus Christ, who is revealed most clearly in them. Again, we see the connection with Christ in death, burial, and resurrection.

Finally, the Father's statement approved all that Jesus had done up to that point. His "hidden years in Nazareth" were years of pleasing the Father. Certainly, the Father's commendation was a great encouragement to the Son as He started His ministry.

Satan (4:1–11)

From the high and holy experience of blessing at the Jordan, Jesus was led into the wilderness for testing. Jesus was not tempted so that the Father could learn anything about His Son, for the Father had already given Jesus His divine approval. Jesus was tempted so that every creature in heaven, on earth, and under the earth might know that Jesus Christ is the Conqueror. He exposed Satan and his tactics, and He defeated Satan. Because of His victory, we can have victory over the tempter.

Just as the first Adam met Satan, so the Last Adam met the enemy (1 Cor. 15:45). Adam met Satan in a beautiful garden, but Jesus met him in a terrible wilderness. Adam had everything he needed, but Jesus was hungry after forty days of fasting. Adam lost the battle and plunged humanity into sin and death. But Jesus won the battle and went on to defeat Satan in more battles, culminating in His final victory on the cross (John 12:31; Col. 2:15).

Our Lord's experience of temptation prepared Him to be our sympathetic High Priest (Heb. 2:16–18; 4:15–16). It is important to note that Jesus faced the enemy *as man,* not as the Son of God. His first word was, *"Man* shall not live by bread alone." We must not think that Jesus used His divine powers to overcome the enemy, because that is just what the enemy wanted Him to do! Jesus used the spiritual resources that are available to us today: the power of the Holy Spirit of God (Matt. 4:1) and the power of the Word of God ("It is written"). Jesus had nothing in His nature that would give Satan a foothold (John 14:30), but His temptations were real just the same. Temptation involves *the will,* and Jesus came to do the Father's will (Heb. 10:1–9).

The first temptation (vv. 1–4). This involved the love of God and the will of God. "Since You are God's beloved Son, why doesn't Your Father feed You? Why does He put You into this terrible wilderness?" This temptation sounded like Satan's words to Eve in Genesis 3! It is a subtle suggestion that our Father does not love us.

But there was another suggestion: "Use Your divine powers to meet Your own needs." When we put our physical needs ahead of our spiritual needs, we sin. When we allow circumstances to dictate our actions, instead of following God's will, we sin. Jesus could have turned the stones into bread, but He would have been exercising His powers *independently of the Father,* and He came to obey the Father (John 5:30; 6:38).

The Lord quoted Deuteronomy 8:3 to defeat Satan. Feeding on and obeying God's Word is more important than consuming physical food. In fact, *it is our food* (John 4:32–34).

The second temptation (vv. 5–7). The second temptation was even more subtle. This time Satan also used the Word of God. "So You intend to live by the Scriptures," he implied. "Then let me quote You a verse of Scripture and see if You will obey it!" Satan took the Lord Jesus to the pinnacle of the temple, probably five hundred feet above the Kidron Valley. Satan then quoted from Psalm 91:11–12, where God promised to care for His own. "If You really believe the Scriptures, then jump! Let's see if the Father cares for You!"

Note carefully our Lord's reply: "It is written *again*" (Matt. 4:7, emphasis mine). We must never divorce one part of Scripture from another, but we must always "compare spiritual things with spiritual" (1 Cor. 2:13).

We can prove almost anything by the Bible if we isolate texts from the contexts and turn them into pretexts. Satan had cleverly omitted the phrase "in all thy ways" when he quoted from Psalm 91. When the child of God is in the will of God, the Father will protect him. He watches over those who are "in His ways."

Jesus replied with Deuteronomy 6:16: "Thou shalt not tempt the Lord thy God." We tempt God when we put ourselves into circumstances that force Him to work miracles on our behalf. The diabetic who refuses to take insulin and argues, "Jesus will take care of me," may be tempting the Lord. We tempt God when we try to force Him to contradict His own Word. It is important for us as believers to read *all* Scripture, and study *all* God has to say, for *all* of it is profitable for daily life (2 Tim. 3:16–17).

The third temptation (vv. 8–11). The devil offered Jesus a shortcut to His kingdom. Jesus knew that He would suffer and die before He entered into His glory (Luke 24:26; 1 Peter 1:11; 5:1). If He bowed down and worshipped Satan *just once* (this is the force of the Greek verb), He could enjoy all the glory without enduring the suffering. Satan has always wanted worship, because Satan has always wanted to be God (Isa. 14:12–14). Worshipping the creature instead of the Creator is the lie that rules our world today (Rom. 1:24–25).

There are no shortcuts to the will of God. If we want to share in the glory, we must also share in the suffering (1 Peter 5:10). As the prince of this world, Satan could offer these kingdoms to Christ (John 12:31; 14:30). But Jesus did not need Satan's offer. The Father had already promised Jesus the kingdom! "Ask of me, and I shall give thee the heathen [nations] for thine inheritance" (Ps. 2:8). You find the same promise in Psalm 22:22–31, and this is the psalm of the cross.

Our Lord replied with Deuteronomy 6:13: "Thou shalt worship the Lord thy God, and him only shalt thou serve." Satan had said nothing about service, but Jesus knew that whatever we worship, we will serve. Worship and service must go together.

Satan slunk away, a defeated foe, but he did not cease to tempt Jesus. We could translate Luke 4:13, "And when the devil had ended every possible kind of temptation, he stood off from Him until a suitable season." Through Peter, Satan again tempted Jesus to abandon the cross (Matt. 16:21–23), and through the crowd that had been fed, Satan tempted Jesus to an "easy kingdom" (John 6:15). One victory never guarantees freedom from further temptation. If anything, each victory we experience only makes Satan try harder.

Notice that Luke's account reverses the order of the second and third temptations as recorded in Matthew. The word *then* in Matthew 4:5 seems to indicate sequence. Luke only uses the simple conjunction "and" and does not say he is following a sequence. Our Lord's command at the end of the third temptation ("Get

thee hence, Satan") is proof that Matthew followed the historical order. There is no contradiction since Luke did not claim to follow the actual sequence.

After Jesus Christ had defeated Satan, He was ready to begin His ministry. No man has a right to call others to obey who has not obeyed himself. Our Lord proved Himself to be the perfect King whose sovereignty is worthy of our respect and obedience. But, true to his purpose, Matthew had one more witness to call to prove the kingship of Jesus Christ.

Christ's Ministry of Power (4:12–15)

Matthew has already shown us that every detail of our Lord's life was controlled by the Word of God. Remember that between the end of His temptation and the statement in Matthew 4:12 comes the ministry described in John 1:19 through John 3:36. We must not think that John the Baptist was thrown into prison immediately after our Lord's temptation. Matthew wrote his book *topically* rather than *chronologically*. Consult a good harmony of the Gospels to study the sequence of events.

In Matthew 4:16, Matthew quoted Isaiah (see Isa. 9:1–2). The prophet wrote about people who "walked" in darkness, but by the time Matthew quoted the passage, the situation was so discouraging that the people were *sitting* in darkness! Jesus Christ brought the Light to them. He made His headquarters in Capernaum in "Galilee of the Gentiles," another reference to the universal outreach of the gospel's message. In Galilee there was a mixed population that was somewhat despised by the racially "pure" citizens of Judea.

How did Jesus bring this Light to Galilee? We are told in Matthew 4:23: through His teaching, preaching, and healing. This emphasis is found often in the gospel of Matthew; see 9:35; 11:4–5; 12:15; 14:34–36; 15:30; 19:2. Matthew was quite clear that He healed "all manner of sickness and all manner of disease" (Matt. 4:23). There was no case too difficult for Him!

The result of these great miracles was a tremendous *fame* for Jesus, and a great *following* of people from many areas. "Syria" refers to an area in northern Galilee. "Decapolis" means "ten cities" and was a district made up of ten cities originally built by followers of Alexander the Great. The Decapolis was in the northeastern part of Galilee. "Beyond Jordan" means Perea, the area east of the Jordan. News traveled fast, and those who had afflicted friends or family members brought them to Jesus for healing.

Matthew listed some of the "cases" in Matthew 4:24. "Diseases and torments" could cover almost any disease. Of course, our Lord often delivered people from demons. The term "lunatic" did not refer to people who were insane. Rather, it was used to describe those afflicted with epilepsy (see Matt. 17:15). *Palsy* meant "paralytic."

Miracles of healing were but a part of Christ's ministry throughout Galilee, for He also taught and preached the Word. The "light" that Isaiah promised was the Light of the Word of God, as well as the Light of His perfect life and compassionate ministry. The word *preach* in Matthew 4:17 and 23 means "to announce as a herald." Jesus proclaimed with authority the good news that the kingdom of heaven was at hand.

The phrase *kingdom of heaven* is found thirty-two times in Matthew's gospel. The phrase *kingdom of God* is found only five times (Matt. 6:33; 12:28; 19:24; 21:31, 43). Out of reverence for the holy name of the Lord, the Jews would not mention "God" but would substitute the word *heaven.* The Prodigal Son confessed that he had sinned "against heaven," meaning, of course, against God. In many places where Matthew uses *kingdom of heaven,* the parallel passages in Mark and Luke use *kingdom of God.*

In the New Testament, the word *kingdom* means "rule, reign, authority" rather than a place or a specific realm. The phrase "kingdom of heaven" refers to the rule of God. The Jewish leaders wanted a political leader who would deliver them from Rome, but Jesus came to bring *spiritual* rule to the hearts of people. This does not deny the reality of a future kingdom as we have already noted.

But Jesus not only proclaimed the good news and taught the people God's truth, He also called to Himself a few disciples whom He could train for the work of the kingdom. In Matthew 4:17–22 we read of the call of Peter, Andrew, James, and John, men who had already met Jesus and trusted Him (John 1:29–42). They had gone back to their fishing business, but He came and called them to give up their business and follow Him. The details of this call may be found in Mark 1:16–20 and Luke 5:1–11.

The term "fishers of men" was not new. For centuries, Greek and Roman philosophers had used it to describe the work of the man who seeks to "catch" others by teaching and persuasion. "Fishing for men" is but one of many pictures of evangelism in the Bible, and we must not limit ourselves to it. Jesus also talked about the shepherd seeking the lost sheep (Luke 15:1–7), and the workers in the harvest-field (John 4:34–38). Since these four men were involved in the fishing business, it was logical for Jesus to use this approach.

Jesus had four and possibly seven men in the band of disciples who were professional fishermen (see John 21:1–3). Why would Jesus call so many fishermen to His side? For one thing, fishermen were busy people; usually professional fishermen did not sit around doing nothing. They either sorted their catch, prepared for a catch, or mended their equipment. The Lord needs busy people who are not afraid to work.

Fishermen have to be courageous and patient people. It certainly takes patience and courage to win others to Christ. Fishermen must have skill; they must learn from others where to find the fish and how to catch them. Soul-winning demands skill too. These men had to work together, and the work of the Lord demands cooperation. But most of all, fishing demands

faith: fishermen cannot see the fish and are not sure their nets will enclose them. Soul-winning requires faith and alertness too, or we will fail.

Matthew has presented to us the person of the King. Every witness affirms, "This is the Son of God, this is the King!"

CHAPTER FOUR
Matthew 5
THE KING'S PRINCIPLES: TRUE RIGHTEOUSNESS

The Sermon on the Mount is one of the most misunderstood messages that Jesus ever gave. One group says it is God's plan of salvation, that if we ever hope to go to heaven we must obey these rules. Another group calls it a "charter for world peace" and begs the nations of the earth to accept it. Still a third group tells us that the Sermon on the Mount does not apply to today, but that it will apply at some future time, perhaps during the tribulation or the millennial kingdom.

I have always felt that Matthew 5:20 was the key to this important sermon: "For I say unto you, that except your righteousness shall exceed the righteousness of the scribes and Pharisees, ye shall in no case enter into the kingdom of heaven." The main theme is true righteousness. The religious leaders had an artificial, external righteousness based on law. But the righteousness Jesus described is a true and vital righteousness that begins internally, in the heart. The Pharisees were concerned about the minute details of conduct, but they neglected the major matter of *character.* Conduct flows out of character.

Whatever applications the Sermon on the Mount may have to world problems, or to future events, it is certain that this sermon has definite applications for us today. Jesus gave this message to individual believers, not to the unsaved world at large. What was taught in the Sermon on the Mount is repeated in the New Testament Epistles for the church today. Jesus originally gave these words to His disciples (Matt. 5:1), and they have shared them with us.

In this chapter, Jesus gave three explanations about true, spiritual righteousness.

What True Righteousness Is (5:1–16)
Being a master Teacher, our Lord did not begin this important sermon with a negative criticism of the scribes and Pharisees. He began with a positive emphasis on righteous character and the blessings that it brings to the life of the believer. The Pharisees taught that righteousness was an external thing, a matter of obeying rules and regulations. Righteousness could be measured by praying, giving, fasting, etc. In the Beatitudes and the pictures of

the believer, Jesus described Christian character that flowed from within.

Imagine how the crowd's attention was riveted on Jesus when He uttered His first word: "Blessed." (The Latin word for blessed is *beatus,* and from this comes the word *beatitude.*) This was a powerful word to those who heard Jesus that day. To them it meant "divine joy and perfect happiness." The word was not used for humans; it described the kind of joy experienced only by the gods or the dead. "Blessed" implied an inner satisfaction and sufficiency that did not depend on outward circumstances for happiness. This is what the Lord offers those who trust Him!

The Beatitudes describe the attitudes that ought to be in our lives today. Four attitudes are described here.

Our attitude toward ourselves (v. 3). To be poor in spirit means to be humble, to have a correct estimate of oneself (Rom. 12:3). It does not mean to be "poor spirited" and have no backbone at all! "Poor in spirit" is the opposite of the world's attitudes of self-praise and self-assertion. It is not a false humility that says, "I am not worth anything; I can't do anything!" It is honesty with ourselves: we know ourselves, accept ourselves, and try to be ourselves to the glory of God.

Our attitude toward our sins (vv. 4–6). We mourn over sin and despise it. We see sin the way God sees it and seek to treat it the way God does. Those who cover sin or defend sin certainly have the wrong attitude. We should not only mourn over our sins, but we should also meekly submit to God (see Luke 18:9–14; Phil. 3:1–14).

Meekness is not weakness, for both Moses and Jesus were meek men (Num. 12:3; Matt. 11:29). This word translated "meek" was used by the Greeks to describe a horse that had been broken. It refers to power under control.

Our attitude toward the Lord (vv. 7–9). We experience God's mercy when we trust Christ (Eph. 2:4–7), and He gives us a clean heart (Acts 15:9) and peace within (Rom. 5:1). But having received His mercy, we then *share* His mercy with others. We seek to keep our hearts pure that we might see God in our lives today. We become peacemakers in a troubled world and channels for God's mercy, purity, and peace.

Our attitude toward the world (vv. 10–16). It is not easy to be a dedicated Christian. Our society is not a friend to God nor to God's people. Whether we like it or not, there is *conflict* between us and the world. Why? Because we are different from the world and we have different attitudes.

As we read the Beatitudes, we find that they represent an outlook radically different from that of the world. The world praises pride, not humility. The world endorses sin, especially if you "get away with it." The world is at war with God, while God is seeking to reconcile His enemies and make them His children. We must expect to be persecuted *if* we are living as God wants us to live. But we must be sure that our suffering is not due to our own foolishness or disobedience.

How True Righteousness Comes (5:17–20)

Certainly after the crowd heard our Lord's description of the kind of person God blesses, they said to themselves, "But we could *never* attain that kind of character. How can we have this righteousness? Where does it come from?" They wondered how His teaching related to what they had been taught all their lives. What about Moses and the law?

In the law of Moses, God certainly revealed His standards for holy living. The Pharisees defended the law and sought to obey it. But Jesus said that the true righteousness that pleases God must *exceed* that of the scribes and Pharisees—and to the common people, the scribes and Pharisees were the holiest men in the community! If *they* had not attained, what hope was there for anybody else?

Jesus explained His own attitude toward the law by describing three possible relationships.

We can seek to destroy the law (v. 17a). The Pharisees thought Jesus was doing this. To begin with, His *authority* did not come from any of the recognized leaders or schools. Instead of teaching "from authorities" as did the scribes and Pharisees, Jesus taught *with authority.*

Not only in His authority, but also in His *activity,* Jesus seemed to defy the law. He deliberately healed people on the Sabbath day and paid no attention to the traditions of the Pharisees. Our Lord's *associations* also seemed contrary to the law, for He was the friend of publicans and sinners.

Yet, it was the Pharisees who were destroying the law! By their traditions, they robbed the people of the Word of God; and by their hypocritical lives, they disobeyed the very law that they claimed to protect. The Pharisees thought they were *conserving God's Word,* when in reality they were *preserving God's Word*: embalming it so that it no longer had life! Their rejection of Christ when He came to earth proved that the inner truth of the law had not penetrated their hearts.

Jesus made it clear that He had come to honor the law and help God's people love it, learn it, and live it. He would not accept the artificial righteousness of the religious leaders. Their righteousness was only an external masquerade. Their religion was a dead ritual, not a living relationship. It was artificial; it did not reproduce itself in others in a living way. It made them proud, not humble; it led to bondage, not liberty.

We can seek to fulfill the law (v. 17b). Jesus Christ fulfilled God's law in every area of His life. He fulfilled it in His birth because He was "made under the law" (Gal. 4:4). Every prescribed ritual for a Jewish boy was performed on Him by His parents. He certainly fulfilled the law in His life, for nobody was ever able to accuse Him of sin. While He did not submit to the traditions of the scribes and Pharisees, He always did what God commanded in the law. The Father was "well pleased" with His Son (Matt. 3:17; 17:5).

Jesus also fulfilled the law in His teaching. It was this that brought Him into conflict with the religious leaders. When He began His ministry, Jesus found the Living Word of God encrusted with man-made traditions and interpretations. He broke away this thick crust of "religion" and brought the people back to God's Word. Then, He opened the Word to them in a new and living way—they were accustomed to the "letter" of the law and not the inner "kernel" of life.

But it was in His death and resurrection that Jesus especially fulfilled the law. He bore the curse of the law (Gal. 3:13). He fulfilled the Old Testament types and ceremonies so that they no longer are required of the people of God (see Heb. 9—10). He set aside the old covenant and brought in the new covenant.

Jesus did not destroy the law by fighting it; He destroyed it by *fulfilling it*! Perhaps an illustration will make this clear. If I have an acorn, I can destroy it in one of two ways. I can put it on a rock and smash it to bits with a hammer. Or, I can plant it in the ground and let it *fulfill itself* by becoming an oak tree.

When Jesus died, He rent the veil of the temple and opened the way into the holiest (Heb. 10:19). He broke down the wall that separated the Jews and Gentiles (Eph. 2:11–13). Because the law was fulfilled in Christ, we no longer need temples made with hands (Acts 7:48ff.) or religious rituals (Col. 2:10–13).

How can we fulfill the law? By yielding to the Holy Spirit and allowing Him to work in our lives (Rom. 8:1–3). The Holy Spirit enables us to experience the "righteousness of the law" in daily life. This does not mean we live sinlessly perfect lives, but it does mean that Christ lives out His life through us by the power of His Spirit (Gal. 2:20).

When we read the Beatitudes, we see the perfect character of Jesus Christ. While Jesus never had to mourn over His sins, since He was sinless, He was still a "man of sorrows, and acquainted with grief" (Isa. 53:3). He never had to hunger and thirst after righteousness since He was the holy Son of God, but He did delight in the Father's will and find His satisfaction in doing it (John 4:34). The only way we can experience the righteousness of the Beatitudes is through the power of Christ.

We can seek to do and teach the law (v. 19). This does not mean we major on the Old Testament and ignore the New! Second Corinthians 3 makes it clear that ours is a ministry of the *new* covenant. But there is a proper ministry of the law (1 Tim. 1:9ff.) that is not contrary to the glorious message of God's grace. Jesus wants us to know more of the righteousness of God, obey it, and share it with others. The moral law of God has not changed. Nine of the Ten Commandments are repeated in the New Testament Epistles and commanded to believers. (The exception is the Sabbath commandment, which was given as a sign to Israel; see Neh. 9:14.)

We do not obey an external law because of fear. No, believers today obey an internal law *and live because of love*. The Holy Spirit teaches us the Word and enables us to obey. Sin is still sin, and God still punishes sin. In fact, we in this present age are *more* responsible because we have been taught and given more!

How Righteousness Works in Daily Life (5:21–48)

Jesus took six important Old Testament laws and interpreted them for His people in the light of the new life He came to give. He made a fundamental change without altering God's standards: He dealt with the attitudes and intents of the heart and not simply with the external action. The Pharisees said that righteousness consisted of performing certain actions, but Jesus said it centered in the attitudes of the heart.

Likewise, with sin: The Pharisees had a list of external actions that were sinful, but Jesus explained that sin came from the attitudes of the heart. Anger is murder in the heart; lust is adultery in the heart. The person who says that he "lives by the Sermon on the Mount" may not realize that the Sermon on the Mount is *more difficult* to keep than the original Ten Commandments!

Murder (vv. 21–26; Ex. 20:13). I have read that one out of every thirty-five deaths in Chicago is a murder, and that most of these murders are "crimes of passion" caused by anger among friends or relatives. Jesus did not say that anger *leads* to murder; He said that anger *is* murder.

There is a holy anger against sin (Eph. 4:26), but Jesus talked about an unholy anger against people. The word He used in Matthew 5:22 means "a settled anger, malice that is nursed inwardly." Jesus described a sinful experience that involved several stages. First there was *causeless anger*. This anger then exploded into *words*: "Raca—empty-headed person!" These words added fuel to the fire so that the person said, "You fool—rebel!"

Anger is such a foolish thing. It makes us destroyers instead of builders. It robs us of freedom and makes us prisoners. To hate someone is to commit murder in our hearts (1 John 3:15).

This does not mean that we should go ahead and murder someone we hate, since we have already sinned inwardly. Obviously, sinful feelings are not excuses for sinful deeds. Sinful anger robs us of fellowship with God as well as with our brothers, but it does not put us into jail as murderers. However, more than one person has become a murderer because he failed to control sinful anger.

Sinful anger must be faced honestly and must be confessed to God as sin. We must go to our brother and get the matter settled, and we must do it quickly. The longer we wait, the worse the bondage becomes! We put ourselves into a terrible prison when we refuse to be reconciled. (See Matt. 18:15–20 for additional counsel.) It has well been said that the person who refuses to forgive his brother destroys the very bridge over which he himself must walk.

Adultery (vv. 27–30; Ex. 20:14). Jesus affirmed God's law of purity, and then explained that the intent of this law was to reveal the sanctity of sex and the sinfulness of the human heart. God created sex, and God protects sex. He has the authority to regulate it and to punish those who rebel against His laws. He does not regulate sex because He wants to rob us, but rather, because He wants to bless us. Whenever God says, no it is that He might say yes.

Sexual impurity begins in the desires of the heart. Again, Jesus is not saying that lustful desires are identical to lustful deeds, and therefore a person might just as well go ahead and commit adultery. The desire and the deed are not identical, but, spiritually speaking, they are equivalent. The "look" that Jesus mentioned was not a casual glance, but a constant stare *with the purpose of lusting.* It is possible for a man to glance at a beautiful woman and know that she is beautiful, but not lust after her. The man Jesus described looked at the woman for *the purpose of feeding his inner sensual appetites* as a substitute for the act. It was not accidental; it was planned.

How do we get victory? By purifying the desires of the heart (appetite leads to action) and disciplining the actions of the body. Obviously, our Lord is not talking about literal surgery, for this would not solve the problem in the heart. The eye and the hand are usually the two "culprits" when it comes to sexual sins, so they must be disciplined. Jesus said, "Deal immediately and decisively with sin! Don't taper off—cut off!" Spiritual surgery is more important than physical surgery, for the sins of the body can lead to eternal judgment. We think of passages like Colossians 3:5 and Romans 6:13; 12:1–2; 13:14.

Divorce (vv. 31–32). Our Lord dealt with this in greater detail in Matthew 19:1–12, and we shall consider it there.

Swearing (vv. 33–37; Lev. 19:12; Deut. 23:23). This is not the sin of "cursing," but the sin of using oaths to affirm that what is said is true. The Pharisees used all kinds of tricks to sidestep the truth, and oaths were among them. They would avoid using the holy name of God, but they would come close by using the city of Jerusalem, heaven, earth, or some part of the body.

Jesus taught that our conversation should be so honest, and our character so true, that we would not need "crutches" to get people to believe us. Words depend on character, and oaths cannot compensate for a poor character. "In the multitude of words there wanteth not sin; but he that refraineth his lips is wise" (Prov. 10:19). The more words a man uses to convince us, the more suspicious we should be.

Retaliation (vv. 38–42; Lev. 24:19–22). The original law was a fair one; it kept people from forcing the offender to pay a greater price than the offense deserved. It also prevented people from taking personal revenge. Jesus replaced a law with an attitude: be willing to suffer loss yourself rather than cause another to suffer. Of course, He applied this to *personal insults,* not to groups or nations. The person who retaliates only makes himself and the offender feel worse; and the result is a settled war and not peace.

In order to "turn the other cheek," we must stay where we are and not run away. This demands both

faith and love. It also means that *we* will be hurt, but it is better to be hurt on the outside than to be harmed on the inside. But it further means that *we should try to help the sinner.* We are vulnerable, because he may attack us anew; but we are also victorious, because Jesus is on our side, helping us and building our characters. Psychologists tell us that violence is born of weakness, not strength. It is the strong man who can love and suffer hurt; it is the weak man who thinks only of himself and hurts others to protect himself. He hurts others then runs away to protect himself.

Love of enemies (vv. 43–48; Lev. 19:17–18). Nowhere did the law teach hatred for one's enemies. Passages like Exodus 23:4–5 indicate just the opposite! Jesus defined our enemies as those who curse us, hate us, and exploit us selfishly. Since Christian love is an act of the will, and not simply an emotion, He has the right to command us to love our enemies. After all, He loved us when we were His enemies (Rom. 5:10). We may show this love by blessing those who curse us, doing good to them, and praying for them. When we pray for our enemies, we find it easier to love them. It takes the "poison" out of our attitudes.

Jesus gave several reasons for this admonition. (1) This love is a mark of maturity, proving that we are *sons of* the Father, and not just little children. (2) It is Godlike. The Father shares His good things with those who oppose Him. Matthew 5:45 suggests that our love "creates a climate" of blessings that makes it easy to win our enemies and make them our friends. Love is like the sunshine and rain that the Father sends so graciously. (3) It is a testimony to others. "What do ye more than others?" is a good question. God expects us to live on a much higher plane than the lost people of the world who return good for good and evil for evil. As Christians, we must return good for evil as an investment of love.

The word *perfect* in Matthew 5:48 does not imply *sinlessly* perfect, for that is impossible in this life (though it is a good goal to strive for). It suggests completeness, maturity, as the sons of God. The Father loves His enemies and seeks to make them His children, and we should assist Him!

CHAPTER FIVE
Matthew 6
THE KING'S PRINCIPLES: TRUE WORSHIP

The true righteousness of the kingdom must be applied in the everyday activities of life. This is the emphasis in the rest of the Sermon on the Mount. Jesus related this principle to our relationships to God in worship (Matt. 6:1–18), our relationship to material things (Matt. 6:19–34), and our relationship to other people (Matt. 7:1–20).

Jesus also warned about the danger of hypocrisy (Matt. 6:2, 5, 16), the sin of using religion to cover up sin. A hypocrite is not a person who falls short of his high ideals, or who occasionally sins, because all of us experience these failures. A hypocrite *deliberately* uses religion to cover up his sins and promote his own gains. The Greek word translated *hypocrite* originally meant "an actor who wears a mask."

The righteousness of the Pharisees was insincere and dishonest. They practiced their religion for the applause of men, not for the reward of God. But true righteousness must come from within. We should test ourselves to see whether we are sincere and honest in our Christian commitment. In this chapter, Christ applied this test to four different areas of life.

Our Giving (6:1–4)

Giving alms to the poor, praying, and fasting were important disciplines in the religion of the Pharisees. Jesus did not condemn these practices, but He did caution us to make sure that our hearts are right as we practice them. The Pharisees used almsgiving to gain favor with God and attention from men, both of which were wrong motives. No amount of giving can purchase salvation, for salvation is the gift of God (Eph. 2:8–9). And to live for the praise of men is a foolish thing because the glory of man does not last (1 Peter 1:24). It is the glory and praise of God that really counts!

Our sinful nature is so subtle that it can defile even a good thing like sharing with the poor. If our motive is to get the praise of men, then like the Pharisees, we will call attention to what we are doing. But if our motive is to serve God in love and please Him, then we will give our gifts without calling attention to them. As a result, we will grow spiritually; God will be glorified; and others will be helped. But if we give with the wrong motive, we rob ourselves of blessing and reward and rob God of glory, even though the money we share might help a needy person.

Does this mean that it is wrong to give openly? Must all giving be anonymous? Not necessarily, for everyone in the early church knew that Barnabas had given the income from the sale of his land (Acts 4:34–37). When the church members laid their money at the apostles' feet, it was not done in secret The difference, of course, was in the *motive* and *manner* in which it was done. A contrast is Ananias and Sapphira (Acts 5:1–11), who tried to use their gift to make people think they were more spiritual than they really were.

Our Praying (6:5–15)

Jesus gave four instructions to guide us in our praying.

We must pray in secret before we pray in public (v. 6). It is not wrong to pray in public in the assembly (1 Tim. 2:1ff.), or even when blessing food (John 6:11) or seeking God's help (John 11:41–42; Acts 27:35). But it is wrong to pray in public if we are not in the habit of praying in private. Observers may think that we are practicing prayer when we are not, and this is hypocrisy. The word translated *closet* means "a private chamber." It could refer to the store-chamber in a house. Our Lord prayed privately (Mark 1:35); so did Elisha (2 Kings 4:32ff.) and Daniel (Dan. 6:10ff.).

We must pray sincerely (vv. 7–8). The fact that a request is repeated does not make it a "vain repetition," for both Jesus and Paul repeated their petitions (Matt. 26:36–46; 2 Cor. 12:7–8). A request becomes a "vain repetition" if it is only a babbling of words without a sincere heart desire to seek and do God's will. The mere reciting of memorized prayers can be vain repetition. The Gentiles had such prayers in their pagan ceremonies (see 1 Kings 18:26).

My friend Dr. Robert A. Cook has often said, "All of us have one routine prayer in our system; and once we get rid of it, then we can really start to pray!" I have noticed this, not only in my own praying, but often when I have conducted prayer meetings. With some people, praying is like putting the needle on a phonograph record *and then forgetting about it.* But God does not answer insincere prayers.

We must pray in God's will (vv. 9–13). This prayer is known familiarly as "The Lord's Prayer," but "The Disciples' Prayer" would be a more accurate title. Jesus did not give this prayer to us to be memorized and recited a given number of times. In fact, he gave this prayer *to keep us from* using vain repetitions. Jesus did not say, "Pray in these words." He said, "Pray after this manner"; that is, "Use this prayer as a pattern, not as a substitute."

The purpose of prayer is to glorify God's name and to ask for help to accomplish His will on earth. This prayer begins with *God's* interests, not ours: God's name, God's kingdom, and God's will. Robert Law has said, "Prayer is a mighty instrument, not for getting man's will done in heaven, but for getting God's will done on earth." We have no right to ask God for anything that will dishonor His name, delay His kingdom, or disturb His will on earth.

It is worth noting that there are *no singular pronouns* in this prayer; they are all plural. It begins with "*Our* Father." When we pray, we must remember that we are part of God's worldwide family of believers. We have no right to ask for ourselves anything that would harm another member of the family. If we are praying in the will of God, the answer will be a blessing to all of God's people in one way or another.

If we put God's concerns first, then we can bring our own needs. God is concerned about our needs and knows them even before we mention them (Matt. 6:8). If this is the case, then why pray? Because prayer is the God-appointed way to have these needs met (see James 4:1–3). *Prayer prepares us for the proper use of the answer.* If we know our need, and if we voice it to God, trusting Him for His provision, then we will make better use of the answer than if God forced it on us without our asking.

It is right to pray for daily physical needs, for forgiveness, and for guidance and protection from evil. "Lead us not into temptation" does not mean that God tempts His children (James 1:13–17). In this petition we are asking God to guide us so that we will not get out of His will and get involved in a situation of temptation (1 John 5:18), or even in a situation of tempting God so that He must miraculously rescue us (Matt. 4:5–7).

We must pray, having a forgiving spirit toward others (vv. 14–15). In this "appendix" to the prayer, Jesus expanded the last phrase of Matthew 6:12, "as we forgive our debtors." He later repeated this lesson to His disciples (Mark 11:19–26). He was not teaching that believers earned God's forgiveness by forgiving others, for this would be contrary to God's free grace and mercy. However, if we have truly *experienced* God's forgiveness, then we will have a readiness to forgive others (Eph. 4:32; Col. 3:13). Our Lord illustrated this principle in the parable of the unmerciful servant (Matt. 18:21–35).

We have seen that true praying is a "family affair" ("Our Father"). If the members of the family are not getting along with one another, how can they claim to have a right relationship with the Father? The emphasis in 1 John 4 is that we show our love for God by loving our brothers. When we forgive each other, we are not *earning* the right to prayer, for the privilege of prayer is a part of our *sonship* (Rom. 8:15–16). Forgiveness belongs to the matter of *fellowship:* If I am not in fellowship with God, I cannot pray effectively. But fellowship with my brother helps to determine my fellowship with God; hence, forgiveness is important to prayer.

Since prayer involves glorifying God's name, hastening the coming of God's kingdom (2 Peter 3:12), and helping to accomplish God's will on earth, the one praying must not have sin in his heart. If God answered the prayers of a believer who had an unforgiving spirit, He would dishonor His own name. How could God work through such a person to get His will done on earth? If God gave him his requests, He would be encouraging sin! The important thing about prayer is not simply getting an answer, but *being the kind of person whom God can trust with an answer.*

Our Fasting (6:16–18)

The only fast that God actually required of the Jewish people was on the annual day of Atonement (Lev. 23:27). The Pharisees fasted each Monday and Thursday (Luke 18:12) and did so in such a way that people knew they were fasting. Their purpose, of course, was to win the praise of men. As a result, the Pharisees lost God's blessing.

It is not wrong to fast, if we do it in the right way and with the right motive. Jesus fasted (Matt. 4:3); so did the members of the early church (Acts 13:2). Fasting helps to discipline the appetites of the body (Luke 21:34) and keep our spiritual priorities straight. But fasting must never become an opportunity for temptation (1 Cor. 7:7). Simply to deprive ourselves of a natural benefit (such as food or sleep) is not *of itself* fasting. We must devote ourselves to God and worship Him. Unless there is the devotion of the heart (see Zech. 7), there is no lasting spiritual benefit.

As with giving and praying, true fasting must be done in secret; it is between the believer and God. To "make unsightly" our faces (by looking glum and asking for pity and praise) would be to destroy the very purpose of the fast. Our Lord here laid down a basic principle of spiritual living: Nothing that is truly spiritual will violate that which God has given us in nature. God usually does not tear down one good thing in order to build up another. If we have to look miserable to be considered spiritual, then there is something wrong with our views of spirituality.

Remember that *hypocrisy robs us of reality in Christian living.* We substitute reputation for character, mere words for true prayer, money for the devotion of the heart. No wonder Jesus compared the Pharisees to tombs that were whitewashed on the outside, but filthy on the inside (Matt. 23:27–28)!

But hypocrisy not only robs us of character, it also *robs us of spiritual rewards.* Instead of the eternal approval of God, we receive the shallow praise of men. We pray, but there are no answers. We fast, but the inner man shows no improvement. The spiritual life becomes hollow and lifeless. We miss the blessing of God here and now, and also lose the reward of God when Christ returns.

Hypocrisy also *robs us of spiritual influence.* The Pharisees were a negative influence; whatever they touched was defiled and destroyed. The people who admired them and obeyed the Pharisees' words thought they themselves were being helped, when in reality, they were being hurt.

The first step toward overcoming hypocrisy is to be honest with God in our secret life. We must never pray anything that we do not mean from the heart; otherwise, our prayers are simply empty words. Our motive must be to please God alone, no matter what men may say or do. We must cultivate the heart in the secret place. It has well been said, "The most important part of a Christian's life is the part that only God sees." When reputation becomes more important than character, we have become hypocrites.

Our Use of Wealth (6:19–34)

We are accustomed to dividing life into the "spiritual" and the "material"; but Jesus made no such division. In many of His parables, He made it clear that a right attitude toward wealth is a mark of true spirituality (see Luke 12:13ff.; 16:1–31). The Pharisees were covetous (Luke 16:14) and used religion to make money. If we have the true righteousness of Christ in our lives, then we will have a proper attitude toward material wealth.

Nowhere did Jesus magnify poverty or criticize the legitimate getting of wealth. God made all things, including food, clothing, and precious metals. God has declared that all things He has made are good (Gen.

1:31). God knows that we need certain things in order to live (Matt. 6:32). In fact, He has given us "richly all things to enjoy" (1 Tim. 6:17). It is not wrong to possess things, *but it is wrong for things to possess us.* The sin of idolatry is as dangerous as the sin of hypocrisy! There are many warnings in the Bible against covetousness (Ex. 20:17; Ps. 119:36; Mark 7:22; Luke 12:15ff.; Eph. 5:5; Col. 3:5).

Jesus warned against the sin of living for the things of this life. He pointed out the sad consequences of covetousness and idolatry.

Enslavement (vv. 19–24). Materialism will enslave the heart (Matt. 6:19–21), the mind (Matt. 6:22–23), and the will (Matt. 6:24). We can become shackled by the material things of life, but we ought to be liberated and controlled by the Spirit of God.

If the heart loves material things and puts earthly gain above heavenly investments, then the result can only be a tragic loss. The treasures of earth may be used for God. But if we gather material things for ourselves, we will lose them; *and we will lose our hearts with them.* Instead of spiritual enrichment, we will experience impoverishment.

What does it mean to lay up treasures in heaven? It means to use *all that we have* for the glory of God. It means to "hang loose" when it comes to the material things of life. It also means measuring life by the true riches of the kingdom and not by the false riches of this world.

Wealth not only enslaves the heart, but it also enslaves the mind (Matt. 6:22–23). God's Word often uses the eye to represent the attitudes of the mind. If the eye is properly focused on the light, the body can function properly in its movements. But if the eye is out of focus and seeing double, it results in unsteady movements. It is most difficult to make progress while trying to look in two directions at the same time.

If our aim in life is to get material gain, it will mean darkness within. But if our outlook is to serve and glorify God, there will be light within. If what should be light is really darkness, then we are being controlled by darkness, and outlook determines outcome.

Finally, materialism can enslave the will (Matt. 6:24). We cannot serve two masters simultaneously. Either Jesus Christ is our Lord, or money is our lord. It is a matter of the will. "But those who want to get rich fall into temptation and a snare" (1 Tim. 6:9). If God grants riches, and we use them for His glory, then riches are a blessing. But if we *will* to get rich, and live with that outlook, we will pay a great price for those riches.

Devaluation (vv. 25–30). Covetousness will not only cheapen our riches, but it will also cheapen *us!* We will start to become worried and anxious, and this anxiety is unnatural and unspiritual. The person who pursues money thinks that riches will solve his problems, when in reality, riches will create more problems! Material wealth gives a dangerous, false sense of security, and that feeling ends in tragedy. The birds

and lilies do not fret and worry, yet they have God's wealth in ways that man cannot duplicate. All of nature depends on God, and God never fails. Only mortal man depends on money, and money always fails.

Jesus said that worry is sinful. We may dignify worry by calling it by some other name—concern, burden, a cross to bear—but the results are still the same. Instead of helping us live longer, anxiety only makes life shorter (Matt. 6:27). The Greek word translated "take no thought" literally means "to be drawn in different directions." Worry pulls us apart. Until man interferes, everything in nature works together, because all of nature trusts God. Man, however, is pulled apart because he tries to live his own life by depending on material wealth.

God feeds the birds and clothes the lilies. He will feed and clothe us. It is our "little faith" that hinders Him from working as He would. He has great blessings for us if only we will yield to Him and live for the riches that last forever.

Loss of testimony (vv. 31–33). To worry about material things is to live like the heathen! If we put God's will and God's righteousness first in our lives, He will take care of everything else. What a testimony it is to the world when a Christian dares to practice Matthew 6:33! What a tragedy it is when so many of us *fail* to practice it.

Loss of joy today (v. 34). Worrying about tomorrow does not help either tomorrow or today. If anything, it robs us of our effectiveness today—which means we will be even less effective tomorrow. Someone has said that the average person is crucifying himself between two thieves: the regrets of yesterday and the worries about tomorrow. It is right to plan for the future and even to save for the future (2 Cor. 12:14; 1 Tim. 5:8). But it is a sin to worry about the future and permit tomorrow to rob today of its blessings.

Three words in this section point the way to victory over worry: (1) *faith* (Matt. 6:30), trusting God to meet our needs; (2) *Father* (Matt. 6:32), knowing He cares for His children; and (3) *first* (Matt. 6:33), putting God's will first in our lives so that He might be glorified. If we have faith in our Father and put Him first, He will meet our needs.

Hypocrisy and anxiety are sins. If we practice the true righteousness of the kingdom, we will avoid these sins and live for God's glory.

CHAPTER SIX
Matthew 7
THE KING'S PRINCIPLES: TRUE JUDGMENT

The scribes and Pharisees were guilty of exercising a false judgment about themselves, other people, and even the Lord. Their false righteousness helped to encourage this false judgment. This explains why our Lord closed this important sermon with a discussion of judgment. In it He discussed three different judgments.

Our Judgment of Ourselves (7:1–5)

The first principle of judgment is that we begin with ourselves. Jesus did not forbid us to judge others, for careful discrimination is essential in the Christian life. Christian love is not blind (Phil. 1:9–10). The person who believes all that he hears and accepts everyone who claims to be spiritual will experience confusion and great spiritual loss. But before we judge others, we must judge ourselves. There are several reasons for this.

We shall be judged (v. 1). The tense of the verb *judged* signifies a once-for-all final judgment. If we first judge ourselves, then we are preparing for that final judgment when we face God. The Pharisees "played God" as they condemned other people, but they never considered that God would one day judge them.

We are being judged (v. 2). The parallel passage in Luke 6:37–38 is helpful here. Not only will God judge us at the end, but people are also judging us right now, and we receive from people exactly what we give. The kind of judgment, and the measure of judgment, comes right back to us. We reap what we have sown.

We must see clearly to help others (vv. 3–5). The purpose of self-judgment is to prepare us to serve others. Christians are obligated to help each other grow in grace. When we do not judge ourselves, we not only hurt ourselves, but we also hurt those to whom we could minister. The Pharisees judged and criticized *others* to make themselves look good (Luke 18:9–14). But Christians should judge *themselves* so that they can help others look good. There is a difference!

Let's look at our Lord's illustration of this point. Jesus chose the symbol of the eye because this is one of the most sensitive areas of the human body. The picture of a man with a two-by-four stuck in his eye, trying to remove a speck of dust from another man's eye, is ridiculous indeed! If we do not honestly face up to our own sins and confess them, we blind ourselves to ourselves, and then we cannot see clearly enough to help others. The Pharisees saw the sins of other people, but they would not look at their own sins.

In Matthew 6:22–23, Jesus used the illustration of the eye to teach us how to have a spiritual outlook on life. *We must not pass judgment on others' motives.* We should examine their actions and attitudes, but we cannot judge their motives—for only God can see their hearts. It is possible for a person to do a good work with a bad motive. It is also possible to fail in a task and yet be very sincerely motivated. When we stand before Christ at the judgment seat, He will examine the secrets of the heart and reward us accordingly (Rom. 2:16; Col. 3:22–25).

The image of the eye teaches us another truth: We must exercise love and tenderness when we seek to help others (Eph. 4:15). I have had extensive eye examinations, and once had surgery to remove an imbedded speck of steel, and I appreciated the tenderness of the physicians. Like eye doctors, we should minister to people we want to help with tender loving care. We can do more damage than a speck of dirt in the eye if we approach others with impatience and insensitivity.

Two extremes must be avoided in this matter of spiritual self-examination. The first is the deception of a shallow examination. Sometimes we are so sure of ourselves that we fail to examine our hearts honestly and thoroughly. A quick glance into the mirror of the Word will never reveal the true situation (James 1:22–25).

The second extreme is what I call a "perpetual autopsy." Sometimes we get so wrapped up in self-examination that we become unbalanced. But we should not look only at ourselves, or we will become discouraged and defeated. We should look by faith to Jesus Christ and let Him forgive and restore us. Satan is the accuser (Rev. 12:10), and he enjoys it when we accuse and condemn ourselves!

After we have judged ourselves honestly before God, and have removed those things that blind us, then we can help others and properly judge their works. But if we know there are sins in our lives, and we try to help others, we are hypocrites. In fact, it is possible for ministry to be a device to cover up sin! The Pharisees were guilty of this, and Jesus denounced them for it.

Our Judgment of Others (7:6–20)

Christians must exercise discernment, for not everyone is a sheep. Some people are dogs or hogs, and some are wolves in sheep's clothing! We are the Lord's sheep, but this does not mean we should let people pull the wool over our eyes!

The reason we must judge (v. 6). As God's people, we are privileged to handle the "holy things" of the Lord. He has entrusted to us the precious truths of the Word of God (2 Cor. 4:7), and we must regard them carefully. No dedicated priest would throw meat from the altar to a filthy dog, and only a fool would give pearls to a pig. While it is true that we must carry the gospel "to every creature" (Mark 16:15), it is also true that we must not cheapen the gospel by a ministry that lacks discernment. Even Jesus refused to talk to Herod (Luke 23:9), and Paul refused to argue with people who resisted the Word (Acts 13:44–49).

The reason for judgment, then, is not that we might condemn others, but that we might be able to minister to them. Notice that Jesus always dealt with individuals according to their needs and their spiritual condition. He did not have a memorized speech that He used with everybody. He discussed the new birth with Nicodemus, but He spoke of living water to the Samaritan woman. When the religious leaders tried to trap Him, He refused to answer their question (Matt. 21:23–27). It is a wise Christian who first assesses the condition of a person's heart before sharing the precious pearls.

The resources God gives us (vv. 7–11). Why did

our Lord discuss prayer at this point in His message? These verses seem to be an interruption, but they are not. You and I are human and fallible; we make mistakes. Only God can judge perfectly. Therefore, we must pray and seek His wisdom and direction. "If any of you lack wisdom, let him ask of God" (James 1:5).

Young King Solomon knew that he lacked the needed wisdom to judge Israel, so he prayed to God, and the Lord graciously answered (1 Kings 3:3ff.). If we are to have spiritual discernment, we must keep on asking God, keep on seeking His will, keep on knocking at the door that leads to greater ministry. God meets the needs of His children.

The guiding principle (v. 12). This is the so-called "Golden Rule," one of the most misunderstood statements in the Bible. This statement is not the sum total of Christian truth, nor is it God's plan of redemption. We should no more build our theology on the Golden Rule than we should build our astronomy on "Twinkle, Twinkle Little Star."

This great truth is a principle that ought to govern our attitudes toward others. It only applies to believers, and it must be practiced in every area of life. *The person who practices the Golden Rule refuses to say or do anything that would harm himself or others.* If our judging of others is not governed by this principle, we will become proud and critical, and our own spiritual character will degenerate.

Practicing the Golden Rule releases the love of God in our lives and enables us to help others, even those who want to hurt us.

But remember that practicing the Golden Rule means paying a price. If we want God's best for ourselves and others, but others resist God's will, then they will oppose us. We are salt, and salt stings the open wound. We are light, and light exposes dirt.

The basis for judging (vv. 13–20). Since there are false prophets in the world, we must be careful of deception. But the greatest danger is *self-deception.* The scribes and Pharisees had fooled themselves into believing that they were righteous and others were sinful. It is possible for people to know the right language, believe intellectually the right doctrines, obey the right rules, and still not be saved. Jesus used two pictures to help us judge ourselves and others.

The two ways (vv. 13–14). These are, of course, the way to heaven and the way to hell. The broad way is the easy way; it is the popular way. But we must not judge spiritual profession by statistics; the majority is not always right. The fact that "everybody does it" is no proof that what they are doing is right.

Quite the contrary is true: God's people have always been a remnant, a small minority in this world. The reason is not difficult to discover: The way of life is narrow, lonely, and costly. We can walk on the broad way and keep our "baggage" of sin and worldliness. But if we enter the narrow way, we must give up those things.

Here, then, is the first test: *Did your profession of faith in Christ cost you anything?* If not, then it was not a true profession. Many people who "trust" Jesus Christ never leave the broad road with its appetites and associations. They have an easy Christianity that makes no demands on them. Yet Jesus said that the narrow way was *hard.* We cannot walk on two roads, in two different directions, at the same time.

The two trees (vv. 15–20). These show that true faith in Christ changes the life and produces fruit for God's glory. Everything in nature reproduces after its kind, and this is also true in the spiritual realm. Good fruit comes from a good tree, but bad fruit comes from a bad tree. The tree that produces rotten fruit is cut down and thrown into the fire. "Wherefore, by their fruits you shall know them" (Matt. 7:20).

The second test is this: *Did my decision for Christ change my life?* False prophets who teach false doctrine can produce only a false righteousness (see Acts 20:29). Their fruit (the results of their ministry) is false and cannot last. The prophets themselves are false; the closer we get to them, the more we see the falsity of their lives and doctrines. They magnify themselves, not Jesus Christ; and their purpose is to exploit people, not to edify them. The person who believes false doctrine, or who follows a false prophet, will never experience a changed life. Unfortunately, some people do not realize this until it is too late.

God's Judgment of Us (7:21–29)

From picturing two ways and two trees, our Lord closed His message by picturing two builders and their houses. The two ways illustrate the *start* of the life of faith; the two trees illustrate the *growth* and results of the life of faith here and now; and the two houses illustrate the *end* of this life of faith, when God shall call everything to judgment. There are false prophets at the gate that leads to the broad way, making it easy for people to enter. But at the end of the way, there is destruction. The final test is not what we think of ourselves, or what others may think. The final test is: *What will God say?*

How can we prepare for this judgment? *By doing God's will.* Obedience to His will is the test of true faith in Christ. The test is not words, not saying, "Lord, Lord," and not obeying His commands. How easy it is to learn a religious vocabulary, and even memorize Bible verses and religious songs, and yet not obey God's will. When a person is truly born again, he has the Spirit of God living within (Rom. 8:9), and the Spirit enables him to know and do the Father's will. God's love in his heart (Rom. 5:5) motivates him to obey God and serve others.

Words are not a substitute for obedience, and neither are religious works. Preaching, casting out demons, and performing miracles can be divinely inspired, but they give no assurance of salvation. It is likely that even Judas participated in some or all of these activities, and yet he was not a true believer. In the last days, Satan will use "lying wonders" to deceive people (2 Thess. 2:7–12).

We are to *hear* God's words and *do* them (see James 1:22–25). We must not stop with only hearing (or studying) His words. Our hearing must result in doing. This is what it means to build on the rock foundation. We should not confuse this symbol with the "rock" in 1 Corinthians 3:9ff. Paul founded the local church in Corinth on Jesus Christ when he preached the gospel and won people to Christ. This is the only foundation for a local church.

The foundation in this parable is *obedience to God's Word*—obedience that is an evidence of true faith (James 2: 14ff.). The two men in this story had much in common. Both had desires to build a house. Both built houses that looked good and sturdy. But when the judgment came (the storm), one of the houses collapsed. What was the difference? Not the mere external looks, to be sure. The difference was in the foundation: The successful builder "dug deep" (Luke 6:48) and set his house on a solid foundation.

A false profession will last until judgment comes. Sometimes this judgment is in the form of the trials of life. Like the person who received the seed of God's Word into a shallow heart (Matt. 13:4–9), the commitment fails when the testing comes. Many people have professed faith in Christ, only to deny their faith when life becomes spiritually costly and difficult.

But the judgment illustrated here probably refers to the final judgment before God. We must not read into this parable all the doctrine that we are taught in the Epistles, for the Lord was illustrating one main point: *profession will ultimately be tested before God.* Those who have trusted Christ, and have proved their faith by their obedience, will have nothing to fear. Their house is founded on the Rock, and it will stand. But those who have professed to trust Christ, yet who have not obeyed God's will, will be condemned.

How shall we test our profession of faith? By popularity? No, for there are many on the broad road to destruction. And there are many who are depending on words, saying, "Lord, Lord"—but this is no assurance of salvation. Even religious activities in a church organization are no assurance. How then shall we judge ourselves and others who profess Christ as Savior?

The two ways tell us to examine the cost of our profession. Have we paid a price to profess faith in Christ? *The two trees* tell us to investigate whether our lives have really changed. Are there godly fruits from our lives? And *the two houses* remind us that true faith in Christ will last, not only in the storms of life, but also in the final judgment.

The congregation was astonished at this sermon. Why? Because Jesus spoke with divine authority. The scribes and Pharisees spoke "from authorities," always quoting the various rabbis and experts of the law. Jesus needed no human teacher to add authority to His words, for He spoke as the Son of God. We cannot lightly dismiss this sermon, for it is God who gave it to us! We must bow before Him and submit to His authority, or we will be condemned.

CHAPTER SEVEN
Matthew 8—9
THE KING'S POWER

We have been introduced to the person of the King (Matt. 1—4) and the principles of the King (Matt. 5—7), and now we are ready for the power of the King. After all, if a king does not have the power to accomplish anything, what good are his credentials or his principles? In chapters 8 and 9, Matthew reported ten miracles. They are not given in chronological order, except for the last four, since Matthew followed his own approach of grouping messages or events.

Before we survey these miracles, however, we must pause to answer the obvious question: Why did our Lord perform miracles? Certainly He wanted to meet human needs. God is concerned about the temporal well-being of His creatures as well as their eternal happiness. It is wrong to separate ministry to the body and ministry to the soul, since we must minister to the whole person (see Matt. 4:23–25).

Certainly our Lord's miracles were additional credentials to prove His claim as the Messiah of Israel. "The Jews require a sign" (1 Cor. 1:22). While miracles of themselves are not proof that a man has been sent by God (even Satan can perform miracles [2 Thess. 2:9]), they do add weight to his claim, especially if his character and conduct are godly. In the case of Jesus Christ, His miracles also fulfilled Old Testament prophecies (see Isa. 29:18–19; 35:4–6). Matthew 8:17 refers us to Isaiah 53:4, and Jesus Himself in Matthew 11:1–5 referred John the Baptist to the Old Testament promises. These same "signs and wonders" would be the credentials of His followers in their ministries (Matt. 10:8; Heb. 2:1–4).

Along with His compassion and credentials, there was a third reason for miracles: His concern to reveal saving truth to people. The miracles were "sermons in action." Even Nicodemus was impressed with them (John 3:1–2). It is worth noting that five of these miracles were performed at Capernaum, and yet the city rejected Him (Matt. 11:21–23). Even the rejection by the nation of Israel fulfilled Old Testament prophecy (see John 12:37–41). Like the judgments against Egypt in Moses' day, the miracles of the Lord were judgments in Israel, for the people had to face facts and make decisions. The religious leaders decided that Jesus was working for Satan (Matt. 9:31–34; 12:24).

One thing is certain: Jesus did not perform miracles to "get a crowd." He usually avoided the crowd. Time after time, Jesus instructed those whom He had healed not to talk too much (Matt. 8:4, 18; 9:30; Luke 8:56). He did not want people trusting Him simply on the basis of spectacular deeds (see John 4:46–54). Faith must be based on His Word (Rom. 10:17).

The miracles in these chapters are recorded in three

groups, with an event relating to discipleship separating the groups. Matthew did not tell his readers why he used this arrangement, but we will follow it. To help us grasp some of the spiritual lessons, I have characterized each section with a special emphasis.

Grace to the Outcasts (8:1–22)

Lepers, Gentiles, and women were considered outcasts by many Jewish people, especially the Pharisees. Many Pharisees would pray each morning, "I give thanks that I am a man and not a woman, a Jew and not a Gentile, a free-man and not a slave."

Cleansing the leper (vv. 1–4). There were a number of afflictions that our Bible categorizes as leprosy. This dreaded infection forced the victim to live apart from others and to cry, "Unclean! Unclean!" when others approached, so they would not be defiled. That the leper ran up to Jesus and violated the code is evidence of his great faith that Jesus would heal him.

Leprosy is an illustration of sin (Isa. 1:5–6). The instructions given to the priests in Leviticus 13 help us understand the nature of sin: Sin is deeper than the skin (Lev. 13:3); it spreads (Lev. 13:8); it defiles and isolates (Lev. 13:45–46); and it is fit only for the fire (Lev. 13:52, 57).

When Jesus touched the leper, He contracted the leper's defilement, *but He also conveyed His health!* Is this not what He did for us on the cross when He was made sin for us (2 Cor. 5:21)? The leper did not question His *ability* to heal; he only wondered if He were willing. Certainly God is willing to save! He is "God our Savior, who will have all men to be saved" (1 Tim. 2:3–4). God is "not willing that any should perish" (2 Peter 3:9).

Jesus commanded the man not to tell others but to go to the priests and have them declare him restored and fit for society. This ceremony is described in Leviticus 14 and is another beautiful picture of Christ's work for sinners. The bird slain pictures the death of Christ; the bird released pictures His resurrection. Putting the bird into the jar pictures the Incarnation, when Christ took a human body that He might die for us. The application of the blood to the ear, thumb, and toe illustrates the need for personal faith in His death. The oil on the blood reminds us of the Spirit of God, who enters the person when he trusts the Savior.

The man did not obey Christ; he told everybody what the Lord had done! (Christ tells us to tell everybody, *and we keep quiet!*) Mark 1:45 tells us that the healed leper's witness forced Jesus to avoid the city, and yet the crowds came to Him.

The centurion's servant healed (vv. 5–13). A centurion was an officer over one hundred men in the Roman army. Every centurion mentioned in the Gospels and Acts was a gentleman of high character and sense of duty, and this man was no exception. The fact that he was concerned about a lowly servant-boy indicates this. The word *palsy* indicates a kind of paralysis.

It would seem that everything about this man would prevent him from coming to Jesus. He was a professional soldier, and Jesus was a Man of peace. He was a Gentile, and Jesus was a Jew. But this soldier had one thing working for him: he was a man of great faith. This centurion understood that Jesus, like himself, was under authority. All Christ had to do was speak the word and the disease would obey Him the way a soldier obeyed his officer. It is worth noting that only those who are *under* authority have the right to *exercise* authority.

Twice in the Gospels it is recorded that Jesus marveled: here, at the *great faith* of the Gentile centurion, and in Mark 6:6, at the *great unbelief* of the Jews. Matthew recorded two "Gentile" miracles: this one and the healing of the daughter of the Syrophoenician woman (Matt. 15:21–28). In both cases, the Lord was impressed with their great faith. This is an early indication that the Jews would not believe, but the Gentiles would. Also, in both of these miracles, our Lord healed from *a distance*. This was a reminder of the spiritual position of the Gentiles "afar off" (Eph. 2:12).

Peter's mother-in-law healed (vv. 14–17). She was in bed with a fever, and Peter and Andrew told Jesus about her need when they all arrived home after the synagogue service (Mark 1:21). Women did not hold a high position in Israel, and it is doubtful that a Pharisee would have paid much attention to the need in Peter's home. Jesus healed her with a touch, and she responded by serving Him and the other men.

This seems like a "minor miracle," but the results were major, for after sundown (when the Sabbath ended), *the whole city* gathered at the door that the Lord might meet their needs (Mark 1:32–34). Blessing in the home ought to lead to blessing in the community. The change in one woman's life led to miracles in the lives of many people.

Matthew saw this as a fulfillment of Isaiah 53:4. Please note that Jesus fulfilled this prophecy *in His life* and not on the cross. He bore man's sicknesses and infirmities *during His ministry on earth.* To say that there is "healing in the atonement," and that every believer has the "right" to claim it, is to misinterpret Scripture. First Peter 2:24 applies this same truth to the forgiving of our sins, which He bore on the cross. Sin and sickness do go together (see Ps. 103:3), since sickness is a consequence of Adam's sin and also an illustration of sin. But God is not obligated to heal all sicknesses. He is obligated to save all sinners who call on Him.

First "discipleship" interlude (vv. 18–22). Because great crowds followed Jesus, and opposition had not yet begun, many would-be disciples wanted to follow Him. However, they would not pay the price. This is the first use of "Son of man" in Matthew as a name for Jesus. It comes from Daniel 7:13 and is definitely a messianic title and a claim to kingship. Matthew 8:22 might be expressed, "Let the spiritually dead bury the physically dead." Jesus was not asking the man to be disrespectful to his father (who was not yet dead), but to have the right priorities in life. It is better to preach the gospel and give life to the spiritually dead than to wait for your father to die and bury him.

Peace to the Disturbed (8:23—9:17)

The persons involved in these three miracles all had a need for peace, and Jesus provided that peace.

Peace in the storm (8:23–27). The Sea of Galilee is about thirteen miles long and eight miles wide. It was not unusual for violent storms suddenly to sweep across the water. Jesus undoubtedly knew the storm was coming and certainly could have prevented it. But He permitted it that He might teach His disciples some lessons.

The storm came because they *obeyed* the Lord, and not because (like Jonah) they *disobeyed* Him. Jesus was asleep because He rested confidently in the will of His Father, and this is what the disciples should have done. Instead, they became frightened and accused Jesus of not caring! Matthew wanted his readers to contrast the "little faith" of the disciples with the "great faith" of the Gentile centurion.

Peace in a community (8:28–34). This dramatic incident is most revealing. It shows what *Satan* does for a man: robs him of sanity and self-control; fills him with fears; robs him of the joys of home and friends; and (if possible) condemns him to an eternity of judgment. It also reveals what *society* does for a man in need: restrains him, isolates him, threatens him, but society is unable to change him. See, then, what Jesus Christ can do for a man whose whole life—within and without—is bondage and battle. What Jesus did for these two demoniacs, He will do for anyone else who needs Him.

Christ came to them, and even braved a storm to do it. This is the grace of God! *He delivered them* by the power of His Word. *He restored them* to sanity, society, and service. The account in Mark 5:1–21 shows that one of the men asked to become a disciple of the Lord. But, instead of granting his request, Jesus sent him home to be a witness. Christian service must begin at home.

There are three prayers in this event: (1) the demons besought Jesus to send them into the swine; (2) the citizens besought Him to leave; and (3) the one man besought Him to let him follow (see Mark 5:18–20). Jesus answered the prayers of the demons and the citizens, but not the prayer of the healed man!

We can construct a "statement of faith" from the words of the demons. (Demons do have faith; see James 2:19.) They believed in the existence of God and the deity of Christ, as well as the reality of future judgment. They also believed in prayer. They knew Christ had the power to send them into the swine.

The fact that the demons destroyed two thousand pigs is nothing compared with the fact that Jesus delivered two men from the powers of Satan. God owns everything (Ps. 50:10–11) and can do with it as

He pleases. Jesus values men more than pigs or sheep (Matt. 12:12). He brought peace to these men's lives and to the community where, for a long time, they had been causing trouble.

Peace in the conscience (9:1–8). The Lord had shown Himself powerful over sickness and storms, but what could He do about *sin?* Palsy was a gradual paralysis. This man was unable to help himself, but fortunately he had four friends with love, faith, and hope. They brought him to Jesus and permitted nothing to stand in their way. Was the man's physical condition the result of his sin? We do not know. But we do know that Jesus dealt with the sin problem first, for this is always the greatest need.

We must not conclude from this miracle that all sickness is caused by sin, or that forgiveness automatically means physical healing. A pastor of mine often says, "God can heal every sickness *except the last one.*" More important than the healing of this man's body was the cleansing of his heart. He went home with both a sound body and a heart at peace with God. "'There is no peace,' saith my God, 'to the wicked'" (Isa. 57:21).

Second "discipleship" interlude (9:9–17). We have covered the call of Matthew in the first chapter of this study. We need only to comment on the four pictures of His ministry that Jesus gave in this message. As the *Physician,* He came to bring spiritual health to sick sinners. As the *Bridegroom,* He came to give spiritual joy. The Christian life is a feast, not a funeral. The illustration of the *cloth* reminds us that He came to bring spiritual wholeness; He did not come to "patch us up" and then let us fall apart. The image of the *wineskins* teaches that He gives spiritual fullness. Jewish religion was a worn-out wineskin that would burst if filled with the new wine of the gospel. Jesus did not come to renovate Moses or even mix law and grace. He came with new life!

Restoration to the Broken (9:18–38)

In this section Matthew recorded four miracles involving five persons.

A broken home (vv. 18–19, 23–26). It must have been difficult for Jairus to come to Jesus, since he was a devout Jew and the leader in the synagogue. But Jairus's love for his dying daughter compelled him to seek Jesus' help, even if the religious leaders were opposing Him. When Jairus first came to Jesus, his daughter was close to death. The delay caused by the healing of the woman gave "the last enemy" opportunity to do its work. The ruler's friends came and told him that his daughter had died.

Jesus quickly reassured the man and went with him. In fact, the delay should have helped to strengthen Jairus's faith, for he saw what the woman's meager faith had accomplished in her own life. We must learn to trust Christ and His promises no matter how we feel, no matter what others say, and no matter how the circumstances may look. The scene at home must have frightened Jairus, yet Jesus took command and raised the girl from the dead.

A broken hope (vv. 20–22). Mark 5:26 informs us that this woman had tried many physicians, but none could help her. Imagine the despair and discouragement she felt. Her hopes were shattered. Because of this hemorrhage, the woman was ceremonially unclean (Lev. 15:25ff.), which only added to her hopelessness. The "hem" refers to the special tassels that the Jews wore on their garments to remind them they were God's people (Num. 15:37–41; Deut. 22:12).

It is interesting that Jairus and this woman—two opposite people—met at the feet of Jesus. Jairus was a leading Jewish man; she was an anonymous woman with no prestige or resources. He was a synagogue leader, while her affliction kept her from worship. Jairus came pleading for his daughter; the woman came with a need of her own. The girl had been healthy for twelve years, and then died; the woman had been ill for twelve years and was now made whole. Jairus's need was public—all knew it; the woman's need was private—only Jesus understood. Both Jairus and the woman trusted Christ, and He met their needs.

Jairus may have resented the woman, because she kept Jesus from getting to his daughter before the girl died. But his real problem was not the woman, *but himself:* He needed faith in Christ. Jesus forced the woman to give her testimony (see Mark's account) both for her sake and for the sake of Jairus. The fact that God has helped others ought to encourage us to trust Him more. We ought not to be so selfish in our praying that we cannot wait on the Lord, knowing He is never late.

This woman's faith was almost superstitious, and yet Jesus honored it and healed her. People must "touch Christ" where they are able, even if they must start at the hem of His garment. The Pharisees enlarged their hems and tassels in order to appear more spiritual, but they lacked the power to heal (Matt. 23:5). Others touched the hem of Christ's garment and were also healed (Matt. 14:34–36).

When Sir James Simpson, the inventor of chloroform, was dying, a friend said to him, "You will soon be resting on His bosom." The scientist replied: "I don't know as I can do that, but I think I have hold of the hem of His garment." It is not the strength of our faith that saves us, but faith in a strong Savior.

Broken bodies (vv. 27–34). We are not told why these men were blind. Blindness was a serious problem in the East in that day. The records state that Jesus healed at least six blind men, and each case was different. These two blind men acknowledged Christ as the Son of David (see Matt. 1:1) and persisted in following Him right into the house. (No doubt they had friends who helped guide them.) It was their faith that Christ honored. Their "Yes, Lord" was the confession that released the power for their healing, and their sight was restored.

Blindness is a picture of spiritual ignorance and unbelief (Isa. 6:10; Matt. 15:14; Rom. 11:25). The sinner must be born again before he can see the things of God (John 3:3). And the believer must be careful to grow spiritually or he will damage his spiritual vision (2 Peter 1:5–9).

The final miracle in this series involved a demon (Matt. 9:32–34). While there is a difference between sicknesses and demonic workings (Matt. 10:8), the demons do have the power to cause physical afflictions. In this case, the demon made the man mute. Think of what a handicap this would be! Jesus delivered him, and the people admitted that this was a new thing in Israel.

But the religious leaders would not admit that Jesus was the Messiah. How, then, could they explain His miracles? Only by saying that His miracles were wrought in the power of the wicked one. They would repeat this charge later, and Jesus would refute it (Matt. 12:22ff.). In their unbelief, the Pharisees were playing right into Satan's hands!

Third "discipleship" interlude (vv. 35–38). Not only did Jesus heal, He also taught and preached. But He could not do the work alone—He needed others to help Him. He requested that His disciples pray that God would provide the needed workers. It was not long before the disciples themselves were involved in the ministry of preaching, teaching, and healing (see Matt. 10). In the same way, when we pray as He commanded, we will see what He saw, feel what He felt, and do what He did. God will multiply our lives as we share in the great harvest that is already ripe (John 4:34–38).

CHAPTER EIGHT
Matthew 10
THE KING'S AMBASSADORS

The work of salvation could be accomplished only by Jesus Christ, and He did it alone. But the *witness* of this salvation could only be accomplished by His people, those who have trusted Him and been saved. The King needed ambassadors to carry the message—and He *still* needs them. "Whom shall I send, and who will go for us?" (Isa. 6:8). It is not enough that we *pray* for laborers (Matt. 9:36–38). We must also make ourselves available to serve Him.

Before Jesus sent His ambassadors out to minister, He preached an "ordination sermon" to encourage and prepare them. In this sermon, the King had something to say to *all* of His servants—past, present, and future. Unless we recognize this fact, the message of this chapter will seem hopelessly confused.

Instructions for Past Apostles (10:1–15)
A "disciple" is a learner, one who follows a teacher and learns his wisdom. Jesus had many disciples, some of

whom were merely "hangers-on," and some who were truly converted (John 6:66). From this large group of followers, Jesus selected a smaller group of twelve men, and these He called "apostles." This word comes from the Greek word *apostello,* which means "to send forth with a commission." It was used by the Greeks for the personal representatives of the king, ambassadors who functioned with the king's authority. To make light of the king's envoys was to be in danger of insubordination.

A man had to meet certain qualifications to be an apostle of Jesus Christ. He must have seen the risen Christ (1 Cor. 9:1) and fellowshipped with Him (Acts 1:21–22). He had to be chosen by the Lord (Eph. 4:11). The apostles laid the foundation of the church (Eph. 2:20) and then passed from the scene. While all believers are sent forth to represent the King (John 17:18; 20:21), no believer today can honestly claim to be an apostle, for none of us has seen the risen Christ (1 Peter 1:8).

These apostles were given special power and authority from Christ to perform miracles. These miracles were a part of their "official credentials" (Acts 2:43; 5:12; 2 Cor. 12:12; Heb. 2:1–4). They healed the sick (and note that this included *all* kinds of diseases), cleansed the lepers, cast out demons, and even raised the dead. These four ministries paralleled the miracles that Jesus performed in Matthew 8 and 9. In a definite way, the apostles represented the King and extended His work.

Christ's commission to these twelve men is not our commission today. He sent them only to the people of Israel. "To the Jew first" is the historic pattern, for "Salvation is of the Jews" (John 4:22). These twelve ambassadors announced the coming of the kingdom just as John the Baptist had done (Matt. 3:2) and Jesus Himself (Matt. 4:17). Sad to say, the nation rejected both Christ and His ambassadors, and the kingdom was taken from them (Matt. 21:43).

The apostles depended on the hospitality of others as they ministered from town to town. In those days, for a town to refuse a guest was a breach of etiquette. However, the ambassadors were to remain only with those who were "worthy," those who trusted Christ and received His message of peace and forgiveness. The apostles were not to compromise. If a town rejected their words, they were to warn the people and depart. To shake off the dust was an act of judgment (Acts 13:51).

We do not know how long this "evangelistic campaign" lasted. Jesus Himself went out to preach (see Matt. 11:1), and later the apostles returned to Him and reported what had happened (Luke 9:10). Mark 6:7 tells us that Jesus had sent the men out in pairs, which explains why their names are listed in pairs in Matthew 10:2–4. Revelation 21:14 tells us that the names of the apostles will be on the foundations of the heavenly walls. The name of Judas will, of course, be replaced by Matthias (Acts 1:26).

While we may learn from the spiritual principles in this paragraph, we should not apply these instructions to our lives. The Lord's commission to us includes "all the world" (Matt. 28:19–20), not just the nation of Israel. We preach the gospel of the grace of God (Acts 20:24). Our message is "Christ died for our sins," and not "The kingdom of heaven is at hand." The King has come; He has already suffered, died, and risen from the dead. Now He offers His salvation to all who will believe.

Instructions for Future Disciples (10:16–23)

The "atmosphere" of this section is different from that in the previous section. Here the Lord spoke of persecution, but we have no record that the Twelve suffered during their tour. Jesus also spoke of a ministry to the Gentiles (Matt. 10:18). The Holy Spirit had not been given, yet Jesus talked about the Spirit speaking in them (Matt. 10:20). Matthew 10:22 seems to indicate a worldwide persecution, yet the apostles were ministering only in their own land. Finally, Matthew 10:23 speaks about the return of the Lord, which certainly moves these events into the future. It is difficult to escape the conclusion that these instructions apply to witnesses at some future time.

But, *what* time? To some degree, some of these events took place in the book of Acts, yet Jesus Christ did not return at that time. And the ministry in Acts was not limited to "the cities of Israel" (Matt. 10:23). It seems that the period described in this section closely parallels the time of tribulation that Jesus described in His "Olivet Discourse" (Matt. 24—25). In fact, the statement "He that shall endure unto the end, the same shall be saved" (Matt. 10:13) is definitely a part of our Lord's prophetic discourse (Matt. 24:13; Mark 13:13). It does not refer to a person keeping himself saved, but rather enduring persecution and being faithful.

If, then, these instructions apply to that future time of tribulation, we can easily understand why Jesus said so much about hatred and persecution. The tribulation period will be a time of *opposition.* God's servants will be like sheep in the midst of wolves. They will need to be "tough-minded but tenderhearted." This opposition will come from organized religion (Matt. 10:17), government (Matt. 10:18), and even the family (Matt. 10:21).

While believers in scattered parts of the world are experiencing some of this persecution today, the indication is that this opposition will be worldwide. "Religion" has always persecuted true believers. Even the apostle Paul persecuted the church when he was the unconverted Saul of Tarsus. Church history reveals that "organized religion" that has no gospel has opposed men and women who have dared to witness boldly for Christ.

Matthew 10:18 states that *government* will also share in this program of persecution. The prophetic Scriptures teach that, in the last days, government and religion will work together to control the world. Revelation 13 describes a time during the tribulation period when a world ruler (the Antichrist) will force the world to worship him and his image. He will control world religion, economics, and government; and he will use all three to persecute those who stand true to Christ.

There will also be a decay of *family* love and loyalty. "Without natural affection" is one of the marks of the end times (2 Tim. 3:3). Jesus quoted Micah 7:6 to prove this point (Matt. 10:21). The three institutions that God established in this world are the home, human government, and the church. In the last days, all three of these institutions will oppose the truth instead of promote it.

But the tribulation period will also be a time of *opportunity*. The believers will be able to witness to governors and kings (Matt. 10:18). Their enemies will try to trip them up, but the Spirit of God will teach the witnesses what to say. Believers today must not use Matthew 10:19–20 as an excuse not to study the Word in preparation for witnessing, teaching, or preaching. These verses describe an emergency situation; they are not God's regular pattern for ministry today. Even during the days of the apostles, the Spirit gave them their messages when they faced their enemies (Acts 4:8). This unusual ministry of the Spirit will be evident during the tribulation period.

The tribulation will be a time of opposition and opportunity, but it will also be a time of *obligation*. The ambassadors of the King must "endure to the end" and faithfully perform their ministry, even if it costs them their lives. In spite of scourging, rejection by their families, persecution from city to city, and trials before leaders, the servants must remain true to their Lord. Their witness will be used by God to win others. Revelation 7:1–8 indicates that 144,000 Jewish witnesses will carry God's Word throughout the world during the tribulation, and as a result, great multitudes will come to Christ (Rev. 7:9ff.).

No doubt these words in Matthew 10 will become very precious and meaningful to witnesses during that time. We, today, can learn from these words, even though their primary interpretation and application are for God's servants at a future time. No matter how difficult our circumstances may be, we can turn opposition into opportunities for witness. We can trust the Spirit of God to help us remember what the Lord has taught us (John 14:26). Instead of fleeing and looking for an easier place, we can "endure to the end," knowing that God will help us and see us through.

Instructions for Present Disciples (10:24–42)

While the truths in this section would apply to God's servants during any period of Bible history, they seem to have a special significance for the church today. The emphasis is, "Fear not!" (Matt. 10:26, 28, 31). The particular fear Christ discussed is explained in Matthew 10:32–33: the fear of confessing Christ openly before men. God has no "secret service." The public confession of faith in Christ is one evidence of true salvation (Rom. 10:9–10). Several reasons show why we must

not be afraid to openly confess Christ. Let's examine these reasons that are found in Matthew 10.

Suffering is to be expected (vv. 24–25). Men persecuted Jesus Christ when He was ministering on earth, so why should we expect anything different? We are His disciples, and the disciple does not "outrank" the Master. They said that Jesus was in league with Satan (Beelzebub: lord of the dung; lord of the house), so they will say the same thing about His followers. However, we should count it a privilege to suffer *for* Him and *with* Him (Acts 5:41; Phil. 3:10).

God will bring everything to light (vv. 26–27). The enemies of Christ use secret and deceptive means to oppose the gospel. But true believers are open and courageous in their lives and witness. We have nothing to hide. "In secret have I said nothing," said Jesus (John 18:20). False witnesses lied about Jesus during His trial, but God saw to it that the truth came out. We have nothing to fear because the Lord will one day reveal the secrets of men's hearts (Rom. 2:16) and expose them and judge them. Our task is not to please men, but to proclaim God's message. The present judgment of men does not frighten us, because we are living in the light of the future judgment of God.

We fear God alone (v. 28). All that men can do is kill the body, and, if they do, the believer's soul goes home to be with the Lord. But God is able to destroy *both* body and soul in hell! Of course, God will never condemn one of His own children (John 5:24; Rom. 8:1). Martin Luther caught this truth when he wrote

> Let goods and kindred go,
> This mortal life also;
> The body they may kill:
> God's truth abideth still;
> His kingdom is forever.

The person who fears God alone need never fear any man or group of men. The fear of God is the fear that cancels fear.

God cares for His own (vv. 29–31). It did not cost much to purchase sparrows in the market. If we compare these verses with Luke 12:6, we discover that sparrows were so cheap that the dealer threw in an extra one! Yet the Father knows when a sparrow falls to the ground, *and the Father is there*. If God cares for sparrows in such a marvelous way, will He not also care for His own who are serving Him? He certainly will! To God, we are of greater value than many sparrows.

God is concerned about all of the details of our lives. Even the hairs of our head are numbered—not "counted" in a total, but numbered individually! God sees the sparrow fall to the ground, and God sees when a hair falls from the head of one of His children. When He protects His own, He protects them down to the individual hairs (Luke 21:18). There is no need for us to fear when God is exercising such wonderful care over us.

Christ honors those who confess Him (vv. 32–33). To confess Him means much more than to make a statement with the lips. It also means to back up that statement with the life. It is one thing to say, "Jesus Christ is Lord," and quite another thing to surrender to Him and obey His will. The walk and the talk must go together.

In heaven, Jesus has two special ministries. As our High Priest, He gives us grace to keep us from sinning. As our Advocate, He forgives and restores us when we do sin (1 John 2:1–2). The *merits* of His heavenly intercessory work do not depend on our faithfulness, for He is faithful even if we are not (2 Tim. 2:12–13). But the *benefits* of His heavenly ministry are for those who are faithful to Him. When Christ confesses us before the Father, He is securing for us the benefits of His sacrificial work on the cross. When He denies us before the Father, He is unable to share these graces with us. The fault is ours, not His.

But something else is involved. One day we shall stand before His judgment seat, where the rewards will be distributed (2 Cor. 5:10; Rom. 14:10). If we have denied Him, we will lose rewards and the joy of hearing His "Well done." To be sure, anyone who denies Him on earth may be forgiven. Peter denied the Lord three times, was forgiven, and was restored.

We cannot escape conflict (vv. 34–39). Once we have identified with Jesus Christ and confessed Him, we are part of a war. We did not start the war; God declared war on Satan (Gen. 3:15). On the night our Lord was born, the angels declared, "On earth peace" (Luke 2:14). But Jesus seemed to deny this truth. "I came not to send peace, but a sword" (Matt. 10:34). Had Israel accepted Him, He would have given them peace. But the people refused Him, and the result was "a sword." Instead of there being "peace on earth," there is "peace in heaven" (Luke 19:38). He has made peace through the blood of His cross (Col. 1:20) so that men can be reconciled to God and to each other.

The only way a believer can escape conflict is to deny Christ and compromise his witness, and this would be sin. Then the believer would be at war with God and with himself. We will be misunderstood and persecuted even by those who are the closest to us, yet we must not allow this to affect our witness. It is important that we suffer for Jesus' sake, and for righteousness's sake, and not because we ourselves are difficult to live with. There is a difference between the "offense of the cross" (Gal. 5:11) and offensive Christians.

Each believer must make the decision once and for all to love Christ supremely and take up his cross and follow Christ. The love in Matthew 10:37 is the motive for the cross in Matthew 10:38. To "carry the cross" does not mean to wear a pin on our lapel or put a sticker on our automobile. It means to confess Christ and obey Him in spite of shame and suffering. It means to die to self daily. If the Lord went to a cross for us, the least we can do is carry a cross for Him.

Matthew 10:39 presents us with only two alternatives: spare your life or sacrifice your life. There is no middle ground. If we protect our own interests, we will be losers; if we die to self and live for His interests, we will be winners. Since spiritual conflict is inevitable in this world, why not die to self and let Christ win the battle *for us* and in us? After all, the real war is *inside*—selfishness versus sacrifice.

We can be a blessing to others (vv. 40–42). Not everyone will reject our witness. There are those who will welcome us and receive a blessing. After all, we are the ambassadors of the King! Our King will see to it that they are rewarded for what they do. When people receive us, they welcome the King, for we are His representatives. Read 2 Samuel 10 for an example of what happens when people mistreat the envoys of the King.

The blessing, however, is not automatic. It all depends on the attitude of the host. If he receives the ambassador as a prophet (a spokesman for God), then he gets one reward; if he receives him only as a righteous man, there is another reward. But even a cup of cold water, given with the right spirit, brings its own reward.

Keep in mind that the theme of this last section is discipleship, not sonship. We become the children of God through faith in Christ; we are disciples as we faithfully follow Him and obey His will. Sonship does not change, but discipleship does change as we walk with Christ. There is a great need today for faithful disciples, believers who will learn from Christ and live for Him.

This brings us to the close of the first major division of Matthew, The Revelation of the King. We have seen His person (Matt. 1—4), His principles (Matt. 5—7), and His power (Matt. 8—10). How will the nation respond to this revelation?

CHAPTER NINE
Matthew 11—12
THE KING'S CONFLICTS

All of the evidence had been presented. John the Baptist had introduced the King to the nation. Jesus had revealed His person, principles, and power. It was now up to the leaders of the nation to make their decision. Instead of receiving their King, they began to rebel against Him. In these two chapters four areas of rebellion are presented.

Rebellion against His Prophet (11:1–30)

Explanation (vv. 1–15). John the Baptist was in prison in the fortress of Machaerus because he had courageously denounced the adulterous marriage of Herod Antipas and Herodias (Luke 3:19–20). It seems that the Jewish leaders would have opposed Herod and sought to free John, but they did nothing. Their attitude toward John reflected their feeling toward Jesus, for John had pointed to Jesus and honored Him.

It is not difficult to sympathize with John as he suffered in prison. He was a man of the desert, yet he was confined indoors. He was an active man, with a divine mandate to preach, yet he was silenced. He had announced judgment, and yet that judgment was slow in coming (Matt. 3:7–12). He received only partial reports of Jesus' ministry and could not see the total picture.

Our Lord's reply to John revealed both tact and tenderness. He reminded John of the Old Testament prophecies about the works of Messiah (Isa. 29:18–19; 35:4–6). John's disciples had already told him what Jesus was doing (Luke 7:18), but Jesus asked them to "show John again." John had come in the spirit and power of Elijah (Luke 1:17), and even Elijah had his days of discouragement! Jesus assured John that He was fulfilling the Father's will.

After answering John, Jesus then praised him. John was not a "popular preacher" who catered to the crowd, nor was he a reed in the wind who vacillated with every change. He was a man of conviction and courage, the greatest of the prophets. The fact that John was privileged to announce the Messiah gave him this high position. His ministry marked the climax of the law and the prophets.

In what sense was John "Elijah who was to come" (Matt. 11:14)? He came in the spirit and power of Elijah (Luke 1:17) and even dressed and ministered like Elijah (2 Kings 1:7–8; Matt. 3:4). Like Elijah, John had a message of judgment for the apostate nation of Israel. His ministry was prophesied (Isa. 40:3), and he fulfilled it. But Malachi 4:5 prophesied the coming of Elijah "before the coming of the great and dreadful day of the Lord." This "day of the Lord" is the time of tribulation that will come on all the earth (see Matt. 24:15). But no such judgments followed the ministry of John the Baptist. Why?

John's ministry was to prepare the nation for Jesus and to present Jesus to the nation (Luke 1:15–17; John 1:29–34). Had the people received John's witness and accepted their Messiah, John would have fulfilled the prophecies literally. Instead, they were fulfilled in a spiritual sense in the lives of those who trusted Christ. Jesus made this clear in Matthew 17:10–13. Many Bible students believe that Malachi 4:5 will be fulfilled literally when Elijah comes as one of the "two witnesses" spoken of in Revelation 11.

The common people held John in high regard (Matt. 21:26), and many of them had repented and been baptized by John. But the leaders refused to honor John, and this proved their unbelief and hardness of heart. Instead of being *childlike* and humbling themselves, the leaders were *childish* and stubborn, like children pouting because they could not have their way. The parable in Matthew 11:16–19 revealed the spiritual condition of the leaders, and unfortunately it also reveals the hearts of unbelievers today.

Condemnation (vv. 16–24). How unusual to find the word *woe* on the lips of Jesus! This word means judgment, but it also includes pity and sorrow. How tragic that these cities should treat lightly their opportunities to see and hear the Christ of God, and be saved! The Gentile cities of Tyre and Sidon, and the godless cities of Sodom and Gomorrah, would have repented had they seen the miracles that Jesus and His disciples performed. Capernaum had been "exalted to heaven" by being privileged to have the Messiah live there. Yet her greater privileges only brought greater responsibilities and greater judgment. Five of the ten miracles recorded in Matthew 8—9 were performed in Capernaum.

Invitation (vv. 25–30). Why did the religious leaders rebel against John and Jesus? Because they (the leaders) were intellectually and spiritually proud and would not become little babes in humility and honesty. There is a vast difference between the spoiled children of the parable (Matt. 11:16–19) and the submissive children of this statement of praise. The Father reveals Himself to the Son, and the Son reveals Himself and the Father to those who are willing to come to the Son in faith. These verses indicate both the sovereignty of the Father and the responsibility of the sinner. Three commands summarize this invitation.

"Come." The Pharisees all said "Do!" and tried to make the people follow Moses and the traditions. But true salvation is found only in a person, Jesus Christ. To come to Him means to trust Him. This invitation is open to those who are exhausted and burdened down. That is exactly how the people felt under the yoke of pharisaical legalism (Matt. 23:4; Acts 15:10).

"Take." This is a deeper experience. When we come to Christ by faith, *He gives* us rest. When we take His yoke and learn, *we find* rest, that deeper rest of surrender and obedience. The first is "peace with God" (Rom. 5:1); the second is "the peace of God" (Phil. 4:6–8). To "take a yoke" in that day meant to become a disciple. When we submit to Christ, we are yoked to Him. The word *easy* means "well-fitting"; He has just the yoke that is tailor-made for our lives and needs. The burden of doing His will is not a heavy one (John 5:3).

"Learn." The first two commands represent a crisis as we come and yield to Christ, but this step is a *process.* As we learn more about Him, we find a deeper peace, because we trust Him more. Life is simplified and unified around the person of Christ. This invitation is for "all"—not just the people of Israel (Matt. 10:5–6).

Rebellion against His Principles (12:1–21)

Jesus deliberately violated the Sabbath traditions on several occasions. He had taught the people that mere external laws could never save them or make them holy; true righteousness had to come from the heart. The Hebrew word *sabat* means "repose or rest," which explains why Matthew introduced these Sabbath conflicts at this point. Jesus offers rest to all who will come to Him; there is no rest in mere religious observances.

It was lawful to satisfy your hunger from your neighbor's field (Deut. 23:24–25). But to do it on the Sabbath was a breach of the law according to the traditions of the scribes and Pharisees, for it meant doing work. Jesus gave a threefold reply to their accusation.

He appealed to a king (vv. 3–4). The consecrated bread was to be eaten only by the priests, yet David and his soldiers ate it. Certainly the Son of David had a right to eat His Father's grain from the field! And if David broke the law and was not condemned, surely Jesus could break man's traditions and be guiltless (see 1 Sam. 21:1ff.).

He appealed to the priests (vv. 5–6). The priests had to offer a given number of sacrifices on the Sabbath (Num. 28:9–10) and yet were not condemned. In fact, their service was in obedience to the law given by God. This suggests that man's traditions about the Sabbath were wrong, for they contradicted God's own law.

He appealed to a prophet (v. 7). The quotation is from Hosea 6:6, one that Jesus had already quoted (Matt. 9:13). The Sabbath law was given to Israel as a mark of her relationship to God (Ex. 20:9–11; 31:13–17; Neh. 9:12–15). But it was also an act of mercy for both man and beast, to give them needed rest each week. Any religious law that is contrary to mercy and the care of nature should be looked on with suspicion. God wants mercy, not religious sacrifice. He wants love, not legalism. The Pharisees who sacrificed to obey their Sabbath laws thought they were serving God. When they accused Christ and His disciples, they thought they were defending God. How like religious legalists today!

Note that Jesus appealed to prophet, priest, and king, for He is Prophet, Priest, and King. Note too the three "greater" statements that He made: as the *Priest,* He is "greater than the temple" (Matt. 12:6); as *Prophet,* He is "greater than Jonah" (Matt. 12:41); and as *King,* He is "greater than Solomon" (Matt. 12:42).

In declaring Himself "Lord of the Sabbath," Jesus was actually affirming equality with God, for God had established the Sabbath (Gen. 2:1–3). He then proved this claim by healing the man with the paralyzed hand. It is sad that the religious leaders used this man and his handicap as a weapon to fight against Jesus. But the Lord was not afraid of their threats. Not doing good on the Sabbath day (or any other day) is the same as doing evil. Jesus argued that if a farmer could care for his animals on the Sabbath, shouldn't we care for man, made in the image of God?

They responded to this deliberate challenge by plotting to kill Him. They had accused Him of blasphemy when He healed the paralytic (Matt. 9:1–8),

and of lack of separation when He ate with Matthew's friends (Matt. 9:11–13). But this deed was even worse. He had deliberately violated the law of God! He had *worked* on the Sabbath by harvesting grain and healing a man.

Our Lord's response to their hatred was withdrawal. He did not openly fight His enemies, but fulfilled the prophecy in Isaiah 42:1–4. His enemies were but broken reeds and smoking flax. Note the double mention of the Gentiles, another hint from Matthew that Israel would reject her King and the kingdom would go to the Gentiles.

The Lord's withdrawal at this point is an anticipation of His "retirement" described in Matthew 14—20. During that time, Jesus avoided direct conflict with His enemies that He might stay on the "divine timetable" and be crucified on schedule. Also, during that time, He taught His disciples and prepared them for His crucifixion.

Rebellion against His Power (12:22–37)

The accusation (vv. 22–24). The man who was brought to Jesus was certainly in a sad state, for he was blind, unable to speak, and possessed with a demon. Jesus delivered the man, something the Pharisees could not do. Their accusation was that He worked by the power of Satan and not by the power of God. They did not agree with Nicodemus's evaluation of His miracles (John 3:2).

The answer (vv. 25–30). Jesus pointed out that their statement was illogical and impractical. Why would Satan fight against himself? Jesus affirmed that Satan had a kingdom, for he is the god of this age (Matt. 4:8–9; John 12:31). He also stated that Satan had a "house," which seems to refer to the body of the man who was possessed (Matt. 12:43–44). If Satan casts out his own demonic helpers, then he is opposing himself, dividing his kingdom, and destroying his house.

Their accusation was also illogical from their own point of view, though they did not see it. There were Jewish exorcists (see Acts 19:13–16) who apparently were successful. By whose power did *they* cast out demons? If it was by Satan's power, they were in league with the devil! Of course, no Pharisee was about to draw that conclusion.

Jesus was able to cast out demons because He had first defeated Satan, the prince of the demons. Jesus entered Satan's kingdom, overcame his power, and claimed his spoils. His victory was through the Spirit of God ("the finger of God," Luke 11:20) and not in the power of the evil one. This means that God is Victor over Satan, and that men must decide on whose side they will stand. There can be no compromise. We are either with God or against God.

The admonition (vv. 31–37). Jesus warned them that their words gave evidence of the evil in their hearts. The sin against the Holy Spirit is not a matter of speech; the words spoken are only "fruit" from the sinful heart. If the heart is a treasury of good, that good will overflow through the lips and do good to others. But if the heart is a treasury of evil, that evil will spill over through the lips and do harm to the person speaking and those listening.

But what is this terrible "sin against the Holy Spirit"? Can it be committed today, and, if so, how? Our Lord said that God will forgive evil words spoken against the Son, but not against the Spirit. Does this mean that the Holy Spirit is more important than Jesus Christ, God's Son? Surely not. We often hear the name of God or Jesus Christ used in blasphemy, but rarely if ever the name of the Holy Spirit. How can God forgive words spoken against His Son, and yet not forgive words spoken against the Spirit?

It appears that this situation existed *only while Christ was ministering on earth.* Jesus did not appear to be different from any other Jewish man (Isa. 53:2). To speak against Christ could be forgiven *while He was on earth.* But when the Spirit of God came at Pentecost as proof that Jesus was the Christ, and was alive, to reject the witness of the Spirit was final. The only consequence would be judgment.

When the leaders rejected John the Baptist, they were rejecting *the Father* who sent him. When they rejected Jesus, they were rejecting *the Son.* But when they rejected the ministry of the apostles, they rejected *the Holy Spirit*—and that is the end. There is no more witness. Such rejection cannot be forgiven.

The phrase "idle word" in Matthew 12:36 means "words that accomplish nothing." If God is going to judge our "small talk," how much more will He judge our deliberate words? It is by our conversation *at unguarded moments* that we reveal our true character.

Is there an "unpardonable sin" today? Yes, the final rejection of Jesus Christ. Jesus made it clear that *all* sins can be forgiven (Matt. 12:31). Adultery, murder, blasphemy, and other sins can all be forgiven; they are not unpardonable. But God cannot forgive the rejection of His Son. It is the Spirit who bears witness to Christ (John 15:26) and who convicts the lost sinner (John 16:7–11).

Rebellion against His Person (12:38–50)

"The Jews require a sign" (1 Cor. 1:22). To ask for a sign was evidence of unbelief: They wanted Him to *prove* that He was the Messiah. We wonder what further proof could have been given! Had they searched their own Scriptures, and sincerely examined His life, they would have concluded, "This is the Son of God!" But for Jesus to have given them a sign would have been wrong. He would have catered to their unbelief and allowed them to set the standards for faith. No matter what miracle He performed, it would not have pleased them.

Jesus gave three responses to their challenge.

He reviewed their history (vv. 39–42). The prophet Jonah was a Jew sent to the Gentiles, and the Queen of Sheba was a Gentile who came to visit Solomon, a Jew (2 Chron. 9:1–12). Because of the bitterness between the Jews and the Gentiles, this reference to the Gentiles must have irritated the Pharisees. But we have noted other occasions when either Jesus or Matthew mentioned the Gentiles.

Jonah was a sign to the people of Nineveh because he had experienced (in the great fish) "death," burial, and resurrection. The only sign Jesus would give to His nation was death, burial, and resurrection. The messages in the first seven chapters of Acts center on the resurrection of Christ, not on His death on the cross. The Jews of that day believed that He had died, for this was the chief topic of conversation (Luke 24:18). *But they did not believe that He was alive* (Matt. 28:11–15). In Acts 2—7, the Holy Spirit gave to the nation of Israel abundant witness that Jesus was alive. This was the only sign they needed.

Jesus is greater than Jonah in many ways. He is greater in His person, for Jonah was a mere man. He was greater in His obedience, for Jonah disobeyed God and was chastened. Jesus actually died, while Jonah's "grave" was in the belly of the great fish. Jesus arose from the dead under His own power. Jonah ministered only to one city, while Jesus gave His life for the whole world. Certainly Jesus was greater in His love, for Jonah did not love the people of Nineveh—he wanted them to die. Jonah's message saved Nineveh from judgment; he was a messenger of the wrath of God. Jesus' message was that of grace and salvation. When we trust Christ, we are not only saved from judgment, but we receive eternal, abundant life.

Jesus is also greater than Solomon in His wisdom, wealth, and works. The Queen of Sheba was amazed at what she saw in Solomon's kingdom, but what we have in the kingdom of God through Christ far surpasses Solomon's glories. To sit at Christ's table and hear His words, and to share His blessings, is much more satisfying than to visit and admire the most spectacular kingdom, even that of Solomon.

The main lesson behind this history lesson is this: The citizens of Nineveh will witness against the rulers of Israel, for they repented at Jonah's preaching. The Queen of Sheba will also witness against them. She traveled a long distance to hear Solomon's wisdom, yet the Jewish leaders rejected the wisdom of Christ, *who was in their very midst!* The greater the opportunity, the greater the judgment. It is a tragic feature in the history of Israel that the nation rejected their deliverers the first time, but accepted them the second time. This was true with Joseph, Moses, David, the prophets (Matt. 23:29), and Jesus Christ.

He revealed their hearts (vv. 43–45). We must connect these verses with Matthew 12:24–29. Satan's "house" is the body of the person who is possessed by the demon. It appears that the demons are restless and seek bodies in which to reside (Matt. 8:28–31). When the demon left, this man's life was changed for the better, *but his life was still empty.* When the demon returned, he brought others with him, and the man's life ended in tragedy.

The primary application is to the nation of Israel, especially that generation present when Jesus ministered on earth. The nation had been purged of the demon of idolatry, which had plagued them in the Old Testament. But reformation was not enough. Reformation could cleanse, but it could not fill. The nation should have received the Savior and been filled with spiritual life. Instead, the people rejected Him, and the end was destruction.

There is a personal application. It is not enough to clean house; we must also invite in the right tenant. The Pharisees were proud of their "clean houses," *but their hearts were empty!* Mere religion, or reformation, will not save. There must be regeneration, the receiving of Christ into the heart (see Rev. 3:20). We cannot be neutral about Jesus Christ.

He rejected their honor (vv. 46–50). Even our Lord's earthly family did not fully understand Him or His ministry (John 7:1–5). Some of His friends thought He was mad (Mark 3:21). But Jesus did not want the honor that comes from people. While He was not disrespectful toward His physical family, He did emphasize the family of God.

Note His use of the word *whosoever* (Matt. 12:50). This paralleled His beautiful invitation in Matthew 11:28–30, where He encouraged all to trust Him. If the nation would not receive Him, at least individuals within the nation—and among the Gentiles—could trust Him. But what will happen to the promised kingdom?

CHAPTER TEN
Matthew 13
THE KING'S SECRETS

This chapter records the events of a crisis day in the ministry of Jesus Christ. He knew that the growing opposition of the religious leaders would lead to His crucifixion. This fact He had to explain to His disciples. But their logical question would be, "What will happen to the kingdom about which we have been preaching?" That question is answered in this series of parables. So, He first explained the truth concerning the kingdom, and then later explained to them the facts about the cross.

Our Lord's use of parables puzzled the disciples. He had used some parables in His teaching already, but on that day He gave a series of seven interrelated parables, then added an eighth. The word *parable* means "to cast alongside." It is a story, or comparison, that is put alongside something else to help make the lesson clear. But these are not ordinary parables; Jesus called them "the mysteries of the kingdom of heaven" (Matt. 13:11). In the New Testament, a "mystery" is a

spiritual truth understood only by divine revelation. It is a "sacred secret" known only to those "on the inside" who learn from the Lord and obey Him.

In this series of parables, Jesus explained the course of the gospel in the world. If Israel had received Him as King, the blessings would have flowed out from Jerusalem to the ends of the earth. But the nation rejected Him, and God had to institute a new program on earth. During this present age, "the kingdom of heaven" is a mixture of true and false, good and bad, as pictured in these parables. It is "Christendom," professing allegiance to the King, and yet containing much that is contrary to the principles of the King.

Why did Jesus teach in parables? Two reasons were given: because of the sluggishness of the people (Matt. 13:10–17) and because it was prophesied in Psalm 78:2 (Matt. 13:34–35). Jesus did not teach in parables to confuse or condemn the people. Rather, He sought to excite their interest and arouse their curiosity. These parables would give light to those with trusting, searching hearts. But they would bring darkness to the unconcerned and unrepentant.

The seven parables describe for us the spiritual course of "the kingdom of heaven" in this present age. In them we see three stages of spiritual development.

The Beginning of the Kingdom (13:1–9, 18–23)
The parable of the sower does not begin with "The kingdom of heaven is like" because it describes how the kingdom begins. It begins with the preaching of the Word, the planting of the seed in the hearts of people. When we say, "Let me plant this thought in your mind," we express the idea of this parable. The seed is God's Word; the various soils represent different kinds of hearts; and the varied results show the different responses to the Word of God. Jesus explained this parable so there is no doubt of its meaning.

Why compare God's Word to seed? Because the Word is "living and powerful" (Heb. 4:12 SCO). Unlike the words of men, the Word of God has life in it, and that life can be imparted to those who will believe. The truth of God must take root in the heart, be cultivated, and be permitted to bear fruit. It is shocking to realize that three fourths of the seed did not bear fruit. Jesus did not describe an age of great harvest, but one in which the Word would be rejected. He was not impressed with the "great multitudes" that followed Him, for He knew that most of the people would not receive His Word within and bear fruit.

Fruit is the test of true salvation (Matt. 7:16). This would include holiness (Rom. 6:22), Christian character (Gal. 5:22–23), good works (Col. 1:10), winning others to Christ (Rom. 1:13), sharing what we have (Rom. 15:25–28), and praising God (Heb. 13:15). If a plant is to bear fruit, it must be rooted in soil and exposed to sunshine.

In the parable, the sun represents persecution that comes because of the Word. *Persecution helps believers grow.* But the sunshine will kill a plant with no roots.

This explains why some "believers" do not last: Their faith was weak, their understanding was meager, and their decision was not sincere. It is possible to "believe" and yet not be saved (John 2:23–25). Unless there is fruit in the life, there is not saving faith in the heart.

Nineteen times in Matthew 13 we find the word *hear*" The parable of the sower is found in the first three Gospels, and in each one, the closing admonition is different. It is important that we hear God's Word, because "Faith cometh by hearing, and hearing by the Word of God" (Rom. 10:17). Jesus said, "Who hath ears to hear" (Matt. 13:9), "Take heed *what* ye hear" (Mark 4:24 my emphasis), and "Take heed *how* ye hear" (Luke 8:18 my emphasis).

Opposition to the Kingdom (Matt. 13:24–43)

Satan opposes the kingdom by trying to snatch the Word from hearts (Matt. 13:4, 19). But when that fails, he has other ways of attacking God's work. These three parables reveal that Satan is primarily an *imitator:* He plants false Christians, he encourages a false growth, and he introduces false doctrine.

The tares—false Christians (vv. 24–30, 36–43). Satan cannot uproot the plants (true Christians), so he plants counterfeit Christians in their midst. In this parable, the good seed is not the Word of God. It represents people converted through trusting the Word. The field is not human hearts; the field is the world. Christ is sowing true believers in various places that they might bear fruit (John 12:23–26). But, wherever Christ sows a true Christian, Satan comes and sows a counterfeit.

We must beware of Satan's counterfeits. He has counterfeit Christians (2 Cor. 11:26) who believe a counterfeit gospel (Gal. 1:6–9). He encourages a counterfeit righteousness (Rom. 10:1–3), and even has a counterfeit church (Rev. 2:9). At the end of the age, he will produce a counterfeit Christ (2 Thess. 2:1–12).

We must also stay awake to make sure that Satan's ministers do not get into the true fellowship and do damage (2 Peter 2; 1 John 4:1–6). It is when God's people go to sleep that Satan works. Our task is not to pull up the false, but to plant the true. (This does not refer to discipline within the local church.) We are not detectives but evangelists! We must oppose Satan and expose his lies. But we must also sow the Word of God and bear fruit in the place where He has planted us.

What will happen to the tares? God will gather them together and burn them. It is interesting to see that some of this "bundling" is already going on as various religious groups merge and strive for union. Spiritual unity among true Christians is one thing, but religious uniformity among mere professing Christians is quite another. It is difficult to tell the false from the true today, but at the end of the age, the angels will separate them.

The mustard seed—false growth (vv. 31–32). In the East, the mustard seed symbolizes something small and insignificant. It produces a large plant, but not a "tree" in the strictest sense. However, the plant is large enough for birds to sit in the branches.

Since Jesus did not explain this parable, we must use what He did explain in the other parables to find its meaning. The birds in the parable of the sower represented Satan (Matt. 13:19). Passages like Daniel 4:12 and Ezekiel 17:23 indicate that a tree is a symbol of a world power. These facts suggest that the parable teaches an abnormal growth of the kingdom of heaven, one that makes it possible for Satan to work in it. Certainly "Christendom" has become a worldwide power with a complex organization of many branches. What started in a humble manner today boasts of material possessions and political influences.

Some make this parable teach the worldwide success of the gospel. But that would contradict what Jesus taught in the first parable. If anything, the New Testament teaches a growing decline in the ministry of the gospel as the end of the age draws near.

The leaven—false doctrine (v. 33). The mustard seed illustrates the false *outward* expansion of the kingdom, while the leaven illustrates the *inward* development of false doctrine and false living. Throughout the Bible, leaven is a symbol of evil. It had to be removed from the Jewish homes during Passover (Ex. 12:15–19; 13:7). It was excluded from the sacrifices (Ex. 34:35), with the exception of the loaves used at the Feast of Pentecost (Lev. 23:15–21). But there the loaves symbolized Jews and Gentiles in the church, and there is sin in the church.

Jesus used leaven to picture hypocrisy (Luke 12:1), false teaching (Matt. 16:6–12), and worldly compromise (Matt. 22:16–21). Paul used leaven to picture carnality in the church (1 Cor. 5:6–8) as well as false doctrine (Gal. 5:9). Sin is like leaven (yeast): It quietly grows, it corrupts, and it "puffs up" (1 Cor. 4:18–19; 5:2; 8:1). It would seem that making the growth of the leaven a picture of the spread of the gospel throughout the world would violate the meaning of this important symbol. It would also contradict the other parables.

Satan has worked hard to introduce false doctrine and false living into the ministry of the Word of God. From the very early days of the church, true believers have battled false doctrine and hypocrisy. How sad it is that some churches and schools that were once true to the Word have turned from the truth to fables. "Prove all things; hold fast that which is good" is sound counsel (1 Thess. 5:21).

The kingdom of heaven began with the sowing of the Word of God in the hearts of men. Much of the seed did not bear fruit, but some was fruitful. Satan opposed the work of God by sowing counterfeit Christians, by encouraging a false growth, and by introducing false doctrine. It would seem that Satan is winning! But the test is at *the end* of the age, not *during* the age.

The Outcome of the Kingdom (13:44–50)

At the close of this age, God will have three peoples:

the Jews (the hidden treasure), the church (the pearl), and the saved Gentile nations who will enter into the kingdom (the dragnet).

The hidden treasure (v. 44). The common interpretation of this parable is that the sinner finds Christ and gives up all that he possesses to gain Him and be saved. But this interpretation presents several problems. To begin with, Jesus Christ is not a hidden treasure. He is perhaps the best-known Person of history. In the second place, the sinner cannot "find Christ" for he is blind and stubborn (Rom. 3:10ff.). It is the Savior who finds the lost sinner (Luke 19:10). And no sinner could ever *purchase* salvation! Please note that the man in the parable did not purchase the treasure; he purchased *the whole field*. "The field is the world" (Matt. 13:38). Must the lost sinner purchase the world to gain Christ? Does he hide Him again?

Once again, Old Testament symbolism assists us in our interpretation. The treasure is the nation of Israel (Ex. 19:5; Ps. 135:4). That nation was placed in the world to bring glory to God, but it failed. It became a nation hidden, a treasure not being invested to produce dividends for God. Jesus Christ gave His all to purchase the whole world in order to save the nation (John 11:51). On the cross, Jesus died for the whole world, but in a special way, He died for Israel (Isa. 53:8). The nation suffered judgment and seeming destruction, but in God's sight it is "hidden" and will be revealed again in glory.

There is, then, a future for Israel. Politically, the nation was reborn on May 14, 1948. But the nation is far from what it ought to be spiritually. God sees Israel as His treasure, and one day He will establish her in her glorious kingdom.

The pearl of great price (vv. 45–46). A well-known gospel song perpetuates the interpretation that this pearl is Jesus Christ and His salvation. But the same objections apply to this interpretation as applied to the previous parable. The sinner does not find Christ; Christ finds the sinner. No sinner is able to pay for salvation, even though he sells all that he has.

The pearl represents the church. The Bible makes a distinction between Jews, Gentiles, and the church (1 Cor. 10:32). Today, the church, the body of Christ, is composed of believing Jews and Gentiles (Eph. 2:11ff.). Unlike most other gems, the pearl is a *unity*—it cannot be carved like a diamond or emerald. The church is a unity (Eph. 4:4–6), even though the professing church on earth is divided. Like a pearl, the church is the product of suffering. Christ died for the church (Eph. 5:25) and His suffering on the cross made possible her birth.

A pearl grows gradually, and the church grows gradually as the Spirit convicts and converts sinners. No one can see the making of the pearl, for it is hidden in the shell of the oyster under the waters. No one can see the growth of His church in the world. The church is among the nations today (waters in the Bible represent nations; Dan. 7:1–3; Rev. 13:1; 17:15) and one day will be revealed in its beauty.

So, in spite of Satan's subtle working in this world, Christ is forming His church. He sold all that He had to purchase His church, and nothing Satan can do will cause Him to fail. There is but one church, a pearl of great price, though there are many local churches. Not everyone who is a member of a local church belongs to the one church, the body of Christ. It is only through repentance and faith in Christ that we become a part of His church. Of course, all true believers ought to identify with a local assembly where they can worship and serve.

The net (vv. 47–50). The preaching of the gospel in the world does not convert the world. It is like a huge dragnet that gathers all kinds of fish, some good and some bad. The professing church today has in it both true and false believers (the parable of the tares) and good and bad. At the end of the age, God will separate the true believers from the false and the good from the bad. When Jesus Christ returns to earth to fight the battle of Armageddon (Rev. 19:11ff.), He will separate believers and unbelievers *already on the earth.* These are living people who are not a part of the church (which was already in heaven) or Israel. These Gentiles will be dealt with in righteousness: The saved will enter into the kingdom, but the unsaved will be cast into the furnace of fire. The same idea is found in the "sheep and goats" parable (Matt. 25:31ff.).

Twice in this series of parables Jesus used the phrase "the end of the world" (Matt. 13:39, 49). He was not referring to the end of this "church age," because the truth about the church was not shared with the disciples until later (Matt. 16:18). The "age" He referred to is the Jewish age at the close of the great tribulation described in Matthew 24:1–31 and Revelation 6—19. We must be careful not to "read into" these passages in Matthew the truths later given through Paul and the other apostles.

When Jesus had completed this series of parables, He asked His disciples if they understood them, and they confidently replied, "Yes, Lord." Understanding involves responsibility. To explain this, the Lord added a final parable (Matt. 13:51–52) to remind them of their responsibilities.

They must be scribes who discover the truth. The scribes began as a noble group under the leadership of Ezra. Their purpose was to preserve the law, study it, and apply its truths to daily life. Over the years, their noble cause degenerated into a routine task of preserving traditions and man-made interpretations, and adding burdens to the lives of the people (Luke 11:46–52). They were so wrapped up in the past that they ignored the present! Instead of sharing living truth from God's Word, they merchandised dead doctrines and "embalmed" traditions that could not help the people.

As believers, we do not search *after* truth, because we have truth in God's Son (John 14:6) and God's

Word (John 17:17). We are taught by the Spirit of Truth (John 16:13) who is truth (1 John 5:6). We search *into* truth that we might discover more truth. We are scribes—students—who sit at the feet of Jesus and listen to His words. One joy of the Christian life is the privilege of learning God's truth from God's Word. But we must not stop there.

They must be disciples who do the truth. "Therefore every scribe who becomes a disciple of the kingdom of heaven" is a more accurate translation of Matthew 13:52. The scribe emphasizes *learning,* but the disciple emphasizes *living.* Disciples are doers of the Word (James 1:22ff.), and they learn by doing.

It is difficult to keep our lives balanced. We often emphasize learning at the expense of living. Or, we may get so busy serving God that we do not take time to listen to His Word. Every scribe must be a disciple, and every disciple must be a scribe.

They must be stewards who dispense the truth. The scribes preserved the law but did not invest it in the lives of the people. The treasure of the law was encrusted by man's traditions. The seed was not planted so it could bear fruit. The "spiritual gold and silver" was not put to work so it could produce dividends. As Christians we should be conservative but not preservative.

The steward guards the treasure, but he also dispenses it as it is needed. He dispenses both the old and the new. New principles and insights are based on old truths. The new cannot contradict the old because the old comes out of the new (Lev. 26:10). The new without the old is mere novelty and will not last. But the old does no good unless it is given new applications in life today. We need both.

When Jesus finished these parables, He went across the sea in a storm and delivered the demoniacs in the country of the Gadarenes. Matthew recorded this in 8:28–34. It was then that Jesus went to His hometown of Nazareth, and this event Matthew recorded in 13:53–58.

Two things amazed the people of Nazareth: the Lord's words and His works. However, they did not trust in Him, and this limited His ministry. What caused the people to doubt Him? They were too familiar with Him in a human way, for He had grown up in their midst. It was a case of knowing Him after the flesh (see 2 Cor. 5:16) and not having the spiritual discernment that God gives to those who will yield to Him (Matt. 11:25–30). These people walked by sight and not by faith.

But, if His own friends and family did not trust Him, what hope was there that the nation would believe on Him? Early in His ministry, Jesus had preached at Nazareth (Luke 4:16–31) and had been rejected, and now He was rejected again. This was His final visit to Nazareth; those villagers had no more opportunities. Jesus would be known as "Jesus of Nazareth," and His followers would be called "Nazarenes," but Nazareth would not receive Him.

Matthew chose this event as a fitting close to the section "Rebellion against the King."

CHAPTER ELEVEN
Matthew 14
THE KING'S WITHDRAWAL

Chapters 14—20 I have called "The Retirement of the King." During the period of time recorded by Matthew in these chapters, Jesus often withdrew from the crowds and spent time alone with His disciples (see Matt. 14:13; 15:21, 29; 16:13; 17:1–8). There were several reasons for these withdrawals: the growing hostility of His enemies, the need for physical rest, and the need to prepare His disciples for His future death on the cross. Unfortunately, the disciples were often caught up in the excitement generated by the crowds that wanted to make Jesus their King (see John 6:15).

However, we must not think that these withdrawals, or periods of retirement from the crowds, were periods of inactivity. Often the crowds followed Jesus and He was unable to remain alone. He would unselfishly minister to their needs in spite of His own need for rest and solitude. In Matthew 14—20, we will see these three groups of people: Christ's enemies, the needy multitudes, and the disciples. As the story reaches its climax, it appears that the enemies have won, but this is not true. In the closing chapter, Matthew describes the risen King commissioning His disciples to go into all the world and share the good news with the multitudes!

We see these same three groups of people in this chapter and our Lord's responses to them.

His Enemies: Caution (14:1–13)
The Herod family looms large in the four gospels and the book of Acts, and it is easy to confuse the various rulers.

Herod the Great founded the dynasty and ruled from 37 BC to 4 BC. He was not a true Jew by birth, but was an Edomite, a descendant of Esau. "He was a heathen in practice, and a monster in character" *(Unger's Bible Dictionary).* He had nine wives (some say ten), and he thought nothing of slaying his own sons or wives if they got in the way of his plans. It was he who had the infants slain in Bethlehem (Matt. 2:13–18).

Herod Antipas, the Herod of this chapter, was a son of Herod the Great. His title was "tetrarch," which means "ruler over the fourth part of the kingdom." He ruled from 4 BC to AD 39, and his rule was deceptive and selfish. He loved luxury and was very ambitious to become a great ruler.

Herod Agrippa is the Herod who imprisoned Peter and killed James (Acts 12). He was a grandson of Herod the Great.

Herod Agrippa II was the Herod who tried Paul (Acts 25:13ff.). He was a son of Agrippa I.

All of the Herods had Edomite blood in them, and, like their ancestor Esau, they were hostile to the Jews (Gen. 25:19ff.). They practiced the Jewish religion when it helped fulfill their plans for gaining more power and wealth.

Herod Antipas was guilty of gross sin: He had eloped with Herodias, the wife of his half-brother Philip I, divorcing his own wife and sending her back to her father, the king of Petra (Lev. 18:16; 20:21). Herod listened to the voice of temptation and plunged himself into terrible sin.

But there were other voices that God sent to warn Herod.

The voice of the prophet (vv. 3–5). Boldly, John the Baptist warned Herod and called him to repent. John knew that the sin of a ruler would only pollute the land and make it easier for others to sin, and that God would judge the sinners (Mal. 3:5). We must commend John for his courage in naming sin and denouncing it. Israel was God's covenant nation, and the sins of the rulers (even though they were unbelievers) would bring the chastening of God.

Instead of listening to God's servant and obeying God's Word, Herod arrested John and imprisoned him. John was put in the fortress of Machaerus, located about four miles east of the Dead Sea. It stood thirty-five hundred feet above sea level on a rocky ridge that was accessible from only one side.

It was Herodias, Herod's wife, who held the grudge against John (see Mark 6:19 NASB); and she influenced her husband. She plotted to have her teenage daughter perform a lascivious dance at Herod's birthday feast. Herodias knew that her husband would succumb to her daughter's charms and make some rash promise to her. She also knew that Herod would want to "save face" before his friends and officials. The plot worked, and John the Baptist was slain.

The voice of conscience (vv. 1–2). When Herod heard of the marvelous works of Jesus, he was sure that John had been raised from the dead. His conscience was troubling him, and neither his wife nor his friends could console him. The voice of conscience is a powerful voice, and it can be the voice of God to those who will listen.

Instead of heeding his conscience, Herod determined to kill Jesus just as he had killed John. Some Pharisees (probably in on the plot) warned Jesus that Herod wanted to kill Him (Luke 13:31–32). But Jesus was not disturbed by the report. The word *fox* in Luke 13:32 is feminine. Jesus said, "Go, tell that vixen." Was He perhaps referring to Herodias, the real power behind the throne?

The voice of Jesus (Luke 23:6–11). When he finally did meet Jesus, Herod found that the Son of God was *silent to him!* Herod had silenced the voice of God! "Today, if you will hear his voice, harden not your hearts" (Heb. 3:7–8).

The voice of history. Herod should have known that he could not get away with his sin. History records that Herod lost prestige and power. His armies were defeated by the Arabs, and his appeals to be made a king (urged by his wife) were refused by Emperor Caligula. Herod was banished to Gaul (France) and then Spain, where he died.

Herod is remembered as a weak ruler whose only concern was his own pleasure and position. He did not serve the people, he served himself. He has the dubious honor of being the man who killed the greatest prophet ever sent to proclaim God's Word.

What was our Lord's response to the news of John's murder? *Caution:* He quietly withdrew from that area and went to a "lonely place." He lived according to a divine timetable (see John 2:4; 7:6, 30; 8:20; 12:23, 27; 13:1; 17:1), and He did not want to deliberately provoke trouble with Herod. Because Herod's agents were all around, the Lord had to exercise wisdom and caution.

Certainly Jesus was deeply moved when He heard that John had been killed. The Jewish nation *permitted* John to be slain because they did nothing to assist him. But these same leaders would *ask* for Jesus to be slain! Jesus would never permit the Jewish rulers to forget the witness of John (Matt. 21:23ff.). Because they rejected John's witness, they rejected their own Messiah and King.

The Multitudes: Compassion (14:14–21)

Jesus and His disciples desperately needed rest (Mark 6:31), yet the needs of the multitudes touched His heart. The word translated "moved with compassion" literally means "to have one's inner being (viscera) stirred." It is stronger than sympathy. The word is used twelve times in the Gospels, and eight of these references are to Jesus Christ.

Jesus was "moved with compassion" when He saw the needy multitudes (Matt. 9:36). They were like sheep that had been lacerated from brutal fleecing—torn, exhausted, and wandering. Twice He was "moved with compassion" when He beheld the hungry multitudes without food (Matt. 14:14; 15:32). The two blind men (Matt. 20:34) and the leper (Mark 1:41) also stirred His compassion, as did the sorrow of the widow at Nain (Luke 7:13).

Jesus used this word in three of His parables. The king had compassion on his bankrupt servant and forgave him his debt, and we ought to forgive one another (Matt. 18:21–35). The Samaritan had compassion on the Jewish victim and cared for him in love (Luke 10:25–37). The father had compassion on his wayward son and ran and greeted him when he came home (Luke 15:20). If our heavenly Father has such compassion toward us, should we not have compassion toward others?

The miracle of the feeding of the five thousand is recorded in all four gospels (Matt. 14:13–21; Mark 6:35–44; Luke 9:12–17; John 6:4–13). It was definitely a miracle. Those who teach that Jesus only encouraged the people to bring out their own hidden lunches have ignored the clear statements of God's Word. John 6:14 definitely calls the event a "sign" or "miracle." Would the crowd have wanted to crown Jesus King simply because He tricked them into sharing their lunches (John 6:14–15)? Not likely!

It takes little imagination to picture the embarrassing plight of the disciples. Here were more than five thousand hungry people, and they had nothing to feed them! Certainly the disciples knew that Jesus was powerful enough to meet the need, yet they did not turn to Him for help. Instead, they took inventory of their own food supply (a lad had five barley loaves and two fish) and their limited treasury. When they considered the time (evening) and the place (a desolate place), they came to the conclusion that nothing could be done to solve the problem. Their counsel to the Lord was: "Send them away!"

How like many of God's people today. For some reason, it is never the right time or place for God to work. Jesus watched His frustrated disciples as they tried to solve the problem, but "He Himself knew what He was intending to do" (John 6:6 NASB). He wanted to teach them a lesson in faith and surrender. Note the steps we must take in solving life's problems.

Start with what you have. Andrew found a lad who had a small lunch, and he brought the lad to Jesus. Was the boy willing to give up his lunch? Yes, he was! God begins where we are and uses what we have.

Give what you have to Jesus. Jesus took the simple lunch, blessed it, and shared it. The miracle of multiplication was in His hands! "Little is much if God is in it." Jesus broke the bread and gave the pieces to the disciples, and they, in turn, fed the multitudes.

Obey what He commands. The disciples had the people sit down as Jesus ordered. They took the broken pieces and distributed them, and discovered that there was plenty for everybody. As His servants, we are "distributors," not "manufacturers." If we give what we have to Him, He will bless it and give it back to us for use in feeding others.

Conserve the results. There were twelve baskets filled with pieces of bread and fish after the people had eaten all they wanted. But these pieces were carefully collected so that nothing was wasted (Mark 6:43; John 6:12). I wonder how many of the pieces the lad took back home with him? Imagine his mother's amazement when the boy told her his story!

The apostle John recorded a sermon on "the Bread of Life" that Jesus gave the next day in the synagogue in Capernaum (John 6:22ff.). The people were willing to receive the physical bread, but they would not receive the living Bread—the Son of God come down from heaven. The miracle of the feeding of the five thousand was actually a sermon in action. Jesus is the Bread of Life, and only He can satisfy the spiritual hunger in man's heart. The tragedy is, men waste their time and money on "that which is not bread" (Isa. 55:1–7). People today are making the same mistake.

Jesus still has compassion on the hungry multitudes, and He still says to His church: "Give them something to eat." How easy it is for us to send people away, to make excuses, to plead a lack of resources. Jesus asks that we give Him all that we have and let Him use it as He sees fit. A hungry world is feeding on empty substitutes while we deprive them of the Bread of Life. When we give Christ what we have, we never lose. We always end up with more blessing than when we started.

The Disciples: Care and Concern (14:22–36)
John recorded the reason why Jesus was in such a hurry to dismiss the crowd and send the disciples back in the boat: The crowd wanted to make Jesus King (John 6:14–15). The Lord knew that their motives were not spiritual and that their purposes were out of God's will. If the disciples had stayed, they would certainly have fallen in with the plans of the crowd, for as yet, the disciples did not fully understand Christ's plans. They were guilty of arguing over "who was the greatest," and a popular uprising would have suited them perfectly.

This experience of the disciples in the storm can be an encouragement to us when we go through the storms of life. When we find ourselves in the storm, we can rest on several assurances.

"He brought me here." The storm came because they were *in* the will of God and not (like Jonah) out of the will of God. Did Jesus know that the storm was coming? Certainly! Did He deliberately direct them into the storm? Yes! They were safer in the storm in God's will than on land with the crowds out of God's will. We must never judge our security on the basis of circumstances alone.

As we read our Bibles, we discover that there are two kinds of storms: storms of *correction,* when God disciplines us, and storms of *perfection,* when God helps us to grow. Jonah was in a storm because he disobeyed God and had to be corrected. The disciples were in a storm because they obeyed Christ and had to be perfected. Jesus had tested them in a storm before, when He was in the boat with them (Matt. 8:23–27). But now He tested them by being *out of the boat.*

Many Christians have the mistaken idea that obedience to God's will produces "smooth sailing." But this is not true. "In the world ye shall have tribulation," Jesus promised (John 16:33). When we find ourselves in the storm because we have obeyed the Lord, we must remember that He brought us here and He can care for us.

"He is praying for me." This entire scene is a dramatic picture of the church and the Lord today. God's people are on the sea, in the midst of a storm. Yet Jesus Christ is in heaven "making intercession for us" (Rom. 8:34). He saw the disciples and knew their plight (Mark 6:48), just as He sees us and knows our needs. He feels the burdens that we feel and knows what we are going through (Heb. 4:14–16). Jesus was praying for His disciples, that their faith would not fail.

If you knew that Jesus Christ was in the next room, praying for you, would it not give you new courage to endure the storm and do His will? Of course it would. He is not in the next room, but He is in heaven interceding for you. He sees your need, He knows your fears, and He is in control of the situation.

"He will come to me." Often we feel like Jesus has deserted us when we are going through the hard times of life. In the psalms, David complained that God seemed far away and unconcerned. Yet he knew that God would ultimately rescue him. Even the great apostle Paul got into a situation so difficult he felt "burdened excessively, beyond our strength, so that we despaired even of life" (2 Cor. 1:8 NASB).

Jesus always comes to us in the storms of life. "When you pass through the waters, I will be with you" (Isa. 43:2 NASB). He may not come at the time we think He should come, because He knows when we need Him the most. He waited until the ship was as far from land as possible, so that all human hope was gone. He was testing the disciples' faith, and this meant removing every human prop.

Why did Jesus walk on the water? To show His disciples that the very thing they feared (the sea) was only a staircase for Him to come to them. Often we fear the difficult experiences of life (such as surgery or bereavement), only to discover that these experiences bring Jesus Christ closer to us.

Why did they not recognize Jesus? Because they were not looking for Him. Had they been waiting by faith, they would have known Him immediately. Instead, they jumped to the false conclusion that the appearance was that of a ghost. Fear and faith cannot live in the same heart, for fear always blinds the eyes to the presence of the Lord.

"He will help me grow." This was the whole purpose of the storm, to help the disciples grow in their faith. After all, Jesus would one day leave them, and they would face many storms in their ministries. They had to learn to trust Him even though He was not present with them, and even though it looked as though He did not care.

Now our center of interest shifts to Peter. Before we criticize Peter for sinking, let's honor him for his magnificent demonstration of faith. He dared to be different. Anybody can sit in the boat and watch. But it takes a person of real faith to leave the boat and walk on the water.

What caused Peter to sink? His faith began to waver because he took his eyes off the Lord and began to look at the circumstances around him. "Why did you doubt?" Jesus asked him (Matt. 14:31). This word translated *doubt* carries the meaning of "standing uncertainly at two ways." Peter started out with great faith but ended up with little faith because he saw *two* ways instead of *one*.

We must give Peter credit for *knowing* that he was sinking and for crying out to the Lord for help. He cried out when he was "beginning to sink" and not when he was drowning. Perhaps this incident came to Peter's mind years later when he wrote in his first epistle: "For the eyes of the Lord are over the righteous, and his ears are open unto their prayers" (1 Peter 3:12).

This experience was difficult for Peter, but it helped him to grow in his knowledge of himself and of the Lord. The storms of life are not easy, but they *are* necessary. They teach us to trust Jesus Christ alone and to obey His Word no matter what the circumstances may be. It has been said, "Faith is not believing in spite of evidence, but obeying in spite of consequence."

"He will see me through." If Jesus says, "Come," then that word is going to accomplish its intended purpose. Since He is the "author and finisher of our faith" (Heb. 12:2), whatever He starts, He completes. We may fail along the way, but in the end, God will succeed. Jesus and Peter walked on the water *together* and went to the ship.

Peter's experience turned out to be a blessing to the other disciples as well as to himself. When they saw the power of Jesus Christ, in conquering and calming the storm, they could only fall down and worship Him. When Jesus calmed the first storm (Matt. 8:23–27), the disciples said, "What manner of man is this?" But now their clear testimony was, "Thou art the Son of God!"

The disciples had helped to feed five thousand people, and then God permitted them to go through a storm. In the book of Acts, they won five thousand people (Acts 4:4), and then *the storm of persecution began.* No doubt Peter and the disciples recalled their storm experience with the Lord and took courage.

This miracle magnifies the kingship of Jesus Christ. In fact, when Matthew wrote Peter's request, "Bid me to come," he used a Greek word that means "the command of a king." Peter knew that Jesus Christ was King over all nature, including the wind and the waves. His word is law and the elements must obey.

The ship landed at Gennesaret, near Capernaum and Bethsaida, and there Jesus healed many people. Did these people know that He had come through a storm to meet their needs? Do *we* remember that He endured the storm of judgment to save our souls (Ps. 42:7)? He endured the storm for us that we might never face the judgment of God. We ought to imitate the disciples, bow at His feet, and acknowledge that He is King of Kings and Lord of Lords!

CHAPTER TWELVE
Matthew 15
THE KING'S CONCERN

As in the previous chapter, we see the Lord in conflict with His enemies (Matt. 15:1–11), teaching His own disciples (Matt. 15:12–20), and ministering to the needy multitudes (Matt. 15:21–31). This is the pattern during this period of withdrawal.

Our Lord's great concerns are *truth* and *love*. He taught the Jewish leaders the *truth* and exposed their hypocrisy, and He showed the Gentile crowds *love* as He met their needs. By studying these two concerns, we can understand the message of this chapter.

Truth: He Rejected Jewish Tradition (15:1–20)

This dramatic event involved three requests and three replies.

The scribes and Pharisees (vv. 1–11). The fact that the scribes and Pharisees united in this attack, and came all the way from Jerusalem to speak to Jesus, indicates the seriousness of their purpose. It is likely that this committee represented the leaders of the Sanhedrin in Jerusalem.

Their accusation about "washing hands" had nothing to do with cleanliness. They were referring to the ceremonial washings of the rigidly orthodox Jews (see Mark 7:1–4). It was bad enough that Jesus and His disciples mingled with outcasts, but they did not even seek to be purified! Of course, in making this accusation, these religious leaders were forcing Jesus to deal with the *very foundation* of their religious faith. If Jesus rejected the sacred traditions of the nation, then He was a heretic!

Where did these traditions come from? They were handed down from the teachers of previous generations. These traditions were originally the "oral law" that (said the rabbis) Moses gave to the elders, and they passed down to the nation. This oral law was finally written down and became the *Mishnah*. Unfortunately, the *Mishnah* became more important and more authoritative than the original law of Moses.

Our Lord's reply to their charge began with *an accusation* (Matt. 15:3). It was *they* who were breaking God's law by practicing their traditions! He then proceeded with an illustration (Matt. 15:4–6), their practice of "Corban" (see Mark 7:11). The Hebrew word *Corban* means "a gift." If a Jew wanted to escape some financial responsibilities, he would declare his goods to be "Corban—a gift to God." This meant he was free from other obligations, such as caring for his parents. But in so doing, the person was losing the power of God's Word in his life, and thus hurting his character and missing God's blessing.

Jesus concluded His reply with an *application* (Matt. 15:7–11), quoting Isaiah 29:13. Jesus made it clear that obedience to tradition made a person disobedient to the Word of God, and this proved the tradition to be false. Exodus 20:12 taught a man to "honor" father and mother. But the "Corban" rule would make a person dishonor his parents, and, at the same time, disobey God.

Tradition is something *external*, while God's truth is *internal*, in the heart. People obey tradition to please men and gain status (Gal. 1:14), but we obey the Word to please God. Tradition deals with *ritual*, while God's truth deals with *reality*. Tradition brings empty words to the lips, but truth penetrates the heart and changes the life. Actually, tradition robs a person of the power of the Word of God.

Unfortunately, there are many "evangelical traditions" in churches today, man-made teachings that are often considered as authoritative as the Word of God—*even though they contradict His Word.* By obeying these traditions, Christians rob themselves of the power of God's Word.

God wants us to give Him our hearts, and not just our lip service. We *believe* in the heart (Rom, 10:9–10), *love* from the heart (Matt. 22:37), *sing* from the heart (Col. 3:16), *obey* from the heart (Rom. 6:17; Eph. 6:6), and *give* from the heart (2 Cor. 9:7). No wonder David prayed, "Create in me a clean heart, O God" (Ps. 51:10).

Jesus declared boldly to the multitudes that sin comes from the heart, not from the diet. It is what comes out of the mouth that defiles us, not what goes in.

The disciples (vv. 12–14). The disciples were astounded by what Jesus taught about foods. After all, they had been raised good Jews (see Acts 10:14 for Peter's testimony). They knew the difference between the "clean" and "unclean" foods (Lev. 11).

But the disciples had another concern: This teaching had offended the Pharisees and was certain to create serious problems. But Jesus was not worried about the Pharisees. Neither they nor their teachings had been planted by God, and therefore would not last. While there are isolated groups that seek to maintain the traditions, for the most part, pharisaeism is gone. However, the *spirit* of pharisaeism (tradition, legalism, hypocrisy, externals) is still with us, what Jesus called "the leaven of the Pharisees" (Matt. 16:6).

Jesus also pointed out that the Pharisees were blind and could only lead their converts into the ditch. In Matthew 23:16, He called them "blind guides"—quite a graphic description. Why be afraid of rootless plants that are dying, or blind guides who cannot see where they are going?

Peter (vv. 15–20). Peter was not content until he had an explanation of the saying about foods. Patiently our Lord explained the lesson again. The meaning seems obvious to us, but it was astonishingly new to orthodox Jews. Whatever enters the mouth eventually goes into the stomach and comes out in human waste. Food never touches the heart. But what comes out of the mouth *begins* in the heart, and these things defile a person. Of course, *actions* are included with *words;* often actions speak louder than words.

The Lord had to repeat this lesson on foods to Peter a few years later when He was going to call him to preach to the Gentiles (Acts 10). Paul repeated it in 1 Timothy 4:3–6. He also dealt with it in Romans 14—15.

Compassion: He Responded to Gentile Needs (15:21–39)

Not only did Jesus *teach* that no foods were unclean,

but He practiced His teaching by going into Gentile territory. He left Israel and withdrew again, this time into the area of Tyre and Sidon. The Gentiles were "unclean" as far as the Jews were concerned. In fact, Jews referred to the Gentiles as "dogs." That Jesus would minister to Gentiles was no surprise (Matt. 12:17–21), though at that time, the emphasis was on ministering to Israel (Matt. 10:5–6).

The demonized (vv. 21–28). Jesus was trying to remain hidden (Mark 7:24), but somehow this Canaanite woman heard where He was and came to Him with her need. Keep in mind that our Lord responded to this woman as He did, not to destroy her faith, but to develop it. Her own replies showed that she was growing in faith and unwilling to let Him go without getting an answer. Godly Samuel Rutherford stated this principle perfectly: "It is faith's work to claim and challenge loving-kindness out of all the roughest strokes of God."

When she approached Him as "Son of David," she was definitely putting herself on Jewish ground, and this she could not do, because she was a Gentile. Of course, this title did reveal her faith in Him as the Messiah of God, for "Son of David" was a name for the Messiah (Matt. 22:42). Since she came to Him on Jewish terms, He was silent. Of course, He knew her heart, and even His silence encouraged her to continue asking.

Impatient with her persistent following and crying out, the disciples said, "Send her away!" We are not sure whether they meant, "Give her what she wants and get rid of her" or just "Get rid of her!" In either case, they were not showing much compassion for either her or her demonized daughter. Our Lord's reply in Matthew 15:24 indicates that they probably wanted Him to answer her request.

We cannot but admire the patience and persistence of this Gentile mother. "Lord, help me!" was her next plea, and this time she avoided any messianic titles. She came as a sinner needing help, and she offered no argument. In His reply, Jesus did not call her a "dog" the way the Pharisees would have addressed a Gentile. The Greek word means "a little pet dog" and not the filthy curs that ran the streets and ate the garbage. "The children" referred, of course, to the people of Israel.

Jesus was not playing games with the woman, nor was He trying to make the situation more difficult. He was drawing out of her a growing response of faith. She immediately seized on His illustration about the children's bread, *which was exactly what He wanted her to do*. We may paraphrase her reply: "It is true that we Gentiles do not sit at the table as children and eat the bread. But even the pet dogs under the table can eat some of the crumbs!" What a tremendous testimony of faith!

It was this faith that Jesus acknowledged, and immediately He healed her daughter. It is worth noting that both of the persons in the gospel of Matthew who had "great faith" were Gentiles: this Canaanite

woman and the Roman centurion (Matt. 8:5–13). In both cases, Jesus healed the one in need *from a distance*. Spiritually speaking, the Gentiles were "afar off" until Calvary, when Jesus Christ died for both Jews and Gentiles and made reconciliation possible (Eph. 2:11ff.).

This woman's faith was great because she persisted in asking and trusting when everything seemed against her. Certainly her race was against her: She was a Gentile. Her sex was against her, for most Jewish rabbis paid little attention to women. It seemed that the disciples were against her, and Christ's words might have led her to believe that even *He* was against her. All of these obstacles only made her persist in asking.

The sick and handicapped (vv. 29–31). Jesus departed from the borders of Tyre and Sidon and went to the region of the Decapolis. The Decapolis included ten cities that were in a league and were authorized by the Romans to mint their own coins, run their own courts, and have their own armies. This was predominantly Gentile territory.

Jesus healed there a man who was deaf and dumb (Mark 7:31–37). Even though the Lord cautioned the man to be silent, he and his friends spread the account of the miracle abroad. This apparently caused a great crowd to gather—including people who were lame, blind, dumb, and crippled (maimed). Jesus healed these people, and the Gentiles "glorified the God of Israel."

We cannot help but marvel at the contrast between these Gentiles and the Jewish leaders who knew the Old Testament Scriptures. The Gentiles glorified Israel's God, but the Jewish leaders said that Jesus was in league with Satan (Matt. 12:22–24). Our Lord's miracles did not cause the Jewish cities to repent (Matt. 11:20ff.), yet the Gentiles believed in Him. The very miracles that He performed should have convinced the Jews that He was the Messiah (Isa. 29:18–19; 35:4–6; Matt. 11:1–6). Jesus marveled at the faith of a Gentile soldier and a Gentile mother. Yet He was amazed at the unbelief of His own people (Mark 6:6).

The hungry (vv. 32–39). Critics have accused the gospel writers of deliberately falsifying the records in order to prove that Jesus performed more miracles. They claim that the feeding of the four thousand was merely an adaptation of the previous miracle of feeding five thousand. A careful examination of the records shows that this accusation is false and that the critics are wrong. This chart shows the differences between the two events.

Feeding 5,000	Feeding 4,000
Primarily Jews	Primarily Gentiles
Galilee, near Bethsaida	The Decapolis
5 loaves, 2 fish	7 loaves, "a few fish"
12 baskets over	7 baskets over
Crowd with Him 1 day	Crowd with Him 3 days
Spring of year (green grass)	Summer season
Tried to make Him King	No popular response

Since the crowd of four thousand had been with Him three days, they had used up their own supplies of food. Our Lord's compassionate heart would not permit Him to send them on their way hungry, lest they faint along the way. The first motive for this miracle was simply the meeting of human needs. The people had already seen His miracles and glorified God, so the miracle was not for the purpose of preaching a sermon or authenticating His ministry.

However, this miracle did have a special purpose for His disciples. We are amazed that they had forgotten the miracle of the feeding of the five thousand. (Read carefully Matt. 16:6–12.) The Twelve were perplexed when they should have been saying, "Jesus is able to multiply loaves and fish, so we have no need to worry!" Of course, it may be that they thought He would not perform that kind of a miracle in Gentile territory. Or, perhaps the fact that the previous crowd had tried to make Him King would cause Jesus to avoid repeating the miracle.

As in the feeding of the five thousand, this miracle took place in His hands. As Jesus broke the bread and gave it to His disciples, the bread multiplied. Everybody ate and everybody was satisfied. Again, Jesus ordered the fragments to be collected so that nothing be wasted. The ability to perform miracles does not grant the authority to waste God's gifts.

The word translated *baskets* in Matthew 15:37 means "a large hamper." It is the same kind of basket that was used to lower Paul over the Damascus wall (Acts 9:25). The word for *basket* in Matthew 14:20 means "a wicker basket," the kind a person carried with food or other goods in it. The fact that these two different words are used is further proof that the two miracles are different.

Jesus did not preach a sermon to this crowd on "the Bread of Life" as He did to the Jews in Capernaum, following the feeding of the five thousand (John 6:22ff.). The facts about the Old Testament manna and the "bread of God" would have been foreign to these Gentiles. Jesus always adapted His teaching to the needs and the understanding of the people to whom He ministered.

Before leaving Matthew 15, let's review several spiritual lessons that it contains for us.

(1) The enemies of truth are often religious people who live according to man's traditions. Satan often uses "religion" to blind the minds of sinners to the simple truths of God's Word.

(2) We must beware of any religious system that gives us an excuse to sin and disobey God's Word.

(3) We must also beware of worship that comes from the lips only, and not from the heart.

(4) If we major on the inner man, the outer man will be what God wants it to be. True holiness comes from within.

(5) It is difficult to break free from tradition. There is something in us that wants to hold to the past and make no changes. Even Peter had to learn his lesson twice!

(6) We dare not limit Christ to any one nation or people. The gospel came "to the Jew first" (Rom. 1:16), but today is for all men in all nations. "Whosoever shall call upon the name of the Lord shall be saved" (Rom. 10:13).

CHAPTER THIRTEEN
Matthew 16
THE KING'S SURPRISE

The events recorded in Matthew 16 form a dramatic turning point in our Lord's ministry. For the first time, He mentioned the church (Matt. 16:18) and openly spoke about His death on the cross (Matt. 16:21). He began to prepare the disciples for His arrest, crucifixion, and resurrection. But, as we shall see, they were slow to learn their lessons.

The theme of *faith* runs through the events in this chapter. In these events, we see four different levels of faith and how they relate to Christ.

No Faith—Tempting Christ (16:1–4)

Their desire to silence Jesus had caused the two opposing religious parties to unite in one common effort. They were waiting for Him when He returned to Galilee. The Pharisees, of course, were the traditionalists of their day, while the Sadducees were quite liberal (see Acts 23:6–10). They united to issue a challenge to Jesus: "Show us a sign from heaven and we will believe You are the Christ."

The word translated *sign* means much more than simply a miracle or a demonstration of power. It means "a wonder by which one may recognize a person or confirm who he is."

This was the fourth time the religious leaders had asked for a sign (Matt. 12:38ff.; John 2:12; 6:30). Later, they did it again (Luke 11:14ff.). But miracles do not convince people of sin or give a desire for salvation (Luke 16:27–31; John 12:10–11; Acts 14:8–20). Miracles will give confirmation where there is faith, but not where there is willful unbelief.

Why did our Lord talk about the weather? To reveal to His enemies their own dishonesty and stubborn blindness. They could examine the evidence in God's world and draw valid conclusions, but they would not examine the evidence He had presented. His enemies *would not* believe, and therefore they *could not* believe (John 12:37ff.). The Pharisees and Sadducees did not lack evidence; they lacked honesty and humility.

Their demand for a sign revealed the sad condition of their hearts: they were evil and adulterous. He did not accuse them of being guilty of physical adultery, but of spiritual adultery (Isa. 57; James 4:4). These men were worshipping a false god of their own manufacture, and this was spiritual adultery. Had they been worshipping the true God, they would have recognized His Son when He came.

Jesus had mentioned the sign of Jonah before (see Matt. 12:38–45). This was the sign of death, burial, and resurrection. Our Lord's crucifixion, burial, and resurrection were actually a sign to Israel that He was their Messiah. It was this sign that Peter preached about at Pentecost (Acts 2:22ff.).

Matthew 16:4 records the Lord's third departure from Galilee. He departed before to avoid Herod (Matt. 14:13) and to avoid the Pharisees (Matt. 15:21). It was certainly an act of judgment.

Little Faith—Misunderstanding Christ (16:5–12)
The disciples had but one loaf of bread with them (Mark 8:14). We are not told what happened to the many baskets of leftover food that resulted from His feeding the four thousand just a short time before. Perhaps they gave it away. Jesus used this embarrassing event as an occasion to teach an important spiritual truth: Beware of the false teachings of the Pharisees and Sadducees.

The disciples misunderstood Him; they thought He was talking about material bread. Often in the ministry of Jesus, people misconstrued His words by interpreting them literally rather than spiritually. Nicodemus thought that Jesus was talking about an actual physical birth (John 3:4), and the Samaritan woman thought He was referring to material water from the well (John 4:11). The Jewish crowd in the synagogue thought Jesus was speaking about eating actual flesh and blood (John 6:52ff.) when He was describing a spiritual experience (John 6:63).

As we noted in our study of Matthew 13, leaven was to the Jews a symbol of evil. Both the Pharisees and the Sadducees had infected the religious beliefs of Israel with false doctrine. The Pharisees were legalists who taught that only obedience to the law and the traditions would please God and usher in His kingdom for Israel. The Sadducees were liberal in their thinking and denied that there would be such a kingdom on earth. They even denied the truth of the resurrection and the existence of angels.

Why would the Lord's mention of leaven cause the disciples to discuss their lack of bread? Possibly they were planning to purchase bread on the other side of the sea, and they thought Jesus was cautioning them not to buy unclean bread, which Jews could not eat. If they had remembered how Jesus had multiplied bread on two occasions, they certainly would not have worried. Their "little faith" kept them from understanding His teaching and depending on His power to meet their needs.

"Little faith" was one of our Lord's favorite names for His disciples (Matt. 6:30; 8:26; 14:31). Of course, "little faith" is better than *no* faith. The disciples had many lessons to learn before they would graduate to "great faith."

Saving Faith—Confessing Christ (16:13–20)
Jesus took His disciples to Gentile territory, in the region of Caesarea Philippi. They were about 120 miles from Jerusalem in the northern part of Palestine. The region was strongly identified with various religions: It had been a center for Baal worship; the Greek god Pan had shrines there; and Herod the Great had built a temple there to honor Augustus Caesar. It was in the midst of this pagan superstition that Peter confessed Jesus as the Son of God. And it was probably within sight of Caesar's temple that Jesus announced a surprise: He would not yet establish His kingdom, but He would build His church.

If anyone else asked, "Whom do men say that I am?" we would think him either mad or arrogant. But in the case of Jesus, a right confession of who He is is basic to salvation (Rom. 10:9–10; 1 John 2:18–23; 4:1–3). His person and His work go together and must never be separated. It is amazing to see how confused the public was about Jesus (John 10:19–21). Perhaps, like Herod, the people thought Jesus was John raised from the dead.

It had been prophesied that Elijah would come again (Mal. 4:5), and some thought that this prediction was fulfilled in Christ. However, Jesus did not minister as did Elijah; it was John the Baptist who came "in the spirit and power of Elias" (Luke 1:13–17). Jeremiah was the weeping prophet whose tender heart was broken at the sight of the decay of the nation. Certainly this attitude was seen in Jesus, the Man of Sorrows.

One thing is clear: We can never make a true decision about Jesus Christ by taking a poll of the people. (But some people *do* get their "spiritual knowledge" this way!) The important thing is not what others say, but what do you and I personally say? The decisions of the crowd (wrong or right) can never substitute for personal decisions.

Peter had the correct response: "Thou art the Christ [the Messiah], the Son of the living God!" This confession was Peter's response to the revelation God the Father had given him. Jesus Himself explained this experience in Matthew 11:25–27. This revelation was not the result of Peter's own investigation. It came as the gracious act of God. God had hidden these things from the proud Pharisees and Sadducees and revealed them to "babes," the humble disciples.

It should be noted that there had been other confessions of faith prior to this one. Nathanael had confessed Christ as the Son of God (John 1:49), and the disciples had declared Him God's Son after He stilled the storm (Matt. 14:33). Peter had given a confession of faith when the crowds left Jesus after His sermon on the Bread of Life (John 6:68–69). In fact, when Andrew had brought his brother Simon to Jesus, it was on the basis of this belief (John 1:41).

How, then, did *this* confession differ from those that preceded it? To begin with, *Jesus explicitly asked for this confession.* It was not an emotional response from people who had seen a miracle, but the studied and sincere statement of a man who had been taught by God.

Also, Jesus *accepted this confession* and built on it to teach them new truth. It must have rejoiced His heart to hear Peter's words. The Lord knew that Peter could now be led into new steps of deeper truth and service. All of our Lord's ministry to His disciples had prepared the way for this experience. Let's look at these great words and concepts individually.

Rock. These Jewish men, steeped in Old Testament Scripture, recognized the rock as a symbol of God. "He is the Rock, his work is perfect" (Deut. 32:4). "The Lord is my rock, and my fortress" (Ps. 18:2). "For who is God save the Lord? Or who is a rock save our God?" (Ps. 18:31).

But let's investigate the Greek words that the Holy Spirit led Matthew to use. "Thou art *petros* [a stone], and upon this rock [*petra*—a large rock] I will build my church." Jesus had given Simon the new name of *Peter* (John 1:42) which means "a stone." The Aramaic form is *Cephas,* which also means "a stone." Everyone who believes in Jesus Christ and confesses Him as the Son and God and Savior, is a "living stone" (1 Peter 2:5 NASB).

Jesus Christ is the foundation rock on which the church is built. The Old Testament prophets said so (Ps. 118:22; Isa. 28:16). Jesus Himself said this (Matt. 21:42) and so did Peter and the other apostles (Acts 4:10–12). Paul also stated that the foundation for the church is Jesus Christ (1 Cor. 3:11). This foundation was laid by the apostles and prophets as they preached Christ to the lost (1 Cor. 2:1–2; 3:11; Eph. 2:20).

In other words, when the evidence is examined, the total teaching of Scripture is that the church, God's temple (Eph. 2:19–22), is built on Jesus Christ—not on Peter. How could God build His church on a fallible man like Peter? Later, the same Peter who confessed Christ became an adversary and entertained Satan's thoughts (Matt. 16:22ff.). "But that was before Peter was filled with the Spirit," some argue. Then consider Peter's doctrinal blunders recorded in Galatians 2, blunders that had to be dealt with by Paul. This event occurred *after* Peter was filled with the Spirit.

Church. This is the first occurrence of this important word in the New Testament. It is the Greek word *ekklesia* (ek-klay-SEE-uh) from which we get our English word *ecclesiastical,* referring to things that pertain to the church. The literal meaning is "a called-out assembly." The word is used 114 times in the New Testament, and in ninety of these references, a local church (assembly) is in view. However, in this first use of *ekklesia,* it seems likely that Jesus had the whole church in mind. He was not just building a local assembly, but a universal church composed of all who make the same confession of faith that Peter made.

The word *ekklesia* was not new to the disciples. This word was applied to the popular assembly of Greek citizens that helped to govern a city or district (Acts 19:32, 39, 41). Also, the Greek translation of the Old Testament (the Septuagint) used *ekklesia* to describe the congregation of Israel when it was gathered for religious activity (Deut. 31:30; Judg. 20:2). However, this does not mean that the Old Testament congregation of Israel was a "church" in the same sense as the churches of the New Testament. Rather, Jesus was introducing something new to His disciples.

Jesus spoke about "my church" in contrast to these other assemblies. This was to be something new and different, for in His church, Jesus Christ would unite believing Jews and Gentiles and form a new temple, a new body (Eph. 2:11—3:12). In His church, natural distinctions would be unimportant (Gal. 3:28). Jesus Christ would be the Builder of this church, the Head of this church (Eph. 1:22; Col. 1:18).

Each believer in this church is a "living stone" (1 Peter 2:5). Believers would meet in local congregations, or assemblies, to worship Christ and to serve Him, but they would also belong to a universal church, a temple being built by Christ. There is a oneness to the people of God (Eph. 4:1–6) that ought to be revealed to the world by love and unity (John 17:20–26).

Gates of hell. A better translation would be "gates of hades." Hell is the final destiny of all unsaved people after the judgment of the Great White Throne (Rev. 20:11–15). *Hades* is simply "the realm of the dead." It holds the spirits of the unsaved dead and releases them at the resurrection (Rev. 20:13; where "hell" ought to read "hades"). According to Jesus, hades is down (Matt. 11:23), and it is a prison to which He holds the keys (Rev. 1:18).

On the basis of Luke 16:19–31, some people believe that *all* the dead went to hades prior to the death and resurrection of Christ—believers to a paradise portion and unbelievers to a punishment portion. We are certain that believers today, when they die, go immediately into the presence of Christ (2 Cor. 5:6–8; Phil. 1:23).

"Gates" represent, in the Bible, authority and power. The city gate was to a Jew what city hall is to people in the Western world. Important business was transacted at the city gate (Deut. 16:18; 17:8; Ruth 4:11). "The gates of hades" then would symbolize the organized power of death and Satan. By His death and resurrection, Jesus Christ would conquer death, so that death would not be able to hold any of His people. Christ would "storm the gates" and deliver the captives! This declaration certainly is verified by 1 Corinthians 15:50ff., Hebrews 2:14–15, and other Scriptures.

Keys of the kingdom. A key is a badge of authority (Isa. 22:15, 22; Luke 11:52). "The kingdom of heaven" is *not* heaven, for no man on earth carries the keys to heaven! (All of the jokes about "St. Peter at the gate" stem from this misunderstanding. They are both unbiblical and in bad taste.) We use keys to open doors. Peter was given the privilege of opening "the door of faith" to the Jews at Pentecost (Acts 2), to the Samaritans (Acts 8:14ff.), and to the Gentiles (Acts 10). But the other apostles shared this authority

(Matt. 18:18), and Paul had the privilege of "opening the door of faith" to the Gentiles outside of Palestine (Acts 14:27).

Nowhere in this passage, or in the rest of the New Testament, are we told that Peter or his successors had any special position or privilege in the church. Certainly Peter in his two epistles claimed to be nothing more than an apostle (1 Peter 1:1), an elder (1 Peter 5:1), and a servant of Jesus Christ (2 Peter 1:1).

Binding and loosing. This was a very familiar phrase to the Jews, for their rabbis often spoke of "binding and loosing," that is, forbidding or permitting. Our Lord's statement in Matthew 16:19 referred to Peter. But His statement later in Matthew 18:18 included all of the apostles. As the representatives of their Lord, they would exercise authority according to His Word.

The Greek verbs in Matthew 16:19 are most important. The *Expanded Translation* by Dr. Kenneth S. Wuest reads, "And whatever you bind on earth [forbid to be done], shall have been already bound in heaven; and whatever you loose on earth [permit to be done], shall have already been loosed in heaven." Jesus did not say that God would obey what they did on earth, but that they should do on earth whatever God had already willed. The church does not get man's will done in heaven; it obeys God's will on earth.

The apostles were not to share this truth about Jesus being the Son of God with other people until after His resurrection and ascension. Then the "sign of Jonah" would be completed, the Spirit would be given, and the message could be proclaimed. The nation in general, and certainly the religious leaders in particular, were not yet ready for this message. Read Peter's sermon at Pentecost and see how he proclaimed Jesus as the Christ (Acts 2).

Serving Faith—Following Christ (16:21–28)

Having declared His person, Jesus now declared His work, for the two must go together. He would go to Jerusalem, suffer and die, and be raised from the dead. This was His first clear statement of His death, though He had hinted at this before (Matt. 12:39–40; 16:4; John 2:19; 3:14; 6:51). "And He was stating the matter plainly" (Mark 8:32 NASB).

Peter's response to this shocking statement certainly represented the feelings of the rest of the disciples: "Pity thyself, Lord! This shall never happen to thee!" Jesus turned His back on Peter and said, "Get behind me, adversary! You are a stumbling block to me!" (literal translation). Peter the "stone" who had just been blessed (Matt. 16:18) became Peter the stumbling block who was not a blessing to Jesus!

What was Peter's mistake? He was thinking like a *man,* for most men want to escape suffering and death. He did not have God's mind in the matter. Where do we find the mind of God? In the Word of God. Until Peter was filled with the Spirit, he had a tendency to argue with God's Word. Peter had enough faith to confess that Jesus is the Son of God, but he did not have the faith to believe that it was right for Jesus to suffer and die. Of course, Satan agreed with Peter's words, for he used the same approach to tempt Jesus in the wilderness (Matt. 4:8–10).

Today the cross is an accepted symbol of love and sacrifice. But in that day the cross was a horrible means of capital punishment. The Romans would not mention the cross in polite society. In fact, no Roman citizen could be crucified; this terrible death was reserved for their enemies. Jesus had not yet specifically stated that He would be crucified (He did this in Matt. 20:17–19). But His words that follow emphasize the cross.

He presented to the disciples two approaches to life:

deny yourself	live for yourself
take up your cross	ignore the cross
follow Christ	follow the world
lose your life for His sake	save your life for your own sake
forsake the world	gain the world
keep your soul	lose your soul
share His reward and glory	lose His reward and glory

To deny self does not mean to deny things. It means to give yourself wholly to Christ and share in His shame and death. Paul described this in Romans 12:1–2 and Philippians 3:7–10, as well as in Galatians 2:20. To take up a cross does not mean to carry burdens or have problems. (I once met a lady who told me her asthma was the cross she had to bear!) To take up the cross means to identify with Christ in His rejection, shame, suffering, and death.

But suffering always leads to glory. This is why Jesus ended this short sermon with a reference to His glorious kingdom (Matt. 16:28). This statement would be fulfilled within a week on the Mount of Transfiguration, described in the next chapter.

CHAPTER FOURTEEN
Matthew 17
THE KING'S GLORY

The chapter begins with a glorious scene on a mountaintop, and ends with Peter catching a fish in order to pay his taxes. What a contrast! Yet, Jesus Christ the King is the theme of the entire chapter. The three events in this chapter give us three pictures of the King.

The King in His Glory (17:1–13)

Matthew and Mark state that the Transfiguration took place "six days later," while Luke says "some eight days after" (Luke 9:28). There is no contradiction; Luke's statement is the Jewish equivalent of "about a week later." During that week, the disciples must have pondered and discussed what Jesus meant by His death and resurrection. No doubt they were also wondering what would happen to the Old Testament promises about the kingdom. If Jesus were going to build a church, what would happen to the promised kingdom?

The text does not name the place where this miracle took place. It was probably on Mount Hermon, which is close to Caesarea Philippi.

The Transfiguration revealed four aspects of the glory of Jesus Christ the King.

The glory of His person. As far as the record is concerned, this is the only time Jesus revealed His glory in this way while He was on the earth. The word translated *transfigured* gives us our English word "metamorphosis." A metamorphosis is a change on the outside that comes from the inside. When a caterpillar builds a cocoon and later emerges as a butterfly, it is due to the process of metamorphosis. Our Lord's glory was not *reflected* but *radiated* from within. There was a change on the outside that came from within as He allowed His essential glory to shine forth (Heb. 1:3).

Certainly this event would strengthen the faith of the disciples, particularly Peter, who had so recently confessed Jesus to be the Son of God. Had Peter made his confession *after* the Transfiguration, it would not have been so meaningful. Peter believed, confessed his faith, and then received assurance (see John 11:40; Heb. 11:6).

Many years later, John recalled this event as the Spirit guided him to write: "And we beheld his glory, the glory as of the only begotten of the Father, full of grace and truth" (John 1:14). In his gospel, John emphasized the deity of Christ and the glory of His person (John 2:11; 7:39; 11:4; 12:23; 13:31–32; 20:31).

Jesus Christ laid aside His glory when He came to earth (John 17:5). Because of His finished work on the cross, He has received back His glory and now shares it with us (John 17:22, 24). However, we do not have to wait for heaven to share in this "transfiguration glory." When we surrender ourselves to God, He will "transfigure" our minds (Rom. 12:1–2). As we yield to the Spirit of God, He changes (transfigures) us "from glory to glory" (2 Cor. 3:18). As we look into the Word of God, we see the Son of God and are transfigured by the Spirit of God into the glory of God.

The glory of His kingdom. At the close of His sermon about cross-bearing, Jesus promised that some of the disciples would see "the Son of man coming in his kingdom" (Matt. 16:28). He selected Peter, James, and John as witnesses to this event. These three friends and business partners (Luke 5:10) had been with Jesus in the home of Jairus (Luke 8:51), and they would go with Him into the arden of Gethsemane before His crucifixion (see Matt. 26:37).

Dr. G. Campbell Morgan has pointed out that these three occasions all had to do with *death*. Jesus was teaching these three men that He was victor over death (He raised Jairus' daughter) and surrendered to death (in the garden). The Transfiguration taught them that He was glorified in death.

The presence of Moses and Elijah was significant. Moses represented the law and Elijah the prophets. All of the law and prophets point to Christ and are fulfilled in Christ (Luke 24:27; Heb. 1:1). Not one word of the Old Testament Scriptures will be unfulfilled. The promised kingdom would be established (Luke 1:32–33, 68–77). Just as the three disciples saw Jesus glorified *on earth,* so God's people would see Him in His glorious kingdom on earth (Rev. 19:11—20:6).

Peter caught this message and never forgot it. "We were eyewitnesses of his majesty. And so we have the prophetic word made more sure" (see 2 Peter 1:12ff.). The experience Peter had on the mount only fortified his faith in the Old Testament prophecies. The important thing is not seeing wonderful sights, but hearing God's Word. "This is my beloved Son, in whom I am well pleased; hear ye him" (Matt. 17:5).

All who are born again belong to the kingdom of God (John 3:3–5). This is a spiritual kingdom that is separate from the material things of this world (Rom. 14:17). But one day, when Jesus returns to this earth, there will be a glorious kingdom for one thousand years (Rev. 20:1–7) with Jesus Christ reigning as King. Those who have trusted Him shall reign on the earth with Him (Rev. 5:10).

The glory of His cross. The disciples had to learn that suffering and glory go together. Peter had opposed His going to Jerusalem to die, so Jesus had to teach him that, apart from His suffering and death, there could be no glory. Peter certainly learned the lesson, for in his first epistle he repeatedly emphasized "suffering and glory" (1 Peter 1:6–8, 11; 4:12—5:11).

Moses and Elijah talked with Jesus about His "exodus" that He would accomplish at Jerusalem (Luke 9:31). His suffering and death would not be an accident, but an accomplishment. Peter used the word *exodus* in describing his own impending death (2 Peter 1:15). For the believer, death is not a one-way street into oblivion. It is an exodus—a release—from the bondage of this life into the glorious liberty of the life in heaven.

Because Jesus died and paid the price, we have been redeemed—purchased and set free. The two Emmaus disciples had hoped that Jesus would set the nation free from Roman bondage (Luke 24:21). What He died to accomplish was not *political* freedom, but *spiritual* freedom: freedom from the world system (Gal. 1:4); freedom from a vain and empty life (1 Peter 1:18); and freedom from iniquity (Titus 2:14). Our redemption in Christ is final and permanent.

The glory of His submission. Peter could not understand why the Son of God would submit to evil men and willingly suffer. The Transfiguration was God's way of teaching Peter that Jesus is glorified when we deny ourselves, take up our cross, and follow

Him. The world's philosophy is "Save yourself!" but the Christian's philosophy is "Yield yourself to God!" As He stood there in glory, Jesus proved to the three disciples that surrender always leads to glory. First the suffering, then the glory; first the cross, then the crown.

Each of the three disciples would have a need for this important truth. James would be the first of the disciples to die (Acts 12:1–2). John would be the last of the disciples to die, but he would go through severe persecution on the Isle of Patmos (Rev. 1:9). Peter would experience many occasions of suffering and would, in the end, give his life for Christ (John 21:15–19; 2 Peter 1:12).

Peter opposed the cross when Jesus first mentioned His death (Matt. 16:22ff.). In the garden, he used his sword to defend Jesus (John 18:10). In fact, even on the Mount of Transfiguration Peter tried to tell Jesus what to do. He wanted to build three booths for Jesus, Moses, and Elijah so that all of them could remain there and enjoy the glory! But the Father interrupted Peter and gave other directions: "Hear him!" The Father will not permit His beloved Son to be put on the same level as Moses and Elijah. "Jesus only" (Matt. 17:8) is God's pattern.

As Jesus and His three disciples came down from the mountaintop, He cautioned them not to reveal what they had seen, not even to the other nine disciples. But the three men were still perplexed. They had been taught that Elijah would come first to prepare for the establishing of the kingdom. Was the presence of Elijah on the mountain the fulfillment of this prophecy (Mal. 4:5–6)?

Jesus gave a twofold answer to their question. Yes, Elijah would come as Malachi 4:5–6 promised. But spiritually speaking, Elijah already came in the person of John the Baptist (see Matt. 11:10–15; Luke 1:17). The nation permitted John to be killed, and would ask for Jesus to be slain. Yet God's program would be fulfilled in spite of the deeds of sinful leaders.

When will Elijah come to restore all things? Some people believe that Elijah will be one of the "two witnesses" whose ministry is described in Revelation 11. Others believe that the prophecy was fulfilled in the ministry of John the Baptist so that there will be no future coming of Elijah.

The King in His Power (17:14–21)

We move from the mountain of glory to the valley of need. The sudden appearance of Jesus and the three disciples startled the multitudes (Mark 9:15). The distraught father had brought his demonized son to the nine disciples, begging them to deliver him, but they could not. The scribes had noticed their failure and were using it as a reason for argument. And while the disciples were defending themselves, and the scribes were accusing them, the demon was all but killing the helpless boy.

When we compare the gospel accounts of this dramatic scene, we discover that this only son was indeed in great trouble and danger. Matthew recorded that the boy was an epileptic (lunatic), very ill, and suicidal, falling into the fire and the water. Mark described him as a mute, who often fell to the ground foaming at the mouth and grinding his teeth. After this display, the boy would go into a kind of *rigor mortis.* Dr. Luke said that the boy was an only son and that he would scream as he went into these convulsions. While some of these symptoms can have natural causes, this boy was at the mercy of a demon. The disciples had been helpless to do anything. No wonder the father rushed to Jesus' feet.

Our Lord's first response was one of sorrow. As He beheld the embarrassed disciples, the arguing scribes, and the needy father and son, He groaned inwardly and said, "How long shall I be with you, and put up with you?" (Luke 9:41 NASB). Their unbelief and spiritual perversity were a burden to Him. What must our Lord feel as He looks at powerless believers today?

Jesus delivered the boy and commanded the spirit never to return to him (Mark 9:25). The demon tried "one last throw" (as Spurgeon put it) so that the crowd thought the boy was dead (Mark 9:26). But Jesus raised the lad up and gave him to his father, while the crowds marveled and gave glory to God (Luke 9:43).

The nine disciples should have been able to cast out the demon. Jesus had given them this power and authority (Matt. 10:1, 8). But somehow, they had lost their power! When they asked Jesus the cause of their shameful failure, He told them: their lack of faith (Matt. 17:20), their lack of prayer (Mark 9:29), and their lack of discipline (Matt. 17:21, though this verse is not found in many manuscripts).

The nine were perhaps jealous because they had not been called to go to the mountaintop with Jesus. During the Lord's absence, they began to grow self-indulgent. They neglected prayer; their faith weakened. Then, when the crisis came, they were unprepared. Like Samson, they went out to battle without realizing that their power was gone (Judg. 16:20). From their example, we see the importance of staying spiritually healthy.

"Faith as a grain of mustard seed" suggests not only *size* (God will honor even a little faith), but also *life* and *growth.* Faith like a mustard seed is *living* faith that is nurtured and caused to grow. Faith must be cultivated so that it grows and does even greater exploits for God (1 Thess. 3:10; 2 Thess. 1:3). Had the nine disciples been praying, disciplining themselves, and meditating on the Word, they would have been able to cast out the demon and rescue the boy.

This entire scene illustrates what Jesus will do when He leaves the glory of heaven to come to this earth. He will defeat Satan and bind him for one thousand years (Rev. 20:1–6).

The King in His Humility (17:22–27)

For a second time, Jesus mentioned His death and resurrection. The disciples were deeply grieved and were afraid to ask Him about it. In fact, His disciples did not believe the reports of His resurrection because they had forgotten His promises (Mark 16:14). But the enemy remembered what He said (John 2:19) and acted accordingly (Matt. 27:62–66).

What a paradox: a king too poverty-stricken to pay the annual temple tax of only a half-shekel! The unique characteristics of this miracle are worth noting.

It is recorded only by Matthew. Matthew, a former tax collector, wrote the gospel of the King, and this miracle affirms our Lord's kingship. The kings of the earth do not take tribute from their own sons. Jesus affirmed Himself to be free from this tribute because He was the Son of the King, the Son of God. Yet, as the Son of God, He was too poor to pay even a half-shekel, and His disciples were as poor as He was. He exercised His kingship over nature to provide what was needed.

God gave Adam and Eve dominion over nature, and this included the fish in the sea (Gen. 1:26; Ps. 8:6–8). Man lost this dominion because of sin, so Peter was not able to command the fish and find the money. Jesus Christ exercised dominion over not only the fish, but also over the animals (Matt. 21:1–7) and the birds (Matt. 26:34, 74–75). What Adam lost because of his disobedience, Jesus Christ regained through His obedience (Heb. 2:6).

While today believers do not have complete dominion over nature, one day we shall reign with Christ and exercise dominion with Him. Meanwhile, God cares for His own and makes sure that all of nature is working for those who trust and obey.

It is the only miracle He performed to meet His own needs. Satan had tempted Christ to use His divine powers for Himself (Matt. 4:3–4), but He had refused. However, in this case, He did not use His power selfishly, for others were involved in this miracle. "Lest we cause them to stumble," was our Lord's explanation for the miracle. He did not want the people to be offended because He, being a Jew, did not support the temple ministry. While Jesus did not hesitate to break the man-made traditions of the Pharisees, He was careful to obey the law of God.

As Christians, we must never use our freedom in Christ to hurt or destroy others. Technically, Jesus did not have to pay the tax, but for practical reasons, He paid it. He also included Peter so that their testimony would not be hurt.

It is the only miracle using money. Since Matthew had been a tax collector, we would expect him to be interested in this miracle. This tax had its origin in the days of Moses (Ex. 30:11ff.). The original tax money was used to make the silver sockets on which the tabernacle poles were erected (Ex. 38:25–27). Subsequent taxes were used to support the ministry of the tabernacle and then the temple. The money was to be a reminder to the Jews that they had been redeemed from Egyptian slavery. We have been redeemed by the precious blood of Christ (1 Peter 1:18–19).

It is the only miracle using one fish. Jesus had multiplied the fish for Peter (Luke 5:1–11), and He would repeat that miracle (John 21:1ff.). But in this case, He used only one fish. When we consider the complexity of this miracle, it amazes us. First, someone had to lose a coin in the water. Then, a fish had to take that coin in its mouth and retain it. That same fish then had to bite on Peter's hook—with an impediment in its mouth—and be caught. You cannot explain all of this in a natural way. It is too complex for an accident, and too difficult for human management.

It was performed for Peter. How the other disciples paid their taxes, we are not told. This was one of many miracles that Jesus performed for Peter. He healed Peter's mother-in-law (Mark 1:29–34), helped Peter to catch fish (Luke 5:1–11), enabled him to walk on the water (Matt. 14:22–33), healed Malchus' ear (Matt. 26:47–56), and delivered Peter from prison (Acts 12:1ff.). No wonder Peter wrote, "Casting all your care upon him, for he cares for you" (1 Peter 5:7).

Jesus knew Peter's need and was able to meet that need. Peter thought he had the problem solved when he entered the house. But before he could tell Jesus what to do, Jesus told *him* what to do! God the Father had interrupted Peter on the mountain (Matt. 17:5), and now God the Son interrupted him in the house. If only we would let Jesus give the directions, we would see Him meet our needs for His glory.

It is the only miracle that does not have the results recorded. We would expect another verse that would read: "And Peter went to the sea, cast in a hook, and drew up a fish; and when he had opened its mouth, he found there a coin, and used it to pay the temple tax for himself and for Jesus." But Matthew 17:28 is not there. Then, how do we know that the miracle took place? *Because Jesus said it would!* "There hath not failed one word of all his good promise" (1 Kings 8:56).

We must commend Peter for his faith. The people at the seashore were accustomed to seeing Peter with a net in his hand, not a hook and line. But Peter had faith in God's Word, and God honored that faith. If we trust the King, He will meet our needs as we obey His Word.

CHAPTER FIFTEEN
Matthew 18
THE KING'S REBUKE

Why do some of God's children have such a difficult time getting along with each other? A poem I heard states the problem perfectly:

To live above, with saints we love
Will certainly be glory.
To live below, with saints we know—
Well, that's another story!

With so much division and dissension among professing Christians these days, we desperately need what Matthew 18 has to teach. Jesus rebuked His disciples for their pride and desire for worldly greatness, and He taught them the three essentials for unity and harmony among God's people.

Humility (18:1–14)

Someone has accurately defined humility as "that grace that, when you know you have it, you've lost it!" It has well been said, "True humility is not thinking meanly of oneself; it is simply not thinking of oneself at all."

The need for humility (v. 1). "Which one of us is the greatest?" was a repeated topic of discussion among the disciples, for we find it mentioned often in the gospel records. Recent events would have aggravated the problem, particularly with reference to Peter. After all, Peter had walked on the water, had been on the mountaintop with the Lord, and had even had his taxes paid by means of a miracle.

The fact that Jesus had been sharing with the disciples the truth about His coming suffering and death did not affect them. They were thinking only of themselves and what position they would have in His kingdom. So absorbed were the disciples in this matter that they actually *argued* with each other (Luke 9:46)!

The selfishness and disunity of God's people is a scandal to the Christian faith. What causes these problems? Pride—thinking ourselves more important than we really are. It was pride that led man into sin at the beginning (Gen. 3:5). When Christians are living for themselves and not for others, then there is bound to be conflict and division (Phil. 2:1ff.).

The example of humility (vv. 2–6, 10–14). The disciples waited breathlessly for Jesus to name the greatest man among them. But He bypassed them completely and called a little child into their midst. This child was the example of true greatness.

True humility means knowing yourself, accepting yourself, and being yourself—your *best* self—to the glory of God. It means avoiding two extremes: thinking *less* of yourself than you ought to (as did Moses when God called him, Ex. 3:11ff.), or thinking *more* of yourself than you ought to (Rom. 12:3). The truly humble person does not deny the gifts God has given him, but uses them to the glory of God.

An unspoiled child has the characteristics that make for humility: trust (Matt. 18:6), dependence, the desire to make others happy, an absence of boasting or selfish desire to be greater than others. By nature, all of us are rebels who want to be celebrities instead of servants. It takes a great deal of teaching for us to learn the lessons of humility.

The disciples wanted to know who was greatest *in* the kingdom. But Jesus warned them that, apart from humility, they could not even *enter* the kingdom! They had to be converted—turned around in their thinking—or they would never make it.

It seems that Jesus is, in these verses, blending two concepts: the human child as an example of humility, and the child of God no matter what his age might be. As Christians, we must not only accept the little children for Jesus' sake, but we must also receive *all* of God's children and seek to minister to them (Rom. 14:1ff.). It is a serious matter to cause a child to sin or to lead him astray. It is equally as serious to cause another believer to stumble because of our poor example (Rom. 14:13ff.; 1 Cor. 8:9ff.). True humility thinks of others, not of self.

Jesus explained that we can have four different attitudes toward the children and, consequently, toward true humility. We can seek to *become like the children* (Matt. 18:3–4) in true humility, as to the Lord. Or, we can only *receive them* (Matt. 18:5) because Jesus told us to. If we are not careful, we will *cause them to stumble* (Matt. 18:6), and even end up *despising them* (Matt. 18:10).

It is a dangerous thing to look down on the children, because God values them highly. When we welcome a child (or a Christian believer), we welcome Christ (Matt. 18:5). The Father cares for them and the angels watch over them (Matt. 18:10). Like the good shepherd, God seeks the lost and saves them, and we must not cause them to perish. If the shepherd goes after an adult sheep, how much more important is it that he protect the lambs!

In these days of child neglect and child abuse, we need to take Christ's warning seriously. It is better to drown with a heavy millstone around one's neck, than to abuse a child and face the judgment of God (Matt. 18:6).

The cost of humility (vv. 7–9). The truly humble person helps to build up others, not to tear them down. He is a stepping-stone, not a stumbling block. Therefore, anything that makes me stumble must be removed from my life, for if it is not, I cause others to stumble. Jesus had uttered similar words in the Sermon on the Mount (Matt. 5:29–30). Paul used the eye, hand, and foot to illustrate the mutual dependence of members of the body of Christ (1 Cor. 12:14–17).

Humility begins with self-examination, and it continues with self-denial. Jesus was not suggesting that we maim our bodies, for harming our physical bodies can never change the spiritual condition of our hearts. Rather, He was instructing us to perform "spiritual surgery" on ourselves, removing anything that causes us to stumble or that causes others to stumble. The humble person lives for Jesus first and others next—he puts himself last. He is happy to deprive himself even of good things, if it will make others happy. Perhaps the best commentary on this is Philippians 2:1–18.

Honesty (18:15–20)

We don't always practice humility. There are times when, deliberately or unconsciously, we offend others and hurt them. Even the Old Testament law recognized "sins of ignorance" (Num. 15:22), and David prayed to be delivered from "secret faults" (Ps. 19:12), meaning "faults that are even hidden from my own eyes." What should we do when another Christian has sinned against us or caused us to stumble? Our Lord gave several instructions.

Keep the matter private. Approach the person who sinned and speak with him alone. It is possible that he does not even realize what he has done. Or, even if he did it deliberately, your own attitude of submission and love will help him to repent and apologize. Above all else, go to him with the idea of winning your brother, not winning an argument. It is possible to win the argument and lose your brother.

We must have a spirit of meekness and gentleness when we seek to restore a brother or sister (Gal. 6:1). We must not go about condemning the offender, or spreading gossip. We must lovingly seek to help him in the same way we would want him to help us if the situation were reversed. The word *restore* in Galatians 6:1 is a Greek medical word that means "to set a broken bone." Think of the patience and tenderness that requires!

Ask for help from others. If the offender refuses to make things right, then we may feel free to share the burden with one or two dependable believers. We should share the facts as we see them and ask the brethren for their prayerful counsel. After all, it may be that *we* are wrong. If the brethren feel the cause is right, then together we can go to the offender and try once again to win him. Not only can these men assist in prayer and persuasion, but they can be witnesses to the church of the truth of the conversation (Deut. 19:15; 2 Cor. 13:1).

When sin is not dealt with honestly, it always spreads. What was once a matter between two people has now grown to involve four or five people. No wonder Jesus and Paul both compared sin to leaven (yeast), because leaven spreads.

Ask the church for help. Remember, our goal is not the winning of a case but the winning of a brother. The word *gained* in Matthew 18:15 is used in 1 Corinthians 9:19–22 to refer to winning the lost, but it is also important to win the saved. This is our Lord's second mention of the church (see Matt. 16:18), and here it has the meaning of a local assembly of believers. Our Lord's disciples were raised in the Jewish synagogue, so they were familiar with congregational discipline.

What started as a private problem between two people is now out in the open for the whole church to see. Church discipline is a neglected ministry these days, yet it is taught here and in the Epistles (see 1 Cor. 5; 2 Thess. 3:6–16; 2 Tim. 2:23–26; Titus 3:10). Just as children in the home need discipline, so God's children in the church need discipline. If by the time the matter comes to the whole church, the offender has not yet changed his mind and repented, then he must be disciplined. He cannot be treated as a spiritual brother, for he has forfeited that position. He can only be treated as one outside the church, not hated, but not held in close fellowship.

Keep the local church spiritual (vv. 18–20). It is important that the local assembly be at its best spiritually before it seeks to discipline a member. When a church disciplines a member, it is actually examining itself and disciplining itself. This is why our Lord added these words about authority, prayer, and fellowship. We cannot discipline others if we ourselves are not disciplined. Whatever we loose (permit) in the assembly must first have been permitted by God (see the comments on Matt. 16:19).

The church must be under the authority of God's Word. Church discipline does not refer to a group of Christian policemen throwing their weight around. Rather, it means God exercising His authority in and through a local body, to restore one of His erring children.

Not only must there be the authority of the Word, but there must also be prayer (Matt. 18:19). The word *agree* in the Greek gives us our English word *symphony*." The church must agree in prayer as it seeks to discipline the erring member. It is through prayer and the Word that we ascertain the will of the Father in the matter.

Finally, there must be fellowship (Matt. 18:20). The local church must be a worshipping community, recognizing the presence of the Lord in their midst. The Holy Spirit of God can convict both the offender and the church, and He can even judge sin in the midst (Acts 5).

There is a desperate need for honesty in the church today. "Speaking the truth in love" is God's standard (Eph. 4:15). If we practice love without truth, it is hypocrisy. But if we try to have truth without love, it may be brutality. Jesus always taught the truth in love. If the truth hurts, it is because "Faithful are the wounds of a friend" (Prov. 27:6).

But keep in mind that *humility* must come before *honesty*. A proud Christian cannot speak the truth in love. He will use a brother's faults as a weapon to fight with and not as a tool to build with. The result will be only greater disharmony and disagreement.

The first internal problem of the New Testament church was dishonesty (Acts 5). Ananias and Sapphira tried to make the church members believe that they were more spiritual than they really were. They lied to themselves in thinking they could get away with the masquerade; they lied to their fellow Christians and the church leaders; and they tried to lie to the Holy Spirit. The result was judgment and death. God may not kill every hypocrite in the church today, but hypocrisy certainly helps to kill the church.

The second internal problem (Acts 6) had to do with people being neglected. The members and leaders faced this problem with truth and love, and the result was blessing. It takes both truth and love, and both must be used with humility.

Forgiveness (18:21–35)

When we start living in an atmosphere of humility and honesty, we must take some risks and expect some dangers. Unless humility and honesty result in forgiveness, relationships cannot be mended and strengthened. Peter recognized the risks involved and asked Jesus how he should handle them in the future.

But Peter made some serious mistakes. To begin with, he lacked humility himself. He was sure his brother would sin against him, but not he against his brother! Peter's second mistake was in asking for limits and measures. Where there is love, there can be no limits or dimensions (Eph. 3:17–19). Peter thought he was showing great faith and love when he offered to forgive at least seven times. After all, the rabbis taught that three times was sufficient.

Our Lord's reply, "Until seventy times seven" (490 times) must have startled Peter. Who could keep count for that many offenses? But that was exactly the point Jesus was making: Love "keeps no record of wrongs" (1 Cor. 13:5 NIV). By the time we have forgiven a brother that many times, we are in the habit of forgiving.

But Jesus was not advising careless or shallow forgiveness. Christian love is not blind (Phil. 1:9–10). The forgiveness Christ requires is on the basis of the instructions He gave in Matthew 18:15–20. If a brother is guilty of a repeated sin, no doubt he would find strength and power to conquer that sin through the encouragement of his loving and forgiving brethren. If we condemn a brother, we bring out the worst in him. But if we create an atmosphere of love and forgiveness, we can help God bring out the best in him.

The parable illustrates the power of forgiveness. It is important to note that *this parable is not about salvation,* for salvation is wholly of grace and is unconditionally given. To make God's forgiveness a temporary thing is to violate the very truth of Scripture (Rom. 5:8; Eph. 2:8–9; Titus 3:3–7). The parable deals with forgiveness between *brothers,* not between lost sinners and God. The emphasis in this chapter is on brother forgiving brother (Matt. 18:15, 21).

The main character in this parable went through three stages in his experience of forgiveness.

He was a debtor (vv. 23–27). This man had been stealing funds from the king and, when the books were audited, his crime was discovered. The total tax levy in Palestine was about 800 talents a year, so you can see how dishonest this man was. In terms of today's buying power, this was probably equivalent to over $10 million.

But this man actually thought he could get out of the debt. He told the king that, given enough time, he could pay it back. We detect two sins here: pride and a lack of sincere repentance. The man was not ashamed because he stole the money; he was ashamed because he got caught. And he actually thought he was big enough to earn the money to repay the king's account. In the economy of that day, a man would have had to work twenty years to earn one talent.

His case was hopeless, except for one thing: The king was a man of compassion. He assumed the loss and forgave the servant. This meant that the man was free and that he and his family would not be thrown into a debtor's prison. The servant did not deserve this forgiveness; it was purely an act of love and mercy on the part of the master.

He was a creditor (v. 28–30). The servant left the presence of the king and went and found a fellow servant who owed him one hundred pence. The average worker earned one penny a day, so this debt was insignificant compared to what the servant had owed the king. Instead of sharing with his friend the joy of his own release, the servant mistreated his friend and demanded that he pay the debt. The debtor used the same approach as the servant: "Have patience with me and I will pay you all of it!" But the unjust servant was unwilling to grant to others what he wanted others to grant to him.

Perhaps he had the *legal* right to throw the man in prison, but he did not have the *moral* right. He had been forgiven himself—should he not forgive his fellow servant? He and his family had been spared the shame and suffering of prison. Should he not spare his friend?

He became a prisoner (vv. 31–34). The king originally delivered him from prison, but the servant put himself back in. The servant exercised justice and cast his friend into prison. "So you want to live by justice?" asked the king. "Then you shall have justice! Throw the wicked servant in prison and torment him! I will do to him as he has done to others." (There is no suggestion that the entire family was sentenced. After all, it was the father who abused the other servant and ignored the king's kindness.)

The world's worst prison is the prison of an unforgiving heart. If we refuse to forgive others, then we are only imprisoning ourselves and causing our own torment. Some of the most miserable people I have met in my ministry have been people who would not forgive others. They lived only to imagine ways to punish these people who had wronged them. But they were really only punishing themselves.

What was wrong with this man? The same thing that is wrong with many professing Christians: They have *received* forgiveness, but they have not really *experienced* forgiveness deep in their hearts. Therefore, they are unable to *share* forgiveness with those who have wronged them. If we live only according to justice, always seeking to get what is ours, we will put ourselves into prison. But if we live according to forgiveness, sharing with others what God has shared with us, then we will enjoy freedom and joy. Peter asked for a just measuring rod; Jesus told him to practice forgiveness and forget the measuring rod.

Our Lord's warning is serious. He did not say that God *saves* only those who forgive others. The theme of this parable is forgiveness between brothers, not salvation for lost sinners. Jesus warned us that God cannot forgive us *if we do not have humble and repentant hearts.*

We reveal the true condition of our hearts by the way we treat others. When our hearts are humble and repentant, we will gladly forgive our brothers. But where there is pride and a desire for revenge, there can be no true repentance, and this means God cannot forgive.

In other words, it is not enough to *receive* God's forgiveness, or even the forgiveness of others. We must *experience* that forgiveness in our hearts so that it humbles us and makes us gentle and forgiving toward others. The servant in the parable did not have a deep experience of forgiveness and humility. *He was simply glad to be "off the hook."* He had never really repented.

"And be ye kind one to another, tenderhearted, forgiving one another, even as God for Christ's sake hath forgiven you" (Eph. 4:32). "Forbearing one another, and forgiving one another, if any man have a quarrel against any: even as Christ forgave you, so also do ye" (Col. 3:13).

CHAPTER SIXTEEN
Matthew 19:1–15
THE KING'S INSTRUCTIONS

The King's "retirement" from the crowds was about to come to an end. But the attacks of the enemy would grow more intense, culminating in His arrest and crucifixion. The religious leaders had already tried to ensnare Him with questions about the Sabbath and signs, and they had failed. They tried again, this time with a most controversial issue—divorce.

This subject is both important and controversial today. The divorce rate continues to climb (at this writing, one divorce for every 1.8 marriages), and divorce has invaded even the homes of Christian leaders. Someone has commented that couples "are married for better or for worse, but not for long." We need to examine again what Jesus taught about this subject. He explained four different laws relating to marriage and divorce.

The Original Creation Law (19:3–6)
Instead of going back to Deuteronomy, Jesus went back to Genesis. What God did when He established the first marriage teaches us *positively* what He had in mind for a man and a woman. If we build a marriage after God's ideal pattern, we will not have to worry about divorce laws.

The reasons for marriage. The only thing that was not "good" about creation was the fact that the man was alone (Gen. 2:18). The woman was created to meet this need. Adam could not find fellowship with the animals. He needed a companion who was equal to him and with whom he could find fulfillment. God's answer to this need was Eve.

Marriage makes possible the continuation of the race. "Be fruitful, and multiply" was God's mandate to the first married couple (Gen. 1:28). From the beginning it was God's command that sex be practiced in the commitment of marriage. Outside of marriage, sex becomes a destructive force; but within the loving commitment of marriage, sex can be creative and constructive.

Marriage is one way to avoid sexual sins (1 Cor. 7:1–6). Of course, a man should not marry simply to legalize lust! If he is lustful outside of marriage, he will no doubt be lustful after he is married. He should not think that getting married will solve all of his personal problems with lust. But marriage is God's appointed way for a man and a woman to share the physical joys of sex.

Paul used marriage as an illustration of the intimate relationship between Christ and the church (Eph. 5:22–23). Just as Eve was taken from the side of Adam (Gen. 2:21), so the church was born from the suffering and death of Christ on the cross. Christ loves His church, nourishes it with His Word, cleanses it, and cares for it. Christ's relationship to His church is the example for all husbands to follow.

The characteristics of marriage. By going back to the original Edenic law, Jesus reminded His listeners of the true characteristics of marriage. If we remember these characteristics, we will better know how to build a happy and enduring marriage.

It is a divinely appointed union. God established marriage, and therefore only God can control its character and laws. No court of law can change what God has established.

It is a physical union. The man and woman become "one flesh." While it is important that a husband and wife be of one mind and heart, the basic union in marriage is physical. If a man and woman became "one spirit" in marriage, then death would not dissolve the marriage, for the spirit never dies. Even if a man and woman disagree, are "incompatible," and cannot get along, they are still married, for the union is a physical one.

It is a permanent union. God's original design was that one man and one woman spend one life together. God's original law knows nothing of "trial marriages." God's law requires that the husband and wife enter into marriage without reservations.

It is a union between one man and one woman. God did not create two men and one woman, two women and one man, two men, or two women. "Group marriages," "gay marriages," and other variations are contrary to the will of God, no matter what some psychologists and jurists may say.

The Seventh Commandment (5:27–30)
While Jesus did not refer to the seventh commandment in this discussion, He did quote it in the Sermon on the Mount (Matt. 5:27–32). Let's examine what He said.

Jesus and the New Testament writers affirm the authority of "Thou shalt not commit adultery" (Ex.

20:14). While the word *fornication* seems to cover many kinds of sexual sins (see Mark 7:21; Rom. 1:29; 1 Cor. 6:13), *adultery* involves only married people. When a married person has intercourse with someone other than his or her mate, that is adultery. God has declared that it is wrong and it is sin. There are numerous warnings in the New Testament against sexual sins, including adultery (Acts 15:20; 1 Cor. 6:15–18; Gal. 5:19ff.; Eph. 4:17ff.; 5:3–12; Col. 3:5; 1 Thess. 4:3–7; Heb. 13:4).

This commandment affirms the sanctity of sex. God created it, God protects it, and God punishes when His law is violated. Nine of the Ten Commandments are repeated in the New Testament for us to heed. (The Sabbath commandment was given only to Israel and does not apply to the church today.) We must not think that because we are "under grace" we can flaunt God's law and get away with it. "Fornicators and adulterers God will judge" (Heb. 13:4 NASB).

However, Jesus went much deeper in His discussion of adultery. He showed that this can be a sin of the heart as well as a sin of the body. It is not enough simply to control the body; we must also control the inner thoughts and desires. To look at a woman *for the purpose of lusting after her* is to commit adultery in the heart. This does not mean that we cannot admire a beautiful person or picture, for it is possible to do that and not sin. It is when we look *with the intention* of satisfying lustful desires that we commit adultery in the heart.

A sanctified sex life begins with the inner desires. Jesus singled out the eye and the hand, because seeing and feeling are usually the first steps toward sexual sin. Of course, He did not command us to perform *physical* surgery, since He was clearly dealing with the *inner* desires. He commanded us to deal drastically with sin, to remove from our lives anything that would pamper our wrong desires. We must "hunger and thirst after righteousness."

Jesus did not alter the original Edenic law of marriage, nor did He annul the seventh commandment What He taught was based solidly on God's creation and God's moral law.

The Mosaic Law of Divorce (19:7–8)

Like many people who "argue religion," these Pharisees were not interested in discovering truth. They were interested only in defending themselves and what they believed. This was why they asked about the Jewish law of divorce recorded in Deuteronomy 24:1–4.

I suggest you read this important passage in the New American Standard Bible to distinguish the tenses of the verbs. This translation makes it clear that Moses gave *only one commandment:* The divorced wife could not return to her first husband if she was put away by a second husband. *Moses did not command divorce;* he permitted it. He commanded that the husband give his ex-wife a legal bill of divorcement. But the wife could not return to her first husband after being remarried and divorced.

What a wise law this was. To begin with, the husband would think twice before hastily putting away his wife, since he could not get her back again. Furthermore, it would have taken time to find a scribe (not everyone could write legal documents), and during that time the two estranged people might have been reconciled. The Pharisees were interpreting Moses' law as though it were a commandment. Jesus made it clear that Moses was only giving *permission* for divorce.

But what did Moses mean by "some uncleanness in her"? The Hebrew means "some matter of nakedness," but this need not refer to sexual sin. That phrase is the equivalent of "some shameful thing" (see Gen. 2:25; 3:7, 10). It is the interpretation of this phrase that divided the two schools of Rabbi Hillel and Rabbi Shammai, famous first-century Jewish scholars. Hillel took a very lax view and said that the husband could divorce his wife for almost any reason, while Shammai took the stricter view and said Moses was speaking only about sexual sin. No matter which side Jesus took, He would surely offend somebody.

There were several laws of marriage given to the Jews, and we must examine them in order to get some perspective. For example, if a man married a woman and discovered that she was not a virgin, he could expose her sin and have her stoned (Deut. 22:13–21). Of course, he had to have proof, and if he did not, he was fined and had to live with the woman all of his life. This law was as much a protection to the woman as to the man.

If a man suspected his wife of unfaithfulness, he followed the procedure outlined in Numbers 5:11ff. We cannot follow that procedure today (which certainly included elements of divine judgment) since there is no priesthood or tabernacle.

Remember that the law of Moses demanded *the death penalty* for those who committed adultery (Lev. 20:10; Deut. 22:22). Our Lord's enemies appealed to this law when they tried to trap Him (John 8:1). While we have no record in the Old Testament that anyone was stoned for committing adultery, this was the divine law. The experience of Joseph (Matt. 1:18–25) indicates that the Jews used divorce rather than stoning in dealing with an adulterous wife.

Why did God command that the adulterer or adulteress be stoned to death? Certainly as an example to warn the people, for adultery undermines the very fabric of society and the home. There must be commitment in marriage, and faithfulness to each other and to God, if there is to be stability in society and in the church. God had to preserve Israel because the promised Savior would come through that nation. God opposed divorce in Israel because it weakened the nation and threatened the birth of the Messiah (see Mal. 2:10–16).

But there was another reason for capital punishment:

This left the other party free to marry again. Death breaks the marriage bond, since marriage is a physical union (Rom. 7:1–3). It was important that families be continued in Israel that they might protect their inheritance (Num. 36).

We must note one final fact before leaving this section: The divorce that Moses permitted in Deuteronomy 24 *actually severed the original marriage relationship.* God permitted the woman to marry again, and her second marriage was not considered adulterous. The second man she married was called a "husband" and not an adulterer. This explains how the woman of Samaria could have had five *husbands,* and yet be living with a man not her husband (John 4:16–18). Apparently all five of those marriages had been legal and scriptural.

This means that scriptural divorce does sever the marriage relationship. *Man* cannot break this relationship by his laws, but *God can break it.* The same God who gives the laws that join people together can also give laws to put them asunder. God can do it, but man cannot.

Finally, Jesus made it clear that this Mosaic law of divorce was a concession on God's part. God's original law of marriage left no room for divorce, but that law was laid down before man had sinned. Rather than have two people living together in constant conflict, with one or both of them seeking fulfillment elsewhere and thus commit sin, God permitted divorce. *This divorce included the right to remarriage.* The Pharisees did not ask about remarriage, for this was no problem. They accepted the fact that the parties would seek other mates, and this was allowed by Moses.

Our Lord's Law of Marriage (19:9–12; 5:31–32)

When Jesus said "And I say unto you," He was claiming to be God, for only God can establish or alter the laws of marriage. He declared that marriage was a permanent union that could only be broken by sexual sin. The word *fornication* in the New Testament covers many kinds of sexual sins. The definition of fornication as "sexual sin between two unmarried persons" would not apply here, for Jesus was talking about married persons. Are we to believe that the 23,000 men who committed fornication under the enticement of Baalam (Num. 25) were all unmarried men? Was the admonition of Acts 15:20, 29 sent only to single church members?

Marriage is a permanent physical union that can be broken only by a physical cause: death or sexual sin. (I would take it that homosexuality and bestiality would qualify.) Man cannot break the union, but God can. Under the Old Testament law, the sinner was stoned to death. But the church today does not bear the sword (Rom. 13:1–4). Were adultery and fornication more serious under the law than the same sins are today? Of course not! If anything, such sins are even worse today in the light of the full revelation of God's grace and holiness that we now have in Jesus Christ.

The conclusion seems to be that divorce in the New Testament is the equivalent of death in the Old Testament: It permitted the innocent party freedom to remarry.

Notice that our Lord's new law of marriage and divorce was based on the three previous laws. From the Edenic law He took the principle that marriage was a physical union that could only be broken by a physical cause, and that only God could permit the breaking of the union. From the seventh commandment He took the principle that sexual sin did indeed break the marriage union. From the Mosaic law of divorce He took the principle that God could ordain divorce and effectively break the marriage union, and that the freed party could remarry and not be guilty of adultery.

Our Lord's teaching is that there is only one scriptural basis for divorce, and that is sexual sin (fornication). If two people are divorced on any other basis, and marry other mates, they are committing adultery.

Jesus did not teach that the offended mate *had* to get a divorce. Certainly there can be forgiveness, patient healing, and a restoration of the broken relationship. This would be the Christian approach to the problem. But, sad to say, because of the hardness of our hearts, it is sometimes impossible to heal the wounds and save the marriage. Divorce is the *final* option, not the first option.

Happy marriages are not accidents. They are the result of commitment, love, mutual understanding, sacrifice, and hard work. If a husband and wife are fulfilling their marriage vows, they will enjoy a growing relationship that will satisfy them and keep them true to each other. Except for the possibility of sudden temptation, no husband or wife would think of a relationship with another person, so long as their relationship at home is growing and satisfying. And the pure love of a husband or wife is a great protection against even sudden temptation.

The disciples' response to Christ's teaching showed that they disagreed with Him. "If there is no way to get out of a bad marriage, then you are better off staying single!" was their argument. Jesus did not want them to consider divorce as an "out" because then they would not have a serious attitude toward marriage.

In Matthew 19:12, Jesus made it clear that each man (and woman) must consider God's will concerning marriage. Some people should not get married because of physical or emotional problems from birth. Others should not get married because of their responsibilities in society; they have been "made eunuchs by man." An only child who must care for aged parents might be an example of this category. Some, like the apostle Paul, stay single that they might better serve the Lord (1 Cor. 7:7).

It is fitting that our Lord's teaching about marriage should be followed by His blessing of the children, for children are the happy heritage of those who are married. Jesus did not look on the children as a curse or a burden. "Two shall become one flesh" is fulfilled in the birth of children, and the love of the parents is deepened and matured as it is shared with others in the home.

The parents brought the children to Jesus that He might bless them. There is no thought here of baptism or even of salvation. Children who have not reached the age of accountability (Isa. 7:16) are surely covered by the death of Christ (Rom. 5:17–21). Children are born sinners (Ps. 51:5), but if they die before they are accountable, they are regenerated and taken to heaven (2 Sam. 12:23; Ps. 23:6).

The children were certainly privileged to have Jesus take them in His arms and pray for them. Our practice of baby dedication today seeks to follow this example. How happy those children are whose parents are married in the will of God, and who are seeking to obey God, and who bring them to Jesus for His blessing.

CHAPTER SEVENTEEN
Matthew 19:16—20:34
THE KING'S DEMANDS

We cannot follow the King without paying a price. After all, He went to the cross for us! Have we the right to escape sacrifice and suffering? In this section, our Lord explains the rightful demands that He makes on those who want to trust Him and be His disciples.

We Must Love Christ Supremely (19:16–26)
Each of the first three Gospels records this event. When we combine the facts, we learn that this man was rich, young, and a ruler—probably the ruler of a synagogue. We can certainly commend this young man for coming publicly to Christ and asking about external matters. He seemed to have no ulterior motive and was willing to listen and learn. Sadly, he made the wrong decision.

The event seems to develop around several important questions.

"What good thing shall I do, that I may have eternal life?" (vv. 16–17). The man was obviously sincere, though his approach to salvation was centered on works and not faith. But this was to be expected among the Jews of that day. However, in spite of his position in society, his morality, and his religion, he felt a definite need for something more.

But our Lord's reply did not focus on salvation. He forced the young man to think seriously about the word *good* that he had used in addressing Jesus. "Only God is good," Jesus said. "Do you believe that I am good and therefore that I am God?" If Jesus is only one of many religious teachers in history, then His words carry no more weight than the pronouncements of any other religious leader. But if Jesus is good, then He is God, and we had better heed what He says.

Why did Jesus bring up the commandments? Did He actually teach that people receive eternal life by obeying God's law? If anyone *could* keep the commandments, he certainly would enter into life. But no one can keep God's law perfectly. "Therefore by the deeds of the law there shall no flesh be justified in his sight: for by the law is the knowledge of sin" (Rom. 3:20). Jesus did not introduce the law to show the young man how to be saved, but to show him that *he needed to be saved.* The law is a mirror that reveals what we are (James 1:22ff.).

"Which commandments?" (vv. 18–19). Was the young man being evasive? I don't think so. But he was making a mistake, for one part of God's law cannot be separated from another part. To classify God's laws into "lesser" and "greater" is to miss the whole purpose of the law. "For whosoever shall keep the whole law, and yet offend in one point, he is guilty of all" (James 2:10). The law represents the authority of God, and to disobey what we may think is a minor law is still to rebel against His authority.

Of course, the young man thought only of external obedience. He forgot about the attitudes of the heart. Jesus had taught in the Sermon on the Mount that hatred was the moral equivalent of murder, and that lust was the equivalent of adultery. We rejoice that this young man had such good manners and morals. But we regret that he did not see his sin, repent, and trust Christ.

The one commandment that especially applied to him, Jesus did not quote: "Thou shalt not covet" (Ex. 20:17). The young man should have pondered *all* of the commandments and not just the ones that Jesus quoted. Was he looking for easy discipleship? Was he being dishonest with himself? I believe that his testimony was sincere, *as far as he knew.* But he did not permit the light of the Word to penetrate deeply enough. Jesus felt a sudden love for this young man (Mark 10:21), so He continued to try to help him.

"What lack I yet?" (vv. 20–22). Nowhere in the Bible are we taught that a sinner is saved by selling his goods and giving the money away. Jesus never told Nicodemus to do this, or any other sinner whose story is recorded in the Gospels. Jesus knew that this man was covetous; he loved material wealth. By asking him to sell his goods, Jesus was forcing him to examine his own heart and determine his priorities. With all of his commendable qualities, the young man still did not truly love God with *all* of his heart. Possessions were his god. He was unable to obey the command, "Go and sell … come and follow."

The young man went away grieved, but he could have gone away in great joy and peace. We cannot love and serve two masters (Matt. 6:24ff.). We can be sure that, apart from Christ, even the material possessions of life give no lasting joy or pleasure. It is good to have the things money can buy provided we do not lose the things that money cannot buy. Unless this rich ruler eventually turned to Christ, he died without salvation, one of the "richest" men in the cemetery.

"Who then can be saved?" (vv. 23—26). The Jewish people of that day believed that riches were an evidence of God's blessing. They based this on the promises God gave the Jewish nation at the beginning of their history. It is true that God *did* promise material blessing if they obeyed, and material loss if they disobeyed (see Deut. 26—28). But in the infancy of the race, the only way God could teach them was through rewards and punishments. We teach young children in the same manner.

However, the highest kind of obedience is not based on a desire for reward or the fear of punishment. It is motivated by love. In His life and His teaching, Jesus tried to show the people that the inner spiritual blessings are far more important than the material gains. God sees the heart, and God wants to build character. Salvation is the gift of God in response to man's faith. Material riches are not a guarantee that God is pleased with a man.

The disciples, being good Jews, were amazed at the Lord's statement about riches. Their question reflected their theology: "If a rich man cannot be saved, what hope is there for the rest of us?" Of course, Jesus did not say that the *possessing* of wealth kept a man from the kingdom. Some manuscripts of Mark 10:24 read, "How hard it is for those who trust in riches to enter the kingdom of God." This is certainly the import of our Lord's teaching. Abraham was a very wealthy man, yet he was a man of great faith. It is good to possess wealth if wealth does not possess you.

We cannot follow the King and live for worldly wealth. We cannot serve God and money. The love of money is the root of all kinds of evil (1 Tim. 6:6–10). Jesus Christ demands of all who will follow Him that they love Him supremely.

We Must Obey Him Unreservedly (19:27—20:16)

Peter was quick to see the contrast between the wealthy ruler and poor disciples. "We have forsaken all, and followed thee; what shall we have therefore?" Jesus gave them a marvelous promise of rewards in this life and in the next. They would even share thrones when He established His kingdom. Whatever good things they had forsaken for His sake would be returned to them a hundredfold. In other words, they were not making sacrifices—they were making investments. But not all of the dividends would be received in this life.

However, Jesus detected in Peter's question the possibility of a wrong motive for service. This was why He added the warning that some who were first in their own eyes would be last in the judgment, and some who were last would end up first. This truth was amplified in the parable of the workers in the vineyard.

This parable has nothing to do with salvation. The penny (a day's wages in that time) does not represent salvation, for nobody works for his salvation. Nor is the parable talking about rewards, for we are not all

going to receive the same reward. "And every man shall receive his own reward according to his own labor" (1 Cor. 3:8).

The parable is emphasizing *a right attitude in service.* It is important to note that there were actually two kinds of workers hired that day: those who wanted a contract and agreed to work for a penny a day, and those who had no contract and agreed to take whatever the owner thought was right. The first laborers that he hired insisted on a contract.

This explains why the householder paid the workers as he did: He wanted those who were hired first (who insisted on a contract) to see how much he paid the workers who were hired later. It was one way the owner could show those workers how really generous he was.

Put yourself in the place of those workers who were hired first but paid last. They each expected to get a penny, because that was what they agreed to accept. But imagine their surprise when they saw the laborers who were hired *last* each receiving a penny! This meant their own wages should have been twelve pennies each!

But the three o'clock workers also received a penny—for only three hours of work. The men last in line quickly recalculated their wages: four pennies for the day's work. When the men hired at noon also were paid a penny, this cut the salary of the contract workers considerably, for now they would earn only two pennies.

But the owner gave them one penny each. Of course, they complained! But they had no argument, because *they had agreed to work for a penny.* They received what they asked for. Had they trusted the goodness of the owner, they would have received far more. But they insisted on a contract.

The lesson for Christ's disciples is obvious. We should not serve Him because we want to receive an expected reward, and we should not insist on knowing what we will get. God is infinitely generous and gracious and will always give us better than we deserve.

Now we can understand the perils that were hidden in Peter's question in Matthew 19:27. For one thing, we must not "suppose" (Matt. 20:10) that we will get something more if we really do not deserve it. It is possible to do the Father's work and yet not do His will from the heart (Eph. 6:6). If we serve Him only for the benefits (temporal and eternal), then we will miss the best blessings He has for us. We must trust Him unreservedly and believe that He will always give what is best.

There is the danger of pride. "What shall we have?" asked Peter. This parable warned him, "How do you know you will have anything?" Beware of overconfidence when it comes to the rewards God will give, for those first in their own eyes (and in the eyes of others) may end up last! Likewise, do not get discouraged, for those who consider themselves "unprofitable servants" may end up first.

Beware of the danger of watching other workers and

measuring yourself by them. "Judge nothing before the time," Paul warns in 1 Corinthians 4:5. We see the worker and the work, but God sees the heart.

Finally, we must beware of criticizing God and feeling that we have been left out. Had the early morning workers trusted the owner and not asked for an agreement, the owner would have given them much more. He was generous, but they would not trust him. They did not rejoice that others received more; instead, they were jealous and complained. The goodness of the owner did not lead them to repentance (Rom. 2:4). It revealed the true character of their hearts: They were selfish! Whenever we find a complaining servant, we know he has not fully yielded to the master's will.

We Must Glorify Him Completely (20:17–34)

For the third time, Jesus announced His arrest, crucifixion, and resurrection (see Matt. 16:21; 17:22). In the previous announcements, He had not specified how He would die. But now He clearly mentioned the cross. He also clearly mentioned His resurrection, but the message did not penetrate the disciples' hearts.

In contrast to this announcement of suffering and death, we have the request of James and John and their mother, Salome. Jesus spoke about a cross, but they were interested in a crown. They wanted reserved seats on special thrones! We get the impression that the mother, Salome, was the real inspiration behind this request, and that she was interested in promoting her sons.

Before we criticize what they did, let's notice some commendable features in this event. For one thing, they *did* believe in prayer, and they dared to believe the promise Jesus had given about sitting on thrones (Matt. 19:28). The word *regeneration* in that verse means "new birth," and refers to the new world over which Jesus and His followers will reign when He returns to earth. It must have taken faith on their part to believe He would establish these thrones, because He had just told them that He was going to die.

But there were several things wrong with their request. To begin with, it was born in ignorance. "Ye know not what ye ask," Jesus replied. Little did Salome realize that the path to the throne is a difficult one. James was the first of the disciples to be martyred, and John had to endure hard days on the Isle of Patmos. These three believers wanted *their* will, not God's will, and they wanted it *their* way.

Another factor was their lack of heavenly direction. They were thinking like *the world:* James and John wanted to "lord it over" the other disciples the way the unsaved Gentile rulers lorded it over their subjects. Their request was *fleshly* (sensual), because they were selfishly asking for glory for themselves, not for the Lord. No doubt they felt relieved that they had gotten to Jesus with this request before Peter did!

Finally, the request was not only of the world and the flesh, but it was of *the devil.* It was motivated by pride. Satan had sought a throne (Isa. 14:12–15) and had been cast down. Satan had offered Jesus a throne and had been refused (Matt. 4:8–11). Satan magnifies *the end* (a throne) but not *the means to* that end. Jesus warned Salome and her sons that the special thrones were available to those who were worthy of them. There are no shortcuts in the kingdom of God.

The result of this request was "indignation" on the part of the other disciples—probably because they had not thought of it first! The wisdom from above always leads to peace; the wisdom of this world leads to war (James 3:13—4:3). Selfishness will only result in dissension and division.

This disagreement gave Jesus the opportunity to teach a practical lesson on leadership. In His kingdom, we must not follow the examples of the world. Our example is Jesus, not some corporation president or wealthy celebrity. Jesus came as a servant; therefore, we should serve one another. He came to give His life; therefore, we should give our lives in service to Him and others.

The word *minister* in Matthew 20:26 means "a servant." Our English word *deacon* comes from it. The word *servant* in Matthew 20:27 means "a slave." Not every servant was a slave, but every slave was a servant. It is sad to note in the church today that we have many celebrities, but very few servants. There are many who want to "exercise authority" (Matt. 20:25), but few who want to take the towel and basin and wash feet.

The key to greatness is not found in position or power, but in character. We get a throne by paying with our lives, not by praying with our lips. We must identify with Jesus Christ in His service and suffering, for even He could not reach the throne except by way of the cross. The best commentary on this is Philippians 2:1–18.

To improve our praying we must improve our serving. If we are serving Him and others, then we will not be praying selfishly. If we honestly can say, "Speak, Lord, for thy servant heareth," then He will say to us, "Speak, servant, for thy Lord heareth." If our prayers do not make us better servants, then there is something wrong with them.

Do our prayers make us easier to live with? The two disciples prayed selfishly and threw the fellowship into an uproar! Do our prayers make us more like Jesus Christ? *Do our prayers cost us anything?* Prayer in the will of God does not mean escape; it means involvement. If our prayers do not bring us nearer to the cross, they are out of God's will.

Salome learned her lesson. When Jesus was crucified, she was standing near the cross (John 19:25, "his mother's sister") and sharing in His sorrow and pain. She did not see two thrones on either side of her Lord—she saw two thieves on two crosses. And she heard Jesus give her son, John, to His mother, Mary. Salome's selfishness was rebuked, and she meekly accepted it.

The closing event of Matthew 20 is the healing of Bartimaeus and his friend, both of whom were blind (see Mark 10:46–52). Here Jesus put into practice what He had just taught the disciples. He became a servant to two rejected blind beggars. The crowds around Jesus tried to silence the two men. After all, what claim did they have on the great Teacher? But Jesus had compassion on them and healed them. He was the servant even of beggars.

This chapter contains some hard things for us to receive and practice. If we love the things of this world, we cannot love God supremely. If we are not yielded completely to His will, we cannot obey Him unreservedly. If we seek glory for ourselves, or if we compare ourselves with other believers, then we cannot glorify Him.

We cannot acknowledge Jesus as our King unless we love Him supremely, obey Him unreservedly, and glorify Him completely. But if we do these things, we will share in His life and joy, and one day reign with Him!

CHAPTER EIGHTEEN
Matthew 21:1—22:14
THE KING'S JUDGMENTS

We now enter the fourth major section of Matthew's gospel, "The Rejection of the King." In this section (Matt. 21:1—22:14), the Lord Jesus revealed the sins of Israel and explained why the religious leaders rejected Him and His message.

Spiritual Blindness (21:1–11)
Since it was Passover, there were probably about two million people in and around Jerusalem. This was the only time in His ministry that Jesus actually planned and promoted a public demonstration. Up to this time, He had cautioned people not to tell who He was, and He had deliberately avoided public scenes.

Why did Jesus plan this demonstration? For one thing, He was obeying the Word and fulfilling the prophecy recorded in Zechariah 9:9. This prophecy could apply only to Jesus Christ, for He is the only One with credentials that prove He is Israel's King. We usually do not associate the lowly donkey with kingship, but this was the royal animal of Jewish monarchs (1 Kings 1:32–35). There were actually two animals involved, the mother and the colt (foal). Jesus sat on the colt with the mother walking beside.

By comparing Matthew's quotation with the original prophecy in Zechariah, we discover some interesting facts. Zechariah's prophecy opens with, "Rejoice greatly" but Matthew omitted this phrase. When Jesus approached the city, He wept! How could He (or the people) rejoice when judgment was coming?

Mathew also omitted "He is just, and having salvation." Our Lord's coming to Jerusalem was an act of mercy and grace, not an act of justice or judgment. He did have salvation for them, but they refused to accept it (John 1:11). The next time Israel sees the King, He will ride in great power and glory (Rev. 19:11ff.).

This colt had never been ridden (Mark 11:2), yet he meekly bore his burden. The presence of the mother helped, of course. But keep in mind that his rider was the King who has "dominion over … all sheep and oxen, yea, and the beasts of the field" (Ps. 8:6–7). The fact that Jesus rode this beast and kept him in control is another evidence of His kingship.

There was a second reason for this public presentation: It forced the Jewish leaders to act. When they saw the spontaneous demonstration of the people, they concluded that Jesus had to be destroyed (see John 12:19). The prophetic Scriptures required that the Lamb of God be crucified on Passover. This demonstration of Christ's popularity incited the rulers to act.

The people acclaimed Jesus as their King both by their words and their deeds. They shouted *Hosanna,* which means, "Save now!" They were quoting from Psalm 118:25–26, and this psalm is definitely messianic in character. Later that week, Jesus Himself would refer to this psalm and apply it to Himself (Ps. 118:22–23; Matt. 21:42).

Keep in mind that this Passover crowd was composed of at least three groups: the Jews who lived in Jerusalem, the crowd from Galilee, and the people who saw Jesus raise Lazarus from the dead (John 12:17–18). Sharing the news of this miracle undoubtedly helped to draw such a large crowd. The people wanted to see this miracle-worker for themselves.

But the Jews still did not recognize Jesus as their King. What caused Israel's spiritual blindness? For one thing, their religious leaders had robbed them of the truth of their own Word and had substituted man-made traditions (Luke 11:52). The leaders were not interested in truth; they were concerned only with protecting their own interests (John 11:47–53). "We have no king but Caesar!" was their confession of willful blindness. Even our Lord's miracles did not convince them. And the longer they resisted the truth, the blinder they became (John 12:35ff.).

Hypocrisy (21:12–22)
Jesus performed two acts of judgment: He cleansed the temple, and He cursed a fig tree. Both acts were contrary to His usual manner of ministry, for He did not come to earth to judge, but to save (John 3:17). Both of these acts revealed the hypocrisy of Israel: The temple was a den of thieves, and the nation (symbolized by the fig tree) was without fruit. Inward corruption and outward fruitlessness were evidences of their hypocrisy.

Cleansing the temple (vv. 12–16). Jesus had opened His ministry with a similar act (John 2:13–25). Now, three years later, the temple was defiled again by the "religious business" of the leaders. They had turned the court of the Gentiles into a place where foreign Jews could exchange money and purchase sacrifices. What had begun as a service and convenience for visitors from other lands soon turned into a lucrative business. The dealers charged exorbitant prices and no one could compete with them or oppose them. Historians tell us that Annas, the former high priest, was the manager of this enterprise, assisted by his sons.

The purpose of the court of the Gentiles in the temple was to give the "outcasts" an opportunity to enter the temple and learn from Israel about the true God. But the presence of this "religious market" turned many sensitive Gentiles away from the witness of Israel. The court of the Gentiles was used for mercenary business, not missionary business.

When Jesus called the temple "my house," He was affirming that He is God. When He called it "my house of prayer," He was quoting Isaiah 56:7. The entire fifty-sixth chapter of Isaiah denounces the unfaithful leaders of Israel. The phrase "den of robbers" comes from Jeremiah 7:11 and is part of a long sermon that Jeremiah delivered in the gate of the temple, rebuking the people for the same sins that Jesus saw and judged in His day.

Why did Jesus call the temple "a den of thieves"? Because the place where thieves hide is called a den. The religious leaders, and some of the people, were using the temple and the Jewish religion to cover up their sins.

What does God want in His house? God wants *prayer* among His people (1 Tim. 2:1ff.), for true prayer is an evidence of our dependence on God and our faith in His Word. He also wants *people* being helped (Matt. 21:14). The needy should feel welcome and should find the kind of help they need. There should be *power* in God's house, the power of God working to change people. *Praise* is another feature of God's house (Matt. 21:15–16). Here Jesus quoted from Psalm 8:2.

Cursing the tree (vv. 17–22). That Jesus would curse a tree may surprise us. The same power that killed the tree could also have given it new life and fruit. Jesus certainly would not hold a tree morally responsible for being fruitless.

When we consider the time and place of this event, we understand it better. Jesus was near Jerusalem in the last week of His public ministry to His people. The fig tree symbolized the nation of Israel (Jer. 8:13; Hos 9:10, 16; Luke 13:6–9). Just as this tree had leaves but no fruit, so Israel had a show of religion but no practical experience of faith resulting in godly living. Jesus was not angry at the tree. Rather, He used this tree to teach several lessons to His disciples.

God wants to produce fruit in the lives of His people. Fruit is the product of life. The presence of leaves usually indicates the presence of fruit, but this was not the case. In the parable of the fig tree (Luke 13:6–9), the gardener was given more time to care for the tree, but now the time was up. This tree was taking up space and doing no good.

While we can make a personal application of this event, the main interpretation has to do with Israel. The time of judgment had come. The sentence was pronounced by the Judge, but it would not be executed for about forty years. Then Rome would come and destroy the city and temple and scatter the people.

Jesus used this event to teach His disciples a practical lesson about faith and prayer. The temple was supposed to be a "house of prayer," and the nation was to be a believing people. But both of these essentials were missing. We too must beware of the peril of fruitlessness.

Disobedience to the Word (21:23—22:14)

This series of three parables grew out of the demand of the chief priests and elders for Jesus to explain what authority He had for cleansing the temple. As the custodians of the spiritual life of the nation, they had the right to ask this question. But we are amazed at their ignorance. Jesus had given them three years of ministry, and they still would not face the facts. They wanted more evidence.

In taking them back to the ministry of John, Jesus was not trying to avoid the issue. John had prepared the way for Jesus. Had the rulers received John's ministry, they would have received Jesus. Instead, the leaders permitted Herod to arrest John and then to kill him. If they would not accept the authority of John, they would not accept the authority of Jesus, for both John and Jesus were sent by God.

It is a basic principle of Christian living that we cannot learn new truth if we disobey what God has already told us. "If any man is willing to do His will, he shall know of the teaching, whether it is of God" (John 7:17 NASB). The religious rulers had rejected the truth preached by John, and therefore Jesus could not impart new truth. Both He and John were under the same authority.

They rejected God the Father (21:23–32). The vineyard, of course, speaks of the nation of Israel (Ps. 80:8–16; Isa. 5). The two sons represent the two classes of people in that nation: the self-righteous religious people, and the publicans and sinners. When John came ministering, the religious crowd showed great interest in his work, but they would not repent and humble themselves and be baptized (Matt. 3:7–12; John 1:19–28). The nonreligious crowd, however, confessed their sins and obeyed John's words and were baptized.

The leaders committed two sins: They would not believe John's message and they would not repent of their sins. Of course, the leaders felt that they had no need to repent (Luke 18:9–14). But when they saw what repentance did for the publicans and sinners, they should have been convinced that John's message was true and salvation was real. Again and again, the religious rulers rejected the clear evidence God gave them.

Their rejection of John was actually a rejection of the Father who had sent him. But God is gracious, and instead of sending judgment, He sent His Son. This leads to the next parable.

They rejected the Son (21:33–46). We are still

at the vineyard. This parable is based on Isaiah 5:1–7, and in it Jesus reminded the Jews of God's goodness to them as a nation. God delivered them from Egypt and planted them in a rich land of milk and honey. He gave them material and spiritual blessings and asked only that they bear fruit for His glory. From time to time, God sent His servants (the prophets) to the people to receive the fruit. But the people mistreated the servants, and even killed some of them.

What should the householder do? He could have sent his armies to destroy these wicked men. But instead he sent his own son to them. The reference, of course, is to Jesus Christ, the Son of God. He is the "heir" (Heb. 1:2). Instead of receiving and honoring the son, the men cast him out of the vineyard and killed him. Jesus was crucified "outside the gate" (Heb. 13:12–13 NASB), rejected by His own nation.

The people listening to the parable were caught up in the drama and did not realize that they passed sentence on themselves. Jesus quoted Psalm 118:22–23 to explain that He was that Son and the religious leaders were the husbandmen (Matt. 21:45). The crowds had quoted from Psalm 118:26 when they had welcomed Jesus into the city, so this Scripture was fresh in the minds of the rulers.

Often in the Old Testament, God is referred to as a rock or a stone (Deut. 32:4, 18, 30–31; Ps. 18:2, 31, 46). The stone is also a messianic title. To Israel, Jesus was a stumbling stone (Isa. 8:14–15; Rom. 9:32–33; 1 Cor. 1:23). Israel rejected the Messiah, but in His death and resurrection He created the church. To the church, Jesus is the foundation stone, the head of the corner (Eph. 2:20–22; 1 Peter 2:4–5). At the end of the age, Jesus will come as the smiting stone (Dan. 2:34), destroy Gentile kingdoms, and establish His own glorious kingdom.

Of course, the Jewish leaders knew the messianic import of the Scripture Jesus quoted. They were the *builders* who rejected the stone (Acts 4:11). What were the consequences? For one thing, the kingdom would be taken from Israel and given to another nation, the church (1 Peter 2:9, and note the context, 1 Peter 2:6–10). Those who would attack this stone would be "pulverized"; those whom Christ judges will be crushed to bits.

They rejected the Holy Spirit (22:1–14). This parable must not be confused with the parable of the great supper (Luke 14:16–24) even though they have elements in common. Again we meet the Father and the Son, and the Son is alive (in spite of what the husbandmen did) and has a bride. The suggestion is that the Lord Jesus and His church are depicted (Eph. 5:22–33). The period described in this parable must be after His resurrection and ascension and the coming of the Holy Spirit.

The Father is still inviting the people of Israel to come, in spite of what they did to His Son. When we study the first seven chapters of Acts, we discover that the message is going out to none but Jews (Acts 2:5, 10,

14, 22, 36; 3:25; 6:7). "To the Jew first" was God's plan (Acts 3:26; Rom. 1:16). How did the nation's leaders respond to the ministry of the Holy Spirit through the apostles? They rejected the Word and persecuted the church. The same rulers who permitted John to be killed, and who asked for Jesus to be killed, themselves killed Stephen! Later, Herod killed James (Acts 12:1ff.).

How did the king in the parable respond to the way the people treated his servants? He became angry and sent his armies to destroy them and their city. He then turned to other people and invited them to come to the feast. This is a picture of God's dealing with Israel. They rejected the Father when they refused to obey John the Baptist's preaching. Israel rejected the Son when they arrested Him and crucified Him. In His grace and patience, God sent other witnesses. The Holy Spirit came on the early believers and they witnessed with great power that Jesus was alive and the nation could be saved (Acts 2:32–36; 3:19–26). The miracles they did were proof that God was at work in and through them.

But Israel also rejected the Holy Spirit! This was Stephen's indictment against the nation: "You do always resist the Holy Ghost" (Acts 7:51). With the stoning of Stephen, God's patience with Israel began to end, though He delayed the judgment for almost forty years. In Acts 8 we read that the message went to the Samaritans, and in Acts 10 we read that it even went to the Gentiles.

This final rejection is, to me, the awful "blasphemy against the Holy Spirit" that Jesus spoke about in Matthew 12:22–32. This was a national sin, committed by Israel. When they rejected John, they rejected the Father who sent him, but there remained the ministry of the Son. When they rejected the Son, *they were forgiven* because of their ignorance (Luke 23:34; Acts 3:17). No sinner *today* can be forgiven for rejecting Christ, for this rejection is what condemns the soul (John 3:16–22).

But there remained the ministry of the Holy Spirit. The Spirit came on the church at Pentecost, and the apostles performed great signs and wonders (Acts 2:43; Heb. 2:1–4). The rulers rejected the witness of the Spirit, *and this brought final judgment.* They had rejected the Father, the Son, and the Spirit, and there were no more opportunities left.

This "sin against the Holy Spirit" cannot be committed today in the same way as Israel committed it, because the situation is different. The Spirit of God is bearing witness through the Word to the person and work of Jesus Christ. It is the Spirit who convinces the world of sin (John 16:7–11). The Spirit can be resisted by unbelievers (Acts 7:51), but nobody knows that crisis hour (if there is one) when the Spirit stops dealing with a lost sinner.

Matthew 22:11–14 seems like an appendix to the parable, but it is vitally important. The wedding garment was provided by the host so that everybody was properly attired and the poor did not feel conspicuous.

Salvation is personal and individual. We must accept what God gives to us—the righteousness of Christ—and not try to make it on our own. Since these parables had a definite *national* emphasis, this *personal* emphasis at the end was most important.

The nation's leaders were guilty of spiritual blindness, hypocrisy, and deliberate disobedience to the Word. Instead of accepting this indictment from Jesus, and repenting, they decided to attack Him and argue with Him. The result: judgment. We should be careful not to follow their example of disobedience.

CHAPTER NINETEEN
Matthew 22:15–46
THE KING'S DEFENSE

On Tuesday of Passover week, our Lord's enemies tried to trap Him by using a series of "loaded" questions. These men were still smarting from the treatment they had received in the series of parables He had given. He had exposed their evil intentions and warned them that they were only asking for judgment. The religious leaders did not enjoy being humiliated before the crowds. They were wholeheartedly bent on destroying Jesus, and they hoped to trap Him into saying something that would permit them to arrest Him.

But there was another reason for the questions, one that His enemies did not realize. Jesus was going to die as the Lamb of God, and it was necessary for the lamb to be examined before Passover (Ex. 12:3–6). If any blemish whatsoever was found on the lamb, it could not be sacrificed. Jesus was examined publicly by His enemies, and they could find no fault in Him.

Of course, this personal interchange between our Lord and the religious leaders was also an opportunity for them to believe and be saved. In fact, one Pharisee came very close to the kingdom (Mark 12:32–34). Even at the last minute, there is hope for the lost sinner, if he will receive the truth, repent, and believe.

There are four questions involved in this public discussion, three of them from the enemy, and one from Jesus Christ.

A Political Question about Taxes (22:15–22)
The Pharisees and the Herodians were enemies; but their common foe brought them together. The Pharisees opposed the Roman poll tax for several reasons: (1) They did not want to submit to a Gentile power; (2) Caesar was revered as a god; and (3) they had better uses for the money than to give it to Rome. Since the Herodians were the party supporting Herod, they were in favor of the tax. After all, Herod's authority was given to him by Caesar, and Herod would have had a difficult time staying in power without Rome's support.

Palestine was an occupied nation, and the Jews had no special love for their conquerors. Every tax the poor

people had to pay was another reminder that they were not free. The Zealots, an "underground" organization of fanatical Jews, often staged protests against Rome. They would oppose any Roman tax.

It is easy to see why the Pharisees and Herodians chose the poll tax as the bait for their trap. It appeared that no matter which side Jesus took, He would create problems for Himself and His ministry. If He opposed the tax, He would be in trouble with Rome. If He approved the tax, He would be in trouble with the Jews.

Jesus immediately saw through their scheme. He knew that their real purpose was not to get an answer to a question, but to try to trap Him. They were only acting a part, and this made them hypocrites. On this basis alone, He could have refused to answer them. But He knew the people around Him would not understand. Here was an opportunity for Him to silence His enemies and, at the same time, teach the people an important spiritual truth.

Each ruler minted his own coins and put his own image on them. The "penny" (denarius) had Caesar's image on it, so it belonged to Caesar. "Give back to Caesar what belongs to Caesar," was His reply. "And give back to God what belongs to God." In this simple, but profound reply, Jesus taught several important truths.

Christians must honor and obey rulers. This is taught elsewhere in the New Testament (Rom. 13; 1 Peter 2:13–17; 1 Tim. 2:1ff.). Christians have a dual citizenship, in heaven (Phil. 3:20) and on earth. We must respect our earthly rulers (or elected leaders), obey the law, pay taxes, and pray for all who are in authority.

Christians must honor and obey God. Caesar was not God. While governments cannot enforce religion (Acts 5:29), neither should they restrict freedom of worship. The best citizen honors his country because he worships God.

Man bears God's image and owes God his all. Caesar's image was on the coin; God's image is on man (Gen. 1:26–27). Sin has marred that image, but through Jesus Christ, it can be restored (Eph. 4:24; Col. 3:10).

The relationship between religion and government is personal and individual. It is right for the people of God to serve in government (remember Daniel and Joseph). But it is wrong for government to control the church, or for the church to control government.

A Doctrinal Question about the Resurrection (22:23–33)
In spite of the fact that the Pharisees and Herodians had been worsted, the Sadducees entered the field and tried *their* attack. Keep in mind that this group accepted only the authority of the five Books of Moses. The Sadducees did not believe in a spirit world or in the doctrine of the resurrection (Acts 23:8). They had often challenged the Pharisees to prove the doctrine of

the resurrection from Moses, but the Pharisees were not too successful with their arguments.

The Sadducees' hypothetical illustration was based on the Jewish law of "levirate marriage" from Deuteronomy 25:5–10. (The word *levirate* comes form the Latin word *levir* which means "a husband's brother." It has nothing to do with the tribe of Levi.) The purpose of this custom was to preserve a man's name should he die without a male heir. In a nation like Israel, where family inheritance was a major thing, it was important that each home have an heir. It was considered a disgrace for a man to refuse to raise up a family for his dead brother.

The Sadducees based their disbelief of the resurrection on the fact that no woman could have seven husbands in the future life. Like many people today, they conceived of the future life as an extension of their present life—only better.

But Jesus told them that they were ignorant. They did not know the Scriptures, nor did they know the power of God, which inferred that they really did not know God. There will be no need for marriage in the next life because there will be no death. Therefore it will not be necessary to bear children to replace those who die.

Jesus did *not* say that we would be angels when we are glorified in heaven. He said we would be *"as the angels"* in that we would be sexless and not married or given in marriage. The foolish stories we hear and the cartoons we see about people dying and becoming angels are certainly unbiblical.

Our Lord was not content to refute the Sadducees' foolish views about the future life. He also wanted to answer their claim that there was no resurrection, *and He did it by referring to Moses!* He knew that Moses was the only authority they would accept. He reminded them of Exodus 3:6 where God said to Moses, "I am the God of Abraham, and the God of Isaac, and the God of Jacob." He did not say, "I *was* the God of Abraham," for that would mean that Abraham was no more. By saying "I am," the Lord made it clear that these three men of faith were *at that time alive.* And by repeating "the God of," the Lord was saying that He knew them and loved them personally and individually.

It is a dangerous thing to speculate about the future life. We must rest on the authority of the Word of God, for only there do we have truth that answers man's questions about the future. The Bible does not tell us everything about the future life, but it does encourage and enlighten us. Jesus answered the foolish, ignorant Sadducees so completely that they were "muzzled" (the word *silence* in Matt. 22:34). Even the crowds were astonished and amazed at His answer.

An Ethical Question about the Law (22:34–40)

The Pharisees probably enjoyed the embarrassment of their enemies, the Sadducees. One of their number showed respect for the Lord and His answer (Mark 12:28) and asked a question of his own: "Teacher, which is the great commandment in the Law?" (Matt. 22:36 NASB). We have every reason to believe that he asked the question in sincerity and with a humble attitude.

This was not a new question, for the scribes had been debating it for centuries. They had documented 613 commandments in the law, 248 positive and 365 negative. No person could ever hope to know and fully obey all of these commandments. So, to make it easier, the experts divided the commandments into "heavy" (important) and "light" (unimportant). A person could major on the "heavy commandments" and not worry about the trivial ones.

The fallacy behind this approach is obvious: You need only break *one law,* heavy or light, to be guilty before God. "For whosoever shall keep the whole law, and yet offend in one point, he is guilty of all" (James 2:10).

Jesus quoted the "Shema" (Deut. 6:4), a statement of faith that was recited daily by every orthodox Jew. (The word *Shema* comes from the Hebrew word that means "to hear.") The confession of faith begins with, "Hear, O Israel!") The greatest commandment is to love God with all that we are and have—heart, soul, mind, strength, possessions, service. To love God is not to "have good feelings about Him," for true love involves the will as well as the heart. Where there is love, there will be service and obedience.

But love for God cannot be divorced from love for one's neighbor, so Jesus also quoted Leviticus 19:18 and put it on the same level as the Shema. All of the law and the prophets hang on *both* of these commandments. We might add that the teachings of the Epistles in the New Testament agree with this statement. If a man really loves God, he must also love his brother and his neighbor (1 John 3:10–18; 4:7–21).

If we have a right relationship with God, we will have no problems with His commandments. Love is the basis for obedience, In fact, all of the law is summed up in love (Rom. 13:8–10). If we love God, we will love our neighbor, and if we love our neighbor, we will not want to do anything to harm him.

But Jesus had a deeper meaning to convey in this marvelous answer. The Jews were afraid of idolatry. When Jesus claimed to be God, they opposed Him because they could not believe it was right to worship a creature. Jesus received worship and did not rebuke those who honored Him. Was this idolatry? No, because He is God! But if the law commands us to love God *and our neighbor,* then it would not be wrong for the Jews to love Jesus. Instead, they were plotting to kill Him. He had said to them one day, "If God were your Father, ye would love me" (John 8:42). They accepted the authority of the law, yet they refused to obey it in their lives.

The scribe who had asked the original question seemed to be an honest and sincere man. Not all of the Pharisees were hypocrites. He publicly agreed with Jesus (Mark 12:32–33). This must have given his fellow Pharisees a fright. Jesus discerned that the man's heart was sincere, and He commended him for his intelligence and honesty. Did the man ever get all the way into the kingdom, when he was so very near? We trust so.

Jesus had now answered three difficult questions. He had dealt with the relationship between religion and government, between this life and the next life, and between God and our neighbors. These are fundamental relationships, and we cannot ignore our Lord's teachings. But there is a question more fundamental than these, and Jesus asked it of His enemies.

A Personal Question about the Messiah (22:41–46)

Jesus did not phrase this question as He had when He asked His disciples, "Whom say you that I am?" (Matt. 16:15). These men who had been arguing with Him were not sympathetic with His cause, nor were they honest in their assessment of His credentials. Jesus had to take an indirect approach with His enemies. He made this sound like another theological question, when in reality it was the most important *personal* question they would ever face.

"Whose Son is the Messiah?" He asked them. As trained experts in the law, they knew the answer: "He is the Son of David." Had they been asked, they could have referred to numbers of Old Testament Scriptures, including 2 Samuel 7:12–13, Psalm 78:68–72, and Micah 5:2. Once they had given this answer, Jesus asked a second question, this time quoting from Psalm 110:1—"The Lord [Jehovah] said unto my Lord [Hebrew "Adonai"], 'Sit thou at my right hand, until I make thine enemies thy footstool.'"

Every orthodox Jewish scholar interpreted this to refer to the Messiah. Only the Messiah could sit at the right hand of Jehovah God. Jesus believed in the inspiration and accuracy of the Old Testament Scriptures, for He said that David spoke these words "in the Spirit" (Matt. 22:43 NASB). Nobody dared to question the accuracy or the authority of the text.

"If Messiah is David's Son," Jesus asked, "then how could Messiah also be David's Lord?" There is only one answer to this question. As God, Messiah is David's Lord; as man, He is David's Son. He is both "the root and the offspring of David" (Rev. 22:16). Psalm 110:1 teaches the deity and the humanity of Messiah. He is David's Lord and He is David's Son.

When He was ministering on earth, Jesus often accepted the messianic title "Son of David" (see Matt. 9:27; 12:23; 15:22; 20:30–31; 21:9, 15). The rulers had heard the multitudes proclaim Him as "Son of David" when He rode into Jerusalem. The fact that He accepted this title is evidence that Jesus knew Himself to be the Messiah, the Son of God. As God, He was David's Lord, but as man, He was David's Son, for He was born into the family of David (Matt. 1:1, 20).

The scholars in that day were confused about the Messiah. They saw two pictures of Messiah in the Old Testament and could not reconcile them. One picture showed a Suffering Servant, the other a conquering and reigning Monarch. Were there two Messiahs? How could God's servant suffer and die? (See 1 Peter 1:10–12.)

Had they listened to what Jesus said, they would have learned that there was only one Messiah, but that He would be both human and divine. He would suffer and die as a sacrifice for sins. He would then rise from the dead in triumph, and one day return to defeat His enemies. However, these religious leaders had their own ideas, and they did not want to change. If they had accepted His teaching, then they would also have to accept Him as the Messiah, and this they were unwilling to do.

The result of this day of dialogue was silence on the part of His enemies. They dared not ask Jesus any more questions, not because they had believed the truth, but because they were afraid to face the truth. "For they did not have courage to question Him any longer about anything" (Luke 20:40 NASB). But neither did they have courage to face the truth and act on it.

Making a decision about Jesus Christ is a matter of life or death. The evidence is there for all to examine. We can examine it defensively and miss the truth. Or we can examine it honestly and humbly, and discover the truth, believe, and be saved. The religious leaders were so blinded by tradition, position, and selfish pride that they could not—and *would* not—see the truth and receive it. We dare not make the same mistake today.

CHAPTER TWENTY
Matthew 23
THE KING'S DENUNCIATION

This was our Lord's last public message. It is a scathing denunciation of false religion that paraded under the guise of truth. Some of the common people no doubt were shocked at His words, for they considered the Pharisees to be righteous.

Perhaps we should remind ourselves that not all of the Pharisees were hypocrites. There were about six thousand Pharisees in that day, with many more who were "followers" but not full members of the group. Most of the Pharisees were middle-class businessmen, and no doubt they were sincere in their quest for truth and holiness. The name "Pharisees" came from a word that means "to separate." The Pharisees were separated from the Gentiles, the "unclean" Jews who did not practice the law ("publicans and sinners," Luke 15:1–2), and from any who opposed the tradition that governed their lives.

Among the Pharisees were a few members who sought for true spiritual religion. Nicodemus (John 3; 7:50–53), Joseph of Arimathea (John 19:38ff.), and the unnamed man mentioned in Mark 12:32–34 come to mind. Even Gamaliel showed a great deal of tolerance toward the newly formed church (Acts 5:34ff.). But for the most part, the Pharisees used their religion to promote themselves and their material gain. No wonder Jesus denounced them. Note the three divisions in this message.

Explanation to the Crowd (23:1–12)

In this section, Jesus explained the basic flaws of pharisaical religion.

They had a false concept of righteousness (vv. 2–3). To begin with, they had assumed an authority not their own. "The scribes and the Pharisees *have seated themselves* in Moses' seat" is the literal translation. There is no record in the Scriptures that God assigned any authority to this group. Their only authority was the Word of God. Therefore, the people were to obey whatever the Pharisees taught *from the Word*. But the people were not to obey the traditions and the man-made rules of the Pharisees.

To the Pharisee, righteousness meant outward conformity to the law of God. They ignored the inward condition of the heart. Religion consisted in obeying numerous rules that governed every detail of life, including what you did with the spices in your cupboard (Matt. 23:23–24). The Pharisees were careful to say the right words and follow the right ceremonies, but they did not *inwardly* obey the law. God desired truth in the inward parts (Ps. 51:6). To preach one thing and practice another is only hypocrisy.

They had a false concept of ministry (v. 4). To them, ministry meant handing down laws to the people and adding to their burdens. In other words, the Pharisees were harder on others than they were on themselves. Jesus came to lighten men's burdens (Matt. 11:28–30), but legalistic religion always seeks to make burdens heavier. Jesus never asks us to do anything that He has not first done. The Pharisees commanded, but they did not participate. They were hypocritical religious dictators, not spiritual leaders.

They had a false concept of greatness (vv. 5–12). To them, success meant recognition by men and praise from men. They were not concerned about the approval of God. They used their religion to attract attention, not to glorify God (Matt. 5:16). This even meant using religious ornaments to display their piety. "Phylacteries" were small leather boxes into which the Pharisees placed portions of the Scriptures. They wore these boxes on their foreheads and arms, in literal obedience to Deuteronomy 6:8 and 11:18. They also increased the size of their "tassels" on the hems of their garments (Num. 15:38; see Matt. 9:20).

The Pharisees also thought that *position* was a mark of greatness, so they sought the best seats in the synagogue and at the public dinners. Where a man sits bears no relationship to what a man is. Albert Einstein wrote, "Try not to become a man of success, but rather try to become a man of value."

They also thought that *titles of honor* were a mark of greatness. The title "rabbi" means "my great one" and was coveted by the religious leaders. (Today religious leaders covet honorary doctor's degrees.) Jesus forbad His disciples to use the title *rabbi* because all of them were brothers, and Jesus alone was their Teacher ("Master" in Matt. 23:8). There is a spiritual equality among the children of God, under the lordship of Jesus Christ.

Jesus also forbad them to use the title *father* with reference to spiritual things. Certainly it is not wrong to call one's biological father by that name, but it is wrong to use it when addressing a spiritual leader. Paul referred to himself as a "spiritual father" because he had begotten people through the gospel (1 Cor. 4:15), but he did not ask them to use that term when addressing him.

A third title that was forbidden was *master* (Matt. 23:10), which means "guide, instructor, leader." This is not the same word that is translated "Master" in Matthew 23:8 in the King James Version. That word means "teacher," while this one means "one who goes before and guides." Perhaps a modern equivalent would be "authority." God has placed spiritual leaders in the church, but they must not replace God in our lives. A true spiritual leader directs his people into freedom and a closer fellowship with Christ, not into bondage to his ideas and beliefs.

True greatness is found in serving others, not in forcing others to serve us (John 3:30; 13:12–17). True greatness is not manufactured; it can only come from God as we obey Him. If we exalt ourselves, God will humble us. But if we humble ourselves, in due time God will exalt us (1 Peter 5:6).

Denunciation of the Pharisees (23:13–36)

We must not read this series of denunciations with the idea that Jesus lost His temper and was bitterly angry. Certainly He was angry at their sins and what those sins were doing to the people. But His attitude was one of painful sorrow that the Pharisees were blinded to God's truth and to their own sins.

Perhaps the best way to deal with these eight "woes" is to contrast them with the eight beatitudes found in Matthew 5:1–12. In the Sermon on the Mount the Lord described true righteousness; here He described a false righteousness.

Entering the kingdom—shutting up the kingdom (v. 13; 5:3). The poor in spirit enter the kingdom, but the proud in spirit keep themselves out and even keep others out. The Greek verb indicates people trying to get in who cannot. It is bad enough to keep yourself out of the kingdom, but worse when you stand in the way of others. By teaching man-made traditions instead of God's truth, they "took away the key of knowledge" and closed the door to salvation (Luke 11:52).

Mourners comforted—destroyers condemned (v. 14; 5:4). While this verse is not in some manuscripts of Matthew, it is found in Mark 12:40 and Luke 20:47. Instead of mourning over their own sins, and mourning with needy widows, the Pharisees took advantage of people in order to rob them. They used their religion as a "cloak of covetousness" (1 Thess. 2:5).

Meek inherit the earth—proud send souls to hell (v. 15; 5:5). A proselyte is a convert to a cause. The Pharisees were out to win others to their legalistic system, yet they could not introduce these people to the living God. Instead of saving souls, the Pharisees were condemning souls!

A "child of hell" is the equivalent of "child of the devil," which is what Jesus called the Pharisees (Matt. 12:34; 23:33; John 8:44). A "child of the devil" is a person who has rejected God's way of salvation (righteousness through faith in Christ). This person parades his own self-righteousness through whatever religious system he belongs to. The convert usually shows more zeal than his leader, and this "double devotion" only produces double condemnation. How tragic that people can think they are going to heaven, when actually they are going to hell!

Hungering for holiness—greedy for gain (vv. 16–22; 5:6). "Blind guides" is a perfect description, one that must have brought a smile to the lips of the listeners. Jesus had used it before (Matt. 15:14). The Pharisees were blind to the true values of life. Their priorities were confused. They would take an oath and use some sacred object to substantiate that oath—the gold in the temple, for example, or the gift on the altar. But they would not swear by the temple itself or the altar. It was the temple that sanctified the gold and the altar that sanctified the gift. They were leaving God out of their priorities.

Jesus knew that the Pharisees wanted both the gold and the gifts on the altar. This is why the Pharisees practiced "Corban"—anything dedicated to God could not be used for others (Matt. 15:1–9; Mark 7:10–13). These men were not seeking for the righteousness of God; they were greedy for gain. They worked out a "religious system" that permitted them to rob God and others and still maintain their reputations.

Obtaining mercy—rejecting mercy (vv. 23–24; 5:7). The Pharisees majored on minors. They had rules for every minute area of life, while at the same time they forgot about the important things. It is usually the case that legalists are sticklers for details, but blind to great principles. This crowd thought nothing of condemning an innocent man, yet they were afraid to enter Pilate's judgment hall lest they be defiled (John 18:28).

There is no question that the Old Testament law required tithing (Lev. 27:30; Deut. 14:22ff.). Abraham had practiced tithing long before the law was given (Gen. 14:20), and Jacob followed his grandfather's example (Gen. 28:20–22). The principles of Christian giving under grace are given in 2 Corinthians 8—9. We are not content simply to give a tithe (10 percent), but we also want to bring offerings to the Lord out of hearts filled with love.

Justice, mercy, and faithfulness are the important qualities God is seeking. Obeying the rules is no substitute. While it is good to pay attention to details, we must never lose our sense of priorities in spiritual matters. Jesus did not condemn the practice of tithing. But He did condemn those who allowed their legalistic scruples to keep them from developing true Christian character.

Pure in heart—defiled in heart (vv. 25–28; 5:8). Jesus used two illustrations: the cup and platter, and the sepulcher. They both stated the same truth: it is possible to be clean on the outside and at the same time defiled on the inside. Imagine using dishes that were defiled! Whatever you put into the dish or cup would also become defiled. The Pharisees were careful to keep the outside very clean, because that was the part that men would see, and they wanted the praise of men. But God sees the heart (1 Sam. 16:7). When God looked within, He saw "greed and self-indulgence" (Matt. 23:25 NIV).

Jewish people were careful not to touch dead bodies or anything relating to the dead, because this would make them ceremonially unclean (Num. 19:11ff.). They would whitewash the tombs lest someone accidentally get defiled, and this was done especially at Passover season. What a graphic picture of the hypocrite: white on the outside, but filled with defilement and death on the inside!

"Blessed are the pure in heart" was our Lord's promise. "Watch over your heart with all diligence, for from it flow the springs of life" (Prov. 4:23 NASB). D. L. Moody used to say, "If I take care of my character, my reputation will take care of itself." The Pharisees lived for reputation, not character.

Peacemakers and persecuted are God's children—persecutors are the devil's children (vv. 29–33; 5:9–12). When Jesus called the Pharisees "serpents generation of vipers," He was identifying them with Satan, who is the serpent (Gen. 3:1ff.). In His parable of the tares, Jesus made it clear that *Satan has a family* (Matt. 13:38). Satan is a murderer and a liar (John 8:44), and his children follow his example. The Pharisees were liars (Matt. 23:30) and murderers (Matt. 23:34).

It was traditional for the Pharisees to build, improve, and embellish the tombs of the martyrs. But it was "their fathers" who killed the martyrs! Not their biological fathers, of course, but their "spiritual fathers"—the hypocrites of the past ages.

There have always been counterfeit believers in the world, starting with Cain (Gen. 4:1–15; 1 John 3:10–15). The Pharisees and their kind are guilty of all the righteous blood shed in the name of "religion." The first martyr recorded in Old Testament Scripture was Abel (Gen. 4), and the last one recorded was the prophet Zechariah (2 Chron. 24:20–22—the Hebrew Bible ends with 2 Chronicles, not Malachi).

What will be the result of this long history of murders? Terrible judgment! "This generation" (the "generation of vipers," Matt. 23:33) would taste the wrath of God when the cup of iniquity was full (Gen. 15:16; Matt. 23:32). Some of this judgment came when Jerusalem was destroyed, and the rest will be meted out in eternity.

As we review these tragic *woes* from the lips of our Lord, we can see why the Pharisees were His enemies. He emphasized the inner man; they were concerned with externals. He taught a spiritual life based on principles, while the Pharisees majored on rules and regulations. Jesus measured spirituality in terms of character, while the Pharisees measured it in terms of religious activities and conformity to external laws. Jesus taught humility and sacrificial service, but the Pharisees were proud and used people to accomplish their own purposes. The holy life of Jesus exposed their artificial piety and shallow religion. Instead of coming out of the darkness, the Pharisees tried to put out the Light, and they failed.

Lamentation over Jerusalem (23:37–39)

Jesus spoke these words of lamentation as a sincere expression of His love for Jerusalem, and His grief over the many opportunities for salvation that they had passed by. "Jerusalem" refers to the entire nation of Israel. The nation's leaders had been guilty of repeated crimes as they rejected God's messengers, and even killed some of them. But in His grace, Jesus came to gather the people and save them.

"I would have ye would not" summarizes the tragedy of final rejection of the truth. There is no argument here about divine sovereignty and human responsibility, for both are included. God could not force His salvation on the people; neither could He change the consequences of their stubborn rejection. "You will not come to me that you may have life" (John 5:40).

The image of the mother bird gathering and covering her brood is a familiar one. Moses used it in his farewell sermon (Deut. 32:11). It is a picture of love, tender care, and a willingness to die to protect others. Jesus did die for the sins of the world, including the nation of Israel: but "his own received him not" (John 1:11).

"Your house" probably means both the temple and the city, both of which would be destroyed in AD 70 by invading Roman armies. The temple was "my house" in Matthew 21:13, but now it has been abandoned and left empty. Jesus left both the temple and the city and went out to the Mount of Olives (Matt. 24:1–3).

Yet, Jesus left the nation with a promise: He would one day return, and the nation would see Him and say, "Blessed be he that cometh in the name of the Lord!" This is a quotation from Psalm 118:26, that great messianic psalm that was quoted so many times in His last week of ministry. The crowds had used those words on Palm Sunday (Matt. 21:9).

When would this promise be fulfilled? At the end of the age when Jesus Christ returns to earth to deliver Israel and defeat their enemies (Zech. 12; Rom.

11:25–27). The fact that Israel rejected the King would not hinder God's great plan of redemption. Instead of establishing His glorious kingdom on earth, Jesus would build His church (Matt. 16:18; Eph. 2:11–22). When that work is finished, He will return and take His church to heaven (1 Thess. 4:13–18). Then there will be a time of judgment on earth ("the day of the Lord," "the time of Jacob's trouble"), at the end of which He will return to deliver Israel.

We cannot read this severe denunciation without marveling at the patience and goodness of the Lord. No nation has been blessed like Israel, and yet no nation has sinned against God's goodness as has Israel. They have been the channel of God's blessing to the world, for "salvation is of the Jews" (John 4:22). Yet they have suffered greatly in this world.

Jesus was born a Jew, and He loved His nation. We who are Gentiles ought to thank God for the Jews, for they gave us the witness of the one true God, they gave us the Bible, and they gave us Jesus Christ the Savior. Like Jesus, we ought to love the Jews, seek to win them, pray for the peace of Jerusalem, and encourage them every way we can.

CHAPTER TWENTY-ONE
Matthew 24:1–44
THE KING'S RETURN—PART 1

The Olivet Discourse grew out of some questions the disciples asked when Jesus told them that the temple would one day be destroyed. First, they wanted to know *when*. This answer is not recorded in Matthew but is given in Luke 21:20–24. Second, they asked about the sign of Christ's return. This is answered in Matthew 24:29–44. In their final question, they asked about the sign of the end of the age. Christ's reply is in Matthew 24:4–8.

We must keep in mind that the "atmosphere" of this discourse is *Jewish*. Jesus talked about Judea (Matt. 24:16), the Sabbath (Matt. 24:20), and the prophecies of Daniel concerning the Jewish people (Matt. 24:15). The full truth about the rapture of the church (1 Cor. 15:51ff.; 1 Thess. 4:13–18) had not yet been revealed, for it was a mystery (Eph. 3:1–12).

Matthew 24:1–44 indicates that our Lord was discussing events that will take place on earth during the time of tribulation. (See Matt. 24:8, where "birthpangs" are a symbol of the tribulation, and see also Matt. 24:21, 29). After the church has been suddenly taken out of the world, there will be a period of "peace and safety" (1 Thess. 5:1–4) followed by a time of terrible suffering. Many Bible scholars believe this period will last seven years (Dan. 9:24–27). It is this period of "tribulation" that Jesus described in the Olivet Discourse. At the end of that period, Jesus will return to the earth, defeat His foes, and establish the promised kingdom.

In the section before us, Jesus explained three different periods in the time of the tribulation.

The Beginning of the Tribulation (24:4–14)

The events described in this section are "the beginning of birth-pangs" (Matt. 24:8). The image of a woman in travail is a picture of the tribulation period (Isa. 13:6–11; 1 Thess. 5:5). Let's consider some of the significant events that will occur at the beginning of this period.

Religious deception (vv. 4–5). The Jews have often been led astray by false prophets and false christs. The rider on the white horse in Revelation 6:1–2 is the Antichrist, that final world dictator who will lead the nations astray. He will begin his career as a peacemaker, signing a covenant with Israel to protect her from her enemies (Dan. 9:27). Israel will welcome this man as their great benefactor (John 5:43).

Wars (v. 6). Note that wars are not a sign of the end. There have always been wars in the world, and will be until the very end. Wars of themselves do not announce the end of the age or the coming of the Lord.

Famines (v. 7a). War and famine usually go together. Revelation 6:6 suggests terribly high prices for staple foods, for a "penny" was a day's wages.

Death (vv. 7b–8). Earthquakes help to create famines, and both help to cause epidemics that take many lives.

Martyrs (v. 9). Christians have always been hated by the world, but here we have an acceleration of persecutions and murders. All nations will be involved. This certainly was not true in the history of the early church.

Worldwide chaos (vv. 10–13). Those who once were true to each other will betray each other. This suggests that marriages, homes, and nations will be torn asunder because of lack of loyalty. Lawlessness will abound (Matt. 24:12), for even the law enforcement agencies will not be able to keep the peace. Matthew 24:13 has nothing to do with personal salvation in this present age of grace. "The end" does not mean the end of this life; it refers to the end of the age (Matt. 24:14). Those believers on earth during this terrible period, who endure in their faith, will be saved when the Lord comes at the end and delivers them.

Worldwide preaching (v. 14). Revelation 7:1–8 teaches that God will choose and seal 144,000 Jewish evangelists who will carry the kingdom message to the ends of the earth. This verse does not teach that the gospel of God's grace must be spread to every nation today before Jesus can return for His church. It is the Lord's return *at the end of the age* that is in view here.

The Middle of the Tribulation (24:15–22)

The midpoint of the tribulation period is most important, for at that time an event will take place that was prophesied centuries ago by Daniel (Dan. 9:24–27). Please notice that this prophecy concerns only the Jews and the city of Jerusalem ("thy people and … thy holy city," Dan. 9:24). To apply it to the church or to any other people or place is to misinterpret God's Word.

The prophecy involves seventy weeks, and the Hebrew word *week* means "a week of years," or seven years. Seventy sevens would equal 490 years. But this period of 490 years is broken up into three parts:

(1) During seven weeks (forty-nine years) the city of Jerusalem would be rebuilt and the worship reestablished.

(2) After sixty-three weeks (434 years) Messiah would come to Jerusalem and die for the sins of the world.

(3) The prince will make an agreement with the Jews for one week (seven years) to protect them from their enemies.

The decree to rebuild Jerusalem was given in 445 BC by Cyrus (2 Chron. 36:22–23; Ezra 1). The city was rebuilt in troubled times. Sir Robert Anderson in his classic book *The Coming Prime* (Kregel, 1975) has proved that there were exactly 482 prophetic years (of 360 days each) between the giving of the decree and the day that Jesus rode into Jerusalem as the King.

But we must account for the remaining "week" of seven years. Where does it fit in? Note that the same city that was rebuilt will also be destroyed "by the people of the prince that shall come" (Dan. 9:26), that is, the Romans. ("The prince that shall come" is a name for the Antichrist.) This event took place in AD 70. But the Jewish nation would be spared and the city restored again. For at some future date, the prince that shall come (Antichrist) will make a covenant with the Jews *for seven years.* This is where the missing "week" fits in. He will agree to protect them from their enemies and permit them to rebuild their temple. (Dan. 9:27 talks about a restoration of the sacrifices, and this would demand a temple.)

The logical place for this seven-year period is after the rapture of the church. "The time of Jacob's trouble," the tribulation period, will be seven years long. Second Thessalonians 2:1–12 indicates that the Antichrist cannot be revealed until the *restrainer* is taken out of the midst. That restrainer is the Holy Spirit in the church. Once the church is out of the world, then Satan can produce his masterpiece, the Antichrist.

He will make the agreement for seven years, but after three-and-one-half years ("in the midst of the week") he will break that agreement. He will then move into the Jewish temple himself and proclaim that he is God (2 Thess. 2:3–4; Rev. 13).

The Antichrist will cause a living statue of himself to be put into the temple, and his associate (the false prophet, Rev. 20:10) will cause the whole earth to worship it. Satan has always wanted the world's worship, and in the middle of the tribulation he will begin to receive it (Matt. 4:8–11). Jesus called this statue "the abomination of desolation" (Dan. 9:27; Matt. 24:15).

An interesting parenthesis occurs at the end of Matthew 24:15—"whoso readeth, let him understand." This statement indicates that what Jesus was teaching would have greater significance for people reading Matthew's gospel in the latter days. By reading the prophet Daniel and the words of Jesus, these believers will understand the events and know what to do. This is another evidence that the Olivet Discourse applies to people during the tribulation period.

Prophetic scholars have speculated as to why the Antichrist would break his covenant with the Jews after three-and-one-half years. It has been suggested that the invasion of Israel by Russia, prophesied in Ezekiel 38—39, would occur at that point. Certainly Israel will be at ease and dwelling in safety at that time, for she will be protected by the Antichrist (Ezek. 38:11). At that time, he will be the ruler of a ten-nation alliance, "The United States of Europe" (Rev. 17:12–13). Russia, of course, will be soundly beaten, not by Israel, but by Almighty God. When the Antichrist sees that his great enemy, Russia, has been beaten, he will take advantage of the opportunity and move into Israel, breaking his covenant and taking over the temple.

The readers of this prophecy in the latter days will know what to do: Get out of Judea! These instructions are similar to those given in Luke 21:20ff., but they refer to a different time period. Luke's instructions apply to the siege of Jerusalem in AD 70, and the "sign" was the gathering of the armies around the city. Matthew's instructions apply to Jewish believers in the middle of the tribulation, and the "sign" is the desecration of the temple by the image of the Antichrist. Those who have confused those two "sign events" have ended up believing that Jesus Christ returned in AD 70!

This entire paragraph relates only to Jews, for no Christian believer would worry about breaking a Sabbath law. This event ushers in "the Great Tribulation," the last half of Daniel's seventieth week, when the judgments of God will be hurled on the earth. During the first three-and-one-half years of the tribulation, the judgments were natural: wars, famines, earthquakes, etc. But during the last half, the judgments will be supernatural and devastating.

During this period, God will care for His elect (Matt. 24:22), referring to Jews and Gentiles who believe and are converted. "The elect" here does not refer to the church since the church will have been raptured at least three-and-one-half years previously.

The End of the Tribulation (24:23–44)

World conditions will be so terrible that men will wonder if any relief will come, and this will give false christs opportunities to deceive many. Satan is capable of performing "lying wonders" (2 Thess. 2:9–12; Rev. 13:13–14). The fact that a religious leader performs miracles is no assurance that he has come from God. Many Jews will be deceived, for "the Jews require a sign" (1 Cor. 1:22). Jesus performed true signs in His Father's name, and the nation rejected Him (John 12:37ff.). Satan's miracles they will accept.

Matthew 24:27 indicates that the return of Jesus to the earth will be sudden, like a stroke of lightning. The event that precedes His return is the gathering of the Gentile nations at Armageddon (Rev. 16:13–16; 19:11ff.). The eagles flying around the carcass picture the awful carnage that will result from this great battle (Rev. 19:17–19). The cosmic changes mentioned in Matthew 24:29 precede the return of Jesus Christ to the earth.

We are not told what "the sign of the Son of man in heaven" is, but the people on earth at that time will recognize it. When Jesus comes for the church, He will come in the air and His people will be caught up to meet Him in the air (1 Thess. 4:17). But our Lord's second coming at the end of the tribulation will be a great public event, with every eye seeing Him (Rev. 1:7).

This event will have special meaning for Israel. Jesus will return at that hour when Israel is about to be defeated by the Gentile armies (Zech. 12). He will rescue His people, and they will see Him and recognize that He is their Messiah (Zech. 12:9–14). There will be a national repentance, national cleansing, and national restoration under the gracious leadership of their Messiah.

We must not confuse the trumpet of Matthew 24:31 with the "trump of God" mentioned in 1 Thessalonians 4:16. "His elect" in Matthew 24:31 refers to people on earth, Jews and Gentiles, who have trusted Christ and been saved. In the Old Testament, Israel's movements were announced by trumpet signals (Num. 10; Joel 2:1ff.). Israel has been a scattered people for many centuries. The angels will gather Israel with trumpets just as the priests did in Old Testament times (Lev. 23:23–25).

Scholars of prophecy do not agree on all the details of future events. But the following summary is a fair representation of what many prophetic scholars believe as to the order of events:

1. The rapture of the church (1 Cor. 15:51–58; 1 Thess. 4:13–18). This can occur at any time.

2. The leader of the ten European nations makes a seven-year agreement with Israel (Dan. 9:26–27).

3. After three-and-one-half years, he breaks the agreement (Dan. 9:27).

4. He moves to Jerusalem and sets up his image in the temple (2 Thess. 2:34; Rev. 13).

5. The Antichrist begins to control the world and forces all people to worship and obey him. At this time God sends great tribulation upon the earth (Matt. 24:21).

6. The nations gather at Armageddon to fight the Antichrist and Israel, but see the sign of Christ's coming and unite to fight Him (Zech. 12; Rev. 13:13–14; 19:11ff.).

7. Jesus returns to the earth, defeats His enemies, is received by the Jews, and establishes His kingdom on

earth (Rev. 19:11ff.; Zech 12:7—13:1). He will reign on earth for one thousand years (Rev. 20:1–5).

The purpose of prophecy is not to entertain the curious, but to encourage the consecrated. Jesus closed this section of His discourse with three practical admonitions, built around three illustrations: a fig tree, Noah, and a thief in the night. Matthew 24:36 makes it clear that no one will know the day or the hour of the Lord's coming. But they can be aware of the movements of events and not be caught by surprise.

The fig tree (vv. 32–35). Luke 21:29 reads, "Behold the fig tree and all the trees" (NASB). The fig tree in the Bible is often a picture of Israel (Hos. 9:10; Luke 13:6–10), and the other trees would picture the nations of the world. Perhaps our Lord was suggesting that increased nationalism will be one of the signs of the end times. Certainly future events cast their shadows before them. "And when these things *begin* to come to pass" (Luke 21:28, italics mine) suggests that a sign need not be full-blown before it is important to God's people.

The budding of the trees indicates that summer is near. The beginning of these signs indicates that the Lord's coming is near. The generation alive on earth at that time will see these events take place. Our generation sees a foreshadowing of these signs. We do not look for signs as such: we look for the Savior (Phil. 3:20). Jesus can come for His church at *any* time.

The days of Noah (vv. 36–42). Here the emphasis is on the fact that the people did not know *the day* when judgment would strike. Noah and his family in the ark are a picture of God's miraculous preservation of Israel during the awful time of the tribulation. (Enoch is a picture of the church, which is raptured before the tribulation—Gen. 5:21–24; Heb. 11:5; 1 Thess. 1:10; 5:1–10.)

What kept the people from listening to Noah's message and obeying? The common interests of life— eating, drinking, marrying, giving in marriage. They lost the *best* by living for the *good*. It is a dangerous thing to get so absorbed in the pursuits of life that we forget Jesus is coming.

The verb "taken" in Matthew 24:39–41 means "taken away in judgment." *Do not apply these verses to the rapture of the church* when believers are caught up in the air to meet the Lord. During the tribulation, a division will take place: Some people will perish in judgment (be taken away), while others will remain to enter into the kingdom. The use of "took them all away" in Matthew 24:39 makes this clear.

The thief in the night (vv. 42–44). Jesus used Noah to warn that men will not know *the day,* and He used the picture of the burglar to warn that they will not know *the hour.* After the rapture of the church, there will be a time of peace and safety on earth (1 Thess. 5:1ff.). Then suddenly God's judgments will fall (2 Peter 3:10ff.).

People alive on earth during the tribulation period will be able, from the Scriptures, to tell the drift of events, but they will not be able to calculate the exact day or hour of Christ's return. Added to this is the fact that the days will be "shortened … for the elect's sake" (Matt. 24:22). This may mean fewer days of tribulation, or it may mean fewer hours so that the people on earth suffer a bit less (Rev. 8:12).

When we combine the exhortations found in these three pictures, we end up with: "Know that he is near! Watch therefore! Be ye also ready!" Believers alive during that period of history will certainly find great comfort in the promises of the Word of God.

While the interpretation of this section relates to Israel during the tribulation, we may apply the Word to our own hearts. We do not know when our Lord will return for His church. Therefore, we must be alert, watchful, and faithful. Jesus dealt with this in detail in the next section of the Olivet Discourse (Matt. 24:45—25:30).

How grateful we ought to be that God has not appointed us to wrath, but to obtain salvation when Jesus Christ appears. He has saved us from the wrath to come (1 Thess. 1:10; 5:9–10). As the people of God, we will certainly go through tribulation (John 16:33; Acts 14:22), but not *the* tribulation.

CHAPTER TWENTY-TWO
Matthew 24:45—25:46
THE KING'S RETURN—PART 2

We noted that the "atmosphere" of the first section of the Olivet Discourse was definitely Jewish. A careful reading of this section indicates that the "atmosphere" has changed. Jesus had been describing the sign-events of the tribulation period, and had named one judgment after another, culminating in His return to earth. But in this section, the emphasis is on *the Lord delaying His return* (Matt. 24:48; 25:5, 19).

It seems reasonable to assign Matthew 24:45— 25:30 to our present age of the church, during which time it appears that the Lord is delaying His return (2 Peter 3). The closing section (Matt. 25:31–46) describes the judgment the Lord will execute when He returns to earth. In general, the teachings in the Olivet Discourse relate to the Jews (Matt. 24:4–44), the professing church (Matt. 24:45—25:30), and the Gentile nations (Matt. 25:31–46). This corresponds with the threefold division of mankind mentioned by Paul in 1 Corinthians 10:32. We have already studied in detail our Lord's coming as it relates to Israel, so let us look at it in the two remaining relationships.

Christ's Coming and the Professing Church (24:45—25:30)
We must not be surprised that our Lord suddenly changed from discussing His return as it relates

to Israel to His return as it relates to the church. It is not uncommon in Scripture for a speaker or writer to change emphasis right in the middle of a sentence. For example, the entire church age occurs in the time period between the words *given* and *and* in Isaiah 9:6. A similar "leap" is seen in Isaiah 61:2, where the church age takes place in the period between the "year of the Lord" and the "day of vengeance."

In the section devoted to Israel, Jesus described primarily the outward events of the period; in this section, He described inward attitudes. While everyone who has trusted Jesus Christ as Savior is going to heaven (John 3:16–18; 17:24), not every believer is ready to meet the Lord.

When Jesus Christ returns and takes His church to heaven, He will sit on His judgment seat and judge His own people (Rom. 14:10–12; 2 Cor. 5:8–11). He will not judge our sins, because these have already been judged on the cross (Rom. 8:1–4). But He will judge our works and will give rewards to those who have earned them (1 Cor. 3:9–15). These parables suggest that Jesus will judge three different groups of professed believers.

Obedient and disobedient servants (24:45–51). God's people on earth are called a household (Gal. 6:10; Eph. 2:19). God has put servants over each household to feed the members. This suggests to us the local church family with its spiritual leaders. The purpose of spiritual leadership is that the leaders feed the people, not that the people feed the leaders! The apostle Peter caught this truth and emphasized it in his first letter (1 Peter 5:1–4).

It is a serious thing to be a pastor or other officer in a local church. We must take care that our motives are right and that we serve Christ and His people in love. Both in word and deed, we must lead the family in the right way (Heb. 13:7–8). The members of the family should submit to spiritual leadership, because one day both people and leaders will face the judgment seat of Christ (Heb. 13:17).

The servant's task is not to be popular, but to be obedient. He must feed the family the food that it needs, when it needs it. He should bring out of his "spiritual cupboard" things new and old (Matt. 13:52). Some Bible teachers, in their search for something new and exciting, forget the nutrition of the old truths of the Word. But other ministers are so wrapped up in the old that they fail to discover the new insights and new applications of the old truths. The new grows out of the old, and the old is made more meaningful by the new.

If the spiritual leader is obediently doing his job when the Lord returns, he shall be rewarded. But if that leader is not doing his job when the Lord returns, he will be dealt with in a severe way. I prefer to translate Matthew 24:51: "And shall punish him severely and appoint him his portion with the hypocrites." (Even in that day of despotic rule, it would be unthinkable for a master to cut his servant in half.) The whole picture is one of pain and loss. This does not suggest punitive measures at the judgment seat of Christ, because there we will have glorified bodies. But it does suggest loss of reward and loss of opportunity.

Jesus did not amplify the truth here, but from other Scriptures we learn that one reward for obedient service will be ministry in the kingdom that He will establish on earth (Luke 19:11ff.). The reward for obedient service is the capacity for greater service. Not to have a place of ministry in His kingdom would, to me, be a tremendous loss.

What caused this servant's downfall? *Something went wrong in his heart:* He ceased to expect his Lord to return (Matt. 24:48). He lived like the world and mistreated his fellow servants. Whenever God's servants cannot work together, it is often because somebody has forgotten that the Lord will return. Looking for His appearing, and loving His appearing, should motivate us to be faithful and loving (1 Thess. 2:19–20; 1 John 2:28).

Wise and foolish witnesses (25:1–13). A wedding in that day had two parts. First, the bridegroom and his friends would go from his house to claim the bride from her parents. Then the bride and groom would return to the groom's house for the marriage feast. The suggestion here is that the groom has already claimed his bride and is now on his way back home. However, we must not press the image of the church as a bride too far, because much of this truth was not revealed until the ministry of Paul (Eph. 5:22ff.).

The church has known for two thousand years that Jesus is coming again, and yet many believers have become lethargic and drowsy. They are no longer excited about the soon-coming of the Lord. As a result, there is little effective witness given that the Lord is returning.

The oil for burning reminds us of the special oil used in the tabernacle services (Ex. 27:20–21). Oil is usually a symbol of the Spirit of God, but I wonder if this particular oil is not also a symbol of the Word of God. The church should be "holding forth the word of life" in this dark and wicked world (Phil. 2:12–16). We need to keep the word of His patience (Rev. 3:10) and keep witnessing of the return of Jesus Christ.

When the bridegroom and bride appeared, half of the bridesmaids were unable to light their lamps because they had no oil. "Our lamps are going out!" they cried. The bridesmaids who had oil were able to light their lamps and keep them shining bright. It was they who entered into the wedding feast and not the foolish girls who had no oil. This suggests that not every professing Christian will enter heaven, for some really have not trusted Jesus Christ sincerely. Without the Spirit of God and the Word of God, there can be no true salvation.

Jesus ended this parable with the warning He had uttered before: "Watch" (Matt. 24:42; 25:13). This does not mean standing on a mountaintop gazing at the heavens (Acts 1:9–11). It means "to stay awake and be alert" (Matt. 26:38–41).

Profitable and unprofitable servants (25:14–30). This parable must not be confused with the parable of the pounds (Luke 19:11–27), though the two parables do have similarities. Please note that each servant in this parable was given money (a talent was worth about twenty years' wages) according to his ability. The man with much ability was given five talents; the man with average ability received two talents; the man with minimal ability received one talent.

The talents represent opportunities to use our abilities. If five talents were given to a person with minimal ability, he would be destroyed by the heavy responsibility. But if only one talent were given to a man of great ability, he would be disgraced and degraded. God assigns work and opportunity according to ability. We are living in the period of time between Matthew 25:18 and 19. We have been assigned our ministries according to the abilities and gifts God has given us. It is our privilege to serve the Lord and multiply His goods.

The three servants fell into two categories: faithful and unfaithful. The faithful servants took their talents and put them to work for their Lord. The unfaithful servant hid his talent in the earth. Instead of using his opportunities, he buried them! He did not purposely do evil. But by doing nothing, he was committing sin and robbing his Lord of service and increase.

The two men who put their money to work each received the same commendation (Matt. 25:21, 23). It was not the *portion* but the *proportion* that made the difference. They started as servants, but their Lord promoted them to rulers. They were faithful with a few things, so the Lord trusted them with many things. They had worked and toiled, and now they entered into joy. Their faithfulness gave each of them a capacity for greater service and responsibility.

The third servant was unfaithful and therefore was unrewarded. Because this man was afraid he might fail, he never tried to succeed. He feared life and his responsibilities. This paralyzed him with anxiety, so he buried the talent to protect it. The least he could have done was put the money in a bank and collect some interest. There was no real risk in that.

What we do not use for the Lord, we are in danger of losing. The master reprimanded the unfaithful, unprofitable servant, and then took his talent from him. The man with the most talents received the extra talent.

Some feel that this unprofitable servant was not a true believer. But it seems that he *was* a true servant, even though he proved to be unprofitable. The "outer darkness" of Matthew 25:30 need not refer to hell, even though that is often the case in the Gospels (Matt. 8:12; 22:13). It is dangerous to build theology on parables, for parables illustrate truth in vivid ways. The man was dealt with by the Lord, he lost

his opportunity for service, and he gained no praise or reward. To me, that is outer darkness.

It is possible that the one-talent man thought that his one talent was not really very important He did not have five talents, or even two. Why worry about one? *Because he was appointed as a steward by the Lord.* Were it not for the one-talent people in our world, very little would get accomplished. His one talent could have increased to two and brought glory to his master.

These three parables encourage us to love His appearing, look for His appearing, and labor faithfully until He comes. We should be watching, witnessing, and working. We may not be successful in the eyes of men, or even popular with others. But if we are faithful and profitable, we shall receive our reward.

Christ's Coming and the Gentile Nations (25:31–46)

This section explains to us how Jesus Christ will judge the Gentile nations. The word *nations* in Matthew 25:32 means "Gentiles," and it is in the neuter gender in the Greek. The word *them* in that same verse is in the masculine. This means that the nations will be gathered before Jesus Christ, but He will judge them as *individuals.* This will not be a judgment of groups (Germany, Italy, Japan, etc.) but of individuals within these nations.

We must not confuse this judgment with the Great White Throne Judgment described in Revelation 20:11–15. Some scholars merge both passages and call this "the general judgment." The Bible knows nothing of a "general judgment." This judgment takes place on earth immediately after the Battle of Armageddon. The White Throne Judgment takes place in space somewhere ("the earth and the heaven fled away," Rev. 20:11). The judgment here in Matthew 25 takes place *before* the kingdom is established on earth, for the saved are told to "inherit the kingdom" (Matt. 25:34). The White Throne Judgment will take place *after* the one thousand–year reign of Christ (Rev. 20:7ff.).

There is another error we must avoid. We must not force this passage to teach salvation by good works. A superficial reading would give the impression that helping one's neighbor is sufficient to earn salvation and go to heaven. But this is not the message of this passage. Nobody at any time in the history of the world was ever saved by good works.

The Old Testament saints were saved by faith (Heb. 11); the New Testament saints were saved by faith in Jesus Christ (Eph. 2:8–10). People today are saved the same way. The gospel of "do good" is not a scriptural message. It is right for *believers* to do good (Gal. 6:10; Heb. 13:16), but this is not the way unbelievers can be saved.

If we keep in mind the three groups in the account, it will help to solve this problem: There were sheep, goats, and brethren. Who are these people that the King dares to call "my brethren"? It seems likely that they are the believing Jews from the tribulation period.

These are people who will hear the message of the 144,000 and trust Jesus Christ. Since these believing Jews will not receive the "mark of the beast" (Rev. 13:16–17), they will be unable to buy or sell. How, then, can they survive? Through the loving care of the Gentiles who have trusted Christ and who care for His brethren.

The interesting thing about this judgment is that the *sheep* individuals are surprised at what they hear. They will not remember having seen the Lord Jesus Christ and ministering to His needs. But just as they lovingly ministered to the believing Jews, they did it to Christ. Their motive was not reward, but sacrificial love. In fact, these Gentiles took their own lives in their hands when they welcomed the homeless Jews and cared for them. "He that receiveth you receiveth me," Jesus said to His disciples (Matt. 10:40); and surely this would also apply to His brethren.

The individuals designated *goats* were judged because they did not trust Jesus Christ and give evidence of that faith by caring for His brethren. They apparently received the mark of the beast and took care of themselves and their own, but they had no time for the Jewish remnant that was suffering on earth (Rev. 12:17). There are sins of omission as well as sins of commission (James 4:17). Not doing good is the moral equivalent of doing evil.

When we compare the two judicial sentences (Matt. 25:34, 41), we discover some interesting truths. To being with, the sheep were blessed of the Father, but it does not say that the goats were "cursed of the Father." The sheep *inherit* the kingdom, and inheritance is based on birth. Because they had been born again through faith, they inherited the kingdom.

This kingdom was prepared for these saved individuals, but Matthew 25:41 does not state that the everlasting fire was prepared for the goats. It was prepared for the devil and his angels (Rev. 20:10). God never prepared hell for people. There is no evidence from Scripture that God predestines people to go to hell. If sinners listen to Satan, and follow his ways, they will end up where he ends up—in the torments of hell. There are only two eternal destinies: everlasting punishment for those who reject Christ or eternal life for those who trust Him.

The sheep will be ushered into the kingdom to share in Christ's glory. The church will be reigning with Christ, and Israel will enjoy the fulfillment of the promises made through the prophets. All of creation will share in the glorious liberty of God's children (Rom. 8:19–21). Jesus Christ will rule from David's throne in Jerusalem (Luke 1:30–33), and peace will reign for one thousand years (Isa. 11).

As we look back over the Olivet Discourse, we should review several facts. To begin with, God is not finished with the people of Israel. Jesus made it clear in this sermon that Israel would be purified and brought to faith in the Messiah. God has not cast away His people (Rom. 11:1).

Second, the Old Testament promises of the kingdom will be fulfilled. The tribulation period will be a very difficult time for people on the earth. But it will be "travail" in preparation for the birth of the kingdom. The suffering will lead to glory.

Third, God is going to judge this world. He is not sending cataclysmic judgments today because this is a day of grace when His message is, "Be ye reconciled to God" (2 Cor. 5:14ff.). The heavens are silent because man's sins have already been judged at the cross. God has spoken once and for all through His Son, and He will not speak to this earth again until He sends His judgments during the tribulation.

Fourth, we as Christians and members of His church are not looking for signs. "The Jews require a sign" (1 Cor. 1:22). There will be no signs given prior to the sudden return of Christ in the air for His church. However, as we see some of these tribulation signs *beginning* ("When these things begin to take place," Luke 21:28 NASB), we feel that the end is not far away. It seems that international tensions and problems are increasing to the point where the world will cry out for a dictator, and Satan will have his candidate ready.

Finally, no matter what view of prophecy we take, we know that Jesus is coming again. As Christians, we must be alert and ready. We must not waste our opportunities. We may not have a great deal of ability or a great many gifts, but we can still be faithful in the calling He has given us.

CHAPTER TWENTY-THREE
Matthew 26:1–56
THE KING'S PREPARATION

Events were now moving to a climax. The King was preparing to suffer and die. This preparation was in three stages and at three different locations. As we examine these stages, we can see the growing conflict between Christ and the enemy.

At Bethany: Worship versus Waste (26:1–16)
Matthew does not claim to give us a chronological account of the events of the last week. At this point he inserted a flashback to describe the feast in Bethany and the beautiful act that Mary performed. The religious leaders were meeting to plot against Jesus, but His friends were meeting to show their love and devotion to Him. Also, by joining these two accounts, Matthew showed the connection between Mary's worship and Judas's betrayal. It was after the feast in Bethany that Judas went to the priests and offered his help (Mark 14:10–11). The Lord's rebuke triggered Judas's response.

The feast at Bethany took place "six days before the Passover" (John 12:1) in the house of Simon the leper. Apparently he had been healed by the Lord Jesus. There were at least seventeen people at this dinner:

Simon, Mary, Martha, Lazarus, Jesus, and the twelve apostles. True to her character as the "doer" in the family, Martha did the serving (Luke 10:38–42). The three key persons in this event are Mary, Judas, and Jesus.

Mary (v. 7). Only John identifies this woman as Mary, sister of Martha and Lazarus. She is found only three times in the Gospels, and in each instance she is at the feet of Jesus. She sat at His feet and listened to the Word (Luke 10:38–42); she came to His feet in sorrow after the death of Lazarus (John 11:28–32); and she worshipped at His feet when she anointed Him with the ointment (John 12:1ff.). Mary was a deeply spiritual woman. She found at His feet her blessing, she brought to His feet her burdens, and she gave at His feet her best.

When we combine the gospel records, we learn that she anointed both His head and His feet, and wiped His feet with her hair. A woman's hair is her glory (1 Cor. 11:15). She surrendered her glory to the Lord and worshipped Him with the precious gift that she brought. It was an act of love and devotion that brought fragrance to the whole house.

Because she had listened to His word, Mary knew that soon Jesus would die and be buried. She also knew that His body would not need the traditional care given to the dead because His body would not see corruption (Ps. 16:10; Acts 2:22–28). Instead of anointing His body *after* His death, she did so *before* His death. It was an act of faith and love.

Judas (vv. 8–9). The disciples did not know the true character of Judas. His criticism of Mary sounded so "spiritual" that they joined him in attacking her. We know the real reason Judas wanted the ointment sold: The money would go into the treasury and he would be able to use it (John 12:6).

Judas is a tragic figure. He was called to be one of Christ's disciples and was named an apostle along with the others (Mark 3:13–19). He received power to heal (Matt. 10:1–4), and he probably used this power. It is not the power to do miracles that is proof of salvation (Matt. 7:21–29), but obedience to God's Word.

In spite of his affiliation with the band of disciples, and his association with Christ, Judas was not a true believe. When Jesus washed the disciples' feet, He made it clear that one of them (Judas) was not cleansed (John 13:10–11). Like many professing Christians today, Judas was *in* the group of believers but not *of* them.

Notice that every time Mary sought to do something for Jesus, she was misunderstood. Her sister Martha misunderstood her when Mary sat at Jesus' feet to hear Him teach the Word. Judas and the other disciples misunderstood her when she anointed Jesus. Her friends and neighbors misunderstood her when she came out of the house to meet Jesus after Lazarus had been buried (John 11:28–31). When we give Jesus Christ first place in our lives, we can expect to be misunderstood and criticized by those who claim to follow Him.

Why did Judas follow Jesus for three years, listen to His Word, share His ministry, and then turn traitor? One thing is certain: Judas was not the victim of circumstances or the passive tool of providence. It was prophesied that one of Messiah's close associates would betray Him, (Ps. 41:9; 55:12–14), but this fact does not relieve Judas of responsibility. We must not make him a martyr because he fulfilled this prophecy.

While we can never fully understand the mind and heart of Judas, we do know that he had every opportunity to be saved. He was often warned by Jesus in the Upper Room, Jesus even washed Judas' feet. Probably, Judas saw in Jesus the hope for Israel's political freedom. If Jesus established His kingdom, Judas, as treasurer, would have had an important position. When Jesus repeatedly refused to become a political Messiah, Judas turned against Him. Satan found a willing tool in Judas. Satan put the ideas into Judas's mind (John 13:2) and then entered into Judas to use him to betray Jesus to the enemy (John 13:27).

Judas's life is a warning to those who pretend to serve Christ but whose hearts are far from God. He is also a warning to those who waste their opportunities and their lives. "Why this waste?" asked Judas when he saw that expensive ointment poured out on Jesus. Yet Judas wasted his opportunities, his life, and his soul! Jesus called him "son of perdition" (John 17:12) which literally means "son of waste."

Jesus (vv. 10–16). He immediately came to the defense of Mary, for He always protects His own. He rebuked Judas and the other disciples and praised Mary for her loving act of devotion. *Nothing given to Jesus in love is ever wasted.* Her act of worship not only brought joy to the heart of Jesus and fragrance to the house, but also blessing to the whole world. Her devotion encourages us to love and serve Christ with our very best. Such service brings blessings to others that perhaps we will know nothing about until we see Him.

Jesus did not criticize the disciples because they were concerned about the poor. He was concerned about the poor, and we should be too. He was cautioning them against missing their opportunity to worship Him. They would always have opportunities to help the poor. But they would not always have the opportunity to worship at His feet and prepare Him for burial.

In the Upper Room: Faithfulness versus Betrayal (26:17–30)

Preparation for Passover (vv. 17–19). It was necessary to purchase and prepare the materials needed for the Passover feast. It was also necessary to find a place in crowded Jerusalem where the feast could be held. Jesus sent Peter and John to make these important preparations (Luke 22:8). They were to follow a man who was carrying a pitcher of water, and he would show them a large upper room. It would be most unusual for a *man* to be carrying the water, for this was usually done by the women.

Peter and John would have had to secure the bread

and bitter herbs, as well as the wine, for the feast. They would have had to find a perfect lamb, and then have had the lamb slain in the court of the temple and the blood put on the altar. The lamb would be roasted whole, and then the feast would be ready.

Announcement of a betrayer (vv. 20–25). Up to the very end, the disciples did not realize that one of their own number, Judas, was the traitor. They did not see any difference in the way Jesus treated Judas, which is remarkable testimony to our Lord's patience and love. It was during the Passover feast, as they were eating, that Jesus announced the presence of a traitor. The disciples looked at one another, wondering who the traitor might be. Then they asked Jesus, "It is not I, is it?" The construction of the question indicates they expected *No* as the answer.

Judas was reclining to our Lord's left; this was a place of honor at a feast. (This may explain why the disciples *again* started arguing over who was the greatest. See Luke 22:24–30.) John was reclining at our Lord's right, and thus was able to rest on His breast (John 13:23). It was an act of friendship to eat bread together, especially bread that had been dipped into the dish of herbs. It was also an honor to be given a morsel of bread by your host. Jesus gave the bread to Judas (Ps. 41:9), and Judas accepted it, *knowing full well that he was betraying his Lord.* For Jesus, giving the bread was a gracious act of hospitality; for Judas, accepting the bread was an evil act of treachery.

Matthew 26:24 presents both the human and the divine sides of this event. From the divine point of view, Judas's treachery was predicted in Scripture and was part of the plan of God. But from the human point of view, Judas was guilty of a base crime and was completely responsible for what he did. Divine sovereignty and human responsibility are not in conflict, even though we may not be able to understand how they work together to fulfill God's will.

After Judas took the morsel of bread, Satan entered into him (John 13:27). He then went out to keep his promise to the religious leaders in delivering Jesus into their hands, and even then, the other disciples did not know what he was doing. "He went immediately out; and it was night" (John 13:30). For Judas, it is still night.

Institution of the Lord's Supper (vv. 26–30). It was after Judas had left the room that Jesus instituted something new, the Lord's Supper (1 Cor. 11:23–34). He took two elements from the Passover feast, the unleavened bread and the cup, and He used these to picture His own death. The broken bread pictured His body given for the sins of the world. The "fruit of the vine" (Matt. 26:29) pictured His blood, shed for the remission of sins. The text does not indicate that anything special or mysterious happened to these two elements. They remained bread and the "fruit of the vine" but they now conveyed a deeper meaning: the body and the blood of Jesus Christ.

The Lord's Supper reminds us to *look ahead* for Christ's return. We will observe this supper until He comes (1 Cor. 11:26). The Passover pointed ahead to the Lamb of God who would take away the sins of the world (John 1:29). The Lord's Supper announces that this great work has been accomplished.

In Matthew 26:29, Jesus added the note of future glory in the kingdom. Jesus did eat bread, fish, and honey after His resurrection (Luke 24:41–43; John 21:9–15). But there is no record that He drank the fruit of the vine. Even as He faced the rejection of His nation and the suffering of the cross, He was looking ahead to the kingdom that would be established because of His sacrifice. There were traditionally four cups drunk at the Passover feast, each cup relating to one of the four promises in Exodus 6:6–7. Jesus instituted the Lord's Supper between the third and fourth cups.

The hymn that Jesus and His disciples sang before they left the Upper Room was part of the traditional Hallel, Psalms 116—118. Read those psalms in the light of Christ's death and resurrection and see how they take on new meaning. Imagine our Lord being able to sing praises to God in the face of rejection, suffering, and death.

Gethsemane: Submission versus Resistance (26:31–56)

At the Mount of Olives was a private garden that Jesus often had used as a retreat (John 18:2). *Gethsemane* means "oil press," a significant name in the light of our Lord's agony in that garden.

The disciples' failure announced (vv. 31–35). This announcement was probably made as the band of men made their way to the garden. We usually point to Peter as the one who had failed the Lord, but *all* of the disciples were involved. Jesus referred to Zechariah 13:7 in warning His disciples, but He also added a word of promise: He would rise again and meet them in Galilee. Unfortunately, the men paid little attention to the promise of His resurrection. On resurrection day, the angels reminded them of the meeting in Galilee (Matt. 28:7, 10).

When Peter disagreed with the Lord, this was the beginning of his sin of denying the Lord. Peter was unwilling to apply the word *all* to himself. Instead of reassuring Peter, the Lord gave him a personal warning: He would deny Christ three times! Peter thought he was *better* than the other men, and Jesus told him he would be even more cowardly than the others.

Peter's response was to deny Christ's word even more fervently, and the other disciples joined in this protest. Had Peter listened to the word and obeyed it, he would not have denied his Lord three times.

Jesus' surrender accomplished (vv. 36–46). He left eight of the disciples at the entrance to the garden, while He and Peter, James, and John went further into the garden. This was the third time He had taken these three men with Him. They were with Him on the Mount of Transfiguration (Matt. 17:1ff.) and in the home of Jairus where He raised Jairus's daughter from the dead (Luke 8:49ff.). He wanted them to watch and pray. He was entering into a difficult time, and the presence of His disciples would be an encouragement to Him.

We must not think that it was the fear of death that made our Lord so agonize in the garden. He did not fear death, but faced it with courage and peace. He was about to "drink the cup" that His Father had prepared for Him, and this meant bearing on His body the sins of the world (John 18:11; 1 Peter 2:24). Many godly people have been arrested, beaten, and slain because of their faith. But only Jesus experienced being made sin and a curse for mankind (2 Cor. 5:21; Gal. 3:13). The Father has never forsaken any of His own, yet He forsook His Son (Matt. 27:46). This was the cup that Jesus willingly drank for us.

Jesus was not wrestling with God's will or resisting God's will. He was yielding Himself to God's will. As perfect Man, He felt the awful burden of sin, and His holy soul was repelled by it. Yet as the Son of God, He knew that this was His mission in the world. The mystery of His humanity and deity is seen vividly in this scene.

Peter and his fellow disciples had promised to be faithful to death, *and yet they went to sleep!* They needed to pray for themselves, because danger was around the corner. And how much it would have meant to their Lord if they had watched and prayed with Him. They had failed, but their Lord had succeeded.

The arrest achieved (vv. 47–56). Jesus knew that Judas and the arresting officers were near, so He awakened the sleeping disciples and prepared them for what was coming. The fact that this band of soldiers and temple guards carried weapons and lanterns shows that Judas did not really understand Jesus. Judas thought they would have to search for Him in the garden and fight off His disciples in order to arrest Him. But Jesus came to them and calmly surrendered. It would not even have been necessary for Judas to betray Jesus with a kiss, for Jesus told the soldiers who He was.

It is tragic to see how Judas cheapened everything that he touched. His name means *praise* (Gen. 29:35), yet who would name a son "Judas" today? He used the kiss as a weapon, not as a sign of affection. In that day, it was customary for disciples to kiss their teacher. But in this case, it was not a mark of submission or respect. The Greek verbs indicate that Judas kissed Jesus repeatedly.

At this point, some of the other disciples asked, "Shall we strike with the sword?" When He was with them in the Upper Room, Jesus had talked to them about swords (Luke 22:31–38). Jesus was preparing them for a different kind of life. They would need to use whatever means He provided for their care and safety. They would be in a hostile world, and He would not always perform miracles to help them.

The problem was, the disciples misunderstood what He taught them. As usual, they took Him literally. "'Lord, look, here are two swords.' And He said to them, 'It is enough'" (Luke 22:38 NASB). Peter had

argued with the Word, denied the Word, and disobeyed the Word (when he went to sleep). Now he ran ahead of the Word. In his zeal to help Jesus, Peter cut off Malchus's ear with a sword. He did not wait for the Lord to tell him what to do, but (like Moses in Egypt, Ex. 2:11–15) Peter rushed ahead and trusted the arm of flesh. Had Jesus not healed the ear of Malchus, there probably would have been *four* crosses on Calvary!

The fact that the guards had not arrested Him in the temple indicates that there was a divine timetable controlling His life. These things were not happening by accident, but by appointment. It was all part of God's plan, yet evil men were responsible for the deed. "This Man, delivered up by the predetermined plan and foreknowledge of God, you nailed to a cross by the hands of godless men and put Him to death" (Acts 2:23 NASB).

Of course, they had no right to arrest Jesus. He had broken no laws. He had committed no crimes. They were treating Him like a common thief—and yet it was *Judas* who was the thief! The disciples who bravely promised to deliver Him deserted Him. "Behold, the hour cometh, yea, is now come, that you shall be scattered, every man to his own, and shall leave me alone; and yet I am not alone, because the Father is with me" (John 16:32). Later, even the Father would leave Him!

Each of us must decide: Will it be the sword or the cup? Will I resist God's will or submit to God's will? The cup usually involves suffering, but that suffering ultimately leads to glory. We need not fear the cup, for it has been prepared by the Father especially for us. He knows how much we can take, and He mixes the contents in wisdom and love.

CHAPTER TWENTY-FOUR
Matthew 26:57—27:26
THE KING'S TRIAL

After Jesus was arrested, He was taken to the house of Annas, the former high priest who was the father-in-law of Caiaphas, the high priest (John 18:13ff.). Annas, a shrewd politican, was something of a "godfather" in the temple establishment. Jesus then was taken to Caiaphas and, in the morning, to the meeting of the Sanhedrin. They turned Him over to Pilate who tried to put Him under Herod's jurisdiction (Luke 23:6–12). But Herod sent Him back to Pilate.

Matthew centered his attention on four persons who were involved in the trial and suffering of the Lord.

Caiaphas (26:57–68)
According to Old Testament law, the high priest was to serve until death. But when the Romans took over the nation of Israel, they made the high priesthood an appointed office. This way they could be certain of having a religious leader who would cooperate with

their policies. Annas served as high priest from AD 6–15, and five of his sons, as well as Caiaphas his son-in-law succeeded him. Caiaphas was high priest from AD 18–36, but Annas was still a power behind the throne (see Luke 3:2).

Both Annas and Caiaphas were Sadducees, which meant they did not believe in the resurrection, the spirit world, or the authority of any of the Old Testament except the five Books of Moses. It was the high priestly family that managed the "temple business," which Jesus had overthrown twice during His ministry. Of course, these men were most happy to lay hands on their enemy. Caiaphas had already made it clear that he intended to sacrifice Jesus in order to save the nation (John 11:47–54).

The high priest hastily assembled the Sanhedrin, composed of the chief priests, the elders, and the scribes (Mark 14:53). While the men were gathering, Caiaphas and his assistants were seeking for witnesses to testify against the prisoner. They had already determined that He was guilty, but they wanted to go through the motions of a legal trial.

Since no honest witnesses could be found (which in itself proves our Lord's innocence), the leaders arranged for false witnesses to testify. The law of Moses warned against false witnesses (Deut. 19:15–21), but even the religious leaders twisted God's Word to accomplish their selfish purposes. That there were *two* witnesses fulfilled the letter of the law. But that they deliberately lied broke both the letter and the spirit of the law. These witnesses cited a statement Jesus had made early in His ministry: "Destroy this temple, and in three days I will raise it up" (John 2:19). It was a serious matter to speak against the temple; this very charge later led to the death of Stephen (Acts 6:12–14; 7:45–50).

When confronted with this charge, Jesus remained silent. This was a fulfillment of Isaiah 53:7. Jesus could not deny that He made the statement, and yet neither could He explain the spiritual meaning of the statement to this group of worldly minded men. In His attitude toward His enemies, Jesus set an example for us to follow (1 Peter 2:18–23).

When Caiaphas saw that the false charges were not incriminating Jesus, he took another approach. He put Jesus under oath. In our day of repeated perjury and carelessness with the truth, we cannot appreciate the solemn importance that the Jews gave to oaths. This, of course, was according to their law (Ex. 20:7; Lev. 19:12; Num. 30:2). Caiaphas knew that Jesus claimed to be the Son of God (John 10:30–33), so he put Him under oath to declare this. The clever priest knew that Jesus could not avoid replying.

Jesus *did* affirm that He is the Son of God. He applied to Himself Psalm 110:1 and Daniel 7:13, both of which are messianic passages. In these two quotations, Jesus predicted His resurrection and ascension and His return in glory. This would mean salvation to those who trust Him, but for Caiaphas it would mean condemnation.

Without even considering the evidence, Caiaphas passed the sentence. The treatment given Jesus after the verdict had been reached was certainly illegal and inhumane. Of course, all of this only revealed the wickedness of the priest's heart. At the same time, it fulfilled the messianic prophecies (Isa. 50:6).

Peter (26:69–75)

Peter has been criticized for following "afar off" (Matt. 26:58), but that was not his mistake. His mistake was that he followed at all. He was supposed to get out! Jesus had warned Peter that he would deny Him. Jesus had also quoted Zechariah 13:7, which states that the "sheep shall be scattered." Finally, Jesus had expressly commanded the disciples not to follow: "Let these go their way" (John 18:8–9). If Peter had listened to the Word and obeyed it, he would never have failed the Lord in such a humiliating way.

The apostle John was also a part of this failure, for he had followed with Peter and gotten both of them entrance into the high priest's house (John 18:15–16). Jesus had warned them to "watch and pray" lest they enter into temptation (Matt. 26:41). But they had gone to sleep instead. Consequently, they entered into temptation, and Peter fell.

Peter's denial of Christ was the climax of a series of failures. When the Lord first warned Peter that he would be tested by Satan, Peter affirmed his faith and his ability to remain true to the Lord. In pride, Peter argued with the Word of God! He even dared to compare himself to the other disciples and affirmed that, though they might fall, *he* would remain true.

The fact that Peter was standing by the enemy's fire, warming himself, indicates how defeated he was. The denial was even more humiliating because two of the interrogators were servant girls. The third challenge came from a man, one of the bystanders, but Peter failed again. This man was a relative of Malchus, the man Peter had wounded (John 18:26). So Peter's impulsive deed caught up with him even after Jesus had repaired the damage.

Mark's account of this event indicates that the cock would crow twice (Mark 14:30). After the third denial, the cock crowed for the second time (Mark 14:72). This means that the first cock-crowing was a warning to Peter, and he should have left the scene immediately. The third denial and the second cock-crow climaxed the test, and Peter had failed.

The crowing of the cock reminded Peter of the word of Jesus. Had Peter remembered and obeyed the word, he would never have denied his Lord. It was at that time that Jesus turned and looked at Peter (Luke 22:61), and that look of love broke the apostle's heart. Peter went out and wept bitterly.

After His resurrection, Jesus met privately with Peter and restored him to his discipleship (Mark 16:7; 1 Cor. 15:5). Jesus also restored him publicly (John 21:15–19). Peter learned some important lessons during that difficult experience. He learned to pay attention to the Word, to watch and pray, and to put no confidence in his own strength.

Judas (27:1–10)

The Jewish council reconvened in the morning and delivered the official verdict against Jesus, so that people could not say that their hastily called night meeting was unlawful. Now *all* were able to attend. It is likely that Nicodemus and Joseph of Arimathea either did not attend or abstained from voting (John 19:38–42). But the Jews did not have the authority to exercise capital punishment (John 18:31), so the prisoner went to Pilate, the Roman procurator. Only he could sentence the prisoner to death.

At this point, Judas returned to the scene. He witnessed the official trial and sentencing of Jesus and realized that He was condemned to die. Judas's response was one of remorse and regret. The Greek word translated "repented himself" in Matthew 27:3 indicates, not a sorrow for sin that leads to a change of mind and action, but a regret at being caught, a remorse that leads to despair. Peter truly repented, and Jesus restored him. But Judas did not repent, and this led him to suicide.

Judas had sold Jesus for the price of a slave (Ex. 21:32). In desperation, he threw the money on the temple floor and left. The law would not permit the use of this kind of *tainted* money for temple purposes (Deut. 23:18). The leaders were careful to observe the law even while they were guilty of breaking it. They used the money to buy a "potter's field" where Jewish strangers who died could be buried properly.

Acts 1:18–19 adds to our understanding of the event. Judas went off by himself, brooded over his terrible crime, and finally hanged himself. Apparently his body was not discovered for some days, because it became bloated and his bowels gushed out. Perhaps the tree limb on which he was hanging also broke and helped to cause this.

Acts 1:18 does not say that Judas committed suicide in the field that the priests bought with the money. That act would have defiled the land and the priests would never have purchased it. Matthew 27:7 states that the priests bought a field; Acts 1:18 states that the money Judas acquired was used to buy it. Judas could not have purchased a field with that money because he gave the money back to the priests. The priests called the cemetery "the field of blood" because it was purchased with "blood money." Judas's suicide added more "blood" to the name, since it was he who contributed the money.

But, why did Matthew relate this event to a prophecy in Jeremiah, when the prophecy is found in Zechariah 11:12–13? One possible solution is that his prophecy was *spoken* by Jeremiah (note Matt. 27:9) and became a part of the Jewish oral tradition. It was later *written* by Zechariah. The prophet Jeremiah definitely was involved in the purchase of a field (Jer. 32:6ff.), and also with a potter's house (Jer. 18:1ff.), and a burial ground (Jer. 19:1–12). Matthew may have been referring to these general facts as background for the specific prophecy written by Zechariah.

Pilate (27:11–6)

Pontius Pilate was the sixth Roman procurator to serve in Judea. He was not liked by the Jews because he did things that deliberately violated their law and provoked them. He was not above killing people to accomplish his purposes (Luke 13:1). Pilate's position was always rather precarious because of his bad relationship with Israel and because of Rome's changing policy with the Jews.

The Jewish leaders accused Jesus of three crimes. They claimed that He was guilty of misleading the nation, forbidding the paying of taxes, and claiming to be a king (Luke 23:2). These were definitely political charges, the kind that a Roman governor could handle. Pilate focused on the third charge—that Jesus claimed to be a king—because this was a definite threat to Rome. If he could deal with this "revolutionary" properly, Pilate could please the Jews and impress the emperor at the same time.

"Are You the King of the Jews?" Pilate asked. Jesus gave him a clear reply: "It is as you say." However, Jesus then asked Pilate a question about his question (John 18:34–37). Was Pilate thinking of "kingship" in the Roman sense? If so, then Jesus is not that kind of a king. Jesus explained to the governor that His kingdom was not of this world, that He had no armies, that His followers did not fight. Rather, His kingdom was a reign of truth.

This conversation convinced Pilate that Jesus was not a dangerous revolutionary. "I find no fault in Him," was Pilate's decision. But the Jewish rulers were insistent that Pilate condemn Jesus. They repeated their charges and, as they enlarged on them, mentioned that Jesus was from Galilee. When Pilate heard that, he saw a way out of his dilemma, since Galilee was under Herod's jurisdiction. It is possible that Herod was displeased with Pilate because Pilate had slain some of Herod's citizens (Luke 13:1). This would have been an opportunity for Pilate to become reconciled to Herod.

Matthew did not record the trial held before Herod Antipas (Luke 23:6–12). Herod was the one who had murdered John the Baptist and had threatened to kill Jesus (Luke 13:31–32). Jesus was silent before Herod, for Herod had silenced the voice of God. All the king could do was mock Jesus and send Him back to Pilate. If Pilate had hoped to get rid of the problem, he was disappointed. However, this maneuver did patch up the quarrel between the two rulers.

Pilate wanted to solve the problem but not make any definite decision about Jesus. As a Roman governor, he was pledged to uphold the law. But as a politician, he knew he had to get along with the people. Every decision Pilate made forced him to make another decision, until he was the prisoner of his own evasions. He questioned Jesus further, but He made no reply.

Pilate had one more scheme: He would follow the tradition of releasing a prisoner. Instead of selecting some unknown prisoner, Pilate deliberately chose the most notorious prisoner he had, Barabbas. This man was a robber (John 18:40) and a murderer (Mark 15:7). Pilate reasoned that the crowd would reject Barabbas and ask for Jesus to be released, for who wants a convicted murderer and robber turned loose into society?

But Pilate was wrong. In spite of the fact that Jesus had ministered by healing the sick and even raising the dead, the people rejected Him and chose a murderer to be released. Pilate realized that a riot was in the making, and he could not afford to let this happen. The very thing the rulers wanted to prevent—a riot at Passover season (Matt. 26:5)—they engineered themselves in order to force Pilate to act. The governor *did* act, purely out of expediency and not on the basis of integrity. He released a guilty man and condemned an innocent Man, and that innocent Man is the Son of God.

Pilate took three steps in an attempt to exonerate himself. First, he washed his hands and declared that he was innocent of any guilt. Second, he stated clearly that Jesus was a just person, that is, not worthy of death. Third, he offered to punish Jesus and then release Him, but the rulers would accept no compromise. Finally, the religious rulers used the one weapon against which Pilate had no defense: "If you release this Man, you are no friend of Caesar; everyone who makes himself out to be a king opposes Caesar" (John 19:12 NASB). At this, Pilate capitulated, had Jesus scourged, and delivered Him to be crucified.

Since the Jews could not execute criminals, it was necessary for the Roman officials to assist, and Pilate issued the order. Of course, all of this was in fulfillment of prophecy. The Jews did not crucify; they used stoning to execute criminals. Psalm 22, written by a Jew, is a vivid picture of crucifixion. "They pierced my hands and my feet" (Ps. 22:16). Jesus was made a curse for us, for "cursed is every one that hangeth on a tree" (Gal. 3:13; Deut. 21:23). But still God was at work in fulfilling His divine purposes.

Pilate knew what was right, but refused to do anything about it. He was "willing to please the people" (Mark 15:15). Judas yielded to *the devil* in his great sin (John 13:2, 27); Peter yielded to *the flesh* when he denied his Lord; but Pilate yielded to *the world* and listened to the crowd. Pilate looked for the easy way, not the right way. He has gone down in history as the man who condemned Jesus.

CHAPTER TWENTY-FIVE
Matthew 27:27–66
THE KING'S SUFFERING AND DEATH

Matthew and the other gospel writers recorded the historical facts of our Lord's suffering and death. It remained for the writers of the New Testament Epistles to explain the theological meaning of this event. History states that "Christ died," but theology explains, "Christ died for our sins" (1 Cor. 15:3). Let's consider the various kinds of suffering that our Lord endured that day.

Mocked by the Soldiers (27:27–30)

The official indictment against Jesus was that He claimed to be the King of the Jews (Matt. 27:37). The soldiers took advantage of this accusation and paid "homage" to the King. It was a cruel way to treat an innocent prisoner who had already been scourged. But Pilate did nothing to restrain them. He was glad to get the prisoner off of his hands.

First, the soldiers disrobed Jesus and dressed Him in an old "soldier's cloak." Imagine attiring the Prince of Peace (Isa. 9:6) in a discarded military uniform! Matthew described the robe as *scarlet,* while Mark used the word *purple.* There is no contradiction; "reddish-purple" would be a good description of an old faded garment. Imagine how our Lord must have felt when this robe was thrown on His bleeding body.

A king must have a crown, so they wove together the thorny twigs of a plant and pushed it on His head. They gave Him a reed as a scepter, and then bowed before Him, saying, "Hail, King of the Jews!" They repeated this mock homage not realizing that the One they were mocking was indeed King of Kings and Lord of Lords.

Then they did something that no subject would ever do to his king: They spat on Him and hit Him with the reed. While some of the soldiers were bowing before Him, others were hitting Him on the head or spitting on Him (Isa. 50:6). Jesus took all of this humiliation and pain without speaking or fighting back (1 Peter 2:18ff.). His submission was not a sign of weakness; it was a sign of strength.

Crucified (27:31–38)

Crucifixion was the most shameful and painful way to execute a criminal. Jesus did not simply die; He died "even the death of a cross" (Phil. 2:8). Roman citizens ordinarily were not crucified. In fact, crucifixion was never mentioned in polite society, so degrading was this form of capital punishment.

Jesus was led outside the city to the place of execution (Heb. 13:12–13). It was required that the prisoner carry his own cross (or at least the crossbeam), and that he wear a placard around his neck announcing his crime. That placard was then hung over his head on the cross for all to see.

While the record does not state so expressly, it appears that Jesus was unable to carry the cross, and this was slowing down the progress of the group. When we remember that He had been awake all night, scourged, and abused by the soldiers, we can conclude that He was exhausted. Jesus started out bearing His cross (John 19:17). Mark 15:22 says, "And they bring him to Golgotha" (literal translation). This suggests that the soldiers had to assist Jesus in the procession, for the word *bring* has the meaning of "to carry, to bear."

There was to be no delay in this execution. The Passover was about to be celebrated, and the Jewish leaders did not want their holy day desecrated by the dead bodies of criminals (John 19:31). In order to hasten the procession, the soldiers drafted a visitor to Jerusalem, Simon from Cyrene. He had come to Jerusalem to celebrate Passover, and now he was humiliated by being forced to carry the cross of an unknown criminal! Roman soldiers had the authority to draft citizens (Matt. 5:41).

Mark referred to Simon as though the people reading his gospel would recognize him: "the father of Alexander and Rufus" (Mark 15:21). Apparently these two sons were well-known members of the church. It seems likely that this humiliating experience resulted in Simon's conversion as well as in the conversion of his family. Simon came to Jerusalem to sacrifice his Passover lamb, and he met the Lamb of God who was sacrificed for him.

It was customary to give a narcotic drink to those about to be crucified, for this would help to ease the pain. Jesus refused this drink; He did the will of God in complete control of His faculties. Also this act fulfilled Psalm 69:21.

It was customary for the soldiers to share the loot at an execution. This was a fulfillment of Psalm 22:18. After they had finished gambling for His clothing (John 19:23–25), they sat down and "guarded him there" (Matt. 27:36). After all, this Jesus was known to be a miracle-worker. Nobody knew how many followers He had, and perhaps they were even then preparing to rescue Him. He had one man in His band of disciples who had been a Zealot (Matt. 10:4—"Simon the Zealot"), and that fanatical group stopped at nothing when it came to opposing Roman authority.

By combining the gospel records, we arrive at the full accusation that was put over His head: "This is Jesus of Nazareth the King of the Jews." The Jewish rulers did not approve of what Pilate wrote, but for once the governor did not vascillate (John 19:21–22). In one sense, this title proved to be the first "gospel tract" ever written. It announced to one of the thieves crucified with Him that He was the Savior and a King. He dared to believe this message and asked Jesus to save him!

Mocked by Jews (27:39–44)

Jesus was not executed in a quiet building, away from the city's noise and activity. He was executed on a public highway, on a day when perhaps hundreds of people were traveling. The fact that His indictment was written in three languages—Greek, Hebrew, and Latin—indicates that a cosmopolitan crowd passed by Golgotha, "the place of the skull." This in itself was humiliating, for the passers-by could stare and shout bitter mockery at the victims. Again, this mockery from the crowd had been predicted (Ps. 22:6–8).

It was bad enough that the common rabble mocked Him, but even the Jewish leaders joined the attack. They reminded Him of His promise to rebuild the temple in three days (Matt. 26:61; John 2:19). "If You can do that, You can come down from the cross and prove to us that You are God's Son!" In reality, it was the fact that He *stayed* on the cross that proved His divine sonship.

The Jewish rulers mocked His claim to be the Savior. "He saved others; He cannot save Himself" (Matt. 27:42 nasb). He *had* saved others. But if He saved Himself, then nobody else could be saved! He did not come to save His life, but to give it as a ransom for sinners.

Rejected by the Father (27:45–56)

Jesus was crucified at nine o'clock in the morning; and from nine until noon, He hung in the light. But at noon, a miraculous darkness covered the land. This was not a sandstorm or an eclipse, as some liberal writers have suggested. It was a heaven-sent darkness that lasted for three hours. It was as though all of creation was sympathizing with the Creator. There were three days of darkness in Egypt before Passover (Ex. 10:21–23), and there were three hours of darkness before the Lamb of God died for the sins of the world.

Jesus had spoken at least three times before this darkness fell. While they were crucifying Him, He repeatedly prayed, "Father, forgive them, for they know not what they do" (Luke 23:34). He had spoken to the repentant thief and assured him a place in paradise (Luke 23:39–43). He had also given His mother into the care of His beloved disciple, John (John 19:18–27). But when the darkness came, Jesus was silent for three hours.

After three hours, the darkness left. Then Jesus cried, "My God, my God, why hast thou forsaken me?" This was a direct quotation from Psalm 22:1. It was during the time of darkness that Jesus had been made sin for us (2 Cor. 5:21). He had been forsaken by the Father! That darkness was a symbol of the judgment that He endured when He was "made a curse" for us (Gal. 3:13). Psalm 22:2 suggests a period of light and a period of darkness, and Psalm 22:3 emphasizes the holiness of God. How could a holy God look with favor on His Son who had become sin?

Jesus spoke these words in Hebrew, and the spectators did not understand Him. They thought He was calling for Elijah to help Him. Had they listened carefully and consulted Psalm 22 in its entirety, they would have understood the truth.

In rapid succession, the Lord spoke three more times. He said, "I thirst" (John 19:28), and this fulfilled Psalm 69:21. Someone took pity on Him and moistened His lips with some sour wine. The others waited to see if perhaps Elijah would come to His rescue.

Then Jesus shouted, "It is finished! Father, into thy

hands I commit my spirit!" The fact that Jesus shouted with a loud voice indicates that He was in complete control of His faculties. Then He voluntarily yielded up His spirit and died.

Though He was "crucified through weakness" (2 Cor. 13:4), He exercised wonderful power when He died. Three miracles took place simultaneously: The veil of the temple was torn in two from top to bottom; an earthquake opened many graves; some saints arose from the dead. The rending of the veil symbolized the wonderful truth that the way was now open to God (Heb. 10:14–26). There was no more need of temples, priests, altars, or sacrifices. Jesus had finished the work of salvation on the cross.

The earthquake reminds us of what happened at Mount Sinai when God gave the law to Moses (Ex. 19:16ff.). The earthquake at Calvary signified that the demands of the law had been met and the curse of the law forever abolished (Heb. 12:18–24). The torn veil indicates that He conquered sin; the earthquake suggests that He conquered the law and fulfilled it; and the resurrections prove that He defeated death.

We are not told who these saints were; they were simply believers who had died. The King James Version suggests that they did not come out of the graves until *after* His resurrection; the New American Standard Bible agrees with this. It is difficult to believe that they were given life on Friday afternoon and yet remained in their tombs until Sunday. The New International Version suggests that these saints were resurrected immediately and came out of their tombs, but that they did not visit in Jerusalem until after Jesus had been raised from the dead. It is not likely that many Jews would be in the cemetery on Passover, since they might be defiled by the dead. These resurrections could have taken place with nobody finding out at that time.

The result of all of this was the testimony of the centurion and those watching. "Truly this was the Son of God." Did this indicate saving faith? Not necessarily. But certainly it indicated hearts that were open to the truth.

The only disciple at the cross when Jesus died was John (John 19:35). But many women were watching from a distance, undoubtedly those who had assisted Him in His ministry (Luke 8:2). Three women were named: Mary Magdalene, who had been delivered of seven demons (Luke 8:2); Mary, the mother of James and Joses, who also was at the tomb on resurrection morning (Matt. 28:1; Mark 16:1); and Salome, the mother of James and John. Salome had asked Jesus for special thrones for her sons. We wonder how she felt as she saw Him hanging on a cross.

His Guarded Tomb (27:57–66)
Were it not for the intervention of Jospeh of Arimathea and Nicodemus (John 19:38), the body of Jesus might not have had a decent burial. Joseph and Nicodemus had come to believe in Jesus, even though they had not openly testified of their faith. God kept them hidden, as it were, that they might care for the body of Jesus. Since Joseph was a rich man, and he prepared the new tomb, he helped in the fulfillment of prophecy, Isaiah 53:9—"He was assigned a grave with the wicked, and with the rich in his death" (NIV).

It is not likely that Joseph prepared that tomb for himself. He was a wealthy man and certainly would not want to be buried so near a place of execution. He prepared that tomb for Jesus, and he selected a site near Golgotha so that he and Nicodemus could bury Christ's body quickly. Joseph and Nicodemus could very well have been in the garden waiting for Jesus to die. When they took Him from the cross, they defiled themselves and were not able to eat the Passover. But, what difference did it make? They had found the Lamb of God!

In contrast to the loving care given by Jesus' friends, notice the plottings and maneuvering of the Jewish leaders. The disciples had forgotten that Jesus promised to rise from the dead on the third day, but His enemies remembered. Pilate permitted the leaders to set a guard at the tomb. This guard put an official Roman seal on the stone. All of this was of God, for now it was impossible for anyone—friend or foe—to steal the body. Without realizing it, the Jewish leaders and the Roman government joined forces to help prove the resurrection of Jesus Christ.

CHAPTER TWENTY-SIX
Matthew 28
THE KING'S VICTORY

If anything proves the kingship of Jesus Christ, it is His resurrection from the dead. The final chapter in Matthew's gospel is a record of victory. It is a thrilling fact that believers today share in that victory.

Notice the various stages in the experience of the believers with reference to His resurrection.

They Thought He Was Dead (28:1)
The women who had lingered at the cross came early to the tomb, bringing spices that they might anoint His body. They thought He was dead. In fact, they wondered how they would move the huge stone that blocked the entrance to the tomb (Mark 16:3). It is remarkable that they did not believe in His resurrection when He had taught this truth repeatedly (Matt. 16:21; 17:23; 20:19; 26:32).

We must never underestimate the importance of the resurrection of Jesus Christ. The world believes that Jesus died, but the world does not believe that He arose from the dead. Peter's message at Pentecost emphasized the resurrection. In fact, it is emphasized throughout the book of Acts. What is the significance of the resurrection?

It proves that Jesus is God's Son. Jesus stated that He had authority to lay down His life and to take it up again (John 10:17–18).

It verifies the truth of Scripture. Both in the Old Testament and in the teaching of Jesus, His resurrection is clearly taught (see Ps. 16:10; 110:1). If Jesus had not come out of the tomb, then these Scriptures would not be true.

It assures our own future resurrection. Because Jesus died and rose again, we shall one day be raised to be like Him (1 Thess. 4:13–18). In fact, the entire structure of the Christian faith rests on the foundation of the resurrection. If we do away with His resurrection, we have no hope.

It is the proof of a future judgment. "Because he hath appointed a day, in the which he will judge the world in righteousness by that man who he hath ordained; whereof he hath given assurance unto all men, in that he hath raised him from the dead" (Acts 17:31).

It is the basis for Christ's heavenly priesthood. Because He lives by the power of an endless life, He is able to save us "to the uttermost" (Heb. 7:23–28). He lives to intercede for us.

It gives power for Christian living. We cannot live for God by our own strength. It is only as His resurrection power works in and through us that we can do His will and glorify His name (see Rom. 6:4).

It assures our future inheritance. Because we have a living hope, we can experience hopeful living. A dead hope grows weaker and weaker before it eventually dies. But because Jesus Christ is alive, we have a glorious future (see 1 Peter 1:3–5).

Whenever God's people gather on the Lord's Day they bear witness that Jesus is alive and that the church has received spiritual blessings. When the followers of the Lord gathered that first Lord's Day, they were discouraged and defeated.

They Heard He Was Alive (28:2–8)

"And behold, a severe earthquake had occurred" (Matt. 28:2 NASB). Two angels had appeared (Luke 24:4), and one of them had rolled the stone away from the door. Of course, the soldiers on duty were greatly frightened by this sudden demonstration of supernatural power. The stone was not rolled away to permit Jesus to come out, for He had already left the tomb. It was rolled back so that the people could see for themselves that the tomb was empty.

One of the angels spoke to the women and calmed their fears. "He is not here! Come, and see!" Keep in mind that these women, as well as the disciples, did not expect Jesus to be alive.

What did they see in the tomb? The graveclothes lying on the stone shelf, still wrapped in the shape of the body (John 20:5–7). Jesus had passed through the graveclothes and left them behind as evidence that He was alive. They lay there like an empty cocoon. There was no sign of struggle; the graveclothes were not in disarray. Even the napkin (which had been wrapped around His face) was folded carefully in a place by itself.

We cannot examine this evidence in the same way the believers did that first Easter Sunday. But we do have the evidence of the Word of God. Jesus was not held by the bonds of death (Acts 2:24). He had promised to arise from the dead, and His Word was never broken.

The remarkable change in the early believers is another proof of His resurrection. One day they were discouraged and hiding in defeat. The next day they were declaring His resurrection and walking in joyful victory. In fact, they were willing to die for the truth of the resurrection. If all of this were a manufactured tale, it could never have changed their lives or enabled them to lay down their lives as martyrs.

Over five hundred witnesses saw Jesus alive at one time (1 Cor. 15:3–8). These appearances of the risen Christ were of such a nature that they could not be explained as hallucinations or self-deception. The people who saw Him were surprised. It would have been impossible for over five hundred people to suffer hallucinations at the same time. Even the apostle Paul, who was an enemy of the church, saw the risen Christ; that experience transformed his life (Acts 9).

The existence of the church, the New Testament, and the Lord's Day add further proof that Jesus is alive. For centuries, the Jews had been God's people, and they had honored the seventh day, the Sabbath. Then a change took place: Jews and Gentiles united in the church and became God's people; they met on the first day of the week, the Lord's Day. The New Testament is a lie if Jesus is dead, for every part of it points to a risen Christ.

Of course, Christians have experienced His resurrection power in their own lives. While the inward, subjective experience *alone* would not prove our Lord's historic resurrection, when combined with the other evidences, it adds great weight to the case. Still it is possible for people to be self-deluded. "Believers" in all kinds of cults will claim their way is true because of what they have experienced. But Christians have the weight of church history, Scripture, and dependable witnesses to back up their own personal experiences of faith.

"Come and see!" was followed by "Go and tell!" We must not keep the resurrection news to ourselves. The angel sent the women to tell (of all people) Christ's own disciples. They should have been expecting the news, but instead, they questioned it even when they heard it.

They Met the Living Christ Personally (28:9–15)

It is when we are obeying God's Word that He comes to us. Jesus had already appeared to Mary Magdalene in the garden (John 20:11–18; Mark 16:9). Notice that our Lord's first two resurrection appearances were to believing women. These faithful women were not only the last to leave Calvary, but they were also the first to come to the tomb. Their devotion to Jesus was rewarded.

"All hail!" can be translated, *Grace.* What a marvelous

greeting for the resurrection day! The women fell at His feet, took hold of Him, and worshipped Him. There must have been some fear in their hearts, for He immediately assured them with His typical, "Be not afraid!"

Not only had the angel commissioned them, but the Lord also commissioned them. The phrase "my brethren" reveals the intimate relationship between Christ and His followers. Jesus had spoken similar words to Mary Magdalene earlier that morning (John 20:17). Jesus reinforced the instructions of the angel that the disciples meet Him in Galilee (see Matt. 28:7). In the garden, Jesus had told His disciples that He would rise from the dead and meet them in Galilee, but they had forgotten (Matt. 26:31–32).

While the believers were worshipping the living Christ, the unbelievers were plotting to destroy the witness of the resurrection of Jesus Christ. By now, some of the soldiers had realized that they were in a desperate plight. The Roman seal had been broken, the stone had been rolled away, and the body was not in the tomb. For a Roman soldier to fail in his duty was an offense punishable by death (Acts 12:19; 16:27–28). But the soldiers were shrewd: They did not report to Pilate or to their superior officers; they reported to the Jewish chief priests. They knew that these men were as anxious to cover up the miracle as were the soldiers themselves! Between the chief priests, the elders, and the soldiers, they put together a story that would explain the empty tomb: The body was stolen.

By examining this story, we see that it actually *proves* the resurrection of Jesus Christ. If Jesus' body was stolen, then it was taken either by His friends or His enemies. His friends could not have done it since they had left the scene and were convinced that Jesus was dead. His enemies would not steal His body because belief in His resurrection was what they were trying to prevent. They would have defeated their own purposes if they had removed His body. And, if they had taken it, why did they not produce it and silence the witness of the early church?

Anyone who stole the body would have taken the body *in the graveclothes*. Yet the empty graveclothes were left in the tomb in an orderly manner. This was hardly the scene of a grave robbery.

The religious leaders had given money to Judas to betray Jesus. They also gave money to the soldiers to say that the body had been stolen. These Romans would have demanded a large price, for their lives were at stake. If their superiors heard that these soldiers had failed, they could have been executed. Even if the story got to Pilate, he was not likely to do much about it. He was sure that Jesus was dead (Mark 15:43–45), and that was all that mattered to him. The disappearance of Jesus' body created no problems for Pilate.

Mark Twain once wrote that a lie can go around the world while truth is still lacing up her boots. There is something in human nature that makes it easy for people to believe lies. It was not until the coming of the Spirit at Pentecost, and the powerful witness of the apostles, that the Jews in Jerusalem discovered the truth: Jesus Christ is alive! Any sincere person who studies this evidence with an open heart will conclude that the resurrection of Jesus Christ is a historic fact that cannot be refuted.

Our Lord also appeared to the two Emmaus disciples that day (Luke 24:13–32), and also to the ten disciples in the Upper Room in Jerusalem (John 20:19–25). A week later, He appeared to the eleven disciples and dealt with Thomas's unbelief (John 20:19–25). On that first Easter Sunday, Jesus also made a special appearance to Peter (Luke 24:33–35; 1 Cor. 15:5).

That day began with the disciples and the women thinking Jesus was dead. Then they were told that He was alive. Following that announcement, they met Him personally. There was one more stage in their experience.

They Shared the Good News with Others (28:16–20)

Some Bible scholars equate this "mountain meeting" in Galilee with the appearance of the Lord to "more than five hundred brethren at one time" (1 Cor. 15:6). The fact that some of the people present doubted His resurrection would suggest that more than the eleven apostles were present, for these men were now confirmed believers. Our Lord's ascension did not take place at this time, but later, after He had ministered to His disciples in Jerusalem (Luke 24:44–53).

Matthew 28:18–20 is usually called "the Great Commission," though this statement is no greater than that in any of the other Gospels, nor is it the last statement Jesus made before He returned to heaven. However, this declaration does apply to us as believers, so we should understand the factors that are involved.

An authority (v. 18). In this verse, the word *power* means "authority," the right to use power. The entire gospel of Matthew stresses the authority of Jesus Christ. There was authority to His teaching (Matt. 7:29). He exercised authority in healing (Matt. 8:1–13), and even in forgiving sins (Matt. 9:6). He had authority over Satan, and He delegated that authority to His apostles (Matt. 10:1). At the close of his gospel, Matthew made it clear that Jesus has *all* authority.

Since Jesus Christ today has all authority, we may obey Him without fear. No matter where He leads us, no matter what circumstances we face, He is in control. By His death and resurrection, Jesus defeated all enemies and won for Himself all authority.

Christianity is a missionary faith. The very nature of God demands this, for God is love, and God is not willing that any should perish (2 Peter 3:9). Our Lord's death on the cross was for the whole world. If we are the children of God and share His nature, then we will want to tell the good news to the lost world.

When we read the book of Acts, we see that the early church operated on the basis of the Lord's sovereign authority. They ministered in His name. They depended on His power and guidance. They did not face a lost world on the basis of their own authority, but on the authority of Jesus Christ.

An activity (vv. 19–20a). The Greek verb translated *go* is actually not a command but a present participle (going). The only command in the entire Great Commission is "make disciples" ("teach all nations"). Jesus said, "While you are going, make disciples of all the nations." No matter where we are, we should be witnesses for Jesus Christ and seek to win others to Him (Acts 11:19–21).

The term "disciples" was the most popular name for the early believers. Being a disciple meant more than being a convert or a church member. *Apprentice* might be an equivalent term. A disciple attached himself to a teacher, identified with him, learned from him, and lived with him. He learned, not simply by listening, but also by doing. Our Lord called twelve disciples and taught them so that they might be able to teach others (Mark 3:13ff.).

A disciple, then, is one who has believed on Jesus Christ and expressed this faith by being baptized. He remains in the fellowship of the believers that he might be taught the truths of the faith (Acts 2:41–47). He is then able to go out and win others and teach them. This was the pattern of the New Testament church (2 Tim. 2:1–2).

In many respects, we have departed from this pattern. In most churches, the congregation pays the pastor to preach, win the lost, and build up the saved—while the church members function as cheerleaders (if they are enthusiastic) or spectators. The "converts" are won, baptized, and given the right hand of fellowship, then they join the other spectators. How much faster our churches would grow, and how much stronger and happier our church members would be, if each one were discipling another believer. The only way a local church can "be fruitful and multiply" (instead of growing by "additions") is with a systematic discipleship program. This is the responsibility of *every* believer, and not just a small group who have been "called to go."

Jesus had opened the minds of His disciples to understand the Scriptures (Luke 24:44–45). They knew what He wanted them to teach to their own converts. It is not enough to win people to the Savior; we must also teach them the Word of God. This is also a part of the Great Commission.

An ability (v. 20b). Jesus is not only "in the midst" when His people gather together (Matt. 18:20), but He is also present with them as they scatter into the world to witness. Had He remained on earth, Jesus could not have fulfilled this promise. It was when the Spirit came that Jesus could be with His people no matter where they were.

Dr. G. Campbell Morgan told about an experience in his life that involved this statement. Early in his Christian life, Morgan used to visit several ladies once a week to read the Bible to them. When he came to the end of Matthew's gospel, Morgan read, "Lo, I am with you always, even unto the end of this age." He added, "Isn't that a wonderful promise?" One of the ladies quickly replied, "Young man, that is not a promise—it is a fact!"

There are no conditions for us to meet, or even to believe, for *Jesus Christ is with us.* Paul discovered this to be true when he was seeking to establish a church in the difficult city of Corinth. Obeying this commission, Paul came to the city (Acts 18:1), won people to Christ and baptized them (Acts 18:8) and taught them the Word (Acts 18:11). When the going was tough, Paul had a special visit from the Lord: "Be not afraid … for I am with thee" (Acts 18:9–10).

The phrase "the end of the age" indicates that our Lord has a plan; He is the Lord of history. As the churches follow His leading and obey His Word, they fulfill His purposes in the world. It will all come to a climax one day; meanwhile, we must all be faithful.

MARK

OUTLINE

Key theme: Jesus Christ the servant
Key verse: Mark 10:45

I. THE PRESENTATION OF THE SERVANT (1:1–13)

II. THE SERVANT'S MINISTRY IN GALILEE (1:14—9:50)
  A. Period of popularity—1:14—6:29
  B. Period of withdrawal—6:30—9:32
  C. Period of completion—9:33–50

III. THE SERVANT'S JOURNEY TO JERUSALEM (10)

IV. THE SERVANT'S MINISTRY IN JERUSALEM (11—16)
  A. Public teaching and controversy—11:1—12:44
  B. Private teaching and ministry—13:1—14:31
  C. Arrest, trial, and crucifixion—14:32—15:47
  D. Resurrection and ascension—16

CONTENTS

CHAPTER ONE
Mark 1

GOD'S SERVANT IS HERE!

T he gospel is neither a discussion nor a debate," said Dr. Paul S. Rees. "It is an announcement!"

Mark wasted no time giving that announcement, for it is found in the opening words of his book. Matthew, who wrote primarily for the Jews, opened his book with a genealogy. After all, he had to prove to his readers that Jesus Christ is indeed the rightful Heir to David's throne. Since Luke focused mainly on the sympathetic ministry of the Son of Man, he devoted the early chapters of his book to a record of the Savior's birth. Luke emphasized Christ's humanity, for he knew that his Greek readers would identify with the perfect Babe who grew up to be the perfect Man.

John's gospel begins with a statement about eternity! Why? Because John wrote to prove to the whole world that Jesus Christ of Nazareth is the Son of God (John 20:31). The *subject* of John's gospel is the deity of Christ, but the *object* of his gospel is to encourage his readers to believe on this Savior and receive the gift of eternal life.

Where does Mark's gospel fit in? Mark wrote for the Romans, and his theme is *Jesus Christ the Servant.* If we had to pick a "key verse" in this gospel, it would be Mark 10:45—"For even the Son of man came not to be ministered unto, but to minister, and to give his life a ransom for many."

The fact that Mark wrote with the Romans in mind helps us understand his style and approach. The emphasis in this gospel is on *activity.* Mark describes Jesus as He busily moves from place to place and meets the physical and spiritual needs of all kinds of people. One of Mark's favorite words is "straightway," meaning "immediately." He uses it forty-one times. Mark does not record many of our Lord's sermons because his emphasis is on what Jesus did rather than what Jesus said. He reveals Jesus as God's Servant, sent to minister to suffering people and to die for the sins of the world. Mark gives us no account of our Lord's birth, nor does he record a genealogy, unnecessary in regard to a servant.

In this opening chapter, Mark shares three important facts about God's Servant.

The Servant's Identity (1:1–11)

How does Mark identify this Servant? He records the testimonies of several dependable witnesses to assure us that Jesus is all that He claims to be.

John Mark, the author of the book, is the first witness (v. 1). He states boldly that Jesus Christ is the Son of God. It is likely that Mark was an eyewitness of some of the events that he wrote about. He lived in Jerusalem with his mother, Mary, and their home was a meeting place for believers in the city (Acts 12:1–19).

Several scholars believe that Mark was the young man described in Mark 14:51–52. Since Peter called Mark "my son" (1 Peter 5:13), it is probable that it was Peter who led Mark to faith in Jesus Christ. Church tradition states that Mark was "Peter's interpreter," so that the gospel of Mark reflects the personal experiences and witness of Simon Peter.

The word *gospel* simply means "the good news." To the Romans, Mark's special target audience, *gospel* meant "joyful news about the emperor." The "gospel of Jesus Christ" is the good news that God's Son has come into the world and died for our sins. It is the good news that our sins can be forgiven, that we can belong to the family of God and one day go to live with God in heaven. It is the announcement of victory over sin, death, and hell (1 Cor. 15:1–8, 51–52; Gal. 1:1–9).

The second witness is that of the prophets (vv. 2–3). Mark cites two quotations from the Old Testament prophets, Malachi 3:1 and Isaiah 40:3 (note also Ex. 23:20). The words *messenger* and *voice* refer to John the Baptist, the prophet God sent to prepare the way for His Son (Matt. 3; Luke 3:1–18; John 1:19–34). In ancient times, before a king visited any part of his realm, a messenger was sent before him to prepare the way. This included both repairing the roads and preparing the people. By calling the nation to repentance, John the Baptist prepared the way for the Lord Jesus Christ. Isaiah and Malachi join voices in declaring that Jesus Christ is the Lord, Jehovah God.

John the Baptist is the next witness (vv. 4–8). Jesus called him the greatest of the prophets (Matt. 11:1–15). In his dress, manner of life, and message of repentance, John identified with Elijah (2 Kings 1:8; Mal. 4:5; Matt. 17:10–13; and note Luke 1:13–17). The "wilderness" where John ministered is the rugged wasteland along the western shore of the Dead Sea. John was telling the people symbolically that they were in a "spiritual wilderness" far worse than the physical wilderness that their ancestors had endured for forty years. John called the people to leave their spiritual wilderness, trust their "Joshua" (Jesus), and enter into their inheritance.

John was careful to magnify Jesus and not himself (see John 3:25–30). John would baptize repentant sinners in water, but "the coming One" would baptize them with the Spirit (Acts 1:4–5). This did not mean that John's baptism was unauthorized (see Matt. 21:23–27), or that water baptism would one day be replaced by Spirit baptism (see Matt. 28:19–20). Rather, John's message and baptism were *preparation* so that the people would be ready to meet and trust the Messiah, Jesus Christ. Our Lord's apostles were no doubt baptized by John (see John 4:1–2; Acts 1:21–26).

The Father and the Holy Spirit are Mark's final witnesses to the identity of God's Servant (vv. 9–11). When Jesus was baptized, the Spirit came on Him as a dove, and the Father spoke from heaven and identified His beloved Son. The people who were there did not hear the voice or see the dove, but Jesus and John did (see John 1:29–34). The word *beloved* not only declares affection, but it also carries the meaning of "the only one." The Father's announcement from heaven reminds us of Psalm 2:7 and Isaiah 42:1.

You will want to note these references in Mark's gospel to Jesus Christ as the Son of God—Mark 1:1, 11; 3:11; 5:7; 9:7; 12:1–11; 13:32; 14:61–62; and 15:39. Mark did not write his book about just any Jewish servant. He wrote his book about the very Son of God who came from heaven to die for the sins of the world.

Yes, Jesus is the Servant—but He is a most unusual Servant. After all, it is the servant who prepares the way for others and announces their arrival. But *others* prepared the way for Jesus and announced that He had come! Even heaven itself took note of Him! This Servant is God the Son.

The Servant's Authority (1:12–28)

We expect a servant to be *under* authority and to *take* orders, but God's Servant *exercises* authority and *gives* orders—even to demons—and His orders are obeyed. In this section, Mark describes three scenes that reveal our Lord's authority as the Servant of God.

Scene one—His temptation (vv. 12–13). Mark does not give as full an account of the Temptation as do Matthew (4:1–11) and Luke (4:1–13), but Mark adds some vivid details that the others omit. The Spirit "driveth him" into the wilderness. This is a strong word that Mark used eleven times to describe the casting out of demons. It is *impelled* in the New American and *sent* in the New International. It does not suggest that our Lord was either unwilling or afraid to face Satan. Rather, it is Mark's way of showing the intensity of the experience. No time was spent basking in the glory of the heavenly voice or the presence of the heavenly dove. The Servant had a task to perform and He immediately went to do it.

In concise form, Mark presents us with two symbolic pictures. Our Lord's forty *days* in the wilderness remind us of Israel's forty *years* in the wilderness. Israel failed when they were tested, but our Lord succeeded victoriously. Having triumphed over the enemy, Jesus could now go forth and call a new people who would enter into their spiritual inheritance. Since the name *Jesus* is the Greek form of "Joshua," we can see the parallel.

The second picture is that of the "last Adam" (1 Cor. 15:45). The first Adam was tested in a beautiful Garden and failed, but Jesus was tempted in a dangerous wilderness and won the victory. Adam lost his "dominion" over creation because of his sin (Gen. 1:28; Ps. 8), but in Christ, that dominion has been restored for all who trust Him (Heb. 2:6–8). Jesus was with the wild beasts and they did not harm Him. He gave a demonstration of that future time of peace and righteousness, when the Lord shall return and establish His kingdom (Isa. 11:9; 35:9). Indeed, He is a Servant with authority!

Scene two—His preaching (vv. 14–22). If ever a man spoke God's truth with authority, it was Jesus Christ (see Matt. 7:28–29). It has been said that the scribes spoke *from* authorities but that Jesus spoke *with* authority. Mark was not recording here the beginning of our Lord's ministry, since He had already ministered in other places (John 1:35–4:4). He is telling us why Jesus left Judea and came to Galilee: Herod had arrested John the Baptist, and wisdom dictated that Jesus relocate. By the way, it was during this journey that Jesus talked with the Samaritan woman (John 4:1–45).

Our Lord's message was the gospel of the kingdom of God, or "the gospel of God" as some texts read. No doubt most of the Jews read "political revolution" into the phrase "kingdom of God," but that was not what Jesus had in mind at all. His kingdom has to do with His reign in the lives of His people; it is a spiritual realm and not a political organization. The only way to enter God's kingdom is by believing the good news and being born again (John 3:1–7).

The gospel is called "the gospel of God" because it comes from God and brings us to God. It is "the gospel of the kingdom" because faith in the Savior brings you into His kingdom. It is the "gospel of Jesus Christ" because He is the heart of it; without His life, death, and resurrection, there would be no good news. Paul called it "the gospel of the grace of God" (Acts 20:24) because there can be no salvation apart from grace (Eph. 2:8–9). There is only one gospel (Gal. 1:1–9), and it centers in what Jesus Christ did for us on the cross (1 Cor. 15:1–11).

Jesus preached that people should repent (change their minds) and believe (see Acts 20:21). Repentance alone is not enough to save us, even though God expects believers to turn from their sins. We must also put positive faith in Jesus Christ and believe His promise of salvation. Repentance without faith could become remorse, and remorse can destroy people who carry a burden of guilt (see Matt. 27:3–5; 2 Cor. 7:8–10).

Because Jesus preached with authority, He was able to call men from their regular occupations and make them His disciples. Who else could interrupt four fishermen at their work and challenge them to leave their nets and follow Him? Several months before, Jesus had already met Peter, Andrew, James, and John, and they had come to trust Him (see John 1:35–49). This was not their initial call to faith and salvation; it was an initial call to discipleship. The fact that Zebedee had hired servants suggests that his fishing business was successful and that he was a man of means. It also assures us that James and John did not mistreat their father when they heeded Christ's call. With the help of his servants, Zebedee could still manage the business.

Jesus did not invent the term "fishers of men." In that day, it was a common description of philosophers and other teachers who "captured men's minds" through teaching and persuasion. They would "bait the hook" with their teachings and "catch" disciples. It is likely that as many as seven of our Lord's disciples were fishermen (John 21:1–3). Surely the good qualities of successful fishermen would make for success in the difficult ministry of winning lost souls: courage, the ability to work together, patience, energy, stamina, faith, and tenacity. Professional fishermen simply could not afford to be quitters or complainers!

Jesus ministered not only in the open air but also in the synagogues. The Jewish synagogues developed during the nation's exile when the people were in Babylon after the temple had been destroyed. Wherever there were ten Jewish men above the age of twelve, a synagogue could be organized. The synagogue was not a place of sacrifice—that was done at the temple—but of reading the Scriptures, praying, and worshipping God. The services were led, not by priests, but by laymen, and the ministry was supervised by a board of elders that was presided over by a "ruler" (Mark 5:22). It was customary to ask visiting rabbis to read the Scriptures and teach, which explains why Jesus had such freedom to minister in the synagogues. The apostle Paul also took advantage of this privilege (Acts 13:14–16; 14:1; 17:1–4).

Our Lord had set up His headquarters in Capernaum, possibly in or near the home of Peter and Andrew (Mark 1:29). You may see the remains of a Capernaum synagogue when you visit the Holy Land today, but it is not the one in which Jesus worshipped. The people assembled for services on the Sabbath as well as on Mondays and Thursdays. Being a faithful Jew, Jesus honored the Sabbath by going to the synagogue, and when He taught the Word, the people were astonished at His authority.

You will discover as you read Mark's gospel that he delights in recording the emotional responses of people. The congregation in the synagogue was "astonished" at His teaching and "amazed" at His healing powers (Mark 1:27; also note 2:12; 5:20, 42; 6:2, 51; 7:37; 10:26; 11:18). You even find Mark recording our Lord's amazement at the unbelief of the people in Nazareth (Mark 6:6). There is certainly nothing monotonous about this narrative!

Scene three—His command (vv. 23–28). We wonder how many synagogue services that man had attended without revealing that he was demonized. It took the presence of the Son of God to expose the demon, and Jesus not only exposed him, but He also commanded him to keep quiet about His identity and to depart from the man. The Savior did not want, nor did He need, the assistance of Satan and his army to tell people who He is (see Acts 16:16–24).

The demon certainly knew exactly who Jesus is (see Acts 19:13–17) and that he had nothing in common with Him. The demon's use of plural pronouns shows how closely he was identified with the man through whom he was speaking. The demon clearly identified

Christ's humanity ("Jesus of Nazareth") as well as His deity ("the Holy One of God"). He also confessed great fear that Jesus might judge him and send him to the pit. There are people today just like this demonized man: in a religious meeting, able to tell who Jesus is, and even trembling with fear of judgment—yet lost (see James 2:19)!

"Hold thy peace!" literally means "Be muzzled!" Jesus would use the same words when stilling the storm (Mark 4:39). The demon tried one last convulsive attack, but then had to submit to the authority of God's Servant and come out of the man. The people in the synagogue were amazed and afraid. They realized that something new had appeared on the scene—a new doctrine and a new power. Our Lord's *words and works* must always go together (John 3:2). The people kept on talking about both, and the fame of Jesus began to spread. Our Lord did not encourage this kind of public excitement lest it create problems with both the Jews and the Romans. The Jews would want to follow Him only because of His power to heal them, and the Romans would think He was a Jewish insurrectionist trying to overthrow the government. This explains why Jesus so often told people to keep quiet (Mark 1:44; 3:12; 5:43; 7:36–37; 8:26, 30; 9:9). The fact that they did not obey created problems for Him.

The Servant's Sympathy (1:29–45)

Two miracles of healing are described in this section, both of which reveal the compassion of the Savior for those in need. In fact, so great was His love for the needy that the Savior ministered to great crowds of people after the Sabbath had ended, when it was lawful for them to come for help. It would appear that God's Servant was at the beck and call of all kinds of people, including demoniacs and lepers, and He lovingly ministered to them all.

Jesus and the four disciples left the synagogue and went to Peter and Andrew's house for their Sabbath meal. Perhaps Peter was a bit apologetic because his wife had to care for her sick mother and was unable to entertain them in the usual manner. We do not know about the other disciples, but we do know that Peter was a married man (Mark 1:30).

Peter and Andrew not only brought their friends James and John home with them from the service, but they also brought the Lord home. That is a good example for us to follow: don't leave Jesus at the church—take Him home with you and let Him share your blessings and your burdens. What a privilege it was for Peter and his family to have the very Son of God as guest in their humble home. Before long, the Guest became the Host, just as one day the Passenger in Peter's boat would become the Captain (Luke 5:1–11).

By faith, the men told Jesus about the sick woman, no doubt expecting Him to heal her. That is exactly what He did! The fever left her immediately, and she was able to go to the kitchen and serve the Sabbath meal. If you have ever had a bad fever, then you know how painful and uncomfortable it is. You also know that after the fever leaves you, it takes time for you to regain your strength. But not so in this case! She was able to serve the Lord immediately. And isn't service to our Lord one of the best ways to thank Him for all He has done for us?

What was the result of this miracle? When the Sabbath ended at sundown, the whole city showed up at Peter's door! They brought their sick and afflicted, and the Lord (who was no doubt weary) healed them all. The Greek verb indicates that they "kept on bringing" people to Him, so that He must have gone to sleep at a very late hour. Note in Mark 1:32 the clear distinction made between the diseased and the demonized. While Satan can cause physical affliction, not all sickness is caused by demonic power,

Late hours did not keep Jesus from His appointed meeting with His Father early the next morning. Read Isaiah 50:4 for a prophetic description of God's righteous Servant as He meets the Father morning by morning. What an example for us to follow! It is no surprise that Jesus had such authority and power when His prayer life was so disciplined (see Mark 9:28–29; 6:46; 14:32–38).

However, the crowds wanted to see Jesus again, not to hear His word, but to experience His healing and see Him perform miracles. Peter was surprised that Jesus did not hasten to meet the crowds but instead left for other towns where He might preach the gospel. Peter did not realize the shallowness of the crowds, their unbelief, and their lack of appetite for the Word of God. Jesus said it was more important for Him to preach the gospel in other places than to stay there and heal the sick. He did not permit popular acclaim to change His priorities.

Perhaps we can understand our Lord's concern for a feverish woman, but that He would meet *and touch* a leper is somewhat beyond our understanding. Lepers were supposed to keep their distance and warn everyone that they were coming, lest others would be defiled (Lev. 13:45–46). This man knew that Jesus was *able* to heal him, but he was not sure the Master was *willing* to heal him. Lost sinners today have the same unnecessary concern, for God has made it abundantly clear that He is not willing that sinners perish (2 Peter 3:9) and that He is willing that all men be saved (1 Tim. 2:4).

When you read the "tests" for leprosy described in Leviticus 13, you can see how the disease is a picture of sin. Like sin, leprosy is deeper than the skin (Lev. 13:3); it spreads (Lev. 13:5–8); it defiles and isolates (Lev. 13:44–46); and it renders things fit only for the fire (Lev. 13:47–59). Anyone who has never trusted the Savior is spiritually in worse shape than this man was physically.

Jesus had compassion on the man (note Mark 6:34; 8:2; 9:22) and healed him. He did it with His touch and with His word. No doubt this was the first loving touch this leper had felt in a long time. As with the fever, so with the leprosy: it was gone instantly!

For reasons already stated, Jesus commanded the man not to tell everybody. He was to go to the priests and follow the instructions given in Leviticus 14, so that he might be declared clean and received back into the social and religious life of the community. However, the man disobeyed orders. Jesus told this man to keep quiet, and yet he told everybody. Jesus commands us to tell everybody—and we keep quiet! The crowds that came to get help from Jesus created a serious problem for Him and probably hindered Him from teaching the Word as He intended to do (Mark 1:38).

The ceremony described in Leviticus 14 presents a beautiful picture in type of the work of redemption. The two birds represent two different aspects of our Lord's ministry: His incarnation and death (the bird put into the jar and then killed), and His resurrection and ascension (the bird stained with the blood and then set free). The blood was applied to the man's right ear (God's Word), right thumb (God's work), and right great toe (God's walk). Then the oil was put on the blood, symbolizing the Holy Spirit of God. The Holy Spirit cannot come on human flesh until first the blood has been applied.

We should learn some important spiritual lessons from this chapter. To begin with, if the Son of God came as a servant, then being a servant is the highest of all callings. We are never more like the Lord Jesus than when we are serving others. Second, God shares His authority with His servants. Only those who are *under* authority have the right to *exercise* authority. Finally, if you are going to be a servant, be sure you have compassion, because people will come to you for help and rarely ask if it is convenient!

Yet, what a privilege it is to follow in the steps of Jesus Christ and meet the needs of others by being one of God's compassionate servants.

CHAPTER TWO
Mark 2:1—3:12
WHAT THE SERVANT OFFERS YOU

With amazing speed the news spread that a miracle-working Teacher had come to Capernaum, and wherever our Lord went, great crowds gathered. They wanted to see Him heal the sick and cast out demons. Had they been interested in His message of the gospel, these multitudes would have been an encouragement to Jesus, but He knew that most of them were shallow in their thinking and blind to their own needs. Often the Lord found it necessary to leave the city and go out into the wilderness to pray (Luke 5:15–16). Every servant of God should follow His example and take time away from people in order to meet the Father and be refreshed and revitalized through prayer.

Now the time had come for Jesus to demonstrate

to the people what His ministry was all about. After all, He had come to do much more than relieve the afflictions of the sick and the demonized. Those miracles were wonderful, but there was something greater for the people to experience—they could enter into the kingdom of God! They needed to understand the spiritual lessons that lay behind the physical miracles He was performing.

In this section, our Lord makes it clear that He came to bring to all who would trust Him three wonderful gifts: forgiveness (Mark 2:1–12), fulfillment (Mark 2:13–22), and freedom (Mark 2:23—3:12).

Forgiveness (2:1–12)

Whether this event took place in His own house ("He was at home" NASB) or Peter's house is not made clear. Since hospitality is one of the basic laws of the East, the people of Capernaum did not wait for an invitation but simply came to the house in droves. This meant that some of the truly needy people could not get close enough to Jesus to receive His help. However, four friends of a palsied man decided to lower their friend through the roof, trusting that Jesus would heal him, and Jesus did. This miracle of healing gave our Lord the opportunity to teach an important lesson about forgiveness.

Consider this scene through the eyes of the Lord Jesus. When He *looked up,* He saw the four men on the roof with their sick friend. Houses had flat roofs that were usually accessible by means of an outside stairway. It would not be difficult to remove the tiles, laths, and grass that comprised the roof and make an opening large enough to fit their friend through on his mat.

We must admire several characteristics of these men, qualities that ought to mark us as "fishers of men." For one thing, they were deeply concerned about their friend and wanted to see him helped. They had the faith to believe that Jesus could and would meet his need. They did not simply "pray about it," but they put some feet to their prayers, and they did not permit the difficult circumstances to discourage them. They worked together and dared to do something different, and Jesus rewarded their efforts. How easy it would have been for them to say, "Well, there is no sense trying to get to Jesus today! Maybe we can come back tomorrow."

When our Lord *looked down,* He saw the palsied man lying on his mat, and immediately Jesus went to the heart of the man's problem—sin. Not all sickness is caused by sin (see John 9:1–3), but evidently this man's condition was the result of his disobedience to God. Even before He healed the man's body, Jesus spoke peace to the man's heart and announced that his sins were forgiven! Forgiveness is the greatest miracle that Jesus ever performs. It meets the greatest need; it costs the greatest price; and it brings the greatest blessing and the most lasting results.

Then Jesus *looked around* and saw the critics who had come to spy on Him (see Luke 5:17). These religious leaders certainly had every right to investigate the ministry of this new teacher, since the religious life of the nation was under their supervision (Deut. 13). But they should have come with open minds and hearts, seeking truth, instead of with critical minds, seeking heresy. Some of the negative attitude that had been present in Judea (John 4:1–4) had now invaded Galilee, and this was the beginning of the official opposition that ultimately led to our Lord's arrest and death. He was now so popular that the Jewish leaders dared not ignore Him. In fact, they must have arrived early for the meeting, because they were right at the scene of action! Or perhaps Jesus graciously gave them front row seats.

When the Lord *looked within,* He saw the critical spirit in their hearts and knew that they were accusing Him of blasphemy. After all, only God *can* forgive sins, and Jesus had just told the paralytic that his sins were forgiven. Jesus was claiming to be God!

But the next instant, He *proved* Himself to be God by reading their hearts and telling them what they were thinking (see John 2:25; Heb. 3:13). Since they wanted to "reason" about things, He gave them something to ponder: Which is easier, to heal the man or to tell him he is forgiven? Obviously, it is easier to say, "Your sins are forgiven!" *because nobody can prove whether or not the forgiveness really took place.* So, to back up His words, Jesus immediately healed the man and sent him home. The healing of the man's body was but an illustration and demonstration of the healing of his soul (Ps. 103:3). The scribes and Pharisees, of course, could neither heal the man nor forgive his sins, so they were caught in their own trap and condemned by their own thoughts.

Jesus affirmed His deity not only by forgiving the man's sins and healing his body, but also by applying to Himself the title "Son of man." This title is used fourteen times in Mark's gospel, and twelve of these references are found after Mark 8:29, when Peter confessed Jesus as the Christ of God (Mark 2:10, 28; 8:31, 38; 9:9, 12, 31; 10:33, 45; 13:26, 34; 14:21, 41, 62). It was definitely a messianic title (Dan. 7:13–14), and the Jews would have interpreted it that way. Jesus used this title about eighty times in the Gospels.

Suppose the religious leaders had opened their hearts to the truth that day, what could they have learned? For one thing, they could have learned that sin is like sickness and that forgiveness is like having your health restored. This was not a new truth, for the Old Testament Scriptures had said the same thing (Ps. 103:3; Isa. 1:5–6, 16–20); but now it had been demonstrated before their very eyes. They also could have learned that Jesus Christ of Nazareth is indeed the Savior with authority to forgive sins—and their own sins could have been forgiven! What an opportunity they missed when they came to the meeting with a critical spirit instead of with a repentant heart!

Fulfillment (2:13–22)

It soon became evident that Jesus was deliberately

associating Himself with the outcasts of Jewish society. He even called a tax collector to become one of His disciples! We do not know that Levi was a dishonest man, though most of the tax collectors were, but the fact that he worked for Herod Antipas and the Romans was enough to disgrace him among loyal Jews. However, when Jesus called him, Levi did not argue or delay. He got up and followed Jesus, even though he knew that Rome would never give him back his job. He burned his bridges ("And he left everything behind"—Luke 5:28 NASB), received a new name ("Matthew, the gift of God"), and enthusiastically invited some of his "sinner" friends to meet the Lord Jesus. These were Jewish people like himself who did not follow the law or appear to have much interest in things religious. It was exactly the kind of people Jesus wanted to reach.

Of course, the critics had to be there, but our Lord used their questions to teach the guests about Himself and the spiritual work He came to do. He explained His mission by using three interesting comparisons.

The Physician (vv. 16–17). Jesus did not consider these people "rejects," even though they had been excommunicated by the religious leaders. Matthew's friends were *patients* who needed a physician, and Jesus was that Physician. We have already seen that sin may be compared to sickness and forgiveness to having your health restored. Now we see that our Savior may be compared to a physician: He comes to us in our need; He makes a perfect diagnosis; He provides a final and complete cure; and *He pays the bill!* What a physician!

But there are three kinds of "patients" whom Jesus cannot heal of their sin sickness: (1) those who do not know about Him; (2) those who know about Him but refuse to trust Him; and (3) those who will not admit that they need Him. The scribes and Pharisees were in that third category, as are all self-righteous sinners today. Unless we admit that we are sinners, deserving of God's judgment, we cannot be saved. Jesus saves only sinners (Luke 19:10).

In Jesus' day, as in the days of the prophets, there were those who claimed to bring spiritual healing to the people, but whose remedies were ineffective. Jeremiah rebuked the priests and false prophets of his day because they were worthless physicians who gave only a false hope to the nation. "They have healed also the hurt of the daughter of my people slightly, saying, 'Peace, peace'; when there is no peace" (Jer. 6:14; 8:11). They applied their weak medicines to the surface symptoms and did not get down deep into the basic problem—the sinful heart (Jer. 17:9). We must beware of such worthless physicians today.

The Bridegroom (vv. 18–20). While the first question they asked had to do with the kind of company Jesus was keeping, their second question raised the issue of why Jesus was having such a good time with these people at the table. His conduct, to them, seemed inappropriate. John the Baptist was an austere man, somewhat of a recluse, but Jesus accepted invitations to meals, played with the children, and enjoyed social gatherings (Matt. 11:16–19). No doubt John's disciples were a bit scandalized to see Jesus at a party, and the pious disciples of the Pharisees (see Matt. 23:15) were quick to join them in their perplexity.

Jesus had already made it clear that He came to convert the sinners, not to compliment the self-righteous. Now He told them that he had come to bring gladness, not sadness. Thanks to the legalism imposed by the scribes and Pharisees, the Jewish religion had become a burdensome thing. The poor people were weighed down by rules and regulations that were impossible to obey (Matt. 23:4). "Life is not supposed to be a funeral!" Jesus told them. "God wants life to be a wedding feast! I am the Bridegroom and these people are My wedding guests. Are not wedding guests supposed to have a good time?"

The Jews knew that marriage was one of the pictures used in the Old Testament to help explain Israel's relationship to the Lord. They had been "married to Jehovah" and they belonged only to Him (Isa. 54:5; Jer. 31:32). When the nation turned to foreign gods, as they often did, they committed "spiritual adultery." They were unfaithful to their Husband, and they had to be disciplined. The major theme of Hosea is God's love for His adulterous wife and His desire to restore the nation to His favor once again.

John the Baptist had already announced that Jesus was the Bridegroom (John 3:29), and our Lord had performed His first miracle at a joyous marriage feast (John 2:1–11). Now He was inviting people to come to the wedding! After all, becoming a Christian is not unlike entering into the marriage relationship (see Rom. 7:4—"that ye should be married to another"). Two people are not married just because they know each other, or even because they have strong feelings about each other. In order to be married, they must commit themselves to each other and make this commitment known. In most societies, the man and woman publicly affirm this commitment when each says, "I do!"

Salvation from sin involves much more than a person knowing about Christ, or even having "good feelings" toward Christ. Salvation comes when the sinner commits himself or herself to Jesus Christ and says, "I do!" Then the believer immediately enters into the joys of this spiritual marriage relationship: bearing His name, sharing His wealth and power, enjoying His love and protection, and one day living in His glorious home in heaven. When you are "married to Christ," life becomes a wedding feast, in spite of trials and difficulties.

Mark 2:20 is a hint of our Lord's anticipated death, resurrection, and return to heaven. It is unlikely that His disciples, at that early stage in their training, even understood what He meant. However, Jesus was not suggesting that His absence from earth would mean that His followers would have to replace the feast with a funeral! He was only pointing out that occasional fasting would be proper at a future time, but that joyful celebration should be the normal experience of believers.

The garment and the wineskins (vv. 21–22). Jesus taught two important lessons about His ministry: (1) He came to save sinners, not to call the religious; and (2) He came to bring gladness and not sadness. The third lesson is this: He came to introduce the new, not to patch up the old.

The religious leaders were impressed with our Lord's teaching, and perhaps they would have been happy to make some of His ideas a part of their own religious tradition. They were hoping for some kind of compromise that would retain the best of pharisaic Judaism and the best of what Christ had to offer. But Jesus exposed the folly of that approach. It would be like tearing patches from a new unshrunk garment and sewing them on an old garment You would ruin the new garment, and when the old garment was washed, the patches would shrink, rip away, and ruin that garment too (note Luke 5:36–39). Or, it would be like putting new unfermented wine in old brittle wineskins. As soon as the wine began to ferment and the gases formed, the old skins would burst—and you would lose both the wine and the skins.

Jesus came to usher in the new, not to unite with the old. The Mosaic economy was decaying, getting old, and ready to vanish away (Heb. 8:13). Jesus would establish a new covenant in His blood (Luke 22:19–20). The law would be written on human hearts, not on stones (2 Cor. 3:1–3; Heb. 10:15–18), and the indwelling Holy Spirit would enable God's people to fulfill the righteousness of the law (Rom. 8:1–4).

By using this illustration, Jesus refuted once and for all the popular idea of a compromising "world religion." Well-meaning but spiritually blind leaders have suggested that we take "the best" from each religion, blend it with what is "best" in the Christian faith, and thus manufacture a synthetic faith that would be acceptable to everybody. But the Christian faith is *exclusive* in character; it will not accept any other faith as its equal or its superior. "There is none other name under heaven, given among men, whereby we must be saved" (Acts 4:12).

Salvation is not a partial patching up of one's life; it is a whole new robe of righteousness (Isa. 61:10; 2 Cor. 5:21). The Christian life is not a mixing of the old and the new; rather, it is a fulfillment of the old in the new. There are two ways to destroy a thing: you can smash it or you can permit it to fulfill itself. An acorn, for example, can be smashed with a hammer, or it can be planted and allowed to grow into an oak. In both instances, the destruction of the acorn is accomplished, but in the second instance, the acorn is destroyed by being fulfilled.

Jesus fulfilled the prophecies, types, and demands of the law of Moses. The law was ended at Calvary when the perfect sacrifice was once offered for the sins of the world (Heb. 8—10). When you trust Jesus Christ, you become part of a new creation (2 Cor. 5:17), and there are always new experiences of grace and glory. How tragic when people hold on to dead religious tradition when they could lay hold of living spiritual truth. Why cherish the shadows when the reality has come (Heb. 10:1ff.)? In Jesus Christ we have the fulfillment of all that God promised (2 Cor. 1:20).

Freedom (2:23—3:12)

The Sabbath was cherished by the Jews as a sacred institution. God gave the people of Israel the Sabbath after they came out of Egypt (Ex. 20:8–11; Neh. 9:14), and it was a special sign between Israel and Jehovah (Ex. 31:13–17). There is no record in Scripture that God ever gave the Sabbath to any other nation. So, when Jesus began openly to violate the Sabbath traditions, it was like declaring war against the religious establishment. He began His campaign by healing a man who had been sick for thirty-eight years (John 5), and then followed with the events recorded in this section.

Jewish tradition stated that there were thirty-nine acts that were strictly forbidden on the Sabbath. Moses had prohibited work on the Sabbath, but he did not give many specifics (Ex. 20:10). It was wrong to kindle a fire for cooking (Ex. 35:3), gather fuel (Num. 15:32ff.), carry burdens (Jer. 17:21ff.), or transact business (Neh. 10:31; 13:15, 19). But Jewish tradition went into great detail and even informed the people how far they could travel on the Sabbath (two hundred cubits, based on Josh. 3:4). In short, the Sabbath day had become a crushing burden, a symbol of the galling religious bondage that had captured the nation.

After healing the man at the Pool of Bethesda, our Lord's next act of "Sabbath defiance" was to walk through the fields on the Sabbath and permit His disciples to pluck the grain, rub it between their hands, and eat it. It was not illegal for a hungry person to take some of his neighbor's fruit or grain, provided he did not fill a vessel or use a harvesting implement (Deut. 23:24–25). However, that was not what upset the Pharisees. What upset them was that the disciples had worked on the Sabbath day!

When you read Matthew's account of this event, you note that Jesus gave three arguments to defend His disciples: what David did (Matt. 12:3–4), what the priests did (Matt. 12:5–6), and what the prophet Hosea said (Matt. 12:7–8). Mark's Roman readers would not be interested in Jewish prophets and priests, so Mark focused on David, whom the Romans would recognize as a great hero and king. The argument is reasonable: if a hungry king and his men were permitted to eat the holy bread from the tabernacle (1 Sam. 21:1–6), then it was right for the Lord of the Sabbath to permit His men to eat the grain from His fields. David broke a definite law given by Moses, for the showbread was for the priests only (Lev. 24:5–9), but the disciples had violated only a man-made tradition. God is surely more concerned with meeting the needs of people than He is with protecting religious tradition. The Pharisees had their priorities confused.

Did Jesus make a mistake when He mentioned Abiathar as the high priest? The record in 1 Samuel 21 names Abimelech, the father of Abiathar (1 Sam. 22:20), as high priest, so our Lord's words appear to be a contradiction. They are not. It is possible that father and son each had both names (1 Chron. 18:16 and 24:6; 1 Sam. 22:20 and 2 Sam. 8:17). Also it is likely that our Lord used "Abiathar" to refer to the Old Testament *passage* about Abiathar rather than to the man. This is the way the Jews identified sections of the Word since their manuscripts did not have chapters and verses such as we have today in our Bibles (see Mark 12:26).

On that same Sabbath day, Jesus went into the synagogue to worship, and while He was there, He deliberately healed a man. Certainly He could have waited one more day, but once again He wanted to challenge the pharisaical legalistic traditions. This time the Pharisees (Luke 6:7) were expecting Him to heal, so they kept their eyes wide open. Our Lord's questions in Mark 3:4 were never answered by His enemies. Since *evil* is at work every day, including the Sabbath day, why should *good* not be at work as well? Death is always at work, but that should not hinder us from seeking to save life.

Jesus could see "the hardening of their hearts" (literal translation), and their sin made Him angry. Our Lord never became angry at the publicans and sinners, but He did express anger toward the self-righteous Pharisees (Matt. 23). They would rather protect their traditions than see a man healed! The man, of course, knew little about this spiritual conflict. He simply obeyed our Lord's command, stretched out his hand, and was healed.

So incensed were the Pharisees over what Jesus had done that they united with the Herodians and started making plans to arrest Jesus and destroy Him. The Herodians were not a religious party; they were a group of Jews who were sympathetic to King Herod and supported his rule. Most of the Jews despised Herod and obeyed his laws reluctantly, so it was surprising that the Pharisees, who were strict Jews, would join themselves with these disloyal politicians. But it was a common enemy—Jesus—that brought the two groups together.

In response to this united opposition, Jesus simply withdrew from there, but He could not prevent the great crowds from following Him. These crowds were dangerous to His cause, of course, because they were not spiritually motivated, and the authorities could accuse Him of leading a popular revolt against the Romans. Yet Jesus received the people, healed the sick, and delivered the demonized. Once again, He warned the demons not to reveal who He was (Mark 1:23–26).

Our Lord had now reached a crisis in His ministry. Great crowds were following Him, but their interest was not in things spiritual. The religious leaders wanted to destroy Him, and even some of Herod's friends were getting involved. His next step would be to spend a night in prayer (Luke 6:12), call twelve men to assist Him as His apostles, and preach a sermon—the Sermon on the Mount—explaining the spiritual basis of His kingdom.

He offered them forgiveness, fulfillment, and freedom, but they refused His offer.

Have *you* accepted His offer?

CHAPTER THREE
Mark 3:13—4:34
THE SERVANT, THE CROWDS, AND THE KINGDOM

No matter where He went, God's Servant was thronged by excited crowds (Mark 3:7–9, 20, 32; 4:1). Had Jesus been a "celebrity" and not a servant, He would have catered to the crowds and tried to please them (see Matt. 11:7–15). Instead, He withdrew from the crowds and began to minister especially to His disciples. Jesus knew that most of the people who pushed to get near Him were shallow and insincere, but His disciples did not know this. Lest they take all of this "success" seriously, Jesus had to teach these men the truth about the crowds and the kingdom. In this section, we see our Lord's three responses to the pressure of the crowd.

He Founded a New Nation (3:13—19)
The number of the disciples is significant because there were twelve tribes in the nation of Israel. In Genesis, God started with Jacob's twelve sons, and in Exodus, He built them into a mighty nation. Israel was chosen to bring the Messiah into the world so that through Him all the nations of the earth could be blessed (Gen. 12:1–3). However, the nation of Israel was now spiritually decayed and ready to reject her own Messiah. God had to establish "a holy nation, a peculiar [purchased] people" (1 Peter 2:9), and the twelve apostles were the nucleus of this new "spiritual" nation (Matt. 21:43).

Jesus spent all night in prayer before choosing these twelve men (Luke 6:12). When He selected them, He had three purposes in mind: (1) training them by personal example and teaching, (2) sending them out to preach the gospel, and (3) giving them authority to heal and cast out demons (see Mark 1:14–15, 38–39; 6:7–13). These twelve men would thus be able to continue His work when He returned to the Father, and they would also be able to train others to carry on the ministry after them (2 Tim. 2:2).

In the New Testament, you will find three other lists of the names of the twelve disciples: Matthew 10:2–4; Luke 6:14–16; and Acts 1:13. Luke tells us that Jesus gave them the special name "apostles." A disciple is one who learns by doing; our modern equivalent might be an "apprentice." An "apostle" is one who is sent on official service with a commission. Jesus had many disciples but only twelve apostles, His special "ambassadors."

When you compare the lists, it appears that the names are arranged in pairs: Peter and Andrew; James and John; Philip and Bartholomew (Nathanael [John 1:45]); Thomas and Matthew (Levi); James, the son of Alphaeus, and Thaddaeus (Judas, son of James, not Iscariot [John 14:22]); Simon the Zealot and Judas Iscariot. Since Jesus sent His apostles out two by two, this was a logical way to list them (Mark 6:7).

Simon's name was changed to Peter, "the rock" (John 1:40–42), and Levi's was changed to Matthew, "the gift of God." James and John were given the nicknames, "Boanerges—the sons of thunder." We commonly think of John as the apostle of love, but he certainly did not begin with that kind of reputation, nor did James his brother (Mark 9:38–41; 10:35–39; Luke 9:54–55). It is encouraging to see what Jesus was able to do with such a diversified group of unlikely candidates for Christian service. There is still hope for us!

Mark defined the Hebrew word *Boanerges* because he was writing for Roman readers. In his gospel you will find several of these "special notes for Gentiles" (Mark 5:41; 7:11, 34; 11:9; 14:36; 15:22, 34). The word *Canaanite* in Mark 3:18 has nothing to do with national or racial origin. It is the Hebrew word *cananaean,* which comes from a word that means "to be jealous, to be zealous." The Zealots were a group of Jewish extremists organized to overthrow Rome, and they used every means available to advance their cause. The historian Josephus called them "daggermen." It would be interesting to know how Simon the Zealot responded when he first met Matthew, a former employee of Rome.

If you consult a harmony of the Gospels, you will see that between Mark 3:19 and 20, Jesus preached the Sermon on the Mount (Matt. 5—7) and participated in the events described in Luke 7:1—8:3. Mark's gospel does not include that famous sermon because his emphasis is on what Jesus did rather than what Jesus said.

He Established a New Family (3:20–21, 31–35)

Our Lord's friends were sure that Jesus was confused, and possibly deranged! The great crowds they saw following Him, and the amazing reports they heard about Him, convinced them that He desperately needed help. He simply was not living a normal life, so His friends came to Capernaum to "take charge of him." Then his mother and "brethren" (Mark 6:3) traveled thirty miles from Nazareth to plead with Him to come home and get some rest, but even they were unable to get near Him. This is the only place in the gospel of Mark where Mary is seen, and her venture was a failure.

History reveals that God's servants are usually misjudged by their contemporaries, and often misunderstood by their families. D. L. Moody was called

"Crazy Moody" by many people in Chicago, and even the great apostle Paul was called mad (Acts 26:24–25). Emily Dickinson wrote:

> Much madness is divinest sense
> To a discerning eye;
> Much sense the starkest madness.
> 'Tis the majority
> In this, as all, prevails.
> Assent, and you are sane;
> Demur—you're straightway dangerous,
> And handled with a chain.

Our Lord was not being rude to His family when He remained in the house and did not try to see them. He knew that their motives were right but their purpose was definitely wrong. If Jesus had yielded to His family, He would have played right into the hands of the opposition. The religious leaders would have said, "See, He agreed with His family—He needs help! Don't take Jesus of Nazareth too seriously." Instead of giving in, He used this crisis as an opportunity to teach a spiritual lesson: His "family" is made up of all those who do the will of God. Our Lord's half-brothers were not believers (John 7:1–5), and Jesus felt closer to the believing publicans and sinners than He did to James, Joses, Judah, and Simon, His half-brothers.

Our Lord was not suggesting that believers ignore or abandon their families in order to serve God, but only that they put God's will above everything else in life. Our love for God should be so great that our love for family would seem like hatred in comparison (Luke 14:26). Certainly it is God's will that we care for our families and provide for them (see 1 Tim. 5:8), but we must not permit even our dearest loved ones to influence us away from the will of God. When you consider the importance of the family in the Jewish society, you can imagine how radical Christ's words must have sounded to those who heard them.

How does one enter into the family of God? By means of a new birth, a spiritual birth from above (John 3:1–7; 1 Peter 1:22–25). When the sinner trusts Jesus Christ as Savior, he experiences this new birth and enters into God's family. He shares God's divine nature (2 Peter 1:3–4) and can call God "Father" (Rom. 8:15–16). This spiritual birth is not something that we accomplish for ourselves, nor can others do it for us (John 1:11–13). It is God's work of grace; all we can do is believe and receive (Eph. 2:8–9).

He Announced a New Kingdom (3:22–30; 4:1–34)

The crowds hoped that Jesus would deliver the nation and defeat Rome. Instead, He called twelve ordinary men and founded a "new nation," a spiritual nation whose citizens had their names written down in heaven (Luke 10:20; Phil. 3:20). The crowds wanted Jesus to behave like a loyal Jew and honor His family, but Jesus established a "new family" made up of all those who trusted Him and did the will of God. The crowds also expected Him to restore the kingdom and bring back Israel's lost glory, but His response was to announce a new kingdom, a spiritual kingdom.

"Kingdom" is a key word in this section (Mark 3:24; 4:11, 26, 30). John the Baptist had announced that the arrival of the King was near, and he had warned the people to prepare to meet Him (Mark 1:1–8). Jesus took up John's message and preached the good news of the kingdom and the necessity for sinners to repent and believe (Mark 1:14–15). But what is this kingdom like? If the Lord was not going to restore Israel and set up a political kingdom, what kind of kingdom was He planning to establish?

At this point, Mark introduced a new word—*parables* (see Mark 3:23; 4:2, 10–11, 13, 33–34). Jesus explained the kingdom, not by giving a lecture on theology, but by painting pictures that captured the attention of the people and forced them to use their imaginations and think. Our English word *parable* comes from two Greek words that mean "to cast alongside" (*para*—alongside; *ballo*—to throw or cast). A parable is a story or figure placed alongside a teaching to help us understand its meaning. It is much more than "an earthly story with a heavenly meaning," and it certainly is not an "illustration" such as a preacher would use in a sermon. A true parable gets the listener deeply involved and compels that listener to make a personal decision about God's truth and his or her life. So penetrating and personal are parables that, after they heard several of them, the religious leaders wanted to kill the Lord Jesus! (See Matt. 21:45–46.)

A parable begins innocently as *a picture* that arrests our attention and arouses our interest. But as we study the picture, it becomes *a mirror* in which we suddenly see ourselves. If we continue to look by faith, the mirror becomes *a window* through which we see God and His truth. How we respond to that truth will determine what further truth God will teach us.

Why did Jesus teach in parables? His disciples asked Him that very question (Mark 4:10–12; and see Matt. 13:10–17). A careful study of His reply reveals that Jesus used parables both to hide the truth and to reveal it. The crowd did not judge the parables; the parables judged the crowd. The careless listener, who thought he knew everything, would hear only a story that he did not really understand, and the result in his life would be judgment (see Matt. 11:25–30). The sincere listener, with a desire to know God's truth, would ponder the parable, confess his ignorance, submit to the Lord, and then begin to understand the spiritual lesson Jesus wanted to teach.

Jesus placed a great deal of importance on *the hearing of the Word of God.* In one form or another, the word *hear* is used thirteen times in Mark 4:1–34. Obviously, our Lord was speaking, not about physical hearing, but about hearing with spiritual discernment. To "hear" the Word of God means to understand it and obey it (see James 1:22–25).

Our Lord gave several parables to help the people

(and that included His disciples) understand the nature of His kingdom.

The strong man (3:22–30). Jesus healed a demoniac who was both blind and dumb (Matt. 12:22–24), and the scribes and Pharisees used this miracle as an opportunity to attack Him. The crowd was saying, "Perhaps this Man is indeed the Son of David, the Messiah." But the religious leaders said, "No, He is in league with Beelzebub! It is Satan's power that is at work in Him, not God's power."

"Beelzebub" (or "Beelzebul") is a name for the devil, and it means "master of the house." Jesus picked up on this meaning and gave a parable about a strong man guarding his house. To plunder the house, one must first overcome the strong man.

Jesus exposed both their bad theology and their faulty logic. If it was by the power of Satan that He had cast out the demon, then Satan was actually fighting against himself! This meant that Satan's house and kingdom were divided and therefore on the verge of collapse. Satan had been guarding that man carefully because the devil does not want to lose any of his territory. The fact that Jesus delivered the man was proof that He was stronger than Satan and that Satan could not stop Him.

Jesus did much more than answer their false accusation. He went on to explain the seriousness of what they had said. After all, our words reveal what is hidden in our hearts (Matt. 12:35), and what is in our hearts determines our character, conduct, and destiny. We sometimes say, "Talk is cheap!" But in reality, what we say can be very costly. Jesus warned the Jewish religious leaders that they were in danger of committing an eternal and unforgivable sin (Matt. 12:32).

When you ask people, "What is the unpardonable sin?" they usually reply, "It is blaspheming the Holy Spirit" or "It is the sin of attributing to the devil the works of the Holy Spirit." Historically speaking, these statements are true, but they do not really answer the question. How do we *today* blaspheme the Spirit of God? What miracles is the Holy Spirit performing *today* that might be carelessly or even deliberately attributed to Satan? Must a person see a miracle in order to commit this terrible sin?

Jesus made it clear that God would forgive *all* sin and *all* blasphemy, *including blasphemy against the very Son of God Himself* (Matt. 12:32)! Does this mean that God the Son is less important than the Holy Spirit? Why would a sin against God the Son be forgivable and yet a sin against the Holy Spirit be unforgivable?

The answer lies in the nature of God and in His patient dealings with the nation of Israel. God the Father sent John the Baptist to prepare the nation for the coming of their Messiah. Many of the common people responded to John's call and repented (Matt. 21:32), but the religious leaders *permitted* John to be arrested and eventually killed. God the Son came as promised and called the nation to trust Him, but those same religious leaders *asked for* Jesus to be killed. On the cross, our Lord prayed, "Father, forgive them, for they know not what they do" (Luke 23:34).

The Holy Spirit came at Pentecost and demonstrated God's power in many convicting ways. How did those same religious leaders respond? By arresting the apostles, ordering them to keep silent, and then *killing Stephen themselves!* Stephen told them what their sin was: "Ye do always resist the Holy Ghost" (Acts 7:51). They had sinned against the Father and the Son, but had been graciously forgiven. When they sinned against the Holy Spirit, they had reached "the end of the line," and there could be no more forgiveness.

People today cannot commit the "unpardonable sin" in the same way the Jewish religious leaders did when Jesus was ministering on earth. The only sin today that God cannot forgive is rejection of His Son (John 3:16–21, 31). When the Spirit of God convicts the sinner and reveals the Savior, the sinner may resist the Spirit and reject the witness of the Word of God, but that does not mean he has forfeited all his opportunities to be saved. If he will repent and believe, God can still forgive him. Even if the sinner so hardens his heart that he seems to be insensitive to the pleadings of God, so long as there is life, there is hope. Only God knows if and when any "deadline" has been crossed. You and I must never despair of any sinner (1 Tim. 2:4; 2 Peter 3:9).

The sower and the soils (4:1–20). This parable helped the disciples understand why Jesus was not impressed by the large crowds that followed Him. He knew that most of them would never produce fruit from changed lives, because the Word He was teaching them was like seed falling into poor soil.

The seed represents God's Word (Luke 8:11), and the sower is the servant of God who shares that Word with others (see 1 Cor. 3:5–9). The human heart is like soil: it must be prepared to receive the seed before that seed can take root and produce a harvest. Like seed, the Word is alive and able to produce spiritual fruit, but the seed must be planted and cultivated before that harvest will come.

As in that day, so today, there are four kinds of hearts, and they respond to God's message in four different ways. The *hard heart* (Mark 4:4, 15) resists the Word of God and makes it easy for Satan (the birds) to snatch it away. Soil becomes hard when too many feet tread on it. Those who recklessly "open their hearts" to all kinds of people and influences are in danger of developing hard hearts (see Prov. 4:23). Hard hearts must be "plowed up" before they can receive the seed, and this can be a painful experience (Jer. 4:3; Hos. 10:12).

The *shallow heart* (vv. 5–6, 16–17). This heart is like thin soil on a rock, very typical to Palestine. Since there is no depth, whatever is planted cannot last because it has no roots. This represents the "emotional hearer" who joyfully accepts God's Word but does not really understand the price that must be paid

to become a genuine Christian. There may be great enthusiasm for several days or weeks, but when persecution and difficulties begin, the enthusiasm wanes and the joy disappears. It is easy for fallen human nature to counterfeit "religious feelings" and give a professed Christian a feeling of false confidence.

The *crowded heart (vv. 7, 18–19).* This heart pictures the person who receives the Word but does not truly repent and remove the "weeds" out of his or her heart. This hearer has too many different kinds of "seeds" growing in the soil—worldly cares, a desire for riches, a lust for things—and the good seed of the Word has no room in which to grow. To change the image, this person wants to walk the "broad way" and the "narrow way" at the same time (Matt. 7:13–14); and it cannot be done.

The *fruitful heart (vv. 8, 20).* This heart pictures the true believer, because fruit—a changed life—is the evidence of true salvation (2 Cor. 5:17; Gal. 5:19–23). The other three hearts produced no fruit, so we conclude that they belong to persons who have never been born again. Not all true believers are equally as productive, but from every genuine Christian's life, there will be some evidence of spiritual fruit.

Each of the three fruitless hearts is influenced by a different enemy: the hard heart—the devil himself snatches the seed; the shallow heart—the flesh counterfeits religious feelings; the crowded heart—the things of the world smother the growth and prevent a harvest. These are the three great enemies of the Christian: the world, the flesh, and the devil (Eph. 2:1–3).

The lamp (4:21–25). In this parable, our Lord used a common object (a lamp) in a familiar scene (a home). The lamp was a clay dish filled with oil, with a wick put into the oil. In order to give light, the lamp had to "use itself up"; and the oil had to be replenished. If the lamp was not lit, or if it was covered up, it did the home no good.

The apostles were like that lamp: they were called to shed God's light and reveal His truth. But they could not "give out" without first "taking in"; hence, the admonition of Mark 4:24–25. The more we hear the Word of God, the better we are able to share it with others. The moment we think that we know it all, what we think we know will be taken from us. We must take heed *what* we hear (Mark 4:24) as well as take heed *how* we hear (Luke 8:18). Our spiritual hearing determines how much we have to give to others. There is no sense trying to "cover things up" because God will one day reveal all things.

The seed growing (4:26–34). The first parable reminds us that we cannot make the seed grow; in fact, we cannot even explain *how* it grows. There is a mystery to the growth of the seed and the development of the harvest. It takes a good deal of faith to be a farmer, and also a good deal of patience. In the parable of the sower and the soils, the Lord suggested that much of the seed scattered would fall on unproductive soil. This fact could discourage His workers; so, in this parable,

He reassured them "in due season we shall reap if we faint not" (Gal. 6:9).

The second parable gave the disciples both warning and encouragement. The encouragement was that, from very small beginnings, the kingdom would eventually grow in size and in influence. While a mustard seed is not the smallest seed in the world, it was probably the smallest seed that the Jews sowed in their gardens. It was a traditional symbol of that which is tiny. Our Lord began with twelve apostles. Later, there were as many as five hundred believers (1 Cor. 15:6). Peter won three thousand at Pentecost, and throughout the book of Acts, that number steadily increased (Acts 4:4; 5:14; 6:1, 7). In spite of the sins and weaknesses of the church, the message has been carried to other nations, and one day, saints from *every* nation shall worship before His throne (Rev. 5:9).

But the growth of the seed is only one part of the story; we must also account for the birds in the branches. In the parable of the sower and soils, the birds stood for Satan, who snatches the seed (Mark 4:15). If we are to be consistent in our interpretation, we must take this into consideration, for both parables were taught on the same day. The growth of the kingdom will not result in the conversion of the world. In fact, some of the growth will give opportunity for Satan to get in and go to work! There was Judas in the disciple band, and Ananias and Sapphira were in fellowship with the Jerusalem church (Acts 5:1–11). Simon Magus was part of the church in Samaria (Acts 8:1–24), and Satan's ministers boldly invaded the Corinthian church (2 Cor. 11:13–15). The bigger the net, the greater the possibility of catching both good and bad fish (Matt. 13:47–50).

Through faith in Jesus Christ, we become citizens of the heavenly nation, children in God's family, and subjects of the King of Kings and Lord of Lords. What a privilege it is to know the Lord Jesus Christ!

CHAPTER FOUR
Mark 4:35—5:43
THE SERVANT CONQUERS!

God's Servant, Jesus Christ, is the Master of every situation and the Conqueror of every enemy. If we trust Him and follow His orders, we need never be afraid. *Victory* is the major theme that binds this long section together. Mark recorded four miracles that Jesus performed, and each miracle announces even to us today the defeat of an enemy.

Victory over Danger (4:35–41)

"The same day" refers to the day on which Jesus gave the "parables of the kingdom." He had been teaching His disciples the Word, and now He would give them a practical test to see how much they had really learned. After all, the hearing of God's Word

is intended to produce faith (Rom. 10:17), and faith must always be tested. It is not enough for us merely to learn a lesson or be able to repeat a teaching. We must also be able to practice that lesson by faith, and that is one reason why God permits trials to come to our lives.

Did Jesus know that the storm was coming? Of course He did! The storm was a part of that day's curriculum. It would help the disciples understand a lesson that they did not even know they needed to learn: Jesus can be trusted in the storms of life. Many people have the idea that storms come to their lives only when they have disobeyed God, but this is not always the case. Jonah ended up in a storm because of his disobedience, but the disciples got into a storm because of their *obedience* to the Lord.

The geographic location of the Sea of Galilee is such that sudden violent storms are not unusual. While crossing this very sea one summer afternoon, I asked an Israeli tour guide if he had ever been in such a storm. "I certainly have!" he replied, throwing up his hands and shaking his head. "And I never want to be in one like it again!"

The storm described here must have been especially fierce if it frightened experienced fishermen like the disciples. There were at least three good reasons why none of the men in the ship should have been disturbed, even though the situation appeared to be threatening.

To begin with, they had His promise that they were going to the other side (Mark 4:35). His commandments are always His enablements, and nothing can hinder the working out of His plans. He did not promise an easy trip, but He did promise a guaranteed arrival at their destination.

Second, the Lord Himself was with them, so what was there to fear? They had already seen His power demonstrated in His miracles, so they should have had complete confidence that He could handle the situation. For some reason, the disciples did not yet understand that He was indeed the Master of every situation.

Finally, they could see that Jesus was perfectly at peace, even in the midst of the storm. This fact alone should have encouraged them. Jesus was in God's will and knew that the Father would care for Him, so He took a nap. Jonah slept during a storm because he had a false sense of security, even though he was running from God. Jesus slept in the storm because He was truly secure in God's will. "I will both lay me down in peace, and sleep, for thou, Lord, only makest me dwell in safety" (Ps. 4:8).

How often in the trials of life we are prone to imitate the faithless disciples and cry out, "Lord, don't You care?" Of course, He cares! He arose and rebuked the storm, and immediately there was a great calm. But Jesus did not stop with the calming of the elements, for the greatest danger was not the wind or the waves: it was the unbelief in the hearts of the disciples. Our greatest problems are within us, not around us. This explains why Jesus gently rebuked them and called them "men of little faith." They had heard Him teach the Word and had even seen Him perform miracles, and yet they still had no faith. It was their unbelief that caused their fear, and their fear made them question whether Jesus really cared. We must beware of "an evil heart of unbelief" (Heb. 3:12).

This was only one of many lessons Jesus would teach His disciples in the familiar environs of the Sea of Galilee, and each lesson would reveal some wonderful new truth about the Lord Jesus. They already knew that He had the authority to forgive sins, to cast out demons, and to heal diseases. Now they discovered that He even had authority over the wind and the sea. This meant that they had no reason ever again to be afraid, for their Lord was in constant control of every situation.

Victory over Demons (5:1–20)

When Jesus and the disciples landed on the other side, they encountered two demoniacs, one of whom was especially vocal (see Matt. 8:28). This entire scene seems very unreal to us who live in so-called "modern civilization," but it would not be unreal on many mission fields. In fact, some Bible teachers believe that demon possession is becoming even more prevalent in today's "modern society."

We see in this scene three different forces at work: Satan, society, and the Savior. These same three forces are still at work in our world, trying to control the lives of people.

First, we see what *Satan* can do to people. Satan is a thief whose ultimate purpose is to destroy (John 10:10; and see Rev. 9:11). We are not told how the demons entered these men and took control, but possibly it was the result of their yielding to sin. Demons are "unclean spirits" and can easily get a foothold in the lives of people who cultivate sinful practices.

Because they yielded to Satan, the thief, these two men lost everything! They lost their homes and the fellowship of their families and friends. They lost their decency as they ran around in the tombs naked. They lost their self-control and lived like wild animals, screaming, cutting themselves, and frightening the citizens. They lost their peace and their purpose for living, and they would have remained in that plight had Jesus not come through a storm to rescue them.

Never underestimate the destructive power of Satan. He is our enemy and would destroy all of us if he could. Like a roaring lion, he seeks to devour us (1 Peter 5:8–9). It is Satan who is at work in the lives of unbelievers, making them "children of disobedience" (Eph. 2:1–3). The two men in the Gerasene graveyard were no doubt extreme examples of what Satan can do to people, but what they reveal is enough to make us want to resist Satan and have nothing to do with him.

The second force at work on these men was *society,* but society was not able to accomplish very much. About all that society can do for problem people is to isolate them, put them under guard and, if necessary, bind them (Luke 8:29). Often these men had been

chained, but the demons had given them strength to break the chains. Even the attempts to tame these men had failed. With all of its wonderful scientific achievements, society still cannot cope with the problems caused by Satan and sin. While we thank God that society does offer a limited amount of restraint and protection, we must confess that society cannot permanently solve these problems and deliver Satan's terrorized victims.

This brings us to the third force, that of *the Savior.* What did Jesus Christ do for these men? To begin with, He graciously came to them in love, and even went through a storm to do it. Some think that the storm itself may have been satanic in origin, since Jesus used the same words to calm the sea as He did to cast out demons (compare Mark 1:25 and 4:39). Perhaps Satan was trying to destroy Jesus, or at least prevent Him from coming to the men who needed Him. But nothing could stop the Lord from coming to that graveyard and bringing deliverance to those men.

Not only did Jesus come to them, but He spoke to them and permitted them to speak to Him. The citizens of that area avoided the two demoniacs, but Jesus treated them with love and respect. He came "to seek and to save that which was lost" (Luke 19:10).

It is interesting to note that, as the demons spoke through the man, they confessed what they really believed. Demons have faith and even tremble because of what they believe (James 2:19), but neither their faith nor their fear can save them. Demons believe that Jesus is the Son of God and that He has authority over them. They believe in the reality of judgment and that one day they will be cast into hell (see Matt. 8:29). This is more than many religious people believe today!

Nowhere does the Bible explain either the psychology or the physiology of demon possession. The man who spoke to Jesus was under the control of *a legion* of demons, and a Roman legion could consist of as many as six thousand men! It is frightening to think of the horrors this man experienced day and night as thousands of unclean spirits tormented him. No doubt the other demonized man experienced his share of agony too.

Satan tried to destroy these men, but Jesus came to deliver them. By the power of His word, He cast out the demons and set the men free. Demons even believe in prayer, for they begged Jesus not to send them into the abyss, the place of torment (Mark 5:7; Luke 8:31). It is encouraging to note that the demons did not know what Jesus planned to do. This suggests that Satan can know God's plans only if God reveals them. In fact, there is no evidence in Scripture that Satan can read the mind of a believer, let alone the mind of God.

Mark 5 tells of three requests: the demons requested that Jesus send them into the pigs (Mark 5:12); the citizens requested that Jesus leave the area (Mark 5:17); and one of the former demoniacs requested that Jesus allow him to follow Him (Mark 5:18). Our Lord granted the first two requests but not the third one.

Did Jesus have the right to destroy two thousand pigs and possibly put their owners out of business? If these men were Jews, then they had no right to be raising and selling unclean pigs anyway. However, this was Gentile territory, so the owners were probably Gentiles.

Certainly, Jesus was free to send the demons wherever He desired—into the abyss, into the swine, or to any other place that He chose. Then why send them into the swine? For one thing, by doing it that way, Jesus gave proof to all the spectators that a miracle of deliverance had really taken place. The destruction of the pigs also gave assurance to the two men that the unclean spirits were actually gone. But more than anything else, the drowning of the two thousand swine was a vivid object lesson to this Christ-rejecting crowd that, to Satan, a pig is as good as a man! In fact, Satan will make a man into a pig! The Lord was warning the citizens against the powers of sin and Satan. It was a dramatic sermon before their very eyes: "The wages of sin is death!"

The swineherds did not want to be blamed for the loss of the pigs, so they immediately ran to tell the owners what had happened. When the owners arrived at the scene, they were afraid as they beheld the dramatic changes that had taken place in the two men. Instead of running around naked, the men were clothed, seated, and in their right minds. They were new creatures (2 Cor. 5:17)!

Why would the owners ask Jesus to leave? Why not ask Him to stay and perform similar cures for others who were also in need? The owners had one main interest—business—and they were afraid that if Jesus remained any longer, He would do even more "damage" to the local economy! Our Lord does not stay where He is not wanted, so He left. What an opportunity these people missed!

Why did Jesus not permit the healed demoniac to follow Him? The man's request was certainly motivated by love for the Lord Jesus, and what a testimony he had! But Jesus knew that the man's place was in his own home, with his loved ones, where he could bear witness to the Savior. After all, effective Christian living must begin at home, where people know us the best. If we honor God there, then we can consider offering ourselves for service elsewhere. This man became one of the earliest missionaries to the Gentiles. Jesus had to leave, but the man remained and bore faithful witness to the grace and power of Jesus Christ. We trust that many of those Gentiles believed on the Savior through his witness.

Victory over Disease (5:21–34)

One crowd sighed with relief as they saw Jesus leave, but another crowd was waiting to welcome Him when He returned home to Capernaum. In that latter crowd stood two people who were especially anxious to see Him—Jairus, a man with a dying daughter; and an anonymous woman suffering from an incurable disease.

It was Jairus who approached Jesus first, but it was the woman who was first helped, so we shall begin with her.

The contrast between these two needy people is striking and reveals the wideness of Christ's love and mercy. Jairus was an important synagogue officer, and the woman was an anonymous "nobody," yet Jesus welcomed and helped both of them. Jairus was about to lose a daughter who had given him twelve years of happiness (Mark 5:42), and the woman was about to lose an affliction that had brought her twelve years of sorrow. Being a synagogue officer, Jairus was no doubt wealthy, but his wealth could not save his dying daughter. The woman was already bankrupt! She had given the doctors all of her money, and yet none of them could cure her. Both Jairus and the poor woman found the answers to their needs at the feet of Jesus (Mark 5:22, 33).

The woman had a hemorrhage that was apparently incurable and was slowly destroying her. One can only imagine the pain and emotional pressure that sapped her strength day after day. When you consider her many disappointments with the doctors and the poverty it brought her, you wonder how she endured as long as she did. But there was one added burden: according to the law, she was ceremonially unclean, which greatly restricted both her religious and her social life (Lev. 15:19ff.). What a burden she carried!

However, she let nothing stand in her way as she pushed through the crowd and came to Jesus. She could have used any number of excuses to convince herself to stay away from Him. She might have said, "I'm not important enough to ask Jesus for help!" or "Look, He's going with Jairus, so I won't bother Him now." She could have argued that nothing else had helped her, so why try again? Or she might have concluded that it was not right to come to Jesus as a last resort, after visiting all those physicians. However, she laid aside all arguments and excuses and came by faith to Jesus.

What kind of faith did she have? It was weak, timid, and perhaps somewhat superstitious. She kept saying to herself that she had to touch His clothes in order to be healed (see Mark 3:10; 6:56). She had heard reports of others being healed by Jesus (Mark 5:27), so she made this one great attempt to get through to the Savior. She was not disappointed: Jesus honored her faith, weak as it was, and healed her body.

There is a good lesson here for all of us. Not everybody has the same degree of faith, but Jesus responds to faith no matter how feeble it might be. When we believe, He shares His power with us and something happens in our lives. There were many others in that crowd who were close to Jesus and even pressing against Him, but they experienced no miracles. Why? Because they did not have faith. It is one thing to throng Him and quite something else to trust Him.

The woman planned to slip away and get lost in the crowd, but Jesus turned and stopped her. Tenderly, He elicited from her a wonderful testimony of what the Lord had done for her. Why did Jesus deal with her publicly? Why did He not simply permit her to remain anonymous and go her way?

For one thing, He did it for her own sake. He wanted to be to her something more than a healer: He wanted to be her Savior and Friend as well. He wanted her to look into His face, feel His tenderness, and hear His loving words of assurance. By the time He finished speaking to her, she experienced something more than physical healing. He called her "daughter" and sent her on her way with a benediction of peace (Mark 5:34). To "be made whole" meant much more than receiving mere physical healing. Jesus had given her spiritual healing as well!

He dealt with her publicly not only for her sake, but also for the sake of Jairus. His daughter was close to death, and he needed all the encouragement he could get. It was bad enough that the crowd was impeding their progress, but now this woman had to interfere and stop Jesus! When one of Jairus's friends arrived and announced that the girl had died, no doubt Jairus felt that the end had come. The Lord's words to the woman about faith and peace must have encouraged Jairus as much as they encouraged her.

Finally, Jesus dealt with her publicly that she might have the opportunity to share her testimony and glorify the Lord. "Let the redeemed of the Lord say so, whom he hath redeemed from the hand of the enemy … he sent his word, and healed them.… Oh, that men would praise the Lord for his goodness, and for his wonderful works to the children of men!" (Ps. 107:2, 20–21). No doubt some people in that crowd heard her words and trusted in the Savior, and when she arrived home, she already knew what it meant to witness for Christ.

Victory over Death (5:35–43)

It was not easy for Jairus to come to Jesus publicly and ask for His help. The religious leaders who were opposed to Jesus would certainly not approve, nor would some of the other synagogue leaders. The things that Jesus had done and taught in the synagogues had aroused the anger of the scribes and Pharisees, some of whom were probably Jairus's friends. But Jairus was desperate, as many people are when they come to Jesus. He would rather lose his friends and save his beloved daughter.

It is beautiful to watch Jesus deal with Jairus and lead him to joyful victory. Throughout this entire event, it was our Lord's *words* that made the difference. Consider the three statements that He made.

The word of faith (v. 36). At this point, Jairus had to believe either his friend or the Lord Jesus. No doubt all of his being responded with convulsive sorrow when he heard that his beloved daughter was dead. But Jesus assured him, "Be not afraid, go on believing" (literal translation). In other words, "You had a certain amount of faith when you came to Me, and your faith was helped when you saw what I did for that woman. Don't quit! Keep on believing!"

It was easier for Jairus to trust the Lord while his daughter was still alive, and while Jesus was still walking with him to his house. But when Jesus stopped to heal the woman, and when the friend came with the bad news, Jairus just about lost his faith. Let's not be too hard on him. We have probably given way to doubts when circumstances and feelings have overwhelmed us. Sometimes God has delayed, and we have wondered why. That is when we need that special "word of faith" from the Lord, and we receive it as we spend time in His Word.

The word of hope (v. 39). When Jesus and Jairus arrived at the house, they saw and heard the professional Jewish mourners who were always summoned when a death occurred. It was traditional for them to wail loudly, to weep, and to lead the family and friends in lamentation. The presence of the mourners in the home is proof that the girl was actually dead, for the family would not have called them if there had been even the slightest hope that the girl was still alive.

"The child is not dead but sleeps!" were our Lord's words of hope to Jairus and his wife. To the believer, death is only sleep, for the body rests until the moment of resurrection (1 Thess. 4:13–18). The spirit does not sleep, for in death, the spirit of the believer leaves the body (James 2:26) and goes to be with Christ (Phil. 1:20–23). It is the body that sleeps, awaiting the return of the Lord and the resurrection (1 Cor. 15:51–58). This truth is a great encouragement to all of us who have had Christian loved ones and friends depart in death. It is His word of hope to us.

The word of love and power (v. 41). Unbelief laughs at God's Word, but faith lays hold of it and experiences the power of God. Jesus did not make a spectacle of this miracle. He was sensitive to the feelings of the parents and grieved by the scornful attitude of the mourners. *Talitha cumi* is Aramaic for "Little girl, get up!" Jesus added, "I say unto thee" (with the emphasis on the *I*), because it was by His authority that her spirit returned to her body (Luke 8:55). The words were not some magic formula that anybody might use to raise the dead.

The girl not only came back to life, but was also healed of her sickness, for she was able to get out of bed and walk around. Always the loving Physician, Jesus instructed the astounded parents to give her some food lest she have a relapse. Divine miracles never replace common sense human care, otherwise we are tempting God.

As with previous miracles, Jesus told the witnesses to keep quiet (Mark 1:44; 3:12). Perhaps the word got out from the mourners that the girl had been "in a coma" and had not actually been dead. According to them, there had not been a miracle after all! However, there had been witnesses to the miracle. The law required only two or three witnesses for confirmation of truth (Deut. 17:6; 19:15), but for this miracle there were *five* witnesses! We have reason to conclude that Jairus and his wife became believers in Jesus Christ, though there is no further mention of them in the gospel record. All her life, the daughter was a witness to the power of Jesus Christ.

Yes, God's Servant is the conqueror over danger, demons, disease, and death. This series of miracles illustrates how Jesus met and helped all kinds of people, from His own disciples to a pair of demoniacs, and it assures us that He is able to help us today.

This does not mean that God *always* must rescue His people from danger (see Acts 12) or heal every affliction (see 2 Cor. 12:1–10), but it does mean that He holds the ultimate authority and that we need never fear. We are "more than conquerors through him who loved us" (Rom. 8:37).

CHAPTER FIVE
Mark 6:1–56
WILL ANYONE TRUST GOD'S SERVANT?

Charles Darwin said that *belief* was "the most complete of all distinctions between man and the lower animals." If this observation is true, it suggests that lack of faith on man's part puts him on the same level as the animals! Agnostic orator Col. Robert Ingersoll took a different point of view, for he once described a believer as "a songless bird in a cage." You would probably agree that his words better describe an *un*believer!

One of the central themes in this section of Mark's gospel is the unbelief of people who came into contact with God's Servant. All of these people had every reason to trust Jesus Christ, yet all of them failed to do so, including His own disciples! As you study this chapter, keep in mind the solemn admonition of Hebrews 3:12: "Take heed, brethren, lest there be in any of you an evil heart of unbelief, in departing from the living God." God takes unbelief seriously, and so should we.

The Unbelief of His Acquaintances (6:1–6)
Jesus returned to Nazareth, where a year before He had been rejected by the people and evicted from the synagogue (Luke 4:16–30). It was certainly an act of grace on His part to give the people another opportunity to hear His Word, believe, and be saved, and yet their hearts were still hard. This time, they did not evict Him: they simply did not take Him seriously.

Our Lord's reputation had once again preceded Him, so He was permitted to teach in the synagogue. Keep in mind that He was ministering to people who knew Him well, because Nazareth was His "hometown." However, these acquaintances had no spiritual perception at all. In fact, Jesus reminded them of what He had told them at that first dramatic visit, that a

prophet is without honor in his own country and among his own people (Mark 6:4; Luke 4:24; John 4:44).

Two things astonished these people: His mighty works and His wonderful wisdom. Actually, Jesus did not do any mighty works while He was there, so the people must have been referring to the reports they had heard about His miracles (see Mark 1:28, 45; 3:7–8; 5:20–21). In fact, their unbelief hindered Jesus from having a greater ministry among them.

What was their problem? Why were they unable to trust Him and experience the wonders of His power and grace as had others? *They thought that they really knew Him.* After all, He had been their neighbor for nearly thirty years, they had seen Him at work in the carpenter's shop, and He appeared to be just another Nazarene. He was a "commoner," and the people saw no reason to commit themselves to Him!

"Familiarity breeds contempt" is a well-known maxim that goes all the way back to Publius the Syrian, who lived in 2 BC. Aesop wrote a fable to illustrate it. In Aesop's fable, a fox had never before seen a lion, and when he first met the king of the beasts, the fox was nearly frightened to death. At their second meeting, the fox was not frightened quite as much; and the third time he met the lion, the fox went up and chatted with him! "And so it is," Aesop concluded, "that familiarity makes even the most frightening things seem quite harmless."

The maxim, however, must be taken with a grain of salt. For example, can you imagine a loving husband and wife thinking less of each other because they know each other so well? Or two dear friends starting to despise each other because their friendship has deepened over the years? Phillips Brooks said it best: "Familiarity breeds contempt, only with contemptible things or among contemptible people." The contempt shown by the Nazarenes said nothing about Jesus Christ, but it said a great deal about them!

A tourist, eager to see everything in the art gallery, fled from picture to picture, scarcely noticing what was in the frames. "I didn't see anything very special here," he said to one of the guards as he left. "Sir," the guard replied, "it is not the pictures that are on trial here—it is the visitors."

A carpenter was a respected artisan in that day, but nobody expected a carpenter to do miracles or teach profound truths in the synagogue. Where did He get all this power and wisdom? From God or from Satan (see Mark 3:22)? And why did His brothers and sisters not possess this same power and wisdom? Even more, why did His brothers and sisters not believe in Him? The people who called Him "the son of Mary" were actually insulting Him, because in that day you identified a man by calling him the son of his father, not the son of his mother.

The people of Nazareth were "offended at him," which literally means "they stumbled over him." The Greek word gives us our English word *scandalize*. Kenneth Wuest wrote in his book *Wuest's Word*

Studies (Eerdmans), "They could not explain Him, so they rejected Him." Jesus was certainly a "stone of stumbling" to them because of their unbelief (Isa. 8:14; Rom. 9:32–33; 1 Peter 2:8).

Twice in the gospel record you find Jesus marveling. As this passage reveals, He marveled at the unbelief of the Jews, and He marveled at the great faith of a Roman centurion, a Gentile (Luke 7:9). Instead of remaining at Nazareth, Jesus departed and made another circuit of the towns and villages in Galilee. His heart was broken as He saw the desperate plight of the people (Matt. 9:35–38), so He decided to send out His disciples to minister with His authority and power.

The Unbelief of His Enemies (6:7–29)

When the Lord originally called the twelve apostles, His purpose was to teach and train them so that they might assist Him and eventually be able to take His place when He returned to the Father (Mark 3:13–15). Before sending them out, He reaffirmed their authority to heal and to cast out demons (Mark 6:7), and He gave them some pointed instructions (see Matt. 10 for a more detailed account of this sermon).

He told them to take what they already owned and not go out and buy special equipment for their itinerant travels. They were not to be loaded down with extra baggage. (You cannot miss the note of urgency in this "commissioning sermon.") Jesus wanted them to be adequately supplied, but not to the point of ceasing to live by faith. The word *bag* means "a beggar's bag." They were definitely not to beg for either food or money.

As they ministered from place to place, they would encounter both hospitality and hostility, both friends and enemies. He cautioned them to stay at one house in each community and not to "pick and choose" when it came to their food and accommodations. After all, they were there to be profitable servants, not pampered guests. If a house or a village did not receive them, they had His permission to declare God's judgment on those people. It was customary for the Jews to shake the dust off their feet whenever they left Gentile territory, but for Jews to do this to their fellow Jews would be something new (Luke 10:10–11; Acts 13:51).

The word translated "send" in Mark 6:7 is *apostello* in the Greek and gives us our English word *apostle*. It means "to send someone with a special commission to represent another and to accomplish his work." Jesus gave these twelve men both the apostolic authority and the divine ability to do the job He sent them to do. They were not "on their own"; they represented Him in all that they did and said.

We noted before (Mark 3:16–19) that a comparison of the lists of the apostles' names reveals that the names are given in several pairs: Peter and Andrew, James and John, Philip and Bartholomew, etc. Jesus sent them out in pairs because it is always easier and safer for servants to travel and work together. "Two are better than one" (Eccl. 4:9), and the law, as

previously observed, required two witnesses to verify a matter (Deut. 17:6; 19:15; 2 Cor. 13:1). They would not only help each other; they would also learn from each other.

The men went out and did what Jesus told them to do. It is remarkable that a band of ordinary men could go out in this way to represent Almighty God, and that they could demonstrate their authority by performing miracles. God's commandments always include His enablements (2 Cor. 3:5–6). They proclaimed the good news of the kingdom, called on sinners to repent, and healed many who were sick (Mark 6:12–13; Luke 9:6).

The reports of Christ's ministry, augmented by that of His disciples (Luke 9:7), even reached into the palace of Herod Antipas. Mark called him "King," which is what Herod wanted to be called, but in reality, godless Herod was only a tetrarch, the ruler of a fourth part of the nation. When Herod the Great died, the Romans divided his territory among his three sons, and Antipas was made tetrarch of Perea and Galilee.

Herod Antipas had married the daughter of King Aretas IV and then had divorced her so he could marry Herodias, the wife of his half-brother, Herod Philip. It was a wicked alliance that was contrary to the law of Moses (Lev. 18:16; 20:21), and the fearless John the Baptist had denounced the king for his sins. When Herod heard about the wonderful works of Jesus, he was sure that John the Baptist had come back from the dead to haunt him and condemn him! Herod's conscience was bothering him, but he was unwilling to face his sins honestly and repent.

At this point, Mark shifted into a flashback to explain how John the Baptist had been cruelly and unjustly arrested and slain. Even in this brief account, we sense the tension in the palace, for Herod feared John, privately listened to him preach, and was in a state of perplexity over what he should do. "Queen" Herodias, on the other hand, hated John, wanted to kill him, and patiently waited for the most convenient time. In their evil character and lawless deeds, these two remind us of Ahab and Jezebel (1 Kings 18—21).

The "strategic day" came (Mark 6:21 NASB) for Herodias to put her plan into action: the celebration of Herod's birthday. Royal feasts were extravagant both in their display of wealth and in their provision for pleasure. The Jews would not have permitted a woman to dance before a group of men, and most Gentile mothers would have forbidden a daughter to do what the daughter of Herodias did. (History informs us that the girl's name was Salome.) But the girl was a part of the mother's plan to get rid of John the Baptist, and Salome played her part well.

When Herod heard the girl's macabre request, he was "greatly distressed" (see Mark 14:34, where the same verb is used of Jesus), but he had to be true to his promise or lose face before a group of influential people. The word *oath* in Mark 6:26 is actually in the plural—"for his many oaths' sake"—because Herod had repeatedly declared his desire to reward the girl for her performance. This was one way he had of impressing his guests, but it backfired. Herod had not been courageous enough to obey John's word, but now he had to obey his own word! The result was the death of an innocent man.

It is remarkable that there is no evidence that any of the Jewish leaders did anything to rescue John the Baptist after he had been arrested. The common people considered John a prophet sent from God, but the religious leaders did not obey John's message (Mark 11:27–33). John's death was the first of three notable violent deaths in the history of Israel. The other two are the crucifixion of Christ and the stoning of Stephen (Acts 7). For the significance of these events, review the comments on Mark 3:22–30. Herod had feared that John's messages would stir up a revolt among the people, something he wanted to avoid. Also, he wanted to please his wife, even though it meant the murdering of a godly man.

John's disciples were permitted to take the body of their leader and bury it, and then they went to tell Jesus what had happened (Matt. 14:12). No doubt the report of John's death deeply stirred our Lord, for He knew that one day His own life would be laid down.

We meet Herod Antipas one more time in the Gospels, when he "tried" Jesus and hoped to see the Lord perform a miracle (Luke 23:6–12). Jesus would not even speak to this adulterer and murderer, let alone please him by doing a miracle! Jesus called Herod a "fox" (Luke 13:31–35), an apt description of this crafty man. In AD 39, Herod Agrippa (Acts 12:1), nephew of Herod Antipas, denounced his uncle to the Roman emperor, and Antipas was deposed and sent into exile. "For what shall it profit a man, if he shall gain the whole world, and lose his own soul?" (Mark 8:36).

The Unbelief of His Disciples (6:30–56)
Jesus took His disciples to a secluded place so that they might rest after their labors. He wanted to discuss their ministry with them and prepare them for their next mission. As Vance Havner has said, "If you don't come apart and rest, you will come apart." Even God's Servant-Son needed time to rest, fellowship with His friends, and find renewal from the Father.

Another factor was the growing opposition of both the political and the religious leaders. Herod's murder of John the Baptist was evidence enough that the "climate" was now changing and that Jesus and His disciples had to be careful. In the next chapter, we shall encounter the hostility of the Jewish religious leaders, and, of course, the political enthusiasm of the crowds was always a problem (John 6:15ff.). The best thing to do was to get away.

But the overzealous crowds would not leave Him alone. They followed Him to the area near Bethsaida, hoping to see Him perform some miraculous cures (Luke 9:10–11; John 6:1ff.). In spite of the interruption to His plans, the Lord welcomed them, taught them the Word, and healed those who were afflicted.

Having experienced interruptions many times in my own life and ministry, I marvel at His patience and grace! What an example for us to follow!

Mark recorded two miracles that Jesus performed. **The feeding of the five thousand (vv. 33–44).** Jesus sent the twelve apostles out to minister because He had compassion on the needy multitudes (Matt. 9:36–38). This time, the needy multitudes came to them—and the disciples wanted to send them away! As yet, they had not learned to look at life through the eyes of their Master. To them, the crowds were a problem, perhaps even a nuisance, but to Jesus, they were as sheep without a shepherd.

When D. L. Moody was building his great Sunday school in Chicago, children came to him from everywhere. They often passed by other churches and Sunday schools to be with Mr. Moody. When asked why he walked so far to attend Moody's Sunday school, one boy replied, "Because they love a fella over there!" The children could tell the difference.

The disciples had two suggestions for solving the problem: either send the people away to find their own food, or raise enough money to buy a bit of bread for everybody. As far as the disciples were concerned, they were in the wrong place at the wrong time, and nothing could be done! With that kind of approach, they would have made ideal committee members! Someone has defined a committee as a group of people who individually can do nothing and collectively decide that nothing can be done.

Jesus looked at the situation, not as a problem, but as an opportunity to trust the Father and glorify His name. An effective leader is someone who sees potential in problems and is willing to act by faith. Acting on the basis of human wisdom, His disciples saw the problem but not the potential. How many times God's people have complained, "If we only had enough money, we could do something!" Two hundred pence (denarii) would be the equivalent of a year's wages for the average laborer! The first step is not to measure *our* resources, but to determine God's will and trust Him to meet the need.

It was Andrew who found the lad with the lunch (John 6:8–9). The Lord had the people sit down in organized groups on the green grass (see Ps. 23:2; 78:19), quite a contrast to Herod's glittering sensual feast. Jesus took the little lunch, blessed it, broke it, and gave it to the disciples to distribute to the hungry people. The miracle took place in His hands, not in theirs, for whatever we give to Him, He can bless and multiply. We are not manufacturers; we are only distributors.

John tells us that Jesus used this miracle as the basis for a sermon on "the bread of life" (John 6:22ff.). After all, He did not perform miracles just to meet human needs, though that was important. He wanted each miracle to be a revelation of Himself, a sermon in action. For the most part, the people were amazed at the miracles, appreciated the help He gave them, but failed to get the spiritual message (John 12:37). They wanted the gift but not the Giver, the enjoyment of physical blessings but not the enrichment of spiritual blessings.

The stilling of the storm (vv. 45–56). A number of miracles were involved in this event: Jesus walking on the water, Peter walking on the water (Mark did not record this; see Matt. 14:28–32), Jesus stilling the storm, and the boat arriving on shore the instant Jesus entered it (John 6:21). It was certainly a "night of wonders" for the Twelve!

Why did Jesus compel His disciples to leave? Because the crowd was getting restless, and there was danger they might start a popular uprising to make Jesus king (John 6:14–15). The Twelve were not ready to face this kind of test, because their ideas of the kingdom were still too national and political.

There was a second reason: He wanted to teach them a lesson on faith that would help prepare them for the work that lay ahead of them after He was gone. The disciples had just completed a very successful mission, healing the sick and preaching the gospel. They had shared in the miraculous feeding of five thousand people. They were on a "spiritual high," and this in itself was dangerous. It is good to be on the mountaintop if you don't get careless and step off a cliff.

Spiritual blessings must be balanced with burdens and battles, otherwise, we may become pampered children instead of mature sons and daughters. On a previous occasion, Jesus had led His disciples into a storm following an exciting day of teaching (Mark 4:35–41). Now, after a time of miraculous ministry, He again led them into a storm. In the book of Acts, it is interesting to note that the "storm" of official persecution began after the disciples had won five thousand people to Christ (Acts 4:1–4). Perhaps while they were in confinement, the apostles recalled the storm that followed the feeding of the five thousand, and they must have encouraged themselves with the assurance that Jesus would come to them and see them through.

Each new experience of testing demands of us more faith and courage. In that first storm experience, the disciples had Jesus in the boat with them, but this time, He was on the mountain praying for them. He was teaching them to live by faith. (For that matter, even when He was in the ship with them, they were still afraid!) The scene illustrates the situation of God's people today: We are in the midst of this stormy world, toiling and seemingly ready to sink, but He is in glory interceding for us. When the hour seems the darkest, He will come to us—and we will reach shore!

The waves that frightened the disciples (including the fishermen in the group) were only stairsteps to bring the Lord Jesus to them. He waited until their situation was so desperate that they could do nothing to help themselves. But why did He act as though He would pass them by? Because He wanted them to recognize Him, trust Him, and invite Him into the ship.

They did not recognize Him, but instead screamed with fear because they thought He was a ghost!

Jesus reassured them with His word: "Take courage; it is I, do not be afraid" (Mark 6:50 NASB). At this point, Peter asked Jesus to let him walk on the water, but Mark omits this detail. Tradition says that Mark wrote as Peter's spokesman, so perhaps Peter was reticent to include this experience lest it give people the wrong impression. It is easy to criticize Peter for sinking—but have you ever gotten out of the boat yourself?

The disciples had failed their test because they lacked spiritual insight and receptive hearts. The miracle of the loaves and fishes had made no lasting impression on them. After all, if Jesus could multiply food and feed thousands of people, then surely He could protect them in the storm. Even a disciple of Jesus Christ can develop a hard heart if he fails to respond to the spiritual lessons that must be learned in the course of life and ministry.

As you review these two miracles, you see that Jesus Christ brings *provision* and *protection.* "The Lord is my shepherd; I shall not want … I will fear no evil" (Ps. 23:1, 4). If we trust Him, we will always have sufficiency and security, no matter what the situation might be. The important thing is that we trust Him.

Mark closed this section on a positive note as he described the people who brought their sick for Jesus to heal. These people had faith and their faith was rewarded. This scene is in contrast to that in Nazareth, where very few were healed because the people lacked faith.

"And this is the victory that overcomes the world, even our faith" (1 John 5:4). Trust the Servant! He never fails.

CHAPTER SIX
Mark 7:1—8:26
THE SERVANT-TEACHER

Throughout his gospel, Mark's emphasis is primarily on what Jesus did. However, in this section of our study you will find Mark recording some of the important *teachings* of the Lord. Mark also describes His ministry among the Gentiles, which would be of special interest to Roman readers. We see in this section three ministries of Jesus, the Servant-Teacher.

Teaching the Jews (7:1–23)
There are four stages in this drama, and the first is *accusation* (Mark 7:1–5). The Jewish religious leaders were now openly hostile toward the Lord and His ministry. It was not unusual for them to follow Him from place to place simply to watch for something to criticize. In this case, they accused the disciples of failing to practice the Jewish ceremonial washing. These washings had nothing to do with personal hygiene, nor

were they commanded in the law. They were a part of the tradition that the scribes and Pharisees had given to the people to add to their burdens (Matt. 23:4).

Our Lord had already violated their Sabbath traditions (Mark 2:23—3:5), so the Jews were eager to accuse Him when they saw the disciples eat "with defiled hands." Why would such a seemingly trivial matter upset these religious leaders? Why would they feel compelled to defend their ceremonial washings? For one thing, these leaders resented it when our Lord openly flaunted their authority. After all, these practices had been handed down from the fathers and carried with them the authority of the ages! The Jews called tradition "the fence of the law." It was not the law that protected the tradition, but the tradition that protected the law!

But something much more important was involved. Whenever the Jews practiced these washings, they declared that they were "special" and that other people were "unclean"! If a Jew went to the marketplace to buy food, he might be "defiled" by a Gentile or (God forbid!) a Samaritan. This tradition had begun centuries before to remind the Jews that they were God's elect people and therefore had to keep themselves separated. However, a good reminder had gradually degenerated into an empty ritual, and the result was pride and religious isolation.

These washings not only indicated a wrong attitude toward people, but they also conveyed a wrong idea of the nature of sin and personal holiness. Jesus made it clear in the Sermon on the Mount that true holiness is a matter of inward affection and attitude and not just outward actions and associations. The pious Pharisees thought they were holy because they obeyed the law and avoided external defilement. Jesus taught that a person who obeys the law externally can still break the law *in his heart,* and that external "defilement" has little connection with the condition of the inner person.

So the conflict was not only between God's truth and man's tradition, but also between two divergent views of sin and holiness. This confrontation was no incidental skirmish; it got to the very heart of true religious faith. Each new generation must engage in a similar conflict, for human nature is prone to hold on to worn-out man-made traditions and ignore or disobey the living Word of God. It is true that some traditions are helpful as reminders of our rich heritage, or as "cement" to bind generations, but we must constantly beware lest tradition take the place of truth. It does us good to examine our church traditions in the light of God's Word and to be courageous enough to make changes. (Note that the word *tradition* in 2 Thess. 2:15 refers to the body of doctrinal truth "handed down" from the apostles to leaders in the church. See also 2 Tim. 2:2.)

The next stage can be labeled *condemnation* (Mark 7:6–13) as Jesus defended His disciples and exposed the hypocrisy of their accusers. The first thing He did was to quote from the prophet Isaiah (Isa. 29:13),

and then He brought in the law of Moses (Ex. 20:12; 21:17; Lev. 20:9). How could the Pharisees argue with the law and the prophets?

In defending their tradition, the Pharisees eroded their own characters and also the character of the Word of God. They were hypocrites, "playactors," whose religious worship was practiced in vain. True worship must come from the heart, and it must be directed by God's truth, not man's personal ideas. What a tragedy that religious people would ignorantly practice their religion and become the worse for doing it!

But they were not only destroying their character; they were also destroying the influence and authority of the very Word of God that they claimed to be defending. Note the tragic sequence: teaching their doctrines as God's Word (Mark 7:7); laying aside God's Word (Mark 7:8); rejecting God's Word (Mark 7:9); finally, robbing God's Word of its power (Mark 7:13). People who revere man-made traditions above the Word of God eventually lose the power of God's Word in their lives. No matter how devout they may appear, their hearts are far from God.

History reveals that the Jewish religious leaders came to honor their traditions far above the Word of God. Rabbi Eleazer said, "He who expounds the Scriptures in opposition to the tradition has no share in the world to come." The *Mishnah,* a collection of Jewish traditions in the *Talmud,* records, "It is a greater offense to teach anything contrary to the voice of the Rabbis than to contradict Scripture itself." But before we criticize our Jewish friends, perhaps we should examine what influence "the church fathers" are having in our own Christian churches. We also may be guilty of replacing God's truth with man's traditions.

Once He had exposed their hypocrisy, Jesus then turned to the law of Moses and indicted them for breaking the fifth commandment. They had an ingenious way of breaking the law and not feeling guilty. Instead of using their wealth to support their parents, the Pharisees dedicated that wealth to God ("Corban" = "an offering, a gift"; see Num. 30) and claimed that the wealth could now be used only for "spiritual purposes." However, they continued to get the benefit of that wealth, even though it technically belonged to God. These men claimed to love God, but they had no love for their parents!

The third stage is *declaration* (Mark 7:14–16). Jesus announced to the whole crowd that the source of holy living is from within, not from without. Actually, he was declaring null and void the entire Mosaic system of "clean and unclean" foods, but at that time, He did not explain this radical truth to the crowd. Later, He did explain it in private to His own disciples.

But this declaration was surely understood by His enemies. They realized that He was breaking down one of the "walls" that separated the Jews from the Gentiles. Of course, the law itself was not set aside until Jesus died on the cross (Eph. 2:14–15; Col. 2:14), but the principle Jesus announced had been true throughout the ages. In every period of history, true holiness has always been a matter of the heart, a right relationship with God by faith. Ceremonial purity was a matter of external obedience to a law as evidence of that faith (Ps. 51:6, 10, 16–17). Moses made it clear in Deuteronomy that God wanted love and obedience to come from the heart, and not be merely outward obedience to rules (note Deut. 6:4–5; 10:12; 30:6, 20).

Our Lord's *explanation* (Mark 7:17–23) was given privately to His disciples when they asked Him "concerning the parable." His explanation seems obvious to us, but we must remember that these twelve men had been brought up under the strict Jewish dietary code that categorized all foods as either "clean" or "unclean" (Lev. 11). In fact, Acts 10:14 suggests that Peter kept a kosher household for years even after he had heard this truth. It is not easy to change our religious traditions.

The human heart is sinful and produces all manner of evil desires, thoughts, and actions, everything from murder to envy ("an evil eye"). Jesus had no illusions about human nature, as do some liberal theologians and humanistic teachers today. He realized that man is a sinner, unable to control or change his own nature, *and that is why Jesus came to earth—to die for lost sinners.*

The Jewish dietary laws were given by God to teach His chosen people to make a difference between what was clean and what was unclean. (No doubt there were also some practical reasons involved, such as sanitation and health.) To disobey these laws was a matter of ceremonial defilement, and that was an external matter. Food *ends up* in the stomach, but sin *begins* in the heart. The food we eat is digested and the waste evacuated, but sin remains and it produces defilement and death.

This dramatic lesson on "truth vs. tradition" could only irritate the Jewish religious leaders more and make them want to silence Jesus. This increased opposition was the reason why He departed from the crowded places and took His disciples into Gentile territory.

Before we leave this section, however, it might be good for us to contrast man's traditions and God's truth.

Man's traditions	God's truth
Outward forms—bondage	Inward faith—liberty
Trifling rules	Fundamental principles
Outward piety	True inward holiness
Neglect, replace the Word	Exalts the Word of God

Helping the Gentiles (7:24—8:9)

Mark records three miracles that Jesus performed as He ministered to the Gentiles in the region of Tyre and Sidon. This is the only recorded instance of our Lord actually leaving Palestine. He was practicing what he had just taught the disciples: there is no difference between Jews and Gentiles, for all are sinners and need the Savior.

Casting out a demon (7:24–30). Of the thirty-five recorded miracles in the Gospels, four directly involve women: the healing of Peter's mother-in-law (Mark 1:30–31); the raising of the widow's son (Luke 7:11–17); the raising of Lazarus (John 11); and the casting out of the demon as recorded here.

Jesus came to this area (about forty miles from Capernaum) so that He might have some privacy, but a concerned mother discovered He was there and came to Him for help. There were many obstacles in her way, yet she overcame them all by faith and got what she needed.

To begin with, her nationality was against her: she was a Gentile and Jesus was a Jew. Besides that, she was a woman, and society in that day was dominated by the men. Satan was against her, for one of his demons had taken control in her daughter's life. The disciples were against her; they wanted Jesus to send her away and let Him (and them) have some rest. For a time, it looked as though even Jesus was against her! It was not an easy situation, and yet she triumphed because of her great faith.

Samuel Rutherford, the saintly Scottish minister who suffered greatly for Christ, once wrote to a friend: "It is faith's work to claim and challenge loving-kindnesses out of all the roughest strokes of God." That is exactly what this Gentile mother did, and we today have much that we can learn from her about faith.

When she first asked Him for help, Jesus did not even answer her! Encouraged by His silence, the disciples urged Him to send her away. When Jesus did speak, it was not to the woman but to the disciples, and His words seem to exclude her completely: "I am not sent but unto the lost sheep of the house of Israel" (Matt. 15:24). However, none of these barriers stopped her from pressing on with her plea.

The first time she cried for help, the mother addressed Jesus as "Son of David," a Jewish title, but the next time she cried out for help, she simply said, "Lord, help me" (Matt. 15:25). It was then that Jesus spoke about feeding the children (Israel) first and not throwing their food to "the little pet puppies." Jesus was not calling the Gentiles "dirty scavenger dogs" as did many of the proud Jews; He was giving her hope, and she took hold of it.

Her reply revealed that faith had triumphed. She did not deny the special place of the "children" (Jews) in God's plan, nor did she want to usurp it. All she wanted were a few crumbs of blessing from the table, for, after all, "Salvation is of the Jews" (John 4:22). It must have rejoiced His heart when she took *His very words* and used them as a basis for her plea! She accepted her place, she believed His Word, and she persisted in her plea, and Jesus not only met her need, but commended her for her faith.

It is significant that the two times in the gospel record when Jesus commended "great faith," He was responding to the faith of Gentiles and not Jews: this Syrophoenician woman and the Roman centurion

(Matt. 8:5–13). It is also worth noting that in both situations, Jesus healed *at a distance,* suggesting the spiritual distance between Jews and Gentiles at that time (Eph. 2:11–22). Finally, the people of Tyre and Sidon were not known for their faith (Matt. 11:21–22), yet this woman dared to believe that Jesus could deliver her daughter.

Great faith is faith that takes God at His Word and will not let go until God meets the need. Great faith can lay hold of even the slightest encouragement and turn it into a fulfilled promise. "Lord, increase our faith."

Healing a deaf man (7:31–37). The region of Decapolis ("ten cities") was also Gentile territory, but before Jesus left the region, the people were glorifying the God of Israel (Matt. 15:30–31). The man they brought to Jesus was handicapped both by deafness and an impediment in his speech, and Jesus healed him. This miracle is recorded only by Mark and would be especially appreciated by his Roman readers, since the "ten cities" region was like a "Rome away from Rome."

Jesus took the man away from the crowd so that the healing would be private and the man would not become a public attraction. Since the man was deaf, he could not hear our Lord's words, but he could feel Jesus' fingers in his ear and the touch on his tongue, and this would encourage the man's faith. The "sigh" was an inward groan, our Lord's compassionate response to the pain and sorrow sin has brought into the world. It was also a prayer to the Father on behalf of the handicapped man. (The same word is used in connection with prayer in Rom. 8:23, and the noun in Rom. 8:26.)

Ephphatha is an Aramaic word that means "be opened, be released." The man did not hear Jesus speak, but the creation heard the command of the Creator, and the man was healed. Both the tongue and the ears functioned normally again. In spite of our Lord's strict command for the people to keep quiet about the miracles, they told the news everywhere (see Mark 1:34, 44; 3:12; 5:43), and this resulted in a large crowd gathering and bringing people who were ill or handicapped. Even though Jesus was trying to enjoy some rest, He took time to heal them all. The result? These Gentiles "glorified the God of Israel" (Matt. 15:31).

Feeding the four thousand (8:1–9). Those who try to find contradictions in the Bible often confuse this miracle with the feeding of the five thousand, which is recorded in all four gospels. Only Matthew and Mark record this event, and it is not difficult to distinguish it from the other miracle of the multiplying of bread and fish. The first miracle took place in Galilee, near Bethsaida, and involved predominantly Jews. This miracle took place near Decapolis and involved mostly Gentiles. In the first miracle, Jesus started with five loaves and two fish, while here He had seven loaves "and a few fish." The five thousand had been with Him one day, but the four thousand had been with him three days. Twelve baskets of fragments were left over after the five thousand were fed, but only seven baskets after the four thousand were fed. There were even two different lands of baskets used: for the five thousand, small wicker lunch baskets *(kophinos), for* the four thousand, large hampers, big enough to hold a man *(spuris,* see Acts 9:25).

Once again, we are encouraged by our Lord's compassion and His complete control over the situation. However, we are discouraged by the blindness and unbelief of the disciples. Had they completely forgotten the previous miracle? Let's not be too hard on them. How many times have *we* forgotten the mercies of the Lord? We need to remind ourselves that Jesus Christ is still the same and has the solution to every problem. All we need do is trust Him, give Him our all, and obey.

Warning the Disciples (8:10–26)

Jesus and the disciples crossed to the western side of the Sea of Galilee, where they were met by the Pharisees who were still angry at Him because of His earlier indictment of their hypocrisy (Mark 7:1–23). This time they tempted Him to prove His divine authority by giving them a sign from heaven. They did not want an earthly miracle, such as the healing of a sick person. They wanted Him to do something spectacular, like bring fire from heaven or bread from heaven (John 6:30–31). This would prove He was indeed sent from God.

Our Lord's response was one of deep grief and disappointment (see Mark 7:34). How tragic that the religious leaders of God's chosen people should be so hardhearted and spiritually blind! Their desire for a sign from heaven was but another evidence of their unbelief, for faith does not ask for signs. True faith takes God at His Word and is satisfied with the inward witness of the Spirit.

Since Mark was writing primarily for Gentile readers, he did not include our Lord's words concerning the sign of the prophet Jonah (Matt. 16:4; and see Matt. 12:38–41). What is "the sign of Jonah"? Death, burial, and resurrection. The proof that Jesus is what He claimed to be is the fact of His own death, burial, and resurrection (Acts 2:22–36; 3:12–26).

Jesus left them and crossed to the east side of the Sea of Galilee, and en route taught His disciples an important spiritual lesson. It appears that they were almost as blind as the Pharisees! The men were having a private discussion about their food supply, because somebody had forgotten to pack bread. Who was to blame?

It must have grieved Jesus that His hand-picked helpers were so spiritually obtuse. The fact that He had multiplied bread on two occasions and fed over ten thousand people had apparently made little impression on them! Why worry and argue over one loaf of bread when you have Jesus in the boat with you? Their minds were dull, their hearts were hard (see Mark 6:52), their eyes were blind, and their ears were deaf (see Mark 4:11–12).

God's people often have a tendency to forget His blessings (Ps. 103:1–2). He meets our needs, but then when the next problem arises, we complain or become frightened. As long as we are with Him, we can be sure He will care for us. It would do us all good to pause occasionally and remind ourselves of His goodness and faithfulness.

But the main lesson had to do with *leaven* (yeast) and not with bread. In the Bible, leaven is consistently a symbol of evil. Each Passover season, the Jews had to remove all leaven from their dwellings (Ex. 12:18–20), and leaven was not allowed with the offerings (Ex. 23:18; 34:25; Lev. 2:11; 6:17). Evil, like leaven, is small and hidden, but it spreads and soon infects the whole (Gal. 5:9).

The Bible uses leaven as a picture of false doctrine (Gal. 5:1–9), unjudged sin in the church (1 Cor. 5), and hypocrisy (Luke 12:1). In this context, Jesus warned them about the teaching (false doctrine) of the Pharisees and the followers of Herod. The Pharisees "said but they did not"; in other words, they practiced and encouraged hypocrisy (note Mark 7:6). The Herodians were a worldly group who catered to Herod, accepted the Roman way of life, and saw in Herod and his rule the promised kingdom for the Jewish nation. If this false teaching got into the hearts and minds of the disciples, it would infect them and pollute the truth Jesus had given them to proclaim about Himself and His kingdom.

We can never be too careful about detecting and avoiding false doctrine. Only a small deviation from the Word may get into an individual or a church, but before long it will grow and infect everything. Our Lord did not often say "Beware!" but when He did, it was important!

In this section, Mark recorded two miracles that are not found in the other Gospels: the healing of the deaf man who had a speech impediment (Mark 7:31–37), and the healing of the blind man outside Bethsaida (Mark 8:22–26). Perhaps we can see in these two men illustrations of the disciples' spiritual condition described in Mark 8:18! Jewish readers would connect these two miracles with the messianic promises in Isaiah 35.

In both these situations, friends brought the men to Jesus, and in both situations, Jesus led the men away from the crowds. In fact, in the latter case, He took the man *outside the city.* Why? Probably because the city of Bethsaida had already been judged because of its unbelief (Matt. 11:21–24). No more evidence would be given to them.

The unique thing about this miracle of healing is that it occurred *gradually* and not instantly. The Gospels record the healing of at least seven blind men, and they show that our Lord used a variety of approaches. Perhaps it was the atmosphere of unbelief in Bethsaida that hindered Him (see Mark 6:5–6), or it

may have been the spiritual condition of the man himself. For some reason not given, the man was not ready for instant sight, so Jesus restored him gradually. The fact that the man recognized men and trees suggests that he had not been born blind but had been blinded by accident or disease.

The man was not from Bethsaida, for Jesus sent him home and cautioned him not to enter that town. Now that he had been healed, why go to unbelieving Bethsaida where Jesus had been rejected? His job was to go home and spread the good news of the kingdom, and to demonstrate its power by showing others what Jesus had done for him (see Mark 2:11; 5:34; 10:52). Should he not give another opportunity to the people in Bethsaida? Perhaps they would believe if they heard how Jesus had restored his sight. No, Bethsaida had been given adequate evidence, but still had refused to believe. It is a dangerous thing for anybody to reject the message of God and harden his or her heart in unbelief.

The disciples learned some valuable lessons on this trip, lessons that they would need to remember and apply in later years of ministry. We today need to learn these same lessons; (1) don't seek after signs, but live by faith in His Word; (2) trust Jesus to meet needs; (3) avoid the leaven of false doctrine; (4) let Jesus work as He wills, and expect variety in His working.

Mark recorded the events of some busy days in the ministry of God's Servant! Next he will take us "behind the scenes" as the Servant instructs His disciples and prepares them for His death on the cross.

CHAPTER SEVEN
Mark 8:27—9:50
THE SERVANT'S SECRETS

A secret has been defined as "something you tell one person at a time." From time to time, Jesus shared special "secrets" with His disciples, and three of them are given here. Believers today need to understand and apply these spiritual secrets if their own lives are to be all that God wants them to be.

Suffering Leads to Glory (8:27—9:13)
Jesus had been preparing His disciples for this private meeting at which He intended to reveal to them what would happen to Him at Jerusalem. He had given hints along the way, but now He would explain matters to them more fully. For the site, He selected Caesarea Philippi, a town about twenty-five miles north of Bethsaida, sitting at the foot of beautiful Mount Hermon. The town was named after Augustus Caesar and Herod Philip, and it contained a marble temple dedicated to Augustus. It was a place dedicated to the glory of Rome, and that glory is now gone, but the glory of Jesus Christ remains and will go on eternally.

Confession (8:27–30). If you were to go around

asking your friends, "What do people say about me?" they would take it as an evidence of pride. What difference does it really make what people think or say about us? We are not that important! But what people believe and say about Jesus Christ *is* important, for He is the Son of God and the only Savior of sinners.

Your confession concerning Jesus Christ is a matter of life or death (John 8:21, 24; 1 John 2:22–27; 4:1–3). The citizens of Caesarea Philippi would say, "Caesar is lord!" That confession might identify them as loyal Roman citizens, but it could never save them from their sins and from eternal hell. The only confession that saves us is "Jesus is Lord!" (1 Cor. 12:1–3) when that confession comes from a heart that truly believes in Him (Rom. 10:9–10).

It is remarkable the number of different opinions the people held about Jesus, though the same situation probably exists today. That some thought He was John the Baptist is especially perplexing, since John and Jesus had been seen publicly together. They were quite different in personality and ministry (Matt. 11:16–19), so it seems strange that the people would confuse them.

John the Baptist came "in the spirit and power of Elijah" (Luke 1:17), in a ministry of judgment, whereas Jesus came in a spirit of meekness and service. John performed no miracles (John 10:41), but Jesus was a miracle-worker. John even dressed like the prophet Elijah (2 Kings 1:8; Mark 1:6). How could the people confuse the two?

Some said that Jesus was one of the prophets, perhaps Jeremiah (Matt. 16:14). Jeremiah was "the weeping prophet," and Jesus was a Man of Sorrows, so there is a definite parallel. Jeremiah called the people to true repentance from the heart, and so did Jesus. Both men were misunderstood and rejected by their own people, both condemned the false religious leaders and the hypocritical worship in the temple, and both were persecuted by those in authority.

In His words and His works, Jesus gave every evidence to the people that He was the Son of God, the Messiah, and yet they did not get the message. Instead of diligently seeking for the truth, the people listened to popular opinion and followed it, just as many people do today. They had opinions instead of convictions, and this is what led them astray. Elbert Hubbard defined public opinion as "the judgment of the incapable many, opposed to that of the discerning few." Thank God for the discerning few!

Peter's confession was bold and uncompromising, just as ours should be: "Thou art the Christ, the Son of the living God" (Matt. 16:16). The word *Christ* means "the Anointed One, the promised Messiah." Prophets, priests, and kings were all anointed when installed in their offices, and our Lord holds all three offices.

Why did Jesus warn them to keep quiet about Him? For one thing, the disciples themselves still had much to learn about Him and what it truly meant to follow Him. The religious leaders of the nation had already made up their minds about Him, and to proclaim Him as Messiah now would only upset God's plans. The common people wanted to see His miracles, but they had little desire to submit to His message. To announce Him as Messiah might well result in a political uprising that would only do harm.

Confusion (vv. 31–38). Now that they had confessed their faith in Christ (but see John 6:66–71), the disciples were ready for the "secret" Jesus wanted to share with them: He was going with them to Jerusalem, where He would die on a cross. From this point on, Mark will focus on their journey to Jerusalem, and the emphasis will be on Jesus' approaching death and resurrection (Mark 9:30–32; 10:32–34).

This announcement stunned the disciples. If He is indeed the Christ of God, as they had confessed, then why would He be rejected by the religious leaders? Why would these leaders crucify Him? Did not the Old Testament Scriptures promise that Messiah would defeat all their enemies and establish a glorious kingdom for Israel? There was something wrong somewhere and the disciples were confused.

True to character, it was Peter who expressed their concern. One minute Peter was led by God to confess his faith in Jesus Christ (Matt. 16:17), and the next minute he was thinking like an unbelieving man and expressing the thoughts of Satan! This is a warning to us that when we argue with God's Word, we open the door for Satan's lies. Peter began rebuking his Master, and Mark used the same word that describes our Lord's rebuking of the demons (Mark 1:25; 3:12).

Peter's protest was born out of his ignorance of God's will and his deep love for his Lord. One minute Peter was a "rock," and the next minute he was a stumbling block! Dr. G. Campbell Morgan said, "The man who loves Jesus, but who shuns God's method, is a stumbling block to Him." Peter did not yet understand the relationship between suffering and glory. He would eventually learn this lesson and would even emphasize it in his first epistle (note 1 Peter 1:6–8; 4:13—5:10).

Note, however, that when Jesus rebuked Peter, He also "looked on his disciples," because they agreed with Peter's assessment of the situation! Steeped in Jewish traditional interpretation, they were unable to understand how their Messiah could ever suffer and die. To be sure, some of the prophets had written about Messiah's sufferings, but much more had been written about Messiah's glory. Some of the rabbis even taught that there would be *two* Messiahs, one who would suffer and one who would reign (see 1 Peter 1:10–12). No wonder the disciples were confused.

But the problem was more than theological; it was very practical. Jesus had called these men to follow Him, and they knew that whatever happened to Him would happen to them. If there was a cross in *His* future, there would be one in *their* future as well. That would be reason enough to disagree with Him! In spite of their devotion to Him, the disciples were still ignorant of the true relationship between the cross and the crown. They were following Satan's philosophy (glory without suffering) instead of God's philosophy (suffering transformed into glory). Which philosophy you accept will determine how you live and how you serve.

Mark 8:34 indicates that, though Jesus and His disciples had met in private, the crowds were not far away. Jesus summoned the people and taught them what He taught His own disciples: *there is a price to pay for true discipleship.* He knew that the crowds were following Him only because of the miracles, and that most of the people were unwilling to pay the price to become true disciples.

Jesus laid down three conditions for true discipleship: (1) we must surrender ourselves completely to Him; (2) we must identify with Him in suffering and death; and (3) we must follow Him obediently, wherever He leads. If we live for ourselves, we will lose ourselves, but if we lose ourselves for His sake and the gospel's, we will find ourselves.

Denying self is not the same as self-denial. We practice self-denial when, for a good purpose, we occasionally give up things or activities. But we deny self when we surrender ourselves to Christ and determine to obey His will. This once-for-all dedication is followed by a daily "dying to self" as we take up the cross and follow Him. From the human point of view, we are losing ourselves, but from the divine perspective, we are finding ourselves. When we live for Christ, we become more like Him, and this brings out our own unique individuality.

But note the motivation for true discipleship: "for my sake and the gospel's" (Mark 8:35). To lose yourself is not an act of desperation; it is an act of devotion. But we do not stop there: personal devotion should lead to practical duty, the sharing of the gospel with a lost world. "For my sake" could lead to selfish religious isolationism, so it must be balanced with "and the gospel's." Because we live for Him, we live for others.

Discipleship is a matter of profit and loss, a question of whether we will *waste* our lives or *invest* our lives. Note the severe warning Jesus gives us here: once we have spent our lives, we cannot buy them back! Remember, He was instructing His *disciples*, men who had already confessed Him as the Son of God. He was not telling them how to be saved and go to heaven, but how to save their lives and make the most of their opportunities on earth. "Losing your soul" is the equivalent of wasting your life, missing the great opportunities God gives you to make your life count. You may "gain the whole world" and be a success in the eyes of men, and yet have nothing to show for your life when you stand before God. If that happens, though you did own the whole world, it would not be a sufficient price to give to God to buy another chance at life.

Is there any reward for the person who is a true disciple? Yes, there is: he becomes more like Jesus Christ and one day shares in His glory. Satan promises you glory, but in the end, you receive suffering. God promises you suffering, but in the end, that suffering is transformed into glory. If we acknowledge Christ and live for Him, He will one day acknowledge us and share His glory with us.

Confirmation (9:1–8). It takes faith to accept and practice this lesson on discipleship, so six days later, the Lord gave a dazzling proof that God indeed does transform suffering into glory. (Luke's "about eight days" is inclusive of the day of the lesson and the day of the glory, Luke 9:28.) He took Peter, James, and John to the top of a mountain (it may have been Mount Hermon), and there He revealed His glory. This event was a vivid confirmation of His words as recorded in Mark 8:38 as well as a demonstration of the glory of the future kingdom (Mark 9:1; John 1:14; 2 Peter 1:12–21). The message was clear: first the suffering, then the glory.

Moses represented the law and Elijah the prophets, both of which find their fulfillment in Jesus Christ (Luke 24:25–27; Heb. 1:1–2). Moses had died and his body was buried, but Elijah had been raptured to heaven (2 Kings 2:11). When Jesus returns, He will raise the bodies of the saints who died and will rapture the living saints (1 Thess. 4:13–18). Jesus will one day establish His glorious kingdom and fulfill the many promises made through the prophets. Christ's sufferings and death would not *prevent* God from establishing His kingdom; rather, by solving the sin problem in God's world, the cross would help to make the kingdom possible.

The word *transfigured* describes a change on the outside that comes from the inside. It is the opposite of "masquerade," which is an outward change that does not come from within. Jesus allowed His glory to radiate through His whole being, and the mountaintop became a Holy of Holies! As you meditate on this event, keep in mind that He has shared this glory with us and promised us a glorious home forever (John 17:22–24). According to Romans 12:1–2 and 2 Corinthians 3:18, believers today can experience this same transfiguration glory.

The three disciples had gone to sleep while Jesus was praying (Luke 9:29, 32), a failure they would repeat in the garden of Gethsemane (Mark 14:32–42). They almost missed seeing Moses and Elijah and Jesus in His glory! Peter's suggestion reflects again human thinking and not divine wisdom. How wonderful it would be to stay on the mountaintop and bask in His glory! But discipleship means denying self, taking up a cross, and following Him, and you cannot do that and selfishly stay on the mount of glory. There are needs to be met in the valley below. If we want to share the glory of Christ on the mountaintop, we must be willing to follow Him into the sufferings of the valley below.

The Father interrupted Peter's speech and focused their attention, not on the vision, but on the Word of God: "Hear him!" The memory of visions will fade, but the unchanging Word abides forever. The glorious vision was not an end in itself; it was God's way of confirming the Word (see 2 Peter 1:12–21). Discipleship is not built on spectacular visions but on the inspired, unchanging Word of God. Nor do we put Moses, Elijah, and Jesus on the same level, as Peter hinted. It is "Jesus only"—His Word, His will, His kingdom, and His glory.

The three men were not allowed to tell the other nine what they had seen on the mount. No doubt their explanation after His resurrection brought great encouragement to the believers who themselves would experience suffering and death for His sake.

Correction (vv. 11–13). The disciples now understood God's plan much better, but they were still confused about the coming of Elijah to prepare the way for the Messiah. They knew the prophecies in Malachi 3:1 and 4:5–6, and that their teachers expected these prophecies to be fulfilled before the Messiah appeared (John 1:21). Had Elijah already come and they missed him, or was he yet to come? Perhaps the appearing of Elijah on the mount was the fulfillment of the prophecy.

Jesus made two facts clear. First, for those who had trusted in Him, this "Elijah" was John the Baptist, for John had indeed prepared the way before Him. John had denied that he was Elijah come from the dead (John 1:21, 25), but he did minister in the "spirit and power of Elijah" (Luke 1:16–17). Second, there would be a future coming of Elijah, just as Malachi had predicted (Matt. 17:11), before the time of great tribulation. Some students connect this with Revelation 11:2–12. The nation did not accept John's ministry. Had they received John, he would have served as the "Elijah" God sent, and they also would have received Jesus. Instead, they rejected both men and allowed them to be slain.

Power Comes from Faith (9:14–29)

The Christian life is "a land of hills and valleys" (Deut. 11:11). In one day, a disciple can move from the glory of heaven to the attacks of hell. When our Lord and His three friends returned to the other nine disciples, they found them involved in a dual problem: they were unable to deliver a boy from demonic control, and the scribes were debating with them and perhaps even taunting them because of their failure. As always, it was Jesus who stepped in to solve the problem.

The boy was both deaf and dumb (Mark 9:17, 25), and the demon was doing his best to destroy him. Imagine what it would be like for that father to try to care for the boy and protect him! Jesus had given His disciples authority to cast out demons (Mark 6:7, 13), and yet their ministry to the boy was ineffective. No wonder the Lord was grieved with them! How often He must be grieved with us when we fail to use the spiritual resources He has graciously given to His people!

Since the disciples had failed, the desperate father was not even sure that Jesus could succeed; hence his statement, "If you can do anything" (Mark 9:22 NASB). However, the father was honest enough to admit his own unbelief and to ask the Lord to help him and his son. Jesus did cast out the demon and restore the boy to his father.

The main lesson of this miracle is the power of faith to overcome the enemy (Mark 9:19, 23–24; and see Matt. 17:20). Why had the nine disciples failed? Because they had been careless in their personal spiritual walk and had neglected prayer and fasting (Mark 9:29). The authority that Jesus had given them was effective only if exercised by faith, but faith must be cultivated through spiritual discipline and devotion. It may be that the absence of their Lord, or His taking the three disciples with Him and leaving them behind, had dampened their spiritual fervor and diminished their faith. Not only did their failure embarrass them, but it also robbed the Lord of glory and gave the enemy opportunity to criticize. It is our faith in Him that glorifies God (Rom. 4:20).

Service Leads to Honor (9:30–50)

Jesus was still leading His disciples to Jerusalem, and as they went, He reminded them of what would happen to Him there. Note that He also reminded them of His resurrection, but they were unable to understand what He was saying (see Matt. 17:9). They were "exceedingly sorry" ("deeply grieved," Matt. 17:23 NASB).

However, they were not grieved enough to set aside their personal dispute over which of them was the greatest! After they heard what Jesus had said about His own suffering and death, you would think they would have forgotten their own selfish plans and concentrated on Him. Perhaps the fact that Peter, James, and John had gone on the mount with Jesus had added some fuel to the fires of competition.

To teach them (and us) a lesson on honor, Jesus set a child before them and explained that the way to be first is to be last, and the way to be last is to be the servant of all. The unspoiled child is an example of submission and humility. A child knows he is a child and acts like a child, and that is his secret of attracting love and care. The child who tries to impress us by acting like an adult does not get the same attention.

True humility means knowing yourself, accepting yourself, being yourself—your *best* self—and giving of yourself for others. The world's philosophy is that you are "great" if others are working for you, but Christ's message is that greatness comes from our serving others. Since the words *child* and *servant* are the same in the Aramaic language, it is easy to see why Jesus connected the two. If we have the heart of a child, we will have little difficulty being servants, and if we have the attitude of servants, we will welcome the children as the representatives of Jesus Christ and the Father.

At this point, John felt it necessary to defend the disciples (Mark 9:38–41) by pointing out their zeal. Imagine telling a man to stop casting out demons when the nine disciples had failed to deliver the deaf and dumb boy from Satan's power! To use the name of Jesus is the same as working under His authority, so the men had no right to stop the man. "To his own master he stands or falls" (Rom. 14:4).

Mark 9:40 should be compared with Matthew

12:30: "He that is not with me is against me." Both statements declare the impossibility of neutrality when it comes to our relationship with Jesus Christ. Since we cannot be neutral, if we are not for Him, we must be against Him; if we are not against Him, we must be for Him. The anonymous exorcist was bringing glory to His name, so he had to be *for* the Savior and not against Him.

But it is not necessary to perform great miracles to prove our love for Christ. When we lovingly receive a child or compassionately share a cup of cold water, we are giving evidence that we have the humble heart of a servant. After all, we are serving Christ, and that is the highest service in the world (Matt. 25:31–46).

Jesus did not treat John's statement lightly; in fact, He went on to explain the danger of causing others to stumble and therefore stop serving the Lord (Mark 9:42–50). "These little ones" refers to all God's children who follow Christ and seek to serve Him. The way believers treat others in the family of God is a serious thing, and God wants us to "have peace one with another" (Mark 9:50). The disciples did not get along with each other, nor did they get along with other believers!

This solemn message about hell carries a warning to all of us to deal drastically with sin. Whatever in our lives makes us stumble, and therefore causes others to stumble, must be removed as if by surgery. The hand, foot, and eye would be considered valuable parts of the body, yet they must be removed if they are causing sin. Of course, the Lord is not commanding literal physical surgery, since He had already made it clear that sin comes from the heart (Mark 7:20–23). What He is teaching is that sin is to the inner person what a cancerous tumor is to the body, and it must be dealt with drastically.

Some people are shocked to hear from the lips of Jesus such frightening words about hell (see Isa. 66:24). Jesus believed in a place called hell, a place of eternal torment and righteous punishment (see Luke 16:19ff.). After an army chaplain told his men that he did not believe in hell, some of them suggested that his services were not needed. After all, if there is no hell, then why worry about death? But if there is a hell, then the chaplain was leading them astray! Either way, they would be better off without him!

The word translated "hell" is *gehenna.* It comes from a Hebrew phrase "the valley *[ge]* of Hinnon," referring to an actual valley outside Jerusalem where wicked King Ahaz worshipped Molech, the fire god, and even sacrificed his children in the fire (2 Chron. 28:1–3; Jer. 7:31; 32:35).

Some manuscripts do not have Isaiah 66:24 quoted in Mark 9:44 and 46, but the statement is quoted in verse 48, and that one verse is sufficient. Hell is not temporary; it is forever (see Rev. 20:10). How essential it is for sinners to trust Jesus Christ and be delivered from eternal hell, and how important it is for believers to get the message out to a lost world!

"But isn't that too great a sacrifice to ask from us?"

someone might argue. "To deal that drastically with sin would cost us too much!" In Mark 9:49–50, Jesus used the concept of "living sacrifices" to illustrate His point (see Rom. 12:1–2). The sacrifice ends up on the altar and is consumed by the fire. Would you rather endure the fires of hell as a lost sinner or the purifying fires of God as a sacrifice for His glory? Remember, Satan promises you glory now, but the pain comes later. Jesus calls us to suffering now, and then we will enjoy the glory.

The Jews were not allowed to put leaven or honey on their sacrifices, but they were required to use salt (Lev. 2:11, 13). Salt speaks of purity and preservation. It was used in Old Testament days in the establishing of covenants. The disciples were God's salt (Matt. 5:13), but they were in danger of losing their flavor and becoming worthless. Our salt today is purified and does not lose its taste, but the salt of that day contained impurities and could lose its flavor. Once you have lost that precious Christian character, how will you restore it?

Instead of rebuking others, the disciples should have been examining their own hearts! It is easy to lose our "saltiness" and become useless to God. Christians will experience the fire of trials and persecutions (1 Peter 1:6–7; 4:12) and they need to stand together, no matter who is the greatest! Commitment and character are the essentials if we are to glorify Him and have peace with each other.

The three lessons Jesus taught in this section are basic to Christian living today. If we are yielded to Him, then suffering will lead to glory, faith will produce power, and our sacrificial service will lead to honor. In spite of his impetuousness and occasional mistakes, Peter got the message and wrote: "But the God of all grace, who hath called us unto his eternal glory by Christ Jesus, after that ye have suffered a while, make you perfect, stablish, strengthen, settle you. To him be glory and dominion for ever and ever" (1 Peter 5:10–11).

CHAPTER EIGHT
Mark 10
THE SERVANT'S PARADOXES

As a master Teacher, our Lord used many different approaches in sharing God's Word: symbols, miracles, types, parables, proverbs, and paradoxes. A paradox is a statement that seems to contradict itself and yet expresses a valid truth or principle. "When I am weak, then am I strong" is a paradox (2 Cor. 12:10; also see 2 Cor. 6:8–10). There are times when the best way to state a truth is by means of paradox, and this chapter describes our Lord doing just that. He could have preached long sermons, but instead, He gave us these five important lessons that can be expressed in five succinct, paradoxical statements.

Two Shall Be One (10:1–12)

Jesus completed His ministry in Galilee, left Capernaum, and came to the Trans-Jordan area, still on His way to the city of Jerusalem (Mark 10:32). This district was ruled by Herod Antipas, which may explain why the Pharisees tried to trap Him by asking a question about divorce. After all, John the Baptist had been slain because he preached against Herod's adulterous marriage (Mark 6:14–29).

But there was more than politics involved in their trick question, because divorce was a very controversial subject among the Jewish rabbis. No matter what answer Jesus gave, He would be sure to displease somebody, and this might give opportunity to arrest Him. The verbs indicate that the Pharisees "kept asking him," as though they hoped to provoke Him to say something incriminating.

In that day there were two conflicting views on divorce, and which view you espoused depended on how you interpreted the phrase "some uncleanness" in Deuteronomy 24:1–4. The followers of Rabbi Hillel were quite lenient in their interpretation and permitted a man to divorce his wife for any reason, even the burning of his food. But the school of Rabbi Shimmai was much more strict and taught that the critical words "some uncleanness" referred only to premarital sin. If a newly married husband discovered that his wife was not a virgin, then he could put her away.

As He usually did, Jesus ignored the current debates and focused attention on the Word of God, in this case, the law of Moses in Deuteronomy 24:1–4. As you study this passage, it is important to note two facts. First, it was *the man* who divorced the wife, not the wife who divorced the husband, for women did not have this right in Israel. (Roman women did have the right of divorce.) Second, the official "bill of divorcement" was given to the wife to declare her status and to assure any prospective husband that she was indeed free to remarry. Apart from the giving of this document, the only other requirement was that the woman not return to her first husband if her second husband divorced her. Among the Jews, the question was not, "May a divorced woman marry again?" because remarriage was permitted and even expected. The big question was, "What are the legal grounds for a man to divorce his wife?"

The law of Moses did not give adultery as grounds for divorce, for, in Israel, the adulterer and adulteress were stoned to death (Deut. 22:22; Lev. 20:10; also see John 8:1–11). Whatever Moses meant by "some uncleanness" in Deuteronomy 24:1, it could not have been adultery.

Jesus explained that Moses gave the divorce law because of the sinfulness of the human heart. The law protected the wife by restraining the husband from impulsively divorcing her and abusing her like an unwanted piece of furniture, instead of treating her like a human being. Without a bill of divorcement, a woman could easily become a social outcast and be treated like a harlot. No man would want to marry her, and she would be left defenseless and destitute.

By giving this commandment to Israel, God was not putting His approval on divorce or even encouraging it. Rather, He was seeking to restrain it and make it more difficult for men to dismiss their wives. He put sufficient regulations around divorce so that the wives would not become victims of their husbands' whims.

The Lord then took them back beyond Moses to the record of the original creation (Gen. 1:27; 2:21–25). After all, in the beginning, it was *God* who established marriage; and He has the right to make the rules. According to Scripture, marriage is between a man and a woman, not two men or two women, and the relationship is sacred and permanent. It is the most intimate union in the human race, for the two become one flesh. This is not true of a father and son or a mother and daughter, but it is true of a man and wife.

While the spiritual element is vitally important in marriage, the emphasis here is that marriage is a *physical* union: the two become one *flesh,* not one spirit. Since marriage is a physical union, only a physical cause can break it—either death (Rom. 7:1–3) or fornication (Matt. 5:32; 19:9). Mark did not include the "exception clause" found in Matthew, but neither did he say that death breaks the marriage union.

Privately, the Lord further explained the matter to His questioning disciples, who by now were convinced that it was a dangerous thing to get married. To remarry after divorce, *other than one granted on the grounds of fornication,* would make the person guilty of committing adultery, and this is a serious thing. Note that Jesus included the women in His warning, which certainly elevated their status in society and gave them equality of responsibility with the men. The rabbis would not have gone this far.

Mark 10:9 warns us that *man* cannot separate those who have been united in marriage, *but God can.* Since He established marriage, He has the right to lay down the rules. A divorce may be legal according to our laws and yet not be right in the eyes of God. He expects married people to practice commitment to each other (Mark 10:7) and to remain true to each other. Too many people view divorce as "an easy way out," and do not take seriously their vows of commitment to each other and to the Lord.

Adults Shall Be as Children (10:13–16)

First marriage, then children; the sequence is logical. Unlike many "moderns" today, the Jews of that day looked on children as a blessing and not a burden, a rich treasure from God and not a liability (Ps. 127—128). To be without children brought a couple both sorrow and disgrace.

It was customary for parents to bring their children to the rabbis for a blessing, and so it was reasonable that they would bring the little ones to Jesus. Some were infants in arms (Luke 18:15), while others were young children able to walk, and He welcomed them all.

Why would the disciples rebuke the people and try to keep the children away from Jesus? (See Matt. 15:23 and Mark 6:36 for other instances of the disciples' seeming hardness of heart.) They probably thought they were doing Him a favor by helping Him protect His time and conserve His strength. In other words, *they did not consider the children to be important!* Their attitude was strange, because Jesus had already taught them to receive the children in His name and to be careful not to cause any of them to stumble (Mark 9:36ff.). Once again, they forgot what He had taught them.

The phrase "much displeased" is too tame. Our Lord actually became indignant as He openly rebuked His disciples for standing in the way. Then He announced that the children were better kingdom examples than were the adults. We tell the children to behave like adults, but Jesus tells the adults to model themselves after the children!

In what ways are children a pattern? In their humble dependence on others, their receptivity, their acceptance of themselves and their position in life. Of course, Jesus was speaking about an unspoiled child, not one who was trying to act like an adult. A child enjoys much but can explain very little. Children live by faith. By faith they accept their lot, trusting others to care for them and see them through.

We enter God's kingdom by faith, like little children: helpless, unable to save ourselves, totally dependent on the mercy and grace of God. We enjoy God's kingdom by faith, believing that the Father loves us and will care for our daily needs. What does a child do when he or she has a hurt or a problem? Take it to Father and Mother! What an example for us to follow in our relationship with our heavenly Father! Yes, God wants us to be childlike, but not childish!

There is no suggestion here that Jesus baptized these children, for Jesus did not even baptize adults (John 4:1–2). If the disciples had been accustomed to baptizing infants, they certainly would not have turned the people away. Jesus took these precious little ones in His loving arms and blessed them—and what a blessing that must have been!

The First Shall Be Last (10:17–31)

Of all the people who ever came to the feet of Jesus, this man is the only one who went away worse than he came. And yet he had so much in his favor! He was a young man (Matt. 19:22) with great potential. He was respected by others, for he held some ruling office, perhaps in a local court (Luke 18:18). Certainly he had manners and morals, and there was enough desire in his heart for spiritual things that he ran up to Jesus and bowed at His feet. In every way, he was an ideal young man, and when Jesus beheld him, He loved him.

With all of his fine qualities, the young man was very superficial in his views of spiritual things. He certainly had a shallow view of salvation, for he thought that he could *do something* to earn or merit eternal

life. This was a common belief in that day among the Jews (John 6:28), and it is very common today. Most unsaved people think that God will one day add up their good works and their bad works, and if their good works exceed their bad works, they will get into heaven.

Behind this good-works approach to salvation is a superficial view of sin, man, the Bible, Jesus Christ, and salvation. Sin is rebellion against the holy God. It is not simply an action; it is an inward attitude that exalts man and defies God. Did this young man actually think that he could do a few religious works and settle his account with the holy God?

The young man had a superficial view of Jesus Christ. He called Him "Good Master" (Teacher), but we get the impression that he was trying to flatter the Lord, for the Jewish rabbis did not allow the word *good* to be applied to men. Only God was good, and the word must be reserved for Him alone. Jesus was not denying that He was God; rather, He was affirming it. He just wanted to be sure that the young man really knew what he was saying and that he was willing to accept the responsibilities involved.

This explains why Jesus pointed the young man to the law of Moses: He wanted him to see himself as a sinner bowed before the holy God. We cannot be saved from sin by keeping the law (Gal. 2:16–21; Eph. 2:8–10). The law is a mirror that shows us how dirty we are, but the mirror cannot wash us. One purpose of the law is to bring the sinner to Christ (Gal. 3:24), which is what it did in this man's case. The law can bring the sinner to Christ, but the law cannot make the sinner like Christ. Only grace can do that.

The young ruler did not see himself as a condemned sinner before the holy God. He had a superficial view of the law of God, for he measured obedience only by external actions and not by inward attitudes. As far as his actions were concerned, he was blameless (see Phil. 3:6), but his inward attitudes were not blameless, because he was covetous. He may have kept some of the commandments, but the last commandment caught him: "Thou shalt not covet!" Covetousness is a terrible sin; it is subtle and difficult to detect, and yet it can cause a person to break all the other commandments. "For the love of money is a root of all sorts of evil" (1 Tim. 6:10 NASB). Looking at this young man, you would conclude that he had everything, but Jesus said that one thing was lacking: *a living faith in God.* Money was his god: he trusted it, worshipped it, and got his fulfillment from it. His morality and good manners only concealed a covetous heart.

Our Lord's directions in Mark 10:21 are not to be applied to everyone who wants to become a disciple, because Jesus was addressing the specific needs of the rich young ruler. The man was rich, so Jesus told him to liquidate his estate and give the money to the poor. The man was a ruler, so Jesus told him to take up a cross and follow Him, which would be a humbling experience. Jesus offered this man the gift of eternal life, but he turned it down. It is difficult to receive a gift when your fist is clenched around money and the things money can buy. The Greek word translated "grieved" gives the picture of storm clouds gathering. The man walked out of the sunshine and into a storm! He wanted to get salvation on his terms, and he was disappointed.

The disciples were shocked at the Lord's declaration about wealth, because most Jews thought that the possession of great wealth was the evidence of God's special blessing. Many people today still cling to this error, in spite of the message of Job, the example of Christ and the apostles, and the clear teaching of the New Testament. In the case of this young man, his wealth *robbed him* of God's greatest blessing, eternal life. Today, wealth continues to make rich people poor and the first last (see 1 Cor. 1:26–31).

Money is a marvelous servant but a terrible master. If you possess money, be grateful and use it for God's glory; but if money possesses you, beware! It is good to have the things that money can buy, provided you don't lose the things that money cannot buy. The deceitfulness of riches had so choked the soil of this young man's heart that he was unable to receive the good seed of the Word and be saved (Matt. 13:22). What a bitter harvest he would reap one day!

However, Peter's response indicated that there were a few problems in his own heart. "What then will there be for us?" (Matt. 19:27 NASB). This statement reveals a rather commercial view of the Christian life: "We have given up everything for the Lord; now, what will we get in return?" Contrast Peter's words with those of the three Hebrew men in Daniel 3:16–18, and with Peter's later testimony in Acts 3:6. He certainly came a long way from "What will I get?" to "What I have, I will give!"

Jesus assured His disciples that no one who follows Him will ever lose what is really important, either in this life or in the life to come. God will reward each one. However, we must be sure our motives are right: "For my sake and the gospel's" (see Mark 8:35). The well-known Christian industrialist of the twentieth century, R. J. LeTourneau, used to say, "If you give because it pays, it won't pay!" If we sacrifice only to get a reward, that reward will never come.

Note that Jesus also promised "persecutions." He had already told His disciples what both the Jews and Gentiles would do to Him in Jerusalem, and now He informed them that they would have their share of persecution. God balances blessings with battles, developing mature sons and daughters.

To the general public, the rich ruler stood first and the poor disciples stood last. But God saw things from the perspective of eternity—and the first became last while the last became first! Those who are first in their own eyes will be last in God's eyes, but those who are last in their own eyes will be rewarded as first! What an encouragement for true disciples!

Servants Shall Be Rulers (10:32–45)

The destination was still Jerusalem, and Jesus was still leading the way. As Mark wrote his account of the Savior's journey to Calvary, he must have meditated much on the great "Servant Songs" in Isaiah 42—53. "For the Lord God will help me; therefore shall I not be confounded: therefore I have set my face like a flint, and I know that I shall not be ashamed" (Isa. 50:7). We cannot but admire the courage of God's Servant as He made His way to Calvary, and we should adore Him all the more because He did it for us.

We must try to understand the bewilderment and fear of His followers, for this was a difficult experience for them and not at all what they had planned or expected. Each new announcement of His death only added to their perplexity. In the first two announcements (Mark 8:31; 9:31), Jesus had told them *what* would occur, but now He told them *where* His passion will take place—in the Holy City of Jerusalem! In this third announcement, He also included the part that the Gentiles would play in His trial and death, and for the fourth time, He promised that He would rise again (note Mark 9:9). He told His disciples the truth, but they were in no condition to understand it.

In the light of our Lord's announcement of His death, we are embarrassed and ashamed to read of James and John asking for thrones. How could they and their mother (Matt. 20:20–21) be so callous and selfish? Peter had responded to the first announcement by arguing with Jesus; after the second announcement, the disciples responded by arguing among themselves over who was the greatest (Mark 9:30–34). These men seemed blind to the meaning of the cross.

Actually, Salome and her two sons were claiming the promise Jesus had given that, in the future kingdom, the disciples would sit on twelve thrones with the Lord Jesus. (See Matt. 19:28. Since Mark was writing especially for the Gentiles, he did not include this promise.) It took a great deal of faith on their part to claim the promise, especially since Jesus had just reminded them of His impending death. The three of them were in agreement (Matt. 18:19), and they had His Word to encourage them, so there was no reason why Jesus should not grant their request.

Except for one thing: they were praying selfishly, and God does not answer selfish prayers (James 4:2–3). If He does, it is only that He might discipline us and teach us how to pray in His will (Ps. 106:15; 1 John 5:14–15). James, John, and Salome did not realize that *it costs something to get answers to prayer.* For Jesus to grant their request, He would have to suffer and die. Why should He pay such a great price just so they could enjoy free thrones? Is that the way to glorify God?

Jesus compared His approaching suffering and death to the drinking of a cup (Mark 14:32–36) and the experiencing of a baptism (Luke 12:50; also see Ps. 41:7; 69:2, 15). It would be a devastating experience—and yet James and John said they were able to go through it with Jesus! Little did they realize what they were saying, for in later years they would indeed have their share of the baptism and the cup. James would be the first of the disciples to be martyred (Acts 12:1–2), and John would experience great persecution.

Because their prayer was motivated by earthly wisdom, not heavenly wisdom, James and John aroused the anger of the other disciples and brought disunity to the group (see James 3:13—4:1). No doubt the men were unhappy because they had not thought of asking first! Once again, Jesus tried to teach them what it means to be an "important person" in the kingdom of God (see Mark 9:33–37).

Like many people today, the disciples were making the mistake of following the wrong examples. Instead of modeling themselves after Jesus, they were admiring the glory and authority of the Roman rulers, men who loved position and authority. While there is nothing wrong with aspiring to greatness, we must be careful how we define "greatness" and why we want to achieve it. Jesus said, "Whoever wishes to become great among you shall be your servant; and whoever wishes to be first among you shall be slave of all" (Mark 10:43–44 NASB).

God's pattern in Scripture is that a person must first be a servant before God promotes him or her to be a ruler. This was true of Joseph, Moses, Joshua, David, Timothy, and even our Lord Himself (Phil. 2:1–11). Unless we know how to obey orders, we do not have the right to give orders. Before a person exercises authority, he or she must know what it means to be under authority. If Jesus Christ followed this pattern in accomplishing the great work of redemption, then surely there is no other pattern for us to follow.

The Poor Become Rich (10:46–52)

A large crowd of Passover pilgrims followed Jesus and His disciples to Jericho, about eighteen miles from Jerusalem. There were actually two cities named Jericho: the old city in ruins, and the new city a mile away, where Herod the Great and his successors built a lavish winter palace. This may help explain the seeming contradiction between Mark 10:46 and Luke 18:35.

There were two blind beggars sitting by the road (Matt. 20:30), one of whom was named Bartimaeus. Both Mark and Luke focused attention on him since he was the more vocal of the two. The beggars heard that Jesus of Nazareth, the Healer, was passing by; they did their best to get His attention so that they might receive His merciful help and be healed.

At first, the crowd tried to silence them, but when Jesus stopped and called for the men, the crowd encouraged them! Desperate people do not permit the crowd to keep them from Jesus (see Mark 5:25–34). Bartimaeus threw off his garment so it would not trip him, and he hastened to the Master. No doubt some of the pilgrims or disciples helped him.

"What do you want Me to do for you?" seems like a strange question to ask a blind man. (It was the same question He had asked James, John, and Salome; Mark 10:36.) But Jesus wanted to give the man opportunity to express himself and give evidence of his own faith. What did he really believe Jesus *could* do for him?

When Bartimaeus called Jesus "Lord," he used the title *Rabboni,* meaning "my Master." The only other person in the Gospels who used it was Mary (John 20:16). The beggar had twice called him "Son of David," a national messianic title, but "Rabboni" was an expression of personal faith.

Matthew tells us that Jesus was moved with compassion and touched their eyes (Matt. 20:34), and immediately they were healed. Out of gratitude to Jesus, the men joined the pilgrim band and started toward Jerusalem, following Jesus. This is the last healing miracle recorded in Mark, and it certainly fits into Mark's "Servant" theme. We see Jesus Christ, God's Suffering Servant, on His way to the cross, and yet He stops to serve two blind beggars! What love, what mercy, and what grace!

CHAPTER NINE
Mark 11:1—12:44
THE SERVANT IN JERUSALEM

Jerusalem at Passover season was the delight of the Jews and the despair of the Romans. Thousands of devout Jews from all over the world arrived in the Holy City, their hearts filled with excitement and nationalistic fervor. The population of Jerusalem more than tripled during the feast, making it necessary for the Roman military units to be on special alert. They lived with the possibility that some enthusiastic Jewish Zealot might try to kill a Roman official or incite a riot, and there was always potential for disputes among the various Jewish religious groups.

Into this situation came God's Servant with less than a week remaining before He would be crucified outside the city walls. In this section, we see God's Servant ministering in three different official roles.

The Servant-King (11:1–11)

On the road Jesus took, a traveler would arrive first at Bethany and then come to Bethphage, about two miles from Jerusalem. The elevation at this point is about 2,600 feet, and from it you have a breathtaking view of the Holy City. The Lord was about to do something He had never done before, something He had repeatedly cautioned others not to do for Him: He was going to permit His followers to give a public demonstration in His honor.

Jesus sent two of His disciples to Bethphage to get the colt that He needed for the event. Most people today think of a donkey as nothing but a humble beast of burden, but in that day, it was looked on as an animal fit for a king to use (1 Kings 1:33). Our Lord needed this beast so that He might fulfill the messianic prophecy found in Zechariah 9:9. Mark does not quote this verse or refer to it because he was writing primarily for Gentile readers.

In fulfilling this prophecy, Jesus accomplished two purposes: (1) He declared Himself to be Israel's King and Messiah; and (2) He deliberately challenged the religious leaders. This set in motion the official plot that led to His arrest, trial, and crucifixion. The Jewish leaders had decided not to arrest Him during the feast, but God had determined otherwise. The Lamb of God must die at Passover.

Many patriotic Jews from the crowd of pilgrims eagerly joined the procession that proclaimed Jesus as the King, the Son of David come in the name of the Lord. The visitors from Galilee were most prominent in the procession, along with the people who had witnessed the raising of Lazarus from the dead (John 12:12–18). You sometimes hear it said that the same people who cried "Hosanna!" on Palm Sunday ended up crying "Crucify Him!" on Good Friday, but this is not true. The crowd that wanted Him crucified came predominantly from Judea and Jerusalem, whereas the Galilean Jews were sympathetic with Jesus and His ministry.

When welcoming a king, it was customary for people to lay their outer garments on the road, and then add festal branches (2 Kings 9:13). The shout "Hosanna!" means "Save now!" and comes from Psalm 118:25–26. Of course, Jesus knew that the people were quoting from a messianic psalm (relate Ps. 118:22–23 with Matt. 21:42–44 and Acts 4:11), but He allowed them to go right ahead and shout. He was openly affirming His kingship as the Son of David.

What were the Romans thinking as they watched this festive demonstration? After all, the Romans were experts at parades and official public events. We call this event "the triumphal entry," but no Roman would have used that term. An official "Roman Triumph" was indeed something to behold! When a Roman general came back to Rome after a complete conquest of an enemy, he was welcomed home with an elaborate official parade. In the parade he would exhibit his trophies of war and the illustrious prisoners he had captured. The victorious general rode in a golden chariot, priests burned incense in his honor, and the people shouted his name and praised him. The procession ended at the arena, where the people were entertained by watching the captives fight with the wild beasts. That was a "Roman Triumph."

Our Lord's "triumphal entry" was nothing like that, but it was a triumph just the same. He was God's anointed King and Savior, but His conquest would be spiritual and not military. A Roman general had to kill at least five thousand enemy soldiers to merit a Triumph, but in a few weeks, the gospel would "conquer" some five thousand Jews and transform their lives (Acts 4:4). Christ's "triumph" would be the victory of love over hatred, truth over error, and life over death.

After looking into the temple area, where He would return the next day, Jesus left the city and spent the night in Bethany, where it was safer and quieter. No doubt He spent time in prayer with His disciples, seeking to prepare them for the difficult week that lay ahead.

The Servant-Judge (11:12–26)

Our Lord's condemning of the tree and cleansing of the temple were both symbolic acts that illustrated the sad spiritual condition of the nation of Israel. In spite of its many privileges and opportunities, Israel was outwardly fruitless (the tree) and inwardly corrupt (the temple). It was unusual for Jesus to act in judgment (John 3:17), yet there comes a time when this is the only thing God can do (John 12:35–41).

Cursing the fig tree (vv. 12–14, 20–26). The fig tree produces leaves in March or April and then starts to bear fruit in June, with another crop in August and possibly a third crop in December. The presence of leaves could mean the presence of fruit, even though that fruit was "left over" from the previous season. It is significant that in this instance Jesus did not have special knowledge to guide Him; He had to go to the tree and examine things for Himself.

If He had power to kill the tree, why didn't He use that power to restore the tree and make it produce fruit? Apart from the drowning of the pigs (Mark 5:13), this is the only instance of our Lord using His miraculous power to destroy something in nature. He did it because He wanted to teach us two important lessons.

First, there is a lesson on *failure:* Israel had failed to be fruitful for God. In the Old Testament, the fig tree is associated with the nation of Israel (Jer. 8:13; Hos. 9:10; Nah. 3:12). Like the fig tree our Lord cursed, Israel had "nothing but leaves." Note that the tree dried up "from the roots" (Mark 11:20). Three years before, John the Baptist had put the ax to the roots of the tree (Matt. 3:10), but the religious leaders would not heed his message. Whenever an individual or a group "dries up" spiritually, it is usually from the roots.

The disciples would probably connect this miracle with the parable that Jesus gave some months before (Luke 13:1–9), and they would see in the miracle a vivid picture of God's judgment on Israel. They might also recall Micah 7:1–6, where the prophet declares that God is seeking "the first ripe fruit" from His people. Christ is still seeking fruit from His people, and for us to be fruitless is sin (John 15:16). We must carefully cultivate our spiritual roots and not settle for "leaves."

Jesus also used this miracle to teach us a lesson on *faith.* The next morning, when the disciples noticed the dead tree, Jesus said, "Have faith in God," meaning, "Constantly be trusting God; live in an attitude of dependence on Him." In Jewish imagery, a mountain signifies something strong and immovable, a problem that stands in the way (Zech. 4:7). We can move these mountains only by trusting God.

Of course, this is not the only lesson Jesus ever

gave on prayer, and we must be careful not to isolate it from the rest of Scripture. Prayer must be in the will of God (1 John 5:14–15), and the one praying must be abiding in the love of God (John 15:7–14). Prayer is not an emergency measure that we turn to when we have a problem. Real prayer is a part of our constant communion with God and worship of God.

Nor should we interpret Mark 11:24 to mean, "If you pray hard enough and *really believe,* God is obligated to answer your prayers, no matter what you ask." That kind of faith is not faith in God; rather, it is nothing but faith in faith, or faith in feelings. True faith in God is based on His Word (John 15:7; Rom. 10:17), and His Word reveals His will to us. It has well been said that the purpose of prayer is not to get man's will done in heaven, but to get God's will done on earth.

True prayer involves forgiveness as well as faith. I must be in fellowship with both my Father in heaven and my brethren on earth if God is to answer my prayers (see Matt. 5:21–26; 6:14–15; 18:15–35). The first word in "The Lord's Prayer" is *our*—"*Our* Father which art in heaven" and not "*My* Father which art in heaven." Though Christians may pray in private, no Christian ever prays alone, for all of God's people are part of a worldwide family that unites to seek God's blessing (Eph. 3:14–15). Prayer draws us together.

We do not earn God's blessing by forgiving one another. Our forgiving spirit is one evidence that our hearts are right with God and that we want to obey His will, and this makes it possible for the Father to hear us and to answer prayer (Ps. 66:18). Faith works by love (Gal. 5:6). If I have faith in God, I will also have love for my brother.

Cleansing the temple (vv. 15–19). Jesus had cleansed the temple during His first Passover visit (John 2:13–22), but the results had been temporary. It was not long before the religious leaders permitted the money changers and the merchants to return. The priests received their share of the profits, and, after all, these services were a convenience to the Jews who traveled to Jerusalem to worship. Suppose a foreign Jew carried his own sacrifice with him and then discovered that it was rejected because of some blemish? The money rates were always changing, so the men who exchanged foreign currency were doing the visitors a favor, even though the merchants were making a generous profit. It was easy for them to rationalize the whole enterprise.

This "religious market" was set up in the court of the Gentiles, the one place where the Jews should have been busy doing serious missionary work. If a Gentile visited the temple and saw what the Jews were doing *in the name of the true God,* he would never want to believe what they taught. The Jews might not have permitted idols of wood and stone in their temple, but there were idols there just the same. The court of the Gentiles should have been a place for praying, but it was instead a place for preying and paying.

Mark especially mentioned the people who sold doves. The dove was one of the few sacrifices that the poor people could afford (Lev. 14:22). It was the sacrifice Joseph and Mary brought when they dedicated Jesus in the temple (Luke 2:24). Even the poor people were victimized by the merchants in the temple, and this in itself must have grieved the Lord Jesus, for He was always sensitive to the poor (see Mark 12:41–44).

Jesus quoted two Scriptures to defend what He did—Isaiah 56:7 and Jeremiah 7:11. At the same time, He exposed the sins of the religious leaders. The Jews looked on the temple primarily as a place of sacrifice, but Jesus saw it as a place of prayer. True prayer is in itself a sacrifice to God (Ps. 141:1–2). Jesus had a spiritual view of the Jewish religion, while the leaders promoted a traditional view that was cluttered with rules and regulations.

Campbell Morgan points out that "a den of thieves" is the place to which thieves run *when they want to hide.* The chief priests and scribes were using the temple and its religious services to "cover up" their sin and hypocrisy. Both Isaiah (Isa. 1:10–17) and Jeremiah (Jer. 7:1–16) had warned the people of their day that the presence of the physical temple was no guarantee of blessing from God. It was what the people did in the temple *from their hearts* that was really important. The nation had not heeded the warning of the prophets, nor would they heed our Lord's warning.

When the scribes and chief priests heard the report of our Lord's activities, they kept seeking some way to arrest Him (see Mark 14:1–2). Judas would solve the problem for them. Before we quickly condemn the Jewish religious leaders for their sins, we should examine our own ministries to see if perhaps we are making merchandise of the gospel. Do the outsiders in our community think of our church buildings as houses of prayer? Are all nations welcomed there? Do we as church members flee to church on Sundays in an attempt to cover up our sins? Do we "go to church" in order to maintain our reputation or to worship and glorify God? If the Lord Jesus were to show up in our house of worship, what changes would He make?

The Servant-Prophet (11:27—12:44)

In the days that followed, the representatives of the religious and political establishment descended on Jesus as He ministered in the temple, trying their best to trip Him up with their questions. He answered four questions, and then He asked them a question that silenced them for good.

A question of authority (11:27—12:12). As the official guardians of the law, the members of the Sanhedrin had both the right and the responsibility to investigate anyone who claimed to be sent by God, and that included Jesus (see Deut. 18:15–22). However, these men did not have open minds or sincere motives. They were not seeking truth; they were looking for evidence to use to destroy Him (Mark 11:18). Jesus knew what they were doing, so He countered their question with another question and exposed their hypocrisy.

Why take them all the way back to John the Baptist? For a very good reason: God does not teach us new truth if we have rejected the truth He has already revealed. This basic principle is expressed in John 7:17: "If any man is willing to do His will, he shall know of the teaching, whether it is of God, or whether I speak from Myself" (NASB). "Obedience is the organ of spiritual knowledge," said the British preacher F. W. Robertson. The Jewish religious leaders had not accepted what John had taught, so why should God say anything more to them? Had they obeyed John's message, they would have gladly submitted to Christ's authority, for John came to present the Messiah to the nation.

The Jewish leaders were caught in a dilemma of their own making. They were not asking "What is true?" or "What is right?" but "What is safe?" This is always the approach of the hypocrite and the crowd-pleaser. It certainly was not the approach of either Jesus (Mark 12:14) or John the Baptist (Matt. 11:7–10). Jesus did not refuse to answer their question; He only refused to accept and endorse their hypocrisy. He was not being evasive; He was being honest.

Before they had opportunity to escape, He told them a parable that revealed *where their sins were leading them.* They had already permitted John the Baptist to be killed, but soon they would ask for the crucifixion of God's Son!

The vineyard was a familiar image of Israel (Ps. 80:8–16; Isa. 5:1–7). According to Leviticus 19:23–25, a farmer would not use the fruit until the fifth year, though we are not sure the Jews were obeying this regulation at that time. In order to retain his legal rights to the property, the owner had to receive produce from the tenants, even if it was only some of the vegetables that grew between the rows of trees or vines. This explains why the tenants refused to give him anything: they wanted to claim the vineyard for themselves. It also explains why the owner continued to send agents to them; it was purely a question of authority and ownership.

If Mark 12:2–5 covers the three years when the fruit was not used, then it was in the fourth year that the beloved Son was sent. *This is the year when the fruit was devoted to the Lord* (Lev. 19:24), and it makes the sending of the Son even more meaningful. If the tenants could do away with the heir, they would have a clear claim to the property, so they cast him out (see Heb. 13:12–13) and killed him. They wanted to preserve their own position and were willing even to kill to accomplish their evil purpose (John 11:47–53).

Jesus then asked, "What shall, therefore, the lord of the vineyard do?" The leaders answered the question first and thereby condemned themselves (Matt. 21:41), and then Jesus repeated their answer as a solemn verdict from the Judge. But before they could appeal the case, He quoted what they knew was a messianic prophecy, Psalm 118:22–23. We met this same psalm at His triumphal entry (Mark 11:9–10). "The Stone"

was a well-known symbol for the Messiah (Ex. 17:6; Dan. 2:34; Zech. 4:7; Rom. 9:32–33; 1 Cor. 10:4; 1 Peter 2:6–8). The Servant-Judge announced a double verdict: they had not only rejected the Son, but they had also refused the Stone! There could be only one consequence—judgment (Matt. 22:1–14).

A question of responsibility (vv. 13–17). A common threat forced two enemies to unite, the Pharisees and the Herodians. The Herodians supported the family of Herod as well as the Romans who gave them the authority to rule. The Pharisees, however, considered the Herod clan to be the evil usurpers of the throne of David, for, after all, Herod was an Edomite and not a Jew. The Pharisees also opposed the poll tax that the Romans had inflicted on Judea, and they resented the very presence of Rome in their land.

Their temporary alliance was a subtle trap, for no matter how Jesus replied to their question, He was in trouble with either Rome or Herod! But Jesus moved the discussion from politics to principle and caught the hypocrites in their own trap. We might state our Lord's reply something like this: "Caesar's image is on his coins, so they must be minted by his authority. The fact that you possess these coins and use them indicates that you think they are worth something. Therefore, you are already accepting Caesar's authority, or you would not use his money! But don't forget that you were created in the image of God and therefore must live under God's authority as well."

I once carried on a brief correspondence with a man who objected to my interpretation of Romans 13. He said that all government was of the devil and that Christians must not bow to the authority of "the powers that be." I pointed out to him that even his use of the United States mail service was an acceptance of governmental authority. The money he spent buying the paper and stamps also came from the "powers that be." For that matter, the very freedom he had to express himself was a right guaranteed by—the government!

The word translated "render" in Mark 12:17 means "to pay a debt, to pay back." Jesus looked on taxes as the citizens' debt to the government in return for the services performed. Today those services would include, among other things, fire and police protection, national defense, the salaries of the officials who manage the affairs of state, special programs for the poor and underprivileged, etc. The individual Christian citizen might not agree with the way all of his tax money is used, and he can express himself with his voice and his vote, but he must accept the fact that God has established human government for our good (Rom. 13; 1 Tim. 2:1–6; 1 Peter 2:13–17). Even if we cannot respect the people in office, we must respect the office.

A question about eternity (vv. 18–27). This is the only place in Mark where the Sadducees are mentioned. This group accepted only the law of Moses as their religious authority; so, if a doctrine could not be defended from the first five books of the Old

Testament, they would not accept it. They did not believe in the existence of the soul, life after death, resurrection, final judgment, angels, or demons (see Acts 23:8). Most of the Sadducees were priests and were wealthy. They considered themselves the "religious aristocrats" of Judaism and tended to look down on everybody else.

They brought a hypothetical question to Jesus, based on the law of marriage given in Deuteronomy 25:7–10. This woman had a series of seven husbands during her lifetime, all brothers, and all of whom had died. "If there is such a thing as a future resurrection," they argued, "then she must spend eternity with seven husbands!" It seemed a perfect argument, as most arguments are that are based on hypothetical situations.

The Sadducees thought that they were smart, but Jesus soon revealed their ignorance of two things: the power of God and the truth of Scripture. Resurrection is not the restoration of life as we know it; it is the entrance into a new life that is different. The same God who created the angels and gave them their nature is able to give us the new bodies we will need for new life in heaven (1 Cor. 15:38ff.). Jesus did not say that we would become angels or be like the angels in everything, for God's children are higher than the angels (John 17:22–24; 1 John 3:1–2). He said that in our resurrection bodies, we would be sexless like the angels, and therefore marriage would no longer exist. In the eternal state, where our new bodies are perfect and there is no death, there will be no need for marriage, procreation, and the continuance of the race.

The Sadducees were also ignorant of the Scriptures. They claimed to accept the authority of Moses, but they failed to notice that Moses taught the continuation of life after death. Once again, our Lord went back to Scripture (note Mark 2:25; 10:19; 12:10), in this case to the passage about the burning bush (Ex. 3). God did not tell Moses that He *was* (past tense) the God of Abraham, Isaac, and Jacob. He said, "I am the God of Abraham, and the God of Isaac, and the God of Jacob." The patriarchs were *alive* when God spoke those words to Moses; therefore, Moses does teach that there is life after death.

A question of priority (vv. 28–34). The next challenger was a scribe who was also a Pharisee (see Matt. 22:34–35). The scribes had determined that the Jews were obligated to obey 613 precepts in the law, 365 negative precepts and 248 positive. One of their favorite exercises was discussing which of these divine commandments was the greatest.

The Lord quoted Deuteronomy 6:4–5, the great confession of faith that even today pious Jews recite each morning and evening. It is called the "Shema" from the first word of the confession which means "hear." Then He quoted Leviticus 19:18, which emphasizes love for one's neighbor. Jesus made love the most important thing in life, because "love is the fulfilling of the law" (Rom. 13:8–10). If we love God,

we will experience His love within and will express that love to others. We do not live by rules but by relationships, a loving relationship to God that enables us to have a loving relationship with others.

When he started this conversation, the scribe was only the tool of the Pharisees who were trying to get evidence against Jesus (note Matt. 22:35). But after he heard our Lord's answer, the scribe stood and dared to commend the Lord for His reply. The Word had spoken to the man's heart, and he was beginning to get a deeper spiritual understanding of the faith he thought he understood. Even the Old Testament Scriptures taught that there was more to the Jewish religion than offering sacrifices and keeping laws (see 1 Sam. 15:22; Ps. 51:16–17; 141:1–2; Jer. 7:22–23; Hos. 6:6; Mic. 6:6–8).

What does it mean when a person is "not far from the kingdom of God"? It means he or she is facing truth honestly and is not interested in defending a "party line" or even personal prejudices. It means the person is testing his or her faith by what the Word of God says and not by what some religious group demands. People close to the kingdom have the courage to stand up for what is true even if they lose some friends and make some new enemies.

A question of identity (vv. 35–37). Now it was our Lord's turn to ask the questions, and He focused on the most important question of all: Who is the Messiah? "What think ye of Christ? Whose Son is he?" (Matt. 22:42). This is a far more important question than the ones His enemies had asked Him, for if we are wrong about Jesus Christ, we are wrong about salvation. This means we end up condemning our own souls (John 3:16–21; 8:24; 1 John 2:18–23).

Jesus quoted Psalm 110:1 and asked them to explain how David's son could also be David's Lord. The Jews believed that the Messiah would be David's son (John 7:41–42), but the only way David's son could also be David's Lord would be if Messiah were *God come in human flesh.* The answer, of course, is our Lord's miraculous conception and virgin birth (Isa. 7:14; Matt. 1:18–25; Luke 1:26–38).

This section closes with two warnings from the Lord: a warning against the pride of the scribes (Mark 12:38–40) and against the pride of the rich (Mark 12:41–44). If a person is "important" only because of the uniform he wears, the title he bears, or the office he holds, then his "importance" is artificial. It is *character* that makes a person valuable, and nobody can give you character: you must develop it yourself as you walk with God.

There were thirteen trumpet-shaped chests around the walls of the court of the women, and here the people dropped in their offerings. The rich made a big production out of their giving (see Matt. 6:1–4), but Jesus rejected them and their gifts. It is not the *portion* but the *proportion* that is important: the rich gave out of their abundance, but the poor widow gave all that she had. For the rich, their gifts were a small contribution, but for the widow, her gift was true consecration of her whole life.

Pride of living and pride of giving are sins we must avoid at all cost. How tragic that the leaders depended on a religious system that shortly would pass off the scene. How wonderful that the common people gladly listened to Jesus and obeyed His Word.

In which group are you?

CHAPTER TEN
Mark 13
THE SERVANT UNVEILS THE FUTURE

The Jews were proud of their temple, in spite of the fact that it was built by the Herod family in order to placate the Jews. Jesus had already given His estimate of the temple (Mark 11:15–17), but His disciples were fascinated by the magnificence of the structure. Imagine how shocked they were when Jesus informed them that the building they admired so much would one day be demolished. The Jewish leaders had defiled it; Jesus would depart from it and leave it desolate (Matt. 23:38); the Romans would destroy it.

Once away from the crowds, Jesus' disciples asked Him when this momentous event would take place and what would happen to indicate it was soon to occur. Their questions revealed that their understanding of prophecy was still quite confused. They thought that the destruction of the temple coincided with the end of the age and the return of their Lord (Matt. 24:3). But their questions gave Jesus the opportunity to deliver a prophetic message that is generally called "The Olivet Discourse" (Matt. 24—25; Luke 21:5–36).

As we study this important sermon, we must follow some practical guidelines. To begin with, we must study this discourse in the light of the rest of Scripture, especially the book of Daniel. The prophetic Scriptures harmonize if we consider all that God has revealed.

Second, we must see the practical application of the discourse. Jesus did not preach this sermon to satisfy the curiosity of His disciples, or even to straighten out their confused thinking. At least four times He said, "Take heed!" (Mark 13:5, 9, 23, 33), and He closed the address with the admonition, "Watch!" While studying this address can help us better understand future events, we must not make the mistake of setting dates (Mark 13:32)!

Third, as we study, we must keep in mind the "Jewish atmosphere" of the discourse. The Olivet Discourse grew out of some questions asked of a Jewish rabbi by four Jewish men, about the future of the Jewish temple. The warnings about "false Christs" would especially concern Jews (Mark 13:5–6, 21–22), as would the warning about Jewish courts and trials (Mark 13:9). The Jews would especially appreciate the reference to "Daniel the prophet" and the admonition to flee from Judea (Mark 13:14).

Finally, we must remember that this chapter describes a period of time known as "the tribulation" (Mark 13:19, 24; also see Matt. 24:21, 29). The Old Testament prophets wrote about this period and called it "the time of Jacob's trouble" (Jer. 30:7), a time of wrath (Zeph. 1:15–18), and a time of indignation and punishment (Isa. 26:20–21). As we shall see, it is Daniel the prophet who gives us the "key," resulting in a better understanding of the sequence of events.

In Mark 13, Jesus described three stages in this tribulation period: (1) the beginning (Mark 13:5–13), (2) the middle (Mark 13:14–18), and (3) the events that lead to the end (Mark 13:19–27). He then closed with two parables that urge believers to watch and take heed (Mark 13:28–37). Matthew's gospel is more detailed but has the same basic outline: the beginning of sorrows (Matt. 24:4–14), the middle of the tribulation (Matt. 24:15–28), the end (Matt. 24:29–31), closing parabolic application (Matt. 24:32–44).

I must point out that it is the conviction of many students of prophecy that believers in this present age of the church will be raptured by Christ and taken to heaven *before the tribulation begins* (1 Thess. 4:13—5:11; Rev. 3:10–11). At the close of the tribulation, they will return to earth with Christ and reign with Him (Rev. 19:11—20:6). I agree with this interpretation, but I do not make it a test of orthodoxy or spirituality.

The First Half of the Tribulation (13:5–13)

The key statement is at the end of Mark 13:8: "These are the beginnings of sorrows." The word translated "sorrows" means "birth pangs," suggesting that the world at that time will be like a woman in travail (see Isa. 13:6–8; Jer. 4:31; 6:24; 13:21; 22:20–23; 1 Thess. 5:3). The birth pangs will come suddenly, build up gradually, and lead to a time of terrible sorrow and tribulation for the whole world.

"Don't be deceived." Jesus listed the things that must *not* be taken as the "signs" of His coming. Rather, they are indications that the tribulation "birth pangs" are just beginning. These signs are the success of false Christs (Mark 13:5–6), nations in conflict (Mark 13:7–8a), natural disturbances (Mark 13:8b), and religious persecutions (Mark 13:9–13). They have been always been with us, but since these events are compared to "birth pangs," our Lord may be saying that *an acceleration of these things* would be significant.

False messiahs. The pages of history are filled with the tragic stories of false messiahs, false prophets, and their enthusiastic but deluded disciples. Jesus warned about false prophets (Matt. 7:15–20), as did Paul (Acts 20:28–31) and John (1 John 4:1–6). There is something in human nature that loves a lie and refuses to believe the costly lessons of the past. Mark Twain said that a lie runs around the world while Truth is putting on her shoes! How easy it is for spiritually blind people to follow popular leaders and gullibly accept their simple but erroneous solutions for the problems of life.

Jesus warned His disciples not to be deceived by these imposters, and that warning holds good today.

Political conflicts. He also warned them not to be disturbed by political conflicts among the nations. The Roman Empire had enjoyed a measure of peace for many years, but it would not last. As the empire decayed and nationalism developed, it was inevitable that nations would come into conflict. The "Pax Romana" would be gone forever.

Natural disasters. War often leaves famine in its wake (2 Kings 25:2–3; Ezek. 6:11). Famine is also caused by man's abuse of the environment, or it can be sent by God as a judgment (1 Kings 17:1). There have always been earthquakes, and some are evidences of God's wrath (Rev. 6:12; 8:5; 11:13; 16:18). Since natural disasters have many causes, it is dangerous to dogmatically make them "the signs of the times."

"Don't be discouraged!" Not only were the believers to take heed and avoid the deceivers, but they were also to *take heed to themselves* (Mark 13:9–13). Why? Because they would face increasing opposition and persecution from sources both official (Mark 13:9–11) and personal (Mark 13:12–13). It was important that the believers use these experiences as opportunities to witness for Jesus Christ. Persecution would begin in the local Jewish courts, but it would move to the higher courts where governors and kings would be involved. You see a similar development recorded in the book of Acts (Acts 4—5; 7; 12; 16; 21—28).

But persecution would only result in proclamation! The believers would suffer *for His sake* and in that way declare His gospel. "We multiply whenever we are mown down by you," said Tertullian to his persecutors. "The blood of Christians is seed!" While I do not think that taking the gospel to all nations (Mark 13:10) is a *condition* for our Lord's return, it is certainly Christ's commission to His people (Matt. 28:19–20). The "end" here means "the end of the age," the tribulation period.

It would not be easy for these "common people" to face courts, governors, and kings, but Jesus assured them that the Holy Spirit would minister through them whenever they had opportunity to witness (Mark 13:11). This passage should not be used as an excuse or a crutch for poorly prepared preachers. It is an encouragement for all believers who sincerely want to witness for Christ and honor Him (John 14:26; Acts 4:8). If we are walking in the Spirit, we will have no trouble bearing witness for Christ when the opportunities arrive (John 15:26–27).

We can understand official persecution, but why would friends and family members create problems for believers (see Mic. 7:4ff.; John 15:18–27)? You would think that Jewish families in particular would be loyal to each other. But the Christian faith was looked on as heresy and blasphemy by both the Jews and the Gentiles. Twice daily, orthodox Jews affirmed, "Hear, O Israel! The Lord our God is one Lord" (Deut. 6:4). The Jew who said, "Jesus is Lord!" blasphemed and was

worthy of death. Rome expected its citizens to declare "Caesar is lord!" or suffer the consequences. Thus, families and friends would be torn between their loyalty to their "ancient faith" and their nation, and their devotion to loved ones.

The real cause for persecution is stated in Mark 13:13: "for my name's sake." If we identify with Jesus Christ, we can expect the world to treat us the way it treated Him (John 15:20ff.). You can belong to all sorts of weird religious groups today and not suffer much opposition from family and friends, but the minute you bring the name of Jesus into the picture, and share the gospel, somebody will start to oppose you. His name is still hated.

Do not interpret Mark 13:13 as a condition for salvation, for it applies primarily to witnesses during the tribulation. In any period a person lives, if he is truly born again God will love him (John 13:1; Rom. 8:35–38) and keep him (John 10:27–29; Rom. 8:29–34). Since "the end" in Mark 13:7 means "the end of the age," that is likely what it means in Mark 13:13. During the tribulation, the true believers will prove their faith by their faithfulness. They will not give in to the godless pressures of false religion (Rev. 13).

The Middle of the Tribulation (13:14–18)

The phrase "abomination of desolation" comes from the book of Daniel and refers to the idolatrous pollution of the Jewish temple by the Gentiles. To the Jews, all idolatry is an abomination (Deut. 29:17; 2 Kings 16:3). The Jewish temple was defiled in 167 BC by the Syrian king Antiochus IV (also called "Epiphanes," meaning "illustrious") when he poured swine's blood on the altar. This event was predicted in Daniel 11:31. The temple was also defiled by the Romans in AD 70 when they captured and destroyed the city of Jerusalem. However, these events were but anticipations of the final "abomination of desolation" prophesied in Daniel 9:27 and 12:11.

In order to understand Daniel 9:24–27, we must remember that the Jewish calendar is built on a series of sevens. The seventh day of the week is the Sabbath, and the seventh week after Passover brings Pentecost. The seventh month brings the Feast of Trumpets, the day of Atonement, and the Feast of Booths. The seventh year is a sabbatical year, and after seven sabbatical years comes the Year of Jubilee.

Daniel saw seventy weeks, or periods of seven years, divinely determined for the Jews and for their Holy City, Jerusalem. This period of 490 years began with the decree of Artaxerxes in 445 BC, permitting the Jews to return to their land and rebuild Jerusalem (Ezra 1:1–4). Why must the city be restored? Because 483 years later (7 x 69), Messiah would come to the city and give His life for sinners.

Now we must do some simple calculating. Most historians agree that Jesus was born in 5 BC, for Herod the Great was still living at the time, and he died in

March, 4 BC. If our Lord died at about the age of 33, that would take us to AD 27 or 28, and this would be 483 years after 445 BC when the decree was given!

We have accounted for 483 of Daniel's 490 years, but what about the remaining 7 years? Daniel 9:27 assigns them to the tribulation period that we are now studying. (Note that Dan. 9:26 also predicts the destruction of Jerusalem—by the Romans, commentators conclude—but these two events must not be confused.) "The time of Jacob's trouble" will last seven years.

But what signals the beginning of this awful seven-year period? The signing of a covenant between the nation of Israel and "the prince that shall come" (Dan. 9:26). This "prince" is the coming world dictator that we usually call "the Antichrist." In the book of Revelation, he is called "the Beast" (Rev. 13—14). He will agree to protect Israel from her many enemies for seven years, and will even allow the Jews to rebuild their temple and restore their ancient liturgy and sacrifices. The Jews rejected their true Messiah but will accept a false messiah (John 5:43). However, after three and a half years, Antichrist will break this covenant, invade the temple, set up his own image, and force the world to worship Satan (see 2 Thess. 2:1–12; Rev. 13). This is Daniel's "abomination of desolation," and it will usher in the last half of the tribulation period, a time known as "the Great tribulation" (Matt. 24:21). Note in Mark 13:14 that Mark's parenthesis is for *readers* at a future time, not *hearers* when Jesus gave this message. This message will have special meaning to them as they see these events taking place.

Jesus gave a special warning to the Jewish believers in Jerusalem and Judea: "Get out as fast as you can!" This same warning applied when Rome attacked Jerusalem in AD 70. (See Luke 21:20–24, and remember that Daniel 9:26 predicted the invasion.) What happened in AD 70 foreshadowed what will happen in the middle of the tribulation. Dr. Harry Rimmer used to say, "Coming events cast their shadows before. Straight ahead lies yesterday!" The warnings in Mark 13:14–18 do not apply to believers today, but they do remind us that God's people in every age must know the prophetic Word and be prepared to obey God at any time.

The Last Half of the Tribulation (13:19–27)

In the book of Revelation, the last half of the tribulation is called "the wrath of God" (Rev. 14:10, 19; 15:1, 7; 16:1, 19; 19:15). During this time, God will judge the world and prepare Israel for the coming of her Messiah. It will be a time of intensive judgment such as the world has never seen or will ever see again. In it, God will be working out His purposes and setting the stage for the coming of the Conqueror (Rev. 19:11ff.).

Even in the midst of His wrath, God remembers mercy (Hab. 3:2), and for the sake of His elect, He shortens the days of the tribulation. (The "elect" refers to Israel and the Gentiles who believe during the tribulation. See Rev. 14.) To "shorten the days" means that He limits them to the three and a half years already determined and stops on time.

Satanic deception will continue to the very end, and false Christs and false prophets will lead people astray. In fact, they will even do miracles (Matt. 7:21–23; 2 Thess. 2:9–12; Rev. 13:13–14). So deceptive will be these miracles that even the elect will be tempted to believe their lies. Of themselves, miracles are not a proof of divine calling and approval (Deut 13:1–5). The final test is the Word of God.

The tribulation period will climax with the appearing of terrifying signs in the heavens and worldwide chaos on the earth (Luke 21:25–26). These signs, which have been predicted by the prophets (Isa. 13:10; 34:4; Joel 2:10; 3:15), will prepare the way for the coming of Jesus Christ to the earth. It will be a revelation of His great glory (see Dan. 7:13–14; Mark 8:38) as He comes to establish His rule on the earth (Acts 1:11; Rev. 1:7).

Mark 13:27 describes the regathering of Israel from the nations to which they have been scattered throughout the world (Deut. 30:3–6; Isa. 11:12; Jer. 31:7–9). They will see their Messiah and trust Him, and the nation will be created in holiness and glory (Zech. 12:9—13:1; 14:4–11). That there is a glorious future for Israel is stated by Paul in Romans 11.

Jesus did not want His disciples to get so involved in the prophecies of the future that they would neglect the responsibilities of the present, so He closed the Olivet Discourse with two parables. (Matt. 25 adds three other parables—the bridesmaids, the talents, and the sheep and goats.) Note that the first parable (Mark 13:28–31) emphasizes knowing that His coming is near, while the second parable emphasizes *not knowing* the time of His return. Is this a contradiction? No, because they were addressed to two different groups of people—the first, to the tribulation saints, and the second, to all believers of every age.

The fig tree has a special association with the nation of Israel (see Mark 11:12–14, but note that Luke 21:29 adds "and all the trees"). Most of the trees in Palestine are evergreens and do not change dramatically with the seasons. Not so the fig tree; it is one of the latest to leaf out in spring, so its shoots are an indication that summer is indeed near.

As Christian believers today, we are not looking for "signs" of His coming; we are looking for Him! But people living during the tribulation will be able to watch these things occur and will know that His coming is near. This assurance will help them to endure (Mark 13:13) and to be good witnesses.

We think of a "generation" as a body of people living at the same time in history. But to what "generation" was Jesus referring in Mark 13:30? Not the generation then living in Judea, because they did not see "all these things" actually take place. Perhaps He meant the generation living during the tribulation period. But since the tribulation covers only seven years, why refer to an entire generation? For that matter, several different generations live together during every period of history.

The Greek word translated "generation" can also mean "race, stock, family." On several occasions, Jesus used it to refer to the Jewish nation (Mark 8:12, 38; 9:19), and that is probably how He used it in Mark 13:30. The chosen nation, God's elect, would be preserved to the very end, and God would fulfill His promises to them. His Word will never fail (Josh. 21:45; 1 Kings 8:56; Matt. 24:35). We as believers do not depend on signs; we depend on His unchanging Word, the "sure word of prophecy" (2 Peter 1:19–21).

The parable of the fig tree cautions tribulation saints to watch and to know the "signs of the times." But the parable of the householder warns *all of us today* (Mark 13:37) to be alert, because we do not know when He will return to take us to heaven (1 Cor. 15:51–52). Like the householder in the story, before our Lord went from us back to heaven, He gave each of us work to do. He expects us to be faithful while He is gone and to be working when He returns. "Take heed, watch and pray" is His admonition.

To "watch" means to be alert, to stay at one's best, to stay awake. (The English name "Gregory" comes from this Greek word translated "watch.") Why must we stay alert? Because nobody knows when Jesus Christ will return. When He was on earth in His humiliation, Jesus did not know the day or hour of His coming again. Even the angels do not know. The unsaved world scoffs at us because we continue to cling to this "blessed hope," but He will return as He promised (2 Peter 3). Our task is to be faithful and to be busy, not to speculate or debate about the hidden details of prophecy.

Watchfulness has nothing to do with going to heaven. It is purely a matter of pleasing Him, hearing His loving commendation, and receiving His reward (Matt. 25:14–30). There is no suggestion here that, when He returns, Jesus will take only the faithful to heaven and leave the others on earth to suffer the tribulation. His family is one, and He is now preparing a home for all of them, even the least worthy (John 14:1–6). We go to heaven because of His grace, not because of our faithfulness or good works (Eph. 2:8–10).

The Christians who read Mark's gospel eventually had to face intense persecution from Rome (1 Peter 4:12ff.), and this particular message must have brought comfort and strength to them. After all, if God is able to help His people witness during the Great tribulation, the worst persecution of all, then surely He could strengthen the saints in the Roman Empire as they faced their fiery trial.

While Christians today will not experience the terrible sufferings described in this chapter, we will have our share of persecution and tribulation in this world before the Lord returns (John 16:33; Acts 14:22). But the warnings of this message in Mark 13 may be applied to our own lives: "Take heed that you are not deceived" (Mark 13:5, 23); "Take heed that you do not become discouraged and quit" (Mark 13:9); "Take heed, watch and pray" (Mark 13:33).

"And what I say unto you, I say unto all, 'Watch'" (Mark 13:37).

CHAPTER ELEVEN
Mark 14:1—15:20
THE SERVANT SUFFERS

While thousands of Passover pilgrims were preparing for the joys of the feast, Jesus was preparing for the ordeal of His trial and crucifixion. Just as He had steadfastly set His face to go to Jerusalem (Luke 9:51), so He steadfastly set His heart to do the Father's will. The Servant was "obedient unto death, even the death of the cross" (Phil. 2:8).

Follow His footsteps during the days and hours of the last week, and you will be amazed to see the responses of various people to the Lord Jesus Christ.

In Bethany—Adored (14:1–11)
This event took place six days before Passover, which would put it on the Friday before the triumphal entry (John 12:1). By placing this story between the accounts of the plot to arrest Jesus, Mark contrasted the treachery of Judas and the leaders with the love and loyalty of Mary. The ugliness of their sins makes the beauty of her sacrifice even more meaningful.

Neither Mark nor Matthew names the woman, but John tells us that it was Mary of Bethany, the sister of Martha and Lazarus (John 11:1–2). Mary is found three times in the gospel story, and each time, she is at the feet of Jesus (Luke 10:38–42; John 11:31–32; 12:1–8). Mary had a close fellowship with the Lord as she sat at His feet and listened to His Word. She is a good model for all of us to follow.

Mary's anointing of the Lord must not be confused with a similar event recorded in Luke 7:36–50. The unnamed woman in the house of Simon the Pharisee was a converted harlot who expressed her love to Christ because of His gracious forgiveness of her many sins. In the house of Simon the (healed) leper, Mary expressed her love to Christ because He was going to the cross to die for her. She prepared His body for burial as she anointed His head (Mark 14:3) and His feet (John 12:3). She showed her love for Jesus while He was still alive.

It was an expensive offering that she gave to the Lord. Spikenard was imported from India, and a whole jar would have cost the equivalent of a common worker's annual income. Mary gave lavishly and lovingly. She was not ashamed to show her love for Christ openly.

There were three consequences to her act of worship. First, the house was filled with the beautiful fragrance of the ointment (John 12:3; also note 2 Cor.

2:15–16). There is always a "spiritual fragrance" in that home where Jesus Christ is loved and worshipped.

Second, the disciples, led by Judas, criticized Mary for wasting her money! It sounded so pious for Judas to talk about the poor, when in reality he wanted the money for himself (John 12:4–6)! Even in the Upper Room, six days later, the disciples still thought Judas was concerned about helping the poor (John 13:21–30). It is interesting that the word translated "waste" in Mark 14:4 is translated "perdition" in John 17:12 *and applied to Judas!* Judas criticized Mary for "wasting money," but he wasted his entire life!

Third, Jesus commended Mary and accepted her gracious gift. He knew the heart of Judas and understood why the other disciples followed his bad example. He also knew Mary's heart and quickly defended her (Rom. 8:33–39). No matter what others may say about our worship and service, the most important thing is that we please the Lord. The fact that others misunderstand and criticize us should not keep us from showing our love to Christ. Our concern should be His approval alone.

When Mary gave her best at the feet of Jesus, she started a "wave of blessing" that has been going on ever since. She was a blessing to Jesus as she shared her love, and she was a blessing to her home as the fragrance spread. Were it not for Mary, her village, Bethany, would probably have been forgotten. The account of her deed was a blessing to the early church that heard about it and, because of the records in three of the Gospels, Mary has been a blessing to the whole world—and still is! The Lord's prediction has certainly been fulfilled.

Mary gave her best in faith and love; Judas gave his worst in unbelief and hatred. He solved the problem of how the Jewish leaders could arrest Jesus without causing a riot during the feast. He sold his Master for the price of a slave (see Ex. 21:32), the basest act of treachery in history.

In the Upper Room—Betrayed (14:12–26)

The Passover lamb was selected on the tenth day of the month Nisan (our March-April), examined for blemishes, and then slain on the fourteenth day of the month (Ex. 12:3–6). The lamb had to be slain in the temple precincts and the supper eaten within the Jerusalem city limits. For the Jews, the Passover feast was the memorial of a past victory, but Jesus would institute a new supper that would be the memorial of His death.

Peter and John saw to it that the supper was prepared (Luke 22:8). It would not be difficult to locate the man carrying the jar of water because the women usually performed this task. Was this man John Mark's father? Did Jesus eat the Passover in an upper room in John Mark's home? These are fascinating speculations, but we have no evidence that can confirm them. However, we do know that John Mark's home was a center for Christian fellowship in Jerusalem (Acts 12:12).

The original Passover feast consisted of the roasted lamb, the unleavened bread, and the dish of bitter herbs (Ex. 12:8–20). The lamb reminded the Jews of the blood that was applied to the doorposts in Egypt to keep the angel of death from slaying their firstborn. The bread reminded them of their haste in leaving Egypt (Ex. 12:39), and the bitter herbs spoke of their suffering as Pharaoh's slaves. At some time in the centuries that followed, the Jews had added to the ceremony the drinking of four cups of wine diluted with water.

Since for the Jews the new day began with sundown, it would be Friday when Jesus and His disciples met in the Upper Room. This was His last Passover, and on that day, He would fulfill the Passover by dying on the cross as the spotless Lamb of God (John 1:29; 1 Cor. 5:7; 1 Peter 2:21–24).

Between Mark 14:17 and 18 are details of the washing of the disciples' feet and the lesson on humility (John 13:1–20). Following that lesson, Jesus became deeply troubled and announced that one of the disciples was a traitor. This announcement stunned all the disciples except Judas, who knew that Jesus was speaking about him. Until the very end, Jesus hid from the other disciples the identity of His betrayer, for He wanted to give Judas every opportunity to turn from sin. He even washed Judas's feet! Had Peter known the truth about Judas, he might have been tempted to kill him.

Some people try to defend Judas by arguing that he betrayed Jesus in order to force Him into revealing His power and setting up the Jewish kingdom. Others say that he was nothing but a servant who obediently fulfilled God's Word. Judas was neither a martyr nor a robot. He was a responsible human being who made his own decisions but, in so doing, fulfilled the Word of God. He must not be made into either a hero ("After all, somebody had to betray Jesus!") or a helpless victim of merciless predestination. Judas was lost for the same reason millions are lost today: he did not repent of his sins and believe on Jesus Christ (John 6:64–71; 13:10–11). If you have never been born again, one day you will wish you had not been born at all.

None of the other disciples really thought himself to be the traitor, for their questions imply a negative answer: "It is not I, is it?" The men had often debated over which of them was the greatest, but now they were discussing which of them was the vilest. To make matters worse, Jesus said that His betrayer had even eaten bread with Him at the table! In the East, to break bread with someone means to enter into a pact of friendship and mutual trust. It would be an act of the basest treachery to break bread and then betray your host. However, even this was the fulfillment of the Word of God (Ps. 41:9).

Judas was sitting in the place of honor at our Lord's left, while John was reclining to His right (John 13:23). When Jesus gave Judas the bread dipped in the herbs, it was the gracious act of a host to a special guest. Even this did not break Judas's heart, for after Judas took the morsel, Satan possessed him. Judas left the Upper Room to go to make the final arrangements to arrest the Lord Jesus. But even then the disciples did not know the truth about Judas (John 13:27–30), and they would not find out the truth until they met him later in the garden of Gethsemane.

After Judas left the scene, Jesus instituted what Christians commonly call "the Lord's Supper" or "the Eucharist." (The word *Eucharist* comes from a Greek word which means "to give thanks.") Before the cup, Jesus took one of the unleavened loaves, blessed it, broke it, and told the men, "This is My body." He then took the Passover cup, blessed it, and gave it to them, saying, "This is my blood" (see 1 Cor. 11:23–26).

Bread and wine were two common items that were used at practically every meal, but Jesus gave them a wonderful new meaning. When Jesus said, "This is my body," and, "This is my blood," He did not transform either the bread or the wine into anything different. When the disciples ate the bread, it was still bread; when they drank the wine, it was still wine. However, the Lord gave a new meaning to the bread and the wine, so that, from that hour, they would serve as memorials of His death.

What, then, did Jesus accomplish by His death? On the cross, Jesus fulfilled the old covenant and established a new covenant (Heb. 9—10). The old covenant was ratified with the blood of animal sacrifices, but the new covenant was ratified by the blood of God's Son. The new covenant in His blood would do what the old covenant sacrifices could not do—take away sin and cleanse the heart and conscience of the believer. We are not saved from our sins by participating in a religious ceremony, but by trusting Jesus Christ as our Savior.

Our Lord's command was, "This do in remembrance of me" (1 Cor. 11:24–25). The word translated "remembrance" means much more than "in memory of," for you can do something in memory of a dead person—yet Jesus is alive! The word carries the idea of a present participation in a past event. Because Jesus is alive, as we celebrate the Lord's Supper, by faith we have communion with Him (1 Cor. 10:16–17). This is not some "magical" experience produced by the bread and cup. It is a spiritual experience that comes through our discerning of Christ and the meaning of the Supper (1 Cor. 11:27–34).

The last thing Jesus and His disciples did in the Upper Room was to sing the traditional Passover hymn based on Psalms 115—118. Imagine our Lord *singing* when the cross was only a few hours away!

In the Garden—Forsaken (14:27–52)
On the way to the garden of Gethsemane ("oil press"), Jesus warned the disciples that they would all forsake Him, but He then assured them that He would meet them again in Galilee after His resurrection. He even quoted Zechariah 13:7—"Smite the shepherd, and the sheep shall be scattered"—to back up His warning. Their minds and hearts were unable to receive and retain His words, for three days later, they did not believe the reports of His resurrection! And the angel had to give them a special reminder to meet Him in Galilee (Mark 16:6–7). Had they listened to His word and believed it, they would have saved themselves a great deal of anxiety, and Peter would not have denied the Lord.

The quotation from Zechariah told the disciples what to do when the Jews arrested Jesus: *scatter!* In fact, at the very time of His arrest, Jesus said, "Let these [disciples] go their way" (John 18:8). In other words, "Men, get out of here!" I have read eloquent sermons blaming Peter for "following afar off," but they completely miss the point. He was not supposed to follow at all! Had he obeyed the Lord, he would not have attacked a man with his sword or denied the Lord three times.

Peter seemed to have a difficult time applying Jesus' commands to himself. The other men might forsake Jesus, but Peter would stand true and, if necessary, go with Him to prison and to death. Of course, the other disciples echoed Peter's boast, so he was not the only self-confident one in the group. In the end, all of them failed.

When about to experience great suffering, most people want to have someone with them, to help share the burden. Often in my pastoral ministry, I have sat with people at the hospital, waiting for the surgeon to come with a report. Being perfectly human, Jesus wanted companionship as He faced the cross, and He selected Peter, James, and John, the same men who had accompanied Him to the home of Jairus (Mark 5:37) and to the Mount of Transfiguration (Mark 9:2). These three experiences parallel Philippians 3:10: "That I may know him [Mount of Transfiguration], and the power of his resurrection [home of Jairus], and the fellowship of his sufferings [garden of Gethsemane]."

Our Lord's struggle in the Garden can be understood only in the light of what would happen to Him on the cross: He would be made sin for us (2 Cor. 5:21) and bear the curse of the law (Gal. 3:13). It was not the physical suffering that almost overwhelmed Him with "anguish and sorrow," but the contemplation of being forsaken by His Father (Mark 15:34). This was "the cup" that He would drink (John 18:11). According to Hebrews 5:7–9, He asked to be saved, not "from death" but *out of death*—that is, raised from the dead—and the Father granted His request.

Abba is an Aramaic word that means "papa" or "daddy." It reveals the intimate relationship between our Lord and His Father. While believers today would probably not use that term in public, it does belong to us because we belong to Him (Rom. 8:15; Gal. 4:6). Note that Jesus did not tell the Father what to do; He had perfect confidence in God's will. Three times He prayed about the matter, and each time He yielded to the Father's will in loving surrender.

What were the three disciples doing? Sleeping! And Peter had vowed that he would die with his Lord—yet he could not even watch with Him! How gently Jesus rebuked the disciples and warned them. "Watch and pray" is an admonition that is often repeated in Scripture (Neh. 4:9; Mark 13:33; Eph. 6:18; Col. 4:2). It means, "Be alert as you pray! Keep your spiritual eyes open, for the enemy is near!"

The third time our Lord returned to the sleeping men, He said, "Are you still sleeping and taking your rest? It is enough; the hour has come" (Mark 14:41 NASB). It was the hour of His sacrifice, when He would die for the sins of the world. At that moment, Judas and the temple guards arrived to arrest Jesus, and Judas kissed Jesus repeatedly as the sign that He was the one to arrest. What hypocrisy!

The fact that Judas brought such a large group of armed men is evidence that neither he nor the religious leaders really understood Jesus. They thought that Jesus would try to escape, or that His followers would put up a fight, or that perhaps He might do a miracle. Our Lord's words in Mark 14:49 were proof that He was in control, for they could have arrested Him many times earlier, except that His hour had not yet come.

Peter did a foolish thing by attacking Malchus (John 18:10), for we do not fight spiritual battles with physical weapons (2 Cor. 10:3–5). He used the wrong weapon, at the wrong time, for the wrong purpose, with the wrong motive. Had Jesus not healed Malchus, Peter would have been arrested as well, and there might have been four crosses on Calvary.

At this point, the disciples forsook Jesus and fled, and so did an unknown young man who came into the Garden and witnessed the arrest. Was this John Mark? We do not know, but since the gospel of Mark is the only one of the four gospels that records this event, the author could well have been writing about himself. If the Upper Room was in the home of John Mark, then perhaps Judas led the soldiers there first. John Mark may have hastily put on an outer garment and followed the mob to the Garden. The soldiers may have even tried to arrest him, so he fled.

The disciples were scattered and the Servant was now alone, "and yet I am not alone, because the Father is with me" (John 16:32). Soon, even the Father would forsake Him!

In the High Priest's Palace—Rejected (14:53–72)

Both the Jewish trial and the Roman trial were in three stages. The Jewish trial was opened by Annas, the former high priest (John 18:13–24). It then moved to the full council to hear witnesses (Mark 14:53–65), and then to an early morning session for the final vote of condemnation (Mark 15:1). Jesus was then sent to Pilate (Mark 15:1–5; John 18:28–38), who sent Him to Herod (Luke 23:6–12), who returned Him to Pilate (Mark 15:6–15; John 18:39–19:6). Pilate yielded to the cry of the mob and delivered Jesus to be crucified.

By the time the soldiers arrived at the palace of the high priest, Peter and John, heedless of the Lord's repeated warnings, followed the mob and even went into the courtyard. Jesus that night had sweat "as it were great drops of blood" (Luke 22:44), but Peter was cold and sat by the enemy fire! The two disciples could not witness the actual trial, but at least they were near enough to see the outcome (Matt. 26:58; John 18:15).

After questioning and insulting Jesus, Annas sent Jesus bound to his son-in-law Caiaphas, the high priest. The Sanhedrin was assembled and the witnesses were ready. It was necessary to have at least two witnesses before the accused could be declared guilty and worthy of death (Deut. 17:6). Many witnesses testified against Jesus, but since they did not agree, their testimony was invalid. How tragic that a group of religious leaders would encourage people to lie, and during a special holy season!

Throughout this time of false accusation, our Lord said nothing (Isa. 53:7; 1 Peter 2:23). But when the high priest put Him under oath, Jesus had to reply, and He testified clearly that he was indeed the Son of God. The title "Son of man" is messianic (Dan. 7:13), and the members of the council knew exactly what Jesus was saying: He was claiming to be God come in human flesh! This claim, of course, was blasphemy to the Jews, and they declared Him guilty and worthy of death. Since it was irregular for the Sanhedrin to vote on capital cases at night, the council met again early the next morning and gave the official sentence (Mark 15:1).

While the Lord was being mocked and abused, Peter was in the courtyard below, trying to escape detection. Had he heeded the Lord's warnings, he would have avoided walking into temptation and denying his Master three times. He is a warning to all of us, for, after all, if an apostle who walked with Christ denied his Lord, what might we do in similar circumstances? The Roman believers who read Mark's gospel no doubt learned from this account, for they would soon be entering the furnace of persecution themselves.

First, one of the high priest's servant girls spoke to Peter, and he denied knowing anything about Jesus. Then the cock crowed. Another servant girl pointed Peter out to some of the bystanders, and again Peter denied knowing Jesus. Finally, a man accused him of being one of the disciples, and some of the bystanders joined in, but Peter vehemently denied knowing Jesus, and even put himself under a curse. Then the cock crowed for the second time and the Lord's prediction was fulfilled (see Mark 14:30).

However, it was not the crowing of the cock that convicted Peter; it was the remembering of Christ's words. It is always the Word that penetrates the heart and brings about true repentance. Peter pondered what Jesus had said and what he himself had done, and then Jesus, on His way to Pilate's hall, turned and looked at Peter. It was a look of love, to be sure, but *injured* love (Luke 22:61). His heart broken, Peter went out quickly and wept bitterly.

Before we judge Peter too severely, we need to

examine our own lives. How many times have we denied the Lord and lost opportunities to share the gospel with others? Do we, like Peter, talk when we should listen, argue when we should obey, sleep when we should pray, and fight when we should submit? Peter at least was sorry for his sins and wept over them, and the Lord did forgive him. After His resurrection, Jesus had a private meeting with Peter (Luke 24:34); then Jesus helped Peter make a public confession when He met the disciples in Galilee (John 21).

In Pilate's Hall—Condemned (15:1–20)

As soon as their early morning meeting was over, and the verdict officially recorded, the Jewish leaders delivered Jesus to the Roman governor, Pontius Pilate. The governor usually resided at Caesarea, but it was his custom to be in Jerusalem each year for the feast. His presence pleased some of the Jews, and he could be on hand if any problems arose among the thousands of people crowded into Jerusalem. Roman governors held court early in the morning, so he was quite prepared when they brought the prisoner to him.

The Jewish council had to convince Pilate that Jesus was guilty of a capital crime and therefore worthy of death (John 18:31–32). In spite of their political corruption, many Roman officials had an appreciation for justice and tried to deal fairly with prisoners. Furthermore, Pilate had no great love for the Jews and was not about to do them any favors. He knew that the Jewish leaders were not interested in seeing justice done; what they really wanted was vengeance (Mark 15:10).

John gives us the most details of the Roman trial, and when you combine the gospel records, you discover that Pilate repeatedly stated that he found no fault in Jesus (John 18:38; Luke 23:14; John 19:4; Luke 23:22; Matt. 27:24). His problem was that he lacked the courage to stand for what he believed. He wanted to avoid a riot (Matt. 27:24), so he was "willing to content the people" (Mark 15:15). Pilate did not ask, "Is it right? Is it safe? Is it popular?"

The council had only one capital crime that they might be able to present to Pilate: Jesus claimed to be a king and He stirred up the people. They tried to pass Him off as a dangerous revolutionary who was undermining the authority of Rome. As Pilate questioned Jesus, the Lord said nothing, but the chief priests kept accusing Him and trying to wear down the governor's resistance.

Pilate thought he could avoid making a decision by sending Jesus to Herod, the ruler of Galilee (Luke 23:6–12), but Herod only sent Jesus back after mocking Him. Then the governor offered the people a choice—Jesus the Nazarene, or Barabbas, the murderer and insurrectionist—thinking that surely sanity would prevail and they would ask to have Jesus released. But the chief priests had prepared the crowd carefully (Mark 15:11), and they asked for Barabbas to be set free and Jesus to be crucified.

The governor then tried a third ruse: he had Jesus scourged, hoping that the sight of the suffering prisoner would somehow arouse their pity (Mark 15:15; John 19:1ff.). But the plan did not work. The governor gave in and delivered Jesus to be crucified.

Then followed the disgraceful mockery by the soldiers, as they beat Him, spat on Him, and bowed in mock homage. Roman soldiers would certainly laugh at a Jew who claimed to be a king! "We have no king but Caesar!" (John 19:12–15). Our Lord quietly suffered and did not fight back, a lesson that Mark's readers would need to learn as they faced official persecution (1 Peter 2:21–24).

But men had not yet done their worst to God's Son. Now they would lead Him outside the city and nail Him to a cross, and the Servant would die for the sins of the very people who were crucifying Him.

CHAPTER TWELVE
Mark 15:21—16:20
THE SERVANT FINISHES HIS WORK

Cecil Rhodes devoted his life to British expansion in South Africa, plus making a fortune in diamonds. He was not yet fifty years old when he died, and his last words were, "So little done, so much to do."

"I have glorified thee on the earth," Jesus said to His Father; "I have finished the work which thou gavest me to do" (John 17:4). It would be wonderful if all of us could give that same kind of report when we get to the end of life's journey. To know that we have accomplished His work and glorified His name would certainly make us look back with thanksgiving and ahead with excitement and anticipation.

The four events described in this final section of Mark give us the climax of the gospel story and the historical basis for the message of the gospel (1 Cor. 15:1–8).

The Servant's Death (15:21–41)

Three specific hours are mentioned in this section of Mark: the third (Mark 15:25), the sixth (Mark 15:33), and the ninth (Mark 15:33–34). The Jews reckoned time from 6 a.m. to 6 p.m., so this means that the third hour was 9 a.m., the sixth hour noon, and the ninth hour 3 p.m. Mark followed the Jewish system, whereas the apostle John used Roman time in his gospel. This means that "the sixth hour" in John 19:14 is 6 a.m.

The third hour (vv. 21–32). According to law, the guilty victim had to carry his cross, or at least the crossbeam, to the place of execution, and Jesus was no exception. He left Pilate's hall bearing His cross (John 19:16–17), but He could not continue, so the soldiers "drafted" Simon of Cyrene to carry the cross for Him. Roman officers had the privilege of "impressing" men for service, and the way they used this privilege irritated the Jews (Matt. 5:41).

When you consider all that our Lord had endured since His arrest, it is not surprising that His strength failed. Indeed, "He could have called ten thousand angels," yet He willingly bore the suffering on our behalf. There was a higher purpose behind this act: the victim carried the cross because he had been found guilty, *but our Lord was not guilty.* We are the guilty ones, and Simon carried that cross on our behalf. Simon Peter boasted that he would go with Jesus to prison and to death (Luke 22:33), but it was Simon of Cyrene, not Simon Peter, who came to the aid of the Master.

In one of his folksy letters to his mother, Harry Truman wrote, "I went to the White House to see the President and discovered I was the President." Simon had come to Jerusalem to celebrate the Passover (Acts 2:10; 6:9), and he ended up meeting the Passover Lamb! We have good reason to believe that Simon trusted the Savior and went home and led his two sons to the Lord. No doubt many of Mark's Roman readers knew Alexander and Rufus (Rom. 16:13), and perhaps they had even known Simon.

Golgotha is a Hebrew word that means "skull," though nowhere does the text explain why the place bore that name. Visitors to the Holy Land today are shown "Gordon's Calvary," which does have the appearance of a skull, but guides also point out another possible site in the Church of the Holy Sepulchre. We do not know the exact place where our Lord was crucified, nor is it important that we know. He was crucified outside the city walls, the place of rejection (Heb. 13:12–13), and He died for the sins of the world.

It was customary for the victims to be given a narcotic potion that would help deaden the pain (Prov. 31:6), but our Lord refused it. For one thing, He wanted to be in full possession of His faculties as He did the Father's will and accomplished the work of redemption. He would enter fully into His sufferings on our behalf and take no shortcuts. He refused the cup of sympathy so that He might better drink the cup of iniquity (Matt. 26:36–43). What an example for us to follow as we do God's will and share "the fellowship of his sufferings" (Phil. 3:10).

None of the gospel writers gives us a description of crucifixion, nor is one necessary. Their aim is not to arouse our pity but to assure our faith. Many of their readers had probably witnessed crucifixions, so any details would have been unnecessary. Crucifixion was such a detestable thing that it was not mentioned in decent society, any more than today we would discuss the gas chamber or the electric chair. Suffice it to say, crucifixion is one of the most horrible forms of death ever devised by man. Read Psalm 22 for a description of some of our Lord's agonies as He hung on the cross.

The victim usually wore a placard that declared his offense. Pilate wrote the one that Jesus wore and that was later hung above Him on the cross: "This is Jesus of Nazareth, the King of the Jews." The Jewish leaders protested, but Pilate for once stood his ground (John 19:19–22). It may be that the message of this sign first aroused the hopes of the repentant thief (Luke 23:39–43). He may have reasoned: "If His name is Jesus, then He is a Savior. If He is from Nazareth, then He would identify with rejected people (John 1:46). If He has a kingdom, then perhaps there is room for me!"

The soldiers at the execution were not only doing their duty, but they were also fulfilling prophecy as they gambled for our Lord's garments (Ps. 22:18). The fact that the innocent Son of God was placed between two guilty criminals also fulfilled prophecy (Isa. 53:12; and see Luke 22:37). The word used for "thieves" is rendered *robber* in John 18:40 in reference to Barabbas, so perhaps these two men had been members of his rebel band.

It seems incredible that the religious leaders so hated Jesus that they even went out to Golgotha to mock Him. Thomas Carlyle called ridicule "the language of the devil," and in this case, that definition is certainly true. The idle spectators who passed by were only too eager to follow the bad example of their leaders, so enduring mockery was added to the sufferings of our Lord. They mocked Him as Prophet (Mark 15:29), as Savior (Mark 15:31), and as King (Mark 15:32). It is possible that their sarcastic "He saved others!" may have encouraged the one thief to trust Him. The thief may have reasoned, "If He saved others, then He can save me!" So God uses even the wrath of man to praise Him (Ps. 76:10).

The sixth hour (v. 33). At noon, a miraculous darkness came over the land, and all creation sympathized with the Creator as He suffered. This was indeed a miracle and not some natural phenomenon, such as a sand storm or an eclipse. It would not be possible to have an eclipse during full moon at Passover. By means of this darkness, God was saying something to the people.

For one thing, the Jews would certainly think about the first Passover. The ninth plague in Egypt was a three-day darkness, followed by the last plague, the death of the firstborn (Ex. 10:22—11:9). The darkness at Calvary was an announcement that God's Firstborn and Beloved Son, the Lamb of God, was giving His life for the sins of the world. It was also an announcement that judgment was coming and men had better be prepared.

The ninth hour (vv. 34–41). Our Lord made seven statements from the cross, three of them before the darkness came: "Father, forgive them, for they know not what they do" (Luke 23:34); "Today shalt thou be with me in paradise" (Luke 23:43); and "Woman, behold thy son.… Behold thy mother" (John 19:26–27). When the darkness came, there was silence on His cross, for it was then that He was made sin for us (2 Cor. 5:21).

At the ninth hour, Jesus expressed the agony of His soul when He cried out from the cross, "My God, my God, why hast thou forsaken me?" (see Ps. 22:1). The darkness symbolized the judgment Jesus experienced when the Father forsook Him. As was so often the case, the people did not understand His words; they thought

He was calling for Elijah the prophet. There was not only darkness over the land, but there was darkness in the minds and hearts of the people (2 Cor. 4:3–6; John 3:16–21; 12:35–41).

Then Jesus said, "I thirst" (John 19:28), and the kind act of the soldier in giving Jesus a sip of vinegar (see Ps. 69:21) assisted Him in uttering two more wonderful statements: "It is finished!" (John 19:30) and "Father, into thy hands I commit my spirit" (Luke 23:46;and see Ps. 31:5). Jesus was not murdered; He willingly laid down His life for us (John 10:11, 15, 17–18). He was not a martyr; He was a willing sacrifice for the sins of the world.

Two remarkable events occurred at His death: there was an earthquake (Matt. 27:51), and the veil in the temple was torn in two. The veil had separated man from God, but now, through His death, Jesus had opened for the whole world a "new and living way" (Heb. 10:12–22; also see John 14:6). There had been an earthquake at Sinai when the law was given (Ex. 19:16–18), but now the law was fulfilled in Jesus Christ and its curse removed (Rom. 10:4; Gal. 3:10–14). Through His sacrifice, Jesus had purchased not only freedom from the law, but also freedom from the entire sacrificial system.

It is thrilling to read the witness of the Roman centurion, especially when you consider that his words could have gotten him into trouble with both the Jews and the Romans. That Jesus Christ is the Son of God is one of Mark's important themes (Mark 1:1, 11; 3:11; 5:7; 9:7; 14:61–62). This makes His servanthood even more wonderful (Phil. 2:1–11).

It is touching to see how the women stood near the cross until the very end. John had also been there, but he had taken Mary, our Lord's mother, to his own home where he could care for her (John 19:25–27). Faithful women were the last at the cross on Friday and the first at the tomb on Sunday. What a contrast to the disciples, who had boasted that they would die for Him! The church of Jesus Christ owes much to the sacrifice and devotion of believing women.

The Servant's Burial (15:42–47)

The Jews recognized two evenings: "early evening," from three to six o'clock, and "evening," after six o'clock, when the new day would begin. This explains how both Matthew (27:57) and Mark could call late Friday afternoon "evening." It was important that the place of execution be quickly cleared, because the Jewish Sabbath was about to begin, and that Sabbath was a "high day" because of the Passover (John 19:31).

God had a wealthy member of the Sanhedrin, Joseph of Arimathea, ready to take care of the body of Jesus (Matt. 27:57). He was assisted by Nicodemus, also a member of the council (John 19:38–42). We must not think that these two men suddenly decided to bury Jesus, because what they did demanded much preparation.

To begin with, Joseph had to prepare the tomb in a garden near the place where Jesus died. This tomb was probably not for Joseph himself, since a wealthy man would not likely choose to be buried near a place of execution. The men also had to obtain a large quantity of spices (John 19:39), and this could not be done when the shops were closed for Passover. And all of this had to be done without the council's knowledge.

It seems evident that God prepared these two men and directed them in their activities. Nicodemus had come to Jesus privately (John 3) and had even defended Him before the council (John 7:45–53). I believe that Joseph and Nicodemus searched the Scriptures together and discovered, led by the Spirit, that the Lamb would die at Passover. It is possible that they were hiding in the new tomb when Jesus died. It was a simple matter for Joseph to go to Pilate for permission to take the body, and for Nicodemus to guard the body until the official release was given. Had these men not acted boldly, the body of Jesus might have been disposed of like rubbish.

It was important that His body be prepared for burial so that the empty graveclothes could be left behind in the tomb (John 20:1–10). Also, the way He was buried fulfilled prophecy (Isa. 53:9). The fact that He was buried is proof that Jesus actually died on the cross, for the Roman officials would not have released the body without proof that Jesus was dead.

The Servant's Resurrection (16:1–18)

Jesus Christ was "delivered for our offenses, and was raised again for our justification" (Rom. 4:25). A dead Savior cannot save anybody. The resurrection of Jesus Christ from the dead is as much a part of the gospel message as His sacrificial death on the cross (1 Cor. 15:1–8). In fact, in the book of Acts, the church gave witness primarily to the resurrection (Acts 1:22; 4:2, 33).

The resurrection proves that Jesus Christ is what He claimed to be, the very Son of God (Rom. 1:4). He had told His disciples that He would be raised from the dead, but they had not grasped the meaning of this truth (Mark 9:9–10, 31; 10:34). Even the women who came early to the tomb did not expect to see Him alive. In fact, they had purchased spices to complete the anointing that Joseph and Nicodemus had so hastily begun.

When you combine the accounts in the Gospels, you arrive at the following probable order of resurrection appearances on that first day of the week: (1) to Mary Magdalene (John 20:11–18 and Mark 16:9–11), (2) to the other women (Matt. 28:9–10), (3) to Peter (Luke 24:34 and 1 Cor. 15:5), (4) to the two men going to Emmaus (Mark 16:12 and Luke 24:13–32), and (5) to ten of the disciples in the Upper Room (Mark 16:14 and John 20:19–25).

It was still dark when Mary Magdalene, Mary the mother of James, Salome, and Joanna (Luke 24:10) started out for the tomb (John 20:1), and they arrived at early dawn (Luke 24:1). Their first surprise was finding the stone already rolled away from the door (Matt. 28:2–4) so that they were able to enter into the tomb. The second surprise was meeting two angels in the tomb (Luke 24:4; Mark focused on only one angel), and the third surprise was hearing the message they delivered. No wonder the women were amazed!

The message was that Jesus was not there: He had risen from the dead, and He was going before them into Galilee where He would meet them. The women were the first messengers of the glorious resurrection message! Note that there was a special word of encouragement for Peter (Mark 16:7), and keep in mind that Mark wrote his gospel with Peter's assistance.

Mary Magdalene ran to tell Peter and John what she had discovered (John 20:2–10), and then she lingered at the tomb after they left. It was then that Jesus appeared to her (John 20:11–18). From her conversation with Jesus, it seems that Mary did not fully grasp what the angels had said, but she was the first believer to see the risen Christ. Mark 16:8 may give the idea that all the women fled, but Mark 16:9 states that Mary met Jesus personally.

After He appeared to Mary, Jesus met the other women as they were on their way to report their conversation with Jesus to the disciples (Matt. 28:9–10). Initially, the women were both joyful and afraid, but after they met the risen Christ, they found the disciples and shared the good news (Matt. 28:8). It is one thing to hear the message and quite something else to meet the risen Lord personally. When you meet Him, you have something to share with others.

The emphasis in Mark 16:9–14 is on the unbelief of the disciples, who were mourning and weeping instead of rejoicing at the good news. Was it because they were prejudiced against the witness of the women? Perhaps, for the testimony of a woman was not accepted in a Jewish court. But even when the two Emmaus disciples gave their witness, not everybody believed. (Compare Mark 16:13 with Luke 24:33–35.) Apparently there was division in the Upper Room until Jesus Himself appeared.

But when He did appear, He reproached them for their unbelief, which was caused by their hardness of heart (see Mark 6:52; 8:17). He was making it clear that the witnesses of His resurrection could and should be trusted. The phrase "the Eleven" in Mark 16:14 simply means "the apostles," because there were only ten of them together at that time, since Thomas was absent (John 20:19–25).

Before His ascension forty days later, the Lord gave several commissions to His followers (Matt. 28:18–20; Luke 24:47–49; John 20:21; 21:15–17; Acts 1:4–8). The one Mark gives probably is a part of the Great Commission that Jesus gave on a mountain in Galilee (Matt. 28:16–20).

In this commission, Jesus pointed out our message and our ministry, and then backed it up with the miraculous credentials that only He could give. The message is the gospel, the good news of salvation through faith in Jesus Christ. The ministry is to share this message with the whole world.

A superficial reading of Mark 16:15–16 would suggest that sinners must be baptized to be saved, but this misinterpretation disappears when you note that the emphasis is on *believing*. If a person does not believe, he is condemned, even if he has been baptized (see John 3:16–18, 36). It was expected in the early church that believers would be baptized (Acts 2:41; 10:44–48).

When God sent Moses to challenge Pharaoh in Egypt, He gave him special miracles to perform as his divine credentials, proving that he was sent from God (Ex. 4:1–9). This was also true of some of the prophets (1 Kings 18; 2 Kings 2:14–25). The apostles were also given special "signs" that enforced their message (Acts 19:11–12; 2 Cor. 12:12; Heb. 2:3–4). Of themselves, miracles do not prove that a person has been sent by God, for the message must also be true to God's Word (see 2 Thess. 2; Rev. 13).

Most of the signs listed here did take place in the days of the apostles and are recorded in the book of Acts. The closest thing we have to taking up serpents is Paul's experience on Malta (Acts 28:3–6), but we have no biblical record of anyone drinking poison and surviving. No doubt God has performed many wonders for His own that we know nothing about, but we shall learn about them in heaven.

It is tragic when well-meaning but untaught people claim these signs for themselves and then die because of snake bites or poison. Of course, the excuse is given that they did not have enough faith! But whatever is not of faith is sin (Rom. 14:23); therefore, they should not have done it in the first place.

The person who takes up serpents just to prove his or her faith is yielding to the very temptation Satan presented to Jesus on the pinnacle of the temple (Matt. 4:5–7): "Cast Yourself down and see if God will take care of You," Satan said in effect. He wants us to "show off" our faith and force God to perform unnecessary miracles. Jesus refused to tempt God, and we should follow His example. Yes, God cares for His children when, in His will, they are in dangerous places, but He is not obligated to care for us when we foolishly get out of His will. We are called to live by faith, not by chance, and to trust God, not tempt Him.

The Servant's Ascension (16:19–20)

In a remarkable way, the gospel of Mark parallels the great "Servant passage" in Philippians 2.

> He came as a Servant (Phil. 2:1–7)—Mark 1—13
> He died on a cross (Phil. 2:8)—Mark 14—15
> He was exalted to glory (Phil. 2:9)—Mark 16

Both Paul and Mark emphasize the need for God's people to get the message out to all nations (Mark 16:15–16; Phil. 2:10–11), and there is the added assurance that God is at work in and through them (Mark 16:19–20; Phil. 2:12–13).

Our Lord's ascension marked the completion of

His earthly ministry and the beginning of His new ministry in heaven as High Priest and Advocate for His people (Heb. 7—10; 1 John 2:1–3). The "right hand of God" is the place of honor and authority (Ps. 110:1; 1 Peter 3:22). Our Lord is like Melchizedek, King of Righteousness and King of Peace (Gen. 14:17–19; Heb. 7:2).

One of His heavenly ministries is that of enabling His people to do His will (Heb. 13:20–21). It is fitting that the gospel of the Servant should end with this reference to work, just as it is fitting for Matthew, the gospel of the King, to end with a reference to His great authority. By His Holy Spirit, the Lord wants to work *in* us (Phil. 2:12–13), *with* us (Mark 16:20), and *for* us (Rom. 8:28).

The apostles and prophets laid the foundation for the church (Eph. 2:20), so their work is finished and the apostolic signs have ceased. But the Lord's working has not ceased, and He is still working in and through His people to save a lost world. His Servant-Son Jesus returned to heaven, but He still has His people on earth who can be His servants, if they will.

What a privilege to have the Lord working with us!

What an opportunity and obligation we have to carry the gospel to the whole world!

"For even the Son of man came not to be ministered unto, but to minister, and to give his life a ransom for many" (Mark 10:45).

Are you serving—or are you expecting others to serve you?

LUKE

OUTLINE

Key theme: Our Lord's journeys as the Son of Man
Key verse: Luke 19:10

I. JOURNEY FROM HEAVEN TO EARTH (1:5—4:13)
   A. Birth announcements—1:5–56
   B. The babies are born—1:57—2:20
   C. Jesus' childhood and youth—2:21–52
   D. Jesus' baptism and temptation—3:1—4:13

II. THE JOURNEY THROUGHOUT GALILEE (4:14—9:17)

III. THE JOURNEY TO JERUSALEM (9:18—19:27)

IV. THE MINISTRY IN JERUSALEM (19:28—24:53)

CONTENTS

CHAPTER ONE
Luke 1

HEAR THE GOOD NEWS!

If ever a man wrote a book filled with good news for everybody, Dr. Luke is that man. His key message is, "For the Son of man is come to seek and to save that which was lost" (Luke 19:10). He presents Jesus Christ as the compassionate Son of Man, who came to live among sinners, love them, help them, and die for them.

In this gospel you meet individuals as well as crowds, women and children as well as men, poor people as well as rich people, and sinners along with saints. It's a book with a message for *everybody,* because Luke's emphasis is on the universality of Jesus Christ and His salvation: "good tidings of great joy, which shall be to all people" (Luke 2:10).

Dr. Luke is named only three times in the New Testament: in Colossians 4:14; 2 Timothy 4:11; and Philemon 24. He wrote Acts (compare Luke 1:1–4 with Acts 1:1) and traveled with Paul (note the "we" sections in Acts 16:10–17; 20:4–15; 21:1–18, and 27:1—28:16). He was probably a Gentile (compare Colossians 4:11 and 14) and was trained as a physician. No wonder he began his book with detailed accounts of the births of two important babies! No wonder he emphasized Christ's sympathy for hurting people! He wrote with the mind of a careful historian and with the heart of a loving physician.

The gospel of Luke was written for Theophilus ("lover of God"), probably a Roman official who had trusted Christ and now needed to be established in the faith. It's also possible that Theophilus was a seeker after truth who was being taught the Christian message, because the word translated *instructed* in Luke 1:4 gives us our English word *catechumen,* "someone who is being taught the basics of Christianity."

The life and message of Christ were so important that many books had already been written about Him, but not everything in them could be trusted. Luke wrote his gospel so that his readers might have an accurate and orderly narrative of the life, ministry, and message of Jesus Christ. Luke had carefully researched his material, interviewed eyewitnesses, and listened to those who had ministered the Word. Most important, he had the guidance of the Holy Spirit. The phrase *from the very first* (Gk. *anothen*) can be translated "from above," as it is in John 3:31 and 19:11. It speaks of the inspiration of the Spirit of God on the message that Luke wrote.

In this first chapter, Luke tells us how God's wonderful news came to different people and how they responded to it. You will discover four different responses.

Unbelief (1:5–25)

It was indeed a dark day for the nation of Israel. The people had heard no prophetic word from God for four hundred years, not since Malachi had promised the coming of Elijah (Mal. 4:5–6). The spiritual leaders were shackled by tradition and, in some instances, corruption; and their king, Herod the Great, was a tyrant. He had nine (some say ten) wives, one of whom he had executed for no apparent reason. But no matter how dark the day, God always has His devoted and obedient people.

A faithful priest (vv. 5–7). Zacharias ("Jehovah has remembered") and Elizabeth ("God is my oath") were a godly couple who both belonged to the priestly line. The priests were divided into twenty-four courses (1 Chron. 24), and each priest served in the temple two weeks out of the year. In spite of the godlessness around them, Zacharias and Elizabeth were faithful to obey the Word of God and live blamelessly.

Their only sorrow was that they had no family, and they made this a matter of constant prayer. Little did they know that God would answer their prayers and give them, not a priest, but a prophet! And no ordinary prophet, for their son would be the herald of the coming King!

A fearful priest (vv. 8–17). The priests on duty drew lots to see which ministries they would perform, and Zacharias was chosen to offer incense in the holy place. This was a high honor that was permitted to a priest but once in a lifetime. The incense was offered daily before the morning sacrifice and after the evening sacrifice, about three o'clock in the afternoon. It was probably the evening offering that was assigned to Zacharias.

You have probably noticed that God often speaks to His people and calls them while they are busy doing their daily tasks. Both Moses and David were caring for sheep, and Gideon was threshing wheat. Peter and his partners were mending nets when Jesus called them. It is difficult to steer a car when the engine is not running. When we get busy, God starts to direct us.

Luke mentions angels twenty-three times in his gospel. There are innumerable angels (Rev. 5:11), only two of which are actually named in Scripture: Michael (Dan. 10:13, 21; 12:1; Jude 9; Rev. 12:7) and Gabriel (Dan. 8:16; 9:21; Luke 1:19, 26). When Gabriel appeared by the altar, Zacharias was frightened, for the angel's appearance could have meant divine judgment.

"Fear not" is a repeated statement in the gospel of Luke (1:13, 30; 2:10; 5:10; 8:50; 12:7, 32). Imagine how excited Zacharias must have been when he heard that he and Elizabeth were to have a son! "Rejoicing" is another key theme in Luke, mentioned at least nineteen times. Good news brings joy!

Gabriel instructed him to name his son John ("Jehovah is gracious") and to dedicate the boy to God to be a Nazarite all of his life (Num. 6:1–21). He would be filled with the Spirit before birth (Luke 1:41) and would be God's prophet to present His Son to the people of Israel (see John 1:15–34). God would use

John's ministry to turn many people back to the Lord, just as Isaiah had promised (Isa. 40:1–5).

A faithless priest (vv. 18–22). You would think that the presence of an angel and the announcement of God's Word would encourage Zacharias's faith, but they did not. Instead of looking to God by faith, the priest looked at himself and his wife and decided that the birth of a son was impossible. He wanted some assurance beyond the plain word of Gabriel, God's messenger, perhaps a sign from God.

This, of course, was unbelief, and unbelief is something God does not accept. Zacharias was really questioning God's ability to fulfill His own Word! Had he forgotten what God did for Abraham and Sarah (Gen. 18:9–15; Rom. 4:18–25)? Did he think that his physical limitations would hinder Almighty God? But before we criticize Zacharias too much, we should examine ourselves and see how strong our own faith is.

Faith is blessed, but unbelief is judged, and Zacharias was struck dumb (and possibly deaf, Luke 1:62) until the Word was fulfilled. "I believed, and therefore have I spoken" (2 Cor. 4:13). Zacharias did not believe; therefore he could not speak. When he left the holy place, he was unable to give the priestly benediction to the people (Num. 6:22–27) or even tell them what he had seen. Indeed, God had given him a very personal "sign" that he would have to live with for the next nine months.

A favored priest (vv. 23–25). Zacharias must have had a difficult time completing his week of ministry, not only because of his handicap, but also because of his excitement. He could hardly wait to return "to the hill country" (Luke 1:39) where he lived, to tell his wife the good news.

God kept His promise and Elizabeth conceived a son in her old age. "There is nothing too hard for the Lord" (Jer. 32:17). Apparently the amazement and curiosity of the people forced her to hide herself even as she praised the Lord for His mercy. Not only was she to have a son, but the birth of her son was evidence that *the Messiah was coming!* These were exciting days indeed!

Faith (1:26–38)

In the sixth month of Elizabeth's pregnancy, Gabriel brought a second birth announcement, this time to a young virgin in Nazareth named Mary. At least there was variety in his assignments: an old man, a young woman; a priest, a descendent of David the king; the temple, a common home; Jerusalem, Nazareth; unbelief, faith.

The people in Judah disdained the Jews in Galilee and claimed they were not "kosher" because of their contacts with the Gentiles there (Matt. 4:15). They especially despised the people from Nazareth (John 1:45–46). But God in His grace chose a girl from Nazareth in Galilee to be the mother of the promised Messiah!

When it comes to Mary, people tend to go to one of two extremes. They either magnify her so much that Jesus takes second place (Luke 1:32), or they ignore her and fail to give her the esteem she deserves (Luke 1:48). Elizabeth, filled with the Spirit, called her "the mother of my Lord" (Luke 1:43), and that is reason enough to honor her.

What do we know about Mary? She was a Jewess of the tribe of Judah, a descendant of David, and a virgin (Isa. 7:14). She was engaged to a carpenter in Nazareth named Joseph (Matt. 13:55), and apparently both of them were poor (Lev. 12:8; Luke 2:24). Among the Jews at that time, engagement was almost as binding as marriage and could be broken only by divorce, to fact, the man and the woman were called "husband" and "wife" even before the marriage took place (compare Matt. 1:19 and Luke 2:5). Since Jewish girls married young, it is likely that Mary was a teenager when the angel appeared to her.

Mary's surprise (vv. 26–33). When you consider Gabriel's greeting, you can well understand why Mary was perplexed and afraid: "Greetings, you who are highly favored! The Lord is with you!" (The phrase *Blessed art thou among women* is not found here in many Greek manuscripts. You find it in Luke 1:42.) Why would an angel come to greet *her?* In what way was she "highly favored" ("greatly graced") by God? How was God with her?

Mary's response reveals her humility and honesty before God. She certainly never expected to see an angel and receive special favors from heaven. There was nothing unique about her that such things should happen. If she had been different from other Jewish girls, as some theologians claim she was, then she might have said, "Well, it's about time! I've been expecting you!" No, all of this was a surprise to her.

Gabriel then gave her the good news: she would become the mother of the promised Messiah whom she would name *Jesus* ("Jehovah is salvation"; see Matt. 1:21). Note that Gabriel affirmed both the deity and the humanity of Jesus. As Mary's son, He would be human; as Son of the Highest (Luke 1:32), He would be the Son of God (Luke 1:35). "For unto us a child is born [His humanity], unto us a son is given [His deity]" (Isa. 9:6). The emphasis is on the greatness of the Son (cf. Luke 1:15), not the greatness of the mother.

But He would also be a king, inherit David's throne, and reign over Israel forever! If we interpret literally what Gabriel said in Luke 1:30–31, then we should also interpret literally what he said in Luke 1:32–33. He was referring to God's covenant with David (2 Sam. 7) and His kingdom promises to the people of Israel (Isa. 9:1–7; 11–12; 61; 66; Jer. 33).

Jesus came to earth to be the Savior of the world, but He also came to fulfill the promises God made to the Jewish fathers (Rom. 15:14). Today, Jesus is enthroned in heaven (Acts 2:29–36), but it is not on *David's* throne. One day Jesus will return and establish His righteous kingdom on earth, and then these promises will be fulfilled.

Mary's surrender (vv. 34–48). Mary knew *what* would happen, but she did not know *how* it would happen. Her question in Luke 1:34 was not an evidence of unbelief (cf. Luke 1:18); rather, it was an expression of faith. She believed the promise, but she did not understand the performance. How could a virgin give birth to a child?

First, Gabriel explained that this would be a miracle, the work of the Holy Spirit of God. Joseph, her betrothed, would not be the father of the child (Matt. 1:18–25), even though Jesus would be legally identified as the son of Joseph (Luke 3:23; 4:22; John 1:45; 6:42). It's possible that some people thought Mary had been unfaithful to Joseph and that Jesus was "born of fornication" (John 8:41). This was a part of the pain that Mary had to bear all her life (Luke 2:35).

Gabriel was careful to point out that the Baby would be a "holy thing" and would not share the sinful human nature of man. Jesus knew no sin (2 Cor. 5:21), He did no sin (1 Peter 2:22), and He had no sin (1 John 3:5). His body was prepared for Him by the Spirit of God (Heb. 10:5) who "overshadowed" Mary. That word is applied to the presence of God in the Holy of Holies in the Jewish tabernacle and temple (Ex. 40:35). Mary's womb became a Holy of Holies for the Son of God!

The angel ended his message by giving Mary a word of encouragement: her aged relative Elizabeth was with child, proving that "with God nothing shall be impossible." God gave a similar word to Abraham when He announced the birth of Isaac (Gen. 18:14). That our God can do anything is the witness of many, including Job (Job 42:2), Jeremiah (Jer. 32:17), and even our Lord Jesus (Matt. 19:26). I personally like the translation of this verse found in the 1901 American Standard Version: "For no word of God shall be void of power." God accomplishes His purposes through the power of His Word (Ps. 33:9).

Mary's believing response was to surrender herself to God as His willing servant. She experienced the grace of God (Luke 1:30) and believed the Word of God, and therefore she could be used by the Spirit to accomplish the will of God. A "handmaid" was the lowest kind of female servant, which shows how much Mary trusted God. She belonged totally to the Lord, body (Luke 1:38), soul (Luke 1:46), and spirit (Luke 1:47). What an example for us to follow (Rom. 12:1–2)!

Joy (1:39–56)

Now that Mary knew she was to become a mother, and that her kinswoman Elizabeth would give birth in three months, she wanted to see Elizabeth so they could rejoice together. "Joy" is the major theme of this section as you see three persons rejoicing in the Lord.

The joy of Elizabeth (vv. 39–45). As Mary entered the house, Elizabeth heard her greeting, was filled with the Spirit, and was told by the Lord why Mary was there. The one word that filled her lips was "blessed." Note that she did not say that Mary was blessed *above* women but *among* women, and certainly this is true. While we don't want to ascribe to Mary that which only belongs to God, neither do we want to minimize her place in the plan of God.

The thing that Elizabeth emphasized was Mary's *faith*: "Blessed is she that believed" (Luke 1:45). We are saved "by grace … through faith" (Eph. 2:8–9). Because Mary believed the Word of God, she experienced the power of God.

The joy of the unborn son, John (vv. 41, 44). This was probably the time when he was filled with the Spirit as the angel had promised (Luke 1:15). Even before his birth, John rejoiced in Jesus Christ, just as he did during his earthly ministry (John 3:29–30). As John the Baptist, he would have the great privilege of introducing the Messiah to the Jewish nation.

The joy of Mary (vv. 46–56). Hers was a joy that compelled her to lift her voice in a hymn of praise. The fullness of the Spirit should lead to joyful praise in our lives (Eph. 5:18–20), and so should the fullness of the Word (Col. 3:16–17). Mary's song contains quotations from and references to the Old Testament Scriptures, especially the Psalms and the song of Hannah in 1 Samuel 2:1–10. Mary hid God's Word in her heart and turned it into a song.

This song is called "The Magnificat" because the Latin version of Luke 1:46 is *Magnificat anima mea Dominum.* Her great desire was to magnify the Lord, not herself. She used the phrase "He hath" eight times as she recounted what God had done for three recipients of His blessing.

What God did for Mary (vv. 46–49). To begin with, God had saved her (Luke 1:47), which indicates that Mary was a sinner like all of us and needed to trust the Lord for her eternal salvation. Not only had He saved her, but He had also chosen her to be the mother of the Messiah (Luke 1:48). He had "regarded" her, which means He was mindful of her and looked with favor on her. No doubt there were others who could have been chosen, but God chose her! The Lord had indeed showered His grace on her (see 1 Cor. 1:26–28).

Not only was God mindful of her, but He was also mighty for her, working on her behalf (Luke 1:49). Mary would have no problem singing "great things he hath done" (see Luke 8:39; 1 Sam. 12:24; 2 Sam. 7:21–23; and Ps. 126:2–3). Because she believed God and yielded to His will, He performed a miracle in her life and used her to bring the Savior into the world.

What God did for us (vv. 50–53). In the second stanza of her song, Mary included *all* of God's people who fear Him from generation to generation. We have all received His mercy and experienced His help. Mary named three specific groups to whom God had been merciful: the helpless (Luke 1:51), the humble (Luke 1:52), and the hungry (Luke 1:53).

The common people of that day were almost helpless when it came to justice and civil rights. They were often hungry, downtrodden, and discouraged (Luke

4:16–19), and there was no way for them to "fight the system." A secret society of patriotic Jewish extremists called "the Zealots" used violent means to oppose Rome, but their activities only made matters worse.

Mary saw the Lord turning everything upside down: the weak dethrone the mighty, the humble scatter the proud, the nobodies are exalted, the hungry are filled, and the rich end up poor! The grace of God works contrary to the thoughts and ways of this world system (1 Cor. 1:26–28). The church is something like that band of men that gathered around David (1 Sam. 22:2).

What God did for Israel (vv. 54–55). "He shall save his people from their sins" (Matt. 1:21). In spite of Israel's destitute condition, the nation was still God's servant, and He would help the people fulfill His purposes. God was on Israel's side! He would remember His mercy and keep His promises (Ps. 98:1–3; see also Gen. 12:1–3; 17:19; 22:18; 26:4; 28:14). Were it not for Israel, Jesus Christ could not have been born into the world.

Mary stayed with Elizabeth until John was born, and then she returned to Nazareth. By then, it was clear that she was pregnant, and no doubt the tongues began to wag. After all, she had been away from home for three months, and why, people were likely asking, had she left in such a hurry? It was then that God gave the good news to Joseph and instructed him what to do (Matt. 1:18–25).

Praise (1:57–80)

God's blessing was resting abundantly on Zacharias and Elizabeth. He sent them a baby boy, just as He promised, and they named him "John" just as God had instructed. The Jews looked on children as a gift from God and a "heritage from the Lord" (Ps. 127:3–5; 128:1–3), and rightly so, for they are. Israel would not follow the practices of their pagan neighbors by aborting or abandoning their children. When you consider that 1.5 million babies are aborted each year in the United States alone, you can see how far we have drifted from the laws of God.

"The greatest forces in the world are not the earthquakes and the thunderbolts," said Dr. E. T. Sullivan. "The greatest forces in the world are babies."

Traditionally, a baby boy would be named after his father or someone else in the family, so the relatives and neighbors were shocked when Elizabeth insisted on the name *John.* Zacharias wrote "His name is John" on a tablet, and that settled it! Immediately God opened the old priest's mouth, and he sang a hymn that gives us four beautiful pictures of what the coming of Jesus Christ to earth really means.

The opening of a prison door (v. 68). The word *redeem* means "to set free by paying a price." It can refer to the releasing of a prisoner or the liberating of a slave. Jesus Christ came to earth to bring "deliverance to the captives" (Luke 4:18), salvation to people in bondage to sin and death. Certainly we are unable to set ourselves free; only Christ could pay the price necessary for our redemption (Eph. 1:7; 1 Peter 1:18–21).

The winning of a battle (vv. 69–75). In Scripture, a horn symbolizes power and victory (1 Kings 22:11; Ps. 89:17, 24). The picture here is that of an army about to be taken captive, but then help arrives and the enemy is defeated. In the previous picture, the captives were set free, but in this picture, the enemy is defeated so *that he cannot capture more prisoners.* It means total victory for the people of God.

The word *salvation* (Luke 1:69, 71) carries the meaning of "health and soundness." No matter what the condition of the captives, their Redeemer brings spiritual soundness. When you trust Jesus Christ as Savior, you are delivered from Satan's power, moved into God's kingdom, redeemed, and forgiven (Col. 1:12–14).

Where did the Redeemer come from? He came from the house of David (Luke 1:69), who himself was a great conqueror. God had promised that the Savior would be a Jew (Gen. 12:1–3), from the tribe of Judah (Gen. 49:10), from the family of David (2 Sam. 7:12–16), born in David's city, Bethlehem (Mic. 5:2). Both Mary (Luke 1:27) and Joseph (Matt. 1:20) belonged to David's line. The coming of the Redeemer was inherent in the covenants God made with His people (Luke 1:72), and it was promised by the prophets (Luke 1:70).

Note that the results of this victory are sanctity and service (Luke 1:74–75). He sets us free, not to do our own will, because that would be bondage, but to do His will and enjoy His freedom.

The canceling of a debt (vv. 76–77). *Remission* means "to send away, to dismiss, as a debt." All of us are in debt to God because we have broken His law and failed to live up to His standards (Luke 7:40–50). Furthermore, all of us are spiritually bankrupt, unable to pay our debt. But Jesus came and paid the debt for us (Ps. 103:12; John 1:29).

The dawning of a new day (vv. 78–79). *Dayspring* means "sunrise." The people were sitting in darkness and death, and distress gripped them when Jesus came; but He brought light, life, and peace. It was the dawn of a new day because of the tender mercies of God (see Matt. 4:16).

The old priest had not said anything for nine months, but he certainly compensated for his silence when he sang this song of praise to God! And how joyful he was that his son was chosen by God to prepare the way for the Messiah (Isa. 40:1–3; Mal. 3:1). John was "prophet of the Highest" (Luke 1:76), introducing to Israel "the Son of the Highest" (Luke 1:32) who was conceived in Mary's womb by "the power of the Highest" (Luke 1:35).

Instead of enjoying a comfortable life as a priest, John lived in the wilderness, disciplining himself physically and spiritually, waiting for the day when God would send him out to prepare Israel for the arrival of the Messiah. People like Simeon and Anna (Luke

2:25–38) had been waiting for this day for many years, and soon it would come.

God calls us today to believe His good news. Those who believe it experience His joy and want to express their praise to Him. It is not enough for us to say that Jesus is *a* Savior, or even *the* Savior. With Mary, we must say, "My spirit hath rejoiced in God *my* Savior" (Luke 1:47, italics mine).

CHAPTER TWO
Luke 2
THE LORD IS COME!

Luke 2 may well be the most familiar and beloved portion in Luke's gospel. My wife and I still read the first twenty verses together each Christmas Eve, just as we did when our children were growing up. The story is old, but it is ever new, and God's people never tire of it.

Dr. Luke gives us three glimpses into the early years of the Lord Jesus Christ.

The Newborn Baby (2:1–20)

"As weak as a baby!" is a common expression that could not be applied to the Baby Jesus in the manger. While He was as weak as any other baby humanly speaking, He was also the center of power as far as heaven was concerned.

His birth drew Mary and Joseph to Bethlehem (vv. 1–7). Augustus Caesar was ruling, but God was in charge, for He used Caesar's edict to move Mary and Joseph eighty miles from Nazareth to Bethlehem to fulfill His Word. Rome took a census every fourteen years for both military and tax purposes, and each Jewish male had to return to the city of his fathers to record his name, occupation, property, and family.

When Mary said "Be it unto me according to thy word" (Luke 1:38), it meant that from then on, her life would be a part of the fulfillment of divine prophecy. God had promised that the Savior would be a human, not an angel (Gen. 3:15; Heb. 2:16), and a Jew, not a Gentile (Gen. 12:1–3; Num. 24:17). He would be from the tribe of Judah (Gen. 49:10), and the family of David (2 Sam. 7:1–17), born of a virgin (Isa. 7:14) in Bethlehem, the city of David (Mic. 5:2).

All of this occurred just as the Scriptures said, and Caesar unknowingly played an important part. A. T. Pierson used to say, "History is His story," and President James A. Garfield called history "the unrolled scroll of prophecy." If God's Word controls our lives, then the events of history only help us fulfill the will of God. "I am watching over My word to perform it," promises the Lord (Jer. 1:12 NASB).

Mary and Joseph were already husband and wife, but since they did not consummate the marriage until after Jesus was born, she is called his "espoused wife" (Matt. 1:18–25). The journey must have been very trying for her, but she rejoiced in doing the will of God, and she was no doubt glad to get away from the wagging tongues in Nazareth.

Mothers in that day wrapped their infants in long bands of cloth to give the limbs strength and protection. The word translated "manger" (Luke 2:7, 12, 16) is translated "stall" in Luke 13:15, and can mean either a feeding trough or an enclosure for animals. You see ancient stone troughs even today as you travel in the Holy Land, and it is probable that such a trough cradled the infant Jesus. Many scholars believe that our Lord was born in a cave where animals were sheltered and not in a wooden shed such as you see in modern manger scenes.

Bethlehem means "house of bread," the ideal birthplace for the Bread of Life (John 6:35). Its rich historic heritage included the death of Rachel and the birth of Benjamin (Gen. 35:16–20; see also Matt. 2:16–18), the marriage of Ruth, and the exploits of David. It is worth noting that the name *Benjamin* means "son of my right hand," and the name *David* means "beloved." Both of these names apply to our Lord, for He is the Beloved Son (Luke 3:22) at God's right hand (Ps. 110:1).

His birth drew the angels from heaven (vv. 8–14). How amazed the angels must have been when they saw the Creator born as a creature, the Word coming as a speechless baby. The best commentary on this is 2 Corinthians 8:9, and the best response from our hearts is wonder and worship. "Great is the mystery of godliness: God was manifest in the flesh" (1 Tim. 3:16).

The first announcement of the Messiah's birth was given by an angel to some anonymous shepherds. Why shepherds? Why not to priests or scribes? By visiting the shepherds, the angel revealed the grace of God toward mankind. Shepherds were really outcasts in Israel. Their work not only made them ceremonially unclean, but it kept them away from the temple for weeks at a time so that they could not be made clean. God does not call the rich and mighty; He calls the poor and the lowly (Luke 1:51–53; 1 Cor. 1:26–29).

The Messiah came to be both the Good Shepherd (John 10) and the Lamb of God sacrificed for the sins of the world (John 1:29). Perhaps these shepherds were caring for the flocks that would provide sacrifices for the temple services. It was fitting that the good news about God's Shepherd and Lamb be given first to humble shepherds.

Shepherds are not easily fooled. They are practical men of the world who have little to do with fantasy. If they said that they saw angels and went and found the Messiah, then you could believe them. God selected hard-working men to be the first witnesses that His Son had come into the world.

First, one angel appeared (Gabriel?) and gave the glad announcement, and then a chorus of angels joined him and gave an anthem of praise. For the first time in centuries, the glory of God returned to earth. If brave shepherds were afraid at what they saw and heard, then you can be sure it was real!

"Fear not!" is one of the key themes of the Christmas story (Luke 1:13, 30, 74; and see Matt. 1:20). Literally the angel said, "I announce to you good news, a great joy which shall be to all the people." He used the word that means "to preach the good news," a word Luke uses often in both his gospel and in the book of Acts. We see here Luke's emphasis on a worldwide gospel: the good news is for everybody, not just the Jews.

What was the good news? Not that God had sent a soldier or a judge or a reformer, but that He had sent a Savior to meet man's greatest need. It was a message of peace to a world that had known much war. The famous "Pax Romana" (Roman Peace) had been in effect since 27 BC, but the absence of war doesn't guarantee the presence of peace.

The Stoic philosopher Epictetus said, "While the emperor may give peace from war on land and sea, he is unable to give peace from passion, grief, and envy. He cannot give peace of heart for which man yearns more than even for outward peace."

The Jewish word *shalom* (peace) means much more than a truce in the battles of life. It means well-being, health, prosperity, security, soundness, and completeness. It has to do more with character than circumstances. Life was difficult at that time just as it is today. Taxes were high, unemployment was high, morals were slipping lower, and the military state was in control. Roman law, Greek philosophy, and even Jewish religion could not meet the needs of men's hearts. Then, God sent His Son!

The angels praised God at creation (Job 38:7), and now they praised Him at the beginning of the new creation. The whole purpose of the plan of salvation is "glory to God" (see Eph. 1:6, 12, 14). God's glory had dwelt in the tabernacle (Ex. 40:34) and in the temple (2 Chron. 7:1–3), but had departed because of the nation's sin (1 Sam. 4:21; Ezek. 8:4; 9:3; 10:4, 18; 11:22–23). Now God's glory was returning to earth in the person of His Son (John 1:14). That lowly manger was a Holy of Holies because Jesus was there!

His birth drew the shepherds from the fields (vv. 15–20). The phrase "even unto Bethlehem" suggests that these men were located some distance away, but they were willing to make the trip in order to see the newborn Messiah. Certainly they arranged for others to care for their flocks while they hastened to Bethlehem. Halford Luccock called this "the first Christmas rush," but it was certainly different from the Christmas rushes we see today!

The verb *found* in Luke 2:16 means "found after a search." The shepherds knew what to look for: a newborn Baby wrapped in swaddling clothes and lying in a manger. And they found Him! They worshipped Him and marveled at God's grace and goodness and the miracle He had wrought for them.

These shepherds are good examples for us to imitate today. They received by faith the message God sent them and then responded with immediate obedience. After finding the Baby, they reported the good news to others, "glorifying and praising God." *They took the place of the angels* (Luke 2:13–14)! Then they humbly returned to their duties, new men going back to the same old job.

For some reason, shepherds were not permitted to testify in court, but God used some humble shepherds to be the first human witnesses that prophecy had been fulfilled and the Messiah had been born. The angels have never experienced the grace of God, so they can't bear witness as we can. Telling others about the Savior is a solemn obligation as well as a great privilege, and we who are believers must be faithful.

The Child (2:21–38)

Dr. Luke now tells us about three important meetings in the temple in Jerusalem: the child Jesus met Moses (Luke 2:20–24), Simeon (Luke 2:25–35), and Anna (Luke 2:36–38).

Moses (vv. 21–24). Note that the word *law* is used five times in Luke 2:21–40. Though He came to deliver His people from the bondage of the law, Jesus was "made under the law" and obeyed its commands (Gal. 4:1–7). He did not come to destroy the law but to fulfill it (Matt. 5:17–18).

Jesus' parents obeyed the law first by having the child circumcised when He was eight days old. This was the sign and seal of the covenant that God made with Abraham (Gen. 17), and it was required of every Jewish male who wanted to practice the faith. The Jews were proud to be God's covenant people, and they scornfully called the Gentiles "the uncircumcision" (Eph. 2:11–12). It is unfortunate that circumcision became an empty ritual for many Jews, because it proclaimed an important spiritual truth (Deut. 10:15–20; Rom. 2:28–29).

"His circumcision was His first suffering for us," said the late Donald Grey Barnhouse, a Philadelphia minister and author. It symbolized the work the Savior did on the cross in dealing with our sin nature (Gal. 6:15; Phil. 3:1–3; Col. 2:10–11). In obedience to the Lord, Mary and Joseph gave Him the name *Jesus,* which means "Jehovah is salvation" (Matt. 1:21).

But circumcision was only the beginning. When the child was forty days old, Mary and Joseph had to come to the temple for the purification rites described in Leviticus 12. They also had to "redeem" the boy since He was Mary's firstborn (Ex. 13:1–12). They had to pay five shekels to redeem the Redeemer who would one day redeem us with His precious blood (1 Peter 1:18–19). Their humble sacrifice would suggest that they were too poor to bring a lamb (2 Cor. 8:9). But He was the Lamb!

Our Lord's relationship to the law is an important part of His saving ministry. He was made under the law (Gal. 4:4); and though He rejected man's religious traditions, He obeyed God's law perfectly (John 8:46). He bore the curse of the law for us (Gal. 3:13) and set us free from bondage (Gal. 5:1).

Simeon (vv. 25–35). Simeon and Anna, like Zacharias and Elizabeth, were a part of the faithful Jewish remnant that eagerly looked for their Messiah (Mal. 3:16). Because of his readiness and eagerness to die (Luke 2:29), Simeon is usually pictured as a very old man, but nothing in Scripture supports this. Tradition says he was 113 years old, but it is only tradition.

"The consolation of Israel" means the messianic hope. One of the traditional Jewish prayers is, "May I see the consolation of Israel!" That prayer was answered for Simeon when he saw Jesus Christ in the temple. He was a man who was led by the Spirit of God, taught by the Word of God, and obedient to the will of God, and therefore he was privileged to see the salvation of God. How important it is for people to see God's salvation, Jesus Christ, before they see death.

In Luke 2:29–32 we find Simeon's response to seeing Jesus. This is the fifth and last of the "Christmas songs" in Luke. (Elizabeth, 1:42–45; Mary, 1:46–56; Zacharias, 1:67–79; the angels, 2:13–14.) It is first of all a *worship* hymn as he blesses God for keeping His promise and sending the Messiah. He joyfully praises God that he has been privileged to see the Lord's Christ.

But his song is also a *salvation* hymn: "For mine eyes have seen thy salvation" (Luke 2:30). Now he is ready to die! The word *depart* in the Greek has several meanings, and each of them tells us something about the death of a Christian. It means to release a prisoner, to untie a ship and set sail, to take down a tent (see 2 Cor. 5:1–8), and to unyoke a beast of burden (see Matt. 11:28–30). God's people are not afraid of death because it only frees us from the burdens of this life and leads into the blessings of the next life.

Simeon's song is a *missionary* hymn, which is something unusual for a devout Jew standing in the temple. He sees this great salvation going out to the Gentiles! Jesus has restored the glory to Israel and brought the light to the Gentiles so that all people can be saved (see Luke 2:10). Remember that the compassion of Christ for the whole world is one of Luke's major themes.

Then Simeon stopped praising and started prophesying (Luke 2:34–35), and in his message used three important images: the stone, the sign, and the sword.

The stone is an important Old Testament image of God (Gen. 49:24; Ps. 18:2; 71:3; Deut. 32:31). Messiah would be a "rejected cornerstone" (Ps. 118:22; Luke 20:17–18; Acts 4:11), and the nation of Israel would stumble over Him (Isa. 8:14; Rom. 9:32). Because of Jesus Christ, many in Israel would fall in conviction and then rise in salvation. (Simeon seems to be speaking about one group, not two.) Even today, God's people Israel stumble over the cross (1 Cor. 1:23) and do not understand that Jesus is their Rock (1 Peter 2:1–6).

The word *sign* means "a miracle," not so much as a demonstration of power but as a revelation of divine truth. Our Lord's miracles in John's gospel are called "signs" because they reveal special truths

about Him (John 20:30–31). Jesus Christ is God's miracle, and yet, instead of admiring Him, the people attacked Him and spoke against Him. His birth was a miracle, yet they slandered it (John 8:41). They said His miracles were done in the power of Satan (Matt. 12:22–24) and that His character was questionable (John 8:48, 52; 9:16, 24). They slandered His death (Ps. 22:6–8; Matt. 27:39–44) and lied about His resurrection (Matt. 27:62–66). Today, people are even speaking against His coming again (2 Peter 3).

But the way people speak about Jesus Christ is evidence of what is in their hearts. He is not only the "salvation stone" and the "judgment stone" (Dan. 2:34, 45), but He is also the "touchstone" that exposes what people are really like. "What think ye of Christ?" (Matt. 22:42) is still the most important question for anybody to answer (1 John 4:1–3).

The image of the sword was for Mary alone, and it spoke of the suffering and sorrow she would bear as the mother of the Messiah. (This suggests that Joseph was dead when Jesus began His ministry thirty years later, or Joseph would have been included.) The Greek word means a large sword such as Goliath used (1 Sam. 17:51), and the verb means "constantly keep on piercing."

During our Lord's life and ministry, Mary did experience more and more sorrow until one day she stood by His cross and saw Him suffer and die (John 19:25–27). However, without minimizing her devotion, Mary's personal pain must not in any way be made a part of Christ's redemptive work. Only He could die for the sins of the world (1 Tim. 2:5–6).

How much did Mary and Joseph understand of God's great plan for this miracle Child? We don't know, but we do know that Mary stored up all these things and pondered them (Luke 2:19, 51). The word means "to put things together"; Mary sought for some pattern that would help her understand God's will. There were times when Mary misunderstood Him (Mark 3:31–35), and this would add to her suffering. The last time you find Mary named in Scripture, she is in the Upper Room, praying with the other believers (Acts 1:14).

Anna (vv. 36–38). Her name means "grace," and she was a godly widow of great age. There are forty-three references to women in Luke's gospel, and of the twelve widows mentioned in the Bible, Luke has three (Luke 2:36–40; 7:11–15; 21:1–4; and note 18:1–8). It isn't difficult to see the heart of a physician in Luke's presentation.

Widows didn't have an easy time in that day; often they were neglected and exploited in spite of the commandment of the law (Ex. 22:21–22; Deut. 10:17–18; 14:29; Isa. 1:17). Anna devoted herself to "serving God by worship" through fastings and prayers. She moved from the tribe of Asher and remained in the temple, waiting for the appearing of God's promised Messiah (see 1 Tim. 5:3–16).

God's timing is always perfect. Anna came up just as Simeon was praising the Lord for the Child Jesus, so she joined in the song! I would like to have heard these elderly people singing in the temple! Their praise was inspired by the Spirit of God, and God accepted it. But Anna did much more than sing; she also spread the good news among the other faithful members of "the remnant" who were waiting for the redemption of Israel. The excitement began to spread as more and more people heard the good news.

Anna was a prophetess, which meant she had a special gift of declaring and interpreting God's message. Other prophetesses in Scripture are Miriam (Ex. 15:20), Deborah (Judg. 4:4), Huldah (2 Kings 22:14), Noadiah (Neh. 6:14), and the wife of Isaiah (Isa. 8:3). The evangelist Philip had four daughters who were prophetesses (Acts 21:8–9).

The Youth (2:39–52)

Having obeyed the law in everything, Mary and Joseph returned to Nazareth, which would be our Lord's home until He started His official ministry. There were many Jewish men with the name *Jesus* (Joshua), so He would be known as "Jesus of Nazareth" (Acts 2:22), and His followers would be called "Nazarenes" (Acts 24:5; see Matt. 2:23). His enemies used the name scornfully and Pilate even hung it on the cross (Matt. 21:11), but Jesus was not ashamed to use it when He spoke from heaven (Acts 22:8). That which men scorned (John 1:46), Jesus Christ took to heaven and made glorious!

What did Jesus do during the "hidden years" at Nazareth? Dr. Luke reports that the lad developed physically, mentally, socially, and spiritually (Luke 2:40, 52). In His incarnation, the Son of God set aside the independent use of His own divine attributes and submitted Himself wholly to the Father (Phil. 2:1–11). There are deep mysteries here that no one can fully understand or explain, but we have no problem accepting them by faith.

Jesus did not perform any miracles as a boy, traditions notwithstanding, because the turning of water into wine was the beginning of His miracles (John 2:1–11). He worked with Joseph in the carpenter shop (Matt. 13:55; Mark 6:3) and apparently ran the business after Joseph died. Joseph and Mary had other children during those years (Matt. 13:55–56; John 7:1–10), for the "until" of Matthew 1:25 indicates that the couple eventually had normal marital relations.

Luke gives us only one story from our Lord's youthful years. Joseph and Mary were devout Jews who observed Passover in Jerusalem every year. Three times a year the Jewish men were required to go to Jerusalem to worship (Deut. 16:16), but not all of them could afford to do so. If they chose one feast, it was usually the Passover, and they tried to take their family with them, for it was the most important feast on the Jewish calendar.

People traveled to the feasts in caravans, the women and children leading the way and setting the pace, and the men and young men following behind. Relatives and whole villages often traveled together and kept an eye on each other's children. At the age of twelve, Jesus could easily have gone from one group to another and not been missed. Joseph would think Jesus was with Mary and the other children, while Mary would suppose He was with Joseph and the men, or perhaps with one of their relatives.

They had gone a day's journey from Jerusalem when they discovered that Jesus was missing. It took a day to return to the city and another day for them to find Him. During those three days, Joseph and Mary had been "greatly distressed" (Luke 2:48, "sorrowing"). This word is used to describe Paul's concern for lost Israel (Rom. 9:2) as well as the pain of lost souls in hades (Luke 16:24–25).

It is worth noting that Luke's phrase "Joseph and his mother" (Luke 2:43) suggests the virgin birth, while the phrase "thy father and I" (Luke 2:48) indicates that Joseph was accepted as the legal father of Jesus (see Luke 3:23). To use Luke 2:48 to disprove the virgin birth is stretching a point.

Whether Jesus had spent the entire time in the temple, we don't know. It certainly would have been safe there, and the heavenly Father was watching over Him. We do know that when Joseph and Mary found Him, He was in the midst of the teachers, asking them questions and listening to their answers, and the teachers were amazed at both His questions and His answers.

Mary's loving rebuke brought a respectful but astonished reply from Jesus: "Why is it that you were looking for Me? Did you not know that I had to be in My Father's house?" (Luke 2:49 NASB). It can also be translated "in the things of My Father" (NASB margin), but the idea is the same. Jesus was affirming His divine sonship and His mission to do the will of the Father.

The word *must* was often on our Lord's lips: "I must preach" (Luke 4:43); "The Son of man must suffer" (Luke 9:22); the Son of Man "must be lifted up" (John 3:14). Even at the age of twelve, Jesus was moved by a divine compulsion to do the Father's will.

Since Jesus "increased in wisdom" (Luke 2:52), we wonder how much He understood God's divine plan at that time. We must not assume that at the age of twelve He was omniscient. Certainly He grew in His comprehension of those mysteries as He communed with His Father and was taught by the Spirit.

One thing is sure: Joseph and Mary didn't understand! This was a part of the pain from "the sword" that Simeon had promised her (Luke 2:35), and no doubt it happened again and again as the boy matured. Years later, during His ministry, our Lord's family didn't understand Him (Luke 8:19–21; John 7:1–5).

Jesus is a wonderful example for all young people to follow. He grew in a balanced way (Luke 2:52) without neglecting any part of life, and His priority was to do the will of His Father (see Matt. 6:33). He knew how to listen (Luke 2:46) and how to ask the right questions. He learned how to work, and He was obedient to His parents.

The Boy Jesus grew up in a large family, in a despised city, nurtured by parents who were probably poor. The Jewish religion was at an all-time low, the Roman government was in control, and society was in a state of fear and change. Yet when Jesus emerged from Nazareth, eighteen years later, the Father was able to say of Him, "Thou art my beloved Son; in thee I am well pleased" (Luke 3:22).

May the Father be able to say that about us!

CHAPTER THREE
Luke 3—4
THIS IS THE SON OF GOD!

I f Socrates would enter the room, we should rise and do him honor," said Napoleon Bonaparte. "But if Jesus Christ came into the room, we should fall down on our knees and worship Him."

Dr. Luke would have agreed with the famous French general, for in these two chapters, he makes it clear that Jesus Christ of Nazareth is indeed the Son of God. Notice the witnesses that he presents, all of whom declare that Jesus is God's Son.

John the Baptist (3:1–20)
When he came (vv. 1–2). When John the Baptist appeared on the scene, no prophetic voice had been heard in Israel for four hundred years. His coming was a part of God's perfect timing, for everything that relates to God's Son is always on schedule (Gal. 4:4; John 2:4; 13:1). The fifteenth year of Tiberius Caesar was AD 28/29.

Luke named seven different men in Luke 3:1–2, including a Roman emperor, a governor, three tetrarchs (rulers over a fourth part of an area), and two Jewish high priests. But God's Word was not sent to any of them! Instead, the message of God came to John the Baptist, a humble Jewish prophet.

How he came (v. 3). Resembling the prophet Elijah in manner and dress (Luke 1:17; Matt. 3:4; 2 Kings 1:8), John came to the area near the Jordan River, preaching and baptizing. He announced the arrival of the kingdom of heaven (Matt. 3:3) and urged the people to repent. Centuries before, Israel had crossed the Jordan (a national baptism) to claim their Promised Land. Now God summoned them to turn from sin and enter His spiritual kingdom.

Keep in mind that John did much more than preach against sin; he also proclaimed the gospel. The word *preached* in Luke 3:18 gives us the English word *evangelize* ("to preach the good news"). John introduced Jesus as the Lamb of God (John 1:29) and told people to trust in Him. John was only the best man at the wedding: Jesus was the Bridegroom (John 3:25–30). John rejoiced at the opportunity of introducing people to the Savior, and then getting out of the way.

A unique feature about John's ministry was baptism (Luke 20:1–8; John 1:25–28). Baptism was nothing new to the people, for the Jews baptized Gentile proselytes. But John baptized *Jews,* and this was unusual. Acts 19:1–5 explains that John's baptism *looked forward* to the coming of the Messiah, while Christian baptism *looks back* to the finished work of Christ.

But there was something even beyond John's baptism, and that was the baptism that the Messiah would administer (Luke 3:16). He would baptize believers with the Holy Spirit, and this began at Pentecost (Acts 1:5; 2:1ff.). Today, the moment a sinner trusts Christ, he or she is baptized by the Spirit into the body of Christ (1 Cor. 12:13).

What is the "baptism of fire"? It does not refer to the "tongues of fire" at Pentecost, for tongues over a person's head could hardly be called a "baptism." John's use of the symbol of "fire" in Luke 3:9 and 17 indicates that he is talking about *judgment* and not blessing. In AD 70 the nation experienced a baptism of fire when Titus and the Roman armies destroyed Jerusalem and scattered the people. All unbelievers will experience a baptism of judgment in the lake of fire (Rev. 20:11–15).

Why he came (vv. 4–20). The illustrations used in the chapter help us understand the ministry God gave to John.

To begin with, John the Baptist was *a voice* "crying in the wilderness" (Luke 3:4; see also Isa. 40:1–5, John 1:23). He was like the herald who went before the royal procession to make sure the roads were ready for the king. Spiritually speaking, the nation of Israel was living in a "wilderness" of unbelief, and the roads to spiritual reality were twisted and in disrepair. The corruption of the priesthood (instead of one, there were *two* high priests!) and the legalistic hypocrisy of the scribes and Pharisees had weakened the nation spiritually. The people desperately needed to hear a voice from God, and John was that faithful voice.

It was John's task to prepare the nation for the Messiah and then present the Messiah to them (Luke 1:16–17, 76–77; John 1:6–8, 15–34). He rebuked their sins and announced God's salvation, for without conviction there can be no conversion.

John is also compared to *a farmer* who chops down useless trees (Luke 3:9) and who winnows the grain to separate the wheat from the chaff (Luke 3:17). Like some "religious sinners" today, many of the Jews thought they were destined for heaven simply because they were descendants of Abraham (see John 8:31–34; Rom. 4:12–17; Gal. 3:26–29). John reminded them that God gets to the *root* of things and is not impressed with religious profession that does not produce fruit. In the last judgment, the true believers (wheat) will be gathered by God, while the lost sinners (chaff) will be burned in the fire.

In Luke 3:7, John pictured the self-righteous sinners

as snakes that slithered out of the grass because a fire was coming! Jesus compared the Pharisees to vipers (Matt. 23:33) because their self-righteousness and unbelief made them the children of the devil (John 8:44–45; Rev. 20:2). How tragic that the religious leaders refused to obey John's message and submit to his baptism (Luke 20:1–8). They not only failed to enter the kingdom themselves, but their bad example and false teaching kept other people from entering.

John the Baptist was also *a teacher* (Luke 3:12). He not only preached publicly, but he also had a personal ministry to the people, telling them how to practice their new faith (Luke 3:10–14). He told them not to be selfish but to share their blessings with others (see Acts 2:44–45; 4:32–37).

Even the tax collectors came to John for counsel. These men were despised by their fellow Jews because they worked for the Romans and usually extorted money from the people. Luke emphasized the fact that Jesus was the friend of tax collectors (Luke 5:27ff.; 15:1–2; 19:1–10). John did not tell them to quit their jobs but to do their work honestly.

Likewise, the soldiers were not condemned for their vocation. Rather, John told them to refrain from using their authority to get personal gain. These were probably Jewish soldiers attached to the temple or to the court of one of the Jewish rulers. It was not likely that Roman soldiers would ask a Jewish prophet for counsel.

John was faithful in his ministry to prepare the hearts of the people and then to present their Messiah to them. He clearly stated that Jesus was "the Lord" (Luke 3:4) and the Son of God (John 1:34). Because John rebuked Herod Antipas for his adulterous marriage to Herodias, he was imprisoned by the king and finally beheaded. However, he had faithfully finished his God-given assignment and prepared the people to meet the Messiah, the Son of God.

The Father and the Spirit (3:21–38)

One day, after all the others had been baptized, Jesus presented Himself for baptism at the Jordan, and John at first refused to comply (Matt. 3:13–15). He knew that Jesus of Nazareth was the perfect Son of God who had no need to repent of sin. Why then was the sinless Son of God baptized?

To begin with, in His baptism He identified with the sinners that He came to save. Also, His baptism was the official start of His ministry (Acts 1:21–22; 10:37–38). He was "about thirty years of age" (Luke 3:23), and the Jewish Levites began their work at age thirty (see Num. 4:3, 35). But our Lord's words tell us the main reason for His baptism: "for in this way it is fitting for us to fulfill all righteousness" (Matt. 3:15 NASB). In what way? In the way pictured by His baptism in the Jordan. Many Bible scholars agree that New Testament baptism was by immersion, which is a picture of death, burial, and resurrection. *Our Lord's baptism in water was a picture of His work of redemption* (Matt. 20:22; Luke 12:50). It was through His

baptism of suffering on the cross that God "fulfilled all righteousness." (The "us" in Matthew 3:15 does not mean John and Jesus. It means the Father, the Son, and the Spirit.)

When our Lord came up from the water, the Father spoke from heaven and identified Him as the beloved Son of God, and the Spirit visibly came upon Jesus in the form of a dove. Those who deny the Trinity have a difficult time explaining this event.

This is the first of three recorded occasions when the Father spoke from heaven. The second was when Jesus was transfigured (Luke 9:28–36), and the third was during His last week before the cross (John 12:28).

Only Luke mentions that Jesus was praying, and this was only one of many occasions (Luke 5:16; 6:12; 9:18, 28–29; 11:1; 23:34, 46). As the perfect Son of Man, Jesus depended on His Father to meet His needs, and that was why He prayed.

Luke interrupted his narrative at this point to give us a genealogy of Jesus. Matthew's genealogy (Matt. 1:1–17) begins with Abraham and moves forward to Jesus, while Luke's begins with Jesus and moves backward to Adam. Matthew gives us the genealogy of Joseph, the legal foster-father of Jesus, while Luke gives us the genealogy of His mother, Mary. Luke 3:23 can be translated: "When He began His ministry, Jesus was about thirty years old (being supposedly the son of Joseph), the son of Heli [an ancestor of Mary]." Mary herself would not be mentioned because it was unusual for women to be named in the official genealogies, though Matthew names four of them (Matt. 1:3, 5, 16).

By putting the genealogy here, Luke reminded his readers that the Son of God was also the Son of Man, born into this world, identified with the needs and problems of mankind. And, since Joseph and Mary were both in David's line, these genealogies prove that Jesus of Nazareth has the legal right to David's throne (Luke 1:32–33).

Satan (4:1–13)

Even the enemy must admit that Jesus is the Son of God. "If thou be the Son of God" (Luke 4:3, 9) is not a supposition but an affirmation. It means "in view of the fact that You are the Son of God" (WUEST). In fact, the fact of His deity was the basis for the first of the three temptations. "Since you are the Son of God," Satan argued, "why be hungry? You can change stones into bread!" Satan wanted Jesus to disobey the Father's will by using His divine power for His own purposes.

Why was Jesus tempted? For one thing, it was proof that the Father's approval was deserved (Luke 4:22). Jesus is indeed the "beloved Son" who always does whatever pleases His Father (John 8:29). Also, in His temptation, Jesus exposed the tactics of the enemy and revealed to us how we can overcome when we are tempted. This experience helped prepare our Lord for His present ministry as our sympathetic High Priest, and we may come to Him for the help we need to overcome the tempter (Heb. 2:16–18; 4:14–16). The first

Adam was tempted in a beautiful garden and failed. The Last Adam was tempted in a dangerous wilderness (Mark 1:13) and succeeded.

We have at our disposal the same spiritual resources that Jesus used when He faced and defeated Satan: prayer (Luke 3:22), the Father's love (Luke 3:23), the power of the Spirit (Luke 4:1), and the Word of God ("It is written"). Plus, we have in heaven the interceding Savior who has defeated the enemy completely. Satan tempts us to bring out the worst in us, but God can use these difficult experiences to put the best into us. Temptation is Satan's weapon to defeat us, but it can become God's tool to build us (see James 1:1–8, 13–17).

In the first temptation, Satan suggested that there must be something wrong with the Father's love since His "beloved Son" was hungry. In years past Israel hungered in the wilderness, and God sent them bread from heaven, so surely Jesus could use His divine power to feed Himself and save His life. Satan subtly used this same approach on Eve: "God is holding out on you! Why can't you eat of *every* tree in the garden? If He really loved you, He would share everything with you!"

But the test was even more subtle than that, for Satan was asking Jesus to *separate the physical from the spiritual.* In the Christian life, eating is a spiritual activity, and we can use even our daily food to glorify God (Rom. 14:20–21; 1 Cor. 10:31). Whenever we label different spheres of our lives "physical," "material," "financial," or "spiritual," we are bound to leave God out of areas where He rightfully belongs. Christ must be first in *everything,* or He is first in nothing (Matt. 6:33). It is better to be hungry in the will of God than satisfied out of the will of God.

When our Lord quoted Deuteronomy 8:3, He put the emphasis on the word *man.* As the eternal Son of God, He had *power* to do anything, but as the humble Son of Man, He had *authority* to do only that which the Father willed. (Note carefully John 5:17, 30; 8:28; 10:17–18; 15:10, 15.) As the Servant, Jesus did not use His divine attributes for selfish purposes (Phil. 2:5–8). Because He was man, He hungered, but He trusted the Father to meet His needs in His own time and His own way.

You and I need bread for the body (Matt. 6:11), but we must not live by physical bread alone. We also need food for the inner person to satisfy our spiritual needs. This food is the Word of God (Ps. 119:103; Jer. 15:16; 1 Peter 2:2). What digestion is to the body, meditation is to the soul. As we read the Word and meditate on it, we receive spiritual health and strength for the inner person, and this enables us to obey the will of God.

We do not know why Luke reversed the second and third temptations, but since he did not claim to record the events in order, he is not contradicting Matthew 4:1–11. The word *then* in Matthew 4:5 indicates that Matthew's order is the correct one. We do seem to have in Luke's order a parallel to 1 John 2:16: the lust of the flesh (stones into bread), the lust of the eyes

(the world's kingdoms and glory), and the pride of life (jump from the pinnacle of the temple), but it's doubtful that Luke had this in mind.

The Father had already promised to give the Son all the kingdoms of the world (Ps. 2:7–8), but first the Son had to suffer and die (John 12:23–33; Rev. 5:8–10). The suffering must come first, then the glory (Luke 24:25–27). The adversary offered Jesus these same kingdoms if He would *once* worship him, and this would eliminate the necessity of His going to the cross (note Matt. 16:21–23). Satan has always wanted to take God's place and receive worship (Isa. 14:13–14).

As the prince of this world, Satan has a certain amount of delegated authority from God (John 12:31; 14:30). One day he will share this authority with the Antichrist, the man of sin, who will rule the world for a brief time (Rev. 13). Satan's offer to Christ was valid, but his terms were unacceptable, and the Savior refused.

Again, Jesus quoted God's Word, this time Deuteronomy 6:13. Satan had said nothing about *service,* but Jesus knew that whatever we worship, we will serve. Service to the Lord is true freedom, but service to Satan is terrible bondage. God's pattern is to start with suffering and end with glory (1 Peter 5:10), while Satan's pattern is to start with glory and end with suffering. Satan wants us to sacrifice the eternal for the temporary and take the "easy way."

There are no "shortcuts" in the Christian life, and there is no easy way to spiritual victory and maturity. If the perfect Son of God had to hang on a tree before He could sit on the throne, then His disciples should not expect an easier way of life (see Luke 9:22–26; Acts 24:22).

Satan questioned the Father's love when he tempted Jesus to turn stones into bread. He questioned His hope when he offered Jesus the world's kingdoms this side of the cross (see Heb. 12:1–3). Satan questioned the Father's faithfulness when he asked Jesus to jump from the temple and prove that the Father would keep His promise (Ps. 91:11–12). Thus, the enemy attacked the three basic virtues of the Christian life—faith, hope, and love.

The pinnacle was probably a high point at the southeast corner of the temple, far above the Kidron Valley. Satan can tempt us even in the Holy City at the highest part of the holy temple! Following the example of Jesus, Satan decided to quote Scripture, and he selected Psalm 91:11–12. Of course, he misquoted the promise, and besides, he omitted "in all thy ways."

When a child of God is in the will of God, he can claim the Father's protection and care. But if he willfully gets into trouble and expects God to rescue him, then he is tempting God. (For an example of this, see Ex. 17:1–7.) We tempt God when we "force" Him (or dare Him) to act contrary to His Word. It is a dangerous thing to try God's patience, even though He is indeed long suffering and gracious.

Our Lord's reply was, "on the other hand, it is

written" (Matt. 4:7 NASB), and He quoted Deuteronomy 6:16. *Jesus balanced Scripture with Scripture to get the total expression of God's will.* If you isolate verses from their contexts, or passages from the total revelation of Scripture, you can prove almost anything from the Bible. Almost every false cult claims to be based on the teachings of the Bible. When we get our orders from God by picking out verses from here and there in the Bible, we are not living by faith. We are living by chance and tempting the Lord. "For whatever is not of faith is sin" (Rom. 14:23), and "faith comes by hearing, and hearing by the word of God" (Rom. 10:17 NKJV).

Jesus came out of the wilderness a victor, but Satan did not give up. He watched for other opportunities to tempt the Savior away from the Father's will. "Let us be as watchful after the victory as before the battle," said Andrew Bonar, and he was right.

The Scriptures (4:14–30)

The events recorded in John 1:19—4:45 took place at this time, but Matthew, Mark, and Luke did not record them. They moved right into the Lord's ministry in Galilee, and Luke alone reports His visit to His hometown of Nazareth. By now, the news had spread widely about the miracle-worker from Nazareth, so His family, friends, and neighbors were anxious to see and hear Him.

It was our Lord's custom to attend public worship, a custom His followers should imitate today (Heb. 10:24–25). He might have argued that the "religious system" was corrupt, or that He didn't need the instruction, but instead, He made His way on the Sabbath to the place of prayer.

A typical synagogue service opened with an invocation for God's blessing and then the recitation of the traditional Hebrew confession of faith (Deut. 6:4–9; 11:13–21). This was followed by prayer and the prescribed readings from the law and from the prophets, with the reader paraphrasing the Hebrew Scriptures in Aramaic.

This was followed by a brief sermon given by one of the men of the congregation or perhaps by a visiting rabbi (see Acts 13:14–16). If a priest was present, the service closed with a benediction. Otherwise, one of the laymen prayed and the meeting was dismissed.

Jesus was asked to read the Scripture text and to give the sermon. The passage He read included Isaiah 61:1–2, and He selected it for His "text." The Jewish rabbis interpreted this passage to refer to the Messiah, and the people in the synagogue knew it. You can imagine how shocked they were when Jesus boldly said that it was written about Him and that He had come to usher in the "acceptable year of the Lord."

The reference here is the "Year of Jubilee" described in Leviticus 25. Every seventh year was a "sabbatical year" for the nation, when the land was allowed to rest, and every fiftieth year (after seven sabbaticals) was set apart as the "Year of Jubilee." The main purpose of this special year was the balancing of the economic system:

slaves were set free and returned to their families, property that was sold reverted to the original owners, and all debts were canceled. The land lay fallow as man and beast rested and rejoiced in the Lord.

Jesus applied all of this to His own ministry, not in a political or economic sense, but in a physical and spiritual sense. He had certainly brought good news of salvation to bankrupt sinners and healing to brokenhearted and rejected people. He had delivered many from blindness and from bondage to demons and disease. Indeed, it was a spiritual "Year of Jubilee" for the nation of Israel!

The problem was that His listeners would not believe in Him. They saw Him only as the son of Mary and Joseph, the Boy they had watched grow up in their own city. Furthermore, they wanted Him to perform in Nazareth the same miracles He had done in Capernaum, but He refused. That's the meaning of the phrase, "Physician, heal thyself." Do a miracle!

At first, they admired the way He taught, but it didn't take long for their admiration to turn into antagonism. Why? *Because Jesus began to remind them of God's goodness to the Gentiles!* The prophet Elijah bypassed all the Jewish widows and helped a Gentile widow in Sidon (1 Kings 17:8–16), and his successor Elisha healed a Gentile leper from Syria (2 Kings 5:1–15). Our Lord's message of grace was a blow to the proud Jewish exclusivism of the congregation, and they would not repent. Imagine this hometown Boy saying that Jews had to be saved by grace just like the pagan Gentiles!

The congregation was so angry, they took action to kill Jesus! St. Augustine said, "They love truth when it enlightens them, but hate truth when it accuses them." That applies well to many congregations today, people who want "gracious words" (Luke 4:22) but who don't want to face the truth (see John 1:17).

In spite of the unbelief of the people in Nazareth, the Scriptures declared that Jesus of Nazareth is God's Son, the Messiah sent to fulfill His promises. The people who do not want Him and who reject "the acceptable year of the Lord" will one day face "the day of vengeance of our God" (Isa. 61:2). How significant that Jesus stopped reading at that very place!

The Demons (4:31–44)

Jesus left Nazareth and set up His headquarters in Capernaum (Matt. 4:13–16), the home of Peter, Andrew, James, and John. He taught regularly in the synagogue and astonished the people by the authority of His message (see Matt. 7:28–29). He further astonished them by His authority over the demons.

Why would a demonized man attend the synagogue? Did he know Jesus would be there? Our Lord did not want the demons to bear witness to Him, so He told them to be still and He cast them out. Of course, the demons know that Jesus is the Son of God (Luke 4:34, 41), and knowing this, they tremble (James 2:19).

After the service, Jesus went to Peter's house, and there He healed Peter's mother-in-law. (Dr. Luke noted that she had a "great fever.") At sundown, when the Sabbath had ended and healing was permissible, a host of people brought their sick and afflicted to Peter's house and asked Jesus to help them. Again, He silenced the demons who confessed Him to be the Son of God.

The Lord must have been weary after such a demanding day, and yet He was up early the next morning to pray (Mark 1:35). It was in prayer that He found His strength and power for service, and so must we.

CHAPTER FOUR
Luke 5
THE DIFFERENCE JESUS MAKES

Jesus was concerned about individuals. He preached to great crowds, but His message was always to the individual, and He took time to help people personally. His purpose was to transform them and then send them out to share His message of forgiveness with others. Luke describes in this chapter our Lord's meetings with four individuals and the changes they experienced because they trusted Him.

From Failure to Success (5:1–11)
This event is not parallel to the one described in Matthew 4:18–22 and Mark 1:16–20. In those accounts, Peter and Andrew were busy fishing, but in this account they had fished all night and caught nothing and were washing their nets. (If nets are not washed and stretched out to dry, they rot and break.) Jesus had enlisted Peter, Andrew, James, and John earlier, and they had traveled with Him in Capernaum and Galilee (Mark 1:21–39), but then they went back to their trade. Now He would call them to a life of full-time discipleship.

It is possible that at least seven of the disciples were fishermen (John 21:1–3). Consider the fact that fishermen generally have the qualities that make for success in serving the Lord. It takes courage and daring, patience and determination to work on the seas, and it also takes a great deal of faith. Fishermen must be willing to work together (they used nets, not hooks) and help one another. They must develop the skills necessary to get the job done quickly and efficiently.

If I had fished all night and caught nothing, I would probably be *selling* my nets, not washing them to get ready to go out again! But true fishermen don't quit. Peter kept on working while Jesus used his ship as a platform from which to address the huge crowd on the shore. "Every pulpit is a fishing boat," said Dr. J. Vernon McGee, "a place to give out the Word of God and attempt to catch fish."

But there was another side to this request: Peter was a "captive audience" as he sat in the ship listening to the Word of God. "So then faith comes by hearing, and hearing by the Word of God" (Rom. 10:17 NKJV). In a short time, Peter would have to exercise faith, and Jesus was preparing him. First He said, "Thrust out a little," and then, when Peter was ready, He commanded, "Launch out into the deep." If Peter had not obeyed the first seemingly insignificant command, he would never have participated in a miracle.

Peter must have been surprised when Jesus took command of the ship and its crew. After all, Jesus was a carpenter by trade (Mark 6:3), and what do carpenters know about fishing? It was a well-known fact that, in the Sea of Galilee, you caught fish at night in the shallow water, not in the daytime in the deep water. What Jesus asked Peter to do was contrary to all of his training and experience, but Peter obeyed. The key was his faith in the Word of God: "Nevertheless, at thy word" (Luke 5:5).

The word translated "Master" (Luke 5:5) is used only by Luke and it has a variety of meanings, all of which speak of authority: chief commander, magistrate, governor of a city, and president of a college. Peter was willing to submit to the authority of Jesus, even though he did not understand all that the Lord was doing. And remember, a great crowd was watching from the shore.

How people respond to success is one indication of their true character. Instead of claiming the valuable catch for themselves, Peter and Andrew called their partners to share it. We are not reservoirs, but channels of blessing, to share with others what God has graciously given to us.

From Sickness to Health (5:12–16)
Here was a man who *needed to be changed,* for he was a leper. Among the Jews, several skin diseases were classified as leprosy, including our modern Hansen's disease. In spite of modern medical advances, an estimated ten million people around the world have leprosy. One form of leprosy attacks the nerves so that the victim cannot feel pain. Infection easily sets in, and this leads to degeneration of the tissues. The limb becomes deformed and eventually falls off.

It was the task of the Jewish priest to examine people to determine whether they were lepers (Lev. 13). Infected people were isolated and could not return to normal society until declared "cleansed." Leprosy was used by Isaiah as a picture of sin (Isa. 1:4–6), and the detailed instructions in Leviticus 13—14 would suggest that more was involved in the procedure than maintaining public health.

Like sin, leprosy is deeper than the skin (Lev. 13:3) and cannot be helped by mere "surface" measures (see Jer. 6:14). Like sin, leprosy spreads (Lev. 13:7–8), and as it spreads, it defiles (Lev. 13:44–45). Because of his defilement, a leprous person had to be isolated outside the camp (Lev. 13:46), and lost sinners one day will be isolated in hell. People with leprosy were looked on as "dead" (Num. 12:12), and garments infected with leprosy were fit only for the fire (Lev. 13:52). How important it is for lost sinners to trust Jesus Christ and get rid of their "leprosy"!

This man not only needed to be changed, but *he wanted to be changed.* Lepers were required to keep their distance, but he was so determined that he broke the law and approached the Lord Jesus personally. Throughout his gospel, Luke makes it clear that Jesus was the Friend of the outcast, and they could come to Him for help. The man humbled himself before the Lord and asked for mercy.

By the grace and power of God, this man *was changed!* In fact, Jesus even touched the man, which meant that He became unclean Himself. This is a beautiful picture of what Jesus has done for lost sinners: He became sin for us that we might be made clean (2 Cor. 5:21; 1 Peter 2:24). Jesus is not only willing to save (1 Tim. 2:4; 2 Peter 3:9), but He is also able to save (Heb. 7:25), and He can do it now (2 Cor. 6:2).

Jesus encouraged the man to see the priest and to obey the rules for restoration given in Leviticus 14. The ceremony is a picture of the work of Jesus Christ in His incarnation, His death, and His resurrection. All of this was done over running water, a symbol of the Holy Spirit of God. This sacrifice reminds us that Jesus had to die for us in order to deliver us from our sins.

Jesus instructed the man not to reveal who had healed him, but the cleansed leper became an enthusiastic witness for the Lord. (Jesus commands us to tell everybody, and we keep quiet!) Because of this witness, great multitudes came to Jesus for help, and He graciously ministered to them. But Jesus was not impressed by these great crowds, for He knew that most of the people wanted only His healing power and not His salvation. He often left the crowds and slipped away into a quiet place to pray and seek the Father's help. That's a good example for all of God's servants to follow.

From Guilt to Forgiveness (5:17–26)

Jesus returned to Capernaum, possibly to Peter's house, and the crowd gathered to see Him heal and to hear Him teach. But a new element was added: some of the official religious leaders from Jerusalem were present to investigate what He was doing. They had every right to do this since it was the responsibility of the elders to prevent false prophets from leading the people astray (Deut. 13; 18:15–22). They had interrogated John the Baptist (John 1:19–34), and now they would examine Jesus of Nazareth.

Since this is the first time the scribes and Pharisees are mentioned in Luke's gospel, it would be good for us to get acquainted with them. The word *Pharisee* comes from a Hebrew word that means "to divide, to separate." The scribes and Pharisees probably developed out of the ministry of Ezra, the priest, who taught the Jewish people to obey the law of Moses and be separate from the heathen nations around them (Ezra 9—10; Neh. 8—9). The great desire of the scribes and

Pharisees was to understand and magnify God's law and apply it in their daily lives.

However, the movement soon became quite legalistic, and its leaders laid so many burdens on the people that it was impossible to "serve the Lord with gladness" (Ps. 100:2). Furthermore, many of the Pharisees were hypocrites and did not practice what they preached (see Matt. 15:1–20; 23:1–36). In the Sermon on the Mount (Matt. 5—7), Jesus exposed the shallowness of pharisaical religion. He explained that true righteousness is a matter of the heart and not external religious practices alone.

The scribes and Pharisees picked a good time to attend one of our Lord's meetings, because God's power was present in a special way and Jesus would heal a man with palsy. If leprosy illustrates the corruption and defilement of sin, then palsy is a picture of the paralysis that sin produces in a life. But Jesus would do more than heal the man; He would also forgive his sins and teach the crowd a lesson in forgiveness.

The paralytic was unable to come to Jesus himself, but he was fortunate enough to have four friends who were able to get him to Jesus. These four men are examples of how friends ought to minister to one another and help needy sinners come to the Savior.

To begin with, they had faith that Jesus would heal him (Luke 5:20), and it is faith that God honors. Their love for the man united them in their efforts so that nothing discouraged them, not even the crowd at the door. (How tragic it is when spectators stand in the way of people who want to meet Jesus. Zaccheus would have this problem. See Luke 19:3.) When they could not get in at the door, they went on the roof, removed the tiling, and lowered the man on his mat right in front of the Lord!

Jesus could have simply healed the man and sent him home, but instead, He used the opportunity to teach a lesson about sin and forgiveness. Certainly it was easier to say to the man, "Your sins be forgiven!" than it was to say, "Rise up and walk!" Why? *Because nobody could prove whether or not his sins really were forgiven!* Jesus took the harder approach and healed the man's body, something everybody in the house could witness.

Was the man's affliction the result of his sin? We do not know, but it is probable (see John 5:1–14). The healing of his body was an outward evidence of the spiritual healing within. Jesus astounded the religious leaders by claiming to have authority both to heal the body and to forgive sins. The people had already acknowledged His authority to teach and to cast out demons (Luke 4:32, 36), but now He claimed authority to forgive sins as well. The scribes and Pharisees could not deny the miracle of healing, but they considered His claim to forgive sins nothing less than blasphemy, for only God can forgive sins. For making that kind of statement, Jesus could be stoned, because He was claiming to be God.

In Luke 5:24, we have the first recorded use of the

title Son of man in Luke's gospel, where it is found twenty-three times. Our Lord's listeners were familiar with this title. It was used of the prophet Ezekiel over eighty times, and Daniel applied it to the Messiah (Dan. 7:13, 18). "Son of man" was our Lord's favorite name for Himself; this title is found at least eighty-two times in the gospel record. Occasionally He used the title "Son of God" (Matt. 27:43; Luke 22:70; John 5:25; 9:35; 10:36; 11:4), but "Son of man" was used more. Certainly the Jewish people caught the messianic character of this title, but it also identified Him with the people He came to save (Luke 19:10). Like Ezekiel, the Old Testament "son of man," Jesus "sat where they sat" (Ezek. 3:15).

The healing was immediate and the people glorified God. But even more than receiving healing, the man experienced forgiveness and the start of a whole new life. Our Lord's miracles not only demonstrated His deity and His compassion for needy people, but they also revealed important spiritual lessons about salvation. They were "object lessons" to teach spiritually blind people what God could do for them if only they would believe in His Son.

From the Old to the New (5:27–39)

When Jesus called Levi, He accomplished three things: He saved a lost soul; He added a new disciple to His band; and He created an opportunity to explain His ministry to Levi's friends and to the scribes and Pharisees. This event probably took place shortly after Jesus healed the palsied man, for the "official committee" was still there (Luke 5:17). And it is likely that Jesus at this time gave Levi his new name—"Matthew, the gift of God" (Luke 6:15; see also Matt. 9:9).

Matthew sat at the toll booth and levied duty on the merchandise that was brought through. Since the tax rates were not always clear, it was easy for an unscrupulous man to make extra money for himself. But even if a tax collector served honestly, the Jews still despised him for defiling himself by working for the Gentiles. John the Baptist had made it clear that there was nothing innately sinful in collecting taxes (Luke 3:12–13), and we have no evidence that Matthew was a thief. But to the Jews, Levi was a sinner, and Jesus was suspect for having anything to do with him and his sinner friends.

We wonder how much Matthew knew about Jesus. Our Lord's friendship with Peter and his partners would put Him in touch with the businessmen of Capernaum, and certainly Matthew had heard Jesus preach by the seaside. Matthew instantly obeyed the Lord's call, left everything, and followed Jesus. He was so overjoyed at his salvation experience that he invited many of his friends to rejoice with him (see Luke 15:6, 9, 23).

The scribes and Pharisees criticized Jesus because they did not understand either His message or His ministry. Jesus simply did not fit into their traditional religious life. It is unfortunate when leaders resist change and refuse to try to understand the new things that God is doing. In order to help them understand, Jesus gave four illustrations of what He was doing.

The Physician (vv. 31–32). The scribes and Pharisees saw Matthew and his friends as condemned sinners, but Jesus saw them as spiritually sick "patients" who needed the help of a physician. In fact, He had illustrated this when He cleansed the leper and healed the paralytic. Sin is like a disease: it starts in a small and hidden way; it grows secretly; it saps our strength; and if it is not cured, it kills. It is tragic when sickness kills the body, but it is even more tragic when sin condemns the soul to hell.

The scribes and Pharisees were quick to diagnose the needs of others, but they were blind to their own needs, for they were sinners like everyone else. They appeared righteous on the outside but were corrupt within (Matt. 23:25–28). They may not have been "prodigal sons" who were guilty of sins of the flesh, but they were certainly "elder brothers" who were guilty of sins of the spirit (Luke 15:11–32; 2 Cor. 7:1).

As I was writing this chapter, I received a phone call from a woman in Canada who disagreed with my radio ministry and repeatedly condemned "the judgmental fundamentalists." I tried to reason with her from the Word, but she would not accept it. According to her, there was no hell and I had no right to preach about it. As I quoted Scripture to her, she hung up; all I could do was pause to pray for her, and I did it with a heavy heart.

The first step toward healing sin sickness is admitting that we have a need and that we must do something about it. False prophets give a false diagnosis that leads to a false hope (Jer. 6:14), but the servant of God tells the truth about sin, death, and hell, and offers the only remedy: faith in Jesus Christ. The religion of the scribes and Pharisees could offer no hope to Matthew's friends, but Jesus could.

What a wonderful Physician Jesus is! He comes to us in love; He calls us; He saves us when we trust Him; *and He "pays the bill."* His diagnosis is always accurate and His cure is perfect and complete. No wonder Matthew was so happy and wanted to share the good news with his friends!

The Bridegroom (vv. 33–35). The scribes and Pharisees were not only upset at the disciples' friends, but also at their obvious joy as they fellowshipped with Jesus and the guests. We get the impression that the Pharisees experienced little if any joy in the practice of their religion (see Matt. 6:16; Luke 15:25–32). Jesus was "a man of sorrows" (Isa. 53:3), but He was also filled with joy (Luke 10:21; John 15:11; 17:13).

Jewish weddings lasted a week and were times of great joy and celebration. By using this image, Jesus was saying to His critics, "I came to make life a wedding feast, not a funeral. If you know the Bridegroom, then you can share His joy." He said that one day He would be "taken away," which suggested rejection and death; but meanwhile, there was good reason for joy, for sinners were coming to repentance.

Fasting is found often in the Old Testament, but nowhere is it commanded in the New Testament. However, the example of the prophets and the early church is certainly significant for believers today. Our Lord's words in Matthew 6:16–18 assume that we will fast ("when," not "if"), and passages like Acts 13:1–3 and 14:23 indicate that fasting was a practice of the early church (see also 1 Cor. 7:5; 2 Cor. 6:5; 11:27).

The garment (v. 36). Jesus did not come to patch up the old; He came to give the new. The Pharisees would admit that Judaism was not all it could be, and perhaps they hoped that Jesus would work with them in reviving the old religion. But Jesus showed the foolishness of this approach by contrasting two garments, an old one and a new one. If you take a patch from a new garment and sew it to an old garment, you ruin both of them. The new garment has a hole in it, and the old garment has a patch that does not match and that will tear away when the garment is washed.

In Scripture, garments are sometimes used to picture character and conduct (Col. 3:8–17). Isaiah wrote about a "robe of righteousness" (Isa. 61:10; see also 2 Cor. 5:21), and he warned against our trusting our own good works for salvation (Isa. 64:6). Many people have a "patchwork" religion of their own making, instead of trusting Christ for the robe of salvation that He gives by grace.

The wineskins (vv. 37–39). If unfermented wine is put into brittle old wineskins, the gas will burst the skins, and both the skins and the wine will be lost. The new life of the Spirit could not be forced into the old wineskins of Judaism. Jesus was revealing that the ancient Jewish religion was getting old and would soon be replaced (see Heb. 8:13). Most of the Jews preferred the old and refused the new. It was not until AD 70, when the Romans destroyed Jerusalem and the temple, and scattered the people, that the Jewish religion *as described in the law* came to an end. Today, the Jews do not have a priesthood, a temple, or an altar, so they cannot practice their religion as their ancestors did (see Hos. 3:4).

The things in the ceremonial law were fulfilled by Jesus Christ, so there is no need today for sacrifices, priests, temples, and ceremonies. All of God's people are priests who bring spiritual sacrifices to the Lord (1 Peter 2:5, 9). The tables of law have been replaced by the tables of the human heart, where God's Spirit is writing the Word and making us like Jesus Christ (2 Cor. 3:1–3, 18).

Jesus Christ still offers "all things new" (Rev. 21:5). As the Physician, He offers sinners new life and spiritual health. As the Bridegroom, He brings new love and joy. He gives us the robe of righteousness and the wine of the Spirit (Eph. 5:18; see also Acts 2:13). Life is a feast, not a famine or a funeral, and Jesus Christ is the only one who can make that kind of a difference in our lives.

CHAPTER FIVE
Luke 6
SO WHAT'S NEW? EVERYTHING!

For over a year, Jesus ministered as a popular itinerant Teacher and Healer, and multitudes followed Him. But now the time had come for Him to "organize" His followers and declare just what His kingdom was all about.

In this chapter, we see the Lord Jesus establishing three new spiritual entities to replace that which was now "worn out" in the Jewish religion: a new Sabbath, a new nation, and a new blessing in the new spiritual kingdom.

A New Sabbath (6:1–11)

The sanctity of the seventh day was a distinctive part of the Jewish faith. God gave Israel the Sabbath law at Sinai (Neh. 9:13–14) and made it a sign between Him and the nation (Ex. 20:8–11; 31:12–17). The word *Sabbath* means "rest" and is linked with God's cessation of work after the six days of creation (Gen. 2:2–3). Some of the rabbis taught that Messiah could not come until Israel had perfectly kept the Sabbath, so obeying this law was very important both personally and nationally.

To call Sunday "the Sabbath" is to confuse the first day and the seventh day and what each signifies. The Sabbath is a reminder of the completion of "the old creation," while the Lord's Day is a reminder of our Lord's finished work in "the new creation" (2 Cor. 5:21; Eph. 2:10; 4:24). The Sabbath speaks of rest *after* work and relates to the law, while the Lord's Day speaks of rest *before* work and relates to grace. The Lord's Day commemorates the resurrection of Jesus Christ from the dead as well as the coming of the Holy Spirit and the "birthday" of the church (Acts 2).

The early church met on the first day of the week (Acts 20:7; 1 Cor. 16:1–2). However, some Jewish believers kept the Sabbath, and this sometimes led to division. Paul addressed this problem in Romans 14:1—15:13 where he gave principles to promote both liberty and unity in the church. But Paul always made it clear that *observing special days had nothing to do with salvation* (Gal. 4:1–11; Col. 2:8–17). We are not saved from sin by faith in Christ *plus* keeping the Sabbath. We are saved by faith in Christ alone.

By their strict and oppressive rules, the Pharisees and scribes had turned the Sabbath day into a burden instead of the blessing God meant it to be, and Jesus challenged both their doctrine and their authority. He had announced a new "Year of Jubilee" (Luke 4:19), and now He would declare a new Sabbath. He had already healed a lame man on the Sabbath, and the religious leaders had determined to kill Him (John 5:18; also note John 5:16). Now He was to violate their Sabbath laws on two more occasions.

In the field (vv. 1–5). It was lawful for a Jew to eat from a neighbor's vineyard, orchard, or field, provided he did not fill a container or use a harvesting implement (Deut. 23:24–25). The disciples were hungry, so they picked the heads of wheat, rubbed them in their hands, and ate them. But in so doing, according to the rabbis, they broke the Sabbath law, because they were harvesting, winnowing, and preparing food!

Always alert for something to criticize, some of the Pharisees asked Jesus why He permitted His disciples to violate the Sabbath laws. This was His second offense, and they were sure they had a case against Him. How tragic that their slavish devotion to religious rules blinded them to the true ministry of the law as well as the very presence of the Lord who gave them the law.

Jesus did not argue with them; instead, He took them right to the Word of God (1 Sam. 21:1–6). The "showbread" was comprised of twelve loaves, one for each tribe in Israel, and it stood on the table in the holy place in the tabernacle and then in the temple (Ex. 25:23–30; Lev. 24:5–9). Fresh bread was put on the table each Sabbath, and only the priests were allowed to eat the loaves.

But David and his men ate the loaves, and what Jew would condemn Israel's great king? "He was God's anointed!" they might argue, *but that was exactly what Jesus claimed for Himself* (Luke 4:18). Not only was He God's Anointed, but He was also the Lord of the Sabbath! When Jesus made that statement, He was claiming to be Jehovah God, because it was the Lord who established the Sabbath. If Jesus Christ is indeed Lord of the Sabbath, then He is free to do *on* it and *with* it whatever He pleases. The Pharisees did not miss His meaning, you can be sure.

God is more concerned about meeting human needs than He is about protecting religious rules. Better that David and his men receive strength to serve God than that they perish only for the sake of a temporary law. God desires compassion, not sacrifice (Matt. 12:7, quoting Hos. 6:6). The Pharisees, of course, had a different view of the law (Matt. 23:23).

In the synagogue (vv. 6–11). The Pharisees knew that it was our Lord's practice to be in the synagogue on the Sabbath, so they were there to watch Him and to gather more evidence against Him. Did they know that the handicapped man would also be there? Did they "plant" him there? We do not know, and Jesus probably did not care. His compassionate heart responded to the man's need, and He healed him. Jesus could have waited a few hours until the Sabbath was over, or He could have healed the man in private, but He did it openly and immediately. It was a deliberate violation of the Sabbath traditions.

Our Lord's defense in the field was based on the Old Testament Scriptures, but His defense in the synagogue was based on *the nature of God's Sabbath law*. God gave that law to help people, not to hurt them. "The Sabbath was made for man, and not man for the Sabbath" (Mark 2:27). Every man in the synagogue would rescue a sheep on the Sabbath, so why not rescue a man made in the image of God (Matt. 12:11–12)? The scribes and Pharisees had turned God's gift into a heavy yoke that nobody could bear (Acts 15:10; Gal. 5:1).

This miracle illustrates the power of faith in God's Word. Jesus commanded the man to do the very thing he could not do, and yet *he did it!* "For no word from God shall be void of power" (Luke 1:37 ASV). God's commandments are always God's enablements.

The scribes and Pharisees were filled with fury. It certainly did not do them any good to worship God in the synagogue that morning. So angry were they that they even joined forces with the Herodians (the Jews who supported Herod) in a plot to kill Jesus (Mark 3:6). Jesus knew their thoughts (Matt. 12:15; Luke 6:8), so He merely withdrew to the Sea of Galilee, ministered to the multitudes, and then went up to a mountain alone to pray.

Jesus gives a spiritual "sabbath rest" that is in the heart all the time (Matt. 11:28–30). Unlike the galling yoke of the law, the yoke that Jesus gives is "well-fitting," and His "burden is light." When the sinner trusts the Savior, he has peace with God because his sins are forgiven and he is reconciled to God (Rom. 5:1–11). As the believer yields to Christ in daily experience, he enjoys "the peace of God" in his heart and mind (Phil. 4:6–7).

A New Nation (6:12–19)

Jesus spent the whole night in prayer, for He was about to call His twelve apostles from among the many disciples who were following Him. A *disciple* is a learner, an apprentice; while an *apostle* is a chosen messenger sent with a special commission. Jesus had many disciples (see Luke 10:1) but only twelve handpicked apostles.

Why did He pray all night? For one thing, He knew that opposition against Him was growing and would finally result in His crucifixion, so He prayed for strength as He faced the path ahead. Also, He wanted the Father's guidance as He selected His twelve apostles, for the future of the church rested with them. Keep in mind that one of the Twelve would betray Him, *and Jesus knew who he was from the beginning* (John 6:64). Our Lord had real human emotions (Luke 22:41–44; Heb. 5:7–8), and it was through prayer that He made this difficult choice.

The names of the apostles are also given in Matthew 10:1–4; Mark 3:16–19; and Acts 1:13 (minus Judas). In all the lists, Peter is named first and, except in Acts 1:13, Judas is named last. The Judas in Acts 1:13 is Judas the brother [more likely "the son"] of James, who is also called Thaddeus in Mark 3:18. It was not unusual for one man to have two or more names.

Simon received the name *Peter* (stone) when Andrew brought him to Jesus (John 1:40–42). Bartholomew is the same as Nathanael (John 1:45–49). The other

Simon in the group was nicknamed "Zelotes," which can mean one of two things. It may mean that he belonged to a group of fanatical Jewish patriots known as "the Zealots," whose purpose was to deliver Israel from the tyranny of Rome. They used every means at hand, including terror and assassination, to accomplish their purposes. Or, perhaps the word *Zelotes* translates from the Hebrew word *qanna* which means "Jealous for God, zealous for God's honor." (It is transliterated in Matt. 10:4 as "Simon the Canaanite" *[qanna].*) Whether Simon was known for his zeal to honor God, or his membership in a subversive organization, we cannot be sure—possibly both.

Nor are we sure of the origin of the word *Iscariot.* It probably means "man [*ish* in Hebrew] of Kerioth," a town in southern Judah (Josh. 15:25). Some connect it with the Aramaic word *seqar,* which means "false-hood." Thus, "Judas the false one." The geographical explanation is probably right.

What an interesting group of men! They illustrate what Paul wrote in 1 Corinthians 1:26–29, and they are an encouragement to us today. After all, if God could use them, can He not use us? Perhaps seven of them were fishermen (see John 21:1–3), one was a tax collector, and the other four are anonymous as far as their vocations are concerned. They were ordinary men; their personalities were different, yet Jesus called them to be with Him, to learn from Him, and to go out to represent Him (Mark 3:14).

Why twelve apostles? Because there were twelve tribes in Israel, and Jesus was forming the nucleus for a new nation (see Matt. 21:43; 1 Peter 2:9). The first Christians were Jews because the gospel came "to the Jew first" (Acts 13:46; Rom. 1:16). Later, the Gentiles were added to the church through the witness of the scattered Jewish believers (Acts 11:19ff.) and the ministry of Paul, apostle to the Gentiles. In the church, there is no difference between Jew and Gentile; we are "all one in Christ Jesus" (Gal. 3:28).

It is significant that after Jesus called His twelve apostles, and before He preached this great sermon, He took time to heal many needy people. This was a demonstration of both His power and His compassion. It was also a reminder to His newly appointed assistants that their job was to share His love and power with a needy world. It is estimated that there were three hundred million people in the world in Jesus' day, while there are over five billion today, four-fifths of them in the less-developed nations. What a challenge to the church!

A New Blessing (6:20–49)

This sermon is probably a shorter version of what we call "The Sermon on the Mount" (Matt. 5—7), though some fine evangelical scholars believe these were two different events. If they are the same event, the fact that Matthew locates it on a mountain (Matt. 5:1), while Luke puts it "in the plain" (Luke 6:17), creates no problem. Dr. D. A. Carson points out that the

Greek word translated "plain" can mean "a plateau in a mountainous region" (*Exegetical Fallacies,* Baker, 43).

Jesus went "into the hill country" with His disciples. After a night of prayer, He came down to a level place, ordained the Twelve, ministered to the sick, and then preached this sermon. It was His description of what it means to have a life of "blessing."

To most Jewish people, the word *blessing* evoked images of a long life; wealth; a large, healthy family; a full barn; and defeated enemies. God's covenant with Israel did include such material and physical blessings (Deut. 28; Job 1:1–12; Prov. 3:1–10), for this was how God taught and disciplined them. After all, they were "little children" in the faith, and we teach children by means of rewards and punishments. With the coming of Jesus, Israel's childhood period ended, and the people had to mature in their understanding of God's ways (Gal. 4:1–6).

Jesus was preaching to His disciples as well as to the multitudes (Luke 6:27, 47), for even the Twelve had to unlearn many things before they could effectively serve Him. Furthermore, they had left everything to follow Jesus (Luke 5:11, 28), and no doubt were asking themselves, "What is in store for us?" (See Matt. 19:27.) The Lord explained in this sermon that the truly blessed life comes not from *getting,* or from *doing,* but from *being.* The emphasis is on Godlike character.

This sermon is not "the gospel," and nobody goes to heaven by "following the Sermon on the Mount." Dead sinners cannot obey the living God; they must first be born again and receive God's life (John 3:1–7, 36).

Nor is this sermon a "constitution" for the kingdom God will one day establish on earth (Matt. 20:21; Luke 22:30). The Sermon on the Mount applies to life today and describes the kind of godly character we should have as believers in this world. Certainly our Lord describes a life situation quite unlike that of the glorious kingdom, including hunger, tears, persecution, and false teachers.

What Jesus did was to focus on *attitudes:* our attitude toward circumstances (Luke 6:20–26), people (Luke 6:27–38), ourselves (Luke 6:39–45), and God (Luke 6:46–49). He emphasized four essentials for true happiness: faith in God, love toward others, honesty with ourselves, and obedience toward God.

Circumstances (vv. 20–26). Life was difficult for the people of that day, and there was not much hope their circumstances would be improved. Like people today, many of them thought that happiness came from having great possessions, or holding an exalted position, or enjoying the pleasures and popularity that money can buy. Imagine how surprised they were when they heard Jesus describe happiness in terms *just the opposite of what they expected!* They discovered that what they needed most was not a change in circumstances but a change in their relationship to God and in their outlook on life.

Jesus was not teaching that poverty, hunger,

persecution, and tears were blessings *in themselves.* If that were true, He would never have done all He did to alleviate the sufferings of others. Rather, Jesus was describing the *inner attitudes* we must have if we are to experience the blessedness of the Christian life. We should certainly do what we can to help others in a material way (James 2:15–17; 1 John 3:16–18), but we must remember that no amount of "things" can substitute for a personal relationship with God.

Matthew's account makes this clear: "Blessed are the poor *in spirit* … Blessed are they which do hunger and thirst *after righteousness*" (Matt. 5:3, 6, italics mine). Jesus was not glorifying material poverty; rather, He was calling for that brokenness of heart that confesses spiritual poverty within (Luke 18:9–14; Phil. 3:4–14). The humble person is the only kind the Lord can save (Isa. 57:15; 66:2; 1 Peter 5:6). If you compare "the Beatitudes" with Isaiah 61:1–3 and Luke 4:18, you will see that our Lord's emphasis was on the condition of the heart and not the outward circumstances. Mary expressed this same insight in her song of praise (Luke 1:46–55).

Jesus Himself would experience the persecution described in Luke 6:22, and so would His disciples. How can we rejoice when men attack us? By remembering that it is a privilege to suffer for His sake (Phil. 3:10). When they treat us the way they treated Him, it is evidence that we are starting to live as He lived, and that is a compliment. All of the saints of the ages were treated this way, so we are in good company! Furthermore, God promises a special reward for all those who are faithful to Him, so the best is yet to come!

The four "woes" all share a common truth: you take what you want from life and you pay for it. If you want immediate wealth, fullness, laughter, and popularity, you can get it, but there is a price to pay: *that is all you will get.* Jesus did not say that these things were wrong. He said that *being satisfied with them is its own judgment.*

H. H. Farmer wrote that "to Jesus the terrible thing about having wrong values in life and pursuing wrong things is not that you are doomed to bitter disappointment, but that you are *not;* not that you do not achieve what you want, but that you *do*" (*Things Not Seen,* Nishbet [London], 96). When people are satisfied with the lesser things of life, the good instead of the best, then their successes add up only as failures. These people are spiritually bankrupt and do not realize it.

Life is built on character, and character is built on decisions. But decisions are based on values, *and values must be accepted by faith.* Moses made his life-changing decisions on the basis of values that other people thought were foolish (Heb. 11:24–29), but God honored his faith. The Christian enjoys all that God gives him (1 Tim. 6:17) because he lives "with eternity's values in view."

People (vv. 27–38). Jesus assumed that anybody who lived for eternal values would get into trouble with the world's crowd. Christians are the "salt of the earth" and "the light of the world" (Matt. 5:13–16), and sometimes the salt stings and the light exposes sin. Sinners show their hatred by avoiding us or rejecting us (Luke 6:22), insulting us (Luke 6:28), physically abusing us (Luke 6:29), and suing us (Luke 6:30). This is something we must expect (Phil. 1:29; 2 Tim. 3:12).

How should we treat our enemies? We must love them, do them good, and pray for them. Hatred only breeds more hatred, "for man's anger does not bring about the righteous life that God desires" (James 1:20 NIV). This cannot be done in our own strength, but it can be done through the power of the Holy Spirit (Rom. 5:5; Gal. 5:22–23).

We must not look at these admonitions as a series of rules to be obeyed. They describe an attitude of heart that expresses itself positively when others are negative, and generously when others are selfish, all to the glory of God. It is an inner disposition, not a legal duty. We must have wisdom to know when to turn the other cheek and when to claim our rights (John 18:22–23; Acts 16:35–40). Even Christian love must exercise discernment (Phil. 1:9–11).

Two principles stand out: we must treat others as we would want to be treated (Luke 6:31), which assumes we want the very best spiritually for ourselves; and we must imitate our Father in heaven and be merciful (Luke 6:36). The important thing is not that we are vindicated before our enemies but that we become more like God in our character (Luke 6:35). This is the greatest reward anyone can receive, far greater than riches, food, laughter, or popularity (Luke 6:24–26). Those things will one day vanish, but character will last for eternity. We must believe Matthew 6:33 and practice it in the power of the Spirit.

Luke 6:37–38 reminds us that we reap what we sow and in the amount that we sow. If we judge others, we will ourselves be judged. If we forgive, we shall be forgiven, but if we condemn, we shall be condemned (see Matt. 18:21–35). He was not talking about eternal judgment but the way we are treated in this life. If we live to give, God will see to it that we receive, but if we live only to get, God will see to it that we lose. This principle applies not only to our giving of money, but also to the giving of ourselves in ministry to others.

Self (vv. 39–45). The four striking figures in this section teach us some important lessons about ministry. To begin with, as His disciples, we must be sure that we see clearly enough to guide others in their spiritual walk. While there are blind people who have a keen sense of direction, it is not likely any of them will be hired as airplane pilots or wilderness guides. Jesus was referring primarily to the Pharisees, who were leading the people astray (Matt. 15:14; 23:16). If we see ourselves as excellent guides, but do not realize our blindness, we will only lead people into the ditch (see Rom. 2:17–22).

Luke 6:40 reminds us that we cannot lead others where we have not been ourselves, nor can we be all that our Master is. In fact, the more we strive to be like Him, the more we realize how far short we fall. This is a warning against pride, for nothing blinds a person like pride.

Continuing the image of "the eye," Jesus taught that we must be able to see clearly enough to help our brother see better. It certainly is not wrong to help a brother get a painful speck of dirt out of his eye, *provided we can see what we are doing.* The crowd must have laughed out loud when Jesus described an "eye doctor" with *a plank* in his eye, performing surgery on a patient with *a speck* in his eye!

The emphasis here is on being honest with ourselves and not becoming hypocrites. It is easy to try to help a brother with his faults *just so we can cover up our own sins!* People who are constantly criticizing others are usually guilty of something worse in their own lives.

The illustration of the tree reminds us that fruit is always true to character. An apple tree produces apples, not oranges, and a good person produces good fruit, not evil. Believers do sin, but the witness of their words and works is consistently good to the glory of God. In terms of ministry, servants of God who are faithful will reproduce themselves in people who are in turn true to the Lord (2 Tim. 2:2).

The last image, the treasury, teaches us that what comes out of the lips depends on what is inside the heart. The human heart is like a treasury, and what we speak reveals what is there. A man who apologized for swearing by saying, "It really wasn't in me!" heard a friend say, "It had to be in you or it couldn't have come out of you!"

We must be honest with ourselves and admit the blind spots in our lives, the obstacles that blur our vision, and the areas within that must be corrected. Then we can be used of the Lord to minister to others and not lead them astray.

God (vv. 46—49). Our Lord's emphasis here is on obedience. It is not enough merely to hear His Word and call Him "Lord." We must also obey what He commands us to do. All of us are builders, and we must be careful to build wisely. To "build on the rock" simply means to obey what God commands in His Word. To "build on the sand" means to give Christ lip service, but not obey His will. It may look as if we are building a strong house, but if it has no foundation, it cannot last. The storm here is not the last judgment but the tests of life that come to every professing Christian. Not everybody who professes to know the Lord has had a real experience of salvation. They may have been active in church and other religious organizations, but if they are not saved by faith, they have no foundation to their lives. When difficulties come, instead of glorifying the Lord, they desert Him, and their house of testimony collapses.

Nobody can really call Jesus Christ "Lord" except by the Holy Spirit of God (Rom. 8:16; 1 Cor. 12:3). If Christ is in our hearts, then our mouths must confess Him to others (Rom. 10:9—10). If we are "rooted and built up in him" (Col. 2:7), then our fruits will be good and our house will withstand the storms. We may have our faults and failures, but the steady witness of our lives will point to Christ and honor Him.

This is the "new blessing" that Jesus offered His nation and that He offers us today. We can experience the "heavenly happiness" and true blessedness that only He can give. The basis for all of this is personal saving faith in the Lord Jesus Christ, for, as Dr. H.A. Ironside once said, "We cannot live the life until first we possess it."

CHAPTER SIX
Luke 7
COMPASSION IN ACTION

Compassion has been defined as "your pain in my heart." What pain our Lord must have felt as He ministered from place to place! In this chapter alone, Jesus is confronted with the miseries of a dying servant, a grieving widow, a perplexed prophet, and a repentant sinner, and He helped them all. If a "hardship committee" had been asked to decide which of these persons was "deserving," we wonder who would have been chosen.

Jesus helped them all, because compassion does not measure: it ministers. Bernard of Clairvaux said, "Justice seeks out only the *merits* of the case, but pity only regards the *need.*" It was compassion, not justice, that motivated the Great Physician who came "not to call the righteous, but sinners to repentance" (Luke 5:32). Let's meet these four hurting people and see our Lord's responses to their needs.

The Servant: His Response to Faith (7:1—10)

In the Gospels and the book of Acts, Roman centurions are presented as quality men of character, and this one is a sterling example. The Jewish elders had little love for the Romans in general and Roman soldiers in particular, and yet the elders commended this officer to Jesus. He loved the Jewish people in Capernaum and even built them a synagogue. He loved his servant and did not want him to die. This centurion was not a Stoic who insulated himself from the pain of others. He had a heart of concern, even for his lowly servant boy who was dying from a paralyzing disease (Matt. 8:6).

Matthew's condensed report (Matt. 8:5—13) does not contradict Luke's fuller account. The centurion's friends represented him to Jesus and then represented Jesus to him. When a newscaster reports that the president or the prime minister said something to Congress or Parliament, this does not necessarily mean that the message was delivered by them in person. It was probably delivered by one of their official representatives, but the message would be received as from the president or prime minister personally.

We are impressed not only with this man's great

love, but also his great humility. Imagine a Roman officer telling a poor Jewish rabbi that he was unworthy to have Him enter his house! The Romans were not known for displaying humility, especially before their Jewish subjects.

But the characteristic that most impressed Jesus was the man's faith. Twice in the gospel record we are told that Jesus marveled. Here in Capernaum, He marveled at the faith of a Gentile; and in Nazareth, He marveled at the unbelief of the Jews (Mark 6:6). The only other person Jesus commended for having "great faith" was a Gentile woman whose daughter He delivered from a demon (Matt. 15:28). It is worth noting that in both of these instances, Jesus healed *at a distance* (see Ps. 107:20; Eph. 2:11–13).

The centurion's faith certainly was remarkable. After all, he was a Gentile whose background was pagan. He was a Roman soldier, trained to be self-sufficient, and we have no evidence that he had ever heard Jesus preach. Perhaps he heard about Jesus' healing power from the nobleman whose son Jesus had healed, also at a distance (John 4:46–54). His soldiers may also have brought him reports of the miracles Jesus had performed, for the Romans kept close touch with the events in Jewish life.

The important word in Luke 7:8 is "also." (It should be in Matt. 8:9 as well, but the KJV omits it for some reason. The NASB has "too" in both places.) The officer saw a parallel between the way he commanded his soldiers and the way Jesus commanded diseases. Both the centurion and Jesus were under authority, and because they were under authority, they had the right to exercise authority. *All they had to do was say the word and things happened.* What tremendous faith this man exhibited! No wonder Jesus marveled.

If this Roman, with very little spiritual instruction, had that kind of faith in God's Word, how much greater *our* faith ought to be! We have an entire Bible to read and study, as well as nearly two thousand years of church history to encourage us, and yet we are guilty of "no faith" (Mark 4:40) or "little faith" (Matt. 14:31). Our prayer ought to be, "Lord, increase our faith!" (Luke 17:5).

The Widow: Jesus' Response to Despair (7:11–17)

Nain was about twenty-five miles from Capernaum, a good day's journey away, yet Jesus went there even though He was not requested to come. Since the Jews buried their dead the same day (Deut. 21:23; Acts 5:5–10), it is likely that Jesus and His disciples arrived at the city gate late in the afternoon of the day the boy died. Four special meetings took place at the city gate that day.

Two crowds met. We can only marvel at the providence of God when we see Jesus meet that funeral procession just as it was heading for the burial ground. He lived on a divine timetable as He obeyed the will of His Father (John 11:9; 13:1). The sympathetic Savior always gives help when we need it most (Heb. 4:16).

What a contrast between the crowd that was following Jesus and the crowd following the widow and her dead son. Jesus and His disciples were rejoicing in the blessing of the Lord, but the widow and her friends were lamenting the death of her only son. Jesus was heading for the city while the mourners were heading for the cemetery.

Spiritually speaking, each of us is in one of these two crowds. If you have trusted Christ, you are going to the city (Heb. 11:10, 13–16; 12:22). If you are "dead in sin," you are already in the cemetery and under the condemnation of God (John 3:36; Eph. 2:1–3). You need to trust Jesus Christ and be raised from the dead (John 5:24; Eph. 2:4–10).

Two only sons met. One was alive but destined to die, the other dead but destined to live. The term *only begotten* as applied to Jesus means "unique," "the only one of its kind." Jesus is not a "son" in the same sense that I am, having been brought into existence by conception and birth. Since Jesus is eternal God, He has always existed. The title *Son of God* declares Christ's divine nature and His relationship to the Father, to whom the Son has willingly subjected Himself from all eternity. All the Persons of the Godhead are equal, but in the "economy" of the Trinity, each has a specific place to fill and task to fulfill.

Two sufferers met. Jesus, "the man of sorrows," could easily identify with the widow's heartache. Not only was she in sorrow, but she was now left alone in a society that did not have resources to care for widows. What would happen to her? Jesus felt the pain that sin and death have brought into this world, and He did something about it.

Two enemies met. Jesus faced death, "the last enemy" (1 Cor. 15:26). When you consider the pain and grief that it causes in this world, death is indeed an enemy, and only Jesus Christ can give us victory (see 1 Cor. 15:51–58; Heb. 2:14–15). Jesus had only to speak the word and the boy was raised to life and health.

The boy gave two evidences of life: he sat up and he spoke. He was lying on an open stretcher, not in a closed coffin, so it was easy for him to sit up. We are not told what he said, but it must have been interesting! What an act of tenderness it was for Jesus to take the boy and give him to his rejoicing mother. The whole scene reminds us of what will happen when the Lord returns, and we are reunited with our loved ones who have gone to glory (1 Thess. 4:13–18).

The response of the people was to glorify God and identify Jesus with the prophet the Jews had been waiting for (Deut. 18:15; John 1:21; Acts 3:22–23). It did not take long for the report of this miracle to spread. People were even more enthusiastic to see Jesus, and great crowds followed Him (Luke 8:4, 19, 42).

John the Baptist: His Response to Doubt (7:18–35)

Confusion (vv. 18–20). John had been in prison some months (Luke 3:19–20), but he knew what Jesus was doing because his own disciples kept him informed. It must have been difficult for this man, accustomed to a wilderness life, to be confined in a prison. The physical and emotional strain were no doubt great, and the long days of waiting did not make it easier. The Jewish leaders did nothing to intercede for John, and it seemed that even Jesus was doing nothing for him. If He came to set the prisoners free (Luke 4:18), then John the Baptist was a candidate!

It is not unusual for great spiritual leaders to have their days of doubt and uncertainty. Moses was ready to quit on one occasion (Num. 11:10–15), and so were Elijah (1 Kings 19) and Jeremiah (Jer. 20:7–9, 14–18), and even Paul knew the meaning of despair (2 Cor. 1:8–9).

There is a difference between doubt and unbelief. Doubt is a matter of the mind: we cannot understand what God is doing or why He is doing it. Unbelief is a matter of the will: we refuse to believe God's Word and obey what He tells us to do. "Doubt is not always a sign that a man is wrong," said Oswald Chambers; "it may be a sign that he is thinking." In John's case, his inquiry was not born of willful unbelief, but of doubt nourished by physical and emotional strain.

You and I can look back at the ministry of Christ and understand what He was doing, but John did not have that advantage. John had announced judgment, but Jesus was doing deeds of love and mercy. John had promised that the kingdom was at hand, but there was no evidence of it so far. He had presented Jesus as "the Lamb of God" (John 1:29), so John must have understood something about Jesus' sacrifice, yet how did this sacrifice relate to the promised kingdom for Israel? He was perplexed about God's plan and his place in it. But let's not judge him harshly, for even the prophets were perplexed about some of these things (1 Peter 1:10–12).

Confirmation (vv. 21–23). Jesus did not give the two men a lecture on theology or prophecy. Instead, He invited them to watch as He healed many people of many different afflictions. Certainly these were His credentials as the promised Messiah (Isa. 29:18–19; 35:4–6; 42:1–7). He had not established a political kingdom, but the kingdom of God was there in power.

The Greek word translated "offended" gives us our English word *scandalize,* and it referred originally to the "bait stick" in a trap. John was in danger of being trapped because of his concern about what Jesus was *not* doing. He was stumbling over his Lord and His ministry. Jesus gently told him to have faith, for his Lord knew what He was doing.

There are many people today who criticize the church for not "changing the world" and solving the economic, political, and social problems of society. What they forget is that God changes His world by changing individual people. History shows that the church has often led the way in humanitarian service and reform, but the church's main job is to bring lost sinners to the Savior. Everything else is a by-product

of that. Proclaiming the gospel must always be the church's first priority.

Commendation (vv. 24–30). What we think of ourselves, or what others think of us, is not as important as what God thinks. Jesus waited until the messengers had departed, and then He publicly commended John for his ministry. At the same time, He exposed the sinful hearts of those who rejected John's ministry.

John the Baptist was not a *compromiser,* a reed blowing in the wind (note Eph. 4:14); nor was he a popular *celebrity,* enjoying the friendship of great people and the pleasures of wealth. John did not waver or weaken, no matter what people did to him. John was not only a prophet, but he was a prophet whose ministry was prophesied (see Isa. 40:3 and Mal. 3:1)! The last of the Old Testament prophets, John had the great privilege as God's messenger of introducing the Messiah to Israel.

How is the least person in the kingdom of God greater than John? In position, not in character or ministry. John was the herald of the King, announcing the kingdom; believers today are children of the kingdom and the friends of the King (John 15:15). John's ministry was a turning point in both the nation's history and in God's plan of redemption (Luke 16:16).

Luke 7:29–30 are the words of Jesus, not an explanation from Luke (see Matt. 21:32). They answer the question some of the people were asking: "If John is such a great prophet, why is he in prison?" The answer is, because of the willful unbelief of the religious leaders. The common people accepted John's message and were baptized by him as proof of their repentance. They "justified God," which means they agreed with what God said about them (Ps. 51:4). But the religious leaders justified themselves (Luke 16:15), not God, and rejected John and his message.

Condemnation (vv. 31–35). Jesus compared that generation to people who were childish, not childlike, and nothing pleased them. He was probably referring to the scribes and Pharisees in particular. John was an individual who declared a stern message of judgment, and they said, "He has a demon!" Jesus mingled with the people and preached a gracious message of salvation, and they said, "He's a glutton, a winebibber, and a friend of publicans and sinners!" They wanted neither the funeral nor the wedding, because nothing pleased them.

People who want to avoid the truth about themselves can always find something in the preacher to criticize. This is one way they "justify themselves." But God's wisdom is not frustrated by the arguments of the "wise and prudent." *It is demonstrated in the changed lives of those who believe.* This is how true wisdom is "justified."

A Sinful Woman: His Response to Love (7:36–50)

Jesus not only accepted hospitality from the publicans and sinners but also from the Pharisees. They needed the

Word of God too, whether they realized it or not. We trust that Simon's invitation was a sincere one and that he did not have some ulterior motive for having Jesus in his home. If he did, his plan backfired, because he ended up learning more about himself than he cared to know!

The repentant woman (vv. 36–38). It was customary in that day for outsiders to hover around during banquets so they could watch the "important people" and hear the conversation. Since everything was open, they could even enter the banquet hall and speak to a guest. This explains how this woman had access to Jesus. He was not behind locked doors. In that day women were not invited to banquets.

Jewish rabbis did not speak to women in public, nor did they eat with them in public. A woman of this type would not be welcomed in the house of Simon the Pharisee. Her sins are not named, but we get the impression she was a woman of the streets with a bad reputation.

Do not confuse this event with a similar one involving Mary of Bethany (John 12:1–8), and do not identify this woman with Mary Magdalene (Mark 16:9; Luke 8:2) as many continue to do.

The woman admitted she was a sinner and gave evidence that she was a *repentant* sinner. If you check a harmony of the Gospels, you will discover that just before this event, Jesus had given the gracious invitation, "Come unto me … and I will give you rest" (Matt. 11:28–30). Perhaps that was when the woman turned from her sin and trusted the Savior. Her tears, her humble attitude, and her expensive gift all spoke of a changed heart.

The critical host (vv. 39–43). Simon was embarrassed, both for himself and for his guests. People had been saying that Jesus was a great prophet (Luke 7:16), but He certainly was not exhibiting much prophetic discernment if He allowed a sinful woman to anoint His feet! He must be a fraud.

Simon's real problem was *blindness:* he could not see himself, the woman, or the Lord Jesus. It was easy for him to say, "*She* is a sinner!" but impossible for him to say, "I am also a sinner!" (see Luke 18:9–14). Jesus proved that He was indeed a prophet by reading Simon's thoughts and revealing his needs.

The parable does not deal with the *amount* of sin in a person's life but the *awareness of* that sin in his heart. How much sin must a person commit to be a sinner? Simon and the woman were both sinners. Simon was guilty of sins of the spirit, especially pride, while the woman was guilty of sins of the flesh (see 2 Cor. 7:1). Her sins were known, while Simon's sins were hidden to everyone except God. *And both of them were bankrupt and could not pay their debt to God.* Simon was just as spiritually bankrupt as the woman, only he did not realize it.

Forgiveness is a gift of God's grace; the debt was paid in full by Jesus Christ (Eph. 1:7; 1 Peter 1:18–19). The word *frankly* means "graciously and freely." The woman accepted God's free offer of salvation and

expressed her love openly. Simon rejected that offer and remained unforgiven. He was not only blind to himself, but he was blind to the woman and to his honored guest!

The forgiving Savior (vv. 44–50). The woman was guilty of sins of commission, but Simon was guilty of sins of omission. He had not been a gracious host to the Lord Jesus. (For a contrast, see Abraham in Gen. 18:1–8.) Everything that Simon neglected to do, the woman did—and she did it better!

There are two errors we must avoid as we interpret our Lord's words. First, we must not conclude that this woman was saved by her tears and her gift. Jesus made it clear that it was *her faith* alone that saved her (Luke 7:50), for no amount of good works can pay for salvation (Titus 3:4–7).

Nor should we think that lost sinners are saved by love, either God's love for them or their love for God. God loves the whole world (John 3:16), yet the whole world is not saved. "For by grace you have been saved through faith, and that not of yourselves; it is the gift of God, not of works, lest anyone should boast" (Eph. 2:8–9 NKJV). Grace is love that pays a price, and that price was the death of the Son of God on the cross.

Jesus did not reject either the woman's tears or her gift of ointment, because her works were the evidence of her faith. "Faith without works is dead" (see James 2:14–26). We are not saved by faith plus works; we are saved by a faith that leads to works. This anonymous woman illustrates the truth of Galatians 5:6: "The only thing that counts is faith expressing itself through love" (NIV).

How did the woman know that her sins were forgiven? *Jesus told her.* How do we know today that we have been forgiven? *God tells us so in His Word.* Here are just a few verses to consider: Isaiah 1:18; 43:25–26; 55:6–7; Acts 13:38–39; Romans 4:7–8; Ephesians 4:32; and Hebrews 8:12. Once you understand the meaning of God's grace, you have no trouble receiving His free and full forgiveness and rejoicing in it.

Of course, the legalistic critics at the dinner were shocked when Jesus said, "Her sins, which are many, are forgiven." By saying this, Jesus was claiming to be God (see Luke 5:21)! But He *is God*, and He died for the sins that she committed. His words of forgiveness were not cheap words; they cost Him dearly on the cross.

How was this woman saved? She repented of her sins and put her faith in Jesus Christ. How did she know she was truly forgiven? She had the assurance of His word. What was the proof of her salvation? Her love for Christ expressed in sacrificial devotion to Him. For the first time in her life, she had peace with God (Luke 7:50). Literally it reads, "Go *into* peace," for she had moved out of the sphere of enmity toward God and was now enjoying peace with God (Rom. 5:1; 8:7–8).

When Jesus healed the centurion's servant, it was a great miracle. An even greater miracle was His raising the widow's son from the dead. But in this chapter, the greatest miracle of all was His saving this woman from her sins and making her a new person. The miracle of salvation has to be the greatest miracle of all, for it meets the greatest need, brings the greatest results (and they last forever), and cost the greatest price.

Simon was blind to the woman and blind to himself. He saw her past, but Jesus saw her future. I wonder how many rejected sinners have found salvation through the testimony of this woman in Luke's gospel. She encourages us to believe that Jesus can take any sinner and make him or her into a child of God.

But God's forgiveness is not automatic; we can reject His grace if we will. In 1830, a man named George Wilson was arrested for mail theft, the penalty for which was hanging. After a time, President Andrew Jackson gave Wilson a pardon *but he refused to accept it!* The authorities were puzzled: should Wilson be freed or hanged?

They consulted Chief Justice John Marshall, who handed down this decision: "A pardon is a slip of paper, the value of which is determined by the acceptance of the person to be pardoned. If it is refused, it is no pardon. George Wilson must be hanged."

If you have never accepted God's pardon, now is the time to believe and be saved.

CHAPTER SEVEN
Luke 8
LESSONS ABOUT FAITH

One of the major themes in Luke 8 is how to get faith and use it in the everyday experiences of life. In the first section, Jesus laid the foundation by teaching His disciples that faith comes through receiving the Word of God into an understanding heart. In the second part, He put them through a series of "examinations" to see how much they had really learned. Most of us enjoy Bible study, but we wish we could avoid the examinations that often follow the lessons! However, it is in the tests of life that faith really grows and we get closer to Christ.

The cynical American editor H. L. Mencken defined faith as "an illogical belief in the occurrence of the impossible," and Mark Twain said (through one of his characters) that faith is "believin' what you know ain't so." Of course, these men are describing superstition, not faith, for the faith of a Christian rests on solid foundations.

Everybody lives by faith in something or someone. The difference between the Christian believer and the unsaved person is not that one has faith and the other does not. They *both* have faith. The difference is in *the object of their faith,* for faith is only as good as the object. The Christian believer has put his faith in Jesus Christ, and he bases that faith on the Word of God.

Teaching: Hearing God's Word (8:1–21)
The Lord continued His itinerant ministry in Galilee,

assisted by His disciples and partially supported by some godly women. It was not unusual for Jewish rabbis to receive gifts from grateful people, and these women had certainly benefited from Jesus' ministry. The New Testament church leaders were supported by gifts from friends (2 Tim. 1:16–18) and from churches (Phil. 4:15–17), and Paul supported himself by his own labor (2 Thess. 3:6–10).

The word *hear* is used nine times in this section. It means much more than simply listening to words. "Hearing" means listening with spiritual understanding and receptivity. "So then faith come by hearing, and hearing by the word of God" (Rom. 10:17). With this in mind, we can understand the three admonitions Jesus gave His followers.

Hear and receive the Word (vv. 4–15). Initially, the sower is Jesus Christ, but the sower represents any of God's people who share the Word of God (John 4:35–38). The seed is the Word of God, for, like seed, the Word has life and power (Heb. 4:12) and can produce spiritual fruit (Gal. 5:22–23). But the seed can do nothing until it is planted (John 12:24). When a person hears and understands the Word, then the seed is planted in the heart. What happens after that depends on the nature of the soil.

Jesus called this parable "the parable of the sower" (Matt. 13:18), but it could also be called "the parable of the soils." The seed without the soil is fruitless, and the soil without the seed is almost useless. The human heart is like soil: if it is prepared properly, it can receive the seed of the Word of God and produce a fruitful harvest.

Jesus described four different kinds of hearts, three of which did not produce any fruit. The proof of salvation is *fruit* and not merely hearing the Word or making a profession of faith in Christ. Jesus had already made that clear in His "Sermon on the Mount" (Luke 6:43–49; also note Matt. 7:20).

The hard soil (vv. 5, 12). This soil represents the person who hears the Word but immediately allows the devil to snatch the seed away. How did the heart become hard? The "wayside" was the path that ran through the common field, separating the plots, and the foot traffic hardened the soil. Whatever goes into the ear or eye finally enters the heart, so be careful who is allowed to "walk on your heart."

The shallow soil (vv. 6, 13). This soil illustrates the emotional hearer who quickly responds to the message, but his interest wanes and he does not continue (see John 8:31–32). In many parts of the Holy Land you find a substratum of limestone covered with a thin layer of soil. The shoot can grow up, but the roots cannot go down, and the sun withers the rootless plant. The sun represents the testing that comes to all professing believers to prove their faith. Sun is good for plants *if they have roots.* Persecution can deepen the roots of a true Christian, but it only exposes the shallowness of the false Christian.

The crowded soil (vv. 7, 14). This soil illustrates the

person who does not repent and "weed out" the things that hinder the harvest. There is enough soil so the roots can go down, but not enough room for the plant to grow up and produce fruit. The plant is crowded out and the fruit is choked. "Cares, riches, and the pleasures of this life" are like weeds in a garden that keep the soil from being fruitful. The person with the "crowded heart" comes closest to salvation, but he still does not bring forth "fruit to perfection."

The good soil (vv. 8, 15). This soil alone is fruitful. It illustrates the individual who hears the Word, understands it, receives it within, is truly saved, and proves it by patiently producing fruit (see 1 Thess. 2:13; 1 Peter 1:22–25). Not everybody produces the same amount of fruit (Matt. 13:8), but all true believers will produce some fruit as evidence of spiritual life. That fruit may include winning others to Christ (Rom. 1:13), money given to God's work (Rom. 15:25–28), good works (Col. 1:10), Christian character (Gal. 5:22–23), and praise to the Lord (Heb. 13:15).

This parable shows that Jesus was not impressed by the great crowds that followed Him. He knew that most of the people did not really "hear" the Word and receive it in their hearts. He gave this story to encourage the disciples in their future ministry, and to encourage us today. When you consider how much teaching, preaching, and witnessing goes on in the course of a month or a year, you wonder why there is such a small harvest. The fault does not lie with the sower or the seed. The problem is with the soil. The human heart will not submit to God, repent and receive the Word, and be saved.

"Faith comes first to the hearing ear, not to the cogitating mind," said A. W. Tozer, the much-quoted pastor and author. Faith is not a matter of IQ or education; it is a matter of humbly preparing the heart to receive God's truth (James 1:19–21). The wise and prudent are blind to truths that are easy for the babes to understand (Matt. 11:20–26).

Hear and share the Word (vv. 16–18). The disciples were perplexed because Jesus taught in parables, so they asked Him for an explanation (Luke 8:9–10; also see Matt. 13:10–17). His reply seems to suggest that He used parables in order to *hide* the truth from the crowds, but just the opposite is true, and Luke 8:16–18 makes that clear. His teaching is a light that must be allowed to shine so that sinners may be saved.

The word *parable* means "to cast alongside." A parable is a story that teaches something new by putting the truth alongside something familiar. The people knew about seeds and soil, so the parable of the sower interested them. Those who were indifferent or proud would shrug it off. Our Lord's parables aroused the interest of the concerned.

A parable starts off as a *picture* that is familiar to the listeners. But as you carefully consider the picture, it becomes a *mirror* in which you see yourself, and many people do not like to see themselves. This explains why some of our Lord's listeners became

angry when they heard His parables, and even tried to kill Him. But if we see ourselves as needy sinners and ask for help, then the mirror becomes a *window* through which we see God and His grace. To understand a parable and benefit from it demands honesty and humility on our part, and many of our Lord's hearers lacked both.

It is a serious thing to hear and understand the Word of God, because this puts on us the obligation to share that Word with others. Everyone who receives the seed then becomes a sower, a light-bearer, and a transmitter of God's truth (see 1 Thess. 1:5–8). If we keep it to ourselves, we will lose it, but if we share it, we will receive more.

Hear and obey the Word (vv. 19–21). Our Lord's mother, Mary, and His half-brothers (Matt. 13:55–56; Acts 1:14) were worried about Jesus and wanted to talk with Him. Some of His friends had already said that He was out of His mind (Mark 3:21), and perhaps His family agreed with them. Jesus took this as an opportunity to teach another spiritual lesson: being a part of His spiritual family is much more important than any human relationship and is based on obedience to the Word of God. It is not enough to "hear" the Word of God; we must also "keep it" (Luke 8:15).

In one of my radio series, I emphasized the importance of *doing* the Word of God, putting it into practice in daily life (James 1:22–25). I warned listeners that it is easy to think we are "spiritual" because we listen to one preacher after another, take notes, mark our Bibles, *but never really practice what we learn.* We are only fooling ourselves.

A listener wrote that my words had made her angry, but then she faced up to the fact that she was indeed guilty of being an "auditor" and not a doer of the Word. She began to listen to fewer radio preachers, to listen more carefully, and to practice what she heard. "This new approach to Bible study has transformed me!" she wrote. "The Bible has become a new Book to me and my life has changed!"

As His disciples, we must take heed *what we hear* (Mark 4:24) and *how we hear* (Luke 8:18), because God will hold us accountable. Listening to the wrong things, or listening to the right things with the wrong attitude, will rob us of truth and blessing. If we are faithful to receive the Word and share it, God will give us more, but if we fail to let our light shine, we will lose what we have. It is a solemn thing to hear the Word of God.

Testing: Heeding God's Word (8:22–56)

By the time the Lord had finished giving "the parables of the kingdom" (Matt. 13:1–52), the disciples must have felt like postgraduate students in the School of Faith! They now understood mysteries that were hidden from the scribes and rabbis and even from the Old Testament prophets. What they did not realize (and we are so like them!) is *that faith must be tested before it can be trusted.* It is one thing to learn a new spiritual truth, but quite something else to practice that truth in the everyday experiences of life.

Satan does not care how much Bible truth we learn so long as we do not live it. Truth that is only in the head is purely academic and never will get into the heart until it is practiced by the will. "Doing the will of God from the heart" is what God wants from His children (Eph. 6:6). Satan knows that academic truth is not dangerous, but *active* truth is.

Watch the Lord Jesus Christ as He meets four challenges to faith and comes forth the Victor. His people face these same challenges today and can also overcome by faith.

Dangerous circumstances (vv. 22–25). Jesus was weary from a long day of teaching and went to sleep as the ship left Capernaum for the opposite shore. But before He did, He gave them a word of command that was also a word of promise: they were going to the opposite shore. This word should have encouraged and strengthened the disciples during the storm, but their faith was still small (Matt. 8:26).

While our tour group was sailing from Tiberias to Capernaum, I asked our guide if he had even been in a storm on the Sea of Galilee. His eyes opened wide and he said, "Yes, and I hope it never happens to me again!" The situation is such that sudden squalls occur as winds from the mountains funnel to the lake located six hundred feet below sea level. When the cold air and warm air meet in this natural basin, a storm is sure to develop.

The disciples were afraid, *but Jesus was not!* He kept on sleeping, confident that His Father was completely in control (Ps. 89:8–9). The disciples became so frightened that they awakened Him and begged Him to rescue them. The title *Master* is the same one Peter used in Luke 5:5. Of course, their problem was not the storm around them but the unbelief within them. Actually, their unbelief was more dangerous than the storm!

The word *rebuked* was used by Jesus when dealing with demons (Luke 4:35, 41; 9:42). It is possible that Satan was behind this severe storm, attempting to destroy Jesus or at least hinder Him from reaching the demonized men at Gadara. But Jesus calmed both the wind and the sea by simply speaking the word. Usually after the winds die down, the waves remain rough for hours, but in this instance, everything became calm immediately and stayed that way (Ps. 148:8).

The disciples failed this test of faith because they did not lay hold of His word that He was going to the other side. It has well been said that faith is not believing in spite of circumstances; it is obeying in spite of feelings and consequences. The disciples looked around and saw danger, and looked within and saw fear, but they failed to look up by faith and see God. Faith and fear cannot dwell together in the same heart.

A woman said to D. L. Moody, "I have found a wonderful promise!" and she quoted Psalm 56:3, "What time I am afraid, I will trust in thee."

"Let me give you a better one," said Moody; and he quoted Isaiah 12:2: "Behold God is my salvation; I will trust and not be afraid."

Satan (vv. 26–39). Two demonized men met Jesus when He landed at Gadara (Matt. 8:28), but one of them was the more forward and did all the speaking. Both were pitiful cases: naked, living in the tombs, violent, dangerous, a menace to the area, and controlled by a legion of demons. (A Roman legion could have as many as six thousand men!) Satan is the thief (John 10:10) who robs his people of everything good and then tries to destroy them. No amount of man-made authority or restraint can control or change the devil's servants. Their only hope is in the Savior.

Demons have faith (James 2:19), but it is not saving faith. They believe that Jesus Christ is the Son of God with authority to command them. They believe in a future judgment (Matt. 8:29) and in the existence of a place of torment to which Jesus could send them ("the abyss," Luke 8:31). They also believe in prayer, for the demons begged Jesus not to send them to the abyss. They asked to be sent into the pigs, and Jesus granted their request.

Did Jesus have the right to permit the legion of demons to destroy a herd of two thousand swine and perhaps put the owners out of business? God owns everything (see Ps. 50:10–11) and can dispose of it as He pleases. Furthermore, these two men were worth far more than many pigs (see Matt. 12:12). The community should have thanked Jesus for ridding their neighborhood of these two menaces, but instead, *they begged Him to leave!*

What a transformation in these two men! You would have expected the people who saw the miracle to ask Jesus to stay and heal others who were sick and afflicted. Apparently money was more important to them than mercy, and they asked Jesus to leave.

The one former demoniac kept pleading with Jesus to be allowed to travel with Him and help Him. What a noble desire from a newly converted man! He had more spiritual discernment than all the other citizens put together. The man was not yet ready to become a disciple, but he could serve Jesus as a witness, starting at home among his Gentile relatives and friends. Jesus did not want Jews who had been healed to say too much about it, but it was safe for the Gentiles to tell others what Jesus had done for them, and that is what he did.

Sickness (vv. 40–48). When Jesus returned to Capernaum, the people welcomed Him, particularly a man and a woman who each had heavy burdens to share with Jesus. The contrast here is interesting, for it shows the variety of people who came to Jesus for help. The man's name is given (Jairus), but the woman is anonymous. Jairus was a wealthy leading citizen, but the woman was a lowly person who had spent all her money trying to get well. Here was a man interceding for his child and a woman hoping to get help for herself, and both came to the feet of Jesus. Jairus had been blessed with twelve years of joy with his daughter, and now might lose her, while the woman had experienced twelve years of misery because of her affliction, and now she was hoping to get well.

This woman had a hidden need, a burden she had lived with for twelve long years. It affected her physically and made life difficult. But it also affected her spiritually, because the hemorrhage made her ceremonially defiled and unable to participate in the religious life of the nation (Lev. 15:19–22). She was defiled, destitute, discouraged, and desperate, but she came to Jesus and her need was met.

Her faith was almost superstitious, but the Lord honored it. She knew that He had healed others and she wanted Him to heal her. She could have used many excuses—the crowd was pressing around Him; nothing had worked for twelve years; it was not right to come to Jesus as a last resort; she was not an important person; He was on His way to heal Jairus's daughter—but she allowed nothing to stand in her way.

Jewish men wore tassels of blue twisted cords on the corners of their outer garments, as a reminder that they were to obey God's commandments (Num. 15:37–40; Deut. 22:12). The Pharisees went to extremes in obeying this rule to impress people with their sanctity (Matt. 23:5). Why the woman chose to touch this part of His garment, we do not know, but Jesus knew somebody with faith had touched Him and had been healed by His power. The healing was immediate and complete.

Why did the Lord ask her to give witness publicly? Was this not an embarrassment to her? Not in the least. To begin with, this public confession was for her sake. It was an opportunity for her to confess Christ and glorify God. Had she stolen away in the crowd, she would not have met Jesus personally or heard His words of assurance and comfort (Luke 8:48).

But her confession was also an encouragement to Jairus, who would soon hear that his daughter had died. (Perhaps he wanted to blame the woman for the delay!) The woman's twelve years of trial were ended, and the same Christ who helped her would help Jairus. She was a testimony to the power of faith. True, she did not exercise "great faith," but Christ honored it and healed her body.

Finally, her witness was a rebuke to the multitude. You can be a part of the crowd and never get any blessing from being near Jesus! It is one thing to "press Him" and another thing to "touch Him" by faith. We may not have strong faith, but we do have a strong Savior, and He responds even to a touch at the hem of His garment.

When the inventor of chloroform, Sir James Simpson, was dying, a friend said to him, "You will soon be resting on His bosom." Simpson humbly replied, "I don't know as I can do that, but I think I have hold of the hem of His garment."

Death (vv. 49–56). The ruler of a synagogue was the elder in charge of the public services and the care of the facilities. He saw to it that people were appointed to pray, read the Scriptures, and give the sermon. He presided over the elders of the synagogue and was usually a man of reputation and wealth. It took a great deal of humility and courage for Jairus to approach Jesus and ask His help, for by this time the Jewish religious leaders were plotting to kill Him.

When Jairus left home, his daughter was so sick she was ready to die. By the time Jesus got away from the crowd to go with him, the girl had died. Jairus's friends thought that Jesus could help only living people, so they advised Jairus to drop the matter and come home. But Jesus encouraged the distraught father with a word of hope.

The scene at the home would have discouraged anybody! The professional mourners were already there, weeping and wailing, and a crowd of friends and neighbors had gathered. Jewish people in that day lost no time or energy in showing and sharing their grief. The body of the deceased would be buried that same day, after being washed and anointed.

Jesus took command of the situation and told the crowd to stop weeping because the girl was not dead but asleep. Of course she was dead, for her spirit had left her body (compare Luke 8:55 with James 2:26), but to Jesus, death was only sleep. This image is often used in the New Testament to describe the death of believers (John 11:11–14; Acts 7:59–60; 1 Cor. 15:51; 1 Thess. 4:13–18). Sleep is a normal experience that we do not fear, and we should not fear death. It is the body that sleeps, not the spirit, for the spirit of the believer goes to be with Christ (Phil. 1:20–24; 2 Cor. 5:6–8). At the resurrection, the body will be "awakened" and glorified, and God's people will share the image of Christ (1 John 3:1–2).

The mourners laughed at Jesus because they knew the girl was dead and that death was final. But they failed to realize that Jesus is "the resurrection and the life" (John 11:25–26). Had He not raised the widow's son from the dead? Did He not tell John the Baptist that the dead were being raised (Luke 7:22)? Apparently the mourners did not believe these reports and thought Jesus was a fool.

So He put them all out! This situation was much too tender and special for Him to allow dozens of unbelieving spectators to watch. He took the parents and three of His disciples, Peter, James, and John, and together they entered the room where the little girl lay dead.

He took her by the hand and spoke in Aramaic, "Talitha cumi! Little girl, arise!" (Peter would one day say, "Tabitha cumi!"—Acts 9:40.) This was not a magic formula but a word of command from the Lord of life and death (Rev. 1:17–18). Her spirit returned to her body and she arose and began to walk around the room! Jesus told them to give her something to eat, for it is likely that during her illness she had eaten little or nothing. Jesus also instructed them not to spread the news, but still the word got around (Matt. 9:26).

Resurrection is a picture of the way Jesus Christ saves lost sinners and raises them from spiritual death (John 5:24; Eph. 2:1–10). The Gospels record three such resurrections, though Jesus probably performed more. In each instance, the person raised gave evidence of life. The widow's son began to speak (Luke 7:15), Jairus's daughter walked and ate food, and Lazarus was loosed from the graveclothes (John 11:44). When a lost sinner is raised from the dead, you can tell it by his speech, his walk, his appetite, and his "change of clothes" (Col. 3:1ff.). You cannot hide life!

Peter, James, and John accompanied Jesus on three special occasions, and this was the first. The second was on the Mount of Transfiguration (Luke 9:28ff.), and the third was in the garden of Gethsemane (Mark 14:33ff.). Campbell Morgan has pointed out that each of these events has something to do with death and that the three disciples learned from these experiences some valuable lessons about Jesus and death.

In the home of Jairus, they learned that Jesus is victorious over death. On the Mount of Transfiguration, they discovered that He would be glorified in His death, and in the garden , they saw that He was surrendered to death. James was the first of the Twelve to die (Acts 12:1–2), John the last to die, and Peter's death was predicted by Jesus (John 21:18–19; 2 Peter 1:13–21). All three men needed these lessons, and we need them today.

CHAPTER EIGHT
Luke 9
A MANY-SIDED MINISTRY

I t was an exasperating evening. I was studying and writing, and the phone was ringing every half hour. Had the calls been from friends, I would have enjoyed taking a break and chatting, but they came from people wanting to sell me everything from dance tickets to investments. By the time I got to bed that night, I had just about decided to get an unlisted number and start protecting my privacy.

At eleven o'clock, a man phoned who was contemplating committing suicide, and with the Lord's help, I was able to encourage him to get a new grip on life. When I hung up, I gave thanks that I did not have an unlisted number. As I lay down to go back to sleep, I thought of the Lord Jesus and the kind of schedule He must have had. He was available to all kinds of people at all times, and He did not turn anyone away. He probably would not have had an unlisted number.

In this chapter, Dr. Luke described the busy life of the compassionate Son of Man as He performed four ministries.

Sending (9:1–11)
The commission (vv. 1–6). The Twelve had been ordained some months before (Luke 6:13–16) and had

been traveling with Jesus as His helpers. Now He was going to send them out in pairs (Mark 6:7) to have their own ministry and to put into practice what they had learned. This was their "solo flight."

But before He sent them out, He gave them the equipment needed to get the job done, as well as the instructions to follow. The parallel passage in Matthew 10 reveals that the Twelve were sent only to the people of Israel (Matt. 10:5–6). Luke does not mention this since he wrote primarily for the Gentiles and emphasized the worldwide outreach of the gospel.

Power is the ability to accomplish a task, and *authority* is the right to do it, and Jesus gave both to His apostles. They were able to cast out demons and heal the sick, but the most important ministry He gave them was that of preaching the gospel. The word *preach* in Luke 9:6 describes a herald proclaiming a message from the king, and in Luke 9:6 it means "to preach the good news." They were heralds of the good news!

The apostles' ability to heal was a special gift that authenticated their ministry (see Rom. 15:18–19; 2 Cor. 12:12; Heb. 2:1–4). Miracles were one evidence that the Lord had sent them and was working through them (Mark 16:20). Today we test a person's ministry by the truth of the Word of God (1 John 2:18–29; 4:1–6). Miracles alone are not proof that a person is truly sent of God, for Satan can enable his false ministers to do amazing things (Matt. 24:24; 2 Cor. 11:13–15; 2 Thess. 2:9–10).

Jesus told the apostles what to take on their journey, with an emphasis on urgency and simplicity. They were not to take a "begging bag" along but were to trust God to open up homes for their hospitality. Matthew 10:11–15 tells how they were to select these homes. If they were refused, they should shake off the dust from their feet, a familiar act performed by orthodox Jews whenever they left Gentile territory (see Luke 10:10–11; Acts 13:51).

The confusion (vv. 7–9). When the disciples left, Jesus also departed and ministered for a time in Galilee (Matt. 11:1), and together they attracted a great deal of attention. In fact, their work was even discussed in the highest levels of government! Herod Antipas (Luke 3:1) was a son of Herod the Great and the man who had John the Baptist killed (Matt. 14:1–12; Luke 3:19–20).

Who was this miracle worker? John the Baptist had done no miracles (John 10:41), but that might change if he were raised from the dead. The Jews expected Elijah to come, so perhaps the prophecy was being fulfilled (see Mal. 4:5; Matt. 11:10–14; 17:11–13; Luke 1:17). Herod's conscience was no doubt convicting him, and he was wondering if perhaps God had sent John back to judge him.

Herod kept trying to see Jesus, but Jesus, unlike some modern "religious celebrities," did not make it a point to go out of His way to mingle with the high and mighty. Jesus called the evil king a "fox" and was not intimidated by his threats (Luke 13:31–32). When Herod and Jesus did finally meet, the king hoped to see a miracle, but the Son of God did nothing and said nothing to him. Evil King Herod had silenced God's voice to him (Luke 23:6–12).

The conclusion (vv. 10–11). The apostles returned and gave a glowing report of their ministry, and Jesus suggested that they all take some time off for rest (Mark 6:30–32). As the popular speaker Vance Havner used to say, "If we don't come apart and rest, we'll just come apart." Their mission of preaching and healing had been demanding, and they all needed time alone for physical and spiritual renewal. This is a good example for busy (and sometimes overworked) Christian workers to imitate.

Attracted by the signs Jesus was doing, the crowds would not leave Him alone, but followed Him from the cities. When Jesus and the Twelve landed, the crowd was already there to meet them, and Jesus had compassion on them and ministered to them (Matt. 14:13–14). The Son of Man could not even take a day off!

Feeding (9:12–17)

Our Lord was not the kind of person who could teach the Word and then say to hungry people, "Depart in peace, be ye warm and filled" (James 2:16). The disciples were only too eager to see the crowd leave (Luke 18:15; see Matt. 15:23). They had not yet caught the compassion of Christ and the burden He had for the multitudes, but one day they would.

When you combine all four accounts of this miracle, you find that Jesus first asked Philip where they could buy enough bread to feed such a great crowd. (There could well have been ten thousand people there.) He was only testing Philip, "for He Himself knew what He was intending to do" (John 6:6 NASB). In the crisis hours of life, when your resources are low and your responsibilities are great, it is good to remember that God already has the problem solved; Jesus started with what they had, a few loaves and fishes that were generously donated by a lad found by Andrew (John 6:8–9). Did Andrew know the boy? Or did the boy offer his little lunch without being asked? Before we ask God to do the impossible, let's start with the possible and give Him what we have. And while we are at it, let's give thanks for mothers who give their sons something to give to Jesus.

The Lord looked up to heaven, the source of our daily bread (Matt. 6:11), gave thanks, and blessed the food, and then He multiplied the few loaves and fishes. Jesus was the "producer" and His disciples were the "distributors." The amazing thing is that *everybody* was served and satisfied, and there were twelve baskets of leftovers, one for each of the disciples. Jesus takes good care of His servants.

This miracle was more than an act of mercy for hungry people, though that was important. It was also a sign of our Lord's messiahship and an illustration of God's gracious provision for man's salvation. The next day, Jesus preached a sermon on "the bread of life" and urged the people to receive Him just as they had received the bread (John 6:22–59). But the people were more interested in their stomachs than their souls, and completely missed the spiritual impact of the miracle. Their desire was to make Jesus king so He could give them bread for the rest of their lives (John 6:14–15)!

After Jesus returned to heaven, the disciples must often have been encouraged by remembering this miracle. It teaches us to have compassion, to look on problems as opportunities for God to work, and to give Him all that we have and trust Him to meet the needs. If we do all we can, He will step in and do the rest. "Let God's promises shine on your problems," said Corrie ten Boom, and that is good counsel for us.

Teaching (9:18–36)

In Luke's gospel, the feeding of the five thousand marks the end of what is called the "Great Galilean Ministry" (Luke 4:14–:17). Jesus now begins His journey to Jerusalem (see Luke 9:51; 13:22; 17:11; 18:31; 19:11, 28). This would be a time of relative retirement with His disciples as He prepared them for what lay ahead. There is a parallel between this account and the account in Acts of Paul's last journey to Jerusalem. In both books we have "a tale of two cities": in Luke, from Nazareth to Jerusalem; and in Acts, from Jerusalem to Rome.

In this section, you see Jesus teaching them three basic lessons about His person, His sacrifice, and His kingdom.

His person (vv. 18–21). If any of us asked our friends what people were saying about us, it would be an evidence of pride, but not so with Jesus Christ. People had better know who He is, because what we think about Jesus determines our eternal destiny (John 8:24; 1 John 4:1–3). It is impossible to be wrong about Jesus and right with God.

Jesus had prayed all night before choosing His disciples (Luke 6:12–13), and now He prayed before asking for their personal confession of faith. The crowd would have its opinions (see Luke 9:7–8), but His disciples must have convictions. Peter was the spokesman for the group and gave a clear witness to the deity of Jesus Christ. This was the second time that he confessed Christ publicly (John 6:68–69). Except for Judas (John 6:70–71), all of the Twelve had faith in Jesus Christ.

Jesus commanded them (the word means "an order from a military officer") not to spread this truth openly. To begin with, the message of His messiahship could not be divorced from the fact of His death and resurrection, and He was now going to teach this to the Twelve. They had a difficult time grasping this new lesson and did not really understand it until after He was raised from the dead (Luke 24:44–48). The Jewish people saw Jesus primarily as a healer and a potential deliverer. If the apostles began preaching that He was indeed the Messiah, it might cause a popular uprising against Rome.

His sacrifice (vv. 22–26). Jesus had already given a number of "hints" about His sacrificial death, but now He began to teach this truth clearly to His disciples. John the Baptist had presented Him as the "Lamb of God" (John 1:29), and Jesus had predicted the "destruction" of the temple of His body (John 2:19). When He compared Himself to the serpent in the wilderness (John 3:14) and to Jonah (Matt. 12:38–40), Jesus was making statements about His suffering and death.

This is the first of three statements in Luke about His coming passion in Jerusalem (Luke 9:43–45; 18:31–34). It is clear that the Twelve did not understand, partly because of their unbelief and immaturity, and partly because it was "hidden" from them by God. Jesus taught them as they were able to receive the truth (John 16:12). It must have shocked the men to hear that their own religious leaders would kill their Master.

But Jesus did not stop with a private announcement of His own death. He also made a public declaration about a cross for *every* disciple. In his gospel, Matthew tells us that this was necessary because of Peter's desire to protect Jesus from suffering (Matt. 16:22ff.). Keep in mind that Jesus is talking about *discipleship* and not *sonship.* We are not saved from our sins because we take up a cross and follow Jesus, but because we trust the Savior who died on the cross for our sins. After we become children of God, then we become disciples.

The closest contemporary word to "disciple" is probably "apprentice." A disciple is more than a student who learns lessons by means of lectures and books. He is one who learns by living and working with his teacher in a daily "hands on" experience. Too many Christians are content to be listeners who gain a lot of knowledge but who have never put that knowledge into practice.

In the Roman world, the cross was a symbol of shame, guilt, suffering, and rejection. There could be no more despicable way to die. Crucifixion was not mentioned in polite conversation, and the people would no more think of wearing crosses on their person than we would think of wearing gold or silver electric chairs. Jesus laid down the stern requirements for discipleship. We must first say no to ourselves—not simply to pleasures or possessions, but to *self*—and then take up our cross and follow Christ daily. This means to be identified with Him in surrender, suffering, and sacrifice. You cannot crucify yourself; you can only yield your body (Rom. 12:1–2) and let God do the rest.

Of course, this kind of life seems foolish to the world; but to the Christian, it is wisdom. To save your life is to lose it, and how can you ever get it back again? But to give your life to Christ is to save it and to live it in fullness. If a person owned the whole world, he would still be too poor to buy back a lost life.

Discipleship is a daily discipline: we follow Jesus a step at a time, a day at a time. A weary cleaning woman said to a friend of mine, "The trouble with life is that it's so daily!" But she was wrong. One of the *best* things about life is that we can take it a day at a time (Deut. 33:25).

Our motive should be to glorify Christ. Anyone who is ashamed of Christ will never take up a cross and follow Him. But if we are ashamed of Him now, He will be ashamed of us when He comes again (Mark 8:38; 2 Tim. 2:11–13) and we will be ashamed before Him (1 John 2:28).

His kingdom (vv. 27–36). As far as the gospel record is concerned, the Transfiguration was the only occasion during Christ's earthly ministry when He revealed the glory of His person. Luke did not use the word *transfigure,* but he described the same scene (Matt. 17:2; Mark 9:2). The word means "a change in appearance that comes from within," and it gives us the English word *metamorphosis.*

What were the reasons behind this event? For one thing, it was God's seal of approval to Peter's confession of faith that Jesus is the Son of God (John 1:14). It was also the Father's way of encouraging the Son as He began to make His way to Jerusalem. The Father had spoken at the baptism (Luke 3:22) and would speak again during that final week of the Son's earthly ministry (John 12:23–28). Beyond the suffering of the cross would be the glory of the throne, a lesson that Peter emphasized in his first epistle (1 Peter 4:12—5:4).

Our Lord's own words in Luke 9:27 indicate that the event was a demonstration (or illustration) of the promised kingdom of God. This seems logical, for the disciples were confused about the kingdom because of Jesus' words about the cross. (We must not be too hard on them, because the prophets were also confused—1 Peter 1:10–12.) Jesus was reassuring them that the Old Testament prophecies would be fulfilled, but first He had to suffer before He could enter into His glory (note especially 2 Peter 1:12–21).

But there is also a practical lesson here, for we can have a spiritual "transfiguration" experience each day as we walk with the Lord. Romans 12:1–2 and 2 Corinthians 3:18 tell us how. As we surrender body, mind, and will, the Lord transforms us from within so that we are not conformed to the world. As we behold Him in the Word (the mirror), we are "transfigured" by the Spirit "from glory to glory." The theological name for this experience is *sanctification,* the process by which we become more like the Lord Jesus Christ, which is the Father's goal for each of His children (Rom. 8:19; 1 John 3:2). Note that our Lord was once again praying, which suggests that prayer is one of the keys to a transformed life.

Peter, James, and John had accompanied Jesus when He raised Jairus's daughter from the dead (Luke 8:51ff.), and they would accompany Him when He prayed in the garden (Matt. 26:36–46). These three occasions remind me of Philippians 3:10: "That I may know him [the Transfiguration], and the power of his resurrection [raising the girl], and the fellowship of his sufferings [in the garden]."

This may well have been the greatest "Bible conference" ever held on earth! Even apart from the great glory that was involved, here you certainly had the greatest speakers: Moses, the law; Elijah, the prophets; and Jesus, who came to fulfill the law and the prophets. You had the greatest topic: Jesus' "decease" (the Greek is *exodus)* that He would accomplish at Jerusalem. Moses had led Israel out of bondage to Egypt, and Elijah had delivered them from bondage to false gods, but Jesus would die to set *a sinful world* free from bondage to sin and death (Gal. 1:4; Col. 1:13; Heb. 2:14–15).

And while all of this was going on, the three privileged disciples were sleeping! (They would repeat this failure in the garden .) Peter's suggestion reminds us of the Jewish "Feast of Booths" that in the Bible is related to the future kingdom (Lev. 23:33–44; Zech. 14:16–21). Peter wanted Jesus to hold on to the glory *apart from the suffering,* but this is not God's plan.

The Father interrupted Peter by bathing the scene in a cloud of glory (Ex. 13:21–22; 40:35, 38) and speaking out of the cloud. (Peter would one day be interrupted by the Son [Matt. 17:24–27] and by the Spirit [Acts 10:44].) These arresting words from heaven remind us of Deuteronomy 18:15; Psalm 2:7; and Isaiah 42:1. When the cloud was gone, Elijah and Moses were also gone.

As wonderful as these experiences are, they are not the basis for a consistent Christian life. That can come only through the Word of God. Experiences come and go, but the Word remains. Our recollection of past experiences will fade, but God's Word never changes. The farther we get from these events, the less impact they make on our lives. That was why the Father said, "Hear him!" and why Peter made this same emphasis on the Word in his report (2 Peter 1:12–21). Our own personal "transfiguration" comes from inner renewal (Rom. 12:1–2), and that comes from the Word (2 Cor. 3:18).

Enduring (9:37–62)

"How long shall I stay with you and put up with you?" (Luke 9:41 niv). You might expect that lament to come from an overworked kindergarten teacher or an impatient army drill instructor, but it was made by the sinless Son of God! We are prone to forget how long suffering our Lord had to be while He was ministering on earth, especially with His own disciples.

When you analyze this section of Luke's gospel, you can better understand why Jesus spoke those words: *He was grieved over the failures of His followers.* He had given His apostles authority over Satan, yet they were too weak to cast out a demon (Luke 9:37–45). In feeding the five thousand, Jesus gave them an example of compassion, yet they persisted in manifesting selfishness and lack of love (Luke 9:46–56). He taught clearly what it meant to follow Him, yet the volunteers

turned out to be "me first" disciples (Luke 9:57–62). No wonder He was grieved!

Lack of power (vv. 37–45). We dare not stay on the glorious mountaintop when there are battles to fight in the valley below. Here was another "only child" needing the help of the Lord (Luke 7:12; 8:42), and even more so because His own disciples had failed. They had the power and the authority (Luke 9:1) but they did not have the success. Why?

When you study all three reports (Matt. 17; Mark 9), you discover what was lacking in their lives. First on the list was *faith* (Matt. 17:19–20); they were part of an unbelieving generation and had lost the confidence that they needed in order to use their power. But *prayer* and *fasting* were also lacking (Mark 9:29), which indicates that the nine men had allowed their devotional disciplines to erode during their Lord's brief absence. No matter what spiritual gifts we may have, their exercise is never automatic.

The devil tried one last throw (a wrestling term in the Greek), but Jesus rebuked the demon and cast him out. The Lord lovingly gave the boy back to his father (see Luke 7:15) and then took the Twelve aside for another lesson about the cross. After all, it was at the cross that Jesus would give Satan that final blow of defeat (John 12:31–32; Col. 2:15).

Lack of love (vv. 46–56). The disciples did not have much love for each other, or they would not have argued over who was the greatest (Luke 9:46–48). Perhaps this debate started because of envy (three of the disciples had been with Jesus on the mount), or because of pride (the other nine had failed to cast out the demon). Also, just before this, Jesus had paid Peter's temple tax for him (Matt. 17:24–27), and this may have aroused some envy.

In His kingdom, the example of greatness is a little child—helpless, dependent, without status, living by faith. The only thing worse than a child trying to act like an adult is an adult acting like a child! There is a great difference between being childlike and childish (see 1 Cor. 13:4–5; 14:20)!

They also showed a lack of love for believers outside their own group (Luke 9:49–50). This is what we would expect from a "son of thunder" (Mark 3:17)! Perhaps John was trying to impress Jesus with his zeal for protecting His name, but the Lord was not impressed. Believers who think that their group is the only group God recognizes and blesses are in for a shock when they get to heaven.

Nor did the apostles love their enemies (Luke 9:51–56). James and John had seen the prophet Elijah on the mount, so they thought they might imitate him and call down fire from heaven (2 Kings 1)! The Samaritans and Jews had been enemies for centuries (2 Kings 17:24–41), so it was understandable that this village would reject Jesus as He traveled toward Jerusalem (John 4:9, 20). Jesus rebuked their vengeful spirit and simply went to another village (Matt. 5:37–48). Later, Samaria would be reached with the gospel (Acts 8).

Lack of discipline (vv. 57–62). Three men could have become disciples, but they would not meet the conditions that Jesus laid down. The first man was a scribe (Matt. 8:19) who volunteered to go until he heard the cost: he had to deny himself. Apparently he was accustomed to a comfortable home.

The second man was called by Jesus (what an honor!), but he was rejected because he would not take up the cross and die to self. He was worried about somebody else's funeral when he should have been planning his own! Jesus is not suggesting here that we dishonor our parents, but only that we not permit our love for family to weaken our love for the Lord. We should love Christ so much that our love for family would look like hatred in comparison (Luke 14:26).

The third man also volunteered, but he could not follow Christ because he was looking back instead of ahead. There is nothing wrong with a loving farewell (1 Kings 19:19–21), but if it gets in the way of obedience, it becomes sin. Jesus saw that this man's heart was not wholly with Him, but that he would be plowing and looking back (see Gen. 19:17, 26; Phi. 3:13–14).

No wonder the laborers are few (Luke 10:2)!

It would appear that what Jesus taught His disciples and the multitudes had done them little good. They lacked power, love, and discipline, and they grieved His heart. If we today lack these spiritual essentials, we can never truly be His disciples, but they are available to us from the Lord. "For God did not give us a spirit of timidity, but of power, of love and of self-discipline" (2 Tim. 1:7 NIV).

Are we a joy to Jesus Christ, or are we breaking His heart?

CHAPTER NINE
Luke 10
WHAT IN THE WORLD DOES A CHRISTIAN DO?

The three scenes in Luke 10 illustrate the threefold ministry of every Christian believer, and they answer the question, "What in the world does a Christian do?"

To begin with, we are the Lord's *ambassadors,* sent to represent Him in this world (Luke 10:1–24). We are also *neighbors,* looking for opportunities to show mercy in the name of Christ (Luke 10:25–37). But at the heart of all our ministry is devotion to Christ, so we must be *worshippers* who take time to listen to His Word and commune with Him (Luke 10:38–42).

Whether we are in the harvest field, on the highway, or in the home, our highest privilege and our greatest joy is to do the will of God.

Ambassadors: Representing the Lord (10:1–24)

This event should not be confused with the sending out of the Twelve (Matt. 10; Luke 9:1–11). There are similarities in the charges given, but this is to be expected since both groups were sent by the same Master to do the same basic job. The twelve apostles ministered throughout Galilee, but these men were sent into Judea, and the men in this chapter are not called apostles. They were anonymous disciples.

Why is this event recorded only by Luke, and why did Jesus select seventy men instead of some other number? (Some texts say seventy-two, and the textual evidence is about even.) Just as the Twelve were associated in number with the twelve sons of Jacob and the twelve tribes of Israel, so the Seventy may be associated with the seventy nations listed in Genesis 10. Luke's emphasis is on the universality of the gospel message, so it seems reasonable that he would be led by the Holy Spirit to include this event. It was a symbolic way of saying, "Jesus wants the message spread to all nations."

Explanation (vv. 1–12). These men were not called "apostles," but they were still "sent *[aposello]* with a commission" to represent the Lord. They were therefore truly ambassadors of the King. Not only were they sent *by* Him, but they were also sent *before* Him to prepare the way for His coming. Their calling was certainly a dignified one.

It was also a difficult calling (Luke 10:2). Harvesting is hard work, even when there are many people helping you, but these men were sent into a vast field with very few workers to help them reap a great harvest. Instead of praying for an easier job, they were to pray for more laborers to join them, and we today need to pray that same prayer. (Please note that it is *laborers,* not spectators, who pray for more laborers! Too many Christians are praying for somebody else to do a job they are unwilling to do themselves.)

Their calling was a dangerous one. As they invaded enemy territory (Luke 10:17), they would be like "lambs among wolves" (Luke 10:3). But as long as they relied on the Lord, they would win the battle. "Any man who takes Jesus Christ seriously becomes the target of the devil," Vance Havner often told audiences. "Most church members do not give Satan enough trouble to arouse his opposition."

It would require discipline and faith for them to do the job (Luke 10:4–8). There was an urgency about the work, and the Lord did not want them to be overburdened with extra supplies or be delayed on the road by elaborate Eastern greetings. They had to trust God to provide homes and food for them, and they were not to be embarrassed to accept hospitality. After all, they were laboring for the Lord and bringing blessing into the home, and "the laborer is worthy of his hire" (Luke 10:7; see also 1 Cor. 9:14; 1 Tim. 5:18).

They were ambassadors of peace, bringing healing to the sick, deliverance to the possessed, and the good news of salvation to lost sinners. Like Joshua's army of old, they first proclaimed peace to the cities. If a city rejected the offer of peace, then it chose judgment

(Deut. 20:10–18). It is a serious thing to reject the ambassadors God sends.

It is important to note that the special power that Jesus gave to His apostles (Luke 9:1) and to the Seventy is not ours to claim today. These two preaching missions were very special ministries, and God did not promise to duplicate them in our age. Our Lord's commission to us emphasizes the proclamation of the message, not the performing of miracles (Matt. 28:19–20; Luke 24:46–49).

Denunciation (vv. 13–16). This seems like harsh language from the lips of the Son of God, but we dare not ignore it or try to explain it away. He named three ancient cities that had been judged by God—Sodom (Gen. 19), and Tyre and Sidon (Ezek. 26–28; Isa. 23)—and used them to warn three cities of His day: Chorazin, Bethsaida, and Capernaum. These three cities had been given more privileges than the three ancient cities, and therefore they had more responsibility. If Sodom, Tyre, and Sidon were destroyed, how could Chorazin, Bethsaida, and Capernaum escape?

To hear Christ's ambassadors means to hear Him, and to despise His representatives means to despise Him. "As my Father hath sent me, even so send I you" (John 20:21; see also 2 Cor. 5:18–21). The way a nation treats an ambassador is the way it treats the government the ambassador represents. For an interesting illustration of this truth, read 2 Samuel 10.

Jubilation (vv. 17–24). There is a threefold joy here: the joy of service (Luke 10:17–19), the joy of salvation (Luke 10:20), and the joy of sovereignty (Luke 10:21–24).

We can well understand the joy of the Seventy as they returned to report their victories to Jesus. He had given them power and authority to heal, to cast out demons, and to preach the Word, and they were successful! In the midst of their great joy, they were careful to give God the glory ("in thy name").

They had seen individual victories from city to city, but Jesus saw these victories as part of a war that dethroned and defeated Satan (note Isa. 14:4–23; John 12:31–32; Rev. 12:8–9). As believers, we are weak in ourselves, but we can be "strong in the Lord, and in the power of his might" (Eph. 6:10ff.). Each victory is important to the Lord, no matter how insignificant it may seem in our eyes. Satan will not finally be judged until Jesus casts him into the lake of fire (Rev. 20:10), but God's people can today claim Christ's Calvary victory by faith (Col. 2:15).

But the enemy will not give up! Satan would certainly attack Christ's servants and seek to destroy them. That is why our Lord added the words of encouragement in Luke 10:19. He assured them that their authority was not gone now that the preaching mission had ended, and that they could safely tread on the "old serpent" without fear (Gen. 3:15; Rev. 12:9).

The Lord cautioned them not to "go on rejoicing" over their victories but to rejoice because their names had been written in heaven. (The verb means "they

have been written and they stand written." It is a statement of assurance. See Phil. 4:3; Rev. 20:12–15.) As wonderful as their miracles were, the greatest miracle of all is still the salvation of a lost soul. The Greek word translated "written" means "to inscribe formally and solemnly." It was used for the signing of a will, a marriage document, or a peace treaty, and also for the enrolling of a citizen. The perfect tense in the Greek means "it stands written."

But our highest joy is not found in service or even in our salvation, but in being submitted to the sovereign will of the heavenly Father, for this is the foundation for both service and salvation. Here we see God the Son rejoicing through God the Holy Spirit because of the will of God the Father! "I delight to do thy will, O my God" (Ps. 40:8).

Jesus was not rejoicing because sinners were blind to God's truth, for God is "not willing that any should perish" (2 Peter 3:9). He rejoiced because *the understanding of that truth* did not depend on natural abilities or education. If that were the case, most of the people in the world would be shut out of the kingdom. When the Twelve and the Seventy were preaching, they did not see the "wise and learned" humbling themselves to receive God's truth and grace, but they saw the "common people" trusting the Word (Luke 7:29–30; 1 Cor. 1:26–29). In His sovereign will, God has ordained that sinners must humble themselves before they can be lifted up (James 4:6; 1 Peter 5:6).

Christ's ambassadors were indeed privileged people. They were able to see and hear things that the greatest saints in the Old Testament ages yearned to see and hear but could not. The Messiah was at work, and they were a part of His work!

Neighbors: Imitating the Lord (10:25–37)

It was expected that rabbis would discuss theological matters in public, and the question this scribe (lawyer) asked was one that was often debated by the Jews. It was a good question asked with a bad motive, because the lawyer hoped to trap our Lord. However, Jesus trapped the lawyer!

Our Lord sent the man back to the law, not because the law saves us (Gal. 2:16, 21; 3:21), but because the law shows us that we need to be saved. There can be no real conversion without conviction, and the law is what God uses to convict sinners (Rom. 3:20).

The scribe gave the right answer, but he would not apply it personally to himself and admit his own lack of love for both God and his neighbor. So, instead of *being justified* by throwing himself on the mercy of God (Luke 18:9–14), he tried *to justify himself* and wriggle out of his predicament. He used the old debating tactic: "Define your terms! What do you mean by 'neighbor'? Who is my neighbor?"

Jesus did not say that this story was a parable, so it could well be the report of an actual occurrence. For Jesus to tell a story that made the Jews look bad and the Samaritans look good would either be dangerous or self-defeating. "You just made that up!" they could say. "We all know that nothing like that would ever happen!" So it is possible that some of His listeners, including the lawyer, knew that such a thing had really happened. Either way, the account is realistic.

The worst thing we can do with any parable, especially this one, is turn it into an allegory and make everything stand for something. The victim becomes the lost sinner who is half-dead (alive physically, dead spiritually), helplessly left on the road of life. The priest and Levite represent the law and the sacrifices, neither of which can save the sinner.

The Samaritan is Jesus Christ who saves the man, pays the bill, and promises to come again. The inn stands for the local church where believers are cared for, and the "two pence" are the two ordinances, baptism and Communion. If you take this approach to Scripture, you can make the Bible say almost anything you please, and you are sure to miss the messages God wants you to get.

The road from Jerusalem down to Jericho was indeed a dangerous one. Since the temple workers used it so much, you would have thought the Jews or Romans would have taken steps to make it safe. It is much easier to maintain a religious system than it is to improve the neighborhood.

Most of us can think up excuses for the priest and Levite as they ignored the victim. (Maybe we have used them ourselves!) The priest had been serving God at the temple all week and was anxious to get home. Perhaps the bandits were still lurking in the vicinity and using the victim as "bait." Why take a chance? Anyway, it was not his fault that the man was attacked. The road was busy, so somebody else was bound to come along and help the man. The priest left it to the Levite, and then the Levite did what the priest did—nothing! Such is the power of the bad example of a religious man.

By using a Samaritan as the hero, Jesus disarmed the Jews, for the Jews and Samaritans were enemies (John 4:9; 8:48). It was not a Jew helping a Samaritan but a Samaritan helping a Jew *who had been ignored by his fellow Jews!* The Samaritan loved those who hated him, risked his own life, spent his own money (two days' wages for a laborer), and was never publicly rewarded or honored as far as we know.

What the Samaritan did helps us better understand what it means to "show mercy" (Luke 10:37), and it also illustrates the ministry of Jesus Christ. The Samaritan identified with the needs of the stranger and had compassion on him. There was no logical reason why he should rearrange his plans and spend his money just to help an "enemy" in need, but mercy does not need reasons. Being an expert in the law, the scribe certainly knew that God required His people to show mercy, even to strangers and enemies (Ex. 23:4–5; Lev. 19:33–34; Mic. 6:8).

See how wisely Jesus "turned the tables" on the lawyer. Trying to evade responsibility, the man asked, "Who is my neighbor?" But Jesus asked, "Which of these three men was neighbor to the victim?" The big question is, "To whom can I be a neighbor?" and this has nothing to do with geography, citizenship, or race. Wherever people need us, there we can be neighbors and, like Jesus Christ, show mercy.

The lawyer wanted to discuss "neighbor" in a general way, but Jesus forced him to consider a specific man in need. How easy it is for us to talk about abstract ideals and fail to help solve concrete problems. We can discuss things like "poverty" and "job opportunities" and yet never personally help feed a hungry family or help somebody find a job.

Of course, the lawyer wanted to make the issue somewhat complex and philosophical, but Jesus made it simple and practical. He moved it from *duty* to *love,* from *debating* to *doing.* To be sure, our Lord was not condemning discussions or debates; He was only warning us not to use these things as excuses for doing nothing. Committees are not always committed!

One of my favorite D. L. Moody stories illustrates this point. Attending a convention in Indianapolis, Mr. Moody asked singer Ira Sankey to meet him at six o'clock one evening at a certain street corner. When Sankey arrived, Mr. Moody put him on a box and asked him to sing, and it was not long before a crowd gathered. Moody spoke briefly, inviting the crowd to follow him to the nearby opera house. Before long, the auditorium was filled, and the evangelist preached the gospel to the spiritually hungry people.

When the delegates to the convention started to arrive, Moody stopped preaching and said, "Now we must close as the brethren of the convention wish to come and to discuss the question, 'How to Reach the Masses.'" *Touché!*

We may read this passage and think only of "the high cost of caring," but it is far more costly *not* to care. The priest and the Levite lost far more by their neglect than the Samaritan did by his concern. They lost the opportunity to become better men and good stewards of what God had given them. They could have been a good influence in a bad world, but they chose to be a bad influence. *The Samaritan's one deed of mercy has inspired sacrificial ministry all over the world.* Never say that such ministry is wasted! God sees to it that no act of loving service in Christ's name is ever lost.

It all depends on your outlook. To the thieves, this traveling Jew was a victim to exploit, so they attacked him. To the priest and Levite, he was a nuisance to avoid, so they ignored him. But to the Samaritan, he was a neighbor to love and help, so he took care of him. What Jesus said to the lawyer, He says to us: "Go and *keep on doing it* likewise" (literal translation).

Worshippers: Listening to the Lord (10:38–42)

Worship is at the heart of all that we are and all that we do in the Christian life. It is important that we be busy ambassadors, taking the message of the gospel to lost souls. It is also essential to be merciful Samaritans, seeking to help exploited and hurting people who need God's mercy. But before we can represent Christ as we should, or imitate Him in our caring ministry, we must spend time with Him and learn from Him. We must "take time to be holy."

Mary of Bethany is seen three times in the gospel record, and on each occasion, she is in the same place: at the feet of Jesus. She sat at His feet and listened to His Word (Luke 10:39), fell at His feet and shared her woe (John 11:32), and came to His feet and poured out her worship (John 12:3). It is interesting to note that in each of these instances, there is some kind of fragrance: in Luke 10, it is food; in John 11, it is death (John 11:39); and in John 12, it is perfume.

Mary and Martha are often contrasted as though each believer must make a choice: be a *worker* like Martha or a *worshipper* like Mary. Certainly our personalities and gifts are different, but that does not mean that the Christian life is an either/or situation. Charles Welsey said it perfectly in one of his hymns:

> Faithful to my Lord's commands,
> I still would choose the better part;
> Serve with careful Martha's hands,
> And loving Mary's heart.

It seems evident that the Lord wants each of us to imitate Mary in our worship and Martha in our work. Blessed are the balanced!

Consider Martha's situation. She received Jesus into her home *and then neglected Him as she prepared an elaborate meal that He did not need!* Certainly a meal was in order, but what we do *with* Christ is far more important than what we do *for* Christ. Again, it is not an either/or situation; it is a matter of balance. Mary had done her share of the work in the kitchen and then had gone to "feed" on the Lord's teachings. Martha felt neglected after Mary left the kitchen, and she began to complain and to suggest that neither the Lord nor Mary really cared!

Few things are as damaging to the Christian life as trying to work for Christ without taking time to commune with Christ. "For without me ye can do nothing" (John 15:5). Mary chose the better part, the part that could not be taken from her. She knew that she could not live "by bread alone" (Matt. 4:4).

Whenever we criticize others and pity ourselves because we feel overworked, we had better take time to examine our lives. Perhaps in all of our busyness, we have been ignoring the Lord. Martha's problem was not that she had too much work to do, but that she allowed her work to distract her and pull her apart. She was trying to serve two masters! If serving Christ makes us difficult to live with, then something is terribly wrong with our service!

The key is to have the right priorities: Jesus Christ first, then others, then ourselves. It is vitally important that we spend time "at the feet of Jesus" every single day, letting Him share His Word with us. *The most important part of the Christian life is the part that only God sees.* Unless we meet Christ personally and privately each day, we will soon end up like Martha: busy but not blessed.

Often in my pastoral ministry, I have asked people with serious problems, "Tell me about your devotional life." The usual response has been an embarrassed look, a bowed head, and the quiet confession, "I stopped reading my Bible and praying a long time ago." And they wondered why they had problems!

According to John 12:1–2, Martha must have learned her lesson, for she prepared a feast for Jesus, the Twelve, and her brother and sister—that's fifteen people—*and did not utter one word of complaint!* She had God's peace in her heart because she had learned to sit at the feet of Jesus.

We are ambassadors, neighbors, and worshippers, these three, and the greatest of these is worshippers.

CHAPTER TEN
Luke 11
LEARNING LIFE'S LESSONS

Our Lord's teaching in Luke 11 grew out of a prayer meeting, a miracle, and an invitation to dinner. Jesus used these occasions to give instructions about four important topics: prayer, Satan, spiritual opportunity, and hypocrisy. It is important that we today understand these topics and apply these truths to our own lives.

Prayer (11:1–13)
The priority of prayer (v. 1). We usually think of John the Baptist as a prophet and martyr, and yet our Lord's disciples remembered him as a man of prayer. John was a "miracle baby," filled with the Holy Spirit before he was born, and yet he had to pray. He was privileged to introduce the Messiah to Israel, and yet he had to pray. Jesus said that John was the greatest of the prophets (Luke 7:28), and yet John had to depend on prayer. If prayer was that vital to a man who had these many advantages, how much more important it ought to be to us who do not have these advantages!

John's disciples had to pray, and Jesus' disciples wanted to learn better how to pray. They did not ask the Master to teach them how to preach or do great signs; they asked Him to teach them to pray. We today sometimes think that we would be better Christians if only we had been with Jesus when He was on earth, but this is not likely. The disciples were with him and yet they failed many times! They could perform miracles, and yet they wanted to learn to pray.

But the greatest argument for the priority of prayer is the fact that our Lord was a Man of prayer. Thus far we have seen that He prayed at His baptism (Luke 3:21), before He chose the Twelve (Luke 6:12), when the crowds increased (Luke 5:16), before He asked the Twelve for their confession of faith (Luke 9:18), and at His Transfiguration (Luke 9:29). The disciples knew that He often prayed alone (Mark 1:35), and they wanted to learn from Him this secret of spiritual power and wisdom.

If Jesus Christ, the perfect Son of God, had to depend on prayer during "the days of his flesh" (Heb. 5:7), then how much more do you and I need to pray! Effective prayer is the provision for every need and the solution for every problem.

Pattern for prayer (vv. 2–4). We call this "the Lord's Prayer," not because Jesus prayed it (He never had to ask for forgiveness), but because Jesus taught it. There is nothing wrong with praying this prayer personally or as part of a congregation, so long as we do it from a believing heart that is sincere and submitted. How easy it is to "recite" these words and not really mean them, but that can happen even when we sing and preach! The fault lies with us, not with this prayer.

This is a "pattern prayer," given to guide us in our own praying (see Matt. 6:9–15 for the parallel). It teaches us that true prayer depends on a spiritual relationship with God that enables us to call Him "Father," and this can come only through faith in Jesus Christ (Rom. 8:14–17; Gal. 4:1–7).

Lyndon Johnson's press secretary, Bill Moyers, was saying grace at a staff lunch, and the president shouted, "Speak up, Bill! I can't hear a thing!" Moyers quietly replied, "I wasn't addressing you, Mr. President." It is good to remind ourselves that when we pray, we talk to God.

True prayer also involves *responsibilities:* honoring God's kingdom and doing God's will (Luke 11:2). It has well been said that the purpose of prayer is not to get man's will done in heaven, but to get God's will done on earth. Prayer is not telling God what we want and then selfishly enjoying it. Prayer is asking God to use us to accomplish *what He wants* so that His name is glorified. His kingdom is extended and strengthened, and His will is done. I must test all of my personal requests by these overruling concerns if I expect God to hear and answer my prayers.

It is important for Christians to know the Word of God, for there we discover the will of God. We must never separate prayer and the Word (John 15:7). During my ministry, I have seen professing Christians disobey God and defend themselves by saying, "I prayed about it and God said it was all right!" This includes a girl who married an unsaved man (2 Cor. 6:14–18), a fellow living with a girl who was not his wife (1 Thess. 4:1–8), and a preacher who started his own church because all the other churches were wrong and only he had true "spiritual insight" (Phil. 2:1–16).

Once we are secure in our relationship with God and His will, then we can bring our *requests* to Him (Luke 11:3–4). We can ask Him to provide our needs (not our greeds!) for today, to forgive us for what we have done yesterday, and to lead us in the future. All of our needs may be included in these three requests:

material and physical provision, moral and spiritual perfection, and divine protection and direction. If we pray this way, we can be sure of praying in God's will.

Persistence in prayer (vv. 5–8). In this parable, Jesus did not say that God is like this grouchy neighbor. In fact, He said just the opposite. If a tired and selfish neighbor finally meets the needs of a bothersome friend, how much more will a loving heavenly Father meet the needs of His own dear children! He is arguing from the lesser to the greater.

We have already seen that prayer is based on *sonship* ("Our Father"), not on friendship, but Jesus used friendship to illustrate persistence in prayer. God the Father is not like this neighbor, for He never sleeps, never gets impatient or irritable, is always generous, and delights in meeting the needs of His children. The friend at the door had to keep on knocking in order to get what he needed, but God is quick to respond to His children's cries (Luke 18:1–8).

The argument is clear. If persistence finally paid off as a man beat on the door of a reluctant friend, how much more would persistence bring blessing as we pray to a loving heavenly Father! After all, we are the children *in the house with Him!*

The word translated "importunity" means "shamelessness" or "avoidance of shame." It can refer to the man at the door who was not ashamed to wake up his friend, but it can also refer to the friend in the house. Hospitality to strangers is a basic law in the East (Gen. 18:1ff.). If a person refused to entertain a guest, he brought disgrace on the whole village and the neighbors would have nothing to do with him. The man in the house knew this and did not want to embarrass himself, his family, or his village, so he got up and met the need.

Why does our Father in heaven answer prayer? Not just to meet the needs of His children, but to meet them in such a way that it brings glory to His name. "Hallowed be thy name." *When God's people pray, God's reputation is at stake.* The way He takes care of His children is a witness to the world that He can be trusted. Phillips Brooks said that prayer is not overcoming God's reluctance; it is laying hold of His highest willingness. Persistence in prayer is not an attempt to change God's mind ("thy will be done") but to get ourselves to the place where He can trust us with the answer.

Promises for prayer (vv. 9–13). The tenses of the verbs are important here: "Keep on asking … keep on seeking … keep on knocking." In other words, don't come to God only in the midnight emergencies, but keep in constant communion with your Father. Jesus called this "abiding" (John 15:1ff.), and Paul exhorted, "Pray without ceasing" (1 Thess. 5:17). As we pray, God will either answer or show us why He cannot answer. Then it is up to us to do whatever is necessary in our lives so that the Father can trust us with the answer.

Note that the lesson closes with an emphasis on God

as Father (Luke 11:11–13). Because He knows us and loves us, *we never need to be afraid of the answers that He gives.* Again, Jesus argued from the lesser to the greater: if an earthly father gives what is best to his children, surely the Father in heaven will do even more. This even includes "the good things of the Holy Spirit" (compare Luke 11:13 with Matt. 7:11), blessings that in the Old Testament were reserved only for a special few.

Satan (11:14–28)

Accusation (vv. 14–16). This is the third miracle of deliverance our Lord performed that elicited from His enemies the accusation that He was in league with Satan (see Matt. 9:32–34; 12:22–37). Instead of rejoicing that God had sent a Redeemer, the religious leaders were rebelling against the truth of God's Word and seeking to discredit Christ's work and character. Imagine people being so blind that they could not distinguish a work of God from a work of Satan!

"Beelzebub" was one of the names of the Philistine god Baal (2 Kings 1:1–3); it means "lord of flies." A variant is "Beelzebul," which means "lord of the dwelling" and ties in with Christ's illustrations in Luke 11:18–26. The Jews often used this name when referring to Satan.

The request in Luke 11:16 was a part of the accusation. "If you are really working for God," they were saying in effect, "prove it by giving us a sign from heaven, not just a miracle on earth." They were tempting God, which is a dangerous thing to do.

Refutation (vv. 17–22). Jesus answered their charges with three arguments. First, their accusation was illogical. Why would Satan fight against himself and divide his own kingdom? (Note that Jesus believed in a real devil who has a kingdom that is strong and united. See Eph. 2:1–3; 6:10ff.) Second, their charges were self-incriminating: by what power were the Jews casting out demons? How do their works differ from Christ's works? On the contrary, Christ's miracles show that the kingdom of *God* is present, not the kingdom of *Satan!*

Finally, their accusation was really an admission of His power, for He could not defeat Satan unless He were stronger than Satan. Jesus pictured Satan as a strong man in armor, guarding his palace and his goods. But Jesus invaded Satan's territory, destroyed his armor and weapons, and claimed his spoils (see John 12:31–33; Col. 2:15; 1 John 3:8). Our Lord has "led captivity captive" (Eph. 4:8) and set the prisoners free (Luke 4:18). Though he is permitted limited authority, Satan is a defeated enemy.

Application (vv. 23–28). It is impossible to be neutral in this spiritual war (Luke 11:23; see also 9:50), for neutrality means standing against Him. There are two spiritual forces at work in the world, and we must choose between them. Satan is scattering and destroying, but Jesus Christ is gathering and building. We must make a choice, and if we choose to make *no* choice, we are really choosing against Him.

Jesus illustrated the danger of neutrality by telling the story of the man and the demon. The man's body was the demon's "house" (Luke 11:24; and note vv. 17 and 21). For some unknown reason, the demonic tenant decided to leave his "house" and go elsewhere. The man's condition improved immediately, *but the man did not invite God to come and dwell within.* In other words, the man remained neutral. What happened? The demon returned with seven other demons worse than himself, and the man's condition was abominable.

"Neutrality in religion is always cowardice," wrote Oswald Chambers. "God turns the cowardice of a desired neutrality into terror."

Taking sides with Jesus means much more than saying the right things, like the woman who cried, "Blessed is the womb that bore You, and the breasts which nursed You" (Luke 11:27 NKJV). She was certainly sincere, but that was not enough. *We take sides with Jesus Christ when we hear His Word and obey it* (see Luke 6:46–49; 8:19–21).

Opportunity (11:29–36)

Because He knew what was in their hearts, Jesus was not impressed by the big crowds, but the disciples were. In order to keep the Twelve from being swayed by "success," Jesus gave them some insights into what was really happening as they ministered the Word. He used three illustrations to show the seriousness of spiritual opportunities.

Jonah (vv. 29–30, 32). The leaders kept asking Jesus for a sign to prove that He was the Messiah. The only sign He promised was "the sign of Jonah the prophet," which is *death, burial, and resurrection.* It is the resurrection of our Lord that proves He is the Messiah, the Son of God (Rom. 1:4), and this is what Peter preached to Israel on the day of Pentecost (Acts 2:22ff.). The witness of the early church was centered on Christ's resurrection (Acts 1:22; 3:15; 5:30–32; 13:32–33). Jonah was a living miracle and so is our Lord Jesus Christ.

Solomon (v. 31). The emphasis here is on the wisdom of a king, not the works of a prophet. The Queen of Sheba traveled many miles to hear the wisdom of Solomon (1 Kings 10), but here was the very Son of God *in their midst,* and the Jews would not believe His words! Even if Jesus had performed a sign, it would not have changed their hearts. They needed the living wisdom of God, but they were content with their stale religious tradition.

The important thing about these illustrations is that *they involved Gentiles.* When Jonah preached to the Gentiles in Nineveh, they repented and were spared. When a Gentile queen heard Solomon's wisdom, she marveled and believed. If, with all their privileges, the Jews did not repent, then the people of Nineveh and the Queen of Sheba would bear witness against them in the last judgment. The Lord gave Israel so many opportunities, yet they would not believe (Luke 13:34–35; John 12:35–41).

Light (vv. 33–36). The third illustration was from daily life, not from history, and was one Jesus had used before (Matt. 6:22–23). God's Word is a light that shines in this dark world (Ps. 119:105; Prov. 6:23). But it is not enough that the light be shining *externally,* it must enter our lives before it can do any good. "The entrance of thy words giveth light; it giveth understanding unto the simple" (Ps. 119:130). The brightest sun cannot enable a blind man to see.

When we trust Jesus Christ, our eyes are opened, the light shines in, and we become children of light (John 8:12; 2 Cor. 4:3–6; Eph. 5:8–14). The important thing is that we take advantage of the light and have a *single outlook of faith.* If we keep one eye on the things of God and the other eye on the world (1 John 2:16), the light will turn into darkness! There is no "twilight living" for the Christian, for God demands total submission and obedience (Luke 11:23).

Three men in the Bible illustrate this truth. They began in the light and ended up in the darkness because they were double-minded. The name *Samson* probably means "sunny," yet he ended up a blind slave in a dark dungeon because he yielded to the "lust of the flesh" (Judg. 16). Lot began as a pilgrim with his uncle Abraham. He ended as a drunk in a cave, committing incest (Gen. 19:30–38), because he yielded to "the lust of the eyes" (Gen. 13:10–11). Lot wanted to serve two masters and look in two directions!

King Saul began his reign as a humble leader, but his pride led him to a witch's cave (1 Sam. 28), and he died of suicide on the field of battle (1 Sam. 31). His sin was "the pride of life"; he would not humble himself and obey the will of God.

Each of us is controlled either by light or darkness. The frightening thing is that some people have so hardened themselves against the Lord that *they cannot tell the difference!* They think they are following the light when, in reality, they are following the darkness. The scribes and Pharisees claimed to "see the light" as they studied the law, but they were living in the darkness (see John 12:35–50).

Hypocrisy (11:37–54)

At this stage in Christ's ministry, when the religious leaders were bent on destroying Him, why would a Pharisee invite Him to his home for a meal? If he had been sincerely seeking truth, he would have talked with our Lord privately. It seems obvious that he was looking for an opportunity to accuse Jesus, and he thought he had it when Jesus did not practice the ceremonial washing before eating (Mark 7:2–3). Knowing what the host was thinking, Jesus responded by giving a "spiritual analysis" of the Pharisees.

He exposed their folly (vv. 37–41). The basic error of the Pharisees was thinking that righteousness was only a matter of external actions, and they minimized internal attitudes. They were very careful to keep the outside clean, but they ignored the wickedness within. They seemed to forget that the same God who created the outside also created the inside, the "inner person" that also needs cleansing (Ps. 51:6, 10).

The Pharisees boasted of their giving (Matt. 6:1–4; Luke 18:11–12), but they did not give *what was within* to the Lord. The way to make the *outside* pure is to make the *inside* pure (Luke 11:41). Kenneth Wuest translates this verse, "Rather, the things which are inside give as alms, and behold, all things are clean to you" (WUEST). The way to clean up a dirty vocabulary is not to brush your teeth but to cleanse your heart.

He denounced their sins (vv. 42–52). These six "woes" parallel the "woes" in Matthew 23. Jesus started with the sins of the Pharisees (Luke 11:42–44) and then turned to the sins of the scribes, for it was their interpretations of the law that formed the basis for the whole pharisaical system (Luke 11:45–52).

The first three "woes" denounce the Pharisees for their *wrong priorities.* They were careful about tithing even the tiny leaves and seeds from the herbs, but they forgot about important things like justice and love (Mic. 6:7–8). They majored on the minors! Jesus did not say they should stop tithing but that they should put their religious activities into proper perspective.

They also put *reputation* above *character.* They thought that sitting in the right seats and being acknowledged by the right people would make them spiritual. Reputation is what people think we are; character is what God knows we are.

The comparison in Luke 11:44 must have infuriated the host and the other Pharisees who were present. The Jews had to be especially careful about ceremonial defilement from dead bodies (Num. 19:11–22; note especially v. 16), so they made sure the graves were carefully marked. But the Pharisees were like *unmarked graves* that did not look like graves at all! This meant that they were *unconsciously defiling others when they thought they were helping them become holier!* Instead of helping people, the Pharisees were harming them.

The scribes felt the sting of our Lord's words and tried to defend themselves. Jesus used three vivid illustrations in answering them: burdens, tombs, and keys.

The scribes were good at adding to the burdens of the people, but they had no heart for helping them carry those burdens. What a tragedy when "ministers" of God's Word create more problems for people who already have problems enough! A pastor friend of mine prays daily, "Lord, help me today not to add to anybody's problems." Jesus had these "religious burdens" in mind when He gave the gracious invitation recorded in Matthew 11:28–30.

The scribes were also good at "embalming" the past and honoring the prophets who had been martyred by the religious establishment *to which they belonged.* Both Bible history and church history reveal that true servants of God are usually rejected by the people who most need their ministry, but the next generation will come along and honor these people. The Pharisees were like "hidden graves," but the scribes built elaborate tombs!

The first recorded martyrdom in the Old Testament is that of Abel, and the last is that of Zechariah (see Gen. 4:1–15; 2 Chron. 24:20–27, and remember that 2 Chronicles is the last book in the Hebrew Bible). Jesus did not suggest that the scribes and Pharisees were *personally* responsible for killing the Old Testament prophets. Rather, He was affirming that *people just like the scribes and Pharisees* did these terrible things to God's servants. Their ultimate crime would be the crucifixion of the Son of God.

Finally, the scribes were guilty of robbing the common people of the knowledge of the Word of God. It was bad enough that they would not enter the kingdom themselves, but they were hindering others from going in! It is a serious thing to teach God's Word, and not everyone is supposed to do it (James 3:1). Unfortunately, what some people call "Bible study" is too often just a group of unprepared people exchanging their ignorance.

But there is another side to this: the scribes convinced the people that nobody could understand and explain the law except the trained and authorized teachers. We have some of that arrogant attitude showing itself today. Teachers who overemphasize the Bible languages give people the impression that the Holy Spirit cannot teach anyone who does not know Greek and Hebrew. There are so many "study Bibles" these days (and many of them are helpful) that you wonder if a student can learn anything from a simple text Bible. We must not despise true Christian scholarship, but we must also keep things in balance.

Jesus is the key to the Scriptures (Luke 24:44–48). When you take away that key, you cannot understand what God has written. As helpful and necessary as theological studies are, the most important requirements for Bible study are a yielded heart and an obedient will. Some of the best Bible teachers I have known in my own ministry were men and women who learned the truth of God's Word on their knees and on the battlefield of life. They were Spirit-taught, not man-taught.

He aroused their anger (vv. 53–54). Hypocrites do not want their sins exposed; it hurts their reputation. Instead of opposing the Lord, these men should have been seeking His mercy. They deliberately began to attack Him with "catch questions" in hopes they could trap Him in some heresy and then arrest Him. What a disgraceful way to treat the Son of God.

But there are religious systems today that are very much like the system defended by the scribes and Pharisees. The leaders interpret and apply the Word for the followers and you are not permitted to ask embarrassing questions or raise objections. The leaders exploit the people and do little or nothing to ease their burdens. Worst of all, the leaders use the system to cover up their own sins. God's truth should set us free, but these groups only lead people into more and more bondage.

God has given teachers to His church (Eph. 4:11), and we should listen to them. But we should also test what we hear by the Scriptures to make sure they are teaching the truth (1 Thess. 5:19–21), and we should not permit anyone to bring us into bondage and exploit us (2 Cor. 11:20).

It is a privilege to have the light of the Word of God and the privilege of prayer. The enemy wants to rob us of the blessings of spiritual growth and freedom. His plan is to substitute hypocrisy for reality and to encourage us to be more concerned about the outside than the inside: reputation and not character.

So serious is this danger that Jesus will have more to say about it in Luke 12. Meanwhile, let us beware!

CHAPTER ELEVEN
Luke 12
BELIEVER, BEWARE!

Our Lord's disciples may not have realized it, but they were in great danger. For one thing, they were surrounded by immense crowds of people whose major concern was not to hear spiritual truth but to see Jesus do a miracle or meet some personal need. At the same time, the scribes and Pharisees were plotting against Jesus and trying to get Him out of the way. The snare of popularity and the fear of man has brought ruin to more than one servant of God.

In Luke 12, Luke recorded five warnings from our Lord. Four of these warnings must be heeded by God's people today if we are to be faithful disciples, and the fifth warning should be heeded by a lost world.

Beware of Hypocrisy (12:1–12)

The word *hypocrite* comes from a Greek word that means "an actor," "one who plays a part." There are hypocrites in every walk of life, people who try to impress others in order to hide their real selves. In the Christian life, a hypocrite is somebody who tries to appear more spiritual than he or she really is. These people know that they are pretending, and they hope they will not be found out. Their Christian life is only a shallow masquerade.

It is easy to see why Jesus gave this warning at this particular time. The disciples might be tempted either to gain popularity by pleasing the crowds, or avoid trouble by pleasing the scribes and Pharisees. All of us want people to like us, and it seems such an easy thing to "act the part" that others want to see.

How can we keep hypocrisy out of our lives?

We must understand what hypocrisy really is (v. 1). Jesus compared it to leaven (yeast), something that every Jew would associate with evil. (See Ex. 12:15–20. Paul also used leaven to symbolize sin. See 1 Cor. 5:6–8; Gal. 5:9.) Like yeast, hypocrisy begins very small but grows quickly and quietly. As it grows, it infects the whole person. Hypocrisy does to the ego what yeast does to bread dough: it puffs it up (see

1 Cor. 4:6, 18–19; 5:2). Soon pride takes over and the person's character deteriorates rapidly.

If we want to keep hypocrisy out of our lives, we must avoid that first bit of "leaven." Once we start to pretend, the process goes on quickly, and the longer we wait, the worse it gets. Sir Walter Scott wrote:

O what a tangled web we weave
When first we practice to deceive.

Hypocrisy is foolish and futile (vv. 2–3). Why? Because nothing can really be hidden. Jesus referred here primarily to His own teachings, but the principle applies to other areas of life. The Twelve might be tempted to cover or compromise the truth so that neither the crowds nor the Pharisees would be offended (see Luke 8:16–18; 11:33). God's truth is like light, not leaven, and it must not be hidden. The lies of the hypocrite will one day be revealed, so why go on pretending? Let your light shine!

We must understand what causes hypocrisy (vv. 4–7). Jesus mentioned "fear" five times in these verses, so He is teaching us that a basic cause of hypocrisy is *the fear of man.* When we are afraid of what others may say about us or do to us, then we try to impress them in order to gain their approval. If necessary, we will even lie to accomplish our purposes, and this is hypocrisy. Unfortunately, many of the scribes and Pharisees were more concerned about reputation than character, what people *thought* about them than what God *knew* about them. The fear of man always brings a snare (Prov. 29:25), and Jesus wanted His disciples to avoid that snare.

The remedy for hypocrisy is to forget about what people may say and do and *fear God alone.* The fear of God is the fear that conquers all other fears, for the person who truly fears God need fear nothing else. All that men can do is kill the body, but God can condemn the soul! Since He is the final Judge, and He judges for eternity, it is logical that we put the fear of God ahead of everything else. Our God knows us and cares for us. He cares for the sparrows, and we are of more value than they, so what do we have to fear from men?

We must confess Christ openly (vv. 8–9). Once we have done this, we will have an easier time living the truth and avoiding hypocrisy. How can we fear men when we know Jesus Christ is confessing us before the Father in heaven? It is not important that men praise our names on earth, but it is important that God acknowledges us in heaven (see 2 Tim. 2:8–14).

We must depend on the Holy Spirit (vv. 10–12). Jesus appears to be contradicting Himself. In Luke 12:8–9, He demands that we openly confess Him, but in Luke 12:10, He says we can speak against Him and be forgiven. However, if we speak against the Spirit, there is no forgiveness! Does this mean that the Holy Spirit is more important than the Son of God?

Note that this statement is connected with the ministry of the Spirit in and through the apostles (Luke 12:11–12). The Jewish nation rejected *God the Father* when they refused to obey John the Baptist and repent, for John was sent by the Father. They rejected *God the Son* when they asked Pilate to crucify Him. But that sin could be forgiven because there was still the ministry of the Spirit.

God did not judge the nation immediately. Instead, Jesus prayed for them as He hung on the cross (Luke 23:34; see also Acts 3:17). Then God sent the Holy Spirit, who ministered through the apostles and other believers in the church. *This was the last opportunity for the nation, and they failed by rejecting the witness of the Spirit* (Acts 7:51). Luke 12:11–12 was fulfilled during the first chapters of Acts, when the message went "to the Jew first" (Acts 3:26; 13:46; Rom. 1:16). Israel's third "national sin" was the stoning of Stephen (Acts 7), after which the message went out to the Samaritans (Acts 8), and then the Gentiles (Acts 10). Note that Stephen said, "You always resist the Holy Spirit!" (Acts 7:51 niv).

I do not believe that the "sin against the Holy Spirit" is committed by people today as it was by Israel centuries ago. I believe that the only "unpardonable sin" today is the final rejection of Jesus Christ (John 3:36). The Spirit of God witnesses through the Word, and it is possible for sinners to reject that witness and resist the Spirit. But the Spirit bears witness to Christ (John 16:7–15), so the way people treat the Spirit is the way they treat the Son of God.

Beware of Covetousness (12:13–21)

At this point, a man in the crowd interrupted Jesus and asked Him to solve a family problem. Rabbis were expected to help settle legal matters, but Jesus refused to get involved. Why? Because He knew that no answer He gave would solve the *real* problem, which was covetousness in the hearts of the two brothers. (The "you" in Luke 12:14 is plural.) As long as both men were greedy, *no* settlement would be satisfactory. Their greatest need was to have their hearts changed. Like too many people today, they wanted Jesus to serve them but not to save them.

Covetousness is an unquenchable thirst for getting more and more of something we think we need in order to be truly satisfied. It may be a thirst for money or the things that money can buy, or even a thirst for position and power. Jesus made it clear that true life does not depend on an abundance of possessions. He did not deny that we have certain basic needs (Matt. 6:32; 1 Tim. 6:17). He only affirmed that we will not make life richer by acquiring *more* of these things.

Mark Twain once defined "civilization" as "a limitless multiplication of unnecessary necessities," and he was right. In fact, many Christians are infected with covetousness and do not know it. They think that Paul's admonition in 1 Timothy 6 applies only to the "rich and famous." Measured by the living standards of the rest of the world, most believers in America are indeed wealthy people.

Jesus told this parable to reveal the dangers that lurk in a covetous heart. As you read it, test your own responses to this farmer's various experiences.

How do you respond to the wealthy farmer's *dilemma?* Here was a man who had a problem with too much wealth! If we say, "I certainly wish I had that problem!" we may be revealing covetousness in our hearts. If suddenly you inherited a great deal of wealth, would it create a problem for you? Or would you simply praise God and ask Him what He wanted you to do with it?

There are perils to prosperity (Prov. 30:7–9). Wealth can choke the Word of God (Matt. 13:22), create snares and temptations (1 Tim. 6:6–10, 17–19), and give you a false sense of security. People say that money does not satisfy, but it does satisfy *if you want to live on that level.* People who are satisfied only with the things that money can buy are in great danger of losing the things that money cannot buy.

This farmer saw his wealth as an opportunity to please himself. He had no thoughts of others or of God.

How do you respond to the *decisions* of the rich man? Are you saying, "Now that is shrewd business! Save and have it ready for the future!" But Jesus saw selfishness in all that this man did (note the eleven personal pronouns), and He said the man was a fool. The world's philosophy is "Take care of Number One!" But Jesus does not endorse that philosophy.

There is certainly nothing wrong with following good business principles, or even with saving for the future (1 Tim. 5:8). Jesus does not encourage waste (John 6:12). But neither does He encourage selfishness motivated by covetousness.

How do you respond to the farmer's *desires?* Are you saying, "This is the life! The man has success, satisfaction, and security! What more could he want?" But Jesus did not see this farmer enjoying life; He saw him facing death! Wealth cannot keep us alive when our time comes to die, nor can it buy back the opportunities we missed while we were thinking of ourselves and ignoring God and others.

Jesus made it clear that true life does not come from an abundance of things, nor do true success or security. This man had a false view of both life and death. He thought that life came from accumulating things, and that death was far away. On March 11, 1856, Henry David Thoreau wrote in his journal, "That man is the richest whose pleasures are cheapest." He also said, "A man is rich in proportion to the number of things which he can afford to let alone."

Finally, how do you respond to the *death* of the boastful farmer? We are prone to say, "Too bad this fellow died just when he had everything going for him! How tragic that he could not finish his great plans." But the greatest tragedy is not what the man left behind but what lay *before* him: eternity without God! The man lived without God and died without God, and his wealth was but an incident in his life. God is not impressed with our money.

What does it mean to be "rich toward God"? It means to acknowledge gratefully that everything we have comes from God, and then make an effort to use what He gives us for the good of others and the glory of God. Wealth can be *enjoyed* and *employed* at the same time if our purpose is to honor God (1 Tim. 6:10ff.). To be rich toward God means spiritual enrichment, not just personal enjoyment. How tragic when people are rich in this world but poor in the next (see Matt. 6:19–34)!

Beware of Worrying (12:22–34)

The rich farmer worried because he had too much, but the disciples might be tempted to worry because they did not have enough! They had given up all they had in order to follow Christ. They were living by faith, and faith is always tested.

Worry is destructive. The word translated "anxious" in Luke 12:22 means "to be torn apart," and the phrase "doubtful mind" (Luke 12:29) means "to be held in suspense." It is the picture of a ship being tossed in a storm. Our English word *worry* comes from an old Anglo-Saxon word that means "to strangle." "Worry does not empty tomorrow of its sorrow," said Corrie ten Boom, "it empties today of its strength."

Worry is also deceptive. It gives us a false view of life, of itself, and of God. Worry convinces us that life is made up of what we eat and what we wear. We get so concerned about *the means* that we totally forget about *the end,* which is to glorify God (Matt. 6:33). There is a great difference between making a living and making a life.

Worry blinds us to the world around us and the way God cares for His creation. God makes the flowers beautiful, and He even feeds the unclean ravens, who have no ability to sow or reap. He ought to be able to care for men *to whom He has given the ability to work.* Jesus was not suggesting that we sit around and let God feed us, for the birds themselves work hard to stay alive. Rather, He encourages us to trust Him and cooperate with Him in using the abilities and opportunities that He gives us (2 Thess. 3:6–15).

But worry even blinds us to itself. We can get to the place where we actually think that worry accomplishes good things in our lives! In Luke 12:25, Jesus pointed out that our worries do not add one extra minute to our lives (Ps. 39:5) or one extra inch to our height. The rich farmer's fretting certainly did not lengthen his life! Instead of adding to our lives, our worries take away from our lives. People can worry themselves into the hospital or into the grave!

Once again, Jesus argued from the lesser to the greater. If God feeds the birds, He will surely feed His children. If He beautifies the plants that grow up one day and are cut down the next, surely He will clothe His own people. The problem is not His little power, for He can do anything; the problem is our little faith.

Worry is deformative. It keeps us from growing and it makes us like the unsaved in the world (Luke

12:30). In short, worry is unchristian; worry is a sin. How can we witness to a lost world and encourage them to put faith in Jesus Christ if we ourselves are doubting God and worrying? Is it not inconsistent to preach faith and yet not practice it? Late chaplain of the United States Senate Peter Marshall once prayed "that ulcers would not become the badge of our faith." Too often they are!

How do we win over worry? The first step is to realize that *God knows our needs,* so we can trust Him to meet them. We are sheep in His little flock, children in His family, and servants in His kingdom, and He will see to it that our needs are fully met. It is His *pleasure* to give us His kingdom, so will He not give us everything that we need (see Rom. 8:32)?

But God's pleasures and our treasures must go together. We must look at earth from heaven's point of view and make sure that we put God's kingdom first in everything. The main question is, "Where is your heart?" If our hearts are fixed on the transient things of earth, then we will always worry. But if we are fixed on the eternal, then God's peace will guard our minds and hearts (Phil. 4:6–9). We must "hang loose" when it comes to this world's goods, and be willing even to sell what we have in order to help others (Acts 2:44–45; 4:34–35). It is not wrong to own things so long as things do not own us.

Beware of Carelessness (12:35–53)

Jesus shifted the emphasis from being worried about the present to being watchful about the future. The themes in Luke 12 all go together, for one of the best ways to conquer hypocrisy, covetousness, and worry is to look for the Lord's return. When you are "living in the future tense," it is difficult for the things of the world to ensnare you. In this section, Jesus explained how we can be ready for His return.

Waiting and watching (vv. 35–40). Jewish weddings were held at night, and a bridegroom's servants would have to wait for their master to come home with his bride. The new husband would certainly not want to be kept waiting at the door with his bride! But the servants had to be sure they were ready to go to work, with their robes tucked under their girdles so they were free to move (see 1 Peter 1:13ff.).

But the remarkable thing in this story is that the master serves the servants! In Jewish weddings, the bride was treated like a queen and the groom like a king, so you would not expect the "king" to minister to his staff. Our King will minister to His faithful servants when He greets us at His return, and He will reward us for our faithfulness.

To "watch" means to be alert, to be ready, not to be caught by surprise. That is the attitude we must have toward the second coming of Jesus Christ. His coming will be like that of a thief: unannounced and unexpected (Matt. 24:43; 1 Thess. 5:2; Rev. 16:15). We must be ready!

The saintly Presbyterian pastor Robert Murray McCheyne sometimes asked people, "Do you believe that Jesus is coming today?" If they replied in the negative, he would say, "Then you had better be ready, for He is coming at an hour when you think not!"

Working (vv. 41–48). Lest we get the idea that watching and waiting are all that He requires, Jesus added this parable to encourage us to be working when He comes. The apostles had a special responsibility to feed God's household, His church, but each of us has some work to do in this world, assigned to us by the Lord. Our responsibility is to be faithful when He comes. We may not appear successful in our own eyes, or in the eyes of others, but that is not important. The thing God wants is faithfulness (1 Cor. 4:2).

Once a believer starts to think his Master is *not* coming back, his life begins to deteriorate. Our relationship with others depends on our relationship to the Lord, so if we stop looking for Him, we will stop loving His people. The motive for Christian life and service must be a desire to please the Lord and be found faithful at His return.

I do not think that Luke 12:46 teaches that unfaithful believers lose their salvation, because our going to heaven depends on faith in Jesus Christ and not good works (Eph. 2:8–10; 2 Tim. 2:11–13). The phrase "cut him in sunder" means "cut him off, separate him," and "unbelievers" can also be translated "unfaithful." Our Lord will separate the faithful believers from the unfaithful; He will reward the faithful, but the unfaithful servants will lose their rewards (1 Cor. 3:13–15).

God's judgment will be fair. It will be based on what the servants know of God's will. This is not to suggest that the more ignorant we are, the easier time we will have at the judgment seat of Christ! We are admonished to know God's will (Rom. 12:2; Col. 1:9) and to grow in our knowledge of Jesus Christ (2 Peter 3:18). Jesus is stating a general principle: the more we have from God, the greater our accountability before God.

Warring (vv. 49–53). As we wait, watch, and work, we will not have an easy time, because we are aliens in enemy territory. The images Jesus used—fire, baptism, division—speak of opposition and conflict. To the Jews, fire was a symbol of judgment, and our Lord's coming into this world did bring judgment (John 9:39–41).

Our Lord's "baptism" in Luke 12:50 refers to His suffering and death, which was pictured by His baptism in the Jordan. (See Ps. 42:7 and Jonah 2:3, and note His reference to Jonah in Luke 11:29–30.) The apostles certainly received a baptism of suffering as they witnessed for Christ after Pentecost.

Luke opened his book announcing "peace on earth" (Luke 2:14), but now he has the Lord seemingly contradicting this promise. Jesus does give peace to those who trust Him (Rom. 5:1), but often their confession of faith becomes a declaration of war among their family and friends. Jesus is a cause of division (see John 7:12, 43; 9:16; 10:19). But even if there is not "peace on earth," there is "peace in heaven" (Luke 19:38) because of the finished work of Jesus Christ on the cross.

After instructing His disciples, Jesus turned and gave a final warning to the people around Him.

Beware of Spiritual Dullness (12:54–59)

Jesus used two illustrations to impress on the crowds the importance of discernment and diligence in spiritual matters. First, He talked about the weather, and then He talked about a lawsuit.

Discernment (vv. 54–57). If people were as discerning about spiritual things as they are about the weather, they would be better off! The crowd could predict a storm, but it could not foresee the coming judgment. It knew that the temperature was about to change, but it could not interpret the "signs of the times." The Jewish nation had the prophetic Scriptures for centuries and should have known what God was doing, but their religious leaders led them astray.

How tragic that men today can predict the movements of the heavenly bodies, split atoms, and even put men on the moon, but they are blind to what God is doing in the world. They know how to get to the stars, but they do not know how to get to heaven! Our educated world possesses a great deal of scientific knowledge but not much spiritual wisdom.

Diligence (vv. 58–59). Anyone will do whatever is necessary to stay out of prison, but how many people will apply that same concern and diligence to stay out of hell? If lawyers and judges would examine God's Word as diligently as they examine their law books, they will gain a wisdom that the law cannot give.

The nation of Israel was marching to judgment, and the Judge was Almighty God, yet they would not seek for terms of peace (Luke 13:34–35). Jesus knew that the Roman armies would come to destroy the city and the temple (Luke 19:41–44), but He could not convince the people to repent. Their debt was mounting up and they would pay the last mite.

We must apply these truths to our own lives personally. If we knew a storm was coming, we would prepare for it. If we knew the officer was coming to take us to court, we would get a lawyer and try to settle the case out of court. The storm of God's wrath is coming, and the Judge is already standing before the door (James 5:9).

"Behold, now is the accepted time; behold, now is the day of salvation" (2 Cor. 6:2).

CHAPTER TWELVE
Luke 13
QUESTIONS AND ANSWERS

A Jewish student asked his teacher, "Rabbi, why is it that when I ask you a question, you always reply by asking me another question?" The rabbi

replied, "So why shouldn't I?" As Jesus continued His journey toward Jerusalem, He encountered four situations involving questions that had to be answered. "To question a wise man is the beginning of wisdom," says a German proverb. Not everyone who questioned the Lord did so from a right motive, but that did not stop Jesus from teaching them what they needed to know. As you study His replies in Luke 13, you can learn more about Him and His ministry, and also more about living the Christian life so as to please Him.

A Political Question about Justice (13:1–9)

Pontius Pilate, the Roman governor, did not get along with the Jews because he was insensitive to their religious convictions. For example, he brought the official Roman ensigns into Jerusalem and infuriated the Jews who resented having Caesar's image in the Holy City. Pilate threatened to kill the protesters *and they were willing to die!* Seeing their determination, the governor relented and moved the ensigns to Caesarea, but that did not stop the hostilities.

The atrocity mentioned in Luke 13:1 may have taken place when Pilate "appropriated" money from the temple treasury to help finance an aqueduct. A large crowd of angry Jews gathered in protest, so Pilate had soldiers *in civilian clothes* mingle with the mob. Using concealed weapons, the soldiers killed a number of innocent and unarmed Jews, and this only added to the Jews' hatred for their governor.

Since Jesus was going up to Jerusalem, anything He said about Pilate was sure to get there before Him. If He ignored the issue, the crowd would accuse Him of being pro-Roman and disloyal to His people. If He defended the Jews and accused Pilate, He would be in trouble with the Romans, and the Jewish leaders would have a good excuse to get Him arrested.

Our Lord moved the whole issue to a higher level and avoided politics completely. Instead of discussing *Pilate's* sins, He dealt with the sins of the people questioning Him. He answered their question by asking a question!

To begin with, He made it clear that human tragedies are not always divine punishments and that it is wrong for us to "play God" and pass judgment. Job's friends made this mistake when they said that Job's afflictions were evidence that he was a sinner. If we take that approach to tragedy, then we will have a hard time explaining the sufferings of the prophets and apostles, and even of our Lord Himself.

"How would you explain the deaths of the people on whom the tower in Siloam fell?" He asked. "That was not the fault of Pilate. Was it God's fault? Shall we blame Him? The eighteen who were killed were just doing their job, yet they died. They were not protesting or creating trouble."

When the blind English poet John Milton was old and obscure, he was visited one day by Charles II, son of the king that the Puritans had beheaded. "Your blindness is a judgment from God for the part you took against my father," said the king. Milton replied, "If I have lost my *sight* through God's judgment, what can you say of your father who lost his *head?*"

Jesus went on to show the logical conclusion of their argument: if God *does* punish sinners in this way, then they themselves had better repent because all men are sinners! The question is not, "Why did these people die?" but, "What right do you have to live?" None of us is sinless, so we had all better get prepared.

It is easier to talk about other people's deaths than it is to face our own sin and possible death. The American publishing tycoon William Randolph Hearst would not permit anyone to mention death in his presence, *yet he died.* I asked a friend of mine what the death rate was in his city, and he replied, "One apiece." Then he added, "People are dying who never died before."

According to Leviticus 19:23–25, fruit from newly planted trees was not eaten the first three years, and the fourth year the crops belonged to the Lord. A farmer would not get any figs for himself until the fifth year, but this man had now been waiting for *seven* years! No wonder he wanted to cut down the fruitless tree!

The parable has an application to individuals and to the nation of Israel. God is gracious and long suffering toward people (2 Peter 3:9) and does more than enough to encourage us to repent and bear fruit (Matt. 3:7–10). He has had every right to cut us down, but in His mercy, He has spared us. Yet we must not presume upon the kindness and long suffering of the Lord, for the day of judgment will finally come.

But the tree also reminds us of God's special goodness to Israel (Isa. 5:1–7; Rom. 9:1–5) and His patience with them. God waited three years during our Lord's earthly ministry, but the nation did not produce fruit. He then waited about forty years more before He allowed the Roman armies to destroy Jerusalem and the temple, and during those years, the church gave to the nation a powerful witness of the gospel message. Finally, the tree was cut down.

It is significant that the parable was "open-ended," so that the listeners had to supply the conclusion. (The book of Jonah is another example of this approach.) Did the tree bear fruit? Did the special care accomplish anything? Was the tree spared or cut down? We have no way to know the answers to these questions, *but we can answer as far as our own lives are concerned!* Again, the question is not "What happened to the tree?" but "What will happen to *me?*"

God is seeking fruit. He will accept no substitutes, and the time to repent is *now.* The next time you hear about a tragedy that claims many lives, ask yourself, "Am I just taking up space, or am I bearing fruit to God's glory?"

A Legal Question about the Sabbath (13:10–21)
Liberation (vv. 10–13). If I had been crippled for eighteen years, I wonder if I would be faithful to worship God week after week in the synagogue. Surely this woman had prayed and asked God for help, and yet she was not delivered. However, God's seeming unconcern did not cause her to become bitter or resentful. There she was in the synagogue.

Ever sensitive to the needs of others, Jesus saw the woman and called her to come forward. It may have seemed heartless to the congregation for Him to do this and expose her handicap publicly (see Matt. 12:13), but He knew what He was doing. For one thing, Satan was in the synagogue and He wanted to expose him and defeat him. But He also wanted the woman to help Him teach the people an important lesson about freedom.

Not only does Satan bow people down, but so do sin (Ps. 38:6), sorrow (Ps. 42:5), and suffering (Ps. 44:25). Jesus Christ is the only one who can set the prisoner free. He spoke the word, laid His hands on her, and she was healed and gave glory to God! That was a synagogue service the people never forgot.

Indignation (v. 14). Instead of rejoicing and giving God the glory, the ruler of the synagogue (see Luke 8:41) became very angry. He did not have the courage to express his anger to Jesus, so he scolded the congregation! But the more you ponder his tirade, the more laughable it becomes. Suppose they *did* bring their sick to be healed; who would heal them? Did *he* have that kind of power, and, if he did, why had he not used it to help people before? What a cowardly hypocrite!

The bondage of the ruler of the synagogue was worse than that of the woman. Her bondage affected only her body, but his bondage shackled his mind and heart. He was so bound and blinded by tradition that he ended up opposing the Son of God! Elbert Hubbard called tradition "a clock that tells us what time it was." The ruler of the synagogue could not "discern this time" (Luke 13:12:56) and he stood condemned.

Vindication (vv. 15–17). Jesus could have healed this woman on any other day of the week. After all, she had been bound for eighteen painful years, and one more day would have made little difference. But He deliberately chose the Sabbath day because He wanted to teach a lesson about freedom. Note the repetition of the word *loose* (Luke 13:12, 15–16).

First, the Lord defended the woman and rebuked the ruler of the synagogue. Jesus reminded him that he treated his animals far better than he treated this poor woman. This indictment included the people in the congregation as well. Our Lord was arguing from the lesser to the greater: if God permits people to help their thirsty animals on the Sabbath, would He not want us to care for needy people made in the image of God? Any tradition that keeps us from helping others is not from God. In fact, it is easy to use tradition as an excuse for not caring for others.

Jesus said that the woman was a "daughter of Abraham," referring to her spiritual condition and not her physical birth (Luke 19:9; Gal. 3:7). All the Jewish women present would have been "daughters of Abraham." Does this mean that she was a converted person *before* the Lord healed her? If so, then she is the only *believer* in the New Testament who was physically afflicted because of demonic attack. (We are not sure what Paul's "thorn in the flesh" was or exactly how Satan used it to buffet Paul. See 2 Cor. 12.)

Perhaps it is a matter of semantics, but I prefer to speak of demonic work in believers as "demon oppression" rather than "demon possession." In fact, the Greek word is "demonized," so we need not think of "possession" in spatial terms. Certainly Satan can and does attack the bodies and minds of God's people. Some satanic oppression could last for many years until someone detects that Satan is at work. Not all sickness is caused by demons (Luke 6:17–19), so we must not blame everything on Satan.

There were people in the congregation who hoped to use this Sabbath violation to accuse Jesus, but He left them so ashamed that they said nothing. The lesson that He taught was clear: Satan puts people into bondage, but true freedom comes from trusting Christ. The Sabbath that God wants to give us is a "heart rest" that comes through His grace and not from obeying traditions (Matt. 11:28–30).

The parables in Luke 13:18–21 were probably spoken to the congregation just before Jesus and the Twelve departed from the synagogue. He had used these parables before and the disciples understood them (Matt. 13:31–33, 51). Some see in them a picture of the visible outward growth of the kingdom (the mustard seed) and the invisible inward influence of the kingdom (the leaven). By using these parables, Jesus was saying, "You Jewish religious leaders may hold to your dead traditions and oppose the truth, but God's living kingdom will still increase. Satan will be defeated!"

But, we must keep two other considerations in mind. First, Jesus had already used leaven as a picture of evil (Luke 12:1), and He was not likely to contradict Himself. Second, the context of Matthew 13 indicates opposition and seeming defeat for God's kingdom, not worldwide conquest. Yes, there will be ultimate victory; but meanwhile, much of the seed sown will bear no fruit, Satan will sow counterfeits, and the net will catch all kinds of fish, good and bad. I cannot find either in church history or in contemporary reports any proof that the kingdom of God has "permeated the whole world." In view of the population increase, we are losing ground!

The Jews knew their Scriptures and recognized the images that Jesus used. Leaven represented evil (Ex. 12:14–20), and a mighty tree pictured a great world kingdom (Ezek. 17:22–24; 31:3–9; Dan. 4:20–22). A mustard seed produces a shrub, not a great tree. The kingdom would be infected with false teaching (Gal. 5:1–9), and the small seed ("little flock," Luke 12:32) would grow into an organization that would be a home for Satan. (The birds represent the evil one, Matt. 13:19.) The professing church today fits both descriptions.

A Theological Question about Salvation (13:22–30)

The events recorded in John 9—10 fit between Luke

13:21 and 22. Note in John 10:40–42 that Jesus then left Judea and went beyond the Jordan into Perea. The events of Luke 13:22—17:10 took place in Perea as the Lord gradually moved toward Jerusalem.

The scribes often discussed the question of how many people would be saved, and somebody asked Jesus to give His thoughts on the issue. As with the question about Pilate, Jesus immediately made the matter personal. "The question is not how many will be saved, but whether or not *you* will be saved! Get that settled first, and then we can discuss what you can do to help get others saved."

I sometimes receive "theological letters" from radio listeners who want to argue about predestination, election, and other difficult doctrines. When I reply, I usually ask them about their prayer life, their witnessing, and their work in the local church. That often ends the correspondence. Too many professed Christians want to discuss these profound doctrines, but they do not want to put them into practice by seeking to win people to Jesus Christ! D. L. Moody prayed, "Lord, save the elect, and then elect some more!"

"Many … will seek to enter in, and shall not be able" (Luke 13:24). Why? The parable tells us why, and it focuses primarily on the Jewish people of that day. However, it has a personal application to all of us today.

Jesus pictured the kingdom as a great feast, with the patriarchs and prophets as honored guests (Luke 13:28). But many of the people who were invited waited too long to respond, and, when they arrived at the banquet hall, it was too late and the door was shut (see Matt. 22:1–14; Luke 14:15–24).

But why did they wait so long? The parable suggests several reasons. To begin with, salvation is not easy; the sinner must enter a narrow gate and walk a narrow way (Luke 13:24; also see 9:23ff.). The world's crowd is on the easy way, the way that leads to destruction (Matt. 7:13–14), and it is much easier to walk with them.

Another reason for their delay was their false sense of security. Jesus had been among them; they had even eaten with Him and enjoyed His fellowship, *yet they had never trusted Him.* God gave the nation many privileges and opportunities, but they wasted them (see Luke 10:13–16). God is long suffering; however, there comes a time when even God shuts the door.

Pride also played a big part: they would not humble themselves before God. In their own eyes, they were first, but in God's eyes, they were last—*and the Gentiles would come and take their place* (see Matt. 21:43)! Imagine the "unclean Gentile dogs" sitting at the feast with Abraham, Isaac, and Jacob, while the unbelieving Jews were outside!

These people were lost because they depended on their ancient religion to save them, but Jesus saw them as "workers of iniquity," not doers of righteousness (Isa. 64:4; Titus 1:16). It takes more than reverence for tradition to get into God's kingdom!

But the major reason was given by Jesus Himself:

"Ye would not" (Luke 13:34). Their minds had been instructed by the Word (Luke 13:26), and their hearts had been stirred by His mighty works, but their wills were stubborn and would not submit to Him. *This is the deadly consequence of delay.* The longer sinners wait, the harder their hearts become. "Today, if you will hear His voice, do not harden your hearts" (Heb. 4:7 NKJV).

The Spanish composer Manuel de Falla was notorious for not answering his mail. When he heard that a friend had died, the composer said, "What a pity! He died before I answered his letter, which he sent me five years ago!"

When sinners fail to answer *God's* invitation to His feast, *they are the ones who die.* They are "thrust out" of the joys of the kingdom and are punished with "weeping and gnashing of teeth" (Luke 13:28). It is a picture of people who are overwhelmed with regret because they see how foolish they were to delay, but, alas, it is too late. One of the agonies of hell will be the remembrance of opportunities wasted.

What is the answer? "Strive to enter in at the narrow gate" (Luke 13:24). The word *strive* comes from the sports arena and describes an athlete giving his best to win the contest. Our English word *agonize* comes from this word. If people today would put as much effort into things spiritual as they do things athletic, they would be much better off.

A Personal Question about Danger (13:31–35)

Jesus was in Perea, which was ruled by Herod Antipas, son of Herod the Great. The Pharisees wanted to get Jesus back into Judea, where the religious leaders could watch Him and ultimately trap Him, so they tried to frighten Him away.

Herod had been perplexed by our Lord's ministry and was afraid that John the Baptist, whom he murdered, had come back from the dead (Luke 9:7–9). In fact, at one point, Herod wanted to meet Jesus so he could see Him perform a miracle (Luke 23:8)! But it appears that Herod's heart was getting harder, for now he threatened to kill Jesus. The warning the Pharisees gave (Luke 13:31) was undoubtedly true or Jesus would not have answered as He did.

Our Lord was not afraid of danger. He followed a "divine timetable" and nothing could harm Him. He was doing the will of God according to the Father's schedule (see John 2:4; 7:30; 8:20; 13:1; 17:1). It had been decreed from eternity that the Son of God would be crucified in Jerusalem at the Passover (1 Peter 1:20; Rev. 13:8), and even Herod Antipas could not hinder the purposes of God. Quite the contrary, our Lord's enemies only helped *fulfill* the will of God (Acts 2:23; 3:13–18).

Jesus used a bit of "holy sarcasm" in His reply. He compared Herod to a fox, an animal that was not held in high esteem by the Jews (Neh. 4:3). Known for its cunning, the fox was an apt illustration of the crafty Herod. Jesus had work to do, and He would

accomplish it. After all, Jesus walked in the light (John 9:4; 11:9–10), and foxes went hunting in the darkness!

But Jesus also had a word to say about His nation: "It cannot be that a prophet perish out of Jerusalem" (Luke 13:33). This parallels what He had said to the scribes and Pharisees in Luke 11:47–51. The nation not only rejected God's loving invitation to His feast, but they even killed the servants who brought them the invitation (see Acts 13:27)!

Our Lord's heart was grieved as He saw the unbelief and rebellion around Him, and He broke out in a lamentation over the sad plight of the Jewish nation. It was a sob of anguish, not an expression of anger. His compassionate heart was broken.

The image of the hen and her chicks would be a familiar one to an agricultural people like the Jews (see Ps. 91:4). Some of the Old Testament references to "wings" refer to the wings of the cherubim in the Holy of Holies in the tabernacle or temple (see Ex. 25:20; Ruth 2:12; Ps. 36:7–8; 61:4). The hen gathers her chicks when she sees danger is coming. The Pharisees told Jesus that He was in danger, when in reality *they* were in danger!

In this lament, Jesus was addressing the whole nation and not just the Pharisees who had tried to provoke Him. The people had been given many opportunities to repent and be saved, but they had refused to heed His call. "House" refers both to the "family" of Jacob ("the house of Israel") and to the temple ("the house of God"), both of which would be "left desolate." The city and temple were destroyed and the people were scattered.

But there is a future for Israel. The time will come when their Messiah will return and be recognized and received by the people. They will say, "Blessed is he that cometh in the name of the Lord" (Luke 13:35; also see Ps. 118:26). Some of the people would use these words at His "triumphal entry" (Luke 19:38), but they will not have their fulfillment until His coming in glory (see Zech. 12:10; 14:4ff.; Matt. 24:30–31).

Israel's house has been left desolate. The nation has no king or priest, no temple or sacrifice (Hos. 3:4–5). But the nation has God's promise that she has not been forsaken (Rom. 11:1ff.). There can be no peace on earth until the Prince of Peace (Isa. 9:6) is seated on David's throne (Isa. 11:1ff.).

"Pray for the peace of Jerusalem" (Ps. 122:6).

Strive to enter in at the narrow gate!

CHAPTER THIRTEEN
Luke 14
THE MAN WHO CAME TO DINNER

Sabbath day hospitality was an important part of Jewish life, so it was not unusual for Jesus to be invited to a home for a meal after the weekly synagogue service. Sometimes the host invited Him sincerely because he wanted to learn more of God's truth. But many times Jesus was asked to dine only so His enemies could watch Him and find something to criticize and condemn. That was the case on the occasion described in Luke 14 when a leader of the Pharisees invited Jesus to dinner.

Jesus was fully aware of what was in men's hearts (John 2:24–25), so He was never caught off guard. In fact, instead of hosts or guests judging Jesus, it was Jesus who passed judgment on them when they least expected it. Indeed, in this respect, He was a dangerous person to sit with at a meal or to follow on the road! In Luke 14, we see Jesus dealing with five different kinds of people and exposing what was false in their lives and their thinking.

The Pharisees: False Piety (14:1–6)

Instead of bringing them to repentance, Jesus' severe denunciation of the Pharisees and scribes (Luke 11:39–52) only provoked them to retaliation, and they plotted against Him. The Pharisee who invited Jesus to his home for dinner also invited a man afflicted with dropsy. This is a painful disease in which, because of kidney trouble, a heart ailment, or liver disease, the tissues fill with water. How heartless of the Pharisees to "use" this man as a tool to accomplish their wicked plan, but if we do not love the Lord, neither will we love our neighbor. Their heartless treatment of the man was far worse than our Lord's "lawless" behavior on the Sabbath.

This afflicted man would not have been invited to such an important dinner were it not that the Pharisees wanted to use him as "bait" to catch Jesus. They knew that Jesus could not be in the presence of human suffering very long without doing something about it. If He ignored the afflicted man, then He was without compassion, but if He healed him, then He was openly violating the Sabbath and they could accuse Him. They put the dropsied man right in front of the Master so He could not avoid him, and then they waited for the trap to spring.

Keep in mind that Jesus had already "violated" their Sabbath traditions on at least seven different occasions. On the Sabbath day, He had cast out a demon (Luke 4:31–37), healed a fever (Luke 4:38–39), allowed His disciples to pluck grain (Luke 6:1–5), healed a lame man (John 5:1–9), healed a man with a paralyzed hand (Luke 6:6–10), delivered a crippled woman who was afflicted by a demon (Luke 13:10–17), and healed a man born blind (John 9). Why our Lord's enemies thought that one more bit of evidence was necessary, we do not know, but we do know that their whole scheme backfired.

When Jesus asked what their convictions were about the Sabbath day, He used on them the weapon they had forged for Him. To begin with, they couldn't heal anybody on *any day,* and everybody knew it. But even more, if the Pharisees said that nobody should be healed on the Sabbath, the people would consider them heartless; if they gave permission for healing,

their associates would consider them lawless. The dilemma was now theirs, not the Lord's, and they needed a way to escape. As they did on more than one occasion, the scribes and Pharisees evaded the issue by saying nothing.

Jesus healed the man and let him go, knowing that the Pharisee's house was not the safest place for him. Instead of providing evidence against *Jesus,* the man provided evidence against the *Pharisees,* for he was "exhibit A" of the healing power of the Lord Jesus Christ.

The Lord knew too much about this legalistic crowd to let them escape. He knew that on the Sabbath day they would deliver their farm animals from danger, so why not permit Him to deliver a man who was made in the likeness of God? Seemingly, they were suggesting that animals were more important than people. (It is tragic that some people even today have more love for their pets than they do for their family members, their neighbors, or even for a lost world.)

Jesus exposed the false piety of the Pharisees and the scribes. They claimed to be defending God's Sabbath laws, when in reality they were denying God by the way they abused people and accused the Savior. There is a big difference between protecting God's truth and promoting man's traditions.

The Guests: False Popularity (14:7–11)

Experts in management tell us that most people wear an invisible sign that reads, "Please make me feel important"; if we heed that sign, we can succeed in human relations. On the other hand, if we say or do things that make others feel insignificant, we will fail. Then people will respond by becoming angry and resentful, because everybody wants to be noticed and made to feel important.

In Jesus' day, as today, there were "status symbols" that helped people enhance and protect their high standing in society. If you were invited to the "right homes" and if you were seated in the "right places," then people would know how important you really were. The emphasis was on reputation, not character. It was more important to sit in the right places than to live the right kind of life.

In New Testament times, the closer you sat to the host, the higher you stood on the social ladder and the more attention (and invitations) you would receive from others. Naturally, many people rushed to the "head table" when the doors were opened because they wanted to be important.

This kind of attitude betrays a false view of success. "Try not to become a man of success," said Albert Einstein, "but try to become a man of value." While there may be some exceptions, it is usually true that valuable people are eventually recognized and appropriately honored. Success that comes only from self-promotion is temporary, and you may be embarrassed as you are asked to move down (Prov. 25:6–7).

When Jesus advised the guests to take the lowest

places, He was not giving them a "gimmick" that guaranteed promotion. The false humility that takes the lowest place is just as hateful to God as the pride that takes the highest place. God is not impressed by our status in society or in the church. He is not influenced by what people say or think about us, because He sees the thoughts and motives of the heart (1 Sam. 16:7). God still humbles the proud and exalts the humble (James 4:6).

British essayist Francis Bacon compared fame to a river that easily carried "things light and swollen" but that drowned "things weighty and solid." It is interesting to scan old editions of encyclopedias and see how many "famous people" are "forgotten people" today.

Humility is a fundamental grace in the Christian life, and yet it is elusive; if you know you have it, you have lost it! It has well been said that humility is not thinking meanly of ourselves; it is simply not thinking of ourselves at all. Jesus is the greatest example of humility, and we would do well to ask the Holy Spirit to enable us to imitate Him (Phil. 2:1–16).

The Host: False Hospitality (14:12–14)

Jesus knew that the host had invited his guests for two reasons: (1) to pay them back because they had invited him to past feasts, or (2) to put them under his debt so that they would invite him to future feasts. Such hospitality was not an expression of love and grace but rather an evidence of pride and selfishness. He was "buying" recognition.

Jesus does not prohibit us from entertaining family and friends, but He warns us against entertaining *only* family and friends exclusively and habitually. That kind of "fellowship" quickly degenerates into a "mutual admiration society" in which each one tries to outdo the others and no one dares to break the cycle. Sad to say, too much church social life fits this description.

Our motive for sharing must be the praise of God and not the applause of men, the eternal reward in heaven and not the temporary recognition on earth. A pastor friend of mine used to remind me, "You can't get your reward twice!" and he was right (see Matt. 6:1–18). On the day of judgment, many who today are first in the eyes of men will be last in God's eyes, and many who are last in the eyes of men will be first in the eyes of God (Luke 13:30).

In our Lord's time, it was not considered proper to ask poor people and handicapped people to public banquets. (The women were not invited either!) But Jesus commanded us to put these needy people at the top of our guest list *because they cannot pay us back.* If our hearts are right, God will see to it that we are properly rewarded, though getting a reward must not be the motive for our generosity. When we serve others from unselfish hearts, we are laying up treasures in heaven (Matt. 6:20) and becoming "rich toward God" (Luke 12:21).

Our modern world is very competitive, and it is easy for God's people to become more concerned about profit and loss than they are about sacrifice and service. "What will *I* get out of it?" may easily become life's most important question (Matt. 19:27ff.). We must strive to maintain the unselfish attitude that Jesus had and share what we have with others.

The Jews: False Security (14:15–24)

When Jesus mentioned "the resurrection of the just," one of the guests became excited and said, "Blessed is he that shall eat bread in the kingdom of God!" The Jewish people pictured their future kingdom as a great feast with Abraham, Isaac, Jacob, and the prophets as the honored guests (Luke 13:28; see Isa. 25:6). This anonymous guest was confident that he would one day be at the "kingdom feast" with them! Jesus responded by telling him a parable that revealed the sad consequences of false confidence.

In Jesus' day when you invited guests to a dinner, you told them the day but not the exact hour of the meal. A host had to know how many guests were coming so he could butcher the right amount of animals and prepare sufficient food. Just before the feast was to begin, the host sent his servants to each of the guests to tell them the banquet was ready and they should come (see Esth. 5:8; 6:14). In other words, *each of the guests in this parable had already agreed to attend the banquet.* The host expected them to be there.

But instead of eagerly coming to the feast, all of the guests insulted the host by refusing to attend, and they all gave very feeble excuses to defend their change in plans.

The first guest begged off because he had to "go and see" a piece of real estate he had purchased. In the East, the purchasing of property is often a long and complicated process, and the man would have had many opportunities to examine the land he was buying. Anybody who purchases land that he has never examined is certainly taking a chance. Since most banquets were held in the evening, the man had little daylight left even for a cursory investigation.

The second man had also made a purchase—ten oxen that he was anxious to prove. Again, who would purchase that many animals without first testing them? Not many customers in our modern world would buy a used car that they had not taken out for a "test drive." Furthermore, how could this man really put these oxen to the test when it was so late in the day? His statement "I go to prove them!" suggests that he was already on his way to the farm when the servant came with the final call to the dinner.

The third guest really had no excuse at all. Since they involved so much elaborate preparation, Jewish weddings were never surprises, so this man knew well in advance that he was taking a wife. That being the case, he should not have agreed to attend the feast in the first place. Since only Jewish men were invited to banquets, the host did not expect the wife to come anyway. Having a new wife could have kept the man from the battlefield (Deut. 24:5) but not from the festive board.

Of course, these were only excuses. I think it was Billy Sunday who defined an excuse as "the skin of a reason stuffed with a lie." The person who is good at excuses is usually not good at anything else. These three guests actually expected to get another invitation in the future, *but that invitation never came.*

Having prepared a great dinner for many guests, the host did not want all that food to go to waste, so he sent his servant out to gather a crowd and bring them to the banquet hall. What kind of men would be found in the streets and lanes of the city or in the highways and hedges? The outcasts, the loiterers, the homeless, the undesirables, *the kind of people that Jesus came to save* (Luke 15:1–2; 19:10). There might even be some Gentiles in the crowd!

These men may have had only one reason for refusing the kind invitation: they were unprepared to attend such a fine dinner. So, the servant constrained them to accept (see 2 Cor. 5:20). They had no excuses. The poor could not afford to buy oxen; the blind could not go to examine real estate; and the poor, maimed, lame, and blind were usually not given in marriage. This crowd would be hungry and lonely and only too happy to accept an invitation to a free banquet.

Not only did the host get other people to take the places assigned to the invited guests, but he also *shut the door so that the excuse-makers could not change their minds and come in* (see Luke 13:22–30). In fact, the host was angry. We rarely think of God expressing judicial anger against those who reject His gracious invitations, but verses like Isaiah 55:6 and Proverbs 1:24–33 give a solemn warning that we not treat His calls lightly.

This parable had a special message for the proud Jewish people who were so sure they would "eat bread in the kingdom of God." Within a few short years, the gospel would be rejected by the official religious leaders, and the message would go out to the Samaritans (Acts 8) and then to the Gentiles (Acts 10; 13ff.).

But the message of this parable applies to all lost sinners today. God still says, "All things are now ready. Come!" Nothing more need be done for the salvation of your soul, for Jesus Christ finished the work of redemption when He died for you on the cross and arose from the dead. The feast has been spread, the invitation is free, and you are invited to come.

People today make the same mistake that the people in the parable made: they delay in responding to the invitation *because they settle for second best.* There is certainly nothing wrong with owning a farm, examining purchases, or spending an evening with your wife. But if these *good* things keep you from enjoying the *best* things, then they become *bad* things. The excuse-makers were actually successful people in the eyes of their friends, but they were failures in the eyes of Jesus Christ.

The Christian life is a feast, not a funeral, and all are invited to come. Each of us as believers must herald abroad the message, "Come, for all things are now ready!" God wants to see His house filled, and "yet there is room." He wants us to go home (Mark 5:19), go into the streets and lanes (Luke 14:21), go into the highways and hedges (Luke 14:23), and go into all the world (Mark 16:15) with the gospel of Jesus Christ.

This parable was the text of the last sermon D. L. Moody preached, "Excuses." It was given on November 23, 1899 in the Civic Auditorium in Kansas City, and Moody was a sick man as he preached. "I must have souls in Kansas City," he told the students at his school in Chicago. "Never, never have I wanted so much to lead men and women to Christ as I do this time!"

There was a throbbing in his chest, and he had to hold to the organ to keep from falling, but Moody bravely preached the gospel, and some fifty people responded to trust Christ. The next day, Moody left for home, and a month later he died. Up to the very end, Moody was "compelling them to come in."

The Multitudes: False Expectancy (14:25–35)

When Jesus left the Pharisee's house, great crowds followed Him, but He was not impressed by their enthusiasm. He knew that most of those in the crowd were not the least bit interested in spiritual things. Some wanted only to see miracles, others heard that He fed the hungry, and a few hoped He would overthrow Rome and establish David's promised kingdom. They were expecting the wrong things.

Jesus turned to the multitude and preached a sermon that deliberately thinned out the ranks. He made it clear that, when it comes to personal discipleship, He is more interested in *quality* than *quantity*. In the matter of saving lost souls, He wants His house to be filled (Luke 14:23), but in the matter of personal discipleship, He wants only those who are willing to pay the price.

A "disciple" is a learner, one who attaches himself or herself to a teacher in order to learn a trade or a subject. Perhaps our nearest modern equivalent is "apprentice," one who learns by watching and by doing. The word *disciple* was the most common name for the followers of Jesus Christ and is used 264 times in the Gospels and the book of Acts.

Jesus seems to make a distinction between salvation and discipleship. Salvation is open to all who will come by faith, while discipleship is for believers willing to pay a price. Salvation means coming to the cross and trusting Jesus Christ, while discipleship means carrying the cross and following Jesus Christ. Jesus wants as many sinners saved as possible ("that my house may be filled"), but He cautions us not to take discipleship lightly, and in the three parables He gave, He made it clear that there is a price to pay.

To begin with, we must love Christ supremely, even more than we love our own flesh and blood (Luke 14:26–27). The word *hate* does not suggest positive antagonism but rather "to love less" (see Gen. 29:30–31; Mal. 1:2–3; and Matt. 10:37). Our love for Christ must be so strong that all other love is like hatred in comparison. In fact, we must hate our own lives and be willing to bear the cross after Him.

What does it mean to "carry the cross"? It means daily identification with Christ in shame, suffering, and surrender to God's will. It means death to self, to our own plans and ambitions, and a willingness to serve Him as He directs (John 12:23–28). A "cross" is something we willingly accept from God as part of His will for our lives. The Christian who called his noisy neighbors the "cross" he had to bear certainly did not understand the meaning of dying to self.

Jesus gave three parables to explain why He makes such costly demands on His followers: the man building a tower, the king fighting a war, and the salt losing its flavor. The usual interpretation is that believers are represented by the man building the tower and the king fighting the war, and we had better "count the cost" before we start, lest we start and not be able to finish. But I agree with Campbell Morgan that the builder and the king represent not the believer but Jesus Christ. *He is the one who must "count the cost" to see whether we are the kind of material He can use to build the church and battle the enemy.* He cannot get the job done with halfhearted followers who will not pay the price.

As I write this chapter, I can look up and see on my library shelves hundreds of volumes of Christian biographies and autobiographies, the stories of godly men and women who made great contributions to the building of the church and the battle against the enemy. They were willing to pay the price, and God blessed them and used them. They were people with "salt" in their character.

Jesus had already told His disciples that they were "the salt of the earth" (Matt. 5:13). When the sinner trusts Jesus Christ as Savior, a miracle takes place and "clay" is turned into "salt." Salt was a valued item in that day; in fact, part of a soldier's pay was given in salt. (The words *salt* and *salary* are related; hence, the saying, "He's not worth his salt.")

Salt is a preservative, and God's people in this world are helping to retard the growth of evil and decay. Salt is also a purifying agent, an antiseptic that makes things cleaner. It may sting when it touches the wound, but it helps to kill infection. Salt gives flavor to things and, most of all, makes people thirsty. By our character and conduct, we ought to make others thirsty for the Lord Jesus Christ and the salvation that He alone can give.

Our modern salt is pure and does not lose its flavor, but the salt in Jesus' day was impure and could lose its flavor, especially if it came in contact with earth. Once the saltiness was gone, there was no way to restore it, and the salt was thrown out into the street to be walked on. When a disciple loses his Christian character, he is "good for nothing" and will eventually be "walked on" by others and bring disgrace to Christ

Discipleship is serious business. If we are not true disciples, then Jesus cannot build the tower and fight the war. "There is always an *if* in connection with discipleship," wrote Oswald Chambers, "and it implies that we need not [be disciples] unless we like. There is never any compulsion; Jesus does not coerce us. There is only one way of being a disciple, and that is by being devoted to Jesus."

If we tell Jesus that we want to take up our cross and follow Him as His disciples, then He wants us to know exactly what we are getting into. He wants no false expectancy, no illusions, no bargains. He wants to use us as stones for building His church, soldiers for battling His enemies, and salt for bettering His world, *and He is looking for quality.*

After all, He was on His way to Jerusalem when He spoke these words, and look what happened to Him there! He does not ask us to do anything for Him that He has not already done for us.

To some, Jesus says, "You cannot be My disciples!" Why? Because they will not forsake all for Him, bear shame and reproach for Him, and let their love for Him control them.

And they are the losers.

Will *you* be His disciple?

CHAPTER FOURTEEN
Luke 15
THE JOYS OF SALVATION

When D. L. Moody was directing his Sunday school in Chicago, one boy walked several miles to attend; and somebody asked him, "Why don't you go to a Sunday school closer to home?"

His reply might have been used by the publicans and sinners in Jesus' day: "Because they love a feller over there."

It is significant that Jesus *attracted* sinners while the Pharisees *repelled* them. (What does this say about some of our churches today?) Lost sinners came to Jesus, not because He catered to them or compromised His message, but because He cared for them. He understood their needs and tried to help them, while the Pharisees criticized them and kept their distance (see Luke 18:9–14). The Pharisees had a knowledge of the Old Testament law and a desire for personal purity, yet they had no love for lost souls.

Three words summarize the message of this chapter: *lost, found,* and *rejoice.* Jesus spoke these parables to answer the accusations of the Pharisees and scribes who were scandalized at His behavior. It was bad enough that Jesus *welcomed* these outcasts and taught them, but He went so far as to *eat with them!* The Jewish religious leaders did not yet understand that the Son of Man had "come to seek and to save that which was lost" (Luke 19:10). Even more, they were still blind to the fact that *they themselves were among the lost.*

This chapter makes it clear that there is one message of salvation: God welcomes and forgives repentant sinners. But these parables also reveal that there are *two aspects to this salvation.* There is *God's* part: the shepherd seeks the lost sheep, and the woman searches for the lost coin. But there is also *man's* part in salvation, for the wayward son willingly repented and returned home. To emphasize but one aspect is to give a false view of salvation, for both the sovereignty of God and the responsibility of man must be considered (see John 6:37; 2 Thess. 2:13–14).

Since one of the major themes of this chapter is joy, let's consider the three different joys that are involved in salvation. C. S. Lewis wrote, "Joy is the serious business of heaven," and it is a joy in which you and I can share.

The Joy of Finding (15:1–10)

The story about the lost sheep would touch the hearts of the men and boys in the crowd, and the women and girls would appreciate the story about the coin that was lost from the wedding necklace. Jesus sought to reach everybody's heart.

The lost sheep (vv. 3–7). The sheep was lost because of foolishness. Sheep have a tendency to go astray, and that is why they need a shepherd (Isa. 53:6; 1 Peter 2:25). The scribes and Pharisees had no problem seeing the publicans and sinners as "lost sheep," but they would not apply that image to themselves! And yet the prophet made it clear that all of us have sinned and gone astray, and that includes religious people.

The shepherd was responsible for each sheep; if one was missing, the shepherd had to pay for it unless he could prove that it was killed by a predator (see Gen. 31:38–39; Ex. 22:10–13; Amos 3:12). This explains why he would leave the flock with the other shepherds, go and search for the missing animal, and then rejoice when he found it. Not to find the lost sheep meant money out of his own pocket, plus the disgrace of being known as a careless shepherd.

By leaving the ninety-nine sheep, the shepherd was not saying they were unimportant to him. They were safe, but the lost sheep was in danger. The fact that the shepherd would go after *one* sheep is proof that each animal was dear to him. Jesus was not suggesting that the scribes and Pharisees were not in need of salvation, for they certainly were. We must not make every part of the parable mean something, otherwise we will turn it into an allegory and distort the message.

There is a fourfold joy expressed when a lost sinner comes to the Savior. Though nothing is said in the story about how the sheep felt, there is certainly joy in the heart of the *person found.* Both Scripture (Acts 3:8; 8:39) and our own personal experience verify the joy of salvation.

But there is also the joy of the person who does the finding. Whenever you assist in leading a lost soul to faith in Christ, you experience a wonderful joy within. Others join with us in rejoicing as we share the good news of a new child of God in the family, and there is also joy in heaven (Luke 15:7, 10). The angels know better than we do what we are saved *from* and *to,* and they rejoice with us.

The lost coin (vv. 8–10). The sheep was lost because of its foolishness, but the coin was lost because of the carelessness of another. It is a sobering thought that our carelessness *at home* could result in a soul being lost.

When a Jewish girl married, she began to wear a headband of ten silver coins to signify that she was now a wife. It was the Jewish version of our modern wedding ring, and it would be considered a calamity for her to lose one of those coins. Palestinian houses were dark, so she had to light a lamp and search until she found the lost coin, and we can imagine her joy at finding it.

We must not press parabolic images too far, but it is worth noting that the coin would have on it the image of the ruler (Luke 20:19–25). The lost sinner bears the image of God, even though that image has been marred by sin. When a lost sinner is "found," God begins to restore that divine image through the power of the Spirit, and one day, the believer will be like Jesus Christ (Rom. 8:29; 2 Cor. 3:18; Col. 3:10; 1 John 3:1–2).

These two parables help us understand something of what it means to be lost. To begin with, it means being *out of place.* Sheep belong with the flock, coins belong on the chain, and lost sinners belong in fellowship with God. But to be lost also means *being out of service.* A lost sheep is of no value to the shepherd, a lost coin has no value to the owner, and a lost sinner cannot experience the enriching fulfillment God has for him in Jesus Christ.

But to turn this around, to be "found" (saved) means that you are back in place (reconciled to God), back in service (life has a purpose), and out of danger. No wonder the shepherd and the woman rejoiced and invited their friends to rejoice with them!

It is easy for us today to read these two parables and take their message for granted, but the people who first heard them must have been shocked. *Jesus was saying that God actually searches for lost sinners!* No wonder the scribes and Pharisees were offended, for there was no place in their legalistic theology for a God like that. They had forgotten that God had sought out Adam and Eve when they had sinned and hidden from God (Gen. 3:8–9). In spite of their supposed knowledge of Scripture, the scribes and Pharisees forgot that God was like a father who pitied his wayward children (Ps. 103:8–14).

There are few joys that match the joy of finding the lost and bringing them to the Savior. "The church has nothing to do but to save souls," said John Wesley, the founder of Methodism. "Therefore, spend and be spent in this work."

The Joy of Returning (15:11–24)

We call this story "the parable of the prodigal son"

(the word *prodigal* means "wasteful"), but it could also be called "the parable of the loving father," for it emphasizes the graciousness of the father more than the sinfulness of the son. Unlike the shepherd and the woman in the previous parables, the father did not go out to seek the son, but it was the memory of his father's goodness that brought the boy to repentance and forgiveness (see Rom. 2:4). Note in the story the three experiences of the younger son.

Rebellion—he went to the far country (vv. 11–16). According to Jewish law, an elder son received twice as much as the other sons (Deut. 21:17), and a father could distribute his wealth during his lifetime if he wished. It was perfectly legal for the younger son to ask for his share of the estate and even to sell it, but it was certainly not a very loving thing on his part. It was as though he were saying to his father, "I wish you were dead!" Thomas Huxley said, "A man's worst difficulties begin when he is able to do just as he likes." How true!

We are always heading for trouble whenever we value things more than people, pleasure more than duty, and distant scenes more than the blessings we have right at home. Jesus once warned two disputing brothers, "Take heed and beware of covetousness" (Luke 12:15). Why? Because the covetous person can never be satisfied, no matter how much he acquires, and a dissatisfied heart leads to a disappointed life. The prodigal learned the hard way that you cannot enjoy the things money can buy if you ignore the things money cannot buy.

"The far country" is not necessarily a distant place to which we must travel, because "the far country" exists first of all *in our hearts.* The younger son dreamed of "enjoying" his freedom far from home and away from his father and older brother. If the sheep was lost through foolishness and the coin through carelessness, then the son was lost because of willfulness. He wanted to have his own way, so he rebelled against his own father and broke his father's heart.

But life in the far country was not what he expected. His resources ran out, his friends left him, a famine came, and the boy was forced to do for a stranger what he would not do for his own father—go to work! This scene in the drama is our Lord's way of emphasizing what sin really does in the lives of those who reject the Father's will. Sin promises freedom, but it only brings slavery (John 8:34); it promises success, but brings failure; it promises life, but "the wages of sin is death" (Rom. 6:23). The boy thought he would "find himself," but he only lost himself! When God is left out of our lives, enjoyment becomes enslavement.

Repentance—he came to himself (vv. 17–19). To "repent" means "to change one's mind," and that is exactly what the young man did as he cared for the pigs. (What a job for a Jewish boy!) He "came to himself," which suggests that up to this point he had not really "been himself." There is an "insanity" in sin that seems to paralyze the image of God within us and liberate the "animal" inside. Students of Shakespeare like to contrast two quotations that describe this contradiction in man's nature.

> What a piece of work is a man! How
> noble in reason! how infinite in faculty!
> in form, in moving, how express and
> admirable! in action how like an angel! in
> apprehension how like a god!
> —HAMLET, II, II

> When he is best, he is a little worse than
> a man; and when he is worst, he is little
> better than a beast.
> —THE MERCHANT OF VENICE, I, II

The young man changed his mind about himself and his situation, and he admitted that he was a sinner. He confessed that his father was a generous man and that service at home was far better than "freedom" in the far country. It is God's goodness, not just man's badness, that leads us to repentance (Rom. 2:4). If the boy had thought only about himself—his hunger, his homesickness, his loneliness—he would have despaired. But his painful circumstances helped him to see his father in a new way, and this brought him hope. If his father was so good to *servants,* maybe he would be willing to forgive a *son.*

Had he stopped there, the boy would have experienced only regret or remorse (2 Cor. 7:10), but true repentance involves the will as well as the mind and the emotions—"I will arise … I will go … I will say…." Our resolutions may be noble, but unless we act on them, they can never of themselves bring about any permanent good. If repentance is truly the work of God (Acts 11:18), then the sinner will obey God and put saving faith in Jesus Christ (Acts 20:21).

Rejoicing—he came to the father (vv. 20–24). Here Jesus answered the accusations of the scribes and Pharisees (Luke 15:2), for the father not only ran to welcome his son, but he honored the boy's homecoming by preparing a great feast and inviting the village to attend. The father never did permit the younger son to finish his confession; he interrupted him, forgave him, and ordered the celebration to begin!

Of course, the father pictures to us the attitude of our heavenly Father toward sinners who repent: He is rich in His mercy and grace, and great in His love toward them (Eph. 2:1–10). All of this is possible because of the sacrifice of His Son on the cross. No matter what some preachers (and singers) claim, we are not saved by God's love; God loves the whole world, and the whole world is not saved. We are saved by God's grace, and grace is *love that pays a price.*

In the East, old men do not run, yet the father ran to meet his son. Why? One obvious reason was his love for him and his desire to show that love. But there is something else involved. This wayward son had brought disgrace to his family and village and, according to Deuteronomy 21:18–21, he should have been stoned to death. *If the neighbors had started to stone him, they would have hit the father who was embracing him!* What a picture of what Jesus did for us on the cross!

Everything the younger son had hoped to find in the far country, he discovered back home: clothes, jewelry, friends, joyful celebration, love, and assurance for the future. What made the difference? Instead of saying, "Father, *give* me!" he said, "Father, *make* me!" He was willing to be a servant! Of course, the father did not ask him to "earn" his forgiveness, because no amount of good works can save us from our sins (Eph. 2:8–10; Titus 3:3–7). In the far country, the prodigal learned the meaning of misery, but back home, he discovered the meaning of mercy.

The ring was a sign of sonship, and the "best robe" (no doubt the father's) was proof of his acceptance back into the family (see Gen. 41:42; Isa. 61:10; 2 Cor. 5:21). Servants did not wear rings, shoes, or expensive garments. The feast was the father's way of showing his joy and sharing it with others. Had the boy been dealt with according to the law, there would have been a funeral, not a feast. What a beautiful illustration of Psalm 103:10–14!

It is interesting to consider the father's description of his son's experience: he was dead, and was now alive; he was lost, and now was found. This is the spiritual experience of every lost sinner who comes to the Father through faith in Jesus Christ (John 5:24; Eph. 2:1–10). Note the parallels between the prodigal's coming to the father and our coming to the Father through Christ (John 14:6):

The Prodigal	*Jesus Christ*
He was lost (v. 24)	"I am the way"
He was ignorant (v. 17)	"I am the truth"
He was dead (v. 24)	"I am the life"

There is only one way to come to the Father, and that is through faith in Jesus Christ. Have you come home?

The Joy of Forgiving (15:25–32)
At this point in the parable, the scribes and Pharisees felt confident that they had escaped our Lord's judgment, for He had centered His attention on the publicans and sinners, pictured by the prodigal son. But Jesus continued the story and introduced the elder brother, who is a clear illustration of the scribes and Pharisees. The publicans and sinners were guilty of the obvious sins of the flesh, but the Pharisees and scribes were guilty of sins of the spirit (2 Cor. 7:1). Their outward actions may have been blameless, but their inward attitudes were abominable (see Matt. 23:25–28).

We must admit that the elder brother had some virtues that are commendable. He worked hard and always obeyed his father. He never brought disgrace either to the home or to the village, and apparently he had enough friends so that he could have planned an enjoyable party (Luke 15:29). He seems like a good

solid citizen and, compared to his younger brother, almost a saint.

However, important as obedience and diligence are, they are not the only tests of character. Jesus taught that the two greatest commandments are to love God and to love others (Luke 10:25–28), but the elder brother broke both of these divine commandments. He did not love God (represented in the story by the father), and he did not love his brother. The elder brother would not forgive his brother who wasted the family inheritance and disgraced the family name. But neither would he forgive his father who had graciously forgiven the young man those very sins!

When you examine the sins of the elder brother, you can easily understand why he pictures the scribes and Pharisees. To begin with, he was *self-righteous.* He openly announced the sins of his brother, but he could not see his own sins (see Luke 18:9–14). The Pharisees defined sin primarily in terms of outward actions, not inward attitudes. They completely missed the message of the Sermon on the Mount and its emphasis on inward attitudes and holiness of heart (Matt. 5—7).

Pride was another one of his failings. Just think, he had served his father all those years and had *never* disobeyed his will! What a testimony! But his heart was not in his work, and he was always dreaming of throwing a big party at which he and his friends could enjoy themselves. He was only a drudge. Like the prophet Jonah, the elder brother did God's will *but not from the heart* (Jonah 4; Eph. 6:6). He was a hard worker and a faithful worker—qualities to be commended—but his work was not a "labor of love" that would please his father.

You cannot help but notice his *unconcern for his missing brother.* Imagine having to be told that his brother had come home! The father watched for the younger son day after day and finally saw him afar off, but the elder brother did not know his brother was home until one of the servants told him.

Even though he knew it would make his father happy, the elder brother did not want his younger brother to come home. Why should he share his estate with somebody who had wasted his own inheritance? Why should he even share the father's love with somebody who had brought shame to the family and the village? Reports of the prodigal's lifestyle only made the elder brother look good, and perhaps this would make the father love his obedient son even more. No doubt about it—the arrival of the younger son was a threat to the older son.

Perhaps the most disturbing thing about the elder son was his fierce *anger.* He was angry at both his father and his brother and would not go into the house and share in the joyful celebration.

Anger is a normal emotion and it need not be sinful. "Be ye angry, and sin not" (Eph. 4:26, quoting Ps. 4:4). Moses, David, the prophets, and our Lord Jesus displayed holy anger at sin, and so should we today. The Puritan preacher Thomas Fuller said that anger was one of the "sinews of the soul." Aristotle gave good advice when he wrote, "Anybody can become angry. That is easy. But to be angry with the right person and to the right degree and at the right time and for the right purpose and in the right way—that is not within everybody's power and is not easy."

The elder brother was angry with his father because his father had given the younger son the feast that the elder brother had always wanted. "You never gave me so much as a goat," he said to his father, "but you killed for him the valuable fatted calf!" The elder brother's dreams were all shattered because the father had forgiven the prodigal.

Of course the elder brother was angry at his younger brother for getting all that attention and receiving the father's special gifts. As far as the elder brother was concerned, *the younger brother deserved none of it.* Had he been faithful? No! Had he obeyed the father? No! Then why should he be treated with such kindness and love?

The Pharisees had a religion of good works. By their fasting, studying, praying, and giving, they hoped to earn blessings from God and merit eternal life. They knew little or nothing about the grace of God. However, it was not what they did, but what they did not do, that alienated them from God (see Matt. 23:23–24). When they saw Jesus receiving and forgiving irreligious people, they rebelled against it. Even more, they failed to see that *they themselves also needed the Savior.*

The same father who ran to meet the prodigal came out of the house of feasting to plead with the older son. How gracious and condescending our Father is, and how patient He is with our weaknesses! The father explained that he would have been willing to host a feast for the older boy and his friends, but the boy had never asked him. Furthermore, ever since the division of the estate, the elder brother owned everything, and he could use it as he pleased.

The elder brother refused to go in; he stayed outside and pouted. He missed the joy of forgiving his brother and restoring the broken fellowship, the joy of pleasing his father and uniting the family again. How strange that the elder brother could speak peaceably to a servant boy, but he could not speak peaceably to his brother or father!

If we are out of fellowship with God, we cannot be in fellowship with our brothers and sisters and, conversely, if we harbor an unforgiving attitude toward others, we cannot be in communion with God (see Matt. 5:21–26; 1 John 4:18–21). When they show true repentance, we must forgive those who sin, and we should seek to restore them in grace and humility (Matt. 18:15–35; Gal. 6:1–5; Eph. 4:32).

The father had the last word, so we do not know how the story ended. (See Jonah 4 for a parallel narrative.) We do know that the scribes and Pharisees continued to oppose Jesus and separate themselves from His followers, and that their leaders eventually brought about our Lord's arrest and death. In spite of the Father's pleading, they would not come in.

Everybody in this chapter experienced joy except the elder brother. The shepherd, the woman, and their friends all experienced the joy of finding. The younger son experienced the joy of returning and being received by a loving, gracious father. The father experienced the joy of receiving his son back safe and sound. But the elder brother would not forgive his brother, so he had no joy. He could have repented and attended the feast, but he refused, so he stayed outside and suffered.

In my years of preaching and pastoral ministry, I have met elder brothers (and sisters!) who have preferred nursing their anger to enjoying the fellowship of God and God's people. Because they will not forgive, they have alienated themselves from the church and even from their family; they are sure that everyone else is wrong and they alone are right. They can talk loudly about the sins of others, but they are blind to their own sins.

"I never forgive!" General Oglethorpe said to John Wesley, to which Wesley replied, "Then, sir, I hope you never sin."

Don't stand outside! Come in and enjoy the feast!

CHAPTER FIFTEEN
Luke 16
THE RIGHT AND WRONG OF RICHES

The *Wall Street Journal* quoted an anonymous wit who defined *money* as "an article which may be used as a universal passport to everywhere except heaven, and as a universal provider for everything except happiness." The writer might have added that money is also a provoker of covetousness and competition, a wonderful servant but a terrible master. The love of money is still "a root of all kinds of evil" (1 Tim. 6:10 NKJV) and has helped fill our world with corruption and lust (1 Peter 1:4).

When you read our Lord's sermons and parables, you are struck with the fact that He had a great deal to say about material wealth. He ministered to people who, for the most part, were poor and who thought that acquiring more wealth was the solution to all their problems. Jesus was not blind to the needs of the poor, and by His example and teaching, He encouraged His followers to share what they had with others. The early church was a fellowship of people who willingly shared their possessions with the less fortunate (Acts 2:44–47; 4:33–37).

In His portrait of the prodigal and the elder brother, Jesus described two opposite philosophies of life. Prior to his repentance, the prodigal *wasted* his life, but his elder brother only *spent* his life as a faithful drudge. Both attitudes are wrong, for the Christian approach to life is that we should *invest* our lives for the good of others and the glory of God. This chapter emphasizes that truth: life is a stewardship, and we must use our God-given opportunities faithfully. One day we must give an account to the Lord of what we have done with all He has given to us, so we had better heed what Jesus says in this chapter about the right and wrong use of wealth.

Neither of the two accounts in this chapter is called a parable either by Jesus or by Luke, so it is likely that our Lord was describing actual happenings. However, whether they are actual events or only parables, the spiritual values are the same.

The Right Use of Wealth (16:1–13)

A foolish steward (vv. 1–2). A steward is someone who manages another's wealth. He does not own that wealth himself, but he has the privilege of enjoying it and using it for the profit of his master. The most important thing about a steward is that he serve his master faithfully (1 Cor. 4:2). When he looks at the riches around him, the steward must remember that they belong to his master, not to him personally, and that they must be used in a way that will please and profit the master.

This particular steward *forgot* that he was a steward and began to act as if he were the owner. He became a "prodigal steward" who wasted his master's wealth. His master heard about it and immediately asked for an inventory of his goods and an audit of his books. He also fired his steward.

Before we judge this man too severely, let's examine our own lives to see how faithful we have been as stewards of what God has given us. To begin with, we are stewards of the *material wealth* that we have, whether much or little, and we will one day have to answer to God for the way we have acquired it and used it.

Christian stewardship goes beyond paying God a tithe of our income and then using the remainder as we please. True stewardship means that we thank God for *all* that we have (Deut. 8:11–18) and use it as He directs. Giving God 10 percent of our income is a good way to begin our faithful stewardship, but we must remember that God should control what we do with the remaining 90 percent as well.

We are also stewards of *our time* (Eph. 5:15–17). The phrase "redeeming the time" comes from the business world and means "buying up the opportunity." Time is eternity, minted into precious minutes and handed to us to use either wisely or carelessly. The main lesson of this narrative is that the steward, as dishonest as he was, used his opportunity wisely and prepared for the future. Life ceased to be "enjoyment" and became "investment."

Christians are stewards of the *gifts and abilities* God has given them (1 Peter 4:10), and we must use those gifts and abilities to serve others. The thief says, "What's yours is mine—I'll take it!" The selfish man says, "What's mine is mine—I'll keep it!" But the Christian must say, "What's mine is a gift from God—I'll share it!" We are stewards, and we must use our abilities to win the lost, encourage the saints, and meet the needs of hurting people.

Finally, God's people are stewards of the gospel (1 Thess. 2:4). God has committed the treasure of His truth to us (2 Cor. 4:7), and we must guard this treasure (1 Tim. 6:20) and invest it in the lives of others (2 Tim. 2:2). The enemy wants to rob the church of this treasure (Jude 3–4), and we must be alert and courageous.

Like this steward, we will one day have to give an account of our stewardship (Rom. 14:10–12; 2 Cor. 5:10ff.). If we have been faithful, the Lord will give us His commendation and reward (Matt. 25:21; 1 Cor. 4:5); but if we have not been faithful, we will lose those blessings, even though we will be saved and enter heaven (1 Cor. 3:13–15).

Vance Havner often said, "God called us to play the game, not keep the score." If we are faithful stewards, God will reward us generously, and that reward will bring glory to His name.

A wise steward (vv. 3–8). The steward knew he would lose his job. He could not change the past, but he could prepare for the future. How? By making friends of his master's creditors so that they would take him in when his master threw him out. He gave each of them a generous discount, provided they paid up immediately, and they were only too glad to cooperate. Even his master complimented him on his clever plan (Luke 16:8).

Jesus did not commend the steward for robbing his master or for encouraging others to be dishonest. *Jesus commended the man for his wise use of opportunity.* "The children of this world" are experts at seizing opportunities for making money and friends and getting ahead. God's people should take heed and be just as wise when it comes to managing the spiritual affairs of life. "The children of this world" are wiser only "in their generation"; they see the things of time, but not the things of eternity. Because the child of God lives "with eternity's values in view," he should be able to make far better use of his opportunities.

The application (vv. 9–13). Jesus gave three admonitions, based on the experience of the steward.

First, He admonishes us to *use our opportunities wisely* (Luke 16:9). One of these days, life will end, and we will not be able to earn or use money. Therefore, while we have the opportunity, we must invest our money in "making friends" for the Lord. This means winning people to Christ, who will one day welcome us to heaven. Our lives and our resources will one day end, so it behooves us to use them wisely.

It is tragic to see how God's wealth is being wasted by Christians who live as though Jesus never died and judgment is never coming. The old couplet is certainly true:

> The only difference between men and boys
> Is that men buy more expensive toys.

The heritage of the past must be used wisely in the

present to guarantee spiritual dividends in the future. All of us should want to meet people in heaven who trusted Christ because we helped to pay the bill for gospel witness around the world, starting at home. Thoreau wrote that a man is wealthy in proportion to the number of things he can afford to do without, and he was right. I once heard the late Jacob Stam pray, "Lord, the only thing we know about sacrifice is how to spell the word." I wonder if today some of us can even spell the word!

Our Lord's second admonition is *be faithful in the way you use your material wealth* (Luke 16:10–12). He makes it clear that you cannot divorce the "spiritual" from the "material." Notice the contrasts:

The material	The spiritual
the god "Mammon"	the true God
that which is least	that which is much
false riches	true riches
that which is another's	that which is yours

Why is our Lord so concerned about the way we use money? Because money is not neutral; it is basically evil ("the mammon of unrighteousness"), and only God can sanctify it and use it for good. It is significant that both Paul and Peter called money "filthy lucre" (1 Tim. 3:3, 8; Titus 1:7, 11; 1 Peter 5:2). Apparently by its very nature, money defiles and debases those who love it and let it control their lives. "We cannot safely use mammon," writes Richard Foster, "until we are absolutely clear that we are dealing, not just with mammon, but with unrighteous mammon" (*Money, Sex and Power,* Harper & Row, 57).

People who are unfaithful in the way they use money are also unfaithful in the way they use the "true riches" of God's kingdom. We cannot be orthodox in our theology and at the same time heretical in the way we use money. God will not commit His true riches to individuals or ministries that waste money and will not give an honest accounting to the people who have supported them. When it came to money, Paul was very careful that everything was honest "not only in the sight of the Lord, but also in the sight of men" (2 Cor. 8:21).

Finally, the Lord admonishes us to *be wholly devoted to God and single-minded* (Luke 16:13; and see Matt. 6:19–24). We cannot love or serve two masters, any more than we can walk in two directions at one time. If we choose to serve money, then we cannot serve God. If we choose to serve God, then we will not serve money. Jesus is demanding *integrity,* total devotion to God that puts Him first in everything (Matt. 6:33).

If God is our Master, then money will be our servant, and we will use our resources in the will of God. But if God is not our Master, then *we will become the servants of money,* and money is a terrible master! We will start *wasting* our lives instead of *investing* them, and we will one day find ourselves "friendless" as we enter the gates of glory.

Henry Fielding wrote, "Make money your god and

it will plague you like the devil!" Jesus said, "Make money your servant and use today's opportunities as investments in tomorrow's dividends." Be a wise steward! There are souls to win to the Savior, and our money can help get the job done.

The Wrong Use of Money (16:14–31)

Jesus had been speaking primarily to His disciples, but the Pharisees had been listening, and their response was anything but spiritual. They sneered at Him! (The Greek word means "to turn up one's nose.") In spite of their strict religious practices, they loved money and cultivated values that were godless. They professed to trust God, but they measured life by wealth and possessions, the same as the unbelieving worldly crowd. *Far too many professed Christians today are making the same mistake.* With their lips, they honor the Lord, but with their wealth, they live like the world.

The Pharisees needed to stop "drifting" with the crowd and start "pressing into the kingdom" as many others were doing. The Pharisees had rejected the ministry of John the Baptist and permitted him to be killed, even though they knew he was God's prophet. They were also rejecting the ministry of Jesus Christ and would ultimately ask Pilate to have Him crucified. When your life is controlled by the love of money, you open the door to every kind of sin.

The law and the prophets were "until John," for John introduced the Savior to the nation and announced the arrival of the kingdom. But that did not mean that the law was discredited or destroyed, for in Jesus Christ, the law has been fulfilled (Matt. 5:17–20). The Pharisees prided themselves in their faithful obedience to the law of Moses, but they did not receive the Savior of whom Moses wrote!

Why did Jesus talk about divorce and remarriage when His basic discussion was about covetousness? The scribes and Pharisees were divided on this question, and perhaps they wanted to provoke Jesus into an argument, but He thwarted their plans. (In most marriages and divorces, money is involved, so the topic was not completely foreign to the discussion.) Some of the Jews were very lax in their views of divorce and remarriage, while others were very strict. Jesus had spoken about this subject before, so it was not a new teaching (Matt. 5:31–32).

Having silenced the sneering Pharisees, Jesus then gave them a vivid description of what would happen to them if they continued in their covetousness and unbelief. The account focuses on an anonymous rich man and a beggar named Lazarus ("God is my help"), and it warns us against covetousness by presenting several contrasts.

A contrast in life (vv. 19–21). This man was indeed rich if he could afford daily to wear expensive clothes and host splendid feasts. The one word that best describes his lifestyle is "flamboyant." He was definitely among "the rich and famous," and other people admired and envied him.

Why is one man wealthy and another man poor? Had the Jewish people obeyed God's commandments concerning the sabbatical year and the Year of Jubilee, there would have been little or no poverty in the land, for the wealth and real estate could not have fallen into the hands of a few wealthy people (see Lev. 25; and note Ex. 23:11; Deut. 14:28–29). The Old Testament prophets denounced the rich for amassing great estates and exploiting the widows and the poor (Isa. 3:15; 10:2; Amos 2:6; 4:1; 5:11–12; 8:4–6; Hab. 2:9–13). In Jesus' day, Palestine was under the rule of Rome, and life was very difficult for the common people.

Lazarus was sick and possibly crippled, because he was "laid" at the rich man's gate daily (see Acts 3:1–2). The only attention he got was from the dogs! The rich man could easily have assisted Lazarus, but he ignored him and went on enjoying his recognition and his riches. Life was comfortable for him and he felt secure.

The rich man obviously had no concept of stewardship, or he would have used part of his wealth to help Lazarus. It is a mystery why he even allowed the beggar to camp at his front door. Perhaps he thought that providing a place for the man was ministry enough, and it may be that some of his wealthy guests occasionally gave Lazarus alms. Did any of them ever recall what the Old Testament had to say about the care of the poor, such as Proverbs 14:21; 19:17; 21:13; or 28:27?

A contrast in death (v. 22). "The rich and poor meet together: the Lord is the maker of them all" (Prov. 22:2). As John Donne said, death is the "great leveler." The rich man died in spite of his wealth (Ps. 49:6–9) and "was buried," no doubt with an expensive funeral. But when Lazarus died, he was carried to Abraham's bosom. What a difference! Perhaps the beggar's body did not even have a decent burial, though the Jews were usually compassionate in such cases. Lazarus certainly did not have the traditional Jewish funeral, with its paid mourners, costly spices, and elaborate tomb. After Lazarus' body was taken away, the neighbors probably said, "Well, we're glad he's not around anymore!"

Death takes place when the spirit leaves the body (James 2:26). But death is not the end; it is the beginning of a whole new existence in another world. For the Christian, death means to be present with the Lord (2 Cor. 5:1–8; Phil. 1:21). For the unbeliever, death means to be away from God's presence and in torment.

A contrast in eternity (vv. 23–31). The King James Version uses the word *hell* in Luke 16:23, but the Greek word is not "hell" but "hades." It is the temporary realm of the dead as they await the judgment. The permanent place of punishment for the lost is "hell," the lake of fire. One day, death will give up the bodies and hades will give up the souls (Rev. 20:13, where "hell" should be "hades"), and the lost will stand before Christ in judgment (Rev. 20:10–15).

From our Lord's description, we learn that hades had two sections: a paradise portion called "Abraham's bosom," and a punishment portion. It is believed by many theologians that our Lord emptied the paradise part of hades when He arose from the dead and returned to the Father (John 20:17; Eph. 4:8–10). We know that today "paradise" is in heaven, where Jesus reigns in glory (Luke 23:43; 2 Cor. 12:1–4). There is no indication in Scripture that souls in heaven can communicate with people in hades or with people on earth.

This narrative refutes so-called "soul sleep," for both the rich man and Lazarus were conscious, one enjoying comfort and the other suffering torment. It is a solemn thing to ponder one's eternal destiny and realize the reality of divine punishment.

C. S. Lewis was told about a gravestone inscription that read: "Here lies an atheist—all dressed up and no place to go." Lewis quietly replied, "I bet he wishes that were so!"

The interesting thing is that, in hades, the rich man began to pray! First, he prayed for himself, that Abraham would have mercy on him and allow Lazarus to bring him some comfort (Luke 16:23–26). Even a drop of cool water would be welcomed. What a change from his sumptuous feasts when slaves ran to do his bidding!

The word *torment* is used four times in this account, and it speaks of definite pain. This is the same word that is used for the doom feared by the evil spirits (Mark 5:7) and the judgments God will send on an unrepentant world (Rev. 9:5; 11:10; 20:10). If hell is the permanent prison of the damned, then hades is the temporary jail, and the suffering in both is very real.

People ask, "How can a loving God even permit such a place as hell to exist, let alone send people there?" But in asking that question, they reveal that they do not understand either the love of God or the wickedness of sin. God's love is a *holy* love ("God is light," 1 John 1:5), not a shallow sentiment, and sin is rebellion against a holy and loving God. God does not "send people to hell." They send themselves there by refusing to heed His call and believe on His Son. The "unbelieving" are named second on the list of the people who go to hell, even before the murderers and the liars (Rev. 21:8; also see John 3:18–21, 36).

Abraham gave two reasons why Lazarus could not bring the comfort that was requested: the character of the rich man and the character of the eternal state. The rich man had lived for the "good things" of earth, and had experienced abundant temporal blessings. He had his reward (Matt. 6:2, 5, 16). He had determined his own destiny by leaving God out of his life, and now neither his character nor his destiny could be changed. Lazarus could not leave his place of comfort and make even a brief visit to the place of torment.

Then the rich man prayed for his brothers (Luke 16:27–31). He did not say, "I'm glad my brothers will also come here. We'll have a wonderful time together!" Occasionally you hear a lost person say, "Well, I don't mind if I go to hell. I'll have a lot of company!" *But there is no friendship or "company" in hell!* Hell is a place of torment and loneliness. It is not an eternal New Year's Eve party at which sinners have a good time doing what they used to do on earth.

Luke 16:28 suggests that Lazarus had testified to the rich man and probably to his brothers, but none of them had taken his witness seriously. But now, Lazarus' testimony is very important! The brothers knew that Lazarus had died, so if the beggar appeared to them, they would be frightened and would listen to his witness. *People in hades have a concern for the lost, but they cannot do anything about it.*

Abraham explained that only one thing could prevent the five men from eventually joining their brother: they needed to hear the Word of God and respond to it by faith. Moses and the prophets tell sinners how to repent and be saved, and the Jews heard them read every Sabbath in the synagogue. Though miracles can attest to the authority of the preacher, they cannot produce either conviction or conversion in the hearts of the lost. Faith that is based solely on miracles is not saving faith (John 2:23–25). A man named Lazarus *did* come back from the dead, *and some of the people wanted to kill him* (see John 11:43–57; 12:10)! Those who claim that there can be no effective evangelism without "signs and wonders" need to ponder this passage and also John 10:41–42.

In the rich man's lifetime, God had spoken to him in many ways. God had permitted him to have riches, yet he did not repent (Rom. 2:4–5). Lazarus had witnessed to the rich man, and so had the Old Testament Scriptures that were familiar to the Jews, but his heart remained unbelieving. The fact that Lazarus died first was a strong witness to the rich man, a reminder that one day he would also die, but even a death at his very doorstep did not melt the man's heart.

In spite of the fact that he was in torment in hades, the rich man did not change; he was still self-centered. He prayed, but it was for his comfort and the safety of *his* family. He was not concerned about other lost sinners; his only concern was his five brothers. He argued with God instead of submitting to His will. This indicates that the punishment of lost sinners is not remedial; it does not improve them. Hades and hell are not hospitals for the sick; they are prisons for the condemned.

Dr. Luke does not tell us how the covetous Pharisees responded to this account. They certainly knew Moses and the prophets, and this meant even greater responsibility—*and greater condemnation* (John 12:35–41).

We must remind ourselves that the rich man was not condemned because he was rich, nor was Lazarus saved because he was poor. Abraham was a very wealthy man, yet he was not in torment in hades. The rich man trusted in his riches and did not trust in the Lord.

"The safest road to hell," wrote C. S. Lewis, "is the gradual one—the gentle slope, soft underfoot, without sudden turnings, without milestones, without signposts."

"For what shall it profit a man, if he shall gain the whole world, and lose his own soul?" (Mark 8:36).

Jesus asked that question.

What is your answer?

CHAPTER SIXTEEN
Luke 17
THINGS THAT REALLY MATTER

As Jesus made His way to Jerusalem, He continued to teach His disciples and prepare them for what He would suffer there. But He was also preparing them for the time when He would no longer be with them and they would be ministering to others in His place. It was a critical period in their lives.

In this chapter, Luke recorded lessons that Jesus gave His disciples about some of the essentials of the Christian life: forgiveness (Luke 17:1–6), faithfulness (Luke 17:7–10), thankfulness (Luke 17:11–19), and preparedness (Luke 17:20–37).

Forgiveness (17:1–6)

After Jesus warned the Pharisees about the sin of loving money (Luke 16:14–31), He then turned to His disciples to warn them about possible sins in their lives, for occasions to stumble ("offenses") are an unfortunate part of life. After all, we are all sinners living in a sinful world. But we must take heed not to cause others to stumble, for it is a serious thing to sin against a fellow believer and tempt him or her to sin (Rom. 14:13; 1 Cor. 10:32; 1 John 2:10).

By "these little ones" (Luke 17:2), Jesus was referring not only to children but also to young believers who were learning how to follow the Lord (Matt. 18:1–6; Luke 10:21). Since Luke 17:1–10 is part of a context that begins with Luke 15:1, "little ones" would include the publicans and sinners who had come to believe in Jesus Christ. The Pharisees had criticized Jesus, and this might well have caused these new believers to stumble. So serious is this sin that a person would be better off cast alive into the sea, never to be seen again, than to deliberately cause others to stumble and sin.

But suppose *you* are not the one who does the sinning. Suppose another believer sins against you. Jesus anticipated this question in Luke 17:3–4 and instructed us what to do. First, we must have a personal concern for each other and obey His warning, "Take heed to yourselves." This means that we should lovingly watch over each other and do all we can to keep one another from sinning.

If a brother or sister does sin against us, we should give a private, loving rebuke. Our tendency might be to feel hurt down inside, nurse a grudge, and then tell others what happened to us, but this is the wrong approach (see Matt. 18:15–20). "Speaking the truth in love" (Eph. 4:15) is the first step toward solving personal differences.

Our aim is not to embarrass or hurt the offender, but to encourage him or her to repent (Gal. 6:1). If the offender does repent, then we must forgive (Eph. 4:32; and see Matt. 5:43–48). In fact, we must be *in the habit of forgiving,* for others might sin against us seven times a day—or even seventy times seven (Matt. 18:21ff.)! No one is likely to commit that much sin in one day, but this use of hyperbole emphasized the point Jesus was making: do not enumerate the sins of others, for love "keeps no record of wrongs" (1 Cor. 13:4–6). We should always be ready to forgive others, for one day we may want them to forgive us!

We might have expected the disciples to respond with the prayer, "Increase our love!" Certainly love is a key element in forgiveness, but faith is even more important. *It takes living faith to obey these instructions and forgive others.* Our obedience in forgiving others shows that we are trusting God to take care of the consequences, handle the possible misunderstandings, and work everything out for our good and His glory.

Mature Christians understand that forgiveness is not a cheap exchange of words, the way squabbling children often flippantly say "I'm sorry" to each other. True forgiveness always involves pain; somebody has been hurt and there is a price to pay in healing the wound. Love *motivates* us to forgive, but faith *activates* that forgiveness so that God can use it to work blessings in the lives of His people.

Our Lord's image of the mustard seed conveys the idea of life and growth. The mustard seed is very small, but it has life in it and, therefore, it can grow and produce fruit (Mark 4:30–32). If our faith is a *living* faith (James 2:14–26), it will grow and enable us to obey God's commands. "Commit thy way unto the Lord; trust also in him; and he shall bring it to pass" (Ps. 37:5). Forgiveness is a test of both our faith and our love.

Human nature being what it is, there will always be offenses that can easily become opportunities for sin. God's people must get into the habit of facing these offenses honestly and lovingly, and forgiving others when they repent. The Anglican pastor and poet George Herbert wrote, "He who cannot forgive breaks the bridge over which he himself must pass."

Faithfulness (17:7–10)

The introductory word *but* indicates that Jesus was now going to balance one lesson with another. There was a danger that the Twelve might get so carried away with transplanting trees that they would ignore the everyday responsibilities of life! Faith that does not result in faithfulness will not accomplish God's work. It is good to have faith to do the *difficult* (Luke 17:1–3) and the *impossible* (Luke 17:4–6), but it is essential that we have faith to do even the *routine tasks* our Master has committed to us. Privileges must always be balanced with responsibilities.

The servant in the story was evidently a "jack-of-all-trades," for he was responsible for farming,

shepherding, and cooking. It was not unusual for people with only modest means to hire at least one servant, but Jesus described a situation which in that day was unthinkable: a master ministering to his servant! In fact, He introduced the story with a phrase that means, "Can any of you imagine …?" Their answer had to be, "No, we cannot imagine such a thing!"

Jesus had already discussed His relationship to His servants *and had promised to serve them if they were faithful* (Luke 12:35–38). He Himself was among them as a servant (Luke 22:27), even though He was Master of all. This story emphasizes faithfulness to duty no matter what the demands might be, and the argument is from the lesser to the greater. If a common servant is faithful to obey the orders of his master who does not reward (thank) him, how much more ought Christ's disciples obey their loving Master, who has promised to reward them graciously!

A faithful servant should not expect any special reward, since he did only what he was told to do. The word translated "unprofitable" means "without need"—that is, "nobody owes us anything." The servant was indeed profitable; after all, he cared for his master's fields, flocks, and food. The statement means, "My master does not owe me anything extra." *The fact that Jesus will reward His servants is wholly a matter of God's grace.* We do not deserve anything because we have obeyed Him and served Him.

As His servants, we must beware lest we have the wrong attitude toward our duties. There are two extremes to avoid: merely doing our duty in a slavish way *because we have to,* or doing our duty *because we hope to gain a reward.* Christian industrialist R. G. LeTorneau used to say, "If you give because it pays, *it won't pay.*" This principle also applies to service. Both extremes are seen in the attitudes of the elder brother (Luke 15:25–32) who was miserably obedient, always hoping that his father would let him have a party with his friends.

What then is the proper attitude for Christian service? "Doing the will of God from the heart" (Eph. 6:6). "If you love Me, keep My commandments" (John 14:15 NKJV). To the person who is born again, "his commandments are not grievous" (1 John 5:3). Serving Him is a delight, not just a duty, and we obey Him because we love Him. "I delight to do thy will, O my God: yea, thy law is within my heart" (Ps. 40:8).

Thankfulness (17:11–19)

Between Luke 17:10 and 11, the events of John 11 occurred as the Lord Jesus made His way to Jerusalem. At the border of Samaria and Judea, Jesus healed ten lepers at one time, and the fact that the miracle involved a Samaritan made it even more significant (see Luke 10:30–37). Jesus used this event to teach a lesson about gratitude to God.

The account begins with *ten unclean men* (Luke 17:11–13), all of whom were lepers (see the comments on Luke 5:12–15). The Jews and Samaritans would not normally live together, but misery loves company and all ten were outcasts. What difference does birth make if you are experiencing a living death? But these men had hope, for Jesus was there, and they cried out for mercy. The word translated "master" is the same one Peter used (Luke 5:5) and means "chief commander." They knew that Jesus was totally in command of even disease and death, and they trusted Him to help them.

The account continues by referring to *nine ungrateful men* (Luke 17:17). Jesus commanded the men to go show themselves to the priest, which in itself was an act of faith, for they had not yet been cured. When they turned to obey, they were completely healed, for their obedience was evidence of their faith (see 2 Kings 5:1–14).

You would have expected all ten men to run to Jesus and thank Him for a new start in life, but only one did so—and he was not even a Jew. How grateful the men should have been for the providence of God that brought Jesus into their area, for the love that caused Him to pay attention to them and their need, and for the grace and power of God that brought about their healing. They should have formed an impromptu men's chorus and sung Psalm 103 together!

But before we judge them too harshly, what is our own "GQ"—"Gratitude Quotient"? How often do we take our blessings for granted and fail to thank the Lord? "Oh that men would praise the Lord for his goodness, and for his wonderful works to the children of men" (Ps. 107:8, 15, 21, 31). Too often we are content to enjoy the gift but we forget the Giver. We are quick to pray but slow to praise.

The next time you sing "Now Thank We All Our God," try to remember that Martin Rinkhart wrote it during the Thirty Years' War, when his pastoral duties were most difficult. He conducted as many as forty funerals a day, including that of his own wife, yet he wrote those beautiful words as a table grace for his family. In spite of war and plague around him and sorrow within him, he was able to give thanks to the Lord from a grateful heart.

Luke's account closes with *one unusual man* (Luke 17:15–19). The Samaritan shouted "Glory to God!" and fell at Jesus' feet to praise Him and give thanks. It would have been logical for him to have followed the other men and gone to the temple, but he first came to the Lord Jesus with his sacrifice of praise (Ps. 107:22; Heb. 13:15). This pleased the Lord more than all the sacrifices the other men offered, even though they were obeying the law (Ps. 51:15–17). Instead of *going to* the priest, the Samaritan *became* a priest, and he built his altar at the feet of Jesus (read Ps. 116:12–19).

By coming to Jesus, the man received something greater than physical healing: he was also saved from his sins. Jesus said, "Your faith has saved you" (literal translation), the same words He spoke to the repentant woman who anointed His feet (Luke 7:50). The Samaritan's nine friends were declared clean by the priest, but he was declared *saved* by the Son of God! While it is wonderful to experience the miracle of physical healing, it is even more wonderful to experience the miracle of eternal salvation.

Every child of God should cultivate the grace of gratitude. It not only opens the heart to further blessings but glorifies and pleases the Father. An unthankful heart is fertile soil for all kinds of sins (Rom. 1:21ff.).

Preparedness (17:20–37)

The Jewish people lived in an excited atmosphere of expectancy, particularly at the Passover season when they commemorated their deliverance from Egypt. They longed for another Moses who would deliver them from their bondage. Some had hoped that John the Baptist would be the deliverer, and then the attention focused on Jesus (John 6:15). The fact that He was going to Jerusalem excited them all the more (Luke 19:11). Perhaps He would establish the promised kingdom!

The Pharisees were the custodians of the law (Matt. 23:2–3), so they had the right to ask Jesus when He thought the kingdom of God would appear. It was customary for Jewish teachers to discuss these subjects publicly, and Jesus gave them a satisfactory answer. However, He reserved His detailed lessons for His disciples.

The word translated "observation" (Luke 17:20) is used only here in the New Testament and means in classical Greek "to observe the future by signs." It carries the idea of spying, lying in wait, and even scientific investigation. The point Jesus made was that God's kingdom would not come with great "outward show" so that people could predict its arrival and plot its progress.

The Pharisees' question was legitimate, but it was also tragic, for Jesus had been ministering among them for some three years, and these men were still in spiritual darkness. They did not understand who Jesus was or what He was seeking to accomplish. Their views of the kingdom were political, not spiritual; Jewish, not universal. Jesus did not deny that there would be a future earthly kingdom, but He did emphasize the importance of the *spiritual* kingdom that could be entered only by the new birth (John 3:1–8).

The statement "the kingdom of God is within you" has challenged Bible translators and interpreters for centuries, and many explanations have been given. One thing we can be sure of is that He was not telling the unbelieving Pharisees that they had the kingdom of God in their hearts!

The Greek preposition can mean "within," "among," or "in the midst of." Jesus was saying, "Don't look for the kingdom 'out there' unless it is first in your own heart" (see Rom. 14:17). At the same time, He may also have been saying, "The fact that I am here in your midst is what is important, for I am the King. How can you enter the kingdom if you reject the King?" (see Luke 19:38–40). The Pharisees were preoccupied with the great events of the future but were ignoring the opportunities of the present (Luke 12:54–57).

Having answered the Pharisees, Jesus then turned to His disciples to instruct them about the coming of the kingdom. He warned them not to become so obsessed with His return that they ended up doing nothing else but trying to track Him down. This is a good warning to believers who do nothing but study prophecy. Certainly we should look for His return and long to see Him come, but at the same time, we should be busy doing His work when He comes (note Acts 1:6–11).

To begin with, His coming will affect the whole world, so it is foolish for anyone to follow false prophets who say, "He is here!" or "He is there!" Furthermore, His coming will be as sudden as a flash of lightning (Matt. 24:27, 30). While a study of the prophetic Scriptures will help us understand the general characteristics of the time of His coming, we cannot know the day or the hour (Matt. 25:13; Luke 12:40, 46). It is futile to investigate signs and try to calculate the day of His coming.

Jesus then used two Old Testament events to illustrate the certainty and the suddenness of His coming: the flood (Gen. 6—8) and the destruction of Sodom (Gen. 19). In both examples, the people of the world were caught unprepared as they engaged in their everyday activities of eating and drinking, marrying, buying, and selling. Noah witnessed to his generation in the years preceding the flood (2 Peter 2:5), but his preaching did not convert them. Noah and his wife, his three sons, and their wives—only eight people—were saved from destruction because they entered the ark. Peter saw this as an illustration of the salvation Christians have through faith in Jesus Christ (1 Peter 3:18–22).

Both Noah and Lot lived in days of religious compromise and moral declension, not unlike our present time. During "the days of Noah," population growth was significant (Gen. 6:1), lawlessness was on the increase (Gen. 6:5), and the earth was given over to violence (Gen. 6:11, 13). In Lot's day, the unnatural lusts of Sodom and Gomorrah were so abhorrent to God that He completely destroyed the cities. Only Lot, two of his daughters, and his wife (who later was destroyed) were saved from the terrible judgment.

Luke 17:30–36 describes what will occur when Jesus Christ returns in judgment to defeat His enemies and establish His kingdom on earth (Rev. 19:11–20:6). Believers in every age of the church can take warning from these verses, but they apply in a special way to Israel at the end of the age (see Matt. 24:29–44). When Jesus comes for His church and takes it to heaven, it will happen "in a moment, in the twinkling of an eye" (1 Cor. 15:52). Nobody taking part in the rapture of the church need worry about being on a housetop or in a field and wanting to get

something out of the house! However, when the Lord returns *to the earth,* His coming will first be preceded by a "sign" in heaven (Matt. 24:30–31), and some people might try to hurry home to rescue something. "Remember Lot's wife!"

The verb *taken* in Luke 17:34–36 does not mean "taken to heaven" but "taken away in judgment" (Matt. 24:36–41). The person "left" is a believer who enters into the kingdom. Noah and his family were "left" to enjoy a new beginning, while the whole population of the earth was "taken" in the flood. In spite of their sins, Lot and his daughters were "left" while the people in Sodom and Gomorrah were "taken" when the fire and brimstone destroyed the cities.

The fact that it is night in Luke 17:34 but day in Luke 17:35–36 indicates that the whole world will be involved in the return of Jesus Christ in glory. "Behold, he cometh with clouds; and every eye shall see him" (Rev. 1:7).

Three times the disciples had heard Jesus talk about people being "taken" and "left," so they asked Him a most logical question: "Where, Lord?" Our Lord's reply has the sound of a familiar proverb: "Just as the eagles [and vultures, Matt. 24:28] gather at a corpse, so the lost will be gathered together for judgment." The description of the last battle in Revelation 19:17–21 certainly parallels the image of carrion-eating birds gorging themselves on flesh.

In other words, when the Lord Jesus returns to judge His enemies, there will be a separation of the saved and the lost. Whether it be day or night, whether people are working or sleeping, the separation and judgment will come. Those who are saved will be left to enter the glorious kingdom, while those who are lost will be taken away in judgment.

Even though the primary interpretation of these verses is for Israel in the end times, they do emphasize for the church the importance of being ready when Jesus returns. We must not be like Lot's wife, whose heart was so in Sodom that she looked back in spite of the angels' warning (Gen. 19:17, 26). There are many professed Christians today whose plans would be interrupted if Jesus returned (note 1 Thess. 5:1–11)! Our Lord's warning in Luke 17:33 finds parallels in Matthew 10:39; Luke 9:24; and John 12:25, and is a fundamental principle of the Christian life. The only way to save your life is to lose it for the sake of Christ and the gospel.

Jesus pictured civilization as a "rotting corpse" that would one day be ripe for judgment. The discerning believer sees evidence of this on every hand and realizes that the "days of Noah" and the "days of Lot" are soon on us. Our Lord can return for His church at any time, so we are not looking for signs, but we do know that "coming events cast their shadows before." As we see many of these things begin to come to pass (Luke 21:28), we know that His return is nearing.

Are we looking for His return, and do we really want to see Him come?

CHAPTER SEVENTEEN
Luke 18
PEOPLE TO MEET, LESSONS TO LEARN

Lord Chesterfield, the English statesman, wrote, "Learning … is only to be acquired by reading men, and studying all the various editions of them."

He was referring to "the knowledge of the world," but what he said applies to *spiritual* knowledge as well. Much can be learned from reading the "book of humanity," whether in daily life, history, biography, or even fiction.

There are several "editions" of mankind introduced in this chapter, and each one has a spiritual lesson to teach us. Being a compassionate physician, Dr. Luke wrote about widows and politicians, Pharisees and publicans, little children and adults, rich men and beggars. From this colorful cast of characters, I have selected four "editions" for us to "read." The lessons they teach us are important.

A Demanding Widow (18:1–8)
Luke mentions widows more than do all the other gospel writers combined (Luke 2:37–38; 4:25–26; 7:11–17; 18:1–8; 20:45–47; 21:1–4). In that day, widows usually had a difficult time making ends meet, in spite of the care God instructed His people to give them (Ex. 22:22–24; Deut. 14:28–29; 16:9–15; Ps. 146:9; Isa. 1:17, 23; Jer. 7:6). The early church was serious about the care of Christian widows (Acts 6:1; 1 Tim. 5:3–10; James 1:27), a good example for us to follow today.

As you study this parable, try to see it in its Eastern setting. The "courtroom" was not a fine building but a tent that was moved from place to place as the judge covered his circuit. The judge, not the law, set the agenda, and he sat regally in the tent, surrounded by his assistants. Anybody could watch the proceedings from the outside, but only those who were approved and accepted could have their cases tried. This usually meant bribing one of the assistants so that he would call the judge's attention to the case.

The widow had three obstacles to overcome. First, being a woman she, therefore, had little standing before the law. In the Palestinian society of our Lord's day, women did not go to court. Since she was a widow, she had no husband to stand with her in court. Finally, she was poor and could not pay a bribe even if she wanted to. No wonder poor widows did not always get the protection the law was supposed to afford them!

Now that we understand something of the setting of this parable, we can better understand what Jesus was teaching. Basically, He was encouraging His disciples to pray, and He did this by presenting three contrasts.

Praying contrasted with fainting (v. 1). If we don't pray, we will faint; it's as simple as that! The word *faint* describes a believer who loses heart and gets so discouraged that he or she wants to quit. I can recall two occasions when I have fainted physically, and it is the most helpless feeling I have ever experienced. I felt myself "going," but I couldn't seem to do a thing about it!

There is a connection between what our Lord said in Luke 18:1 and His statement in Luke 17:37. If society is like a rotting corpse, then the "atmosphere" in which we live is being slowly polluted, and this is bound to affect our spiritual lives. But when we pray, we draw on the "pure air" of heaven, and this keeps us from fainting.

But what does it mean "always to pray" or to "pray without ceasing" (1 Thess. 5:17)? It certainly doesn't mean that we should constantly be repeating prayers, because Jesus warned against that kind of praying (Matt. 6:5–15). Rather, it means to make prayer as natural to us as our regular breathing. Unless we are sick or smothering, we rarely think about our breathing; we just do it. Likewise with prayer—it should be the natural habit of our lives, the "atmosphere" in which we constantly live.

Prayer is much more than the words of our lips; it is the desires of our hearts, *and our hearts are constantly "desiring" before Him,* even if we never speak a word. So, to "pray without ceasing" means to have such holy desires in our hearts, in the will of God, that we are constantly in loving communion with the Father, petitioning Him for His blessing.

Take your choice: do you want to pray—or faint?

The widow contrasted with God's elect (vv. 2–5). Jesus did not say that God's people are like this woman; in fact, He said just the opposite. Because we are *not* like her, we should be encouraged in our praying. He argued from the lesser to the greater: "If a poor widow got what she deserved from a selfish judge, how much more will God's children receive what is right from a loving heavenly Father!"

Consider the contrasts. To begin with, the woman was a stranger, *but we are the children of God,* and God cares for His children (Luke 11:13). The widow had no access to the judge, but God's children have an open access into His presence and may come at any time to get the help they need (Eph. 2:18; 3:12; Heb. 4:14–16; 10:19–22).

The woman had no friend at court to help get her case on the docket. All she could do was walk around outside the tent and make a nuisance of herself as she shouted at the judge. But when Christian believers pray, they have in heaven a Savior who is Advocate (1 John 2:1) and High Priest (Heb. 2:17–18), who constantly represents them before the throne of God.

When we pray, we can open the Word and claim the many promises of God, but the widow had no promises that she could claim as she tried to convince the judge to hear her case. We not only have God's unfailing promises, but we also have the Holy Spirit, who assists us in our praying (Rom. 8:26–27).

Perhaps the greatest contrast is that the widow came to a court of law, but God's children come to a throne of grace (Heb. 4:14–16). She pled out of her poverty, but we have all of God's riches available to us to meet our every need (Phil. 4:19). The point is clear: if we fail to pray, our condition spiritually will be just like that of the poor widow. That should encourage us to pray!

The judge contrasted with the Father (vv. 6–8). Unless you see that Jesus is pointing out contrasts, you will get the idea that God must be "argued" or "bribed" into answering prayer! God is *not* like this judge, for God is a loving Father, who is attentive to our every cry, generous in His gifts, concerned about our needs, and ready to answer when we call. The only reason the judge helped the widow was because he was afraid she would "weary" him, which literally means "give me a black eye"—i.e., ruin his reputation. God answers prayer for His glory and for our good, and He is not vexed when we come.

How, then, do we explain *delays* in answers to prayer, especially when Jesus said that God would "avenge [give them justice] speedily" (Luke 18:8)? Remember that God's delays are not the delays of inactivity but of preparation. God is always answering prayer, otherwise Romans 8:28 could not be in the Bible. God works in all things at all times, causing all things to work together to accomplish His purposes. The moment we send Him a request that is in His will (see 1 John 5:14–15), God begins to work. We may not see it now, but one day the answer will come.

The question in Luke 18:8 ties in with what Jesus taught in Luke 17:22–37: "Shall he find [that kind of] faith on the earth?" The end times will not be days of great faith. Eight people were saved in Noah's day, and only four out of Sodom (and one of them perished on the way). Passages like 1 Timothy 4 and 2 Timothy 3 paint a dark picture of the last days.

A Deluded Pharisee (18:9–17)

Throughout His public ministry, Jesus exposed the self-righteousness and unbelief of the Pharisees (see Luke 11:39–54). He pictured them as debtors too bankrupt to pay what they owed God (Luke 7:40–50), guests fighting for the best seats (Luke 14:7–14), and sons proud of their obedience but unconcerned about the needs of others (Luke 15:25–32). The sad thing is that the Pharisees were completely deluded and thought they were right and Jesus was wrong. This is illustrated in this parable.

The Pharisee was deluded about prayer, for he prayed with himself and told God (and anybody else listening) how good he was. The Pharisees used prayer as a means of getting public recognition and not as a spiritual exercise to glorify God (Matt. 6:5; 23:14).

He was deluded about himself, for he thought he was accepted by God because of what he did or what he did not do. The Jews were required to fast only once a year, on the day of Atonement (Lev. 16:29), but he fasted twice a week. He tithed everything that came

into his possession, even the tiny herbs from his garden (Matt. 23:23).

He was deluded about the publican who was also in the temple praying. The Pharisee thought that the publican was a great sinner, but the publican went home justified by God, while the proud Pharisee went home only self-satisfied. To be "justified" means to be declared righteous by God on the basis of the sacrifice of Jesus Christ on the cross (Rom. 3:19—4:25).

The publican repeatedly smote his breast, for he knew where his greatest problem was, and he called to God for mercy. The publican knew the enormity of his sins, but the Pharisee was blissfully ignorant of his own heart. The Pharisee's pride condemned him, but the publican's humble faith saved him (see Luke 14:11; Isa. 57:15). It is the prodigal son and elder brother over again (Luke 15:11ff.).

In contrast to the proud Pharisee are the children who were brought to Jesus (Luke 18:15–17). It was customary for the Jews to bring little children to the rabbis to receive their special blessing, so it is strange that the disciples would stand in the way. Perhaps they thought Jesus was weary and needed rest, or they may have decided that He was not really interested in children. How wrong they were!

However, this was not the first time the disciples had attempted to "get rid of people." They wanted to send the crowd away hungry, but Jesus fed them (Matt. 14:15ff.), and they tried to stop the Canaanite woman from asking Jesus to heal her daughter (Matt. 15:21ff.), but Jesus answered her prayer. The Twelve did not yet have the compassion of their Master, but it would come in due time.

Jesus wants us to be *childlike* but not *childish.* An unspoiled child illustrates humility, faith, and dependence. A child has a sense of wonder that makes life exciting. The only way to enter God's kingdom is to become like a child and be born again (John 3). If the proud Pharisee had become like a child, he too would have gone home justified.

A Dishonest Youth (18:18–34)

The rich young ruler (Matt. 19:20) may be the only man in the Gospels who came to the feet of Jesus and went away in worse condition than when he came. And yet he had so much in his favor! He was moral and religious, earnest and sincere, and probably would have qualified for membership in the average church. Yet he refused to follow Jesus Christ and instead went his own way in great sorrow.

What was wrong with him? In a word: *dishonesty.* In spite of the fact that he came to the right Person, asked the right question, and received the right answer, *he made the wrong decision.* Why? Because he was not honest with God or with himself. Therefore, he would not do what he was commanded to do. He was a superficial young man who said one thing but did another. Consider the areas in which he was dishonest.

His view of Christ (vv. 18–19). The rabbis were

called "Master" (Teacher), but it was most unusual for a rabbi to be called "good." The Jews reserved the word *good* for God (Ps. 25:8; 34:8; 86:5; 106:1). This explains why our Lord asked the young man what he meant, for if he really believed that Jesus was "good," *then he had to confess that Jesus was God.* By asking this question, our Lord was not denying His deity but affirming it. He was testing the young man to see if he really understood what he had just said.

His subsequent behavior proved that the young ruler did not believe that Jesus Christ was God. If he really thought he was in the presence of Almighty God, why did he argue politely about the law, brag about his character, and then refuse to obey the Word? Surely he knew that God sees the heart and knows all things!

His view of sin (vv. 20–21). He also had a superficial view of his own sin. No doubt the young man sincerely tried to keep the law; in fact, this may have been what brought him to the feet of Jesus (Gal. 3:24). Jesus did not quote the law to him as a means of salvation, because obedience to the law does not save us. He held the law before the young man as a mirror to reveal his sins (Rom. 3:19–20; Gal. 2:21; 3:21).

But the young man looked into the mirror and would not see the stains and blemishes in his life. When Jesus quoted from the second table of the law, He did not quote the last commandment, "Thou shalt not covet" (Ex. 20:17). Jesus knew the young man's heart, so instead of preaching to him about covetousness, He asked him to do something that a covetous person would not do.

Nobody is saved by giving all his wealth to the poor, but nobody can be saved who will not repent of his sins and turn away from them. This young man was possessed by the love of money and he would not let go.

His view of salvation (vv. 22–34). The young man thought that eternal life came to those who "did something" (Luke 18:18), which was a typical Jewish conviction (Luke 18:9–12). But when Jesus gave him something to do, he refused to obey! He wanted salvation on his terms, not God's, so he turned and went away in great sorrow.

The disciples were shocked when Jesus announced that it was difficult for rich people to be saved. They were Jews and the Jews believed that riches were a mark of God's blessing. "If rich people can't be saved," they reasoned, "what hope is there for the rest of us?" John D. Rockefeller would have agreed with them, for he once said that riches were "a gift from heaven signifying, 'This is My beloved son, in whom I am well pleased.'"

It is not possessing riches that keeps people out of heaven, for Abraham, David, and Solomon were wealthy men. It is *being possessed* by riches and *trusting* them that makes salvation difficult for the wealthy. Wealth gives people a false sense of success and security, and when people are satisfied with themselves, they feel no need for God.

Peter's comment in Luke 18:28 suggests that he had a rather commercial view of discipleship: "What then will there be for us?" (Matt. 19:27 NASB). Jesus promised all of them ("you" in Luke 18:29 is plural) blessings in this life and reward in the life to come, but then He balanced His words with another announcement about His impending suffering and death. How could Peter be thinking about personal gain when his Lord was going to Jerusalem to be crucified?

The rich young ruler is a warning to people who want a Christian faith that does not change their values or upset their lifestyle. Jesus does not command every seeking sinner to sell everything and give to the poor, but He does put His finger of conviction on any area in our lives about which we are dishonest.

A Determined Beggar (18:35–43)

Matthew tells us that there were *two* blind beggars who met Jesus as He *left* Jericho (Matt, 20:29–30), but Luke introduces us to one blind beggar, Bartimaeus, who called out as Jesus *approached* Jericho. There were two Jerichos, the old ruined city and the new one built by Herod the Great, and they stood about a mile apart. The two men, one of whom was more outspoken, were sitting at the entrance to the new city, so there is no contradiction (note Mark 10:46).

In that day, blindness was a common affliction for which there was no cure, and all a blind person could do was beg. These two men had not been born blind, for their prayer was to "regain" their sight (Luke 18:41 NASB; and note Matt. 20:34 NASB). They persisted in crying out to the Lord, in spite of the obstacles in their way: their inability to see Jesus, the opposition of the crowd, and our Lord's delay in responding to them. They were not going to let Jesus pass them without first pleading for mercy.

The fact that they addressed Him as "Son of David," a messianic title, indicates that these two Jewish beggars knew that Jesus could give sight to the blind (Isa. 35:5; and see Luke 4:18). Jesus responded to their faith and healed them, and what a change took place! They went from darkness to light, from begging to following Jesus, and from crying to praising the Lord. They joined the pilgrim crowd going to Jerusalem and lifted their voices in praising the Lord.

The contrast is obvious between these two beggars and the rich young ruler (Luke 18:18–27). The beggars were poor, yet they became rich, while the young man was rich and became eternally poor. The beggars claimed no special merit and openly admitted their need, while the young man lied about himself and bragged about his character. The young man would not believe, so he went away from Jesus very sad, but the two beggars believed in Jesus and followed Him with songs of praise. "He hath filled the hungry with good things; and the rich he hath sent empty away" (Luke 1:53).

The "human editions" we have "read" in this chapter encourage us to put our faith in Jesus Christ, no matter what others may say or do. The widow was not discouraged by the indifferent attitude of the judge, nor the publican by the hypocritical attitude of the Pharisee. The parents brought their little ones to Jesus in spite of the selfish attitude of the apostles, and the blind men came to Jesus even though the crowd told them to keep quiet and stay put. Jesus always responds to faith and rewards those who believe.

But the rich young ruler stands as a warning to all who depend on character to save them from sin. This young man shows us how close a person may come to salvation and yet turn away in unbelief. John Bunyan closed his *Pilgrim's Progress* with the warning, "Then I saw that there was a way to hell, even from the gates of heaven, as well as from the City of Destruction." Heed that warning today!

CHAPTER EIGHTEEN
Luke 19
JERUSALEM AT LAST!

When Christopher Columbus made his voyage west in 1492, he kept two log books, one of which contained falsified information. He wanted his men to believe that they were closer to land than they really were. Apparently Columbus felt that the morale of the crew was more important than the integrity of the captain.

As Jesus journeyed to Jerusalem, He told His disciples what would happen there, but they could not grasp what their Lord was saying (Luke 18:31–34). Some of the people in the crowd thought He was going to Jerusalem to deliver Israel from Roman bondage and usher in the kingdom of God. Still others followed Him just to see the next miracle He would perform.

In this chapter, Dr. Luke focuses on who Jesus really is as he presents Him in a threefold ministry.

The Savior Who Seeks the Lost (19:1–10)
The name *Zaccheus* means "righteous one," but this supervisor of tax collectors was not living up to his name. Certainly the Jewish religious community in Jericho would not have considered him righteous, for he not only collected taxes from his own people but also worked for the unclean Gentiles! And publicans were notorious for collecting more taxes than required; the more money they collected, the more income they enjoyed (Luke 3:12–13). Though Zaccheus was a renegade in the eyes of the Jews, he was a precious lost sinner in the eyes of Jesus.

It is interesting to see the changes Zaccheus experienced that day, all because Jesus visited Jericho.

A man became a child (vv. 2–4). In the East, it is unusual for a man to run, especially a wealthy government official, yet Zaccheus ran down the street like a little boy following a parade. And he even climbed a tree! Curiosity is certainly characteristic

of most children, and Zaccheus was motivated by curiosity that day.

John Calvin wrote, "Curiosity and simplicity are a sort of preparation for faith." This is often the case, and it was certainly true of Zaccheus. Why the big crowd? Who is this Jesus of Nazareth they are following? What am I missing?

Jesus said, "Whosoever shall not receive the kingdom of God like a little child shall in no way enter therein" (Luke 18:17). Perhaps more than anything else, it is pride that keeps many "successful" people from trusting Jesus Christ.

A seeking man became found (v. 5). Zaccheus thought he was seeking Jesus (Luke 19:3), but Jesus was seeking him (Luke 19:10)! By nature, the lost sinner does not seek the Savior (Rom. 3:11). When our first parents sinned, they hid from God, but God came and sought them (Gen. 3:1–10). When Jesus was ministering on earth, He sought out the lost; and today the Holy Spirit, through the church, is searching for lost sinners.

We do not know how God had worked in the heart of Zaccheus to prepare him for this meeting with Jesus. Was Levi, the former publican (Luke 5:27–39), one of his friends? Had he told Zaccheus about Jesus? Was he praying for Zaccheus? Had Zaccheus become weary of wealth and started yearning for something better? We cannot answer these questions, but we can rejoice that a seeking Savior will always find a sinner who is looking for a new beginning.

A small man became big (vv. 7–8). It was not Zaccheus's fault that he was "little of stature" and could not see over the crowd. He did what he could to overcome his handicap by putting aside his dignity and climbing a tree. In a spiritual sense, all of us are "little of stature," for "all have sinned and come short of the glory of God" (Rom. 3:23). No one measures up to God's high standards; we are all "too little" to enter into heaven.

The tragedy is, many lost sinners think they are "big." They measure themselves by man's standards—money, position, authority, popularity—things that are an "abomination in the sight of God" (Luke 16:15). They think they have everything when really they have nothing (Rev. 3:17).

Zaccheus trusted Jesus Christ and became a true "son of Abraham," meaning, of course, a child of faith (Rom. 4:12; Gal. 3:7). That is as big as you can get!

A poor man became rich (vv. 9–10). The people thought Zaccheus was a wealthy man, but actually he was only a bankrupt sinner who needed to receive God's gift of eternal life, the most expensive gift in the world. This is the only instance in the four gospels of Jesus inviting Himself to someone's home, and it illustrates the words of Revelation 3:20.

Zaccheus was not saved because he promised to do good works. He was saved because he responded by faith to Christ's gracious word to him. Having trusted the Savior, he then gave evidence of his faith by promising to make restitution to those he had wronged. Saving faith is more than pious words and devout feelings. It creates a living union with Christ that results in a changed life (James 2:14–26).

Under the Mosaic law, if a thief voluntarily confessed his crime, he had to restore what he took, add one fifth to it, and bring a trespass offering to the Lord (Lev. 6:1–7). If he stole something he could not restore, he had to repay fourfold (Ex. 22:1), and if he was caught with the goods, he had to repay double (Ex. 22:4). Zaccheus did not quibble over the terms of the law; he offered to pay the highest price because his heart had truly been changed.

The child of God is born rich, for he shares "every spiritual blessing" in Jesus Christ (Eph. 1:3). We have the riches of God's mercy and grace (Eph. 1:7; 2:4) as well as the riches of His glory (Phil. 4:19) and wisdom (Rom. 11:33). These are "unsearchable riches" that can never be fully understood or completely exhausted (Eph. 3:8).

The host became the guest (v. 6). Jesus invited Himself to Zaccheus's house, and Zaccheus received Him joyfully. *Joy* is one of the key themes in the gospel of Luke, and the word is found over twenty times in one form or another. The experience of salvation certainly ought to produce joy in the believer's heart.

Zaccheus became the guest in his own house, for Jesus was now his Master. He was ready to obey the Lord and do whatever was necessary to establish a genuine testimony before the people. To be sure, the people criticized Jesus for visiting in a publican's house (Luke 5:27–32), but the Lord paid no attention to their words. The critics also needed to be saved, but there is no evidence that they trusted Jesus.

When a day begins, you never know how it will end. For Zaccheus, that day ended in joyful fellowship with the Son of God, for he was now a changed man with a new life. Jesus is still seeking the lost and yearning to save them. Has He found you?

The Master Who Rewards the Faithful (19:11–27)

Passover season was always an emotionally charged time for the Jews, because it reminded them of their deliverance from the slavery of Egypt. This annual celebration aggravated the misery of their bondage to Rome and made them yearn all the more for a deliverer. Of course, there were subversive groups like the Zealots who used commando tactics against Rome, and politicians like the Herodians who compromised with Rome, but most of the Jews rejected those approaches. They wanted God to fulfill the Old Testament prophecies and send them their promised King.

Jesus knew that many of the people in the crowd were hoping to see Him establish the kingdom, so He gave this parable to clarify things. Many of the people who listened no doubt connected it with an event in Jewish history that had occurred many years before. When Herod the Great died in 4 BC, he left Judea to his son Archelaus, who had to go to Rome to have the inheritance approved. Not wanting Archelaus as their ruler, the Jews sent fifty men to argue their case before Augustus Caesar, who did ratify the inheritance without giving Archelaus the title of "king."

Jesus explained that the kingdom would not come until a future time, but that His servants had better be faithful now to do the job assigned to them. In the parable, you see three different responses to the Master.

Faithful obedience (vv. 16–19, 24). Each of the servants received an amount of money equal to three months' wages for a laboring man, so you can figure out its buying power today. *Occupy* means "do business, put my money to work." They could give the money to investors and earn interest, or purchase goods and sell them for a profit. The important thing was that they give back to their master more than he had given to them. How they did it was up to them, so long as it was legal and profitable.

We are given a report on only three of the ten servants, and the first two proved to be successful. The first servant brought ten pounds more, the second brought five pounds more, and both were rewarded accordingly. These men did their job faithfully even though they were promised no rewards and had no assurance that their master would even return, let alone secure the kingdom that he sought.

The parable of the talents (Matt. 25:14–30) is similar to the parable of the pounds, but their lessons must not be confused. In this parable, each of the ten servants received the same amount but different rewards, while in the parable of the talents, the servants received different amounts but the same reward, the approval and joy of the Lord (Matt. 25:21).

The parable of the talents teaches us to be faithful to use our different gifts as God gives us opportunities to serve. Some people have a great deal of ability, so God gives them greater opportunity. The important thing is not how much ability you have but how faithful you are to use what you have for the Lord. The person with the least ability, if he or she is faithful, will receive the same reward as the most gifted church leader.

In the parable of the pounds, each servant has the same deposit, which probably represents the message of the gospel (1 Thess. 2:4; 1 Tim. 1:11; 6:20). Our gifts and abilities are different, but our job is the same: to share the Word of God so that it multiplies and fills the world (1 Thess. 1:8; 2 Thess. 3:1). Only 120 believers met together on the day of Pentecost (Acts 1:15), but before that day ended, there were 3,000 more (Acts 2:41). And before long, there were 5,000 believers (Acts 4:4). In time, the Jewish leaders accused the disciples of "filling Jerusalem" with the message (Acts 5:28)!

When it comes to witnessing, all believers start on the same level, so the reward is according to faithfulness and achievement. The faithful servants were rewarded by being made *rulers* of various cities. The reward for faithful work is always—more work! But what a compliment to be entrusted with the management of so many cities! How we serve the Lord today will help determine our reward and ministry when He comes to establish His kingdom on earth. Faithfulness now is preparation for blessed service then.

Unfaithful disobedience (vv. 20–23). At least one of the ten men did not obey his master and as a result lost even the pound that the master gave him. It is a basic principle of the Christian life that wasted opportunity means loss of reward *and possibly loss of the privilege of service.* If we do not use the gifts God gives us under His direction, why should we even have them? Somebody else can make better use of the gifts to the glory of God (see Matt. 13:12 and Luke 8:18).

"It is always so," wrote Charles Haddon Spurgeon; "the gracious and faithful man obtains more grace and more means of usefulness, while the unfaithful man sinks lower and lower and grows worse and worse. We must either make progress or else lose what we have attained. There is no such thing as standing still in religion."

This servant was unfaithful because his heart was not right toward his master. He saw his master as a hard man who was demanding and unfair. The servant had no love for his master; in fact, he feared him and dreaded to displease him. Rather than lose the pound and incur his master's anger, he guarded it so that he would at least have something to give the master if he returned and asked for a reckoning.

It is sad when a Christian is motivated by slavish fear instead of loving faith. While there is a proper "fear of the Lord" that should be in every Christian's heart, that "fear" should be the respect of a loving child and not the dread of a frightened slave. "Nothing twists and deforms the soul more than a low or unworthy conception of God," wrote Dr. A. W. Tozer. How important it is that we do the will of God from our hearts (Eph. 6:6).

Outright rebellion (vv. 14–27). The "citizens" or "enemies" are mentioned at the beginning and the ending and are an important part of the story, for most of the people in the crowd that day were in that category. Jesus was near Jerusalem, and in a few days He would hear the mob shout, "We have no king but Caesar" (John 19:15). In other words, "We will not have this Man to reign over us!"

God was gracious to Israel and gave the nation nearly forty years of grace before judgment fell (Luke 19:41–44). But we must be careful to see in this a warning to all who reject Jesus Christ—Jew or Gentile—for during this time while He is away in heaven, Jesus Christ is calling men everywhere to repent and submit to Him.

The faithful servants obeyed because they trusted their master and wanted to please him. The unfaithful servant disobeyed because he feared his master. But these citizens rebelled because they hated their king (Luke 19:14). Jesus quoted Psalm 69:4 and told His disciples, "They hated me without a cause" (John 15:25).

We are living today in the period between Luke 19:14 and 15 when our Master is absent but will return according to His promise. We have been given a task to perform, and we must be faithful until He comes. What will the King say to us when He returns? Will His words mean reward, rebuke, or possibly retribution? "Moreover it is required in stewards, that a man be found faithful" (1 Cor. 4:2).

The King Who Offers Peace (19:28–48)

The traditional calendar for the events of our Lord's last week of ministry looks like this:

Sunday—Triumphal entry into Jerusalem
Monday—Cleansing the temple
Tuesday—Controversies with the Jewish leaders
Wednesday—Apparently a day of rest
Thursday—Preparation for Passover
Friday—Trial and crucifixion
Saturday—Jesus rests in the tomb
Sunday—Jesus raised from the dead

Keep in mind that the Jewish day went from sundown to sundown, so that our Thursday evening would be their Friday, the day of Passover.

Preparation (vv. 28–36). The owners of the donkey and the colt were disciples of the Lord and had everything ready for Him. The plan was executed quietly because the Jewish leaders had let it be known that anyone confessing Christ would be excommunicated (John 9:22). The fact that the rulers planned to kill Jesus made it even more important that the owners be protected (John 7:1, 19, 25; 8:37; 11:47–57).

We think of the donkey as a lowly animal, but to the Jew it was a beast fit for a king (1 Kings 1:33, 44). Jesus rode the colt (Luke 19:35) while the mother walked along with it. The fact that the colt had never been ridden and yet submitted to Jesus indicates our Lord's sovereignty over His creation. The laying of garments on the animals and on the road and the waving and spreading of branches were all part of a traditional Jewish reception for royalty.

Celebration (vv. 37–40). This is the only time that Jesus permitted a public demonstration on His behalf, and He did so for at least two reasons. First, He was fulfilling prophecy and presenting Himself as Israel's king (Zech. 9:9). How much of this the crowd really understood we cannot tell, even though they responded by quoting their praises from a messianic psalm (Ps. 118:25–26). No doubt many of the Passover pilgrims thought that Jesus would now get rid of the Roman invaders and establish the glorious kingdom.

The second reason for this demonstration was to force the Jewish religious leaders to act. They had hoped to arrest Him *after* the Passover (Matt. 26:3–5), but God had ordained that His Son be slain *on* Passover as the "Lamb of God, which taketh away the sin of the world" (John 1:29; and see 1 Cor. 5:7). Every previous attempt to arrest Jesus had failed because "his hour was not yet come" (John 7:30; 8:20; also see John 13:1; 17:1). When they saw this great public celebration, the leaders knew that they had to act, and the willing cooperation of Judas solved their problem for them (Matt. 26:14–16).

The theme of the celebration was *peace.* Dr. Luke opened his gospel with the angel's announcement of "peace on earth" (Luke 2:14), but now the theme is "peace in heaven." Because the King was rejected, there could be no peace on earth. Instead, there would be constant bitter conflict between the kingdom of God and the kingdom of evil (Luke 12:49–53). There would be no peace on earth but, thanks to Christ's work on the cross, there is "peace with God" in heaven (Rom. 5:1; Col. 1:20). The appeal today is, "Be ye reconciled to God" (2 Cor. 5:17–21).

Lamentation (vv. 41–44). While the crowd was rejoicing, Jesus was weeping! This is the second occasion on which our Lord wept openly, the first being at the tomb of Lazarus (John 11:35). There He wept quietly, but here He uttered a loud lamentation like one mourning over the dead. In this, He was like the prophet Jeremiah, who wept bitterly over the destruction of Jerusalem (Jer. 9:1ff.; see also the book of Lamentations). Jonah looked on Nineveh and hoped it would be destroyed (Jonah 4), while Jesus looked at Jerusalem and wept because it had destroyed itself.

No matter where Jesus looked, He found cause for weeping. If He looked *back,* He saw how the nation had wasted its opportunities and been ignorant of their "time of visitation." If He looked *within,* He saw spiritual ignorance and blindness in the hearts of the people. They should have known who He was, for God had given them His Word and sent His messengers to prepare the way.

As He looked *around,* Jesus saw religious activity that accomplished very little. The temple had become a den of thieves, and the religious leaders were out to kill Him. The city was filled with pilgrims celebrating a festival, but the hearts of the people were heavy with sin and life's burdens.

As Jesus looked *ahead,* He wept as He saw the terrible judgment that was coming to the nation, the city, and the temple. In AD 70, the Romans would come and, after a siege of 143 days, kill 600,000 Jews, take thousands more captive, and then destroy the temple and the city. Why did all of this happen? Because the people did not know that God had visited them! "He came unto his own, and his own received him not" (John 1:11). "We will not have this man to reign over us" (Luke 19:14).

Denunciation (vv. 45–48). Jesus lodged in Bethany that night (Matt. 21:17) and came into the city early the next morning. It was then that He cursed the fig tree (Mark 11:12–14) and cleansed the temple for the second time. (See John 2:13–22 for the record of the first cleansing of the temple.)

The court of the Gentiles was the only place in the temple that was available to the Gentiles. There the

Jews could witness to their "pagan" neighbors and tell them about the one true and living God. But instead of being devoted to evangelism, the area was used for a "religious marketplace" where Jews from other lands could exchange money and purchase approved sacrifices. The priests managed this business and made a good profit from it.

Instead of *praying* for the people, the priests were *preying* on the people! The temple was not a "house of prayer" (Isa. 56:7); it was a "den of thieves" (Jer. 7:11). Campbell Morgan reminds us that a "den of thieves" is a place where thieves *run to hide* after they have committed their wicked deeds. The religious leaders were using the services of the holy temple to cover up their sins (see Isa. 1:1–20). But before we condemn them too harshly, have we ever gone to church and participated in religious worship just to give people the impression that we were godly?

Jesus remained in the temple and used it as a gathering place for those who needed help. He healed many who were sick and afflicted, and He taught the people the Word of God. The hypocritical religious leaders tried to destroy Him, but His hour had not yet come and they could not touch Him. In the days that followed, they argued with Him and tried to catch Him in His words (Luke 20), but they failed. When His hour came, He would surrender to them and they would crucify Him.

The courageous Son of God had set His face like a flint and come to Jerusalem. During His last week of ministry, He would courageously face His enemies and then bravely go to the cross to die for the sins of the world.

He still summons us to *be courageous!*

CHAPTER NINETEEN
Luke 20
ISSUES AND ANSWERS

Jesus had already told the Twelve to expect conflict and suffering when they arrived in the Holy City. "The Son of man must suffer many things, and be rejected of the elders and chief priests and scribes, and be slain, and be raised the third day" (Luke 9:22). Jesus knew fully what was coming, and He was not afraid.

In this chapter, you meet the three groups of religious leaders (Luke 20:1) and witness their conflict with Jesus. They challenged Him because He had cleansed the temple and called them "thieves." They tried to catch Him in His words so they could trump up some charge against Him and have Him arrested as an enemy of the state.

But there was more to this series of questions than mere guile. The word translated "rejected" in Luke 9:22 (and also Luke 20:17) means "to reject after investigation." It was required that the Jews carefully examine the Passover lambs from the tenth day to the fourteenth day to make sure they had no blemishes (Ex. 12:1–6). Jesus Christ, the Lamb of God (John 1:29), was watched and tested by His enemies during that final week, and yet in spite of what they saw and learned, they rejected Him.

However, *Jesus was also examining them!* For as they questioned Him, He questioned them, and their responses revealed the ignorance, hatred, and unbelief of their hearts.

Our Lord's questions centered on four different men.

A Question about John the Baptist (20:1–19)

The cleansing of the temple was a dramatic event that both captured the attention of the people and aroused the anger of the religious establishment. The fact that Jesus daily made the temple His headquarters for ministry only made the members of the Sanhedrin more indignant, so they decided to question Him. "What authority do You have to do these things?" they asked. "And if You do have authority, who gave it to You?"

Authority is important for the success of any social, political, or religious organization; without authority, you have confusion. The chief priests claimed their authority from Moses, for the law set the tribe of Levi apart to serve in the sanctuary. The scribes were students of the law and claimed their authority from the rabbis whose interpretations they studied. The elders of Israel were the leaders of the families and clans, chosen usually for their experience and wisdom. All of these men were sure of their authority and were not afraid to confront Jesus.

They wanted to push our Lord into a dilemma so that no matter how He answered, He would be in trouble. If He said that He had *no* authority, then He was in trouble with the Jews for invading their temple and acting like a prophet. If He said that His authority came from God, then He would be in trouble with the Romans, who were always alert to would-be messiahs, especially during Passover season (see Acts 5:34–39; 21:37–39).

Note our Lord's wise approach as He turned things around and put them completely on the defensive. First, *He asked a question* (Luke 20:3–8); then *He gave a parable* (Luke 20:9–16); and finally, *He quoted a prophecy* (Luke 20:17–18). In each of these approaches, He revealed the sins of the nation of Israel.

Their past rejection (vv. 3–8). Jesus took them back to John the Baptist for two reasons. First, John had pointed to Jesus and introduced Him to the nation (John 1:15–34), so their rejection of John was actually a rejection of the Lord Jesus Christ. Second, it is a spiritual principle that if we disobey truth we already know, God cannot reveal new truth to us (see John 7:14–17). Why answer their question when they had refused to submit to John's message?

Now it was the religious leaders who were in the dilemma! No matter what answer they gave, they were in trouble, so they decided to "play dumb" and not answer at all. They were deceitful in asking the question and dishonest in the way they avoided answering it. Even if Jesus *had* given them an answer, *their hearts were not prepared to receive it.* If they had disobeyed God's message given by John the Baptist (Luke 7:24–30), they would disobey the message given by God's Son. That was the theme of the parable Jesus told.

Their present rebellion (vv. 9–16). These men knew the Scriptures and recognized that Jesus was speaking about the "vineyard" of Israel (Ps. 80:8ff.; Isa. 5:1–7). God the Father blessed the nation abundantly and gave the Jews a land that was rich and pleasant. All He asked was that they obey His statutes and give Him the "spiritual harvest" He deserved.

Instead of being grateful for their blessings and joyfully giving the Lord His due, the nation proceeded to rob God and reject His messengers (see Neh. 9:26; Jer. 7:25–26; 25:4). God was patient and sent them one servant after another, but they refused to obey (Matt. 23:29–39). Finally, He sent His beloved Son (Luke 3:22), and they killed Him. In this story, Jesus gave His own death announcement.

Under Jewish law, any man could lay claim to ownerless property. The tenants may have concluded that the owner was dead; otherwise he would have come himself. If they killed the son, then they could claim the vineyard for themselves. *This is exactly the way the religious leaders were thinking as they stood there before Jesus* (see John 11:47–54)!

Their future ruin (vv. 17–18). Jesus fixed a steady gaze on them and quoted Psalm 118:22. The rulers knew that this was a messianic psalm, and they had heard it shouted by the crowd when Jesus rode into the city (compare Luke 19:38 with Ps. 118:26). By applying this verse to Himself, Jesus was clearly claiming to be the Messiah. The "builders," of course, were the Jewish religious leaders (Acts 4:11).

In the Old Testament, the "stone" is a familiar symbol of God and of the promised Messiah (see Gen. 49:24; Ex. 17:6; 33:22; Deut. 32:4, 15, 30–31; Isa. 8:14; 28:16; 1 Cor. 10:4). Because the Jews did not believe, they stumbled over Him and were judged. Those who trust Jesus Christ find Him to be the foundation stone and the chief cornerstone of the church (1 Cor. 3:11; Eph. 2:20).

But Jesus also referred to Daniel 2:34–35, 44–45, where the Messiah is pictured as a "smiting stone" that crushes all that gets in its way. He was warning the Sanhedrin that they would only destroy themselves if they condemned Him. The same principle applies today, and unbelievers should carefully heed His warning.

When the rulers rejected John the Baptist, they sinned against the Father who sent Him. When they crucified Jesus, they sinned against the Son. Jesus had told them that they could sin against Him and still be forgiven, but when they sinned against the Holy Spirit, there could be no forgiveness (Matt. 12:24–37). Why? *Because that was the end of God's witness to the nation.* This is the so-called "unpardonable sin," and it was committed by the Jewish leaders when they finally rejected the witness of the Spirit of God through the apostles. The evidence of their rejection was the stoning of Stephen (Acts 7:51–60). Then the gospel went from the Jews to the Samaritans (Acts 8) and then to the Gentiles (Acts 10).

In this parable, Jesus illustrated the insidious nature of sin: *the more we sin, the worse it becomes.* The tenants started off beating some of the servants and wounding others, but they ended up becoming murderers! The Jewish leaders *permitted* John the Baptist to be killed, they *asked* for Jesus to be crucified, and then *they themselves stoned Stephen.* They sinned against the Father and the Son and the Holy Spirit, and that was the end of God's witness to them.

It is a serious thing to reject the message of God and the messengers of God (see John 12:35–43; Heb. 2:1–4).

A Question about Caesar (20:20–26)

Jesus knew that the men who questioned Him were spies sent by the Pharisees and the Herodians (Mark 12:13), but He patiently listened and replied. These two groups were usually fighting each other, but now they had a common enemy, and this brought them together. They wanted to discuss taxes and Roman authority, hoping to provoke Jesus into offending either the Jews ("Pay the poll tax!") or the Romans ("Don't pay the poll tax!"). But Jesus lifted the discussion to a much higher level and forced the spies to think about the relationship between the kingdom of God and the kingdoms of men.

Governmental authority is instituted by God and must be respected (Prov. 8:15; Dan. 2:21, 37–38; Rom. 13; 1 Peter 2:11–17). Yes, our citizenship is in heaven (Phil. 3:20), and we are strangers and pilgrims on earth, but that does not mean we should ignore our earthly responsibilities. Human government is essential to a safe and orderly society, for man is a sinner and must be kept under control.

Jesus was not suggesting that we divide our loyalties between God and government. Since "the powers that be are ordained of God" (Rom. 13:1), *we live as good citizens when we obey the authorities for the Lord's sake.* When obedience to God conflicts with obedience to man, then we must put God first (Acts 4:19–20; 5:29), but we must do it in a manner that is honorable and loving. Even if we cannot respect the people in office, *we must respect the office.* The counsel that Jeremiah gave to the Jewish exiles in Babylon is a good one for God's "strangers and pilgrims" to follow today (Jer. 29:4–7): "Seek the peace of the city!"

Caesar's image and name were on the coins, so it was basically *his* currency. To pay the poll tax meant simply to give Caesar back that which belonged to him. God's image is stamped on us; therefore, He has the right to command our lives as citizens in His kingdom. We should seek to be such good citizens that God will be glorified and the unsaved will be attracted to the gospel and want to become Christians (1 Peter 2:9–12; 3:8–17).

It is unfortunate that some Christians have the mistaken idea that the more obnoxious they are as citizens, the more they please God and witness for Christ. We must never violate our conscience, but we should seek to be peacemakers and not troublemakers. Daniel is an example to follow (Dan. 1).

A Question about Moses (20:27–40)

Next in line were the Sadducees with a hypothetical question based on the Jewish law of "levirate marriage" (Gen. 38; Deut. 25:5–10). The word *levirate* comes from the Latin *levir,* which means "a husband's brother." The Sadducees accepted as Scripture only the five books of Moses, and they did not believe in angels, spirits, or the resurrection of the dead (Acts 23:8). They claimed that Moses did not write about any of these doctrines. The priestly party in Israel was composed of Sadducees, which explains why the priests opposed the apostles' preaching of the resurrection (Acts 4:1–2) and why they wanted to kill Lazarus, who was raised from the dead (John 12:10–11).

Jesus pointed out that His opponents were wrong and that their question revealed assumptions that limited God's power and denied God's Word. Resurrection is not reconstruction; it is the miraculous granting of a new body that has continuity with the old body but not identity. Paul compared our present body to a planted seed and the future resurrection body to the glorious flower and fruit (1 Cor. 15:35–50). Our Lord's resurrection body was the same as before His death and yet different! His friends recognized Him and even felt Him; He could eat food, and yet He could also walk through closed doors, change His appearance, and vanish suddenly.

The future life with God is not a mere continuation of the present life only on "a higher scale." We will maintain our identities and know each other, but there will be no more death—hence, no need for marriage and procreation. Christians do not become angels. In heaven we will share the image of Jesus Christ and be much higher than the angels (1 John 3:2). Angels appear in Scripture as men, but they are spirit beings without sexuality. It is in this regard that we will be like them; there will be no marriage or childbearing in heaven.

Is not God powerful enough to raise the dead and give them new bodies suited to their new environment? If today He can give different bodies to the various things in creation, why can He not give people new bodies at the resurrection (1 Cor. 15:35–44)? In their attempt to be "rational," the Sadducees denied the very power of God!

But Jesus went beyond logic and referred them to the Word of God, particularly what happened to Moses as recorded in Exodus 3. There God identified Himself with Abraham, Isaac, and Jacob, and thus affirmed that these three patriarchs were very much alive. But if they were alive, then they were "out of the body," for they had died (James 2:26). There must be a real world of spirit beings or Moses would not have written these words. (By the way, Moses also affirmed the existence of angels: Gen. 19:1, 15; 28:12; 32:1.)

But Jesus said that Exodus 3:6, 15–16 taught not only the truth of life after death but also the reality of the resurrection. In what way? Not by direct statement but by inference. God is the God of the whole person—spirit, soul, and body (1 Thess. 5:23)—because He created the whole person. He does not simply "save our souls" and ignore the rest of our being. Inherent in the very nature of God's creative act is His concern for the total person. Hence, He will not keep us disembodied spirits forever but will give us glorious bodies to match our heavenly perfection.

Another factor is God's covenental relationship with the patriarchs. He made promises of earthly blessing to them and their descendants, but He cannot fulfill these promises if His people are going to live forever only as disembodied spirits. Can there be a glorious new heaven and earth but no corporeal glory for the people of God?

Jesus affirmed what the Sadducees denied: the existence of angels, the reality of life after death, and the hope of a future resurrection—and He did it with only one passage from Moses! Of course, He could have referred to other passages that teach a future resurrection, but He met His adversaries on their own ground (see Job 14:14; 19:25–27; Ps. 16:9–10; 17:15; Isa. 26:19; Ezek. 37; Dan. 12:2).

A Question about David (20:41–44)

While the Pharisees were still gathered together, Jesus asked them a final question: "What do you think about the Christ? Whose Son is He?" (Matt. 22:41–42 NKJV). This is the *key* question for every generation and each individual, for our salvation and eternal destiny are dependent on what we think about Christ (1 John 2:21–25; 4:1–6; 5:1).

Of course, they knew the expected reply: "The Son of David." They based this on such verses as 2 Samuel 7:13–14; Isaiah 11:1; and Jeremiah 23:5. God had ordained that the Messiah should come from the family of David and be born in David's city, Bethlehem (Mic. 5:2). The fact that the Jewish people identified Jesus with Nazareth, not Bethlehem, indicates that they had not really looked into the facts connected with His birth (John 7:40–53).

Jesus then referred them to Psalm 110, which is quoted in the New Testament more than any other psalm. The Jewish religious leaders in that day identified Psalm 110 as a prophetic psalm and said that David was speaking of the Messiah. But if the Messiah is David's *Lord,* how can He be David's *son?* Here was an enigma for them to solve!

The only explanation is that Messiah must be both God and man. As eternal God, Messiah is David's Lord, but as man, He is David's son (Rom. 1:3; 9:4–5; Acts 2:32–36; 13:22–23).

On Palm Sunday, the multitudes had acclaimed Jesus as the Son of David, and He had not rebuked them (Matt. 21:9; Mark 11:10). By applying Psalm 110:1 to Himself, Jesus claimed to be Israel's promised Messiah, the Son of God.

Then why did the Pharisees not believe in Him? Because their minds were made up, their hearts were hardened, and their eyes were blind (John 12:37–50). They did not have the courage to confess the truth, and they persecuted those who did affirm faith in Jesus Christ. Christ's question silenced His enemies (Matt. 22:46) and ended their public challenges, but they would not admit defeat.

Because of their hypocrisy and dishonesty, the scribes and Pharisees were dangerous to have around, so Jesus warned the people about them (Luke 20:45–47; see Matt. 23). Men see the outside, but God sees the heart (1 Sam. 16:7; Heb. 4:12).

These religious leaders did not desire personal holiness; they wanted public recognition. Therefore, they wore special garments, expected special titles and greetings, and looked for special seats at public gatherings.

There is a double tragedy here. First of all, their deliberate hypocrisy was only a cover-up that enabled them to fool people and exploit them. Of all rackets, religious rackets are the worst. The religious leaders had turned the temple of God into a den of thieves and religious devotion into playacting. The general public actually thought that their leaders were godly men, when in reality they were defiling and destroying souls (Matt. 23:13–36).

The second tragedy is that they rejected their own Messiah and voted to crucify Him. They led the nation into ruin because they would not admit their sins and confess Jesus Christ. Keep in mind that these men were "experts" in the Bible, yet they did not apply its truths to their own lives. Their religion was a matter of external observance, not internal transformation.

At this point according to Matthew (Matt. 23:37–39), Jesus once again uttered a lamentation over the blind unbelief of the nation and their unwillingness to trust in Him.

He had given them many opportunities, but they had wasted them.

Now it was too late.

This same tragedy is reenacted today. This is why the Holy Spirit warns, "Today, if you will hear His voice, do not harden your hearts" (Heb. 3:7–8 NKJV).

"How often I wanted to … but you were not willing" (Matt. 23:37 NKJV).

CHAPTER TWENTY
Luke 21
QUESTIONS ABOUT TOMORROW

Now it was the disciples' turn to ask the questions! It all started with the arrival in the temple of a poor widow with an offering for the Lord (Luke 21:1–4). Compared to the gifts of the rich men, her two copper coins seemed insignificant, but Jesus said that she gave more than all the others combined. "The widow's mite" does not represent *the least* we can give, but *the most,* our very all. When we sing, "Take my silver and my gold / Not a mite will I withhold," we are telling God that everything we have belongs to Him.

When it comes to our giving, God sees more than the *portion;* He also sees the *proportion.* Men see *what is given,* but God sees *what is left,* and by that He measures the gift and the condition of our hearts. Winston Churchill said, "We make a living by what we get, but we make a life by what we give." He may have learned that from Jesus (Luke 6:38) or perhaps from Paul (2 Cor. 8:1–15).

The temple was a beautiful structure, embellished with many costly decorations that a poor widow could never give, and the disciples mentioned this to Jesus. But our Lord was not impressed. He told them that the day would come when the beautiful Jewish temple would be demolished (Luke 21:5–6). He had already announced that the city would be destroyed (Luke 19:41–44), but now He specifically mentioned the destruction of the temple.

Jesus left the temple and went to the Mount of Olives, and there Peter, James, and John asked Him three questions: (1) When would the temple be destroyed? (2) What would be the sign of His coming? (3) What would be the sign of the end of the age? (See Mark 13:3–4; Matt. 24:3.) The disciples thought that these three events would occur at the same time, but Jesus explained things differently. Actually, the temple would be destroyed first, and then there would be a long period of time before He would return and establish His kingdom on earth (see Luke 19:11–27).

Our Lord's reply comprises what we call "The Olivet Discourse," the greatest prophetic sermon He ever preached. It is recorded in greater detail in Matthew 24—25 and Mark 13, and you will want to compare the three passages. Since Luke wrote with the Gentile reader in mind, he omitted some of the strong Jewish elements of the sermon while retaining the essential truths that we must consider and apply.

Keep in mind that this was a message given to Jews by a Jew about the future of the Jewish nation. Though there are definite applications to God's people today, the emphasis is on Jerusalem, the Jews, and the temple. Our Lord was not discussing His coming for the church, for that can occur at any time and no signs need precede it (1 Cor. 15:51–58; 1 Thess. 4:13–18).

"For the Jews require a sign" (1 Cor. 1:22); the church looks for a Savior (Phil. 3:20–21).

The sermon focuses on a period in God's program called "the tribulation," when God will pour out His wrath on the nations of the world. Many Bible students believe that the tribulation will begin after the Lord comes *in the air* and takes His church to heaven (1 Thess. 4:13—5:11). It will climax with the return of Jesus Christ *to the earth,* at which time He will defeat His foes and establish His kingdom (Rev. 19:1—20:6).

It is helpful to see the development of the sermon as a whole, so here is a suggested outline:

> *The first half of the tribulation*
> (Matt. 24:4–14; Mark 13:5–13; Luke 21:8–19)
> *The middle of the tribulation*
> (Matt. 24:15–28; Mark 13:14–18; note Dan. 9:24–27)
> *The last half of the tribulation*
> (Matt. 24:29–31; Mark 13:19–27; Luke 21:25–27)
> *Closing admonitions*
> (Matt. 24:32—25:51; Mark 13:28–37; Luke 21:28–36)

Jesus answered the disciples' questions by discussing four topics relating to the future of the nation of Israel.

The Description of the Age (21:8–19)

The characteristics Jesus stated can be seen in *every* age of the church, for from the beginning there have been counterfeit messiahs, national and international upheavals, and religious persecution. But these things will *increase and intensify* as the time of Jesus' coming draws near. Thomas Campbell, British poet and educator, said that "coming events cast their shadows before" and he was right.

There will be *religious delusion* (Luke 21:8), and even God's people will be in danger of being deceived. Satan is a counterfeiter who for centuries has led people astray by deceiving their minds and blinding their hearts (2 Cor. 4:1–6; 11:1–4, 13–15). Israel was often seduced into sin by false prophets, and the church has had its share of false teachers (2 Peter 2).

Most people are naturally concerned about the future, especially when world events are threatening; therefore, religious racketeers can prey on them and take advantage of them. In every age, there are those who either claim to be the Christ or claim to know when He will return. These false prophets often "use" the Scriptures to "prove" the accuracy of their predictions, in spite of the fact that Jesus clearly stated that nobody knows the time of His return (Matt. 24:36–44).

"Be not deceived!" is our Lord's admonition, and we must take it to heart. The only sure way to keep our balance in a deceptive world is to know the Scriptures and obey what God tells us to do (2 Peter 3:17–18). It is foolish and hurtful to become so obsessed with Bible prophecy that we start to neglect the practical things of the Christian life. Blessed are the balanced!

There will also be *international distress* (Luke 21:9–11). I have a friend who has been keeping track of the earthquakes that have occurred in recent years. Another prophetic student has a list of all the wars and attempted invasions. Both have overlooked the fact that Jesus said that wars, earthquakes, pestilences, and famines *by themselves* are not signs of His soon return. These things have been going on throughout the history of the world.

However, during the first half of the tribulation, these events will multiply and intensify. Matthew 24:1–14 lists them in detail, and if you compare Revelation 6, you will see the parallel:

Events	Matthew	Revelation
false Christs	24:4–5	6:1–2
wars	24:6	6:3–4
famines	24:7a	6:5–6
death	24:7b–8	6:7–8
martyrs	24:9	6:9–11
worldwide chaos	24:10–13	6:12–17

In fact, most of Revelation 6—19, describes the tribulation period in detail and follows the outline of Matthew 24: (1) first half of the tribulation, chapters 6—9; (2) middle of the tribulation, chapters 10—14; (3) last half of the tribulation, chapters 15—19.

Our Lord's admonition to His people is, "Don't be terrified!" These things must come to pass; there is nothing anyone can do to prevent them. This does not mean that God's people are submitting to blind fate; rather, it means they are yielding to the plan of a loving Father who works all things "after the counsel of his own will" (Eph. 1:11).

Finally, there will be *religious persecution,* both official (Luke 21:12–15) and personal (Luke 21:16–19). Of course, there has been religious persecution ever since Cain killed Abel (Matt. 23:34–36; and see Acts 4:1ff.; 5:17ff.; 6:9ff.; 8:1ff.). Jesus promised that His people would suffer (John 15:18—16:4, 32–33), and that promise holds true today (2 Tim. 3:12). But the persecution in the end times will be much more severe, and many will give their lives for Christ.

Notice the encouragements Jesus gives to all who suffer persecution. To begin with, we must remember that when we are persecuted, we suffer *for His name's sake* (Luke 21:12), and this is a high honor (Acts 5:41). It is not important what people say about our names, but it is important that the name of Christ be glorified.

Second, times of suffering provide opportunities for witness (Luke 21:13–15). The apostles made good use of the witness stand when they were arrested and taken before the council (Acts 4—5), and Christ's servants and martyrs down through the centuries have followed their example. The English word *martyr* comes from the Greek word *martus,* which means "a witness" (see 1 Peter 3:13–17).

Because of official persecution, God's witnesses will stand before important people, and when that happens, they must not panic, for God will give them the words to speak. This promise is not an excuse for lazy preachers or Sunday school teachers who do not want to study! Rather, it is an assurance to faithful witnesses that God will always give them the words they need when they need them.

Not only will the saints endure official persecution from the government, but there will also be opposition from family and friends. Relatives will even follow in the footsteps of Judas and betray their Christian loved ones to be killed. Hatred, arrest, and death will be the lot of many of God's children during the tribulation.

But they must not despair, for God is in control. Not a hair on their head can perish apart from His sovereign will (Matt. 10:28–31). Knowing this, they can have endurance and be able to face the challenge with faith and courage.

While many Christians today enjoy freedom from official persecution, or even family opposition, there are others who suffer greatly for their faith, and what our Lord said here is an encouragement to them. A friend of mine ministered in Eastern Europe, and a believer in Poland said to him, "We are praying for you Christians in the Western world *because you have it too easy.* The Lord must help you not to compromise."

Remember, the things Jesus described here are not signs of His soon return, because they have been going on for centuries. However, as the coming of the Lord draws near, these things will multiply and intensify. No matter what our views may be of the coming of the Lord, we all need to heed His three admonitions: "Don't be deceived! Don't be afraid! Don't worry!"

The Destruction of the Temple (21:20–24)

This paragraph is peculiar to Luke; there is no parallel in Matthew or Mark, in spite of the similar language in Matthew 24:16–21 and Mark 13:14–17. However, it is clear that both Matthew and Mark were referring to events in the middle of the tribulation when "the abomination of desolation" would be set up in the Jewish temple and the Antichrist (the world ruler) would begin to persecute Israel (Dan. 9:24–27; Rev. 13). Jesus warned the people to flee and go into hiding, for "great tribulation" was about to fall.

Luke's account refers not to a distant event to occur during the tribulation but to the destruction of Jerusalem by Titus and the Roman army in AD 70, just forty years from that time (see Luke 19:41–44). This terrible event was in many respects a "dress rehearsal" for what will happen when Satan vents his anger on Israel and the believing Gentiles during the last half of the tribulation (Rev. 12:7–17). The Jewish historian Josephus claimed that nearly a million people were killed by the Romans, and over one hundred thousand taken captive, when Titus captured the city.

This was not the first time Jerusalem would be "trodden down of the Gentiles," for the Babylonians had destroyed the city in 586 BC when "the times of the Gentiles" began. This significant period in God's plan will end when Jesus Christ returns to the earth, destroys all Gentile power, and sets up His own righteous kingdom (Dan. 2:34–36, 44–45; Rev. 19:11ff.).

Believers today who are looking for their Lord's return should not apply Luke 21:20–24 to their own situation. Jesus was talking about Jerusalem in AD 70. In Matthew 24:15–28 and Mark 13:14–23, He was speaking about Israel's situation at the middle of the tribulation. Since our Lord's coming for the church will take place "in the twinkling of an eye" (1 Cor. 15:52), no one will have time to go back home for a coat; nor will we have to worry about traveling on the Sabbath or caring for nursing babies.

Thus far in His message, our Lord has told the disciples when the temple would be destroyed and what signs would point to the end of the age. Now He tells them about His own coming at the end of the tribulation period.

The Return of the Lord (21:25–28)

Revelation 15—19 describes the frightening judgment signs that God will send on the earth during the last half of the "time of Jacob's trouble" (Jer. 30:7). When these things occur, it will be evidence that the Lord's coming is drawing near. The image of "waves roaring" describes nations rising and falling like waves in a storm (Ps. 46:1–6; Rev. 17:15). It will be an awesome time, and the population of the earth will tremble with fear, but men will not repent of their sins and turn to God by faith (Rev. 9:20–21; 16:9–11).

Matthew 24:29 informs us that the sun and moon will be darkened and the stars will fall (Isa. 13:10; 34:4; Joel 2:10, 31; 3:15). Matthew 24:30 states that "the sign of the Son of man" will appear in heaven. We do not know what this "sign" is, but it will produce fear among the nations of the earth. However, then Jesus Christ will appear, and every eye will see Him (Rev. 1:7). The nation of Israel will at last recognize their Messiah, repent, believe, and be saved (Zech. 12:10–14; and see Mark 14:61–62).

These awesome signs will bring terror to the lost people of the world, but hope to those who have trusted the Lord during the tribulation period (Rev. 7), for these believers know that the Lord's coming will be soon. Believers today look for the Savior, not signs. However, as we see "coming events casting their shadows," we believe that the Lord's return is near.

Christ's appearing will be sudden, glorious, and with great power (Luke 21:27). The image here is taken from Daniel 7:13–14, a messianic passage that must have been familiar to the disciples. The angels promised that Jesus would return to earth in the same way He departed (Acts 1:9–11), and He will (Rev. 1:7).

There are those who ignore and even ridicule the doctrine of the return of Christ. After all, the church has been waiting for the Lord for two thousand years, and He has not returned yet! Peter answered that

accusation in 2 Peter 3. He pointed out that God keeps His promises whether we believe them or not, and that God measures time differently from the way men measure it. Furthermore, the reason He waits is so that *unsaved sinners may repent, be saved, and be ready when Jesus comes.* While His seeming delay is a trial to the church, it is an opportunity for the lost.

Having answered their questions, the Lord then "applied" the message to their hearts by giving them two closing admonitions: "Know!" and "Watch!"

The Responsibilities of the Believers (21:29–38)

In the Bible, the fig tree is often an image of Israel (Hos. 9:10; Luke 13:6–10). Some students interpret this parable to mean that the emergence of the State of Israel on May 15, 1948 was the "sign" that the Lord would soon return. Surely it is a significant thing that Israel is now a free nation after so many centuries of political bondage. But Luke added "and all the trees" (Luke 21:29), suggesting that more than one nation is involved. Perhaps Jesus was saying that *the rise of nationalism around the world* is the thing to watch. In recent years we have certainly seen the growth of nationalism and the emerging of new nations, and this may be a "sign" that the coming of the Lord is near.

However, the basic idea here is that of *knowing what is going on.* As the budding of the trees indicates that summer is near, so the occurring of these signs indicates that the Lord's return is near (see Luke 12:54–57 for a similar passage). The important thing is that the believer *knows* that God is keeping His promises and that His Word will not fail (Josh. 23:14).

To what "generation" does Luke 21:32 apply? Some who doubt that Jesus will literally return say that this statement applies to the generation of the apostles, so that "the coming of the Lord" was either the coming of the Spirit at Pentecost (Acts 2) or the destruction of Jerusalem in AD 70. *But none of the signs Jesus mentioned took place before or during those events.* Nor did they climax with the deliverance of Israel and the establishing of the kingdom.

Jesus was probably referring to the generation that would be alive on earth at the time all these things take place. He was not suggesting that it would take a whole generation to accomplish these things, for they will occur with swiftness once they begin. The Greek word translated "generation" can also mean "race" and could refer to the people of Israel. Jesus used it that way in Mark 8:12, 38; 9:19. Jesus was assuring the disciples that, in spite of all the difficulties Israel would endure, the nation would be protected by God and not be destroyed. Satan has wanted to destroy the nation of Israel, but he will not succeed.

His first admonition was "Know!" and His second was "Watch!" (Luke 21:34–36). Both admonitions apply to God's people in every age, though they will have a special meaning for the Jews of the tribulation period. "Watch!" does not mean to stand around looking for signs. It means, "Be awake! Be alert! Don't get caught unprepared!" This admonition carries a warning for us today, because it is so easy for us to "get weighted down" with the cares of this life and the temptations of the world and the flesh (see Luke 12:35–48).

During difficult times, it is easy to give up and start living like the unsaved world, and believers during the tribulation period will face that temptation. They must "watch and pray" and resist the temptations around them, for they want to be ready when their Lord returns.

Luke 21:36 refers primarily to believers standing before the Lord at the judgment when He returns to earth to establish His kingdom (Matt. 25:31–46). The sheep will enter into the kingdom, while the goats will be cast out. While some of God's people will die during the tribulation judgments and persecutions, some will "escape" and see Jesus Christ when He returns in glory.

If believers during that *difficult* age will be tempted to yield to the world and the flesh, Christians in this present age of comfort and affluence must face even greater dangers. We today do not know when our Lord will return, and it behooves us to be faithful and to be ready.

"I'm not looking for signs," said the late Vance Havner; "I'm listening for a sound."

The sound of the trumpet! The shout of the archangel!

"Even so, come, Lord Jesus!" (Rev. 22:20).

CHAPTER TWENTY-ONE
Luke 22:1–38
IN THE UPPER ROOM

Jesus had "steadfastly set his face to go to Jerusalem" (Luke 9:51), knowing full well what would happen to Him there, and now those events were about to occur.

They were appointments, not accidents, for they had been determined by the Father and written centuries ago in the Old Testament Scriptures (Luke 24:26–27). We cannot but admire our Savior and love Him more as we see Him courageously enter into this time of suffering and eventual death. We must remember that He did it for us.

The Passover supper in the Upper Room gives us the focus for our present study.

Before the Supper: Preparation (22:1–13)
Passover, Pentecost, and Tabernacles were the three most important feasts on the Jewish calendar (Lev. 23), and all the Jewish men were expected to go to Jerusalem each year to celebrate (Deut. 16:16). The Feast of Passover commemorated the deliverance of Israel from Egypt, and it was a time for both remembering and rejoicing (Ex. 11—12). Thousands of

excited pilgrims crowded in and around Jerusalem during that week, causing the Romans to always be nervous about possible uprisings. Passover had strong political overtones, and it was the ideal time for some would-be messiah to attempt to overthrow Rome. This explains why King Herod and Pontius Pilate, the Roman governor, were in Jerusalem instead of being at Tiberius and Caesarea respectively. They wanted to help keep the peace.

The religious leaders prepared for a crime (vv. 1–6). It is incredible that these men perpetrated history's greatest crime during Israel's holiest festival. During Passover, the Jews were expected to remove all leaven (yeast) from their houses (Ex. 12:15) as a reminder that their ancestors left Egypt in haste and had to eat unleavened bread. Jesus had warned His disciples about the "leaven of the Pharisees, which is hypocrisy" (Luke 12:1; also see Matt. 16:6; 1 Cor. 5:1–8), and now we see this hypocrisy at work.

The religious leaders had cleansed their homes but not their hearts (see Matt. 23:25–28). For a long time now, they had wanted to arrest Jesus and get Him out of the way, but they had not been able to work out a safe plan that would protect them from the people. Judas solved their problem for them. He guaranteed to deliver Jesus to them privately so there would be no uproar from the people. The last thing the Jewish Sanhedrin wanted was a messianic uprising at Passover season (see Luke 19:11).

Judas was motivated and energized by Satan (John 13:2, 27), for he never was a true believer in Jesus Christ. His sins had never been cleansed by the Lord (John 13:10–11), and he had never believed and received eternal life (John 6:64–71). Yet none of the other apostles had the least suspicion that Judas was a traitor. We have every reason to believe that Judas had been given the same authority as the other men and that he had preached the same message and performed the same miracles. It shows how close a person can come to God's kingdom and still be lost (Matt. 7:21–29).

Why did Judas betray the Lord Jesus? We know that he was a thief (John 12:4–6) and that money played a part in his terrible deed. But thirty pieces of silver was not a large payment for such a great crime, and there had to be something more involved. It is possible that Judas saw in Jesus the salvation of the Jewish nation and, therefore, he followed Him because he hoped to hold an office in the kingdom. Keep in mind that the Twelve often argued over who was the greatest in the kingdom, and Judas, the treasurer, surely participated in those important discussions.

When Judas understood that Jesus would not establish the kingdom but rather would surrender to the authorities, he turned against Him in bitter retaliation. The "leaven" in his life grew quietly and secretly until it produced "malice and wickedness" (1 Cor. 5:6–8). When you cooperate with Satan, you pay dearly, and Judas ended up destroying himself (Matt. 27:3–5).

Satan is a liar and a murderer (John 8:44), and he reproduced himself perfectly in Judas.

Jesus prepared for the Passover (vv. 7–13). The way our Lord arranged for the Passover feast indicates that He knew there were plots afoot. Until the disciples arrived at the Upper Room, only Jesus and Peter and John had known where the feast would be held. Had Judas known, he might have been tempted to inform the authorities.

Peter and John would have no trouble locating the man with the water pitcher, because men rarely carried pitchers of water. This was the task of the women. Like the men who owned the ass and colt (Luke 19:28–34), this anonymous man was a disciple of Jesus who made his house available to the Master for His last Passover.

Peter and John would purchase an approved lamb and take it to the temple to be slain. Then they would take the lamb and the other elements of the supper to the house where they planned to meet, and there the lamb would be roasted. The table would be furnished with wine, unleavened bread, and the paste of bitter herbs that reminded the Jews of their long and bitter bondage in Egypt (see Ex. 12:1–28).

There is a chronological question here that must be addressed or it will appear that the gospel writers are contradicting each other. According to John 18:28, the Jewish leaders had not yet eaten the Passover, and the day Jesus was tried and condemned was "the preparation of the Passover" (John 19:14). But our Lord and His disciples had already eaten the Passover!

In their excellent *Harmony of the Gospels* (Harper & Row), Robert Thomas and Stanley Gundry suggest a possible solution to the dilemma (320–23). The Jews at that time reckoned days in one of two ways: from sunset to sunset or from sunrise to sunrise. The first approach was traditionally Jewish (Gen. 1:5), while the second was Roman, though it had biblical precedent (see Gen. 8:22).

If Matthew, Mark, and Luke used the Jewish reckoning, and John the Roman, then there is no contradiction. There was an "overlapping" of days that permitted both groups to celebrate on the same *date* but a different *day.* The temple priests permitted the Jews to bring their lambs for sacrifice either the earlier or the later time. Apparently the Jewish leaders followed the Roman form of reckoning (John 18:28), while Jesus and the disciples followed the Jewish form. Our Lord was crucified on Passover at the time when the lambs were being slain, becoming a fulfillment of Old Testament type.

During the Supper: Revelation (22:14–16, 21–38)

The disciples did not know what to expect as they met in the Upper Room, but it turned out to be an evening of painful revelation. Jesus, the Host of the supper, met them with the traditional kiss of peace (He kissed Judas!), and then the men reclined around the table, Judas at our Lord's left and John at His right (John 13:23).

Jesus revealed His love (vv. 14–16). He did this by what He *said* and by what He *did.* He told His friends that He had a great desire to share this last Passover with them before He suffered. Passover commemorated the Exodus of Israel from Egypt centuries before, but He would accomplish a greater "exodus" on the cross. He would purchase redemption from sin for a world of lost sinners (Luke 9:31).

Then He arose, girded Himself with a towel, and washed the disciples' feet, including Judas' (John 13:1–20). Later that evening, the Twelve would argue over which of them was the greatest, so this lesson on humility and service did not penetrate their hearts. Perhaps Peter had this scene in mind when years later he admonished his readers to "be clothed with humility" (1 Peter 5:5; and see Phil. 2:1–11).

Our Lord's words in Luke 22:16 indicate that there would be no more Passover on God's calendar. The next feast would be the great "kingdom feast" when He would return to establish His rule on earth (Luke 22:28–30; 13:24–30; Matt. 8:11–12). He saw beyond the suffering to the glory, beyond the cross to the crown, and in His love, He reached out to include His friends.

Jesus revealed the presence of treachery (vv. 21–23). He had already hinted to His disciples that one of their number was not truly with Him (John 6:66–71), but now He openly spoke about a traitor in their midst. However, He did not do this just for the sake of the disciples, but more for the sake of Judas. Jesus had kissed Judas and washed his feet, and now He was giving Judas another opportunity to repent. It is most significant that Jesus did not openly identify Judas as the traitor but protected him until the very end.

If Jesus knew that Judas would betray Him, why did He choose him in the first place? And, if *somebody* had to betray the Lord, why condemn Judas? After all, he simply did God's will and fulfilled the Old Testament prophecy (see Ps. 41:9; 55:12–14; compare Ps. 69:25 and 109:8 with Acts 1:15–20).

Before He chose His twelve apostles, Jesus spent a whole night in prayer (Luke 6:12–16), so we must believe that it was the Father's will that Judas be among them (John 8:29). But the selection of Judas did not seal his fate; rather, it gave him opportunity to watch the Lord Jesus closely, believe, and be saved. God in His sovereignty had determined that His Son would be betrayed by a friend, *but divine foreknowledge does not destroy human responsibility or accountability.* Judas made each decision freely and would be judged accordingly, even though he still fulfilled the decree of God (Acts 2:23).

The fact that the disciples were puzzled by this strange announcement reveals that they did not know Judas' true character, their own hearts ("Which of us could do such a terrible thing?"), or the prophecies in the psalms. Nor did they remember the Lord's statements that He would be betrayed into the hands of the enemy (Matt. 17:22; 20:18). If Peter had fully understood what was happening, he might have used his sword on Judas!

Much about Judas remains a mystery to us, and we must not speculate too much. Judas is certainly a witness to the sinlessness of Jesus Christ, for if anybody could have given witness against Him, it was Judas. However, the authorities had to find false witnesses in order to build their case against Jesus. Judas admitted that he had "betrayed innocent blood" (Matt. 27:4).

At this point, Judas left the Upper Room to go to the religious leaders and get ready for the arrest of Jesus in the garden. Judas went out "and it was night" (John 13:30), for he was obeying the prince of darkness (Luke 22:53). Alas, for Judas, *it is still night and always will be night!*

Jesus revealed the disciples' worldliness (vv. 24–30). This was not the first time the disciples had committed this sin (Matt. 20:20–28; Mark 9:33–37; Luke 9:46–48), but in the light of what their Lord had said and done that evening, this latest exhibition was inexcusable. Perhaps the argument grew out of their speculating over who would betray Him, or there may have been some jealousy over the way they had been seated at the table. When you are interested in promoting yourself, it doesn't take much to start an argument.

Jesus had to explain that they were thinking like the unsaved Gentiles and not like God's children. The Romans in particular vied for honors and did all they could, legally and illegally, to win promotion and recognition, but they are not the examples for us to follow. As in all things, Jesus is our example, and He has completely reversed the measure of true greatness.

True greatness means to be like Jesus, and that means being a servant to others. A servant does not argue over who is the greatest, because he knows that he is the least, and he accepts this from the hand of God. Since all Christians are to be servants, there is no reason for us to compete with one another for honors and recognition. It is too bad that this competitive spirit is so strong in the church today as people promote themselves and their ministries as "the greatest."

Jesus closed this lesson on servanthood by reminding them of their future reward in the kingdom (Luke 22:28–30). In spite of their weaknesses and failures, the disciples had stood by Jesus during His earthly ministry, and God would honor them for their faithfulness. We should not mind being servants today, for we shall sit on thrones in the future kingdom! For that matter, our faithful service today is preparing us for the rewards we shall receive. Jesus has set the example: first the cross, then the crown.

Jesus revealed Peter's denial (vv. 31–38). It is interesting that this word of warning followed the dispute over who was the greatest! Imagine how the disciples must have felt when they heard that not only would one of their number betray Him, but that their spokesman and leader would publicly deny Him! If a strong man like Peter was going to fail the Lord, what hope was there for the rest of them?

The word *you* in Luke 22:31 is plural; Satan asked to have all the disciples so he might sift them like wheat. These men had been with Jesus in His trials (Luke 22:28), and He would not forsake them in their trials. This was both a warning and an encouragement to Peter and the other men, and our Lord's prayers were answered. Peter's courage failed but not his faith; he was restored to fellowship with Christ and was greatly used to strengthen God's people.

Peter's self-confident boasting is a warning to us that none of us really knows his own heart (Jer. 17:9) and that we can fail *in the point of our greatest strength.* Abraham's greatest strength was his faith, and yet his faith failed him when he went down to Egypt and lied about Sarah (Gen. 12:10—13:4). Moses' strength was in his meekness (Num. 12:3), yet he lost his temper, spoke rashly with his lips, and was not allowed to enter Canaan (Num. 20). Peter was a brave man, but his courage failed him and he denied his Lord three times. "Therefore let him who thinks he stands take heed lest he fall" (1 Cor. 10:12 NKJV).

The word *converted* in Luke 22:32 means "turned around." Peter was already a *saved* man, but he would soon start going in the wrong direction and would have to be turned around. He would not lose the gift of eternal life, but he would disobey the Lord and jeopardize his discipleship. Actually, all of the disciples would forsake Jesus, but Peter would also deny Him. It is a humbling lesson for all of us.

Our Lord's counsel in Luke 22:35–38 was not fully understood by the disciples, because they interpreted what He said quite literally. Peter's use of the sword in the garden is evidence of this (Luke 22:49–51). The point He was making was this: "You are now moving into a whole new situation. If they arrest Me, they will one day arrest you. If they treat Me like a common criminal (Isa. 53:12), they will do the same to you; so, be prepared!"

During their ministry with Jesus, the disciples had been sent out with special authority, and they were treated with respect and appreciation (Luke 9:1ff.; 10:1ff.). At that time, Jesus was still a very popular rabbi, and the authorities were not able to attack His disciples. But now "his hour had come" and the situation would change radically. Today, God's people are aliens in enemy territory, and we must use our faith and sanctified common sense as we serve the Lord. This is a good warning to zealous people who foolishly get themselves into tight spots and then expect God to perform miracles for them. The apostle Paul knew how to use the "sword" of human government to protect him and the gospel (Acts 16:35–40; 21:37–40; 25:11; Rom. 13).

Their words, "Here are two swords!" must have grieved the Lord, for they indicated that the disciples had missed the meaning of His words. Did they think that He needed their protection or that He would now overthrow Rome and establish the kingdom? "It is enough!" means "Don't say anything more about the matter" (Deut. 3:26). His kingdom does not advance by means of men's swords (John 18:36–37) but by the power of God's truth, the Word of God that is sharper than any human sword (Eph. 6:17; Heb. 4:12).

After the Supper: Commemoration (22:17–20)

It was when the Passover meal was drawing to a close (Matt. 26:25; Luke 22:20) that Jesus instituted the ordinance that the church calls "the Communion" (1 Cor. 10:16), or "the Lord's Supper" (1 Cor. 11:20), or "the Eucharist," from the Greek word that means "to give thanks."

The Passover feast opened with a prayer of thanksgiving, followed by the drinking of the first of four cups of wine. (The wine was diluted with water and was not intoxicating.)

Next they ate the bitter herbs and sang Psalms 113—114. Then they drank the second cup of wine and began eating the lamb and the unleavened bread. After drinking the third cup of wine, they sang Psalms 115—118, and then the fourth cup was passed among them. It is likely that between the third and fourth cups of wine, Jesus instituted the Supper.

Paul gave the order of the Supper in 1 Corinthians 11:23–26. First, Jesus broke a piece from the unleavened loaf, gave thanks, and shared it with the disciples, saying that it represented His body, which was given for them. He then gave thanks for the cup and shared it, saying that it represented His blood. It was a simple observance that used the basic elements of a humble Jewish meal. Jesus sanctified the simple things of life and used them to convey profound spiritual truths.

Jesus stated one of the purposes for the Supper: "in remembrance of me" (1 Cor. 11:24–25). It is a memorial feast to remind the believer that Jesus Christ gave His body and blood for the redemption of the world. There is no suggestion in the accounts of the Supper that anything "miraculous" took place when Jesus blessed the bread and the cup. The bread remained bread and the wine remained wine, and the physical act of receiving the elements did not do anything special to the eleven disciples. When we partake, we identify ourselves with His body and blood (1 Cor. 10:16), but there is no suggestion here that we receive His body and blood.

A second purpose for the supper is the proclaiming of His death until He returns (1 Cor. 11:26). The Supper encourages us to *look back* with love and adoration to what He did for us on the cross and to *look forward* with hope and anticipation to His coming again. Since we must be careful not to come to the Lord's table with known sin in our lives, the Supper should also be an occasion for *looking within,* examining our hearts, and confessing our sins (1 Cor. 11:27–32).

A third blessing from the Supper is the reminder of the unity of the church: we are "one loaf" (1 Cor. 10:17). It is "the *Lord's* Supper" and is not the exclusive property of any Christian denomination. Whenever we share in the Supper, we are identifying with Christians everywhere and are reminded of our obligation to "keep the unity of the Spirit in the bond of peace" (Eph. 4:3).

For us to receive a spiritual blessing from the Supper, it takes more than mere physical participation. We must also be able to "discern the body" (1 Cor. 11:29), that is, see the spiritual truths that are inherent in the bread and the cup. This spiritual discernment comes through the Spirit using the Word. The Holy Spirit makes all of this real to us as we wait before the Lord at the table.

Following the instituting of the Supper, Jesus taught His disciples many of the basic truths they desperately needed to know in order to have effective ministries in a hostile world (John 14—16). He prayed for His disciples (John 17); then they sang a hymn and departed from the Upper Room for the garden of Gethsemane. Judas knew they would go there and he would have the arresting officers all prepared.

As you review this passage, you cannot help but be impressed with the calmness and courage of the Savior. It is He who is in control, not Satan or Judas or the Sanhedrin. It is He who encourages the apostles! And He is able even to sing a hymn before He goes out to die on a cross! Isaac Watts has best expressed what our response should be:

> Love so amazing, so divine,
> Demands my soul, my life, my all.

CHAPTER TWENTY-TWO
Luke 22:39–71
THE NIGHT THEY ARRESTED GOD

Perhaps the best way to grasp the spiritual lessons behind the tragic events of that night is to focus on the *symbols* that appear in the narrative. The Bible is a picture book as well as a book of history and biography, and these pictures can say a great deal to us. In this passage, there are six symbols that can help us better understand our Lord's suffering and death. They are: a lonely garden , a costly cup, a hypocritical kiss, a useless sword, a crowing cock, and a glorious throne.

A Lonely Garden (22:39)

The Son of Man left the Upper Room and went with His disciples to the garden of Gethsemane on the Mount of Olives. This was His customary place of retirement when in Jerusalem (Luke 21:37). Knowing that the Lord would be there (John 18:1–2), Judas led his band of Roman soldiers and temple guards into the garden to arrest Jesus, who willingly yielded Himself into their hands.

But why a garden? Human history began in a garden (Gen. 2:7–25) and so did human sin (Gen. 3). For the redeemed, the whole story will climax in a "garden city" where there will be no sin (Rev. 21:1–22:7). But between the garden where man failed and the garden where God reigns is Gethsemane, the garden where Jesus accepted the cup from the Father's hand.

John informs us that when Jesus went to the garden, He crossed the Kidron brook (John 18:1). John may have had in mind King David's experience when he left Jerusalem and fled from his son Absalom (2 Sam. 15; and note especially v. 23). Both David and Jesus were throneless kings, accompanied by their closest friends and rejected by their own people. The name *Kidron* means "murky, dark," and *Gethsemane* means "olive press." Surely these names are significant.

Guides in modern Jerusalem can take visitors to four different sites that lay claim to being the ancient garden of Gethsemane. Perhaps the most widely accepted one, and surely the most popular, is outside the east wall of Jerusalem near the Church of All Nations. The olive trees there are indeed very old, but it is not likely that they go back as far as the time of Christ, since the Romans destroyed all the trees in their invasion of Judea in AD 70.

The geographical location of the garden of Gethsemane is not as important as the spiritual message that we receive from what Jesus did there when He accepted "the cup" from His Father's hand. The first Adam rebelled in the garden of Eden and brought sin and death into the world, but the Last Adam (1 Cor. 15:45) submitted in the garden of Gethsemane and brought life and salvation for all who will believe.

A Costly Cup (22:40–46)

Jesus left eight of His disciples somewhere in the garden and took Peter, James, and John with Him to a private place to pray (Mark 14:32–33). This is the third time He has shared a special occasion with these three men. The first was when Jesus raised Jairus's daughter from the dead (Luke 8:41–56), and the second was when He was transfigured before them (Luke 9:28–36). There must be a spiritual message here.

Dr. G. Campbell Morgan, the British expositor, has pointed out that each of these occasions had something to do with death. In Jairus's house, Jesus proved Himself to be victorious over death; and on the Mount of Transfiguration, He was glorified through death. (He and Moses and Elijah were talking about His "exodus" in Jerusalem [Luke 9:31].) Here in the garden, Jesus was surrendered to death. Since James was the first of the apostles to die (Acts 12:1–2), John the last to die, and Peter experienced great persecution and eventually was crucified, these three lessons were very practical for their own lives.

Jesus is the Son of God and knew full well that He would be raised from the dead, and yet His soul experienced agony as He anticipated what lay before Him. In the hours ahead, He would be humiliated and abused, and suffer shame and pain on the cross. But even more, He would be made sin for us and separated from His Father. He called this solemn experience "drinking the cup." (For parallel uses of this image, see Ps. 73:10; 75:8; Isa. 51:17, 22; Jer. 25:15–28.)

A comparison of the gospel accounts reveals that Jesus prayed three times about the cup and returned three times to the disciples, only to find them asleep. How little they realized the testing and danger that lay before them! And how much it would have meant to Jesus to have had their prayer support as He faced Calvary (see Heb. 5:7–8)!

Dr. Luke is the only gospel writer who mentions "sweat.... like great drops of blood." His use of the word *like* may suggest that the sweat merely fell to the ground like clots of blood. But there is a rare physical phenomenon known as *hematidrosis,* in which, under great emotional stress, the tiny blood vessels rupture in the sweat glands and produce a mixture of blood and sweat. The first Adam sinned in a garden and was condemned to living by the sweat of his brow (Gen. 3:19). Jesus, the Last Adam, obeyed the Father in a garden and conquered Adam's sin (Rom. 5:12–21).

Luke is also the only writer to mention the ministry of the angel (Luke 22:43). In fact, both the gospel of Luke and the book of Acts give angels a prominent place in the work of the Lord. Angels could not come to die for our sins, but they could strengthen our Savior as He courageously accepted the cup from His Father's hand. Dr. George Morrison said, "Every life has its Gethsemane, and every Gethsemane has its angel." What an encouragement to God's people when they wrestle and pray about difficult and costly decisions!

A Hypocritical Kiss (22:47–48)

Someone has defined "kiss" as "the contraction of the mouth due to the enlargement of the heart." But not all kisses are born out of a loving heart, for kisses can also be deceitful. In the case of Judas, his kiss was the basest kind of hypocrisy and treachery.

It was customary in that day for disciples to greet their teachers with a loving and respectful kiss. Judas used the kiss as a sign to tell the arresting officers who Jesus was (Matt. 26:48–49). Jesus had taught in the temple day after day, and yet the temple guards could not recognize Him!

The presence of such a large group of armed soldiers shows how little Judas really knew about the Lord Jesus. Did he think that Jesus would try to run away or perhaps hide somewhere in the garden? Judas must have expected Jesus and the disciples to resist arrest; otherwise he would not have enlisted so much help. Perhaps he feared that Jesus might perform a miracle, but even if He did, what can a group of armed men do against the power of Almighty God?

Judas was deceitful; he was a liar just like Satan who entered into him (John 8:44; 13:27). He defiled almost everything that he touched: his name (*Judah* = "praise"), the disciple band (Luke 6:13–16), gifts given to Christ (John 12:1–8), and the kiss. He even invaded a private prayer meeting, defiled it with his presence, and betrayed the Savior *with a kiss.* "Faithful are the wounds of a friend, but the kisses of an enemy are deceitful" (Prov. 27:6).

A Useless Sword (22:49–53)

The disciples remembered (and misunderstood) His words about the sword (Luke 22:35–38), so they asked Him if now was the time to make use of their two swords. Without waiting for the answer, Peter rushed ahead and attacked a man who turned out to be Malchus, a servant to the high priest (John 18:10, 26–27).

Why did Peter do this? For one thing, he had to back up the boastful words he had spoken in the Upper Room (Luke 22:33) and again on the way to the garden (Matt. 26:30–35). Peter had been sleeping when he should have been praying, talking when he should have been listening, and boasting when he should have been fearing. Now he was fighting when he should have been surrendering!

Peter made a number of serious mistakes when he attacked Malchus with his sword. To begin with, Peter was fighting the wrong enemy with the wrong weapon. Our enemies are not flesh and blood, and they cannot be defeated with ordinary weapons (2 Cor. 10:3–6; Eph. 6:10–18). In His wilderness temptations, Jesus defeated Satan with the Word of God (Matt. 4:1–11), and that is the weapon we must use (Eph. 6:17; Heb. 4:12).

Peter also revealed the wrong attitude and trusted the wrong energy. While Jesus was surrendering, Peter was busy declaring war! And he was depending on "the arm of flesh." His whole approach to the situation was not at all Christlike (John 18:36) and stands as a good warning to us today. The lost world may act this way, but it is not the way God's servants should act (Matt. 12:19; 2 Tim. 2:24).

It is just like Jesus to act in grace when others are acting in malice (Ps. 103:10). He showed grace to Peter by rebuking his presumptuous sin and repairing the damage he had done. He showed grace to Malchus, a lowly slave, by healing his ear, and He showed grace to the whole world by willingly yielding Himself to the mob and going to Calvary. He did not come to judge but to save (Luke 19:10; John 3:17).

Our Lord's last miracle before the cross was not a big flashy thing that attracted attention. It is likely that very few of the men who were there that night even knew what Peter and Jesus had done. Jesus could have summoned twelve legions of angels (Matt. 26:53), one legion (six thousand soldiers) for each of the eleven disciples and one for Himself, but He did not. Instead of performing some spectacular feat, He lovingly healed the ear of an obscure slave and then presented His hands to be bound.

Each of us must decide whether we will go through life *pretending,* like Judas; or *fighting,* like Peter; or *yielding to God's perfect will,* like Jesus. Will it be the kiss, the sword, or the cup?

A Crowing Cock (22:54–62)

Our Lord endured six different "trials" before He was condemned to be crucified, three before the Jews and three before the Roman authorities. First, He was taken to Annas, the former high priest who was an influential man in the nation and retained his former title (John 18:12–13). Annas sent Jesus to Caiaphas, his son-in-law, who was the official high priest (Matt. 26:57). Finally, at daybreak, He was tried before the Sanhedrin and found guilty (Luke 22:66–71).

The Jews did not have the right of capital punishment (John 18:31–32), so they had to take Jesus to the Roman authorities to get Him crucified. First, they took Him to Pilate (Luke 23:1–4), who tried to avoid a decision by sending Him to Herod (Luke 23:6–12), who sent Him back to Pilate (Luke 23:13–25)! When Pilate saw that he could not escape making a decision, he gave the Sanhedrin what they asked for and condemned Jesus to die on a Roman cross.

It was during the second Jewish "trial," the one before Caiaphas, that Peter in the courtyard denied his Lord three times. How did it happen? To begin with, Peter did not take the Lord's warnings seriously (Matt. 26:33–35; Luke 22:31–34), nor did he "watch and pray" as Jesus had instructed in the garden (Mark 14:37–38). For all of his courage and zeal, the apostle Peter was totally unprepared for Satan's attacks.

Jesus was led out of the garden , and "Peter followed afar off" (Luke 22:54). This was the next step toward his defeat. In spite of all the sermons that have been delivered on this text, criticizing him for walking at a distance, *Peter was not intended to follow at all.* The "sheep" were supposed to scatter and then meet Jesus later in Galilee (Matt. 26:31). In fact, when He was arrested, Jesus said to the guards, "Let these [disciples] go their way" (John 18:8–9), a clear signal that they were not to follow Him.

Peter and John followed the mob and gained entrance into the courtyard of Caiaphas's house (John 18:15–16). It was a cold night (though Jesus had been sweating!), and Peter first *stood* by the fire (John 18:18) and then *sat down* with the servants and officers (Luke 22:55). Sitting there in enemy territory (Ps. 1:1), Peter was an easy target. While he was thinking only of his own comfort, his Master was being abused by the soldiers (Luke 22:63–65).

First, it was one of the high priest's servant girls who challenged Peter. She accused him of being with Jesus and of being one of His disciples. Peter lied and said, "Woman, I am not one of His disciples! I don't know Him and I don't know what you are talking about!" He left the fire and went out to the porch (Matt. 26:71), and the cock crowed the first time (Mark 14:68). This in itself should have warned him to get out, but he lingered.

Peter could not escape notice, and a second servant

girl told the bystanders, "This man was with Jesus of Nazareth! He is one of them!" For a second time, Peter lied and said, "I am not! I don't know the man!"

The bystanders were not convinced, especially when one of Malchus's relatives showed up and asked, "Didn't I see you in the garden with Him?" Others joined in and said, "Surely you are one of them, because the way you talk gives you away. You talk like a Galilean." (The Galileans had a distinctive dialect.) At this point Peter used an oath and said, "I don't know the man! I don't know what you are talking about!" It was then that the cock crowed for the second time and the Lord's prediction was fulfilled (Mark 14:30).

At that moment, Jesus, being led away to the next trial, turned and looked at Peter, and His look broke Peter's heart. While the bystanders were watching Jesus, Peter slipped out and went off and wept bitterly. It is to Peter's credit that all the Lord had to do was *look* at him to bring him to the place of repentance.

For one cock to crow at the right time while the other birds in the city remained silent was certainly a miracle. But the crowing of the cock was much more than a miracle that fulfilled our Lord's words; it was also a special message to Peter, a message that helped to restore him to fellowship again. What encouragements did the crowing of the cock give to the apostle Peter?

First, it was an assurance to him that Jesus Christ was still in control of things even though He was a prisoner, bound and seemingly helpless before His captors. Peter could recall witnessing his Lord's authority over the fish, the winds, and the waves, and even over disease and death. No matter how dark the hour was for Peter, Jesus was still in control!

Second, the crowing of the cock assured Peter that he could be forgiven. Peter had not been paying close attention to the Word of God. He had argued with it, disobeyed it, and even run ahead of it, but now he "remembered the word of the Lord" (Luke 22:61), and this brought him hope. Why? Because with the word of warning was also a promise of restoration! Peter would be converted and strengthen his brethren (Luke 22:32).

Finally, the miracle of the cock told Peter that a new day was dawning, for after all, that is what the rooster's call means each day. It was not a new day for Judas or for the enemies of the Lord, but it was a new day for Peter as he repented and wept bitterly. "A broken and a contrite heart, O God, thou wilt not despise" (Ps. 51:17). On resurrection morning, the angel sent a special message to encourage Peter (Mark 16:7), and the Lord Himself appeared to Peter that day and restored him to fellowship (Luke 24:34).

Each one of us, at one time or another, will fail the Lord and then hear (in one way or another) "the crowing of the cock." Satan will tell us that we are finished, that our future has been destroyed, but that is not God's message to us. It was certainly not the end for Peter! His restoration was so complete that he was able to say to the Jews, "But you denied the Holy One and the Just" (Acts 3:14 NKJV). Peter did not have 1 John 1:9 to read, but he did experience it in his own heart.

A Glorious Throne (22:63–71)

Jesus had not yet officially been declared guilty, and yet the soldiers were permitted to mock Him and abuse Him. Here they mocked His claim to being a prophet; later they would mock His claim to being a king (John 19:1–3). But their mockery, sinful as it was, actually fulfilled Christ's own promise (Matt. 20:19). He is an example to us of how we should behave when sinners ridicule us and our faith (see 1 Peter 2:18–25).

It is generally believed that the Jewish council could not vote on capital offenses at night, so the chief priests, scribes, and elders had to assemble again as soon as it was day. Whether this ruling was in force in our Lord's day, we are not sure, but it does explain the early morning meeting of the Sanhedrin.

This was the climax of the religious trial, and the key issue was, "Is Jesus of Nazareth the Christ of God?" They were sure His claims were false and that He was guilty of blasphemy, and the penalty for blasphemy was death (Lev. 24:10–16).

Jesus knew the hearts of His accusers, their unbelief, and intellectual dishonesty (Luke 20:1–8). It was futile to preach a sermon or enter into a debate. They had already rejected the evidence He had given them (John 12:37–43), and more truth would only have increased their responsibility and their judgment (John 9:39–41).

Our Lord called Himself "Son of man," a messianic title found in Daniel 7:13–14. He also claimed to have the right to sit "on the right hand of the power of God" (Luke 22:69), a clear reference to Psalm 110:1, another messianic passage. It was this verse that He quoted earlier that week in His debate with the religious leaders (Luke 20:41–44). Jesus saw beyond the sufferings of the cross to the glories of the throne (Phil. 2:1–11; Heb. 12:2).

That our Lord is seated at the right hand of the Father is a truth that is often repeated in the New Testament (Heb. 1:3; 8:1; 10:12; 12:2; 1 Peter 3:22; Acts 2:33; 5:31; 7:55–56; Rom. 8:34; Eph. 1:20; Col. 3:1). This is the place of honor, authority, and power, and by claiming this honor, Jesus was claiming to be God.

Only Luke records the direct question in Luke 22:70 and our Lord's direct answer, which literally was "You say that I am." They would use this testimony later when they brought Him to Pilate (John 19:7). Some liberal theologians say that Jesus never claimed to be God, and we wonder what they do with this official trial. The Jewish religious leaders knew what Jesus was talking about, and this is why they condemned Him for blasphemy.

The "religious trial" was now over. The next step was to put Him through a civil trial and convince the Roman governor that Jesus of Nazareth was a criminal worthy of death. The Son of God was to be crucified, and only the Romans could do that.

Referring to the Jewish authorities, William Stalker wrote in *The Trial and Death of Jesus Christ,* "It may be said that they walked according to their light, but the light that was in them was darkness."

"None so blind as those that will not see," wrote Matthew Henry, the noted Bible commentator.

"While you have the light, believe in the light, that you may become sons of light" (John 12:36 NKJV).

CHAPTER TWENTY-THREE
Luke 23
CONDEMNED AND CRUCIFIED

The trial and death of Jesus Christ revealed both the wicked heart of man and the gracious heart of God. When men were doing their worst, God was giving His best. "But where sin abounded, grace did much more abound" (Rom. 5:20). Jesus was not crucified because evil men decided to get Him out of the way. His crucifixion was "by the determinate counsel and foreknowledge of God" (Acts 2:23), an appointment made from eternity (1 Peter 1:20; Rev. 13:8).

As you study this chapter, notice the six encounters our Lord experienced during those critical hours.

Jesus and Pilate (23:1–25)
Pontius Pilate served as governor of Judea from AD 26 to 36, at which time he was recalled to Rome and then passed out of official Roman history. He was hated by the orthodox Jews and never really understood them. Once he aroused their fury by putting up pagan Roman banners in the Jewish temple, and he was not beneath sending armed spies into the temple to silence Jewish protesters (Luke 13:1–3).

In his handling of the trial of Jesus, the governor proved to be indecisive. The gospel of John records seven different moves that Pilate made as he went *out* to meet the people and then went *in* to question Jesus (John 18:29, 33, 38; 19:1, 4, 9, 13). He kept looking for a loophole, but he found none. Pilate has gone down in history as the man who tried Jesus Christ, three times declared Him not guilty, and yet crucified Him just the same.

Pilate affirming (vv. 1–5). Roman officials were usually up early and at their duties, but Pilate was probably surprised that morning to learn that he had a capital case on his hands, and on Passover at that. The Jewish leaders knew that their religious laws meant nothing to a Roman official, so they emphasized the political aspects of their indictment against Jesus. There were three charges: He perverted the nation, opposed paying the poll tax to Caesar, and claimed to be a king.

Pilate privately interrogated Jesus about His kingship because that was the crucial issue, and he concluded that He was guilty of no crime. Three times during the trial, Pilate clearly affirmed the innocence

of Jesus (Luke 23:4, 14, 22). Dr. Luke reported three other witnesses besides Pilate who also said, "Not guilty!": King Herod (Luke 23:15), one of the malefactors (Luke 23:40–43), and a Roman centurion (Luke 23:47).

Pilate deferring (vv. 6–12). The Jews rejected his verdict and began to accuse Jesus all the more. When they mentioned Galilee, Pilate, astute politician that he was, immediately saw an opportunity to get Jesus off his hands. He sent Him to Herod Antipas, ruler of Galilee, the man who had murdered John the Baptist, who was anxious to see Jesus (Luke 9:7–9). Perhaps the wily king could find some way to please the Jews.

Herod must have been shocked and perhaps nervous when the guards brought Jesus in, but the more he questioned Him, the bolder he became. Perhaps Jesus might even entertain the king with a miracle! In spite of the king's persistent interrogation and the Jews' vehement accusations, Jesus said nothing. *Herod had silenced the voice of God.* It was not Herod who was judging Jesus; it was Jesus who was judging Herod.

The king finally became so bold as to mock Jesus and permit his soldiers to dress Him in "an elegant robe," the kind that was worn by Roman candidates for office. Herod did not issue an official verdict about Jesus (Luke 23:15), but it was clear that he did not find Him guilty of any crime worthy of death (Luke 23:15).

The only thing accomplished by this maneuver was the mending of a broken friendship. Herod was grateful to Pilate for helping him to see Jesus and for honoring him by seeking his counsel. The fact that Herod sent Jesus back to Pilate without issuing a verdict could be interpreted as, "Since we are not in Galilee, Pilate, you have the authority to act, and I will not interfere. Jesus is *your* prisoner, not mine. I know you will do the right thing." Finally, the fact that the two men met over a common threat (or enemy) helped them to put aside their differences and become friends again.

Pilate bargaining (vv. 13–23). He met the Jewish leaders and announced for the second time that he did not find Jesus guilty of the charges they had made against Him. The fact that Herod backed Pilate's decision would not have impressed the Jews very much, because they despised Herod almost as much as they despised the Romans.

Since it was customary at Passover for the governor to release a prisoner, Pilate offered the Jews a compromise: he would chastise Jesus and let Him go. He had another prisoner on hand, Barabbas, but Pilate was sure the Jews would not want him to be released. After all, Barabbas was a robber (John 18:40), a murderer, and an insurrectionist (Luke 23:19). He may have been a leader of the Jewish Zealots, who at that time was working for the overthrow of Rome.

We must not think that the general populace of the city was gathered before Pilate and crying out for the blood of Jesus, though a curious crowd no doubt gathered. It was primarily the official religious leaders of the nation, the chief priests in particular (Luke 23:23), who shouted Pilate down and told him to crucify Jesus. To say that the people who cried "Hosanna!" on Palm Sunday ended up crying "Crucify Him!" on Good Friday is not completely accurate.

Pilate yielding (vv. 24–25). Pilate realized that his mishandling of the situation had almost caused a riot, and a Jewish uprising was the last thing he wanted during Passover. So, he called for water and washed his hands before the crowd, affirming his innocence (Matt. 27:24–25). He was a compromiser who was "willing to content the people" (Mark 15:15). Barabbas was released and Jesus was condemned to die on a Roman cross.

Pilate was a complex character. He openly said that Jesus was innocent, yet he permitted Him to be beaten and condemned Him to die. He carefully questioned Jesus and even trembled at His answers, but the truth of the Word did not make a difference in his decisions. He wanted to be popular and not right; he was more concerned about reputation than he was character. If Herod had silenced the voice of God, then Pilate smothered the voice of God. He had his opportunity and wasted it.

Jesus and Simon (23:26)

It was a part of the prisoner's humiliation that he carry his own cross to the place of execution, so when Jesus left Pilate's hall, He was carrying either the cross or the crossbeam (John 19:17). Apparently, He was unable to go on, for the soldiers had to "draft" Simon of Cyrene to carry the cross for Him. (This was a legal Roman procedure. See Matt. 5:41.) When you consider all that Jesus had endured since His arrest in the garden , it is not difficult to imagine Him falling under the load. But there is something more involved: carrying the cross was a sign of guilt, *and our Lord was not guilty!*

Thousands of Jews came to Jerusalem from other nations to celebrate the feasts (Acts 2:5–11), and Simon was among them. He had traveled over eight hundred miles from Africa to celebrate Passover, and now he was being humiliated on a most holy day! What would he say to his family when he got home?

What looked to Simon like a catastrophe turned out to be a wonderful opportunity, for it brought him in contact with Jesus Christ. (By the way, where was the *other* Simon—Simon Peter—who had promised Jesus to go with Him to prison and to death?) Simon may have come into the city to attend the 9 a.m. prayer meeting in the temple, but the soldiers rearranged his schedule for him.

We have good reason to believe that Simon was converted because of this encounter with Jesus. Mark identified him as "the father of Alexander and Rufus" (Mark 15:21), two men that Mark assumed his Roman readers would know. A Christian named Rufus was greeted by Paul in Romans 16:13, and it is possible that he was the son of Simon of Cyrene. Apparently Simon and his two sons became well-known Christians who were held in honor in the church.

Before Simon met Jesus, he had religion and devotion, but after he met Jesus, he had reality and salvation. He did both a physical and spiritual "about face" that morning, and it transformed his life. God can still use unexpected and difficult situations, even humiliating situations, to bring people to the Savior.

Jesus and the Jerusalem Women (23:27–31)

Public executions drew crowds of spectators, and one involving Jesus would especially attract attention. Add to this the fact that Jerusalem was crowded with pilgrims, and it is not difficult to believe that a "great multitude" was following the condemned man to Calvary.

In that crowd was a group of women who openly wept and lamented as they sympathized with Jesus and contemplated the terrible spiritual condition of their nation. It has been pointed out that, as far as the gospel records are concerned, no woman was ever an enemy of Jesus. Nor was Jesus ever the enemy of womankind. His example, His teachings, and most of all, His redemption have done much to dignify and elevate women. The news of His birth was shared with a Jewish maiden, His death was witnessed by grieving women, and the good news of His resurrection was announced first to a woman who had been demon-possessed.

Jesus appreciated their sympathy and used it to teach them and us an important lesson. While they were weeping over the injustice of *one man's death,* He was looking ahead and grieving over the terrible destruction of *the entire nation,* a judgment that was wholly justified (see Luke 19:41–4). Alas, it would be the women and children who would suffer the most, a fact supported by history. The Romans attempted to starve the Jews into submission, and hungry men, defending their city, took food from their suffering wives and children and even killed and ate their own flesh and blood.

The nation of Israel was like a "green tree" during the years when Jesus was on earth. It was a time of blessing and opportunity, and it should have been a time of fruitfulness. But the nation rejected Him and became like a "dry tree," fit only for the fire. Jesus often would have gathered His people together, but they would not. In condemning Him, they only condemned themselves.

We might paraphrase His words: "If the Roman authorities do this to one who is innocent, what will they do to you who are guilty? When the day of judgment arrives, can there be any escape for you?"

Jesus and the Malefactors (23:32–43)

It had been prophesied that the Suffering Servant would be "numbered with the transgressors" (Isa. 53:12; Luke 22:37), and two criminals were crucified with Jesus, men who were robbers (Matt. 27:38). The Greek word means "one who uses violence to rob openly," in contrast to the thief who secretly enters a house and steals. These two men may have been guilty of armed robbery involving murder.

The name *Calvary* comes from the Latin *calvaria,* which means "a skull." (The Greek is *kranion,* which gives us the English word *cranium,* and the Aramaic word is *Golgotha.)* The name is not explained in the New Testament. The site may have resembled a skull, as does "Gordon's Calvary" near the Damascus Gate in Jerusalem. Or perhaps the name simply grew out of the ugly facts of execution.

Our Lord was crucified about 9 a.m. and remained on the cross until 3 p.m.; and from noon to 3 p.m., there was darkness over all the land (Mark 15:25, 33). Jesus spoke seven times during those six terrible hours:

1. "Father, forgive them" (Luke 23:34)
2. "Today shalt thou be with me in paradise" (Luke 23:43)
3. "Woman, behold thy son" (John 19:25–27) [Three hours of darkness; Jesus is silent]
4. "Why hast thou forsaken me?" (Matt. 27:46)
5. "I thirst" (John 19:28)
6. "It is finished!" (John 19:30)
7. "Father, into thy hands" (Luke 23:46)

Luke recorded only three of these seven statements, the first, the second, and the last. Our Lord's prayer for His enemies, and His ministry to a repentant thief, fit in well with Luke's purpose to show Jesus Christ as the sympathetic Son of Man who cared for the needy.

While they were nailing Him to the cross, He repeatedly prayed, "Father, forgive them; for they know not what they do" (Luke 23:34). Not only was He practicing what He taught (Luke 6:27–28), but He was fulfilling prophecy and making "intercession for the transgressors" (Isa. 53:12).

We must not infer from His prayer that ignorance is a basis for forgiveness, or that those who sinned against Jesus were automatically forgiven because He prayed. Certainly both the Jews and the Romans were ignorant of the *enormity* of their sin, but that could not absolve them. The law provided a sacrifice for sins committed ignorantly, but there was no sacrifice for deliberate presumptuous sin (Ex. 21:14; Num. 15:27–31; Ps. 51:16–17). Our Lord's intercession postponed God's judgment on the nation for almost forty years, giving them additional opportunities to be saved (Acts 3:17–19).

It was providential that Jesus was crucified *between* the two thieves, for this gave both of them equal access to the Savior. Both could read Pilate's superscription, "This is Jesus of Nazareth the King of the Jews," and both could watch Him as He graciously gave His life for the sins of the world.

The one thief imitated the mockery of the religious leaders and asked Jesus to rescue him from the cross, but the other thief had different ideas. He may have reasoned, "If this Man is indeed the Christ, and if He has a kingdom, and if He has saved others, then He can

meet my greatest need, which is salvation from sin. I am not ready to die!" It took courage for this thief to defy the influence of his friend and the mockery of the crowd, and it took faith for him to trust a dying King! When you consider all that he had to overcome, the faith of this thief is astounding.

The man was saved wholly by grace; it was the gift of God (Eph. 2:8–9). He did not deserve it, and he could not earn it. His salvation was personal and secure, guaranteed by the word of Jesus Christ. The man hoped for some kind of help in the future, but Jesus gave him forgiveness that very day, and he died and went with Jesus to paradise (2 Cor. 12:1–4).

It should be noted that the people at Calvary fulfilled Old Testament prophecy in what they did: gambling for our Lord's clothing (Ps. 22:18), mocking Him (Ps. 22:6–8), and offering Him vinegar to drink (Ps. 69:21). God was still on the throne and His Word was still in control.

Jesus and the Father (23:44–49)

We must keep in mind that what our Lord accomplished on the cross was an eternal transaction that involved Him and the Father. He did not die as a martyr who had failed in a lost cause. Nor was He only an example for people to follow. Isaiah 53 makes it clear that Jesus did not die for His own sins, because He had none; He died for our sins. He made His soul an offering for sin (Isa. 53:4–6, 10–12).

The three hours of darkness was a miracle. It was not an eclipse, because that would have been impossible during the Passover season when there is a full moon. It was a God-sent darkness that shrouded the cross as the Son of God was made sin for us (2 Cor. 5:21). It was as though all nature was sympathizing with the Creator as He suffered and died. When Israel was in Egypt, three days of darkness preceded the first Passover (Ex. 10:21ff.). When Jesus was on the cross, three hours of darkness preceded the death of God's Lamb for the sins of the world (John 1:29).

Both Matthew 27:45–46 and Mark 15:33–34 record our Lord's cry at the close of the darkness, a Hebrew quotation from Psalm 22:1, "My God, My God, why hast thou forsaken me?" What this abandonment was and how Jesus felt it are not explained to us, but certainly it involves the fact that He became sin for us.

Our Lord cried with a loud voice, "It is finished!" (John 19:30), a declaration of victory. He had finished the work the Father gave Him to do (John 17:4). The work of redemption was completed, the types and prophecies were fulfilled (Heb. 9:24ff.), and the Savior could now rest.

He then addressed His Father in the final statement from the cross, "Father, into thy hands I commend my spirit" (Ps. 31:5). This was actually a bedtime prayer used by Jewish children, and it tells us how our Lord died: confidently, willingly (John 10:17–18), and victoriously. Those who know Jesus as their Savior may die with the same confidence and assurance (2 Cor. 5:1–8; Phil. 1:20–23).

When our Lord released His spirit, the veil of the temple was torn in two "from the top to the bottom" (Mark 15:38). This miracle announced to the priests and people that the way into God's presence was open for all who would come to Him by faith through Jesus Christ (Heb. 9:1—10:25). No more do sinners need earthly temples, altars, sacrifices, or priests, for all had now been fulfilled in the finished work of the Son of God.

Luke recorded three responses to the events of the last moments of Christ's death. The centurion who was in charge of the execution testified, "Certainly this was a righteous [innocent] man, the Son of God" (Mark 15:39; Luke 23:47). He was greatly impressed by the darkness, the earthquake (Matt. 27:54), and certainly the way Jesus suffered and died. He must have been shocked when Jesus shouted and then instantly died, for victims of crucifixion often lingered for days and did not have the strength to speak.

The people who came to "see the spectacle" began to drift away one by one, some of them beating their breasts as they felt their guilt (Luke 18:13). Were these people believers? Probably not. They were spectators who were attracted to the execution, but certainly they saw and heard enough to convict them of their own sins.

Finally, our Lord's friends were there, including the women who followed Jesus (Luke 8:1–3; 24:22). It is significant that the women were the last at the cross and the first at the tomb on Easter morning.

Jesus and Joseph of Arimathea (23:50–56)

Joseph and his friend Nicodemus (John 19:38–42) were both members of the Jewish council, but they had not been present to vote against Jesus. Mark 14:64 states that the whole council condemned Him, and that could not have happened if Joseph and Nicodemus had been there.

It is likely that Joseph and Nicodemus had learned from the Old Testament Scriptures how Jesus would die, so they agreed to take care of His burial. The new tomb was likely Joseph's, prepared in a garden near Golgotha but not for himself; it was for Jesus. No rich man would prepare his own burial place so near a place of execution and so far from his own home. The two men could well have been hiding in the tomb while Jesus was on the cross, waiting for that moment when He would yield up His life. They would have the spices and the winding sheets all prepared, for they would probably not be able to go shopping for these items on Passover.

When Jesus died, Joseph immediately went to Pilate for permission to have the body, and Nicodemus stayed at Calvary to keep watch. They tenderly took Jesus from the cross, quickly carried Him to the garden, washed the body, and wrapped it with the spices. It was a temporary burial; they would return after the Sabbath to do the job properly. When they laid Jesus into the new tomb, they fulfilled Isaiah 53:9, and they kept the Romans from throwing His body on the garbage dump outside the city. Condemned criminals lost the right to proper burial, but God saw to it that His Son's body was buried with dignity and love.

It was important that the body be buried properly, for God would raise Jesus from the dead. If there were any doubt about His death or burial, that could affect the message and the ministry of the gospel (1 Cor. 15:1–8).

When after six days God finished the work of the "old creation," He rested (Gen. 2:1–3). After six hours, our Lord finished the work of the "new creation" (2 Cor. 5:17), and He rested on the Sabbath in Joseph's tomb.

But that was not the end of the story.

He would rise again!

CHAPTER TWENTY-FOUR
Luke 24
THE SON OF MAN TRIUMPHS!

Christianity is in its very essence a resurrection religion," says Dr. John Stott. "The concept of resurrection lies at its heart. If you remove it, Christianity is destroyed." The resurrection of Jesus Christ affirms to us that He is indeed the Son of God, just as He claimed to be (Rom. 1:4). It also proves that His sacrifice for sin has been accepted and that the work of salvation is completed (Rom. 4:24–25). Those who trust Him can "walk in newness of life" because He is alive and imparts His power to them (Rom. 6:4; Gal. 2:20). Our Lord's resurrection also declares to us that He is the Judge who will come one day and judge the world (Acts 17:30–31).

It is no surprise, then, that Satan has attacked the truth of the resurrection. The first lie that he spawned was that the disciples came and stole Christ's body (Matt. 28:11–15), but it is difficult to imagine how they could have done this. To begin with, the tomb was carefully guarded (Matt. 27:61–66), and it would have been next to impossible for the frightened apostles to overpower the soldiers, open the tomb, and secure the body. But the biggest obstacle is the fact that the apostles themselves *did not believe that He would be resurrected!* Why, then, would they steal His body and try to perpetrate a hoax?

A second lie is that Jesus did not really die on the cross but only swooned, and when He was put into the cool tomb, He revived. But Pilate carefully checked with the centurion to see whether Jesus was dead (Mark 15:44), and the Roman soldiers who broke the legs of the two thieves knew that Jesus had died (John 19:31–34). Furthermore, how could a "cool tomb" transform Christ's body so that He could appear and disappear and walk through closed doors?

The message of the gospel rests on the death of Jesus Christ *and His resurrection* (1 Cor. 15:1–8). The apostles were sent out as witnesses of His resurrection (Acts 1:22), and the emphasis in the book of Acts is on the resurrection of Jesus Christ.

This explains why Luke climaxed his book with a report of some of the appearances of Jesus after He had been raised from the dead. He first appeared to Mary Magdalene (John 20:11–18), then to the "other women" (Matt. 28:9–10), and then to the two men on the way to Emmaus (Luke 24:13–22). At some time, He also appeared to Peter (Luke 24:34) and to His half-brother James (1 Cor. 15:7).

That evening, He appeared to the apostles (Luke 24:36–43), but Thomas was not with them (John 20:19–25). A week later, He appeared to the apostles again, especially for the sake of Thomas (John 20:26–31). He appeared to seven of the apostles when they were fishing at the Sea of Galilee (John 21). He appeared several times to the apostles before His ascension, teaching them and preparing them for their ministry (Acts 1:1–12).

When the believers discovered that Jesus was alive, it made a tremendous difference in their lives.

Perplexed Hearts: He Opens the Tomb (24:1–12)

We do not know at what time Jesus arose from the dead on the first day of the week, but it must have been very early. The earthquake and the angel (Matt. 28:2–4) opened the tomb, not to let Jesus out but to let the witnesses in. "Come and see, go and tell!" is the Easter mandate for the church.

Mary Magdalene had been especially helped by Jesus and was devoted to Him (Luke 8:2). She had lingered at the cross (Mark 15:47), and then she was first at the tomb. With her were Mary the mother of James, Joanna, and other devout women (Luke 24:10), hoping to finish preparing their Lord's body for burial. It was a sad labor of love that was transformed into gladness when they discovered that Jesus was alive.

"Who will roll the stone away?" was their main concern. The Roman soldiers would not break the Roman seal, especially for a group of mourning Jewish women. But God had solved the problem for them; the tomb was open *and there was no body to prepare!*

At this point two angels appeared on the scene. Matthew 28:2 and Mark 16:5 mention only one of the two, the one who gave the message to the women. There was a kind rebuke in his message as he reminded them of their bad memories! More than once, Jesus had told His followers that He would suffer and die and be raised from the dead (Matt. 16:21; 17:22–23; 20:17–19; Luke 9:22, 44; 18:31–34). How sad it is when God's people forget His Word and live defeated lives. Today, the Spirit of God assists us to remember His Word (John 14:26).

Obedient to their commission, the women ran to tell the disciples the good news, but the men did not believe them! (According to Mark 16:14, Jesus later

rebuked them for their unbelief.) Mary Magdalene asked Peter and John to come to examine the tomb (John 20:1–10), and they too saw the proof that Jesus was not there. However, all that the evidence said was that the body was gone and that apparently there had been no violence.

As Mary lingered by the tomb weeping, Jesus Himself appeared to her (John 20:11–18). It is one thing to see the empty tomb and the empty grave-clothes, but quite something else to meet the risen Christ. We today cannot see the evidence in the tomb, but we do have the testimony of the witnesses found in the inspired Word of God. And we can live out our faith in Jesus Christ and know *personally* that He is alive in us (Gal. 2:20).

Keep in mind that these women did not expect to see Jesus alive. They had forgotten His resurrection promises and went to the tomb only to finish anointing His body. To say that they had hallucinations and only thought they saw Jesus is to fly in the face of the evidence. And would this many people hallucinate about the same thing at the same time? Not likely. They became excited witnesses, even to their leaders, that Jesus Christ is alive!

Discouraged Hearts: He Opens Their Eyes (24:13–35)

Emmaus was a small village eight miles northwest of Jerusalem. The two men walking from Jerusalem to Emmaus were discouraged disciples who had no reason to be discouraged. They had heard the reports of the women that the tomb was empty and that Jesus was alive, but they did not believe them. They had hoped that Jesus would redeem Israel (Luke 24:21), but their hopes had been shattered. We get the impression that these men were discouraged and disappointed because God did not do what they wanted Him to do. They saw the glory of the kingdom, but they failed to understand the suffering.

Jesus graciously walked with them and listened to their "animated heated conversation" (Luke 24:17 wuest). No doubt they were quoting various Old Testament prophecies and trying to remember what Jesus had taught, but they were unable to put it all together and come up with an explanation that made sense. Was He a failure or a success? Why did He have to die? Was there a future for the nation?

There is a touch of humor in Luke 24:19 when Jesus asked, "What things?" *He had been at the heart of all that had happened in Jerusalem, and now He was asking them to tell Him what occurred!* How patient our Lord is with us as He listens to us tell Him what He already knows (Rom. 8:34). But we may come "boldly" ("with freedom of speech") to His throne and pour out our hearts to Him, and He will help us (Ps. 62:8; Heb. 4:16).

The longer Cleopas talked, the more he indicted himself and his friend for their unbelief. What more evidence could they want? Witnesses (including apostles) had seen the tomb empty. Angels had announced that Jesus was alive. Witnesses had seen Him alive and heard Him speak. The proof was there!

"Faith comes by hearing, and hearing by the word of God" (Rom. 10:17 NKJV). This explains why Jesus opened the Word to these two men as the three of them walked to Emmaus. Their real problem was not in their heads but in their hearts (see Luke 24:25, 32; and note v. 38). They could have discussed the subject for days and never arrived at a satisfactory answer. What they needed was a fresh understanding of the Word of God, and Jesus gave that understanding to them. He opened the Scriptures and then opened their eyes, and they realized that Jesus was not only alive *but right there with them!*

What was their basic problem? They did not believe all that the prophets had written about the Messiah. That was the problem with most of the Jews in that day: they saw Messiah as a conquering Redeemer, but they did not see Him as a Suffering Servant. As they read the Old Testament, they saw the glory but not the suffering, the crown but not the cross. The teachers in that day were not unlike some of the "success preachers" today, blind to the *total* message of the Bible.

That was some Bible conference, and I wish I could have been there! Imagine the greatest Teacher explaining the greatest themes from the greatest Book and bringing the greatest blessings to men's lives: eyes open to see Him, hearts open to receive the Word, and lips open to tell others what Jesus said to them!

Perhaps Jesus started at Genesis 3:15, the first promise of the Redeemer, and traced that promise through the Scriptures. He may have lingered at Genesis 22, which tells of Abraham placing his only beloved son on the altar. Surely He touched on Passover, the Levitical sacrifices, the tabernacle ceremonies, the day of Atonement, the serpent in the wilderness, the Suffering Servant in Isaiah 53, and the prophetic messages of Psalms 22 and 69. *The key to understanding the Bible is to see Jesus Christ on every page.* He did not teach them only doctrine or prophecy; He taught "the things concerning himself" (Luke 24:27).

These men had talked to Jesus and listened to Jesus, and when He made as though He would go on alone, they asked Jesus to come home with them. *They had been won by the Word of God,* and they did not even know who the Stranger was. All they knew was that their hearts were "burning" within them, and they wanted the blessing to last.

The more we receive the Word of God, the more we will want to fellowship with the God of the Word. The hymn writer expressed it perfectly: "Beyond the sacred page / I seek Thee, Lord." Understanding Bible knowledge can lead to a "big head" (1 Cor. 8:1), but receiving Bible truth and walking with the Savior will lead to a burning heart.

Jesus opened the Scriptures to them, and then He opened their eyes so that they recognized Him.

Now they knew for themselves that Jesus was alive. They had the evidence of the open tomb, the angels, the witnesses, the Scriptures and now their own personal experience with the Lord. The fact that Jesus vanished did not mean that He abandoned them, for He was with them even though they could not see Him, and they would see Him again.

The best evidence that we have understood the Bible and met the living Christ is that we have something exciting to share with others. The two men immediately left Emmaus and returned to Jerusalem to tell the believers that they had met Jesus. But when they arrived, the apostles and the others *told them* that Jesus was alive and had appeared to Peter! What a difference it would make in our church services if everybody who gathered came to tell about meeting the living Christ! If our services are "dead" it is probably because we are not really walking with and listening to the living Savior.

The "breaking of bread" (Luke 24:30, 35) refers to a meal and not to the Lord's Supper. As far as we know, the apostles were the only ones Jesus had instructed about the Lord's Supper, and it was not likely that our Lord would celebrate it at this time. Jesus revealed Himself to them during a common meal, and that is often how He works. We must learn to see Him in the everyday things of life. However, as we do celebrate the Lord's Supper from time to time, we want Jesus to reveal Himself to us in a new way, and we must not be satisfied with anything less.

Troubled Hearts: He Opens Their Minds (24:36–46)

So many exciting things had happened that day and so much was unexplained that ten of the apostles, plus other believers, met together that evening and shared their witness with one another. While Cleopas and his friend were telling their story, *Jesus Himself appeared in the room!* And the doors were shut (John 20:19)!

You would have expected the believers to heave a great sigh of relief and sing a hymn of praise, but instead they became terrified, frightened, and troubled (Luke 24:37–38). They thought a ghost had appeared! It all happened so suddenly that they were totally unprepared, even though several of them had already seen the risen Christ. Mark 16:14 suggests that the condition of their hearts had something to do with the expression of their fears.

Jesus sought to calm them. The first thing He did was to give them His blessing: "Peace be unto you!" He even repeated the blessing (John 20:19–21). "The God of peace" had raised Jesus from the dead, and there was nothing for them to fear (Heb. 13:20–21). Because of His sacrifice on the cross, men and women could now have peace with God (Rom. 5:1) and enjoy the peace of God (Phil. 4:6–7).

The next thing He did to calm them was to show them His wounded hands and feet (Ps. 22:16) and assure them that He was not a ghost. Songwriters sometimes mention His "scars," but the record says nothing about "scars." The "prints" of Calvary were on His glorified body (John 20:24–29), and they are still there (Rev. 5:6, 9, 12). It has well been said that the only work of man now in heaven is the marks of Calvary on the body of the exalted Savior.

Jesus even ate some honey and fish to prove to His doubting followers that He was indeed alive and real, and He even invited them to *feel* His body (Luke 24:39; 1 John 1:1). With our limited knowledge, we cannot explain how a human body can be solid flesh and bones and still pass through closed doors and appear and disappear, or how it can be glorified and still carry the marks of the cross. We do know that we shall one day be like Him and share His glory (1 John 3:1–2).

Luke 24:41 describes a perplexing emotion: "they believed not for joy." It was just too good to be true! Jacob had this same feeling when he got the news that Joseph was alive (Gen. 45:26–28), and the nation of Israel experienced it when God gave them a great deliverance (Ps. 126:1–3). Jesus had told His disciples that they would rejoice when they saw Him again, and the promise was fulfilled (John 16:22).

The final source of peace and assurance is the Word of God, so our Lord "opened their understanding" of the Old Testament Scriptures, just as He had done with the Emmaus disciples. After all, the believers were not being sent into the world to share their own personal experiences but to share the truths of the Word of God. We today cannot touch and feel the Lord Jesus, nor is it necessary that we do so, but we can rest our faith on the Word of God (1 John 1:1–5).

Jesus not only enabled them to understand the law, the prophets, and the psalms, but He also reminded them of what He had taught them, and He explained how it all fit together. Now they began to understand the necessity for His suffering and death and how the cross related to the promise of the kingdom (see 1 Peter 1:10–12). What a privilege it was for them to listen to Jesus expound the Word!

Joyful Hearts: He Opens Their Lips (24:47–53)

But privilege always brings responsibility; they were to be witnesses of all that He had said and done (Acts 1:8). A witness is somebody who sincerely tells what he has seen and heard (Acts 4:20), and the word *witness* is used in one way or another twenty-nine times in the book of Acts. As Christians, we are not judges or prosecuting attorneys sent to condemn the world. We are witnesses who point to Jesus Christ and tell lost sinners how to be saved.

How could a group of common people ever hope to fulfill that kind of a commission? God promised to provide the power (Luke 24:49; Acts 1:8), and He did. On the day of Pentecost, the Holy Spirit came upon the church and empowered them to preach the Word (Acts 2). After Pentecost, the Spirit continued to fill them with great power (see Acts 4:33).

Witnessing is not something that we do for the Lord; it is something that He does through us, *if* we are filled with the Holy Spirit. There is a great difference between a "sales talk" and a Spirit-empowered witness. "People do not come to Christ at the end of an argument," said Vance Havner. "Simon Peter came to Jesus because Andrew went after him with a testimony." We go forth in the authority of His name, in the power of His spirit, heralding His gospel of His grace.

Luke 24:50–52 should be compared with Mark 16:19–20 and Acts 1:9–12. For some reason, our Lord's ascension is not given the prominence in the church that it deserves. Think of what it meant to Him to return to heaven and sit on the throne of glory (John 17:5, 11)! His ascension is proof that He has conquered every enemy and that He reigns supremely "far above all" (Eph. 1:18–23).

In heaven today, our Lord ministers as our High Priest (Heb. 7:25) and our Advocate (1 John 2:1). As High Priest, He gives us the grace we need to face testing and temptation (Heb. 4:14–16); and if we fail, as Advocate He forgives and restores us when we confess our sins (1 John 1:6–10). As the glorified Head of the church, Jesus Christ is equipping His people to live for Him and serve Him in this present world (Eph. 4:7–16; Heb. 13:20–21). Through the Word of God and prayer, He is ministering to us by His Spirit and making us more like Himself.

Of course, He is also preparing in heaven a home for His people (John 14:1–6), and one day He will return and take us to be with Him forever.

The last thing our Lord did was to bless His people, and the first thing they did was to worship Him! The two always go together, for as we truly worship Him, He will share His blessings. He not only opened their lips to witness, but He also opened their lips to worship and praise Him!

Dr. Luke opened his gospel with a scene in the temple (Luke 1:8ff.), and he closed his gospel the same way (Luke 24:53). But what a contrast between the unbelieving, silent priest and the trusting, joyful saints! Luke has explained how Jesus went to Jerusalem and accomplished the work of redemption. His book begins and ends in Jerusalem. But his next book, The Acts of the Apostles, would explain how that gospel traveled from Jerusalem to Rome!

Is the gospel going out to the ends of the earth from your Jerusalem?

JOHN

OUTLINE

Key theme: Jesus is the Christ; believe and live!
Key verse: John 20:31

I. OPPORTUNITY (1:15—6:71)
He presents Himself to
A. His disciples—1:19—2:12
B. The Jews—2:13—3:36
C. The Samaritans—4:1–54
D. The Jewish leaders—5:1–47
E. The multitudes—6:1–71

II. OPPOSITION (7—12)
There is conflict with the Jewish leaders over
A. Moses—7:1—8:11
B. Abraham—8:12–59
C. Who Messiah is—9:1—10:42
D. His miraculous power—11:1—12:36
E. They would not believe on Him—12:37–50

III. OUTCOME (13—21)
A. The faith of the disciples—13—17
B. The unbelief of the Jews—18—19
C. The victory of Christ—20—21

CONTENTS

CHAPTER ONE
John 1

GOD IS HERE!

But will God indeed dwell on the earth?" asked Solomon as he dedicated the temple (1 Kings 8:27). A good question, indeed! God's glory had dwelt in the tabernacle (Ex. 40:34), and in the temple (1 Kings 8:10–11), but that glory had departed from disobedient Israel (Ezek. 9:3; 10:4, 18; 11:22–23).

Then a marvelous thing happened: the glory of God came to His people again, in the person of His Son, Jesus Christ. The writers of the four gospels have given us "snapshots" of our Lord's life on earth, for no complete biography could ever be written (John 21:25). Matthew wrote with his fellow Jews in mind and emphasized that Jesus of Nazareth had fulfilled the Old Testament prophecies. Mark wrote for the busy Romans. Whereas Matthew emphasized the King, Mark presented the Servant, ministering to needy people. Luke wrote his gospel for the Greeks and introduced them to the sympathetic Son of Man.

But it was given to John, the beloved disciple, to write a book for both Jews and Gentiles, presenting Jesus as the Son of God. We know that John had Gentiles in mind as well as Jews, because he often "interpreted" Jewish words or customs for his readers (John 1:38, 41–42; 5:2; 9:7; 19:13, 17; 20:16). His emphasis to the Jews was that Jesus not only fulfilled the Old Testament prophecies, but He also fulfilled the *types.* Jesus is the Lamb of God (John 1:29) and the Ladder from heaven to earth (John 1:51; and see Gen. 28). He is the New Temple (John 2:19–21), and He gives a new birth (John 3:4ff.). He is the serpent lifted up (John 3:14) and the Bread of God that came down from heaven (John 6:35ff.).

Whereas the first three Gospels major on describing *events* in the life of Christ, John emphasized the *meaning* of these events. For example, all four gospels record the feeding of the five thousand, but only John records Jesus' sermon on "The Bread of Life," which followed that miracle when He interpreted it for the people.

But there is one major theme that runs throughout John's gospel: Jesus Christ is the Son of God, and if you commit yourself to Him, He will give you eternal life (John 20:31). In this first chapter, John recorded seven names and titles of Jesus that identify Him as eternal God.

The Word (1:1–3, 14)

Much as our words reveal to others our hearts and minds, so Jesus Christ is God's "Word" to reveal His heart and mind to us. "He that hath seen me hath seen the Father" (John 14:9). A word is composed of letters, and Jesus Christ is "Alpha and Omega" (Rev. 1:11), the first and last letters of the Greek alphabet. According to Hebrews 1:1–3, Jesus Christ is God's *last* Word to mankind, for He is the climax of divine revelation.

Jesus Christ is the eternal Word (vv. 1–2). He existed in the beginning, not because He had a beginning as a creature, but because He is eternal. He *is God* and He was *with* God. "Before Abraham was, I am" (John 8:58).

Jesus Christ is the creative Word (v. 3). There is certainly a parallel between John 1:1 and Genesis 1:1, the "new creation" and the "old creation." God created the worlds through His word: "And God said, 'Let there be …'"/ "For he spake, and it was done; he commanded, and it stood fast" (Ps. 33:9). God created all things through Jesus Christ (Col. 1:16), which means that Jesus is not a created being. He is eternal God.

The verb *was made* is perfect tense in the Greek, which means a "completed act." Creation is finished. It is not a process still going on, even though God is certainly at work in His creation (John 5:17). Creation is not a process; it is a finished product.

Jesus Christ is the incarnate Word (v. 14). He was not a phantom or a spirit when He ministered on earth, nor was His body a mere illusion. John and the other disciples each had a personal experience that convinced them of the reality of the body of Jesus (1 John 1:1–2). Even though John's emphasis is the deity of Christ, he makes it clear that the Son of God came *in the flesh* and was subject to the sinless infirmities of human nature.

In his gospel, John points out that Jesus was weary (John 4:6) and thirsty (John 4:7), He groaned within (John 11:33) and openly wept (John 11:35). On the cross, He thirsted (John 19:28), died (John 19:30), and bled (John 19:34). After His resurrection, He proved to Thomas and the other disciples that He still had a real body (John 20:24–29), howbeit, a glorified body.

How was the "Word made flesh"? By the miracle of the Virgin Birth (Isa. 7:14; Matt. 1:18–25; Luke 1:26–38). He took on Himself sinless human nature and identified with us in every aspect of life from birth to death. "The Word" was not an abstract concept of philosophy, but a real Person who could be seen, touched, and heard. Christianity is Christ, and Christ is God.

The revelation of God's glory is an important theme in the gospel. Jesus revealed God's glory in His person, His works, and His words. John recorded seven wonderful signs (miracles) that openly declared the glory of God (John 2:11). The glory of the old covenant of law was a fading glory, but the glory of the new covenant in Christ is an increasing glory (see 2 Cor. 3). The law could reveal sin, but it could never remove sin. Jesus Christ came with *fullness* of grace and truth, and this fullness is available to all who will trust Him (John 1:16).

The Light (1:4–13)

Life is a key theme in John's gospel; it is used thirty-six times. What are the essentials for human life? There are at least four: light (if the sun went out, everything would die), air, water, and food. Jesus is all of these! He is the Light of life and the Light of the world (John 8:12). He is the "Sun of righteousness" (Mal. 4:2). By His Holy Spirit, He gives us the "breath of life" (John 3:8; 20:22), as well as the Water of life (John 4:10, 13–14; 7:37–39). Finally, Jesus is the Living Bread of Life that came down from heaven (John 6:35ff.*).* He not only has life and gives life, but he is life (John 14:6).

Light and darkness are recurring themes in John's gospel. God is light (1 John 1:5), while Satan is "the power of darkness" (Luke 22:53). People love either the light or the darkness, and this love controls their actions (John 3:16–19). Those who believe on Christ are the "sons of light" (John 12:35–36). Just as the first creation began with "Let there be light!" so the new creation begins with the entrance of light into the heart of the believer (2 Cor. 4:3–6). The coming of Jesus Christ into the world was the dawning of a new day for sinful man (Luke 1:78–79).

You would think that blind sinners would welcome the light, but such is not always the case. The coming of the true light brought conflict as the powers of darkness opposed it. A literal translation of John 1:5 reads, "And the light keeps on shining in the darkness, and the darkness has not overcome it or understood it." The Greek verb can mean "to overcome" or "to grasp, to understand." Throughout the gospel of John, you will see both attitudes revealed: people will not understand what the Lord is saying and doing and, as a result, they will oppose Him. John 7—12 records the growth of that opposition, which ultimately led to the crucifixion of Christ.

Whenever Jesus taught a spiritual truth, His listeners interpreted it in a material or physical way. The light was unable to penetrate the darkness in their minds. This was true when He spoke about the temple of His body (John 2:19–21), the new birth (John 3:4),

the living water (John 4:11), eating His flesh (John 6:51ff.), spiritual freedom (John 8:30–36), death as sleep (John 11:11–13), and many other spiritual truths. Satan strives to keep people in the darkness, because darkness means death and hell, while light means life and heaven.

This fact helps explain the ministry of John the Baptist (John 1:6–8). John was sent as a witness to Jesus Christ, to tell people that the Light had come into the world. The nation of Israel, in spite of all its spiritual advantages, was blind to their own Messiah! The word *witness* is a key word in this book; John uses the noun fourteen times and the verb thirty-three times. John the Baptist was one of many people who bore witness to Jesus,: "This is the Son of God!" Alas, John the Baptist was martyred and the Jewish leaders did nothing to prevent it.

Why did the nation reject Jesus Christ? Because they "knew him not." They were spiritually ignorant. Jesus is the "true Light"—the original of which every other light is a copy—but the Jews were content with the copies. They had Moses and the law, the temple and the sacrifices, but they did not comprehend that these "lights" pointed to the true Light who was the fulfillment, the completion, of the Old Testament religion.

As you study John's gospel, you will find Jesus teaching the people that He is the fulfillment of all that was typified in the law. It was not enough to be born a Jew; they had to be born again, born from above (John 3). He deliberately performed two miracles on the Sabbath to teach them that He had a new rest to give them (John 5; 9). He was the satisfying manna (John 6) and the life-giving Water (John 7:37–39). He is the Shepherd of a new flock (John 10:16), and He is a new Vine (John 15). But the people were so shackled by religious tradition that they could not understand spiritual truth. Jesus came to His own world that He had created, but His own people, Israel, could not understand Him and would not receive Him.

They saw His works and heard His words. They observed His perfect life. He gave them every opportunity to grasp the truth, believe, and be saved. Jesus is the way, but they would not walk with Him (John 6:66–71). He is the truth, but they would not believe Him (John 12:37ff.). He is the life, and they crucified Him!

But sinners today need not commit those same blunders. John 1:12–13 gives us the marvelous promise of God that anyone who receives Christ will be born again and enter the family of God! John says more about this new birth in John 3, but he points out here that it is a spiritual birth from God, not a physical birth that depends on human nature.

The Light is still shining! Have you *personally* received the Light and become a child of God?

The Son of God (1:15–28, 49)

John the Baptist is one of the most important persons

in the New Testament. He is mentioned at least eighty-nine times. John had the special privilege of introducing Jesus to the nation of Israel. He also had the difficult task of preparing the nation to receive their Messiah. He called them to repent of their sins and to prove that repentance by being baptized and then living changed lives.

John summarized what John the Baptist had to say about Jesus Christ (John 1:15–18). First, *He is eternal* (John 1:15). John the Baptist was actually born six months before Jesus (Luke 1:36), so in this statement he is referring to our Lord's preexistence, not His birth date. Jesus existed before John the Baptist was ever conceived.

Jesus Christ *has fullness of grace and truth* (John 1:16–17). Grace is God's favor and kindness bestowed on those who do not deserve it and cannot earn it. If God dealt with us only according to truth, none of us would survive, but He deals with us on the basis of grace *and* truth. Jesus Christ, in His life, death, and resurrection, met all the demands of the law; now God is free to share fullness of grace with those who trust Christ. Grace without truth would be deceitful, and truth without grace would be condemning.

In John 1:17, John did not suggest that there was no grace under the law of Moses, because there was. Each sacrifice was an expression of the grace of God. The law also revealed God's truth. But in Jesus Christ, grace and truth reach their fullness, and this fullness is available to us. We are saved by grace (Eph. 2:8–9), but we also live by grace (1 Cor. 15:10) and depend on God's grace in all that we do. We can receive one grace after another, for "He giveth more grace" (James 4:6). In John 1:17, John hinted that a whole new order had come in, replacing the Mosaic system.

Finally, *Jesus Christ reveals God to us* (John 1:18). As to His essence, God is invisible (1 Tim. 1:17; Heb. 11:27). Man can see God revealed in nature (Ps. 19:1–6; Rom. 1:20) and in His mighty works in history; but he cannot see God Himself. Jesus Christ reveals God to us, for He is "the image of the invisible God" (Col. 1:15) and "the express image of his person" (Heb. 1:3). The word translated "declared" gives us our English word *exegesis,* which means "to explain, to unfold, to lead the way." Jesus Christ explains God to us and interprets Him for us. We simply cannot understand God apart from knowing His Son, Jesus Christ.

The word *Son* is used for the first time in John's gospel as a title for Jesus Christ (John 1:18). The phrase "only-begotten" means "unique, the only one of its kind." It does not suggest that there was a time when the Son was not, and then the Father brought Him into being. Jesus Christ is eternal God; He has always existed.

At least nine times in John's gospel, Jesus is called "the Son of God" (John 1:34, 49; 3:18; 5:25; 10:36; 11:4, 27; 19:7; 20:31). You will recall that John had as his purpose in writing to convince us that Jesus is the Son of God (John 20:31). At least nineteen times,

Jesus is referred to as "the Son." He is not only the Son of God, but He is God the Son. Even the demons admitted this (Mark 3:11; Luke 4:41).

John the Baptist is one of six persons named in the gospel of John who gave witness that Jesus is God. The others are Nathanael (John 1:49), Peter (John 6:69), the blind man who was healed (John 9:35–38), Martha (John 11:27), and Thomas (John 20:28). If you add our Lord Himself (John 5:25; 10:36), then you have seven clear witnesses.

John gave the record of four days in the life of John the Baptist, Jesus, and the first disciples. He continues this sequence in John 2 and presents, as it were, a "week" in the "new creation" that parallels the creation week in Genesis 1.

On the first day (John 1:19–24), a committee from the Jewish religious leaders interrogated John the Baptist. These men had every right to investigate John and his ministry, since they were the custodians and guardians of the faith. They asked him several questions and he clearly answered them.

"Who are you?" was a logical question. Was he the promised Messiah? Was he the prophet Elijah who was supposed to come before the Messiah appeared (Mal. 4:5)? Great crowds had gathered to hear John, and many people had been baptized. Though John did no miracles (John 10:41), it was possible the people thought that he was the promised Messiah.

John denied being either Elijah or the Messiah. (In one sense, he was the promised Elijah. See Matt. 17:10–13.) John had nothing to say about himself because he was sent to talk about Jesus! Jesus is the Word; John was but "a voice"—and you cannot see a voice! John pointed back to Isaiah's prophecy (Isa. 40:1–3) and affirmed that he was the fulfillment.

Having ascertained who John was, the committee then asked what he was doing. "Why are you baptizing?" John got his authority to baptize, not from men, but from heaven, because he was commissioned by God (Matt. 21:23–32). The Jewish religious leaders in that day baptized Gentiles who wanted to adopt the Jewish faith, *but John baptized Jews!*

John explained that his baptism was in water, but that the Messiah would come and baptize with a spiritual baptism. Again, John made it clear that he was not establishing a new religion or seeking to exalt himself. He was pointing people to the Savior, the Son of God (John 1:34). We shall learn later that it was through baptism that Jesus Christ would be presented to the people of Israel.

Lamb of God (1:29–34)

This is the second day of the week that the apostle John recorded, and no doubt some of the same committee members were present to hear John the Baptist's message. This time, he called Jesus "the Lamb of God," a title he would repeat the next day (John 1:35–36). In one sense, the message of the Bible can be summed up in this title. The question in the Old Testament is,

"Where is the lamb?" (Gen. 22:7). In the four gospels, the emphasis is "Behold the Lamb of God!" Here He is! After you have trusted Him, you sing with the heavenly choir, "Worthy is the Lamb" (Rev. 5:12).

The people of Israel were familiar with lambs for the sacrifices. At Passover, each family had to have a lamb, and during the year, two lambs a day were sacrificed at the temple altar, plus all the other lambs brought for personal sacrifices. Those lambs were brought by men to men, but here is God's Lamb, given by God to men! Those lambs could not take away sin, but the Lamb of God can take away sin. Those lambs were for Israel alone, but this Lamb would shed His blood for the whole world!

What does John's baptism have to do with Jesus as the Lamb of God? It is generally agreed by scholars of all denominations that, in the New Testament, baptism was by immersion. It pictured death, burial, and resurrection. When John the Baptist baptized Jesus, Jesus and John were picturing the "baptism" Jesus would endure *on the cross* when He would die as the sacrificial Lamb of God (Isa. 53:7; Luke 12:50). It would be through death, burial, and resurrection that the Lamb of God would "fulfill all righteousness" (Matt. 3:15).

Perhaps John was mistaken. Perhaps John was not sure that Jesus of Nazareth was the Lamb of God or the Son of God. But the Father made it clear to John just who Jesus is by sending the Spirit like a dove to light on Him. What a beautiful picture of the Trinity!

The Messiah (1:35–42)

This is now the third day in the sequence. The seventh day included the wedding at Cana (John 2:1), and since Jewish weddings traditionally were on Wednesdays, it would make this third day the Sabbath day. But it was not a day of rest for either John the Baptist or Jesus, for John was preaching and Jesus was gathering disciples.

The two disciples of John who followed Jesus were John, the writer of the gospel, and his friend Andrew. John the Baptist was happy when people left him to follow Jesus, because his ministry focused on Jesus. "He must increase, but I must decrease" (John 3:30).

When Jesus asked them, "What are you seeking?" He was forcing them to define their purposes and goals. Were they looking for a revolutionary leader to overthrow Rome? Then they had better join the Zealots! Little did Andrew and John realize that day how their lives would be transformed by the Son of God.

"Where are You dwelling?" may have suggested, "If You are too busy now, we can visit later." But Jesus invited them to spend the day with Him (it was 10 a.m.), and no doubt He told them something of His mission, revealed their own hearts to them, and answered their questions. They were both so impressed that they found their brothers and brought them to Jesus. Andrew found Simon and John brought James.

Indeed, they *were* their brothers' keepers (Gen. 4:9)! Whenever you find Andrew in John's gospel, he is bringing somebody to Jesus: his brother, the lad with the loaves and fishes (John 6:8), and the Greeks who wanted to see Jesus (John 12:20–21). No sermons from Andrew are recorded, but he certainly preached great sermons by his actions as a personal soul winner!

"We have found the Messiah!" was the witness Andrew gave to Simon. *Messiah* is a Hebrew word that means "anointed," and the Greek equivalent is "Christ." To the Jews, it was the same as "Son of God" (see Matt. 26:63–64; Mark 14:61–62; Luke 22:67–70). In the Old Testament, prophets, priests, and kings were anointed and thereby set apart for special service. Kings were especially called "God's anointed" (1 Sam. 26:11; Ps. 89:20); so, when the Jews spoke about their Messiah, they were thinking of the king who would come to deliver them and establish the kingdom.

There was some confusion among the Jewish teachers as to what the Messiah would do. Some saw Him as a suffering sacrifice (as in Isa. 53), while others saw a splendid king (as in Isa. 9 and 11). Jesus had to explain even to His own followers that the cross had to come before the crown, that He must suffer before He could enter into His glory (Luke 24:13–35). Whether or not Jesus was indeed the Messiah was a crucial problem that challenged the Jews in that day (John 7:26, 40–44; 9:22; 10:24).

Simon's interview with Jesus changed his life. It also gave him a new name—*Peter* in the Greek, *Cephas* in the Aramaic that Jesus spoke—both of which mean "a rock." It took a great deal of work for Jesus to transform weak Simon into a rock, but He did it! "Thou art … thou shalt be" is a great encouragement to all who trust Christ. Truly, He gives us the "power to become" (John 1:12).

It is worth noting that Andrew and John trusted Christ through the faithful preaching of John the Baptist. Peter and James came to Christ because of the compassionate personal work of their brothers. Later on, Jesus would win Philip personally, and then Philip would witness to Nathanael and bring him to Jesus. Each man's experience is different, because God uses various means to bring sinners to the Savior. The important thing is that we trust Christ and then seek to bring others to Him.

The King of Israel (1:43–49)

Jesus called Philip personally and Philip trusted Him and followed Him. We do not know what kind of heart preparation Philip experienced, for usually God prepares a person before He calls him. We do know that Philip proved his faith by seeking to share it with his friend Nathanael.

John 21:2 suggests that at least seven of our Lord's disciples were fishermen, including Nathanael. Fishermen are courageous and stick to the job, no matter how difficult it may be. But Nathanael started out a doubter: he did not believe that anything worthwhile could come out of Nazareth. Our Lord was born in Bethlehem, but He grew up in Nazareth and bore that stigma (Matt. 2:19–23). To be called "a Nazarene" (Acts 24:5) meant to be looked down on and rejected.

When Nathanael hesitated and argued, Philip adopted our Lord's own words: "Come and see" (John 1:39). Later on, Jesus would invite, "Come … and drink" (John 7:37) and, "Come and dine" (John 21:12). "Come" is the great invitation of God's grace.

When Nathanael came to Jesus, he discovered that the Lord already knew all about him! What a shock! By calling him "an Israelite in whom is no guile," Jesus was certainly referring to Jacob, the ancestor of the Jews, a man who used guile to trick his brother, his father, and his father-in-law. Jacob's name was changed to "Israel, a prince with God." The reference to "Jacob's ladder" in John 1:51 confirms this.

When Jesus revealed His knowledge of Nathanael, where he had been and what he had been doing, this was enough to convince the man that Jesus indeed was "the Son of God, the King of Israel." His experience was like that of the Samaritan woman at the well. "When he [Messiah] is come, he will tell us all things.… Come, see a man who told me all things that ever I did" (John 4:25, 29). The revealing of the human heart should also take place in the ministry of local churches (1 Cor. 14:23–35).

When Philip witnessed to Nathanael, the evidence he gave was Moses and the prophets (John 1:45). Perhaps Jesus gave Philip a "quick course" in the Old Testament messianic prophecies, as He did with the Emmaus disciples (Luke 24:13ff.). It is always good to tie our personal witness to the Word of God.

"King of Israel" would be a title similar to "Messiah, anointed One," for the kings were always God's anointed (see Ps. 2, especially vv. 2, 6–7). At one point in His ministry, the crowds wanted to make Jesus king, but He refused them (John 6:15ff.). He did present Himself as King (John 12:10ff.), and He affirmed to Pilate that He was born a king (John 18:33–37).

Some students believe that Nathanael and Bartholomew are the same person. John never mentions Bartholomew in his gospel, but the other three writers name Bartholomew and not Nathanael. Philip is linked with Bartholomew in the lists of names (Matt. 10:3; Mark 3:18; Luke 6:14), so it is possible that the two men were "paired off" and served together. It was not unusual in that day for one man to have two different names.

The Son of Man (1:50–51)

"Son of man" was one of our Lord's favorite titles for Himself; it is used eighty-three times in the Gospels and at least thirteen times in John. The title speaks of both the deity and humanity of Jesus. The vision in Daniel 7:13 presents the "Son of man" in a definite messianic setting, and Jesus used the title in the same way (Matt. 26:64).

As Son of Man, Jesus is the "living link" between heaven and earth. This explains His reference to "Jacob's ladder" in Genesis 28. Jacob the fugitive thought he was alone, but God had sent the angels to guard and guide him. Christ is God's "ladder" between heaven and earth. "No man cometh to the Father, but by me" (John 14:6). Often in this gospel, you will find Jesus reminding people that He came down from heaven. The Jewish people knew that "Son of man" was a name for their Messiah (John 12:34).

At the close of that fourth day, Jesus had six believing men who were His disciples. They did not immediately "forsake all and follow him"; that was to come later. But they had trusted Him and experienced His power. In the three years that lay ahead, they would grow in their faith, learn more about Jesus, and one day take His place on the earth so that the Word might be carried to all mankind.

Jesus of Nazareth is God come in the flesh. When Philip called Him "the son of Joseph," he was not denying Jesus' virgin birth or divine nature. That was merely His legal identification, for a Jewish person was identified according to who his father was (John 6:42). The witness of this entire chapter is clear: Jesus of Nazareth is God come in the flesh!

God is here!

CHAPTER TWO
John 2
LEARNING ABOUT JESUS

The six disciples who now trusted Jesus started on their lifelong walk with Him and from the beginning began to learn more about Him. We who read the gospel record in its entirety are prone to take these events for granted, but to the disciples, each day and each new event brought marvels that were difficult to understand. In this chapter alone, John recorded three wonderful revelations of Jesus Christ.

His Glory (2:1–12)

"The third day" means three days after the call of Nathanael (John 1:45–51). Since that was the fourth day of the week recorded in John (John 1:19, 29, 35, 43), the wedding took place on "the seventh day" of this "new creation week." Throughout his gospel, John makes it clear that Jesus was on a divine schedule, obeying the will of the Father.

Jewish tradition required that virgins be married on a Wednesday, while widows were married on a Thursday. Being the "seventh day" of John's special week, Jesus would be expected to rest, just as God rested on the seventh day (Gen. 2:1–3). But sin had interrupted God's Sabbath rest, and it was necessary for both the Father and the Son to work (John 5:17; 9:4). In fact, John recorded two specific miracles that Jesus deliberately performed on Sabbath days (John 5; 9).

At this wedding, we see Jesus in three different roles: the Guest, the Son, and the Host.

Jesus the Guest (vv. 1–2). Our Lord was not a recluse, as was John the Baptist (Matt. 11:16–19). He accepted invitations to social events, even though His enemies used this practice to accuse Him (Luke 15:1–2). Our Lord entered into the normal experiences of life and sanctified them by His presence. Wise is that couple who invite Jesus to their wedding!

He was accompanied by His mother and His six disciples. Perhaps it was the addition of seven more people that helped create the crisis, but it must have been a small wedding feast if this were the case. We have reason to believe that our Lord's earthly family was not prosperous, and it is likely that their friends were not wealthy people. Perhaps the shortage of wine was related to a low-budget feast.

Were Jesus and His disciples invited because of Mary, or because of Nathanael (John 21:2)? Our Lord was not yet well known; He had performed no miracles as yet. It was not likely that He was invited because the people knew who He was. It was probably His relationship with Mary that brought about the invitation.

Jesus the Son (vv. 3–5). Since Jewish wedding feasts lasted a week, it was necessary for the groom to have adequate provisions. For one thing, it would be embarrassing to run out of either food or wine, and a family guilty of such gaucherie could actually be fined! So, to run out of wine could be costly both financially and socially.

Why did Mary approach Jesus about the problem? Did she actually expect Him to do something special to meet the need? Certainly she knew who He was, even though she did not declare this wonderful truth to others. She must have been very close to either the bride or the bridegroom to have such a personal concern for the success of the festivities, or even to know that the supply of wine was depleted. Perhaps Mary was assisting in the preparation and serving of the meal.

Mary did not tell Jesus what to do; she simply reported the problem. (Compare the message of Mary and Martha to Jesus, when Lazarus was sick—John 11:3.) Jesus' reply seems a bit abrupt, and even harsh, but such is not the case. "Woman" was a polite way to address her (John 19:26; 20:13), and His statement merely means, "Why are you getting Me involved in this matter?" He was making it clear to His mother that He was no longer under her supervision (it is likely that Joseph was dead), but that from now on, He would be doing what the Father wanted Him to do. There had been a hint of this some years before (Luke 2:40–52).

At this point, John introduced one of the key elements of his record, the idea of "the hour." Jesus lived on a "heavenly timetable," marked out for Him by the Father. (See John 7:30; 8:20; 12:23; 13:1; 17:1; and note also the words of Jesus as recorded in John 11:9–10.) As you study John's gospel, you will observe how this concept of "the hour" is developed.

Mary's words to the servants reveal that she was willing to let her Son do whatever He pleased, and that she trusted Him to do what was right. It would be wise for all of us to obey what she said! It is worth noting that it was Jesus, not Mary, who took command and solved the problem; and that Mary pointed, not to herself, but to Jesus.

Jesus the Host (vv. 6–12). Our Lord's first miracle was not a spectacular event that everybody witnessed. Mary, the disciples, and the servants knew what had happened, but nobody else at the feast had any idea that a miracle had taken place. His first miracle was a quiet event at a wedding in contrast to His last miracle recorded by John (John 11), a public event after a funeral.

Each of the six stone waterpots could contain about twenty gallons each. However, we are not told that all of the available water in the jars turned into wine. Only that which the servants drew out and served was transformed into wine. The quality of this new wine was so superior that the man in charge of the banquet highly praised it, and, of course, the groom's family basked in the glory of the compliments.

The fact that this was "the beginning of miracles" automatically declares as false the stories about the miracles performed by Jesus when He was an infant or a young child. They are nothing but superstitious fables and ought to be rejected by anyone who accepts the authority of the Bible.

The miracle did something for His disciples. It revealed His glory (John 1:14) and gave them a stronger foundation for their faith. Though miracles *alone* are insufficient evidence for declaring Jesus to be the Son of God (2 Thess. 2:9–10), the cumulative effect of miracle after miracle should certainly convince them of His deity. The disciples had to begin somewhere, and over the months, their faith deepened as they got to know Jesus better.

But there is certainly more to this miracle than simply meeting a human need and saving a family from social embarrassment. The gospel of John, unlike the other three Gospels, seeks to share the *inner meaning*—the spiritual significance—of our Lord's works, so that each miracle is a "sermon in action." We must be careful not to "spiritualize" these events so that they lose their historical moorings, but, at the same time, we must not be so shackled to history that we are blind to (as A.T. Pierson used to say) "His story."

To begin with, the word John used in his book is not *dunamis,* which emphasizes power, but *sĩmeion,* which means "a sign." What is a sign? Something that points beyond itself to something greater. It was not enough for people to believe in Jesus' works; they had to believe in Him and in the Father who sent Him (John 5:14–24). This explains why Jesus often added a sermon to the miracle and in that sermon interpreted the sign. In John 5, the healing of the paralytic on the Sabbath opened the way for a message on His deity, "the Lord of the Sabbath." The feeding of the five thousand (John 6) led naturally into a sermon on the Bread of Life.

If our Lord had preached a sermon after He turned the water into wine, what might He have said? For one thing, He likely would have told the people that the world's joy always runs out and cannot be regained, but the joy He gives is ever new and ever satisfying. (In the Scriptures, wine is a symbol of joy. See Judg. 9:13; Ps. 104:15.) The world offers the best at the first, and then, once you are "hooked," things start to get worse. But Jesus continues to offer that which is best until we one day enjoy the finest blessings in the eternal kingdom (Luke 22:18).

But our Lord would certainly have a special message here for His people, Israel. In the Old Testament, the nation is pictured as "married" to God and unfaithful to her marriage covenant (Isa. 54:5; Jer. 31:32; Hos. 2:2ff.). The wine ran out, and all Israel had left were six empty waterpots! They held water for *external* washings, but they could provide nothing for internal cleaning and joy. In this miracle, our Lord brought fullness where there was emptiness, joy where there was disappointment, and something *internal* for that which was only external (water for ceremonial washings).

When John mentioned "the third day" (John 2:1), he may have been giving us a hint of our Lord's resurrection. All of these blessings are possible because of His sacrifice on the cross and His resurrection from the dead (John 2:19).

Interestingly Moses' first miracle was a plague—turning water into blood (Ex. 7:19ff.), which speaks of judgment. Our Lord's first miracle spoke of grace.

This miracle also presents a practical lesson in service for God. The water turned into wine because the servants cooperated with Jesus and obeyed His commands. Several of the signs in John's gospel involve the cooperation of man and God: the feeding of the five thousand (John 6), the healing of the man born blind (John 9), and the raising of Lazarus (John 11). Whether we pass out bread, wash away mud, or roll away the stone, we are assisting Him in performing a miracle.

It is significant that the servants knew the source of this special wine (John 2:9). When Jesus healed the nobleman's son (John 4:46–54), it was the servants who were in on the secret. We are not just His servants; we are also His friends, and we know what He is doing (John 15:15).

Wine was the normal drink of the people in that day, and we must not use this miracle as an argument for the use of alcoholic beverages today. A man given to drink once said to me, "After all, Jesus turned water into wine!"

My reply was, "If you use Jesus as your example for drinking, why don't you follow His example in everything else?" Then I read Luke 22:18 to him. This verse clearly states that, in heaven now, Jesus is a teetotaler!

Sincere Christians of our day consider such verses as 1 Corinthians 8:9; 10:23, 31 before concluding that the use of alcoholic beverages is a wise thing today. I am reminded of the story of the drunken coal miner who was converted and became a vocal witness for Christ. One of his friends tried to trap him by asking, "Do you believe that Jesus turned water into wine?"

"I certainly do!" the believer replied. "In my home, He has turned wine into furniture, decent clothes, and food for my children!"

Finally, it is worth noting that the Jews always diluted the wine with water, usually to the proportion of three parts water to one part wine. While the Bible does not command total abstinence, it certainly *magnifies* it and definitely warns against drunkenness.

His Zeal (2:12–22)

Jesus, His family, and His disciples remained in Capernaum a few days, and then He went to Jerusalem for the Passover feast. Each Jewish man was required to attend three annual feasts at the Holy City: Passover, Pentecost, and Tabernacles (Deut. 16:16). The feasts mentioned in the gospel of John are Passover (John 2:13; 6:4; 12:1), Tabernacles (John 7:2), and Dedication (John 10:22). The unnamed feast in John 5:1 may have been Purim (Est. 9:26, 31).

Though He deliberately violated the man-made religious traditions of the Pharisees, our Lord obeyed the statutes of the law and was faithful to uphold the law. In His life and death, He fulfilled the law so that, today, believers are not burdened by that "yoke of bondage" (Acts 15:10).

Jesus revealed His zeal for God first of all by *cleansing the temple* (John 2:13–17). The priests had established a lucrative business of exchanging foreign money for Jewish currency, and also selling the animals needed for the sacrifices. No doubt, this "religious market" began as a convenience for the Jews who came long distances to worship in the temple, but in due time the "convenience" became a business, not a ministry. The tragedy is that this business was carried on in the court of the Gentiles in the temple, the place where the Jews should have been meeting the Gentiles and telling them about the one true God. Any Gentile searching for truth would not likely find it among the religious merchants in the temple.

Our Lord suddenly appeared in the temple and cleaned house! He was careful not to destroy anyone's property (He did not release the doves, for example), but He made it clear that He was in command. The temple was His Father's house, and He would not have the religious leaders pollute it with their money-making enterprises.

The condition of the temple was a vivid indication of the spiritual condition of the nation. Their religion was a dull routine, presided over by worldly minded men whose main desire was to exercise authority and get rich. Not only had the wine run out at the wedding feast but the glory had departed from the temple.

When they saw His courageous zeal, the disciples remembered Psalm 69:9 "The zeal of [for] thine house hath eaten me up." Psalm 69 is definitely a messianic psalm that is quoted several times in the New Testament: Psalm 69:4 (John 15:25); Psalm 69:8 (John 7:3–5); Psalm 69:9 (John 2:17; Rom. 15:3); Psalm 69:21 (Matt. 27:34, 48); and Psalm 69:22 (Rom. 11:9–10).

There was still a godly remnant in Israel who loved God and revered His temple (Luke 1:5–22; 2:25–38), but most religious leaders were false shepherds who exploited the people. When Jesus cleansed the temple, He "declared war" on the hypocritical religious leaders (Matt. 23), and this ultimately led to His death. Indeed, His zeal for God's house *did* eat Him up!

He also revealed His zeal by *giving His life* (John 2:18–22). It was logical for the religious leaders to ask Him to show the source of His authority. After all, they were the guardians of the Jewish faith, and they had a right to test any new prophet who appeared. "The Jews require a sign" (1 Cor. 1:22). Often, during His ministry, the leaders asked Jesus to give them a sign, and He refused to do so, *except* for the sign of Jonah (Matt. 12:39ff.). The "sign of Jonah" is death, burial, and resurrection.

Jesus used the image of the temple to convey this truth. "Destroy this temple [My body], and in three days I will raise it up" (John 2:19). Being spiritually blind, those who heard misunderstood what He was saying. Throughout the gospel of John, you will find people misunderstanding *spiritual* truth and interpreting in material or physical terms (John 3:4; 4:11; 6:52). Herod's temple was started in 20 BC and not completed until AD 64. How could one man "raise it up" in three days?

This statement was, of course, a prediction of His own death and resurrection, and His disciples remembered it after He was raised from the dead. But His enemies also remembered it and used it at His trial (Matt. 26:59–61), and some of the people mocked Him with it when He was dying on the cross (Matt. 27:40).

In writing this gospel, John included a number of vivid pictures of the death of the Savior. The first is the slaying of the Lamb in John 1:29, indicating that His death would be that of a substitute for sinners. The destroying of the temple is the second picture (John 2:19), suggesting a violent death that would end in victorious resurrection.

The third picture is that of the serpent lifted up (John 3:14), a reference to Numbers 21:5–9. The Savior would be made sin for us (1 Peter 2:24). His death would be voluntary (John 10:11–18): the Shepherd would lay down His life for the sheep. Finally, the planting of the seed (John 12:20–25) teaches that His death would produce fruit to the glory of God. His death and burial would look like failure, but in the end, God would bring victory.

The temple was an important element of the Jewish faith, for in it God was supposed to dwell. All of the ceremonies and sacrifices of the Jewish religion centered in the temple. When Jesus suggested that their precious building would be destroyed, their angry reaction was predictable. After all, if *His* body is the temple, then the Jewish temple would be needed no more. In this cryptic statement, our Lord actually predicted the end of the Jewish religious system.

But that was one of the purposes John had in mind when he wrote his gospel: the legal system has ended, and "grace and truth" have come through Jesus Christ. He is the new sacrifice (John 1:29) and the new temple (John 2:19). John will tell us later that the new worship will depend on inward integrity, not outward geography (John 4:19–24).

His Knowledge (2:23–25)

While in Jerusalem for the Passover, Jesus performed miracles that are not given in detail in any of the Gospels. It must have been these signs that especially attracted Nicodemus (John 3:2). Because of the miracles, many people professed to believe in Him, but Jesus did not accept their profession. No matter what the people themselves said, or others said about them, He did not accept human testimony. Why? Because, being God, He knew what was in each person's heart and mind.

The words *believed* in John 2:23 and *commit* in John 2:24 are the same Greek word. These people believed in Jesus, but He did not believe in them! They were "unsaved believers"! It was one thing to respond to a miracle but quite something else to commit oneself to Jesus Christ and continue in His Word (John 8:30–31).

John was not discrediting the importance of our Lord's signs, because he wrote his book to record these signs and to encourage his readers to trust Jesus Christ and receive eternal life (John 20:30–31). However, throughout the book, John makes it clear that it takes more than believing in miracles for a person to be saved. Seeing the signs and believing in them would be a great beginning; in fact, even the disciples started that way and had to grow in their faith (compare John 2:11 and 22).

Throughout the gospel of John, you see the Jewish people divided over the meaning of these miracles (John 9:16; 11:45–46). The same miracles that attracted Nicodemus to Jesus caused some of the other religious leaders to want to kill Him! They even asserted that His miracles were done in the power of Satan! Our Lord's miracles were testimonies (John 5:36), giving evidence of His divine sonship, but they were also *tests,* exposing the hearts of the people (John 12:37ff.). The same events that opened some eyes only made other eyes that much more blind (John 9:39–41).

It is important to see that Jesus tied His miracles to the truth of His message. He knew that the human heart is attracted to the sensational. The five thousand that He fed wanted to make Him King—until He preached a sermon on the Bread of Life, and then they left Him in droves! "Grace and truth came by Jesus Christ" (John 1:17). In grace, Jesus fed the hungry; in truth, He taught the Word. The people wanted the physical food but not the spiritual truth, so they abandoned Him.

"He knew what was in man" is a statement that is proved several times in John's gospel. Jesus knew the character of Simon (John 1:42). He knew what Nathanael was like (John 1:46ff.), and He told the Samaritan woman "all things" that she had ever done (John 4:29). He knew that the Jewish leaders did not have God's love in their hearts (John 5:42), and that one of His disciples was not truly a believer (John 6:64). He saw the repentance in the heart of the adulteress (John 8:10–11) and the murder in the hearts of His enemies (John 8:40ff.). Several times in the Upper Room message, Jesus revealed to His disciples their own inner feelings and questions.

As you follow our Lord's ministry in John's gospel, you see Him moving gradually out of the bright light of popularity and into the dark shadows of rejection. At the beginning, it was easy for people to follow the crowd and watch His miracles. But then, His words began to penetrate hearts, with conviction following, and conviction leads either to conversion or opposition. It is impossible to be neutral. People had to decide, and most of them decided against Him.

Yes, Jesus knows the human heart. "Except ye see signs and wonders, ye will not believe" (John 4:48). People who want His works but not His Word can never share His life. "Seeing is believing" is not the Christian approach (John 11:40; 20:29). First we believe; then we see. Miracles can only lead us to the Word (John 5:36–38), and the Word generates saving faith (Rom. 10:17).

Our Lord's accurate knowledge of the human heart is another evidence of His deity, for only God can see the inner person. This brief paragraph prepares us for the important interview with Nicodemus recorded in the next chapter. Note the repetition of the word *man* from John 2:25 to 3:1. Nicodemus wanted to learn more about Jesus, but he ended up learning more about himself!

CHAPTER THREE
John 3
A MATTER OF LIFE AND DEATH

Not only was Benjamin Franklin a great statesman and inventor, but he was also a great correspondent and received letters from famous people from all over the world. One day he received what could well have been the most important letter ever to come to his desk. It was from the well-known British preacher George Whitefield.

"I find that you grow more and more famous in the learned world," Whitefield wrote. "As you have made

such progress in investigating the mysteries of electricity, I now humbly urge you to give diligent heed to the mystery of the new birth. It is a most important and interesting study and, when mastered, will richly repay you for your pains."

The new birth is one of the key topics in John 3. In addition, in this chapter we see Jesus Christ in three different roles: the Teacher (John 3:1–21), the Bridegroom (John 3:22–30), and the Witness (John 3:31–36).

Jesus Christ the Teacher (3:1–21)

We have already noted the connection between John 2:23–25 and 3:1. Nicodemus was initially attracted to Jesus because of the miracles He did. He wanted to know more about Jesus and the doctrines that He taught. Nicodemus himself was *"the* teacher of the Jews" (John 3:10, literal translation), and he had great respect for the Teacher from Galilee.

Nicodemus was a Pharisee, which meant he lived by the strictest possible religious rules. Not all of the Pharisees were hypocrites (as one may infer from Jesus' comments recorded in Matt. 23), and evidence indicates that Nicodemus was deeply sincere in his quest for truth. He came to Jesus by night, not because he was afraid of being seen, but most likely because he wanted to have a quiet uninterrupted conversation with the new Teacher "come from God." The fact that Nicodemus used the plural pronoun "we," and Jesus responded with the plural "ye" (John 3:7) may indicate that Nicodemus was representing the religious leaders. He was a man of high moral character, deep religious hunger, and yet profound spiritual blindness.

In order to instruct Nicodemus in the basics of salvation, our Lord used four quite different illustrations.

Birth (vv. 1–7). Our Lord began with that which was familiar, birth being a universal experience. The word translated "again" also means "from above." Though all human beings have experienced natural birth on earth, if they expect to go to heaven, they must experience a supernatural spiritual birth from above.

Once again, we meet with the blindness of sinners: this well-educated religious leader, Nicodemus, did not understand what the Savior was talking about! Jesus was speaking about a spiritual birth, but Nicodemus thought only of a physical birth. The situation is no different today. When you talk with people about being born again, they often begin to discuss their family's religious heritage, their church membership, religious ceremonies, and so on.

Being a patient teacher, our Lord picked up on Nicodemus's words and further explained the new birth. To be "born of water" is to be born physically ("enter a second time into his mother's womb") but to be born again means to be born of the Spirit. Just as there are two parents for physical birth, so there are two "parents" for spiritual birth: the Spirit of God (John 3:5) and the Word of God (James 1:18; 1 Peter

1:23–25). The Spirit of God takes the Word of God and, when the sinner believes, imparts the life of God.

Jesus was not teaching that the new birth comes through water baptism. In the New Testament, baptism is connected with *death,* not birth, and no amount of physical water can effect a spiritual change in a person. The emphasis in John 3:14–21 is on *believing,* because salvation comes through faith (Eph. 2:8–9). The evidence of salvation is the witness of the Spirit within (Rom. 8:9), and the Spirit enters your life when you believe (Acts 10:43–48; Eph. 1:13–14).

Water baptism is certainly a part of our obedience to Christ and our witness for Christ (Matt. 28:18–20; Acts 2:41). But it must not be made an essential for salvation; otherwise, none of the Old Testament saints was ever saved, nor was the thief on the cross (Luke 23:39–43). In every age, there has been but one way of salvation—faith in God's promise—though the *outward evidence* of that faith has changed from age to age.

Human birth involves travail (John 16:21), and so does the birth from above. Our Savior had to travail on the cross so that we might become members of the family of God (Isa. 53:11). Concerned believers have to travail in prayer and witness as they seek to lead sinners to Christ (1 Cor. 4:15; Gal. 4:19).

The child inherits the nature of the parents, and so does the child of God. We become "partakers of the divine nature" (2 Peter 1:4). Nature determines appetite, which explains why the Christian has an appetite for the things of God (1 Peter 2:2–3). He has no desire to go back to the foul things of the world that once appealed to him (2 Peter 2:20–22). He feeds on the Word of God and grows into spiritual maturity (Heb. 5:11–14).

Of course, birth involves life, and spiritual birth from above involves *God's* life. John uses the word *life* thirty-six times in his gospel. The opposite of life is death, and the person who has not believed on Jesus Christ does not have God's life, eternal life, abundant life. *You do not manufacture Christians any more than you manufacture babies!* The only way to enter God's family is through the new birth (John 1:11–13).

Birth involves a future, and we are "born again to a living hope" (1 Peter 1:3 NASB). A newborn baby cannot be arrested because he or she has no past! When you are born again into God's family, your sins are forgiven and forgotten, and your future is bright with a living hope.

Nicodemus must have had a surprised and yet bewildered look on his face, for the Lord had to say, "You must not be surprised that I told you that all of you must be born again" (John 3:7 PH). But Nicodemus was born a Jew! He was a part of God's covenant people (Rom. 9:4–5)! Certainly his birth was better than that of a Gentile or a Samaritan! And his life was exemplary, for he was a faithful Pharisee! He could well understand Jesus telling the *Romans* that they had to be born again, but certainly not the *Jews!*

The wind (vv. 8–13). It is likely that the evening wind was blowing just then as Nicodemus and Jesus sat on the housetop conversing. The word *wind* in both Hebrew and Greek can also be translated "spirit." One of the symbols of the Spirit of God in the Bible is the wind or breath (Job 33:4; John 20:22; Acts 2:2). Like the wind, the Spirit is invisible but powerful, and you cannot explain or predict the movements of the wind.

When Jesus used this symbol, Nicodemus should have readily remembered Ezekiel 37:1–14. The prophet saw a valley full of dead bones, but when he prophesied to the wind, the Spirit came and gave the bones life. Again, it was the combination of the Spirit of God and the Word of God that gave life. The nation of Israel (including Nicodemus and his fellow council members) was dead and hopeless, but in spite of the morality and religion of the people, they needed the life of the Spirit.

The new birth from above is a necessity ("Ye must be born again"), but it is also a mystery. Everyone who is born of the Spirit is like the wind: you cannot fully explain or predict either the wind or the child of God! For that matter, human birth is still a mystery, in spite of all that we know about anatomy and physiology. Each new life is exciting and different.

Nicodemus came "by night," and he was still in the dark! He could not understand the new birth even after Jesus had explained it to him. Our Lord stated clearly that Nicodemus's knowledge of the Old Testament should have given him the light he needed (John 3:10). Alas, "the teacher of the Jews" knew the *facts* recorded in the Scriptures, but he could not understand the *truths.*

What was the problem? For one thing, the religious leaders would not submit to the authority of Christ's witness (John 3:11). We will see this "authority conflict" increase as we continue in our studies. The religious leaders claimed to believe Moses, yet they could not believe Jesus (John 5:37–47). The Pharisees were more concerned about the praise of men than the praise of God (John 12:37–50).

"I have used earthly illustrations," said Jesus, "and you cannot understand. If I began to share the deep spiritual truths, you still would not believe" (John 3:12).

The serpent on the pole (vv. 14–18). The story in Numbers 21:4–9 was certainly familiar to Nicodemus. It is a story of sin, for the nation rebelled against God and had to be punished. God sent fiery serpents that bit the people so that many died. It is also a story of grace, for Moses interceded for the people and God provided a remedy. He told Moses to make a brass serpent and lift it up on a pole for all to see. Any stricken person who looked at the serpent would immediately be healed. So, it is also a story of faith: when the people looked by faith, they were saved.

The verb *lifted up* has a dual meaning: to be crucified (John 8:28; 12:32–34) and to be glorified and exalted. In his gospel, John points out that our Lord's crucifixion was actually the means of His glorification

(John 12:23ff.). The cross was not the end of His glory; it was the means of His glory (Acts 2:33).

Much as the serpent was lifted up on that pole, so the Son of God would be lifted up on a cross. Why? To save us from sin and death. In the camp of Israel, the solution to the "serpent problem" was not in killing the serpents, making medicine, pretending they were not there, passing antiserpent laws, or climbing the pole. The answer was in looking by faith at the uplifted serpent.

The whole world has been bitten by sin, and "the wages of sin is death" (Rom. 6:23). God sent His Son to die, not only for Israel, but for a whole world. How is a person born from above? How is he or she saved from eternal perishing? By believing on Jesus Christ; by looking to Him in faith.

On January 6, 1850, a snowstorm almost crippled the city of Colchester, England, and a teenage boy was unable to get to the church he usually attended. So he made his way to a nearby Primitive Methodist chapel, where an ill-prepared layman was substituting for the absent preacher. His text was Isaiah 45:22—"Look unto me, and be ye saved, all the ends of the earth." For many months this young teenager had been miserable and under deep conviction, but though he had been reared in church (both his father and grandfather were preachers), he did not have the assurance of salvation.

The unprepared substitute minister did not have much to say, so he kept repeating the text. "A man need not go to college to learn to look," he shouted. "Anyone can look—a child can look!" About that time, he saw the visitor sitting to one side, and he pointed at him and said, "Young man, you look very miserable. Young man, look to Jesus Christ!"

The young man did look by faith, and that was how the great preacher Charles Haddon Spurgeon was converted.

The difference between perishing and living, and between condemnation and salvation, is faith in Jesus Christ. Jesus could well have come to this world as a judge and destroyed every rebellious sinner, but in love, He came to this world as our Savior, *and He died for us on the cross!* He became the "uplifted serpent." The serpent in Moses' day brought physical life to dying Jews, but Jesus Christ gives eternal life to anyone who trusts Him. He has salvation for a whole world!

Light and darkness (vv. 19–21). This is one of the major images used in this gospel (John 1:4–13). Why will sinners not come into the "light of life"? Because they love the darkness! They want to persist in their evil deeds, and this keeps them from coming to the light, for the closer the sinner gets to the light, the more his sins are exposed. It is not "intellectual problems" that keep people from trusting Christ; it is the moral and spiritual blindness that keeps them loving the darkness and hating the light.

Please note that Nicodemus finally did "come to the light." He was in the "midnight of confusion" (John 3:1–21), but eventually he came out into the "sunlight of confession" when he identified with Christ at Calvary (John 19:38–42). He realized that the uplifted Savior was indeed the Son of God.

Jesus the Bridegroom (3:22–30)

Until John the Baptist was arrested by Herod and put into prison, his ministry overlapped that of the Lord Jesus. John did not want anyone to follow him; his ministry was to point to the Lamb of God and urge people to trust Him. But when two popular preachers are involved in similar work, it is easy for both friends and enemies to get caught up in competition and comparison.

It appears that some of John's disciples started the argument. It began on doctrinal grounds—the matter of purifying—but soon moved to personal grounds. In John 3:25, some manuscripts read "a Jew" instead of "the Jews." Could this unnamed Jew have possibly been Nicodemus? We cannot say, but it is a possibility.

The matter of purifying was important to the Jews (Mark 7:1–23). Under the Old Testament law, it was necessary for them to keep themselves ceremonially clean if they were to serve God and please Him. Unfortunately, the Pharisees added so many extra traditions to the law that the observing of it became a burden.

Without realizing it, John's disciples were putting him into a situation of competing against the Lord Jesus! "All men come to him!" (John 3:26) sounds like a wail of despair. It is interesting to note that four of the greatest men in the Bible faced this problem of comparison and competition: Moses (Num. 11:26–30), John the Baptist (John 3:26–30), Jesus (Luke 9:46–50), and Paul (Phil. 1:15–18). A leader often suffers more from his zealous disciples than from his critics!

How did John the Baptist handle this controversy? To begin with, he stated a conviction: all ministry and blessing come from God, so there can be no competition (John 3:27). Paul would have agreed with this (1 Cor. 3:1–9; 4:1–7). Our gifts and opportunities come from God, and He alone must get the glory.

Then John used a beautiful illustration. He compared Jesus to the bridegroom and himself only to the best man (John 3:29). Once the bridegroom and bride had been brought together, the work of the best man was completed. What a foolish thing it would be for the best man to try to "upstage" the bridegroom and take his place. John's joy was to hear the voice of the Bridegroom and know that He had claimed His bride.

Even before his birth, John the Baptist rejoiced in the Lord (Luke 1:44). John was content to be the voice announcing Jesus to be the Word (John 1:23). Jesus was the Light, and John the Baptist was the witness pointing to the Light (John 1:6–8).

Often press releases and book reviews cross my desk, along with conference folders, and at times I am perturbed by what I read. Very few speakers and writers are ordinary people. They are "world travelers" or "noted lecturers" who have addressed "huge audiences." They are always in "great demand," and their ministries are described in such ways that they make the apostle Paul a midget by comparison.

A Presbyterian pastor in Melbourne, Australia introduced J. Hudson Taylor by using many superlatives, especially the word *great.* Taylor stepped to the pulpit and quietly said, "Dear friends, I am the little servant of an illustrious Master." If John the Baptist in heaven heard that statement, he must have shouted "Hallelujah!"

The image of the Bridegroom would have been significant to the Jewish people, for Jehovah had a "marriage covenant" with the nation (Isa. 54:5; 62:4ff.; Jer. 2:2; 3:20; Ezek. 16:8; Hos. 2:19ff.). Alas, Israel had been unfaithful to her vows, and God had to put her away temporarily. Today, God is calling out a people for His name, the church, the bride of Christ (2 Cor. 11:1–3; Eph. 5:22–33). One day the Bridegroom will come to claim His bride and take her to her home in heaven (Rev. 19:6–9; 21:9ff.).

The word *must* is used in three significant ways in this chapter. There is the "must" of the sinner (John 3:7), the "must" of the Savior (John 3:14), and the "must" of the servant (John 3:30).

Jesus the Witness (3:31–36)

Bible scholars do not agree as to who is speaking in John 3:31–36, John the apostle or John the Baptist. For that matter, some students believe that John 3:16–21 came from the apostle John and not the Lord Jesus. There were no quotation marks in early manuscripts, but since all Scripture is inspired, it really makes little difference who said the words.

The emphasis in this paragraph is on witness ("testimony"), one of the key subjects in John's gospel. The Greek word translated "witness" or "testimony" is used forty-seven times. John bore witness to Jesus (John 1:7; 5:33), but Jesus was also a witness to the truth. Why should we heed His witness? For several reasons.

He came from heaven (v. 31). He was not simply called from heaven, or empowered by heaven; He *came* from heaven. It was this claim that the Jews disputed, because they knew it was His claim that He was God (John 6:38–42). John the Baptist certainly was not "from above," nor did he claim to be. No earthly messenger of God came "from above." Only Jesus Christ can make that claim and prove it to be true.

Since Jesus came from heaven, He represents the Father; and to reject His witness is to reject the Father (John 5:23). We know that His witness is true because He is the true God. We can trust it and rely on it.

It comes from Him firsthand (vv. 32–33). He shares what He has seen and heard from the Father (John 8:38). Those who receive His witness *and act on it* know by personal experience that His witness is true (John 7:17). Our Lord's teachings are not to be studied intellectually, separated from everyday life. It is when

we obey His Word and put it into practice that we see its truth and experience its power.

The Father has authorized His Son (vv. 34–35). God sent Him (another key theme in John's gospel); God gave Him the Word; God gave Him the Spirit; and God gave Him all things (John 13:3). What a commissioning! To reject the Son's witness is to rebel against the highest authority in the universe.

We usually think of God's love for a lost world (John 3:16), but John reminds us of the Father's love for His Son. Jesus is the Father's "beloved Son" (Matt. 3:17; Mark 1:11; Luke 3:22). Because the Father loves the Son, He has given Him all things, and He shows Him all things (John 5:20). It is a love that can hold nothing back.

Therefore, when we receive His witness, we share in His love and His wealth. To reject Christ's witness is to sin against love and light. No wonder our Lord wept over the city of Jerusalem (Matt. 23:37–39). They had rejected His witness—both His messages and His miracles—and their rejection led to judgment.

We might escape the wrath of God (v. 36). This is the only place in any of John's epistles or his gospel that he uses the word *wrath.* (He uses it six times in the book of Revelation.) This verse parallels John 3:18 and makes it clear that there can be no neutrality when it comes to the witness of Jesus Christ: we either trust Him or we reject Him.

"Everlasting life" does not simply mean eternity in heaven. The believer possesses that life right now! It is the life of God in the believer. The opposite of eternal life is eternal death, the wrath of God. A person does not have to die and go to hell to be under the wrath of God. "He that believeth not is condemned already" (John 3:18). The verdict has already been given, but the sentence has not yet been executed. Why? Because God is patient and long suffering, and continues to call sinners to repentance (2 Peter 3:9).

As you review John 3, you can see that the apostle John is emphasizing a personal relationship with Jesus Christ.

It is a *living relationship* that begins with the new birth, the birth from above. When we receive Jesus Christ into our lives, we share His very life and become children in the family of God.

It is also a *loving relationship,* for He is the Bridegroom and we are a part of the bride. Like John the Baptist, we desire that Jesus Christ increase as we decrease. He must receive all the honor and glory.

It is a *learning relationship,* for He is the faithful Witness who shares God's truth with us. What a delight it is to receive His Word, meditate on it, and make it part of our very lives.

But we must never forget the cost of these blessings. For us to be born into God's family, Jesus Christ had to die. For us to enter into the loving relationship of salvation, He had to endure the hatred and condemnation of men. He had to be lifted up on the cross so that we might experience forgiveness and eternal life.

May we never take this for granted!

"He must increase, but I must decrease" (John 3:30).

CHAPTER FOUR
John 4
THE BAD SAMARITAN

In John 4, our Lord ministers to a variety of people: the sinful Samaritan woman, His own disciples, the many Samaritans who trusted in Him, and finally, a nobleman and his household. What did these have in common? *Faith* in Jesus Christ. John was fulfilling the purpose of his gospel in showing his readers how various kinds and classes of people came to believe in Jesus as the Son of God.

Let's meet these various persons and discover how their faith began, how it grew, and what it did for them and for others.

The Samaritan Woman (4:1–30)

Because the Pharisees were trying to incite competition between Jesus and John the Baptist (John 3:25–30), Jesus left Judea and started north for Galilee. He could have taken one of three possible routes: along the coast, across the Jordan and up through Perea, or straight through Samaria. Orthodox Jews avoided Samaria because there was a longstanding, deep-seated hatred between them and the Samaritans.

The Samaritans were a mixed race, part Jew and part Gentile, that grew out of the Assyrian captivity of the ten northern tribes in 727 BC. Rejected by the Jews because they could not prove their genealogy, the Samaritans established their own temple and religious services on Mount Gerizim. This only fanned the fires of prejudice. So intense was their dislike of the Samaritans that some of the Pharisees prayed that no Samaritan would be raised in the resurrection! When His enemies wanted to call Jesus an insulting name, they called Him a Samaritan (John 8:48).

Because He was on a divinely appointed schedule, it was necessary that Jesus go through Samaria. Why? Because He would meet a woman there and lead her into saving faith, the kind of true faith that would affect an entire village. Our Lord was no respecter of persons. Earlier, He counseled a moral Jewish man (John 3), and now He would witness to an immoral Samaritan woman!

He arrived at Jacob's well at six o'clock in the evening, the usual time for women to come for water. The disciples went to the nearby town for food while Jesus deliberately waited at the well. He was weary, hungry, and thirsty. John not only presents Jesus as the Son of God but also as true man. Our Lord entered into all the normal experiences of our lives and is able to identify with us in each of them.

As you read our Lord's interview with this woman, notice how her knowledge of Jesus increases until she acknowledges that He is the Christ. There were four stages in this experience.

He is "a Jew" (vv. 7–10). In that day, it was not considered proper for any man, especially a rabbi, to speak in public to a strange woman (John 4:27). But our Lord set social customs aside because a soul's eternal salvation was at stake. It certainly surprised her when He asked for a drink of water. She surmised that He was a Jewish rabbi, and perhaps she tried to "read between the lines" to find another meaning to His request. What was He *really* seeking?

The information in John's parenthesis at the end of John 4:9 was for the benefit of his Gentile readers. Since the disciples had gone into the city to purchase food, it is obvious that the Jews did have *some* "dealings" with the Samaritans, so John was not trying to exaggerate. The phrase can be translated "ask no favors from the Samaritans" or "use no vessels in common with the Samaritans." Why would Jesus, a Jew, want to use her "polluted" vessel to get a drink of water?

Of course, our Lord's request was simply a way to open the conversation and share with her the truth about "living water." Whenever He witnessed to people, Jesus did not use a "sales talk" that He adapted to meet every situation. To Nicodemus, He spoke about new birth, but to this woman, He spoke about living water.

Jesus pointed out to her that she was ignorant of three important facts: who He was, what He had to offer, and how she could receive it. Here was eternal God speaking to her, offering her eternal life! The Samaritans were as blind as the Jews (John 1:26). But our Lord's words had aroused her interest, so she pursued the conversation.

"Greater than Jacob" (vv. 11–15). Jesus was speaking about spiritual water, but she interpreted His words to mean literal water. Again, we see how easily people confuse the material and the spiritual. Furthermore, this woman was concerned about *how* He would obtain this water, instead of simply asking Him to give her a drink of it.

Of course Jesus *is* greater than Jacob—and greater than the well itself! To paraphrase His reply: "Whosoever *continues to drink* of this material water (or anything the world has to offer) will thirst again. But whosoever *takes one drink* of the water I give will never thirst again" (see John 4:13–14). How true it is that the things of this world never completely satisfy. In hell today, people are crying, "I thirst!"

We have noted before that *life* is one of John's key concepts. He uses the word at least thirty-six times. Campbell Morgan has pointed out that mankind needs air, water, and food in order to have life. (We might also add that he needs light.) All of these are provided in Jesus Christ. He provides the "breath" (Spirit) of God (John 3:8; 20:22). He is the Bread of Life (John 6:48) and the Light of Life (John 1:4–5), and He gives us the water of life.

The woman's immediate response was to ask for this gift, but she did not know what she was saying. The seed of the Word fell on shallow soil, and the shoots that sprang up had no root (Matt. 13:20–21). She had made progress, but she still had a long way to go, so Jesus patiently dealt with her.

"A prophet" (vv. 16–24). The only way to prepare the soil of the heart for the seed is to plow it up with conviction. That was why Jesus told her to go get her husband: He forced her to admit her sin. There can be no conversion without conviction. There must first be conviction and repentance, and then there can be saving faith. Jesus had aroused her mind and stirred her emotions, but He also had to touch her conscience, and that meant dealing with her sin.

"I have no husband" was the shortest statement she made during the entire conversation! Why? Because now she was under conviction and her "mouth was stopped" (Rom. 3:19). But this was the best thing that could have happened to her!

However, instead of listening to Jesus, she tried to get Him on a "detour" by discussing the differences between the Jewish and the Samaritan religions. It is much more comfortable to discuss religion than to face one's sins! However, Jesus once again revealed her spiritual ignorance: she did not know who to worship, where to worship, or how to worship! He made it clear that all religions are not equally acceptable before God, that some worshippers act in ignorance and unbelief.

The only faith that God will accept is that which came through the Jews. The Bible is of Jewish origin, and our Savior was a Jew. The first Christians were Jews. A religious worker in an airport told me that the world's deliverer came from Korea, but Jesus said, "Salvation is of the Jews." Only those who have the indwelling Holy Spirit, and who obey the truth, can worship God acceptably.

It was a devastating statement to say that worship would no longer be limited to the Jewish temple. This ties in with John 2:19–21 and also Stephen's statement in Acts 7:48–50. John's gospel clearly reveals that there is a new sacrifice (John 1:29), a new temple (John 2:19–21; 4:20–24), a new birth (John 3:1–7), and a new water (John 4:11). Jews reading this gospel should realize that God has established in Jesus Christ a whole new economy. The old covenant law has been fulfilled and set aside.

"The Christ" (vv. 25–30). In spite of her ignorance, there was one truth this woman did know: the Messiah was coming and would reveal the secrets of hearts. Where did she learn this truth? We do not know, but that seed had lain buried in her heart until that very hour, and now it was going to bear fruit. Our Lord's response to her statement was, literally, "I that speak to thee, I am!" He dared to utter the holy name of God!

At this point, the woman put her faith in Jesus Christ and was converted. Immediately she wanted to share her faith with others, so she went into the village and told the men she had met the Christ. When you consider how little spiritual truth this woman knew, her zeal and witness put us to shame. But God used her simple testimony, and many of the people came out to the well to meet Jesus. The rabbis said, "It is better that the words of the law be burned than be delivered to a woman!" But Jesus did not agree with that narrow prejudice.

Why did she leave her waterpot when she hurried into the city? For one thing, she had the living water within and was now satisfied. Also, she intended to come back, and perhaps in the interim, the disciples and Jesus could use the vessel to satisfy their thirst. Gone were the racial barriers and battles that had existed before! They were all one in faith and love!

This woman did not come to faith in Christ immediately. Jesus was patient with her, and in this, He sets a good example for us in our own personal work. Certainly she was the least likely prospect for salvation, yet God used her to win almost an entire village!

The Disciples (4:31–38)

When the disciples returned from obtaining food, they were shocked that Jesus was conversing with a woman, and especially a Samaritan, but they did not interrupt. They were learning that their Master knew what He was doing and did not need their counsel. But, after the woman left, they urged Jesus to share the meal with them, because they knew that He was hungry.

"I have food to eat that ye know not of" was His reply, and, as usual, they did not understand it. They thought He was speaking of literal food, and they wondered where He got it. Then He explained that doing the Father's will—in this case, leading the woman to salvation—was true nourishment for His soul. The disciples were satisfied with bread, but He was satisfied with accomplishing the Father's work.

"Seek your life's nourishment in your life's work," said Phillips Brooks. The will of God ought to be a source of strength and satisfaction to the child of God, just as if he sat down to a sumptuous feast. If what we are doing tears us down instead of builds us up, then we may well question whether it is the will of God for us.

Our Lord did not look on the Father's will as a heavy burden or a distasteful task. He viewed His work as the very nourishment of His soul. Doing the Father's will fed Him and satisfied Him inwardly. "I delight to do thy will, O my God: yea, thy law is within my heart" (Ps. 40:8). The Samaritan woman was now doing the Father's will and finding excitement and enrichment in it.

Jesus then changed the image from that of food to that of the harvest, which is the source of the food. He quoted the familiar Jewish proverb about waiting for the harvest, and then pointed to the villagers even then coming out to the well to meet Him, thanks to the witness of the woman. The disciples went into the village to get food for themselves, but they did no evangelizing. The woman took their place!

The image of the harvest is a familiar one in the Bible and is often applied to the ministry of winning lost souls. Both the parable of the sower and the parable of the tares (Matt. 13:1–30) relate to this theme, and Paul used it in his letters (Rom. 1:13; 1 Cor. 3:6–9; Gal. 6:9). We plant the seed of God's Word in the hearts of people who hear it, and we seek to cultivate that seed by our love and prayers. In due time, that seed may bear fruit to the glory of God.

No doubt the disciples had said, as they approached the city of Sychar, "There can be no harvest here! These people despise us Jews and would have no use for our message." But just the opposite was true: the harvest was ready and only needed faithful workers to claim it. For some reason, when it comes to witnessing for Christ, it is always the wrong time and the wrong place! It takes faith to sow the seed, and we must do it even when the circumstances look discouraging. Read Ecclesiastes 11:4 and take it to heart!

There is no competition in the Lord's harvest. Each of us has an assigned task and we are all a part of each other's labors (1 Cor. 3:6–9). One sows, one reaps, but each worker gets his honest reward for the work he has done.

John 4:38 indicates that others had labored in Samaria and had prepared the way for this harvest. We do not know who these faithful workers were, nor do we need to know, for God will reward them. Perhaps some of these people had heard John the Baptist preach, or perhaps some of John's followers had reached into this difficult field. Some archeologists have located "Aenon near Salim" where John baptized (John 3:23) near the biblical Shechem, which is close to Sychar and Jacob's well. If this is the case, then John the Baptist prepared the soil and planted the seed, and Jesus and the disciples reaped the harvest. Of course, the woman herself planted some of the seed through her witness to the men.

The disciples were learning a valuable lesson that would encourage them in the years to come. They were not alone in the work of the Lord, and they must never look on any opportunity for witness as wasted time and energy. It takes faith to plow the soil and plant the seed, but God has promised a harvest (Ps. 126:5–6; Gal. 6:9). In a few years, Peter and John would participate in another harvest among the Samaritans (Acts 8:5–25). Those who sow may not see the harvest, but those who reap will see it and give thanks for the faithful labors of the sowers.

The Greek word translated "labor" in John 4:38 is translated "wearied" in John 4:6. Sowing, cultivating, and harvesting are difficult tasks, not only in the physical realm, but also in the spiritual. There is no place in the harvest for lazy people. The work is too difficult and the laborers are too few.

The Samaritans (4:39–42)
Many of the Samaritans believed because of the testimony of the woman, and then many more believed

when they heard Jesus personally. So excited were they about Him that they begged Him to stay with them, and He stayed for two days. During that short time, His word produced fruit in their lives.

It is important that new converts be grounded in the Word—the Bible. These Samaritans began their spiritual walk by trusting in what the woman said, but they soon learned to trust the Word taught by the Savior. Theirs was no "secondhand" salvation. They knew that they were saved because they had believed His message. "Now we know!" was their happy testimony.

You would have thought that these Samaritans would have been narrow in their faith, seeing Jesus as the Savior of the Jews and the Samaritans. But they declared that He was "the Savior of the world" (John 4:42). They had been converted only a few days, but they already had a missionary vision! In fact, their vision was wider than that of the apostles!

It is interesting to trace our Lord's movements that brought Him to Samaria. He was in Jerusalem (John 2:23) and then came into Judea (John 3:22). From Judea He went into Samaria (John 4:4), and the Samaritans declared Him to be "the Savior of the world." This is a perfect parallel to Acts 1:8—"And ye shall be witnesses unto me both in Jerusalem, and in all Judea, and in Samaria, and unto the uttermost part of the earth." Our Lord has set the example. If we follow, He will give us the harvest.

This unnamed Samaritan woman was a fruitful believer: she bore fruit ("many believed"), more fruit ("many more believed"), and today continues to bear "much fruit" to the glory of God (see John 15:1–5). Nobody knows how many lost sinners have come to the Savior because of the witness of this woman recorded in John 4.

The Nobleman (4:43–54)
Our Lord continued His journey to Galilee (John 4:3) and came again to Cana. Galilee was known as *"Galil ha goyim*—Galilee of the Gentiles." Apparently Jesus had detected in Judea (His own country) the increasing hostility of the religious leaders, though the real opposition would not yet appear for some months. Our Lord was really never identified with Judea even though He had been born in Bethlehem. He was known as the prophet from Galilee (Matt. 21:11; John 7:52). Jesus knew that the public response to His ministry in Jerusalem had been insincere and shallow (John 2:23–25), and that it was not honoring to Him at all.

Why did Jesus return to Cana? Perhaps He wanted to cultivate the "seed" He had planted there when He attended the wedding feast. Nathanael came from Cana, so perhaps there was a personal reason for this visit. Jesus was met at Cana by a nobleman from Capernaum, some twenty miles away. The man had heard about His miracles and came all that distance to intercede for his son, who was dying. The first miracle at Cana came at the request of His mother (John

2:1–5), and this second miracle at Cana at the request of a father (John 4:47).

Was this man a Jew or a Gentile? We do not know. Nor do we know his exact position in the government. He may have been a member of Herod's court, but whatever his national or social standing, he was clearly at his wit's end and desperately needed the help of the Savior. He "kept beseeching him" to travel to Capernaum to heal his son.

John 4:48 was not a rebuke of this nobleman. Rather, it was our Lord's lament at the spiritual condition of the people in general, both in Judea and Galilee. "Seeing is believing" has always been the "pragmatic" philosophy of the lost world, even the religious world. The nobleman believed that Jesus could heal his son, but he made two mistakes in his thinking: that Jesus had to go to Capernaum to save the lad, and that if the boy died meanwhile, it was too late.

We must admire this man's faith. Jesus simply said, "Go thy way; thy son liveth" (John 4:50). And the man believed Jesus and started to return home! Both the Samaritan woman and this anonymous nobleman must have rejoiced the heart of Jesus as they believed the Word and acted on it.

The boy was healed the instant Jesus spoke those words, so the man's servants started out to find him so they could share the good news. (Again, it is the servants who know what is going on. See John 2:9; 15:15.) The boy had been healed at the seventh hour, which, in Roman time, would be seven o'clock in the evening. The father certainly would not have traveled at night, for that would have been dangerous; nor would the servants have taken that risk. The father's faith was so strong that he was willing to delay going home, even though his heart yearned to see his beloved son.

When the father and the servants met the next day, their report confirmed his faith. Note that the father thought the healing would be gradual ("began to improve"), but the servants reported a complete, instant recovery.

This man began with *crisis faith*. He was about to lose his son and he had no other recourse but the Lord Jesus Christ. Many people came to Jesus with their crises, and He did not turn them away. The nobleman's crisis faith became *confident* faith: he believed the Word and had peace in his heart. He was even able to delay his trip home, knowing that the boy was out of danger.

His confident faith became *confirmed* faith. Indeed, the boy had been completely healed! And the healing took place at the very time when Jesus spoke the Word. It was this fact that made a believer out of the nobleman and his household. He believed that Jesus was the Christ, the Son of God, and he shared this faith with his family. He had *contagious* faith and shared his experience with others.

This is one of several miracles that Jesus performed "at a distance." He healed the centurion's servant from a distance (Matt. 8:5–13, and note that he too lived in Capernaum), and He healed the daughter of the Canaanite woman in the same manner (Matt. 15:21–28). These two were Gentiles and, spiritually speaking, were "at a distance" (Eph. 2:12–13). Perhaps this nobleman was also a Gentile. We do not know.

John 4:54 does not state that this healing was the second miracle that Jesus ever performed, for that would contradict John 2:23 and 3:2. This was the second miracle He performed *in Cana of Galilee* (see John 2:1, 11). He certainly gave those people special privileges.

But we must note that both miracles were "private" rather than public. Mary, the disciples, and the servants knew where the excellent wine had come from, but the guests did not. (Of course, it is possible that the servants told the story to others.) The nobleman's son was healed at Capernaum, not Cana, but news traveled rapidly in those days and certainly the word got out.

Jesus' first miracle at the wedding revealed His power over *time*. The Father is always making water into wine, but He takes a season or two to finish the work. Jesus made the wine instantly. In this sense, our Lord's miracles were only *instantaneous* copies of what the Father is always doing. "My Father worketh hitherto, and I work" (John 5:17). The Father is constantly multiplying bread, season after season, but the Son multiplied it instantly.

In the second recorded miracle, Jesus showed His power over *space*. He was not limited simply because He was in Cana and the sick boy was in Capernaum. The fact that the father believed the Word and did not know the results until the next day is evidence that he had confident faith. He trusted the word that Jesus spoke, and so should we.

CHAPTER FIVE
John 5
THE MAN WHO WAS EQUAL WITH GOD

Our Lord's first two miracles recorded by John were somewhat private in nature. The servants and the disciples knew that He transformed the water into wine, and the servants and the nobleman's family knew that He had healed the sick son. The miracle recorded in John 5 was not only public, but it was performed on the Sabbath day and incited the opposition of the religious leaders. We see here the beginning of "official persecution" against the Savior.

There are three exciting "acts" in this drama.

The Cure (5:1–15)
When you visit St. Anne's Church in Jerusalem, they will show you the deep excavation that has revealed the ancient Pool of Bethesda. The Hebrew name *Bethesda* has been spelled various ways and given differing

meanings. Some say it means "house of mercy" or "house of grace," but others say it means "place of the two outpourings." There is historical and archeological evidence that two adjacent pools of water served this area in ancient times.

The pool is situated near the northeast corner of the Old City, close to the Sheep Gate (Neh. 3:1; 12:39). Perhaps John saw some spiritual significance to this location, for he had already told his readers that Jesus Christ is "the Lamb of God" (John 1:29).

We do not know which feast Jesus was observing when He went to Jerusalem, and it is not important that we know. His main purpose for going was not to maintain a religious tradition but to heal a man and use the miracle as the basis for a message to the people. The miracle illustrated what He said in John 5:24—the power of His Word and the gift of life.

While it is true that some manuscripts omit the end of John 5:3 and all of verse 4, it is also true that the event (and the man's words in John 5:7) would make little sense if these words are eliminated. Why would anybody, especially a man sick for so many years, remain in one place if nothing special were occurring? You would think that after thirty-eight years of nothing happening to *anybody,* the man would go elsewhere and stop hoping! It seems wisest for us to accept the fact that something extraordinary kept all these handicapped people at this pool, hoping for a cure.

John described these people as "impotent, blind, lame, paralyzed." What havoc sin has wrought in this world! But the healing of these infirmities was one of the prophesied ministries of the Messiah (Isa. 35:3–6). Had the religious leaders known their own Scriptures, they would have recognized their Redeemer, but they were spiritually blind.

No matter how you look at this miracle, it is an illustration of the grace of God. It was grace that brought Jesus to the Pool of Bethesda, for who would want to mingle with a crowd of helpless people! Jesus did not heal all of them; He singled out one man and healed him. The fact that Jesus came to the man, spoke to him, healed him, and then met him later in the temple is proof of His wonderful grace and mercy.

John noted that the man had been ill for thirty-eight years. Perhaps he saw in this a picture of his own Jewish nation that had wandered in the wilderness for thirty-eight years (Deut. 2:14). Spiritually speaking, Israel was a nation of impotent people, waiting hopelessly for something to happen.

Jesus knew about the man (see John 2:23–24) and asked him if he wanted to be healed. You would think that the man would have responded with an enthusiastic, "Yes! I want to be healed!" But, instead, he began to give excuses! He had been in that sad condition for so long that his will was as paralyzed as his body. But if you compare John 5:6 with verse 40, you will see that Jesus had a spiritual lesson in mind as well. Indeed, this man did illustrate the tragic spiritual state of the nation.

The Lord healed him through the power of His spoken word. He commanded the man to do the very thing he was unable to do, but in His command was the power of fulfillment (see Mark 3:5; Heb. 4:12). The cure was immediate and certainly some of the many people at the pool must have witnessed it. Jesus did not pause to heal anyone else; instead, He "moved away" (John 5:13) so as not to create a problem. (The Greek word means "to dodge.")

The miracle would have caused no problem except that it occurred on the Sabbath day. Our Lord certainly could have come a day earlier, or even waited a day, but He wanted to get the attention of the religious leaders. Later, He would deliberately heal a blind man on the Sabbath (John 9:1–14). The scribes had listed thirty-nine tasks that were prohibited on the Sabbath, and carrying a burden was one of them. Instead of rejoicing at the wonderful deliverance of the man, the religious leaders condemned him for carrying his bed and thereby breaking the law.

It is not easy to understand the relationship between this man and Jesus. There is no evidence that he believed on Christ and was converted, yet we cannot say that he was opposed to the Savior. In fact, he did not even know who it was that healed him until Jesus met him in the temple. No doubt the man went there to give thanks to God and to offer the appropriate sacrifices. It seems strange that the man did not actively seek a closer relationship with the One who healed him, but more than one person has gratefully accepted the gift and ignored the Giver.

Did the man "inform" on Jesus because of fear? We do not know. The Jewish leaders at least turned from him and aimed their accusations at Jesus Christ, and, unlike the healed blind man in John 9, this man was not excommunicated. The Lord's words (John 5:14) suggest that the man's physical plight had been the result of sin, but Jesus did not say that the man's sins had been forgiven as He did in dealing with the sick man lowered through the roof (see Mark 2:1–12). It is possible to experience an exciting miracle and still not be saved and go to heaven!

The Controversy (5:16–18)

The Jewish leaders did not prosecute the man who was healed, even though he had broken the law, but they did begin to persecute the Lord Jesus. As the guardians of the faith, the members of the Jewish Sanhedrin (the religious ruling council) had the responsibility of investigating new preachers and teachers who appeared in the land, lest some false prophet come along and lead the people astray. They had looked into the ministry of John the Baptist (John 1:19ff.) and more recently had been scrutinizing the ministry of Jesus.

Jesus had healed a demoniac on the Sabbath (Luke 4:31–37), so the Sanhedrin was already suspicious. In the days following the miracle recorded in John 5, Jesus would defend His disciples for picking grain on the Sabbath (Matt. 12:1–8), and He would heal a man's withered hand on the Sabbath (Matt. 12:9–14). He deliberately challenged the legalistic traditions of the scribes and Pharisees. They had taken the Sabbath—God's gift to man—and had transformed it into a prison house of regulations and restrictions.

When they confronted Jesus with His unlawful conduct, He simply replied that He was doing only what His Father was doing! God's Sabbath rest had been broken by man's sin (see Gen. 3), and ever since the fall of man, God has been seeking lost sinners and saving them. But when Jesus said "my Father" instead of the usual "our Father," used by the Jews, He claimed to be equal with God.

The Jewish leaders instantly understood His claim, and they changed their accusation from that of Sabbath-breaking to blasphemy, because Jesus claimed to be God. Liberal theologians who say that Jesus never claimed to be God have a difficult time with this passage.

Of course, the penalty for such blasphemy was death. It is here that the "official persecution" of Jesus began, culminating in His crucifixion. In the days that followed, our Lord often confronted His enemies with their evil desire to kill Him (John 7:19, 25; 8:37, 59). They hated Him without a cause (John 15:18–25). They ignored the good deeds that He performed for the helpless and hopeless, and centered their attention on destroying Him.

Jesus made Himself equal with God because He is God. This is the theme of John's gospel. The Jewish leaders could not disprove His claims, so they tried to destroy Him and get Him out of the way. Both in His crucifixion and His resurrection, Jesus openly affirmed His deity and turned His enemies' weapons against them.

British writer George MacDonald pointed out that John 5:17 gives us a profound insight into our Lord's miracles. Jesus did *instantly* what the Father is always doing slowly. For example, in nature, as mentioned earlier, the Father is slowly turning water into wine, but Jesus did it instantly. Through the powers in nature, the Father is healing broken bodies, but Jesus healed them immediately. Nature is repeatedly multiplying bread, from sowing to harvest, but Jesus multiplied it instantly in His own hands.

The Claims (5:19–47)

In response to their accusations, Jesus made three significant claims that proved His sonship.

He claimed to be equal with God (vv. 19–23). Instead of denying their accusation, He endorsed it! If today a man made this kind of a claim, we would conclude that he was joking or mentally disturbed. Jesus was certainly not insane, and there is every evidence that He was deadly serious when He spoke these words. Either He is what He claims to be, or He is a liar, and if He is a liar, how do you explain all the good He has done in the lives of needy people? Nobody wants to trust a liar; Jesus' disciples were willing to die for Him.

Jesus claimed to be one with His Father in *His works*. If healing a man on the Sabbath was a sin, then the Father was to blame! Jesus did nothing "of himself" but only that which the Father was doing. The Father and the Son worked together, doing the same deeds in the same way. "I and the Father are one" (John 10:30).

When our Lord came to earth as man, He submitted Himself to the Father in everything. "Lo, I come to do thy will, O God" (Heb. 10:9). He veiled His glory and laid aside the independent exercise of His divine attributes. In the wilderness, Satan tempted Him to use His divine powers for Himself, but He refused to act independently. He was totally dependent on the Father and the power of the Holy Spirit of God.

Not only did the Father show the Son His works and enable Him to do them, but the Father also shared His love (John 5:20). The first three Gospels open with the Father calling Jesus "My beloved Son," and John echoed this statement in John 3:35. We usually think of the Father's love for the lost world, as in John 3:16, but we must also remember the Father's love for His dear Son.

Because the Father loves the Son, the Father shows Him His works. The blind religious leaders could not see what Jesus was doing, because they did not know the Father or the Son. In fact, even greater works were in the Father's plan, works that would cause them to marvel. Perhaps He had in mind the healing of Lazarus, for in John 5:21, He mentioned the raising of the dead.

For Jesus to claim to have power to raise the dead was a blasphemous thing in the eyes of the Jewish leaders; they gave that power to God alone. They said that Jehovah held the three great keys: the key to open the heavens and give rain (Deut. 28:12); the key to open the womb and give conception (Gen. 30:22); and the key to open the grave and raise the dead (Ezek. 37:13). As far as the gospel records are concerned, Jesus had not yet raised anyone from the dead, so to make this claim was to invite even more opposition.

John 5:21 certainly can mean much more than the physical raising of people from the dead, for certainly Jesus was referring to His gift of spiritual life to the spiritually dead. He amplified this truth further as recorded in John 5:24–29.

So, Jesus claimed to be equal with the Father in His works, but He also claimed to be equal with the Father in *executing judgment* (John 5:22). To the orthodox Jew, Jehovah God was "the Judge of all the earth" (Gen. 18:25), and no one dared to apply that august title to himself. But Jesus did! By claiming to be the Judge, He claimed to be God. "Because he [God] hath appointed a day in the which he will judge the world in righteousness by that man whom he hath ordained" (Acts 17:31).

Our Lord claimed equality in another area, namely, *equal honor with the Father* (John 5:23). The fact that He is the appointed Judge should cause men to honor Him. What a tremendous claim: if you do not honor the Son, you are not honoring the Father! The "religious" people who say that they worship God, but who deny the deity of Christ, have neither the Father nor the Son! Apart from Jesus Christ, we cannot know the Father, worship the Father, or serve the Father.

He claimed to have authority to raise the dead (vv. 24–29). For a second time, Jesus introduced His words with the solemn "verily, verily" (see John 5:19, 24–25). More than twenty times in John's gospel you will find Jesus using this solemn form of address. It is as though He was saying, "Pay attention to this! What I am about to say is important!"

In this fascinating paragraph, Jesus spoke about four different resurrections. He described the resurrection of lost sinners into eternal life (see John 5:24–25; Eph. 2:1–10). The lost sinner is as lifeless and helpless as a corpse. No matter how an undertaker may prepare a corpse, it is still dead, and no corpse is "deader" than any other corpse. If you are dead, you are dead! The lost sinner is helpless to save himself, and he certainly cannot give himself life.

How are dead sinners raised from the dead? By hearing God's Word and believing on God's Son. Jesus healed the paralyzed man at the pool by His Word (John 5:8). Each time He raised somebody from the dead, He spoke the Word (Luke 7:11–17; 8:49–56; John 11:41–44). His Word is "living and powerful" (Heb. 4:12) and can raise sinners from spiritual death. "Everlasting life" means that they can never die spiritually again, nor can they ever come into judgment (Rom. 8:1). To hear His Word and believe means salvation; to reject His Word means condemnation (John 12:48).

The second resurrection mentioned is the resurrection of our Lord Himself (John 5:26). Our life is derived, but His life is original, "in himself." "In him was life" (John 1:4). The grave could not hold Him because He is "the Prince of life" (Acts 2:24; 3:15). Jesus laid down His life and then took it up again (John 10:17–18). Because He has life in Himself, He can share that life with all who will trust Him.

The third resurrection named is the future resurrection of life, when believers are raised from the dead (John 5:28–29a). This wonderful truth is explained in 1 Thessalonians 4:13–18 and 1 Corinthians 15. Keep in mind that resurrection is not reconstruction. It does not imply that God "puts the pieces back together again." The resurrection body is a new body, a glorified body, suited to the new heavenly environment. Death is not the end for the believer, nor will he live in heaven as a disembodied spirit. God saves the whole person, and this includes the body (Rom. 8:23; Phil. 3:20–21). This resurrection of life will take place when Jesus Christ returns in the air and calls His people to Himself.

The fourth resurrection He mentioned is the resurrection of condemnation (John 5:29b). This resurrection involves only the lost, and it will take place just before Jesus Christ ushers in the new heaven and the new earth (Rev. 20:11–15). What an awesome event that will be, when the dead "small and great" stand before Jesus Christ! The Father has committed all judgment to the Son (John 5:22) and has given Him the authority to execute judgment (John 5:27). Today Jesus Christ is the Savior, but one day He shall sit as the Judge.

The title "Son of man" used in John 5:27 refers to Daniel 7:13–14 and is a definite messianic title. It is used twelve times in John's gospel and over eighty times in all four gospels. The Jews would know this title from their reading of the book of Daniel, and they would know that by using it, Jesus was claiming to be the Messiah, and the Judge.

Believers will be given resurrection bodies so that they might reign with Christ in glory. Unbelievers will be given resurrection bodies—but not glorified bodies—that they might be judged and then suffer punishment in those bodies. Bodies that were used for sin will suffer the consequences of that sin.

The fact that Jesus has the authority to raise the dead is proof that He is equal with the Father, and therefore He is God.

He claimed that there are valid witnesses who support His claim to deity (vv. 30–47). The word *witness* is a key word in John's gospel; it is used forty-seven times. Jesus did bear witness to Himself, but He knew they would not accept it, so He called in three other witnesses.

The first was John the Baptist (John 5:30–35), whom the religious leaders had interrogated carefully (John 1:15ff.). In fact, at the very end of His ministry, our Lord pointed the rulers back to the witness of John the Baptist (Matt. 21:23–27). John knew who Jesus was and faithfully declared what he knew to the people of Israel. John told the people that Jesus was the Lord (John 1:23), the Lamb of God (John 1:29, 36), and the Son of God (John 1:34).

John was a "burning and a shining lamp" (Jesus is the Light, John 8:12), and the Jewish people were excited about his ministry. However, their enthusiasm cooled, and nobody lifted a finger to try to deliver John when he was arrested by Herod. The leaders looked on John as a "local celebrity" (Matt. 11:7–8), but they did not want to receive his message of repentance. The publicans and sinners accepted John's message and were converted, but the religious leaders refused to submit (Matt. 21:28–32).

Whenever God raises up a spiritual leader who commands attention, there is always the danger of attracting people who want to bask in his popularity but not submit to his authority. A "mixed multitude" followed Moses and Israel out of Egypt, people who were impressed with the miracles but not yielded to the Lord. The prophets and apostles, as well as the great leaders in church history, all had to put up with shallow people who followed the crowd but refused to obey the truth. We have them in churches today.

Our Lord's second witness was the witness of His

miracles (John 5:36). You will remember that John selected seven of these "signs" to include in his gospel as proof that Jesus is the Son of God (John 20:30–31). Jesus made it clear that His works were the works of the Father (John 5:17–20; 14:10). Even Nicodemus had to admit that our Lord's miracles identified Him as "sent from God" (John 3:2).

But the Bible also records miracles performed by ordinary men, such as Moses, Elijah, and Paul. Do these miracles prove that they are also sent of God? Yes, they do (see Heb. 2:3–4), but none of these men ever claimed to be the very Son of God. No servant of God able to perform God's mighty works would ever claim to be God Himself. The fact that Jesus made this claim, backed up by His mighty works and perfect life, is evidence that His claim is true.

Jesus indicated that the Father gave Him a specific ministry to finish while He was here on earth. "I have finished the work which thou gavest me to do" (John 17:4). He was not only on a divine timetable, but He followed a divine agenda. He had specific works to accomplish in the Father's will.

Since the Old Testament law required the testimony of two or three witnesses (Num. 35:30; Deut. 17:6), the Lord met that requirement by giving three trustworthy witnesses.

The third and final witness our Lord summoned was *the Word of the Father* (John 5:37–47). The Jewish people highly revered the written Word of God, particularly the law that was given through Moses. Moses heard God's voice and saw God's glory, but we have that same voice and glory in the inspired Word of God (see 2 Peter 1:12–21). The Old Testament Scriptures bear witness to Jesus Christ, yet the people who received and preserved that Word were blind to their own Messiah. Why?

For one thing, they did not permit that Word to generate faith in their hearts (John 5:38). John 5:39 is probably a statement of fact and not a command and could be rendered: "Ye search the scriptures, for in them ye think ye have eternal life." The Jewish scribes sought to know the Word of God, but they did not know the God of the Word! They counted the very letters of the text, but they missed the spiritual truths that the text contained.

Because of my radio ministry, I often receive letters from people who disagree with my interpretations or applications of Scripture, and sometimes these letters are quite angry. (I will not quote here the language I have seen in letters from professed Christians!) It is unfortunate when our "study" of the Bible makes us arrogant and militant instead of humble and anxious to serve others, even those who disagree with us. The mark of true Bible study is not knowledge that puffs up, but love that builds up (1 Cor. 8:1).

So, there was something wrong with the *minds* of these Jewish leaders: they did not see Christ in their own Scriptures (see 2 Cor. 3:14–18; 4:3–6). But there was also something wrong with their *wills:* they would not trust in the Savior. Because they did not have the Word in their hearts, they did not want Christ in their hearts. They were religious and self-righteous, but they were not saved.

These leaders had a third problem, and this was the lack of love in their *hearts.* "Ye have not the love of God in you" (John 5:42). This means the experience of God's love for them as well as their expression of love for God. They claimed to love God, but their attitude toward Jesus Christ proved that their love was counterfeit.

Their attitude toward God's Word hindered their faith, but so also did their attitude toward themselves and one another. The Pharisees enjoyed being honored by men (see Matt. 23:1–12), and they did not seek for the honor that comes from God alone. They did not honor the Son (John 5:23) because He did not honor them! Because they rejected the true Son of God who came in the Father's name, they would one day accept a false messiah, the Antichrist, who would come in his own name (John 5:43; and see 2 Thess. 2; Rev. 13). If we reject that which is true, we will ultimately receive that which is false.

Our Lord closed this penetrating sermon by warning the Jewish leaders that Moses, whom they honored, would be their judge, not their savior. The very Scriptures that they used to defend their religion would one day bear witness against them. The Jews *knew* what Moses wrote, but they did not really *believe* what he wrote. It is one thing to have the Word in our hands or our heads, but quite another thing to have it in our hearts. Jesus is the Word made flesh (John 1:14), and the written Word bears witness to the Incarnate Word. "And beginning at Moses and all the prophets, he expounded unto them in all the Scriptures the things concerning himself" (Luke 24:27).

The witness of John the Baptist, the witness of the divine miracles, and the witness of the Word of God all unite to declare that Jesus Christ is indeed one with the Father and the very Son of God.

Our Lord was not intimidated by the accusations of the religious leaders. If you check a harmony of the Gospels, you will see that after the events recorded in John 5, Jesus deliberately violated the Sabbath again! He permitted His disciples to pick grain on the Sabbath, and He healed a man with a withered hand (Matt. 12:1–14). These events probably took place in Galilee, but the news would certainly reach the leaders in Jerusalem and Judea.

The healing of the man on the Sabbath would come up again (John 7:21–23). The leaders would persist in protecting tradition instead of understanding truth (see Mark 7:1–13). But before we judge them, perhaps we ought to examine our own lives and churches. Are we permitting religious tradition to blind us to the truth of God's Word? Are we so involved in "Bible study" that we fail to see Jesus Christ in the Word? Does our knowledge of the Bible give us a "big head" or a "burning heart"?

CHAPTER SIX
John 6
JESUS LOSES HIS CROWD

Since John's gospel is selective (John 20:30–31), he does not record events in the life of Jesus that do not help him fulfill his purpose. Between the healing of the paralytic (John 5) and the feeding of the five thousand, you have many events taking place, some of which are mentioned in Luke 6:1—9:10 and Mark 3:1—6:30. During this period our Lord preached "the Sermon on the Mount" (Matt. 5—7) and gave the parables of the kingdom (Matt. 13).

The feeding of the five thousand was a miracle of such magnitude that it is recorded in all four gospels. A great multitude had been following Jesus for several days, listening to His teaching and beholding His miracles. Jesus had tried to "get away" to rest, but the needs of the crowd pressed on Him (Mark 6:31–34). Because of His compassion, He ministered to the multitude in three different ways.

Jesus Feeds the Multitude (6:1–14)
The problem, of course, was how to meet the needs of such a vast crowd of people. Four solutions were proposed.

First, the disciples suggested that Jesus send the people away (Mark 6:35–36). Get rid of the problem (see Matt. 15:23). But Jesus knew that the hungry people would faint on the way if somebody did not feed them. It was evening (Matt. 14:15), and that was no time for travel.

The second solution came from Philip in response to our Lord's "test question" (John 6:5): raise enough money to buy food for the people. Philip "counted the cost" and decided they would need the equivalent of two hundred days' wages! And even that would not provide bread enough to satisfy the hunger of all the men, women, and children (Matt. 14:21). Too often, we think that money is the answer to every need. Of course, Jesus was simply testing the strength of Philip's faith.

The third solution came from Andrew, but he was not quite sure how the problem would be solved. He found a little boy who had a small lunch: two little fish and five barley cakes. Once again, Andrew is busy bringing somebody to Jesus (see John 1:40–42; 12:20–22). We do not know how Andrew met this lad, but we are glad he did! Though Andrew does not have a prominent place in the Gospels, he was apparently a "people person" who helped solve problems.

The fourth solution came from our Lord, and it was the true solution. He took the little boy's lunch, blessed it, broke it, handed it out to His disciples, and they fed the whole crowd! The miracle took place in the hands of the Savior, not in the hands of the disciples. He multiplied the food; they only had the joyful privilege of passing it out. Not only were the people fed and satisfied, but the disciples salvaged twelve baskets of fragments for future use. The Lord wasted nothing.

The practical lesson is clear: whenever there is a need, give all that you have to Jesus and let Him do the rest. Begin with what you have, but be sure you give it all to Him. That little lad is to be commended for sharing his lunch with Christ, and his mother is to be commended for giving him something to give to Jesus. The gift of that little snack meant as much to Jesus as the pouring out of the expensive ointment (John 12:1ff.).

But did Jesus really perform a miracle? Perhaps the generosity of the boy only embarrassed the other people so that they brought out their hidden lunches and shared them all around. Nonsense! Jesus knows the hearts of men (John 2:24; 6:61, 64, 70) and He declared that the people were hungry. Surely He would have known of the existence of hidden food! Furthermore, the people themselves declared that this was a miracle and even wanted to crown Him King (John 6:14–16)! Had this event been only the result of mass psychology, the crowd would not have responded that way. John would never have selected this as one of the "signs" if it were not an authentic miracle.

It is significant that twice John mentioned the fact that Jesus gave thanks (John 6:11, 23). Matthew, Mark, and Luke all state that Jesus looked up to heaven when He gave thanks. By that act, He reminded the hungry people that God is the source of all good and needful gifts. This is a good lesson for us: instead of complaining about what we do not have, we should give thanks to God for what we do have, and He will make it go further.

Jesus Leaves the Multitude (6:15–21)
Jesus compelled the disciples to get into the boat (Matt. 14:22; Mark 6:45) because He knew they were in danger. The crowd was now aroused, and there was a movement to make Him King. Of course, some of the disciples would have rejoiced at the opportunity to become famous and powerful! Judas would have become treasurer of the kingdom, and perhaps Peter would have been named prime minister! But this was not in the plan of God, and Jesus broke up the meeting immediately. Certainly the Roman government would have stepped in had a movement begun.

Did Jesus know that a storm was coming? Of course. Then why did He deliberately send His friends into danger? Quite the opposite is true: He was rescuing them from greater danger, the danger of being swept along by a fanatical crowd. But there was another reason for that storm: the Lord has to balance our lives, otherwise we will become proud and then fall. The disciples had experienced great joy in being part of a thrilling miracle. Now they had to face a storm and learn to trust the Lord more. The feeding of the five thousand was the lesson, but the storm was the examination after the lesson.

Sometimes we are caught in a storm because we have disobeyed the Lord. Jonah is a good example. But sometimes the storm comes because we have *obeyed* the Lord. When that happens, we can be sure that our Savior will pray for us, come to us, and deliver us. In writing the account of this event years later, perhaps John saw in it a picture of Christ and His church. Christ is in heaven interceding for us, but we are in the midst of the storms of life, trying to reach the shore. One day, He will come for us and we shall reach the port safely, the storms all past.

Actually, there were several miracles involved in this event. Jesus walked on the water, and so did Peter (Matt. 14:28–32). Jesus stilled the storm, and instantly the boat was on the other shore. Of course, all of this happened at night so that only Jesus and His disciples knew what had occurred. Jesus had led His people into the green pastures (John 6:10), and now He brought them into the still waters (Ps. 23:2). What a wonderful Shepherd He is!

As you read the gospel records, note that our Lord was never impressed by the great crowds. He knew that their motives were not pure and that most of them followed Him in order to watch His miracles of healing. "Bread and circuses" was Rome's formula for keeping the people happy, and people today are satisfied with that kind of diet. Give them food and entertainment and they are happy. Rome set aside ninety-three days each year for public games at government expense. It was cheaper to entertain the crowds than to fight them or jail them.

We must never be deceived by the "popularity" of Jesus Christ among certain kinds of people today. Very few want Him as Savior and Lord. Many want Him only as Healer or Provider, or the One who rescues them from problems they have made for themselves. "And ye will not come to me, that ye might have life" (John 5:40).

Jesus Teaches the Multitude (6:22–71)

The purpose of the sign was that He might preach the sermon. Again, it was a ministry of "grace and truth" (John 1:17). In grace, our Lord fed the hungry people, but in truth, He gave them the Word of God. They wanted the food but they did not want the truth, and, in the end, most of them abandoned Jesus and refused to walk with Him. He lost His crowd with one sermon!

The next day began with a mystery: how did Jesus get to Capernaum? The crowd saw the disciples embark to go across the Sea of Galilee to Capernaum, and then the men were lost in the storm. The crowd also saw Jesus leave the place and go by Himself to a mountain. But the next morning, here were Jesus and His disciples *together* in Capernaum! Certainly He had not walked around the lake, and there was no evidence that He had taken another boat. Other boats had arrived, no doubt driven in by the storm, but Jesus had not been in any of them.

No doubt some of the people who had been fed simply went away to their homes, while others stayed to see what Jesus would do next. Our Lord's sermon probably began outdoors, and then the discussion moved into the synagogue (John 6:59). It would be impossible for a huge crowd to participate in the synagogue service, though the overflow could remain outside and hear what was being said.

This sermon on "the bread of life" is actually a dialogue between Christ and the people, especially the religious leaders ("the Jews"). We see four responses of the crowd to the Lord Jesus in John 6: seeking (vv. 22–40), murmuring (vv. 41–51), striving (vv. 52–59), and departing (vv. 60–71).

Seeking (vv. 22–40). The disciples may have been impressed that so many people stayed through a storm in order to seek their Master, but Jesus was not impressed. He knows the human heart. He knew that the people originally followed Him because of His miracles (John 6:2), but now their motive was to get fed! Even if they were attracted only by the miracles, at least there was still a possibility they might be saved. After all, that is where Nicodemus started (John 3:1–2). But now their interest had degenerated to the level of food.

Jesus pointed out that there are two kinds of food: food for the body, which is necessary but not the most important, and food for the inner man, the spirit, which is essential. What the people needed was not food but *life,* and life is a gift. Food only *sustains* life, but Jesus *gives* eternal life. The words of Isaiah come to mind: "Why do you spend money for what is not bread, and your wages for what does not satisfy?" (Isa. 55:2 NASB).

The people picked up the word *labor* and misinterpreted it to mean they had to *work* for salvation. They completely missed the word *give.* Steeped in legalistic religion, they thought they had to "do something" to merit eternal life. Jesus made it clear that only one "work" was necessary—to believe on the Savior. When a person believes on Christ, he is not performing a good work that earns him salvation. There is certainly no credit in believing, for it is what God does *in response to our faith* that is important (see Eph. 2:8–10).

The crowd began by seeking Christ, but then started to seek a sign from Him. "For the Jews require a sign" (1 Cor. 1:22). The rabbis taught that, when Messiah came, He would duplicate the miracle of the manna (see Ex. 16). If Jesus was truly sent by God (see John 6:29, 38, 57), then let Him prove it by causing manna to fall from heaven. They wanted to "see and believe." But faith that is based on signs alone, and not on the truth of the Word, can lead a person astray, for even Satan is able to perform "lying wonders" (2 Thess. 2:8–10). Note also John 2:18–25; 4:48.

The quotation in John 6:31 is from Psalm 78:24, a psalm that records the unbelief and rebellion of the nation of Israel.

In His reply, our Lord sought to deepen the people's understanding of the truth. It was *God,* not Moses, who gave the manna, so they must take their eyes off Moses and focus them on God. Also, God *gave* the manna in the past, but the Father is *now giving* the true bread in the person of Jesus Christ. The past event is finished, but the present spiritual experience goes on!

Then Jesus clearly identified what the bread is: He is the true Living Bread that came down from heaven. But He came, not only for Israel but for the whole world. And He came, not just to *sustain* life, but to *give* life! Seven times in this sermon, our Lord referred to His "coming down from heaven" (John 6:33, 38, 41–42, 50–51, 58), a statement that declared Him to be God. The Old Testament manna was but a type of the "true bread," the Lord Jesus Christ.

This dialogue began with the crowd seeking Christ and then seeking a sign, but listeners soon began to seek the "true bread" that Jesus talked about. However, like the woman of Samaria, they were not ready for salvation (see John 4:15). She wanted the living water so she would not have to keep going to the well. The crowd wanted the bread so they would not have to toil to maintain life. People today still want Jesus Christ only for the benefits He is able to give.

In His reply to their impetuous request, Jesus used two key words that often appear in this sermon: *come and believe.* To come to Jesus means to believe on Him, and to believe on Him means to come to Him. Believing is not merely an intellectual thing, giving mental assent to some doctrine. It means to come to Christ and yield yourself to Him. At the close of His sermon, Jesus illustrated *coming* and *believing* by speaking about *eating* and *drinking.* To come to Christ and believe on Him means to receive Him within, just as you receive food and drink.

John 6:35 contains the first of seven great "I am" statements recorded by John, statements that are found nowhere else in the Gospels. (For the other six, see John 8:12; 10:7–9, 11–14; 11:25–26; 14:6; 15:1, 5.) God revealed Himself to Moses by the name I AM (Jehovah) (Ex. 3:14). God is the self-existent One who "is, and … was, and … is to come" (Rev. 1:8). When Jesus used the name "I am," He was definitely claiming to be God.

John 6:37–40 contains Jesus' explanation of the process of personal salvation. These are among the most profound words He ever spoke, and we cannot hope to plumb their depths completely. He explained that salvation involves both divine sovereignty and human responsibility. The Father *gives* men and women to the Son (John 6:37, 39; 17:2, 6, 9, 11–12, 24), but these men and women must *come* to Him, that is, *believe* on Him. He assured them that nobody who came to Him would ever be lost but would be raised at the last day. Even death cannot rob us of salvation! (In regard to the "last day," see John 6:40, 44, 54. Jesus was referring to His return and the final events that climax God's program for mankind.)

From our human and limited perspective, we cannot see how divine sovereignty and human responsibility can work together, but from God's perspective, there is no conflict. When a church member asked Charles Spurgeon how he reconciled these two, he replied, "I never try to reconcile friends." It is the Father's will that sinners be saved (1 Tim. 2:4; 2 Peter 3:9) and that those who trust Christ be secure in their salvation. Believers receive eternal life, and Jesus can never lose them.

Murmuring (vv. 41–51). Our Lord's statement "For I came down from heaven" (John 6:38) disturbed the religious leaders, for they knew it was a claim of deity. They thought they knew Jesus, who He was and where He came from (see Matt. 13:53–58; John 7:40–43). Jesus, of course, was the *legal* son of Joseph but not his natural son, for He was born of a virgin (Luke 1:34–38). The leaders identified Jesus with Nazareth in Galilee, not Bethlehem in Judea, and they thought that Joseph was His natural father. Had they investigated the matter, they would have learned who Jesus really is.

Even in the days of Moses, the Jews were known for their murmuring (Ex. 15:24; 17:3; Num. 14:2). Perhaps the leaders and some of the crowd had now moved into the synagogue to continue the discussion. The main issue was, "Where did He come from?" Five times Jesus used the phrase "came down from heaven," but they would not accept it.

Jesus further explained how the sinner can come to God: it is through the truth of the Word (John 6:44–45). The Father draws the sinner by His Word. Jesus quoted Isaiah 54:13 (or perhaps Jer. 31:33–34) to prove His point: "And they shall all be taught of God." It is through the teaching of the Word that God draws people to the Savior. (Note John 5:24 and its emphasis on hearing the Word.) The sinner hears, learns, and comes as the Father draws him. A mystery? Yes! A blessed reality? Yes!

This was basically the same message He gave after He had healed the paralytic (see John 5:37–40). The crowd wanted to *see* something, but their real need was to *learn* something. It is by the Word that we "see" God and receive the faith to come to Christ and trust Him (Rom. 10:17).

When Jesus called Himself "the Living Bread," He was not claiming to be exactly like the manna. *He was claiming to be even greater!* The manna only *sustained* life for the Jews, but Jesus *gives life* to the whole world. The Jews ate the daily manna and eventually died, but when you receive Jesus Christ within, you live forever. When God gave the manna, He gave only a gift, but when Jesus came, He gave Himself. There was no cost to God in sending the manna each day, but He gave His Son at great cost. The Jews had to eat the manna every day, but the sinner who trusts Christ *once* is given eternal life.

It is not difficult to see in the manna a picture of our Lord Jesus Christ. The manna was a mysterious thing to the Jews; in fact, the word *manna* means "What is it?" (see Ex. 16:15). Jesus was a mystery to those who saw Him. The manna came at night from heaven, and Jesus came to this earth when sinners were in moral and spiritual darkness. The manna was small (His humility), round (His eternality), and white (His purity). It was sweet to the taste (Ps. 34:8), and it met the needs of the people adequately.

The manna was given to a rebellious people; it was the gracious gift of God. All they had to do was stoop and pick it up. If they failed to pick it up, *they walked on it.* The Lord is not far from any sinner. All the sinner has to do is humble himself and take the gift that God offers.

Jesus closed this part of His message by referring to His *flesh,* a word that will be used six more times before the dialogue is concluded. John 6:51 is a declaration that the Son of God will give Himself as a sacrifice "for the life of the world." The substitutionary death of Jesus Christ is a key doctrine in John's gospel. Jesus would die for the world (John 3:16; 6:51), for His sheep (John 10:11, 15), for the nation (John 11:50–52), and for His friends (John 15:12). Paul made it personal, and so should we: "who loved me, and gave himself for me" (Gal. 2:20). We must not limit the work of Christ on the cross. He is the sacrifice not for our sins only, but also for the sins of the whole world (1 John 2:2).

Striving (vv. 52–59). The word striving means "to fight and quarrel." Being orthodox Jews, the listeners knew the divine prohibition against eating human flesh or any kind of blood (Gen. 9:3–4; Lev. 17:10–16; 19:26). Here we have another example in John's gospel of the people misunderstanding a spiritual truth by treating it literally (see John 2:19–21; 3:4; 4:11). All Jesus said was, "Just as you take food and drink within your body and it becomes a part of you, so you must receive Me within your innermost being so that I can give you life."

Some interpreters tell us that Jesus was speaking about the Lord's Supper, and that we eat His flesh and drink His blood when we partake of the elements at the table, the bread and the cup. I do not believe that Jesus had the Communion (or Eucharist) in mind when He spoke these words.

For one thing, why would He discuss the Lord's Supper with a group of disagreeable unbelievers? He had not even shared that truth with His own disciples! Why would He cast this precious pearl before the swine?

Second, he made it clear that He was not speaking in literal terms (John 6:63). He was using a human analogy to convey a spiritual truth, just as He did with Nicodemus and the Samaritan woman.

Third, Jesus made it plain that this eating and drinking were *absolutely essential* for eternal life. He made no exceptions. If, then, He was speaking about a church ordinance (or sacrament), then everybody who has never shared in that experience is spiritually dead

and is going to hell. This would include all the Old Testament saints, the thief on the cross, and a host of people who have trusted Christ in emergency situations (hospitals, accidents, foxholes, etc.). I personally cannot believe that our gracious God has excluded from salvation all who cannot participate in a church ceremony.

Another factor is the tense of the Greek verbs in John 6:50–51 and 53. It is the aorist tense, which signifies a once-for-all action. The Communion service is a repeated thing; in fact, it is likely that the early church observed the Lord's Supper daily (Acts 2:46).

It is significant that the word *flesh* is never used in any of the reports of the Lord's Supper, either in the Gospels or in 1 Corinthians 11:23–34. The word used is *body.*

If a person holds that our Lord was speaking about the Communion service, then he must believe that somehow the two elements, the bread and the fruit of the vine, turn into the very body and blood of Christ, for He said, "So he that eateth *me,* even he shall live by *me"* (John 6:57, italics mine). How does this "miracle" take place? What is the secret of accomplishing it? Why is it not apparent?

Our Lord's messages recorded in the gospel of John are filled with symbolism and imagery. To take them literally is to make the same mistake the people made who first heard them.

Departing (vv. 60–71). Our Lord's teaching was not hard to understand but hard to accept once you understood it. The Jewish religious leaders both misunderstood His words and rejected them. They were "offended" by what He taught. (The Greek word is "scandalized.") They stumbled over the fact that He claimed to come down from heaven. They also stumbled over the idea that they had to eat His flesh and drink His blood in order to be saved. But if they stumbled over these two matters, what would they do if they saw Him ascend back into heaven (John 6:62)?

Jesus explained that His language was figurative and spiritual, not literal. There is no salvation in "flesh." In fact, the New Testament has nothing good to say about "the flesh." There is nothing good in it (Rom. 7:18), and we must not have confidence in it (Phil. 3:3).

How, then, do we "eat His flesh and drink His blood"? *Through the Word.* "The words that I speak unto you, they are spirit and they are life" (John 6:63). "And the Word was made flesh" (John 1:14). Our Lord said the same thing: "He that heareth my word and believeth on him that sent me, hath everlasting life" (John 5:24). The scribes who knew Jeremiah 31:31–34 would have understood the concept of receiving God's Word into one's inner being.

The result of this message was the loss of most of our Lord's disciples. They went back to the old life, the old religion, and the old hopeless situation. Jesus Christ is "the way" (John 14:6), but they would not walk with Him. This was no surprise to the Lord, because He knows the hearts of all people.

When Jesus asked His twelve apostles if they planned to desert Him too, it was Peter who spoke up and declared their faith. Where else could they go? "Thou hast the words of eternal life." Peter got the message! He knew that Jesus was speaking about *the Word* and not about literal flesh and blood.

Peter was one of several people who declared their belief that Jesus is the Son of God (see John 1:34, 49; 3:18; 5:25; 9:35; 10:36; 11:4, 27; 19:7; 20:31). The only mistake he made was to bear witness for the entire group. Peter was sure that *all* of the apostles were believers, which shows how convincing Judas was. Even Peter did not know that Judas was an unbeliever!

The preaching of the Word of God always leads to a sifting of the hearts of the listeners. God draws sinners to the Savior through the power of truth, His Word. Those who reject the Word will reject the Savior. Those who receive the Word will receive the Savior and experience the new birth, eternal life.

Do you feel your need because there is a spiritual hunger within? Are you willing to admit that need and come to the Savior? If you will, He will save you and satisfy you *forever!*

CHAPTER SEVEN
John 7
FEAST FIGHT

The Feast of Tabernacles looked back to Israel's journey through the wilderness, and looked forward to the promised kingdom of Messiah. The Jews lived in booths made of branches to remind them of God's providential care of the nation for nearly forty years (Lev. 23:33–44).

Following the Feast of Trumpets and the solemn day of Atonement, Tabernacles was a festive time for the people. The temple area was illumined by large candlesticks that reminded the people of the guiding pillar of fire, and each day the priests would carry water from the Pool of Siloam and pour it out from a golden vessel, reminding the Jews of the miraculous provision of water from the rock.

The feast may have been a jubilant time for the people, but it was a difficult time for Jesus, for it marked the beginning of open and militant opposition to Him and His ministry. Ever since He had healed the paralytic on the Sabbath day, Jesus had been targeted by the Jewish leaders who wanted to kill Him (John 7:1, 19–20, 25, 30, 32, 44; and note 8:37, 40). He remained in Galilee, where He would be safer, but He could not remain in Galilee and also observe the feast.

John 7 has three time divisions: before the feast (vv. 1–10), in the midst of the feast (vv. 11–36), and on the last day of the feast (vv. 37–52). The responses during each of those periods can be characterized by three words: disbelief, debate, and division.

Before the Feast: Disbelief (7:1–10)

Mary bore other children, with Joseph as their natural father (Matt. 13:55–56; Mark 6:1–6), so Jesus would have been their half-brother. It seems incredible that His brothers could have lived with Him all those years and not realized the uniqueness of His person. Certainly they knew about His miracles (see John 7:3–4) since everybody else did. Having been in the closest contact with Him, they had the best opportunity to watch Him and test Him, yet they were still unbelievers.

Here were men going up to a religious feast, yet rejecting their own Messiah! How easy it is to follow tradition and miss eternal truth. The publicans and sinners were rejoicing at His message, but His own half-brothers were making fun of Him.

These men certainly had the world's point of view: if you want to get a following, use your opportunities to do something spectacular. Jerusalem would be crowded with pilgrims, and this would give Jesus the ideal "platform" to present Himself and win disciples. No doubt the brothers knew that the multitude of disciples had deserted Jesus (John 6:66). This was His opportunity to recoup His losses. Satan had offered a similar suggestion three years before (Matt. 4:1ff.).

Jesus had already turned down the crowd's offer to make Him king (John 6:15), and He was not about to yield to them in any way. Celebrities might ride to success on the applause of the crowd, but God's servants know better. By doing miracles during the feast, at the "official city," Jesus could muster a crowd, reveal Himself as Messiah, and overcome the enemy. The suggestion, of course, came from hearts and minds blinded by unbelief. This unbelief had been prophesied in Psalm 69:8—"I am become a stranger unto my brethren, and an alien unto my mother's children." (Since Jesus was not Joseph's natural son, He could not say "My father's children.")

It was not the right time for Jesus to show Himself to the world (John 14:22ff.). One day He shall return, and "every eye shall see him" (Rev. 1:7). We have noticed that our Lord lived on a "divine timetable" that was marked out by the Father (John 2:4; 7:6, 8, 30; 8:20; 12:23; 13:1; 17:1).

Jesus was exercising caution because He knew that the Jewish leaders wanted to kill Him. Though they were "religious" leaders, they were a part of "the world" that hated Jesus because He exposed their evil works. By His character and His ministry, He revealed the shallowness and emptiness of their futile religious system; He called the people back to the reality of life in God. History reveals that the "religious system" often persecutes the very prophets of God who are sent to save it!

Some manuscripts do not have the word *yet* in John 7:8, but its absence does not alter the thrust of the statement. Jesus was certainly not lying or being evasive; rather, He was exercising sensible caution. Suppose He told His brothers His plans, and they told somebody else? Could the information possibly get to the leaders? "I am going to the feast when the right time comes," is what He said. After His family had gone, Jesus went to Jerusalem "under cover," so as not to call attention to Himself.

In our Lord's actions, we see a beautiful illustration of divine sovereignty and human responsibility. The Father had a plan for His Son, and nothing could spoil that plan. Jesus did not tempt the Father by rushing to the feast, nor did He lag behind when the proper time had come for Him to attend the feast. It requires spiritual discernment to know God's timing.

In the Midst of the Feast: Debate (7:11–36)

Note that this public debate about the Lord Jesus involved three different groups of people. First, of course, were the Jewish leaders ("the Jews") who lived in Jerusalem and were attached to the temple ministry. This would include the Pharisees and the chief priests (most of whom were Sadducees) as well as the scribes. These men differed theologically, but they agreed on one thing: their opposition to Jesus Christ and their determination to get rid of Him. The exceptions would be Nicodemus and Joseph of Arimathea (John 19:38–42).

The second group would be "the people" (John 7:12, 20, 31–32). This would be the festival crowd that had come to Jerusalem to worship. Many of them would not be influenced by the attitude of the religious leaders at Jerusalem. You will note in John 7:20 that "the people" were amazed that anybody would want to kill Jesus! They were not up to date on all the gossip in the city and had to learn the hard way that Jesus was considered a lawbreaker by the officials.

The third group was composed of the Jews who resided in Jerusalem (John 7:25). They, of course, would have likely sided with the religious leaders.

The debate began before Jesus even arrived at the city, and it centered on *His character* (John 7:11–13). The religious leaders "kept seeking" Jesus, while the crowd kept arguing whether He was a good man or a deceiver. He would have to be one or the other, because a truly good man would not deceive anybody. Yes, Jesus is either what He claims to be, or He is a liar.

But when Jesus began to teach openly in the temple, the debate shifted to *His doctrine* (John 7:14–19). Character and doctrine go together, of course. It would be foolish to trust the teachings of a liar! The Jews were amazed at what He taught because He did not have any credentials from their approved rabbinical schools. But since He lacked this "proper accreditation," His enemies said that His teachings were nothing but private opinions and not worth much. It has often been said that Jesus taught with authority, while the scribes and Pharisees taught from authorities, quoting all the famous rabbis.

Jesus explained that His doctrine came from the Father. He had already made it clear that He and the Father were one in the works that He performed (John 5:17) and in the judgment that He executed (John 5:30). Now He claimed that His teachings also came from the Father, and He would make that astounding claim again (John 8:26, 38). When I teach the Word of God, I can claim authority for the Bible but not for all of my interpretations of the Bible. Jesus rightly could claim absolute authority for everything that He taught!

But does not *every* religious teacher make a similar claim? How, then, can we know that Jesus is teaching us the truth? *By obeying what He tells us to do.* God's Word proves itself true to those who will sincerely do it. The British preacher F.W. Robertson said that "obedience is the organ of spiritual knowledge." John 7:17 literally reads, "If any man is willing to do His [God's] will, he shall know." This explains why the Jewish leaders did not understand Jesus' teachings: they had stubborn wills and would not submit to Him (John 5:40).

Is our Lord suggesting here a "pragmatic test" for divine truth? Is He saying, "Try it! If it works, it must be true!" and thus suggesting that if it does not work it must be false? This kind of a test would lead to confusion, for almost any cultist could say, "I tried what the cult teaches, and it works!"

No, our Lord's statement goes much deeper. He was not suggesting a shallow "taste test" but rather the deep personal commitment of the person to truth. The Jews depended on education and authorities and received their doctrine secondhand, but Jesus insisted that we experience the authority of truth *personally.* The Jewish leaders were attempting to *kill Jesus*, yet at the same time they claimed to understand God's truth and obey it. This proves that an enlightened and educated mind is no guarantee of a pure heart or a sanctified will. Some of the world's worst criminals have been highly intelligent and well-educated people.

Satan offered Adam and Eve knowledge, but it was knowledge based on disobedience (Gen. 3:5). Jesus offered knowledge as the result of obedience: first the yoke of responsibility, then the joy of knowing God's truth. Dr. G. Campbell Morgan said it perfectly: "When men are wholly, completely consecrated to the will of God and want to do that above everything else, then they find out that Christ's teaching is divine, that it is the teaching of God."

If we really seek God's will, then we will not worry over who gets the glory. All truth is God's truth, and God alone deserves the glory for what He has taught us. No teacher or preacher can take the credit for what only can come from God. If he does go after the glory, then it is proof that his teaching is self-generated and not received from God. This is the origin of many cults and church splits: somebody "invents" a doctrine, takes credit for it, and uses it to divide God's people.

The first "debate" was with the Jews: but the visitors to the city entered into the discussion (John 7:20). Jesus had boldly announced that the leaders wanted to kill Him because He had violated the Sabbath and then claimed to be God (see John 5:10–18). The orthodox Jews broke the Sabbath laws when they had their sons circumcised on the Sabbath, so why could He not heal a man on the Sabbath? "Why go ye about to kill me?"

The visitors, of course, did not know that their leaders were out to kill Jesus, so they challenged His statement. But their reply contained a serious accusation—that Jesus had a demon. This was not a new accusation, for the leaders had said it before (Matt. 9:32ff.; 10:25; 11:18–19; 12:24ff.). "You must be crazy to think that anybody wants to kill You!"

Our Lord used the very law of Moses to refute the enemy's argument, but He knew that they would not give in. Why? Because their standard of judgment was not honest. They evaluated things on the basis of superficial examination of the facts. They judged on the basis of "seems" and not "is." Unfortunately, too many people make that same mistake today. John 7:24 is the opposite of verse 17, where Jesus called for sincere devotion to truth.

The residents of Jerusalem entered the conversation (John 7:25). They knew that the rulers wanted to kill Jesus, and they were amazed that He was teaching openly and getting away with it! Perhaps the rulers had been convinced that indeed He is the Messiah, sent from God! Then why were they not worshipping Him and leading others to worship Him?

Their question (John 7:25) suggested a negative answer: "No, the rulers do not believe that He is the Christ, do they?" They were able to defend their conclusion with logic:

1. Nobody knows where the Christ comes from.
2. We know where Jesus of Nazareth came from.
3. Conclusion: Jesus cannot be the Messiah.

Once again, the people could not see the truth because they were blinded by what they thought were dependable facts. Jesus had met this same kind of resistance in the synagogue in Capernaum (John 6:42ff.). Even the learned teachers—the "expert builders"—would not be able to identify the Chief Cornerstone, even though they had studied the God-given "blueprints" for centuries (Acts 4:11)!

At this point, our Lord raised His voice so that everybody could hear (note also John 7:37). He was probably speaking in a tone revealing irony: "Yes, you think you know Me and where I came from! But really, you do not!" Then He explained why they did not know Him: *they did not know the Father!* This was a serious accusation to make against an orthodox Jew, for the Jews prided themselves in knowing the true God, the God of Israel.

But Jesus went even further He boldly asserted that He not only knew the Father, but was sent by Him! He

was once again claiming to be God! He was not simply *born* into this world like any other human; He was *sent* to earth by the Father. This means that He existed before He was born on the earth.

This was certainly a crisis hour in His ministry, and some of the leaders tried to have Him arrested, but "his hour was not yet come." Many of the pilgrims put their faith in Him. It was a faith based on miracles, but at least it was a beginning (see John 2:23; 6:2, 26). Nicodemus first became interested in Jesus because of His miracles (John 3:1–2), and eventually he openly professed faith in Christ.

The Pharisees and chief priests, who presided over the Jewish religious establishment, resented the fact that the people were trusting in Jesus. Apparently these "believers" were not afraid to tell what they had done (John 7:13, 32). This time, the rulers sent members of the temple guard to arrest Jesus, but it was Jesus who "arrested" them! He warned them that they had but "a little while" to hear the truth, believe, and be saved (see John 12:35ff.). It was not Jesus who was in danger, but those who wanted to arrest Him!

As in previous messages, the people misunderstood what Jesus was saying. Within six months, Jesus would go back to the Father in heaven, and the unsaved Jews would not be able to follow Him. What a contrast between "where I am, there ye cannot come" (John 7:34) and "that where I am, there ye may be also" (John 14:3)!

Had these men been willing to do God's will, they would have known the truth. Soon it would be too late.

The End of the Feast: Division (7:37–52)

The last day of the feast would be the seventh day, a very special day on which the priests would march seven times around the altar, chanting Psalm 118:25. It would be the last time they would draw the water and pour it out. No doubt just as they were pouring out the water, symbolic of the water Moses drew from the rock, Jesus stood and shouted His great invitation to thirsty sinners.

It has been pointed out that this "great day," the twenty-first of the seventh month, is the same date on which the prophet Haggai made a special prediction about the temple (Hag. 2:1–9). While the ultimate fulfillment must await the return of Christ to this earth, certainly there was a partial fulfillment when Jesus came to the temple. Haggai 2:6–7 is quoted in Hebrews 12:26–29 as applying to the return of the Lord.

Jesus was referring to the experience of Israel recorded in Exodus 17:1–7. That water was but a picture of the Spirit of God. Believers would not only drink the living water, but they would become channels of living water to bless a thirsty world! The "artesian well" that He promised in John 4:14 has now become a flowing river! While there are no specific prophetic Scriptures that indicate "rivers of water" flowing from the believer, there are a number of verses that parallel this thought: Isaiah 12:3; 15; 32:2; 44:3; and 58:11; and Zechariah 14:8. Note that Zechariah 14:16ff. speaks about the future Feast of Tabernacles, when the Lord is King.

Water for drinking is one of the symbols of the Holy Spirit in the Bible. (Water for washing is a symbol of the Word of God; see John 15:3; Eph. 5:26.) Just as water satisfies thirst and produces fruitfulness, so the Spirit of God satisfies the inner person and enables us to bear fruit. At the feast, the Jews were reenacting a tradition that could never satisfy the heart. Jesus offered them living water and eternal satisfaction!

What was the result of this declaration and invitation? The people were divided: some defended Him and some wanted to arrest Him. Is He a "good man" or "a deceiver" (John 7:12)? Is He "the Christ" (John 7:31)? Is He the promised "Prophet" (John 7:40; Deut. 18:15)? If only they had honestly examined the evidence, they would have discovered that, indeed, He was the Christ, the Son of God. They identified Jesus with Galilee (John 1:45–46; 7:52) when in reality He was born in Bethlehem (see John 6:42 for similar reasoning).

The temple officers returned to the Jewish council meeting empty-handed. It certainly should have been relatively easy for them to arrest Jesus, yet they failed to do so. What stopped them? "Never man spake like this man!" was their defense. In other words, "This Jesus is more than a man! No mere man speaks as He does!" They were "arrested" by the Word of God, spoken by the Son of God.

Again, the leaders refused to face facts honestly but passed judgment on the basis of their prejudices and their superficial examination of the facts. It is much easier to label people (and *libel* people!) than to listen to the facts they present. "So some of the people have believed on Jesus! So what? These common people know nothing about the law anyway! Have any *important* people—like ourselves—believed on Him? Of course not!" They would use a similar argument to try to discredit the witness of the blind man that Jesus healed (John 9:34).

We should not be surprised when "the intelligentsia" refuses to trust Jesus Christ, or when religious leaders reject Him. God has hidden His truth from "the wise and prudent" and revealed it to "spiritual babes," the humble people who will yield to Him (Matt. 11:25–27). Paul was a very intelligent rabbi when God saved him, yet he had to be "knocked down" before he would acknowledge that Jesus Christ was the resurrected Son of God. Read 1 Corinthians 1:26–31 to learn Paul's explanation for the difficulty of winning "smart religious people" to the Savior.

No doubt the rulers would have sent the guard out again, but Nicodemus spoke up. This man is found three times in John's gospel, and each time he is identified as the one "who came to Jesus by night" (see John 3:1–2; 19:39). No doubt Nicodemus had been doing a great deal of thinking and studying since that first interview with Jesus, and he was not afraid to take his stand for truth.

Nicodemus was sure that the council was not giving Jesus an honest hearing. The rulers had already passed judgment and were trying to arrest Him before He had even been given a fair and lawful trial! Perhaps Nicodemus had in mind such Old Testament Scriptures as Exodus 23:1 and Deuteronomy 1:16–17; 19:15–21.

What did Nicodemus want them to consider about Jesus? His word and His works. It was Jesus the Teacher and the miracle worker who had attracted Nicodemus's interest in the first place (John 3:2). In fact, Jesus had pointed to His works as proof of His deity (John 5:32), and He repeatedly urged the people to pay attention to His words. The two go together, for the miracles point to the messages, and the messages interpret the spiritual meaning of the miracles.

You can hear the sarcasm and disdain in the reply of the rulers: "Are you a lowly and despised Galilean too?" They refused to admit that Nicodemus was right in asking for a fair trial, but the only way they could answer him was by means of ridicule. This is an ancient debate trick: when you cannot answer the argument, attack the speaker.

They challenged Nicodemus to search the prophecies to see if he could find any statement that a prophet would come out of Galilee. Of course, Jonah was from Galilee, and Jesus said that Jonah was a picture of Himself in death, burial, and resurrection (Matt. 12:38–41). Perhaps Nicodemus read Isaiah 9:1–2 (see Matt. 4:12–16) and began to trace the great messianic prophecies in the Old Testament. If he did, then he became convinced that Jesus of Nazareth was the very Son of God.

You cannot help but feel sorry for the people described in this chapter, people who responded to Jesus in the wrong ways. His half-brothers responded with disbelief, various people responded with debate, and the result was division. Had they willingly received the truth, and had they acted with sincere obedience, they would have ended up at the feet of Jesus, confessing Him as Messiah and Son of God.

But people *today* commit the same blunder and permit their prejudices and superficial evaluations to blind them to the truth.

Don't let it happen to you!

CHAPTER EIGHT
John 8
CONTRASTS AND CONFLICTS

I s the story of the woman taken in adultery a part of Scripture? If it is, where does it belong in the gospel record? John 7:53—8:11 is not found in some of the ancient manuscripts; where it is found, it is not always in this location in John's gospel. Most scholars seem to agree that the passage is a part of inspired Scripture ("a fragment of authentic gospel material," says Dr. F. F. Bruce) regardless of where it is placed.

To many of us, the story fits right here! In fact, the development of the entire chapter can easily be seen to grow out of this striking event in the temple. Our Lord's declaration on His being the Light of the World (John 8:12) certainly fits, and so do His words about true and false judgment (John 8:15–16, 26). The repeated phrase "die in your sins" (John 8:21, 24) would clearly relate to the judgment of the woman, and the fact that the chapter ends with an attempt to stone Jesus shows a perfect parallel to the opening story. The transition from John 7:52 to 8:12 would be too abrupt without a transitional section.

Our Lord found Himself again in conflict with the Jewish religious leaders, but this time, they set a trap, hoping to get enough evidence to arrest Jesus and get Him out of the way. However, their plot failed, but a controversy followed. In this chapter we see a series of contrasts that reveal the graciousness of Christ and the wickedness of man.

Grace and Law (8:11)

The Feast of Tabernacles had ended, but Jesus took advantage of the opportunity to minister to the pilgrims in the temple. During the feast, word had quickly spread that Jesus was not only attending but openly teaching in the temple (see Luke 21:37). He taught in the court of the women at the place where the treasury was situated (John 8:20). The scribes and Pharisees knew where He would be, so they hatched their plot together.

They would not be likely to catch a couple in the "very act" of adultery, so we wonder if the man (who never was indicted!) was part of the scheme. The law required that both guilty parties be stoned (Lev. 20:10; Deut. 22:22) and not just the woman. It does seem suspicious that the man went free. The scribes and Pharisees handled the matter in a brutal fashion, even in the way they interrupted the Lord's teaching and pushed the woman into the midst of the crowd.

The Jewish leaders, of course, were trying to pin Jesus on the horns of a dilemma. If He said, "Yes, the woman must be stoned!" then what would happen to His reputation as the "friend of publicans and sinners"? The common people would no doubt have abandoned Him and would never have accepted His gracious message of forgiveness.

But, if He said, "No, the woman should not be stoned!" then He was openly breaking the law and subject to arrest. On more than one occasion, the religious leaders had tried to pit Jesus against Moses, and now they seemed to have the perfect challenge (see John 5:39–47; 6:32ff.; 7:40ff.).

Instead of passing judgment on the woman, Jesus passed judgment on the judges! No doubt He was indignant at the way they treated the woman. He was also concerned that such hypocrites should condemn another person and not judge themselves. We do not know what He wrote on the dirt floor of the temple. Was He simply reminding them that the Ten Commandments had been originally written "by the finger of God" (Ex. 31:18), and that He is God? Or was He perhaps reminding them of the warning in Jeremiah 17:13?

It was required by Jewish law that the accusers cast the first stones (Deut. 17:7). Jesus was not asking that sinless men judge the woman, for He was the only sinless Person present. If our judges today had to be perfect, judicial benches would be empty. He was referring to the particular sin of the woman, a sin that can be committed in the heart as well as with the body (Matt. 5:27–30). Convicted by their own consciences, the accusers quietly left the scene, and Jesus was left alone with the woman. He forgave her and warned her to sin no more (John 5:14).

We must not misinterpret this event to mean that Jesus was "easy on sin" or that He contradicted the law. For Jesus to forgive this woman meant that He had to one day die for her sins. Forgiveness is free but it is not cheap. Furthermore, Jesus perfectly fulfilled the law so that no one could justly accuse Him of opposing its teachings or weakening its power. By applying the law to the woman and not to themselves, the Jewish leaders were violating both the letter and the spirit of the law—and they thought they were defending Moses!

The law was given to reveal sin (Rom. 3:20), and we must be condemned by the law before we can be cleansed by God's grace. Law and grace do not compete with each other; they complement each other. Nobody was ever saved by keeping the law, but nobody was ever saved by grace who was not first indicted by the law. There must be conviction before there can be conversion.

Nor is Christ's gracious forgiveness an excuse to sin. "Go, and sin no more!" was our Lord's counsel. "But there is forgiveness with thee, that thou mayest be feared" (Ps. 130:4). Certainly the experience of gracious forgiveness would motivate the penitent sinner to live a holy and obedient life to the glory of God.

Light and Darkness (8:12–20)

This second great "I am" statement certainly fits into the context of the first eleven verses of John 8. Perhaps the sun was then appearing (John 8:2) so that Jesus was comparing Himself to the rising sun. But this would mean He was once again claiming to be God, for to the Jew, the sun was a symbol of Jehovah God (Ps. 84:11; Mal. 4:2). There is, for our galaxy, only one sun, and it is the center and the source of life. So there is but one God who is the center of all and the source of all life (John 1:4). "God is light" (1 John 1:5), and wherever the light shines, it reveals man's wickedness (Eph. 5:8–14).

Our Lord's "I am" statement was also related to the Feast of Tabernacles, during which the huge candelabra were lighted in the temple at night to remind the people of the pillar of fire that had guided Israel in their wilderness journey. In fact, John has combined three "wilderness images": the manna (John 6), the water from the rock (John 7), and the pillar of fire (John 8).

To "follow" the Lord Jesus means to believe on Him, to trust Him, and the results are *life* and *light* for the believer. The unsaved are walking in darkness because they love darkness (John 3:17ff.). One of the major messages in this gospel is that the spiritual light is now shining, but people cannot comprehend it—and they try to put it out (John 1:4–5).

Not all of the Jewish leaders had left the group, and others had no doubt come along after the woman left. As usual, they debated with Jesus. This time, they accused Him of bearing witness to Himself by claiming to be the Light of the world, and Jewish courts would not permit a person to bear witness to himself.

But light *has to* bear witness to itself! The only people who cannot see the light are *blind* people!

I recall the first time I flew at night. I was fascinated by the changing textures of colored lights in the cities below me. When our plane left the New York area and headed out into the night, I was amazed that I could see pinpoints of light miles away. Then I understood why it was necessary to have blackouts during the war, for the enemy pilots could see the smallest evidence of light and thus find the target. Light bears witness to itself; it tells you it is there.

Perhaps the Pharisees were quoting our Lord's own words (see John 5:31ff.), but He quickly refuted *their* argument. One of the key words in this section is *witness;* it is used seven times. Jesus made it clear that their witness was not dependable because their judgment was faulty. They judged on the basis of externals, mere human judgment, but He judged on the basis of spiritual knowledge. The way they judged the woman taken in adultery proved that they neither understood the law nor their own sinful hearts.

Since they wanted to use the law to condemn the woman and trap the Savior, Jesus also used the law to answer them. He quoted a principle found in Deuteronomy 17:6 and 19:15, as well as Numbers 35:30, that the testimony of two men was required to validate a judgment. Jesus had those two testimonies: *He* gave witness and so did *His Father*. We have seen from John 5:37–47 that the witness of the Father is found in the Word of God.

How tragic that these experts in the law did not even know their own Messiah as He stood before them! They claimed to know the law of God, but they did not know the God of the law. They did not have His Word abiding in their hearts (John 5:38), nor did they experience His love (John 5:42). They did not know the Father, and therefore did not know the Son.

Jesus never really answered their question, "Where is thy Father?" The word *father* is used twenty-one times in this chapter, so Jesus did not avoid the issue but faced it honestly. He knew that their "father" was

not God—but the devil! These men were religious, and yet they were the children of the devil!

Their further attempts to arrest Jesus were again thwarted by the Father, for it was not yet our Lord's hour when He should give His life. When the servant of God is in the will of God, he can have courage and peace as he does his duty.

Life and Death (8:21–30)

Jesus had already mentioned His leaving them (John 7:34), but the Jews had misunderstood what He said. Once again, He warned them: He would leave them, they would not be able to follow Him, and they would die in their sins! They were wasting their God-given opportunities by arguing with Him instead of trusting Him, and one day soon, their opportunities would end.

Once again, the people misunderstood His teaching. They thought He was planning to kill Himself! Suicide was an abhorrent thing to a Jew, for the Jews were taught to honor all life. If Jesus committed suicide, then He would go to a place of judgment, and this, they reasoned, was why they could not follow Him.

Actually, just the opposite was true: it was *they* who were going to the place of judgment! Jesus was returning to His Father in heaven, and nobody can go there who has not trusted the Savior. The reason Jesus and the Jewish leaders were going to different destinations was because they had different *origins:* Jesus came from heaven, but they belonged to the earth. Jesus was *in* the world, but He did not belong to the world (see John 17:14–16).

The true believer has his citizenship in heaven (Luke 10:20; Phil. 3:20–21). His affection and attention are fixed heavenward. But the unsaved belong to this world; in fact, Jesus called them "the children of this world" (Luke 16:8). Since they have not trusted Christ and had their sins forgiven, their destiny is to die in their sins. The Christian dies "in the Lord" because he lives "in the Lord" (Rev. 14:13), but the unbeliever dies in his sins because he lives in his sins.

It seems incredible that these religious "experts" should ask, "Who are You?" He had given them every evidence that He is the Son of God, yet they had deliberately rejected the evidence. Our Lord's reply may be expressed, "I am exactly what I said!" In other words, "Why should I teach you *new* things, or give you *new* proof, when you have not honestly considered the witness I have already given?"

Jesus boldly made several claims to deity (John 8:26). He said He would judge, and judgment (to the Jews) belonged only to God. He claimed to be sent by God, and He claimed to have heard from God the things that He taught. How did the religious leaders respond to these clear affirmations of deity? They did not understand! God reveals His truth to the "babes" and not to the "wise and prudent" (Luke 10:21).

Now Jesus spoke about His own death, when He

would be "lifted up" on the cross (John 3:14; 12:32). The word translated "lifted up" has a dual meaning: "lifted up in crucifixion," and "lifted up in exaltation and glorification." Jesus often combined the two, for He saw His crucifixion in terms of glory and not just suffering (John 12:23; 13:30–31; 17:1). This same combination of "suffering and glory" is repeated in Peter's first letter.

It would be in His death, burial, resurrection, and ascension that Jesus would be revealed to the Jewish nation. This was the message Peter preached at Pentecost (Acts 2), not only the death of Jesus but also His resurrection and exaltation to glory. Even a Roman soldier, beholding the events at Golgotha would confess, "Truly this man was the Son of God" (Mark 15:39). The early church, following the example of their Lord (Luke 24:25–27), would show from the Old Testament prophecies both the sufferings and the glory of the Messiah.

Jesus made two more stupendous claims: not only was He sent by the Father, but the Father was with Him because He always did what pleased the Father (John 8:29). No doubt, His enemies reacted violently to these words: but some of the listeners put their faith in Him. Whether this was true saving faith or not (see John 2:23–25), we cannot tell, but our Lord's words to them would indicate that they knew what they were doing.

Salvation is a matter of life or death. People who live in their sins and reject the Savior must die in their sins. There is no alternative. We either receive salvation by grace or experience condemnation under God's law. We either walk in the light and have eternal life, or walk in the darkness and experience eternal death. There is a fourth contrast.

Freedom and Bondage (8:31–47)

What listeners are represented by the pronoun *they* in John 8:33? In the previous verses, Jesus addressed the "believers" mentioned in John 8:30, and He warned them that continuance in the Word—discipleship— was proof of true salvation. When we obey His Word, we grow in spiritual knowledge, and as we grow in spiritual knowledge, we grow in freedom from sin. Life leads to learning, and learning leads to liberty.

It is not likely that the pronoun *they* refers to these new believers, for they would probably not argue with their Savior! If John 8:37 is any guide, "they" probably refers to the same unbelieving Jewish leaders who had opposed Jesus throughout this conversation (John 8:13, 19, 22, 25). As before, they did not understand His message. Jesus was speaking about true spiritual freedom, freedom from sin, but they were thinking about political freedom.

Their claim that Abraham's descendants had never been in bondage was certainly a false one that was refuted by the very record in the Old Testament Scriptures. The Jews had been enslaved by seven mighty nations, as recorded in the book of Judges.

The ten northern tribes had been carried away captive by Assyria, and the two southern tribes had gone into seventy years of captivity in Babylon. And at that very hour, the Jews were under the iron heel of Rome! How difficult it is for proud religious people to admit their failings and their needs!

Jesus explained that the difference between spiritual freedom and bondage is a matter of whether one is a son or a servant. The servant may live in the house, but he is not a part of the family, and he cannot be guaranteed a future. (Jesus may have had Isaac and Ishmael in mind here; see Gen. 21.) "Whosoever keeps on practicing sin [literal translation] is the servant of sin." These religious leaders would not only *die* in their sins (John 8:21, 24), but they were right then *living* in bondage to sin!

How can slaves of sin be set free? Only by the Son. How does He do it? Through the power of His Word. Note the emphasis on the Word in John 8:38–47, and He had already told them, "The truth shall make you free" (John 8:32). They would not "make room" for His Word in their hearts.

In the rest of this section, you see the debate centering around the word *father*. Jesus identified Himself with the Father in heaven, but He identified them with the father from hell, Satan. Of course, the Jews claimed Abraham as their father (Luke 3:8ff.), but Jesus made a careful distinction between "Abraham's seed" (physical descendants) and "Abraham's children" (spiritual descendants because of personal faith; Gal. 3:6–14).

These Jewish leaders, who claimed to belong to Abraham, were very unlike Abraham. For one thing, they wanted to kill Jesus; Abraham was the "friend of God" and fellowshipped with Him in love (Isa. 41:8). Abraham listened to God's truth and obeyed it, but these religious leaders rejected the truth.

Nature is determined by birth, and birth is determined by paternity. If God is your Father, then you share God's nature (2 Peter 1:1–4), but if Satan is your father, then you share in his evil nature. Our Lord did not say that *every* lost sinner is a "child of the devil," though every lost sinner is certainly a child of wrath and disobedience (Eph. 2:1–3). Both here and in the parable of the tares (Matt. 13:24–32, 36–43), Jesus said that the Pharisees and other "counterfeit" believers were the children of the devil. Satan is an imitator (2 Cor. 11:13–15), and he gives his children a false righteousness that can never gain them entrance into heaven (Rom. 10:1–4).

What were the characteristics of these religious leaders who belonged to the devil? For one thing, they rejected the truth (John 8:40) and tried to kill Jesus because He spoke the truth. They did not love God (John 8:42), nor could they understand what Jesus taught (John 8:43, 47). Satan's children may be well versed in their religious traditions, but they have no understanding of the Word of God.

Satan is a liar and a murderer. He lied to our first

parents ("Yea, hath God said?") and engineered their deaths. Cain was a child of the devil (1 John 3:12), for he was both a liar and a murderer. He killed his brother Abel and then lied about it (Gen. 4). Is it any wonder that these religious leaders lied about Jesus, hired false witnesses, and then had Him killed?

The worst bondage is the kind that the prisoner himself does not recognize. He thinks he is free, yet he is really a slave. The Pharisees and other religious leaders thought that they were free, but they were actually enslaved in terrible spiritual bondage to sin and Satan. They would not face the truth, and yet it was the truth alone that could set them free.

Honor and Dishonor (8:48–59)

The leaders could not refute our Lord's statements, so they attacked His person. Some students think that the leaders' statement in John 8:41—"We are not born of fornication"—was a slur on our Lord's own birth and character. After all, Mary was with child before she and Joseph were married. But the personal attacks in John 8:48 are quite obvious. For a Jew to be called a Samaritan was the grossest of insults, and then to be called a demon-possessed person only added further insult.

Note that Jesus did not even dignify the racial slur with an answer. (No doubt there was also in this the suggestion that, like the Samaritans, Jesus was a heretic.) They were dishonoring Him, but He was honoring the Father. You will recall that He made it clear that it was impossible to honor the Father without honoring the Son (John 5:23). They were seeking their own glory (see John 5:41–44), but He was seeking the glory that belongs to God alone. Tradition-centered religion, without Christ, is often a "mutual admiration society" for people who want the praise of men.

Jesus had warned them that they would die in their sins because of their unbelief, and now He invited them to trust His Word and "never see death" (John 8:51). He had said this before in His synagogue sermon (John 6:39–40, 44, 54). Once again, the leaders lacked the spiritual insight to understand what He was saying. Abraham was dead, yet he was a godly man, and the faithful prophets were also dead. This kind of talk only convinced them the more that He had a demon (John 7:20)!

By claiming to be the Lord of death, He was claiming to be God (John 5:21–29). This was not an honor He made for Himself; the Father gave it to Him. In fact, Abraham (whom they claimed as their father) saw His day and rejoiced! Instead of rejoicing, they were revolting and trying to kill Him.

How did Abraham "see" our Lord's day, that is, His life and ministry on earth? The same way he saw the future city: by faith (Heb. 11:10, 13–16). God did not give Abraham some special vision of our Lord's life and ministry, but He did give him the spiritual perception to "see" these future events. Certainly Abraham saw the birth of the Messiah in the miraculous birth of his own son, Isaac. He certainly saw Calvary when he offered Isaac to God (Gen. 22). In the priestly ministry of Melchizedek (Gen. 14:17–24), Abraham could see the heavenly priesthood of the Lord. In the marriage of Isaac, Abraham could see a picture of the marriage of the Lamb (Gen. 24).

His statement found in John 8:58 can be translated, "Before Abraham came into being, I Am." Again, this was another affirmation of His divine sonship, and the Jewish leaders received it as such. He had once again made Himself equal with God (John 5:18), and this was the sin of blasphemy, worthy of death (Lev. 24:16). Jesus was divinely protected and simply walked away. His hour had not yet come. We cannot help but admire His courage as He presented the truth and invited blind religious men to trust Him and be set free.

The most difficult people to win to the Savior are those who do not realize that they have a need. They are under the condemnation of God, yet they trust their religion to save them. They are walking in the darkness and not following the light of life. They are sharing a "living death" because of their bondage to sin, and, in spite of their religious deeds, they are dishonoring the Father and the Son. These are the people who crucified Jesus Christ, and Jesus called them the children of the devil.

Whose child are you? Is God your Father because you have received Jesus Christ into your life (John 1:12–13)? Or is Satan your father because you are depending on a counterfeit righteousness, a "works righteousness," not the righteousness that comes through faith in Jesus Christ?

If God is your Father, then heaven is your home. If He is not your Father, then hell is your destiny.

It is truly a matter of life or death!

CHAPTER NINE
John 9
THE BLIND MAN CALLS THEIR BLUFF

Our Lord performed miracles in order to meet human needs. But He also used those miracles as a "launching pad" for a message conveying spiritual truth. Finally, His miracles were His "credentials" to prove that He was indeed the Messiah. "The blind receive their sight" was one such messianic miracle (Matt. 11:5), and we see it demonstrated in this chapter. Jesus used this miracle as the basis for a short sermon on spiritual blindness (John 9:39–41) and a longer sermon on true and false shepherds (John 10:1–18).

I am told that in the United States somebody goes blind every twenty minutes. The man we meet in this chapter was *born* blind; he had never seen the beauty of God's creation or the faces of his loved ones. When Jesus arrived on the scene, everything changed, and the man was made to see. However, the greatest miracle was not the opening of his eyes but the opening of his heart to the Savior. It cost him everything to confess Jesus as the Son of God, but he was willing to do it.

The easiest way to grasp the message of this chapter is to note the stages in this man's growing understanding of who Jesus is.

"A Man Called" (9:1–12)

About the only thing a blind man could do in that day was beg, and that is what this man was doing when Jesus passed by (John 9:8). No doubt there were many blind people who would have rejoiced to be healed, but Jesus selected this man (see Luke 4:25–27). Apparently the man and his parents were well known in the community. It was on the Sabbath when Jesus healed the man (John 9:14), so that once again He was upsetting and deliberately challenging the religious leaders (John 5:9ff.).

The disciples did not look at the man as an object of mercy but rather as a subject for a theological discussion. It is much easier to discuss an abstract subject like "sin" than it is to minister to a concrete need in the life of a person. The disciples were sure that the man's congenital blindness was caused by sin, either his own or his parents', but Jesus disagreed with them.

In the final analysis, *all* physical problems are the result of our fall in Adam, for his disobedience brought sin and death into the world (Rom. 5:12ff.). But afterward, to blame a specific disability on a specific sin committed by specific persons is certainly beyond any man's ability or authority. Only God knows why babies are born with handicaps, and only God can turn those handicaps into something that will bring good to the people and glory to His name.

Certainly both the man and his parents had at some time committed sin, but Jesus did not see their sin as the cause of the man's blindness. Nor did He suggest that God deliberately made the man blind so that, years later, Jesus could perform a miracle. Since there is no punctuation in the original manuscripts, we are free to read John 9:3–4 this way: Neither has this man sinned nor his parents. But that the works of God should be made manifest in him, I must work the works of Him that sent Me, while it is day.

Our Lord's method of healing was unique: He put clay on the man's eyes and told him to go wash. Once Jesus healed two blind men by merely touching their eyes (Matt. 9:27–31), and He healed another blind man by putting spittle on his eyes (Mark 8:22–26). Though the healing power was the same, our Lord varied His methods lest people focus on the *manner* of healing and miss the *message* in the healing.

There were at least two reasons for our Lord's use of the clay. For one thing, it was a picture of the *incarnation*. God made the first man out of the dust, and God sent His Son as a real Man. Note the emphasis on the meaning of "Siloam"—"sent." And relate this to John 9:4: "The works of him that sent me" (see also John 3:17, 34; 5:36; 7:29; 8:18, 42). Jesus gave

a little illustration of His own coming to earth, sent by the Father.

The second reason for the clay was *irritation;* it encouraged the man to believe and obey! If you have ever had an irritation in your eyes, you know how quickly you seek *irrigation* to cleanse it out! You might compare this "irritation" to the convicting work of the Holy Spirit as He uses God's law to bring the lost sinner under judgment.

But the illumination now led to a problem in *identification:* was this really the blind beggar, and who caused him to see? Throughout the rest of John 9, a growing conflict takes place around these two questions. The religious leaders did not want to face the fact that Jesus had healed the man, or even that the man had been healed!

Four times in this chapter people asked, "How were you healed?" (John 9:10, 15, 19, 26). First the neighbors asked the man, and then the Pharisees asked him. Not satisfied with his reply, the Pharisees then asked the man's parents and then gave the son one final interrogation. All of this looked very official and efficient, but it was really a most evasive maneuver on the part of both the people and the leaders. The Pharisees wanted to get rid of the evidence, and the people were afraid to speak the truth!

They were all asking the wrong question! They should not have asked "How?" but "Who?" (Simply rearrange the letters!) But we are so prone to ask "How?" We want to understand the mechanics of a miracle instead of simply trusting the Savior, who alone can perform the miracle. Nicodemus wanted to know how he could reenter his mother's womb (John 3:4, 9). "How can this man give us his flesh to eat?" (John 6:52). Understanding the process, even if we could, is no guarantee that we have experienced the miracle.

When asked to describe his experience, the man simply told what had happened. All he knew about the person who had done the miracle was that He was "a man called Jesus." He had not seen our Lord, of course, but he had heard His voice. Not only was the beggar ignorant of Jesus' identity, but he did not know where Jesus had gone. At this point, the man has been healed, but he has not been saved. The light had dawned, but it would grow brighter until he saw the face of the Lord and worshipped Him (see Prov. 4:18).

At least twelve times in the gospel of John, Jesus is called "a man" (see John 4:29; 5:12; 8:40; 9:11, 24; 10:33; 11:47, 50; 18:14, 17, 29; 19:5). John's emphasis is that Jesus Christ is God, but the apostle balances it beautifully by reminding us that Jesus is also true man. The incarnation was not an illusion (1 John 1:1–4).

"A Prophet" (9:13–23)

Since the Pharisees were the custodians of the faith, it was right that the healed man be brought to them for investigation. The fact that they studied this miracle in such detail is only further proof that Jesus did indeed heal the man. Since the man was *born* blind, the miracle was even greater, for blindness caused by sickness or injury might suddenly go away. Our Lord's miracles can bear careful scrutiny by His enemies.

But Jesus' act of deliberately healing the man on the Sabbath day caused the Pharisees great concern. It was illegal to work on the Sabbath, and by making the clay, applying the clay, and healing the man, Jesus had performed three unlawful "works." The Pharisees should have been praising God for a miracle; instead, they sought evidence to prosecute Jesus.

When people refuse to face evidence honestly, but in fear evade the issue (see John 9:22), then it is impossible to come to a united conclusion. Once again, Jesus was the cause of division (John 9:16; see also 7:12, 43). The religious leaders were judging on the basis of one thing: nobody who breaks the Sabbath could possibly be a true prophet of God. They were "one-issue" thinkers, not unlike some religious people today. The Pharisees did not realize that Jesus was offering the people something greater than the Sabbath—the true spiritual rest that comes from God (Matt. 11:28–30).

But the beggar was not intimidated by the threats of the Pharisees. When asked who he thought Jesus was, the man boldly said, "He is a prophet!" (Note John 4:19 for a parallel.) Some of the Old Testament prophets, such as Moses, Elijah, and Elisha, did perform miracles. The Jewish people would look on their prophets as men of God who could do wonderful things by the power of God.

But the religious leaders did not want to see Jesus given that kind of high designation. "This man is not of God" (John 9:16). Perhaps they could discredit the miracle. If so, then they could convince the people that Jesus had plotted the whole thing and was really deceiving the people. He had craftily "switched" beggars so that the sighted man was not the man who had been known as the blind beggar.

The best way to get that kind of evidence would be to interrogate the parents of the beggar, so they called them in and asked them two questions: (1) "Is this your son?" And (2) "If he is, how does he now see?" In they refused to answer either question, they were in trouble, or if they answered with replies contrary to what the leaders wanted, they were in trouble. What a dilemma!

They answered the first question honestly: he was their son and he had been born blind. They answered the second question evasively: they did not know how he was healed or who healed him. They then used the old-fashioned tactic called "passing the buck" by suggesting that the Pharisees ask the man himself. After all, he was of age!

What lay behind all of this questioning and these furtive replies? *The fear of people.* We met it at the Feast of Tabernacles (John 7:13), and we shall meet it again at our Lord's last Passover (John 12:42). These people were seeking the honor of men and not the honor that comes from God (John 5:44). To be sure,

it was a serious thing to be excommunicated from the synagogue, but it was far more serious to reject the truth and be lost forever. "The fear of man brings a snare" (Prov. 29:25 NASB). The Pharisees were trying to trap Jesus, and the parents were trying to avoid a trap, but all of them were only ensnaring themselves! The parents should have heeded the counsel of Isaiah 51:7 and 12.

The Pharisees could present a "good case" for their position. After all, they did have the law of Moses as well as centuries of Jewish tradition. What they failed to understand was that Jesus Christ had fulfilled all of this ceremonial law and was now bringing in something new. In Moses, you have preparation, but in Jesus Christ, you have consummation (see John 1:17).

"A Man of God" (9:24–34)

Anxious to settle the case, the Pharisees did call the man in, and this time, they put him under oath. "Give God the praise" is a form of Jewish "swearing in" at court (see Josh. 7:19).

But the "judges" prejudiced everybody from the start! "We know that this man is a sinner!" They were warning the witness that he had better cooperate with the court, or he might be excommunicated. But the beggar was made of sturdier stuff than to be intimidated. He had experienced a miracle, and he was not afraid to tell them what had happened.

He did not debate the character of Jesus Christ, because that was beyond his knowledge and experience. But one thing he did know: now he could see. His testimony (John 9:25) reminds me of Psalm 27. Read that psalm in the light of this chapter, from the viewpoint of the healed beggar, and see how meaningful it becomes.

For the fourth time, the question is asked, "How did He open your eyes?" (see John 9:10, 15, 19, and 26). I can imagine the man getting quite impatient at this point. After all, he had been blind all his life, and there was so much now to see. He certainly did not want to spend much longer in a synagogue court, looking at angry faces and answering the same questions!

We admire the boldness of the man in asking those irate Pharisees if they wanted to follow Jesus! The man expected a negative answer, but he was courageous even to ask it. Unable to refute the evidence, the judges began to revile the witness, and once again Moses is brought into the picture (John 5:46). The Pharisees were cautious men who would consider themselves conservatives, when in reality they were "preservatives." A true conservative takes the best of the past and uses it, but he is also aware of the new things that God is doing. The new grows out of the old (Matt. 13:52). A "preservative" simply embalms the past and preserves it. He is against change and resists the new things that God is doing. Had the Pharisees really understood Moses, they would have known who Jesus was and what He was doing.

The leaders were sure about Moses, but they were not sure about Jesus. They did not know where He came from. He had already told them that He had come from heaven, sent by the Father (John 6:33, 38, 41–42, 50–51). They were sure that He was the natural son of Mary and Joseph, and that He was from the city of Nazareth (John 6:42; 7:41–42). They were judging "after the flesh" (John 8:15) and not exercising spiritual discernment.

It seemed incredible to the healed man that the Pharisees would not know this Man who had opened his eyes! How many people were going around Jerusalem, opening the eyes of blind people? Instead of investigating the miracle, these religious leaders should have been investigating the One who did the miracle and learning from Him. The "experts" were rejecting the Stone that was sent to them (Acts 4:11).

The beggar then gave the "experts" a lesson in practical theology. Perhaps he had Psalm 66:18 in mind: "If I regard iniquity in my heart, the Lord will not hear me." The leaders called Jesus a sinner (John 9:24), yet Jesus was used of God to open the blind man's eyes.

He added another telling argument: Jesus healed a man *born* blind. Never, to their knowledge, had this occurred before. So, God not only heard Jesus, but He enabled Him to give the man sight. How, then, could Jesus be a sinner?

Religious bigots do not want to face either evidence or logic. Their minds are made up. Had the Pharisees honestly considered the facts, they would have seen that Jesus is the Son of God, and they could have trusted Him and been saved.

Again, the leaders reviled the man and told him he was born in sin. However, he would not *die* in his sins (see John 8:21, 24); because before this chapter ends, the beggar will come to faith in Jesus Christ. All of us are born in sin (Ps. 51:5), but we need not live in sin (Col. 3:6–7) or die in our sins. Faith in Jesus Christ redeems us from sin and gives us a life of joyful liberty.

The religious leaders officially excommunicated this man from the local synagogue. This meant that the man was cut off from friends and family and looked on by the Jews as a "publican and sinner." But Jesus came for the "outcasts" and never let them down.

"The Son of God" (9:35–41)

The Good Shepherd always cares for His sheep. Jesus knew that the man had been excommunicated, so He found him and revealed Himself to him. Remember, the man knew our Lord's voice, but he had never seen His face.

The man now reached the climax of his knowledge of Jesus Christ and his faith in Him. It is not enough to believe that He is "a man called Jesus," or even "a prophet" or "a man of God." "Whosoever believeth that Jesus is the Christ is born of God" (1 John 5:1). John wrote his gospel to prove that Jesus is the Son of God, and to present to his readers the testimonies of people who met Jesus and affirmed that He is God's Son. This beggar is one such witness.

Jesus identified Himself as the Son of God (see John 9:35; also 5:25), and the beggar believed and was saved (John 9:38). "My sheep hear my voice" (John 10:27). He did not "see and believe"; he *heard* and believed. Not only did he trust the Savior, but he worshipped Him. If Jesus Christ is not God, then why did He accept worship? Peter, Paul, and Barnabas certainly didn't accept worship (see Acts 10:25–26; 14:11–15).

John the Baptist affirmed that Jesus is the Son of God (John 1:34) and so did Nathanael (John 1:49). Jesus stated that He is the Son of God (John 5:25; 9:35), and Peter also affirmed it (John 6:69). Now the healed blind beggar has joined this group of witnesses.

Wherever Jesus went, some of the Pharisees tried to be present so they could catch Him in something He said or did. Seeing them, Jesus closed this episode by preaching a brief but penetrating sermon on spiritual blindness.

John 9:39 does not contradict John 3:16–17. The *reason* for our Lord's coming was salvation, but the *result* of His coming was condemnation of those who would not believe. The same sun that brings beauty out of the seeds also exposes the vermin hiding under the rocks. The religious leaders were blind and would not admit it; therefore, the light of truth only made them blinder. The beggar admitted his need, and he received both physical and spiritual sight. No one is so blind as he who will not see, the one who thinks he has "all truth" and there is nothing more for him to learn (John 9:28, 34).

The listening Pharisees heard what Jesus said and it disturbed them. "Are we blind also?" they asked, expecting a negative answer. Jesus had already called them "blind leaders of the blind" (Matt. 15:14), so they had their answer. They were blinded by their pride, their self-righteousness, their tradition, and their false interpretation of the Word of God.

Our Lord's reply was a paradox. "If you were blind, you would be better off. But you claim to see. Therefore, you are guilty!" Blindness would at least be an excuse for not knowing what was going on. But they *did* know what was going on. Jesus had performed many miracles, and the religious leaders ignored the evidence to make a right decision.

Jesus is the Light of the World (John 8:12; 9:5). The only people who cannot see the light are blind people and those who refuse to look, those who make themselves blind. The beggar was physically blind and spiritually blind, yet both his eyes and his heart were opened. Why? Because he listened to the Word, believed it, obeyed, and experienced the grace of God. The Pharisees had good physical vision, but they were blind spiritually. Had they listened to the Word and sincerely considered the evidence, they too would have believed on Jesus Christ and been born again.

In what sense did the Pharisees "see"? They saw the change in the blind beggar and could not deny that he had been healed. They saw the mighty works that Jesus performed. Even Nicodemus, one of their number, was impressed with the Lord's miracles (John 3:2). If they had examined the evidence with honesty, they would have seen the truth clearly. "If any man wills to do His [God's] will, he shall know of the doctrine" (John 7:17, literal translation). "And ye will not come to me, that ye might have life" (John 5:40).

John 10 is actually a continuation of our Lord's ministry to the Pharisees. The healing of the blind beggar is the background (John 10:21). In fact, the word translated "cast out" in John 9:35 is translated "puts forth" in John 10:4. The beggar was cast out of the synagogue but taken by the Good Shepherd and added to His flock! The emphasis in John 10 is on Jesus Christ, the Good and True Shepherd, as opposed to the Pharisees, who were false shepherds.

We never meet this healed beggar again, but surely the man followed Jesus closely and was among those who witnessed for Him. We hope that he was able to win his fearful parents to the Lord. While being excommunicated from the synagogue was certainly a painful experience for him, he certainly found in his fellowship with Jesus Christ much more spiritual help and encouragement than he could ever have found in the Jewish traditions.

Even today, there are people who must choose between Christ and family, or Christ and their traditional religion.

This blind beggar made the right choice, even though the cost was great.

"The path of the just is as the shining light, that shineth more and more unto the perfect day" (Prov. 4:18).

CHAPTER TEN
John 10
THE GOOD SHEPHERD AND HIS SHEEP

Perhaps you remember the episode of *Candid Camera* that took place at an exclusive prep school where all of the students were well above average. The *Candid Camera* people posed as career consultants who were going to advise these brilliant young men concerning the careers that would be best suited to them, on the basis of "tests" and "interviews" that seemed (to the students) quite authentic.

One young man eagerly awaited the "counselor's" verdict. Surely the adviser would tell the boy to be a college president or a bank president, or perhaps a research scientist. But, no, the "counselor" had other ideas. You should have seen the look on the boy's face when the "counselor" said: "Son, after evaluating your tests and interview, I've decided that the best job for you is—a shepherd."

The student did not know whether to laugh or cry. After all, who in his right mind would want to be a shepherd? Why devote your life to "stupid sheep"

who do not seem to have sense enough to find their way home?

John 10 focuses on the image of sheep, sheepfolds, and shepherds. It is a rural and Eastern image, to be sure, but it is an image that can say a great deal to us today, even in our urban industrialized world. Paul used this image when admonishing the spiritual leaders in the church at Ephesus (Acts 20:28ff.). The truths that cluster around the image of the shepherd and the sheep are found throughout the Bible, and they are important to us today. The symbols that Jesus used help us understand who He is and what He wants to do for us.

Perhaps the easiest way to approach this somewhat complex chapter of John's gospel is to note the three declarations that Jesus made about Himself.

"I Am the Door" (10:1–10)

This sermon grew out of our Lord's confrontation with Jewish leaders, following the excommunication of the beggar (John 9). He had briefly spoken to them about light and darkness, but now He changed the image to that of the shepherd and the sheep. Why? Because to the Jewish mind, a "shepherd" was any kind of leader, spiritual or political. People looked on the king and prophets as shepherds. Israel was privileged to be "the flock of the Lord" (Ps. 100:3). For background, read Isaiah 56:9–12; Jeremiah 23:1–4; 25:32–38; Ezekiel 34; and Zechariah 11.

Jesus opened His sermon with *a familiar illustration* (John 10:1–6), one that every listener would understand. The sheepfold was usually an enclosure made of rocks, with an opening for the door. The shepherd (or a porter) would guard the flock, or flocks, at night by lying across the opening. It was not unusual for several flocks to be sheltered together in the same fold. In the morning, the shepherds would come, call their sheep, and assemble their own flocks. Each sheep recognized his own master's voice.

The true shepherd comes in through the door, and the porter recognizes him. The thieves and robbers could never enter through the door, so they have to climb over the wall and enter the fold through deception. But even if they did get in, they would never get the sheep to follow them, for the sheep follow only the voice of their own shepherd. The false shepherds can never *lead* the sheep, so they must *steal* them away.

It is clear that the listeners did not understand what Jesus said or why He said it. (The word translated "parable" means "a dark saying, a proverb." Our Lord's teaching in John 10 is not like the parables recorded in the other Gospels.) The occasion for this lesson was the excommunication of the beggar from the synagogue (John 9:34). The false shepherds did not care for this man; instead, they mistreated him and threw him out. But Jesus, the Shepherd, came to him and took him in (John 9:35–38).

It is unfortunate that John 10:1 is often used to teach that the sheepfold is heaven, and that those who try to get in by any way other than Christ are destined to fail. While the teaching is true (Acts 4:12), it is not based on this verse. Jesus made it clear that the fold is the nation of Israel (John 10:16). The Gentiles are the "other sheep" not of the fold of Israel.

When Jesus came to the nation of Israel, He came the appointed way, just as the Scriptures promised. Every true shepherd must be called of God and sent by God. If he truly speaks God's Word, the sheep will "hear his voice" and not be afraid to follow him. The true shepherd will love the sheep and care for them.

Since the people did not understand His symbolic language, Jesus followed the illustration with an *application* (John 10:7–10). Twice He said, "I am the door." He is the Door of the sheepfold and makes it possible for the sheep to *leave* the fold (the religion of Judaism) and to *enter* His flock. The Pharisees *threw* the beggar out of the synagogue, but Jesus *led* him out of Judaism and into the flock of God!

But the Shepherd does not stop with leading the sheep out; He also leads them *in*. They become a part of the "one flock" (not "fold"), which is His church. He is the Door of salvation (John 10:9). Those who trust Him enter into the Lord's flock and fold, and they have the wonderful privilege of going "in and out" and finding pasture. When you keep in mind that the shepherd actually was the "door" of the fold, this image becomes very real.

As the Door, Jesus delivers sinners from bondage and leads them into freedom. They have salvation! This word *saved* means "delivered safe and sound." It was used to say that a person had recovered from severe illness, come through a bad storm, survived a war, or was acquitted at court. Some modern preachers want to do away with an "old-fashioned" word like "saved," but Jesus used it!

Jesus was referring primarily to the religious leaders of that day (John 10:8). He was not condemning every prophet or servant of God who ever ministered before He came to earth. The statement "are thieves and robbers" (not "were") makes it clear that He had the present religious leaders in mind. They were not true shepherds nor did they have the approval of God on their ministry. They did not love the sheep, but instead exploited them and abused them. The beggar was a good example of what the "thieves and robbers" could do.

It is clear in the gospel record that the religious rulers of Israel were interested only in providing for themselves and protecting themselves. The Pharisees were coveteous (Luke 16:14) and even took advantage of the poor widows (Mark 12:40). They turned God's temple into a den of thieves (Matt. 21:13), and they plotted to kill Jesus so that Rome would not take away their privileges (John 11:49–53).

The True Shepherd came to save the sheep, but the false shepherds take advantage of the sheep and exploit them. Behind these false shepherds is "the thief" (John 10:10), probably a reference to Satan. The thief wants to steal the sheep from the fold, slaughter them, and destroy them. We shall see later that the sheep are safe in the hands of the Shepherd and the Father (John 10:27–29).

When you go through "the Door," you receive life and you are saved. As you go "in and out," you enjoy *abundant* life in the rich pastures of the Lord. His sheep enjoy fullness and freedom. Jesus not only gave His life *for* us, but He gives His life *to* us right now!

The emphasis in this first section is on "the door." Our Lord then shifted the emphasis to "the shepherd" and made a second declaration.

"I Am the Good Shepherd" (10:11–21)

This is the fourth of our Lord's "I am" statements in John's gospel (John 6:35; 8:12; 10:9). Certainly in making this statement, He is contrasting Himself to the false shepherds who were in charge of the Jewish religion of that day. He had already called them "thieves and robbers," and now He would describe them as "hirelings."

The word translated "good" means "intrinsically good, beautiful, fair." It describes that which is the ideal, the model that others may safely imitate. Our Lord's goodness was inherent in His nature. To call Him "good" is the same as calling Him "God" (Mark 10:17–18).

Some of the greatest people named in the Bible were shepherds by occupation: Abel, the patriarchs, Moses, and David, to name a few. Even today in the Holy Land, you may see shepherds leading flocks and revealing how intimately they know each sheep, its individual traits, and its special needs. Keep in mind that Jewish shepherds did not tend the sheep in order to slaughter them, unless they were used for sacrifice. Shepherds tended them that the sheep might give wool, milk, and lambs.

Jesus pointed out four special ministries that He performs as the Good Shepherd.

He dies for the sheep (vv. 11–13). Under the old dispensation, the sheep died for the shepherd, but now the Good Shepherd dies for the sheep! Five times in this sermon, Jesus clearly affirmed the sacrificial nature of His death (John 10:11, 15, 17–18). He did not die as a martyr, killed by men; He died as a substitute, willingly laying down His life for us.

The fact that Jesus said that He died "for the sheep" must not be isolated from the rest of biblical teaching about the cross. He also died for the nation Israel (John 11:50–52) and for the world (John 6:51). While the blood of Jesus Christ is *sufficient* for the salvation of the world, it is *efficient* only for those who will believe.

Jesus contrasted Himself to the hireling who watches over the sheep only because he is paid to do so. But when there is danger, the hireling runs away, while the true shepherd stays and cares for the flock. The key phrase is "whose own the sheep are not." The Good Shepherd *purchases the sheep,* and they are His because He died for them. They belong to Him, and He cares for them. By nature, sheep are stupid and prone to get into danger, and they need a shepherd to care for them.

Throughout the Bible, God's people are compared to sheep, and the comparison is a good one. Sheep are clean animals, unlike pigs and dogs (2 Peter 2:20–22). They are defenseless and need the care of the shepherd (Ps. 23). They are, to use Wesley's phrase, "prone to wander," and must often be searched for and brought back to the fold (Luke 15:3–7). Sheep are peaceful animals, useful to the shepherd. In these, and other ways, they picture those who have trusted Jesus Christ and are a part of God's flock.

The Pharisees, in contrast to good shepherds, had no loving concern for the beggar, so they put him out of the synagogue. Jesus found him and cared for him.

He knows His sheep (vv. 14–15). In the gospel of John, the word *know* means much more than intellectual awareness. It speaks of an intimate relationship between God and His people (see John 17:3). The Eastern shepherd knows his sheep personally and therefore knows best how to minister to them.

To begin with, our Lord knows our names (see John 10:3). He knew Simon (John 1:42) and even gave him a new name. He called Zaccheus by name (Luke 19:5), and when He spoke Mary's name in the garden, she recognized her Shepherd (John 20:16). If you have ever had your identity "lost" in a maze of computer operations, then you can appreciate the comforting fact that the Good Shepherd knows each of His sheep by name.

He also knows our natures. While all sheep are alike in their essential nature, each sheep has its own distinctive characteristics, and the loving shepherd recognizes these traits. One sheep may be afraid of high places, another of dark shadows. A faithful shepherd will consider these special needs as he tends the flock.

Have you ever noticed how different the twelve apostles were from one another? Peter was impulsive and outspoken, while Thomas was hesitant and doubting. Andrew was a "people person" who was always bringing somebody to Jesus, while Judas wanted to "use" people in order to get their money for himself. Jesus knew each of the men personally, and He knew exactly how to deal with them.

Because He knows our natures, He also knows our needs. Often, *we* do not even know our own needs! Psalm 23 is a beautiful poetic description of how the Good Shepherd cares for His sheep. In the pastures, by the waters, and even through the valleys, the sheep need not fear, because the shepherd is caring for them and meeting their needs. If you connect Psalm 23:1 and 6, you get the main theme of the poem: "I shall not want … all the days of my life."

As the shepherd cares for the sheep, the sheep get to know their shepherd better. The Good Shepherd knows His sheep and His sheep know Him. They get to know Him better by listening to His voice (the Word) and experiencing His daily care. As the sheep follow the Shepherd, they learn to love and to trust Him. He loves "his own" (John 13:1) and He shows that love in the way He cares for them.

The Good Shepherd brings other sheep into the flock (v. 16). The "fold" is Judaism (John 10:1), but there is another fold—the Gentiles who are outside the covenants of Israel (Eph. 2:11ff.). In our Lord's early ministry, He concentrated on the "lost sheep of the house of Israel" (Matt. 10:5–6; 15:24–27). The people converted at Pentecost were Jews and Jewish proselytes (Acts 2:5, 14), but the church was not to remain a "Jewish flock." Peter took the gospel to the Gentiles (Acts 10—11), and Paul carried the message to the Gentiles in the far reaches of the Roman Empire (Acts 13: 1ff.).

The phrase "one fold" should read "one flock." There is but one flock, the people of God who belong to the Good Shepherd. God has His people all over this world (see Acts 18:1–11), and He will call them and gather them together.

The missionary message of the gospel of John is obvious: "For God so loved the world" (John 3:16). Jesus Himself defied custom and witnessed to a Samaritan woman. He refused to defend the exclusivist approach of the Jewish religious leaders. He died for a lost world, and His desire is that His people reach a lost world with the message of eternal life.

The Good Shepherd takes up His life again (vv. 17–21). His voluntary death was followed by His victorious resurrection. From the human point of view, it appeared that Jesus was executed; but from the divine point of view, He laid down His life willingly. When Jesus cried on the cross, "It is finished," He then voluntarily yielded up His spirit to the Father (John 19:30). Three days later, He voluntarily took up His life again and arose from the dead. The Father gave Him this authority in love.

Sometimes the Scriptures teach that it was the Father who raised the Son (Acts 2:32; Rom. 6:4; Heb. 13:20). Here, the Son stated that He had authority to take up His life again. Both are true, for the Father and the Son worked together in perfect harmony (John 5:17, 19). In a previous sermon, Jesus had hinted that He had power to raise Himself from the dead (John 5:26). Of course, this was a claim that the Jews would protest; because it was tantamount to saying "I am God!"

How did the listeners respond to this message? "There was a division therefore again among the Jews" (John 10:19). Note that word *again* (John 7:43; 9:16). The old accusation that Jesus was a demoniac was hurled at Him again (John 7:20; 8:48, 52). People will do almost anything to avoid facing the truth!

Since Jesus Christ is "the Door," we would expect a division, because a door shuts some people in and others out! He is the Good Shepherd, and the shepherd must separate the sheep from the goats. It is impossible to be neutral about Jesus Christ, for what we believe about Him is a matter of life or death (John 8:24).

His third declaration was the most startling of all.

"I Am the Son of God" (10:22–42)

The events in this section occurred about two and a half months after those described in John 10:1–21.

John put them together because in both messages, Jesus used the imagery of the shepherd and the sheep.

The encounter (vv. 22–24). The "Feast of the Dedication" (Hanukkah, "the feast of lights") takes place in December, near the time of the Christian Christmas celebration. The feast commemorates the rededication of the temple by Judas Maccabeus in 164 BC, after it had been desecrated by the Romans. This historical fact may bear a relationship to the words of Jesus in John 10:36, for He had been set apart (dedicated) by the Father and sent into the world. The Jewish leaders were celebrating a great event in history yet passing by a great opportunity right in their own temple!

The leaders surrounded Jesus in the temple so that He had to stop and listen to them. They had decided that it was time for a "showdown," and they did not want Him to evade the issue any longer. "How long are You going to hold us in suspense?" they kept saying to Him. "Tell us plainly—are You the Messiah?"

The explanation (vv. 25–42). Jesus reminded them of what He had already taught them. He emphasized the witness of His *words* ("I told you") and His *works* (see John 5:17ff., and 7:14ff. for similar replies).

But our Lord went much deeper in His explanation this time, for He revealed to the Jewish leaders *why* they did not understand His words or grasp the significance of His works: they were not His sheep. From the human standpoint, we become His sheep by believing, but from the divine standpoint, we believe because we are His sheep. There is a mystery here that we cannot fathom or explain, but we can accept it and rejoice (Rom. 11:33–36). God has His sheep and He knows who they are. They will hear His voice and respond.

The lost sinner who hears God's Word knows nothing about divine election. He hears only that Christ died for the sins of the world, and that he may receive the gift of eternal life by trusting the Savior. When he trusts the Savior, he becomes a member of God's family and a sheep in the flock. Then he learns that he was "chosen … in him [Christ] before the foundation of the world" (Eph. 1:4). He also learns that each saved sinner is the Father's "love gift" to His Son (see John 10:29; 17:2, 6, 9, 11–12, 24).

In the Bible, divine election and human responsibility are perfectly balanced, and what God has joined together, we must not put asunder.

Jesus went on to explain that His sheep are secure in His hand and in the Father's hand. "They shall never perish" is His promise (John 3:16; 6:39; 17:12; 18:9). The false shepherds bring destruction (John 10:10, same Greek word), but the Good Shepherd sees to it that His sheep shall never perish.

The security of God's sheep is assured here in several ways. First, by definition—we have "eternal life," and that cannot be conditional and still be eternal. Second, this life is a gift, not something that we earn or merit. If we were not saved by our own good works, but by His grace, then we cannot be lost by our "bad

works" (Rom. 11:6). But most important, Jesus gave us His promise that His sheep do not perish and that His promise cannot be broken.

It is important to keep in mind that Jesus was talking about sheep—true believers—and not counterfeits. The dog and the pig will go back into sin (2 Peter 2:20–22), but the sheep, being a clean animal, will follow the Shepherd into the green pastures. The false professor will talk about his faith and even his works, but he will never make it into heaven (Matt. 7:13–29). Most of us know people who professed to be saved and then went back into sin, but their doing so only proved that they never really trusted Christ to begin with. Jesus did not promise security to anyone but His true sheep.

As you review our Lord's teaching about His ministry as the Good Shepherd, you note that He has a threefold relationship to His sheep. He has a *loving* relationship because He died for the sheep, as well as a *living* relationship because He cares for the sheep. It is also a *lasting* relationship, for He keeps His sheep and not a one is lost.

Our Lord made a statement that He knew would startle His enemies and give them more reason to oppose Him (John 10:30). It was the "plain answer" that the religious leaders had asked for. "I and my Father are one" is as clear a statement of His deity as you will find anywhere in Scripture. This was even stronger than His statement that He had come down from heaven (John 6) or that He existed before Abraham ever lived (John 8:58).

The word *one* does not suggest that the Father and the Son are identical persons. Rather, it means that they are one in essence: the Father is God and the Son is God, but the Father is not the Son and the Son is not the Father. He is speaking about unity, not identity. (See John 17:21–24 for similar language.)

The Jewish leaders understood clearly what He was saying! Some modern liberal theologians would water down our Lord's statement, but the people who heard it knew exactly what He was saying: "I am God!" (Note John 10:33.) To speak this way, of course, was blasphemy, and according to Jewish belief, blasphemy had to be punished by being put to death (see Lev. 24:16; Num. 15:30ff.; Deut. 21:22).

Our Lord used Psalm 82:6 to refute their accusation and halt their actions. The picture in Psalm 82 is that of a court, where God has assembled the judges of the earth, to warn them that they too will one day be judged. The Hebrew word *elohim* can be translated as "god" or as "judges," as in Exodus 21:6 and 22:8–9. It is also one of the Old Testament names for God. The Jewish rulers certainly knew their own language and they knew that Jesus was speaking the truth. If God called human judges "gods," then why should they stone Him for applying the same title to Himself?

John 10:36 is crucial because it gives a double affirmation of the deity of Christ. First, the Father sanctified (set apart) the Son and sent Him into the world, and second, Jesus stated boldly, "I am the Son of God" (see John 5:25). He gave them the "plain answer" they asked for, but they would not believe it!

Could they have believed? Jesus *invited* them, urged them, to believe, if only on the basis of His miracles (John 10:37–38). If they would believe the miracles, then they would know the Father, and that would open the way for them to know the Son and believe on Him. It was simply a matter of examining the evidence honestly and being willing to accept the truth.

Once again, they tried to arrest Him (see John 7:44; 8:59), but He escaped and left the area completely. He did not return to Jerusalem until "Palm Sunday," when He presented Himself as Israel's King.

John the Baptist had ministered at Bethabara (John 1:28), but we are not sure where this was. It was on the other side of the Jordan River, perhaps eighteen to twenty miles from Jerusalem. Some maps put it almost directly across from Jerusalem, just east of Jericho.

Why did Jesus go there? For one thing, it was a safe retreat; the Jewish religious leaders were not likely to follow Him there. Also, it was a good place to prepare for His final week of public ministry when He would lay down His life for the sheep. As He remembered His own baptism by John, and all that He had experienced at that time (Matt. 3:13–17; John 1:20–34), it must have fortified Him for the suffering that He knew He must endure.

The common people continued to seek Jesus, and He continued to minister to them. It is worth noting that John the Baptist's witness was still bearing fruit long after he was dead! His witness to Jesus Christ led many to trust the Savior. John was not a miracle worker, but he was a faithful witness who pointed to Jesus Christ. "He must increase, but I must decrease" (John 3:30).

Have you responded personally to our Lord's three great declarations recorded in this chapter?

He is the Door. Have you "entered in" by faith so that you are saved?

He is the Good Shepherd. Have you heard His voice and trusted Him? After all, He laid down His life for you!

He is the Son of God. Do you believe that? Have you given yourself to Him and received eternal life?

Remember His stern warning: "If ye believe not that I am he, ye shall die in your sins" (John 8:24).

CHAPTER ELEVEN
John 11
THE LAST MIRACLE—THE LAST ENEMY

The raising of Lazarus from the dead was not our Lord's last miracle before the cross, but it was certainly His greatest and the one that aroused the most response both from His friends and His enemies. John selected this miracle as the seventh in the series recorded in his book because it was really the climactic miracle of our Lord's earthly ministry. He had raised others from the dead, but Lazarus had been in the grave four days. It was a miracle that could not be denied or avoided by the Jewish leaders.

If Jesus Christ can do nothing about death, then whatever else He can do amounts to nothing. "If in this life only we have hope in Christ, we are of all men most miserable" (1 Cor. 15:19). Death is man's last enemy (1 Cor. 15:26), but Jesus Christ has defeated this horrible enemy totally and permanently.

The emphasis in John 11 is on faith; you find some form of the word *believe* at least eight times in this account. Another theme is "the glory of God" (John 11:4, 40). In what Jesus said and did, He sought to strengthen the faith of three groups of people.

The Disciples (11:1–16)
We sometimes think of the disciples as "supersaints," but such was not the case. They often failed their Lord, and He was constantly seeking to increase their faith. After all, one day He would leave them and they would have the responsibility of carrying on the ministry. If their faith was weak, their work could never be strong.

Jesus was at Bethabara, about twenty miles from Bethany (John 1:28; 10:40). One day, a messenger arrived with the sad news that our Lord's dear friend Lazarus was sick. If the man had traveled quickly, without any delay, he could have made the trip in one day. Jesus sent him back the next day with the encouraging message recorded in John 11:4. Then Jesus waited two more days before He left for Bethany, and by the time He and His disciples arrived, Lazarus had been dead for four days. This means that Lazarus had died *the very day* the messenger left to contact Jesus!

The schedule of events would look something like this, allowing one day for travel:

> Day 1—The messenger comes to Jesus (Lazarus dies).
> Day 2—The messenger returns to Bethany.
> Day 3—Jesus waits another day, then departs.
> Day 4—Jesus arrives in Bethany.

When the messenger arrived back home, he would find Lazarus already dead. What would his message convey to the grieving sisters now that their brother was already dead and buried? Jesus was urging them to believe His word no matter how discouraging the circumstances might appear.

No doubt the disciples were perplexed about several matters. First of all, if Jesus loved Lazarus so much, why did He permit him to get sick? Even more, why did He delay to go to the sisters? For that matter, could He not have healed Lazarus at a distance, as He did the nobleman's son (John 4:43–54)? The record makes it clear that there was a strong love relationship between

Jesus and this family (John 11:3, 5, 36), and yet our Lord's behavior seems to contradict this love.

God's love for His own is not a pampering love; it is a perfecting love. The fact that He loves us and we love Him is no guarantee that we will be sheltered from the problems and pains of life. After all, the Father loves His Son: and yet the Father permitted His beloved Son to drink the cup of sorrow and experience the shame and pain of the cross. We must never think that love and suffering are incompatible. Certainly they unite in Jesus Christ.

Jesus could have prevented Lazarus' sickness or even healed it from where He was, but He chose not to. He saw in this sickness an opportunity to glorify the Father. It is not important that we Christians are comfortable, but it is important that we glorify God in all that we do.

In their "prayer" to Jesus, the two sisters did not tell Him what to do. They simply informed Him that there was a need, and they reminded Him of His love for Lazarus. They knew that it was dangerous for Jesus to return to Judea because the Jewish leaders were out to destroy Him. Perhaps they hoped that He would "speak the word" and their brother would be restored to health.

Our Lord's message to the sisters did not say that their brother would not die. It promised only that death would not be the *ultimate* result, for the ultimate result would be the glory of God. (Note that once again, Jesus called Himself "the Son of God.") He wanted them to lay hold of this promise; in fact, He reminded Martha of this message when she balked at having the tomb opened (John 11:40).

When we find ourselves confronted by disease, disappointment, delay, and even death, our only encouragement is the Word of God. We must live by faith and not by sight. Their situation seemed hopeless, yet the sisters knew that Jesus was the Master of every situation. The promise in Psalm 50:15 finds a parallel here: "And call upon me in the day of trouble: I will deliver thee, and thou shalt glorify me."

What about our Lord's delay? He was not waiting for Lazarus to die, for he was already dead. Jesus lived on a divine timetable (John 11:9), and He was waiting for the Father to tell Him when to go to Bethany. The fact that the man had been dead four days gave greater authenticity to the miracle and greater opportunity for people to believe, including His own disciples (see John 11:15).

When our Lord announced that He was returning to Judea, His disciples were alarmed, because they knew how dangerous it would be. (Bethany is only about two miles from Jerusalem.) But Jesus was willing to lay down His life for His friends (John 15:13). He knew that His return to Judea and the miracle of raising Lazarus would precipitate His own arrest and death.

The Lord calmed their fears by reminding them that He was on the Father's schedule, and that nothing could harm them. As we have seen, this is an important theme in the gospel of John (John 2:4; 7:6, 8, 30; 8:20; 12:23; 13:1; 17:1). But the disciples not only misunderstood the schedule, they also misunderstood the reason for the visit. They thought that, if Lazarus was sleeping, he was getting better! It was another example of their inability to grasp spiritual truth. "If he is sleeping, he must be improving—so let's not bother to go to Bethany!"

Then He told them openly that Lazarus was dead. (Death for the believer is compared to sleep. See Acts 7:60; 1 Cor. 15:51; 1 Thess. 4:13–18.) He did not say He was glad that His friend died, but that He was glad He had not been there, for now He could reveal to His disciples His mighty power. The result would be glory to God and the strengthening of their faith.

If Thomas's attitude was any indication, the faith of the disciples certainly needed strengthening! The name Thomas means "twin" in the Aramaic language; the Greek equivalent is Didymus. We do not know whose twin he was, but there are times when *all of us* seem to be his twin when we consider our unbelief and depressed feelings! It was Thomas who demanded evidence before he would accept the truth of our Lord's resurrection (John 20:24–28).

Thomas was a doubting man, but we must confess that he was a devoted man: he was willing to go with Jesus into danger and risk his own life. We may not admire his faith, but we can certainly applaud his loyalty and courage.

The Sisters (11:17–40)

Jesus was concerned not only about the faith of His own disciples, but also about the faith of Mary and Martha (John 11:26, 40). Each experience of suffering and trial ought to increase our faith, but this kind of spiritual growth is not automatic. We must respond positively to the ministry of the Word and the Spirit of God. Jesus had sent a promise to the two sisters (John 11:4), and now He would discover how they had received it.

The event recorded in Luke 10:38–42 makes it clear that Mary and Martha were quite different in their personalities. Martha was the worker, the active one, while Mary was the contemplative one who sat at the feet of Jesus and listened to His words. Jesus did not condemn Martha's service, but He did rebuke her for being "torn apart" by so many things. She needed to have priorities and center her activities on the things that God would approve. As an old Wesley hymn puts it, we need to have a balanced life:

> Faithful to my Lord's commands,
> I still would choose the better part:
> Serve with careful Martha's hands
> And loving Mary's heart.

We would expect Martha to rush out to meet Jesus while Mary sat in the house, weeping with her friends.

Since Mary later echoed Martha's words of greeting (John 11:32), it is likely that the sisters often said these words to each other as they waited for Jesus to arrive. While there may have been a tinge of disappointment in the statement, there was also evidence of faith, for nobody ever died in the presence of Jesus Christ. "If" is such a big word! How futile it is to imagine what might have been, if—!

Martha was quick to affirm her faith in Jesus Christ (John 11:22), and Jesus responded to that faith by promising her that her brother would rise again. He was thinking of the immediate situation, but she interpreted His words to mean the future resurrection in the last day (Dan. 12:2–3; John 5:28–29). Here is another instance in John's gospel of people lacking spiritual perception and being unable to understand the words of Jesus.

Our Lord's reply is the fifth of the "I am" statements. It is important to note that Jesus did not deny what Martha said about the future resurrection. The resurrection of the human body is a cardinal doctrine in the orthodox Jewish faith. But in His great "I am" statement, our Lord completely transformed the doctrine of the resurrection and, in so doing, brought great comfort to Martha's heart.

To begin with, He brought the doctrine of the resurrection out of the shadows and into the light. The Old Testament revelation about death and resurrection is not clear or complete; it is, as it were, "in the shadows." In fact, there are some passages in Psalms and Ecclesiastes that almost make one believe that death is the end and there is no hope beyond the grave. False teachers like to use these passages to support their heretical teachings, but they ignore (or misinterpret) the clear teachings found in the New Testament. After all, it was not David or Solomon who "brought life and immortality to light through the gospel" (2 Tim. 1:10), but Jesus Christ!

By His teaching, His miracles, and His own resurrection, Jesus clearly taught the resurrection of the human body. He has declared once for all that death is real, that there is life after death, and that the body will one day be raised by the power of God.

He transformed this doctrine in a second way: He took it out of a book and put it into a person, Himself. "I am the resurrection and the life" (John 11:25)! While we thank God for what the Bible teaches (and all Martha had was the Old Testament), we realize that we are saved by the Redeemer, Jesus Christ, and not by a doctrine written in a book. When we know Him by faith, we need not fear the shadow of death.

When you are sick, you want a doctor and not a medical book or a formula. When you are being sued, you want a lawyer and not a law book. Likewise, when you face your last enemy, death, you want the Savior and not a doctrine written in a book. In Jesus Christ, every doctrine is made personal (1 Cor. 1:30). When you belong to Him, you have all that you ever will need in life, death, time, or eternity!

But perhaps the greatest transformation Jesus performed was to move the doctrine of the resurrection out of the future and into the present. Martha was looking to the future, knowing that Lazarus would rise again and she would see him. Her friends were looking to the past and saying, "He could have prevented Lazarus from dying" (John 11:37)! But Jesus tried to center their attention on the *present:* wherever He is, God's resurrection power is available *now* (Rom. 6:4; Gal. 2:20; Phil. 3:10).

Jesus affirmed that believers would one day be raised from the dead (John 11:25). Then He immediately revealed the added truth that some believers would never die (and it is a double negative, "never never die!") (John 11:26). How is this possible? The answer is found in 1 Thessalonians 4:13, 18. When Jesus Christ returns in the air to take His people home, those who are alive at His coming shall never die. They shall be changed and caught up to meet Him in the air!

Martha did not hesitate to affirm her faith. She used three different titles for Jesus: Lord, Christ (Messiah), and Son of God. The words "I believe" are in the perfect tense, indicating a fixed and settled faith. "I have believed and I will continue to believe!"

Our Lord dealt with Martha's faith; now He had to help Mary. Why did Martha call Mary "secretly"? Possibly because of the danger involved: they knew that the Jewish leaders were out to arrest Jesus. When Mary arose to go to meet Jesus, her friends misunderstood her actions and thought she was going to the tomb to weep. They wanted to weep with her, so they followed along. Imagine their surprise when they met Jesus!

Mary is found three times in the gospel record, and each time she is at the feet of Jesus (Luke 10:39; John 11:32; 12:3). She sat at His feet and listened to His word; she fell at His feet and poured out her sorrow, and she came to His feet to give Him her praise and worship. Mary's only recorded words in the Gospels are given in John 11:32, and they echo what Martha had already said (John 11:21).

Mary did not say much because she was overcome with sorrow and began to weep. Her friends joined in the weeping, as Jewish people are accustomed to do. The word used means "a loud weeping, a lamentation." Our Lord's response was to groan within and "be moved with indignation." At what was He indignant? At the ravages of sin in the world that He had created. Death is an enemy, and Satan uses the fear of death as a terrible weapon (Heb. 2:14–18). No wonder Jesus was indignant!

The mystery of our Lord's incarnation is seen by His question in John 11:34. Jesus knew that Lazarus had died (John 11:11), but He had to ask where he was buried. Our Lord never used His divine powers when normal human means would suffice.

"Jesus wept" is the shortest and yet the deepest verse in Scripture. His was a silent weeping (the Greek word is used nowhere else in the New Testament) and not the loud lamentation of the mourners. But why did

He weep at all? After all, He knew that He would raise Lazarus from the dead (John 11:11).

Our Lord's weeping reveals the humanity of the Savior. He has entered into all of our experiences and knows how we feel. In fact, being the perfect God-Man, Jesus experienced these things in a deeper way than we do. His tears also assure us of His sympathy; He is indeed "a man of sorrows and acquainted with grief" (Isa. 53:3). Today, He is our merciful and faithful High Priest, and we may come to the throne of grace and find all the gracious help that we need (Heb. 4:14–16).

We see in His tears the tragedy of sin but also the glory of heaven. Perhaps Jesus was weeping *for* Lazarus, as well as *with* the sisters, because He knew He was calling His friend from heaven and back into a wicked world where he would one day have to die again. Jesus had come down from heaven; He knew what Lazarus was leaving behind.

The spectators saw in His tears an evidence of His love. But some of them said, "If Jesus loved Lazarus so much, why did He not prevent his death?" Perhaps they were thinking, "Jesus is weeping because He was unable to do anything. They are tears of deep regret." In other words, *nobody present really expected a miracle!* For this reason, nobody could accuse Jesus of "plotting" this event and being in collusion with the two sisters and their friends. Even the disciples did not believe that Jesus would raise Lazarus from the dead!

The one person who declared her faith was Martha (John 11:27), and she failed at the last minute. "Open the tomb? By now he smells!" Jesus gently reminded her of the message He had sent at least three days before (John 11:4), and He urged her to believe it. True faith relies on God's promises and thereby releases God's power. Martha relented, and the stone was rolled away.

The Jews (11:41–57)

The emphasis from this point on was on the faith of the spectators, the people who had come to comfort Mary and Martha. Jesus paused to pray (John 11:41; see also 6:11) and thanked the Father that the prayer had already been heard. When had He prayed? Probably when He received the message that His friend was sick (John 11:4). The Father then told Him what the plan was, and Jesus obeyed the Father's will. His prayer now was for the sake of the unbelieving spectators, that they might know that God had sent Him.

A quaint Puritan writer said that if Jesus had not named Lazarus when He shouted, He would have emptied the whole cemetery! Jesus called *Lazarus* and raised him from the dead. Since Lazarus was bound, he could not walk to the door of the tomb, so God's power must have carried him along. It was an unquestioned miracle that even the most hostile spectator could not deny.

The experience of Lazarus is a good illustration of what happens to a sinner when he trusts the Savior (Eph. 2:1–10). Lazarus was dead, and all sinners are dead. He was decayed, because death and decay go

together. All lost people are spiritually dead, but some are more "decayed" than others. No one can be "more dead" than another.

Lazarus was raised from the dead by the power of God, and all who trust Christ have been given new life and lifted out of the graveyard of sin (see John 5:24). Lazarus was set free from the graveclothes (see Col. 3:1ff.) and given new liberty. You find him seated with Christ at the table (John 12:2), and all believers are "seated with Christ" in heavenly places (Eph. 2:6), enjoying spiritual food and fellowship.

Because of the great change in Lazarus, many people desired to see him, and his "living witness" was used by God to bring people to salvation (John 12:9–11). There are no recorded words of Lazarus in the Gospels, but his daily walk is enough to convince people that Jesus is the Son of God. Because of his effective witness, Lazarus was persecuted by the religious leaders who wanted to kill him and get rid of the evidence.

As with the previous miracles, the people were divided in their response. Some did believe and on "Palm Sunday" gave witness of the miracle Jesus had performed (John 12:17–18). But others immediately went to the religious leaders and reported what had happened in Bethany. These "informers" were so near the kingdom, yet there is no evidence that they believed. If the heart will not yield to truth, then the grace of God cannot bring salvation. These people could have experienced a spiritual resurrection in their own lives!

It was necessary that the Jewish council (Sanhedrin) meet and discuss what to do with Jesus. They were not seeking after truth; they were seeking for ways to protect their own selfish interests. If He gathered too many followers, He might get the attention of the Roman authorities, and this could hurt the Jewish cause.

The high priest, Caiaphas, was a Sadducee, not a Pharisee (Acts 23:6–10), but the two factions could always get together to fight a common enemy. Unknown to himself and to the council, Caiaphas uttered a divine prophecy: Jesus would die for the nation so that the nation would not perish. "For the transgression of my people was he stricken" (Isa. 53:8). True to his vision of a worldwide family of God, John added his inspired explanation: Jesus would die not only for the Jews, but for all of God's children who would be gathered together in one heavenly family. (Note John 4:42; 10:16.)

The official decision that day was that Jesus must die (see Matt. 12:14; Luke 19:47; John 5:18; 7:1, 19–20, 25). The leaders thought that *they* were in control of the situation, but it was God who was working out His predetermined plan (Acts 2:23). Originally, they wanted to wait until after the Passover, but God had decreed otherwise.

Jesus withdrew to Ephraim, about fifteen miles north of Jerusalem, and there He remained in quiet retirement with His disciples. The crowd was gathering in Jerusalem for the Passover feast, and the pilgrims were wondering if Jesus would attend the feast even though He was in danger. He was now on the "wanted" list, because the council had made it known that anyone who knew where Jesus was must report it to the officials.

John 11 reveals the deity of Jesus Christ and the utter depravity of the human heart. The rich man in hades had argued, "If one went unto them from the dead, they will repent" (Luke 16:30). Lazarus came back from the dead, and the officials wanted to kill him! Miracles certainly reveal the power of God, but of themselves they cannot communicate the grace of God.

The stage had been set for the greatest drama in history, during which man would do his worst and God would give His best.

CHAPTER TWELVE
John 12
CHRIST AND THE CRISIS

John 12 records the second major crisis in the ministry of our Lord as seen by John the apostle. The first occurred when many of His disciples would no longer walk with Him (John 6:66), even though He is "the way" (John 14:6). In this chapter, John tells us that many would not believe in Him (John 12:37ff.), even though He is "the truth." The third crisis will come in John 19: even though He is "the life," the leaders crucified Him.

John opened his book by telling us that Jesus "came unto his own [world], and his own [people] received him not" (John 1:11). In the first twelve chapters, John presented one witness after another, and one proof after another, to convince us that Jesus is indeed the Christ, the Son of God. All of this evidence was seen firsthand by the leaders of the nation, and yet they rejected His claims. Having been rejected by "His own" nation, Jesus then retired with "his own" disciples (John 13:1), whom He loved to the uttermost.

We see in John 12 the Lord Jesus Christ as He relates to four different groups of people, and there are lessons that we can learn as we study this section.

Jesus and His Friends (John 12:1–11)
Our Lord knew that the Jewish leaders were out to arrest Him and kill Him (John 11:53, 57), but He still returned to Bethany, only two miles from the very citadel of His enemies. Why? So that He might spend a quiet time with His dear friends Mary, Martha, and Lazarus. True to their personalities, Martha busily served and Mary worshipped at the feet of Jesus (see Luke 10:38–42).

The account of Mary's anointing of her Lord is found also in Matthew 26:6–13 and Mark 14:3–9. But it must not be confused with the account given in Luke 7:36–50, where a former harlot anointed Jesus in the house of Simon the Pharisee. Mary was a virtuous woman, and she anointed Jesus in the house of Simon the (former) leper (Mark 14:3). The Luke 7 event took place in Galilee, while the account we are now considering occurred in Judea. The fact that there are two "Simons" involved should not surprise us, for Simon was a common name in that day.

When you combine all three accounts, you learn that Mary anointed both His head and His feet. It was an act of pure love on her part, for she knew her Lord was about to endure suffering and death. Because she sat at Jesus' feet and listened to Him speak, she knew what He was going to do. It is significant that Mary of Bethany was not one of the women who went to the tomb to anoint the body of Jesus (Mark 16:1).

In a sense, Mary was showing her devotion to Jesus *before* it was too late. She was "giving the roses" while He was yet alive, and not bringing them to the funeral! Her act of love and worship was public, spontaneous, sacrificial, lavish, personal, and unembarrassed. Jesus called it "a good work" (Matt. 26:10; Mark 14:6) and both commended and defended her.

It would have required a year's wages from a common laborer to purchase that ointment. Like David, Mary would not give to the Lord that which cost her nothing (2 Sam. 24:24). Her beautiful act of worship brought a fragrance to the very house in which they were dining, and the blessing of her deed has spread around the world (Matt. 26:13; Mark 14:9). Little did Mary realize that night that her love for Christ would be a blessing to believers around the world for centuries to come!

When she came to the feet of Jesus, Mary took the place of a slave. When she undid her hair (something Jewish women did not do in public), she humbled herself and laid her glory at His feet (see 1 Cor. 11:15). Of course, she was misunderstood and criticized, but that is what usually happens when somebody gives his or her best to the Lord.

It was Judas who started the criticism, and, sad to say, the other disciples took it up. They did not know that Judas was a devil (John 6:70), and they admired him for his concern for the poor. After all, he was the treasurer, and especially at Passover season, he would want to share with those who were less fortunate (see John 13:21–30). Until the very end, the disciples believed that Judas was a devoted follower of the Lord.

John 12:4 records Judas's first words found anywhere in the four gospels. His last words are found in Matthew 27:4. Judas was a thief and was in the habit of stealing money from the money box that he carried. (The Greek word translated "bag" meant originally a small case in which mouthpieces were kept for wind instruments. Then it came to mean any small box, and especially a money box. The Greek version of the Old Testament uses this word in 2 Chron. 24:8–10 for King Joash's money chest.) No doubt Judas had already decided to abandon Jesus, and he wanted to get what he could out of what he considered a bad situation. Perhaps he had hoped that Jesus would defeat Rome and set up the kingdom; in which case, Judas would have been treasurer of the kingdom!

What Mary did was a blessing to Jesus and a blessing to her own life. She was also a blessing to the home, filling it with fragrance (see Phil. 4:18), and today, she is a blessing to the church around the world. Her one act of devotion in the little village of Bethany still sends "ripples of blessing."

But not so Judas! We call our daughters "Mary," but no parent would call a son "Judas." His very name is listed in the dictionary as a synonym for treachery. Mary and Judas are seen in contrast in Proverbs 10:7—"The memory of the just is blessed, but the name of the wicked shall rot." "A good name is better than precious ointment," says Ecclesiastes 7:1, and Mary had both.

Matthew 26:14 gives the impression that immediately after this rebuke, Judas went to the priests and bargained to deliver Jesus into their hands. But it is likely that the events recorded in Matthew 21—25 took place first. No doubt the Lord's rebuke of Judas at Bethany played an important part in his decision actually to betray Jesus. Also, the fact that Jesus once again openly announced His death would motivate Judas to escape while the opportunity was there.

As we look at this event, we see some "representative people" who are examples to us. Martha represents *work* as she served the dinner she had prepared for the Lord. This was just as much a "fragrant offering" as was Mary's ointment (see Heb. 13:16). Mary represents *worship,* and Lazarus represents *witness* (John 11:9–11). People went to Bethany just to be able to see this man who had been raised from the dead!

As mentioned we have no recorded words from Lazarus in the New Testament, but his miraculous life was an effective witness for Jesus Christ. (In contrast, John the Baptist did no miracles, yet his words brought people to Jesus. See John 10:40–42.) We today ought to "walk in newness of life" (Rom. 6:4) because we have been "raised from the dead" (Eph. 2:1–10; Col. 3:1ff.). Actually, the Christian life ought to be a beautiful balance of worship, work, and witness.

But the fact that Lazarus was a walking miracle put him into a place of danger: the Jewish leaders wanted to kill *him* as well as Jesus! Our Lord was right when He called them children of the devil, for they were murderers indeed (John 8:42–44). They threw the healed blind man out of the synagogue rather than permit him to bear witness to Christ every Sabbath, and they tried to put Lazarus back into the tomb because he was leading people to faith in Christ. If you will not accept the evidence, you must try to get rid of it!

This quiet evening of fellowship—in spite of the cruel way the disciples treated Mary—must have brought special encouragement and strength to the Savior's heart as He faced the demands of that last week before the cross. We should examine our own hearts and homes to ask whether we are bringing joy to His heart by our worship, work, and witness.

Jesus and the Passover Pilgrims (12:12–19)

John shifted the scene from a quiet dinner in Bethany to a noisy public parade in Jerusalem. All four gospels record this event, and their accounts should be compared. This was the only "public demonstration" that our Lord allowed while He was ministering on earth. His purpose was to fulfill the Old Testament prophecy (Zech. 9:9). The result was a growing animosity on the part of the religious leaders, leading eventually to the crucifixion of the Savior.

There were three different groups in the crowd that day: (1) the Passover visitors from outside Judea (John 12:12, 18); (2) the local people who had witnessed the raising of Lazarus (John 12:17); and (3) the religious leaders who were greatly concerned about what Jesus might do at the feast (John 12:19). At each of the different feasts, the people were in keen expectation, wondering if Jesus would be there and what He would do. It looked as though Jesus was actually seeking to incite a revolution and establish Himself as king, but that was not what He had in mind.

What did this event mean to Jesus? For one thing, it was a part of His obedience to the Father's will. The prophet Zechariah (Zech. 9:9) prophesied that the Messiah would enter Jerusalem in that manner, and He fulfilled the prophecy. "Daughter of Zion" is another name for the city of Jerusalem (Jer. 4:31; Lam. 2:4, 8, 10). Certainly Jesus was openly announcing to the people that He indeed is the King of Israel (John 1:49), the promised Messiah. No doubt many of the pilgrims hoped that *now* He would defeat the Romans and set the nation of Israel free.

What did this demonstration mean to the Romans? Nothing is recorded about the Roman viewpoint, but it is certain that they kept a close watch that day. During the annual Passover feast, it was not uncommon for some of the Jewish nationalists to try to arouse the people, and perhaps they thought this parade was that kind of an event. I imagine that some of the Roman soldiers must have smiled at the "triumphal entry," because it was nothing like their own "Roman triumph" celebrations in the city of Rome.

Whenever a Roman general was victorious on foreign soil, killing at least five thousand of the enemy, and gaining new territory, he was given a "Roman triumph" when he returned to the city. It was the Roman equivalent of the American "ticker-tape parade," only with much more splendor. The victor would be permitted to display the trophies he had won and the enemy leaders he had captured. The parade ended at the arena, where some of the captives entertained the people by fighting wild beasts. Compared to a "Roman triumph," our Lord's entry into Jerusalem was nothing.

What did the "triumphal entry" mean to the people of Israel? The pilgrims welcomed Jesus, spread their garments before Him, and waved palm branches as symbols of peace and victory (Rev. 7:9). They quoted from Psalm 118:26, which is a messianic psalm, and they proclaimed Him the "King of Israel." But while they were doing this, Jesus was weeping (Luke 19:37–44)!

The name *Jerusalem* means "city of peace" or "foundation of peace," and the people were hoping that Jesus would bring them the peace that they needed. However, He wept because He saw what lay ahead of the nation—war, suffering, destruction, and a scattered people. At His birth, the angels announced "peace on earth" (Luke 2:13–14), but in His ministry Jesus announced "war on earth" (Luke 12:51ff.). It is significant that the crowds shouted "peace in heaven" (Luke 19:38), because that is the only place where there is peace today!

The nation had wasted its opportunities; their leaders did not know the time of God's visitation. They were ignorant of their own Scriptures. The next time Israel sees the King, the scene will be radically different (Rev. 19:11ff.)! He will come in glory, not in humility, and the armies of heaven will accompany Him. It will be a scene of victory as He comes to defeat His enemies and establish His kingdom.

It is a repeated theme in Scripture that there can be no glory unless first there is suffering. Jesus knew that He must die on the cross before He could enter into His glory (Luke 24:26). The Jewish theologians were not clear in their minds concerning the sufferings of the Messiah and the glorious kingdom that the prophets announced. Some teachers held that there were two Messiahs, one who would suffer and one who would reign. Even our Lord's own disciples were not clear as to what was going on (see John 11:16).

How did the Jewish leaders respond to the "Triumphal Entry" of the Lord? As they watched the great crowd gather and honor Jesus, the Pharisees were quite sure that Jesus had won the day. They were anticipating some kind of general revolt during the Passover season. Perhaps Jesus would perform a great miracle and in that way capture the minds and hearts of the restless people. How little they really understood the mind and heart of the Master! What they did not realize was that Jesus was "forcing their hand" so that the Sanhedrin would act *during the feast.* The Lamb of God had to give His life when the Passover lambs were being slain.

The statement, "Behold, the world is gone after him!" (John 12:19) was both an exaggeration and a prophecy. In the next section, we meet some visitors from outside Israel.

Jesus and the Gentile Visitors (12:20–36)

Following His entry into Jerusalem, our Lord cleansed the temple for the second time. He quoted Isaiah 56:7 and Jeremiah 7:11: "Is it not written, my house shall be called of all nations the house of prayer? but ye have made it a den of thieves" (Mark 11:17). Perhaps these Greeks heard that word and were encouraged by it.

One of John's major themes is that Jesus is the Savior of the world, not simply the Redeemer of Israel. He is the Lamb of God who takes away the sin of the world (John 1:29). "For God so loved the world" (John 3:16). The Samaritans rightly identified Him as "the Savior of the world" (John 4:42). He gave His life *for* the world and He gives life *to* the world (John 6:33). He is the Light of the World (John 8:12). The universal emphasis of John's gospel is too obvious to miss. Jesus will bring the "other sheep" who are outside the Jewish fold (John 10:16; and see 11:51–52).

The original text indicates that these Greeks "were accustomed to come and worship at the feast." They were not curious visitors or one-time investigators. No doubt they were "God-fearers," Gentiles who attended the Jewish synagogue and sought the truth, but who had not yet become proselytes. Gentiles came to see Jesus when He was a young child (Matt. 2), and now Gentiles came to see Him just before His death.

These men "kept asking" Philip for the privilege of an interview with Jesus. Philip finally told Andrew (who was often bringing people to Jesus), and Andrew gave the request to the Lord. No doubt there were many people who wanted private interviews with the Lord, but they were afraid of the Pharisees (John 9:22). Being from out of the country, the Gentile visitors either did not know about the danger, or did not fear the consequences.

We can commend these Greeks for wanting to see Jesus. The Jews would say, "We would see a sign!" (Matt. 12:38; 1 Cor. 1:22) but these men said, "We would see [have an interview with] Jesus." There is no record that Jesus did talk with these men, but the message that He gave in response contains truths that all of us need.

The central theme of this message is the glory of God (John 12:23, 28). We would have expected Jesus to say, "The hour is come, that the Son of man should be crucified." But Jesus saw beyond the cross to the glory that would follow (see Luke 24:26; Heb. 12:2). In fact, the glory of God is an important theme in the remaining chapters of John's gospel (see John 13:31–32; 14:13; 17:1, 4–5, 22, 24).

Jesus used the image of a seed to illustrate the great spiritual truth that there can be no glory without suffering, no fruitful life without death, no victory without surrender. Of itself, a seed is weak and useless, but when it is planted, it "dies" and becomes fruitful. There is both beauty and bounty when a seed "dies" and fulfills its purpose. If a seed could talk, it would no doubt complain about being put into the cold, dark earth. But the only way it can achieve its goal is by being planted.

God's children are like seeds. They are small and insignificant, but they have life in them, God's life. However, that life can never be fulfilled unless we yield ourselves to God and permit Him to "plant us." We must die to self so that we may live unto God (Rom. 6; Gal. 2:20). The only way to have a fruitful life is to follow Jesus Christ in death, burial, and resurrection.

In these words, Jesus challenges us today to surrender our lives to Him. Note the contrasts: loneliness or fruitfulness; losing your life or keeping your life; serving self or serving Christ; pleasing self or receiving God's honor.

I read about some Christians who visited a remote mission station to see how the ministry was going. As they watched the dedicated missionary team at work, they were impressed with their ministry, but admitted that they missed "civilization."

"You certainly have buried yourself out here!" one of the visitors exclaimed.

"We haven't buried ourselves," the missionary replied. "We were planted!"

Our Lord knew that He was facing suffering and death, and His humanity responded to this ordeal. His soul was troubled, not because He was questioning the Father's will, but because He was fully conscious of all that the cross involved. Note that Jesus did not say, "What shall I do?" because He knew what He was ordained to do. He said, "What shall I say?" In the hour of suffering and surrender, there are only two prayers we can pray, either "Father, save me!" or "Father, glorify Thy name!"

In one of my radio messages, I made the statement, "God does not expect us to be comfortable, but He does expect us to be conformable." No sooner had the program ended than my office phone rang and an anonymous listener wanted to argue with me about that statement.

"Conformable to what?" the voice thundered. "Haven't you read Romans 12:2—'Be not conformed to this world'?"

"Sure I've read Romans 12:2," I replied. "Have you read Romans 8:29? God has predestined us 'to be conformed to the image of his Son.'"

After a long pause (I was glad he was paying the phone bill), he grunted and said, "OK."

Comfortable or *conformable:* that is the question. If we are looking for comfortable lives, then we will protect our plans and desires, save our lives, and never be planted. But if we yield our lives and let God plant us, we will never be alone but will have the joy of being fruitful to the glory of God. "If any man [Jew or Greek] serve me, let him follow me." This is the equivalent of Matthew 10:39 and Mark 8:36.

The prayer, "Father, glorify thy name!" received a reply from heaven! God the Father spoke to His Son and gave Him a double assurance: the Son's past life and ministry had glorified the Father, and the Son's future suffering and death would glorify the Father. It is significant that the Father spoke to the Son at the beginning of the Son's ministry (Matt. 3:17), as the Son began His journey to Jerusalem (Matt. 17:5), and now as the Son entered the last days before the cross. God always gives that word of assurance to those who willingly suffer for His sake.

The people heard a sound but did not know the message that had been conveyed. Yet if the voice was for their sakes and they could not understand it, what good was it? In that the voice assured Jesus, who was to die for their sakes, the voice was for their good. They heard Him pray and they heard a sound from heaven in response to that prayer. That should have convinced them that Jesus was in touch with the Father. We might translate John 12:30, "That voice came more for your sake than for Mine."

Jesus then openly spoke about the cross. It was an hour of judgment for the world and for Satan, the prince of the world. The death of Jesus Christ would seem like a victory for the wicked world, but it would really be a judgment of the world. On the cross, Jesus would defeat Satan and his world system (Gal. 6:14). Even though he is permitted to go to and fro on the earth, Satan is a defeated enemy. As we serve the Lord, we overcome the wicked one (Luke 10:17–19). One day Satan shall be cast out of heaven (Rev. 12:10), and eventually he will be judged and imprisoned forever (Rev. 20:10).

We have met the phrase "lifted up" before (John 3:14; 8:28). Its basic meaning is *crucifixion* (note John 12:33), but it also carries the idea of *glorification*. "Behold, My servant will prosper. He will be high and lifted up, and greatly exalted" (Isa. 52:13 NASB). The Son of Man was *glorified* by being *crucified!*

The phrase "all men" does not suggest universal salvation. It means "all people without distinction," that is, Jews and Gentiles. He does not force them; He draws them (see John 6:44–45). He was "lifted up" that men might find the way (John 12:32), know the truth (John 8:28), and receive the life (John 3:14). The cross reminds us that God loves a whole world and that the task of the church is to take the gospel to the whole world.

The people did not understand what He was teaching. They knew that "Son of man" was a title for Messiah, but they could not understand why Messiah would be crucified! Did not the Old Testament teach that the Messiah would live forever? (See Ps. 72:17; 89:36; 110:4; Isa. 9:7.)

But that was no time to be discussing the fine points of theology! It was an hour of crisis (see John 12:31, where the Greek word *krisis* means judgment) and an hour of opportunity. The light was shining and they had better take advantage of their opportunity to be saved! We have met this image of light and darkness before (John 1:4–9; 3:17–20; 8:12; 9:39–41). By a simple step of faith, these people could have passed out of spiritual darkness and into the light of salvation.

This marked the end of our Lord's public ministry as far as John's record is concerned. Jesus departed and hid Himself. It was judgment on the nation that saw His miracles, heard His messages, and scrutinized His ministry, and yet refused to believe on Him.

Jesus and Unbelieving Jews (12:37–49)

The key word in this section is *believe;* it is used eight times. First, John explained the unbelief of the people.

They *would not* believe (John 12:37–38, with a quotation from Isa. 53:1); they *could not* believe (John 12:39); and they *should not* believe (John 12:40–41, with a quotation from Isa. 6:9–10).

In spite of all the clear evidence that was presented to them, the nation would not believe. The "arm of the Lord" had been revealed to them in great power, yet they closed their eyes to the truth. They had heard the message ("report") and seen the miracles, and yet would not believe.

When a person starts to resist the light, something begins to change within him, and he comes to the place where he cannot believe. There is "judicial blindness" that God permits to come over the eyes of people who do not take the truth seriously. (This quotation is found in a number of places in the New Testament. See Matt. 13:14–15; Mark 4:12; Luke 8:10; Acts 28:25–27; Rom. 11:8.) It is a serious thing to treat God's truth lightly, for a person could well miss his opportunity to be saved. "Seek ye the Lord while he may be found, call ye upon him while he is near" (Isa. 55:6).

There were those who would not believe, and there were those who would not openly confess Christ even though they had believed (John 12:42–43). Nicodemus and Joseph of Arimathea belonged to this group initially, but eventually came out openly in their confession of Christ (John 19:38ff.). In the early church, there were numbers of Pharisees (Acts 15:5) and even priests (Acts 6:7). It was the old struggle between the glory of God and the praise of men (John 12:25–26). It was a costly thing to be excommunicated (John 9:22), and these "secret believers" wanted the best of both worlds. Note John 5:44 in this regard.

In John 12:44–50 we have our Lord's last message before He "hid himself" from the people. Again, the emphasis was on faith. A number of the basic themes in John's gospel run through this message: God sent the Son; to see the Son means to see the Father; Jesus is the Light of the World; His words are the very words of God; faith in Him brings salvation; to reject Him is to face eternal judgment. In fact, the very Word that He spoke will judge those who have rejected it and Him!

It is an awesome thought that the unbeliever will face at the judgment every bit of Scripture he has ever read or heard. The very Word that he rejects becomes his judge! Why? Because the written Word points to the Living Word, Jesus Christ (John 1:14).

Many people reject the truth simply because of the fear of man (John 12:42–43). Among those who will be in hell are "the fearful" (Rev. 21:8). Better to fear God and go to heaven than to fear men and go to hell!

The word *judge* is repeated four times in the closing words of this message, and a solemn word it is. Jesus did not come to judge; He came to save (John 3:18; 8:15). But if the sinner will not trust the Savior, the Savior must become the Judge. The sinner is actually passing judgment on himself, not on the Lord!

As you have studied these twelve chapters of the gospel of John, you have seen Jesus Christ in His life, His ministry, His miracles, His message, and His desire to save lost sinners.

You have considered the evidence. Have you come to the conviction that Jesus Christ is indeed the Son of God, the Savior of the world?

Have *you* trusted Him and received everlasting life?

"While you have the light, believe in the light, that you may become sons of light" (John 12:36 NKJV).

CHAPTER THIRTEEN
John 13:1–35
THE SOVEREIGN SERVANT

Three times in my ministry I have had to deliver "farewell messages" to congregations I had served, and it is not an easy thing to do. I may not have succeeded, but my purpose was always to prepare them for the future. This included warning as well as instruction. They would call a new pastor and enter into a new phase of ministry, and I wanted them to be at their best.

John 13—17 is our Lord's "farewell message" to His beloved disciples, climaxing with His intercessory prayer for them and for us. Other farewell addresses in Scripture were delivered by Moses (Deut. 31—33), Joshua (Josh. 23—24), and Paul (Acts 20). However, Jesus added a significant "action section" to His message when He washed His disciples' feet. It was an object lesson they would never forget.

In this passage, we see our Lord in a fourfold relationship: to His heavenly Father (John 13:1–5), to Simon Peter (John 13:6–11), to all of the disciples (John 13:12–17), and to Judas (John 13:18–35). In each of these sections of John's gospel, you will discover a special message, a spiritual truth to help you in your own Christian life.

Humility: Jesus and the Father (13:1–5)

Jesus had entered Jerusalem on Sunday, and on Monday had cleansed the temple. Tuesday was a day of conflict as the religious leaders sought to trip Him up and get evidence to arrest Him. These events are recorded in Matthew 21—25. Wednesday was probably a day of rest, but on Thursday He met in the Upper Room with His disciples in order to observe Passover.

The emphasis in John 13:1–3 is on *what our Lord knew*, and in John 13:4–5 on *what our Lord did*.

Jesus knew that "his hour was come." More than any of the gospel writers, John emphasized the fact that Jesus lived on a "heavenly timetable" as He did the Father's will. Note the development of this theme:

2:4—"Mine hour is not yet come."
7:30—"His hour was not yet come."
8:20—"His hour was not yet come."
12:23—"The hour is come that the Son of man should be glorified."
13:1—"Jesus knew that his hour was come."
17:1—"Father, the hour is come."

What was this divinely appointed "hour"? It was the time when He would be glorified through His death, resurrection, and ascension. From the human point of view, it meant suffering, but from the divine point of view, it meant glory. He would soon leave this world and return to the Father who sent Him, Jesus having finished His work on earth (John 17:4). When the servant of God is in the will of God, he is immortal until his work is done. They could not even arrest Jesus, let alone kill Him, until the right hour had arrived.

Jesus also knew that Judas would betray Him. Judas is mentioned eight times in John's gospel, more than in any of the other Gospels. Satan had entered into Judas (Luke 22:3), and now he would give him the necessary thought to bring about the arrest and crucifixion of the Son of God. The word translated "put" in John 13:2 literally means "to throw." It reminds us of the fiery darts of the wicked one (Eph. 6:16). Judas was an unbeliever (John 6:64–71), so he did not have a "shield of faith" to use to ward off Satan's attacks.

Finally, Jesus knew that the Father had given Him all things (John 13:3). This statement parallels John 3:35, and it also reminds us of Matthew 11:27. Even in His humiliation, our Lord had all things through His Father. He was poor and yet He was rich. Because Jesus knew who He was, where He came from, what He had, and where He was going, He was complete master of the situation. You and I as believers know that we have been born of God, that we are one day going to God, and that in Christ we have all things; therefore, we ought to be able to follow our Lord's example and serve others.

What Jesus knew helped determine *what Jesus did* (John 13:4–5). The disciples must have been shocked when they saw their Master rise from supper, lay aside His outer garments, wrap a towel around His waist, take a basin of water, and wash their feet. Jewish servants did not wash their masters' feet, though Gentile slaves might do it. It was a menial task, and yet Jesus did it! As a special mark of affection, a host or hostess might wash a guest's feet, but it was not standard operating procedure in most homes.

Jesus knew that there was a competitive spirit in the hearts of His disciples. In fact, within a few minutes, the men were disputing over which of them was the greatest (Luke 22:24–30). He gave them an unforgettable lesson in humility, and by His actions rebuked their selfishness and pride. The more you think about this scene, the more profound it becomes. It is certainly an illustration of what Paul wrote years later in Philippians 2:1–16. Peter must have recalled the event when he wrote his first epistle and urged his readers to "be clothed with humility" (1 Peter 5:5).

Too often we confuse "the poor in spirit" (Matt. 5:3) with the "poor-spirited," and true humility with timidity and inferiority. The British literary giant Samuel Johnson was once asked to prepare a funeral sermon for a girl who had died, and he asked what her special virtues were. He was told that she was kind to her inferiors. Johnson replied that this was commendable, but that it would be difficult to determine who her inferiors were!

The Father had put all things into the Son's hands, *yet Jesus picked up a towel and a basin!* His humility was not born of poverty, but of riches. He was rich, yet He became poor (2 Cor. 8:9). A Malay proverb says, "The fuller the ear is of rice-grain, the lower it bends."

It is remarkable how the gospel of John reveals the humility of our Lord even while magnifying His deity: "The Son can do nothing of himself" (John 5:19, 30). "For I came down from heaven, not to do mine own will" (John 6:38). "My doctrine is not mine" (John 7:16). "And I seek not mine own glory" (John 8:50). "The word which ye hear is not mine" (John 14:24). His ultimate expression of humility was His death on the cross.

Jesus was the Sovereign, yet He took the place of a servant. He had all things in His hands, yet He picked up a towel. He was Lord and Master, yet He served His followers. It has well been said that humility is not thinking meanly of yourself; it is simply not thinking of yourself at all. True humility grows out of our relationship with the Father. If our desire is to know and do the Father's will so that we might glorify His name, then we will experience the joy of following Christ's example and serving others.

We today, just like the disciples that night, desperately need this lesson on humility. The church is filled with a worldly spirit of competition and criticism as believers vie with one another to see who is the greatest. We are growing in knowledge, but not in grace (see 2 Peter 3:18). "Humility is the only soil in which the graces root," wrote Andrew Murray. "The lack of humility is the sufficient explanation of every defect and failure."

Jesus served His disciples because of His humility and because of His love. Contrast John 13:1 with 1:11 and 3:16: Jesus came "unto his own [world], and his own [people] received him not." "For God so loved the world." In the Upper Room, Jesus ministered in love to His own disciples, and they received Him and what He had to say. The Greek text says, "He loved them to the uttermost."

Holiness: Jesus and Peter (13:6–11)

As Peter watched the Lord wash his friends' feet, he became more and more disturbed and could not understand what He was doing. As you read the life of Christ in the Gospels, you cannot help but notice how Peter often spoke impulsively out of his ignorance and had to be corrected by Jesus. Peter opposed Jesus going to the cross (Matt. 16:21–23), and he tried to manage our Lord's affairs at the Transfiguration (Matt. 17:1–8). He expressed the faith of the disciples (John 6:66–71) without realizing that one of the number was a traitor.

The word translated "wash" in John 13:5–6, 8, 12, and 14 is *niptō* and means "to wash a part of the body."

But the word translated "washed" in John 13:10 is *louō* and means "to bathe all over." The distinction is important, for Jesus was trying to teach His disciples the importance of a holy walk.

When the sinner trusts the Savior, he is "bathed all over" and his sins are washed away and forgiven (see 1 Cor. 6:9–11; Titus 3:3–7; and Rev. 1:5). "And their sins and iniquities will I remember no more" (Heb. 10:17). However, as the believer walks in this world, it is easy to become defiled. He does not need to be bathed all over again; he simply needs to have that defilement cleansed away. God promises to cleanse us when we confess our sins to Him (1 John 1:9).

But why is it so important that we "keep our feet clean"? Because if we are defiled, we cannot have communion with our Lord. "If I wash thee not, thou hast no part with me" (John 13:8). The word translated "part" is *meros,* and it carries the meaning here of "participation, having a share in someone or something." When God "bathes us all over" in salvation, He brings about our *union* with Christ, and that is a settled relationship that cannot change. (The verb *wash* in John 13:10 is in the perfect tense. It is settled once and for all.) However, our *communion* with Christ depends on our keeping ourselves "unspotted from the world" (James 1:27). If we permit unconfessed sin in our lives, we hinder our walk with the Lord, and that is when we need to have our feet washed.

This basic truth of Christian living is beautifully illustrated in the Old Testament priesthood. When the priest was consecrated, he was bathed all over (Ex. 29:4), and that experience was never repeated. However, during his daily ministry, he became defiled, so it was necessary that he wash his hands and feet at the brass laver in the courtyard (Ex. 30:18–21). Only then could he enter the holy place and trim the lamps, eat the holy bread, or burn the incense.

The Lord cleanses us through the blood of Christ, that is, His work on the cross (1 John 1:5–10), and through the application of His Word to our lives (Ps. 119:9; John 15:3; Eph. 5:25–26). The "water of the Word" can keep our hearts and minds clean so that we will avoid the pollutions of this world. But if we do sin, we have a loving Advocate in glory who will hear our prayers of confession and forgive us (1 John 2:1–2).

Peter did not understand what his Lord was doing, but instead of waiting for an explanation, he impulsively tried to tell the Lord what to do. There is a strong double negative in John 13:8. The Greek scholar Kenneth Wuest translated Peter's statement, "You shall by no means wash my feet, no, never" (WUEST). Peter really meant it! Then when he discovered that to refuse the Lord would mean to lose the Lord's fellowship, he went in the opposite direction and asked for a complete bath!

We can learn an important lesson from Peter: don't question the Lord's will or work, and don't try to change it. He knows what He is doing. Peter had a difficult time accepting Christ's ministry to him *because*

Peter was not yet ready to minister to the other disciples. It takes humility and grace to serve others, but it also takes humility and grace to allow others to serve us. The beautiful thing about a submissive spirit is that it can both give and receive to the glory of God.

John was careful to point out that Peter and Judas were in a different relationship with Jesus. Yes, Jesus washed Judas's feet! But it did Judas no good because he had not been bathed all over. Some people teach that Judas was a saved man who sinned away his salvation, but that is not what Jesus said. Our Lord made it very clear that Judas had never been cleansed from his sins and was an unbeliever (John 6:64–71).

It is a wonderful thing to deepen your fellowship with the Lord. The important thing is to be honest with Him and with ourselves and keep our feet clean.

Happiness: Jesus and the Disciples (13:12–17)

John 13:17 is the key—"If ye know these things, happy are ye if ye do them." The sequence is important: humbleness, holiness, then happiness. Aristotle defined happiness as "good fortune joined to virtue … a life that is both agreeable and secure." That might do for a philosopher, but it will never do for a Christian believer! Happiness is the byproduct of a life that is lived in the will of God. When we humbly serve others, walk in God's paths of holiness, and do what He tells us, then we will enjoy happiness.

Jesus asked the disciples if they understood what He had done, and it is not likely that they did. So, He explained it: He had given them a lesson in humble service, an example for them to follow. The world thinks that happiness is the result of others serving us, but real joy comes when we serve others in the name of Christ. The world is constantly pursuing happiness, but that is like chasing a shadow: it is always just beyond your reach.

Jesus was their Master, so He had every right to command their service. Instead, He served them! He gave them an example of true Christian ministry. On more than one occasion during the previous three years, He had taught them lessons about humility and service, but now He had demonstrated the lesson to them. Perhaps the disciples remembered His lesson about the child (Matt. 18:1–6) or the rebuke He gave James and John when they asked for thrones (Matt. 20:20–28). Now it was all starting to fall into place.

The servant (slave) is not greater than his master; so, if the master becomes a slave, where does that put the slave? *On the same level as the master!* By becoming a servant, our Lord did not push us down: He lifted us up! He dignified sacrifice and service. You must keep in mind that the Romans had no use for humility, and the Greeks despised manual labor. Jesus combined these two when He washed the disciples' feet.

The world asks, "How many people work for you?" but the Lord asks, "For how many people do you work?" When I was ministering at a conference in Kenya, an African believer shared one of their proverbs with me: "The chief is servant of all." How true it is that we need leaders who will serve and servants who will lead. G. K. Chesterton said that a really great man is one who makes others feel great, and Jesus did this with His disciples *by teaching them to serve.*

However, it is not enough just to *know* this truth; we must put it into practice. James 1:22–27 makes it clear that the blessing comes in the *doing* of the Word, not the hearing. Wuest translates the last phrase in James 1:25, "This man shall be prospered spiritually in his doing." Even studying this section in John's gospel can stir us emotionally or enlighten us intellectually, but it cannot bless us spiritually until we do what Jesus told us to do. This is the only way to lasting happiness.

Be sure to keep these lessons in their proper sequence: humbleness, holiness, happiness. Submit to the Father, keep your life clean, and serve others. This is God's formula for true spiritual joy.

Hypocrisy: Jesus and Judas (13:18–35)

A dark shadow now fell across the scene as Jesus dealt with Judas, the traitor. It is important to note that Judas was not a true believer; he was a hypocrite. He had never believed in Jesus (John 6:64–71), he had not been bathed all over (John 13:10–11), and he had not been among the chosen ones whom the Father gave to the Son (John 13:18; 17:12). How close a person can come to salvation and yet be lost forever! Judas was even the treasurer of the group (John 12:6) and was certainly held in high regard by his fellow disciples.

At that hour, Jesus had two great concerns: to fulfill the Word of God (John 13:18–30) and to magnify the glory of God (John 13:31–35).

The Scripture Jesus quoted was Psalm 41:9—"Yea, mine own familiar friend, in whom I trusted, which did eat of my bread, hath lifted up his heel against me." When David wrote the psalm, he was probably referring to his counselor Ahithophel, who turned traitor and joined Absalom's rebellion (see 2 Sam. 15—17). It is significant that both Judas and Ahithophel committed suicide by hanging themselves (2 Sam. 17:23; Matt. 27:3–10; Acts 1:18). However, Judas did not commit suicide in order to fulfill biblical prophecy, for that would make God the author of his sin. Judas was responsible for his own decisions, and those decisions fulfilled God's Word.

Jesus was concerned that Judas's treachery would not weaken His disciples' faith. This is why He related it to the Word of God: when the disciples saw all of this fulfilled, it would make their faith stronger (see John 8:28). Judas had been disloyal, but He expected them to be loyal to Him and His cause. After all, He was God the Son sent by God the Father. They were Christ's chosen representatives; to receive them would be the same as receiving the Father and the Son. What a privilege, to be ambassadors of the King!

The remarkable thing is that the others at the table with Jesus did not know that Judas was an unbeliever and a traitor. Up to the very hour of his treachery,

Judas was protected by the Savior whom he betrayed. Had Jesus openly revealed what He knew about Judas, it is likely that the men would have turned on him. Remember what Peter did to Malchus when soldiers came to take Jesus!

From the very beginning, Jesus knew what Judas would do (John 6:64), but He did not compel him to do it. Judas was exposed to the same spiritual privileges as the other disciples, yet they did him no good. The same sun that melts the ice only hardens the clay. In spite of all that our Lord said about money, and all of His warning about covetousness, Judas continued to be a thief and steal from the treasury. In spite of all our Lord's warning about unbelief, Judas persisted in his rejection. *Jesus even washed Judas's feet!* Yet his hard heart did not yield.

Jesus had spoken before about a traitor (John 6:70), but the disciples did not take it to heart. Now when He spoke openly about it at the table, His disciples were perplexed.

Peter signaled to John, who was the closest to Jesus at the table, and asked him to find out who the traitor was. The Lord's reply to John was certainly not heard by all the men; in fact, they were carrying on discussions among themselves about who the traitor might be (Luke 22:23). When Jesus gave the bread to Judas, it was interpreted as an act of love and honor. In fact, Judas was seated at the place of honor, so our Lord's actions were seen in that light. He was bestowing a special honor on Judas. No wonder, after Judas left the room, the disciples got into an argument over who was the greatest (Luke 22:24–30).

John was no doubt stunned by this revelation, but before he could say or do anything, Jesus had sent Judas on his way. Even though Satan had entered Judas, it was Jesus who was in charge. He lived on the timetable given to Him by the Father, and He wanted to fulfill what was written in the Word. Since Judas was the treasurer, it was logical for the disciples to conclude that he had been sent on a special mission by the Lord. Judas had hypocritically expressed an interest in the poor (John 12:4–6), so perhaps he was on an errand of mercy to help the poor.

Keep in mind that Judas knew what he was doing and that he did it deliberately. He had already met with the Jewish religious leaders and agreed to lead them to Jesus in such a way that there would not be any public disturbance (Luke 21:37—22:6). He heard Jesus say, "Woe unto that man by whom the Son of man is betrayed! It had been good for that man if he had not been born" (Matt. 26:24). Yet, he persisted in his unbelief and treachery.

John's little phrase "and it was night" carries a tremendous impact when you remember that *light* and *darkness* are important spiritual images in his gospel. Jesus is the Light of the World (John 8:12), but Judas rejected Jesus and went out into darkness, and for Judas, *it is still night!* Those who do evil hate the light (John 3:18–21). Our Lord's warning in John 12:25–26 went unheeded by Judas—and it goes unheeded by lost sinners today, people who will go where Judas went unless they repent and trust the Savior.

The instant Judas was gone, the atmosphere was cleared, and Jesus began to instruct His disciples and prepare them for His crucifixion and His ultimate return to heaven. It was after Judas's departure that He instituted the Lord's Supper, something that Judas as an unbeliever certainly could not share. Judas was out in the night, controlled by the prince of darkness, Satan, but Jesus was in the light, sharing love and truth with His beloved disciples. What a contrast!

The theme now changes to the glory of God (John 13:31–35). From the human perspective, the death of Christ was a dastardly deed involving unspeakable suffering and humiliation, but from the divine perspective it was the revelation of the glory of God. "The hour is come that the Son of man should be glorified" (John 12:23). Twelve times in this gospel, the title "Son of man" appears, and this one in John 12:31 is the final instance. Daniel 7:13 identifies this title as messianic, and Jesus sometimes used it this way (Matt. 26:64).

What did it mean for Jesus to glorify the Father? He tells us in His prayer, "I have glorified thee on the earth; I have finished the work which thou gavest me to do" (John 17:4). This is the way all of us glorify God, by faithfully doing what He calls us to do. In our Lord's case, the Father's will was that the Son die for lost sinners, be raised from the dead, and then ascend to heaven. The Son glorified the Father and the Father glorified the Son (John 17:1, 5).

There would come a time when the Son would be glorified in these disciples (John 17:10), but they could not follow Him at that time. Peter boasted that he would follow the Lord even to death (Luke 22:33), but unfortunately ended up denying Him three times.

Jesus had said to the Jews on two occasions that they would seek Him but not be able to find Him or follow Him (John 7:33–36; 8:21–24). Note that He did not tell His disciples that they would not be able to find Him, but He did say that to the unbelieving Jews. One day the believing disciples would go to be with Him (John 14:1–3), and they would also see Him after His resurrection. But during this time of His suffering and death, it was important that they not try to follow Him.

I have heard eloquent sermons about the sin of Peter who "followed afar off" (Luke 22:54), and the emphasis was that he should have followed nearer. The simple fact is that he should not have followed at all! The statement in John 13:33 is proof enough, and when you add Matthew 26:31 (quoted from Zech. 13:7) and our Lord's words in John 18:8, the evidence is conclusive. Because Peter disregarded this warning, he got into trouble.

The disciples' responsibility was to love one another just as Christ had loved them. They would certainly need this love in the hours to follow, when their Master would be taken from them and their brave spokesman, Peter, would fail Him and them. In fact, all of them would fail, and the only thing that would bring them together would be their love for Christ and for each other.

The word *love* is used only twelve times in John 1—12, but in John 13—21 it is used forty-four times! It is a key word in Christ's farewell sermon to His disciples, as well as a burden in His high priestly prayer (John 17:26). The word *new* does not mean "new in time," because love has been important to God's people even from Old Testament times (see Lev. 19:18). It means "new in experience, fresh." It is the opposite of "worn out." Love would take on a new meaning and power because of the death of Christ on the cross (John 15:13). With the coming of the Holy Spirit, love would have a new power in their lives.

This section begins and ends with love: Jesus' love for His own (John 13:1) and the disciples' love for one another. It is love that is the true evidence that we belong to Jesus Christ. The church leader Tertullian (AD 155–220) quoted the pagans as saying of the Christians, "See how they love one another?" And how do we evidence that love? By doing what Jesus did: laying down our lives for the brethren (1 John 3:16). And the way to start is by getting down and washing one another's feet in sacrificial service.

CHAPTER FOURTEEN
John 13:36—14:31
HEART TROUBLE

This section opens and closes with our Lord's loving admonition, "Let not your heart be troubled" (John 14:1, 27). We are not surprised that the apostles were troubled. After all, Jesus had announced that one of them was a traitor, and then He warned Peter that he was going to deny his Lord three times. Self-confident Peter was certain that he could not only follow his Lord, but even die with Him and for Him. Alas, Peter did not know his own heart, nor do we really know *our* hearts, except for one thing: our hearts easily become troubled.

Perhaps the heaviest blow of all was the realization that Jesus was going to leave them (John 13:33). Where was He going? Could they go with Him? How could they get where He was going? These were some of the perplexing questions that tumbled around in their minds and hearts and were tossed back and forth in their conversation at the table.

How did Jesus calm their troubled hearts? By giving them six wonderful assurances to lay hold of, assurances that we today may claim and thus enjoy untroubled hearts. If you are a believer in Jesus Christ, you may claim every single one of these assurances.

You Are Going to Heaven (13:36—14:6)
Jesus did not rebuke Peter for asking Him where He

was going, but His reply was somewhat cryptic. One day Peter would "follow" Jesus to the cross (John 21:18–19; 2 Peter 1:12–15), and then he would follow Him to heaven. Tradition tells us that Peter was crucified, though he asked to be crucified head-downward because he did not feel worthy to die as his Master died.

Just as Peter was beginning to feel like a hero, Jesus announced that he himself would soon become a casualty. The message not only shocked Peter, but it also stunned the rest of the disciples. After all, if brave Peter denied the Lord, what hope was there for the rest of them? It was then that Jesus gave His message to calm their troubled hearts.

According to Jesus, heaven is a real place. It is not a product of religious imagination or the result of a psyched-up mentality, looking for "pie in the sky by and by." Heaven is the place where God dwells and where Jesus sits today at the right hand of the Father. Heaven is described as a kingdom (2 Peter 1:11), an inheritance (1 Peter 1:4), a country (Heb. 11:16), a city (Heb. 11:16), and a home (John 14:2).

The word *Father* is used fifty-three times in John 13—17. Heaven is "my Father's house," according to the Son of God. It is "home" for God's children! Some years ago, a London newspaper held a contest to determine the best definition of "home." The winning entry was "Home is the place where you are treated the best and complain the most." The poet Robert Frost said that home is the place that, when you arrive there, they have to take you in. A good definition!

The Greek word *monē* is translated "mansions" in John 14:2 and "abode" in John 14:23. It simply means "rooms, abiding places," so we must not think in terms of manor houses. It is unfortunate that some unbiblical songs have perpetuated the error that faithful Christians will have lovely mansions in glory, while worldly saints will have to be content with little cottages or even shacks. Jesus Christ is now preparing places for all true believers, and each place will be beautiful. When He was here on earth, Jesus was a carpenter (Mark 6:3). Now that He has returned to glory, He is building a church on earth and a home for that church in heaven.

John 14:3 is a clear promise of our Lord's return for His people. Some will go to heaven through the valley of the shadow of death, but those who are alive when Jesus returns will *never* see death (John 11:25–26). They will be changed to be like Christ and will go to heaven (1 Thess. 4:13–18).

Since heaven is the Father's house, it must be a place of love and joy. When the apostle John tried to describe heaven, he almost ran out of symbols and comparisons (Rev. 21—22)! Finally, he listed the things that would not be there: death, sorrow, crying, pain, night, etc. What a wonderful home it will be—and we will enjoy it forever!

Thomas's question revealed his keen desire to be with Jesus (see John 11:16), and this meant that he had to know where the Master was going and how he himself would get there. The Lord made it clear that He was going to the Father, and that He was the only way to the Father. Heaven is a real place, a loving place, and an exclusive place. Not everybody is going to heaven, but rather only those who have trusted Jesus Christ (see Acts 4:12; 1 Tim. 2:4–6).

Jesus does not simply teach the way or point the way; *He is the way.* In fact, "the Way" was one of the early names for the Christian faith (Acts 9:2; 19:9, 23; 22:4; 24:14, 22). Our Lord's statement, "No man cometh unto the Father but by me," wipes away any other proposed way to heaven—good works, religious ceremonies, costly gifts, etc. There is only one way, and that way is Jesus Christ.

How would this assurance of going to heaven help to calm the disciples' troubled hearts? Dr. James M. Gray put it beautifully in a song he wrote years ago: "Who could mind the journey, when the road leads home?" The assurance of a heavenly home at the end of life's road enables us to bear joyfully with the obstacles and battles along the way. It was this assurance that even encouraged our Lord, "who for the joy that was set before him endured the cross" (Heb. 12:2). Paul had this truth in mind when he wrote, "For I reckon that the sufferings of this present time are not worthy to be compared with the glory which shall be revealed in us" (Rom. 8:18).

You Know the Father Right Now (14:7–11)

We do not have to wait until we enter heaven to get to know the Father. We can know Him today and receive from Him the spiritual resources we need to keep going when the days are difficult.

What does it mean to "know the Father"? The word *know* is used 141 times in John's gospel, but it does not always carry the same meaning. In fact, there are four different "levels" of *knowing* according to John. The lowest level is simply knowing a fact. The next level is to understand the truth behind that fact. However, you can know the fact and know the truth behind it and still be lost in your sins. The third level introduces *relationship;* "to know" means "to believe in a person and become related to him or her." This is the way "know" is used in John 17:3. In fact, in Scripture, "to know" is used of the most intimate relationship between man and wife (Gen. 4:1).

The fourth use of "know" means "to have a deeper relationship with a person, a deeper communion." It was this level Paul was referring to when he wrote, "That I may know him" (Phil. 3:10). Jesus will describe this deeper relationship in John 14:19–23, so we will save any further comment until we deal with that section.

When Jesus said that knowing Him and seeing Him was the same as knowing and seeing the Father, He was claiming to be God. From now on, they would understand more and more about the Father, even though Jesus was leaving them.

I appreciate Philip's desire to know the Father. He had come a long way since that day Jesus found him and called him (John 1:43–45). The burning desire of every believer ought to be to know God better. We read and study the Word of God so that we might better know the God of the Word.

The Greek construction of the question in John 14:10 indicates that the Lord expected a yes answer from Philip: he *did* believe that Jesus was in the Father and the Father in Him. That being the case, Philip should have realized that the words of Jesus, as well as His works, came from the Father and revealed the Father. Believers today have not seen the Lord Jesus in the flesh (1 Peter 1:8), but we do see Him and His works in the Word. The emphasis throughout John's gospel is that you cannot separate Christ's words and works, for both come from the Father and reveal the Father.

The "believe" in John 14:10 is singular, for Jesus was addressing Philip, but in John 14:11, it is plural and He addresses all of the disciples. The tense of both is "go on believing." Let your faith grow!

Four hundred years before Christ was born, the Greek philosopher Plato wrote, "To find out the Father and Maker of all this universe is a hard task, and when we have found Him, to speak of Him to all men is impossible." But Plato was wrong! We *can* know the Father and Maker of the universe, for Jesus Christ revealed Him to us. Why should our hearts be troubled when the Creator and Governor of the universe is *our own Father?*

The very Lord of heaven and earth is our Father (Luke 10:21). There is no need for us to have troubled hearts, for He is in control.

You Have the Privilege of Prayer (14:12–15)

"Why pray when you can worry?" asks a plaque that I have seen in many homes. One of the best remedies for a troubled heart is prayer.

> O what peace we often forfeit,
> O what needless pain we bear;
> All because we do not carry
> Everything to God in prayer.

However, if God is going to answer our prayers and give us peace in our hearts, there are certain conditions that we must meet. In fact, the meeting of these conditions is a blessing in itself!

We must pray in faith (v. 12). This is a promise for us to claim, and the claiming of it demands faith. The double "verily" assures us that this is a solemn announcement. The fact that Jesus did return to the Father is an encouragement, for there He is interceding for us. He will have more to say about this intercessory work later in His discourse.

The "greater works [things]" would apply initially to the apostles who were given the power to perform special miracles as the credentials of their office

(Rom. 15:18–19; Heb. 2:3–4). These miracles were not greater in *quality,* for "the servant is not greater than his lord" (John 13:16), but rather in scope and quantity. Peter preached one sermon and three thousand sinners were converted in one day! The fact that ordinary people performed these signs made them even more wonderful and brought great glory to God (Acts 5:13–16).

Of course, it is not the believer *himself* who does these "greater things"; it is God working in and through the believer: "The Lord working with them" (Mark 16:20). "For it is God which worketh in you" (Phil. 2:13). Faith and works must always go together, for it is faith that releases the power of God in our lives.

Both love and obedience are part of effective prayer. "If I regard [see and approve] iniquity in my heart, the Lord will not hear me" (Ps. 66:18).

We do not obey the Lord simply because we want our prayers answered, somewhat like the attitude of a child just before Christmas. We obey Him because we love Him, and the more we obey Him, the more we experience His love. To "keep" His commandments means to value them, treasure them, guard them, and do them. "I have esteemed the words of his mouth more than my necessary food" (Job 23:12).

Believing prayer is wonderful medicine to soothe a troubled heart. Meditate on Philippians 4:6–7—and then put it into practice!

We must pray in Christ's name (vv. 13–14). This is not a "magic formula" that we automatically attach to our prayer requests, guaranteeing that God will answer. To ask anything of the Father, in the name of Jesus, means that we ask what Jesus would ask, what would please Him, and what would bring Him glory by furthering His work. When a friend says to you, "You may use my name!" he is handing you a great privilege as well as a tremendous responsibility.

The "whatsoever" in John 14:13 is qualified by all that God has revealed in His Word about prayer; likewise, the "anything" in John 14:14. God is not giving us *carte blanche;* "in My name" is the controlling element. To know God's name means to know His nature, what He is, and what He wants to do. God answers prayer in order to honor His name; therefore, prayer must be in His will (1 John 5:14–15). The first request in "the Lord's Prayer" is, "Hallowed be thy name" (Matt. 6:9). Any request that does not glorify God's name should not be asked in His name.

We must pray in loving obedience (v. 15). When you love someone, you honor his or her name, and you would never use that name in a demeaning manner. *Love* is an important theme in the gospel of John; it is used as a verb or noun a total of fifty-six times.

We Have the Holy Spirit (14:16–18)

Jesus had a great deal to say about the Holy Spirit in His Upper Room message, for apart from the help of the Spirit of God, we cannot live the Christian life as

God would have us live it. We must know who the Holy Spirit is, what He does, and how He does it.

The Holy Spirit is given two special names by our Lord: "another Comforter" and "the Spirit of truth." The Greek word translated "Comforter" is *paraklētos* and it is used only by John (14:16, 26; 15:26; 16:7; 1 John 2:1). It means "called alongside to assist." The Holy Spirit does not work instead of us, or in spite of us, but in us and through us.

Our English word *comfort* comes from two Latin words meaning "with strength." We usually think of "comfort" as soothing someone, consoling him or her, and to some extent this is true. But true comfort strengthens us to face life bravely and keep on going. It does not rob us of responsibility or make it easy for us to give up. Some translations call the Holy Spirit "the Encourager," and this is a good choice of words. *Paraklētos* is translated "Advocate" in 1 John 2:1. An "advocate" is one who represents you at court and stands at your side to plead your case.

As "the Spirit of Truth," the Holy Spirit is related to Jesus, the Truth, and the Word of God, which of itself is the truth (John 14:6; 17:17). The Spirit inspired the Word and also illumines the Word so we may understand it. Later on in this message, Jesus will explain the teaching ministry of the Holy Spirit. Since He is the "Spirit of truth," the Holy Spirit cannot lie or be associated with lies. He never leads us to do anything contrary to the Word of God, for again God's Word is truth.

If we want the Holy Spirit to work in our lives, we must seek to glorify Christ, and we must make much of the Word of God. When you compare Ephesians 5:18—6:9 with Colossians 3:16—4:1, you will see that both passages describe the same kind of Christian life—joyful, thankful, and submissive. To be filled with the Spirit is the same as to be controlled by the Word. The Spirit of truth uses the Word of truth to guide us into the will and the work of God.

The Holy Spirit abides in the believer. He is a gift from the Father in answer to the prayer of the Son. During His earthly ministry, Jesus had guided, guarded, and taught His disciples, but now He was going to leave them. The Spirit of God would come to them *and dwell in them,* taking the place of their Master. Jesus called the Spirit "another Comforter," and the Greek word translated "another" means "another of the same kind." The Spirit of God is not different from the Son of God, for both are God. The Spirit of God had dwelt *with* the disciples in the person of Jesus Christ. Now He would dwell *in* them.

Of course, the Spirit of God had been on earth before. He empowered men and women in the Old Testament to accomplish God's work. However, during the Old Testament Age, the Spirit of God would come on people and then leave them. God's Spirit departed from King Saul (1 Sam. 16:14; 18:12), and David, when confessing his sin, asked that the Spirit not be taken from him (Ps. 51:11). When the Holy Spirit was given at Pentecost, He was given

to God's people to remain with them forever. Even though we may grieve the Spirit, He will not leave us.

The way we treat the Holy Spirit is the way we treat the Lord Jesus Christ. The believer's body is the temple of the Spirit (1 Cor. 6:19–20), so what he or she does with that body affects the indwelling Holy Spirit. The Spirit wrote the Word of God, and the way we treat the Bible is the way we treat the Spirit of God and the Son of God.

The world cannot receive the Spirit because the world lives "by sight" and not by faith. Furthermore, the world does not know Jesus Christ, and you cannot have knowledge of the Spirit apart from the Son. The presence of the Spirit in this world is actually an indictment against the world, for the world rejected Jesus Christ.

The word translated "comfortless" in John 14:18 means "orphans." We are not alone, abandoned, helpless, and hopeless! Wherever we go, the Spirit is with us, so why should we feel like orphans? There is no need to have a troubled heart when you have the very Spirit of God dwelling within you!

We Enjoy the Father's Love (14:19–24)

"The love of God is shed abroad in our hearts by the Holy Spirit which is given unto us" (Rom. 5:5). Orphans feel unwanted and unloved, but our Father shares His love with us. Jesus explained a threefold manifestation of God's love.

There was a past manifestation to the disciples (vv. 19–20). John 14:19 focuses on His resurrection and post-resurrection appearances to His disciples and other believers. The last time the world saw Jesus was when Joseph and Nicodemus took Him from the cross and buried Him. The next time the world sees Him, He will come in power and great glory to judge lost sinners.

John 14:20 centers especially on the coming of the Spirit at Pentecost and the oneness of the believers with their Lord. Jesus returned to heaven as the exalted Head of the church (Eph. 1:19–23). Then He sent the Spirit so that the members of the body would be joined to their Head in a living union. Believers today, of course, did not see Jesus after His resurrection or in His ascension, but we are united to Him by the indwelling Holy Spirit.

There is a present manifestation of Himself to believers (vv. 21, 23–24). Note the repetition of the word *love.* If we treasure His Word and obey it, then the Father and the Son will share Their love with us and make Their home in us. The word translated "abode" in John 14:23 means "make our home" and is related to "mansions" in John 14:2.

When the sinner trusts Christ, he is born again, and the Spirit immediately enters his body and bears witness that he is a child of God. The Spirit is resident and will not depart. But as the believer yields to the Father, loves the Word, prays, and obeys, there is a deeper relationship with the Father, Son, and Spirit. Salvation means we are going to heaven, but submission means that heaven comes to us!

This truth is illustrated in the experiences of Abraham and Lot, recorded in Genesis 18 and 19. When Jesus and the two angels visited Abraham's tent, they felt right at home. They even enjoyed a meal, and Jesus had a private talk with Abraham. But our Lord did not go to Sodom to visit Lot, because He did not feel at home there. Instead, He sent the two angels.

Our experience with God ought to go deeper and deeper, and it will as we yield to the Spirit of truth and permit Him to teach us and guide us. If we love God and obey Him, He will manifest His love to us in a deeper way each day.

There will be a future manifestation when Jesus Christ returns (v. 19). Judas (not Iscariot) recalled that Jesus had said He would not manifest Himself to the world (John 14:22). But this seemed to contradict other statements He had made, such as recorded in Matthew 24:30. His question was, "What has come to pass that You are no longer going to reveal Yourself to the world?" Has there been a change in the divine plan?

Jesus had been rejected by His own people, so He could not manifest Himself to them. In fact, it was an act of mercy that He did not manifest Himself to the world, because that would have meant judgment. He has revealed Himself to His church and left the church in the world to be a witness of God's love. He is patiently waiting, still giving lost sinners opportunity to repent and be saved (2 Peter 3:1–10). One day He will return (Rev. 1:7), and the world will behold Him.

One of the best ways to ease a troubled heart is to bathe it in the love of God. When you feel like an "orphan," let the Spirit of God reveal God's love to you in a deeper way. Charles Spurgeon said, "Little faith will take your soul to heaven, but great faith will bring heaven to your soul." Your heart can become a "heaven on earth" as you commune with the Lord and worship Him.

You Have His Gift of Peace (14:25–31)

Shalom—peace—is a precious word to the Jewish people. It means much more than just the absence of war or distress. *Shalom* means wholeness, completeness, health, security, even prosperity in the best sense. When you are enjoying God's peace, there is joy and contentment. But God's peace is not like the "peace" that the world offers.

The world bases its peace on its *resources,* while God's peace depends on *relationships.* To be right with God means to enjoy the peace of God. The world depends on personal ability, but the Christian depends on spiritual adequacy in Christ. In the world, peace is something you hope for or work for, but to the Christian, peace is God's wonderful gift, received by faith. Unsaved people enjoy peace when there is an absence of trouble; Christians enjoy peace *in spite of trials* because of the presence of power, the Holy Spirit.

People in the world walk by sight and depend on the externals, but Christians walk by faith and depend on the eternals. The Spirit of God teaches us the Word and guides us (not drags us!) into the truth. He also reminds us of what He has taught us so that we can depend on God's Word in the difficult times of life. The Spirit uses the Word to give us His peace (John 14:27), His love (John 15:9–10), and His joy (John 15:11). If that does not calm a troubled heart, nothing will!

Again, Jesus assured them that they would see Him again (John 14:28). Why rejoice because He returned to the Father? Because His return made possible His wonderful intercessory ministry on our behalf, our great High Priest in heaven (Heb. 2:17–18; 4:14–16). We have the Spirit within us, the Savior above us, and the Word before us! What tremendous resources for peace!

In John 14:30–31, the Lord named two of our great spiritual enemies—the world and the devil. Jesus overcame the world and the devil (John 12:31), and the devil has no claim on Him. There is no point in Jesus Christ where the devil can get a foothold. Since we are "in Christ," Satan can get no foothold in the believer's life, unless we permit it. Neither Satan nor the world can trouble our hearts if we are yielded to the "peace of God" through the Holy Spirit.

When Jesus said, "My Father is greater than I" (John 14:28), He was not denying His own deity or His equality with God, for then He would have been contradicting Himself (John 10:30). When Jesus was here on earth, He was necessarily limited by having a human body. He voluntarily laid aside the independent exercise of His divine attributes and submitted Himself to the Father. In that sense, the Father was greater than the Son. Of course, when the Son returned to heaven, all He had laid aside was restored once again (John 17:1, 5).

Jesus showed His love for the Father (and for the world) by voluntarily going to the cross. He did not hide or flee. He willingly laid down His life. He and the disciples may have left the Upper Room at this point (John 14:31) so that what Jesus said from that point on was spoken on the way to the garden. Or, they may have arisen from the table and lingered awhile as He instructed them. We can easily imagine the allegory of the vine being given as they walked that night through the vineyards.

His own perfect peace assures us that He alone can give true peace. Jesus was always the Master of the situation, and He enables us to take control of our lives as we surrender to Him and receive His legacy of peace.

CHAPTER FIFTEEN
John 15:1–17
RELATIONSHIPS AND RESPONSIBILITIES

This is the seventh and last of the "I am" statements of Christ recorded in the gospel of John. However, Jesus did not stop with this image, but went on to use the picture of "the friend." These two pictures of the believer—branches and friends—reveal both our privileges and our responsibilities. As *branches,* we have the privilege of sharing His life, and the responsibility of abiding. As *friends,* we have the privilege of knowing His will, and the responsibility of obeying.

Branches—We Must Abide (15:1–11)

The cultivation of vineyards was important to the life and economy of Israel. A golden vine adorned Herod's temple. When our Lord used this image, He was not introducing something new; it was familiar to every Jew. There are four elements in this allegory that we must understand to benefit from His teaching.

The vine. There are actually three different vines found in Scripture. The *past* vine was the nation of Israel (see Ps. 80:8–19; Isa. 5:1–7; Jer. 2:21; Ezek. 19:10–14; Hos. 10:1). In an act of wonderful grace, God "transplanted" Israel into Canaan and gave the nation every possible benefit. "What could have been done more to my vineyard, that I have not done in it?" God asked (Isa. 5:4). If ever a nation had everything it needed to succeed, it was Israel.

But the vine produced wild grapes! Instead of practicing justice, it practiced oppression; instead of producing righteousness, it produced unrighteousness and cries of distress from the victims. God had to deal with the nation Israel and chasten it, but even that did not produce lasting results. When God's own Son came to the vineyard, they cast Him out and killed Him (Matt. 21:33–46).

There is also a *future* vine, "the vine of the earth" described in Revelation 14:14–20. This is the Gentile world system ripening for God's judgment. Believers are branches in "the vine of heaven," but the unsaved are branches in "the vine of the earth." The unsaved depend on this world for their sustenance and satisfaction, while believers depend on Jesus Christ. The "vine of the earth" will be cut down and destroyed when Jesus Christ returns.

The *present* Vine is our Lord Jesus Christ, and, of course, the vine includes the branches. He is the "true Vine," that is, "the original of which all other vines are a copy." As Christians, we do not live on substitutes! The symbolism of the Vine and branches is similar to that of the Head and the body: we have a living relationship to Christ and belong to Him.

When we lived in Chicago, we had a small grape arbor in our backyard, but what we cultivated was nothing like what is even today cultivated in the Holy Land. Ours was a very fragile plant and it was easy to break off a branch. The vines I saw in the Holy Land were large and strong, and it was next to impossible for anyone to break off a mature branch *without injuring the vine itself.* Our union with Christ is a *living* union, so we may bear fruit; a *loving* union, so that we may enjoy Him; and a *lasting* union, so that we need not be afraid.

The branches. Of itself, a branch is weak and useless. It is good for either bearing or burning, but not for building (read Ezek. 15). The branch cannot produce its own life; it must draw that life from the vine. It is our communion with Christ through the Spirit that makes possible the bearing of the fruit.

Many of the images of Christ and the believer given in Scripture emphasize this important concept of *union and communion:* the body and its members (1 Cor. 12), the bride and the Bridegroom (Eph. 5:25–33), the sheep and the Shepherd (John 10). A member of the body cut off from the body would die. The marriage creates the union, but it takes daily love and devotion to maintain the communion. The shepherd brings the sheep into the flock, but the sheep must follow the shepherd in order to have protection and provision.

The sooner we as believers discover that we are but branches, the better we will relate to the Lord, for we will know our own weakness and confess our need for His strength.

The key word is *abide;* it is used eleven times in John 15:1–11 ("continue" in John 15:9 and "remain" in John 15:11). What does it mean to "abide"? It means to keep in fellowship with Christ so that His life can work in and through us to produce fruit. This certainly involves the Word of God and the confession of sin so that nothing hinders our communion with Him (John 15:3). It also involves obeying Him because we love Him (John 15:9–10).

How can we tell when we are "abiding in Christ"? Is there a special feeling? No, but there are special evidences that appear and they are unmistakably clear. For one thing, when you are abiding in Christ you produce fruit (John 15:2). What that "fruit" is, we will discuss later. Also, you experience the Father's "pruning" so that you will bear more fruit (John 15:2). The believer who is abiding in Christ has his prayers answered (John 15:7) and experiences a deepening love for Christ and for other believers (John 15:9, 12–13). He also experiences joy (John 15:11).

This abiding relationship is natural to the branch and the vine, but it must be cultivated in the Christian life. It is not automatic. Abiding in Christ demands worship, meditation on God's Word, prayer, sacrifice, and service—but what a joyful experience it is! Once you have begun to cultivate this deeper communion with Christ, you have no desire to return to the shallow life of the careless Christian.

The vinedresser. The vinedresser is in charge of caring for the vines, and Jesus said that this is the work of His Father. It is He who "purges" or prunes the branches so they will produce more fruit. Note the progression here: no fruit (John 15:2), fruit, more fruit, much fruit (John 15:5, 8). Many Christians pray that God will make them more fruitful, but they do not enjoy the pruning process that follows!

The vinedresser prunes the branches in two ways: he cuts away dead wood that can breed disease and insects, and he cuts away living tissue so that the life of the vine will not be so dissipated that the quality of the crop will be jeopardized. In fact, the vinedresser will even cut away whole bunches of grapes so that the rest of the crop will be of higher quality. God wants both quantity and quality.

This pruning process is the most important part of the whole enterprise, and the people who do it must be carefully trained or they can destroy an entire crop. Some vineyards invest two or three years in training the "primers" so they know where to cut, how much to cut, and even at what angle to make a cut.

The greatest judgment God could bring to a believer would be to let him alone, let him have his own way. Because God loves us, He "prunes" us and encourages us to bear more fruit for His glory. If the branches could speak, they would confess that the pruning process hurts, but they would also rejoice that they will be able to produce more and better fruit.

Your heavenly Father is never nearer to you than when He is pruning you. Sometimes He cuts away the dead wood that might cause trouble, but often He cuts off the living tissue that is robbing you of spiritual vigor. Pruning does not simply mean spiritual surgery that removes what is bad. It can also mean cutting away the good and the better so that we might enjoy the best. Yes, pruning hurts, but it also helps. We may not enjoy it, but we need it.

How does the Father prune us? Sometimes He simply uses the Word to convict and cleanse us. (The word translated "purge" in John 15:2 is the same as "clean" in John 13:10. See Eph. 5:26–27.) Sometimes He must chasten us (Heb. 12:1–11). At the time, it hurts when He removes something precious from us, but as the "spiritual crop" is produced, we see that the Father knew what He was doing.

The more we abide in Christ, the more fruit we bear, and the more fruit we bear, the more the Father has to prune us so that the quality keeps up with the quantity. Left to itself, the branch might produce many clusters, but they will be inferior in quality. God is glorified by a bigger crop that is also a *better* crop.

The fruit. The word *results* is often heard in conversations among Christian workers, but this is not actually a Bible concept. A machine can produce results, and so can a robot, but it takes a *living organism* to produce fruit. It takes time and cultivation to produce fruit; a good crop does not come overnight.

We must remember that the branches do not eat the fruit: others do. We are not producing fruit to please ourselves but to serve others. We should be the kind of people who "feed" others by our words and our works. "The lips of the righteous feed many" (Prov. 10:21).

Several different kinds of spiritual fruit are named in the Bible. We bear fruit when we win others to Christ (Rom. 1:13). We are a part of the harvest (John 4:35–38). As we grow in holiness and obedience, we are bearing fruit (Rom. 6:22). Paul considered

Christian giving to be fruit from a dedicated life (Rom. 15:28). "The fruit of the Spirit" (Gal. 5:22–23) is the kind of Christian character that glorifies God and makes Christ real to others. Even our good works, our service, grow out of our abiding life (Col. 1:10). The praise that comes from our hearts and lips is actually fruit to the glory of God (Heb. 13:15).

Many of these things could be counterfeited by the flesh, but the deception would eventually be detected, for real spiritual fruit has in it *the seeds for more fruit*. Man-made results are dead and cannot reproduce themselves, but Spirit-produced fruit will go on reproducing from one life to another. There will be fruit—more fruit—much fruit.

A true branch, united with the vine, will always bear fruit. Not every branch bears a bumper crop, just as not every field has a bumper harvest (Matt. 13:8, 23), but there is always fruit where there is life. If there is no fruit, the branch is worthless and it is cast away and burned. I do not believe our Lord is teaching here that true believers can lose their salvation, for this would contradict what He taught in John 6:37 and 10:27–30. It is unwise to build a theological doctrine on a parable or allegory. Jesus was teaching one main truth—the fruitful life of the believer—and we must not press the details too much. Just as an unfruitful branch is useless, so an unfruitful believer is useless, and both must be dealt with. It is a tragic thing for a once-fruitful believer to backslide and lose his privilege of fellowship and service. If anything, John 15:6 describes divine discipline rather than eternal destiny. "There is [for believers] a sin unto death" (1 John 5:16).

Our Lord had spoken about peace (John 14:27); now He mentions love and joy (John 15:9–11). Love, joy, and peace are the first three "fruit of the Spirit" named in Galatians 5:22–23. Our abiding in Christ certainly ought to produce His love, joy, and peace in our hearts. Because we love Him, we keep His commandments, and, as we keep His commandments, we abide in His love and experience it in a deeper way.

Several times in John's gospel you will find Jesus speaking about the Father's love for Him. We so emphasize God's love for the world and the church that we forget that the Father loves the Son. Because the Father does love the Son, He has put all things into the Son's hand (John 3:35) and has revealed all things to the Son (John 5:20). The Father loved the Son before the foundation of the world (John 17:24); He loved the Son when the Son died on the cross (John 10:17). The amazing thing is believers today can experience personally that same love! Jesus prayed "that the love with which thou hast loved me may be in them [the disciples and believers today]" (John 17:26).

As branches in the Vine, we have the privilege of abiding and the responsibility of bearing fruit. Now we turn to the second picture, that of *friends.*

Friends—We Must Obey (15:12–17)

Most of us have many acquaintances but very few friends, and even some of our friends may prove unfriendly or even unfaithful. What about Judas? "Yes, mine own familiar friend, in whom I trusted, which did eat of my bread, hath lifted up his heel against me" (Ps. 41:9). Even a devoted friend may fail us when we need him most. Peter, James, and John went to sleep in the garden when they should have been praying, and Peter even denied the Lord three times. Our friendship to each other and to the Lord is not perfect, but His friendship to us is perfect.

However, we must not interpret this word *friend* in a limited way, because the Greek word means "a friend at court." It describes that "inner circle" around a king or emperor. (In John 3:29, it refers to the "best man" at a wedding.) The "friends of the king" would be close to him and know his secrets, but they would also be subject to him and have to obey his commands. There is thus no conflict between being a friend and being a servant.

The perfect illustration of this in Scripture is Abraham, "the friend of God" (2 Chron. 20:7; Isa. 41:8; James 2:23), who was also the servant of God (Gen. 26:24). In Genesis 18, our Lord and two angels came to visit Abraham as they were on their way to investigate the sin of Sodom. Even though Abraham was nearly one hundred years old, he interrupted his noonday rest, greeted the visitors, saw to their comfort, and fed them a lovely meal. In the first fifteen verses of this chapter, Abraham is on the move, and twice he refers to himself as a servant (Gen. 18:3, 5). Note that this old man "hastened" and "ran" and encouraged others to perform their work quickly, a perfect example of a servant. Nor did Abraham sit and eat with them. Like a true servant, he stood nearby, ready to do their bidding.

In the last half of the chapter, the atmosphere changes, and Abraham is quietly standing still, communing with the Lord. He is still a servant, but now he is being a friend. "Shall I hide from Abraham that which I do?" the Lord asked. As a friend of God, Abraham shared God's secrets.

It is this kind of a relationship that Jesus described when He called His disciples "friends." It was certainly a relationship of *love,* both for Him and for each other. The "friends of the King" could not compete with each other for attention or promotion. They were a part of the "inner circle," not to promote themselves, but to serve their King. What a rebuke this must have been to the selfish disciples, who often argued over who was the greatest!

How is it possible for Jesus to *command* us to love one another? Can true love be commanded? You must keep in mind that Christian love is not basically a "feeling"; it is an act of the will. The proof of our love is not in our feelings but in our actions, even to the extent of laying down our lives for Christ and for one another (1 John 3:16). Jesus laid down His life for both His friends and His enemies (Rom. 5:10)! While the emotions are certainly involved, real Christian love is an act of the will. It means treating others the way God treats us.

So, our friendship with Christ involves love and obedience. But it also involves knowledge: He "lets us in on" His plans. Indeed, He is our Master (John 13:13, 16), but he does not treat us as servants. He treats us as friends, *if* we do what He commands. Abraham was God's friend because he obeyed God (Gen. 18:19). If we have friendship with the world, we then experience enmity with God (James 4:1–4). Lot in Sodom was not called God's friend, even though Lot was a saved man (2 Peter 2:7). God told Abraham what He planned to do to the cities of the plain, and Abraham was able to intercede for Lot and his family.

It is interesting to note that, in John's gospel, it was the servants who knew what was going on! The servants at the wedding feast in Cana knew where the wine came from (John 2:9), and the nobleman's servants knew when the son was healed (John 4:51–53).

One of the greatest privileges we have as His friends is that of learning to know God better and "getting in on" God's secrets. I can never forget the impact on my own heart when I heard Dr. Oswald Sanders say to the Back to the Bible staff, "Each of us is as close to God as we choose to be." We are His friends, and we ought to be near the throne, listening to His Word, enjoying His intimacy, and obeying His commandments.

One day while he was a fugitive, David was near Bethlehem, his home city, and he longed for a drink of water from the well by the gate. Three of his mighty men were close enough to David to hear his sigh, and they risked their lives to bring their king the water that he wanted (2 Sam. 23:15–17). That is what it means to be a friend of the king.

In John 14:16, Jesus reminded the men that they had this privileged position only because of His grace. They did not choose Him; He chose them! He chose them out of the world (John 14:19) and ordained them to do His will. Again, we find this important word *fruit*. As branches, we share His life and bear fruit, and as friends, we share His love and bear fruit. As branches, we are pruned by the Father; as friends, we are instructed by the Son, and His Word controls our lives.

The word *ordained* simply means "appointed." It refers to the act of setting someone apart for special service. We have graciously been chosen and set apart by the Lord in order to go into the world and bear fruit. He has sent us into the world (John 17:18) as His personal ambassadors to tell others about the King and His great salvation. When we witness to others and win them to Christ, this is bringing forth fruit to the glory of God.

As I mentioned before, the evidence of true sonship, discipleship (John 15:8), and friendship (John 15:15) is *fruit.* "Wherefore by their fruits ye shall know them" (Matt. 7:20). Where there is true fruit, it remains; man-made "results" eventually disappear. Fruit has in it the seed for more fruit, so the process goes on and on. Whatever is born of the Spirit of God has the mark of eternity on it, and it will last.

Once again, Jesus brought up the privilege of prayer. The friends of the king certainly speak to their sovereign and share their burdens and needs with him. In the days of monarchies, it was considered a very special honor to be invited to speak to the king or queen, yet the friends of Jesus Christ can speak to Him at any time. The throne of grace is always available to them.

John 15:15–16 summarize for us what it means to be a friend of the King of Kings. It is a humbling experience, for He chose us and we did not choose Him. We must keep this in mind lest we become proud and presumptuous. It means that we keep our ears open and listen to what He says to us. "Hast thou heard the secret of God?" (Job 15:8). "The secret of the Lord is with them that fear him; and he will show them his covenant" (Ps. 25:14). We must be attentive and alert.

But the purpose for all of this is that we might obey Him and get His work done. The King has tasks that must be performed, and if we love Him, we will obey His commands. We will seek to bear fruit that will please Him and glorify the Father. Our joy should be to please Him.

Jesus closed this part of His message by reminding them (and us) of the most important commandment of all: love one another. There are dozens of "one another" statements in the New Testament, but all of them are summarized in "love one another." Jesus had already given this commandment to the Eleven (John 13:34–35), and now He has repeated it twice (John 15:12, 17). It will be stated in one way or another many more times in the New Testament letters, especially by John in his first epistle. The friends of the King must not only love Him, but also one another. What joy it brings to His heart when He sees His friends loving one another and working together to obey His commands.

This study began in the vineyard and ended in the throne room! The next study will take us to the battlefield, where we experience the hatred of the lost world. If we are not abiding as branches and obeying as friends, we will never be able to face the opposition of the world. If we do not love one another, how can we ever hope to love lost men and women in the world? If we are not marching together as the friends of the King, we will never present a united front to the enemy.

"Without me, ye can do nothing" (John 15:5).

We are not simply handicapped or hindered. We are hopelessly paralyzed! We can do *nothing!*

But if we abide in Him, if we stay close to the throne, we can do *anything* that He commands us to do!

What a privilege—and what a responsibility!

CHAPTER SIXTEEN
John 15:18—16:16
WHAT IN THE WORLD IS THE SPIRIT DOING?

This long section, John 15:18—16:16, is tied together by two important themes: the opposition of the world against the church, and the ministry of the Spirit to and through the church. Our Lord had been talking about love (John 15:9–13, 17), but now He is talking about *hatred,* and He used the word seven times. It seems incredible that anyone would hate Jesus Christ and His people, but that is exactly what the situation is today, and *some of that hatred comes from religious people.* In a few hours, the religious leaders of Israel would be condemning their Messiah and crying out for His blood.

Our Lord had openly taught His disciples that one day persecution would come. He mentioned it in the Sermon on the Mount (Matt. 5:10–12, 44) and in His "commissioning sermon" when He sent out the disciples to minister (Matt. 10:16–23). In His sermon denouncing the Pharisees, Jesus openly said that they would persecute and kill God's servants (Matt. 23:34–35), and there was a similar warning given in His prophetic message on Mount Olivet (Mark 13:9–13).

Throughout the gospel of John, it is evident that the religious establishment not only opposed Jesus, but even sought to kill Him (John 5:16; 7:19, 25; 8:37, 59; 9:22; also note 11:8). As He continued His ministry, there was a tide of resentment, then hatred, and then open opposition toward Him. So, the disciples should not have been surprised when Jesus brought up the subject of persecution, for they had heard Him warn them and they had seen Him face men's hatred during His ministry.

Until the Lord returns, or until we die, we must live in this hostile world and face continued opposition. How can we do it? What is the secret of victory? It is the presence and power of the Holy Spirit of God in our lives. This is the key section in the Upper Room message about the Holy Spirit and His ministry.

Before we study this passage and see the threefold ministry of the Spirit to the church in the world, we must pause to remind ourselves just who the Holy Spirit is. The Holy Spirit of God is a person; Jesus referred to the Spirit as "He" and not "it." The Holy Spirit has a mind (Rom. 8:27), a will (1 Cor. 12:11), and emotional feelings (Gal. 5:22–23).

In John 15:26 all three Persons of the Godhead are mentioned: Jesus the Son will send the Spirit from the Father. Because the Holy Spirit is a person, and is God, it means that the Christian has God indwelling his body! If we did not have the Holy Spirit within, we would not be able to serve the Lord in this present evil world. We are to walk in the Spirit (Gal. 5:16), worship in the Spirit (Phil. 3:3), and witness in the Spirit (Acts 1:8).

Christians can stand and withstand in the midst of the world's hatred because of the special ministries of the Holy Spirit.

The Spirit as Comforter Encourages the Church (15:18—16:4)

We should begin by clarifying what Jesus means by "the world," because the term is used in Scripture in at least three different ways. It can mean *the created world* ("the world was made by him"—John 1:10), the world of *humanity* ("For God so loved the world"—John 3:16), or *society apart from God and opposed to God*. We sometimes use the phrase "the world system" to define this special meaning.

For example, when you listen to the radio news, you may hear the announcer say, "And now the news from the world of sports!" Obviously, "the world of sports" is not a special country or planet where everybody lives who is connected in some way with sports. "The world of sports" refers to all the organizations, people, plans, activities, philosophies, etc. that are a part of sports. Some of these things are visible and some are invisible, but all of them are organized around one thing—sports.

"The world" from a Christian point of view involves all the people, plans, organizations, activities, philosophies, values, etc. that belong to society without God. Some of these things may be very cultural; others may be very corrupt; but all of them have their origins in the heart and mind of sinful man and promote what sinful man wants to enjoy and accomplish. As Christians, we must be careful not to love the world (1 John 2:15–17) or be conformed to the world (Rom. 12:1–2).

Jesus pulls no punches when He tells His disciples that their situation in the world will be serious and even dangerous. Note the progress in the world's opposition: hatred (John 15:18–19), persecution (John 15:20), excommunication, and even death (John 16:2). You can trace these stages of resistance as you read the book of Acts.

Why does the world system, including the "religious world," hate the Christian, the one who believes on Jesus Christ and seeks to follow Him? Jesus gave several reasons.

We are identified with Christ (15:18, 20). If they hated Him, they will also hate those of us who are identified with Him. In John 15:20, Jesus quoted the statement He had made earlier (John 13:16), and the logic of it is clear. He is the Master; we are the servants. He is greater than we are, so He must receive the praise and glory. But the world will not give Him praise and glory! The world hates Him, and therefore the world must hate us. If with all of His greatness and perfection, Jesus does not escape persecution, what hope is there for us with our imperfections?

This principle is seen in some of the other images of the relationship between Christ and His own. He is the Shepherd and we are the sheep, and when they attack the Shepherd, it affects the sheep (Matt. 26:31). He is the Master (Teacher) and we are the disciples, the learners. But it is encouraging to know that when God's people are persecuted, our Lord enters into their suffering, for He is the Head of the body and we are the members. "Saul, Saul, why persecutest thou me?" (Acts 9:4). Anything that the enemy can do to us has already been done to Jesus Christ, and He is "with us" as we suffer.

We do not belong to the world (15:19). When we trusted Christ, we moved into a new spiritual position: we are now "in Christ" and "out of the world." To be sure, we are *in* the world physically, but not *of* the world spiritually. Now that we are "partakers of the heavenly calling" (Heb. 3:1), we are no longer interested in the treasures or pleasures of sin in this world. This does not mean that we are isolated from reality or insulated from the world's needs, so "heavenly minded that we are no earthly good." Rather, it means that we look at the things of earth from heaven's point of view.

The world system functions on the basis of conformity. As long as a person follows the fads and fashions and accepts the values of the world, he or she will "get along." But the Christian refuses to be "conformed to this world" (Rom. 12:2). The believer is a "new creation" (2 Cor. 5:17) and no longer wants to live the "old life" (1 Peter 4:1–4). We are the light of the world and the salt of the earth (Matt. 5:13–16), but a dark world does not want light and a decaying world does not want salt! In other words, the believer is not just "out of step"; he is out of place! (See John 17:14, 16; 1 John 4:5.)

The world is spiritually ignorant and blind (15:21). If you had asked the religious leaders in Jerusalem if they knew the God they were seeking to defend, they would have said, "Of course we know Him! Israel has known the true God for centuries!" But Jesus said that they *did not* know the Father and, therefore, they could not know the Son (see John 16:3). The religious leaders knew a great deal about Jehovah God and could quote chapter and verse to defend their doctrines, but they did not personally know God.

This was not a new theme for our Lord to discuss, because He had mentioned it before to the religious leaders who opposed Him. "Ye neither know me, nor my Father; if ye had known me, ye should have known my Father also" (John 8:19). "Yet ye have not known him; but I know him" (John 8:55). Jesus had taught them the Word and had demonstrated His deity in miraculous signs and a godly walk, and yet the religious leaders of the nation were blind to His identity: "The world knew him not" (John 1:10).

The religious world today claims to know God, but it does not want to bow the knee to Jesus Christ as the Son of God and the only Savior of the world. Satan has blinded their minds (2 Cor. 4:3–4), and sin has blinded their hearts (Eph. 4:17–19). Like Saul of Tarsus, they are so convinced that their "religion" and "righteousness" are satisfactory that *in the name of that religion* they persecute God's people!

The world will not be honest about its own sin (15: 22–24; 16:1–4). Once again, Jesus emphasized His words and His works. We have seen this emphasis throughout the gospel of John (3:2; 5:36–38; 10:24–27; 14:10–11). The people had no excuse ("cloak") for their sin. They had seen His works and heard His word, but they would not admit the truth. All of the evidence had been presented, but they were not honest enough to receive it and act on it.

This statement is parallel to what Jesus told the Pharisees after He had healed the blind man (John 9:39–41). They had to admit that Jesus had healed the man born blind, but they would not follow the evidence to its logical conclusion and put *their* trust in Him. Jesus told them that they were the ones who were blind! But since they admitted that they had seen a miracle, this made their sin even worse. They were not sinning in ignorance; they were sinning against a flood of light. Why? Because that light revealed their own sin and they did not want to face their sin honestly. Their attitude was similar to that described in 2 Peter 3:5—"For this they *willingly are* ignorant" (italics mine).

How does the Holy Spirit encourage believers when they are experiencing the hatred and opposition of the world? It is primarily through the Word of God. For one thing, the Spirit reminds us that this opposition is clearly expressed by various writers in the Scriptures. In John 15:25, Jesus quoted Psalms 35:19 and 69:4. The Word assured Him that the hatred of the world was not because of anything He had done to deliberately incite such opposition. We today can turn to passages like Philippians 1:28–30; 2 Timothy 2:9–12; Hebrews 12:3–4; and 1 Peter 4:12ff. We also have the encouraging words of our Lord found in the Gospels.

The Spirit also witnesses to us and through us during times of persecution (John 15:26–27). He reminds us that what we are experiencing is "the fellowship of his [Christ's] sufferings" (Phil. 3:10) and that it is a privilege to bear reproach for His name. (Read *carefully* 1 Peter 4:12–19.)

Times of persecution have always been times of proclamation and witness for the church. We must be "ready always to give an answer" when unsaved people attack us (1 Peter 3:15). The Spirit witnesses to us so that we can witness to the world (Mark 13:11). Apart from the power of the Spirit of God, we cannot give a clear witness for Christ (Acts 1:8).

There is no reason for the believer to stumble ("be offended," John 16:1) when the world stokes up the furnace of persecution. He should expect persecution, if only because his Lord told him it was coming. (Note especially John 13:19 and 14:29, where the Lord warned His disciples in advance.) Furthermore, they must not stumble when this persecution comes from religious people who actually think they are serving God. The word translated "service" in John 16:2 means "priestly service." This statement is certainly a description of Saul of Tarsus, who thought he was serving God by destroying the church (see Acts 7:57—8:3; 22:3–4; 26:912).

It is tragic when "religious" people persecute and murder in the name of God. While it is true that "the blood of the martyrs is the seed of the church" (Tertullian), it is also true that their blood is the stain on the pages of history.

The Spirit as Reprover Witnesses through the Church (16:5–11)

For three years, Jesus had been with them to protect them from attack, but now He was about to leave them. He had told them this earlier in the evening (John 13:33), and Peter had asked Him where He was going (John 13:36). However, Peter's question revealed more concern about *himself* than about the Lord Jesus! Also, his question centered on the immediate, not the ultimate. It was necessary for Jesus to explain why it was important *for them* that He return to the Father.

The major reason, of course, is that the Holy Spirit might come to empower the church for life and witness. Also, the ascended Savior would be able to intercede for His people at the heavenly throne of grace. With all of their faults, the disciples dearly loved their Master, and it was difficult for them to grasp these new truths.

It is important to note that the Spirit comes to *the church* and not to the world. This means that He works in and through the church. The Holy Spirit does not minister in a vacuum. Just as the Son of God had to have a body in order to do His work on earth, so the Spirit of God needs a body to accomplish His ministries, and that body is the church. Our bodies are His tools and temples, and He wants to use us to glorify Christ and to witness to a lost world.

Sometimes we hear people pray, "Lord, send Your Spirit to speak to the lost! May the Spirit go from heart to heart." Such praying is no doubt sincere, but is it biblical? The Spirit does not "float" in some ghostly way up and down the rows of a church building, seeking to win the lost. The Holy Spirit works through the people in whom He lives. When the Holy Spirit came at Pentecost, He empowered Peter to preach, and the preaching of the Word brought conviction to those who heard.

The key word here is *reprove* (John 16:8). It is a legal word that means "to bring to light, to expose, to refute, to convict and convince." It could be translated "pronounce the verdict." The world may think that it is judging Christians, but it is the Christians who are passing judgment on the world as they witness to Jesus Christ! Believers are the witnesses, the Holy Spirit is the "prosecuting attorney," and the unsaved are the guilty prisoners. However, the purpose of this indictment is not to condemn but to bring salvation.

The Holy Spirit convicts the world of one particular sin, the sin of *unbelief.* The law of God and the conscience of man will convict the sinner of his *sins* (plural) specifically, but it is the work of the Spirit, through the witness of the believers, to expose the unbelief of the lost world. After all, it is unbelief that condemns the lost sinner (John 3:18–21), not the committing of individual sins. A person could "clean up his life" and quit his or her bad habits and still be lost and go to hell.

The Spirit also convicts the sinner of *righteousness,* not unrighteousness. Whose righteousness? The righteousness of Jesus Christ the perfect Lamb of God. The world would not receive the Son of God (John 1:10), so He has returned to the Father. When He was here on earth, He was accused by men of being a blasphemer, a lawbreaker, a deceiver, and even a demoniac. The Spirit of God reveals the Savior in the Word and in this way glorifies Him (John 16:13–14). The Spirit also reveals Christ in the lives of believers. The world cannot receive or see the Spirit of God, but they can see what He does as they watch the lives of dedicated believers.

The Spirit convicts the lost sinner of *judgment.* Do not confuse this statement with Acts 24:25 ("of righteousness, temperance, and judgment to come"). Jesus was referring to His judgment of Satan that was effected by His death on the cross (John 12:31). Satan is the prince of this world, but he is a defeated prince. Satan has already been judged and the verdict announced. All that must take place is the executing of the sentence, and that will occur when Jesus returns.

When a lost sinner is truly under conviction, he will see the folly and evil of unbelief; he will confess that he does not measure up to the righteousness of Christ, and he will realize that he is under condemnation because he belongs to the world and the devil (Eph. 2:1–3). The only person who can rescue him from such a horrible situation is Jesus Christ, the Son of God. There can be no conversion without conviction, and there can be no conviction apart from the Spirit of God using the Word of God and the witness of the child of God.

Witnessing is a great privilege, but it is also a serious responsibility. It is a matter of life or death! How we need to depend on the Holy Spirit to guide us to the right persons, give us the right words, and enable us patiently to glorify Jesus Christ.

The Spirit as Teacher Guides the Church (16:12–15)

Our Lord was always careful to give His disciples the right amount of truth at the best time. This is always the mark of a great teacher. The Holy Spirit is our Teacher today, and He follows that same principle: He teaches us the truths we need to know, when we need them, and when we are ready to receive them.

When you compare John 14:26 with 16:13, you see the wonderful way that God arranged for the writing of the New Testament Scriptures. The Spirit would remind them of what Jesus had taught them; this gives us the four gospels. The Spirit would also "guide" them into all truth, and this would result in the Epistles. "He will show you things to come" refers to the prophetic Scriptures, especially the book of Revelation.

It is essential that we see that the work of the Spirit of God is never divorced from Jesus Christ or the Word of God. "He shall testify of me" (John 15:26); "He shall glorify me" (John 16:14). People who claim that the Spirit of God led them to do things contrary to the example of Christ or the teaching of the Word are mistaken and are being led astray by Satan. Jesus is the truth (John 14:6), and the Word is truth (John 17:17), and the Holy Spirit is "the Spirit of truth." Where the Holy Spirit is at work, there must be truth.

The phrase "He [the Spirit] shall not speak of himself" (John 16:13) does not mean that the Spirit never refers to Himself, for when He wrote the Bible, the Spirit often mentioned Himself. Rather, it means that He does not speak apart from the Father and the Son; He does not "manufacture" a different message. You have the entire Godhead mentioned in John 16:13, because the Spirit of God does not ignore either the Father or the Son. They work harmoniously together.

The teaching of the Spirit through the apostles was not different from the teaching of the Spirit through Jesus Christ. Some theologians like to contrast the "Christianity of Christ" with the "Christianity of Paul." They claim that Paul "ruined" Christianity by making it so theological and complicating the "simple message" of Jesus Christ. What a sad interpretation this is. What Jesus said in John 14:26 and 16:13 completely refutes this false teaching. The same Holy Spirit communicated the truths found in the four gospels, the Epistles, and the book of Revelation, and He also wrote the history and doctrine found in Acts.

It is the ministry of the Spirit to enrich us with the treasures of God's truth. He enlightens us with God's truth and enriches us with God's treasures. The Word of God is a rich mine of gold, silver, and precious jewels (Prov. 3:13–15; 8:10–21). What a joy it is to have the Spirit illumine His Word.

We do not study the Word of God to order to "argue religion" with people, or to show off our grasp of spiritual things. We study the Word to see Jesus Christ, to know God better, to glorify Him in our lives. As we witness in this hostile world, the Spirit uses the Word He has taught us, and we share Jesus Christ with the lost. It is our job to witness; it is the Spirit's job to convict.

Perhaps some of us need to quit acting like prosecuting attorneys—or judges—so that the Spirit can use us as faithful witnesses.

CHAPTER SEVENTEEN
John 16:16–33
LET THERE BE JOY!

This section—John 16:16–33—concludes the Upper Room Discourse and deals primarily with the emotions of the disciples. They were sorrowing, they were confused about some of Jesus' teaching, and they were afraid. It is an encouragement to me to know that the disciples were real men with real problems, yet the Lord was able to use them. We sometimes get the false impression that these men were different from us, especially endowed with spiritual knowledge and courage, but such was not the case. They were human!

One of the recurring themes in this section is *joy* (John 16:20–22, 24, 33). The Eleven were certainly not experiencing much joy that night! But what Jesus said to them eventually made a difference in their lives, just as it can make a difference in our lives today. Tenderly and patiently, our Lord explained how His people can have joy in their lives.

There Is a Principle to Grasp (16:16–22)
The principle is simply this: God brings joy to our lives, not by substitution, but by transformation. His illustration of the woman giving birth makes this clear. *The same baby that caused the pain also caused the joy.* In birth, God does not substitute something else to relieve the mother's pain. Instead, He uses what is there already but transforms it.

Every parent knows what it is like to have an unhappy child because a toy is broken or a playmate has gone home. The parent can do one of two things: substitute something else for the broken toy or absent friend, or transform the situation into a new experience for the unhappy child. If Mother always gets a new toy for the child each time a toy is broken, that child will grow up expecting every problem to be solved by substitution. If Mother always phones another playmate and invites him or her over, the child will grow up expecting people to come to his rescue whenever there is a crisis. The result either way is a spoiled child who will not be able to cope with reality.

The way of substitution for solving problems is the way of immaturity. The way of transformation is the way of faith and maturity. We cannot mature emotionally or spiritually if somebody is always replacing our broken toys.

Jesus did not say that the mother's sorrow (pain) was replaced by joy, but that the sorrow was transformed into joy. The same baby that caused the pain also caused the joy! And so it is in the Christian life: God takes seemingly impossible situations, adds the miracle of His grace, and transforms trial into triumph and sorrow into joy. "The Lord thy God turned the curse into a blessing" (Deut. 23:5; see Neh. 13:2).

Joseph's brothers sold him as a slave, and Potiphar put him into prison as a criminal, but God transformed that hopeless situation of defeat into victory. Egypt's persecution of Israel only caused them to multiply and prosper the more. King Saul's murderous pursuit of David only made him more a man of God and helped produce the psalms that encourage our hearts today. Even Jesus took the cross, a symbol of defeat and shame, and transformed it into a symbol of victory and glory.

Now that we understand this principle, we can better understand the problems and questions of the disciples.

In John 16:16, Jesus announced that in a little while, they would not see Him; then, in a little while, they would see Him. It was a deliberately puzzling statement (John 16:25, He spoke in proverbs ["dark sayings"]), and the disciples did not understand. This also encourages me as I study my Bible and find statements that I cannot understand. Even the disciples had their hours of spiritual ignorance!

What did Jesus mean? Possibly He was talking about the soon-to-occur events in connection with His death and resurrection. After His burial, they would not see Him for a little while, but then He would rise from the dead and they would see Him again. He had told them on previous occasions that He would rise from the dead after three days, but His words did not sink into their minds and hearts.

However, I think that Jesus was speaking primarily about His return to the Father ("Because I go to the Father"—John 16:16). This ties in with John 16:10—"Because I go to my Father, and ye see me no more." The disciples did not live to see the return of Christ, but they did die and see Him when they arrived in glory. In comparison to eternity, the time that the church has been awaiting the Lord's return has really been but "a little while" (see 2 Cor. 4:16–18). In fact, the phrase "a little while" is used in this very sense in Hebrews 10:37—"For yet a little while, and he that shall come will come, and will not tarry."

Instead of asking Jesus to explain His words, the men began to discuss it among themselves, almost as though they were embarrassed to admit their ignorance. However, you do not get very far by exchanging your ignorance! It is when we come to the Lord and ask for His help that we learn the important lessons of life.

Egypt was glad when Israel departed (Ps. 105:38), and the world was glad when Jesus Christ moved off the scene. Both the religious and political leaders of that day expected to see the early believers die out and the "Christian movement" disappear, but such was not the case. Jesus sent His Holy Spirit to His church, and the church is carrying the Word of His grace to the ends of the earth. The early believers even rejoiced when they were persecuted (Acts 5:41).

To the mother experiencing birth pains, every minute may seem an hour. Our concept of time changes with our feelings. Thirty minutes in the dentist chair may seem like hours, while hours fishing or dining with friends may seem like a very short time. The mother feels as though the birth is taking a long time, when really it may be only "a little while." When the baby has been born, pain is forgotten as joy fills her heart.

The world today does not want Jesus Christ or His church. The world is rejoicing while we are suffering, longing for our Lord to return. In fact, all of creation is suffering "birth pangs" because of sin, awaiting His return (Rom. 8:22). When the Bridegroom is away, the bride mourns (Matt. 9:15). But, in "a little while" He shall return, and we shall go with Him to heaven to enjoy the Father's house.

While the immediate application may have been to the sorrowing hearts of the disciples, the ultimate application is to all of God's people as they await the coming of Jesus Christ. To us, it seems like a long wait, but God does not measure time as we do (see 2 Peter 3). But while we are waiting, we must deal with our trials and hurts on the basis of *transformation* and not *substitution,* if we expect to mature in the Christian life.

There Is a Promise to Believe (16:23–28)

The central theme of this paragraph is prayer: "Ask, and ye shall receive, that your joy may be full" (John 16:24). It is important to note that the text uses two different words for "ask," although they can be used interchangeably. The word used in John 16:19, 23a, and 26 means "to ask a question" or "to ask a request." It is used when someone makes a request of someone equal. The word translated "ask" in John 16:23b, 24, and 26b ("pray") means "to request something of a superior." This latter word was never used by Jesus in His prayer life because He is equal to the Father. We come as inferiors to God, asking for His blessing, but He came as the very Son of God, equal with the Father.

In John 16:23, what period of time did Jesus mean by "in that day"? I think He was referring to the time after the coming of the Spirit. He promised them in John 16:22 that He would see them again, and He kept His promise. He spent forty days with them after His resurrection, teaching them clearly the truths they needed to know in order to take His place and minister on earth (Acts 1:3ff.). "That day" cannot refer to the day of His return for His church, because there is no evidence in Scripture that we shall pray to Him after we get to heaven.

Jesus knew that they wanted to ask Him a question (John 16:19). He assured them that a day would soon come when they would not ask Him questions. Instead, they would pray to the Father and He would meet their needs. This was the promise that they desperately needed to believe: that the Father loved them and would hear their requests and meet their needs. While Jesus was on earth, He met all the needs of His disciples. Now He would return to the Father, but the Father would meet their needs. Here is the wonderful promise and privilege of prayer.

Our Lord had mentioned prayer many times in His ministry, and He had set the example for prayer in His own life. He was indeed a man of prayer. In His Upper Room message, Jesus emphasized prayer (John 14:12–14; 15:7, 16; 16:23–26). He made it clear that believing prayer is one of the secrets of a fruitful Christian life.

In John 16:25–27, Jesus explained that there would be a new situation because of His resurrection and ascension, and because of the coming of the Holy Spirit He would no longer speak to them in terms that demanded spiritual insight for their understanding. He would speak to them plainly and reveal the Father to them. There in the Upper Room, He had used a number of symbolic images to get His message across: the washing of their feet, the "Father's house," the vine and branches, and the birth of a baby. In the days that followed, these images would become clearer to the disciples as they would be taught by the Spirit of God.

The purpose of Bible study is not simply to understand profound truths, but to get to know the Father better. "I will show you plainly of the Father" (John 16:25). If our reading and Bible study falls short of this, it does more harm than good.

There would be not only a new situation in teaching, but also a new situation in their praying. He had already intimated this in John 16:23. Jesus would return to heaven to be with the Father, and there He would minister as our High Priest, making intercession for us (Rom. 8:34; Heb. 7:25). He would also minister as our Advocate (1 John 2:1). As our High Priest, Jesus gives us grace to keep us from sinning. As our Advocate, He restores us when we confess our sins. His ministry in heaven makes possible our ministry of witness on earth, through the power of the Spirit.

When you read the book of Acts, you discover that the early church depended on prayer. They believed the promises of God and asked God for what they needed. It would do all of God's people good if they reviewed regularly what Jesus taught about prayer in this Upper Room Discourse. There is indeed joy in praying and in receiving answers to prayer. There is joy in meeting the conditions Jesus has laid down for successful praying. I think it was George Müller who said that true prayer was not overcoming God's reluctance, but overcoming God's willingness.

There is joy in prayer, and there is joy in realizing the principle of *transformation.* Jesus shared a third kind of joy, the joy of sharing His victory over the world.

There Is a Position to Claim (16:29–33)

In John 16:29–30, the disciples suddenly moved out of their spiritual stupor and made a tremendous affirmation of faith. First, they claimed to understand what He had been teaching them, though this claim was probably presumptuous, as their subsequent actions proved. They seemed unable to grasp the meaning of His promised resurrection. They were bewildered even after His resurrection as to the future of Israel (Acts 1:6ff.). I am not criticizing them, because we today have just as many blind spots when it comes to understanding His Word. All I am suggesting is that their affirmation was a bit presumptuous.

They not only affirmed their understanding, but they also affirmed their faith and assurance. "Now we are sure … by this we believe." It was quite a statement of faith, and I believe the Lord accepted it. In His prayer recorded in the next chapter, Jesus told the

Father about His disciples and reported on their spiritual condition (John 17:6–8). Certainly He knew their weaknesses, but He was quick to approve their growing evidences of faith and assurance.

But it is possible to have faith, understanding, and assurance *and still fail the Lord.* Unless we practice that faith, apply that understanding, and rest on that assurance, we will fail when the time of testing comes. That is what happened to the disciples, and Jesus warned them that it would happen.

He had already warned Peter that he would deny Him, but now He warned the entire band of disciples that they would all forsake Him. John does not quote the Old Testament prophecy (Zech. 13:7); it is quoted in Matthew 26:31. This statement from the Lord should have been a warning to Peter not to follow Jesus when He was arrested. "Let these go their way!" was our Lord's word in the garden (John 18:8). He knew that it was not safe for them to tarry.

Jesus has promised never to leave us alone (Matt. 28:20; Heb. 13:5), yet His own disciples left Him alone. Peter, James, and John went into the garden with Him, but then fell asleep. Jesus knew that the Father would be with Him. "I am not alone, but I and the Father that sent me" (John 8:16). "And he that sent me is with me. The Father hath not left me alone" (John 8:29). What an encouragement it was to the Son to know that He was doing the Father's will and that He could depend on the Father's help.

At one point, however, Jesus did feel the absence of the Father: "My God, my God, why hast thou forsaken me?" (Matt. 27:46; Ps. 22:1). When He was made sin for us, He was separated from the Father. He was alone that we might never be alone. He was forsaken that we might never be forsaken.

John 16:33 is the summary and climax of the Upper Room message. Why did He give this message? So that the disciples might have peace in a world of tribulation. Note the contrast between "in me" and "in the world." In Christ there is peace; in the world there is tribulation. This is the position we need to claim: we are *in Christ,* and therefore we can overcome the world and all of its hatred.

George Morrison defined peace as "the possession of adequate resources." In Jesus Christ, we have all the resources that we need. But peace depends also on appropriate relationships, because spiritual resources depend on spiritual relationships. "In me" is the key. In ourselves, we have nothing, but "in Christ" we have all that we need.

Every believer is either *overcome* or an *overcomer.* "And this is the victory that overcometh the world, even our faith" (1 John 5:4). The world wants to overcome us; this is why Satan uses the world to persecute and pressure believers. The world wants us to conform; it does not want us to be different. When we yield ourselves to Christ and trust Him, He enables us to be overcomers. We must claim our spiritual position in Christ and believe Him for victory.

"Be of good cheer!" is one of our Lord's repeated statements of encouragement. Literally it means, "Cheer up!" There is the "good cheer" of His pardon (Matt. 9:1–8), His power (Matt. 9:18–22), and His presence (Matt. 14:22–27). Here in John 16:33, He announces the "good cheer" of His victory over the world. We are overcomers because He has first overcome for us.

As we review this section, we can see how these three explanations our Lord gave all fit together. He revealed a wonderful principle—God transforms sorrow into joy. But this principle will not work in our lives unless we believe His promise and pray. God has ordained that His work is accomplished through believing prayer. But we will not be able to pray effectively if we do not claim our position as conquerors in Jesus Christ.

But John 16:33 is also a preface to His great High Priestly Prayer. He had taught them the Word; now He would pray for them. The Word and prayer must always go together (Acts 6:4). He used the word *world* nineteen times in this prayer, for in it He shows us how to overcome the world. He Himself was facing the hatred of the world *and the devil,* yet He would be able to endure the suffering and win the victory.

There is joy when we permit God to transform sorrow into joy. There is joy when God answers prayer. There is joy when we overcome the world.

Let there be joy!

CHAPTER EIGHTEEN
John 17
THE PRAYER OF THE OVERCOMER

Most scholars who have sought to harmonize the accounts in the four gospels have the Lord Jesus praying the prayer of John 17 in the Upper Room after He had finished His instructions to the disciples. Then He and the disciples sang the traditional Passover psalms, left the Upper Room, and headed for the garden of Gethsemane, where Jesus had been accustomed to meet with them and pray (see Matthew 26:30–46 and Mark 14:26–42).

Whether He prayed it in the Upper Room or en route to the garden, this much is sure: it is the greatest prayer ever prayed on earth and the greatest prayer recorded anywhere in Scripture. John 17 is certainly the " Holy of Holies" of the gospel record, and we must approach this chapter in a spirit of humility and worship. To think that we are privileged to listen in as God the Son converses with His Father just as He is about to give His life as a ransom for sinners!

No matter what events occurred later that evening, this prayer makes it clear that Jesus was and is the Overcomer. He was not a "victim"; He was and is the Victor! "Be of good cheer," He had encouraged His disciples; "I have overcome the world" (John 16:33).

The word *world* is used nineteen times in this prayer, so it is easy to see the connection between the prayer and John 16:33. If you and I will understand and apply the truths revealed in this profound prayer, it will enable us to be overcomers too.

The progression of thought in this prayer is not difficult to discover. Jesus first prayed for Himself and told the Father that His work on earth had been finished (John 17:1–5). Then He prayed for His disciples, that the Father would *keep them* and *sanctify them* (John 17:6–19). He closed His prayer by praying for you and me and the whole church, that we might be unified in Him and one day share His glory (John 17:20–26).

Why did Jesus pray this prayer? Certainly He was preparing Himself for the sufferings that lay ahead. As He contemplated the glory that the Father promised Him, He would receive new strength for His sacrifice (Heb. 12:1–3). But He also had His disciples in mind (John 17:13). What an encouragement this prayer should have been to them! He prayed about their security, their joy, their unity, and their future glory! He also prayed it for us today, so that we would know all that He has done for us and given to us, and all that He will do for us when we get to heaven.

In this prayer, our Lord declares four wonderful privileges we have as His children, privileges that help to make us overcomers.

We Share His Life (17:1–5)

Our Lord began this prayer by praying for Himself, but in praying for Himself, He was also praying for us. "A prayer for self is not by any means necessarily a selfish prayer," wrote Dr. R. A. Torrey, and an examination of Bible prayers shows that this is true. Our Lord's burden was the glory of God, and this glory would be realized in His finished work on the cross. The servant of God has every right to ask his Father for the help needed to glorify His name. "Hallowed be thy name" is the first petition in the Lord's Prayer (Matt. 6:9), and it is the first emphasis in this prayer.

"Father, the hour is come," reminds us of the many times in John's gospel when "the hour" is mentioned, beginning at John 2:4. Jesus had lived on a "divine timetable" while on earth and He knew He was in the will of the Father. "My times are in thy hand" (Ps. 31:15).

The important word *glory* is used five times in these verses, and we must carefully distinguish the various "glories" that Jesus mentions. In John 17:5, He referred to His preincarnate glory with the Father, the glory that He laid aside when He came to earth to be born, to serve, to suffer, and to die. In John 17:4, He reported to the Father that His life and ministry on earth had glorified Him, because He (Jesus) had finished the work the Father gave Him to do. In John 17:1 and 5, our Lord asked that His preincarnate glory be given to Him again, so that the Son might glorify the Father in His return to heaven.

The word *glory* is used eight times in this prayer, so it is an important theme. He glorified the Father in His miracles (John 2:11; 11:40), to be sure, but He brought the greatest glory to the Father through His sufferings and death (see John 12:23–25; 13:31–32). From the human point of view, Calvary was a revolting display of man's sin, but from the divine point of view, the cross revealed and magnified the grace and glory of God. Jesus anticipated His return to heaven when He said, "I have finished the work which thou gavest me to do" (John 17:4). This "work" included His messages and miracles on earth (John 5:17–19), the training of the disciples for future service, and most of all, His sacrifice on the cross (Heb. 9:24–28; 10:11–18).

It is on the basis of this "finished work" that we as believers have the gift of eternal life (John 17:2–3). The word *give* is used in one form or another in this prayer at least seventeen times. Seven times Jesus states that believers are the Father's gift to His Son (John 17:2, 6, 9, 11–12, 24). We are accustomed to thinking of Jesus as the Father's love gift to us (John 3:16), but the Lord affirms that believers are the Father's "love gift" to His beloved Son!

"Eternal [everlasting] life" is an important theme in John's gospel; it is mentioned at least seventeen times. Eternal life is God's free gift to those who believe on His Son (John 3:15–16, 36; 6:47; 10:28). The Father gave His Son the authority to give eternal life to those whom the Father gave to the Son. From the human viewpoint, we receive the gift of eternal life when we believe on Jesus Christ. But from the divine viewpoint, we have already been given to the Son in divine election. This is a mystery that the human mind cannot fully understand or explain; we must accept it by faith.

What is "eternal life"? It is knowing God personally. Not just knowing *about* Him, but having a personal relationship with Him through faith in Jesus Christ. We cannot know the Father apart from the Son (John 14:6–11). It is not enough simply to "believe in God"; this will never save a lost soul from eternal hell. "The devils [demons] also believe, and tremble" (James 2:19). Our Lord's debate with the Jewish leaders (John 8:12ff.) makes it clear that people may be devoutly religious and still not know God. Eternal life is not something we earn by character or conduct; it is a gift we receive by admitting we are sinners, repenting, and believing on Jesus Christ and Jesus Christ alone.

The Father answered His Son's request and gave Him the glory. There is in heaven today a glorified Man, the God-Man, Jesus Christ! Because He has been glorified in heaven, sinners can be saved on earth. Anyone who trusts Jesus Christ will receive the gift of eternal life.

Because we share His life, we are overcomers, for we also share His victory! "For whatsoever is born of God overcometh the world; and this is the victory that overcometh the world, even our faith" (1 John 5:4). When you were born the first time, you were born "in Adam" and were a loser. When you are born again through faith in Christ, you are born a winner!

Satan has tried to obscure the precious truth of the finished work of Jesus Christ, because he knows it is a basis for spiritual victory. "And they overcame him [Satan] by the blood of the Lamb" (Rev. 12:11). Don't let Satan rob you of your overcoming power through Christ's finished work.

We Know His Name (John 17:6–12)

Christ has given His own eternal life (John 17:2), but He has also given them the revelation of the Father's name (John 17:6). The Old Testament Jew knew his God as "Jehovah," the great I AM (Ex. 3:11–14). Jesus took this sacred name "I AM" and made it meaningful to His disciples: "I am the bread of life" (John 6:35); "I am the light of the world" (John 8:12); "I am the good shepherd" (John 10:11); etc. In other words, Jesus revealed the Father's gracious name by showing His disciples that He was everything they needed.

But the Father's name includes much more than this, for Jesus also taught His disciples that God—the great I AM—was their heavenly Father. The word *Father* is used fifty-three times in John 13—17, and 122 times in John's gospel! In His messages to the Jews, Jesus made it clear that the Father sent Him, that He was equal to the Father, and that His words and works came from the Father. It was a clear claim to deity, but they refused to believe.

In the Bible, "name" refers to "nature," because names so often were given to reveal something special about the nature of the person bearing the name. Jacob was a schemer, and his name comes from a Hebrew root that means "to take by the heel," i.e., to trip up, to deceive (Gen. 25:26). The name *Isaac* means "laughter" (Gen. 21:6) because he brought joy to Abraham and Sarah. Even the name Jesus reveals that He is the Savior (Matt. 1:21).

"I have manifested thy name" means "I have revealed the nature of God." One of the ministries of the Son was to declare the Father (John 1:18). The Greek word translated "declared" means, "to unfold, to lead, to show the way." Jesus did not instantly reveal the Father in a blaze of blinding glory, because His disciples could not have endured that kind of experience. Gradually, by His words and His deeds, He revealed to them the nature of God, as they were able to bear it (John 16:12).

The emphasis in this section is on the safety of the believer; God keeps His own (John 17:11–12). Our safety depends on the nature of God, not our own character or conduct. When He was on earth, Jesus kept His disciples and they could depend on Him. "I kept them in thy name" (John 17:12). If the limited Savior, in a human body, could keep His own while He was on earth, should He not be able to keep them now that He is glorified in heaven? He and the Father, together with the Holy Spirit, are surely able to guard and secure God's people!

Furthermore, God's people are the Father's gift to His Son. Would the Father present His Son with a gift that would not last? The disciples had belonged to the Father by creation and by covenant (they were Jews), but now they belonged to the Son. How precious we are in His sight! How He watches over us and even now prays for us! Whenever you feel as though the Lord has forgotten you, or that His love seems far away, read Romans 8:28–39—and rejoice!

Our security rests in another fact: we are here to glorify Him (John 17:10). With all of their failures and faults, the disciples still receive this word of commendation: "I am glorified in them." Would it bring glory to God if one of His own, who trusted in the Savior, did not make it to heaven? Certainly not! This was Moses' argument when the nation of Israel sinned: "Wherefore should the Egyptians speak, and say, 'For mischief did he bring them out, to slay them in the mountains, and to consume them from the face of the earth?'" (Ex. 32:12). Certainly God knows all things, so why save them at all if He knows they will fail along the way? Whatever God starts, He finishes (Phil. 1:6).

God has provided the divine resources for us to glorify Him and be faithful. We have His Word (John 17:7–8), and His Word reveals to us all that we have in Jesus Christ. The Word gives us faith and assurance. We have the Son of God interceding for us (John 17:9; Rom. 8:34; Heb. 4:14–16). Since the Father always answers the prayers of His Son (John 11:41–42), this intercessory ministry helps to keep us safe and secure.

We also have the fellowship of the church: "that they may be one, as we are" (John 17:11). The New Testament knows nothing of isolated believers; wherever you find saints, you find them in fellowship. Why? Because God's people need each other. Jesus opened His Upper Room message by washing the disciples' feet and teaching them to minister to one another. In the hours that would follow, these men (including confident Peter!) would discover how weak they were and how much they needed each other's encouragement.

The believer, then, is secure in Christ for many reasons: the very nature of God, the nature of salvation, the glory of God, and the intercessory ministry of Christ. But what about Judas? Was he secure? How did he fall? Why did Jesus not keep him safe? For the simple reason that *Judas was never one of Christ's own.* Jesus faithfully kept all that the Father gave to Him, but Judas had never been given to Him by the Father. Judas was not a believer (John 6:64–71); he had never been cleansed (John 13:11); he had not been among the chosen (John 13:18); he had never been given to Christ (John 18:8–9).

No, Judas is not an example of a believer who "lost his salvation." He is an example of an unbeliever who *pretended to have salvation* but was finally exposed as a fraud. Jesus keeps all whom the Father gives to Him (John 10:26–30).

We are overcomers because we share His life. There is a third privilege that enables us to overcome.

We Have His Word (17:13–19)

"I have given them thy word" (John 17:14; and see v. 8). The Word of God is the gift of God to us. The Father gave the words to His Son (John 17:8), and the Son gave them to His disciples who, in turn, have passed them along to us as they were inspired by the Spirit (2 Tim. 3:16; 2 Peter 1:20–21). The Word is divine in origin, a precious gift from heaven. We must never take God's Word for granted, for those who are overcomers know the Word and how to use it in daily life.

How does the Word of God enable us to overcome the world? To begin with, *it gives us joy* (John 17:13), and this inward joy gives us the strength to overcome (Neh. 8:10). We commonly think of Jesus Christ as "a man of sorrows" (Isa. 53:3), and indeed He was; but He was also a person of deep abiding joy. John 17:13 is the very heart of this prayer, *and its theme is joy!*

Jesus had referred to His joy already (John 15:11) and had explained that joy comes by transformation and not substitution (John 16:20–22). Joy also comes from answered prayer (John 16:23–24). Now He made it clear that joy comes from the Word also. The believer does not find his joy in the world but in the Word. Like John the Baptist, we should rejoice greatly when we hear the Bridegroom's voice (John 3:29)!

We must never picture Jesus going around with a long face and a melancholy disposition. He was a man of joy, and He revealed that joy to others. His joy was not the fleeting levity of a sinful world but the abiding enjoyment of the Father and the Word. He did not depend on outward circumstances but on inward spiritual resources that were hidden from the world. This is the kind of joy He wants us to have, and we can have it through His Word. "Thy word was unto me the joy and rejoicing of mine heart" (Jer. 15:16). "I have rejoiced in the way of thy testimonies, as much as in all riches" (Ps. 119:14). "I rejoice at thy word, as one that findeth great spoil" (Ps. 119:162).

The Word not only imparts the joy of the Lord, but it also *assures us of His love* (John 17:14). The world hates us, but we are able to confront this hatred with God's own love, a love imparted to us by the Spirit through the Word. The world hates us because we do not belong to its system (John 15:18–19) and will not be conformed to its practices and standards (Rom. 12:2). The Word reveals to us what the world is really like; the Word exposes the world's deceptions and dangerous devices.

The world competes for the Father's love (1 John 2:15–17), but the Word of God enables us to enjoy the Father's love. One of the first steps toward a worldly life is the neglect of the Word of God. D. L. Moody wrote in the front of his Bible, "This book will keep you from sin or sin will keep you from this book." Just as the pillar of fire was darkness to the Egyptians but

light to Israel, so God's Word is our light in this dark world, but the world cannot understand the things of God (Ex. 14:20; 1 Cor. 2:12–16).

The Word of God not only brings us God's joy and love, but it also imparts God's power for holy living (John 17:15–17). The burden of our Lord's prayer in John 17:6–12 was *security,* but here it is *sanctity,* practical holy living to the glory of God. We are *in* the world but not *of* the world, and we must not live *like* the world. Sometimes we think it would be easier if we were "out of the world," but this is not true. Wherever we go, we take our own sinful self with us, and the powers of darkness will follow us. I have met people who have gone into "spiritual isolation" in order to become more holy, only to discover that it does not always work.

True sanctification (being set apart for God) comes through the ministry of the Word of God. "Now ye are clean through the word which I have spoken unto you" (John 15:3). When you were saved, you were set apart for God. As you grow in your faith, you are more and more experiencing sanctification. You love sin less and you love God more. You want to serve Him and be a blessing to others. All of this comes through the Word.

God's truth has been given to us in three "editions": His Word is truth (John 17:17); His Son is the truth (John 14:6); and His Spirit is the truth (1 John 5:6). We need all three if we are to experience true sanctification, a sanctification that touches every part of our inner person. With the mind, we *learn* God's truth through the Word. With the heart, we *love* God's truth, His Son. With the will, we yield to the Spirit and *live* God's truth day by day. It takes all three for a balanced experience of sanctification.

It is not enough merely to study the Bible and learn a great deal of doctrinal truth. We must also love Jesus Christ more as we learn all that He is and all He has done for us. Learning and loving should lead to living, allowing the Spirit of God to enable us to obey His Word. This is how we glorify Him in this present evil world.

The Word gives us joy, love, and power to live a holy life. It also gives us what we need to serve Him as witnesses in this world (John 17:18–19). Sanctification is not for the purpose of selfish enjoyment or boasting; it is so that we might represent Christ in this world and win others to Him. Jesus set Himself apart for us, and now He has set us apart for Him. The Father sent Him into the world, and now He sends us into the world. We are people "under orders" and we had better obey! Jesus is now "set apart" in heaven, praying for us, that our witness will bear fruit as many repent of their sins and turn to the Lord.

How can we be overcome by the world when we have the Word of God to enlighten us, enable us, and encourage us?

We Share His Glory (17:20–26)

Here our Lord focuses our attention on the future.

He begins to pray for us who live today, for the whole church throughout all ages. He has already prayed about security and sanctity; now the burden of His prayer is *unity.* He is concerned that His people experience a spiritual unity that is like the oneness of the Father and the Son. Christians may belong to different fellowships, but they all belong to the Lord and to each other.

The disciples had often exhibited a spirit of selfishness, competition, and disunity, and this must have broken the Savior's heart. I wonder how He feels when He sees the condition of the church today! The Puritan preacher Thomas Brooks wrote: "Discord and division become no Christian. For wolves to worry the lambs is no wonder, but for one lamb to worry another, this is unnatural and monstrous."

What is the basis for true Christian unity? The person and work of Jesus Christ and His glory (John 17:2–5). He has already given His glory to us, and He promises that we will further experience that glory when we get to heaven! All true believers have God's glory within, no matter what they may look like on the outside. Christian harmony is not based on the externals of the flesh but the internals and eternals of the Spirit in the inner person. We must look beyond the elements of our first birth—race, color, abilities, etc.—and build our fellowship on the essentials of our new birth.

We already possess His glory within (John 17:22; and note Rom. 8:29), and one day we shall behold His glory in heaven (John 17:24). As we grow in the Lord, the glory within begins to grow and to reveal itself in what we say and do and the way we say and do it. People do not see us and glorify us; they see the Lord and glorify Him (Matt. 5:16; 1 Cor. 6:19–20).

One of the things that most impresses the world is the way Christians love each other and live together in harmony. It is this witness that our Lord wants in the world "that the world may believe that thou hast sent me" (John 17:21). The lost world cannot see God, but they can see Christians, and what they see in us is what they will believe about God. If they see love and unity, they will believe that God is love. If they see hatred and division, they will reject the message of the gospel.

Jesus has assured us that some will believe because of our witness (John 17:20), but we must make sure that our witness is true and loving. Some Christians are prosecuting attorneys and judges instead of faithful witnesses, and this only turns lost sinners away from the Savior.

There is every reason why believers should love one another and live in unity. We trust the same Savior and share the same glory. We will one day enjoy the same heaven! We belong to the same Father and seek to do the same work, witnessing to a lost world that Jesus Christ alone saves from sin. We believe the same truth, even though we may have different views of minor doctrinal matters, and we follow the same example that Jesus set for His people, to live a holy life. Yes, believers

do have their differences, but we have much more in common, and this should encourage us to love one another and promote true spiritual unity.

I have often used John 17:24 as a text for funeral meditations. How do we know that Christians go to heaven? Because of the price that Jesus paid (1 Thess. 5:9–10), and the promise that Jesus made (John 14:1–6), and the prayer that Jesus prayed (John 17:24). The Father always answers His Son's prayers, so we know that believers who die do go to heaven to behold the glory of God.

In John 17:25–26, there are no petitions. Jesus simply reported to His Father about the ministry in the world, and He made several declarations that are important to us. He declared that the world does not know the Father, but that we believers know Him because the Son has revealed the Father to us. The world certainly has many opportunities to get to know the Father, but it prefers to go on in blindness and hardness of heart. Our task as Christians is to bear witness to the lost world and share God's saving message.

He also declares the importance of truth and love in the church. Believers know God's name (nature) and even share in that divine nature. Jesus makes it clear that *truth* and *love* must go together (see Eph. 4:15). It has well been said that truth without love is brutality, but love without truth is hypocrisy. The mind grows by taking in truth, but the heart grows by giving out in love. Knowledge alone can lead to pride (1 Cor. 8:1), and love alone can lead to wrong decisions (see Phil. 1:9–10). Christian love must not be blind!

As you review this prayer, you see the spiritual priorities that were in the Savior's heart: the glory of God; the sanctity of God's people; the unity of the church; the ministry of sharing the gospel with a lost world. We today would be wise to focus on these same priorities.

One day, each of us will have to give an account of his or her ministry. It is a solemn thought that we shall stand before the judgment seat of Christ and give our "final report."

I trust that we will be able to say, "I have glorified thee on the earth; I have finished the work which thou gavest me to do" (John 17:4).

CHAPTER NINETEEN
John 18:1–27
GUILT AND GRACE IN THE GARDEN

The private ministry of our Lord with His disciples has now ended, and the public drama of redemption is about to begin. Man will do his worst, and God will respond with His very best. "But where sin abounded, grace did much more abound" (Rom. 5:20).

Perhaps the best way to see the truths in John 18:1–27, and grasp the lessons they convey, is to pay attention to the symbolism that is involved. John's gospel is saturated with symbols, some more obvious than others, and these symbols convey some important spiritual truths. There are five such symbols in this section.

The Garden—Obedience (18:1)

The Kidron Valley is located east of Jerusalem, between the city wall and the Mount of Olives, and the garden of Gethsemane is on the western slope of Olivet. Jesus often went to this garden with His disciples, no doubt to rest, meditate, and pray (Luke 22:39). Jerusalem was filled with pilgrims attending the Passover, and Jesus would want to get away from the crowded city to a private place. He knew that Judas would come for Him there, and He was ready.

Human history began in a garden (Gen. 2:8ff.), and the first sin of man was committed in that garden. The first Adam disobeyed God and was cast out of the garden, but the Last Adam (1 Cor. 15:45) was obedient as He went into the garden of Gethsemane. In a garden, the first Adam brought sin and death to mankind, but Jesus, by His obedience, brought righteousness and life to all who will trust Him. He was "obedient unto death, even the death of the cross" (Phil. 2:8).

History will one day end in another garden, the heavenly city that John describes in Revelation 21 and 22. In that garden, there will be no more death and no more curse. The river of the water of life will flow ceaselessly, and the tree of life will produce bountiful fruit. Eden was the garden of disobedience and sin; Gethsemane was the garden of obedience and submission; and heaven shall be the eternal garden of delight and satisfaction, to the glory of God.

The name *Gethsemane* means "oil press." Even today there are ancient olive trees in Gethsemane, though certainly not the ones that were there in Jesus' day. The olives would be picked and put into the press for their oil. What a picture of suffering! So our Lord would go through the "oil press" and the "winepress" (Isa. 63:3) and taste our judgment for us.

The brook Kidron is also significant. The name means "dusky, gloomy," referring to the dark waters that were often stained by the blood from the temple sacrifices. Our Lord and His disciples were about to go through "dark waters," and Jesus would experience the "waves and billows" of God's wrath (Ps. 42:7; also note Jonah 2:3).

The Kidron had special historical significance, for King David crossed the Kidron when he was rejected by his nation and betrayed by his own son, Absalom (2 Sam. 15; also note John 18:23). Jesus had been rejected by His people and at that very moment was being betrayed by one of His own disciples! It is interesting that David's treacherous counselor Ahithophel hanged himself (2 Sam. 17:23), and David's treacherous son Absalom was caught in a tree and killed while hanging there (2 Sam. 18:9–17). Judas, of course, went out and hanged himself (Matt. 27:3–10).

Jesus fully knew what lay before Him, yet He went to the garden in obedience to the Father's will. He left eight of the men near the entrance, and took Peter, James, and John and went to another part of the garden to pray (Matt. 26:36–46; Mark 14:32–42). His human soul longed for the kind of encouragement and companionship they could give Him at this critical hour, but, alas, they went to sleep! It was easy for the men to boast about their devotion to Christ, but when the test came, they failed miserably. Before we judge them too severely, however, we had better examine our own hearts.

The Kiss—Treachery (18:2–9)

Judas had lived with the Lord Jesus for perhaps three years, and had listened to Him teach, yet he knew very little about Him. The traitor actually brought a company of temple guards, armed with swords and clubs (Matt. 26:55)! Just think of the privileges Judas despised and the opportunities he wasted! The word *band* in John 18:3 could be translated "cohort." A Roman cohort was a tenth of a legion, and this would be six hundred men! It is not likely that Judas brought that many to the garden, but apparently a full cohort was made available to him had he needed it. Did he not realize that the Lamb of God would meekly submit and that there would be no need to battle?

Jesus was in full control; He knew what would happen (see John 13:1, 3, 11; 16:19). Judas expected some kind of deception, so he arranged to identify Jesus by kissing Him (Matt. 26:48–49). But Jesus shocked both Judas and the arresting officers by boldly presenting Himself to them. He had nothing to fear and nothing to hide; He would *willingly* lay down His life for His sheep. Furthermore, by surrendering to the officers, Jesus helped to protect His disciples. He kept them safe not only spiritually (John 17:11–12) but also physically.

Why did the arresting soldiers draw back and fall to the ground when Jesus told them, "I am he"? The Jews present would be struck by His "I am" statement, an affirmation of deity. The Romans, who were in the majority, would be struck by His bearing, for it was obvious that He was in command. It was an emotionally charged situation, and we do not know what Judas had told them about Jesus to help prepare them for this confrontation. The Jewish leaders had tried to have Jesus arrested before and always without success. The band was prepared for conflict, and when they met with surrender and calm, they were overwhelmed.

Perhaps it was a manifestation of divine power, or an exhibition of the majesty of Jesus Christ. "When the wicked, even mine enemies and my foes, came upon me to eat up my flesh, they stumbled and fell" (Ps. 27:2).

Judas's kiss, which was given repeatedly to the Lord, was certainly one of the basest acts of treachery recorded anywhere in sacred or secular history. In that day, a kiss was a sign of affection and devotion.

Members of the family kissed each other in meeting and in parting, but Judas was not a member of God's family. Disciples greeted a rabbi by kissing him; it was a sign of devotion and obedience. But Judas was not truly a disciple of Jesus Christ, though he belonged to the disciple band. In the garden, Judas stood with the enemy, not with Jesus' friends!

When people today pretend to know and love the Lord, they are committing the sin of Judas. It is bad enough to betray Christ, but to do it with *a kiss*, a sign of affection, is the basest treachery of all. It was born in the pit of hell.

The Sword—Rebellion (18:10)

All of the disciples had courageously affirmed their devotion to Christ (Matt. 26:35), and Peter decided to prove it, so he quickly drew out a small sword and started to fight! He certainly misunderstood what Jesus had said about swords earlier that evening (Luke 22:35–38). He had warned them that from now on the situation would change, and men would treat them as transgressors. He was not suggesting that they use material swords to fight spiritual battles, but that they get a new mind-set and expect opposition and even danger. He had provided for them and protected them while He was with them on earth, but now He was returning to the Father. They would have to depend on the Holy Spirit and exercise wisdom. Peter apparently took His words literally and thought he was supposed to declare war!

Peter's sword symbolizes rebellion against the will of God. Peter should have known that Jesus would be arrested and that He would willingly surrender to His enemies (Matt. 16:21ff.; 17:22–23; 20:17–19). Peter made every mistake possible! He fought the wrong enemy, used the wrong weapon, had the wrong motive, and accomplished the wrong result! He was openly resisting the will of God and hindering the work that Jesus came to accomplish! While we admire his courage and sincerity, it was certainly a demonstration of zeal without knowledge.

Why did Peter fail so miserably? For one thing, he had argued with the Lord when Jesus warned him that he would deny his Master that very night. Peter had slept when he should have been praying, and he talked when he should have been listening. He imitated the very enemies who came to arrest Jesus, for they too were armed with swords. Peter would discover that the sword of the Spirit is the weapon God's servants use in fighting their spiritual battles (Heb. 4:12; Eph. 6:17). He would use that sword at Pentecost and "slay" three thousand souls!

Jesus did not need Peter's protection. He could have summoned legions of angels had He wanted to be delivered (Matt. 26:52–54). Luke tells us that Jesus healed Malchus's ear (John 22:51), which was certainly an act of grace on His part. It was gracious from Peter's point of view, for had He not healed Malchus, Peter might have been arrested and crucified! Peter

was acting like one of the Jewish Zealots and not like a disciple of Jesus Christ.

But it was also an act of grace toward Malchus. After all, he was only a servant, and why worry about what happens to a servant? He was also an enemy, standing with the men who came to arrest Jesus, so he ought to suffer! Is it possible that Malchus had actually laid hold of Jesus? We do not know, but if he did, he laid hands on the holy Son of God. However, our Lord did not judge Malchus, though he was a sinner deserving the wrath of God. Instead, He healed him! It was our Lord's last public miracle before the cross.

Keep in mind that this miracle reveals His grace toward us. If Jesus had the power to stun an armed mob and heal a severed ear, He could have saved Himself from arrest, trial, and death. *But He willingly submitted!* And He did it for us!

It is a sad thing when well-meaning but ignorant Christians take up the sword to "defend" the Lord Jesus Christ. Peter hurt Malchus, something no believer should do. Peter hurt the testimony of Christ and gave the false impression that His disciples hate their enemies and try to destroy them. (Note our Lord's reply to Pilate in John 18:36.)

The Cup—Submission (18:11–14)

Peter had a sword in his hand, but our Lord had a cup in His hand. Peter was resisting God's will but the Savior was accepting God's will. Earlier, Jesus had prayed, "O my Father, if it be possible, let this cup pass from me; nevertheless, not as I will, but as thou wilt" (Matt. 26:39). The cup represented the suffering He would endure and the separation from the Father that He would experience on the cross. He prayed this prayer three times, evidence that His whole being was sensitive to the price He would pay for our salvation. His holy soul must have been stirred to the depths when He contemplated being made sin!

The drinking of a cup is often used in Scripture to illustrate experiencing suffering and sorrow. When Babylon captured Jerusalem, the city had "drunken the dregs of the cup of trembling" (Isa. 51:17). Jeremiah pictured God's wrath against the nations as the pouring out of a cup (Jer. 25:15–28). There is also a cup of consolation (Jer. 16:7) and the overflowing cup of joy (Ps. 23:5).

Jesus had compared His own sufferings to the drinking of a cup and the experiencing of a baptism (Matt. 20:22–23). When He instituted the supper, He compared the cup to His blood, shed for the remission of sins (Matt. 26:27–28). The image was a familiar one to His disciples, and it is not an unfamiliar image today. To "drink the cup" means to go through with a difficult experience, and "not my cup of tea" means saying no to a certain course of action. The fact that some trophies are designed like cups suggests that winners have been through demanding experiences and had to "swallow a lot."

Jesus was able to accept the cup because it was mixed

by the Father and given to Him from the Father's hand. He did not resist the Father's will, because He came to do the Father's will and finish the work the Father gave Him to do. "I delight to do thy will, O my God: yea, thy law is within my heart" (Ps. 40:8). Since the Father had mixed and measured the contents of the cup, Jesus knew He had nothing to fear.

This is a good lesson to us: we need never fear the cups that the Father hands to us. To begin with, our Savior has already drunk the cup before us, and we are only following in His steps. We need never fear what is in the cup because the Father has prepared it for us in love. If we ask for bread, He will never give us a stone, and the cup He prepares will never contain anything that will harm us. We may suffer pain and heartbreak, but He will eventually transform that suffering into glory.

Jesus deliberately gave Himself to His enemies. They bound Him and led Him to the house of Annas, which was not too far away. Annas had served as high priest until he was deposed by the Romans; now his son-in-law Caiaphas was the high priest. God had ordained that one man should serve as high priest for a lifetime, so it is easy to see that the Jewish religious establishment was in sad condition. It is generally believed that the high priest's family was in charge of the temple "business," and the fact that Jesus twice cleansed the temple must have aroused their anger against Him.

The "trial" before Annas was more like an informal hearing. It was illegal and it was brutal. Imagine a guard being allowed to strike a prisoner! Imagine a man not holding an office interrogating a prisoner!

Annas, of course, was looking for some kind of evidence on which to base an accusation that would lead to a verdict of capital punishment. What doctrine was Jesus teaching? Was it subversive? Jesus told him to ask the people who listened to Him, because He had said nothing secretly. In fact, Annas himself could have come and listened!

What about our Lord's disciples? Were they organized to overthrow the government? Did not one of them use his sword in the garden? Jesus was careful to say nothing about His disciples. Think of it: while Peter was in the courtyard denying his Lord, Jesus was on trial protecting Peter!

Jewish law demanded that witnesses be called before a prisoner was questioned. Annas defied this law, and eventually the council hired *false* witnesses. Jesus knew His rights ("bear witness of the evil"—John 18:23), but He did not insist on them. He is an example to us when we suffer wrongfully (1 Peter 2:19–25; 4:12–19).

The Fire—Denial (18:15–27)

Jesus had predicted that Peter would deny Him three times (Matt. 26:34; John 13:38), but that he would be restored to fellowship and service (Luke 22:32). Peter followed the crowd when he should have been fleeing

(John 18:8; and see Matt. 26:30–32). Had he gone his way, he would never have denied the Lord. While we certainly admire his love and courage, we cannot agree with his actions, for he walked right into temptation. This is what Jesus warned him about in the garden (Matt. 26:41).

We do not know who the other disciple was who went with Peter into the courtyard of the home of the high priest. It was probably John, though it is difficult to understand how a fisherman could be acquainted with the high priest and his household. Was this "other disciple" possibly Nicodemus or Joseph of Arimathea? They would certainly have access to this home.

As you watch Peter, you see him gradually moving into the place of temptation and sin, and his actions parallel the description in Psalm 1:1. First, Peter walked "in the counsel of the ungodly" when he followed Jesus and went into the high priest's courtyard. Peter should have followed the counsel of Jesus and gotten out of there in a hurry! Then, Peter stood with the enemy by the fire (John 18:16, 18), and before long, he *sat* with the enemy (Luke 22:55). It was now too late, and within a short time, he would deny his Lord three times.

First, a servant girl asked, "Art not thou also one of this man's disciples?" The Greek text indicates that she expected a negative answer, and that is what she got! Peter denied Christ by denying that he belonged to the band of disciples.

Peter remained by the fire, so it is no wonder that he was approached again. (That same night, Jesus had been perspiring as He had prayed in the garden!) Another servant girl asked the same question, again expecting a negative reply. The pronoun *they* in John 18:25 suggests that others in the circle around the fire took up the question and one by one hurled it at Peter.

The third question came from one of Malchus's relatives! The Greek construction indicates that he expected an *affirmative* answer: "I saw you in the garden with Jesus, didn't I? Yes, I did!" After all, this man had gotten a good look at Peter because he was probably standing with Malchus when Jesus was arrested. Some of the bystanders took up the discussion (Matt. 26:73; Mark 14:70) so that Peter may have been surrounded by challengers.

At that point, Peter's resistance broke down completely. He began to "curse and swear" (Matt. 26:74). This does not mean that Peter let loose a volley of blasphemies, but rather that he put himself under a curse in order to emphasize his statement. He was on trial, so he put himself under an oath to convince his accusers that he was telling the truth.

It was at that point that the cock began to crow (John 18:27) just as Jesus had predicted (Matt. 26:34). There were four "watches": evening (6–9 p.m.), midnight (9–12), cockcrowing (12 midnight to 3 a.m.), and morning (3–6 a.m.) (see Mark 13:35). The crowing of the cock reminded Peter of the Lord's words, and he went out and wept bitterly.

The crowing of the cock was assurance to Peter that Jesus was totally in control of the situation, even though He was bound and being harassed by the authorities. By controlling one bird, Jesus affirmed His sovereignty. According to Genesis 1:26, God gave man authority over the fish, the fowl, and the animals. Peter had seen Jesus exercise authority over the fish (Matt. 17:24–27; Luke 5:1–11) and the animals (Matt. 21:1–11), but now he recognized His authority over the birds.

But the cockcrowing was also an invitation to repentance. "When thou art converted, strengthen thy brethren" (Luke 22:32). Luke tells us that Jesus turned and looked at Peter (Luke 22:61), and this look of love broke Peter's heart. Peter had been a witness of Christ's sufferings (1 Peter 5:1), and by his own denials he added to those sufferings.

Keep in mind that the crowing of the cock was the announcement of the dawning of a new day! "Weeping may endure for a right, but joy cometh in the morning" (Ps. 30:5). It is worthwhile to contrast Peter and Judas. Peter wept over his sins and repented, while Judas admitted his sins but never really repented. Judas experienced remorse, not repentance. When Judas went out from the Upper Room, "it was night" (John 13:30), but when Peter went out to weep bitterly, there was the dawning of a new day. It is the contrast between godly sorrow that leads to true repentance, and the sorrow of the world (regret and remorse) that leads to death (2 Cor. 7:9–10). We will discover that Jesus restored Peter (John 21) and enabled him to serve with great power and blessing.

In the garden that night, you would find both guilt and grace. Peter was guilty of resisting God's will. Judas was guilty of the basest kind of treachery. The mob was guilty of rejecting the Son of God and treating Him as though He were the lowest kind of criminal.

But Jesus was gracious! Like King David, He crossed the Kidron, fully conscious that Judas was betraying Him. He went into the garden of Gethsemane surrendered to the Father's will. He healed Malchus's ear. He protected His disciples. He yielded Himself into the hands of sinners that He might suffer and die for us.

"Love so amazing, so divine / Demands my soul, my life, my all!"

What is in your hand today—the sword, or the cup?

CHAPTER TWENTY
John 18:28—19:16
"SUFFERED UNDER PONTIUS PILATE"

Long before the Jewish leaders had Jesus arrested in the garden, they had determined to kill Him (John 11:47–54). However, the Jewish council did not have the right to execute prisoners, so it was necessary to get the cooperation and approval of Rome. This meant a visit to the Roman procurator, Pontius Pilate.

There were three stages in both the Jewish "trial" and the Roman "trial." After His arrest, Jesus was taken to the home of Annas and there interrogated informally (John 18:12–14, 19–23). Annas hoped to get information that would implicate Jesus as an enemy of the state. He wanted to prove that both His doctrine and His disciples were anti-Roman, for then He would be worthy of death.

Stage two of the Jewish trial took place before Caiaphas and whatever members of the Sanhedrin the high priest could assemble at that hour of the night (Matt. 26:57–68; Mark 14:53–65). When Jesus confessed clearly that He was the Christ, the council found Him guilty of blasphemy and therefore, according to their law, worthy of death. However, it was necessary for the council to meet early the next morning and give their verdict, since it was not considered legal to try capital cases at night. So, stage three of the Jewish trial took place as early as possible, and the leaders condemned Jesus to death (Matt. 27:1; Luke 22:66–71).

The three stages of the Roman trial were the first appearance before Pilate (John 18:28–38), the appearance before Herod (Luke 23:6–12), and the second appearance before Pilate (John 18:39—19:16; and see Matt. 27:15–26; Mark 15:6–15; Luke 23:13–25). As you can see, the apostle John records only the interrogations by Annas and Pilate, and mentions Caiaphas only in passing. He focuses primarily on the Roman trial. By the time he wrote this gospel, the Jewish nation had been scattered by Rome, Jerusalem had been destroyed, and Roman power was all that really mattered.

Pontius Pilate was in office from AD 26–36 and was not greatly liked by the Jews. He could be ruthless when he wanted to be (see Luke 13:1–2), but he also understood the Jewish power structures and knew how to use them. His handling of the trial of Jesus reveals an indecisive man, a weak man, a compromising man. Rome's motto was, "Let justice be done though the heavens fall!" Pilate was not concerned about justice; his only concern was to protect himself, his job, and Rome. Alas, he failed in all three!

As you read John's account, you see Pilate seeking to find some "loophole" that would please both sides. He was afraid of the crowd, but then he grew more and more afraid of the prisoner! At least three times he announced that Jesus was not guilty of any crime (Luke 23:14; John 19:4; Luke 23:22; John 19:6). Yet he refused to release Him!

The Roman "trial," conducted by Pilate, revolved around four key questions.

"What Is the Accusation?" (18:28–32)

As soon as the Sanhedrin had voted to condemn Jesus, the officers took Him to the palace where Pilate was living during the Passover season. It was customary for the Roman governor to be in Jerusalem during Passover in case there were any outbursts of Jewish nationalism. The religious leaders did not hesitate to condemn an innocent man, but they were careful not to be defiled by walking on Gentile ground! It would be tragic to be ceremonially defiled during the seven days of Passover!

It was logical for Pilate to ask for the official accusation. Instead of stating the charges clearly, the Jewish leaders "beat around the bush" and probably made the astute politician suspicious. Luke 23:2 lists three "official charges": (1) He led the nation astray; (2) He opposed paying tribute to Caesar; and (3) He claimed to be the Jewish Messiah and King.

Pilate was not anxious to get involved in a Jewish court case, especially at Passover, so he tried to evade the issue. After all, if the prisoner was creating problems for the Jews, let the Jews try Him under their own law. Rome had permitted the Jews to retain a certain amount of jurisdiction, especially in matters relating to their religious laws and customs. (See Acts 18:12–16 for another example.)

But had the Jews *alone* judged Jesus and found Him guilty, He would have been killed by stoning, and God had determined that the Son would be crucified (see John 3:14; 8:28; 12:32–33). Jesus was to bear the curse of the law and become a curse for us, and in order to do this, He had to hang on a tree (Deut. 21:22–23; Gal. 3:13). The fact that the Romans allowed the Jews to stone Stephen to death indicates that Rome was lenient with the Sanhedrin on some capital cases (Acts 7:57–60).

When you seriously consider the three accusations against Jesus, you quickly see that they were completely unsupportable. For one thing, He had not "subverted" the nation, either politically or religiously. Of course, He had publicly denounced the Pharisees and their hypocritical religious system, but He was not the first one—or the only one—to do that. Jesus had blessed the nation and brought them new hope. The fact that some of the militant Jews saw in Him a potential king (John 6:15) was not our Lord's fault, and He fled from all such political demonstrations.

As for opposing paying tribute to Caesar, *He taught just the opposite!* "Render therefore unto Caesar the things which are Caesar's," He said, "and unto God the things that are God's" (Matt. 22:21).

He did claim to be King but not in a political sense. Even His own disciples did not fully understand these truths until after His resurrection (Acts 1:1–8). It is no wonder the common people sometimes misunderstood Him (Luke 19:11). Of course, the Jewish religious leaders were groping for any piece of evidence they could find on which they could build a case, and they were even willing to secure false witnesses!

"Are You the King of the Jews?" (18:33–38)
The question asking Jesus if He was King of the Jews is recorded by each of the gospel writers. As Roman governor, Pilate would certainly be interested in the claims of any king. Messianic expectations always ran high at Passover season, and it would be easy for a Jewish pretender to incite the people into a riot or a rebellion against Rome. Pilate no doubt felt himself on safe ground when he asked about Christ's kingship.

However, he was not prepared for His answer. "It is as you say" (Matt. 27:11 NASB). But then Jesus added a question of His own: "Are you saying this on your own initiative, or did others tell you about Me?" (John 18:34 NASB). What was our Lord really asking? "What kind of a king do you have in mind? A Roman king or a Jewish king? A political king or a spiritual king?" Jesus was not evading the issue; He was forcing Pilate to clarify the matter for *his own sake*. After all, it was not Jesus who was on trial; it was Pilate!

If Pilate had a Roman king in mind, then Jesus could be considered a rebel. If the governor was thinking about a Jewish kind of king, then political matters could be set aside. It is interesting that Pilate called Jesus "king" at least four times during the trial, and even used that title for the placard he hung on the cross (John 18:39; 19:3, 14–15, 19).

Pilate's reply to Jesus showed what the Romans thought of the Jews: "Am I a Jew?" No doubt there was an obvious note of disdain and sarcasm in his voice. Jesus was not a prisoner because Pilate had arrested him, but because His own nation's leaders had arrested Him! Where there is smoke there must be fire, so Pilate asked, "What have You done?"

Graciously, Jesus consented to explain Himself and His kingdom. Yes, He admitted that He is a king, but His kingdom (reign) does not come from the authority of the world. The Jews were under Roman authority, and Pilate was under the authority of the emperor, but Jesus derived His authority from God. His kingdom is spiritual, in the hearts of His followers, and He does not depend on worldly or fleshly means to advance His cause. If His kingdom were from the world, by now His followers would have assembled an army and fought to release Him.

Jesus did not say that He had no kingdom in this world, or that He would never rule on earth. He does have a kingdom in this world, wherever there are people who have trusted Him and yielded to His sovereignty. One day He shall return and establish a righteous kingdom on earth (Dan. 7:13–28). Pilate's concern was the source of this kingdom: where did Jesus derive His authority?

In John 18:37, Jesus explained who He is and what kind of kingdom belonged to Him. Pilate probably did not grasp the significance of these profound words, but we today can discern some of the meaning Jesus had in mind. He was "born," which indicates His humanity, but He also "came into the world," which indicates His deity. The fact that Jesus came "into the world" means that He had existed before His birth at Bethlehem, and this is an important and repeated truth in John's gospel (John 1:9–10; 3:17, 19; 9:39; 10:36; 12:46; 16:28; 17:18).

But Jesus not only told Pilate of His origin; He also explained His ministry: to bear witness unto the truth. His was a spiritual kingdom of truth, and He won people to His cause, not through force, but through conviction and persuasion. He spoke the truth of God's Word, and all who were His people would respond to His call (see John 8:47; 10:27). Rome's weapon was the sword; but our Lord's weapon was the truth of God, the sword of the Spirit (Eph. 6:17).

We do not know with what attitude Pilate asked his now-famous question, "What is truth?" In his classic essay "Of Truth," Francis Bacon wrote, "'What is Truth?' said jesting Pilate; and would not stay for an answer." But we are not certain that Pilate was jesting. Perhaps he was sincere. For centuries, Roman and Greek philosophers had discussed and debated this very question and had come to no settled conclusions. Whether Pilate was sneering or sighing as he asked the question, we do not know, so it would be unwise to pass judgment.

At least he had the courage to face the crowd and declare his verdict: "I find in Him no fault at all." But he did not get the response he desired, for the chief priests and elders only began to accuse Jesus all the more (see Matt. 27:12–14)! Jesus was silent before His accusers (1 Peter 2:21–23), and this silence amazed Pilate. Could this King not even defend Himself? If He did not speak, how could anyone secure any evidence? Pilate faced a dilemma.

But the chief priests and elders solved his problem when they shouted that Jesus had stirred up the people even in Galilee (Luke 23:5). Galilee! That was Herod's responsibility, so why not send the prisoner to Herod, who was also in Jerusalem for the feast? Between John 18:38 and 39 you have the events recorded in Luke 23:6–12. Pilate's maneuver did not solve his problem, because Herod sent Jesus back! All that it accomplished was the healing of the breach between these two rulers. Pilate still had to deal with Jesus and the Jews.

"Shall I Release the King of the Jews?" (18:39—19:7)

The fact that Herod had found nothing worthy of death in Jesus encouraged Pilate to confront the Jewish leaders and seek to release the prisoner. He summoned the chief priests and rulers and told them that he found no guilt in Jesus, that Herod had found no guilt in Jesus, and that the next step would be to punish Jesus and release Him. The Jews had already made it clear that they wanted Jesus to die (John 18:31), but Pilate was feebly trying to do the noble thing.

Hoping to strengthen this suggestion, Pilate offered to bargain with the Jewish leaders. It was a custom at Passover for the governor to release a prisoner and please the Jews; so, why not release Jesus? Or, he could release Barabbas, but why would the Jews want Barabbas set free? After all, he was a robber (John 18:40), a notorious prisoner (Matt. 27:16), an

insurrectionist, and a murderer (Luke 23:19). Who would want *that* kind of a prisoner turned loose?

Incredible as it seems, the crowd asked for Barabbas! The people were persuaded by the chief priests and elders (Matt. 27:20), whose religious convictions did not motivate them toward justice and equity. National feelings always increased during Passover, and a vote *for* Barabbas was a vote *against* Rome. Even though Jesus had been a popular figure among the people, many of them no doubt were disappointed that He had not led a popular uprising to overthrow Rome. Perhaps they had even hoped that His "triumphal entry" a few days before would be the start of Jewish liberation.

There is no explaining how a mob chooses its heroes. No doubt many of the Jews admired Barabbas for his cunning and courage, and they rejoiced that he was fighting Rome. Had they honestly compared and contrasted the two "candidates," the people would have had to vote for Jesus Christ. But when a mob is manipulated by crafty leaders, in an atmosphere of patriotic fervor, it loses itself and starts to think with its feelings instead of its brains. Their condemning vote said nothing about the Son of God, but it said a great deal about them.

Never at a loss for an idea, Pilate tried a new approach—sympathy. The crowd had cried "Crucify him!" (Mark 15:14), but perhaps they would be placated if Jesus were scourged. What man could behold a scourged prisoner and still want the victim crucified? The scourge was a leather whip, knotted and weighted with pieces of metal or bone, and many a prisoner never survived the whipping. It pains us to think that the sinless Son of God was subjected to such cruelty. He was innocent, yet He was treated as though He were guilty, and He did it for us. He was slapped in the face before Annas (John 18:22), and spat on and beaten before Caiaphas and the council (Matt. 26:67). Pilate scourged Him and the soldiers smote Him (John 19:1–3), and before they led Him to Calvary, the soldiers mocked Him and beat Him with a rod (Mark 15:19). How much He suffered for us!

Pilate had called Him "King of the Jews" (John 18:39), so the soldiers decided that the "king" should have a crown and a robe. The Jews had mocked His claim to being a prophet (Matt. 26:67–68), and now the Gentiles mocked His claim to being a king. The verb tenses in the Greek text in John 19:3 indicate that the soldiers *repeatedly* came to Him, mocked Him, and beat Him with their hands. The forces of hell were having a heyday in Pilate's hall.

Sin had brought thorns and thistles into the world (Gen. 3:17–19), so it was only fitting that the Creator wear a crown of thorns as He bore the sins of the world on the cross. The very metal He had created and placed in the ground was used to make nails to pound through His hands and feet.

For the third time, Pilate went out to face the people (John 18:29, 38; 19:4), this time bringing Jesus with him. Surely the sight of this scourged and humiliated prisoner would arouse some pity in their hearts, but it did not. For the second time, Pilate declared that he found no fault in Jesus, but his words only aroused their hateful passions more. "Behold the man!" carries the idea, "Look at this poor fellow! Hasn't He suffered enough? Take pity on Him and let me release Him." It was a noble effort on Pilate's part, but it failed.

The failure of Pilate's plan teaches us an important lesson: it takes more than human sentiment to bring the lost sinner to salvation. There is a view of the Atonement called "the moral influence theory" that would fit right into the governor's approach. It states that the realization of our Lord's sufferings moves the heart of the sinner so that he turns from sin and begins to love God. It is purely subjective and has no bearing on the holiness of God or the importance of satisfying divine justice.

If any crowd should have been moved by pity, it was the Jewish crowd that waited on Pilate. What nation has suffered more than the Jews? Here was one of their own, a Jewish prophet, suffering unjustly at the hands of the Romans, and the Jews did not repent or even show any touch of pity! If sinners who actually saw Christ in His suffering did not repent, what hope is there for people twenty centuries later who only read about His agonies?

The cross involves much more than an exhibition of innocent suffering. On that cross, the Son of God paid the price for the sins of the world and thereby declared the love of God and defended the holiness and justice of God. We are not saved by feeling pity for Jesus. We are saved by repenting of our sins and trusting Jesus, the sinless substitute. "If Christ was not actually doing something by His death," wrote Dr. Leon Morris, "then we are confronted with a piece of showmanship, nothing more."

This does not mean that it is wrong for the believer to contemplate the cross and meditate on Christ's sufferings. The familiar hymn "When I Survey the Wond'rous Cross" helps us realize afresh the price that Jesus paid for us, but we must not confuse sentimentality with true spiritual emotion. It is one thing to shed tears during a church service and quite something else to sacrifice, suffer, and serve after the meeting has ended. We do not simply contemplate the cross; we carry it.

For the third time, Pilate announced, "I find no fault in Him!" The crowd might well have shouted, "Then why did you have Him scourged?" Pilate's actions belied his words. He was a weak-willed man who, like many politicians, hoped to find a happy compromise that would please everybody. The Chinese teacher Confucius defined "cowardice" as "to know what is right and not do it."

The religious leaders were not at a loss for a powerful reply: "We have a law, and by our law he ought to die, because he made himself the Son of God" (John 19:7). This statement is not found in the other Gospels

(but see Matt. 26:63–64); however, it fits right into John's purpose in writing his gospel (John 20:31).

"Where Are You From?" (19:8–16)

The Romans and Greeks had numerous myths about the gods coming to earth as men (note Acts 14:8–13), so it is likely that Pilate responded to the phrase "Son of God" with these stories in mind. Already the governor had been impressed by the words and demeanor of our Lord; he had never met a prisoner like Him before. Was He indeed a god come to earth? Did He have supernatural powers? No wonder Pilate was starting to be afraid! Also, Pilate's wife had sent him a strange message that he should have nothing to do with Jesus (Matt. 27:19). Jesus had even come into her dreams!

Why did Jesus not answer Pilate's question? Because He had already answered it (John 18:36–37). It is a basic spiritual principle that God does not reveal new truth to us if we fail to act on the truth we already know. Furthermore, Pilate had already made it clear that he was not personally interested in spiritual truth. All he was concerned about was maintaining peace in Jerusalem as he tried to expedite the trial of Jesus of Nazareth. Pilate did not deserve an answer!

Fear and anger often go together. When we are afraid we are weak, we go to the other extreme and try to appear strong. This is what Pilate did as he reminded Jesus of his Roman authority. But his statement did not demonstrate his power; it demonstrated his weakness. For if he had the authority to release Jesus, *why did he not do it?* He condemned himself with his own boastful words.

Of course, our Lord's silence before both Herod and Pilate was a fulfillment of Isaiah 53:7. Peter later used this as an example for suffering Christians to follow (1 Peter 2:18–23).

John 19:11 records our Lord's last words to Pilate, words that reveal His faith in the Father and His surrender to His will (see 1 Peter 2:23; 4:19). All authority comes from God (Rom. 13:1ff.). Jesus was able to surrender to Rome and the Jews because He was first of all yielded to God. Pilate was boasting about his authority (John 19:10), but Jesus reminded him that his so-called authority was only delegated to him from God. One day God would call him to account for the way he had used his privileges and responsibilities.

To whom was Jesus referring when He said "he that delivered me up unto thee"? Certainly not God, because God does not and cannot sin. Jesus was referring to Caiaphas, the corrupt high priest who had long before determined that Jesus must die (John 11:47–54). Caiaphas knew the Scriptures and had been given every opportunity to examine the evidence. He had willfully closed his eyes and hardened his heart. He had seen to it that Jesus was not given a fair trial. It was his associates who were inciting the mob to cry, "Let Him be crucified!" Pilate was a spiritually blind pagan, but Caiaphas was a Jew who had a knowledge of

Scripture. Therefore, it was Caiaphas, not Pilate, who had the greater sin.

What a dilemma Pilate was in! How would he go about investigating the claim that Jesus was "the Son of God"? And there was no evidence that He was a troublemaker or a seditionist. In a final burst of courage, Pilate tried to release Jesus. John does not tell us what steps Pilate took (the Greek text says "he kept seeking to release Him"), but they all failed. In fact, the crowd started to accuse *Pilate* of being a traitor to Caesar! This was too much for the governor, so he gave his official verdict and delivered Jesus to be crucified. Matthew tells us that Pilate washed his hands before the crowd (Matt. 27:24), but this did not cleanse his heart. Alas, it was Pilate who was on trial, not Jesus!

It is likely that John used Roman time, so that "the sixth hour" would have been 6 a.m. Mark tells us that Jesus was crucified "the third hour," which, in Jewish reckoning, would have been 9 a.m. Since John wrote *"about* the sixth hour," we need not try to figure out why it took three hours to get Jesus from Pilate's hall to Calvary.

The "preparation" refers to the preparation for the Sabbath (see John 19:31), which would begin at sundown that day (Friday). Being the Passover Sabbath, it was an especially holy day. The religious leaders were more concerned about their traditions than they were knowing the truth and obeying the will of God. On a high and holy day, they crucified their own Messiah, Jesus the Son of God!

The crowd had the last word: "We have no king but Caesar!" "We will not have this man to reign over us" (Luke 19:14). Well-meaning preachers have often said that the crowd that on Palm Sunday shouted "Hosanna!" turned right around and shouted "Crucify Him!" on Good Friday. However, it was two different crowds. The Palm Sunday crowd came primarily from Galilee, where Jesus was very popular. The crowd at Pilate's hall was from Judea and Jerusalem, where the religious leaders were very much in control. If the Galilean disciples had had their way, they would have revolted and delivered Jesus!

From the human standpoint, the trial of Jesus was the greatest crime and tragedy in history. From the divine viewpoint, it was the fulfillment of prophecy and the accomplishment of the will of God. The fact that God had planned all of this did not absolve the participants of their responsibility. In fact, at Pentecost, Peter put both ideas together in one statement (Acts 2:23).

When Israel asked to have a king, and God gave them Saul, the nation rejected God the Father (1 Sam. 8:5–7). When they asked for Barabbas, they rejected God the Son. Today, they are rejecting the pleading of God the Holy Spirit (Acts 7:51; Rom. 10:21). Yet there will come a day when they shall see their King, believe, and be saved (Zech. 12:10–11; Matt. 24:30; Rev. 1:7).

Both the nation and the governor were on trial, and both failed miserably.

May we not fail!

CHAPTER TWENTY-ONE
John 19:17–42
"EVEN THE DEATH OF THE CROSS"

The Apostle's Creed states it without embellishment: "He was crucified, dead, and buried." These three events are described in John 19:17–42, momentous events that we should understand not only from the historical point of view but also from the doctrinal. *What* happened is important; *why* it happened is also important, if you hope to go to heaven.

Crucified (19:17–27)
Pilate delivered Jesus to the chief priests, and they, with the help of the Roman soldiers, took Jesus to be crucified. "It was the most cruel and shameful of all punishments," said the Roman statesman-philosopher Cicero. "Let it never come near the body of a Roman citizen; nay, not even near his thoughts or eyes or ears."

Crucifixion probably had its origin among the Persians and Phoenicians, but it was the Romans who made special use of it. No Roman citizen could be crucified, though there were exceptions. This mode of capital punishment was reserved for the lowest kind of criminals, particularly those who promoted insurrection. Today, we think of the cross as a symbol of glory and victory, but in Pilate's day, the cross stood for the basest kind of rejection, shame, and suffering. It was Jesus who made the difference.

It was customary for the criminal to carry his cross, or at least the crossbeam, from the hall of judgment to the place of execution. Jesus began the mile-long walk carrying His cross, but He was relieved by Simon of Cyrene, whom the Roman soldiers "drafted" to do the job. We do not know why Jesus was relieved of this burden; the Scriptures are silent. Was He too weak from the scourgings to carry the load? Was His weakness holding back the procession at a time when the Jews were anxious to get it over with so they could celebrate their Passover Sabbath? One thing is sure: the bearing of the cross was a mark of guilt, *and Jesus was not guilty* (see Mark 15:20–21; Rom. 16:13).

It was also required that the criminal wear a placard announcing his crime. The only announcement recorded in the Gospels is the one that Pilate wrote: "This is Jesus of Nazareth the King of the Jews." The chief priests protested the title, but Pilate refused to change it. It was his final thrust against the Jewish religious establishment. He knew that the priests and elders envied Jesus and wanted to destroy Him (Matt. 27:18). A shrewd politician like Pilate well understood the workings of the Jewish religious establishment. He knew that his placard would insult and embarrass them, and that is exactly what he wanted.

The fact that this title was written in Hebrew

(Aramaic), Greek, and Latin is significant. For one thing, it shows that our Lord was crucified in a place where many peoples and nations met, a cosmopolitan place. Hebrew is the language of religion, Greek of philosophy, and Latin of law, and all three combined to crucify the Son of God. But what He did on the cross, He did for the whole world! In this gospel, John emphasizes the worldwide dimensions of the work of Christ. Without realizing it, Pilate wrote a "gospel tract" when he prepared this title, for one of the thieves discovered that Jesus was King, and he asked entrance into His kingdom.

Jesus was crucified outside the city (Heb. 13:11–13) between two other victims, possibly associates of Barabbas. We do not know where our Savior's cross stood. There have been so many changes in the topography of Jerusalem since AD 70, when Titus and the Romans destroyed it, that it is impossible to determine accurately either our Lord's route to the cross or where the cross stood. Pilgrims to the Holy Land today are shown both the Church of the Holy Sepulcher and "Gordon's Calvary" near the garden tomb.

The Hebrew word *Golgotha* means "cranium, skull"; Calvary is the Latin equivalent. We are not told why it had this peculiar name. Certainly Jewish people would not permit unclean skulls to be left at a place of public execution! For that matter, the bodies (with heads intact) were usually disposed of by burial (if the victims had friends) or by throwing them on the public garbage dump. "Gordon's Calvary" does resemble a skull, but did the terrain look like that two thousand years ago?

That Jesus was crucified with two notorious thieves only added to the shame. But it also fulfilled Isaiah 53:12: "He was numbered with the transgressors." He was treated like a common criminal!

Modern executions are usually carried out in almost clinical privacy, but Jesus was nailed to a cross and hung up for everyone to see. It was Passover season and there were thousands of visitors in the city. The place of execution was outside the city where many people would pass. Jesus was a well-known figure, so His arrest and condemnation would be topics for discussion. It was natural for people to gather and watch the grim scene.

Of course, the soldiers had to be there; that was their job. At most Roman executions, a centurion would be assigned with four soldiers to assist him. Since Jesus was a popular teacher with many followers, Pilate may have assigned more guards to Golgotha. It was the privilege of the soldiers to share whatever personal belongings the victims had, so they divided up all that Jesus owned—His personal clothing. He would have had a turban, a pair of sandals, an undergarment (the seamless robe), an outer garment, and a girdle. The four men each took a piece of clothing, and then they gambled for the seamless robe. This fulfilled Psalm 22:18.

John does not record it, but the other gospel writers tell us that some of the people passing by reviled Jesus, no doubt at the instigation of the chief priests and scribes (Mark 15:29–32). When you read Psalm 22, you see how David used the image of *animals* to describe the people who persecuted our Lord: bulls (Ps. 22:12), lions (Ps. 22:13, 21), and dogs (Ps. 22:16, 20). When men reject their Lord, they become like animals.

A group of women, along with the apostle John, stood near the cross. (Later, they would move farther away and join other friends of Jesus [Matt. 27:55–56; Mark 15:40–41].) John specifies four women: Mary, the mother of Jesus; His mother's sister, Salome, the mother of James and John; Mary, the wife of Clopas (Cleophas); and Mary Magdalene. It took courage to stand there in the midst of such hatred and ridicule, but their being there must have encouraged our Lord.

The first time we meet Mary in the gospel of John, she is attending a wedding (John 2:1–11); now she is preparing for a burial. The hour had come! She was experiencing "the sword" that had been predicted years before (Luke 2:35). Her silence is significant, for if anyone could have rescued Jesus, it was His mother. All she had to do was announce that His claims were false—but she said nothing! What a testimony to the deity of Christ.

Jesus assured her of His love, and He gave His choicest disciple, who rested on His bosom, to be her adopted son and to care for her. Whether that moment John took Mary away from the scene and took her home, we do not know. We do know that he cared for her and that she was among the believers in the Upper Room as they awaited Pentecost (Acts 1:14). Even while He was performing the great work of redemption, Jesus was faithful to His responsibilities as a son. What an honor it was for John to take his Lord's place in Mary's life!

Do not confuse Mary Magdalene with the "sinful woman" described in Luke 7:36ff. Jesus had delivered Mary Magdalene from demons (Mark 16:9; Luke 8:2), and she used her resources to assist Jesus in His ministry. Salome had asked Jesus for thrones for her two sons (Matt. 20:20–29), and He had denied her request. You wonder what she was thinking about as she stood there and beheld Jesus dying on the cross. The scene must have rebuked her selfishness.

Dead (19:28–30)

Our Lord knew what was going on; He was fully in control as He obeyed the Father's will. He had refused to drink the pain-deadening wine that was always offered to those about to be crucified (Matt. 27:34). In order to fulfill the Scriptures (Ps. 69:21), He said, "I thirst." He was enduring real physical suffering, for He had a real human body. He had just emerged from three hours of darkness when He felt the wrath of God and separation from God (Matt. 27:45–49). When you combine darkness, thirst, and isolation, you have—hell! There were physical reasons for His thirst (Ps. 22:15), but there were also spiritual reasons (Ps. 42:1–2).

One of the soldiers took pity on Jesus and moistened His lips with the cheap vinegar wine the soldiers drank. We must not imagine Jesus hanging many feet up in the air, almost inaccessible. His feet were perhaps three or four feet from the ground, so it would be easy for the man to put a sponge at the end of a reed and give Jesus a drink. You and I today can "give Jesus a drink" by sharing what we have with those in need (Matt. 25:34–40).

Psalm 69 has strong messianic overtones. Note Psalm 69:3: "My throat is dried." Psalm 69:4 is referred to by Jesus in John 15:25, and Psalm 69:8 should be connected with John 7:3–5. Psalm 69:9 is quoted in John 2:17, and Psalm 69:21 is referred to in John 19:28–29. Note the emphasis on "reproach" (Ps. 69:7–10, 19–20) and the image of the "deep waters" (Ps. 69:14–15; and see Luke 12:50).

Our Lord made seven statements while He was on the cross; they are known as "the seven words from the cross." First, He thought of others: those who crucified Him (Luke 23:34), the believing thief (Luke 23:39–43), and His mother (John 19:25–27). The central word had to do with His relationship to the Father (Matt. 27:45–49), and the last three statements focused on Himself: His body (John 19:28–29), His soul (John 19:30; and see Isa. 53:10), and His spirit (Luke 23:46).

The drink of vinegar did not fully quench His thirst, but it did enable Him to utter that shout of triumph, in a loud voice, "It is finished!" In the Greek text, it is *telelestai,* and it means, "It is finished, it stands finished, and it always will be finished!" While it is true that our Lord's sufferings were now finished, there is much more included in this dramatic word. Many of the Old Testament types and prophecies were now fulfilled, and the once-for-all sacrifice for sin had now been completed.

The word *tetelestai* is unfamiliar to us, but it was used by various people in everyday life in those days. A servant would use it when reporting to his or her master, "I have completed the work assigned to me" (see John 17:4). When a priest examined an animal sacrifice and found it faultless, this word would apply. Jesus, of course, is the perfect Lamb of God, without spot or blemish. When an artist completed a picture, or a writer a manuscript, he or she might say, "It is finished!" The death of Jesus on the cross "completes the picture" that God had been painting, the story that He had been writing, for centuries. Because of the cross, we understand the ceremonies and prophecies in the Old Testament.

Perhaps the most meaningful sense of *tetelestai* was that used by the merchants: "The debt is paid in full!" When He gave Himself on the cross, Jesus fully met the righteous demands of a holy law; He paid our debt in full. None of the Old Testament sacrifices could take away sins; their blood only *covered* sin. But the Lamb of God shed His blood, and that blood can *take away* the sins of the world (John 1:29; Heb. 9:24–28).

There was once a rather eccentric evangelist named Alexander Wooten, who was approached by a flippant young man who asked, "What must I do to be saved?"

"It's too late!" Wooten replied, and went about his work.

The young man became alarmed. "Do you mean that it's too late for me to be saved?" he asked. "Is there nothing I can do?"

"Too late!" said Wooten. *"It's already been done! The only thing you can do is believe."*

The death of Jesus Christ is a major theme in the gospel of John. It was announced by John the Baptist even before Jesus had officially begun His ministry (John 1:29, 35–36). Our Lord's first mention is in John 3:14, where the image is certainly that of crucifixion (and see John 8:28; 12:32). Jesus often spoke of "taking up the cross" (Matt. 10:38; 16:24). After Peter's confession of faith, Jesus clearly announced that He would be killed (Matt. 16:21), and later He told the disciples that He would be crucified (Matt. 20:17–19).

In John's gospel, you find a number of pictures of our Lord's death: the slaying of the lamb (John 1:29); the destroying of the temple (John 2:19); the lifting up of the serpent (John 3:14); the shepherd laying down his life for the sheep (John 10:11–18); and the planting of the seed in the ground (John 12:20–25). These pictures make it clear that Jesus' death was not an accident; it was a divine appointment. He was not murdered in the strictest sense: He willingly gave His life for us. His death was an atonement, not just an example. He actually accomplished the work of redemption on the cross.

Some unbelievers have invented the idea that Jesus did not really die, that He only "swooned" on the cross and was then revived in the "cool tomb." But there are too many witnesses that Jesus Christ actually died: the centurion (Mark 15:44–45); all the gospel writers; the angels (Matt. 28:5, 7); the Jews (Acts 5:28); Christ Himself (Luke 24:46; Rev. 1:18); and even the worshipping hosts in heaven (Rev. 5:9, 12). Of course, Paul, Peter, and John mention the death of Christ in their letters.

His death was voluntary: He willingly dismissed His spirit (John 19:30; and note 10:17–18). He "gave himself" (Gal. 2:20). He offered Himself as a ransom (Mark 10:45), as a sacrifice to God (Eph. 5:2), and as a propitiation for sin (1 John 2:2). In Luke 9:31, His death is called a "decease," which in the Greek is "exodus," suggesting the Passover lamb and the deliverance from bondage. It will take eternity to reveal all that happened when Jesus Christ died on the cross.

Buried (19:31–42)

Two groups of people were involved in our Lord's burial: the Roman soldiers (John 19:31–37) and the Jewish believers (John 19:38–42). It was not unusual for victims to remain on the cross in a lingering death, so the Jewish religious leaders did all they could to hasten the death of Jesus and the two thieves. However, our Lord was in control, and He dismissed His spirit at "the ninth hour," which was 3 p.m. (see Matt. 27:45–50). The last three "words from the cross" were spoken within a short period of time just before He laid down His life.

It is remarkable that the Roman soldiers *did not do* what they were commanded to do—break the victims' legs—but they *did do* what they were not supposed to do—pierce the Savior's side! In both matters, they fulfilled the very Word of God! The bones of the Passover lamb were not to be broken (Ex. 12:46; Num. 9:12; and note Ps. 34:20), so our Lord's bones were protected by the Lord. His side was to be pierced (Zech. 12:10; Rev. 1:7), so that was done by one of the soldiers.

John saw a special significance to the blood and water that came from the wound in the side. For one thing, it proved that Jesus had a real body (see 1 John 1:1–4) and experienced a real death. By the time John wrote this book, there were false teachers in the church claiming that Jesus did not have a truly human body. There may also be a symbolic meaning: the blood speaks of our justification, the water of our sanctification and cleansing. The blood takes care of the guilt of sin; the water deals with the stain of sin. Some students connect John 19:34 with 1 John 5:6, but perhaps the connection is weak. In 1 John 5, John deals with evidence that Jesus Christ is God come in the flesh, and he presents three witnesses: the Spirit, the water, and the blood (1 John 5:6, 8). The Spirit relates to Pentecost, the water to His baptism, and the blood to His crucifixion. In each of these events, God made it clear that Jesus Christ is what He claimed to be, God come in the flesh. In fact, in John 19:35, the apostle makes it clear that the water and blood should encourage his readers to believe that Jesus is the Christ (see John 20:31).

When the soldiers were through with their gruesome work, our Lord's friends took over, and from that point on, as far as the record is concerned, no unbelievers touched the body of Jesus. God had prepared two high-ranking men to prepare His body for burial and to place it in a proper tomb. Had Joseph and Nicodemus not been there, it is likely that the body of Jesus would have been "carried off to some obscure and accursed ditch," as James Stalker states in his classic *The Trial and Death of Jesus Christ*. If the friends of any victims appeared, the Romans were only too happy to give them the bodies and get them off their hands.

When you assemble the data available about Joseph of Arimathea, you learn that he was rich (Matt. 27:57), a prominent member of the Jewish council (Mark 15:43), a good and righteous man who had not consented to what the council did (Luke 23:50–51), a member of that "believing minority" of Jews who were praying for Messiah to come (Mark 15:43; and note Luke 2:25–38), and a disciple of Jesus Christ (John 19:38). It was he who asked for the body of Jesus and, with his friend Nicodemus, gave the Savior a decent burial.

But there are some mysteries about Joseph that perplex us and invite closer investigation. Why did he have a tomb so near to a place of execution? Most pious Jews wanted to be buried in the Holy City, but a rich man like Joseph could certainly afford a better site for his final resting place. Imagine his relatives coming to pay their respects and having to listen to the curses and cries of criminals on crosses not far away! (Note John 19:41.)

Matthew, Luke, and John all tell us that the tomb was new and had never been used. It was "his [Joseph's] own new tomb" (Matt. 27:60); he had hewn it out for himself. *Or did he hew it out for Jesus?*

John informs us that Joseph was a "secret disciple for fear of the Jews." The Greek word translated "secretly" is a perfect passive participle and could be translated "having been secreted." In Matthew 13:35, this same verb form is translated "have been kept secret." In other words, Joseph was God's "secret agent" in the Sanhedrin! From the human standpoint, Joseph kept "under cover" because he feared the Jews (John 7:13; 9:22; 12:42), but from the divine standpoint, he was being protected so he could be available to bury the body of Jesus.

We have already met Nicodemus in our study of John 1—12. Note that each time he is named, he is identified as the man who came to Jesus by night (John 3:1ff.; 7:50–53). But the man who started off with confusion at night (John 3) ended up with open confession in the daylight! Nicodemus came out of the dark and into the light and, with Joseph, was not ashamed to publicly identify with Jesus Christ. Of course, when the two men touched His dead body, they defiled themselves and could not participate in Passover. But, what difference did it make? They had found the Lamb of God!

It seems evident that Joseph and Nicodemus carefully planned their activities at Calvary. They certainly could not secure a tomb at the last minute, nor would they be able to purchase sixty-five pounds of costly spices so quickly during the Passover, when many merchants would not be doing business. No sooner had Jesus died than Joseph went to Pilate and received permission to take the body. Nicodemus stayed at the cross to make sure nothing happened to his Lord's body. The two men might even have been waiting *in the new tomb,* with the spices and wrappings, ready for the moment when the Savior would lay down His life.

Haste was important, and the men worked quickly. They could not give Jesus' body the full ministry of washing and anointing that was traditional, but they did the best they could. It was important to get the body safely away from the Romans and the Jewish leaders. Of course, Mary of Bethany had already anointed His body for burial (Mark 14:8; John 12:1–8). Some of the other women watched the two men minister to Jesus, and they witnessed His burial (Matt. 27:61; Mark 15:47). They planned to return after the Sabbath and complete the burial procedures (Luke 23:55—24:1).

All of this raises the question, "How did Joseph and Nicodemus know to prepare for His burial?" What follows is only conjecture on my part but, to me, it seems reasonable.

When Nicodemus first visited Jesus, he was impressed with His miracles and His teachings, but he could not understand what it meant to be born again. Certainly after that interview, Nicodemus searched the Scriptures and asked God for guidance concerning these important spiritual matters.

At the critical council meeting recorded in John 7:45–53, Nicodemus boldly stood up and defended the Savior! His associates ridiculed him for thinking that a prophet could come out of Galilee! "Search, and look!" they said—and that is exactly what Nicodemus did. It is likely that Joseph quietly joined him and revealed the fact that he too was more and more convinced that Jesus of Nazareth was indeed Israel's Messiah, the Son of God.

As Nicodemus and Joseph searched the Old Testament, they would find the messianic prophecies and discover that many of them had been fulfilled in Jesus Christ. Certainly they would see Him as the "Lamb of God" and conclude that He would be sacrificed at Passover. Jesus had already told Nicodemus that He would be "lifted up" (John 3:14), and this meant crucifixion. Since the Passover lambs were slain about 3 p.m., the two men could know almost the exact time when God's Lamb would die on the cross! Surely they would read Isaiah 53 and notice verse 9—"And he made his grave with the wicked, and with the rich in his death." Jesus would be buried in a rich man's tomb!

Joseph arranged to have the tomb hewn out, and the men assembled the cloths and spices needed for the burial. They may have been hiding in the tomb all during the six hours of our Lord's agony on the cross. When they heard, "It is finished! Father, into thy hands I commend my spirit!" they knew that He was dead, and they went to work. They boldly identified with Jesus Christ at a time when He seemed like a failure and His cause hopelessly defeated. As far as we know, of all the disciples, only John was with them at the cross.

The Sabbath was about to dawn. Jesus had finished the work of the "new creation" (2 Cor. 5:17), and now He would rest.

CHAPTER TWENTY-TWO
John 20:1–18
THE DAWNING OF A NEW DAY

If the gospel of John were an ordinary biography, there would be no chapter 20. I am an incurable reader of biographies, and I notice that almost all of them conclude with the death and burial of the subject. I have yet to read one that describes the subject's

resurrection from the dead! The fact that John continued his account and shared the excitement of the resurrection miracle is proof that Jesus Christ is not like any other man. He is, indeed, the Son of God.

The resurrection is an essential part of the gospel message (1 Cor. 15:1–8) and a key doctrine in the Christian faith. It proves that Jesus Christ is the Son of God (Acts 2:32–36; Rom. 1:4) and that His atoning work on the cross has been completed and is effective (Rom. 4:24–25). The empty cross and the empty tomb are God's "receipts" telling us that the debt has been paid. Jesus Christ is not only the Savior, but He is also the Sanctifier (Rom. 6:4–10) and the Intercessor (Rom. 8:34). One day He shall return as Judge (Acts 17:30–31).

From the very beginning, the enemies of the Lord tried to deny the historic fact of the resurrection. The Jewish leaders claimed that the Lord's body had been stolen from the tomb. This statement is absurd, for if the body was stolen by His followers, how did they do it? The tomb was guarded by Roman soldiers and the stone sealed by an official Roman seal. Furthermore, His disciples *did not believe* that He was to be raised from the dead; it was His enemies who remembered His words (Matt. 27:62–66). *They* certainly would not have taken the body! The last thing they wanted was anyone believing that Jesus had indeed risen from the dead. If His friends *could not* steal the body, and His enemies *would not,* then who took it?

Perhaps the disciples had "visions" of the risen Lord and interpreted them as evidences for the resurrection. But they did not *expect* to see Him, and that is not the land of psychological preparation from which hallucinations are made. And how could more than five hundred people have the same hallucination at the same time (1 Cor. 15:6)?

Did the followers of our Lord perhaps go to the wrong tomb? Not likely. They carefully watched where He was buried (Matt. 27:61; Mark 15:47; Luke 23:55–57). They loved the Master and were not likely to get confused about His resting place. In fact, as the women approached the tomb, they were worried about who would roll back the heavy stone (Mark 16:1–3), so they were acquainted with the situation.

As to the foolish argument that Jesus did not die, but only swooned and was later revived, little need be said. It was proved by many witnesses that Jesus was dead when His body was taken from the cross. Later, He was seen alive by dependable witnesses. The only logical conclusion is that He kept His promise and arose from the dead.

But the glorious truth of the resurrection was not understood immediately by even His closest followers. It gradually dawned on these grieving people that their Master was not dead, but alive! And what a difference it made when the full realization of His resurrection took hold of them! For Mary Magdalene it meant moving from tears to joy (John 20:1–18), for the ten disciples it meant going from fear to courage (John

20:19–23); and for Thomas it meant moving from doubt to assurance (John 20:24–31). With Mary, the emphasis is on love; with the ten, the emphasis is on hope; and with Thomas, the emphasis is on faith.

As we consider Mary Magdalene's experience that Lord's Day morning, we can see three stages in her comprehension of the truth of the resurrection. Peter and John are also a part of this experience.

Faith Eclipsed (20:1–2)

Mary Magdalene and several other women agreed to go to the tomb early on the first day of the week, so that they might show their love for Christ in completing the burial preparations. Joseph of Arimathea and Nicodemus had been forced by circumstances to prepare His body hastily, and the women wanted to finish the task. Their great concern was how to get into the tomb. Perhaps the Roman soldiers would take pity on them and give them a hand.

What they did not know was that an earthquake had occurred and the stone had been rolled back by an angel! It seems that Mary Magdalene went ahead of the other women and got to the tomb first. When she saw the stone rolled away from the door of the tomb, she concluded that somebody had broken into the tomb and stolen the body of her Lord. We may criticize Mary for jumping to conclusions, but when you consider the circumstances, it is difficult to see how she would have reached any other conclusion. It was still dark, she was alone, and, like the other followers of Jesus, she did not believe that He would return from the dead.

She ran to give the news to Peter and John, who must have been living together at a place known to the other believers. Perhaps it was the Upper Room where they had met with Jesus. Mary's use of the pronoun "we" is interesting, for it included the other women who at that moment were discovering that Jesus was alive (see Mark 16:1–8; Luke 24:1–8)! The women left the tomb and carried the angels' message to the other disciples.

It is significant that the first witnesses of the resurrection of Christ were *believing women*. Among the Jews in that day, the testimony of women was not held in high regard. "It is better that the words of the law be burned," said the rabbis, "than be delivered to a woman." But these Christian women had a greater message than that of the law, for they knew that their Savior was alive.

Mary's faith was not extinguished; it was only eclipsed. The light was still there, but it was covered. Peter and John were in the same spiritual condition, but soon all three of them would move out of the shadows and into the light.

Faith Dawning (20:3–10)

John 20:3 suggests that Peter started off first to run to the tomb, but John 20:4 reports that John got there first. Perhaps John was a younger man in better

physical condition, or perhaps John was just a better runner. It is tempting to "spiritualize" this footrace and relate it to Isaiah 40:31 and Hebrews 12:1–2. When a believer is out of fellowship with the Lord, it is difficult to run the race of faith. However, both men deserve credit for having the courage to run into enemy territory, not knowing what lay before them. The whole thing could have been a clever trap to catch the disciples.

When John arrived at the tomb, he cautiously remained outside and looked in. Perhaps he wanted Peter to be with him when he went into the burial chamber. What did John see? The graveclothes lying on the stone shelf without any evidence of violence or crime. *But the graveclothes were empty!* They lay there like an empty cocoon, still retaining the shape of Jesus' body.

Peter arrived and impulsively went into the tomb, just as we would expect him to do. He also saw the linen clothes lying there empty and the cloth for the head carefully rolled and lying by itself. Grave robbers do not carefully unwrap the corpse and then leave the graveclothes neatly behind. In fact, with the presence of the spices in the folds of the clothes, it would be almost impossible to unwrap a corpse without damaging the wrappings. The only way those linen clothes could be left in that condition would be if Jesus passed *through them* as He arose from the dead.

John then entered the tomb and looked at the evidence. "He saw, and believed."

When John wrote this account, he used three different Greek words for *seeing*. In John 20:5, the verb simply means "to glance in, to look in." In John 20:6, the word means "to look carefully, to observe." The word *saw* in John 20:8 means "to perceive with intelligent comprehension." Their resurrection faith was now dawning!

It seems incredible that the followers of Jesus did not expect Him to come out of the tomb alive. After all, He had told them many times that He would be raised from the dead. Early in His ministry He had said, "Destroy this temple, and in three days I will raise it up" (John 2:19). After His resurrection, the disciples remembered that He had said this (John 2:22); however, His enemies remembered it too (Matt. 27:40, 63–64).

He compared Himself to Jonah (Matt. 12:40), and on two occasions clearly announced His resurrection after three days (Matt. 16:21; 20:19). On Thursday of His last week of ministry He again promised to be raised up and meet them in Galilee (Matt. 26:32; and see Luke 24:6–7).

What kind of faith did Peter and John have at that stage in their spiritual experience? They had faith based on evidence. They could see the graveclothes; they knew that the body of Jesus was not there. However, as good as evidence is to convince the mind, it can never change the life. Those of us who live centuries later cannot examine the evidence, for the material evidence (the tomb, the graveclothes) is no longer there for us to inspect.

But we have the record in the Word of God (John 20:9), and that record is true (John 19:35; 21:24). In fact, it is faith *in the Word* that the Lord really wanted to cultivate in His disciples (see John 2:22; 12:16; 14:26). Peter made it clear that the Word of God, not personal experiences, should be the basis for our faith (1 Peter 1:12–21).

The disciples had only the Old Testament Scriptures, so that is what is referred to in John 20:9. The early church used the Old Testament to prove to both Jews and Gentiles that Jesus is the Christ, that He died for sinners, and that He arose again (Acts 9:22; 13:16ff.; 17:1–4; etc.). The gospel includes "and that he arose again the third day according to the Scriptures" (1 Cor. 15:4). What Scriptures did Paul and John have in mind?

Paul saw the resurrection in Psalm 2:7 (Acts 13:33). Peter saw it in Psalm 16:8–11 (Acts 2:23–36, and note 13:35). Peter also referred to Psalm 110:1 (Acts 2:34–35). The statement "he shall prolong his days" in Isaiah 53:10 is also interpreted as a prediction of Christ's resurrection. Jesus Himself used the prophet Jonah to illustrate His own death, burial, and resurrection (Matt. 12:38–40), and this would include the "three days" part of the message. Paul saw in the Feast of Firstfruits a picture of the resurrection (Lev. 23:9–14; 1 Cor. 15:20–23), and again, this would include "the third day." Some students see the resurrection and "the third day" in Hosea 6:2.

After His resurrection, our Lord did not reveal Himself to everyone, but only to selected witnesses who would share the good news with others (Acts 10:39–43). This witness is now found in Scripture, the New Testament, and both the Old Testament and the New Testament agree in their witness. The law, the psalms, the prophets, and the apostles together bear witness that Jesus Christ is alive!

Peter and John saw the evidence and believed. Later, the Holy Spirit confirmed their faith through the Old Testament Scriptures. That evening, they would meet the Master personally! Faith that was eclipsed has now started to dawn, and the light will get brighter.

Faith Shining (20:11–18)

When I think of Mary Magdalene lingering alone in the garden, I recall Proverbs 8:17—"I love them that love me; and those that seek me early shall find me." Mary loved her Lord and came early to the garden to express that love. Peter and John had gone home by the time Mary got back to the tomb, so they did not convey to her what conclusion they had reached from the evidence they had examined. Mary still thought that Jesus was dead. Another verse comes to mind—Psalm 30:5: "Weeping may endure for a night, but joy cometh in the morning."

Mary's weeping was the loud lamentation so characteristic of Jewish people when they express their sorrow (John 11:31, 33). There is certainly nothing wrong with sincere sorrow, because God made us to shed tears, and weeping is good therapy for broken hearts. The sorrow of the Christian, however, must be different from the hopeless sorrow of the world (1 Thess. 4:13–18), because we have been born again "unto a living hope by the resurrection of Jesus Christ from the dead" (1 Peter 1:3 NASB). We weep—not because our believing loved ones have gone to heaven—but because they have left us and we miss them.

When Mary looked into the sepulcher, she saw two men in white. Their position at either end of the shelf where the body had been lying makes us think of the cherubim on the mercy seat (Ex. 25:17–19). It is as though God is saying, "There is now a new mercy seat! My Son has paid the price for sin, and the way is open into the presence of God!" Mary apparently was not disturbed at seeing these men, and there is no evidence that she knew they were angels. The brief conversation neither dried her tears nor quieted her mind. She was determined to find the body of Jesus.

Why did Mary turn back and not continue her conversation with the two strangers? Did she hear a sound behind her? Or did the angels stand and recognize the presence of their Lord? Perhaps both of these speculations are true or neither is true. She was certain that the Lord's body was not in the tomb, so why linger there any longer?

Why did she not recognize the One for whom she was so earnestly searching? Jesus may have deliberately concealed Himself from her, as He would later do when He walked with the Emmaus disciples (Luke 24:13–32). It was still early and perhaps dark in that part of the garden. Her eyes were probably blinded by her tears as well.

Jesus asked her the same question that the angels had asked, "Why are you weeping?" How tragic that she was weeping when she could have been praising, had she realized that her Lord was alive! Then He added, "Whom are you seeking?" (He had asked the mob the same question in the garden—John 18:4.) It is encouraging to us to know that "Jesus knows all about our sorrows." The Savior knew that Mary's heart was broken and that her mind was confused. He did not rebuke her; tenderly, He revealed Himself to her.

All He had to do was to speak her name, and Mary immediately recognized Him. His sheep hear [recognize] His voice, and He calls them by name (John 10:3). Apparently Mary had turned away from Jesus, for when He spoke her name, she had to turn back to look at Him again. What a blessed surprise it was to see the face of her beloved Master!

All she could say was, "Rabboni—my Master, my Teacher." The title *Rabboni* is used in only one other place in the Gospels, Mark 10:51 (in the Greek text "Lord" is "Rabboni"). "Rabbi" and "Rabboni" were equivalent terms of respect. In later years, the Jews recognized three levels of teachers: rab (the lowest), rabbi, and rabboni (the highest).

Mary not only spoke to Him, but she grasped His feet and held on to Him. This was a natural gesture: now that she had found Him, she did not want to lose Him. She and the other believers still had a great deal to learn about His new state of glory; they still wanted to relate to Him as they had done during the years of His ministry before the cross.

Jesus permitted the other women to hold His feet (Matt. 28:9), and He did not forbid them. Why did He say to Mary, "Do not cling to me"? One reason was that she would see Him again because He had not yet ascended to the Father. He remained on earth for forty days after His resurrection and often appeared to the believers to teach them spiritual truth (Acts 1:1–9). Mary had no need to panic; this was not her last and final meeting with the Lord.

A second reason is that she had a job to do—to go tell His brethren that He was alive and would ascend to the Father. "He is not ashamed to call them brethren" (Heb. 2:11). "I will declare thy name unto my brethren" (Ps. 22:22). He had called His own *servants* (John 13:16) and *friends* (John 15:15), but now He called them *brethren*. This meant that they shared His resurrection power and glory.

Some students feel that Jesus did return to the Father on that morning, and that was the ascension He was referring to, but no other New Testament passage corroborates this interpretation. To say that He was fulfilling the symbolism of the day of Atonement and presenting the blood to the Father is, I think, stretching a type too far (Lev. 16). For that matter, *He had no blood to present;* He had presented that on the cross when He was made sin for us. In His resurrection glory, Jesus was "flesh and bones" (Luke 24:39), not "flesh and blood." The resurrection itself was proof that the work of redemption had been completed ("raised because of our justification"—Rom. 4:24–25 NASB). What more could He do?

Our Lord never used the phrases "our Father" or "our God." His relationship to the Father was different from that of the disciples, and He was careful to make that distinction. We say "our Father" and "our God" because all believers belong to the same family and have an equal standing before God. He reminded Mary and the other believers that God was their Father and that He would be with the Father in heaven after His ascension. In His Upper Room message, He had taught them that He would return to the Father so that the Spirit might come to them.

Though it was the same Jesus, only in a glorified body, it was not quite the same relationship. We must be careful not to relate to Christ "after the flesh" (1 Cor. 5:16), that is, relate to Him as though He were still in His state of humiliation. He is today the exalted Son of God in glory, and we must honor Him as such. The juvenile familiarity that some people display in public when they testify, pray, or sing only reveals that they have little understanding of Paul's words in 2 Corinthians 5:16. When John was with Jesus at the table, he leaned against His bosom (John 13:23), but when John saw Jesus on the Isle of Patmos, he fell at His feet as dead (Rev. 1:17)!

It would have been selfish and disobedient for Mary to have clung to Jesus and kept Him to herself. She arose and went to where the disciples were gathered and gave them the good news that she had seen Jesus alive. "I have seen the Lord!" (Note John 20:14, 18, 20, 25, 29.) Mark reports that these believers were mourning and weeping—and that they would not believe her (Mark 16:9–11)! Mary herself had been weeping, and Jesus had turned her sorrow into joy. If they had believed, their sorrow would also have turned to joy. Unbelief has a terribly deadening effect on a person. No wonder God warns us against "an evil heart of unbelief" (Heb. 3:12).

Mary not only shared the fact of His resurrection and that she had seen Him personally, but she also reported the words that He had spoken to her. Again, we see the importance of the Word of God. Mary could not transfer her experience over to them, but she could share the Word, and it is the Word that generates faith (Rom. 10:17). The living Christ shared His living Word (1 Peter 1:23–25).

It is good to have faith that is based on solid evidence, but the evidence should lead us to the Word, and the Word should lead us to the Savior. It is one thing to accept a doctrine and defend it; it is something else to have a personal relationship to the living Lord. Peter and John believed that Jesus was alive, but it was not until that evening that they met the risen Christ in person along with the other disciples. (Jesus appeared to Peter sometime during the afternoon, Luke 24:34; 1 Cor. 15:5.) Evidence that does not lead to experience is nothing but dead dogma. The key is faith in the Word of God.

Dr. Robert W. Dale, who was one of Great Britain's leading Congregational pastors and theologians, was one day preparing an Easter sermon when a realization of the risen Lord struck him with new power.

"Christ is alive!" he said to himself. "Alive—alive—alive!" He paused, and then said, "Can that really be true? *Living* as really as I myself am?"

He got up from his desk and began to walk about the study, repeating, "Christ is living! Christ is living!"

Dr. Dale had known and believed this doctrine for years, but the reality of it overwhelmed him that day. From that time on, "the living Christ" was the theme of his preaching, and he had his congregation sing an Easter hymn every Sunday morning. "I want my people to get hold of the glorious fact that Christ is alive, and to rejoice over it; and Sunday, you know, is the day on which Christ left the dead."

Historical faith says, "Christ lives!"
Saving faith says, "Christ lives *in me!*"
Do you have saving faith?

CHAPTER TWENTY-THREE
John 20:19–31
THE POWER OF HIS RESURRECTION

The news that Jesus was alive began to spread among His followers, at first with hesitation, but then with enthusiasm. Even His disciples did not believe the first reports, and Thomas demanded proof. But wherever people were confronted with the reality of His resurrection, their lives were transformed. In fact, that same transforming experience can be yours today. As you see in John 20:19–31 the changes that took place in the lives of people, ask yourself, "Have I personally met the risen Christ? Has He changed *my* life?"

From Fear to Courage (20:19–25)
Our Lord rested in the tomb on the Sabbath and arose from the dead on the first day of the week. Many people sincerely call Sunday "the Christian Sabbath," but Sunday is not the Sabbath day. The seventh day of the week, the Sabbath, commemorates God's finished work of creation (Gen. 2:1–3). The Lord's Day commemorates Christ's finished work of redemption, the "new creation." God the Father worked for six days and then rested. God the Son suffered on the cross for six hours and then rested.

God gave the Sabbath to Israel as a special "sign" that they belonged to Him (Ex. 20:8–11; 31:13–17; Neh. 9:14). The nation was to use that day for physical rest and refreshment both for man and beast, but for Israel, it was not commanded as a special day of assembly and worship. Unfortunately, the scribes and Pharisees added all kinds of restrictions to the Sabbath observance until it became a day of bondage instead of a day of blessing. Jesus deliberately violated the Sabbath traditions, though He honored the Sabbath day.

There were at least five resurrection appearances of our Lord on that first day of the week: to Mary Magdalene (John 20:11–18), the other women (Matt. 28:9–10), Peter (1 Cor. 15:5; Luke 24:34), the two Emmaus disciples (Luke 24:13–32), and the disciples minus Thomas (John 20:19–25). The next Sunday, the disciples met again and Thomas was with them (John 20:26–31). It would appear that the believers from the very first met together on Sunday evening, which came to be called "the Lord's day" (Rev. 1:10). It appears that the early church met on the first day of the week to worship the Lord and commemorate His death and resurrection (Acts 20:7; 1 Cor. 16:1–2).

The Sabbath was over when Jesus arose from the dead (Mark 16:1). He arose on the first day of the week (Matt. 28:1; Luke 24:1; John 20:1). The change from the seventh day to the first day was not effected by some church decree; it was brought about from the beginning by the faith and witness of the first believers. For centuries, the Jewish Sabbath had been associated with law: six days of work, and then you rest. But the Lord's Day, the first day of the week, is associated with grace: first there is faith in the living Christ, then there will be works.

There is no evidence in Scripture that God ever gave the original Sabbath command to the Gentiles, or that it was repeated for the church to obey. Nine of the Ten Commandments are repeated in the church epistles, but the Sabbath commandment is not repeated. However, Paul makes it clear that believers must not make "special days" a test of fellowship or spirituality (Rom. 14:5ff.; Col. 2:16–23).

How did our Lord transform His disciples' fear into courage? For one thing, *He came to them.* We do not know where these ten frightened men met behind locked doors, but Jesus came to them and reassured them. In His resurrection body, He was able to enter the room without opening the doors! It was a solid body, for He asked them to touch Him—and He even ate some fish (Luke 24:41–43). But it was a different kind of body, one that was not limited by what we call "the laws of nature."

It is remarkable that these men were actually afraid. The women had reported to them that Jesus was alive, and the two Emmaus disciples had added their personal witness (Luke 24:33–35). It is likely that Jesus had appeared personally to Peter sometime that afternoon (Mark 16:7; Luke 24:34; 1 Cor. 15:5), though Peter's *public* restoration would not take place until later (John 21). No wonder Jesus reproached them at that time "with their unbelief and hardness of heart" (Mark 16:14).

But His first word to them was the traditional greeting, "Shalom—peace!" He could have rebuked them for their unfaithfulness and cowardice the previous weekend, but He did not. "He hath not dealt with us after our sins; nor rewarded us according to our iniquities" (Ps. 103:10). The work of the cross is peace (Rom. 5:1; Eph. 2:14–17), and the message they would carry would be the gospel of peace (Rom. 10:15). Man had declared war on God (Ps. 2; Acts 4:23–30), but God would declare "Peace!" to those who would believe.

Not only did Jesus come to them, but *He reassured them.* He showed them His wounded hands and side and gave them opportunity to discover that it was indeed their Master, and that He was not a phantom. (The Gospels do not record wounds in His feet, but Psalm 22:16 indicates that His feet were also nailed to the cross.)

But the wounds meant more than identification; they also were evidence that the price for salvation had been paid and man indeed could have "peace with God." The basis for all our peace is found in the person and work of Jesus Christ. He died for us, He arose from the dead in victory, and now He lives for us. In our fears, we cannot lock Him out! He comes to us in grace and reassures us through His Word. "Faithful are the wounds of a friend" (Prov. 27:6).

When Jesus saw that the disciples' fear had now turned to jo,.*he commissioned them:* "As my Father hath sent me, even so send I you" (John 20:21). Keep in mind that the original disciples were not the only ones present; others, including the Emmaus disciples, were also in the room. This commission was not the "formal ordination" of a church order; rather, it was the dedication of His followers to the task of world evangelism. We are to take His place in this world (John 17:18). What a tremendous privilege and what a great responsibility! It is humbling to realize that Jesus loves us as the Father loves Him (John 15:9; 17:26), and that we are in the Father just as He is (John 17:21–22). It is equally as humbling to realize that He has sent us into the world just as the Father sent Him. As He was about to ascend to heaven, He again reminded them of their commission to take the message to the whole world (Matt. 28:18–20).

It must have given the men great joy to realize that, in spite of their many failures, their Lord was entrusting them with His Word and His work. They had forsaken Him and fled, but now He was sending them out to represent Him. Peter had denied Him three times, and yet in a few days, Peter would preach the Word (and accuse the Jews of denying Him—Acts 3:13–14!) and thousands would be saved.

Jesus came to them and reassured them, but He also *enabled them* through the Holy Spirit. John 20:22 reminds us of Genesis 2:7, when God breathed life into the first man. In both Hebrew and Greek, the word for "breath" also means "spirit." The breath of God in the first creation meant physical life, and the breath of Jesus Christ in the new creation meant spiritual life. The believers would receive the baptism of the Spirit at Pentecost and be empowered for ministry (Acts 1:4–5; 2:1–4). Apart from the filling of the Spirit, they could not go forth to witness effectively. The Spirit had dwelt *with* them in the person of Christ, but now the Spirit would be *in* them (John 14:17).

John 20:23 must not be interpreted to mean that Jesus gave to a select body of people the right to forgive sins and let people into heaven. Jesus had spoken similar words before (Matt. 16:19), but He was not setting aside the disciples (and their successors) as a "spiritual elite" to deal with the sins of the world. Remember, there were others in the room besides the disciples, and Thomas was missing!

A correct understanding of the Greek text helps us here. Some years ago, I corresponded with the eminent Greek scholar Dr. Julius R. Mantey (now deceased) about this verse, and he assured me that the correct translation both here and in Matthew 16:19 should be: "Whosoever sins you remit [forgive] shall have already been forgiven them, and whosoever sins you retain [do not forgive] shall have already not been forgiven them." In other words, the disciples did not provide forgiveness; they proclaimed forgiveness on the basis of the message of the gospel. Another Greek scholar, Dr. Kenneth Wuest, translates it "they have been previously forgiven them."

As the early believers went forth into the world, they announced the good news of salvation. If sinners would repent and believe on Jesus Christ, their sins would be forgiven them! "Who can forgive sins but God only?" (Mark 2:7). All that the Christian can do is announce the message of forgiveness; God performs the miracle of forgiveness. If sinners will believe on Jesus Christ, we can authoritatively declare to them that their sins have been forgiven, but we are not the ones who provide the forgiveness.

By now, their fears had vanished. They were sure that the Lord was alive and that He was caring for them. They had both "peace with God" and the "peace of God" (Phil. 4:6–7). They had a high and holy commission and the power provided to accomplish it. And they had been given the great privilege of bearing the good news of forgiveness to the whole world. All they now had to do was tarry in Jerusalem until the Holy Spirit would be given.

From Unbelief to Confidence (20:26–28)

Why was Thomas not with the other disciples when they met on the evening of resurrection day? Was he so disappointed that he did not want to be with his friends? But when we are discouraged and defeated, we need our friends all the more! Solitude only feeds discouragement and helps it grow into self-pity, which is even worse.

Perhaps Thomas was afraid. But John 11:16 seems to indicate that he was basically a courageous man, willing to go to Judea and die with the Lord! John 14:5 reveals that Thomas was a spiritually minded man who wanted to know the truth and was not ashamed to ask questions. There seems to have been a "pessimistic" outlook in Thomas. We call him "Doubting Thomas," but Jesus did not rebuke him for his doubts. He rebuked him for unbelief: "Be not faithless, but believing." Doubt is often an intellectual problem: we want to believe, but the faith is overwhelmed by problems and questions. Unbelief is a moral problem; we simply will not believe.

What was it that Thomas would not believe? The reports of the other Christians that Jesus Christ was alive. The verb *said* in John 20:25 means that the disciples "kept saying to him" that they had seen the Lord Jesus Christ alive. No doubt the women and the Emmaus pilgrims also added their witness to this testimony. On the one hand, we admire Thomas for wanting *personal* experience, but on the other hand, we must fault him for laying down conditions for the Lord to meet.

Like most people in that day, he had two names: "Thomas" is Aramaic, "Didymus" is Greek, and they both mean "twin." Who was Thomas's twin? We do not know—but sometimes you and I feel as if we might be his twins! How often we have refused to believe and have insisted that God prove Himself to us!

Thomas is a good warning to all of us not to miss meeting with God's people on the Lord's Day (Heb. 10:22–25). Because Thomas was not there, he missed seeing Jesus Christ, hearing His words of peace, and receiving His commission and gift of spiritual life. He had to endure a week of fear and unbelief when he could have been experiencing joy and peace! Remember Thomas when you are tempted to stay home from church. You never know what special blessing you might miss!

But let's give him credit for showing up the next week. The other ten men had told Thomas that they had seen the Lord's hands and side (John 20:20), so Thomas made that the test. Thomas had been there when Jesus raised Lazarus, so why should he question our Lord's own resurrection? But, he still wanted proof; "seeing is believing."

Thomas's words help us to understand the difference between *doubt* and *unbelief.* Doubt says, "I cannot believe! There are too many problems!" Unbelief says, "I *will not* believe unless you give me the evidence I ask for!" In fact, in the Greek text, there is a double negative: "I positively will not believe!"

Jesus had heard Thomas's words; nobody had to report them to Him. So, the next Lord's Day, the Lord appeared in the room (again, the doors were locked) and dealt personally with Thomas and his unbelief. He still greeted them with "Shalom—peace!" Even Thomas's unbelief could not rob the other disciples of their peace and joy in the Lord.

How gracious our Lord is to stoop to our level of experience in order to lift us where we ought to be. The Lord granted Gideon the "tests of faith" that he requested (Judg. 6:36–40), and He granted Thomas his request as well. There is no record that Thomas ever accepted the Lord's invitation. When the time came to prove his faith, Thomas needed no more proof!

Our Lord's words translate literally, "Stop becoming faithless but become a believer." Jesus saw a dangerous process at work in Thomas's heart, and He wanted to put a stop to it. The best commentary on this is Hebrews 3, where God warns against "an evil heart of unbelief" (Heb. 3:12).

It is not easy to understand the psychology of doubt and unbelief. Perhaps it is linked to personality traits; some people are more trustful than others. Perhaps Thomas was so depressed that he was ready to quit, so he "threw out a challenge" and never really expected Jesus to accept it. At any rate, Thomas was faced with his own words, and he had to make a decision.

John 20:29 indicates that Thomas's testimony did not come from his *touching* Jesus, but from his *seeing* Jesus. "My Lord and my God!" is the last of the testimonies that John records to the deity of Jesus Christ. The others are John the Baptist (John 1:34); Nathanael (John 1:49); Jesus Himself (John 5:25; 10:36); Peter (John 6:69); the healed blind man (John 9:35); Martha

(John 11:27); and, of course, John himself (John 20:30–31).

It is an encouragement to us to know that the Lord had a personal interest in and concern for "Doubting Thomas." He wanted to strengthen his faith and include him in the blessings that lay in store for His followers. Thomas reminds us that unbelief robs us of blessings and opportunities. It may sound sophisticated and intellectual to question what Jesus did, but such questions are usually evidence of hard hearts, not of searching minds. Thomas represents the "scientific approach" to life—and it did not work! After all, when a skeptic says, "I will not believe unless—" he is already admitting that he does believe! He believes in the validity of the test or experiment that he has devised! If he can have faith in his own "scientific approach," why can he not have faith in what God has revealed?

We need to remind ourselves that everybody lives by faith. The difference is in the *object* of that faith. Christians put their faith in God and His Word, while unsaved people put their faith in themselves.

From Death to Life (20:29–31)

John could not end his book without bringing the resurrection miracle to his own readers. We must not look at Thomas and the other disciples and envy them, as though the power of Christ's resurrection could never be experienced in our lives today. *That was why John wrote this gospel*—so that people in *every* age could know that Jesus is God and that faith in Him brings everlasting life.

It is not necessary to "see" Jesus Christ in order to believe. Yes, it was a blessing for the early Christians to see their Lord and know that He was alive; but that is not what saved them. They were saved, not by seeing, but by believing. The emphasis throughout the gospel of John is on *believing.* There are nearly one hundred references in this gospel to believing on Jesus Christ.

You and I today cannot see Christ, nor can we see Him perform the miracles (signs) that John wrote about in this book. But the record is there, and that is all that we need. "So then faith cometh by hearing, and hearing by the word of God" (Rom. 10:17; and note 1 John 5:9–13). As you read John's record, you come face to face with Jesus Christ, how He lived, what He said, and what He did. All of the evidence points to the conclusion that He is indeed God come in the flesh, the Savior of the world.

The signs that John selected and described in this book are proof of the deity of Christ. They are important. But sinners are not saved by believing in miracles; they are saved by believing on Jesus Christ. Many of the Jews in Jerusalem believed on Jesus because of His miracles, but He did not believe in them (John 2:23–25)! Great crowds followed Him because of His miracles (John 6:2), but in the end, most of them left Him for good (John 6:66). Even the religious leaders who plotted His death believed that He did miracles, but this "faith" did not save them (John 11:47ff.).

Faith in His miracles should lead to faith in His Word, and to personal faith in Jesus as Savior and Lord. Jesus Himself pointed out that faith in His works (miracles) was but *the first step* toward faith in the Word of God (John 5:36–40). The sinner must "hear" the Word if he is to be saved (John 5:24).

There was no need for John to decribe every miracle that our Lord performed; in fact, he supposed that a complete record could never be written (John 21:25). The life and ministry of Jesus Christ were simply too rich and full for any writer, even an inspired one, to give a complete record. But a complete record is not necessary. All of the basic facts are here for us to read and consider. There is sufficient truth for any sinner to believe and be saved!

The *subject* of John's gospel is "Jesus is the Christ, the Son of God." He presented a threefold proof of this thesis: our Lord's works, our Lord's walk, and our Lord's words. In this gospel, you see Jesus performing miracles; you watch Him living a perfect life in the midst of His enemies; and you hear Him speaking words that nobody else could speak.

Either Jesus was a madman, or He was deluded, or He was all that He claimed to be. While some of His enemies did call Him deranged and deluded, the majority of people who watched Him and listened to Him concluded that He was unique, unlike anyone else they had ever known. How could a madman or a deluded man accomplish what Jesus accomplished? *When people trusted Him, their lives were transformed!* That does not happen when you trust a madman or a deceiver.

He claimed to be God come in the flesh, the Son of God, the Savior of the world. That is what He is!

John was not content simply to explain a subject. He was an evangelist who wanted to achieve an object. He wanted his readers to believe in Jesus Christ and be saved! He was not writing a biography to entertain or a history to enlighten. He was writing an evangel to change men's lives.

"Life" is one of John's key words; he uses it at least thirty-six times. Jesus offers sinners abundant life and eternal life, and the only way they can get it is through personal faith in Him.

If sinners need life, then the implication is that they are *dead*. "And you hath he quickened [made alive, resurrected] who were dead in trespasses and sins" (Eph. 2:1). Salvation is not resuscitation; it is resurrection (John 5:24). The lost sinner is not sick or weak; *he is dead*.

This life comes "through his name." What is his name? In John's gospel, the emphasis is on his name "I am." Jesus makes seven great "I am" statements in this gospel, offering the lost sinner all that he needs.

Eternal life is not "endless time," for even lost people are going to live forever in hell. "Eternal life" means *the very life of God experienced today.* It is a quality of life, not a quantity of time. It is the spiritual experience of "heaven on earth" today. The Christian does not have to die to have this eternal life; he possesses it in Christ today.

The ten disciples were changed from fear to courage, and Thomas was changed from unbelief to confidence. Now, John invites *you* to trust Jesus Christ and be changed from death to eternal life.

If you have already made this life-changing decision, give thanks to God for the precious gift of eternal life.

If you have never made this decision, *do so right now.*

"He that believeth on the Son hath everlasting life; and he that believeth not the Son shall not see life, but the wrath of God abideth on him" (John 3:36).

CHAPTER TWENTY-FOUR
John 21
TRANSFORMED TO SERVE

The average reader would conclude that John completed his book with the dramatic testimony of Thomas (John 20:28–31), and the reader would wonder why John added another chapter. The main reason is the apostle Peter, John's close associate in ministry (Acts 3:1). John did not want to end his gospel without telling his readers that Peter was restored to his apostleship. Apart from the information in this chapter, we would wonder why Peter was so prominent in the first twelve chapters of the book of Acts.

John had another purpose in mind: he wanted to refute the foolish rumor that had spread among the believers that John would live until the return of the Lord (John 21:23). John made it clear that our Lord's words had been greatly misunderstood.

I think John may have had another purpose in mind: he wanted to teach us how to relate to the risen Christ. During the forty days between His resurrection and ascension, our Lord appeared and disappeared at will, visiting with the disciples and preparing them for the coming of the Spirit and their future ministries (Acts 1:1–9). They never knew when He would appear, so they had to stay alert! (The fact that He may return for His people *today* ought to keep us on our toes!) It was an important time for the disciples because they were about to take His place in the world and begin to carry the message to others.

I see in this chapter three pictures of the believer and a responsibility attached to each picture.

We Are Fishers of Men—Obey Him (21:1–8)
The Lord had instructed His disciples to meet Him in Galilee, which helps to explain why they were at the Sea of Galilee, or Sea of Tiberias (Matt. 26:32; 28:7–10; Mark 16:7). But John did not explain why Peter decided to go fishing, and Bible students are not in agreement in their suggestions. Some claim that he was perfectly within his rights, that he needed to pay

his bills and the best way to get money was to go fishing. Why sit around idle? Get busy!

Others believe that Peter had been called *from* that kind of life (Luke 5:1–11) and that it was wrong for him to return. Furthermore, when he went fishing, Peter took six other men with him! If he was wrong, they were wrong too, and it is a sad thing when a believer leads others astray.

By the way, it is interesting that at least seven of the twelve disciples were probably fishermen. Why did Jesus call so many fishermen to follow Him? For one thing, fishermen are courageous, and Jesus needs brave people to follow Him. They are also dedicated to one thing and cannot easily be distracted. Fishermen do not quit! (We are thinking, of course, of professional fishermen, not people relaxing on vacation!) They know how to take orders, and they know how to work together.

Whether Peter and his friends were right or wrong we cannot prove—though I personally think that they were wrong—but we do know this: their efforts were in vain. Had they forgotten the Lord's words, "For without me, ye can do nothing" (John 15:5)? They toiled all night and caught nothing. Certainly, Peter must have remembered what happened two years before, when Jesus called him into full-time discipleship (Luke 5:1–11). On that occasion, Peter had fished all night and caught nothing, but Jesus had turned his failure into success.

Perhaps Peter's impulsiveness and self-confidence were revealing themselves again. He was sincere, and he worked hard, but there were no results. How like some believers in the service of the Lord! They sincerely believe that they are doing God's will, but their labors are in vain. They are serving without direction from the Lord, so they cannot expect blessing from the Lord.

After His resurrection, our Lord was sometimes not recognized (Luke 24:16; John 20:14), so it was that His disciples did not recognize Him when, at dawning, He appeared on the shore. His question expected a negative reply: "You have not caught anything to eat, have you?" Their reply was brief and perhaps a bit embarrassed: "No."

It was time for Jesus to take over the situation, just as He did when He called Peter into discipleship. He told them where to cast the net; they obeyed, and they caught 153 fish! The difference between success and failure was the width of the ship! We are never far from success when we permit Jesus to give the orders, and we are usually closer to success than we realize.

It was John who first realized that the stranger on the shore was their own Lord and Master. It was John who leaned on the Lord's breast at the table (John 13:23) and who stood by the cross when his Lord suffered and died (John 19:26). It is love that recognizes the Lord and shares that good news with others: "It is the Lord!"

With characteristic impulsiveness, Peter quickly put on his outer garment ("naked" simply means "stripped for work") and dove into the water! He wanted to get to Jesus! This is in contrast to Luke 5:8, where Peter told the Lord to depart from him. The other six men followed in the boat, bringing the net full of fish. In the experience recorded in Luke 5, the nets began to break, but in this experience, the net held fast.

Perhaps we can see in these two "fishing miracles" an illustration of how the Lord helps His people fish for lost souls. All of our efforts are useless apart from His direction and blessing. During this present age, we do not know how many fish we have caught, and it often appears that the nets are breaking! But at the end of the age, when we see the Lord, not one fish will be lost and we will discover how many there are.

Jesus called the disciples and us to be "fishers of men." This phrase was not invented by Jesus; it had been used for years by Greek and Roman teachers. To be a "fisher of men" in that day meant to seek to persuade men and "catch" them with the truth. A fisherman catches living fish, but when he gets them, they die. A Christian witness seeks to catch "dead fish" (dead in their sins), and when he or she "catches" them, they are made alive in Christ!

Now we can understand why Jesus had so many fishermen in the disciple band. Fishermen know how to work. They have courage and faith to go out "into the deep." They have much patience and persistence, and they will not quit. They know how to cooperate with one another, and they are skilled in using the equipment and the boat. What examples for us to follow as we seek to "catch fish" for Jesus Christ!

We are indeed "fishers of men," and there are "fish" all around us. If we obey His directions, we will catch the fish.

We Are Shepherds—Love Him (21:9–18)

Jesus met His disciples on the beach where He had already prepared breakfast for them. This entire scene must have stirred Peter's memory and touched his conscience. Surely he was recalling that first catch of fish (Luke 5:1–11) and perhaps even the feeding of the five thousand with bread and fish (John 6). It was at the close of the latter event that Peter had given his clearcut witness of faith in Jesus Christ (John 6:66–71). The "fire of coals" would certainly remind him of the fire at which he denied the Lord (John 18:18). It is good for us to remember the past; we may have something to confess.

Three "invitations" stand out in John's gospel: "Come and see" (John 1:39); "Come and drink" (John 7:37); and "Come and dine" (John 21:12). How loving of Jesus to feed Peter before He dealt with his spiritual needs. He gave Peter opportunity to dry off, get warm, satisfy his hunger, and enjoy personal fellowship. This is a good example for us to follow as we care for God's people. Certainly the spiritual is more important than the physical, but caring for the physical can prepare the way for spiritual ministry. Our Lord does not so emphasize "the soul" that He neglects the body.

Peter and his Lord had already met privately and no doubt taken care of Peter's sins (Luke 24:34; 1 Cor. 15:5), but since Peter had denied the Lord *publicly,* it was important that there be a public restoration. Sin should be dealt with only to the extent that it is known. Private sins should be confessed in private, public sins in public. Since Peter had denied his Lord three times, Jesus asked him three personal questions. He also encouraged him by giving a threefold commission that restored Peter to his ministry.

The key issue is Peter's love for the Lord Jesus, and that should be a key matter with us today. But what did the Lord mean by "more than these"? Was He asking, "Do you love Me more than you love these other men?" Not likely, because this had never been a problem among the disciples. They all loved the Lord Jesus supremely, even though they did not always obey Him completely. Perhaps Jesus meant, "Do you love Me more than you love these boats and nets and fish?" Again, this is not likely, for there is no evidence that Peter ever desired to go back permanently into the fishing business. Fishing did not seem to compete with the Savior's love.

The question probably meant, "Do you love Me—as you claimed—more than these other disciples love Me?" Peter had boasted of his love for Christ and had even contrasted it with that of the other men. "I will lay down my life for thy sake" (John 13:37). "Though all men shall be offended because of thee, yet will I never be offended" (Matt. 26:33). There is more than a hint in these boastful statements that Peter believed that he loved the Lord more than did the other disciples.

Many commentaries point out that, in this conversation, two different words are used for "love." In His questions in John 21:15–16, our Lord used *agape,* which is the Greek word for the highest kind of love, sacrificing love, divine love. Peter always used *phileo,* which is the love of friend for friend, fondness for another. In John 21:17, Jesus and Peter both used *phileo.*

However, it is doubtful that we should make too much of an issue over this, because the two words are often used interchangeably in the gospel of John. In John 3:16, God's love for man is *agape* love, but in John 16:27, it is *phileo* love. The Father's love for His Son is *agape* love in John 3:35 but *phileo* love in John 5:20. Christians are supposed to love one another. In John 13:34, this love is *agape* love, but in John 15:19, it is *phileo* love. It would appear that John used these two words as synonyms, whatever fine distinctions there might have been between them.

Before we judge Peter too severely, two other matters should be considered. When answering the first two questions, Peter did affirm his *agape* love when he said, "Yes, Lord!" The fact that Peter himself used *phileo* did not negate his wholehearted assent to the Lord's use of *agape.* Second, Peter and Jesus undoubtedly spoke in Aramaic, even though the Holy Spirit

recorded the conversation in common Greek. It might be unwise for us to press the Greek too far in this case.

In spite of his faults and failures, Peter did indeed love the Lord, and he was not ashamed to admit it. The other men were certainly listening "over Peter's shoulder" and benefiting from the conversation, for they too had failed the Lord after boasting of their devotion. Peter had already confessed his sin and been forgiven. Now he was being restored to apostleship and leadership.

The image, however, changes from that of the fisherman to that of the shepherd. Peter was to minister both as an evangelist (catching the fish) and a pastor (shepherding the flock). It is unfortunate when we divorce these two because they should go together. Pastors ought to evangelize (2 Tim. 4:5) and then shepherd the people they have won so that they mature in the Lord.

Jesus gave three admonitions to Peter: "Feed My lambs," "Shepherd My sheep," and "Feed My sheep." Both the lambs and the more mature sheep need feeding and leading, and that is the task of the spiritual shepherd. It is an awesome responsibility to be a shepherd of God's flock (1 Peter 5:2)! There are enemies that want to destroy the flock, and the shepherd must be alert and courageous (Acts 20:28–35). By nature, sheep are ignorant and defenseless, and they need the protection and guidance of the shepherd.

While it is true that the Holy Spirit equips people to serve as shepherds, and gives these people to churches (Eph. 4: 11ff.), it is also true that each individual Christian must help to care for the flock. Each of us has a gift or gifts from the Lord, and we should use what He has given us to help protect and perfect the flock. Sheep are prone to wander, and we must look after each other and encourage each other.

Jesus Christ is the Good Shepherd (John 10:11), the Great Shepherd (Heb. 13:20–21), and the Chief Shepherd (1 Peter 5:4). Pastors are "under-shepherds" who must obey Him as they minister to the flock. *The most important thing the pastor can do is to love Jesus Christ.* If he truly loves Jesus Christ, the pastor will also love His sheep and tenderly care for them. The Greek word for "sheep" at the end of John 21:17 means "dear sheep." Our Lord's sheep are dear to Him and He wants His ministers to love them and care for them personally and lovingly. (See Ezek. 34 for God's indictment of unfaithful shepherds, the leaders of Judah.) A pastor who loves the flock will serve it faithfully, no matter what the cost.

We Are Disciples—Follow Him (21:19–25)

Jesus had just spoken about Peter's life and ministry, and now He talks about Peter's death. This must have been a shock to Peter, to have the Lord discuss his death in such an open manner. No doubt Peter was rejoicing that he had been restored to fellowship and apostleship. Why bring up martyrdom?

The first time Jesus spoke about His own death,

Peter had opposed it (Matt. 16:21ff.). Peter had even used his sword in the garden in a futile attempt to protect his Lord. Yet Peter had boasted he would die for the Lord Jesus! But when the pressure was on, Peter failed miserably. (You and I probably would have done worse!) Anyone who yields himself to serve the Lord must honestly confront this matter of death.

When a person has settled the matter of death, then he is ready to live and to serve! Our Lord's own death is a repeated theme in John's gospel: He knew that His "hour" would come, and He was prepared to obey the Father's will. We as His followers must yield ourselves—just as He yielded Himself for us—and be "living sacrifices" (Rom. 12:1–2) who are "ready to be offered" (2 Tim. 4:6–8) if it is the will of God.

Earlier that morning, Peter had "girded himself" and hurried to shore to meet Jesus (John 21:7). The day would come when another would take charge of Peter—and kill him (see 2 Peter 1:13–14). Tradition tells us that Peter was indeed crucified, but that he asked to be crucified upside down, because he was not worthy to die exactly as his Master had died.

But Peter's death would not be a tragedy; it would glorify God! The death of Lazarus glorified God (John 11:4, 40) and so did the death of Jesus (John 12:23ff.). Paul's great concern was that he glorify God, whether by life or by death (Phil. 1:20–21). This should be our desire as well.

Our Lord's words, "Follow me!" must have brought new joy and love to Peter's heart. Literally, Jesus said, "Keep on following Me." Immediately, Peter began to follow Jesus, just as he had done before his great denial. However, for a moment *Peter took his eyes off the Lord Jesus,* a mistake he had made at least two other times. After that first great catch of fish, Peter took his eyes off his Lord and looked at *himself.* "Depart from me; for I am a sinful man, O Lord" (Luke 5:8). When he was walking on the stormy sea with Jesus, Peter looked away from the Lord and began to look at the wind and waves, and immediately he began to sink (Matt. 14:30). It is dangerous to look at the circumstances instead of looking to the Lord.

Why did Peter look away from his Lord and start to look back? He heard somebody walking behind him. It was the apostle John, who was also following Jesus Christ. Peter did a foolish thing and asked Jesus, "What shall this man do?" In other words, "Lord, you just told me what will happen to me; now, what will happen to John?"

The Lord rebuked Peter and reminded him that his job was to follow, not to meddle into the lives of other believers. Beware when you get your eyes off the Lord and start to look at other Christians! "Looking unto Jesus" should be the aim and practice of every believer (Heb. 12:1–2). To be distracted by ourselves, our circumstances, or by other Christians is to disobey the Lord and possibly get detoured out of the will of God. Keep your eyes of faith on Him and on Him alone.

This does not mean that we ignore others, because we do have the responsibility of caring for one another (Phil. 2:1–4). Rather, it means that we must not permit our curiosity about others to distract us from following the Lord. God has His plan for us; He also has plans for our Christian friends and associates. How He works in their lives is His business. Our business is to follow Him as He leads us (see Rom. 14:1–13).

I recall a critical time in my own ministry when I was disturbed because other ministers were apparently getting God's "blessing" in abundance, while I seemed to be reaping a meager harvest. I must confess that I envied them and wished that God had given their gifts to me. But the Lord tenderly rebuked me with, "What is that to thee? Follow thou me." It was just the message I needed, and I have tried to heed it ever since.

Jesus did not say that John would live until His return, but that is the way some of the misguided believers understood it. More problems are caused by confused saints than by lost sinners! Misinterpreting the Word of God only creates misunderstanding about God's people and God's plans for His people.

However, there is a somewhat enigmatic quality to what the Lord said about John. Jesus did not say that John would live until He returned, nor did He say that John would die before He returned. As it was, John lived the longest of all the disciples and did witness the Lord's return when he saw the visions that he recorded in the book of Revelation.

As John came to the close of his book, he affirmed again the credibility of his witness. (Remember, *witness* is a key theme in the gospel of John. The word is used forty-seven times.) John witnessed these events himself and wrote them for us as he was led by the Holy Spirit. He could have included so much more, but he wrote only what the Spirit told him to write.

The book ends with Peter and John together following Jesus, and He led them right into the book of Acts! What an exciting thing it was to receive the power of the Spirit and to bear witness of Jesus Christ! Had they not trusted Him, been transformed by Him, and followed Him, they would have remained successful fishermen on the Sea of Galilee, and the world would never have heard of them.

Jesus Christ is transforming lives today. Wherever He finds a believer who is willing to yield to His will, listen to His Word, and follow His way, He begins to transform that believer and accomplish remarkable things in that life. He also begins to do wonderful things through that life.

Peter and John have been off the scene (except for their books) for centuries, but you and I are still here. We are taking His place and taking their place. What a responsibility! What a privilege!

We can succeed only as we permit Him to transform us.

Acts

OUTLINE

Key theme: The expansion of the church in the world

Key verse: Acts 1:8

I. THE MINISTRY OF PETER (1—12)

Jerusalem the center
Ministry primarily to Israel
A. Peter and the Jews—1—7
B. Peter and the Samaritans—8
C. The conversion of Paul—9
D. Peter and the Gentiles—10—11
E. Peter's arrest and deliverance—12

II. THE MINISTRY OF PAUL (13—28)

Syrian Antioch the center
Ministry primarily to the Gentiles
A. Paul's first missionary journey—13—14
B. The Jerusalem Conference—15
C. Paul's second missionary journey—
16:1—18:22
D. Paul's third missionary journey—
18:23—21:17
E. Paul's arrest and voyage to Rome—21:18—
28:31

CONTENTS

CHAPTER ONE
Acts 1
THE FAITH OF THE FIRST CHRISTIANS

A famous Hollywood producer once said that for a movie to be successful, it must start with an earthquake and work up to a climax. Luke certainly didn't follow that formula when he wrote the book of Acts. Except for the ascension of Jesus Christ, events recorded in Acts 1 are anything but dramatic. After all, what is exciting about a business meeting?

Then why record these events? Why didn't Luke just start with the story of Pentecost? For several reasons.

To begin with, Luke was writing volume two of a work that started with what we call the gospel of Luke (see Luke 1:1–4), and he had to begin with the proper salutation and introduction. We don't know who Theophilus was or even if he was a believer, but Luke's salutation suggests that he may have been an important Roman official (see Acts 23:26; 24:3; 26:25). Likely Theophilus was a Christian or at least a seeker who was carefully studying the Christian faith. His name means "friend of God," and we hope he lived up to his name.

But even more important, Luke had to build a bridge between his gospel and the book of Acts (Luke 24:50–53). At the close of his gospel, he had left the believers in the temple, praising God. Now he had to pick up the story and explain what happened next. Imagine how confused you would be if, in reading your New Testament, you turned the last page of the gospel of John and discovered—Romans! "How did the church get to Rome?" you would ask yourself; the answer is found in the book of Acts.

The book of Acts is also the account of the work of the Holy Spirit *in* and *through* the church. The gospel of Luke records what Jesus "began both to do and teach" in His human body, and the book of Acts tells us what Jesus *continued* to do and teach through His spiritual body, the church. Even today, congregations can learn much about church life and ministry from this book, and this even includes the business meetings!

In this chapter, we see the believers taking care of "unfinished business" and getting ready for Pentecost. What they said and did reveals to us the faith of the church. In what did they really believe?

They Believed in the Risen Christ (1:1–11)

After His resurrection, Jesus remained on earth for forty days and ministered to His disciples. He had already opened their minds to understand the Old Testament message about Himself (Luke 24:44–48), but there were other lessons they needed to learn before they could launch out in their new ministry. Jesus appeared and disappeared during those forty days, and the believers never knew when He might show up. It was excellent preparation for the church because the days were soon coming when He would no longer be on earth to instruct them personally. We believers today never know when our Lord may return, so our situation is somewhat similar to theirs.

The Lord taught them several important lessons during that time of special ministry.

The reality of His resurrection (v. 3a). Some of the believers may have had their doubts forty days before (Mark 16:9–14), but there could be no question now that Jesus had indeed been raised from the dead. To strengthen their faith, He gave them "many infallible proofs," which Luke did not explain. We know that when Jesus met His disciples, He invited them to touch His body, and He even ate before them (Luke 24:38–43). Whatever proofs He gave, they were convincing.

Faith in His resurrection was important to the church because their own spiritual power depended on it. Also, the message of the gospel involves the truth of the resurrection (Rom. 10:9–10; 1 Cor. 15:1–8), and, if Jesus were dead, the church would be speechless. Finally, the official Jewish position was that the disciples had stolen Jesus' body from the tomb (Matt. 28:11–15), and the believers had to be able to refute this as they witnessed to the nation.

These believers were chosen to be special witnesses of Christ's resurrection, and that was the emphasis in their ministry (Acts 1:22; 2:32; 3:15; 5:30–32). Most of the people in Jerusalem knew that Jesus of Nazareth had been crucified, but they did not know that He had been raised from the dead. By their words, their walk, and their mighty works, the believers told the world that Jesus was alive. This was "the sign of Jonah" that Jesus had promised to the nation (Matt. 12:38–41)—His death, burial, and resurrection.

The coming of His kingdom (v. 3b). This refers to the reign of God over the hearts and lives of those who have trusted Him (see Matt. 6:33; Rom. 14:17; 1 John 3:1–9). When you read the four gospels, you discover that the apostles had a strongly political view of the kingdom and were especially concerned about their own positions and privileges. Being loyal Jews, they longed for the defeat of their enemies and the final establishment of the glorious kingdom under the rule of King Messiah. They did not realize that there must first be a spiritual change in the hearts of the people (see Luke 1:67–79).

Jesus did not rebuke them when they "kept asking" about the future Jewish kingdom (Acts 1:7). After all, He had opened their minds to understand the Scriptures (Luke 24:44), so they knew what they were asking. But God has not revealed His timetable to us, and it is futile for us to speculate. The important thing is not to be curious about the future but to be busy in the present, sharing the message of God's *spiritual* kingdom. This is another emphasis in the book of Acts (see Acts 8:12; 14:22; 20:25; 28:23, 31).

The power of His Holy Spirit (vv. 4–8). John the Baptist had announced a future baptism of the Holy Spirit (Matt. 3:11; Mark 1:8; Luke 3:16; John 1:33; and see Acts 11:16), and now that prophecy would be fulfilled. Jesus had also promised the coming of the Spirit (John 14:16–18, 26; 15:26–27; 16:7–15). It would be an enduement of power for the disciples so that they would be able to serve the Lord and accomplish His will (Luke 24:49). John had spoken about "the Holy Spirit and fire," but Jesus said nothing about fire. Why? Because the "baptism of fire" has to do with future judgment, when the nation of Israel will go through tribulation (Matt. 3:11–12). The appearing of "tongues of fire" at Pentecost (Acts 2:3) could not be termed a "baptism."

Acts 1:8 is a key verse. To begin with, it explains that the power of the church comes from the Holy Spirit and not from man (see Zech. 4:6). God's people experienced repeated fillings of the Spirit as they faced new opportunities and obstacles (Acts 2:4; 4:8, 31; 9:17; 13:9). Ordinary people were able to do extraordinary things because the Spirit of God was at work in their lives. The ministry of the Holy Spirit is not a luxury; it is an absolute necessity.

"Witness" is a key word in the book of Acts and is used twenty-nine times as either a verb or a noun. A witness is somebody who tells what he has seen and heard (Acts 4:19–20). When you are on the witness stand in court, the judge is not interested in your ideas or opinions; he only wants to hear what you know. Our English word *martyr* comes from the Greek word translated "witness," and many of God's people have sealed their witness by laying down their lives.

We hear a great deal these days about "soul winning," and the emphasis is a good one. However, while *some* of God's people have a calling to evangelism (Eph. 4:11), *all* of God's people are expected to be witnesses and tell the lost about the Savior. Not every Christian can bring a sinner to the place of faith and decision (though most of us could do better), but every Christian can bear faithful witness to the Savior. "A true witness delivereth souls" (Prov. 14:25).

Acts 1:8 also gives us a general outline of the book of Acts as it describes the geographical spread of the gospel: from Jerusalem (Acts 1—7) to Judea and Samaria (Acts 8—9), and then to the Gentiles and to the ends of the earth (Acts 10—28). No matter where we live, as Christians we should begin our witness at home and then extend it "into all the world." As Dr. Oswald J. Smith used to say, "The light that shines the farthest will shine the brightest at home."

The assurance of His coming again (vv. 9–11). Our Lord's ascension into heaven was an important part of His ministry, for if He had not returned to the Father, He could not have sent the promised gift of the Holy Spirit (John 16:5–15). Also, in heaven today, the Savior is our interceding High Priest, giving us the grace that we need for life and service (Heb. 4:14–16). He is also our Advocate before the Father, forgiving us when we confess our sins (1 John 1:9—2:2). The exalted and glorified Head of the church is now working with His people on earth and helping them accomplish His purposes (Mark 16:19–20).

As the believers watched Jesus being taken up to glory, two angels appeared and gently rebuked them. Angels play an important role in the ministry described in Acts, just as they do today, even though we cannot see them (see Acts 5:19–20; 8:26; 10:3–7; 12:7–10, 23; 27:23). The angels are the servants of the saints (Heb. 1:14).

The two messengers gave the believers assurance that Jesus Christ would come again, just as He had been taken from them. This seems to refer to His public "coming in the clouds" (Matt. 24:30; 26:64; Rev. 1:7) rather than to His coming for His church "in a moment, in the twinkling of an eye" (1 Cor. 15:51–52; 1 Thess. 4:13–18). Regardless of what views different people may take of God's prophetic program, Christians agree that Jesus is coming again and that He can come at any time. This in itself is a great motivation for faithful Christian service (Luke 12:34–48).

They Believed in Each Other (1:12–14)

They obeyed their Lord's commandment and returned to Jerusalem "with great joy" (Luke 24:52). It is likely that the group met in the Upper Room where the last Passover had been celebrated, but they were also found at worship in the temple (Luke 24:53).

What a variety of people made up that first assembly of believers! There were men and women, apostles and "ordinary" people, and even members of the Lord's earthly family (see Matt. 13:55; Mark 6:3). His "brethren" had not believed in Him during His ministry (John 7:5), but they did come to trust Him after the resurrection (Acts 1:14). Mary was there as a member of the assembly, participating in worship and prayer along with the others. The center of their fellowship was the risen Christ, and all of them adored and magnified Him.

How easy it would have been for someone to bring division into this beautiful assembly of humble people! The members of the Lord's family might have claimed special recognition, or Peter could have been criticized for his cowardly denial of the Savior. Or perhaps Peter might have blamed John, because it was John who brought him into the high priest's house (John 18:15–16). John might well have reminded the others that *he* had faithfully stood at the cross, and had even been chosen by the Savior to care for His mother. But there was none of this. In fact, nobody was even arguing over who among them was the greatest!

The key phrase is "with one accord," a phrase that is found six times in Acts (1:14; 2:1, 46; 4:24; 5:12; 15:25; and note also 2:44). There was among these believers a wonderful unity that bound them together in Christ (Ps. 133; Gal. 3:28), the kind of unity that Christians need today. "I do not want the walls of separation between different orders of Christians to be destroyed," said the godly British preacher Rowland Hill, "but only lowered, that we may shake hands a little easier over them!"

It is not enough for Christians to have faith in the Lord; they must also have faith in one another. To these 120 people (Acts 1:15) the Lord had given the solemn responsibility of bearing witness to a lost world, and none of them could do the job alone. They would experience severe persecution in the days ahead, and one of them, James, would lay down his life for Christ. It was not a time for asking, "Who is the greatest?" or, "Who committed the greatest sin?" It was a time for praying together and standing together in the Lord. As they waited and worshipped together, they were being better prepared for the work that lay before them.

They Believed in Prayer (1:15, 24–25)

Prayer plays a significant role in the story of the church as recorded in the book of Acts. The believers prayed for guidance in making decisions (Acts 1:15–26) and for courage to witness for Christ (Acts 4:23–31). In fact, prayer was a normal part of their daily ministry (Acts 2:42–47; 3:1; 6:4). Stephen prayed as he was being stoned (Acts 7:55–60). Peter and John prayed for the Samaritans (Acts 8:14–17), and Saul of Tarsus prayed after his conversion (Acts 9:11). Peter prayed before he raised Dorcas from the dead (Acts 9:36–43). Cornelius prayed that God would show him how to be saved (Acts 10:1–4), and Peter was on the housetop praying when God told him how to be the answer to Cornelius's prayers (Acts 10:9).

The believers in John Mark's house prayed for Peter when he was in prison, and the Lord delivered him both from prison and from death (Acts 12:1–11). The church at Antioch fasted and prayed before sending out Barnabas and Paul (Acts 13:1–3; and note 14:23). It was at a prayer meeting in Philippi that God opened Lydia's heart (Acts 16:13), and another prayer meeting in Philippi opened the prison doors (Acts 16:25ff.). Paul prayed for his friends before leaving them (Acts 20:36; 21:5). In the midst of a storm, he prayed for God's blessing (Acts 27:35), and after a storm, he prayed that God would heal a sick man (Acts 28:8). In almost every chapter in Acts you find

a reference to prayer, and the book makes it very clear that something happens when God's people pray.

This is certainly a good lesson for the church today. Prayer is both the thermometer and the thermostat of the local church, for the "spiritual temperature" either goes up or down, depending on how God's people pray. John Bunyan, author of *Pilgrim's Progress,* said, "Prayer is a shield to the soul, a sacrifice to God, and a scourge to Satan." In the book of Acts, you see prayer accomplishing all of these things.

They Believed in God's Leading (1:16–23)

The Lord Jesus was no longer with them to give them personal directions, but they were not without the leading of the Lord, for they had the Word of God and prayer. In fact, the Word of God and prayer formed the foundation for the ministry of the church as recorded in the book of Acts (Acts 6:4).

Peter has been criticized for taking charge, but I believe he was doing the will of God. Jesus had made it clear that Peter was to be their leader (Matt. 16:19; Luke 22:31–32; John 21:15–17). Peter was "first among equals," but he was their recognized leader. His name is mentioned first in each listing of the apostles, including Acts 1:13.

But should Peter and the others have waited until the Spirit had been given? We must not forget that the Lord had previously "breathed" on them and imparted the Spirit to them (John 20:22). When the Spirit came at Pentecost, it was for the purpose of filling them with power and baptizing them into one body in Christ.

We must also remember that the Lord had opened up their minds to understand the Scriptures (Luke 24:45). When Peter referred to Psalms 69:25 and 109:8, he was not doing this on his own, but was being led by the Spirit of God. These people definitely believed in the divine inspiration of the Old Testament Scriptures (Acts 1:16; and see 3:18; 4:25), and they also believed that these Scriptures had a practical application to their situation.

A radio listener once wrote to ask me, "Why do you teach from the Old Testament? After all, it's ancient history and it's all been fulfilled by Jesus!" I explained that the only "Bible" the early church had was the Old Testament, and yet they were able to use it to discover the will of God. We need both the Old and the New; in fact, the New Testament writers often quote from the Old Testament to prove their point. St. Augustine said, "The New is in the Old concealed; the Old is by the New revealed."

Certainly we must interpret the Old by the New, but we must not think that God no longer speaks to His people through the Old Testament Scriptures. *"All"* Scripture is given by inspiration of God, and is profitable" (2 Tim. 3:16, italics mine). "Man shall not live by bread alone, but by *every* word that proceedeth out of the mouth of God" (Matt. 4:4, italics mine). We must use the whole Bible and balance Scripture with Scripture as we seek to discover the mind of God.

"But it was wrong for them to select a new apostle," some claim, "because Paul was the one who was chosen by God to fill up the ranks. They chose Matthias and he was never heard of again!"

Except for Peter and John, *none of the original Twelve* are mentioned by name in the book of Acts after 1:13! Paul could not have "filled up the ranks" because he could never have met the divine qualifications laid down in Acts 1:21–22. Paul was not baptized by John the Baptist; he did not travel with the apostles when Jesus was with them on earth; and, though he saw the glorified Christ, Paul was not a witness of the resurrection as were the original apostles.

Paul made it clear that he was *not* to be classified with the Twelve (1 Cor. 15:8; Gal. 1:15–24), and the Twelve knew it. If the Twelve thought that Paul was supposed to be one of them, they certainly did not show it! In fact, they refused to admit Paul into the Jerusalem fellowship until Barnabas came to his rescue (Acts 9:26–27)! The twelve apostles ministered primarily to the twelve tribes of Israel, while Paul was sent to the Gentiles (Gal. 2:1–10).

No, Paul was not meant to be the twelfth apostle. Peter and the other believers were in the will of God when they selected Matthias, and God gave His endorsement to Matthias by empowering him with the same Spirit that was given to the other men whom Jesus had personally selected (Acts 2:1–4, 14).

It was necessary that twelve men witness at Pentecost to the twelve tribes of Israel, and also that twelve men be prepared to sit on twelve thrones to judge the twelve tribes (Luke 22:28–30). From Acts 2—7, the witness was primarily to Israel, "to the Jew first" (see Rom. 1:16; Acts 3:26; 13:46). Once the message had gone to the Gentiles (Acts 10—11), this Jewish emphasis began to decline. When the apostle James was martyred, he was not replaced (Acts 12). Why? Because the official witness to Israel was now completed, and the message was going out to Jews and Gentiles alike. There was no more need for twelve apostles to give witness to the twelve tribes of Israel.

Peter's account of the purchase of the land and the death of Judas appears to contradict the record in Matthew 27:3–10, but actually it complements it. Judas did not buy the field personally, but since it was his money that paid for it, in that sense, he was the buyer. And, since the thirty pieces of silver were considered "blood money," the field was called "the field of blood" (Matt. 27:8). It was not Judas's blood that gave the field its name, for the Jews would not use as a sacred cemetery a place that had been defiled by a suicide. Judas hanged himself, and apparently the rope broke and his body (possibly already distended) burst open when it hit the ground.

The believers prayed for God's guidance before they "voted," because they wanted to select the man that God had already chosen (Prov. 16:33). Their exalted Lord was working in them and through them from heaven. This is the last instance in the Bible of the casting of lots, and there is no reason why believers today should use this approach in determining God's will. While it is not always easy to discover what God wants us to do, if we are willing to obey Him, He will reveal His will to us (John 7:17). What is important is that we follow the example of the early church by emphasizing the Word of God and prayer.

Not all our Lord's followers were in the Upper Room, for there were only 120 present and 1 Corinthians 15:6 states that at least 500 persons saw the risen Christ at one time. Bible scholars do not agree on the size of the population of Palestine at that time, and their estimates run from 600,000 to 4 million. But regardless of what figure you select, the 120 believers were still a minority, yet they turned their world upside down for Christ!

What was their secret? The power of the Holy Spirit!

Dr. Luke explains this in Acts 2.

CHAPTER TWO
Acts 2
POWER FROM HEAVEN!

W e are not going to move this world by criticism of it nor conformity to it, but by the combustion within it of lives ignited by the Spirit of God."

Vance Havner made that statement and he was right. The early church had none of the things that we think are so essential for success today—buildings, money, political influence, social status—and yet the church won multitudes to Christ and saw many churches established throughout the Roman world. Why? Because the church had the power of the Holy Spirit energizing its ministry. They were a people who "were ignited by the Spirit of God."

That same Holy Spirit power is available to us today to make us more effective witnesses for Christ. The better we understand His working at Pentecost, the better we will be able to relate to Him and experience His power. The ministry of the Spirit is to glorify Christ in the life and witness of the believer (John 16:14), and that is what is important. Acts 2 helps us understand the Holy Spirit by recording four experiences in the life of the church.

The Church Waiting for the Spirit (2:1)

Pentecost means "fiftieth" because this feast was held fifty days after the Feast of Firstfruits (Lev. 23:15–22). The calendar of Jewish feasts in Leviticus 23 is an outline of the work of Jesus Christ. Passover pictures His death as the Lamb of God (John 1:29; 1 Cor. 5:7), and the Feast of Firstfruits pictures His resurrection from the dead (1 Cor. 15:20–23). Fifty days after Firstfruits is the Feast of Pentecost, which pictures the formation of the church. At Pentecost, the Jews celebrated the giving of the law, but Christians celebrate it because of the giving of the Holy Spirit to the church.

The Feast of Firstfruits took place on the day after the Sabbath following Passover, which means it was always on the first day of the week. (The Sabbath is the seventh day.) Jesus arose from the dead on the first day of the week and "became the firstfruits of them that slept" (1 Cor. 15:20). Now, if Pentecost was fifty days later—seven weeks plus one day—then Pentecost also took place on the first day of the week. Christians assemble and worship on Sunday, the first day of the week, because on that day our Lord arose from the dead, but it was also the day on which the Holy Spirit was given to the church.

On the Feast of Firstfruits, the priest waved a sheaf of grain before the Lord, but on Pentecost, he presented two loaves of bread. Why? Because at Pentecost, the Holy Spirit baptized the believers and united them into one body. The Jewish believers received this baptism at Pentecost, and the Gentile believers received this baptism in the home of Cornelius (Acts 10). This explains the presence of two loaves of bread (see 1 Cor. 10:17). The fact that there was leaven (yeast) in the loaves indicates the presence of sin in the church on earth. The church will not be perfect until it gets to heaven.

We must not conclude that this ten-day prayer meeting brought about the miracles of Pentecost, or that we today may pray as they did and experience "another Pentecost." Like our Lord's death at Calvary, Pentecost was a once-for-all event that will not be repeated. The church may experience new fillings of the Spirit, and certainly patient prayer is an essential element to spiritual power, but we would not ask for another Pentecost any more than we would ask for another Calvary.

The Church Worshipping the Lord (2:2–13)

As we study the events of Pentecost, it is important that we separate the accidentals from the essentials. The Spirit *came* and the people heard the sound of rushing wind and saw tongues of fire. The Spirit *baptized* and *filled* the believers, and then *spoke* as they praised God in various languages. The Spirit *empowered* Peter to preach, and then He *convicted* the listeners so that three thousand of them trusted Christ and were saved. Let's consider these ministries one by one.

The Spirit came (vv. 2–3). The Holy Spirit had been active prior to Pentecost and had worked in creation (Gen. 1:1–2), in Old Testament history (Judg. 6:34; 1 Sam. 16:13), and in the life and ministry of Jesus (Luke 1:30–37; 4:1, 14; Acts 10:38). However, now there would be two changes: the Spirit would dwell in people and not just come on them, and His presence would be permanent, not temporary (John 14:16–17). The Spirit could not have come sooner, for it was essential that Jesus die, be raised from the dead, and return to heaven before the Spirit could be given (John 7:37–39; 16:7ff.). Remember the Jewish calendar in Leviticus 23: Passover, Firstfruits, and then Pentecost.

There were three startling signs that accompanied the coming of the Spirit: the sound of a rushing wind, tongues of fire, and the believers praising God in various languages. The word *Spirit* is the same as "wind" in both the Hebrew and the Greek (John 3:8). The people did not *feel* the wind; they heard *the sound* of a mighty wind. It is likely the believers were in the temple when this occurred (Luke 24:53). The word *house* in Acts 2:2 can refer to the temple (see Acts 7:47). The tongues of fire symbolized the powerful witness of the church to the people. Campbell Morgan reminds us that our tongues can be set on fire either by heaven or by hell (James 3:5–6)! Combine wind and fire and you have—a blaze!

The Spirit baptized (1:5). The Greek word *baptizo* has two meanings, one literal and the other figurative. The word literally means "to submerge," but the figurative meaning is "to be identified with." The baptism of the Spirit is that act of God by which He identified believers with the exalted Head of the church, Jesus Christ, and formed the spiritual body of Christ on earth (1 Cor. 12:12–14). Historically, this took place at Pentecost; today, it takes place whenever a sinner trusts Jesus Christ and is born again.

When you read about "baptism" in the New Testament, you must exercise discernment to determine whether the word is to be interpreted literally or symbolically. For example, in Romans 6:3–4 and Galatians 3:27–28, the reference is symbolic since water baptism cannot put a sinner into Jesus Christ. Only the Holy Spirit can do that (Rom. 8:9; 1 Cor. 12:13; see Acts 10:44–48). Water baptism is a public witness of the person's identification with Jesus Christ, while Spirit baptism is the personal and private experience that identifies the person with Christ.

It is important to note that historically, the baptism of the Spirit took place in two stages: the Jewish believers were baptized at Pentecost, and the Gentiles were baptized and added to the body in the home of Cornelius (Acts 10:44–48; 11:15–17; and see Eph. 2:11–22).

The Spirit filled (v. 4). The filling of the Spirit has to do with power for witness and service (Acts 1:8). We are not exhorted to be baptized by the Spirit, for this is something God does once and for all when we trust His Son. But we are commanded to be filled with the Spirit (Eph. 5:18), for we need His power constantly if we are to serve God effectively. At Pentecost, the Christians were filled with the Spirit and experienced the baptism of the Spirit, but after that, they experienced many fillings (Acts 4:8, 31; 9:17; 13:9) but no more baptisms.

Occasionally someone says, "What difference does it make what words we use? The important thing is that we have the experience!" I doubt that they would apply that same approach to any other area of life such as medicine, cooking, or mechanics. What difference does it make if the pharmacist uses arsenic or aspirin in the prescription, just so long as you get well? Or if the mechanic installs an alternator or a carburetor, just so long as the car works?

The Holy Spirit has revealed God's truth to us in *words* (1 Cor. 2:12–13), and these words have definite meanings that must not be changed. Regeneration must not be confused with justification, nor propitiation with adoption. Each of these words is important in God's plan of salvation and must be defined accurately and used carefully.

The baptism of the Spirit means that I belong to His body; the fullness of the Spirit means that my body belongs to Him. The baptism is final; the fullness is repeated as we trust God for new power to witness. The baptism involves all other believers, for it makes us one in the body of Christ (Eph. 4:1–6); while the fullness is personal and individual. These are two distinct experiences and they must not be confused.

The Spirit spoke (vv. 5–13). Note that the believers were praising God, not preaching the gospel, and that they used known languages, not an "unknown tongue" (Acts 2:6, 8). Luke named fifteen different geographical locations and clearly stated that the citizens of those places heard Peter and the others declare God's wonderful works *in languages they could understand.* The Greek word translated "language" in Acts 2:6 and "tongue" in Acts 2:8 is *dialektos* and refers to a language or dialect of some country or district (Acts 21:40; 22:2; 26:14). Unless we are instructed otherwise in Scripture, we must assume that when "speaking in tongues" is mentioned elsewhere in Acts, or in 1 Corinthians, it refers to an identical experience: believers praising God in the Spirit in languages that are known.

Why did God do this? For one thing, Pentecost was a reversal of the judgment at the Tower of Babel when God confused man's language (Gen. 11:1–9). God's judgment at Babel scattered the people, but God's blessing at Pentecost united the believers in the Spirit. At Babel, the people were unable to understand each other, but at Pentecost, men heard God's praises and understood what was said. The Tower of Babel was a scheme designed to praise men and make a name for men, but Pentecost brought praise to God. The building of Babel was an act of rebellion, but Pentecost was a ministry of humble submission to God. What a contrast!

Another reason for this gift of tongues was to let the people know that the gospel was for the whole world. God wants to speak to every person in his or her own language and give the saving message of salvation in Jesus Christ. The emphasis in the book of Acts is on worldwide evangelization, "unto the uttermost part of the earth" (Acts 1:8). "The Spirit of Christ is the spirit of missions," said Henry Martyn, "and the nearer we get to Him, the more intensely missionary we must become."

Apparently the sound of the wind drew the people to the temple where the believers were gathered, but it was the praise by the believers that really captured their attention. The careless listeners mocked and accused the believers of being drunk, but others were sincerely concerned to find out what was going on. The people were perplexed (Acts 2:6), amazed (Acts 2:7, 12), and they marveled (Acts 2:7).

It is interesting that the mockers should accuse the believers of being drunk, for wine is associated with the Holy Spirit (Eph. 5:18). Paul relates the two *in contrast,* for when a man is filled with strong drink, he loses control of himself and ends up being ashamed, but when a person is filled with the Spirit, he has self-control and glorifies God. Strong drink can bring a temporary exhilaration, but the Spirit gives a deep satisfaction and a lasting joy.

The Church Witnessing to the Lost (2:14–41)

Peter did not preach in tongues; he addressed his audience in the everyday Aramaic that they understood. The message was given by a Jew, to Jews (Acts 2:14, 22, 29, 36), on a Jewish holy day, about the resurrection of the Jewish Messiah whom their nation had crucified. The Gentiles who were there were proselytes to the Jewish religion (Acts 2:10). Peter would not open the door of faith to the Gentiles until he visited Cornelius (Acts 10).

There are three explanations in Peter's sermon.

He explained what happened: the Spirit had come (vv. 14–21). The joyful worship of the believers was not the result of too much wine; it was the evidence of the arrival of God's Holy Spirit to dwell in His people. Orthodox Jews did not eat or drink before 9 a.m. on the Sabbath or on a holy day, nor did they usually drink wine except with meals.

Peter did not say that Pentecost was the *fulfillment* of the prophecy of Joel 2:28–32, because the signs and wonders predicted had not occurred. When you read Joel's prophecy in context, you see that it deals with the nation of Israel in the end times, in connection with "the day of the Lord." However, Peter was led by the Spirit to see in the prophecy an application to the church. He said, "This is that same Holy Spirit that Joel wrote about. He is here!" Such an announcement would seem incredible to the Jews, because they thought God's Spirit was given only to a few select people (see Num. 11:28–29). But here were 120 of their fellow Jews, men and women, enjoying the blessing of the same Holy Spirit that had empowered Moses, David, and the prophets.

It was indeed the dawning of a new age, the "last days" in which God would bring to completion His plan of salvation for mankind. Jesus had finished the great work of redemption, and nothing more had to be done except to share the good news with the world, beginning with the nation of Israel. The invitation is, "Whosoever shall call on the name of the Lord shall be saved" (Acts 2:21).

He explained how it happened: Jesus was alive (vv. 22–35). News travels fast in the East, and probably most of the adults in Jerusalem, residents and visitors, knew about the arrest, trial, and crucifixion of Jesus of Nazareth. They also had heard rumors of an "official announcement" that His followers had stolen the body of Jesus just to make people think that He had kept His word and been raised from the dead.

But Peter told them the truth: Jesus of Nazareth

had indeed been raised from the dead, and the resurrection proves that He is the Messiah! Peter gave them four proofs of the resurrection of Jesus Christ of Nazareth, and then he called on them to believe on Christ and be saved.

His first proof was the person of Jesus Christ (vv. 22–24). Peter's audience knew that Jesus was a real Person from the town of Nazareth and that He had performed many signs and miracles. (On "Jesus of Nazareth," see Acts 2:22; 3:6; 4:10; 6:14; 10:38; 22:8; 26:9; also 24:5.) It was clear that God's hand was on Him. They had heard Him speak and had watched His life. They had even seen Him raise the dead, yet they could find no fault in Him—and these things were not "done in a corner" (Acts 26:26)!

It was incredible that such a Man should be defeated by death. From one point of view, the crucifixion of Jesus was a terrible crime (Acts 2:23), but from another point of view it was a wonderful victory (Acts 2:24). The word translated "pains" means "birth pangs," suggesting that the tomb was a "womb" out of which Jesus was "born" in resurrection glory (see Acts 13:33).

Peter's second proof was the prophecy of David (vv. 25–31). He quoted Psalm 16:8–11, verses that obviously could not apply to David who was already dead and buried. Being a prophet of God, David wrote about the Messiah, that His soul would not remain in hades (the realm of the dead) or His body in the grave where it would decay.

The third proof was the witness of the believers (v. 33). After His resurrection, Jesus did not appear to the world at large, but to His own followers whom He had commissioned to give witness to others that He was alive (Acts 1:3, 22). But were these people dependable witnesses? Can we trust them? We certainly can! Prior to Christ's resurrection, the disciples did not even believe that He would be raised from the dead, and they themselves had to be convinced (Mark 16:9–14; Acts 1:3). They had nothing to gain by preaching a lie, because their message aroused official opposition and even led to the imprisonment and death of some of the believers. A few fanatics might be willing to believe and promote a lie for a time, but when thousands believe a message, and when that message is backed up by miracles, you cannot easily dismiss it. These witnesses were trustworthy.

Peter's fourth proof of the resurrection of Christ was the presence of the Holy Spirit (vv. 33–35). Follow his logic. If the Holy Spirit is in the world, then God must have sent Him. Joel promised that one day the Spirit would come, and Jesus Himself had promised to send the gift of the Holy Spirit to His people (Luke 24:49; John 14:26; 15:26; Acts 1:4). But if Jesus is dead, He cannot send the Spirit; therefore, He must be alive. Furthermore, He could not send the Spirit unless He had returned to heaven to the Father (John 16:7); so, Jesus has ascended to heaven! To back up this statement, Peter quoted Psalm 110:1, a verse that certainly could not be applied to David (note Matt. 22:41–46).

Peter's conclusion was both a declaration and an accusation: Jesus is your Messiah, *but you crucified Him* (see Acts 2:23)! Peter did not present the cross as the place where the sinless substitute died for the world, but where Israel killed her own Messiah! They committed the greatest crime in history! Was there any hope? Yes, for Peter gave a third explanation that was good news to their hearts.

He explained why it happened: to save sinners (vv. 36–41). The Holy Spirit took Peter's message and used it to convict the hearts of the listeners. (In Acts 5:33 and 7:54, a different Greek word is used that suggests anger rather than conviction for sin.) After all, if they were guilty of crucifying their Messiah, what might God do to them! Note that they addressed their question to the other apostles as well as to Peter, for all twelve were involved in the witness that day, and Peter was only first among equals.

Peter told them how to be saved: they had to repent of their sins and believe on Jesus Christ. They would give proof of the sincerity of their repentance and faith by being baptized in the name of Jesus Christ, thus identifying themselves publicly with their Messiah and Savior. Only by repenting and believing on Christ could they receive the gift of the Spirit (Gal. 3:2, 14), and this promise was for both the Jews and the "far off" Gentiles (Eph. 2:13–19).

It is unfortunate that the translation of Acts 2:38 in the King James Version suggests that people must be baptized in order to be saved, because this is not what the Bible teaches. The Greek word *eis* (which is translated "for" in the phrase "for the remission of sins") can mean "on account of or "on the basis of." In Matthew 3:11, John the Baptist baptized on the basis that people had repented. Acts 2:38 should not be used to teach salvation by baptism. If baptism is essential for salvation, it seems strange that Peter said nothing about baptism in his other sermons (Acts 3:12–26; 5:29–32; 10:34–43). In fact, the people in the home of Cornelius received the Holy Spirit *before they were baptized* (Acts 10:44–48)! Since believers are commanded to be baptized, it is important that we have a clean conscience by obeying (1 Peter 3:21), but we must not think that baptism is a part of salvation. If so, then nobody in Hebrews 11 was saved, because none of them was ever baptized.

Acts 2:40 indicates that the apostles continued to share the Word and to urge the people to trust Jesus Christ. They looked on the nation of Israel as a "crooked generation" that was under condemnation (Matt. 16:4; 17:17; Phil. 2:15). Actually, the nation would have about forty years before Rome would come and destroy the city and the temple and scatter the people. History was repeating itself. During the forty years in the wilderness, the new generation "saved itself" from the older generation that rebelled against God. Now, God would give His people another forty years of grace, and on that day, three thousand people repented, believed, and were saved.

The Church Walking in the Spirit (2:42–47)

The believers continued to use the temple for their place of assembly and ministry, but they also met in various homes. The three thousand new converts needed instruction in the Word and fellowship with God's people if they were to grow and become effective witnesses. The early church did more than make converts; they also made *disciples* (Matt. 28:19–20).

Two phrases in Acts 2:42 may need explanation. "Breaking of bread" probably refers to their regular meals, but at the close of each meal, they probably paused to remember the Lord by observing what we call "the Lord's Supper." Bread and wine were the common fare at a Jewish table. The word *fellowship* means much more than "being together." It means "having in common" and probably refers to the sharing of material goods that was practiced in the early church. This was certainly not a form of modern communism, for the program was totally voluntary, temporary (Acts 11:27–30), and motivated by love.

The church was unified (Acts 2:44), magnified (Acts 2:47a), and multiplied (Acts 2:47b). It had a powerful testimony among the unsaved Jews, not only because of the miracles done by the apostles (Acts 2:43), but also because of the way the members of the fellowship loved each other and served the Lord. The risen Lord continued to work with them (Mark 16:20), and people continued to be saved. What a church!

The Christians you meet in the book of Acts were not content to meet once a week for "services as usual." They met daily (Acts 2:46), cared daily (Acts 6:1), won souls daily (Acts 2:47), searched the Scriptures daily (Acts 17:11), and increased in number daily (Acts 16:5). Their Christian faith was a day-to-day reality, not a once-a-week routine. Why? Because the risen Christ was a living reality to them, and His resurrection power was at work in their lives through the Spirit.

The promise is still good: "Whosoever shall call on the name of the Lord shall be saved" (Acts 2:21; Rom. 10:13). Have you called? Have you trusted Jesus Christ to save you?

CHAPTER THREE
Acts 3:1—4:4
THE POWER OF HIS NAME

The emphasis in Acts 3 and 4 is on the name of the Lord Jesus (Acts 3:6, 16; 4:7, 10, 12, 17–18, 30). A name, of course, implies much more than identification; it carries with it authority, reputation, and power. When somebody says, "You can use my name!" you sincerely hope the name is worth using. If an order is given in the name of the President of the United States or the Prime Minister of Great Britain, those who receive the order know that they are obligated to obey. If I were to issue orders at the White House or at No. 10 Downing Street (even if I could get in), nobody would pay much attention because my name has no official authority behind it.

But the name of the Lord Jesus has *all authority* behind it, for He is the Son of God (Matt. 28:18). Because His name is "above every name" (Phil. 2:9–11), He deserves our worship and obedience. The great concern of the first Christians was that the name of Jesus Christ, God's Son, be glorified, and believers today should have that same concern.

As we study this section, we should note that the Jewish emphasis is very pronounced. Peter addressed Jewish men (Acts 3:12) and called them "children of the prophets and of the covenant" (Acts 3:25). He referred to the Jewish fathers (Acts 3:13) as well as to the prophets (Acts 3:18, 21–25). The phrase "times of restitution" (Acts 3:21) is definitely Jewish and refers to the messianic kingdom promised in the prophets. The message is still going out "to the Jew first" (Acts 3:26) and is presented in Jewish terms.

There are three stages in this event, and each stage reveals something wonderful about Jesus Christ.

Amazement: Jesus the Healer (3:1–10)

The believers were still attached to the temple and to the traditional hours of prayer (Ps. 55:17; Dan. 6:10; Acts 10:30). Keep in mind that Acts 1—10 describes a gradual transition from Israel to the Gentiles and from "Jewish Christianity" (note Acts 21:20) to the "one body" made up of both Jews and Gentiles. It took several years before many of the Jewish believers really understood the place of the Gentiles in God's program, and this understanding did not come without its conflicts.

The contrast between Acts 2 and 3 is interesting: Peter the preacher—Peter the personal worker; multitudes—one poor man; ministry resulting in blessing—ministry resulting in arrest and persecution. The events in Acts 3 are an illustration of the last phrase in Acts 2:47, showing us how the Lord added to His church daily. While the Holy Spirit is not named in this chapter, He was certainly at work in and through the apostles, performing His ministry of glorifying Jesus Christ (John 16:14).

Peter and John are often found together in Scripture. They were partners in the fishing business (Luke 5:10); they prepared the last Passover for Jesus (Luke 22:8); they ran to the tomb on the first Easter Sunday morning (John 20:3–4); and they ministered to the Samaritans who believed on Jesus Christ (Acts 8:14). Now that they were filled with the Holy Spirit, the apostles were no longer competing for greatness, but were at last working faithfully together to build the church (Ps. 133).

That Peter noticed the lame beggar is another evidence of the Spirit's ministry. No doubt thousands of people were near the temple (Acts 4:4), and perhaps scores of beggars, but the Lord told Peter to heal a lame man lying at the Beautiful Gate. There were nine gates that led from the court of the Gentiles into the temple itself. Scholars are not agreed, but the Beautiful Gate was probably the "Eastern Gate" that led into the court of the women. Made of Corinthian bronze, the gate looked like gold, and it certainly was a choice place for a lame man to beg.

The giving of alms was an important part of the Jewish faith, so beggars found it profitable to be near the temple. Since the believers had pooled their resources (Acts 2:44–45), the two apostles had no money to give, but money was not what the man needed most. He needed salvation for his soul and healing for his body, and money could provide neither. Through the power of the name of Jesus, the beggar was completely healed, and he was so happy and excited that he acted like a child, leaping and praising God.

It is easy to see in this man an illustration of what salvation is like. He was born lame, and all of us are born unable to walk so as to please God. Our father Adam had a fall and passed his lameness on to all of his descendants (Rom. 5:12–21). The man was also poor, and we as sinners are bankrupt before God, unable to pay the tremendous debt that we owe Him (Luke 7:36–50). He was "outside the temple," and all sinners are separated from God, no matter how near to the door they might be. The man was healed wholly by the grace of God, and the healing was immediate (Eph. 2:8–9). He gave evidence of what God had done by "walking, and leaping, and praising God" (Acts 3:8) and by publicly identifying himself with the apostles, both in the temple (Acts 3:11) and in their arrest (Acts 4:14). Now that he could stand, there was no question *where* this man stood!

Indictment: Jesus, the Son of God (3:11–16)

The healing of the lame beggar drew a crowd around the three men. Solomon's Porch, on the east side of the temple, was a corridor where our Lord had ministered (John 10:23) and where the church worshipped (Acts 5:12).

In his sermon at Pentecost, Peter had to refute the accusation that the believers were drunk. In this sermon, he had to refute the notion that he and John had healed the man by their own power. (Paul and Barnabas would face a similar situation after healing a lame man. See Acts 14:8–18.) Peter immediately identified the source of the miracle—Jesus Christ, the Son of God. Wisely, Peter said that this was the God of their fathers, the God of Abraham, Isaac, and Jacob.

The Spirit certainly gave Peter boldness as he reminded the Jews of the way they had treated Jesus. They had denied Him and delivered Him up to be crucified. Even worse, they had asked for a guilty man, Barabbas, to be set free so that an innocent prisoner might be crucified! In order to convince them of their crimes, Peter used several different names and titles for our Lord: God's Son, Jesus, the Holy One, the Just One, the Prince (Pioneer) of life. This was no ordinary man that they had handed over to the Romans to crucify!

Calvary may have been man's last word, but the empty tomb was God's last word. He glorified His Son by raising Him from the dead and taking Him back to heaven. The enthroned Christ had sent His Holy Spirit and was working through His church. The healed beggar was proof that Jesus was alive. If ever a people were guilty, it was the people Peter addressed in the temple. They were guilty of killing their own Messiah!

This is probably not the kind of message we would give at an evangelistic meeting today, because it was designed especially for Peter's Jewish audience. As at Pentecost, Peter was addressing people who knew the Scriptures and were acquainted with the recent events in Jerusalem (see Luke 24:18). It was not a group of ignorant pagans with no religious background. Furthermore, the Jewish leaders had indeed perpetrated a great injustice when they arrested and condemned Jesus and asked Pilate to have Him crucified. How many citizens agreed with their decision, we do not know, but you can imagine the remorse of the people when they learned that they had betrayed and killed their own Messiah!

There must be conviction before a sinner can experience conversion. Unless a patient is convinced that he is sick, he will never accept the diagnosis or take the treatment. Peter turned the temple into a courtroom and laid all the evidence out for everybody to see. How could two ordinary fishermen perform such a great miracle unless God was with them? Nobody would dare deny the miracle because the beggar stood there before them all in "perfect soundness" (Acts 3:16; 4:14). To accept the miracle would have been to admit that Jesus Christ is indeed the living Son of God and that His name has power.

Encouragement: Jesus, the Savior (3:17—4:4)

But Peter did not leave the people without hope. In fact, he almost seemed to defend them by pointing out that they had acted in ignorance (Acts 3:17) while at the same time they had fulfilled the Word of God (Acts 3:18).

In the Old Testament law, there is a difference between deliberate sins and sins of ignorance (see Lev. 4—5; Num. 15:22–31). The person who sinned presumptuously was a rebel against God and was guilty of great sin. He was to be "cut off" from his people (Num. 15:30–31), which could mean excommunication and even death. The defiant "high-handed" sinner was condemned, but the person who sinned unwittingly and without deliberate intent was given opportunity to repent and seek God's forgiveness. Ignorance does not remove the sinner's guilt, but it does mitigate the circumstances.

Jesus had prayed, "Father, forgive them; for they know not what they do" (Luke 23:34), and God had answered that prayer. Instead of sending judgment, He sent the Holy Spirit to empower His church and to convict lost sinners. Israel's situation was something like that of the "manslayer" who killed his neighbor without prior malicious intent, and fled to the nearest city of refuge (Num. 35:9–34). So long as he remained in the city, he was safe, for then the avengers could not reach him and kill him. He was free to go home only after the death of the high priest. Peter invited these "murderers" to flee by faith to Jesus Christ and find refuge in Him (Heb. 6:18).

In his previous sermon, Peter had explained that the cross was the meeting place of divine sovereignty and human responsibility (Acts 2:23), and he repeated this truth in this second sermon (Acts 3:17–18). There are mysteries here that the human mind cannot fully understand, so we must accept them by faith. God had a plan from all eternity, yet His plan did not force men to act against their own will. The prophets had foretold the sufferings and death of the Messiah, and the nation fulfilled these prophecies without realizing what they were doing. When God cannot rule, He overrules and always accomplishes His divine purposes and decrees.

Having announced the crime, presented the evidence, and explained the nature of their sin, Peter then offered them pardon (Acts 3:19–26)! What a strange thing for the prosecuting attorney to become the defense attorney and the pardoning judge! Peter's burden was to encourage his people to trust Christ and experience His gracious salvation.

What did he tell them to do? First of all, *they had to repent of their sins* (see Acts 2:38; 5:31; 17:30), which means to have a change of mind about themselves, their sin, and Jesus Christ. Repentance is much more than "feeling sorry for your sins." As the little Sunday school girl said, "It means feeling sorry enough to quit!" False sorrow for sin could be mere regret ("I'm sorry I got caught!") or remorse ("I feel terrible!"), and such feelings have a tendency to pass away. Repentance is not the same as "doing penance," as though we have to make a special sacrifice to God to prove that we are sincere. True repentance is admitting that what God says is true, and because it is true, to change our mind about our sins and about the Savior.

The message of repentance was not new to the Jews, for John the Baptist had preached it and so had Jesus (Matt. 3:2; 4:17). In one sense, repentance is a gift from God (Acts 11:18); in another sense, it is the heart's response to the convicting ministry of the Spirit of God (Acts 26:20). The person who sincerely repents will have little problem putting his faith in the Savior.

Second, they had to *be converted,* "to turn again," and exercise saving faith in Jesus Christ. The biblical message is "repentance toward God, and faith toward our Lord Jesus Christ" (Acts 20:21), and the two go together. Unless we turn from our sins, we cannot put saving faith in Jesus Christ. It is unfortunate that some preachers have so ignored the doctrine of repentance that their "converts" lack a true sense of conviction of sin. Balanced evangelism presents to the sinner both repentance and faith.

Peter announced what would happen if they repented and turned to Jesus Christ: "in order that your sins may be blotted out, in order that the times of refreshing may come from the presence of the Lord, in order that He may send Jesus Christ" (literal translation). There was a promise for the individual (sins forgiven) and a promise for the nation (times of spiritual refreshing). Peter was actually calling for *national repentance,* for the nation through its leaders had denied its Messiah and condemned Him to die. The declaration is that, if the nation repented and believed, the Messiah would return and establish the promised kingdom. The nation did not repent—and certainly God knew this would happen—so the message eventually moved from the Jews to the Samaritans (Acts 8) and to the Gentiles (Acts 10).

The emphasis in Acts 3:22–25 is on *the prophets* who had announced the coming of the Messiah. Peter quoted from Moses (Deut. 18:15, 18–19) and reminded his listeners that Moses had predicted the arrival of a prophet, and this prophet was the Messiah (see Luke 24:19; John 1:19–28; 6:14). Not to obey ("hear") this prophet meant condemnation. But Moses was not the only one who foretold the coming of Jesus Christ, for all the prophets united in their witness to Him (see Luke 24:25–27, 44–48).

When Peter spoke about "these days," to what "days" was he referring? The days of the life and ministry of Jesus Christ, the days when God's prophet would speak to His people and offer them salvation. The nation's rejection of Him made them especially guilty because the Jews were the privileged "sons of the prophets and of the covenant." They had sinned against a flood of light!

When God called Abraham, He made an unconditional covenant with him and his descendants that through them the nations of the world would be blessed (Gen. 12:1–3). This promise was fulfilled when Jesus Christ came into the world through the Jewish nation (Gal. 3:6–14). The gospel message came "to the Jew first" because the Jews were God's chosen instrument through whom the Gentiles would be blessed (Acts 3:26; 13:46; Rom. 1:16). The first Christians were Jews, and the first missionaries were Jews.

But notice that Peter did not permit the "national blessings" to overshadow the personal responsibility of the individuals listening to his message (Acts 3:26). God raised up Jesus Christ and sent Him to *each one* who would turn away from his iniquities (note Acts 3:20). National repentance depends on personal repentance, the response of individual sinners to the message of salvation. Peter was addressing a large crowd, but he still made the application personal.

His message produced two opposite results: (1) some two thousand Jews believed the Word and were converted, and (2) the religious leaders of the nation rejected the message and tried to silence the apostles. We have here the beginning of the persecution about which Jesus had already warned His followers (Matt. 10:17–18; Luke 21:12–15; John 15:18—16:4).

We would expect the Sadducees to oppose the message because they did not believe in the resurrection of the human body (Acts 23:6–8). Peter's fearless declaration that Jesus Christ had been raised from the dead ran contrary to their religious beliefs. If the common people questioned the theology of their spiritual leaders, it could undermine the authority of the whole Jewish council. Instead of honestly examining the evidence, the leaders arrested the apostles and kept them in custody overnight, intending to try them the next day. However, the arrival of the temple guards could not prevent two thousand men from trusting Jesus Christ and identifying themselves with the believers in Jerusalem.

As you review this section of Acts, you cannot help but be impressed with some practical truths that should encourage all of us in our witnessing for Christ.

1. God is long suffering with lost sinners. The leaders of Israel had rejected the ministry of John the Baptist (Matt. 21:23–27) and the ministry of Jesus, and yet God gave them another opportunity to repent and be saved. They had denied and slain their own Messiah, and yet God patiently held back His judgment and sent His Spirit to deal with them. God's people today need patience as we witness to a lost world.

2. True witness involves the "bad news" of sin and guilt as well as the "good news" of salvation through faith in Jesus Christ. There can be no true faith in Christ unless first there is repentance from sin. It is the ministry of the Holy Spirit to convict lost sinners (John 16:7–11), and He will do this if we faithfully witness and use God's Word.

3. The way to reach the masses is by helping the individual sinner. Peter and John won the crippled beggar, and his transformed life led to the conversion of two thousand men! The servant of God who has no time for personal work with individual sinners will not be given many opportunities for ministering to great crowds. Like Jesus, the apostles took time for individuals.

4. The best defense of the truth of the Christian faith is a changed life. The healed beggar was "exhibit A" in Peter's defense of the resurrection of Jesus Christ. In his evangelistic ministries, the Methodist preacher Samuel Chadwick used to pray for "a Lazarus" in every campaign, some "great sinner" whose conversion would shock the community. He got the idea from John 12:9–11. God answered his prayers in meeting after meeting as infamous wicked men trusted Christ and became witnesses through their changed lives. Let's go after the "hard cases" and see what God can do!

5. Whenever God blesses, Satan shows up to oppose the work and silence the witness, and often he uses religious people to do his work. The same crowd that opposed the ministry of Jesus Christ also opposed the work of the apostles, and they will oppose our ministry today. Expect it—but don't let it stop you! The important thing is not that we are comfortable, but that the name of the Lord is glorified through the preaching of the gospel.

6. God has promised to bless and use His Word, so let's be faithful to witness. Jesus even prayed that our witness would have success (John 17:20), so we have every reason to be encouraged. There is power in the name of Jesus, so we need not fear to witness and call sinners to repent.

7. The name of Jesus Christ still has power! While we may not perform the same apostolic miracles today that were seen in the early church, we can still claim the authority of Jesus Christ as He has instructed us in the Word.

We can preach the "remission of sins" in His name (Luke 24:47) so that people might believe and have "life through his name" (John 20:31). We can give someone a cup of cold water in His name (Mark 9:41), and we can receive a child in His name (Matt. 18:5). These ministries may not seem as spectacular as healing a cripple, but they are still important to the work of God.

We can ask in His name as we pray (John 14:13–14; 15:16; 16:23–26). When we ask the Father for something "in the name of Jesus Christ," it is as though Jesus Himself were asking it. If we remember this, it will help to keep us from asking for things unworthy of His name.

Yes, the name of Jesus Christ still has authority and power. Let's go forth in His name and conquer!

CHAPTER FOUR
Acts 4:5–31
PERSECUTION, PRAYER, AND POWER

The early church had none of the "advantages" that some ministries boast of and depend on today. They did not have big budgets provided by wealthy donors. Their pastors lacked credentials from the accepted schools, nor did they have the endorsement of the influential political leaders of that day. Most of their ministers had jail records and would probably have a hard time today *joining* our churches, let alone *leading* them. What really was the secret of their success? This chapter provides the answer: the Christians of the early church knew how to pray so that God's hand could work in mighty power.

When asked to explain the secret of his remarkable ministry, the noted British preacher Charles Haddon Spurgeon replied, "My people pray for me." St. Augustine said, "Pray as though everything depended on God, and work as though everything depended on you." Prayer is not an escape from responsibility; it is our *response* to God's *ability*. True prayer energizes us for service and battle.

Once again, the focus of attention is on the name of the Lord Jesus Christ (Acts 4:7, 10, 12, 17–18). In this chapter, we see what three groups of people do with His name.

The Apostles: Defending His Name (4:5–14)
The court (vv. 5–7). The court was essentially composed of the high priest's family. The Jewish religious

system had become so corrupt that the offices were passed from one relative to another without regard for the Word of God. When Annas was deposed from the priesthood, Caiaphas his son-in-law was appointed. In fact, five of Annas's sons held the office at one time or another. Somebody has defined a "nepotist" as "a man who, being evil, knows how to give good gifts to his children." Annas certainly qualified.

This was an official meeting of the Sanhedrin (Acts 4:15), the same council that a few months before had condemned Jesus to die. In fact, these officials recognized Peter and John as the associates of Jesus (Acts 4:13). The Sanhedrin was charged with the responsibility of protecting the Jewish faith, and this meant that they had to examine every new teacher and teaching that appeared in the land (see Deut. 13). They certainly had the right to investigate what the church was doing, but they did not have the right to arrest innocent men and then refuse to honestly examine the evidence.

Their question was legal, but they did everything they could to avoid admitting that a miracle had taken place (Acts 4:14). They were evasive and merely referred to the miracle as "this." They were probably scornful as well, so that their question might be paraphrased, "Where did common people like you get the power and authority to do a thing like this?" It was once again the question of "By whose name?" After all, the apostles might be in league with the devil! Even Satan can perform miracles!

The case (vv. 8–14). Peter spoke in the power of the Holy Spirit of God. Note that Peter was again filled with the Spirit (see Acts 2:4) and would experience another filling before the day ended (Acts 4:31). There is one baptism of the Spirit, and this is at conversion (1 Cor. 12:13), but there must be many fillings of the Spirit if the believer is to be an effective witness for Jesus Christ (Eph. 5:18ff.).

Peter respectfully began with an explanation of how the miracle occurred. Certainly the members of the Sanhedrin had seen the crippled beggar many times, and perhaps they had even given alms to him and piously prayed for him. How was this well-known man healed? "By the name of Jesus Christ of Nazareth!" Those words must have pierced the hearts of the members of the council! They thought they had finished with the prophet from Nazareth, and now His followers were telling everybody that Jesus was alive! Since the Sadducees did not believe in the resurrection of the dead, Peter's statement was almost a declaration of war!

But the Spirit was telling Peter what to say (see Luke 21:12–15), and the apostle quoted Psalm 118:22, definitely a messianic reference (see Matt. 21:42; 1 Peter 2:4–8). He made it clear that the members of the council were "the builders" and that they had rejected God's Stone, Jesus, the Son of God.

The image of "the stone" was not new to these men who were experts in the Old Testament Scriptures. They knew that the "rock" was a symbol of God (Deut. 32:4, 15, 18, 31; 2 Sam. 22:2; Ps. 18:2; Isa.

28:16), and that the prophet Daniel had used the rock to picture Messiah and the coming of His kingdom on earth (Dan. 2:31–45). The Jews stumbled over the Rock (Rom. 9:32; 1 Cor. 1:23) and rejected Him, just as Psalm 118:22 had predicted. However, to those who have trusted Him, Jesus Christ is the precious Cornerstone (1 Peter 2:4–8) and the chief Cornerstone (Eph. 2:20).

Peter went on to explain that Jesus is not only the Stone, but He is also the Savior (Acts 4:12). Peter saw in the healing of the beggar a picture of the spiritual healing that comes in salvation. "Made whole" in Acts 4:9 is a translation of the same Greek word that is translated "saved" in Acts 4:12, for salvation means wholeness and spiritual health. Jesus Christ is the Great Physician who alone can heal mankind's greatest malady, the sickness of sin (Mark 2:14–17). Of course, Peter also had "all the people of Israel" in mind as he spoke (see Acts 4:10) because the message was still going out exclusively to the Jews. Even Psalm 118, from which Peter quoted, speaks of a future national salvation for Israel.

The Council: Opposing His Name (4:15–22)

Their problem (vv. 13–14). They were in a dilemma; no matter which way they turned, they were "trapped." They could not deny the miracle, because the man was standing before them, and yet they could not explain how "uneducated and untrained men" (NASB) could perform such a mighty deed. Peter and John were ordinary fishermen, not professional scribes or authorized ministers of the Jewish religion. They were disciples of Jesus of Nazareth, but—He was dead! The council took notice of the courage and confidence of Peter and John, as well as the power of Peter's words, and it all added up to perplexity.

It is important to note that, of itself, the miracle was not proof of the resurrection of Christ or even of the truth of Peter's message. Satan can perform miracles (2 Thess. 2:9–10) and false prophets can do wonders (Deut. 13:1–5). The miracle and the message, *in the context of all that had been going on since Pentecost,* was one more evidence that Jesus Christ was alive and at work in the church by His Holy Spirit. In both sermons, Peter used the Old Testament to support and explain his claims, and this is one evidence of a true prophet of God (Deut. 13:1–5; Isa. 8:20). Miracles are not a substitute for the Word of God (Luke 16:27–31).

Their deliberation (vv. 15–18). The council did not seek for truth, but rather sought for some way to avoid the truth! Had they honestly considered the evidence and meekly listened to the message, they might have been saved, but their pride and hardness of heart stood in the way. Some of the chief priests and elders had experienced a similar dilemma during Passover when they had tried to trap Jesus in the temple (Matt. 21:23–27). Some people never learn! But their response is proof that miracles alone can never convict or convert the lost sinner. Only the Word of God can do that (see John 11:45–53; Acts 14:1–20).

Their conclusion. They wanted to "let the thing die a natural death." This meant threatening the apostles and forbidding them to teach and preach in the name of Jesus. This official sentence shows how much the enemy fears the witness of the church, for Satan has been trying to silence God's people from the very beginning. Sad to say, he has succeeded with far too many Christians, the "silent witnesses" of the church. Even the existential philosopher Albert Camus said, "What the world expects of Christians is that Christians should speak out, loud and clear … in such a way that never a doubt, never the slightest doubt, could arise in the heart of the simplest man."

The council did not want the gospel message to spread, and yet that is exactly what happened! From 120 praying men and women in Acts 1, the church increased to more than 3,000 on the day of Pentecost, and now there were more than 5,000 disciples in the fellowship. In the days that followed, "believers were the more added to the Lord, multitudes both of men and women" (Acts 5:14; and see 6:1, 7). Satan's attempts to silence the church only led to a stronger witness for the Lord.

The failure of the council (vv. 19–22). This was evident when Peter refused to be intimidated by their threats. All of us need to follow Peter's example and make our decisions on the basis of "Is it right?" and not "Is it popular?" or "Is it safe?" However, we must be sure that we have the clear teaching of the Word of God on our side before we take a stand against the authority of the government. Peter knew what the Lord had commanded the believers to do (Acts 1:8), and he was going to obey Him at any cost.

It is popular today to promote various causes by defying the government, disobeying the law, and defending these actions on the basis of conscience. Since even some Christians are involved in this approach to social action, it is important to understand the kind of "civil disobedience" practiced by people in the Bible. Peter and John are not the only ones who disobeyed the authorities in order to serve God. A list of "dedicated conscientious objectors" would include, among others, the Jewish midwives (Ex. 1), Moses' parents (Heb. 11:23), Daniel (Dan. 1; 6), and the three Hebrew children (Dan. 3). When you examine the records, you discover the biblical principles by which they operated, principles that are not always followed today.

To begin with, each of these "objectors" had a message from God that could not be questioned. The midwives and Moses' parents knew that it was wrong to murder the babies. Daniel and his friends, and the three Hebrew men, knew that it was wrong to eat food offered to idols or to bow down to idols in worship. Peter and John knew that they were under orders from their Master to preach the gospel to the ends of the earth, and that it would be wrong to obey the

Sanhedrin. All of these people were faithfully obeying a clear word from God and not just following some selfish personal whim of their own.

Second, their convictions touched every area of their lives, In other words, they did everything "with conscience toward God" (1 Peter 2:19) because they belonged to God. The university student today whose conscience permits him to cheat on exams or drive while drunk, but not register for military service, does not convince me that he is really cultivating a healthy conscience. When a person's *total life* is under the direction of a godly conscience, then I find it easier to have confidence in his unpopular decisions.

Note also that our examples from the Bible acted with respect and courtesy, even when they defied the law. It is possible for Christians to respect authority and at the same time disobey the authorities (see Rom. 13; Titus 3:1–2; 1 Peter 2:13–25). Daniel tried to avoid getting his guard into trouble, and the apostles used their arrests as opportunities for witness. This is quite a contrast to some of the modern "Christian objectors" who seem to major on denunciation and accusation rather than loving witness.

Of course, the greatest example of unjust suffering is that of Jesus Christ, and we must imitate Him (see 1 Peter 2:13–25). Jesus teaches us that righteous protest against injustice always involves sacrifice and suffering, and must be motivated by love. God's people must be careful not to clothe their prejudice in the garments of "righteous indignation" and pass themselves off as courageous soldiers of conscience. We must examine our own hearts honestly to make certain we are not conducting a "holy war" just to satisfy inner frustrations.

Because they had no real case to offer, the council could only threaten the men and let them go. After all, when you have a living miracle before you, as well as an approving public around you, you must be careful what you do!

The Church: Calling on His Name (4:23–31)

The greatest concentration of power in Jerusalem that day was in the prayer meeting that followed the trial. This is one of the truly great prayers recorded in the Bible, and it is a good example for us to follow.

To begin with, it was a prayer that was born out of witness and service for the Lord. Peter and John had just come in "from the trenches," and the church met to pray in order to defeat the enemy. Too often today, believers gather for prayer as though attending a concert or a party. There is little sense of urgency and danger because most of us are comfortable in our Christian walk. If more of God's people were witnessing for Christ in daily life, there would be more urgency and blessing when the church meets for prayer.

It was a united prayer meeting as they "lifted up their voice to God with one accord" (Acts 4:24; see 1:14). The people were of one heart and mind, and God was pleased to answer their requests. Division in the church always hinders prayer and robs the church of spiritual power.

Their praying was based solidly on the Word of God, in this case, Psalm 2. The Word of God and prayer must always go together (John 15:7). In His Word, God speaks to us and tells us what He wants to do. In prayer, we speak to Him and make ourselves available to accomplish His will. True prayer is not telling God what to do, but asking God to do His will in us and through us (1 John 5:14–15). It means getting God's will done on earth, not man's will done in heaven.

They did not pray to have their circumstances changed or their enemies put out of office. Rather, they asked God to empower them to make the best use of their circumstances and to accomplish what He had already determined (Acts 4:28). This was not "fatalism" but faith in the Lord of history who has a perfect plan and is always victorious. They asked for divine enablement, not escape, and God gave them the power that they needed.

"Do not pray for easy lives," wrote Phillips Brooks. "Pray to be stronger men and women. Do not pray for tasks equal to your powers. Pray for powers equal to your tasks." That is the way the early Christians prayed, and that is the way God's people should pray today.

They addressed God as "Sovereign Lord," the God who is in control of all things. The Greek word gives us our English word *despot,* a ruler who exercises absolute power, either benevolently or abusively. Simeon used this same title when he prayed in the temple (Luke 2:29). It is good to know the Sovereign Lord when you are experiencing persecution.

They also approached Him as the Creator, for, after all, if your Father is "Lord of heaven and earth," what have you to fear (see Matt. 11:25–30)? Nehemiah approached God on this same basis (Neh. 9:6), and so did the psalmist (see Ps. 145) and the prophet Isaiah (Isa. 42). Years later, when he wrote his first epistle, Peter encouraged suffering saints to yield themselves to the faithful Creator (1 Peter 4:19).

Psalm 2 describes the revolt of the nations against the Lord and His Christ. The psalm originally grew out of the crowning of a new king in Israel, perhaps David, but its ultimate message points to the King of Kings, Jesus Christ. Whenever a new king was enthroned, the vassal rulers around were required to come and submit to him, but some of them refused to do this. God only laughed at their revolt, for He knew that they could never stand up against His King.

The early believers applied the message of this psalm to their own situation and identified their adversaries as Herod, Pilate, the Romans, and the Jews. These enemies had "ganged up" against Jesus Christ and even crucified Him, yet God raised Him from the dead and enthroned Him in heaven. All of this was a part of God's perfect plan (see Acts 2:23; 3:18), so there was no need to fear.

The early church strongly believed in God's sovereignty and His perfect plan for His people. But note that they did not permit their faith in divine sovereignty to destroy human responsibility, for they were faithful to witness and pray. It is when God's people get out of balance and overemphasize either sovereignty or responsibility that the church loses power. Again, we are reminded of Augustine's wise words, "Pray as though everything depends on God, and work as though everything depended on you." Faith in a sovereign Lord is a tremendous encouragement for God's people to keep serving the Lord when the going is difficult.

They did not ask for protection; they asked for power. They did not ask for fire from heaven to destroy the enemy (see Luke 9:51–56) but for power from heaven to preach the Word and heal the sick (see Matt. 5:10–12, 43–48). Their great desire was for boldness in the face of opposition (see Acts 4:17). The emphasis is on the hand of God at work in the life of the church (Acts 4:28, 30), not the hand of man at work for God. Believing prayer releases God's power and enables God's hand to move (Isa. 50:2; 64:1–8).

Finally, note that they wanted to glorify God's Child (Servant) Jesus Christ (Acts 4:27, 30). It was His name that gave them power to minister the Word and to perform miracles, and His name alone deserved the glory. The glory of God, not the needs of men, is the highest purpose of answered prayer.

God's answer was to shake the place where they were meeting and to fill the people once again with the Spirit of God (Acts 4:31). This gave them the boldness that they needed to continue to serve God in spite of official opposition. This was not a "second Pentecost" because there cannot be another Pentecost any more than there can be another Calvary. It was a new filling of the Spirit to equip the believers to serve the Lord and minister to the people.

We will consider Acts 4:32–37 in our next study, but it is worth noting that the new fullness of the Spirit also created a deeper unity among the people (Acts 4:34) and a greater desire to sacrifice and share with one another. They enjoyed "great power" and "great grace," which ought to be the marks of a "great" church. This led to a great ingathering of souls for the Lord.

"Lord, thou art God!" What a declaration of faith and what a practical application of good theology! However, if their lives had not been submitted to His control, they could not have prayed that way. Boldness in prayer is the result of faithfulness in life and service. The sovereignty of God is not an abstract doctrine that we accept and defend. It is a living truth that we act on and depend on for every need. When you are loyal to the Lord and put Him first (Acts 4:19), then you can trust Him to be faithful to you and see you through.

The name of Jesus Christ has not lost its power, but many of God's people have lost their power because they have stopped praying to the sovereign God.

"Nothing lies beyond the reach of prayer except that which lies outside the will of God." I don't know who first said that, but the statement is absolutely true. Dr. R. A. Torrey, the noted evangelist and educator, said, "Pray for great things, expect great things, work for great things, but above all—pray."

The early church prayed, and God answered in mighty power.

CHAPTER FIVE
Acts 4:32—5:16
BEWARE OF THE SERPENT!

Satan had failed completely in his attempt to silence the witness of the church. However, the enemy never gives up; he simply changes his strategy. His first approach had been to attack the church from the outside, hoping that arrest and threats would frighten the leaders. When that failed, Satan decided to attack the church *from the inside* and use people who were a part of the fellowship.

We must face the fact that Satan is a clever foe. If he does not succeed as the "devouring lion" (1 Peter 5:8), then he attacks again as the "deceiving serpent" or an "angel of light" (2 Cor. 11:3, 13–14). Satan is both a murderer and a liar (John 8:44), and the church must be prepared for both attacks.

The Generosity of the Believers (4:32–37)
The believers had prayed and God's Spirit had filled them and given them new power. The church that depends on believing prayer will know the blessing of the Holy Spirit in its ministry. How can we tell when a local church is really filled with the Spirit? When you go back to the record of the first filling at Pentecost (Acts 2:44–47), you discover three outstanding characteristics of a Spirit-filled church.

It is unified (2:44, 46). This is a God-given spiritual unity, not a man-made organizational uniformity. The church is an organism that is held together by life, and that life comes through the Holy Spirit. Of course, the church must be organized, for if an organism is not organized, it will die. However, when the organization starts to hinder spiritual life and ministry, then the church becomes just another religious institution that exists to keep itself going. When the Holy Spirit is at work, God's people will be united in their doctrinal beliefs, as well as in fellowship, giving, and worship (Acts 4:42).

A Spirit-filled church is magnified and will have "favor with all the people" (2:47). In spite of the opposition of the rulers, the common people were drawn to the believers because something new and exciting was happening. When the religious leaders tried to silence the church, it was their fear of the people that restrained them (Acts 4:21; 5:26). Yes, a Spirit-filled church will have its enemies, but what the

Lord is doing will attract the attention and the admiration of people who are hungry to know God.

A Spirit-filled church is multiplied, because the Lord will daily add new believers to the church (2:47). Evangelism will not be the work of a chosen few, but the daily delight and ministry of the whole congregation. In the early church, each member sought to be an effective witness for Jesus Christ, no matter where he happened to be. No wonder the church grew from 120 to over 5,000 in just a short time!

How did Satan's attack affect the spiritual condition of the church? It had no affect at all! The fact that Peter and John were arrested, tried, and threatened had absolutely no effect on the spiritual life of the church, for the church was still unified (Acts 4:32), magnified (Acts 4:33), and multiplied (Acts 4:32)!

One evidence of the unity of the church was the way they sacrificed and shared with one another. When the Holy Spirit is at work, giving is a blessing and not a burden. We must keep in mind that this "Christian communism" was very unlike the political Communism of our day. What the believers did was purely voluntary (Acts 5:4) and was motivated by love. No doubt many of the new believers were visitors in Jerusalem, having come for the feasts, and they had to depend on their Christian friends to help meet their daily needs.

Nor should we think that every believer sold all his goods and brought the money to the apostles. Acts 4:34 indicates that some of the members "from time to time" sold various pieces of property and donated to the common treasury. When the assembly had a need, the Spirit directed someone to sell something and meet the need.

While the early church's spirit of sacrifice and loving generosity is worthy of our emulation, believers today are not required to imitate these practices. The principles of Christian giving are outlined in the Epistles, especially in 2 Corinthians 8—9, and nowhere are we instructed to bring our money and lay it at the pastor's feet (Acts 4:35) as though he were an apostle. It is the *spirit* of their giving that is important to us today and not the "letter" of their system.

Joseph, nicknamed "Barnabas" (son of encouragement), is introduced at this point for several reasons. First, he was a generous giver and illustrated the very thing Dr. Luke was describing. Second, his noble act apparently filled Ananias and Sapphira with envy so that they attempted to impress the church with their giving and ended up being killed. Third, Barnabas had a most important ministry in the church and is mentioned at least twenty-five times in the book of Acts and another five times in the Epistles. In fact, it is Barnabas who encouraged Paul in his early service for the Lord (Acts 9:26–27; 11:19–30; 13:1–5) and who gave his cousin John Mark the encouragement he needed after his failure (Acts 13:13; 15:36–41; Col. 4:10).

Levites were not permitted to own land, so it is

difficult to understand how Barnabas acquired the property that he sold. Perhaps that particular law (Num. 18:20; Deut. 10:9) applied only in Palestine and the property was in Cyprus, or perhaps the corrupt religious leaders had become lax in enforcing the law. There is much we do not know about Joseph Barnabas, but this we do know: he was a Spirit-filled man who was an encouragement to the church because he gave his all to the Lord. Not every believer can be like Peter and John, but we can all be like Barnabas and have a ministry of encouragement.

The Hypocrisy of Ananias and Sapphira (5:1–11)

George MacDonald wrote, "Half of the misery in the world comes from trying to *look,* instead of trying to *be,* what one is not." The name that Jesus gave to this practice is "hypocrisy," which simply means "wearing a mask, playing the actor." We must not think that failure to reach our ideals is hypocrisy, because no believer lives up to all that he or she knows or has in the Lord. Hypocrisy is *deliberate* deception, trying to make people think we are more spiritual than we really are.

When I was pastoring my first church, the Lord led us to build a new sanctuary. We were not a wealthy congregation, so our plans had to be modest. At one point in the planning, I suggested to the architect that perhaps we could build a simple edifice with a more elaborate facade at the front to make it look more like an expensive church.

"Absolutely not!" he replied. "A church stands for truth and honesty, and any church I design will not have a facade! A building should tell the truth and not pretend to be what it isn't."

Years later, I ran across this poem, which is a sermon in itself:

> They build the front just like St. Mark's,
> Or like Westminster Abbey;
> And then, as if to cheat the Lord,
> They make the back parts shabby.

That was the sin of Ananias and Sapphira: putting on a lovely "front" in order to conceal the shabby sin in their lives, sin that cost them their lives.

Ananias means "God is gracious," but he learned that God is also holy, and Sapphira means "beautiful," but her heart was ugly with sin. No doubt some people are shocked when they read that God killed two people just because they lied about a business transaction and about their church giving. But when you consider the features connected with this sin, you have to agree that God did the right thing by judging them.

It is worth noting that the Lord judges sin severely *at the beginning of a new period in salvation history.* Just after the tabernacle was erected, God killed Nadab and Abihu for trying to present "false fire" to the Lord (Lev. 10). He also had Achan killed for disobeying orders after Israel had entered the Promised Land (Josh. 7). While God was certainly not responsible for their sins,

He did use these judgments as warnings to the people, and even to us (1 Cor. 10:11–12).

To begin with, the sin of Ananias and Sapphira was *energized by Satan* (Acts 5:3), and that is a serious matter. If Satan cannot defeat the church by attacks from the outside, he will get on the inside and go to work (Acts 20:28–31). He knows how to lie to the minds and hearts of church members, even genuine Christians, and get them to follow his orders. We forget that the admonition about the spiritual armor (Eph. 6:10–18) was written to God's people, not to unbelievers, because it is the Christians who are in danger of being used by Satan to accomplish his evil purposes.

Oliver Wendell Holmes wrote, "Sin has many tools, but a lie is the handle which fits them all." Satan is a liar and a murderer (John 8:44). He lied to and *through* this couple, and the lie led to their deaths. When God judged Ananias and Sapphira, He was also judging Satan. He was letting everybody know that He would not tolerate deception in His church.

Their sin was *motivated by pride,* and pride is a sin that God especially hates and judges (Prov. 8:13). No doubt the church was praising God for the generous offering that Barnabas had brought when Satan whispered to the couple, "You can also bask in this kind of glory! You can make others think that you are as spiritual as Barnabas!" Instead of resisting Satan's approaches, they yielded to him and planned their strategy.

Jesus made it very clear that we must be careful how we give, lest the glory that belongs to God should be given to us (Matt. 6:1–4, 19–34). The Pharisees were adept at calling attention to their gifts, and they received the praises of men—but that's all they received! Whatever we possess, God has given to us; we are stewards, not owners. We must use what He gives us for His glory alone (see John 5:44).

Daniel Defoe called pride "the first peer and president of hell." Indeed, it was pride that transformed Lucifer into Satan (Isa. 14:12–15), and it was pride ("Ye shall be as gods") that caused our first parents to sin (Gen. 3). Pride opens the door to every other sin, for once we are more concerned with our reputation than our character, there is no end to the things we will do just to make ourselves "look good" before others.

A third feature of their sin was especially wicked: their sin was *directed against God's church.* We have reason to believe that Ananias and Sapphira were believers. The spiritual level of the church at that time was so high that it is doubtful that a mere "professor" could have gotten into the fellowship without being detected. The fact that they were able to lie to the Spirit (Acts 5:3) and tempt the Spirit (Acts 5:9) would indicate that they had the Spirit of God living within.

God loves His church and is jealous over it, for the church was purchased by the blood of God's Son

(Acts 20:28; Eph. 5:25) and has been put on earth to glorify Him and do His work. Satan wants to destroy the church, and the easiest way to do it is to use those who are within the fellowship. Had Peter not been discerning, Ananias and Sapphira would have become influential people in the church! Satan would have been working through them to accomplish his purposes!

The church is "the pillar and ground of the truth" (1 Tim. 3:15), and Satan attacks it with his lies. The church is God's temple in which He dwells (1 Cor. 3:16), and Satan wants to move in and dwell there too. The church is God's army (2 Tim. 2:1–4), and Satan seeks to get into the ranks as many traitors as he can. The church is safe so long as Satan is attacking from the outside, but when he gets on the inside, the church is in danger.

It is easy for us to condemn Ananias and Sapphira for their dishonesty, but we need to examine our own lives to see if our profession is backed up by our practice. Do we really mean everything we pray about in public? Do we sing the hymns and gospel songs sincerely or routinely? "These people honor me with their lips, but their hearts are far from me" (Matt. 15:8 NIV). If God killed "religious deceivers" today, how many church members would be left?

What is described in this chapter is not a case of church discipline. Rather it is an example of God's personal judgment. "The Lord shall judge his people. It is a fearful thing to fall into the hands of the living God" (Heb. 10:30–31). Had Ananias and Sapphira judged their own sin, God would not have judged them (1 Cor. 11:31), but they agreed to lie, and God had to deal with them.

Ananias was dead and buried, and Sapphira did not even know it! Satan always keeps his servants in the dark, while God guides His servants in the light (John 15:15). Peter accused her of tempting God's Spirit, that is, deliberately disobeying God and seeing how far God would go (Ex. 17:2; Deut. 6:16). They were actually defying God and daring Him to act—and He acted, with swiftness and finality. "Thou shalt not tempt the Lord thy God" (Matt. 4:7).

We must keep in mind that their sin was not in robbing God of money but in lying to Him and robbing Him of glory. They were not required to sell the property, and, having sold it, they were not required to give any of the money to the church (Acts 5:4). Their lust for recognition conceived sin in their hearts (Acts 5:4, 9), and that sin eventually produced death (James 1:15).

The result was a wave of godly fear that swept over the church and over all those who heard the story (Acts 5:11). We have moved from "great power" and "great grace" (Acts 4:33) to "great fear," and all of these ought to be present in the church. "Let us have grace, whereby we may serve God acceptably with reverence and godly fear: for our God is a consuming fire" (Heb. 12:28–29).

The Ministry of the Apostles (5:12–16)

We have learned that the Spirit-filled church is unified, magnified, and multiplied. Satan wants to divide the church, disgrace the church, and decrease the church, and he will do it, if we let him.

But the church described here completely triumphed over the attacks of Satan! The people were still unified (Acts 5:12), magnified (Acts 5:13), and multiplied (Acts 5:14). Multitudes were added to the Lord, and for the first time, Luke mentions the salvation of women. Both in his gospel and in Acts, Luke has a great deal to say about women and their relationship to Christ and the church. There are at least a dozen references in Acts to women, as Luke shows the key role women played in the apostolic church. This is a remarkable thing when you consider the general position of women in the culture of that day (see Gal. 3:26–28).

God gave the apostles power to perform great miracles. While it is true that some of the ordinary members exercised miraculous powers (Acts 6:8), it was primarily the apostles who did the miracles. These "signs and wonders" were God's way of authenticating their ministry (Rom. 15:18–19; 2 Cor. 12:12; Heb. 2:4).

Just as there were special judgments at the beginning of a new era, so there were also special miracles. We find no miracles performed in Genesis, but at the beginning of the age of law, Moses performed great signs and wonders. Elijah and Elisha were miracle workers at the beginning of the great era of the prophets, and Jesus and the apostles performed signs and wonders when the Gospel Age was inaugurated. Each time God opened a new door, He called man's attention to it. It was His way of saying, "Follow these leaders, because I have sent them."

The mighty wonders performed by the apostles were the fulfillment of the Lord's promise that they would do "greater works" in answer to believing prayer (John 14:13–14). When Jesus performed miracles during His ministry on earth, He had three purposes in mind: (1) to show compassion and meet human need; (2) to present His credentials as the Son of God; and (3) to convey spiritual truth. For example, when He fed the five thousand, the miracle met their physical need, revealed Him as the Son of God, and gave Him opportunity to preach a sermon about the Bread of Life (John 6).

The apostolic miracles followed a similar pattern. Peter and John healed the crippled beggar and met his need, but Peter used that miracle to preach a salvation sermon and to prove to the people and the council that he and John were indeed the servants of the living Christ. One of the qualifications for an apostle was that he had seen the risen Christ (Acts 1:22; 1 Cor. 9:1), and, since nobody can claim that experience today, there are no apostles in the church. The apostles and prophets laid the foundation for the church (Eph. 2:20), and the pastors, teachers, and evangelists are building on it. If there are no apostles, there can be no "signs of an apostle" as are found in the book of Acts (2 Cor. 12:12).

This certainly does not mean that God is limited and can no longer perform miracles for His people! But it does mean that the need for confirming miracles has passed away. We now have the completed Word of God, and we test teachers by their message, not by miracles (1 John 2:18–29; 4:1–6). And we must keep in mind that Satan is a counterfeiter and well able to deceive the unwary. In the Old Testament, any prophet who performed miracles but, at the same time, led the people away from God's Word, was considered a false prophet and was killed (Deut. 13). The important thing was not the miracles, but whether his message was true to the Word of God.

A radio listener wrote me and wanted to debate this issue with me, insisting that there were instances today of people being raised from the dead. I wrote him a kind letter and asked him to send me the testimonies of the witnesses, the kind of evidence that could be presented in court. He wrote back and honestly admitted that that kind of evidence was not available, but he still believed it because he had heard a TV preacher say it was so. Most of the miracles recorded in the Bible were out in the open for everybody to see, and it would not be difficult to prove them in a court of law.

Peter and the other apostles found themselves ministering as their Lord had ministered, with people coming from all over, bringing their sick and afflicted (Matt. 4:23–25; Mark 1:45; 2:8–12). The Twelve must have found it very difficult to walk down the street, for people crowded around them and laid before them sick people on their pallets. Some of the people even had the superstitious belief that there was healing in Peter's shadow.

It is significant that *all of these people were healed.* There were no failures and nobody was sent away because he or she "did not have faith to be healed." These were days of mighty power when God was speaking to Israel and telling them that Jesus of Nazareth was indeed their Messiah and Savior. "For the Jews require a sign" (1 Cor. 1:22), and God gave signs to them. The important thing was not the healing of the afflicted, but the winning of lost souls, as multitudes were added to the fellowship. The Spirit gave them power for wonders and power for witness (Acts 1:8), for miracles apart from God's Word cannot save the lost.

The greatest miracle of all is the transformation of a lost sinner into a child of God by the grace of God. That is the miracle that meets the greatest need, lasts the longest, and costs the greatest price—the blood of God's Son.

And that is one miracle we can all participate in as we share the message of the gospel, "the power of God unto salvation to every one that believeth" (Rom. 1:16).

CHAPTER SIX
Acts 5:17–42
TRUTH AND CONSEQUENCES

After Pentecost, the message of the resurrection of Jesus Christ spread rapidly in Jerusalem as Spirit-empowered witnesses shared the gospel with the lost. Signs and wonders accompanied the preaching of the Word, and no one could deny that God was at work in a new way among His ancient people.

But not everybody was happy with the success of the church. The "religious establishment" that had opposed the ministry of Jesus, and then crucified Him, took the same hostile approach toward the apostles. "If they persecuted Me, they will also persecute you," said Jesus. "They will put you out of the synagogues; yes, the time is coming that whoever kills you will think that he offers God service" (John 15:20; 16:2 NKJV). These words were beginning to be fulfilled.

It was the age-old conflict between living truth and dead tradition. The new wine could not be put into the old wineskins, nor could the new cloth be sewn on the worn-out garments (Matt. 9:14–17). The English martyr Hugh Latimer said, "Whenever you see persecution, there is more than a probability that truth is on the persecuted side."

We see in this account four different responses to God's truth, responses we still see today.

The Council: Attacking the Truth (5:17–28)

The high priest and his associates had three reasons for arresting the apostles (this time it was *all* of the apostles) and bringing them to trial. To begin with, Peter and John had not obeyed the official orders to stop preaching in the name of Jesus Christ. They were guilty of defying the law of the nation. Second, the witness of the church was refuting the doctrines held by the Sadducees, giving every evidence that Jesus Christ was alive. Third, the religious leaders were filled with envy ("indignation") at the great success of these untrained and unauthorized men (see Matt. 27:18; Acts 13:45). The traditions of the fathers had not attracted that much attention or gained that many followers in such a short time. It is amazing how much envy can be hidden under the disguise of "defending the faith."

The apostles did not resist arrest or organize a public protest. They quietly went along with the temple guard and actually spent a few hours in the public jail. But during the night, an angel set them free and told them to return to their witnessing in the temple. (The Sadducees, of course, did not believe in angels. See Acts 23:8.) In the book of Acts, you will find several instances of angelic ministries as God cared for His people (Acts 8:26; 10:3, 7; 12:7–11, 23; 27:23). The angels are servants who minister to us as we serve the Lord (Heb. 1:14).

As in Peter's deliverance (Acts 12:7–11), neither

the guards nor the leaders knew that the prisoners had been liberated. You are tempted to smile as you imagine the surprised looks on the faces of the guards when they discovered that their most important prisoners were gone. And just imagine the astonishment of the envious members of the Sanhedrin when they heard the report! Here they were trying to *stop* the miracles, but their actions only *multiplied* the miracles!

What a contrast between the apostles and the members of the council. The council was educated, ordained, and approved, and yet they had no ministry of power. The apostles were ordinary laymen, yet God's power was at work in their lives. The council was trying desperately to protect themselves and their dead traditions, while the apostles were risking their lives to share the living Word of God. The dynamic church was enjoying the new; the dead council was defending the old.

You find a variety of emotions in this section: envy (Acts 5:17), bewilderment (Acts 5:24), and fear (Acts 5:26; see 4:21 and Matt. 21:26). Yet, when the apostles came in, the high priest boldly accused them of defying the law and causing trouble. He would not even use the name of Jesus Christ, but instead said "this name" and "this man's blood," lest by speaking His name he would defile his lips or bring down the wrath of God (see John 15:21).

But even this hateful indictment was an admission that the church was increasing and getting the job done! The wrath of man was bringing praise to the Lord (Ps. 76:10). The high priest realized that if the apostles were right, then the Jewish leaders had been wrong in condemning Jesus Christ. Indeed, if the apostles were right, then the council was guilty of His blood (Matt. 27:25; 1 Thess. 2:14–16). As this "trial" progressed, the apostles became the judges and the council became the accused.

The Apostles: Affirming the Truth (5:29–32)

The apostles did not change their convictions (Acts 4:19–20). They obeyed God and trusted Him to take care of the consequences. They could not serve two masters, and they had already declared whose side they were on. Had they been diplomats instead of ambassadors (2 Cor. 5:20), they could have pleased everybody and escaped a beating. But they stood firmly for the Lord, and He honored their courage and faith.

Neither did they change their message (Acts 5:30–32). Peter indicted the leaders for the death of Jesus (see Acts 3:13–14; 4:10), and boldly affirmed once again that Jesus Christ had been raised from the dead. Not only was Jesus raised from the dead, but He was also exalted by God to heaven. The work of the Holy Spirit in recent days was evidence that Jesus had returned to heaven and sent His Spirit as He promised. The Sadducees certainly did not rejoice to hear the apostles speak about resurrection from the dead.

That Jesus Christ is at God's right hand is a key theme in the Scriptures. The right hand is, of course, the place of honor, power, and authority. Psalm 110:1 is the basic prophecy, but there are numerous references: Matthew 22:44; Mark 14:62; 16:19; Acts 2:33–34; 5:31; Romans 8:34; Ephesians 1:20; Colossians 3:1; Hebrews 1:3; 8:1; 10:12; 12:2; and 1 Peter 3:22. Soon, Stephen would see Jesus standing at God's right hand (Acts 7:55).

In his second sermon, Peter had called Jesus "the Prince of life" (Acts 3:15); and here he called Him "a Prince and a Savior." The word *Prince* means "a pioneer, one who leads the way, an originator." The Sanhedrin was not interested in pioneering anything; all they wanted to do was protect their vested interests and keep things exactly as they were (see John 11:47–52). As the "Pioneer of life," Jesus saves us and leads us into exciting experiences as we walk "in newness of life" (Rom. 6:4). There are always new trails to blaze.

Hebrews 2:10 calls Him "the Pioneer [captain] of their salvation," for our salvation experience must never become static. The Christian life is not a parking lot; it is a launching pad! It is not enough just to be born again; we must also grow spiritually (2 Peter 3:18) and make progress in our walk. In Hebrews 12:2, Jesus is called "the Pioneer [author] … of our faith," which suggests that He leads us into new experiences that test our faith and help it to grow. One of the major themes of Hebrews is "let us press on to maturity" (Heb. 6:1 NASB), and we cannot mature unless we follow Christ, the Pioneer, into new areas of faith and ministry.

The title *Savior* was not new to the members of the council, for the word was used for physicians (who save people's lives), philosophers (who solve people's problems), and statesmen (who save people from danger and war). It was even applied to the emperor. But only Jesus Christ is the true and living Savior who rescues from sin, death, and judgment all who will trust Him.

Peter again called the nation to repentance (Acts 2:36; 3:19–26; 4:10–12) and promised that the gift of the Spirit would be given to all who "obey Him." This does not imply that the gift of the Spirit is a reward for obedience, for a gift can be received only by faith. The phrase "obey him" is the same as "obedient to the faith" in Acts 6:7, and means "to obey God's call and trust God's Son." God does not *suggest* that sinners repent and believe; He *commands* it (Acts 17:30).

It was a bold witness that the apostles gave before the highest Jewish religious court. The Spirit of God enabled them and they were not afraid. After all, Jesus had promised to be with them and, through His Holy Spirit, empower them for witness and service. They were His witnesses of His resurrection (Acts 1:22; 2:24, 32; 3:15, 26; 4:10), and He would see them through.

Gamaliel: Avoiding the Truth (5:33–39)

Gamaliel was a Pharisee who probably did not want to see the Sadducees win any victories. He was a scholar highly esteemed by the people, rather liberal in his applications of the law, and apparently moderate in his approach to problems. "When Rabban Gamaliel the Elder died," said the Jews, "the glory of the law ceased and purity and abstinence died." Paul was trained by Gamaliel (Acts 22:3). Gamaliel's "counsel" was unwise and dangerous, but God used it to save the apostles from death. That the Sadducees would heed the words of a Pharisee shows how distinguished a man Gamaliel was.

In spite of the fact that Gamaliel tried to use cool logic rather than overheated emotions, his approach was still wrong. To begin with, he automatically classified Jesus with two rebels, which means *he had already rejected the evidence.* To him, this "Jesus of Nazareth" was just another zealous Jew, trying to set the nation free from Rome. But did Theudas or Judas ever do the things that Jesus did? Were they raised from the dead? With a clever twist of bad logic, Gamaliel convinced the council that there was really nothing to worry about! Troublemakers come and go, so be patient.

Furthermore, Gamaliel assumed that "history repeats itself." Theudas and Judas rebelled, were subdued, and their followers were scattered. Give these Galileans enough time and they too will disband, and you will never again hear about Jesus of Nazareth. While some students do claim to see "cycles" in history, these "cycles" are probably only in the eyes of the beholder. By selecting your evidence carefully, you can prove almost anything from history. The birth, life, death, and resurrection of Jesus Christ had never happened before and would never happen again. God had broken into history and visited this earth!

Gamaliel also had the mistaken idea that, if something is not of God, it must fail. But this idea does not take into consideration the sinful nature of man and the presence of Satan in the world. Mark Twain said that a lie runs around the world while truth is still putting on her shoes. In the end, God's truth will be victorious, but meanwhile, Satan can be very strong and influence multitudes of people.

Success is no test of truth, in spite of what the pragmatists say. False cults often grow faster than God's church. This world is a battlefield on which truth and error are in mortal combat, and often it looks as if truth is "on the scaffold," while wrong sits arrogantly on the throne. How long should the council wait to see if the new movement would survive? What tests would they use to determine whether or not it was successful? What is success? No matter how you look at it, Gamaliel's "wisdom" was foolish.

But the biggest weakness of his advice was his motive: he encouraged neutrality when the council was facing a life-and-death issue that demanded decision. "Wait and see!" is actually not neutrality; *it is a definite decision.* Gamaliel was voting "No!" but he was preaching "maybe someday."

There are many matters in life that do not demand a courageous decision of conscience. I had a friend in seminary who became emotionally disturbed because he tried to make every decision a matter of conscience,

including the cereal he ate at breakfast and the route he took when he walked to the store. But when we face a serious matter of conscience, we had better examine the evidence carefully. This, Gamaliel refused to do. He lost an opportunity for salvation because he turned the meeting into a petty discussion about Jewish insurrectionists.

Jesus made it clear that it is impossible to be neutral about Him and His message. "He that is not with me is against me; and he that gathereth not with me scattereth abroad" (Matt. 12:30). The members of the council knew the words of Elijah, "How long will you waver between two opinions?" (1 Kings 18:21 NIV). There are times when being neutral means making a quiet (and perhaps cowardly) decision to reject God's offer. It is significant that the first group named among those who go to hell is "the fearful" (Rev. 21:8), the people who knew the truth but were afraid to take their stand.

If Gamaliel was really afraid of fighting against God, why did he not honestly investigate the evidence, diligently search the Scriptures, listen to the witnesses, and ask God for wisdom? This was the opportunity of a lifetime! Daniel Defoe, author of *Robinson Crusoe,* claimed that nobody was born a coward. "Truth makes a man of courage," he wrote, "and guilt makes that man of courage a coward." What some men call caution, God would call cowardice. The apostles were true ambassadors; Gamaliel was really only a "religious politician."

The Church: Announcing the Truth (5:40–42)

Part of the council wanted to kill the apostles (Acts 5:33), but Gamaliel's speech tempered their violence. In a compromise move, the council decided to have the apostles beaten, so the men were given thirty-nine strokes (see Deut. 25:1–3; 2 Cor. 11:24). Then the apostles were commanded to stop speaking in the name of Jesus Christ lest something worse happen to them. (Review Acts 2:22; 3:6, 16; 4:10, 12, 17–18, 30.)

When people refuse to deal with disagreements on the basis of principle and truth, they often resort to verbal or physical violence, and sometimes both. The sad thing is that this violence often masquerades as patriotism or as religious zeal. When understanding fails, violence starts to take over, and people begin to destroy each other in the name of their nation or their God. It is tragic that even the history of religion is punctuated with accounts of persecutions and "holy wars." William Temple said that Christians are "called to the hardest of all tasks: to fight without hatred, to resist without bitterness, and in the end, if God grant it so, to triumph without vindictiveness."

How did the apostles respond to this illegal treatment from their nation's religious leaders? They rejoiced! Jesus had told them to expect persecution and had instructed them to rejoice in it (Matt. 5:10–12). The opposition of men meant the approval of God, and it was actually a privilege to suffer for His name (Phil. 1:29).

To paraphrase Phillips Brooks, the purpose of life is to glorify God by the building of character through truth. The Sanhedrin thought that it had won a great victory, when actually the council had experienced a crushing defeat. No doubt they congratulated each other for doing such a good job of defending the faith! But it was the apostles who were the winners, because they grew in godliness as they yielded to God's will and suffered for their Master. In later years, Peter would have much to say in his first epistle about the meaning of suffering in the life of the believer, but now he was learning the lessons.

Neither the threats nor the beatings stopped them from witnessing for Jesus Christ. If anything, this persecution only made them trust God more and seek greater power in their ministry. True believers are not "quitters." The apostles had a commission to fulfill, and they intended to continue as long as their Lord enabled them. Acts 5:42 summarizes the apostolic pattern for evangelism, an excellent pattern for us to follow.

To begin with, they witnessed "daily." This meant that they took advantage of witnessing opportunities no matter where they were (Eph. 5:15–16). *Every* Christian is a witness, either a good one or a bad one, and our witness either draws others to Christ or drives them away. It is a good practice to start each day asking the Lord for the wisdom and grace needed to be a loving witness for Christ that day. If we sincerely look for opportunities and expect God to give them to us, we will never lack for open doors.

D. L. Moody was fearless in his witness for Christ and sought to speak about spiritual matters to at least one soul each day. "How does your soul prosper today?" he would ask; or, "Do you love the Lord? Do you belong to Christ?" Some were offended by his blunt manner, but not a few were led to Christ then and there. "The more we use the means and opportunities we have," he said, "the more will our ability and our opportunities be increased." He also said, "I live for souls and for eternity; I want to win some soul to Christ." He was not satisfied only to address great crowds; he also felt constrained to speak to people personally and urge them to trust Jesus Christ.

The believers witnessed "in the temple." After all, that was where the "religious" people gathered, and it was easier to reach them there. For several years, the church was looked on as another "sect" of the Jewish faith, and both the temple and the many synagogues were open to believers. In his missionary journeys, Paul always went first to the local synagogue or Jewish place of prayer, and he witnessed there until he was thrown out.

My counsel to new Christians has usually been, "Go back to your home and church, be a loving witness for Christ, and stay until they ask you to leave" (see 1 Cor. 7:17–24). The apostles did not abandon the Jewish temple, though they knew the old dispensation was ended and that one day the temple would be destroyed. They were not compromising; they were "buying up the opportunity" to reach more people for Christ.

While I was ministering at the Moody Church in Chicago, it was my joy to lead a pastor to Christ, a gifted man who ministered to a wealthy congregation. He went back to his church and began to share Christ, and numbers of his people were saved. Then the denominational leaders stepped in and started to threaten him with dismissal.

"What do I do?" he asked, and I said, "Stay there until they throw you out. Be loving and kind, but don't give in!" Eventually he was forced out of the church, but not before his witness had influenced many both in the church and in the community. Today, God is using him in a remarkable way to witness for Christ and to train others to witness. He is able to get into churches and groups that might never invite me!

The early Christians also witnessed "in every house." Unlike congregations today, these people had no buildings that were set aside for worship and fellowship. Believers would meet in different homes, worshipping the Lord, listening to teaching, and seeking to win the lost (see Acts 2:46). Paul referred to a number of "house fellowships" when he greeted the saints in Rome (Rom. 16:5, 10–11, 14). The early church took the Word right into the homes, and we should follow their example. This does not mean that it is wrong to have special buildings set aside for church ministry, but only that we must not confine the ministry to the four walls of a church building.

Their ministry went on without ceasing. The authorities had told them to stop witnessing, but they only witnessed all the more! Their motive was not defiance to the law but rather obedience to the Lord. It was not something they turned on and off, depending on the situation. They were "always at it," and they kept at it as long as God gave them opportunities.

The witness of the church included both teaching and preaching, and that is a good balance. The word translated "preach" gives us our English word *evangelize*, and this is the first of fifteen times it is used in Acts. It simply means "to preach the gospel, to share the good news of Jesus Christ." (See 1 Cor. 15:1–8 for the official statement of the gospel message.)

However, proclamation must be balanced with instruction (see Acts 2:42) so that the sinners know *what* to believe and the new converts understand *why* they believed. The message cannot produce fruit unless the person understands it and can make an intelligent decision (Matt. 13:18–23). Believers cannot grow unless they are taught the Word of God (1 Peter 2:1–3).

Finally, it was Jesus Christ who was the center of their witness. That was the very name that the Sanhedrin had condemned! The early church did not go about arguing religion or condemning the establishment: they simply told people about Jesus Christ and urged them to trust in Him. "For we preach not ourselves, but Christ Jesus the Lord" (2 Cor. 4:5). "Ye shall be witnesses unto me" (Acts 1:8).

It was my privilege to speak at a service celebrating the fortieth anniversary of a pastor friend whose ministry has blessed many. A number of his friends shared in the service and quite candidly expressed their love for him and their appreciation for his ministry. My friend became more and more embarrassed as the meeting progressed, and when it came time for me to bring the message, he leaned over and whispered in my ear, "Warren, please tell them about Jesus!"

In his clever and convicting book *The Gospel Blimp,* the late Joe Bayly wrote: "Jesus Christ didn't commit the gospel to an advertising agency; He commissioned disciples."

That commission still stands.

In your life, is it commission—or omission?

CHAPTER SEVEN
Acts 6—7
STEPHEN, THE MAN GOD CROWNED

There are two words for "crown" in the New Testament: *diadema,* which means "a royal crown" and gives us the English word *diadem*; and *stephanos,* the "victor's crown," which gives us the popular name Stephen. You can inherit a *diadema,* but the only way to get a *stephanos* is to earn it.

Acts 6 and 7 center on the ministry and martyrdom of Stephen, a Spirit-filled believer who was crowned by the Lord. "Be thou faithful unto death, and I will give thee a crown of life" (Rev. 2:10). He was faithful both in life and in death and therefore is a good example for us to follow.

These chapters present Stephen as a faithful believer in four different areas of ministry.

Stephen the Servant (6:1–7)

The church was experiencing "growing pains," and this was making it difficult for the apostles to minister to everybody. The "Grecians" were the Greek-speaking Jews who had come to Palestine from other nations, and therefore may not have spoken Aramaic, while the "Hebrews" were Jewish residents of the land who spoke both Aramaic and Greek. The fact that the "outsiders" were being neglected created a situation that could have divided the church. However, the apostles handled the problem with great wisdom and did not give Satan any foothold in the fellowship.

When a church faces a serious problem, this presents the leaders and the members with a number of opportunities. For one thing, problems give us the opportunity to examine our ministry and discover what changes must be made. In times of success, it is easy for us to maintain the *status quo,* but this is dangerous.

Henry Ward Beecher called success "a last-year's nest from which the birds have flown." Any ministry or organization that thinks its success will go on automatically is heading for failure. We must regularly examine our lives and our ministries lest we start taking things for granted.

The apostles studied the situation and concluded that *they* were to blame: they were so busy serving tables that they were neglecting prayer and the ministry of the Word of God. They had created their own problem because they were trying to do too much. Even today, some pastors are so busy with secondary tasks that they fail to spend adequate time in study and in prayer. This creates a "spiritual deficiency" in the church that makes it easy for problems to develop.

This is not to suggest that serving tables is a menial task, because *every* ministry in the church is important. But it is a matter of priorities; the apostles were doing jobs that others could do just as well. D. L. Moody used to say that it was better to put ten men to work than to try to do the work of ten men. Certainly it is better for you, for the workers you enlist, and for the church as a whole.

Church problems also give us an opportunity to exercise our faith, not only faith in the Lord, but also faith in each other. The leaders suggested a solution, and all the members agreed with it. The assembly selected seven qualified men, and the apostles set them apart for ministry. The church was not afraid to adjust their structure in order to make room for a growing ministry. When structure and ministry conflict, this gives us an opportunity to trust God for the solution. It is tragic when churches destroy ministry because they refuse to modify their structure. The apostles were not afraid to share their authority and ministry with others.

Problems also give us the opportunity to express our love. The Hebrew leaders and the predominantly Hebrew members selected six men who were Hellenists and one man who was both a Gentile and a proselyte! What an illustration of Romans 12:10 and Philippians 2:1–4! When we solve church problems, we must think of others and not of ourselves only.

We commonly call these seven men of Acts 6 "deacons" because the Greek noun *diakonos* is used in Acts 6:1 ("ministration"), and the verb *diakoneo* ("serve") is used in Acts 6:2. However, this title is not given to them in this chapter, although you find deacons mentioned in Philippians 1:1 and their qualifications given in 1 Timothy 3:8–13. The word simply means "a servant." These seven men were humble servants of the church, men whose work made it possible for the apostles to carry on their important ministries among the people. Stephen was one of these men. The emphasis in Stephen's life is on *fullness:* he was full of the Holy Spirit and wisdom (Acts 6:3, 10), full of faith (Acts 6:5), and full of power (Acts 6:8). In Scripture, to be "full of" means "to be controlled by." This man was controlled by the Spirit, faith, wisdom, and power. He was a God-controlled man yielded to the Holy Spirit, a man who sought to lead people to Christ.

What was the result? The blessing of God continued and increased! The church was still unified (Acts 6:5), multiplied (Acts 6:7), and magnified (Acts 6:8). Acts 6:7 is one of several "summaries" found in the book, statements that let us know that the story has reached an important juncture (see Acts 2:41; 4:4; 5:12–16; 6:7; 9:31; 12:24; 16:5; 19:20; and 28:31). In Acts 6:7, Dr. Luke describes the climax of the ministry in Jerusalem, for the persecution following Stephen's death will take the gospel to the Samaritans and then to the Gentiles. It has been estimated that there were eight thousand Jewish priests attached to the temple ministry in Jerusalem, and "a great company" of them trusted Jesus Christ as Savior!

Stephen the Witness (6:8–15)

This Spirit-filled man did not limit his ministry to the serving of tables; he also won the lost and even did miracles. Up to this point, it was the apostles who performed the miracles (Acts 2:43; 5:12), but now God gave this power to Stephen also. This was part of His plan to use Stephen to bear witness to the leaders of Israel. Stephen's powerful testimony would be the climax of the church's witness to the Jews. Then the message would go out to the Samaritans and then to the Gentiles.

Jews from many nations resided in Jerusalem in their own "quarters," and some of these ethnic groups had their own synagogues. The freedmen ("libertines") were the descendants of Jews who had previously been in bondage but had won their freedom from Rome. Since Paul came from Tarsus in Cilicia (Acts 21:39), it is possible that he heard Stephen in the synagogue and may have debated with him. However, nobody could match or resist Stephen's wisdom and power (see Luke 21:15). Their only alternative was to destroy him.

Their treatment of Stephen parallels the way the Jewish leaders treated Jesus. First, they hired false witnesses to testify against him. Then, they stirred up the people who accused him of attacking the law of Moses and the temple. Finally, after listening to his witness, they executed him (see Matt. 26:59–62; John 2:19–22).

The Jews were jealous over their law and could not understand how Christ had come to fulfill the law and to bring in the new age. They were proud of their temple and refused to believe that God would permit it to be destroyed. Stephen faced the same spiritual blindness that Jeremiah faced in his ministry (see Jer. 7). The church faced the opposition of Jewish tradition for many years to come, from within its own ranks (Acts 15) and from false teachers coming in from the outside (Gal. 2:4).

The enemy surprised Stephen and arrested him while he was ministering ("having came upon him suddenly" is Wuest's translation of Acts 6:12), and they took him before the same council that had tried Jesus

and the apostles. It was not even necessary for Stephen to speak in order to give witness, for the very glow on his face told everybody that he was a servant of God. Certainly the members of the Sanhedrin would recall Moses' shining face (Ex. 34:29–30). It was as though God was saying, "This man is not against Moses! He is like Moses—he is My faithful servant!"

Stephen the Judge (7:1–53)

This is the longest address in the book of Acts and one of the most important. In it, Stephen reviewed the history of Israel and the contributions made by their revered leaders:

Abraham (Acts 7:2–8), Joseph (Acts 7:9–17), Moses (Acts 7:18–44), Joshua (Acts 7:45), and David and Solomon (Acts 7:46–50). But this address was more than a recitation of familiar facts; it was also a refutation of their indictments against Stephen and a revelation of their own national sins. Stephen proved from their own Scriptures that the Jewish nation was guilty of worse sins than those they had accused him of committing. What were these sins?

They misunderstood their own spiritual roots (vv. 1–8). Stephen's address opens with "the God of glory" and closes with the glory of God (Acts 7:55), and all the time he spoke, his face radiated that same glory! Why? Because Israel was the only nation privileged to have the glory of God as a part of its inheritance (Rom. 9:4). Alas, the glory of God had departed, first from the tabernacle (1 Sam. 4:19–22) and then from the temple (Ezek. 10:4, 18). God's glory had come in His Son (John 1:14), but the nation had rejected Him.

Abraham was the founder of the Hebrew nation, and his relationship to God was one of *grace* and *faith*. God had graciously appeared to him and called him out of heathen darkness into the light of salvation, and Abraham had responded by faith. Abraham was saved by grace, through faith, and not because he was circumcised, kept a law, or worshipped in a temple. All of those things came afterward (see Rom. 4; Gal. 3). He believed the promises of God and it was this faith that saved him.

God promised the land to Abraham's descendants, and then told Abraham that his descendants would suffer in Egypt before they would enter and enjoy the land, and this took place just as God promised. From the very beginning, God had a wise plan for His people, and that plan would be fulfilled as long as they trusted His Word and obeyed His will.

The Jews greatly revered Abraham and prided themselves in being his "children." But they confused physical descent with spiritual experience and depended on their national heritage rather than their personal faith. John the Baptist had warned them about this sin (Matt. 3:7–12) and so had Jesus (John 8:33–59). The Jews were blind to the simple faith of Abraham and the patriarchs, and they had cluttered it with man-made traditions that made salvation a matter of good works, not faith. God has no grand-children. Each of us must be born into the family of God through personal faith in Jesus Christ (John 1:11–13).

The Jews prided themselves in their circumcision, failing to understand that the rite was symbolic of an inner spiritual relationship with God (Deut. 10:16; Jer. 4:4; 6:10; Acts 7:51; Gal. 5:1–6; Phil. 3:3; Col. 2:11–12). Over the years, the fulfilling of ritual had taken the place of the enjoyment of reality. This happens in churches even today.

They rejected their God-sent deliverers (vv. 9–36). I have combined the sections dealing with Joseph and Moses because these two Jewish heroes have this in common: they were both rejected as deliverers the first time, but were accepted the second time. Joseph's brethren hated their brother and sold him into servitude, yet later he became their deliverer. They recognized Joseph "at the second time" (Acts 7:13) when they returned to Egypt for more food. Israel rejected Moses when he first tried to deliver them from Egyptian bondage, and he had to flee for his life (Ex. 2:11–22). But when Moses came to them the second time, the nation accepted him and he set them free (Acts 7:35).

These two events illustrate how Israel treated Jesus Christ. Israel rejected their Messiah when He came to them the first time (John 1:11), but when He comes again, they will recognize Him and receive Him (Zech. 12:10; Rev. 1:7). In spite of what they did to His Son, God has not cast away His people (Rom. 11:1–6). Israel today is suffering from a partial spiritual blindness that one day will be taken away (Rom. 11:25–32). Individual Jews are being saved, but the nation as a whole is blind to the truth about Jesus Christ.

Before leaving this section, we must deal with some seeming contradictions between Stephen's address and the Old Testament Scriptures.

Genesis 46:26–27 states that seventy people made up the household of Jacob, including Joseph's family already in Egypt, but Stephen claimed that there were seventy-five (Acts 7:14; and see Ex. 1:1–5). The Hebrew text has seventy in both Genesis and Exodus, but the Septuagint (Greek translation of the Old Testament) has seventy-five. Where did the number seventy-five come from in the Septuagint? In their count, the translators included Joseph's grandchildren (1 Chron. 7:14–15, 20–25). Being a Hellenistic Jew, Stephen would naturally use the Septuagint. There is no real contradiction; your total depends on the factors you include.

Acts 7:16 suggests that Jacob was buried at Shechem, but Genesis 50:13 states that he was buried in the cave of Machpelah at Hebron, along with Abraham, Isaac, and Sarah (Gen. 23:17). It was Joseph who was buried at Shechem (Josh. 24:32). It is likely that the children of Israel carried out of Egypt the remains of all the sons of Jacob, and not just Joseph alone, and buried them

together in Shechem. The "fathers" mentioned in Acts 7:15 would be the twelve sons of Jacob.

But who purchased the burial place in Shechem—Abraham or Jacob? Stephen seems to say that Abraham bought it, but the Old Testament record says that Jacob did (Gen. 33:18–20). Abraham purchased the cave of Machpelah (Gen. 23:14–20). The simplest explanation is that Abraham actually purchased *both* pieces of property and that Jacob later had to purchase the Shechem property again. Abraham moved around quite a bit, and it would be very easy for the residents of the land to forget or ignore the transactions he had made.

They disobeyed their law (vv. 37–43). Stephen's opponents had accused him of speaking against the sacred law of Moses, but the history of Israel revealed that the nation had repeatedly *broken* that law. God gave the law to His congregation ("church") in the wilderness at Mount Sinai, His living Word through the mediation of angels (see Acts 7:53; Gal. 3:19). No sooner had the people received the law than they disobeyed it by asking Aaron to make them an idol (Ex. 32), and thereby broke the first two of the Ten Commandments (Ex. 20:1–6).

The Jews had worshipped idols in Egypt (Josh. 24:14; Ezek. 20:7–8), and after their settlement in the Promised Land they gradually adopted the gods of the pagan nations around them. God repeatedly disciplined His people and sent them prophets to warn them, until finally He carried them off to Babylon, where they were finally cured of idolatry.

Acts 7:42 should be compared with Romans 1:24–28, for all of these verses describe the judgment of God when He "takes His hands off" and permits sinners to have their own way. When Stephen quoted Amos 5:25–27, he revealed what the Jews had really been doing all those years: in outward form, they were worshipping Jehovah, but in their hearts, they were worshipping foreign gods! The form of the question in Acts 7:42 demands a negative reply: "No, you were not offering those sacrifices to the Lord!"

In this day of "pluralism" of religions and an emphasis on "toleration," we must understand why God hated the pagan religions and instructed Israel to destroy them. To begin with, these religions were unspeakably obscene in their worship of sex and their use of religious prostitutes. Their practices were also brutal, even to the point of offering children as sacrifices to their gods. It was basically demon worship, and it opened the way for all kinds of godless living on the part of the Jews. Had the nation turned from the true God and succumbed to idolatry, it could have meant the end of the godly remnant and the fulfillment of the promise of the Redeemer.

God's law was given to the Jews to protect them from the pagan influence around them, and to enable them to enjoy the blessings of the land. It was the law that made them a holy people, different from the other nations. When Israel broke down that wall of distinction by disobeying God's law, they forfeited the blessing of God and had to be disciplined.

They despised their temple (vv. 44–50). The witnesses accused Stephen of seeking to destroy the temple, but that was exactly what the Jewish nation did! Moses built the tabernacle and God's glory graciously dwelt in the Holy of Holies (Ex. 40:34–38). Solomon built the temple, and once again God's glory came in (1 Kings 8:10–11). But over the years, the worship at the temple degenerated into mere religious formality, and eventually there were idols placed in the temple (2 Kings 21:1–9; Ezek. 8:7–12). Jeremiah warned people against their superstitious faith in the temple and told them that they had turned God's house into a den of thieves (Jer. 7:1–16).

Had the nation heeded their own prophets, they would have escaped the horrors of the Babylonian siege (see the book of Lamentations) and the destruction of their city and temple. Even Solomon recognized the truth that God did not live in buildings (1 Kings 8:27), and the prophet Isaiah made it even clearer (Isa. 66:1–2). We really make nothing for God, because everything comes from Him, and how can the Creator of the universe be contained in a man-made building (Acts 17:24)? The Jewish defense of their temple was both illogical and unscriptural.

They stubbornly resisted their God and His truth (vv. 51–53). This is the climax of Stephen's speech, the personal application that cut his hearers to the heart. Throughout the centuries, Israel had refused to submit to God and obey the truths He had revealed to them. Their ears did not hear the truth, their hearts did not receive the truth, and their necks did not bow to the truth. As a result, they killed their own Messiah!

The nation refused to accept the new truth that God was revealing from age to age. Instead of seeing God's truth as seed that produces fruit and more seed, the religious leaders "embalmed" the truth and refused to accept anything new. By the time Jesus came to earth, the truth of God was encrusted with so much tradition that the people could not recognize God's truth when He did present it. Man's dead traditions had replaced God's living truth (see Matt. 15:1–20).

Stephen the Martyr (7:54–60)

You wonder what kind of a world we live in when good and godly men like Stephen can be murdered by religious bigots! But we have similar problems in our "enlightened" age today: taking hostages, bombings that kill or maim innocent people, assassinations, and all in the name of politics or religion. The heart of man has not changed, nor can it be changed apart from the grace of God.

What were the results of Stephen's death? For Stephen, death meant *coronation* (Rev. 2:10). He saw the glory of God and the Son of God standing to receive him to heaven (see Luke 22:69). Our Lord sat down when He ascended to heaven (Ps. 110:1; Mark 16:19), but He stood up to welcome to glory the first

Christian martyr (Luke 12:8). This is the last time the title "Son of man" is used in the Bible. It is definitely a messianic title (Dan. 7:13–14), and Stephen's use of it was one more witness that Jesus is indeed Israel's Messiah.

Stephen was not only tried in a manner similar to that of our Lord, but he also died with similar prayers on his lips (Luke 23:34, 46; Acts 7:59–60). A heckler once shouted to a street preacher, "Why didn't God do something for Stephen when they were stoning him?" The preacher replied, "God did do something for Stephen. He gave him the grace to forgive his murderers and to pray for them!" A perfect answer!

For Israel, Stephen's death meant *condemnation.* This was their third murder: they had *permitted* John the Baptist to be killed; they had *asked* for Jesus to be killed; and now they were killing Stephen themselves. When they allowed Herod to kill John, the Jews sinned against God the Father who had sent John (Matt. 21:28–32). When they asked Pilate to crucify Jesus, they sinned against God the Son (Matt. 21:33–46). When they stoned Stephen, Israel sinned against the Holy Spirit who was working in and through the apostles (Matt. 10:1–8; Acts 7:51). Jesus said that this sin could never be forgiven (Matt. 12:31–32). Judgment finally came in AD 70 when Titus and the Roman armies destroyed Jerusalem and the temple.

For the church in Jerusalem, the death of Stephen meant *liberation.* They had been witnessing "to the Jew first" ever since Pentecost, but now they would be directed to take the message out of Jerusalem to the Samaritans (Acts 8) and even to the Gentiles (Acts 11:19–26). The opposition of the enemy helped prevent the church from becoming a Jewish "sect" and encouraged them to fulfill the commission of Acts 1:8 and Matthew 28:18–20.

Finally, as far as Saul (Acts 7:58) was concerned, the death of Stephen eventually meant *salvation.* He never forgot the event (Acts 22:17–21), and no doubt Stephen's message, prayers, and glorious death were used of the Spirit to prepare Saul for his own meeting with the Lord (Acts 9). God never wastes the blood of His saints. Saul would one day see the same glory that Stephen saw and would behold the Son of God and hear Him speak!

When Christians die, they "fall asleep" (John 11:11; 1 Thess. 4:13). The body sleeps and the spirit goes to be with the Lord in heaven (Acts 7:59; 2 Cor. 5:6–9; Phil. 1:23; Heb. 12:22–23). When Jesus returns, He will bring with Him the spirits of those who have died (1 Thess. 4:14), their bodies will be raised and glorified, and body and spirit will be united in glory to be "forever with the Lord." Even though we Christians weep at the death of a loved one (Acts 8:2), we do not sorrow hopelessly, for we know we shall meet again when we die or when the Lord returns.

God does not call all of us to be martyrs, but He does call us to be "living sacrifices" (Rom. 12:1–2). In some respects, it may be harder to *live* for Christ than to *die* for Him, but if we are living for Him, we will be prepared to die for Him if that is what God calls us to do.

In 1948, Auca martyr Jim Elliot wrote in his journal, "I seek not a long life, but a full one, like You, Lord Jesus." Two years later, he wrote: "I must not think it strange if God takes in youth those whom I would have kept on earth till they were older. God is peopling Eternity, and I must not restrict Him to old men and women."

Like Stephen, Jim Elliot and his four comrades were called on January 8, 1956, to "people Eternity" as they were slain by the people they were seeking to reach. What has happened to the Aucas since then is proof that the blood of the martyrs is indeed the seed of the church. Many Aucas are now Christians.

"Be thou faithful unto death, and I will give thee a crown of life" (Rev. 2:10).

CHAPTER EIGHT
Acts 8
A CHURCH ON THE MOVE

There is one thing stronger than all the armies in the world," wrote Victor Hugo, "and that is an idea whose time has come."

The gospel of Jesus Christ is much more than an idea. The gospel is "the power of God to salvation for everyone who believes" (Rom. 1:16 NKJV). It is God's "dynamite" for breaking down sin's barriers and setting the prisoners free. Its time had come and the church was on the move. The "salt" was now leaving the "Jerusalem saltshaker" to be spread over all Judea and Samaria, just as the Lord had commanded (Acts 1:8).

The events in Acts 8 center around four different men.

A Zealous Persecutor—Saul (8:1–3)
The book of Acts and the Epistles give sufficient data for a sketch of Saul's early life. He was born in Tarsus in Cilicia (Acts 22:3), a "Hebrew of the Hebrews" (see 2 Cor. 11:22; Phil. 3:5), the "son of a Pharisee" (Acts 23:6), and a Roman citizen (Acts 16:37; 22:25–28). He was educated in Jerusalem by Gamaliel (Acts 22:3) and became a devoted Pharisee (Acts 26:4–5; Phil. 3:5). Measured by the law, his life was blameless (Phil. 3:6). He was one of the most promising young Pharisees in Jerusalem, well on his way to becoming a great leader for the Jewish faith (Gal. 1:14).

Saul's zeal for the law was displayed most vividly in his persecution of the church (Gal. 1:13–14; Phil. 3:6). He really thought that persecuting the believers was one way of serving God, so he did it with a clear conscience (2 Tim. 1:3). He obeyed the light that he had, and, when God gave him more light, he obeyed that and became a Christian!

In what ways did Saul persecute the church? He "made havoc of the church," and the verb here describes a wild animal mangling its prey. When Christ spoke to Saul on the Damascus road, He compared him to a beast (Acts 9:5)! The stoning of Stephen, which Saul approved, shows the lengths to which he would go to achieve his purpose. He persecuted both men and women "unto the death" (Acts 22:4), entering both houses and synagogues (Acts 22:19). He had the believers imprisoned and beaten (Acts 22:19; 26:9–11). If they renounced their faith in Jesus Christ ("compelling them to blaspheme"—Acts 26:11), they were set free; if they did not recant, they could be killed.

In later years, Paul described himself as "exceedingly mad against them" (Acts 26:11), "a blasphemer [he denounced Jesus Christ], and a persecutor, and injurious [violent]" (1 Tim. 1:13). He was a man with great authority whose devotion to Moses completely controlled his life, and almost destroyed his life. He did it "ignorantly in unbelief" (1 Tim. 1:13), and God showed him mercy and saved him. Saul of Tarsus is the last person in Jerusalem you would have chosen to be the great apostle to the Gentiles!

A Faithful Preacher—Philip (8:4–8)
Persecution does to the church what wind does to seed: it scatters it and only produces a greater harvest. The word translated "scattered" (*diaspeiro*, Acts 8:1, 4) means "to scatter seed." The believers in Jerusalem were God's seed, and the persecution was used of God to plant them in new soil so they could bear fruit (Matt. 13:37–38). Some went throughout Judea and Samaria (see Acts 1:8), and others went to more distant fields (Acts 11:19ff.).

The Samaritans were a "half-breed" people, a mixture of Jew and Gentile. The nation originated when the Assyrians captured the ten northern tribes in 732 BC, deported many of the people, and then imported others who intermarried with the Jews. The Samaritans had their own temple and priesthood and openly opposed fraternization with the Jews (John 4:9).

We have no reason to believe that God permitted this persecution because His people were negligent and had to be "forced" to leave Jerusalem. The fact that Saul persecuted believers "even unto strange [foreign] cities" (Acts 26:11) would suggest that their witness was bearing fruit even beyond Jerusalem. Nor should we criticize the apostles for remaining in the city. If anything, we should commend them for their courage and devotion to duty. After all, somebody had to remain there to care for the church.

Because of the witness and death of Stephen, it is possible that the focus of the persecution was against the Hellenistic Jews rather than the "native" Jews. It would be easier for Saul and his helpers to identify the Hellenistic believers since many of the "native" Jews were still very Jewish and very much attached to the temple. Peter was still keeping a "kosher home" when he was sent to evangelize the household of Cornelius (Acts 10:9–16).

Philip was chosen as a deacon (Acts 6:5) but, like Stephen, he grew in his ministry and became an effective evangelist (see Acts 21:8). God directed him to evangelize in Samaria, an area that had been prohibited to the apostles (Matt. 10:5–6). Both John the Baptist and Jesus had ministered there (John 3:23; 4:1ff.), so Philip entered into their labors (John 4:36–38).

The word for preaching in Acts 8:4 means "to preach the gospel, to evangelize"; while the word in Acts 8:5 means "to announce as a herald." Philip was God's commissioned herald to deliver His message to the people of Samaria. To reject the messenger would mean to reject the message and rebel against the authority behind the herald, Almighty God. How people respond to God's messenger and God's message is serious business.

Philip not only declared God's Word, but he also demonstrated God's power by performing miracles. It was the apostles who had majored on miracles (Acts 2:43; 5:12), yet both Stephen and Philip did signs and wonders by the power of God (Acts 6:8). However, the emphasis here is on the Word of God: the people gave heed to the Word because they saw the miracles, and by believing the Word, they were saved. Nobody was ever saved simply because of miracles (John 2:23–25; 12:37–41).

Great persecution (Acts 8:1) plus the preaching of the gospel resulted in great joy! Both in his gospel and in the book of Acts, Luke emphasizes the joy of salvation (Luke 2:10; 15:7, 10; 24:52; Acts 8:8; 13:52; 15:3). The people of Samaria who heard the gospel and believed were delivered from physical affliction, demonic control, and, most important, from their sins. No wonder there was great joy!

The gospel had now moved from "Jewish territory" into Samaria where the people were part Jew and part Gentile. God in His grace had built a bridge between two estranged peoples and made the believers one in Christ, and soon He would extend that bridge to the Gentiles and include them as well. Even today, we need "bridge builders" like Philip, men and women who will carry the gospel into pioneer territory and dare to challenge ancient prejudices. "Into all the world … the gospel to every creature" is still God's commission to us.

A Clever Deceiver—Simon the Sorcerer (8:9–25)

It is a basic principle in Scripture that wherever God sows His true believers, Satan will eventually sow his counterfeits (Matt. 13:24–30, 36–43). This was true of the ministry of John the Baptist (Matt. 3:7ff.) and Jesus (Matt. 23:15, 33; John 8:44), and it would be true of Paul's ministry also (Acts 13:6ff.; 2 Cor. 11:1–4, 13–15). The enemy comes as a lion to devour, and when that approach fails, he comes as a serpent to deceive. Satan's tool in this case was a sorcerer named Simon.

The word translated "bewitched" in Acts 8:9 and 11 simply means "astounded, confounded." It is translated "wondered" in Acts 8:13. The people were amazed at the things that Simon did and, therefore, they believed the things that he said. They considered him "the great power of God." Simon's sorcery was energized by Satan (2 Thess. 2:1–12) and was used to magnify himself, while Philip's miracles were empowered by God and were used to glorify Christ. Simon started to lose his following as the Samaritans listened to Philip's messages, believed on Jesus Christ, were born again, and were baptized.

What does it mean that "Simon himself believed" (Acts 8:13)? We can answer that question best by asking another one: What was the basis of his "faith"? His faith was not in the Word of God, but in the miracles he saw Philip perform, and there is no indication that Simon repented of his sins. He certainly did not believe with *all* his heart (Acts 8:37). His faith was like that of the people of Jerusalem who witnessed our Lord's miracles (John 2:23–25), or even like that of the demons (James 2:19). Simon continued with Philip, not to hear the Word and learn more about Jesus Christ, but to witness the miracles and perhaps learn how they were done.

It is important to note that the Samaritans did not receive the gift of the Holy Spirit when they believed. It was necessary for two of the apostles, Peter and John, to come from Jerusalem, put their hands on the converts, and impart to them the gift of the Spirit. Why? Because God wanted to unite the Samaritan believers with the original Jewish church in Jerusalem. He did not want two churches that would perpetuate the division and conflict that had existed for centuries. Jesus had given Peter the "keys of the kingdom of heaven" (Matt. 16:13–20), which meant that Peter had the privilege of "opening the door of faith" to others. He opened the door to the Jews at Pentecost, and now he opened the door to the Samaritans. Later, he would open the door of faith to the Gentiles (Acts 10).

Remember too that the first ten chapters of Acts record a period of transition, from the Jew to the Samaritan to the Gentile. God's pattern for today is given in Acts 10: the sinner hears the gospel, believes, receives the gift of the Spirit, and then is baptized. It is dangerous to base any doctrine or practice *only* on what is recorded in Acts 1—10, for you might be building on that which was temporary and transitional. Those who claim we must be baptized to receive the gift of the Spirit (Acts 2:38) have a hard time explaining what happened to the Samaritans, and those who claim we must have "the laying on of hands" to receive the Spirit have a difficult time with Acts 10. Once you accept Acts 1—10 as a transitional period in God's plan, with Acts 10 being the climax, the problems are solved.

The wickedness of Simon's heart was fully revealed by the ministry of the two apostles. Simon not only wanted to perform miracles, but he also wanted the power to convey the gift of the Holy Spirit to others—and he was quite willing to pay for this power! It is this passage that gives us the word *simony,* which means "the buying and selling of church offices or privileges."

As you study the book of Acts, you will often find the gospel in conflict with money and "big business." Ananias and Sapphira lost their lives because they lied about their gift (Acts 5:1–11). Paul put a fortune-teller out of business in Philippi and ended up in jail (Acts 16:16–24). He also gave the silversmiths trouble in Ephesus and helped cause a riot (Acts 19:23–41). The early church had its priorities straight: it was more important to preach the Word than to win the support of the wealthy and influential people of the world.

Peter's words to Simon give every indication that the sorcerer was not a converted man. "Thy money perish with thee!" is pretty strong language to use with a believer. He had neither "part or lot in this matter" ("this word") and his heart was not right before God. While it is not out of place for believers to repent (see Rev. 2–3), the command to repent is usually given to unbelievers. The word *thought* in Acts 8:22 means "plot or scheme" and is used in a bad sense. The fact that Simon was "in the gall of bitterness" (Deut. 29:18; Heb. 12:15) and "the bond of iniquity" would indicate that he had never truly been born again.

Simon's response to these severe words of warning was not at all encouraging. He was more concerned about avoiding judgment than getting right with God! There is no evidence that he repented and sought forgiveness. A sinner who wants the prayers of others but who will not pray himself is not going to enter God's kingdom.

This episode only shows how close a person can come to salvation and still not be converted. Simon heard the gospel, saw the miracles, gave a profession of faith in Christ, and was baptized, and yet he was never born again. He was one of Satan's clever counterfeits, and, had Peter not exposed the wickedness of his heart, Simon would have been accepted as a member of the Samaritan congregation!

Even though the persecution was still going on, Peter and John returned to Jerusalem, preaching the gospel in "many villages of the Samaritans" as they went their way. They lost no opportunity to share the good news with others now that the doors were open in Samaria.

A Concerned Seeker—an Ethiopian (8:26–40)

Philip was not only a faithful preacher, he was also an obedient personal worker. Like his Master, he was willing to leave the crowds and deal with one lost soul. The angel could have told this Ethiopian official how to be saved, but God has not given the commission to angels: He has given it to His people. Angels have never personally experienced God's grace; therefore, they can never bear witness of what it means to be saved.

D. L. Moody once asked a man about his soul, and the man replied, "It's none of your business!" "Oh, yes, it is my business!" Moody said, and the man immediately exclaimed, "Then you must be D. L. Moody!" It

is every Christian's business to share the gospel with others, and to do it without fear or apology.

Philip's experience ought to encourage us in our own personal witness for the Lord. To begin with, God directed Philip to the right person at the right time. You and I are not likely to have angels instruct us, but we can know the guidance of the Holy Spirit in our witnessing, if we are walking in the Spirit and praying for God's direction.

Late one afternoon, I was completing my pastoral calling and I felt impressed to make one more visit to see a woman who was faithfully attending church but was not a professed Christian. At first, I told myself that it was foolish to visit her that late in the day, since she was probably preparing a meal for her family. But I went anyway and discovered that she had been burdened about her sins all that day! Within minutes, she opened her heart to Christ and was born again. Believe me, I was glad I obeyed the leading of the Spirit!

This court official did not come from what we know today as Ethiopia; his home was in ancient Nubia, located south of Egypt. Since he was a eunuch, he could not become a full Jewish proselyte (Deut. 23:1), but he was permitted to become a "God fearer" or "a proselyte of the gate." He was concerned enough about his spiritual life to travel over two hundred miles to Jerusalem to worship God, but his heart was still not satisfied.

This Ethiopian represents many people today who are religious, read the Scriptures, and seek the truth, yet do not have saving faith in Jesus Christ. They are sincere, but they are lost! They need someone to show them the way.

As Philip drew near to the chariot, he heard the man reading from the prophet Isaiah. (It was customary in those days for students to read out loud.) God had already prepared the man's heart to receive Philip's witness! If we obey the Lord's leading, we can be sure that God will go before us and open the way for our witness.

Isaiah 53 was the passage he was reading, the prophecy of God's Suffering Servant. Isaiah 53 describes our Lord Jesus Christ in His birth (Isa. 53:1–2), life and ministry (Isa. 53:3), substitutionary death (Isa. 53:4–9), and victorious resurrection (Isa. 53:10–12). Isaiah 53:4 should be connected with 1 Peter 2:24; Isaiah 53:7 with Matthew 26:62–63; Isaiah 53:9 with Matthew 27:57–60; and Isaiah 53:12 with Luke 23:34, 37.

The Ethiopian focused on Isaiah 53:7–8, which describes our Lord as the willing Sacrifice for sinners, even to the point of losing His human rights. As Philip explained the verses to him, the Ethiopian began to understand the gospel because the Spirit of God was opening his mind to God's truth. It is not enough for the lost sinner to desire salvation; he must also understand God's plan of salvation. It is the heart that understands the Word that eventually bears fruit (Matt. 13:23).

The idea of substitutionary sacrifice is one that is found from the beginning of the Bible to the end. God killed animals so that He might clothe Adam and Eve (Gen. 3:21). He provided a ram to die in the place of Isaac (Gen. 22:13). At Passover, innocent lambs died for the people of Israel (Ex. 12), and the entire Jewish religious system was based on the shedding of blood (Lev. 17, especially v. 11). Jesus Christ is the fulfillment of both the Old Testament types and the prophecies (John 1:29; Rev. 5).

"Faith cometh by hearing, and hearing by the Word of God" (Rom. 10:17). The Ethiopian believed on Jesus Christ and was born again! So real was his experience that he insisted on stopping the caravan and being baptized immediately! He was no "closet Christian"; he wanted everybody to know what the Lord had done for him.

How did he know that believers were supposed to be baptized? Perhaps Philip had included this in his witness to him, or perhaps he had even seen people baptized while he was in Jerusalem. We know that Gentiles were baptized when they became Jewish proselytes. Throughout the book of Acts, baptism is an important part of the believer's commitment to Christ and witness for Christ.

While Acts 8:37 is not found in all the New Testament manuscripts, there is certainly nothing in it that is unbiblical (Rom. 10:9–10). In the days of the early church, converts were not baptized unless they first gave a clear testimony of their faith in Jesus Christ. And keep in mind that the Ethiopian was speaking not only to Philip but also to those in the caravan who were near his chariot. He was an important man, and you can be sure that his attendants were paying close attention.

Philip was caught away to minister elsewhere (compare 1 Kings 18:12), but the treasurer "went on his way rejoicing" (see Acts 8:8). God did not permit Philip to do the necessary discipling of this new believer, but surely He provided for it when the man arrived home. Even though he was a eunuch, the Ethiopian was accepted by God (see Isa. 56:3–5)!

Philip ended up at Azotus, about twenty miles from Gaza, and then made his way to Caesarea, a journey of about sixty miles. Like Peter and John, Philip "preached his way home" (Acts 8:25) as he told others about the Savior. Twenty years later, we find Philip living in Caesarea and still serving God as an evangelist (Acts 21:8ff.).

As you trace the expansion of the gospel during this transition period (Acts 2—10), you see how the Holy Spirit reaches out to the whole world. In Acts 8, the Ethiopian who was converted was a descendant of Ham (Gen. 10:6, where "Cush" refers to Ethiopia). In Acts 9, Saul of Tarsus will be saved, a Jew and therefore a descendant of Shem (Gen. 10:21ff.). In Acts 10, the Gentiles find Christ, and they are the descendants of Japheth (Gen. 10:2–5). The whole world was peopled by Shem, Ham, and Japheth (Gen. 10:1), and God wants the whole world—all of their descendants—to hear the message of the gospel (Matt. 28:18–20; Mark 16:15).

In October 1857, J. Hudson Taylor began to minister in Ningpo, China, and he led a Mr. Nyi to Christ. The man was overjoyed and wanted to share his faith with others.

"How long have you had the good tidings in England?" Mr. Nyi asked Hudson Taylor one day. Taylor acknowledged that England had known the gospel for many centuries.

"My father died seeking the truth," said Mr. Nyi. "Why didn't you come sooner?"

Taylor had no answer to that penetrating question.

How long have *you* known the gospel?

How far have you shared it personally?

CHAPTER NINE
Acts 9:1–31
GOD ARRESTS SAUL

The conversion of Saul of Tarsus, the leading persecutor of the Christians, was perhaps the greatest event in church history after the coming of the Spirit at Pentecost. The next great event would be the conversion of the Gentiles (Acts 10), and Saul (Paul) would become the apostle to the Gentiles. God was continuing to work out His plan to bring the gospel to the whole world.

"Paul was a great man," said Charles Spurgeon, "and I have no doubt that on the way to Damascus he rode a very high horse. But a few seconds sufficed to alter the man. How soon God brought him down!"

The account of the conversion of Saul of Tarsus is given three times in Acts, in chapters 9, 22, and 26. According to the record before us, Saul experienced four meetings that together transformed his life.

He Met Jesus Christ (9:1–9)
When you look at Saul *on the road* (Acts 9:1–2), you see a very zealous man who actually thought he was doing God a service by persecuting the church. Had you stopped him and asked for his reasons, he might have said something like this:

"Jesus of Nazareth is dead. Do you expect me to believe that a crucified nobody is the promised Messiah? According to our law, anybody who is hung on a tree is cursed [Deut. 21:23]. Would God take a cursed false prophet and make him the Messiah? No! His followers are preaching that Jesus is both alive and doing miracles through them. But their power comes from Satan, not God. This is a dangerous sect, and I intend to eliminate it before it destroys our historic Jewish faith!"

In spite of his great learning (Acts 26:24), Saul was spiritually blind (2 Cor. 3:12–18) and did not understand what the Old Testament really taught about the Messiah. Like many others of his country-men, he stumbled over the cross (1 Cor. 1:23) because he depended on his own righteousness and not on the righteousness of God (Rom. 9:30–10:13; Phil. 3:1–10). Many self-righteous religious people today do not see their need for a Savior and resent it if you tell them they are sinners.

Saul's attitude was that of an angry animal whose very breath was dangerous (see Acts 8:3)! Like many other rabbis, he believed that the law had to be obeyed before Messiah could come, and yet these "heretics" were preaching against the law, the temple, and the tra-ditions of the fathers (Acts 6:11–13). Saul wasted the churches in Judea (Gal. 1:23) and then got authority from the high priest to go as far as Damascus to hunt down the disciples of Jesus. This was no insignificant enterprise, for the authority of the highest Jewish coun-cil was behind him (Acts 22:5).

Damascus had a large Jewish population, and it has been estimated that there could well have been thirty to forty synagogues in the city. The fact that there were already believers there indicates how effec-tive the church had been in getting out the message. Some of the believers may have fled the persecution in Jerusalem, which explains why Saul wanted authority to bring them back. Believers were still identified with the Jewish synagogues, for the break with Judaism would not come for a few years. (See James 2:2, where "assembly" is "synagogue" in the original Greek.)

Saul suddenly found himself *on the ground* (Acts 9:4)! It was not a heat stroke or an epileptic seizure that put him there, but a personal meeting with Jesus Christ. At midday (Acts 22:6), he saw a bright light from heaven and heard a voice speaking his name (Acts 22:6–11). The men with him also fell to the earth (Acts 26:14) and heard the sound, but they could not understand the words spoken from heaven. They stood to their feet in bewilderment (Acts 9:7), hearing Saul address someone, but not knowing what was happening.

Saul of Tarsus made some wonderful discoveries that day. To begin with, he discovered to his surprise that Jesus of Nazareth was actually *alive!* Of course, the believers had been constantly affirming this (Acts 2:32; 3:15; 5:30–32), but Saul had refused to accept their testimony. If Jesus was alive, then Saul had to change his mind about Jesus and His message. He had to repent, a difficult thing for a self-righteous Pharisee to do.

Saul also discovered that he was a lost sinner who was in danger of the judgment of God. "I am Jesus, whom you are persecuting" (Acts 9:5 NKJV). Saul thought he had been serving God, when in reality he had been persecuting the Messiah! When measured by the holiness of Jesus Christ, Saul's good works and legalistic self-righteousness looked like filthy rags (Isa. 64:6; Phil. 3:6–8). All of his values changed. He was a new person because he trusted Jesus Christ.

The Lord had a special work for Saul to do

(Acts 26:16–18). The Hebrew of the Hebrews would become the apostle to the Gentiles; the persecutor would become a preacher; and the legalistic Pharisee would become the great proclaimer of the grace of God. Up to now, Saul had been like a wild animal, fighting against the goads, but now he would become a vessel of honor, the Lord's "tool," to preach the gospel in the regions beyond. What a transformation!

Some thirty years later, Paul wrote that Christ had "apprehended him" on the Damascus road (Phil. 3:12). Saul was out to arrest others when the Lord arrested him. He had to lose his religion before he could gain the righteousness of Christ. His conversion experience is unique, because sinners today certainly do not hear God's voice or see blinding heavenly lights. However, Paul's experience is an example of how Israel will be saved when Jesus Christ returns and reveals Himself to them (Zech. 12:10; Matt. 24:29ff.; 1 Tim. 1:12–16). His salvation is certainly a great encouragement to any lost sinner, for if "the chief of sinners" could be saved, surely anybody can be saved!

It is worth noting that the men who were with Saul saw the light, but did not see the Lord, and they heard the sound, but did not hear the voice speaking the words (note John 12:27–29). We wonder if any of them later trusted in Christ because of Saul's testi-mony. He definitely saw the glorified Lord Jesus Christ (1 Cor. 15:7–10).

The men led Saul *into the city* (Acts 9:8–9), for the angry bull (Acts 9:1) had now become a docile lamb! The leader had to be led because the vision had left him blind. His spiritual eyes had been opened, but his physical eyes were closed. God was thoroughly humbling Saul and preparing him for the ministry of Ananias. He fasted and prayed (Acts 9:11) for three days, during which time he no doubt started to "sort out" what he believed. He had been saved by grace, not by law, through faith in the living Christ. God began to instruct Saul and show him the relation-ship between the gospel of the grace of God and the traditional Mosaic religion that he had practiced all his life.

He Met Ananias (9:10–19)

Ananias was a devout Jew (Acts 22:12) who was a believer in Jesus Christ. He knew what kind of repu-tation Saul had and that he was coming to Damascus to arrest believers. It was up to a week's journey from Jerusalem to Damascus, but some of the Jerusalem Christians had gotten to the city first in order to warn the saints.

It is interesting to note in Acts 9 the different names used for God's people: disciples (Acts 9:1, 10, 19, 25–26, 36, 38), those of the way (Acts 9:2), saints (Acts 9:13, 32, 41), all that call on God's name (Acts 9:14, 21), and brethren (Acts 9:17, 30). We use the word *Christian* most frequently, and yet that name did not appear on the scene until later (Acts 11:26). "Disciples" is the name that is used most in the book of Acts, but you do not find it used in the Epistles. There the name "saints" is the most frequently used title for God's people.

Ananias was available to do God's will, but he certainly was not anxious to obey! The fact that Saul was "praying" instead of "preying" should have encouraged Ananias. "Prayer is the autograph of the Holy Ghost upon the renewed heart," said Charles Spurgeon (Rom. 8:9, 14–16). Instead of trusting himself, Saul was now trusting the Lord and waiting for Him to show him what to do. In fact, Saul had already seen a vision of a man named Ananias (Hananiah = "the Lord is gracious") coming to minister to him; so, how could Ananias refuse to obey?

Acts 9:15 is a good summary of Paul's life and ministry. It was all of grace, for he did not choose God; it was God who chose him (1 Tim. 1:14). He was God's vessel (2 Tim. 2:20–21), and God would work in and through him to accomplish His purposes (Eph. 2:10; Phil. 2:12–13). God's name would be glorified as His servant would take the gospel to Jews and Gentiles, kings and commoners, and as he would suffer for Christ's sake. This is the first reference in the book of Acts to the gospel going to the Gentiles (see also Acts 22:21; 26:17).

Once convinced, Ananias lost no time going to the house of Judas and ministering to the waiting Saul. The fact that he called him "brother" must have brought joy to the heart of the blinded Pharisee. Saul not only heard Ananias's voice, but he felt his hands (Acts 9:12, 17). By the power of God, his eyes were opened and he could see! He was also filled with the Holy Spirit and baptized, and then he ate some food.

The King James Version of Acts 22:16 conveys the impression that it was necessary for Saul to be baptized in order to be saved, but that was not the case. Saul washed away his sins by "calling on the Lord" (Acts 2:21; Rom. 10:13). Kenneth Wuest translates Acts 22:16, "Having arisen, be baptized and wash away your sins, having previously called upon His name." In the Greek, it is not a present participle ("calling"), but an aorist participle ("having called"). His calling on the Lord preceded his baptism.

Saul tarried with the believers in Damascus and no doubt learned from them. Imagine what it would be like to disciple the great apostle Paul! He discovered that they were loving people, undeserving of the persecution he had inflicted on them, and that they knew the truth of God's Word and only wanted to share it with others.

Before we leave this section, we should emphasize some practical lessons that all believers ought to learn.

To begin with, *God can use even the most obscure saint.* Were it not for the conversion of Saul, we would never have heard of Ananias, and yet Ananias had an important part to play in the ongoing work of the church. Behind many well-known servants of God are lesser-known believers who have influenced them. God keeps the books and will see to it that each servant will get a just reward. The important thing is not fame but faithfulness (1 Cor. 4:1–5).

The experience of Ananias also reminds us that we *should never be afraid to obey God's will.* Ananias at first argued with the Lord and gave some good reasons why he should not visit Saul. But the Lord had everything under control, and Ananias obeyed by faith. When God commands, we must remember that He is working "at both ends of the line," and that His perfect will is always the best.

There is a third encouragement: *God's works are always balanced.* God balanced a great public miracle with a quiet meeting in the house of Judas. The bright light and the voice from heaven were dramatic events, but the visit of Ananias was somewhat ordinary. The hand of God pushed Saul from his "high horse," but God used the hand of a man to bring Saul what he most needed. God spoke from heaven, but He also spoke through an obedient disciple who gave the message to Saul. The "ordinary" events were just as much a part of the miracle as were the extraordinary.

Finally, *we must never underestimate the value of one person brought to Christ.* Peter was ministering to thousands in Jerusalem, and Philip had seen a great harvest among the Samaritan people, but Ananias was sent to only one man. Yet what a man! Saul of Tarsus became Paul the apostle, and his life and ministry have influenced people and nations ever since. Even secular historians confess that Paul is one of the significant figures in world history.

On April 21, 1855, Edward Kimball led one of the young men in his Sunday school to faith in Christ. Little did he realize that Dwight L. Moody would one day become the world's leading evangelist. The ministry of Norman B. Harrison in an obscure Bible conference was used of God to bring Theodore Epp to faith in Christ, and God used Theodore Epp to build the Back to the Bible ministry around the world. Our task is to lead men and women to Christ; God's task is to use them for His glory; and every person is important to God.

He Met the Opposition (9:20–25)

Saul immediately began to proclaim the Christ that he had persecuted, declaring boldly that Jesus is the Son of God. This is the only place in Acts that you find this title, but Paul used it in his Epistles at least fifteen times. It was a major emphasis in his ministry. The dramatic change in Saul's life was a source of wonder to the Jews at Damascus. Every new convert's witness for Christ ought to begin right where he is, so Saul began his ministry first in Damascus (Acts 26:20).

It is likely that Saul's visit to Arabia (Gal. 1:17) took place about this time. Had Dr. Luke included it in his account, he would have placed it between Acts 9:21 and 22. We do not know how long he remained in Arabia, but we do know that after three years, Saul was back in Jerusalem (Gal. 1:18).

Why did he go to Arabia? Probably because the

Lord instructed him to get alone so that He might teach Saul His Word. There were many things that would have to be clarified in Saul's mind before he could minister effectively as an apostle of Jesus Christ. If Saul went to the area near Mount Sinai (Gal. 4:25), it took considerable courage and strength for such a journey. Perhaps it was then that he experienced "perils of robbers" and "perils in the wilderness" (2 Cor. 11:26). It is also possible that he did some evangelizing while in Arabia, because when he returned to Damascus, he was already a marked man.

The important thing about this Arabian sojourn is the fact that Saul did not "confer with flesh and blood" but received his message and mandate directly from the Lord (see Gal. 1:10–24). He did not borrow anything from the apostles in Jerusalem, because he did not even meet them until three years after his conversion.

When Saul returned to Damascus, he began his witness afresh, and the Jews sought to silence him. Now he would discover what it meant to be the hunted instead of the hunter! This was but the beginning of the "great things" he would suffer for the name of Christ (Acts 9:16). How humiliating it must have been for Saul to be led into Damascus as a blind man and then smuggled out like a common criminal (see 2 Cor. 11:32–33).

Throughout his life, the great apostle was hated, hunted, and plotted against by both Jews and Gentiles ("in perils of my own countrymen, in perils of the Gentiles"—2 Cor. 11:26 NKJV). As you read the book of Acts, you see how the opposition and persecution increase, until the apostle ends up a prisoner in Rome (Acts 13:45, 50; 14:19; 17:5, 13; 18:12; 20:3, 19; 21:10–11, 27ff.). But he counted it a privilege to suffer for the sake of Christ, and so should we. "Yea, and all that will live godly in Christ Jesus shall suffer persecution" (2 Tim. 3:12).

He Met the Jerusalem Believers (9:26–31)

There were two stages in Saul's experience with the church in Jerusalem.

Saul rejected (v. 26). At first, the believers in the Jerusalem church were afraid of him. Saul "kept trying" (literal Greek) to get into their fellowship, but they would not accept him. For one thing, they were afraid of him and probably thought that his new attitude of friendliness was only a trick to get into their fellowship so he could have them arrested. They did not believe that he was even a disciple of Jesus Christ, let alone an apostle who had seen the risen Savior.

Their attitude seems strange to us, for surely the Damascus saints had gotten word to the church in Jerusalem that Saul had been converted and was now preaching the Word. Perhaps Saul's "disappearance" for almost three years gave an air of suspicion to his testimony. Where had he been? What was he doing? Why had he waited so long to contact the Jerusalem elders? Furthermore, what right did he have to call himself an apostle when he had not been selected by

Jesus Christ? There were many unanswered questions that helped create an atmosphere of suspicion and fear.

Saul accepted (vv. 27–31). It was Barnabas who helped the Jerusalem church accept Saul. We met Joseph, the "son of encouragement," in Acts 4:36–37, and we will meet him again as we continue to study Acts. Barnabas "took hold" of Saul, brought him to the church leaders, and convinced them that Saul was both a believer and a chosen apostle. He had indeed seen the risen Christ (1 Cor. 9:1). It is not necessary to invent some "hidden reason" why Barnabas befriended Saul. This was just the nature of the man: he was an encouragement to others.

There seems to be a contradiction between Acts 9:27 and Galatians 1:18–19. How could Barnabas introduce Saul to "the apostles" (plural) if Peter was the only apostle Saul met? Dr. Luke is obviously using the word "apostle" in the wider sense of "spiritual leader." Even Galatians 1:19 calls James, the brother of the Lord, an apostle, and Barnabas is called an apostle in Acts 14:4 and 14. In his epistles, Paul sometimes used "apostle" to designate a special messenger or agent of the church (Rom. 16:7; 2 Cor. 8:23; Phil. 2:25, original Greek). So, there really is no contradiction; it is the leaders of the Jerusalem church that Saul met.

Saul began to witness to the Greek-speaking Jews, the Hellenists that had engineered the trial and death of Stephen (Acts 6:9–15). Saul was one of them, having been born and raised in Tarsus, and no doubt he felt an obligation to take up the mantle left by Stephen (Acts 22:20). The Hellenistic Jews were not about to permit this kind of witness, so they plotted to kill him.

At this point, we must read Acts 22:17–21. God spoke to Saul in the temple and reminded him of his commission to take the message to the Gentiles (Acts 9:15). Note the urgency of God's command: "Quick! Leave Jerusalem immediately, because they will not accept your testimony about me" (Acts 22:18 NIV). Saul shared this message with the church leaders, and they assisted him in returning to his native city, Tarsus. The fact that they believed Saul's testimony about the vision is proof that he had been fully accepted by the church.

We will not meet Saul again until Acts 11:25, when once more it is Barnabas who finds him and brings him to the church at Antioch where they ministered together. That took place about seven years after Saul left Jerusalem, about ten years after his conversion. We have every reason to believe that Saul used Tarsus as his headquarters for taking the gospel to the Gentiles in that part of the Roman Empire. He ministered "in the regions of Syria and Cilicia" (Gal. 1:21) and established churches there (Acts 15:41). Some Bible scholars believe that the Galatian churches were founded at this time.

It is likely that some of the trials listed in 2 Corinthians 11:24–26 occurred during this period. Only one Roman beating is recorded in Acts (16:22), which leaves two not accounted for. Likewise, the five

Jewish beatings are not recorded either in Acts or the Epistles. Luke tells us about only one shipwreck (Acts 27), but we have no record of the other two. Anyone who thinks that the apostle was taking a vacation during those years is certainly in error!

Acts 9:31 is another of Luke's summaries that he regularly dropped into the book (Acts 2:46–47; 4:4, 32; 5:12–14). Note that the geographic locations parallel those given in Acts 1:8. Luke is telling us that the message was going out just as the Lord had commanded. Soon, the center would be Antioch, not Jerusalem, and the key leader Paul, not Peter, and the gospel would be taken to the uttermost part of the earth.

It was a time of "peace" for the churches, but not a time of complacency, for they grew both spiritually and numerically. They seized the opportunity to repair and strengthen their sails before the next storm began to blow! The door of faith had been opened to the Jews (Acts 2) and to the Samaritans (Acts 8), and soon it would be opened to the Gentiles (Acts 10). Saul has moved off the scene, and Peter now returns. Soon, Peter will move off the scene (except for a brief mention in Acts 15), and Paul will fill the pages of the book of Acts.

God changes His workmen, but His work goes on.

And you and I are privileged to be a part of that work today!

CHAPTER TEN
Acts 9:32—10:48
PETER'S MIRACLE MINISTRY

What is the greatest miracle that God can do for us? Some would call the healing of the body God's greatest miracle, while others would vote for the raising of the dead. However, I think that the greatest miracle of all is the salvation of a lost sinner. Why? Because salvation costs the greatest price, it produces the greatest results, and it brings the greatest glory to God.

In this section, we find Peter participating in all three miracles: he heals Aeneas, he raises Dorcas from the dead, and he brings the message of salvation to Cornelius and his household.

A Great Miracle—Healing the Body (9:32–35)
The apostle Peter had been engaged in an itinerant ministry (Acts 8:25) when he found himself visiting the saints in Lydda, a largely Gentile city about twenty-five miles from Jerusalem. It is possible that the area had first been evangelized by people converted at Pentecost, or perhaps by faithful believers who had been scattered far and wide during the great persecution. No doubt Philip the evangelist had also ministered there (Acts 8:40).

We know very little about Aeneas. How old was

he? Did he believe on Jesus Christ? Was he a Jew or a Gentile? All that Dr. Luke tells us is the man had been palsied for eight years, which meant he was crippled and helpless. He was a burden to himself and a burden to others, and there was no prospect that he would ever get well.

Peter's first miracle had been the healing of a crippled man (Acts 3), and now that miracle was repeated. As you read the book of Acts, you will see parallels between the ministries of Peter and Paul. Both healed cripples. Both were arrested and put into jail and were miraculously delivered. Both were treated like gods (Acts 10:25–26; 14:8–18), and both gave a bold witness before the authorities. Both had to confront false prophets (Acts 8:9–24; 13:6–12). No one reading the book of Acts could end up saying, "I am for Paul!" or "I am for Peter!" (1 Cor. 1:12). "But it is the same God which worketh all in all" (1 Cor. 12:6).

The resurrected Christ, by the authority of His name, brought perfect soundness to Aeneas (see Acts 3:6, 16; 4:10). The healing was instantaneous, and the man was able to get up and make his bed. He became a walking miracle! Acts 9:35 does not suggest that the entire population of Lydda and Sharon were saved, but only all those who had contact with Aeneas. Just seeing him walk around convinced them that Jesus was alive and they needed to trust in Him. (See John 12:10–11 for a similar instance.)

You can be sure that Peter did much more in Lydda than heal Aeneas, as great and helpful as that miracle was. He evangelized, taught and encouraged the believers, and sought to establish the church in the faith. Jesus had commissioned Peter to care for the sheep (John 21:15–17), and Peter was faithful to fulfill that commission.

A Greater Miracle—Raising the Dead (9:36–43)
Joppa, the modern Jaffa, is located on the seacoast, some ten miles beyond Lydda. The city is important in Bible history as the place from which the prophet Jonah embarked when he tried to flee from God (Jonah 1:1–3). Jonah went to Joppa to avoid going to the Gentiles, but Peter in Joppa received his call to go to the Gentiles! Because Jonah disobeyed God, the Lord sent a storm that caused the Gentile sailors to fear. Because Peter obeyed the Lord, God sent the "wind of the Spirit" to the Gentiles and they experienced great joy and peace. What a contrast!

It seemed so tragic that a useful and beloved saint like Dorcas (Tabitha = gazelle) should die when she was so greatly needed by the church. This often happens in local churches, and it is a hard blow to take. In my own pastoral ministry, I have experienced the loss of choice saints who were difficult to replace in the church, yet, all we can say is, "The Lord gave, and the Lord hath taken away; blessed be the name of the Lord" (Job 1:21).

The believers in Joppa heard that Peter was in the area, and they sent for him immediately. There is no record in Acts that any of the apostles had raised the dead, so their sending for Peter was an evidence of their faith in the power of the risen Christ. When our Lord ministered on earth. He raised the dead, so why would He not be able to raise the dead from His exalted throne in glory?

We usually think of the apostles as leaders who told other people what to do, but often the people commanded them! (For Peter's "philosophy of ministry" read 1 Peter 5.) Peter was a leader who served the people and was ready to respond to their call. Peter had the power to heal, and he used the power to glorify God and help people, not to promote himself.

It was a Jewish custom first to wash the dead body, and then to anoint it with spices for burial. When Peter arrived in the upper room where Dorcas lay in state, he found a group of weeping widows who had been helped by her ministry. Keep in mind that there was no "government aid" in those days for either widows or orphans, and needy people had to depend on their "network" for assistance. The church has an obligation to help people who are truly in need (1 Tim. 5:3–16; James 1:27).

The account of Peter's raising of Dorcas should be compared with the account of our Lord's raising of Jairus's daughter (Mark 5:34–43). In both cases, the mourning people were put out of the room, and the words spoken are almost identical: *"talitha cumi: little girl, arise"*; *"Tabitha cumi: Tabitha, arise."* Jesus took the girl by the hand before He spoke to her, for He was not afraid of becoming ceremonially defiled, and Peter took Dorcas by the hand after she had come to life. In both instances, it was the power of God that raised the person from the dead, for the dead person certainly could not exercise faith.

As with the healing of Aeneas, the raising of Dorcas attracted great attention and resulted in many people trusting Jesus Christ. During the "many days" that he tarried in Joppa, Peter took the opportunity to ground these new believers in the truth of the Word, for faith built on miracles alone is not substantial.

It was a good thing Peter tarried in Joppa, because God met with him there in a thrilling new way. God's servants need not always be "on the go." They should take time to be alone with God, to reflect and meditate and pray, especially after experiencing great blessings. Yes, there were plenty of sick people Peter might have visited and healed, but God had other plans. He deliberately detained His servant in Joppa to prepare him for his third use of "the keys."

It is significant that Peter stayed in the home of a tanner, because tanners were considered "unclean" by the Jewish rabbis (see Lev. 11:35–40). God was moving Peter a step at a time from Jewish legalism into the freedom of His wonderful grace.

The Greatest Miracle—Winning Lost Sinners (10:1–48)

Chapter 10 is pivotal in the book of Acts, for it records

the salvation of the Gentiles. We see Peter using "the keys of the kingdom" for the third and last time. He had opened the door of faith for the Jews (Acts 2) and also for the Samaritans (Acts 8), and now he would be used of God to bring the Gentiles into the church (see Gal. 3:27–28; Eph. 2:11–22).

This event took place about ten years after Pentecost. Why did the apostles wait so long before going to the lost Gentiles? After all, in His Great Commission (Matt. 28:19–20), Jesus had told them to go into *all* the world, and it would seem logical for them to go to their Gentile neighbors as soon as possible. But God has His times as well as His plans, and the transition from the Jews to the Samaritans to the Gentiles was a gradual one.

The stoning of Stephen and the subsequent persecution of the church marked the climax of the apostles' witness to the Jews. Then the gospel moved to the Samaritans. When God saved Saul of Tarsus, He got hold of His special envoy to the Gentiles. Now was the time to open the door of faith (Acts 14:27) to the Gentiles and bring them into the family of God.

There were four acts to this wonderful drama.

Preparation (vv. 1–22). Before He could save the Gentiles, God had to prepare Peter to bring the message and Cornelius to hear the message. Salvation is a divine work of grace, but God works through human channels. Angels can deliver God's messages to lost men, but they cannot preach the gospel to them. That is our privilege—and responsibility.

Caesarea is sixty-five miles northwest of Jerusalem and thirty miles north of Joppa (Jaffa). At that time, Caesarea was the Roman capital of Judea and boasted of many beautiful public buildings. In that city lived Cornelius, the Roman centurion, whose heart had tired of pagan myths and empty religious rituals, and who had turned to Judaism in hopes he could find salvation. Cornelius was as close to Judaism as he could get without becoming a proselyte. There were many "God fearers" like him in the ancient world (Acts 13:16), and they proved to be a ready field for spiritual harvest.

It is interesting to see how religious a person can be and still not be saved. Certainly, Cornelius was sincere in his obedience to God's law, his fasting, and his generosity to the Jewish people (compare this to Luke 7:1–10). He was not permitted to offer sacrifices in the temple, so he presented his prayers to God as his sacrifices (Ps. 141:1–2). In every way, he was a model of religious respectability—and yet he was not a saved man.

The difference between Cornelius and many religious people today is this: he knew that his religious devotion was not sufficient to save him. Many religious people today are satisfied that their character and good works will get them to heaven, and they have no concept either of their own sin or of God's grace. In his prayers, Cornelius was asking God to show him the way of salvation (Acts 11:13–14).

In many respects, John Wesley was like Cornelius.

He was a religious man, a church member, a minister, and the son of a minister. He belonged to a "religious club" at Oxford, the purpose of which was the perfecting of the Christian life. Wesley served as a foreign missionary, but even as he preached to others, he had no assurance of his own personal salvation.

On May 24, 1738, Wesley reluctantly attended a small meeting in London where someone was reading aloud from Martin Luther's commentary on Romans. "About a quarter before nine," Wesley wrote in his journal, "while he was describing the change which God works in the heart through faith in Christ, I felt my heart strangely warmed, I felt I did trust in Christ, Christ alone for salvation; and an assurance was given me that He had taken away my sins, even mine, and saved me from the law of sin and death." The result was the great Wesleyan revival that not only swept many into the kingdom, but also helped transform British society through Christian social action.

God sent an angel to instruct Cornelius and, in true military fashion, Cornelius immediately obeyed. But why send for Peter, who was thirty miles away in Joppa, when Philip the evangelist was already in Caesarea (Acts 8:40)? Because it was Peter, not Philip, who had been given the "keys." God not only works at the right time, but He also works through the right servant, and both are essential.

Peter also had to be prepared for this event since he had lived as an orthodox Jew all of his life (Acts 10:14). The law of Moses was a wall between the Jews and the Gentiles, and this wall had been broken down at the cross (Eph. 2:14–18). The Gentiles were considered aliens and strangers as far as the Jewish covenants and promises were concerned (Eph. 2:11–13). But now, all of that would change, and God would declare that, as far as the Jew and the Gentile were concerned, "There is no difference" either in condemnation (Rom. 3:22–23) or in salvation (Rom. 10:12–13).

Why did God use a vision about food to teach Peter that the Gentiles were not unclean? For one thing, Peter was hungry, and a vision about food would certainly "speak to his condition," as the Quakers say. Second, the distinction between "clean and unclean foods" was a major problem between the Jews and the Gentiles in that day. In fact, Peter's Christian friends criticized him for eating with the Gentiles (Acts 11:1–3)! God used this centuries-old regulation (Lev. 11) to teach Peter an important spiritual lesson.

A third reason goes back to something Jesus had taught Peter and the other disciples when He was ministering on earth (Mark 7:1–23). At that time, Peter did not fully understand what Jesus was saying, but now it would all come together. God was not simply changing Peter's diet; He was changing His entire program! The Jew was not "clean" and the Gentile "unclean," but *both Jew and Gentile were "unclean" before God!* "For God hath concluded them all in unbelief, that he might have mercy on all" (Rom. 11:32).

This meant that a Gentile did not have to become a Jew in order to become a Christian.

Even though Peter's refusal was in the most polite terms, it was still wrong. Dr. W. Graham Scroggie wrote, "You can say 'No,' and you can say 'Lord'; but you cannot say 'No, Lord!'" If He is truly our Lord, then we can only say "Yes!" to Him and obey His commands.

God's timing is always perfect, and the three men from Caesarea arrived at the door just as Peter was pondering the meaning of the vision. The Spirit commanded Peter to meet the men and go with them. The phrase "nothing doubting" (Acts 10:20) means "making no distinctions." You find it again in Acts 11:12, and a similar word is used in Acts 11:2 ("contended with him" = "made a difference"). Peter was no longer to make any distinctions between the Jews and the Gentiles.

Explanation (vv. 23–33). The fact that Peter allowed the Gentiles to lodge with him is another indication that the walls were coming down. Peter selected six Jewish believers to go along as witnesses (Acts 11:12), three times the official number needed. It would take at least two days to cover the thirty miles between Joppa and Caesarea. When Peter arrived, he discovered that Cornelius had gathered relatives and friends to hear the message of life. He was a witness even before he became a Christian!

How easy it would have been for Peter to accept honor and use the situation to promote himself, but Peter was a servant, not a celebrity (1 Peter 5:1–6). When he announced that he did not consider the Gentiles unclean, this must have amazed and rejoiced the hearts of his listeners. For centuries the Jews, on the basis of Old Testament law, had declared the Gentiles to be unclean, and some Jews even referred to the Gentiles as "dogs."

The remarkable thing in this section is Peter's question, "I ask, therefore, for what intent ye have sent for me?" (Acts 10:29). Didn't Peter know that he had been summoned there to preach the gospel? Had he forgotten the Acts 1:8 commission to go to "the uttermost part of the earth"? Today, we can look back at developing events in the church and understand what God was doing, but it might not have been that easy had we been living in the midst of those events. In fact, the Jerusalem church questioned Peter about his actions (Acts 11:1–18), and later called a conference to deal with the place of the Gentiles in the church (Acts 15).

Cornelius rehearsed his experience with the angel and then told Peter why he had been summoned: to tell him, his family, and his friends how they could be saved (Acts 11:14). They were not interested Gentiles asking for a lecture on Jewish religion. They were lost sinners begging to be told how to be saved.

Before we leave this section, some important truths must be emphasized. First, the idea that "one religion is as good as another" is completely false. Those who tell us that we should worship "the God of many names" and not "change other people's religions" are going contrary to Scripture. "Salvation is of the Jews" (John 4:22), and there can be no salvation apart from faith in Jesus Christ, who was born a Jew. Cornelius had piety and morality, but he did not have salvation. Some might say, "Leave Cornelius alone! His religion is a part of his culture, and it's a shame to change his culture!" God does not see it that way. Apart from hearing the message of the gospel and trusting Christ, Cornelius had no hope.

Second, the seeking Savior (Luke 19:10) will find the seeking sinner (Jer. 29:13). Wherever there is a searching heart, God responds. This is why it is essential that we as God's children obey His will and share His Word. You never know when your witness for Christ is exactly what somebody has been waiting and praying for.

Third, Peter certainly was privileged to minister to a model congregation (Acts 10:33). They were all present, they wanted to hear the Word, and they listened, believed, and obeyed. What more could a preacher ask?

Proclamation (vv. 34–43). There can be no faith apart from the Word (Rom. 10:17), and Peter preached that Word. God is no respecter of persons as far as nationality and race are concerned. When it comes to sin and salvation, "there is no difference" (Rom. 2:11; 3:22–23; 10:1–13). All men have the same Creator (Acts 17:26), and all men need the same Savior (Acts 4:12). Acts 10:35 does not teach that we are saved by works, otherwise Peter would be contradicting himself (Acts 10:43). To "fear God and work righteousness" is a description of the Christian life. To fear God is to reverence and trust Him (Mic. 6:8). The evidence of this faith is a righteous walk.

Peter then summarized the story of the life, death, and resurrection of Jesus Christ. Cornelius and his friends knew about Christ's life and death, for "this thing was not done in a corner" (Acts 26:26). Peter made it clear that Israel was God's instrument for accomplishing His work (Acts 10:36), but that Jesus is "Lord of all," and not just Lord of Israel. From the very founding of the nation of Israel, God made it clear that the blessing would be from Israel to the whole world (Gen. 12:1–3).

The public at large knew about Christ's life, ministry, and death, but only the apostles and other believers were witnesses of His resurrection. As in his previous sermons, Peter laid the blame for the crucifixion on the Jewish leaders (Acts 3:15; 4:10; 5:30), as did Stephen (Acts 7:52). Paul would pick up this same emphasis (1 Thess. 2:14–16).

Having finished this recitation of the historical basis for the gospel message, Christ's death and resurrection, Peter then announced the good news: "Whosoever believeth in him shall receive remission of sin" (Acts 10:43; see 2:21). His hearers laid hold of that word "whosoever," applied it to themselves, believed on Jesus Christ, and were saved.

Vindication (vv. 44–48). Peter was just getting

started in his message when his congregation believed and the Holy Spirit interrupted the meeting (Acts 11:15). God the Father interrupted Peter on the Mount of Transfiguration (Matt. 17:4–5), and God the Son interrupted him in the matter of the temple tax (Matt. 17:24–27). Now, God the Spirit interrupted him—and Peter never was able to finish his sermon! Would that preachers today had interruptions of this kind!

The Holy Spirit was giving witness to the six Jews who were present that these Gentiles were truly born again. After all, these men had not seen the vision with Peter, and they needed to understand that the Gentiles were now on an equal footing with the Jews. This does not suggest that every new believer gives evidence of salvation by speaking in tongues, though every true believer will certainly use his or her tongue to glorify God (Rom. 10:9–10). This was an event parallel to Pentecost: the same Spirit who had come on the Jewish believers had now come on the Gentiles (Acts 11:15–17; 15:7–9). No wonder the men were astonished!

With this event, the period of transition in the early history of the church comes to an end. Believers among the Jews, Samaritans, and Gentiles have all received the Spirit of God and are united in the body of Christ (1 Cor. 12:13; Gal. 3:27).

These Gentiles were not saved by being baptized; they were baptized because they gave evidence of being saved. To use Acts 2:38 to teach salvation by baptism, or Acts 8:14–16 to teach salvation by the laying on of hands, is to ignore the transitional character of God's program. Sinners have always been saved by faith; that is one principle God has never changed. But God does change His methods of operation, and this is clearly seen in Acts 1—10. The experience of Cornelius and his household makes it very clear that baptism is not essential for salvation. From now on, the order will be hear the Word, believe on Christ, and receive the Spirit, and then be baptized and unite with other believers in the church to serve and worship God.

Peter tarried in Caesarea and helped to ground these new believers in the truth of the Word. Perhaps Philip assisted him. This entire experience is an illustration of the commission of Matthew 28:19–20. Peter went where God sent him and made disciples ("teach") of the Gentiles. Then he baptized them and taught them the Word.

That same commission applies to the church today. Are we fulfilling it as we should?

CHAPTER ELEVEN
Acts 11
MAKING ROOM FOR THE GENTILES

Acts 11 describes how the church in Jerusalem related to "the saints below," the Gentiles in Caesarea and Antioch who had trusted Jesus

Christ as their Savior and Lord. Having fellowship with the Gentiles was a new experience for these Jewish Christians, who all their lives had looked on the Gentiles as pagans and outsiders. Tradition said that a Gentile had to "become a Jew" in order to be accepted, but now Jews and Gentiles were united in the church through faith in Jesus Christ (Gal. 3:26–28).

Acts 11 describes three responses of the Jewish believers to the Gentile Christians. As you study these responses, you will better understand how Christians today ought to relate to one another.

They Accepted the Gentiles (11:1–18)

Peter no sooner returned to Jerusalem when he was met by members of the strong legalistic party in the church of Judea ("they that were of the circumcision") who rebuked him for fellowshipping with Gentiles and eating with them. Keep in mind that these Jewish believers did not yet understand the relationship between law and grace, Jews and Gentiles, and Israel and the church. Most Christians today understand these truths, but, after all, we have Romans, Galatians, Ephesians, and Hebrews! There were many converted priests in the church who would be zealous for the law (Acts 6:7), and even the ordinary Jewish believer would have a difficult time making the transition (Acts 21:20). It was not only a matter of religion, but also of culture, and cultural habits are very hard to break.

The phrase "contended with him" comes from the same word translated "doubting nothing" in Acts 10:20 and 11:12. It means "to make a difference." These legalists were making a difference between the Gentiles and the Jews after Peter had demonstrated that "there is no difference!" God had declared the Gentiles "clean," that is, accepted before God on the same basis as the Jews—through faith in Jesus Christ.

Peter had nothing to fear. After all, he had only followed orders from the Lord, and the Spirit had clearly confirmed the salvation of the Gentiles. Peter reviewed the entire experience from beginning to end, and, when he was finished, the Jewish legalists dropped their charges and glorified God for the salvation of the Gentiles (Acts 11:18). However, this did not end the matter completely, for this same legalistic party later debated with Paul about the salvation of the Gentiles (Acts 14:26—15:2). Even after the Jerusalem Conference, legalistic teachers continued to attack Paul and invade the churches he founded. They wanted to woo the believers into a life of obedience to the law (Gal. 1:6ff.; Phil. 3:1–3, 17–21). It is possible that many of these legalists were genuine believers, but they did not understand their freedom in Jesus Christ (Gal. 5:1ff.).

In his personal defense in Acts 11, Peter presented three pieces of evidence: the vision from God (Acts 11:5–11), the witness of the Spirit (Acts 11:12–15, 17), and the witness of the Word (Acts 11:16). Of course, none of these men had seen the vision, but they trusted Peter's report, for they knew that he had been as orthodox as they in his personal life (Acts 10:14). He was not likely to go to the Gentiles on his own and then invent a story to back it up.

The witness of the Spirit was crucial, for this was God's own testimony that He had indeed saved the Gentiles. It is interesting that Peter had to go *all the way back to Pentecost* to find an example of what happened in the home of Cornelius! This suggests that a dramatic "baptism of the Spirit" (Acts 11:16), accompanied by speaking in tongues, was not an everyday occurrence in the early church. Peter could not use the experience of the Samaritans as his example, because the Samaritans received the gift of the Spirit through the laying on of the apostles' hands (Acts 8:14–17). Cornelius and his household received the Spirit the moment they trusted Christ. This is the pattern for today.

"What was I, that I could withstand God?" asked Peter, and to this question, the legalists had no answer. From beginning to end, the conversion of the Gentiles was God's gracious work. He gave them the gift of repentance and the gift of salvation when they believed. In later years, God would use the letters of Paul to explain the "one body," how believing Jews and believing Gentiles are united in Christ (Eph. 2:11—3:12). But at that time, this "mystery" was still hidden, so we must not be too hard on those saints who were uneasy about the place of the Gentiles in the church.

Christians are to receive one another and not dispute over cultural differences or minor matters of personal conviction (Rom. 14—15). Some of the Jewish Christians in the early church wanted the Gentiles to become Jews, and some of the Gentile believers wanted the Jews to stop being Jews and become Gentiles! This attitude can create serious division in the church even today, so it is important that we follow the example of Acts 11:18 and the admonition of Romans 14:1, and receive those whom God has also received.

They Encouraged the Gentiles (11:19–26)

When the saints were scattered abroad during Saul's persecution of the church (Acts 8:1), some of them ended up in Antioch, the capital of Syria, three hundred miles north of Jerusalem. (Don't confuse this city with Antioch in Pisidia, Acts 13:14.) There were at least sixteen Antiochs in the ancient world, but this one was the greatest.

With a population of half a million, Antioch ranked as the third largest city in the Roman Empire, following Rome and Alexandria. Its magnificent buildings helped give it the name "Antioch the Golden, Queen of the East." The main street was more than four miles long, paved with marble, and lined on both sides by marble colonnades. It was the only city in the ancient world at that time that had its streets lighted at night.

A busy port and a center for luxury and culture, Antioch attracted all kinds of people, including wealthy retired Roman officials who spent their days chatting in the baths or gambling at the races. With its large cosmopolitan population and its great commercial and political power, Antioch presented to the church an exciting opportunity for evangelism.

Antioch was a wicked city, perhaps second only to Corinth. Though all the Greek, Roman, and Syrian deities were honored, the local shrine was dedicated to Daphne, whose worship included immoral practices. "Antioch was to the Roman world what New York City is to ours," writes James A. Kelso in *An Archaeologist Follows the Apostle Paul*. "Here where all the gods of antiquity were worshipped, Christ must be exalted." Not only was an effective church built in Antioch, but it became the church that sent Paul out to win the Gentile world for Christ.

When the persecuted believers arrived in Antioch, they did not at all feel intimidated by the magnificence of the buildings or the pride of the citizens. The Word of God was on their lips and the hand of God was on their witness, and "a great number" of sinners repented and believed. It was a thrilling work of God's wonderful grace.

The church leaders in Jerusalem had a responsibility to "shepherd" the scattered flock, which now included Gentile congregations as far away as Syria. Apparently the apostles were ministering away from Jerusalem at the time, so the elders commissioned Barnabas to go to Antioch to find out what was going on among the Gentiles. This proved to be a wise choice, for Barnabas lived up to his nickname, "son of encouragement" (Acts 4:36).

Acts 11:24 gives us a "spiritual profile" of Barnabas, and he appears to be the kind of Christian all of us would do well to emulate. He was a righteous man who obeyed the Word in daily life so that his character was above reproach. He was filled with the Spirit, which explains the effectiveness of his ministry. That he was a man of faith is evident from the way he encouraged the church and then encouraged Saul. New Christians and new churches need people like Barnabas to encourage them in their growth and ministry.

How did Barnabas encourage these new Gentile believers? For one thing, he rejoiced at what he saw. Worshipping with Gentiles was a new experience for him, but he approached it positively and did not look for things to criticize. It was a work of God, and Barnabas gave thanks for God's grace.

He emphasized dedication of the heart as he taught the people the Word of God. The phrase "cleave [cling] to the Lord" does not suggest that they were to "keep themselves saved." The same grace that saves us can also keep us (1 Cor. 15:10; Heb. 13:9). The phrase reminds us of Joshua's admonition to Israel in Joshua 22:5. To "cleave to the Lord" includes loving the Lord, walking in His ways, obeying His Word, and serving Him wholeheartedly. It means that we belong to Him alone and that we cultivate our devotion to Him. "No man can serve two masters" (Matt. 6:24).

There were two wonderful results from Barnabas's work in Antioch. First, the church's witness made a great impact on the city so that "many people were added to the Lord" (Acts 11:24). When the saints are grounded in the Word, they will have a strong witness to the lost, and there will be a balance in the church between edification and evangelism, worship and witness, teaching and testifying.

Second, the growth of the church meant that Barnabas needed help, so he went to Tarsus and enlisted Saul. But why go so far away just to find an assistant? Why not send to Jerusalem and ask the deacon Nicolas, who was from Antioch (Acts 6:5)? Because Barnabas knew that God had commissioned Saul to minister to the Gentiles (Acts 9:15; 22:21; 26:17). You recall that Barnabas befriended Saul in Jerusalem (Acts 9:26–27), and no doubt the two of them often talked about Saul's special call from God.

Saul had been converted about ten years when Barnabas brought him to Antioch. The New Testament does not tell us what Saul did back home in Tarsus after he left Jerusalem (Acts 9:28–30), but it is likely he was busy evangelizing both Jews and Gentiles. It may have been during this period that he founded the churches in Cilicia (Acts 15:23, 41; Gal. 1:21), and that he experienced some of the sufferings listed in 2 Corinthians 11:23–28. As he witnessed in the synagogues, you can be sure he would not have had an easy time of it!

What Barnabas did for Saul needs to be practiced in our churches today. Mature believers need to enlist others and encourage them in their service for the Lord. It was one of D. L. Moody's policies that each new Christian be given a task soon after conversion. At first, it might be only passing out hymnals or ushering people to their seats, but each convert had to be busy. As previously mentioned, he said, "It is better to put ten men to work than to do the work of ten men." Many of Mr. Moody's "assistants" became effective Christian workers in their own right, and this multiplied the witness.

It was at Antioch that the name *Christian* was first applied to the disciples of Jesus Christ. The Latin suffix *-ian* means "belonging to the party of." In derision, some of the pagan citizens of Antioch joined this Latin suffix to the Hebrew name "Christ" and came up with *Christian*. The name is found only three times in the entire New Testament: Acts 11:26; 26:28; 1 Peter 4:16.

Unfortunately, the word *Christian* has lost a great deal of significance over the centuries and no longer means "one who has turned from sin, trusted Jesus Christ, and received salvation by grace" (Acts 11:21–23). Many people who have never been born again consider themselves "Christians" simply because they say they are not "pagans." After all, they may belong to a church, attend services somewhat regularly, and even occasionally give to the work of the church! But it takes more than that for a sinner to become a child of God. It takes repentance from sin and faith in Jesus Christ, who died for our sins on the cross and rose again to give us eternal life.

The believers in the early church *suffered* because they were Christians (1 Peter 4:16). Dr. David Otis Fuller has asked, "If you were arrested for being a Christian, would there be enough evidence to convict you?" A good question! And the answer is a matter of life or death!

They Received Help from the Gentiles (11:27–30)

The foundation for the church was laid by the apostles and prophets (Eph. 2:20), and then both eventually moved off the scene. After all, you don't keep laying the foundation! The New Testament prophets received their messages from the Lord by the Holy Spirit, and delivered them to the people, sometimes in a tongue. The message would then have to be interpreted, after which the people would evaluate the message to make sure it came from God (note 1 Cor. 12:10; 14:27–33; 1 Thess. 5:19–21).

The New Testament prophets received their messages from the Lord *immediately,* but ministers and teachers today get their messages *mediately* through the Scriptures. We today have the completed Word of God from which the Holy Spirit teaches and guides us. First Corinthians 12:10 ties together the gifts of prophecy, discernment, and tongues and the interpretation of tongues. Of course, the Spirit is sovereign and can give to a believer any gift He desires (1 Cor. 12:11), but the passing of apostles and prophets from the scene, and the completing of God's revelation in the Word, suggest that a change has taken place.

There are people today who claim to receive special "words of revelation" or "words of wisdom" from the Lord, but such revelations are suspect and even dangerous. "To the law and to the testimony; if they speak not according to this word, it is because there is no light in them" (Isa. 8:20). "Hearken not unto the words of the prophets that prophesy unto you," warned Jeremiah. "They make you vain [fill you with false hopes]; they speak a vision of their own heart, and not out of the mouth of the Lord" (Jer. 23:16).

The Spirit told Agabus (see Acts 21:10–11) that a great famine was soon to come, and it did come during the reign of Claudius Caesar (AD 41–54), when crops were poor for many years. Ancient writers mention at least four famines: two in Rome, one in Greece, and one in Judea. The famine in Judea was especially severe, and the Jewish historian Josephus records that many people died for lack of money to buy what little food was available.

Agabus delivered his message to the Antioch believers, and they determined to help their fellow Christians in Judea. The purpose of true prophecy is not to satisfy our curiosity about the future but to stir up our hearts to do the will of God. The believers could not stop the famine from coming, but they could send relief to those in need.

An important spiritual principle is illustrated in this passage: if people have been a spiritual blessing to us, we should minister to them out of our material possessions.

"Let him who is taught in the word share in all good things with him who teaches" (Gal. 6:6 NKJV). The Jewish believers in Jerusalem had brought the gospel to Antioch. Then they had sent Barnabas to encourage the new believers. It was only right that the Gentiles in Antioch reciprocate and send material help to their Jewish brothers and sisters in Judea. Some years later, Paul would gather a similar offering from the Gentile churches and take it to the saints in Jerusalem (Acts 24:17; and see Rom. 15:23–28).

It is important to note that a change had taken place in the Jerusalem church. At one time, nobody in the church had any need (Acts 4:34), nor was it necessary to ask others for help. Those early years were "days of heaven on earth" as God richly blessed His people and used them as witnesses to the unbelieving nation. They were "times of refreshing" from the Lord (Acts 3:19). But when the message moved from the Jews to the Samaritans and the Gentiles, the Jerusalem "sharing program" gradually faded away and things became more normal.

The pattern for Christian giving today is not Acts 2:44–45 and 4:31–35, but Acts 11:29, "every man according to his ability." It is this pattern that Paul taught in 2 Corinthians 8—9. The practice of "Christian communism" was found only in Jerusalem and was a temporary measure while the message was going "to the Jew first." Like God's care of the Jews in the wilderness, it was a living exhibition of the blessings God would bestow if the nation would repent and believe.

The fact that the church elected Barnabas and Saul to take the relief offering to Jerusalem is evidence that they had confidence in them. The men had been working together in the teaching of the Word, and now they joined hands in the practical ministry of relieving the wants of the Jerusalem believers. No doubt they also ministered the Word along the way as they made the long journey from Antioch to Jerusalem. In a short time, the Spirit would call these two friends to join forces and take the gospel to the Gentiles in other lands (Acts 13:1ff.), and they would travel many miles together.

Another significant result from this ministry was the addition of John Mark to their "team" (Acts 12:25). It is likely that Mark was converted through the ministry of Peter (1 Peter 5:13). His mother's house was a gathering place for the Jerusalem believers (Acts 12:12), and she and Barnabas were related (Col. 4:10). Even though John Mark failed in his first "term" as a missionary (Acts 13:13), and helped cause a rift between Barnabas and Paul (Acts 15:38–40), he later became an effective assistant to Paul (2 Tim. 4:11) and was used of God to write the gospel of Mark.

The word *elders* in Acts 11:30 has not been used before in Acts, except to refer to the Jewish leaders (Acts 4:5, 23; 6:12). In the church, the elders were mature believers who had the spiritual oversight of the ministry (1 Peter 5:1; 2 John 1). When you compare

Acts 20:17 and 28, and Titus 1:5 and 7, you learn that "elder" and "bishop" [overseer] are equivalent titles. The elders/bishops were the "pastors" of the flocks, assisted by the deacons, and the qualifications for both are found in 1 Timothy 3.

Wherever Paul established churches, he saw to it that qualified elders were ordained to give leadership to the assemblies (Acts 14:23; Titus 1:5). In the Jerusalem church, the apostles and elders gave spiritual oversight (Acts 15:2, 4, 6, 22). The delegation from the Antioch church did not ignore the spiritual leaders in Jerusalem, but delivered the gift to them for distribution to the needy members. This is an important principle and should be heeded in this day when so many organizations want to get support from local churches.

Was it a humbling experience for the Jewish believers to receive help from the Gentiles? Perhaps, but it was also a beautiful demonstration of love and a wonderful testimony of unity. Sir Winston Churchill said, "We make a living by what we get, but we make a life by what we give." It was an enriching experience for the churches in Jerusalem and in Antioch, for there is blessing both in giving and receiving when God's grace is in control.

It is unfortunate when individual Christians and local churches forget those who have been a spiritual blessing to them. The church at Antioch is a splendid example of how we as believers ought to show gratitude in a practical way to those who have helped us in our Christian life. Phillips Brooks was asked what he would do to revive a dead church, and he replied, "I would take up a missionary offering!"

Sincerely thinking of others is still the best formula for a happy and useful Christian life, both for individuals and for churches.

CHAPTER TWELVE
Acts 12
WAKE UP TO A MIRACLE!

Imagine waking up to a miracle and having an angel for your alarm clock!

That's what happened to Peter when he was in prison for the third time, awaiting trial and certain death. Years later, when he wrote his first epistle, Peter may have had this miraculous experience in mind when he quoted Psalm 34:15–16: "For the eyes of the Lord are over the righteous, and his ears are open unto their prayers; but the face of the Lord is against them that do evil" (1 Peter 3:12). That quotation certainly summarizes what God did for Peter, and it reveals to us three wonderful assurances to encourage us in the difficult days of life.

God Sees Our Trials (12:1–4)
"The eyes of the Lord are over the righteous" (1 Peter 3:12).

God watched and noted what Herod Agrippa I was doing to His people. This evil man was the grandson of Herod the Great, who ordered the Bethlehem children to be murdered, and the nephew of Herod Antipas, who had John the Baptist beheaded. A scheming and murderous family, the Herods were despised by the Jews, who resented having Edomites ruling over them. Of course, Herod knew this, so he persecuted the church to convince the Jewish people of his loyalty to the traditions of the fathers. Now that the Gentiles were openly a part of the church, Herod's plan was even more agreeable to the nationalistic Jews who had no place for "pagans."

Herod had several believers arrested, among them James, the brother of John, whom he beheaded. Thus James became the first of the apostles to be martyred. When you ponder his death in the light of Matthew 20:20–28, it takes on special significance. James and John, with their mother, had asked for thrones, but Jesus made it clear that there can be no glory apart from suffering. "Are ye able to drink of the cup that I shall drink of, and to be baptized with the baptism that I am baptized with?" He asked (Matt. 20:22). Their bold reply was, "We are able."

Of course, they did not know what they were saying, but they eventually discovered the high cost of winning a throne of glory: James was arrested and killed, and John became an exile on the Isle of Patmos, a prisoner of Rome (Rev. 1:9). Indeed, they did drink of the cup and share in the baptism of suffering that their Lord had experienced!

If it pleased the Jews when James was killed, just think how delighted they would be if Peter were slain! God permitted Herod to arrest Peter and put him under heavy guard in prison. Sixteen soldiers, four for each watch, kept guard over the apostle, with two soldiers chained to the prisoner and two watching the doors. After all, the last time Peter was arrested, he mysteriously got out of jail, and Herod was not about to let that happen again.

Why was James allowed to die, while Peter was rescued? After all, both were dedicated servants of God, needed by the church. The only answer is *the sovereign will of God,* the very thing Peter and the church had prayed about after their second experience of persecution (Acts 4:24–30). Herod had "stretched forth" his hand to destroy the church, but God would stretch forth His hand to perform signs and wonders and glorify His Son (Acts 4:28–30). God allowed Herod to kill James, but He kept him from harming Peter. It was the throne in heaven that was in control, not the throne on earth.

Please note that the Jerusalem church did not replace James as they had replaced Judas (Acts 1:15–26). As long as the gospel was going "to the Jew first," it was necessary to have the full complement of twelve apostles to witness to the twelve tribes of Israel. The stoning of Stephen ended that special witness to Israel, so the number of official witnesses was no longer important.

It is good to know that, no matter how difficult the trials or how disappointing the news. God is still on the throne and has everything under control. We may not always understand His ways, but we know His sovereign will is best.

God Hears Our Prayers (12:5–17)

"And his ears are open unto their prayers" (1 Peter 3:12).

The phrase "but prayer" is the turning point in the story. Never underestimate the power of a praying church! "The angel fetched Peter out of prison," said the Puritan preacher Thomas Watson, "but it was prayer that fetched the angel." Follow the scenes in this exciting drama in Acts 12.

Peter sleeping (vv. 5–6). If you were chained to two Roman soldiers and facing the possibility of being executed the next day, would you sleep very soundly? Probably not, but Peter did. In fact, Peter was so sound asleep that the angel had to strike him on the side to wake him up!

The fact that Peter had been a prisoner twice before is not what gave him his calm heart. For that matter, this prison experience was different from the other two. This time, he was alone, and the deliverance did not come right away. The other two times, he was able to witness, but this time, no special witnessing opportunities appeared. Peter's previous arrests had taken place after great victories, but this one followed the death of James, his dear friend and colleague. It was a new situation altogether.

What gave Peter such confidence and peace? To begin with, many believers were praying for him (Acts 12:12), and kept it up day and night for a week, and this helped to bring him peace (Phil. 4:6–7). Prayer has a way of reminding us of the promises of God's Word, such as, "I will both lay me down in peace, and sleep; for thou, Lord, only makest me to dwell in safety" (Ps. 4:8). Or, "Fear thou not, for I am with thee. Be not dismayed, for I am thy God. I will strengthen thee; yea, I will help thee; yea, I will uphold thee with the right hand of my righteousness" (Isa. 41:10).

But the main cause of Peter's peace was the knowledge that Herod could not kill him. Jesus had promised Peter that he would live to be an old man and end his life crucified on a Roman cross (John 21:18–19). Peter simply laid hold of that promise and committed the entire situation to the Lord, and God gave him peace and rest. He did not know how or when God would deliver him, but he did know that deliverance was coming.

Peter obeying (vv. 7–11). Once again we behold the ministry of angels (Acts 5:19; 8:26; 10:3, 7) and are reminded that the angels care for God's children (Ps. 34:7). The angel brought light and liberty into the prison cell, but the guards had no idea that anything was going on. However, if Peter was going to be delivered, he had to obey what the angel commanded. He probably thought it was a dream or a vision, but he

arose and followed the angel out of the prison and into the street Only then did he come to himself and realize that he had been a part of another miracle.

The angel commanded Peter to bind his garments with his girdle, and then to put on his sandals. These were certainly ordinary tasks to do while a miracle is taking place! But God often joins the miraculous with the ordinary just to encourage us to keep in balance. Jesus multiplied the loaves and fishes, but then commanded His disciples to gather up the leftovers. He raised Jairus's daughter from the dead, then told her parents to give her something to eat. Even in miracles, God is always practical.

God alone can do the extraordinary, but His people must do the ordinary. Jesus raised Lazarus from the dead, but the men had to roll the stone from the tomb. The same angel that removed the chains from Peter's hands could have put the shoes on Peter's feet, but he told Peter to do it. God never wastes miracles.

Peter had to stoop before he could walk. It was a good lesson in humility and obedience. In fact, from that night on, every time Peter put on his shoes, it must have reminded him of the prison miracle and encouraged him to trust the Lord.

This deliverance took place at Passover season, the time of year when the Jews celebrated their exodus from Egypt. The word *delivered* in Acts 12:11 is the same word Stephen used when he spoke about the Jewish exodus (Acts 7:34). Peter experienced a new kind of "exodus" in answer to the prayers of God's people.

Peter knocking (vv. 12–16). As Peter followed the angel, God opened the way, and when Peter was free, the angel vanished. His work was done, and now it was up to Peter to trust the Lord and use his common sense in taking the next step. Since it was the prayers of God's people that had helped to set him free, Peter decided that the best place for him would be in that prayer meeting at Mary's house. Furthermore, he wanted to report the good news that God had answered their prayers. So Peter headed for the house of Mary, mother of John Mark.

When you remember that (a) many people were praying, (b) they were praying earnestly, (c) they prayed night and day for perhaps as long as a week, and (d) their prayers were centered specifically on Peter's deliverance, then the scene that is described here is almost comical. The answer to their prayers is standing at the door, but they don't have faith enough to open the door and let him in! God could get Peter out of a prison, but Peter can't get himself into a prayer meeting!

Of course, the knock at the door might have been that of Herod's soldiers, coming to arrest more believers. It took courage for the maid Rhoda ("rose") to go to the door, but imagine her surprise when she recognized Peter's voice! She was so overcome that she forgot to open the door! Poor Peter had to keep knocking and calling while the "believers" in the prayer meeting decided what to do! And the longer he stood at the gate, the more dangerous his situation became.

The exclamation, "It is his angel" (Acts 12:15) reveals their belief in "guardian angels" (Matt. 18:10; Heb. 1:14). Of course, the logical question is, "Why would an angel bother to knock?" All he had to do was simply walk right in! Sad to say, good theology plus unbelief often leads to fear and confusion.

We must face the fact that even in the most fervent prayer meetings there is sometimes a spirit of doubt and unbelief. We are like the father who cried to Jesus, "Lord, I believe; help thou mine unbelief" (Mark 9:24). These Jerusalem saints believed that God could answer their prayers, so they kept at it night and day. But, when the answer came right to their door, they refused to believe it. God graciously honors even the weakest faith, but how much more He would do if only we would trust Him.

Note the plural pronouns in Acts 12:16: "They ... opened the door and ... they were astonished." I get the impression that, for safety's sake, they decided to open the door *together* and face *together* whatever might be on the other side. Rhoda would have done it by herself, but she was too overcome with joy. It is commendable that a lowly servant girl recognized Peter's voice and rejoiced that he was free. Rhoda surely was a believer who knew Peter as a friend.

Peter declaring (v. 17). Apparently everybody began to speak at once, and Peter had to silence them. He quickly gave an account of the miracle of his deliverance and no doubt thanked them for their prayer help. He instructed them to get the word to James, the half-brother of the Lord, who was the leader of the Jerusalem assembly (Matt. 13:55; Acts 15:13ff.; Gal. 1:19). James was also the author of the epistle of James.

Where Peter went when he left the meeting, nobody knows to this day! It certainly was a well-kept secret. Except for a brief appearance in Acts 15, Peter walks off the pages of the book of Acts to make room for Paul and the story of his ministry among the Gentiles. First Corinthians 9:5 tells us that Peter traveled in ministry with his wife, and 1 Corinthians 1:12 suggests that he visited Corinth. There is no evidence in Scripture that Peter ever visited Rome. In fact, if Peter had founded the church in Rome, it is unlikely that Paul would have gone there, for his policy was to work where other apostles had not labored (Rom. 15:18–22). Also, he certainly would have said something to or about Peter when he wrote his letter to the Romans.

Before we leave this section, it would be profitable to consider how Christians can best pray for those in prison, for even today there are many people in prison only because they are Christians. "Remember them that are in bonds, as bound with them" commands Hebrews 13:3. In other words, pray for them as you would want them to pray for you if your situations were reversed.

We ought to pray that God will give them grace to bear with suffering so that they might have a triumphant witness for the Lord. We should ask the Spirit to minister the Word to them and bring it to their remembrance. It is right to ask God to protect His own and to give them wisdom as they must day after day deal with a difficult enemy. We must ask God that, if it is His will, they be delivered from their bondage and suffering and reunited with their loved ones.

God Deals with Our Enemies (12:18–25)

"But the face of the Lord is against them that do evil" (1 Peter 3:12).

If the account had ended with Peter's departure, we would find ourselves wondering, "What happened to the prison guards and to Herod?" We do not know at what time the angel delivered Peter, but when the next quaternion arrived at the cell, imagine their consternation when they discovered that the guards were there but the prisoner was gone! If the new watch awakened the old watch, it was certainly a rude awakening for them! If the old watch was already awake and alert, they must have had a difficult time explaining the situation to the new watch. How could a chained prisoner escape when there were four guards present and the doors were locked?

If a guard permitted a prisoner to escape, Roman law required that he receive the same punishment that the prisoner would have received, even if it was death (see Acts 16:27; 27:42). This law did not strictly apply in Herod's jurisdiction, so the king was not forced to kill the guards, but, being a Herod, he did it anyway. Instead of killing one man to please the Jews, he killed four and perhaps hoped it would please them more.

"The righteous is delivered out of trouble, and the wicked cometh in his stead" (Prov. 11:8). This truth is illustrated in the death of Herod. While God does not always bring retribution this quickly, we can be sure that the Judge of all the earth will do what is right (Gen. 18:25; Rev. 6:9–11).

The people of Tyre and Sidon, who depended on the Jews for food (see Ezra 3:7), had in some way displeased King Herod and were in danger of losing this assistance. In true political fashion, they bribed Blastus, who was in charge of the king's bed chamber, and thus a trusted official; he in turn convinced the king to meet the delegation. It was an opportunity for the proud king to display his authority and glory, and for the delegates to please him with their flattery.

The Jewish historian Josephus said that this scene took place during a festival honoring Claudius Caesar, and that the king wore a beautiful silver garment in honor of the occasion. We do not know what Herod said in his oration, but we do know why he said it: he wanted to impress the people. And he did! They played on his Herodian ego and told him he was a god, and he loved every minute of it.

But he did not give the glory to the Lord, so this whole scene was nothing but idolatry. "I am the Lord: that is my name: and my glory will I not give to another" (Isa. 42:8; see 48:11). Instead of Peter being killed by Herod, it was Herod who was killed by Peter's God! Perhaps the same angel who delivered Peter also smote the king. Herod contracted some affliction in his bowels and died five days later, according to Josephus. This was in AD 44.

This event is more than a slice of ancient history, because it typifies the world and its people today. The citizens of Tyre and Sidon were concerned about one thing only—getting sufficient food to feed their stomachs. To be sure, food is essential to life, but when we pay any price to get that food, we are doing wrong. By flattering the king and calling him a god, the delegation knew they could get what they wanted.

I cannot help but see in King Herod an illustration of the future "man of sin" who will one day rule the world and persecute God's people (2 Thess. 2; Rev. 13). This "man of sin" (or Antichrist) will make himself god and will command the worship of the whole world. But Jesus Christ will return and judge him and those who follow him (Rev. 19:11–21).

The world still lives for praise and pleasure. Man has made himself his own god (Rom. 1:25). The world still lives on the physical and ignores the spiritual (see 1 John 2:15–17). It lives by force and flattery instead of faith and truth, and one day it will be judged.

The church today, like Israel of old, suffers because of people like Herod who use their authority to oppose the truth. Beginning with Pharaoh in Egypt, God's people have often suffered under despotic rulers and governments, and God has always preserved His witness in the world. God has not always judged evil officials as He judged Herod, but He has always watched over His people and seen to it that they did not suffer and die in vain. Our freedom today was purchased by their bondage.

The early church had no "political clout" or friends in high places to "pull strings" for them. Instead, they went to the highest throne of all, the throne of grace. They were a praying people, for they knew that God could solve their problems. God's glorious throne was greater than the throne of Herod, and God's heavenly army could handle Herod's weak soldiers any day or night! The believers did not need to bribe anyone at court. They simply took their case to the highest court and left it with the Lord!

And what was the result? "But the word of God grew and multiplied" (Acts 12:24). This is another of Luke's summaries, or "progress reports," that started with Acts 6:7 (see 9:31; 16:5; 19:20; 28:31). Luke is accomplishing the purpose of his book and showing us how the church spread throughout the Roman world from its small beginnings in Jerusalem. What an encouragement to us today!

At the beginning of Acts 12, Herod seemed to be in control, and the church was losing the battle. But at the end of the chapter, Herod is dead and the church—very much alive—is growing rapidly!

The secret? A praying church!

Missionary Isobel Kuhn used to pray when in trouble, "If this obstacle is from thee, Lord, I accept it; but if it is from Satan, I refuse him and all his works in the name of Calvary!" And Dr. Alan Redpath has often said, "Let's keep our chins up and our knees down—we're on the victory side!"

God works when churches pray, and Satan still trembles "when he sees the weakest saint upon his knees."

CHAPTER THIRTEEN
Acts 13—14
GOD OPENS THE DOORS

We usually identify the preaching of the gospel with the quiet rural villages of Palestine where the Lord Jesus ministered. For this reason, many Christians are surprised to learn that the church in the book of Acts was almost entirely *urban*. Historian Wayne A. Meeks writes that "within a decade of the crucifixion of Jesus, the village culture of Palestine had been left behind, and the Greco-Roman city became the dominant environment of the Christian movement" (*The First Urban Christians*, 11).

The church began in Jerusalem and then spread to other cities, including Samaria, Damascus, Caesarea, and Antioch in Syria. At least forty different cities are named in Acts. From Antioch, Paul and his helpers carried the gospel throughout the then-known world. In fact, the record given in Acts 13—28 is almost a review of ancient geography. About the year 56, the apostle Paul was able to write, "So that from Jerusalem, and round about unto Illyricum, I have fully preached the gospel of Christ" (Rom. 15:19). What a record!

In these two chapters, Dr. Luke described Paul's ministry in six different cities, beginning and ending at Antioch.

Antioch in Syria—Decision (13:1–5)
That sainted missionary to India and Persia Henry Martyn once said, "The Spirit of Christ is the spirit of missions, and the nearer we get to Him, the more intensely missionary we must become." Paul (Saul) and Barnabas had that experience as they ministered in Antioch and were called by the Spirit to take the gospel to the Roman world.

Until now, Jerusalem had been the center of ministry, and Peter had been the key apostle. But from this point on, Antioch in Syria would become the new center (Acts 11:19ff.), and Paul the new leader. The gospel was on the move!

Luke listed five different men who were ministering in the church: *Barnabas*, whom we have already met (Acts 4:36–37; 9:27; 11:22–26); *Simeon*, who may have been from Africa since he was nicknamed "Black"; *Lucius*, who came from Cyrene and may have been one of the founders of the church in Antioch (Acts 11:20); *Manaen*, who was an intimate friend (or perhaps an adopted foster brother) of Herod Antipas, who had killed John the Baptist; and *Saul* (Paul), last on the list but soon to become first.

These men were serving as "prophets and teachers" in a local church. The prophets helped lay the foundation for the church as they proclaimed the Word of God (Eph. 2:20; 1 Cor. 14:29–32). They were more "forth-tellers" than "foretellers," though at times the prophets did announce things to come (Acts 11:27–30). The teachers helped to ground the converts in the doctrines of the faith (2 Tim. 2:2).

God had already called Paul to minister to the Gentiles (Acts 9:15; 21:17–21), and now He summoned Barnabas to labor with him. The church confirmed their calling, commissioned the men, and sent them forth. It is the ministry of the Holy Spirit, working through the local church, to equip and enlist believers to go forth and serve. The modern mission board is only a "sending agency" that expedites the work authorized by the local church.

Barnabas and Paul took John Mark with them as their assistant. He was a cousin to Barnabas (Col. 4:10), and his mother's home in Jerusalem was a gathering place for the believers (Acts 12:12). It is likely that it was Peter who led John Mark to faith in Christ (1 Peter 5:13). John Mark no doubt helped Barnabas and Paul in numerous ways, relieving them of tasks and details that would have interfered with their important ministry of the Word.

Paphos—Deception (13:6–12)

It was logical to go first to Cyprus, for this was the home of Barnabas (Acts 4:36). Luke gives us no details of the ministry in Salamis, the great commercial center at the east end of the island. We trust that some people did believe the gospel and that a local assembly was formed. The men then moved ninety miles to Paphos on the west end of the island, and there they met their first opposition.

Paphos was the capital of Cyprus, and the chief Roman official there was Sergius Paulus, "an understanding man" who wanted to hear the Word of God. He was opposed by a Jewish false prophet named "Son of Jesus [Joshua]." It is unusual to find a *Jewish* false prophet and sorcerer, for the Jews traditionally shunned such demonic activities. The name *Elymas* means "sorcerer" or "wise man" (cf. the "wise men" of Matt. 2).

This event is an illustration of the lesson that Jesus taught in the parable of the tares (Matt. 13:24–30, 36–43): wherever the Lord sows His true children (the wheat), Satan comes along and sows a counterfeit (the tares), a child of the devil. Paul recognized that Elymas was a child of the devil (John 8:44), and he inflicted blindness on the false prophet as a judgment from God. This miracle was also evidence to Sergius Paulus that Paul and Barnabas were servants of the true God and preached the true message of salvation (Heb. 2:4). The Roman official believed and was saved.

Acts 13:9 is the first place you find the familiar name *Paul* in the New Testament. As a Jewish Roman citizen, the apostle's full name was probably "Saul Paulus," for many Jews had both Jewish and Roman names.

Perga—Desertion (13:13)

Why did John Mark desert his friends and return to Jerusalem? Perhaps he was just plain homesick, or he may have become unhappy because Paul had begun to take over the leadership from Mark's cousin Barnabas (note "Paul and his company" in Acts 13:13). Mark was a devoted Jew, and he may have felt uncomfortable with the saved Gentiles. Some students think that John Mark's return to Jerusalem helped start the opposition of the legalistic Judaizers who later opposed Paul (see Acts 15 and the epistle to the Galatians).

Another possibility is the fear of danger as the party moved into new and difficult areas. But whatever the cause of his defection, John Mark did something so serious that Paul did not want him back on his "team" again (Acts 15:36ff.)! Later, Paul would enlist Timothy to take John Mark's place (Acts 16:1–5). John Mark did redeem himself and was eventually accepted and approved by Paul (2 Tim. 4:11).

During my years of ministry as a pastor and as a member of several mission boards, I have seen first-term workers do what John Mark did, and it has always been heartbreaking. But I have also seen some of them restored to missionary service, thanks to the prayers and encouragement of God's people. A. T. Robertson said that Mark "flickered in the crisis," but the light did not completely go out. This is an encouragement to all of us.

Antioch in Pisidia—Disputation (13:14–52)

Paul and Barnabas traveled 100 miles north and about 3,600 feet up to get to this important city on the Roman road. As you follow Paul's journeys in Acts, you will notice that he selected strategic cities, planted churches in them, and went on from the churches to evangelize the surrounding areas. You will also notice that, where it was possible, he started his ministry in the local synagogue, for he had a great burden for his people (Rom. 9:1–5; 10:1), and he found in the synagogue both Jews and Gentiles ready to hear the Word of God.

This is the first of Paul's sermons recorded in the book of Acts, and it may be divided into three parts, each of which is introduced by the phrase "men and brethren."

Preparation (vv. 16–25). In this section, Paul reviewed the history of Israel, climaxing with the ministry of John the Baptist and the coming of their Messiah. He made it clear that it was God who was at work in and for Israel, preparing the way for the coming of the promised Messiah. He also reminded his hearers that the nation had not always been faithful to the Lord and the covenant, but had often rebelled.

Every pious Jew knew that the Messiah would come from David's family, and that a prophet would announce His coming beforehand. John the Baptist was that prophet.

Declaration (vv. 26–37). As Paul addressed both the Jews and the Gentile "God-fearers" in the congregation, he changed his approach from third person ("they") to second person ("you"). He explained to them why their leaders in Jerusalem rejected and crucified the nation's Messiah. It was not because they had not read or heard the message of the prophets, but because they did not understand the message. Furthermore, the crucifixion of Jesus of Nazareth was even promised in the prophets. (Peter took this same approach in his second message, Acts 3:12–18.)

It was the resurrection of Jesus Christ that was the crucial event: "But God raised him from the dead" (Acts 13:30). (See Acts 13:33–34, 37, and note that "raised" in Acts 13:22–23 means "brought") Paul has declared the gospel to them, "the word of this salvation" (Acts 13:26) and "the glad tidings" (Acts 13:32). Christ died, He was buried, and He arose again!

Since Paul was addressing a synagogue congregation, he used the Old Testament Scriptures to support his argument. In Acts 13:33, Psalm 2:7 is quoted; note that it refers to the *resurrection* of Christ, not to the birth of Christ. The "virgin tomb" (John 19:41) was like a "womb" that gave birth to Jesus Christ in resurrection glory.

Then he quoted Isaiah 55:3, referring to the covenant that God made with David, "the sure mercies of David." God had promised David that from him the Messiah would come (2 Sam. 7:12–17). This was an "everlasting covenant" with a throne to be established forever (2 Sam. 7:13, 16). If Jesus is the Messiah, and He died and remained dead, this covenant could never be fulfilled. Therefore, Jesus had to be raised from the dead or the covenant would prove false.

His third quotation was from Psalm 16:10, the same passage Peter quoted in his message at Pentecost (Acts 2:24–28). The Jews considered Psalm 16 to be a messianic psalm, and it was clear that this promise did not apply to David, who was dead, buried, and decayed. It had to apply to Jesus Christ, the Messiah.

Application (vv. 38–52). Paul had declared the good news to them (Acts 13:32), and now all that remained was to make the personal application and "draw the net." He told them that through faith in Jesus Christ, they could have two blessings that the law could never provide: the forgiveness of their sins and justification before the throne of God.

Justification is the act of God whereby He declares the believing sinner righteous in Jesus Christ. It has to do with the believer's standing before the throne of God. The Jews were taught that God justified the righteous and punished the wicked (2 Chron. 6:22–23). But God justifies the ungodly who will put their faith in Jesus Christ (Rom. 4:1–8).

The law cannot justify the sinner; it can only condemn him (Rom. 3:19–20; Gal. 2:16). God not only forgives our sins, but He also gives us the very righteousness of Christ and puts it on our account! This was certainly good news delivered by Paul to that searching congregation of Jews and Gentiles who had no peace in their hearts, even though they were religious.

Paul closed his message with a note of warning taken from Habakkuk 1:5 (and see Isa. 29:14). In Habakkuk's day, the "unbelievable work" God was doing was the raising up of the Chaldeans to chasten His people, a work so remarkable that nobody would believe it. After all, why would God use an evil pagan nation to punish His own chosen people, sinful though they might be? God was using Gentiles to punish Jews! But the "wonderful work" in Paul's day was that God was using the Jews to save the Gentiles!

What was the result? Many Jews and Gentile proselytes believed and associated with Paul and Barnabas. The Gentiles were especially excited about Paul's message and wanted him to tell them more, which he did the next Sabbath. The people had done a good job of spreading the news, because a great crowd gathered. They were probably predominantly Gentiles, which made the Jews envious and angry.

Paul's final message in the synagogue declared that God had sent the Word to the Jews first (Acts 3:26; Rom. 1:16), but they had now rejected it. Therefore, Paul would now take the good news to the Gentiles, and he quoted Isaiah 49:6 to back up his decision. (Note also Luke 2:29–32.) He was ready to go to the ends of the earth to win souls to Christ!

Acts 13:48 gives us the divine side of evangelism, for God has His elect people (Eph. 1:4). The word translated *ordained* means "enrolled," and indicates that God's people have their names written in God's book (Luke 10:20; Phil. 4:3). But Acts 13:49 is the human side of evangelism: if we do not preach the Word, then nobody can believe and be saved. It takes both (see 2 Thess. 2:13–14; Rom. 10:13–15).

The unbelieving Jews were not going to sit back and let Paul and Barnabas take over. First, they disputed with them, and then they brought legal action against them and expelled them from their borders. The missionaries were not discouraged: they shook off the dust of their feet against them (Luke 9:5; 10:11) and went to the next town, leaving behind them a group of joyful disciples.

Iconium—Division (14:1–7)

This city, more Greek than Roman, was in the Roman province of Galatia. Paul's ministry in the synagogue was singularly blessed and a multitude of Jews and Gentiles believed. Once again, the unbelieving Jews stirred up hatred and opposition, but the missionaries stayed on and witnessed boldly for Christ. (Note the "therefore" in Acts 14:3.)

God also enabled the men to perform signs and wonders as their "credentials" that they were indeed the servants of the true God (see Acts 15:12; Gal. 3:5; Heb. 2:4). Faith is not based on miracles (Luke 16:27–31; John 2:23–25), but faith can be bolstered by miracles. The important thing is "the word of his grace" that performs the work of His grace (Acts 14:26).

The result? The city was divided and the Christians were threatened with public disgrace and stoning. Obedient to their Lord's counsel in Matthew 10:23, they fled from that area into a different Roman district and continued to minister the Word of God.

Lystra—Delusion (14:8–20)

Lystra was in the Roman province of Galatia, about eighteen miles southwest of Iconium. This was the first of three visits Paul made to this city, and an eventful visit it was! On his second missionary journey, Paul enlisted Timothy in Lystra (Acts 16:1–5), and he made a visit to this church on his third journey as well (Acts 18:23). We should note four different responses during this visit.

The crippled man's response to the Word (vv. 8–10). Both Peter and Paul healed men who were lame from birth (Acts 3). Had their lameness been caused by disease or accident, the cure might have been attributed to a sudden change in their health. As it was, the cure was obviously miraculous.

The word translated "speak" in Acts 14:9 means ordinary conversation, though it can refer to formal speaking. It is likely that Paul was simply conversing with some of the citizens in the marketplace, telling them about Jesus, and the lame man overheard what he said. The Word produced faith (Rom. 10:17) and faith brought healing.

The crowd's response to the crippled man (vv. 11–13). Miracles by themselves do not produce either conviction or faith. They must be accompanied by the Word (Acts 14:3). This was a superstitious crowd that interpreted events in the light of their own mythology. They identified Barnabas as Jupiter (Zeus), the chief of the gods; and Paul, the speaker, they identified with Mercury (Hermes), the messenger of the gods. Jupiter was the patron deity of the city, so this was a great opportunity for the priest of Jupiter to become very important and lead the people in honoring their god.

The apostles' response to the crowd (vv. 14–19). How easy it would have been to accept this worship and try to use the honor as a basis for teaching the people the truth, but that is not the way God's true servants minister (2 Cor. 4:1–2; 1 Thess. 2:1–5). Paul and Barnabas opposed what they were doing and boldly told the people that the gods of Lystra were "vanities."

Paul's message was not based on the Old Testament, because this was a pagan Gentile audience. He started with the witness of God in creation (see Acts 17:22ff.). He made it clear that there is but one God who is the living God, the giving God, and the forgiving God. And He has been patient with the sinning nations

(Acts 17:30) and has not judged them for their sins as they deserve.

The crowd quieted down, but when some troublemaking Jews arrived from Antioch and Iconium, the crowd followed their lead and stoned Paul. One minute, Paul was a god to be worshipped; the next minute, he was a criminal to be slain! Emerson called a mob "a society of bodies voluntarily bereaving themselves of reason." Often this is true.

The disciples' response to Paul (v. 20). There were new believers in Lystra, and this was a crisis situation for them. They were a minority, their leader had been stoned, and their future looked very bleak. But they stood by Paul! It is likely that they joined hearts and prayed for him, and this is one reason God raised him up. Was Paul dead? We are not told. This is the only stoning he ever experienced (2 Cor. 11:25), but from it came glory to God. It may have been this event that especially touched Timothy and eventually led to his association with Paul (2 Tim. 3:10).

Antioch in Syria—Declaration (14:21–28)

On their return trip to Antioch, the missionaries were engaged in several important ministries.

First, they preached the gospel and made disciples ("taught many"). It is difficult to understand how they got back into the cities from which they had been expelled, but the Lord opened the doors.

Second, they strengthened ("confirmed") the believers in the things of Christ and encouraged ("exhorted") them to continue in the faith. Continuance is a proof of true faith in Jesus Christ (John 8:31–32; Acts 2:42). Paul made it very clear that living the Christian life was not an easy thing and that they would all have to expect trials and sufferings before they would see the Lord in glory.

Third, they organized the churches (Acts 14:23–25). The local church is both an organism and an organization, for if an organism is not organized, it will die! Paul and Barnabas ordained spiritual leaders and gave them the responsibility of caring for the flock. If you compare Titus 1:5 and 7, you will see that "elder" and "bishop" (overseer) refer to the same office, and both are equivalent to "pastor" (shepherd).

The word translated *ordained* means "to elect by a show of hands." It is possible that Paul chose the men and the congregation voted its approval, or that the people selected them by vote and Paul ordained them (see Acts 6:1–6).

Finally, they reported to their "sending church" on the work God had done (Acts 14:26–28). They had been gone at least a year, and it must have been exciting for them and for the church when they arrived back home. They had, by the grace of God, fulfilled the work God had given them to do, and they joyfully reported the blessings to the church family.

This is perhaps the first "missionary conference" in church history, and what a conference it must have been! A church officer once said to me, "I don't care how much money you want for missions, I'll give it, but *just don't make me listen to missionaries speak!*" I felt sorry for him that his spiritual temperature was so low that he could not listen to reports of what God was doing in the difficult corners of the harvest field.

As you review Paul's first missionary journey, you can see the principles by which he operated, principles that are still applicable today.

He worked primarily in the key cities and challenged the believers to take the message out to the more remote areas. The gospel works in the population centers, and we must carry it there.

He used one approach with the synagogue congregations and another with the Gentiles. He referred the Jews and Jewish proselytes to the Old Testament Scriptures, but when preaching to the Gentiles, he emphasized the God of creation and His goodness to the nations. His starting point was different, but his finishing point was the same: faith in the Lord Jesus Christ.

He majored on establishing and organizing local churches. Jesus had the local church in mind when He gave what we call the "Great Commission" (Matt. 28:19–20). After we make disciples ("teach"), we must baptize them (the responsibility primarily of a local church) and then teach them the Word of God. Merely winning people to Christ is but fulfilling one-third of the commission! It takes the local assembly of believers to help us fulfill all of what Jesus commanded us to do.

He grounded the believers in the Word of God. This is the only source of strength and stability when persecution comes, as it inevitably does come. Paul did not preach a popular "success gospel" that painted a picture of an easy Christian life.

The amazing thing is that Paul and his associates did all of this without the modern means of transportation and communication that we possess today. Dr. Bob Pierce used to say to us in Youth for Christ, "Others have done so much with so little, while we have done so little with so much!" The wasted wealth of American believers alone, if invested in world evangelization, might lead to the salvation of millions of lost people.

Paul and Barnabas announced that the "door of faith" had been opened to the Gentiles.

That door is still open, to Jews and Gentiles alike—to a whole world! Walk through that open door and help take the gospel to others.

Be daring!

CHAPTER FOURTEEN
Acts 15:1–35
DON'T CLOSE THE DOORS!

The progress of the gospel has often been hindered by people with closed minds who stand in front of open doors and block the way for others.

In 1786, when William Carey laid the burden of world missions before a ministerial meeting in Northampton, England, the eminent Dr. Ryland said to him, "Young man, sit down! When God pleases to convert the heathen, He will do it without your aid or mine!" More than one Spirit-filled servant of God has had to enter open doors of opportunity without the support of churches and religious leaders.

Paul and his associates faced this same challenge at the Jerusalem Conference about twenty years after Pentecost. Courageously, they defended both the truth of the gospel and the missionary outreach of the church. There were three stages in this event.

The Dispute (15:1–5)

It all started when some legalistic Jewish teachers came to Antioch and taught that the Gentiles, in order to be saved, had to be circumcised and obey the law of Moses. These men were associated with the Jerusalem congregation but not authorized by it (Acts 15:24). Identified with the Pharisees (Acts 15:5), these teachers were "false brethren" who wanted to rob both Jewish and Gentile believers of their liberty in Christ (Gal. 2:1–10; 5:1ff.).

It is not surprising that there were people in the Jerusalem church who were strong advocates of the law of Moses but ignorant of the relationship between law and grace. These people were Jews who had been trained to respect and obey the law of Moses, and after all, Romans, Galatians, and Hebrews had not yet been written! There was a large group of priests in the Jerusalem assembly (Acts 6:7), as well as people who still followed some of the Old Testament practices (see Acts 21:20–26). It was a time of transition, and such times are always difficult.

What were these legalists actually doing and why were they so dangerous? They were attempting to mix law and grace and to pour the new wine into the ancient brittle wineskins (Luke 5:36–39). They were stitching up the rent veil (Luke 23:45) and blocking the new and living way to God that Jesus had opened when He died on the cross (Heb. 10:19–25). They were rebuilding the wall between Jews and Gentiles that Jesus had torn down on the cross (Eph. 2:14–16). They were putting the heavy Jewish yoke on Gentile shoulders (Acts 15:10; Gal. 5:1) and asking the church to move out of the sunlight into the shadows (Col. 2:16–17; Heb. 10:1). They were saying, "A Gentile must first become a Jew before he can become a Christian! It is not sufficient for them simply to trust Jesus Christ. They must also obey Moses!"

Several important issues are involved here, not the least of which is the work of Christ on the cross as declared in the message of the gospel (1 Cor. 15:1–8; Heb. 10:1–18). God pronounces a solemn anathema on anyone who preaches any other gospel than the gospel of the grace of God found in Jesus Christ His Son (Gal. 1:1–9). When any religious leader says, "Unless you belong to our group, you cannot be saved!" or,

"Unless you participate in our ceremonies and keep our rules, you cannot be saved!" he is adding to the gospel and denying the finished work of Jesus Christ. Paul wrote his epistle to the Galatians to make it clear that salvation is wholly by God's grace, through faith in Christ, *plus nothing!*

Another issue involved was the nature of the church's missionary program. If these legalists (we call them "the Judaizers") were correct, then Paul and Barnabas had been all wrong in their ministry. Along with preaching the gospel, they should have been teaching the Gentiles how to live as good Jews. No wonder Paul and Barnabas debated and disputed with these false teachers (Acts 15:2, 7)! The Antioch believers were being "troubled" and "subverted" (Acts 15:24), and this same confusion and disruption would soon spread to the Gentile churches Paul and Barnabas had founded. This was a declaration of war that Paul and Barnabas could not ignore.

God gave Paul a revelation instructing him to take the whole matter to the Jerusalem church leaders (Gal. 2:2), and to this the Antioch assembly agreed ("they" in Acts 15:2). The gathering was not a "church council" in the denominational sense, but rather a meeting of the leaders who heard the various groups and then made their decision. Though the "mother church" in Jerusalem did have great influence, each local church was autonomous.

The Defense (15:6–18)

It appears that at least four different meetings were involved in this strategic conference: (1) a public welcome to Paul and his associates, Acts 15:4; (2) a private meeting of Paul and the key leaders, Galatians 2:2; (3) a second public meeting at which the Judaizers presented their case, Acts 15:5–6 and Galatians 2:3–5; and (4) the public discussion described in Acts 15:6ff. In this public discussion, four key leaders presented the case for keeping the doors of grace open to the lost Gentiles.

Peter reviewed the past (vv. 6–11). We get the impression that Peter sat patiently while the disputing ("questioning") was going on, waiting for the Spirit to direct him. "He who answers a matter before he hears it, it is folly and shame to him" (Prov. 18:13 NKJV). Peter reminded the church of four important ministries that God had performed for the Gentiles, ministries in which he had played an important part.

First, God made a choice that Peter should preach the gospel to the Gentiles (Acts 15:7). Jesus had given the keys of the kingdom to Peter (Matt. 16:19), and he had used them to open the door of faith to the Jews (Acts 2), the Samaritans (Acts 8:14–17), and the Gentiles (Acts 10). The apostles and brethren in Judea had censured Peter for visiting the Gentiles and eating with them, but he had satisfactorily defended himself (Acts 11:1–18). Note that Peter made it clear that Cornelius and his household were saved by hearing and believing, not by obeying the law of Moses.

Second, God gave the Holy Spirit to the Gentiles to bear witness that they truly were born again (Acts 15:8). Only God can see the human heart; so, if these people had not been saved, God would never have given them the Spirit (Rom. 8:9). But they did not receive the Spirit by keeping the law, but by believing God's Word (Acts 10:43–46; see Gal. 3:2). Peter's message was "whoever believes in Him will receive remission of sins" (Acts 10:43 NKJV), not "whoever believes and obeys the law of Moses."

Third, God erased a difference (Acts 15:9, 11). For centuries, God had put a difference between Jews and Gentiles, and it was the task of the Jewish religious leaders to protect and maintain that difference (Lev. 10:10; Ezek. 22:26; 44:23). Jesus taught that the Jewish dietary laws had nothing to do with inner holiness (Mark 7:1–23), and Peter had learned that lesson again when he had that vision on the housetop in Joppa (Acts 10:1ff.).

Ever since the work of Christ on Calvary, God has made no difference between Jews and Gentiles as far as sin (Rom. 3:9, 22) or salvation (Rom. 10:9–13) are concerned. Sinners can have their hearts purified only by faith in Christ; salvation is not by keeping the law (Acts 15:9). We would expect Peter to conclude his defense by saying, "They [the Gentiles] shall be saved even as we Jews," but he said just the reverse! "We [Jews] shall be saved, even as they!"

God's fourth ministry—and this was Peter's strongest statement—was the removing of the yoke of the law (Acts 15:10). The law was indeed a yoke that burdened the Jewish nation, but that yoke has been taken away by Jesus Christ (see Matt. 11:28–30; Gal. 5:1ff.; Col. 2:14–17). After all, the law was given to the Jewish nation to protect them from the evils of the Gentile world and prepare them to bring the Messiah into the world (Gal. 4:1–7). The law cannot purify the sinner's heart (Gal. 2:21), impart the gift of the Holy Spirit (Gal. 3:2), or give eternal life (Gal. 3:21). What the law could not do, God did through His own Son (Rom. 8:1–4). Those who have trusted Christ have the righteousness of God's law in their hearts and, through the Spirit, obey His will. They are not motivated by fear, but by love, for "love is the fulfilling of the law" (Rom. 13:8–10).

Paul and Barnabas reported on the present (v. 12). Peter's witness made a great impact on the congregation because they sat in silence after he was finished. Then Paul and Barnabas stood up and told the group what God had done among the Gentiles through their witness. Dr. Luke devoted only one summary sentence to their report since he had already given it in detail in Acts 13—14. Paul and Barnabas were greatly respected by the church (see Acts 15:25–26), and their testimony carried a great deal of weight.

Their emphasis was on the miracles that God had enabled them to perform among the Gentiles. These miracles were proof that God was working with them (Mark 16:20; Acts 15:4) and that they were God's chosen messengers (Rom. 15:18–19; Heb. 2:24). "Does God give you his Spirit and work miracles among you because you observe the law, or because you believe what you heard?" (Gal. 3:5 NIV). They had preached grace, not law, and God had honored this message.

If you will review the record of the first missionary journey (Acts 13—14), you will see that the emphasis is on what God did in response to men's faith. See Acts 13:8, 12, 39, 41, 48; 14:1, 22–23, 27. Note also the emphasis on grace (Acts 13:43; 14:3, 26). God opened for the Gentiles "the door of faith," not "the door of law." For that matter the Antioch church, which commissioned Paul and Barnabas, was founded by people who "believed and turned unto the Lord" (Acts 11:21) and experienced the grace of God (Acts 11:23). They were saved the same way sinners are saved today, "by grace, through faith" (Eph. 2:8–9).

Both Peter and Paul received from God special visions directing them to go to the Gentiles (Acts 10:1ff.; 22:21). However, it was Paul whom God set apart as the apostle to the Gentiles (Rom. 11:13; Gal. 2:6–10; Eph. 3:1–12). If Gentile sinners had to obey the law of Moses in order to be saved, then why did God give Paul the gospel of grace and send him off to the Gentiles? God could just as well have sent Peter!

Peter reviewed God's ministries to the Gentiles in the past, and Paul and Barnabas reported on God's work among the Gentiles in that present day. James was the final speaker, and he focused on the future.

James related it all to the future (vv. 13–18). James was a brother to Jesus (Matt. 13:55; Gal. 1:19) and the writer of the epistle of James. He and his brethren were not believers in Christ until after the resurrection (John 7:5; 1 Cor. 15:7; Acts 1:14). James had strong leanings toward the law (there are at least ten references to law in his epistle), so he was most acceptable to the legalistic party in the Jerusalem church.

The key idea in James' speech is *agreement*. First, he expressed his full agreement with Peter that God was saving the Gentiles by grace. It must have startled the Judaizers when James called these saved Gentiles "a people for his [God's] name," because for centuries the Jews had carried that honorable title (see Deut. 7:6; 14:2; 28:10). Today, God is graciously calling out a people, the church, from both Jews and Gentiles. In fact, the Greek word for "church" *(ekklesia)* means "a called-out assembly" *(kaleo* = to call; *ek* = out). But if they are called out, then their salvation is all of grace and not through the keeping of the law!

The Judaizers did not understand how the Gentiles and the Jews related to each other in the church, or how the church fit into God's promise to establish a kingdom for Israel. The Old Testament declared both the salvation of the Gentiles (Isa. 2:2; 11:10) and the future establishing of a glorious kingdom for Israel (Isa. 11—12; 35; 60), but it did not explain how they related to each other. The legalists in the church were jealous for both the future glory of Israel and the past glory of Moses and the law. It seemed to them that

their acceptance of the Gentiles as "spiritual equals" jeopardized the future of Israel.

We today have a better grasp of this truth because Paul explained it in Ephesians 2—3 and Romans 9—11. Saved Jews and Gentiles are both members of the same body and "one in Christ Jesus" (Gal. 3:28). The truth about the church, the body of Christ, was a "mystery" (a sacred secret) hidden in past ages and revealed to the church by the Spirit. God's "mystery program" for the church does not cancel His great "prophecy program" for Israel. Paul makes it clear in Romans 9—11 that there is a future for Israel and that God will keep His "kingdom promises" to His people.

James stated that the prophets also agreed with this conclusion, and he cited Amos 9:11–12 to prove his point. Note that he did not state that what Peter, Paul, and Barnabas had said was a *fulfillment* of this prophecy. He said that what Amos wrote *agreed with their testimony*. A careful reading of Amos 9:8–15 reveals that the prophet is describing events in the end times, when God will regather His people Israel to their land and bless them abundantly. If we "spiritualize" these promises, we rob them of their plain meaning and James' argument falls apart.

Amos also prophesied that the fallen house ("tent") of David would be raised up and God would fulfill His covenant with David that a king would sit on his throne (see 2 Sam. 7:25–29). This future King, of course, will be Jesus Christ the Son of David (2 Sam. 7:13, 16; Isa. 9:6–7; Luke 1:32), who will reign over Israel during the kingdom. In fact, the only Jew alive today who can prove His genealogy and defend His kingship is Jesus Christ!

God revealed these truths gradually to His people, but His plan had been settled from the beginning. Neither the cross nor the church were afterthoughts with God (Acts 2:23; 4:27–28; Eph. 1:4). The Judaizers thought that Israel had to "rise" in her glorious kingdom before the Gentiles could be saved, but God revealed that it was through Israel's "fall" that the Gentiles would find salvation (Rom. 11:11–16). At the time of the Jerusalem Conference, David's house and throne indeed were fallen, but they would be restored one day and the kingdom established.

The Decision (15:19–35)

The leaders and the whole church (Acts 15:22), directed by the Holy Spirit (Acts 15:28), made a two-fold decision: a doctrinal decision about salvation, and a practical decision about how to live the Christian life.

The doctrinal decision we have already examined. The church concluded that Jews and Gentiles are all sinners before God and can be saved only by faith in Jesus Christ. There is one need, and there is but one gospel to meet that need (Gal. 1:6–12). God has today but one program: He is calling out a people for His name. Israel is set aside but not cast away (Rom. 11:1ff.), and when God's program for the church is completed, He will begin to fulfill His kingdom promises to the Jews.

But all doctrine must lead to duty. James emphasized this in his epistle (James 2:14–26), and so did Paul in his letters. It is not enough for us simply to accept a biblical truth; we must apply it personally in everyday life. Church problems are not solved by passing resolutions, but by practicing the revelations God gives us from His Word.

James advised the church to write to the Gentile believers and share the decisions of the conference. This letter asked for obedience to two *commands* and a willingness to agree to two personal *concessions.* The two commands were that the believers avoid idolatry and immorality, sins that were especially prevalent among the Gentiles (see 1 Cor. 8—10). The two concessions were that they willingly abstain from eating blood and meat from animals that had died by strangulation. The two commands do not create any special problems, for idolatry and immorality have always been wrong in God's sight, both for Jews and Gentiles. But what about the two concessions concerning food?

Keep in mind that the early church did a great deal of eating together and practicing of hospitality. Most churches met in homes, and some assemblies held a "love feast" in conjunction with the Lord's Supper (1 Cor. 11:17–34). It was probably not much different from our own potluck dinners. If the Gentile believers ate food that the Jewish believers considered "unclean," this would cause division in the church. Paul dealt clearly with this whole problem in Romans 14—15.

The prohibition against eating blood was actually given by God before the time of the law (Gen. 9:4), and it was repeated by Moses (Lev. 17:11–14; Deut. 12:23). If an animal is killed by strangulation, some of the blood will remain in the body and make the meat unfit for Jews to eat. Hence, the admonition against strangulation. "Kosher" meat is meat that comes from clean animals that have been killed properly so that the blood has been totally drained from the body.

It is beautiful to see that this letter expressed the loving unity of people who had once been debating with each other and defending opposing views. The legalistic Jews willingly gave up insisting that the Gentiles had to be circumcised to be saved, and the Gentiles willingly accepted a change in their eating habits. It was a loving compromise that did not in any way affect the truth of the gospel. As every married person and parent knows, there are times in a home when compromise is wrong, but there are also times when compromise is right. Wise Samuel Johnson said, "Life cannot subsist in society but by reciprocal concessions." The person who is always right, and who insists on having his or her own way, is difficult to live with happily.

What did this decision accomplish in a practical way? At least three things. First, it strengthened the unity of the church and kept it from splitting into two extreme "law" and "grace" groups. President Eisenhower

called the right kind of compromise "all of the usable surface. The extremes, right or left, are in the gutters." Again, this is not *doctrinal* compromise, for that is always wrong (Jude 3). Rather, it is learning to give and take in the practical arrangements of life so that people can live and work together in love and harmony.

Second, this decision made it possible for the church to present a united witness to the lost Jews (Acts 15:21). For the most part, the church was still identified with the Jewish synagogue, and it is likely that in some cities, entire synagogue congregations believed on Jesus Christ—Jews, Gentile proselytes, and Gentile "God-fearers" together. If the Gentile believers abused their freedom in Christ and ate meat containing blood, this would offend both the saved Jews and their unsaved friends whom they were trying to win to Christ. It was simply a matter of not being a stumbling block to the weak or to the lost (Rom. 14:13–21).

Third, this decision brought blessing as the letter was shared with the various Gentile congregations. Paul and Barnabas, along with Judas and Silas, took the good news to Antioch, and the church rejoiced and was encouraged because they did not have to carry the burdensome yoke of the law (Acts 15:30–31). On his second missionary journey, Paul shared the letter with the churches he had founded on his first missionary journey. The result was a strengthening of the churches' faith and an increase of their number (Acts 16:5).

We today can learn a great deal from this difficult experience of the early church. To begin with, problems and differences are opportunities for growth just as much as temptations for dissension and division. Churches need to work together and take time to listen, love, and learn. How many hurtful fights and splits could have been avoided if only some of God's people had given the Spirit time to speak and to work.

Most divisions are caused by "followers" and "leaders." A powerful leader gets a following, refuses to give in on even the smallest matter, and before long there is a split. Most church problems are not caused by doctrinal differences but by different viewpoints on practical matters. What color shall we paint the church kitchen? Can we change the order of the service? I heard of one church that almost split over whether the organ or the piano should be on the right side of the platform!

Christians need to learn the art of loving compromise. They need to have their priorities in order so they know when to fight for what is really important in the church. It is sinful to follow some impressive member of the church who is fighting to get his or her way on some minor issue that is not worth fighting about. Every congregation needs a regular dose of the love described in 1 Corinthians 13 to prevent division and dissension.

As we deal with our differences, we must ask, "How will our decisions affect the united witness of the church to the lost?" Jesus prayed that His people might be united so that the world might believe on

Him (John 17:20–21). Unity is not uniformity, for unity is based on love and not law. There is a great need in the church for diversity in unity (Eph. 4:1–17), for that is the only way the body can mature and do its work in the world.

God has opened a wonderful door of opportunity for us to take the gospel of God's grace to a condemned world. But there are forces in the church even today that want to close that door. There are people who are preaching "another gospel" that is not the gospel of Jesus Christ.

Help keep that door open—and reach as many as you can!

Be daring!

CHAPTER FIFTEEN
Acts 15:36—16:40
MORE OPEN DOORS

For the apostle Paul, the church at Antioch was not a parking lot: it was a launching pad. He could never settle down to a "comfortable ministry" anywhere as long as there were open doors for the preaching of the gospel.

Paul would have agreed enthusiastically with the words of Robertson McQuilken from his book *The Great Omission:* "In a world in which nine out of every ten people are lost, three out of four have never heard the way out, and one of every two cannot hear, the church sleeps on. Could it be we think there must be some other way? Or perhaps we don't really care that much." Paul cared—and so should we.

There were several new elements in this second journey that indicated that God was still at work, in spite of the seeming obstacles and personal difficulties that arose.

A New Partner (15:36–41)
Paul and Barnabas agreed on the importance of the trip, but they could not agree on the composition of the "team." Here were two dedicated men who had just helped bring unity to the church, and yet they could not settle their own disagreements! Disturbing and painful as these conflicts are, they are often found in church history, and yet God is able to overrule them and accomplish His purposes.

That Barnabas would champion John Mark is certainly no surprise. He and Mark were cousins (Col. 4:10 NASB), and the family ties would be strong. But even more, Barnabas was the kind of man who eagerly tried to help others, which is why the early church named him "son of encouragement" (Acts 4:36). He was ready to give John Mark an opportunity to serve the Lord and to prove himself. Barnabas "kept on insisting" (WUEST) that they take Mark along.

But Paul was just as adamant that they *not* take

Mark! After all, on the first missionary journey, John Mark had deserted them to return home (Acts 13:13), and this was a mark of weakness. The ministry was too important, and the work too demanding, to enlist someone who might prove unreliable.

As the discussion continued, it turned into a real argument (the word *paroxysm* comes from the word translated "contention"), and it seemed like the only solution was for the friends to divide the territory and separate. Barnabas took Mark and went to his native Cyprus, and Paul took Silas and headed for Syria and Celicia (note Acts 15:23).

Who was right? It really doesn't make much difference. Perhaps both men were right on some things and wrong on other things. We know that John Mark ultimately did succeed in the ministry and that Paul came to love and appreciate him (see Col. 4:10; 2 Tim. 4:11; Philem. 23–24). Good and godly people in the church do disagree; this is one of the painful facts of life that we must accept. Paul looked at people and asked, "What can they do for God's work?" while Barnabas looked at people and asked, "What can God's work do for them?" Both questions are important to the Lord's work, and sometimes it is difficult to keep things balanced.

Paul selected a new partner, Silas, a chief man in the church, a prophet (Acts 15:22, 32), and one chosen to take the Jerusalem Conference decrees to the churches (Acts 15:27). "Silas" is probably a Greek version of the name *Saul.* He was coauthor with Paul of the Thessalonian epistles, and he was the secretary for Peter's first epistle (1 Peter 5:12). Like Paul, he was a Roman citizen (Acts 16:37).

God changes His workmen, but His work goes right on. Now there were *two* missionary teams instead of one! If God had to depend on perfect people to accomplish His work, He would never ever get anything done. Our limitations and imperfections are good reasons for us to depend on the grace of God, for our sufficiency is from Him alone (2 Cor. 3:5).

A New Helper (16:1–5)
Paul and Silas approached their destination from the east, so they came first to Derbe and then to Lystra, just the reverse of the first journey (Acts 14:6–20). The preachers went from church to church, delivering the decrees and helping establish the believers in the faith. The result was fruit from the witness of the believers so that the churches increased in number daily (see Acts 2:47). It was certainly a most successful tour, but I wonder if any of the believers asked about Barnabas. And what did Paul tell them?

Perhaps the best thing that happened at Lystra was the enlistment of Timothy to replace John Mark as Paul's special assistant. Timothy was probably converted through Paul's ministry when the apostle first visited Lystra, for Paul called him "my beloved son" (1 Cor. 4:17) and "my own son in the faith" (1 Tim. 1:2). Timothy's mother and grandmother had prepared the way for his decision by being the first in the family to trust Christ (2 Tim. 1:5). Young Timothy undoubtedly witnessed Paul's sufferings in Lystra (Acts 14:19–20; 2 Tim. 3:10–11) and was drawn by the Lord to the apostle. Timothy was Paul's favorite companion and coworker (Phil. 2:19–23), perhaps the son Paul never had but always wanted.

Because he had a good report from the churches (1 Tim. 3:7), Timothy was ordained by Paul and added to his "team" (1 Tim. 4:14; 2 Tim. 1:6). Paul's next step was to have Timothy circumcised, an action that seems to contradict the decision of the Jerusalem Conference. However, there was an important spiritual principle behind Paul's decision.

The decision at the Jerusalem Conference was that it was not necessary to be circumcised *in order to be saved.* Paul did not allow Titus to be circumcised lest the enemy think he was promoting their cause (Gal. 2:1–5). The battle in Jerusalem was over the truth of the gospel, not over the fitness of a man to serve. Paul's concern with Timothy was not his salvation but his fitness for service.

Timothy would be working with both Jews and Gentiles in the churches, and it was essential that he not offend them. That was why Paul had Timothy circumcised (see 1 Cor. 9:19–23). Again, it was not a matter of Timothy's salvation or personal character, but rather of avoiding serious problems that would surely become stumbling blocks as the men sought to serve the Lord (Rom. 14:13–15). It is a wise spiritual leader who knows how and when to apply the principles of the Word of God, when to stand firm and when to yield.

In the years that followed, Timothy played an important part in the expansion and strengthening of the churches. He traveled with Paul and was often his special ambassador to the "trouble spots" in the work, such as Corinth. He became shepherd of the church in Ephesus (1 Tim. 1:3) and probably joined Paul in Rome shortly before the apostle was martyred (2 Tim. 4:21).

A New Vision (16:6–40)
In this section, we see three wonderful "openings."

God opened the way (vv. 6–12). After visiting the churches he had founded, Paul tried to enter new territory for the Lord by traveling east into Asia Minor and Bythinia, but the Lord closed the door. We don't know how God revealed His will in this matter, but we can well imagine that Paul was disappointed and perhaps a bit discouraged. Everything had been going so smoothly on this second journey that these closed doors must have come as a great surprise. However, it is comforting to know that even apostles were not always clear as to God's will for their ministries! God planned for the message to get there another time (Acts 18:19—19:41; see 1 Peter 1:1).

In His sovereign grace, God led Paul west into Europe, not east into Asia. It is interesting to speculate how world history might have been changed had Paul been sent to Asia instead of to Europe. At Troas, Paul was called to Macedonia by a man whom he saw in a night vision. "Nothing makes a man strong like a call for help," wrote George MacDonald, and Paul was quick to respond to the vision (compare Acts 26:19).

Note the pronoun *we* in Acts 16:10, for Dr. Luke, who wrote the book of Acts, joined Paul and his party at Troas. There are three "we" sections in Acts: 16:10–17; 20:5–15; and 27:1—28:16. Luke changed from "we" to "they" in Acts 17:1, which suggests that he may have remained in Philippi to pastor the church after Paul left. The next "we" section begins in Acts 20:5 in connection with Paul's trip from Macedonia. Luke devoted a good deal of space to Paul's ministry in Philippi, so perhaps he was a resident of that city. Some students think Luke may have been the man Paul saw in the vision.

From Troas to Neapolis, the port of Philippi was a distance of about 150 miles, and it took them two days to make the journey. Later, the trip in the opposite direction would take five days, apparently because of contrary winds (Acts 20:6). Philippi lay ten miles inland from Neapolis, and the way Luke described the city would suggest that he was indeed one of its proudest citizens.

Philippi was a Roman colony, which meant that it was a "Rome away from Rome." The emperor organized "colonies" by ordering Roman citizens, especially retired military people, to live in selected places so there would be strong pro-Roman cities in these strategic areas. Though living on foreign soil, the citizens were expected to be loyal to Rome, to obey the laws of Rome, and to give honor to the Roman emperor. In return, they were given certain political privileges, not the least of which was exemption from taxes. This was their reward for leaving their homes in Italy and relocating elsewhere.

God opened Lydia's heart (vv. 13–15). Paul and his friends did not plunge immediately into evangelizing the city, even though they knew God had called them there. No doubt they needed to rest and pray and make their plans together. It is not enough to know *where* God wants us to work; we must also know *when* and *how* He wants us to work.

The Jewish population in Philippi must have been very small since there was no synagogue there, only a place of prayer by the river outside the city. (It required ten men for the founding of a synagogue.) Paul had seen a *man* in the vision at Troas, but here he was ministering to a group of *women!* "It is better that the words of the law be burned than be delivered to a woman!" said the rabbis, but that was no longer Paul's philosophy. He had been obedient and the Lord had gone before to prepare the way.

Lydia was a successful businesswoman from Thyatira, a city renowned for its purple dye. She probably was in charge of a branch office of her guild in Philippi. God brought her all the way to Greece so that she might hear the gospel and be converted. She was "a worshipper of God," a Gentile who was not a full Jewish proselyte but who openly worshipped with the Jews. She was seeking truth.

Paul shared the Word ("spoken" in Acts 16:14 means personal conversation, not preaching), God opened her heart to the truth, and she believed and was saved. She boldly identified herself with Christ by being baptized, and she insisted that the missionaries stay at her house. All of her household had been converted, so this was a good opportunity for Paul and his associates to teach them the Word and establish a local church. (We will deal with "household salvation" when we get to Acts 16:31.)

We must not conclude that because *God* opened Lydia's heart, Lydia's part in her conversion was entirely passive. She listened attentively to the Word, and it is the Word that brings the sinner to the Savior (John 5:24). The same God who ordained the end, Lydia's salvation, also ordained the *means to the end,* Paul's witness of Jesus Christ. This is a beautiful illustration of 2 Thessalonians 2:13–14.

God opened the prison doors (vv. 16–40). No sooner are lost people saved than Satan begins to hinder the work. In this case, he used a demonized girl who had made her masters wealthy by telling fortunes. As Paul and his "team" went regularly to the place of prayer, still witnessing to the lost, this girl repeatedly shouted after them, "These men are the servants of the Most High God, who show us the way of salvation!" Paul did not want either the gospel or the name of God to be "promoted" by one of Satan's slaves, so he cast out the demon. After all, Satan may speak the truth one minute and the next minute tell a lie, and the unsaved would not know the difference.

The owners had no concern for the girl; they were interested only in the income she provided, and now that income was gone. (The conflict between money and ministry appears often in Acts: 5:1–11; 8:18–24; 19:23ff.; 20:33–34.) Their only recourse was the Roman law, and they thought they had a pretty good case because the missionaries were Jewish and were propagating a religion not approved by Rome. Moved by both religious and racial prejudices, the magistrates acted rashly and did not investigate the matter fully. This neglect on their part later brought them embarrassment.

Why didn't Paul and Silas plead their Roman citizenship (see Acts 22:25–29; 25:11–12)? Perhaps there was not time, or perhaps Paul was saving that weapon for better use later on. He and Silas were stripped and beaten (see 2 Cor. 11:23, 25) and put in the city prison. It looked like the end of their witness in Philippi, but God had other plans.

Instead of complaining or calling on God to judge their enemies, the two men prayed and praised God. When you are in pain, the midnight hour is not the easiest time for a sacred concert, but God gives "songs in the night" (Job 35:10; also see Ps. 42:8). "Any fool can sing in the day," said Charles Haddon Spurgeon. "It is easy to sing when we can read the notes by daylight; but the skilful stager is he who can sing when there is not a ray of light to read by … Songs in the night come only from God; they are not in the power of men."

Prayer and praise are powerful weapons (2 Chron. 20:1–22; Acts 4:23–37). God responded by shaking the foundations of the prison, opening all the doors, and loosening the prisoners' bonds. They could have fled to freedom, but instead they remained right where they were. For one thing, Paul immediately took command and, no doubt, the fear of God was on these pagan men. The prisoners must have realized that there was something very special about those two Jewish preachers!

Paul's attention was fixed on the jailer, the man he really wanted to win to Christ. It was a Roman law that if a guard lost a prisoner, he was given the same punishment the prisoner would have received, so there must have been some men in the prison who had committed capital crimes. The jailer would rather commit suicide than face shame and execution. A hard-hearted person seeking vengeance would have let the cruel jailer kill himself, but Paul was not that kind of a man (see Matt. 5:10–12, 43–48). It was the jailer who was the prisoner, not Paul, and Paul not only saved the man's life, but pointed him to eternal life in Christ.

"What must I do to be saved?" is the cry of lost people worldwide, and we had better be able to give them the right answer. The legalists in the church would have replied, "Unless you are circumcised according to the custom of Moses, you cannot be saved" (Acts 15:1 NKJV). But Paul knew the right answer—faith in Jesus Christ. In the book of Acts, the emphasis is on faith in Jesus Christ alone (Acts 2:38–39; 4:12; 8:12, 37; 10:10–43; 13:38–39).

The phrase "and thy house" does not mean that the faith of the jailer would automatically bring salvation to his family. Each sinner must trust Christ personally in order to be born again, for we cannot be saved "by proxy." The phrase means "and your household will be saved if they will also believe." We must not read into this statement the salvation of infants (with or without baptism), because it is clear that Paul was dealing with people old enough to hear the Word (Acts 16:32), to believe, and to rejoice (Acts 16:34).

So-called "household salvation" has no basis in the Word of God—that is, that the decision of the head of the household brings salvation to the members of the household. The people in the household of Cornelius were old enough to respond to his call (Acts 10:24) and to understand the Word and believe (Acts 10:44; 11:15–17; 15:7–9). The household of Crispus was composed of people old enough to hear and believe God's Word (Acts 18:8). There is no suggestion here that the adults made decisions for infants or children.

It is touching to see the change in the attitude of the jailer as he washed the wounds of these two prisoners who were now his brothers in Christ. One of the evidences of true repentance is a loving desire to make restitution and reparation wherever we have hurt others. We should not only wash one another's feet (John 13:14–15), but we should also cleanse the wounds we have given to others.

What about the other prisoners? Luke doesn't give us the details, but it is possible that some of them were also born again through the witness of Paul and Silas and the jailer. Some of these prisoners may have been waiting for execution, so imagine their joy at hearing a message of salvation! Paul and Silas thought nothing of their own pains as they rejoiced in what God did in that Philippian jail! No doubt the jailer later joined with Lydia in the assembly.

The city officials knew that they had no convincing case against Paul and Silas, so they sent word to the jailer to release them. Paul, however, was unwilling to "sneak out of town," for that kind of exit would have left the new church under a cloud of suspicion. People would have asked, "Who were those men? Were they guilty of some crime? Why did they leave so quickly? What do their followers believe?" Paul and his associates wanted to leave behind a strong witness of their own integrity as well as a good testimony for the infant church in Philippi.

It was then that Paul made use of his Roman citizenship and boldly challenged the officials on the legality of their treatment. This was not personal revenge but a desire to give protection and respect for the church. While the record does not say that the magistrates officially and publicly apologized, it does state that they respectfully came to Paul and Silas, escorted them out of the prison, and politely asked them to leave town. Paul and Silas remained in Philippi long enough to visit the new believers and encourage them in the Lord.

As you review this chapter, you can see that the work of the Lord progresses through difficulties and challenges. Sometimes the workers have problems with each other, and sometimes the problems come from the outside. It is also worth noting that not every sinner comes to Christ in exactly the same manner. Timothy was saved partly through the influence of a godly mother and grandmother. Lydia was converted through a quiet conversation with Paul at a Jewish prayer meeting, while the jailer's conversion was dramatic. One minute he was a potential suicide, and the next minute he was a child of God!

Different people with different experiences, and yet all of them changed by the grace of God.

Others just like them are waiting to be told God's simple plan of salvation.

Will you help them hear?

In your own witness for Christ, will you be daring?

CHAPTER SIXTEEN
Acts 17
RESPONDING TO GOD'S WORD

This chapter describes Paul's ministry in three cities and how some of the people in those cities responded to the Word of God. These pictures are snapshots, not murals, for Dr. Luke did not give us many details. However, as we study these three different responses, we can certainly see our modern world and better understand what to expect as we seek to witness for Christ today.

Thessalonica—Resisting the Word (17:1–9)

Following the famous Egnatian Way, Paul and Silas went one hundred miles from Philippi to Thessalonica. (Timothy is not mentioned again until Acts 17:14, so he may have remained in Philippi.) As far as we can tell, they did not pause to minister in either Amphipolis or Apollonia. Perhaps there were no synagogues in those cities, and Paul certainly expected the new believers in Philippi to carry the message to their neighbors. It was Paul's policy to minister in the larger cities and make them centers for evangelizing a whole district (see Acts 19:10, 26; 1 Thess. 1:8).

Paul knew that Thessalonica (our modern Salonika) was a strategic city for the work of the Lord. Not only was it the capital of Macedonia, but it was also a center for business, rivaled only by Corinth. It was located on several important trade routes, and it boasted an excellent harbor. The city was predominantly Greek, even though it was controlled by Rome. Thessalonica was a "free city," which meant that it had an elected citizens' assembly, it could mint its own coins, and it had no Roman garrison within its walls.

Paul labored at his tentmaking trade (Acts 18:3; 1 Thess. 2:9; 2 Thess. 3:7–10), but on the Sabbath ministered in the Jewish synagogue where he knew he would find both devout Jews and Gentiles, "God-seekers" and proselytes. This witness went on for only three Sabbaths; then he had to minister outside the synagogue. We do not know exactly how long Paul remained in Thessalonica, but it was long enough to receive financial help twice from the church in Philippi (Phil. 4:15–16). Read 1 Thessalonians 1 to learn how God blessed Paul's ministry and how the message spread from Thessalonica to other places. It was not a long ministry, but it was an effective one.

Four key words in Acts 17:2–3 describe Paul's approach to the synagogue congregation. First, he *reasoned,* which means he dialogued with them through questions and answers. He *explained* ("opening") the Scriptures to them and *proved* ("alleging") that Jesus is indeed the Messiah. The word translated "alleging" means "to lay down alongside, to prove by presenting the evidence." The apostle set before them one Old Testament proof after another that

Jesus of Nazareth is Messiah God. Paul was careful to *announce* ("preach") the death and resurrection of Jesus Christ, which is the message of the gospel (1 Cor. 15:1ff.). In the sermons in Acts, you will find an emphasis on the resurrection, for the believers were called to be witnesses of His resurrection (Acts 1:21–22; 2:32; 3:15; 5:32). "Christianity is in its very essence a resurrection religion," says Dr. John Stott. "The concept of resurrection lies at its heart. If you remove it, Christianity is destroyed."

As the result of three weeks' ministry, Paul saw a large number of people believe, especially Greek proselytes and influential women. Among the men were Aristarchus and Secundus, who later traveled with Paul (Acts 20:4). Luke's phrase "not a few" (Acts 17:4, 12) is one way of saying, "It was a big crowd!"

But these results did not bring joy to everybody. The unbelieving Jews envied Paul's success and were grieved to see the Gentiles and the influential women leaving the synagogue. Paul hoped that the salvation of the Gentiles would "provoke" the Jews into studying the Scriptures and discovering their promised Messiah (Rom. 11:13–14), but in this case, it only provoked them into persecuting the infant church.

The Jews wanted to drag the missionaries before their city assembly ("the people," Acts 17:5; see 19:30), so they manufactured a riot to get the attention of the magistrates. Unable to find the missionaries, the mob seized Jason, host to Paul and his friends, and took him and some of the believers instead. The Jews' accusations were similar to the ones used at the trial of Jesus: disturbing the peace and promoting treason (Luke 23:2). Their crime was that of "saying that there is another king, one Jesus."

The Greek word translated "another" means "another of a different kind," that is, a king unlike Caesar. When you read Paul's two Thessalonian letters, you see the strong emphasis he gave in Thessalonica on the kingship of Christ and the promise of His return. Of course, our Lord's kingdom is neither political nor "of this world" (John 18:36–37), but we cannot expect unsaved pagans to understand this.

The kingship of Jesus Christ is unlike that of the rulers of this world. He conquers with ambassadors, not armies, and His weapons are truth and love. He brings men peace by upsetting the peace and turning things upside down! He conquers through His cross, where He died for a world of lost sinners. He even died for His enemies (Rom. 5:6–10)!

The mob was agitated because they could not find Paul and Silas, so they settled for second best and obtained a peace bond against them. Jason had to put up the money and guarantee that Paul and Silas would leave the city and not return. It is possible that Jason was a relative of Paul's, which would make the transaction even more meaningful (Rom. 16:21). Paul saw this prohibition as a device of Satan to hinder the work (1 Thess. 2:18), but it certainly did not hinder the Thessalonian church

from "sounding out the word" and winning the lost (1 Thess. 1:6–9).

Berea—Receiving the Word (17:10–15)

Under cover of night, Paul and Silas left the city and headed for Berea, about forty-five miles away. It does not appear that Timothy was with them, as he was probably working in Philippi. Later, he would join Paul in Athens (Acts 17:15) and then be sent to Thessalonica to encourage the church in its time of persecution (1 Thess. 3: 1ff.). Since Timothy was a Gentile, and had not been present when the trouble erupted, he could minister in the city freely. The peace bond could keep Paul out, but it would not apply to Paul's young assistant.

Paul went into the synagogue and there discovered a group of people keenly interested in the study of the Old Testament Scriptures. In fact, they met *daily* to search the Scriptures to determine whether or not what Paul was saying was true. Paul had been overjoyed at the way the people in Thessalonica had received the Word (1 Thess. 2:13), so these "noble Bereans" must have really encouraged his heart. All of us should imitate these Bereans by faithfully studying God's Word daily, discussing it, and testing the messages that we hear.

God used His Word so that many people trusted Christ. One of the men who was converted was Sopater, who later assisted Paul (Acts 20:4). He may be the same man (Sosipater) who later sent greetings to the Christians in Rome (Rom. 16:21).

Once again, Satan brought the enemy to the field as the unbelieving Jews from Thessalonica came to Berea and stirred up the people (note 1 Thess. 2:13–20). How did these men hear that Paul and Silas were ministering in Berea? Perhaps the growing witness of the Berean believers reached as far as Thessalonica, or it may be that some troublemaker took the message to his friends in Thessalonica. Satan also has his "missionaries" and they are busy (2 Cor. 11:13–15).

The believers in Berea outwitted the enemy by taking Paul to the sea and putting him on a ship bound for Athens. Once more, Paul had to leave a place of rich ministry and break away from dear people he had come to love. Silas and Timothy later joined Paul in Athens, and then Timothy was sent to Thessalonica to help the saints there (1 Thess. 3:1–6). Silas was also sent on a special mission somewhere in Macedonia (Philippi?), and later both men met Paul in Corinth (Acts 18:1–5).

Athens—Ridiculing the Word (17:16–34)

Paul arrived in the great city of Athens, not as a sightseer, but as a soul-winner. The late Noel O. Lyons, for many years director of the Greater Europe Mission, used to say, "Europe is looked over by millions of visitors and is overlooked by millions of Christians." Europe needs the gospel today just as it did in Paul's day, and we dare not miss our opportunities. Like Paul, we must have open eyes and broken hearts.

The city. Athens was in a period of decline at this time, though still recognized as a center of culture and education. The glory of its politics and commerce had long since faded. It had a famous university and numerous beautiful buildings, but it was not the influential city it once had been. The city was given over to a "cultured paganism" that was nourished by idolatry, novelty (Acts 17:21), and philosophy.

"The Greek religion was a mere deification of human attributes and the powers of nature," wrote Conybeare and Howson in their classic *Life and Epistles of St. Paul.* "It was a religion which ministered to art and amusement, and was entirely destitute of moral power" (280–281). The Greek myths spoke of gods and goddesses that, in their own rivalries and ambitions, acted more like humans than gods, and there were plenty of deities to choose from! One wit jested that in Athens it was easier to find a god than a man. Paul saw that the city was "wholly given to idolatry," and it broke his heart.

We today admire Greek sculpture and architecture as beautiful works of art, but in Paul's day, much of this was directly associated with their religion. Paul knew that idolatry was demonic (1 Cor. 10:14–23) and that the many gods of the Greeks were only characters in stories who were unable to change men's lives (1 Cor. 8:1–6). With all of their culture and wisdom, the Greeks did not know the true God (1 Cor. 1:18–25).

As for novelty, it was the chief pursuit of both the citizens and the visitors (Acts 17:21). Their leisure time was spent telling or hearing "some new thing." Eric Hoffer wrote that "the fear of becoming a 'has been' keeps some people from becoming anything." The person who chases the new and ignores the old soon discovers that he has no deep roots to nourish his life. He also discovers that nothing is really new; it's just that our memories are poor (Eccl. 1:8–11).

The city was also devoted to philosophy. When you think of Greece, you automatically think of Socrates and Aristotle and a host of other thinkers whose works are still read and studied today. Newspaper columnist Franklin P. Adams once defined philosophy as "unintelligible answers to insoluble problems," but the Greeks would not have agreed with him. They would have followed Aristotle, who called philosophy "the science which considers truth."

Paul had to confront two opposing philosophies as he witnessed in Athens, those of the Epicureans and the Stoics. We today associate the word *Epicurean* with the pursuit of pleasure and the love of "fine living," especially fine food. But the Epicurean philosophy involved much more than that. In one sense, the founder Epicurus was an "existentialist" in that he sought truth by means of personal experience and not through reasoning. The Epicureans were materialists and atheists, and their goal in life was pleasure. To some, "pleasure" meant that which was grossly physical, but to others, it meant a life of refined serenity, free from pain and anxiety. The true Epicurean avoided extremes and sought to enjoy life by keeping things in balance, but pleasure was still his number one goal.

The Stoics rejected the idolatry of pagan worship and taught that there was one "World God." They were pantheists, and their emphasis was on personal discipline and self-control. Pleasure was not good and pain was not evil. The most important thing in life was to follow one's reason and be self-sufficient, unmoved by inner feelings or outward circumstances. Of course, such a philosophy only fanned the flames of pride and taught men that they did not need the help of God. It is interesting that the first two leaders of the Stoic school committed suicide.

The Epicureans said "Enjoy life!" and the Stoics said "Endure life!" but it remained for Paul to explain how they could enter into life through faith in God's risen Son.

The witness. "Left at Athens alone" (1 Thess. 3:1), Paul viewed the idolatrous city and his spirit was "stirred" (same word as "contention" in Acts 15:39—"paroxysm"). Therefore, he used what opportunities were available to share the good news of the gospel. As was his custom, he "dialogued" in the synagogue with the Jews, but he also witnessed in the marketplace *(agora)* to the Greeks. Anyone who was willing to talk was welcomed by Paul to his daily "classes."

It did not take long for the philosophers to hear about this "new thing" that was going on in the *agora,* and they came and listened to Paul and probably debated with him. As they listened, they gave two different responses. One group ridiculed Paul and his teachings and called him a "babbler." The word literally means "birds picking up seed," and it refers to someone who collects various ideas and teaches as his own the secondhand thoughts he borrows from others. It was not a very flattering description of the church's greatest missionary and theologian.

The second group was confused but interested. They thought Paul believed as they themselves did in many gods, because he was preaching "Jesus and Anastasis" (the Greek word for "resurrection"). The word translated "preached" in Acts 17:18 means "to preach the gospel." Those who say that Paul modified his evangelistic tactics in Athens, hoping to appeal to the intellectuals, have missed the point. He preached the gospel as boldly in Athens as he did in Berea and would do in Corinth.

The defense. The Council of the Aeropagus was responsible to watch over both religion and education in the city, so it was natural for them to investigate the "new doctrine" Paul was teaching. They courteously invited Paul to present his doctrine at what appears to have been an informal meeting of the council on Mars' Hill. Paul was not on trial; the council members only wanted him to explain what he had been telling the people in the *agora.* After all, life in Athens consisted in hearing and telling new things, and Paul had something new!

Paul's message is a masterpiece of communication.

He started where the people were by referring to their altar dedicated to an unknown god. Having aroused their interest, he then explained who that God is and what He is like. He concluded the message with a personal application that left each council member facing a moral decision, and some of them decided for Jesus Christ.

Paul opened his address with a compliment: "I see that in every way you are very religious" (Acts 17:22 NIV). They were so religious, in fact, that they even had an altar to "the unknown god," lest some beneficent deity be neglected. If they did not know this god, how could they worship him? Or how could he help them? It was this God that Paul declared.

In this message, which is similar to his sermon at Lystra (Acts 14:15–17), Paul shared four basic truths about God.

The greatness of God: He is Creator (v. 24). Every thinking person asks, "Where did I come from? Why am I here? Where am I going?" Science attempts to answer the first question, and philosophy wrestles with the second, but only the Christian faith has a satisfactory answer to all three. The Epicureans, who were atheists, said that all was matter and matter always was. The Stoics said that everything was God, "the Spirit of the Universe." God did not create anything; He only organized matter and impressed on it some "law and order."

But Paul boldly affirmed, "In the beginning, God!" God made the world and everything in it, and He is Lord of all that He has made. He is not a distant God, divorced from His creation, nor is He an imprisoned God, locked in creation. He is too great to be housed in man-made temples (1 Kings 8:27; Isa. 66:1–2; Acts 7:48–50), but He is not too great to be concerned about man's needs (Acts 17:25). We wonder how the Council members reacted to Paul's statement about temples, for right there on the Acropolis were several shrines dedicated to Athena.

The goodness of God: He is Provider (v. 25). Men may pride themselves in serving God, but it is God who serves man. If God is God, then He is self-sufficient and needs nothing that man can supply. Not only do the temples not contain God, but the services in the temples add nothing to God! In two brief statements, Paul completely wiped out the entire religious system of Greece!

It is God who gives to us what we need: "life, and breath, and all things." God is the source of every good and perfect gift (James 1:17). He gave us life and He sustains that life by His goodness (Matt. 5:45). It is the goodness of God that should lead men to repentance (Rom. 2:4). But instead of worshipping the Creator and glorifying Him, men worship His creation and glorify themselves (Rom. 1:18–25).

The government of God: He is Ruler (vv. 26–29). The gods of the Greeks were distant beings who had no concern for the problems and needs of men. But the God of creation is also the God of history and geography! He created mankind "from one man" (Acts 17:36 NIV) so that all nations are made of the same stuff and have the same blood. The Greeks felt that they were a special race, different from other nations, but Paul affirmed otherwise. Even their precious land that they revered came as a gift from God. It is not the power of man, but the government of God, that determines the rise and fall of nations (Dan. 4:35).

God is not a distant deity; "He [is] not far from every one of us" (Acts 17:27). Therefore, men ought to seek God and come to know Him in truth. Here Paul quoted from the poet Epimenides: "For in him we live, and move, and have our being." Then he added a quotation from two poets, Aratus and Cleanthes: "For we are also his offspring." Paul was not saying that all people on earth are the spiritual children of God, for sinners become God's children only by faith in Jesus Christ (John 1:11–13). Rather, he was affirming the "Fatherhood of God" in a *natural* sense, for man was created in the image of God (Gen. 1:26). In this sense, Adam was a "son of God" (Luke 3:38).

This led to Paul's logical conclusion: God made us in His image, so it is foolish for us to make gods in our own image! Greek religion was nothing but the manufacture and worship of gods who were patterned after men and who acted like men. Paul not only showed the folly of temples and the temple rituals, but also the folly of all idolatry.

The grace of God: He is Savior (vv. 30–34). As he brought his message to a close, Paul summarized the clear evidences of God's grace. For centuries, God was patient with man's sin and ignorance (see Acts 14:16; Rom. 3:25). This does not mean that men were not guilty (Rom. 1:19–20), but only that God held back divine wrath. In due time, God sent a Savior, and now He commands all men to repent of their foolish ways. This Savior was killed and then raised from the dead, and one day, He will return to judge the world. The proof that He will judge is that He was raised from the dead.

It was the doctrine of the resurrection that most of the members of the Council could not accept. To a Greek, the body was only a prison, and the sooner a person left his body, the happier he would be. Why raise a dead body and live in it again? And why would God bother with a personal judgment of each man? This kind of teaching was definitely incompatible with Greek philosophy. They believed in immortality, but not in resurrection.

There were three different responses to the message. Some laughed and mocked and did not take Paul's message seriously. Others were interested but wanted to hear more. A small group accepted what Paul preached, believed on Jesus Christ, and were saved. We wonder if the others who postponed their decision eventually trusted Christ. We hope they did.

When you contrast the seeming meager results in Athens with the great harvests in Thessalonica and Berea, you are tempted to conclude that Paul's ministry there was a dismal failure. If you do, you might find yourself drawing a hasty and erroneous conclusion. Paul was not told to leave, so we assume he lingered in Athens and continued to minister to both believers and unbelievers. Proud, sophisticated, wise Athens would not take easily to Paul's humbling message of the gospel, especially when he summarized all of Greek history in the phrase "the times of this ignorance." The soil here was not deep and it contained many weeds, but there was a small harvest.

And, after all, one soul is worth the whole world!

We still need witnesses who will invade the "halls of academe" and present Christ to people who are wise in this world but ignorant of the true wisdom of the world to come. "Not many wise men after the flesh, not many mighty, not many noble are called" (1 Cor. 1:26), but some *are* called, and God may use you to call them.

Take the gospel to your "Athens."

CHAPTER SEVENTEEN
Acts 18:1–22
IT'S ALWAYS TOO SOON TO QUIT

A man was shoveling snow from his driveway when two boys carrying snow shovels approached him. "Shovel your snow, Mister?" one of them asked. "Only two dollars!"

Puzzled, the man replied, "Can't you see that I'm doing it myself?"

"Sure," said the enterprising lad; "that's why we asked. We get most of our business from people who are half through and feel like quitting!"

Dr. V. Raymond Edman used to say to the students at Wheaton (Illinois) College, "It's always too soon to quit!" And Charles Spurgeon reminded his London congregation, "By perseverance, the snail reached the ark."

Corinth, with its 200,000 people, would not be the easiest city in which to start a church, and yet that's where Paul went after leaving Athens. And he went alone! The going was tough, but the apostle did not give up.

Corinth's reputation for wickedness was known all over the Roman Empire. (Rom. 1:18–32 was written in Corinth!) Thanks to its location, the city was a center for both trade and travel. Money and vice, along with strange philosophies and new religions, came to Corinth and found a home there. Corinth was the capital of Achaia and one of the two most important cities Paul visited. The other was Ephesus.

When God opens doors, the enemy tries to close them, and there are times when we close the doors on ourselves because we get discouraged and quit. As Paul ministered in Corinth, the Lord gave him just the encouragements that he needed to keep him going, and these same encouragements are available to us today.

Devoted Helpers (18:1–5)

Paul came to Corinth following his ministry to the philosophers in Greece, and he determined to magnify Jesus Christ and the cross, to depend on the Holy Spirit, and to present the gospel in simplicity (1 Cor. 2:1–5). There were many philosophers and itinerant teachers in Corinth, preying on the ignorant and superstitious population, and Paul's message and ministry could easily be misunderstood.

One way Paul separated himself from the "religious hucksters" was by supporting himself as a tentmaker. By the providence of God, he met a Jewish couple, Aquila and Priscilla ("Prisca," 2 Tim. 4:19), who were workers in leather as was Paul. Jewish rabbis did not accept money from their students but earned their way by practicing a trade. All Jewish boys were expected to learn a trade, no matter what profession they might enter. "He who does not teach his son to work, teaches him to steal!" said the rabbis, so Saul of Tarsus learned to make leather tents and to support himself in his ministry (see Acts 18:3; 1 Cor. 9:6–15; 2 Cor. 11:6–10).

Were Aquila and Priscilla Christian believers at that time? We don't know for certain, but it's likely that they were. Perhaps they were even founding members of the church in Rome. We do know that this dedicated couple served most faithfully and even risked their lives for Paul (Rom. 16:3–4). They assisted him in Ephesus (Acts 18:18–28), where they even hosted a church in their home (1 Cor. 16:19). Aquila and Priscilla were an important part of Paul's "team," and he thanked God for them. They are a good example of how "lay ministers" can help to further the work of the Lord. Every pastor and missionary thanks God for people like Aquila and Priscilla, people with hands, hearts, and homes dedicated to the work of the Lord.

Paul lived and worked with Aquila and Priscilla, but on the Sabbath days witnessed boldly in the synagogue. After all, that was why he had come to Corinth. When Silas and Timothy arrived from Macedonia (Acts 17:14–15; 18:5), they brought financial aid (2 Cor. 11:9), and this enabled Paul to devote his full time to the preaching of the gospel. What a joy it must have been for Paul to see his friends and to hear from them the good news of the steadfastness of the Christians in the churches they had planted together (1 Thess. 3).

Everyone agrees that Paul was a great Christian and a great missionary evangelist, but how much would Paul have accomplished *alone?* Friends like Aquila and Priscilla, Silas and Timothy, and the generous believers in Macedonia, made it possible for Paul to serve the Lord effectively. His Christian friends, new and old, encouraged him at a time when he needed it the most.

Of course, this reminds us that we should encourage our friends in the work of the Lord. Ralph Waldo Emerson wrote, "God evidently does not intend us all to be rich or powerful or great, but He does intend us all to be friends." "Bear ye one another's burdens, and so fulfill the law of Christ" is the way Paul expressed it

(Gal. 6:2). Humanly speaking, there would have been no church in Corinth were it not for the devotion and service of many different people.

Opposition (18:6–8)

Whenever God is blessing a ministry, you can expect increased opposition as well as increased opportunities. "For a great and effective door has opened to me, and there are many adversaries" (1 Cor. 16:9 NKJV). After all, the enemy gets angry when we invade his territory and liberate his slaves. As in Thessalonica and Berea (Acts 17:5–13), the unbelieving Jews who rejected the Word stirred up trouble for Paul and his friends (see 1 Thess. 2:14–16). Such opposition is usually proof that God is at work, and this ought to encourage us. Spurgeon used to say that the devil never kicks a dead horse!

Jewish opposition had forced Paul to leave Thessalonica and Berea, but in Corinth, it only made him determined to stay there and get the job done. It is always too soon to quit! Like the undaunted Christopher Columbus, Paul could write in his journal, "Today we sailed on!"

Two interesting Old Testament images are found in Acts 18:6. To shake out one's garments was an act of judgment that said, "You have had your opportunity, but now it's over!" Today we might say that we were washing our hands of a situation. (See Neh. 5:13; and compare Acts 13:51 and Matt. 10:14.) While Paul never ceased witnessing to the Jews, his primary calling was to evangelize the Gentiles (Acts 13:46–48; 28:28).

To have blood *on your hands* means that you bear the responsibility for another's death because you were not faithful to warn him. The image comes from the watchman on the city walls whose task it was to stay alert and warn of coming danger (see Ezek. 3:17–21; 33:1–9). But to have blood *on your head* means that you are to blame for your own judgment. You had the opportunity to be saved, but you turned it down (see Josh. 2:19). Paul's hands were clean (Acts 20:26) because he had been faithful to declare the message of the gospel. The Jews had their own blood on their own heads because they rejected God's truth.

At just the right time, God brought another friend into Paul's life—Gentile, God-fearing Titus Justus. Some Bible students think his full name was Gaius Titus Justus and that he was the "Gaius my host" referred to in Romans 16:23. The connection between Gaius and Crispus in Acts 18:7–8 and 1 Corinthians 1:14 is certainly significant.

Paul departed from the synagogue and began using the house of Titus Justus as his preaching station, right next to the synagogue! This was certainly a wise decision on Paul's part, because it gave him continued contact with the Jews and Gentile proselytes, and as a result, even the chief ruler of the synagogue was converted! It was the ruler's job to see to it that the synagogue building was cared for and that the services were held in a regular and orderly manner. We have here another instance of an entire family turning to the Lord (Acts 10:24, 44; 16:15, 34). How that must have stirred the Jewish population in Corinth!

When you examine Paul's ministry in Corinth, you will see that he was fulfilling the Lord's commission given in Matthew 28:19–20. Paul came to Corinth ("Go"), he won sinners to Christ ("make disciples"), he baptized, and he taught them (note Acts 18:11). He even experienced the assurance of the Lord's "Lo, I am with thee always" (Acts 18:9–10).

Paul's associates baptized most of the new converts (1 Cor. 1:11–17), just as our Lord's disciples did when He ministered on earth (John 4:1–2; and note Acts 10:46–48). The important thing is the believer's obedience to the Lord and not the name of the minister who does the baptizing. When I became senior pastor at the Moody Church in Chicago, an older member boastfully said to me, "I was baptized by Dr. Ironside!" He was surprised that I was not impressed. I was sure that Dr. Ironside would have lovingly rebuked him for speaking like that, for Dr. Ironside was a humble man who wanted Christ's name exalted, not his own.

To walk by faith means to see opportunities even in the midst of opposition. A pessimist sees only the problems; an optimist sees only the potential; but a realist sees the potential in the problems. Paul did not close his eyes to the many dangers and difficulties in the situation at Corinth, but he did look at them from the divine point of view.

Faith simply means obeying God's will in spite of feelings, circumstances, or consequences. There never was an easy place to serve God, and if there is an easy place, it is possible that something is wrong. Paul reminded Timothy, "Yes, and all who desire to live godly in Christ Jesus will suffer persecution" (2 Tim. 3:12 NKJV).

"Prosperity is the blessing of the Old Testament," wrote Francis Bacon; "adversity is the blessing of the New." Paul did not allow adversity to keep him from serving God.

The Word of Assurance (18:9–17)

The conversion of Crispus, an important Jewish leader, opened up more opportunities for evangelism and brought more opposition from the enemy! The Jewish community in Corinth was no doubt furious at Paul's success and did everything possible to silence him and get rid of him. Dr. Luke does not give us the details, but I get the impression that between Acts 18:8 and 9, the situation became especially difficult and dangerous. Paul may have been thinking about leaving the city when the Lord came to him and gave him the assurance that he needed.

It is just like our Lord to speak to us when we need Him the most. His tender "Fear not!" can calm the storm in our hearts regardless of the circumstances around us. This is the way He assured Abraham (Gen. 15:1), Isaac (Gen. 26:24), and Jacob (Gen. 46:3), as well as Jehoshaphat (2 Chron. 20:15–17), Daniel

(Dan. 10:12, 19), Mary (Luke 1:30), and Peter (Luke 5:10). The next time you feel alone and defeated, meditate on Hebrews 13:5 and Isaiah 41:10 and 43:1–7, and claim by faith the presence of the Lord. He is with you!

When he was a young man, the famous British preacher G. Campbell Morgan used to read the Bible each week to two elderly women. One evening, when he finished reading the closing words of Matthew 28, Morgan said to the ladies, "Isn't that a wonderful promise!" and one of them replied, "Young man, that is not a promise—it is a fact!"

Jesus had already appeared to Paul on the Damascus road (Acts 9:1–6; 26:12–18) and also in the temple (Acts 22:17–18). Paul would be encouraged by Him again when he was imprisoned in Jerusalem (Acts 23:11) and later in Rome (2 Tim. 4:16–17). Our Lord's angel would also appear to Paul in the midst of the storm and give him a word of assurance for the passengers and crew (Acts 27:23–25). One of our Lord's names is "Emmanuel—God with us" (Matt. 1:23), and He lives up to His name.

Paul was encouraged not only by the presence of the Lord, but also by His promises. Jesus assured Paul that no one would hurt him and that he would bring many sinners to the Savior. The statement "I have many people in this city" implies the doctrine of divine election, for "the Lord knows those who are His" (2 Tim. 2:19 NKJV). God's church is made up of people who were "chosen … in him [Christ] before the foundation of the world" (Eph. 1:4; and see Acts 13:48).

Please note that divine sovereignty in election is not a deterrent to human responsibility in evangelism. Quite the opposite is true! Divine election is one of the greatest encouragements to the preaching of the gospel. Because Paul knew that God already had people set apart for salvation, he stayed where he was and preached the gospel with faith and courage. Paul's responsibility was to obey the commission; God's responsibility was to save sinners. If salvation depends on sinful man, then all of our efforts are futile, but if "salvation is of the Lord" (Jonah 2:9), then we can expect Him to bless His Word and save souls.

"Scripture nowhere dispels the mystery of election," writes John Stott in *God's New Society* (InterVarsity, 37), "and we should beware of any who try to systematize it too precisely or rigidly. It is not likely that we shall discover a simple solution to a problem which has baffled the best brains of Christendom for centuries."

The important thing is that we accept God's truth and act on it. Paul did not spend his time speculating about divine sovereignty and human responsibility, the way some ivory-tower Christians do today. *He got busy and tried to win souls to Christ!* You and I do not know who God's elect are, so we take the gospel to every creature and let God do the rest. And we certainly do not discuss election with the lost! D. L. Moody once told some unconverted people, "You have no more to

do with the doctrine of election than you have with the government of China!"

Before leaving this theme, we should note that it is our personal responsibility to make sure that we are among God's elect. "Therefore, brethren, be even more diligent to make your calling and election sure" (2 Peter 1:10 NKJV). To the inquisitive theorist who asked about the number of the elect, Jesus replied, "Strive to enter in at the narrow gate" (Luke 13:23–24). In other words, "What you need is salvation for yourself, not speculation about others! Be sure you are saved yourself; then we can talk about these wonderful truths."

Paul continued in Corinth, knowing that God was with Him and that people would be saved. During those eighteen months of witness, Paul saw many victories in spite of Satan's opposition. The church was not made up of many mighty and noble people (1 Cor. 1:26–31), but of sinners whose lives were transformed by the grace of God (1 Cor. 6:9–11).

Dr. Luke shared only one example of divine protection during Paul's ministry in Corinth (Acts 18:12–17), but it is a significant one. The arrival of a new proconsul gave the unbelieving Jews hope that Rome might declare this new "Christian sect" illegal. They broke the law by attacking Paul and forcing him to go to court. This was not the first time that fanatical Jews had tried to prove that Paul was breaking the Roman law (Acts 16:19–24; 17:6–7).

Being a Roman citizen, Paul was prepared to defend himself, but this turned out to be unnecessary because Gallio defended Paul! The proconsul immediately saw that the real issue was not the application of the Roman law but the interpretation of the Jewish religion, so he refused to try the case!

But that was not the end of the matter. The Greeks who were witnessing the scene got hold of Sosthenes, the man who replaced Crispus as ruler of the synagogue, and beat him right before the eyes of the proconsul! It was certainly a flagrant display of anti-Semitism, but Gallio looked the other way. If this is the same Sosthenes mentioned by Paul in 1 Corinthians 1:1, then he too got converted, and the Jews had to find another ruler for their synagogue! It would be interesting to know exactly how it happened. Did Paul and some of the believers visit Sosthenes and minister to him? Perhaps his predecessor Crispus helped "wash the wounds" (Acts 16:33) and used this as an opportunity to share the love of Christ.

How strange and wonderful are the providences of God! The Jews tried to force the Roman proconsul to declare the Christian faith illegal, but Gallio ended up doing just the opposite. By refusing to try the case, Gallio made it clear that Rome would not get involved in cases involving Jewish religious disputes. As far as he was concerned, Paul and his disciples had as much right as the Jews to practice their religion and share it with others.

In the book of Acts, Luke emphasizes the relationship between the Roman government and the

Christian church. While it was true that the *Jewish* council prohibited the apostles to preach (Acts 4:17–21; 5:40), there is no evidence in Acts that Rome ever did so. In fact, in Philippi (Acts 16:35–40), Corinth, and Ephesus (Acts 19:31), the Roman officials were not only tolerant but almost cooperative. Paul knew how to use his Roman citizenship wisely so that the government worked for him and not against him, and he was careful not to accuse the government or try to escape its authority (Acts 25:10–12).

God's Will (18:18–22)

"If God will" (Acts 18:21) was more than a religious slogan with Paul; it was one of the strengths and encouragements of his life and ministry. Knowing and doing God's will is one of the blessings of the Christian life (Acts 22:14). In some of his letters, Paul identified himself as "an apostle of Jesus Christ by the will of God" (1 Cor. 1:1; 2 Cor. 1:1; Eph. 1:1; Col. 1:1; 2 Tim. 1:1). At a most critical time in his life and ministry, Paul found courage in affirming, "The will of the Lord be done" (Acts 21:14).

After eighteen months of ministry, Paul decided that it was God's will for him to leave Corinth and return to his home church in Antioch. His friends Priscilla and Aquila (note how Luke varies the order of their names) accompanied him to Ephesus and remained there when he departed for Caesarea. In Acts 18:24, we will pick up the story of the church in Ephesus and the important part played by Aquila and Priscilla.

Cenchraea was the seaport for Corinth, and there was a Christian congregation there (Rom. 16:1). Here Paul had his head shorn, "for he had a vow." This probably refers to the Nazarite vow described in Numbers 6. Since the Nazarite vow was purely voluntary, Paul was not abandoning grace for law when he undertook it. The vow was not a matter of salvation but of personal devotion to the Lord. He allowed his hair to grow for a specific length of time and then cut it when the vow was completed. He also abstained from using the fruit of the vine in any form.

We are not told why Paul took this vow. Perhaps it was a part of his special dedication to God during the difficult days of the early ministry in Corinth. Or perhaps the vow was an expression of gratitude to God for all that He had done for him and his associates. According to Jewish law, the Nazarite vow had to be completed in Jerusalem with the offering of the proper sacrifices. The hair was shorn at the completion of the vow, not at the beginning, and it was not necessary for one to be in Jerusalem to make the vow.

Luke does not tell us how long Paul was in Ephesus, but the time was evidently very short. The Jews there were much more receptive to the gospel and wanted Paul to stay, but he wanted to get to Jerusalem to complete his vow, and then to Antioch to report to the church. However, he did promise to return, and he kept that promise (Acts 19:1).

The statement "I must by all means keep this feast that cometh in Jerusalem" (Acts 18:21) must not be interpreted to mean that Paul and the early Christians felt obligated to observe the Jewish feasts (see Acts 20:16). Being in Jerusalem during the important feasts (in this case, Passover) would give Paul opportunity to meet and witness to key Jewish leaders from throughout the Roman Empire. He would also be able to minister to Christian Jews who returned to their homeland.

Paul taught clearly that the observing of religious feasts was neither a means of salvation nor an essential for sanctification (Gal. 4:1–11). Christians are at liberty to follow their own conscience so long as they do not judge others or cause others to stumble (Rom. 14:1—15:7). Also, keep in mind Paul's personal policy with regard to these matters of Jewish practice (1 Cor. 9:19–23).

Arriving at Caesarea, Paul went up to Jerusalem and greeted the believers there. He then went to Antioch and reported to his home church all that God had done on this second missionary journey. He had been gone from Antioch perhaps two years or more, and the saints were no doubt overjoyed to see him and hear about the work of God among the Gentiles.

There's no proof, but likely Paul kept reminding the believers in Antioch, "It's always too soon to quit!"

That's a good reminder for us to heed today.

CHAPTER EIGHTEEN
Acts 18:23—19:41
EXCITEMENT IN EPHESUS

We don't know how long Paul remained in Antioch before leaving on his third missionary journey, but perhaps it was as long as a year. As in his second journey, he visited the churches and strengthened the believers. Luke does not describe this journey in detail because his main purpose is to get Paul to Ephesus. He wants to share with his readers the marvelous ministry God gave to Paul in that strategic city so steeped in idolatry and the occult.

Ephesus, with its 300,000 inhabitants, was the capital city of the Roman province of Asia and its most important commercial center. Thanks to a large harbor, Ephesus grew wealthy on trade, and, thanks to the temple of Diana, it attracted hosts of visitors who wanted to see this building that was one of the seven wonders of the world.

The temple was probably four centuries old in Paul's day. It measured 418 feet by 239 feet, and boasted of 100 columns that stood over 50 feet high. In the sacred enclosure of the temple stood the "sacred image" of Artemis (Diana) that was supposed to have fallen from heaven (Acts 19:35). It was probably a meteorite. Since Artemis was a fertility goddess, cultic prostitution was an important part of her worship, and hundreds of "priestesses" were available in the temple.

Paul's three years in Ephesus (Acts 20:31)—the longest he stayed in any city—were certainly exciting and fruitful. Let's meet some of the people who were involved.

A Man with an Incomplete Message (18:23–28)

When Paul departed from Ephesus for Jerusalem, he left his friends Aquila and Priscilla behind to carry on the witness in the synagogue. Imagine their surprise one Sabbath to hear a visiting Jewish teacher named Apollos preach many of the truths that they themselves believed and taught!

Apollos was certainly an exceptional man in many ways. He came from Alexandria, the second most important city in the Roman Empire. A center for education and philosophy, the city was founded by (and named after) Alexander the Great, and it boasted a university with a library of almost 700,000 volumes. The population of Alexandria (about 600,000) was quite cosmopolitan, being made up of Egyptians, Romans, Greeks, and Jews. At least a quarter of the population was Jewish, and the Jewish community was very influential.

Apollos knew the Old Testament Scriptures well and was able to teach them with eloquence and power. He was fervent ("boiling") in his spirit and diligent in his presentation of the message. He was bold enough to enter the synagogue and preach to the Jews. The only problem was that this enthusiastic man was declaring an incomplete gospel. His message got as far as John the Baptist and then stopped! He knew nothing about Calvary, the resurrection of Christ, or the coming of the Holy Spirit at Pentecost. He had zeal, but he lacked spiritual knowledge (Rom. 10:1–4).

The ministry of John the Baptist was an important part of God's redemptive plan. God sent John to prepare the nation of Israel for their Messiah (John 1:15–34). John's baptism was a baptism of repentance; those who were baptized looked forward to the coming Messiah (Acts 19:4). John also announced a future baptism of the Holy Spirit (Matt. 3:11; Mark 1:8), which took place on the day of Pentecost (Acts 1:5). Apollos knew about the promises, but he did not know about their fulfillment.

Where did Apollos get his message to begin with? Since Alexandria was a famous center for learning, it is possible that some of John the Baptist's disciples (Matt. 14:12; Luke 11:1) had gone there while Christ was still ministering on earth, and shared with the Jews as much as they knew. The word *instructed* in Acts 18:25 means "catechized" and suggests that Apollos had personal formal training in the Scriptures. However, that training was limited to the facts about the ministry of John the Baptist. Apollos' message was not inaccurate or insincere; it was just incomplete.

When I travel in conference ministry, I depend on my wife to plan the routes and do the navigating. (I can get lost in a parking lot!) On one particular trip, we got confused because we could not find a certain road. Then we discovered that our map was out of date! We quickly obtained a new map and everything was fine. Apollos had an old map that had been accurate in its day, but he desperately needed a new one. That new map was supplied by Aquila and Priscilla.

Aquila and Priscilla did not instruct him in public because that would have only confused the Jews. They took him home to a Sabbath dinner and then told him about Jesus Christ and the coming of the Holy Spirit. They led him into a deeper knowledge of Christ, and the next Sabbath, Apollos returned to the synagogue and gave the Jews the rest of the story! In fact, so effective was his ministry that the believers in Ephesus highly recommended him to the churches in Achaia. Here Apollos not only strengthened the saints, but he also debated with the unbelieving Jews and convinced many of them that Jesus is the Messiah.

Apollos ministered for a time to the church in Corinth (Acts 19:1), where his learning and eloquence attracted attention (1 Cor. 1:12; 3:4–6, 22; 4:6). It is unfortunate that a clique gathered around him and helped bring division to the church, because he was definitely one of Paul's friends and a trusted helper (1 Cor. 16:12; Titus 3:13).

Twelve Men with an Inconsistent Witness (19:1–10)

When Paul arrived back in Ephesus, he met twelve men who professed to be Christian "disciples" but whose lives gave evidence that something was lacking. Paul asked them, "Did you receive the Holy Spirit when you believed?" (Acts 19:2 NIV, NASB, NKJV). The question was important because *the witness of the Spirit is the one indispensable proof that a person is truly born again* (Rom. 8:9, 16; 1 John 5:9–13), and you receive the Spirit when you believe on Jesus Christ (Eph. 1:13).

Their reply revealed the vagueness and uncertainty of their faith, for they did not even know that the Holy Spirit had been given! As disciples of John the Baptist, they knew that there was a Holy Spirit, and that the Spirit would one day baptize God's people (Matt. 3:11; Luke 3:16; John 1:32–33). It is possible that these men were Apollos' early "converts" and therefore did not fully understand what Christ had done.

Why did Paul ask about their baptism? Because in the book of Acts, a person's baptismal experience is an indication of his or her spiritual experience. Acts 1—10 records a transition period in the history of the church, from the apostles' ministry to the Jews to their ministry to the Gentiles. During this transition period, Peter used "the keys of the kingdom" (Matt. 16:19) and opened the door of faith to the Jews (Acts 2), the Samaritans (Acts 8:14ff.), and finally to the Gentiles (Acts 10).

It is important to note that God's pattern for today is given in Acts 10:43–48: sinners hear the Word, they believe on Jesus Christ, they *immediately* receive the

Spirit, and then they are baptized. The Gentiles in Acts 10 did not receive the Spirit by means of water baptism or by the laying on of the apostles' hands (Acts 8:14–17).

The fact that these men did not have the Spirit dwelling within was proof that they had never truly been born again. But they had been baptized by John's baptism, the same baptism that the apostles had received (see Acts 1:21–22)! What was wrong with them?

Some people say that these men were already saved, but they lacked the fullness of the Spirit in their lives. So Paul explained how to be "baptized in the Spirit," and this led to a new life of victory. But that's not what the record says. Paul sensed that these men did not have the witness of the Spirit in their lives, and therefore they were not converted men. He certainly would not discuss the fullness of the Spirit with unsaved people! No, these twelve men had been baptized and were seeking to be religious, but something was missing. Alas, we have people just like them in our churches today!

Paul explained to them that John's baptism was a baptism of repentance that *looked forward* to the coming of the promised Messiah, while Christian baptism is a baptism that *looks back* to the finished work of Christ on the cross and His victorious resurrection. John's baptism was on "the other side" of Calvary and Pentecost. It was correct for its day, but now that day was ended.

Keep in mind that John the Baptist was a prophet who ministered under the old dispensation (Matt. 11:7–14). The old covenant was ended, not by John at the Jordan, but by Jesus Christ at Calvary (Heb. 10:1–18). The baptism of John was important to the Jews of that time (Matt. 21:23–32), but it is no longer valid for the church today. In a very real sense, these twelve men were like "Old Testament believers" who were anticipating the coming of the Messiah. Certainly Paul explained to the men many basic truths that Luke did not record. Then he baptized them, for their first "baptism" was not truly Christian baptism.

Why was it necessary for Paul to lay hands on these men before they could receive the Spirit? Didn't this contradict the experience of Peter recorded in Acts 10:44–48? Not if you keep in mind that this was a special group of men who would help form the nucleus of a great church in Ephesus. By using Paul to convey the gift of the Spirit, God affirmed Paul's apostolic authority and united the Ephesian church to the other churches as well as to the "mother church" in Jerusalem. When Peter and John laid hands on the believing Samaritans, it united them to the Jerusalem church and healed a breach between Jews and Samaritans that had existed for centuries.

What God did through Paul for these twelve men was not normative for the church today. How do we know? Because it was not repeated. The people who were converted in Ephesus under Paul's ministry all received the gift of the Holy Spirit *when they trusted the Savior*. Paul makes this clear in Ephesians 1:13–14, and this is the pattern for us today.

In Acts 19:6, we have the last instance of the gift of tongues in the book of Acts. The believers spoke in tongues at Pentecost and praised God, and their listeners recognized these tongues as known languages (Acts 2:4–11) and not as some "heavenly speech." The Gentile believers in the house of Cornelius also spoke in tongues (Acts 10:44–46), and their experience was identical to that of the Jews in Acts 2 (see Acts 11:15). This was of historic significance since the Spirit was baptizing Jews (Acts 2) and Gentiles (Acts 10) into the body of Christ (see 1 Cor. 12:13).

Today, the gift of tongues is not an evidence of the baptism of the Spirit or the fullness of the Spirit. Paul asked, "Do all speak with tongues?" (1 Cor. 12:30), and the Greek construction demands no as an answer. When Paul wrote to his Ephesian friends about the filling of the Holy Spirit, he said nothing about tongues (Eph. 5:18ff.). Nowhere in Scripture are we admonished to seek a baptism of the Holy Spirit, or to speak in tongues, but we are commanded to be filled with the Spirit. Read Paul's letter to the Ephesian church and note the many references to the Holy Spirit of God and His work in the believer.

Seven Men with Inadequate Power (19:11–20)

It is remarkable that Paul was able to witness in the synagogue for three months before he had to leave. No doubt the faithful ministry of Aquila and Priscilla played an important part in this success. However, hardness of heart set in (Heb. 3:7ff.), so Paul left the synagogue and moved his ministry to a schoolroom, taking his disciples with him. He probably used the room during the "off hours" each day (11 a.m. to 4 p.m.), when many people would be resting. Paul ministered in this way for about two years and "all they who dwelt in Asia heard the word of the Lord Jesus, both Jews and Greeks" (Acts 19:10).

What a victorious ministry! It appears that everybody knew what Paul was saying and doing (see Acts 19:17, 20)! Even Paul's enemies had to admit that the Word was spreading and people were being saved (Acts 19:26). Two factors made this possible: the witness of the believers as they went from place to place, and the "special miracles" that God enabled Paul to perform in Ephesus (Acts 19:11).

In Bible history, you will find three special periods of miracles: (1) the time of Moses; (2) the time of Elijah and Elisha; and (3) the time of Jesus and His apostles. Each period was less than one hundred years. Depending on how some of these events are classified, the total number of miracles for all three periods is less than one hundred. Of course, not all the miracles were recorded (see John 20:30–31).

When our Lord performed miracles, He usually had at least three purposes in mind: (1) to show His compassion and meet human needs; (2) to teach a spiritual truth; and (3) to present His credentials as the Messiah. The apostles followed this same pattern in their miracles. In fact, the ability to do miracles was one of the proofs of apostolic authority (Mark 16:20; Rom. 15:18–19; 2 Cor. 12:12; Heb. 2:1–4). Miracles *of themselves* do not save lost sinners (Luke 16:27–31; John 2:23–25). Miracles must be tied to the message of the Word of God.

God enabled Paul to perform "special miracles" because Ephesus was a center for the occult (Acts 19:18–19), and Paul was demonstrating God's power right in Satan's territory. But keep in mind that wherever God's people minister the truth, Satan sends a counterfeit to oppose the work. Jesus taught this truth in His parable of the tares (Matt. 13:24–30, 36–43); Peter experienced it in Samaria (Acts 8:9ff.); and Paul experienced it at Paphos (Acts 13:4–12). Satan imitates whatever God's people are doing, because he knows that the unsaved world cannot tell the difference (2 Cor. 11:13–15).

It was not unusual for Jewish priests to seek to cast out demons (Luke 11:19), but it was unusual for them to use the name of Jesus Christ. Since these men had no personal relationship with the Savior, they had to invoke the name of Paul as well, but their scheme did not work. The demon said, "Jesus I recognize, and Paul I am acquainted with; but who are you?" (literal translation). The demonized man then attacked the seven priests and drove them from the house.

Had this exorcism succeeded, it would have discredited the name of Jesus Christ and the ministry of the church in Ephesus. (Paul faced a similar situation in Philippi. See Acts 16:16ff.) However, God used the scheme to defeat Satan and to bring conviction to the believers who were still involved in magical arts. Instead of disgracing the name of Jesus, the event magnified His name and caused the Word of God to spread even more rapidly.

The tense of the verbs in Acts 19:18 indicates that the people "kept coming … kept confessing … kept showing." These believers apparently had not made a clean break with sin and were still practicing their magic, but the Lord had dealt with them. The total value of the magical books and spells that they burned was equivalent to the total salaries of 150 men working for a whole year! These people did not count the cost but repented and turned from their sins.

A Mob of Indignant Citizens (19:21–41)
In Acts 19:21, we have the first mention of Paul's plan to go to Rome. The fulfilling of this plan will be described in the last third of the book of Acts. Paul would soon write to the saints in Rome and express this desire to them (Rom. 1:13–15; 15:22–29). But first he had to visit the churches in Macedonia and Achaia in order to complete the "love offering" that he was taking for the poor saints in Jerusalem (Acts 24:17; Rom. 15:25–33; 1 Cor. 16:3–7). While he remained in Ephesus (1 Cor. 16:8–9), he sent Timothy to help him finish the job (1 Cor. 4:17; 16:10–11).

It was at this point that Satan attacked again, not as the deceiver (2 Cor. 11:3–4), but as the destroyer (1 Peter 5:8) and the murderer (John 8:44). Satan incited the guild of silversmiths to stage a public protest against Paul and the gospel. Paul may have been referring to this riot when he wrote, "I have fought with beasts at Ephesus" (1 Cor. 15:32). The enemy had been repeatedly defeated throughout Paul's three years of ministry in Ephesus. It would have been a master stroke on Satan's part to climax that ministry with a citywide attack that could result in Paul's arrest, or even his death.

Wherever the gospel is preached in power, it will be opposed by people who make money from superstition and sin. Paul did not arouse the opposition of the silversmiths by picketing the temple of Diana or staging anti-idolatry rallies. All he did was teach the truth daily and send out his converts to witness to the lost people in the city. As more and more people got converted, fewer and fewer customers were available.

"For the love of money is a root of all kinds of evil" (1 Tim. 6:10 NKJV). Demetrius and his silversmiths were promoting idolatry and immorality in order to make a living, while Paul was declaring the true God and pointing people to cleansing and purity through the free grace of God. The silversmiths were really more concerned about their jobs and their income than they were about Diana and her temple, but they were wise enough not to make this known.

Benjamin Franklin said that a mob was "a monster with heads enough, but no brains." How sad it is when people permit themselves to be led by a few selfish leaders who know the art of manipulation. Demetrius made use of the two things the Ephesians loved the most: the honor of their city and the greatness of their goddess and her temple. Without the help of radio, TV, or newspaper, he got his propaganda machine going and soon had the whole city in an uproar.

Max Lerner wrote in *The Unfinished Country,* "Every mob, in its ignorance and blindness and bewilderment, is a League of Frightened Men that seeks reassurance in collective action." It was a "religious mob" that shouted "Crucify Him! Crucify Him!" to Pilate, and eventually got its way. Had this Ephesian mob succeeded in its plans, Paul would have been arrested and executed before the law could have stepped in to protect him.

The confused crowd, some twenty-five thousand shouting people, finally filled up the amphitheater; most of them did not know what was happening or why they were there. Since the mob could not find Paul, they seized two of his helpers, Gaius (not the Gaius of Acts 20:4; Rom. 16:23; 1 Cor. 1:14) and Aristarchus (Acts 20:4). Paul wanted to enter the theater—what an opportunity for preaching the gospel!—but the believers and some of the city leaders wisely counseled him to stay away (Acts 19:30–31).

Before long, race prejudice entered the picture, when a Jew named Alexander tried to address the crowd (Acts 19:33–34). No doubt he wanted to explain to them that the Jews living in Ephesus did not endorse Paul's message or ministry, and, therefore, must not be made scapegoats just to satisfy the crowd. But his very presence only aroused the mob even more, and they shouted for two more hours, "Great is Diana of the Ephesians!" The crowd knew that the Jews did not approve of idols and would not honor Diana. The only thing that protected the Jews was the Roman law that gave them freedom of religion.

It was the city clerk who finally got matters under control, and he did it primarily for political reasons. Ephesus was permitted by Rome to exist as a "free city" with its own elected assembly, but the Romans would have rejoiced to find an excuse for removing these privileges (Acts 19:40). The same tactics that the silversmiths used to arouse the mob, the clerk used to quiet and reassure them—the greatness of their city and of their goddess.

Luke records the official statement that the believers were innocent of any crime, either public (Acts 19:37) or private (Acts 19:38). Paul had this same kind of "official approval" in Philippi (Acts 16:35–40) and in Corinth (Acts 18:12–17), and he would receive it again after his arrest in Jerusalem. Throughout the book of Acts, Luke makes it clear that the persecution of the Christian church was incited by the unbelieving Jews and not by the Romans. If anything, Paul used his Roman citizenship to protect himself, his friends, and the local assemblies.

The crowd was dismissed, and no doubt the people went home congratulating themselves that they had succeeded in defending their great city and their famous goddess. It is doubtful that many of them questioned the truthfulness of their religion or determined to investigate what Paul had been preaching for three years. It is much easier to believe a lie and follow the crowd.

But Ephesus is gone, and so is the worldwide worship of Diana of the Ephesians. The city and the temple are gone, and the silversmiths' guild is gone. Ephesus is a place visited primarily by archeologists and people on Holy Land tours. Yet the gospel of God's grace and the church of Jesus Christ are still here! We have four inspired letters that were sent to the saints in Ephesus—Ephesians, 1 and 2 Timothy, and Revelation 2:1–7. The name of Paul is honored, but the name of Demetrius is forgotten. (Were it not for Paul, we would not have met Demetrius in the first place!)

The church ministers by persuasion, not propaganda. We share God's truth, not man's religious lies. Our motive is love, not anger; and the glory of God, not the praise of men. This is why the church goes on, and we must keep it so.

CHAPTER NINETEEN
Acts 20
A MINISTER'S FAREWELL

In the final third of the book of Acts, Dr. Luke records Paul's journey to Jerusalem, his arrest there, and his voyage to Rome. The gospel of Luke follows a similar pattern as Luke describes Christ's journey to Jerusalem to die (Luke 9:53; 13:33; 18:31; 19:11, 28). Much as Jesus set His face "like a flint" to do the Father's will (Isa. 50:7; Luke 9:51), so Paul determined to finish his course with joy, no matter what the cost might be (Acts 20:24).

This chapter describes three "farewell events" as Paul closed his ministry in Macedonia, Achaia, and Asia.

A Farewell Journey (20:1–5)
"I do not expect to visit this country again!" D. L. Moody spoke those words in 1867 when he made his first trip to England. He was so seasick during the voyage that he decided he would never sail again, but he made five more visits to England, seasickness notwithstanding.

Paul was ready for another journey. He wanted to make at least one more visit to the churches the Lord had helped him to found, because Paul was a man with a concerned heart. "The care of all the churches" was his greatest joy as well as his heaviest burden (2 Cor. 11:23–28).

After the riot, Paul left Ephesus and headed toward Macedonia and Achaia (see Acts 19:21). He expected to meet Titus at Troas and get a report on the problems in Corinth, but Titus did not come (2 Cor. 2:12–13). The men finally met in Macedonia and Paul rejoiced over the good news Titus brought (2 Cor. 7:5–7). Paul had originally planned to make two visits to Corinth (2 Cor. 1:15–16), but instead he made one visit that lasted three months (Acts 20:3; 1 Cor. 16:5–6). During that visit, he wrote his epistle to the Romans.

Paul had two goals in mind as he visited the various churches. His main purpose was to encourage and strengthen the saints so that they might stand true to the Lord and be effective witnesses. His second purpose was to finish taking up the collection for the needy believers in Jerusalem (Rom. 15:25–27; 1 Cor. 16:1–9; 2 Cor. 8—9). The men who accompanied him (Acts 20:4) were representatives of the churches, appointed to travel with Paul and help handle the funds (2 Cor. 8:18–24).

Once again, Paul had to change his plans, this time because of a Jewish plot to kill him at sea. Instead of sailing from Corinth, he traveled overland through Achaia and Macedonia, sailing from Philippi to Troas, where his "team" agreed to rendezvous. As a person who dislikes travel and changes in plans, I admire Paul for his courage, stamina, and adaptability. In spite of the complications and delays in travel today, we have a much easier time than Paul did—and we complain! He kept going!

A Farewell Service (20:6–12)

Paul was not able to make it to Jerusalem for the annual Passover celebration, so now his goal was to arrive there at least by Pentecost (Acts 20:16). Note the pronoun change to "us" and "we," for Dr. Luke has now joined the party (see Acts 16:17). He had probably been ministering at Philippi where he joined Paul for the last leg of the journey. Paul must have rejoiced to have Luke, Titus, and Timothy at his side again. The men remained at Troas a week so that they might fellowship with the believers there. Perhaps they were also waiting for the departure of the next ship.

Luke gives us a brief report of a local church service in Troas, and from it we learn something of how they met and worshipped the Lord. Consider the elements involved.

The Lord's Day. To begin with, they met on the first day of the week and not on the seventh day, which was the Sabbath (see also 1 Cor. 16:1–2). The first day came to be called "the Lord's Day" because on it the Lord Jesus Christ arose from the dead (Rev. 1:10). We should also remember that the church was born on the first day of the week when the Spirit came at Pentecost. During the early years of the church, the believers did maintain some of the Jewish traditions, such as the hours of prayer (Acts 3:1). But as time went on, they moved away from the Mosaic calendar and developed their own pattern of worship as the Spirit taught them.

The Lord's people. The church met in the evening because Sunday was not a holiday during which people were free from daily employment. Some of the believers would no doubt be slaves, unable to come to the assembly until their work was done. The believers met in an upper room because they had no church buildings in which to gather. This room may have been in the private home of one of the believers. The assembly would have been a cosmopolitan group, but their social and national distinctions made no difference: they were "all one in Christ Jesus" (Gal. 3:28).

The Lord's Supper. The early church shared a "potluck" meal called the "love feast" *(agape),* after which they would observe the Lord's Supper (Acts 2:42; 1 Cor. 11:17–34). The "breaking of bread" in Acts 20:7 refers to the Lord's Supper, whereas in Acts 20:11 it describes a regular meal. By sharing and eating with one another, the church enjoyed fellowship and also gave witness of their oneness in Christ. Slaves would actually eat at the same table with their masters, something unheard of in that day.

It is likely that the church observed the Lord's Supper each Lord's Day when they met for fellowship and worship. In fact, some believers probably ended many of their regular meals at home by taking the bread and wine and remembering the Lord's death. While Scripture does not give us specific instructions

in the matter ("as often," 1 Cor. 11:26), the example of the early church would encourage us to meet at the Lord's table often. However, the Communion must not become routine, causing us to fail to receive the blessings involved.

The Lord's message. The Word of God was always declared in the Christian assemblies, and this included the public reading of the Old Testament Scriptures (1 Tim. 4:13) as well as whatever apostolic letters had been received (Col. 4:16). It is sad to see how the Word is neglected in church services today. Knowing that this would probably be his last meeting with the saints at Troas, Paul preached a long sermon, after which he ate and conversed with the people until morning. It's doubtful that anybody complained. How we today wish we could have been there to hear the apostle Paul preach!

The Word of God is important to the people of God, and the preaching and teaching of the Word must be emphasized. The church meets for edification as well as for celebration, and that edification comes through the Word. "Preach the word!" is still God's admonition to spiritual leaders (2 Tim. 4:2). According to Dr. D. Martyn Lloyd-Jones, "the decadent periods and eras in the history of the church have always been those periods when preaching has declined" *(Preachers and Preaching,* Zondervan, 24).

The Lord's power. Whether it was the lateness of the hour or the stuffiness of the room (surely not the dullness of Paul's sermon!), Eutychus ("Fortunate") fell asleep and then fell out the window, and was killed by the fall. However, Paul raised him from the dead and left him and the church comforted. God's power was present to work for His people.

How old was Eutychus? The Greek word *manias* in Acts 20:9 means a man from twenty-four to forty years of age. The word *pais* in Acts 20:12 means a young child or youth. Dr. Howard Marshall, an eminent Greek scholar, says he was a "young lad of eight to fourteen years. Since the word *pais* can mean "a servant," Eutychus may have been a young man who was also a servant. He may have worked hard that day and was weary. No wonder he fell asleep during the lengthy sermon!

Let's not be too hard on Eutychus. At least he was there for the service, and he did try to keep awake. He sat near ventilation, and he must have tried to fight off the sleep that finally conquered him. The tense of the Greek verb indicates that he was gradually overcome, not suddenly.

Also, let's not be too hard on Paul. After all, he was preaching his farewell sermon to this assembly, and he had a great deal to tell them for their own good. Those sitting near should have been watching Eutychus, but, of course, they were engrossed in what Paul was saying. Paul did interrupt his sermon to rush downstairs to bring the young man back to life. His approach reminds us of Elijah (1 Kings 17:21–22) and Elisha (2 Kings 4:34–35).

Perhaps each of us should ask ourselves, "What really keeps me awake?" Christians who slumber during one hour in church somehow manage to stay awake during early-morning fishing trips, lengthy sporting events and concerts, or late-night TV specials. Also, we need to prepare ourselves physically for public worship to make sure we are at our best. "Remember," said Spurgeon, "if we go to sleep during the sermon and die, there are no apostles to restore us!"

A Farewell Message (20:13–38)

Paul chose to walk from Troas to Assos, a distance of about twenty miles. Why? For one thing, it enabled him to stay longer with the saints in Troas, while he sent Luke and the party on ahead (Acts 20:13). It would take the ship at least a day to sail from Troas to Assos, and Paul could probably walk it in ten hours or less. Also, Paul probably wanted time alone to commune with the Lord about his trip to Jerusalem. The apostle must have sensed already that difficult days lay ahead of him. He may also have been pondering the message he would give to the Ephesian elders. Finally, the exercise was certainly beneficial! Even inspired apostles need to care for their bodies. I personally would prefer walking to sailing!

There were fifty days between Passover (Acts 20:6) and Pentecost (Acts 20:16), and Paul's trip from Philippi to Troas had already consumed twelve of them (Acts 20:6). It took another four days to get to Miletus, so Paul decided not to go to Ephesus lest he lose any more valuable time. Instead, he invited the leaders of the Ephesian church to travel about thirty miles and meet him at Miletus, where the ship was waiting to unload cargo and take on more. Paul was not one to waste time or to lose opportunities.

In the book of Acts, Luke reports eight messages given by the apostle Paul to various people: a Jewish synagogue congregation (Acts 13:14–43), Gentiles (Acts 14:14–18; 17:22–34), church leaders (Acts 20:17–38), a Jewish mob (Acts 22:1–21), the Jewish council (Acts 23:1–10), and various government officials (Acts 24:10–21; 26:1–32). His address to the Ephesian elders is unique in that it reveals Paul the pastor rather than Paul the evangelist or Paul the defender of the faith. The message enables us to get a glimpse of how Paul ministered in Ephesus for three years.

The word *elder* is *presbutos* in the Greek ("presbyter") and refers to a mature person who has been selected to serve in office (Acts 14:23). These same people are called "overseers" in Acts 20:28, which is *episkopos* or "bishop." They were chosen to "feed the church" (Acts 20:28), which means "to shepherd." Paul called the local church "a flock" (Acts 20:28–29), so these men were also pastors. (The word *pastor* means "shepherd.") Thus in the New Testament churches, the three titles *elder, bishop,* and *pastor* were synonymous. The qualifications for this office are given in 1 Timothy 3:1–7 and Titus 1:5–9.

There were three parts to Paul's farewell message.

First he reviewed the past (Acts 20:18–21); then he discussed the present (Acts 20:22–27); and finally, he spoke about the future (Acts 20:28–35). In the first part, he emphasized his faithfulness to the Lord and to the church as he ministered for three years in Ephesus. The second section reveals Paul's personal feelings in view of both the past and the future. In the third part, he warned them of the dangers that the churches faced.

A review of the past (vv. 18–21). Paul was not one to work into his ministry gradually like a diplomat feeling his way. "From the first day" he gave himself unsparingly to the work of the Lord in Ephesus, for Paul was an ambassador and not a diplomat.

The *motive* for Paul's ministry is found in the phrase "serving the Lord" (Acts 20:19). He was not interested in making money (Acts 20:33) or in enjoying an easy life (Acts 20:34–35), for he was the bondslave of Jesus Christ (Acts 20:24; Rom. 1:1). Paul was careful to let people know that his motives for ministry were spiritual and not selfish (1 Thess. 2:1–13).

The *manner* of his ministry was exemplary (Acts 20:18–19). He lived a consistent life that anybody could inspect, for he had nothing to hide. He served in humility and not as a "religious celebrity" demanding that others serve him. But his humility was not a sign of weakness, for he had the courage to face trials and dangers without quitting. Paul was not ashamed to admit to his friends that there had also been times of tears (see also Acts 20:31, 37; Rom. 9:1–2; 2 Cor. 2:4; Phil. 3:18).

The *message* of his ministry (Acts 20:20–21) was also widely known, because he announced it and taught it publicly (Acts 19:9) as well as in the various house churches of the fellowship. He told sinners to repent of their sins and believe in Jesus Christ. This message was "the gospel of the grace of God" (Acts 20:24), and it is the *only* message that can save the sinner (1 Cor. 15:1–8; Gal. 1:6–12).

Furthermore, Paul reminded them that, in his ministry, he had not held back anything that was profitable to them. He declared to them "all the counsel of God" (Acts 20:27). His was a balanced message that included the doctrines and duties, as well as the privileges and responsibilities, that belonged to the Christian life. In his preaching, he neither compromised nor went to extremes, but kept things in balance. Paul also kept his outlook and congregation balanced, witnessing both to Jews and to Gentiles.

A testimony of the present (vv. 22–27). The phrase "And now, behold" shifts the emphasis from the past to the present as Paul opens his heart and tells his friends just how he feels. He did not hide from them the fact that he was bound in his spirit (Acts 19:21) to go to Jerusalem, even though he knew that danger and possible death awaited him there. The Holy Spirit had witnessed this message to him in city after city. A lesser man would have found some way to escape, but not Paul. He was too gripped by his calling and his devotion to Jesus Christ to look for some safe and easy way out. In his testimony, Paul used six graphic pictures of his ministry to explain why he would not quit but would go to Jerusalem to die for Jesus Christ if necessary. Paul could say, "None of these things move me!" because he knew what he was as a minister of Jesus Christ.

Paul saw himself as *an accountant* (Acts 20:24) who had examined his assets and liabilities and decided to put Jesus Christ ahead of everything else. He had faced this kind of reckoning early in his ministry and had willingly made the spiritual the number one priority in his life (Phil. 3:1–11).

He also saw himself as a *runner* who wanted to finish his course in joyful victory (Phil. 3:12–14; 2 Tim. 4:8). The three phrases "my life, my course, the ministry" are the key. Paul realized that his life was God's gift to him, and that God had a special plan for his life that would be fulfilled in his ministry. Paul was devoted to a great Person ("serving the Lord") and motivated by a great purpose, the building of the church.

Paul's third picture is that of the *steward,* for his ministry was something that he had "received of the Lord." The steward owns little or nothing, but he possesses all things. His sole purpose is to serve his master and please him. "Moreover it is required in stewards that one be found faithful" (1 Cor. 4:2 NKJV). The steward must one day give an account of his ministry, and Paul was ready for that day.

The next picture is that of the *witness,* "testifying of the gospel of the grace of God" (Acts 20:24; and note v. 21). The word means "to solemnly give witness," and it reminds us of the seriousness of the message and of the ministry. As we share the gospel with others, it is a matter of life or death (2 Cor. 2:15–16). Paul was a faithful witness both in the life that he lived (Acts 20:18) and the message that he preached.

Picture number five is the *herald* (Acts 20:25). The word *preaching* means "to declare a message as the herald of the king." The witness tells what has happened to him, but the herald tells what the king tells him to declare. He is a man commissioned and sent with a message, and he must not change that message in any way. And since he is sent by the king, the people who listen had better be careful how they treat both the messenger and the message.

The final picture, and perhaps the most dramatic, is that of the *watchman* (Acts 20:26). As in Acts 18:6, this is a reference to the "watchman on the walls" in Ezekiel 3:17–21; 33:1–9. What a serious calling it was to be a watchman! He had to stay awake and alert, ready to sound the alarm if he saw danger approaching. He had to be faithful, not fearful, because the safety of many people rested with him. Paul had been a faithful watchman (Acts 20:31), for he had declared to sinners and saints all the counsel of God. Unfortunately, we have today many unfaithful watchmen who think only of themselves (Isa. 56:10–13).

A group of servicemen asked their new chaplain if he believed in a real hell for lost sinners, and he smiled and told them that he did not. "Then you are wasting your time," the men replied. "If there is no hell, we don't need you; and if there is a hell, you are leading us astray. Either way, we're better off without you!"

A warning about the future (vv. 28–38). Paul brought his farewell message to a close by warning the leaders of the dangers they had to recognize and deal with if they were to protect and lead the church. Never underestimate the great importance of the church. The church is important to God the Father because His name is on it—"the church of God." It is important to the Son because He shed His blood for it, and it is important to the Holy Spirit because He is calling and equipping people to minister to the church. It is a serious thing to be a spiritual leader in the church of the living God.

To begin with, there are dangers *around us,* "wolves" that want to ravage the flock (Acts 20:29). Paul was referring to false teachers, the counterfeits who exploit the church for personal gain (Matt. 7:15–23; 10:16; Luke 10:3; 2 Peter 2:1–3). How important it is that believers know the Word of God and be able to detect and defeat these religious racketeers.

But there are also dangers *among us* (Acts 20:30), because of people within the church who are ambitious for position and power. Church history, ancient and modern, is filled with accounts of people like Diotrephes who love to have preeminence (3 John 9–11). It is shocking to realize that more than one false prophet got his or her start within the Christian church family! Read 1 John 2:18–19 and take heed.

There are also dangers *within us* (Acts 20:31–35), and this seems to be where Paul put the greatest emphasis. "Take heed, therefore, unto yourselves" (Acts 20:28). He names five sins that are especially destructive to the life and ministry of spiritual leaders in the church.

The first is *carelessness* (Acts 20:31), failing to stay alert and forgetting the price that others have paid so that we might have God's truth. "Watch and remember!" are words we had better heed. It is so easy for us today to forget the toil and tears of those who labored before us (Heb. 13:7). Paul's warning and weeping should be constant reminders to us to take our spiritual responsibilities seriously.

The second sin is *shallowness* (Acts 20:32). We cannot build the church unless God is building our lives daily. There is a balance here between prayer ("I commend you to God") and the Word of God ("the word of his grace"), because these two must always work together (1 Sam. 12:23; John 15:7; Acts 6:4). The Word of God alone is able to edify and enrich us, and the spiritual leader must spend time daily in the Word of God and prayer. *Covetousness* is the third sin we must avoid (Acts 20:33). It means a consuming and controlling desire for what others have and for more of what we ourselves already have. "Thou shalt not covet" is the last of the Ten Commandments, but if we do covet, we will end up breaking all the other nine! Those who covet will steal, lie, and murder to get what they want, and even dishonor their own parents. Covetousness is idolatry (Eph. 5:5; Col. 3:5). In the qualifications for an elder, it is expressly stated that he must not be guilty of the sin of covetousness (1 Tim. 3:3).

Paul also mentioned *laziness* (Acts 20:34). Paul earned his own way as a tentmaker, even though he could have used his apostolic authority to demand support and thereby have an easier life. It is not wrong for Christian workers to receive salaries, for "the laborer is worthy of his hire" (Luke 10:7; 1 Tim. 5:18). But they should be certain that they are really *earning* those salaries! (Read Prov. 24:30–34.)

Finally, Paul warned about *selfishness* (Acts 20:35). True ministry means giving, not getting; it means following the example of the Lord Jesus Christ. Dr. Earl V. Pierce used to call this "the supreme beatitude" because, unlike the other beatitudes, it tells us how to be *more* blessed! These words of Jesus are not found anywhere in the Gospels, but they were a part of the oral tradition, and Paul memorized them.

This beatitude does not suggest that people who receive are "less blessed" than people who give. (The beggar in Acts 3 would argue about that!) It could be paraphrased, "It's better to share with others than to keep what you have and collect more." In other words, the blessing does not come in accumulating wealth, but in sharing it. After all, Jesus became poor that we might become rich (2 Cor. 8:9). One of the best commentaries on this statement is Luke 12:16–31.

Paul closed this memorable occasion by kneeling down and praying for his friends, and then they all wept together. It is a difficult thing to say good-bye, especially when you know you will not see your friends again in this life. But we have the blessed assurance that we will one day see our Christian friends and loved ones in heaven, when Jesus Christ returns (1 Thess. 4:13–18).

Meanwhile, there is a job to be done—so, let's do it!

CHAPTER TWENTY
Acts 21:1—22:29
THE MISUNDERSTOOD MISSIONARY

Is it so bad, then, to be misunderstood?" asked Ralph Waldo Emerson. "Pythagoras was misunderstood, and Socrates, and Jesus, and Luther, and Copernicus, and Galileo, and Newton … To be great is to be misunderstood."

Emerson might have added that the apostle Paul was misunderstood, by friends and foes alike. Three of these misunderstandings—and their consequences—are recorded in these chapters.

Paul's Friends Misunderstood His Plans (21:1–17)

Paul had to tear himself away from the Ephesian elders, so great was his love for them. He and his party

sailed from Miletus to Cos, then to Rhodes, and then to Patera, a total of three days' journey. But Paul was uncomfortable with a "local coastal" ship that stopped at every port, so when he found a boat going directly to Phoenicia, he and his friends boarded it. It would be a voyage of about four hundred miles.

Tyre (vv. 3–6). This would have been Paul's first contact with the believers in Tyre, though it is likely that his persecution of the Jerusalem believers helped to get this church started (Acts 11:19). The men had to seek out the believers, so it must not have been a large assembly, and apparently there was no synagogue in the town. They stayed a week with the saints while their ship unloaded its cargo and took on new cargo.

Paul had devoted a good part of his third missionary journey to taking up a love gift for the Jews in Judea. It was a practical way for the Gentiles to show their oneness with their Jewish brothers and sisters, and to repay them for sharing the gospel with the Gentiles (Rom. 15:25–27). There was in the church a constant threat of division, for the Jewish extremists (the Judaizers) wanted the Gentiles to live like Jews and follow the law of Moses (Acts 15:1ff.). Wherever Paul ministered, these extremists tried to hinder his work and steal his converts. Paul hoped that his visit to Jerusalem with the offering would help to strengthen the fellowship between Jews and Gentiles.

Now, Paul began to get messages from his friends that his visit to Jerusalem would be difficult and dangerous. Of course, he had already suspected this, knowing how the false teachers operated (Rom. 15:30–31), but these messages were very personal and powerful. In Tyre, the believers "kept on saying to him" (literal Greek) that he should not set foot in Jerusalem.

After a week in Tyre, Paul and his party departed. It is touching to see how the believers had come to love Paul, though they had known him only a week. The first stop was Ptolemais, where they visited the believers for a day, and then they sailed to Caesarea, their final destination.

Caesarea (vv. 7–14). The men stayed with Philip, one of the original deacons (Acts 6:1–6) who also served as an evangelist (Acts 8:5ff.). It was now some twenty years since he had come to Caesarea and made it his headquarters (Acts 8:40). Since Philip had been an associate of Stephen, and Paul had taken part in Stephen's death, this must have been an interesting meeting.

While Paul rested in Caesarea, the prophet Agabus came to give him a second warning message from the Lord. Some fifteen years before, Paul and Agabus had worked together in a famine relief program for Judea (Acts 11:27–30), so they were not strangers. Agabus delivered his message in a dramatic way as he bound his own hands and feet with Paul's girdle and told the apostle that he would be bound in Jerusalem.

As did the saints in Tyre, so the believers in Caesarea begged Paul not to go to Jerusalem. Surely the men chosen by the churches could deliver the love offering to James and the Jerusalem elders, and it would not be necessary for Paul to go personally. But Paul silenced them and told them that he was prepared ("ready") not only to be bound, but also to die if necessary for the name of the Lord Jesus Christ.

Now we must pause to consider whether Paul was right or wrong in making that trip to Jerusalem. If it seems improper, or even blasphemous, so to examine the actions of an apostle, keep in mind that he was a human being like anyone else. His epistles were inspired, but this does not necessarily mean that everything he did was perfect. Whether he was right or wrong, we can certainly learn from his experience.

On the *con* side, these repeated messages do sound like warnings to Paul to stay out of Jerusalem. For that matter, over twenty years before, the Lord had commanded Paul to get out of Jerusalem because the Jews would not receive his testimony (Acts 22:18). Paul had already written to the Romans about the dangers in Judea (Acts 15:30–31), and he had shared these same feelings with the Ephesian elders (Acts 20:22–23), so he was fully aware of the problems involved.

On the *pro* side, the prophetic utterances can be taken as warnings ("Get ready!") rather than as prohibitions ("You must not go!"). The statement in Acts 21:4 does not use the Greek negative *ou*, which means absolute prohibition, but *me*, used "where one *thinks* a thing is not" *(Manual Greek Lexicon of the New Testament,* by G. Abbott-Smith, 289). Agabus did not forbid Paul to go to Jerusalem; he only told him what to expect if he did go. As for the Lord's command in Acts 22:18, it applied to that particular time and need not be interpreted as a prohibition governing the rest of Paul's life. While it is true that Paul avoided Jerusalem, it is also true that he returned there on other occasions: with famine relief (Acts 11:27–30); to attend the Jerusalem Conference (Acts 15:1ff.); and after his second missionary journey (Acts 18:22—"going up to greet the church" refers to Jerusalem).

In view of Paul's statement in Acts 23:1, and the Lord's encouraging words in Acts 23:11, it is difficult to believe that the apostle deliberately disobeyed the revealed will of God. God's prophecy to Ananias (Acts 9:15) certainly came true in the months that followed as Paul had opportunity to witness for Christ.

Instead of accusing Paul of compromise, we ought to applaud him for his courage. Why? Because in going to Jerusalem, he took his life in his hands in order to try to solve the most pressing problem in the church: the growing division between the "far right" legalistic Jews and the believing Gentiles. Ever since the Jerusalem Conference (Acts 15), trouble had been brewing, and the legalists had been following Paul and seeking to capture his converts. It was a serious situation, and Paul knew that he was a part of the answer as well as a part of the problem. But he could not solve the problem by remote control through representatives; he had to go to Jerusalem personally.

Jerusalem (vv. 15–17). A company of believers left Caesarea and traveled with Paul to Jerusalem, probably to celebrate the feast. It was a journey of sixty-five miles that took at least three days by foot—two days if they had animals. What fellowship they must have enjoyed as they recounted what God had done in and through them! What a great encouragement it was for Paul to have these friends at his side as he faced the challenge of Jerusalem.

The city would be crowded with pilgrims, but Paul and his party planned to live with Mnason, "an early disciple," who lived in Jerusalem and had been visiting Caesarea. Was he perhaps converted under Peter's preaching at Pentecost? Or did his fellow Cypriot Barnabas win him to Christ (Acts 4:36)? We are not told, but we do know that Mnason was a man given to hospitality, and his ministry helped Paul at a strategic time in the apostle's ministry.

We could wish that Dr. Luke had told us more about that first meeting with the church leaders in Jerusalem. James and the other leaders did receive them gladly, but how did they respond to the gift from the Gentiles? Nothing is said about it. Were some of them perhaps a bit suspicious? A few years later, the Roman writer Martial would say, "Gifts are like hooks!" and perhaps some of the Jerusalem elders felt that way about this gift. Certainly the legalistic wing of the church would question anything that Paul said or did.

The Jerusalem Church Misunderstood His Message (21:18–26)

Apparently that first meeting was devoted primarily to fellowship and personal matters, because the second meeting was given over to Paul's personal report of his ministry to the Gentiles. The Jerusalem leaders had agreed years before that Paul should minister to the Gentiles (Gal. 2:7–10), and the elders rejoiced at what they heard. The phrase "declared particularly" means "reported in detail, item by item." Paul gave a full and accurate account, not of what he had done, but of what the Lord had done through his ministry (see 1 Cor. 15:10).

You get the impression that the legalists had been working behind the scenes. No sooner had Paul finished his report than the elders brought up the rumors that were then being circulated about Paul among the Jewish Christians. It has well been said that, though a rumor doesn't have a leg to stand on, it travels mighty fast!

What were his enemies saying about Paul? Almost the same things they said about Jesus and Stephen: he was teaching the Jews to forsake the laws and customs given by Moses and the fathers. They were not worried about what Paul taught the Gentile believers, because the relationship of the Gentiles to the law had been settled at the Jerusalem Conference (Acts 15). In fact, the elders carefully rehearsed the matter (Acts 21:25), probably for the sake of Paul's Gentile companions. The leaders were especially concerned that Paul's presence in the city not cause division or disruption among the "thousands of Jews ... zealous of the law" (Acts 21:20).

But, why were so many believing Jews still clinging to the law of Moses? Had they not read Romans and Galatians? Probably not, and even if they had, old customs are difficult to change. In fact, one day God would have to send a special letter to the Jews, the epistle to the Hebrews, to explain the relationship between the old and new covenants. As Dr. Donald Grey Barnhouse used to say, "The book of Hebrews was written to the Hebrews to tell them to stop being Hebrews!" It was not until the city and the temple were destroyed in AD 70 that traditional Jewish worship ceased.

Paul did warn the Gentiles not to get involved in the old Jewish religion (Gal. 4:1–11), but he nowhere told the Jews that it was wrong for them to practice their customs, *so long as they did not trust in ceremony or make their customs a test of fellowship* (Rom. 14:1—15:7). There was freedom to observe special days and diets, and believers were not to judge or condemn one another. The same grace that gave the Gentiles freedom to abstain also gave the Jews freedom to observe. All God asked was that they receive one another and not create problems or divisions.

It seems incredible that Paul's enemies would accuse him of these things, for all the evidence was against them. Paul had Timothy circumcised before taking him along on that second missionary journey (Acts 16:1–3). Paul had taken a Jewish vow while in Corinth (Acts 18:18), and it was his custom not to offend the Jews in any way by deliberately violating their customs or the law of Moses (1 Cor. 9:19–23). However, rumors are not usually based on fact, but thrive on half-truths, prejudices, and outright lies.

The leaders suggested that Paul demonstrate publicly his reverence for the Jewish law. All they asked was that he identify himself with four men under a Nazarite vow (Num. 6), pay for their sacrifices, and be with them in the temple for their time of purification. He agreed to do it. If it had been a matter involving somebody's personal salvation, you can be sure that Paul would never have cooperated, for that would have compromised his message of salvation by grace, through faith. But this was a matter of personal conviction on the part of Jewish believers, who were given the freedom to accept or reject the customs.

Paul reported to the priest the next day and shared in the purification ceremony, but he himself did not take any vows. He and the men had to wait seven days and then offer the prescribed sacrifices. The whole plan appeared to be safe and wise, but it did not work. Instead of bringing peace, it caused an uproar, and Paul ended up a prisoner.

The Jews Misunderstood Paul's Ministry (21:27—22:29)

In the temple, separating the court of the Gentiles from the other courts, stood a wall beyond which no Gentile was allowed to go (note Eph. 2:14). On the wall was this solemn inscription: "No foreigner may enter within the barricade which surrounds the sanctuary and enclosure. Anyone who is caught so doing will have himself to blame for his ensuing death." The Romans had granted the Jewish religious leaders authority to deal with anybody who broke this law, and this included the right of execution. This law plays an important role in what happened to Paul a week after he and the four Nazarites began their purification ceremonies.

Some Jews from Asia saw Paul in the temple and jumped to the conclusion that he had polluted their sacred building by bringing Gentiles past the barricade. It is likely that these Jews came from Ephesus, because they recognized Paul's friend Trophimus, who came from Ephesus. With their emotions running at full speed, and their brains in neutral, these men argued: (1) wherever Paul went, his Gentile friends went; (2) Paul was seen in the temple; therefore, his friends had been in the temple too! Such is the logic of prejudice.

They seized Paul and would have killed him had the Roman guards not intervened in the nick of time. (At least one thousand soldiers were stationed in the Antonia Fortress at the northwest corner of the temple area.) The temple crowd was in an uproar, completely ignorant of what was going on. The scene reminds you of the riot in Ephesus. (Compare Acts 21:30 with Acts 19:29, and Acts 21:34 with Acts 19:32.) It required the chief captain (Claudius Lysias, Acts 23:26), two centurions, and perhaps two hundred soldiers to get the mob under control and to rescue Paul. The captain actually thought Paul was an Egyptian rebel who was wanted by the Romans for inciting a revolt (Acts 21:38). This explains why he had Paul bound with two chains (see Acts 21:11).

When Claudius interrogated the people, they could not explain what caused the riot because they did not really know. The original troublemakers must have escaped during the great excitement, knowing that they could not actually substantiate their charges. Since Claudius could get no help from the people in the temple, he decided to interrogate Paul, so his soldiers carried Paul from the court of the Gentiles up the stairs into the barracks. As Paul was borne away, the crowd shouted angrily, "Away with him!" This again reminds us of our Lord's arrest and trial (Luke 23:18, 21; John 19:15).

At this point, Paul decided it was time to speak up, and the captain was amazed that his dangerous prisoner could speak Greek. When Paul asked for permission to address the Jews, Claudius consented, hoping that perhaps he would get enough information for an official report. He never did (see Acts 23:23–30). Paul spoke to the Jews in their native Aramaic, and this helped quiet them down. He was never able to finish his speech, but he did get to explain three important aspects of his life and ministry.

His early conduct (22:3–5). Paul had been a

leading rabbi in his day (Gal. 1:13–14), so he was certainly known to some of the people in the crowd. Note how Paul piled up his Jewish credentials: he was a Jew, a native of Tarsus, brought up in Jerusalem, trained by Gamaliel, a follower of the law, a zealous persecutor of the church, and a representative of the Sanhedrin. How could his countrymen not respectfully listen to a man with that kind of record!

Instead of accusing them of participating in a riot, he commended them for being "zealous toward God." (He had used a similar approach with the Athenians; Acts 17:22.) He admitted that he too had been guilty of having people arrested and bound, and even killed. The Christian faith was known as "the way" (Acts 9:2; 19:9, 23; 24:14, 22), probably a reference to our Lord's statement, "I am the way" (John 14:6).

His wonderful conversion (22:6–16). Luke recorded Paul's conversion experience in Acts 9, and Paul would repeat the account later for Felix and Agrippa (Acts 26:1–32). It is difficult to imagine a comparable crowd today quietly listening to that kind of a testimony. However, people in that day expected miraculous things to happen and were no doubt fascinated by Paul's story (see Acts 23:9). Also, Paul was on official Sanhedrin business when these events took place, which at least gave it some aura of authority.

In his testimony, Paul affirmed that Jesus of Nazareth was alive. Paul saw His glory and heard His voice. The people listening in the temple courts knew the official Jewish position that Jesus of Nazareth was an impostor who had been crucified and His body stolen from the tomb by His disciples, who then started the rumor that Jesus had been raised from the dead. Of course, Paul himself had believed this story when he was persecuting the church.

The men with Paul saw the bright light, but were not blinded as he was, and they heard a sound, but could not understand what was being said (Acts 9:7). Imagine Paul's amazement to discover that Jesus was alive! Instantly, he had to change his whole way of thinking (repentance) and let the risen Lord have control.

Note Paul's wisdom as he identified himself with Ananias, a devout Jew who kept the law and who called him "brother." Note also that Ananias attributed Paul's great experience to "the God of our fathers." In quoting Ananias, Paul gave reason for his listeners to accept his salvation experience and his call to service. Paul had seen "the Just [Righteous] One," which was a title for Messiah (see Acts 3:14; 7:52). Paul was now commissioned by God to take His message to "all men." This would include the Gentiles, but Paul did not say so until later.

Acts 22:16 in the King James Version seems to suggest that baptism is required for the washing away of our sins, but such is not the case. In his *Expanded Translation of the New Testament*, Greek scholar Kenneth Wuest puts it, "Having arisen, be baptized and wash away your sins, having previously called upon His Name." We are saved by calling on the Lord by faith (Acts 2:21; 9:14), and we give evidence of that faith by being baptized. According to Acts 9:17, Paul was filled with the Spirit *before* he was baptized, and this would indicate that he was already born again. It is the "calling," not the baptizing, that effects the cleansing.

Certainly many of Paul's listeners knew about the new "Christian sect" that had sprung up, the baptisms that had taken place, the stoning of Stephen, and the miracles that these "people of the way" had wrought. Paul was not speaking to ignorant people, because these things had not been "done in a corner" (Acts 26:26).

His special calling (22:17–29). After his conversion, Paul had ministered in Damascus and then had gone to Arabia, perhaps to evangelize and to meditate on God's Word (Acts 9:19–25; Gal. 1:16–17). When Paul did return to Jerusalem, the church leaders did not accept him until Barnabas interceded and got him in (Acts 9:26–29). Note how Paul again emphasized the Jewish elements in his experience, for the Jews would be impressed with a man who prayed in the temple and had a vision from God.

The Lord told Paul to leave Jerusalem quickly, because the people would not receive his witness. By obeying this command, Paul saved his life, because the Hellenistic Jews had plotted to kill him (Acts 9:29–30). But first, Paul debated with the Lord! He wanted to show the Jews that he was a new person and tell them that Jesus was the Messiah, and He was alive. If Paul won some of them to the Lord, it would perhaps help to compensate for all the damage he had done, especially in the killing of Stephen.

The Lord's command was, "Depart, for I will send you far from here to the Gentiles" (Acts 22:21 NKJV). Paul was about to explain why he was involved with the Gentiles, but the Jews in the temple courts would not permit him to go on. No devout Jew would have anything to do with the Gentiles! Had Paul not uttered that one word, he might have later been released, *and perhaps he knew this.* However, he had to be faithful in his witness, no matter what it cost him. Paul would rather be a prisoner than give up his burden for lost souls and for missions! We could use more Christians like that today.

When Claudius saw that the riot was starting again, he took Paul into the barracks for "examination by torture." The apostle had already mentioned that he was born in Tarsus, but he had not told them that his citizenship was Roman. It was unlawful for a Roman citizen to be scourged. We do not know how people proved their citizenship in those days; perhaps they carried the first-century equivalent of an ID card.

Claudius must have been shocked that this little Jewish troublemaker who spoke Aramaic and Greek was actually a Roman citizen. "With great sum I obtained this freedom," Claudius boasted, indicating that he had gotten his citizenship by bribing the Roman officials, for it could not be actually purchased. But Paul was ahead of the Roman captain, for he had been born into freedom and Roman citizenship, thanks to his father. How Paul's father obtained his freedom, we do not know. We do know that Paul knew how to make use of his Roman citizenship for the cause of Christ.

The soldiers had made two mistakes, and they were quick to undo them: they had bound Paul and had planned to scourge him. No doubt Claudius and his men were especially kind to Paul now that they knew he was a Roman citizen. God was using the great power of the empire to protect His servant and eventually get him to Rome.

Paul's entire time in Jerusalem was one filled with serious misunderstandings, but he pressed on. Perhaps at this point some of his friends were saying, "We told him so! We warned him!" For Paul and his associates, it may have looked like the end of the road, but God had other plans for them. Paul would witness again and again, and to people he could never have met had he not been a Roman prisoner. God's missionary did get to Rome—and the Romans paid the bill!

That's what happens when God's people are willing to be daring!

CHAPTER TWENTY-ONE
Acts 22:30 – 23:35
PAUL THE PRISONER

I was once called to be a character witness in a child custody case involving a man who had served time in prison. This was a new experience for me, and I was completely unprepared for the first question the attorney asked me: "Reverend, do you think that a man who has been a prisoner is fit to raise a child?"

"That depends on the man," I replied bravely. "Some of the greatest men in history have been prisoners—John the Baptist, John Bunyan, and even the apostle Paul."

"Simply answer yes or no!" said the judge curtly, and that was the end of my sermon.

"Paul the prisoner" (Acts 23:18) was the name the Roman soldiers used for the apostle, a designation he himself often used (Eph. 3:1; 4:1; 2 Tim. 1:8; Philem. 1, 9). Paul was under "military custody," which meant he was bound to a Roman soldier who was responsible for him. Prisoners under "public custody" were put in the common jail, a horrible place for any human being to suffer (Acts 16:19–24).

Paul's friends could visit him and help meet his personal needs. It is sad that we don't read, "And prayer was made fervently by the church for Paul" (see Acts 12:5). There is no record that the Jerusalem church took any steps to assist him, either in Jerusalem or during his two years in Caesarea.

This is an exciting chapter, and in it we read of three confrontations that Paul experienced.

Paul and the Jewish Council (22:30—23:10)

Having discovered that Paul was a Roman citizen, the Roman captain now had two serious problems to solve. First, he needed to let the prisoner know what the official charges were against him, since that was Paul's right as a Roman citizen. Second, he also needed to have some official charges for his own records and to share with his superiors. He was sure that Paul had done something notorious, otherwise why would so many people want to do away with him? Yet nobody seemed to know what Paul's crimes were. What a plight for a Roman official to be in!

The logical thing was to let Paul's own people try him, so the captain arranged for a special meeting of the Jewish council (Sanhedrin). This group was composed of seventy (or seventy-one) of the leading Jewish teachers, with the high priest presiding. It was their responsibility to interpret and apply the sacred Jewish law to the affairs of the nation, and to try those who violated that law. The Romans gave the council permission to impose capital punishment where the offense deserved it.

The captain and his guard (Acts 23:10) brought Paul into the council chamber and stepped aside to watch the proceedings. Knowing how the Jews in the temple had treated Paul, Claudius remained there on guard lest his prisoner be taken from him and killed. No Roman soldier could afford to lose a prisoner, for that might mean the forfeiting of his own life. The loss of a prisoner against whom the charges were nebulous would be especially embarrassing for any Roman officer.

As Paul faced the council and examined it carefully, he decided to start with a personal approach. "Men and brethren" immediately identified him as a Jew and no doubt helped win the attention of his countrymen.

The Greek word translated "lived" means "to live as a citizen." It gives us the English word *politics*. Paul affirmed that he was a loyal Jew who had lived as a good Jewish citizen and had not broken the law. His conscience did not condemn him even though the Jews had condemned him.

"Conscience" is one of Paul's favorite words; he used it twice in Acts (23:1; 24:16) and twenty-one times in his letters. The word means "to know with, to know together." Conscience is the inner "judge" or "witness" that approves when we do right and disapproves when we do wrong (Rom. 2:15). Conscience does not *set* the standard; it only *applies* it. The conscience of a thief would bother him if he told the truth about his fellow crooks just as much as a Christian's conscience would convict him if he told a lie about his friends. Conscience does not make the standards; it only applies the standards of the person, whether they are good or bad, right or wrong.

Conscience may be compared to a window that lets in the light. God's law is the light, and the cleaner the window is, the more the light shines in. As the window gets dirty, the light gets dimmer, and finally the light becomes darkness. A good conscience, or pure conscience (1 Tim. 3:9), is one that lets in God's light so that we are properly convicted if we do wrong and encouraged if we do right. A defiled conscience (1 Cor. 8:7) is one that has been sinned against so much that it is no longer dependable. If a person continues to sin against his conscience, he may end up with an evil conscience (Heb. 10:22) or a seared conscience (1 Tim. 4:2). Then he would feel convicted if he did what was *right* rather than what was wrong!

Paul had persecuted the church and had even caused innocent people to die, so how could he claim to have a good conscience? *He had lived up to the light that he had,* and that is all that a good conscience requires. After he became a Christian and the bright light of God's glory shone into his heart (2 Cor. 4:6), Paul then saw things differently and realized that he was "the chief of sinners" (1 Tim. 1:15).

Ananias the high priest (not to be confused with Annas in Acts 4:6) was so incensed at Paul's saying that he had "lived in all good conscience" that he ordered the nearest Jewish council members to slap Paul across the mouth. (Jesus had been treated in a similar way— John 18:22.) This was, of course, illegal and inhumane, for, after all, Paul had not even been proven guilty of anything. Certainly the high priest would be expected to show honesty and fairness, if not compassion and concern (Lev. 19:15; Heb. 5:2).

Paul responded with what appears to me to be justified anger, though many disagree about this. When called to account for what he had said, Paul did not apologize. Rather, he showed respect for the *office* but not for the *man.* Ananias was indeed one of the most corrupt men ever to be named high priest. He stole tithes from the other priests and did all he could to increase his authority. He was known as a brutal man who cared more for Rome's favor than for Israel's welfare.

In calling the high priest a "whited wall," Paul was simply saying that the man was a hypocrite (Matt. 23:27; see Ezek. 13:10–12). Paul spoke prophetically, because God did indeed smite this wicked man. When the Jews revolted against Rome in the year 66, Ananias had to flee for his life because of his known sympathies with Rome. The Jewish guerrillas found him hiding in an aqueduct at Herod's palace, and they killed him. It was an ignominious death for a despicable man.

Paul's reply in Acts 23:5 has been variously interpreted. Some say that Paul did not know who the high priest was. Or perhaps Paul was speaking in holy sarcasm: "Could such a man actually be the high priest?" Since this was an informal meeting of the council, perhaps the high priest was not wearing his traditional garments and sitting in his usual place. For that matter, Paul had been away from the Jewish religious scene for many years and probably did not know many people in the council.

The quoting of Exodus 22:28 would indicate that Paul may not have known that it was the high priest who ordered him to be smitten. Again, note that Paul showed respect for the office, but not for the man who held the office. There is a difference.

Having failed in his personal approach, Paul then used a doctrinal approach. He declared that the real issue was his faith in the doctrine of the resurrection, a doctrine over which the Pharisees and Sadducees violently disagreed. Paul knew that by defending this important doctrine, he would divide the council and soon have the members disputing among themselves, which is exactly what happened. So violent was the response that Claudius and his men had to rush down to the floor of the council chamber and rescue their prisoner for the second time!

Was Paul "playing politics" when he took this approach? I don't think so. After his unfortunate clash with the high priest, Paul realized that he could never get a fair trial before the Sanhedrin. If the trial had continued, he might well have been condemned and taken out and stoned as a blasphemer. The Asian Jews, if given opportunity to testify, could well have added fuel to the fire with their false witness. No, the wisest thing to do was to end the hearing as soon as possible and trust God to use the Roman legions to protect him from the Jews.

There is a second consideration: Paul was absolutely right when he said that the real issue was the doctrine of the resurrection, not "the resurrection" in general, but the resurrection of Jesus Christ (see Acts 24:21; 26:6–8; 28:20). Had he been given the opportunity, Paul would have declared the gospel of "Jesus Christ and the resurrection" just as he had declared it before Jewish congregations in many parts of the empire. The witness in Acts centers on the resurrection (see Acts 1:22; 2:32; 3:15).

Jesus had stood trial before the Sanhedrin, and so had His apostles, and now Paul had witnessed to them. What great opportunities the council had, and yet they would not believe!

Paul and the Lord Jesus (23:11)

A few years after Paul's conversion, when Paul's life was in danger in Jerusalem, Jesus appeared to him in the temple and told him what to do (Acts 22:17–21). When Paul was discouraged in Corinth and contemplated going elsewhere, Jesus appeared to him and encouraged him to stay (Acts 18:9–10). Now, when Paul was certainly at "low ebb" in his ministry, Jesus appeared once again to encourage and instruct him. Paul would later receive encouragement during the storm (Acts 27:22–25) and during his trial in Rome (2 Tim. 4:16–17). "Lo, I am with you always" is a great assurance for every situation (Matt. 28:20).

The Lord's message to Paul was one of *courage.* "Be of good cheer!" simply means "Take courage!" Jesus often spoke these words during His earthly ministry. He spoke them to the palsied man (Matt. 9:2) and to the woman who suffered with the hemorrhage (Matt. 9:22). He shouted them to the disciples in the storm (Matt. 14:27) and repeated them in the Upper Room

(John 16:33). As God's people, we can always take courage in times of difficulty because the Lord is with us and will see us through.

It was also a message of *commendation.* The Lord did not rebuke Paul for going to Jerusalem. Rather, He commended him for the witness he had given, even though that witness had not been received. When you read the account of Paul's days in Jerusalem, you get the impression that everything Paul did failed miserably. His attempt to win over the legalistic Jews only helped cause a riot in the temple, and his witness before the Sanhedrin left the council in confusion. But the Lord was pleased with Paul's testimony, and that's what really counts.

Finally, it was a message of *confidence:* Paul would go to Rome! This had been Paul's desire for months (Acts 19:21; Rom. 15:22–29), but events in Jerusalem had made it look as though that desire would not be fulfilled. What encouragement this promise gave to Paul in the weeks that followed, difficult weeks when leaders lied about him, when fanatics tried to kill him, and when government officials ignored him. In all of this, the Lord was with him and fulfilling His perfect plan to get His faithful servant to Rome.

Paul and the Jewish Conspirators (23:12–35)

Paul's life had been in danger from the very beginning of his ministry, when he witnessed for Christ in Damascus (Acts 9:22–25). During his first visit to Jerusalem after his conversion, the Hellenistic Jews tried to kill him (Acts 9:29). The Jews drove him out of Antioch in Pisidia (Acts 13:50–51) and threatened to stone him in Iconium (Acts 14:5). Paul was stoned in Lystra (Acts 14:19–20), and in Corinth, the Jews tried to get him arrested (Acts 18:12–17). In Ephesus, the Jews had a plot to kill him (Acts 20:19), and they even planned to kill him at sea (Acts 20:3). Paul's words in 1 Thessalonians 2:14–16 take on special meaning when you consider all that Paul suffered at the hands of his own countrymen.

Perhaps it was the Asian Jews who conspired to kill Paul (Acts 21:27–29). Certain of the chief priests and elders agreed to cooperate with them and try to influence Claudius. It was a natural thing for the council to want further information from Paul, and it would have been an easy thing to ambush Paul's party and kill the apostle. If this got the captain in trouble with his superiors, the high priest could protect him. The Romans and the Jews had cooperated this way before (Matt. 28:11–15).

But the forty fasting men and the scheming religious leaders had forgotten that Paul was an apostle of Jesus Christ, and that the exalted Lord was watching from heaven. At Paul's conversion, the Lord had told him that he would suffer, but He had also promised that He would deliver him from his enemies (Acts 9:15–16; 26:16–17). Paul held on to that promise all of his life, and God was faithful.

We know nothing about Paul's sister and nephew except what is recorded here. Philippians 3:8 suggests that Paul lost his family when he became a Christian, but we do not know if any of his relatives were converted later. (The word *kinsman* in Rom. 16:7 and 11 means "fellow Jew," as in Rom. 9:3.) Since Paul's family had long been connected with the Pharisees (Acts 23:6), his sister was no doubt in touch with the "powers that be" and able to pick up the news that was passed along. Wives do chat with each other, and a secret is something you tell one person at a time!

It is not likely that either the sister or the nephew were believers, for that certainly would have shut them out of the official religious circle in Jerusalem. But they were devout Jews and knew that the plot was evil (Ex. 23:2). It was in the providence of God that they were able to hear the news and convey it privately to Claudius. St. Augustine said, "Trust the past to the mercy of God, the present to His love, and the future to His providence."

We certainly must admire the integrity and courage of Claudius Lysias, the captain. How did he know the boy was even telling the truth? Paul had already caused Claudius so much trouble that it might be a relief to get rid of him! The Jews did not know that Claudius was aware of their plot, so he could have used his "inside knowledge" for his own profit. No Roman soldier could afford to lose a prisoner, but there were always ways to work things out.

Throughout the book of Acts, Dr. Luke speaks favorably of the Roman military officers, beginning with Cornelius in Acts 10 and ending with Julius (Acts 27:1, 3, 43). There is no record in Acts of *official* Roman persecution against the church; the opposition was instigated by the unbelieving Jews. While the empire had its share of corrupt political opportunists, for the most part, the military leaders were men of quality who respected the Roman law.

Claudius's plan was simple and wise. He knew that he had to get Paul out of Jerusalem or there would be one murderous plot after another, and one of them just might succeed. He also knew that he had better determine the charges against Paul or he might be accused of illegally holding a Roman citizen. He could solve both problems by sending Paul to Caesarea and putting him under the authority of Felix, the Roman governor.

If Paul had been a private citizen, attempting to travel from Jerusalem to Caesarea (about sixty-five miles), he would have been an easy target for the conspirators. But God arranged for 470 Roman soldiers to protect him, almost half of the men in the temple garrison! Once again in his career, Paul was smuggled out of a city under cover of night (Acts 9:25; 17:10).

The captain's official letter is most interesting. Of course, Claudius put himself and his men in the best light, which is to be expected. While it is true they prevented Paul from being killed, it was not because they knew he was a Roman. Claudius thought Paul was an Egyptian and almost had him scourged!

Acts 23:29 is another of Luke's "official statements" from Roman officials, proving that Christians were not considered criminals. The officials in Philippi had almost apologized to Paul (Acts 16:35–40), and Gallio in Corinth had refused to try him (Acts 18:14–15). In Ephesus, the town clerk told twenty-five thousand people that the Christians were innocent of any crime (Acts 19:40), and now the Roman captain from the temple fortress was writing the same thing. Later, Festus (Acts 25:24–25) and Herod Agrippa (Acts 26:31–32) would also affirm that Paul should have been set free. Even the Jewish leaders in Rome had to confess that they had had no official news against Paul (Acts 28:21).

Leaving at nine o'clock that night, Paul and his escort went from Jerusalem to Antiparis, about thirty-seven miles away. This must have been an all-night forced march for that many people to cover that much ground in that short a time. The cavalry then continued with Paul while the two hundred soldiers returned to the barracks, since the dangerous part of the trip was now over. They traveled another twenty-seven miles to Caesarea, where Paul was officially turned over to Felix. Paul was safe from the Jewish plotters, but was he safe from Felix?

Antonius Felix was governor (procurator) of Judea. He was married to Drusilla, a Jewess who was daughter of Herod Agrippa I (Acts 12:1) and who left her husband to become Felix's third wife. She was sister of Herod Agrippa II (Acts 25:13ff.). The Roman historian Tacitus said that Felix "exercised the power of a king in the spirit of a slave." Felix was called "a vulgar ruffian" and lived up to the name.

Not only was Paul protected by an escort fit for a king, but he was put, not in the common prison, but in the palace built by Herod the Great, where the governor had his official headquarters. We wonder if any of the believers in Caesarea knew about Paul's presence and sought to bring him personal aid and encouragement. They would certainly remember the visit of Agabus and realize that his dire prophecy had been fulfilled (Acts 21:10–14).

As you review the events recorded in this chapter, you cannot help but be impressed with the commitment of the apostle Paul to his calling. "None of these things move me" (Acts 20:24). If ever a man dared to follow Christ, come what may, he was that man. Paul did not look for the easy way but for the way that would most honor the Lord and win the lost. He was even willing to become a prisoner if that would further the work of the gospel.

You are also impressed with the amazing providence of God in caring for His servant. "The angel of the Lord encamps all around those who fear Him, and delivers them" (Ps. 34:7 NKJV). "Let us trust in God, and be very courageous for the gospel," wrote Charles Spurgeon, "and the Lord Himself will screen us from all harm."

God's people can afford to be daring, in the will of God, because they know their Savior will be dependable and work out His perfect win. Paul was alone—but not alone! His Lord was with him and he had nothing to fear.

CHAPTER TWENTY-TWO
Acts 24
PAUL THE WITNESS

L aw was the most characteristic and lasting expression of the Roman spirit," wrote historian Will Durant in *Caesar and Christ*. "The first person in Roman law was the citizen." In other words, it was the responsibility of the court to protect the citizen from the State, but too often various kinds of corruption infected the system and made justice difficult for the common man. Paul would soon discover how corrupt a Roman governor could be.

"The secret of Roman government was the principle of indirect rule," wrote Arnold Toynbee. This meant that the real burden of administration was left pretty much on the shoulders of the local authorities. Imperial Rome got involved only if there was danger from without or if the local governing units were at odds with one another.

In this chapter we see the Roman legal system at work and three men each making his contribution.

Tertullus: False Accusations (24:1–9)

In the Bible record, when people go to Jerusalem, they always go up, but when they go *from* Jerusalem, they always go down. This explains why the official Jewish party "descended" when they came to Caesarea. With Ananias the high priest were some of the Jewish elders as well as a lawyer to present the case and defend their charges. Roman law was as complex as our modern law, and it took an expert to understand it and know how to apply it successfully to his client's case.

Tertullus began with the customary *flattery,* a normal part of the judicial routine. After all, before you can win your case, you must win over your judge. Tacitus, the Roman orator and politician, called flatterers "those worst of enemies," and Solomon wrote that "a flattering mouth works ruin" (Prov. 26:28 NKJV).

The lawyer complimented Felix because the governor's many reforms had brought quietness to the land. (Question: Why did it require nearly five hundred soldiers to protect one man in transit from Jerusalem to Caesarea?) It was true that Felix had put down some revolts, but he had certainly not brought peace to the land. In fact, during the time Felix was suppressing robbers in his realm, he was also hiring robbers to murder the high priest Jonathan! So much for his reforms.

But the prosecutor's accusations against Paul were no more truthful than his flattery. He brought three charges: a personal charge ("he is a pestilent fellow"), a political charge (sedition and leading an illegal religion), and a doctrinal charge (profaning the temple).

As for Paul being "a pest," it all depends on one's point of view. The Jews wanted to maintain their ancient traditions, and Paul was advocating something new. The Romans were afraid of anything that upset their delicate "peace" in the empire, and Paul's record of causing trouble was long and consistent. As Vance Havner used to say, "Wherever Paul went, there was either a riot or a revival!"

This personal charge was based on the Jews' conflicts with Paul in different parts of the Roman world. I have already pointed out that it was his own countrymen, not the Roman authorities, who caused Paul trouble from city to city. The Jews from Asia (Acts 21:27) would certainly have stories to tell about Lystra, Corinth, and Ephesus! This first accusation reminds us of the charges brought against the Lord Jesus at His trial (Luke 23:1–2, 5).

The political charge was much more serious, because no Roman official wanted to be guilty of permitting illegal activities that would upset the *Pax Romana* (Roman Peace). Rome had given the Jews freedom to practice their religion, but the Roman officials kept their eyes on them lest they use their privileges to weaken the empire. When Tertullus called Paul "an instigator of insurrections among all the Jews throughout the Roman Empire" (WUEST), he immediately got the attention of the governor. Of course, his statement was an exaggeration, but how many court cases have been won by somebody stretching the truth?

Tertullus knew that there was some basis for this charge because Paul had preached to the Jews that Jesus Christ was their King and Lord. To the Romans and the unbelieving Jews, this message sounded like treason against Caesar (Acts 16:20–21; 17:5–9). Furthermore, it was illegal to establish a new religion in Rome without the approval of the authorities. If Paul indeed was a "ringleader of the sect of the Nazarenes," then his enemies could easily build a case against him.

At that time, the Christian faith was still identified with the Jews, and they were permitted by the Romans to practice their religion. There had been Gentile seekers and God-fearers in the synagogues, so the presence of Gentiles in the churches did not create legal problems. Later, when the number of Gentile believers increased and more of the congregations separated from the Jewish synagogues, then Rome saw the difference between Jews and Christians and trouble began. Rome did not want a rival religion thriving in the empire and creating problems.

Tertullus's third accusation had to be handled with care because it implicated a Roman officer who had saved a man's life. For the most part, Roman officials like Felix did not want anything to do with cases involving Jewish law (John 18:28–31; Acts 16:35–40; 18:12–17). The fewer Jews who ended up in Roman courts, the better it would be for the empire. Tertullus had to present this third charge in a way that made the Jews look good without making the Romans look too bad, and he did a good job.

To begin with, he softened the charge. The accusation given by the Asian Jews was that Paul had polluted the temple (Acts 21:28), but Tertullus said, "He even tried to profane the temple" (Acts 24:6 NKJV). Why the change? For at least two good reasons. To begin with, Paul's accusers realized that the original charge could never be substantiated if the facts were investigated. But even more, the Asian Jews who started the story seemed to have vanished from the scene! If there were no witnesses, there could be no evidence or conviction.

When you compare Luke's account of Paul's arrest (Acts 21:27–40) with the captain's account (Acts 23:25–30) and the lawyer's account (Acts 24:6–8), you can well understand why judges and juries can get confused. Tertullus gave the impression that Paul had actually been guilty of profaning the temple, that the Jews had been within their rights in seizing him, and that the captain had stepped out of line by interfering. It was Claudius, not the Jews, who was guilty of treating a Roman citizen with violence! But Felix had the official letter before him and was more likely to believe his captain than a paid Hellenistic Jewish lawyer.

Tertullus knew that the Jews had authority from Rome to arrest and prosecute those who violated Jewish law. True, the Romans thought that the Jews' devotion to their traditions was excessive and superstitious, yet Rome wisely let them have their way. The Jews were even permitted to execute guilty offenders in capital cases, such as Paul's "offense" of permitting Gentiles to cross the protective barricade in the temple (Acts 21:28–29). Tertullus argued that if Claudius had not interfered, the Jews would have tried Paul themselves, and this would have saved Felix and Rome a great deal of trouble and expense.

In closing his argument, Tertullus hinted that Claudius Lysias should have been there personally and had not just sent the Jewish leaders to present the case. Why was he absent? Could he not defend his case? Was he trying to "pass the buck" to others? As far as we know, during the two years Paul was detained in Caesarea, Claudius never did show up to tell his side of the story. We wonder why.

But Paul was there and Felix could get the truth out of him! "If you examine Paul," the clever lawyer said, "you will find that what I am saying is true." The other members of the Jewish delegation united in agreeing with their lawyer, which was no surprise to anybody.

Paul: Faithful Answers (24:10–21)

But the governor did not examine Paul. He merely nodded his head as a signal that it was now Paul's turn to speak. Paul did not flatter Felix (see 1 Thess. 2:1–6); he merely acknowledged that the governor was a man of experience and therefore a man of knowledge. After this brief but honest introduction, Paul then proceeded to answer the charges of Tertullus (Acts 24:10–16), the Asian Jews (Acts 24: 17–19), and the Jewish council (Acts 24:20–21).

As far as the temple charge was concerned, Paul was

in the temple to worship and not to lead a disturbance. In fact, the temple records would show that Paul was registered to pay the costs for four Jews who had taken a Nazarite vow. Paul had not preached in the temple or the synagogues, nor had he preached anywhere in the city. (Years before, Paul had made an agreement with Peter and the Jerusalem elders that he would not evangelize the Jews in Jerusalem. See Gal. 2:7–10.) Nobody could prove that he was guilty of leading any kind of rebellion against the Jews or the Romans.

Furthermore, since he had been in Jerusalem only a week (the twelve days of Acts 24:11, minus the five days of Acts 24:1), there had hardly been time to organize and lead an assault on the temple! While students of Paul's life do not agree on every detail, the order of events was probably something like this:

Day 1—Paul arrived in Jerusalem (21:17)
Day 2—Met with James and the elders (21:18)
Day 3—In the temple with the Nazarites (21:26)
Day 4—In the temple
Day 5—In the temple
Day 6—Arrested in the temple (21:27)
Day 7—Met with the Jewish council (23:1–10)
Day 8—Threatened; taken to Caesarea (23:12, 23)
Day 9—Arrived in Caesarea (23:33)
Day 10—Waited (Felix sent for the Jewish leaders)
Day 11—Waited for the Jewish leaders to arrive
Day 12—Waited—they arrived—hearing scheduled
Day 13—The hearing conducted

The four men who had taken the Nazarite vow were evidently already involved in their temple duties when James suggested that Paul pay their costs (Acts 21:24). If they had started the day before Paul arrived in Jerusalem, then the day of Paul's arrest would have been the seventh day of their obligations (Acts 21:27). The New American Standard Bible translates Acts 21:27, "And when the seven days were almost over." This implies that the events occurred on the seventh day of their schedule, Paul's sixth day in the city.

It would probably take two days for the official Roman messenger to get from Caesarea to Jerusalem, and another two days for Ananias and his associates to make it to Caesarea. They were not likely to linger; the case was too important.

Having disposed of the temple charges, Paul then dealt with the charges of sedition and heresy. Even though the high priest was a Sadducee, there were certainly Pharisees in the official Jewish delegation, so Paul appealed once again to their religious roots in the Scriptures. The fact that Paul was a Christian did not mean that he worshipped a different God from the God of his fathers. It only meant he worshipped the God of his fathers in a new and living way, for the only acceptable way to worship the Father is through Jesus Christ (John 5:23). His faith was still founded on the Old Testament Scriptures, and they bore witness to Jesus Christ.

The Sadducees accepted the five Books of Moses (the law), but not the rest of the Old Testament. They rejected the doctrine of the resurrection because they said it could not be found anywhere in what Moses wrote. (Jesus had refuted that argument, but they chose to ignore it. See Matt. 22:23–33.) By declaring his personal faith in the resurrection, Paul affirmed his orthodox convictions and identified himself with the Pharisees. Once again, the Pharisees were caught on the horns of a dilemma, for if Paul's faith was that of a heretic, then they were heretics too!

Paul and the early Christians did not see themselves as "former Jews" but as "fulfilled Jews." The Old Testament was a new book to them because they had found their Messiah. They knew that they no longer needed the rituals of the Jewish law in order to please God, but they saw in these ceremonies and ordinances a revelation of the Savior. Both as a Pharisee and a Christian, Paul had "taken pains" always to have a good conscience and to seek to please the Lord.

Having replied to the false charges of Tertullus, Paul then proceeded to answer the false accusation of the Asian Jews that he had profaned the temple (Acts 24:17–19). He had not come to Jerusalem to defile the temple but to bring needed help to the Jewish people and to present his own offerings to the Lord. (This is the only mention in Acts of the special offering.) When the Asians saw him in the temple, he was with four men who were fulfilling their Nazarite vows. How could Paul possibly be *worshipping* God and *profaning* God's house at the same time? A Jewish priest was in charge of Paul's temple activities, so, if the holy temple was defiled, the priest was responsible. Paul was only obeying the law.

Now Paul reached the heart of his defense, for it was required by Roman law that the accusers face the accused at the trial, or else the charges would be dropped. Ananias had wisely not brought any of the Hellenistic Jews with him, for he was sure that their witness would fall down under official examination. These men were good at inciting riots; they were not good at producing facts.

Paul closed his defense by replying to the members of the Jewish council (Acts 24:20–21). Instead of giving him a fair hearing, the high priest and the Sanhedrin had abused him and refused to hear him out. Ananias was no doubt grateful that Paul said nothing about his slap in the face, for it was not legal for a Roman citizen to be treated that way.

Do we detect a bit of holy sarcasm in Paul's closing statement? We might paraphrase it, "If I have done anything evil, it is probably this: I reminded the Jewish council of our great Jewish doctrine of the resurrection." Remember, the book of Acts is a record of the early church's witness to the resurrection of Jesus Christ (Acts 1:22). The Sadducees had long abandoned the doctrine, and the Pharisees did not give it the practical importance it deserved. Of course, Paul would have related this doctrine to the resurrection of Jesus Christ, and the Sanhedrin did not want that.

They had accused Paul of being anti-Jewish and anti-Roman, but they could not prove their charges. If the Jewish leaders had further pursued any of these charges, their case would have collapsed. But there was enough circumstantial evidence to plant doubts in the minds of the Roman officials, and perhaps there was enough race prejudice in them to water that seed and encourage it to grow. After all, had not the Emperor Claudius expelled the Jews from Rome (Acts 18:2)? Perhaps Paul would bear watching.

Felix: Foolish Attitudes (24:22–27)

If ever a man failed both personally and officially, that man was Felix, procurator of Judea. He certainly could not plead ignorance of the facts, because he was "well acquainted with the Way" (Acts 24:22 NIV). His wife, Drusilla, was a Jewess and perhaps kept him informed of the activities among her people, and as a Roman official, he would carefully (if privately) investigate these things. He saw the light, but he preferred to live in the darkness.

Felix saw to it that Paul was comfortably cared for while at the same time safely guarded. "Liberty" in Acts 24:23 means that he was not put in the common jail or kept in close confinement. He had limited freedom in the palace, chained to a soldier. (The guards were changed every six hours, a perfect captive congregation!) Paul's friends were permitted to minister to him (Greek: "wait on him as personal servants"), so people could come and go to meet his needs. What Paul's ministry was during those two years in Caesarea, we do not know, but we can be sure he gave a faithful witness for the Lord.

The record of one such witness is given by Luke, and it makes Felix's guilt even greater. Not only was Felix's mind informed, but his heart was moved by fear, and yet he would not obey the truth. It is not enough for a person to know the facts about Christ, or to have an emotional response to a message. He or she must willingly repent of sin and trust the Savior. "But you are not willing to come to Me that you may have life" (John 5:40 NKJV).

It must have been the curiosity of his wife, Drusilla, that prompted Felix to give Paul another hearing. She wanted to hear Paul, for, after all, her family had been involved with "the Way" on several occasions. Her great-grandfather tried to kill Jesus in Bethlehem (Matt. 2); her great-uncle killed John the Baptist and mocked Jesus (Luke 23:6–12); and Acts 12:1–2 tells of her father killing the apostle James.

Dr. Luke has given us only the three points of Paul's sermon to this infamous couple: righteousness, self-control, and the judgment to come. But what an outline! Paul gave them three compelling reasons why they should repent and believe on Jesus Christ.

First, they had to do something about *yesterday's*

sin ("righteousness"). In 1973, Dr. Karl Menninger, one of the world's leading psychiatrists, published a startling book, *Whatever Became of Sin?* He pointed out that the very word *sin* has gradually dropped out of our vocabulary, "the word, along with the notion." We talk about mistakes, weaknesses, inherited tendencies, faults, and even errors, but we do not face up to the fact of sin.

"People are no longer sinful," said Phyllis McGinley, noted American writer and poet. "They are only immature or underprivileged or frightened or, more particularly, sick." But a holy God demands righteousness; that's the bad news. Yet the good news is that this same holy God *provides* His own righteousness to those who trust Jesus Christ (Rom. 3:21–26). We can never be saved by our own righteousness of good works. We can be saved only through Christ's righteousness made available by His finished work of salvation on the cross.

The second point in Paul's sermon dealt with self-control: we must do something about *today's temptations*. Man can control almost everything but himself. Here were Felix and Drusilla, prime illustrations of lack of self-control. She divorced her husband to become Felix's third wife, and though a Jewess, she lived as though God had never given the Ten Commandments at Sinai. Felix was an unscrupulous official who did not hesitate to lie, or even to murder, in order to get rid of his enemies and promote himself. Self-control was something neither of them knew much about.

Paul's third point was the clincher "judgment to come." *We must do something about tomorrow's judgment.* Perhaps Paul told Felix and Drusilla what he told the Greek philosophers: God has "appointed a day, in which he will judge the world in righteousness" by the Lord Jesus Christ (Acts 17:31). Jesus Christ is either your Savior or your Judge. How do we know that Jesus Christ is the Judge? "He has given assurance of this to all by raising Him from the dead" (Acts 17:31 NKJV). Once again, the resurrection!

"Felix trembled" (Acts 24:25), which literally means "Felix became terrified." Roman leaders prided themselves in their ability to be stoical and restrain their emotions under all circumstances, but a conviction from God gripped Felix's heart, and he could not hide it. Paul had diagnosed the case and offered the remedy. It was up to Felix to receive it.

What did Felix do? *He procrastinated!* "When I have a convenient time, I will call for you," he told the apostle. "Procrastination is the thief of time," wrote Edward Young. Perhaps he was thinking about the English proverb, "One of these days is none of these days." Procrastination is also the thief of souls. The most "convenient season" for a lost sinner to be saved is *right now.* "Behold, now is the accepted time; behold, now is the day of salvation" (2 Cor. 6:2).

"I think there's a special time for each person to be saved," a man argued to whom I was witnessing. "I can't get saved until that time comes."

"What are the signals that your special time has come?" I asked. "Well," he drawled, "I don't rightly know." "Then how will you know when you are supposed to be saved?" I asked. But the stupidity of his position never bothered him. I do hope he was saved before he died.

Consider Felix's foolish attitudes. He had a foolish attitude toward God's Word, thinking that he could "take it or leave it." But God "now *commands* all men everywhere to repent" (Acts 17:30 NKJV, italics mine). When God speaks, men and women had better listen and obey.

Felix had a foolish attitude toward his sins. He knew he was a sinner, yet he refused to break with his sins and obey the Lord. He had a foolish attitude toward God's grace. The Lord had been long suffering toward Felix, yet the governor would not surrender. Felix was not sure of another day's life, yet he foolishly procrastinated. "Do not boast about tomorrow, for you do not know what a day may bring forth" (Prov. 27:1 NIV).

Instead of listening to Paul, Felix tried to "use" Paul as a political pawn, either to get money from the church or to gain favor with the Jews. The fact that Felix had further discussions with Paul is no indication that his heart was interested in spiritual things. Paul's friends were coming and going, and perhaps some of them had access to the large offering sent by the Gentile churches. Certainly Paul gave further witness to the governor, but to no avail. When Felix was replaced, he left Paul a prisoner, but it was Felix who was really the prisoner.

The governor's mind was enlightened (Acts 24:22), his emotions were stirred (Acts 24:25), but his will would not yield. He tried to gain the world, but, as far as we know, he lost his soul. He procrastinated himself into hell.

Dr. Clarence Macartney told a story about a meeting in hell. Satan called his four leading demons together and commanded them to think up a new lie that would trap more souls. "I have it!" one demon said. "I'll go to earth and tell people there is no God."

"It will never work," said Satan. "People can look around them and see that there is a God."

"I'll go and tell them there is no heaven!" suggested a second demon, but Satan rejected that idea. "Everybody knows there is life after death and they want to go to heaven."

"Let's tell them there is no hell!" said a third demon.

"No, conscience tells them their sins will be judged," said the devil. "We need a better lie than that."

Quietly, the fourth demon spoke. "I think I've solved your problem," he said. "I'll go to earth and tell everybody *there is no hurry.*"

The best time to trust Jesus Christ is—*now!*

And the best time to tell others the good news of the gospel is—*now!*

CHAPTER TWENTY-THREE
Acts 25—26
PAUL THE DEFENDER

The new governor, Porcius Festus, was a better man than his predecessor and took up his duties with the intention of doing what was right. However, he soon discovered that Jewish politics was not easy to handle, especially the two-year-old case of the apostle Paul, a prisoner with no official charges against him. Paul was a Jew whose countrymen wanted to kill him, and he was a Roman whose government did not know what to do with him.

What a dilemma! If Festus released Paul, the Jews would cause trouble, and that was something the new governor dared not risk. However, if he held Paul prisoner, Festus would have to explain why a Roman citizen was being held without definite official charges. Festus knew that it was smart for him to act quickly and take advantage of the fact that he was a newcomer on the scene. To delay would only make the problem worse, and it was bad enough already.

These two chapters present Festus in three different situations, each of which related to the apostle Paul.

Conciliation: Festus and the Jewish Leaders (25:1–12)

Knowing how important it was for him to get along well with the Jewish leaders, Festus lost no time in visiting the Holy City and paying his respects, and the leaders lost no time in bringing up Paul's case. The new high priest was Ishmael; he had replaced Jonathan, who had been killed by Felix. Ishmael wanted to resurrect the plot of two years before and remove Paul once and for all (Acts 23:12–15).

It is not likely that the new governor knew anything about the original plot or even suspected that the Jewish religious leaders were out for blood. Since a Roman court could meet in Jerusalem as well as in Caesarea, transferring Paul would be a normal procedure. Festus would probably not demand that a large retinue go with him, so an ambush would be easy. Finally, since it was a matter involving a Jewish prisoner and the Jewish law, the logical place to meet would be Jerusalem.

"Kill Paul!" had been the cry of the unbelieving Jews ever since Paul had arrived in Jerusalem (Acts 21:27–31; 22:22; 23:10–15; 25:3); however, Festus knew nothing of this. Paul had been warned of this danger, but he had also been assured that the Lord would protect him, use his witness, and then take him safely to Rome (Acts 23:11; 26:17). The situation was growing more serious, for now it was the council itself, and not a group of outsiders, that was plotting Paul's death. You would think that their anger would have subsided after two years, but it had not. Satan the murderer was hard at work (John 8:44).

Festus was wise not to cooperate with their scheme, but he did invite the leaders to accompany him to Caesarea and face Paul once again. This would give Festus opportunity to review the case and get more facts. The Jews agreed, but the hearing brought out nothing new. The Jewish delegation (this time without their lawyer) only repeated the same unfounded and unproved accusations, hoping that the governor would agree with them and put Paul to death (Acts 25:15–16).

What did Paul do? He once again affirmed that he was innocent of any crime against the Jewish law, the temple, or the Roman government. Festus saw that no progress was being made, so he asked Paul if he would be willing to be tried in Jerusalem. He did this to please the Jews and probably did not realize that he was jeopardizing the life of his famous prisoner. But a Roman judge could not move a case to another court without the consent of the accused, *and Paul refused to go!* Instead, he claimed the right of every Roman citizen to appeal to Caesar.

What led Paul to make that wise decision? For one thing, he knew that his destination was Rome, not Jerusalem, and the fastest way to get there was to appeal to Caesar. Paul also knew that the Jews had not given up their hopes of killing him, so he was wise to stay under the protection of Rome. By appealing to Caesar, Paul forced the Romans to guard him and take him to Rome. Finally, Paul realized that he could never have a fair trial in Jerusalem anyway, so why go?

It must have infuriated the Jewish leaders when Paul, by one statement, took the case completely out of their hands. He made it clear that he was willing to die *if* he could be proved guilty of a capital crime, but first they had to find him guilty. Festus met with his official council, and they agreed to send Paul to Nero for trial. No doubt the new governor was somewhat embarrassed that he had handled one of his first cases so badly that the prisoner was forced to appeal to Caesar, and to Caesar he must go!

Consultation: Festus and Agrippa (25:13–22)

But the new governor's problems were not over. He had managed not to offend the Jews, but he had not determined the legal charges against his prisoner. How could he send such a notable prisoner to the emperor and not have the man's crimes listed against him?

About that time, Festus had a state visit from Herod Agrippa II and Herod's sister, Bernice. This youthful king, the last of the Herodians to rule, was the great-grandson of the Herod who killed the Bethlehem babes, and the son of the Herod who killed the apostle James (Acts 12). The fact that his sister lived with him created a great deal of suspicion on the part of the Jewish people, for their law clearly condemned incest (Lev. 18:1–18; 20:11–21). Rome had given Herod Agrippa II legal jurisdiction over the temple in Jerusalem, so it was logical that Festus share Paul's case with him.

Festus was smart enough to understand that the Jewish case against Paul had nothing to do with civil law. It was purely a matter of "religious questions" (Acts 18:14–15; 23:29), which the Romans were unprepared to handle, especially the doctrine of the resurrection. Acts 25:19 proves that Paul was defending much more than the resurrection in general. He was declaring and defending the resurrection of Jesus Christ. As we have noted in our studies, this is the key emphasis of the witness of the church in the book of Acts.

Festus gave the impression that he wanted to move the trial to Jerusalem because the "Jewish questions" could be settled only by Jewish people in Jewish territory (Acts 25:20). It was a pure fabrication, of course, because his real reason was to please the Jewish leaders, most of whom King Herod knew. Festus needed something definite to send to the emperor Nero, and perhaps Agrippa could supply it. ("Augustus" in Acts 25:21, 25 is a title, "the august one," and not a proper name.)

The king was an expert in Jewish matters (Acts 26:2–3) and certainly would be keenly interested in knowing more about this man who caused a riot in the temple. Perhaps Herod could assist Festus in finding out the real charges against Paul, and perhaps Festus could assist Herod in learning more about Jewish affairs in the Holy City.

Confrontation: Festus, Agrippa, and Paul (25:23—26:32)

It seems incredible that all of this pomp and ceremony was because of one little Jewish man who preached the gospel of Jesus Christ! But the Lord had promised Paul he would bear witness before "Gentiles and kings" (Acts 9:15), and that promise was being fulfilled again. Once Paul was finished with his witness, all his hearers would know how to be saved and would be without excuse.

They met in an "audience room" in the palace, and the key military men and officers of the Roman government were there. Paul's case had probably been discussed by various official people many times over the past two years, so very few of those present were ignorant of the affair.

Festus was certainly exaggerating when he said that "all the multitude of the Jews" had pressed charges against Paul, but that kind of statement would make the Jews present feel much better. Acts 25:25 gives us the second of Luke's "official statements" declaring Paul's innocence (see Acts 23:29), and there will be others before his book is completed.

In his flowery speech before Agrippa, Festus indicated that he wanted the king to examine Paul (Acts 25:26), but there is no record that he did. In fact, before the session ended, Paul became the judge, and Festus, King Agrippa, and Bernice became the defendants! Paul was indeed defending himself (Acts 26:24 NKJV), but at the same time, he was presenting the truth of the gospel and witnessing to the difference Jesus Christ can make in a person's life. This is the longest of Paul's speeches found in Acts.

King Agrippa was in charge and told Paul that

he was free to speak. In his brief introduction, Paul sincerely gave thanks that Agrippa was hearing his case, because he knew the king was an expert in Jewish religious matters. Paul did not mention it then, but he also knew that the king believed the Old Testament prophets (Acts 26:27). Paul also hinted that his speech might be a long one and that he would appreciate the king's patience in hearing him out.

Five key statements summarize Paul's defense.

"I lived a Pharisee" (vv. 4–11). Paul's early life in Jerusalem was known to the Jews, so there was no need to go into great detail. He was a devout Pharisee (Phil. 3:5) and the son of a Pharisee (Acts 23:6), and his peers had likely realized he would accomplish great things as a rabbi (Gal. 1:13–14 NIV). It was because of his convictions about the resurrection and "the hope of Israel" that he was now a prisoner (see Acts 23:6; 24:15). Once again, Paul appealed to Jewish orthodoxy and loyalty to the Hebrew tradition.

It is worth noting that Paul mentioned "our twelve tribes" (Acts 26:7). While it is true that the ten northern tribes (Israel) were conquered by Assyria in 722 BC and assimilated to some extent, it is not true that these ten tribes were "lost" or annihilated. Jesus spoke about all twelve tribes (Matt. 19:28), and so did James (James 1:1) and the apostle John (Rev. 7:4–8; 21:12). God knows where His chosen people are, and He will fulfill the promises He has made to them.

The pronoun *you* in Acts 26:8 is plural, so Paul must have looked around at the entire audience as he spoke. The Greeks and Romans, of course, would not believe in the doctrine of the resurrection (Acts 17:31–32), nor would the Sadducees who were present (Acts 23:8). To Paul, this was a crucial doctrine, for if there is no resurrection, then Jesus Christ was not raised and Paul had no gospel to preach. (For Paul's argument about the resurrection and the gospel, see 1 Cor. 15).

Paul was not only a Pharisee, but he had also been a zealous persecutor of the church. He had punished the believers and tried to force them to deny Jesus Christ, and some of them he had helped send to their death. The phrase "gave my voice" (Acts 26:10) literally means "registered my vote." This suggests that Paul had been an official member of the Sanhedrin, but surely if that were true, seemingly he would have mentioned it in one of his speeches. The phrase probably means nothing more than he "voted against them" as a special representative of the high priest (Acts 9:2, 14).

In the early days of the church, the Jewish believers continued to meet in the synagogues, and that was where Paul found them and punished them (Matt. 10:17; 23:34). What Paul in his early years looked on as "religious zeal" (Gal. 1:13–14), in his later years he considered to be "madness" (Acts 26:11). Like a wild animal, he had "made havoc of the church" (Acts 8:3), "breathing out threatenings and slaughter" (Acts 9:1).

"I saw a light" (vv. 12–13). Not content to limit his work to Jerusalem, Paul had asked for authority to visit the synagogues in distant cities. His zeal had driven out many of the believers and they had taken their message to Jews in other communities (Acts 8:4).

Paul considered himself an enlightened man, for, after all, he was a Jew (Rom. 9:4–5), a scholar (Acts 22:3), and a Pharisee. In reality, Paul had lived in gross spiritual darkness. He knew the law in his preconversion days, but he had not realized that the purpose of the law was to bring him to Christ (Gal. 3:24). He had been a self-righteous Pharisee who needed to discover that his good works and respectable character could never save him and take him to heaven (Phil. 3:1–11).

The light that Paul saw was supernatural, for it was the glory of God revealed from heaven (compare Acts 7:2, 55–56). It actually had blinded Paul for three days (Acts 9:8–9), but his spiritual eyes had been opened to behold the living Christ (2 Cor. 4:3–6). But seeing a light was not enough; he also had to hear the Word of God.

"I heard a voice" (vv. 14–18). Paul's companions had seen the light, but not the Lord, and they had heard a sound, but they could not understand the words. They all fell to the earth, but only Paul remained there (Acts 9:7). Jesus Christ spoke to Paul in the familiar Aramaic tongue of the Jews, called him by name, and told him it was futile for him to continue fighting the Lord. In that moment, Paul had made two surprising discoveries: Jesus of Nazareth was alive, and He was so united to His people that their suffering was His suffering! Paul was persecuting not only the church, but also his own Messiah!

How encouraging it is to know that God in His grace speaks to those who are His enemies. God had been dealing with Paul, but Paul had been resisting Him, kicking against the "goads." What were these "goads"? Certainly the testimony and death of Stephen (Acts 22:20), plus the faithful witness of the other saints who had suffered because of Paul. Perhaps Paul had also struggled with the emptiness and weakness of Judaism and his own inability to meet the demands of the law. Even though he could now say he was "blameless" in conduct and conscience (Acts 23:1; Phil. 3:6), yet within his own heart, he certainly knew how far short he came of meeting God's holy standards (Rom. 7:7–16).

The word *minister* in Acts 26:16 means "an underrower" and refers to a lowly servant on a galley ship. Paul had been accustomed to being an honored leader, but after his conversion he became a subordinate worker, and Jesus Christ became his Master. The Lord had promised to be with Paul and protect him, and He also promised to reveal Himself to him. Paul saw the Lord on the Damascus road, and again three years later while in the temple (Acts 22:17–21). Later, the Lord appeared to him in Corinth (Acts 18:9) and in Jerusalem (Acts 23:11), and He would appear to him again.

No doubt it was a surprise to Paul after his conversion to hear that the Lord was sending him to the Gentiles. He had a great love for his own people and would gladly have lived and died to win them to Christ

(Rom. 9:1–3), but that was not God's plan. Paul would always be "the apostle to the Gentiles."

Acts 26:18 describes both the spiritual condition of the lost and the gracious provision of Christ for those who will believe. You will find parallels in Isaiah 35:5; 42:6ff.; and 61:1. The lost sinner is like a blind prisoner in a dark dungeon, and only Christ can open his eyes and give him light and freedom (2 Cor. 4:3–6). But even after he is set free, what about his court record and his guilt? The Lord forgives his sins and wipes the record clean! He then takes him into His own family as His own child and shares His inheritance with him!

What must the sinner do? He must trust Jesus Christ ("faith that is in me"—Acts 26:18). Paul had to lose his religion to gain salvation! He discovered in a moment of time that all of his righteousnesses were but filthy rags in God's sight, and that he needed the righteousness of Christ (Isa. 64:6).

"I was not disobedient" (vv. 19–21). When Paul had asked, "Lord, what wilt thou have me to do?" (Acts 9:6) he meant it sincerely, and when the Lord told him, he obeyed orders immediately. He began right at Damascus and it almost cost him his life (Acts 9:20–25). Likewise, when he had witnessed to the Jews in Jerusalem, they attempted to kill him (Acts 9:29–30). In spite of repeated discouragements and dangers, Paul had remained obedient to the call and the vision that Jesus Christ gave him. Nothing moved him (Acts 20:24)!

In Acts 26:21, Paul clearly explained to Agrippa and Festus what had really happened in the temple and why it had happened. It was "on account of these things" that Paul had been attacked and almost killed: his declaration that Jesus of Nazareth was alive and was Israel's Messiah, his ministry to the Gentiles, and his offer of God's covenant blessings to both Jews and Gentiles *on the same terms of repentance and faith* (see Acts 20:21). The proud nationalistic Israelites would have nothing to do with a Jew who treated Gentiles like Jews!

"I continue unto this day" (vv. 22–32). It is one thing to have a great beginning, with visions and voices, but quite another thing to keep on going, especially when the going is tough. The fact that Paul continued was proof of his conversion and evidence of the faithfulness of God. He was saved by God's grace and enabled to serve by God's grace (1 Cor. 15:10).

The one word that best summarizes Paul's life and ministry is "witnessing" (see Acts 26:16). He simply shared with others what he had learned and experienced as a follower of Jesus Christ. His message was not something he manufactured, for it was based solidly on the Old Testament Scriptures. We must remind ourselves that Paul and the other apostles did not have the New Testament, but used the Old Testament to lead sinners to Christ and to nurture the new believers.

Acts 26:23 is a summary of the gospel (1 Cor. 15:3–4), and each part can be backed up from the Old Testament. See, for example, Isaiah 52:13—53:12 and

Psalm 16:8–11. Paul could even defend his call to the Gentiles from Isaiah 49:6 (see also Acts 13:47). Jesus was not the first person to be raised from the dead, but He was the first one to be raised and never die again. He is "the firstfruits of them that slept" (1 Cor. 15:20).

In his message in the temple, when Paul got to the word *Gentiles,* the crowd exploded (Acts 22:21–22). That is the word Paul spoke when Festus responded and loudly accused Paul of being mad. How strange that Festus did not think Paul was mad when he was persecuting the church (Acts 26:11)! Nobody called D. L. Moody crazy when he was energetically selling shoes and making money, but when he started winning souls, people gave him the nickname "Crazy Moody." This was not the first time Paul had been called "crazy" (2 Cor. 5:13), and he was only following in the footsteps of his Master (Mark 3:20–21; John 10:20).

Paul had been addressing King Agrippa, but the emotional interruption of the governor forced him to reply. He reminded Festus that the facts about the ministry of Jesus Christ, including His death and resurrection, were public knowledge and "not done in a corner." The Jewish Sanhedrin was involved and so was the Roman governor, Pilate. Jesus of Nazareth had been a famous public figure for at least three years, and huge crowds had followed Him. How then could the governor plead ignorance?

Festus had not interrupted because he really thought Paul was mad. Had that been the case, he would have treated Paul gently and ordered some of his guards to escort him to a place of rest and safety. Furthermore, what official would send a raving madman to be tried before the emperor? No, the governor was only giving evidence of conviction in his heart. Paul's words had found their mark, and Festus was trying to escape.

But Paul did not forget King Agrippa, a Jew who was an expert in these matters. When Paul asked if Agrippa believed the prophets, he was forcing him to take a stand. Certainly the king would not repudiate what every Jew believed! But Agrippa knew that if he affirmed his faith in the prophets, he must then face the question, "Is Jesus of Nazareth the one about whom the prophets wrote?"

Festus avoided decision by accusing Paul of being mad. King Agrippa eluded Paul's question (and the dilemma it presented) by adopting a superior attitude and belittling Paul's witness. His reply in Acts 26:28 can be stated, "Do you think that in such a short time, with such few words, you can persuade *me* to become a Christian?" Perhaps he spoke with a smirk on his face and a sneer in his voice. But he certainly spoke his own death warrant (John 3:18–21, 36).

Paul was polite in his reply. "I would to God, that whether in a short or long time, not only you, but also all who hear me this day, might become such as I am, except for these chains" (Acts 26:29 NASB). Festus and Agrippa knew that their prisoner had a compassionate concern for them, and they could not easily escape his challenge. The best thing to do was to end the hearing, so the king stood up, and this told everybody that the audience was over.

Both Agrippa and Festus declared that Paul was innocent of any crime deserving of death. Luke continues to accumulate these official statements so that his readers will understand that Paul was an innocent man (see Acts 16:35–40; 18:12–17; 23:29; 25:25). In fact, Paul might have been set free, had he not appealed to Caesar. Was he foolish in making his appeal? No, he was not, for it was the appeal to Caesar that finally ended the repeated accusations of the Jewish leaders. They knew they could not successfully fight against Rome.

What Agrippa and Festus did not understand was that *Paul* had been the judge and *they* had been the prisoners on trial. They had been shown the light and the way to freedom, but they had deliberately closed their eyes and returned to their sins. Perhaps they felt relieved that Paul would go to Rome and trouble them no more. The trial was over, but their sentence was still to come; and come it would.

What a wonderful thing is the opportunity to trust Jesus Christ and be saved! What a terrible thing is wasting that opportunity and perhaps never having another.

CHAPTER TWENTY-FOUR
Acts 27—28
PAUL ARRIVES IN ROME

I must also see Rome!" Those were Paul's words during his ministry in Ephesus (Acts 19:21), and little did he realize all that would happen to him before he would arrive in the imperial city: illegal arrest, Roman and Jewish trials, confinement, and even shipwreck. He had long wanted to preach the gospel in Rome (Rom. 1:14–16) and then go on into Spain (Rom. 15:28), but he had not planned to travel as a prisoner. Through it all, Paul trusted God's promise that he would witness in Rome (Acts 23:11), and the Lord saw him through.

Why would Luke devote such a long section of his book to a description of a voyage and shipwreck? Surely he could have summarized the account for us! But Luke was a skilled writer, inspired by the Spirit of God, and he knew what he was doing. For one thing, this exciting report balances the speeches that we have been reading and brings more drama into the account. Also, Luke was an accurate historian who presented the important facts about his hero and his voyage to Rome.

But perhaps the major purpose Luke had in mind was the presenting of Paul as the courageous leader who could take command of a difficult situation in a time of great crisis. Future generations would love and appreciate Paul all the more for what he did en route to Rome.

Since ancient times, writers have pictured life as a journey or a voyage. *Pilgrim's Progress* by John Bunyan is based on this theme, and so is Homer's *Odyssey.*

We sometimes use the "voyage" metaphor in everyday conversation: "Smooth sailing!" or "Don't make shipwreck!" or "Sink or swim!" When a Christian dies, we might say, "She has reached the other shore." Dr. Luke was certainly not writing an allegory, but he did use this exciting event to show how one man's faith can make a big difference for him and others "in the storms of life." What an encouragement to our own faith!

In Paul's journey to Rome, we see the great apostle in four important roles.

Paul the Counselor (27:1–20)

Luke had not included himself since Acts 21:18, but now he joined Paul and Aristarchus (Acts 19:29; 20:2, 4) for the voyage to Rome. It is possible that Luke was allowed to go as Paul's physician and Aristarchus as Paul's personal attendant. How Paul must have thanked God for his faithful friends who gave up their liberty, and even risked their lives, that he might have the help he needed. There is no evidence that either of these men had been arrested, yet Paul referred to Aristarchus as a "fellow prisoner" (Col. 4:10). This could refer to a voluntary imprisonment on his part in order to assist Paul.

Paul was not the only prisoner that Julius and his men were taking to Rome, for there were "certain other prisoners" with them. The Greek word means "others of a different kind" and may suggest that, unlike Paul, these men were going to Rome to die and not to stand trial. What mercy that they met Paul who could tell them how to go to heaven when they died!

The centurion found a coastal ship leaving Caesarea, so they embarked and covered the eighty miles from Caesarea to Sidon in one day. In Sidon, Paul was permitted to visit his friends and put together the things needed for the long trip. Luke records the kindness of a Roman officer to the apostle Paul (Acts 24:23), as well as the encouragement of the anonymous believers in Sidon. Their names are in God's book and they shall be rewarded one day (Phil. 4:3).

From Sidon to Myra, the voyage became difficult because of the westerly winds. At Myra, Julius, a Roman officer, found a ship going to Italy, so he abandoned the slower coastal ship and put Paul and the others on board this large grain ship from Egypt that carried 276 passengers (Acts 27:37–38). Rome depended on Egypt for much of its grain supply, and the Roman government gave special consideration to those who ran these ships.

The strong winds again hindered their progress so that "many days" were required to cover the 130 miles from Myra to Cnidus. The pilot then steered south-southwest to Crete, passing Salmone and finally struggling into Fair Havens. It had been a most difficult voyage, a portent of things to come.

The centurion now had to decide whether to winter at Fair Havens or set sail and try to reach the port of Phoenix (Phoenicia, Acts 27:12) on the southern coast of Crete, about forty miles away. His approach to making this decision is a classic illustration of how *not* to determine the will of God.

Paul admonished them to stay in Fair Havens. They had already encountered adverse winds, and it was now the start of the stormy season. "The fast" refers to the day of Atonement, which fell in September/October, and every sailor knew that sailing was difficult from mid-September to mid-November, and impossible from mid-November to February.

Acts 27:10 sounds so much like a prophecy that we are prone to believe God gave Paul a premonition of danger. Paul had already experienced three shipwrecks (2 Cor. 11:25), so he was certainly speaking from experience. (The Greek word translated "perceive" in Acts 27:10 means "to perceive from past experience.") However, the men in charge gave little value to Paul's warning, an attitude they lived to regret.

What were the factors that governed Julius's decision? To begin with, Fair Havens was not a comfortable place to settle down because it was too open to the winter storms. Phoenix had a more sheltered harbor. Julius also listened to the "expert advice" of the pilot and captain ("master and owner") of the ship. They advised that the ship head for Phoenix as fast as possible. Surely they could cover forty miles safely, and already they had lost too much time (Acts 27:9). When Julius added up the votes, it was three to one that the ship set sail. After all, the majority cannot be wrong, especially when it includes the experts!

But the clinching argument came with an encouraging change in the weather, for the south wind began to blow gently, and that was just what they needed. As the ship left the harbor, perhaps Julius, the pilot, and the captain smiled tolerantly at Paul and his two friends as if to say, "See, you were wrong!"

However, it was not long before Paul was proved right, for the "soft wind" became a stormy wind. The word translated "tempestuous" gives us the English word *typhoon.* Sailors called this special wind *Euroclydon,* a hybrid Greek and Latin word that means "a northeasterner." The crew had to let the ship drift because it was impossible to steer it, and the wind drove it twenty-three miles to the south, to the island of Cauda. Here the sailors pulled in the small boat that was towed behind larger ships, lest they lose it or it be driven against the ship and cause damage.

As the storm grew worse, the crew did all it could to keep the ship afloat. They wrapped ropes (or chains) around the hull so the boat would not come apart, and they took down some of the sails. The second day, they started throwing some of the wheat overboard, and the third day they jettisoned the furnishings. (Note Luke's use of "we" in Acts 27:19.) Because of the storm, they could not see the sun or the stars, so it was impossible to determine their position. The situation seemed hopeless, and it all happened because one man would not listen to God's messenger.

Sometimes we get ourselves into storms for the same reasons: impatience (Acts 27:9), accepting expert advice that is contrary to God's will, following the majority, and trusting "ideal" conditions (Acts 27:13). "He that believeth shall not make haste" (Isa. 28:16). It pays to listen to God's Word.

Paul the Encourager (27:21–44)

"Paul began as a prisoner," said Joseph Parker; "he ended as the captain." Paul "took over" the situation when it was obvious that nobody else knew what to do. A crisis does not make a person; a crisis shows what a person is made of, and it tends to bring true leadership to the fore. Paul gently rebuked the centurion, pilot, and captain for ignoring his warning. Soon they would discover that God had spared all of them only because of Paul.

Consider Paul's four ministries of encouragement to the passengers and crew.

He shared God's Word with them (vv. 22–26). A messenger from the Lord had visited Paul and told him that the ship and cargo would be lost, but that all the passengers would be spared and cast on an island. Once again, the Lord gave him a special word of encouragement at the right time (Acts 18:9–10; 23:11). Today, we are not likely to have visions, but we do have the promises in His Word to encourage us (Isa. 41:10; 43:1–5; Rom. 15:4). It was for Paul's sake that God did this, and it was Paul's faith that God honored. What a testimony he was to the people on that storm-tossed ship!

He warned them (vv. 27–32). During the two weeks they had been at sea, the ship had been driven over five hundred miles off course and was now adrift in the Adrian Sea. (It is now called the Ionian Sea and must not be confused with the Adriatic Sea.) As the crew took soundings, they discovered that the water was getting shallower (from 120 feet to 90 feet), indicating that land was near. From the roar of the waves, it appeared that the ship was headed for the rocks.

In order to keep the prow headed toward shore, some of the crew dropped four anchors from the stern. But others of the crew tried to escape from the ship in the dinghy that had been brought on board (Acts 27:16). This was not only an act of selfishness and revolt on their part, but it was also an act of unbelief. Paul had told everybody God's promise that He would keep all those safe who sailed with him on the voyage (Acts 27:24). For the men to abandon ship was to take their lives in their own hands and threaten the lives of others. Whether the soldiers acted wisely in cutting the boat free, it is difficult to determine, but in an emergency, you take emergency measures.

He set a good example before them (vv. 33–38). What a difference it makes when a person has faith in God! Instead of vainly wishing for a change (Acts 27:29) or selfishly trying to escape (Acts 27:30), Paul got ready for the demands that would come at daybreak. It is not difficult to understand why everyone had fasted those two weeks, but now it was time to eat. Caring for one's health is an important part of the Christian life, and even an apostle must not abuse his body.

Paul took the bread and openly prayed and gave thanks to God. (This is a good example for us to follow when we are eating in public places.) His example encouraged the others to join him, and before long, everybody felt better. There are times when one dedicated believer can change the whole atmosphere of a situation simply by trusting God and making that faith visible.

He rescued them (vv. 39–44). When it was day, the pilot saw where they were and made every effort to get the ship to shore. But it was all futile; the ship was grounded and the waves began to beat the stern to pieces. The only thing the passengers could do was jump into the water and make for land.

The soldiers, of course, were concerned about their prisoners, for if a prisoner escaped, the soldier was held accountable and could be killed. Once again, it was Paul whose presence saved their lives. Just as the Lord promised, all of them made it safely to shore, and not one was lost. I have a feeling that Paul had been sharing the gospel with his fellow passengers and that some of them had trusted in the Lord as a result of this experience. Luke does not give us the details, but would you expect Paul to do otherwise?

Before leaving this exciting section of Acts, we should note some practical lessons that it teaches us. First of all, storms often come when we disobey the will of God. (Jonah is a good example of this truth.) However, it was not Paul who was at fault, but the centurion in charge of the ship. We sometimes suffer because of the unbelief of others.

Second, storms have a way of revealing character. Some of the sailors selfishly tried to escape; others could only hope for the best; but Paul trusted God and obeyed His will.

Third, even the worst storms cannot hide the face of God or hinder the purposes of God. Paul received the word of assurance that they needed, and God overruled so that His servant arrived safely in Rome.

Finally, storms can give us opportunities to serve others and bear witness to Jesus Christ. Paul was the most valuable man on that ship! He knew how to pray, he had faith in God, and he was in touch with the Almighty.

Paul the Helper (28:1–10)

God had brought them to the Isle of Malta (which means "refuge"), where the native people welcomed all 276 of them and did their best to make them comfortable. To the Greeks, anybody who did not speak Greek was a "barbarian." These people proved to be kind and sympathetic. The storm abated, but the weather was cold, so the natives built a fire.

After all he had done for the passengers, Paul could well have requested a throne and insisted that everybody serve him! Instead, he did his share of the work and helped gather fuel for the fire. No task is too small for the servant of God who has "the mind of Christ" (Phil. 2:1–13).

One rainy day, a man accompanied by two women arrived at Northfield, hoping to enroll his daughter in D. L. Moody's school for young women. The three needed help in getting their luggage from the railway depot to the hotel, so the visitor "drafted" a rather common-looking man with a horse and wagon, assuming he was a local cabby. The "cabby" said he was waiting for students, but the visitor ordered him to take them to the hotel. The visitor was shocked when the "cabby" did not charge him, and was even more shocked to discover that the "cabby" was D. L. Moody himself! Moody was a leader because he knew how to be a servant.

The episode of the viper reminds us of Paul's experience in Lystra (Acts 14:6–18). First, the people thought that Justice, one of their goddesses, had caught up with this notorious prisoner who was supposed to drown in the sea but had somehow escaped. (If only they knew!) When Paul failed to swell up and die, they decided that he must be a god himself! Such are the reasonings of people who judge by appearances.

Was the viper a weapon of Satan to get Paul out of the way? The storm did not drown him, but a hidden trap might catch him. As Christians, we must constantly be alert, for either the serpent or the lion will attack us (2 Cor. 11:3; 1 Peter 5:8). We should also keep in mind that we are being watched, and we must use every opportunity to magnify Christ.

Paul and the party remained on Malta for three months, and, thanks to Paul, they were treated graciously and sent on their way with generous gifts. Since they had lost everything in the shipwreck, the passengers were grateful to have their needs supplied. Luke says nothing about evangelism on the island, but we must believe that Paul shared the gospel with anybody who would listen. His miraculous deliverance from the sea and from the viper, and his power to heal, would certainly arouse the interest of the people, and Paul would want to give the glory to the Lord (Matt. 5:16).

Paul the Preacher (28:11–31)

Whether all 276 people boarded the Alexandrian ship, or just Julius and his guard and prisoners, we do not know; nor do we know why Luke took such care to identify the ship. In Greek mythology, "Castor and Pollux" were the names of the twin sons of Zeus and were revered as the protectors of men on the sea. Many Roman ships bore their image as a plea for safety. It was eighty miles to Syracuse, another seventy to Rhegium, and about 180 to Puteoli, the port of Naples. This time the "south wind" was exactly what they needed in order to make the voyage quickly and safely.

In Puteoli, Paul and his friends, along with Julius and the other prisoners and guards, were urged by the believers to stay and rest for a week, and Julius gave his consent. The centurion knew that Paul had saved their lives, and perhaps he was even getting interested in what these Christians had to offer.

Word had gotten to Rome that Paul was coming; how, we do not know. Perhaps Aristarchus did not go with Paul and Luke on the grain ship, but made his way instead overland to Rome where he met Paul's friends. (At least twenty-six are named in Rom. 16.) Or, perhaps a delegation from Caesarea headed for Rome as soon as Paul appealed to Caesar.

Julius and his party took the famous Appian Way and traveled 125 miles from Puteoli to Rome. The first group of Christians met Paul at the Forum of Appius, about forty-three miles from Rome, and the second group met him at the Three Taverns, ten miles nearer to the city. (Some saints will go farther than others!) Paul was greatly encouraged when he met them, as well he might be. Now he could fellowship with the saints and they could be a blessing to one another.

Paul's greatest concern was his witness to the Jews in Rome. They had received no special word about Paul, but they did know that the "Christian sect" was being spoken against in many places (Acts 28:21–22). When you read Paul's letter to the Romans, you get the impression that the Jews in Rome had misunderstood some of his teachings (Rom. 3:8; 14:1ff.). The apostle made it clear that his appeal to Caesar must not be interpreted as an indictment against his nation. Actually, he was a prisoner *on behalf of* his nation and "the hope of Israel."

On the day appointed, Paul spent "from morning till evening" explaining the Scriptures and revealing Christ in the law and the prophets. He had "dialogued" this way with the Jews in one synagogue after another, and now he was sharing the Word with the leaders of many synagogues in Rome.

The result? Some were persuaded and some were not. When the Jewish leaders left Paul's house, they were still arguing among themselves! But Paul had faithfully given his witness to the Jews in Rome, and now he would turn to the Gentiles.

Paul quoted the words of Isaiah to these men (Isa. 6:9–10), words that described their tragic spiritual condition. Jesus had used this passage in connection with His parables of the kingdom (Matt. 13:13–15; Mark 4:12; Luke 8:10). The apostle John in his gospel applied them to Israel (John 12:39–40), and Paul quoted them in his Roman epistle (Rom. 11:7–8). It is one thing to *listen* and quite something else to *hear,* and there is a great difference between *seeing* and *perceiving.* If anybody should have possessed spiritual understanding, it was these Jewish leaders, but their hearts were dull and hard. Too often those who enjoy the most spiritual privileges are not ready when they must make spiritual decisions.

But their unbelief did not put an end to Paul's ministry of the gospel! He announced that the gospel some of the Jews had rejected would be proclaimed to the Gentiles, "and they will hear it!" This is one of the major themes of Acts, how the gospel moved from the Jews to the Gentiles and from Jerusalem to Rome. Without the book of Acts, we would turn in the New Testament from the gospel of John to Romans and ask, "How did the gospel ever get from the Jews in Jerusalem to the Gentiles in Rome?"

Paul kept "open house" and received anybody who wanted to discuss the things of the kingdom of God. He was chained to a guard who was relieved every six hours, but who was forced to listen as Paul preached and taught and prayed. No wonder some of them were saved (Phil. 1:12–14; 4:22)!

During these two years in Rome, Paul wrote Philippians, Ephesians, Colossians, and Philemon. He expected to be released (Phil. 1:23–27; 2:24; Philem. 22), and most students agree that he was. During this time, he had Timothy with him (Phil. 1:1; 2:19; Col. 1:1), as well as John Mark, Luke, Aristarchus, Epaphras, Justus, and Demas (Col. 4:10–14; Philem. 24). He also met Philemon's runaway slave Onesimus and led him to faith in Christ (Philem. 10–21). Epaphroditus brought a gift to him from the Philippian church and almost died ministering to Paul (Phil. 2:25–30; 4:18). Tychicus was Paul's "mailman" who delivered Ephesians (Eph. 6:21), Colossians, and Philemon (Col. 4:7–9).

Dr. Luke ended his book before Paul's case had been heard, so he could not give us the results of the trial. We have every reason to believe that Paul was indeed released and that he resumed his ministry, probably traveling as far as Spain (Rom. 15:24, 28). During this period (AD 63–66/67), he wrote letters to Timothy and Titus. He left Titus in Crete (Titus 1:5), Trophimus sick in Miletus (2 Tim. 4:20), and Timothy in Ephesus (1 Tim. 1:3). He planned to meet some of his helpers at Nicopolis (Titus 3:12–13) after he had visited some of the churches he had established. Wherever he went, he sought to bring Jews and Gentiles to faith in Jesus Christ.

He was arrested again, probably about the year 67, and this time his situation was changed drastically. He did not live in a house, but was chained in a prison and treated like a criminal (2 Tim. 1:16; 2:9). Winter was coming, and he asked Timothy to bring him his cloak (2 Tim. 4:13). But the saddest thing about this second imprisonment was his being forsaken by the believers in Rome (2 Tim. 4:16–17). The great apostle to the Gentiles was abandoned by the very people he came to assist.

Even Demas forsook him, and only Luke was with him (2 Tim. 4:10–11). The family of Onesiphorus ministered to his needs (2 Tim. 1:16–18), but he longed for Timothy and Mark to come to be at his side (2 Tim. 1:4; 4:9, 21). Paul knew that the end was coming (2 Tim. 4:6–8). Tradition tells us that he was beheaded at Rome in AD 67/68.

Luke did not write his book simply to record ancient history. He wrote to encourage the church in every age to be faithful to the Lord and carry the gospel to the ends of the earth. "What was begun with so much heroism ought to be continued with ardent zeal," said Charles Spurgeon, "since we are assured that the same Lord is mighty still to carry on His heavenly designs."

"Lo, I am with you always!"

ROMANS

OUTLINE

Key theme: The righteousness of God
Key verse: Romans 1:17

I. INTRODUCTION (1:1–17)

II. SIN—RIGHTEOUSNESS DEMANDED (1:18—3:20)
A. The Gentiles guilty—1:18–32
B. The Jews guilty—2:1–3:8
C. The whole world guilty—3:9–20

III. SALVATION—RIGHTEOUSNESS DECLARED (3:21—5:21)
A. Justification stated—3:21–31
B. Justification illustrated in Abraham—4
C. Justification explained in Adam—5

IV. SANCTIFICATION—RIGHTEOUSNESS DEFENDED (6—8)
A. Victory—the flesh—6
B. Liberty—the Law—7
C. Security—the Spirit—8

V. SOVEREIGNTY—RIGHTEOUSNESS DECLINED (9—11)
A. Israel's past riches—9
B. Israel's present rejection—10
C. Israel's future restoration—11

VI. SERVICE—RIGHTEOUSNESS DEMONSTRATED (12:1—15:7)
A. In the church body—12
B. In society—13
C. Toward the weaker believer—14:1—15:7

VII. CONCLUSION (15:8—16:27)

CONTENTS

CHAPTER ONE
Romans 1:1–17
READY FOR ROME

On May 24, 1738, a discouraged missionary went "very unwillingly" to a religious meeting in London. There a miracle took place. "About a quarter before nine," he wrote in his journal, "I felt my heart strangely warmed. I felt I did trust in Christ, Christ alone, for salvation; and an assurance was given me that He had taken away my sins, even mine, and saved me from the law of sin and death."

That missionary was John Wesley. The message he heard that evening was the preface to Martin Luther's commentary on Romans. Just a few months before, John Wesley had written in his journal: "I went to America to convert the Indians; but Oh! who shall convert me?" That evening in Aldersgate Street, his question was answered. And the result was the great Wesleyan Revival that swept England and transformed the nation.

Paul's epistle to the Romans is still transforming people's lives, just the way it transformed Martin Luther and John Wesley. The one Scripture above all others that brought Luther out of mere religion into the joy of salvation by grace, through faith, was Romans 1:17: "The just shall live by faith." The Protestant Reformation and the Wesleyan Revival were both the fruit of this wonderful letter written by Paul from Corinth about the year AD 56. The letter was carried to the Christians at Rome by one of the deaconesses of the church at Cenchrea, Sister Phebe (Rom. 16:1).

Imagine! You and I can read and study the same inspired letter that brought life and power to Luther and Wesley! And the same Holy Spirit who taught them can teach us! You and I can experience revival in our hearts, homes, and churches if the message of this letter grips us as it has gripped men of faith in centuries past.

In the opening verses of the letter, Paul introduces himself to the believers in Rome. Some of them must have known him personally, since he greets them in the final chapter, but many of them he had never met. So, in these first seventeen verses, Paul seeks to link himself to his Roman readers in three ways.

He Presented His Credentials (1:1–7)

In ancient days, the writer of a letter always opened with his name. But there would be many men named Paul in that day, so the writer had to further identify himself and convince the readers that he had a right to send the letter. What were Paul's credentials?

He was a servant of Jesus Christ (v. 1a). The word Paul used for *servant* would be meaningful to the Romans, because it is the word *slave*. There were an estimated sixty million slaves in the Roman Empire, and a slave was looked on as a piece of property, not a person. In loving devotion, Paul had enslaved himself to Christ, to be His servant and obey His will.

He was an apostle (v. 1b). This word means "one who is sent by authority with a commission." It was applied in that day to the representatives of the emperor or the emissaries of a king. One of the requirements for an apostle was the experience of seeing the risen Christ (1 Cor. 9:1–2). Paul saw Christ when he was on the road to Damascus (Acts 9:1–9), and it was then that Christ called him to be His apostle to the Gentiles. Paul received from Christ divine revelations that he was to share with the churches.

He was a preacher of the gospel (vv. 1c–4). When he was a Jewish rabbi, Paul was separated as a Pharisee to the laws and traditions of the Jews. But when he yielded to Christ, he was separated to the gospel and its ministry. *Gospel* means "the good news." It is the message that Christ died for our sins, was buried and rose again, and now is able to save all who trust Him (1 Cor. 15:1–4). It is "the gospel of God" (Rom. 1:1) because it originates with God; it was not invented by man. It is "the gospel of Christ" (Rom. 1:16) because it centers in Christ, the Savior. Paul also calls it "the gospel of his Son" (Rom. 1:9), which indicates that *Jesus Christ is God!* In Romans 16:25–26, Paul called it "my gospel." By this he meant the special emphasis he gave in his ministry to the doctrine of the church and the place of the Gentiles in the plan of God.

The gospel is not a new message; it was promised in the Old Testament, beginning in Genesis 3:15. The prophet Isaiah certainly preached the gospel in passages such as Isaiah 1:18, and chapters 53 and 55. The salvation we enjoy today was promised by the prophets, though they did not fully understand all that they were preaching and writing (1 Peter 1:10–12).

Jesus Christ is the center of the gospel message. Paul identified Him as a man, a Jew, and the Son of God. He was born of a virgin (Isa. 7:14; Matt. 1:18–25) into the family of David, which gave Him the right to David's throne. He died for the sins of the world, and then was raised from the dead. It is this miraculous event of substitutionary death and victorious resurrection that constitutes the gospel, and it was this gospel that Paul preached.

He was a missionary to the Gentiles (vv. 5–7). *Missionary* is the Latin form of "apostle—one who is sent." There were probably several assemblies of believers in Rome and not just one church, since in Romans 16 Paul greets a number of "home church" groups (Rom. 16:5, 10–11, 14). We do not know for certain how these churches began, but it is likely that believers from Rome who were at Pentecost established the assemblies on their return to Rome (Acts 2:10). There were both Jews and Gentiles in these fellowships, because Paul addresses both in this letter. (Jews: Rom. 2:17–29; 4:1; 7:1. Gentiles: Rom. 1:13; 11:13–24; 15:15–21.) The churches in Rome were not founded by Peter or any other apostle. If they had been, Paul would not have planned to visit Rome, because his policy was to minister only where no other apostle had gone (Rom. 15:20–21).

Note the repetition of the word *called:* Paul was called to be an apostle; the believers were the called of Jesus Christ; and they were also called saints. (Not "to be" saints; they already were saints! A saint is a set-apart one, and the person who trusts Jesus Christ is set apart and is a saint.) Salvation is not something that we do for God; it is God who calls us in His grace (2 Thess. 2:13–14). When you trust Christ, you are saved by His grace and you experience His peace.

Paul's special commission was to take the gospel to the Gentiles (the word *nations* means Gentiles), and this is why he was planning to go to Rome, the very capital of the empire. He was a preacher of the gospel, and the gospel was for all nations. In fact, Paul was anxious to go to Spain with the message of Christ (Rom. 15:28).

Having presented his credentials, Paul proceeded to forge a second link between himself and the believers in Rome.

He Expressed His Concern (1:8–15)

We can well understand Paul's concern for the churches that *he* founded, but why would he be concerned about the believers at Rome? He was unknown to many of them, yet he wanted to assure them that he was deeply concerned about their welfare. Note the evidences of Paul's concern.

He was thankful for them (v. 8). "The whole world"—meaning the whole Roman Empire—knew of the faith of the Christians at Rome. Travel was relatively common in that day and "all roads led to Rome." It is no wonder that the testimony of the church spread abroad, and this growing witness made Paul's ministry easier as he went from place to place and was able to point to this testimony going out from the heart of the Roman Empire.

He prayed for them (vv. 9–10). They did not know of Paul's prayer support, but the Lord knew about it and honored it. (I wonder how many of us know the people who are praying for us?) One of the burdens of Paul's prayer was that God would permit him to visit Rome and minister to the churches there. He would have visited them sooner, but his missionary work had kept him busy (Rom. 15:15–33). He was about to leave Corinth for Jerusalem to deliver the special offering received from the Gentile churches for the poor Jewish saints. He hoped he would be able to travel from Jerusalem to Rome, and then on to Spain, and he was hoping for a prosperous journey.

Actually, Paul had a very perilous journey, and he arrived in Rome a prisoner as well as a preacher. In Jerusalem he was arrested in the temple, falsely accused by the Jewish authorities, and eventually sent to Rome as the emperor's prisoner to be tried before Caesar. When Paul wrote this letter, he had no idea that he would go through imprisonment and even shipwreck before arriving in Rome! At the close of the letter (Rom. 15:30–33), he asked the believers in Rome to pray for him as he contemplated this trip, and it is a good thing that they did pray!

He loved them (vv. 11–12). "I long to see you!" This is the pastor's heart in Paul the great missionary. Some of the saints in Rome were very dear to Paul, such as Priscilla and Aquila (Rom. 16:3–4), who risked their lives for him, "the beloved Persis" (Rom. 16:12), and others who had labored and suffered with Paul. But he also loved the believers that he did not know, and he longed to be able to share some spiritual gift with them. He was looking forward to a time of mutual blessing in the love of Christ.

He was in debt to them (vv. 13–14). As the apostle to the Gentiles, Paul had an obligation to minister in Rome. He would have fulfilled that obligation sooner, but his other labors had hindered him. Sometimes Paul was hindered because of the work of Satan (1 Thess. 2:17–20), but in this case he was hindered because of the work of the Lord. There was so much to do in Asia Minor and Greece that he could not immediately spare time for Rome. But Paul had to pay his debt; he was under orders from the Lord.

The Greeks considered every non-Greek a barbarian. Steeped in centuries of philosophy, the Greeks saw themselves as wise and everyone else as foolish. But Paul felt an obligation to *all* men, just as we need to feel a burden for the whole world. Paul could not be free from his debt until he had told as many people as possible the good news of salvation in Christ.

He was eager to visit them (v. 15). Two different Greek words are translated "ready" in the King James Version. One means "prepared," as in Acts 21:13. "I am ready ... to die at Jerusalem for the name of the Lord Jesus." The other one, used in Romans 1:15, means "eager, with a ready mind." Paul was not eager to die, though he was prepared to die. But he was eager to visit Rome that he might minister to the believers there. It was not the eagerness of a sightseer, but the eagerness of a soul-winner.

After reading these five evidences of Paul's concern for the Christians at Rome, these saints could not but give thanks to God for the apostle Paul and his burden to come and minister to them. Actually, the epistle to the Romans, in which Paul explained the gospel he preached, was his letter of introduction that prepared the believers for his visit. No doubt the false teachers had already gotten to Rome and were seeking to poison the Christians against Paul (see Rom. 3:8). Some would accuse him of being anti-law; others would say he was a traitor to the Jewish nation. Still others would twist his teaching about grace and try to prove that he taught loose living. No wonder Paul was eager to get to Rome! He wanted to share with them the fullness of the gospel of Christ.

But would the gospel of Christ work in the great city of Rome as it had in other places? Would Paul succeed there, or would he fail? The apostle no doubt felt these objections and raised these questions in his own mind, which is why he forged a third link between himself and his readers.

He Affirmed His Confidence (1:16–17)

What a testimony: "I am debtor! I am eager! I am not ashamed!" Why would Paul even be tempted to be ashamed of the gospel as he contemplated his trip to Rome? For one thing, the gospel was identified with a poor Jewish carpenter who was crucified. The Romans had no special appreciation for the Jews, and crucifixion was the lowest form of execution given a criminal. Why put your faith in a Jew who was crucified?

Rome was a proud city, and the gospel came from Jerusalem, the capital city of one of the little nations that Rome had conquered. The Christians in that day were not among the elite of society; they were common people and even slaves. Rome had known many great philosophers and philosophies; why pay any attention to a fable about a Jew who arose from the dead (1 Cor. 1:18–25)? Christians looked on each other as brothers and sisters, all one in Christ, which went against the grain of Roman pride and dignity. To think of a little Jewish tentmaker, going to Rome to preach such a message, is almost humorous.

But Paul was not ashamed of the gospel. He had confidence in his message, and he gave us several reasons that explain why he was not ashamed.

The origin of the gospel: it is the gospel of Christ (v. 16a). Any message that was handed down from Caesar would immediately get the attention of the Romans. But the message of the gospel is from and about the very Son of God! In his opening sentence, Paul called this message "the gospel of God" (Rom. 1:1). How could Paul be ashamed of such a message, when it came from God and centered in His Son, Jesus Christ?

During my years in high school, I was chosen to be an office monitor. The other hall monitors sat at various stations around the building, but I was privileged to sit right outside the door of the main high school office. I was entrusted with important messages that I had to deliver to different teachers and staff members, and on occasion even to other schools. Believe me, it was fun to walk into a classroom and even interrupt a lesson! No teacher ever scolded me, because all of them knew I carried messages from the principal. I never had to be afraid or ashamed, because I knew where my messages came from.

The operation of the gospel: it is the power of God (v. 16b). Why be ashamed of power? Power is the one thing that Rome boasted of the most. Greece might have its philosophy, but Rome had its power. The fear of Rome hovered over the empire like a cloud. Were they not the conquerors? Were not the Roman legions stationed all over the known world? But with all of her military power, Rome was still a weak nation. The philosopher Seneca called the city of Rome "a cesspool of iniquity"; and the writer Juvenal called it a "filthy sewer into which the dregs of the empire flood."

No wonder Paul was not ashamed: he was taking to sinful Rome the one message that had the power to change men's lives! He had seen the gospel work in other wicked cities, such as Corinth and Ephesus, and he was confident that it would work in Rome. It had transformed his own life, and he knew it could transform the lives of others. There was a third reason why Paul was not ashamed.

The outcome of the gospel: it is the power of God unto salvation (v. 16c). That word *salvation* carried tremendous meaning in Paul's day. Its basic meaning is "deliverance," and it was applied to personal and national deliverance. The emperor was looked on as a savior, as was the physician who healed you of illness. The gospel delivers sinners from the penalty and power of sin. "Salvation" is a major theme in this letter; salvation is the great need of the human race (see Rom. 10:1, 9–10). If men and women are to be saved, it must be through faith in Jesus Christ as proclaimed in the gospel.

The outreach of the gospel: "to everyone that believeth" (vv. 16d–17). This was not an exclusive message for either the Jew or the Gentile; it was for all men, *because all men need to be saved.* "Go ye into all the world and preach the Gospel," was Christ's commission (Mark 16:15). "To the Jew first" does not suggest that the Jew is better than the Gentile, for there is "no difference" in condemnation or in salvation (Rom. 2:6–11; 10:9–13). The gospel came "to the Jew first" in the ministry of Jesus Christ (Matt. 10:5–7) and the apostles (Acts 3:26). How marvelous it is to have a message of power that can be taken to *all* people!

God does not ask men to *behave* in order to be saved, but to *believe.* It is faith in Christ that saves the sinner. Eternal life in Christ is one gift that is suitable for all people, no matter what their need may be or what their station in life.

Romans 1:17 is the key verse of the letter. In it Paul announces the theme: "the righteousness of God." The word *righteousness* is used in one way or another over sixty times in this letter (*righteous, just,* and *justified*). God's righteousness is revealed in the gospel; for in the death of Christ, God revealed His righteousness by punishing sin; and in the resurrection of Christ, He revealed His righteousness by making salvation available to the believing sinner. The problem "How can a holy God ever forgive sinners and still be holy?" is answered in the gospel. Through the death and resurrection of Christ, God is seen to be "both just and justifier" (Rom. 3:26).

The gospel reveals a righteousness that is *by faith.* In the Old Testament, righteousness was *by works,* but sinners soon discovered they could not obey God's law and meet His righteous demands. Here Paul refers to Habakkuk 2:4: "The just shall live by his faith." This verse is quoted three times in the New Testament: Romans 1:17; Galatians 3:11; and Hebrews 10:38.

Romans explains "the just"; Galatians explains "shall live"; and Hebrews explains "by faith." There are more than sixty references to faith or unbelief in Romans.

When you study Romans, you walk into a courtroom. First, Paul called Jews and Gentiles to the stand and found both guilty before God. Then he explained God's marvelous way of salvation—justification by faith. At this point, he answered his accusers and defended God's salvation. "This plan of salvation will encourage people to sin!" they cry. "It is against the very law of God!" But Paul refuted them, and in so doing explained how the Christian can experience victory, liberty, and security.

Chapters 9—11 are not a parenthesis or a detour. There were Jewish believers in the Roman assemblies and they would naturally ask, "What about Israel? How does God's righteousness relate to them in this new age of the church?" In these three chapters, Paul gave a complete history of Israel, past, present, and future.

Then he concluded with the practical outworking of God's righteousness in the life of the believer. This begins with dedication to God (Rom. 12:1–2), continues with ministry in the church (Rom. 12:3–21), and then obedience to the government (Rom. 13:1–14). He also told Jews and Gentiles, strong and weak, how to live together in harmony and joy. In the closing section (Rom. 15:14–16:27), Paul explained his plans and greeted his friends.

When you sum it all up, the book of Romans is saying to us—*"Be right!"* Be right with God, with yourself, and with others! The righteousness of God received by faith makes it possible for us to live right lives. Rome needed this message, and we need it today: *Be right!*

CHAPTER TWO
Romans 1:18—3:20
WHEN GOD GIVES UP

Hear ye! Hear ye! Court is now in session!" Paul could have used those awesome words at this point in his letter, because Romans 1:18 is the door that leads us into God's courtroom. The theme of Romans is the righteousness of God, but Paul had to begin with the unrighteousness of man. Until man knows he is a sinner, he cannot appreciate the gracious salvation God offers in Jesus Christ. Paul followed the basic Bible pattern: first law and condemnation, then grace and salvation.

In this section, God makes three declarations that together prove that all men are sinners and need Jesus Christ.

The Gentile World Is Guilty! (1:18–32)
The picture Paul paints here is an ugly one. I confess that there are some neighborhoods that I dislike driving through, and I avoid them if I can. My avoiding

them does not change them or eliminate them. God's description of sinners is not a pretty one, but we cannot avoid it. This section does not teach evolution (that man started low and climbed high), but *devolution:* he started high and, because of sin, sank lower than the beasts. Four stages mark man's tragic devolution.

Intelligence (vv. 18–20). Human history began with man knowing God. Human history is not the story of a beast that worshipped idols, and then evolved into a man worshipping one God. Human history is just the opposite: man began knowing God, but turned from the truth and rejected God. God revealed Himself to man through creation, the things that He made. From the world around him, man knew that there was a God who had the wisdom to plan and the power to create. Man realized too that this Creator was eternal … "His eternal power and Godhead" (Rom. 1:20), since God could not be created if He is the Creator. These facts about God are not hidden in creation; they are "clearly seen" (Rom. 1:20). "The heavens declare the glory of God, and the firmament showeth his handiwork" (Ps. 19:1).

The word translated "hold" in Rom. 1:18 can also be translated "hold down, suppress." Men knew the truth about God, but they did not allow this truth to work in their lives. They suppressed it in order that they might live their own lives and not be convicted by God's truth. The result, of course, was refusing the truth (Rom. 1:21–22), and then turning the truth into a lie (Rom. 1:25). Finally, man so abandoned the truth that he became like a beast in his thinking and in his living.

Ignorance (vv. 21–23). Man knew God; this is clear. But man did not *want* to know God or honor Him as God. Instead of being thankful for all that God had given him, man refused to thank God or give Him the glory He deserves. Man was willing to use God's gifts, but he was not willing to worship and praise God for His gifts. The result was an empty mind and a darkened heart. Man the worshipper became man the philosopher, but his empty wisdom only revealed his foolishness. Paul summarized all of Greek history in one dramatic statement: "the times of this ignorance" (Acts 17:30). First Corinthians 1:18–31 is worth reading at this point.

Having held down God's truth and refusing to acknowledge God's glory, man was left without a god, and man is so constituted that he must worship something. If he will not worship the true God, he will worship a false god, *even if he has to manufacture it himself!* This fact about man accounts for his propensity to idolatry. Man exchanged the glory of the true God for substitute gods that he himself made. He exchanged glory for shame, incorruption for corruption, truth for lies.

Note that first on the list of false gods is *man.* This fulfilled Satan's purpose when he told Eve, "You will be like God" (Gen. 3:5 NASB). "Glory to man in the highest!" Satan encouraged man to say. Instead of man being made in God's image, man made gods in his own image—and then descended so low as to worship birds, beasts, and bugs!

Indulgence (vv. 24–27). From idolatry to immorality is just one short step. If man is his own god, then he can do whatever he pleases and fulfill his desires without fear of judgment. We reach the climax of man's battle with God's truth when man exchanges the truth of God for "the lie" and abandons truth completely. "The lie" is that man is his own god, and he should worship and serve himself and not the Creator. It was "the lie" Satan used in the garden to lead Eve into sin: "Ye shall be as God!" Satan has always wanted the worship that belongs only to God (Isa. 14:12–15; Matt. 4:8–10), and in idolatry, he receives that worship (1 Cor. 10:19–21).

The result of this self-deification was self-indulgence, and here Paul mentions a vile sin that was rampant in that day and has become increasingly prevalent in our own day: homosexuality. This sin is repeatedly condemned in Scripture (Gen. 18:20ff.; 1 Cor. 6:9–10; Jude 7). Paul characterizes it as "vile" and "unnatural," as well as "against nature." Not only were the men guilty, but "even the women."

Because of their sin "God gave them up" (Rom. 1:24, 26), which means that He permitted them to go on in their sins and reap the sad consequences. They received "in their own persons the due penalty of their error" (Rom. 1:27 NASB). This is the meaning of Romans 1:18: "The wrath of God is being revealed from heaven" (literal translation). God revealed His wrath, not by sending fire from heaven, but by abandoning sinful men to their lustful ways. But there was one more stage.

Impenitence (vv. 28–32). When man began to feel the tragic consequences of his sins, you would think he would repent and seek God, but just the opposite was true. Because he was abandoned by God, he could only become worse. Man did not even want to retain God in his knowledge! So, "God gave them over" this time to a "depraved mind" (Rom. 1:28 NASB), which means a mind that cannot form right judgments. They now abandoned themselves to sin. Paul names twenty-four specific sins, all of which are with us today. (For other lists, see Mark 7:20–23; Gal. 5:19–21; 1 Tim. 1:9–10; 2 Tim. 3:2–5.)

But the worst is yet to come. Men not only committed these sins in open defiance of God, but encouraged others and applauded them when they sinned. How far man fell! He began glorifying God but ended exchanging that glory for idols. He began knowing God but ended refusing to keep the knowledge of God in his mind and heart. He began as the highest of God's creatures, made in the image of God, but he ended lower than the beasts and insects, because he worshiped them as his gods. The verdict? "They are without excuse" (Rom. 1:20).

This portion of Scripture gives ample proof that the heathen are lost. Dan Crawford, British missionary to Africa, said: "The heathen are sinning against a flood of light." There is a desperate need for us to carry the gospel to all men, for this is the only way they can be saved.

The Jewish World Is Guilty! (2:1—3:8)

Bible scholars do not agree on whom Paul was addressing in Romans 2:1–16. Some think he was dealing with the moral pagan who did not commit the sins named in Romans 1:18–32, but who sought to live a moral life. But it seems to me that Paul was addressing his Jewish readers in this section. To begin with, his discussion of the law in Romans 2:12–16 would have been more meaningful to a Jew than to a Gentile. And in Romans 2:17, he openly addressed his reader as "a Jew." This would be a strange form of address if in the first half of the chapter he were addressing Gentiles.

It would not be an easy task to find the Jews guilty, since disobedience to God was one sin they did not want to confess. The Old Testament prophets were persecuted for indicting Israel for her sins, and Jesus was crucified for the same reason. Paul summoned four witnesses to prove the guilt of the Jewish nation.

The Gentiles (2:1–3). Certainly the Jews would applaud Paul's condemnation of the Gentiles in Romans 1:18–32. In fact, Jewish national and religious pride encouraged them to despise the "Gentile dogs" and have nothing to do with them. Paul used this judgmental attitude to prove the guilt of the Jews, for the very things they condemned in the Gentiles, they themselves were practicing! They thought that they were free from judgment because they were God's chosen people. But Paul affirmed that God's election of the Jews made their responsibility and accountability even greater.

God's judgment is according to truth. He does not have one standard for the Jews and another for the Gentiles. One who reads the list of sins in Romans 1:29–32 cannot escape the fact that each person is guilty of at least one of them. There are "sins of the flesh and of the spirit" (2 Cor. 7:1); there are "prodigal sons" and "elder brothers" (Luke 15:11–32). In condemning the Gentiles for their sins, the Jews were really condemning themselves. As the old saying puts it, "When you point your finger at somebody else, the other three are pointing at you."

God's blessing (2:4–11). Instead of giving the Jews special treatment from God, the blessings they received from Him gave them greater responsibility to obey Him and glorify Him. In His goodness, God had given Israel great material and spiritual riches: a wonderful land, a righteous law, a temple and priesthood, God's providential care, and many more blessings. God had patiently endured Israel's many sins and rebellions, and had even sent them His Son to be their Messiah. Even after Israel crucified Christ, God gave the nation nearly forty more years of grace and withheld His judgment. It is not the judgment of

God that leads men to repentance, but the goodness of God—but Israel did not repent.

In Romans 2:6–11, Paul was not teaching salvation by character or good deeds. He was explaining another basic principle of God's judgment: God judges according to deeds, just as He judges according to truth. Paul was dealing here with the consistent actions of a person's life, the total impact of his character and conduct. For example, David committed some terrible sins, but the total emphasis of his life was obedience to God. Judas confessed his sin and supplied the money for buying a cemetery for strangers, yet the total emphasis of his life was disobedience and unbelief.

True saving faith results in obedience and godly living, even though there may be occasional falls. When God measured the deeds of the Jews, He found them to be as wicked as those of the Gentiles. The fact that the Jews occasionally celebrated a feast or even regularly honored the Sabbath day did not change the fact that their consistent daily life was one of disobedience to God. God's blessings did not lead them to repentance.

God's law (1:12–24). Paul's statement in Romans 2:11, "For there is no respect of persons with God," would shock the Jew, for he considered himself deserving of special treatment because he was chosen by God. But Paul explained that the Jewish law only made the guilt of Israel that much greater! God did not give the law to the Gentiles, so they would not be judged by the law. Actually, the Gentiles had "the work of the law written in their hearts" (Rom. 2:15). Wherever you go, you find people with an inner sense of right and wrong, and this inner judge, the Bible calls "conscience." You find among all cultures a sense of sin, a fear of judgment, and an attempt to atone for sins and appease whatever gods are feared.

The Jew boasted in the law. He was different from his pagan neighbors who worshipped idols! But Paul made it clear that it was not the *possession* of the law that counted, but the *practice* of the law. The Jews looked on the Gentiles as blind, in the dark, foolish, immature, and ignorant! But if God found the "deprived" Gentiles guilty, how much more guilty were the "privileged" Jews! God not only judges according to truth (Rom. 2:2), and according to men's deeds (Rom. 2:6), but He also judges "the secrets of men" (Rom. 2:16). He sees what is in the heart!

The Jewish people had a religion of outward action, not inward attitude. They may have been moral on the outside, but what about the heart? Our Lord's indictment of the Pharisees in Matthew 23 illustrates the principle perfectly. God not only sees the deeds but He also sees the "thoughts and intents of the heart" (Heb. 4:12). It is possible for a Jew to be guilty of theft, adultery, and idolatry (Rom. 2:21–22) even if no one saw him commit these sins outwardly. In the Sermon on the Mount we are told that such sins can be committed in the heart.

Instead of glorifying God among the Gentiles, the Jews were dishonoring God, and Paul quoted Isaiah 52:5 to prove his point. The pagan Gentiles had daily contact with the Jews in business and other activities, and they were not fooled by the Jews' devotion to the law. The very law that the Jews claimed to obey only indicted them!

Circumcision (2:25–29). This was the great mark of the covenant, and it had its beginning with Abraham, the father of the Jewish nation (Gen. 17). To the Jews, the Gentiles were "uncircumcised dogs." The tragedy is that the Jews depended on this physical mark instead of the spiritual reality it represented (Deut. 10:16; Jer. 9:26; Ezek. 44:9). A true Jew is one who has had an inward spiritual experience in the heart, and not merely an outward physical operation. People today make this same mistake with reference to baptism or the Lord's Supper, or even church membership.

God judges according to "the secrets of the heart" (Rom. 2:16), so that He is not impressed with mere outward formalities. An obedient Gentile with no circumcision would be more acceptable than a disobedient Jew with circumcision. In fact, a disobedient Jew turns his circumcision into uncircumcision in God's sight, for God looks at the heart. The Jews praised each other for their obedience to the law, but the important thing is the "praise of God" and not the praise of men (Rom. 2:29). When you recall that the name "Jew" comes from "Judah," which means "praise," this statement takes on new meaning (Gen. 29:35; 49:8).

Paul's summation (3:1–8). All of Paul's four witnesses agreed: the Jews were guilty before God. In Romans 3:1–8, Paul summed up the argument and refuted those Jews who tried to debate with him. They raised three questions: (1) "What advantage is it to be a Jew?" Reply: Every advantage, especially possessing the Word of God; (2) "Will Jewish unbelief cancel God's faithfulness?" Reply: Absolutely not—it establishes it; (3) "If our sin commends his righteousness, how can he judge us?" Reply: We do not do evil that good may come of it. God judges the world righteously.

The Whole World Is Guilty! (3:9–20)

The third declaration was obvious, for Paul had already proved (charged) both Jews and Gentiles to be guilty before God. Next he declared that all men were sinners, and proved it with several quotations from the Old Testament. Note the repetition of the words *none* and *all*, which in themselves assert the universality of human guilt.

His first quotation was from Psalm 14:1–3. This psalm begins with, "The fool hath said in his heart, 'There is no God.'" The words "there is" are in italics, meaning they were added by the translators, so you can read the sentence, "The fool hath said in his heart, 'No, God!'" This parallels the description of man's devolution given in Romans 1:18–32, for it all started with man saying no to God.

These verses indicate that the whole of man's inner being is controlled by sin: his mind ("none that understandeth"), his heart ("none that seeketh after God"), and his will ("none that doeth good"). Measured by God's perfect righteousness, no human being is sinless. No sinner seeks after God. Therefore, God must seek the sinner (Gen. 3:8–10; Luke 19:10). Man has gone astray and has become unprofitable both to himself and to God. Our Lord's parables in Luke 15 illustrate this perfectly.

In Romans 3:13–18, Paul gave us an X-ray study of the lost sinner, from head to foot. His quotations are as follows: verse 13a—Psalm 5:9; verse 13b—Psalm 140:3; verse 14—Psalm 10:7; verses 15–17—Isaiah 59:7–8; verse 18—Psalm 36:1. These verses need to be read in their contexts for the full impact.

Romans 3:13–14 emphasize human speech—the throat, tongue, lips, and mouth. The connection between words and character is seen in Matthew 12:34: "For out of the abundance of the heart the mouth speaketh." The sinner is spiritually dead by nature (Eph. 2:1–3), therefore only death can come out of his mouth. The condemned mouth can become a converted mouth and acknowledge that "Jesus Christ is Lord" (Rom. 10:9–10). "For by thy words thou shalt be justified, and by thy words thou shalt be condemned" (Matt. 12:37).

In Romans 3:15–16, Paul pictured the sinner's feet. Just as his words are deceitful, so his ways are destructive. The Christians' feet are shod with the gospel of peace (Eph. 6:15), but the lost sinner brings death, destruction, and misery wherever he goes. These tragedies may not occur immediately, but they will come inevitably. The lost sinner is on the broad road that leads to destruction (Matt. 7:13–14); he needs to repent, trust Jesus Christ, and get on the narrow road that leads to life.

Romans 3:17 deals with the sinner's mind: he does not know the way of God's peace. This is what caused Jesus to weep over Jerusalem (Luke 19:41–44). The sinner does not want to know God's truth (Rom. 1:21, 25, 28); he prefers to believe Satan's lie. God's way of peace is through Jesus Christ: "Therefore being justified by faith, we have peace with God through our Lord Jesus Christ" (Rom. 5:1).

In Romans 3:18, which cites Psalm 36:1, the sinner's arrogant pride is prescribed: "There is no fear of God before their eyes." The entire psalm should be read to get the full picture. The ignorance mentioned in Romans 3:17 is caused by the pride of verse 18, for it is "the fear of the Lord" that is the beginning of knowledge (Prov. 1:7).

These quotations from God's law, the Old Testament Scriptures, lead to one conclusion: the whole world is guilty before God! There may be those who want to argue or defense, but every mouth is stopped. There is no debate or defense. The whole world is guilty, Jews and Gentiles. The Jews stand condemned by the law of which they boast, and the Gentiles stand condemned on the basis of creation and conscience.

The word *therefore* in Romans 3:20 carries the meaning of "because," and gives the reason why the whole world is guilty. No flesh can obey God's law and be justified (declared righteous) in His sight. It is true that "the doers of the law shall be justified" (Rom. 2:13), but nobody can do what the law demands! This inability is one way that men know they are sinners. When they try to obey the law, they fail miserably and need to cry out for God's mercy. Neither Jew nor Gentile can obey God's law; therefore God must save sinners by some other means. The explanation of that means by which man can be saved occupied Paul for the rest of his letter.

The best way to close this section would be to ask a simple question: Has your mouth ever been stopped? Are you boasting of your own self-righteousness and defending yourself before God? If so, then perhaps you have never been saved by God's grace. It is only when we stand silent before Him as sinners that He can save us. As long as we defend ourselves and commend ourselves, we cannot be saved by God's grace. The whole world is guilty before God—and that includes you and me!

CHAPTER THREE
Romans 3:21—4:25
FATHER ABRAHAM

Paul's theme in the second section of his letter was *Salvation—Righteousness Declared*. He had proved that all men are sinners; next he was to explain how sinners can be saved. The theological term for this salvation is justification by faith. Justification is the act of God whereby He declares the believing sinner righteous in Christ on the basis of the finished work of Christ on the cross. Each part of this definition is important, so we must consider it carefully.

To begin with, justification is an act, not a process. There are no degrees of justification; each believer has the same right standing before God. Also, justification is something God does, not man. No sinner can justify himself before God. Most important, justification does not mean that God makes us righteous, but that He declares us righteous. Justification is a legal matter. God puts the righteousness of Christ on our record in the place of our own sinfulness. And nobody can change this record.

Do not confuse justification and sanctification. Sanctification is the process whereby God makes the believer more and more like Christ. Sanctification may change from day to day. Justification never changes. When the sinner trusts Christ, God declares him righteous, and that declaration will never be repealed. God looks on us and deals with us as though we had never sinned at all!

But, how can the holy God declare sinners righteous? Is justification merely a "fictional idea" that has no real foundation? In this section of Romans, Paul answered these questions in two ways. First, he explained justification by faith (Rom. 3:21–31); then he illustrated justification by faith from the life of Abraham (Rom. 4:1–25).

Justification Explained (3:21–31)

"But now the righteousness of God … has been manifested" (Rom. 3:21, literal translation). God had revealed His righteousness in many ways before the full revelation of the gospel: His law, His judgments against sin, His appeals through the prophets, His blessing on the obedient. But in the gospel, a new kind of righteousness has been revealed (Rom. 1:16–17), and the characteristics of this righteousness are spelled out in this section.

Apart from the law (v. 21). Under the Old Testament law, righteousness came by man behaving, but under the gospel, righteousness comes by believing. The law itself reveals the righteousness of God, because the law is "holy and just and good" (Rom. 7:12). Furthermore, the law bore witness to this gospel righteousness even though it could not provide it. Beginning at Genesis 3:15, and continuing through the entire Old Testament, witness is given to salvation by faith in Christ. The Old Testament sacrifices, the prophecies, the types, and the great "gospel Scriptures" (such as Isa. 53) all bore witness to this truth. The law could witness to God's righteousness, but it could not provide it for sinful man. Only Jesus Christ could do that (see Gal. 2:21).

Through faith in Christ (v. 22a). Faith is only as good as its object. All men trust something, if only themselves, but the Christian trusts Christ. Law righteousness is a reward for works. Gospel righteousness is a gift through faith. Many people say, "I trust in God!" But this is not what saves us. It is personal, individual faith in Jesus Christ that saves and justifies the lost sinner. Even the demons from hell believe in God and tremble, yet this does not save them (James 2:19).

For all men (vv. 22b–23). God gave His law to the Jews, not to the Gentiles, but the good news of salvation through Christ is offered to all men. All men need to be saved. There is no difference between the Jew and the Gentile when it comes to condemnation. "All have sinned, and are coming short of the glory of God" (Rom. 3:23, literal translation). God declared all men guilty so that He might offer to all men His free gift of salvation.

By grace (v. 24). God has two kinds of attributes: absolute (what He is in Himself), and relative (how He relates to the world and men). One of His absolute attributes is love: "God is love" (1 John 4:8). When God relates that love to you and me, it becomes grace and mercy. God in His mercy does not give us what we do deserve, and God in grace gives us what we do not deserve. The Greek word translated "freely" is translated in John 15:25 as "without a cause." We are justified without a cause! There is no

cause in us that would merit the salvation of God! It is all of grace!

At great cost to God (vv. 24b–25). Salvation is free, but it is not cheap. Three words express the price God paid for our salvation: propitiation, redemption, and blood. In human terms, "propitiation" means appeasing someone who is angry, usually by a gift. But this is not what it means in the Bible. "Propitiation" means the satisfying of God's holy law, the meeting of its just demands, so that God can freely forgive those who come to Christ. The word *blood* tells us what the price was. Jesus had to die on the cross in order to satisfy the law and justify lost sinners.

The best illustration of this truth is the Jewish day of Atonement described in Leviticus 16. Two goats were presented at the altar, and one of them was chosen for a sacrifice. The goat was slain and its blood taken into the Holy of Holies and sprinkled on the mercy seat, that golden cover on the ark of the covenant. This sprinkled blood covered the two tablets of the law inside the ark. The shed blood met (temporarily) the righteous demands of the holy God.

The priest then put his hands on the head of the other goat and confessed the sins of the people. Then the goat was taken out into the wilderness and set free to symbolize the carrying away of sins. "As far as the east is from the west, so far hath he removed our transgressions from us" (Ps. 103:12). In the Old Testament period, the blood of animals could never take away sin; it could only cover it until the time when Jesus would come and purchase a finished salvation. God had "passed over" the sins that were past (Rom. 3:25, literal translation), knowing that His Son would come and finish the work. Because of His death and resurrection, there would be "redemption"—a purchasing of the sinner and setting him free.

Dr. G. Campbell Morgan was trying to explain "free salvation" to a coal miner, but the man was unable to understand it. "I have to pay for it," he kept arguing. With a flash of divine insight, Dr. Morgan asked, "How did you get down into the mine this morning?" "Why, it was easy," the man replied. "I just got on the elevator and went down."

Then Morgan asked, "Wasn't that too easy? Didn't it cost you something?"

The man laughed. "No, it didn't cost me anything, but it must have cost the company plenty to install that elevator." Then the man saw the truth: "It doesn't cost me anything to be saved, but it cost God the life of His Son."

In perfect justice (vv. 25a–26). God must be perfectly consistent with Himself. He cannot break His own law or violate His own nature. "God is love" (1 John 4:8), and "God is light" (1 John 1:5). A God of love wants to forgive sinners, but a God of holiness must punish sin and uphold His righteous law. How can God be both "just and the justifier"? The answer is in Jesus Christ. When Jesus suffered the wrath of God on the cross for the sins of the world, He fully met the demands of God's law and also fully expressed the love of God's heart. The animal sacrifices in the Old Testament never took away sin, but when Jesus died, He reached all the way back to Adam and took care of those sins. No one (including Satan) could accuse God of being unjust or unfair because of His seeming passing over of sins in the Old Testament time.

To establish the law (vv. 27–31). Because of his Jewish readers, Paul wanted to say more about the relationship of the gospel to the law. The doctrine of justification by faith is not against the law, because it establishes the law. God obeyed His own law in working out the plan of salvation. Jesus in His life and death completely fulfilled the demands of the law. God does not have two ways of salvation, one for the Jews and one for the Gentiles, for He is one God. He is consistent with His own nature and His own law. If salvation is through the law, then men can boast, but the principle of faith makes it impossible for men to boast. The swimmer, when he is saved from drowning, does not brag because he trusted the lifeguard. What else could he do? When a believing sinner is justified by faith, he cannot boast of his faith, but he can boast in a wonderful Savior.

In Romans 4—8, Paul explained how God's great plan of salvation was in complete harmony with the Old Testament Scriptures. He began first with the father of the Jewish nation, Abraham.

Justification Illustrated (4:1–25)

The Jewish Christians in Rome would immediately have asked, "How does this doctrine of justification by faith relate to our history? Paul, you say that this doctrine is witnessed to by the law and the prophets. Well, what about Abraham?"

Paul accepted the challenge and explained how Abraham was saved. Abraham was called "our father," referring primarily to the Jews' natural and physical descent from Abraham. But in Romans 4:11, Abraham was also called "the father of all them that believe," meaning, all who have trusted Christ (see Gal. 3:1–18). Paul stated three important facts about Abraham's salvation that prove that the patriarch's spiritual experience was like that of believers today.

He was justified by faith, not works (vv. 1–8). Paul called two witnesses to prove that statement: Moses (Gen. 15:6) and David (Ps. 32:1–2). In Romans 4:1–3, Paul examined the experience of Abraham as recorded in Genesis 15. Abraham had defeated the kings (Gen. 14) and was wondering if they would return to fight again. God appeared to him and assured him that He was his shield and "exceeding great reward." But the thing that Abraham wanted most was a son and heir. God had promised him a son, but as yet the promise had not been fulfilled.

It was then that God told him to look at the stars. "So shall thy seed [descendants] be!" God promised, and Abraham believed God's promise. The Hebrew word translated believed means "to say amen." God

gave a promise, and Abraham responded with "Amen!" It was this faith that was counted for righteousness.

The word counted in Romans 4:3 is a Greek word that means "to put to one's account." It is a banking term. This same word is used eleven times in this chapter, translated "reckoned" (Rom. 4:4, 9–10) and "imputed" (Rom. 4:6, 8, 11, 21–24), as well as "counted." When a man works, he earns a salary and this money is put to his account. But Abraham did not work for his salvation; he simply trusted God's Word. It was Jesus Christ who did the work on the cross, and His righteousness was put on Abraham's account.

Romans 4:5 makes a startling statement: God justifies the ungodly! The law said, "I will not justify the wicked" (Ex. 23:7). The Old Testament judge was commanded to "justify the righteous, and condemn the wicked" (Deut. 25:1). When Solomon dedicated the temple, he asked God to condemn the wicked and justify the righteous (1 Kings 8:31–32)! But God justifies the ungodly—because there are no godly for Him to justify! He put our sins on Christ's account that He might put Christ's righteousness on our account.

In Romans 4:6–8, Paul used David as a witness, quoting from one of David's psalms of confession after his terrible sin with Bathsheba (Ps. 32:1–2). David made two amazing statements: (1) God forgives sins and imputes righteousness apart from works; (2) God does not impute our sins. In other words, once we are justified, our record contains Christ's perfect righteousness and can never again contain our sins. Christians do sin, and these sins need to be forgiven if we are to have fellowship with God (1 John 1:5–7), but these sins are not held against us. God does keep a record of our works, so that He might reward us when Jesus comes, but He is not keeping a record of our sins.

He was justified by grace, not law (vv. 9–17). As we have seen, the Jews gloried in circumcision and the law. If a Jew was to become righteous before God, he would have to be circumcised and obey the law. Paul had already made it clear in Romans 2:12–29 that there must be an inward obedience to the law, and a "circumcision of the heart." Mere external observances can never save the lost sinner.

But Abraham was declared righteous when he was in the state of uncircumcision. From the Jewish point of view, Abraham was a Gentile. Abraham was ninety-nine years old when he was circumcised (Gen. 17:23–27). This was more than fourteen years after the events in Genesis 15. The conclusion is obvious: circumcision had nothing to do with his justification.

Then why was circumcision given? It was a sign and a seal (Rom. 4:11). As a sign, it was evidence that he belonged to God and believed His promise. As a seal, it was a reminder to him that God had given the promise and would keep it. Believers today are sealed by the Holy Spirit of God (Eph. 1:13–14). They have also experienced a spiritual circumcision in the heart (Col. 2:10–12), not just a minor physical operation, but the putting off of the old nature through the death and resurrection of Christ. Circumcision did not add to Abraham's salvation; it merely attested to it.

But Abraham was also justified before the law was given, and this fact Paul discusses in Romans 4:13–17. The key word here is "promise." Abraham was justified by believing God's promise, not by obeying God's law, for God's law through Moses had not yet been given. The promise to Abraham was given purely through God's grace. Abraham did not earn it or merit it. So today, God justifies the ungodly because they believe His gracious promise, not because they obey His law. The law was not given to save men, but to show men that they need to be saved (Rom. 4:15).

The fact that Abraham was justified by grace and not law proves that salvation is for all men. Abraham is the father of all believers, both Jews and Gentiles (Rom. 4:16; Gal. 3:7, 29). Instead of the Jew complaining because Abraham was not saved by law, he ought to rejoice that God's salvation is available to all men, and that Abraham has a spiritual family (all true believers) as well as a physical family (the nation of Israel). Paul saw this as a fulfillment of Genesis 17:5: "I have made thee a father of many nations."

He was justified by resurrection power, not human effort (vv. 18–25). These verses are an expansion of one phrase in Romans 4:17: "who quickeneth the dead." Paul saw the rejuvenation of Abraham's body as a picture of resurrection from the dead, and then he related it to the resurrection of Christ.

One reason why God delayed in sending Abraham and Sarah a son was to permit all their natural strength to decline and then disappear. It was unthinkable that a man ninety-nine years old could beget a child in the womb of his wife who was eighty-nine years old! From a reproductive point of view, both of them were dead.

But Abraham did not walk by sight; he walked by faith. What God promises, He performs. All we need do is believe. Abraham's initial faith in God as recorded in Genesis 15 did not diminish in the years that followed. In Genesis 17—18, Abraham was "strong in faith." It was this faith that gave him strength to beget a son in his old age.

The application to salvation is clear: God must wait until the sinner is "dead" and unable to help himself before He can release His saving power. As long as the lost sinner thinks he is strong enough to do anything to please God, he cannot be saved by grace. It was when Abraham admitted that he was "dead" that God's power went to work in his body. It is when the lost sinner confesses that he is spiritually dead and unable to help himself that God can save him.

The gospel is "the power of God unto salvation" (Rom. 1:16) because of the resurrection of Jesus Christ from the dead. Romans 4:24 and Romans 10:9–10 parallel each other. Jesus Christ was "delivered up to die on account of our offenses, and was raised up because of our justification" (Rom. 4:25, literal translation). This means that the resurrection of Christ is the proof that God accepted His Son's sacrifice, and that

now sinners can be justified without God violating His own law or contradicting His own nature.

The key, of course, is "if we believe" (Rom. 4:24). There are over sixty references to faith or unbelief in Romans. God's saving power is experienced by those who believe in Christ (Rom. 1:16). His righteousness is given to those who believe (Rom. 3:22). We are justified by faith (Rom. 5:1). The object of our faith is Jesus Christ who died for us and rose again.

All of these facts make Abraham's faith that much more wonderful. He did not have a Bible to read; he had only the simple promise of God. He was almost alone as a believer, surrounded by heathen unbelievers. He could not look back at a long record of faith; in fact, he was helping to write that record. Yet Abraham believed God. People today have a complete Bible to read and study. They have a church fellowship, and can look back at centuries of faith as recorded in church history and the Bible. Yet many refuse to believe!

Dr. Harry Ironside, for eighteen years pastor of the Moody Church in Chicago, told of visiting a Sunday school class while on vacation. The teacher asked, "How were people saved in Old Testament times?"

After a pause, one man replied, "By keeping the law."

"That's right," said the teacher.

But Dr. Ironside interrupted: "My Bible says that by the deeds of the law shall no flesh be justified."

The teacher was a bit embarrassed, so he said, "Well, does somebody else have an idea?"

Another student replied, "They were saved by bringing sacrifices to God."

"Yes, that's right!" the teacher said, and tried to go on with the lesson.

But Dr. Ironside interrupted, "My Bible says that the blood of bulls and goats cannot take away sin."

By this time the unprepared teacher was sure the visitor knew more about the Bible than he did, so he said, "Well, you tell us how people were saved in the Old Testament!"

And Dr. Ironside explained that they were saved by faith—the same way people are saved today! Twenty-one times in Hebrews 11 you find the same words, "by faith."

If you are a Jew, you are a child of Abraham physically, but are you a child of Abraham spiritually? Abraham is the father of all who believe on Jesus Christ and are justified by faith. If you are a Gentile, you can never be a natural descendant of Abraham, but you can be one of his spiritual descendants. Abraham "believed God and it was counted unto him for righteousness."

CHAPTER FOUR
Romans 5
LIVE LIKE A KING!

Since Romans is a book of logic, it is a book of "therefores." We have the "therefore" of condemnation in Romans 3:20, justification in Romans

5:1, no condemnation in Romans 8:1, and dedication in Romans 12:1. In presenting his case, Paul has proved that the whole world is guilty before God, and that no one can be saved by religious deeds, such as keeping the law. He has explained that God's way of salvation has always been "by grace, through faith" (Eph. 2:8–9), and he has used Abraham as his illustration. If a reader of the letter stopped at this point, he would know that he needed to and could be saved.

But there is much more the sinner needs to know about justification by faith. Can he be sure that it will last? How is it possible for God to save a sinner through the death of Christ on the cross? Romans 5 is Paul's explanation of the last two words in Romans 4: "our justification." He explained two basic truths: the blessings of our justification (Rom. 5:1–11), and the basis for our justification (Rom. 5:12–21).

The Blessings of Our Justification (5:1–11)

In listing these blessings, Paul accomplished two purposes. First, he told how wonderful it is to be a Christian. Our justification is not simply a guarantee of heaven, as thrilling as that is, but it is also the source of tremendous blessings that we enjoy here and now.

His second purpose was to assure his readers that justification is a lasting thing. His Jewish readers in particular would ask, "Can this spiritual experience last if it does not require obedience to the law? What about the trials and sufferings of life? What about the coming judgment?" When God declared us righteous in Jesus Christ, He gave to us seven spiritual blessings that assure us that we cannot be lost.

Peace with God (v. 1). The unsaved person is at "enmity with God" (Rom. 5:10; 8:7) because he cannot obey God's law or fulfill God's will. Two verses from Isaiah make the matter clear: "There is no peace, saith the Lord, unto the wicked" (Isa. 48:22); "And the work of righteousness shall be peace" (Isa. 32:17). Condemnation means that God declares us sinners, which is a declaration of war. Justification means that God declares us righteous, which is a declaration of peace, made possible by Christ's death on the cross. "Mercy and truth are met together; righteousness and peace have kissed each other" (Ps. 85:10). "Because the law worketh wrath" (Rom. 4:15), nobody condemned by the law can enjoy peace with God. But when you are justified by faith, you are declared righteous, and the law cannot condemn you or declare war!

Access to God (v. 2a). The Jew was kept from God's presence by the veil in the temple, and the Gentile was kept out by a wall in the temple with a warning on it that any Gentile who went beyond would be killed. But when Jesus died, He tore the veil (Luke 23:45) and broke down the wall (Eph. 2:14). In Christ, believing Jews and Gentiles have access to God (Eph. 2:18; Heb. 10:19–25), and they can draw on the inexhaustible riches of the grace of God (Eph. 1:7; 2:4; 3:8). We stand "in grace" and not "in law." Justification has to do with our standing; sanctification has to do with our state. The child of a king can enter his father's presence no matter how the child looks. The word *access* here means "entrance to the king through the favor of another."

Glorious hope (v. 2b). "Peace with God" takes care of the past: He will no longer hold our sins against us. "Access to God" takes care of the present: we can come to Him at any time for the help we need. "Hope of the glory of God" takes care of the future: one day we shall share in His glory! The word *rejoice* can be translated "boast," not only in Romans 5:2, but also in Romans 5:3 and 11 ("joy"). When we were sinners, there was nothing to boast about (Rom. 3:27), because we fell short of the glory of God (Rom. 3:23). But in Christ, we boast in His righteousness and glory! Paul will amplify this in Romans 8:18–30.

Christian character (vv. 3–4). Justification is no escape from the trials of life. "In this world ye shall have tribulation" (John 16:33). But for the believer, trials work for him and not against him. No amount of suffering can separate us from the Lord (Rom. 8:35–39); instead, trials bring us closer to the Lord and make us more like the Lord. Suffering builds Christian character. The word *experience* in Romans 5:4 means "character that has been proved." The sequence is tribulation—patience—proven character—hope. Our English word *tribulation* comes from a Latin word *tribulum*. In Paul's day, a tribulum was a heavy piece of timber with spikes in it, used for threshing the grain. The tribulum was drawn over the grain and it separated the wheat from the chaff. As we go through tribulations, and depend on God's grace, the trials only purify us and help to get rid of the chaff.

God's love within (vv. 5–8). "Hope deferred maketh the heart sick" (Prov. 13:12). But as we wait for this hope to be fulfilled, the love of God is "poured out into our hearts" (literal translation). Note how the first three of the "fruit of the Spirit" are experienced: love (Rom. 5:5), joy (Rom. 5:2), and peace (Rom. 5:1). Before we were saved, God proved His love by sending Christ to die for us. Now that we are His children, surely He will love us more. It is the inner experience of this love through the Spirit that sustains us as we go through tribulations.

For many months I visited a young man in a hospital who had almost burned to death. I do not know how many operations and skin grafts he had during those months, or how many specialists visited him. But the thing that sustained him during those difficult months was not the explanations of the doctors but the promises they gave him that he would recover. That was his hope. And the thing that sustained his hope was the love of his family and many friends as they stood by him. The love of God was channeled through them to him. He did recover and today gives glory to God.

Faith (Rom. 5:1), hope (Rom. 5:2), and love (Rom. 5:5) all combine to give the believer patience in the trials of life. And patience makes it possible for the believer to grow in character and become a mature child of God (James 1:1–4).

Salvation from future wrath (vv. 9–10). Paul argued from the lesser to the greater. If God saved us when we were enemies, surely He will keep on saving us now that we are His children. There is a "wrath to come," but no true believer will experience it (1 Thess. 1:9–10; 5:8–10). Paul further argued that if Christ's death accomplished so much for us, how much more will He do for us in His life as He intercedes for us in heaven! "Saved by his life" refers to Romans 4:25: "raised again for [on account of] our justification." Because He lives, we are eternally saved (Heb. 7:23–25).

A will is of no effect until the death of the one who wrote it. Then an executor takes over and sees to it that the will is obeyed and the inheritance distributed. But suppose the executor is unscrupulous and wants to get the inheritance for himself? He may figure out many devious ways to circumvent the law and steal the inheritance.

Jesus Christ wrote us into His will, and He wrote the will with His blood. "This cup is the new testament in my blood, which is shed for you" (Luke 22:20). He died so that the will would be in force, but then He arose from the dead and returned to heaven that He might enforce the will Himself and distribute the inheritance. Thus, we are "saved by his life."

Reconciliation with God (v. 11). The word *atonement* means "reconciliation, brought back into fellowship with God." The term is mentioned also in Romans 5:10. In Romans 1:18–32, Paul explained how men declared war on God and, because of this, deserved to be condemned eternally. But God did not declare war on man. Instead, He sent His Son as the Peacemaker (Eph. 2:11–18), that men might be reconciled to God.

A review of these seven blessings of justification shows how certain our salvation is in Christ. Totally apart from law, and purely by grace, we have a salvation that takes care of the past, the present, and the future. Christ died for us; Christ lives for us; Christ is coming for us! Hallelujah, what a Savior!

The Basis of Our Justification (5:12–21)

How is it possible for God to save sinners in the person of Jesus Christ? We understand that somehow Christ took our place on the cross, but how was such a substitution possible?

Paul answered the question in this section, and these verses are the very heart of the letter. To understand these verses a few general truths about this section need to be understood. First, note the repetition of the little word *one*. It is used eleven times. The key idea here is our identification with Adam and with Christ. Second, note the repetition of the word *reign*, which is used five times. Paul saw two men—Adam and Christ—each of them reigning over a kingdom. Finally, note that the phrase *much more* is repeated five times. This means that in Jesus Christ we have gained much more than we ever lost in Adam!

In short, this section is a contrast of Adam and Christ. Adam was given dominion over the old creation; he sinned; and he lost his kingdom. Because of Adam's sin, all mankind is under condemnation and death. Christ came as the King over a new creation (2 Cor. 5:17). By His obedience on the cross, He brought in righteousness and justification. Christ not only undid all the damage that Adam's sin effected, but He accomplished "much more" by making us the very sons of God. Some of this "much more" Paul has already explained in Romans 5:1–11.

Skeptics sometimes ask, "Was it fair for God to condemn the whole world just because of one man's disobedience?" The answer, of course, is that it was not only fair, but it was also wise and gracious. To begin with, if God had tested each human being individually, the result would have been the same: disobedience. But even more important, by condemning the human race through one man (Adam), God was then able to save the human race through one Man (Jesus Christ)! Each of us is racially united to Adam, so that his deed affects us. (See Heb. 7:9–10 for an example of this racial headship.) The fallen angels cannot be saved because they are not a race. They sinned individually and were judged individually. There can be no representative to take their judgment for them and save them. But because you and I were lost in Adam, our racial head, we can be saved in Christ, the Head of the new creation. God's plan was both gracious and wise.

Our final question must be answered: How do we know that we are racially united to Adam? The answer is in Romans 5:12–14, and the argument runs like this: We know that all men die. But death is the result of disobeying the law. There was no law from Adam to Moses, but men still died. A general result demands a general cause. What is that cause? It can be only one thing: the disobedience of Adam. When Adam sinned, he ultimately died. All of his descendants died (Gen. 5), yet the law had not yet been given. Conclusion: they died because of Adam's sin. "For that all have sinned" (Rom. 5:12) means "all have sinned in Adam's sin." Men do not die because of their own acts of sin; otherwise, babies would not die (Rom. 9:11). Men die because they are united racially to Adam, and "in Adam all men die" (1 Cor. 15:22).

Having understood these general truths about the passage, we may now examine the contrasts that Paul gives between Adam and Christ and between Adam's sin and Christ's act of obedience on the cross.

Adam's offense is contrasted with Christ's free gift (v. 15). Because of Adam's trespass, many died; because of Christ's obedience, the grace of God abounds to many bringing life. The word *many* (literally "the many") means the same as "all men" in Romans 5:12 and 18. Note the "much more," for the grace of Christ brings not only physical life, but also spiritual life and abundant life. Christ did conquer death and one day will raise the bodies of all who have died "in Christ." If He stopped there, He would only reverse the effects of Adam's sin, but He went on to do "much more." He gives eternal life abundantly to all who trust Him (John 10:10).

The effect of Adam's sin is contrasted with the effect of Christ's obedience (v.16). Adam's sin brought judgment and condemnation, but Christ's work on the cross brings justification. When Adam sinned, he was declared unrighteous and condemned. When a sinner trusts Christ, he is justified—declared righteous in Christ.

The two "reigns" are contrasted (v. 17). Because of Adam's disobedience, death reigned. Read the "book of the generations of Adam" in Genesis 5, and note the solemn repetition of the phrase "and he died." In Romans 5:14, Paul argued that men did not die "from Adam to Moses" for the same reason that Adam died—breaking a revealed law of God—for the law had not yet been given. "The wages of sin is death" (Rom. 6:23). Because sin was reigning in men's lives (Rom. 5:21), death was also reigning (Rom. 5:14, 17).

But in Jesus Christ we enter a new kingdom: "For the kingdom of God is not meat and drink; but righteousness, and peace, and joy in the Holy Ghost" (Rom. 14:17). "Therefore being justified by faith," we are declared righteous, we have peace with God, and we rejoice in the hope of the glory of God. Note that it is we who reign! "Much more they … shall reign in life by one, Jesus Christ." In Adam we lost our kingship, but in Jesus Christ we reign as kings. And we reign "much more"! Our spiritual reign is far greater than Adam's earthly reign, for we share "abundance of grace and of the gift of righteousness" (Rom. 5:17).

The two "one acts" are contrasted (vv. 18–19). Adam did not have to commit a series of sins. In one act God tested Adam, and he failed. It is termed an "offense" and an act of "disobedience." The word *offense* means "trespass—crossing over the line." God told Adam how far he could go, and Adam decided to go beyond the appointed limit. "Of every tree of the garden thou mayest freely eat: but of the tree of the knowledge of good and evil, thou shalt not eat of it: for in the day that thou eatest thereof, thou shalt surely die" (Gen. 2:16–17).

In contrast to "the trespass of one" is "the righteousness of one," meaning the righteous work of Christ on the cross. In Romans 5:19 Paul calls it "the obedience of one" (see Phil. 2:5–12). Christ's sacrifice on the cross not only made possible "justification," but also "justification *of life*" (italics mine). Justification is not merely a legal term that describes our position before God ("just as if I'd never sinned"), but it results in a certain kind of life. "Justification of life" in Romans 5:18 is parallel to "be made righteous" in Romans 5:19. In other words, our justification is the result of a living union with Christ. And this union ought to result in a new kind of life, a righteous life of obedience to God. Our union with Adam made us sinners; our union with Christ enables us to "reign in life."

Law and grace are contrasted (vv. 20–21). "Then law crept in" (Williams); or, "Then the law came in beside" (literal translation). Grace was not an addition to God's plan; grace was a part of God's plan from the very beginning. God dealt with Adam and Eve in grace; He dealt with the patriarchs in grace; and He dealt with the nation of Israel in grace. He gave the law through Moses, not to replace His grace, but to reveal man's need for grace. Law was temporary, but grace is eternal.

But as the law made man's sins increase, God's grace abounded even more. God's grace was more than adequate to deal with man's sins. Even though sin and death still reign in this world, God's grace is also reigning through the righteousness of Christ. The Christian's body is subject to death and his old nature tempts him to sin, but in Jesus Christ, he can "reign in life" because he is a part of the gracious kingdom of Christ.

An Old Testament story helps us understand the conflict between these two "reigns" in the world today. God rejected Saul as the king of Israel and anointed David. Those who trusted David eventually shared his kingdom of peace and joy. Those who trusted Saul ended in shame and defeat.

Like David, Jesus Christ is God's anointed King. Like Saul, Satan is still free to work in this world and seek to win men's allegiance. Sin and death are reigning in the "old creation" over which Adam was the head, but grace and righteousness are reigning in "the new creation" over which Christ is the Head. And as we yield to Him, we "reign in life."

In Romans 5:14, Adam is called "the figure of him that was to come." Adam was a type, or picture, of Jesus Christ. Adam came from the earth, but Jesus is the Lord from heaven (1 Cor. 15:47). Adam was tested in a garden, surrounded by beauty and love; Jesus was tempted in a wilderness, and He died on a cruel cross surrounded by hatred and ugliness. Adam was a thief, and was cast out of Paradise, but Jesus Christ turned to a thief and said, "Today shalt thou be with me in paradise" (Luke 23:43). The Old Testament is "the book of the generations of Adam" (Gen. 5:1), and it ends with "a curse" (Mal. 4:6). The New Testament is "the book of the generation of Jesus Christ" (Matt. 1:1), and it ends with "no more curse" (Rev. 22:3).

You cannot help being "in Adam," for this came by your first birth over which you had no control. But you can help staying "in Adam," for you can experience a second birth—a new birth from above—that will put you "in Christ." This is why Jesus said, "Ye must be born again" (John 3:7).

CHAPTER FIVE
Romans 6
DYING TO LIVE

During a court session, an attorney will often rise to his feet and say, "Your Honor, I object!" Some of the Roman Christians must have felt like objecting as they heard Paul's letter being read, and Paul seemed to anticipate their thinking. In Romans 6—8 Paul defended his doctrine of justification by faith. He anticipated three objections: (1) "If God's grace abounds when we sin, then let's continue sinning so we might experience more grace" (Rom. 6; 1–14); (2) "If we are no longer under the law, then we are free to live as we please" (Rom. 6:15—7:6); and (3) "You have made God's law sinful" (Rom. 7:7–25).

These objections prove that the readers did not understand either law or grace. They were going to extremes: legalism on the one hand and license on the other. So as Paul defended justification he also explained sanctification. He told how we can live lives of victory (Rom. 6), liberty (Rom. 7), and security (Rom. 8). He explained our relationship to the flesh, the law, and the Holy Spirit. In Romans 6, Paul gave three instructions for attaining victory over sin.

Know (6:1–10)
The repetition of the word *know* in Romans 6; 1, 6, and 9 indicates that Paul wanted us to understand a basic doctrine. Christian living depends on Christian learning; duty is always founded on doctrine. If Satan can keep a Christian ignorant, he can keep him impotent.

The basic truth Paul was teaching is the believer's identification with Christ in death, burial, and resurrection. Just as we are identified with Adam in sin and condemnation, so we are now identified with Christ in righteousness and justification. At Romans 5:12, Paul made a transition from discussing "sins" to discussing "sin"—from the actions to the principle, from the fruit to the root. Jesus Christ not only died for our sins, but He also died unto sin, and we died with Him. Perhaps a chart will explain the contrasts better.

Romans 3:21—5:21	Romans 6—8
Substitution: He died for me	Identification: I died with Him
He died for my sins	He died unto sin
He paid sin's penalty	He broke sin's power
Justification: righteousness	Sanctification: righteousness

In other words, justification by faith is not simply a legal matter between me and God; it is a living relationship. It is "a justification which brings life" (Rom. 5:18, literal translation). I am in Christ and identified with Him. Therefore, whatever happened to Christ has happened to me. When He died, I died. When He arose, I arose in Him. I am now seated with Him in the heavenlies (see Eph. 2:1–10; Col. 3:1–3)! Because of this living union with Christ, the believer has a totally new relationship to sin.

He is dead to sin (vv. 2–5). Paul's illustration is baptism. The Greek word has two basic meanings: (1) a literal meaning—to dip or immerse; and (2) a figurative meaning—to be identified with. An example of the latter would be 1 Corinthians 10:2: "And were all baptized unto Moses in the cloud and in the sea." The nation of Israel was identified with Moses as their leader when they crossed the Red Sea.

It appears that Paul had both the literal and the figurative in mind in this paragraph, for he used the readers' experience of water baptism to remind them of their identification with Christ through the baptism of the Holy Spirit. To be "baptized into Jesus Christ" (Rom. 6:3) is the same as "For by one Spirit are we all baptized into one body" (1 Cor. 12:13). There is a difference between water baptism and the baptism of the Spirit (John 1:33). When a sinner trusts Christ, he is immediately born into the family of God and receives the gift of the Holy Spirit. A good illustration of this is the household of Cornelius when they heard Peter preach (Acts 10:34–48). When these people believed on Christ, they immediately received the Holy Spirit. After that, they were baptized. Peter's words, "Whosoever believeth in him shall receive remission of sins" gave to them the promise that they needed. They believed—and they were saved!

Historians agree that the mode of baptism in the early church was immersion. The believer was "buried" in the water and brought up again as a picture of death, burial, and resurrection. Baptism by immersion (which is the illustration Paul is using in Rom. 6) pictures the believer's identification with Christ in His death, burial, and resurrection. It is an outward symbol of an inward experience. Paul is not saying that their immersion in water put them "into Jesus Christ," for that was accomplished by the Spirit when they believed. Their immersion was a picture of what the Spirit did: the Holy Spirit identified them with Christ in His death, burial, and resurrection.

This means that the believer has a new relationship to sin. He is "dead to sin." "I am crucified with Christ" (Gal. 2:20). If a drunk dies, he can no longer be tempted by alcohol because his body is dead to all physical senses. He cannot see the alcohol, smell it, taste it, or desire it. In Jesus Christ we have died to sin so that we no longer want to "continue in sin." But we are not only dead to sin; we are also alive in Christ. We have been raised from the dead and now walk in the power of His resurrection. We walk in "newness of life" because we share His life. "I am crucified with Christ, nevertheless I live" (Gal. 2:20).

This tremendous spiritual truth is illustrated in the miracle of the resurrection of Lazarus (John 11). When

Jesus arrived at Bethany, Lazarus had been in the tomb four days, so there was no question about his death. By the power of His word ("Lazarus, come forth!") Jesus raised His friend from the dead. But when Lazarus appeared at the door of the tomb, he was wrapped in graveclothes. So Jesus commanded, "Loose him, and let him go!" He had been raised to walk "in newness of life." In John 12, Lazarus was seated with Christ at the table, in fellowship with Him. Dead—raised from the dead—set free to walk in newness of life—seated with Christ: all of these facts illustrate the spiritual truths of our identification with Christ as given in Ephesians 2:1–10.

Too many Christians are "betweeners": they live between Egypt and Canaan, saved but never satisfied; or they live between Good Friday and Easter, believing in the cross but not entering into the power and glory of the resurrection. Romans 6:5 indicates that our union with Christ assures our future resurrection should we die. But Romans 6:4 teaches that we share His resurrection power today. "Since, then, you have been raised with Christ, set your hearts on things above … For you died, and your life is now hidden with Christ in God" (Col. 3:1, 3 niv).

It is clear, then, that the believer cannot deliberately live in sin since he has a new relationship to sin because of his identification with Christ. The believer has died to the old life; he has been raised to enjoy a new life. The believer does not want to go back into sin any more than Lazarus wanted to go back into the tomb dressed again in his graveclothes! Then Paul introduced a second fact.

He should not serve sin (vv. 6–10). Sin is a terrible master, and it finds a willing servant in the human body. The body is not sinful; the body is neutral. It can be controlled either by sin or by God. But man's fallen nature, which is not changed at conversion, gives sin a beachhead from which it can attack and then control. Paul expressed the problem: "For I know that in me (that is, in my flesh) dwelleth no good thing: for to will is present with me; but how to perform that which is good I find not" (Rom. 7:18).

A tremendous fact is introduced here: the old man (the old ego, self) was crucified with Christ so that the body need not be controlled by sin. The word *destroyed* in Romans 6:6 does not mean annihilated; it means "rendered inactive, made of no effect." The same Greek word is translated "loosed" in Romans 7:2. If a woman's husband dies, she is "loosed" from the law of her husband and is free to marry again. There is a change in relationship. The law is still there, but it has no authority over the woman because her husband is dead.

Sin wants to be our master. It finds a foothold in the old nature, and through the old nature seeks to control the members of the body. But in Jesus Christ, we died to sin, and the old nature was crucified so that the old life is rendered inoperative. Paul was not describing an experience; he was stating a fact. The practical experience was to come later. It is a fact of history that Jesus

Christ died on the cross. It is also a fact of history that the believer died with Him, and "he that is dead is freed from sin" (Rom. 6:7). Not "free to sin" as Paul's accusers falsely stated, but "freed from sin."

Sin and death have no dominion over Christ. We are "in Christ"; therefore, sin and death have no dominion over us. Jesus Christ not only died "for sin," but He also died "unto sin." That is, He not only paid the penalty for sin, but He broke the power of sin. This idea of dominion takes us back to Romans 5:12–21, where Paul dealt with the "reigns" of sin, death, and grace. Through Christ we "reign in life" (Rom. 5:17) so that sin no longer controls our lives.

The big question now is, "I believe the facts of history, but how do I make this work in daily experience?" This leads to Paul's second instruction.

Reckon (6:11)

In some parts of the United States, "to reckon" means "to think" or "to guess." "I reckon" is also the equivalent of "I suppose." But none of these popular meanings can apply to this verse. The word *reckon* is a translation of a Greek word that is used forty-one times in the New Testament—nineteen times in Romans alone. It appears in Romans 4, where it is translated as "count, reckon, impute." It means "to take into account, to calculate, to estimate." The word *impute*—"to put to one's account"—is perhaps the best translation.

To reckon means "to put to one's account." It simply means to believe that what God says in His Word is really true in your life.

Paul didn't tell his readers to *feel* as if they were dead to sin, or even to *understand* it fully, but to *act* on God's Word and claim it for themselves. Reckoning is a matter of faith that issues in action. It is like endorsing a check: if we really believe that the money is in the checking account, we will sign our name and collect the money. Reckoning is not claiming a promise, but acting on a fact. God does not command us to become dead to sin. He tells us that we *are* dead to sin and alive unto God, and then commands us to act on it. Even if we do not act on it, the facts are still true.

Paul's first instruction ("know") centered in the *mind,* and this second instruction ("reckon") focuses on the *heart.* His third instruction touches the *will.*

Yield (6:12–23)

The word *yield* is found five times in this section (Rom. 6:13, 16, 19) and means "to place at one's disposal, to present, to offer as a sacrifice." According to Romans 12:1, the believer's body should be presented to the Lord as "a living sacrifice" for His glory. The Old Testament sacrifices were dead sacrifices. The Lord may ask some of us to die for Him, but He asks all of us to *live* for Him.

How we are to yield (vv. 12–13). This is an act of the will based on the knowledge we have of what Christ has done for us. It is an intelligent act—not the impulsive decision of the moment based on some emotional stirring. It is important to notice the tenses of the verbs in these verses. A literal translation is "Do not constantly allow sin to reign in your mortal body so that you are constantly obeying its lusts. Neither constantly yield your members of your body as weapons [or tools] of unrighteousness to sin; but once and for all yield yourselves to God." That once-and-for-all surrender is described in Romans 12:1.

There must be in the believer's life that final and complete surrender of the body to Jesus Christ. This does not mean there will be no further steps of surrender, because there will be. The longer we walk with Christ, the deeper the fellowship must become. But there can be no subsequent steps without that first step. The tense of the verb in Romans 12:1 corresponds with that in Romans 6:13—a once-and-for-all yielding to the Lord. To be sure, we daily surrender afresh to Him, but even that is based on a final and complete surrender.

Why does the Lord want your body? To begin with, the believer's body is God's temple, and He wants to use it for His glory (1 Cor. 6:19–20; Phil. 1:20–21). But Paul wrote that the body is also God's tool and God's weapon (Rom. 6:13). God wants to use the members of the body as tools for building His kingdom and weapons for fighting His enemies.

The Bible tells of people who permitted God to take and use their bodies for the fulfilling of His purposes. God used the rod in Moses' hand and conquered Egypt. He used the sling in David's hand to defeat the Philistines. He used the mouths and tongues of the prophets. Paul's dedicated feet carried him from city to city as he proclaimed the gospel. The apostle John's eyes saw visions of the future, his ears heard God's message, and his fingers wrote it all down in a book that we can read.

But you can also read in the Bible accounts of the members of the body being used for sinful purposes. David's eyes looked on his neighbor's wife; his mind plotted a wicked scheme; his hand signed a cowardly order for the woman's husband to be killed. As you read Psalm 51, you see that his whole body was affected by sin: his eyes (Ps. 51:3), mind (Ps. 51:6), ears (Ps. 51:8), heart (Ps. 51:10), and lips and mouth (Ps. 51:14–15). No wonder he prayed for a *thorough* cleansing (Ps. 51:2)!

Why we are to yield (vv. 14–23). Three words summarize the reasons for our yielding: *favor* (Rom. 6:14–15), *freedom* (Rom. 6:16–20), and *fruit* (Rom. 6:21–23).

Favor (vv. 14–15). It is because of God's grace that we yield ourselves to Him. Paul has proved that we are not saved by the law and that we do not live under the law. The fact that we are saved by grace does not give us an excuse to sin, but it does give us a reason to obey. Sin and law go together. "The sting of death is sin; and the strength of sin is the law" (1 Cor. 15:56). Since we are not under law, but under grace, sin is robbed of its strength.

Freedom (vv. 16–20). The illustration of the master and servant is obvious. Whatever you yield to becomes your master. Before you were saved, you were the slave of sin. Now that you belong to Christ, you are freed from that old slavery and made the servant of Christ. Romans 6:19 suggests that the Christian ought to be as enthusiastic in yielding to the Lord as he was in yielding to sin. A friend once said to me, "I want to be as good a saint as I was a sinner!" I knew what he meant because in his unconverted days he was almost "the chief of sinners."

The unsaved person is free—free *from* righteousness (Rom. 6:20). But his bondage to sin only leads him deeper into slavery so that it becomes harder and harder to do what is right. The Prodigal Son is an example of this (Luke 15:11–24). When he was at home, he decided he wanted his freedom, so he left home to find himself and enjoy himself. But his rebellion only led him deeper into slavery. He was the slave of wrong desires, then the slave of wrong deeds, and finally he became a literal slave when he took care of the pigs. He wanted to find himself, but he lost himself! What he thought was freedom turned out to be the worst kind of slavery. It was only when he returned home and *yielded to his father* that he found true freedom.

Fruit (vv. 21–23). If you serve a master, you can expect to receive wages. Sin pays wages—death! God also pays wages—holiness and everlasting life. In the old life, we produced fruit that made us ashamed. In the new life in Christ, we produce fruit that glorifies God and brings joy to our lives. We usually apply Romans 6:23 to the lost, and certainly it does apply, but it also has a warning for the saved. (After all, it was written to Christians.) "There is a sin unto death" (1 John 5:17). "For this reason many among you are weak and sick, and a number sleep" (1 Cor. 11:30 NASB). Samson, for example, would not yield himself to God, but preferred to yield to the lusts of the flesh, and the result was death (Judg. 16). If the believer refuses to surrender his body to the Lord, but uses its members for sinful purposes, then he is in danger of being disciplined by the Father, and this could mean death. (See Heb. 12:5–11; and note the end of v. 9 in particular.)

These three instructions need to be heeded each day that we live. *Know* that you have been crucified with Christ and are dead to sin. *Reckon* this fact to be true in your own life. *Yield* your body to the Lord to be used for His glory.

Now that you *know* these truths, *reckon* them to be true in *your* life, and then *yield* yourself to God.

CHAPTER SIX
Romans 7
CHRISTIANS AND THE LAW

Something in human nature makes us want to go to extremes, a weakness from which Christians are not wholly free. "Since we are saved by grace," some argue, "we are free to live as we please," which is the extreme of *license.*

"But we cannot ignore God's law," others argue. "We are saved by grace, to be sure; but we must live under law if we are to please God." This is the extreme expression of *legalism.*

Paul answered the first group in Romans 6; the second group he answered in Romans 7. The word *law* is used twenty-three times in this chapter. In Romans 6, Paul told us how to stop doing bad things; in Romans 7 he told how *not* to do good things. "You were not justified by keeping the law," he argued, "and you cannot be sanctified by keeping the law."

Every growing Christian understands the experience of Romans 6 and 7. Once we learn how to "know, reckon, and yield," we start getting victory over the habits of the flesh, and we feel we are becoming more spiritual. We set high standards and ideals for ourselves and for a while seem to attain them.

Then everything collapses! We start to see deeper into our own hearts, and we discover sins that we did not know were there. God's holy law takes on a new power, and we wonder if we can ever do anything good! Without realizing it, we have moved into "legalism" and have learned the truth about sin, the law, and ourselves.

What really is "legalism"? It is the belief that I can become holy and please God by obeying laws. It is measuring spirituality by a list of dos and don'ts. The weakness of legalism is that it sees *sins* (plural) but not *sin* (the root of the trouble). It judges by the outward and not the inward. Furthermore, the legalist fails to understand the real purpose of God's law and the relationship between law and grace.

In my pastoral experience, I have counseled many people who have suffered severe emotional and spiritual damage because they have tried to live holy lives on the basis of a high standard. I have seen the consequences of these attempts: either the person becomes a pretender, or he suffers a complete collapse and abandons his desires for godly living. I have seen too that many legalists are extremely hard on other people—critical, unloving, unforgiving. Paul wanted to spare his readers this difficult and dangerous experience. In Romans 7, he discussed three topics, which, if understood and applied, will deliver us from legalism.

The Authority of the Law (7:1–6)

These verses actually continue the discussion that Paul began in Romans 6:15, answering the question, "Shall we sin because we are not under the law, but under grace?" He used the illustration of a master and servant to explain how the Christian should yield himself to God. In this passage he used the illustration of a husband and wife to show that the believer has a new relationship to the law because of his union with Jesus Christ.

The illustration is a simple one, but it has a profound application. When a man and woman marry, they are united for life. Marriage is a physical union ("They two shall be one flesh" Gen. 2:24) and can only be broken by a physical cause. One such cause is *death.* (Matt. 5:31–34; 19:1–12 indicate that unfaithfulness also breaks the marriage bond, but Paul does not bring this up. He is not discussing marriage and divorce; he is using marriage to illustrate a point.)

As long as they live, the husband and wife are under the authority of the law of marriage. If the woman leaves the man and marries another man, she commits adultery. But if the husband dies, she is free to remarry because she is no longer a wife. It is death that has broken the marriage relationship and set her free.

Paul's *application* in Romans 7:4–6 clinches the argument. He states two marvelous facts that explain the believer's relationship to the law.

We died to the law (vv. 4–5). It appears that Paul has confused his illustration, but he has not. When we were unsaved ("in the flesh," Rom. 7:5), we were under the authority of God's law. We were condemned by that law. When we trusted Christ and were united to Him, *we died to the law* just as we died to the flesh (Rom. 6:1–10). The law did not die; *we* died.

But in Paul's illustration from marriage, it was the *husband* who died and the wife who married again. If you and I are represented by the wife, and the law is represented by the husband, then the application does not follow the illustration. If the wife died in the illustration, the only way she could marry again would be to come back from the dead. But that is exactly what Paul wants to teach! When we trusted Christ, we died to the law; but in Christ, we arose from the dead and now are "married" (united) to Christ to live a new kind of life!

The law did not die, because God's law still rules over men. We died to the law, and it no longer has dominion over us. But we are not "lawless"; we are united to Christ, sharing His life, and thus walking "in newness of life." Romans 8:4 climaxes the argument: "That the righteousness of the law might be fulfilled in us, who walk not after the flesh but after the Spirit." In the old life of sin, we brought forth fruit "unto death," but in the new life of grace, we "bring forth fruit unto God." To be "dead to the law" does not mean that we lead lawless lives. It simply means that the *motivation* and *dynamic* of our lives does not come from the law: it comes from God's grace through our union with Christ.

We are delivered from law (v. 6). This is the logical conclusion: the law cannot exercise authority over a dead person. The Authorized Version reads as though the law died, but Paul wrote, "We having died to that wherein we were held." Death means deliverance (note Rom. 6:9–10). But we were delivered that we might serve. The Christian life is not one of independence and rebellion. We died to the law that we might be "married to Christ." We were delivered from the law that we might serve Christ. This truth refutes the false accusation that Paul taught lawlessness.

What is different about Christian service as opposed to our old life of sin? To begin with, the Holy Spirit of God energizes us as we seek to obey and serve the Lord. (The word *spirit* ought to be capitalized in Romans 7:6—"newness of Spirit.") Under law, no enablement was given. God's commandments were written on stones and read to the people. But under grace, God's Word is written in our hearts (2 Cor. 3:1–3). We "walk in newness of life" (Rom. 6:4) and serve "in newness of Spirit." The believer, then, is no longer under the authority of the law.

The Ministry of the Law (7:7–13)

Paul's objectors were ready! "What good is the law if we don't need it anymore? Why, a teaching such as yours turns the law into sin!" In answering that objection, Paul explained the ministries of the law, ministries that function even today.

The law reveals sin (v. 7). "By the law is the knowledge of sin" (Rom. 3:20). "Where no law is, there is no transgression" (Rom. 4:15). The law is a mirror that reveals the inner man and shows us how dirty we are (James 1:22–25). Note that Paul did not use murder, stealing, or adultery in his discussion; he uses *coveting*. This is the last of the Ten Commandments, and it differs from the other nine in that it is an inward attitude, not an outward action. Covetousness leads to the breaking of the other commandments! It is an insidious sin that most people never recognize in their own lives, but God's law reveals it.

The rich ruler in Mark 10:17–27 is a good example of the use of the law to reveal sin and show a man his need for a Savior. The young man was very moral outwardly, but he had never faced the sins within. Jesus did not tell him about the law because the law would save him; He told him about the law because the young man did not realize his own sinfulness. True, he had never committed adultery, robbed anyone, given false witness, or dishonored his parents, but what about covetousness? When Jesus told him to sell his goods and give to the poor, the man went away in great sorrow. The commandment, "Thou shalt not covet," had revealed to him what a sinner he really was! Instead of admitting his sin, he rejected Christ and went away unconverted.

The law arouses sin (vv. 8–9). Since Paul was a devout Pharisee, seeking to obey the law before his conversion, it is easier to understand these verses. (Read Phil. 3:1–11 and Gal. 1 for other autobiographical data on Paul's relationship to the law in his unconverted days.) Keep in mind too that "the strength of sin is the law" (1 Cor. 15:56). Since we have a sinful nature, the law is bound to arouse that nature the way a magnet draws steel.

Something in human nature wants to rebel whenever a law is given. I was standing in Lincoln Park in Chicago, looking at the newly painted benches; and I noticed a sign on each bench: "Do Not Touch." As I watched, I saw numbers of people deliberately reach out and touch the wet paint! Why? Because the sign told them not to! Instruct a child not to go near the water, and that is the very thing he will do! Why? "Because the carnal mind is enmity against God: for it is not subject to the law of God, neither indeed can be" (Rom. 8:7).

Believers who try to live by rules and regulations discover that their legalistic system only arouses more sin and creates more problems. The churches in Galatia were very legalistic, and they experienced all kinds of trouble. "But if ye bite and devour one another, take heed that ye be not consumed one of another" (Gal. 5:15). Their legalism did not make them more spiritual; it made them more sinful! Why? Because the law arouses sin in our nature.

The law kills (vv. 10–11). "For if there had been a law given which could have given life, verily righteousness should have been by the law" (Gal. 3:21). But the law cannot give life: it can only show the sinner that he is guilty and condemned. This explains why legalistic Christians and churches do not grow and bear spiritual fruit. They are living by law, and the law always kills. Few things are more dead than an orthodox church that is proud of its "high standards" and tries to live up to them in its own energy. Often the members of such a church start to judge and condemn one another, and the sad result is a church fight and then a church split that leaves members—or former members—angry and bitter.

As the new Christian grows, he comes into contact with various philosophies of the Christian life. He can read books, attend seminars, listen to tapes, and get a great deal of information. If he is not careful, he will start following a human leader and accept his teachings as law. This practice is a very subtle form of legalism, and it kills spiritual growth. No human teacher can take the place of Christ; no book can take the place of the Bible. Men can give us information, but only the Spirit can give us illumination and help us understand spiritual truths. The Spirit enlightens us and enables us; no human leader can do that.

The law shows the sinfulness of sin (vv. 12–13). Unsaved people know that there is such a thing as sin, but they do not realize the sinfulness of sin. Many Christians do not realize the true nature of sin. We excuse our sins with words like "mistakes" or "weaknesses," but God condemns our sins and tries to get us to see that they are "exceedingly sinful." Until we realize how wicked sin really is, we will never want to oppose it and live in victory.

Paul's argument here is tremendous: (1) the law is not sinful—it is holy, just, and good; (2) but the law reveals sin, arouses sin, and then uses sin to slay us; if something as good as the law accomplishes these results, then something is radically wrong somewhere; (3) conclusion: see how sinful sin is when it can use something good like the law to produce such tragic results. Sin is indeed "exceedingly sinful." The problem is not with the law; the problem is with my sinful nature. This prepares the way for the third topic in this chapter.

The Inability of the Law (7:14–25)

Having explained what the law is supposed to do, Paul now explains what the law cannot do.

The law cannot change you (v. 14). The character of the law is described in four words: holy, just, good, and spiritual. That the law is holy and just, nobody can deny, because it came from the holy God who is perfectly just in all that He says and does. The law is good. It reveals God's holiness to us and helps us to see our need for a Savior.

What does it mean that the law is "spiritual"? It means that the law deals with the inner man, the spiritual part of man, as well as with the outer actions. In the original giving of the law in Exodus, the emphasis was on the outward actions. But when Moses restated the law in Deuteronomy, he emphasized the inner quality of the law as it relates to man's heart. This spiritual emphasis is stated clearly in Deuteronomy 10:12–13. The repetition of the word *love* in Deuteronomy also shows that the deeper interpretation of the law relates to the inner man (Deut. 4:37; 6:4–6; 10:12; 11:1; 30:6, 16, 20).

Our nature is carnal (fleshly), but the law's nature is spiritual. This explains why the old nature responds as it does to the law. It has well been said, "The old nature knows no law, the new nature needs no law." The law cannot transform the old nature; it can only reveal how sinful that old nature is. The believer who tries to live under law will only *activate* the old nature; he will not eradicate it.

The law cannot enable you to do good (vv. 15–21). Three times in this passage Paul stated that sin dwells in us (Rom. 7:14, 18, 20). He was referring, of course, to the old nature. It is also true that the Holy Spirit dwells in us; and in Romans 8, Paul explained how the Spirit of God enables us to live in victory, something the law cannot help us do.

The many pronouns in this section indicate that the writer is having a problem with *self*. This is not to say that the Christian is a split personality, because he is not. Salvation makes a man whole. But it does indicate that the believer's mind, will, and body can be controlled either by the old nature or the new nature, either by the flesh or the Spirit. The statements here indicate that the believer has two serious problems: (1) he cannot do the good he wants to do, and (2) he does the evil that he does not want to do.

Does this mean that Paul could not stop himself from breaking God's law, that he was a liar and thief and murderer? Of course not! Paul was saying that of *himself* he could not obey God's law, and that even when he did, evil was still present with him. No matter what he did, his deeds were tainted by sin. Even after he had done his best, he had to admit that he was "an unprofitable servant" (Luke 17:10). "So I find this law at work: when I want to do good, evil is right there

with me" (Rom. 7:21 NIV). This, of course, is a different problem from that in Romans 6. The problem there was, "How can I stop doing bad things?" while the problem here is, "How can I ever do anything good?"

The legalist says, "Obey the law and you will do good and live a good life." But the law only reveals and arouses sin, showing how sinful it is! It is impossible for me to obey the law because I have a sinful nature that rebels against the law. Even if I think I have done good, I know that evil is present. The law is good, but by nature, I am bad! So, the legalist is wrong: the law cannot enable us to do good.

The law cannot set you free (vv. 21–25). The believer has an old nature that wants to keep him in bondage; "I will get free from these old sins!" the Christian says to himself. "I determine here and now that I will not do this any longer." What happens? He exerts all his willpower and energy, and for a time succeeds, but then when he least expects it, he falls again. Why? Because he tried to overcome his old nature with law, and the law cannot deliver us from the old nature. When you move under the law, you are only making the old nature stronger because "the strength of sin is the law" (1 Cor. 15:56). Instead of being a dynamo that gives us power to overcome, the law is a magnet that draws out of us all kinds of sin and corruption. The inward man may delight in the law of God (Ps. 119:35), but the old nature delights in breaking the law of God. No wonder the believer under law becomes tired and discouraged, and eventually gives up! He is a captive, and his condition is "wretched." (The Greek word indicates a person who is exhausted after a battle.) What could be more wretched than exerting all your energy to try to live a good life, only to discover that the best you do is still not good enough!

Is there any deliverance? Of course! "I thank God that there is Someone who shall deliver me—Jesus Christ our Lord!" Because the believer is united to Christ, he is dead to the law and no longer under its authority. But he is alive to God and able to draw on the power of the Holy Spirit. The explanation of this victory is given in Romans 8.

The final sentence in the chapter does not teach that the believer lives a divided life: sinning with his flesh but serving God with his mind. This would mean that his body was being used in two different ways *at the same time,* and this is impossible. The believer realizes that there is a struggle within him between the flesh and the Spirit (Gal. 5:16–18), but he knows that one or the other must be in control.

By "the mind" Paul meant "the inward man" (Rom. 7:22) as opposed to "the flesh" (Rom. 7:18). He amplified this thought in Romans 8:5–8. The old nature cannot do anything good. Everything the Bible says about the old nature is negative: "no good thing" (Rom. 7:18); "the flesh profiteth nothing" (John 6:63); "no confidence in the flesh" (Phil. 3:3). If we depend on the energy of the flesh, we cannot serve God, please

God, or do any good thing. But if we yield to the Holy Spirit, then we have the power needed to obey His will. The flesh will never serve the law of God because the flesh is at war with God. But the Spirit can only obey the law of God! Therefore, the secret of doing good is to yield to the Holy Spirit.

Paul hinted at this in the early verses of this chapter when he wrote, "That we should bring forth fruit unto God" (Rom. 7:4). Just as we are dead to the old nature, so we are dead to the law. But we are united to Christ and alive in Christ, and therefore can bring forth fruit unto God. It is our union with Christ that enables us to serve God acceptably. "For it is God which worketh in you, both to will and to do of his good pleasure" (Phil. 2:13). That solved Paul's problem in Romans 7:18: "For to will is present with me; but how to perform that which is good I find not."

The old nature knows no law and the new nature needs no law. Legalism makes a believer wretched because it grieves the new nature and aggravates the old nature! The legalist becomes a Pharisee whose outward actions are acceptable, but whose inward attitudes are despicable. No wonder Jesus called them "whited sepulchres, which indeed appear beautiful outward, but are within full of dead men's bones, and of all uncleanness" (Matt. 23:27). How wretched can you get!

The best is yet to come! Romans 8 explains the work of the Holy Spirit in overcoming the bad and producing the good.

CHAPTER SEVEN
Romans 8
FREEDOM AND FULFILLMENT

On January 6, 1941, President Franklin Delano Roosevelt addressed Congress on the state of the war in Europe. Much of what he said that day has been forgotten. But at the close of his address, he said that he looked forward "to a world founded upon four essential human freedoms." He named them: freedom of speech, freedom of worship, freedom from want, and freedom from fear. These words are still remembered, even though their ideals have not yet been realized everywhere in the world.

Romans 8 is the Christian's "Declaration of Freedom," for in it Paul declares the four spiritual freedoms we enjoy because of our union with Jesus Christ. A study of this chapter shows the emphasis on the Holy Spirit, who is mentioned nineteen times. "Where the Spirit of the Lord is, there is liberty" (2 Cor. 3:17).

Freedom from Judgment—No Condemnation (8:1–4)

Romans 3:20 shows the "therefore" of condemnation, but Romans 8:1 gives the "therefore" of *no* condemnation—a tremendous truth and the conclusion of a marvelous argument. (The words "who walk not

… etc." do not belong here according to the best manuscripts. There are no conditions for us to meet.) The basis for this wonderful assurance is the phrase "in Christ Jesus." In Adam, we were condemned. In Christ, there is no condemnation!

The verse does not say "no mistakes" or "no failures," or even "no sins." Christians *do* fail and make mistakes, and they do sin. Abraham lied about his wife; David committed adultery; Peter tried to kill a man with his sword. To be sure, they suffered consequences because of their sins, but they did not suffer condemnation.

The law condemns, but the believer has a new relationship to the law, and therefore he cannot be condemned. Paul made three statements about the believer and the law, and together they add up to *no condemnation.*

The law cannot claim you (v. 2). You have been made free from the law of sin and death. You now have life in the Spirit. You have moved into a whole new sphere of life in Christ. "The law of sin and death" is what Paul described in Romans 7:7–25. "The law of the Spirit of life" is described in Romans 8. The law no longer has any jurisdiction over you: you are dead to the law (Rom. 7:4) and free from the law (Rom. 8:2).

The law cannot condemn you (v. 3). Why? Because Christ has already suffered that condemnation for you on the cross. The law could not save; it can only condemn. But God sent His Son to save us and do what the law could not do. Jesus did not come as an angel; He came as a man. He did not come "in sinful flesh," for that would have made Him a sinner. He came *in the likeness* of sinful flesh, as a man. He bore our sins in His body on the cross.

The "law of double jeopardy" states that a man cannot be tried twice for the same crime. Since Jesus Christ paid the penalty for your sins, and since you are "in Christ," God will not condemn you.

The law cannot control you (v. 4). The believer lives a righteous life, not in the power of the law, but in the power of the Holy Spirit. The law does not have the power to produce holiness; it can only reveal and condemn sin. But the indwelling Holy Spirit enables you to walk in obedience to God's will. The righteousness that God demands in His law is fulfilled in you through the Spirit's power. In the Holy Spirit, you have life and liberty (Rom. 8:2) and "the pursuit of happiness" (Rom. 8:4).

The legalist tries to obey God in his own strength and fails to measure up to the righteousness that God demands. The Spirit-led Christian, as he yields to the Lord, experiences the sanctifying work of the Spirit in his life. "For it is God that worketh in you, both to will and to do of his good pleasure" (Phil. 2:13). It is this fact that leads to the second freedom we enjoy as Christians.

Freedom from Defeat—No Obligation (8:5–17)

"Therefore, brethren, we are debtors, not to the flesh,

to live after the flesh" (Rom. 8:12). There is no obligation to the old nature. The believer can live in victory. In this section, Paul described life on three different levels, and he encouraged his readers to live on the highest level.

"You have not the Spirit" (vv. 5–8). Paul is not describing two kinds of Christians, one carnal and one spiritual. He is contrasting the saved and the unsaved. There are four contrasts.

In the flesh—in the Spirit (v. 5). The unsaved person does not have the Spirit of God (Rom. 8:9) and lives *in* the flesh and *for* the flesh. His mind is centered on the things that satisfy the flesh. But the Christian has the Spirit of God within and lives in an entirely new and different sphere. His mind is fixed on the things of the Spirit. This does not mean that the unsaved person never does anything good, or that the believer never does anything bad. It means that the bent of their lives is different. One lives for the flesh, the other lives for the Spirit.

Death—life (v. 6). The unsaved person is alive physically, but dead spiritually. The inner man is dead toward God and does not respond to the things of the Spirit. He may be moral, and even religious, but he lacks spiritual life. He needs "the Spirit of life in Christ Jesus" (Rom. 8:2).

War with God—peace with God (vv. 6–7). In our study of Romans 7, we have seen that the old nature rebels against God and will not submit to God's law. Those who have trusted Christ enjoy "peace with God" (Rom. 5:1), while the unsaved are at war with God. "'There is no peace,' saith the Lord, 'unto the wicked'" (Isa. 48:22).

Pleasing self—pleasing God (v. 8). To be "in the flesh" means to be lost, outside Christ. The unsaved person lives to please himself and rarely if ever thinks about pleasing God. The root of sin is selfishness—"I will" and not "Thy will."

To be unsaved and not have the Spirit is the lowest level of life. But a person need not stay on that level. By faith in Christ he can move to the second level.

"You have the Spirit" (vv. 9–11). "But ye are not in the flesh, but in the Spirit, if so be that the Spirit of God dwell in you" (Rom. 8:9). The evidence of conversion is the presence of the Holy Spirit within, witnessing that you are a child of God (Rom. 8:16). Your body becomes the very temple of the Holy Spirit (1 Cor. 6:19–20). Even though the body is destined to die because of sin (unless, of course, the Lord returns), the Spirit gives life to that body today so that we may serve God. If we should die, the body will one day be raised from the dead, because the Holy Spirit has sealed each believer (Eph. 1:13–14).

What a difference it makes in your body when the Holy Spirit lives within. You experience new life, and even your physical faculties take on a new dimension of experience. When evangelist D. L. Moody described his conversion experience, he said: "I was in a new world. The next morning the sun shone brighter and the birds sang sweeter … the old elms waved their branches for joy, and all nature was at peace." Life in Christ is abundant life.

But there is a third level of experience for which the other two are preparation.

"The Spirit has you!" (vv. 12–17). It is not enough for us to have the Spirit; the Spirit must have us! Only then can He share with us the abundant, victorious life that can be ours in Christ. We have no obligation to the flesh, because the flesh has only brought trouble into our lives. We do have an obligation to the Holy Spirit, for it is the Spirit who convicted us, revealed Christ to us, and imparted eternal life to us when we trusted Christ. Because He is "the Spirit of Life," He can empower us to obey Christ, and He can enable us to be more like Christ.

But He is also the Spirit of death. He can enable us to "put to death" (mortify) the sinful deeds of the body. As we yield the members of our body to the Spirit (Rom. 6:12–17), He applies to us and in us the death and resurrection of Christ. He puts to death the things of the flesh, and He reproduces the things of the Spirit.

The Holy Spirit is also "the Spirit of adoption" (Rom. 8:14–17). The word *adoption* in the New Testament means "being placed as an adult son." We come into God's family by birth. But the instant we are born into the family, God adopts us and gives us the position of an adult son. A baby cannot walk, speak, make decisions, or draw on the family wealth. But the believer can do all of these the instant he is born again.

He can walk and be "led of the Spirit" (Rom. 8:14). The verb here means "willingly led." We yield to the Spirit, and He guides us by His Word day by day. We are not under bondage to law and afraid to act. We have the liberty of the Spirit and are free to follow Christ. The believer can also speak: "We cry, Abba, Father" (Rom. 8:15). Would it not be amazing if a newborn baby looked up and greeted his father! First, the Spirit says, "Abba, Father" to us (Gal. 4:6), and then we say it to God. ("Abba" means "papa"—a term of endearment.)

A baby cannot sign checks, but the child of God by faith can draw on his spiritual wealth because he is an heir of God and a joint-heir with Christ (Rom. 8:17). The Spirit teaches us from the Word, and then we receive God's wealth by faith. What a thrilling thing it is to have "the Spirit of adoption" at work in our lives!

There is no need for the believer to be defeated. He can yield his body to the Spirit and by faith overcome the old nature. The Spirit of life will empower him. The Spirit of death will enable him to overcome the flesh. And the Spirit of adoption will enrich him and lead him into the will of God.

Freedom from Discouragement—No Frustration (8:18–30)

Paul in this section dealt with the very real problem of suffering and pain. Perhaps the best way to understand this section is to note the three "groans" that are discussed.

Creation groans (vv. 18–22). When God finished His creation, it was a good creation (Gen. 1:31), but today it is a groaning creation. There is suffering and death; there is pain, all of which is, of course, the result of Adam's sin. It is not the fault of creation. Note the words that Paul used to describe the plight of creation: suffering (Rom. 8:18), vanity (Rom. 8:20), bondage (Rom. 8:21), decay (Rom. 8:21), and pain (Rom. 8:22). However, this groaning is not a useless thing: Paul compared it to a woman in travail. There is pain, but the pain will end when the child is delivered. One day creation will be delivered, and the groaning creation will become a glorious creation! The believer does not focus on today's sufferings; he looks forward to tomorrow's glory (Rom. 8:18; 2 Cor. 4:15–18). Today's groaning bondage will be exchanged for tomorrow's glorious liberty!

We believers groan (vv. 23–25). The reason we groan is because we have experienced "the firstfruits of the Spirit," a foretaste of the glory to come. Just as the nation of Israel tasted the firstfruits of Canaan when the spies returned (Num. 13:23–27), so we Christians have tasted of the blessings of heaven through the ministry of the Spirit. This makes us want to see the Lord, receive a new body, and live with Him and serve Him forever. We are waiting for "the adoption," which is the redemption of the body when Christ returns (Phil. 3:20–21). This is the thrilling climax to "the adoption" that took place at conversion when "the Spirit of adoption" gave us an adult standing in God's family. When Christ returns, we shall enter into our full inheritance.

Meanwhile, we wait and hope. "For we are saved by that hope" (Rom. 8:24, literal translation). What hope? "That blessed hope and the glorious appearing of the great God and our Savior Jesus Christ" (Titus 2:13). The best is yet to come! The believer does not get frustrated as he sees and experiences suffering and pain in this world. He knows that the temporary suffering will one day give way to eternal glory.

The Holy Spirit groans (vv. 25–30). God is concerned about the trials of His people. When He was ministering on earth, Jesus groaned when He saw what sin was doing to mankind (Mark 7:34; John 11:33, 38). Today the Holy Spirit groans with us and feels the burdens of our weaknesses and suffering. But the Spirit does more than groan. He prays for us in His groaning so that we might be led into the will of God. We do not always know God's will. We do not always know how to pray, but the Spirit intercedes so that we might live in the will of God in spite of suffering. The Spirit "shares the burden."

The believer never need faint in times of suffering and trial because he knows that God is at work in the world (Rom. 8:28), and that He has a perfect plan (Rom. 8:29). God has two purposes in that plan: our good and His glory. Ultimately, He will make us like Jesus Christ! Best of all, God's plan is going to succeed!

It started in eternity past when He chose us in Christ (Eph. 1:4–5). He predetermined that one day we would be like His Son. Predestination applies only to saved people. Nowhere are we taught that God predestines people to be eternally condemned. If they are condemned, it is because of their refusal to trust Christ (John 3:18–21). Those whom He chose, He called (see 2 Thess. 2:13–14); when they responded to His call, He justified them, and He also glorified them. This means that the believer has already been glorified in Christ (John 17:22); the revelation of this glory awaits the coming of the Lord (Rom. 8:21–23).

How can we Christians ever be discouraged and frustrated when we already share the glory of God? Our suffering today only guarantees that much more glory when Jesus Christ returns!

Freedom from Fear—No Separation (8:31–39)

There is no condemnation because we share the righteousness of God and the law cannot condemn us. There is no obligation because we have the Spirit of God who enables us to overcome the flesh and live for God. There is no frustration because we share the glory of God, the blessed hope of Christ's return. There is no separation because we experience the love of God: "What shall separate us from the love of Christ?" (Rom. 8:35).

The emphasis in this final section is on the security of the believer. We do not need to fear the past, present, or future because we are secure in the love of Christ. Paul presented five arguments to prove that there could be no separation between the believer and the Lord.

God is for us (v. 31). *The Father* is for us and proved it by giving His Son (Rom. 8:32). *The Son* is for us (Rom. 8:34) and so is *the Spirit* (Rom. 8:26). God is making all things work for us (Rom. 8:28). In His person and His providence, God is for us. Sometimes, like Jacob, we lament, "All these things are against me" (Gen. 42:36), when actually everything is working for us. The conclusion is obvious: "If God be for us, who can be against us?"

The believer needs to enter into each new day realizing that God is for him. There is no need to fear, for his loving Father desires only the best for His children, even if they must go through trials to receive His best. "'For I know the plans that I have for you,' declares the Lord, 'plans for welfare and not for calamity to give you a future and a hope'" (Jer. 29:11 NASB).

Christ died for us (v. 32). The argument here is from the lesser to the greater. If when we were sinners, God gave us His best, now that we are God's children, will He not give us all that we need? Jesus used this same argument when He tried to convince people that it was foolish to worry and fear. God cares for the birds and sheep, and even for the lilies; surely He will care for you! God is dealing with His own on the basis of Calvary grace, not on the basis of law. God freely gives all things to His own!

God has justified us (v. 33). This means that He has declared us righteous in Christ. Satan would like to accuse us (Zech. 3:1–7; Rev. 12:10), but we stand righteous in Jesus Christ. We are God's elect—chosen in Christ and accepted in Christ. God will certainly not accuse us, since it is He who has justified us. For Him to accuse us would mean that His salvation was a failure and we are still in our sins.

Understanding the meaning of justification brings peace to our hearts. When God declares the believing sinner righteous in Christ, that declaration never changes. Our Christian experience changes from day to day, but justification never changes. We may accuse ourselves, and men may accuse us, but God will never take us to court and accuse us. Jesus has already paid the penalty and we are secure in Him.

Christ intercedes for us (v. 34). A dual intercession keeps the believer secure in Christ: the Spirit intercedes (Rom. 8:26–27) and the Son of God intercedes (Rom. 8:34). The same Savior who died for us is now interceding for us in heaven. As our High Priest, He can give us the grace we need to overcome temptation and defeat the enemy (Heb. 4:14–16). As our Advocate, He can forgive our sins and restore our fellowship with God (1 John 1:9—2:2). Intercession means that Jesus Christ represents us before the throne of God and we do not have to represent ourselves.

Paul hinted at this ministry of intercession in Romans 5:9–10. We are not only saved by His death, but we are also saved by His life. "Therefore he is able to save completely those who come to God through him, because he always lives to intercede for them" (Heb. 7:25 NIV). Peter sinned against the Lord, but he was forgiven and restored to fellowship because of Jesus Christ. "Simon, Simon, listen! Satan has asked permission to sift all of you like wheat, but I have prayed especially for you that your own faith may not utterly fail" (Luke 22:31–32, Williams). He is interceding for each of us, a ministry that assures us that we are secure.

Christ loves us (vv. 35–39). In Romans 8:31–34 Paul proved that God cannot fail us, but is it possible that we can fail Him? Suppose some great trial or temptation comes, and we fail? Then what? Paul deals with that problem in this final section and explains that nothing can separate us from the love of Jesus Christ.

To begin with, God does not shelter us from the difficulties of life because we need them for our spiritual growth (Rom. 5:3–5). In Romans 8:28 God assures us that the difficulties of life are working *for* us and not *against* us. God permits trials to come that we might use them for our good and His glory. We endure trials for His sake (Rom. 8:36), and since we do, do you think that He will desert us? Of course not! Instead, He is closer to us when we go through the difficulties of life.

Furthermore, He gives us the power to conquer (Rom. 8:37). We are "more than conquerors," literally, "we are superconquerors" through Jesus Christ! He gives us victory and more victory! We need not fear

life or death, things present or things to come, because Jesus Christ loves us and gives us the victory. This is not a promise with conditions attached: "If you do this, God will do that." This security in Christ is an established fact, and we claim it for ourselves because we are in Christ. Nothing can separate you from His love! Believe it—and rejoice in it!

A review of this wonderful chapter shows that the Christian is completely victorious. We are free from judgment because Christ died for us and we have His righteousness. We are free from defeat because Christ lives in us by His Spirit and we share His life. We are free from discouragement because Christ is coming for us and we shall share His glory. We are free from fear because Christ intercedes for us and we cannot be separated from His love.

No condemnation! No obligation! No frustration! No separation!

If God be for us, who can be against us?

CHAPTER EIGHT
Romans 9
DID GOD MAKE A MISTAKE?

It seems strange that Paul would interrupt his discussion of salvation and devote a long section of three chapters to the nation of Israel. Why didn't he move from the doctrinal teaching of Romans 8 to the practical duties given in Romans 12—15? A careful study of Romans 9—11 reveals that this section is not an interruption at all; it is a necessary part of Paul's argument for justification by faith.

To begin with, Paul was considered a traitor to the Jewish nation. He ministered to Gentiles, and he taught freedom from the law of Moses. He had preached in many synagogues and caused trouble, and no doubt many of the Jewish believers in Rome had heard of his questionable reputation. In these chapters, Paul showed his love for Israel and his desire for their welfare. This is the personal reason for this discussion.

But there was a doctrinal reason. Paul had argued in Romans 8 that the believer is secure in Jesus Christ and that God's election would stand (Rom. 8:28–30). But someone might ask, "What about the Jews? They were chosen by God, and yet now you tell us they are set aside and God is building His church. Did God fail to keep His promises to Israel?" In other words, the very character of God was at stake. If God was not faithful to the Jews, how do we know He will be faithful to the church?

The emphasis in Romans 9 is on Israel's past election, in Romans 10 on Israel's present rejection, and in Romans 11 on Israel's future restoration. Israel is the only nation in the world with a complete history—past, present, and future. In Romans 9, Paul defended the character of God by showing that

Israel's past history actually magnified the attributes of God. He specifically named four attributes of God: His faithfulness (Rom. 9:1–13), righteousness (Rom. 9:14–18), justice (Rom. 9:19–29), and grace (Rom. 9:30–33). You will note that these divisions correspond with Paul's three questions: "Is there unrighteousness with God?" (Rom. 9:14), "Why doth he find fault?" (Rom. 9:19), and "What shall we say then?" (Rom. 9:30).

God's Faithfulness (9:1–13)

It is remarkable how Paul moved from the joy of Romans 8 into the sorrow and burden of Romans 9. When he looked at Christ, he rejoiced, but when he looked at the lost people of Israel, he wept. Like Moses (Ex. 32:30–35), he was willing to be cursed and separated from Christ if it would mean the salvation of Israel. What a man this Paul was! He was willing to stay out of heaven for the sake of the saved (Phil. 1:22–24), and willing to go to hell for the sake of the lost.

His theme was God's election of Israel, and the first thing he dealt with was the blessing of their election (Rom. 9:4–5). Israel was adopted by God as His own people (Ex. 4:22–23). He gave them His glory in the tabernacle and the temple (Ex. 40:34–38; 1 Kings 8:10–11). The glory Moses beheld on Mount Sinai came to dwell with Israel (Ex. 24:16–17). God gave Israel His covenants, the first to Abraham, and then additional covenants to Moses and to David. He also gave them His law to govern their political, social, and religious life, and to guarantee His blessing if they obeyed. He gave them "the service of God," referring to the ministry in the tabernacle and the temple. He gave them the promises and the patriarchs ("the fathers" in Rom. 9:5). The purpose of all of this blessing was that Jesus Christ, through Israel, might come into the world. (Note that Rom. 9:5 affirms that Jesus Christ is God.) All of these blessings were given freely to Israel and to no other nation.

But in spite of these blessings, Israel failed. When the Messiah appeared, Israel rejected Him and crucified Him. No one knew this better than Paul, because in his early days he had persecuted the church. Does Israel's failure mean that God's Word has failed? (The Greek word translated "taken none effect" pictures a ship going off its course.) The answer is, "No! God is faithful no matter what men may do with His Word." Here Paul explains the basis for Israel's election.

It was not of natural descent (vv. 6–10). As we saw in Romans 2:25–29, there is a difference between the natural seed of Abraham and the spiritual children of Abraham. Abraham actually had two sons, Ishmael (by Hagar) and Isaac (by Sarah). Since Ishmael was the firstborn, he should have been chosen, but it was Isaac that God chose. Isaac and Rebecca had twin sons, Esau and Jacob. As the firstborn, Esau should have been chosen, but it was Jacob that God chose. And Esau and Jacob had the same father and mother, unlike Ishmael and Isaac, who had the same father but different mothers. God did not base His election on the physical. Therefore, if the nation of Israel—Abraham's physical descendants—has rejected God's Word, this does not nullify God's elective purposes at all.

It is not of human merit (vv. 11–13). God chose Jacob before the babies were born. The two boys had done neither good nor evil, so God's choice was not based on their character or conduct. Romans 9:13 is a reference to Malachi 1:2–3 and refers to nations (Israel and Edom) and not individual sinners. God does not hate sinners. John 3:16 makes it clear that He loves sinners. The statement here has to do with national election, not individual. Since God's election of Israel does not depend on human merit, their disobedience cannot nullify the elective purposes of God. God is faithful even though His people are unfaithful.

God's Righteousness (9:14–18)

The fact that God chose one and not the other seems to indicate that He is unrighteous. "Is there unrighteousness with God?" Paul asked, and then he replied, "God forbid!" It is unthinkable that the holy God should ever commit an unrighteous act. Election is always totally a matter of grace. If God acted only on the basis of righteousness, nobody would ever be saved. Paul quoted Exodus 33:19 to show that God's mercy and compassion are extended according to God's will and not man's will. All of us deserve condemnation—not mercy. The reference in Exodus 33 deals with Israel's idolatry while Moses was on the mount receiving the law. The whole nation deserved to be destroyed, yet God killed only three thousand people—not because they were more wicked or less godly, but purely because of His grace and mercy.

Paul then quoted Exodus 9:16, using Pharaoh as an illustration. Moses was a Jew; Pharaoh was a Gentile, yet both were sinners. In fact, both were murderers! Both saw God's wonders. Yet Moses was saved and Pharaoh was lost. God raised up Pharaoh that He might reveal His glory and power, and He had mercy on Moses that He might use him to deliver the people of Israel. Pharaoh was a ruler, and Moses was a slave, yet it was Moses who experienced the mercy and compassion of God—because God willed it that way. God is sovereign in His work and acts according to His own will and purposes. So it was not a matter of righteousness but of the sovereign will of God.

God is holy and must punish sin, but God is loving and desires to save sinners. If everybody is saved, it would deny His holiness, but if everybody is lost, it would deny His love. The solution to the problem is God's sovereign election.

A seminary professor once said to me, "Try to explain election, and you may lose your mind; but explain it away and you will lose your soul!"

God chose Israel and condemned Egypt, because this was His sovereign purpose. Nobody can condemn

God for the way He extends His mercy, because God is righteous.

Before leaving this section, we need to discuss the "hardening" of Pharaoh (Rom. 9:18). This hardening process is referred to at least fifteen times in Exodus 7—14. Sometimes we are told that Pharaoh hardened his heart (Ex. 8:15, 19, 32), and other times that God hardened Pharaoh's heart (Ex. 9:12; 10:1, 20, 27). By declaring His Word and revealing His power, God gave Pharaoh opportunity to repent, but instead, Pharaoh resisted God and hardened his heart. The fault lay not with God but Pharaoh. The same sunlight that melts the ice also hardens the clay. God was not unrighteous in His dealings with Pharaoh because He gave him many opportunities to repent and believe.

God's Justice (9:19–29)

But this fact of God's sovereign will only seems to create a new problem. "If God is sovereign, then who can resist Him? And if one does resist Him, what right does He have to judge?" It is the age-old question of the justice of God as He works in human history.

I recall sharing in a street meeting in Chicago and passing out tracts at the corner of Madison and Kedzie. Most of the people graciously accepted the tracts, but one man took the tract and with a snarl crumpled it up and threw it in the gutter. The name of the tract was "Four Things God Wants You to Know."

"There are a few things I would like God to know!" the man said. "Why is there so much sorrow and tragedy in this world? Why do the innocent suffer while the rich go free? Bah! Don't tell me there's a God! If there is, then God is the biggest sinner that ever lived!" And he turned away with a sneer and was lost in the crowd.

We know that God by nature is perfectly just. "Shall not the Judge of all the earth do right?" (Gen. 18:25). It is unthinkable that God would will an unjust purpose or perform an unjust act. But at times it seems that He does just that. He had mercy on Moses but condemned Pharaoh. Is this just? He elected Israel and rejected the other nations. Is this just? Paul gives three answers to this charge.

Who are we to argue with God (vv. 19–21)? This is a logical argument. God is the Potter and we are the clay. God is wiser than we are, and we are foolish to question His will or to resist it. (The reference here is to Isa. 45:9.) To be sure, the clay has no life and is passive in the potter's hand. We have feelings, intellect, and willpower, and we can resist Him if we choose. (See Jer. 18, where this thought is developed.) But it is God who determines whether a man will be a Moses or a Pharaoh. Neither Moses, nor Pharaoh, nor anyone else, could choose his parents, his genetic structure, or his time and place of birth. We have to believe that these matters are in the hands of God.

However, this does not excuse us from responsibility. Pharaoh had great opportunities to learn about the true God and trust Him, and yet he chose to rebel.

Paul did not develop this aspect of truth because his theme was divine sovereignty, not human responsibility. The one does not deny the other, even though our finite minds may not fully grasp them both.

God has His purposes (vv. 22–24). We must never think that God enjoyed watching a tyrant like Pharaoh. He endured it. God said to Moses, "I have surely seen the affliction of my people … and have heard their cry … for I know their sorrows" (Ex. 3:7). The fact that God was long suffering indicates that He gave Pharaoh opportunities to be saved (see 2 Peter 3:9). The word *fitted* in Romans 9:22 does not suggest that *God* made Pharaoh a "vessel of wrath." The verb is in what the Greek grammarians call the middle voice, making it a reflexive action verb. So, it should read: *"fitted himself for* destruction." God prepares men for glory (Rom. 9:23), but sinners prepare themselves for judgment. In Moses and Israel, God revealed the riches of His mercy; in Pharaoh and Egypt, He revealed His power and wrath. Since neither deserved any mercy, God cannot be charged with injustice.

Ultimately, of course, God's purpose was to form His church from both Jews and Gentiles (Rom. 9:24). Believers today are, by God's grace, "vessels of mercy" that He is preparing for glory, a truth that reminds us of Romans 8:29–30.

All of this was prophesied (vv. 25–29). First Paul quoted Hosea 2:23, a statement declaring that God would turn from the Jews and call the Gentiles. Then he cited Hosea 1:10 to prove that this new people being called would be God's people and "children of the living God." He then quoted Isaiah 10:22–23 to show that only a remnant of Israel would be saved, while the greater part of the nation would suffer judgment. Romans 9:28 probably refers to God's work of judgment during the tribulation, when the nation of Israel will be persecuted and judged, and only a small remnant left to enter into the kingdom when Jesus Christ returns to earth. But the application for today is clear: only a remnant of Jews is believing, and they, together with the Gentiles, are the "called of God" (Rom. 9:24). The final quotation from Isaiah 1:9 emphasized the grace of God in sparing the believing remnant.

Now, what does all of this prove? That God was not unjust in saving some and judging others, because He was only fulfilling the Old Testament prophecies given centuries ago. He would be unjust if He did not keep His own Word. But even more than that, these prophecies show that God's election has made possible the salvation of the Gentiles. This is the grace of God. At the Exodus, God rejected the Gentiles and chose the Jews, so that, through the Jews, He might save the Gentiles. The nation of Israel rejected His will, but this did not defeat His purposes. A remnant of Jews does believe and God's Word has been fulfilled.

So far, Paul had defended the character of God by showing His faithfulness, His righteousness, and His justice. Israel's rejection had not canceled God's election; it had only proved that He was true to His character and His purposes.

God's Grace (9:30–33)

Paul moved next from divine sovereignty to human responsibility. Note that Paul did not say "elect" and "nonelect," but rather emphasized faith. Here is a paradox: the Jews sought for righteousness but did not find it, while the Gentiles, who were not searching for it, found it! The reason? Israel tried to be saved by works and not by faith. They rejected "grace righteousness" and tried to please God with "law righteousness." The Jews thought that the Gentiles had to *come up* to Israel's level to be saved; when actually the Jews had to *go down* to the level of the Gentiles to be saved. "For there is no difference: for all have sinned and come short of the glory of God" (Rom. 3:22–23). Instead of permitting their religious privileges (Rom. 9:1–5) to lead them to Christ, they used these privileges as a substitute for Christ.

But see the grace of God: Israel's rejection means the Gentiles' salvation! Paul's final quotation was from Isaiah 28:16. It referred to Christ, God's Stone of salvation (see Ps. 118:22). God gave Christ to be a Foundation Stone, but Israel rejected Him and He became a stumbling stone. Instead of "rising" on this Stone, Israel fell (Rom. 11:11), but, as we shall see, their fall made possible the salvation of the Gentiles by the grace of God.

We need to decide what kind of righteousness we are seeking, whether we are depending on good works and character, or trusting Christ alone for salvation. God does not save people on the basis of birth or behavior. He saves them "by grace, through faith" (Eph. 2:8–9). It is not a question of whether or not we are among God's elect. That is a mystery known only to God. He offers us His salvation by faith. The offer is made to "whosoever will" (Rev. 22:17). After we have trusted Christ, then we have the witness and evidence that we are among His elect (Eph. 1:4–14; 1 Thess. 1:1–10). But first we must trust Him and receive by faith His righteousness that alone can guarantee heaven.

No one will deny that there are many mysteries connected with divine sovereignty and human responsibility. Nowhere does God ask us to choose between these two truths, because they both come from God and are a part of God's plan. They do not compete; they cooperate. The fact that we cannot fully understand *how* they work together does not deny the fact that they do. When a man asked Charles Spurgeon how he reconciled divine sovereignty and human responsibility, Spurgeon replied: "I never try to reconcile friends!"

But the main thrust of this chapter is clear: Israel's rejection of Christ does not deny the faithfulness of God. Romans 9 does not negate Romans 8. God is still faithful, righteous, just, and gracious, and He can be depended on to accomplish His purposes and keep His promises.

CHAPTER NINE
Romans 10
THE WRONG RIGHTEOUSNESS

The theme of this chapter is Israel's present rejection. Paul moved from divine sovereignty (Rom. 9) to human responsibility. He continued the theme of righteousness introduced at the end of the previous chapter (Rom. 9:30–33) and explains three aspects of Israel's rejection.

The Reasons for Their Rejection (10:1–13)

You would think that Israel as a nation would have been eagerly expecting the arrival of their Messiah and been prepared to receive Him. For centuries they had known the Old Testament prophecies and had practiced the law, which was "a schoolmaster" to lead them to Christ (Gal. 3:24). God had sought to prepare the nation, but when Jesus Christ came, they rejected Him. "He came unto his own [world] and his own [people] received him not" (John 1:11). To be sure, there was a faithful remnant in the nation that looked for His arrival, such as Simeon and Anna (Luke 2:25–38), but the majority of the people were not ready when He came.

How do we explain this tragic event? Paul gives several reasons why Israel rejected their Messiah.

They did not feel a need for salvation (v. 1). There was a time when Paul would have agreed with his people, for he himself opposed the gospel and considered Jesus Christ an impostor. Israel considered the Gentiles in need of salvation, but certainly not the Jews. In several of His parables, Jesus pointed out this wrong attitude: the elder brother (Luke 15:11–32) and the Pharisee (Luke 18:9–14) are two examples. Israel would have been happy for political salvation from Rome, but she did not feel she needed spiritual salvation from her own sin.

They were zealous for God (v. 2). Ever since Israel returned to their land from Babylonian captivity, the nation had been cured of idolatry. In the temple and the local synagogues, only the true God was worshipped and served, and only the true law was taught. So zealous were the Jews that they even "improved upon God's law" and added their own traditions, making them equal to the law. Paul himself had been zealous for the law and the traditions (Acts 26:1–11; Gal. 1:13–14).

But their zeal was not based on knowledge; it was heat without light. Sad to say, many religious people today are making the same mistake. They think that their good works and religious deeds will save them, when actually these practices are keeping them from being saved. Certainly many of them are sincere and devout, but sincerity and devotion will never save the soul. "Therefore by the deeds of the law there shall no flesh be justified in his sight" (Rom. 3:20).

They were proud and self-righteous (v. 3). Israel was ignorant of God's righteousness, not because they had never been told, but because they refused to learn. There is an ignorance that comes from lack of opportunity, but Israel had had many opportunities to be saved. In their case, it was an ignorance that stemmed from willful, stubborn resistance to the truth. They would not submit to God. They were proud of their own good works and religious self-righteousness, and would not admit their sins and trust the Savior. Paul had made the same mistake before he met the Lord (Phil. 3:1–11).

The godly Presbyterian preacher Robert Murray McCheyne was passing out tracts one day and handed one to a well-dressed lady. She gave him a haughty look and said, "Sir, you must not know who I am!"

In his kind way, McCheyne replied, "Madam, there is coming a day of judgment, and on that day it will not make any difference who you are!"

They misunderstood their own law (vv. 4–13). Everything about the Jewish religion pointed to the coming Messiah—their sacrifices, priesthood, temple services, religious festivals, and covenants. Their law told them they were sinners in need of a Savior. But instead of letting the law bring them to Christ (Gal. 3:24), they worshipped their law and rejected their Savior. The law was a signpost, pointing the way. But it could never take them to their destination. The law cannot give righteousness; it only leads the sinner to the Savior who can give righteousness.

Christ is "the end of the law" in the sense that through His death and resurrection, He has terminated the ministry of the law for those who believe. The law is ended as far as Christians are concerned. The righteousness of the law is being fulfilled in the life of the believer through the power of the Spirit (Rom. 8:4), but the reign of the law has ended (see Eph. 2:15; Col. 2:14). "For ye are not under the law, but under grace" (Rom. 6:14).

Paul quoted from the Old Testament to prove to his readers that they did not even understand their own law. He began with Leviticus 18:5, which states the purpose of the law: if you obey it, you live.

"But we did obey it!" they would argue.

"You may have obeyed it *outwardly,*" Paul would reply, "but you did not believe it from your heart." He then quoted Deuteronomy 30:12–14 and gave the passage a deeper spiritual meaning. The theme of Moses' message was "the commandment" (Deut. 30:11), referring to the Word of God. Moses argued that the Jews had no reason to disobey the Word of God because it had been clearly explained to them and it was not far from them. In fact, Moses urged them to receive the Word in their hearts (see Deut. 5:29; 6:5–12; 13:3; 30:6). The emphasis in Deuteronomy is on the heart, the inner spiritual condition, and not mere outward acts of obedience.

Paul gave us the spiritual understanding of this admonition. He saw "the commandment" or "the

Word" as meaning "Christ, God's Word." So, he substituted "Christ" for "the commandment." He told us that God's way of salvation was not difficult and complicated. We do not have to go to heaven to find Christ, or into the world of the dead. He is near to us. In other words, the gospel of Christ— the Word of faith—is available and accessible. The sinner need not perform difficult works in order to be saved. All he has to do is trust Christ. The very Word on the lips of the religious Jews was the Word of faith. The very law that they read and recited pointed to Christ.

At this point Paul quoted Isaiah 28:16 to show that salvation is *by faith:* "Whosoever believeth on him shall not be ashamed." He quoted this verse before in Romans 9:33. He made it clear in Romans 10:9–10 that salvation is *by faith*—we believe in the heart, receive God's righteousness, and then confess Christ openly and without shame.

Paul's final quotation was from Joel 2:32, to prove that this salvation is open to everyone: "For whosoever shall call upon the name of the Lord shall be saved." Paul had already proved that "there is no difference" in condemnation (Rom. 3:20–23); now he affirms that "there is no difference" in salvation. Instead of the Jew having a special righteousness of his own through the law, he was declared to be as much a sinner as the Gentile he condemned.

This entire section emphasizes the difference between "law righteousness" and "faith righteousness." The contrasts are seen in the following summary:

Law Righteousness	*Faith Righteousness*
Only for the Jew	For "whosoever"
Based on works	Comes by faith alone
Self-righteousness	God's righteousness
Cannot save	Brings salvation
Obey the Lord	Call on the Lord
Leads to pride	Glorifies God

Having explained the reasons for Israel's rejection of God's righteousness, Paul moves into the next aspect of the subject.

The Remedy for Their Rejection (10:14–17)

This passage is often used as the basis for the church's missionary program, and rightly so, but its first application is to the nation of Israel. The only way unbelieving Jews can be saved is by calling on the Lord. But before they can call on Him, they must believe. For the Jew, this meant believing that Jesus Christ of Nazareth truly is the Son of God and the Messiah of Israel. It also meant believing in His death and resurrection (Rom. 10:9–10). But in order to believe, they must hear the Word, for it is the Word that creates faith in the heart of the hearer (Rom. 10:17). This meant that a herald of the Word must be sent, and it is the Lord who does the sending. At this point, Paul could well have been remembering his own call to preach the Word to the Gentiles (Acts 13:1–3).

The quotation in Romans 10:15 is found in Isaiah 52:7 and Nahum 1:15. The Nahum reference had to do with the destruction of the Assyrian Empire, the hated enemies of the Jews. Nineveh was their key city, a wicked city to which God had sent Jonah some 150 years before Nahum wrote. God had patiently dealt with Nineveh, but now His judgment was going to fall. It was this "good news" that the messenger brought to the Jews, and this is what made his feet so beautiful.

Isaiah used this statement for a *future* event—the return of Christ and the establishing of His glorious kingdom. "Thy God reigneth!" (Read Isa. 52:7–10.) The messenger with the beautiful feet announced that God had defeated Israel's enemies and that Messiah was reigning from Jerusalem.

But Paul used the quotation in a *present* application: the messengers of the gospel taking the good news to Israel today. The "peace" spoken of is "peace with God" (Rom. 5:1) and the peace Christ has effected between Jews and Gentiles by forming the one body, the church (Eph. 2:13–17). The remedy for Israel's rejection is in hearing the Word of the gospel and believing on Jesus Christ.

Isaiah 53:1 was Paul's next quotation, proving that not all of Israel would obey His Word. This verse introduced one of the greatest messianic chapters in the Old Testament. Traditionally, Jewish scholars have applied Isaiah 53 to the nation of Israel rather than to Messiah, but many ancient rabbis saw in it a picture of a suffering Messiah bearing the sins of His people (see Acts 8:26–40). In Isaiah's day, the people did not believe God's Word, nor do they believe it today. John 12:37–41 cites Isaiah 53:1 to explain how the nation saw Christ's miracles and still refused to believe. Because they would not believe, judgment came on them and they could not believe.

Note that trusting Christ is not only a matter of believing, but also obeying. Not to believe on Christ is to disobey God. God "commandeth all men everywhere to repent" (Acts 17:30). Romans 6:17 also equates "believing" and "obeying." True faith must touch the will and result in a changed life.

We must never minimize the missionary outreach of the church. While this passage relates primarily to Israel, it applies to all lost souls around the world. They cannot be saved unless they call on the Lord Jesus Christ. But they cannot call unless they believe. Faith comes by hearing, so they must hear the message. How will they hear? A messenger must go to them with the message. But this means that God must call the messenger and the messenger must be sent. What a privilege it is to be one of His messengers and have beautiful feet!

As I was writing this chapter, my phone rang and one of the businessmen in our city reported another soul led to Christ. My caller had had serious spiritual problems a few years ago and I was able to help him.

Since that time, he has led many to Christ, including some in his office. His phone call was to give me the good news that one of his associates had led a friend to Christ, another miracle in a spiritual chain reaction that has been going on for three years now. My friend has beautiful feet, and wherever he goes he shares the good news of the gospel.

Some of us share the news here at home, but others are sent to distant places. In spite of some closed doors, there are still more open doors for the gospel than ever before, and we have better tools to work with. My friend, the late Dr. E. Meyers Hamson, veteran missionary and professor of missions, said that there are four reasons why the church must send out missionaries: (1) *the command from above*—"go ye into all the world" (Mark 16:15); (2) *the cry from beneath*—"send him to my father's house" (Luke 16:27); (3) *the call from without*—"come over and help us" (Acts 16:9); and (4) *the constraint from within*—"the love of Christ constraineth us" (2 Cor. 5:14).

There remains a third aspect of Israel's rejection for Paul to discuss.

The Results of Their Rejection (10:18–21)

There are three results, and each of them is supported by a quotation from the Old Testament.

Israel is guilty (v. 18). Someone might have argued with Paul: "But how do you know that Israel really heard?" His reply would have been Psalm 19:4, a psalm that emphasizes the revelation of God in the world. God reveals Himself in creation (Ps. 19:1–6) and in His Word (Ps. 19:7–11). The "book of Nature" and the "book of Revelation" go together and proclaim the glory of God. Israel had the benefit of both books, for she saw God at work in nature and she received God's written Word. Israel heard, but she would not *heed*. No wonder Jesus often had to say to the crowds, "He that hath ears to hear, let him hear!"

The message goes to the Gentiles (vv. 19–20). What marvelous grace! When Israel rejected her Messiah, God sent the gospel to the Gentiles that they might be saved. This was predicted by Moses in Deuteronomy 32:21. Paul had mentioned this truth before in Romans 9:22–26. One reason why God sent the gospel to the Gentiles was that they might provoke the Jews to jealousy (Rom. 10:19; 11:11). It was an act of grace both to the Jews and to the Gentiles. The prophet Isaiah predicted too that God would save the Gentiles (Isa. 65:1).

As you study the New Testament, you discover that "to the Jew first" is a ruling principle of operation. Jesus began His ministry with the Jews. He forbad His disciples to preach to the Gentiles or the Samaritans when He sent them on their first tour of ministry (Matt. 10:1–6). After His resurrection, He commanded them to wait in Jerusalem and to start their ministry there (Luke 24:46–49; Acts 1:8). In the first seven chapters of Acts, the ministry is to Jews and to Gentiles who were Jewish proselytes. But when the nation stoned Stephen and persecution broke loose, God sent the gospel to the Samaritans (Acts 8:1–8) and then to the Gentiles (Acts 10).

The Jewish believers were shocked when Peter went to the Gentiles (Acts 11:1–18). But he explained that it was God who sent him and that it was clear to him that Jews and Gentiles were both saved the same way—by faith in Christ. But the opposition of the legalistic Jews was so great that the churches had to call a council to discuss the issue. The record of this council is given in Acts 15. Their conclusion was that Jews and Gentiles were all saved by faith in Christ, and that a Gentile did not have to become a Jewish proselyte before he could become a Christian.

God still yearns over His people (v. 21). This quotation is from Isaiah 65:2. "All day long" certainly refers to this present "day of salvation" or day of grace in which we live. While Israel as a nation has been set aside, individual Jewish people can be saved and are being saved. The phrase "all day long" makes us think of Paul's ministry to the Jews in Rome when he arrived there as a prisoner. "From morning till evening" Paul expounded the Scriptures to them and sought to convince them that Jesus is the Messiah (Acts 28:23). Through Paul, God was stretching out His arms of love to His disobedient people, yearning over them, and asking them to return. God's favor to the Gentiles did not change His love for the Jews.

God wants to use us to share the gospel with both Jews and Gentiles. God can use our feet and our arms just as He used Paul's. Jesus Christ wept over Jerusalem and longed to gather His people in His arms! Instead, those arms were stretched out on a cross where He willingly died for Jews and Gentiles alike. God is long suffering and patient "not willing that any should perish, but that all should come to repentance" (2 Peter 3:9). Will God's patience with Israel wear out? Is there any future for the nation? Yes, there is, as the next chapter will show.

CHAPTER TEN
Romans 11
GOD IS NOT THROUGH WITH ISRAEL!

For centuries people have been puzzled by the nation of Israel. The Roman government recognized the Jewish religion, but it still called the nation *secta nefaria*—"a nefarious sect." The great historian Arnold Toynbee classified Israel as "a fossil civilization" and did not know what to do with it. For some reason, the nation did not fit into his historical theories.

Paul devoted all of Romans 11 to presenting proof that God is not through with Israel. We must not apply this chapter to the church today, because Paul is discussing a literal future for a literal nation. He called five witnesses to prove there was a future in God's plan for the Jews.

Paul Himself (11:1)

"Hath God cast away his people? God forbid! For I also am an Israelite!" If God has cast away His people, then how can the conversion of the apostle Paul be explained? The fact that his conversion is presented three times in the book of Acts is significant (Acts 9, 22, 26). Certainly Dr. Luke did not write these chapters and repeat the story just to exalt Paul. No, they were written to show Paul's conversion as an illustration of the future conversion of the nation of Israel. Paul called himself "one born out of due time" (1 Cor. 15:8). In 1 Timothy 1:16 he stated that God saved him "that in me first Jesus Christ might show forth all long suffering, for a pattern to them which should hereafter believe on him to life everlasting."

The accounts of Paul's conversion tell very little that parallels our salvation experience today. Certainly none of us has seen Christ in glory or actually heard Him speak from heaven. We were neither blinded by the light of heaven nor thrown to the ground. In what way, then, is Paul's conversion "a pattern"? It is a picture of how the nation of Israel will be saved when Jesus Christ returns to establish His kingdom on earth. The details of Israel's future restoration and salvation are given in Zechariah 12:10—13:1. The nation shall see Him as He returns (Zech. 14:4; Acts 1:11; Rev. 1:7), recognize Him as their Messiah, repent, and receive Him. It will be an experience similar to that of Saul of Tarsus when he was on his way to Damascus to persecute Christians (Acts 9).

This is why Paul used himself as the first witness. The *fact* that he was saved does not prove that there is a future for Israel. Rather, what is important is the *way* he was saved.

The Prophet Elijah (11:2–10)

Israel is God's elect nation; He foreknew them, or chose them, and they are His. The fact that most of the nation has rejected Christ is no proof that God has finished with His people. In his day, Elijah thought that the nation had totally departed from God (see 1 Kings 19). But Elijah discovered that there was yet a remnant of true believers. He thought he was the only faithful Jew left and discovered that there were seven thousand more.

Paul referred to this "remnant" in Romans 9:27, a quotation from Isaiah 10:22–23. At no time has the entire nation of Israel been true to the Lord. God makes a distinction between Abraham's natural children and his spiritual children (Rom. 2:25–29). The fact that the Jews shared in the covenant by being circumcised did not guarantee their salvation. Like Abraham, they had to believe God in order to receive His righteousness (Rom. 4:1–5).

Note that this remnant is saved by grace and not by works (Rom. 11:5–6). Note also the parallel in Romans 9:30–33. It is impossible to mix grace and works, for the one cancels the other. Israel's main concern had always been in trying to please God with good works (Rom. 9:30—10:4). The nation refused to submit to Christ's righteousness, just as religious, self-righteous people refuse to submit today.

If a remnant had been saved, thus proving that God was not through with His people, then what had happened to the rest of the nation? They had been hardened (a better translation than "blinded" in Rom. 11:7). This was the result of their resisting the truth, just as Pharaoh's heart was hardened because he resisted the truth. Paul quoted Isaiah 29:10 to support his statement, and also referred to Deuteronomy 29:4. We would expect a pagan ruler to harden himself against the Lord, but we do not expect God's people to do so.

Romans 11:9–10 are cited from Psalm 69:22–23. This psalm is one of the most important of the messianic psalms and is referred to several times in the New Testament. (Note especially Romans 11:4, 9, 21–22.) Their "table to become a snare" means that their blessings turn into burdens and judgments. This is what happened to Israel: their spiritual blessings should have led them to Christ, but instead they became a snare that kept them from Christ. Their very religious practices and observances became substitutes for the real experience of salvation. Sad to say, this same mistake is made today when people depend on religious rituals and practices instead of trusting in the Christ who is pictured in these activities.

Paul made it clear that the hardening of Israel is neither total nor final, and this is proof that God has a future for the nation. "Hardness in part is happened to Israel, until the fullness of the Gentiles be come in" (Rom. 11:25). The existence of the believing Jewish remnant today, as in Elijah's day, is evidence that God still has a plan for His people. Paul did not imitate Elijah's mistake and say, "I only am left!" He knew that there was a remnant of Israel in this world who trusted God.

The Gentiles (11:11–15)

In Romans 2:1–3 Paul used the Gentiles to prove the Jews guilty of sin, but here he used the Gentiles to assure Israel of a future restoration. His logic here is beautiful. When the Jews rejected the gospel, God sent it to the Gentiles and they believed and were saved. Three tragedies occurred in Israel: the nation *fell* (Rom. 11:11), was *lost* (Rom. 11:12, "diminished"), and was *cast away* (Rom. 11:15). None of these words suggests a *final* judgment on Israel But the amazing thing is that through Israel's fall, salvation came to the Gentiles. God promised that the Gentiles would be saved (Rom. 9:25–26), and He kept His promise. Will He not also keep His promise to the Jews?

It is important to understand that the Old Testament promises to the Gentiles were linked to Israel's "rise"—her entering into her kingdom. Prophecies like Isaiah 11 and Isaiah 60 make it clear that the Gentiles will share in Israel's kingdom. But Israel did not "rise"; *she fell!* What would God then do with the Gentiles? God introduced a new factor—the

church—in which believing Jews and Gentiles are one in Christ (Eph. 2:11–22). In Ephesians 3, Paul called this new program "the mystery," meaning "the sacred secret" that was not revealed in the Old Testament. Does this mean that God has abandoned His kingdom program for Israel? Of course not! Israel is merely set aside until the time comes for God's plans for Israel to be fulfilled.

Paul stated that the Gentiles had a vital ministry to Israel. Today, the saved Gentiles provoke Israel "to jealousy" (see Rom. 10:19) because of the spiritual riches they have in Christ. Israel today is spiritually bankrupt, while Christians have "all spiritual blessings" in Christ (Eph. 1:3). (If an unsaved Jew visited the average church service, would he be provoked to *jealousy* and wish he had what we have—or would he just be provoked?)

There is a future for Israel. Paul calls it "their fullness" (Rom. 11:12) and their "receiving" (Rom. 11:15). Today, Israel is fallen spiritually, but when Christ returns, the nation will rise again. Today, Israel is cast away from God, but one day they shall be received again. God will never break His covenant with His people, and He has promised to restore them. (See Jer. 31:35–37, where God links His promises to Israel to the sun, moon, and stars.)

The Patriarchs (11:16–24)

From looking at the future, Paul next looked to the past to show Israel's spiritual heritage. From the beginning, Israel was a special people, set apart by God. Paul used two illustrations to prove his argument that God was not finished with the Jews.

The lump of dough (v. 16a). The reference here is to Numbers 15:17–21. The first part of the dough was to be offered up to God as a symbol that the entire lump belonged to Him. The same idea was involved in the Feast of Firstfruits, when the priest offered a sheaf to the Lord as a token that the entire harvest was His (Lev. 23:9–14). The basic idea is that when God accepts the part He sanctifies the whole.

Applying this to the history of Israel, we understand Paul's argument. God accepted the founder of the nation, Abraham, and in so doing set apart his descendants as well. God also accepted the other patriarchs, Isaac and Jacob, in spite of their sins or failings. This means that God must accept the "rest of the lump"—the nation of Israel.

The olive tree (vv. 16b–24). This is a symbol of the nation of Israel (Jer. 11:16–17; Hos. 14:4–6). Please keep in mind that Paul was not discussing the relationship of individual believers to God, but the place of Israel in the plan of God. The roots of the tree support the tree; again, this was a symbol of the patriarchs who founded the nation. God made His covenants with Abraham, Isaac, and Jacob, and He cannot deny them or change them. Thus, it is God's promise to Abraham that sustains Israel even today.

Many of the Jewish people did not believe. Paul pictured them as branches broken off the tree. But he saw an amazing thing taking place: other branches were grafted into the tree to share in the life of the tree. These branches were the Gentiles. In Romans 11:24, Paul described this "grafting in" as "contrary to nature." Usually a cultivated branch is grafted into a wild tree and shares its life without producing its poor fruit. But in this case, it was the "wild branch" (the Gentiles) that was grafted into the good tree! "Salvation is of the Jews" (John 4:22).

To say that the olive tree, with its natural and grafted branches, is a picture of the church would be a great mistake. In the church, "there is no difference"; believers are "all one in Christ Jesus" (Gal. 3:28). God does not look on the members of Christ's body and see them as Jews or Gentiles. The olive tree illustrates the relationship between Jew and Gentile in the program of God. The "breaking off of the branches" is the equivalent of "the fall" (Rom. 11:11), "the diminishing" (Rom. 11:12), and "the casting away" (Rom. 11:15). To read into this illustration the matter of the eternal destiny of the individual believer is to abuse the truth Paul was seeking to communicate.

Paul warned the Gentiles that they were obligated to Israel, and therefore they dared not boast of their new spiritual position (Rom. 11:18–21). The Gentiles entered into God's plan because of faith, and not because of anything good they had done. Paul was discussing the Gentiles collectively, and not the individual experience of one believer or another.

It is worth noting that, according to Bible prophecy, the professing Gentile church will be "cut off" because of apostasy. First Timothy 4 and 2 Timothy 3, along with 2 Thessalonians 2, all indicate that the professing church in the last days will depart from the faith. *There is no hope for the apostate church, but there is hope for apostate Israel!* Why? Because of the roots of the olive tree. God will keep His promises to the patriarchs, but God will break off the Gentiles because of their unbelief.

No matter how far Israel may stray from the truth of God, the roots are still good. God is still the "God of Abraham, and the God of Isaac, and the God of Jacob" (Ex. 3:6; Matt. 22:23). He will keep His promises to these patriarchs. This means that the olive tree will flourish again!

God Himself (11:25–36)

Paul saved his best witness for the last. He proved that the very character and work of God were involved in the future of Israel. Men may dispute about prophecy and differ in their interpretations, but let every man realize that he is dealing with *God's people,* Israel.

God's timing (v. 25). What has happened to Israel is all a part of God's plan, and He knows what He is doing. The blinding (or hardening, Rom. 11:7) of Israel as a nation is neither total nor final: it is partial and temporary. How long will it last? "Until the fullness of the Gentiles be come in" (Rom. 11:25). There is a "fullness" for Israel (Rom. 11:12) and for

the Gentiles. Today, God in His grace is visiting the Gentiles and taking out a people for His name (Acts 15:12–14). Individual Jews are being saved, of course, but this present age is primarily a time when God is visiting the Gentiles and building His church. When this present age has run its course, and the fullness of the Gentiles has come in, then God will once more deal with the nation of Israel.

Romans 11:25 is one of several *"until* verses" in the Bible, all of which are important. (Read Matthew 23:32–39; Luke 21:24; and Psalm 110:1 for other references.) It is reassuring that God knows what time it is and that He is never late in fulfilling His will.

God's promise (v. 26). The reference here is Isaiah 59:20–21, and you ought to read Isaiah 60 to complete the picture. God has promised to save His people, and He will keep His promise. There are those who interpret this as meaning salvation to individuals through the gospel, but it is my conviction that the prophet has national conversion in mind. "All Israel shall be saved" does not mean that every Jew who has ever lived will be converted, but that the Jews living when the Redeemer returns will see Him, receive Him, and be saved. Zechariah 12—13 give the details. It seems to me that there are too many details in these Old Testament prophecies of national restoration for Israel for us to spiritualize them and apply them to the church today.

God's covenant (vv. 27–28). This is, of course, a continuation of the quotation from Isaiah 59, but the emphasis is on the covenant of God with Israel. God chose Israel in His grace and not because of any merit in her (Deut. 7:6–11; 9:1–6). If the nation was not chosen because of its goodness, can it be rejected because of its sin? "Election" means grace, not merit. The Jewish people are "enemies" to the believing Gentiles because of their hostile attitude toward the gospel. But to God, the Jewish people are "beloved for the fathers' sakes." God will not break His covenant with Abraham, Isaac, and Jacob.

God's nature (v. 29). "I am the Lord, I change not" (Mal. 3:6). "God is not a man that he should lie; neither the son of man, that he should repent" (Num. 23:19). God's gifts to Israel, and God's calling of Israel, cannot be taken back or changed, or God would cease to be true to His own perfect nature. The fact that Israel may not enjoy her gifts, or live up to her privileges as an elect nation, does not affect this fact one bit. God will be consistent with Himself and true to His Word no matter what men may do. "Shall their unbelief make the faithfulness of God without effect?" (Rom. 3:3, literal translation).

God's grace (vv. 30–32). "Because of the unbelief of the Jews, you Gentiles were saved," said Paul. "Now, may it be that through your salvation Israel will come to know Christ." Note that Paul repeatedly reminded the saved Gentiles that they had a spiritual obligation to Israel to "provoke them to jealousy" (Rom. 10:19; 11:11, 14). Israel's hardness is only "in part" (Rom. 11:25), which means that individual Jews can be saved. God has included "all in unbelief—Jews and Gentiles—so that *all* might have the opportunity to be saved by grace. "There is no difference." If God can save Jews by His grace and mercy today, why can He not save them in the future?

We must remember that God chose the Jews so that the Gentiles might be saved. "In thee shall all families of the earth be blessed," was God's promise to Abraham (Gen. 12:1–3). The tragedy was that Israel became exclusive and failed to share the truth with the Gentiles. They thought that the Gentiles had to become Jews in order to be saved. But God declared both Jews and Gentiles to be lost and condemned. This meant that He could have mercy on all because of the sacrifice of Christ on the cross.

God's wisdom (vv. 33–36). Having contemplated God's great plan of salvation for Jews and Gentiles, all Paul could do was sing a hymn of praise. As someone has remarked, "Theology becomes doxology!" Only a God as wise as our God could take the fall of Israel and turn it into salvation for the world! His plans will not be aborted, nor will His purposes lack fulfillment. No human being can fully know the mind of the Lord, and the more we study His ways, the more we offer Him praise. Are we to conclude that God does *not* know what He is doing, and that the nation of Israel completely ruined His plans? Of course not! God is too wise to make plans that will not be fulfilled. Israel did not allow Him to rule, so He overruled!

Paul summoned five witnesses, and they all agreed: there is a future for Israel. When Israel recovers from her "fall" and enters into her "fullness," the world will experience the riches of God's grace as never before. When Jesus Christ returns and sits on David's throne to reign over His kingdom, then Israel will be "reconciled" and "received," and it will be like a resurrection!

CHAPTER ELEVEN
Romans 12—13
RIGHT RELATIONSHIPS MEAN RIGHT LIVING

In all of his letters, Paul concluded with a list of practical duties that were based on the doctrines he had discussed. In the Christian life, doctrine and duty always go together. What we believe helps to determine how we behave. It is not enough for us to understand Paul's doctrinal explanations. We must translate our *learning* into *living* and show by our daily lives that we trust God's Word.

The key idea in this section is *relationships*. The term "relational theology" is a relatively new one, but the idea is not new. If we have a right relationship to God, we will have a right relationship to the people who are a part of our lives. "If a man say, I love God, and hateth his brother, he is a liar" (1 John 4:20).

Our Relationship to God (12:1–2)

This is the fourth "therefore" in the letter. Romans 3:20 is the "therefore" of condemnation, declaring that the whole world is guilty before God. Romans 5:1 is the "therefore" of justification, and Romans 8:1 the "therefore" of assurance. In Romans 12:1, we have the "therefore" of dedication, and it is this dedication that is the basis for the other relationships that Paul discussed in this section.

What is true dedication? As Paul described it here, Christian dedication involves three steps.

You give God your body (v. 1). Before we trusted Christ, we used our body for sinful pleasures and purposes, but now that we belong to Him, we want to use our body for His glory. The Christian's body is God's temple (1 Cor. 6:19–20) because the Spirit of God dwells within him (Rom. 8:9). It is our privilege to glorify Christ in our body and magnify Christ in our body (Phil. 1:20–21).

Just as Jesus Christ had to take on Himself a body in order to accomplish God's will on earth, so we must yield our bodies to Christ that He might continue God's work through us. We must yield the members of the body as "instruments of righteousness" (Rom. 6:13) for the Holy Spirit to use in the doing of God's work. The Old Testament sacrifices were dead sacrifices, but we are to be living sacrifices.

There are two "living sacrifices" in the Bible, and they help us understand what this really means. The first is Isaac (Gen. 22); the second is our Lord Jesus Christ. Isaac willingly put himself on the altar and would have died in obedience to God's will, but the Lord sent a ram to take his place. Isaac "died" just the same—he died to self and willingly yielded himself to the will of God. When he got off that altar, Isaac was a "living sacrifice" to the glory of God.

Of course, our Lord Jesus Christ is the perfect illustration of a "living sacrifice," because He actually died as a sacrifice, in obedience to His Father's will. But He arose again. And today He is in heaven as a "living sacrifice," bearing in His body the wounds of Calvary. He is our High Priest (Heb. 4:14–16) and our Advocate (1 John 2:1) before the throne of God.

The verb "present" in this verse means "present once and for all." It commands a definite commitment of the body to the Lord, just as a bride and groom in their wedding service commit themselves to each other. It is this once-for-all commitment that determines what they do with their bodies. Paul gives us two reasons for this commitment: (1) it is the right response to all that God has done for us—"I beseech you *therefore,* brethren, *by the mercies of God*" (italics mine); and (2) this commitment is our "reasonable service" or our "spiritual worship." This means that every day is a worship experience when your body is yielded to the Lord.

You give Him your mind (v. 2a). The world wants to control your mind, but God wants to transform your mind (see Eph. 4:17–24; Col. 3:1–11). This word *transform* is the same as *transfigure* in Matthew 17:2.

It has come into our English language as the word *metamorphosis*. It describes a change from within. The world wants to change your mind, so it exerts pressure from without. But the Holy Spirit changes your mind by releasing power from within. If the world controls your thinking, you are a *conformer;* if God controls your thinking, you are a *transformer.*

God transforms our minds and makes us spiritually minded by using His Word. As you spend time meditating on God's Word, memorizing it, and making it a part of your inner man, God will gradually make your mind more spiritual (see 2 Cor. 3:18).

You give Him your will (v. 2b). Your mind controls your body, and your will controls your mind. Many people think they can control their will by "willpower," but usually they fail. (This was Paul's experience as recorded in Rom. 7:15–21). It is only when we yield the will to God that His power can take over and give us the willpower (and the won't power!) that we need to be victorious Christians.

We surrender our wills to God through disciplined prayer. As we spend time in prayer, we surrender our will to God and pray, with the Lord, "Not my will, but thy will be done." We must pray about everything, and let God have His way in everything.

For many years I have tried to begin each day by surrendering my body to the Lord. Then I spend time with His Word and let Him transform my mind and prepare my thinking for that new day. Then I pray, and I yield the plans of the day to Him and let Him work as He sees best. I especially pray about those tasks that upset or worry me—and He always sees me through. To have a right relationship with God, we must start the day by yielding to Him our bodies, minds, and wills.

Relationship to Other Believers (12:3–16)

Paul was writing to Christians who were members of local churches in Rome. He described their relationship to each other in terms of the members of a body. (He used this same picture in 1 Cor. 12; Eph. 4:7–16.) The basic idea is that each believer is a living part of Christ's body, and each one has a spiritual function to perform. Each believer has a gift (or gifts) to be used for the building up of the body and the perfecting of the other members of the body. In short, we belong to each other, we minister to each other, and we need each other. What are the essentials for spiritual ministry and growth in the body of Christ?

Honest evaluation (v. 3). Each Christian must know what his spiritual gifts are and what ministry (or ministries) he is to have in the local church. It is not wrong for a Christian to recognize gifts in his own life and in the lives of others. What *is* wrong is the tendency to have a false evaluation of ourselves. Nothing causes more damage in a local church than a believer who overrates himself and tries to perform a ministry that he cannot do. (Sometimes the opposite is true, and people undervalue themselves. Both attitudes are wrong.)

The gifts that we have came because of God's grace.

They must be accepted and exercised by faith. We were saved "by grace, through faith" (Eph. 2:8–9), and we must live and serve "by grace through faith." Since our gifts are from God, we cannot take the credit for them. All we can do is accept them and use them to honor His name. (See 1 Cor. 15:10 for Paul's personal testimony about gifts.)

I once ministered with two men who had opposite attitudes toward their gifts: the one man constantly belittled his gifts and would not use them, and the other man constantly boasted about gifts that he did not possess. Actually, both of them were guilty of pride, because both of them refused to acknowledge God's grace and let Him have the glory. Moses made a similar mistake when God called him (Ex. 4:1–13). When the individual believers in a church know their gifts, accept them by faith, and use them for God's glory, then God can bless in a wonderful way.

Faithful cooperation (vv. 4–8). Each believer has a different gift, and God has bestowed these gifts so the local body can grow in a balanced way. But each Christian must exercise his or her gift by faith. We may not see the result of our ministry, but the Lord sees it and He blesses. Note that "exhortation" (encouragement) is just as much a spiritual ministry as preaching or teaching. Giving and showing mercy are also important gifts. To some people, God has given the ability to rule, or to administer the various functions of the church. Whatever gift we have must be dedicated to God and used for the good of the whole church.

It is tragic when any one gift is emphasized in a local church beyond all the other gifts. "Are all apostles? are all prophets? are all teachers? are all workers of miracles? Have all the gifts of healing? do all speak with tongues? do all interpret?" (1 Cor. 12:29–30). The answer to all these questions is no! And for a Christian to minimize the other gifts while he emphasizes his own gift is to deny the very purpose for which gifts are given: the benefit of the whole body of Christ. "Now to each man the manifestation of the Spirit is given for the common good" (1 Cor. 12:7 NIV).

Spiritual gifts are tools to build with, not toys to play with or weapons to fight with. In the church at Corinth, the believers were tearing down the ministry because they were abusing spiritual gifts. They were using their gifts as ends in themselves and not as a means toward the end of building up the church. They so emphasized their spiritual gifts that they lost their spiritual graces! They had the gifts of the Spirit but were lacking in the fruit of the Spirit—love, joy, peace, etc. (Gal. 5:22–23).

Loving participation (vv. 9–16). Here the emphasis is on the attitudes of those who exercise the spiritual gifts. It is possible to use a spiritual gift in an unspiritual way. Paul makes this same point in 1 Corinthians 13, the great "love chapter" of the New Testament. Love is the circulatory system of the spiritual body, which enables all the members to function in a healthy, harmonious way. This must be an honest love, not a hypocritical love (Rom. 11:9), and it must be humble, not proud (Rom. 11:10). "Preferring one another" means treating others as more important than ourselves (Phil. 2:1–4).

Serving Christ usually means satanic opposition and days of discouragement. Paul admonished his readers to maintain their spiritual zeal because they were serving the Lord and not men. When life becomes difficult, the Christian cannot permit his zeal to grow cold. "Be joyful in hope, patient in affliction, faithful in prayer" (Rom. 12:12 NIV).

Finally, Paul reminded them that they must enter into the feelings of others. Christian fellowship is much more than a pat on the back and a handshake. It means sharing the burdens and the blessings of others so that we all grow together and glorify the Lord. If Christians cannot get along with one another, how can they ever face their enemies? A humble attitude and a willingness to share are the marks of a Christian who truly ministers to the body. Our Lord ministered to the common people, and they heard Him gladly (Mark 12:37). When a local church decides it wants only a certain "high class" of people, it departs from the Christian ideal for ministry.

Our Relationship to Our Enemies (12:17–21)

The believer who seeks to obey God is going to have his enemies. When our Lord was ministering on earth, He had enemies. No matter where Paul and the other apostles traveled, there were enemies who opposed their work. Jesus warned His disciples that their worst enemies might be those of their own household (Matt. 10:36). Unfortunately, some believers have enemies because they lack love and patience, and not because they are faithful in their witness. There is a difference between sharing in "the offense of the cross" (Gal. 5:11; 6:12–15) and being an offensive Christian!

The Christian must not play God and try to avenge himself. Returning evil for evil, or good for good, is the way most people live. But the Christian must live on a higher level and return good for evil. Of course, this requires *love,* because our first inclination is to fight back. It also requires *faith,* believing that God can work and accomplish His will in our lives and in the lives of those who hurt us. We must give place to "the wrath"—the wrath of God (Deut. 32:35).

A friend of mine once heard a preacher criticize him over the radio and tell things that were not only unkind, but also untrue. My friend became very angry and was planning to fight back, when a godly preacher said, "Don't do it. If you defend yourself, then the Lord can't defend you. Leave it in His hands." My friend followed that wise counsel, and the Lord vindicated him.

The admonition in Romans 12:20 reminds us of Christ's words in Matthew 5:44–48. These words are easy to read but difficult to practice. Surely we need to pray and ask God for love as we try to show kindness to our enemies. Will they take advantage of us? Will they hate us more? Only the Lord knows. Our task is not to protect ourselves but to obey the Lord and leave the results with Him. Paul referred to Proverbs 25:21–22 as he urged us to return good for evil in the name of the Lord. The "coals of fire" refer perhaps to the feeling of shame our enemies will experience when we return good for evil.

As children of God, we must live on the highest level—returning good for evil. Anyone can return good for good and evil for evil. The only way to overcome evil is with good. If we return evil for evil, we only add fuel to the fire. And even if our enemy is not converted, we have still experienced the love of God in our own hearts and have grown in grace.

Our Relationship to the State (13:1–14)

God has established three institutions: the home (Gen. 2:18–25), government (Gen. 9:1–17), and the church (Acts 2). Paul was writing to believers at the very heart of the Roman Empire. As yet, the great persecutions had not started, but were on the way. Christianity was still considered a Jewish sect, and the Jewish religion was approved by Rome. But the day would come when it would be very difficult, if not impossible, for a Christian to be loyal to the emperor. He could not drop incense on the altar and affirm, "Caesar is god!"

In our own day, we have people who teach riot and rebellion *in the name of Christ!* They would have us believe that the Christian thing to do is to disobey the law, rebel against the authorities, and permit every man to do that which is right in his own eyes. Paul refuted this position in this chapter by explaining four reasons why the Christian must be in subjection to the laws of the State.

For wrath's sake (vv. 1–4). It is God who has established the governments of the world (see Acts 17:24–28). This does not mean that He is responsible for the sins of tyrants, but only that the authority to rule comes originally from God. It was this lesson that Nebuchadnezzar had to learn the hard way. (See Dan. 4, and especially vv. 17, 25, 32.) To resist the law is to resist the God who established government in the world, and this means inviting punishment.

Rulers must bear the sword; that is, they have the power to afflict punishment and even to take life. God established human government because man is a sinner and must have some kind of authority over him. God has given the sword to rulers, and with it the authority to punish and even to execute. Capital punishment was ordained in Genesis 9:5–6, and it has not been abolished. Even though we cannot always respect the man in office, we must respect the office, for government was ordained by God.

On more than one occasion in his ministry, Paul used the Roman law to protect his life and to extend his work. The centurions mentioned in the book of Acts appear to be men of character and high ideals. Even though government officials are not believers, they are still the "ministers of God" because He established the authority of the State.

For conscience's sake (vv. 5–7). We move a bit higher in our motivation now. Any citizen can obey the law because of fear of punishment, but a Christian ought to obey because of conscience. Of course, if the government interferes with conscience, then the Christian must obey God rather than men (Acts 5:29). But when the law is right, the Christian must obey it if he is to maintain a good conscience (1 Tim. 1:5, 19; 3:9; 4:2; Acts 24:16).

The United States Government maintains a "Conscience Fund" for people who want to pay their debts to the Government and yet remain anonymous. Some city governments have a similar fund. I read about a city that had investigated some tax frauds and announced that several citizens were going to be indicted. They did not release the names of the culprits. That week, a number of people visited the City Hall to "straighten out their taxes"—and many of them were not on the indictment list. When conscience begins to work, we cannot live with ourselves until we have made things right.

Romans 13:7 commands us to pay what we owe: taxes, revenue, respect, honor. If we do not pay our taxes, we show disrespect to the law, the officials, and the Lord. And this cannot but affect the conscience of the believer. We may not agree with all that is done with the money we pay in taxes, but we dare not violate our conscience by refusing to pay.

For love's sake (vv. 8–10). Paul enlarged the circle of responsibility by including other people besides government officials. "Love one another" is the basic principle of the Christian life. It is the "new commandment" that Christ gave to us (John 13:34). When we practice love, there is no need for any other laws, because love covers it all! If we love others, we will not sin against them. This explained why the Ten Commandments were not referred to often in the New Testament. In fact, the Sabbath commandment is not quoted at all in any of the Epistles. As believers, we do not live under the law; we live under grace. Our motive for obeying God and helping others is the love of Christ in our hearts.

Does "owe no man anything" refer also to the Christian's financial practices? Some people believe that it does, and that it is a sin to have a debt. J. Hudson Taylor, the godly missionary to China, would never incur a debt, basing his conviction on this verse. Charles Spurgeon, the great Baptist preacher, had the same conviction. However, the Bible does not forbid borrowing or legal financial transactions that involve interest. What the Bible does forbid is the charging of high interest, robbing the brethren, and failing to pay honest debts (see Ex. 22:25–27; Neh. 5:1–11). Matthew 25:27 and Luke 19:23 indicate that banking and investing for gain are not wrong. Certainly no one should get into unnecessary debt, or sign contracts he cannot maintain. "Thou shalt not steal." But to make Romans 13:8 apply to all kinds of legal obligations involving money is, to me, stretching a point.

In this section, Paul has centered on the very heart of the problem—the human heart. Because the heart of man is sinful, God established government. But laws cannot change the heart; man's heart is still selfish and can be changed only by the grace of God.

For Jesus' sake (vv. 11–14). We have come a long way in our reasons for obeying the law: from fear to conscience to love to our devotion to Jesus Christ! The emphasis is on the imminent return of Christ. As His servants, we want to be found faithful when He returns. The completion of our salvation is near! The light is dawning! Therefore, be ready!

Paul gave several admonitions in the light of the Lord's soon return. The first is, "Wake up!" Relate this with 1 Thessalonians 5:1–11, and also Matthew 25:1–13. The second is, "Clean up!" We do not want to be found dressed in dirty garments when the Lord returns (1 John 2:28—3:3). The Christian wears the armor of light, not the deeds of darkness. He has no reason to get involved in the sinful pleasures of the world. Finally, Paul admonished, "Grow up" (Rom. 13:14). To "put on" the Lord Jesus Christ means to become more like Him, to receive by faith all that He is for our daily living. We grow on the basis of the food we eat. This is why God warns us not to make provisions for the flesh. If we feed the flesh, we will fail, but if we feed the inner man the nourishing things of the Spirit, we will succeed.

In other words, a Christian citizen ought to be the best citizen. Christians may not always agree on politics or parties, but they can all agree on their attitude toward human government.

CHAPTER TWELVE
Romans 14:1—15:7
WHEN CHRISTIANS DISAGREE

Disunity has always been a major problem with God's people. Even the Old Testament records the civil wars and family fights among the people of Israel, and almost every local church mentioned in the New Testament had divisions to contend with. The Corinthians were divided over human leaders, and some of the members were even suing each other (1 Cor. 1:10–13; 6:1–8). The Galatian saints were "biting and devouring" one another (Gal. 5:15), and the saints in Ephesus and Colosse had to be reminded of the importance of Christian unity (Eph. 4:1–3; Col. 2:1–2). In the church at Philippi, two women were at odds with each other and, as a result, were splitting the church (Phil. 4:1–3). No wonder the psalmist wrote, "Behold, how good and how pleasant it is for brethren to dwell together in unity" (Ps. 133:1).

Some of these problems stemmed from the backgrounds of the believers in the churches. The Jews, for example, were saved out of a strict legalistic background that would be difficult to forget. The Gentiles never had to worry about diets and days. The first church council in history debated the issue of the relationship of the Christian to the law (Acts 15).

The believers in Rome were divided over special diets and special days. Some of the members thought it was a sin to eat meat, so they ate only vegetables. Other members thought it a sin not to observe the Jewish holy days. If each Christian had kept his convictions to himself, there would have been no problem, but they began to criticize and judge one another. The one group was sure the other group was not at all spiritual.

Unfortunately, we have similar problems today with many "gray areas" of life that are not clearly right or wrong to every believer. Some activities we know are wrong, because the Bible clearly condemns them. Other activities we know are right, because the Bible clearly commands them. But when it comes to areas that are not clearly defined in Scripture, we find ourselves needing some other kind of guidance. Paul gave principles of this guidance. He explained how believers could disagree on nonessentials and still maintain unity in the church. He gave his readers three important admonitions.

Receive One Another (14:1–12)

You will note that this section begins and ends with this admonition (Rom. 15:7). Paul was addressing those who were "strong in the faith," that is, those who understood their spiritual liberty in Christ and were not enslaved to diets or holy days. The "weak in faith" were immature believers who felt obligated to obey legalistic rules concerning what they ate and when they worshipped. Many people have the idea that the Christians who follow strict rules are the most mature, but this is not necessarily the case. In the Roman assemblies, the weak Christians were those who clung to the law and did not enjoy their freedom in the Lord. The weak Christians were judging and condemning the strong Christians, and the strong Christians were despising the weak Christians.

"Welcome one another!" was Paul's first admonition, and he gave four reasons why they should.

God has received us (vv. 1–3). It is not our responsibility to decide the requirements for Christian fellowship in a church; only the Lord can do this. To set up man-made restrictions on the basis of personal prejudices (or even convictions) is to go beyond the Word of God. Because God has received us, we must receive one another. We must not argue over these matters, nor must we judge or despise one another. Perhaps St. Augustine put the matter best: "In essentials, unity; in nonessentials, liberty; in all things, charity."

When God sent Peter to take the gospel to the Gentiles, the church criticized Peter because he ate with these new Christians (Acts 11:1–3). But God had clearly revealed His acceptance of the Gentiles by giving them the same Holy Spirit that He bestowed on the Jewish believers at Pentecost (Acts 10:44–8; 11:15–18). Peter did not obey this truth consistently, for later on he refused to fellowship with the Gentile Christians in Antioch, and Paul had to rebuke him (Gal, 2:11–13). God showed both Peter and Paul that Christian fellowship was not to be based on food or religious calendars.

In every church there are weak and strong believers. The strong understand spiritual truth and practice it, but the weak have not yet grown into that level of maturity and liberty. The weak must not condemn the strong and call them unspiritual. The strong must not despise the weak and call them immature. God has received both the weak and the strong; therefore, they should receive one another.

God sustains His own (v. 4). The strong Christian was judged by the weak Christian, and this Paul condemned because it was wrong for the weak Christian to take the place of God in the life of the strong Christian. God is the Master; the Christian is the servant. It is wrong for anyone to interfere with this relationship.

It is encouraging to know that our success in the Christian life does not depend on the opinions or attitudes of other Christians. God is the Judge, and He is able to make us stand. The word *servant* here suggests that Christians ought to be busy working for the Lord; then they will not have the time or inclination to judge or condemn other Christians. People who are busy winning souls to Christ have more important things to do than to investigate the lives of the saints!

Jesus Christ is Lord (vv. 5–9). The word *Lord* is found eight times in these verses. No Christian has the right to "play God" in another Christian's life. We can pray, advise, and even admonish, but we cannot take the place of God. What is it that makes a dish of food "holy" or a day "holy"? It is the fact that we relate it to the Lord. The person who treats a special day as "holy" does so "unto the Lord." The person who treats every day as sacred, does so "unto the Lord." The Christian who eats meat gives thanks to the Lord, and the Christian who abstains from meat abstains "unto the Lord." To be "fully persuaded [or assured] in his own mind" (Rom. 14:5) means: Let every man see to it that he is really doing what he does for the Lord's sake, and not merely on the basis of some prejudice or whim.

Some standards and practices in our local churches are traditional but not necessarily scriptural. Some of us can remember when dedicated Christians opposed Christian radio "because Satan was the prince of the power of the air!" Some people even make Bible translations a test of orthodoxy. The church is divided and weakened because Christians will not allow Jesus Christ to be Lord.

An interesting illustration of this truth is given in John 21:15–25. Jesus had restored Peter to his place as an apostle, and once again He told him, "Follow me." Peter began to follow Christ, but then he heard someone walking behind him. It was the apostle John.

Then Peter asked Jesus, "Lord, what shall this man do?"

Notice the Lord's reply: "What is that to thee?

Follow thou me!" In other words, "Peter, you make sure you have made Me Lord of your life. Let Me worry about John." Whenever I hear believers condemning other Christians because of something they disagree with, something that is not essential or forbidden in the Word, I feel like saying, "What is that to thee? Follow Christ! Let Him be the Lord!"

Paul emphasized the believer's union with Christ: "Whether we live, therefore, or whether we die, we are the Lord's" (Rom. 14:8). Our first responsibility is to the Lord. If Christians would go to the Lord in prayer instead of going to their brother with criticism, there would be stronger fellowship in our churches.

Jesus Christ is Judge (vv. 10–12). Paul asked the weak Christian, "Why are you judging your brother?" Then he asked the strong Christian, "Why are you despising your brother?" Both strong and weak must stand at the judgment seat of Christ, and they will not judge each other—they will be judged by the Lord.

The judgment seat of Christ is that place where Christians will have their works judged by the Lord. It has nothing to do with our sins, since Christ has paid for them and they can be held against us no more (Rom. 8:1). The word for "judgment seat" in the Greek is *bema,* meaning the place where the judges stood at the athletic games. If during the games they saw an athlete break the rules, they immediately disqualified him. At the end of the contests, the judges gave out the rewards (see 1 Cor. 9:24–27). First Corinthians 3:10–15 gives another picture of the judgment seat of Christ. Paul compared our ministries with the building of a temple. If we build with cheap materials, the fire will burn them up. If we use precious, lasting materials, our works will last. If our works pass the test, we receive a reward. If they are burned up, we lose the reward, but we are still saved "yet so as by fire."

How does the Christian prepare for the judgment seat of Christ? By making Jesus Lord of his life and faithfully obeying Him. Instead of judging other Christians, we had better judge our own lives and make sure we are ready to meet Christ at the *bema* (see Luke 12:41–48; Heb. 13:17; 1 John 2:28).

The fact that our sins will never be brought up against us should not encourage us to disobey God. Sin in our lives keeps us from serving Christ as we should, and this means loss of reward. Lot is a good example of this truth (Gen. 18—19). Lot was not walking with the Lord as was his uncle, Abraham, and as a result, he lost his testimony even with his own family. When the judgment finally came, Lot was spared the fire and brimstone, but everything he lived for was burned up. He was saved "yet so as by fire."

Paul explained that they did not have to give an account for anyone else but themselves. So they were to make sure that their account would be a good one. He was stressing the principle of lordship—make Jesus Christ the Lord of your life, and let Him be the Lord in the lives of other Christians as well.

Two of the most famous Christians in the Victorian Era in England were Charles Spurgeon and Joseph Parker, both of them mighty preachers of the gospel. Early in their ministries they fellowshipped and even exchanged pulpits. Then they had a disagreement, and the reports even got into the newspapers. Spurgeon accused Parker of being unspiritual because he attended the theater. Interestingly enough, Spurgeon smoked cigars, a practice many believers would condemn. Who was right? Who was wrong? Perhaps *both* of them were wrong! When it comes to questionable matters in the Christian life, cannot dedicated believers disagree without being disagreeable? "I have learned that God blesses people I disagree with!" a friend of mine told me one day, and I have learned the same thing. When Jesus Christ is Lord, we permit Him to deal with His own servants as He wishes.

Edify One Another (14:13–23)

If we stopped with the first admonition, it might give the impression that Christians were to leave each other alone and let the weak remain weak. But this second admonition explains things further. The emphasis is not on "master-servant" but on "brother." It is the principle of brotherly love. If we love each other, we will seek to edify each other, build each other up in the faith. Paul shared several facts to help his readers help their brethren.

Christians affect each other (vv. 13–15). Note the possible ways we can affect each other. We can cause others to stumble, grieve others, or even destroy others. Paul was speaking of the way the strong Christian affected the weak Christian. Paul dealt with a similar problem in 1 Corinthians 8—9, where the question was, "Should Christians eat meat that has been offered to idols in heathen temples?" There he pointed out that knowledge and love must work together. "Knowledge puffs up, but love builds up" (1 Cor. 8:1 NIV). The strong Christian has spiritual knowledge, but if he does not practice love, his knowledge will hurt the weak Christian. Knowledge must be balanced by love.

Often little children are afraid of the dark and think there is something hiding in the closet. Of course, Mother knows that the child is safe, but her knowledge alone cannot assure or comfort the child. You can never argue a child into losing fear. When the mother sits at the bedside, talks lovingly to the child, and assures him that everything is secure, then the child can go to sleep without fear. Knowledge plus love helps the weak person grow strong.

"There is nothing unclean of itself," Paul wrote (Rom. 14:14). No foods are unclean, no days are unclean, no people are unclean. (Read Acts 10 to see how Peter learned this lesson.) What something *does* to a person determines its quality. One man may be able to read certain books and not be bothered by them, while a weaker Christian reading the same books might be tempted to sin. But the issue is not, "How does it affect me?" so much as, "If I do this, how will it affect my brother?" Will it make him stumble? Will it grieve him or even destroy him by encouraging him to sin? Is it really worth it to harm a brother just so I can enjoy some food? No!

Christians must have priorities (vv. 16–18). Like the Pharisees of old, we Christians have a way of majoring on the minor things (Matt. 23:23–24). I have seen churches divided over matters that were really insignificant when compared with the vital things of the Christian faith. I have heard of churches being split over such minor matters as the location of the piano in the auditorium and the serving of meals on Sundays. "The kingdom of God is not meat and drink" (Rom. 14:17). "But food does not bring us near to God; we are no worse if we do not eat, and no better if we do" (1 Cor. 8:8 NIV)

Not the externals, but the eternals must be first in our lives: righteousness, peace, and joy. Where do they come from? The Holy Spirit of God at work in our lives (see Rom. 5:1–2). If each believer would yield to the Spirit and major in a godly life, we would not have Christians fighting with each other over minor matters. Spiritual priorities are essential to harmony in the church.

Christians must help each other grow (vv. 19–21). Both the strong believer and the weak believer need to grow. The strong believer needs to grow in *love;* the weak believer needs to grow in *knowledge.* So long as a brother is weak in the faith, we must lovingly deal with him in his immaturity. But if we really love him, we will help him to grow. It is wrong for a Christian to remain immature, having a weak conscience.

An illustration from the home might help us better understand what is involved. When a child comes into a home, everything has to change. Mother and Father are careful not to leave the scissors on the chair or anything dangerous within reach. But as the child matures, it is possible for the parents to adjust the rules of the house and deal with him in a more adult fashion. It is natural for a child to stumble when he is learning to walk. But if an adult constantly stumbles, we know something is wrong.

Young Christians need the kind of fellowship that will protect them and encourage them to grow. But we cannot treat them like "babies" all their lives! The older Christians must exercise love and patience and be careful not to cause them to stumble. But the younger Christians must "grow in grace and in the knowledge of our Lord and Savior Jesus Christ" (2 Peter 3:18). As they mature in the faith, they can help other believers to grow. To gear the ministry of a Sunday school class or local church only to the baby Christians is to hinder their growth as well as the ministry of the more mature saints. The weak must learn from the strong, and the strong must love the weak. The result will be peace and maturity to the glory of God.

Christians must not force their opinions on others (vv. 22–23). There are certain truths that all Christians must accept because they are the foundation for the faith. But areas of honest disagreement must not be made a test of fellowship. If you have a sincere conviction from God about a matter, keep it to yourself and do not try to force everybody else to accept it. No Christian can "borrow" another Christian's convictions and be honest in his Christian life. Unless he can hold them and practice them "by faith," he is sinning. Even if a person's convictions are immature, he must never violate his conscience. This would do great damage to his spiritual life. For example, the mature Christian knows that an idol is nothing. But a young Christian, just converted out of pagan idolatry, would still have fears about idols. If the strong believer forced the new Christian to eat meat sacrificed to an idol, the younger Christian would experience problems in his conscience that would only further weaken it (see 1 Cor. 8—9).

Conscience is strengthened by knowledge. But knowledge must be balanced by love; otherwise it tears down instead of building up. The truth that "all foods are clean" (Rom. 14:14, 20) will not of itself make a Christian grow. When this truth is taught in an atmosphere of love, then the younger Christian can grow and develop a strong conscience. Believers may hold different convictions about many matters, but they must hold them in love.

Please One Another (15:1–7)

Paul classified himself with the strong saints as he dealt with a basic problem—*selfishness.* True Christian love is not selfish; rather, it seeks to share with others and make others happy. It is even willing to carry the younger Christians, to help them along in their spiritual development. We do not endure them. We encourage them!

Of course, the great example in this is our Lord Jesus Christ. He paid a tremendous price in order to minister to us. Paul quoted Psalm 69:9 to prove his point. Does a strong Christian think he is making a great sacrifice by giving up some food or drink? Then let him measure his sacrifice by the sacrifice of Christ. No sacrifice we could ever make could match Calvary.

A person's spiritual maturity is revealed by his discernment. He is willing to give up his rights that others might be helped. He does this, not as a burden, but as a blessing. Just as loving parents make sacrifices for their children, so the mature believer sacrifices to help younger Christians grow in the faith.

Paul shared the two sources of spiritual power from which we must draw if we are to live to please others: the Word of God (Rom. 15:4) and prayer (Rom. 15:5–6). We must confess that we sometimes get impatient with younger Christians, just as parents become impatient with their children. But the Word of God can give us the "patience and encouragement" that we need. Paul closed this section praying for his readers, that they might experience from God that spiritual unity that He alone can give.

This suggests to us that the local church must major in the Word of God and prayer. The first real danger to the unity of the church came because the apostles were too busy to minister God's Word and pray (Acts 6:1–7). When they found others to share their burdens, they returned to their proper ministry, and the church experienced harmony and growth.

The result of this is, of course, glory to God (Rom. 15:7). Disunity and disagreement do not glorify God; they rob Him of glory. Abraham's words to Lot are applicable to today: "Let there be no strife, I pray thee, between me and thee … for we be brethren" (Gen. 13:8). The neighbors were watching! Abraham wanted them to see that he and Lot were different from them because they worshipped the true God. In His prayer in John 17, Jesus prayed for the unity of the church to the glory of God (John 17:20–26). Receive one another; edify one another; and please one another—all to the glory of God.

CHAPTER THIRTEEN
Romans 15:8—16:27
MAN ON THE MOVE

One of the key words in the closing chapters of Romans is *ministry* In fact, Paul used three different Greek words to discuss the theme. In Romans 15:8, 25, 31; and 16:1, it is the simple word for a servant or service. Our English word *deacon* comes from this word. In Romans 15:16 and 27 (the word *minister*), he used the ordinary word for service in public office or in the temple. In Romans 15:16 he used a word that is found nowhere else in the Greek New Testament, and it means "to perform sacred rites, to minister in a priestly service."

In this section, Paul explained four different ministries.

The Ministry of Jesus Christ to the Gentiles (15:8–13)
The supreme example of ministry must always be Jesus Christ. "But I am among you as he that serveth" (Luke 22:27). He came first of all to minister to the Jews, that through Israel He might be able to minister to the Gentiles. "To the Jew first" is a principle that was followed in the earthly ministry of Christ and in the early ministry of the church.

For example, John the Baptist came to minister to the nation of Israel to prepare them for their Messiah. When Jesus began His ministry, it was only to the people of Israel. When He sent out the apostles on their first evangelistic mission, He ordered them, "Go not into the way of the Gentiles, and into any city of the Samaritans enter ye not; but go rather to the lost sheep of the house of Israel" (Matt. 10:5–6). This does not mean that He ignored individual Gentiles, because He did minister to a few (Matt. 8:5–13; 15:21–28), but His major emphasis was on Israel.

After His resurrection, He commanded the apostles

to remain in Jerusalem and begin their ministry there (Luke 24:44–49). The period covered by Acts 1—7 is characterized by a ministry only to Jews or Jewish proselytes. It was not until Acts 8 that the gospel went to the Samaritans; in Acts 10 it went to the Gentiles. Then, through the ministry of Paul, it went throughout the Roman Empire (Acts 13:1–3).

When He came and died, Jesus Christ confirmed the promises that God made to Abraham and the other "fathers" of the Jewish nation (see Luke 1:30–33, 46–55, 67–80). Some of these promises have already been fulfilled, but many await fulfillment when He returns to earth to establish His kingdom.

Was it selfish of God to emphasize the Jews? No, because through the Jews, He would send the good news of salvation to the Gentiles. The first Christians were Jewish believers! "Salvation is of the Jews" (John 4:22). In the Old Testament period, God chose Israel to be a minister to the Gentiles, but instead, Israel copied the idolatrous ways of the Gentiles and had to be chastened. In the New Testament period, God chose Jewish believers to carry the good news to the Gentiles, and they obeyed Him.

There is a beautiful progression in the promises that Paul quoted in Romans 15:9–12.

- The Jews glorify God *among* the Gentiles (Rom. 15:9, quoting Ps. 18:49)
- The Gentiles rejoice *with* the Jews (Rom. 15:10, quoting Deut. 32:43)
- All the Jews and Gentiles *together* praise God (Rom. 15:11, quoting Ps. 117:1)
- Christ shall reign over Jews and Gentiles (Rom. 15:12, quoting Isa. 11:10)

Romans 15:8 covers the period of the Gospels and Acts 1—7. Romans 15:9 describes the ministry of Paul as he witnessed among the Gentiles. Romans 15:10 could be applied to the church council in Acts 15 when the Gentiles were given equal status "with his people." Today, Jews and Gentiles in the church are praising God together.

The word *trust* at the end of Romans 15:12 is actually the word *hope*. At one time the Gentiles were "without hope" (Eph. 2:12 NIV), but now in Christ they have hope. Not only do believers have hope, but they also have joy and peace and power (Rom. 15:13). The Holy Spirit of God shares these blessings with them as they yield to Him.

Because the Jewish Christians were faithful to take the gospel to the Gentiles, the nations of the world today have the opportunity to trust Christ as Savior.

Paul's Ministry to the Gentiles (15:14–24)
Unless we understand the distinctive ministry of Paul, we will not fully appreciate the message of God's grace. Paul explained the characteristics of his ministry.

It was received by grace (vv. 14–15). When he was Saul of Tarsus, the crusading rabbi, Paul knew little of the grace of God. He persecuted the church and sought to destroy it. When Paul met Jesus Christ on the Damascus road (Acts 9), he experienced the grace of God. It was God's grace that saved him, and it was God's grace that called him and made him an apostle (1 Cor. 15:8–11). "We have received grace and apostleship, for obedience to the faith among all nations, for his name" (Rom. 1:5). In Ephesians 3, Paul explained his ministry to the Gentiles in greater detail.

It was centered in the gospel (v. 16). As mentioned before, Paul used two different words for *minister* in this verse, but the emphasis is on priestly service. Paul looked on himself as a priest at the altar, offering up to God the Gentiles he had won to Christ. They were a "spiritual sacrifice" to the glory of God (see 1 Peter 2:5). Even his preaching of the gospel was a "priestly duty" (NIV). This insight into ministry certainly adds dignity and responsibility to our service. It was important that the priests offer to God only that which was the best (see Mal. 1:6–14).

Note the involvement of the Trinity in the ministry of the Word. Paul was the minister of Jesus Christ; he preached "the gospel of God"; and he served in the power of the Holy Spirit of God who sanctified his ministry. What a privilege, and yet what a responsibility, to be the servant of the Triune God, winning the lost to Jesus Christ! We must remember that soul-winning is a priestly ministry, a sacred obligation. And we must serve the Lord with dedication and devotion just as the priest in the temple.

It was done for God's glory (v. 17). "Therefore I glory in Christ Jesus in my service to God" (NIV). The word translated "glory" carries the idea of "boast, take pride in." Paul used it before in Romans 2:17, 23; 5:2–3, 11 ("joy"); 3:27; and 4:2. Paul was not bragging about his ministry. He was boasting in what the Lord had done. The apostle did not serve and suffer as he did just to make a name for himself, for he had a much higher purpose in mind. He wanted to bring glory to Jesus Christ. "That in all things he might have the preeminence" (Col. 1:18).

It was done by God's power (vv. 18–19). The Holy Spirit empowered Paul to minister, and enabled him to perform mighty signs and wonders. The miracles God gave Paul to do were "signs" in that they came from God and revealed Him to others. And they were "wonders" in that they aroused the wonder of the people. But their purpose was always to open the way for the preaching of the gospel. Miracles were given to authenticate the messenger and the message (Heb. 2:1–4). Miracles *by themselves* can never save the lost. When Paul healed the crippled man at Lystra (Acts 14), the immediate response was pagan: the people called Paul and Barnabas gods and tried to worship them! When Paul shared the gospel with them, they did not respond so enthusiastically. Finally, the people stoned Paul and left him for dead outside the city walls.

The Spirit of God empowered Paul to share the Word, and the purpose was to "make the Gentiles obedient" (Rom. 15:18). It was "by word and deed" that the apostle shared the good news.

We may not be able to perform miracles today, since this was a special apostolic gift. But "by word and deed" we can share the love of God with the lost around us. Changes in conduct and character are just as much miracles as the healing of the sick.

It was according to God's plan (vv. 20–24). God had a special plan for Paul to follow: he was not to preach where any other apostle had ministered. (This is one evidence that Peter had not founded the churches at Rome, or had been to Rome, for this would have prevented Paul from going there.) "From Jerusalem and round about unto Illyricum" (Rom. 15:19) covers about fourteen thousand miles! When you consider the slowness of travel and the dangers involved (2 Cor. 11:26–27), you can appreciate the tremendous achievement of Paul's missionary ministry. While it is not wrong to enter into another man's labors (John 4:38), it is also good to have a pioneer ministry and take the gospel to new territory. Paul cited Isaiah 52:15 as the divine approval for this kind of ministry.

The vast area of opportunity in other parts of the empire kept Paul from visiting Rome sooner. He was not hindered from going to Rome by satanic opposition or physical obstacles, but by the challenge of completing his work right where he was. He was so faithful in his evangelistic outreach that he was able to say that he had no more places to minister in those parts. This did not mean that Paul personally witnessed to every person in that area, but that he took the gospel and left behind witnessing churches and Christians who would carry on the work. Paul finished one job before he started another one, a good example for our evangelistic ministry today.

Paul's desire for many years had been to visit Rome and then move on to Spain, but there is no record that he ever did. Tradition says that he did go to Spain, and possibly to Britain, after he was released, but church tradition is not always to be trusted.

The Gentiles' Ministry to the Jews (15:25–33)

Paul and his associates had received a special offering from the Gentile churches in Greece for the suffering Jewish saints in Jerusalem. Details about this collection are recorded in 2 Corinthians 8—9. There were several purposes behind this special offering. To begin with, it was an expression of love on the part of the Gentiles toward their Jewish brethren. Second, it meant practical relief at a time when the poor Jewish believers needed it the most. Third, it helped to unite Jews and Gentiles in the church. It was a bond that brought them closer together.

Paul looked on this offering as the paying of a debt. The Gentiles had received *spiritual* wealth from the Jews. They now returned *material* wealth, paying their debt. Paul considered himself a "debtor" to the whole world (Rom. 1:14). He also considered the Gentile Christians debtors to the Jews, for it was the Jews who gave to the Gentiles the Word of God and the Son of God. We Christians ought to feel an obligation to Israel, and to pay that debt by praying for Israel, sharing the gospel, and helping in a material way. Anti-Semitism has no place in the life of a dedicated Christian.

Not only was this offering a payment of a debt, but it was also "fruit" (Rom. 15:28). It was not "loot" that Paul stole from the churches! It was fruit—the natural result of their walk with the Lord (see John 15:1–8).

When the life of the Spirit flows through a church, giving is no problem. Paul, in 2 Corinthians 8:1–5, described the miracle of grace that occurred in the churches of Macedonia.

Paul was anxious that this offering be received by the Jewish believers and be acceptable to them. He wanted to bring about, under God, a closer bond between the mother church at Jerusalem and the daughter churches in other parts of the empire. Unfortunately, there were still Jews who opposed the message of grace to the Gentiles and who wanted the Gentiles to become Jews and accept the Jewish law. (Bible students call these people "Judaizers." They followed Paul wherever he went and tried to steal his churches from him. The epistle to the Galatians was written to combat their evil works.)

The words "strive together" in Romans 15:30 suggest an athlete giving his best in the contest. Perhaps the words "wrestling together" better express the idea. This same term is used of the praying of Epaphras in Colossians 4:12. This verse does not mean that we must fight with God to get what we need. Rather, it means our praying must not be a casual experience that has no heart or earnestness. We should put as much fervor into our praying as a wrestler does into his wrestling!

The Believers' Ministry to Paul (16:1–27)

What a remarkable chapter! In it Paul greeted at least twenty-six people by name, as well as two unnamed saints, and he also greeted several churches that were meeting in homes. He closed with greetings from nine believers who were with him in Corinth when he wrote the letter. What is the significance of this? It shows that Paul was a friend maker as well as a soul winner. He did not try to live an isolated life; he had friends in the Lord, and he appreciated them. They were a help to him personally and to his ministry. In my own reading of Christian biography, I have discovered that the servants whom God has used the most were people who could make friends. They multiplied themselves in the lives of their friends and associates in the ministry. While there may be a place for the secluded saint who lives alone with God, it is my conviction that most of us need each other. We are sheep, and sheep flock together.

Some friends to greet (vv. 1–16). He began with Phebe, a member of the church at Cenchrea, and the lady who carried the letter to the saints at Rome.

Never did a messenger carry a more important letter! Cenchrea was the seaport of Corinth, so Phebe was probably won to Christ during Paul's year and a half of ministry in Corinth. The word *servant* is the feminine of *deacon,* and some students believe she was a "deaconess" in the church. This is possible, because there were women in the early church who served by visiting the sick, assisting the young women, and helping the poor. Paul confessed that Phebe had been a helper (literally "protectress") of himself and other Christians. And he encouraged the church to care for her.

How we wish we had the details of the stories behind each of these names! We have met Priscilla and Aquila in the book of Acts (18:1–3, 18–19, 26). Where and when they risked their lives for Paul, we do not know, but we are glad they did it (see also 1 Cor. 16:19; 2 Tim 4:19)! At the time of this writing, they were in Rome and a church met in their house. In this chapter, Paul greeted a number of such assemblies (Rom. 16:10–11, 14–15).

Four persons are called "beloved" by Paul: Epenetus (Rom. 16:5), Amplias (Rom. 16:8), Stachys (Rom. 16:9), and Persis (Rom. 16:12). Paul would remember Epenetus in particular, for he was the first of the converts in Asia. Apparently he belonged to the household of Stephanas, for in 1 Corinthians 16:15 these people are also called "the firstfruits of Achaia."

Andronicus and Junias are called "kinsmen," which may mean blood relatives of Paul, or only that they too were Jewish, possibly of the tribe of Benjamin like Paul. At one time they had been in prison with Paul. The word *apostle* here does not imply that they held the same office as Paul, but rather that they were "messengers" of the Lord. The word *apostle* has both a narrow and a broad meaning.

The Rufus mentioned in Romans 16:13 may be the same as the one named in Mark 15:21, but we cannot be certain. If so, then Simon's experience at Calvary led to his conversion and that of his household. Paul and Rufus were not related. "His mother and mine" means only that Rufus's mother had been like a mother to Paul (see Mark 10:30).

This list shows the parts that people played in Paul's ministry and the ministry of the churches. Phebe was a "succourer" of many. Priscilla and Aquila were "helpers" and "laid down their own necks" for Paul. The conversion of Epenetus led to the salvation of others in Asia. Mary "bestowed much labor." Andronicus and Junias went to prison with Paul. One can only give thanks for these devoted saints who fulfilled their ministries to the glory of God. May we follow in their train!

Some foes to avoid (vv. 17–20). Not everyone was working with Paul for the spreading of the gospel. There were some who, for selfish reasons, were dividing the churches by teaching false doctrine. These people were probably the same Judaizers who had given Paul trouble in other churches (see Phil. 3:17–21). Instead of preaching the truth, these men spread their own religious propaganda, using deceit and clever speeches. We have the same problem today, and Christians must beware of false teachers. They come to your front door with magazines, books, and tapes, trying to convince you that they are teaching the truth. Paul gives two instructions: mark them (identify them), and avoid them.

It is a matter of obedience to the Lord and testimony to others. The issue is not making or keeping friends, but pleasing the Lord and maintaining a consistent testimony. Romans 16:20 suggests that these false teachers really come from Satan, and one day even he shall be completely defeated.

Some faithful servants to honor (vv. 21–27). What a roll call of heroes! Timothy was mentioned often in the book of Acts and the Epistles. He was Paul's "son in the faith" and labored with Paul in many difficult places (see Phil. 2:19–24). Lucius was a fellow Jew, as were Jason and Sosipater. We have no proof that this is the same Jason who protected Paul in Thessalonica (Acts 17:1–9). That Jason was probably a Gentile.

Tertius was the secretary who wrote the letter as Paul dictated it. Gaius was the man in whose home Paul was residing at Corinth. First Corinthians 1:14 told how Paul won Gaius to Christ and baptized him when he founded the church in Corinth. Apparently there was an assembly of believers meeting in his house. Erastus held a high office in the city, probably the treasurer. The gospel reached into high places in Corinth as well as into low places (1 Cor. 1:26–31; 6:9–11).

Romans 16:24 was probably written by Paul's own hand, since this was his "official seal" in every letter (see 2 Thess. 3:17–18).

The closing benediction is the longest one Paul ever wrote. It reflects his special ministry to the Gentiles. "The mystery" has to do with God's program of uniting believing Jews and Gentiles in the one body, the church (see Eph. 3). This was Paul's special message. It was because of this message that the Judaizers persecuted Paul, because they wanted to maintain Jewish privileges. Both Jews and Gentiles in the Roman churches needed to know what God's program was. Some of this Paul had explained in Romans 9—11.

Christians are established by the truth, which explains why Paul wrote this letter: to explain God's plan of salvation to Christians so they would be established, and so they would share the truth with the lost. After all, we cannot really share with others something we do not have ourselves.

This means that our own study of Romans should make us more stable in the faith, and more excited to share Christ with others. And the result? "To God only wise, be glory through Jesus Christ for ever!"

1 CORINTHIANS

OUTLINE

Key theme: God's wisdom
Key verses: 1 Corinthians 2:6–8

I. GREETING (1:1–3)

II. REPROOF: THE REPORT OF SIN IN THE CHURCH (1:4—6:20)

   A. Divisions in the church—1:4—4:21
   B. Discipline in the church—5
   C. Disputes in the courts—6:1–8
   D. Defilement in the world—6:9–20

III. INSTRUCTION: THE REPLY TO THEIR QUESTIONS (7:1—16:12)

   A. Marriage—7
   B. Food offered to idols—8—10
   C. Church ordinances—11
   D. Spiritual gifts—12:1—14:40
   E. The Resurrection—15
   F. The offering—16:1–12

IV. CONCLUSION (16:13–24)

CONTENTS

CHAPTER ONE
1 Corinthians 1
BE WISE ABOUT THE CHRISTIAN'S CALLING

"Jesus, yes! The church, no!" Remember when that slogan was popular among young people in the '60s? They certainly could have used it with sincerity in Corinth back in AD 56, because the local church there was in serious trouble. Sad to say, the problems did not stay within the church family; they were known by the unbelievers outside the church.

To begin with, the church at Corinth was a *defiled* church. Some of its members were guilty of sexual immorality; others got drunk; still others were using the grace of God to excuse worldly living. It was also a *divided* church, with at least four different groups competing for leadership (1 Cor. 1:12). This meant it was a *disgraced* church. Instead of glorifying God, it was hindering the progress of the gospel.

How did this happen? The members of the church permitted the sins of the city to get into the local assembly. Corinth was a polluted city, filled with every kind of vice and worldly pleasure. About the lowest accusation you could make against a man in that day would be to call him a "Corinthian." People would know what you were talking about.

Corinth was also a proud, philosophical city, with many itinerant teachers promoting their speculations. Unfortunately, this philosophical approach was applied to the gospel by some members of the church, and this fostered division. The congregation was made up of different "schools of thought" instead of being united behind the gospel message.

If you want to know what Corinth was like, read Romans 1:18–32. Paul wrote the Roman epistle while in Corinth, and he could have looked out the window and seen the very sins that he listed!

Of course, when you have proud people depending on human wisdom, adopting the lifestyle of the world, you are going to have problems. In order to help them solve their problems, Paul opened his letter by reminding them of their *calling in Christ*. He pointed out three important aspects of this calling.

Called to Be Holy (1:1–9)

Paul first attacked the serious problem of defilement in the church, yet he said nothing about the problem itself. Instead, he took the positive approach and reminded the believers of their high and holy position in Jesus Christ. In 1 Corinthians 1:1–9, he described the church that God sees; in 1 Corinthians 1:10–31, he described the church that men see. What we are in Jesus Christ *positionally* ought to be what we practice in daily life, but often we fail.

Note the characteristics of the church because of our holy calling in Jesus Christ.

Set apart by God (vv. 1–3). The word *church* in the Greek language means "a called-out people." Each church has two addresses: a geographic address ("at Corinth") and a spiritual address ("in Christ Jesus"). The church is made up of saints, that is, people who have been "sanctified" or "set apart" by God. A saint is not a dead person who has been honored by men because of his or her holy life. No, Paul wrote to *living* saints, people who, through faith in Jesus Christ, had been set apart for God's special enjoyment and use.

In other words, every true believer is a saint because every true believer has been set apart by God and for God.

A Christian photographer friend told me about a lovely wedding that he "covered." The bride and groom came out of the church, heading for the limousine, when the bride suddenly left her husband and ran to a car parked across the street! The motor was running and a man was at the wheel, and off they drove, leaving the bridegroom speechless. The driver of the "get-away car" turned out to be an old boyfriend of the bride, a man who had boasted that "he could get her any time he wanted her." Needless to say, the husband had the marriage annulled.

When a man and woman pledge their love to each other, they are set apart for each other; and any other relationship outside of marriage is sinful. Just so, the Christian belongs completely to Jesus Christ; he is set apart for Him and Him alone. But he is also a part of a worldwide fellowship, the church, "all that in every place call upon the name of Jesus Christ" (1 Cor. 1:2). A defiled and unfaithful believer not only sins against the Lord, but he also sins against his fellow Christians.

Enriched by God's grace (vv. 4–6). Salvation is a gracious gift from God; but when you are saved, you are also given spiritual gifts. (Paul explained this in detail in 1 Cor. 12–14.) The Greek word translated "enriched" gives us our English word *plutocrat*, "a very wealthy person." The Corinthians were especially rich in spiritual gifts (2 Cor. 8:7), but were not using these gifts in a spiritual manner. The fact that God has called us, set us apart, and enriched us ought to encourage us to live holy lives.

Expecting Jesus to return (v. 7). Paul will have a great deal to say about this truth in 1 Corinthians 15. Christians who are looking for their Savior will want to keep their lives above reproach (1 John 2:28—3:3).

Depending on God's faithfulness (vv. 8–9). The work of God was confirmed *in* them (1 Cor. 1:6), but it was also confirmed *to* them in the Word. This is a legal term that refers to the guarantee that settles a transaction. We have the witness of the Spirit within us and the witness of the Word before us, guaranteeing that God will keep His "contract" with us and save us to the very end. This guarantee is certainly not an excuse for sin! Rather, it is the basis for a growing relationship of love, trust, and obedience.

Now, in the light of these great truths, how could the people in the Corinthian assembly get involved in the sins of the world and the flesh? They were an elect people, an enriched people, and an established people. They were saints, set apart for the glory of God! Alas, their practice was not in accord with their position.

When Paul mentioned the word *fellowship* in 1 Corinthians 1:9, he introduced a second aspect of the Christian's calling.

Called into Fellowship (1:10–25)

Having mentioned the problem of defilement in the church, now Paul turned to the matter of division in the church. Division has always been a problem among God's people, and almost every New Testament epistle deals with this topic or mentions it in one way or another. Even the twelve apostles did not always get along with each other.

In 1 Corinthians 1:13, Paul asked his readers three important questions, and these three questions are the key to this long paragraph.

Is Christ divided (vv. 10–13a)? The verb means, "Has Christ been divided and different parts handed out to different people?" The very idea is grotesque and must be rejected. Paul did not preach one Christ, Apollos another, and Peter another. There is but one Savior and one gospel (Gal. 1:6–9). How, then, did the Corinthians create this four-way division? Why were there quarrels ("contentions") among them?

One answer is that they were looking at the gospel from a philosophical point of view. Corinth was a city filled with teachers and philosophers, all of whom wanted to share their "wisdom."

Another answer is that human nature enjoys following human leaders. We tend to identify more with spiritual leaders who help us and whose ministry we understand and enjoy. Instead of emphasizing the *message* of the Word, the Corinthians emphasized the *messenger.* They got their eyes off the Lord and on the Lord's servants, and this led to competition.

Paul will point out in 1 Corinthians 3 that there can be no competition among true servants of God. It is sinful for church members to compare pastors, or for believers to follow human leaders as disciples of men and not disciples of Jesus Christ. The "personality cults" in the church today are in direct disobedience to the Word of God. Only Jesus Christ should have the place of preeminence (Col. 1:18).

Paul used several key words in this section to emphasize the unity of the saints in Christ. He called his readers *brethren,* reminding them that they belonged to one family. The phrase "perfectly joined together" is a medical term that describes the unity of the human body *knit together.* So, they had a *loving* union as members of the body. They were also identified by the name of Jesus Christ. This was probably a reference to their baptism.

We do not know who the people were who belonged to "the house of Chloe," but we commend them for their courage and devotion. They did not try to hide the problems. They were burdened about

them; they went to the right person with them; and they were not afraid to be mentioned by Paul. This was not the kind of "cloak and dagger" affair that we often see in churches—activities that usually make the problem worse and not better.

Paul was the minister who founded the church, so most of the members would have been converted through his ministry. Apollos followed Paul (Acts 18:24–28) and had an effective ministry. We have no record that Peter (Cephas) ever visited Corinth, unless 1 Corinthians 9:5 records it. Each of these men had a different personality and a different approach to the ministry of the Word; *yet they were one* (1 Cor. 3:3–8; 4:6).

Were you baptized in the name of Paul (vv. 13b–17)? Keep in mind that baptism was an important matter in the New Testament church. When a sinner trusted Christ and was baptized, he cut himself off from his old life and often was rejected by his family and friends. It cost something to be baptized in that day.

Just as Jesus did not baptize people (John 4:1–2), so both Peter (Acts 10:48) and Paul allowed their associates to baptize the new converts. Until the church grew in Corinth, Paul did some of the baptizing; but that was not his main ministry. In this section, Paul was not minimizing baptism, but rather was putting it into its proper perspective, because the Corinthians were making too much of it. "I was baptized by Apollos!" one would boast, while another would say, "Oh, but I was baptized by Paul!"

It is wrong to identify any man's name with your baptism other than the name of Jesus Christ To do so is to create division. I have read accounts about people who had to be baptized by a certain preacher, using special water (usually from the Jordan River), on a special day, as though these are the matters that are important! Instead of honoring the Lord Jesus Christ and promoting the unity of the church, these people exalt men and create disunity.

Crispus had been the ruler of the synagogue in Corinth (Acts 18:8); and Gaius was probably the man Paul lived with when he wrote Romans (Rom. 16:23). "The household of Stephanas" (1 Cor. 1:16) is probably described in part in 1 Corinthians 16:15–18. Apparently Paul did not carry with him a record of the names of all the people he baptized. It was sufficient that they were written in God's book.

Was Paul crucified for you (vv. 18–25)? The mention of the cross in 1 Corinthians 1:17 introduced this long section on the power of the gospel versus the weakness of man's wisdom. It is interesting to see how Paul approached this problem of division in the church. First, he pointed to the unity of Christ: there is one Savior and one body. Then he reminded them of their baptism, a picture of their spiritual baptism into Christ's body (1 Cor. 12:13). Then he took them to the cross.

Crucifixion was not only a horrible death; it was a

shameful death. It was illegal to crucify a Roman citizen. Crucifixion was never mentioned in polite society, any more than we today would discuss over dinner the gas chamber or the electric chair.

The key word in this paragraph is *wisdom;* it is used eight times. The key idea that Paul expressed is that we dare not mix man's wisdom with God's revealed message. The entire section on wisdom (1 Cor. 1:17–2:16) presents a number of contrasts between the revealed Word of God and the wisdom of men.

God's wisdom is revealed primarily in the cross of Jesus Christ, but not everybody sees this. Paul pointed out that there are three different attitudes toward the cross.

Some stumble at the cross (v. 23a). This was the attitude of the Jews, because their emphasis was on miraculous signs and the cross appears to be weakness. Jewish history is filled with miraculous events, from the exodus out of Egypt to the days of Elijah and Elisha. When Jesus was ministering on earth, the Jewish leaders repeatedly asked Him to perform a sign from heaven; but He refused.

The Jewish nation did not understand their own sacred Scriptures. They looked for a Messiah who would come like a mighty conqueror and defeat all their enemies. He would then set up His kingdom and return the glory to Israel. The question of the apostles in Acts 1:6 shows how strong this hope was among the Jews.

At the same time, their scribes noticed in the Old Testament that the Messiah would suffer and die. Passages like Psalm 22 and Isaiah 53 pointed toward a different kind of Messiah, and the scholars could not reconcile these two seemingly contradictory prophetic images. They did not understand that their Messiah had to suffer and die before He could enter into His glory (see Luke 24:13–35), and that the future messianic kingdom was to be preceded by the age of the church.

Because the Jews were looking for power and great glory, they stumbled at the weakness of the cross. How could anybody put faith in an unemployed carpenter from Nazareth who died the shameful death of a common criminal? But the gospel of Jesus Christ is "the power of God unto salvation" (Rom. 1:16). Rather than a testimony of weakness, the cross is a tremendous instrument of power! After all, the "weakness of God [in the cross] is stronger than men" (1 Cor. 1:25).

Some laugh at the cross (v. 23b). This was the response of the Greeks. To them, the cross was foolishness. The Greeks emphasized wisdom; we still study the profound writings of the Greek philosophers. But they saw no wisdom in the cross, for they looked at the cross from a human point of view. Had they seen it from God's viewpoint, they would have discerned the wisdom of God's great plan of salvation.

Paul called on three men to bear witness: the wise (the expert), the scribe (the interpreter and writer), and the disputer (the philosopher and debater). He asked them one question: Through your studies into man's wisdom, have you come to know God in a personal way? They all must answer no! The fact that they laugh at the cross and consider it foolishness is evidence that they are perishing.

Paul quoted Isaiah 29:14 in 1 Corinthians 1:19, proving that God has written a big "0—Failure!" over the wisdom of men. In his address on Mars Hill, Paul dared to tell the philosophers that Greek and Roman history were but "times of this ignorance" (Acts 17:30). He was not suggesting that they knew nothing, because Paul knew too well that the Greek thinkers had made some achievements. However, their wisdom did not enable them to find God and experience salvation.

Some believe and experience the power and the wisdom of the cross (v. 24). Paul did not alter his message when he turned from a Jewish audience to a Greek one: he preached Christ crucified. "The foolishness of preaching" (1 Cor. 1:21) does not mean that the *act* of preaching is foolish, but rather the content of the message. The New International Version states it, "Through the foolishness of what was preached," and this is correct.

Those who have been called by God's grace, and who have responded by faith (see 2 Thess. 2:13–14), realize that Christ is God's power and God's wisdom. Not the Christ of the manger, or the temple, or the marketplace—but the Christ of the cross. It is in the death of Christ that God has revealed the foolishness of man's wisdom and the weakness of man's power.

We are called into fellowship because of our union with Jesus Christ: He died for us; we were baptized in His name; we are identified with His cross. What a wonderful basis for spiritual unity!

Called to Glorify God (1:26–31)

The Corinthians had a tendency to be "puffed up" with pride (1 Cor. 4:6, 18–19; 5:2). But the gospel of God's grace leaves no room for personal boasting. God is not impressed with our looks, our social position, our achievements, our natural heritage, or our financial status. Note that Paul wrote *many,* not *any.* In the New Testament, we do meet some believers with "high social standing," but there are not many of them. The description Paul gave of the converts was certainly not a flattering one (1 Cor. 6:9–11).

Paul reminded them of what they were (v. 26). They were not wise, mighty, or noble. God called them, not *because of* what they were, but *in spite of* what they were! The Corinthian church was composed primarily of ordinary people who were terrible sinners. Before his conversion, Paul had been very self-righteous; he had to give up his religion in order to go to heaven! The Corinthians were at the other end of the spectrum, and yet they were not too sinful for God to reach and save them.

Paul reminded the Corinthians of why God

called them (vv. 27–29). God chose the foolish, the weak, the base ("low born"), and the despised to show the proud world their need and His grace. The lost world admires birth, social status, financial success, power, and recognition. But none of these things can guarantee eternal life.

The message and miracle of God's grace in Jesus Christ utterly confounds ("puts to shame") the high and mighty people of this world. The wise of this world cannot understand how God changes sinners into saints, and the mighty of this world are helpless to duplicate the miracle. God's "foolishness" confounds the wise; God's "weakness" confounds the mighty!

The annals of church history are filled with the accounts of great sinners whose lives were transformed by the power of the gospel. In my own ministry, as in the ministry of most pastors and preachers, I have seen amazing things take place that the lawyers and psychologists could not understand. We have seen delinquent teenagers become successful students and useful citizens. We have seen marriages restored and homes reclaimed, much to the amazement of the courts.

And why does God reveal the foolishness and the weakness of this present world system, even with its philosophy and religion? "That no flesh should glory in his presence" (1 Cor. 1:29). Salvation must be wholly of grace; otherwise, God cannot get the glory.

It is this truth that Paul wanted to get across to the Corinthians, because they were guilty of glorying in men (1 Cor. 3:21). If we glory in men—even godly men like Peter and Paul and Apollos—we are robbing God of the glory that He alone deserves. It was this sinful attitude of pride that was helping to cause division in the church.

Finally, Paul reminded the Corinthians of all they had in Jesus Christ (vv. 30–31). Since every believer is "in Christ," and he has all that he needs, why compete with each other or compare yourselves with each other? It is the Lord who has done it all! "He that glorieth, let him glory in the Lord" (1 Cor. 1:31, a quotation from Jer. 9:24, quoted again in 2 Cor. 10:17).

The spiritual blessings that we need are not abstractions that elude our grasp; they are all in a Person, Jesus Christ. He is our wisdom (Col. 2:3), our righteousness (2 Cor. 5:21), our sanctification (John 17:19), and our redemption (Rom. 3:24).

Actually, the emphasis here is that God shows His wisdom by means of the righteousness, sanctification, and redemption that we have in Christ. Each of these theological words carries a special meaning for Christians. *Righteousness* has to do with our standing before God. We are justified: God declares us righteous in Jesus Christ. But we are also *sanctified,* set apart to belong to God and to serve Him. *Redemption* emphasizes the fact that we are set free because Jesus Christ paid the price for us on the cross. This will lead to complete redemption when Christ returns.

So, in one sense, we have the three tenses of salvation given here: we *have been saved* from the penalty of sin (righteousness); we *are being saved* from the power of sin (sanctification); and we *shall be saved* from the presence of sin (redemption). And every believer has all of these blessings in Jesus Christ!

Therefore, why glory in men? What does Paul have that you do not have? Does Peter have more of Jesus Christ than you do? (It was likely that Jesus Christ had more of Peter, but that is another matter!) We should glory in the Lord and not in ourselves or our spiritual leaders.

As you review this chapter, you can see the mistakes that the Corinthians were making, mistakes that helped to create problems in their church. They were not living up to their holy calling, but were instead following the standards of the world. They ignored the fact that they were called into a wonderful spiritual fellowship with the Lord and with each other. Instead, they were identifying with human leaders and creating divisions in the church. Instead of glorifying God and His grace, they were pleasing themselves and boasting about men.

They were a defiled church, a divided church, a disgraced church!

But, before we pass judgment on them, we should examine our own churches and our own lives. We have been called to be holy, called into fellowship, and called to glorify God.

Are we living up to this calling?

CHAPTER TWO
1 Corinthians 2
BE WISE ABOUT THE CHRISTIAN MESSAGE

My wife was at the wheel of our car as we drove to Chicago, and I was in the copilot's seat reading the page proofs of another author's book that a publisher had asked me to review. Occasionally I would utter a grunt, and then a groan, and finally I shook my head and said, "Oh, no! I can't believe it!"

"I take it you don't like the book," she said. "Something wrong with it?"

"You bet there is!" I replied. "Just about everything is wrong with it, because this man does not know what the message of the gospel really is!"

There was a time, however, when that author had been faithful to the gospel. But over the years, he had begun to take a philosophical (and, I fear, political) approach to the gospel. The result was a hybrid message that was no gospel at all.

It is worth noting that when Paul ministered in Corinth, he obeyed our Lord's commission and preached the gospel. There is a beautiful parallel between Matthew 28:18–20 and Acts 18:1–11.

Christ's Commission (Matt. 28:18–20)	Paul's Ministry (Acts 18:1–11)
"Go ye therefore" (v. 19)	Paul came to Corinth (v. 1)
"make disciples" [teach] (v. 19)	many heard and believed (v. 8)
"baptizing them" (v. 19)	and were baptized (v. 8)
"teaching them" (v. 20)	for a year and six months he taught the Word (v. 11)
"Lo, I am with you" (v. 20)	"For I am with thee" (v. 10)

What had happened at Corinth is happening in churches today: men are mixing philosophy (man's wisdom) with God's revealed message, and this is causing confusion and division. Different preachers have their own "interpretation" to God's message, and some even invent their own vocabulary!

Paul explained the three fundamentals of the gospel message and urged his readers to return to these fundamentals.

The Gospel Centers in the Death of Christ (2:1–5)

Paul reminded the Corinthians of his approach (vv. 1–2). The opening words, "And I," can be translated "Accordingly," on the basis of 1 Corinthians 1:31—the glory of God. Paul had not come to Corinth to glorify himself or to start a religious "fan club." He had come to glorify God.

The itinerant philosophers and teachers depended on their wisdom and eloquence to gain followers. The city of Corinth was filled with such "spellbinders." Paul did not depend on eloquent speech or clever arguments; he simply declared God's Word in the power of the Spirit. He was an ambassador, not a "Christian salesman."

Had he used spectacular speech and philosophy, Paul would have exalted himself and hidden the very Christ he came to proclaim! God had sent him to preach the gospel "not with wisdom of words, lest the cross of Christ should be made of no effect" (1 Cor. 1:17).

A certain church had a beautiful stained-glass window just behind the pulpit. It depicted Jesus Christ on the cross. One Sunday there was a guest minister who was much smaller than the regular pastor. A little girl listened to the guest for a time, then turned to her mother and asked, "Where is the man who usually stands there so we can't see Jesus?"

Too many preachers of the Word so magnify themselves and their gifts that they fail to reveal the glory of Jesus Christ. Paul gloried in the cross of Christ (Gal. 6:14) and made it the center of his message.

Then Paul reminded the Corinthians of his attitude (vv. 3–4). Though he was an apostle, Paul came to them as a humble servant. He did not depend on himself; he became nothing that Christ might be everything. In later years, Paul brought this up again and contrasted himself to the false teachers who had invaded Corinth (2 Cor. 10:1–12). Paul had learned that when he was weak, then God made him strong.

Paul depended on the power of the Holy Spirit. It was not his experience or ability that gave his ministry its power; it was the work of the Spirit of God. His preaching was a "demonstration," not a "performance." The word translated "demonstration" means "legal proof presented in court." The Holy Spirit used Paul's preaching to change lives, and that was all the proof Paul needed that his message was from God. Wicked sinners were transformed by the power of God (1 Cor. 6:9–11)!

However, we must note that Paul is not telling ministers deliberately to preach poorly, or to avoid using the gifts God gave them. Men like Charles Spurgeon and George Whitefield were gifted orators whose words carried power, *but they did not depend on their natural talents.* They trusted the Spirit of God to work in the hearts of their hearers, and He did. Those who minister the Word must prepare and use every gift God has given them—but they must not put their confidence in themselves (see 2 Cor. 3:5).

Finally, Paul reminded them of his aim (v. 5). He wanted them to trust in God and not in the messenger God sent. Had he depended on human wisdom and presented the plan of salvation as a philosophical system, then the Corinthians would have put their trust in an *explanation.* Because Paul declared the Word of God in the power of God, his converts put their faith in a *demonstration:* they experienced God at work in their own lives.

Years ago, a wise Christian said to me, "When you are leading people to Christ, never tell them that they are saved because they have done this or that. It is the job of the Holy Spirit to witness to people that they are saved. Unless He is at work, there can be no salvation." Wise counsel, indeed!

I recall a fine professional man who faithfully attended a church I pastored—a man who was unsaved, but not antagonistic to the gospel. Many of us prayed for him as he continued to listen to the Word. One day a Christian friend of his decided to win him to Christ, or else! He spent several hours presenting argument after argument, and finally the man "prayed the sinner's prayer." Then he stopped attending church! Why? Because he had been talked into something that was not real, and he knew he could not follow through. Later on, he *did* trust Christ and, through the Spirit, have the assurance of salvation. Up to that point, if anybody asked him if he were saved, he would reply, "Sure—Tom told me I was saved!" What a difference when the Spirit gives the assurance!

The gospel is still God's power to change men's lives (Rom. 1:16). Effectiveness in evangelism does not depend on our arguments or persuasive gimmicks, but on the power of the Spirit of God at work in our lives and through the Word that we share.

The Gospel Is Part of the Father's Eternal Plan (2:6–9)

Salvation was purchased by the Son, but it was planned by the Father. Those who talk about "the simple gospel" are both right and wrong. Yes, the message of the gospel is simple enough for an illiterate pagan to understand, believe, and be saved. But it is also so profound that the most brilliant theologian cannot fathom its depths.

There is a "wisdom of God" in the gospel that challenges the keenest intellect. However, this wisdom is not for the masses of lost sinners, nor is it for the immature believers. It is for the mature believers who are growing in their understanding of the Word of God. (The word *perfect* in 1 Cor. 2:6 means "mature." See 1 Cor. 3:1–4.) Perhaps here Paul was answering those in the church who were promoting Apollos, who was an eloquent and profound preacher (Acts 18:24–28).

Let's notice the characteristics of this wisdom.

This wisdom comes from God, not man (v. 7). This wisdom tells the mature saint about the vast eternal plan that God has for His people and His creation. The wisest of the "princes of this world [age]" could not invent or discover this marvelous wisdom that Paul shared from God.

This wisdom has been hidden (v. 7). That is why it is called a mystery, for in the New Testament, a mystery is a "sacred secret," a truth hidden in past ages but now revealed to the people of God. It was Paul whom God used in a special way to share the various "mysteries" that are related to the gospel (see Eph. 3); but note the repetition of the pronoun "we." Paul did not leave out the other apostles.

This wisdom involves God's ordination (v. 7). This means that God made the plan, set it in motion, and will see to it that it will succeed. The great plan of redemption was not a hasty afterthought on the part of God after He saw what man had done. Though all of this boggles our minds, we must accept the Bible truth of divine election and predestination. Even the death of Jesus Christ was ordained of God (Acts 2:22–23; 1 Peter 1:18–20), though men were held responsible for the wicked deed. One of the secrets of an effective prayer life is to lay hold of God's purposes by faith (Acts 4:23–31).

This wisdom results in the glory of God's people (v. 7). One of the greatest expositions of this "plan of the ages" is in Ephesians 1. Three times in that passage, Paul explained that all of this is done for God's glory (Eph. 1:6, 12, 14). It is a staggering thought that we shall one day share in the very glory of God (see John 17:22–24; Rom. 8:28–30)!

This wisdom is hidden from the unsaved world (v. 8). Who are "the princes of this world [age]" that Paul mentions? Certainly the men who were in charge of government when Jesus was on earth did not know who He was (Acts 3:17; 4:25–28). When Jesus on the cross prayed, "Father, forgive them: for they know not what they do" (Luke 23:34), He was echoing this truth. Their ignorance did not *excuse* their sin, of course, because every evidence had been given by the Lord and they should have believed.

But there is another possibility. Paul may have been referring to the *spiritual and demonic rulers of this present age* (Rom. 8:38; Col. 2:15; Eph. 6:12ff.). This would make more sense in 1 Corinthians 2:6, for certainly Pilate, Herod, and the other rulers were not recognized for any special wisdom. The wisdom of this age has its origin in the rulers of this age, of which Satan is the prince (John 12:31; 14:30; 16:11). Of course, the spiritual rulers would have to work in and through the human rulers. So perhaps we must not press the distinction (John 13:2, 27).

But if this interpretation is true, then it opens up a challenging area of consideration. The satanic forces, including Satan himself, did not understand God's great eternal plan! They could understand from the Old Testament Scriptures that the Son of God would be born and die, but they could not grasp the full significance of the cross because these truths were hidden by God. In fact, it is now, through the church, that these truths are being revealed to the principalities and powers (Eph. 3:10).

Satan thought that Calvary was God's great defeat; but it turned out to be God's greatest victory and *Satan's defeat* (Col. 2:15)! From the time of our Lord's birth into this world, Satan had tried to kill Him, because Satan did not fully understand the vast results of Christ's death and resurrection. Had the demonic rulers known, they would not have "engineered" the death of Christ. (Of course, all of this was part of God's eternal plan. It was God who was in control, not Satan.)

Finally, this wisdom applies to the believer's life today (v. 9). This verse is often used at funerals and applied to heaven, but the basic application is to the Christian's life *today*. The next verse makes it clear that God is revealing these things to us here and now.

This verse is a quotation (with adaptation) from Isaiah 64:4. The immediate context relates it to Israel in captivity, awaiting God's deliverance. The nation had sinned and had been sent to Babylon for chastening. They cried out to God that He would come down to deliver them, and He did answer their prayer after seventy years of their exile. God had plans for His people, and they did not have to be afraid (Jer. 29:11).

Paul applied this principle to the church. Our future is secure in Jesus Christ no matter what our circumstances may be. In fact, God's plans for His own are so wonderful that our minds cannot begin to conceive of them or comprehend them! God has ordained this for our glory (1 Cor. 2:7). It is glory all the way from earth to heaven!

For those who love God, every day is a good day

(Rom. 8:28). It may not *look* like a good day, or *feel* like it; but when God is working His plan, we can be sure of the best. It is when we fail to trust Him or obey Him, when our love for Him grows cold, that life takes on a somber hue. If we walk in God's wisdom, we will enjoy His blessings.

We have considered two fundamental truths of the gospel: this message centers in the death of Christ, and it is part of the Father's vast eternal plan. The believers at Corinth had forgotten the cost of their salvation; they had gotten their eyes off of the cross. They were also involved in minor matters—"baby toys"—because they had lost the wonder of the greatness of God's plan for them. They needed to return to the ministry of the Holy Spirit, and this would be Paul's next point.

The Gospel Is Revealed by the Spirit through the Word (2:10–16)

Our salvation involves all three Persons in the Godhead (Eph. 1:3–14; 1 Peter 1:2). You cannot be saved apart from the Father's electing grace, the Son's loving sacrifice, and the Spirit's ministry of conviction and regeneration. It is not enough to say, "I believe in God." What God? Unless it is "the God and Father of our Lord Jesus Christ" (Eph. 1:3), there can be no salvation.

This trinitarian aspect of our salvation helps us to understand better some of the mysteries of our salvation. Many people get confused (or frightened) when they hear about election and predestination. As far as the Father is concerned, I was saved when He chose me in Christ before the foundation of the world (Eph. 1:4); but I knew nothing about that the night I was saved! It was a hidden part of God's wonderful eternal plan.

As far as God the Son is concerned, I was saved when He died for me on the cross. He died for the sins of the whole world, yet the whole world is not saved. This is where the Spirit comes in: as far as the Spirit is concerned, I was saved in May 1945 at a Youth for Christ rally where I heard Billy Graham (then a young evangelist) preach the gospel. It was then that the Holy Spirit applied the Word to my heart, I believed, and God saved me.

Paul pointed out four important ministries of the Holy Spirit of God.

The Spirit indwells believers (v. 12). The very moment you trusted Jesus Christ, the Spirit of God entered your body and made it His temple (1 Cor. 6:19–20). He baptized you (identified you) into the body of Christ (1 Cor. 12:13). He sealed you (Eph. 1:13–14) and will remain with you (John 14:16). He is God's gift to you.

The Holy Spirit is the Spirit of liberty (2 Cor. 3:17). We have not received the "spirit of the world" because we have been called out of this world and no longer belong to it (John 17:14, 16). We are no longer under the authority of Satan and his world system.

Nor have we received a "spirit of bondage again to fear" (Rom. 8:15). The Holy Spirit ministers to us and makes the Father real to us. This ties in with 2 Timothy 1:7—"For God hath not given us the spirit of fear; but of power, and of love, and of a sound [disciplined] mind." We have a wealth of spiritual resources because the Spirit lives within us!

The Spirit searches (vv. 10–11). I cannot know what is going on within your personality, but your human spirit within you knows. Neither can I know "the deep things of God" unless somehow I can enter into God's personality. I cannot do that—but by His Spirit, God has entered into my personality. Through the Holy Spirit, each believer becomes a sharer of the very life of God.

The Holy Spirit knows "the deep things of God" and reveals them to us. First Corinthians 2:10 makes it clear that "the deep things of God" is another description of "the things which God hath prepared for them that love him" (1 Cor. 2:9). God wants us to know *today* all the blessings of His grace that He has planned for us.

The Spirit teaches (v. 13). Jesus promised that the Spirit would teach us (John 14:26) and guide us into truth (John 16:13). But we must note carefully the sequence here: the Spirit taught Paul from the Word, and Paul then taught the believers. The truth of God is found in the Word of God. And it is very important to note that these spiritual truths are given in specific *words*. In the Bible, we have much more than inspired thoughts; we have inspired *words*. "For I have given unto them the words which thou gavest me" (John 17:8).

Each of our four children has a different vocation. We have a pastor, a nurse, an electronics designer, and a secretary in a commercial real estate firm. Each of the children had to learn a specialized vocabulary in order to succeed. The only one I really understand is the pastor.

The successful Christian learns the vocabulary of the Spirit and makes use of it. He knows the meaning of justification, sanctification, adoption, propitiation, election, inspiration, and so forth. In understanding God's vocabulary, we come to understand God's Word and God's will for our lives. If the engineering student can grasp the technical terms of chemistry, physics, or electronics, why should it be difficult for Christians, taught by the Spirit, to grasp the vocabulary of Christian truth?

Yet I hear church members say, "Don't preach doctrine. Just give us heartwarming sermons that will encourage us!" Sermons based on what? If they are not based on doctrine, they will accomplish nothing! "But doctrine is so dull!" people complain. Not if it is presented the way the Bible presents it. Doctrine to me is exciting! What a thrill to be able to study the Bible and let the Spirit teach us "the deep things of God" (1 Cor. 2:10).

How does the Spirit teach the believer? He compares "spiritual things with spiritual." He reminds us of what He has taught us (John 14:26), relates that truth to something new, and then leads us into new truth and new applications of old truth. What a joy it is to sit before the pages of the Bible and let the Spirit reveal God's truth. The trouble is, many Christians are too busy for this kind of quiet meditation. What enrichment they are missing!

The Holy Spirit is like a householder who "bringeth forth out of his treasure things new and old" (Matt. 13:52). The new always comes out of the old and helps us better understand the old. God gives us new insights into old truths as we compare one part of Scripture with another. Jesus based His teaching on the Old Testament, yet people were amazed at what He taught because it was so fresh and exciting.

I suggest that you make time every day to read the Word and meditate on it. Follow a regular schedule in your reading, and give yourself time to pray, think, and meditate. Let the Spirit of God search the Word and teach you. The study and application of basic Bible doctrine can transform your life.

The Spirit matures the believer (vv. 14–16). The contrast here is between the saved person (called "spiritual" because he is indwelt by the Spirit) and the unsaved person (called "natural" because he does not have the Spirit within). In 1 Corinthians 3:1–4, Paul will introduce a third kind of person, the "carnal man." He is the immature Christian, the one who lives on a childhood level because he will not feed on the Word and grow.

At one time, every Christian was "natural," having only the things of nature. When we trusted the Savior, the Spirit came in and we moved into the plane of "spiritual"—able to live in the realm of the Spirit. *Then we had to grow!* The unsaved man cannot receive the things of the Spirit because he does not believe in them and cannot understand them. But as the Christian day by day receives the things of the Spirit, he grows and matures.

One of the marks of maturity is discernment—the ability to penetrate beneath the surface of life and see things as they really are. Unsaved people "walk by sight" and really see nothing. They are spiritually blind. The maturing Christian grows in his spiritual discernment and develops the ability (with the Spirit's help) to understand more and more of the will and mind of God. The Corinthians lacked this discernment; they were spiritually ignorant.

To "have the mind of Christ" does not mean we are infallible and start playing God in the lives of other people. Nobody instructs God! (Paul quoted Isa. 40:13. Also see Rom. 11:33–36.) To "have the mind of Christ" means to look at life from the Savior's point of view, having His values and desires in mind. It means to think God's thoughts and not think as the world thinks.

The unsaved person does not understand the Christian; they live in two different worlds. But the Christian understands the unsaved person. First

Corinthians 2:15 does not suggest that unsaved people cannot point out flaws in the believer's life (they often do), but that the unsaved man really cannot penetrate into the full understanding of what the Christian's life is all about. I like the New American Standard Bible's translation: "But he who is spiritual appraises all things, yet he himself is appraised by no man." That "no man" includes other Christians as well. We must be very careful not to become spiritual dictators in the lives of God's people (2 Cor. 1:24).

The Corinthian Christians were so wrapped up in the miraculous gifts of the Spirit that they were neglecting the basic ministries of the Spirit. And in their emphasis on the Spirit, they were also neglecting the Father and the Son.

Blessed are the balanced! And blessed are they who understand and share "all the counsel of God" (Acts 20:27).

CHAPTER THREE
1 Corinthians 3
BE WISE ABOUT THE LOCAL CHURCH

British Bible teacher Dr. G. Campbell Morgan had four sons; all became ministers. Someone asked one of the grandsons if he also would become a minister, and he replied, "No, I plan to work for a living."

What is a pastor supposed to do? What really is "the work of the ministry"? If we don't know, we will never know how to evaluate the minister's work. Perhaps no issue creates more problems in the local church than this one: how do we know when the pastor and church leaders are really doing their job?

Paul painted three pictures of the church in this chapter and, using these pictures, pointed out what the ministry is supposed to accomplish. The church is a *family* and the goal is *maturity* (1 Cor. 3:1–4). The church is a *field* and the goal is *quantity* (1 Cor. 3:5–9a). The church is a *temple* and the goal is *quality* (1 Cor. 3:9b–23).

The Family—Maturity (3:1–4)

Paul already explained that there are two kinds of people in the world—natural (unsaved) and spiritual (saved). But now he explained that there are two kinds of saved people: mature and immature (carnal). A Christian matures by allowing the Spirit to teach him and direct him by feeding on the Word. The immature Christian lives for the things of the flesh *(carnal* means "flesh") and has little interest in the things of the Spirit. Of course, some believers are immature because they have been saved only a short time, but that is not what Paul was discussing here.

Paul was the "spiritual father" who brought this family into being (1 Cor. 4:15). During the eighteen months he ministered in Corinth, Paul had tried to feed his spiritual children and help them mature in the faith. Just as in a human family, everybody helps the new baby grow and mature, so in the family of God we must encourage spiritual maturity.

What are the marks of maturity? For one thing, you can tell the mature person by his *diet*. As I write this chapter, we are watching our grandson and our granddaughter grow up. Becky is still being nursed by her mother, but Jonathan now sits at the table and uses his little cup and (with varying degrees of success) his tableware. As children grow, they learn to eat different food. They graduate (to use Paul's words) from milk to meat.

What is the difference? The usual answer is that "milk" represents the easy things in the Word, while "meat" represents the hard doctrines. But I disagree with that traditional explanation, and my proof is Hebrews 5:10–14. That passage seems to teach that "milk" represents what Jesus Christ did on earth, while "meat" concerns what He is doing now in heaven. The writer of Hebrews wanted to teach his readers about the present heavenly priesthood of Jesus Christ, but his readers were so immature, he could not do it (note Heb. 6:1–4).

The Word of God is our spiritual food: milk (1 Peter 2:2), bread (Matt. 4:4), meat (Heb. 5:11–14), and even honey (Ps. 119:103). Just as the physical man needs a balanced diet if his body is to be healthy, so the inner man needs a balanced diet of spiritual food. The baby begins with milk, but as he grows and his teeth develop, he needs solid food.

It is not difficult to determine a believer's spiritual maturity, or immaturity, if you discover what kind of "diet" he enjoys. The immature believer knows little about the present ministry of Christ in heaven. He knows the *facts* about our Lord's life and ministry on earth, but not the *truths* about His present ministry in heaven. He lives on "Bible stories" and not Bible doctrines. He has no understanding of 1 Corinthians 2:6–7.

In my itinerant ministry, I have preached in hundreds of churches and conferences; and I have always been grateful for congregations that wanted to be enlightened and edified, not entertained. It is important that we preach the gospel to the lost; but it is also important that we *interpret* the gospel to the saved. The entire New Testament is an interpretation and application of the gospel. Paul did not write Romans, for example, to tell the Romans how to be saved—for they were already saints. He wrote to explain to them what was really involved in their salvation. It was an explanation of the "deep things of God" and how they applied to daily life.

There is another way to determine maturity: the mature Christian practices love and seeks to get along with others. Children like to disagree and fuss. And children like to identify with heroes, whether sports heroes or Hollywood heroes. The "babes" in Corinth were fighting over which preacher was the greatest—Paul, Apollos, or Peter. It sounded like children on the playground: "My father can fight better than your father! My father makes more money than your father!"

When immature Christians, without spiritual discernment, get into places of leadership in the church, the results will be disastrous. More than one brokenhearted pastor has phoned me, or written me, asking what to do with church officers who talk big but live small. (In all fairness, I should say that sometimes it is the *officers* who write asking what to do with an immature pastor!)

The work of the pastor is to help the church grow spiritually and mature in the Lord. This is done by the steady, balanced ministry of the Word. Ephesians 4:1–16 explains how this is done: It is necessary for each member of the body to make his own contribution. God gives spiritual gifts to His people, and then He gives these gifted people to the various churches to build up the saints. As the believers grow, they build the church.

Paul will have more to say about spiritual gifts in 1 Corinthians 12—14, but this should be said now: A mature Christian uses his gifts as tools to build with, while an immature believer uses gifts as toys to play with or trophies to boast about. Many of the members of the Corinthian church enjoyed "showing off" their gifts, but they were not interested in serving one another and edifying the church.

What is the ministry all about? It involves loving, feeding, and disciplining God's family so that His children mature in the faith and become more like Jesus Christ.

The Field—Quantity (3:5–9a)

Paul was fond of agricultural images and often used them in his letters. "Ye are God's husbandry" simply means, "You are God's cultivated field, God's garden." In the parable of the sower, Jesus compared the human heart to soil and the Word of God to seed (Matt. 13:1–9, 18–23). Paul took this *individual* image and made it *collective:* the local church is a field that ought to bear fruit. The task of the ministry is the sowing of the seed, the cultivating of the soil, the watering of the plants, and the harvesting of the fruit.

How did this image of the church as a "field" apply to the special problems of the Corinthians? To begin with, the emphasis must be on God and not on the laborers. Paul and Apollos were only servants who did their assigned tasks. It was God who gave life to their efforts. Even the faith of the believers was a gift from God (1 Cor. 3:5). It is wrong to center attention on the servants. Look instead to the Lord of the harvest, the source of all blessing.

Note the emphasis in this paragraph on *increase* or *growth*. Why compare preachers or statistics? God is the source of the growth; no man can take the credit. Furthermore, no one man can do *all* the necessary work. Paul planted the seed, Apollos watered it, but only God could make it grow (1 Cor. 3:6).

Three main lessons appear from this image.

First, diversity of ministry. One laborer plows the soil, another sows the seed, a third waters the seed.

As time passes, the plants grow, the fruit appears, and other laborers enjoy reaping the harvest. This emphasis on diversity will also show up when Paul compares the church to a body with many different parts.

Second, unity of purpose. No matter what work a person is doing for the Lord, he is still a part of the harvest. "Now he that planteth and he that watereth are one" (1 Cor. 3:8). Paul, Apollos, and Peter were not competing with each other. Rather, each was doing his assigned task under the lordship of Jesus Christ. Even though there is diversity of ministry, there is unity of purpose; and there ought to be unity of spirit.

Third, humility of spirit. It is not the human laborers who produce the harvest, but the Lord of the harvest. "God gave the increase.… God that giveth the increase" (1 Cor. 3:6–7). Granted, God has ordained that human beings should be His ministers on earth; but their efforts apart from God's blessing would be failures. The Corinthians were proud of their church, and various groups in the assembly were proud of their leaders. But this attitude of being "puffed up" was dividing the church because God was not receiving the glory.

Jesus expressed the same idea as recorded in John 4:34–38. The sower and the reaper not only work together, but one day they shall rejoice together and receive their own rewards. There can be no such thing as isolated ministry, because each worker enters into the labors of others. I have had the privilege of leading people to Christ who were total strangers to me, but others had sown the seed and watered it with their love and prayers.

"And every man shall receive his own reward according to his own labor" (1 Cor. 3:8). What men may think of our ministry is not important; what God may think is of supreme importance. Our reward must not be the praise of men, but the "Well done!" of the Lord of the harvest.

God wants to see increase in His field. He wants each local church to produce the fruit of the Spirit (Gal. 5:22–23), holiness (Rom. 6:22), giving (Rom. 15:26), good works (Col. 1:10), praise to the Lord (Heb. 13:15), and souls won to Christ (Rom. 1:13). Along with spiritual growth, there should be a measure of numerical growth. *Fruit has in it the seed for more fruit.* If the fruit of our ministry is genuine, it will eventually produce "more fruit … much fruit" to the glory of God (John 15:1–8).

Those who serve in ministry must constantly be caring for the "soil" of the church. It requires diligence and hard work to produce a harvest. The lazy preacher or Sunday school teacher is like the slothful farmer Solomon wrote about in Proverbs 24:30–34. Satan is busy sowing discord, lies, and sin; and we must be busy cultivating the soil and planting the good seed of the Word of God.

The Temple—Quality (3:9b–23)

The usual explanation of this passage is that it describes the building of the Christian life. We all build on Christ, but some people use good materials, while others use poor materials. The kind of material you use determines the kind of reward you will get.

While this may be a valid *application* of this passage, it is not the basic *interpretation.* Paul was discussing the building of the local church, the temple of God. (In 1 Cor. 6:19–20 the individual believer is God's temple; but here it is the local assembly that is in view. In Eph. 2:19–22, the whole church is compared to a temple of God.) Paul pointed out that one day God will judge our labors as related to the local assembly. "The fire will test the quality of each man's work" (1 Cor. 3:13 NIV).

God is concerned that we build with quality. The church does not belong to the preacher or to the congregation. It is *God's* church. "Ye are God's building" (1 Cor. 3:9). If we are going to build the local church the way God wants it built, we must meet certain conditions.

First, we must build on the right foundation (vv. 10–11). That foundation is Jesus Christ. When Paul came to Corinth, he determined to preach only Christ and Him crucified (1 Cor. 2:1–2). He laid the only foundation that would last. In more than thirty years of ministry, I have seen "churches" try to build on a famous preacher or a special method or a doctrinal emphasis they felt was important; but these ministries simply did not last. The Corinthians were emphasizing personalities—Paul, Peter, Apollos—when they should have been glorifying Christ.

The foundation is laid by the proclaiming of the gospel of Jesus Christ. The foundation is the most important part of the building, because it determines the size, shape, and strength of the superstructure. A ministry may seem to be successful for a time, but if it is not founded on Christ, it will eventually collapse and disappear.

I am thinking now of a pastor who "discovered a great truth" in the Bible (actually, he read it in some books) and decided to build his church on the promotion of that "great truth." He split his church and took a group with him who were "devoted to the truth" he had discovered. But the new church never succeeded. Now his group is scattered and he goes from church to church, trying to get converts to his cause. He built on the wrong foundation.

Second, we must build with the right materials (vv. 12–17). Paul described two opposite kinds of materials, as the chart reveals.

Gold, Silver, Precious Stones	Wood, Hay, Stubble
Permanent	Passing, temporary
Beautiful	Ordinary, even ugly
Valuable	Cheap
Hard to obtain	Easy to obtain

What did Paul want to symbolize by his choice of materials? He was not talking about *people,* because Christians are the "living stones" that make up God's temple (1 Peter 2:5). I personally believe Paul was referring to the *doctrines of the Word of God*. In each section of this chapter, the Word is symbolized in a way that fits the image of the church Paul used. The Word is food for the family, seed for the field, and materials for the temple.

The book of Proverbs presents the wisdom of the Word of God as treasure to be sought, protected, and invested in daily life. Consider these passages:

Happy is the man that findeth wisdom, and the man that getteth understanding. For the merchandise of it is better than the merchandise of silver, and the gain thereof than fine gold. She is more precious than rubies. (3:13–15a)

My son, if thou wilt receive my words, and hide my commandments with thee; so that thou incline thine ear unto wisdom, and apply thine heart to understanding; yea, if thou criest after knowledge, and liftest up thy voice for understanding; if thou seekest her as silver, and searchest for her as for hid treasures; then shalt thou understand the fear of the Lord, and find the knowledge of God. (2:1–5)

Receive my instruction, and not silver; and knowledge rather than choice gold. For wisdom is better than rubies; and all the things that may be desired are not to be compared to it. (8:10–11)

When you remember that Paul has been writing about *wisdom* in these first three chapters, you can easily see the connection. The Corinthians were trying to build their church by man's wisdom, the wisdom of this world, when they should have been depending on the wisdom of God as found in the Word.

This says to me that ministers of the Word must dig deep into the Scriptures and mine out the precious gold, silver, and jewels, and then build these truths into the lives of the people. D. L. Moody used to say that converts should be weighed as well as counted. God is interested in *quality* as well as *quantity,* and Paul made it clear that it is possible to have both. The faithful minister can work in the field and see increase, and he can build with the Word of God and see beauty and lasting blessings.

It is a serious thing to be a part of the building of God's temple. First Corinthians 3:16–17 warn us that if we destroy ("defile") God's temple by using cheap materials, God will destroy us! This does not mean eternal condemnation, of course, because 1 Corinthians 3:15 assures us that each worker will be saved, even if he loses a reward. I think Paul is saying that each of us builds into the church *what we build into our own lives.* Veteran missionary to India Amy Carmichael used to say, "The work will never go

deeper than we have gone ourselves." So we end up tearing down our own lives if we fail to build into the church the values that will last. We may look very successful to men, but "the day shall declare it," and on that day, some ministers will go up in smoke.

It is unwise to compare and contrast ministries. Paul warned in 1 Corinthians 4:5, "Therefore, judge nothing before the time."

Young ministers often asked Dr. Campbell Morgan the secret of his pulpit success. Morgan replied, "I always say to them the same thing—work; hard work; and again, work!" Morgan was in his study at six o'clock each morning, digging treasures out of the Bible. You can find wood, hay, and stubble in your backyard, and it will not take too much effort to pick it up. But if you want gold, silver, and jewels, *you have to dig for them.* Lazy preachers and Sunday school teachers will have much to answer for at the judgment seat of Christ—and so will preachers and teachers who *steal* materials from others instead of studying and making it their own.

Third, we must build according to the right plan (vv. 18–20). It comes as a shock to some church members that you cannot manage a local church the same way you run a business. This does not mean we should not follow good business principles, but the operation is totally different. There is a wisdom of this world that works for the world, but it will not work for the church.

The world depends on promotion, prestige, and the influence of money and important people. The church depends on prayer, the power of the Spirit, humility, sacrifice, and service. The church that imitates the world may seem to succeed in time, but it will turn to ashes in eternity. The church in the book of Acts had none of the "secrets of success" that seem to be important today. They owned no property; they had no influence in government; they had no treasury ("Silver and gold have I none," said Peter); their leaders were ordinary men without special education in the accepted schools; they held no attendance contests; they brought in no celebrities; and yet they turned the world upside down!

God has a specific plan for each local church (Phil. 2:12–13). Each pastor and church leader must seek the mind of God for His wisdom. First Corinthians 3:19 warns that man's wisdom will only trap him (a quotation from Job 5:13); and 1 Corinthians 3:20 warns that man's wisdom only leads to vanity and futility (a quotation from Ps. 94:11). Though the church must be identified with the *needs* of the world, it must not imitate the *wisdom* of the world.

Finally, we must build with the right motive (vv. 21–23). That motive is the glory of God. The members of the Corinthian church were glorying in men, and this was wrong. They were comparing men (1 Cor. 4:6) and dividing the church by such carnal deeds. Had they been seeking to glorify God alone, there would have been harmony in the assembly.

Paul closed this appeal by pointing out that each

believer possesses all things in Christ. Each one of God's servants belongs to *each* believer. No member of the church should say, "I belong to Paul!" or "I like Peter!" because each servant belongs to each member equally. Perhaps we cannot help but have our personal preferences when it comes to the way different men minister the Word. But we must not permit our personal preferences to become divisive prejudices. In fact, the preacher I may enjoy the least may be the one I need the most!

"All are yours"—the world, life, death, things present, things to come! How rich we are in Christ! If all things belong to all believers, then why should there be competition and rivalry? "Get your eyes off of men!" Paul admonished. "Keep your eyes on Christ, and work with Him in building the church!"

"Ye are Christ's"—this balances things. I have all things in Jesus Christ, but I must not become careless or use my freedom unwisely. "All things are yours"— that is Christian *liberty.* "And ye are Christ's"—that is Christian *responsibility.* We need both if we are to build a church that will not turn to ashes when the fire falls.

How we need to pray for ministers of the Word! They must feed the family and bring the children to maturity. They must sow the seed in the field and pray for an increase. They must mine the treasures of the Word and build these treasures into the temple. No wonder Paul cried, "And who is sufficient for these things?" But he also gave the answer: "Our sufficiency is of God" (2 Cor. 2:16; 3:5).

CHAPTER FOUR
1 Corinthians 4
BE WISE ABOUT THE CHRISTIAN MINISTRY

In 1 Corinthians 3, Paul presented three pictures of the local church. Now he presents three pictures of the minister—a steward (1 Cor. 4:1–6), a spectacle (1 Cor. 4:7–13), and a father (1 Cor. 4:14–21). He wanted his readers to understand how God measures and evaluates a Christian's service. First Corinthians 4:6 explains Paul's purpose: "That no one of you be puffed up for one against another."

We must avoid extremes when it comes to evaluating men and their ministries. On the one hand, we can be so indifferent that we accept anybody who comes along. But the other extreme is to be so hypercritical that Paul himself would fail the test. It is important that we "try the spirits" (1 John 4:1–6; and note 2 John), but we must be careful not to grieve the Spirit as we do so.

In these three pictures of ministry, Paul presented three characteristics of a true minister of Jesus Christ.

Faithfulness—The Steward (4:1–6)
Paul answered the leaders of the various factions in the church when he called himself, Peter, and Apollos "ministers of Christ." The word translated "ministers" is literally "under-rowers." It described the slaves who rowed the huge Roman galleys. "We are not the captains of the ship," said Paul, "but only the galley slaves who are under orders. Now, is one slave greater than another?"

Then Paul explained the image of the *steward.* A steward is a servant who manages everything for his master, but who himself owns nothing. Joseph was a chief steward in Potiphar's household (Gen. 39). The church is the "household of faith" (Gal. 6:10), and the ministers are stewards who share God's wealth with the family (Matt. 13:52). Paul called this spiritual wealth "the mysteries of God." We met this important word *mystery* in 1 Corinthians 2:7, so you may want to review it.

The responsibility of the steward is to be *faithful to his master.* A steward may not please the members of the household; he may not even please some of the other servants; but if he pleases his own master, he is a good steward. This same idea is expressed in Romans 14:4.

So, the main issue is not, "Is Paul popular?" or, "Is Apollos a better preacher than Paul?" The main issue is, "Have Paul, Apollos, and Peter been faithful to do the work God assigned to them?" Jesus had this same test in mind when He told the parable recorded in Luke 12:41–48. If a servant of God is faithful in his personal life, in his home, and in his ministry of the Word, then he is a good steward and will be adequately rewarded.

But a servant is constantly being judged. There is always somebody criticizing something he does. Paul pointed out that there are three judgments in the life of the steward.

There is man's judgment (v. 3a). Paul did not get upset when people criticized him, for he knew that his Master's judgment was far more important. The phrase *man's judgment* is literally "man's day." This is in contrast to *God's* day of judgment yet to come (1 Cor. 1:8; 3:13).

There is the servant's own self-judgment (vv. 3b–4a). Paul knew nothing that was amiss in his life and ministry, but even that did not excuse him. Sometimes we do not really know ourselves. There can be a fine line between a clear conscience and a self-righteous attitude, so we must beware.

The most important judgment is God's judgment (v. 4b). Certainly God judges us today through His Word (Heb. 4:12) and by the ministry of the Spirit. Sometimes He uses the ministry of a loving friend to help us face and confess sin (Matt. 18:15–17). But the main reference here is to the final evaluation when each Christian stands at the judgment seat of Christ (Rom. 14:10; 2 Cor. 5:10). Then the true facts will be revealed and the faithful servants rewarded.

These verses must not be used to cultivate a self-righteous independence of people. The local church is a family, and members of the family must help each other to grow. There is a place for honest, loving criticism (Eph. 4:15). If the critic is right, then he has helped us. If he is wrong, then we can help him. Either way, the truth is strengthened.

Paul's "therefore" in 1 Corinthians 4:5 alerts us that he is about to make a personal application of the truths just discussed. He closed this section with a threefold rebuke.

First, "you are judging God's servants at the wrong time" (v. 5). It is when the Lord returns that He will evaluate their lives and ministries, so wait until then. In fact, you cannot see into men's hearts; you cannot begin to judge their motives. Only God can do that. "Man looketh on the outward appearance, but the Lord looketh on the heart" (1 Sam. 16:7).

The Corinthians who were passing judgment on Paul were actually "playing God" and assuming to themselves the privileges that only God has. How often in my own ministry I have made this mistake! How easy it is to misread a situation and misjudge a person.

Second, "you are judging by the wrong standard" (v. 6a). The Corinthians were measuring different men by their own personal preferences and prejudices. They were even comparing ministers with one another. The only true basis for evaluation is "that which is written"—the Word of God.

The Bible clearly reveals what kind of life and service is required of God's ministers. There is no need for us to devise new standards. Often I receive letters from churches seeking pastors, asking if I could recommend candidates to them. Too often their "requirements" have gone beyond what God requires in His Word. Again, it is the problem Paul discussed in 1 Corinthians 1 and 2—the wisdom of men versus the wisdom of God.

Third, "you are judging with the wrong motive" (v. 6b). Each group in the church was tearing down the other preachers in order to build up the man they liked. Their motive was not at all spiritual. They were promoting division in the church by being partisan to one man as opposed to the others. They needed to examine their own hearts and get rid of the pride that was destroying the church.

God's servants are stewards of His truth, and the key test is *Have they been faithful to obey and to teach the Word of God?* Not just faithful *preaching,* but faithful *practicing* as well. The testimony of Samuel (1 Sam. 12:1–5) and Paul (Acts 20:17ff.) will bear witness to this truth.

Humbleness—The Spectacle (4:7–13)

When Paul called himself and other apostles "a spectacle unto the world" (1 Cor. 4:9), he was using an image familiar to people in the Roman Empire. The government kept the people pacified by presenting entertainments in the different cities. The amphitheaters would be filled with citizens, eager to see men compete in the games and prisoners fight with the beasts. (In fact, the Greek word translated "spectacle" gives us our English word *theater.*) The Coliseum at Rome became the center for these "entertainments."

When the "main events" were ended, then the poorest and weakest prisoners were brought in to fight with the beasts. Nobody expected too much from their performance.

What a picture of the apostles of Jesus Christ! But it forms the background for a series of contrasts that Paul presented for the purpose of trying to humble the Corinthians.

Kings—prisoners (vv. 7–9). The questions in 1 Corinthians 4:7 ought to make all of us stop and think. I like the New American Standard Bible's translation of the first question: "Who regards you as superior?" A young preacher once said to a friend of mine, "Please pray that I will stay humble." My friend replied, "Tell me, what do you have to be proud about?" Why would anybody regard us as superior? Perhaps it is our own biased opinion that makes us feel so important. The best commentary on 1 Corinthians 4:7 is the witness of John the Baptist: "A man can receive nothing, except it be given him from heaven.… He [Christ] must increase, but I must decrease" (John 3:27, 30).

Paul used a bit of sanctified sarcasm in 1 Corinthians 4:8 when he described the Corinthians as kings. "I wish I could reign with you and be important!" he wrote. "But instead, I must go into the arena and suffer for the Lord Jesus Christ. You are first in men's eyes, but we apostles are last." In the eyes of God, the apostles were first (1 Cor. 12:28), but in the eyes of men they were last.

There is no place for pride in the ministry. If a truly great leader like Paul considered himself "on exhibition last in the program," where does this leave the rest of us? Church members are wrong when they measure ministers other than by the standards God has given. They are also wrong when they boast about their favorite preachers. This is not to say that faithful servants cannot be recognized and honored, but in all things God must be glorified (1 Thess. 5:12–13).

Wise men—fools (v. 10a). Paul was a fool according to the standards of men. Had he remained a Jewish rabbi, he could have attained great heights in the Jewish religion (Gal. 1:14). Or had he sided with the Jewish legalists in the Jerusalem church and not ministered to the Gentiles, he could have avoided a great deal of persecution (Acts 15; 21:17ff.). But when Paul asked the Lord, "What wilt thou have me to do?" (Acts 9:6) he really meant it.

The Corinthians were wise in their own eyes, but they were actually fools in the sight of God. By depending on the wisdom and the standards of the world, they were acting like fools. The way to be spiritually wise is to become a fool in the eyes of the world (1 Cor. 3:18). I often find myself quoting those words of martyred Jim Elliot: "He is no fool who gives what he cannot keep to gain what he cannot lose."

Strong men—weak (v. 10b). There was a time when Paul gloried in his strengths; but then he met

Jesus Christ and discovered that what he thought were assets were really liabilities (Phil. 3). It was through his own personal suffering that Paul discovered that his spiritual strength was the result of personal weakness (2 Cor. 12:7–10). Strength that knows itself to be strength is weakness; but weakness that knows itself to be weakness becomes strength.

The Corinthians were proud of their spiritual achievements. The factions in the church were proud of their human leaders and favorite preachers. But all of this was only weakness. There is strength only when God gets the glory. "My strength is made perfect in weakness" (2 Cor. 12:9).

Honorable—despised (vv. 10c–13). This was the crux of the whole matter: The Christians in Corinth wanted the honor that comes from men, not the honor that comes from God. They were trying to "borrow" glory by associating themselves with "great men." Paul answered, "If you associate with us, you had better be ready for suffering. We apostles are not held in honor—we are despised!"

Paul then described the privations and sufferings that he had to endure as a servant of God. The fact that he worked with his own hands as a tentmaker would have lowered him in the eyes of many, because the Greeks despised manual labor.

Paul also described how he responded to the way people treated him; and this, in itself, helped to make him great. What life does to us depends on what life finds in us. When Paul was reviled, he blessed—just as Jesus commanded (Matt. 5:44). When persecuted, he endured it by the grace of God and did not retaliate. When he was slandered, Paul tried to conciliate. In all things, he sought to respond in love.

What was the result? Men treated him "as the filth of the world … the offscouring of all things" (1 Cor. 4:13). "Away with such a fellow from the earth: for it is not fit that he should live" (Acts 22:22). Paul and the other apostles were treated just as their Lord was treated; but God vindicated them and brought glory to His name.

Faithfulness in service and humbleness of mind: these are two important characteristics of a minister of Jesus Christ. He must be willing to work and willing to suffer. It is one thing to be faithful and quite another to be popular. But there is a third characteristic that helps to balance the others.

Tenderness—The Father (4:14–21)

Paul had already compared the local church to a family (1 Cor. 3:1–4). But now the emphasis is on the minister as a "spiritual father." In none of his letters did Paul ever call himself "father." He was mindful of the Lord's teaching in Matthew 23:8–12. But in comparing himself to a "spiritual father," Paul reminded the church of the important ministries he had performed on their behalf.

First, Paul had founded the family (vv. 14–15). The Corinthians were Paul's beloved children in the faith. Whenever we share the gospel with someone and have the joy of leading him to faith in Christ, we become a "spiritual parent" in his life. This does not give us any special authority over his faith (2 Cor. 1:24), but it *does* create a special relationship that God can use to help him grow. The local church is God's family for helping the newborn Christians develop.

It is important to note that Paul did not take the credit for their conversion. Their spiritual birth was *in Christ* and *through the gospel.* Sinners are born again through the ministry of the Spirit of God and the Word of God (John 3:6; 1 Peter 1:23–25). Paul was the "father" who stood by and assisted at their birth.

A child may have many guardians and teachers, but he can have only one father. He has a special relationship to his father that must not be preempted by anyone else. There had been no church in Corinth before Paul came, so that even the second-generation believers in the church were the results of Paul's effective ministry.

Paul founded the church and Apollos followed him and taught the people. In some way that is not made clear in the Scriptures, Peter also ministered at Corinth. (Perhaps he had not been there personally, but other teachers from Jerusalem had ministered in Corinth as "representatives" of Peter.) God's children need the ministry of different teachers, but they must never forget the "spiritual father" who brought them to Christ.

Second, Paul was an example to the family (vv. 16–17). Children have a way of imitating their parents, either for good or for ill. Researchers tell us that teenagers learn to drink at home and not from their peers. My guess is that other bad habits are learned the same way.

The word *followers* literally is "mimics." Paul gave the same admonition in Philippians 3:17, but we must not think that he was exalting himself. Little children learn first by example, then by explanation. When Paul pastored the church in Corinth, he set the example before them in love, devotion to Christ, sacrifice, and service. "Be ye followers of me, even as I also am of Christ" (1 Cor. 11:1). Paul was a good example because he was following the greatest Example of all, Jesus Christ.

But Paul was also a good teacher. It takes both example and instruction to bring a child to maturity. Paul sent Timothy (also one of his spiritual children) to remind the church of the doctrines and practices that Paul always taught. Timothy did not carry the letter to the church (1 Cor. 16:10), but apparently went ahead to prepare the way for the letter.

God does not have one standard for one church and a different standard for another church. He may work out His will in different ways (Phil. 2:12–13), but the basic doctrines and principles are the same. Because churches have gotten away from God's wisdom and have substituted man's wisdom, we have serious doctrinal differences among various churches.

Men have gone beyond "that which is written" (1 Cor. 4:6), and this has brought division into the church.

Third, Paul was faithful to discipline the family (vv. 18–21). A child's will must be broken, but not destroyed. Until a colt is broken, it is dangerous and useless; but once it learns to obey, it becomes gentle and useful. Pride is a terrible thing in the Christian life and in the church. The yeast of sin (leaven, 1 Cor. 5:6–8) had made the Corinthians "puffed up," even to the point of saying, "Paul will not come to us! His bark is worse than his bite!" (2 Cor. 10:8–11)

Paul had been patient with their disobedience, but now he warned them that the time had come for discipline. Paul was not like the tolerant modern mother who shouted at her spoiled son, "This is the last time I'm going to tell you for the last time!"

A faithful parent must discipline his children. It is not enough to teach them and be an example before them; he must also punish them when they rebel and refuse to obey. Paul would have preferred to come with meekness and deal with their sins in a gentle manner, but their own attitude made this difficult. They were puffed up—and even proud of their disobedience (1 Cor. 5:1–2)!

The contrast in this paragraph is between *speech* and *power,* words and deeds. The arrogant Corinthians had no problem "talking big," the way children often will do; but they could not back up their talk with their "walk." Their religion was only in words. Paul was prepared to back up his talk with power, with deeds that would reveal their sins and God's holiness.

This section prepared the way for the next two chapters that deal with discipline in the local church. There was much sin in the Corinthian congregation, and Paul was prepared to deal with it. He had already written them a letter about the matter (1 Cor. 5:9), but the congregation had not obeyed him. It was then that some of the more spiritual members contacted Paul (1 Cor. 1:11; 16:17) and shared the burdens with him. Some of the church leaders had written Paul for counsel (1 Cor. 7:1), and Paul prayed that they might obey the counsel he wrote to them.

It is a principle of life that those who will not govern themselves must be governed. Insurance companies and medical authorities urged drivers to wear seat belts, but many of them refused. So the government passed a law *requiring* drivers to wear seat belts. If you fail to obey, you will be punished.

Paul gave the Corinthian church opportunity to set their household in order. In the following chapters, he explained how the local church ought to be governed in the will of God. Unfortunately, the church did not immediately obey. Paul had to make a quick visit to Corinth, and his experience during that visit was very painful (2 Cor. 2:1; 12:14; 13:1). He then had to write them a very strong letter (1 Cor. 7:8–12); possibly it was carried by Titus.

To the glory of God, the matters did get settled for the most part. There was still some mopping up to do (2 Cor. 12:20—13:5), but the crisis was now over.

It is not an easy thing to be a minister of Jesus Christ. As a steward, you must be faithful to your Master no matter what men may say to you or do to you. You will be treated as refuse by the people of the world. Your own spiritual children may break your heart and have to be disciplined.

God's faithful servants deserve our love, respect, obedience, and prayer support.

CHAPTER FIVE
1 Corinthians 5—6
BE WISE ABOUT CHURCH DISCIPLINE

The church at Corinth was not only a divided church, but it was also a disgraced church. There was sin in the assembly and, sad to say, everybody knew about it. But the church was slow to *do* anything about it.

No church is perfect, but human imperfection must never be an excuse for sin. Just as parents must discipline their children in love, so local churches must exercise discipline over the members of the assembly. Church discipline is not a group of "pious policemen" out to catch a criminal. Rather, it is a group of brokenhearted brothers and sisters seeking to restore an erring member of the family.

Since some of the members at Corinth did not want to face the situation and change it, Paul presented to the church three important considerations.

Consider the Church (5:1–13)
"What will this sin do to the church?" is certainly an important consideration. Christians are "called to be saints" (1 Cor. 1:2), and this means holy living to the glory of God. If a Christian loves his church, he will not stand by and permit sin to weaken it and perhaps ruin its testimony.

How should we respond? Paul gave three specific instructions for the church to follow.

Mourn over the sin (vv. 1–2). This is the word used for mourning over the dead, which is perhaps the deepest and most painful kind of personal sorrow possible. Instead of mourning, the people at Corinth were puffed up. They were boasting of the fact that their church was so "open-minded" that even fornicators could be members in good standing!

The sin in question was a form of incest: a professed Christian (and a member of the church) was living with his stepmother in a permanent alliance. Since Paul does not pass judgment on the woman (1 Cor. 5:9–13), we assume that she was not a member of the assembly and probably not even a Christian. This kind of sin was condemned by the Old Testament law (Lev. 18:6–8; 20:11) as well as by the laws of the Gentile nations. Paul shamed the church by saying,

"Even the unsaved Gentiles don't practice this kind of sin!"

While it is true that the Christian life is a feast (1 Cor. 5:8), there are times when it becomes a funeral. Whenever a Christian brother or sister sins, it is time for the family to mourn and to seek to help the fallen believer (Gal. 6:1–2). The offending brother in Corinth was "dead" as far as the things of the Lord were concerned. He was out of fellowship with the Lord and with those in the church who were living separated lives.

Judge the sin (vv. 3–5). While Christians are not to judge one another's motives (Matt. 7:1–5) or ministries (1 Cor. 4:5), we are certainly expected to be honest about each other's conduct. In my own pastoral ministry, I have never enjoyed having to initiate church discipline; but since it is commanded in the Scriptures, we must obey God and set personal feelings aside.

Paul described here an official church meeting at which the offender was dealt with according to divine instructions. Public sin must be publicly judged and condemned. (For our Lord's instructions about discipline, study Matt. 18:15–20.) The sin was not to be swept under the rug; for, after all, it was known far and wide even among the unsaved who were outside the church.

The church was to gather together and expel the offender. Note the strong words that Paul used to instruct them: "taken away from among you" (1 Cor. 5:2), "deliver such an one unto Satan" (1 Cor. 5:5), "purge out" (1 Cor. 5:7), and "put away" (1 Cor. 5:13). Paul did not suggest that they handle the offender gently. Of course, we assume that first the spiritual leaders of the church sought to restore the man personally.

This was to be done by the authority of Jesus Christ—in His name—and not simply on the authority of the local church. Church membership is a serious thing and must not be treated carelessly or lightly.

What does it mean to deliver a Christian "unto Satan"? It does not mean to deprive him of salvation, since it is not the church that grants salvation to begin with. When a Christian is in fellowship with the Lord and with the local church, he enjoys a special protection from Satan. But when he is out of fellowship with God and excommunicated from the local church, he is "fair game" for the enemy. God could permit Satan to attack the offender's body so that the sinning believer would repent and return to the Lord.

Purge the sin (vv. 6–13). The image here is that of the Passover supper (Ex. 12). Jesus is the Lamb of God who shed His blood to deliver us from sin (John 1:29; 1 Peter 1:18–25). The Jews in Egypt were delivered from death by the application of the blood of the lamb. Following the application of the blood, the Jewish families ate the Passover supper. One of the requirements was that no yeast (leaven) be found anywhere in their dwellings. Even the bread at the feast was to be unleavened.

Leaven is a picture of sin. It is small but powerful; it

works secretly; it "puffs up" the dough; it spreads. The sinning church member in Corinth was like a piece of yeast: he was defiling the entire loaf of bread (the congregation). It was like a cancer in the body that needed to be removed by drastic surgery.

The church must purge itself of "old leaven"—the things that belong to the "old life" before we trusted Christ. We must also get rid of malice and wickedness (there was a great deal of hard feelings between members of the Corinthian church) and replace them with sincerity and truth. As a loaf of bread (1 Cor. 10:17), the local church must be as pure as possible.

However, the church must not judge and condemn those who are *outside* the faith. That judgment is future, and God will take care of it. In 1 Corinthians 5:9–13, Paul emphasized once again the importance of separation from the world. Christians are not to be *isolated,* but separated. We cannot avoid contact with sinners, but we can avoid contamination by sinners.

If a professed Christian is guilty of the sins named here, the church must deal with him. Individual members are not to "company" with him (1 Cor. 5:9—"get mixed up with, associate intimately"). They are not to *eat* with him, which could refer to private hospitality or more likely the public observance of the Lord's Supper (see 1 Cor. 11:23–34).

Church discipline is not easy or popular, but it is important. If it is done properly, God can use it to convict and restore an erring believer. Second Corinthians 2:1–11 indicates that this man did repent and was restored to fellowship.

Consider Lost Sinners (1–8)

The church at Corinth was rapidly losing its testimony in the city. Not only did the unsaved know about the immorality in the assembly, but they were also aware of the lawsuits involving members of the church. Not only were there sins of the flesh, but also sins of the spirit (2 Cor. 7:1).

The Greeks in general, and the Athenians in particular, were known for their involvement in the courts. The Greek playwright Aristophanes has one of his characters look at a map and ask where Greece is located. When it is pointed out to him, he replies that there must be some mistake—because he cannot see any lawsuits going on! However, the United States is rapidly getting a similar reputation: over two hundred thousand civil suits were filed in the federal courts in one recent twelve-month period. Nearly one million lawyers (their number is increasing) are handling them. In one year, more than twelve million suits were filed in the state courts.

Paul detected three tragedies in this situation. First, *the believers were presenting a poor testimony to the lost.* Even the unbelieving Jews dealt with their civil cases in their own synagogue courts. To take the problems of Christians and discuss them before the "unjust" and "unbelievers" was to weaken the testimony of the gospel.

Second, *the congregation had failed to live up to its full position in Christ.* Since the saints will one day participate in the judgment of the world and even of fallen angels, they ought to be able to settle their differences here on earth. The Corinthians boasted of their great spiritual gifts. Why, then, did they not use them in solving their problems?

Bible students are not agreed on the meaning of Paul's statement in 1 Corinthians 6:4. Some think he is using a bit of sarcasm: "You are better off asking the weakest member of your church to settle the matter, than to go before the most qualified unsaved judge!" Others take the phrase "who are least esteemed in [or 'by'] the church" to refer to the pagan judges. Or it may be that Paul is saying that God can use even the least member of the church to discern His will. The result is still the same: It is wrong for Christians to take their civil suits to court.

Sometimes there are "friendly suits" that are required by law to settle certain issues. That is not what Paul was referring to. It seems that the church members were at each other's throats, trying to get their way in the courts. I am happy to see that there is a trend in our churches today for Christian lawyers to act as arbitrators in civil cases, and help to settle these matters out of court.

There was a third tragedy: *the members suing each other had already lost.* Even if some of them won their cases, they had incurred a far greater loss in their disobedience to the Word of God. "Now, therefore, there is utterly a fault among you" (1 Cor. 6:7) can be translated, "It is already a complete defeat for you." Paul was certainly referring to our Lord's teaching in Matthew 5:39–42. Better to lose money or possessions than to lose a brother and lose your testimony as well.

Over the years of my own ministry, I have seen the sad results of churches and church members trying to solve personal problems in court. Nobody really wins—except the devil! The Corinthians who were going to court were disgracing the name of the Lord and the church just as much as the man who was guilty of incest, and they needed to be disciplined.

I recall a ministerial student who phoned me to tell me he was going to sue his school. Apparently the administration would not allow him to do something he felt was very necessary to his education. I advised him to cool off, talk to his faculty counselor, and get the idea out of his mind. He took my advice and in so doing not only avoided a bad testimony, but grew spiritually through the experience.

Consider the Lord (6:9–20)

There was a great deal of sexual laxness in the city of Corinth. It was a permissive society with a philosophy similar to that which the world has today: Sex is a normal physical function, so why not use it as you please? Paul pointed out that God created sex when He made the first man and woman, and therefore He has the

right to tell us how to use it. The Bible is the "owner's manual" and it must be obeyed.

God condemns sexual sins; Paul named some of them in 1 Corinthians 6:9. In that day, idolatry and sensuality went together. "Effeminate" and "abusers" describe the passive and active partners in a homosexual relationship. (Paul dealt with this and with lesbianism in Rom. 1:26–27.) In 1 Corinthians 6:10, Paul pointed his finger at the members guilty of sins of the spirit, those suing each other because of their covetous attitude.

But God can also cleanse sexual sins and make sinners into new creatures in Christ. "Ye are washed, but ye are sanctified, but ye are justified" (1 Cor. 6:11). The tenses of these verbs indicate a completed transaction. Now, because of all that God had done for them, they had an obligation to God to use their bodies for His service and His glory.

Consider God the Father (vv. 12–14). He created our bodies, and one day He will resurrect them in glory. (More about the resurrection in 1 Cor. 15.) In view of the fact that our bodies have such a wonderful origin, and an even more wonderful future, how can we use them for such evil purposes?

The Corinthians had two arguments to defend their sensuality. First, "All things are lawful unto me" (1 Cor. 6:12). This was a popular phrase in Corinth, based on a false view of Christian freedom. We have not been set free so that we can enter into a new kind of bondage! As Christians, we must ask ourselves, "Will this enslave me? Is this activity really profitable for my spiritual life?"

Their second argument was, "Meats for the belly, and the belly for meats" (1 Cor. 6:13). They treated sex as an appetite to be satisfied and not as a gift to be cherished and used carefully. Sensuality is to sex what gluttony is to eating; both are sinful and both bring disastrous consequences. Just because we have certain normal desires, given by God at creation, does not mean that we must give in to them and always satisfy them. Sex outside of marriage is destructive, while sex in marriage can be creative and beautiful.

There may be excitement and enjoyment in sexual experience outside of marriage, *but there is not enrichment.* Sex outside of marriage is like a man robbing a bank: he gets something, but it is not his and he will one day pay for it. Sex within marriage can be like a person putting money into a bank: there is safety, security, and he will collect dividends. Sex within marriage can build a relationship that brings joys in the future; but sex apart from marriage has a way of weakening future relationships, as every Christian marriage counselor will tell you.

Consider God the Son (vv. 15–18). The believer's body is a member of Christ (see 1 Cor. 12:12ff.). How can we be joined to Christ and joined to sin at the same time? Such a thought astounds us. Yet some of the Corinthians saw no harm in visiting the temple prostitutes (there were a thousand of them at the temple of Aphrodite) and committing fornication.

Jesus Christ bought us with a price (1 Cor. 6:20), and therefore our bodies belong to Him. We are one spirit with the Lord, and we must yield our bodies to Him as living sacrifices (Rom. 12:1–2). If you begin each day by surrendering your body to Christ, it will make a great deal of difference in what you do with your body during the day.

Paul referred to the creation account (Gen. 2:24) to explain the seriousness of sexual sin. When a man and woman join their bodies, *the entire personality is involved.* There is a much deeper experience, a "oneness" that brings with it deep and lasting consequences. Paul warned that sexual sin is the most serious sin a person can commit against his body, for it involves the whole person (1 Cor. 6:18). Sex is not just a part of the body. Being "male" and "female" involves the total person. Therefore, sexual experience affects the total personality.

Paul did not suggest that being joined to a harlot was the equivalent of marriage, for marriage also involves *commitment.* The man and woman leave the parental home to begin a new home. This helps us to understand why sex *within marriage* can be an enriching experience of growth, because it is based on commitment. When two people pledge their love and faithfulness to each other, they lay a strong foundation on which to build. Marriage protects sex and enables the couple, committed to each other, to grow in this wonderful experience.

Consider God the Holy Spirit (vv. 19–20). God the Father created our bodies; God the Son redeemed them and made them part of His body; and God the Spirit indwells our bodies and makes them the very temple of God. How can we defile God's temple by using our bodies for immorality?

The word *your* is plural, but the words *body* and *temple* are singular (1 Cor. 6:19). It may be that Paul was here describing not only the individual believer, but also the local church. Each local assembly is a "body" of people united to Jesus Christ. The conduct of individual members affects the spiritual life of the entire church.

In both cases, the lesson is clear: "Glorify God in your body!" The Holy Spirit was given for the purpose of glorifying Jesus Christ (John 16:14). The Spirit can use our bodies to glorify Him and to magnify Him (Phil. 1:20–21). Our special relationship to the Holy Spirit brings with it a special responsibility.

So God the Father, God the Son, and God the Holy Spirit are all involved in what we do with our bodies. If we break God's laws, then we must pay the penalty (Rom. 1:24–27).

As you review this section, you will see that sexual sins affect the entire personality. They affect the *emotions,* leading to slavery (1 Cor. 6:12b). It is frightening to see how sensuality can get ahold of a person and defile his entire life, enslaving him to habits that

destroy. It also affects a person *physically* (1 Cor. 6:18). The fornicator and adulterer, as well as the homosexual, may forget their sins, *but their sins will not forget them.*

In my pastoral counseling, I have had to help married couples whose relationship was falling apart because of the consequences of *pre*marital sex, as well as *extra*marital sex. The harvest of sowing to the flesh is sometimes delayed, but it is certain (Gal. 6:7–8). How sad it is to live with the consequences of *forgiven* sin.

Having said all this, we must also realize that there are *eternal* consequences for people who practice sexual sins. In 1 Corinthians 6:9–10, Paul *twice* stated that people who *practice* such sins will not inherit God's kingdom. A Christian may fall into these sins and be forgiven, as was David; but no Christian would *practice* such sins (1 John 3:1–10).

Finally, in all fairness, we must note that there are other sins besides sexual sins. For some reason, the church has often majored on condemning the sins of the prodigal son and has forgotten the sins of the elder brother (see Luke 15:11–32). There are sins of the spirit as well as sins of the flesh—Paul names some of them in 1 Corinthians 6:10. Covetousness can send a man to hell just as easily as can adultery.

We must remember that the grace of God can change the sinner's life. "And such *were* some of you" (1 Cor. 6:11 emphasis mine). It is wonderful how faith in Christ makes a sinner into a "new creation" (2 Cor. 5:17, 21). And it is important that we *live* like those who are a part of God's new creation. We are not our own. We belong to the Father who made us, the Son who redeemed us, and the Spirit who indwells us. We also belong to the people of God, the church, and our sins can weaken the testimony and infect the fellowship.

"Be ye holy, for I am holy" (1 Peter 1:16).

CHAPTER SIX
1 Corinthians 7
BE WISE ABOUT CHRISTIAN MARRIAGE

Up to this point, Paul had been dealing with the sins reported to be known in the Corinthian congregation. Now he takes up the questions about which they had written to him: marriage (1 Cor. 7:1, 25), food offered to idols (1 Cor. 8:1), spiritual gifts (1 Cor. 12:1), the resurrection of the dead (1 Cor. 15:1), and the missionary offering for the Jews (1 Cor. 16:1). As you study 1 Corinthians 7, please keep in mind that Paul is replying to definite questions. He is not spelling out a complete "theology of marriage" in one chapter. It is necessary to consider as well what the rest of the Bible has to say about this important subject.

Some liberal critics have accused Paul of being against both marriage and women. These accusations are not true, of course. Nor is it true that in 1 Corinthians 7:6, 10, 12, and 25 Paul was disclaiming divine inspiration for what he wrote. Rather, he was referring to what Jesus taught when He was on earth (Matt. 5:31–32; 19:1–12; Mark 10:1–12; Luke 16:18). Paul had to answer some questions that Jesus never discussed; but when a question arose that the Lord had dealt with, Paul referred to His words. Instead of disclaiming inspiration, Paul claimed that what he wrote was equal in authority to what Christ taught.

Paul explained God's will concerning Christian marriage, and he addressed his counsel to three different groups of believers.

Christians Married to Christians (7:1–11)

Apparently one of the questions the church asked was, "Is celibacy [remaining unmarried] more spiritual than marriage?" Paul replied that it is good for a man or a woman to have the gift of celibacy, but the celibate state is not better than marriage, nor is it the best state for everybody. Dr. Kenneth Wuest translated Paul's reply, "It is perfectly proper, honorable, morally befitting for a man to live in strict celibacy."

First Corinthians 7:6 makes it clear that celibacy is permitted, but it is not commanded; and 1 Corinthians 7:7 informs us that not everybody has the gift of remaining celibate. This ties in with our Lord's teaching in Matthew 19:10–12, where "eunuchs" refers to those who abstain from marriage. "It is not good that the man should be alone" (Gen. 2:18) is generally true for most people; but some have been called to a life of singleness for one reason or another. Their singleness is not "subspiritual" or "superspiritual." It all depends on the will of God.

One purpose for marriage is "to avoid fornication." First Corinthians 7:2 makes it clear that God does not approve either of polygamy or homosexual "marriages." One man married to one woman has been God's pattern from the first. However, the husband and wife must not abuse the privilege of sexual love that is a normal part of marriage. The wife's body belongs to the husband, and the husband's body to the wife; and each must be considerate of the other. Sexual love is a beautiful tool to build with, not a weapon to fight with. To refuse each other is to commit robbery (see 1 Thess. 4:6) and to invite Satan to tempt the partners to seek their satisfaction elsewhere.

As in all things, the spiritual must govern the physical; for our bodies are God's temples. The husband and wife may abstain in order to devote their full interest to prayer and fasting (1 Cor. 7:5); but they must not use this as an excuse for prolonged separation. Paul is encouraging Christian partners to be "in tune" with each other in matters both spiritual and physical.

In 1 Corinthians 7:8–9, Paul applied the principle stated in 1 Corinthians 7:1 to single believers and widows: If you cannot control yourself, then marry.

Not only did the church ask about celibacy, but they also asked Paul about divorce. Since Jesus had dealt with this question, Paul cited His teaching: Husbands and wives are not to divorce each other (see also 1 Cor. 7:39). If divorce does occur, the parties should remain unmarried or seek reconciliation.

This is, of course, the ideal for marriage. Jesus did make one exception: If one party was guilty of fornication, this could be grounds for divorce. Far better that there be confession, forgiveness, and reconciliation; but if these are out of the question, then the innocent party may get a divorce. However, divorce is the last option; first, every means available should be used to restore the marriage.

It has been my experience as a pastor that when a husband and wife are yielded to the Lord, and when they seek to please each other in the marriage relationship, the marriage will be so satisfying that neither partner would think of looking elsewhere for fulfillment. "There are no sex problems in marriage," a Christian counselor once told me, "only personality problems with sex as one of the symptoms." The present frightening trend of increased divorces among Christians (and even among the clergy) must break the heart of God.

Christians Married to Non-Christians (7:12–24)

Some of the members of the Corinthian church were saved after they had been married, but their mates had not yet been converted. No doubt, some of these believers were having a difficult time at home; and they asked Paul, "Must we remain married to unsaved partners? Doesn't our conversion alter things?"

Paul replied that they were to remain with their unconverted mates so long as their mates were willing to live with them. Salvation does not alter the marriage state; if anything, it ought to enhance the marriage relationship. (Note Peter's counsel to wives with unsaved husbands in 1 Peter 3:1–6.) Since marriage is basically a physical relationship ("they shall be one flesh," Gen. 2:24), it can only be broken by a physical cause. Adultery and death would be two such causes (1 Cor. 7:39).

It is an act of disobedience for a Christian knowingly to marry an unsaved person (note "only in the Lord" in 1 Cor. 7:39; 2 Cor. 6:14). But if a person becomes a Christian after marriage, he should not use that as an excuse to break up the marriage just to avoid problems. In fact, Paul emphasized the fact that the Christian partner could have a spiritual influence on the unsaved mate. First Corinthians 7:14 does not teach that the unsaved partner is *saved* because of the believing mate, since each person must individually decide for Christ. Rather, it means that the believer exerts a spiritual influence in the home that can lead to the salvation of the lost partner.

What about the children? Again, the emphasis is on the influence of the godly partner. The believing husband or wife must not give up. In my own ministry, I have seen devoted Christians live for Christ in divided homes and eventually see their loved ones trust the Savior.

Salvation does not change the marriage state. If the wife's becoming a Christian annulled the marriage, then the children in the home would become illegitimate ("unclean" in 1 Cor. 7:14). Instead, these children may one day be saved if the Christian mate is faithful to the Lord.

It is difficult for us who are accustomed to the Christian faith to realize the impact that this new doctrine had on the Roman world. Here was a teaching for every person, regardless of race or social status. The church was perhaps the only assembly in the Roman Empire where slaves and freemen, men and women, rich and poor, could fellowship on an equal basis (Gal. 3:28). However, this new equality also brought with it some misunderstandings and problems; and some of these Paul dealt with in 1 Corinthians 7:17–24.

The principle that Paul laid down was this: Even though Christians are all one in Christ, each believer should remain in the same calling he was in when the Lord saved him. Jewish believers should not try to become Gentiles (by erasing the physical mark of the covenant), and Gentiles should not try to become Jews (by being circumcised). Slaves should not *demand* freedom from their Christian masters, just because of their equality in Christ. However, Paul *did* advise Christian slaves to secure their freedom if at all possible, probably by purchase. This same principle would apply to Christians married to unsaved mates.

But suppose the unsaved mate leaves the home? First Corinthians 7:15 gives the answer: The Christian partner is not obligated to keep the home together. We are called to peace, and we should do all we can to live in peace (Rom. 12:18); but there comes a time in some situations where peace is impossible. If the unsaved mate separates from his or her partner, there is little the Christian can do except to pray and continue faithful to the Lord.

Does separation then give the Christian mate the right to divorce and remarriage? Paul did not say so. What if the unconverted mate ends up living with another partner? That would constitute adultery and give grounds for divorce. But even then, 1 Corinthians 7:10–11 would encourage forgiveness and restoration. Paul did not deal with every possible situation. He laid down spiritual principles, not a list of rules.

We are prone to think that a change in circumstances is always the answer to a problem. But the problem is usually *within* us and not *around* us. The heart of every problem is the problem in the heart. I have watched couples go through divorce and seek happiness in new circumstances, only to discover that they carried their problems with them. A Christian lawyer once told me, "About the only people who profit from divorces are the attorneys!"

Unmarried Christians (7:25–40)

Paul had already addressed a brief word to this group

in 1 Corinthians 7:8–9, but in this closing section of the chapter, he went into greater detail. Their question was, *"Must* a Christian get married? What about the unmarried women in the church who are not getting any younger?" (see 1 Cor. 7:36). Perhaps Paul addressed this section primarily to the parents of marriageable girls. Since Jesus did not give any special teaching on this topic, Paul gave his counsel as one taught of the Lord. He asked them to consider several factors when they made their decision about marriage.

First, consider the present circumstances (vv. 25–31). It was a time of distress (1 Cor. 7:26) when society was going through change (1 Cor. 7:31). There was not much time left for serving the Lord (1 Cor. 7:29). It is possible that there were political and economic pressures in Corinth about which we have no information. In view of the difficulties, it would be better for a person to be unmarried. However, this did not mean that married people should seek a divorce (1 Cor. 7:27). Paul's counsel was to the unmarried.

This did not mean that *nobody* should get married; but those who do marry must be ready to accept the trials that will accompany it (1 Cor. 7:28). In fact, the situation might become so difficult that even those already married will have to live as though they were not married (1 Cor. 7:29). Perhaps Paul was referring to husbands and wives being separated from each other because of economic distress or persecution.

To consider the circumstances is good counsel for engaged people today. The average age for first-time brides and grooms is climbing, which suggests that couples are waiting longer to get married. In my pastoral premarital counseling, I used to remind couples that the cheapest thing in a wedding was the marriage license. From then on, the prices would go up!

Second, face the responsibilities honestly (vv. 32–35). The emphasis in this paragraph is on the word *care,* which means "to be anxious, to be pulled in different directions." It is impossible for two people to live together without burdens of one kind or another, but there is no need to rush into marriage and create more problems. Marriage requires a measure of maturity, and age is no guarantee of maturity.

Once again, Paul emphasized living for the Lord. He did not suggest that it was impossible for a man or a woman to be married and serve God acceptably, because we know too many people who have done it. But the married servant of God must consider his or her mate, as well as the children God may give them; and this could lead to distraction. It is a fact of history that both John Wesley and George Whitefield might have been better off had they remained single—Wesley's wife finally left him, and Whitefield traveled so much that his wife was often alone for long periods of time.

It is possible to please both the Lord and your mate, if you are yielded to Christ and obeying the Word. Many of us have discovered that a happy home and satisfying marriage are a wonderful encouragement in the difficulties of Christian service. A well-known

Scottish preacher was experiencing a great deal of public criticism because of a stand he took on a certain issue, and almost every day there was a negative report in the newspapers. A friend met him one day and asked, "How are you able to carry on in the face of this opposition?" The man replied quietly, "I am happy at home."

Unmarried believers who feel a call to serve God should examine their own hearts to see if marriage will help or hinder their ministry. They must also be careful to wed mates who feel a like call to serve God. Each person has his own gift and calling from God and must be obedient to His Word.

Third, each situation is unique (vv. 36–38). Paul addressed here the fathers of the unmarried girls. In that day, it was the parents who arranged the marriages, the father in particular (2 Cor. 11:2). Paul had already said in 1 Corinthians 7:35 that he was not laying down an ironclad rule for everybody to follow, regardless of circumstances. Now he made it clear that the father had freedom of choice whether or not he would give his daughter in marriage.

I have noticed that often in churches marriages come in "packs." One couple gets engaged and before long four couples are engaged. If all of these engagements are in the will of God, it can be a very exciting and wonderful experience; but I fear that some couples get engaged just to keep up with the crowd. Sometimes in Christian colleges, couples get what I call "senior panic" and rush out of engagement and into marriage immediately after graduation, lest they be left "waiting at the church." Sad to say, not all of these marriages are successful.

Even though our modern approach to dating and marriage was completely foreign to the Corinthians, the counsel Paul gave them still applies today. It is a wise thing for couples to counsel with their parents and with their Christian leaders in the church, lest they rush into something which afterward they regret.

Paul hit on a key problem in 1 Corinthians 7:36 when he mentioned "the flower of her age." This is a delicate phrase that simply means the girl is getting older. Dr. Kenneth Wuest translates it "past the bloom of her youth." She is starting to become one of the "unclaimed blessings" in the church. The danger, of course, is that she would rush into marriage just to avoid becoming a spinster, and she might make a mistake. A pastor friend of mine likes to say to couples, "Better to live in single loneliness than in married cussedness!"

Each situation is unique, and parents and children must seek the Lord's will. It takes more than two Christian people to make a happy marriage. Not every marriage that is scriptural is necessarily sensible.

Finally, remember that marriage is for life (vv. 39–40). It is God's will that the marriage union be permanent, a lifetime commitment. There is no place in Christian marriage for a "trial marriage," nor is there any room for the "escape hatch" attitude: "If the marriage doesn't work, we can always get a divorce."

For this reason, marriage must be built on something sturdier than good looks, money, romantic excitement, and social acceptance. There must be Christian commitment, character, and maturity. There must be a willingness to grow, to learn from each other, to forgive and forget, to minister to one another. The kind of love Paul described in 1 Corinthians 13 is what is needed to cement two lives together.

Paul closed the section by telling the widows that they were free to marry, but "only in the Lord" (1 Cor. 7:39). This means that they must not only marry believers, but marry in the will of God. Paul's counsel (for the reasons already given) was that they remain single, but he left the decision to them.

God has put "walls" around marriage, not to make it a prison, but to make it a safe fortress. The person who considers marriage a prison should not get married. When two people are lovingly and joyfully committed to each other—and to their Lord—the experience of marriage is one of enrichment and enlargement. They grow together and discover the richness of serving the Lord as a team in their home and church.

As you review this chapter, you cannot help but be impressed with the seriousness of marriage. Paul's counsel makes it clear that God takes marriage seriously, and that we cannot disobey God's Word without suffering painful consequences. While both Paul and Jesus leave room for divorce under certain conditions, this can never be God's first choice for a couple. God hates divorce (Mal. 2:14–16), and certainly no believer should consider divorce until all avenues of reconciliation have been patiently explored.

While a person's marital failure may hinder him from serving as a pastor or deacon (1 Tim. 3:2, 12), it need not keep him from ministering in other ways. Some of the best personal soul-winners I have known have been men who, before their conversion, had the unfortunate experience of divorce. A man does not have to hold an office in order to have a ministry.

In summary, each person must ask himself or herself the following questions if marriage is being contemplated:
1. What is my gift from God?
2. Am I marrying a believer?
3. Are the circumstances such that marriage is right?
4. How will marriage affect my service for Christ?
5. Am I prepared to enter into this union for life?

CHAPTER SEVEN
1 Corinthians 8; 10
BE WISE ABOUT CHRISTIAN LIBERTY

After answering their questions about marriage, Paul turned to one of the most controversial subjects in the letter he received from the Corinthian church: "Can Christians eat meat that has been sacrificed to idols?" The immediate question does not interest believers today since we do not face that problem. But the wider issue of "Christian liberty" *does* apply to us, because we face questions that Paul never faced. Is it right for Christians to attend the theater? Should a believer have a television set in his home? To what extent can a Christian get involved in politics?

In 1 Corinthians 8—10, Paul enunciated four basic principles that would guide believers in making personal decisions about those "questionable" areas of the Christian life. The four principles are as follows:

Knowledge must be balanced by love (1 Cor. 8)
Authority must be balanced by discipline
　(1 Cor. 9)
Experience must be balanced by caution
　(1 Cor. 10:1–22)
Freedom must be balanced by responsiblity
　(1 Cor. 10:23–33)

As you can see, Paul addressed himself primarily to the strong Christians in the church, believers who had spiritual knowledge and experience and who understood their authority and freedom in Christ. It is the strong who must care for the weak (Rom. 14—15).

The question of meats offered to idols is dealt with in 1 Corinthians 8; 10, so we will examine it in this chapter. In 1 Corinthians 9, Paul illustrated this principle of the right use of authority by explaining his own financial policy; so we will consider that in our next study.

Knowledge Must Be Balanced by Love (8:1–13)
There were two sources of meat in the ancient world: the regular market (where the prices were higher) and the local temples (where meat from the sacrifices was always available). The strong members of the church realized that idols could not contaminate food, so they saved money by purchasing the cheaper meat available from the temples. Furthermore, if unconverted friends invited them to a feast at which sacrificial meat was served, the strong Christians attended it whether at the temple or in the home.

All of this offended the weaker Christians. Many of them had been saved out of pagan idolatry, and they could not understand why their fellow believers would want to have anything to do with meat sacrificed to idols. (In Rom. 14—15, the weak Christians had problems over diets and holy days, but it was the same basic issue.) There was a potential division in the church, so the leaders asked Paul for counsel.

Paul called to their attention three important factors.

Knowledge (vv. 1–2). The Corinthians were enriched in spiritual knowledge (1 Cor. 1:5) and were, in fact, rather proud of their achievements. They knew that an idol was nothing, merely the representation of a false god who existed only in the darkened minds of those who worshiped it. The presence of an idol in a temple was no solid proof that the god existed. (Later, Paul would point out that idolatry was basically the

worship of demons.) So the conclusion was logical: A nonexistent god could not contaminate food offered on his altar.

So far, it is the strong Christians who are ahead. Why, then, are the weak Christians upset with them, when their position is so logical? Because you don't always solve every problem with logic. The little child who is afraid of the dark will not be assured by arguments, especially if the adult (or older brother) adopts a superior attitude. Knowledge can be a weapon to fight with or a tool to build with, depending on how it is used. If it "puffs up" then it cannot "build up [edify]."

A know-it-all attitude is only an evidence of ignorance. The person who really knows truth is only too conscious of how much he does not know. Furthermore, it is one thing to know *doctrine* and quite something else to know *God.* It is possible to grow in Bible knowledge and yet not grow in grace or in one's personal relationship with God. The test is *love,* which is the second factor Paul discussed.

Love (vv. 3–6). Love and knowledge must go together, "speaking the truth in love" (Eph. 4:15). It has well been said, "Truth without love is brutality, but love without truth is hypocrisy." Knowledge is power and it must be used in love. But love must always be controlled by knowledge (see Paul's prayer in Phil. 1:9–11). The strong believers in the church had knowledge, but they were not using their knowledge in love. Instead of building up the weak saints, the strong Christians were only puffing up themselves.

Paul's great concern was that the strong saints help the weaker saints to grow and to stop being weak saints. Some people have the false notion that the *strong* Christians are the ones who live by rules and regulations and who get offended when others exercise their freedom in Christ; but such is not the case. It is the *weak* Christians who must have the security of law and who are afraid to use their freedom in Christ. It is the weak Christians who are prone to judge and criticize stronger believers and to stumble over what they do. This, of course, makes it difficult for the strong saints to minister to their weaker brothers and sisters.

It is here that love enters the picture, for "love builds up" and puts others first. When spiritual knowledge is used in love, the stronger Christian can take the hand of the weaker Christian and help him to stand and walk so as to enjoy his freedom in Christ. *You cannot force-feed immature believers and transform them into giants.* Knowledge must be mixed with love; otherwise, the saints will end up with "big heads" instead of enlarged hearts. A famous preacher used to say, "Some Christians grow; others just swell."

Knowledge and love are two important factors, for knowledge must be balanced by love if we are to use our Christian freedom in the right way. But there is a third factor.

Conscience (vv. 7–13). The word *conscience* simply means "to know with," and it is used thirty-two times in the New Testament. Conscience is that internal court where our actions are judged and are either approved or condemned (Rom. 2:14–15). Conscience is not the law; it bears witness to God's moral law. But the important thing is this: *conscience depends on knowledge.* The more spiritual knowledge we know and *act on,* the stronger the conscience will become.

Some Christians have weak consciences because they have been saved only a short time and have not had opportunity to grow. Like little babes in the home, they must be guarded carefully. Other saints have weak consciences because they *will not* grow. They ignore their Bibles and Christian fellowship and remain in a state of infancy (1 Cor. 3:1–4; Heb. 5:11–14). But some believers remain weak because they are afraid of freedom. They are like a child old enough to go to school, who is afraid to leave home and must be taken to school each day.

The conscience of a weak Christian is easily defiled (1 Cor. 8:7), wounded (1 Cor. 8:12), and offended (1 Cor. 8:13). For this reason, the stronger saints must defer to the weaker saints and do nothing that would harm them. It might not harm the mature saint to share a feast in an idolatrous temple, but it might harm his weaker brother. First Corinthians 8:10 warns that the immature believer might decide to imitate his stronger brother and thus be led into sin.

It is important to note that the stronger believer defers to the weaker believer in love *only that he might help him to mature.* He does not "pamper" him; he seeks to edify him, to help him grow. Otherwise, *both* will become weak.

We are free in Christ, but we must take care that our spiritual knowledge is tempered by love, and that we do not tempt the weaker Christian to run ahead of his conscience. Where knowledge is balanced by love, the strong Christian will have a ministry to the weak Christian, and the weak Christian will grow and become strong.

Experience Must Be Balanced by Caution (10:1–22)

Paul reminded the experienced believers who were strong in the faith that they had better not grow overconfident in their ability to overcome temptation. "Wherefore let him that thinketh he standeth take heed lest he fall" (1 Cor. 10:12). Paul used the nation of Israel as his example to warn the mature believers that their experience must be balanced by caution. He gave three warnings.

First, he warned that privileges were no guarantee of success (vv. 1–4). Israel had been delivered from Egypt by the power of God, just as the Christian believer has been redeemed from sin. (In 1 Cor. 5:7–8, Paul had already related Passover to salvation.) Israel was identified with Moses in their Red Sea "baptism," just as the Corinthians had been identified with Christ in their Christian baptism. Israel ate the manna from heaven and drank the water God provided, just as Christians nourish themselves on the spiritual sustenance God supplies (John 6:63, 68; 7:37–39).

However, these spiritual privileges did not prevent the Jews from falling into sin.

There are dangers to maturity as well as to immaturity, and one of them is overconfidence. When we think we are strong, we discover that we are weak. The strong believer who eats in the temple may find himself struggling with an enemy who is too strong for him.

Paul did not suggest in 1 Corinthians 10:4 that an actual rock accompanied the Jews throughout their wilderness journey, though some Jewish rabbis taught this idea. It was a *spiritual* rock that supplied what they needed, and that Rock was Christ. Sometimes the water came from a rock (Ex. 17:1–7; Num. 20:7–11) and at other times from a well (Num. 21:16–18). God provided the water.

Paul issued a second warning: good beginnings do not guarantee good endings (vv. 5–12). The Jews experienced God's miracles, and yet they failed when they were tested in the wilderness. Experience must always be balanced with caution, for we never come to the place in our Christian walk where we are free from temptation and potential failure. All of the Jews twenty years old and upward who were rescued from Egypt, except for Joshua and Caleb, died in the wilderness during their years of wandering (Num. 14:26ff.).

We can hear some of the "strong" Corinthians asking, "But what does that have to do with us?" Paul then pointed out that the Corinthian church was guilty of the same sins that the Jews committed. Because of their lust for evil things, the Corinthians were guilty of immorality (1 Cor. 6), idolatry (1 Cor. 8; 10), and murmuring against God (2 Cor. 12:20–21). Like the nation of Israel, they were tempting God and just "daring Him" to act.

Paul certainly knew his Old Testament, and his readers would recognize the events referred to. The "lusting" is found in Numbers 11:4ff., the idolatry in Exodus 32, and the fornication in Numbers 25. The Israelites often tempted God, but perhaps Numbers 21:4–6 was the reference Paul had in mind. For their complaining, see Numbers 14 and 16.

This kind of sin is serious and God must judge it. Not only did some of these rebels immediately die (see 1 Cor. 11:29–31), but those who remained were not permitted to enter the Promised Land. They were saved from Egypt but were not privileged to claim their rich inheritance. Paul was not suggesting that his readers might lose their salvation, but he was afraid that some of them would be "castaways" (1 Cor. 9:27), disapproved of God and unable to receive any reward.

I heard about a pastor who gave a series of sermons on "The Sins of the Saints." One member of the church, apparently under conviction, disapproved of the series and told the pastor so. "After all," she said, "sin in the life of a Christian is different from sin in the life of an unsaved person."

"Yes, it is," the pastor replied. "It's *worse!*"

We must not think that because the Jews were under the law that their sins were worse than ours and therefore dealt with more severely. Sin in the church today is far more serious, because we have Israel's example to learn from, and we are living "at the end of the ages." To sin against the law is one thing; to sin against grace is quite something else.

Paul's third warning was that God can enable us to overcome temptation if we heed His Word (vv. 13–22). God permits us to be tempted because He knows how much we can take; and He always provides a way to escape if we will trust Him and take advantage of it. The believer who thinks he can stand may fall; but the believer who flees will be able to stand.

Paul had already told his readers to "flee fornication" (1 Cor. 6:18); and now his warning is "Flee from idolatry" (1 Cor. 10:14). He explained the reason why: the idol itself is nothing, but it can be used by Satan to lead you into sin. Idolatry is demonic (Deut. 32:17; Ps. 106:37). To sit at an idol's table could mean fellowship ("communion, partakers") with demons. Paul was again enforcing the important doctrine of separation from sin (2 Cor. 6:1—7:1).

He used the Lord's Supper as an illustration. When the believer partakes of the cup and loaf at the Lord's table, he is, in a spiritual way, having fellowship with the body and blood of Christ. By remembering Christ's death, the believer enters into a communion with the risen Lord. In 1 Corinthians 10:18, Paul pointed to the temple altar and sacrifices as another illustration of this truth. The application is clear: A believer cannot partake of the Lord's food (the Old Testament sacrifice, the New Testament supper) and the devil's food (the idol's table) without exposing himself to danger and provoking the Lord.

"Are we stronger than he?" (1 Cor. 10:22) is directed at the strong Christian who was sure he could enjoy his liberty in the pagan temple and not be harmed. "You may be stronger than your weaker brother," Paul intimated, "but you are not stronger than God!" It is dangerous to play with sin and tempt God.

Freedom Must Be Balanced by Responsibility (10:23–33)

At no time did Paul deny the freedom of the mature Christian to enjoy his privileges in Christ. "All things are lawful"—*but* not everything is profitable, and some things lead to slavery (1 Cor. 6:12). "All things are profitable"—*but* some activities can cause your weaker brother to stumble (1 Cor. 8:11–13). In other words, it is a mark of maturity when we balance our freedom with responsibility; otherwise, it ceases to be freedom and becomes anarchy, lawlessness.

To begin with, we have a responsibility to our fellow Christians in the church (1 Cor. 10:23–30). We are responsible to build others up in the faith and to seek their advantage. Philippians 2:1–4 gives the same admonition. While we do have freedom in Christ, we are not free to harm another believer.

Paul applied this truth to the impending question of meat offered to idols. He had already warned against a believer *publicly* participating in pagan feasts (1 Cor.

8:9–13), so now he dealt with *private* meals. In 1 Corinthians 10:25–26, he instructed the believers to ask no questions about the meat purchased at the market for use in their own homes. After all, everything comes from God (he quoted Ps. 24:1), and all food is permissible to the believer (see Mark 7:14–23; Acts 10:9–16, 28; 1 Tim. 4:3–5). The mature believer can enjoy in his own home even meat sacrificed to idols. Even if meat purchased at the regular market originally came from the temple (which was often the case), he would not be harmed.

But what about those times when the believer is the guest in the home of an unbeliever? Paul handled that problem in 1 Corinthians 10:27–30. If the Christian feels disposed to go (Paul did not make this decision a matter of great import), he should eat whatever is set before him and ask no questions (see Luke 10:8; 1 Tim. 6:17). However, there may be present at the meal one of the weaker brothers or sisters who wants to avoid meat offered to idols, and who has done some investigating. If this weaker saint informs the stronger Christian that the meat indeed has been offered to idols, then the stronger saint must not eat it. If he did, he would cause the weaker believer to stumble and possibly to sin.

Paul anticipated the objections. "Why should I not enjoy food for which I give thanks? Why should my liberty be curtailed because of another person's weak conscience?" His reply introduced the second responsibility we have: *We are responsible to glorify God in all things* (1 Cor. 10:31). We cannot glorify God by causing another Christian to stumble. To be sure, our own conscience may be strong enough for us to participate in some activity and not be harmed. But we dare not use our freedom in Christ in any way that will injure a fellow Christian.

But there is a third responsibility that ties in with the first two: *We are responsible to seek to win the lost* (1 Cor. 10:32–33). We must not make it difficult either for Jews or Gentiles to trust the Lord, or for other members of the church to witness for the Lord. We must not live to seek our own benefit ("profit"), but also the benefit of others, that they might be saved.

When Paul wrote, "I please all men in all things" (1 Cor. 10:33), he was not suggesting that he was a compromiser or a man-pleaser (see Gal. 1:10). He was affirming the fact that his life and ministry were centered on helping others rather than on promoting himself and his own desires.

Before we leave this important section, we ought to note the fact that Paul probably appeared inconsistent to those who did not understand his principles of Christian living. At times, he would eat what the Gentiles were eating. At other times, he would eat only "kosher" food with the Jews. But instead of being inconsistent, he was actually living *consistently* by the principles he laid down in these chapters. A weather vane seems inconsistent, first pointing in one direction and then in another. But a weather vane is always consistent: it always points toward the direction where the wind is blowing. That is what makes it useful.

Are there some things that a mature Christian can do in the privacy of his own home that he would not do in public? Yes, provided they do not harm him personally and he does not tempt the Lord. I know a couple who, when their children were small, eliminated all games from their home that used either cards or dice. When their children were more mature, they were permitted to play those games.

As Christians, we *do* have freedom. This freedom was purchased for us by Jesus Christ, so it is very precious. Freedom comes from knowledge: "And ye shall know the truth, and the truth shall make you free" (John 8:32). The more we understand about the atom, for example, the more freedom we have to use it wisely. However, knowledge must be balanced by love; otherwise, it will tear down instead of build up.

The strong Christian not only has knowledge, but he also has experience. He can look back and see how the Lord has dealt with him through the years. But he must be careful, for experience must be balanced with caution. Take heed, lest you fall!

The strong Christian knows that he has this freedom, but he also knows that freedom involves responsibility. I have the freedom, for example, to take my car out of the garage and drive it on the highway; *but I must drive it responsibly.* I am not free to drive at any speed on my street; nor am I free to ignore the traffic signs along the way.

Out of these chapters come several "tests" we may apply to our own decisions and activities.

"All things are lawful," *but*—
1. Will they lead to freedom or slavery? (1 Cor. 6:12)
2. Will they make me a stumbling block or a stepping-stone? (1 Cor. 8:13)
3. Will they build me up or tear me down? (1 Cor. 10:23)
4. Will they only please me, or will they glorify Christ? (1 Cor. 10:31)
5. Will they help to win the lost to Christ or turn them away? (1 Cor. 10:33)

The way we use our freedom and relate to others indicates whether we are mature in Christ. Strong and weak Christians need to work together in love to edify one another and glorify Jesus Christ.

CHAPTER EIGHT
1 Corinthians 9
BE WISE ABOUT PERSONAL PRIORITIES

This chapter deals with Paul's policy of financial support, and it appears to be an interruption of his discussion of "meats offered to idols." Actually, it is not an interruption; it is an illustration of the very principles that he presents in 1 Corinthians 8 and 10. Paul used himself as an illustration of the mature use of liberty: he was free to receive financial support from the Corinthian church, yet he set aside that right in order to achieve a higher goal.

Keep in mind that, for the most part, the Greeks despised manual labor. They had slaves to do manual labor so that the citizens could enjoy sports, philosophy, and leisure. The Jews, of course, magnified honest labor. Even the learned rabbis each practiced a trade, and they taught the people, "He who does not teach his son to work, teaches him to be a thief." Paul was trained as a tentmaker, a worker in leather.

In order to illustrate the Christian use of personal rights, Paul presented a twofold defense of his financial policy as a servant of Christ.

He Defended His Right to Receive Support (9:1–14)
In this first half of the chapter, Paul proved that he had the right to receive financial support from the church at Corinth. He gave five arguments to support this contention.

His apostleship (vv. 1–6). The word *apostle* means "one sent under commission" and refers primarily to the twelve apostles and Paul. These men had a special commission, along with the New Testament prophets, to lay the foundation of the church (Eph. 2:20). One of the qualifications for being an apostle was a personal experience of seeing the resurrected Christ (Acts 1:21–22). Paul saw the Lord when he was traveling to Damascus to arrest Christians (Acts 9:1–9). The apostles were to be witnesses of Christ's resurrection (Acts 2:32; 3:15; 5:32; 10:39–43).

The apostles also were given the ability to perform special signs and wonders to attest the message that they preached (Heb. 2:4). Paul had performed such miracles during his ministry in Corinth (2 Cor. 12:12). In fact, Paul considered the Corinthian church a very special "seal" of his ministry as an apostle. Corinth was a difficult city to minister in, and yet Paul accomplished a great work because of the Lord's enablement (see Acts 18:1–17).

Therefore, as an apostle, Paul had the right to receive support from the people to whom he ministered. (The word *power* is used six times in this chapter, and means "authority, right.") The apostle was the representative of Christ; he deserved to be welcomed and cared for. Paul was unmarried; but if he'd had a wife, she too would have had the right to be supported by the church. Peter was a married man (Mark 1:30), and his wife traveled with him. Paul had the same right, but he did not use it.

Paul also had the right to devote his full time to the ministry of the Word. He did not have to make tents. The other apostles did not work to support themselves because they gave themselves completely to the ministry of the Word. However, both Paul and Barnabas labored with their own hands to support not only themselves, but also the men who labored with them.

Human experience (v. 7). Everyday experience teaches us that a workman deserves some reward for his labors. If a man is drafted to be a soldier, the government pays his wages and provides a certain amount of supplies for him. The man who plants a vineyard gets to eat the fruit, just as the shepherd or herdsman has the right to use the milk from the animals.

Perhaps in the back of his mind, Paul was comparing the church to an army, a vineyard, and a flock. As an apostle, Paul was in the very front line of the battle. He had already compared the church at Corinth to a cultivated field (1 Cor. 3:6–9), and the Lord Himself had used the image of the vine and branches (John 15) as well as the flock (John 10). The lesson was clear: The Christian worker has the right to expect benefits for his labors. If this is true in the "secular" realm, it is also true in the spiritual realm.

The Old Testament law (vv. 8–12). The Old Testament was the "Bible" of the early church, since the New Testament was in the process of being written. The first believers found guidance in the spiritual principles of the law, even though they had been liberated from obeying the commandments of the law. Saint Augustine said, "The New is in the Old concealed; the Old is by the New revealed."

Paul quoted Deuteronomy 25:4 to prove his point. (He quoted this same verse when he wrote to Timothy and encouraged the church to pay their ministers adequately, 1 Tim. 5:17–18.) Since oxen cannot read, this verse was not written for them. Nor was it written only for the farmer who was using the labors of the ox. It would be cruel for the farmer to bind the mouth of the ox and prevent him from eating the available grain. After all, the ox was doing the work.

Paul correctly saw a spiritual principle in this commandment: The laborer has the right to share in the bounties. The ox had plowed the soil in preparation for sowing, and now he was treading out the grain that had been harvested. Paul had plowed the soil in Corinth. He had seen a harvest from the seed he had planted. It was only right that he enjoyed some of the fruits of that harvest.

First Corinthians 9:11 enunciates a basic principle of the Christian life: If we receive *spiritual* blessings, we should in turn share *material* blessings. For example, the Jews gave spiritual blessings to the Gentiles; so the Gentiles had an obligation to share materially with the Jews (Rom. 15:25–27). Those who teach us the Word have the right to expect us to support them (Gal. 6:6–10).

We have reason to believe that Paul did accept financial support from other churches. The Philippian believers sent him two gifts when he went to Thessalonica (Phil. 4:15–16). "I robbed other churches, taking wages of them, to do you service," Paul reminded the Corinthians (2 Cor. 11:8). Apparently other ministers had accepted support at Corinth (1 Cor. 9:12), but Paul preferred to remain independent "lest we should hinder the gospel of Christ." He wanted to be the best example possible to other believers (2 Thess. 3:6–9).

Old Testament practice (v. 13). The priests and Levites lived off of the sacrifices and offerings that were brought to the temple. The regulations governing their part of the offerings, and the special tithes they received also are found in Numbers 18:8–32; Leviticus 6:14—7:36; and 27:6–33. The application is clear: If the Old Testament ministers under law were supported by the people to whom they ministered, should not God's servants who minister under grace also be supported?

The teaching of Jesus (v. 14). Paul was no doubt referring to our Lord's words recorded in Luke 10:7–8 and Matthew 10:10. The Corinthians did not have a copy of either gospel to refer to, but the Lord's teaching would have been given to them as a part of the oral tradition shared by the apostles. *The laborer is worthy of his hire* is a fundamental principle that the church dare not neglect.

Paul certainly proved his point. His five arguments proved conclusively that he had the right to expect the Corinthian believers to support him in his ministry when he was with them. Yet he had deliberately refused their support. Why? This he explained in the second part of his defense.

He Defended His Right to Refuse Support (9:15–27)

Paul had the authority (right) to receive material support, but being a mature Christian, he balanced his authority with discipline. He did not have the right to give up his liberty in Christ, but he did have the liberty to give up his rights. Now we understand why he wrote as he did: he gave the Corinthian believers a living example of the very principles he was writing about. Should not the stronger believers in the church be able to set aside their rights for the sake of the weaker saints? Was eating meat more important than edifying the church?

Paul was talking about *priorities,* the things that are really important to us in our lives. It is unfortunate that some Christians have their personal priorities confused and, as a result, are hindering the work of Christ. If each believer were practicing Matthew 6:33, there would be plenty of money for missions, plenty of manpower for service, and the work of the Lord would prosper. But not every Christian is practicing Matthew 6:33.

A lady sent a gift to a ministry and explained that it was money she had saved because she had turned off the hot water tank in her house. She also did without a daily paper so that she might have more to give to the Lord's work. When she took a bath, she heated the water on the stove, "just the way we did it when we were kids." The Lord may not call all of us to this kind of sacrifice, but her example is worthy of respect.

Paul gave three reasons that explained why he had refused support from the Corinthian church.

For the gospel's sake (vv. 15–18). Paul did not want to "hinder the gospel of Christ" (1 Cor. 9:12). In that day, the Greek cities were filled with all kinds of itinerant teachers and preachers, most of whom were out to make money. Not only had Paul refused to use the kind of oratory and arguments that these teachers used (1 Cor. 2:1–5), but he also refused to accept money from those to whom he ministered. He wanted the message of the gospel to be free from any obstacles or hindrances in the minds of lost sinners.

For that matter, when Paul added "neither have I written these things" (1 Cor. 9:15), he was making sure that his readers did not get the idea that he was "hinting" that they should support him!

Paul could not claim any credit for preaching the gospel, because he had been called of God to preach. "Necessity is laid upon me; yea, woe is unto me, if I preach not the gospel!" (1 Cor. 9:16). God had given him a divine stewardship ("dispensation"), and "it is required in stewards, that a man be found faithful" (1 Cor. 4:2). God would see to it that Paul would receive his wages (*reward*—same word translated "hire" in Luke 10:7).

What was Paul's reward? The joy of preaching the gospel without charge! This meant that no man could accuse him of underhanded motives or methods as he shared the good news of Jesus Christ.

It is unfortunate when the ministry of the gospel is sometimes hindered by an overemphasis on money. The unsaved world is convinced that most preachers and missionaries are only involved in "religious rackets" to take money from innocent people. No doubt there are religious racketeers in the world today (1 Tim. 6:3–16), people who use religion to exploit others and control them. We would certainly not agree with their purposes or their practices. We must make sure that nothing we do in our own ministry gives the impression that we are of their number.

A wrong attitude toward money has hindered the gospel from the earliest days of the church. Ananias and Sapphira loved money more than they loved the truth, and God killed them (Acts 5). Simon the magician thought he could buy the gift of the Spirit with money (Acts 8:18–24). His name is now in the dictionary. *Simony* is the practice of buying and selling religious offices and privileges.

For eighteen fruitful years, Dr. H. A. Ironside pastored the Moody Church in Chicago. I recall the first time I heard him announce an offering. He said, "We ask God's people to give generously. If you are not a believer in Jesus Christ, we do not ask you to give. We have a gift for you—eternal life through faith in Christ!" He made it clear that the offering was for believers, lest the unsaved in the congregation stumble over money and then reject the gospel.

For the sinners' sake (vv. 19–23). What a paradox: free from all men, yet the servant of all men! "Ourselves your servants for Jesus' sake" (2 Cor. 4:5).

Because he was free, Paul was able to serve others and to set aside his own rights for their sake.

It is unfortunate that the phrase "all things to all men" (1 Cor. 9:22) has been used and abused by the world and made to mean what Paul did not intend for it to mean. Paul was not a chameleon who changed his message and methods with each new situation. Nor was Paul a compromiser who adjusted his message to please his audience. He was an ambassador, not a politician!

Paul was a Jew who had a great burden for his own people (Rom. 9:1–3; 10:1). But his special calling was to minister to the Gentiles (Eph. 3:8). Whenever he went into a new city (and he always went where the gospel had not yet been preached, Rom. 15:20), he headed straight for the synagogue, if there was one, and boldly shared the gospel. If he was rejected by the Jews, then he turned to the Gentiles.

What separated Jews and Gentiles in that day? The law and the covenants (Eph. 2:11–15). In his personal life, Paul so lived that he did not offend either the Jews or the Gentiles. He did not parade his liberty before the Jews, nor did he impose the law on the Gentiles.

Was Paul behaving in an inconsistent manner? Of course not. He simply adapted his approach to different groups. When you read his sermons in the book of Acts, you see this wise adaptation. When he preached to Jews, he started with the Old Testament patriarchs; but when he preached to Gentiles, he began with the God of creation. Paul did not have a "stock sermon" for all occasions.

It is worth noting that our Lord followed the same approach. To the highborn Jew, Nicodemus, He talked about spiritual birth (John 3); but to the Samaritan woman, He spoke about living water (John 4). Jesus was flexible and adaptable, and Paul followed His example. Neither Jesus nor Paul had an inflexible "evangelistic formula" that was used in every situation.

It takes tact to have contact. When the people I witness to tell me about their experience of confirmation, I tell them that I too was confirmed. I express my appreciation for the pastor who taught me and prayed for me. Then I tell them, "A year after I was confirmed, I met Jesus Christ personally and was born again." A good witness tries to build bridges, not walls.

To immature people, Paul's lifestyle probably looked inconsistent. In reality, he was very consistent, for his overriding purpose was to win people to Jesus Christ. Consistency can become a very legalistic thing, and a man can become so bound by man-made rules and standards that he has no freedom to minister. He is like young David trying to battle in Saul's armor.

Paul had the right to eat whatever pleased him, but he gave up that right so that he might win the Jews. Paul revered the law (see Rom. 7:12), but set that aside so that he might reach the lost Gentiles. He even identified himself with the legalistic weak Christians so that he might help them to grow. It was not compromise, but rather total abandonment to the higher law of love.

Paul followed the example of the Savior and humbled himself to become the servant of all.

For his own sake (vv. 24–27). Paul was fond of athletic images and used them often in his letters. The Corinthians would have been familiar with the Greek Olympic Games as well as their own local Isthmian Games. Knowing this, Paul used a metaphor very close to their experience.

An athlete must be disciplined if he is to win the prize. Discipline means giving up the good and the better for the best. The athlete must watch his diet as well as his hours. He must smile and say "No, thank you" when people offer him fattening desserts or invite him to late-night parties. There is nothing wrong with food or fun, but if they interfere with your highest goals, then they are hindrances and not helps.

The Christian does not run the race in order to get to heaven. He is in the race because he has been saved through faith in Jesus Christ. Only Greek citizens were allowed to participate in the games, and they had to obey the rules both in their training and in their performing. Any contestant found breaking the training rules was automatically disqualified.

In order to give up his rights and have the joy of winning lost souls, Paul had to discipline himself. That is the emphasis of this entire chapter: Authority (rights) must be balanced by discipline. If we want to serve the Lord and win His reward and approval, we must pay the price.

The word *castaway* (1 Cor. 9:27) is a technical word familiar to those who knew the Greek games. It means "disapproved, disqualified." At the Greek games, there was a herald who announced the rules of the contest, the names of the contestants, and the names and cities of the winners. He would also announce the names of any contestants who were disqualified.

Paul saw himself as both a "herald" and a "runner." He was concerned lest he get so busy trying to help others in the race that he ignore himself and find himself disqualified. Again, it was not a matter of losing personal salvation. (The disqualified Greek athlete did not lose his citizenship, only his opportunity to win a prize.) The whole emphasis is on *rewards*, and Paul did not want to lose his reward.

Only one runner could win the olive-wreath crown in the Greek games, but *every* believer can win an incorruptible crown when he stands before the judgment seat of Christ. This crown is given to those who discipline themselves for the sake of serving Christ and winning lost souls. They keep their bodies under control and keep their eyes on the goal.

In recent years, evangelical Christians have rediscovered the importance of personal discipline and the relationship between a disciplined body and a Spirit-filled life. We must, of course, avoid extremes. On the one hand, religious asceticism is unhealthy and of no value spiritually (Col. 2:18–23). But on the other hand, there is something to be said for disciplined eating, exercising, and resting, and a Spirit-directed

balanced life. We smugly congratulate ourselves that we do not smoke or use alcohol, but what about our overeating and overweight? And many Christians cannot discipline their time so as to have a consistent devotional life or Bible-study program.

Paul had one great goal in life: to glorify the Lord by winning the lost and building up the saints. To reach this goal, he was willing to pay any price. *He was willing even to give up his personal rights!* He sacrificed immediate gains for eternal rewards, immediate pleasures for eternal joys.

CHAPTER NINE
1 Corinthians 11
BE WISE ABOUT CHURCH ORDER

Since Paul had some negative things to say to the church later in this section, he opened it on a positive note by praising the church. Two matters in particular merited praise: the church remembered Paul and appreciated him, and the church was faithful to keep the teaching that had been given them. The word *ordinances* simply means "traditions," teachings that were passed on from one person to another (2 Tim. 2:2). The traditions of men should be avoided (Matt. 15:2–3; Col. 2:8), but the traditions that are given in the Word of God must be observed.

One of the biggest problems in the Corinthian church was disorder in the public meetings. Some of the women were assuming more freedom than they should have; there was disorder at the Lord's Supper; and there was confusion in the use of the spiritual gifts. The church had been greatly enriched with spiritual *gifts,* but they were sadly lacking in spiritual *graces.*

Paul could have tried to solve these problems by issuing apostolic edicts, but instead he patiently explained the spiritual principles that supported the teachings he had given the church. He founded his arguments on the Word of God.

Paul dealt with three particular areas of confusion in their public worship.

Women Praying and Prophesying (11:3–16)

The Christian faith brought freedom and hope to women, children, and slaves. It taught that all people, regardless of race or sex, were equal before their Creator, and that all believers were one in Jesus Christ (Gal. 3:28). As we have noted before, the local church was perhaps the only fellowship in the Roman Empire that welcomed all people, regardless of nationality, social status, sex, or economic position.

It was to be expected that there would be some who would carry this newfound freedom to excess. A new movement always suffers more from its disciples than from its enemies, and this was true in Corinth. Some of the women flaunted their "freedom" in the public meetings by refusing to cover their heads when they participated.

Paul did not forbid the women to pray or to prophesy. (Prophesying is not quite the same as our "preaching" or "expounding the Word." A person with the gift of prophecy proclaimed God's message as it was given to him *immediately* by the Spirit. The modern preacher studies the Word and prepares his message.) While the New Testament does not seem to permit women elders (1 Tim. 3:2), women in the early church who had the gift of prophecy were allowed to exercise it. They were also permitted to pray in the public meetings. However, they were not permitted to usurp authority over the men (1 Tim. 2:11–15) or to judge the messages of the other prophets (1 Cor. 14:27–35). If they had any questions, they were to ask their husbands (or other men) outside of the church meeting.

Eastern society at that time was very jealous over its women. Except for the temple prostitutes, the women wore long hair and, in public, wore a covering over their heads. (Paul did not use the word *veil,* i.e., a covering over the face. The woman put the regular shawl over her head, and this covering symbolized her submission and purity.) For the Christian women in the church to appear in public without the covering, let alone to pray and share the Word, was both daring and blasphemous.

Paul sought to restore order by reminding the Corinthians that God had made a difference between men and women, that each had a proper place to God's economy. There were also appropriate customs that symbolized these relationships and reminded both men and women of their correct places in the divine scheme. Paul did not say, or even hint, that *difference* meant *inequality* or *inferiority.* If there is to be peace in the church (1 Cor. 15:33), then there must be some kind of order; and order of necessity involves rank. However, *rank* and *quality* are two different things. The captain has a higher rank than the private, but the private may be a better man.

God's order to the church is based on three fundamentals that Paul considered to be self-evident.

Redemption (vv. 3–7). There is a definite order of "headship" to the church: the Father is the Head over Christ, Christ is the Head of the man, and the man is the head of the woman. Some interpret *head* to mean "origin," but this would mean that the Father originated Christ—something we cannot accept. In His redemptive ministry, the Son was subject to the Father even though He is equal to the Father (John 10:30; 14:28). Likewise, the woman is subject to the man even though to Christ she is equal to the man (1 Cor. 3:21–23; Gal. 3:28; Eph. 5:21–33).

Keep in mind that Paul was writing about the relationship *within the local assembly,* not in the world at large. It is God's plan that in the home and in the local church, the men should exercise headship under the authority of Jesus Christ.

The important fact is this: both women and men must honor the Lord by respecting the symbols of this headship—hair and the head-covering. Whenever a woman prays or prophesies in the assembly, she must have long hair and must wear a covering. The man should have short hair and not wear any covering. (This would be a change for Paul, for devout Jewish men always wore a cap when they prayed.) The man honors his Head (Christ) by being uncovered, while the woman honors her head (the man) by being covered. She is showing her submission both to God and to the man.

The Corinthian women who appeared in the assembly without the head-covering were actually putting themselves on the low level of the temple prostitutes. The prostitutes wore their hair very short, and they did not wear a head-covering in public. Their hairstyle and manner announced to others just what they were and what they were offering. "If you are going to abandon the covering," wrote Paul, "then why not go all the way and cut your hair?"

In Jewish law, a woman proved guilty of adultery had her hair cut off (Num. 5:11–31). Paul used two different words in 1 Corinthians 11:5–6: *shaved* means exactly that, all the hair shaved off; *shorn* means "cut short." Either one would be a disgrace to a woman.

Both man and woman are made in the image of God and for the glory of God; but since the woman was made from the man (Gen. 2:18–25), she is also the "glory of the man." She glorifies God and brings glory to the man by submitting to God's order and keeping her head covered in public worship. Thus, Paul tied together both local custom and biblical truth, the one pointing to the other.

Creation (vv. 8–12). We have already touched briefly on this truth. God's order is based on the fact that man was created first (1 Tim. 2:13), and that the woman was created for the man. Again, priority does not imply inferiority; for Paul made it clear in 1 Corinthians 11:11–12 that there is *partnership* as well as headship in God's creation. The man and the woman are spiritually one in the Lord (Gal. 3:28), and one cannot do without the other. Furthermore, the woman may have come from the man at the beginning, but today, it is the man who is born of the woman. Man and woman belong to each other and need each other.

Why did Paul bring up the angels in 1 Corinthians 11:10? He was arguing from the facts of creation, and the angels were a part of that creation. The angels also know their place and show respect when they worship God, for they cover their faces (Isa. 6:2). Finally, in some special way, the angels share in the public worship of the church and learn from the church (Eph. 3:10; 1 Peter 1:12). Public worship is a serious thing, for the angels are present; and we ought to conduct ourselves *as if we were in heaven.*

Nature (vv. 13–16). In a general way, it is true that nature gives women longer hair and men shorter hair. The Romans, Greeks, and Jews (except for the

Nazarites) pretty much followed this custom. Nowhere does the Bible tell us how long our hair should be. It simply states that there ought to be a noticeable difference between the length of the men's hair and the women's hair so that there be no confusion of the sexes. It is shameful for the man to look like a woman or the woman to look like a man.

The woman's long hair is her glory, and it is given to her *"instead of* a covering" (literal translation). In other words, if local custom does not dictate a head-covering, her long hair can be that covering. I do not think that Paul meant for all women in every culture to wear a shawl for a head-covering; but he did expect them to use their long hair as a covering and as a symbol of their submission to God's order. This is something that every woman can do.

In my ministry in different parts of the world, I have noticed that the basic principle of headship applies in every culture; but the means of demonstrating it differs from place to place. The important thing is the submission of the heart to the Lord and the public manifestation of obedience to God's order.

Selfishness at the "Love Feasts" (11:17–22)

Since the beginning of the church, it was customary for the believers to eat together (Acts 2:42, 46). It was an opportunity for fellowship and for sharing with those who were less privileged. No doubt they climaxed this meal by observing the Lord's Supper. They called this meal "the love feast" since its main emphasis was showing love for the saints by sharing with one another.

The "agape feast" (from the Greek word for "love") was part of the worship at Corinth, but some serious abuses had crept in. As a result, the love feasts were doing more harm than good to the church. For one thing, there were various cliques in the church, and people ate with their own "crowd" instead of fellowshipping with the whole church family. While Paul condemned this selfish practice, he did take a positive view of the results: at least God would use this to reveal those who were true believers.

Another fault was selfishness: the rich people brought a great deal of food for themselves, while the poorer members went hungry. The original idea of the agape feast was sharing, but that idea had been lost. Some of the members were even getting drunk. It is likely that the weekly agape feast was the only decent meal some of the poorer members regularly had; and to be treated so scornfully by the richer members not only hurt their stomachs, but also their pride.

Of course, the divisions at the dinner were but evidence of the deeper problems in the church. The Corinthians thought they were advanced believers, when in reality they were but little children. Paul did not suggest that they abandon the feast, but rather that they restore its proper meaning. "Let the rich eat at home if they are hungry. When you abuse believers who are less fortunate than you are, then you are actually despising the church!" The agape feast should

have been an opportunity for edification, but they were using it as a time for embarrassment.

I recall an incident at a Sunday school picnic when I was just a teenager. The person in charge of the games set up a relay that involved various people throwing eggs to each other as they backed farther and farther apart. Of course, the farther the teams went from each other, the harder the participants had to throw the eggs, and the results were hilarious.

However, some of us noticed two Sunday school children watching the eggs with great fascination. They came from a poor family that probably rarely ate eggs because they could not afford them. The little girl went to the lady leading the games and asked, "If there are any eggs left over, can my brother and I take them home?" Wisely, the lady stopped the game before it was really over, awarded the prizes, and gave all the eggs to the two children. She knew that it was wrong for some of the saints to have a good time at the expense of others.

A drinking party is hardly the best way to prepare for the Lord's Supper. Scorning others is certainly not the way to remember the Savior who died for all sinners, rich and poor. How important it is that we prepare our hearts when we come to the Lord's Table!

Abuses at the Lord's Supper (11:23–34)

Evangelical churches recognize two ordinances established by Jesus Christ for His people to observe: baptism and the Lord's Supper. (The Supper is also called *the Communion* as in 1 Corinthians 10:16, and *the Eucharist,* which means "the giving of thanks.") Jesus Christ took the cup and the loaf—the ingredients of a common meal in that day—and transformed them into a meaningful spiritual experience for believers. However, the value of the experience depends on the condition of the hearts of those who participate; and this was the problem at Corinth.

It is a serious thing to come to the Communion with an unprepared heart. It is also a serious thing to receive the Supper in a careless manner. Because the Corinthians had been sinning in their observing of the Lord's Supper, God had disciplined them. "For this cause many are weak and sickly among you, and many sleep [have died]" (1 Cor. 11:30).

The Lord's Supper gives us an opportunity for spiritual growth and blessings if we approach it in the right attitude. What, then, must we do if the Supper is to bring blessing and not chastening?

First, we should look back (vv. 23–26a). The broken bread reminds us of Christ's body, given for us; and the cup reminds us of His shed blood. It is a remarkable thing that Jesus wants His followers to remember His *death.* Most of us try to forget how those we love died, but Jesus wants us to remember how He died. Why? Because everything we have as Christians centers in that death.

We must remember *that* He died, because this is a part of the gospel message: "Christ died … and was buried" (1 Cor. 15:3–4). It is not the life of our Lord, or His teachings, that will save sinners—but His death. Therefore, we also remember *why* He died: Christ died for our sins; He was our substitute (Isa. 53:6; 1 Peter 2:24), paying the debt that we could not pay.

We should also remember *how* He died: willingly, meekly, showing forth His love for us (Rom. 5:8). He gave His body into the hands of wicked men, and He bore on His body the sins of the world.

However, this "remembering" is not simply the recalling of historical facts. It is a participation in spiritual realities. At the Lord's Table, we do not walk around a monument and admire it. We have fellowship with a living Savior as our hearts reach out by faith.

Second, we should look ahead (v. 26b). We observe the Supper "till he come." The return of Jesus Christ is the blessed hope of the church and the individual Christian. Jesus not only died for us, but He arose again and ascended to heaven; and one day He shall return to take us to heaven. Today, we are not all that we should be; but when we see Him, "we shall be like him" (1 John 3:2).

Third, we should look within (vv. 27–28, 31–32). Paul did not say that we had to be *worthy* to partake of the Supper, but only that we should partake *in a worthy manner.* At a Communion service in Scotland, the pastor noted that a woman in the congregation did not accept the bread and cup from the elder, but instead sat weeping. The pastor left the table and went to her side and said, "Take it, my dear, *it's for sinners!*" And, indeed, it is; but sinners saved by God's grace must not treat the Supper in a sinful manner.

If we are to participate in a worthy manner, we must examine our own hearts, judge our sins, and confess them to the Lord. To come to the Table with unconfessed sin in our lives is to be guilty of Christ's body and blood, for it was sin that nailed Him to the cross. If we will not judge our own sins, then God will judge us and chasten us until we do confess and forsake our sins.

The Corinthians neglected to examine themselves, but they were experts at examining everybody else. When the church gathers together, we must be careful not to become "religious detectives" who watch others, but who fail to acknowledge our own sins. If we eat and drink in an unworthy manner, we eat and drink judgment (chastening) to ourselves, and that is nothing to take lightly.

Chastening is God's loving way of dealing with His sons and daughters to encourage them to mature (Heb. 12:1–11). It is not a judge condemning a criminal, but a loving Father punishing His disobedient (and perhaps stubborn) children. Chastening proves God's love for us, and chastening can, if we cooperate, perfect God's life in us.

Finally, we should look around (vv. 33–34). We should not look around in order to criticize other believers, but in order to discern the Lord's body (1 Cor. 11:29). This perhaps has a dual meaning: we

should discern His body in the loaf, but also in the church around us—for the church is the body of Christ. "For we being many are one bread, and one body" (1 Cor. 10:17). The Supper should be a demonstration of the unity of the church—but there was not much unity in the Corinthian church. In fact, their celebration of the Lord's Supper was only a demonstration of their disunity.

The Lord's Supper is a family meal, and the Lord of the family desires that His children love one another and care for one another. It is impossible for a true Christian to get closer to his Lord while at the same time he is separated from his fellow believers. How can we remember the Lord's death and not love one another? "Beloved, if God so loved us, we ought also to love one another" (1 John 4:11).

No one ought to come to the Table who is not a true believer. Nor should a true believer come to the Table if his heart is not right with God and with his fellow Christians. This is why many churches have a time of spiritual preparation before they observe the Lord's Supper, lest any of the participants bring chastening on themselves. I recall one church member who approached me and shared with me a personal defeat that had not only hurt him spiritually, but had been "advertised" by others and was about to bring reproach on him and the church.

"What can I do to make this right?" he asked, convincing me that he had indeed judged the sin and confessed it. I reminded him that the next week we were going to observe the Lord's Supper, and I suggested that he ask the Lord for direction. The evening of the Supper, I opened the service in a way I had not done before. "Is there anyone here who has anything to share with the church?" I asked, and my repentant friend stood to his feet and walked forward, meeting me at the table. In a quiet, concise manner, he admitted that he had sinned, and he asked the church's forgiveness. We felt a wave of Spirit-given love sweep over the congregation, and people began to weep openly. At that observance of the Supper, we truly discerned the Lord's body.

The Communion is not supposed to be a time of "spiritual autopsy" and grief, even though confession of sin is important. It should be a time of thanksgiving and joyful anticipation of seeing the Lord! Jesus gave thanks, even though He was about to suffer and die. Let us give thanks also.

CHAPTER TEN
1 Corinthians 12—13
BE WISE ABOUT THE CHURCH BODY

One of the marks of an individual's maturity is a growing understanding of, and appreciation for, his own body. There is a parallel in the spiritual life: as we mature in Christ, we gain a better understanding of the church, which is Christ's body. The emphasis in recent years on "body life" has been a good one. It has helped to counteract the wrong emphasis on "individual Christianity" that can lead to isolation from the local church.

Of course, the image of the body is not the only one Paul used in discussing the church, and we must be careful not to press it too far. The church is also a family, an army, a temple, and even a bride; and each image has important lessons to teach us. However, in three of his letters, Paul gave emphasis to the church as a body; and, in each of these passages, he brought out the same three important truths: unity, diversity, and maturity. The following chart makes this clear.

	Unity	Diversity	Maturity
1 Corinthians	12:1–13	12:14–31	13:1–13
Romans	12:1–5	12:6–8	12:9–21
Ephesians	4:1–6	4:7–12	4:13–16

It is impossible to discuss the body without also discussing the ministry of the Holy Spirit. It was the Spirit who gave birth to the body at Pentecost and who ministers in and through the body. In the Corinthian church, unfortunately, the members were grieving the Holy Spirit by the carnal ways in which they were using spiritual gifts. They were like children with toys instead of adults with valuable tools, and they needed to mature.

Unity: The Gift of the Spirit (12:1–13)

Since there was division in the Corinthian church, Paul began with an emphasis on the oneness of the church. He pointed out four wonderful bonds of spiritual unity.

We confess the same Lord (vv. 1–3). Paul contrasted their experience as unconverted idolaters with their present experience as Christians. They had worshipped dead idols, but now they belonged to the living God. Their idols never spoke to them, but God spoke to them by His Spirit, and He even spoke *through* them in the gift of prophecy. When they were lost, they were under the control of the demons (1 Cor. 10:20) and were led astray ("carried away," 1 Cor. 12:2). But now the Spirit of God lived in them and directed them.

It is only through the Spirit that a person can *honestly* say, "Jesus is Lord." A sneering sinner may mouth the words, but he is not giving a true confession. (Perhaps Paul was referring to things they had said when influenced by the demons prior to conversion.) It is important to note that the believer is always in control of himself when the Holy Spirit is at work (1 Cor. 14:32) because Jesus Christ *the Lord* is in charge. Any so-called "Spirit manifestation" that robs a person of self-control is not of God; for "the fruit of the Spirit is … self-control" (Gal. 5:22–23 NASB).

If Jesus Christ truly is Lord in our lives, then there should be unity in the church. Division and dissension among God's people only weakens their united testimony to a lost world (John 17:20–21).

We depend on the same God (vv. 4–6). There is a trinitarian emphasis here: "the same Spirit … the same Lord … the same God." We individually may have different gifts, ministries, and ways of working, but "it is God which worketh in you both to will and to do of his good pleasure" (Phil. 2:13). The source of the gift is God; the sphere for administering the gift is from God; and the energy to use the gift is from God. Why, then, glorify men? Why compete with one another?

We minister to the same body (vv. 7–11). The gifts are given for the good of the whole church. They are not for individual enjoyment, but for corporate employment. The Corinthians especially needed this reminder, because they were using their spiritual gifts selfishly to promote themselves and not to prosper the church. When we accept our gifts with humility, then we use them to promote harmony, and this helps the whole church.

The various gifts are named in 1 Corinthians 12:8–10 and 28, and also in Ephesians 4:11 and Romans 12:6–8. When you combine the lists, you end up with nineteen different gifts and offices. Since the listing in Romans is not identical with the listing in 1 Corinthians, we may assume that Paul was not attempting to exhaust the subject in either passage. While the gifts named are adequate for the ministry of the church, God is not limited to these lists. He may give other gifts as He pleases.

We have already discussed *apostles* (1 Cor. 9:1–6). *Prophets* were New Testament spokesmen for God whose messages came immediately from God by the Spirit. Their ministry was to edify, encourage, and comfort (1 Cor. 14:3). Their messages were tested by the listeners to determine whether they were truly from God (1 Cor. 14:29; 1 Thess. 5:19–21). Ephesians 2:20 makes it clear that apostles and prophets worked together to lay the foundation of the church, and we may assume that they were no longer needed once that foundation was completed.

Teachers (also pastor-teacher) instructed converts in the doctrinal truths of the Christian life. They taught from the Word and from the teachings of the apostles (tradition). Unlike the prophets, they did not get their messages immediately by the Spirit, though the Spirit helped them in their teaching. James 3:1 indicates that this is a serious calling.

The *evangelist* majored on sharing the good news of salvation with the lost. All ministers should do the work of an evangelist (2 Tim. 4:5) and seek to win souls, but some men have been given evangelism as a special calling.

In the early church, *miracles* were a part of the credentials of God's servants (Heb. 2:1–4). In fact, miracles, healings, and tongues all belong to what theologians call "the sign gifts" and belonged in a special way to the infancy of the church. The book of Acts, as well as church history, indicates that these miraculous gifts passed off the scene.

Helps and *governments* have to do with the serving of others and the guiding of the church. Without spiritual leadership, the church flounders. *Ministry* (Rom. 12:7) and *ruling* belong to this same category. In my three pastorates, I was grateful for people with the gifts of helps and leadership.

There were several "speaking gifts": *tongues* and the *interpretation of tongues* (about which more will be said later), the *word of wisdom* and the *word of knowledge* (the ability to understand and apply God's truth to a definite situation), and *exhortation* (encouragement, rebuke if necessary).

Giving and *showing mercy* relate to sharing material aid with those in need, as well as supporting God's servants in ministry. The gift of *faith* has to do with believing God for what He wants to accomplish in the church's ministry, that He will lead and provide. The *discerning of spirits* was important in the early church, since Satan tried to counterfeit the work of God and the Word of God. Today, the Spirit especially uses the written Word to give us discernment (1 John 2:18–24; 4:1–6). Since there are no prophets in the church today, we need not worry about false prophets; but we do have to beware of false *teachers* (2 Peter 2:1).

Some students have categorized the various gifts as the speaking gifts, the sign gifts, and the serving gifts. However, we should not be so fascinated by the individual gifts that we forget the main reason why Paul listed them: to remind us that they unite us in our ministries to the one body. The Holy Spirit bestows these gifts "as he will" (1 Cor. 12:11), not as we will. No Christian should complain about his or her gifts, nor should any believer boast about his or her gifts. We are many members in one body, ministering to each other.

We have experienced the same baptism (vv. 12–13). It is unfortunate that the term "baptism of the Spirit" has been divorced from its original New Testament meaning. God has spoken to us in Spirit-given *words* that we must not confuse (1 Cor. 2:12–13). The baptism of the Spirit occurs at conversion when the Spirit enters the believing sinner, gives him new life, and makes his body the temple of God. *All* believers have experienced this once-for-all baptism (1 Cor. 12:13). Nowhere does the Scripture command us to *seek* this baptism, because we have already experienced it and it need not be repeated.

The "filling of the Spirit" (Eph. 5:18ff.) has to do with the Spirit's control of our lives. (In Scripture, to be *filled by* something means "to be controlled by.") We are *commanded* to be filled, and we can be if we yield all to Christ and ask Him for the Spirit's filling. This is a repeated experience, for we constantly need to be filled with spiritual power if we are to glorify Christ. To be baptized by the Spirit means that we belong to *Christ's body*. To be filled with the Spirit means that *our bodies* belong to Christ.

The evidence of the Spirit's baptism at conversion is the witness of the Spirit within (Rom. 8:14–16). It is not "speaking in tongues." *All* of the believers in the Corinthian assembly had been baptized by the Spirit, but not all of them spoke in tongues (1 Cor. 12:30). The evidences of the Spirit's filling are power for witnessing (Acts 1:8), joyfulness and submission (Eph. 5:19ff.), Christlikeness (Gal. 5:22–26), and a growing understanding of the Word (John 16:12–15).

Because of the gift of the Spirit, which is received at conversion, we are all members of the body of Christ. Race, social status, wealth, or even sex (Gal. 3:28) are neither advantages nor handicaps as we fellowship and serve the Lord.

Diversity: The Gifts of the Spirit (12:14–31)

Unity without diversity would produce uniformity, and uniformity tends to produce death. Life is a balance between unity and diversity. As a human body weakens, its systems slow down and everything tends to become uniform. The ultimate, of course, is that the body itself turns to dust.

This helps to explain why some churches (and other Christian ministries) have weakened and died: there was not sufficient diversity to keep unity from becoming uniformity. Dr. Vance Havner has expressed it: "First there is a man, then a movement, then a machine, and then a monument." Many ministries that began as a protest against "dead orthodoxy" became dead themselves, because in their desire to remain pure and doctrinally sound, they stifled creativity and new ideas.

However, if diversity is not kept under control, it could destroy unity; and then you have anarchy. We shall discover in 1 Corinthians 13 that it is *maturity* that balances unity and diversity. The tension in the body between individual members and the total organism can only be solved by maturity.

Using the human body as his illustration, Paul explained three important facts about diversity in the body of Christ. Why are there different members?

The body needs different functions if it is to live, grow, and serve (vv. 14–20). No member should compare or contrast itself with any other member, because each one is different and each one is important. I suppose I could learn to walk on my hands, but I prefer to use my feet, even though I have not yet learned to type or to eat with my feet. The ear cannot see and the eye cannot hear, yet each organ has an important ministry. And have you ever tried to smell through your ears?

There is a tendency today for some people to magnify the "sensational" gifts. Some believers feel very guilty because they possess gifts that do not put them into the limelight. It is this attitude that Paul opposed and refuted in this paragraph. Diversity does not suggest inferiority. Are we to believe that the sovereign Lord made a mistake when He bestowed the gifts?

The members promote unity as they discover their dependence on one another (vv. 21–26).

Diversity in the body is an evidence of the wisdom of God. Each member needs the other members, and no member can afford to become independent. When a part of the human body becomes independent, you have a serious problem that could lead to sickness and even death. In a healthy human body, the various members cooperate with each other and even compensate for each other when a crisis occurs. The instant any part of the body says to any other part, "I don't need you!" it begins to weaken and die and create problems for the whole body.

A famous preacher was speaking at a ministers' meeting, and he took time before and after the meeting to shake hands with the pastors and chat with them. A friend asked him, "Why take time for a group of men you may never see again?" The world-renowned preacher smiled and said, "Well, I may be where I am because of them! Anyway, if I didn't need them on the way up, I might need them on the way down!" No Christian servant can say to any other servant, "My ministry can get along without you!"

Paul may be referring to the private parts of the body in 1 Corinthians 12:23–24. If so, then to "bestow honor" on them refers to the use of attractive clothing. The more beautiful parts of the body need no special help.

God's desire is that there be no division ("schism") in the church. Diversity leads to disunity when the members compete with one another; but diversity leads to unity when the members care for one another. How do the members care for each other? By each one functioning according to God's will and helping the other members to function. If one member suffers, it affects every member. If one member is healthy, it helps the others to be strong.

Diversity of members fulfills the will of God in the body (vv. 27–31). It is God who bestows the gifts and assigns the offices. He has a perfect plan, not only for the church as a whole, but also for each local congregation. We have no reason to believe that each congregation in the New Testament possessed all of the gifts. The church at Corinth was an especially gifted assembly (1 Cor. 1:4–7; 2 Cor. 8:7). However, God gives to each congregation just the gifts it needs when they are needed.

In this paragraph, Paul pointed out that there is a "priority list" for the gifts, that some have more significance than others. But this fact does not contradict the lesson already shared—that each gift is important and each individual believer is important. Even in the human body, there are some parts that we can do without, even though their absence might handicap us a bit.

The apostles and prophets, of course, appeared first on the scene because they had a foundational ministry (Eph. 2:20). Teachers were needed to help establish believers in the faith. The other gifts were needed from time to time to help individual believers and to build the church.

The construction of the Greek in 1 Corinthians 12:29–30 demands *no* as the answer to each of these questions. No individual believer possesses all the spiritual gifts. Each believer has the gift (or gifts) assigned to him by the Lord and needed at that time.

The word translated "best" in 1 Corinthians 12:31 simply means "greater." Some spiritual gifts are greater in significance than others, and it is proper for the believer to desire these gifts (1 Cor. 14:1). Paul put a high value on prophecy, but the Corinthians valued the gift of tongues. Paul put tongues at the end of the list.

Unity and diversity must be balanced by maturity, and that maturity comes with love. It is not enough to have the *gift* of the Spirit and *gifts* from the Spirit. We must also have the *graces* of the Spirit as we use our gifts to serve one another.

Maturity: The Graces of the Spirit (13:1–13)

It was Jonathan Swift, the satirical author of *Gulliver's Travels,* who said, "We have just enough religion to make us hate, but not enough to make us love one another." Spiritual gifts, no matter how exciting and wonderful, are useless and even destructive if they are not ministered in love. In all three of the "body" passages in Paul's letters, there is an emphasis on love. The main evidence of maturity in the Christian life is a growing love for God and for God's people, as well as a love for lost souls. It has well been said that love is the "circulatory system" of the body of Christ.

Few chapters in the Bible have suffered more misinterpretation and misapplication than 1 Corinthians 13. Divorced from its context, it becomes "a hymn to love" or a sentimental sermon on Christian brotherhood. Many people fail to see that Paul was still dealing with the Corinthians' problems when he wrote these words: the abuse of the gift of tongues, division in the church, envy of others' gifts, selfishness (remember the lawsuits?), impatience with one another in the public meetings, and behavior that was disgracing the Lord.

The only way spiritual gifts can be used creatively is when Christians are motivated by love. Paul explained three characteristics of Christian love that show why it is so important in ministry.

Love is enriching (vv. 1–3). Paul named five spiritual gifts: tongues, prophecy, knowledge, faith, and giving (sacrifice). He pointed out that, without love, the exercise of these gifts is *nothing.* Tongues apart from love is just a lot of noise! It is love that enriches the gift and that gives it value. Ministry without love cheapens both the minister and those who are touched by it; but ministry with love enriches the whole church. "Speaking the truth in love" (Eph. 4:15).

Christians are "taught of God to love one another" (1 Thess. 4:9). God the Father taught us to love by sending His Son (1 John 4:19), and God the Son taught us to love by giving His life and by commanding us to love each other (John 13:34–35). The Holy Spirit teaches us to love one another by pouring out God's love in our hearts (Rom. 5:5). The most important lesson in the school of faith is to love one another. Love enriches all that it touches.

Love is edifying (vv. 4–7). "Knowledge puffeth up, but love edifieth [builds up]" (1 Cor. 8:1). The purpose of spiritual gifts is the edification of the church (1 Cor. 12:7; 14:3, 5, 12, 17, 26). This means we must not think of ourselves, but of others; and this demands love.

The Corinthians were impatient in the public meetings (1 Cor. 14:29–32), but love would make them long suffering. They were envying each other's gifts, but love would remove that envy. They were "puffed up" with pride (1 Cor. 4:6, 18–19; 5:2), but love would remove pride and self-vaunting and replace it with a desire to promote others. "Be kindly affectioned one to another with brotherly love, in honor preferring one another" (Rom. 12:10).

At the "love feast" and the Lord's Table, the Corinthians were behaving in a very unseemly manner. If they had known the meaning of real love, they would have behaved themselves in a manner pleasing to the Lord. They were even suing one another! But love "seeketh not [its] own, is not easily provoked, thinketh no evil" (1 Cor. 13:5). The phrase *thinketh no evil* means "does not keep any record of wrongs." One of the most miserable men I ever met was a professed Christian who actually kept in a notebook a list of the wrongs he felt others had committed against him. Forgiveness means that we wipe the record clean and never hold things against people (Eph. 4:26, 32).

Love does not rejoice in iniquity, yet the Corinthians were boasting about sin in their church (1 Cor. 5). Love "shall cover the multitude of sins" (1 Peter 4:8). Like Noah's sons, we should seek to hide the sins of others, and then help them make things right (Gen. 9:20–23).

Read 1 Corinthians 13:4–7 carefully and compare this with the fruit of the Spirit listed in Galatians 5:22–23. You will see that all of the characteristics of love show up in that fruit. This is why love edifies: it releases the power of the Spirit in our lives and churches.

Love is enduring (vv. 8–13). Prophecy, knowledge, and tongues were not permanent gifts. (*Knowledge* does not mean "education," but the immediate imparting of spiritual truth to the mind.) These three gifts went together. God would impart knowledge to the prophet, and he would give the message in a tongue. Then an interpreter (sometimes the prophet himself) would explain the message. These were gifts that some of the Corinthians prized, especially the gift of tongues.

These gifts will fail (be abolished) and cease, but love will endure forever; for "God is love" (1 John 4:8, 16). The Corinthians were like children playing with toys that would one day disappear. You expect a child to think, understand, and speak like a child; but you also expect the child to mature and start thinking and

speaking like an adult. The day comes when he must "put away childish things" (1 Cor. 13:11).

In the New Testament (which at that time was not completed) we have a complete revelation, but our understanding of it is partial. (Review 1 Cor. 8:1–3 if you think otherwise.) There is a maturing process for the church as a whole (Eph. 4:11–16) and also for the individual believer (1 Cor. 14:20; 2 Peter 3:18). We will not be fully completed until Jesus returns, but we ought to be growing and maturing now. Children live for the temporary; adults live for the permanent. Love is enduring, and what it produces will endure.

Note that all three of the Christian graces will endure, even though "faith will become sight and hope will be fulfilled." But the greatest of these graces is love; because when you love someone, you will trust him and will always be anticipating new joys. Faith, hope, and love go together, but it is love that energizes faith and hope.

Unfortunately, some of the emphasis today on the Holy Spirit has not been *holy* (because it has ignored Scripture) and has not been *spiritual* (because it has appealed to the carnal nature). We must not tell other believers what gifts they should have or how they can obtain them. This matter is in the sovereign will of God. We must not minimize gifts, but neither should we neglect the *graces* of the Spirit. In my itinerant ministry, I have run across too many local church problems created by people who were zealous for the gifts, but careless of the graces.

Unity—diversity—maturity; and maturity comes through love.

CHAPTER ELEVEN
1 Corinthians 14
BE WISE ABOUT USING SPIRITUAL GIFTS

Paul had discussed the gift of the Spirit, the gifts of the Spirit, and the graces of the Spirit; and now he concluded this section by explaining the government of the Spirit in the public worship services of the church. Apparently there was a tendency for some of the Corinthians to lose control of themselves as they exercised their gifts, and Paul had to remind them of the fundamental principles that ought to govern the public meetings of the church. There are three principles: edification, understanding, and order.

Edification (14:1–5, 26b)
This was one of Paul's favorite words, borrowed, of course, from architecture. *To edify* means "to build up." This concept is not alien to the "body" image of the church; even today, we speak about "bodybuilding exercises." There is an overlapping of images here, for

the body of Christ is also the temple of the living God. Paul's choice of the word *edify* was a wise one.

The mistake the Corinthians were making was to emphasize their own personal edification to the neglect of the church. They wanted to build themselves up, but they did not want to build up their fellow believers. This attitude, of course, not only hurt the other Christians, but it also hurt the believers who were practicing it. After all, if we are all members of the same body, the way we relate to the other members must ultimately affect us personally. "The eye cannot say unto the hand, I have no need of thee" (1 Cor. 12:21). If one member of the body is weak or infected, it will affect the other members.

Paul detected that the church was neglecting prophecy and giving a wrong emphasis to tongues. We must not think of a New Testament prophet as a person who foretold the future, for even the Old Testament prophets did more than that. Prophets received God's message immediately, through the Holy Spirit, and communicated that message to the church, usually in a tongue, but not always. Prophecy was not the same as our modern-day "preaching," because today's preachers study the Bible and prepare their messages. No preacher today should claim that he has immediate inspiration from God.

Paul explained the supreme value of prophecy over tongues by contrasting the two gifts.

Prophecy speaks to men, tongues to God (vv. 1–3). "If you are zealous for spiritual gifts, at least desire the best gifts," was Paul's counsel. Prophecy was best because it built up the church. It gave the listeners encouragement and comfort—something that everybody needs.

It is unfortunate that our translators inserted *unknown* in 1 Corinthians 14:2, because the New Testament knows nothing of an "unknown tongue." From the very beginning of the church, tongues were *known* languages, recognized by the listeners (Acts 2:4, 6, 8, 11). The tongue would be unknown *to the speaker* and to the listeners, but it was not unknown in the world (1 Cor. 14:10–11, 21).

It is also unfortunate that people have the idea that tongues were used to preach the gospel to the lost. Quite the contrary was true: Paul was afraid that the excessive tongues-speaking in the church would convince the lost that the Christians were crazy (1 Cor. 14:23)! At Pentecost, the believers extolled "the wonderful works of God," but Peter preached the gospel in the Aramaic language his listeners could all understand.

The believer who speaks in a tongue speaks to God in praise and worship; but the believer who prophesies shares the Word with the church and helps those who listen. This leads to the second contrast.

Prophecy edifies the church, tongues edify only the speaker (vv. 4–5). Paul did not deny the value of tongues to the speaker, but he did place a greater value on building up the church. "Greater is he that prophesieth than he that speaketh with tongues"

(1 Cor. 14:5). Unless the tongues are interpreted (1 Cor. 12:10, 30), the message can do the church no good. Paul pointed out that an interpreter must be present before the gift of tongues may be exercised (1 Cor. 14:28).

Keep in mind that the members of the Corinthian church did not sit in the services with Bibles on their laps. The New Testament was being written, and the Old Testament scrolls were expensive and not available to most believers. God spoke to His people directly through the prophets, and the message was sometimes given in a tongue. The three gifts of knowledge, prophecy, and tongues worked together to convey truth to the people (1 Cor. 13:1–2, 8–11).

Paul emphasized the importance of doctrinal teaching in the church. Our worship must be based on truth, or it may become superstitious emotionalism. Christians need to know what they believe and why they believe it. The prophet shared truth with the church, and thereby edified the assembly. The person speaking in tongues (unless there is an interpreter) is enjoying his worship of God, but he is not edifying the church.

In my own ministry, I have shared in many local church services and conferences, and I have always tried to communicate biblical truth to the people. Sometimes the music has not been edifying, and at other times, the music communicated the Word of God in a powerful way. Whenever all of us as ministers have aimed at edification, and not entertainment, God has blessed and the people have been helped. A ministry that does not build up will tear down, no matter how "spiritual" it may seem. When we explain and apply the Word of God to individual lives, we have a ministry of edification.

Understanding (14:6–25)

Eight times in this section, Paul used the word *understanding*. It is not enough for the minister to impart information to people; the people must *receive* it if it is to do them any good. The seed that is received in the good ground is the seed that bears fruit, but this means that there must be an *understanding* of the Word of God (Matt. 13:23). If a believer wants to be edified, he must prepare his heart to receive the Word (1 Thess. 2:13). Not everybody who *listens* really *hears*.

The famous Congregationalist minister Dr. Joseph Parker preached at an important meeting and afterward was approached by a man who pointed out an error in the sermon. Parker listened patiently to the man's criticism, and then asked, "And what *else* did you get from the message?" This remark simply withered the critic, who then disappeared into the crowd. Too often we are quick to judge the sermon instead of allowing the Word of God to judge us.

Illustration (vv. 6–11). Paul used three simple illustrations to prove his point that there must be understanding if there is to be an edifying spiritual ministry: musical instruments, a bugle call in battle, and daily conversation.

If a musical instrument does not give a clear and distinct sound, nobody will recognize the music being played. Everyone knows how uncomfortable one feels when a performer *almost* plays the right note because the instrument is defective or out of tune. Large pipe organs must be constantly serviced lest their reeds fail to perform properly. I was in a church service one evening during which the organ pitch gradually changed because of atmospheric conditions, and by the close of the service, the organ could not be played with the piano because of the radical change that had occurred.

If the bugler is not sure whether he is calling "Retreat!" or "Charge!" you can be sure none of the soldiers will know what to do either. Half of them will rush forward, while the other half will run back! The call must be a clear one if it is to be understood.

But this fact is also true in everyday conversation. I recall the first time my wife and I visited Great Britain and were confronted with the variety of local dialects there. We asked directions of a friendly gentleman in London and, quite frankly, could understand very little of what he said. (Perhaps he had a difficult time understanding us!)

First Corinthians 14:10 gives us good reason to believe that, when Paul wrote about tongues, he was referring to known languages and not some "heavenly" language. Each language is different and yet each language has its own meaning. No matter how sincere a speaker may be, if I do not understand his language, he cannot communicate with me. To the Greeks, a *barbarian* was the lowest person on the social or national ladder. In fact, anybody who was not a Greek was considered a barbarian.

The musician, the bugler, and the everyday conversationalist cannot be understood unless their messages are communicated in a manner that is meaningful to the listener. Having illustrated the principle of understanding, Paul then applied it to three different persons.

Application (vv. 12–25). Paul first applied the principle of understanding to the speaker himself (1 Cor. 14:12–15). Again, he reminded the Corinthians that it is better to be a blessing to the church than to experience some kind of personal "spiritual excitement." If the believer speaks in a tongue, his spirit (inner person) may share in the experience, but his mind is not a part of the experience. It is not wrong to pray or sing "in the spirit," but it is better to include the mind and understand what you are praying or singing. (Note that the word *spirit* in 1 Cor. 14:14–15 does not refer to the Holy Spirit, but to the inner person, as in 1 Cor. 2:11.) If the speaker is to be edified, he must understand what he is saying.

What, then, is the speaker to do? He must ask God for the interpretation of the message. Paul assumed that an interpreter would be present (1 Cor. 14:27–28)

or that the speaker himself had the gift of interpreting. Of course, all of this discussion emphasized once again the superiority of prophecy over tongues: prophecy needs no interpretation and can therefore be a blessing to everybody.

Paul then applied the principle to other believers in the assembly (1 Cor. 14:16–20). He assumed that they would listen to the message and respond to it. But if they did not understand the message, how could they respond? (Apparently, saying *Amen!* in church was not frowned on in those days.) The "unlearned" person was probably a new believer, or possibly an interested "seeker." He could not be edified unless he understood what was being said.

Again, it was a matter of priorities. While Paul did not oppose the ministry of tongues, he did try to put it into a right perspective. The issue was not quantity of words, but quality of communication. The Corinthians were acting like children playing with toys. When it came to knowing about sin, Paul wanted them to be "babes"; but when it came to spiritual understanding, he wanted them to be mature men (1 Cor. 3:1–4; 13:11–13).

Some people have the idea that speaking in a tongue is an evidence of spiritual maturity, but Paul taught that it is possible to exercise the gift in an unspiritual and immature manner.

Paul's final application was to the unsaved person who happened to come into the assembly during a time of worship (1 Cor. 14:21–25). Paul made here another point for the superiority of prophecy over tongues: a message in tongues (unless interpreted) could never bring conviction to the heart of a lost sinner. In fact, the unsaved person might leave the service before the interpretation was given, thinking that the whole assembly was crazy. Tongues were not used for evangelism, neither at Pentecost nor in the meetings of the early church.

However, tongues did have a "message" for the lost Jews in particular: they were a sign of God's judgment. Paul quoted Isaiah 28:11–12, a reference to the invading Assyrian army whose "barbaric" language the Jews would not understand. The presence of this "tongue" was evidence of God's judgment on the nation. God would rather speak to His people in clear language they could understand, but their repeated sins made this impossible. He *had* spoken to them through His messengers in their own tongue, and the nation would not repent. Now He had to speak in a foreign tongue, and this meant judgment.

As a nation, the Jews were always seeking a sign (Matt. 12:38; 1 Cor. 1:22). At Pentecost, the fact that the apostles spoke in tongues was a sign to the unbelieving Jews who were there celebrating the feast. The miracle of tongues aroused their interest, but it did not convict their hearts. It took Peter's preaching (in Aramaic, which the people all understood) to bring them to the place of conviction and conversion.

The principle of *edification* encourages us to major

on sharing the Word of God so that the church will be strengthened and grow. The principle of *understanding* reminds us that what we share must be understood if it is to do any good. The private use of spiritual gifts may edify the user, but it will not edify the church; and Paul admonished us to "excel to the edifying of the church" (1 Cor. 14:12).

But a third principle must be applied: the principle of order.

Order (14:26–40)

Two statements in this section go together: "Let all things be done unto edifying" (1 Cor. 14:26), and, "Let all things be done decently and in order" (1 Cor. 14:40). When a building is constructed, there must be a plan, or everything will be in chaos. I know of a church that had terrible problems building their parsonage, until someone discovered that the lumberyard had a different set of plans from that of the contractor. It was no wonder that the materials shipped to the site did not fit into the building!

The Corinthian church was having special problems with disorder in their public meetings (1 Cor. 11:17–23). The reason is not difficult to determine: They were using their spiritual gifts to please themselves and not to help their brethren. The key word was not *edification,* but *exhibition.* If you think that *your* contribution to the service is more important than your brother's contribution, then you will either be impatient until he finishes, or you will interrupt him. Add to this problem the difficulties caused by the "liberated women" in the assembly, and you can understand why the church experienced carnal confusion.

First Corinthians 14:26 gives us a cameo picture of worship in the early church. Each member was invited to participate as the Lord directed. One would want to sing a psalm (Eph. 5:19; Col. 3:16). Another would be led to share a doctrine. Someone might have a revelation that would be given in a tongue and then interpreted. Apart from some kind of God-given order, there could never be edification.

Note that the tongues speakers were the ones causing the most trouble, so Paul addressed himself to them and gave several instructions for the church to obey in their public meetings.

First, speaking and interpreting, along with judging (evaluating the message) must be done in an orderly manner (1 Cor. 14:27–33). There must not be more than three speakers at any one meeting, and each message must be interpreted and evaluated in order. If no interpreter was present, then the tongues speaker must keep silent. Paul's admonitions to the Thessalonian congregation would apply here: "Quench not the Spirit. Despise not prophesyings. Prove all things; hold fast that which is good" (1 Thess. 5:19–21).

Why were the messages evaluated? To determine whether the speaker had truly communicated the Word of God through the Holy Spirit. It was

possible for a speaker, under the control of his own emotions, to imagine that God was speaking to him and through him. It was even possible for Satan to counterfeit a prophetic message (see 2 Cor. 11:13–14). The listeners would test the message, then, by Old Testament Scriptures, apostolic tradition, and the personal guidance of the Spirit ("discerning of spirits," 1 Cor. 12:10).

If while a person is speaking, God gives a revelation to another person, the speaker must be silent while the new revelation is shared. If God is in charge, there can be no *competition* or *contradiction* in the messages. If, however, the various speakers are "manufacturing" their messages, there will be confusion and contradiction.

When the Holy Spirit is in charge, the various ministers will have self-control; for self-control is one fruit of the Spirit (Gal. 5:23). I once shared a Bible conference with a speaker who had "poor terminal facilities." He often went fifteen to twenty minutes past his deadline, which meant, of course, that I had to condense my messages at the last minute. He excused himself to me by saying, "You know, when the Holy Spirit takes over, you can't worry about clocks!" My reply was to quote 1 Corinthians 14:32: "And the spirits of the prophets are subject to the prophets."

Our own self-control is one of the evidences that the Spirit is indeed at work in the meeting. One of the ministries of the Spirit is to bring order out of chaos (Gen. 1). Confusion comes from Satan, not from God (James 3:13–18). When the Spirit is leading, the participants are able to minister "one by one" so that the total impact of God's message may be received by the church.

How do we apply this instruction to the church today since we do not have New Testament prophets, but we do have the completed Scripture? For one thing, we must use the Word of God to test every message that we hear, asking the Spirit to guide us. There are false teachers in the world and we must beware (2 Peter 2; 1 John 4:1–6). But even true teachers and preachers do not know everything and sometimes make mistakes (1 Cor. 13:9, 12; James 3:1). Each listener must evaluate the message and apply it to his own heart.

Our public meetings today are more formal than those of the early church, so it is not likely that we need to worry about the order of the service. But in our more informal meetings, we need to consider one another and maintain order. I recall being in a testimony meeting where a woman took forty minutes telling a boring experience and, as a result, destroyed the spirit of the meeting.

Evangelist D. L. Moody was leading a service and asked a man to pray. Taking advantage of his opportunity, the man prayed on and on. Sensing that the prayer was killing the meeting instead of blessing it, Moody spoke up and said, "While our brother finishes his prayer, let us sing a hymn!" Those who are in charge of public meetings need to have discernment—and courage.

Second, the women in the meeting were not to speak (1 Cor. 14:34–35). Paul had already permitted the women to pray and prophesy (1 Cor. 11:5), so this instruction must apply to the immediate context of evaluating the prophetic messages. It would appear that the major responsibility for doctrinal purity in the early church rested on the shoulders of the men, the elders in particular (1 Tim. 2:11–12).

The context of this prohibition would indicate that some of the women in the assembly were creating problems by asking questions and perhaps even generating arguments. Paul reminded the married women to be submitted to their husbands and to get their questions answered at home. (We assume that the unmarried women could counsel with the elders or with other men in their own families.) Sad to say, in too many Christian homes today, it is the wife who has to answer the questions for the husband because she is better taught in the Word.

What "law" was Paul referring to in 1 Corinthians 14:34? Probably Genesis 3:16. (The word *law* was a synonym for the Old Testament Scriptures, especially the first five books.) In 1 Corinthians 11, Paul had discussed the relationship of men and women in the church, so there was no need to go into detail.

Third, participants must beware of "new revelations" that go beyond the Word of God (1 Cor. 14:36–40). "To the law and to the testimony; if they speak not according to this word, it is because there is no light in them" (Isa. 8:20). The church had the Old Testament as well as the oral tradition given by the apostles (2 Tim. 2:2), and this was the standard by which all revelations would be tested. We today have the completed Scriptures as well as the accumulated teachings of centuries of church history to help us discern the truth. The historic evangelical creeds, while not inspired, do embody orthodox theology that can direct us.

In these verses, Paul was answering the church member who might say, "We don't need Paul's help! The Spirit speaks to us. We have received new and wonderful revelations from God!" This is a dangerous attitude, because it is the first step toward rejecting God's Word and accepting counterfeit revelations, including the doctrines of demons (1 Tim. 4:1ff.). "The Word did not originate in your congregation!" Paul replied. "One of the marks of a true prophet is his obedience to apostolic teaching." In this statement, Paul claimed that what he wrote was actually inspired Scripture, "the commandments of the Lord" (1 Cor. 14:37).

First Corinthians 14:38 does not suggest that Paul wanted people to remain ignorant; otherwise, he would not have written this letter and answered their questions. The New International Version translates it, "If he ignores this [Paul's apostolic authority], he himself will be ignored [by Paul and the churches]."

Fellowship is based on the Word, and those who willfully reject the Word automatically break the fellowship (1 John 2:18–19).

Paul summarized the main teachings of 1 Corinthians 14 in verses 39–40. Prophecy is more important than tongues, but the church should not prohibit the correct exercise of the gift of tongues. The purpose of spiritual gifts is the edification of the whole church, and therefore, gifts must be exercised in an orderly manner. Public worship must be carried on "in a seemly manner," that is, with beauty, order, and spiritual motivation and content.

Before leaving this chapter, it might be helpful to summarize what Paul wrote about the gift of tongues. It is the God-given ability to speak in a known language with which the speaker was not previously acquainted. The purpose was not to win the lost, but to edify the saved. Not every believer had this gift, nor was this gift an evidence of spirituality or the result of a "baptism of the Spirit."

Only three persons were permitted to speak in tongues in any one meeting, and they had to do so in order and with interpretation. If there was no interpreter, they had to keep silent. Prophecy is the superior gift, but tongues were not to be despised if they were exercised according to Scripture.

When the foundational work of the apostles and prophets ended, it would seem that the gifts of knowledge, prophecy, and tongues would no longer be needed. "Whether there be tongues, they shall cease" (1 Cor. 13:8). Certainly God could give this gift today if He pleased, but I am not prepared to believe that every instance of tongues is divinely energized. Nor would I go so far as to say that all instances of tongues are either satanic or self-induced.

It is unfortunate when believers make tongues a test of fellowship or spirituality. That in itself would alert me that the Spirit would not be at work. Let's keep our priorities straight and major on winning the lost and building the church.

CHAPTER TWELVE
1 Corinthians 15
BE WISE ABOUT THE RESURRECTION

Corinth was a Greek city, and the Greeks did not believe in the resurrection of the dead. When Paul had preached at Athens and declared the fact of Christ's resurrection, some of his listeners actually laughed at him (Acts 17:32). Most Greek philosophers considered the human body a prison, and they welcomed death as deliverance from bondage.

This skeptical attitude had somehow invaded the church, and Paul had to face it head-on. The truth of the resurrection had doctrinal and practical implications for life that were too important to ignore. Paul dealt with the subject by answering four basic questions.

Are the Dead Raised? (15:1–19)

It is important to note that the believers at Corinth did believe in the resurrection of Jesus Christ; so Paul started his argument with that fundamental truth. He presented three proofs to assure his readers that Jesus Christ indeed had been raised from the dead.

Proof #1—their salvation (vv. 1–2). Paul had come to Corinth and preached the message of the gospel, and their faith had transformed their lives. But an integral part of the gospel message was the fact of Christ's resurrection. After all, a dead Savior cannot save anybody. Paul's readers had received the Word, trusted Christ, been saved, and were now standing on that Word as the assurance of their salvation. The fact that they were standing firm was proof that their faith was genuine and not empty.

Proof #2—the Old Testament Scriptures (vv. 3–4). *First of all* means "of first importance." The gospel is the most important message that the church ever proclaims. While it is good to be involved in social action and the betterment of mankind, there is no reason why these ministries should preempt the gospel. "Christ died … He was buried … He rose again … He was seen" are the basic historical *facts* on which the gospel stands (1 Cor. 15:3–5). "Christ died *for our sins*" (author's italics) is the theological explanation of the historical facts. Many people were crucified by the Romans, but only one "victim" ever died for the sins of the world.

When Paul wrote "according to the Scriptures" (1 Cor. 15:3) he was referring to the Old Testament Scriptures. Much of the sacrificial system in the Old Testament pointed to the sacrifice of Christ as our substitute and Savior. The annual day of Atonement (Lev. 16) and prophecies like Isaiah 53 would also come to mind.

But where does the Old Testament declare His resurrection on the third day? Jesus pointed to the experience of Jonah (Matt. 12:38–41). Paul also compared Christ's resurrection to the "firstfruits," and the firstfruits were presented to God on the day following the Sabbath after Passover (Lev. 23:9–14; 1 Cor. 15:23). Since the Sabbath must always be the seventh day, the day after Sabbath must be the *first* day of the week, or Sunday, the day of our Lord's resurrection. This covers three days on the Jewish calendar. Apart from the Feast of Firstfruits, there were other prophecies of Messiah's resurrection in the Old Testament: Psalm 16:8–11 (see Acts 2:25–28); Psalm 22:22ff. (see Heb. 2:12); Isaiah 53:10–12; and Psalm 2:7 (see Acts 13:32–33).

Proof #3—Christ was seen by witnesses (vv. 5–11). On the cross, Jesus was exposed to the eyes of unbelievers; but after the resurrection, He was seen by believers who could be witnesses of His resurrection (Acts 1:22; 2:32; 3:15; 5:32). Peter saw Him and so did the disciples collectively. James was a half-brother of the Lord who became a believer after the Lord appeared to him (John 7:5; Acts 1:14). The five hundred *plus* brethren all saw Him at the same time (1 Cor. 15:6), so it could not have been a hallucination or a deception. This event may have been just before His ascension (Matt. 28:16ff.).

But one of the greatest witnesses of the resurrection was Paul himself, for as an unbeliever he was soundly convinced that Jesus was dead. The radical change in his life—a change that brought him persecution and suffering—is certainly evidence that the Lord had indeed been raised from the dead. Paul made it clear that his salvation was purely an act of God's grace; but that grace worked in and through him as he served the Lord. "Born out of due time" probably refers to the future salvation of Israel when they, like Paul, see the Messiah in glory (Zech. 12:10—13:6; 1 Tim. 1:16).

At this point, Paul's readers would say, "Yes, we agree that *Jesus* was raised from the dead." Then Paul would reply, "If you believe that, then you must believe in the resurrection of *all* the dead!" Christ came as a man, truly human, and experienced all that we experience, except that He never sinned. If there is no resurrection, then Christ was not raised. If He was not raised, there is no gospel to preach. If there is no gospel, then you have believed in vain and you are still in your sins! If there is no resurrection, then believers who have died have no hope. We shall never see them again!

The conclusion is obvious: Why be a Christian if we have only suffering in this life and no future glory to anticipate? (In 1 Cor. 15:29–34, Paul expanded this idea.) The resurrection is not just important; it is "of first importance," because all that we believe hinges on it.

When Are the Dead Raised? (15:20–28)

Paul used three images to answer this question.

Firstfruits (vv. 20, 23). We have already noted this reference to the Old Testament feast (Lev. 23:9–14). As the Lamb of God, Jesus died on Passover. As the sheaf of firstfruits, He arose from the dead three days later on the first day of the week. When the priest waved the sheaf of the firstfruits before the Lord, it was a sign that the entire harvest belonged to Him. When Jesus was raised from the dead, it was God's assurance to us that we shall also be raised one day as part of that future harvest. To believers, death is only "sleep." The body sleeps, but the soul is at home with the Lord (2 Cor. 5:1–8; Phil. 1:21–23). At the resurrection, the body will be "awakened" and glorified.

Adam (vv. 21–22). Paul saw in Adam a type of Jesus Christ *by the way of contrast* (see also Rom. 5:12–21). The first Adam was made from the earth, but the Last Adam (Christ, 1 Cor. 15:45–47) came from heaven. The first Adam disobeyed God and brought sin and death into the world, but the Last Adam obeyed the Father and brought righteousness and life.

The word *order* in 1 Corinthians 15:23 originally

referred to military rank. God has an order, a sequence, in the resurrection. Passages like John 5:25–29 and Revelation 20 indicate that there is no such thing taught in Scripture as a "general resurrection." When Jesus Christ returns in the air, He will take His church to heaven and at that time raise from the dead all who have trusted Him and have died in the faith (1 Thess. 4:13–18). Jesus called this "the resurrection of life" (John 5:29). When Jesus returns to the earth in judgment, then the lost will be raised in "the resurrection of damnation" (John 5:29; Rev. 20:11–15). Nobody in the first resurrection will be lost, but nobody in the second resurrection will be saved.

The kingdom (vv. 24–28). When Jesus Christ comes to the earth to judge, He will banish sin for a thousand years and establish His kingdom (Rev. 20:1–6). Believers will reign with Him and share His glory and authority. This kingdom, prophesied in the Old Testament, is called "the millennium" by prophetic teachers. The word comes from the Latin: *mille*—thousand, *annum*—year.

But even after the millennium, there will be one final rebellion against God (Rev. 20:7–10), which Jesus Christ will put down by His power. The lost will then be raised, judged, and cast into the lake of fire. Then death itself shall be cast into hell, and the last enemy shall be destroyed. Jesus Christ will have put all things under His feet! He will then turn the kingdom over to the Father and then the eternal state—the new heavens and new earth—shall be ushered in (Rev. 21—22).

Good and godly students of the Word have not always agreed on the details of God's prophetic program, but the major truths seem to be clear. Jesus Christ reigns in heaven today, and all authority is "under his feet" (Ps. 110; Eph. 1:15–23). Satan and man are still able to exercise choice, but God is sovereignly in control. Jesus Christ is enthroned in heaven today (Ps. 2). The resurrection of the saved has not yet taken place, nor the resurrection of the lost (2 Tim. 2:17–18).

When will Jesus Christ return for His church? Nobody knows; but when it occurs, it will be "in a moment, in the twinkling of an eye" (1 Cor. 15:52). It behooves us to be ready (1 John 2:28—3:3).

Why Are the Dead Raised? (15:29–34, 49–58)

The resurrection of the human body is a future event that has compelling implications for our personal lives. If the resurrection is not true, then we can forget about the future and live as we please! But the resurrection *is* true! Jesus *is* coming again! Even if we die before He comes, we shall be raised at His coming and stand before Him in a glorified body.

Paul cited four areas of Christian experience that are touched by the fact of the resurrection.

Evangelism (v. 29). What does it mean to be "baptized for the dead"? Some take this to mean "proxy baptism," where a believer is baptized on behalf of a dead relative; but we find no such teaching in the New Testament. In the second century, there were some heretical groups that practiced "vicarious baptism," but the church at large has never accepted the practice. To begin with, salvation is a personal matter that each must decide for himself; and, second, nobody needs to be baptized to be saved.

The phrase probably means "baptized to take the place of those who have died." In other words, if there is no resurrection, why bother to witness and win others to Christ? Why reach sinners who are then baptized and take the place of those who have died? If the Christian life is only a "dead-end street," get off of it!

Each responsible person on earth will share in either the resurrection of life and go to heaven, or the resurrection of judgment and go to hell (John 5:28–29). We weep for believers who have died, but we ought also to weep for unbelievers who still have opportunity to be saved! The reality of the resurrection is a motivation for evangelism.

Suffering (vv. 30–32). *I die daily* does not refer to "dying to self," as in Romans 6, but to the physical dangers Paul faced as a servant of Christ (2 Cor. 4:8—5:10; 11:23–28). He was in constant jeopardy from his enemies and on more than one occasion had been close to death. Why endure suffering and danger if death ends it all? "Let us eat and drink, for tomorrow we shall die" (Isa. 22:13).

What we do in the body in this life comes up for review at the judgment seat of Christ (2 Cor. 5:10). God deals with the *whole* person, not just with the "soul." The body shares in salvation (Rom. 8:18–23). The suffering endured in the body will result in glory at the resurrection (2 Cor. 4:7–18). If there is no future for the body, then why suffer and die for the cause of Christ?

Separation from sin (vv. 33–34). If there is no resurrection, then what we do with our bodies will have no bearing on our future. Immorality was a way of life in Corinth, and some of the believers rejected the resurrection in order to rationalize their sin. "Evil company corrupts good morals" is a quotation from the Greek poet Menander, a saying no doubt familiar to Paul's readers. The believer's body is the temple of God and must be kept separated from the sins of the world (2 Cor. 6:14—7:1). To fellowship with the "unfruitful works of darkness" (Eph. 5:6–17) is only to corrupt God's temple.

It was time for the Corinthians to *wake up* and *clean up* (see 1 Thess. 5:4–11). The believer who is compromising with sin has no witness to the lost around him, those who "have not the knowledge of God." What a shameful thing to be selfishly living in sin while multitudes die without Christ!

Death (vv. 49–57). The heavenly kingdom is not made for the kind of bodies we now have, bodies of flesh and blood. So when Jesus returns, the bodies of living believers will instantly be transformed to be like His body (1 John 3:1–3), and the dead believers shall be raised with new glorified bodies. Our new bodies will not be subject to decay or death.

Sigmund Freud, the founder of psychiatry, wrote, "And finally there is the painful riddle of death, for which no remedy at all has yet been found, nor probably ever will be." Christians have victory *in* death and *over* death! Why? Because of the victory of Jesus Christ in His own resurrection. Jesus said, "Because I live, ye shall also" (John 14:19).

Sin, death, and the law go together. The law reveals sin, and the "wages of sin is death" (Rom. 6:23). Jesus bore our sins on the cross (1 Peter 2:24), and also bore the curse of the law (Gal. 3:13). It is through Him that we have this victory, and we share the victory *today*. The literal translation of 1 Corinthians 15:57 is, "But thanks be to God who *keeps on giving us the victory* through our Lord Jesus Christ." We experience "the power of his resurrection" in our lives as we yield to Him (Phil. 3:10).

First Corinthians 15:58 is Paul's hymn of praise to the Lord, as well as his closing admonition to the church. Because of the assurance of Christ's victory over death, we know that nothing we do for Him will ever be wasted or lost. We can be steadfast in our service, unmovable in suffering, abounding in ministry to others, because we know our labor is not in vain. First Corinthians 15:58 is the answer to Ecclesiastes, where thirty-eight times Solomon used the sad word *vanity*. "Vanity of vanities, all is vanity!" wept Solomon; but Paul sang a song of victory!

How Are the Dead Raised? (15:35–48)

Being philosophers, the Greeks reasoned that the resurrection of the human body was an impossibility. After all, when the body turned to dust, it became soil from which other bodies derived nourishment. In short, the food that we eat is a part of the elements of the bodies of generations long gone. When the body of the founder of Rhode Island, Roger Williams, was disinterred, it was discovered that the roots of a nearby apple tree had grown through the coffin. To some degree, the people who ate the apples partook of his body. At the resurrection, then, who will claim the various elements?

Paul's reply to this kind of reasoning was very blunt: "You fool!" Then he made the important point that *resurrection is not reconstruction.* Nowhere does the Bible teach that, at the resurrection, God will "put together the pieces" and return to us our former bodies. There is *continuity* (it is *our* body), but there is not *identity* (it is not the *same* body).

Paul knew that such miracles cannot be explained, so he used three analogies to make the doctrine clear.

Seeds (vv. 35–38, 42–48). When you sow seed, you do not expect that same seed to come up at the harvest. The seed dies, but from that death there comes life. (See John 12:23–28 for our Lord's use of this same analogy.) You may sow a few grains of wheat, but you will have many grains when the plant

matures. Are they the same grains that were planted? No, but there is still continuity. You do not sow wheat and harvest barley.

Furthermore, what comes up at the harvest is usually more beautiful than what was planted. This is especially true of tulips. Few things are as ugly as a tulip bulb, yet it produces a beautiful flower. If at the resurrection, all God did was to put us back together again, there would be no improvement. Furthermore, flesh and blood cannot inherit God's kingdom. The only way we can enjoy the glory of heaven is to have a body suited to that environment.

Paul discussed the details of this marvelous change in 1 Corinthians 15:42–48. The body is sown (in burial) in corruption, because it is going to decay; but it is raised with such a nature that it cannot decay. There is no decay or death in heaven. It is buried in humility (in spite of the cosmetic skill of the mortician); but it is raised in glory. In burial, the body is weak; but in resurrection, the body has power. We shall be like Jesus Christ!

Today, we have a "natural body," that is, a body suited to an earthly environment. We received this body from our first parent, Adam: he was made of dust, and so are we (Gen. 2:7). But the resurrection body is suited to a spiritual environment. In His resurrection body, Jesus was able to move quickly from place to place, and even walk through locked doors; yet He was also able to eat food, and His disciples were able to touch Him and feel Him (Luke 24:33–43; John 20:19–29).

The point Paul was making was simply this: The resurrection body completes the work of redemption and gives to us the image of the Savior. We are made in the image of God as far as personality is concerned, but in the image of Adam as far as the body is concerned. One day we shall bear the image of the Savior when we share in His glory.

First Corinthians 15:46 states an important biblical principle: first the "natural" (earthly), and then the "spiritual" (heavenly). The first birth gives us that which is natural, but the second birth gives us that which is spiritual. God rejects the first birth, the natural, and says, "You must be born again!" He rejected Cain and chose Abel. He rejected Abraham's firstborn, Ishmael, and chose Isaac, the second-born. He rejected Esau and chose Jacob. If we depend on our first birth, we shall be condemned forever; but if we experience the new birth, we shall be blessed forever.

Flesh (v. 39). Paul anticipated here the discovery of science that the cell structure of different kinds of animals is different; and therefore, you cannot breed various species indiscriminately. The human body has a nature of one kind, while animals, birds, and fish have their own particular kind of flesh. The conclusion is this: If God is able to make different kinds of bodies for men, animals, birds, and fish, why can He not make a different kind of body for us at the resurrection? (Pet lovers take note: Paul did not teach here that animals will be resurrected. He only used them as an example.)

Heavenly bodies (vv. 40–41). Not only are there earthly bodies, but there are also heavenly bodies; and they differ from one another. In fact, the heavenly bodies differ from each other in glory as far as the human eye is concerned. Paul is suggesting here that believer may differ from believer in glory, even though all Christians will have glorified bodies. Every cup in heaven will be filled, but some cups will be bigger than others, because of the faithfulness and sacrifice of those saints when they were on earth.

These illustrations may not answer every question that we have about the resurrection body, but they do give us the assurances that we need. God will give to us a glorified body suited to the new life in heaven. It will be as unlike our present body in quality as the glory of the sun is unlike a mushroom in the cellar. We will use this new body to serve and glorify God for all eternity.

We must remember that this discussion was not written by Paul merely to satisfy the curiosity of believers. He had some practical points to get across, and he made them very clear in 1 Corinthians 15:29–34. If we really believe in the resurrection of the body, then we will use our bodies today to the glory of God (1 Cor. 6:9–14).

Finally, the lost will be given bodies suited to their environment in hell. They will suffer forever in darkness and pain (Matt. 25:41; 2 Thess. 1:7–10; Rev. 20:11–15). It behooves us who are saved to seek to rescue them from judgment! "Knowing therefore the terror of the Lord, we persuade men" (2 Cor. 5:11).

If you have never trusted the Savior, do so now—before it is too late!

CHAPTER THIRTEEN
1 Corinthians 16
BE WISE ABOUT CHRISTIAN STEWARDSHIP

It is to the credit of the believers at Corinth that, when they wrote their questions to Paul, they asked him about the collection he was taking for the poor saints in Jerusalem. Paul answered their question and then closed the letter by informing the church of his personal travel plans and also the plans for his associates in the ministry.

This chapter may seem unrelated to our needs today, but actually it deals in a very helpful way with three areas of stewardship: money (1 Cor. 16:1–4), opportunities (1 Cor. 16:5–9), and people (1 Cor. 16:10–24). These are probably the greatest resources the church has today, and they must not be wasted.

Money (16:1–4)
One of the most important ministries Paul had during his third journey was the gathering of a special "relief offering" for the poor believers in Jerusalem. He wanted to achieve several purposes in this offering. For one thing, the Gentiles owed material help to the Jews in return for the spiritual blessings the Jews had given them (Rom. 15:25–27). At the Jerusalem Conference years before, Paul had agreed to "remember the poor," so he was keeping his pledge (Gal. 2:10). Paul not only preached the gospel, but he also tried to assist those who had physical and material needs.

Why was there such a great need in the Jerusalem church? It is likely that many of the believers had been visiting Jerusalem at Pentecost when they heard the Word and were saved. This meant that they were strangers, without employment, and the church would have to care for them. In the early days of the church, the members had gladly shared with each other (Acts 2:41–47; 4:33–37); but even their resources were limited. There had also been a famine (Acts 11:27–30), and the relief sent at that time could not last for too long a time.

Apart from keeping his promise and meeting a great need, Paul's greatest motive for taking up the offering was to help unite Jewish and Gentile believers. Paul was a missionary to the Gentiles, and this bothered some of the Jewish believers (Acts 17:21–25). Paul hoped that this expression of Gentile love would help to heal some wounds and build some bridges between the churches. (For more information about this offering, read 2 Cor. 8—9.)

Even though this was a special missionary offering, from Paul's instructions we may learn some basic principles that relate to Christian stewardship.

Giving is an act of worship. Each member was to come to the Lord's Day gathering prepared to give his share for that week. The early church met on the first day of the week in commemoration of the resurrection of Jesus Christ (The Holy Spirit came on the church at Pentecost on the first day of the week.) It is tragic when church members give only as a duty and forget that our offerings are to be "spiritual sacrifices" presented to the Lord (Phil. 4:18). Giving should be an act of worship to the resurrected and ascended Savior.

Giving should be systematic. Some students have suggested that many people were paid on the first day of the week during that time in history. But even if they were not, each believer was to set aside his offering at home and then bring it to the assembly on the first day. Paul did not want to have to take up a number of collections when he arrived in Corinth. He wanted the whole contribution to be ready. If today's church members were as systematic in their giving as they are in handling their other financial matters, the work of the Lord would not suffer as it sometimes does.

Giving was personal and individual. Paul expected each member to share in the offering, the rich and poor alike. Anyone who had an income was privileged to share and to help those in need. He wanted all to share in the blessing.

Giving is to be proportionate. "As God hath prospered him" (1 Cor. 16:2) suggests that believers who have more should give more. The Jewish believers in the church would have been accustomed to the tithe, but Paul did not mention any special proportion. Certainly the tithe (10 percent of one's income) is a good place to *begin* our stewardship, but we must not remain at that level. As the Lord gives us more, we should plan to give more.

The trouble is, too many saints, as they earn more, involve themselves in more and more financial obligations; and then they do not have more to give to the Lord. Instead of finding a suitable "level" and remaining there, they keep trying to "go higher," and their income is *spent* rather than *invested*. As the old saying goes, "When your outgo exceeds your income, then your upkeep is your downfall."

Paul made it clear in 2 Corinthians 8—9 that Christian giving is a *grace,* the outflow of the grace of God in our lives and not the result of promotion or pressure. An open heart cannot maintain a closed hand. If we appreciate the grace of God extended to us, we will want to express that grace by sharing with others.

Money is to be handled honestly. The various churches involved in this special offering appointed delegates to help Paul manage it and take it safely to Jerusalem. (See 2 Cor. 8:16–24 for more information on the "finance committee" that assisted Paul.) It is unfortunate when Christian ministries lose their testimony because they mismanage funds entrusted to them. Every ministry ought to be businesslike in its financial affairs. Paul was very careful not to allow anything to happen that would give his enemies opportunity to accuse him of stealing funds (2 Cor. 8:20–21).

This explains why Paul encouraged the *churches* to share in the offering and to select dependable representatives to help manage it. Paul was not against *individuals* giving personally; in this chapter, as well as in Romans 16, he named various individuals who assisted him personally. This no doubt included helping him with his financial needs. But generally speaking, Christian giving is church-centered. Many churches encourage their members to give designated gifts through the church budget.

It is interesting that Paul mentioned the offering just after his discussion about the resurrection. There were no "chapter breaks" in the original manuscripts, so the readers would go right from Paul's hymn of victory into his discussion about money. Doctrine and duty go together; so do worship and works. Our giving is "not in vain" because our Lord is alive. It is His resurrection power that motivates us to give and to serve.

Opportunities (16:5–9)

"Be very careful, then, how you live—not as unwise but as wise, making the most of every opportunity, because the days are evil" (Eph. 5:15–16 NIV). Paul was as careful in his use of time as he was in his use of money. Someone has said that killing time is the chief occupation of modern society, but no Christian can afford to kill time or waste opportunities.

Paul informed his friends at Corinth of his plans for future travel and ministry. It is worth noting that his statements were very tentative: "It may be suitable … it may be … wherever I go … but I trust." Of course, the entire plan was dependent on God's providential leading: "if the Lord permit." Paul's attitude toward his future plans agreed with the injunctions in James 4:13–17.

Paul was at Ephesus when he wrote this letter. His plan was to travel to Macedonia for a time of ministry (*pass through* in 1 Cor. 16:5 means "travel in a systematic ministry"), winter at Corinth, and then go to Judea with the collection. From November to February, it was impossible to travel by ship; so it would have been convenient for Paul to stay at Corinth and be with his friends. There were some problems to solve in the church, and Paul had promised to come to help the leaders (1 Cor. 11:34).

However, various circumstances forced Paul to revise his plans at least twice. His plan B was to visit Corinth, then travel through Macedonia, passing through Corinth a second time on his way to Judea (2 Cor. 1:15–16). Instead of one long visit, he planned two shorter visits; but even this plan did not materialize. Plan C turned out to be a quick and painful visit to Corinth, after which he returned to Ephesus. He then went to Troas to wait for Titus (who had been sent to Corinth, 2 Cor. 2:12–13; 7:5ff.), visited Macedonia, and then went to Judea. He did not spend as much time at Corinth as he had hoped or as they had expected.

What do we learn from this difficult experience of Paul's? For one thing, a Christian must use his common sense, pray, study the situation, and seek the best he can to determine the will of God. Proverbs 3:5–6 ("lean not unto thine own understanding") must not be interpreted to mean "Put your brain in neutral and don't think!" God gave us our minds and He expects us to think, but He does not want us to *depend* only on our own reasoning. We must pray, meditate on the Word, and even seek the counsel of mature Christian friends.

Second, our decisions may not always be in the will of God. We may make promises that we cannot keep and plans that we cannot fulfill. Does this mean that we are liars or failures? (Some of the believers at Corinth thought Paul was deceptive and not to be trusted. See 2 Cor. 1:12—2:13.) In my own ministry, I have had to change my plans and alter my schedule because of situations over which I had no control. Did this mean I had been out of the will of God in making my plans? Not necessarily. Even an apostle (who had been to heaven and back) occasionally had to revise his datebook.

There are two extremes we must avoid in this

important matter of seeking God's will. One is to be so frightened at making a mistake that we make no decisions at all. The other is to make impulsive decisions and rush ahead, without taking time to wait on the Lord. After we have done all we can to determine the leading of the Lord, we must decide and act, and leave the rest to the Lord. If we are in some way out of His will, He will so work that we will finally have His guidance. The important thing is that we sincerely *want* to do His will (John 7:17). After all, He guides us "for his name's sake" (Ps. 23:3), and it is *His* reputation that is at stake.

Paul had an open door of ministry in Ephesus, and this was important to him. He wanted to win the lost in Ephesus, not go to Corinth to pamper the saved. (On "open doors," see Acts 14:27; 2 Cor. 2:12; Col. 4:3; Rev. 3:8.) Paul was neither an optimist nor a pessimist; he was a realist. He saw both the opportunities and the obstacles. God had opened "a great door for effective work," and Paul wanted to seize the opportunities while they were still there.

An ancient Roman proverb says, "While we stop to think, we often miss our opportunity." Once we know what to do, we must do it and not delay. We can usually think of many reasons (or excuses) not to act. Even though Paul was in danger in Ephesus (1 Cor. 15:32), he planned to remain there while the door was open. Like a wise merchant, he had to "buy up the opportunity" before it vanished and would never return.

The stewardship of opportunity is important. The individual believer, and the church family, must constantly ask, *What opportunities is God giving us today?* Instead of complaining about the obstacles, we must take advantage of the opportunities, and leave the results with the Lord.

People (16:10–24)

Often at the close of his letters, Paul named various people who were a part of his life and his ministry; and what a variety they were! He was not only a soul-winner, but he was a friend maker; and many of his friends found their way into dedicated service for the Lord. Evangelist Dwight L. Moody possessed this same gift of making friends and then enlisting them for the Lord's service. Some of the greatest preachers and musicians of the late nineteenth and early twentieth centuries were "found" by Moody, including Ira Sankey, G. Campbell Morgan, Henry Drummond, and F. B. Meyer.

Money and opportunities are valueless without people. The church's greatest asset is people, and yet too often the church takes people for granted. Jesus did not give His disciples money, but He did invest three years training them for service so they might seize the opportunities He would present them. If *people* are prepared, then God will supply both the *opportunities* and the *money* so that His work will be accomplished.

Timothy (vv. 10–11). Timothy, along with Titus, was one of Paul's special assistants, usually sent to the most difficult places. Timothy had been brought up in a godly home (2 Tim. 1:5), but it was Paul who had led the young man to Christ. Paul usually referred to him as "my own son in the faith" (1 Tim. 1:2). When John Mark abandoned Paul and returned to Jerusalem, it was Timothy who was called to work as Paul's assistant (Acts 16:1–5).

Timothy learned his lessons well and made great progress in Christian life and service (Phil. 2:20–22). Eventually, Timothy took Paul's place at Ephesus, a most difficult place to minister. (It would not be easy to be Paul's successor!) At one point, Timothy wanted to leave the city, but Paul encouraged him to stay (1 Tim. 1:3).

The advice Paul gave the Corinthians about Timothy (1 Cor. 16:10) would suggest that the young man had some physical and emotional problems (1 Tim. 5:23; 2 Tim. 1:4). He needed all the encouragement he could get. The important thing was that he was doing God's work and laboring with God's servant. A church should not expect every servant of God to be an apostle Paul. Young men starting out in service have great potential, and the church should encourage them. "Let no man despise thee!"

Apollos (vv. 12–14). Apollos was an eloquent Jew who was brought into the full understanding of the gospel by Priscilla and Aquila (Acts 18:24–28). He had ministered with great power at Corinth, and there was a segment of the church there that felt attached to him (1 Cor. 1:12; 3:4–8). It is unlikely that Apollos promoted this division, for his great concern seemed to be to preach Christ. In spite of the division ("The Apollos Fan Club"), Paul did not hesitate to encourage Apollos to return to Corinth for further ministry. It is clear that there was no envy on Paul's part or sense of competition on the part of Apollos.

Paul did not have the authority to place men against their will. Apollos did not feel he should go to Corinth at that time, and Paul had to concur with his decision. It is wonderful the way these different men worked together.

Perhaps it was in the light of the divisions in the church that Paul gave the admonitions in 1 Corinthians 16:13–14. *Watch* simply means "Be alert! Be vigilant!" The enemy is always at hand, and we are never safe from attack. Satan would certainly attack the church and try to hinder the ministry of Timothy or Apollos.

To *stand fast in the faith* means to have mature stability. Paul had already warned them that they were immature children who needed to grow up (1 Cor. 3:1ff.). No wonder Paul added, *Quit you like men,* which means, "Act like men, not children." (The word *quit* is short for "acquit"—to perform or act.) It was a call to courageous manliness at an hour when mature leadership was needed.

But even manliness needs to be balanced with love, lest leadership become dictatorship. Paul had expounded the value and virtues of love in 1 Corinthians 13. Carl

Sandburg, when addressing the United States Congress, said that Abraham Lincoln was a man of "velvet steel." That is a good image for the Christian to borrow, for true manliness does not exclude tenderness.

Stephanas and his household (vv. 15–18). These were the first people to be won to Christ in Achaia, and Paul had baptized them himself, instead of leaving it to one of his helpers (1 Cor. 1:16). They became important leaders in the church, for they "devoted themselves" to Christ's service. The verb means "they appointed themselves," but it does not suggest that they pushed their way into leadership. Rather, whenever they saw a need, they went to work to meet it without waiting to be asked. They were Paul's helpers, and they labored ("toiled to the point of exhaustion") for the Lord. What a wonderful thing it is when an entire family serves the Lord faithfully in the local church.

Stephanas was joined by Fortunatus and Achaicus as an official committee sent from Corinth to Ephesus to confer with Paul about church problems. Paul saw in them a representation of the entire church; their love to Paul compensated for Paul's absence from Corinth. But these men did more than share problems with Paul; they also refreshed his spirit and brought him blessing.

This is a good place to encourage church members to refresh and encourage their pastor. Too often, believers share only problems and burdens with their spiritual leaders, and rarely share the blessings. Who is the pastor's pastor? To whom does the pastor turn for spiritual refreshment and encouragement? Every church member, if he will, can help refresh the pastor and make his burdens lighter.

Paul encouraged the church to honor this very special family and submit to their spiritual leadership. It is right to honor faithful Christians if God gets the glory.

Aquila and Priscilla (vv. 19–20). These two were a dedicated husband-and-wife team whose lives and ministries intersected and intertwined with Paul's. The apostle met them at Corinth because, like Paul, they were tentmakers (Acts 18:1–3). This godly couple had been expelled from Rome because Aquila was a Jew; but that was only part of God's providence to get them to Corinth where they could assist Paul.

Priscilla must have been a remarkable woman. This couple's names occur in the New Testament six times, and in four of these instances, Priscilla's name stands first. (The best texts put Priscilla first in Acts 18:26.) We get the impression that she was the stronger of the two, a devoted leader and witness. They worked together in serving the Lord and helping Paul.

When Paul moved from Corinth to Ephesus, Aquila and Priscilla packed up and moved their business with him and assisted in founding the church in that needy city (Acts 18:18ff.). So capable were they that Paul left them to oversee the ministry while he returned to Antioch. It was while they were at Ephesus that they assisted Apollos in better understanding the truth of the gospel.

Every local church can be thankful for husbands and wives like Aquila and Priscilla, people who work together in serving the Lord and helping the preacher. The fact that his wife was a better leader did not hinder Aquila from standing with her in their united ministry. (I am sure that Priscilla submitted to her husband and did not try to act important.) One of the Ephesian assemblies met in their house, which shows they were people given to hospitality. Romans 16:4 states that, at one time, this dedicated couple risked their own lives to help save Paul. (See Acts 19:29–30; 20:19 for possible situations where this rescue might have occurred.)

But Priscilla and Aquila did not remain in Ephesus; for when Paul wrote to the saints at Rome, he greeted this couple there (Rom. 16:3). Once again, they had a church meeting in their house (Rom. 16:5). In my itinerant ministry, I have more than once preached to an assembly that had been founded in somebody's living room.

In Paul's last letter, he sent greetings to Prisca (alternate spelling) and Aquila by way of Timothy, who was then overseeing the work in Ephesus (2 Tim. 4:19). This remarkable couple had left Rome and were now back in Ephesus, this time to assist Timothy as they had assisted Paul.

How many couples today would move as often as did Priscilla and Aquila, just to be able to serve the Lord better? And whenever they moved, they had to move their business as well. People with this kind of dedication and sacrifice are not easy to find, but they are great assets to the local church.

Paul's closing words need not detain us. The "holy kiss" (1 Cor. 16:20) was a common mode of greeting, the men kissing the men and the women kissing the women (Rom. 16:16; 2 Cor. 13:12; 1 Thess. 5:26; 1 Peter 5:14). If Paul were writing to Western churches, he would say, "Shake hands with one another."

Paul usually dictated his letters and then took the pen and added his signature. He also added his "benediction of grace" as a mark that the letter was authentic (see Gal. 6:11; 2 Thess. 3:17).

The word *anathema* is Aramaic and means "accursed" (see 1 Cor. 12:3). Not to love Christ means not to believe in Him, and unbelievers are accursed (John 3:16–21). The word *maranatha* is Greek and means "our Lord comes" or (as a prayer) "our Lord, come!" (see Rev. 22:20). If a person loves Jesus Christ, he will also love His appearing (2 Tim. 4:8).

Paul had been stern with the Corinthian believers, but he closed his letter by assuring them of his love. After all, "Faithful are the wounds of a friend" (Prov. 27:6).

Paul has shared a great deal of spiritual wisdom with us. May we receive it with meekness and put it into practice to the glory of God!

2 CORINTHIANS

OUTLINE

Key theme: God's encouragement
Key verses: 2 Corinthians 4:1, 6

I. PAUL EXPLAINS HIS MINISTRY (1—7)
    A. Triumphant—1—2
    B. Glorious—3
    C. Sincere—4
    D. Believing—5
    E. Loving—6—7

II. PAUL ENCOURAGES THEIR GENEROSITY— (8—9)
(He was receiving an offering for the Jewish saints.)
    A. Principles of "grace giving"—8
    B. Promises for "grace givers"—9

III. PAUL ENFORCES HIS AUTHORITY (10—13)
    A. The warrior, attacking the opposition—10
    B. The spiritual father, protecting the church—11:1–15
    C. The "fool," boasting of suffering—11:16—12:10
    D. The apostle, exercising loving authority—12:11—13:14

CONTENTS

CHAPTER ONE
2 Corinthians 1:1–11
DOWN—BUT NOT OUT!

"**Y**ou seem to imagine that I have no ups and downs, but just a level and lofty stretch of spiritual attainment with unbroken joy and equanimity. By no means! I am often perfectly wretched and everything appears most murky."

So wrote the man who was called in his day "The Greatest Preacher in the English-speaking World"—Dr. John Henry Jowett. He pastored leading churches, preached to huge congregations, and wrote books that were bestsellers.

"I am the subject of depressions of spirit so fearful that I hope none of you ever get to such extremes of wretchedness as I go to."

Those words were spoken in a sermon by Charles Haddon Spurgeon whose marvelous ministry in London made him perhaps the greatest preacher England ever produced.

Discouragement is no respecter of persons. In fact, discouragement seems to attack the successful far more than the unsuccessful; for the higher we climb, the farther down we can fall. We are not surprised then when we read that the great apostle Paul was "pressed out of measure" and "despaired even of life" (2 Cor. 1:8). Great as he was in character and ministry, Paul was human just like the rest of us.

Paul could have escaped these burdens except that he had a call from God (2 Cor. 1:1) and a concern to help people. He had founded the church at Corinth and had ministered there for a year and a half (Acts 18:1–18). When serious problems arose in the church after his departure, he sent Timothy to deal with them (1 Cor. 4:17) and then wrote the letter that we call 1 Corinthians.

Unfortunately, matters grew worse, and Paul had to make a "painful visit" to Corinth to confront the troublemakers (2 Cor. 2:1ff.). Still, no solution. He then wrote "a severe letter," which was delivered by his associate Titus (2 Cor. 2:4–9; 7:8–12). After a great deal of distress, Paul finally met Titus and got the good report that the problem had been solved. It was then that he wrote the letter we call 2 Corinthians.

He wrote the letter for several reasons. First, he wanted to encourage the church to forgive and restore the member who had caused all the trouble (2 Cor. 2:6–11). He also wanted to explain his change in plans (2 Cor. 1:15–22) and enforce his authority as an apostle (2 Cor. 4:1–2; 10–12). Finally, he wanted to encourage the church to share in the special "relief offering" he was taking up for the needy saints in Judea (2 Cor. 8—9).

One of the key words in this letter is *comfort* or *encouragement.* The Greek word means "called to one's side to help." The verb is used eighteen times in this letter, and the noun eleven times. In spite of all the trials he experienced, Paul was able (by the grace of God) to write a letter saturated with encouragement.

What was Paul's secret of victory when he was experiencing pressures and trials? His secret was God. When you find yourself discouraged and ready to quit, get your attention off of yourself and focus it on God. Out of his own difficult experience, Paul tells us how we can find encouragement in God. He gives us three simple reminders.

Remember What God Is to You (1:3)
Paul began his letter with a doxology. He certainly could not sing about his circumstances, but he could sing about the God who is in control of all circumstances. Paul had learned that praise is an important factor in achieving victory over discouragement and depression. "Praise changes things" just as much as "Prayer changes things."

Praise Him because He is God! You find this phrase "blessed be God" in two other places in the New Testament, in Ephesians 1:3 and 1 Peter 1:3. In Ephesians 1:3 Paul praised God for what He did in the past, when He "chose us in [Christ]" (Eph. 1:4) and blessed us "with all spiritual blessings" (NASB). In 1 Peter 1:3 Peter praised God for future blessings and "a living hope" (NASB). But in 2 Corinthians Paul praised God for present blessings, for what God was accomplishing then and there.

During the horrors of the Thirty Years' War, Pastor Martin Rinkart faithfully served the people in Eilenburg, Saxony. He conducted as many as forty funerals a day, a total of over four thousand during his ministry. Yet out of this devastating experience, he wrote a "table grace" for his children, which today we use as a hymn of thanksgiving:

Now thank we all our God,
With heart and hands and voices,
Who wondrous things hath done,
In whom His world rejoices!

Praise Him because He is the Father of our Lord Jesus Christ! It is because of Jesus Christ that we can call God "Father" and even approach Him as His children. God sees us in His Son and loves us as He loves His Son (John 17:23). We are "beloved of God" (Rom. 1:7) because we are "accepted in the beloved" (Eph. 1:6).

Whatever the Father did for Jesus when He was ministering on earth, He is able to do for us today. We are dear to the Father because His Son is dear to Him and we are citizens of "the kingdom of his dear Son [the Son of his love]" (Col. 1:13). We are precious to the Father, and He will see to it that the pressures of life will not destroy us.

Praise Him because He is the Father of mercies! To the Jewish people, the phrase *father of* means "originator of." Satan is the father of lies (John 8:44) because lies originated with him. According to Genesis 4:21, Jubal was the father of musical instruments because he originated the pipe and the harp. God is the Father of mercies because all mercy originates with Him and can be secured only from Him.

God in His grace gives us what we do not deserve, and in His mercy He does not give us what we do deserve. "It is of the Lord's mercies that we are not consumed" (Lam. 3:22). God's mercy is *manifold* (Neh. 9:19), *tender* (Ps. 25:6), and *great* (Num. 14:19). The Bible frequently speaks of the "multitude of God's mercies" so inexhaustible is the supply (Ps. 5:7; 51:1; 69:13, 16; 106:7, 45; Lam. 3:32).

Praise Him because He is the God of all comfort! The words *comfort* or *consolation* (same root word in the Greek) are repeated ten times in 2 Corinthians 1:1–11. We must not think of *comfort* in terms of "sympathy," because sympathy can weaken us instead of strengthen us. God does not pat us on the head and give us a piece of candy or a toy to distract our attention from our troubles. No, He puts strength into our hearts so we can face our trials and triumph over them. Our English word *comfort* comes from two Latin words meaning "with strength." The Greek word means "to come alongside and help." It is the same word used for the Holy Spirit ("the Comforter") in John 14—16.

God can encourage us by His Word and through His Spirit, but sometimes He uses other believers to give us the encouragement we need (2 Cor. 2:7–8; 7:6–7). How wonderful it would be if all of us had the nickname "Barnabas—son of encouragement" (Acts 4:36)!

When you find yourself discouraged because of difficult circumstances, it is easy to look at yourself and your feelings, or to focus on the problems around you. But the first step we must take is to look by faith to the Lord and realize all that God is to us. "I will lift up mine eyes unto the hills, from whence cometh my help. My help cometh from the Lord, which made heaven and earth" (Ps. 121:1–2).

Remember What God Does for You (1:4a, 8–11)

He permits the trials to come. There are ten basic words for suffering in the Greek language, and Paul used five of them in this letter. The most frequently used word is *thlipsis,* which means "narrow, confined, under pressure," and in this letter is translated "affliction" (2 Cor. 2:4; 4:17), "tribulation" (2 Cor. 1:4), and "trouble" (2 Cor. 1:4, 8). Paul felt hemmed in by difficult circumstances, and the only way he could look was up.

In 2 Corinthians 1:5–6, Paul used the word *pathêma,* "suffering," which was also used for the sufferings of our Savior (1 Peter 1:11; 5:1). There are some sufferings that we endure simply because we are human and subject to pain; but there are other sufferings that come because we are God's people and want to serve Him.

We must never think that trouble is an accident. For the believer, everything is a divine appointment. There are only three possible outlooks a person can take when it comes to the trials of life. If our trials are the products of "fate" or "chance," then our only recourse is to give up. Nobody can control fate or chance. If *we* have to control everything ourselves, then the situation is equally as hopeless. But if *God* is in control, and we trust Him, then we can overcome circumstances with His help.

God encourages us in all our tribulations by teaching us from His Word that it is He who permits trials to come.

He is in control of trials (v. 8). "We were under great pressure, far beyond our ability to endure, so that we despaired even of life" (NIV). Paul was weighed down like a beast of burden with a load too heavy to bear. But God knew just how much Paul could take, and He kept the situation in control.

We do not know what the specific "trouble" was, but it was great enough to make Paul think he was going to die. Whether it was peril from his many enemies (see Acts 19:21ff.; 1 Cor. 15:30–32), serious illness, or special satanic attack, we do not know; but we do know that God controlled the circumstances and protected His servant. When God puts His children into the furnace, He keeps His hand on the thermostat and His eye on the thermometer (1 Cor. 10:13; 1 Peter 1:6–7). Paul may have despaired of life, but God did not despair of Paul.

God enables us to bear our trials (v. 9). The first thing He must do is show us how weak we are in ourselves. Paul was a gifted and experienced servant of God, who had been through many different kinds of trials (see 2 Cor. 4:8–12; 11:23ff.). Surely all of this experience would be sufficient for him to face these new difficulties and overcome them.

But God wants us to trust *Him*—not our gifts or abilities, our experience, or our "spiritual reserves." Just about the time we feel self-confident and able to meet the enemy, we fail miserably. "For when I am weak, then am I strong" (2 Cor. 12:10).

When you and I die to self, then God's resurrection power can go to work. It was when Abraham and Sarah were as good as dead physically that God's resurrection power enabled them to have the promised son (Rom. 4:16–25). However, "dying to self" does not mean idle complacency, doing nothing and expecting God to do everything. You can be sure that Paul prayed, searched the Scriptures, consulted with his associates, and trusted God to work. The God who raises the dead is sufficient for *any* difficulty of life! He is able, but we must be available.

Paul did not deny the way he felt, nor does God want us to deny our emotions. "We were troubled on every side; without were fightings, within were fears" (2 Cor. 7:5). The phrase "sentence of death" in 2 Corinthians 1:9 could refer to an official verdict, perhaps an order for Paul's arrest and execution. Keep in mind that the unbelieving Jews hounded Paul's trail and wanted to eliminate him (Acts 20:19). "Perils by my own countrymen" must not be overlooked in the list of dangers (2 Cor. 11:26).

God delivers us from our trials (v. 10). Paul saw God's hand of deliverance whether he looked back, around, or ahead. The word Paul used means "to help out of distress, to save and protect." God does not always deliver us immediately, nor in the same way. James was beheaded, yet Peter was delivered from prison (Acts 12). *Both* were delivered, but in different ways. Sometimes God delivers us *from* our trials, and at other times He delivers us *in* our trials.

God's deliverance was in response to Paul's faith, as well as to the faith of praying people in Corinth (2 Cor. 1:11). "This poor man cried, and the Lord heard him, and saved him out of all his troubles" (Ps. 34:6).

God is glorified through our trials (v. 11). When Paul reported what God had done for him, a great chorus of praise and thanksgiving went up from the saints to the throne of God. The highest service you and I can render on earth is to bring glory to God, and sometimes that service involves suffering. "The gift bestowed" refers to Paul's deliverance from death, a wonderful gift indeed!

Paul was never ashamed to ask Christians to pray for him. In at least seven of his letters, he mentioned his great need for prayer support (Rom. 15:30–32; Eph. 6:18–19; Phil. 1:19; Col. 4:3; 1 Thess. 5:25; 2 Thess. 3:1; Philem. 22). Paul and the believers in Corinth were helping each other (2 Cor. 1:11, 24).

A missionary friend told me about the miraculous deliverance of his daughter from what was diagnosed as a fatal disease. At the very time the girl was so ill, several friends in the United States were praying for the family; and God answered prayer and healed the girl. The greatest help we can give to God's servants is "helping together by prayer."

The word *sunupourgeo* translated "helping together" is used only here in the Greek New Testament and is composed of three words: *with, under, work.* It is a picture of laborers under the burden, working together to get the job accomplished. It is encouraging to know that the Holy Spirit also assists us in our praying and helps to carry the load (Rom. 8:26).

God works out His purposes in the trials of life, if we yield to Him, trust Him, and obey what He tells us to do. Difficulties can increase our faith and strengthen our prayer lives. Difficulties can draw us closer to other Christians as they share the burdens with us. Difficulties can be used to glorify God. So, when you find yourself in the trials of life, remember what God is to you and what God does for you.

Remember What God Does through You (1:4b–7)

In times of suffering, most of us are prone to think only of ourselves and to forget others. We become cisterns instead of channels. Yet one reason for trials is so that you and I might learn to be channels of blessing to comfort and encourage others. Because God has encouraged us, we can encourage them.

One of my favorite preachers is Dr. George W. Truett, who pastored the First Baptist Church of Dallas, Texas, for nearly fifty years. In one of his sermons, he told about an unbelieving couple whose baby died suddenly. Dr. Truett conducted the funeral and later had the joy of seeing them both trust Jesus Christ.

Many months later, a young mother lost her baby; and again, Dr. Truett was called to bring her comfort. But nothing he shared with her seemed to help her. But at the funeral service, the newly converted mother stepped to the girl's side and said, "I passed through this, and I know what you are passing through. God called me, and through the darkness I came to Him. He has comforted me, and He will comfort you!"

Dr. Truett said, "The first mother did more for the second mother than I could have done, maybe in days and months; for the first young mother had traveled the road of suffering herself."

However, Paul made it clear that we do not need to experience *exactly* the same trials in order to be able to share God's encouragement. If we have experienced God's comfort, then we can "comfort them which are in any trouble" (2 Cor. 1:4b). Of course, if we have experienced similar tribulations, they can help us identify better with others and know better how they feel; but our experiences cannot alter the comfort of God. That remains sufficient and efficient no matter what our own experiences may have been.

Later in 2 Corinthians 12, Paul will give us an example of this principle. He was given a "thorn in the flesh"—some kind of physical suffering that constantly buffeted him. We do not know what this thorn in the flesh was, nor do we need to know. What we do know is that Paul experienced the grace of God and then shared that encouragement with us. No matter what your trial may be, "My grace is sufficient for thee" (2 Cor. 12:9) is a promise you can claim. We would not have that promise if Paul had not suffered.

The subject of human suffering is not easy to understand, for there are mysteries to the working of God that we will never grasp until we get to heaven. Sometimes we suffer because of our own sin and rebellion, as did Jonah. Sometimes we suffer to keep us from sinning, as was the case with Paul (2 Cor. 12:7). Suffering can perfect our character (Rom. 5:1–5) and help us to share the character of God (Heb. 12:1–11).

But suffering can also help us to minister to others. In every church, there are mature saints of God who have suffered and experienced God's grace, and they are the great "encouragers" in the congregation. Paul experienced trouble, not as punishment for something he had done, but as preparation for something he was yet *going to do*—minister to others in need. Just think of the trials that King David had to endure in order to give us the great encouragement that we find in the Psalms.

Second Corinthians 1:7 makes it clear that there was always the possibility that the situation might be reversed: the Corinthian believers might go through trials and receive God's grace so that they might encourage others. God sometimes calls a church family to experience special trials in order that He might bestow on them special abundant grace.

God's gracious encouragement helps us *if we learn to endure.* "Patient endurance" is an evidence of faith. If we become bitter or critical of God, if we rebel instead of submit, then our trials will work *against* us instead of *for* us. The ability to endure difficulties patiently, without giving up, is a mark of spiritual maturity (Heb. 12:1–7).

God has to work *in* us before He can work *through* us. It is much easier for us to grow in knowledge than to grow in grace (2 Peter 3:18). Learning God's truth and getting it into our heads is one thing, but living God's truth and getting it into our character is quite something else. God put young Joseph through thirteen years of tribulation before He made him second ruler of Egypt, and what a great man Joseph turned out to be! God always prepares us for what He is preparing for us, and a part of that preparation is suffering.

In this light, 2 Corinthians 1:5 is very important: even our Lord Jesus Christ had to suffer! When we suffer in the will of God, we are sharing the sufferings of the Savior. This does not refer to His "vicarious sufferings" on the cross, for only He could die as a sinless substitute for us (1 Peter 2:21–25). Paul was referring here to "the fellowship of his sufferings" (Phil. 3:10), the trials that we endure because, like Christ, we are faithfully doing the Father's will. This is suffering "for righteousness' sake" (Matt. 5:10–12).

But as the sufferings increase, so does the supply of God's grace. The word *abound* suggests the picture of a river overflowing. "But he giveth more grace" (James 4:6). This is an important principle to grasp: God has ample grace for our every need, *but He will not bestow it in advance.* We come by faith to the throne of grace "that we may obtain mercy, and find grace to help in time of need" (Heb. 4:16). The Greek word means "help when you need it, timely help."

I read about a devoted believer who was arrested for his faith and condemned to be burned at the stake. The night before the execution, he wondered if he would have enough grace to become a human torch; so he tested his courage by putting his finger into the flame of the candle. Of course, it burned him and he pulled his hand back in pain. He was certain that he would never be able to face martyrdom without failing. But the next day, God gave him the grace he needed, and he had a joyful and triumphant witness before his enemies.

Now we can better understand 2 Corinthians 1:9; for, if we could store up God's grace for emergency use, we would be prone to trust ourselves and not "the God of all grace" (1 Peter 5:10). All the resources God gives us may be kept for future use—money, food, knowledge, and so forth—but the grace of God cannot be stored away.

Rather, as we experience the grace of God in our daily lives, it is *invested into our lives as godly character* (see Rom. 5:1–5). This investment pays dividends when new troubles come our way, for godly character enables us to endure tribulation to the glory of God.

There is a "companionship" to suffering: it can draw us closer to Christ and to His people. But if we start to wallow in self-pity, suffering will create isolation instead of involvement We will build walls and not bridges.

The important thing is to fix your attention on God and not on yourself. Remember *what God is to you*—"the Father of our Lord Jesus Christ, the Father of mercies, and the God of all comfort" (2 Cor. 1:3). Remember *what God does for you*—that He is able to handle your trials and make them work out for your good and His glory. Finally, remember *what God does through you*—and let Him use you to be an encouragement to others.

CHAPTER TWO
2 Corinthians 1:12—2:17
YOU DON'T HAVE TO FAIL!

In his book *Profiles in Courage,* John F. Kennedy wrote, "Great crises produce great men and great deeds of courage." While it is true that a crisis helps to make a person, it is also true that a crisis helps to reveal what a person is made of. Pilate faced a great crisis, but his handling of it did not give him either courage or greatness. How we handle the difficulties of life will depend largely on what kind of character we have; for what life does to us depends on what life finds in us.

In this very personal letter, Paul opened his heart to the Corinthians (and to us) and revealed the trials he had experienced. To begin with, he had been severely criticized by some of the people in Corinth because he had changed his plans and apparently not kept his promise. When Christians misunderstand each other, the wounds can go very deep. Then, there was the problem of opposition to his apostolic authority in the church. One of the members—possibly a leader—had to be disciplined, and this gave Paul great sorrow. Finally, there were the difficult circumstances Paul had to endure in Asia (2 Cor. 1:8–11), a trial so severe that he despaired of life.

What kept Paul from failing? Other people, facing these same crises, would have collapsed! Yet Paul not only triumphed over the circumstances, but out of them produced a great letter that even today is helping God's people experience victory. What were the spiritual resources that kept Paul going?

A Clear Conscience (1:12–24)
Our English word *conscience* comes from two Latin words: *com,* meaning "with," and *scire,* meaning "to know." Conscience is that inner faculty that "knows with" our spirit and approves when we do right, but accuses when we do wrong. Conscience is not the law

of God, but it bears witness to that law. It is the window that lets in the light; and if the window gets dirty because we disobey, then the light becomes dimmer and dimmer (see Matt. 6:22–23; Rom. 2:14–16).

Paul used the word *conscience* twenty-three times in his letters and spoken ministry as given in Acts. "And herein do I exercise myself, to have always a conscience void of offense toward God, and toward men" (Acts 24:16). When a person has a good conscience, he has integrity, not duplicity; and he can be trusted.

Why were the Corinthians accusing Paul of deception and carelessness? Because he had been forced to change his plans. He had originally promised to spend the winter in Corinth "if the Lord permit" (1 Cor. 16:2–8). Paul wanted to gather the offerings that the Corinthians collected for the poor Jewish believers and give the church the privilege of sending him and his associates on their way to Jerusalem.

Much to Paul's regret and embarrassment, he had to change those plans. I sympathize with him, for in my own limited ministry I have sometimes had to change plans and even cancel meetings—and without benefit of apostolic authority! "Plans get you into things," said Will Rogers, "but you have to work your way out." Paul now planned to make *two* visits to Corinth, one on his way into Macedonia, and the other on his way from Macedonia. He would then add the Corinthian collection to that of the Macedonian churches and go on his way to Jerusalem.

Alas, even Plan B had to be scrapped. Why? Because his own loving heart could not endure another "painful visit" (2 Cor. 1:23; 2:1–3). Paul had informed the church about his change in plans, but even this did not silence the opposition. They accused him of following "fleshly wisdom" (2 Cor. 1:12), of being careless with the will of God (2 Cor. 1:17), and of making plans just to please himself. They were saying, "If Paul says or writes one thing, he really means another! His yes is no, and his no is yes."

Misunderstandings among God's people are often very difficult to untangle, because one misunderstanding often leads to another. Once we start to question the integrity of others or distrust their words, the door is opened to all kinds of problems. But, no matter what his accusers might say, Paul stood firm because he had a clear conscience. What he wrote, what he said, and what he lived were all in agreement. And, after all, he had added to his original plan "if the Lord permit" (1 Cor. 16:7; and note James 4:13–17).

When you have a clear conscience, you will live in the light of the return of Jesus Christ (v. 14). "The day of Jesus Christ" refers to that time when Christ appears and takes His church to heaven. Paul was certain that, at the judgment seat of Christ, he would rejoice over the Corinthian believers and they would rejoice over him. Whatever misunderstandings there may be today, when we stand before Jesus Christ, all will be forgiven, forgotten, and transformed into glory, to the praise of Jesus Christ.

When you have a clear conscience, you will be serious about the will of God (vv. 15–18). Paul did not make his plans carelessly or haphazardly; he sought the leading of the Lord. Sometimes he was not sure what God wanted him to do (Acts 16:6–10), but he knew how to wait on the Lord. His motives were sincere: he was seeking to please the Lord and not men. When we stop to consider how difficult both transportation and communication were in that day, we can marvel that Paul did not have *more* problems with his busy schedule.

Jesus instructed us to mean what we say. "Say just a simple, 'Yes, I will' or 'No, I won't.' Your word is enough. To strengthen your promise with a vow shows that something is wrong" (Matt. 5:37 TLB). Only a person with bad character uses extra words to strengthen his yes or no. The Corinthians knew that Paul was a man of true character, because he was a man with a clear conscience. During his eighteen months of ministry among them, Paul had proved himself faithful; and he had not changed.

When you have a clear conscience, you glorify Jesus Christ (vv. 19–20). You cannot glorify Christ and practice deception at the same time. If you do, you will violate your conscience and erode your character; but eventually the truth will come out. The Corinthians were saved because Paul and his friends preached Jesus Christ to them. How could God reveal truth *through false instruments?* The witness and the walk of the minister must go together, for the work that we do flows out of the lives that we live.

There is no yes-and-no about Jesus Christ. He is God's "eternal yes" to those who trust Him. "For no matter how many promises God has made, they are yes in Christ. And so through him the Amen is spoken by us to the glory of God" (2 Cor. 1:20 NIV). Jesus Christ reveals the promises, fulfills the promises, and enables us to claim the promises! One of the blessings of a good conscience is that we are not afraid to face God or men, or to claim the promises God gives in His Word. Paul was not guilty of "manipulating" the Word of God in order to support his own sinful practices (see 2 Cor. 4:2).

Finally, when you have a clear conscience, you will be on good terms with the Spirit of God (vv. 21–24). The word *established* is a business term and refers to the guarantee of the fulfilling of a contract. It was the assurance that the seller gave to the buyer that the product was as advertised, or that the service would be rendered as promised.

The Holy Spirit is God's guarantee that He is dependable and will accomplish all that He has promised. Paul was careful not to grieve the Holy Spirit; and, because the Spirit was not convicting him, he knew that his motives were pure and his conscience was clear.

All Christians have been anointed by the Spirit (2 Cor. 1:21). In the Old Testament, the only persons who were anointed by God were prophets, priests, and kings. Their anointing equipped them for service.

As we yield to the Spirit, He enables us to serve God and to live godly lives. He gives us the special spiritual discernment that we need to serve God acceptably (1 John 2:20, 27).

The Spirit has also sealed us (2 Cor. 1:22; Eph. 1:13) so that we belong to Christ and are claimed by Him. The witness of the Spirit within guarantees that we are authentic children of God and not counterfeit (Rom. 5:5; 8:9). The Spirit also assures us that He will protect us, because we are His property.

Finally, the Holy Spirit enables us to serve others (2 Cor. 1:23–24), not as "spiritual dictators" who tell others what to do, but as servants who seek to help others grow. The false teachers who invaded the Corinthian church were guilty of being dictators (see 2 Cor. 11), and this had turned the hearts of the people away from Paul, who had sacrificed so much for them.

The Spirit is God's "earnest" (down payment, guarantee, security) that one day we shall be with Him in heaven and possess glorified bodies (see Eph. 1:14). He enables us to enjoy the blessings of heaven in our hearts today! Because of the indwelling Holy Spirit, Paul was able to have a clear conscience and face misunderstandings with love and patience. If you live to please people, misunderstandings will depress you; but if you live to please God, you can face misunderstandings with faith and courage.

A Compassionate Heart (2:1–11)

One of the members of the Corinthian church caused Paul a great deal of pain. We are not sure if this is the same man Paul wrote about in 1 Corinthians 5, the man who was living in open fornication, or if it was another person, someone who publicly challenged Paul's apostolic authority. Paul had made a quick visit to Corinth to deal with this problem (2 Cor. 12:14; 13:1) and had also written a painful letter about the situation. In all of this, he revealed a compassionate heart. Note the evidences of Paul's love.

Love puts others first (vv. 1–4). He did not think of his own feelings, but of the feelings of others. In Christian ministry, those who bring us great joy can also create for us great sorrow; and this was what Paul was experiencing. He wrote them a stern letter, born out of the anguish of his own heart, and bathed in Christian love. His great desire was that the church might obey the Word, discipline the offender, and bring purity and peace to the congregation.

"Faithful are the wounds of a friend; but the kisses of an enemy are deceitful" (Prov. 27:6). Paul knew that his words would wound those he loved, and this brought pain to his heart. But he also knew (as every loving parent knows) that there is a big difference between *hurting* someone and *harming* him. Sometimes those who love us must hurt us in order to keep us from harming ourselves.

Paul could have exercised his apostolic authority and commanded the people to respect him and obey him; but he preferred to minister with patience and love. God knew that Paul's change in plans had as its motive the sparing of the church from further pain (2 Cor. 1:23–24). Love always considers the feelings of others and seeks to put their good ahead of everything else.

Love also seeks to help others grow (vv. 5–6). It is worth noting that Paul did not mention the name of the man who had opposed him and divided the church family. However, Paul did tell the church to discipline this man *for his own good.* If the person referred to is the fornicator mentioned in 1 Corinthians 5, then these verses indicate that the church did hold a meeting and discipline the man, and that he repented of his sins and was restored.

True discipline is an evidence of love (see Heb. 12). Some young parents with "modern views" of how to raise children refuse to discipline their disobedient offspring because these parents claim they love their children too much. But if they really loved their children, they would chasten them.

Church discipline is not a popular subject or a widespread practice. Too many churches sweep such things under the rug instead of obeying the Scriptures and confronting the situation boldly by "speaking the truth in love" (Eph. 4:15). "Peace at any price" is not a biblical principle, for there cannot be true spiritual peace without purity (James 3:13–18). Problems that are swept under the rug have a way of multiplying and creating even worse problems later on.

The man whom Paul confronted, and whom the church disciplined, was helped by this kind of loving attention. When I was a child, I didn't always appreciate the discipline that my parents gave me, though I must confess that I deserved far more than I received. But now that I look back, I can thank God that they loved me enough to hurt me and hinder me from harming myself. Now I understand what they really meant when they said, "This hurts us more than it hurts you."

Love forgives and encourages (vv. 7–11). Paul urged the church family to forgive the man, and he gave solid reasons to back up this admonition. To begin with, they were to forgive him *for his own sake,* "lest [he] be swallowed up with overmuch sorrow" (2 Cor. 2:7–8). Forgiveness is the medicine that helps to heal broken hearts. It was important that the church assure this repentant member of their love.

In my own pastoral ministry, I have shared in meetings where disciplined members have been forgiven and restored to fellowship; and they have been high and holy hours in my life. When a church family assures a forgiven brother or sister that the sin is forgotten and the fellowship restored, there is a sense of the Lord's presence that is wonderful to experience. Every parent who disciplines a child must follow that discipline with assurance of love and forgiveness, or the discipline will do more harm than good.

They should confirm their love to the forgiven brother *for the Lord's sake* (2 Cor. 2:9–10). After all, discipline is as much a matter of obedience to the Lord as it is obligation to a brother. The problem was not simply between a sinning brother and a grieving apostle: it was also between a sinning brother and a grieving Savior. The man had sinned against Paul and the church, but he had most of all sinned against the Lord. When timid church leaders try to whitewash situations instead of facing them honestly, they are grieving the heart of the Lord.

Paul gave a third reason: they must forgive the offender *for the church's sake* (2 Cor. 2:11). When there is an unforgiving spirit in a congregation because sin has not been dealt with in a biblical manner, it gives Satan a "beachhead" from which he can operate in the congregation. We grieve the Holy Spirit and "give place to the devil" when we harbor an unforgiving spirit (Eph. 4:27–32).

One of Satan's "devices" is to accuse believers who have sinned so that they feel their case is hopeless. I have had people write me or phone me to ask for help because they have been under satanic oppression and accusation. The Holy Spirit convicts us of sin so that we will confess it and turn to Christ for cleansing; but Satan accuses us of sin so that we will despair and give up.

When an offending brother or sister is disciplined according to the Bible, and repents, then the church family must forgive and restore the member, and the matter must be forgotten and never brought up again. If the church family—or any person in the family—carries an unforgiving spirit, then Satan will use that attitude as a beachhead for new assaults against the church.

Paul was able to overcome the problems that he faced because he had a clear conscience and a compassionate heart. But there was a third spiritual resource that gave him victory.

A Conquering Faith (2:12–17)
It appeared in Asia that Paul's plans had completely fallen apart. Where was Titus? What was going on at Corinth? Paul had open doors of ministry at Troas, but he had no peace in his heart to walk through those doors. Humanly speaking, it looked like the end of the battle, with Satan as the victor.

Except for one thing: Paul had a conquering faith! He was able to break out in praise and write, "Thanks be unto God" (2 Cor. 2:14). This song of praise was born out of the assurances Paul had because he trusted the Lord.

Paul was sure that God was leading him (v. 14a). The circumstances were not comfortable, and Paul could not explain the detours and disappointments, but he was sure that God was in control. The believer can always be sure that God is working everything together for good, so long as we love Him and seek to obey His will (Rom. 8:28). This promise is not an excuse for carelessness, but it is an encouragement for confidence.

A friend of mine was to meet a Christian leader behind the iron curtain and arrange for the publishing of a certain book, but all the arrangements fell through. My friend was alone in a dangerous place wondering what to do next, when he "chanced" to make contact with a stranger—who took him right to the very leaders he wanted to reach! It was the providence of God at work, the fulfilling of Romans 8:28.

Paul was also sure that God was leading him in triumph (v. 14b). The picture here is that of the "Roman Triumph," the special tribute that Rome gave to their conquering generals. It was their equivalent of the American ticker-tape parade.

If a commander in chief won a complete victory over the enemy on foreign soil, and if he killed at least five thousand enemy soldiers and gained new territory for the emperor, then that commander in chief was entitled to a Roman Triumph. The processional would include the commander riding in a golden chariot, surrounded by his officers. The parade would also include a display of the spoils of battle, as well as the captive enemy soldiers. The Roman priests would also be in the parade, carrying burning incense to pay tribute to the victorious army.

The procession would follow a special route through the city and would end at the Circus Maximus, where the helpless captives would entertain the people by fighting wild beasts. It was a very special day in Rome when the citizens were treated to a full-scale Roman Triumph.

How does this piece of history apply to the burdened believer today? Jesus Christ, our great Commander in chief, came to foreign soil (this earth) and completely defeated the enemy (Satan). Instead of killing five thousand persons, He gave life to more than five thousand persons—to three thousand plus at Pentecost and to another two thousand plus shortly after Pentecost (Acts 2:41; 4:4). Jesus Christ claimed the spoils of battle—lost souls who had been in bondage to sin and Satan (Luke 11:14–22; Eph. 4:8; Col. 2:15). What a splendid victory!

The victorious general's sons would walk behind their father's chariot, sharing in his victory; and that is where believers are today—following in Christ's triumph. We do not fight *for* victory; we fight *from* victory. Neither in Asia nor in Corinth did the situation look like victory to Paul, but he believed God—and God turned defeat into victory.

Paul was sure that God was using him as He was leading him (vv. 14c–17). As the Roman priests burned the incense in the parade, that odor affected different people in different ways. To the triumphant soldiers, it meant life and victory; but to the conquered enemy, it meant defeat and death. They were on their way to be killed by the beasts.

Using this image of the incense, Paul pictured the Christian ministry. He saw believers as incense, giving forth the fragrance of Jesus Christ in their lives and labors. To God, believers are the very fragrance of Jesus Christ. To other believers, we are the fragrance of life;

but to unbelievers, we are the fragrance of death. In other words, the Christian life and ministry are matters of life and death. The way we live and work can mean life or death to a lost world around us.

No wonder Paul cried out, "And who is sufficient for these things?" (2 Cor. 2:16). He gave his answer in the next chapter: "our sufficiency is of God" (2 Cor. 3:5). He reminded the Corinthians that his heart was pure and his motives sincere. After all, there was no need to be clever and "peddle" the Word of God, when he was following in the triumphant train of the victorious Savior! They might misunderstand him, but God knew his heart.

We don't have to fail! Circumstances may discourage us, and people may oppose us and misunderstand us; but we have in Christ the spiritual resources to win the battle: a clear conscience, a compassionate heart, and a conquering faith.

"If God be for us, who can be against us? … Nay, in all these things we are more than conquerors through him that loved us" (Rom. 8:31, 37).

CHAPTER THREE
2 Corinthians 3
FROM GLORY TO GLORY

Wherever you find the genuine, you will find somebody promoting the counterfeit. Even art critics have been fooled by fake "masterpieces," and sincere publishers have purchased "valuable manuscripts," only to discover them to be forgeries. Henry Ward Beecher was right when he said, "A lie always needs a truth for a handle to it."

No sooner did the gospel of God's grace begin to spread among the Gentiles than a counterfeit "gospel" appeared, a mixture of law and grace. It was carried by a zealous group of people that we have come to call the "Judaizers." Paul wrote his letter to the Galatians to refute their doctrines, and you will find him referring to them several times in 2 Corinthians.

Their major emphasis was that salvation was by faith in Christ *plus* the keeping of the law (see Acts 15:1ff.). They also taught that the believer is perfected in his faith by obeying the law of Moses. Their "gospel of legalism" was very popular, since human nature enjoys achieving religious goals instead of simply trusting Christ and allowing the Holy Spirit to work. It is much easier to measure "religion" than true righteousness.

Paul looked on these false teachers as "peddlers" of the Word of God (see 2 Cor. 2:17 NIV), "religious racketeers" who preyed on ignorant people. He rejected their devious methods of teaching the Bible (2 Cor. 4:2) and despised their tendency to boast about their converts (2 Cor. 10:12–18). One reason why the Corinthians were behind in their contribution to the special offering was that the Judaizers had "robbed" the church (2 Cor. 11:7–12, 20; 12:14).

How did Paul refute the doctrines and practices of these legalistic false teachers? By showing the surpassing glory of the ministry of the gospel of the grace of God. In 2 Corinthians 3, Paul contrasted the ministry of the old covenant (law) with the ministry of the new covenant (grace), and he proved the superiority of the new covenant ministry. Note the contrasts that he presented.

Tablets of Stone—Human Hearts (3:1–3)
The Judaizers boasted that they carried "letters of recommendation" (2 Cor. 3:1 NIV) from the "important people" in the Jerusalem church, and they pointed out that Paul had no such credentials. It is a sad thing when a person measures his worth by what people say about him instead of by what God knows about him. Paul needed no credentials from church leaders: his life and ministry were the only recommendations needed.

When God gave the law, He wrote it on tablets of stone, and those tablets were placed in the ark of the covenant. Even if the Israelites could read the two tablets, this experience would not change their lives. The law is an external thing, and people need an *internal* power if their lives are to be transformed. The legalist can admonish us with his "Do this!" or "Don't do that!" but he cannot give us the power to obey. If we do obey, often it is not from the heart—and we end up worse than before!

The ministry of grace changes the heart. The Spirit of God uses the Word of God and writes it on the heart. The Corinthians were wicked sinners when Paul came to them, but his ministry of the gospel of God's grace completely changed their lives (see 1 Cor. 6:9–11). Their experience of God's grace certainly meant more to them than the letters of commendation carried by the false teachers. The Corinthian believers were lovingly written on Paul's heart, and the Spirit of God had written the truth on their hearts, making them "living epistles of Christ."

The test of ministry is changed lives, not press releases or statistics. It is much easier for the legalist to boast, because he can "measure" his ministry by external standards. The believer who patiently ministers by the Spirit of God must leave the results with the Lord. How tragic that the Corinthians followed the boastful Judaizers and broke the heart of the man who had rescued them from judgment.

Death—Life (3:4–6)
Paul was quick to give the glory to God and not to himself. His confidence ("trust") was in God, and his sufficiency came from God. Paul was a brilliant and well-educated man; yet he did not depend on his own adequacy. He depended on the Lord.

The legalists, of course, told people that any person could obey the law and become spiritual. A legalistic ministry has a way of inflating the egos of people. When you emphasize the grace of God, you must tell people that they are lost sinners who cannot save themselves. Paul's testimony was, "But by the grace of God I am what I am" (1 Cor. 15:10). No one is sufficient of himself to minister to the hearts of people. That sufficiency can only come from God.

As you read this chapter, note the different names that Paul used for the old covenant and the new covenant as he contrasted them. In 2 Corinthians 3:6, "the letter" refers to the old covenant law, while "the spirit" refers to the new covenant message of grace. Paul was not contrasting two approaches to the Bible, a "literal interpretation" and a "spiritual interpretation." He was reminding his readers that the old covenant law could not give life; it was a ministry of death (see Gal. 3:21). The gospel gives life to those who believe because of the work of Jesus Christ on the cross.

Paul was not suggesting that the law was a mistake or that its ministry was unimportant. Far from it! Paul knew that the lost sinner must be slain by the law and left helplessly condemned before he can be saved by God's grace. John the Baptist came with a message of judgment, preparing the way for Jesus and His message of saving grace.

A legalistic ministry brings death. Preachers who major on rules and regulations keep their congregations under a dark cloud of guilt, and this kills their joy, power, and effective witness for Christ. Christians who are constantly measuring each other, comparing "results," and competing with each other soon discover that they are depending on the flesh and not the power of the Spirit. There never was a standard that could transform a person's life, and that includes the Ten Commandments. Only the grace of God, ministered by the Spirit of God, can transform lost sinners into living epistles that glorify Jesus Christ.

Paul's doctrine of the new covenant was not something that he invented for the occasion. As a profound student of the Scriptures, Paul certainly had read Jeremiah 31:27–34, as well as Ezekiel 11:14–21. In the New Testament, Hebrews 8—10 is the key passage to study. The old covenant law, with its emphasis on external obedience, was preparation for the new covenant message of grace and the emphasis on internal transformation of the heart.

Fading Glory—Increasing Glory (3:7–11)

This paragraph is the heart of the chapter, and it should be studied in connection with Exodus 34:29–35. Paul did not deny the glory of the old covenant law, because in the giving of the law and the maintaining of the tabernacle and temple services, there certainly was glory. What he affirmed, however, was that the glory of the new covenant of grace was far superior, and he gave several reasons to support his affirmation.

The new covenant glory means spiritual life, not death (vv. 7–8). When Moses descended from the mountain, after conversing with God, his face shone with the glory of God. This was a part of the glory of the giving of the law, and it certainly impressed the people. Paul then argued from the lesser to the greater: if there was glory in the giving of a law that brought death, how much more glory is there in a ministry that brings life!

Legalists like the Judaizers like to magnify the glory of the law and minimize its weaknesses. In his letter to the Galatian churches, Paul pointed out the deficiencies of the law: the law cannot justify the lost sinner (Gal. 2:16), give a sinner righteousness (Gal. 2:21), give the Holy Spirit (Gal. 3:2), give an inheritance (Gal. 3:18), give life (Gal. 3:21), or give freedom (Gal. 4:8–10). The glory of the law is really the glory of a ministry of death.

The new covenant glory means righteousness, not condemnation (vv. 9–10). The law was not given for the purpose of salvation, for there is no salvation through obedience to the law. The law produces condemnation and is the mirror that reveals how dirty our faces really are. But we cannot wash our faces in the mirror.

The ministry of the new covenant produces righteousness and changes lives to the glory of God. Man's greatest need is righteousness, and God's greatest gift is righteousness through faith in Jesus Christ. "For if righteousness [comes] by the law, then Christ is dead in vain" (Gal. 2:21). The person who tries to live under the law will find himself feeling more and more guilty, and this can produce a feeling of hopelessness and rejection. It is when we trust Christ, and live by faith in God's grace, that we experience acceptance and joy.

Second Corinthians 3:10 states that the law really "lost its glory" when compared to the surpassing glory of the ministry of God's grace. There simply is no comparison. Sad to say, there are some people who cannot "feel spiritual" unless they carry a weight of guilt. The law produces guilt and condemnation, for it is like a bond of indebtedness (Col. 2:14), a guardian who disciplines us (Gal. 4:1–5), and a yoke too heavy to bear (Gal. 5:1; Acts 15:10).

The new covenant glory is permanent, not temporary (v. 11). The tense of the verb here is very important: "that which is passing away." Paul wrote at a period in history when the ages were overlapping. The new covenant of grace had come in, but the temple services were still being carried on and the nation of Israel was still living under law. In AD 70, the city of Jerusalem and the temple would be destroyed by the Romans, and that would mark the end of the Jewish religious system.

The Judaizers wanted the Corinthian believers to go back under the law, to "mix" the two covenants. "Why go back to that which is temporary and fading away?" Paul asked. "Live in the glory of the new covenant, which is getting greater and greater." The glory of the law is but the glory of past history, while the glory of the new covenant is the glory of present experience. As believers, we can be "changed … from glory to glory" (2 Cor. 3:18), something that the law can never accomplish.

The glory of the law was fading in Paul's day, and today that glory is found only in the records in the Bible. The nation of Israel has no temple or priesthood. If they did build a temple, there would be no Shekinah glory dwelling in the Holy of Holies. The law of Moses is a religion with a most glorious past, but it has no glory today. The light is gone; all that remain are shadows (Col. 2:16–17).

Paul has pointed out that the ministry of grace is internal (2 Cor. 3:1–3), it brings life (2 Cor. 3:4–6), and it involves increasing glory (2 Cor. 3:7–11). He presented one final contrast to prove the superiority of the new covenant ministry of grace.

Concealment—Openness (3:12–18)

The Bible is basically a "picture book," because it uses symbols, similes, metaphors, and other literary devices to get its message across. In this paragraph, Paul used the experience of Moses and his veil to illustrate the glorious freedom and openness of the Christian life under grace. Paul saw in Moses' experience a deeper spiritual meaning than you and I would have seen as we read Exodus 34:29–35.

The historical event (vv. 12–13). When you are a part of a ministry of increasing glory, you can be bold in what you say; and Paul did not hide his boldness. Unlike Moses, Paul had nothing to conceal.

When Moses came down from communing with God, his face shone, reflecting the glory of God. When he spoke to the people, they could see the glory on his face, and they were impressed by it. But Moses knew that the glory would fade away; so, when he finished teaching the people, he put on a veil. This prevented them from seeing the glory disappear; for, after all, who wants to follow a leader who is losing his glory?

The word translated "end" in 2 Corinthians 3:13 has two meanings: "purpose" and "finish." The veil prevented the people from seeing the "finish" of the glory as it faded away. But the veil also prevented them from understanding the "purpose" behind the fading glory. The law had just been instituted, and the people were not ready to be told that this glorious system was only temporary. The truth that the covenant of law was a preparation for something greater was not yet made known to them.

The national application (vv. 14–17). Paul had a special love for Israel and a burden to see his people saved (Rom. 9:1–3). Why were the Jewish people rejecting their Christ? As the missionary to the Gentiles, Paul was seeing many Gentiles trust the Lord, but the Jews—his own people—were rejecting the truth and persecuting Paul and the church.

The reason? There was a "spiritual veil" over their minds and hearts. Their spiritual eyes were blinded, so that when they read the Old Testament Scriptures, they did not see the truth about their own Messiah. Even though the Scriptures were read systematically in the synagogues, the Jewish people did not grasp the spiritual message God had given to them. They were blinded by their own religion.

Is there any hope for the lost children of Israel? Yes, there is! "Nevertheless, when it [the heart] shall turn to the Lord [by trusting Jesus Christ], the veil shall be taken away" (2 Cor. 3:16).

In each of the three churches I have pastored, it has been my joy to baptize Jewish people who have trusted Jesus Christ. It is amazing how their minds open to the Scriptures after they have been born again. One man told me, "It's like scales falling from your eyes. You wonder why everybody doesn't see what you see!" The veil is removed by the Spirit of God and they receive spiritual vision.

But no sinner—Jew or Gentile—can turn to Christ apart from the ministry of the Holy Spirit of God. "Now the Lord is that Spirit" (2 Cor. 3:17). This statement is a bold declaration of the deity of the Holy Spirit: He is God. The Judaizers who had invaded the church at Corinth were depending on the law to change men's lives, but only the Spirit of God can bring about spiritual transformation. The law can bring only bondage, but the Spirit introduces us into a life of liberty. "For ye have not received the spirit of bondage again to fear; but ye have received the Spirit of adoption, whereby we cry, 'Abba, Father'" (Rom. 8:15).

As a nation, Israel today is spiritually blind; but this does not mean that individual Jews cannot be saved. The church today needs to recover its lost burden for Israel. We are their debtors, because all the spiritual blessings we have came through Israel. "Salvation is of the Jews" (Jonn 4:22). The only way we can "pay off" this debt is by sharing the gospel with them and praying that they might be saved (Rom. 10:1).

The personal application (v. 18). "But we all, with open face beholding as in a glass the glory of the Lord, are changed into the same image from glory to glory, even as by the Spirit of the Lord." This verse is the climax of the chapter, and it presents a truth so exciting that I marvel so many believers have missed it—or ignored it. You and I can share the image of Jesus Christ and go "from glory to glory" through the ministry of the Spirit of God!

Under the old covenant, only Moses ascended the mountain and had fellowship with God; but under the new covenant, all believers have the privilege of communion with Him. Through Jesus Christ, we may enter into the very Holy of Holies (Heb. 10:19–20)—and we don't have to climb a mountain!

The "mirror" is a symbol of the Word of God (James 1:22–25). As we look into God's Word and see God's Son, the Spirit transforms us into the very image of God. It is important, however, that we hide nothing from God. We must be open and honest with Him and not "wear a veil."

The word translated "changed" is the same word translated "transfigured" in the accounts of our Lord's transfiguration (Matt. 17; Mark 9). It describes a change on the outside that comes from the inside. Our

English word *metamorphosis* is a transliteration of this Greek word. Metamorphosis describes the process that changes an insect from a larva into a pupa and then into a mature insect. The changes come from within.

Moses *reflected* the glory of God, but you and I may *radiate* the glory of God. When we meditate on God's Word and in it see God's Son, then the Spirit transforms us! We become more like the Lord Jesus Christ as we grow "from glory to glory." *This wonderful process cannot be achieved by keeping the law.* The glory of the law faded away, but the glory of God's grace continues to increase in our lives.

Keep in mind that Paul was contrasting, not only the old covenant with the New, but also the old covenant *ministry* with the ministry of grace. The goal of old covenant ministry is obedience to an external standard, but this obedience cannot change human character. The goal of new covenant ministry is likeness to Jesus Christ. Law can bring us to Christ (Gal. 3:24), but only grace can make us like Christ. Legalistic preachers and teachers may get their listeners to conform to some standard, but they can never transform them to be like the Son of God.

The means for old covenant ministry is the law, but the means for new covenant ministry is the Spirit of God using the Word of God. (By the "law" I do not mean the Old Testament, but rather the whole legal system given by Moses. Certainly, the Spirit can use both the Old and New Testaments to reveal Jesus Christ to us.) Since the Holy Spirit wrote the Word, He can teach it to us. Even more, because the Spirit lives in us, He can enable us to obey the Word from our hearts. This is not legal obedience, born of fear, but filial obedience born of love.

Finally, the result of old covenant ministry is bondage; but the result of new covenant ministry is freedom in the Spirit. Legalism keeps a person immature, and immature people must live by rules and regulations (see Gal. 4:1–7). God wants His children to obey, not because of an external code (the law), but because of internal character. Christians do not live under the law, but this does not mean that we are lawless! The Spirit of God writes the Word of God on our hearts, and we obey our Father because of the new life He has given us within.

The lure of legalism is still with us. False cults prey on professed Christians and church members, as did the Judaizers in Paul's day. We must learn to recognize false cults and reject their teachings. But there are also gospel-preaching churches that have legalistic tendencies and keep their members immature, guilty, and afraid. They spend a great deal of time dealing with the externals, and they neglect the cultivation of the inner life. They exalt standards and they denounce sin, but they fail to magnify the Lord Jesus Christ. Sad to say, in some New Testament churches we have an Old Testament ministry.

Paul has now explained two aspects of his own ministry: it is triumphant (2 Cor. 1—2) and it is glorious (2 Cor. 3). The two go together: "Therefore seeing we have this [kind of] ministry, as we have received mercy, we faint not" (2 Cor. 4:1).

When your ministry involves the glory of God—you cannot quit!

CHAPTER FOUR
2 Corinthians 4:1—5:8
COURAGE FOR THE CONFLICT

The key theme of this section is repeated in 1 Corinthians 4:1 and 16: "We faint not!" Literally, Paul said, "We do not lose heart!" There were certainly plenty of reasons for discouragement in Paul's situation, yet the great apostle did not quit. What was it that kept him from fainting in the conflicts of life? *He knew what he possessed in Jesus Christ!* Instead of complaining about what he did not have, Paul rejoiced in what he did have; and you and I can do the same thing.

We Have a Glorious Ministry (4:1–6)
"Therefore, seeing we have *this kind* of ministry" is the literal translation of what Paul wrote. What kind of ministry? The kind described in the previous chapter: a glorious ministry that brings men life, salvation, and righteousness; a ministry that is able to transform men's lives. This ministry is a gift—we receive it from God. It is given to us because of God's mercy, not because of anything we are or we have done (see 1 Tim. 1:12–17).

The way you look at your ministry helps to determine how you will fulfill it. If you look on serving Christ as a burden instead of a privilege, you will be a drudge and do only what is required of you. Some people even look on service as a punishment from God. When Paul considered the fact that he was a minister of Jesus Christ, he was overwhelmed by the grace and mercy of God. His positive attitude toward the ministry had some practical consequences in his life.

It kept him from being a quitter (v. 1). He confessed to the Corinthians that his trials in Asia had almost brought him to despair (2 Cor. 1:8). In spite of his great gifts and vast experience, Paul was human and subject to human frailties. But how could he lose heart when he was involved in such a wonderful ministry? Would God have entrusted this ministry to him so that he might fail? Of course not! With the divine calling came the divine enabling; he knew that God would see him through.

A discouraged Methodist preacher wrote to the great Scottish preacher Alexander Whyte to ask his counsel. Should he leave the ministry? "Never think of giving up preaching!" Whyte wrote to him. "The angels around the throne envy you your great work!" That was the kind of reply Paul would have written, the kind of reply all of us need to ponder whenever we feel our work is in vain.

It kept him from being a deceiver (vv. 2–4).
"But we have renounced the things hidden because of shame, not walking in craftiness or adulterating the Word of God, but by the manifestation of the truth commending ourselves to every man's conscience in the sight of God" (2 Cor. 4:2 NASB). Paul was certainly alluding to the Judaizers when he wrote these words. Many false teachers today claim to base their doctrine on the Word of God, but false teachers handle God's Word in deceptive ways. You can prove anything by the Bible, provided you twist the Scriptures out of context and reject the witness of your own conscience. The Bible is a book of literature, and it must be interpreted according to the fundamental rules of interpretation. If people treated other books the way they treat the Bible, they would never learn anything.

Paul had nothing to hide, either in his personal life or in his preaching of the Word. Everything was open and honest; there was no deception or distortion of the Word. The Judaizers were guilty of twisting the Scriptures to fit their own preconceived interpretations, and ignorant people were willing to follow them.

If Paul was such a faithful teacher of the Word, then why did not more people believe his message? Why were the false teachers so successful in winning converts? Because the mind of the lost sinner is blinded by Satan, and fallen man finds it easier to believe lies than to believe truth. The gospel "is hid to them that are lost: in whom the god of this world hath blinded the minds of them which believe not, lest the light of the glorious gospel of Christ, who is the image of God, should shine unto them" (2 Cor. 4:3–4).

Paul had already explained that the minds of the Jews were "veiled" because of the blindness of their hearts (Rom. 11:25; 2 Cor. 3:14–16). The minds of the Gentiles are also blinded! Those who are lost ("perishing") cannot understand the message of the gospel. Satan does not want the glorious light of salvation to shine into their hearts. As the god of this age and the prince of this world (John 12:31), Satan keeps lost sinners in the dark. The sad thing is that Satan uses *religious* teachers (like the Judaizers) to deceive people. Many of the people who today belong to cults were originally members of Christian churches.

It kept him from being a self-promoter (vv. 5–6).
The awesome fact that Paul had received this ministry from Christ kept him from being a quitter and a deceiver; but it also kept him from being a self-promoter (2 Cor. 4:5–6). "We preach not ourselves" (2 Cor. 4:5). The Judaizers enjoyed preaching about themselves and glorying in their achievements (2 Cor. 10:12–18). They were not servants who tried to help people; they were dictators who exploited people.

Paul was certainly a man who practiced genuine humility. He did not trust in himself (2 Cor. 1:9) or commend himself (2 Cor. 3:1–5) or preach himself (2 Cor. 4:5). He sought only to lead people to Jesus Christ and to build them up in the faith. It would have been easy for Paul to build a "fan club" for himself and

take advantage of weak people who thrive on associating with great men. The Judaizers operated in that way, but Paul rejected that kind of ministry.

What happens when you share Jesus Christ with lost sinners? The light begins to shine! Paul compared conversion to creation as described in Genesis 1:3. Like the earth of Genesis 1:2, the lost sinner is formless and empty; but when he trusts Christ, he becomes a new creation (2 Cor. 5:17). God then begins to *form* and *fill* the life of the person who trusts Christ, and he begins to be fruitful for the Lord. God's "Let there be light!" makes everything new.

We Have a Valuable Treasure (4:7–12)
From the glory of the new creation, Paul moved to the humility of the clay vessel. The believer is simply a "jar of clay"; it is the treasure *within the vessel* that gives the vessel its value. The image of the vessel is a recurring one in Scripture, and from it we can learn many lessons.

To begin with, God has made us the way we are so that we can do the work He wants us to do. God said of Paul, "He is a chosen vessel unto me, to bear my name before the Gentiles" (Acts 9:15). No Christian should ever complain to God because of his lack of gifts or abilities, or because of his limitations or handicaps. Psalm 139:13–16 indicates that our very genetic structure is in the hands of God. Each of us must accept himself and be himself.

The important thing about a vessel is that it be clean, empty, and available for service. Each of us must seek to become "a vessel unto honor, sanctified [set apart], and meet for the master's use, and prepared unto every good work" (2 Tim. 2:21). We are vessels so that God might use us. We are *earthen* vessels so that we might depend on God's power and not our own.

We must focus on the treasure and not on the vessel. Paul was not afraid of suffering or trial, because he knew that God would guard the vessel so long as Paul was guarding the treasure (see 1 Tim. 1:11; 6:20). God permits trials, God controls trials, and God uses trials for His own glory. *God is glorified through weak vessels.* The missionary who opened inland China to the gospel, J. Hudson Taylor, used to say, "All God's giants have been weak men who did great things for God because they reckoned on Him being with them."

Sometimes God permits our vessels to be jarred so that some of the treasure will spill out and enrich others. Suffering reveals not only the weakness of man but also the glory of God. Paul presented a series of paradoxes in this paragraph: earthen vessels—power of God; the dying of Jesus—the life of Jesus; death working—life working. The natural mind cannot understand this kind of spiritual truth and therefore cannot understand why Christians triumph over suffering.

Not only must we focus on the treasure and not on the vessel, but we must also focus on the Master and not on the servant. If we suffer, it is for Jesus' sake. If we die to self, it is so that the life of Christ might be revealed in us. If we go through trials, it is so that

Christ might be glorified. And all of this is for the sake of others. As we serve Christ, death works in us—but life works in those to whom we minister.

Dr. John Henry Jowett said, "Ministry that costs nothing, accomplishes nothing." He was right. A pastor friend and I once heard a young man preach an eloquent sermon, but it lacked something. "There was something missing," I said to my friend; and he replied, "Yes, and it won't be there until his heart is broken. After he has suffered awhile, he will have a message worth listening to."

The Judaizers did not suffer. Instead of winning lost souls, they stole converts from Paul's churches. Instead of sacrificing for the people, they made the people sacrifice for them (2 Cor. 11:20). The false teachers did not have a treasure to share. All they had were some museum pieces from the old covenant, faded antiques that could never enrich a person's life.

It has been my experience that many churches are ignorant of the price a pastor pays to be faithful to the Lord in serving His people. This section is one of three sections in 2 Corinthians devoted to a listing of Paul's sufferings. The other two are 6:1–10 and 11:16—12:10. The test of a true ministry is not stars, but scars. "From henceforth let no man trouble me: for I bear in my body the marks [brands] of the Lord Jesus" (Gal. 6:17).

How can we keep from giving up? By remembering that we are privileged to have the treasure of the gospel in our vessels of clay!

We Have a Confident Faith (4:13–18)

The phrase *spirit of faith* means "attitude or outlook of faith." Paul was not referring to a special gift of faith (1 Cor. 12:9), but rather to that attitude of faith that ought to belong to every believer. He saw himself identified with the believer who wrote Psalm 116:10: "I believed, and therefore have I spoken." True witness for God is based on faith in God, and this faith comes from God's Word (Rom. 10:17). Nothing closes a believer's mouth like unbelief (see Luke 1:20).

Of what was Paul so confident? That he had nothing to fear from life or death! He had just listed some of the trials that were a part of his life and ministry, and now he was affirming that his faith gave him victory over all of them. Note the assurances that he had because of his faith.

He was sure of ultimate victory (v. 14). If Jesus Christ has conquered death, the last enemy, then why fear anything else? Men do everything they can to penetrate the meaning of death and prepare for it, yet the world has no answer to death. Until a person is prepared to die, he is not really prepared to live. The joyful message of the early church was the victory of Christ over death, and we need to return to that victorious emphasis. Note too that Paul saw a future reunion of God's people when he wrote, "and shall present us with you." Death is the great divider, but in Jesus Christ there is assurance that His people shall be reunited in His presence (1 Thess. 4:13–18).

He was sure God would be glorified (v. 15). This verse parallels Romans 8:28 and gives us the assurance that our sufferings are not wasted: God uses them to minister to others and also to bring glory to His name. How is God glorified in our trials? By giving us the "abundant grace" we need to maintain joy and strength when the going gets difficult. Whatever begins with grace, leads to glory (see Ps. 84:11; 1 Peter 5:10).

He was sure his trials were working for him, not against him (vv. 16–17). "We faint not" (see 2 Cor. 4:1) was Paul's confident testimony. What does it matter if the "outward person" is perishing, so long as the "inward person" is experiencing daily spiritual renewal? Paul was not suggesting that the body is not important, or that we should ignore its warnings and needs. Since our bodies are the temples of God, we must care for them; but we cannot control the natural deterioration of human nature. When we consider all the physical trials that Paul endured, it is no wonder he wrote as he did.

As Christians, we must live a day at a time. No person, no matter how wealthy or gifted, can live two days at a time. God provides for us "day by day" as we pray to Him (Luke 11:3). He gives us the strength that we need according to our daily requirements (Deut. 33:25). We must not make the mistake of trying to "store up grace" for future emergencies, because God gives us the grace that we need when we need it (Heb. 4:16). When we learn to live a day at a time, confident of God's care, it takes a great deal of pressure off of our lives.

Yard by yard, life is hard!
Inch by inch, life's a cinch!

When you live by faith in Christ, you get the right perspective on suffering. Note the contrasts Paul presented in 2 Corinthians 4:17: light affliction—weight of glory; momentary—eternal; working against us—working for us. Paul was writing with eternity's values in view. He was weighing the present trials against the future glory, and he discovered that his trials were actually working *for him* (see Rom. 8:18).

We must not misunderstand this principle and think that a Christian can live any way he pleases and expect everything to turn into glory in the end. Paul was writing about trials experienced in the will of God as he was doing the work of God. God can and does turn suffering into glory, but He cannot turn sin into glory. Sin must be judged, because there is no glory in sin.

Second Corinthians 4:16 should be related to 3:18, because both verses have to do with the spiritual renewal of the child of God. Of itself, suffering will not make us holier men and women. Unless we yield to the Lord, turn to His Word, and trust Him to work, our suffering could make us far worse Christians. In my own pastoral ministry, I have seen some of God's people grow critical and bitter, and go from bad to worse instead of "from glory to glory." We need that "spirit of faith" that Paul mentioned in 2 Corinthians 4:13.

He was sure the invisible world was real (v. 18). Dr. A. W. Tozer used to remind us that the invisible world described in the Bible was the only "real world." If we would only see the visible world the way God wants us to see it, we would never be attracted by what it offers (1 John 2:15–17). The great men and women of faith mentioned in Hebrews 11 achieved what they did because they "saw the invisible" (Heb. 11:10, 13–14, 27).

The things of this world seem so real because we can see them and feel them; but they are all temporal and destined to pass away. Only the eternal things of the spiritual life will last. Again, we must not press this truth into extremes and think that "material" and "spiritual" oppose each other. When we use the material in God's will, He transforms it into the spiritual, and this becomes a part of our treasure in heaven. (More on this in 2 Cor. 8—9.) We value the material *because* it can be used to promote the spiritual, and not for what it is in itself.

How can you look at things that are invisible? By faith, when you read the Word of God. We have never seen Christ or heaven, yet we know they are real because the Word of God tells us so. Faith is "the evidence of things not seen" (Heb. 11:1). Because Abraham looked for the heavenly city, he separated himself from Sodom; but Lot chose Sodom because he walked by sight and not by faith (Gen. 13; Heb. 11:10).

Of course, the unsaved world thinks we are odd—perhaps even crazy—because we insist on the reality of the invisible world of spiritual blessing. Yet Christians are content to govern their lives by eternal values, not temporal prices.

We Have a Future Hope (5:1–8)

"We have this ministry…. We have this treasure…. We [have] the same spirit of faith…. We have a building of God" (2 Cor. 4:1, 7, 13; 5:1). What a testimony Paul gave to the reality of the Christian faith!

This "building of God" is not the believer's heavenly home, promised in John 14:1–6. It is his glorified body. Paul was a tentmaker (Acts 18:1–3), and here he used a tent as a picture of our present earthly bodies. A tent is a weak, temporary structure, without much beauty; but the glorified body we shall receive will be eternal, beautiful, and never show signs of weakness or decay (see Phil. 3:20–21). Paul saw the human body as an earthen vessel (2 Cor. 4:7) and a temporary tent; but he knew that believers would one day receive a wonderful glorified body, suited to the glorious environment of heaven.

It is interesting to trace Paul's testimony in this paragraph.

We know (v. 1). How do we know? Because we trust the Word of God. No Christian has to consult a fortune-teller, a Ouija board, a spiritist, or a deck of cards to find out what the future holds or what lies on the other side of death. God has told us all that we need to know in the pages of His Word. Paul's "we know" connects with his "knowing" in 2 Corinthians 4:14, and this relates to the resurrection of Jesus Christ. We know that He is alive; therefore, we know that death cannot claim us. "Because I live, ye shall live also" (John 14:19).

If our tent is "taken down" ("dissolved"), we need not fear. The body is only the house we live in. When a believer dies, the body goes to the grave, but the spirit goes to be with Christ (Phil. 1:20–25). When Jesus Christ returns for His own, He will raise the dead bodies in glory, and body and spirit shall be joined together for a glorious eternity in heaven (1 Cor. 15:35–58; 1 Thess. 4:13–18).

We groan (vv. 2–5). Paul was not expressing a morbid desire for death. In fact, his statement is just the opposite: he was eager for Jesus Christ to return so that he would be "clothed upon" with the glorified body. He presented three possibilities, using the image of the body as a tent: (1) *alive*—residing in the tent; (2) *dead*—unclothed, out of the tent, "naked"; (3) *clothed upon*—the transformation of the body at the return of Christ. Paul was hoping that he would be alive and on the earth at the return of Christ, so that he might not have to go through the experience of death. Paul used a similar picture in 1 Corinthians 15:51–58, and he used the idea of "groaning" in Romans 8:22–26.

The glorified body is called "a building of God, a house not made with hands" in 2 Corinthians 5:1, and "our house which is from heaven" in 2 Corinthians 5:2. This is in contrast to our mortal bodies, which came from the dust of the earth. "And as we have borne the image of the earthy, we shall also bear the image of the heavenly" (1 Cor. 15:49). It is important to note that Paul was not groaning because he was in a human body, but because he longed to see Jesus Christ and receive a glorified body. He was groaning for glory!

This explains why death holds no terrors for the Christian. Paul called his death a "departure" (2 Tim. 4:6). One meaning of this Greek word is "to take down one's tent and move on." But how can we be sure that we shall one day have new bodies like the glorified body of our Savior? We can be sure because the Spirit lives within us. Paul mentioned the sealing and the earnest of the Spirit in 2 Corinthians 1:22 (see also Eph. 1:13–14). The Holy Spirit dwelling in the believer's body is the "down payment" that guarantees the future inheritance, including a glorified body. In modern Greek, the word translated "earnest" means "engagement ring." The church is engaged to Jesus Christ and is waiting for the Bridegroom to come to take her to the wedding.

We are always confident (vv. 6–8). The people of God can be found in one of two places: either in heaven or on earth (Eph. 3:15). None of them is in the grave, in hell, or in any "intermediate place" between earth and heaven. Believers on earth are "at home in the body," while believers who have died are "absent from the body." Believers on earth are "absent from the Lord," while believers in heaven are "present with the Lord."

Because he had this kind of confidence, Paul was not afraid of suffering and trials, or even of dangers. This is not to suggest that he tempted the Lord by taking unnecessary risks, but it does mean that he was willing to "lose his life" for the sake of Christ and the ministry of the gospel. He walked by faith and not by sight. He looked at the eternal unseen, not the temporal seen (2 Cor. 4:18). Heaven was not simply a *destination* for Paul: it was a *motivation*. Like the heroes of faith in Hebrews 11, he looked for the heavenly city and governed his life by eternal values.

As we review this section of 2 Corinthians, we can see how Paul had courage for the conflict and would not lose heart. He had a glorious ministry that transformed lives. He had a valuable treasure in the earthen vessel of his body, and he wanted to share that treasure with a bankrupt world. He had a confident faith that conquered fear, and he had a future hope that was both a destination and a motivation.

No wonder Paul was "more than conqueror" (Rom. 8:37)!

Every believer in Jesus Christ has these same marvelous possessions and can find through them courage for the conflict.

CHAPTER FIVE
2 Corinthians 5:9–21
MOTIVES FOR MINISTRY

What we believe and how we behave must always go together. Paul usually connected *duty* and *doctrine*, because what God has done for us must motivate us to do something for God. Phillips Brooks said, "Christianity knows no truth which is not the child of love and the parent of duty."

"You would have preached a marvelous sermon," a woman said to her pastor, "except for all those 'therefores' at the end!"

Paul would have agreed with the pastor, for he usually used "therefores" and "wherefores" liberally in his letters. In fact, you find them in this section of 2 Corinthians 5 in verses 9, 11, and 16–17. Paul moved from explanation to application, and his theme was *motivation for ministry*. His enemies had accused him of using the ministry of the gospel for his own selfish purposes, when in reality *they* were the ones who were "merchandising" the gospel (see 2 Cor. 2:17; 4:2).

What is the ministry of the Christian? To persuade sinners to be reconciled to God (2 Cor. 5:11, 20). We must never force people to trust Christ, or coerce them by some devious approach. "Our message to you is true, our motives are pure, our conduct is absolutely aboveboard" (1 Thess. 2:3, Phillips). The Christian worker must have the right motive for ministry as well as the right message.

In this section, Paul stated three acceptable motives for ministry.

The Fear of the Lord (5:9–13)
"Knowing, therefore, the terror [fear] of the Lord" (2 Cor. 5:11). This kind of attitude is often lacking in ministry. The famous Bible scholar B. F. Westcott once wrote, "Every year makes me tremble at the daring with which people speak of spiritual things." Phillips Brooks used to warn about "clerical jesters" whose jesting about the Bible robbed that inspired Book of some of its glory and power. Too often there is a sad absence of reverence in the public meetings of the church, so that it is no surprise that the younger generation is not taking the things of God seriously.

Paul explained this motive by sharing his own testimony in three powerful statements.

We labor (v. 9). This means "we are ambitious." There is an ambition that is selfish and worldly, but there is also a holy ambition that honors the Lord. Paul's great ambition was to be well pleasing to Jesus Christ. The Judaizers ministered to please men and enlisted them in their cause; but Paul ministered to please Jesus Christ alone (Gal. 1:10). A man-pleasing ministry is a carnal, compromising ministry; and God cannot bless it.

The word translated "accepted" ("well pleasing") is used in several other places in the New Testament, and each of these references helps us better understand what it is that pleases the Lord. It is well pleasing to Him when we present our bodies to Him as living sacrifices (Rom. 12:1), and when we live so as to help others and avoid causing them to stumble (Rom. 14:18). God is well pleased when His children separate themselves from the evil around them (Eph. 5:10), as well as when they bring their offerings to Him (Phil. 4:18). He is pleased with children who submit to their parents (Col. 3:20), as well as with saints who permit Jesus Christ to work out His perfect will in their lives (Heb. 13:20–21).

There is nothing wrong with godly ambition. "Yea, so have I strived [been ambitious] to preach the gospel" was Paul's testimony in Romans 15:20; it was this godly ambition that compelled him to take the message where it had never been heard. Paul commanded the Thessalonian believers to "study [be ambitious] to be quiet" (1 Thess. 4:11). If, led by the Spirit, believers would put as much drive into Christian living and service as they do athletics or business, the gospel would make a greater impact on the lost world. "I want to be as zealous for God as I was for the devil!" a new Christian told me, and his life was greatly used of God.

We must all appear (v. 10). Not every believer is ambitious for the Lord, but every believer is going to appear before the Lord; and now is the time to prepare. The judgment seat of Christ is that future event when God's people will stand before the Savior as their works are judged and rewarded (see Rom. 14:8–10). Paul was ambitious for the Lord because he wanted to meet Him with confidence and not shame (1 John 2:28).

The term "judgment seat" comes from the Greek word *bema,* which was the platform in Greek towns where orations were made or decisions handed down by rulers (see Matt. 27:19; Acts 12:21; 18:12). It was also the place where the awards were given out to the winners in the annual Olympic Games. This "judgment seat" must not be confused with the Great White Throne from which Christ will judge the wicked (Rev. 20:11–15). Because of the gracious work of Christ on the cross, believers will not face their sins (John 5:24; Rom. 8:1); but we will have to give an account of our works and service for the Lord.

The judgment seat of Christ will be a place of *revelation;* for the word *appear* means "be revealed." As we live and work here on earth, it is relatively easy for us to hide things and pretend; but the true character of our works will be exposed before the searching eyes of the Savior. He will reveal whether our works have been good or bad ("worthless"). The character of our service will be revealed (1 Cor. 3:13) as well as the motives that impelled us (1 Cor. 4:5).

It will also be a place of *reckoning* as we give an account of our ministries (Rom. 14:10–12). If we have been faithful it will be a place of *reward* and *recognition* (1 Cor. 3:10–15; 4:1–6). For those of us who have been faithful, it will be a time of *rejoicing* as we glorify the Lord by giving our rewards back to Him in worship and in praise.

Is the desire for reward a proper motive for service? The fact that God does promise rewards is proof that the motive is not a sinful one, even though it may not be the highest motive. Just as parents are happy when their children achieve recognition, so our Lord is pleased when His people are *worthy* of recognition and reward. The important thing is not the reward itself, but the joy of pleasing Christ and honoring Him.

We persuade men (vv. 11–13). If God judges His own people, then what will happen to the lost? "And if the righteous scarcely be saved, where shall the ungodly and the sinner appear?" (1 Peter 4:18). The word *terror* does not mean fright, dread, or horror. After all, we are going to see our Savior—and He loves us. But Paul did not minimize the awesomeness of the occasion. We shall stand before Christ, "and there is no respect of persons" (Col. 3:23–25). Christ has commanded us to spread the gospel to all nations, and we must be obedient. Someone asked the Duke of Wellington what he thought of foreign missions, and his reply was "What are your marching orders?"

How can the Christian prepare for the judgment seat of Christ? To begin with, he must maintain a clear conscience (2 Cor. 5:11). No doubt some of the enemies at Corinth were saying, "Just wait until Paul stands before the Lord!" But Paul was not afraid, because he knew that his conscience was clear (see 2 Cor. 1:12). The truth about each one of us shall be revealed, and Jesus Christ will commend us for those things that have pleased Him.

Second, we must take care not to depend on the praise of men (2 Cor. 5:12). This verse relates to 2 Corinthians 3:1, where Paul referred to the "letters of commendation" that the Judaizers prized so highly. If we live only for the praise of men, we will not win the praise of God at the judgment seat of Christ. To live for man's praise is to exalt reputation over character, and it is character that will count when we see Christ. Actually, the Corinthians should have commended Paul! Instead, they were "promoting" the Judaizers, who gloried in appearance (see 2 Cor. 11:18), but were unspiritual in heart.

Finally, we must ignore the criticisms of men (2 Cor. 5:13). Paul's enemies said that he was crazy. Paul said that he was "mad" when he was persecuting the church (Acts 26:11), but his enemies said he was mad since he had become a believer himself (Acts 26:24). But people said that our Lord was mad, so Paul was in good company (see Mark 3:21). "If I am mad," Paul was saying, "it is for your good and the glory of God— so that makes it worthwhile!"

When Dwight L. Moody was ministering at his large Sunday school and church in Chicago, people often called him "Crazy Moody." In the eyes of the unsaved world, Moody was crazy to have given up a successful business career to become a Sunday school worker and evangelist; but time has proved his decision to be a wise one. Today, we don't know the names of the people who laughed at him, but we do know—and honor—the name of D. L. Moody.

It behooves every Christian to examine his own life regularly to see if he is ready for the judgment seat of Christ. Wanting to give a good account before Christ is a worthy motive for Christian service.

The Love of Christ (5:14–17)

How can such opposite emotions as fear and love dwell in the same heart? Certainly they are found in the hearts of children who love their parents and yet respect them and their authority. "Serve the Lord with fear, and rejoice with trembling" (Ps. 2:11).

The phrase "the love of Christ" means His love for us as seen in His sacrificial death. "We love him, because he first loved us" (1 John 4:19). He loved us when we were unlovely; in fact, He loved us when we were ungodly, sinners, and enemies (see Rom. 5:6–10). When He died on the cross, Christ proved His love for the world (John 3:16), the church (Eph. 5:25), and individual sinners (Gal. 2:20). When you consider the reasons why Christ died, you cannot help but love Him.

He died that we might die (v. 14). The tense of the verb gives the meaning "then all died." This truth is explained in detail in Romans 6, the believer's identification with Christ. When Christ died, we died in Him and with Him. Therefore, the old life should have no hold on us today. "I am crucified with Christ" (Gal. 2:20).

He died that we might live (vv. 15–17). This is the positive aspect of our identification with Christ: we not only died with Him, but we also were raised with Him that we might "walk in newness of life" (Rom. 6:4). Because we have died with Christ, we can overcome sin; and because we live with Christ, we can bear fruit for God's glory (Rom. 7:4).

He died that we might live *through* Him: "God sent his only begotten Son into the world, that we might live through him" (1 John 4:9). This is our experience of salvation, eternal life through faith in Jesus Christ. But He also died that we might live *for* Him, and not live unto ourselves (2 Cor. 5:15). This is our experience of service. It has well been said, "Christ died our death for us that we might live His life for Him." If a lost sinner has been to the cross and been saved, how can he spend the rest of his life in selfishness?

In 1858, Frances Ridley Havergal visited Germany with her father, who was getting treatment for his afflicted eyes. While in a pastor's home, she saw a picture of the crucifixion on the wall, with the words under it: "I did this for thee. What hast thou done for Me?" Quickly she took a piece of paper and wrote a poem based on that motto; but she was not satisfied with it, so she threw the paper into the fireplace. The paper came out unharmed! Later, her father encouraged her to publish it; and we sing it today to a tune composed by Philip P. Bliss.

> I gave My life for thee,
> My precious blood I shed,
> That thou might'st ransomed be,
> And quickened from the dead;
> I gave, I gave My life for thee,
> What hast thou given for Me?

Christ died that we might live *through* Him and *for* Him, and that we might live *with* Him. "Who died for us, that, whether we wake or sleep, we should live together with him" (1 Thess. 5:10). Because of Calvary, believers are going to heaven to live with Christ forever!

He died that we might die, and He died that we might live. But He also died that we might *share in the new creation* (2 Cor. 5:16–17). Our new relationship to Christ has brought about a new relationship to the world and the people around us. *We no longer look at life the way we used to.* To know Christ "after the flesh" means to evaluate Him from a human point of view. But "the days of his flesh" are ended (Heb. 5:7) because He has ascended to heaven and is now glorified at the Father's right hand.

Adam was the head of the old creation, and Christ (the Last Adam, 1 Cor. 15:45) is the Head of the new creation. The old creation was plunged into sin and condemnation because of the disobedience of Adam. The new creation means righteousness and salvation because of the obedience of Jesus Christ. (See Rom. 5:12–21 for the explanation of the "two Adams.")

Because we are a part of the new creation, everything has become new.

For one thing, we have a new view of Christ. It is unfortunate that too great an emphasis is given in music and art on Christ "after the flesh." The facts about the earthly life of Jesus are important, because the Christian message is grounded in history. But we must interpret the manger by the throne. We do not worship a Babe in a manger; we worship a glorified Savior on the throne.

Because "all things are become new," we also have a new view of people around us. We see them as sinners for whom Christ died. We no longer see them as friends or enemies, customers or coworkers; we see them the way Christ sees them, as lost sheep who need a shepherd. When you are constrained by the love of Christ, you want to share His love with others.

During an especially controversial presidential election, a church officer came into a Sunday school class wearing a large pin that promoted one of the candidates. The pastor stopped him and advised him to take it off until he was out of church.

"Why take it off?" he argued. "He's a perfectly good candidate!"

"But suppose the pin is seen by an unsaved man of the other party?" the pastor replied. "Will it upset him and maybe keep him from hearing the Word and getting saved?"

Sullenly, the man removed the pin; and then he smiled and said, "I guess I should remember that people aren't Republicans or Democrats. They're sinners who need a Savior—and that's more important than winning an election."

But we should also look at other Christians as a part of the new creation, and not evaluate them on the bases of education, race, finances, or position in society. "There is neither Jew nor Greek, there is neither bond nor free, there is neither male nor female: for ye are all one in Christ Jesus" (Gal. 3:28).

The Commission of Christ (5:18–21)

The key idea in this paragraph is *reconciliation.* Because of his rebellion, man was the enemy of God and out of fellowship with Him. Through the work of the cross, Jesus Christ has brought man and God together again. God has been reconciled and has turned His face in love toward the lost world. The basic meaning of the word *reconcile is* "to change thoroughly." It refers to a changed relationship between God and the lost world.

God does not have to be reconciled to man, because that was accomplished by Christ on the cross. It is sinful man who must be reconciled to God. "Religion" is man's feeble effort to be reconciled to God, efforts that are bound to fail. The Person who reconciles us to God is Jesus Christ, and the place where He reconciles us is His cross.

Another key idea in this section is *imputation.* This is a word borrowed from banking; it simply means "to put to one's account." When you deposit money in the bank, the computer (or the clerk) puts that amount to your account, or to your credit. When Jesus died on the cross, all of our sins were imputed to Him—put to His account. He was treated by God as though He had actually committed those sins.

The result? All of those sins have been paid for, and God no longer holds them against us, because we have trusted Christ as our Savior. But even more: God has put to our account the very righteousness of Christ! "For he hath made him [Christ] to be sin for us, who knew no sin; that we might be made the righteousness of God in him" (2 Cor. 5:21).

Reconciliation is based on imputation: because the demands of God's holy law have been fully met on the cross, God can be reconciled to sinners. Those who believe on Jesus Christ as their Savior will never have their sins imputed against them again (Ps. 32:1–2; Rom. 4:1–8). As far as their records are concerned, they share the righteousness of Jesus Christ!

There is a lovely illustration of this truth in the little letter Paul wrote to his friend Philemon. Philemon's slave, Onesimus, stole from his master and then fled to Rome. Because of his crimes, he could have been crucified. But in the providence of God, Onesimus met Paul and was converted. Paul wrote the Letter to Philemon to encourage his friend to forgive Onesimus and receive him home. "Receive him as myself," wrote Paul (Philem. 17); "if he … oweth thee aught, put that on mine account" (Philem. 18). Paul was willing to pay the bill (imputation) so that Onesimus and Philemon could be reconciled.

How does this wonderful doctrine of reconciliation motivate us to serve Christ? We are ambassadors with a message. God has committed to us the ministry and the word of reconciliation (2 Cor. 5:18–19).

In the Roman Empire, there were two kinds of provinces: senatorial provinces and imperial provinces. The senatorial provinces were made up of people who were peaceful and not at war with Rome. They had surrendered and submitted. But the imperial provinces were not peaceful; they were dangerous because they would rebel against Rome if they could. It was necessary for Rome to send ambassadors to the imperial provinces to make sure that rebellion did not break out.

Since Christians in this world are the ambassadors of Christ, this means that the world is in rebellion against God. This world is an "imperial province" as far as God is concerned. He has sent His ambassadors into the world to declare peace, not war. "Be ye reconciled to God!" We represent Jesus Christ (John 20:21; 2 Cor. 4:5). If sinners reject us and our message, it is Jesus Christ who is actually rejected. What a great privilege it is to be heaven's ambassadors to the rebellious sinners of this world!

When I was a young pastor, it used to embarrass me somewhat to make visits and confront people with the claims of Christ. Then it came to me that I was a privileged person, an ambassador of the King of Kings!

There was nothing to be embarrassed about. In fact, the people I visited should have been grateful that one of Christ's ambassadors came to see them.

God has not declared war on the world; at the cross He declared peace. But one day, He *will* declare war; and then it will be too late for those who have rejected the Savior (2 Thess. 1:3–10). Satan is seeking to tear everything apart in this world, but Christ and His church are involved in the ministry of reconciliation, bringing things back together again, and back to God.

Ministry is not easy. If we are to succeed, we must be motivated by the fear of the Lord, the love of Christ, and the commission that He has given to us. What a privilege it is to serve Him!

CHAPTER SIX
2 Corinthians 6—7
HEART TO HEART

These two chapters bring to a heartfelt conclusion Paul's explanation of his ministry. He has told his readers that, in spite of trials, his was a triumphant ministry (2 Cor. 1—2) and a glorious ministry (2 Cor. 3), and that he could not ever think of quitting. His enemies had accused him of using the ministry for personal gain, but he had proved his ministry to be sincere (2 Cor. 4) and based on faith in God (2 Cor. 5). All that remained now was to challenge the hearts of the Corinthians and assure them of his love; and this he did by presenting them with three loving appeals.

An Appeal for Appreciation (6:1–10)

Principles of Psychology by William James has been a classic text and certainly was a pioneer work in that field. But the author admitted that there was "an immense omission" in the book. "The deepest principle of human nature is the craving to be appreciated," he wrote; and yet he had not dealt with this principle in his book.

As you read 2 Corinthians, you get the strong impression that the church did not really appreciate Paul and the work he had done among them. They should have been defending Paul and not forcing him to defend himself. The Corinthians were boasting about the Judaizers who had invaded the church, and yet the Judaizers had done nothing for them. So Paul reminded them of the ministry God had given him at Corinth.

Paul the evangelist (vv. 1–2). It was Paul who had gone to Corinth with the good news of the gospel; and through his ministry, the church had been founded. He had fulfilled the work of the "ambassador" described in 2 Corinthians 5:18–21. It was not the Judaizers who had won them to Christ; it was Paul.

But even now, Paul was not certain that everybody in the church who professed to be saved was truly a child of God (see 2 Cor. 13:5). He quoted Isaiah 49:8

as his appeal for them to receive God's grace. Because of the reconciling work of Christ on the cross (2 Cor. 5:18–19), today is indeed "the day of salvation." There is no guarantee that any sinner will have the opportunity to be saved *tomorrow.* "Seek ye the Lord while he may be found" (Isa. 55:6).

A pastor was dealing with a young lady who was arguing that she had plenty of time to decide for Jesus Christ. He handed her a piece of paper and said, "Would you sign a statement that you would be willing to postpone salvation for a year?" No, she would not do that. Six months? No again. One month? She hesitated, but said no. Then she began to see the folly of her argument because she had assurance of opportunity *only for today;* and she trusted Christ without delay.

Paul the example (vv. 3–10). One of the greatest obstacles to the progress of the gospel is the bad example of people who profess to be Christians. Unsaved people like to use the inconsistencies of the saints—especially preachers—as an excuse for rejecting Jesus Christ. Paul was careful not to do anything that would put a stumbling block in the way of either sinners or saints (see Rom. 14). He did not want the ministry to be discredited ("blamed") in any way because of his life.

Paul reminded his readers of *the trials he had endured for them* (2 Cor. 6:4–5). He had been a man of endurance ("patience") and had not quit when things were tough. *Afflictions* are trials under pressure, when you are pressed down by circumstances. *Necessities* are the everyday hardships of life, and *distresses* refer to experiences that push us into a corner where there seems to be no escape. The Greek word means "a narrow place."

But even unsaved people go through those experiences, so Paul then listed a few of the trials he endured because of the opposition of people: stripes, imprisonments, and tumults (riots). These he experienced because he was faithfully serving the Lord. He then named some of the sacrifices he made voluntarily for the sake of the ministry: labors (work resulting in weariness), watchings (sleepless nights), fastings (willingly going without food). Of course, Paul had not announced these things publicly. The only reason he mentioned them in this letter was to assure the Corinthians of his love for them.

He further reminded them of *the tools he had used in his ministry* (2 Cor. 6:6–7). *Pureness* means "chastity" (see 2 Cor. 11:2). Paul kept himself morally clean. *Longsuffering* refers to patience with difficult people, while *patience* (2 Cor. 6:4) refers to endurance in difficult circumstances. Paul depended on the power of the Spirit so that he might manifest the fruit of the Spirit, such as kindness and sincere love. He used the Word of God to convey spiritual knowledge, and he wore the armor of God (see Eph. 6:10ff.) to protect him from satanic attacks.

Finally, he reminded them of *the testimony that he bore* (2 Cor. 6:8–10). Paul listed a series of paradoxes, because he knew that not everybody really understood him and his ministry. Paul's enemies gave an evil report of him as a man who was a dishonorable deceiver. But God gave a good report of Paul as a man who was honorable and true. Paul was well known and yet, at the same time, unknown.

What a price Paul paid to be faithful in his ministry! And yet how little the Corinthians really appreciated all he did for them. They brought sorrow to his heart, yet he was "always rejoicing" in Jesus Christ. He became poor that they might become rich (see 1 Cor. 1:5; 2 Cor. 8:9). The word translated "poor" means "the complete destitution of a beggar."

Was Paul wrong in appealing for their appreciation? I don't think so. Too many churches are prone to take for granted the sacrificial ministry of pastors, missionaries, and faithful church officers. Paul was not begging for praise, but he was reminding his friends in Corinth that his ministry to them had cost him dearly.

Of course, in all of this personal testimony, Paul was refuting the malicious accusations of the Judaizers. How much had *they* suffered for the people at Corinth? What price did *they* pay for their ministry? Like most "cultists" today, these false teachers stole another man's converts; they did not seek to win the lost themselves.

It has well been said, "If you want to find gratitude, look in the dictionary." Are we showing gratitude to those who have ministered to us?

An Appeal for Separation (6:11—7:1)

In spite of all the problems and heartaches the church had caused him, Paul still loved the believers at Corinth very much. He had spoken honestly and lovingly to them; now he tenderly asked them to open their hearts to him. He felt like a father whose children were robbing him of the love that he deserved (see 1 Cor. 4:15).

Why were they withholding their love? Because they had divided hearts. The false teachers had stolen their hearts, and now they were cool toward Paul. They were like a daughter engaged to be married, but being seduced by an unworthy suitor (see 2 Cor. 11:1–3). The Corinthians were compromising with the world, so Paul appealed to them to separate themselves to God, the way a faithful wife is separated to her husband.

It is unfortunate that the important doctrine of separation has been misunderstood and abused in recent years, for it is an essential truth. Some sincerely zealous Christians have turned separation into isolation, until their fellowship has become so narrow that they cannot even get along with themselves. In reaction to this extreme position, other believers have torn down all the walls and will fellowship with anybody, regardless of what he believes or how he lives. While we applaud their desire to practice Christian love, we want to remind them that even Christian love must exercise discernment (Phil. 1:9–11).

Paul presented three arguments to try to convince these believers that they must separate themselves from that which is contrary to God's will.

The nature of the believer (6:14–16). It is nature that determines association. Because a pig has a pig's nature, it associates with other pigs in the mud hole. Because a sheep has a sheep's nature, it munches grass with the flock in the pasture. The Christian possesses a divine nature (2 Peter 1:3–4), and therefore he should want to associate himself only with that which pleases the Lord.

The concept of the "unequal yoke" comes from Deuteronomy 22:10: "Thou shalt not plow with an ox and an ass together." The ox was a clean animal to the Jews, but the ass was not (Deut. 14:1–8); and it would be wrong to yoke them together. Furthermore, they have two opposite natures and would not even work well together. It would be cruel to bind them to each other. In the same way, it is wrong for believers to be yoked together with unbelievers.

Note the nouns that Paul used: *fellowship, communion, concord* (harmony), *part, agreement.* Each of these words speaks of having something in common. The word *concord* gives us our English word "symphony," and it speaks of beautiful music that comes when the players are reading the same score and obeying the same leader. What chaos we would have if each instrumentalist played his own tune in his own way!

God's desires for His people are seen in these words. He wants us to *share* with each other (fellowship) and *have in common* (communion) the blessings of the Christian life. He wants us to enjoy *harmony* and *agreement* as we live and work together. When we try to walk with the world and with the Lord at the same time, we break this spiritual fellowship and create discord and division.

Paul saw believers and unbelievers in stark contrast to each other: righteousness—unrighteousness, light—darkness, Christ—Belial (Satan), belief—infidelity (unbelief), God's temple—idols. How could you possibly bring these opposites together? The very nature of the Christian demands that he be separated from that which is unholy. When a saved person marries an unsaved partner, it sets up an impossible situation; and the same thing applies to business partnerships and religious "fellowship."

Note that the word *ye* is plural in 2 Corinthians 6:16. Paul is here referring to the local church as a whole, and not to the individual believer only, as in 1 Corinthians 6:19–20. The local church is the dwelling place of God because believers are the people of God (see Ex. 6:7; 25:8; Lev. 26:12; Ezek. 37:26–27). For a local church to compromise its testimony is like a holy temple being defiled.

The command of Scripture (6:17). The major part of this quotation is from Isaiah 52:11, but there are also echoes in it of Ezekiel 20:34, 41. The reference in Isaiah is to the captive nation leaving Babylon and returning to their own land, but the spiritual application is to the separation of the people of God today.

God commands His people to "come out," which implies a definite act on their part. "Be ye separate" suggests devotion to God for a special purpose. Separation is not just a negative act of departure; it is also a positive act of dedication to God. We must separate *from* sin and *unto* God. "Touch not the unclean thing" is a warning against defilement. The Old Testament Jew was defiled if he touched a dead body or the issue from a festering sore. Of course, Christians today do not contract spiritual defilement by touch, but the principle is the same: we must not associate with that which will compromise our testimony or lead us into disobedience.

God's command of separation is found throughout Scripture. He warned Israel not to mingle with the pagan nations in the land of Canaan (Num. 33:50–56); yet they repeatedly disobeyed His Word and were punished because of it. The prophets repeatedly pled with the people to forsake their heathen idols and devote themselves wholly to the Lord. Finally, God had to send Israel into Assyrian captivity and Judah into Babylonian captivity. Our Lord rejected the false "separation" of the Pharisees, but He did warn His disciples against the leaven (false doctrine) of the Pharisees and Sadducees, and He prayed that they would be kept from the defilement of the world (Matt. 16:6, 11; John 17:14–17).

The apostles in their letters to the churches also emphasized doctrinal and personal purity. The believer was *in* the world, but he must be careful not to become like the world. The church must also separate itself from those who reject the doctrine given by Christ and the apostles (Rom. 12:1–2; 16:17–20; Col. 3:1–2; 1 Tim. 6:10–11; Titus 2:14; 1 Peter 4:3–6; 1 John 4:6). Even in the book of Revelation, there is an emphasis on God's people being separated from that which is false and contrary to holy living (Rev. 2:14–16, 20–24; 18:4ff.).

In our desire for doctrinal and personal purity, we must not become so self-centered that we ignore the needy world around us. Our Lord was "holy, harmless, undefiled, separate from sinners" (Heb. 7:26), and yet He was "a friend of publicans and sinners" (Luke 7:34). Like a skillful physician, we must practice "contact without contamination." Otherwise, we will isolate ourselves from the people who need our ministry the most.

The promise of God's blessing (6:17—7:1). God becomes our Father when we trust Jesus Christ as our Savior, but He cannot *be to us* a Father unless we obey Him and fellowship with Him. He longs to receive us in love and treat us as His precious sons and daughters. Salvation means we share the Father's life, but separation means that we enter fully into the Father's love. Jesus promised this "deeper love" in John 14:21–23.

God blesses those who separate themselves from sin and unto the Lord. Abraham separated himself from Ur of the Chaldees and God blessed him. When Abraham compromised and went to Egypt, God had to chasten him (Gen. 11:31—12:20). As long as Israel was separated from the sinful nations in Canaan, God blessed them; but when they began to mingle with the heathen, God had to discipline them. Both Ezra and Nehemiah had to teach the people again the meaning of separation (Ezra 9—10; Neh. 9:2; 10:28; 13:1–9, 23–31).

Because of God's gracious promises, we have some spiritual responsibilities (2 Cor. 7:1). We must cleanse ourselves once and for all of anything that defiles us. It is not enough to ask God to cleanse us; we must clean up our own lives and get rid of those things that make it easy for us to sin. No believer can legislate for any other believer; each one knows the problems of his own heart and life.

Too often Christians deal with symptoms and not causes. We keep confessing the same sins because we have not gotten to the root of the trouble and "cleansed ourselves." Perhaps there is "filthiness of the flesh," some pet sin that "feeds" the old nature (Rom. 13:14). Or it may be "filthiness of the spirit," an attitude that is sinful. The prodigal son was guilty of sins of the flesh, but his "moral" elder brother was guilty of sins of the spirit. He could not even get along with his own father (see Luke 15:11–21).

But cleansing ourselves is only half of the responsibility; we must also be "perfecting holiness in the fear of God" (2 Cor. 7:1). This is a constant process as we grow in grace and knowledge (2 Peter 3:18). It is important to be balanced. The Pharisees were keen on putting away sin, but they neglected to perfect holiness. But it is foolish to try to perfect holiness if there is known sin in our lives.

Paul had appealed for appreciation and for separation. He gave one final appeal in his attempt to regain the love and devotion of the believers in Corinth.

An Appeal for Reconciliation (7:2–16)

"Open wide your hearts to us!" (see 2 Cor. 6:13). "Receive us" (2 Cor. 7:2). "Can two walk together, except they be agreed?" (Amos 3:3). If the Corinthians would only cleanse their lives and their church fellowship, God would receive them (2 Cor. 6:17) and they could again have close fellowship with Paul.

The emphasis in this section is on the way God encouraged Paul after he had experienced such great trials in Asia and Troas (see 2 Cor. 1:8–10; 2:12–13). There is actually a threefold encouragement recorded in these verses.

Paul encouraged the church (vv. 2–4). The church had received Titus; now they should receive Paul (2 Cor. 7:13). Paul asked them to trust him, for he had never done anything to wrong them. This is certainly a reference to the false teachers who had accused Paul, especially the use of the word *defrauded* ("exploits," see 2 Cor. 11:20 NIV). "Paul is taking up this missionary offering so he can use the money himself!" they were saying.

Why is it so difficult to assure people of our love?

What more could Paul do to convince them? He was willing to die for them if necessary, for they were in his heart (see 2 Cor. 3:1ff.; 6:11–13). He was boasting of them to others ("glorying of you"), but they were criticizing him.

But, in spite of these problems, Paul had good reason to encourage the church, because the visit of Titus had been successful; and now there was opportunity to "mend the fences" and restore fellowship. This leads to the second encouragement.

Titus encouraged Paul (vv. 5–10). The first encouragement Paul received was the coming of Titus after they had been separated from each other. It was not easy to communicate or to travel in those days, and Paul had to depend on the providence of God for his plans to work out regarding the visit of Titus to Corinth. (Even with our modern means of transportation and communication, we still need to depend on God's providence.)

But Paul was encouraged by the report that Titus gave of his reception at Corinth. They had read Paul's "painful letter" and had repented of their sins and disciplined the members who had created the problems. It is unfortunate that the King James Version translates two different Greek words as "repent," for they have different meanings. The word *repent* in 2 Corinthians 7:8 means "regret," and *repented* in 2 Corinthians 7:10 means "to be regretted."

Paul had written them a stern letter, and then had regretted it. But the letter achieved its purpose and the Corinthians repented, and this made Paul rejoice. Their repentance was not merely a passing "regret"; it was a true godly sorrow for sin. "Godly sorrow brings repentance that leads to salvation and leaves no regret, but worldly sorrow brings death" (2 Cor. 7:10 NIV). The difference is seen in Judas and Peter. Judas "repented himself" (was full of regret) and went and committed suicide, while Peter wept and repented of his fall (Matt. 26:75—27:5).

Do Christians need to repent? Jesus said that we do (Luke 17:3–4), and Paul agreed with Him (2 Cor. 12:21). Four of the seven churches of Asia Minor, listed in Revelation 2 and 3, were commanded to repent. To repent simply means "to change one's mind," and disobedient Christians need to repent, not in order to be saved, but in order to restore their close fellowship with God.

The Corinthians encouraged Titus (vv. 11–16). They went to great lengths to do the will of God. First of all, they received Titus and refreshed him by their fellowship (2 Cor. 7:13). They rejoiced his heart as they proved to be all that Paul boasted that they were. They accepted his message from Paul and acted on it.

In 2 Corinthians 7:11, Paul spelled out their handling of the matter of discipline. "For behold what earnestness this very thing, this godly sorrow, has produced in you; what vindication of yourselves, what indignation, what fear, what longing, what zeal, what avenging of wrong! In everything you demonstrated yourselves to be innocent in the matter" (NASB). Paul was encouraged when Titus told him of the way they repented and showed concern and zeal to do what was right. Paul assured them that the purpose of his letter was not only to rebuke the offender and help the offended, but to prove his love for the church. Paul had suffered a great deal because of this situation, but his suffering was worth it all now that the problem was solved.

One of the most difficult things to do is to rebuild a shattered relationship. This Paul tried to do in 2 Corinthians, and especially in chapters 6 and 7. Unfortunately, there are many shattered relationships today—in homes, churches, and ministries—and they can be repaired and strengthened only when people face problems honestly, deal with them biblically and lovingly, and seek to get right with God.

As you and I examine our own lives, we must determine to be a part of the answer and not a part of the problem. We must show appreciation, practice separation, and encourage reconciliation if God is to use us to restore broken relationships.

CHAPTER SEVEN
2 Corinthians 8
THE GRACE OF GIVING—PART 1

One of the major ministries of Paul's third missionary journey was the taking up of a special "relief offering" for the poor Christians in Judea. Once before Paul had assisted in this way (Acts 11:27–30), and he was happy to do it again. It is significant that it was Paul who remembered the "forgotten beatitude" of our Lord: "It is more blessed to give than to receive" (Acts 20:35).

But Paul had other blessings in mind besides the material assisting of the poor. He wanted this offering to strengthen the unity of the church as the Gentile churches shared with the Jewish congregations across the sea. Paul saw the Gentiles as "debtors" to the Jews (Rom. 15:25–28), and the special collection was one way to pay that debt.

This offering was also evidence to the Jewish believers (some of whom were still zealous for the law) that Paul was not the enemy of the Jews or of Moses (Acts 20:17ff.). Early in his ministry, Paul had promised to remember the poor (Gal. 2:6–10), and he labored to keep that promise; but at the same time, he hoped that the generosity of the Gentiles would silence the jealousy of the Jews.

Unfortunately, the Corinthians were not doing their part. Like many people, they had made promises, but they failed to keep them. In fact, an entire year had been wasted (2 Cor. 8:10). What was the cause of this serious delay? The low spiritual level of the church. When a church is not spiritual, it is not generous. Another factor was the invasion of the Judaizers, who

probably siphoned off as much money as they could (2 Cor. 11:7–12, 20; 12:14).

Paul knew that it would be difficult to get the Corinthians to participate, so he lifted his appeal to the highest spiritual level possible: he taught them that giving was an act of grace. Paul used nine different words to refer to the offering, but the one he used the most was *grace*. Giving is truly a *ministry* and *fellowship* (2 Cor. 8:4) that helps others, but the motivation must be from the grace of God in the heart. Paul knew that this collection was a *debt* owed by the Gentiles (Rom. 15:27) and *fruit* from their Christian lives (Rom. 15:28); but it was even more: it was the working of the grace of God in human hearts.

It is a wonderful thing when Christians enter into the grace of giving, when they really believe that giving is more blessed than receiving. How can we tell when we are practicing "grace giving"? Paul indicated that there were a number of evidences that appear when our giving is motivated by grace.

When We Give in Spite of Circumstances (8:1–2)
The Macedonian churches that Paul was using as an example had experienced severe difficulties, and yet they had given generously. They had not simply gone through "affliction"; they had experienced a "great trial of affliction" (2 Cor. 8:2). They were in *deep poverty,* which means "rock-bottom destitution." The word describes a beggar who has absolutely nothing and has no hope of getting anything. Their difficult situation may have been caused in part by their Christian faith, for they may have lost their jobs or been excluded from the trade guilds because they refused to have anything to do with idolatry.

But their circumstances did not hinder them from giving. In fact, they gave joyfully and liberally! No computer could analyze this amazing formula: great affliction and deep poverty *plus grace* equals abundant joy and abounding liberality! It reminds us of the paradox in Paul's ministry: "as poor, yet making many rich" (2 Cor. 6:10). It also reminds us of the generous offerings that were taken at the building of the tabernacle (Ex. 35:5–6) and the temple (1 Chron. 29:6–9).

When you have experienced the grace of God in your life, you will not use difficult circumstances as an excuse for not giving. For that matter, are circumstances *ever* an encouragement to giving? In my first pastorate, we had a great need for a new church building; but some of the people opposed a building program because of the "economic situation." Apparently the steel mills were planning to go on strike, and the refineries were going to shut down, and the railroads were having problems … and it seemed like a risky time to build. But there were enough people who believed in "grace giving" so that the church did erect a new sanctuary—in spite of the strikes, shutdowns, layoffs, and other economic problems. Grace giving means giving in spite of circumstances.

When We Give Enthusiastically (8:3–4)

It is possible to give generously but not give enthusiastically. "The preacher says I should give until it hurts," said a miserly church member, "but for me, it hurts just to think about giving!" The Macedonian churches needed no prompting or reminding, as did the church at Corinth. They were more than willing to share in the collection. In fact, *they begged to be included* (2 Cor. 8:4)! How many times have you heard a Christian *beg* for somebody to take an offering?

Their giving was voluntary and spontaneous. It was of grace, not pressure. They gave because they wanted to give and because they had experienced the grace of God. Grace not only frees us from our sins, but it frees us from ourselves. The grace of God will open your heart *and your hand.* Your giving is not the result of cold calculation, but of warmhearted jubilation!

When We Give as Jesus Gave (8:5–9)

Jesus Christ is always the preeminent example for the believer to follow, whether in service, suffering, or sacrifice. Like Jesus Christ, the Macedonian Christians *gave themselves to God and to others* (2 Cor. 8:5). If we give ourselves to God, we will have little problem giving our substance to God. If we give ourselves to God, we will also give of ourselves for others. It is impossible to love God and ignore the needs of your neighbor. Jesus Christ gave Himself for us (Gal. 1:4; 2:20). Should we not give ourselves to Him? He died so that we might not live for ourselves, but for Him and for others (2 Cor. 5:15).

The Macedonians' giving was, like Christ's, *motivated by love* (2 Cor. 8:7–8). What a rebuke to the Corinthians, who were so enriched with spiritual blessings (1 Cor. 1:4–5). They were so wrapped up in the *gifts* of the Spirit that they had neglected the *graces* of the Spirit, including the grace of giving. The Macedonian churches had an "abundance of deep poverty" (2 Cor. 8:2), and yet they abounded in their liberality. The Corinthians had an abundance of spiritual gifts, yet they were lax in keeping their promise and sharing in the collection.

We must never argue that the ministry of our spiritual gifts is a substitute for generous giving. "I teach a Sunday school class, so I don't have to give!" is not an explanation—it's an excuse. The Christian who remembers that his gifts are *gifts* will be motivated to give to others and not "hide" behind his ministry for the Lord. I have met pastors and missionaries who have argued that, since they devote their whole time in serving the Lord, they are not obligated to give. Paul argued just the opposite: since you are wonderfully gifted from God, you ought to want to give even more!

Paul was careful that they understood that he was not *ordering* them to give. Actually, he was contrasting the attitude of the Macedonians with that of the Corinthians. He was pointing out that the Macedonians were following the example of the Lord: they were poor, yet they gave. The Corinthians said that they loved Paul; now he asked them to prove that love by sharing in the offering. Grace giving is an evidence of love—love for Christ, love for God's servants who have ministered to us, and love for those who have special needs that we are able to help meet.

Finally, *their giving was sacrificial* (2 Cor. 8:9). In what ways was Jesus rich? Certainly He was rich in His person, for He is eternal God. He is rich in His possessions and in His position as King of Kings and Lord of Lords. He is rich in His power, for He can do anything. Yet, in spite of the fact that He had all these riches—and more—*He became poor.*

The tense of the verb indicates that it is His incarnation, His birth at Bethlehem, that is meant here. He united Himself to mankind and took on Himself a human body. He left the throne to become a servant. He laid aside all His possessions so that He did not even have a place to lay His head. His ultimate experience of poverty was when He was made sin for us on the cross. Hell is eternal poverty, and on the cross Jesus Christ became the poorest of the poor.

Why did He do it? That we might become rich! This suggests that we were poor before we met Jesus Christ, and we were—totally bankrupt. But now that we have trusted Him, we share in all of His riches! We are now the children of God, "heirs of God, and joint-heirs with Jesus Christ" (Rom. 8:17). Since this is true, *how can we refuse to give to others?* He became poor to make us rich! Can we not follow His example, as did the Macedonian churches, who out of their deep poverty abounded in liberality?

When We Give Willingly (8:10–12)

There is a great difference between *promise* and *performance.* The Corinthians had boasted to Titus a year before that they would share in the special collection (2 Cor. 8:6), but they did not keep their promise. Note that in 2 Corinthians 8:10–12 Paul emphasized *willingness.* Grace giving must come from a willing heart; it cannot be coerced or forced.

During my years of ministry, I have endured many offering appeals. I have listened to pathetic tales about unbelievable needs. I have forced myself to laugh at old jokes that were supposed to make it easier for me to part with my money. I have been scolded, shamed, and almost threatened, and I must confess that none of these approaches has ever stirred me to give more than I planned to give. In fact, more than once I gave *less* because I was so disgusted with the worldly approach. (However, I have never gotten like Mark Twain, who said that he was so sickened by the long appeal that he not only did not give what he planned to give, but he took a bill out of the plate!)

We must be careful here not to confuse *willing* with *doing,* because the two must go together. If the willing is sincere and in the will of God, then there must be "a performance also" (2 Cor. 8:11; Phil. 2:12–13).

Paul did not say that *willing* was a substitute for *doing,* because it is not. But if our giving is motivated by grace, we will give willingly, and not because we have been forced to give.

God sees the "heart gift" and not the "hand gift." If the heart wanted to give more, but was unable to do so, God sees it and records it accordingly. But if the hand gives more than the heart wants to give, God records what is in the heart, no matter how big the offering in the hand might be.

A friend of mine was leaving for a business trip, and his wife reminded him before church that she needed some extra money for household expenses. Just before the offering, he slipped some money into her hand; and she, thinking it was their weekly offering, put it all in the plate. It was the expense money for the week.

"Well," said my friend, "we gave it to the Lord and He keeps the records."

"How much did you *intend* to give?" asked their pastor, and my friend gave an amount. "Then that's what God recorded," said the pastor, "because He saw the intent of your heart!"

God sees, not the portion, but the proportion. If we could have given more, and did not, God notes it. If we wanted to give more, and could not, God also notes that. When we give willingly, according to what we have, we are practicing grace giving.

When We Give by Faith (8:13–24)
Paul did not suggest that the rich become poor so that the poor might become rich. It would be unwise for a Christian to go into debt in order to relieve somebody else's debt, unless, of course, he was able to handle the responsibility of paying the debt back. Paul saw an "equality" in the whole procedure: the Gentiles were enriched spiritually by the Jews, so the Jews should be enriched materially by the Gentiles (see Rom. 15:25–28). Furthermore, the Gentile churches at that time were enjoying some measure of material wealth, while the believers in Judea were suffering. That situation could one day be reversed. There might come a time when the Jewish believers would be assisting the Gentiles.

Who does the equalizing? God does. Paul used the miracle of the manna as an illustration of the principle (Ex. 16:18). No matter how much manna the Jews gathered each day, they always had what they needed. Those who tried to hoard the manna discovered that it was impossible, because the manna would decay and smell (Ex. 16:20). The lesson is clear: gather what you need, share what you can, and don't try to hoard God's blessings. God will see to it that you will not be in need if you trust Him and obey His Word.

Our *motive* for giving is God's spiritual blessing in our lives, but our *measure* for giving is God's material blessing. Paul made this clear when he wrote to the Corinthians in his first letter, "Let every one of you lay by him in store, as God hath prospered him" (1 Cor. 16:2). Paul did not lay down any mathematical formula, because grace giving is not limited by a tithe (10 percent). Grace giving is systematic, but it is not legalistic. It is not satisfied with only the minimum, whatever that minimum might be.

Since it is God who does the "balancing of the books," we cannot accuse Paul of teaching some form of communism. In fact, 2 Corinthians 8:13 is a direct statement against communism. The so-called "communism" of the early church (Acts 2:44–47; 4:32–37) has no relationship to the communistic political and economic systems that are promoted today. The early Christians (like many Christians today) *voluntarily* shared what they had, but did not force people to participate. The entire program was temporary; and the fact that Paul had to take up a special collection to relieve their needs is proof that the program was never meant to be imitated by later generations of Christians.

Grace giving is a matter of faith: we obey God and believe that He will meet our needs as we help to meet the needs of others. As the Jews gathered the manna each day, so we must depend on God to "give us this day our daily bread" (Matt. 6:11). We must not waste or squander what God gives us, neither must we hoard it. In the will of God, it is right to save. (The Jews saved Friday's manna to eat on the Sabbath, and the manna did not decay [Ex. 16:22–26].) But out of God's will, the wealth that we hoard will harm us rather than help us (see James 5:1–6).

Beginning in 2 Corinthians 8:16, Paul suddenly turned from a profound spiritual principle to some practical counsel on how the special collection would be handled. While it is true that grace giving means giving by faith, it is also true that grace giving does not mean giving by chance. The Christian who shares with others must be sure that what he gives is managed honestly and faithfully.

Over the years, I have tried to encourage God's people to support ministries that could be trusted. On more than one occasion, I have warned a church member not to give to an unworthy organization, only to discover that he gave anyway. Then he would come to me a few months later and say, "I sent a check to that outfit, and now I discover that it's a fake!"

"I warned you not to give anything," I would reply very gently.

"Well, the Lord knows my heart," he would argue. "Even though the money was wasted, I got credit for the gift in heaven!"

Grace giving is not foolish giving. Even in a local church, the people who handle the funds must possess certain qualifications. Paul was very careful how he handled money entrusted to him, because he did not want to get the reputation of being a "religious thief." The churches that contributed to the collection chose certain representatives to travel with Paul, so that everything would be done honestly, decently, and in order.

I noted in one of our Sunday school classes in

a church I pastored that *one* young man was taking up the offering, counting it, recording it, and then taking it to the Sunday school office. In a nonthreatening way, I suggested that he was putting himself in a dangerous position if anybody accused him of anything, because he could not prove that he was handling the money honestly. "I trust you," I said, "but I don't trust the people who may be watching you and looking for something to criticize." Instead of following my suggestion, he became very angry and left the church.

The men and women in every Christian ministry—a local church, a missionary organization, an evangelistic meeting—should possess the following qualifications if they are to handle God's money.

A God-given desire to serve (vv. 16–17). Paul did not "draft" Titus; the young man had a desire in his heart to assist in the gathering of the special offering. Too often in local churches, men and women are put on the finance committee who do not have a sincere desire to serve God in this way. Above all else, a person who handles the Lord's money must have a heart that is right with God.

A burden for lost souls (v. 18). We do not know who this brother was, but we thank God he had a testimony that he shared the gospel. Perhaps he was an evangelist; at least he was known to the churches as a man burdened for souls. Local church nominating committees put the good "soul-winners" on the evangelism committee or on the missions committee, which is fine; but some of them also ought to be on the finance committee or the board of trustees. Why? *To keep the priorities straight.* I have seen committees approve large sums for buildings and equipment who would not release funds for a soul-winning ministry.

A discouraged young pastor sought my counsel one day. "My finance committee is running scared," he said. "The economic situation has made them so tightfisted, they won't spend any money—and we have a big surplus in the bank!" I had never met his committee, but I knew one thing about them: they needed a burden for lost souls.

A desire to honor God (v. 19). Too often, financial reports glorify the church, or a group of special donors, and do not glorify God. There is no such thing in the church as "secular and sacred," "business and ministry." All that we do is "sacred business" and ministry for the Lord. When the church constitution says that the deacons (or elders) handle the "spiritual affairs" of the church, and the trustees handle the "material and financial affairs," it is making an unbiblical distinction. *The most spiritual thing a church can do is use its money wisely for spiritual ministry.*

We glorify God by using what He gives us the way He wants it used. If the people who manage church finances are not burdened to glorify God, they will soon be using those funds in ways that dishonor God.

A reputation for honesty (vv. 20–22). Paul made it clear that he welcomed the representatives from the cooperating churches. He wanted to avoid any blame. It is not enough to say, "Well, the Lord sees what we're doing!" We should make certain that *men* can see what we are doing. I like the way J. B. Phillips translated 2 Corinthians 8:21: "Naturally we want to avoid the slightest breath of criticism in the distribution of their gifts, and to be absolutely aboveboard not only in the sight of God but in the eyes of men."

Personally, I would not support a missionary or Christian worker who was not identified in some way with a reputable committee or board, or a reputable organization. Nor would I give support to any ministry that did not have its books audited and the report available to the donors. I am not saying that all "free-lance" Christian workers are irresponsible; but I would have more confidence in their ministries if they were attached to a board or an organization that supervised their financial support.

Note the emphasis in 2 Corinthians 8:22 on *diligence.* If there is one quality that is needed when handling finances, it is diligence. I have heard of church treasurers who did not keep up-to-date accurate records of income and expenditures, and who handed in careless annual reports with the excuse that they were "too busy to keep up with the books." Then they should not have taken the office!

A cooperative spirit (vv. 23–24). Titus not only had a heart for this ministry (2 Cor. 8:16), but he knew how to be a good "team member." Paul called him his "partner" and "fellow helper." Titus was not like the committee member I heard about who said at the first meeting, "As long as I am on this committee, there will be no unanimous votes!"

Finance committee members do not *own* the money; it belongs to the Lord. The committee is but a steward, managing the money honestly and carefully for the service of the Lord. Note too that Paul saw the committee as special servants of the *churches.* The raising of this special "relief fund" was a cooperative effort of the Gentile churches, and Paul and the representatives were but "messengers" of the churches. The Greek word is *apostolos,* from which we get "apostle—one sent with a special commission." These dedicated Christians felt an obligation to the churches to do their work honestly and successfully.

Grace giving is an exciting adventure! When you learn to give "by grace, through faith" (just the way you were saved, Eph. 2:8–9), you start to experience a wonderful liberation from things and from circumstances. Instead of *things* possessing you, you start to control them; you develop a new set of values and priorities. You no longer measure life or other people on the basis of money or possessions. If money is the best test of success, then Jesus was a failure, because He was a poor Man!

Grace giving enriches you as you enrich others.

Grace giving makes you more like Jesus Christ.

Have you discovered the thrill of grace giving?

CHAPTER EIGHT
2 Corinthians 9
THE GRACE OF GIVING—PART 2

It seems strange that we Christians need encouragement to give, when God has given so much to us. God had enriched the Corinthians in a wonderful way, and yet they were hesitant to share what they had with others. They were not accustomed to *grace* giving, so Paul had to explain it to them. Having explained grace giving to them, Paul then tried to motivate them to get involved in the special offering; he did this by sharing five encouragements that relate to grace giving.

Your Giving Will Provoke Others (9:1–5)
While Christians must not compete with each other in their service for Christ, they ought to "consider one another to provoke unto love and to good works" (Heb. 10:24). When we see what God is doing in and through the lives of others, we ought to strive to serve Him better ourselves. There is a fine line between fleshly imitation and spiritual emulation, and we must be careful in this regard. But a zealous Christian can be the means of stirring up a church and motivating people to pray, work, witness, and give.

The interesting thing is this: Paul had used the zeal of the Corinthians to challenge the Macedonians; but now he was using the Macedonians to challenge the Corinthians! A year before, the Corinthians had enthusiastically boasted that they would share in the offering, but then they had done nothing. The Macedonians had followed through on their promise, and Paul was afraid that his boasting would be in vain.

Paul sent Titus and the other brothers to Corinth to stir them up to share in the offering. Far more important than the money itself was the spiritual benefit that would come to the church as they shared in response to God's grace in their lives. Paul had written to the church before to tell them how to take up the contributions (1 Cor. 16:1–4), so there was no excuse for their delay. Paul wanted the entire contribution to be ready when he and his "finance committee" arrived, so that there might not be any last-minute collections that might appear to be forced on the church.

What did Paul want to avoid? Embarrassment to himself and to the church if the offering was not ready. For, after all, there were several representatives from the Macedonian churches on the special committee (see Acts 20:4). Paul had boasted to the Macedonians about Corinth, and now he feared that his boasting might be in vain.

Apparently, Paul did not see anything wrong or unspiritual about asking people to promise to give. He did not tell them *how much* they had to promise, but he did expect them to keep their promise. When a person signs up for a telephone, he promises to pay a certain amount each month. If it is acceptable to make

financial commitments for things like telephones, cars, and credit cards, certainly it ought to be acceptable to make commitments for the work of the Lord.

Notice the words that Paul used as he wrote about the collection. It was "ministering to the saints," a service to fellow believers. It was also a "bounty" (2 Cor. 9:5), which means "a generous gift." Was Paul perhaps hinting that the Corinthians give more than they had planned?

However, Paul was careful not to put on any pressure. He wanted their gift to be "a matter of bounty [generosity], and not as of covetousness [something squeezed out of them]." High-pressure offering appeals do not belong to grace giving.

Our greatest encouragement for giving is that it pleases the Lord, but there is nothing wrong with practicing the kind of giving that provokes others to give. This does not mean that we should advertise what we do as individuals, because that kind of practice would violate one of the basic principles of giving: give secretly to the Lord (Matt. 6:1–4). However, Paul was writing to *churches;* and it is not wrong for congregations to announce what they have given collectively. If our motive is to boast, then we are not practicing grace giving. But if our desire is to provoke others to share, then God's grace can work through us to help others.

Your Giving Will Bless You (9:6–11)
"Give, and it shall be given unto you," was our Lord's promise; and it still holds true (Luke 6:38). The "good measure" He gives back to us is not always money or material goods, but it is always worth far more than we gave. Giving is not something we *do,* but something we *are.* Giving is a way of life for the Christian who understands the grace of God. The world simply does not understand a statement like Proverbs 11:24: "There is that scattereth, and yet increaseth; and there is that withholdeth more than is meet, but it tendeth to poverty." In grace giving, our motive is not "to get something," but receiving God's blessing is one of the fringe benefits.

If our giving is to bless us and build us up, we must be careful to follow the principles that Paul explained in this section.

The principle of increase: we reap in measure as we sow (v. 6). This principle needs little explanation, because we see it operating in everyday life. The farmer who sows much seed will have a better chance for a bigger harvest. The investor who puts a large sum of money in the bank will certainly collect more dividends. The more we invest in the work of the Lord, the more "fruit" will abound to our account (Phil. 4:10–20).

Whenever we are tempted to forget this principle, we need to remind ourselves that God was unsparing in His giving. "He that spared not his own Son, but delivered him up for us all, how shall he not with him also freely give us all things?" (Rom. 8:32). In both nature and grace, God is a generous Giver; and he who would be godly must follow the divine example.

The principle of intent: we reap as we sow with right motives (v. 7). Motive makes absolutely no difference to the farmer! If he sows good seed and has good weather, he will reap a harvest whether he is working for profit, pleasure, or pride. It makes no difference how he plans to use the money that he earns; the harvest will probably come just the same.

But not so with the Christian: motive in giving (or in any other activity) is vitally important. Our giving must come from the heart, and the motive in the heart must please God. We must not be "sad givers" who give grudgingly, or "mad givers" who give because we have to ("of necessity"); but we should be "glad givers" who cheerfully share what we have because we have experienced the grace of God. "He that hath a bountiful eye shall be blessed" (Prov. 22:9).

If we cannot give joyfully (the Greek word gives us our English word *hilarious),* then we must open our hearts to the Lord and ask Him to grant us His grace. Certainly God can bless a gift that is given out of a sense of duty, but God cannot bless the giver unless his heart is right. Grace giving means that God blesses the giver as well as the gift, and that the giver is a blessing to others.

The principle of immediacy: we reap even while we are sowing (vv. 8–11). The farmer has to wait for his harvest, but the believer who practices grace giving begins to reap the harvest immediately. To be sure, there are long-range benefits from our giving, but there are also immediate blessings.

To begin with, we start to share God's abundant grace (2 Cor. 9:8). The "universals" in this verse are staggering: *all* grace; *always; all* sufficiency, *every* good work. This does not mean that God makes every Christian wealthy in material things; but it does mean that the Christian who practices grace giving will always have what he needs when he needs it. Furthermore, the grace of God enriches him morally and spiritually so that he grows in Christian character. In his walk and his work, he depends wholly on the sufficiency of God.

It is disturbing to see how many Christians today are totally dependent on others for their spiritual resources. Preachers cannot get sermons unless they borrow them from a book or a other resource. Church officers are bewildered about what to do with a problem unless they phone two or three well-known preachers for advice. Far too many church members have to consult with the pastor once a week or they fall apart spiritually.

The word *sufficiency* means "adequate resources within" (see Phil. 4:11). Through Jesus Christ, we can have the adequacy to meet the demands of life. As Christians, we do need to help and encourage one another; but we must not depend on one another. Our dependence must be on the Lord. He alone can give us that "well of water" in the heart that makes us sufficient for life (John 4:14).

We not only share God's grace, but we also share His righteousness (2 Cor. 9:9). Paul quoted Psalm 112:9 to prove his point. That psalm describes the righteous man who has no fears because his heart is sincere and obedient to the Lord. Paul did not suggest that we *earn* righteousness by our giving, because the only way to get righteousness is by faith in Jesus Christ. However, if our hearts are right, our giving will be used by God to make our character righteous. Grace giving builds Christian character.

We reap as we sow, and we share God's miracle multiplication of what we give and do (2 Cor. 9:10). The farmer has to decide how much seed he will keep for food and how much he will plant. If the harvest has been lean, there is less seed available both for eating and planting. But the Christian who believes in grace giving never has to worry about this decision: God supplies all that he needs. There is always spiritual and material "bread" for the eating and spiritual and material "seed" for the sowing.

Paul referred here to Isaiah 55:10–11, a passage that uses "seed" and "bread" to refer to both the Word of God and to the literal harvest in the field. There is no such thing as "secular" and "sacred" in the Christian life. The giving of money is just as spiritual an act as the singing of a hymn or the handing out of a gospel tract. *Money is seed.* If we give it according to the principles of grace, it will multiply to the glory of God and meet many needs. If we use it in ways other than God desires, the harvest will be poor.

Finally, as we sow, we are enriched and we enrich others (2 Cor. 9:11). The farmer reaps immediate physical benefits as he works in his field, but he has to wait for the harvest. The Christian who is motivated by grace reaps the blessings of personal enrichment in his or her own life and character, and this enrichment benefits others. The final result is glory to God as others give thanks to Him. Paul was careful to point out that grace giving does not bring credit to us; it brings thanksgiving to God. We are but channels through whom God works to meet the needs of others.

But 2 Corinthians 9:11 teaches another truth: God enriches us so that we may give even more bountifully. One of the joys of grace giving is the joy of giving more and more. Everything we have—not just our income—belongs to God, is given to God, and is used by God to accomplish His work. We are enriched in everything because we share everything with Him and with others.

As a pastor, I have watched young Christians lay hold of these principles of grace giving and start to grow. It has been a great joy to see them trust God as their giving is motivated by grace. At the same time, I have seen other believers smile at these principles and gradually impoverish themselves. Some of them "prospered" financially, but their income was their downfall: it did not enrich them. They had their reward, but they lost their opportunities for spiritual enrichment.

Grace giving means that we really believe that God is the great Giver, and we use our material and spiritual resources accordingly. You simply cannot outgive God!

Your Giving Will Meet Needs (9:12)

Paul introduced a new word for the offering: *service.* It means "priestly service," so once again, Paul lifted the offering to the highest level possible. He saw this collection as a "spiritual sacrifice" presented to God, the way a priest presented a costly sacrifice on the altar.

Christians no longer bring animals as sacrifices to God, because the work of Christ on the cross has ended the Levitical system (Heb. 10:1–14). But the material gifts we bring to the Lord become "spiritual sacrifices" if they are given in the name of Jesus (Phil. 4:10–20; Heb. 13:15–16; 1 Peter 2:5).

But the emphasis in 2 Corinthians 9:12 is on the fact that their offering would meet the needs of poor saints in Judea. "For the administration of this service not only supplieth the want of the saints, but is abundant also by many thanksgivings unto God" (2 Cor. 9:12). The Gentile believers could have given a number of excuses for not giving. "It's not our fault that they had a famine and are poor!" might have been one of them. Or, "The churches closer to Judea ought to give them help." Or, "We believe in giving, but we think we should first take care of our own."

When a Christian starts to think of excuses for not giving, he automatically moves out of the sphere of grace giving. *Grace never looks for a reason; it only looks for an opportunity.* If there is a need to be met, the grace-controlled Christian will do what he can to meet it.

"As we have therefore opportunity, let us do good unto all men, especially unto them who are of the household of faith" (Gal. 6:10). Paul admonished the wealthy Christians "that they do good, that they be rich in good works, ready to distribute, willing to communicate [share]" (1 Tim. 6:18). Most of us would not consider ourselves "wealthy," but the rest of the world does.

However, *we* are not the ones who get the glory; it is the Lord who is glorified (Matt. 5:16). Many people will give thanksgiving to God because of our sharing in the meeting of their needs. We may not hear that thanksgiving on earth today, but we will hear it in heaven when the church is gathered together.

It might be profitable here to notice Paul's use of the concept of *abundance* as he wrote this letter. He opened the letter with abundant suffering that was matched by abundant comfort (2 Cor. 1:5). He also mentioned abundant grace (2 Cor. 4:15) and abundant joy and liberality (2 Cor. 8:2). Because of God's abundant grace, we can abound always in every good work (2 Cor. 9:8). The apostle saw the Christian life as one of abundance, for Jesus Christ can make us adequate for every situation.

Our giving ought to provide for necessities, not subsidize luxuries. There are needs to be met, and our limited resources must not be squandered. It is true that the need itself is not the only reason for giving, for there are always more needs than any one Christian or church can meet; but the need is important. Some needs are greater than others, and some needs are more strategic than others. We need accurate information as well as spiritual illumination as we seek to meet the many needs that are pressing on us today.

Your Giving Will Glorify God (9:13)

"Let your light so shine before men," said our Lord, "that they may see your good works, and glorify your Father which is in heaven" (Matt. 5:16). This is one of the beauties of church giving: no individual gets the glory that belongs only to God.

For what would the grateful Jewish believers give thanks? Of course, they would praise God for the generosity of the Gentile churches in meeting their physical and material needs. But they would also praise God for the spiritual submission of the Gentiles, their obedience to the Spirit of God who gave them the desire to give. They would say, "Those Gentiles not only preach the gospel, but they also practice it!"

The little phrase *and unto all men* at the end of this verse (2 Cor. 9:13) is significant. The Jewish believers would give thanks that *others* were also being assisted by the Gentile churches. Each little congregation that received aid would be thankful for that aid and for the aid being given to others. Instead of saying, "Why didn't *we* get more?" they would be praising God that others in need were also being helped. That is the way grace giving works.

It might be good for our churches to take inventory to see if anybody is giving thanks to God for our obedience and generosity. No amount of evangelistic zeal or worship activity can compensate for lost opportunities in serving others and meeting their practical needs. It is not a matter of choosing one and ignoring the other. There must be a balance of sharing the gospel and meeting practical needs, if our light is to shine brightly and steadily. It has well been said that it is difficult to preach the gospel to a hungry man (see James 2:15–16).

I recall reading about a wealthy Christian who daily, at family devotions, prayed for the needs of the missionaries that his church supported. One morning, after he had concluded family prayers, his little boy said, "Dad, if I had your checkbook, I could answer your prayers!" A discerning lad, indeed!

Your Giving Will Unite God's People (9:14–15)

This, of course, was one of the major purposes that Paul had on his heart when he challenged the Gentile churches to assist the Jewish believers. The extreme legalists in the church had accused Paul of being anti-Jewish and even anti-law. The Gentile churches were removed from the "mother church" in Jerusalem both by distance and culture. Paul wanted to prevent a division in the church, and the "relief offering" was a part of that prevention program.

In what ways would this offering bind the Jewish and Gentile congregations more closely? For one thing, the offering was an expression of love. The Gentiles were not obligated to share (though Paul did see the offering as the payment of a "spiritual debt," Rom. 15:25–27), but they did so because of the grace of God. The Jews, in turn, would feel themselves bound to their Gentile brothers and sisters.

Another spiritual bond would be prayer. "And in their prayers for you their hearts will go out to you, because of the surpassing grace God has given you" (2 Cor. 9:14 NIV). Were the Gentile churches "buying" the prayer support of the Jewish churches? Not in the least! Paul envisioned a spontaneous expression of love, praise, and prayer as he shared the offering in Judea.

I have had the experience of visiting several mission fields and hearing believers there say, "We are praying for you." I recall chatting with a fine Christian from eastern Europe, who said, "We are praying for you in the United States, because in some ways, you have a more difficult time being spiritual Christians than we do." When I asked him to explain, he smiled and said, "You have relatively easy lives, and comfort is an enemy of the spiritual life. In eastern Europe, we know who our enemies are, and we know who our friends are. Where you live, it is easy to be fooled. Yes, we are praying for you!"

Both the Jewish and the Gentile churches would be drawn closer to Jesus Christ. "Thanks [grace] be unto God for his unspeakable [indescribable] gift" (2 Cor. 9:15). In Jesus Christ, all human distinctions are erased, and we no longer see each other as Jews or Gentiles, rich or poor, givers or recipients. "For ye are all one in Christ Jesus" (Gal. 3:28).

It is sad when our giving becomes a substitute for our living. A church officer once complained to me, "I'll give any amount of money you want for missions. Just don't make me listen to a missionary speak!" When a Christian practices grace giving, his money is not a substitute for either his concern or his service. He first gives himself to the Lord (2 Cor. 8:5) and then he gives what he has. His gift is a symbol, as it were, of the surrender of his heart. You cannot separate the gift and the giver when your giving is motivated by God's grace.

I suggest you read 2 Corinthians 8 and 9 again, and that you note the emphasis on the grace of God. If our churches and other ministries would get back to grace giving, there would be fewer high-pressure offering appeals, fewer gimmicks to raise funds, and fewer complaints from the people of God. Instead, there would be plenty of money available for the ministries that truly magnify the grace of God. And I think that the unsaved people in the world would sit up and take notice!

You and I are saved because God believed in grace giving.

How much do *we* believe in grace giving?

CHAPTER NINE
2 Corinthians 10
MINISTERIAL MISUNDERSTANDINGS

Whenever I receive a critical letter from a reader or a radio listener, I usually set it aside in a special file until I feel I am really ready to answer it. On a few occasions, I have replied to letters too quickly, and I have regretted it. By waiting, I give myself time to think and pray, to read between the lines, and to prepare a reply that would do the most good and the least damage.

The Spirit led Paul to use a wise approach as he wrote to the Corinthians. He was writing to a divided church (1 Cor. 1:11ff.), a church that was resisting his authority, and a church that was being seduced by false teachers. So, first he explained his ministry so that they would no longer doubt his sincerity. He then encouraged them to share in the offering, for he knew that this challenge would help them grow in their spiritual lives. Grace giving and grace living go together.

Now, in the last section of the letter, Paul challenged the rebels in the church—including the false teachers—and enforced his apostolic ministry. As you read 2 Corinthians 10—13, you will find Paul referring directly to his accusers (2 Cor. 10:7, 10–12; 11:4, 20–23, for example) and answering their false charges. He does not hide the fact that the Judaizers in the church are ministers of Satan who want to destroy the work of God (2 Cor. 11:12–15).

Paul used one word twenty times in 2 Corinthians 10—13, the word translated "boast" or "glory." When you first read these chapters, you get the impression that Paul was bragging about himself; but such was not the case. Paul "gloried in Jesus Christ" and not in himself or his achievements (Rom. 5:11; Gal. 6:14; Phil. 3:3). He boasted to others about the Corinthians, but it seemed that his boasting might be in vain (2 Cor. 7:4, 14; 8:24).

Keep in mind that Paul was not defending himself personally; he was defending his ministry and his apostolic authority. He was not involved in a "personality contest" with other ministers. His enemies did not hesitate to accuse him falsely, nor did they hesitate to promote themselves (2 Cor. 11:12). It was the worldly attitude of the Corinthians that *forced* Paul to defend himself by reminding them of his life and ministry. Paul never hesitated to talk about Jesus Christ, but he did refuse to talk about himself, unless there was good reason to do so.

Finally, when Paul did *boast*, he limited himself to the ministry God had given him (2 Cor. 10:13), and then he emphasized his *sufferings,* not his successes. When this letter was read in the Corinthian assembly, it must have brought shame to the hearts of those who had criticized Paul—and it must have made the Judaizers look foolish.

Paul's first step in enforcing his ministry was to correct the misunderstandings that existed in the minds of the people with reference to his work. They did not understand three important areas of ministry.

How to Wage Spiritual Warfare (10:1–6)

The accusation (vv. 1–2). This is not difficult to find. The rebels in the church (led by the Judaizers) said that Paul was very courageous when he wrote letters from a distance, but very timid and even weak when he was present with the Corinthians (see also 2 Cor. 10:9–11). The Judaizers, of course, were consistently overbearing in their attitudes—and the people loved them (2 Cor. 11:20). Paul's "inconsistent" manner of life paralleled his "yes and no" approach to making promises (2 Cor. 1:15–20).

When Paul founded the church at Corinth, his purpose was to exalt Christ and not himself (1 Cor. 2:1–5). Christians usually grow the way they are born. If they are born in an atmosphere of dictatorial leadership, they grow up depending on man's wisdom and strength. If they are born in an atmosphere of humility and love, they learn to depend on the Lord. Paul wanted his converts to trust the Lord, and not the servant; so he deliberately "played down" his own authority and ability.

How ignorant the Corinthians were, even after all that Paul had taught them. They failed to realize that true spiritual power is in "meekness and gentleness" (2 Cor. 10:1), not in "throwing weight around." Paul's very attitude in these opening verses disarmed his opponents. (In fact, his use of his own name is significant; for *Paul* means "little.") If Paul was a weakling, then so was Jesus Christ; for Jesus exhibited meekness and gentleness (Matt. 11:29). However, our Lord could also be stern and even angry when the occasion demanded it (see Matt. 15:1–2; 23:13–33; Mark 11:15–17; John 2:13–16). Paul was warning them in a loving way, "Please don't force me to come and show how bold I can be!"

The answer (vv. 3–6). This reveals what spiritual warfare is all about. Because the Corinthians (led by the false teachers) judged Paul's ministry by the outward appearance, they completely missed the power that was there. They were evaluating things "according to the flesh" (2 Cor. 10:2) and not according to the Spirit. The Judaizers, like some "great" religious personalities today, impressed the people with their overpowering abilities, their oratorical powers, and their "commendations" from church leaders.

Paul took a different approach; for, though he was as human as anyone else, he did not depend on the human but on the divine, the spiritual weapons provided by the Lord. His warfare was not according to the flesh, because he was not fighting against flesh and blood (see Eph. 6:10ff.). You cannot fight spiritual battles with carnal weapons.

The word *warfare* in 2 Corinthians 10:4 means "campaign." Paul was not simply fighting a little skirmish in Corinth; the attack of the enemy there was part of a large satanic campaign. The powers of hell are still trying to destroy the work of God (Matt. 16:18), and it is important that we not yield any ground to the enemy, not even one church!

There are walls of resistance in the minds of people, and these walls (like the walls of Jericho) must be pulled down. What are these "mental walls"? Reasonings that are opposed to the truth of God's Word. Pride of intelligence that exalts itself. Paul was not attacking intelligence, but intellectualism, the high-minded attitude that makes people think they know more than they really do (Rom. 12:16). Paul had faced this "wisdom of men" when he founded the church (1 Cor. 1:18ff.), and it had surfaced again with the coming of the Judaizers.

Paul's attitude of humility was actually one of his strongest weapons, for pride plays right into the hands of Satan. The meek Son of God had far more power than Pilate (see John 19:11), and He proved it. Paul used spiritual weapons to tear down the opposition—prayer, the Word of God, love, the power of the Spirit at work in his life. He did not depend on personality, human abilities, or even the authority he had as an apostle. However, he was ready to punish the offenders, if necessary, once the congregation had submitted to the Lord.

Many believers today do not realize that the church is involved in warfare, and those who do understand the seriousness of the Christian battle do not always know how to fight the battle. They try to use human methods to defeat demonic forces, and these methods are doomed to fail. When Joshua and his army marched around Jericho for a week, the spectators thought they were mad. When the Jews trusted God and obeyed orders, they brought down the high walls and conquered the enemy (Josh. 6:1–20).

When I was pastoring in Chicago, I met weekly with three pastor friends, and together we united in "warfare praying." We claimed God's promise to cast down the wrong thinking that was keeping people from surrendering to God; and God did great things in the lives of many people for whom we interceded. Once the walls in the mind have been torn down, the door to the heart can be opened.

How to Use Spiritual Authority (10:7–11)

One of the most difficult lessons Christ's disciples had to learn was that, in the kingdom of God, position and power were no evidence of authority. Jesus warned His followers not to pattern their leadership after that of the Gentiles who loved to "lord it over" others and to act important (see Mark 10:35–45). The example we must follow is that of Jesus Christ, who came as a servant and ministered to others. Paul followed that example.

But the Corinthians were not spiritually minded enough to discern what Paul was doing. They contrasted his meekness with the "personality power" of the Judaizers, and they concluded that Paul had no authority at all. To be sure, he wrote powerful letters; but his physical appearance was weak, and his speech "unimpressive." They were judging by the outward appearance and were not exercising spiritual discernment.

Some friends and I once listened to a man preach whose entire sermon was made up of impressive "big" words, an occasional quotation from the Bible (usually taken out of context), and many references to world events and the "signs of the times." As we left the meeting, one of my friends said, "First Kings 19:11 describes that performance perfectly: 'The Lord was not in the wind.'" Yet people around us were saying that it was "the most wonderful sermon" they had ever heard. I seriously doubt that ten minutes later they were able to recall one concrete thing that the preacher had said.

Paul did not deny that he had authority, but he did refuse to exercise that authority in an unspiritual manner. The purpose for his authority was to build them up, not tear them down; and it requires much more skill to build than to destroy. Furthermore, it takes love to build up (1 Cor. 8:1); and the Corinthians interpreted Paul's love and meekness as a sign of weakness.

The difference between Paul and the Judaizers was this: Paul used his authority to build up the church, while the Judaizers used the church to build up their authority.

In my many years of pastoral and itinerant ministry, I have never ceased to be amazed at how some local churches treat their pastors. If a man shows love and true humility, they resist his leadership and break his heart. The next pastor will be a "dictator" who "runs the church"—and he gets just what he wants. And the people love him and brag about him! Our Lord was treated the same way, so perhaps we should not be surprised.

The opponents in the church were accusing Paul of not being a true apostle; for, if he were a true apostle, he would show it by using his authority. On the other hand, if Paul *had* thrown his weight around, they would have found fault with that. No matter what course Paul took, they were bound to condemn him. This is what always happens when church members are not spiritually minded, but evaluate ministry from a worldly viewpoint.

But their accusation backfired. If Paul was not an apostle, then he was a counterfeit and not even a believer. But if that were true, then the church at Corinth was not a true church. Paul had already made it clear that nobody could separate his ministry and his personal life (2 Cor. 1:12–14). If he were a deceiver, then the Corinthians were the deceived!

Paul also pointed out that there was no contradiction between his preaching and his writing. He was bold in his letters because that was what was needed at the time. How much more would he have enjoyed being able to write with gentleness. But it would not have achieved the desired purpose. And, even when he wrote "weighty and powerful" letters, he wrote from a heart of love. "You had better prepare for my next visit," he was saying, "because if it is necessary, I will show you how powerful I can be."

How a Christian uses authority is an evidence of his spiritual maturity and character. An immature person *swells* as he uses his authority, but a mature person *grows* in the use of authority, and others grow with him. The wise pastor, like the wise parent, knows when to wait in loving patience and when to act with determined power. It takes more power to wait than to strike. A mature person does not use authority to *demand* respect, but to *command* respect. Mature leaders suffer while they wait to act, while immature leaders act impetuously and make others suffer.

The false teachers depended on "letters of recommendation" for their authority, but Paul had a divine commission from heaven. The life that he lived and the work that he did were "credentials" enough, for it was evident that the hand of God was on his life. Paul could dare to write, "From henceforth let no man trouble me; for I bear in my body the marks of the Lord Jesus" (Gal. 6:17).

When my wife and I have ministered in England, we have always tried to arrange our schedule so that we might visit in London. We especially enjoy shopping in Selfridge's and Harrod's, London's two leading department stores. H. Gordon Selfridge, who built the great store that bears his name, always claimed that he was a success because he was a leader and not a "boss." The leader says, "Let's go!" while the boss says, "Go!" The boss *knows* how it is done, but the leader *shows* how it is done. The boss inspires fear; the leader inspires enthusiasm based on respect and goodwill. The boss fixes the *blame* for the breakdown, while the true leader fixes the breakdown. The boss keeps saying, "I," while the leader says, "We." Mr. Selfridge's philosophy of management would certainly agree with the apostle Paul's philosophy of leadership.

How to Measure Spiritual Ministry (10:12–18)

I suppose more problems have been caused by people "measuring the ministry" than by any other activity in the church. If the work of the church is the work of God, and if the work of God is a miracle, how do we go about measuring a miracle? In His personal examination of the seven churches named in Revelation 2 and 3, the Lord Jesus measured them far differently than they measured themselves. The church that thought it was poor, He considered to be rich; and the church that boasted of its wealth, He declared to be poor (Rev. 2:8–11; 3:14–22).

Some people measure ministry only by statistics. While it is true that the early church did take note of numbers (Acts 2:41; 4:4), it is also true that uniting with the church at that time was a much more difficult (and dangerous) thing (see Acts 5:13). Some years ago, one of America's large denominations had as its theme, "A Million More in '64, and Every One a Tither!" I heard one of their leading preachers comment, "If we get a million more like the last million, God help us!" Quantity is no guarantee of quality.

False measurement (v. 12). The Judaizers were great on measuring their ministry, because a religion of external activities is much easier to measure than one of internal transformation. The legalist can measure what he does and what he does not do, but the Lord is the only One who can see spiritual growth in a believer's heart. Sometimes those who are growing the most feel like they are less than the least.

In a sense, the Judaizers belonged to a "mutual admiration society" that set up its own standards and measured everybody by them. Of course, those inside the group were successful; those outside were failures. Paul was one of the outsiders, so he was considered a failure. Unfortunately, they did not measure themselves by Jesus Christ (see Eph. 4:12–16). If they had, it would have made a difference.

True measurement (vv. 13–18). Paul suggests three questions we may ask ourselves as we seek to measure our ministries by the will of God.

Am I where God wants me to be (vv. 13–14)? God "assigned a field" in which Paul was to work: he was the apostle to the Gentiles (Acts 9:15; 22:21; Eph. 3). He was also to go where no other apostle had ministered; he was to be a "pioneer preacher" to the Gentiles.

Paul used a bit of sanctified sarcasm in his defense. "The area God assigned to me included even you Corinthians!" (see 2 Cor. 10:13). It was not the Judaizers who had come to Corinth with the gospel. They, like the cultists today, arrived on the scene only after the church had already been established (see Rom. 15:15–22).

Churches and ministers are not competing with each other; they are competing with themselves. God is not going to measure us on the basis of the gifts and opportunities that He gave to Charles Spurgeon or Billy Sunday. He will measure my work by what He assigned to me. God requires faithfulness above everything else (1 Cor. 4:2).

There is something intimidating about attending a pastors' conference or a denominational convention, because the people on the program are usually the "front-runners" with the best records. Young pastors and older men in narrow places often go home carrying feelings of guilt because their faithful work does not seem to produce as much fruit. Some of these discouraged men then try all kinds of programs and promotions, only to have more disappointment; and then they contemplate leaving the ministry. If only they would realize that God measures their ministries on the basis of where He has put them, and not on the basis of what is going on in some other city, it would encourage them to stay on the job and keep being faithful.

Is God glorified by my ministry (vv. 15–17)? This is another jibe at the Judaizers, who stole other men's converts and claimed them as their own. Paul would not boast about another man's work, nor would he invade another man's territory. Whatever work he did, God did through him, and God alone should receive the glory.

I once listened to a man give a lecture on how to build a large Sunday school. Everything in the lecture was correct and certainly had worked in some of the large ministries in the United States. The only problem was, *the man had never built a large Sunday school himself!* He had visited many of the large ministries, interviewed the pastors and staff members, and developed his lecture. After he finished his lecture, people flocked to his side to ask questions and get autographs. I happened to be standing next to a pastor who had built one of the finest churches—and one of the largest—in America.

"Those people ought to be talking to you," I said to him. "You've done it and you know more about Sunday school work than he does!"

"Let him enjoy himself," said my friend with a kind smile. "We're all doing the same work, and all that counts is that God is glorified."

Paul added another bit of "holy irony" when he told the Corinthians that the only thing that had kept him from going to "the regions beyond" them was their own lack of faith. Had they been submissive to his leadership and obedient to the Word, he could have reached other lost souls; but they created so many problems for him that he had to take time from missionary evangelism to solve the problems in the church. "I would have better statistics to report," he was saying, "but you hindered me."

Paul quoted Jeremiah 9:24 in 2 Corinthians 10:17, a statement he had also quoted in 1 Corinthians 1:31. The Corinthians were prone to glory in men, especially now that the Judaizers had taken over in the church. When the Corinthians heard the "reports" of what these teachers had done, and when they saw the "letters of recommendation" that they carried, the church was quite carried away with them. As a result, Paul and his ministry looked small and unsuccessful.

But the final test is not when the reports are published for the annual meeting. The final test comes at the judgment seat of Christ, "and then shall every man have praise of God" (1 Cor. 4:5). If men get the glory, then God cannot be glorified. "I am the Lord: that is my name: and my glory will I not give to another" (Isa. 42:8).

This is not to suggest that well-known ministers with flourishing works are robbing God of glory. As we grow and bear "much fruit," we bring glory to the Father (John 15:1–8). But we must be careful that it is "fruit" that comes from spiritual life and not "results" that appear when we manipulate people and manufacture statistics.

Can the Lord commend my work (v. 18)? We may commend ourselves or be commended by others and still not deserve the commendation of God. How does God approve our work? By testing it. The word *approved* in 2 Corinthians 10:18 means "to approve by testing." There is a future testing at the judgment seat of Christ (1 Cor. 3:10ff.), but there is also a present testing of the work that we do. God permits difficulties to come to local churches in order that the work might be tested and approved.

Over the years, I have seen ministries tested by financial losses, the invasion of false doctrine, the emergence of proud leaders who want to run the church, and the challenge of change. Some of the churches have fallen apart and almost died because the work was not spiritual. Other ministries have grown because of the trials and have become purer and stronger; and, through it all, God was glorified.

Certainly our ministries must keep records and issue reports, but we must not fall into the "snare of statistics" and think that numbers are the only measurement of ministry. Each situation is unique, and no ministry can honestly be evaluated on the basis of some other ministry. The important thing is that we are where God wants us to be, doing what He wants us to do so that He might be glorified. Motive is as much a part of God's measurement of our work as is growth. If we are seeking to glorify and please God alone, and if we are not afraid of His evaluation of our hearts and lives, then we need not fear the estimates of men or their criticisms.

"But he that glorieth, let him glory in the Lord" (2 Cor. 10:17).

CHAPTER TEN
2 Corinthians 11
FATHER KNOWS BEST

If you were a Christian minister, how would you go about convincing the people in your congregation that you really loved them?

This was the problem Paul faced as he wrote this epistle. If he reminded the people of the work he did among them, they would only reply, "Paul is bragging!" If he said nothing about his ministry at Corinth, the Judaizers would say, "See, we told you Paul didn't accomplish anything!"

So what did Paul do? He was led by the Spirit of God to use a beautiful image—a comparison—that was certain to reach the hearts of the believers at Corinth. He compared himself to a "spiritual father" caring for his family. He had used this image before to remind the Corinthians that, as a "father" he had begotten them through the gospel, and that he could discipline them if he felt it was necessary (1 Cor. 4:14–21). They were his beloved spiritual children, and he wanted the very best for them.

Paul gave them three evidences of his fatherly love for them.

His Jealousy over the Church (11:1–6, 13–15)
True love is never envious, but it has a right to be jealous over those who are loved. A husband is jealous over his wife and rightfully resents and resists any rivalry that threatens their love for each other. A true patriot has every right to be jealous over his freedom and will fight to protect it. Likewise, a father (or a mother) is jealous over his or her children and seeks to protect them from anything that will harm them.

The *picture* here is that of a loving father who has a daughter engaged to be married. He feels it is his privilege and duty to keep her pure, so that he can present her to her husband with joy and not with sorrow. Paul saw the local church as a bride, engaged to be married to Jesus Christ (see Eph. 5:22ff.; Rom. 7:4). That marriage will not take place until Jesus Christ has come for His bride (Rev. 19:1–9). Meanwhile, the church—and this means individual Christians—must keep herself pure as she prepares to meet her Beloved.

The *peril,* then, is that of unfaithfulness to her fiancé. The engaged woman owes her love and allegiance to but one—her betrothed. If she shares herself with any other man, she is guilty of unfaithfulness. The word translated "simplicity" in 2 Corinthians 11:3 means "sincerity, singleness of devotion." A divided heart leads to a defiled life and a destroyed relationship.

The image of love and marriage, and the need for faithfulness, is often used in the Bible. The prophet Jeremiah saw the people of Judah losing their love for God, and he warned them: "Thus saith the Lord; 'I remember thee, the kindness of thy youth, the love of thine espousals'" (Jer. 2:2). The nation of Judah had lost its "honeymoon love" and was guilty of worshipping idols. Jesus used the same image when He warned the church at Ephesus: "Nevertheless I have somewhat against thee, because thou hast left thy first love" (Rev. 2:4).

The *person behind the peril* was Satan, pictured here as the serpent. The reference is to Genesis 3. It is worth noting that Paul had a great deal to say about our adversary, the devil, when he wrote this letter to the Corinthians. He warned that Satan has several devices for attacking believers. He can burden the consciences of believers who have sinned (2 Cor. 2:10–11), blind the minds of unbelievers (2 Cor. 4:4) or beguile the minds of believers (2 Cor. 11:3), and even buffet the bodies of God's ministers (2 Cor. 12:7).

The focus here is on the mind, for Satan is a liar and tries to get us to listen to his lies, ponder them, and then believe them. This is what he did with Eve. First, he *questioned* God's word ("Yea, hath God said?"), then he *denied* God's word ("Ye shall not surely die"), and then he *substituted his own lie* ("Ye shall be as gods") (see Gen. 3:1, 4–5).

Satan, of course, is crafty. He knows that believers will not immediately accept a lie, so the enemy has to "bait the hook" and make it easy for us to accept what he has to offer. Basically, Satan is an imitator: he copies what God does and then tries to convince us that his offer is better than God's. How does he do this? By using counterfeit ministers who pretend to serve God, but who are really the servants of Satan.

Satan has a counterfeit gospel (Gal. 1:6–12) that involves a different savior and a different spirit. Unfortunately, the Corinthians had "welcomed" this "new gospel," which was a mixture of law and grace and not a true gospel at all. There is only one gospel and, therefore, there can be only one Savior (1 Cor. 15:1ff.). When you trust the Savior, you receive the Holy Spirit of God within, and there is only one Holy Spirit.

The *preachers* of this false gospel (and they are with us yet today) are described in 2 Corinthians 11:13–15. They claimed to have divine authority as God's servants, but their authority was bogus. They claimed that the true servants of God were all impostors; in Paul's day, they said this about him. They even claimed to be "super-apostles," on a much higher level than Paul. With their clever oratory, they mesmerized the ignorant believers, while at the same time they pointed out that Paul was not a very gifted speaker (2 Cor. 11:6; 10:10). How tragic it is when unstable believers are swayed by the "fair speech" of Satan's ministers, instead of standing firm on the basic truths of the gospel taught to them by faithful pastors and teachers.

"They are not 'super-apostles' at all!" warned Paul. "They are *pseudo* apostles—false apostles! Their motive is not to glorify God, but to get personal gain by capturing converts. Their methods are deceitful" (2 Cor. 2:17; 4:2). The basic idea here is that of using bait to catch fish. They offer church members a Christian life that is "superior" to that described in the New Testament, a life that is an unbiblical mixture of law and grace.

Instead of being empowered by the Spirit, these ministers are energized by Satan. Three times, Paul used the word *transform* in referring to their work (see 2 Cor. 11:13–15). This Greek word simply means "to disguise, to masquerade." There is a change on the outside, but there is no change on the inside. Satan's workers, like Satan himself, never appear in their true character; they always wear a disguise and hide behind a mask.

As I was writing this book, several of Satan's "masquerading ministers" appeared at my front door. One of them, an attractive young lady, tried to tell me she was working for world peace; but when I confronted her, she admitted that she belonged to a cult. Two well-dressed young men introduced themselves with, "We are here representing Jesus Christ!" I quickly informed them that I knew what group they represented, and I closed the door. I did not even say goodbye. If you think I was unkind, read 2 John 5—11—and obey it.

Paul proved his love for the church by protecting it from the attacks of false teachers; and yet the members of the church "fell for" the Judaizers and let them come in. The Corinthians had "left their first love" and were no longer giving single-hearted devotion to Jesus Christ. It was not only that they had turned against Paul, but they had turned away from Christ; and that was far more serious.

His Generosity to the Church (11:7–12)

A loving parent provides for the needs of the family, and Paul sacrificed that he might minister to the church at Corinth. While Paul was there, he labored with his own hands as a tentmaker (Acts 18:1–3) and even received gifts from other churches so that he might evangelize Corinth. In other words, it had cost the Corinthians nothing to benefit from the apostolic ministry of this great man of God.

Did the Corinthians appreciate the sacrifices that Paul made for them? No, most of them did not. In fact, the Judaizers even used Paul's financial policy as "proof" that he was not a true apostle. After all, if he *were* a true apostle, he would accept financial support.

Paul had already explained his policy in a previous letter (1 Cor. 9). He had pointed out that he *was* a true apostle because he had seen the risen Christ and had been commissioned by Him. Paul had the right to ask for financial support, just as God's faithful servants do today; but he had deliberately given up that right so that nobody could accuse him of using the gospel simply as a means of making money. He gave up his "financial rights" for the gospel's sake and for the sake of lost sinners who might stumble over anything that gave the impression of being "religious business."

On the other hand, it was the Judaizers who were guilty of "peddling the gospel" for personal profit. Paul had preached the gospel to them *freely* (2 Cor. 11:7, literally "without charge, for nothing"), but the false teachers were preaching a *false* gospel—and robbing the church (2 Cor. 11:20). Paul used a bit of irony in 2 Corinthians 11:8: "Yes, I have been a 'robber.' I 'robbed' other churches so I would not have to 'rob' you!" And now the Judaizers were *really* robbing them.

A loving father does not lay his burdens on his children. Instead, he sacrifices so that the children might have what they need. It is a difficult thing to teach children the difference between "prices" and "values." Children seem to have no idea what it means for parents to go to work and earn the money that provides what the family needs. When one of my nephews was very young, he heard his parents discussing the purchase of some major appliance, and he could not understand why they did not just go out and buy it. "Why don't you just write one of those pieces of paper?" he asked, pointing to his father's checkbook. He did not understand that there has to be money in the bank to back up what you write on those "pieces of paper."

Paul did not bring up this matter of money in order to boast about himself. Rather, he was using every means possible to silence the boasting of the Judaizers. Paul knew that not a single person could accuse him of covetousness or selfishness (see Acts 20:33–35, Paul's testimony to the Ephesian church). His hands were clean. He wanted to "cut off" any opportunity for his enemies to accuse him.

The word *chargeable* in 2 Corinthians 11:9 is worth considering in a special way (see also 2 Cor. 12:13–14). In the Greek, it literally means "to grow numb." The word comes from the image of the electric eel numbing its victim with its shock. A numbed part of the body would be a burden to the victim. Paul had not used any devious tricks to catch the believers by surprise, attack them, or rob them. Both in his preaching of the gospel and his handling of finances, he was open and honest.

In my own travels, I have seen situations in local churches that have broken my heart. I have seen congregations show little or no appreciation to faithful pastors who were laboring sacrificially to see the church grow. Some of these men were underpaid and overworked, yet the churches seemed to have no love for them. However, their successors were treated like kings! Certainly at the judgment seat of Christ, the books will be balanced.

I once heard Dr. W. A. Criswell tell about the faithful missionary couple who returned to the United States on the same ship that brought Teddy Roosevelt home from a safari in Africa. Many reporters and photographers were on the dock, waiting to see Roosevelt and interview him and take pictures; but nobody was on hand to welcome home the veteran missionaries who had spent their lives serving Christ in Africa.

That evening, in their modest hotel room, the couple reviewed their arrival in New York City; and the husband was somewhat bitter.

"It isn't fair," he said to his wife. "Mr. Roosevelt comes home from a hunting trip, and the whole country is out to meet him. We get home after years of service, and nobody was there to greet us."

But his wife had the right answer, "Honey, *we aren't home yet.*"

Paul has presented two pieces of evidence to prove his love for the Corinthians: his jealousy over the church—protecting them from "spiritual unfaithfulness," and his generosity to the church—refusing to accept support from them. He shared a third piece of evidence.

His Anxiety for the Church (11:16–33)

The key to this long section is 2 Corinthians 11:28, which could be paraphrased: "Yes, I have been through many trials, but the greatest trial of all, the heaviest burden of all, is my concern for the churches!" The word translated "care" means "pressure, stress, anxiety." The other experiences were external ("without") and occasional, but the burden of the churches was internal and constant.

"We never know the love of our parents for us till we have become parents," said Henry Ward Beecher, and he was right. When our older son was a tot, he pushed a toy into the electrical outlet and was "zapped" across the room. (We didn't have the word *zap* in those days, but that's still what happened.) One day recently he discovered his own little son playing with the outlet, and father's explosive response nearly frightened the child out of a year's growth. "Now I know how you and Mom felt when I was a kid," he told me over the phone. "Being a parent has its fears as well as its joys."

Before listing the various kinds of trials he had experienced, Paul was careful to explain why he was "boasting" in this way. Paul never had any problem boasting about Christ and telling of His sufferings, but he was always hesitant to speak of his own painful experiences as a servant of God. Paul and John the Baptist would have agreed: "He [Christ] must increase, but I must decrease" (John 3:30). "But he that glorieth, let him glory in the Lord" (2 Cor. 10:17).

It was the immature and unspiritual attitude of the Corinthians that forced Paul to write about himself and "glory" (boast) in these experiences. He had begun this section (2 Cor. 11:1) by apologizing for his boasting, and he repeated this sentiment in 2 Corinthians 11:16. In 2 Corinthians 11:17, Paul was not denying the inspiration of his words; rather, he was admitting that, by boasting, he was being very unlike the Lord (see 2 Cor. 10:1). However, he had to do it to prove his love for the Corinthians and protect them from those who would lead them astray.

To begin with, the false teachers were not ashamed to boast, and the Corinthians were not afraid to accept their boasting. "Since boasting is the 'in thing' in your fellowship," Paul seemed to be saying, "then I will boast." Paul may have had the principle of Proverbs 26:5 in mind: "Answer a fool according to his folly, lest he be wise in his own conceit."

Furthermore, Paul was boasting so that he might *help* the church, while the false teachers boasted so that they might "help themselves" to what they could get out of the church. Paul's motive was pure; theirs was selfish. Second Corinthians 11:20 lists the various ways the Judaizers had taken advantage of the church:

Bondage:	They taught a doctrine of legalism that was contrary to the gospel of grace.
Devour:	They "ate up" all they could get in the church; they took advantage of their privilege of receiving financial support.
Take of you:	"Take you in," fool you. The image is that of a bird caught in a snare or a fish caught on a hook. "They baited you and caught you!"
Exalt:	They exalted themselves, not the Lord Jesus Christ; they loved to be honored and treated as great leaders.
Smite you:	This probably refers to verbal attacks rather than physical violence; the Judaizers did not hesitate to "slap them in the face" and embarrass them in public.

Paul ended this exposure of the unspiritual attitudes and actions of the Judaizers by bringing in some more "inspired irony": "To my shame I admit that we were too weak for that!" (2 Cor. 11:21 NIV). The Corinthians thought that Paul's meekness was weakness, when it was really strength. And they thought that the Judaizers' arrogance was power. How ignorant the saints can sometimes be.

When it came to their Jewish heritage, the false teachers were equal to Paul; but when it came to ministry for Christ, it was Paul who was the "super-apostle" and not the Judaizers. Consider what Paul endured for the cause of Christ and the care of the churches.

Sufferings for Christ (vv. 23–25a). Had Paul not been an apostle, he would not have experienced these trials. He received "stripes above measure" from both the Gentiles and from the Jews. Three times the Gentiles beat him with rods, and five times he was given thirty-nine lashes by the Jews. Only one beating is recorded in the book of Acts (16:22), as well as the one stoning (Acts 14:19).

Paul knew from the outset of his ministry that he would suffer for Jesus' sake (Acts 9:15–16), and God reaffirmed this to him as his ministry continued (Acts 20:23). He who caused others to suffer for their faith, himself had to suffer for his faith.

Natural hardships (vv. 25b–33). Almost any traveler in that day could have experienced some of these hardships; yet we cannot help but believe that they were caused by the enemy in an attempt to hinder the work of the Lord. Acts 27 records one of the three shipwrecks; we know nothing about the other two. We wonder how many of his precious personal possessions Paul lost in this way.

Because he was constantly on the move, Paul was exposed to the perils of travel. The Judaizers visited the safe places; Paul journeyed to the difficult places. But Paul was no ordinary traveler: he was a marked man. He had enemies among both the Jews and the Gentiles, and some would like to have killed him.

Second Corinthians 11:27 describes the personal consequences of all this difficult travel. In my own limited itinerant ministry, I have had the convenience of automobiles and planes, and yet I must confess that travel wears me out. How much more difficult it was for Paul! No wonder he was filled with weariness and pain. He often had to go without food, drink, and sleep; and sometimes he lacked sufficient clothing to keep himself warm.

While any other traveler could have suffered these things, Paul endured them because of his love for Christ and the church. His greatest burden was not *around* him, but *within* him: the care of all the churches. Why did he care so much? Because he identified with the believers (2 Cor. 11:29). Whatever happened to "his children" touched his own heart, and he could not abandon them.

Paul climaxed this narration of his sufferings by telling of his humiliating experience at Damascus, when he—the great apostle—was smuggled out of the city in a basket let over the wall (2 Cor. 11:32–33)! Would any

of the Judaizers ever tell a story like that? Of course not! Even when Paul did narrate his sufferings, he was careful that Christ was glorified, and not Paul.

We cannot read these verses without admiring the courage and devotion of the apostle Paul. Each trial left its mark on his life, and yet he kept moving on, serving the Lord. "But none of these things move me, neither count I my life dear unto myself" (Acts 20:24).

Paul certainly proved his love for the church.

Now the church had to prove its love for Paul.

May we never take for granted the sacrifices that others have made so that we might enjoy the blessings of the gospel today.

CHAPTER ELEVEN
2 Corinthians 12:1–10
A PREACHER IN PARADISE

This section is the climax of Paul's defense of his apostleship and his love for the believers at Corinth. He was reticent to write about these personal experiences, but there was no other way to solve the problem. In fact, to avoid exalting himself, Paul described his experience in the third person rather than the first person. He shared with his readers three experiences from God.

Glory: God Honored Him (12:1–6)

The Judaizers were anxious to receive honors, and they boasted about their "letters of recommendation" (2 Cor. 3:1ff.). But Paul did not look for honor from men; he let God honor him, for that alone is the honor that really counts.

First, God honored Paul by giving him visions and revelations. Paul saw the glorified Christ on the very day he was converted (Acts 9:3; 22:6). He saw a vision of Ananias coming to minister to him (Acts 9:12), and he also had a vision from God when he was called to minister to the Gentiles (Acts 22:17).

During his ministry, he had visions from God to guide him and encourage him. It was by a vision that he was called to Macedonia (Acts 16:9). When the ministry was difficult in Corinth, God encouraged Paul by a vision (Acts 18:9–10). After his arrest in Jerusalem, Paul was again encouraged by a vision from God (Acts 23:11). An angel appeared to him in the midst of the storm and assured him that he and the passengers would be saved (Acts 27:23).

Along with these special visions that related to his call and ministry, spiritual revelations of divine truth were also communicated to Paul (see Eph. 3:1–6). God gave him a profound understanding of the plan of God for this present age. Certainly Paul understood the mysteries of God.

God also honored Paul by taking him to heaven and then sending him back to the earth again. This marvelous experience had taken place fourteen years before the writing of this letter, which would place the experience in about the year AD 43. This would be the period in Paul's life between his departure for Tarsus (Acts 9:30) and his visit from Barnabas (Acts 11:25–26). There is no record of the details of this event, and it is useless for us to speculate.

Jewish rabbis were accustomed to speaking about themselves in the third person, and Paul adopted that approach as he unfolded this experience to his friends (and enemies) at Corinth. So wonderful was this experience that Paul was not quite sure whether God had taken him bodily to heaven, or whether his spirit had left his body. (There is quite a contrast between being "let down" in a basket and being "caught up" to the third heaven!) Paul affirmed here the reality of heaven and the ability of God to take people there. The *third heaven* is the same as "paradise," the heaven of heavens where God dwells in glory. Thanks to modern science, men today have visited the heaven of the clouds (we fly above the clouds) and the heaven of the planets (men have walked on the moon), but man cannot get to God's heaven without God's help.

The interesting thing is that Paul kept quiet about this experience for fourteen years! During those years, he was buffeted by his "thorn in the flesh," and perhaps people wondered why he had such a burdensome affliction. The Judaizers may have adopted the views of Job's comforters and said, "This affliction is a punishment from God." (Actually, it was a *gift* from God.) Some of Paul's good friends may have tried to encourage him by saying, "Cheer up, Paul. One day you'll be in heaven!" Paul could have replied, "That's why I have this thorn—I went to heaven!"

God honored Paul by granting him visions and revelations, and by taking him to heaven; but He honored him further by permitting him to hear "unspeakable words" while he was in heaven. He overheard the divine secrets that are shared only in heaven. These things could be spoken by God and by beings in heaven, but they could not be spoken by men.

Could the Judaizers relate any experiences that were like this one? Even Moses, who was intimate with God, met the Lord on the mountaintop; but Paul met the Lord in paradise. Paul had exercised great spiritual discipline during those fourteen years, for he had told this experience to no one. There is no doubt that this vision of God's glory was one of the sustaining powers in Paul's life and ministry. No matter where he was— in prison, in the deep, in dangerous travels—he knew that God was with him and that all was well.

You and I are not going to heaven till we die or till our Lord returns. But we have a marvelous encouragement in the fact that we are *today* seated with Christ in the heavenly places (Eph. 2:6). We have a position of authority and victory "far above all" (Eph. 2:21–22). While we have not seen God's glory as Paul did, we do share God's glory now (John 17:22), and one day we shall enter into heaven and behold the glory of Christ (John 17:24).

Such an honor as this would have made most people very proud. Instead of keeping quiet for fourteen years, they would have immediately told the world and become famous. But Paul did not become proud. He simply told the truth—it was not empty boasting—and let the facts speak for themselves. His great concern was that nobody rob God of the glory and give it to Paul. He wanted others to have an honest estimate of him and his work (see Rom. 12:3).

How could Paul have such a great experience and still remain humble? Because of the second experience that God brought to his life.

Goodness: God Humbled Him (12:7–8)

The Lord knows how to balance our lives. If we have only blessings, we may become proud; so He permits us to have burdens as well. Paul's great experience in heaven could have ruined his ministry on earth; so God, in His goodness, permitted Satan to buffet Paul in order to keep him from becoming proud.

The mystery of human suffering will not be solved completely in this life. Sometimes we suffer simply because we are human. Our bodies change as we grow older, and we are susceptible to the normal problems of life. The same body that can bring us pleasures can also bring us pains. The same family members and friends who delight us can also break our hearts. This is a part of the "human comedy," and the only way to escape it is to be less than human. But nobody wants to take that route.

Sometimes we suffer because we are foolish and disobedient to the Lord. Our own rebellion may afflict us, or the Lord may see fit to chasten us in His love (Heb. 12:3ff.). King David suffered greatly because of his sin; the consequences were painful and so was the discipline of God (see 2 Sam. 12:1–22; Ps. 51). In His grace, God forgives our sins; but in His government, He must permit us to reap what we sow.

Suffering also is a tool God uses for building godly character (Rom. 5:1–5). Certainly Paul was a man of rich Christian character because he permitted God to mold and make him in the painful experiences of his life. When you walk along the shore of the ocean, you notice that the rocks are sharp in the quiet coves, but polished in those places where the waves beat against them. God can use the "waves and billows" of life to polish us, if we will let Him.

Paul's thorn in the flesh was given to him to keep him from sinning. Exciting spiritual experiences—like going to heaven and back—have a way of inflating the human ego; and pride leads to a multitude of temptations to sin. Had Paul's heart been filled with pride, those next fourteen years would have been filled with failure instead of success.

We do not know what Paul's thorn in the flesh was. The word translated "thorn" means "a sharp stake used for torturing or impaling someone." It was a physical affliction of some kind that brought pain and distress to Paul. Some Bible students think that Paul had an eye affliction (see Gal. 6:11); but we cannot know for sure. It is a good thing that we do not know, because no matter what our sufferings may be, we are able to apply the lessons Paul learned and get encouragement.

God permitted Satan to afflict Paul, just as He permitted Satan to afflict Job (see Job 1—2). While we do not fully understand the origin of evil in this universe, or all the purposes God had in mind when He permitted evil to come, we do know that God controls evil and can use it even for His own glory. Satan cannot work against a believer without the permission of God. Everything that the enemy did to Job and Paul was permitted by the will of God.

Satan was permitted to *buffet* Paul. The word means "to beat, to strike with the fist." The tense of the verb indicates that this pain was either constant or recurring. When you stop to think that Paul had letters to write, trips to take, sermons to preach, churches to visit, and dangers to face as he ministered, you can understand that this was a serious matter. No wonder he prayed three times (as his Lord had done in the Garden, Mark 14:32–41) that the affliction might be removed from him (2 Cor. 12:8).

When God permits suffering to come to our lives, there are several ways we can deal with it. Some people become bitter and blame God for robbing them of freedom and pleasure. Others just give up and fail to get any blessing out of the experience because they will not put any courage into the experience. Still others grit their teeth and put on a brave front, determined to "endure to the very end." While this is a courageous response, it usually drains them of the strength needed for daily living; and after a time, they may collapse.

Was Paul sinning when he prayed to be delivered from Satan's buffeting? I don't think so. It is certainly a normal thing for a Christian to ask God for deliverance from sickness and pain. God has not *obligated* Himself to heal every believer whenever he prays; but He has encouraged us to bring our burdens and needs to Him. Paul did not know whether this "thorn in the flesh" was a temporary testing from God, or a permanent experience he would have to learn to live with.

There are those who want us to believe that an afflicted Christian is a disgrace to God. "If you are obeying the Lord and claiming all that you have in Christ," they say, "then you will never be sick." I have never found that teaching in the Bible. It is true that God promised the Jews special blessing and protection under the old covenant (Deut. 7:12ff.), but He never promised the New Testament believers freedom from sickness or suffering. If Paul had access to "instant healing" because of his relationship to Christ, then why didn't he make use of it for himself and for others, such as Epaphroditus (Phil. 2:25ff.)?

What a contrast between Paul's two experiences! Paul went from paradise to pain, from glory to suffering. He tasted the blessing of God in heaven and then felt the buffeting of Satan on earth. He went from ecstasy to agony, and yet the two experiences belong together. His one experience of glory prepared him for the constant experience of suffering, for he knew that God was able to meet his need. Paul had gone to heaven—but then he learned that heaven could come to him.

Grace: God Helped Him (12:9–10)

Two messages were involved in this painful experience. The thorn in the flesh was Satan's message to Paul, but God had another message for him, a message of grace. The tense of the verb in 2 Corinthians 12:9 is important: "And He [God] has once-for-all said to me." God gave Paul a message that stayed with him. The words Paul heard while in heaven, he was not permitted to share with us; but he did share the words God gave him on earth—and what an encouragement they are.

It was a message of grace. What is grace? It is God's provision for our every need when we need it. It has well been said that God in His grace gives us what we do not deserve, and in His mercy He does not give us what we do deserve. Someone has made an acrostic of the word grace: God's Riches Available at Christ's Expense. "And of his [Christ's] fullness have all we received, and grace for grace" (John 1:16).

It was a message of *sufficient grace*. There is never a shortage of grace. God is sufficient for our spiritual ministries (2 Cor. 3:4–6) and our material needs (2 Cor. 9:8) as well as our physical needs (2 Cor. 12:9). If God's grace is sufficient to save us, surely it is sufficient to keep us and strengthen us in our times of suffering.

It was a message of *strengthening grace*. God permits us to become weak so that we might receive His strength. This is a continuous process: "My power is [being] made perfect in [your] weakness" (2 Cor. 12:9 niv). Strength that knows itself to be strength is actually weakness, but weakness that knows itself to be weakness is actually strength.

In the Christian life, we get many of our blessings through *transformation,* not *substitution.* When Paul prayed three times for the removal of his pain, he was asking God for a substitution: "Give me health instead of sickness, deliverance instead of pain and weakness." Sometimes God does meet the need by substitution; but other times He meets the need by transformation. He does not remove the affliction, but He gives us His grace so that the affliction works *for* us and not *against* us.

As Paul prayed about his problem, God gave him a deeper insight into what He was doing. Paul learned that his thorn in the flesh was *a gift from God*. What a strange gift! There was only one thing for Paul to do: accept the gift from God and allow God to accomplish His purposes. God wanted to keep Paul from being "exalted above measure," and this was His way of accomplishing it.

When Paul accepted his affliction as the gift of God, this made it possible for God's grace to go to work in his life. It was then that God spoke to Paul and gave him the assurance of His grace. Whenever you are going through suffering, spend extra time in the Word of God; and you can be sure God will speak to you. He always has a special message for His children when they are afflicted.

God did not give Paul any explanations; instead, He gave him a promise: "My grace is sufficient for thee." *We do not live on explanations; we live on promises.* Our feelings change, but God's promises never change. Promises generate faith, and faith strengthens hope.

Paul claimed God's promise and drew on the grace that was offered to him; this turned seeming tragedy into triumph. God did not change the situation by removing the affliction; He changed it by adding a new ingredient: grace. Our God is "the God of all grace" (1 Peter 5:10), and His throne is a "throne of grace" (Heb. 4:16). The Word of God is "the word of his grace" (Acts 20:32), and the promise is that "he giveth more grace" (James 4:6). No matter how we look at it, God is adequate for every need that we have.

But God does not give us His grace simply that we might "endure" our sufferings. Even unconverted people can manifest great endurance. God's grace should enable us to *rise above* our circumstances and feelings and cause our afflictions to work *for us* in accomplishing positive good. God wants to build our character so that we are more like our Savior. God's grace enabled Paul not only to accept his afflictions, but to glory in them. His suffering was not a tyrant that controlled him, but a servant that worked for him.

What benefits did Paul receive because of his suffering? For one thing, he experienced the power of Christ in his life. God transformed Paul's weakness into strength. The word translated "rest" means "to spread a tent over." Paul saw his body as a frail tent (2 Cor. 5:1ff.), but the glory of God had come into that tent and transformed it into a holy tabernacle.

Something else happened to Paul: he was able to glory in his infirmities. This does not mean that he preferred pain to health, but rather that he knew how to turn his infirmities into assets. What made the difference? The grace of God *and* the glory of God. He "took pleasure" in these trials and problems, not because he was psychologically unbalanced and enjoyed pain, but because he was suffering for the sake of Jesus Christ. He was glorifying God by the way he accepted and handled the difficult experiences of life.

"It is a greater thing to pray for pain's conversion than its removal," wrote P. T. Forsyth, and this is true. Paul won the victory, not by substitution, but by transformation. He discovered the sufficiency of the grace of God.

From Paul's experience, we may learn several practical lessons.

1. *The spiritual is far more important to the dedicated believer than the physical.* This is not to suggest that we ignore the physical, because our bodies are the temples of the Spirit of God. But it does mean that we try not to make our bodies an end in themselves. They are

God's tools for accomplishing His work in this world. What God does in developing our Christian character is far more valuable than physical healing without character.

2. *God knows how to balance burdens and blessings, suffering and glory.* Life is something like a prescription: the individual ingredients might hurt us, but when properly blended, they help us.

3. *Not all sickness is caused by sin.* The argument of Job's comforters was that Job had sinned, and that was why he was suffering. But their argument was wrong in Job's case, as well as in Paul's case. There are times when God permits Satan to afflict us so that God might accomplish a great purpose in our lives.

4. *There is something worse than sickness, and that is sin; and the worst sin of all is pride.* The healthy person who is rebelling against God is in worse shape than the suffering person who is submitting to God and enjoying God's grace. It is a paradox—and an evidence of the sovereignty of God—that God used Satan, the proudest of all beings, to help keep Paul humble.

5. *Physical affliction need not be a barrier to effective Christian service.* Today's saints are too prone to pamper themselves and use every little ache or pain as an excuse to stay home from church or refuse to accept opportunities for service. Paul did not permit his thorn in the flesh to become a stumbling block. In fact, he let God turn that thorn into a stepping-stone.

6. *We can always rest in God's Word.* He always has a message of encouragement for us in times of trial and suffering.

The great French mystic, Madame Guyon, once wrote to a suffering friend, "Ah, if you knew what power there is in an accepted sorrow!"

Paul knew about that power, because he trusted the will of God and depended on the grace of God. That same power can be yours today.

CHAPTER TWELVE
2 Corinthians 12:11—13:14
THREE TO GET READY!

As Paul brought his letter to a close, his great love for the Corinthians constrained him to make one last appeal. He did not want his third visit to their church to be another painful experience for them and for him. He had opened his heart to them, explained his ministry, answered their accusations, and urged them to submit to the Word of God and obey the Lord. What more could he say or do?

In this closing section of the letter, Paul used three approaches in his attempt to motivate the Corinthians toward obedience and submission.

He Shamed Them (12:11–21)

When we were children, how many times did we hear, "Shame on you!" from a parent or a neighbor? It is a good thing when people can be ashamed of their bad actions or attitudes. It is evidence of a hard heart and a calloused conscience when a guilty person no longer feels shame. "Were they ashamed when they had committed abomination? Nay, they were not at all ashamed, neither could they blush" (Jer. 6:15).

First, Paul shamed the Corinthians for their *lack of commendation* (2 Cor. 12:11–13). They should have been boasting about him instead of compelling him to boast. Instead, the Corinthians were boasting about the "super-apostles," the Judaizers who had won their affection and were now running their church.

Was Paul inferior to these men? In no way! The Corinthians had seen Paul in action; in fact, they owed their very souls to him. He had done among them the miraculous signs that proved his apostleship (Heb. 2:1–4). He had persevered in his ministry at Corinth in spite of external persecution and internal problems. He had cost the church nothing. Paul used his subtle irony again when he wrote, "How were you inferior to the other churches, except that I was never a burden to you? Forgive me this wrong!" (2 Cor. 12:13 NIV).

One of the dangers of the Christian life is that of getting accustomed to our blessings. A godly pastor or Sunday school teacher can do so much for us that we begin to take the ministry for granted. (To be fair, I must admit that pastors are sometimes guilty of taking their church members for granted.) This attitude led Paul to shame them for their *lack of appreciation* (2 Cor. 12:14–18).

In spite of the difficulties involved, Paul had been faithful to visit the Corinthians; and now he was about to make his third visit (see 2 Cor. 13:1). Instead of being grateful, the Corinthians criticized Paul for changing his plans. Paul had taken no support from the church, but rather had given sacrificially for the church; yet they were unwilling to show their appreciation by sharing with others. It seemed that the more Paul loved them, the less they loved Paul! Why? Because they did not have a sincere love for Christ (2 Cor. 11:3). Paul was willing to "spend and expend" in order to help the church.

The Judaizers had used crafty methods in order to exploit the church (see 2 Cor. 4:2), but Paul had been open and without guile. The only "trick" Paul had played on them was his refusal to receive financial support. In this, he disarmed them so that they could never accuse him of being interested only in money. None of the associates that Paul sent to them exploited them in any way or took advantage of them.

It is a tragic thing when children do not appreciate what their parents do for them. It is also a tragedy when God's children fail to appreciate what their "spiritual parents" do for them. What is the cause of this lack of appreciation? Paul dealt with it in the next paragraph: *lack of consecration* (2 Cor. 12:19–21). There were terrible sins in the church, and Paul wanted them judged and put away before he came for his visit. Otherwise, his visit would just be another painful experience.

Some of the church members were probably saying, "If Paul visits us again, he will just create more problems!" Paul made it clear that his desire was to *solve* problems and strengthen the church. Sins in the church must be faced honestly and dealt with courageously. To sweep them under the rug is to make matters worse. Sin in the church is like cancer in the human body: it must be cut out.

Consider the sins that the church was guilty of, sins that should have been confessed and put away. They were guilty of quarreling (debates) because they envied one another. They had sudden explosions of anger (wraths). They promoted carnal intrigues and plots in the church (strifes), which involved backbitings and whisperings. All of this was born out of pride and an exaggerated sense of importance (swellings) and resulted in disorder in the church (tumults) (2 Cor. 12:20). If you will compare this list of sins with 1 Corinthians 13, you will see that there was a lack of love in the congregation.

Along with these "sins of the spirit" (2 Cor. 7:1), there were also gross sins of the flesh—fornication and lasciviousness (debauchery). Paul had dealt with these sins in 1 Corinthians 5 and 6, but some of the offenders had persisted in their disobedience. They were permitting their old life to take over again (1 Cor. 6:9–11), instead of yielding to the new life.

Paul did not eagerly anticipate this third visit. He feared that he would not find the church as he wanted it to be, and that they would not find him as they wanted him to be. But Paul promised them that, though he would be humbled and grieved (the word means "to grieve for the dead"), he would still use his authority to straighten things out. His love for them was too great for him to ignore these problems and permit them to continue to weaken the church.

The Corinthians should have been ashamed, but they were not. To assure that he would get his message across, Paul used a second approach.

He Warned Them (13:1–8)

There are two warnings here.

"Prepare yourselves!" (vv. 1–4). In dealing with sin in a local church, we must have facts and not rumors. Paul quoted Deuteronomy 19:15, and we find parallels in Numbers 35:30 and Matthew 18:16, as well as 1 Timothy 5:19. The presence of witnesses would help to guarantee the truth about a matter, especially when the church members were at such variance with one another.

Had the church members followed the instructions given by Jesus in Matthew 18:15–20, they would have solved most of their problems themselves. I have seen small disagreements in a church grow into large and complicated problems, only because the believers did not obey our Lord's directions. The pastor and congregation must not get involved in a matter until the individuals involved have sincerely sought a solution.

The Judaizers in the church had accused Paul

of being a weak man (see 2 Cor. 10:7–11). Their approach to ministry was heavy-handed and dictatorial, while Paul's was gentle and humble (see 2 Cor. 1:24). Now Paul assured them that he would show them how strong he could be—*if* that is what it took to solve the problems. "I will not spare!" was his warning, and he used a word that means "to spare in battle." In short, Paul was declaring war on anybody who opposed the authority of God's Word.

"Let Paul prove he is a true apostle!" said his opponents. Paul's reply was, "Like Jesus Christ, I am strong when it appears I am weak." On the cross, Jesus Christ manifested weakness; but the cross is still "the power of God" (1 Cor. 1:18). Paul had already explained his method of spiritual warfare (2 Cor. 10:1–6) and had cautioned his readers not to look on the surface of things, but to look deeper.

By the standards of the world, both Jesus and Paul were weak; but by the standards of the Lord, both were strong. It is a wise and mature worker who knows when to be "weak" and when to be "strong" as he deals with the discipline problems in the local church.

A pastor friend of mine, now in heaven, had a quiet manner of delivery in the pulpit, and a similar approach in his personal ministry. After hearing him preach, a visitor said, "I kept waiting for him to start preaching!" She was accustomed to hearing a loud preacher who generated more heat than light. But my friend built a strong church because he knew the true standards for ministry. He knew how to be "weak in Christ" and also how to be "strong."

How do people measure the ministry today? By powerful oratory or biblical content? By Christian character or what the press releases say? Too many Christians follow the world's standards when they evaluate ministries, and they need to pay attention to God's standards.

"Examine yourselves!" (vv. 5–8). This paragraph is an application of the word *proof* that Paul used in 2 Corinthians 13:3. "You have been examining me," wrote Paul, "but why don't you take time to examine yourselves?" I have noticed in my ministry that those who are quick to examine and condemn others are often guilty of worse sins themselves. In fact, one way to make yourself look better is to condemn somebody else.

To begin with, Paul told the Corinthians that they should examine their hearts to see if they were really born again and members of the family of God. Do you have the witness of the Holy Spirit in your heart (Rom. 8:9, 16)? Do you love the brethren (1 John 3:14)? Do you practice righteousness (1 John 2:29; 3:9)? Have you overcome the world so that you are living a life of godly separation (1 John 5:4)? These are just a few of the tests we can apply to our own lives to be certain that we are the children of God.

In one of the churches I pastored, we had a teenager who was the center of every problem in the youth group. He was a gifted musician and a member of the church, but nevertheless he was a problem. One summer when he went off to our church youth camp, the youth leaders and church officers and I agreed together to pray for him daily. At one of the meetings, he got up and announced that he had been saved that week! His Christian profession up to that time had been counterfeit. He experienced a dramatic change in his life, and today he is serving the Lord faithfully.

No doubt many of the problems in the church at Corinth were caused by people who professed to be saved, but who had never repented and trusted Jesus Christ. Our churches are filled with such people today. Paul called such people *reprobate,* which means "counterfeit, discredited after a test." Paul used this word again in 2 Corinthians 13:6–7, emphasizing the fact that it is important for a person to know for sure that he is saved and going to heaven (see 1 John 5:11–13).

In 2 Corinthians 13:7, Paul made it clear that he did not want the Corinthians to fail the test just to prove that he was right. Nor did he want them to live godly lives just so he could boast about them. He did not mind being despised and criticized for their sakes, so long as they were obeying the Lord. He was not concerned about his own reputation, for the Lord knew his heart; but he was concerned about their Christian character.

The important thing is the truth of the gospel and the Word of God (2 Cor. 13:8). Paul did not state here that it is impossible to attack the truth or hinder the truth, for these things were going on at that time in the Corinthian church. He was affirming that he and his associates wanted the truth to prevail, come what may, and that they were determined to further the truth, not obstruct it. In the end, God's truth will prevail, so why try to oppose it? "There is no wisdom nor understanding nor counsel against the Lord" (Prov. 21:30).

He Encouraged Them (13:9–14)

To begin with, Paul encouraged the Corinthians by his personal prayers on their behalf (2 Cor. 13:9). The word translated "wish" in the King James Version carries the meaning of "pray." Paul prayed for their *perfection,* which does not mean absolute sinless perfection, but "spiritual maturity." The word is part of a word family in the Greek that means "to be fitted out, to be equipped." As a medical term, it means "to set a broken bone, to adjust a twisted limb." It also means "to outfit a ship for a voyage" and "to equip an army for battle." In Matthew 4:21, it is translated "mending nets."

One of the ministries of our risen Lord is that of perfecting His people (Heb. 13:20–21). He uses the Word of God (2 Tim. 3:16–17) in the fellowship of the local church (Eph. 4:11–16) to equip His people for life and service. He also uses suffering as a tool to equip us (1 Peter 5:10). As Christians pray for one another (1 Thess. 3:10) and personally assist one another (Gal. 6:1, where "restore" is this same word *perfect*), the exalted Lord ministers to His church and makes them fit for ministry.

Balanced Christian growth and ministry is impossible in isolation. Someone has said that you can no more raise one Christian than you can raise one bee. Christians belong to each other and need each other. A baby must grow up in a loving family if it is to be balanced and normal. The emphasis today on the individual Christian, as apart from his place in a local assembly, is wrong and very dangerous. We are sheep, and we must flock together. We are members of the same body, and we must minister to one another.

In 2 Corinthians 13:10, Paul gave the Corinthians a second encouragement—the Word of God. Paul wrote this letter to meet the immediate needs of a local congregation, but we today benefit from it because it is a part of the inspired Word of God. This letter carries the same authority as the presence of the apostle himself. Paul's great desire was that the congregation's obedience to the letter solve their problems, so that he would not have to exercise authority when he visited them.

Sometimes the minister of the Word must tear down before he can build up (see Jer. 1:7–10). The farmer must pull up the weeds before he can plant the seeds and get a good crop. Paul had to tear down the wrong thinking in the minds of the Corinthians (2 Cor. 10:4–6) before he could build up the truth in their hearts and minds. The negative attitude of the Corinthians made it necessary for Paul to *destroy,* but his great desire was to *build.*

In my own ministry, I have been through two building programs and two remodeling programs and, in spite of all their demands, building programs to me are much easier. It is much simpler and less expensive to build a new structure on unimproved land than to tear down walls and try to remodel an old building. Likewise, it is much easier to take a new believer and teach him the Word than it is to try to change the wrong thinking of an older saint. Wrong ideas can hold out against the truth for a long time, until the Spirit of God demolishes the walls in the mind.

Paul encouraged the saints *to cultivate grace, love, and peace* (2 Cor. 13:11–12). The word translated "farewell" means "grace," a common form of greeting in that day. It can also be translated "rejoice." The command *be perfect* relates to Paul's prayer in 2 Corinthians 13:9 and carries the idea "be mature, be restored and fitted for life." *Be of good comfort* means "be encouraged." In spite of all their sins and problems, they had every right to be encouraged.

Live in peace was a needed admonition, for there were divisions and dissensions in the church (see 2 Cor. 12:20). If they practiced love and sought to be of one mind, the wars would cease and they would enjoy peace in their fellowship. To *be of one mind* does not mean that we all agree on everything, but that we agree to disagree over matters that are not essential.

Our God is the "God of love and peace" (2 Cor. 13:11). Can the outside world tell that from the way we live and the way we conduct the business of the church? "Behold how they love one another!" was what the lost world said about the early church, but it has been a long time since the church has earned that kind of commendation.

Since ancient times, the kiss has been a form of greeting and a gesture of love and fellowship. However, it was usually exchanged between members of the same sex. The early church used the *kiss of peace* and *kiss of love* as evidences of their affection and concern for one another. It was a "holy kiss," sanctified because of their devotion to Jesus Christ. Members of the early church often kissed new believers after their baptism and thus welcomed them into the fellowship.

The everyday fellowship of God's people is important to the church. We must greet each other in other places as well as the fellowship of the assembly, and we must show concern for each other. In giving this admonition in 2 Corinthians 13:12, Paul was certainly hitting hard at one of the most serious problems in the church: their division and lack of concern for one another.

The closing benediction in 2 Corinthians 13:14 is one of the most beloved used in the church. It emphasizes the Trinity (see Matt. 28:19) and the blessings we can receive because we belong to God. *The grace of our Lord Jesus Christ* reminds us of His birth, when He became poor in order to make us rich (see 2 Cor. 8:9). The *love of God* takes us to Calvary, where God gave His Son as the sacrifice for our sins (John 3:16). The *communion of the Holy Ghost* reminds us of Pentecost, when the Spirit of God came and formed the church (Acts 2).

The Corinthian believers then, and all believers now, desperately needed the blessings of grace, love, and communion. The Judaizers then, and the cultists today, emphasized law instead of grace, exclusiveness instead of love, and independence rather than communion (fellowship). The competition in the Corinthian church, resulting in divisions, would have been solved if the people had only lived by God's grace and love.

The church is a miracle, and it can be sustained only by the miracle ministry of God. No amount of human skill, talents, or programs can make the church what it ought to be. Only God can do that. If each believer is depending on the grace of God, walking in the love of God, and participating in the fellowship of the Spirit, not walking in the flesh, then he will be a part of the answer and not a part of the problem. He will be *living* this benediction—and being a benediction to others!

Ask God to make you that kind of Christian.

Be encouraged—and then encourage others.

GALATIANS

OUTLINE

Key theme: Christian liberty in the grace of God
Key verse: Galatians 5:1

I. PERSONAL: GRACE AND THE GOSPEL (1—2)
    A. Grace declared in Paul's message—1:1–10
    B. Grace demonstrated in Paul's life—1:11–24
    C. Grace defended in Paul's ministry—2:1–21
        1. Before the church collectively—2:1–10
        2. Before Peter personally—2:11–21

II. DOCTRINAL: GRACE AND THE LAW (3—4)
    A. The personal argument—3:1–5
    B. The scriptural argument—3:6–14
    C. The logical argument—3:15–29
    D. The historical argument—4:1–11
    E. The sentimental argument—4:12–18
    F. The allegorical argument—4:19–31

III. PRACTICAL: GRACE AND THE CHRISTIAN LIFE (5—6)
    A. Liberty, not bondage—5:1–12
    B. The Spirit, not the flesh—5:13–26
    C. Others, not self—6:1–10
    D. God's glory, not man's praise—6:11–18

CONTENTS

CHAPTER ONE
Galatians 1:1–10
BAD NEWS ABOUT THE GOOD NEWS

The lad at my front door was trying to sell me a subscription to a weekly newspaper, and he was very persuasive. "It only costs a quarter a week," he said, "and the best thing about this newspaper is that it prints only the good news!"

In a world filled with trouble, it is becoming more and more difficult to find any "good news," so perhaps the newspaper was a bargain after all. To the person who has trusted Christ as Savior, the real "good news" is the gospel: "Christ died for our sins according to the Scriptures … he was buried, and … he rose again the third day according to the Scriptures" (1 Cor. 15:3–4). It is the good news that sinners can be forgiven and go to heaven because of what Jesus Christ did on the cross. The good news of salvation through faith in Christ is the most important message in the world.

This message had changed Paul's life and, through him, the lives of others. But now this message was being attacked, and Paul was out to defend the truth of the gospel. Some false teachers had invaded the churches of Galatia—churches Paul had founded—and were teaching a different message from that which Paul had taught.

As you begin to read Paul's letter to the Galatian Christians, you can tell immediately that something is radically wrong, because he does not open his letter with his usual praise to God and prayer for the saints. He has no time! Paul is about to engage in a battle for the truth of the gospel and the liberty of the Christian life. False teachers are spreading a false "gospel" which is a mixture of law and grace, and Paul is not going to stand by and do nothing.

How does Paul approach the Galatian Christians in his attempt to teach them the truth about the gospel? In these opening verses, the apostle takes three definite steps as he prepares to fight this battle.

He Explains His Authority (1:1–5)

Later on in his letter, Paul will deal with the Galatians on the basis of affection (Gal. 4:12–20); but at the outset he is careful to let them know the authority he has from the Lord. He has three sources of authority.

His ministry (vv. 1–2). "Paul, an apostle." In the early days of the church, God called special men to do special tasks. Among them were the *apostles*. The word means "one who is sent with a commission." While He was ministering on earth, Jesus had many *disciples* ("learners"), and from these He selected twelve *apostles* (Mark 3:13–19). Later, one of the requirements for an apostle was that he have witnessed the resurrection (Acts 1:21–22; 2:32; 3:15). Of course, Paul himself was neither a disciple nor an apostle during Christ's earthly ministry, but he had seen the risen Lord and been commissioned by Him (Acts 9:1–18; 1 Cor. 9:1).

Paul's miraculous conversion and call to apostleship created some problems. From the very beginning, he was apart from the original apostles. His enemies said that he was not a true apostle for this reason. Paul is careful to point out that he had been made an apostle by Jesus Christ just as much as had the original Twelve. His apostleship was not from human selection and approval, but by divine appointment. Therefore, he had the authority to deal with the problems in the Galatian churches.

But in his ministry, Paul had a second basis for authority: *he had founded the churches in Galatia.* He was not writing to them as a stranger, but as the one who had brought them the message of life in the beginning! This letter reveals Paul's affection for these believers (see Gal. 4:12–19). Unfortunately, this affection was not being returned to him.

This matter of the founding of the Galatian churches has kept serious Bible students at work for many years. The problem stems from the meaning of the word *Galatia.* Several hundred years before the birth of Christ, some fierce tribes migrated from Gaul (modern France) into Asia Minor, and founded Galatia, which simply means "the country of the Gauls." When the Romans reorganized the ancient world, they made Galatia a part of a larger province that included several other areas, and they called the entire province Galatia. So, back in Paul's day, when a person talked about Galatia, you could not be sure whether he meant the smaller country of Galatia or the larger Roman province.

Bible students are divided over whether Paul wrote to churches in the *country* of Galatia or in the *province* of Galatia. The former view is called the "north Galatian theory" and the latter the "south Galatian theory." The matter is not finally settled, but the evidence seems to indicate that Paul wrote to churches in the southern part of the province of Galatia—Antioch, Iconium, Lystra, Derbe—churches he founded on his first missionary journey (Acts 13—14).

Paul always had a loving concern for his converts and a deep desire to see the churches he had founded glorify Christ (see Acts 15:36; 2 Cor. 11:28). He was not content to lead men and women to Christ and then abandon them. (For an example of his "after-care," read 1 Thess. 2.)

When Paul heard that false teachers had begun to capture his converts and lead them astray, he was greatly concerned—and rightly so. After all, teaching new Christians how to live for Christ is as much a part of Christ's commission as winning them (Matt. 28:19–20). Sad to say, many of the Galatian Christians had turned away from Paul, their "spiritual father" in the Lord, and were now following legalistic teachers who were mixing Old Testament law with the gospel of God's grace. (We call these false teachers "Judaizers" because they were trying to entice Christians back into the Jewish religious system.)

So, Paul had a ministry as an apostle, and specifically as the founder of the Galatian churches. As such, he had the authority to deal with the problems in the churches. But there was a second source of authority.

His message (vv. 3–4). From the very beginning, Paul clearly stated the message of the gospel, because it was this message that the Judaizers were changing. The gospel centers in a *Person*—Jesus Christ, the Son of God. This Person paid a *price*—He gave Himself to die on the cross. (You will discover that the cross is important in the Galatian letter, see 2:19–21; 3:1, 13; 4:5; 5:11, 24; 6:12–14.) Christ paid the price that He might achieve a *purpose*—delivering sinners from bondage.

"Liberty in Christ" is the dominant theme of Galatians. (Check the word *bondage* in 2:4; 4:3, 9, 24–25; 5:1.) The Judaizers wanted to lead the Christians out of the liberty of grace into the bondage of law. Paul knew that bondage was not a part of the message of the gospel, for Christ had died to set men free.

Paul's ministry and message were sources of spiritual authority.

His motive (v. 5). "To whom be glory forever and ever!" The false teachers were not ministering for the glory of Christ, but for their own glory (see Gal. 6:12–14). Like false teachers today, the Judaizers were not busy winning lost people to Christ. Rather, they were stealing other men's converts and bragging about their statistics. But Paul's motive was pure and godly: he wanted to glorify Jesus Christ (see 1 Cor. 6:19–20; 10:31–33).

Paul has now explained his authority. He is ready for a second step as he begins this battle for the liberty of the Christian.

He Expresses His Anxiety (1:6–7)

"I am amazed that you are so quickly moving away!" This was the first reason for Paul's anxiety: the Galatians were *deserting the grace of God*. (The verb indicates they were in the process of deserting and had not fully turned away.)

Paul struck while the iron was hot. God had called them in His grace and saved them from their sins. Now they were moving from grace back into law. They were abandoning liberty for legalism! And they were doing it so quickly, without consulting Paul, their "spiritual father," or giving time for the Holy Spirit to teach them. They had become infatuated with the religion of the Judaizers, just the way little children follow a stranger because he offers them candy.

"The grace of God" is a basic theme in this letter (Gal. 1:3, 6, 15; 2:9, 21; 5:4; 6:18). Grace is simply God's favor to undeserving sinners. The words *grace* and *gift* go together, because salvation is the gift of God through His grace (Eph. 2:8–10). The Galatian believers were not simply "changing religions" or "changing churches" but were actually abandoning the very grace of God! To make matters worse, they were deserting the very God of grace! God had called them and saved them; now they were deserting Him for human leaders who would bring them into bondage.

We must never forget that the Christian life is a living relationship with God through Jesus Christ. A man does not become a Christian merely by agreeing to a set of doctrines; he becomes a Christian by submitting to Christ and trusting Him (Rom. 11:6). You cannot mix grace and works, because the one excludes the other. Salvation is the gift of God's grace, purchased for us by Jesus Christ on the cross. To turn from grace to law is to desert the God who saved us.

But they were guilty of another sin that gave Paul great anxiety: *they were perverting the gospel of God.* The Judaizers claimed to be preaching "the gospel," but there cannot be two gospels, one centered in works and the other centered in grace. "They are not preaching another gospel," wrote Paul, "but a *different* message—one so different from the true gospel that it is no gospel at all." Like the cultists today, the Judaizers would say, "We believe in Jesus Christ—*but* we have something wonderful *to add* to what you already believe." As if any man could "add" something better to the grace of God!

The word translated "pervert" in Galatians 1:7 is used only three times in the New Testament (Acts 2:20; Gal. 1:7; James 4:9). It means "to turn about, to change into an opposite character." The word could be translated "to reverse." In other words, the Judaizers had reversed the gospel—they had turned it around and taken it back into the law! Later in this letter, Paul explains how the law was preparation for the coming of Christ, but the Judaizers had a different interpretation. To them, the law and the gospel went together. "Except ye be circumcised after the manner [law] of Moses, ye cannot be saved" (Acts 15:1).

What was this "deserting and perverting" doing to the Galatian Christians? It was troubling them (Gal. 1:7). This verb "trouble" carries with it the idea of perplexity, confusion, and unrest. You get some idea of the force of this word when you see how it is used in other places. "Trouble" describes the feelings of the disciples in the ship during the storm (Matt. 14:26). It also describes the feelings of King Herod when he heard that a new King had been born (Matt. 2:3). No wonder Paul was anxious for his converts: they were going through great agitation because of the false doctrines that had been brought to the churches. Grace always leads to peace (see Gal. 1:3), but the believers had deserted grace and therefore had no peace in their hearts.

Keep in mind that God's grace involves something more than man's salvation. We not only are saved by grace, but we are to live by grace (1 Cor. 15:10). We stand in grace; it is the foundation for the Christian life (Rom. 5:1–2). Grace gives us the strength we need to be victorious soldiers (2 Tim. 2:1–4). Grace enables us to suffer without complaining, and even to use that suffering for God's glory (2 Cor. 12:1–10). When a Christian turns away from living by God's grace, he must depend on his own power. This leads to failure and disappointment. This is what Paul meant by "fallen from grace" (Gal. 5:4)—moving out of the sphere of grace into the sphere of law, ceasing to depend on God's resources and depending on our own resources.

No wonder Paul was anxious. His friends in Christ were deserting the God of grace, perverting the grace of God, and reverting to living by the flesh and their own resources. They had begun their Christian lives in the Spirit, but now they were going to try to continue in the power of the flesh (Gal. 3:3).

Having explained his authority and expressed his anxiety, Paul then took the third step.

He Exposes His Adversaries (1:8–10)

"Make love, not war!" may have been a popular slogan, but it is not always feasible. Doctors must make war against disease and death; sanitary engineers must war against filth and pollution; legislators must war against injustice and crime. And they all fight *because of something they love!*

"Ye that love the Lord, hate evil" (Ps. 97:10). "Abhor that which is evil; cleave to that which is good" (Rom. 12:9). Paul waged war against the false teachers because he loved the truth, and because he loved those whom he had led to Christ. Like a loving father who guards his daughter until she is married, Paul watched over his converts lest they be seduced into sin (2 Cor. 11:1–4).

The Judaizers were identified by *the false gospel that they preached.* The test of a man's ministry is not popularity (Matt. 24:11) or miraculous signs and wonders (Matt. 24:23–24), but his faithfulness to the Word of God (see Isa. 8:20; 1 Tim. 4; 1 John 4:1–6; and note that 2 John 5—11 warns us not to encourage those who bring false doctrine). Christ had committed the gospel to Paul (1 Cor. 15:1–8), and he, in turn, had committed it to other faithful servants (1 Tim. 1:11; 6:20; 2 Tim. 1:13; 2:2). But the Judaizers had come along and substituted their false gospel for the true gospel, and for this sin, Paul pronounced them accursed. The word he used is *anathema,* which means "dedicated to destruction." (Read Acts 23:14 for a forceful illustration of the meaning of this word.) No matter who the preacher may be—an angel from heaven or even Paul himself—if he preaches any other gospel, he is accursed!

But there is a second characteristic of Paul's adversaries: *the false motives that they practiced.* His enemies accused Paul of being a compromiser and "adjusting" the gospel to fit the Gentiles. Perhaps they twisted the meaning of Paul's statement, "I am made all things to all men, that I might by all means save some" (1 Cor. 9:22). They said, "When Paul is with the Jews, he lives like a Jew; but when he is with the Gentiles, he lives like the Gentiles. He is a man-pleaser, and therefore you cannot trust him!"

But in reality, it was the false teachers who were the man-pleasers. "These men are paying you special attention, but not sincerely," Paul wrote (Gal. 4:17). "They want to shut you off from me, so that you may keep on paying them special attention" (Williams). Later, Paul also exposed the false teachers as the compromisers, going back to Old Testament practices so that they would not be persecuted by the Jewish people (Gal. 6:12–15). Paul was definitely *not* a man-pleaser. His *ministry* did not come from man (Gal. 1:1), nor did his *message* come from man (Gal. 1:12). Why, then, should he be afraid of men? Why should he seek to please men? His heart's desire was to please Christ.

When Verdi produced his first opera in Florence, the composer stood by himself in the shadows and kept his eye on the face of one man in the audience—the great Rossini. It mattered not to Verdi whether the people in the hall were cheering him or jeering him; all he wanted was a smile of approval from the master musician. So it was with Paul. He knew what it was to suffer for the gospel, but the approval or disapproval of men did not move him. "Therefore also we have as our ambition … to be pleasing to Him" (2 Cor. 5:9 NASB). Paul wanted the approval of Christ.

The servant of God is constantly tempted to compromise in order to attract and please men. When D. L. Moody was preaching in England, a worker came to him on the platform and told him that a very important nobleman had come into the hall. "May the meeting be a blessing to him!" was Moody's reply, and he preached just as before, without trying to impress anybody.

Paul was not a politician; he was an ambassador. His task was not to "play politics" but to proclaim a message. These Judaizers, on the other hand, were cowardly compromisers who mixed law and grace, hoping to please both Jews and Gentiles, but never asking whether or not they were pleasing God.

We have noted three steps Paul took toward engaging these false teachers in battle: He explained his authority, expressed his anxiety, and exposed his adversaries. But how is he going to attack his enemies? What approach will he use to convince the Galatian believers that all they need is faith in God's grace? A quick survey of the entire letter shows that Paul was a master defender of the gospel. Take time to read the entire letter at one sitting, and, as you read, note the three approaches that Paul took.

His first approach was *personal* (Gal. 1—2). He reviewed his own personal experience with Jesus Christ and the message of the gospel. He pointed out that he had received the gospel independently, from the Lord and not from the twelve apostles (Gal. 1:11–24), but that they had approved his message and his ministry (Gal. 2:1–10). Furthermore, Paul had even defended the gospel when Peter, the leading apostle, had compromised his earlier stand (Gal. 2:11–21). The autobiographical section of the letter proves that Paul was not a "counterfeit apostle," but that his message and ministry were true to the faith.

Galatians 3 and 4 are *doctrinal,* and in them Paul presented several arguments to establish that sinners are saved by faith and grace, not by works and law. First he appealed to their own experiences (Gal. 3:1–5). Then he went back to the Old Testament law in Galatians 3:6–14 to show that even Abraham and the prophets understood salvation as being by grace through faith. Having mentioned the law, Paul then explained why the law was given originally (Gal. 3:15—4:18). He then used the story of Sarah and Hagar to illustrate the relationship between law and grace (Gal. 4:19–31).

The final two chapters of the letter are *practical* in emphasis, as Paul turned from argument to application. The Judaizers accused Paul of promoting lawlessness because he preached the gospel of the grace of God; so in this section, Paul explained the relationship between the grace of God and practical Christian living. He showed that living by grace means liberty, not bondage (Gal. 5:1–12); depending on the Spirit, not the flesh (Gal. 5:13–26); living for others, not for self (Gal. 6:1–10); and living for the glory of God, not for man's approval (Gal. 6:11–18). It is either one series of actions or the other—law or grace—but it cannot be both.

CHAPTER TWO
Galatians 1:11–24
BORN FREE!

Whoso would be a man must be a nonconformist." So wrote Emerson, and many a thinker agrees with him.

The English art critic John Ruskin said, "I fear uniformity. You cannot manufacture great men any more than you can manufacture gold."

The German philosopher Schopenhauer wrote, "We forfeit three-fourths of ourselves in order to be like other people."

Francis Asbury, first bishop of the Methodist Church in the United States, once prayed at a deacon ordination, "O Lord, grant that these brethren may never want to be like other people."

Of course, there is a wrong kind of individualism that destroys instead of fulfills; but in a society accustomed to interchanging parts, it is good to meet a man like Paul, who dared to be himself in the will of God. But his freedom in Christ was a threat to those who found safety in conformity.

Paul's enemies pointed to his nonconformity as proof that his message and ministry were not really of God. "He claims to be an apostle," they argued, "but he does not stand in the apostolic tradition." It is this misrepresentation that Paul answered in this section of

Galatians. His nonconformity was divinely deliberate. God had chosen to reveal Himself in a different way to Paul.

In Galatians 1:11–12, Paul stated his theme: His message and ministry are of divine origin. He did not invent the gospel, nor did he receive it from men; but he received the gospel from Jesus Christ. Both his message and his apostolic ministry were divinely given. Therefore, anybody who added anything to Paul's gospel was in danger of divine judgment, because that gospel was given by Jesus Christ from heaven (1 Cor. 15:1–11).

The best way for Paul to prove his point was to reach into his past and remind the Galatian Christians of the way God had dealt with him. Paul stated that his past life was already known to his readers (Gal. 1:13), but it was obvious that they did not fully understand what those experiences meant. So, Paul flashed on the screen three pictures from his past as evidence that his apostleship and his gospel were truly of God.

The Persecutor (1:13–14)
Paul began with his past conduct as an unconverted Jewish rabbi. (For a vivid account of these years from Paul's own lips, read Acts 22 and 26, as well as Acts 9.) In this historical flashback, Paul pointed out his relationship to the church (Gal. 1:13) and to the religion of the Jews (Gal. 1:14). He was persecuting the church and profiting and progressing in the Jewish religion. Everything was going his way, and he was rapidly being recognized as a spiritual leader in Israel.

It is interesting to note the words that are used to describe Paul's activities when he was "Saul of Tarsus" persecuting the church. He "consented" to the murder of Stephen (see Acts 8:1), and then proceeded to "make havoc of the church" (see Acts 8:3) by breaking up families and putting believers in prison. The very atmosphere that he breathed was "threatening and slaughter" (Acts 9:1). So bent on destroying the church was Paul that he voted to kill the believers (Acts 22:4–5; 26:9–11). He mentioned these facts in his letters (1 Cor. 15:9; Phil. 3:6; 1 Tim. 1:13), marveling that God could save such a sinner as he.

Paul actually thought that Jesus was an impostor and His message of salvation a lie. He was sure that God had spoken through Moses, but how could he be sure that God had spoken through Jesus of Nazareth? Steeped in Jewish tradition, young Saul of Tarsus championed his faith. His reputation as a zealous persecutor of "the sect of the Nazarenes" became known far and wide (see Acts 9:13–14). Everybody knew that this brilliant student of Rabbi Gamaliel (Acts 22:3) was well on his way to becoming an influential leader of the Jewish faith. His personal religious life, his scholarship (Acts 26:24), and his zeal in opposing alien religious faiths all combined to make him the most respected young rabbi of his day.

Then something happened: Saul of Tarsus, the persecutor of the church, became Paul the apostle, the preacher of the gospel. This change was not gradual; it happened suddenly and without warning (Acts 9:1–9). Saul was on his way to Damascus to persecute the Christians; a few days later he was in Damascus preaching to the Jews that the Christians are right. How could the Judaizers explain this sudden transformation?

Was Saul's remarkable "about-face" caused by his own people, the Jews? Unthinkable! The Jews were encouraging Saul in his program of persecution, and his conversion was an embarrassment to them.

Was Saul's change caused by the Christians he was persecuting? Certainly the believers prayed for him, and no doubt the death of Stephen—and especially the glorious testimony he had given—affected Paul deeply (Acts 22:19–20). But the Christians ran from Paul (Acts 8:1, 4; 9:10–16), and, as far as we know, they had no idea that the young rabbi would ever become a Christian.

But if the amazing change in Paul was not caused by the Jews or the church, *then who caused it?* It had to have come from God!

No matter how you look at it, the conversion of Paul was a spiritual miracle. It was humanly impossible for Rabbi Saul to become the apostle Paul apart from the miracle of God's grace. And the same God who saved Paul also called him to be an apostle, and gave him the message of the gospel. *For the Judaizers to deny Paul's apostleship and gospel was the same as denying his conversion!* Certainly Paul was preaching the same message that he himself had believed—the truth that had changed him. But no mere human message could effect such a change. Paul's argument was conclusive: His past conduct as a persecutor of the church plus the dramatic change that he experienced proved that his message and ministry were from God.

The Believer (1:15–16b, 24)

Having discussed his past character and conduct, Paul went on to explain his conversion; for, after all, this was the crucial thing in his life. "What I preach to others, I have experienced myself," he was saying to his accusers. "This is the true gospel. Any other gospel is counterfeit." In these verses Paul explained the characteristics of his conversion experience.

God did it (vv. 15a, 16a). "It pleased God … to reveal his Son in me." Whenever Paul spoke or wrote about his conversion, it was always with emphasis on the fact that God did the work. "Salvation is of the Lord" (Jonah 2:9).

God did it by grace (v. 15b). Paul's experience reminds us of young Jeremiah (Jer. 1:4–10) and also of John the Baptist (Luke 1:5–17). Salvation is by God's grace, not man's efforts or character. *Grace* and *called* (Gal. 1:15b) go together, for whomever God chooses in His grace He calls through His Word (1 Thess. 1:4–5). The mysteries of God's sovereign will and man's responsibility to obey are not fully revealed to us. We do know that God is "not willing that any should perish" (2 Peter 3:9), and that those who do

trust Christ discover they have been "chosen … in him before the foundation of the world" (Eph. 1:4).

God did it through Christ (v. 16a). In another letter Paul makes it clear that he had plenty to boast about when he was an unconverted man (Phil. 3). He had religion and self-righteousness, as well as reputation and recognition; *but he did not have Christ!* When, on the Damascus Road, Paul saw his own self-righteous rags contrasted to the righteousness of Christ, he realized what he was missing. "But what things were gain to me, those I counted loss for Christ" (Phil. 3:7).

God revealed Christ *to* Paul, *in* Paul, and *through* Paul. The "Jews' religion" (Gal. 1:14) had been an experience of outward rituals and practices; but faith in Christ brought about an inward experience of reality with the Lord. This "inwardness" of Christ was a major truth with Paul (Gal. 2:20; 4:19).

God did it for the sake of others (v. 16b). God chose Paul, not only to save him, but also to use him to win others. In the Bible, the doctrine of election is never taught with a view to producing pride or selfishness. Election involves responsibility. God chose Paul to preach among the Gentiles the same grace that he had experienced. This, in itself, was evidence that Paul's conversion was of God; for certainly a prejudiced Jewish rabbi would never decide of himself to minister to the despised Gentiles! (See Acts 9:15; 15:12; 22:21–22; Eph. 3:1, 8.)

God did it for His glory (v. 24). As a fanatical rabbi, Paul had all the glory a man could want; but what he was doing did not glorify God. Man was *created* to glorify God (Isa. 43:7), and man is *saved* to glorify God (1 Cor. 6:19–20). Bringing glory to God was ever a compelling motive in Paul's life and ministry (Rom. 11:36; 16:27; 1 Cor. 10:31; Eph. 1:6; 3:20–21; Phil. 4:20). The Judaizers were interested in their own glory (Gal. 6:11–18). That is why they were stealing Paul's converts and leading them astray. If Paul had been interested in glorifying himself, he could have remained a Jewish rabbi and perhaps become Gamaliel's successor. But it was the glory of God that motivated Paul, and this ought to motivate our lives as well.

When Charles Haddon Spurgeon was a young preacher, his father, the Rev. John Spurgeon, suggested that Charles go to college to gain prominence. It was arranged for him to meet Dr. Joseph Angus, the principal of Stepney College, London. They were to meet at Mr. Macmillan's home in Cambridge, and Spurgeon was there at the appointed hour. He waited for two hours, but the learned doctor never appeared. When Spurgeon finally inquired about the man, he discovered that Dr. Angus had been waiting in another room and, because of another appointment, had already departed. Disappointed, Spurgeon left for a preaching engagement. While he was walking along, he heard a voice clearly say to him, "Seekest thou great things for thyself? Seek them not!" (see Jer. 45:5). From that moment, Spurgeon determined to do the will of

God for the glory of God; and God blessed him in an exceptional way.

Paul has pictured himself as a persecutor, and has reviewed his character and conduct. He has also pictured himself as a believer, reviewing his conversion. He now presents a third picture.

The Preacher (1:16c–23)

What were Paul's contacts with other believers after he was converted? This is a question vital to his defense. Paul had no personal contacts with the apostles right after his conversion experience on the Damascus Road. "Immediately I conferred not with flesh and blood" (Gal. 1:16c). The logical thing for Paul to have done after his conversion was to introduce himself to the church at Jerusalem and profit from the spiritual instruction of those who had been "in Christ" before him. But this he did not do—and his decision was led of the Lord. For if he had gone to Jerusalem, his ministry might have been identified with that of the apostles—all Jews—and this could have been a hindrance to his work among the Gentiles.

At this point we need to remind ourselves that the message of the gospel came "to the Jew first" (Acts 3:26; Rom. 1:16). Our Lord's ministry was to the nation of Israel, and so was the ministry of the apostles for the first few years (see Acts 1—7). The death of Stephen was a turning point. As the believers were scattered, they took the good news with them to other places (Acts 8:4; 11:19ff.). Philip took the message to the Samaritans (Acts 8), and then God directed Peter to introduce it to the Gentiles (Acts 10). However, it remained for Paul to carry the gospel to the Gentile masses (Acts 22:21–22; Eph. 3:1, 8), and for this reason God kept him separated from the predominantly Jewish ministry being conducted by the apostles in Jerusalem.

Paul did not immediately go to Jerusalem. Where did he go? He reviewed his contacts and showed that there was no opportunity for him to receive either his message or his apostolic calling from any of the leaders of the church. (Compare this section with Acts 9:10–31, and keep in mind that even the best biblical scholars are not agreed on the chronology of Paul's life. Fortunately, the details of history do not affect the understanding of what Paul has written: we can disagree on chronology and yet agree on theology!)

He went to Arabia (v. 17b). This was after his initial ministry in Damascus (Acts 9:19–20). Instead of "conferring with flesh and blood," Paul gave himself to study, prayer, and meditation, and met with the Lord alone. He may have spent the greater part of three years in Arabia (Gal. 1:18), and no doubt was involved in evangelism as well as personal spiritual growth. The apostles had received three years of teaching from the Lord Jesus, and now Paul was going to have his own opportunity to be taught of the Lord.

He went back to Damascus (v. 17c). It would have been logical to visit Jerusalem at this point, but the Lord directed otherwise. Certainly it was a risky thing for Paul to go back to the city that knew he had become a Christian. The Jewish leaders who had looked to him as their champion against Christianity would definitely be after his blood. Apparently the "basket incident" of Acts 9:23–25 (see 2 Cor. 11:32–33) took place at this time. The return to Damascus and the danger it brought to Paul's life are further proof that the Jewish leaders considered Paul an enemy, and therefore that his experience with Christ was a valid one.

He finally visited Jerusalem (vv. 18–20). This was three years after his conversion, and his main purpose was to visit Peter. But Paul had a tough time getting into the church fellowship (Acts 9:26–28)! If his message and ministry had been from the apostles, this would never have happened; but because Paul's experience had been with the Lord Jesus alone, the apostles were suspicious of him. He stayed in Jerusalem only fifteen days, and he saw only Peter and James (the Lord's brother). Thus he received neither his message nor his apostleship from the Jerusalem church. There simply was not the time nor the opportunity. He had already received them both directly from Christ.

He returned home to Tarsus (vv. 21–23). Again, the record in Acts explains why: His life was in danger in Jerusalem, just as it had been in Damascus (Acts 9:28–30). As Paul went through Syria, he preached the Word, and when he arrived in Cilicia, his home province (Acts 21:39; 22:3), he began to evangelize (see Acts 15:23). Historians have concluded that he remained there perhaps seven years, until Barnabas recruited him for the work in Antioch (Acts 11:19–26). A few believers in Jerusalem knew Paul, but the believers in the churches of Judea did not know him, though they heard that he was now preaching the very faith he had once tried to destroy.

In the light of Paul's conduct, his conversion, and his contacts, how could anybody accuse him of borrowing or inventing either his message or his ministry? Certainly he *did* receive his gospel by a revelation from Jesus Christ. Therefore, we must be careful what we do with this gospel, for it is not the invention of men, but the very truth of God.

Some critical scholars have accused Paul of "corrupting the simple gospel," but the evidence is against this accusation. *The same Christ who taught on earth also taught through Paul from heaven.* Paul did not invent his teaching; he "received" it (Rom. 1:5; 1 Cor. 11:23; 15:3). At the time of Paul's conversion, God said He would appear to him in the future (Acts 26:16), apparently for the purpose of revealing His truths to him. This means that the Christ of the four gospels and the Christ of the epistles is the same Person; there is no conflict between Christ and Paul. When Paul wrote his letters to the churches, he put his own teaching on the same level with that of Jesus Christ (2 Thess. 3:3–15). The apostle Peter even called Paul's letters "scripture" (2 Peter 3:15–16).

Modern-day "Judaizers," like their ancient counterparts, reject the authority of Paul and try to undermine the gospel that he preached. In Paul's day, their message was "the gospel *plus* Moses." In our day it is "the gospel *plus*" any number of religious leaders, religious books, or religious organizations. "You cannot be saved unless …" is their message (Acts 15:1); and that "unless" usually includes joining their group and obeying their rules. If you dare to mention the gospel of grace as preached by Jesus, Paul, and the other apostles, they reply, "But God has given us a new revelation!"

Paul has the answer for them: "If any man preach any other gospel unto you than that ye have received, let him be accursed" (Gal. 1:9). When a sinner trusts Christ and is born again (John 3:1–18), he is "born free." He has been redeemed—purchased by Christ and set free. He is no longer in bondage to sin or Satan, nor should he be in bondage to human religious systems (Gal. 4:1–11; 5:1). "If the Son therefore shall make you free, ye shall be free indeed" (John 8:36).

CHAPTER THREE
Galatians 2:1–10
THE FREEDOM FIGHTER—PART 1

"This will remain the land of the free only so long as it is the home of the brave." So wrote veteran news analyst Elmer Davis in his book *But We Were Born Free,* and his convictions would certainly be echoed by the apostle Paul. To Paul, his spiritual liberty in Christ was worth far more than popularity or even security. He was willing to fight for that liberty.

Paul's first fight for Christian liberty was at the Jerusalem Council (Acts 15:1–35; Gal. 2:1–10); his second was at a private meeting with Peter (Gal. 2:11–21). Had Paul been unwilling to wage this spiritual warfare, the church in the first century might have become only a Jewish sect, preaching a mixture of law and grace. But because of Paul's courage, the gospel was kept free from legalism, and it was carried to the Gentiles with great blessing.

Before we look at the three acts in the first drama, the Council at Jerusalem, we must get acquainted with the participants. *Paul,* of course, we know as the great apostle to the Gentiles.

Barnabas was one of Paul's closest friends. In fact, when Paul tried to get into the fellowship of the Jerusalem church, it was Barnabas who opened the way for him (Acts 9:26–28).

The name *Barnabas* means "son of encouragement," and you will always find Barnabas encouraging somebody. When the gospel came to the Gentiles in Antioch, it was Barnabas who was sent to encourage them in their faith (Acts 11:19–24).

Thus, from the earliest days, Barnabas was associated with the Gentile believers. It was Barnabas who enlisted Paul to help minister at the church in Antioch (Acts 11:25–26), and the two of them worked together, not only in teaching, but also in helping the poor (Acts 11:27–30).

Barnabas accompanied Paul on the first missionary trip (Acts 13:1—14:28) and had seen God's blessings on the gospel that they preached. It is worth noting that it was Barnabas who encouraged young John Mark after he had dropped out of the ministry and incurred the displeasure of Paul (Acts 13:13; 15:36–41). In later years, Paul was able to commend Mark and benefit from his friendship (Col. 4:10; 2 Tim. 4:11).

Titus was a Gentile believer who worked with Paul and apparently was won to Christ through the apostle's ministry (Titus 1:4). He was a product of the apostle's ministry among the Gentiles, and was taken to the Jerusalem conference as "exhibit A" from the Gentile churches. In later years, Titus assisted Paul by going to some of the most difficult churches to help them solve their problems (2 Cor. 7; Titus 1:5).

Three men were the "pillars" of the church in Jerusalem: Peter; John; and James, the brother of the Lord (who must not be confused with the apostle James, who was killed by Herod, Acts 12:1–2). *Peter* we know from his prominent part in the accounts in the Gospels as well as in the first half of the book of Acts. It was to Peter that Jesus gave "the keys," so that it was he who was involved in opening the door of faith to the Jews (Acts 2), the Samaritans (Acts 8), and the Gentiles (Acts 10). *John* we also know from the gospel records as one of Christ's "inner three" apostles, associated with Peter in the ministry of the Word (Acts 3:1ff.).

It is *James* who perhaps needs more introduction. The gospel record indicates that Mary and Joseph had children, and James was among them (Matt. 13:55; Mark 6:3). (Of course, Jesus was born by the power of the Spirit, and not through natural generation, Matt. 1:18–25; Luke 1:26–38.) Our Lord's brothers and sisters did not believe in Him during His earthly ministry (John 7:1–5). Yet we find "his brethren" associated with the believers in the early church (Acts 1:13–14). Paul informed us that the risen Christ appeared to James, and this was the turning point in his life (1 Cor. 15:5–7). James was the leader of the early church in Jerusalem (Acts 15; see also 21:18). He was also the writer of the epistle of James; and that letter, plus Acts 21:18, would suggest that he was very Jewish in his thinking.

Along with these men, and the "apostles and elders" (Acts 15:4, 6), were a group of "false brethren" who infiltrated the meetings and tried to rob the believers of their liberty in Christ (Gal. 2:4). Undoubtedly these were some of the Judaizers who had followed Paul in church after church and had tried to capture his converts. The fact that Paul called them "false brethren" indicates that they were not true Christians, but were only masquerading as such so they could capture the conference for themselves.

This, then, is the cast of characters. Acts 15 should be read along with Galatians 2:1–10 to get the full story of the event.

Act 1—The Private Consultation (2:1–2)

Paul and Barnabas had returned to Antioch from their first missionary journey, excited about the way God had "opened the door of faith unto the Gentiles" (Acts 14:27). But the Jewish legalists in Jerusalem were upset with their report; so they came to Antioch and taught, in effect, that a Gentile had to become a Jew before he could become a Christian (Acts 15:1).

Circumcision, which they demanded of the Gentiles, was an important Jewish rite, handed down from the days of Abraham (Gen. 17). Submitting to circumcision meant accepting and obeying the whole Jewish law. Actually, the Jewish people had forgotten the inner, spiritual meaning of the rite (Deut. 10:16; Jer. 4:1–4; Rom. 2:25–29), just as some churches today have lost the spiritual meaning of baptism and have turned it into an external ritual. The true Christian has experienced an inner circumcision of the heart (Col. 2:10–11) and does not need to submit to any physical operation (Phil. 3:1–3).

When Paul and Barnabas confronted these men with the truth of the gospel, the result was a heated argument (Acts 15:2). It was decided that the best place to settle the question was before the church leaders in Jerusalem. We should not think that this "Jerusalem Conference" was a representative meeting from all the churches, such as a denominational conference; it was not. Paul, Barnabas, Titus, and certain other men from Antioch represented the Gentile Christians who had been saved totally apart from Jewish law; but there were no representatives from the churches Paul had established in Gentile territory.

When the deputation arrived in Jerusalem, they met privately with the church leaders. Paul did not go to Jerusalem because the church sent him; he "went up by revelation"—that is, the Lord sent him (compare Gal. 2:1 and 1:12). And the Lord gave him the wisdom to meet with the leaders first so that they would be able to present a united front at the public meetings.

"Lest by any means I should run, or had run, in vain" (Gal. 2:2) does not mean that Paul was unsure either of his message or his ministry. His conduct on the way to the conference indicates that he had no doubts (Acts 15:3). What he was concerned about was the future of the gospel among the Gentiles, because this was his specific ministry from Christ. If the "pillars" sided with the Judaizers, or tried to compromise, then Paul's ministry would be in jeopardy. He wanted to get their approval *before* he faced the whole assembly; otherwise a three-way division could result.

What was the result of this private consultation? *The apostles and elders approved Paul's gospel.* They added nothing to it (Gal. 2:6b) and thereby declared the Judaizers to be wrong. But this private meeting was only the beginning.

Act 2—The Public Convocation (2:3–5)

The historical account of the Council of Jerusalem is recorded by Luke (Acts 15:6–21). Several witnesses presented the case for the gospel of the grace of God, beginning with Peter (Acts 15:7–11). It was he who had been chosen by God to take the gospel to the Gentiles originally (Acts 10); and he reminded the assembly that God gave the Holy Spirit to the believing Gentiles just as He did to the Jews, so that there was "no difference."

This had been a difficult lesson for the early Christians to learn, because for centuries there had been a difference between Jews and Gentiles (Lev. 11:43–47; 20:22–27). In His death on the cross, Jesus had broken down the barriers between Jews and Gentiles (Eph. 2:11–22), so that in Christ there are no racial differences (Gal. 3:28). In his speech to the conference, Peter made it clear that there is but one way of salvation: faith in Jesus Christ.

Then Paul and Barnabas told the assembly what God had done among the Gentiles (Acts 15:12), and what a "missionary report" that must have been! The "false brethren" who were there must have debated with Paul and Barnabas, but the two soldiers of the cross would not yield. Paul wanted the "truth of the gospel" to continue among the Gentiles (Gal. 2:5).

It seems that Titus became a test case at this point. He was a Gentile Christian who had never submitted to circumcision. Yet it was clear to all that he was genuinely saved. Now, if the Judaizers were right ("Except ye be circumcised after the manner of Moses, ye cannot be saved," Acts 15:1), *then Titus was not a saved man.* But he was a saved man, and gave evidence of having the Holy Spirit; therefore, the Judaizers were wrong.

At this point, it might be helpful if we considered another associate of Paul—Timothy (see Acts 16:1–3). Was Paul being inconsistent by refusing to circumcise Titus, yet agreeing to circumcise Timothy? No, because two different issues were involved. In the case of Timothy, Paul was not submitting to Jewish law in order to win him to Christ. Timothy was part Jew, part Gentile, and his lack of circumcision would have hindered his ministry among the people of Israel. Titus was a full Gentile, and for him to have submitted would have indicated that he was missing something in his Christian experience. To have circumcised Titus would have been cowardice and compromise; *not* to have circumcised Timothy would have been to create unnecessary problems in his ministry.

James, the leader of the church, gave the summation of the arguments and the conclusion of the matter (Acts 15:13–21). As Jewish as he was, he made it clear that a Gentile does *not* have to become a Jew in order to become a Christian. God's program for this day is to "take out of the Gentiles a people for his name." Jews and Gentiles are saved the same way: through faith in Jesus Christ. James then asked that the assembly counsel the Gentiles to do nothing that would offend unbelieving Jews, lest they hinder them from being saved. Paul won the battle.

His view prevailed in the private meeting when the leaders approved his gospel and in the public meeting when the group agreed with Paul and opposed the Judaizers.

Echoes of the Jerusalem Conference are heard repeatedly in Paul's letter to the Galatians. Paul mentioned the "yoke of bondage" (Gal. 5:1), reminding us of Peter's similar warning (Acts 15:10). The themes of liberty and bondage are repeated often (Gal. 2:4; 4:3, 9, 21–31; 5:1), as is the idea of circumcision (Gal. 2:3; 5:3–4; 6:12–13).

Centuries later, today's Christians need to appreciate afresh the courageous stand Paul and his associates took for the liberty of the gospel. Paul's concern was "the truth of the gospel" (Gal. 2:5, 14), not the "peace of the church." The wisdom that God sends from above is "first pure, then peaceable" (James 3:17). "Peace at any price" was not Paul's philosophy of ministry, nor should it be ours.

Ever since Paul's time, the enemies of grace have been trying to add something to the simple gospel of the grace of God. They tell us that a man is saved by faith in Christ *plus* something—good works, the Ten Commandments, baptism, church membership, religious ritual—and Paul made it clear that these teachers are wrong. In fact, Paul pronounced a curse on any person (man or angel) who preaches any other gospel than the gospel of the grace of God, centered in Jesus Christ (Gal. 1:6–9; see 1 Cor. 15:1–7 for a definition of the gospel). It is a serious thing to tamper with the gospel.

Act 3—The Personal Confirmation (2:6–10)

The Judaizers had hoped to get the leaders of the Jerusalem church to disagree with Paul. By contrast, Paul made it clear that he himself was not impressed either by the persons or the positions of the church leaders. He respected them, of course. Otherwise he would not have consulted with them privately. But he did not fear them or seek to buy their influence. All he wanted them to do was recognize "the grace of God" at work in his life and ministry (Gal. 2:9), and this they did.

Not only did the assembly approve Paul's gospel, and oppose Paul's enemies, but they encouraged Paul's ministry and recognized publicly that God had committed the Gentile aspect of His work into Paul's hands. They could add nothing to Paul's message or ministry, and they dared not take anything away. There was agreement and unity: One gospel would be preached to Jews and to Gentiles.

However, the leaders recognized that God had assigned different areas of ministry to different men. Apart from his visit to the household of Cornelius (Acts 10) and to the Samaritans (Acts 8), Peter had centered his ministry primarily among the Jews. Paul had been called as God's special ambassador to the Gentiles. So, it was agreed that each man would minister in the sphere assigned to him by God.

"The gospel of the circumcision" and "the gospel of the uncircumcision" are not two different messages; it had already been agreed that there is only one gospel.

Rather, we have here two different spheres of ministry, one to the Jews and the other to the Gentiles. Peter and Paul would both preach the same gospel, and the same Lord would be at work in and through them (Gal. 2:8), but they would minister to different peoples.

This does not mean that Paul would never seek to win the Jews. To the contrary, he had a great burden on his heart for his people (Rom. 9:1–3). In fact, when Paul came to a city, he would first go to the Jewish synagogue, if there was one, and start his work among his own people. Nor was Peter excluded from ministering to the Gentiles. But each man would concentrate his work in his own sphere assigned to him by the Holy Spirit. James, Peter, and John would go to the Jews; Paul would go to the Gentiles (Gal. 2:9b, where the word *heathen* means "Gentile nations").

The Jerusalem Conference began with a great possibility for division and dissension; yet it ended with cooperation and agreement. "Behold, how good and how pleasant it is for brethren to dwell together in unity" (Ps. 133:1). Perhaps we need to practice some of this same cooperation today.

We need to recognize the fact that God calls people to different ministries in different places; yet we all preach the same gospel and are seeking to work together to build His church. Among those who know and love Christ, there can be no such thing as "competition." Peter was a great man, and perhaps the leading apostle; yet he gladly yielded to Paul—a newcomer—and permitted him to carry on his ministry as the Lord led him. Previously, Paul explained his independence from the apostles (Gal. 1); now in Galatians 2 he points out his interdependence with the apostles. He was free, and yet he was willingly in fellowship with them in the ministry of the gospel.

We move next from the theological to the practical—helping the poor (Gal. 2:10). Certainly these things go together. Correct doctrine is never a substitute for Christian duty (James 2:14–26). Too often our church meetings discuss problems, but they fail to result in practical help for the needy world. Paul had always been interested in helping the poor (Acts 11:27–30), so he was glad to follow the leaders' suggestion.

Even though the conference ended with Paul and the leaders in agreement, it did not permanently solve the problem. The Judaizers did not give up, but persisted in interfering with Paul's work and invading the churches he founded. Paul carried the good news of the council's decision to the churches in Antioch, Syria, and Cilicia (Acts 15:23) and in the other areas where he had ministered (Acts 16:4). But the Judaizers followed at his heels (like yelping dogs, see Phil. 3:1–3), starting at Antioch, where they even swayed Peter to their cause (see Gal. 2:11ff.).

There is little question that the Judaizers went to the churches of Galatia to sow their seeds of discord, and for this reason Paul had to write the letter we are now studying. It may have been written from Antioch shortly after the Council of Jerusalem, though some scholars date it later and have Paul writing from either Ephesus or Corinth. These historical details are important, but they are not vital to an understanding of the letter itself. Suffice it to say that this is probably Paul's earliest letter, and in it we find every major doctrine that Paul believed, preached, and wrote about in his subsequent ministry.

The curtain falls on this drama, but it will go up to reveal another. Once again God's "freedom fighter" will have to defend the truth of the gospel, this time before Peter.

CHAPTER FOUR
Galatians 2:11–21
THE FREEDOM FIGHTER—PART 2

Eternal vigilance is the price of liberty!" Wendell Phillips said that at a Massachusetts antislavery meeting in 1852, but its sentiment is valid today— not only in the realm of the political, but even more so in the realm of the spiritual. Paul had risked his life to carry the gospel of God's grace to the regions beyond, and he was not willing for the enemy to rob him or his churches of their liberty in Christ. It was this "spiritual vigilance" that led Paul into another dramatic encounter, this time with the apostle Peter, Barnabas, and some of the friends of James. Again, the drama is in three acts.

Peter's Relapse (2:11–13)

Apparently, sometime after the important conference described in Acts 15, Peter came from Jerusalem to Antioch. The first thing to note is *Peter's freedom* then. He enjoyed fellowship with *all* the believers, Jews and Gentiles alike. To "eat with the Gentiles" meant to accept them, to put Jews and Gentiles on the same level as one family in Christ.

Raised as an orthodox Jew, Peter had a difficult time learning this lesson. Jesus had taught it while He was with Peter before the crucifixion (Matt. 15:1–20). The Holy Spirit had reemphasized it when He sent Peter to the home of Cornelius, the Roman centurion (Acts 10). Furthermore, the truth had been accepted and approved by the conference of leaders at Jerusalem (Acts 15). Peter had been one of the key witnesses at that time.

Before we criticize Peter, perhaps we had better examine our own lives to see how many familiar Bible doctrines *we* are actually obeying. As you examine church history, you see that, even with a complete Bible, believers through the years have been slow to believe and practice the truths of the Christian faith. When we think of the persecution and discrimination that have been practiced in the name of Christ, it embarrasses us. It is one thing for us to defend a doctrine in a church meeting, and quite something else to put it into practice in everyday life.

Peter's freedom was threatened by *Peter's fear.* While he was in Antioch, the church was visited by some of the associates of James. (You will remember that James was a strict Jew even though he was a Christian believer.) Paul did not suggest that James sent these men to investigate Peter, or even that they were officials of the Jerusalem church. No doubt they belonged to the "circumcision party" (Acts 15:1, 5) and wanted to lead the Antioch church into religious legalism.

After his experience with Cornelius, Peter had been called on the carpet and had ably defended himself (Acts 11). But now, he became afraid. Peter had not been afraid to obey the Spirit when He sent him to Cornelius, nor was he afraid to give his witness at the Jerusalem Conference. But now, with the arrival of some members of "the opposition," Peter lost his courage. "The fear of man bringeth a snare" (Prov. 29:25).

How do we account for this fear? For one thing, we know that Peter was an impulsive man. He could show amazing faith and courage one minute and fail completely the next. He walked on the waves to go to Jesus, but then became frightened and began to sink. He boasted in the Upper Room that he would willingly die with Jesus, and then denied his Lord three times. Peter in the book of Acts is certainly more consistent than in the four gospels, but he was not perfect—*nor are we!* Peter's fear led to Peter's *fall*. He ceased to enjoy the "love feast" with the Gentile believers and separated himself from them.

There are two tragedies to Peter's fall. First, it made him a hypocrite (which is the meaning of the word *dissembled*). Peter pretended that his actions were motivated by faithfulness, when they were really motivated by fear. How easy it is to use "Bible doctrine" to cover up our disobedience.

The second tragedy is that *Peter led others astray with him.* Even Barnabas was involved. Barnabas had been one of the spiritual leaders of the church in Antioch (Acts 11:19–26), so his disobedience would have a tremendous influence on the others in the fellowship.

Suppose Peter and Barnabas had won the day and led the church into legalism? What might the results have been? Would Antioch have continued to be the great missionary church that sent out Paul and Barnabas (Acts 13)? Would they, instead, have sent out the "missionaries" of the circumcision party and either captured or divided the churches Paul had already founded? You can see that this problem was not a matter of personality or party; it was a question of "the truth of the gospel." And Paul was prepared to fight for it.

Paul's Rebuke (2:14–21)

Bible students are not sure just where Paul's conversation with Peter ends and where his letter to the Galatians continues in the passage. It does not really matter, since the entire section deals with the same topic: our liberty in Jesus Christ. We will assume that the entire section represents Paul's rebuke of Peter. It is interesting to note that Paul builds the entire rebuke on doctrine. There are five basic Christian doctrines that were being denied by Peter because of his separation from the Gentiles.

The unity of the church (v. 14). Peter was a Jew, but through his faith in Christ he had become a Christian. Because he was a Christian, he was part of the church, and in the church there are no racial distinctions (Gal. 3:28). We have seen how the Lord taught Peter this important lesson, first in the house of Cornelius and then at the Jerusalem Conference.

Paul's words must have stung Peter: "You are a Jew, yet you have been living like a Gentile. Now you want the Gentiles to live like Jews. What kind of inconsistency is that?"

Peter himself had stated at the Jerusalem Conference that God had "put no difference between us and them" (Acts 15:9). But now *Peter* was putting a difference. God's people are one people, even though they may be divided into various groups. Any practice on our part that violates the Scripture and separates brother from brother is a denial of the unity of the body of Christ.

Justification by faith (vv. 15–16). This is the first appearance of the important word *justification* in this letter, and probably in Paul's writings (if, as we believe, Galatians was the first letter he wrote). "Justification by faith" was the watchword of the Reformation, and it is important that we understand this doctrine.

"How should [a] man be just with God?" (Job 9:2) was a vital question, because the answer determined eternal consequences. "The just shall live by his faith" (Hab. 2:4) is God's answer; and it was this truth that liberated Martin Luther from religious bondage and fear. So important is this concept that three New Testament books explain it to us: Romans (see 1:17), Galatians (see 3:11), and Hebrews (see 10:38). Romans explains the meaning of "the just"; Galatians explains "shall live"; and Hebrews explains "by faith."

But what is justification? *Justification is the act of God whereby He declares the believing sinner righteous in Jesus Christ.* Every word of this definition is important. Justification is an *act* and not a process. No Christian is "more justified" than another Christian. "Having therefore been once-and-for-all justified by faith, we have peace with God" (Rom. 5:1, literal translation). Since we are justified by faith, it is an instant and immediate transaction between the believing sinner and God. If we were justified by works, then it would have to be a gradual process.

Furthermore, justification is an act *of God;* it is not the result of man's character or works. "It is God that justifieth" (Rom. 8:33). It is not by doing the "works of the law" that the sinner gets a right standing before God, but by putting his faith in Jesus Christ. As Paul will explain later in this letter, the law was given to reveal sin and not to redeem from sin (see Rom. 3:20).

God in His grace has put our sins on Christ—and Christ's righteousness has been put to our account (see 2 Cor. 5:21).

In justification, God *declares* the believing sinner righteous; He does not *make* him righteous. (Of course, real justification leads to a changed life, which is what James 2 is all about.) Before the sinner trusts Christ, he stands *guilty* before God; but the moment he trusts Christ, he is declared *not guilty*, and he can never be called *guilty* again!

Justification is not simply "forgiveness," because a person could be forgiven and then go out and sin and become guilty. Once you have been "justified by faith" you can never be held guilty before God.

Justification is also different from "pardon," because a pardoned criminal still has a record. When the sinner is justified by faith, *his past sins are remembered against him no more,* and God no longer puts his sins on record (see Ps. 32:1–2; Rom. 4:1–8).

Finally, God justifies *sinners,* not "good people." Paul declared that God justifies "the ungodly" (Rom. 4:5). The reason most sinners are not justified is because they will not admit they are sinners! And sinners are the only kind of people Jesus Christ can save (Matt. 9:9–13; Luke 18:9–14).

When Peter separated himself from the Gentiles, he was denying the truth of justification by faith, because he was saying, "We Jews are different from—and better than—the Gentiles." Yet both Jews and Gentiles are sinners (Rom. 3:22–23) and can be saved only by faith in Christ.

Freedom from the law (vv. 17–18). At the Jerusalem Conference, Peter had compared the Mosaic law to a burdensome yoke (Acts 15:10; see Gal. 5:1). Now he had put himself under that impossible yoke.

Paul's argument went like this: "Peter, you and I did not find salvation through the law; we found it through faith in Christ. But now, after being saved, you go back into the law! This means that Christ alone did not save you; otherwise you would not have needed the law. So, Christ actually made you a sinner!

"Furthermore, you have preached the gospel of God's grace to Jews and Gentiles, and have told them they are saved by faith and not by keeping the law. By going back into legal-ism, you are building up what you tore down! This means that you sinned by tearing it down to begin with!"

In other words, Paul was arguing from Peter's own experience of the grace of God. To go back to Moses is to deny everything that God had done for him and through him.

The very gospel itself (vv. 19–20). If a man is justified by the works of the law, then why did Jesus Christ die? His death, burial, and resurrection are the key truths of the gospel (1 Cor. 15:1–8). We are *saved* by faith in Christ (He died for us), and we *live* by faith in Christ (He lives in us). Furthermore, we are so identified with Christ by the Spirit that *we died with Him* (see Rom. 6). This means that we are dead to the law. To go back to Moses is to return to the graveyard! We have been "raised to walk in newness of life" (Rom. 6:4); and since we live by His resurrection power, we do not need the "help" of the law.

The grace of God (v. 21). The Judaizers wanted to mix law and grace, but Paul told us that this is impossible. To go back to the law means to "set aside" the grace of God.

Peter had experienced God's grace in his own salvation, and he had proclaimed God's grace in his own ministry. But when he withdrew from the Gentile Christian fellowship, he openly denied the grace of God.

Grace says, "There is no difference! All are sinners, and all can be saved through faith in Christ!"

But Peter's actions had said, "There *is* a difference! The grace of God is not sufficient; we also need the law."

Returning to the law nullifies the cross: "If righteousness came by the law, then Christ is dead in vain" (Gal. 2:21). Law says *do*! Grace says *done*! "It is finished!" was Christ's victory cry (John 19:30). "For by grace are ye saved through faith" (Eph. 2:8).

We have no record of Peter's reply to Paul's rebuke, but Scripture would indicate that he admitted his sin and was restored to the fellowship once again. Certainly when you read his two letters (1 and 2 Peter) you detect no deviation from the gospel of the grace of God. In fact, the theme of 1 Peter is "the true grace of God" (1 Peter 5:12); and the word *grace* is used in every chapter of the letter. Peter is careful to point out that he and Paul were in complete agreement, lest anyone try to "rob Peter to pay Paul" (2 Peter 3:15–16).

So end the two acts of this exciting drama. But the curtain has not come down yet, for there is a third act, which involves you and me.

The Believer's Response

We know what Peter's response was when he was challenged to live up to the truth of the gospel: fear and failure. And we know what Paul's response was when he saw the truth of the gospel being diluted: courage and defense. But the important question *today* is, what is *my* response to the "truth of the gospel"? Perhaps this is a good place to take inventory of ourselves before we proceed into the doctrinal chapters of this letter. Let me suggest some questions for each of us to answer.

Have I been saved by the grace of God? The only gospel that saves is the gospel of the grace of God as revealed in Jesus Christ. Any other gospel is a false gospel and is under a curse (Gal. 1:6–9). Am I trusting in *myself* for salvation—*my* morality, *my* good works, even *my* religion? If so, then I am not a Christian, for a true Christian is one who has trusted Christ *alone*. "For by grace are ye saved through faith; and that not of yourselves: it is the gift of God: not of works, lest any man should boast" (Eph. 2:8–9).

Am I trying to mix law and grace? Law means I must do something to please God, while grace means

that God has finished the work for me and all I need do is believe on Christ. Salvation is not by faith in Christ *plus* something; it is by faith in Christ *alone*. While church membership and religious activities are good in their place as expressions of faith in Christ, they can never be added to faith in Christ in order to secure eternal life. "And if by grace, then is it no more of works: otherwise grace is no more grace. But if it be of works, then it is no more grace: otherwise work is no more work" (Rom. 11:6).

Am I rejoicing in the fact that I am justified by faith in Christ? It has often been said that "justified" means "just as if I'd never sinned," and this is correct. It brings great peace to the heart to know that one has a right standing before God (Rom. 5:1). Just think: the righteousness of Christ has been put to our account! God has not only declared that we are righteous in Christ, but He deals with us as though we had never sinned at all! We need never fear judgment because our sins have already been judged in Christ on the cross (Rom. 8:1).

Am I walking in the liberty of grace? Liberty does not mean license; rather, it means the freedom in Christ to enjoy Him and to become what He has determined for us to become (Eph. 2:10). It is not only "freedom to *do*" but also "freedom *not* to do." We are no longer in bondage to sin and the law. As Paul will explain in the practical section of this letter (Gal. 5—6), we obey God because of love and not because of law. Christians enjoy a wonderful liberty in Christ. Am I enjoying it?

Am I willing to defend the truth of the gospel? This does not mean that we become evangelical detectives investigating every church and Sunday school class in town. But it does mean that we do not fear men when they deny the truths that have brought us eternal life in Christ. "Do I seek to please men? For if I yet pleased men, I should not be the servant of Christ" (Gal. 1:10).

Many people with whom we come in contact actually believe that people are saved by faith in Christ plus "doing good works … keeping the Ten Commandments … obeying the Sermon on the Mount," and any number of other "religious *plusses."* We may not have the same apostolic authority that Paul exercised, but we do have the Word of God to proclaim; and it is our obligation to share the truth.

Am I "walking uprightly according to the truth of the gospel"? The best way to defend the truth is to live the truth. My verbal defense of the gospel will accomplish very little if my life contradicts what I say. Paul is going to explain to us how to live in liberty by the grace of God, and it is important that we obey what he says.

A new employee was instructed how to measure valve parts to make sure they were ready for the final assembly. But after a few hours, his foreman was receiving complaints that the parts he was approving were faulty. "What are you doing?" the foreman asked.

"I showed you how to use that micrometer. You're sending through parts that are oversize!"

The employee replied, "Oh, most of the parts I was measuring were too large, so I opened up the micrometer a bit."

Changing the standards will never make for success, either in manufacturing or ministry. Paul maintained the standards of "the truth of the gospel"—and so should we.

CHAPTER FIVE
Galatians 3:1–14
BEWITCHED AND BOTHERED

The sixty verses that make up Galatians 3 and 4 are some of the strongest writing that Paul ever penned. But, after all, he was in a battle! He was out to prove that salvation is by grace alone, and not by the works of the law. His opponents had used every possible means to try to capture the churches of Galatia, and Paul was not going to fight them half-heartedly. The apostle was no amateur when it came to debate, and in these two chapters he certainly proves his abilities. His logic is unassailable.

Paul used six different arguments to prove that God saves sinners through faith in Christ and not by the works of the law. He began with the *personal argument* (Gal. 3:1–5) in which he asked the Galatians to recall their personal experience with Christ when they were saved. Then he moved into the *scriptural argument* (Gal. 3:6–14), in which he quoted six Old Testament passages to prove his point. In the *logical argument* (Gal. 3:15–29) he reasoned with his readers on the basis of what a covenant is and how a covenant works. He then presented the *historical argument* (Gal. 4:1–11), explaining the place of law in the history of Israel.

At this point, Paul's love for his converts came to the surface. The result is a *sentimental argument* (Gal. 4:12–18) as the apostle appealed to them to remember his love and their happy relationship in days past. But then Paul went right back to his close reasoning, and concluded with the *allegorical argument* (Gal. 4:19–31) based on the life of Abraham and his relationships with Sarah and Hagar. Practical application of his doctrinal argument follows in the last two chapters.

The Personal Argument (3:1–5)

The key to this section is in the word *suffered* (Gal. 3:4), which can be translated "experienced." Paul asked, "Have you experienced so many things in vain?" The argument from Christian experience was a wise one with which to begin, because Paul had been with them when they had trusted Christ. Of course, to argue from experience can be dangerous, because experiences can be counterfeited and they can be misunderstood. Subjective experience must be balanced with objective evidence, because experiences can change, but truth never changes. Paul balanced the subjective experience of the Galatian Christians with the objective teaching of the unchanging Word of God (Gal. 3:6–14).

It was obvious that these people had experienced something in their lives when Paul had first visited them; but the Judaizers had come along and convinced them that their experience was not complete. They needed something else, and that "something else" was obedience to the law of Moses. These false teachers had bewitched them and turned them into fools. In calling them "fools" Paul was not violating Christ's words in the Sermon on the Mount (Matt. 5:22), because two different words are used and two different ideas are expressed. *Foolish* in Galatians 3:1 means "spiritually dull" (see Luke 24:25), while the word Jesus used carries the idea of "a godless person." Paul was declaring a fact; Jesus was warning against verbal abuse.

Paul reminded them that they had truly experienced a meeting with God.

They saw God the Son (v. 1). It was "Christ and him crucified" that Paul had preached in Galatia, and with such effectiveness that the people could almost see Jesus crucified for them on the cross. The words *evidently set forth* translate a Greek word that means "publicly portrayed, or announced on a poster." Just as we put important information on a poster and display it in a public place, so Paul openly presented Christ to the Galatians, with great emphasis on His death for sinners on the cross. They heard this truth, believed it, and obeyed it; and as a result, were born into the family of God.

They received God the Holy Spirit (vv. 2–4). The Holy Spirit is mentioned eighteen times in this epistle and plays an important part in Paul's defense of the gospel of the grace of God. The only real evidence of conversion is the presence of the Holy Spirit in the life of the believer (see Rom. 8:9). Paul asked an important question: Did they receive the Spirit by faith in the Word of God, or by doing the works of the law? Of course, there could be but one answer: The Spirit came into their lives because they trusted Jesus Christ.

It is important that we understand the work of the Spirit in salvation and Christian living. The Holy Spirit *convicts* the lost sinner and reveals Christ to him (John 16:7–11). The sinner can resist the Spirit (Acts 7:51) or yield to the Spirit and trust Jesus Christ. When the sinner believes in Christ, he is then *born of the Spirit* (John 3:1–8) and receives new life. He is also *baptized by the Spirit* so that he becomes a part of the spiritual body of Christ (1 Cor. 12:12–14). The believer is *sealed by the Spirit* (Eph. 1:13–14) as a guarantee that he will one day share in the glory of Christ.

Since the Holy Spirit does so much for the believer, this means that the believer has a responsibility to the Holy Spirit, who lives within his body (1 Cor. 6:19–20). The Christian should *walk in the Spirit* (Gal. 5:16, 25) by reading the Word, praying, and obeying

God's will. If he disobeys God, then he is *grieving the Spirit* (Eph. 4:30), and if he persists in doing this, he may *quench the Spirit* (1 Thess. 5:19). This does not mean that the Holy Spirit will leave him, because Jesus has promised that the Spirit abides forever (John 14:16). But it does mean that the Spirit cannot give him the joy and power that he needs for daily Christian living. Believers should be *filled with the Spirit* (Eph. 5:18–21), which simply means "controlled by the Spirit." This is a continuous experience, like drinking water from a fresh stream (John 7:37–39).

So, in their conversion experience, the believers in Galatia had received the Spirit by faith and not by the works of the law. This led Paul to another question: "If you did not *begin* with the law, why bring it in anyway? If you began with the Spirit, can you go on to maturity without the Spirit, depending on the flesh?" The word *flesh* here does not refer to the human body, but rather to the believer's old nature. Whatever the Bible says about "flesh" is usually negative (see Gen. 6:1–7; John 6:63; Rom. 7:18; Phil. 3:3). Since we were saved through the Spirit and not the flesh, through faith and not law, then it is reasonable that we should continue that way.

The illustration of human birth is appropriate here. Two human parents are required for a child to be conceived and born, and two *spiritual* parents are required for a child to be born into God's family: the Spirit of God and the Word of God (John 3:1–8; 1 Peter 1:22–25). When a normal child is born, he has all that he needs for life; nothing need be added. When the child of God is born into God's family, he has all that he needs spiritually; *nothing need be added!* All that is necessary is that the child have food, exercise, and cleansing that he might grow into maturity. It would be strange if the parents had to take the child to the doctor at one month to receive ears, at two months to receive toes, and so on.

"You have begun in the Spirit," wrote Paul. "Nothing need be added! Walk in the Spirit and you will grow in the Lord."

They experienced miracles from God the Father (v. 5). The *He* in this verse refers to the Father as the One who ministers the Spirit and "worketh miracles among [them]." The same Holy Spirit who came into the believer at conversion continues to work in him and through him so that the whole body is built up (see Eph. 4:16; Col. 2:19). The Father continues to supply the Spirit in power and blessing, and this is done by faith and not by the works of the law. The phrase *among you* can also be translated "within you." These miracles would therefore include wonderful changes *within* the lives of the Christians, as well as signs and wonders within the church fellowship.

"Do you really believe the miracles in the Bible?" a skeptic asked a new Christian who had been a terrible drinker. "Of course I do!" the believer replied. The skeptic laughed. "Do you mean that you really believe that Jesus could turn water into wine?" he asked. "I

sure do! In my home He turned wine into food and clothing and furniture!"

The Scriptural Argument (3:6–14)

Paul turns now from subjective experience to the objective evidence of the Word of God. We never judge the Scriptures by our experience; we test our experience by the Word of God. In the first section, Paul asked six questions; in this section he will quote six Old Testament statements to prove that salvation is by faith in Christ and not by the works of the law. Since the Judaizers wanted to take the believers back into the law, Paul quoted the law! And, since they magnified the place of Abraham in their religion, Paul used Abraham as one of his witnesses.

Abraham was saved by faith (vv. 6–7). Paul began by quoting Moses to show that God's righteousness was placed to Abraham's account only because he believed God's promise (Gen. 15:6). The words *accounted* in Galatians 3:6 and *counted* in Genesis 15:6 mean the same as *imputed* in Romans 4:11, 22–24. The Greek word means "to put to one's account." When the sinner trusts Christ, God's righteousness is put to his account. More than this, the believer's sins are no longer put to his account (see Rom. 4:1–8). This means that the record is always clean before God, and therefore the believer can never be brought into judgment for his sins.

The Jewish people were very proud of their relationship with Abraham. The trouble was, they thought that this relationship guaranteed them eternal salvation. John the Baptist warned them that their *physical* descent did not guarantee *spiritual* life (Matt. 3:9). Jesus made a clear distinction between "Abraham's seed" physically and "Abraham's children" spiritually (John 8:33–47). Some people today still imagine that salvation is inherited. Because mother and father were godly people, the children are automatically saved. But this is not true. It has well been said, "God has no grandchildren."

This salvation is for the Gentiles (vv. 8–9). The word *heathen* (Gal. 3:8), as used here, simply means Gentiles. Paul's quotation of Moses (Gen. 12:3) proves that, from the very beginning of Abraham's relationship with God, the blessing of salvation was promised to all the nations of the world. God preached the "good news" to Abraham centuries ago, and Paul brought that same good news to the Galatians: Sinners are justified through faith and not by keeping the law. The logic here is evident: If God promised to save the Gentiles by faith, then the Judaizers were wrong in wanting to take the Gentile believers back into law. The true "children of Abraham" are not the Jews by physical descent, but Jews and Gentiles who have believed in Jesus Christ. All those who are "of faith" (believers) are blessed with "believing Abraham."

When you read God's great covenant with Abraham in Genesis 12:1–3, you discover that many different blessings were promised—some personal, some national and political, and some universal and spiritual. Certainly God did make Abraham's name great; he is revered not only by Jews, but also by Christians, Muslims, and many others. God did multiply his descendants, and God did bless those who blessed Abraham. He also judged those who cursed his descendants (Egypt, Babylon, and Rome are cases in point). But the greatest blessings that God sent through Abraham and the Jewish nation have to do with our eternal salvation. Jesus Christ is that promised "Seed," through whom all the nations have been blessed (Gal. 3:16).

This salvation is by faith, not law (vv. 10–12). Salvation could never come by obedience to law because the law brings a curse, not a blessing. Here Paul quoted from Deuteronomy 27:26. Law demands obedience, and this means obedience in *all things*. The law is not a "religious cafeteria" where people can pick and choose (see James 2:10–11). Paul next quoted Habakkuk: "The just shall live by his faith" (Hab. 2:4). This statement is so important that the Holy Spirit inspired three New Testament books to explain it, as mentioned before. *Romans* explains "the just" and tells how the sinner can be justified before God (see Rom. 1:17). *Galatians* explains how the just "shall live"; and *Hebrews* discusses "by faith" (see Heb. 10:38). Nobody could ever live "by law" because the law kills and shows the sinner he is guilty before God (Rom. 3:20; 7:7–11).

But someone might argue that it takes faith even to obey the law; so Paul quoted Leviticus to prove that it is *doing* the law, not believing it, that God requires (Lev. 18:5). Law says, "Do and live!" but grace says, "Believe and live!" Paul's own experience (Phil. 3:1–10), as well as the history of Israel (Rom. 10:1–10), proves that works righteousness can never save the sinner; only faith righteousness can do that.

The Judaizers wanted to seduce the Galatians into a religion of legal works, while Paul wanted them to enjoy a relationship of love and life by faith in Christ. For the Christian to abandon faith and grace for law and works is to lose everything exciting that the Christian can experience in his daily fellowship with the Lord. The law cannot justify the sinner (Gal. 2:16); neither can it give him righteousness (Gal. 2:21). The law cannot give the gift of the Spirit (Gal. 3:2), nor can it guarantee that spiritual inheritance that belongs to God's children (Gal. 3:18). The law cannot give life (Gal. 3:21), and the law cannot give liberty (Gal. 4:8–10). Why, then, go back into the law?

This salvation comes through Christ (vv. 13–14). These two verses beautifully summarize all that Paul had been saying in this section. Does the law put sinners under a curse? Then Christ has redeemed us from that curse! Do you want the blessing of Abraham? It comes through Christ! Do you want the gift of the Spirit, but you are a Gentile? This gift is given through Christ to the Gentiles! All that you need is in Christ! There is no reason to go back to Moses.

Paul quoted Deuteronomy again: "He that is hanged is accursed of God" (Deut. 21:33 nkjv). The Jews did not crucify criminals; they stoned them to death. But in cases of shameful violation of the law, the body was hung on a tree and exposed for all to see. This was a great humiliation, because the Jewish people were very careful in their treatment of a dead body. After the body had been exposed for a time, it was taken down and buried (see Josh. 8:29; 10:26; 2 Sam. 4:12).

Of course, Paul's reference to a "tree" relates to the cross on which Jesus died (Acts 5:30; 1 Peter 2:24). He was not stoned and then His dead body exposed; He was nailed alive to a tree and left there to die. But by dying on the cross, Jesus Christ bore the curse of the law for us; so that now the believer is no longer under the law and its awful curse. "The blessing of Abraham" (justification by faith and the gift of the Spirit) is now ours through faith in Jesus Christ.

The word *redeemed* in Galatians 3:13 means to purchase a slave for the purpose of setting him free. It is possible to purchase a slave and keep him as a slave, but this is not what Christ did. By shedding His blood on the cross, He purchased us that we might be set free. The Judaizers wanted to lead the Christians into slavery, but Christ died to set them free. Salvation is not exchanging one form of bondage for another. Salvation is being set free from the bondage of sin and the law *into* the liberty of God's grace through Christ.

This raises an interesting question: How could these Judaizers ever convince the Galatian Christians that the way of law was better than the way of grace? Why would any believer deliberately want to choose bondage instead of liberty? Perhaps part of the answer is found in the word *bewitched* that Paul used in Galatians 3:1. The word means "to cast a spell, to fascinate." What is there about legalism that can so fascinate the Christian that he will turn from grace to law?

For one thing, legalism appeals to the flesh. The flesh loves to be "religious"—to obey laws, to observe holy occasions, even to fast (see Gal. 4:10). Certainly there is nothing wrong with obedience, fasting, or solemn times of spiritual worship, *provided that the Holy Spirit does the motivating and the empowering.* The flesh loves to boast about its religious achievements—how many prayers were offered, or how many gifts were given (see Luke 18:9–14; Phil. 3:1–10).

Another characteristic of religious legalism that fascinates people is the appeal to the senses. Instead of worshipping God "in spirit and in truth" (John 4:24), the legalist invents his own system that satisfies his senses. He cannot walk by faith; he has to walk by sight and hearing and tasting and smelling and feeling. To be sure, true Spirit-led worship does not deny the five senses. We see other believers; we sing and hear the hymns; we taste and feel the elements of the Lord's Supper. But these external things are but windows through which faith perceives the eternal. They are not ends in themselves.

The person who depends on religion can measure himself and compare himself with others. This is another fascination to legalism. But the true believer measures himself with Christ, not other Christians (Eph. 4:11ff.). There is no room for pride in the spiritual walk of the Christian who lives by grace; but the legalist constantly boasts about his achievements and his converts (Gal. 6:13–14).

Yes, there is a fascination to the law, but it is only bait that leads to a trap; and once the believer takes the bait, he finds himself in bondage. Far better to take God at His Word and rest on His grace. We were saved "by grace, through faith"; and we must live "by grace, through faith." This is the way to blessing. The other way is the way to bondage.

CHAPTER SIX
Galatians 3:15–29
THE LOGIC OF LAW

The Judaizers had Paul in a corner. He had just finished proving from the Old Testament that God's plan of salvation left no room for the works of the law. But the fact that Paul quoted six times from the Old Testament raised a serious problem: If salvation does not involve the law, then why was the law given in the first place? Paul quoted from the law to prove the insignificance of the law. If the law is now set aside, then his very arguments are worthless because they are taken from the law.

Our faith is a logical faith and can be defended on rational grounds. While there are divine mysteries in the faith that no man can fully explain, there are also divine reasons that any sincere person can understand. Paul was trained as a Jewish rabbi and was fully equipped to argue his case. In this section, he makes four statements that help us understand the relationship between *promise* and *law*.

The Law Cannot Change the Promise (3:15–18)

The word *promise* is used eight times in these verses, referring to God's promise to Abraham that in him all the nations of the earth would be blessed (Gen. 12:1–3). This promise involved being justified by faith and having all the blessings of salvation (Gal. 3:6–9). It is obvious that the promise to Abraham (and, through Christ, to us today), given about 2000 b.c., preceded by centuries the law of Moses (about 1450 b.c.). The Judaizers implied that the giving of the law *changed* that original covenant of promise. Paul argued that it did not.

To begin with, once two parties conclude an agreement, a third party cannot come along years later and change that agreement. The only persons who can change an original agreement are the persons who made it. To add anything to it or take anything from it would be illegal.

If this is true among sinful men, how much more does it apply to the holy God? Note that Abraham did not make a covenant with God; *God made a covenant with Abraham!* God did not lay down any conditions for Abraham to meet. In fact, when the covenant was ratified *Abraham was asleep!* (see Gen. 15). It was a covenant of grace: God made promises to Abraham; Abraham did not make promises to God.

But Paul revealed another wonderful truth: God made this promise, not only to Abraham, but also to Christ. "And to thy seed, which is Christ" (Gal. 3:16).

The Bible concept of "the seed" goes back to Genesis 3:15, after the fall of man. God states that there will be a conflict in the world between Satan's seed (children of the devil, see John 8:33–44) and the woman's seed (God's children and, ultimately, God's Son). The Scriptures show this conflict: Cain versus Abel (see 1 John 3:10–12); Israel versus the nations; John the Baptist and Jesus versus the Pharisees (Matt. 3:7–9; 23:29–33); the true believer versus the counterfeit (see the parable of the tares, Matt. 13:24–30, 36–43). Satan's goal in the Old Testament was to keep the Seed (Christ) from being born into the world, for Satan knew that God's Son would one day crush his head.

In the final analysis, God made this covenant of promise with Abraham *through Christ,* so that the only two parties who can make any changes are God the Father and God the Son. *Moses cannot alter this covenant!* He can add nothing to it; he can take nothing from it. The Judaizers wanted to add to God's grace (as though anything could be added to grace!) and take from God's promises. They had no right to do this since they were not parties in the original covenant.

The 430 years of Galatians 3:17 has puzzled Bible students for many years. From Abraham's call (Gen. 12) to Jacob's arrival in Egypt (Gen. 46) is 215 years. (This may be computed as follows: Abraham was 75 years old when God called him and 100 when Isaac was born, Gen. 12:4; 21:5. This gives us 25 years. Isaac was 60 when Jacob was born, Gen. 25:26; and Jacob was 130 years old when he arrived in Egypt, Gen. 47:9. Thus, 25 + 60 + 130 = 215 years.) But Moses tells us that Israel sojourned in Egypt 430 years (Ex. 12:40); so the total number of years from Abraham's call to the giving of the law is 645 years, not 430. The length of the stay in Egypt is recorded also in Genesis 15:13 and Acts 7:6, where the round figure of 400 years is used.

Several solutions have been offered to this puzzle, but perhaps the most satisfying is this: Paul was counting from the time Jacob went into Egypt, when God appeared to him and *reaffirmed* the covenant (Gen. 46:1–4). The 430 years is the time from God's confirmation of His promise to Jacob until the giving of the law at Sinai.

Regardless of what solution to the dating question we may choose, the basic argument is clear: a law given centuries later cannot change a covenant made by other parties. But suppose the later revelation, such as the law of Moses, was greater and more glorious than the earlier? What then? Paul made a second statement.

The Law Is Not Greater Than the Promise (3:19–20)

The account of the giving of the law is impressive (Ex. 19). There were thunders and lightnings, and the people were trembling with fear. Even Moses was shaking in his sandals (Heb. 12:18–21). It was a dramatic event in comparison with the giving of the covenant to Abraham (Gen. 15), and, of course, the Judaizers were impressed with these emotional externals. But Paul pointed out that the law is inferior to the covenant of promise in two ways.

The law was temporary (v. 19a). "It was added … until the seed should come." Now it is obvious that a temporary law cannot be greater than a permanent covenant. When you read God's covenant with Abraham, you find no "ifs" in His words. Nothing was conditional; all was of grace. But the blessings of the law were dependent on the meeting of certain conditions. Furthermore, the law had a terminus point: "until the seed [Christ] should come." With the death and resurrection of Christ, the law was done away, and now its righteous demands are fulfilled in us through the Spirit (Rom. 7:4; 8:1–4).

The law required a mediator (vv. 19b–20). When God gave the law to Israel, He did it by means of angels and through the mediation of Moses. Israel "received the law by the disposition of angels" (Acts 7:53). This means that the nation received the law third-hand: from God to angels to Moses. But when God made His covenant with Abraham, He did it personally, without a mediator. God was revealing to Abraham all that He would do for him and his descendants. A mediator stands between two parties and helps them to agree; but there was no need for a mediator in Abraham's case since God was entering into a covenant with him, not Abraham with God. "God is one" (Gal. 3:20), therefore there was no need for a go-between.

The Judaizers were impressed by the *incidentals* of the law—glory, thunder, lightning, angels, and other externals. But Paul looked beyond incidentals to the *essentials*. The law was temporary and required a mediator. The covenant of promise was permanent, and no mediator was required. There could be but one conclusion: The covenant was greater than the law.

The Law Is Not Contrary to the Promise (3:21–26)

You can almost hear the Judaizers shouting the question in Galatians 3:21: "Is the law then *against* the promises of God?" Is God contradicting Himself? Does His right hand not know what His left hand is doing? As he replied to this question, Paul revealed his deep insight into the ways and purposes of God. He did not say that the law *contradicts* the promise, but rather that it *cooperates* with the promise in fulfilling the purposes of God. While *law* and *grace* seem to be contrary to one another, if you go deep enough, you will discover that they actually *complement* one another. Why, then, was the law given?

The law was not given to provide life (v. 21). Certainly the law of Moses regulated the lives of the Jewish people, but it did not and could not provide *spiritual* life to the people. (Gal. 3:21 should be matched with 2:21.) If life and righteousness could have come through the law, then Jesus Christ would never have died on the cross. But Jesus did die; therefore, the law could never give the sinner life and righteousness. It was "worship of the law" that led Israel into a self-righteous religion of works, the result of which was the rejection of Christ (Rom. 9:30—10:13).

The law was given to reveal sin (vv. 19a, 22). It is here that we see the way that law and grace cooperate in bringing the lost sinner to Jesus Christ. law shows the sinner his guilt, and grace shows him the forgiveness he can have in Christ. The law is "holy, and just, and good" (Rom. 7:12), but we are unholy, unjust, and bad. The law does not *make* us sinners; it reveals to us that we already *are* sinners (see Rom. 3:20). The law is a mirror that helps us see our "dirty faces" (James 1:22–25)—*but you do not wash your face with the mirror!* It is grace that provides the cleansing through the blood of Jesus Christ (see 1 John 1:7b).

There is a lawful use of the law, and there is an unlawful use (1 Tim. 1:8–11). The lawful use is to reveal sin and cause men to see their need of a Savior. The unlawful use is to try to achieve salvation by the keeping of the law. When people claim they are saved by "keeping the Ten Commandments," they are revealing their ignorance of the true meaning of the law. The law concludes "all [men] under sin" (Gal. 3:22), Jews and Gentiles alike. But since *all* are under sin, *all* may be saved by grace! God does not have two ways of salvation; He has but one—faith in Jesus Christ.

The law was given to prepare the way for Christ (vv. 23–26). Here Paul uses an illustration that was familiar to all his readers—the child guardian. In many Roman and Greek households, well-educated slaves took the children to and from school and watched over them during the day. Sometimes they would teach the children, sometimes they would protect and prohibit, and sometimes they would even discipline. This is what Paul meant by *schoolmaster* (Gal. 3:24); but please do not read into this word our modern idea of a schoolteacher. The transliteration of the Greek would give us our word *pedagogue*, which literally means "a child conductor."

By using this illustration, Paul was saying several things about the Jews and their law. First, he was saying that the Jews were not *born* through the law, but rather were *brought up* by the law. The slave was not the child's father; he was the child's guardian and disciplinarian. So, the law did not *give* life to Israel; it *regulated* life. The Judaizers taught that the law was necessary for life and righteousness, and Paul's argument shows their error.

But the second thing Paul said is even more important: *the work of the guardian was preparation for the child's maturity.* Once the child came of age, he no longer needed the guardian. So the law was a preparation for the nation of Israel until the coming of the promised Seed, Jesus Christ. The ultimate goal in God's program was His coming (Gal. 3:22), but "before this faith [Christ] came" (Gal. 3:23 NIV), the nation was "imprisoned by the law" (literal translation).

The law separated Israel from the Gentile nations (Eph. 2:12–18); it governed every aspect of their lives. During the centuries of Jewish history, the law was preparing for the coming of Christ. The *demands* of the law reminded the people that they needed a Savior. The *types* and *symbols* in the law were pictures of the coming Messiah (see Luke 24:27).

A good example of this purpose of the law is in the account of the rich young ruler (Matt. 19:16ff.). This young man had everything anybody could desire, but he was not satisfied. He had tried to keep the commandments all his life, but still something was missing. *But these commandments brought him to Christ!* This is one of the purposes of the law, to create in lost sinners a sense of guilt and need. The sad thing is that the young man was not honest as he looked into the mirror of the law, for the last commandment ("Thou shalt not covet") escaped him; and he went away without eternal life.

The law has performed its purpose: the Savior has come and the "guardian" is no longer needed. It is tragic that the nation of Israel did not recognize their Messiah when He appeared. God finally had to destroy the temple and scatter the nation, so that today it is impossible for a devoted Jew to practice the faith of his fathers. He has no altar, no priesthood, no sacrifice, no temple, no king (Hos. 3:4). All of these have been fulfilled in Christ, so that any man—Jew or Gentile—who trusts Christ becomes a child of God.

The law cannot change the promise, and the law is not greater than the promise. But the law is not contrary to the promise: they work together to bring sinners to the Savior.

The Law Cannot Do What the Promise Can Do (3:27–29)

With the coming of Jesus Christ, the nation of Israel moved out of childhood into adulthood. The long period of preparation was over. While there was a certain amount of glory to the law, there was a greater glory in the gracious salvation of God as found in Christ. The law could reveal sin and, to a certain extent, control behavior, but the law could not do for the sinner what Jesus Christ can do.

To begin with, the law could never justify the guilty sinner. "I will not justify the wicked," said the Lord (Ex. 23:7); yet Paul stated that God "justifies the ungodly" (Rom. 4:5). King Solomon, at the dedication of the temple, reminded God to condemn the wicked and justify the righteous (1 Kings 8:32); and this was a proper request in light of the holiness of God. The trouble is, nobody was righteous! It is only through faith in Jesus Christ that the sinner is justified—declared righteous—before God.

Furthermore, the law could never give a person a oneness with God; it separated man from God. There was a fence around the tabernacle and a veil between the holy place and the Holy of Holies.

Faith in Jesus baptizes us "into Christ" (Gal. 3:27). This baptism of the Spirit identifies the believer with Christ and makes him part of His body (1 Cor. 12:12–14). Water baptism is an outward picture of this inner work of the Holy Spirit (see Acts 10:44–48).

The phrase *put on Christ* (Gal. 3:27) refers to a change of garments. The believer has laid aside the dirty garments of sin (Isa. 64:6) and, by faith, received the robes of righteousness in Christ (see Col. 3:8–15). But to the Galatians, this idea of "changing clothes" would have an additional meaning. When the Roman child came of age, he took off the childhood garments and put on the toga of the adult citizen. The believer in Christ is not just a "child of God"; he is also a "son of God" (see Gal. 3:26, where "children" ought to be translated "adult sons"). The believer has an adult status before God—so why go back into the childhood of the law?

"All one in Christ Jesus"—what a tremendous claim! The law created differences and distinctions, not only between individuals and nations, but also between various kinds of foods and animals. Jesus Christ came, not to divide, but to unite.

This must have been glorious news for the Galatian Christians, for in their society slaves were considered to be only pieces of property; women were kept confined and disrespected; and Gentiles were constantly sneered at by the Jews.

The Pharisee would pray each morning, "I thank Thee, God, that I am a Jew, not a Gentile; a man, not a woman; and a freeman, and not a slave." Yet all these distinctions are removed "in Christ."

This does not mean that our race, political status, or sex is changed at conversion; but it does mean that these things are of no value or handicap when it comes to our spiritual relationship to God through Christ. The law perpetuated these distinctions, but God in His grace has declared *all men* to be on the same level that He might have mercy on *all men* (Rom. 11:25–32).

Finally, the law could never make us heirs of God (Gal. 3:29). God made the promise to "Abraham's Seed" (singular, Gal. 3:16), and that Seed is Christ. If we are "in Christ" by faith, then we too are "Abraham's seed" spiritually speaking. This means we are heirs of the spiritual blessings God promised to Abraham. This does not mean that the material and national blessings promised to Israel are set aside, but that Christians today are enriched spiritually because of God's promise to Abraham (see Rom. 11:13ff.).

This section of Galatians is valuable to us as we read the Old Testament Scriptures. It shows us that the spiritual lessons of the Old Testament are not for the Jews only but have application to Christians today (see Rom. 15:4; 1 Cor. 10:11–12). In the Old Testament we have *preparation for Christ;* in the

Gospels, the *presentation of Christ;* and in the Acts through Revelation, the *appropriation of Christ.*

Your Christian life ought to take on new wonder and meaning as you realize all that you have in Christ. And all of this is by grace—not by law! You are an adult son in God's family, an heir of God. Are you drawing on your inheritance? This will be Paul's theme in the next section.

CHAPTER SEVEN
Galatians 4:1–18
IT'S TIME TO GROW UP!

One of the tragedies of legalism is that it gives the appearance of spiritual maturity when, in reality, it leads the believer back into a "second childhood" of Christian experience. The Galatian Christians, like most believers, wanted to grow and go forward for Christ; but they were going about it in the wrong way. Their experience is not too different from that of Christians today who get involved in various legalistic movements, hoping to become better Christians. Their motives may be right, but their methods are wrong.

This is the truth Paul was trying to get across to his beloved converts in Galatia. The Judaizers had bewitched them into thinking that the law would make them better Christians. Their old nature felt an attraction for the law because the law enabled them to *do* things and measure external results. As they measured themselves and their achievements, they felt a sense of accomplishment, and, no doubt, a little bit of pride. They thought they were going forward when actually they were regressing.

Such people are in a situation similar to the airplane passengers who heard their pilot announce: "Our navigator has lost our position, folks, and we have been flying rather aimlessly for over an hour. That's the bad news. But the good news is that we are making very good time."

Paul took three approaches in this section as he sought to convince the Galatians that they did not need legalism in order to live the Christian life. They had all they needed in Jesus Christ.

He Explains Their Adoption (4:1–7)
Among the blessings of the Christian experience is *adoption* (Gal. 4:5; Eph. 1:5). We do not *enter* God's family by adoption, the way a homeless child would enter a loving family in our own society. The only way to get into God's family is by *regeneration,* being "born again" (John 3:3).

The New Testament word for *adoption* means "to place as an adult son." It has to do with our *standing* in the family of God: we are not little children but adult sons with all of the privileges of sonship.

It is unfortunate that many translations of the New Testament do not make a distinction between *children of God* and *sons of God.* We are the children of God by faith in Christ, born into God's family. But every child of God is automatically placed into the family as a *son,* and as a son he has all the legal rights and privileges of a son. When a sinner trusts Christ and is saved, as far as his *condition* is concerned, he is a "spiritual babe" who needs to grow (1 Peter 2:2–3); but as far as his *position* is concerned, he is an adult son who can draw on the Father's wealth and who can exercise all the wonderful privileges of sonship.

We *enter* God's family by regeneration, but we *enjoy* God's family by adoption. The Christian does not have to wait to begin enjoying the spiritual riches he has in Christ. "If a son, then an heir of God through Christ" (Gal. 4:7). Now follows Paul's discussion about adoption. He reminds his readers of three facts.

What we were: children in bondage (vv. 1–3). No matter how wealthy a father may be, his infant son or toddling child cannot really enjoy that wealth. In the Roman world, the children of wealthy people were cared for by slaves. No matter who his father was, the child was still a child, under the supervision of a servant. In fact, the child himself was not much different from the servant who guarded him. The servant was commanded by the master of the house, and the child was commanded by the servant.

This was the spiritual condition of the Jews under the age of the law. The law, you recall, was the "guardian" that disciplined the nation and prepared the people for the coming of Christ (Gal. 3:23–25). So, when the Judaizers led the Galatians back into legalism, they were leading them not only into religious bondage, but also into moral and spiritual infancy and immaturity.

Paul states that the Jews were, like little children, in bondage to "the elements of the world." This word *elements* means "the basic principles, the ABCs." For some fifteen centuries, Israel had been in kindergarten and grade school, learning their "spiritual ABCs," so that they would be ready when Christ would come. Then they would get the full revelation, for Jesus Christ is "the Alpha and the Omega" (Rev. 22:13); He encompasses *all* the alphabet of God's revelation to man. He is God's last Word (Heb. 1:1–3).

Legalism, then, is not a step toward maturity; it is a step back into childhood. The law was not God's final revelation; it was but the preparation for that final revelation in Christ. It is important that a person know his ABCs, because they are the foundation for understanding all of the language. But the man who sits in a library and recites the ABCs, instead of reading the great literature that is around him, is showing that he is immature and ignorant, not mature and wise. Under the law, the Jews were children in bondage, not sons enjoying liberty.

What God did: redeemed us (vv. 4–5). The expression *the fullness of the time* (Gal. 4:4) refers to that time when the world was providentially ready for the birth of the Savior. Historians tell us that the Roman world was in great expectation, waiting for a Deliverer, at the time when Jesus was born. The old religions were dying; the old philosophies were empty and powerless to change men's lives. Strange new mystery religions were invading the empire. Religious bankruptcy and spiritual hunger were everywhere. God was preparing the world for the arrival of His Son.

From the historical point of view, the Roman Empire itself helped prepare the world for the birth of the Savior. Roads connected city with city, and all cities ultimately with Rome. Roman laws protected the rights of citizens, and Roman soldiers guarded the peace. Thanks to both the Greek and Roman conquests, Latin and Greek were known across the empire. Christ's birth at Bethlehem was not an accident; it was an appointment: Jesus came in "the fullness of the time." (And, it is worth noting, He will come again when the time is ready.)

Paul was careful to point out the dual nature of Jesus Christ (Gal. 4:4), that He is both God and man. As God, Jesus "came forth" (John 16:28); but as man, He was "made of a woman." The ancient promise said that the Redeemer would be of "the woman's seed" (Gen. 3:15); and Jesus fulfilled that promise (Isa. 7:14; Matt. 1:18–25).

Paul has told us *who* came—God's Son; he has told us *when* He came and *how* He came. Now he explains *why* He came: "to redeem them that were under the law" (Gal. 4:5). *Redeem* is the same word Paul used earlier (Gal. 3:13); it means "to set free by paying a price." A man could purchase a slave in any Roman city (there were about sixty million slaves in the empire), either to keep the slave for himself or to set him free. Jesus came to set us free. So, to go back into the law is to undo the very work of Christ on the cross. He did not purchase us to make us slaves, but *sons!* Under law, the Jews were mere children, but under grace, the believer is a son of God with an adult standing in God's family.

Perhaps at this point a chart will help us understand better the contrast between being a "child of God" and a "son of God."

The Child	The Son
by regeneration	by adoption
entering the family	enjoying the family
under guardians	the liberty of an adult
cannot inherit	an heir of the Father

What we are: sons and heirs (vv. 6–7). Once again, the entire Trinity is involved in our spiritual experience: God the Father sent the Son to die for us, and God the Son sent His Spirit to live in us. The contrast here is not between immature children and adult sons, but between *servants* and *sons.* Like the prodigal son, the Galatians wanted their Father to accept them as servants, when they really were sons (Luke 15:18–19). The contrasts are easy to see.

The son has the same nature as the father, but the servant does not. When we trust Christ, the Holy Spirit comes to live within us; and this means we are "partakers of the divine nature" (2 Peter 1:4). The law could never give a person God's nature within. All it could do was reveal to the person his desperate need for God's nature. So, when the believer goes back into law, he is denying the very divine nature within, and he is giving the old nature (the flesh) opportunity to go to work.

The son has a father, while the servant has a master. No servant could ever say "Father" to his master. When the sinner trusts Christ, he receives the Holy Spirit within, and the Spirit tells him that he is a child of the Father (Rom. 8:15–16). It is natural for a baby to cry, but not for a baby to talk to his father. When the Spirit enters the heart, He says, "Abba, Father" (Gal. 4:6); and, in response, the believer cries, "Abba, Father" (Rom. 8:15). The word *Abba* is an Aramaic word that is the equivalent of our English word *papa.* This shows the closeness of the child to the Father. No servant has this.

The son obeys out of love, while the servant obeys out of fear. The Spirit works in the *heart* of the believer to quicken and increase his love for God. "The fruit of the Spirit is love" (Gal. 5:22). "The love of God is shed abroad in our hearts by the Holy [Spirit]" (Rom. 5:5). The Judaizers told the Galatians that they would become better Christians by submitting to the law, but the law can never produce obedience. Only love can do that. "If ye love me, keep my commandments" (John 14:15).

The son is rich, while the servant is poor. We are both "sons and heirs." And since we are adopted—placed as adult sons in the family—we may begin drawing on our inheritance right now. God has made available to us the riches of His grace (Eph. 1:7; 2:7), the riches of His glory (Phil. 4:19), the riches of His goodness (Rom. 2:4), and the riches of His wisdom (Rom. 11:33ff.)—and all of the riches of God are found in Christ (Col. 1:19; 2:3).

The son has a future, while the servant does not. While many kind masters did provide for their slaves in old age, it was not required of them. The father always provides for the son (2 Cor. 12:14).

In one sense, our adoption is not yet final, because we are awaiting the return of Christ and the redemption of our bodies (Rom. 8:23). Some scholars think that this second stage in our adoption corresponds to the Roman practice when a man adopted someone outside his family to be his son. First there was a *private* ceremony at which the son was purchased; then there was a *public* ceremony at which the adoption was declared openly before the officials.

Christians have experienced the first stage: we have been purchased by Christ and indwelt by the Spirit. We are awaiting the second stage: the public declaration at the return of Christ when "we shall be like him" (1 John 3:1–3). We are "sons and heirs," and the best part of our inheritance is yet to come (see 1 Peter 1:1–5).

He Laments Their Regression (4:8–11)

What really happened when the Galatians turned from grace to law? To begin with, they abandoned liberty for bondage. When they were ignorant sinners, they had served their false gods and had experienced the tragedy of such pagan slavery. But then they had trusted Christ and been delivered from superstition and slavery. Now they were abandoning their liberty in Christ and going back into bondage. They were dropping out of the school of grace and enrolling in the kindergarten of law! They were destroying all the good work the Lord had done in them through Paul's ministry.

The phrase *weak and beggarly elements* tells us the extent of their regression. They were giving up the power of the gospel for the weakness of law, and the wealth of the gospel for the poverty of law. The law never made anybody rich or powerful; on the contrary, the law could only reveal man's weakness and spiritual bankruptcy. No wonder Paul weeps over these believers, as he sees them abandon liberty for bondage, power for weakness, and wealth for poverty.

How were they doing this? By adopting the Old Testament system of religion with its special observations of "days, and months, and times, and years" (Gal. 4:10).

Does this mean that it is wrong for Christians to set aside one day a year to remember the birth of Christ? Or that a special observance of the coming of the Spirit at Pentecost, or the blessing of the harvest in autumn, is a sin?

Not necessarily. If we observe special days like slaves, hoping to gain some spiritual merit, then we are sinning. But if in the observance, we express our liberty in Christ and let the Spirit enrich us with His grace, then the observance can be a spiritual blessing.

The New Testament makes it clear that Christians are not to legislate religious observances for each other (Rom. 14:4–13). We are not to praise the man who celebrates the day, nor are we to condemn the man who does not celebrate. But if a man thinks he is saving his soul, or automatically growing in grace, because of a religious observance, then he is guilty of legalism.

Our evangelical churches have many different kinds of observances, and it is wrong for us to go beyond the Word of God in comparing, criticizing, or condemning. But all of us must beware of that legalistic spirit that caters to the flesh, leads to pride, and makes the outward event a substitute for the inward experience.

He Seeks Their Affection (4:12–18)

Paul was a wonderful spiritual father; he knew just how to balance rebuke with love. Now he turns from "spanking" to "embracing" as he reminds the believers of their love for him and his love for them. At one point they were willing to sacrifice anything for Paul, so great was their love; but now he had become their enemy. The Judaizers had come in and stolen their affection.

Bible students wish Paul had been more explicit here, because we are not sure just what events he is talking about. When Paul had originally visited them, he was suffering from some physical affliction. If, as noted in Galatians 1, Paul wrote this letter to the churches of south Galatia, then he is referring to his first missionary journey, recorded in Acts 13—14. Apparently Paul had not intended to visit these cities, but was forced to do so because of some bodily infirmity. We can only speculate as to what this was. Some have suggested malaria; others, an affliction of the eyes (see Gal. 4:15). Whatever it was, it must have made Paul somewhat repulsive in appearance, because he commended the Galatians for the way they received him in spite of the way he looked. To them, he was an angel of God. It is a wonderful thing when people accept God's servants, not because of their outward appearance, but because they represent the Lord and bring His message.

Now Paul asked them, "What has happened to that love? What has happened to the blessedness—the happiness—you experienced when you heard the gospel and trusted Christ?" Of course, Paul knew what had happened: the Judaizers had come in and stolen their hearts.

One of the marks of a false teacher is that he tries to attract other men's converts to himself, and not simply to the truth of the Word or to the person of Jesus Christ. It was not the Judaizers who originally came to Galatia and led them to Christ; it was Paul. Like the cultists today, these false teachers were not winning lost sinners to Christ, but were stealing converts from those who were truly serving the Lord. Paul had proved to be their loving friend. He had "become as they were" by identifying himself with them (Gal. 4:12). Now they were turning away from Paul and following false shepherds.

Paul told them the truth, but the Judaizers told them lies. Paul sought to glorify Christ, but the Judaizers glorified themselves and their converts. "Those people are zealous to win you over, but for no good. What they want is to alienate you from us, so that you may be zealous for them" (Gal. 4:17 NIV).

A true servant of God does not "use people" to build up himself or his work; he ministers in love to help people know Christ better and glorify Him. Beware of that religious worker who wants your exclusive allegiance because he is the only one who is right. He will use you as long as he can and then drop you for somebody else—and your fall will be a painful one. The task of the spiritual leader is to get people to love and follow Christ, not to promote himself and his ministry.

"Faithful are the wounds of a friend; but the kisses of an enemy are deceitful" (Prov. 27:6). Paul had proved his love to the Galatians by telling them the truth; but they would not accept it. They were enjoying the "kisses" of the Judaizers, not realizing that these kisses were leading them into bondage and sorrow. Christ had made them sons and heirs, but they were rapidly becoming slaves and beggars.

They had not lost the *experience* of salvation—they were still Christians; but they were losing the *enjoyment* of their salvation and finding satisfaction in their works instead. Sad to say, *they did not realize their losses.* They actually thought they were becoming better Christians by substituting law for grace, and the religious deeds of the flesh for the fruit of the Spirit.

Is *your* Christian life moving forward into liberty or backward into bondage? Think carefully before you answer.

CHAPTER EIGHT
Galatians 4:19–31
MEET YOUR MOTHER

We parents never seem to outgrow our children. "When they're little, they're a handful; but when they're grown, they're a heartful!" I remember hearing my mother say, "When they're little, they step on your toes; but when they're grown, they step on your heart."

This is what Paul was experiencing as he tried to help the Galatian believers with their confused spiritual lives. When he had first come to them with the gospel, he had "travailed" spiritually to see them turn to the Lord. But, after all, the Lord Jesus had travailed on the cross to make possible their salvation (Isa. 53:11), and Paul's travail was nothing in comparison. But now the Galatian Christians were falling back into legalism and a "second childhood" experience; and Paul had to travail over them again. He longed to see Christ formed in them, just as we parents long to see our children mature in the will of God.

Since the Judaizers appealed to the law, Paul accepted their challenge and used the law to prove that Christians are not under the law. He took the familiar story of Ishmael and Isaac (Gen. 16—21) and drew from it basic truths about the Christian's relationship to the law of Moses.

The events described actually happened, but Paul used them as an allegory, which is a narrative that has a deeper meaning behind it. Perhaps the most famous allegory in the English language is John Bunyan's *Pilgrim's Progress,* in which Bunyan traces Christian's experiences from the City of Destruction to heaven. In an allegory, persons and actions represent hidden meanings, so that the narrative can be read on two levels: the literal and the symbolic.

Paul's use of Genesis in this section does not give us license to find "hidden meanings" in all the events of the Old Testament. If we take that approach to the Bible, we can make it mean almost anything we please. This is the way many false teachings arise. The Holy Spirit inspired Paul to discern the hidden meaning of the Genesis story. We must always interpret the Old Testament in the light of the New Testament, and where the New Testament gives us permission, we may search for hidden meanings. Otherwise, we must accept the plain statements of Scripture and not try to "spiritualize" everything.

The Historical Facts (4:19–23)
Perhaps the easiest way to grasp the historical account is to trace briefly Abraham's experiences as recorded in Genesis 12—21. Using his age as our guide, we will trace the events on which Paul based his argument for Christian liberty.

75—Abraham is called by God to go to Canaan; and God promises him many descendants (Gen. 12:1–9). Both Abraham and his wife, Sarah, wanted children, but Sarah was barren. God was waiting until both of them were "as good as dead" before He would perform the miracle of sending them a son (Rom. 4:16–25).

85—The promised son has not yet arrived, and Sarah becomes impatient. She suggests that Abraham marry Hagar, her maid, and try to have a son by her. This act was legal in that society, but it was not in the will of God. Abraham followed her suggestion and married Hagar (Gen. 16:1–3).

86—Hagar gets pregnant and Sarah gets jealous! Things are so difficult in the home that Sarah throws Hagar out. But the Lord intervenes, sends Hagar back, and promises to take care of her and her son. When Abraham is 86, the son is born, and he calls him Ishmael (Gen. 16:4–16).

99—God speaks to Abraham and promises again that he will have a son by Sarah and says to call his name Isaac. Later, God appears again and reaffirms the promise to Sarah as well (see Gen. 17—18).

100—The son is born (Gen. 21:1–7). They name him Isaac ("laughter") as commanded by God. But the arrival of Isaac creates a new problem in the home: Ishmael has a rival. For fourteen years, Ishmael has been his father's only son, very dear to his heart. How will Ishmael respond to the presence of a rival?

103—It was customary for the Jews to wean their children at about the age of three, and to make a great occasion of it. At the feast, Ishmael starts to mock Isaac (Gen. 21:8ff.) and to create trouble in the home. There is only one solution to the problem, and a costly one at that: Hagar and her son have to go. With a broken heart, Abraham sends his son away, because this is what the Lord tells him to do (Gen. 21:9–14).

On the surface, this story appears to be nothing more than a tale of a family problem, but beneath the surface are meanings that carry tremendous spiritual power. Abraham, the two wives, and the two sons represent spiritual realities; and their relationships teach us important lessons.

The Spiritual Truths (4:24–29)
Paul now explained the meanings that lie behind these historical events; perhaps they are best classified as shown in the chart below.

Paul began with the two sons, Ishmael and Isaac

(Gal. 4:22–23), and explained that they illustrate our two births: the physical birth that makes us sinners and the spiritual birth that makes us the children of God. As you think about this and read Genesis 21:1–12, you discover some wonderful spiritual truths about your salvation.

The Old Covenant	The New Covenant
Law	Grace
Hagar the slave	Sarah the free woman
Ishmael, conceived after the flesh	Isaac, miraculously conceived
Earthly Jerusalem in bondage	Heavenly Jerusalem, which is free

Isaac illustrates the believer in several particulars.

He was born by God's power. In fact, God deliberately waited twenty-five years before He granted Abraham and Sarah their son. Isaac was "born after the Spirit" (Gal. 4:29), and, of course, the Christian is "born of the Spirit" (John 3:1–7). Isaac came into the world through Abraham (who represents faith, Gal. 3:9) and Sarah (who represents grace); so that he was born "by grace … through faith" as is every true Christian (Eph. 2:8–9).

He brought joy. His name means "laughter," and certainly he brought joy to his aged parents. Salvation is an experience of joy, not only to the believer himself, but also to those around him.

He grew and was weaned (Gen. 21:8). Salvation is the beginning, not the ending. After we are born, we must grow (1 Peter 2:2; 2 Peter 3:18). Along with maturity comes weaning: we must lay aside "childish things" (1 Cor. 13:11). How easy it is for us to hold the "toys" of our earlier Christian days and fail to lay hold of the "tools" of the mature believer. The child does not enjoy being weaned, but he can never become a man until it happens. (Read Ps. 131 at this point.)

He was persecuted (Gen. 21:9). Ishmael (the flesh) caused problems for Isaac, just as our old nature causes problems for us. (Paul will discuss this in detail in Gal. 5:16ff.) Ishmael created no problems in the home until Isaac was born, just as our old nature creates no problems for us until the new nature enters when we trust Christ. In Abraham's home we see the same basic conflicts that we Christians face today:

Hagar versus Sarah = law versus grace
Ishmael versus Isaac = flesh versus Spirit

It is important to note that *you cannot separate these four factors.* The Judaizers taught that law made the believer more spiritual, but Paul made it clear that law only releases the opposition of the flesh and a conflict within the believer ensues (see Rom. 7:19). There was no law strong enough either to change or to control Ishmael, *but Isaac never needed any law.* It has well been said, "The old nature knows no law and the new nature needs no law."

Having explained the significance of the two sons, Paul turned to an explanation of the two wives, Sarah and Hagar. He was illustrating the contrasts between law and grace and was proving that the believer is not under law but is under the loving freedom that comes through God's grace. Notice, then, the facts about Hagar that prove that the law no longer has power over the Christian.

Hagar was Abraham's second wife. God did not *begin* with Hagar; He began with Sarah.

As far as God's dealings with men are concerned, *God began with grace.* In Eden, God provided for Adam and Eve by grace. Even after they sinned, in His grace He provided them with coats of skins for a covering (Gen. 3:21). He did not give them laws to obey as a way of redemption; instead, He gave them a gracious promise to believe: the promise of a victorious Redeemer (Gen. 3:15).

In His relationship with Israel also, God first operated on the basis of grace, not law. His covenant with Abraham (Gen. 15) was all of grace, because Abraham was in a deep sleep when the covenant was established. When God delivered Israel from Egypt, it was on the basis of grace and not law, for the law had not yet been given. Like Hagar, Abraham's second wife, the law was "added" (Gal. 3:19). Hagar performed a function temporarily, and then moved off the scene, just as the law performed a special function and then was taken away (Gal. 3:24–25).

Hagar was a slave. Five times in this section she is called a "bondmaid" or "bondwoman" (Gal. 4:22–23, 30–31). Sarah was a freewoman, and therefore her position was one of liberty; but Hagar, even though married to Abraham, was still a servant. Likewise, the law was given *as a servant.* "Wherefore then serveth the law?" (Gal. 3:19). It served as a *mirror* to reveal men's sins (Rom. 3:20) and as a *monitor* to control men and ultimately lead them to Christ (Gal. 3:23–25); but the law was never meant to be *a mother!*

Hagar was not meant to bear a child. Abraham's marriage to Hagar was out of the will of God; it was the result of Sarah's and Abraham's unbelief and impatience. Hagar was trying to do what only Sarah could do, and it failed. The law cannot give life (Gal. 3:21) or righteousness (Gal. 2:21) or the gift of the Spirit (Gal. 3:2) or a spiritual inheritance (Gal. 3:18). Isaac was born Abraham's heir (Gen. 21:10), but Ishmael could not share in this inheritance. The Judaizers were trying to make Hagar a mother again, while Paul was in spiritual travail for his converts that they might become more like Christ. No amount of religion or legislation can give the dead sinner life. Only Christ can do that through the gospel.

Hagar gave birth to a slave. Ishmael was "a wild man" (Gen. 16:12), and even though he was a slave, nobody could control him, including his mother. Like Ishmael, the old nature (the flesh) is at war with God, and the law cannot change or control it. By nature, the Spirit and the flesh are "contrary the one to the other" (Gal. 5:17), and no amount of religious activity is going to change the picture. Whoever chooses Hagar (law) for his mother is going to experience bondage (Gal. 4:8–11, 22–25, 30–31; 5:1). But whoever chooses Sarah (grace) for his mother is going to enjoy liberty in Christ. God wants His children to be free (Gal. 5:1).

Hagar was cast out. It was Sarah who gave the order: "Cast out this bondwoman and her son" (Gen. 21:9–10), and God subsequently approved it (Gen. 21:12). Ishmael had been in the home for at least seventeen years, but his stay was not to be permanent; eventually he had to be cast out. There was not room in the household for Hagar and Ishmael with Sarah and Isaac; one pair had to go.

It is impossible for law and grace, the flesh and the Spirit, to compromise and stay together. God did not ask Hagar and Ishmael to make occasional visits to the home; the break was permanent. The Judaizers in Paul's day—and in our own day—were trying to reconcile Sarah and Hagar, and Isaac and Ishmael; such reconciliation is contrary to the Word of God. It is impossible to mix law and grace, faith and works, God's gift of righteousness and man's attempts to earn righteousness.

Hagar was not married again. God never gave the law to any other nation or people, including His church. For the Judaizers to impose the law on the Galatian Christians was to oppose the very plan of God. In Paul's day, the nation of Israel was under bondage to the law, while the church was enjoying liberty under the gracious rule of the "Jerusalem which is above" (Gal. 4:26). The Judaizers wanted to "wed" Mount Sinai and the heavenly Mount Zion (Heb. 12:22), but to do this would be to deny what Jesus did on Mount Calvary (Gal. 2:21). Hagar is not to be married again.

From the human point of view, it might seem cruel that God should command Abraham to send away his own son Ishmael, whom he loved very much. But it was the only solution to the problem, for the "wild man" could never live with the child of promise. In a deeper sense, however, think of what it cost God when He gave His Son to bear the curse of the law to set us free. Abraham's broken heart meant Isaac's liberty; God's giving of His Son means our liberty in Christ.

The Practical Blessings (4:30–31)

We Christians, like Isaac, are the children of promise by grace. The covenant of grace, pictured by Sarah, is our spiritual mother. The law and the old nature (Hagar and Ishmael) want to persecute us and bring us into bondage. How are we to solve this problem?

We can try to change them. This must fail, for we cannot change either the law or the old nature. "That which is born of the flesh is flesh" (John 3:6), and, we might add, *it always will be flesh.* God did not try to change Ishmael and Hagar, either by force or by education; neither can you and I change the old nature and the law.

We can try to compromise with them. This did not work in Abraham's home, and neither will it work in our lives. The Galatians were trying to effect such a compromise, but it was only leading them gradually into bondage. False teachers today tell us, "Don't abandon Christ; simply move into a deeper Christian life by practicing the law along with your faith in Christ." Invite Hagar and Ishmael back home again. But this is a path back into slavery: "How turn ye again to the weak and beggarly elements, whereunto ye desire again to be in bondage?" (Gal. 4:9).

We can cast them out. This is what we are supposed to do. First, Paul applied this to the nation of Israel (Gal. 4:25–27); then he applied it to the individual Christian. The nation of Israel had been in bondage under the law, but this was a temporary thing, preparing them for the coming of Christ. Now that Christ had come, law had to go. Jesus Christ, like Isaac, was a child of promise, born by the miraculous power of God. Once He had come and died for the people, the law had to go. Paul quoted Isaiah 54:1, applying his words to Sarah, who was barren before the birth of Isaac; but also applying it to the church (Gal. 4:27). Note the contrasts.

Israel	*The Church*
earthly Jerusalem	heavenly Jerusalem
bondage	freedom
barren legalism	fruitful grace

Sarah had been barren, and she tried to become fruitful by having Abraham marry Hagar. This failed and brought only trouble. *The law cannot give life or fruitfulness; legalism is barren.* For the early church to go back into bondage would mean barrenness and disobedience to the Word of God. Because it held fast to grace, the church spread across the world in fruitfulness.

But individual churches and Christians can make the same mistake the Galatians were making: they can fail to cast out Hagar and Ishmael. *Legalism* is one of the major problems among Christians today. We must keep in mind that *legalism* does not mean the setting of spiritual standards; it means worshipping these standards and thinking that we are spiritual because we obey them. It also means judging other believers on the basis of these standards. A person can refrain from smoking, drinking, and gambling, for example, *and still not be spiritual.* The Pharisees had high standards; yet they crucified Jesus.

The old nature loves legalism because it gives the old nature a chance to "look good." It costs very little for Ishmael not to do certain bad things, or to do certain religious deeds, just so long as he can remain Ishmael. For seventeen years Ishmael caused no trouble in the home; and then Isaac came along, and there was conflict. Legalism caters to Ishmael. The Christian who claims to be spiritual because of what he doesn't do is only fooling himself. It takes more than negations to make a positive, fruitful spiritual life.

No doubt the Judaizers were attractive people. They carried credentials from religious authorities (2 Cor. 3:1). They had high standards and were careful in what they ate and drank. They were effective in making converts and liked to advertise their accomplishments (Gal. 4:17–18; 6:12–14). They had rules and standards to cover every area of life, making it easy for their followers to know who was "spiritual" and who was not. But the Judaizers were leading the people into bondage and defeat, not liberty and victory, *and the people did not know the difference.*

In the closing chapters of this letter, Paul will point out the greatest tragedy of legalism: it gives opportunity for the flesh to work. The old nature cannot be controlled by law; eventually it has to break out—and when it does, watch out! This explains why legalistic religious groups often have fights and divisions ("ye fight and devour one another," Gal. 5:15), and often are plagued with the defiling sins of the flesh (Gal. 5:19ff.). While every church has its share of these problems, it is especially prominent in those groups where there is an atmosphere of legalism. When you invite Hagar and Ishmael to live with Sarah and Isaac, you are inviting trouble.

Thank God, the Christian is set free from the curse of the law and the control of the law. "Cast out the bondwoman and her son." It may pain us deeply, as it did Abraham; but it must be done. To attempt to mix law and grace is to attempt the impossible. It makes for a frustrated, barren Christian life. But to live by grace, through faith, gives one a free and fulfilling Christian life.

What is the secret? The Holy Spirit. And it is this secret that Paul will share in the closing "practical" chapters of the letter. Meanwhile, you and I need to beware lest Ishmael and Hagar have crept back into our lives. If they have—let us cast them out.

CHAPTER NINE
Galatians 5:1–12
STOP! THIEF!

Paul's doctrine of grace is dangerous!" cried the Judaizers. "It replaces law with license. Why, if we do away with our rules and abandon our high standards, the churches will fall apart."

First-century Judaizers are not the only ones afraid to depend on God's grace. Legalists in our churches today warn that we dare not teach people about the liberty we have in Christ lest it result in religious anarchy. These people misunderstand Paul's teaching about grace, and it is to correct such misunderstanding that Paul wrote the final section of his letter (Gal. 5—6).

Paul turned now from argument to application,

from the doctrinal to the practical. The Christian who lives by faith is not going to become a rebel. Quite the contrary, he is going to experience the *inner discipline* of God that is far better than the outer discipline of man-made rules. No man could become a rebel who depends on God's grace, yields to God's Spirit, lives for others, and seeks to glorify God. The *legalist* is the one who eventually rebels, because he is living in bondage, depending on the flesh, living for self, and seeking the praise of men and not the glory of God.

No, Paul's doctrine of Christian liberty through grace is not the dangerous doctrine. It is *legalism* that is the dangerous doctrine, because *legalism* attempts to do the impossible: change the old nature and make it obey the laws of God. Legalism succeeds for a short time, and then the flesh begins to rebel. The surrendered Christian who depends on the power of the Spirit is not *denying* the law of God or rebelling against it. Rather, that law is *being fulfilled in him* through the Spirit (Rom. 8:1–4). It is easy to see the sequence of thought in these closing chapters:

1. I have been set free by Christ. I am no longer under bondage to the law (Gal. 5:1–12).
2. But I need something—Someone—to control my life from within. That Someone is the Holy Spirit (Gal. 5:13–26).
3. Through the Spirit's love, I have a desire to live for others, not for self (Gal. 6:1–10).
4. This life of liberty is so wonderful, I want to live it to the glory of God; for He is the One making it possible (Gal. 6:11–18).

Now, contrast this with the experience of the person who chooses to live under law, under the discipline of some religious leader:

1. If I obey these rules, I will become a more spiritual person. I am a great admirer of this religious leader, so I now submit myself to his system.
2. I believe I have the strength to obey and improve myself. I do what I am told and measure up to the standards set for me.
3. I'm making progress. I don't do some of the things I used to do. Other people compliment me on my obedience and discipline. I can see that I am better than others in my fellowship. How wonderful to be so spiritual.
4. If only others were like me! God is certainly fortunate that I am His. I have a desire to share this with others so they can be as I am. Our group is growing and we have a fine reputation. Too bad other groups are not as spiritual as we are.

No matter how you look at it, legalism is an insidious, dangerous enemy. *When you abandon grace for law, you always lose.* In this first section (Gal. 5:1–12), Paul explained what the believer loses when he turns from God's grace to man-made rules and regulations.

The Slave—You Lose Your Liberty (5:1)

Paul has used two comparisons to show his readers what the law is really like: a schoolmaster or guardian (Gal. 3:24; 4:2), and a bondwoman (Gal. 4:22ff.). Now he compared it to a yoke of slavery. You will recall that Peter used this same image at the famous conference in Jerusalem (see Acts 15:10).

The image of the yoke is not difficult to understand. It usually represents slavery, service, and control by someone else over your life; it may also represent willing service and submission to someone else. When God delivered Israel from Egyptian servitude, it was the breaking of a yoke (Lev. 26:13). The farmer uses the yoke to control and guide his oxen because they would not willingly serve if they were free.

When the believers in Galatia trusted Christ, they lost the yoke of servitude to sin and put on the yoke of Christ (Matt. 11:28–30). The yoke of religion is hard, and the burdens heavy; Christ's yoke is "easy" and His burden is "light." That word *easy* in the Greek means "kind, gracious." The yoke of Christ *frees* us to fulfill His will, while the yoke of the law *enslaves* us. The unsaved person wears a yoke of sin (Lam. 1:14); the religious legalist wears the yoke of bondage (Gal. 5:1); but the Christian who depends on God's grace wears the liberating yoke of Christ.

It is Christ who has made us free from the bondage of the law. He freed us from the curse of the law by dying for us on the tree (Gal. 3:13). The believer is no longer under law; he is under grace (Rom. 6:14). This does not mean that we are outlaws and rebels. It simply means that we no longer need the *external* force of law to keep us in God's will, because we have the *internal* leading of the Holy Spirit of God (Rom. 8:1–4). Christ died to set us free, not to make us slaves. To go back to law is to become entangled in a maze of "do's and don'ts" and to abandon spiritual adulthood for a "second childhood."

Sad to say, there are some people who feel very insecure with liberty. They would rather be under the tyranny of some leader than to make their own decisions freely. There are some believers who are frightened by the liberty they have in God's grace; so they seek out a fellowship that is legalistic and dictatorial, where they can let others make their decisions for them. This is comparable to an adult climbing back into the crib. The way of Christian liberty is the way of fulfillment in Christ. No wonder Paul issues that ultimatum: "Do not be entangled again in the yoke of bondage. Take your stand for liberty."

The Debtor—You Lose Your Wealth (5:2–6)

Paul used three phrases to describe the losses the Christian incurs when he turns from grace to law: "Christ shall profit you nothing" (Gal. 5:2); "a debtor to do the whole law" (Gal. 5:3); "Christ is become of no effect unto you" (Gal. 5:4). This leads to the sad conclusion in Galatians 5:4: "Ye are fallen from grace." It is bad enough that legalism robs the believer of his liberty, but it also robs him of his spiritual wealth in Christ. The believer living under law becomes a bankrupt slave.

God's Word teaches that when we were unsaved, we owed God a debt we could not pay. Jesus made this clear in His parable of the two debtors (Luke 7:36–50). Two men owed money to a creditor, the one owing ten times as much as the other. But neither was able to pay, so the creditor "graciously forgave them both" (literal translation). No matter how much morality a man may have, he still comes short of the glory of God. Even if his sin debt is one tenth that of others, he stands unable to pay, bankrupt at the judgment bar of God. God in His grace, because of the work of Christ on the cross, is able to forgive sinners, no matter how large their debt may be.

Thus when we trust Christ, *we become spiritually rich.* We now share in the riches of God's grace (Eph. 1:7), the riches of His glory (Eph. 1:18; Phil. 4:19), the riches of His wisdom (Rom. 11:33), and the "unsearchable riches of Christ" (Eph. 3:8). In Christ we have "all the treasures of wisdom and knowledge" (Col. 2:3), and we are "complete in him" (Col. 2:10). Once a person is "in Christ," he has all that he needs to live the kind of Christian life God wants him to live.

The Judaizers, however, want us to believe that we are missing something, that we would be more "spiritual" if we practiced the law with its demands and disciplines. But Paul made it clear that *the law adds nothing—because nothing can be added!* Instead, the law comes in as a thief and robs the believer of the spiritual riches he has in Christ. It puts him back into bankruptcy, responsible for a debt he is unable to pay.

To live by grace means to depend on God's abundant supply of every need. To live by law means to depend on my own strength—the flesh—and be left to get by without God's supply. Paul warned the Galatians that to submit to circumcision in these circumstances would rob them of all the benefits they have in Christ (though circumcision itself is an indifferent matter, Gal. 5:6; 6:15). Furthermore, to submit would put them under obligation to obey *the whole law.*

It is at this point that legalists reveal their hypocrisy, for they fail to keep the *whole* law. They look on the Old Testament law the way a customer surveys the food in a cafeteria: they choose what they want and leave the rest. But this is not honest. To teach that a Christian today should, for example, keep the Sabbath but not the Passover, is to dismember God's law. The same Lawgiver who gave the one commandment also gave the other (James 2:9–11). Earlier, Paul had quoted Moses to prove that the curse of the law is on everyone who fails to keep *all* the law (Gal. 3:10; see Deut. 27:26).

Imagine a motorist driving down a city street and deliberately driving through a red light. He is pulled over by a policeman who asks to see his driver's license. Immediately the driver begins to defend himself. "Officer, I know I ran that red light—but I have never robbed anybody. I've never killed anybody. I've never cheated on my income tax."

The policeman smiles as he writes out the ticket, because he knows that *no amount of obedience can make up for one act of disobedience.* It is one law, and the same law that protects the obedient man punishes the offender. To boast about keeping part of the law while at the same time breaking another part is to confess that I am worthy of punishment.

Now we can better understand what Paul meant by "fallen from grace" (Gal. 5:4). Certainly he was not suggesting that the Galatians had "lost their salvation," because throughout this letter he dealt with them *as believers.* At least nine times he called them *brethren,* and he also used the pronoun *we* (Gal. 4:28, 31). This Paul would never do if his readers were lost. He boldly stated, "And because ye are sons, God hath sent forth the Spirit of his Son into your hearts, crying, 'Abba, Father'" (Gal. 4:6). If his readers were unsaved, Paul could never write those words.

No, to be "fallen from grace" does not mean to lose salvation. Rather, it means "fallen out of the sphere of God's grace." You cannot mix grace and law. If you decide to live in the sphere of law, then you cannot live in the sphere of grace. The believers in Galatia had been *bewitched* by the false teachers (Gal. 3:1) and thus were *disobeying* the truth. They had *removed* toward another gospel (Gal. 1:6–9) and had *turned back* to the elementary things of the old religion (Gal. 4:9). As a result, they had become *entangled* with the yoke of bondage, and this led to their present position: "fallen from grace." And the tragedy of this fall is that they had robbed themselves of all the good things Jesus Christ could do for them.

Paul next presented the life of the believer in the sphere of grace (Gal. 5:5–6). This enables us to contrast the two ways of life. When you live by grace, you depend on the power of the Spirit; but under law, you must depend on yourself and your own efforts. Faith is not dead; faith *works* (see James 2:14–26). But the efforts of the flesh can never accomplish what faith can accomplish through the Spirit. And faith works *through love*—love for God and love for others. Unfortunately, flesh does not manufacture love; too often it produces selfishness and rivalry (see Gal. 5:15). No wonder Paul pictured the life of legalism as a fall!

When the believer walks by faith, depending on the Spirit of God, he lives in the sphere of God's grace; and all his needs are provided. He experiences the riches of God's grace. And, he always has something to look forward to (Gal. 5:5): one day Jesus shall return to make us like Himself in perfect righteousness. The law gives no promise for perfect righteousness in the future. The law prepared the way for the first coming of Christ (Gal. 3:23—4:7), but it cannot prepare the way for the second coming of Christ.

So, the believer who chooses legalism robs himself of spiritual liberty and spiritual wealth. He deliberately puts himself into bondage and bankruptcy.

The Runner—You Lose Your Direction (5:7–12)

Paul was fond of athletic illustrations and used them often in his letters. His readers were familiar with the Olympic Games as well as other Greek athletic contests that always included footraces. It is important to note that Paul never uses the image of the race to tell people how to be saved. He is always talking to Christians about how to live the Christian life. A *contestant in the Greek games had to be a citizen before he could compete.* We become citizens of heaven through faith in Christ; then the Lord puts us on our course, and we run to win the prize (see Phil. 3:12–21). We do not run to be saved; we run because we are already saved and want to fulfill God's will in our lives (Acts 20:24).

"You did run well." When Paul first came to them, they received him "as an angel of God" (Gal. 4:14). They accepted the Word, trusted the Lord Jesus Christ, and received the Holy Spirit. They had a deep joy that was evident to all, and were willing to make any sacrifice to accommodate Paul (Gal. 4:15). But now, Paul was their enemy. What had happened?

A literal translation of Galatians 5:7 gives us the answer: "You were running well. Who cut in on you so that you stopped obeying the truth?" In the races, each runner was to stay in his assigned lane, but some runners would cut in on their competitors to try to get them off course. This is what the Judaizers had done to the Galatian believers: they cut in on them and forced them to change direction and go on a "spiritual detour." It was not God who did this, because He had called them to run faithfully in the lane marked "Grace."

His explanation changes the figure of speech from athletics to cooking, for Paul introduces the idea of yeast (leaven). In the Old Testament, leaven is generally pictured as a symbol of evil. During Passover, for example, no yeast was allowed in the house (Ex. 12:15–19; 13:7). Worshippers were not permitted to mingle leaven with sacrifices (Ex. 34:25), though there were some exceptions to this rule. Jesus used leaven as a picture of sin when He warned against the "leaven of the Pharisees" (Matt. 16:6–12); and Paul used leaven as a symbol of sin in the church at Corinth (1 Cor. 5).

Yeast is really a good illustration of sin: it is small, but if left alone it grows and permeates the whole. The false doctrine of the Judaizers was introduced to the Galatian churches in a small way, but, before long, the "yeast" grew and eventually took over.

The spirit of legalism does not suddenly overpower a church. Like leaven, it is introduced secretly, it grows, and before long poisons the whole assembly. In most cases, the *motives* that encourage legalism are good ("We want to have a more spiritual church"), but the *methods* are not scriptural.

It is not wrong to have standards in a church, but we should never think that the standards will make anybody spiritual, or that the keeping of the standards is an evidence of spirituality. How easy it is for the yeast to grow. Before long, we become proud of our spirituality ("puffed up" is the way Paul put it [1 Cor.

5:2] and that is exactly what yeast does: it puffs up), and then critical of everybody else's lack of spirituality. This, of course, only feeds the flesh and grieves the Spirit, but we go on our way thinking we are glorifying God.

Every Christian has the responsibility to watch for the *beginnings* of legalism, that first bit of yeast that infects the fellowship and eventually grows into a serious problem. No wonder Paul is so vehement as he denounces the false teachers: "I am suffering persecution because I preach the cross, but these false teachers are popular celebrities because they preach a religion that pampers the flesh and feeds the ego. Do they want to circumcise you? I wish that they themselves were *cut off!*" (Gal. 5:11–12, literal translation).

Since the death and resurrection of Christ, there is no spiritual value to circumcision; it is only a physical operation. Paul wished that the false teachers would *operate on themselves*—"castrate themselves"—so that they could not produce any more "children of slavery."

The believer who lives in the sphere of God's grace is free, rich, and running in the lane that leads to reward and fulfillment. The believer who abandons grace for law is a slave, a pauper, and a runner on a detour. In short, he is a loser. And the only way to become a winner is to "purge out the leaven," the false doctrine that mixes law and grace, and yield to the Spirit of God.

God's grace is sufficient for every demand of life. We are saved by grace (Eph. 2:8–10), and we serve by grace (1 Cor. 15:9–10). Grace enables us to endure suffering (2 Cor. 12:9). It is grace that strengthens us (2 Tim. 2:1) so that we can be victorious soldiers. Our God is the God of *all* grace (1 Peter 5:10). We can come to the throne of grace and find grace to help in every need (Heb. 4:16). As we read the Bible, which is "the word of his grace" (Acts 20:32), the Spirit of grace (Heb. 10:29) reveals to us how rich we are in Christ.

"And of his fullness have all we received, and grace for grace" (John 1:16).

How rich we are!

CHAPTER TEN
Galatians 5:13–26
THE FIFTH FREEDOM

At the close of an important speech to Congress on January 6, 1941, President Franklin D. Roosevelt shared his vision of the kind of world he wanted to see after the war was over. He envisioned four basic freedoms enjoyed by all people: freedom of speech, freedom of worship, freedom from want, and freedom from fear. To some degree, these freedoms have been achieved on a wider scale than in 1941, but our world still needs another freedom, a fifth freedom. Man needs to be free from himself and the tyranny of his sinful nature.

The legalists thought they had the answer to the problem in laws and threats, but Paul has explained that no amount of legislation can change man's basic sinful nature. It is not law on the *outside,* but love on the *inside* that makes the difference. We need another power within, and that power comes from the Holy Spirit of God.

There are at least fourteen references to the Holy Spirit in Galatians. When we believe on Christ, the Spirit comes to dwell within us (Gal. 3:2). We are "born after the Spirit" as was Isaac (Gal. 4:29). It is the Holy Spirit in the heart who gives assurance of salvation (Gal. 4:6); and it is the Holy Spirit who enables us to live for Christ and glorify Him. The Holy Spirit is not simply a "divine influence"; He is a divine Person, just as are the Father and the Son. What God the Father *planned* for you, and God the Son *purchased* for you on the cross, God the Spirit *personalizes* for you and applies to your life as you yield to Him.

This paragraph is perhaps the most crucial in the entire closing section of Galatians; for in it Paul explained three ministries of the Holy Spirit that enable the believer to enjoy liberty in Christ.

The Spirit Enables Us to Fulfill the Law of Love (5:13–15)
We are prone to go to extremes. One believer interprets *liberty* as *license* and thinks he can do whatever he wants to do. Another believer, seeing this error, goes to an opposite extreme and imposes law on everybody. Somewhere between *license* on the one hand and *legalism* on the other hand is true Christian liberty.

So, Paul began by explaining *our calling:* we are called to liberty. The Christian is a free man. He is free from the *guilt* of sin because he has experienced God's forgiveness. He is free from the *penalty* of sin because Christ died for him on the cross. And he is, through the Spirit, free from the *power* of sin in his daily life. He is also free from the *law* with its demands and threats. Christ bore the curse of the law and ended its tyranny once and for all. We are "called unto liberty" because we are "called into the grace of Christ" (Gal. 1:6). *Grace* and *liberty* go together.

Having explained our calling, Paul then issued a *caution:* "Don't allow your liberty to degenerate into license!"

This, of course, is the fear of all people who do not understand the true meaning of the grace of God. "If you do away with rules and regulations," they say, "you will create chaos and anarchy."

Of course, that danger is real, not because God's grace fails, but because men fail of the grace of God (Heb. 12:15). If there is a "true grace of God" (1 Peter 5:12), then there is also a *false* grace of God; and there are false teachers who "change the grace of our God into a license for immorality" (Jude 4 NIV). So, Paul's caution is a valid one. Christian liberty is not a license to sin but an opportunity to serve.

This leads to *a commandment:* "By love serve one

another" (Gal. 5:13). The key word, of course, is *love*. The formula looks something like this:

liberty + love = service to others
liberty − love = license (slavery to sin)

"I have an extra day off this week," Carl told his wife as he walked into the kitchen. "I think I'll use it to fix Donna's bike and then take Larry on that museum trip he's been talking about."

"Fixing a bike and visiting a museum hardly sound like exciting ways to spend a day off," his wife replied.

"It's exciting if you love your kids!"

The amazing thing about love is that it takes the place of all the laws God ever gave. "Thou shalt love thy neighbor as thyself" solves every problem in human relations (see Rom. 13:8–14). If you love people (because you love Christ), you will not steal from them, lie about them, envy them, or try in any way to hurt them. Love in the heart is God's substitute for laws and threats.

When our children were small, we lived next to a busy highway, and the children knew they would be spanked if they went near the road. As they grew older, they discovered that obedience brought rewards. They learned to obey not only to escape pain but to gain pleasure. Today they live in different metropolitan areas and all of them drive. But we neither threaten nor bribe them in order to keep them safe. They have a built-in discipline of love that regulates their lives, and they would not deliberately hurt themselves, their parents, or other people. Love has replaced law.

On a much higher level, the Holy Spirit within gives us the love that we need (Rom. 5:5; Gal. 5:6, 22). Apparently the Galatian believers were lacking in this kind of love, because they were "biting and devouring one another" and were in danger of destroying one another (Gal. 5:15). The picture here is of wild animals attacking each other. This in itself is proof that law cannot force people to get along with each other. No matter how many rules or standards a church may adopt, they are no guarantee of spirituality. Unless the Holy Spirit of God is permitted to fill hearts with His love, selfishness and competition will reign. Both extremes in the Galatian churches—the legalists and the libertines—were actually destroying the fellowship.

The Holy Spirit does not work in a vacuum. He uses the Word of God, prayer, worship, and the fellowship of believers to build us up in Christ. The believer who spends time daily in the Word and prayer, and who yields to the Spirit's working, is going to enjoy liberty and will help build up the church. Read 2 Corinthians 3 for Paul's explanation of the difference between a spiritual ministry of grace and a carnal ministry of law.

The Spirit Enables Us to Overcome the Flesh (5:16–21, 24)

The conflict (vv. 16–17). Just as Isaac and Ishmael were unable to get along, so the Spirit and the flesh (the old nature) are at war with each other. By "the flesh," of course, Paul did not mean "the body." The human body is not sinful; it is neutral. If the Holy Spirit controls the body, then we walk in the Spirit; but if the flesh controls the body, then we walk in the lusts (desires) of the flesh. The Spirit and the flesh have different appetites, and this is what creates the conflict.

These opposite appetites are illustrated in the Bible in different ways. For example, the sheep is a clean animal and avoids garbage, while the pig is an unclean animal and enjoys wallowing in filth (2 Peter 2:19–22). After the rain ceased and the ark settled, Noah released a raven, which never came back (Gen. 8:6–7). The raven is a carrion-eating bird and found plenty to feed on. But when Noah released the dove (a clean bird), it came back (Gen. 8:8–12). The last time he released the dove and it did not return, he knew that it had found a clean place to settle down; therefore the waters had receded.

Our old nature is like the pig and the raven, always looking for something unclean on which to feed. Our new nature is like the sheep and the dove, yearning for that which is clean and holy. No wonder a struggle goes on within the life of the believer! The unsaved man knows nothing of this battle because he does not have the Holy Spirit (Rom. 8:9).

Note that the Christian cannot simply *will* to overcome the flesh: "These two are opposed to each other, so that you cannot do anything you please" (Gal. 5:17, Williams). It is this very problem that Paul discusses in Romans: "I do not know what I am doing. For what I want to do I do not do, but what I hate I do…. For what I do is not the good I want to do; no, the evil I do not want to do—this I keep on doing" (Rom. 7:15, 19 NIV). Paul is not denying that there is victory. He is simply pointing out that we cannot win this victory in our own strength and by our own will.

The conquest (v. 18). The solution is not to pit our will against the flesh, but to surrender our will to the Holy Spirit. This verse literally means "But if you are *willingly led* by the Spirit, then you are not under the law." The Holy Spirit writes God's law on our hearts (Heb. 10:14–17; see 2 Cor. 3) so that we *desire* to obey Him in love. "I delight to do thy will, O my God: yea, thy law is within my heart" (Ps. 40:8). Being "'led of the Spirit" and "walking in the Spirit" are the opposites of yielding to the desires of the flesh.

The crucifixion (vv. 19–21, 24). Paul now lists some of the ugly "works of the flesh." (You will find similar lists in Mark 7:20–23; Rom. 1:29–32; 1 Tim. 1:9–10; 2 Tim. 3:2–5.) The flesh is able to manufacture sin, but it can never produce the righteousness of God. "The heart is deceitful above all things, and desperately wicked" (Jer. 17:9). This list in Galatians can be divided into three major categories:

The sensual sins (vv. 19, 21b). Adultery is illicit sex between married people, while *fornication* generally refers to the same sin among unmarried people.

Uncleanness means just that: a filthiness of heart and mind that makes the person defiled. The unclean person sees dirt in everything (see Titus 1:15). *Lasciviousness* is close to our word *debauchery*. It speaks of a wanton appetite that knows no shame. It goes without saying that all of these sins were rampant in the Roman Empire. *Drunkenness* and *revellings* (orgies) need no explanation.

The superstitious sins (v. 20a). Idolatry, like the sins named above, is with us today. Idolatry is simply putting things ahead of God and people. We are to worship God, love people, and use things, but too often we use people, love self, and worship things, leaving God out of the picture completely. Jesus tells us that whatever we worship, we serve (Matt. 4:10). The Christian who devotes more of himself to his car, house, or boat than he does to serving Christ may be in danger of idolatry (Col. 3:5).

The word *witchcraft* is from the Greek word *pharmakeia*, which means "the use of drugs." Our English word *pharmacy* is derived from this word. Magicians in Paul's day often used drugs to bring about their evil effects. Of course, sorcery is forbidden in the Bible as are all activities of the occult (Deut. 18:9–22).

The social sins (vv. 20b–21a). Hatred means "enmity," the attitude of mind that defies and challenges others. This attitude leads to *variance*, which is strife, the outworking of enmity. *Emulations* means jealousies or rivalries. How tragic when Christians compete with one another and try to make one another look bad in the eyes of others. *Wrath* means outbursts of anger, and *strife* carries with it the idea of "self-seeking, selfish ambition," that creates divisions in the church.

Seditions and *heresies* are kindred terms. The first suggests division, and the second cliques caused by a party spirit. *Divisions* and *factions* would be a fair translation. These are the result of church leaders promoting themselves and insisting that the people follow them, not the Lord. (The word *heresy* in the Greek means "to make a choice.") *Envyings* suggests the carrying of grudges, the deep desire for what another has (see Prov. 14:30). *Murders* needs no elucidation.

The person who *practices* these sins shall not inherit the kingdom of God. Paul is not talking about an *act* of sin, but a *habit* of sin. There is a false assurance of salvation that is not based on the Word of God. The fact that the believer is not under law, but under grace, is no excuse for sin (Rom. 6:15). If anything, it is an encouragement to live in obedience to the Lord.

But how does the believer handle the old nature when it is capable of producing such horrible sins? The law cannot *change* or *control* the old nature.

The old nature must be crucified (v. 24). Paul explains that the believer is identified with Christ in His death, burial, and resurrection (Rom. 6). Christ not only died *for* me, but *I died with Christ*. Christ died for me to remove the *penalty* of my sin, but I died with Christ to break sin's *power*.

Paul has mentioned this already in Galatians (see 2:19–20), and he will mention it again (6:14). He does not tell us to crucify ourselves, because this is impossible. (Crucifixion is one death a man cannot inflict on himself.) He tells us that the flesh has already been crucified. It is our responsibility to *believe* this and *act on it*. (Paul calls this "reckoning" in Rom. 6; you have the same truth presented in Col. 3:5ff.)

You and I are not debtors to the flesh, but to the Spirit (Rom. 8:12–14). We must accept what God says about the old nature and not try to make it something that it is not. We must not make "provision for the flesh" (Rom. 13:14) by feeding it the things that it enjoys. In the flesh dwells no good thing (Rom. 7:18), so we should put no confidence in the flesh (Phil. 3:3). The flesh is not subject to God's law (Rom. 8:7) and it cannot please God (Rom. 8:8). Only through the Holy Spirit can we "put to death" the deeds that the flesh would do through our body (Rom. 8:13). The Holy Spirit is not only the Spirit of life (Rom. 8:2; Gal. 5:25), but He is also the Spirit of death: He helps us to reckon ourselves dead to sin.

We have seen two ministries of the Spirit of God: He enables us to fulfill the law, and He enables us to overcome the flesh. He has a third ministry as well.

The Spirit Enables Us to Produce Fruit (5:22–23, 25–26)

It is one thing to overcome the flesh and *not do* evil things, but quite something else *to do* good things. The legalist might be able to boast that he is not guilty of adultery or murder (but see Matt. 5:21–32), but can anyone see the beautiful graces of the Spirit in his life? Negative goodness is not enough in a life; there must be positive qualities as well.

The contrast between *works* and *fruit* is important. A machine in a factory *works* and turns out a product, but it could never manufacture fruit. Fruit must grow out of life, and, in the case of the believer, it is the life of the Spirit (Gal. 5:25). When you think of "works" you think of effort, labor, strain, and toil; when you think of "fruit" you think of beauty, quietness, the unfolding of life. The flesh produces "dead works" (Heb. 9:14), but the Spirit produces living fruit And this fruit has in it the seed for still more fruit (Gen. 1:11). Love begets more love! Joy helps to produce more joy! Jesus is concerned that we produce "fruit … more fruit … much fruit" (John 15:2, 5), because this is the way we glorify Him. The old nature cannot produce fruit; only the new nature can do that.

The New Testament speaks of several different kinds of "fruit": people won to Christ (Rom. 1:13), holy living (Rom. 6:22), gifts brought to God (Rom. 15:26–28), good works (Col. 1:10), and praise (Heb. 13:15). The "fruit of the Spirit" listed in our passage has to do with *character* (Gal. 5:22–23). It is important that we distinguish the *gift* of the Spirit, which is salvation (Acts 2:38; 11:17), and the *gifts* of the Spirit, which have to do with service (1 Cor. 12), from the *graces* of the Spirit, which relate to Christian character. It is unfortunate that an overemphasis on gifts has led some Christians to neglect the graces of the Spirit. Building Christian character must take precedence over displaying special abilities.

The characteristics that God wants in our lives are seen in the ninefold fruit of the Spirit. Paul began with *love* because all of the other fruit is really an outgrowth of love. Compare these eight qualities with the characteristics of love given to the Corinthians (see 1 Cor. 13:4–8). This word for love is *agape,* which means divine love. (The Greek word *eros,* meaning "sensual love," is never used in the New Testament.) This divine love is God's gift to us (Rom. 5:5), and we must cultivate it and pray that it will increase (Phil. 1:9).

When a person lives in the sphere of love, then he experiences *joy*—that inward peace and sufficiency that is not affected by outward circumstances. (A case in point is Paul's experience recorded in Phil. 4:10–20.) This "holy optimism" keeps him going in spite of difficulties. Love and joy together produce *peace,* "the peace of God, which passeth all understanding" (Phil. 4:7). These first three qualities express the *Godward* aspect of the Christian life.

The next three express the *manward* aspect of the Christian life: *long suffering* (courageous endurance without quitting), *gentleness* (kindness), and *goodness* (love in action). The Christian who is long suffering will not avenge himself or wish difficulties on those who oppose him. He will be kind and gentle, even with the most offensive, and will sow goodness where others sow evil. Human nature can never do this on its own; only the Holy Spirit can.

The final three qualities are *selfward: faith* (faithfulness, dependability); *meekness* (the right use of power and authority, power under control); and *temperance* (self-control). Meekness is not weakness. Jesus said, "I am meek and lowly in heart" (Matt. 11:29), and Moses was "very meek" (Num. 12:3); yet no one could accuse either of them of being weak. The meek Christian does not throw his weight around or assert himself. Just as wisdom is the right use of knowledge, so meekness is the right use of authority and power.

It is possible for the old nature to *counterfeit* some of the fruit of the Spirit, but the flesh can never *produce* the fruit of the Spirit. One difference is this: when the Spirit produces fruit, God gets the glory and the Christian is not conscious of his spirituality; but when the flesh is at work, the person is inwardly proud of himself and is pleased when others compliment him. The work of the Spirit is to make us more like Christ for His glory, not for the praise of men.

The cultivation of the fruit is important. Paul warns that there must be a right atmosphere before the fruit will grow (Gal. 5:25–26). Just as fruit cannot grow in every climate, so the fruit of the Spirit cannot grow in every individual's life or in every church.

Fruit grows in a climate blessed with an abundance of the Spirit and the Word. "Walk in the Spirit" (Gal. 5:25) means "keep in step with the Spirit"—not to run ahead and not to lag behind. This involves the Word, prayer, worship, praise, and fellowship with God's people. It also means "pulling out the weeds" so that the seed of the Word can take root and bear fruit. The Judaizers were anxious for praise and "vainglory," and this led to competition and division. Fruit can never grow in that kind of an atmosphere.

We must remember that this fruit is produced *to be eaten,* not to be admired and put on display. People around us are starving for love, joy, peace, and all the other graces of the Spirit. When they find them in our lives, they know that we have something they lack. We do not bear fruit for our own consumption; we bear fruit that others might be fed and helped, and that Christ might be glorified. The flesh may manufacture "results" that bring praise to us, but the flesh cannot bear fruit that brings glory to God. It takes patience, an atmosphere of the Spirit, walking in the light, the seed of the Word of God, and a sincere desire to honor Christ.

In short, the secret is the Holy Spirit. He alone can give us that "fifth freedom"—freedom from sin and self. He enables us to fulfill the law of love, to overcome the flesh, and to bear fruit.

Will you yield to Him and let Him work?

CHAPTER ELEVEN
Galatians 6:1–10
THE LIBERTY OF LOVE

The story has often been told about the message the founder of the Salvation Army sent to their international convention. General William Booth was unable to attend personally because of ill health, so he cabled the delegates a message containing one word: "OTHERS!"

In the popular comic strip "Peanuts," Lucy asks Charlie Brown, "Why are we here on earth?" He replies, "To make others happy." She ponders this for a moment and then asks, "Then why are the others here?"

"One another" is one of the key phrases in the Christian's vocabulary. "Love one another" is found at least a dozen times in the New Testament, along with "pray one for another" (James 5:16), "edify one another" (1 Thess. 5:11), prefer one another (Rom. 12:10), "use hospitality one to another" (1 Peter 4:9), and many other like admonitions.

In the section before us, Paul adds another phrase: "Bear ye one another's burdens" (Gal. 6:2). The Spirit-led Christian thinks of others and how he can minister to them. In this section, Paul described two important ministries that we ought to share with one another.

Bearing Burdens (6:1–5)
The legalist is not interested in bearing burdens.

Instead, he *adds* to the burdens of others (Acts 15:10). This was one of the sins of the Pharisees in Jesus' day: "For they bind heavy burdens and grievous to be borne, and lay them on men's shoulders; but they themselves will not move them with one of their fingers" (Matt. 23:4). The legalist is always harder on other people than he is on himself, but the Spirit-led Christian demands more of himself than he does of others *that he might be able to help others.*

Paul presented a hypothetical case of a believer who is suddenly tripped up and falls into sin. The word *overtaken* carries the idea of being surprised, so it is not a case of deliberate disobedience. Why did Paul use this illustration? *Because nothing reveals the wickedness of legalism better than the way the legalists treat those who have sinned.* Call to mind the Pharisees who dragged a woman taken in adultery before Jesus (John 8). Or that Jewish mob that almost killed Paul because they *thought* he had defiled the temple by bringing in Gentiles (Acts 21:27ff.). (Legalists do not need facts and proof; they need only suspicions and rumors. Their self-righteous imaginations will do the rest.) So, in this paragraph, Paul was really contrasting the way the legalist would deal with the erring brother, and the way the spiritual man would deal with him.

A contrast in aim. The spiritual man would seek to restore the brother in love, while the legalist would exploit the brother. The word *restore* means "to mend, as a net, or to restore a broken bone." If you have ever had a broken bone, you know how painful it is to have it set. The sinning believer is like a broken bone in the body, and he needs to be restored. The believer who is led by the Spirit and living in the liberty of grace will seek to help the erring brother, for "the fruit of the Spirit is love" (Gal. 5:22). "By love serve one another" (Gal. 5:13). When Jesus sought to be a physician to the sinful, He was severely criticized by the Pharisees (Mark 2:13–17), and so the spiritual believer today will be criticized by the legalists.

Instead of trying to restore the erring brother, the legalist will condemn him and then *use the brother to make himself look good.* This is what the Pharisee did in the parable of the Pharisee and the publican (Luke 18:9–14). "[Love] shall cover the multitude of sins" (1 Peter 4:8). The legalist rejoices when a brother falls, and often gives the matter wide publicity, because then he can boast about his own goodness and how much better his group is than the group to which the fallen brother belongs.

This is why Paul admonished us, "Let us not be desirous of vainglory, provoking one another, envying one another" (Gal. 5:26). The word *provoke* means "to challenge to a contest, to compete with." The believer who walks in the Spirit is not *competing* with other Christians or challenging them to become "as good as he is." However, the legalist lives by competition and comparison, and tries to make himself look good by making the other fellow look bad.

A contrast in attitude. The Spirit-led believer approaches the matter in a spirit of meekness and love, while the legalist has an attitude of pride and condemnation. The legalist does not need to "consider himself" because he pretends he could never commit such a sin. But the believer living by grace realizes that no man is immune from falling. "Let him that thinketh he standeth take heed lest he fall" (1 Cor. 10:12). He has an attitude of humility because he realizes his own weaknesses.

But there is a second contrast: he knows the love of Christ in his own heart. "The law of Christ" is "Love one another" (John 13:34; 15:12). Paul has already discussed the "law of love" (Gal. 5:13–15), and now he is applying it. "Tender loving care" is not a modern invention, because Paul is urging it on believers in this passage. How much we appreciate it when the doctor uses tenderness as he sets a broken bone. And how much more should we use "tender loving care" when we seek to restore a broken life.

It takes a great deal of love and courage for us to approach an erring brother and seek to help him. Jesus compared this to eye surgery (Matt. 7:1–5)—and how many of us feel qualified for that?

Paul probably had in mind here our Lord's instructions on reconciliation (Matt. 18:15–35). If your brother sins against you, go talk to him privately, *not* for the purpose of winning an argument, but for the purpose of winning your brother. (That word *gained* is the same word Paul used in 1 Cor. 9:19–22 to refer to winning the lost to Christ. It is important to win the lost, but it is also important to win the saved.) If he hears you, then the matter is settled. But if he will not agree, then ask one or two spiritual people to go with you. If he will still not settle the matter, then the whole church must be informed and take steps of discipline. But Jesus went on to point out that the church must practice prayer (Matt. 18:19–20) and forgiveness (Matt. 18:21–35), or discipline will not be effective.

The legalist, of course, has no time for this kind of spiritual "soul-winning." When he hears that his brother has sinned, instead of going to the brother, he shares the sad news with others ("so you can pray more intelligently about it") and then condemns the brother for not being more spiritual.

Remember, the legalist makes himself look better by making his brother look worse. Thus Paul's warnings here (Gal. 6:3–4). The Judaizers were guilty of boasting about themselves, their achievements, and their converts (Gal. 6:12–14). They usually did this by comparing themselves with others (see 2 Cor. 10:11). But such comparisons are sinful and deceptive. It is easy to find somebody worse off than we are, so that our comparison makes us look better than we really are. Christian love would lead us not to expose a brother's failures or weaknesses, no matter how much better it would make us look.

A man should "prove his own work" (Gal. 6:4) in the light of God's will and not in the shadows of somebody else's achievements. "Each man should test his own actions. Then he can take pride in himself, without comparing himself to somebody else, for each man should carry his own load" (Gal. 6:4–5 NIV). There is no place for competition in the work of God, unless we are competing against sin and Satan. When we see words like "best, fastest-growing, biggest, finest" applied to Christian ministries, we wonder who is getting the glory.

This does not mean that it is wrong to keep records. Charles Haddon Spurgeon used to say, "Those who criticize statistics usually have none to report." But we must be careful that we are not making others look bad just to make ourselves look good. And we should be able to rejoice at the achievements and blessings of others just as if they were our own (Rom. 12:10). After all, if one member of the body is blessed, it blesses the whole body.

There is no contradiction between Galatians 6:2 and 5, because two different Greek words for *burden* are used. In Galatians 6:2 it is a word meaning "a heavy burden," while in Galatians 6:5 it describes "a soldier's pack." We should help each other bear the heavy burdens of life, but there are personal responsibilities that each man must bear for himself. "Each soldier must bear his own pack." If my car breaks down, my neighbor can help drive my children to school, but he cannot assume the responsibilities that only belong to me as their father. That is the difference. It is wrong for me to expect somebody else to be the father in our family; that is a burden (and a privilege) that I alone can bear.

Sharing Blessings (6:6–10)

Just as *one another* is a key phrase in the Christian vocabulary, so is the word *fellowship* (translated "communicate" in Gal. 6:6). From the very beginning of the church, *sharing* was one of the marks of Christian experience (Acts 2:41–47). The Greek word has now worked its way into our English vocabulary, and we see the word *koinonia* here and there in religious publications. It simply means "to have in common," and refers to our common fellowship in Christ (Gal. 2:9), our common faith (Jude 3), and even our sharing in the sufferings of Christ (Phil. 3:10). But often in the New Testament, *koinonia* refers to the sharing of material blessings with one another (Acts 2:42; 2 Cor. 8:4; Heb. 13:16 [Greek text]). It is this that Paul had in mind in these verses.

He began with *a precept* (Gal. 6:6), urging us to share with one another. The teacher of the Word shares spiritual treasures, and those who are taught ought to share material treasures. (Paul used a similar approach when he explained why the Gentile churches ought to give an offering to the Jewish believers, Rom. 15:27.) We must remember that what we do with *material* things is an evidence of how we value *spiritual* things. "For where your treasure is, there will your heart be also" (Matt. 6:21).

Because the apostle Paul did not want money to become a stumbling block to the unsaved, he earned his own living (see 1 Cor. 9), but he repeatedly taught that the spiritual leader in the church was to be supported by the gifts of the people. Jesus said, "The laborer is worthy of his hire" (Luke 10:7), and Paul echoed this statement (1 Cor. 9:11, 14).

But we must realize the spiritual *principle* that lies behind this precept. God does not command believers to give simply that pastors and teachers (and missionaries, Phil. 4:10–19) might have their material needs met, *but that the givers might get a greater blessing* (Gal. 6:7–8). The basic principle of sowing and reaping is found throughout the entire Bible. God has ordained that we *reap what we sow*. Were it not for this law, the whole principle of cause and effect would fail. The farmer who sows wheat can expect to reap wheat. If it were otherwise, there would be chaos in our world.

But God has also told us to be careful *where we sow*, and it is this principle that Paul dealt with here. He looked on our material possessions as seed, and he sees two possible kinds of soil: the flesh and the Spirit. We can use our material goods to promote the flesh, or to promote the things of the Spirit. But once we have finished sowing, *we cannot change the harvest*.

Money sown to the flesh will bring a harvest of corruption (see Gal. 5:19–21). That money is gone and can never be reclaimed. Money sown to the Spirit (such as sharing with those who teach the Word) will produce life, and in that harvest will be seeds that can be planted again for another harvest, and on and on into eternity. If every believer only looked on his material wealth as seed, and planted it properly, there would be no lack in the work of the Lord. Sad to say, much seed is wasted on carnal things and can never bring glory to God.

Of course, there is a much wider application of the principle to our lives; because all that we do is either an investment in the flesh or the Spirit. We shall reap whatever we have sown, and we shall reap *in proportion* as we have sown. "He which soweth sparingly shall reap also sparingly; and he which soweth bountifully shall reap also bountifully" (2 Cor. 9:6). The believer who walks in the Spirit and "sows" in the Spirit is going to reap a spiritual harvest. If his sowing has been generous, the harvest will be bountiful, if not in this life, certainly in the life to come.

Paul's enemies, the Judaizers, did not have this spiritual attitude toward giving and receiving. Paul sacrificed and labored that he might not be a burden to the churches, but the false teachers used the churches to promote their own schemes and fill their own coffers. This is also what happened in the Corinthian church, and Paul had to write them: "In fact, you even put up with anyone who enslaves you or exploits you or takes advantage of you or pushes himself forward or slaps you in the face" (2 Cor. 11:20 NIV).

How many times we have seen the sacrificing godly pastor persecuted and driven out, while the arrogant promoter is honored and gets everything he wants. The carnal believer thrives under the "spiritual dictatorship" of a legalistic promoter-pastor, because it makes him feel secure, successful, and spiritual. The carnal believer will sacrifice what he has to make the work more successful, only to discover that he is sowing to the flesh and not to the Spirit.

Having given us the precept (Gal. 6:6) and the principle behind the precept (Gal. 6:7–8), Paul now gave us a *promise* (Gal. 6:9): "In due season we shall reap if we faint not." Behind this promise is a peril: getting weary in the work of the Lord, and then eventually fainting, and stopping our ministry.

Sometimes spiritual fainting is caused by a lack of devotion to the Lord. It is interesting to contrast two churches that are commended for "work, labor, and patience" (1 Thess. 1:3; Rev. 2:2). The church at Ephesus had actually left its first love and was backslidden (Rev. 2:4–5). Why? The answer is seen in the commendation to the Thessalonian church: "Work of faith, labor of love, patience of hope." Not just work, labor, and patience, but the proper motivation: "faith, love, and hope." How easy it is for us to work for the Lord, but permit the spiritual motivation to die. Like the priests of Israel that Malachi addressed, we serve the Lord but complain, "Behold, what a weariness is it" (Mal. 1:13).

Sometimes we faint because of lack of prayer. "Men ought always to pray, and not to faint" (Luke 18:1). Prayer is to the spiritual life what breathing is to the physical life, and if you stop breathing, you will faint. It is also possible to faint because of lack of nourishment. "Man shall not live by bread alone, but by every word that proceedeth out of the mouth of God" (Matt. 4:4). If we try to keep going without proper food and rest, we will faint. How important it is to "wait upon the Lord" to get the strength we need for each day (Isa. 40:28–31).

But the promise Paul gave us will help to keep us going: "In due season we shall reap." The seed that is planted does not bear fruit immediately. There are seasons to the soul just as there are seasons to nature, and we must give the seed time to take root and bear fruit. How wonderful it is when the plowman overtakes the reaper (Amos 9:13). Each day we ought to sow the seed so that one day we will be able to reap (Ps. 126:5–6). But we must remember that the Lord of the harvest is in charge, and not the laborers.

Sharing blessings involves much more than teaching the Word and giving of our material substance. It also involves doing good "unto all men" (Gal. 6:10). There are those in this world who do evil (Ps. 34:16); in fact, there are those who return evil for good (Ps. 35:12). Most of the people in the world return good for good and evil for evil (see Luke 6:32–35; 1 Thess. 5:15). But the Christian is supposed to return good for evil (Rom. 12:18–21) and to do this in a spirit of Christian love. Actually, the Christian's good works are a spiritual sacrifice that he gives to the Lord (Heb. 13:16).

We are to "do good unto all men." This is how we let our light shine and glorify our Father in heaven (Matt. 5:16). It is not only by *words* that we witness to the lost, but also by our *works.* In fact, our works pave the way for our verbal witness; they win us the right to be heard. It is not a question of asking, "Does this person deserve my good works?" Did we deserve what God did for us in Christ? Nor should we be like the defensive lawyer who tried to argue, "Who is my neighbor?" (Luke 10:25–37). Jesus made it very clear that the question is not "Who is my neighbor?" but "To whom can I be a neighbor?"

As we "do good unto all men," we must give priority to "the household of faith," the fellowship of believers. This does not mean that the local church should become an exclusive clique with the members isolated from the world around them and doing nothing to help the lost. Rather, it is a matter of balance. Certainly the believers in Paul's day would have greater needs than would the outsiders, since many of the believers suffered for their faith (see Heb. 10:32–34). Furthermore, a man always cares for his own family before he cares for the neighborhood (1 Tim. 5:8).

We must remember, however, that we share with other Christians so that all of us might be able to share with a needy world. The Christian in the household of faith is a receiver that he might become a transmitter. As we abound in love for one another, we overflow in love for all men (1 Thess. 3:12).

This is how it was meant to be.

CHAPTER TWELVE
Galatians 6:11–18
THE MARKS OF FREEDOM

It was Paul's custom, after dictating a letter, to take the pen and write his own farewell. His standard signature was "The grace of our Lord Jesus Christ be with you" (1 Thess. 5:28; see 2 Thess. 3:17–18). But so concerned was Paul that the Galatians get the message of this letter that he took the pen and wrote *an entire concluding paragraph* with his own hand. "Look at the large letters I write with my own hand!"

Why did Paul write this paragraph, and why did he use such large letters? The Holy Spirit inspired him to add these closing words to give one more contrast between the legalists and the Spirit-led Christians, to show that the Spirit-led believer lives for the glory of God, not the praise of man. And he wrote in large letters for emphasis: "DON'T MISS THIS!"

Some Bible students believe that Paul's thorn in the flesh (2 Cor. 12:7–10; Gal. 4:14–15) was some kind of eye trouble. This would mean that he would have to write in large letters so that he himself would be able to read what he had written. Whether or not that is true, Paul was making it clear that he had something important to write in conclusion, that he was not simply going to end the letter in some conventional manner. If he did have eye trouble, his willingness to write this closing paragraph with his own hand would certainly appeal to the hearts of the readers.

He has shown them that the believer living under law and the believer living under grace are diametrically opposed to each other. It is not just a matter of "different doctrine," but a matter of two different ways of life. They had to choose between bondage or liberty (Gal. 5:1–12), the flesh or the Spirit (Gal. 5:13–26), and living for self or living for others (Gal. 6:1–10).

Now he presented a fourth contrast: living for the praise of men or the glory of God (Gal. 6:11–18). He was dealing with *motive,* and there is no greater need in our churches today than for an examination of the motives for our ministries. We know *what* we are doing, but do we know *why* we are doing it? A good work is spoiled by a bad motive.

Paul approached this delicate subject in an interesting way. The legalists wanted to subject the Galatian believers to circumcision, so Paul took this up and related it to the work of Christ on the cross, and also to his own ministry. In this paragraph Paul presented three "marked men"—the legalist (Gal. 6:12–13), the Lord Jesus Christ (Gal. 6:14–16), and the apostle Paul himself (Gal. 6:17–18).

The Legalist (6:12–13)

Paul did not have anything good to say about the legalist. He described him and his kind in four ways.

They are braggarts (vv. 12a, 13b). Their main purpose was not to win people to Christ, or even to help the believers grow in grace. Their chief purpose was to win more converts so they could brag about them. They wanted to "make a fine impression outwardly" even though they did no good inwardly. Their work was not done for the good of the church or for the glory of God; it was done for their own glory.

While it is certainly not wrong to want to win people to Christ, or to see the work of the Lord increase, it is definitely wrong to want these blessings for the glory of man. We want to see more people sharing in our ministries, not so that we can count people, but because people count. But we must be careful not to use people to further our own selfish programs for our own glorification.

I receive a number of local church newsletters and newspapers. I was shocked to find an article in one of them in which the pastor named several other churches and proceeded to explain how his church was much better. Some of the churches he mentioned were not evangelical in belief, and I wondered what those members would think of Christ and the gospel if they read his boastful critique. No doubt it made it difficult for the believers to witness to these other people once this pastor had condemned their churches.

They are compromisers (v. 12b). Why did they preach and practice circumcision and all that went with it? *To escape persecution.* Because Paul preached the grace of God and salvation apart from the works of the law, he was persecuted (Gal. 5:11). The Judaizers tried to make the Christians think that they too were Christians, and they tried to make the followers of the Mosaic law think that they too obeyed the law. Consequently, they escaped being persecuted by the legalistic group for their identification with the cross of Christ and its devastating effect on the law.

We are prone to look at the cross (and crucifixion) in a sentimental way. We wear crosses on our lapels or on chains around our necks. But to the first-century citizen, the cross was not a beautiful piece of jewelry; it was the lowest form of death and the ultimate in humiliation. The proper Roman citizen would never mention the cross in polite conversation. It stood for rejection and shame.

When Paul trusted Christ, he identified himself with the cross and took the consequences. To the Jew the cross was a stumbling block, and to the Gentile it was foolishness (1 Cor. 1:18–31). The legalists, emphasizing circumcision rather than crucifixion, won many converts. Theirs was a popular religion because it avoided the shame of the cross.

They are persuaders (v. 12a). The word *constrain* carries with it the idea of strong persuasion and even force. It is translated "compel" in Galatians 2:14. While it does not mean "to force against one's will," it is still a strong word. It indicates that the Judaizers were great persuaders; they had a "sales talk" that convinced the Galatian believers that legalism was the way for them. Whenever Paul presented the Word, it was in truth and sincerity, and he used no oratorical tricks or debater's skills. (See 1 Cor. 2:1–5 and 2 Cor. 4:1–5 to see how Paul presented the Word to his listeners. Paul was not a politician; he was an ambassador.)

They are hypocrites (v. 13). "They want you to submit to the law, but they themselves do not obey the law." The legalists belonged to the same group as the Pharisees about whom Jesus said, "They say and do not" (Matt. 23:3). Of course, Paul was not suggesting that the Judaizers *should* keep the law, because keeping the law is neither possible nor necessary. Rather, he was condemning them for their dishonesty; they had no intention of keeping the law, even if they could. Their reverence for the law was only a mask to cover their real goal: winning more converts to their cause. They wanted to report more statistics and get more glory.

Yes, the legalist is a marked man; so when you detect him, avoid him.

Jesus Christ (6:14–16)

Paul kept coming back to the cross (Gal. 2:20–21; 3:13; 4:5; 5:11, 24; 6:12). "If righteousness come by the law, then Christ is dead in vain" (Gal. 2:21). The wounds of Calvary certainly make Christ a "marked Man," for those wounds mean liberty to those who will trust Him. The Judaizers boasted in circumcision; but Paul boasted in a crucified and risen Savior. He gloried in the cross. Certainly this does not mean that he gloried in the brutality or suffering of the cross. He was not looking at the cross as a piece of wood on which a criminal died. He was looking at the cross of *Christ* and glorying in it. Why would Paul glory in the cross?

He knew the Person of the cross. Jesus Christ is mentioned at least forty-five times in the Galatian letter, which means that one third of the verses contain some reference to Him. The person of Jesus Christ captivated Paul, and it was Christ who made the cross glorious to him. In his early years as a Jewish rabbi, Paul had much to glory in (Gal. 1:13–14; Phil. 3:1–10); but after he met Christ, all his self-glory turned to mere refuse. The legalists did not glory in the cross of Christ *because they did not glory in Christ.* It was Moses—and themselves—who got the glory. They did not really know the Person of the cross.

He knew the power of the cross. To Saul, the learned Jewish rabbi, a doctrine of sacrifice on a cross was utterly preposterous. That the Messiah would come, he had no doubt, but that He would come to die—and to die *on a cursed cross*—well, there was no place for this in Saul's theology. The cross in that day was the ultimate example of weakness and shame. Yet Saul of Tarsus experienced the power of the cross and became Paul the apostle. The cross ceased to be a stumbling block to him and became, instead, the very foundation stone of his message: "Christ died for our sins."

For Paul, the cross meant *liberty:* from self (Gal. 2:20), the flesh (Gal. 5:24), and the world (Gal. 6:14). In the death and resurrection of Christ, the power of God is released to give believers deliverance and victory. It is no longer *we* who live; it is Christ who lives in us and through us. As we yield to Him, we have victory over the world and the flesh. There is certainly no power in the law to give a man victory over self, the flesh, and the world. Quite the contrary, the law *appeals* to the human ego ("I can do something to please God"), and encourages the flesh to work. And the world does not care if we are "religious" just so long as the cross is left out. In fact, the world approves of religion—apart from the gospel of Jesus Christ. So, the legalist inflates the ego, flatters the flesh, and pleases the world; the true Christian crucifies all three.

He knew the purpose of the cross. It was to bring into the world a new "people of God." For centuries, the nation of Israel had been the people of God, and the law had been their way of life. All of this was preparation for the coming of Jesus Christ (Gal. 4:1–7). Now that Christ had come and finished His great work of redemption, God had set aside the nation of Israel and brought into the world a "new creation" and a new nation, "the Israel of God." This does not mean that God is finished with the nation of Israel. Today, God is calling out from both Jews and Gentiles "a people for his name" (Acts 15:14), and in Christ there are no racial or national distinctions (Gal. 3:27–29). Paul clearly taught, however, that there is a future in God's plan for the Jewish nation (Rom. 11).

One purpose of the cross was to bring in *a new creation* (Gal. 6:15 NIV). This "new creation" is the church, the body of Christ. The "old creation" was headed by Adam, and it ended in failure. The new creation is headed by Christ, and it is going to succeed.

To the Romans, Paul explained the doctrine of the two Adams—Adam and Christ (Rom. 5:12–21). The first Adam disobeyed God and brought into the world sin, death, and judgment. The Last Adam (1 Cor. 15:45) obeyed God and brought life, righteousness, and salvation. Adam committed one sin and plunged all of creation into judgment. Christ performed one act of obedience in His death on the cross, and paid for all the sins of the world. Because of Adam's sin, death reigns in this world. Because of Christ's victory, *we can "reign in life"* through Jesus Christ (Rom. 5:17). In other words, the believer belongs to a "new creation," a spiritual creation, that knows nothing of the defects and limitations of the "old creation" (see 2 Cor. 5:17).

Another purpose of the cross was to create a *new nation,* "the Israel of God" (Gal. 6:16). This is one of many names for the church found in the New Testament. Jesus said to the Jewish leaders, "The kingdom of God shall be taken from you, and given to a nation bringing forth the fruits thereof" (Matt. 21:43). Peter identified that nation as the family of God: "But ye are a chosen generation, a royal priesthood, an holy nation" (1 Peter 2:9).

As mentioned previously, this does not mean that the church has permanently replaced the nation of Israel in the program of God, but only that the church is "the people of God" on earth today just as Israel was in centuries past.

What a rebuke to the Judaizers. They wanted to take the church back into Old Testament law, when that law could not even be kept by the nation of Israel! That nation was set aside to make way for God's new people, the church!

Believers today may not be "Abraham's children" in the flesh, but they are "Abraham's seed" through faith in Jesus Christ (Gal. 4:28–29). They have experienced a circumcision of the heart that is far more effective than physical circumcision (Rom. 2:29; Phil. 3:3; Col. 2:11). For this reason, neither circumcision nor the lack of it is of any consequence to God (Gal. 6:15; see also Gal. 5:6).

The Apostle Paul (6:17–18)

There was a time when Paul was proud of his mark of circumcision (Phil. 3:4–6), but after he became a believer, he became a "marked man" in a different way. He now gloried in the scars he had received and in the suffering he had endured in the service of Jesus Christ.

The contrast with the legalists is plain to see: "The Judaizers want to mark your flesh and brag about you, but I bear in my body the brands of the Lord Jesus Christ—for His glory." What a rebuke! "If your religious celebrities have any scars to show for the glory of Christ, then let them be shown. Otherwise—stop bothering me!"

Paul was not claiming that he bore the five wounds of Calvary on his body. Rather he was affirming that he had suffered for Christ's sake (something the legalists never did), and he had on his body the scars to prove it. When you read 2 Corinthians 11:18–33, you have no difficulty understanding this claim of his, for in many ways and in many places Paul suffered physically for Christ.

In Paul's day, it was not unusual for the follower of some heathen god or goddess to be branded with the mark of that idol. He was proud of his god and wanted others to know it. In the same way, Paul was "branded" for Jesus Christ. It was not a temporary mark that could be removed, but a permanent mark that he would take to his grave. Nor did he receive his brands in an easy way: he had to suffer repeatedly to become a marked man for Christ.

It was also the practice in that day to brand slaves, so that everyone would know who the owner was. Paul was the slave of Jesus Christ, and he wore His mark to prove it.

It is worth noting that *sin brands a person.* It may mark his mind, his personality, even his body. Few people are proud of the sin marks they bear, and conversion does not change them. (Thank God, those changes will come when Jesus returns!) How much better it is to love Christ and live for Him and be "branded" for His glory.

Believers today need to remember that it is the Christian leader who has *suffered* for Christ who has something to offer. The Judaizers in Paul's day knew nothing of suffering. They may have been persecuted in some small way for belonging to a religious group, but this is far different from "the fellowship of his [Christ's] sufferings" (Phil. 3:10).

Beware of that religious leader who lives in his ivory tower and knows nothing of battling against the world, the flesh, and the devil, who has no "marks" to show for his obedience to Christ. Paul was no armchair general; he was out in the front lines, waging war against sin, and taking his share of suffering.

So, Paul comes to the end of his letter; and he closes just the way he began: GRACE! Not "the law of Moses," but THE GRACE OF OUR LORD JESUS CHRIST!

No more need be said, because that says it all.

EPHESIANS

OUTLINE

Key theme: The believer's riches in Christ
Key verse: Ephesians 1:3

I. DOCTRINE: OUR RICHES IN CHRIST (1—3)

A. Our spiritual possessions in
   Christ—1:4–14
   1. From the Father—1:4–6
   2. From the Son—1:7–12
   3. From the Spirit—1:13–14
   First Prayer—for enlightenment—1:15–23
B. Our spiritual position in Christ—2:1–22
   1. Raised and seated on the
      throne—2:1–10
   2. Reconciled and set into the tem-
      ple—2:11–22
   Second Prayer—for enablement—3:1–21 (vv.
   2–13 are a parenthesis)

II. DUTY: OUR RESPONSIBILITIES IN CHRIST (4—6)

A. Walk in unity—4:1–16
B. Walk in purity—4:17—5:17
   1. Walk not as other Gentiles—4:17–32
   2. Walk in love—5:1–6
   3. Walk as children of light—5:7–14
   4. Walk carefully—5:15–17
C. Walk in harmony—5:18—6:9
   1. Husbands and wives—5:18–33
   2. Parents and children—6:1–4
   3. Masters and servants—6:5–9
D. Walk in victory—6:10–24

CONTENTS

CHAPTER ONE
Ephesians 1:1–3

SAINTS ALIVE!

She had gone down in history as "America's Greatest Miser," yet when she died in 1916, "Hetty" Green left an estate valued at over $100 million. She ate cold oatmeal because it cost to heat it. Her son had to suffer a leg amputation, because she delayed so long in looking for a free clinic that his case became incurable. She was wealthy, yet she chose to live like a pauper.

Eccentric? Certainly! Crazy? Perhaps—but nobody could prove it. She was so foolish that she hastened her own death by bringing on an attack of apoplexy while arguing about the value of drinking skimmed milk! But Hetty Green is an illustration of too many Christian believers today. They have limitless wealth at their disposal, and yet they live like paupers. It was to this kind of Christian that Paul wrote the epistle to the Ephesians.

The Author (1:1a)

Some names in history we identify immediately, and "Paul" is one of them. His name was originally "Saul" (Acts 7:58), and, since he was from the tribe of Benjamin (Phil. 3:5), it is likely he was named after the first king of Israel (1 Sam. 9). Unlike his namesake, however, Saul of Tarsus was obedient, and faithfully served God. As a devoted rabbi, Saul became the leader of the antichristian movement in Jerusalem (Acts 9:1–2; Gal. 1:13–14). But in the midst of this activity, Saul was "arrested" by Jesus Christ and was converted (Acts 9:3ff.; 26).

Saul of Tarsus became Paul, the apostle to the Gentiles (Acts 9:15). While he was ministering in the church of Antioch, he was called by the Spirit to take the gospel to the Gentiles, and he obeyed (Acts 13:1–3). The book of Acts records three missionary journeys that took Paul throughout the Roman Empire in one of the greatest evangelistic endeavors in church history. About the year 53, Paul first ministered in Ephesus but did not remain there (Acts 18:19–21). Two years later, while on his third journey, Paul stayed in Ephesus for at least two years and saw that whole vast area evangelized (Acts 19:1–20). During these years, he founded a strong church in the city that was dedicated to the worship of the goddess Diana. For a description of Paul's ministry in Ephesus, read Acts 20, and for an explanation of the opposition to Paul's ministry there, read Acts 19:21–41.

It was nearly ten years later when Paul wrote to his beloved friends in Ephesus. Paul was a prisoner in Rome (Eph. 3:1; 4:1; 6:20), and he wanted to share with these believers the great truths the Lord had taught him about Christ and the church. Compare Ephesians 6:21–22 with Colossians 4:7–9 and Philemon to get a better understanding of the historical background. Onesimus, a slave, ran away from Philemon, his master, who lived at Colosse. While in Rome, Onesimus met Paul and was converted. Tychicus, one of the pastors of the church at Colosse, which may have met in Philemon's house, was also in Rome to discuss some problems with Paul. So Paul took advantage of the presence of these two men to send three letters to his friends: the epistle to the Ephesians, the epistle to the Colossians, and the epistle to Philemon. At the same time, he sent Onesimus back to his master.

So, the letter was written from Rome about the year AD 62. Though Paul was on trial for his life, he was concerned about the spiritual needs of the churches he had founded. As an *apostle,* "one sent with a commission," he had an obligation to teach them the Word of God and to seek to build them up in the faith (Eph. 4:11–12).

The Assembly (1:1b–2)

Are you surprised to find Paul addressing his letter to *saints?* After all, saints are dead people who have achieved such spiritual eminence that they have been given that special title, *saints.* Or are they?

No word in the New Testament has suffered more than this word *saint.* Even the dictionary defines a *saint* as a "person officially recognized for holiness of life." Who makes this official recognition? Usually some religious body, and the process by which a person becomes a saint is technically known as *canonization.* The deceased person's life is examined carefully to see whether he qualifies for sainthood. If the candidate's character and conduct are found to be above reproach, if he has been responsible for working at least two miracles, then he is qualified to be made a saint.

As interesting as this procedure is, we do not find it authorized in the Bible. Nine times in this brief letter, Paul addressed his readers as saints (Eph. 1:1, 15, 18; 2:19; 3:8, 18; 4:12; 5:3; 6:18). These saints were alive, not dead, though once they had been "dead in trespasses and sins" (Eph. 2:1–3). And it is clear that they had never performed any miracles, though they had *experienced* a miracle by trusting Christ as Savior (Eph. 2:4–10). The word *saint* is simply one of the many terms used in the New Testament to describe "one who has trusted Jesus Christ as Savior." The person is "alive," not only physically, but also spiritually (Eph. 2:1). You will find Christians called *disciples* (Acts 9:1, 10, 19, 25–26, 36, 38), *people of the Way* (Acts 9:2), and *saints* (Acts 9:13, 32, 41).

The word *saint* means "one who has been set apart." It is related to the word *sanctified,* which means "set apart." When the sinner trusts Christ as his Savior, he is taken out of "the world" and placed "in Christ." The believer is *in* the world physically, but not of the world spiritually (John 17:14–16). Like a scuba diver, he exists in an alien environment because he possesses special equipment—in this case, the indwelling Holy

Spirit of God. Every true believer possesses the Holy Spirit (Rom. 8:9; 1 Cor. 6:19–20), and it is through the Spirit's power that the Christian is able to function in the world.

Now for the important question: How did these people at Ephesus become saints? The answer is found in two words: "faithful" and "grace" (Eph. 1:1–2). When Paul addressed his letter to the "saints … and faithful in Christ Jesus" he was not addressing two different groups of people. The word *faithful* carries the meaning of "believers in Christ Jesus." These people were not saved by living faithful lives; rather they put their faith in Christ and were saved. This is clear from Ephesians 1:12–14, 19.

The word *grace* is used twelve times in Ephesians, and refers to "the kindness of God toward undeserving people." Grace and mercy often are found together in the Bible, and they certainly belong together in the experience of salvation. *Grace* and *faith* go together, because the only way to experience grace and salvation is through faith (Eph. 2:8–9).

The phrase "in Christ Jesus" is used twenty-seven times in this letter! It describes the spiritual position of the believer: He is identified with Christ he is in Christ, and therefore is able to draw on the wealth of Christ for his own daily living.

The Aim (1:3)
Each book in the Bible has its own special theme and message, even though it may deal with many different topics. Genesis is the book of *beginnings;* Matthew is the book of the *kingdom;* Galatians is the book of *liberty.* Ephesians 1:3 states its theme: *the Christian's riches in Christ.*

The source of our blessings. "Blessed be the God and Father of our Lord Jesus Christ." God the Father has made us rich in Jesus Christ! When you were born again into God's family, you were born rich. Through Christ you share in the riches of God's grace (Eph. 1:7; 2:7), God's glory (Eph. 1:18; 3:16), God's mercy (Eph. 2:4), and "the unsearchable riches of Christ" (Eph. 3:8). Our heavenly Father is not poor; He is rich—and He has made us rich in His Son.

J. Paul Getty, one of the richest men in the world, was worth an estimated $1.3 billion. The weekly income of some of the "oil sheiks" runs into the millions. Yet all of this wealth is but "pennies" when compared with the spiritual wealth we have in Christ. In this letter, Paul explained to us what these riches are and how we may draw on them for effective Christian living.

The scope of our blessings. We have "all spiritual blessings." This can be translated "all the blessings of the Spirit," referring to the Holy Spirit of God. In the Old Testament, God promised His earthly people, Israel, material blessings as a reward for their obedience (Deut. 28:1–13). Today, He promises to supply all our needs "according to his riches in glory by Christ Jesus" (Phil. 4:19), but He does not promise to shield

us from either poverty or pain. The Father has given us every blessing of the Spirit, everything we need for a successful, satisfying Christian life. *The spiritual is far more important than the material.*

The Holy Spirit is mentioned many times in this letter, because He is the One who channels our riches to us from the Father, through the Son. Not to know and depend on the Holy Spirit's provision is to live a life of spiritual poverty. No wonder Paul began his Ephesian ministry asking some professed Christians if they really knew the Holy Spirit (Acts 19:1–7). We might ask professed Christians today, "Did you receive the Holy Spirit when you believed?" If the answer is no, then you are not saved. "Now if any man have not the Spirit of Christ, he is none of his" (Rom. 8:9). Unless you have the *witness* of the Spirit (Rom. 8:15–16), you cannot draw on the *wealth* of the Spirit.

The sphere of our blessings. Our blessings are "in heavenly places in Christ." Perhaps a clearer translation would be "in the heavenlies in Christ." The unsaved person is interested primarily in *earthlies,* because this is where he lives. Jesus called them "the children of this world" (Luke 16:8). The Christian's life is centered in *heaven.* His citizenship is in heaven (Phil. 3:20); his name is written in heaven (Luke 10:20); his Father is in heaven; and his attention and affection ought to be centered on the things of heaven (Col. 3:1ff.). Evangelist D. L. Moody used to warn about people who were so "heavenly minded they were no earthly good," but that is not what Paul was describing. "The heavenlies" (literal translation) describes that place where Jesus Christ is right now (Eph. 1:2) and where the believer is seated with Him (Eph. 2:6). The battles we fight are not with flesh and blood on earth, but with satanic powers "in the heavenlies" (Eph. 6:12).

The Christian really operates in two spheres: the human and the divine, the visible and the invisible. Physically, he is on the earth in a human body, but spiritually he is seated with Christ in the heavenly sphere—and it is this heavenly sphere that provides the power and direction for the earthly walk. The president of the United States is not always seated at his desk in the White House, but that executive chair represents the sphere of his life and power. No matter where he is, he is the president, because only he has the privilege of sitting at that desk. Likewise with the Christian: no matter where he may be on this earth, he is seated in the heavenlies with Jesus Christ, and this is the basis of his life and power.

When she was young, Victoria was shielded from the fact that she would be the next ruling monarch of England lest this knowledge spoil her. When her teacher finally did let her discover for herself that she would one day be Queen of England, Victoria's response was, "Then I will be good!" Her life would be controlled by her position. No matter where she was, Victoria was governed by the fact that she sat on the throne of England.

The fact that Paul is writing about wealth would

be significant to his readers, because Ephesus was considered the bank of Asia. One of the seven wonders of the world—the great temple of Diana—was in Ephesus and was not only a center for idolatrous worship, but also a depository for wealth. Some of the greatest art treasures of the ancient world were housed in this magnificent building. In this letter, Paul will compare the church of Jesus Christ to a temple and will explain the great wealth that Christ has in His church. Paul has already used the word *riches*, but you may want to check other "financial" words such as *inheritance* (Eph. 1:11, 14, 18; 5:5) *and fullness, or filled* (Eph. 1:10, 23; 3:19; 4:10, 13; 5:18). Paul is saying to us, "BE RICH!"

The Analysis

Paul's letter to the Ephesians is as carefully structured as that great temple of Diana, and it contains greater beauty and wealth! We *inherit* the wealth by faith and *invest* the wealth by works. Without this balance, our spiritual riches do us no good.

CHAPTER TWO
Ephesians 1:4–14
HOW RICH YOU ARE!

One of the funniest cartoons I ever saw showed a pompous lawyer reading a client's last will and testament to a group of greedy relatives. The caption read, "I, John Jones, being of sound mind and body, *spent it all!*"

When Jesus Christ wrote His last will and testament for His church, He made it possible for us to share His spiritual riches. Instead of spending it all, Jesus Christ paid it all. His death on the cross and His resurrection make possible our salvation.

He wrote us into His will, then He died so the will would be in force. Then He arose again that He might become the heavenly Advocate (lawyer) to make sure the terms of the will were correctly followed!

In this long sentence, Paul named just a few of the blessings that make up our spiritual wealth.

Blessings from God the Father (1:4–6)

He has chosen us (v. 4). This is the marvelous doctrine of *election*, a doctrine that has confused some and confounded others. A seminary professor once said to me, "Try to explain election and you may lose your mind. But try to explain it away and you may lose your soul!" That salvation begins with God, and not with man, all Christians will agree. "Ye have not chosen me, but I have chosen you" (John 15:16). The lost sinner, left to his own ways, does not seek God (Rom. 3:10–11); God in His love seeks the sinner (Luke 19:10).

Note that God chose us even before He created the universe, so that our salvation is wholly of His grace and not on the basis of anything we ourselves have done. He chose us *in Christ,* not in ourselves. And He chose us for a purpose: to be holy and without blame. In the Bible, election is always *unto* something. It is a privilege that carries a great responsibility.

Does the sinner respond to God's grace against his own will? No, he responds because God's grace makes him willing to respond. The mystery of divine sovereignty and human responsibility will never be solved in this life. Both are taught in the Bible (John 6:37). Both are true, and both are essential.

You will note that all three persons in the Godhead are involved in our salvation (see also 1 Peter 1:3). As far as God the Father is concerned, you were saved when He chose you in Christ in eternity past. But that alone did not save you. As far as God the Son is concerned, you were saved when He died for you on the cross. As far as God the Spirit is concerned, you were saved when you yielded to His conviction and received Christ as your Savior. What began in eternity past was fulfilled in time present, and will continue for all eternity!

He has adopted us (v. 5). Here we meet that misunderstood word *predestination*. This word, as it is used in the Bible, refers *primarily* to what God does for saved people. Nowhere in the Bible are we taught that people are predestined to hell, because this word refers only to God's people. The word simply means "to ordain beforehand, to predetermine." Election seems to refer to *people,* while predestination refers to *purposes.* The events connected with the crucifixion of Christ were predestined (Acts 4:25–28). God has predestined our adoption (Eph. 1:5) and our conformity to Christ (Rom. 8:29–30), as well as our future inheritance (Eph. 1:11).

Adoption has a dual meaning, both present and future. You do not get into God's family by adoption. You get into His family by regeneration, the new birth (John 3:1–18; 1 Peter 1:22–25). Adoption is the act of God by which He gives His "born ones" an adult standing in the family. Why does He do this? So that we might *immediately* begin to claim our inheritance and enjoy our spiritual wealth! A baby cannot legally use this inheritance (Gal. 4:1–7), but an adult son can—and should! This means that you do not have to wait until you are an old saint before you can claim your riches in Christ.

The *future* aspect of adoption is found in Romans 8:22–23, the glorified body we will have when Jesus returns. We already have our adult standing before God, but the world cannot see this. When Christ returns, this "private adoption" will be made public for everyone to see!

He has accepted us (v. 6). We cannot make ourselves acceptable to God, but He, by His grace, makes us accepted in Christ. This is our eternal position that will never change. Some translations read "which He freely bestowed on us in the Beloved" (NASB). Or, "He has *be-graced* [literal translation] us in the Beloved." The idea is the same. Because of God's grace in Christ, we are accepted before Him. Paul wrote Philemon to encourage him to accept his runaway slave, Onesimus, using the same argument. "If he owes you anything, I will pay it. Receive him as you would receive me" (Philem. 17–19, paraphrased). The parallel is easy to see.

Blessings from God the Son (1:7–12)

We should not think that each person of the Godhead works independently, because they all worked together to make possible our salvation. But each Person has a special ministry to perform, a special "spiritual deposit" to make in our lives.

He has redeemed us (v. 7a). To *redeem* means "to purchase and set free by paying a price." There were sixty million slaves in the Roman Empire, and often they were bought and sold like pieces of furniture. But a man could purchase a slave and set him free, and this is what Jesus did for us. The price was His own blood (1 Peter 1:18ff.). This means that we are free from the law (Gal. 5:1), free from slavery to sin (Rom. 6), as well as free from the power of Satan and the world (Gal. 1:4; Col. 1:13–14). If we were slaves, we would be poor, but because we are sons, we are rich!

He has forgiven us (v. 7b). The word *forgive* means "to carry away." This reminds us of the ritual on the Jewish day of Atonement, when the high priest sent the scapegoat into the wilderness (Lev. 16). First the priest killed one of the two goats and sprinkled its blood before God on the mercy seat. Then he confessed Israel's sins over the live goat, and had the goat taken into the wilderness to be lost. Christ died to carry away our sins so they might never again be seen (Ps. 103:12; John 1:29). No written accusation stands against us because our sins have been taken away! Sin made us poor, but grace makes us rich.

He has revealed God's will to us (vv. 8–10). This letter has much to say about God's plan for His people, a plan that was not fully understood even in Paul's day. The word *mystery* has nothing to do with things eerie. It means a "sacred secret, once hidden but now revealed to God's people." We believers are a part of God's "inner circle." We are able to share in the secret that God will one day unite everything in Christ. Ever since sin came into the world, things have been falling apart. First, man was separated from God (Gen. 3). Then man was separated from man, as Cain killed Abel (Gen. 4). People tried to maintain a kind of unity by building the Tower of Babel (Gen. 11), but God judged them and scattered them across the world. God called Abraham and put a difference between the Jew and the Gentile, a difference that was maintained until Christ's death on the cross. Sin is tearing everything apart, but in Christ, God will gather everything together in the culmination of the ages. We are a part of this great eternal program.

He has made us an inheritance (vv. 11–12). The King James Version reads, "In whom also we have obtained an inheritance," but "in whom also we were made an inheritance" is also a possible translation. Both are true and the one includes the other. In Christ we have a wonderful inheritance (1 Peter 1:1–4), and in Christ we are an inheritance. We are valuable to Him. Think of the price God paid to purchase us and make us part of His inheritance! God the Son is the Father's love gift to us; and we are the Father's love gift to His Son. Read John 17 and note how many times Christ called us "those whom thou hast given me." The church is Christ's body (Eph. 1:22–23), building (Eph. 2:19–22), and bride (Eph. 5:22–23); Christ's future inheritance is wrapped up in His church. We are "joint-heirs with Christ" (Rom. 8:17), which means that He cannot claim His inheritance apart from us!

Blessings from God the Holy Spirit (1:13–14)

We move now from eternity past (Eph. 1:4–6) and history past (Eph. 1:7–12), to the immediate experience of the Ephesian Christians. The Holy Spirit had worked in their lives, and they knew it.

He has sealed us (v. 13). The entire process of salvation is given in this verse, so we had better examine it carefully. It tells how the sinner becomes a saint. First, he hears the gospel of salvation. This is the good news that Christ died for our sins, was buried and rose again (1 Cor. 15:1ff.). The Ephesians were Gentiles, and the gospel came "to the Jew first" (Rom. 1:16). But Paul, a Jew, brought the gospel to the Gentiles as he shared the Word of God with them.

The Ephesians "heard the gospel" and discovered it was for them—"your salvation" (Eph. 1:13). Even though the Bible teaches election, it also announces, "Go ye into all the world and preach the gospel to every creature" (Mark 16:15). A soul-winner does not discuss election with unsaved people, because it is a family secret that belongs to the saints. He simply announces the truth of the gospel and invites men to trust Christ, and the Holy Spirit does the rest. D. L. Moody used to pray, "Lord, save the elect—and then elect some more!" The same God who ordains the end, the salvation of souls, also ordains the means to the end, the preaching of the gospel in the power of the Spirit.

Having heard the Word, the Ephesians believed, and it is this faith that brought salvation (Eph. 2:8–9). This pattern follows what Paul wrote in Romans 10:13–15, so read that passage carefully. It is God's plan for evangelism. When the Ephesians believed, they were "sealed with the Spirit." "After that ye believed" should read *"when* ye believed." You receive the Spirit immediately on trusting Christ. This is not an experience subsequent to conversion. (Read Acts 10:34–48.)

What is the significance of this sealing of the Holy Spirit? For one thing, it speaks of a *finished transaction.* Even today, when important legal documents are processed, they are stamped with the official seal to signify the completion of the transaction. This sealing also implies *ownership:* God has put his seal on us because

He has purchased us to be His own (1 Cor. 6:19–20). It also means *security and protection.* The Roman seal on the tomb of Jesus carried this meaning (Matt. 27:62–66). So, the believer belongs to God, and is safe and protected because he is a part of a finished transaction. According to John 14:16–17, the Holy Spirit abides with the believer forever. It is possible for us to grieve the Spirit and thereby lose the blessings of His ministry (Eph. 4:30). But He doesn't leave us.

Another use for the seal is as a mark of *authenticity.* Just as a signature on a letter attests to the genuineness of the document, so the presence of the Spirit proves the believer is genuine. "If any man have not the Spirit of Christ, he is none of his" (Rom. 8:9). It is not simply our lip profession, our religious activity, or our good works, but the witness of the Spirit that makes our profession authentic.

He has given us an earnest (v. 14). *Earnest* is a fascinating word! In Paul's day, it meant "the down payment to guarantee the final purchase of some commodity or piece of property." Even today you will hear a real estate agent talk about earnest money. The Holy Spirit is God's first installment to guarantee to His children that He will finish His work and eventually bring them to glory. The "redemption of the purchased possession" refers to the redemption of the body at the return of Christ (Rom. 8:18–23; 1 John 3:1–3). "Redemption" is experienced in three stages:

- We *have been redeemed* through faith in Jesus Christ (Eph. 1:7).
- We *are being redeemed* as the Spirit works in our lives to make us more like Christ (Rom. 8:1–4).
- We *shall be redeemed* when Christ returns and we become like Him.

But the word translated "earnest" also means "engagement ring." In Greece today you would find this word being used that way. But, after all, isn't an engagement ring an assurance—a guarantee—that the promises made will be kept? Our relationship to God through Christ is not simply a *commercial* one, but also a personal experience of love. He is the Bridegroom and His church is the bride. We know that He will come and claim His bride because He has given us His promise and His Spirit as the "engagement ring." What greater assurance could we want?

We have examined a number of basic Bible doctrines in this chapter, all on the theme of our riches in Christ. It would be profitable for us to review what these verses teach us.

1. *True riches come from God.* It is a source of great encouragement to know that Father, Son, and Holy Spirit are all working on my behalf to make me rich. God not only gives us "richly all things to enjoy" (1 Tim. 6:17), but He gives us *eternal* riches without which all other wealth is valueless.

A distraught wife sought out a Christian marriage counselor and told her sad story of a marriage about to dissolve. "But we have so much!" she kept saying.

"Look at this diamond ring on my finger. Why, it's worth thousands! We have an expensive mansion in an exclusive area. We have three cars, and even a cabin in the mountains. Why, we have everything money can buy!"

The counselor replied, "It's good to have the things money can buy provided you don't lose the things money can't buy. What good is an expensive house if there's no home? Or an expensive ring if there's no love?"

In Christ, you and I have "what money can't buy," and these spiritual riches open up to us all the wealth of God's vast creation. We enjoy the gifts because we know and love the Giver.

2. *All of these riches come by God's grace and for God's glory.* Did you notice that after each of the main sections in Ephesians 1:4–14, Paul added the purpose behind these gifts? Why has God the Father chosen us, adopted us, and accepted us? "To the praise of the glory of his grace" (Eph. 1:6). Why has the Son redeemed us, forgiven us, revealed His will to us, and made us part of God's inheritance? "That we should be to the praise of his glory" (Eph. 1:12). Why has God the Spirit, sealed us and become the guarantee of our future blessing? "Unto the praise of his glory" (Eph. 1:14).

We often have the idea that God saves sinners mainly because He pities them, or wants to rescue them from eternal judgment, but God's main purpose is that He might be glorified. His creation reveals His wisdom and power, but His church reveals His love and grace. You cannot deserve or earn these spiritual riches; you can only receive them by grace, through faith.

3. *These riches are only the beginning!* There is always more spiritual wealth to claim from the Lord as we walk with Him. The Bible is our guidebook; the Holy Spirit is our Teacher. As we search the Word of God, we discover more and more of the riches we have in Christ. These riches were planned by the Father, purchased by the Son, and presented by the Spirit. There is really no need for us to live in poverty when all of God's wealth is at our disposal!

My friend was discussing money matters with his wife, and neither of them realized that their little son was listening. Finally the boy broke in with the suggestion, "Why don't you just write one of those pieces of paper?" Junior did not understand that it was necessary to have money in the bank to back up "those pieces of paper." But we never face that problem when it comes to our spiritual wealth.

A little devotional book by Charles Spurgeon is titled *A Checkbook on the Bank of Faith.* A promise from the Bible was given for each day of the year, along with a short devotional message. The author described each promise as being as good as money in the bank to anyone who would claim it by faith, as a person would write a check against his bank account. By faith we can claim God's promises and draw on His limitless wealth to meet every need we may face.

CHAPTER THREE
Ephesians 1:15–23
READ THE BANKBOOK

On January 6, 1822, the wife of a poor German pastor had a son, never dreaming that he would one day achieve world renown and great wealth. When Heinrich Schliemann was seven years old, a picture of ancient Troy in flames captured his imagination. Contrary to what many people believed, Heinrich argued that Homer's great poems, the *Iliad* and the *Odyssey,* were based on historic facts and he set out to prove it. In 1873, he uncovered the ancient site of Troy, along with some fabulous treasure, which he smuggled out of the country, much to the anger of the Turkish government. Schliemann became a famous, wealthy man because he dared to believe an ancient record and act on his faith.

We discovered that we were "born rich" when we trusted Christ. But this is not enough, for we must grow in our understanding of our riches if we are ever going to use them to the glory of God. Too many Christians have never "read the bankbook" to find out the vast spiritual wealth that God has put to their account through Jesus Christ. They are like the late newspaper publisher, William Randolph Hearst, who invested a fortune collecting art treasures from around the world. One day Mr. Hearst found a description of some valuable items that he felt he must own, so he sent his agent abroad to find them. After months of searching, the agent reported that he had finally found the treasures. They were in Mr. Hearst's warehouse. Hearst had been searching frantically for treasures he already owned! Had he read the catalog of his treasures, he would have saved himself a great deal of money and trouble.

Paul desired the Ephesian Christians to understand what great wealth they had in Christ. Paul knew of their faith and love, and in this he rejoiced. The Christian life has two dimensions: faith toward God and love toward men, and you cannot separate the two. But Paul knew that faith and love were just the beginning. The Ephesians needed to know much more. This is why he prayed for them, and for us.

In the prison prayers of Paul (Eph. 1:15–23; 3:14–21; Phil. 1:9–11; Col. 1:9–12), we discover the blessings he wanted his converts to enjoy. In none of these prayers did Paul request material things. His emphasis was on spiritual perception and real Christian character. He did not ask God to give them what they did not have, but rather prayed that God would reveal to them what they already had.

Before we study Paul's four requests in this "prayer for enlightenment," we must notice two facts. First, enlightenment comes from the Holy Spirit. He is the "Spirit of wisdom and revelation" (Isa. 11:2; John 14:25–26; 16:12–14). With his natural mind, man cannot understand the things of God. He needs the Spirit to enlighten him (1 Cor. 2:9–16). The Holy Spirit reveals truth to us from the Word, and then gives us the wisdom to understand and apply it. He also gives us the power—the enablement—to practice the truth (Eph. 3:14–21).

Second, this enlightenment comes to the heart of the believer (Eph. 1:18). Literally this verse reads, "The eyes of your heart being enlightened." We think of the heart as the emotional part of man, but in the Bible, the heart means the inner man, and includes the emotions, the mind, and the will. The inner man, the heart, has spiritual faculties that parallel the physical senses. The inner man can *see* (Ps. 119:18; John 3:3), *hear* (Matt. 13:9; Heb. 5:11), *taste* (Ps. 34:8; 1 Peter 2:3), *smell* (Phil. 4:18; 2 Cor. 2:14), and *touch* (Acts 17:27). This is what Jesus meant when He said of the people, "They seeing see not, and hearing they hear not" (Matt. 13:13). The inability to see and understand spiritual things is not the fault of the intelligence but of the heart. The eyes of the heart must be opened by the Spirit of God.

That They Might Know God (1:17b)

This, of course, is the highest knowledge possible. The *atheist* claims there is no God for us to know, and the *agnostic* states that if there is a God we cannot know Him. But Paul has met God in the person of Jesus Christ, and he knows that a man really cannot understand much of anything else without a knowledge of God.

This willful ignorance of God led mankind into corruption and condemnation. In Romans 1:18ff., Paul described the stages in man's devolution: from willful ignorance of God to idolatry (substituting a lie for the truth) to immorality and indecency. Where does it begin? It begins with an unwillingness to know God as Creator, Sustainer, Governor, Savior, and Judge.

The believer must grow in his knowledge of God. To know God personally is salvation (John 17:3). To know Him increasingly is sanctification (Phil. 3:10). To know Him perfectly is glorification (1 Cor. 13:9–12). Since we are made in the image of God (Gen. 1:26–28), the better we know God, the better we know ourselves and each other. It is not enough to know God only as Savior. We must get to know Him as Father, Friend, Guide, and the better we know Him, the more satisfying our spiritual lives will be.

A believer said to me one day after a Bible lesson, "I'm sure glad I came! You gave me two good verses to use on my wicked neighbor!" Surely there are times when we use God's Word as a sword to defeat the enemy, but that is not the primary purpose behind the writing of the Bible. As the familiar hymn puts it,

> Beyond the sacred page
> I seek Thee, Lord.
> My spirit pants for Thee,
> O living Word.

That We Might Know God's Calling (1:18a)

The word *called* is an important word in the Christian's vocabulary. The word *church* is a combination of two Greek words that mean "called out." Paul never tired of testifying that God called him "by his grace" (Gal. 1:15), and he reminded Timothy that the believer has a "holy calling" (2 Tim. 1:9). We have been "called out of darkness into his marvelous light" (1 Peter 2:9), and have even been "called to glory" (1 Peter 5:10). God calls us by His grace and not because of any merit that we may possess.

Paul wanted us to understand the hope that is ours because of this calling (Eph. 4:4). Some callings offer no hope, but the calling we have in Christ assures us of a delightful future. Keep in mind that the word *hope* in the Bible does not mean "hope so," like a child hoping for a doll or a bike at Christmas. The word carries with it "assurance for the future." The believer's hope is, of course, the return of Jesus Christ for His church (1 Thess. 4:13–18; 1 John 3:1–3). When we were lost, we were "without hope" (Eph. 2:12), but in Jesus Christ, we have a "living hope" (1 Peter 1:3) that encourages us day by day.

Dr. Kenneth Chafin, a well-known Baptist author, tells about the pastor and deacon who were visiting prospective members and drove up to a beautiful suburban home surrounded by a velvet lawn and gorgeous landscaping. Two expensive cars stood in the driveway, and through the picture window, the men saw their prospect, lounging in an easy chair and watching TV. The deacon turned to his pastor and said, "What kind of good news do we have for *him?*"

How prone we are to confuse prices and values. Ephesus was a wealthy city. It boasted the temple of Diana, one of the wonders of the ancient world. Today, Ephesus is an archeologist's paradise, but all of its wealth and splendor are gone. But the Christians who once lived there are today in heaven, enjoying the glory of God!

The hope that belongs to our calling should be a dynamic force in our lives, encouraging us to be pure (1 John 2:28–3:3), obedient (Heb. 13:17), and faithful (Luke 12:42–48). The fact that we shall one day see Christ and be like Him should motivate us to live like Christ today.

That We Might Know God's Riches (1:18b)

This phrase does not refer to our inheritance in Christ (Eph. 1:11), but His inheritance in us. This is an amazing truth—that God should look on us as a part of His great wealth! Just as a man's wealth brings glory to his name, so God will get glory from the church because of what He has invested in us. When Jesus Christ returns, we shall be "to the praise of the glory of his grace" (Eph. 1:6).

God deals with us on the basis of our future, not our past. He said to cowardly Gideon, "The Lord is with thee, thou mighty man of valor" (Judg. 6:12).

Jesus said to Andrew's brother, "Thou art Simon ... thou shalt be called Cephas [a stone]" (John 1:42).

Gideon did become a mighty man of valor, and Simon did become Peter, a rock. We Christians live in the future tense, our lives controlled by what we shall be when Christ returns. Because we are God's inheritance, we live to please and glorify Him.

This truth suggests to us that Christ will not enter into His promised glory until the church is there to share it with Him. He prayed for this before He died, and this prayer will be answered (John 17:24). Christ will be glorified in us (2 Thess. 1:10), and we will be glorified in Him (Col. 3:4). Knowing this should lead the believer into a life of dedication and devotion to the Lord.

That We Might Know God's Power (1:19–23)

By making us His inheritance, God has shown His love. By promising us a wonderful future, He has encouraged our hope. Paul offered something to challenge our faith: "the exceeding greatness of his power to us-ward who believe" (Eph. 1:19). So tremendous is this truth that Paul enlisted many different words from the Greek vocabulary to get his point across: *dunamis*—"power" as in dynamo and dynamite; *energeia*—"working" as in energy; *kratos*—"mighty"; *ischus*—"power." Ephesians 1:19 can be translated, "What is the surpassing greatness of His power toward us who believe, according to the operation of the might of His strength." He is talking about divine dynamic, eternal energy, available to us!

After all, what good is it to have wealth if you are too weak to use it? Or if you are so afraid of robbers that you cannot really enjoy it? John D. Rockefeller was the world's first billionaire. It is said that for many years, he lived on crackers and milk because of stomach troubles caused by worrying about his wealth. He rarely had a good night's sleep, and guards stood constantly at his door. Wealthy—but miserable! When he began to share his wealth with others in great philanthropic endeavors, his health improved considerably and he lived to be an old man.

We Christians need power for several reasons. To begin with, by nature we are too weak to appreciate and appropriate this wealth, and to use it as it should be used. "The spirit indeed is willing, but the flesh is weak" (Matt. 26:41). To turn this vast spiritual wealth over to a mere human being, living by human wisdom and strength, would be like handing an atomic bomb to a two-year-old. God's power enables us to use God's wealth.

But there is a second reason why we need God's power. There are enemies who want to rob us of our wealth (Eph. 1:21; 6:11–12). We could never defeat these spiritual foes in our own power, but we can through the Spirit's power. Paul wanted us to know the greatness of God's power so that we would not fail to use our wealth, and so that the enemy would not deprive us of our wealth.

The power is seen in the resurrection of Jesus Christ. In the Old Testament people measured God's power by His creation (Isa. 40:12–27) or by His miracle at the exodus of Israel from Egypt (Jer. 16:14). But today, we measure God's power by the miracle of Christ's resurrection. Much more was involved than merely raising Him from the dead, for Christ also ascended to heaven and sat down in the place of authority at the right hand of God. He is not only Savior; He is also Sovereign (Acts 2:25–36). No authority or power, human or in the spirit world, is greater than that of Jesus Christ, the exalted Son of God. He is "far above all," and no future enemy can overcome Him, because He has been exalted "far above all" powers.

But how does this apply to you and me today? In Ephesians 1:22–23, Paul explained the practical application. Because we are believers, we are in the church, which is Christ's body—and He is the Head. This means that there is a living connection between you and Christ. Physically speaking, the head controls the body and keeps the body functioning properly. Injure certain parts of the brain and you handicap or paralyze corresponding parts of the body. Christ is our spiritual Head. Through the Spirit, we are united to Him as the members of His body. This means that we share His resurrection, ascension, and exaltation. (Paul will amplify this later.) We too are seated in the heavenlies (Eph. 2:6), and all things are under our feet.

No wonder Paul wants us to know "the exceeding greatness of his power to us-ward"! Apart from this power, we cannot draw on our great wealth in Christ.

I recall going to the hospital with one of our church members to try to get her husband to sign a paper that would authorize her to draw on his private checking account so she could pay his bills. The man was so weak he could not sign the paper. She finally had to get witnesses to verify his "X" on the document. His weakness nearly deprived her of her wealth.

The power of the Holy Spirit, through the resurrected, ascended Christ, is available to all Christians—by faith. His power is to "us-ward who believe" (Eph. 1:19). It is grace that supplies the wealth, but it is faith that lays hold of the wealth. We are saved "by grace, through faith" (Eph. 2:8–9), and we live "by grace," through faith (1 Cor. 15:10).

In the four gospels, we see God's power at work in the ministry of Jesus Christ, but in the book of Acts, we see that same power at work in ordinary men and women, members of the body of Christ. What a transformation took place in Peter's life between the end of the Gospels and the beginning of Acts. What made the difference? The resurrection power of Jesus Christ (Acts 1:8).

The greatest power shortage today is not in our generators or our gas tanks. It is in our personal lives. Will Paul's prayer be answered in your life? Will you, starting today, begin to know by experience God— God's calling—God's riches—and God's power?

CHAPTER FOUR
Ephesians 2:1–10
GET OUT OF THE GRAVEYARD

Having described our spiritual *possessions* in Christ, Paul turned to a complementary truth: our spiritual *position* in Christ. First he explained what God has done for all sinners in general; then he explained what God did for the Gentiles in particular. The sinner who trusts Christ has been raised and seated on the throne (Eph. 2:1–10), and believing Jews and Gentiles have been reconciled and set into the temple (Eph. 2:11–22). What a miracle of God's grace! We are taken out of the great graveyard of sin and placed into the throne room of glory.

Perhaps the easiest way for us to approach this long paragraph is to see in it four specific works.

Sin's Work against Us (2:1–3)

A publisher asked me for a full-length portrait that they could "blow up" and use as a life-size display at their convention booth to promote my tapes. A friend of mine took the picture, and it was a new experience for me. I had been accustomed to sitting for head-and-shoulder photographs, but standing for a full-length photo was something new. I had to watch my posture, the feet had to be placed just right, and the arms and hands—usually forgotten—had to be in just the right position. Fortunately, my photographer friend is an expert, and we managed to get a decent picture in a short time. In these three verses, Paul gave us a full-length picture of the terrible spiritual condition of the unsaved person. Note his characteristics.

He is dead (v. 1). Of course, this means spiritually dead; that is, he is unable to understand and appreciate spiritual things. He possesses no spiritual life, and he can do nothing of himself to please God. Just as a person physically dead does not respond to physical stimuli, so a person spiritually dead is unable to respond to spiritual things. A corpse does not hear the conversation going on in the funeral parlor. He has no appetite for food or drink; he feels no pain; he is dead. Just so with the inner man of the unsaved person. His spiritual faculties are not functioning, and they cannot function until God gives him life. The cause of this spiritual death is "trespasses and sins" (Eph. 2:1). "The wages of sin is death" (Rom. 6:23). In the Bible, *death* basically means "separation," not only physically, as the spirit separated from the body (James 2:26), but also spiritually, as the spirit separated from God (Isa. 59:2).

The unbeliever is not sick; he is dead! He does not need resuscitation; he needs resurrection. All lost sinners are dead, and the only difference between one sinner and another is the state of decay. The lost derelict on skid row may be more decayed outwardly than the unsaved society leader, but both are dead in sin—and one corpse cannot be more dead than another! This means that our world is one vast graveyard, filled with people who are dead while they live (1 Tim. 5:6).

He is disobedient (vv. 2–3a). This was the beginning of man's spiritual death—his disobedience to the will of God. God said, "In the day that thou eatest thereof thou shalt surely die" (Gen. 2:17). Satan said, "Ye shall not surely die" (Gen. 3:4), and because they believed this lie, the first man and woman sinned and experienced immediate spiritual death and ultimate physical death. Since that time, mankind has lived in disobedience to God. There are three forces that encourage man in his disobedience—the world, the devil, and the flesh.

The world, or world-system, puts pressure on each person to try to get him to conform (Rom. 12:2). Jesus Christ was not "of this world" and neither are His people (John 8:23; 17:14). But the unsaved person, either consciously or unconsciously, is controlled by the values and attitudes of this world.

The devil is "the spirit that now worketh in the children of disobedience." This does not mean that Satan is personally at work in the life of each unbeliever, since Satan as a created being is limited in space. Unlike God, who is omnipresent, Satan cannot be in all places at one time. But because of his demonic associates (Eph. 6:11–12) and his power over the world system (John 12:31), Satan influences the lives of all unbelievers, and also seeks to influence believers. He wants to make people "children of disobedience" (Eph. 2:2; 5:6). He himself was disobedient to God, so he wants others to disobey Him too.

One of Satan's chief tools for getting people to disobey God is lies. He is a liar (John 8:44), and it was his lie at the beginning of human history, "Ye shall not surely die," that plunged the human race into sin. The unsaved multitudes in today's world system disobey God because they believe the lies of Satan. When a person believes and practices a lie, he becomes a child of disobedience.

The flesh is the third force that encourages the unbeliever to disobey God. By *the flesh* Paul does not mean the body, because of itself, the body is not sinful. *The flesh* refers to that fallen nature that we were born with, that wants to control the body and the mind and make us disobey God. An evangelist friend of mine once announced as his topic, "Why Your Dog Does What It Does," and, of course, many dog lovers came out to hear him. What he had to say was obvious, but too often overlooked: "A dog behaves like a dog because he has a dog's nature." If somehow you could transplant into the dog the nature of the cat, his behavior would change radically. Why does a sinner behave like a sinner? Because he has the nature of a sinner (Ps. 51:5; 58:3). This sinful nature the Bible calls "the flesh."

Is it any wonder that the unsaved person is disobedient to God? He is controlled by the world, the flesh, and the devil, the three great enemies of God! And he

cannot change his own nature or, of himself, overcome the world and the devil. He needs outside help, and that help can come only from God.

He is depraved (v. 3b). The lost sinner lives to please the "desires of the flesh and the wishes of the mind" (literal translation). His actions are sinful because his appetites are sinful. When you apply the word *depraved* to the unsaved person, you are not saying that he *only* does evil, or that he is incapable of doing good. You are simply saying that he is incapable of doing anything to merit salvation or meet the high standards of God's holiness. Jesus said that lost sinners do good to each other (Luke 6:33) and to their children (Luke 11:13), but they cannot do anything spiritually good to please God. The people on Malta who kindly assisted Paul and his friends after the shipwreck certainly did good works, but they still needed to be saved (Acts 28:1–2).

He is doomed (v. 3c). By nature, children of wrath! By deed, children of disobedience! The unsaved person is condemned already (John 3:18). The sentence has been passed, but God in His mercy is staying the execution of the sentence (2 Peter 3:8–10). Man cannot save himself, but God in His grace steps in to make salvation possible. "But God!"—what a difference those two words make! This leads to the second work.

God's Work for Us (2:4–9)

The focus of attention now is on God, not on sinful man. "Salvation is of the Lord" (Jonah 2:9). We are reminded of four activities that God performed on behalf of sinners to save them from the consequences of their sins.

He loved us (v. 4). By nature, "God is love" (1 John 4:8). But God would love even if there were no sinners, because love is a part of His very being. Theologians call love one of God's attributes. But God has two kinds of attributes: those that He possesses of Himself (intrinsic attributes, such as life, love, holiness) and those by which He relates to His creation, especially to man (relative attributes). For example, by nature God is *truth,* but when He relates to man, God's truth becomes *faithfulness. God* is by nature *holy,* and when He relates that holiness to man, it becomes *justice.*

Love is one of God's intrinsic attributes, but when this love is related to sinners, it becomes *grace* and *mercy.* God is "rich in mercy" (Eph. 2:4) and in "grace" (Eph. 2:7), and these riches make it possible for sinners to be saved. It comes as a shock to some people when they discover that we are not saved "by God's love," but by God's mercy and grace. In His mercy, He does not give us what we do deserve, and in His grace He gives us what we do not deserve. And all of this is made possible because of the death of Jesus Christ on the cross. It was at Calvary that God displayed His hatred for sin and His love for sinners (Rom. 5:8; John 3:16).

He quickened us (v. 5). This means He made us alive, even when we were dead in sins. He accomplished this spiritual resurrection by the power of the Spirit, using the Word. In the four gospels, it is recorded that Jesus raised three people from the dead: the widow's son (Luke 7:11–17), Jairus's daughter (Luke 8:49–56), and Lazarus (John 11:41–46). In each case, He spoke the Word and this gave life. "The Word of God is quick [living] and powerful" (Heb. 4:12). These three physical resurrections are pictures of the spiritual resurrection that comes to the sinner when he hears the Word and believes (John 5:24).

But our spiritual resurrection is much greater because it puts us in union with Christ: God "made us alive together with Christ." As members of His body we are united to Him (Eph. 1:22–23), so that we share His resurrection life and power (Eph. 1:19–20).

He exalted us (v. 6). We are not raised from the dead and left in the graveyard. Because we are united to Christ, we have been exalted with Him and we are sharing His throne in the heavenlies. Our physical position may be on earth, but our spiritual position is "in heavenly places in Christ Jesus." Like Lazarus, we have been called from the grave to sit with Christ and enjoy His fellowship (John 12:1–2).

He keeps us (vv. 7–9). God's purpose in our redemption is not simply to rescue us from hell, as great a work as that is. His ultimate purpose in our salvation is that for all eternity the church might glorify God's grace (Eph. 1:6, 12, 14). So, if God has an eternal purpose for us to fulfill, He will keep us for all eternity. Since we have not been saved by our good works, we cannot be lost by our bad works. Grace means salvation completely apart from any merit or works on our part. Grace means that God does it all for Jesus' sake! Our salvation is the gift of God. (The word *that* in Eph. 2:8, in the Greek, is neuter; while *faith* is feminine. Therefore *that* cannot refer to *faith*. It refers to the whole experience of salvation, including faith.) Salvation is a gift, not a reward.

Salvation cannot be "of works" because the work of salvation has already been completed on the cross. This is the work that God does *for* us, and it is a finished work (John 17:1–4; 19:30). We can add nothing to it (Heb. 10:1–14); we dare take nothing from it. When Jesus died, the veil of the temple was torn in two, from the top to the bottom, signifying that the way to God was now open. There is no more need for earthly sacrifices. One sacrifice—the Lamb of God—has finished the great work of salvation. God did it all, and He did it by His grace.

Sin worked against us and God worked for us, but the great work of conversion is but the beginning.

God's Work in Us (2:10a)

"For we are his workmanship created in Christ Jesus." The Greek word translated "workmanship" is *poiema,* from which we derive our English word *poem.* It means "that which is made, a manufactured product." In other words, our conversion is not the end; it is the beginning. We are a part of God's "new creation" (2

Cor. 5:17), and God continues to work in us to make us what He wants us to be. His purpose is to make us more like Christ (Rom. 8:29).

But how does God work in us? Through His Holy Spirit, "both to will and to do of his good pleasure" (Phil. 2:13). Christ finished His work of redemption on the cross, but He arose from the dead and returned to heaven. There He carries on His unfinished work of perfecting His church (Eph. 4:7–16; Heb. 13:20–21). Christ is equipping us for our walk and our work here on earth. To do this, He uses three special tools: the Word of God (1 Thess. 2:13), prayer (Eph. 3:20–21), and suffering (1 Peter 4:11–14). As we read God's Word, understand it, meditate on it, and feed on it, the Word goes to work in our lives to cleanse us and nourish us. As we pray, God's Spirit works in us to release power. And as we suffer, the Spirit of God ministers to us. Suffering drives us back to the Word and prayer, and the cycle is repeated.

Too many Christians think that conversion is the only important experience, and that nothing follows. But this is wrong. We can use the resurrection of Lazarus as an example. After Jesus raised Lazarus from the dead, He said, "Loose him, and let him go" (John 11:44). In other words, "This man is now alive. Get him out of the graveclothes!" Paul had this concept in mind in Ephesians 4:22–24 when he wrote, "That ye put off concerning the former conversation [behavior] the old man, which is corrupt … and that ye put on the new man, which after God is created in righteousness and true holiness." Colossians 3:1 has the same message: "[Since] ye then be risen with Christ, seek those things which are above."

The same resurrection power that saved you and took you out of the graveyard of sin can daily help you live for Christ and glorify Him. At great expense to Himself, God worked for us on the cross. And today, on the basis of that price paid at Calvary, He is working in us to conform us to Christ. God cannot work in us unless He has first worked for us, and we have trusted His Son. Also, He cannot work through us unless He works in us. This is why it is important for you to spend time daily in the Word and prayer, and to yield to Christ during times of suffering. For it is through the Word, prayer, and suffering that God works in you.

The Bible shows many examples of this principle. God spent forty years working in Moses before He could work through him. At the beginning of his ministry, Moses was impetuous and depended on his own strength. He killed an Egyptian and had to flee Egypt, hardly a successful way to start a ministry. But during those forty years as a humble shepherd in the desert, Moses experienced God's working in his life, a working that prepared him for forty more years of magnificent service.

There are other examples. Joseph suffered for thirteen years before God put him on the throne of Egypt, second to Pharaoh. David was anointed king when he was a youth, but he did not gain the throne until he had suffered many years as an exile. Even the apostle Paul spent three years in Arabia after his conversion, no doubt experiencing God's deeper work to prepare him for his ministry. God has to work in us before He can work through us; and this leads to the fourth work in our passage.

God's Work through Us (2:10b)

We are "created in Christ Jesus unto good works." We are not saved by good works, but saved unto good works. The famous theologian John Calvin wrote, "It is faith alone that justifies, but faith that justifies can never be alone." We are not saved by faith plus good works, but by a faith that works. The basic Scripture on this theme is James 2, where the writer points out that saving faith always results in a changed life. It is not enough to say that we have faith; we must demonstrate this faith by our works.

The Bible speaks of many different kinds of works. There are "the works of the law," which cannot save (Gal. 2:16; 3:11). There are also "the works of the flesh," which are listed in Galatians 5:19–21. Paul spoke of "works of darkness" (Rom. 13:12; Eph. 5:11). The "dead works" in Hebrews 6:1 seem to be "works that lead to death," since "the wages of sin is death" (Rom. 6:23). The "works of righteousness" in Titus 3:5 refer to religious works, or other good deeds, that sinners try to practice as a means of salvation. Isaiah declared that "all our righteousnesses are as filthy rags in his sight" (Isa. 64:6). If our righteousnesses are filthy, what must our sins look like!

The "works" Paul wrote about in Ephesians 2:10 have two special characteristics. First, they are "good" works, in contrast to "works of darkness" and "wicked works." If you contrast Ephesians 2:10 with Ephesians 2:2 you will see that the unbeliever has Satan working in him, and therefore his works are not good. But the believer has God working in him, and therefore his works are good. His works are not good because he himself is good, but because he has a new nature from God, and because the Holy Spirit works in him and through him to produce these good works.

It is too bad that many believers minimize the place of good works in the Christian life. Because we are not saved by good works, they have the idea that good works are evil; and this is a mistake. "Let your light so shine before men, that they may see your good works, and glorify your Father which is in heaven" (Matt. 5:16). We do not perform good works to glorify ourselves, but to glorify God. Paul desired that Christ would be magnified in his body, even if it meant death (Phil. 1:20–21). We should "abound to every good work" (2 Cor. 9:8), and be "fruitful in every good work" (Col. 1:10). One result of a knowledge of the Bible is that the believer is "thoroughly equipped for every good work" (2 Tim. 3:17 NASB). As believers, we are to be "zealous of good works" (Titus 2:14). Our

good works are actually "spiritual sacrifices" that we offer to God (Heb. 13:16).

It is important to note that we do not manufacture these good works. They are the results of the work of God in our hearts. "It is God which worketh in you both to will and to do of his good pleasure" (Phil. 2:13). The secret of Paul's good works was "the grace of God" (1 Cor. 15:10). Our good works are evidence that we have been born again. "Not everyone that saith unto me, 'Lord, Lord,' shall enter into the kingdom of heaven; but he that doeth the will of my Father which is in heaven" (Matt. 7:21). Our good works are also testimonies to the lost (1 Peter 2:12). They win us the right to be heard.

A pastor friend told about a Christian lady who often visited a retirement home near her house. One day she noticed a lonely man sitting, staring at his dinner tray. In a kindly manner she asked, "Is something wrong?"

"Is something wrong!" replied the man in a heavy accent. "Yes, something is wrong! I am a Jew, and I cannot eat this food!"

"What would you like to have?" she asked.

"I would like a bowl of hot soup!"

She went home and prepared the soup and, after getting permission from the office, took it to the man. In succeeding weeks, she often visited him and brought him the kind of food he enjoyed, and eventually she led him to faith in Christ. Yes, preparing soup can be a spiritual sacrifice, a good work to the glory of God.

But these works are not only good; they are also "prepared." "Good works which God hath before ordained [prepared] that we should walk in them" (Eph. 2:10). The only other time this word is used in the New Testament is in Romans 9:23: "vessels of mercy, which he had afore prepared unto glory." The unbeliever walks "according to the course of this world" (Eph. 2:2), but the believer walks in the good works God has prepared for him.

This is an amazing statement. It means that God has a plan for our lives and that we should walk in His will and fulfill His plan. Paul is not talking about "kismet"—an impersonal fate that controls your life no matter what you may do. He is talking about the gracious plan of a loving heavenly Father, who wills the very best for us. The will of God comes from the heart of God. "The counsel of the Lord standeth forever, the thoughts of his heart to all generations" (Ps. 33:11). We discover God's exciting will for our lives as the Spirit reveals it to us from the Word (1 Cor. 2:9–13).

It would be helpful to close this chapter with a personal inventory. Which of these four works are you experiencing? Is sin working against you because you have not yet trusted Christ? Then trust Him now! Have you experienced His work *for* you—*in* you— *through* you?

Are you wearing the "graveclothes" or the "graceclothes"? Are you enjoying the liberty you have in Christ, or are you still bound by the habits of the old life in the graveyard of sin? As a Christian, you have been raised and seated on the throne. Practice your position in Christ! He has worked *for* you; now let Him work *in* you and *through* you, that He might give you an exciting, creative life to the glory of God.

CHAPTER FIVE
Ephesians 2:11–22
THE GREAT PEACE MISSION

"Peace in our time! Peace with honor!" Some of us still remember those words of British Prime Minister, Sir Neville Chamberlain, when he returned from conferences in Germany in September 1938. He was sure that he had stopped Adolf Hitler. Yet one year later, Hitler invaded Poland, and on September 3, 1939, Great Britain declared war on Germany. Chamberlain's great peace mission had failed.

It seems that most peace missions fail. I read somewhere that from 1500 BC. to AD 850 there were 7,500 "eternal covenants" agreed on among various nations with the hope of bringing peace, but that no covenant lasted longer than two years. The only "eternal covenant" that has lasted—and that will last—is the one made by the eternal God, sealed by the blood of Jesus Christ. It is Christ's peace mission that Paul explained in this section, and three very important words summarize this great work: separation, reconciliation, and unification.

Separation: What the Gentiles Were (2:11–12)
In the first ten verses of Ephesians 2, Paul discussed the salvation of sinners in general, but now he turned to the work of Christ for Gentiles in particular. Most of the converts in the Ephesian church were Gentiles, and they knew that much of God's program in the Old Testament involved the Jews. For centuries, the "circumcision" (Jews) had looked down on the "uncircumcision" (Gentiles) with an attitude that God had never intended them to display. The fact that a Jew had received the physical mark of the covenant was no proof he was a man of faith (Rom. 2:25–29; Gal. 5:6; 6:15). Those who have trusted Christ have received a spiritual circumcision "made without hands" (Col. 2:11).

But since the hour that God called Abraham, God made a difference between Jews and Gentiles. He made this difference, not that the Jews might boast, but that they might be a blessing and a help to the Gentiles. God set them apart that He might use them to be a channel of His revelation and goodness to the heathen nations. Sad to say, Israel kept this difference nationally and ritually, but not morally. Israel became like the lost nations around her. For this reason, God often had to discipline the Jews because they would not maintain their spiritual separation and minister to the nations in the name of the true God.

The one word that best describes the Gentiles is *without*. They were "outside" in several respects.

Without Christ. The Ephesians worshipped the goddess Diana and, before the coming of the gospel, knew nothing about Christ. Those who claim that pagan religions are just as acceptable to God as the Christian faith will have a problem here, for Paul cites the Ephesians' Christless state as a definite tragedy. But then, keep in mind that every unsaved person, Jew or Gentile, is "outside Christ," and that means condemnation.

Without citizenship. God called the Jews and built them into a nation. He gave them His laws and His blessings. A Gentile could enter the nation as a proselyte, but he was not born into that very special nation. Israel was God's nation, in a way that was not true of any Gentile nation.

Without covenants. While the blessing of the Gentiles is included in God's covenant with Abraham (Gen. 12:1–3), God did not make any covenants with the Gentile nations. The Gentiles were "aliens" and "strangers"—and the Jews never let them forget it. Many of the Pharisees would pray daily, "O God, I give thanks that I am a Jew, not a Gentile."

Without hope. Historians tell us that a great cloud of hopelessness covered the ancient world. Philosophies were empty; traditions were disappearing; religions were powerless to help men face either life or death. People longed to pierce the veil and get some message of hope from the other side, but there was none (1 Thess. 4:13–18).

Without God. The heathen had gods aplenty, as Paul discovered in Athens (Acts 17:16–23). Someone in that day said that it was easier to find a god than a man in Athens. "There be gods many and lords many," wrote Paul (1 Cor. 8:5). But the pagan, no matter how religious or moral he might have been, did not know the true God. The writer of Psalm 115 contrasted the true God with the idols of the heathen.

It is worth noting that the spiritual plight of the Gentiles was caused not by God but by their own willful sin. Paul said the Gentiles knew the true God but deliberately refused to honor Him (Rom. 1:18–23). Religious history is not a record of man starting with many gods (idolatry) and gradually discovering the one true God.

Rather, it is the sad story of man knowing the truth about God and deliberately turning away from it! It is a story of devolution, not evolution! The first eleven chapters of Genesis give the story of the decline of the Gentiles, and from Genesis 12 on (the call of Abraham), it is the story of the Jews. God separated the Jews from the Gentiles that He might be able to save the Gentiles also. "Salvation is of the Jews" (John 4:22).

God called the Jews, beginning with Abraham, that through them He might reveal Himself as the one true God. With the Jews He deposited His Word, and through the Jews He gave the world the Savior (Rom. 9:1–5). Israel was to be a light to the Gentiles that they too might be saved. But sad to say, Israel became like the Gentiles, and the light burned but dimly. This fact is a warning to the church today. When the church is least like the world, it does the most for the world.

Reconciliation: What God Did for the Gentiles (2:13–18)

The "but now" in Ephesians 2:13 parallels the "but God" in Ephesians 2:4. Both speak of the gracious intervention of God on behalf of lost sinners. "Enmity" is the key word in this section (Eph. 2:15–16), and you will note that it is a twofold enmity: between Jews and Gentiles (Eph. 2:13–15) and between sinners and God (Eph. 2:16–18). Paul described here the greatest peace mission in history: Jesus Christ not only reconciled Jews and Gentiles, but He reconciled both to Himself in the one body, the church.

The word *reconcile* means "to bring together again." A distraught husband wants to be reconciled to his wife who has left him; a worried mother longs to be reconciled to a wayward daughter; and the lost sinner needs to be reconciled to God. Sin is the great separator in this world. It has been dividing people since the very beginning of human history. When Adam and Eve sinned, they were separated from God. Before long, their sons were separated from each other and Cain killed Abel. The earth was filled with violence (Gen. 6:5–13), and the only remedy seemed to be judgment. But even after the flood, men sinned against God and each other, and even tried to build their own unity without God's help. The result was another judgment that scattered the nations and confused the tongues. It was then that God called Abraham, and through the nation of Israel, Jesus Christ came to the world. It was His work on the cross that abolished the enmity between Jew and Gentile and between sinners and God.

The enmity between Jews and Gentiles (vv. 13–15). God had put a difference between Jews and Gentiles so that His purposes in salvation might be accomplished. But once those purposes were accomplished, there was no more difference. In fact, it was His purpose that these differences be erased forever, and they are erased through the work of Christ in reconciliation.

It was this lesson that was so difficult for the early church to understand. For centuries, the Jews had been different from the Gentiles—in religion, dress, diet, and laws. Until Peter was sent to the Gentiles (Acts 10), the church had no problems. But with the salvation of the Gentiles on the same terms as the Jews, problems began to develop. The Jewish Christians reprimanded Peter for going to the Gentiles and eating with them (Acts 11), and representatives of the churches gathered for an important conference on the place of the Gentiles in the church (Acts 15). Must a Gentile become a Jew to become a Christian? Their conclusion was, "No! Jews and Gentiles are saved the same way—by faith in Jesus Christ." The enmity was gone!

The cause of that enmity was the law, because the law made a definite distinction between Jews and Gentiles. The dietary laws reminded the Jews that God had put a difference between the clean and unclean (Lev. 11:44–47). But the Gentiles did not obey these laws; therefore they were unclean. Ezekiel the prophet reminded the priests that their task was to teach the Jews "the difference between the holy and the profane" (Ezek. 44:23). The divine ordinances given by God to Israel stood as a wall between the Jews and the other nations. In fact, there was a wall in the Jewish temple, separating the court of the Gentiles from the rest of the temple areas. Archeologists have discovered the inscription from Herod's temple, and it reads like this:

> No foreigner may enter within the barricade which surrounds the sanctuary and enclosure. Anyone who is caught doing so will have himself to blame for his ensuing death.

It was this wall that the Jews thought Paul and his Gentile friends crossed when the Jews attacked him in the temple and threatened to kill him (Acts 21:28–31).

In order for Jews and Gentiles to be reconciled, this wall had to be destroyed, and this Jesus did on the cross. The cost of destroying the enmity was the blood of Christ. When He died, the veil in the temple was literally torn in two, and the wall of separation (figuratively) was torn down. By fulfilling the demands of the law in His righteous life, and by bearing the curse of the law in His sacrificial death (Gal. 3:10–13), Jesus removed the legal barrier that separated Jew from Gentile. For centuries, there was a difference between them. But today, "there is no difference between the Jew and the Greek. For the same Lord over all is rich unto all that call upon him. For whosoever shall call upon the name of the Lord shall be saved" (Rom. 10:12–13).

In Jesus Christ, Jew and Gentile become one. "He is our peace" (Eph. 2:14). Through Christ, the far-off Gentile is made nigh (Eph. 2:13, 17), and both Jew and Gentile are made one. The consequences of Christ's work are, then, the destroying of the enmity by the abolishing of the law, and the creating of a new *man*—the church, the body of Christ. The word *abolish* simply means "to nullify." The law no longer holds sway over either Jew or Gentile, since in Christ believers are not under law but under grace. The righteousness of the law, revealing God's holiness, is still God's standard. But this is fulfilled in the believer by the Holy Spirit (Rom. 8:1–4). It took the early church a long time to get accustomed to "there is no difference!" In fact, some religious groups have not learned the lesson yet, for they are trying to get Christians back under law (Gal. 4:8–11; 5:1; Col. 2:13–23).

Christ "is our peace" (Eph. 2:14) and He made "peace" (Eph. 2:15). That verb *to make* in Ephesians 2:15 means "to create." The church, the body of Christ, is God's new creation (2 Cor. 5:15). Everything in the old creation is falling apart because of sin, but in the new creation there is unity because of righteousness. "There is neither Jew nor Greek, there is neither bond nor free, there is neither male nor female: for ye are all one in Christ Jesus" (Gal. 3:28). You may contrast the old position of the Gentiles with their new position and see how wonderfully Christ worked on their behalf on the cross:

Old Position	New Position
"without Christ"	"in Christ" (Eph. 2:13)
"aliens"	"a holy nation" (1 Peter 2:9)
"strangers"	"no more strangers" (Eph. 2:19)
"no hope"	"called in one hope" (Eph. 4:4)
"without God" (Eph. 2:12)	"The God and Father of our Lord Jesus Christ" (Eph. 1:3)

The enmity between sinners and God (vv. 16–18). Not only did the Gentiles need to be reconciled to the Jews, but both the Jews and the Gentiles needed to be reconciled to God! This was the conclusion the apostles came to at the Jerusalem Conference recorded in Acts 15. Peter said that God "put no difference between us [Jews] and them [Gentiles], purifying their hearts by faith…. But we believe that through the grace of the Lord Jesus Christ we shall be saved, even as they" (Acts 15:9, 11). It was not a question of the Gentile becoming a Jew to become a Christian, but the Jew admitting he was a sinner like the Gentile. "For there is no difference: for all have sinned and come short of the glory of God" (Rom. 3:22–23). The same law that separated Gentile and Jew also separated men and God, and Christ bore the curse of the law.

A man stopped in my office one day and said he wanted to get help. "My wife and I need a re-cancellation!" he blurted out. I knew he meant "reconciliation." But in one sense, "re-cancellation" was the right word. They had sinned against each other (and the Lord), and there could be no harmony until those sins were cancelled. A God of love wants to reconcile the sinner to Himself, but a God of holiness must see to it that sin is judged. God solved the problem by sending His Son to be the sacrifice for our sins, thereby revealing His love and meeting the demands of His righteousness. It was truly a "re-cancellation" (see Col. 2:13–14).

Jesus Christ "is our peace" (Eph. 2:14). He "made peace" (Eph. 2:15), and He "preached peace" (Eph. 2:17). As the Judge, He could have come to declare war. But in His grace, He came with the message of peace (Luke 2:8–14; 4:16–19). Jew and Gentile are at peace with each other in Christ, and both have open access to God (Rom. 5:1–2). This reminds us of the rent veil at the time of Christ's death (Matt. 27:50–51; Heb. 10:14–25). Reconciliation is complete!

Unification: What Jews and Gentiles Are in Christ (2:19–22)

Paul repeated the word "one" to emphasize the unifying work of Christ: "made both one" (Eph. 2:14); "one new man" (Eph. 2:.15); "one body" (Eph. 2:16); "one Spirit" (Eph. 2:18). All spiritual distance and division have been overcome by Christ. In the closing verses of this chapter, Paul gave three pictures that illustrate the unity of believing Jews and Gentiles in the church.

One nation (v. 19a). Israel was God's chosen nation, but they rejected their Redeemer and suffered the consequences. The kingdom was taken from them and given to "a nation bringing forth the fruits thereof" (Matt. 21:43). This "new nation" is the church, "a chosen generation … a holy nation, a peculiar people" (Ex. 19:6; 1 Peter 2:9). In the Old Testament, the nations were reckoned by their descent from Shem, Ham, or Japheth (Gen. 10). In the book of Acts, we see these three families united in Christ. In Acts 8, a descendant of Ham is saved, the Ethiopian treasurer; in Acts 9, a descendant of Shem, Saul of Tarsus, who became Paul the apostle; and in Acts 10, the descendants of Japheth, the Gentiles in the household of the Roman soldier, Cornelius. Sin has divided mankind, but Christ unites by His Spirit. All believers, regardless of national background, belong to that "holy nation" with citizenship in heaven (Phil. 3:20–21).

One family (v. 19b). Through faith in Christ, we enter into God's family, and God becomes our Father. This wonderful family of God is found in two places, "in heaven and earth" (Eph. 3:15). Living believers are on earth; believers who have died are in heaven. None of God's children are "under the earth" (Phil. 2:10) or in any other place in the universe. We are all brothers and sisters in the one family, no matter what racial, national, or physical distinctions we may possess.

One temple (vv. 20–22). In the book of Genesis, God "walked" with His people (Gen. 5:22, 24; 6:9), but in Exodus, He decided to "dwell" with His people (Ex. 25:8). God dwelt in the tabernacle (Ex. 40:34–38) until Israel's sins caused "the glory to depart" (1 Sam. 4). Then God dwelt in the temple (1 Kings 8:1–11), but, alas, again Israel sinned and the glory departed (Ezek. 10:18–19). God's next dwelling place was the body of Christ (John 1:14), which men took and nailed to a cross. Today, through His Spirit, God dwells in the church, the temple of God. God does not dwell in man-made temples, including church buildings (Acts 7:48–50). He dwells in the hearts of those who have trusted Christ (1 Cor. 6:19–20), and in the church collectively (Eph. 2:20–22).

The foundation for this church was laid by the apostles and New Testament prophets. Jesus Christ is the Foundation (1 Cor. 3:11) and the Chief Cornerstone (Ps. 118:22; Isa. 8:14). The cornerstone binds the structure together; Jesus Christ has united Jews and Gentiles in the church. This reference to the temple would be meaningful to both the Jews and the Gentiles in the Ephesian church: the Jews would think of Herod's temple in Jerusalem, and the Gentiles would think of the great temple of Diana. Both temples were destined to be destroyed, but the temple Christ is building will last forever. "I will build my church" (Matt. 16:18). The Holy Spirit builds this temple by taking dead stones out of the pit of sin (Ps. 40:2), giving them life, and setting them lovingly into the temple of God (1 Peter 2:5). This temple is "fitly framed together" as the body of Christ (Eph. 2:21; 4:16), so that every part accomplishes the purpose God has in mind.

As you look back over this chapter, you cannot help but praise God for what He, in His grace, has done for sinners. Through Christ, He has raised us from the dead and seated us on the throne. He has reconciled and set us into His temple. Neither spiritual *death* nor spiritual *distance* can defeat the grace of God! But He has not only saved us individually, He has also made us a part of His church collectively. What a tremendous privilege it is to be a part of God's eternal program!

This leads to two practical applications as we close this study.

First, have you personally experienced the grace of God? Are you spiritually dead? Are you distant from God? Or have you trusted Christ and received that eternal life that only He can give? If you are not sure of your spiritual position, I urge you to turn to Christ by faith and trust Him. Like the nation of Israel, you may have been given many spiritual privileges, only to reject the God who gave them. Or, like the Gentiles, you may have turned away from God and lived deliberately in sin and disobedience. In either case, "there is no difference, for all have sinned and come short of the glory of God" (Rom. 3:22–23). Call on Christ—He will save you.

Second, if you are a true believer in Christ, are you helping others to trust Him? You have been raised from the dead—do you "walk in newness of life" (Rom. 6:4)? Do you share this good news of eternal life with others? You are no longer at enmity with God, but are you spreading the good news of "peace with God" with those who are still fighting Him?

Jesus Christ died to make reconciliation possible. You and I must live to make the message of reconciliation personal. God has "given to us the ministry of reconciliation" (2 Cor. 5:18). We are His ambassadors of peace (2 Cor. 5:20). Our feet should be shod "with the preparation of the gospel of peace" (Eph. 6:15). "Blessed are the peacemakers, for they shall be called the children of God" (Matt. 5:9).

A missionary was preaching in the village market, and some of the people were laughing at him because he was not a very handsome man. He took it for a time, and then he said to the crowd, "It is true that I do not have beautiful hair, for I am almost bald. Nor do I have beautiful teeth, for they are really not mine; they were made by the dentist. I do not have a beautiful face, nor can I afford to wear beautiful clothes. But this I know: I have beautiful feet!" And

he quoted the verse from Isaiah: "How beautiful upon the mountains are the feet of him that bringeth good tidings, that publisheth peace" (Isa. 52:7). Do you have beautiful feet?

CHAPTER SIX
Ephesians 3:1–13
I KNOW A SECRET

I was once a character witness at a child-custody trial. I was grateful that the case was being tried at a small rural county seat rather than in a big city, because it was my first experience on the witness stand. I have since learned that the location of the court makes little difference. All trials can be difficult and it is no fun to be a witness at any.

The prosecutor's first question caught me unawares, "Reverend, do you think that a man who has been in prison is fit to raise a child?"

I was supposed to answer yes or no, so the reply I gave did not make the judge too happy. "Well," I said slowly, stalling for time, "I guess it depends on the man. Some very famous people have been in jail and have made the world a better place because of their experiences—John Bunyan, for example, and the great apostle Paul." I could have given other examples from the Bible, but I detected that my answer was not acceptable to the court.

Twice in this letter, Paul reminded his readers that he was a prisoner (Eph. 3:1; 4:1), and at the close he called himself an "ambassador in bonds" (Eph. 6:20). No doubt the Ephesians were asking, "Why is Paul a prisoner in Rome? Why would God permit such a thing?" In this paragraph, Paul explained his situation and, in doing so, also explained one of the greatest truths in this letter, the "mystery" of the church. In the New Testament, a *mystery* is not something eerie or inscrutable, but rather "a truth that was hidden by God in times past and is now revealed to those who are in His family." A *mystery* is a "sacred secret" that is unknown to unbelievers, but understood and treasured by the people of God.

Paul explained the mystery—the Gentile believers are now united to the Jewish believers in one body, the church (Eph. 3:6). He had mentioned this new work of God, so his readers were familiar with the concept (Eph. 1:10; 2:11, 22). But now Paul explained the tremendous impact of this "sacred secret" that had so possessed his own life and ministry. Actually, this explanation is almost a parenthesis in the letter, for Paul began this section with the intention of praying for his readers. Compare Ephesians 3:1 and 14. His use of the words *prisoner* and *Gentiles* led him into this important explanation of the "mystery of the church," and in this explanation, Paul showed us that the "mystery" is important to four different groups of persons.

It Was Important to Paul (3:1–5)

The best way to grasp the importance of "the mystery" in Paul's life is to focus on the two descriptions he gave of himself in this section. He began by calling himself "a prisoner" (Eph. 3:1), and then he called himself "a minister" (Eph. 3:7). Paul was a prisoner because he believed in God's new program of uniting believing Jews and Gentiles into one body, the church. The orthodox Jews in Paul's day considered the Gentiles "dogs," but some of the Christian Jews did not have a much better attitude toward the Gentiles.

Paul was a leader in Jewish orthodoxy when Christ saved him (Gal. 1:11–24; Phil. 3:1–11), yet in the providence of God, he began his early ministry in a local church in Antioch that was composed of both Jews and Gentiles (Acts 11:19–26). When the council was held at Jerusalem to determine the status of believing Gentiles, Paul courageously defended the grace of God and the unity of the church (Acts 15; Gal. 2:1–10).

Paul knew from the very beginning of his Christian life that God had called him to take the gospel to the Gentiles (Acts 9:15; 26:13–18), and he was not disobedient to that call. Wherever Paul ministered, he founded local churches composed of believing Jews and Gentiles, all "one in Christ Jesus" (Gal. 3:28).

Because Paul was the "apostle to the Gentiles" (Rom. 11:13; 15:15–16; Eph. 3:8; 1 Tim. 2:7), he was accused of being prejudiced against the Jews, particularly the Jewish believers in Jerusalem and Judea. The special offering Paul collected for the needy believers in Judea should have shown the goodwill that existed between these churches and the churches Paul founded (Rom. 15:25–33). Paul delivered the offering in person (Acts 21:17–19), and from all evidence, it was graciously received by the Judean Christians. Even though Paul took drastic steps to pacify the Jewish believers, there was a riot in the temple and Paul was arrested (Acts 21:30–33). Paul defended himself by giving his personal testimony, and the crowd listened to him until he got to the word "Gentiles" and then they rioted again (Acts 22:22–23). The rest of the book of Acts explains how Paul got from Jerusalem to Rome, "a prisoner of Jesus Christ for you Gentiles" (Eph. 3:1). Had Paul compromised his message and encouraged the selfish prejudices of the Jews he probably would have been released.

Paul was not only a "prisoner" because of "the mystery," but he was also a "minister." God gave him a "dispensation" (stewardship) that he might go to the Gentiles, not only with the good news of salvation through Christ, but also with the message that Jews and Gentiles are now one in Christ. The word *dispensation* comes from two Greek words: *oikos,* meaning "house" and *nomos,* meaning "law." Our English word "economy" is derived directly from the Greek *oikonomia,* "the law of the house," or "a stewardship, a management." God has different ways of managing His program from age to age, and these different "stewardships" Bible students sometimes call "dispensations" (Eph. 1:9–10).

God's principles do not change, but His methods of dealing with mankind do change over the course of history. "Distinguish the ages," wrote Saint Augustine, "and the Scriptures harmonize."

God made Paul a steward of "the mystery" with the responsibility of sharing it with the Gentiles. It was not enough simply to win them to Christ and form them into local assemblies. He was also to teach them their wonderful position in Christ as members of the body, sharing God's grace equally with the Jews. This truth had not been revealed in the Old Testament Scriptures. It was revealed to the New Testament apostles and prophets (see Eph. 4:11) by the Holy Spirit. God revealed it personally to Paul, and it was his responsibility to share it with the Gentile Christians. This was the "dispensation"—or stewardship—that God had given him. And because Paul was a faithful steward, he was now a prisoner in Rome. Like Joseph in the Old Testament, his faithful stewardship resulted in false arrest and imprisonment. But, in the end, it brought great glory to God and salvation to Jews and Gentiles.

It Was Important to the Gentiles (3:6–8)

In Ephesians 2:11–22, we discovered that Christ's work on the cross accomplished much more than the salvation of individual sinners. It reconciled Jews and Gentiles to each other and to God. It is this truth that Paul presented here, and you can imagine what exciting news it would be! The truth of "the mystery" reveals to believing Gentiles that they have a wonderful new relationship through Jesus Christ.

To begin with, they are fellow-heirs with the Jews and share in the spiritual riches God gave them because of His covenant with Abraham (Gal. 3:29). In Christ, being a Jew or a Gentile is neither an asset nor a liability, for together we share the riches of Christ. The Gentiles are also fellow-members of the body of Christ, the church. "There is one body" (Eph. 4:4). Our human birth determines our racial distinctions, but our spiritual birth unites us as members of the same body (1 Cor. 12:12–14). Christ is the Head of this body (Eph. 5:22–23), and each individual member shares in the ministry (Eph. 4:10–13). Finally, in their new relationship, the Gentiles are partakers of God's promises. Once they were outside the covenant, with no claims on the promises of God (Eph. 2:12), but now, in Christ, they share the promises of God with the believing Jews. In Romans 11:13–15, Paul explained that believing Gentiles share in the spiritual riches that God gave to Israel. But in Romans 11:1–12, Paul explained that God has not, because of the church, negated His promises to Israel. The church today shares in the spiritual riches of Israel, but one day God will restore His people and fulfill His promises concerning their land and their kingdom.

"The mystery" not only gives believing Gentiles a new relationship, it also reveals that there is a new power available to them (Eph. 3:7). This power is illustrated in the life of Paul. God saved him by grace and gave him a stewardship, a special ministry to the Gentiles. But God also gave Paul the power to accomplish this ministry. The word *working* here is *energeia* from which we get our word *energy*. The word *power* is *dunamis*, which gives us our words *dynamic* and *dynamite*. Paul has already told us about this mighty power in Ephesians 1:19–23, and he will mention it again in Ephesians 3:20 and Ephesians 4:16. The mighty resurrection power of Christ is available to us for daily life and service.

Finally, there is available to the Gentiles new riches: "the unsearchable riches of Christ" (Eph. 3:8). Paul called them "exceeding riches" (Eph. 2:7), but here he described them as "unfathomable." The words can also be translated "untraceable," which means that they are so vast you cannot discover their end. (Some students suggest that "untraceable" might also carry the idea that "the mystery" cannot be traced in the Old Testament since it was hidden by God.)

Are these riches available to every believer? Yes! In fact, Paul made it clear that he himself had no special claim on God's wealth, for he considered himself "less than the least of all saints" (Eph. 3:8). The name *Paul* (Paulus) means "little" in Latin, and perhaps Paul bore this name because he realized how insignificant he really was (Acts 13:9). He called himself "the least of the apostles" (1 Cor. 15:9), but at least he was an apostle, which is more than we can claim. Here he called himself, not "the least of all saints," but "less than the least of all saints" (Eph. 3:8), and he later calls himself the "chief of sinners" (1 Tim. 1:15). Understanding the deep truths of God's Word does not give a man a big head; it gives him a broken and contrite heart.

It Is Important to the Angels (3:9–10)

Perhaps at this point, you are asking yourself the question, "Why did God keep His secret about the church hidden for so many centuries?" Certainly the Old Testament clearly states that God will save the Gentiles through Israel, but nowhere are we told that both Jews and Gentiles will form a new creation, the church, the body of Christ. It was this mystery that the Spirit revealed to Paul and other leaders in the early church, and that was so difficult for the Jews to accept.

Paul told us that "the principalities and powers" are also involved in this great secret. God is "educating" the angels by means of the church! By "the principalities and powers," Paul meant the angelic beings created by God, both good and evil (Eph. 1:21; 6:12; Col. 1:16; 2:15). Angels are created beings and are not omniscient. In fact, Peter indicated that during the Old Testament period, the angels were curious about God's plan of salvation then being worked out on earth (1 Peter 1:10–12). Certainly the angels rejoice at the repentance of a lost sinner (Luke 15:10), and Paul suggested that the angels watch the activities of the local assembly (1 Cor. 11:10). "We are made a spectacle unto the world, and to angels," Paul wrote (1 Cor. 4:9).

What, then, do the angels learn from the church? "The manifold wisdom of God" (Eph. 3:10). Certainly the angels know about the power of God as seen in His creation. But the wisdom of God as seen in His new creation, the church, is something new to them. Unsaved men, including wise philosophers, look at God's plan of salvation and consider it "foolishness" (1 Cor. 1:18–31). But the angels watch the outworking of God's salvation, and they praise His wisdom. Paul called it *manifold wisdom,* and this word carries the idea of "variegated" or "many-colored." This suggests the beauty and variety of God's wisdom in His great plan of salvation.

But there is another facet to this truth that must be explored. What are the *evil* angels learning from God's "mystery"? That their leader, Satan, does not have any wisdom! Satan knows the Bible, and he understood from the Old Testament Scriptures *that* the Savior would come, *when* He would come, *how* He would come, and *where* He would come. Satan also understood *why* He would come, as far as redemption is concerned. But nowhere in the Old Testament would Satan find any prophecies concerning the church, "the mystery" of Jews and Gentiles united in one body! Satan could see unbelieving Jews rejecting their Messiah, and he could see Gentiles trusting the Messiah, but he could not see both believing Jews and Gentiles united in one body, seated with Christ in the heavenlies, and completely victorious over Satan! Had Satan known the far-reaching results of the cross, no doubt he would have altered his plans accordingly.

God hid this great plan "from the beginning of the world," but now He wants "the mystery" to be known by His church. And this is why He made Paul a "steward" of this great truth. Ephesians 3:9 should read, "And to make all men see what is the stewardship of the mystery." Here is an amazing truth: Now *all believers* are to be faithful stewards of this great truth! This "sacred secret" that was so important to Paul, and to the Gentiles, and to angels, is now in *our* hands!

It Should Be Important to Christians Today (3:11–13)

When God saved Paul, He deposited with him the precious treasures of gospel truth (1 Tim. 1:11). Paul in turn committed these truths to others, exhorting them to commit the truths to faithful men who would guard them and share them (2 Tim. 2:2). "O Timothy! Keep that which is committed to thy trust" (1 Tim. 6:20). At the close of his life, Paul would say, to the glory of God, "I have kept the faith" (2 Tim. 4:7). During those apostolic days, the truths of the gospel and "the mystery" were guarded, preached, and handed down to faithful men.

But a study of church history reveals that, one by one, many of the basic truths of the Word of God were lost during the centuries that followed. God had His faithful people—a minority—at all times, but many of the great truths of the Word were buried under man-made theology, tradition, and ritual. Then, God's Spirit began to open the eyes of seeking souls, and these great truths were unveiled again. Martin Luther championed justification by faith. Other spiritual leaders rediscovered the person and work of the Holy Spirit, the glorious truth of the return of Jesus Christ, and the joy of the victorious Christian life. In recent years, the truth of "the mystery" has again excited the hearts of God's people. We rejoice that we are "all one in Christ Jesus."

Most of us identify Napoleon Bonaparte as the would-be conqueror of Europe. But not many would name him as a patron of arts and sciences. Yet he was. In July 1798, Napoleon began to occupy Egypt, but by September 1801, he was forced to get out. Those three years meant failure as far as his military and political plans were concerned, but they meant success in one area that greatly interested him—archeology. For in August 1799, a Frenchman named Boussand discovered the Rosetta Stone about thirty miles from Alexandria. This discovery gave to archeologists the key to understanding Egyptian hieroglyphics. It opened the door to modern Egyptian studies.

The "mystery" is God's "Rosetta Stone." It is the key to what He promised in the Old Testament, what Christ did in the Gospels, what the early church did in the book of Acts, what Paul and the other writers teach in the Epistles, and what God will do as recorded in the book of Revelation. God's program today is not "the headship of Israel" (Deut. 28:1–13), but the headship of Christ over His church. We today are under a different "stewardship" from that of Moses and the Prophets, and we must be careful not to confuse what God has clarified.

The reason many churches are weak and ineffective is because they do not understand what they have in Christ. And the cause of this is often spiritual leaders who are not good "stewards of the mystery." Because they do not "rightly divide the word of truth" (2 Tim. 2:15), they confuse their people concerning their spiritual position in Christ, and they rob their people of the spiritual wealth in Christ.

This great truth concerning the church is not a divine afterthought. It is a part of God's eternal purpose in Christ (Eph. 3:11). To ignore this truth is to sin against the Father who planned it, the Son whose death made it possible, and the Spirit who today seeks to work in our lives to accomplish what God has planned. When you understand this truth, it gives you great confidence and faith (Eph. 3:12). When you know what God is doing in the world, and you work with Him, you can be sure that He will work *in* you and *for* you. All of His divine resources are available to those who sincerely want to do His will and help Him accomplish His purposes on earth.

The early church thought that the gospel belonged to the Jews because it had come *through* them and *to* them first. Until Peter, by divine direction, went to the Gentiles in Acts 10, the Jewish believers thought that a Gentile had to become a Jew before he could become a Christian! God's Spirit gradually revealed to the churches that God was doing a new thing: He was calling out a people for His name from both the Jews and Gentiles (Acts 15:14). There are no national, racial, political, physical, or social distinctions in the church! "There is neither Jew nor Greek, there is neither bond nor free, there is neither male nor female; for ye are all one in Christ Jesus" (Gal. 3:28).

But an understanding of God's program in this present age not only gives the believer confidence toward God. It also gives him courage in the difficult circumstances of life. Paul's sufferings for the Gentiles would mean glory for the Gentiles. In the Old Testament age, when God's people obeyed, God blessed them materially, nationally, and physically (Deut. 28), and if they disobeyed, He withdrew these blessings. This is not the way He deals with the church today. Our blessings are spiritual, not material (Eph. 1:3); they have *all* been given to us completely in Christ. We appropriate them by faith, but if we disobey God, He does not revoke them. We simply lose the enjoyment and the enrichment of them. Paul was certainly a dedicated, Spirit-filled man, yet he was suffering as a prisoner. Paul made it clear that physical, material blessings are not always the experience of the dedicated Christian (2 Cor. 4:7–12; 11:23—12:10).

I was driving to a preaching engagement, trying to follow a map I had found in the glove compartment of my car. (I am a very poor navigator, so my wife is usually the navigator in our family.) For some reason, I could not locate the interstate highway I needed, so I stopped to get directions at a filling station.

"You've got an ancient map there, Mister!" the attendant told me. "Here's the latest map. Follow it and you'll get where you are going." He was right. I followed the new map and arrived in plenty of time to preach.

People who do not understand God's "mystery" in His church are trying to make spiritual progress with the wrong map. Or, to change the figure, they are trying to build with the wrong blueprints. God's churches on this earth—the local assemblies—are not supposed to be either Gentile culture cliques or Jewish culture cliques. For a German church to refuse fellowship to a Swede is just as unscriptural as for a Jewish congregation to refuse a Gentile. God's church is not to be shackled by culture, class, or any other physical distinction. It is a spiritual entity that must submit to the headship of Jesus Christ in the power of the Spirit.

Yes, God had a "secret"—but God does not want it to be a secret anymore! If you understand your wonderful position in Christ, then live up to it—and share the blessing with others. This "secret" was important to Paul, to the Gentiles, and to the angels—and it ought to be important to you and me today.

CHAPTER SEVEN
Ephesians 3:14–21
GET YOUR HANDS ON YOUR WEALTH

This passage is the second of two prayers recorded in Ephesians, the first one being Ephesians 1:15–23. In the first prayer, the emphasis is on *enlightenment,* but in this prayer, the emphasis is on *enablement.* It is not so much a matter of *knowing* as *being*—laying our hands on what God has for us and by faith making it a vital part of our lives. Paul was saying, "I want you to get your hands on your wealth, realize how vast it is, and start to use it."

It is worth noting that both of these prayers, as well as the other prison prayers (Phil. 1:9–11; Col. 1:9–12), deal with the spiritual condition of the inner man, and not the material needs of the body. Certainly it is not wrong to pray for physical and material needs, but the emphasis in these petitions is on the spiritual. Paul knew that if the inner man is what he ought to be, the outer man will be taken care of in due time. Too many of our prayers focus only on physical and material needs and fail to lay hold of the deeper inner needs of the heart. It would do us good to use these prison prayers as our own, and ask God to help us in our inner person. That is where the greatest needs are.

The Invocation (3:14–15)

The first thing that strikes us is Paul's posture: "I bow my knees." (This must have been quite an experience for the Roman soldier chained to Paul!) The Bible nowhere commands any special posture for prayer. Abraham stood before the Lord when he prayed for Sodom (Gen. 18:22), and Solomon stood when he prayed to dedicate the temple (1 Kings 8:22). David "sat before the Lord" (1 Chron. 17:16) when he prayed about the future of his kingdom. And Jesus "fell on his face" when He prayed in Gethsemane (Matt. 26:39).

You have noticed, no doubt, the emphasis on spiritual posture in Ephesians. As lost sinners, we were buried in the graveyard (Eph. 2:1). But when we trusted Christ, He raised us from the dead and seated us with Christ in the heavenlies (Eph. 2:4–6). Because we are *seated* with Christ, we can *walk* so as to please Him (Eph. 4:1, 17; 5:2, 8, 15) and we can *stand* against the devil (Eph. 6:10–13). But the posture that links "sitting" with "walking" and "standing" is "bowing the knee." It is through prayer that we lay hold of God's riches that enable us to behave like Christians and battle like Christians. Whether we actually bow our knees is not the important thing; that we bow our hearts and wills to the Lord and ask Him for what we need is the vital matter.

Paul's prayer was addressed to "the Father of our Lord Jesus Christ." In the Bible, prayer is addressed to the Father, through the Son, and in the Spirit. This is the usual pattern, though you do find petitions addressed to the Son, and possibly to the Spirit (1 Thess. 3:12–13). In Ephesians 1:3, Paul called the Father "the God and Father of our Lord Jesus Christ." He was the "God … of our Lord Jesus Christ" when Jesus was here on earth, for as man, Jesus lived in total dependence on God. This title reminds us of Christ's humanity. But God is the "Father of our Lord Jesus Christ" because Jesus Christ is eternal God; so this title reminds us of His deity.

There is a sense, however, in which all men in general, and Christians in particular, share in the fatherhood of God. Paul stated that "the whole family in heaven and earth is named" after the divine Father. That word *family* can be translated "fatherhood." Every fatherhood in heaven and on earth gets its origin and name from the Father. He is the great Original; every other fatherhood is but a copy. Adam is called "the son of God" (Luke 3:38), referring to his creation. Believers are the "sons of God" by rebirth (John 1:11–13; 1 John 3:1–2). All men are not children of God by nature. Instead, they are children of disobedience and children of wrath (Eph. 2:2–3). As Creator, God is the Father of each man but as Savior, He is only the Father of those who believe. There is no such thing in Scripture as the universal fatherhood of God that saves all men. "Ye must be born again" (John 3:7).

The Petition (3:16–19)

There are four requests in Paul's prayer, but they must not be looked on as isolated, individual petitions. These four requests are more like four parts to a telescope. One request leads into the next one, and so on. He prays that the inner man might have spiritual strength, which will, in turn, lead to a deeper experience with Christ. This deeper experience will enable them to "apprehend" (get hold of) God's great love, which will result in their being "filled unto all the fullness of God." So, then, Paul was praying for strength, depth, apprehension, and fullness.

Strength (v. 16). The presence of the Holy Spirit in the life is evidence of salvation (Rom. 8:9); but the power of the Spirit is enablement for Christian living, and it is this power that Paul desired for his readers. "Ye shall receive power, when the Holy Spirit is come upon you" (Acts 1:8, literal translation). Jesus performed His ministry on earth in the power of the Spirit (Luke 4:1, 14; Acts 10:38), and this is the only resource we have for Christian living today. As you read the book of Acts, you see the importance of the Holy Spirit in the life of the church, for there are some fifty-nine references to the Spirit in the book, or one fourth of the total references found in the New Testament. Someone has said, "If God took the Holy Spirit out of this world, most of what we Christians are doing would go right on—and nobody would know the difference!" Sad, but true.

The power of the Spirit is given to us "according to the riches of his glory" (Eph. 3:16). Christ returned to glory and sent the Spirit from heaven to indwell and empower His people. It is not necessary for us to "work something up." The power has to be sent down. How marvelous that God does not give the Spirit's power to us "out of his riches," but "according to"—which is a far greater thing. If I am a billionaire and I give you ten dollars, I have given you *out of* my riches; but if I give you a million dollars, I have given to you *according to* my riches. The first is a *portion;* the second is a *proportion.*

This power is available for "the inner man." This means the spiritual part of man where God dwells and works. The inner man of the lost sinner is dead (Eph. 2:1), but it becomes alive when Christ is invited in. The inner man can see (Ps. 119:18), hear (Matt. 13:9), taste (Ps. 34:8), and feel (Acts 17:27), and he must be "exercised" (1 Tim. 4:7–8). He also must be cleansed (Ps. 51:7) and fed (Matt. 4:4). The outer man is perishing, but the inner man can be renewed spiritually in spite of outward physical decay (2 Cor. 4:16–18). It is this inner power that makes him succeed.

What does it mean to have the Holy Spirit empower the inner man? It means that our spiritual faculties are controlled by God, and we are exercising them and growing in the Word (Heb. 5:12–14). It is only when we yield to the Spirit and let Him control the inner man that we succeed in living to the glory of God. This means feeding the inner man the Word of God, praying and worshipping, keeping clean, and exercising the senses by loving obedience.

Depth (v. 17). Paul used three pictures here to convey this idea of spiritual depth, and the three pictures are hidden in the three verbs: "dwell," "rooted," and "grounded." The verb *dwell* literally means (and here I follow Dr. Kenneth Wuest) "to settle down and feel at home." Certainly Christ was already resident in the hearts of the Ephesians, or else Paul would not have addressed them as "saints" in Ephesians 1:1. What Paul was praying for was a deeper experience between Christ and His people. He yearned for Christ to settle down and feel at home in their hearts—not a surface relationship, but an ever-deepening fellowship.

Abraham's life is an illustration of this truth. God was going to bless Abraham with a son, so the Lord Himself came down and visited Abraham's tent, and He brought two angels with Him. They came to the tent, they talked with Abraham, and they even ate a meal with him. They felt very much at home, because Abraham was a man of faith and obedience. But the three guests had another task. They had to investigate the sins of Sodom because God planned to destroy the cities of Sodom and Gomorrah. Lot, a believer, was living in Sodom, and God wanted to warn him to get out before the judgment could fall. But the Lord Himself did not go to Sodom. He sent the two angels (Gen. 18–19). The Lord did not feel at home in Lot's house the way He felt at home in Abraham's tent.

The verb *rooted* moves us into the plant world. The tree must get its roots deep into the soil if it is to have both nourishment and stability, and the Christian must have his spiritual roots deep into the love of God. Psalm 1:1–3 is a perfect description of this word, and Jeremiah 17:5–8 is a good commentary on it. One of the most important questions a Christian can ask himself is, "From what do I draw my nourishment and my stability?" If there is to be power in the Christian life, then there must be depth. The roots must go deeper and deeper into the love of Christ.

Grounded is an architectural term; it refers to the foundations on which we build. In the first two churches I pastored, we were privileged to construct new buildings, and in both projects it seemed we would never get out of the ground. In my second building program, we had to spend several thousand dollars taking soil tests because we were building over an old lake bed. For weeks, the men were laying out and pouring the footings. One day I complained to the architect, and he replied, "Pastor, the most important part of this building is the foundation. If you don't go deep, you can't go high." That sentence has been a sermon to me ever since.

The trials of life test the depth of our experience. If two roommates in college have a falling out, they may seek new roommates, for after all, living with a roommate is a passing experience. But if a husband and wife, who love each other, have a disagreement, the trial only deepens their love as they seek to solve the problems. The storm that blows reveals the strength of the roots. Jesus told the story about the two builders, one of whom did not go deep enough for his foundation (Matt. 7:24–29). Paul prayed that the believers might have a deeper experience with Christ, because only a deep experience could sustain them during the severe trials of life.

Apprehension (vv. 18–19a). The English words *comprehend* and *apprehend* both stem from the Latin word *prehendere* which means "to grasp." We say that a monkey has a "prehensile tail." That is, its tail is able to grasp a tree limb and hold on. Our word *comprehend* carries the idea of mentally grasping something; while *apprehend* suggests laying hold of it for yourself. In other words, it is possible to understand something but not really make it your own. Paul's concern was that we lay hold of the vast expanses of the love of God. He wanted us to live in four dimensions. When God gave the land to Abraham, He told him to "walk through the land in the length of it and in the breadth of it" (Gen. 13:17). Abraham had to step out by faith and claim his inheritance. But we today have an inheritance in four dimensions: breadth, length, depth, and height. God's fourth dimension is love!

But there is a paradox here. Paul wanted us to know personally the love of Christ "which passeth knowledge." There are dimensions, but they cannot be measured. "The love of Christ which passeth knowledge" parallels "the unsearchable riches of Christ" (Eph. 3:8). We are so rich in Christ that our riches cannot be calculated even with the most sophisticated computer.

Perhaps you saw the cartoon that depicted a man chatting with a boat salesman. In the beautiful showroom were yachts and cabin cruisers that glittered with elegance. In the caption, the salesman is saying to the customer, "Sir, if you have to ask how much they are, they are too expensive for you!"

No Christian ever has to worry about having inadequate spiritual resources to meet the demands of life. If he prays for spiritual strength and spiritual depth, he will be able to apprehend—get his hands on—all the resources of God's love and grace. "I can do all things through Christ which strengtheneth me" (Phil. 4:13). And what is the result of all of this?

Fullness (v. 19b). It is said that nature abhors a vacuum. This explains why air or water will automatically flow into an empty place. The *divine* nature abhors a vacuum. God wants us to experience His fullness. "Filled *unto* all the fullness of God" is the more accurate translation. The *means* of our fullness is the Holy Spirit (Eph. 5:18), and the *measure* of our fullness is God Himself (Eph. 4:11–16). It is tragic when Christians use the wrong measurements in examining their own spiritual lives. We like to measure ourselves by the weakest Christians that we know, and then boast, "Well, I'm better than they are." Paul tells us that the measure is Christ, and that we cannot boast about anything (nor should we). When we have reached *His* fullness, then we have reached the limit.

In one sense, the Christian is already "made full in Christ" (Col. 2:9–10, where "complete" means "filled full"). Positionally, we are complete in Him, but practically, we enjoy only the grace that we apprehend by faith. The resources are there. All we need do is accept them and enjoy them. Paul will have more to say about this fullness (Eph. 5:18–21), so we will reserve further comment until we reach that section.

The Benediction (3:20–21)

After contemplating such a marvelous spiritual experience, it is no wonder Paul burst forth in a doxology, a fitting benediction to such a prayer. Note again the trinitarian emphasis in this benediction: Paul prayed to God the Father, concerning the indwelling power of God the Spirit, made available through God the Son.

Perhaps the best way for us to grasp some of the greatness of this doxology is to look at it in outlined form:

> Now unto Him that is
> > able to do *all*
> > > *above* all
> > > > *abundantly* above all
> > > > > *exceeding* abundantly above all

Paul seemed to want to use every word possible to convey to us the vastness of God's power as found in Jesus Christ. He ended each of the two previous chapters with praise to God for His great victory in Christ. He told us that Christ's power is so great He arose from the dead and ascended *far above all* (Eph. 1:19–23). He taught us that His power is so great He has reconciled Jews and Gentiles to each other, and to God, and that He is now building a temple to the eternal glory of God (Eph. 2:19–22). But in the paragraph before us, Paul shared the exciting truth that this *far above all* power is available to us! It is even "above all that we ask or think." In other words, the power of Christ, like the love of Christ, is beyond human understanding or measurement. And this is just the kind of power you and I need if we are to walk and war in victory.

The word *power* is again *dunamis,* which we met back in Ephesians 3:7, and *working* is *energeia* (energy) found in Ephesians 1:11, 19; 2:2; 3:7; and 4:16. Some power is dormant; it is available, but not being used, such as the power stored in a battery. But God's energy is effectual power—power at work in our lives. This power works *in* us, in the inner man (Eph. 3:16). Philippians 2:12–13 are parallel verses, so be sure to read them. It is the Holy Spirit who releases the resurrection power of Christ in our lives.

One winter day, I had an important engagement in Chicago, and the evening before, the area was hit by a severe snowstorm. I did not have a garage, so my car was not only covered with snow, but heavy cakes of ice had formed under the fenders and bumpers. These ice cakes I simply kicked off, after I had swept off the car. I drove to the gas station to fill the tank. When I pushed the button on the dashboard to open the gas cap, it didn't work. No matter how hard or often I pushed, the cap stayed shut. The station attendant looked under the fender and discovered the problem. In kicking off the ice, I had broken the wire that connected the gas cap with the battery.

Apparently this is what has happened to many Christians. They have been cut off from their source of power. Unbelief, unconfessed sin, careless living, worldliness in action or attitude—all of these can rob us of power. And a Christian robbed of power cannot be used of God. "Without me, ye can do nothing" (John 15:5).

Why does God share His power with us? So that we can build great churches for our own glory? So that we can boast of our own achievements? No! "To him be glory in the church!" The Spirit of God was given to glorify the Son of God (John 16:14). The church on earth is here to glorify the Son of God. If our motive is to glorify God by building His church, then God will share His power with us. The power of the Spirit is not a luxury; it is a necessity.

But the amazing thing is that what we do in His power today will glorify Christ "throughout all ages, world without end" (Eph. 3:21). The church's greatest ministry is yet to come. What we do here and now is preparing us for the eternal ages, when we shall glorify Christ forever.

He is able to do all—*above* all—*abundantly* above all—*exceeding* abundantly above all!

Get your hands on your spiritual wealth by opening

your heart to the Holy Spirit, and praying with Paul for strength for the inner man … for a new depth of love … for spiritual apprehension … and for spiritual fullness.

"Ye have not because ye ask not" (James 4:2).

CHAPTER EIGHT
Ephesians 4:1–16
LET'S WALK TOGETHER

All of Paul's letters contain a beautiful balance between doctrine and duty, and Ephesians is the perfect example. The first three chapters deal with doctrine, our riches in Christ, while the last three chapters explain duty, our responsibilities in Christ. The key word in this last half of the book is *walk* (Eph. 4:1, 17; 5:2, 8, 15), while the key idea in the first half is wealth. In these last three chapters, Paul admonished us to walk in *unity* (Eph. 4:1–16), *purity* (Eph. 4:17–5:17), *harmony* (Eph. 5:18–6:9), and *victory* (Eph. 6:10–24).

These four "walks" perfectly parallel the basic doctrines Paul has taught us in the first three chapters.

Before we look at this section in detail, we must note two important words in Ephesians 4:1: *therefore* and *beseech*. The word *therefore* indicates that Paul was basing his exhortations to duty on the doctrines taught in the first three chapters. (Rom. 12:1–2 are parallel verses.) The Christian life is not based on ignorance but knowledge, and the better we understand Bible doctrine, the easier it is to obey Bible duties. When people say, "Don't talk to me about doctrine—just let me live my Christian life!" they are revealing their ignorance of the way the Holy Spirit works in the life of the believer. "It makes no difference what you believe, just as long as you live right" is a similar confession of ignorance. It *does* make a difference what you believe, because what you believe determines how you behave!

Our Wealth	*Our Walk*
Called by grace to belong to His body (chap. 1)	Walk worthy of your calling—the unity of the Body (4:1–16)
Raised from the dead (2:1–10)	Put off the grave-clothes (4:17–5:17); walk in purity
Reconciled (2:11–22)	Walk in harmony (5:18–6:9)
Christ's victory over Satan is the mystery (chap. 3)	Walk in victory (6:10–24)

The word *beseech* indicates that God, in love, urges us to live for His glory. He does not say, as He did to the Old Testament Jews, "If you obey Me, I will bless you." Rather, He says, "I have already blessed you—now, in response to My love and grace, obey Me." He

has given us such a marvelous calling in Christ; now it is our responsibility to live up to that calling.

The main idea in these first sixteen verses is the unity of believers in Christ. This is simply the practical application of the doctrine taught in the first half of the letter: God is building a body, a temple. He has reconciled Jews and Gentiles to Himself in Christ. The oneness of believers in Christ is already a spiritual reality. Our responsibility is to guard, protect, and preserve that unity. To do this, we must understand four important facts.

The Grace of Unity (4:1–3)

Unity is not uniformity. Unity comes from within and is a spiritual grace, while uniformity is the result of pressure from without. Paul used the human body as a picture of Christian unity (1 Cor. 12), and he adapted the same illustration here in this section (Eph. 4:13–16). Each part of the body is different from the other parts, yet all make up one body and work together.

If we are going to preserve the "unity of the Spirit," we must possess the necessary Christian graces, and there are seven of them listed here. The first is *lowliness,* or *humility.* Someone has said, "Humility is that grace that, when you know you have it, you have lost it." Humility means putting Christ first, others second, and self last. It means knowing ourselves, accepting ourselves, and being ourselves to the glory of God. God does not condemn you when you accept yourself and your gifts (Rom. 12:3). He just does not want us to think more *highly* of ourselves than we ought to—or *less highly* than we ought to.

Meekness is not weakness. It is power under control. Moses was a meek man (Num. 12:3), yet see the tremendous power he exercised. Jesus Christ was "meek and lowly in heart" (Matt. 11:29), yet He drove the moneychangers from the temple. In the Greek language, this word was used for a soothing medicine, a colt that had been broken, and a soft wind. In each case you have power, but that power is under control.

Allied with meekness is *longsuffering,* which literally means "long-tempered," the ability to endure discomfort without fighting back. This leads to the mentioning *of forbearance,* a grace that cannot be experienced apart from love. "Love suffereth long and is kind" (1 Cor. 13:4). Actually, Paul was describing some of the "fruit of the Spirit" (Gal. 5:22–23); for the "unity of the Spirit" (Eph. 4:3) is the result of the believer "walking in the Spirit" (Gal. 5:16).

The next grace that contributes to the unity of the Spirit is *endeavor.* Literally it reads "being eager to maintain, or guard, the unity of the Spirit." "It's great that you love each other," I once heard a seasoned saint say to a newly wedded couple, "but if you're going to be happy in marriage, you gotta work at it!" The verb used here is a present participle, which means we must constantly be endeavoring to maintain this unity. In fact, when we think the situation is the best, Satan will move in to wreck it. The spiritual unity of a home, a Sunday school class, or a church is the responsibility of each person involved, and the job never ends.

The final grace is *peace*—"the bond of peace." Read James 3:13—4:10 for the most vivid treatment of war and peace in the New Testament. Note that the reason for war on the outside is war on the inside. If a believer cannot get along with God, he cannot get along with other believers. When "the peace of God" rules in our hearts, then we build unity (Col. 3:15).

The Grounds of Unity (4:4–6)

Many people today attempt to unite Christians in a way that is not biblical. For example, they will say, "We are not interested in doctrines, but in love. Now, let's forget our doctrines and just love one another!" But Paul did not discuss spiritual unity in the first three chapters; he waited until he had laid the doctrinal foundation. While not all Christians agree on some minor matters of Christian doctrine, they all do agree on the foundation truths of the faith. Unity built on anything other than Bible truth is standing on a very shaky foundation. Paul names here the seven basic spiritual realities that unite all true Christians.

One body. This is, of course, the body of Christ in which each believer is a member, placed there at conversion by the Spirit of God (1 Cor. 12:12–31). The one body is the model for the many local bodies that God has established across the world. The fact that a person is a member of the one body does not excuse him from belonging to a local body, for it is there that he exercises his spiritual gifts and helps others to grow.

One Spirit. The same Holy Spirit indwells each believer, so that we belong to each other in the Lord. There are perhaps a dozen references to the Holy Spirit in Ephesians, because He is important to us in the living of the Christian life.

One hope of your calling. This refers to the return of the Lord to take His church to heaven. The Holy Spirit within is the assurance of this great promise (Eph. 1:13–14). Paul was suggesting here that the believer who realizes the existence of the one body, who walks in the Spirit, and who looks for the Lord's return, is going to be a peacemaker and not a troublemaker.

One Lord. This is our Lord Jesus Christ, who died for us, lives for us, and one day will come for us. It is difficult to believe that two believers can claim to obey the same Lord, and yet not be able to walk together in unity. Someone asked Ghandi, the spiritual leader of India, "What is the greatest hindrance to Christianity in India?" He replied, "Christians." Acknowledging the lordship of Christ is a giant step toward spiritual unity among His people.

One faith. There is one settled body of truth deposited by Christ in His church, and this is "the faith." Jude called it "the faith which was once delivered unto the saints" (Jude 3). The early Christians recognized a body of basic doctrine that they taught, guarded, and committed to others (2 Tim. 2:2).

Christians may differ in some matters of interpretation and church practice, but all true Christians agree on "the faith"—and to depart from "the faith" is to bring about disunity within the body of Christ.

One baptism. Since Paul was here discussing the one body, this "one baptism" is probably the baptism of the Spirit, that act of the Spirit when He places the believing sinner into the body of Christ at conversion (1 Cor. 12:13). This is not an experience after conversion, nor is it an experience the believer should pray for or seek after. We are commanded to be filled with the Spirit (Eph. 5:18), but we are never commanded to be baptized with the Spirit, for we have already been baptized by the Spirit at conversion. As far as the one body is concerned, there is one baptism—the baptism of the Spirit. But as far as local bodies of believers are concerned, there are two baptisms: the baptism of the Spirit and water baptism.

One God and Father. Paul liked to emphasize God as Father (Eph. 1:3, 17; 2:18; 3:14; 5:20). The marvelous oneness of believers in the family of God is evident here, for God is over all, and working through all, and in all. We are children in the same family, loving and serving the same Father, so we ought to be able to walk together in unity. Just as in an earthly family the various members have to give and take in order to keep a loving unity in the home, so God's heavenly family must do the same. The "Lord's Prayer" opens with "Our Father"—not "My Father."

Paul was quite concerned that Christians not break the unity of the Spirit by agreeing with false doctrine (Rom. 16:17–20), and the apostle John echoed this warning (2 John 6–11). The local church cannot believe in peace at any price, for God's wisdom is "first pure, then peaceable" (James 3:17). Purity of doctrine of itself does not produce spiritual unity, for there are churches that are sound in faith, but unsound when it comes to love. This is why Paul joined the two: "speaking the truth in love" (Eph. 4:15).

The Gifts for Unity (4:7–11)

Paul moved now from what all Christians have in common to how Christians differ from each other. He was discussing variety and individuality within the unity of the Spirit. God has given each believer at least one spiritual gift (1 Cor. 12:1–12), and this gift is to be used for the unifying and edifying (building up) of the body of Christ. We must make a distinction between "spiritual gifts" and natural abilities. When you were born into this world God gave you certain natural abilities, perhaps in mechanics, art, athletics, or music. In this regard, all men are not created equal, because some are smarter, or stronger, or more talented than others. But in the spiritual realm, each believer has at least one spiritual gift no matter what natural abilities he may or may not possess. A spiritual gift is a God-given ability to serve God and other Christians in such a way that Christ is glorified and believers are edified.

How does the believer discover and develop his

gifts? By fellowshipping with other Christians in the local assembly. Gifts are not toys to play with. They are tools to build with. And if they are not used in love, they become weapons to fight with, which is what happened in the Corinthian church (1 Cor. 12—14). Christians are not to live in isolation, for after all, they are members of the same body.

Paul taught that Christ is the Giver of these gifts, through the Holy Spirit (Eph. 4:8–10). He ascended to heaven as Victor forevermore. The picture here is of a military conqueror leading his captives and sharing the spoil with his followers. Only in this case, the "captives" are not His enemies, but His own. Sinners who once were held captives by sin and Satan have now been taken captive by Christ. Even death itself is a defeated foe! When He came to earth, Christ experienced the depths of humiliation (Phil. 2:5–11), but when He ascended to heaven, He experienced the very highest exaltation possible. Paul quoted Psalm 68:18, applying to Jesus Christ a victory song written by David (Eph. 4:8).

There are three lists of spiritual gifts given in the New Testament: 1 Corinthians 12:4–11, 27–31; Romans 12:3–8; and Ephesians 4:11. Since these lists are not identical, it may be that Paul has not named all the gifts that are available. Paul wrote that some gifts are more important than others, but that all believers are needed if the body is to function normally (1 Cor. 14:5, 39). Paul named, not so much "gifts" as the gifted men God has placed in the church, and there are four of them.

Apostles (v. 11a). The word means "one who is sent with a commission." Jesus had many disciples, but He selected twelve apostles (Matt. 10:1–4). A *disciple* is a "follower" or a "learner," but an *apostle* is a "divinely appointed representative." The apostles were to give witness of the resurrection (Acts 1:15–22), and therefore had to have seen the risen Christ personally (1 Cor. 9:1–2). There are no apostles today in the strictest New Testament sense. These men helped to lay the foundation of the church—"the foundation of the apostles and prophets" (Eph. 2:20), and once the foundation was laid, they were no longer needed. God authenticated their ministry with special miracles (Heb. 2:1–4), so we should not demand these same miracles today. Of course, in a broad sense, all Christians have an apostolic ministry. "As my Father hath sent me, even so send I you" (John 20:21). But we must not claim to be apostles.

Prophets (v. 11b). We commonly associate a prophet with predictions of future events, but this is not his primary function. A New Testament prophet is one who proclaims the Word of God (Acts 11:28; Eph. 3:5). Believers in the New Testament churches did not possess Bibles, nor was the New Testament written and completed. How, then, would these local assemblies discover God's will? His Spirit would share God's truth with those possessing the gift of prophecy. Paul suggested that the gift of prophecy had to do with

understanding "all mysteries and all knowledge" (1 Cor. 13:2), meaning, of course, spiritual truths. The purpose of prophecy is "edification, encouragement, and consolation" (1 Cor. 14:3, literal translation). Christians today do not get their spiritual knowledge *immediately* from the Holy Spirit, but *mediately* through the Spirit teaching the Word. With the apostles, the prophets had a foundational ministry in the early church, and they are not needed today (Eph. 2:20).

Evangelists (v. 11c). "Bearers of the good news." These men traveled from place to place to preach the gospel and win the lost (Acts 8:26–40; 21:28). All ministers should "do the work of an evangelist," but this does not mean that all ministers are evangelists (2 Tim. 4:5). The apostles and prophets laid the foundation of the church, and the evangelists built on it by winning the lost to Christ. Of course, in the early church, every believer was a witness (Acts 2:41–47; 11:19–21), and so should we be witnesses today. But there are people also today who have the gift of evangelism. The fact that a believer may not possess this gift does not excuse him from being burdened for lost souls or witnessing to them.

Pastors and teachers (v. 11d). The fact that the word *some* is not repeated indicates that we have here one office with two ministries. *Pastor* means "shepherd," indicating that the local church is a flock of sheep (Acts 20:28), and it is his responsibility to feed and lead the flock (1 Peter 5:1–4, where "elder" is another name for "pastor"). He does this by means of the Word of God, the food that nourishes the sheep. The Word is the staff that guides and disciplines the sheep. The Word of God is the local church's protection and provision, and no amount of entertainment, good fellowship, or other religious substitutes can take its place.

The Growth of Unity (4:12–16)

Paul was looking at the church on two levels in this section. He saw the body of Christ, made up of all true believers, growing gradually until it reaches spiritual maturity, "the measure of the stature of the fullness of Christ." But he also saw the local body of believers ministering to each other, growing together, and thereby experiencing spiritual unity.

A freelance missionary visited a pastor friend of mine asking for financial support. "What group are you associated with?" my friend asked.

The man replied, "I belong to the invisible church."

My friend then asked, "Well, what church are you a member of?"

Again he got the answer, "I belong to the invisible church!"

Getting a bit suspicious, my friend asked, "When does this invisible church meet? Who pastors it?"

The missionary then became incensed and said, "Well, your church here isn't the true church. I belong to the invisible church!"

My friend replied, "Well, here's some invisible money to help you minister to the invisible church!"

Now, my pastor friend was not denying the existence of the one body. Rather, he was affirming the fact that the *invisible church* (not a biblical term, but I will use it) ministers *through* the visible church.

The gifted leaders are supposed to "equip the saints unto the work of the ministry, unto the building up of the body of Christ" (literal translation). The saints do not call a pastor and pay him to do the work. They call him and follow his leadership as he, through the Word, equips them to do the job (2 Tim. 3:13–17). The members of the church grow by feeding on the Word and ministering to each other. The first evidence of spiritual growth is *Christlikeness*.

The second evidence is *stability*. The maturing Christian is not tossed about by every religious novelty that comes along. There are religious quacks waiting to kidnap God's children and get them into their false cults, but the maturing believer recognizes false doctrine and stays clear of it. The cultists do not try to win lost souls to Christ. They do not establish rescue missions in the slum areas of our cities, because they have no good news for the man on skid row. Instead, these false teachers try to capture immature Christians, and for this reason, most of the membership of the false cults comes from local churches, particularly churches that do not feed their people the Word of God.

The third evidence of maturity is *truth joined with love:* "Speaking the truth in love" (Eph. 4:15). It has well been said that truth without love is brutality, but love without truth is hypocrisy. Little children do not know how to blend truth and love. They think that if you love someone, you must shield him from the truth if knowing the truth will hurt him. It is a mark of maturity when we are able to share the truth with our fellow Christians, and do it in love. "Faithful are the wounds of a friend, but the kisses of an enemy are deceitful" (Prov. 27:6).

One more evidence of maturity is *cooperation* (Eph. 4:16). We realize that, as members of the one body and a local body, we belong to each other, we affect each other, and we need each other. Each believer, no matter how insignificant he may appear, has a ministry to other believers. The body grows as the individual members grow, and they grow as they feed on the Word and minister to each other. Note once again the emphasis on love: "forbearing one another in love" (Eph. 4:2); "speaking the truth in love" (Eph. 4:15); "the edifying of itself in love" (4:16). Love is the circulatory system of the body. It has been discovered that isolated, unloved babies do not grow properly and are especially susceptible to disease, while babies who are loved and handled grow normally and are stronger. So it is with the children of God. An isolated Christian cannot minister to others, nor can others minister to him, and it is impossible for the gifts to be ministered either way.

So, then, spiritual unity is not something we manufacture. It is something we already have in Christ, and

we must protect and maintain it. Truth unites, but lies divide. Love unites, but selfishness divides. Therefore, "speaking the truth in love," let us equip one another and edify one another, that all of us may grow up to be more like Christ.

CHAPTER NINE
Ephesians 4:17–32
TAKE OFF THE GRAVECLOTHES!

The Bible was written to be obeyed, and not simply studied, and this is why the words "therefore" and "wherefore" are repeated so often in the second half of Ephesians (4:1, 17, 25; 5:1, 7, 14, 17, 24). Paul was saying, "Here is what Christ has done for you. Now, in the light of this, here is what we ought to do for Christ." We are to be doers of the Word, and not hearers only (James 1:22). The fact that we have been called in Christ (Eph. 1:18) ought to motivate us to walk in unity (Eph. 4:1–16). And the fact that we have been raised from the dead (Eph. 2:1–10) should motivate us to walk in purity (Eph. 4:17—5:17), or, as Paul told the Romans, "walk in newness of life" (Rom. 6:4). We are alive in Christ, not dead in sins; therefore "put off the old man … and put on the new man (Eph. 4:22, 24). Take off the graveclothes and put on the grace-clothes!

The Admonition (4:17–19)

There are some negatives in the Christian life, and here is one of them: "Walk not as other Gentiles walk." The Christian is not to imitate the life of the unsaved people around him. They are "dead in trespasses and sins" (Eph. 2:1), while he has been raised from the dead and been given eternal life in Christ. Paul explains the differences between the saved and the unsaved.

To begin with, Christians *think* differently from unsaved people. Note the emphasis here on thinking: mind (Eph. 4:17, 23), understanding (Eph. 4:18), ignorance (Eph. 4:18), "learned Christ" (Eph. 4:20). Salvation begins with repentance, which is a change of mind. The whole outlook of a person changes when he trusts Christ, including his values, goals, and interpretation of life. What is wrong with the mind of the unsaved person? For one thing, his thinking is "vain" (futile). It leads to no substantial purpose. Since he does not know God, he cannot truly understand the world around him, nor can he understand himself. The sad story is told in Romans 1:21–25. Our world today possesses a great deal of knowledge, but very little wisdom. Thoreau put it beautifully when he said that we have "improved means to unimproved ends."

The unsaved man's thinking is futile because it is darkened. He thinks he is enlightened because he rejects the Bible and believes the latest philosophies, when in reality he is in the dark. "Professing themselves to be wise, they become fools" (Rom. 1:22). But they think they are wise. Satan has blinded the minds of the unsaved (2 Cor. 4:3–6) because he does not want them to see the truth in Jesus Christ. It is not simply that their eyes are blinded so they cannot see, but that their minds are darkened so that they cannot think straight about spiritual matters.

Of course, the unsaved man is dead because of this spiritual ignorance. The truth and the life go together. If you believe God's truth, then you receive God's life. But you would think that the unbeliever would do his utmost to get out of his terrible spiritual plight. Alas, the hardness of his heart enslaves him. He is "past feeling" because he has so given himself over to sin that sin controls him. Read Romans 1:18–32 for a vivid expansion of these three brief verses.

The Christian cannot pattern himself after the unsaved person, because the Christian has experienced a miracle of being raised from the dead. His life is not futile, but purposeful. His mind is filled with the light of God's Word, and his heart with the fullness of God's life. He gives his body to God as an instrument of righteousness (Rom. 6:13), and not to sin for the satisfaction of his own selfish lusts. In every way, the believer is different from the unbeliever, and therefore the admonition: "Walk not."

The Argument (4:20–24)

Paul reinforced his admonition with an argument from the spiritual experience of his readers. Again the emphasis is on the mind, or the outlook, of the believer. "But ye have not so learned Christ" (Eph. 4:20). He did not say "learned about Christ," because it is possible to learn about Christ and never be saved. To "learn Christ" means to have a personal relationship to Christ so that you get to know Him better each day. I can learn about Sir Winston Churchill because I own many of his books and can secure books about his life. But I can never "learn him" because he is dead. Jesus Christ is alive! Therefore, I can "learn Christ" through a personal fellowship with Him.

This fellowship is based on the Word of God. I can be taught "the truth" as it is in Jesus Christ. The better I understand the Word of God, the better I know the Son of God, for the whole Bible is a revelation of the Lord Jesus Christ (Luke 24:27; John 5:39). The unsaved man is spiritually ignorant, while the Christian is intelligent in the things of the Word. And the unsaved man does not know Christ, while the believer grows in his personal knowledge of Christ day by day. We have believed the truth; we have received the life; therefore, we will walk "in the way" and not walk after the example of the unsaved world.

But this experience of salvation goes much deeper than this, for it has resulted in a whole new position before God. The old man (the former life) has been put away, and we can now walk in newness of life through Christ. Ephesians 4:22–24 is a summary of Romans 5—8, where Paul explained the believer's identification with Christ in death, burial, and resurrection.

He also dealt with this in Ephesians 2:4–6, as well as in Colossians 3. As Christians, we have not simply changed our minds. We have totally changed our citizenship. We belong to God's "new creation" in Christ (2 Cor. 5:17), and therefore, the ideas and desires of the old creation no longer should control our lives.

The simplest illustration of this great truth is given in John 11, the resurrection of Lazarus. Our Lord's friend, Lazarus, had been in the grave four days when Jesus and His disciples arrived at Bethany, and even Martha admitted that, by now, the decaying body would smell (John 11:39). But Jesus spoke the word and Lazarus came forth alive, an illustration of John 5:24. Notice our Lord's next words: "Loose him, and let him go" (John 11:44). Take off the graveclothes! Lazarus no longer belonged to the old dominion of death, for he was now alive. Why go about wearing graveclothes? Take off the old and put on the new!

This was Paul's argument—you no longer belong to the old corruption of sin; you belong to the new creation in Christ. Take off the graveclothes! How do we do this? "Be renewed in the spirit of your mind" (Eph. 4:23). Conversion is a crisis that leads to a process. Through Christ, once and for all, we have been given a new position in His new creation, but day by day, we must by faith appropriate what He has given us. The Word of God renews the mind as we surrender our all to Him (Rom. 12:1–2). "Sanctify them through thy truth: thy Word is truth" (John 17:17). As the mind understands the truth of God's Word, it is gradually transformed by the Spirit, and this renewal leads to a changed life. Physically, you are what you eat, but spiritually, you are what you think. "As he thinketh in his heart, so is he" (Prov. 23:7). This is why it is important for us as Christians to spend time daily meditating on the Word, praying, and fellowshipping with Christ.

The Application (4:25–32)

Paul was not content to explain a principle and then leave it. He always applied it to the different areas of life that need to feel its power. Paul even dared to name sins. Five different sins are named in this section, and Paul told us to avoid them and he explained why.

Lying (v. 25). A lie is a statement that is contrary to fact, spoken with the intent to deceive. If I tell you it is noon, and then discover that my watch is wrong, I did not tell a lie. But if I gave you the wrong time so you would be late to a meeting and I would benefit from it, that would be a lie. Satan is a liar (John 8:44), and he wants us to believe that God is a liar. "Yea, hath God said?" (Gen. 3:1). Whenever we speak truth, the Spirit of God works, but whenever we tell a lie, Satan goes to work. We like to believe that we help people by lying to them, but such is not the case. We may not see the sad consequences immediately, but ultimately they will come. "Ye know that no lie is of the truth" (1 John 2:21). Hell is prepared for "whosoever loveth and maketh a lie" (Rev. 22:15). This does not mean that anybody who ever told a lie will go to hell, but rather that those whose lives are controlled by lies—they love lies and they make lies—are lost forever. The Christian's life is controlled by truth.

Note the reason Paul gave for telling the truth: We belong to each other in Christ. He urged us to build the body in love (Eph. 4:16) and he urged us to build the body in truth. "Speaking the truth in love" (Eph. 4:15). As "members one of another" we affect each other, and we cannot build each other apart from truth. The first sin that was judged in the early church was the sin of lying (Acts 5:1–11).

Anger (vv. 26–27). Anger is an emotional arousal caused by something that displeases us. In itself, anger is not a sin, because even God can be angry (Deut. 9:8, 20; Ps. 2:12). Several times in the Old Testament the phrase appears, "the anger of the Lord" (Num. 25:4; Jer. 4:8; 12:13). The holy anger of God is a part of His judgment against sin, as illustrated in our Lord's anger when He cleansed the temple (Matt. 21:12–13). The Bible often speaks of anger "being kindled" (Gen. 30:2; Deut. 6:15), as though anger can be compared to fire. Sometimes a man's anger smolders, and this we would call *malice,* but this same anger can suddenly burst forth and destroy, and this we would call *wrath.*

It is difficult for us to practice a truly holy anger or righteous indignation because our emotions are tainted by sin, and we do not have the same knowledge that God has in all matters. God sees everything clearly and knows everything completely, and we do not. The New Testament principle seems to be that the believer should be angry at sin but loving toward people. "Ye that love the Lord, hate evil" (Ps. 97:10).

It is possible to be angry and not sin, but if we do sin, we must settle the matter quickly and not let the sun go down on our wrath. "Agree with thine adversary quickly" (Matt. 5:25). "Go and tell him his fault between thee and him alone" (Matt. 18:15). The fire of anger, if not quenched by loving forgiveness, will spread and defile and destroy the work of God. According to Jesus, anger is the first step toward murder (Matt. 5:21–26), because anger gives the devil a foothold in our lives, and Satan is a murderer (John 8:44). Satan hates God and God's people, and when he finds a believer with the sparks of anger in his heart, he fans those sparks, adds fuel to the fire, and does a great deal of damage to God's people and God's church. Both lying and anger "give peace to the devil" (Eph. 4:27).

When I was living in Chicago, one out of every thirty-five deaths was a murder, and most of these murders involved relatives and friends. They are what the law calls "crimes of passion." Two friends get into an argument (often while gambling), one of them gets angry, pulls a gun or knife, and kills his friend. Horace was right when he said, "Anger is momentary insanity."

A woman tried to defend her bad temper by saying, "I explode and then it's all over with."

"Yes," replied a friend, "just like a shotgun—but look at the damage that's left behind."

"Anyone can become angry," wrote Aristotle. "But to be angry with the right person, to the right degree, at the right time, for the right purpose, and in the right way—this is not easy."

Solomon has a good solution: "A soft answer turneth away wrath, but grievous words stir up anger" (Prov. 15:1).

Stealing (v. 28). "Thou shalt not steal" is one of the Ten Commandments, and when God gave that commandment, He instituted the right of private ownership of property. A man has the right to turn his strength into gain, and to keep that gain and use it as he sees fit. God gave numerous laws to the Jews for the protection of their property, and these principles have become a part of our law today. Stealing was particularly a sin of the slaves in Paul's day. Usually they were not well cared for and were always in need, and the law gave them almost no protection. When he wrote to Titus, Paul urged him to admonish the slaves not to "purloin" but to be faithful to their masters (Titus 2:10). But it was not only the slaves, but citizens in general, who were addicted to thievery, for Paul wrote to people in the Ephesian church who were gainfully employed (Eph. 4:28).

Just as Satan is a liar and a murderer, he is also a thief. "The thief cometh not, but for to steal, and to kill, and to destroy" (John 10:10). He turned Judas into a thief (John 12:6), and he would do the same to us if he could. When he tempted Eve, he led her to become a thief, for she took the fruit that was forbidden. And she, in turn, made Adam a thief. The first Adam was a thief and was cast out of Paradise, but the Last Adam, Christ, turned to a thief and said, "Today shalt thou be with me in paradise" (Luke 23:43).

Paul added motive to the admonition. We should tell the truth because we are "members of another." We should control our anger lest we "give place to the devil." We should work, and not steal, so that we might be able "to give to him that needeth." You would expect Paul to have said, "Let him work that he might take care of himself and not be tempted to steal." Instead, he lifted human labor to a much higher level. We work that we might be able to help others. If we steal, we hurt others; therefore, we should work that we might be able to help others. Even honest labor could become a selfish thing, and this Paul seeks to avoid. Of course, it was a fundamental rule in the early church that "if any would not work, neither should he eat" (2 Thess. 3:10). A lazy Christian robs himself, others, and God. Of course, Paul was not writing to believers who could not work because of handicaps, but with those who would not work.

Paul himself was an example of a hard worker, for while he was establishing local churches, he labored as a tentmaker. Every Jewish rabbi was taught a trade, for, said the rabbis, "If you do not teach your son a trade, you teach him to be a thief." The men that God called in the Scriptures were busy working when their call came. Moses was caring for sheep; Gideon was threshing wheat; David was minding his father's flock;

and the first four disciples were either casting nets or mending them. Jesus Himself was a carpenter.

Corrupt speech (v. 29). The mouth and heart are connected. "Out of the abundance of the heart, the mouth speaketh" (Matt. 12:34). We expect a change in speech when a person becomes a Christian. It is interesting to trace the word *mouth* through the book of Romans and see how Christ makes a difference in a man's speech. The sinner's mouth is "full of cursing and bitterness" (Rom. 3:14), but when he trusts Christ, he gladly confesses with his mouth "Jesus Christ is Lord" (Rom. 10:9–10 NIV). As a condemned sinner, his mouth is stopped before the throne of God (Rom. 3:19), but as a believer, his mouth is opened to praise God (Rom. 15:6). Change the heart and you change the speech. Paul certainly knew the difference, for when he was an unsaved rabbi, he was "breathing out threatenings and slaughter against the disciples of the Lord" (Acts 9:1). But when he trusted Christ, a change took place: "Behold, he prayeth" (Acts 9:11). From "preying" to "praying" in one step of faith!

The word *corrupt,* used in Matthew 7:17–18, refers to rotten fruit. It means "that which is worthless, bad, or rotten." Our words do not have to be "dirty" to be worthless. Sometimes we go along with the crowd and try to impress people with the fact that we are not as puritanical as they think. Peter may have had this motive in mind when he was accused by the girl of being one of Christ's disciples. "Then began he to curse and to swear, saying, 'I know not the man'" (Matt. 26:74). The appetites of the old life sometimes show up when we permit "filthy communication" out of the mouth (Col. 3:8). Remember, before we were saved, we lived in spiritual death (Eph. 2:1–3), and, like Lazarus, our personal corruption produced an odor that was not pleasing to God. No wonder Paul wrote, "Their throat is an open sepulchre" (Rom. 3:13).

The remedy is to make sure the heart is full of blessing. So fill the heart with the love of Christ so that only truth and purity can come out of the mouth. Never have to say, "Now, take this with a grain of salt." Paul told us to put the salt of God's grace in everything we say. "Let your speech be always with grace, seasoned with salt" (Col. 4:6). And keep in mind that your words have power, either for good or evil. Paul told us to speak in such a way that what we say will build up our hearers, and not tear them down. Our words should minister grace and help to draw others closer to Christ. Satan, of course, encourages speech that will tear people down and destroy the work of Christ. If you need to be reminded of the power of the tongue, read the third chapter of James.

Bitterness (vv. 30–32). These verses warn us against several sins of the attitude and amplify what Paul wrote about anger. *Bitterness* refers to a settled hostility that poisons the whole inner man. Somebody does something we do not like, so we harbor ill will against him. "Husbands, love your wives and be not bitter against them" (Col. 3:19). Bitterness leads to wrath, which is the explosion on the outside of the feelings on the inside. Wrath and anger often lead to brawling (clamor) or blasphemy (evil speaking). The first is fighting with fists, the second is fighting with words. It is difficult to believe that Christians would act this way, but they do, and this is why Paul warned us. "Behold, how good and how pleasant it is for brethren to dwell together in unity!" (Ps. 133:1).

A handsome elderly man stopped at my study one day and asked me if I would perform a wedding for him. I suggested that he bring the bride in so that we might chat together and get better acquainted, since I hesitate to marry strangers. "Before she comes in," he said, "let me explain this wedding to you. Both of us have been married before—to each other! Over thirty years ago, we got into an argument, I got mad, and we separated. Then we did a stupid thing and got a divorce. I guess we were both too proud to apologize. Well, all these years we've lived alone, and now we see how foolish we've been. Our bitterness has robbed us of the joys of life, and now we want to remarry and see if the Lord won't give us a few years of happiness before we die." Bitterness and anger, usually over trivial things, make havoc of homes, churches, and friendships.

Paul gave three reasons why we must avoid bitterness. First, *it grieves the Holy Spirit.* He lives within the Christian, and when the heart is filled with bitterness and anger, the Spirit grieves. We parents know just a little of this feeling when our children at home fight with each other. The Holy Spirit is happiest in an atmosphere of love, joy, and peace, for these are the "fruit of the Spirit" that He produces in our lives as we obey Him. The Holy Spirit cannot leave us, because He has sealed us until that day when Christ returns to take us home. We do not lose our salvation because of our sinful attitudes, but we certainly lose the joy of our salvation and the fullness of the Spirit's blessing.

Second, our sin *grieves God the Son*, who died for us. Third, it *grieves God the Father*, who forgave us when we trusted Christ. Here Paul put his finger on the basic cause of a bitter attitude: We cannot forgive people. An unforgiving spirit is the devil's playground, and before long it becomes the Christian's battleground. If somebody hurts us, either deliberately or unintentionally, and we do not forgive him, then we begin to develop bitterness within, which hardens the heart. We should be tenderhearted and kind, but instead we are hardhearted and bitter. Actually, we are not hurting the person who hurt us; we are only hurting ourselves. Bitterness in the heart makes us treat others the way Satan treats them, when we should treat others the way God has treated us. In His gracious kindness, God has forgiven us, and we should forgive others. We do not forgive for *our* sake (though we do get a blessing from it) or even for *their* sake, but for *Jesus'* sake. Learning how to forgive and forget is one of the secrets of a happy Christian life.

Review once again the motives for "walking in purity": We are members one of another; Satan wants to get a foothold in our lives; we ought to share with others; we ought to build one another up; and we ought not to grieve God. And, after all, we have been raised from the dead—so why wear the graveclothes? Jesus says of us as He said of Lazarus: "Loose him, and let him go!"

CHAPTER TEN
Ephesians 5:1–17
IMITATING OUR FATHER

The word *followers* in Ephesians 5:1 is the word *mimics,* so that the verse can be translated "Be ye imitators of God as beloved children." This sets the theme for the section. Paul was simply arguing that children are like their parents, a fact that can be both encouraging and embarrassing to those of us who have children. Have you ever seen a child sitting in the front seat of an automobile, trying to drive like his father! Or walking behind him, pretending to mow the lawn? Or, sad to say, imitating Dad smoking a cigarette or taking a drink of alcohol? Children probably learn more by watching and imitating than any other way.

If we are the children of God, then we ought to imitate our Father. This is the basis for the three admonitions in this section. God is love (1 John 4:8); therefore, "walk in love" (Eph. 5:1–2). God is light (1 John 1:5); therefore, walk as children of light (Eph. 5:3–14). God is truth (1 John 5:6); therefore, walk in wisdom (Eph. 5:15–17). Of course, each of these "walks" is a part of Paul's exhortation to "walk in purity."

Walk in Love (5:1–2)
This admonition ties in with the last two verses of the previous chapter where Paul has warned us against bitterness and anger. It is tragic when these attitudes show up in the family of God. As a pastor, I have witnessed malice and bitterness in the lives of people as I have conducted funerals and even weddings. You would think that sharing the sorrow of losing a loved one, or sharing a joy of a marriage, would enable people to forgive past wrongs and try to get along with each other. But such is not the case. It takes a real love in the heart, for "charity [love] shall cover the multitude of sins" (1 Peter 4:8).

Paul gave several reasons why the Christian ought to walk in love.

He is God's child. Having been born again through faith in Christ, he is therefore one of the "partakers of the divine nature" (2 Peter 1:4), and since "God is love" it is logical that God's children will walk in love. When Paul encouraged his readers to "walk in love," he was not asking them to do something that was foreign to the Christian life; for we have received a new nature that wants to express itself in love. The old nature is basically selfish, and

for this reason builds walls and declares war. But the new nature is loving, and therefore builds bridges and proclaims peace.

He is God's beloved child. "Be ye imitators of God as beloved children." Imagine, God speaks of us the same way He spoke of Jesus Christ: "This is my beloved Son" (Matt. 3:17). In fact, the Father loves us as He loves His Son (John 17:23). We are born into a loving relationship with the Father that ought to result in our showing love to Him by the way we live. What more could the Father do to express His love to us? Is it asking too much for us to "walk in love" to please Him?

He was purchased with a great price. "Greater love hath no man than this, that a man lay down his life for his friends" (John 15:13). But He laid down His life for His enemies (Rom. 5:10). Our love for Him is our response to His love for us. Paul compared Christ's sacrifice on the cross to the Old Testament "sweet savor" sacrifices that were presented at the altar of the temple (Lev. 1:9, 13, 17; 2:9). The idea behind "sweet savor" is simply that the sacrifice is well pleasing to God. This does not suggest that God is pleased that sin demands death, and that His Son had to die to save lost sinners. Rather, it indicates that the death of Christ satisfies the holy law of God and therefore is acceptable and pleasing to the Father. The sweet-savor offerings are described in Leviticus 1–3: the burnt offering, the meal offering, and the peace offering. The burnt offering pictures Christ's complete devotion to God; the meal offering, His perfection of character; and the peace offering, His making peace between sinners and God. Since the sin offering and the trespass offering (Lev. 4–5) picture Christ taking the place of the sinner, they are not considered "sweet-savor" offerings. Certainly nothing is beautiful about sin!

Paul began with "walk in love" because love is the fundamental factor in the Christian life. If we walk in love, we will not disobey God or injure men because "he that loveth another hath fulfilled the law" (Rom. 13:8). The Holy Spirit puts this love in our hearts (Rom. 5:5).

Walk As Children of Light (5:3–14)
Since "God is light" and we are imitating our Father, then we should walk in the light and have nothing to do with the darkness of sin. Paul gave three descriptions of believers that prove his point.

We are saints (vv. 3–4). That is, we are "set-apart ones" and no longer belong to the world of darkness around us. We have been "called out of darkness into his marvelous light" (1 Peter 2:9). It is beneath the dignity of a saint to indulge in the sins that belong to the world of darkness, some of which Paul named here. He warned us against the sexual sins (fornication, uncleanness) that were so prevalent in that day—and are prevalent today. Sad to say, these sins have invaded the homes of Christians and brought grief to local churches too. "Covetousness" may seem out of place next to fornication, but the two sins are but different expressions of the same basic weakness of fallen nature—uncontrolled appetite. The fornicator and the covetous person each desire to satisfy the appetite by taking what does not belong to them. "The lust of the flesh and the lust of the eyes" (1 John 2:16) would describe these two sins. "Let there not be even a hint of these sins!" said Paul.

In Ephesians 5:4 he warned against sins of the tongue, which, of course, are really sins of the heart. It is not difficult to see the relationship between the sins named in Ephesians 5:3 and those in Ephesians 5:4. People who have base appetites usually cultivate a base kind of speech and humor, and often people who want to commit sexual sins, or have committed them, enjoy jesting about them. Two indications of a person's character are what makes him laugh and what makes him weep. The saint of God sees nothing humorous in obscene language or jests. "Foolish talking" does not mean innocent humor but rather senseless conversation that cheapens the man and does not edify or minister grace to the hearers (Eph. 4:29). Paul was not condemning small talk because much conversation falls into that classification. He was condemning foolish talk that accomplishes no good purpose.

Jesting is a translation of a word that means "able to turn easily." This suggests a certain kind of conversationalist who can turn any statement into a coarse jest. The gift of wit is a blessing, but when it is attached to a filthy mind or a base motive, it becomes a curse. There are quick-witted people who can pollute any conversation with jests that are always inconvenient (out of place). How much better it is for us to be quick to give thanks! This is certainly the best way to give glory to God and keep the conversation pure.

A Christian woman attended an anniversary dinner in honor of a friend, not knowing that there would be a program of low comedy following the meal. The so-called comedian tried to entertain the crowd with coarse humor that degraded everything that the Christian guest held to be sacred and honorable. At one point in the program, the comedian's throat became dry. "Please bring me a glass of water," he called to a waiter.

At that point the Christian woman added, "And bring a toothbrush and a bar of soap with it!" To be sure, soap in the mouth will never cleanse the conversation, but she made her point.

Christians who have God's Word in their hearts (Col. 3:16) will always season their speech with salt (Col. 4:6), for grace in the heart means grace on the lips.

We are kings (vv. 5–6). When we trusted Christ, we entered into the kingdom of God (John 3:3), but we are also awaiting the full revelation of His kingdom when He returns (2 Tim. 4:1). Paul made it clear that people who deliberately and persistently live in sin will not share in God's kingdom. "They which practice such things shall not inherit the kingdom of God" (Gal. 5:21, literal translation). "Whoremonger" is a translation of the Greek word *pornos*, from which

we get our word *pornography,* and it means "one who practices fornication—illicit sex." The morally unclean and the covetous will join the fornicator in judgment. Paul equated covetousness with idolatry, for it is the worship of something other than God. These warnings deal with the habitual practice of sin, and not the occasional act of sin. David committed adultery, yet God forgave him and one day took him to heaven. Certainly David was disciplined for his sin, but he was not rejected by God.

In Paul's day, there were false Christians who argued that believers could live in sin and get away with it. These deceivers had many arguments to convince ignorant Christians that they could sin repeatedly and still enter God's kingdom. "You were saved by grace!" they argued. "Therefore go ahead and sin that God's grace might abound!" Paul answered that foolish argument in Romans 6. "Sin in the life of a believer is different from sin in the life of an unsaved person!" Yes—*it's worse!* God judges sin no matter where He finds it, and He does not want to find it in the life of one of His own children. I personally believe that no true Christian can ever be lost, but he will prove the reality of his faith by an obedient life.

There are many professors who are not possessors (Matt. 7:21–23). A Christian is not *sinless,* but he does *sin less*—and less—and less! The Christian is a king, and it is beneath his dignity to indulge in the practices of the lost world that is outside the kingdom of God.

We are light (vv. 7–14). This figure is the main thrust of the passage, for Paul was admonishing his readers to "walk as children of light." You will want to read 2 Corinthians 6:14—7:1 for a parallel passage that explains the contrasts that exist between the child of God and the unsaved person. Paul did not say that we were "in the darkness," but that we "were darkness." Now that we are saved, "what communion hath light with darkness?" After all, light produces fruit, but the works of darkness are unfruitful as far as spiritual things are concerned. "For the fruit of the Spirit [or "the light"] is in all goodness and righteousness and truth." It is impossible to be in darkness and light at the same time!

The light produces "goodness," one manifestation of the fruit of the Spirit (Gal. 5:22). Goodness is "love in action." Righteousness means rightness of character before God and rightness of actions before men. Both of these qualities are based on *truth,* which is conformity to the Word and will of God.

Jesus had much to say about light and darkness. "Let your light so shine before men, that they may see your good works, and glorify your Father which is in heaven" (Matt. 5:16). "Everyone that doeth evil hateth the light, neither cometh to the light, lest his deeds should be reproved. But he that doeth truth cometh to the light, that his deeds may be made manifest, that they are wrought in God" (John 3:20–21).

To "walk as children of light" means to live before the eyes of God, not hiding anything. It is relatively easy to hide things from other people because they cannot see our hearts and minds, but "all things are naked and opened unto the eyes of him with whom we have to do" (Heb. 4:13). Every time I take a plane to a meeting, I must surrender myself and my luggage to a special inspection, and I am happy to do so, because this inspection helps to detect bombs. I have never been afraid to walk through the "detection tunnel" or have my luggage pass through the X-ray equipment, because I have nothing to hide.

An author asked Charles Spurgeon for permission to write his life story, and the great preacher replied, "You may write my life in the skies—I have nothing to hide!"

But walking "as children of light" also means revealing God's light in our daily lives. By our character and conduct, we bring God's light into a dark world. As God's lights, we help others find their way to Christ. The mind of the unsaved person is blinded by Satan (2 Cor. 4:3–4) and by sin (Eph. 4:17–19). Only as we witness and share Christ can the light enter in. Just as a healthy person can assist the sickly, so a child of God can lead the lost out of darkness into God's wonderful light.

Light reveals God; light produces fruit; but light also exposes what is wrong. No surgeon would willingly operate in darkness lest he make a false move and take a life. How could an artist paint a true picture in darkness? The light reveals the truth and exposes the true character of things. This explains why the unsaved person stays clear of the church and the Bible. God's light reveals his true character, and the exposure is not very complimentary. As we Christians walk in light, we refuse to fellowship with the darkness, and we expose the dark things of sin for what they really are.

"I am come a light into the world," said Jesus (John 12:46). He also said to His disciples, "Ye are the light of the world" (Matt. 5:14). When He was here on earth, the perfection of His character and conduct exposed the sinfulness of those around Him. This is one reason why the religious leaders hated Him and sought to destroy Him. "If I had not come and spoken unto them, they had not had sin, but now they have no cloak for their sin" (John 15:22). Just as a healthy person unconsciously exposes the handicaps and sicknesses of people he visits in a hospital, so the Christian exposes the darkness and sin around him just by living like a Christian. Paul told us to live balanced lives—positively, to walk in the light; negatively, to denounce and expose the wickedness of those in the darkness. It is not enough simply to expose the wickedness of those in the darkness. It is not enough simply to expose sin. We must also bear fruit.

But Ephesians 5:12 gives us a caution. Be careful how you deal with the "unfruitful works of darkness." The motto today seems to be "Tell it like it is!" And yet that can be a dangerous policy when it comes to exposing the filthy things of darkness, lest we unconsciously advertise and promote sin. Paul said, "It is

a shame even to speak of those things" (Eph. 6:12). Some preachers enjoy reveling in the sensational, so much so that their sermons excite appetites and give to the innocent more information than they need. "But yet I would have you wise unto that which is good, and simple concerning evil" (Rom. 16:19).

I recall a friend in youth work who felt it necessary to read all that the teenagers were reading "in order to understand them better," and it so polluted his mind that he himself fell into sin. It is not necessary for the believer to perform an autopsy on a rotting corpse to expose its rottenness. All he has to do is turn on the light! "For whatsoever doth make manifest is light" (Eph. 5:13).

When you think of light, you think of waking up to a new day, and Paul presented this picture (Eph. 5:14), paraphrasing Isaiah 60:1. You have the same image in Romans 13:11–13 and 1 Thessalonians 5:1–10. That Easter morning, when Christ arose from the dead, was the dawning of a new day for the world. Christians are not sleeping in sin and death. We have been raised from the dead through faith in Him. The darkness of the graveyard is past, and we are now walking in the light of salvation. Salvation is the beginning of a new day, and we ought to live as those who belong to the light, not to the darkness. "Lazarus, come forth!"

The believer has no business in the darkness. He is a *saint,* which means he is a partaker "of the inheritance of the saints in light" (Col. 1:12). He is a *king,* because he has been delivered "from the power of darkness" and has been translated "into the kingdom of his dear Son" (Col. 1:13). He is "light in the Lord" (Eph. 5:8).

Walk in Wisdom (5:15–17)

Circumspect comes from two Latin words that mean "looking around." The Greek word carries the idea of precision and accuracy. "See that you walk carefully, with exactness" is the meaning. The opposite would be walking carelessly and without proper guidance and forethought. We cannot leave the Christian life to chance. We must make wise decisions and seek to do the will of God.

Ephesians 5:14–15 are related to these verses. Paul appeared to be saying, "Don't walk in your sleep! Wake up! Open your eyes! Make the most of the day!" It is sad to see many professed Christians drift through life like sleepwalkers, never really making the most of opportunities to live for Christ and serve Him. Paul presented several reasons why we should be accurate and careful in our walk.

It is a mark of wisdom (v. 15). Only a fool drifts with the wind and tide. A wise man marks out his course, sets his sails, and guides the rudder until he reaches his destination. When a man wants to build a house, he first draws his plans so he knows what he is doing. Yet, how many Christians plan their days so that they use their opportunities wisely? True, we cannot know what a day may bring forth (James 4:13–17). But it is also true that a planned life can better deal with unexpected events. Someone said, "When the pilot does not know what port he is heading for, no wind is the right wind."

Life is short (v. 16a). "Buying up the opportunity—taking advantage of it." An old Chinese adage says, "Opportunity has a forelock so you can seize it when you meet it. Once it is past, you cannot seize it again." Our English word *opportunity* comes from the Latin and means "toward the port." It suggests a ship taking advantage of the wind and tide to arrive safely in the harbor. The brevity of life is a strong argument for making the best use of the opportunities God gives us.

The days are evil (v. 16b). In Paul's time, this meant that Roman persecution was on the way (1 Peter 4:12–19). How foolish to waste opportunities to win the lost, when soon those opportunities might be taken away by the advances of sin in society! If the days were evil when Paul wrote this letter, what must be their condition today?

God has given us a mind (v. 17a). "Understanding" suggests using our minds to discover and do the will of God. Too many Christians have the idea that discovering God's will is a mystical experience that rules out clear thinking. But this idea is wrong—and dangerous. We discover the will of God as He transforms the mind (Rom. 12:1–2); and this transformation is the result of the Word of God, prayer, meditation, and worship. If God gave you a mind, then He expects you to use it. This means that learning His will involves gathering facts, examining them, weighing them, and praying for His wisdom (James 1:5). God does not want us simply to *know* His will; He wants us to *understand* His will.

God has a plan for our lives (v. 17b). Paul alluded to this plan (Eph. 2:10). If God saved me, He has a purpose for my life, and I should discover that purpose and then guide my life accordingly. He reveals His plan through His Word (Col. 1:9–10), His Spirit in our hearts (Col. 3:15), and the working of circumstances (Rom. 8:28). The Christian can walk carefully and accurately because he knows what God wants him to do. Like the builder following the blueprint, he accomplishes what the architect planned.

This completes the section we have called "Walk in Purity." The emphasis is on the new life as contrasted with the old life, imitating God and not the evil world around us. In the next section, "Walk in Harmony," Paul deals with the relationships of life and shows how life in Christ can bring heaven to the home.

CHAPTER ELEVEN
Ephesians 5:18–33
HEAVEN IN YOUR HOME

When home is ruled according to God's Word," said Charles Haddon Spurgeon, "angels might be asked to stay with us, and they would not find themselves out of their element."

The trouble is that many homes are not governed by God's Word—even homes where the members are professing Christians—and the consequences are tragic. Instead of angels being guests in some homes, it seems that demons are the masters. Too many marriages end in the divorce court, and nobody knows how many husbands and wives are emotionally divorced even though they share the same address. The poet William Cowper called the home "the only bliss of Paradise that hast surviv'd the Fall," but too many homes are an outpost of hell instead of a parcel of paradise.

The answer is the Holy Spirit of God! It is only through the power of the Holy Spirit that we can walk in harmony as husbands and wives (Eph. 5:22–33), parents and children (Eph. 6:1–4), and employers and employees (Eph. 6:5–9). The unity of the people of God that Paul described (Eph. 4:1–16) must be translated into daily living if we are to enjoy the harmony that is a foretaste of heaven on earth.

"Be filled with the Spirit" is God's command, and He expects us to obey. The command is plural, so it applies to all Christians and not just to a select few. The verb is in the present tense—"keep on being filled"—so it is an experience we should enjoy constantly and not just on special occasions. And the verb is passive. We do not fill ourselves but permit the Spirit to fill us. The verb "fill" has nothing to do with contents or quantity, as though we are empty vessels that need a required amount of spiritual fuel to keep going. In the Bible, *filled* means "controlled by." "They … were filled with wrath" (Luke 4:28) means "they were controlled by wrath" and for that reason tried to kill Jesus. "The Jews were filled with envy" (Acts 13:45) means that the Jews were controlled by envy and opposed the ministry of Paul and Barnabas. To be "filled with the Spirit" means to be constantly controlled by the Spirit in our mind, emotions, and will.

When a person trusts Christ as his Savior, he is immediately baptized by the Spirit into the body of Christ (1 Cor. 12:13). Nowhere in the New Testament are we commanded to be baptized by the Spirit, because this is a once-for-all experience that takes place at conversion. When the Spirit came at Pentecost, the believers were baptized by the Spirit, and thus the body of Christ was formed (Acts 1:4–5). But they were also "filled with the Spirit" (Acts 2:4), and it was this filling that gave them the power they needed to witness for Christ (Acts 1:8). In Acts 2, the Jewish believers were baptized by the Spirit, and in Acts 10 the Gentile believers had the same experience (Acts 10:44–48; 11:15–17). Thus the body of Christ was made up of Jews and Gentiles (Eph. 2:11–22). That historic baptism, in two stages, has never been repeated any more than Calvary has been repeated. But that baptism is made personal when the sinner trusts Christ and the Spirit enters in to make him a member of the body of Christ. The baptism of the Spirit means that I belong to Christ's body. The filling of the Spirit means that my body belongs to Christ.

We usually think of the power of the Spirit as necessary for preaching and witnessing, and this is true. (See Acts 4:8, 31; 6:3, 5; 7:55; 13:9. The apostles experienced repeated fillings after that initial experience at Pentecost.) But Paul wrote that the Spirit's fullness is also needed in the home. If our homes are to be a heaven on earth, then we must be controlled by the Holy Spirit. But how can a person tell whether or not he is filled with the Spirit? Paul stated that there are three evidences of the fullness of the Spirit in the life of the believer: he is *joyful* (Eph. 5:19), *thankful* (Eph. 5:20), and *submissive* (Eph. 5:21–33). Paul said nothing about miracles or tongues or other special manifestations. He stated that the home can be a heaven on earth if each family member is controlled by the Spirit, and is joyful, thankful, and submissive.

Joyful (5:19)

Joy is one of the fruit of the Spirit (Gal. 5:22). Christian joy is not a shallow emotion that, like a thermometer, rises and falls with the changing atmosphere of the home. Rather, Christian joy is a deep experience of adequacy and confidence in spite of the circumstances around us. The Christian can be joyful even in the midst of pain and suffering. This kind of joy is not a thermometer but a thermostat. Instead of rising and falling with the circumstances, it determines the spiritual temperature of the circumstances. Paul put it beautifully when he wrote, "I have learned in whatsoever state I am, therewith to be content" (Phil. 4:11).

To illustrate this joy, Paul used the familiar image of drunkenness: "Be not drunk with wine ... but be filled with the Spirit" (Eph. 5:18). When the believers at Pentecost were filled with the Spirit, the crowd accused them of being drunk with new wine (Acts 2:13–15). There was such a joyfulness about them that the unbelievers could think of no better comparison. But some practical lessons can be learned from the contrasts. To begin with, the drunk is under the control of another force, since alcohol is actually a depressant. He feels a great sense of release—all his troubles are gone. He can "lick anybody in the house!" The drunk is not ashamed to express himself (though what he says and does is shameful), nor can he hide what is going on in his life.

Transfer this picture to the believer who is filled with the Spirit. God controls his life, and he experiences a deep joy he is not afraid to express to the glory of God. Of course, the drunk is really out of control, since the alcohol affects his brain, while the believer experiences a beautiful self-control that is really God in control. Self-control is among the fruit of the Spirit (Gal. 5:23). "The spirits of the prophets are subject to the prophets" (1 Cor. 14:32). The drunk makes a fool of himself, but the Spirit-filled Christian glorifies God and is willing to be a "fool for Christ's sake" (1 Cor. 4:10). The drunk calls attention to himself, while the Spirit-filled believer is a witness for Christ.

It is certainly not difficult to live or work with someone who is filled with the Spirit and joyful. He has a song in his heart and on his lips. The drunk often sings, but his songs only reveal the corruption in his heart. The Spirit-filled Christian's song comes from God, a song he could never sing apart from the Spirit's power. God even gives us songs in the night (Ps. 42:8). In spite of pain and shame, Paul and Silas were able to sing praises to God in the Philippian jail (Acts 16:25), and the result was the conversion of the jailer and his family. What a happy time they all had that midnight hour—and they did not need to get drunk to enjoy it!

"Your neighborhood tavern is the friendliest place in town!" That slogan appeared in a headline of a special newspaper insert during "National Tavern Month," so I decided to test its veracity. I watched the newspapers for several weeks and cut out items that related to taverns—and all of them were connected with brawls and murders. The friendliest place in town! But this headline reminded me that people who drink together often experience a sympathy and conviviality. This fact is no argument for alcohol, but it does illustrate a point: Christians who are filled with the Holy Spirit enjoy being together and experience a sense of joyful oneness in the Lord. They do not need the false stimulants of the world. They have the Spirit of God—and He is all they need.

Thankful (5:20)

Someone defined the home as "the place where we are treated the best—and complain the most!" How true this is! "My father never talks to me unless he wants to bawl me out or ask about my grades," a teenager once told me. "After all, a guy needs some encouragement once in a while!" Marriage counselors tell us that "taking each other for granted" is one of the chief causes of marital problems. Being thankful to God for each other is a secret of a happy home, and it is the Holy Spirit who gives us the grace of thankfulness.

How does a grateful heart promote harmony in the home? For one thing, the sincerely grateful person realizes that he is enriched because of others, which is a mark of humility. The person who thinks the world owes him a living is never thankful for anything. He thinks he is doing others a favor by permitting them to serve him. The thankful heart is usually humble, a heart that gladly acknowledges God as the "Giver of every good and perfect gift" (James 1:17). Like Mary's gift to Jesus in John 12, gratitude fills the house with fragrance.

To be sure, all of us are grateful for some things at some special occasions, but Paul commanded his readers to be thankful for all things at all times. This exhortation in itself proves our need of the Spirit of God, because in our own strength we could never obey this commandment. Can we really be thankful in times of suffering, disappointment, and even bereavement? Keep in mind that Paul was a prisoner when he wrote those words, yet he was thankful for what God was doing in him and for him (Eph. 1:16; 5:4, 20; Phil. 1:3; Col. 1:3, 12; 2:7; 3:17; 4:2). When a Christian finds himself in a difficult situation, he should immediately give thanks to the Father, in the name of Jesus Christ, by the power of the Spirit, to keep his heart from complaining and fretting. The devil moves in when a Christian starts to complain, but thanksgiving in the Spirit defeats the devil and glorifies the Lord. "In everything give thanks: for this is the will of God in Christ Jesus concerning you" (1 Thess. 5:18).

The word *gratitude* comes from the same root word as *grace*. If we have experienced the grace of God, then we ought to be grateful for what God brings to us. *Thank* and *think* also come from the same root word. If we would think more, we would thank more.

Submissive (5:21–33)

Paul applied the principle of harmony to husbands and wives (Eph. 5:21–33), parents and children (Eph. 6:1–4), and masters and servants (Eph. 6:5–9), and he began with the admonition that each submit to the other (Eph. 5:21). Does this suggest that the children tell the parents what to do, or that the masters obey the servants? Of course not! *Submission* has nothing to do with the *order* of authority, but rather governs the *operation* of authority, how it is given and how it is received. Often Jesus tried to teach His disciples not to throw their weight around, or seek to become great at somebody else's expense. Unfortunately, they failed to learn the lesson, and even at the Last Supper they were arguing over who was the greatest (Luke 22:24–27). When Jesus washed their feet, He taught them that the greatest is the person who uses his authority to build up people and not, like the Pharisees, to build up his authority and make himself important. We are to esteem others "more important than ourselves" (Rom. 12:10; Phil. 2:1–4). By nature, we want to promote ourselves, but the Holy Spirit enables us to submit ourselves.

As you study Paul's words to husbands and wives, remember that he was writing to believers. He was nowhere suggesting that women are inferior to men, or that all women must be in subjection to all men in every situation. The fact that he uses Christ and the church as his illustration is evidence that he has the Christian home in mind.

Wives, submit yourselves (vv. 22–24). He gives two reasons for this command: the lordship of Christ (Eph. 5:22) and the headship of the man in Christ (Eph. 5:23). When the Christian wife submits herself to Christ and lets Him be the Lord of her life, she will have no difficulty submitting to her husband. This does not mean that she becomes a slave, for the husband is also to submit to Christ. And if both are living under the lordship of Christ, there can be only harmony. Headship is not dictatorship. "Each for the other, both for the Lord." The Christian husband and wife should pray together and spend time in the Word, so that they might know God's will for their individual lives and for their home. Most of the marital conflicts I have dealt with as a pastor have stemmed from failure of the husband and/or wife to submit to Christ, spend time in His Word, and seek to do His will each day.

This explains why a Christian should marry a Christian and not become "unequally yoked together" with an unbeliever (2 Cor. 6:14–18). If the Christian is submitted to Christ, he will not try to establish a home that disobeys the Word of God. Such a home invites civil war from the beginning. But something else is important. The Christian couple must be careful to submit to Christ's lordship even before they are married. Unless the couple prays together and sincerely seeks God's will in His Word, their marriage begins on a weak foundation. Sins committed before marriage ("We're Christians—we can get away with this!") have a way of causing problems after marriage. Certainly God is able to forgive, but something very precious is lost just the same. Dr. William Culbertson, former president of Moody Bible Institute, used to warn about "the sad consequences of forgiven sins," and engaged Christian couples need to take that warning to heart.

Husbands, love your wives (vv. 25–33). Paul had much more to say to the Christian husbands than to the wives. He set for them a very high standard: Love your wives "even as Christ also loved the church." Paul was lifting married love to the highest level possible, for he saw in the Christian home an illustration of the relationship between Christ and the church. God established marriage for many reasons. For one thing, it meets man's *emotional* needs. "It is not good that the man should be alone" (Gen. 2:18). Marriage also has a *social* purpose in the bearing of children to continue the race (Gen. 1:28). Paul indicated a *physical* purpose for marriage—to help man and woman fulfill the normal desires given them by God (1 Cor. 7:1–3). But in Ephesians 5, Paul indicated also a *spiritual* purpose in marriage, as the husband and wife experience with each other the submission and the love of Christ (Eph. 5:22–33).

If the husband makes Christ's love for the church the pattern for loving his wife, then he will love her *sacrificially* (Eph. 5:25). Christ gave Himself for the church, so the husband, in love, gives himself for his wife. Jacob so loved Rachel that he sacrificially worked fourteen years to win her. True Christian love "seeketh not her own" (1 Cor. 13:5)—it is not selfish. If a husband is submitted to Christ and filled with the Spirit, his sacrificial love will willingly pay a price that she might be able to serve Christ in the home and glorify Him.

The husband's love will also be a *sanctifying* love (Eph. 5:26–27). The word *sanctify* means "to set apart." In the marriage ceremony, the husband is set apart to belong to the wife, and the wife is set apart to belong to the husband. Any interference with this God-given arrangement is sin. Today, Christ is cleansing His church through the ministry of His Word (John 15:3; 17:17). The love of the husband for his wife ought to be cleansing her (and him) so that both are becoming more like Christ. Even their physical relationship should be so controlled by God that it becomes a means of spiritual enrichment as well as personal enjoyment (1 Cor. 7:3–5). The husband is not to "use" his wife for his own pleasure, but rather is to show the kind of love that is mutually rewarding and sanctifying. The marriage experience is one of constant growth when Christ is the Lord of the home. Love always enlarges and enriches, while selfishness does just the opposite.

The church today is not perfect; it has spots and wrinkles. Spots are caused by defilement on the outside, while wrinkles are caused by decay on the inside. Because the church becomes defiled by the world, it needs constant cleansing, and the Word of God is the cleansing agent. "Keep yourselves unspotted from the world" (James 1:27). Strictly speaking, there should be no wrinkles in the church, because wrinkles are evidence of old age and internal decay. As the church is nourished by the Word, these wrinkles ought to disappear. Like a beautiful bride, the church ought to be clean and youthful, which is possible through the Spirit of God using the Word of God. One day the church will be presented in heaven "a glorious church" at the coming of Jesus Christ (Jude 24).

The husband's love for his wife should be sacrificial and sanctifying, but it should also be *satisfying* (Eph. 5:28–30). In the marriage relationship, the husband and wife become "one flesh." Therefore, whatever each does to the other, he or she does to himself or herself. It is a mutually satisfying experience. The man who loves his wife is actually loving his own body, since he and his wife are one flesh. As he loves her, he is nourishing her. Just as love is the circulatory system of the body of Christ (Eph. 4:16), so love is the nourishment of the home. How many people have confessed, "I am starved for love." There should be no starvation for love in the Christian home, for the husband and wife should so love each other that their physical, emotional, and spiritual needs are met. If both are submitted to the Lord, and to each other, they will be so satisfied that they will not be tempted to look anywhere else for fulfillment.

Our Christian homes are to be pictures of Christ's relationship to His church. Each believer is a member of Christ's body, and each believer is to help nourish the body in love (Eph. 4:16). We are one with Christ. The church is His body and His bride, and the Christian home is a divinely ordained illustration of this relationship. This certainly makes marriage a serious matter.

Paul referred to the creation of Eve and the forming of the first home (Gen. 2:18–24). Adam had to give part of himself in order to get a bride, but Christ gave all of Himself to purchase His bride at the cross. God opened Adam's side, but sinful men pierced Christ's side. So united are a husband and wife that they are "one flesh." Their union is even closer than that of parents and children. The believer's union with Christ is even closer and, unlike human marriage, will last for all eternity. Paul closed with a final admonition that the husband love his wife and that the wife reverence (respect) her husband, both of which require the power of the Holy Spirit.

If Christian husbands and wives have the power of the Spirit to enable them, and the example of Christ to encourage them, why do too many Christian marriages fail? Somebody is out of the will of God. Just because two Christians know each other and get along together does not mean they are supposed to get married. In fact, not every believer is supposed to marry. It is sometimes God's will for a Christian to remain single (Matt. 19:12; 1 Cor. 7:7–9). It is wrong for a believer to marry an unbeliever, but it is also wrong for two Christians to marry out of the will of God.

But even if two Christians marry in the will of God, they must stay in God's will if their home is to be the creative fellowship God wants it to be. "The fruit of the Spirit is love" (Gal. 5:22), and unless both husband and wife are walking in the Spirit they cannot share the love of Christ, the love that is so beautifully described in 1 Corinthians 13. The root of most marital problems is sin, and the root of all sin is selfishness. Submission to Christ and to one another is the only way to overcome selfishness, for when we submit, the Holy Spirit can fill us and enable us to love one another in a sacrificial, sanctifying, satisfying way—the way Christ loves the church.

To experience the fullness of the Spirit a person must first possess the Spirit—be a Christian. Then there must be a sincere desire to glorify Christ, since this is why the Holy Spirit was given (John 16:14). We do not use the Holy Spirit; He uses us. There must be a deep thirst for God's fullness, a confession that we cannot do His will apart from His power. We must claim the promise of John 7:37–39: "If any man thirst, let him come unto me, and drink!" By faith yield yourself to Christ; by faith ask Him for the fullness of the Spirit. By faith receive. When you find yourself joyful, thankful, and submissive, you will know that God has answered.

One more important factor should be considered. The Spirit of God uses the Word of God to work in our lives. Read Colossians 3:16—4:1 and you will see a parallel to our Ephesians passage. And you will note that to be filled with the Word of God produces joy, thanksgiving, and submission. In other words, when you are controlled by the Word of God, you are filled with the Spirit of God. Not only husbands and wives, but all Christians need to spend time daily letting the Word of Christ dwell in them richly, for then the Spirit of God can work in our lives to make us joyful, thankful, and submissive. And this means heaven in the home—or wherever God may put us.

CHAPTER TWELVE
Ephesians 6:1–9
LIVING THE LORDSHIP OF CHRIST

After watching a television presentation about rebellious youth, a husband said to his wife, "What a mess! Where did our generation go wrong?" The wife calmly answered, "We had children."

It seems no matter where we look in modern society, we see antagonism, division, and rebellion. Husbands and wives are divorcing each other; children are rebelling against their parents; and employers and employees are seeking for new ways to avoid strikes and keep the machinery of industry running productively. We have tried education, legislation, and every other approach, but nothing seems to work. Paul's solution to the antagonisms in the home and in society was *regeneration*—a new heart from God and a new submission to Christ and to one another. God's great program is to "gather together in one all things in Christ" (Eph. 1:10). Paul indicated that this spiritual harmony begins in the lives of Christians who are submitted to the lordship of Christ.

In this section Paul admonished four groups of Christians about how they could have harmony in Christ.

Christian Children (6:1–3)

Paul did not tell the parents to admonish the children; he did it himself. Children were present in the assembly when this letter was read. Did they understand all that Paul wrote? Do *we* understand it all? Christian families attended the public worship together, and no doubt the parents explained the Word to the children when they were at home. He gave them four reasons why they should obey their parents.

They are Christians ("in the Lord," v. 1a). This argument is an application of the theme of the entire section, which is "submitting yourselves one to another in the fear of God" (Eph. 5:21). When a person becomes a Christian, he is not released from normal obligations of life. If anything, his faith in Christ ought to make him a better child in the home.

To the Colossians Paul enforced his admonition with "for this is well pleasing unto the Lord" (Col. 3:20). Here is harmony in the home: the wife submits to the husband "as unto Christ"; the husband loves his wife "even as Christ also loved the church"; and the children obey "in the Lord."

Obedience is right (v. 1b). There is an order in nature, ordained of God, that argues for the rightness of an action. Since the parents brought the child into the world, and since they have more knowledge and wisdom than the child, it is right that the child obey his parents. Even young animals are taught to obey. The "modern version" of Ephesians 6:1 would be, "Parents, obey your children, for this will keep them happy and bring peace to the home." But this is contrary to God's order in nature.

Obedience is commanded (v. 2a). Here Paul cited the fifth commandment (Ex. 20:12; Deut. 5:16) and applies it to the New Testament believer. This does not mean that the Christian is "under the law," for Christ has set us free from both the curse and the bondage of the law (Gal. 3:13; 5:1). But the righteousness of the law is still a revelation of the holiness of God, and the Holy Spirit enables us to practice that

righteousness in our daily lives (Rom. 8:1–4). All of the Ten Commandments are repeated in the New Testament epistles for the Christian to observe except "Remember the sabbath day, to keep it holy." It is just as wrong for a New Testament Christian to dishonor his parents as it was for an Old Testament Jew.

To "honor" our parents means much more than simply to obey them. It means to show them respect and love, to care for them as long as they need us, and to seek to bring honor to them by the way we live. A young couple came to see me about getting married, and I asked if their parents agreed to the wedding. They looked at each other in embarrassment, then confessed, "We were hoping you wouldn't ask about that." I spent the next hour trying to convince them that their parents had a right to rejoice in this event, and that to exclude them would cause wounds that might never heal. "Even if they are not believers," I said, "they are your parents, and you owe them love and respect." They finally agreed, and the plans we made together made both families happy. Had we followed the couple's original plans, the two of them would have lost their testimony with their relatives, but, instead, they were able to give a good witness for Jesus Christ.

Obedience brings blessing (vv. 2b–3). The fifth commandment has a promise attached to it: "That thy days may be long upon the land which the Lord thy God giveth thee" (Ex. 20:12). This promise originally applied to the Jews as they entered Canaan, but Paul applied it to believers today. He substituted "earth" for "land" and told us that the Christian child who honors his parents can expect two blessings. It will be well with him, and he will live long on the earth. This does not mean that everyone who died young dishonored his parents. He was stating a principle: when children obey their parents in the Lord, they will escape a good deal of sin and danger and thus avoid the things that could threaten or shorten their lives. But life is not measured only by quantity of time. It is also measured by quality of experience. God enriches the life of the obedient child no matter how long he may live on the earth. Sin always robs us; obedience always enriches us.

So, the child must learn early to obey father and mother, not only because they are his parents, but also because God has commanded it to be so. Disobedience to parents is rebellion against God. The sad situation in homes today is the result of rejecting God's Word (Rom. 1:28–30; 2 Tim. 3:1–5). By nature, a child is selfish, but in the power of the Holy Spirit, a child can learn to obey his parents and glorify God.

Christian Fathers (6:4)

If left to themselves, children will be rebels, so it is necessary for the parents to train their children. Years ago, the then Duke of Windsor said, "Everything in the American home is controlled by switches—except the children!" The Bible records the sad results of parents neglecting their children, either by being bad examples to them or failing to discipline them properly. David pampered Absalom and set him a bad example, and the results were tragic. Eli failed to discipline his sons, and they brought disgrace to his name and defeat to the nation of Israel. In his latter years, even Isaac pampered Esau, while his wife showed favoritism to Jacob; and the result was a divided home. Jacob was showing favoritism to Joseph when God providentially rescued the lad and made a man out of him in Egypt. Paul told us that the father has several responsibilities toward his children.

He must not provoke them. In Paul's day, the father had supreme authority over the family. When a baby was born into a Roman family, for example, it was brought out and laid before the father. If he picked it up, it meant he was accepting it into the home. But if he did not pick it up, it meant the child was rejected. It could be sold, given away, or even killed by exposure. No doubt a father's love would overcome such monstrous acts, but these practices were legal in that day. Paul told the parents, "Don't use your authority to abuse the child, but to encourage and build the child." To the Colossians he wrote, "Fathers, provoke not your children to anger, lest they be discouraged" (Col. 3:21). So, the opposite of "provoke" is "encourage."

I was addressing a group of Christian students on the subject of prayer, and was pointing out that our Father in heaven is always available when we call. To illustrate it, I told them that the receptionist at our church office has a list of names prepared by me, and these people could get to me at any time, no matter what I was doing. Even if I was in a staff meeting or in a counseling session, if any of these people phoned, she was to call me immediately. At the top of this list was my family. Even if the matter seems to me inconsequential, I want my family to know that I am available. After the service, one of the students said to me, "Would you adopt me? I can never get through to my father, and I need his encouragement so much!"

Fathers provoke their children and discourage them by saying one thing and doing another—by always blaming and never praising, by being inconsistent and unfair in discipline, and by showing favoritism in the home, by making promises and not keeping them, and by making light of problems that, to the children, are very important. Christian parents need the fullness of the Spirit so they can be sensitive to the needs and problems of their children.

He must nurture them. The text reads, "But nurture them in the discipline and admonition of the Lord." The verb translated "bring them up" is the same word that is translated "nourisheth" in Ephesians 5:29. The Christian husband is to nourish his wife and his children by sharing love and encouragement in the Lord. It is not enough to nurture the children physically by providing food, shelter, and clothing. He must also nurture them emotionally and spiritually. The development of the Boy Jesus is our example: "And Jesus increased in wisdom and stature, and in favor with God and man" (Luke 2:52). Here is

balanced growth: intellectual, physical, spiritual, and social. Nowhere in the Bible is the training of children assigned to agencies outside the home, no matter how they might assist. God looks to the parents for the kind of training that the children need.

He must discipline them. The word "nurture" carries with it the idea of learning through discipline. It is translated "chastening" in Hebrews 12. Some modern psychologists oppose the old-fashioned idea of discipline, and many educators follow their philosophy. "Let the children express themselves!" they tell us. "If you discipline them, you may warp their characters." Yet discipline is a basic principle of life and an evidence of love. "Whom the Lord loveth he chasteneth" (Heb. 12:6). "He that spareth him chasteneth him diligently" (Prov. 13:24, literal translation).

We must be sure, however, that we discipline our children in the right manner. To begin with, we must discipline in love and not in anger, lest we injure either the body or the spirit of the child, or possibly both. If we are not disciplined, we surely cannot discipline others, and "flying off the handle" never made either a better child or a better parent.

Also, our discipline must be fair and consistent "My father would use a cannon to kill a mosquito!" a teenager once told me. "I either get away with murder, or get blamed for everything!" Consistent, loving discipline gives assurance to the child. He may not agree with us, but at least he knows that we care enough to build some protective walls around him until he can take care of himself.

"I never knew how far I could go," a wayward girl told me, "because my parents never cared enough to discipline me. I figured that if it wasn't important to them, why should it be important to me?"

He must instruct and encourage them. This is the meaning of the word *admonition*. The father and mother not only use actions to raise the child, but also words. In the book of Proverbs, for example, we have an inspired record of a father sharing wise counsel with his son. Our children do not always appreciate our counsel, but that does not eliminate the obligation we have to instruct and encourage them. Of course, our instruction must always be tied to the Word of God (see 2 Tim. 3:13–17).

When the Supreme Court handed down its ruling against required prayer in the public schools, the famous editorial cartoonist Herblock published a cartoon in the *Washington Post* showing an angry father waving a newspaper at his family and shouting, "What do they expect us to do—listen to the kids pray at home?" The answer is yes! Home is the place where the children ought to learn about the Lord and the Christian life. It is time that Christian parents stop passing the buck to Sunday school teachers and Christian day-school teachers, and start nurturing their children.

Christian Servants (6:5–8)

The word *servants* undoubtedly refers to Christian

slaves, but we may certainly apply these words to the Christian employee today. There were probably sixty million slaves in the Roman Empire in that day, and slavery was an accepted institution. Nowhere in the New Testament is slavery *per se* attacked or condemned, though the overall thrust of the gospel is against it. Paul's ministry was not to overthrow the Roman government or any of its institutions, but to preach the gospel and win the lost to Christ. Certainly the results of his evangelism ultimately led to the overthrow of the Roman Empire, but that was not Paul's main motive. Just as the preaching of Wesley and Whitefield resulted in the abolition of slavery and child labor, the elevation of women, and the care of the needy, so Paul's ministry contributed to the death of slavery and the encouragement of freedom. However, he was careful not to confuse the social system with the spiritual order in the church (1 Cor. 7:20–24).

Paul admonished the servants to be obedient, with several good reasons. First, they were really serving Christ. True, they had "masters according to the flesh," but their true Master was in heaven (Eph. 6:9). The fact that an employee and his employer are both Christians is no excuse for either one to do less work. Rather, it is a good reason to be more faithful to each other. The employee should show proper respect for employer, and not try to take advantage of him. He should devote his full attention and energy to the job at hand ("singleness of heart"). The best way to be a witness on the job is to do a good day's work. The Christian worker will avoid "eye service"—working only when the boss is watching, or working extra hard when he is watching, to give the impression he is doing a very good job.

The second reason is that doing a good job is the will of God. Christianity knows nothing of sacred and secular. A Christian can perform any good work as a ministry to Christ, to the glory of God. For this reason, the worker must do his job "from the heart," since he is serving Christ and doing the will of God. There were tasks assigned to these slaves that they detested, but they were to perform them just the same, so long as they were not disobeying the will of God. "Singleness of heart" and "doing the will of God from the heart" both indicate the importance of a right heart attitude on the job.

Paul's third argument is that they will be rewarded by the Lord (Eph. 6:8). In that day, slaves were treated like pieces of property, no matter how well educated they might be. An educated, cultured slave who became a Christian might receive even harsher treatment from his master because of his faith, but harsh treatment was not to keep him from doing his best (1 Peter 2:18–25). We are to serve Christ, not men. We shall receive our rewards from Christ, not from men.

Christian Masters (6:9)

The Christian faith does not bring about harmony by erasing social or cultural distinctions. Servants are still servants when they trust Christ, and masters are still masters. Rather, the Christian faith brings harmony by working in the heart. Christ gives us a new motivation, not a new organization. Both servant and master are serving the Lord and seeking to please Him, and in this way they are able to work together to the glory of God. What are the responsibilities of a Christian master (or employer) to his workers?

He must seek their welfare. "Do the same things unto them." If the employer expects the workers to do their best for him, he must do his best for them. The master must serve the Lord from his heart if he expects his servants to do the same. He must not exploit them.

One of the greatest examples of this in the Bible is Boaz in the book of Ruth. He greeted his workers with "The Lord be with you." And they replied, "The Lord bless thee" (Ruth 2:4). Boaz was sensitive to the needs of his workers and generous to the stranger, Ruth. His relationship with his workers was one of mutual respect and a desire to glorify the Lord. It is unfortunate when an employee says, "My boss is supposed to be a Christian, but you'd never know it!"

He must not threaten. Roman masters had the power and lawful authority to kill a slave who was rebellious, though few of them did so. Slaves cost too much money to destroy them. Paul suggested that the Christian master has a better way to encourage obedience and service than threats of punishment. The negative power of fear could result in the worker doing less instead of more, and this kind of motivation could not be continued over a long period of time. Far better was the positive motivation of "that which is just and equal" (Col. 4:1). Let a man share the results of his labor and he will work better and harder. Even the Old Testament gives this same counsel: "Thou shalt not rule over him with rigor, but shalt fear thy God" (Lev. 25:43).

He must be submitted to the Lord. "Your master also is in heaven" (Eph. 6:9). This is practicing the lordship of Christ. The wife submits to her own husband "as unto the Lord" (Eph. 5:22), and the husband loves the wife "as Christ also loved the church" (Eph. 5:25). Children obey their parents "in the Lord" (Eph. 6:1), and parents raise their children "in the nurture and admonition of the Lord" (Eph. 6:4). Servants are obedient "as unto Christ" (Eph. 6:5), and masters treat their servants as their "Master in heaven" would have them do. Each person, in submission to the Lord, has no problems submitting to those over him.

Jesus said the way to be a ruler is first to be a servant (Matt. 25:21). The person who is not under authority has no right to exercise authority. This explains why many of the great men of the Bible were first servants before God made them rulers: Joseph, Moses, Joshua, David, and Nehemiah are just a few examples. Even after a man becomes a leader, he must still lead by serving. An African proverb says, "The chief is servant of all." "And whosoever will be chief among you, let him be your servant" (Matt. 20:27).

A friend of mine was promoted to a place of executive leadership and, unfortunately, it went to his head. He enjoyed all of his executive privileges and more, and never lost an opportunity to remind his employees who was in charge. But he lost the respect of his workers, and production and efficiency went down so fast that the board had to replace him. Because my friend forgot that he had a "Master in heaven," he failed to be a good "master on earth."

He must not play favorites. God is no respecter of persons. He will judge a master or a servant if he sins, or He will reward a master or a servant if he obeys (Eph. 6:8). A Christian employer cannot take privileges with God simply because of his position; nor should a Christian employer play favorites with those under his authority. Paul warned Timothy to "observe these things without preferring one before another, doing nothing by partiality" (1 Tim. 5:21). One of the fastest ways for a leader to divide his followers and lose their confidence is for the leader to play favorites and show partiality.

This closes the section we have called "Walk in Harmony." If we are filled with the Holy Spirit and are joyful, thankful, and submissive, then we can enjoy harmony in the relationships of life as we live and work with other Christians. We will also find it easier to work with and witness to the unbelievers who may disagree with us. The fruit of the Spirit is love, and love is the greatest adhesive in the world!

CHAPTER THIRTEEN
Ephesians 6:10–24
YOU'RE IN THE ARMY NOW!

Sooner or later every believer discovers that the Christian life is a battleground, not a playground, and that he faces an enemy who is much stronger than he is—apart from the Lord. That Paul should use the military to illustrate the believer's conflict with Satan is reasonable. He himself was chained to a Roman soldier (Eph. 6:20), and his readers were certainly familiar with soldiers and the equipment they used. In fact, military illustrations were favorites with Paul (2 Cor. 10:4; 1 Tim. 6:12; 2 Tim. 2:3; 4:7).

As Christians, we face three enemies: the world, the flesh, and the devil (Eph. 2:1–3). "The world" refers to the system around us that is opposed to God, that caters to "the lust of the flesh, and the lust of the eyes, and the pride of life" (1 John 2:15–17). "Society apart from God" is a simple, but accurate, definition of "the world." "The flesh" is the old nature that we inherited from Adam, a nature that is opposed to God and can do nothing spiritual to please God. By His death and resurrection, Christ overcame the world (John 16:33; Gal. 6:14), and the flesh (Rom. 6:1–6; Gal. 2:20), and the devil (Eph. 1:19–23). In other words, as believers, we do not fight *for* victory—we fight *from* victory!

The Spirit of God enables us, by faith, to appropriate Christ's victory for ourselves.

In these closing verses of the letter, Paul discussed four topics so that his readers, by understanding and applying these truths, might walk in victory.

The Enemy (6:10–12)
The intelligence corps plays a vital part in warfare because it enables the officers to know and understand the enemy. Unless we know who the enemy is, where he is, and what he can do, we have a difficult time defeating him. Not only in Ephesians 6, but throughout the entire Bible, God instructs us about the enemy, so there is no reason for us to be caught off guard.

The leader—the devil. The enemy has many different names. *Devil* means "accuser," because he accuses God's people day and night before the throne of God (Rev. 12:7–11). *Satan* means "adversary," because he is the enemy of God. He is also called the tempter (Matt. 4:3), and the murderer and the liar (John 8:44). He is compared to a lion (1 Peter 5:8), a serpent (Gen. 3:1; Rev. 12:9), and an angel of light (2 Cor. 11:13–15), as well as "the god of this age" (2 Cor. 4:4 NIV).

Where did he come from, this spirit-creature that seeks to oppose God and defeat His work? Many students believe that in the original creation, he was "Lucifer, son of the morning" (Isa. 14:12–15) and that he was cast down because of his pride and his desire to occupy God's throne. Many mysteries are connected with the origin of Satan, but what he is doing and where he is going are certainly no mystery! Since he is a created being, and not eternal (as God is), he is limited in his knowledge and activity. Unlike God, Satan is not all-knowing, all-powerful, or everywhere-present. Then how does he accomplish so much in so many different parts of the world? The answer is in his organized helpers.

Satan's helpers. Paul called them "principalities … powers … rulers … spiritual wickedness in high places" (Eph. 6:12). Charles B. Williams translated it, "For our contest is not with human foes alone, but with the rulers, authorities, and cosmic powers of this dark world; that is, with the spirit forces of evil challenging us in the heavenly contest" (WILLIAMS). This suggests a definite army of demonic creatures that assist Satan in his attacks against believers. The apostle John hinted that one third of the angels fell with Satan when he rebelled against God (Rev. 12:4), and Daniel wrote that Satan's angels struggle against God's angels for control of the affairs of nations (Dan. 10:13–20). A spiritual battle is going on in this world and in the sphere of "the heavenlies," and you and I are a part of this battle. Knowing this makes "walking in victory" a vitally important thing to us—and to God.

The important point is that our battle is not against human beings. It is against spiritual powers. We are wasting our time fighting people when we ought to be fighting the devil who seeks to control people and make them oppose the work of God. During Paul's ministry in Ephesus, a riot took place that could have destroyed the church (Acts 19:21–41). It wasn't caused only by Demetrius and his associates, for behind them were Satan and his associates. Certainly Paul and the church prayed, and the opposition was silenced. The advice of the king of Syria to his soldiers can be applied to our spiritual battle: "Fight neither with small nor great, save only with the king" (1 Kings 22:31).

Satan's abilities. The admonitions Paul gave indicate that Satan is a strong enemy (Eph. 6:10–12) and that we need the power of God to be able to stand against him. Never underestimate the power of the devil. He is not compared to a lion and a dragon just for fun! The book of Job tells what his power can do to a man's body, home, wealth, and friends. Jesus called Satan a thief who comes "to steal, and to kill, and to destroy" (John 10:10). Not only is Satan strong, but he is also wise and subtle, and we fight against "the wiles of the devil." *Wiles* means "cunning, crafty arts, strategems." The Christian cannot afford to be "ignorant of his devices" (2 Cor. 2:11). Some men are cunning and crafty and "lie in wait to deceive" (Eph. 4:14), but behind them is the arch-deceiver, Satan. He masquerades as an angel of light (2 Cor. 11:14) and seeks to blind men's minds to the truth of God's Word. The fact that Paul uses the word *wrestle* indicates that we are involved in a hand-to-hand battle and are not mere spectators at a game. Satan wants to use our external enemy, the world, and our internal enemy, the flesh, to defeat us. His weapons and battle plans are formidable.

The Equipment (6:13–17)

Since we are fighting against enemies in the spirit world, we need special equipment both for offense and defense. God has provided the "whole armor" for us, and we dare not omit any part. Satan looks for that unguarded area where he can get a beachhead (Eph. 4:27). Paul commanded his readers to put on the armor, take the weapons, and withstand Satan, all of which we do by faith. Knowing that Christ has already conquered Satan, and that the spiritual armor and weapons are available, by faith we accept what God gives us and go out to meet the foe. The day is evil, and the enemy is evil, but "if God be for us, who can be against us?" (Rom. 8:31).

The girdle of truth (v. 14a). Satan is a liar (John 8:44), but the believer whose life is controlled by truth will defeat him. The girdle held the other parts of the armor together, and truth is the integrating force in the life of the victorious Christian. A man of integrity, with a clear conscience, can face the enemy without fear. The girdle also held the sword. Unless we practice the truth, we cannot use the Word of truth. Once a lie gets into the life of a believer, everything begins to fall apart. For over a year, King David lied about his sin with Bathsheba, and nothing went right. Psalms 32 and 51 tell of the price he paid.

The breastplace of righteousness (v. 14b). This piece of armor, made of metal plates or chains, covered the body from the neck to the waist, both front and back. It symbolizes the believer's righteousness in Christ (2 Cor. 5:21) as well as his righteous life in Christ (Eph. 4:24). Satan is the accuser, but he cannot accuse the believer who is living a godly life in the power of the Spirit. The life we live either fortifies us against Satan's attacks or makes it easier for him to defeat us (2 Cor. 6:1–10). When Satan accuses the Christian, it is the righteousness of Christ that assures the believer of his salvation. But our positional righteousness in Christ, without practical righteousness in the daily life, only gives Satan opportunity to attack us.

The shoes of the gospel (v. 15). The Roman soldier wore sandals with hobnails in the soles to give him better footing for the battle. If we are going to "stand" and "withstand," then we need the shoes of the gospel. Because we have the peace with God (Rom. 5:1) that comes from the gospel, we need not fear the attack of Satan or men. We must be at peace with God and with each other if we are to defeat the devil (James 4:1–7). But the shoes have another meaning. We must be prepared each day to share the gospel of peace with a lost world. The most victorious Christian is a witnessing Christian. If we wear the shoes of the gospel, then we have the "beautiful feet" mentioned in Isaiah 52:7 and Romans 10:15. Satan has declared war, but you and I are ambassadors of peace (2 Cor. 5:18–21); and, as such, we take the gospel of peace wherever we go.

The shield of faith (v. 16). The shield was large, usually about four feet by two feet, made of wood, and covered with tough leather. As the soldier held it before him, it protected him from spears, arrows, and "fiery darts." The edges of these shields were so constructed that an entire line of soldiers could interlock shields and march into the enemy like a solid wall. This suggests that we Christians are not in the battle alone. The "faith" mentioned here is not saving faith, but rather living faith, a trust in the promises and the power of God. Faith is a defensive weapon that protects us from Satan's fiery darts. In Paul's day, arrows, dipped in some inflammable substance and ignited, were shot at the enemy. Satan shoots "fiery darts" at our hearts and minds: lies, blasphemous thoughts, hateful thoughts about others, doubts, and burning desires for sin. If we do not by faith quench these darts, they will light a fire within and we will disobey God. We never know when Satan will shoot a dart at us, so we must always walk by faith and use the shield of faith.

The helmet of salvation (v. 17). Satan wants to attack the mind, the way he defeated Eve (Gen. 3; 2 Cor. 11:1–3). The helmet refers to the mind controlled by God. It is too bad that many Christians have the idea that the intellect is not important, when in reality it plays a vital role in Christian growth, service, and victory. When God controls the mind, Satan cannot lead the believer astray. The Christian who studies his Bible and learns the meaning of Bible doctrines is not going to be led astray too easily. We need to be "taught by him, as the truth is in Jesus" (Eph. 4:21). We are to "grow in grace, and in the knowledge of our Lord and Saviour Jesus Christ" (2 Peter 3:18). Wherever Paul ministered, he taught the new converts the truths of the Word of God, and this helmet protected them from Satan's lies.

One Sunday afternoon, I visited a man who had been a deacon in a local church, but was at that time involved in a false cult. We sat at the table with open Bibles, and I tried to show him the truth of God's Word, but it seemed his mind was blinded by lies. "How did you happen to turn away from a Bible-preaching church and get involved in this belief?" I asked, and his reply stunned me.

"Preacher, I blame the church. I didn't know anything about the Bible, and they didn't teach me much more. I wanted to study the Bible, but nobody told me how. Then they made me a deacon, and I wasn't ready for it. It was too much for me. I heard this man preaching the Bible over the radio and it sounded as if he knew something. I started reading his magazine and studying his books, and now I'm convinced he's right."

What a tragedy that when his local church took him in, they failed to fit him with the helmet of salvation. Had they practiced the truth found in 2 Timothy 2:2, this man might not have been a casualty in the battle.

The sword of the Spirit (v. 17b). This sword is the offensive weapon God provides us. The Roman soldier wore on his girdle a short sword which was used for close-in fighting. Hebrews 4:12 compares the Word of God to a sword, because it is sharp and is able to pierce the inner man just as a material sword pierces the body. You and I were "cut to the heart" (Acts 2:37; 5:33) when the Word convicted us of our sins. Peter tried to use a sword to defend Jesus in the garden (Luke 22:47–51), but he learned at Pentecost that the "sword of the Spirit" does a much better job. Moses also tried to conquer with a physical sword (Ex. 2:11–15), only to discover that God's Word alone was more than enough to defeat Egypt.

A material sword pierces the body, but the Word of God pierces the heart. The more you use a physical sword, the duller it becomes, but using God's Word only makes it sharper in our lives. A physical sword requires the hand of a soldier, but the sword of the Spirit has its own power, for it is "living and powerful" (Heb. 4:12). The Spirit wrote the Word, and the Spirit wields the Word as we take it by faith and use it. A physical sword wounds to hurt and kill, while the sword of the Spirit wounds to heal and give life. But when we use the sword against Satan, we are out to deal him a blow that will cripple him and keep him from hindering God's work.

When He was tempted by Satan in the wilderness, Christ used the sword of the Spirit and defeated the enemy. Three times Jesus said, "It is written" (Luke 4:1–13). Note that Satan can also quote the Word— "For it is written" (Luke 4:10)—but he does not quote it completely. Satan tries to use the Word of God to confuse us, so it is important that we know every word that God has given us. "You can prove anything by the Bible," someone said. True—if you take verses out of context, leave out words, and apply verses to Christians today that do not really apply. The better you know the Word of God, the easier it will be for you to detect Satan's lies and reject his offers.

In one sense, the "whole armor of God" is a picture of Jesus Christ. Christ is the Truth (John 14:6), and He is our righteousness (2 Cor. 5:21) and our peace (Eph. 2:14). His faithfulness makes possible our faith (Gal. 2:20); He is our salvation (Luke 2:30); and He is the Word of God (John 1:1, 14). This means that when we trusted Christ, we received the armor. Paul told the Romans what to do with the armor (Rom. 13:11–14): wake up (Rom. 13:11), cast off sin, and "put on the armor of light" (Rom. 13:12). We do this by putting "on the Lord Jesus Christ" (Rom. 13:14). By faith, put on the armor and trust God for the victory. Once and for all, we have put on the armor at the moment of salvation. But there must be a daily appropriation. When King David put off his armor and returned to his palace, he was in greater danger than when he was on the battlefield (2 Sam. 11). We are never out of reach of Satan's devices, so we must never be without the whole armor of God.

The Energy (6:18–20)

Prayer is the energy that enables the Christian soldier to wear the armor and wield the sword. We cannot fight the battle in our own power, no matter how strong or talented we may think we are. When Amalek attacked Israel, Moses went to the mountaintop to pray, while Joshua used the sword down in the valley (Ex. 17:8–16). It took both to defeat Amalek—Moses' intercession on the mountain and Joshua's use of the sword in the valley. Prayer is the power for victory, but not just any kind of prayer. Paul told how to pray if we would defeat Satan.

Pray always. This obviously does not mean "always saying prayers." We are not heard for our "much speaking" (Matt. 6:7). "Pray without ceasing" (1 Thess. 5:17) says to us, "Always be in communion with the Lord. Keep the receiver off the hook!" Never have to say when you pray, "Lord, we come into Thy presence," because you never left His presence! A Christian must "pray always" because he is always subject to temptations and attacks of the devil. A surprise attack has defeated more than one believer who forgot to "pray without ceasing."

Pray with all prayer. There is more than one kind of praying: prayer, supplication, intercession, thanksgiving (Phil. 4:6; 1 Tim. 2:1). The believer who prays only to ask for things is missing out on blessings that come with intercessions and giving of thanks. In fact, thanksgiving is a great prayer weapon for defeating Satan. "Praise changes things" as much as "prayer changes things." Intercession for others can bring victory to our own lives. "And the Lord turned the captivity of Job when he prayed for his friends" (Job 42:10).

Pray in the Spirit. The Bible formula is that we pray to the Father, through the Son, and in the Spirit. Romans 8:26–27 tells us that only in the Spirit's power can we pray in the will of God. Otherwise, our praying could be selfish and out of the will of God. In the Old Testament tabernacle, there was a small golden altar standing before the veil, and here the priest burned the incense (Ex. 30:1–10; Luke 1:1–11). The incense is a picture of prayer. It had to be mixed according to God's plan and could not be counterfeited by man. The fire on the altar is a picture of the Holy Spirit, for it is He who takes our prayers and "ignites" them in the will of God. It is possible to pray fervently in the flesh and never get through to God. It is also possible to pray quietly in the Spirit and see God's hand do great things.

Pray with your eyes open. *Watching* means "keeping on the alert." The phrase "watch and pray" occurs often in the Bible. When Nehemiah was repairing the walls of Jerusalem and the enemy was trying to stop the work, Nehemiah defeated the enemy by watching and praying. "Nevertheless we made our prayer unto our God, and set a watch" (Neh. 4:9). "Watch and pray" is the secret of victory over the world (Mark 13:33), the flesh (Mark 14:38), and the devil (Eph. 6:18). Peter went to sleep when he should have been praying, and the result was victory for Satan (Mark 14:29–31, 67–72). God expects us to use our God-given senses, led by the Spirit, so that we detect Satan when he is beginning to work.

Keep on praying. The word *perseverance* simply means "to stick to it and not quit." The early believers prayed this way (Acts 1:14; 2:42; 6:4), and we also should pray this way (Rom. 12:12). Perseverance in prayer does not mean we are trying to twist God's arm, but rather that we are deeply concerned and burdened and cannot rest until we get God's answer. As Robert Law put it, "Prayer is not getting man's will done in heaven; it is getting God's will done on earth" (*Tests of Life*, [Grand Rapids, Mich.: Baker, 1968]). Most of us quit praying just before God is about to give the victory. Not everybody is so constituted that he can sincerely spend a whole night in prayer, but all of us can persevere in prayer far more than we do. The early church prayed without ceasing when Peter was in prison and, at the last moment, God gave them their answer (Acts 12:1–19). Keep on praying until the Spirit stops you or the Father answers you. Just about the time you feel like quitting, God will give the answer.

Pray for all the saints. The Lord's Prayer begins with "Our Father"—not "My Father." We pray as part of a great family that is also talking to God, and we ought to pray for the other members of the family. Even Paul asked for the prayer support of the Ephesians—and he had been to the third heaven and back. If Paul needed the prayers of the saints, how much more do you and I need them! If my prayers help another believer defeat Satan, then that victory will help me too. Note that Paul did not ask them to pray for his comfort or safety, but for the effectiveness of his witness and ministry.

The Encouragement (6:21–24)

We are not fighting the battle alone. There are other believers who stand with us in the fight, and we ought to be careful to encourage one another. Paul encouraged the Ephesians; Tychicus was an encouragement to Paul (Acts 20:4); and Paul was going to send Tychicus to Ephesus to be an encouragement to them. Paul was not the kind of missionary who kept his affairs to himself. He wanted the people of God to know what God was doing, how their prayers were being answered, and what Satan was doing to oppose the work. His motive was not selfish. He was not trying to get something out of them.

What an encouragement it is to be a part of the family of God! Nowhere in the New Testament do we find an isolated believer. Christians are like sheep; they flock together. The church is an army, and the soldiers need to stand together and fight together.

Note the words Paul used as he closed this letter: peace—love—faith—grace! He was a prisoner of Rome, yet he was richer than the emperor. No matter what our circumstances may be, in Jesus Christ we are "blessed with all spiritual blessings"!

PHILIPPIANS

OUTLINE

Key theme: The joy of the Lord
Key verse: Philippians 3:1

I. THE SINGLE MIND (1)
    A. The fellowship of the gospel—1:1–11
    B. The furtherance of the gospel—1:12–26
    C. The faith of the gospel—1:27–30

II. THE SUBMISSIVE MIND (2)
    A. The example of Christ—2:1–11
    B. The example of Paul—2:12–18
    C. The example of Timothy—2:19–24
    D. The example of Epaphroditus—2:25–30

III. THE SPIRITUAL MIND (3)
    A. Paul's past—3:1–11 (the accountant—"I count")
    B. Paul's present—3:12–16 (the athlete—"I press")
    C. Paul's future—3:17–21 (the alien—"I look")

IV. THE SECURE MIND (4)
    A. God's peace—4:1–9
    B. God's power—4:10–13
    C. God's provision—4:14–23

CONTENTS

CHAPTER ONE
Philippians 1:1–11
HOW TO INCREASE YOUR JOY

How about corning over to the house for some fellowship?" "What a golf game! Man, did we have great fellowship!"

"The fellowship at the retreat was just terrific!"

That word *fellowship* seems to mean many things to many different people. Perhaps, like a worn coin, it may be losing its true impression. If so, we had better take some steps to rescue it. After all, a good Bible word like *fellowship* needs to stay in circulation as long as possible.

In spite of his difficult circumstances as a prisoner in Rome, Paul was rejoicing. The secret of his joy was the *single mind;* he lived for Christ and the gospel. (Christ is named eighteen times in Philippians 1, and the gospel is mentioned six times.) "For to me to live is Christ, and to die is gain" (Phil. 1:21). But what really is "the single mind"? It is the attitude that says, "It makes no difference what happens to me, just as long as Christ is glorified and the gospel shared with others." Paul rejoiced in spite of his circumstances, because his circumstances strengthened the *fellowship of the gospel* (Phil. 1:1–11), promoted *the furtherance of the gospel* (Phil. 1:12–26), and guarded *the faith of the gospel* (Phil. 1:27–30).

The word *fellowship* simply means "to have in common" But true Christian fellowship is really much deeper than sharing coffee and pie, or even enjoying a golf game together. Too often what we think is "fellowship" is really only acquaintanceship or friendship. You cannot have fellowship with someone unless you have something in common, and for Christian fellowship, this means the possessing of eternal life within the heart. Unless a person has trusted Christ as his Savior, he knows nothing of "the fellowship of the gospel." In Philippians 2:1, Paul wrote about "the fellowship of the Spirit," because when a person is born again he receives the gift of the Spirit (Rom. 8:9). There is also "the fellowship of his sufferings" (Phil. 3:10). When we share what we have with others, this is also fellowship (Phil. 4:15, translated "communicate" in kjv).

So, true Christian fellowship is much more than having a name on a church roll or being present at a meeting. It is possible to be close to people physically and miles away from them spiritually. One of the sources of Christian joy is this fellowship that believers have in Jesus Christ. Paul was in Rome, his friends were miles away in Philippi, but their spiritual fellowship was real and satisfying. When you have the single mind, you will not complain about circumstances because you know that difficult circumstances will result in the strengthening of the fellowship of the gospel.

Paul used three thoughts in Philippians 1:1–11 that describe true Christian fellowship: I have you in my mind (Phil. 1:3–6), I have you in my heart (Phil. 1:7–8), I have you in my prayers (Phil. 1:9–11).

I Have You in My Mind (1:3–6)

Isn't it remarkable that Paul was thinking of others and not of himself? As he awaited his trial in Rome, Paul's mind went back to the believers in Philippi, and every recollection he had brought him joy. Read Acts 16; you may discover that some things happened to Paul at Philippi, the memory of which could produce sorrow. He was illegally arrested and beaten, was placed in the stocks, and was humiliated before the people. But even those memories brought joy to Paul, because it was through this suffering that the jailer found Christ! Paul recalled Lydia and her household, the poor slave girl who had been demon possessed, and the other dear Christians at Philippi, and each recollection was a source of joy. (It is worth asking, "Am I the kind of Christian who brings joy to my pastor's mind when he thinks of me?")

It is possible that Philippians 1:5 is talking about their *financial* fellowship with Paul, a topic he picks up again in Philippians 4:14–19. The church at Philippi was the only church that entered into fellowship with Paul to help support his ministry. The "good work" of Philippians 1:6 may refer to the sharing of their means; it was started by the Lord, and Paul was sure the Lord would continue it and complete it.

But we will not go astray if we apply these verses to the work of salvation and Christian living. We are not saved by our good works (Eph. 2:8–9). Salvation is the good work God does in us when we trust His Son. In Philippians 2:12–13 we are told that God continues to work in us through His Spirit. In other words, salvation includes a threefold work:

- the work God does *for* us—salvation;
- the work God does *in* us—sanctification;
- the work God does *through* us—service.

This work will continue until we see Christ, and then the work will be fulfilled. "We shall be like him, for we shall see him as he is" (1 John 3:2).

It was a source of joy to Paul to know that God was still working in the lives of his fellow believers at Philippi. After all, this is the real basis for joyful Christian fellowship, to have God at work in our lives day by day.

"There seems to be friction in our home," a concerned wife said to a marriage counselor. "I really don't know what the trouble is."

"Friction is caused by one of two things," said the counselor, and to illustrate he picked up two blocks of wood from his desk. "If one block is moving and one is standing still, there's friction. Or, if both are moving but in opposite directions, there's friction. Now, which is it?"

"I'll have to admit that I've been going backward in my Christian life, and Joe has really been growing," the wife admitted. "What I need is to get back to fellowship with the Lord."

I Have You in My Heart (1:7–8)

Now we move a bit deeper, for it is possible to have others in our minds without really having them in our hearts. (Someone has observed that many people today would have to confess, "I have you on my nerves!") Paul's sincere love for his friends was something that could not be disguised or hidden.

Christian love is "the tie that binds." Love is the evidence of salvation: "We know that we have passed from death unto life, because we love the brethren" (1 John 3:14). It is the "spiritual lubrication" that keeps the machinery of life running smoothly. Have you noticed how often Paul used the phrase "you all" as he wrote? There are at least nine instances in this letter. He did not want to leave anyone out! (Some translations read, "You have me in your heart" in Phil. 1:7, but the basic truth is the same.)

How did Paul evidence his love for them? For one thing, he was suffering on their behalf. His bonds were proof of his love. He was "the prisoner of Jesus Christ for you Gentiles" (Eph. 3:1). Because of Paul's trial, Christianity was going to get a fair hearing before the officials of Rome. Since Philippi was a Roman colony, the decision would affect the believers there. Paul's love was not something he merely talked about; it was something he practiced. He considered his difficult circumstances an opportunity for defending and confirming the gospel, and this would help his brethren everywhere.

But how can Christians learn to practice this kind of love? "I get along better with my unsaved neighbors than I do my saved relatives!" a man confided to his pastor. "Maybe it takes a diamond to cut a diamond, but I've just about had it!" Christian love is not something we work up; it is something that God does in us and through us. Paul longed for his friends "in the bowels [love] of Jesus Christ" (Phil. 1:8). It was not Paul's love channeled through Christ; it was Christ's love channeled through Paul. "God has poured out his love into our hearts by the Holy Spirit, whom he has given us" (Rom. 5:5 NIV). When we permit God to perform His "good work" in us, then we grow in our love for one another.

How can we tell that we are truly bound in love to other Christians? For one thing, we are concerned about them. The believers at Philippi were concerned about Paul and sent Epaphroditus to minister to him. Paul was also greatly concerned about his friends at Philippi, especially when Epaphroditus became ill and could not return right away (Phil. 2:25–28). "My little children, let us not love in word, neither in tongue; but in deed and in truth" (1 John 3:18).

Another evidence of Christian love is a willingness to forgive one another. "And above all things have fervent charity [love] among yourselves: for charity [love] shall cover the multitude of sins" (1 Peter 4:8).

"Tell us some of the blunders your wife has made," a radio quizmaster asked a contestant.

"I can't remember any," the man replied.

"Oh, surely you can remember something!" the announcer said.

"No, I really can't," said the contestant. "I love my wife very much, and I just don't remember things like that." First Corinthians 13:5 states that "love keeps no record of wrongs" (NIV).

Christians who practice love always experience joy; both come as a result of the presence of the same Holy Spirit. "The fruit of the Spirit is love, joy" (Gal. 5:22).

I Have You in My Prayers (1:9–11)

Paul found joy in his memories of the friends at Philippi and in his growing love for them. He also found joy in remembering them before the throne of grace in prayer. The high priest in the Old Testament wore a special garment, the ephod, over his heart. On it were twelve stones with the names of the twelve tribes of Israel engraved on them, a jewel for each tribe (Ex. 28:15–29). He carried the people over his heart in love, and so did Paul. Perhaps the deepest Christian fellowship and joy we can experience in this life is at the throne of grace, praying with and for one another.

This is a prayer for maturity, and Paul began with *love.* After all, if our Christian love is what it ought to be, everything else should follow. He prayed that they might experience *abounding* love and *discerning* love. Christian love is not blind! The heart and mind work together so that we have discerning love and loving discernment. Paul wanted his friends to grow in discernment, in being able to "distinguish the things that differ."

The ability to distinguish is a mark of maturity. When a baby learns to speak, it may call every four-legged animal a "bow-wow." But then the child discovers that there are cats, white mice, cows, and other four-legged creatures. To a little child, one automobile is just like another, but not to a car-crazy teenager! He can spot the differences between models faster than his parents can even name the cars! One of the sure marks of maturity is discerning love.

Paul also prayed that they might have mature Christian *character,* "sincere and without offense." The Greek word translated "sincere" may have several meanings. Some translate it "tested by sunlight." The sincere Christian is not afraid to "stand in the light!"

Sincere may also mean "to whirl in a sieve," suggesting the idea of a winnowing process that removes chaff. In both cases the truth is the same: Paul prayed that his friends would have the kind of character that can pass the test. (Our English word *sincere* comes from a Latin word that means "unadulterated, pure, unmixed.")

Paul prayed for them to have mature Christian love and character, "without offense till the day of Christ" (Phil. 1:10). This means that our lives do not cause others to stumble, and that they are ready for the judgment seat of Christ when He returns (see 2 Cor. 5:10; 1 John 2:28). Here are two good tests for us to follow as we exercise spiritual discernment: (1) Will it make others stumble? (2) Will I be ashamed if Jesus should return?

Paul also prayed that they might have mature

Christian *service.* He wanted them filled and fruitful (Phil. 1:11). He was not interested simply in "church activities," but in the kind of spiritual fruit that is produced when we are in fellowship with Christ. "Abide in me, and I in you. As the branch cannot bear fruit of itself, except it abide in the vine; no more can ye, except ye abide in me" (John 15:4). Too many Christians try to "produce results" in their own efforts instead of abiding in Christ and allowing His life to produce the fruit.

What is the "fruit" God wants to see from our lives? Certainly He wants the "fruit of the Spirit" (Gal. 5:22–23), Christian character that glorifies God. Paul compared winning lost souls to Christ to bearing fruit (Rom. 1:13), and he also names "holiness" as a spiritual fruit (Rom. 6:22). He exhorted us to be "fruitful in every good work" (Col. 1:10), and the writer to the Hebrews reminded us that our praise is the "fruit of our lips" (Heb. 13:15).

The fruit tree does not make a great deal of noise when it produces its crop; it merely allows the life within to work in a natural way, and fruit is the result. "He that abideth in me, and I in him, the same bringeth forth much fruit: for without me ye can do nothing" (John 15:5).

The difference between spiritual fruit and human "religious activity" is that the fruit brings glory to Jesus Christ. Whenever we do anything in our own strength, we have a tendency to boast about it. True spiritual fruit is so beautiful and wonderful that no man can claim credit for it; the glory must go to God alone.

This, then, is true Christian fellowship—a having-in-common that is much deeper than mere friendship. "I have you in my mind … I have you in my heart … I have you in my prayers." This is the kind of fellowship that produces joy, *and it is the single mind that produces this kind of fellowship!*

Jerry had to go to New York City for special surgery, and he hated to go. "Why can't we have it done at home?" he asked his doctor. "I don't know a soul in that big, unfriendly city!" But when he and his wife arrived at the hospital, there was a pastor to meet them and invite them to stay at his home until they got settled. The operation was serious, and the wait in the hospital was long and difficult, but the fellowship of the pastor and his wife brought a new joy to Jerry and his wife. They learned that circumstances need not rob us of joy if we will but permit these circumstances to strengthen the fellowship of the gospel.

CHAPTER TWO
Philippians 1:12–26
PIONEERS WANTED

More than anything else, Paul's desire as a missionary was to preach the gospel in Rome. The hub of the great empire, Rome was the key city

of its day. If Paul could conquer it for Christ, it would mean reaching millions with the message of salvation. It was critically important on Paul's agenda, for he said, "After I have been there [Jerusalem], I must also see Rome" (Acts 19:21). From Corinth he wrote, "So, as much as in me is, I am ready [eager] to preach the gospel to you that are at Rome also" (Rom. 1:15).

Paul wanted to go to Rome as a preacher, but instead he went as *a prisoner!* He could have written a long letter about that experience alone. Instead, he summed it all up as "the things which happened unto me" (Phil. 1:12). The record of these things is given in Acts 21:17—28:31, and it begins with Paul's illegal arrest in the temple in Jerusalem. The Jews thought he had desecrated their temple by bringing in Gentiles, and the Romans thought he was an Egyptian renegade who was on their "most-wanted" list. Paul became the focal point of both political and religious plotting and remained a prisoner in Caesarea for two years. When he finally appealed to Caesar (which was the privilege of every Roman citizen), he was sent to Rome. En route, the ship was wrecked! The account of that storm and Paul's courage and faith is one of the most dramatic in the Bible (Acts 27). After three months of waiting on the Island of Malta, Paul finally embarked for Rome and the trial he had requested before Caesar.

To many, all of this would have looked like failure, but not to this man with a "single mind," concerned with sharing Christ and the gospel. Paul did not find his joy in ideal circumstances; he found his joy in winning others to Christ. And if his circumstances promoted the furtherance of the gospel, that was all that mattered! The word *furtherance* means "pioneer advance." It is a Greek military term referring to the army engineers who go before the troops to open the way into new territory. Instead of finding himself confined as a prisoner, Paul discovered that his circumstances really opened up new areas of ministry.

Everyone has heard of Charles Haddon Spurgeon, the famous British preacher, but few know the story of his wife, Susannah. Early in their married life, Mrs. Spurgeon became an invalid. It looked as though her only ministry would be encouraging her husband and praying for his work. But God gave her a burden to share her husband's books with pastors who were unable to purchase them. This burden soon led to the founding of the "Book Fund." As a work of faith, the "Book Fund" provided thousands of pastors with tools for their work. All this was supervised by Mrs. Spurgeon from her home. It was a pioneer ministry.

God still wants His children to take the gospel into new areas. He wants us to be pioneers, and sometimes He arranges circumstances so that we can be nothing else but pioneers. In fact, that is how the gospel originally came to Philippi! Paul had tried to enter other territory, but God had repeatedly shut the door (Acts 16:6–10). Paul wanted to take the message eastward into Asia, but God directed him to take it westward into Europe. What a difference it would have made in the history of mankind if Paul had been permitted to follow his plan!

God sometimes uses strange tools to help us pioneer the gospel. In Paul's case, there were three tools that helped him take the gospel even into the elite Praetorian Guard, Caesar's special troops: his *chains* (Phil. 1:12–14), his *critics* (Phil. 1:15–19), and his *crisis* (Phil. 1:20–26).

Paul's Chains (1:12–14)

The same God who used Moses' rod, Gideon's pitchers, and David's sling, used Paul's chains. Little did the Romans realize that the chains they affixed to his wrists would *release* Paul instead of *bind* him! Even as he wrote during a later imprisonment, "I suffer trouble, as an evildoer, even unto bonds; but the word of God is not bound" (2 Tim. 2:9). He did not complain about his chains; instead he consecrated them to God and asked God to use them for the pioneer advance of the gospel. And God answered his prayers.

To begin with, these chains gave Paul *contact with the lost.* He was chained to a Roman soldier twenty-four hours a day! The shifts changed every six hours, which meant Paul could witness to at least four men each day! Imagine yourself as one of those soldiers, chained to a man who prayed "without ceasing," who was constantly interviewing people about their spiritual condition, and who was repeatedly writing letters to Christians and churches throughout the empire! It was not long before some of these soldiers put their faith in Christ. Paul was able to get the gospel into the elite Praetorian Guard, something he could not have done had he been a free man.

But the chains gave Paul contact with another group of people: the officials in Caesar's court. He was in Rome as an official prisoner, and his case was an important one. The Roman government was going to determine the official status of this new "Christian" sect. Was it merely another sect of the Jews? Or was it something new and possibly dangerous? Imagine how pleased Paul must have been knowing that the court officials were forced to study the doctrines of the Christian faith!

Sometimes God has to put "chains" on His people to get them to accomplish a "pioneer advance" that could never happen any other way. Young mothers may feel chained to the home as they care for their children, but God can use those "chains" to reach people with the message of salvation. Susannah Wesley was the mother of nineteen children, before the days of labor-saving devices and disposable diapers! Out of that large family came John and Charles Wesley, whose combined ministries shook the British Isles. At six weeks of age, Fanny Crosby was blinded, but even as a youngster she determined not to be confined by the chains of darkness. In time, she became a mighty force for God through her hymns and gospel songs.

The secret is this: When you have the single mind, you look on your circumstances as God-given opportunities for the furtherance of the gospel, and you rejoice at *what God is going to do* instead of complaining about *what God did not do.*

Paul's chains not only gave contact with the lost, but they also gave *courage to the saved.* Many of the believers in Rome took fresh courage when they saw Paul's faith and determination (Phil. 1:14). They were "much more bold to speak the word without fear." That word *speak* does not mean "preach." Rather, it means "everyday conversation." No doubt many of the Romans were discussing Paul's case, because such legal matters were of primary concern to this nation of lawmakers. And the Christians in Rome who were sympathetic to Paul took advantage of this conversation to say a good word for Jesus Christ. Discouragement has a way of spreading, but so does encouragement! Because of Paul's joyful attitude, the believers in Rome took fresh courage and witnessed boldly for Christ.

While recovering in the hospital from a serious auto accident, I received a letter from a total stranger who seemed to know just what to say to make my day brighter. In fact, I received several letters from him, and each one was better than the one before. When I was able to get around, I met him personally. I was amazed to discover that he was blind, a diabetic, handicapped because of a leg amputation (and since then the other leg has been removed), and that he lived with and cared for his elderly mother! If a man ever wore chains, this man did! But if a man ever was free to pioneer the gospel, this man was! He was able to share Christ in high school assemblies, before service clubs, at the "Y," and before professional people in meetings that would have been closed to an ordained minister. My friend had the single mind; he lived for Christ and the gospel. Consequently, he shared the joy of furthering the gospel.

Our chains may not be as dramatic or difficult, but there is no reason why God cannot use them in the same way.

Paul's Critics (1:15–19)

It is hard to believe that anyone would oppose Paul, but there were believers in Rome doing just that. The churches there were divided. Some preached Christ sincerely, wanting to see people saved. Some preached Christ insincerely, wanting to make the situation more difficult for Paul. The latter group was using the gospel to further their own selfish purposes. Perhaps they belonged to the "legalistic" wing of the church that opposed Paul's ministry to the Gentiles and his emphasis on the grace of God as opposed to obedience to the Jewish law. Envy and strife go together, just as love and unity go together.

Paul used an interesting word in Philippians 1:16—*contention.* It means "to canvass for office, to get people to support you." Paul's aim was to glorify Christ and get people to follow Him; his critics' aim was to promote themselves and win a following of their own. Instead of asking, "Have you trusted Christ?" they asked, "Whose side are you on—ours or Paul's?" Unfortunately, this kind of "religious politics" is still seen today. And the people who practice it need to realize that they are only hurting themselves.

When you have the single mind, you look on your critics as another opportunity for the furtherance of the gospel. Like a faithful soldier, Paul was "set [appointed] for the defense of the gospel" (Phil. 1:17). He was able to rejoice, not in the selfishness of his critics, but in the fact that *Christ was being preached!* There was no envy in Paul's heart. It mattered not that some were for him and some were against him. All that mattered was the preaching of the gospel of Jesus Christ!

It is a matter of historic record that the two great English evangelists, John Wesley and George Whitefield, disagreed on doctrinal matters. Both of them were very successful, preaching to thousands of people and seeing multitudes come to Christ. It is reported that somebody asked Wesley if he expected to see Whitefield in heaven, and the evangelist replied, "No, I do not."

"Then you do not think Whitefield is a converted man?"

"Of course he is a converted man!" Wesley said. "But I do not expect to see him in heaven—because he will be so close to the throne of God and I so far away that I will not be able to see him!" Though he differed with his brother in some matters, Wesley did not have any envy in his heart, nor did he seek to oppose Whitefield's ministry.

Criticism is usually very hard to take, particularly when we are in difficult circumstances, as Paul was. How was the apostle able to rejoice even in the face of such diverse criticism? He possessed the single mind! Philippians 1:19 indicates that Paul expected his case to turn out victoriously ("to my salvation") because of the prayers of his friends and the supply of the Holy Spirit of God. The word *supply* gives us our English word *chorus.* Whenever a Greek city was going to put on a special festival, somebody had to pay for the singers and dancers. The donation called for had to be a lavish one, and so this word came to mean "to provide generously and lavishly." Paul was not depending on his own dwindling resources; he was depending on the generous resources of God, ministered by the Holy Spirit.

Paul shared in the pioneer advance of the gospel in Rome through his chains and his critics, but he had a third tool that he used.

Paul's Crisis (1:20–26)

Because of Paul's chains, Christ was *known* (Phil. 1:13), and because of Paul's critics, Christ was *preached* (Phil. 1:18). But because of Paul's crisis, Christ was *magnified!* (Phil. 1:20). It was possible that Paul would be found a traitor to Rome and then executed. His preliminary trial had apparently gone in his favor. The final verdict, however, was yet to come. But Paul's body was not his own,

and his only desire (because he had the single mind) was to magnify Christ in his body.

Does Christ need to be magnified? After all, how can a mere human being ever magnify the Son of God? Well, the stars are much bigger than the telescope, and yet the telescope magnifies them and brings them closer. The believer's body is to be a telescope that brings Jesus Christ close to people. To the average person, Christ is a misty figure in history who lived centuries ago. But as the unsaved watch the believer go through a crisis, they can see Jesus magnified and brought so much closer. To the Christian with the single mind, Christ is with us here and now.

The telescope brings distant things closer, and the microscope makes tiny things look big. To the unbeliever, Jesus is not very big. Other people and other things are far more important. But as the unbeliever watches the Christian go through a crisis experience, he ought to be able to see how big Jesus Christ really is. The believer's body is a "lens" that makes a "little Christ" look very big, and a "distant Christ" come very close.

Paul was not afraid of life or death! Either way, he wanted to magnify Christ in his body. No wonder he had joy!

Paul confessed that he was facing a difficult decision. To remain alive was necessary for the believers' benefit in Philippi, but to depart and be with Christ was far better. Paul decided that Christ would have him remain, not only for the "furtherance of the gospel" (Phil. 1:12) but also for the "furtherance and joy of [their] faith" (Phil. 1:25). He wanted them to make some "pioneer advance" into new areas of spiritual growth. (By the way, Paul admonished Timothy, the young pastor, to be sure to pioneer new spiritual territory in his own life and ministry. See 1 Tim. 4:15, where "profiting" is our phrase "pioneer advance.")

What a man Paul was! He was willing to postpone going to heaven in order to help Christians grow, and he was willing to go to hell in order to win the lost to Christ! (Rom. 9:1–3)

Of course, death had no terrors for Paul. It simply meant "departing." This word was used by the soldiers; it meant "to take down your tent and move on." What a picture of Christian death! The "tent" we live in is taken down at death, and the spirit goes home to be with Christ in heaven. (Read 2 Cor. 5:1–8.) The sailors also used this word; it meant "to loosen a ship and set sail." Lord Tennyson used this figure of death in his famous poem "Crossing the Bar."

But *departure* was also a political term; it described the setting free of a prisoner. God's people are in bondage because of the limitations of the body and the temptations of the flesh, but death will free them. Or they will be freed at the return of Christ (Rom. 8:18–23) if that should come first. Finally, *departure* was a word used by the farmers; it meant "to unyoke the oxen." Paul had taken Christ's yoke, which is an easy yoke to bear (Matt. 11:28–30), but how many burdens he carried in his ministry! (If you need your memory refreshed, read 2 Cor. 11:22—12:10.) To depart to be with Christ would mean laying aside the burdens, his earthly work completed.

No matter how you look at it, nothing can steal a man's joy if he possesses the single mind! "For to me to live is Christ, and to die is gain" (Phil. 1:21). Maltbie Babcock, who wrote "This Is My Father's World," said, "Life is what we are alive to." When my wife and I go shopping, I dread going to the fabric department, but I often have to go because my wife enjoys looking at fabrics. If on the way to the fabric section I spot the book department, I suddenly come alive! The thing that excites us and motivates us is the thing that really is "life" to us. In Paul's case, Christ was his life. Christ excited him and made his life worth living.

Philippians 1:21 becomes a valuable test of our lives. "For to me to live is _____ and to die is _____." Fill in the blanks yourself.

"For to me to live is *money* and to die is *to leave it all behind.*"

"For to me to live is *fame* and to die is *to be forgotten.*"

"For to me to live is *power* and to die is *to lose it all.*"

No, we must echo Paul's convictions if we are going to have joy in spite of circumstances, and if we are going to share in the furtherance of the gospel. "For to me to live is Christ, and to die is gain!"

CHAPTER THREE
Philippians 1:27–30
BATTLE STATIONS!

The Christian life is not a playground; it is a battleground. We are *sons* in the family, enjoying the *fellowship* of the gospel (Phil. 1:1–11); we are *servants* sharing in the *furtherance* of the gospel (Phil. 1:12–26); but we are also *soldiers* defending the *faith* of the gospel. And the believer with the single mind can have the joy of the Holy Spirit even in the midst of battle.

"The faith of the gospel" is that body of divine truth given to the church. Jude called it "the faith which was once delivered unto the saints" (Jude 3). Paul warned in 1 Timothy 4:1 that "in the latter times some shall depart from the faith." God committed this spiritual treasure to Paul (1 Tim. 1:11), and he in turn committed it to others, like Timothy (1 Tim. 6:20), whose responsibility was to commit this deposit to still others (2 Tim. 2:2). This is why the church must engage in a teaching ministry, so that each new generation of believers will know, appreciate, and use the great heritage of the faith.

But there is an enemy who is out to steal the treasure from God's people. Paul had met the enemy in Philippi, and he was now facing him in Rome. If Satan can only rob believers of their Christian faith,

the doctrines that are distinctively theirs, then he can cripple and defeat the ministry of the gospel. It is sad to hear people say, "I don't care what you believe, just so long as you live right." What we believe determines how we behave, and wrong belief ultimately means a wrong life. Each local church is but one generation short of potential extinction. No wonder Satan attacks our young people in particular, seeking to get them away from "the faith."

How can a group of Christians fight this enemy? "For the weapons of our warfare are not of the flesh" (2 Cor. 10:4 NASB). Peter took up a sword in the garden, and Jesus rebuked him (John 18:10–11). We use spiritual weapons—the Word of God and prayer (Eph. 6:11–18; Heb. 4:12), and we must depend on the Holy Spirit to give us the power that we need. But an army must fight *together*, and this is why Paul sent these admonitions to his friends at Philippi. He was explaining in this paragraph that there are three essentials for victory in the battle to protect "the faith."

Consistency (1:27a)
The old English word *conversation*, of course, means *walk* and not *talk*. "Only conduct yourselves in a manner worthy of the gospel of Christ" (NASB). The most important weapon against the enemy is not a stirring sermon or a powerful book; it is the consistent life of believers.

The verb Paul used is related to our word *politics*. He was saying, "Behave the way citizens are supposed to behave." My wife and I were visiting in London and one day decided to go to the zoo. We boarded the bus and sat back to enjoy the ride; but it was impossible to enjoy it because of the loud, coarse conversation of the passengers at the front of the bus. Unfortunately, they were Americans, and we could see the Britishers around us raising their eyebrows and shaking their heads, as though to say, "Oh, yes, they're from America!" We were embarrassed because we knew that these people did not really represent the best of American citizens.

Paul was suggesting that we Christians are the citizens of heaven, and while we are on earth we ought to behave like heaven's citizens. He brought this concept up again in Philippians 3:20. It would be a very meaningful expression to the people in Philippi because Philippi was a Roman colony, and its citizens were actually Roman citizens, protected by Roman law. The church of Jesus Christ is a colony of heaven on earth! And we ought to behave like the citizens of heaven.

"Am I conducting myself in a manner worthy of the gospel?" is a good question for us to ask ourselves regularly. We should "walk … worthy of the calling" that we have in Christ (Eph. 4:1 NASB), which means walking "worthy of the Lord unto all pleasing" (Col. 1:10). We do not behave in order to go to heaven, as though we could be saved by our good works; but we behave because our names are already written in heaven, and our citizenship is in heaven.

It is worth remembering that the world around us knows only the gospel that it sees in our lives.

> You are writing a gospel,
> A chapter each day,
> By the deeds that you do
> And the words that you say.
> Men read what you write,
> Whether faithful or true:
> Just what is the gospel
> According to you?
> —SOURCE UNKNOWN

"The gospel" is the good news that Christ died for our sins, was buried, and rose again (1 Cor. 15:1–8). There is only one "good news" of salvation; any other gospel is false (Gal. 1:6–10). The message of the gospel is the good news that sinners can become the children of God through faith in Jesus Christ, God's Son (John 3:16). To add anything to the gospel is to deprive it of its power. We are not saved from our sins by faith in Christ *plus* something else; we are saved by faith in Christ *alone.*

"We have some neighbors who believe a false gospel," a church member told his pastor. "Do you have some literature I can give them?"

The pastor opened his Bible to 2 Corinthians 3:2: "You are our letter, written in our hearts, known and read by all men" (NASB). He said, "The best literature in the world is no substitute for your own life. Let them see Christ in your behavior, and this will open up opportunities to share Christ's gospel with them."

The greatest weapon against the devil is a godly life. And a local church that practices the truth, that "behaves what it believes," is going to defeat the enemy. This is the first essential for victory in this battle.

Cooperation (1:27b)

Paul now changed the illustration from politics to athletics. The word translated "striving together" gives us our English word *athletics.* Paul pictured the church as a team, and he reminded them that it is teamwork that wins victories.

Keep in mind that there was division in the church at Philippi. For one thing, two women were not getting along with each other (Phil. 4:2). Apparently the members of the fellowship were taking sides, as is often the case, and the resulting division was hindering the work of the church. The enemy is always happy to see internal divisions in a local ministry. "Divide and conquer!" is his motto, and too often he has his way. It is only as believers stand together that they can overcome the wicked one.

Throughout this letter, Paul used an interesting device to emphasize the importance of unity. In the Greek language, the prefix *sun-* means "with, together," and when used with different words, strengthens the idea of unity. (It is somewhat like our prefix *co-.*) At least sixteen times, Paul used this prefix in Philippians,

and his readers could not have missed the message! In Philippians 1:27, the Greek word is *sunathleo*—"striving together as athletes."

Jerry was disgusted, and he decided to tell the coach how he felt. "There's no sense coming out for practice anymore," he complained. "Mike is the team—you don't need the rest of us."

Coach Gardner knew the trouble. "Look, Jerry, just because Mike gets many of the chances to shoot doesn't mean the rest of you guys aren't needed. Somebody has to set things up at the basket, and that's where you come in."

Sometimes a team has a "glory hound" who has to be in the spotlight and get all the praise. Usually he makes it difficult for the rest of the team. They aren't working equally together, but are working to make one person look good. It is this attitude that makes for defeat. Unfortunately, we have some "glory hounds" in the church. John had to deal with a man named Diotrephes because the man "loved to have the preeminence" (3 John 9). Even the apostles James and John asked to have special thrones (Matt. 20:20–28). The important word is *together:* standing firmly together in one spirit, striving together against the enemy, and doing it with one mind and heart.

It would not be difficult to expand this idea of the local church as a team of athletes. Each person has his assigned place and job, and if each one is doing his job, it helps all the others. Not everybody can be captain or quarterback! The team has to follow the rules, and the Word of God is our "rule book." There is one goal—to honor Christ and do His will. If we all work together, we can reach the goal, win the prize, and glorify the Lord. But the minute any one of us starts disobeying the rules, breaking training (the Christian life does demand discipline), or looking for glory, the teamwork disappears and division and competition take over.

In other words, Paul was reminding us again of the need for *the single mind.* There is joy in our lives, even as we battle the enemy, if we live for Christ and the gospel and practice "Christian teamwork." To be sure, there are some people with whom we cannot cooperate (2 Cor. 6:14–18; Eph. 5:11), but there are many with whom we *can*—and should!

We are citizens of heaven and therefore should walk consistently. We are members of the same "team" and should work cooperatively. But there is a third essential for success as we face the enemy, and that is *confidence.*

Confidence (1:28–30)

"Don't be alarmed by your opponents!" The word Paul used pictures a horse shying away from battle. To be sure, nobody blindly runs into a fight, but then, no true believer should deliberately avoid facing the enemy. In these verses, Paul gave us several encouragements that give us confidence in the battle.

First, *these battles prove that we are saved* (Phil. 1:29). We not only believe on Christ but also suffer for Christ. Paul called this "the fellowship of his sufferings" (Phil. 3:10). For some reason, many new believers have the idea that trusting Christ means the end of their battles. In reality, it means the beginning of *new* battles. "In the world ye shall have tribulation" (John 16:33). "Yea, and all that will live godly in Christ Jesus shall suffer persecution" (2 Tim. 3:12).

But the presence of conflict is *a privilege;* we suffer "for his sake." In fact, Paul told us that this conflict is "granted" to us—it is a gift! If we were suffering for ourselves, it would be no privilege, but because we are suffering for and with Christ, it is a high and holy honor. After all, He suffered for us, and a willingness to suffer for Him is the very least we can do to show our love and gratitude.

A third encouragement is this: *others are experiencing the same conflict* (Phil. 1:30). Satan wants us to think we are alone in the battle, that our difficulties are unique, but such is not the case. Paul reminded the Philippians that he was going through the same difficulties they were experiencing hundreds of miles from Rome! A change in geography is usually no solution to spiritual problems, because human nature is the same wherever you go, and the enemy is everywhere. Knowing that my fellow believers are also sharing in the battle is an encouragement for me to keep going and to pray for them as I pray for myself.

Actually, going through spiritual conflict is one way we have *to grow in Christ.* God gives us the strength we need to stand firm against the enemy, and this confidence is proof to him that he will lose and we are on the winning side (Phil. 1:28). The Philippians had seen Paul go through conflict when he was with them (read Acts 16:19ff.), and they had witnessed his firmness in the Lord. The word *conflict* gives us our word *agony (agonia),* and is the same word that is used for Christ's struggle in the garden (Luke 22:44). As we face the enemy and depend on the Lord, He gives us all that we need for the battle. When the enemy sees our God-given confidence, it makes him fear.

So, the single mind enables us to have joy in the midst of battle because it produces in us consistency, cooperation, and confidence. We experience the joy of "spiritual teamwork" as we strive together for the faith of the gospel.

CHAPTER FOUR
Philippians 2:1–11
THE GREAT EXAMPLE

People can rob us of our joy. Paul was facing his problems with people at Rome (Phil. 1:15–18) as well as with people in Philippi, and it was the latter who concerned him the most. When Epaphroditus brought a generous gift from the church in Philippi, and good news of the church's concern for Paul, he also brought the bad news of a possible division in the church family. Apparently there was a double threat

to the unity of the church; false teachers coming in from without (Phil. 3:1–3) and disagreeing members within (Phil. 4:1–3). What Euodia ("fragrance") and Syntyche ("fortunate") were debating about, Paul did not state. Perhaps they both wanted to be president of the missionary guild or the choir!

Paul knew what some church workers today do not know: that there is a difference between *unity* and *uniformity.* True spiritual unity comes from within; it is a matter of the heart. Uniformity is the result of pressure from without. This is why Paul opened this section appealing to the highest possible spiritual motives (Phil. 2:1–4). Since the believers at Philippi were "in Christ," this ought to have encouraged them to work toward unity and love, not division and rivalry. In a gracious way, Paul was saying to the church, "Your disagreements reveal that there is a spiritual problem in your fellowship. It isn't going to be solved by rules or threats; it's going to be solved when your hearts are right with Christ and with each other." Paul wanted them to see that the basic cause was *selfishness,* and the cause of selfishness is *pride.* There can be no joy in the life of the Christian who puts himself above others.

The secret of joy in spite of circumstances is *the single mind.* The secret of joy in spite of people is *the submissive mind.* The key verse is "Let nothing be done through strife or vainglory; but in lowliness of mind let each esteem other better [more important] than themselves" (Phil. 2:3). In Philippians 1, it is "Christ first" and in Philippians 2 it is "others next." Paul the soul-winner in Philippians 1 becomes Paul the servant in Philippians 2.

It is important that we understand what the Bible means by "humility." The humble person is not one who thinks meanly of himself; he simply does not think of himself at all! (I think Andrew Murray said that.) Humility is that grace that, when you know you have it, you have lost it. The truly humble person knows himself and accepts himself (Rom. 12:3). He yields himself to Christ to be a servant, to use what he is and has for the glory of God and the good of others. "Others" is the key idea in this chapter (Phil. 2:3–4); the believer's eyes are turned away from himself and focused on the needs of others.

The "submissive mind" does not mean that the believer is at the beck and call of everybody else or that he is a "religious doormat" for everybody to use! Some people try to purchase friends and maintain church unity by "giving in" to everybody else's whims and wishes. This is not what Paul is suggesting at all. The Scripture puts it perfectly: "ourselves your servants for Jesus' sake" (2 Cor. 4:5). If we have the single mind of Philippians 1, then we will have no problem with the submissive mind of Philippians 2.

Paul gave us four examples of the submissive mind: Jesus Christ (Phil. 2:1–11), Paul himself (Phil. 2:12–18), Timothy (Phil. 2:19–24), and Epaphroditus (Phil. 2:25–30). Of course, the great example is Jesus, and Paul began with Him. Jesus Christ illustrates the four characteristics of the person with the submissive mind.

He Thinks of Others, Not Himself (2:5–6)

The "mind" of Christ means the "attitude" Christ exhibited. "Your attitude should be the same as that of Christ Jesus" (Phil. 2:5 NIV). After all, outlook determines outcome. If the outlook is selfish, the actions will be divisive and destructive. James said the same thing (see James 4:1–10).

These verses in Philippians take us to eternity past. "Form of God" has nothing to do with shape or size. God is Spirit (John 4:24), and as such is not to be thought of in human terms. When the Bible refers to "the eyes of the Lord" or "the hand of the Lord," it is not claiming that God has a human shape. Rather, it is using human terms to describe divine attributes (the characteristics of God) and activities. The word *form* means "the outward expression of the inward nature." This means that in eternity past, *Jesus Christ was God.* In fact, Paul stated that Jesus was "equal with God." Other verses such as John 1:1–4; Colossians 1:15; and Hebrews 1:1–3 also state that Jesus Christ is God.

Certainly as God, Jesus Christ did not need anything! He had all the glory and praise of heaven. With the Father and the Spirit, He reigned over the universe. But Philippians 2:6 states an amazing fact: He did not consider His equality with God as "something selfishly to be held on to." Jesus did not think of Himself; He thought of others. His outlook (or attitude) was that of unselfish concern for others. This is "the mind of Christ," an attitude that says, "I cannot keep my privileges for myself, I must use them for others; and to do this, I will gladly lay them aside and pay whatever price is necessary."

A reporter was interviewing a successful job counselor who had placed hundreds of workers in their vocations quite happily. When asked the secret of his success, the man replied, "If you want to find out what a worker is really like, don't give him responsibilities—give him *privileges.* Most people can handle responsibilities if you pay them enough, but it takes a real leader to handle privileges. A leader will use his privileges to help others and build the organization; a lesser man will use privileges to promote himself." Jesus used His heavenly privileges for the sake of others—for *our* sake.

It would be worthwhile to contrast Christ's attitude with that of Lucifer (Isa. 14:12–15) and Adam (Gen. 3:1–7). Many Bible students believe that the fall of Lucifer is a description of the fall of Satan. He once was the highest of the angelic beings, close to the throne of God (Ezek. 28:11–19), but he desired to be *on* the throne of God! Lucifer said, "I will!" but Jesus said, *"Thy* will." Lucifer was not satisfied to be a creature; he wanted to be the Creator! Jesus was the Creator, yet He willingly became man. Christ's humility is a rebuke to Satan's pride.

Lucifer was not satisfied to be a rebel himself; he invaded Eden and tempted man to be a rebel. Adam had all that he needed; he was actually the "king" of God's creation ("let them have dominion," Gen. 1:26). But Satan said, "You will be like God!" Man deliberately grasped after something that was beyond his reach, and as a result plunged the whole human race into sin and death. Adam and Eve thought only of themselves; Jesus Christ thought of others.

We expect unsaved people to be selfish and grasping, but we do not expect this of Christians, who have experienced the love of Christ and the fellowship of the Spirit (Phil. 2:1–2). More than twenty times in the New Testament, God instructs us how to live with "one another." We are to prefer one another (Rom. 12:10), edify one another (1 Thess. 5:11), and bear each other's burdens (Gal. 6:2). We should not judge one another (Rom. 14:13) but rather admonish one another (Rom. 15:14). *Others* is the key word in the vocabulary of the Christian who exercises the submissive mind.

He Serves (2:7)

Thinking of "others" in an abstract sense only is insufficient; we must get down to the nitty-gritty of true service. A famous philosopher wrote glowing words about educating children but abandoned his own. It was easy for him to love children in the abstract, but when it came down to practice, that was something else. Jesus thought of others *and became a servant!* Paul traced the steps in the humiliation of Christ: (1) He emptied Himself, laying aside the independent use of His own attributes as God; (2) He permanently became a human, in a sinless physical body; (3) He used that body to be a servant; (4) He took that body to the cross and willingly died.

What grace! From heaven to earth, from glory to shame, from Master to servant, from life to death, "even the death of the cross!" In the Old Testament age, Christ had visited earth on occasion for some special ministry (Gen. 18 is a case in point), but these visits were temporary. When Christ was born at Bethlehem, He entered into a *permanent* union with humanity from which there could be no escape. He willingly humbled Himself that He might lift us up! Note that Paul used the word *form* again in Philippians 2:7, "the outward expression of the inward nature." Jesus did not pretend to be a servant; He was not an actor playing a role. *He actually was a servant!* This was the true expression of His innermost nature. He was the God-Man, Deity and humanity united in one, and He came as a servant.

Have you noticed as you read the four gospels that it is Jesus who serves others, not others who serve Jesus? He is at the beck and call of all kinds of people—fishermen, harlots, tax collectors, the sick, the sorrowing. "Even as the Son of man came not to be ministered unto, but to minister, and to give his life a ransom for many" (Matt. 20:28). In the upper room, when His disciples apparently refused to minister, Jesus arose, laid aside His outer garments, put on the long linen towel, and *washed their feet* (John 13)! He took the place of a menial slave! This was the submissive mind in action—and no wonder Jesus experienced such joy!

During the American Civil War, General George B. McClellan was put in charge of the great army of the Potomac, mainly because public opinion was on his side. He fancied himself to be a great military leader and enjoyed hearing the people call him "a young Napoleon." However, his performance was less than sensational. President Lincoln commissioned him General-in-Chief, hoping this would get some action, but still he procrastinated. One evening, Lincoln and two of his staff members went to visit McClellan, only to learn that he was at a wedding. The three men sat down to wait, and an hour later the general arrived home. Without paying any attention to the president, McClellan went upstairs and did not return. Half an hour later, Lincoln sent the servant to tell McClellan that the men were waiting. The servant came back to report McClellan had gone to bed!

His associates angry, Lincoln merely got up and led the way home. "This is no time to be making points of etiquette and personal dignity," the president explained. "I would hold McClellan's horse if he will only bring us success." This attitude of humility was what helped to make Lincoln a great man and a great president. He was not thinking of himself; he was thinking of serving others. Service is the second mark of the submissive mind.

He Sacrifices (2:8)

Many people are willing to serve others *if* it does not cost them anything. But if there is a price to pay, they suddenly lose interest. Jesus "became obedient unto death, even the death of the cross" (Phil. 2:8). His was not the death of a martyr but the death of a Savior. He willingly laid down His life for the sins of the world.

Dr. J. H. Jowett said, "Ministry that costs nothing accomplishes nothing." If there is to be any blessing, there must be some "bleeding." At a religious festival in Brazil, a missionary was going from booth to booth, examining the wares. He saw a sign above one booth: "Cheap Crosses." He thought, "That's what many Christians are looking for these days—cheap crosses. My Lord's cross was not cheap. Why should mine be?"

The person with the submissive mind does not avoid sacrifice. He lives for the glory of God and the good of others, and if paying a price will honor Christ and help others, he is willing to do it. This was Paul's attitude (Phil. 2:17), Timothy's (Phil. 2:20), and also Epaphroditus's (Phil. 2:30). Sacrifice and service go together if service is to be true Christian ministry.

In his book *Dedication and Leadership,* Douglas Hyde explained how the Communists succeeded in their program. A member of the Communist Party himself for twenty years, Hyde understands their philosophy. He pointed out that the Communists never ask a man to do a "mean, little job." They always ask him boldly to undertake something that will cost him. They make big demands, and they get a ready response. Mr. Hyde called "the willingness to sacrifice" one of the most important factors in the success of the Communist program. Even the youths in the movement are expected to study, serve, give, and obey, and this is what attracts and holds them.

A church council was planning the annual "Youth Sunday" program, and one of the members suggested that the teenagers serve as ushers, lead in prayer, bring special music. One of the teens stood up and said, "Quite frankly, we're tired of being asked to do little things. We'd like to do something difficult this year, and maybe keep it going all year long. The kids have talked and prayed about this, and we'd like to work with our trustees in remodeling that basement room so it can be used for a classroom. And we'd like to start visiting our elderly members each week and taking them cassettes of the services. And, if it's OK, we'd like to have a weekly witness on Sunday afternoons in the park. We hope this is OK with you."

He sat down, and the new youth pastor smiled to himself. He had privately challenged the teens to do something that would cost them—and they enthusiastically responded to the challenge. He knew that sacrifice is necessary if there is going to be true growth and ministry.

The test of the submissive mind is not just how much we are willing to take in terms of suffering, but how much we are willing to give in terms of sacrifice. One pastor complained that his men were changing the words of the hymn from "Take my life and let it be" to "Take my wife and let me be!" They were willing for others to make the sacrifices, but they were unwilling to sacrifice for others.

It is one of the paradoxes of the Christian life that the more we give, the more we receive; the more we sacrifice, the more God blesses. This is why the submissive mind leads to joy; it makes us more like Christ. This means sharing His joy as we also share in His sufferings. Of course, when love is the motive (Phil. 2:1), sacrifice is never measured or mentioned. The person who constantly talks about his sacrifices does not have the submissive mind.

Is it costing *you* anything to be a Christian?

He Glorifies God (2:9–11)

This, of course, is the great goal of all that we do—to glorify God. Paul warns us against "vainglory" in Philippians 2:3. The kind of rivalry that pits Christian against Christian and ministry against ministry is not spiritual, nor is it satisfying. It is vain, empty. Jesus humbled Himself for others, and God highly exalted Him; and the result of this exaltation is glory to God.

Our Lord's exaltation began with His resurrection. When men buried the body of Jesus, that was the last thing any human hands did to Him. From that point on, it was God who worked. Men had done their worst to the Savior, but God exalted Him and honored Him. Men gave Him names of ridicule and slander, but the

Father gave Him a glorious name! Just as in His humiliation He was given the name "Jesus" (Matt. 1:21), so in His exaltation He was given the name "Lord" (Phil. 2:11; see Acts 2:32–36). He arose from the dead and then returned in victory to heaven, ascending to the Father's throne.

His exaltation included sovereign authority over all creatures in heaven, on earth, and under the earth. All will bow to Him (see Isa. 45:23). It is likely that "under the earth" refers to the lost, since God's family is either in heaven or on earth (Eph. 3:14–15). One day all will bow before Him and confess that He is Lord. Of course, it is possible for people to bow and confess *today,* and receive His gift of salvation (Rom. 10:9–10). To bow before Him now means salvation; to bow before Him at the judgment means condemnation.

The whole purpose of Christ's humiliation and exaltation is the glory of God (Phil. 2:11). As Jesus faced the cross, the glory of the Father was uppermost in His mind: "Father, the hour is come; glorify thy Son, that thy Son also may glorify thee" (John 17:1). In fact, He has given this glory to us (John 17:22), and one day we shall share it with Him in heaven (John 17:24; see Rom. 8:28–30). The work of salvation is much greater and grander than simply the salvation of a lost soul, as wonderful as that is. Our salvation has as its ultimate purpose the glory of God (Eph. 1:6, 12, 14).

The person with the submissive mind, as he lives for others, must expect sacrifice and service; but in the end, it is going to lead to glory. "Humble yourselves therefore under the mighty hand of God, that he may exalt you in due time" (1 Peter 5:6). Joseph suffered and served for thirteen years, but then God exalted him and made him the second ruler of Egypt. David was anointed king when he was but a youth. He experienced years of hardship and suffering, but at the right time, God exalted him as king of Israel.

The joy of the submissive mind comes not only from helping others and sharing in the fellowship of Christ's sufferings (Phil. 3:10), but primarily from the knowledge that we are glorifying God. We are letting our light shine through our good works, and this glorifies the Father in heaven (Matt. 5:16). We may not see the glory today, but we shall see it when Jesus comes and rewards His faithful servants.

CHAPTER FIVE
Philippians 2:12–18
THE INS AND OUTS OF CHRISTIAN LIVING

Few things are harder to put up with," wrote Mark Twain, "than the annoyance of a good example." Perhaps the thing most annoying about a good example is its inability to accomplish the same achievements in our own lives. Admiration for a great person can inspire us, but it cannot enable us. Unless the person can enter into our own lives and share his skills, we cannot attain to his heights of accomplishment. It takes more than an example on the outside; it takes power on the inside.

Paul has just presented Jesus Christ as our great Example in the exercise of the submissive mind. We read it, and we agree with it, *but how do we go about practicing it?* How could any mortal man ever hope to achieve what Jesus Christ achieved? It seems almost presumptuous to even try! Here we are, trying to develop humility, and we are exercising pride by daring to imitate the Lord Jesus Christ!

The problem is really not that difficult. Paul was not asking us to "reach for the stars," though the higher the goal the more we ought to achieve. Rather, he was setting before us the divine *pattern* for the submissive mind and the divine *power* to accomplish what God has commanded. "It is God which worketh in you" (Phil. 2:13). It is not by imitation, but by incarnation—"Christ liveth in me" (Gal. 2:20). The Christian life is not a series of ups and downs. It is rather a process of "ins and outs." God works *in,* and we work *out.* We cultivate the submissive mind by responding to the divine provisions God makes available to us.

There Is a Purpose to Achieve (2:12, 14–16)

"Work out your own salvation" (Phil. 2:12) does not suggest, "Work *for* your own salvation." To begin with, Paul was writing to people who were already "saints" (Phil. 1:1), which means they had trusted Christ and had been set apart for Him. The verb "work out" carries the meaning of "work to full completion," such as working out a problem in mathematics. In Paul's day it was also used for "working a mine," that is, getting out of the mine all the valuable ore possible; or "working a field" so as to get the greatest harvest possible. The purpose God wants us to achieve is Christlikeness, "to be conformed to the image of his Son" (Rom. 8:29). There are problems in life, but God will help us to "work them out." Our lives have tremendous potential, like a mine or a field, and He wants to help us fulfill that potential.

Cindy did not seem very happy when she arrived home from college to spend the holiday with her family. Her parents noticed her unusual behavior but were wise enough to wait until she was ready to share her problem with them. It happened after dinner.

"Mother, Dad, I have something to tell you, and I'm afraid it's going to hurt you."

"Just tell us what's on your heart," her father said, "and we'll understand. We want to pray with you about it—whatever it is."

"Well, you know that all during high school I talked about becoming a nurse, mainly because Mom is a nurse, and I guess you expected me to follow in her footsteps. But I can't go on. The Lord just doesn't want me to be a nurse!"

Her mother smiled and took Cindy's hand. "Dear,

your father and I want God's will for your life. If you do anything else, we'll *all* be unhappy!"

Cindy had done the courageous thing; she had faced God's will and decided that she wanted to work out *her own salvation*—her own Christian life—and not what somebody else wanted her to do. One of the wonderful things about being a Christian is the knowledge that God has a plan for our lives (Eph. 2:10) and will help us to work it out for His glory. Our God is a God of infinite variety! No two flowers are the same, no two snowflakes are the same; why should two Christians be the same? All of us must be like Christ, *but we must also be ourselves.*

The phrase "work out your own salvation" probably has reference particularly to the special problems in the church at Philippi, but the statement also applies to the individual Christian. We are not to be "cheap imitations" of other people, especially "great Christians." We are to follow only what we see of Christ in their lives. "Be ye followers of me, even as I also am of Christ" (1 Cor. 11:1). Every "great saint" has feet of clay and ultimately may disappoint you, but Jesus Christ can never fail you.

In Philippians 2:14–15, Paul contrasted the life of the believer with the lives of those who live in the world. Unsaved people complain and find fault, but Christians rejoice. Society around us is "twisted and distorted," but the Christian stands straight because he measures his life by God's Word, the perfect standard. The world is dark, but Christians shine as bright lights. The world has nothing to offer, but the Christian holds out the Word of life, the message of salvation through faith in Christ. In other words, as we allow God to achieve this purpose in our lives, we become better witnesses in a world that desperately needs Christ. Apply these characteristics to Jesus and you will see that He lived a perfect life in an imperfect world.

It is important to note that this purpose is achieved "in the midst of a crooked and perverse generation" (Phil. 2:15). Paul did not admonish us to retreat from the world and go into a spiritual isolation ward. It is only as we are confronted with the needs and problems of real life that we can begin to become more like Christ. The Pharisees were so isolated and insulated from reality that they developed an artificial kind of self-righteousness that was totally unlike the righteousness God wanted them to have. Consequently, the Pharisees forced a religion of fear and bondage on the people (read Matt. 23), and they crucified Christ because He dared to oppose that kind of religion. It is not by leaving the world but by ministering to it that we see God's purpose fulfilled in our lives.

There Is a Power to Receive (2:13)

The principle Paul laid down is this: God must work *in* us before He can work *through* us. This principle is seen at work throughout the Bible in the lives of men like Moses, David, the apostles, and others. God had a special purpose for each man to fulfill, and each man

was unique and not an imitation of somebody else. For example, it took God forty years to bring Moses to the place where He could use him to lead the people of Israel. As Moses tended sheep during those forty years, God was working in him so that one day He might work through him. *God is more interested in the workman than in the work.* If the workman is what he ought to be, the work will be what it ought to be.

Too many Christians obey God only because of pressure on the outside, and not power on the inside. Paul warned the Philippians that not his presence with them but their desire to obey God and please Him was the important thing (Phil. 1:27; 2:12). They could not build their lives on Paul because he might not be with them very long. It is sad to see the way some ministries in the church weaken or fall apart because of a change in leadership. We have a tendency to please men and to obey God only when others are watching. But when you surrender to the power of God within you, then obedience becomes a delight and not a battle.

The power that works in us is the power of the Holy Spirit of God (John 14:16–17, 26; Acts 1:8; 1 Cor. 6:19–20). Our English word *energy* comes from the word translated "worketh" in Philippians 2:13. It is God's divine energy at work in us and through us! The same Holy Spirit who empowered Christ when He was ministering on earth can empower us as well. But we must recognize the fact that the energy of the flesh (Rom. 7:5) and of the devil (Eph. 2:2; 2 Thess. 2:7) are also at work. Because of the death, resurrection, and ascension of Christ, God's divine energy is available to us (Eph. 1:18–23). The power is here, but how do we use it? What "tools" does God use, by His Spirit, to work in our lives? There are three "tools": the Word of God, prayer, and suffering.

The Word of God. "For this cause also thank we God without ceasing, because, when ye received the word of God, which ye heard of us, ye received it not as the word of men, but as it is in truth, the word of God, which effectually worketh also in you that believe" (1 Thess. 2:13). God's divine energy is released in our lives through His inspired Word. The same Word that spoke the universe into being can release divine power in our lives! But we have a responsibility to *appreciate* the Word, and not treat it the way we treat the words of men. The Word of God is unique: it is inspired, authoritative, and infallible. If we do not appreciate the Word, then God's power cannot energize our lives.

But we must also *appropriate* the Word—"receive it." This means much more than listening to it, or even reading and studying it. To "receive" God's Word means to welcome it and make it a part of our inner being. God's truth is to the spiritual man what food is to the physical man.

Finally, we must *apply* the Word; it works only in those "that believe." When we trust God's Word and act on it, then God's power is released in our lives. The angel's promise to Mary in Luke 1:37—"For with God nothing shall be impossible"—is translated "For no word from God shall be void of power" in the American Standard Version (1901). God's Word has the power of accomplishment in it, and faith releases that power.

We see this truth operating in the life of Jesus. He commanded the crippled man to stretch out his hand, and the very command gave him the power to obey and be healed (Matt. 12:13). He commanded Peter to walk to Him on the water, and the command enabled Peter to do so, as long as he exercised faith (Matt. 14:22–33). It is faith in God's promises that releases God's power. His commandments are His enablements. The Holy Spirit wrote down the promises for us in the Word, and He gives us the faith to lay hold of these promises. "For no matter how many promises God has made, they are 'Yes' in Christ. And so through him the 'Amen' is spoken by us to the glory of God" (2 Cor. 1:20 NIV).

Prayer. *So,* if we want God's power working in us, we must spend time daily with the Word of God. But we must also pray, because *prayer is* the second "tool" God uses to work in the lives of His children. "Now unto him that is able to do exceeding abundantly above all that we ask or think, according to the power that worketh in us" (Eph. 3:20). The Holy Spirit is closely related to the practice of prayer in our lives (Rom. 8:26–27; Zech. 12:10). The book of Acts makes it clear that prayer is a divinely ordained source of spiritual power (Acts 1:14; 4:23–31; 12:5, 12), and the Word of God and prayer go together (Acts 6:4). Unless the Christian takes time for prayer, God cannot work in him and through him. In the Bible and in church history, the people God used were people who prayed.

Suffering. God's third "tool" is *suffering.* The Spirit of God works in a special way in the lives of those who suffer for the glory of Christ (1 Peter 4:12–19). The "fiery trial" has a way of burning away the dross and empowering the believer to serve Christ. Paul himself had experienced God's power in that Philippian jail when he was beaten and thrust into the stocks in the inner prison, for he was able to sing and praise God in spite of his suffering (Acts 16:19–33). His "fiery trial" also enabled him to forgive the jailer. It was not the earthquake that brought conviction to the man; the earthquake almost led him to suicide! It was Paul's encouraging word, "Don't do it! We are all here!" (TLB). This kind of love broke the man's heart, and he fell before Paul asking how to be saved.

The Word of God, prayer, and suffering are the three tools that God uses in our lives. Just as electricity must run through a conductor, so the Holy Spirit must work through the means God has provided. As the Christian reads the Word and prays, he becomes more like Christ, and the more he becomes like Christ, the more the unsaved world opposes him. This daily "fellowship of his sufferings" (Phil. 3:10) drives the believer back to the Word and prayer, so that all three tools work together to provide the spiritual power he needs to glorify Christ.

If we are to have the submissive mind, and the joy that goes with it, we must recognize that there is a purpose to achieve (God's plan for our lives), a power to receive (the Holy Spirit), and a promise to believe.

There Is a Promise to Believe (2:16–18)

What is this promise? *That joy comes from submission.* The world's philosophy is that joy comes from aggression: fight everybody to get what you want, and you will get it and be happy. The example of Jesus is proof enough that the world's philosophy is wrong. He never used a sword or any other weapon, yet He won the greatest battle in history—the battle against sin and death and hell. He defeated hatred by manifesting love; He overcame lies with truth. *Because He surrendered He was victorious!* And you and I must dare to believe His promise, "For whosoever exalteth himself shall be abased; and he that humbleth himself shall be exalted" (Luke 14:11). "How happy are the humble-minded, for the kingdom of heaven is theirs" (Matt. 5:3 PH).

There is a twofold joy that comes to the person who possesses and practices the submissive mind: a joy hereafter (Phil. 2:16) and a joy here and now (Phil. 2:17–18). In the day of Christ (see Phil. 1:6, 10), God is going to reward those who have been faithful to Him. "The joy of thy Lord" is going to be a part of that reward (Matt. 25:21). The faithful Christian will discover that his sufferings on earth have been transformed into glory in heaven! He will see that his work was not in vain (1 Cor. 15:58). It was this same kind of promise of future joy that helped our Savior in His sufferings on the cross (Heb. 12:1–2).

But we do not have to wait for the return of Christ to start experiencing the joy of the submissive mind. That joy is a present reality (Phil. 2:17–18), and it comes through sacrifice and service. It is remarkable that in two verses that discuss sacrifice, Paul used the words *joy* and *rejoice*—and repeats them! Most people would associate sorrow with suffering, but Paul saw suffering and sacrifice as doorways to a deeper joy in Christ.

In Philippians 2:17, Paul was comparing his experience of sacrifice to that of the priest pouring out the drink offering (Num. 15:1–10). It was possible that Paul's trial would go against him and he would be executed. But this did not rob Paul of his joy. His death would be a willing sacrifice, a priestly ministry, on behalf of Christ and His church, and this would give him joy. "Sacrifice and service" are marks of the submissive mind (Phil. 2:7–8, 21–22, 30), and the submissive mind experiences joy even in the midst of suffering.

It takes faith to exercise the submissive mind. We must believe that God's promises are true and that they are going to work in our lives just as they worked in Paul's life. God works *in* us through the Word, prayer, and suffering, and we work *out* in daily living and service. God fulfills His purposes in us as we receive and believe His Word. Life is not a series of disappointing "ups and downs." Rather, it is a sequence of delightful "ins and outs." God works in—we work out! The example comes from Christ, the energy comes from the Holy Spirit, and the result is—JOY!

CHAPTER SIX
Philippians 2:19–30
A PRICELESS PAIR

A reporter in San Bernardino, California arranged for a man to lie in the gutter on a busy street. Hundreds of people passed the man, but not one stopped to help him or even show sympathy!

Newspapers across the country a few years ago told how thirty-eight people watched a man stalk a young lady and finally attack her—and none of the spectators even picked up a phone to call the police!

A couple of teenagers in Detroit discovered a woman in a telephone booth who had suffered a heart attack. They carried her to a nearby house and rang the bell, asking for help. The only reply they received was, "Get off my porch—and take her with you!"

A Kentucky doctor was driving down the highway to visit a patient when he saw an accident take place. He stopped and gave aid to the injured and then made his visit. One of the drivers he helped sued him!

Is it possible to be a "Good Samaritan" today? Must everybody harden his heart in order to protect himself? Perhaps "sacrifice and service" are ancient virtues that somehow do not fit into our so-called modern civilization. It is worth noting that even in Paul's day mutual concern was not a popular virtue. The Christians at Rome were not too interested in the problems at Philippi; Paul could not find *one person* among them willing to go to Philippi (Phil. 2:19–21). Times have not changed too much.

In this paragraph, Paul was still discussing the submissive mind. He has given us a *description* of the submissive mind in the example of Jesus Christ (Phil. 2:1–11). He has explained the *dynamics* of the submissive mind in his own experience (Phil. 2:12–18). Now he introduced us to two of his helpers in the ministry, Timothy and Epaphroditus, and he did this for a reason. He knew that his readers would be prone to say, "It is impossible for us to follow such examples as Christ and Paul! After all, Jesus is the very Son of God, and Paul is a chosen apostle who has had great spiritual experiences!" For this reason, Paul introduced us to two "ordinary saints," men who were not apostles or spectacular miracle workers. He wanted us to know that the submissive mind is not a luxury enjoyed by a chosen few; it is a necessity for Christian joy, and an opportunity for *all* believers.

Timothy (Phil. 2:19–24)
Paul probably met Timothy on his first missionary journey (Acts 14:6ff.), at which time, perhaps, the youth was converted (1 Cor. 4:17). Apparently, Timothy's mother and grandmother had been converted first (2 Tim. 1:3–5). He was the son of a Jewish mother and Gentile father, but Paul always considered the young man his own "dearly beloved son" in the faith (2 Tim. 1:2). When Paul returned to Derbe and Lystra while on his second journey, he enlisted young Timothy as one of his fellow laborers (Acts 16:1–4). In one sense, Timothy replaced John Mark, whom Paul had refused to take along on the journey because of Mark's previous abandonment of the cause (Acts 13:13; 15:36–41).

In Timothy's experience, we learn that the submissive mind is not something that suddenly, automatically appears in the life of the believer. Timothy had to develop and cultivate the "mind of Christ." It was not natural for him to be a servant; but, as he walked with the Lord and worked with Paul, he became the kind of servant that Paul could trust and God could bless. Notice the characteristics of this young man.

He had a servant's mind (vv. 19–21). To begin with, Timothy naturally cared for people and was concerned about their needs. He was not interested in "winning friends and influencing people"; he was genuinely interested in their physical and spiritual welfare. Paul was concerned about the church at Philippi and wanted to send someone to convey his concern and get the facts. There were certainly hundreds of Christians in Rome (Paul greeted twenty-six of them by name in Rom. 16); yet not one of them was available to make the trip! "All seek their own, not the things which are Jesus Christ's" (Phil. 2:21). In a very real sense, all of us live either in Philippians 1:21 or Philippians 2:21!

But Timothy had a natural concern for the welfare of others; he had a servant's mind. It is too bad that the believers in Rome were so engrossed in themselves and their own internal wranglings (Phil. 1:15–16) that they had no time for the important work of the Lord. This is one of the tragedies of church problems; they divert time, energy, and concern away from the things that matter most. Timothy was not interested in promoting any party or supporting any divisive cause. He was interested only in the spiritual condition of God's people, and this concern was *natural* to him. How did this concern develop? The answer is in the next characteristic of this remarkable young man.

He had a servant's training (v. 22). Paul did not add Timothy to his "team" the very day the boy was saved. Paul was too wise to make an error like that. He left him behind to become a part of the church fellowship in Derbe and Lystra, and it was in that fellowship that Timothy grew in spiritual matters and learned how to serve the Lord. When Paul returned to that area a few years later, he was happy to discover that young Timothy "was well reported of the brethren" (Acts 16:2). Years later, Paul would write to Timothy about the importance of permitting new converts to grow before thrusting them into important places of ministry (1 Tim. 3:6–7).

A popular local nightclub performer visited a pastor and announced that he had been saved and wanted to serve the Lord. "What should I do next?" he asked.

"Well, I'd suggest you unite with a good church and start growing," the pastor replied. "Is your wife a Christian?"

"No, she isn't," the musician replied. "I hope to win her. But, do I have to wait? I mean, I'd like to do something for God right now."

"No, you don't have to wait to witness for the Lord," explained the pastor. "Get busy in a church, and use your talents for Christ."

"But you don't know who I am!" the man protested. "I'm a big performer—everybody knows me. I want to start my own organization, make records, and appear before big crowds!"

"If you go too far too fast," warned the pastor, "you may hurt yourself and your testimony. And the place to start winning people is right at home. God will open up places of service for you as He sees you are ready. Meanwhile, study the Bible and give yourself a chance to grow."

The man did not take the pastor's counsel. Instead, he set up a big organization and started out on his own. His "success" lasted less than a year. Not only did he lose his testimony because he was not strong enough to carry the heavy burdens, but his constant traveling alienated him from his wife and family. He drifted into a "fringe group" and disappeared from public ministry, a broken and bankrupt man.

"His branches went out farther than his roots went deep," the pastor said. "When that happens, you eventually topple."

Paul did not make this mistake with Timothy. He gave him time to get his roots down, and then he enlisted the young man to work with him on his missionary tours. He taught Timothy the Word and permitted him to watch the apostle in his ministry (2 Tim. 3:10–17). This was the way Jesus trained His disciples. He gave personal instruction balanced by on-the-job experience. Experience without teaching can lead to discouragement, and teaching without experience can lead to spiritual deadness. It takes both.

He had a servant's reward (vv. 23–24). Timothy knew the meaning of "sacrifice and service" (Phil. 2:17), but God rewarded him for his faithfulness. To begin with, Timothy had the joy of helping others. To be sure, there were hardships and difficulties, but there were also victories and blessings. Because Timothy was a "good and faithful servant," faithful over a few things, God rewarded him with "many things," and he entered into the joy of the submissive mind (Matt. 25:21). He had the joy of serving with the great apostle Paul and assisting him in some of his most difficult assignments (1 Cor. 4:17ff; Timothy is mentioned at least twenty-four times in Paul's letters).

But perhaps the greatest reward God gave to Timothy was to choose him to be Paul's replacement when the great apostle was called home (see 2 Tim. 4:1–11). Paul himself wanted to go to Philippi, but had had to send Timothy in his place. But, what an honor! Timothy was not only Paul's son and Paul's servant, but he became Paul's substitute! His name is held in high regard by Christians today, something that young Timothy never dreamed of when he was busy serving Christ

The submissive mind is not the product of an hour's sermon, or a week's seminar, or even a year's service. The submissive mind grows in us as, like Timothy, we yield to the Lord and seek to serve others.

Epaphroditus (2:25–30)

Paul was a "Hebrew of the Hebrews"; Timothy was part Jew and part Gentile (Acts 16:1); and Epaphroditus was a full Gentile as far as we know. He was the member of the Philippian church who risked his health and life to carry their missionary offering to the apostle in Rome (Phil. 4:18). His name means "charming," and a charming Christian he is!

He was a balanced Christian (v. 25). Paul could not say enough about this man—"my brother, and companion in labor, and fellow-soldier." These three descriptions parallel what Paul wrote about the gospel in the first chapter of this letter:

"my brother"	the "fellowship in the gospel" (Phil. 1:5)
"my companion in	"the furtherance of the labor gospel" (Phil. 1:12)
"my fellow-soldier	"the faith of the gospel" (Phil. 1:27)

Epaphroditus was a balanced Christian!

Balance is important in the Christian life. Some people emphasize "fellowship" so much that they forget the furtherance of the gospel. Others are so involved in defending the "faith of the gospel" that they neglect building fellowship with other believers. Epaphroditus did not fall into either of these traps. He was like Nehemiah, the man who rebuilt the walls of Jerusalem with his sword in one hand and his trowel in the other (Neh. 4:17). You cannot build with a sword nor battle with a trowel! It takes both to get the Lord's work accomplished.

Dr. H. A. Ironside used to tell about a group of believers who thought only of "fellowship." They had little concern for reaching the lost or for defending the faith against its enemies. In front of their meeting place they hung a sign: JESUS ONLY. But the wind blew away some of the letters, and the sign read—US ONLY. It was a perfect description of a group of people who were not balanced Christians.

He was a burdened Christian (vv. 26–27, 30). Like Timothy, Epaphroditus was concerned about others. To begin with, he was concerned about *Paul.* When he heard in Philippi that Paul was a prisoner in Rome, he volunteered to make that long, dangerous trip to Rome to stand at Paul's side and assist him. He carried the church's love gift with him, protecting it with his own life.

Our churches today need men and women who are burdened for missions and for those in difficult places of Christian service. "The problem in our churches," states one missionary leader, "is that we have too many spectators and not enough participants." Epaphroditus was not content simply to contribute to the offering. He gave *himself to* help carry the offering!

But this man was also burdened for *his own home church.* After arriving in Rome, he became very ill. In fact, he almost died. This delayed his return to Philippi, and the people there became concerned about him. But Epaphroditus was not burdened about himself; he was burdened over the people in Philippi *because they were worried about him!* This man lived in Philippians 1:21, not Philippians 2:21. Like Timothy, he had a natural concern for others. The phrase "full of heaviness" in Philippines 2:26 is the same description used of Christ in Gethsemane (Matt. 26:37). Like Christ, Epaphroditus knew the meaning of sacrifice and service (Phil. 2:30), which are two of the marks of the submissive mind.

He was a blessed Christian (vv. 28–30). What a tragedy it would be to go through life and not be a blessing to anyone! Epaphroditus was a blessing to Paul. He stood with him in his prison experience and did not permit even his own sickness to hinder his service. What times he and Paul must have had together! But he was also a blessing to his own church. Paul admonished the church to honor him because of his sacrifice and service. (Christ gets the glory, but there is nothing wrong with the servant receiving honor. Read 1 Thess. 5:12–13.) There is no contradiction between Philippians 2:7 ("made himself of no reputation") and Philippians 2:29 ("hold such in reputation"). Christ "emptied Himself" in His gracious act of humiliation, and God exalted Him. Epaphroditus sacrificed himself with no thought of reward, and Paul encouraged the church to hold him in honor to the glory of God.

He was a blessing to Paul and to his own church, and he is also a blessing to us *today!* He proves to us that the joyful life is the life of sacrifice and service, that the submissive mind really does work. He and Timothy together encourage us to submit ourselves to the Lord, and to one another, in the Spirit of Christ. Christ is the pattern we follow. Paul shows us the power (Phil. 4:12–19); and Timothy and Epaphroditus are the proof that this mind really works.

Will you permit the Spirit to reproduce "the mind of Christ" in you?

CHAPTER SEVEN
Philippians 3:1–11
LEARNING HOW TO COUNT

Circumstances and people can rob us of joy, but so can *things,* and it is this "thief" that Paul deals with in Philippians 3. It is important to see the total message of this chapter before examining it in detail, so perhaps the following outline will be helpful.

vv. 1–11	*vv. 12–16*	*vv. 17–21*
Paul's past	Paul's present	Paul's future
the accountant	the athlete	the alien
"I count"	"I press"	"I look"
new values	new vigor	new vision

What Paul was describing is the "spiritual mind." In Philippians 3:18–19, he described professed Christians who "mind earthly things," but then in Philippians 3:20 he described the believer with the spiritual mind, who "minds heavenly things." You will recall that the city of Philippi was actually a Roman colony—a "Rome away from Rome." In the same sense, the people of God are a colony of heaven on earth. "Our citizenship is in heaven" (Phil. 3:20 NASB), and we look at earth from heaven's point of view. This is the spiritual mind.

It is easy for us to get wrapped up in "things," not only the tangible things that we can see, but also the intangibles such as reputation, fame, achievement. Paul wrote about "what things were gain" to him (Phil. 3:7); he also mentioned "things which are behind" and "things which are before" (Phil. 3:13). In Paul's case, some of these "things" were intangible, such as religious achievements (Gal. 1:14), a feeling of self-satisfaction, morality. We today can be snared both by tangibles and intangibles, and as a result lose our joy.

But even the tangible things are not in themselves sinful. God made things, and the Bible declares that these things are good (Gen. 1:31). God knows that we need certain things in order to live (Matt. 6:31–34). In fact, He "giveth us richly all things to enjoy" (1 Tim. 6:17). But Jesus warned us that our lives do not consist in the abundance of the things that we possess (Luke 12:15). Quantity is no assurance of quality. Many people who have the things money can buy have lost the things that money cannot buy.

The key word in Philippians 3:1–11 is *count* (Phil. 3:7–8, 13). In the Greek, two different words are used, but the basic idea is the same: to evaluate, to assess. "The unexamined life is not worth living," said Socrates. Yet, few people sit down to weigh seriously the values that control their decisions and directions. Many people today are the slaves of "things," and as a result do not experience real Christian joy.

In Paul's case, the "things" he was living for before he knew Christ seemed to be very commendable: a righteous life, obedience to the law, the defense of the religion of his fathers. But none of these things satisfied him or gave him acceptance with God.

Like most "religious" people today, Paul had enough morality to keep him out of trouble, but not enough righteousness to get him into heaven! It was not bad things that kept Paul away from Jesus— it was good things! He had to lose his "religion" to find salvation.

One day, Saul of Tarsus, the rabbi, met Jesus

Christ, the Son of God, and on that day Saul's values changed (read Acts 9:1–31). When Saul opened his books to evaluate his wealth, he discovered that apart from Jesus Christ, everything he lived for was only refuse. He explained in this section that there are only two kinds of righteousness (or spiritual wealth)—works righteousness and faith righteousness—and only faith righteousness is acceptable to God.

Works Righteousness (3:1–6)

The exhortation (vv. 1–3). "Finally" at this point does not mean Paul is about to close the letter, because he keeps on going. The word means "For the rest," and introduces the new section. Paul's "finally" at Philippians 4:18 is the one that means "I am about to close." Paul has warned the believers at Philippi before, but now he warned them again. "Look out for dogs! Look out for the workers of evil! Look out for the mutilation!" To whom was he referring in this triple warning? The answer takes us back into the early history of the church.

From the very beginning, the gospel came "to the Jew first" (see Acts 3:26; Rom. 1:16), so that the first seven chapters of Acts deal only with Jewish believers or with Gentiles who were Jewish proselytes (Acts 2:10). In Acts 8:5–25, the message went to the Samaritans, but this did not cause too much of an upheaval since the Samaritans were at least partly Jewish. But when Peter went to the Gentiles in Acts 10, this created an uproar. Peter was called on the carpet to explain his activities (Acts 11). After all, the Gentiles in Acts 10 had become Christians *without first becoming Jews,* and this was a whole new thing for the church. Peter explained that it was God who had directed him to preach to the Gentiles, and the matter seemed to be settled.

But it was not settled for long. Paul was sent out by the Holy Spirit to minister especially to the Gentiles (Acts 13:1–3; 22:21). Peter had opened the door of faith to the Gentiles in Acts 10, and Paul followed his example on his first missionary journey (see Acts 14:26–28). It did not take long for the strict Jewish believers to oppose Paul's ministry and come to Antioch teaching that it was necessary for the Gentiles to submit to Jewish rules before they could be saved (Acts 15:1). This disagreement led to the Conference at Jerusalem that is described in Acts 15. The result of the conference was an approval of Paul's ministry and a victory for the gospel of the grace of God. Gentiles did *not* have to become Jewish proselytes in order to become Christians!

But the dissenters were not content. Having failed in their opposition to Paul at Antioch and Jerusalem, they followed him wherever he went and tried to steal his converts and his churches. Bible students call this group of false teachers who try to mix law and grace "Judaizers." The epistle to the Galatians was written primarily to combat this false teaching. It is this group of "Judaizers" that Paul was referring to in Philippians 3:1–2. He used three terms to describe them.

"Dogs." The orthodox Jew would call the Gentile a "dog," but here Paul called orthodox Jews "dogs"! Paul was not just using names; he was comparing these false teachers to the dirty scavengers so contemptible to decent people. Like those dogs, these Judaizers snapped at Paul's heels and followed him from place to place "barking" their false doctrines. They were troublemakers and carriers of dangerous infection.

"Evil workers." These men taught that the sinner was saved by faith *plus* good works, especially the works of the law. But Paul stated that their "good works" are really *evil* works because they are performed by the flesh (old nature) and not the Spirit, and they glorify the workers and not Jesus Christ. Ephesians 2:8–10 and Titus 3:3–7 make it clear that nobody can be saved by doing good works, even religious works. A Christian's good works are the result of his faith, not the basis for his salvation.

"The mutilation." Here Paul used a pun on the word *circumcision*. The word translated "circumcision" literally means "a mutilation." The Judaizers taught that circumcision was essential to salvation (Acts 15:1; Gal. 6:12–18), but Paul stated that circumcision of *itself* is only a mutilation! The true Christian has experienced a spiritual circumcision in Christ (Col. 2:11), and does not need any fleshly operations. Circumcision, baptism, the Lord's Supper, tithing, or any other religious practice cannot save a person from his sins. Only faith in Jesus Christ can do that.

In contrast to the false Christians, Paul described the true Christians, the "true circumcision" (see Rom. 2:25–29 for a parallel).

He worships God in the Spirit. He does not depend on his own good works, which are only of the flesh (see John 4:19–24).

He boasts in Jesus Christ. People who depend on religion are usually boasting about what they have done. The true Christian has nothing of which to boast (Eph. 2:8–10). His boast is only in Christ! In Luke 18:9–14, Jesus gave a parable that describes these two opposite attitudes.

He has no confidence in the flesh. The popular religious philosophy of today is "The Lord helps those who help themselves." It was also popular in Paul's day, and it is just as wrong today as it was then. (By "the flesh" Paul meant "the old nature" that we received at birth.) The Bible has nothing good to say about "flesh," and yet most people today depend entirely on what they themselves can do to please God. Flesh only corrupts God's way on earth (Gen. 6:12). It profits nothing as far as spiritual life is concerned (John 6:63). It has nothing good in it (Rom. 7:18). No wonder we should put no confidence in the flesh!

A lady was arguing with her pastor about this matter of faith and works. "I think that getting to heaven is like rowing a boat," she said. "One oar is faith, and the other is works. If you use both, you get there. If you use only one, you go around in circles."

"There is only one thing wrong with your illustration,"

replied the pastor. "Nobody is going to heaven *in a rowboat!*"

There is only one "good work" that takes the sinner to heaven: the finished work of Christ on the cross (John 17:1–4; 19:30; Heb. 10:11–14).

The example (vv. 4–6). Paul was not speaking from an ivory tower; he personally *knew* the futility of trying to attain salvation by means of good works. As a young student, he had sat at the feet of Gamaliel, the great rabbi (Acts 22:3). His career as a Jewish religious leader was a promising one (Gal. 1:13–14), and yet Paul gave it all up—to become a hated member of the "Christian sect" and a preacher of the gospel! Actually, the Judaizers were compromising in order to avoid persecution (Gal. 6:12–13), while Paul was being true to Christ's message of grace and as a result was suffering persecution.

In this intensely autobiographical section, Paul examined his own life. He became an "auditor" who opens the books to see what wealth he has, and he discovers that *he is bankrupt!*

Paul's relationship to the nation. He was born into a pure Hebrew family and entered into a covenantal relationship when he was circumcised. He was not a proselyte, nor was he descended from Ishmael (Abraham's other son) or Esau (Isaac's other son). The Judaizers would understand Paul's reference to the tribe of Benjamin, because Benjamin and Joseph were Jacob's favorite sons. They were born to Rachel, Jacob's favorite wife. Israel's first king came from Benjamin, and this little tribe was faithful to David during the rebellion under Absalom. Paul's human heritage was something to be proud of! When measured by this standard, he passed with flying colors.

Paul's relationship to the law. "As touching the law, a Pharisee … touching the righteousness which is in the law, blameless" (Phil. 3:5–6). To the Jews of Paul's day, a Pharisee had reached the very summit of religious experience, the highest ideal a Jew could ever hope to attain. If anybody was going to heaven, it was the Pharisee! He held to orthodox doctrine (see Acts 23:6–9) and tried to fulfill the religious duties faithfully (Luke 18:10–14). While we today are accustomed to use the word *Pharisee* as the equivalent of "hypocrite," this usage was not prevalent in Paul's day. Measured by the righteousness of the law, Paul was blameless. He kept the law and the traditions perfectly.

Paul's relationship to Israel's enemies. But it is not enough to believe the truth; a man must also oppose lies. Paul defended his orthodox faith by persecuting the followers of "that pretender," Jesus (Matt. 27:62–66). He assisted at the stoning of Stephen (Acts 7:54–60), and after that he led the attack against the church in general (Acts 8:1–3). Even in later years, Paul admitted his role in persecuting the church (Acts 22:1–5; 26:1–11; see also 1 Tim. 1:12–16). Every Jew could boast of his own blood heritage (though he certainly could not take any credit for it). Some Jews could boast of their faithfulness to the Jewish religion.

But Paul could boast of those things *plus* his zeal in persecuting the church.

At this point we might ask, "How could a sincere man like Saul of Tarsus be so wrong?" The answer is, *he was using the wrong measuring stick!* Like the rich young ruler (Mark 10:17–22) and the Pharisee in Christ's parable (Luke 18:10–14), Saul of Tarsus was looking at the *outside* and not the *inside.* He was comparing himself with standards set by men, not by God. As far as obeying *outwardly* the demands of the law, Paul was a success, but he did not stop to consider the *inward sins* he was committing. In the Sermon on the Mount, Jesus made it clear that there are sinful *attitudes* and *appetites* as well as sinful *actions* (Matt. 5:21–48).

When he looked at himself or looked at others, Saul of Tarsus considered himself to be righteous. But one day he saw himself as compared with Jesus Christ! It was then that he changed his evaluations and values, and abandoned "works righteousness" for the righteousness of Jesus Christ.

Faith Righteousness (3:7–11)

When Paul met Jesus Christ on the Damascus road (Acts 9), he trusted Him and became a child of God. It was an instantaneous miracle of the grace of God, the kind that still takes place today whenever sinners will admit their need and turn to the Savior by faith. When Paul met Christ, he realized how futile were his good works and how sinful were his claims of righteousness. A wonderful transaction took place. Paul lost some things, but he gained much more than he lost!

Paul's losses (v. 7). To begin with, he lost whatever was *gain to him personally apart from God.* Certainly Paul had a great reputation as a scholar (Acts 26:24) and a religious leader. He was proud of his Jewish heritage and his religious achievements. All of these things were valuable to him; he could profit from them. He certainly had many friends who admired his zeal. But he measured these "treasures" against what Jesus Christ had to offer, and he realized that all he held dear was really nothing but "refuse" compared to what he had in Christ. His own "treasures" brought glory to him personally, but they did not bring glory to God. They were "gain" to him only, and as such, were selfish.

This does not mean that Paul repudiated his rich heritage as an orthodox Jew. As you read his letters and follow his ministry in the book of Acts, you see how he valued both his Jewish blood and his Roman citizenship. Becoming a Christian did not make him *less* a Jew. In fact, it made him a *completed* Jew, a true child of Abraham both spiritually and physically (Gal. 3:6–9). Nor did he lower his standards of morality because he saw the shallowness of Pharisaical religion. He accepted the *higher* standard of living—conformity to Jesus Christ (Rom. 12:1–2). When a person becomes a Christian, God takes away the bad, but He also takes the good and makes it better.

Paul's gains (vv. 8–11). Again we are reminded of Jim Elliot's words: "He is no fool who gives what he cannot keep to gain what he cannot lose." This is what Paul experienced: he lost his religion and his reputation, but he gained far more than he lost.

The knowledge of Christ (v. 8). This means much more than knowledge *about* Christ, because Paul had that kind of historical information before he was saved. To "know Christ" means to have a personal relationship with Him through faith. It is this experience that Jesus mentioned in John 17:3. You and I know *about* many people, even people who lived centuries ago, but we know personally very few. "Christianity *is* Christ." Salvation is knowing Him in a personal way.

The righteousness of Christ (v. 9). Righteousness was the great goal of Paul's life when he was a Pharisee, but it was a self-righteousness, a works righteousness, that he never really could attain. But when Paul trusted Christ, he lost his own self-righteousness and gained the righteousness of Christ. The technical word for this transaction is *imputation* (read Rom. 4:1–8 carefully). It means "to put to one's account." Paul looked at his own record and discovered that he was spiritually bankrupt. He looked at Christ's record and saw that He was perfect. When Paul trusted Christ, he saw God put Christ's righteousness *to his own account!* More than that, Paul discovered that his sins had been put on Christ's account on the cross (2 Cor. 5:21). And God promised Paul that He would never write his sins against him anymore. What a fantastic experience of God's grace!

Romans 9:30—10:13 is a parallel passage and you ought to read it carefully. What Paul said about the nation Israel was true in his own life before he was saved. And it is true in the lives of many religious people today; they refuse to abandon their own righteousness that they might receive the free gift of the righteousness of Christ. Many religious people will not even admit they *need* any righteousness. Like Saul of Tarsus, they are measuring themselves by themselves, or by the standards of the Ten Commandments, and they fail to see the *inwardness* of sin. Paul had to give up his religion to receive righteousness, but he did not consider it a sacrifice.

The fellowship of Christ (vv. 10–11). When he became a Christian, it was not the *end* for Paul, but the *beginning.* His experience with Christ was so tremendous that it transformed his life. And this experience continued in the years to follow. It was a *personal* experience ("That I may know him") as Paul walked with Christ, prayed, obeyed His will, and sought to glorify His name. When he was living under law, all Paul had was a set of rules. But now he had a Friend, a Master, a constant Companion! It was also a *powerful* experience ("and the power of his resurrection"), as the resurrection power of Christ went to work in Paul's life. "Christ liveth in me" (Gal. 2:20). Read Ephesians 1:15–23 and 3:13–21 for Paul's estimate of the resurrection power of Christ and what it can do in your life.

It was also a *painful* experience ("and the fellowship of his sufferings"). Paul knew that it was a privilege to suffer for Christ (Phil. 1:29–30). In fact, suffering had been a part of his experience from the very beginning (Acts 9:16). As we grow in our knowledge of Christ and our experience of His power, we come under the attack of the enemy. Paul had been a persecutor at one time, but he learned what it means to be persecuted. But it was worth it! For walking with Christ was also a *practical* experience ("being made conformable unto his death"). Paul lived for Christ because he died to self (Rom. 6 explains this); he took up his cross daily and followed Him. The result of this death was a spiritual resurrection (Phil. 3:11) that caused Paul to walk "in newness of life" (Rom. 6:4). Paul summarized this whole experience in Galatians 2:20, so take time to read it.

Yes, Paul gained far more than he lost. In fact, the gains were so thrilling that Paul considered all other "things" nothing but garbage in comparison! No wonder he had joy—his life did not depend on the cheap things of the world but on the eternal values found in Christ. Paul had the "spiritual mind" and looked at the things of earth from heaven's point of view. People who live for things are never really happy, because they must constantly protect their treasures and worry lest they lose their value. Not so the believer with the spiritual mind; his treasures in Christ can never be stolen and they never lose their value.

Maybe now is a good time for you to become an accountant and evaluate in your life the "things" that matter most to you.

CHAPTER EIGHT
Philippians 3:12–16
LET'S WIN THE RACE!

Most people read biographies to satisfy their curiosity about great people, hoping also that they may discover the "secret" that made them great. I recall sitting in a grade school assembly program many years ago, listening to an aged doctor who promised to tell us the secret of his long, healthy life. (At one time he was a physician to the president of the United States. I've forgotten which one, but at that stage in my life, it seemed it must have been Washington or Jefferson.) All of us sat there with great expectation, hoping to learn the secret of a long life. At the climax of his address, the doctor told us, "Drink eight glasses of water a day!"

In Philippians 3, Paul gave us his spiritual biography, his past (Phil. 3:1–11), his present (Phil. 3:12–16), and his future (Phil. 3:17–21). We have already met Paul "the accountant," who discovered new values when he met Jesus Christ. In this section we meet Paul "the athlete" with his spiritual vigor, pressing toward the finish line in the Christian race. In the final section we will see Paul "the alien," having his citizenship in heaven and looking for the coming of Jesus Christ. In each of these experiences, Paul was exercising the *spiritual mind;* he was looking at things on earth from God's point of view. As a result, he was not upset by things behind him, around him, or before him—*things* did not rob him of his joy!

In his letters, Paul used many illustrations from the world to communicate truth about the Christian life. Four are prominent: the military ("Put on the whole armor of God"), architecture ("You are the temple of God"), agriculture ("Whatsoever a man sows, that shall he also reap"), and athletics. In this paragraph, it is Paul the athlete. Bible students are not agreed as to the exact sport Paul was describing, whether the footrace or the chariot race. Either one will do, but my own preference is the chariot race. The Greek chariot, used in the Olympic Games and other events, was really only a small platform with a wheel on each side. The driver had very little to hold on to as he raced around the course. He had to lean forward and strain every nerve and muscle to maintain balance and control the horses. The verb "reaching forth" in Philippians 3:13 literally means "stretching as in a race."

It is important to note that Paul was not telling us how to be saved. If he were, it would be a picture of salvation by works or self-effort, and this would contradict what he wrote in the first eleven verses of Philippians 3. In order to participate in the Greek games, the athlete had to be a citizen. He did not run the race to gain his citizenship. In Philippians 3:20, Paul reminded us that "our conversation [citizenship] is in heaven." Because we are already the children of God through faith in Christ, we have the responsibility of "running the race" and achieving the goals God has set for us. This is a graphic picture of Philippians 2:12–13: "Work out your own salvation … for it is God which worketh in you." Each believer is on the track; each has a special lane in which to run; and each has a goal to achieve. If we reach the goal the way God has planned, then we receive a reward. If we fail, we lose the reward, but we do not lose our citizenship. (Read 1 Cor. 3:11–15 for the same idea, only using architecture as the symbol.)

All of us want to be "winning Christians" and fulfill the purposes for which we have been saved. What are the essentials for winning the race and one day receiving the reward that is promised?

Dissatisfaction (3:12–13a)

"Not as though I had already attained!" This is the statement of a great Christian who never permitted himself to be satisfied with his spiritual attainments. Obviously, Paul was satisfied with Jesus Christ (Phil. 3:10), but he was not satisfied with his Christian life. A sanctified dissatisfaction is the first essential to progress in the Christian race.

Harry came out of the manager's office with a look on his face dismal enough to wilt the roses on the secretary's desk.

"You didn't get fired?" she asked.

"No, it's not that bad. But he sure did lay into me about my sales record. I can't figure it out; for the past month I've been bringing in plenty of orders. I thought he'd compliment me, but instead he told me to get with it."

Later in the day, the secretary talked to her boss about Harry. The boss chuckled. "Harry is one of our best salesmen and I'd hate to lose him. But he has a tendency to rest on his laurels and be satisfied with his performance. If I didn't get him mad at me once a month, he'd never produce!"

Many Christians are self-satisfied because they compare their "running" with that of other Christians, usually those who are not making much progress. Had Paul compared himself with others, he would have been tempted to be proud and perhaps to let up a bit. After all, there were not too many believers in Paul's day who had experienced all that he had! But Paul did not compare himself with others; he compared himself with *himself* and with *Jesus Christ!* The dual use of the word *perfect* in Philippians 3:12 and 15 explains his thinking. He has not arrived yet at perfection (Phil. 3:12), but he is "perfect" [mature] (Phil. 3:15), and one mark of this maturity is the knowledge that he is *not* perfect! The mature Christian honestly evaluates himself and strives to do better.

Often in the Bible we are warned against a false estimate of our spiritual condition. The church at Sardis had "a name that thou livest, and art dead" (Rev. 3:1). They had reputation without reality. The church at Laodicea boasted that it was rich, when in God's sight it was "wretched, and miserable, and poor, and blind, and naked" (Rev. 3:17). In contrast to the Laodicean church, the believers at Smyrna thought they were poor when they were really rich! (Rev. 2:9). Samson thought he still had his old power, but in reality it had departed from him (Judg. 16:20).

Self-evaluation can be a dangerous thing, because we can err in two directions: (1) making ourselves *better* than we are, or (2) making ourselves *worse* than we really are. Paul had no illusions about himself; he still had to keep "pressing forward" in order to "lay hold of that for which Christ laid hold" of him. A divine dissatisfaction is essential for spiritual progress. "As the hart panteth after the water brooks, so panteth my soul after thee, O God. My soul thirsteth for God, for the living God" (Ps. 42:1–2).

Devotion (3:13b)

"One thing" is a phrase that is important to the Christian life. "One thing thou lackest," said Jesus to the self-righteous rich young ruler (Mark 10:21). "One thing is needful," He explained to busy Martha when she criticized her sister (Luke 10:42). "One thing I know," exclaimed the man who had received his sight by the power of Christ (John 9:25). "One thing have I desired of the Lord, that will I seek after," testified the psalmist (Ps. 27:4). Too many Christians are too involved in "many things," when the secret of progress is to concentrate on "one thing." It was this decision that was a turning point in D. L. Moody's life. Before the tragedy of the Chicago fire in 1871, Mr. Moody was involved in Sunday school promotion, YMCA work, evangelistic meetings, and many other activities, but after the fire, he determined to devote himself exclusively to evangelism. "This one thing I do!" became a reality to him. As a result, millions of people heard the gospel.

The believer must devote himself to "running the Christian race." No athlete succeeds by doing everything; he succeeds by *specializing.* There are those few athletes who seem proficient in many sports, but they are the exception. The winners are those who concentrate, who keep their eyes on the goal and let nothing distract them. They are devoted entirely to their calling. Like Nehemiah the wall-building governor, they reply to the distracting invitations, "I am doing a great work, so that I cannot come down" (Neh. 6:3). "A double-minded man is unstable in all his ways" (James 1:8). Concentration is the secret of power. If a river is allowed to overflow its banks, the area around it becomes a swamp. But if that river is dammed and controlled, it becomes a source of power. It is wholly a matter of values and priorities, living for that which matters most.

Direction (3:13c)

The unsaved person is controlled by the past, but the Christian running the race looks toward the future. Imagine what would happen on the race course if the charioteers (or the runners) started looking behind them! It is bad enough for a plowman to look back (Luke 9:62), but for a charioteer to do so means a possible collision and serious injury.

We are accustomed to saying "past, present, future," but we should view time as flowing from the *future* into the *present* and then into the *past.* At least, the believer should be future-oriented, "forgetting those things which are behind." Please keep in mind that in Bible terminology, "to forget" does not mean "to fail to remember." Apart from senility, hypnosis, or a brain malfunction, no mature person can forget what has happened in the past. We may wish that we could erase certain bad memories, but we cannot. "To forget" in the Bible means "no longer to be influenced by or affected by." When God promises, "And their sins and iniquities will I remember no more" (Heb. 10:17), He is not suggesting that He will conveniently have a bad memory! This is impossible with God. What God is saying is, "I will no longer hold their sins against them. Their sins can no longer affect their standing with Me or influence My attitude toward them."

So, "forgetting those things which are behind" does not suggest an impossible feat of mental and psychological gymnastics by which we try to erase the sins and mistakes of the past. *It simply means that we break the power of the past by living for the future.* We cannot change the past, but we can change the *meaning* of the past. There were things in Paul's past that could have been weights to hold him back (1 Tim. 1:12–17), but they became inspirations to speed him ahead. The events did not change, but his understanding of them changed.

A good example of this principle is Joseph (Gen. 45:1–15). When he met his brothers the second time and revealed himself to them, he held no grudge against them. To be sure, they had mistreated him, but he saw the past from God's point of view. As a result he was unable to hold anything against his brothers. Joseph knew that God had a plan for his life—a race for him to run—and in fulfilling that plan and looking ahead, he broke the power of the past.

Too many Christians are shackled by regrets of the past. They are trying to run the race by looking backward! No wonder they stumble and fall and get in the way of other Christians! Some Christian runners are being distracted by the *successes* of the past, not the failures, and this is just as bad. "The things which are behind" must be set aside and "the things which are before" must take their place.

It is possible to have dissatisfaction, devotion, and direction and still lose the race and the reward. There is a fourth essential.

Determination (3:14)

"I press." This same verb is translated "I follow after" in Philippians 3:12, and it carries the idea of intense endeavor. The Greeks used it to describe a hunter eagerly pursuing his prey. A man does not become a winning athlete by listening to lectures, watching movies, reading books, or cheering at the games. He becomes a winning athlete by getting into the game and determining to win! The same zeal that Paul employed when he persecuted the church (Phil. 3:6), he displayed in serving Christ. Come to think of it, wouldn't it be wonderful if Christians put as much determination into their spiritual life as they do their golfing, fishing, or bowling?

There are two extremes to avoid here: (1) "*I* must do it all" and (2) "*God* must do it all!" The first describes the activist, the second the quietist, and both are heading for failure. "Let go and let God!" is a clever slogan, but it does not fully describe the process of Christian living. What quarterback would say to his team, "OK, men, just let go and let the coach do it all!" On the other hand, no quarterback would say, "Listen to me and forget what the coach says!" Both extremes are wrong.

The Christian runner with the spiritual mind realizes that God must work *in* him if he is going to win the race (Phil. 2:12–13). "Without me ye can do nothing" (John 15:5). God works *in* us that He might work *through* us. As we apply ourselves to the things of the spiritual life, God is able to mature us and strengthen us for the race. "Exercise thyself rather unto godliness" (1 Tim. 4:7–8). Some Christians are so busy "dying to self" that they never come back to life again to run the race! And others are so sure they can make it on their own that they never stop to read the Word, pray, or ask for the power of the Lord.

Toward what goal is the runner pressing with such spiritual determination? "The prize of the high [upward] calling of God in Christ Jesus" (Phil. 3:14). When he reaches the goal he will receive the reward! Again, Paul was not suggesting that we attain to heaven by our own efforts. He was simply saying that just as the athlete is rewarded for his performance, so the faithful believer will be crowned when Jesus Christ returns. (See 1 Cor. 9:24–27 for a parallel, and note that while only *one* athlete may receive a prize, *all* Christians may receive the reward. Furthermore, the laurel wreath of the Olympic Games will fade, but the crown Christ gives will never fade.) The important thing is that we reach the goal He has established for us. No matter how successful we may be in the eyes of men, we cannot be rewarded unless we "take hold of that for which Christ Jesus took hold of [us]" (Phil. 3:12 NIV).

Discipline (3:15–16)

It is not enough to run hard and win the race; the runner must also obey the rules. In the Greek games, the judges were very strict about this. Any infringement of the rules disqualified the athlete. He did not lose his citizenship (though he disgraced it), but he did lose his privilege to participate and win a prize. In Philippians 3:15–16, Paul emphasized the importance of the Christian remembering the "spiritual rules" laid down in the Word.

One of the greatest athletes ever to come out of the United States was Jim Thorpe. At the 1912 Olympics at Stockholm, he won the pentathlon and the decathlon, and was undoubtedly the hero of the games. But the next year officials found that Thorpe had played semiprofessional baseball and therefore had forfeited his amateur standing. This meant that he had to return his gold medals and his trophy, and that his Olympic achievements were erased from the records. It was a high price to pay for breaking the rules. (Thorpe's medals were reinstated in 1985 by the Olympic Committee.)

This was what Paul had in mind in 1 Corinthians 9:24–27. "Any man who enters an athletic contest practices rigid self-control in training" (Phil. 3:25, WMS). If the athlete breaks training, he is disqualified; if he breaks the rules of the game, he is disqualified. "No contestant in the games is crowned, unless he competes according to the rules" (2 Tim. 2:5 WMS). The issue is not what *he* thinks or what the *spectators* think but what the judges say. One day each Christian will stand before the judgment seat of Christ (Rom. 14:10–12). The Greek word for "judgment seat" is *bema,* the very same word used to describe the place where the Olympic judges gave out the prizes! If we have disciplined ourselves to obey the rules, we shall receive a prize.

Bible history is filled with people who began the race with great success but failed at the end because they disregarded God's rules. They did not lose their salvation, but they did lose their rewards (1 Cor. 3:15). It happened to Lot (Gen. 19), Samson (Judg. 16), Saul (1 Sam. 28; 31), and Ananias and Sapphira (Acts 5). And it can happen to us! It is an exciting experience to run the race daily, "looking unto Jesus" (Heb. 12:1–2). It will be even more exciting when we experience that "upward calling" and Jesus returns to take us to heaven! Then we will stand before the *bema* to receive our rewards! It was this future prospect that motivated Paul, and it can also motivate us.

CHAPTER NINE
Philippians 3:17–21
LIVING IN THE FUTURE TENSE

How strange in a letter filled with joy to find Paul *weeping!* Perhaps he was weeping over himself and his difficult situation! No, he was a man with a *single mind,* and his circumstances did not discourage him. Was he weeping because of what some of the Roman Christians were doing to him? No, he had the *submissive mind* and would not permit people to rob him of his joy. These tears were not for himself at all; they were shed because of others. Because Paul had the *spiritual mind,* he was heartbroken over the way some professed Christians were living, people who "mind earthly things."

While we cannot be sure, it is likely that Philippians 3:18–19 describes the Judaizers and their followers. Certainly Paul was writing about professed Christians and not people outside the church. The Judaizers were the "enemies of the cross of Christ" in that they added the law of Moses to the work of redemption that Christ wrought on the cross. Their obedience to the Old Testament dietary laws would make a "god" out of the belly (see Col. 2:20–23), and their emphasis on circumcision would amount to glorying in that about which they ought to be ashamed (see Gal. 6:12–15). These men were not spiritually minded; they were earthly minded. They were holding on to earthly rituals and beliefs that God had given to Israel, and they were opposing the heavenly blessings that the Christian has in Christ (Eph. 1:3; 2:6; Col. 3:1–3).

The word *spiritual* has suffered as much abuse as the word *fellowship.* Too many people think that a "spiritual Christian" is mystical, dreamy, impractical, and distant. When he prays, he shifts his voice into a sepulchral tone *in tremolo* and goes to great lengths to inform God of the things He already knows. Unfortunately, this kind of unctuous piety is a poor example of true spirituality. To be spiritually minded does not require one to be impractical and mystical. Quite the contrary, the spiritual mind makes the believer think more clearly and get things done more efficiently.

To be "spiritually minded" simply means to look at earth from heaven's point of view. "Give your heart to the heavenly things, not to the passing things of earth" (Col. 3:2 ph). "Practice occupying your minds with the things above, not with the things on earth" (Col. 3:2 wms). D. L. Moody used to scold Christians for being "so heavenly minded they were no earthly good," and that exhortation still needs to be heeded. Christians have a dual citizenship—on earth and in heaven—and our citizenship in heaven ought to make us better people here on earth. The spiritually minded believer is not attracted by the things of this world. He makes his decisions on the basis of eternal values and not the passing fads of society. Lot chose the well-watered plain of Jordan because his values were worldly, and ultimately he lost everything. Moses refused the pleasures and treasures of Egypt because he had something infinitely more wonderful to live for (Heb. 11:24–26). "What shall it profit a man, if he shall gain the whole world, and lose his own soul?" (Mark 8:36).

"For our citizenship is in heaven" (Phil. 3:20 nasb). The Greek word translated "conversation" or "citizenship" is the word from which we get the English word *politics*. It has to do with one's behavior as a citizen of a nation. Paul was encouraging us to have the spiritual mind, and he did this by pointing out the characteristics of the Christian whose citizenship is in heaven. Just as Philippi was a colony of Rome on foreign soil, so the church is a "colony of heaven" on earth.

Our Names Are on Heaven's Record

The citizens of Philippi were privileged to be Roman citizens away from Rome. When a baby was born in Philippi, it was important that its name be registered on the legal records. When the lost sinner trusts Christ and becomes a citizen of heaven, his name is written in "the book of life" (Phil. 4:3).

Citizenship is important. When you travel to another country, it is essential that you have a passport that proves your citizenship. None of us wants to suffer the fate of Philip Nolan in the classic tale *The Man Without a Country*. Because he cursed the name of his country, Nolan was sentenced to live aboard ship and never again see his native land or even hear its name or news about its progress. For fifty-six years he was on an endless journey from ship to ship and sea to sea, and finally was buried at sea. He was a "man without a country."

The Christian's name is written in "the book of life," and this is what determines his final entrance into the heavenly country (Rev. 20:15). When you confess Christ on earth, He confesses your name in heaven (Matt. 10:32–33). Your name is written down in heaven (Luke 10:20), and it stands written forever. (The Greek verb "written" in Luke 10:20 is in the perfect tense: "it is once-for-all written and stands written.")

A friend in Washington, D.C., arranged for my oldest son and me to tour the White House. She told us to be at a certain gate at eight o'clock in the morning and to be prepared to show evidence of who we were. David and I walked up to the gate, and the guard politely asked our names. We told him, showing our credentials. He said, "Yes, sir! Mr. Warren Wiersbe and David! You may enter!" We got into the White House because our names were written down on the proper list, and our names got on that list through the intercession of another. So it is with our entrance into heaven: because we have trusted Christ, our names are written down, and we will enter glory on His merits and intercession alone.

We Speak Heaven's Language

Those who "mind earthly things" *talk* about earthly things. After all, what comes out of the mouth reveals what is in the heart (Matt. 12:34–37). The unsaved person does not understand the things of God's Spirit (1 Cor. 2:14–16), so how can he talk about them intelligently? The citizens of heaven understand spiritual things and enjoy discussing them and sharing them with one another.

"They are of the world: therefore speak they of the world, and the world heareth them. We are of God: he that knoweth God heareth us; he that is not of God heareth not us. Hereby know we the spirit of truth, and the spirit of error" (1 John 4:5–6).

But speaking heaven's language not only involves what we say, but also the way we say it. The spiritually minded Christian doesn't go around quoting Bible verses all day! But he is careful to speak in a manner that glorifies God. "Let your speech be alway with grace, seasoned with salt, that ye may know how ye ought to answer every man" (Col. 4:6). No believer ought ever to say, "Now take this with a grain of salt!" *Put the salt into your speech!* Salt prevents corruption. "Let no corrupt communication proceed out of your mouth, but that which is good to the use of edifying, that it may minister grace unto the hearers" (Eph. 4:29).

We Obey Heaven's Laws

The citizens of Philippi were governed by Roman law, not Greek law, even though they were located hundreds of miles away from Rome. In fact, it was this policy that put Paul into jail when he first visited Philippi (Acts 16:16–24). Paul himself used his Roman citizenship to guarantee his protection under Roman law (Acts 16:35–40; 21:33–40; 22:24–30).

In Philippians 3:17, Paul warned the Philippian believers against imitating the wrong kind of citizens. "Be followers together of me." Of course, Paul was a follower of Christ, so his admonition is not egotistical! (1 Cor. 11:1). Paul knew himself to be an "alien" in this world, a "pilgrim and a stranger" (see 1 Peter 2:11). His life was governed by heaven's laws, and this is what made him different. He was concerned about others, not himself. He was interested in giving, not getting. His motive was love (2 Cor. 5:14), not hatred. By faith, Paul obeyed the Word of God, knowing that one day he would be rewarded. Men might oppose him and persecute him now, but in that final day of reckoning, he would be the winner.

Sad to say, there are those today, like the Judaizers in Paul's day, who profess to be citizens of heaven, but whose lives do not show it. They may be zealous in their religious activities and even austere in their disciplines, but there is no evidence of the control of the Spirit of God in their lives. All that they do is energized by the flesh, and they get all the glory. It is bad enough that they are going astray, but they also lead other people astray. No wonder Paul wept over them.

He Is Loyal to Heaven's Cause

The cross of Jesus Christ is the theme of the Bible, the heart of the gospel, and the chief source of praise in heaven (Rev. 5:8–10). The cross is the proof of God's love for sinners (Rom. 5:8) and God's hatred for sin. The cross condemns what the world values. It judges mankind and pronounces the true verdict: *Guilty!*

In what sense were the Judaizers the "enemies of the cross of Christ"? For one thing, the cross ended the Old Testament religion. When the veil of the temple was torn in two, God was announcing that the way to God was open through Christ (Heb. 10:19–25). When Jesus shouted, "It is finished!" He made one sacrifice for sins, and thus ended the whole sacrificial system (Heb. 10:1–14). By His death and resurrection, Jesus accomplished a "spiritual circumcision" that made ritual circumcision unnecessary (Col. 2:10–13). Everything that the Judaizers advocated had been eliminated by the death of Christ on the cross!

Furthermore, everything that they lived for was condemned by the cross. Jesus had broken down the wall that stood between Jews and Gentiles (Eph. 2:14–16), and the Judaizers were rebuilding that wall! They were obeying "carnal [fleshly] ordinances" (Heb. 9:10), regulations that appealed to the flesh and were not directed by the Spirit. But the true believer crucifies the flesh (Gal. 5:24). He also crucifies the world (Gal. 6:14). Yet the Judaizers were minding "earthly things." It is the cross that is central in the life of the believer. He does not glory in men, in religion, or in his own achievements; he glories in the cross (Gal. 6:14).

Paul wept because he knew the future of these men: "whose end is destruction" (Phil. 3:19). This word carries with it the idea of waste and "lostness." (It is translated "waste" in Mark 14:4.) Judas is called "the son of perdition," and this is the word used (John 17:12). A wasted life and an eternity of waste! In contrast, the true child of God, whose citizenship is in heaven, has a bright future.

We Are Looking for Heaven's Lord

The Judaizers were living in the past tense, trying to get the Philippian believers to go back to Moses and the law, but true Christians live in the future tense, anticipating the return of their Savior (Phil. 3:20–21). As the *accountant* in Philippians 3:1–11, Paul discovered

new *values. As* the *athlete* in Philippians 3:12–16, he displayed new *vigor.* Now as the *alien,* he experiences a new *vision:* "We look for the Saviour." It is this anticipation of the coming of Christ that motivates the believer with the spiritual mind.

There is tremendous energy in the present power of a future hope. Because Abraham looked for a city, he was content to live in a tent (Heb. 11:13–16). Because Moses looked for the rewards of heaven, he was willing to forsake the treasures of earth (Heb. 11:24–26). Because of the "joy that was set before him" (Heb. 12:2), Jesus was willing to endure the cross. The fact that Jesus Christ is returning is a powerful motive for dedicated living and devoted service *today.* "And every man that hath this hope in him purifieth himself, even as he is pure" (read 1 John 2:28—3:3).

The citizen of heaven, living on earth, is never discouraged because he knows that his Lord is one day going to return. He faithfully keeps on doing his job lest his Lord return and find him disobedient (Luke 12:40–48). The spiritually minded believer does not live for the things of this world; he anticipates the blessings of the world to come. This does not mean that he ignores or neglects his daily obligations; but it does mean that what he does today is governed by what Christ will do in the future.

Paul mentioned particularly that the believer will receive a glorified body, like the body of Christ. Today we live in a "body of humiliation" (which is the meaning of the word translated "vile" in Phil. 3:21), but when we see Christ, we will receive a body of glory. It will happen in a moment, in the twinkling of an eye! (1 Cor. 15:42–53). At that moment, all the things of this world will be worthless to us—just as they ought to be, relatively, today! If we are living in the future tense, then we will be exercising the spiritual mind and living for the things that really matter.

When Jesus returns, He will "subdue all things unto himself" (Phil. 3:21b). That word *subdue* means "to arrange in ranks." Isn't that our problem today? *We do not arrange things in their proper order.* Our values are twisted. Consequently, our vigor is wasted on useless activities, and our vision is clouded so that the return of Christ is not a real motivating power in our lives. Living in the future tense means letting Christ arrange the things in life according to the proper rank. It means living "with eternity's values in view," and daring to believe God's promise that "he that doeth the will of God abideth forever" (1 John 2:17).

CHAPTER TEN
Philippians 4:1–9
YOU DON'T HAVE TO WORRY!

If anybody had an excuse for worrying, it was the apostle Paul. His beloved Christian friends at Philippi were disagreeing with one another, and he was not there to help them. We have no idea what Euodia and Syntyche were disputing about, but whatever it was, it was bringing division into the church. Along with the potential division at Philippi, Paul had to face division among the believers at Rome (Phil. 1:14–17). Added to these burdens was the possibility of his own death! Yes, Paul had a good excuse to worry—*but he did not!* Instead, he took time to explain to us the secret of victory over worry.

What is worry? The Greek word translated "anxious" (careful) in Philippians 4:6 means "to be pulled in different directions." Our hopes pull us in one direction; our fears pull us the opposite direction; and we are pulled apart! The Old English root from which we get our word *worry* means "to strangle." If you have ever really worried, you know how it does strangle a person! In fact, worry has definite physical consequences: headaches, neck pains, ulcers, even back pains. Worry affects our thinking, our digestion, and even our coordination.

From the spiritual point of view, worry is *wrong thinking* (the mind) and *wrong feeling* (the heart) about circumstances, people, and things. Worry is the greatest thief of joy. It is not enough for us, however, to tell ourselves to "quit worrying" because that will never capture the thief. Worry is an "inside job," and it takes more than good intentions to get the victory. The antidote to worry is the *secure mind:* "And the peace of God … shall keep [garrison, guard like a soldier] your hearts and minds through Christ Jesus" (Phil. 4:7). When you have the secure mind, the peace of God guards you (Phil. 4:7) and the God of peace guides you (Phil. 4:9). With that kind of protection—why worry?

If we are to conquer worry and experience the secure mind, we must meet the conditions that God has laid down. There are three: right praying (Phil. 4:6–7), right thinking (Phil. 4:8), and right living (Phil. 4:9).

Right Praying (4:6–7)

Paul did not write, "Pray about it!" He was too wise to do that. He used three different words to describe "right praying": *prayer, supplication,* and *thanksgiving.* "Right praying" involves all three. The word *prayer* is the general word for making requests known to the Lord. It carries the idea of adoration, devotion, and worship. Whenever we find ourselves worrying, our first action ought to be to get alone with God and worship Him. Adoration is what is needed. We must see the greatness and majesty of God! We must realize that He is big enough to solve our problems. Too often we rush into His presence and hastily tell Him our needs, when we ought to approach His throne calmly and in deepest reverence. The first step in "right praying" is *adoration.*

The second is *supplication,* an earnest sharing of our needs and problems. There is no place for half-hearted, insincere prayer! While we know we are not heard for our "much speaking" (Matt. 6:7–8), still we realize that our Father wants us to be earnest in our

asking (Matt. 7:1–11). This is the way Jesus prayed in the garden (Heb. 5:7), and while His closest disciples were sleeping, Jesus was sweating great drops of blood! Supplication is not a matter of carnal energy but of spiritual intensity (Rom. 15:30; Col. 4:12).

After adoration and supplication comes *appreciation,* giving thanks to God (see Eph. 5:20; Col. 3:15–17). Certainly the Father enjoys hearing His children say, "Thank You!" When Jesus healed ten lepers, only one of the ten returned to give thanks (Luke 17:11–19), and we wonder if the percentage is any higher today. We are eager to ask but slow to appreciate.

You will note that "right praying" is not something every Christian can do immediately, because "right praying" depends on the right kind of mind. This is why Paul's formula for peace is found at the *end* of Philippians and not at the *beginning.* If we have the *single mind* of Philippians 1 then we can give *adoration.* (How can a double-minded person ever praise God?) If we have the *submissive mind* of Philippians 2, we can come with *supplication.* (Would a person with a proud mind ask God for something?) If we have the *spiritual mind* of Philippians 3 we can show our *appreciation.* (A worldly minded person would not know that God had given him anything to appreciate!) In other words, we must practice Philippians 1, 2, and 3 if we are going to experience the *secure mind* of Philippians 4.

Paul counseled us to take "everything to God in prayer." "Don't worry about *anything,* but pray about *everything!*" was his admonition. We are prone to pray about the "big things" in life and forget to pray about the so-called "little things"—until they grow and become big things! Talking to God about *everything* that concerns us and Him is the first step toward victory over worry.

The result is that the "peace of God" guards the heart and the mind. You will remember that Paul was chained to a Roman soldier, guarded day and night. In like manner, "the peace of God" stands guard over the two areas that create worry—the heart (wrong feeling) and the mind (wrong thinking). When we give our hearts to Christ in salvation, we experience "peace with God" (Rom. 5:1), but the "peace of God" takes us a step further into His blessings. This does not mean the absence of trials on the outside, but it does mean a quiet confidence within, regardless of circumstances, people, or things.

Daniel gave us a wonderful illustration of peace through prayer. When the king announced that none of his subjects was to pray to anyone except the king, Daniel went to his room, opened his windows, and prayed as before (Dan. 6:1–10). Note how Daniel prayed. He "prayed, and gave thanks before his God" (Dan. 6:10) and he made "supplication" (Dan. 6:11). Prayer—supplication—thanksgiving! And the result was perfect peace *in the midst of difficulty!* Daniel was able to spend the night with the lions in perfect peace, while the king *in his palace* could not sleep (Dan. 6:18).

The first condition for the secure mind and victory over worry is right praying.

Right Thinking (4:8)

Peace involves the heart *and the mind.* "Thou wilt keep him in perfect peace, whose mind is stayed on thee: because he trusteth in thee" (Isa. 26:3). Wrong thinking leads to wrong feeling, and before long the heart and mind are pulled apart and we are strangled by worry. We must realize that thoughts are real and powerful, even though they cannot be seen, weighed, or measured. We must bring "into captivity every thought to the obedience of Christ" (2 Cor. 10:5).

Sow a thought, reap an action.
Sow an action, reap a habit.
Sow a habit, reap a character.
Sow a character, reap a destiny!

Paul spells out in detail the things we ought to think about as Christians.

Whatever is true. Dr. Walter Cavert reported a survey on worry that indicated that only 8 percent of the things people worried about were legitimate matters of concern! The other 92 percent were either imaginary, never happened, or involved matters over which the people had no control anyway. Satan is the liar (John 8:44), and he wants to corrupt our minds with his lies (2 Cor. 11:3). "Yea, hath God said?" is the way he approaches us, just as he approached Eve (Gen. 3:1ff.). The Holy Spirit controls our minds through truth (John 17:17; 1 John 5:6), but the devil tries to control them through lies. *Whenever we believe a lie, Satan takes over!*

Whatever is honest and just. This means "worthy of respect and right." There are many things that are not respectable, and Christians should not think about these things. This does not mean we hide our heads in the sand and avoid what is unpleasant and displeasing, but it does mean we do not focus our attention on dishonorable things and permit them to control our thoughts.

Whatever is pure, lovely, and of good report. "Pure" probably refers to moral purity, since the people then, as now, were constantly attacked by temptations to sexual impurity (Eph. 4:17–24; 5:8–12). "Lovely" means "beautiful, attractive." "Of good report" means "worth talking about, appealing." The believer must major on the high and noble thoughts, not the base thoughts of this corrupt world.

Whatever possesses virtue and praise. If it has *virtue,* it will motivate us to do better, and if it has *praise,* it is worth commending to others. No Christian can afford to waste "mind power" on thoughts that tear him down or that would tear others down if these thoughts were shared.

If you will compare this list to David's description of the Word of God in Psalm 19:7–9, you will see a parallel. The Christian who fills his heart and mind with God's Word will have a "built-in radar" for detecting wrong thoughts. "Great peace have they which love thy law" (Ps. 119:165). Right thinking is the result of daily meditation on the Word of God.

Right Living (4:9)

You cannot separate outward action and inward attitude. Sin always results in unrest (unless the conscience is seared), and purity ought to result in peace. "And the work of righteousness shall be peace; and the effect of righteousness quietness and peace" (Isa. 32:17). "But the wisdom that is from above is first pure, then peaceable" (James 3:17). Right living is a necessary condition for experiencing the peace of God.

Paul balances four activities: "learned and received" and "heard and seen." It is one thing to *learn* a truth, but quite another to *receive* it inwardly and make it a part of our inner man (see 1 Thess. 2:13). Facts in the head are not enough; we must also have truths in the heart. In Paul's ministry, he not only *taught* the Word but also *lived* it so that his listeners could see the truth in his life. Paul's experience ought to be our experience. We must learn the Word, receive it, hear it, and do it. "But be ye doers of the word, and not hearers only" (James 1:22).

"The peace of God" is one test of whether or not we are in the will of God. "Let the peace that Christ can give keep on acting as umpire in your hearts" (Col. 3:15 WMS). If we are walking with the Lord, then the peace of God and the God of peace exercise their influence over our hearts. Whenever we disobey, we lose that peace and we know we have done something wrong. God's peace is the "umpire" that calls us "out"!

Right praying, right thinking, and right living: these are the conditions for having the secure mind and victory over worry. As Philippians 4 is the "peace chapter" of the New Testament, James 4 is the "war chapter." It begins with a question: "From whence come wars and fightings among you?" James explained the causes of war: *wrong praying* ("Ye ask, and receive not, because ye ask amiss," James 4:3), *wrong thinking* ("purify your hearts, ye double minded," James 4:8), and *wrong living* ("know ye not that the friendship of the world is enmity with God?" James 4:4). There is no middle ground. Either we yield heart and mind to the Spirit of God and practice right praying, thinking, and living; or we yield to the flesh and find ourselves torn apart by worry.

There is no need to worry! And, worry is a sin! (Have you read Matt. 6:24–34 lately?) With the peace of God to guard us and the God of peace to guide us—*why worry?*

CHAPTER ELEVEN
Philippians 4:10–23
THE SECRET OF CONTENTMENT

The trouble with him is that he's a thermometer and not a thermostat!" This statement by one of his deacons aroused the pastor's curiosity. They were discussing possible board members, and Jim's name had come up.

"Pastor, it's like this," the deacon explained. "A thermometer doesn't change anything around it—it just registers the temperature. It's always going up and down. But a thermostat regulates the surroundings and changes them when they need to be changed. Jim is a thermometer—he lacks the power to change things. Instead, they change him!"

The apostle Paul was a thermostat. Instead of having spiritual ups and downs as the situation changed, he went right on, steadily doing his work and serving Christ. His personal references at the close of this letter indicate that he was not the victim of circumstances but the victor over circumstances: I can accept all things (Phil. 4:11); "I can do all things" (Phil. 4:13); I have all things (Phil. 4:18). Paul did not have to be pampered to be content; he found his contentment in the spiritual resources abundantly provided by Christ.

Contentment is not complacency, nor is it a false peace based on ignorance. The complacent believer is unconcerned about others, while the contented Christian wants to share his blessings. Contentment is not escape from the battle, but rather an abiding peace and confidence in the midst of the battle. "I have learned, in whatsoever state I am, therewith to be content" (Phil. 4:11). Two words in that verse are vitally important—"learned" and "content."

The verb "learned" means "learned by experience." Paul's spiritual contentment was not something he had immediately after he was saved. He had to go through many difficult experiences of life in order to learn how to be content. The word *content* actually means "contained." It is a description of the man whose resources are within him so that he does not have to depend on substitutes without. The Greek word means "self-sufficient" and was a favorite word of the stoic philosophers. But the Christian is not sufficient in himself; he is sufficient in Christ. Because Christ lives within us, we are adequate for the demands of life.

In this chapter, Paul named three wonderful spiritual resources that make us adequate and give us contentment.

The Overruling Providence of God (4:10)

In this day of scientific achievement, we hear less and less about the providence of God. We sometimes get the idea that the world is a vast natural machine and that even God Himself cannot interrupt the wheels as they are turning. But the Word of God clearly teaches the providential workings of God in nature and in the lives of His people. The word *providence* comes from two Latin words: *pro,* meaning "before," and *video,* meaning "to see." God's providence simply means that God sees to it beforehand. It does not mean that God simply *knows* beforehand, because providence involves much more. It is the working of God in advance to arrange circumstances and situations for the fulfilling of His purposes.

The familiar story of Joseph and his brothers illustrates the meaning of providence (Gen. 37—50). Joseph's brothers envied him and sold him as a slave when he was only seventeen years old. He was taken to Egypt, and there God revealed that seven years of famine were coming after seven years of plenty. It was through Joseph's interpretation of Pharaoh's dreams that this fact was discovered. Because of that, Joseph was elevated to the position of second ruler in Egypt. After twenty years of separation, Joseph's brothers were reconciled to him, and they understood what the Lord had done.

"God did send me before you to preserve life," said Joseph (Gen. 45:5). "But as for you, ye thought evil against me; but God meant it unto good" (Gen. 50:20). This is the providence of God: His hand ruling and overruling in the affairs of life. Paul experienced this divine providence in his life and ministry, and he was able to write, "And we know that all things work together for good to them that love God, to them that are the called according to his purpose" (Rom. 8:28). God in His providence had caused the church at Philippi to become concerned about Paul's needs, and it came at the very time Paul needed their love most! They had been concerned, but they had lacked the opportunity to help. Many Christians today have the opportunities, but they lack the concern!

Life is not a series of accidents; it is a series of appointments. "I will guide thee with mine eye" (Ps. 32:8). Abraham called God "Jehovah-Jireh," meaning "the Lord will see to it" (Gen. 22:14). "And when he putteth forth his own sheep, he goeth before them" (John 10:4). This is the providence of God, a wonderful source of contentment.

The Unfailing Power of God (4:11–13)

Paul was quick to let his friends know that he was not complaining! His happiness did not depend on circumstances or things; his joy came from something deeper, something apart from either poverty or prosperity. Most of us have learned how to "be abased," because when difficulties come we immediately run to the Lord! But few have learned how "to abound." Prosperity has done more damage to believers than has adversity. "I am rich, and increased with goods, and have need of nothing" (Rev. 3:17).

The word *instructed* in Philippians 4:12 is not the same as "learned" in Philippians 4:11. "Instructed" means "initiated into the secret." This word was used by the pagan religions with reference to their "inner secrets." Through trial and testing, Paul was "initiated" into the wonderful secret of contentment in spite of poverty or prosperity. "I can do all things through Christ which strengtheneth me" (Phil. 4:13). It was the power of Christ within him that gave him spiritual contentment.

Fog had moved into O'Hare Field, the airport that serves Chicago, and my departure had been delayed. I was sitting in the terminal reading a book and quietly asking God to work out His plans for the trip. Near me was a gentleman waiting for the same plane, but he was pacing up and down like a caged lion, and the language he was using to describe the fog was making the atmosphere more dense! I thought, "Here is a man without any inner resources." Later, he asked me how I could be so calm when the planes were all late, and I had the opportunity to share the gospel with him.

While flying back to Chicago from upper New York via New York City, we had to stay in our holding pattern over Kennedy Airport for more than an hour. When the stewardess announced that we would be landing an hour late, a man across the aisle shouted, "Bring out the booze!" This was his only resource when things were going against him.

All of nature depends on hidden resources. The great trees send their roots down into the earth to draw up water and minerals. Rivers have their sources in the snow-capped mountains. The most important part of a tree is the part you cannot see, the root system, and the most important part of the Christian's life is the part that only God sees. Unless we draw on the deep resources of God by faith, we fail against the pressures of life. Paul depended on the power of Christ at work in his life (see Phil. 1:6, 21; 2:12–13; 3:10). "I can— through Christ!" was Paul's motto, and it can be our motto too.

"I am ready for anything through the strength of the One who lives within me," is the way J. B. Phillips translated Philippians 4:13. The Living Bible puts it this way: "I can do everything God asks me to with the help of Christ who gives me the strength and power." No matter which translation you prefer, they all say the same thing: the Christian has all the power *within* that he needs to be adequate for the demands of life. We need only release this power by faith.

Every Christian ought to read *Hudson Taylor's Spiritual Secret* by Dr. and Mrs. Howard Taylor, because it illustrates this principle of inner power in the life of a great missionary to China. For many years, Hudson Taylor worked hard and felt that he was trusting Christ to meet his needs, but somehow he had no joy or liberty in his ministry. Then a letter from a friend opened his eyes to the adequacy of Christ. "It is not by trusting my own faithfulness, but by looking away to the Faithful One!" he said. This was a turning point in his life. Moment by moment, he drew on the power of Christ for every responsibility of the day, and Christ's power carried him through.

Jesus taught this same lesson in the sermon on the vine and branches in John 15. He is the Vine; we are the branches. A branch is good only for bearing fruit; otherwise you may as well burn it. The branch does not bear fruit through its own self-effort, but by drawing on the life of the Vine. "Without me, ye can do nothing" (John 15:5). As the believer maintains his communion with Christ, the power of God is there to see him through. "I am self-sufficient in Christ's sufficiency" (Phil. 4:13, AMP).

The overruling providence of God and the unfailing power of God are two spiritual resources on which we can draw that we might be adequate for the tasks of life. But there is a third resource.

The Unchanging Promise of God (4:14–20)

Paul thanked the church at Philippi for their generous gift. He compared their giving to three very familiar things.

A budding tree (v. 10). The word *flourished* carries the idea of a flower or tree budding or blossoming. Often we go through "winter seasons" spiritually, but then the spring arrives and there is new life and blessing. The tree itself is not picked up and moved; the circumstances are not changed. The difference is *the new life within.*

An investment (vv. 14–17). Paul looked on their missionary gift as an investment that would pay them rich spiritual dividends. The word *communicate* is our familiar word "fellowship. " The church entered into an arrangement of "giving and receiving"; the church gave *materially* to Paul and received *spiritually* from the Lord. The Lord keeps the books and will never fail to pay one spiritual dividend! That church is poor that fails to share materially with others.

A sacrifice (v. 18). Paul looked on their gift as a spiritual sacrifice, laid on the altar to the glory of God. There are such things as "spiritual sacrifices" in the Christian life (see 1 Peter 2:5). We are to yield our bodies as spiritual sacrifices (Rom. 12:1–2), as well as the praise of our lips (Heb. 13:15). Good works are a sacrifice to the Lord (Heb. 13:16), and so are the lost souls that we are privileged to win to Christ (Rom. 15:16). Here, Paul saw the Philippian believers as priests, giving their offering as a sacrifice to the Lord. In the light of Malachi 1:6–14, we need to present the very finest that we have to the Lord.

But Paul did not see this gift as simply coming from Philippi. He saw it as the supply of his need from heaven. Paul's trust was in the Lord. There is an interesting contrast between Philippians 4:18 and 19. We might state it this way if we were to paraphrase Paul: "You met *my* need, and God is going to meet *your* need. You met *one* need that I have, but my God will meet *all* of your needs. You gave out of your *poverty,* but God will supply your needs out of His *riches* in glory!"

God has not promised to supply all our "greeds." When the child of God is in the will of God, serving for the glory of God, then he will have every need met. Hudson Taylor often said, "When God's work is done in God's way for God's glory, it will not lack for God's supply."

A young pastor came to a church that had been accustomed to raising its annual budget by means of suppers, bazaars, and the like. He told his officers he could not agree with their program. "Let's pray and ask God to meet every need," he suggested. "At the end of the month, pay all the bills and leave my salary till the last. If there isn't enough money for my salary, then I'm the one who suffers, and not the church. But I don't think anybody is going to suffer!" The officers were sure that both the pastor and the church would die, but such was not the case. Each month every bill was paid, and at the end of the year there was a surplus in the treasury for the first time in many years.

Contentment comes from adequate resources. Our resources are the providence of God, the power of God, and the promises of God. These resources made Paul sufficient for every demand of life, and they can make us sufficient too.

CHAPTER TWELVE
PUTTING PHILIPPIANS TO WORK

Now that you have completed your study of this exciting and practical letter, *don't lose what you have learned!* The best thing about Bible study isn't the learning but the *living.* So, here are a few suggestions for keeping the joy in your life.

1. Surrender your mind to the Lord at the beginning of each day. This is a part of dedication: "I beseech you therefore, brethren, by the mercies of God, that ye present your *bodies* a living sacrifice.... And be not conformed to this world: but be ye transformed by the renewing of your *mind,* that ye may prove what is that good, and acceptable, and perfect *will* of God" (Rom. 12:1–2). Give God your body, mind, and will—by faith—as you start each day.

2. Let the Holy Spirit renew your mind through the Word. Daily systematic reading of the Bible is a must if you are going to have victory and joy.

3. As you pray, ask God to give you that day a single mind, a submissive mind, a spiritual mind, a secure mind. As you contemplate the day's schedule, be sure that nothing you have planned robs you of the joy God wants you to have. Perhaps you must meet a person you don't especially like. Ask God to give you the submissive mind that you will need. Or, maybe you must go through a difficult experience. Then be sure you have the single mind, concerned with Christ and the gospel, and not only with your own personal likes and dislikes.

4. During the day, "mind your mind!" If you find yourself losing your inner peace and joy, stop and take inventory: *Do I have the single mind? Did I just miss an opportunity to glorify Christ? Or was I a bit pushy, so that I lost the submissive mind?* If you discover you have sinned, then immediately confess it to the Lord (1 John 1:9). If possible, go back and remedy your mistake. If this cannot be done, ask God to give you another opportunity for witness.

5. Guard the gates of your mind. Remember Paul's admonition in Philippians 4:8: "Whatsoever things are true … honest … just … pure … lovely … of good report … think on these things." When an unkind or impure thought enters your mind, *deal with it instantly.* If you cultivate it, it will take root and grow—and rob you of your joy. Sometimes Satan will throw his "fiery darts" at you, and sometimes he will use other people to do it for him. One of the best ways to defeat the wrong kinds of thoughts is to fill your mind with Scripture; so take time to memorize the Word of God.

6. Remember that your joy is not meant to be a selfish thing; it is God's way of glorifying Christ and helping others through you. Jesus first, Others second, Yourself last, and the result is JOY.

COLOSSIANS

OUTLINE

Key theme: Jesus Christ is preeminent
Key verse: Colossians 1:18

I. DOCTRINE: CHRIST'S PREEMINENCE DECLARED (1)

   A. In the gospel message—1:1–12
   B. In redemption—1:13–14
   C. In creation—1:15–17
   D. In the church—1:18–23
   E. In Paul's ministry—1:24–29

II. DANGER: CHRIST'S PREEMINENCE DEFENDED (2)

   A. Beware of empty philosophies—2:1–10
   B. Beware of religious legalism—2:11–17
   C. Beware of man-made disciplines—2:18–23

III. DUTY: CHRIST'S PREEMINENCE DEMONSTRATED (3—4)

   A. In person purity—3:1–11
   B. In Christian fellowship—13:12–17
   C. In the home—3:18–21
   D. In daily work—3:22—4:1
   E. In Christian witness—4:2–6
   F. In Christian service—4:7–18

CONTENTS

CHAPTER ONE
Colossians 1:1–2
FROM PAUL, WITH LOVE

Do the heavenly bodies have any influence over our lives? The millions of people who consult their horoscopes each day would say, "Yes!" In the United States, there are about 1,750 daily newspapers, and 1,220 of them carry astrological data!

Is there any relationship between diet and spiritual living?

Does God speak to us immediately, in our minds, or only through His Word, the Bible?

Do the Eastern religions have something to offer the evangelical Christian?

These questions sound very contemporary. Yet they are the very issues Paul dealt with in his magnificent epistle to the Colossians. We need this important letter today just as they needed it back in AD 60 when Paul wrote it.

The City
Colosse was one of three cities located about one hundred miles inland from Ephesus. The other two cities were Laodicea and Hierapolis (Col. 4:13, 16). This area was a meeting point of East and West because an important trade route passed through there. At one time, all three cities were growing and prosperous, but gradually Colosse slipped into a second-rate position. It became what we would call a small town. Yet the church there was important enough to merit the attention of the apostle Paul.

All kinds of philosophies mingled in this cosmopolitan area, and religious hucksters abounded. There was a large Jewish colony in Colosse, and there was also a constant influx of new ideas and doctrines from the East. It was fertile ground for religious speculations and heresies!

The Church
Colosse probably would never have been mentioned in the New Testament had it not been for the church there. The city is never named in the book of Acts because Paul did not start the Colossian church, nor did he ever visit it. Paul had *heard* of their faith (Col. 1:4, 9), but he had never seen these believers personally (Col. 2:1). Here was a church of unknown people, in a small town, receiving an inspired letter from the great apostle Paul!

How did the Colossian church begin? It was the outgrowth of Paul's three-year ministry in Ephesus (Acts 19; 20:17–38). So effective was the witness of the church at Ephesus that "all they which dwelt in Asia heard the word of the Lord Jesus, both Jews and Greeks" (Acts 19:10). This would include people in Colosse, Laodicea, and Hierapolis.

When we examine the persons involved in the prison correspondence of Paul (see Eph., Phil., Col., Philem., and 2 Tim.), we can just about put the story together of how the Colossian church was founded. During Paul's ministry in Ephesus, at least two men from Colosse were brought to faith in Jesus Christ—Epaphras and Philemon (see Philem. 19). Epaphras apparently was one of the key founders of the church in Colosse, for he shared the gospel with his friends there (Col. 1:7). He also had a ministry in the cities of Hierapolis and Laodicea (Col. 4:12–13).

Philemon had a church meeting in his home (Philem. 2). It is likely that Apphia and Archippus, mentioned in this verse, were respectively the wife and son of Philemon, and that Archippus was the pastor of the church (Col. 4:17).

There is a good lesson for us here: God does not always need an apostle, or a "full-time Christian worker" to get a ministry established. Nor does He need elaborate buildings and extensive organizations. Here were two laymen who were used of God to start ministries in at least three cities. It is God's plan that the Christians in the large urban areas like Ephesus reach out into the smaller towns and share the gospel. Is *your* church helping to evangelize "small-town" mission fields?

The Colossian assembly was predominantly Gentile in its membership. The sins that Paul named (Col. 3:5–9) were commonly associated with the Gentiles, and his statement about the mystery applied more to the Gentiles than to the Jews (Col. 1:25–29). The church was probably about five years old when Paul wrote this letter.

The Crisis
Why did Paul write this letter to the church in Colosse? Because a crisis had occurred that was about to destroy the ministry of the church. By comparing the prison letters, we can arrive at the following reconstruction of events.

Paul was at that time a prisoner in Rome (Acts 21:17—28:31). He met a runaway slave named Onesimus who belonged to Philemon, one of the leaders of the church in Colosse. Paul led Onesimus to Christ. He then wrote his letter to Philemon, asking his friend to forgive Onesimus and receive him back as a brother in Christ.

About the same time, Epaphras showed up in Rome because he needed Paul's help. Some new doctrines were being taught in Colosse and were invading the church and creating problems. So Paul wrote this letter to the Colossians in order to refute these heretical teachings and establish the truth of the gospel.

Epaphras remained with Paul in Rome (Col. 4:12–13). Onesimus and Tychicus carried Paul's epistles to their destinations: Ephesians 6:21; Colossians 4:7–9; and Philemon. Epaphras was called Paul's "fellow prisoner," a title also given to Aristarchus (Col. 4:10; Philem. 23). This suggests that Epaphras *willingly* remained with Paul to assist him. Neither Aristarchus nor Epaphras was a prisoner because he broke the law and was arrested. They were Paul's willing companions, sacrificing their own comfort to help him.

What was the heresy that threatened the peace and purity of the Colossian church? It was a combination of Eastern philosophy and Jewish legalism, with elements of what Bible scholars call gnosticism (NOSti-cism). This term comes from the Greek word *gnosis* (KNOW-sis), which means "to know." (An *agnostic* is one who does not know.) The gnostics were the people who were "in the know" when it came to the deep things of God. They were the "spiritual aristocracy" in the church.

To begin with, this heresy promised people such a close union with God that they would achieve a "spiritual perfection." Spiritual fullness could be theirs only if they entered into the teachings and ceremonies prescribed. There was also a "full knowledge," a spiritual depth, that only the initiated could enjoy. This "wisdom" would release them from earthly things and put them in touch with heavenly things.

Of course, all of this teaching was but man-made philosophy based on traditions and not on divine truth (Col. 2:8). It grew out of the philosophical question *Why is there evil in this world if creation was made by a holy God?* As these philosophers speculated and pondered, they came to the false conclusion that matter was evil. Their next false conclusion was that a holy God could not come into contact with evil matter, so there had to be a series of "emanations" from God to His creation. They believed in a powerful spirit world that used material things to attack mankind. They also held to a form of astrology, believing that angelic beings ruled heavenly bodies and influenced affairs on earth (see Col. 1:16; 2:10, 15).

Added to these Eastern speculations was a form of Jewish legalism. The teachers believed that the rite of circumcision was helpful in spiritual development (Col. 2:11). They taught that the Old Testament law, especially the dietary laws, was also useful in attaining spiritual perfection (Col. 2:14–17). Definite rules and regulations told them what was evil and what was good (Col. 2:21).

Since to them matter was evil, they had to find some way to control their own human natures in this pursuit of perfection. Two different practices resulted. One school of thought held that the only way to conquer evil matter was by means of rigid discipline and asceticism (Col. 2:23). The other view taught that it was permissible to engage in all kinds of sin, since matter was evil anyway! It appears that the first opinion was the predominant one in Colosse.

It is easy to see how this kind of teaching undermined the very foundations of the Christian faith. To begin with, these heretics attacked the person and work of Jesus Christ. To them, He was merely one of God's many "emanations" and not the very Son of God come in the flesh. The Incarnation means God *with us*

(Matt. 1:23), but these false teachers claimed that God was keeping His distance from us! When we trust the Son of God, there is no need for intermediary beings between us and heaven!

In His work on the cross, Jesus Christ settled the sin question (Col. 1:20) and completely defeated all satanic forces (Col. 2:15). He put an end to the legal demands of the law (Col. 2:14–17). In fact, Jesus Christ alone is the Preeminent One (Col. 1:18; 3:11)! All that the believer needs is Jesus!

Matter is not evil, and the human body is not evil. Each person is born with a fallen human nature that wants to control the body and use it for sin, but the body itself is not evil. If that were the case, Jesus Christ would never have come to earth in a human body. Nor would He have enjoyed the everyday blessings of life as He ministered on earth, such as attending wedding feasts and accepting invitations to dinner. Diets and disciplines can be good for one's health, but they have no power to develop true spirituality (Col. 2:20–23).

As for astrology and the influence of angels and heavenly bodies, Paul denounced this with vigor. On the cross, Jesus won a complete victory over all satanic powers (Col. 2:15). Christians do not need to turn to the rudiments of the world (Col. 2:8, 20). This word translated "rudiments" means "elemental beings" or "elementary principles." In this case, it refers to the beings that (according to the gnostics) controlled the heavenly bodies that in turn controlled events on earth. Believers who consult horoscopes substitute superstition for revelation and deny the person and work of Christ.

This false teaching was a deceptive combination of many things: Jewish legalism, Eastern philosophy, pagan astrology, mysticism, asceticism, and even a touch of Christianity. There was something for everybody, and this was what made it so dangerous. The false teachers claimed that they were not *denying* the Christian faith, but only lifting it to a higher level. They offered fullness and freedom, a satisfying life that solved all the problems that people face.

Do we have any of this heresy today? Yes, we do; and it is just as deceptive and dangerous! When we make Jesus Christ and the Christian revelation only *part* of a total religious system or philosophy, we cease to give Him the preeminence. When we strive for "spiritual perfection" or "spiritual fullness" by means of formulas, disciplines, or rituals, we go backward instead of forward. Christian believers must beware of mixing their Christian faith with such alluring things as yoga, transcendental meditation, Eastern mysticism, and the like. We must also beware of "deeper life" teachers who offer a system for victory and fullness that bypasses devotion to Jesus Christ. In all things, He must have the preeminence.

This heresy was in direct contrast to the teaching of Paul. It took a negative view of life: "God is far away, matter is evil, and demonic forces are constantly threatening us." The Christian faith teaches that God is near us, that God made all things good (though they can be used for evil), and that Christ has delivered His people from the powers of darkness (Col. 1:13). This heresy turned the world into a frightful prison, while Jesus made it clear that the Father is at work in this world caring for His own. Finally, these false teachers tried to change people from the outside, by means of diets and disciplines. But true spiritual growth comes from within.

The Correspondence

With this background, we can now look at Paul's letter to the Colossians and get an overview of what he has written. We know that his epistle to the Ephesians was written and sent about the same time as his Colossian letter. Keeping this in mind, we can discover many parallels between these two letters. However, the emphasis in Ephesians is on the church, the body of Christ, but the emphasis in Colossians is on Christ, the Head of the body.

In this letter, Paul used the vocabulary of the false teachers, but he did not use their definitions. He used these words in their true Christian meaning. As we study Colossians, we will find words such as *fullness, perfect,* and *complete,* all of which were used by the gnostic heretics. Over thirty times Paul used the little word *all.* He also wrote about *wisdom,* which was a key term in the gnostic vocabulary; he had a great deal to say about angels and spirit powers too.

His main theme was *the preeminence of Jesus Christ* (Col. 1:18; 3:11). There is no need for us to worry about angelic mediators or spiritual emanations. God has sent His Son to die for us! Every person who believes on Jesus Christ is saved and is a part of His body, the church, of which He is the Head (Col. 1:18). We are united to Christ in a wonderful living relationship!

Furthermore, nothing need be added to this relationship, because each believer is "complete in him" (Col. 2:10). All of God's fullness dwells in Christ (Col. 2:9), and we share that fullness! "For in Christ all the fullness of the Deity lives in bodily form, and you have been given fullness in Christ" (Col. 2:9–10 NIV).

While in an airport waiting for my plane to be called, I was approached by a young man who wanted to sell me a book. One look at the garish cover told me that the book was filled with Eastern myths and philosophies.

"I have a book here that meets all my needs," I told the young man, and I reached into my briefcase and took out my Bible.

"Oh, we aren't against the Bible!" he assured me. "It's just that we have something more, and it makes our faith even better."

"Nobody can give me more than Jesus Christ has already given me," I replied. I turned to Colossians 2, but by that time the young man was hurrying down the corridor.

Sad to say, there are many Christians who actually believe that some person, religious system, or discipline can add something to their spiritual experience. But they already have everything they ever will need in the person and work of Jesus Christ.

Paul did not begin by attacking the false teachers and their doctrines. He began by exalting Jesus Christ and showing His preeminence in five areas: the gospel message, redemption, creation, the church, and Paul's own ministry. The people to whom Paul was writing had become Christians because of the gospel message brought to them by Epaphras. If this message was wrong, then they were not saved at all!

Once he had established the preeminence of Christ, then Paul attacked the heretics on their own ground. In Colossians 2, Paul exposed the false origin of their teachings and showed how their teachings contradicted everything Paul taught about Jesus Christ. The believer who masters this chapter is not likely to be led astray by some alluring and enticing "new-and-improved brand of Christianity."

But Paul did not think his task completed when he had refuted the heretics, for he still had some important words for the church. In Colossians 3—4, Paul explained the greatest antidote to false teaching—*a godly life.* Those who say, "I don't care what you believe, just so long as you live a good life" are not thinking logically. *What we believe determines how we behave.* If we believe that matter is evil, we will use our bodies one way, but if we believe that our bodies are temples of the Holy Spirit, we will live accordingly.

Wrong doctrine always leads to wrong living. Right doctrine should lead to right living. In the two concluding chapters, Paul applied the preeminence of Christ to the daily affairs of life. If Christ is truly preeminent in our lives, then we will glorify Him by keeping pure, by enjoying fellowship with other saints, by loving each other at home and being faithful at work, and by seeking to witness for Christ and serve Him effectively. Unless doctrine leads to duty, it is of no use to us.

Many Bible scholars have concluded that Colossians is the most profound letter Paul ever wrote. This must not keep us from reading and studying this wonderful letter. But we must be cautioned against a superficial approach to these chapters. Unless we depend on the Spirit of God to teach us, we will miss the truths God wants us to learn.

The church today desperately needs the message of Colossians. We live in a day when religious toleration is interpreted to mean "one religion is just as good as another." Some people try to take the best from various religious systems and manufacture their own private religion. To many people, Jesus Christ is only *one* of several great religious teachers, with no more authority than they. He may be prominent, but He is definitely not preeminent.

This is an age of "syncretism." People are trying to harmonize and unite many different schools of thought and come up with a superior religion. Our evangelical churches are in danger of diluting the faith in their loving attempt to understand the beliefs of others. Mysticism, legalism, Eastern religions, asceticism, and man-made philosophies are secretly creeping into churches. They are not denying Christ, but they are dethroning Him and robbing Him of His rightful place of preeminence.

As we study this exciting letter, we must heed Paul's warnings: "Lest any man should beguile you" (Col. 2:4), "Lest any man spoil you" (Col. 2:8), "Let no man therefore judge you" (Col. 2:16).

CHAPTER TWO
Colossians 1:3–8
MIRACLES AT COLOSSE

The famous Scottish preacher Alexander Whyte was known as an appreciator. He loved to write postcards to people, thanking them for some kindness or blessing they had brought to his life. Those messages often brought a touch of encouragement to a heart just when it was needed most. Appreciation is great medicine for the soul.

The apostle Paul was a great encourager, and this epistle is a good example of the grace of thanksgiving. In this section (which is one long sentence in the original Greek), he gave thanks for what Christ has done in the lives of the Colossian Christians. But he also mentioned thanksgiving in five other places in this letter: Colossians 1:12; 2:7; 3:15, 17; and 4:2. When you recall that Paul wrote this letter *in prison,* his attitude of thanksgiving is even more wonderful.

Like Paul, we should be grateful for what God is doing in the lives of others. As Christians, we are all members of one body (1 Cor. 12:12–13). If one member of the body is strengthened, this helps to strengthen the entire body. If one church experiences a revival touch from God, it will help all the churches. In this expression of thanksgiving, Paul traced the stages in the spiritual experience of the Colossian believers.

They Heard the Gospel (1:5b–7)
The good news of the gospel was not native to their city. It had to be brought to them, and in their case, Epaphras was the messenger. He was himself a citizen of Colosse (Col. 4:12–13), but he had come in contact with Paul and had been converted to Jesus Christ. This was probably during Paul's great three-year ministry in Ephesus (Acts 19:10).

Once Epaphras had been saved, he shared this thrilling news with his relatives and friends back home. Perhaps it would have been exciting for Epaphras to stay with Paul in Ephesus, where so many wonderful things were taking place. But his first responsibility was to take the gospel to his own home city (see Mark 5:19).

The gospel is the good news that Jesus Christ has solved the problem of sin through His death, burial, and resurrection. The word *gospel* means "good news." Unfortunately, some people witness as though the gospel is the bad news of condemnation.

I recall one church officer who was more of a prosecuting attorney than a Christian witness. Though he constantly reproved people for their sins, he failed to share the good news of forgiveness through faith in Christ.

But we can learn a lesson from him. In our witnessing, we should remember to emphasize the good news of the gospel (see 1 Cor. 15:1–8). In this section in his Letter to the Colossians, Paul reviews the characteristics of this exciting gospel message.

It centers in a Person—Jesus Christ. The theme of this epistle is the preeminence of Jesus Christ, and He is certainly preeminent in the gospel. The false teachers who had invaded the fellowship in Colosse were trying to remove Jesus Christ from His place of preeminence; but to do this was to destroy the gospel. It is *Christ* who died for us and who arose again. The gospel message does not center in a philosophy, a doctrine, or a religious system. It centers in Jesus Christ, the Son of God.

It is the "Word of truth" (v. 5 NIV**).** This means that it came from God and can be trusted. "Thy word is truth" (John 17:17). There are many messages and ideas that can be called *true,* but only God's Word can be called *truth.* Satan is the liar; to believe his lies is to be led astray into death (John 8:44). Jesus is the Truth (John 14:6); when we trust Him, we experience life. Men have tried to destroy God's truth, but they have failed. The Word of truth still stands!

Everybody has faith in something. But faith is only as good as the object in which a person puts his trust. The jungle pagan worships a god of stone; the educated city pagan worships money or possessions or status. In both cases, faith is empty. The true Christian believer has faith in Jesus Christ, and that faith is based on the Word of truth. Any other kind of faith is but superstition—it cannot save.

It is the message of God's grace (v. 6b). Two words in the Christian vocabulary are often confused: *grace* and *mercy.* God in His grace gives me what I do not deserve. Yet God in His mercy does not give me what I do deserve. Grace is God's favor shown to undeserving sinners. The reason the gospel is *good* news is because of grace: God is willing and able to save all who will trust Jesus Christ.

John Selden (1584–1654) was a leading historian and legal authority in England. He had a library of eight thousand volumes and was recognized for his learning. When he was dying, he said to Archbishop Ussher, "I have surveyed most of the learning that is among the sons of men, and my study is filled with books and manuscripts on various subjects. But at present, I cannot recollect any passage out of all my books and papers whereon I can rest my soul, save this from the sacred Scriptures: 'The grace of God that bringeth salvation hath appeared to all men' (Titus 2:11)."

It is for the whole world (v. 6). When I was a young pastor, one of my favorite preachers was Dr. Walter Wilson of Kansas City. He had a unique way of making old truths seem new and exciting. I once heard him quote John 3:16 and ask, "If you were to give a gift that would be suitable for the whole world, what would you give?"

He then listed several possibilities and showed how those gifts could not suit everybody: books (many people cannot read); foods (people eat different things in different parts of the world); clothing (climates are different); money (not every culture makes use of money). He came to the logical conclusion that only the gospel, with its gift of eternal life, was suitable for the whole world, and he was right.

Paul said that the gospel was bearing fruit in all the world. The Word of God is the only seed that can be planted anywhere in the world and bear fruit. The gospel can be preached "to every creature which is under heaven" (Col. 1:23). Paul's emphasis was on "every man" (Col. 1:28). False teachers do not take their message to all the world. They go where the gospel has already gone and try to lead believers astray. *They have no good news for lost sinners!*

If people are to be saved, they must hear the gospel of Jesus Christ. And if they are to hear, we who are saved must carry the message. Are you doing your part?

They Believed in Jesus Christ (1:4)

It is possible to hear and not believe, even though the Word of God has the power to generate faith in those who hear (Rom. 10:17). Millions of people have heard the good news of salvation and yet not believed. But those who believe in Jesus Christ receive from God the gift of eternal life (John 3:14–18).

We are not saved by faith *in faith*. There is a cult of "believism" today that promotes faith but has little to do with Jesus Christ. Even some popular songs carry the message of "faith in faith." The modern attitude is "If you believe, you are safe." But the obvious question is, "Believe in *what?*" Their answer: "Just believe!"

Nor are we saved by faith *in a set of doctrines*. I have often been told the story about the famous evangelist George Whitefield, who was witnessing to a man. "What do you believe?" Whitefield asked. The man replied, "I believe what my church believes."

"And what does your church believe?" asked the evangelist.

"What I believe," replied the man.

Undaunted, Whitefield tried again and asked, "And what do you *both* believe?"

"Why, we both believe the same thing!" was the man's evasive reply.

Saving faith involves the mind, the emotions, and the will. With the mind we understand the truth of the gospel, and with the heart we feel conviction and the need to be saved. But it is only when we exercise the will and commit ourselves to Christ that the process is complete. Faith is not mental assent to a body of doctrines, no matter how true those doctrines may be. Faith is not emotional concern. *Faith is commitment to Jesus Christ.*

When missionary John G. Paton was translating the Bible in the Outer Hebrides, he searched for the exact word to translate *believe*. Finally, he discovered it: the word meant "lean your whole weight upon." That is what saving faith is—leaning your whole weight upon Jesus Christ.

Saving faith is grounded in the gospel (Col. 1:23). It is the Word of God that gives us assurance. As we grow in the Lord, our faith becomes steadfast (Col. 2:5) and established (Col. 2:7).

The false teachers who had come to Colosse tried to undermine the saints' faith in Christ and the Word. This same kind of undermining goes on today. Any religious teaching that dethrones Jesus Christ, or that makes salvation other than an experience of God's grace through faith, is either confused or anti-Christian and born of Satan.

One final thought: the experience of the believers in Colosse was so wonderful that people talked about it! Paul heard about it from Epaphras; the false teachers heard about it and decided to visit the Colossian assembly to see the remarkable change for themselves.

You cannot keep silent once you have experienced salvation in Jesus Christ. Is your Christian life the kind that encourages others and makes it easy for them to witness? Is your church fellowship so exciting that even the unsaved are taking notice?

They Were Discipled (1:7)

Epaphras did not simply lead the Colossians to Christ and then abandon them. He taught them the Word and sought to establish their faith. The word translated "learned" in Colossians 1:7 is related to the word *disciple* in the Greek language. It is the same word Jesus used: "Learn of me" (Matt. 11:29) or, in effect, "Become My disciple."

These new believers were in danger of turning from the truth and following the false teachers. Paul reminded them that it was Epaphras who led them to Christ, discipled them, and taught them the Word. The word *before* (Col. 1:5) probably means "before these false teachers appeared on the scene." Like the Colossians, we should beware of any religious leader who does not seek to win lost souls, but who devotes himself to "stealing sheep" from the flocks of others.

We should never forget that new Christians must be discipled. Just as the newborn baby needs loving care and protection till he can care for himself, so the new Christian needs discipling. The Great Commission does not stop with the salvation of the lost, for in that commission Jesus commanded us to teach converts the Word as well (Matt. 28:19–20). That is what the fellowship of the local church is all about. The New Testament does not teach the kind of "individual Christianity" that is so prevalent today—people who ignore the local church and who find all their spiritual food in books, radio, TV, or recordings.

Epaphras was a faithful minister. He not only won people to Christ, but he taught them the Word and helped them to grow. He also prayed for them (Col. 4:12–13) that they might become mature in Jesus Christ. When danger threatened the members of the church, Epaphras went to Rome to get counsel from Paul. He loved his people and wanted to protect them from false doctrines that would destroy the fellowship and hinder their spiritual development.

The word *disciple* is found more than 260 times in the Gospels and Acts, and the verb translated, "to learn as a disciple" is found twenty-five times in the New Testament. In that day, a disciple was not simply a person who sat and listened to a teacher. He was someone who lived with the teacher and who learned by listening, looking, and living. Discipleship involved more than enrolling in a school and attending lectures. It meant total surrender to the teacher. It meant learning by living. Perhaps our modern-day medical students or trade apprentices come close to illustrating the meaning of discipleship.

But we who disciple other believers must be careful not to get in the way. We are not to make disciples *for ourselves,* but for Jesus Christ. We must relate people to Him so that they love and obey Him. Epaphras faithfully taught his people and related them to Jesus Christ, but the false teachers came in and tried to "draw away disciples." (For Paul's warning about this problem, see Acts 20:28–30.) Human nature has the tendency to want to follow men instead of God—to want "something new" instead of the basic foundational truths of the gospel.

Now we come to the results of Epaphras's efforts.

They Became Faithful in Christ (1:6, 8)

The Word of God is seed (Luke 8:11). This means the Word has life in it (Heb. 4:12). When it is planted in the heart, it can produce fruit. "All over the world this gospel is bearing fruit and growing" (Col. 1:6 NIV).

Near King's Cross station in London, England, there is a cemetery containing a unique grave, that of the agnostic Lady Ann Grimston. She is buried in a marble tomb, marked by a marble slab. Before she died, she said sarcastically to a friend, "I shall live again as surely as a tree will grow from my body."

An unbeliever, Lady Ann Grimston did not believe that there was life after death. However, *a tree did grow from her grave!* A tiny seed took root, and as it grew, it cracked the marble and even tore the metal railing out of the ground! There is life and power in a seed, and there is life and power in the Word of God.

When God's Word is planted and cultivated, it produces fruit. Faith, hope, and love are among the firstfruits in the spiritual harvest. These spiritual graces are among the evidences that a person has truly been born again (see Rom. 5:1–4; Eph. 1:13–15; 1 Thess. 1:3; Heb. 6:9–12; 1 Peter 1:3–9).

Faith comes through the hearing of God's Word (Rom. 10:17). Our Christian lives start with *saving* faith; but this is only the beginning. We learn to walk by faith (2 Cor. 5:7) and work by faith (1 Thess. 1:3). It is faith that gives power to prayer (Luke 17:5–6). Faith is a shield that protects us from Satan's fiery darts (Eph. 6:16).

Love is another evidence of true salvation, for the unsaved person is wrapped up mainly in himself (Eph. 2:1–3). The fact that these people loved *all* the saints was proof that God had changed them and given them eternal life. Christian love is not a shallow feeling that we manufacture; it is the work of the Holy Spirit in our hearts (Rom. 5:5; Col. 1:8). It is worth noting that Colossians 1:8 is the only verse in the letter that mentions the Holy Spirit, and it is in connection with love.

This Spirit-given love was for "all the saints" (Col. 1:4) and not only for the people of their own fellowship. As Christians, we also need to realize the vastness of God's love and share it with all the saints (Eph. 3:17–19). Believers should be "knit together in love" (Col. 2:2) so that there will be a true spiritual unity to the glory of God. The bond that unites us is love (Col. 3:14). Uniformity is the result of compulsion from the outside; unity is the result of compassion on the inside.

Hope is also a characteristic of the believer. Unsaved people are without hope because they are without God (Eph. 2:11–12). Those outside of Christ have no hope (1 Thess. 4:13). In the Bible, hope does not mean "hope so." Our hope in Christ is as definite and assured as our faith in Christ. Because Christ is in us, we have the "hope of glory" (Col. 1:27).

The false teachers tried to unsettle the Colossian believers and move them away from the hope of the gospel (Col. 1:23). But Paul made it clear that this hope is "laid up" for believers in heaven (Col. 1:5). The word translated "laid up" carries the meaning of "to be reserved, to be set aside for someone." It was used to refer to money laid up or hidden. The tense of the verb indicates that this hope has *once and for all* been reserved so that nothing can take it from us. Not only has this hope (our glorious inheritance in glory) been reserved for us, but we are being kept by God's power so that we can be sure of enjoying heaven one day (1 Peter 1:1–5). We are being guarded for glory!

What is the relationship between faith, hope, and love? Certainly the more we love someone, the more we will trust him. We do not trust a casual acquaintance to the same degree that we trust a confidential friend. As we come to know God better, we trust Him more and we love Him more. Love and faith encourage each other.

But hope also has a valuable contribution to make. Wherever there is a relationship of faith and love, there will be a growing hope. When a man and woman fall in love and learn to trust each other in that love, their future always becomes brighter. In fact, Paul taught that hope is a motivating power for love and for faith:

"the faith and love that spring from the hope that is stored up for you in heaven" (Col. 1:5 NIV).

The blessed hope of seeing Jesus Christ and going to heaven to be with Him is a powerful force in the Christian's life. When we realize the joy we shall have in heaven, it makes us love Him more. The fact that we *know* we shall be with Him in glory encourages us to trust Him more. Even the problems and trials here on earth do not move us away from that hope.

I have noticed that the prospect of a future happiness has a way of making people love one another more. Have you ever watched children just before Christmas or a family vacation? The bright promise of heaven encourages our faith and expands our love. Then faith and love work together to make the present more enjoyable and the future more exciting.

Divisions and dissensions among Christians are tragic. I am not suggesting that we all get together in a "super church," but I do feel that there could be more love and understanding among God's people. The fact that we are going to be together in heaven ought to encourage us to love each other on earth. This is one reason why Christ has already given us His glory within. "And the glory which thou gavest me I have given them; that they may be one, even as we are one" (John 17:22).

The hope of seeing Christ and going to heaven is not only a motivation for faith and love, but it is also a motivation for holy living. "And every man that hath this hope in him purifieth himself, even as he is pure" (1 John 3:3). When I was a young Christian, an older friend warned me, "Don't be caught doing anything that would embarrass you if Jesus returned!" That is a rather negative view of the promise of heaven, even though it does have some merit. In fact, John warned us that if we do not abide in Christ (keep in fellowship with Him in obedience), we may be ashamed when He returns (1 John 2:28).

But there is a positive side to this truth. We should keep our lives clean so that when Jesus Christ *does* return, nothing will cloud our first meeting with Him. We will enter into the joy and glory of His presence with confidence and love! Peter called this a "rich welcome" into the everlasting kingdom (2 Peter 1:11 NIV).

The hope of heaven is also an encouragement in times of suffering (1 Peter 1:4–9). As believers, we have our share of suffering, but in the midst of trials, we can rejoice "with joy unspeakable and full of glory" (1 Peter 1:8). When unbelievers suffer, they get discouraged and they want to give up. But when Christians suffer, their faith can become stronger and their love can deepen because their hope shines brighter.

How do we know that we have this hope? The promise is given in "the Word of the truth of the gospel" (Col. 1:5). We believers do not have to "work up" a good feeling of hope. God's unchanging Word assures us that our hope is secure in Christ. In fact, this hope is compared to an anchor (Heb. 6:19) that can never break or drift.

No wonder Paul was thankful for the believers in Colosse! God had given Paul "special miracles" at Ephesus (Acts 19:11). But no miracle is greater than the salvation of the lost sinner. Through the faithful witness of Epaphras, God performed miracles of grace in Colosse.

Have you experienced the miracle of salvation?

If you have, then keep growing and being fruitful for the Lord. The same Word that gave you life when you trusted Christ will continue to nourish that life and make you a faithful, fruitful Christian.

Are there any "gospel miracles" of grace taking place where you live?

CHAPTER THREE
Colossians 1:9–12
A PRISONER'S PRAYER

The prayers in Paul's prison letters are certainly unique. To begin with, he prayed for others and not for himself. The requests in his prayers center on *spiritual* blessings, not on material or physical matters. Of course, it is not wrong to pray about physical or material needs. But spiritual needs are vastly more important.

How would you pray for a group of people you had never seen? All that Paul knew about the believers in Colosse he learned from their faithful pastor, Epaphras. Paul knew of the false teaching that was threatening the church, so he centered his praying on that problem. In his prayer, Paul made three requests.

He Prayed for Spiritual Intelligence (1:9)
The false teachers promised the Colossian believers that they would be "in the know" if they accepted the new doctrines. Words like *knowledge, wisdom,* and *spiritual understanding* were a part of their religious vocabulary, so Paul used these words in his prayer.

Satan is so deceptive! He likes to borrow Christian vocabulary, but he does not use the Christian dictionary! Long before the false teachers had adopted these terms, the words had been in the Christian vocabulary.

The phrase "for this cause" relates the prayer to what Paul had written in Colossians 1:6: "and knew the grace of God in truth." The report from Epaphras convinced Paul that these believers truly knew Christ and were born again. But there was much more to learn *from* Him and *about* Him! "You do not need a new spiritual experience," Paul was saying. "You only need to grow in the experience you have already had."

When a person is born into God's family by faith in Jesus Christ, he is born with all that he needs for growth and maturity. This is the theme of Colossians: "And you are complete in him" (Col. 2:10). No other experience is needed than the new birth. "Do not look for something new," Paul warned the church.

"Continue to grow in that which you received at the beginning" (author's paraphrase).

Every believer needs to have "the knowledge of his will." The Greek word translated "knowledge" in this verse carries the meaning of "full knowledge." There is always more to learn about God and His will for our lives. No Christian would ever dare to say that he had "arrived" and needed to learn nothing more. Like the college freshman who handed in a ten-page report titled "The History of the Universe," that Christian would only declare his ignorance.

The will of God is an important part of a successful Christian life. God wants us to *know* His will (Acts 22:14) and *understand* it (Eph. 5:17). God is not a distant dictator who issues orders and never explains. Because we are His friends, we can know what He is doing and why He is doing it (John 15:13–15). As we study His Word and pray, we discover new and exciting truths about God's will for His people.

The word *filled* is a key word in Colossians. It was also a key word in the teachings of the false teachers who had invaded the Colossian church. Paul used it many times (see Col. 1:19, 25; 2:2, 9–10; 4:12, 17 [*complete* = "filled full"]). The word carries the idea of being fully equipped. It was used to describe a ship that was ready for a voyage. The believer has in Christ all that he needs for the voyage of life. "And you are complete in him" (Col. 2:10). "And of his fullness have all we received" (John 1:16).

In the language of the New Testament, to be "filled" means to be "controlled by." When we are filled with anger, we are controlled by anger. To be "filled with the Spirit" (Eph. 5:18) means to be "controlled by the Spirit." Paul's prayer, then, is that these believers might be controlled by the full knowledge of God's will.

But how does this take place? How can believers grow in the full knowledge of God's will? Paul's closing words of Colossians 1:9 tell us: "By means of all wisdom and spiritual insight" (literal translation). *We understand the will of God through the Word of God.* The Holy Spirit teaches us as we submit to Him (John 14:26; 16:13). As we pray and sincerely seek God's truth, He gives us through the Spirit the wisdom and insight that we need (Eph. 1:17).

The *general* will of God for all His children is given clearly in the Bible. The *specific* will of God for any given situation must always agree with what He has already revealed in His Word. The better we know God's general will, the easier it will be to determine His specific guidance in daily life. Paul did not encourage the Colossians to seek visions or wait for voices. He prayed that they might get deeper into God's Word and thus have greater wisdom and insight concerning God's will. He wanted them to have "all wisdom"—not that they would know everything, but that they would have all the wisdom necessary for making decisions and living to please God.

Spiritual intelligence is the beginning of a successful, fruitful Christian life. God puts no premium on ignorance. I once heard a preacher say, "I didn't never go to school. I'm just a igerant Christian, and I'm glad I is!" A man does not have to go to school to gain spiritual intelligence, but neither should he magnify his "igerance."

Great men of God like Charles Spurgeon, G. Campbell Morgan, and H. A. Ironside never had the privilege of formal Bible training. But they were devoted students of the Word, learning its deeper truths through hours of study, meditation, and prayer. The first step toward fullness of life is spiritual intelligence—growing in the will of God by knowing the Word of God.

He Prayed for Practical Obedience (1:10)

The false teachers in Colosse attracted people through their offer of "spiritual knowledge," but they did not relate this knowledge to life. In the Christian life, knowledge and obedience go together. There is no separation between *learning* and *living.* The wisdom about which Paul prayed was not simply a head knowledge of deep spiritual truths (see Col. 1:28; 2:3; 3:16; 4:5). True spiritual wisdom must affect the daily life. Wisdom and practical intelligence must go together (see Ex. 31:3; Deut. 4:6; 1 Cor. 1:19).

In my pastoral ministry, I have met people who have become intoxicated with "studying the deeper truths of the Bible." Usually they have been given a book or introduced to some teacher's tapes. Before long, they get so smart they become dumb! The "deeper truths" they discover only detour them from practical Christian living. Instead of getting burning hearts of devotion to Christ (Luke 24:32), they get big heads and start creating problems in their homes and churches. All Bible truths are practical, not theoretical. If we are growing in knowledge, we should also be growing in grace (2 Peter 3:18).

Two words summarize the practicality of the Christian life: *walk* and *work.* The sequence is important: first wisdom; then walk; then work. I cannot work for God unless I am walking with Him, but I cannot walk with Him if I am ignorant of His will. The believer who spends time daily in the Word and prayer (Acts 6:4) will know God's will and be able to walk with Him and work for Him.

After all, our purpose in life is not to please ourselves, but to please the Lord. We should walk *worthy of our calling* (Eph. 4:1) and *worthy of the gospel* (Phil. 1:27), which means we will walk *worthy of God* (1 Thess. 2:12). In short, we should walk to *please* God (1 Thess. 4:1).

It is not we who work for God; it is God who works in us and through us to produce the fruit of His grace (Phil. 2:12–13). Christian service is the result of Christian devotion. The work that we do is the outflow of the life that we live. It is by abiding in Christ that we can produce fruit (John 15:1ff.).

God must make the worker before He can do the work. God spent thirteen years preparing Joseph for his ministry in Egypt, and eighty years preparing Moses to lead Israel. Jesus spent three years teaching His disciples how to bear fruit; and even the learned apostle Paul needed a "postgraduate course" in Arabia before he could serve God with effectiveness. A newborn babe can cry and make its presence known, but it cannot work. A new Christian can witness for Christ and even win others—but he must be taught to walk and learn God's wisdom before he is placed in an office of responsible ministry.

God's wisdom reveals God's will. As we obey God's will in our walk, we can work for Him and bear fruit. We will not just occasionally serve God; we will be "fruitful in every good work" (Col. 1:10). But there is a blessed by-product of this experience: "increasing in the knowledge of God" (Col. 1:10). As we walk with God and work for God, we get to know Him better and better.

Our Christian lives desperately need *balance*. Certainly we get to know God better as we pray in our private rooms and as we meditate on His Word. But we also get to know Him as we walk in our daily lives and work to win others and help His people.

Worship and service are not competitive. They always go together. When He was ministering on earth, our Lord retired to pray—then He went out to serve. We need to avoid the extremes of impractical mysticism and fleshly enthusiasm. As we spend time with God, we get to understand Him and His will for our lives, and as we go out to obey Him, we learn more.

Practical obedience means pleasing God, serving Him, and getting to know Him better. Any doctrine that isolates the believer from the needs of the world around him is not spiritual doctrine. Evangelist D. L. Moody often said, "Every Bible should be bound in shoe-leather." Paul would agree.

Paul has prayed that we might have spiritual intelligence, and that this intelligence might result in practical obedience. But there is a third request that completes these first two; and without it, the Christian life could not be mature.

He Prayed for Moral Excellence (1:11–12)
Wisdom and conduct should always be related to moral character. One of the great problems in our evangelical world today is the emphasis on "spiritual knowledge" and "Christian service," without connecting these important matters to personal character.

For example, some teachers and preachers claim to have God's wisdom—yet they lack love and kindness and the other basic qualities that make the Christian life beautiful and distinctive. Even some "soul-winning Christians" are so busy serving God that they cannot take time to check facts—so they publish lies about other Christians. For some months, I read a certain religious publication. But when I discovered that they had no "Letters to the Editor" column (except for praise), and that they never published a correction or apologized for an error, I stopped reading the magazine.

Knowledge, conduct, service, and character must always go together. We know God's will that we might obey it, and, in obeying it, we serve Him and grow in Christian character. While none of us is perfectly balanced in these four factors, we ought to strive for that balance.

It is God's energy that empowers us. Colossians 1:11 reads, in effect, "With all power being empowered according to the might of His glory." Paul used two different Greek words for God's energy: *dunamis* (from which we get our word *dynamite*) means "inherent power"; and *kratos* means "manifested power," power that is put forth in action. The grace of our Christian lives is but a result of God's power at work in our lives. Spiritual growth and maturity can come only as we yield to God's power and permit Him to work in us.

We usually think of God's glorious power being revealed in great feats of daring—the Israelites crossing the Red Sea, David leading a victorious army, or Paul raising the dead. But the emphasis here is on Christian character: patience, longsuffering, joyfulness, and thanksgiving. The inner victories of the soul are just as great, if not greater, than the public victories recorded in the annals of history. For David to control his temper when he was being maligned by Shimei was a greater victory than his slaying of Goliath (2 Sam. 16:5–13). "He who is slow to anger is better than the mighty, and he who rules his spirit, than he who captures a city" (Prov. 16:32 NASB).

The word *patience* means "endurance when circumstances are difficult." It is the opposite of despondency. This word is never used in reference to God, for God does not face difficult circumstances. Nothing is impossible with God (Jer. 32:27).

Patience is an important characteristic of the maturing Christian life. If we do not learn to be patient, we are not likely to learn anything else. As believers, we are able to rejoice even in our tribulations, because we know that "tribulation brings about perseverance; and perseverance proven character; and proven character, hope" (Rom. 5:3–4 NASB).

We must never think that patience is complacency. Patience is *endurance in action*. It is not the Christian sitting in a rocking chair, waiting for God to do something. It is the soldier on the battlefield, keeping on when the going is tough. It is the runner on the racetrack, refusing to stop because he wants to win the race (Heb. 12:1).

Too many Christians have a tendency to quit when circumstances become difficult. The saintly Dr. V. Raymond Edman, late president of Wheaton College (Illinois), used to remind the students, "It is always too soon to quit."

I have often thought of that statement when I find myself in the midst of trying circumstances. It is not talent or training that guarantees victory: it is perseverance. "By perseverance the snail reached the ark," said Charles Spurgeon.

Along with patience, we need *longsuffering*. This

word means "self-restraint" and is the opposite of revenge. Patience has to do primarily with circumstances, while longsuffering has to do with people. God is longsuffering toward people because of His love and grace (2 Peter 3:9). Longsuffering is one fruit of the Spirit (Gal. 5:22). It is among the "grace garments" that the believer should wear (Col. 3:12).

It is amazing how people can patiently endure trying circumstances, only to lose their tempers with a friend or loved one. Moses was patient during the contest with Pharaoh in Egypt. But he lost his temper with his own people and, as a result, forfeited his right to enter the Promised Land (Num. 20). "Like a city that is broken into and without walls is a man who has no control over his spirit" (Prov. 25:28 NASB).

Patience and longsuffering go together if we are growing spiritually. Paul listed them as the marks of the true minister of Jesus Christ (2 Cor. 6:4–6). Certainly, Paul displayed these graces in his own life (2 Tim. 3:10). The great example of patience and longsuffering in the Old Testament is Job (James 5:10–11). In the New Testament, of course, it is Jesus Christ.

It is easy for God to perform miracles in the realms of the material or physical, because everything in creation obeys His command. Jesus could heal Malchus's ear, but He could not automatically change Peter's heart and remove the hatred and violence that was in it (Luke 22:50–51). God could bring water out of the rock, but He could not force Moses to be patient.

A pastor often visited a Christian young man who had been badly burned. The young man had to lie still for hours, and it was difficult for him to perform even the basic functions of life.

"I wish God would do a miracle and heal me," the young man said to his pastor one day.

"God is doing a miracle," the pastor replied, "but not the kind you are looking for. I have watched you grow in patience and kindness during these weeks. That, to me, is a greater miracle than the healing of your body."

God's power is evidenced in our lives not only in our patience and longsuffering, but also in our *joyfulness.* When circumstances are difficult, we should exhibit *joyful* patience, and when people are hard to live with, we should reveal *joyful* longsuffering. There is a kind of patience that "endures but does not enjoy." Paul prayed that the Colossian Christians might experience *joyful* patience and longsuffering.

We often use the words *joy* and *happiness* interchangeably, but a distinction should be made. Happiness often depends on happenings. If circumstances are encouraging and people are kind, we are happy. But joy is independent of both circumstances and people. The most joyful epistle Paul wrote was Philippians, and he wrote it from jail as he faced the possibility of being martyred for his faith.

Only God's Spirit working within us can give us joy in the midst of problem circumstances and problem people. "The fruit of the Spirit is … joy" (Gal. 5:22).

Joy is not something that we ourselves "work up"; it is something the Spirit Himself "works in"—"joy in the Holy Spirit" (Rom. 14:17 NIV).

I can recall times in my life when all the circumstances around me pointed to difficulty and possible defeat. Yet my heart was filled with a spiritual joy that could only come from God. Sad to say, I also remember times (far too many!) when I gave in to the problems around me, and I lost both the joy and the victory.

The fourth evidence of God's power in our lives is *thankfulness.* Christians who are filled with the Holy Spirit will be joyful and thankful (Eph. 5:18–20). When we lose our joy, we start complaining and becoming critical.

The Colossian epistle is filled with thanksgiving. Paul gave thanks for the church in Colosse (Col. 1:3), and he prayed that they might grow in their own thanksgiving to God (Col. 1:12). The Christian life should abound with thanksgiving (Col. 2:7). One of the evidences of spiritual growth in our Bible study is thanksgiving (Col. 3:15–17). Our prayers should always include thanksgiving (Col. 4:2). The Christian who is filled with the Spirit, filled with the Word, and watching in prayer will prove it by his attitude of appreciation and thanksgiving to God.

Some people are appreciative by nature, but some are not, and it is these latter people who especially need God's power to express thanksgiving. We should remember that every good gift comes from God (James 1:17) and that He is (as the theologians put it) "the Source, Support, and End of all things." The very breath in our mouths is the free gift of God.

Years ago, Northwestern University in Evanston, Illinois had a life-saving squad that assisted passengers on the Lake Michigan boats. On September 8, 1860, a passenger boat, the *Lady Elgin,* floundered near Evanston, and a ministerial student, Edward Spencer, personally rescued seventeen persons. The exertion of that day permanently damaged his health and he was unable to train for the ministry. When he died some years later, it was noted that not one of the seventeen persons he had saved ever came to thank him.

Thankfulness is the opposite of selfishness. The selfish person says, "I *deserve* what comes to me! Other people *ought* to make me happy!" But the mature Christian realizes that life is a gift from God, and that the blessings of life come only from His bountiful hand.

Of course, the one blessing that ought to move us constantly to thanksgiving is that God has made us "meet [fit] to be partakers of the inheritance of the saints in light" (Col. 1:12). The word *fit* means "qualified": God has qualified us for heaven! And, while we are waiting for Christ to return, we enjoy our share of the spiritual inheritance that we have in Him (Eph. 1:11, 18–23).

In the Old Testament, God's people had an *earthly* inheritance, the land of Canaan. Christians today have a *spiritual* inheritance in Christ. Canaan is not a picture of heaven, for there will be no battles or defeats in heaven. Canaan is a picture of our *present* inheritance in Christ. We must claim our inheritance by faith as we step out on the promises of God (Josh. 1:1–9). Day by day, we claim our blessings, and this makes us even more thankful to the Lord.

As we review this marvelous prayer, we can see how penetrating it is. We need spiritual intelligence if we are going to live to please God. We also need practical obedience in our walk and work. But the result of all of this must be spiritual power in the inner man, power that leads to joyful patience and longsuffering, with thanksgiving.

Have you been praying this way lately?

CHAPTER FOUR
Colossians 1:13–20
CROWN HIM LORD OF ALL!

The false teachers in Colosse, like the false teachers of our own day, would not *deny* the importance of Jesus Christ. They would simply *dethrone* Him, giving Him prominence but not preeminence. In their philosophy, Jesus Christ was but one of many "emanations" that proceeded from God and through which men could reach God. It was this claim that Paul refuted in this section.

Probably no paragraph in the New Testament contains more concentrated doctrine about Jesus Christ than this one. We can keep ourselves from going on a detour if we remember that Paul wrote to prove the preeminence of Christ, and he did so by using four unanswerable arguments.

Christ Is the Savior (1:13–14)
Man's greatest problem is sin—a problem that can never be solved by a philosopher or a religious teacher. Sinners need a Savior. These two verses present a vivid picture of the four saving actions of Christ on our behalf.

He delivered us (v. 13a). This word means "rescued from danger." We could not deliver ourselves from the guilt and penalty of sin, but Jesus could and did deliver us. We were in danger of spending eternity apart from God. The sword of God's judgment was hanging over our heads!

But this deliverance involved something else: we were delivered from the authority of Satan and the powers of darkness. The gnostic false teachers believed in an organization of evil spirits that controlled the world (see Col. 1:16; 2:10, 15); angels, archangels, principalities, powers, virtues, dominions, and thrones. John Milton used these titles when describing Satan's forces in his classic *Paradise Lost.*

He translated us (v. 13b). This word was used to describe the deportation of a population from one country into another. History records the fact that Antiochus the Great transported at least two thousand Jews from Babylonia to Colosse.

Jesus Christ did not release us from bondage only to have us wander aimlessly. He moved us into His own kingdom of light and made us victors over Satan's kingdom of darkness. Earthly rulers transported the defeated people, but Jesus Christ transported the winners.

The phrase "his dear Son" can be translated "the Son of His love." At the baptism and transfiguration of Jesus Christ, the Father declared that Jesus was His "beloved Son" (Matt. 3:17; 17:5). This fact reminds us of the price the Father paid when He gave His Son for us. It also reminds us that His kingdom is a kingdom of love as well as a kingdom of light.

The experience of Israel in the Old Testament is an illustration of this spiritual experience; for God delivered them from the bondage of Egypt and took them into the Promised Land of their inheritance. God brings us out that He might bring us in.

He redeemed us (v. 14a). This word means "to release a prisoner by the payment of a ransom." Paul did not suggest that Jesus paid a ransom to Satan in order to rescue us from the kingdom of darkness. By His death and resurrection, Jesus met the holy demands of God's law. Satan seeks to accuse us and imprison us because he knows we are guilty of breaking God's law. But the ransom has been paid on Calvary, and through faith in Jesus Christ, we have been set free.

He has forgiven us (v. 14b). Redemption and forgiveness go together (Eph. 1:7). The word translated "forgiveness" means "to send away" or "to cancel a debt." Christ has not only set us free and transferred us to a new kingdom, but He has canceled every debt so that we cannot be enslaved again. Satan cannot find anything in the files that will indict us!

In recent years, the church has rediscovered the freedom of forgiveness. God's forgiveness of sinners is an act of His grace. We did not deserve to be forgiven, nor can we earn forgiveness. Knowing that we are forgiven makes it possible for us to fellowship with God, enjoy His grace, and seek to do His will. Forgiveness is not an excuse for sin; rather, it is an encouragement for obedience. And, because we have been forgiven, we can forgive others (Col. 3:13). The parable of the unforgiving servant makes it clear that an unforgiving spirit always leads to bondage (Matt. 18:21–35).

Jesus Christ is preeminent in salvation. No other person could redeem us, forgive us, transfer us out of Satan's kingdom into God's kingdom, and do it wholly by grace. The phrase, "through His blood," reminds us of the cost of our salvation. Moses and the Israelites only had to shed the blood of a lamb to be delivered from Egypt. But Jesus had to shed His blood to deliver us from sin.

Christ Is the Creator (1:15–17)
The false teachers were very confused about creation.

They taught that matter was evil, including the human body. They also taught that Jesus Christ did not have a real body, since this would have put Him in contact with evil matter. The results of these false teachings were tragic, including extreme asceticism on the one hand and unbridled sin on the other. After all, if your body is sinful, you either try to enslave it or you enjoy it.

In this section, Paul explained the fourfold relationship of Jesus Christ to creation.

He existed before creation (v. 15). The term "firstborn" does not refer to time, but to place or status. Jesus Christ was not the first being created, since He Himself is the Creator of all things. "Firstborn" simply means "of first importance, of first rank." Solomon was certainly not born first of all of David's sons, yet he was named the firstborn (Ps. 89:27). "Firstborn of every creature" means "prior to all Creation." Jesus Christ is not a created being; He is eternal God.

Paul used the word *image* to make this fact clear. It means "an exact representation and revelation." The writer to the Hebrews affirms that Jesus Christ is "the express image of his person" (Heb. 1:3). Jesus was able to say, "He that hath seen me hath seen the Father" (John 14:9). In His essence, God is invisible, but Jesus Christ has revealed Him to us (John 1:18). Nature reveals the existence, power, and wisdom of God, but nature cannot reveal the very essence of God to us. It is only in Jesus Christ that the invisible God is revealed perfectly. Since no mere creature can perfectly reveal God, Jesus Christ must be God.

He created all things (v. 16a). Since Christ created all things, He Himself is uncreated. The word *for* that introduces this verse could be translated "because." Jesus Christ is the Firstborn of all *because* He created all things. It is no wonder that the winds and waves obeyed Him, and diseases and death fled from Him, for He is Master over all. "All things were made by him" (John 1:3). This includes all things in heaven and earth, visible and invisible. All things are under His command.

All things exist for Him (v. 16b). Everything exists *in* Him, *for* Him, and *through* Him. Jesus Christ is the Sphere in which they exist, the Agent through which they came into being, and the One for whom they were made.

Paul's use of three different prepositions is one way of refuting the philosophy of the false teachers. For centuries, the Greek philosophers had taught that everything needed a primary cause, an instrumental cause, and a final cause. The primary cause is the plan, the instrumental cause the power, and the final cause the purpose. When it comes to creation, Jesus Christ is the primary cause (He planned it), the instrumental cause (He produced it), and the final cause (He did it for His own pleasure).

If everything in creation exists *for* Him, then nothing can be evil of itself (except for Satan and fallen angels, and even those God uses to accomplish His will). Gnostic regulations about using God's creation are all foolish (Col. 2:20–23). It also means that God's creation, even though under bondage to sin (Rom. 8:22), can be used for God's glory and enjoyed by God's people (1 Tim. 6:17).

He holds all things together (v. 17). "In him all things hold together" (NIV). A guide took a group of people through an atomic laboratory and explained how all matter was composed of rapidly moving electric particles. The tourists studied models of molecules and were amazed to learn that matter is made up primarily of space. During the question period, one visitor asked, "If this is the way matter works, what holds it all together?" For that, the guide had no answer.

But the Christian has an answer: Jesus Christ! Because "He is before all things," He can hold all things together. Again, this is another affirmation that Jesus Christ is God. Only God exists before all of creation, and only God can make creation cohere. To make Jesus Christ less than God is to dethrone Him.

It used to bother me to sing the familiar song "This Is My Father's World." I thought Satan and sin were in control of this world. I have since changed my mind, and now I sing the song with joy and victory. Jesus Christ made all things, He controls all things, and by Him all things hold together. Indeed, this *is* my Father's world!

Christ Is the Head of the Church (1:18)

There are many images of the church in the New Testament, and the body is one of the most important (Rom. 12:4ff.; 1 Cor. 12:14; Eph. 4:8–16). No denomination or local assembly can claim to be "the body of Christ," for that body is composed of *all* true believers. When a person trusts Christ, he is immediately baptized by the Holy Spirit into this body (1 Cor. 12:12–13). The baptism of the Spirit is not a postconversion experience—for it occurs the instant a person believes in Jesus Christ.

Each Christian is a member of this spiritual body, and Jesus Christ is the Head. In Greek usage, the word *head* meant "source" and "origin" as well as "leader, ruler." Jesus Christ is the Source of the church, His body, and the Leader. Paul called Him "the beginning," which tells us that Jesus Christ has priority in time as far as His church is concerned. The term *beginning* can be translated "originator."

No matter which name you select, it will affirm the preeminence of Jesus Christ in the church. The church had its origin in Him, and today it has its operation in Him. As the Head of the church, Jesus Christ supplies it with life through His Spirit. He gives gifts to men, and then places these gifted people in His church that they might serve Him where they are needed. Through His Word, Jesus Christ nourishes and cleanses the church (Eph. 5:25–30).

No believer on earth is the head of the church. This position is reserved exclusively for Jesus Christ.

Various religious leaders may have founded churches or denominations, but only Jesus Christ is the Founder of the church that is His body. This church is composed of all true believers, and it was born at Pentecost. It was then that the Holy Spirit came and baptized the believers into one spiritual body.

The fact that there is "one body" in this world (Eph. 4:4) does not eliminate or minimize the need for *local* bodies of believers. The fact that I belong to the universal church does not release me from my responsibilities to the local church. I cannot minister to the whole church, but I can strengthen and build the church by ministering to God's people in a local assembly.

Jesus Christ is the Head of the church, and the Beginning of the church; and He is also the Firstborn from the dead. We saw this word *firstborn* in Colossians 1:15. Paul did not say that Jesus was the first person to be raised from the dead, for He was not. But He is the most important of all who have been raised from the dead; for without His resurrection, there could be no resurrection for others (1 Cor. 15:20ff.).

It seems odd that Paul used the word *born* in connection with death, for the two concepts seem opposed to each other. But the tomb was a womb from which Christ came forth in victory, for death could not hold Him (Acts 2:24). The Son was begotten in resurrection glory (Ps. 2:7; Acts 13:33).

This brings us to the theme of this entire section: "That in all things he might have the preeminence" (Col. 1:18). This was God's purpose in making His Son the Savior, Creator, and Head of the church. The word translated "preeminence" is used nowhere else in the New Testament. It is related to the word translated "firstborn," and it magnifies the unique position of Jesus Christ. "Christ is all, and in all" (Col. 3:11).

In 1893, the World's Columbian Exposition was held in Chicago, and more than twenty-one million people visited the exhibits. Among the features was a "World Parliament of Religions," with representatives of the world's religions, meeting to share their "best points" and perhaps come up with a new religion for the world.

Evangelist D. L. Moody saw this as a great opportunity for evangelism. He used churches, rented theaters, and even rented a circus tent (when the show was not on) to present the gospel of Jesus Christ. His friends wanted Moody to attack the "Parliament of Religions," but he refused. "I am going to make Jesus Christ so attractive," he said, "that men will turn to Him." Moody knew that Jesus Christ was the preeminent Savior, not just one of many "religious leaders" of history. The "Chicago Campaign" of 1893 was probably the greatest evangelistic endeavor in D. L. Moody's life, and thousands came to Christ.

But the false teachers of Colosse could never give Jesus Christ the place of preeminence, for, according to their philosophy, Jesus Christ was only one of many "emanations" from God. He was not the only way to God (John 14:6), rather, He was but one rung on the ladder! It has well been said, "If Jesus Christ is not Lord of all, He cannot be Lord at all."

We have now studied three arguments for the preeminence of Jesus Christ: He is the Savior, He is the Creator, and He is the Head of the church. These arguments reveal His relationship with lost sinners, with the universe, and with believers. But what about His relationship with God the Father?

He Is the Beloved of the Father (1:19–20)

Paul had already called Jesus Christ "his [God's] dear Son" (Col. 1:13). Those who have trusted Jesus Christ as their Savior are "accepted in the beloved" (Eph. 1:6). For this reason, God can call *us* His beloved (Col. 3:12).

Then Paul took a giant step forward in his argument, for he declared that "all fullness" dwelt in Jesus Christ! The word translated "fullness" is the Greek word *pleroma* (pronounced "play-RO-ma"). It was a technical term in the vocabulary of the gnostic false teachers. It meant "the sum total of all the divine power and attributes." We have already noted that Paul used this important word eight times in the Colossian letter, so he was meeting the false teachers on their own ground.

The word *dwell* is equally important. It means much more than merely "to reside." The form of the verb means "to be at home permanently." The late Dr. Kenneth S. Wuest, noted Greek expert, pointed out in his excellent commentary on Colossians that the verb indicates that this fullness was "not something added to His Being that was not natural to Him, but that it was part of His essential Being as part of His very constitution, and that permanently" (*Ephesians and Colossians in the Greek New Testament,* [Grand Rapids, Mich.: Eerdmans], 187).

The Father would not permanently give His *pleroma* to some created being. The fact that it "pleased the Father" to have His fullness in Christ is proof that Jesus Christ is God. "And of his [Christ's] fullness have all we received" (John 1:16). "For in him [Jesus Christ] dwelleth all the fullness of the Godhead bodily" (Col. 2:9).

Because Jesus Christ is God, He is able to do what no mere man could ever do: reconcile lost sinners to a holy God. When the first man and woman sinned, they declared war on God, but God did not declare war on them. Instead, God sought Adam and Eve, and He provided a covering for their sins.

The natural mind of the unsaved sinner is at war with God (Rom. 8:7). The sinner may be sincere, religious, and even moral; but he is still at war with God.

How can a holy God ever be reconciled with sinful man? Can God lower His standards, close His eyes to sin, and compromise with man? If He did, the universe would fall to pieces! God must be consistent with Himself and maintain His own holy law.

Perhaps man could somehow please God. But by nature, man is separated from God, and by his deeds, he is alienated from God (Col. 1:21). The sinner is "dead in trespasses and sins" (Eph. 2:1ff.), and therefore is unable to do anything to save himself or to please God (Rom. 8:8).

If there is to be reconciliation between man and God, the initiative and action must come from God. It is *in Christ* that God was reconciled to man (2 Cor. 5:19). But it was not the incarnation of Christ that accomplished this reconciliation, nor was it His example as He lived among men. It was through His *death* that peace was made between God and man. He "made peace through the blood of his cross" (Col. 1:20).

Of course, the false teachers offered a kind of reconciliation between man and God. However, the reconciliation they offered was not complete or final. The angels and the "emanations" could in some way bring men closer to God, according to the gnostic teachers. But the reconciliation we have in Jesus Christ is perfect, complete, and final. More than that, the reconciliation in Christ *involves the whole universe!* He reconciles "all things unto himself … things in earth, or things in heaven" (Col. 1:20).

However, we must not conclude wrongly that universal reconciliation is the same as universal salvation. "Universalism" is the teaching that all beings, including those who have rejected Jesus Christ, will one day be saved. This was not what Paul believed. "Universal restorationism" was not a part of Paul's theology, for he definitely taught that sinners needed to believe in Jesus Christ to be saved (2 Thess. 1).

Paul wrote that Christ solved the sin problem on the cross once and for all. This means that one day God can bring together in Christ all who belong to Him (Eph. 1:9–10). He will be able to glorify believers and punish unbelievers, *and do it justly,* because of Christ's death on the cross. No one—not even Satan—can accuse God of doing wrong, because sin has been effectively dealt with on the cross.

If Jesus Christ is only a man, or only an emanation from God, He cannot reconcile God and man. The only arbitrator who can bring God and man together is One who is *both God and Man Himself.* Contrary to what the gnostics taught, Jesus Christ was a true human being with a real body. He was God in human flesh (John 1:14). When He died on the cross, He met the just demands of the law because He paid the penalty for man's sins (1 Peter 2:24). Reconciliation was completed on the cross (Rom. 5:11).

A man once came to see me because he had difficulties at home. He was not a very well-educated man and sometimes got his words confused. He told me that he and his wife were having "martial problems" when he meant to say "marital problems." (Later I found out that they really were "at war" with each other, so maybe he was right after all!) But the word that caught my attention was in this sentence: "Pastor, me and my wife need a re-cancellation."

He meant to say *reconciliation,* but the word *re-cancellation* was not a bad choice. There can be peace and a reunion of those who are at war *only when sin has been cancelled.* As sinners before a righteous God, we need a "re-cancellation." Our sins were cancelled on the cross.

As we review this profound section (and this study has only scratched the surface), we notice several important truths.

First, Jesus Christ has taken care of *all things.* All things were created by Him and for Him. He existed before all things, and today He holds all things together. He has reconciled all things through the cross. No wonder Paul declared that "in all things he might have the preeminence" (Col. 1:18).

Second, all that we need is Jesus Christ. We have all of God's fullness in Him, and we are "filled full" (complete) in Him (Col. 2:10). There is no need to add anything to the person or work of Jesus Christ. To add anything is to take away from His glory. To give Him prominence instead of preeminence is to dethrone Him.

Third, God is pleased when His Son, Jesus Christ, is honored and given preeminence. There are people who tell us they are Christians, but they ignore or deny Jesus Christ. "We worship the Father," they tell us, "and that is all that is necessary."

But Jesus made it clear that *the Son* is to be worshipped as well as the Father "that all may honor the Son just as they honor the Father. He who does not honor the Son does not honor the Father, who sent him" (John 5:23–24 NIV).

The late Dr. M. R. DeHaan, noted radio Bible teacher, told about a preacher who was confronted by a cultist who rejected the deity of Jesus Christ.

"Jesus cannot be the eternal Son of God, for a father is always older than his son," the man argued. "If the Father is not eternal, then He is not God. If Jesus is His Son, then He is not eternal."

The preacher was ready with an answer. "The thing that makes a person a father is having a son. But if God is the *eternal* Father, then He must have an *eternal* Son! This means that Jesus Christ is eternal—and that He is God!"

Jesus Christ is the Savior, the Creator, the Head of the church, and the Beloved of the Father. He is eternal God … and in our lives He deserves to have the preeminence.

Is Jesus Christ preeminent in your life?

CHAPTER FIVE
Colossians 1:21—2:3
ONE MAN'S MINISTRY

If you received a letter from a man you had never met, a man who was a prisoner, accused of being a troublemaker, how would you respond?

The Colossian believers faced that exact problem. They knew that Paul had been instrumental in leading their pastor, Epaphras, to saving faith in Christ. They also knew that Epaphras had gone to Rome to consult with Paul and had not yet returned. The church members had received Paul's letter, brought to them by Tychicus and Onesimus. But the false teachers in Colosse had been discrediting Paul and causing doubts in the people's minds. "Why listen to a man who is a political prisoner?" they asked. "Can you trust him?"

Paul no doubt realized that this would be the situation, so he paused in the first part of this letter to give some words of explanation. He had been so wrapped up in exalting Jesus Christ that he had not shown any interest in writing about himself! In this section, Paul explained his three ministries.

Sharing the Gospel (1:21–23)

Even though Paul had not personally evangelized Colosse, it was his ministry in Ephesus that led to the founding of the Colossian church. Paul was "made a minister" (Col. 1:25). A large part of his ministry consisted in preaching the good news of salvation through faith in Jesus Christ. His was a ministry of reconciliation (2 Cor. 5:17–21). Paul reviewed for his readers their own spiritual experience.

Their past alienation (v. 21a). The word translated "alienated" means "estranged." These Gentiles in Colosse were estranged from God and separated from the spiritual blessings of Israel (Eph. 2:11ff.). The gods that they worshipped were false gods, and their religious rituals could not take care of their sin or guilt.

But this estrangement was not only a matter of Gentile position; it was also a matter of sinful practices and attitudes. The Gentiles were *enemies,* which means they were "actively hostile to God." Even though they had not received a divine law, such as God gave to Israel, these Gentiles knew the truth about God through creation and conscience (Rom. 1:18ff.). They could not plead ignorance before the bar of God's justice.

The enmity of their minds led to wicked works. Both in attitude and action, they were at war with God. "Because the carnal mind [the mind of the unbeliever] is enmity against God" (Rom. 8:7). This explains why the unbeliever must repent—change his mind—before he can be saved.

Their present reconciliation (vv. 21b–22). They did not reconcile themselves to God; it was God who took the initiative in His love and grace. The Father sent the Son to die on a cross that sinners might be reconciled to God. Jesus died for us when we were "without strength" (Rom. 5:6) and could do nothing for ourselves. He died for us "while we were yet sinners" and "when we were enemies" (Rom. 5:8, 10).

Paul emphasized the physical body of Jesus Christ that was nailed to the cross. The false teachers denied the Incarnation and taught that Jesus Christ did not have a real human body. Their philosophy that all matter was evil made it necessary for them to draw this false conclusion. But the New Testament makes it clear that Jesus *did* have a fully human body and that He bore our sins on that body on the cross (1 Peter 2:24).

The purpose of this reconciliation is *personal holiness.* God does not make peace (Col. 1:20) so that we can continue to be rebels! He has reconciled us to Himself so that we may share His life and His holiness. We are presented to God "holy and unblameable and unreproveable" (Col. 1:22).

The word *holy* is closely related to the word *saint.* Both of these words express the idea of "being set apart, being devoted to God." In the New Testament, saints are not dead people who during their lives performed miracles and never sinned. New Testament saints were living people who had trusted Jesus Christ. Paul wrote this letter to living saints (Col. 1:2).

Unblameable means "without blemish." The word was applied to the temple sacrifices, which had to be without blemish. It is amazing that God looks at His children and sees no blemish on them! God chose us to be "holy and without blame" (Eph. 1:4).

Unreproveable means "free from accusation." Once we have been reconciled to God, no charges can be brought against us (Rom. 8:31–34). Satan, the accuser of the brethren (Rev. 12:1–12), would like to hurl charges at us, but God will not accept them (see Zech. 3). People may have accusations to bring against us, but they cannot change our relationship with God.

The most important thing in our Christian lives is not how we look in our own sight or in the sight of others (1 Cor. 4:1–4), but how we look in God's sight. I recall counseling a Christian who was in the habit of reminding herself of her past sins and failures. She seemed to enjoy having other people criticize her. I kept reminding her of what she was *in God's sight.* Her constant emphasis on her failures denied the work that Jesus Christ had done for her on the cross. It took time, but eventually she accepted her wonderful new position in Christ and began to get victory over criticism and depression.

Paul's emphasis on our holy standing before God was certainly an attack on the false teachers, for they promised their followers a kind of "perfection" that nothing else could give. "You already have a perfect standing in Christ," Paul wrote, "so why seek for it anywhere else?"

Their future glorification (v. 23). "The hope of the gospel" means that blessed hope of our Lord's return (Titus 2:13). Paul had already mentioned this hope: "The hope which is laid up for you in heaven" (Col. 1:5). Later in the chapter, he called it "the hope of glory" (Col. 1:27).

There was a time when these Gentile Colossians were without hope (Eph. 2:12). The reason? They were without God. But when they were reconciled to God, they were given a wonderful hope of glory. All of God's children will one day be with Christ in heaven (John 17:24). In fact, so secure is our future that Paul stated that we have *already been glorified!* (Rom. 8:30). All we are waiting for is the revelation of this glory when Jesus Christ returns (Rom. 8:17–19).

Paul's statement to the Colossians seems to cast a shadow on the assurance of our future glory (see Col. 1:23). Is it possible for a believer to lose his salvation? No, the *if* clause does not suggest doubt or lay down a condition by which we "keep up our salvation."

Paul used an architectural image in this verse—a house, firmly set on the foundation. The town of Colosse was located in a region known for earthquakes, and the word translated "moved away" can mean "earthquake stricken." Paul was saying, "If you are truly saved, and built on the solid foundation, Jesus Christ, then you will continue in the faith and nothing will move you. You have heard the gospel and trusted Jesus Christ, and He has saved you."

In other words, we are not saved by continuing in the faith. But we continue in the faith and thus prove that we are saved. It behooves each professing Christian to test his own faith and examine his own heart to be sure he is a child of God (2 Cor. 13:5; 2 Peter 1:10ff.).

Suffering for the Gentiles (1:24–27)

Paul's enemies made much of the fact that the great apostle was a prisoner of Rome. The false teachers in Colosse probably ridiculed Paul and used this as a weapon to fight the truth of the gospel. But Paul turned this weapon around and used it to defeat his enemies and to build a closer relationship with the church in Colosse.

Paul's rejoicing (v. 24). "Instead of being ashamed of my suffering, I am rejoicing in it!" How could anyone rejoice in suffering? To begin with, Paul was suffering because of Jesus Christ. It was "the fellowship of his sufferings" (Phil. 3:10). Like the early apostles, Paul rejoiced that he was "counted worthy to suffer shame for his name" (Acts 5:41). A Christian should never suffer "as a thief or as an evildoer," but it is an honor to "suffer as a Christian" (1 Peter 4:15–16). There is a special blessing and reward reserved for the faithful believer who suffers for the sake of Christ (Matt. 5:10–12).

Paul had a second cause for rejoicing in his suffering: he was suffering because of the Gentiles. Paul was the chosen apostle to the Gentiles (Eph. 3:1–13). In fact, he was a prisoner in Rome because of his love for the Gentiles. He was arrested in Jerusalem on false charges, and the Jews listened to his defense until he used the word *Gentiles* (see Acts 22:21ff.). It was that word that infuriated them and drove them to ask for his execution. (The full account is given in Acts 21–28, and an exciting account it is.)

So the Gentile believers in Colosse had every reason to love Paul and be thankful for his special ministry to them. But there was a third cause for Paul's rejoicing: he was suffering for the sake of Christ's body, the church. There was a time when Paul had persecuted the church and caused it to suffer. But now Paul devoted his life to the care of the church. Paul did not ask, as do some believers, "What will I get out of it?" Instead he asked, "How much will God let me put into it?" The fact that Paul was a prisoner did not stop him from ministering to the church.

It is important to note, however, that these sufferings had nothing to do with the sacrificial sufferings of Christ on the cross. Only the sinless Lamb of God could die for the sins of the world (John 1:29). Paul was "filling up in his turn the leftover parts of Christ's sufferings" (Col. 1:24, literal translation). The word *afflictions* refers to the "pressures" of life, the persecutions Paul endured. This word is never used in the New Testament for the sacrificial sufferings of Jesus Christ.

The sacrificial sufferings of Christ are over, but His body, the church, experiences suffering because of its stand for the faith. The Head of the church in heaven feels the sufferings that His people endure. ("Saul, Saul, why persecutest thou me?" [Acts 9:4]) Paul was taking his turn in sharing these afflictions, and others would follow in his train. But Paul did not complain. "For as the sufferings of Christ abound in us, so our consolation also abounds by Christ" (2 Cor. 1:5).

Paul's responsibility (vv. 25–27). Had Paul compromised with the Jews and stopped ministering to the Gentiles, he could have been spared a great deal of suffering. But he could not abandon his calling just for personal safety and comfort. He had been made a minister by God; he had been given a "stewardship" (dispensation) and he had to be faithful to his calling (1 Cor. 4:2). It was not a matter of choice: he was called to fulfill the Word of God. This can mean "I must preach the Word fully and not compromise any truth." It can also mean "I am commissioned by God's Word and I must be faithful to discharge my office."

Paul's special message regarding the Gentiles had to do with what he called "the mystery." To us today, a mystery is something eerie and perhaps frightening, but this was not the way the word was defined in Paul's day. The false teachers used this word to describe the inner secrets of their religions. A mystery is a "sacred secret," hidden in the past and now revealed by the Holy Spirit (see Eph. 3:1–13).

God called the nation of Israel to be His people, He gave them His law (including the priesthood and sacrifices), and He gave them a wonderful land. He promised them a King who would one day establish a glorious kingdom and fulfill the many promises made to Abraham and David. The Old Testament prophets wrote about a Messiah who would suffer, and a Messiah who would reign. They could not explain the seeming contradiction (see 1 Peter 1:9–12). They did not understand that the Messiah first had to suffer before He could enter into glory (Luke 24:13–27).

Jesus Christ came to earth, was rejected by His people, and was crucified. He arose again and returned to heaven. Did this mean that God's promised kingdom for Israel was now abandoned? No, because God had initiated a new program—His *mystery*—that was not explained by the Old Testament prophets. The mystery is that today God is uniting Jews and Gentiles in the church (Eph. 2:11–22). When the church is completed, then Jesus Christ will return and take His people to heaven (1 Thess. 4:13–18). Then He will again deal with Israel as a nation and establish the promised kingdom (Acts 15:12–18).

Imagine what this message meant to the Gentiles. They were no longer excluded from the glory and riches of God's grace! During the Old Testament dispensation, a Gentile had to become a Jewish proselyte in order to share in the blessings of Israel. But in the new dispensation, Jews and Gentiles alike are saved by faith in Jesus Christ (Rom. 10:12–13). No wonder the Jewish false teachers opposed Paul. He dared to say, "There is no difference!"

We who have grown up in somewhat Christian surroundings have a tendency to take all of this for granted. But think of the excitement this message must have generated in a church composed of new believers who had no background in the church. Once they were outside the covenants of God, but now they were members of His family. Once they were living in spiritual ignorance and death, but now they were alive and sharing in the riches of God's wisdom in Christ. Once they had no hope, but now they had a glorious hope because Christ now lived within! It would be good for us today to recapture some of that "first love" excitement.

I was privileged to minister in Africa for three weeks, and there I was introduced to some of the finest Christians I have ever met. I taught the Word to over five hundred national pastors in Kenya for almost a week, and each service was a challenge and blessing to me. Many of the pastors still had the marks of paganism and idolatry on their bodies; yet their faces were aglow with the joy of the Lord. I went to Africa to minister to them, *but they ministered to me!* They reminded me not to take for granted the glorious riches I have in Jesus Christ.

Striving for the Saints (1:28—2:3)

We have met Paul the preacher, sharing the gospel and Paul the prisoner, suffering for the Gentiles.

Now we meet Paul the prayer warrior, striving in prayer for the individual saints that they might mature in the faith. The words *striving* (Col. 1:29) and *conflict* (Col. 2:1) are athletic terms. They refer to the strenuous effort put forth by the runner to win the race. Our English word *agony* comes from this Greek word.

Paul's instruction (v. 28a). "Whom" refers, of course, to Jesus Christ. "For we preach not ourselves, but Christ Jesus the Lord" (2 Cor. 4:5). The false teachers exalted themselves and their great "spiritual" attainments. They preached a system of teaching, but Paul preached a Person. The gnostics preached philosophy and the empty traditions of men (Col. 2:8), but Paul proclaimed Jesus Christ. The false teachers had

lists of rules and regulations (Col. 2:16, 20–21), but Paul presented Christ. What a difference in ministries!

Paul not only *preached* (the word means "to announce with authority as a herald"), but he also *warned.* While it is good to proclaim positive truth, it is also necessary to warn God's people against the lies of the enemy (Acts 20:31). In fact, God's people should be alert to warn one another (*admonish* in Col. 3:16 NIV). Paul considered himself a spiritual father to the local churches, and it was his duty to warn his children (1 Cor. 4:14).

But Paul was also a *teacher* of the truth. It is not enough to warn people; we must also teach them the positive truths of the Word of God. How far would we get in our travels if the highway signs told us where the roads were *not* going? Not very far! It is good to *win* a man to Christ, and then to *warn* him about the dangers ahead; but it is also important to *teach* that convert the basic truths of the Christian life.

Paul not only preached Christ, but he also "taught Christ," for in Christ are "all the treasures of wisdom and knowledge" (Col. 2:3). It was not necessary to introduce any new teaching, for all that a believer needs to know is related to Jesus Christ. "Teaching every man in all wisdom" was Paul's concern (Col. 1:28). Wisdom is the right use of knowledge. The false teachers promised to give people a "hidden wisdom" that would make them "spiritually elite." But all true spiritual wisdom is found only in Jesus Christ.

Paul's intent (v. 28b; 2:2–3). He wanted to present every believer "perfect in Christ Jesus." The word *perfect* was a favorite word with the gnostic teachers. It described the disciple who was no longer a novice, but who had matured and was fully instructed in the secrets of the religion. Paul used it to mean "complete, mature in Christ." This is the goal of all preaching, warning, and teaching.

What are the evidences of this spiritual maturity? Paul described them next (Col. 2:2).

Encouragement—"that their hearts might be comforted." Our English word *encourage* means "with heart." To encourage people is to give them new heart. Shallow sympathy usually makes people feel worse, but true spiritual encouragement makes them feel better. It brings out the best in people.

Endearment—"being knit together in love." The mature Christian loves the brethren and seeks to be a peacemaker, not a troublemaker. He is a part of spiritual unity in the church. An immature person is often selfish and causes division.

Enrichment—"unto all riches of the full assurance of understanding." Paul mentioned the riches of Christ earlier (Col. 1:27). Too many Christians are living like paupers when they could be living like kings. Mature Christians do not complain about what they don't have. Rather, they make use of the vast resources that they do have in Jesus Christ.

Enlightenment—"full assurance of understanding." The mature believer has assurance in his heart that he is a child of God. The spiritual knowledge that he has in Christ constantly enlightens him and directs him daily. I have often counseled believers who told me they lacked assurance of their salvation. Invariably, they have been neglecting God's Word and living in ignorance.

God wants us as His children to have "understanding" and "wisdom and knowledge" (Col. 2:2–3). The word translated "understanding" literally means "to place together." It is the ability to assess things. *Wisdom* implies the ability to defend what we understand. *Knowledge* suggests the ability to grasp truth. All of these terms were also used by the gnostics.

Paul's intercession (1:29—2:1). "For this I labor to the point of exhaustion, agonizing" is a literal translation of the first part of Colossians 1:29. What a picture of prayer! So much of our praying is calm and comfortable, and yet Paul exerted his spiritual muscles the way a Greek runner would exert himself in the Olympic Games. He also taught Epaphras to pray the same way (Col. 4:12).

This does not mean that our prayers are more effective if we exert all kinds of fleshly energy. Nor does it mean that we must "wrestle with God" and wear Him out before He will meet our needs. Paul described a *spiritual* striving: it was God's power at work in his life. True prayer is directed to the Father (Matt. 6:9), through the Son (in His name, John 14:13–14), in the power of the Holy Spirit (Jude 20). When the Spirit is at work in our lives, then we can pray mightily in the will of God.

How does the Spirit assist us in our praying? For one thing, the Spirit teaches us the Word and shows us the will of God (John 16:13–15). Prayer is not our trying to change God's mind. It is learning what is the mind of God and asking accordingly (1 John 5:14–15). The Holy Spirit constantly intercedes for us even though we do not hear His voice (Rom. 8:26–27). He knows the Father's will and He helps us pray in that will.

There are times when we simply do not feel like praying—and that is when we must pray the most! The Spirit gives us divine energy for prayer, in spite of the way we feel. The resurrection power of Jesus Christ is made available to us (Eph. 3:20–21).

In these verses Paul explained his ministry, and in so doing, he silenced the accusations of the enemy. He also stirred the affections of the believers as they realized how much Paul had done for them.

All of us are not called to be apostles, but each one of us does have a God-given ministry. We can share the gospel and be soul-winners. We can suffer for Christ and fulfill the ministry God has given us. We can strive in prayer for God's people and encourage them to mature. Paul took time to minister to *individuals;* note the repetition of "every man" in Colossians 1:28. If we minister to only a few believers, we are helping the whole church.

Are you fulfilling your God-given ministry?

CHAPTER SIX
Colossians 2:4–15
SAINTS ALIVE—AND ALERT

I recall a story about a pastor who was concerned about some unsavory businesses that had opened near a school. His protests finally led to a court case, and the defense attorney did all he could to embarrass the gospel minister.

"Are you not a pastor?" the lawyer asked. "And doesn't the word *pastor* mean 'shepherd'?"

To this definition the minister agreed.

"Well, if you are a shepherd, why aren't you out taking care of the sheep?"

"Because today I'm fighting the wolves!" was the pastor's quick reply, and a good answer it was.

Knowing that there were enemies already attacking the church in Colosse, Paul offered encouragement. By heeding his admonitions, the Colossians would overcome their enemies.

Keep Making Spiritual Progress (2:4–7)
In the Christian life, we never stand still: we either go forward or gradually slip backward. "Let us go on to maturity!" is the call we must obey (Heb. 6:1, literal translation). The Christian who is not making spiritual progress is an open target for the enemy to attack and destroy.

The need for progress (v. 4). Satan is deceptive. He wants to lead believers astray, and to do this, he uses deceptive words. The Greek term used here describes the persuasive arguments of a lawyer. Satan is a liar (John 8:44), and by his lies he leads believers into the wrong path. It is important that we exercise spiritual discernment, and that we continue to grow in our knowledge of spiritual truth.

The nature of progress (vv. 5–7). In order to emphasize his admonition, Paul used several vivid pictures to illustrate spiritual progress.

The army (v. 5). The words *order* and *steadfastness* are military terms. They describe an army that is solidly united against the enemy. *Order* describes the arrangement of the army in ranks, with each soldier in his proper place. Not everybody can be a five-star general, but the general could never fight the battle alone. *Steadfastness* pictures the soldiers in battle formation, presenting a solid front to the enemy. Christians ought to make progress in discipline and obedience, just as soldiers on the battlefield.

The pilgrim (v. 6). The Christian life is compared to a pilgrimage, and believers must learn to walk. Paul had already encouraged his readers to "walk worthy of the Lord" (Col. 1:10), and later he used this image again (Col. 3:7; 4:5). In the Ephesian epistle, the companion letter to the Colossian epistle, Paul used the image at least seven times (Eph. 2:2, 10; 4:1, 17; 5:2, 8, 15).

We are to walk in Christ the same way we originally received Christ—*by faith.* The gnostic teachers wanted to introduce some "new truths" for Christian maturity, but Paul denounced them. "You started with Christ and you must continue with Christ," Paul wrote. "You started with faith and you must continue with faith. This is the only way to make spiritual progress."

The tree (v. 7a). Rooted is an agricultural word. The tense of the Greek word means "once and for all having been rooted." Christians are not to be tumbleweeds that have no roots and are blown about by "every wind of doctrine" (Eph. 4:14). Nor are they to be "transplants" that are repeatedly moved from soil to soil. Once we are rooted by faith in Christ, there is no need to change the soil! The roots draw up the nourishment so that the tree can grow. The roots also give strength and stability.

The building (v. 7b). Built up is an architectural term. It is in the present tense: "being built up." When we trust Christ to save us, we are put on the foundation; from then on, we grow in grace. The word *edify* that is found often in Paul's letters simply means "to build up." To make spiritual progress means to keep adding to the temple to the glory of God.

The school (v. 7c). It is the Word of God that builds and strengthens the Christian. Epaphras had faithfully taught the Colossian believers the truth of the Word (Col. 1:7). But the false teachers were undermining that doctrine. Today, Christians who study the Word become established in the faith. Satan has a difficult time deceiving the Bible-taught believer.

The river (v. 7d). The word *abounding* is often used by Paul. It suggests the picture of a river overflowing its banks. Our first experience in the Lord is that of drinking the water of life by faith, and He puts within us an artesian well of living water (John 4:10–14). But that artesian well should become a "river of living water" (John 7:37–39) that grows deeper and deeper. The image of the river flowing from the sanctuary (Ezek. 47), getting deeper as it flows, probably is what Paul had in mind. Sad to say, many of us are making no progress—our lives are shallow trickles instead of mighty rivers.

Again, Paul mentioned "thanksgiving" (see Col. 1:3, 12). A thankful spirit is a mark of Christian maturity. When a believer is abounding in thanksgiving, he is really making progress!

By reviewing these pictures of spiritual progress, we see how the growing Christian can easily defeat the enemy and not be led astray. If his spiritual roots are deep in Christ, he will not want any other soil. If Christ is his sure foundation, he has no need to move. If he is studying and growing in the Word, he will not be easily enticed by false doctrine. And if his heart is overflowing with thanksgiving, he will not even consider turning from the fullness he has in Christ. A grounded, growing, grateful believer will not be led astray.

Watch Out for Spiritual Perils (2:8–10)

Paul continued the military image with this warning: "Beware lest any man carry you off as a captive" (literal translation). The false teachers did not go out and win the lost, any more than the cultists do today. They "kidnapped" converts from churches! Most of the people I have talked with who are members of antichristian cults were at one time associated with a Christian church of one denomination or another.

How is it possible for false teachers to capture people? The answer is simple: These "captives" are ignorant of the truths of the Word of God. They become fascinated by the philosophy and empty delusion of the false teachers. (This is not to say that *all* philosophy is wrong, because there is a Christian philosophy of life. The word simply means "to love wisdom.") When a person does not know the doctrines of the Christian faith, he can easily be captured by false religions.

This philosophy of the false teachers is "hollow and deceptive" (Col. 2:8 NIV) for several reasons. To begin with, it is the tradition of men and not the truth of God's Word. The word *tradition* means "that which is handed down"; and there is a true Christian tradition (1 Cor. 15:3ff.; 2 Thess. 2:15; 3:6; 2 Tim. 2:2). The important thing about any teaching is its origin: Did it come from God or from man? The religious leaders in our Lord's day had their traditions and were very zealous to obey them and protect them (Matt. 15:1–20). Even the apostle Paul, before he met the Lord, was "exceedingly zealous of the traditions" (Gal. 1:14).

If a new Christian from a distant mission field were to visit many of our churches, he would probably be astounded at the ideas and practices we have that cannot be supported by God's Word. Our man-made traditions are usually more important to us than the God-given doctrines of the Scriptures! While it is not wrong to have church traditions that remind us of our godly heritage, we must be careful not to make these traditions equal to the Word of God.

The false teachers' traditions were "hollow and deceptive" for another reason: they involved "the rudiments of the world." The Greek word translated "rudiments" basically means "one of a row or series." It had several meanings attached to it: (1) the elementary sounds or letters, the ABCs; (2) the basic elements of the universe, as in 2 Peter 3:10–12; (3) the basic elements of knowledge, the ABCs of some system, as in Hebrews 5:12. But in ancient Greece, this word also meant "the elemental spirits of the universe, the angels that influenced the heavenly bodies." It was one of the words in the vocabulary of the religious astrology of that day.

The gnostics believed that the angels and the heavenly bodies influenced people's lives. Paul's warnings to the Colossians about "new moon" and other religious practices determined by the calendar (Col. 2:16) may be related to this gnostic teaching, though the Jewish people also watched the calendar (Gal. 4:10).

One thing is certain: such teachings about demons and angels were not a part of true Christian doctrine. If anything, such teachings were satanic.

The fact that this teaching is not after Christ is sufficient to warn us against horoscopes, astral charts, Ouija boards, and other spiritist practices. The whole zodiac system is contrary to the teaching of the Word of God. The Christian who dabbles in mysticism and the occult is only asking for trouble.

Why follow empty philosophy when we have all fullness in Christ? This is like turning away from the satisfying river to drink at the dirty cisterns of the world (Jer. 2:13). Of course, the false teachers in Colosse did not ask the believers to forsake Christ. They asked them to make Christ a *part* of the new system. But this would only remove Him from His rightful place of preeminence.

So Paul gave the true and lasting antidote to all false teaching: "All fullness is in Christ, and you have been made full in Him. *Why, then, would you need anything else?*" (see Col. 2:9–10).

We have seen the word "fullness" *(pleroma)* before (Col. 1:19). It means "the sum total of all that God is, all of His being and attributes." This word was used by the gnostics, but they did not give it the same meaning as did Paul. To them, the *pleroma* was the source of all the "emanations" through which men could come to God. The highest point in gnostic religious experience was to share in the *pleroma*.

Of course, there are no emanations from God. The gulf between heaven and earth was bridged in the incarnation of Jesus Christ. He is declared to be "Emmanuel, God with us" (Matt. 1:23). Jesus Christ is the fullness of God, and that fullness dwells continually and permanently in Him *bodily*. Once again, Paul refuted the gnostic doctrine that matter was evil and that Jesus did not have a human body.

When Jesus Christ ascended to heaven, He went in a human body. It was a glorified body, to be sure, but it was real. After His resurrection, our Lord was careful to assure His disciples that He was the same Person in the same body; He was not a ghost or a spirit (see John 20:19–29). There is a glorified Man in heaven! The God-Man, Jesus Christ, embodies the fullness of God!

Now, the remarkable thing is this: *every believer shares that fullness!* "And ye are complete in him" (Col. 2:10). The tense of the Greek verb indicates that this fullness is a permanent experience. Dr. Kenneth Wuest's very literal Expanded Translation reads, "And you are in Him, having been completely filled full with the present result that you are in a state of fullness."

When a person is born again into the family of God, he is born complete in Christ. His spiritual growth is not by *addition,* but by *nutrition.* He grows from the inside out. Nothing needs to be added to Christ because He already is the very fullness of God. As the believer draws on Christ's fullness, he is "filled unto all the fullness of God" (Eph. 3:19). What more does he need?

Indeed, there are spiritual perils that the Christian faces. The fundamental test of any religious teaching is "Where does it put Jesus Christ—His person and His work?" Does it rob Him of His fullness? Does it deny either His deity or His humanity? Does it affirm that the believer must have some "new experience" to supplement his experience with Christ? If so, that teaching is wrong and dangerous.

Draw on Your Spiritual Provisions (2:11–15)

Remember that the false teaching that threatened the Colossian church was made up of several elements: Eastern mysticism, astrology, philosophy, and Jewish legalism. It is the latter element that Paul dealt with in this section of his letter. Apparently, the false teachers insisted that their converts submit to circumcision and obey the Old Testament law.

Gnostic legalism was not quite the same as the brand of legalism practiced by the Judaizers whom Paul refuted in his epistle to the Galatians. The Jewish teachers that Paul attacked in Galatians insisted that circumcision and obedience to the law were necessary for salvation. (See Acts 15 for some background on this problem.) Gnostic legalism said that the Jewish law would help the believers become more spiritual. If they were circumcised, and if they watched their diets and observed the holy days, then they would become part of the "spiritual elite" in the church. Unfortunately, we have people with similar ideas in our churches today.

Paul made it clear that the Christian is not subject in any way to the Old Testament legal system, *nor can it do him any good spiritually.* Jesus Christ *alone* is sufficient for our every spiritual need, for all of God's fullness is in Him. We are identified with Jesus Christ because He is the Head of the body (Col. 1:18) and we are the members of the body (1 Cor. 12:12–13). Paul explained our fourfold identification with Jesus Christ that makes it not only unnecessary, but sinful for us to get involved in any kind of legalism.

Circumcised in Him (v. 11). Circumcision was a sign of God's covenant with the Jewish people (Gen. 17:9–14). Though it was a physical operation, it had a spiritual significance. The trouble was that the Jewish people depended on the physical and not the spiritual. A mere physical operation could never convey spiritual grace (Rom. 2:25–29). Often in the Old Testament, God warned His people to turn from their sins and experience a *spiritual* circumcision of the heart (Deut. 10:16; 30:6; Jer. 4:4; 6:10; Ezek. 44:7). People make the same mistake today when they depend on some religious ritual to save them—such as baptism or the Lord's Supper.

It is not necessary for the believer to submit to circumcision, because he has already experienced a spiritual circumcision through his identification with Jesus Christ. But there is a contrast here between

Jewish circumcision and the believer's spiritual circumcision in Christ:

Jews	Believers
external surgery	internal—the heart
only a part of the body	the whole "body of sins"
done by hands	done without hands
no spiritual help in come sin	enables them to over conquering sin

When Jesus Christ died and rose again. He won a complete and final victory over sin. He not only died *for* our sins (salvation), but He "died *unto* sin" (sanctification; see Rom. 6:10ff). What the law could not do, Jesus Christ accomplished for us. The old nature ("the body of the sins of the flesh") was put off—rendered inoperative—so that we need no longer be enslaved to its desires. The old sinful nature is not eradicated, for we can still sin (1 John 1:5—2:6). But the power has been broken as we yield to Christ and walk in the power of the Spirit.

Alive in Him (vv. 12–13). Here Paul used the illustration of baptism. Keep in mind that in the New Testament, the word *baptize* has both a literal and a figurative meaning. The literal meaning is "to dip, to immerse." The figurative meaning is "to be identified with." For example, the Jewish nation was "baptized unto Moses" when it went through the Red Sea (1 Cor. 10:1–2). There was no water involved in this baptism, because they went over on dry land. In this experience, the nation was identified with Moses.

Paul used the word *baptism* in a figurative sense in this section of his letter—for no amount of material water could bury a person with Christ or make him alive in Christ. Water baptism by immersion is a picture of this spiritual experience. When a person is saved, he is immediately baptized by the Spirit into the body of Christ (1 Cor. 12:12–13) and identified with the Head, Jesus Christ. This identification means that *whatever happened to Christ also happened to us.* When He died, we died with Him. When He was buried, we were buried. When He arose again, we arose with Him—and we left the graveclothes of the old life behind (Col. 3:1–14).

All of this took place "through the faith of the operation of God" (Col. 2:12). It was the power of God that changed us, not the power of water. The Spirit of God identified us with Jesus Christ, and we were buried with Him, raised with Him, and made alive with Him! (The Greek verbs are very expressive: co-buried, co-raised, and co-made alive.) Because God raised His Son from the dead, we have eternal life.

The practical application is clear: since we are identified with Christ and He is the fullness of God, *what more do we need?* We have experienced the energy of God through faith in Christ, so why turn to the deadness of the law? God has forgiven us all our trespasses (Col. 2:13b) so that we have a perfect standing before Him.

Free from the law in Him (v. 14). Jesus not only took our sins to the cross (1 Peter 2:24), but He also took the law to the cross and nailed it there, forever out of the way. The law was certainly against us, because it was impossible for us to meet its holy demands. Even though God never gave the Ten Commandments to the Gentiles, the righteous demands of the law—God's holy standards—were "written in their hearts" (Rom. 2:12–16).

When He shed His blood for sinners, Jesus Christ canceled the huge debt that was against sinners because of their disobedience to God's holy law. In Bible days, financial records were often kept on parchment, and the writing could be washed off. This is the picture Paul painted.

How could the holy God be just in canceling a debt? In this way His Son paid the full debt when He died on the cross. If a judge sets a man free who is guilty of a crime, the judge cheapens the law and leaves the injured party without restitution. God paid sin's debt when He gave His Son on the cross, and He upheld the holiness of His own law.

But Jesus Christ did even more than cancel the debt: He took the law that condemned us and set it aside so that we are no longer under its dominion. We are "delivered from the law" (Rom. 7:6). We "are not under the law, but under grace" (Rom. 6:14). This does not mean that we are lawless, because the righteousness of the law is fulfilled in us as we walk in the power of the Spirit (Rom. 8:4). Our relationship with Jesus Christ enables us to obey God out of love, not out of slavish fear.

Victorious in Him (v. 15). Jesus not only dealt with sin and the law on the cross, but He also dealt with Satan. Speaking about His crucifixion, Jesus said, "Now is the judgment of this world; now shall the prince of this world be cast out" (John 12:31). The death of Christ on the cross looked like a great victory for Satan, but it turned out to be a great defeat from which Satan cannot recover.

Jesus had three great victories on the cross. First, He "disarmed the powers and authorities" (Col. 2:15 NIV), stripping Satan and his army of whatever weapons they held. Satan cannot harm the believer who will not harm himself. It is when we cease to watch and pray (as did Peter) that Satan can use his weapons against us.

Second, Jesus "made a public spectacle" (Col. 2:15 NIV) of the enemy, exposing Satan's deceit and vileness. In His death, resurrection, and ascension, Christ vindicated God and vanquished the devil.

His third victory is found in the word *triumph.* Whenever a Roman general won a great victory on foreign soil, took many captives and much loot, and gained new territory for Rome, he was honored by an official parade known as "the Roman Triumph." Paul alluded to this practice in his Second Letter to the Corinthians (see 2 Cor. 2:14). Jesus Christ won a complete victory, and He returned to glory in a great triumphal procession (Eph. 4:8ff.). In this, He disgraced and defeated Satan.

You and I share in His victory over the devil. We need not worry about the elemental forces that govern the planets and try to influence men's lives. The satanic armies of principalities and powers are defeated and disgraced! As we claim the victory of Christ, use the equipment He has provided for us (Eph. 6:10ff.), and trust Him, we are free from the influence of the devil.

What a wonderful position and provision we have in Christ! Are we living up to it by faith?

CHAPTER SEVEN
Colossians 2:16–23
BELIEVER, BEWARE!

From the flashing red signals at a railroad crossing to the skull and crossbones on a bottle of rubbing alcohol, warnings are a part of daily life. Children must be taught to heed warnings, and adults must be reminded not to get too accustomed to them. Warnings are a matter of life or death.

The spiritual life also has its dangers and its warnings. Moses warned the Israelites to beware of forgetting the Lord once they got settled in the Promised Land (Deut. 6:12). The Lord Jesus often used the word *beware* (Matt. 7:15; Mark 12:38; Luke 12:15).

Paul had already warned about the false teachers (Col. 2:8). In this section of his letter, Paul gave three warnings for us to heed if we are to enjoy our fullness in Jesus Christ.

"Let No One Judge You" (2:16–17)
This warning exposes the danger of the *legalism* of the gnostic teachers in Colosse. Their doctrines were a strange mixture of Eastern mysticism, Jewish legalism, and a smattering of philosophy and Christian teaching. Apparently, the Jewish legalism played a very important role. This is no surprise, because human nature thrives in "religious duties." The flesh is weak when it comes to doing spiritual things (Matt. 26:41), but it is very strong when it comes to practicing religious rules and regulations. Somehow, adhering to the religious routine inflates the ego and makes a person content in his self-righteousness. In discussing this problem, Paul presented three important truths.

The basis for our freedom (v. 16a). It is found in the word *therefore,* which relates this discussion to the previous verses. The basis for our freedom is the person and work of Jesus Christ. All the fullness of the Godhead dwells bodily in Him (Col. 2:9). On the cross, He canceled the debt and the dominion of the Law (Col. 2:14). As believers, we are under grace as a rule of life and not under Law (Rom. 6:14ff.).

The believing Gentiles in Colosse never were under the law of Moses, since that law was given only to Israel

(Rom. 9:4). It seems strange that, now that they were Christians, they would want to submit themselves to Jewish legalism! Paul had the same problem with the Gentiles in the churches of Galatia, and he refuted Jewish legalism in his letter to the Galatian believers (Gal. 3:1ff.).

The person who judges a believer because that believer is not living under Jewish laws is really judging Jesus Christ. He is saying that Christ did not finish the work of salvation on the cross, and that we must add something to it. He is also saying that Jesus Christ is not sufficient for all the spiritual needs of the Christian. The false teachers in Colosse were claiming a "deeper spiritual life" for all who would practice the law. Outwardly, their practices seemed to be spiritual; but in actual fact, these practices accomplished nothing spiritual.

The bondage of legalism (v. 16). Let no one tell you otherwise: legalism *is* bondage! Peter called it a "yoke upon the neck" (Acts 15:10). Paul used the same image when he warned the Galatians: "Stand fast therefore in the liberty wherewith Christ hath made us free, and be not entangled again with the yoke of bondage" (Gal. 5:1).

These legalistic regulations had to do with foods and with eating and drinking (partaking or abstaining). Under the Old Testament system, certain foods were classified as "clean" or "unclean" (see Lev. 11). But Jesus made it clear that, of *itself,* food was neutral. It was what came out of the heart that made a person spiritual or unspiritual (Matt. 15:1–20). Peter was reminded of this lesson again when he was on the housetop in Joppa (Acts 10:9ff.) and when he was rebuked in Antioch by Paul (Gal. 2:11ff.). "But food does not bring us near to God; we are no worse if we do not eat, and no better if we do" (1 Cor. 8:8 NIV).

It is likely that God's instructions about foods given through Moses had *physical* reasons behind them as well as spiritual. This point that Paul brought up is a different matter. If a man feels he is healthier for abstaining from certain foods, then he should abstain and care for his body. But he should not judge others who can eat that food, nor should he make it a test of spiritual living. Romans 14 and 15 is the key passage on this subject.

But the legalistic system not only involved diet; it also involved *days.* Once again, this was borrowed from the laws given through Moses. The Old Testament Jew was commanded to keep the weekly Sabbath, which was the seventh day of the week (Ex. 20:9–11). It is wrong to call Sunday "the Christian Sabbath" because it is not so designated in the New Testament. It is "the Lord's Day" (Rev. 1:10), the first day of the week (Acts 20:7; 1 Cor. 16:2), the day that commemorates the victorious resurrection of Jesus Christ from the dead (John 20:1, 19, 26).

The Jews also had their feast days (Lev. 25) and their special "new-moon" celebrations (see Isa. 1:13). Their religion was tied to the calendar. Now, all of this had its proper function under the old dispensation, but it was not meant to be a permanent part of the faith under the new dispensation (see John 1:17). The law was a schoolmaster that helped to train and discipline Israel in the childhood of the nation, preparing the people for the coming of the Messiah. Now that Jesus had come, the schoolmaster was no longer needed to perform the same functions (Gal. 3:24—4:11).

Does this mean that the Old Testament law has no ministry to New Testament Christians? Of course not! The law still reveals the holiness of God, and in the law Jesus Christ can be seen (Luke 24:27). "We know that the law is good if one uses it properly" (1 Tim. 1:8 NIV). The law reveals sin and warns of the consequences of sin—but it has no power to prevent sin or redeem the sinner. Only grace can do that

The blessing of grace (v. 17). The law is but a shadow; but in Christ we have the reality, the substance. "The law is only a shadow of the good things that are coming" (Heb. 10:1 NIV). Why go back into shadows when we have the reality in Jesus Christ? This is like trying to hug a shadow when the reality is at hand!

People who religiously observe diets and days give an outward semblance of spirituality, but these practices cannot change their hearts. Legalism is a popular thing because you can "measure" your spiritual life—and even brag about it! But this is a far cry from measuring up to Christ (Eph. 4:13)!

"Let No Man Beguile You of Your Reward" (2:18–19)

The word translated "beguile" in the King James Version means "to declare unworthy of a prize." It is an athletic term: the umpire disqualifies the contestant because he has not obeyed the rules. The contestant does not cease to be a citizen of the land, but he forfeits the honor of winning a prize. A Christian who fails to obey God's directions does not lose his salvation. But he does lose the approval of the Lord and the rewards He has promised to those who are faithful (1 Cor. 3:8).

It is a gracious act of God that He has promised rewards to those who serve Him. Certainly He does not owe us anything! We ought to be so grateful that He has saved us from judgment that we would serve Him whether or not we received a reward. Most of God's servants probably obey Him out of love and devotion and never think about rewards. Just as there are degrees of punishment in hell (Matt. 23:14), so there will be degrees of glory in heaven—even though all believers will be like Christ in their glorified bodies. The Puritan Thomas Watson said it perfectly: "Though every vessel of mercy shall be full [in heaven], yet one may hold more than another."

There is, then, the danger that our lives today will rob us of reward and glory tomorrow. The peril Paul had in mind here was Eastern *mysticism,* the belief that a person can have an immediate experience with the spiritual world, completely apart from the Word of God or the Holy Spirit. The false teachers in Colosse had visions and made contact with angels. In bypassing the Word of God and the Spirit of God, they were opening themselves to all kinds of demonic activity—because Satan knows how to give counterfeit experiences to people (2 Cor. 11:13–15).

The word translated "intruding" was a technical term used by the mystical religions of that day. It meant "to set foot in the inner shrine, to be fully initiated into the mysteries of the religion." No Christian has to go through any initiation ceremony to get into the presence of God. We may have "boldness to enter into the holiest by the blood of Jesus" (Heb. 10:19). We may "come boldly unto the throne of grace" (Heb. 4:16). And as for worshipping angels, *they are our servants!* The angels are "all ministering spirits, sent forth to minister for them who shall be heirs of salvation" (Heb. 1:14).

Of course, all of this mystical ceremony was wrapped up in a false humility that was actually an expression of pride. "I am not good enough to come directly to God," the gnostic would say, "so I will start with one of the angels."

Trying to reach God the Father through anyone or anything other than His Son, Jesus Christ, is idolatry. Jesus Christ is the one and only Mediator between God and man (John 14:6; 1 Tim. 2:5). The person who worships through angels or saints now in heaven does not prove his humility, for he is not submitting to the authority of God's Word. Actually, he reveals a subtle kind of pride that substitutes man-made traditions for me Word of God. "His unspiritual mind puffs him up with idle notions" (Col. 2:18 NIV).

True worship always humbles a person. The *mind* is awed by the greatness of God; the *heart* is filled with love for God; and the *will* is submitted to the purpose God has for the life. The gnostics, however, were interested primarily in "deeper spiritual knowledge," and they ignored God's truth. Their "inner secrets" gave them big heads, but not burning hearts or submissive wills. "Knowledge puffs up, but love builds up" (1 Cor. 8:1 NIV).

It is worth noting that a true spiritual experience with God leads to submission and service. When Job met the Lord he said, "I have heard of thee by the hearing of the ear, but now mine eye seeth thee. Wherefore I abhor myself, and repent in dust and ashes" (Job 42:5–6). Peter fell down before his Lord and said, "Depart from me; for I am a sinful man, O Lord" (Luke 5:8). Isaiah saw the Lord and confessed how sinful he was (Isa. 6), and when John saw the risen Christ, he fell at His feet like a dead man (Rev. 1:17).

The cheap familiarity with which some people approach God in prayer, or talk about Him in testimony or conversation, sometimes borders on blasphemy. The saintly Bishop Westcott of Great Britain, author of many scholarly commentaries on various books of the Bible, once wrote, "Every year makes me tremble at the daring with which people speak of spiritual things."

Tragically, this "vain religion of the puffed-up fleshly mind" is but a mere substitute for true spiritual nourishment from Jesus Christ, the Head of the body, His church. This is one of several passages in the New Testament that pictures the church as the body of Christ (see Rom. 12:4ff.; 1 Cor. 12–14; Eph. 4:4–16; Col. 1:18, 24). All of us, as believers, are members of the spiritual body, the church, because of the work of the Holy Spirit (1 Cor. 12:12–13). As Christians, we minister to one another in the body just as the various parts of the human body minister to each other (1 Cor. 12:14ff.).

But if a believer does not draw on the spiritual nourishment that comes from Christ and other Christians, he becomes weak. The false teachers were not holding to the Head, and therefore they were spiritually undernourished, but *they* thought they were spiritual experts. Imagine thinking yourself a giant when in reality you are a pygmy!

The false teachers were anxious to win converts to their cause, but the spiritual body grows by *nutrition,* not by *addition.* Every member of Christ's body, including the "ligaments and sinews" (joints and bands), is important to the health and growth of the body. No matter what your spiritual gift may be, you are important to the church. In fact, some people who may not have spectacular public ministries are probably just as important behind the scenes as those out in public.

It is through worship, prayer, and the Word that we draw on the spiritual resources of Christ. All of us must be part of a local church where we can exercise our own spiritual gifts (Eph. 4:11–17). "Now to each one the manifestation of the Spirit is given for the common good" (1 Cor. 12:7 NIV). The New Testament says nothing of "isolated saints" outside of the local church.

But it is possible to be *in* a local church and not draw on the Head and the nourishment of the spiritual body. The false teachers in Colosse sought to introduce their teachings into the local assembly, and if they succeeded, they would have caused the spiritual nourishment to *decrease* instead of *increase.* Unless the members of the local assembly abide in Christ, yield to the Spirit, and obey the Word, they cannot experience the life of the Head, Jesus Christ.

There is a fascination with "religious mysticism" that attracts people. Learning mysteries, being initiated into the inner secrets, and having contact with the spirit world all seem exciting.

But these practices are soundly condemned by God. The true Christian glories in Christ, not in his own experience. He follows the Word, led by the Holy Spirit, and as he abides in Christ, he experiences blessing and fruitfulness. He seeks no other experience than that which relates him to the Head, Jesus Christ.

"Let No One Enslave You!" (2:20–23)

Paul condemned legalism and mysticism; next he attacked and condemned *asceticism.* An ascetic practices rigorous self-denial and even self-mortification in order to become more spiritual. Ascetic practices were popular during the Middle Ages: wearing hair shirts next to the skin, sleeping on hard beds, whipping oneself, not speaking for days (maybe years), going without food or sleep, and so forth.

There is a definite relationship between legalism and asceticism, for the ascetic often subjects himself to rules and regulations: "Touch not, taste not, handle not" (Col. 2:21). Certain foods or practices are unholy and must be avoided. Other practices are holy and must never be neglected. The ascetic's entire life is wrapped up in a system of rules.

As Christians, we admit that physical discipline is needed in our lives. Some of us eat too much and are overweight. Some of us drink too much coffee or cola drinks and are nervous and upset. We believe that our bodies are temples of the Holy Spirit (1 Cor. 6:19–20), yet sometimes we do not care for our bodies as we should. "Physical training is of some value," Paul wrote (1 Tim. 4:8 NIV). Paul disciplined his own body and kept it under control (1 Cor. 9:27). So there is a place in our Christian lives for proper care of our bodies.

But the ascetic hopes to sanctify the soul by his discipline of the body, and it is this heresy that Paul attacked. Just as days and diets have no sanctifying value, neither does fleshly discipline. In this section Paul gave several arguments to warn the Christian against carnal religious asceticism.

The Christian's spiritual position (v. 20). Asceticism has to do with the rudiments of the world and not the riches of the kingdom. Earlier we saw the word *rudiments* and learned that it meant "the fundamentals or ABCs of something" (Col. 2:8). In this case, "the rudiments of the world" refers to rules and regulations about foods. As Christians, we are dead to all of this because of our union with Jesus Christ in death, burial, and resurrection (see Rom. 6; Col. 2:12–15). Though we are *in* the world physically, we are not *of* the world spiritually (John 17:15–16). We have been transferred into God's kingdom (Col. 1:13), and therefore we govern our lives by His laws and not the rules of men.

This is not to suggest that Christians are lawless. A student in a Christian school once told me it was "unspiritual" for him to obey the rules! I reminded him that Christians always respect the authority of those over them (1 Peter 2:11ff.), and that he knew the rules before he arrived on campus. If he did not like them, he should have stayed home! Paul was not counseling us to be rebels, but he was warning us not to think we are spiritual because we obey certain rules and regulations that pertain to the body.

The futility of ascetic rules (vv. 21–22). To begin with, these rules did not come from God; they were the inventions of men. God "giveth us richly all things to enjoy" (1 Tim. 6:17). Foods have been "created to be received with thanksgiving" (1 Tim. 4:3). But the "commandments and doctrines" of the false teachers replaced the inspired Word of God (see Mark 7:6–9). The doctrines were what the false teachers believed; the commandments were the regulations they gave in applying their doctrines to practical daily life.

God gave foods to be used, and they "perish with the using" (Col. 2:22). Jesus explained that food went into the stomach, not the heart (Mark 7:18ff.). The man who refuses certain foods because they will defile him does not understand what either Jesus or Paul taught: "I know, and am persuaded by the Lord Jesus, that there is nothing unclean of itself" (Rom. 14:14).

Many of us are quick to criticize the ancient monks, the Eastern mystics, and the Hindu or Muslim fakirs, but we fail to see this same error in our own churches. While there are automatic connections between physical discipline and health, there is no connection between such discipline and holiness. If we deliberately abstain from some food or drink to keep from hurting a weaker Christian (Rom. 14:13ff.), that is one thing. But we must not say that our abstinence makes us more spiritual than another brother who partakes of that food and gives thanks to God (Rom. 14:6).

The deception of asceticism (v. 23). The people who practice asceticism have a "reputation" for spirituality, but the product does not live up to the promotion. I am amazed at the way educated people in America flock to see and hear gurus and other Eastern spiritual leaders whose teachings cannot change the human heart. This "self-imposed worship" is not the true worship of God, which must be "in spirit and in truth" (John 4:24). Their humility is false, and their harsh disciplines accomplish nothing for the inner man.

While it is certainly better to exercise self-control than to yield to the physical appetites of the body, we must not think that such self-control is necessarily *spiritually* motivated. The ascetics of many non-Christian religions give evidence of remarkable self-control. The stoics and their ascetic philosophy were well known in Paul's day. Their adherents could duplicate any discipline that the gnostic teachers cared to present.

The power of Christ in the life of the believer does more than merely restrain the desires of the flesh: *it puts new desires within him.* Nature determines appetite. The Christian has the very nature of God within (2 Peter 1:4), and this means he has godly ambitions and desires. He does not need *law* on the outside to control his appetites because he has *life* on the inside! The harsh rules of the ascetics "lack any value in restraining sensual indulgence" (Col. 2:23 niv). If anything, they eventually bring out the worst instead of the best. In the closing two chapters of this letter, Paul explained how the new life functions in the believer to give him purity and victory.

This section closes the second chapter of Colossians in which the emphasis was on *danger*. Paul defended the preeminence of Jesus Christ, and he refuted the false doctrines of legalism, mysticism, and asceticism. It now remains for us to believe what he wrote and practice these spiritual principles.

The answer to legalism is the spiritual reality we have in Christ. The answer to mysticism is the spiritual union with Christ, the Head of the church. The answer to asceticism is our position in Christ in death, burial, and resurrection.

We put all of this into daily practice as we fellowship with Christ through worship, the Word, and prayer. As we yield to the indwelling Spirit, we receive the power we need for daily living. It is in our fellowship with other believers that we contribute spiritually to the growth of the body, the church, and the other members of the body contribute to us. What a wonderful way to live!

Is Christ preeminent in your life? Are you drawing on His spiritual power, or depending on some manmade "religious" substitute?

CHAPTER EIGHT
Colossians 3:1–11
HEAVEN ON EARTH

In the final two chapters of Colossians, Paul moved into the practical application of the doctrines he had been teaching. After all, it does little good if Christians *declare* and *defend* the truth, but fail to *demonstrate* it in their lives. There are some Christians who will defend the truth at the drop of a hat, but their personal lives deny the doctrines they profess to love. "They profess that they know God, but in works they deny Him" (Titus 1:16).

We must keep in mind that the pagan religions of Paul's day said little or nothing about personal morality. A worshipper could bow before an idol, put his offering on the altar, and go back to live the same old life of sin. What a person believed had no direct relationship with how he behaved, and no one would condemn a person for his behavior.

But the Christian faith brought a whole new concept into pagan society: what we believe has a very definite connection with how we behave! After all, faith in Christ means being united to Christ, and if we share His life, we must follow His example. He cannot live in us by His Spirit and permit us to live in sin. Paul connected doctrine with duty in this section by giving his readers three instructions.

Seek the Heavenly (3:1–4)
The emphasis is on the believer's relationship with Christ.

We died with Christ (v. 3a). The fullest explanation of this wonderful truth is found in Romans 6—8. Christ not only died *for* us (substitution), but we died *with* Him (identification). Christ not only died *for* sin, bearing its penalty, but He died *unto* sin, breaking its power. Because we are "in Christ" through the work of the Holy Spirit (1 Cor. 12:13), we died with Christ. This means that we can have victory over the old sin nature that wants to control us. "How shall we, that are dead to sin, live any longer therein?" (Rom. 6:2).

We live in Christ (v. 4a). Christ is our life. Eternal life is not some heavenly substance that God imparts when we, as sinners, trust the Savior. Eternal life is Jesus Christ Himself. "He that hath the Son hath life; and he that hath not the Son of God hath not life" (1 John 5:12). We are dead and alive at the same time—dead to sin and alive in Christ.

Someone has said, "Life is what you are alive to." A child may come alive when you talk about a baseball game or an ice cream cone. A teenager may come alive when you mention cars or dates. Paul wrote, "For to me to live is Christ" (Phil. 1:21). Christ was Paul's life and he was alive to anything that related to Christ. So should it be with every believer.

Years ago I heard a story about two sisters who enjoyed attending dances and wild parties. Then they were converted and found new life in Christ. They received an invitation to a party and sent their RSVP in these words: "We regret that we cannot attend because we recently died."

We are raised with Christ (v. 1a). It is possible to be alive and still live in the grave. During World War II, several Jewish refugees hid in a cemetery, and a baby was actually born in one of the graves. However, when Jesus gave us His life, He lifted us out of the grave and set us on the throne in heaven! Christ is seated at the right hand of God, and we are seated there "in Christ."

The word *if* does not suggest that Paul's readers might not have been "risen with Christ", for all of us, as believers, are identified with Christ in death, burial, resurrection, and ascension. The word *since* gives the truer meaning of the word. Our exalted position in Christ is not a hypothetical thing or a goal for which we strive. It is an accomplished fact.

We are hidden in Christ (v. 3b). We no longer belong to the world, but to Christ; and the sources of life that we enjoy come only from Him. "Hidden in Christ" means security and satisfaction. The eminent Greek scholar Dr. A. T. Robertson commented on this: "So here we are in Christ who is in God, and no burglar, not even Satan himself, can separate us from the love of God in Christ Jesus (Rom. 8:31–39)" *(Paul and the Intellectuals,* Broadman, 98).

The Christian life is a "hidden life" as far as the world is concerned, because the world does not know Christ (see 1 John 4:1–6). Our sphere of life is not this earth, but heaven; and the things that attract us and excite us belong to heaven, not to earth. This does not mean that we should ignore our earthly responsibilities. Rather it means that our motives and our strength come from heaven, not earth.

We are glorified in Christ (v. 4b). Christ is now seated at the Father's right hand, but one day He will come to take His people home (1 Thess. 4:13–18). When He does, we shall enter into eternal glory with Christ. When He is revealed in His glory, we shall also be revealed in glory. According to the apostle Paul, *we have already been glorified* (Rom. 8:30)! This glory simply has not yet been revealed. Christ has already given us His glory (John 17:22), but the full revelation of the glory awaits the return of the Savior (Rom. 8:17–25).

Now, in view of our wonderful identification with Christ, we have a great responsibility: "Seek those things which are above" (Col. 3:1). Through Christ's death, burial, resurrection, and ascension, we have been separated from the old life of this world, and we now belong to a new heavenly life.

But how do we "seek those things which are above"? The secret is found in Colossians 3:2: "Habitually set your mind—your attention—on things above, not on things on the earth" (literal translation). Our feet must be on earth, but our minds must be in heaven. This is not to suggest that (as D. L. Moody used to say) we become "so heavenly minded that we are no earthly good." It means that the practical everyday affairs of life get their direction from Christ in heaven. It means further that we look at earth from heaven's point of view.

While attending a convention in Washington, D.C., I watched a Senate committee hearing on television. I believe they were considering a new ambassador to the United Nations. The late Senator Hubert Humphrey was making a comment as I turned on the television set: "You must remember that in politics, how you stand depends on where you sit." He was referring, of course, to the political party seating arrangement in the Senate, but I immediately applied it to my position in Christ. How I stand—and walk—depends on where I sit, *and I am seated with Christ in the heavenlies!*

When the nation of Israel came to the border of the Promised Land, they refused to enter, and, because of their stubborn unbelief, they had to wander in the wilderness for forty years (see Num. 13—14). That whole generation, starting with the twenty-year-olds, died in the wilderness, except for Caleb and Joshua, the only two spies who believed God. How were Caleb and Joshua able to "get the victory" during those forty difficult years in the wilderness? *Their minds and hearts were in Canaan!* They knew they had an inheritance coming, and they lived in the light of that inheritance.

The queen of England exercises certain powers and privileges because she sits on the throne. The president of the United States has privileges and powers because he sits behind the desk in the oval office of the White House. The believer is seated on the throne with Christ. We must constantly keep our affection and our attention fixed on the things of heaven, through the Word and prayer, as well as through worship and service. We can enjoy "days of heaven upon the earth" (Deut. 11:21) if we will keep our hearts and minds in the heavenlies.

Slay the Earthly (3:5–9)

We turn now from the positive to the negative. There are some people who do not like the negative. "Give us positive doctrines!" they say. "Forget about negative warnings and admonitions!" But the negative warnings and commands grow out of the positive truths of Christian doctrine. This is why Paul wrote, "Mortify *therefore.*"

No amount of positive talk about health will cure a ruptured appendix. The doctor will have to "get negative" and take out the appendix. No amount of lecturing on beauty will produce a garden. The gardener has to pull weeds! The positive and the negative go together, and one without the other leads to imbalance.

The word *mortify* means "put to death." Because we have died with Christ (Col. 3:3), we have the spiritual power to slay the earthly, fleshly desires that want to control us. Paul called this "reckoning" ourselves to be dead to sin but alive in Christ (Rom. 6:11). Our Lord used the same idea when He said, "And if thy right eye offend thee, pluck it out" (Matt. 5:29–30).

Obviously, neither Paul nor Jesus was talking about *literal* surgery. Sin does not come from the eye, hand, or foot; it comes from the heart, the evil desires within. Centuries ago in England, if a pickpocket was convicted, his right hand was cut off. If he was convicted a second time, his left hand was amputated. One pickpocket lost both hands and continued his "trade" by using his teeth! Physical surgery can never change the heart.

Not only was Paul negative in this paragraph, but he also *named sins,* and some people do not like that. These sins belong to the old life and have no place in our new life in Christ. Furthermore, God's judgment falls on those who practice these sins, and God is no respecter of persons. God's wrath fell on the Gentile world because of these sins (Rom. 1:18ff.), and His wrath will fall again. "Because of these, the wrath of God is coming," Paul warned (Col. 3:6 NIV).

Fornication refers to sexual immorality in general. *Uncleanness* means "lustful impurity that is connected with luxury and loose living." *Inordinate affection* describes a state of mind that excites sexual impurity. The person who cultivates this kind of appetite can always find opportunity to satisfy it. *Evil concupiscence* means "base, evil desires." It is clear that desires lead to deeds, appetites lead to actions. If we would purify our actions, then we must first purify our minds and hearts.

What we desire usually determines what we do. If I create in my children an appetite for candy, then I must satisfy that appetite. If they become overweight and unhealthy, then I must change their appetites, and I must teach them how to enjoy foods other than sweets. "Create in me a clean heart, O God" (Ps. 51:10) should be our prayer, for it is out of the heart that these evil desires come (Mark 7:21–23).

After he had named these sensual sins, Paul added, "and covetousness, which is idolatry" (Col. 3:5b). *Covetousness* is the sin of always wanting more, whether it be more things or more pleasures. The covetous person is never satisfied with what he has, and he is usually envious of what other people have. This is idolatry, for covetousness puts things in the place of God. "Thou shalt not covet" is the last of the Ten Commandments (Ex. 20:17). Yet this sin can make us break all of the other nine! A covetous person will dishonor God, take God's name in vain, lie, steal, and commit every other sin in order to satisfy his sinful desires.

Do believers in local churches commit such sins? Unfortunately, they sometimes do. Each of the New Testament epistles sent to local churches makes mention of these sins and warns against them. I am reminded of a pastor who preached a series of sermons against the sins of the saints. A member of his congregation challenged him one day and said that it would be better if the pastor preached those messages to the lost. "After all," said the church member, "sin in the life of a Christian is different from sin in the lives of other people."

"Yes" replied the pastor, *"it's worse!"*

After warning us against the sensual sins, Paul then pointed out the dangers of the social sins (Col. 3:8–9). Dr. G. Campbell Morgan called these "the sins in good standing." We are so accustomed to anger, critical attitudes, lying, and coarse humor among believers that we are no longer upset or convicted about these sins. We would be shocked to see a church member commit some sensual sin, but we will watch him lose his temper in a business meeting and call it "righteous indignation."

The picture here is that of a person changing clothes: "Put off … put on" (Col. 3:9–10). This relates to the resurrection of Jesus Christ (Col. 3:1), for when He arose from the dead, Jesus Christ left the graveclothes behind (John 20:1–10). He had entered into a glorious resurrection life and had no need for the graveclothes. Likewise, when Lazarus was raised from the dead, Jesus instructed the people to "loose him, and let him go" (John 11:44).

The graveclothes represent the old life with its sinful deeds. Now that we have new life in Christ, we must walk "in newness of life" by putting off the old deeds and desires (Rom. 6:4). We do this by practicing our position in Christ, by reckoning ourselves to be dead to the old and alive to the new.

Paul began with *anger, wrath, and malice*—sins of bad attitude toward others. The word *anger* is the same as the word *wrath* (Col. 3:6), referring there to the wrath of God. This word describes habitual attitudes, while *wrath* refers to the sudden outburst of anger, God has a right to be angry at sin and to judge it, because He is holy and just. In fact, there is a righteous anger against sin that ought to characterize the saints (Eph. 4:26). But none of us have the right to "play God" and pass final judgment on others by our attitudes. *Malice* is an attitude of ill will toward a person. If we have malice toward a person, we are sad when he is successful, and we rejoice when he has trouble. This is sinful.

Blasphemy describes speech that slanders others and tears them down. Often among Christians this kind of malicious gossip masquerades as a spiritual concern: "I would never tell you what I know about her, except that I know you'll want to pray about it." Evil speaking is caused by malice (1 Peter 2:1). If you have deep-seated ill will toward a person, you will use every opportunity to say something bad about him.

Filthy communication is just that: foul speech, coarse humor, obscene language. For some reason, some Christians think it is manly or contemporary to use this kind of speech. Low humor sometimes creeps into conversations. If someone says, "Now, take this with a grain of salt!" you can remind him of Colossians 4:6: "Let your speech be always with grace, seasoned with salt." Salt is a symbol of purity, and grace and purity go together.

The final sin Paul named was *lying* (Col. 3:9). He wrote this same warning to the believers in Ephesus (Eph. 4:25). Satan is the liar (John 8:44), while the Holy Spirit is the Spirit of Truth (John 14:17; 15:26). When a Christian lies, he is cooperating with Satan; when he speaks the truth in love (Eph. 4:15), he is cooperating with the Spirit of God.

A lie is any misrepresentation of the truth, *even if the words are accurate.* The tone of voice, the look on the face, or a gesture of the hand can alter the meaning of a sentence. So can the motive of the heart. If my watch is wrong and I give a friend the wrong time, that is not a lie. Lying involves the intent to deceive for the purpose of personal gain. An old proverb says, "Half a fact is a whole lie."

Bishop Warren A. Candler was preaching about the lies of Ananias and Sapphira (Acts 5), and asked the congregation, "If God still struck people dead for lying, where would I be?" The congregation snickered a bit, but the smiles disappeared when the Bishop shouted, "I'd be right here—*preaching to an empty church!*"

Strengthen the Christly (3:10–11)

Because we are alive in Christ, we must seek the things that are above. And, because we died with Christ, we must put off the things that belong to the earthly life of past sin. The result is that we can become like Jesus Christ! God wants to renew us and make us into the image of His Son!

The Greek verbs translated "put off" and "put on" (Col. 3:9–10) indicate a once-for-all action. When we trust Christ, we put off the old life and put on the new. The old man has been buried, and the new man is now in control. But the verb translated "renewed" is a present participle—"who is constantly being renewed." The *crisis* of salvation leads to the *process* of sanctification, becoming more like Jesus Christ.

The Greeks had two different words for *new.* The word *neos* means "new in time." We use this word as an English prefix in such words as "neoorthodoxy" and "neoclassicism." The word *kainos* means "new in quality, fresh." Sometimes the two words were used interchangeably in the New Testament, but there is still a fundamental difference.

The believer has once and for all put on the "new man" *(neos),* and, as a consequence, he is being renewed *(kainos).* There is a change in quality, for he is becoming like Jesus Christ. The "new Man" is Jesus Christ, the last Adam (1 Cor. 15:45), the Head of the new creation (2 Cor. 5:17).

How does this renewal come about? Through knowledge. The word *knowledge* was one of the key terms in the vocabulary of the gnostics. But their so-called spiritual knowledge could never change a person's life to make him like Christ. The better he gets to know Christ, the more he becomes like Him (Phil. 3:10).

Man was created in the image of God (Gen. 1:26–27). This involves man's personality (intellect, emotion, will) and man's spirituality (he is more than a body). When man sinned, this image of God was marred and ruined. Adam's children were born in the image of their father (Gen. 5:1, 3). In spite of the ravages of sin, man still bears the image of God (Gen. 9:6; James 3:9).

We were *formed* in God's image, and *deformed* from God's image by sin. But through Jesus Christ, we can be *transformed* into God's image! We must be renewed in the spirit of our minds (Eph. 4:23). As we grow in knowledge of the Word of God, we will be transformed by the Spirit of God to share in the glorious image of God (2 Cor. 3:18). God transforms us by the renewing of our minds (Rom. 12:2), and this involves the study of God's Word. It is the truth that sets us free from the old life (John 8:31–32).

God's purpose for us is that we be "conformed to the image of His Son" (Rom. 8:29). This refers to character, the spiritual quality of the inner man. When we see Jesus Christ, we shall be like Him and have glorified bodies (1 John 3:1–3), but while we are waiting for Him to return, we can become like Him and share His holy image. This is a process of constant renewing as the Spirit of God uses the Word of God.

Human distinctions and differences should be no barrier to holy living in the church. In Jesus Christ, all human distinctions disappear (Col. 3:11). In Christ, there are no nationalities ("neither Greek nor Jew"). There is no recognition of former religious differences ("circumcision nor uncircumcision"). The gnostics taught that circumcision was important to the spiritual life (Col. 2:11ff.). But Paul made it clear that this traditional act of physical surgery gave no advantages in the spiritual life.

There are also no cultural differences in Christ ("barbarian, Scythian"). The Greeks considered all non-Greeks to be barbarians; and the Scythians were the lowest barbarians of all! Yet, in Jesus Christ, a person's cultural status is no advantage or disadvantage. Nor is his economic or political status ("bond or free"). Paul made it clear that a slave should try to get his freedom (1 Cor. 7:20–23), but he should not think he is handicapped *spiritually* because of his social position.

All of these human distinctions belong to the

"old man" and not the "new man." In his letter to the Galatians, Paul added, "There is neither male nor female," and thus erased even differences between the sexes. "Christ is all, and in all" was Paul's conclusion. "For ye are all one in Christ Jesus" (Gal. 3:28).

It is wrong to build the fellowship of the church on anything other than Jesus Christ, His person and His work. Ministries that are built on human distinctions, such as race, color, or social standing, are not biblical. One of the evidences of spiritual growth and the renewing of the mind is this willingness to receive and love all who sincerely know Christ and seek to glorify Him. The gnostic "super saints" were trying to isolate the Colossian believers from the rest of the church, and this was wrong. Even though *physically* we do not lose our national heritage when we become Christians, we do not use that heritage as a test of what is spiritual.

"Christ is all and in all" is the emphasis in this letter. "That in all things he might have the preeminence" (Col. 1:18). Because we are complete in Christ, we can look beyond the earthly differences that separate people and enjoy a spiritual unity in the Lord. The gnostic false teachers, like the false teachers today, tried to rob God's people of the richness of their oneness in Christ. Beware!

We are alive in Christ; therefore, we should seek the heavenly. We are dead in Christ; therefore, we should slay the earthly. We can become like Christ; therefore, we must strengthen the Christly and permit the Spirit to renew our minds, making us more into the image of God.

CHAPTER NINE
Colossians 3:12–17
ALL DRESSED UP AND SOMEPLACE TO GO

This section completes Paul's exhortation to the Christian to live a holy life. It continues the illustration of *garments:* "Put off … put on" (Col. 3:8–10). He exhorted his readers to put off the graveclothes of sin and the old life, and to put on the "grace-clothes" of holiness and the new life in Christ.

The emphasis in this section is on *motives.* Why should we put off the old deeds and put on the qualities of the new life? Paul explained four motives that ought to encourage us to walk in newness of life (Rom. 6:4).

The Grace of Christ (3:12–14)
Grace is God's favor to undeserving sinners. Paul reminded the Colossians of what God's grace had done for them.

God chose them (v. 12a). The word *elect* means "chosen of God." God's words to Israel through Moses help us to understand the meaning of salvation by grace: "The Lord did not set his love upon you, nor choose you, because ye were more in number than any people; for ye were the fewest of all people. But because the Lord loved you … hath the Lord brought you out [of Egypt] with a mighty hand" (Deut. 7:7–8).

This miracle of divine election did not depend on anything that we are or that we have done, for God chose us in Christ "before the foundation of the world" (Eph. 1:4). If God saved a sinner on the basis of merit or works, nobody would be saved. It is all done through God's grace that it might all bring glory to God.

Of course, *election* is a "sacred secret" that belongs to God's children. It is not a doctrine that we believers explain to the unsaved. "The Lord knoweth them that are his" (2 Tim. 2:19), so we must leave the working out of His eternal purposes with Him. Our task is to share the good news of the gospel with a lost world.

God set them apart (v. 12). That is the meaning of the word *holy.* Because we have trusted Christ, we have been set apart from the world unto the Lord. We are not our own; we belong completely to Him (1 Cor. 6:19–20). Just as the marriage ceremony sets apart a man and a woman for each other exclusively, so salvation sets the believer apart exclusively for Jesus Christ. Would it not be a horrible thing, at the end of a wedding, to see the groom run off with the maid of honor? It is just as horrible to contemplate the Christian living for the world and the flesh.

God loves them (v. 12). When an unbeliever sins, he is a creature breaking the laws of the holy Creator and Judge. But when a Christian sins, he is a child of God breaking the loving heart of his Father. Love is the strongest motivating power in the world. As the believer grows in his love for God, he will grow in his desire to obey Him and walk in the newness of life that he has in Christ.

God has forgiven them (vv. 13–14). "Having forgiven you all trespasses" (Col. 2:13). God's forgiveness is complete and final; it is not conditional or partial. How is the holy God able to forgive us guilty sinners? Because of the sacrifice of Jesus Christ on the cross. God has forgiven us "for Christ's sake" (Eph. 4:32), and not for our own sake.

Chosen by God, set apart for God, loved by God, and forgiven by God. They all add up to GRACE! Now, because of these gracious blessings, the Christian has some solemn responsibilities before God. He must put on the beautiful graces of the Christian life. Paul named eight graces.

1. Put on … tender mercies (Col. 3:12). The Greek uses the term *bowels of compassion* because the Greek people located the deeper emotions in the intestinal area, while we locate them in the heart. As believers, we need to display tender feelings of compassion toward one another (see Phil. 2:1ff). This is not something that we turn on and off, like the TV set. It is a constant attitude of heart that makes us easy to live with.

2. Put on … kindness (Col. 3:12). We have been saved because of God's kindness toward us through

Colossians 3

Jesus Christ (Eph. 2:7; Titus 3:4). We, in turn, ought to show kindness toward others. "Be ye kind one to another" (Eph. 4:32) is God's command.

One of the most beautiful pictures of kindness in the Bible is King David's treatment of the crippled prince, Mephibosheth (see 2 Samuel 9). David's desire was to show "the kindness of God" to King Saul's family because of his own love for Saul's son Jonathan. The young man chosen was Mephibosheth, Jonathan's son, a poor cripple. If David had acted according to justice, he would have condemned Mephibosheth, for the man belonged to a condemned family. But David acted on the basis of love and grace.

David sought Mephibosheth and assured him not to be afraid. He invited Mephibosheth to live in the palace as a member of his family, and to eat at the king's bountiful table. This is the kindness of God! You and I have experienced an even greater kindness, for as Christians, we are God's children and shall live with Him in heaven forever!

3. Put on … humbleness of mind (Col. 3:12). The pagan world of Paul's day did not admire humility. Instead, they admired pride and domination. Jesus Christ is the greatest example of humbleness of mind (Phil. 2:1ff.). Humility is not thinking poorly of oneself. Rather, it is having the proper estimate of oneself in the will of God (Rom. 12:3). The person with humbleness of mind thinks of others first and not of himself.

4. Put on … meekness (Col. 3:12). Meekness is not weakness; it is power under control. This word was used to describe a soothing wind, a healing medicine, and a colt that had been broken. In each instance, there is *power:* a wind can become a storm; too much medicine can kill; a horse can break loose. But this power is under control. The meek person does not have to fly off the handle because he has everything under control.

5. Put on … longsuffering (Col. 3:12). This word is literally "long-temper." The short-tempered person speaks and acts impulsively and lacks self-control. When a person is longsuffering, he can put up with provoking people or circumstances without retaliating. It is good to be able to get angry, for this is a sign of holy character. But it is wrong to get angry quickly at the wrong things and for the wrong reasons.

6. Put on … forbearance (Col. 3:13). This word literally means "to hold up" or "to hold back." God is forbearing toward sinners in that He holds back His judgment (Rom. 2:4; 3:25). Meekness, longsuffering, and forbearance go together.

7. Put on … forgiveness (Col. 3:13). This is the logical result of all that Paul has written so far in this section. It is not enough that the Christian must endure grief and provocation, and refuse to retaliate; he must also forgive the troublemaker. If he does not, then feelings of malice will develop in the heart; and these can lead to greater sins.

It is Christlike to forgive (Eph. 4:32), and forgiveness opens the heart to the fullness of the love of God. The very instant we have a complaint against another person, we should forgive him in our hearts. ("Family forgiveness" is another matter. We should go to the offender and seek to help him in love. See Matt. 18:15–35.)

8. Put on … love (Col. 3:14). This is the most important of the Christian virtues, and it acts like a "girdle" that ties all the other virtues together. All of the spiritual qualities Paul has named are aspects of true Christian love, as a reading of 1 Corinthians 13 will reveal. Love is the first of the fruit of the Spirit and the other virtues follow—joy (Col. 3:16), peace (Col. 3:15), longsuffering, gentleness, kindness, and meekness (Col. 3:12).

When love rules in our lives, it unites all these spiritual virtues so that there is beauty and harmony, indicating spiritual maturity. This harmony and maturity keep the life balanced and growing. The gnostic system could never do this.

The Peace of Christ (3:15)

In this verse Paul turned from character to conduct. How can a Christian know when he is doing God's will? One answer is the peace of Christ in the heart and in the church. When the believer loses his inner peace, he knows that he has in some way disobeyed God.

The word translated "rule" is an athletic term. It means "to preside at the games and distribute the prizes." Paul used a variation of this word in his letter to the Colossians: "Let no one declare you unworthy of a prize" (literal translation, Col. 2:18). In the Greek games, there were judges (we would call them "umpires") who rejected the contestants who were not qualified, and who disqualified those who broke the rules.

The peace of God is the "Umpire" in our believing hearts and our churches. When we obey the will of God, we have His peace within, but when we step out of His will (even unintentionally), we lose His peace.

We must beware, however, of a false peace in the heart. Jonah deliberately disobeyed God, yet he was able to go to sleep in the hold of a ship *in a storm!* "I had peace about it!" is not sufficient evidence that we are in the will of God. We must pray, surrender to His will, and seek His guidance in the Scriptures. The peace of heart *alone* is not always the peace of God.

Something else is involved: if we have peace in our hearts, we will be at peace with others in the church. We are called to one body, and our relationship in that body must be one of harmony and peace. If we are out of the will of God, we are certain to bring discord and disharmony to the church. Jonah thought he was at peace, when actually his sins created a storm!

When a Christian loses the peace of God, he begins to go off in directions that are out of the will of God. He turns to the things of the world and the flesh to compensate for his lack of peace within. He tries to escape, but he cannot escape *himself!* It is only when

687

he confesses his sin, claims God's forgiveness, and does God's will that he experiences God's peace within.

When there is peace in the heart, there will be praise on the lips: "And be ye thankful" (Col. 3:15). The Christian out of God's will is never found giving sincere praise to God. When David covered up his sins, he lost his peace and his praise (Ps. 32; 51). When he confessed his sins, then his song returned.

The Word of Christ (3:16)

This means, of course, the Word of God. The false teachers came to Colosse with man-made traditions, religious rules, and human philosophies. They tried to harmonize God's Word with their teachings, but they could not succeed. God's Word always magnifies Jesus Christ.

It was not the word of false teachers that brought salvation to the Colossians; it was the Word of the truth of the gospel (Col. 1:5). This same Word gives us life and sustains and strengthens us (1 Peter 1:22—2:3).

The Word will transform our lives if we will but permit it to "dwell" in us richly. The word *dwell* means "to feel at home." If we have experienced the grace and the peace of Christ, then the Word of Christ will feel at home in our hearts. We will discover how rich the Word is with spiritual treasures that give value to our lives.

However, we must not think that Paul wrote this only to individual Christians; for he directed it to the entire church body. "Let the Word of Christ dwell among you" is a possible translation. As it dwells richly in each member of the church, it will dwell richly in the church fellowship.

There is a danger today, as there was in Paul's day, that local churches minimize the Word of God. There seems to be a lack of simple Bible teaching in Sunday school classes and pulpits. Far more interest is shown in movies, musical performances, and various entertainments than in God's Word. Many saved people cannot honestly say that God's Word dwells in their hearts richly because they do not take time to read, study, and memorize it.

There is (according to Paul) a definite relationship between our knowledge of the Bible and our expression of worship in song. One way we teach and encourage ourselves and others is through the singing of the Word of God. But if we do not know the Bible and understand it, we cannot honestly sing it from our hearts.

Perhaps this "poverty of Scripture" in our churches is one cause of the abundance of unbiblical songs that we have today. A singer has no more right to sing a lie than a preacher has to preach a lie. The great songs of the faith were, for the most part, written by believers who knew the doctrines of the Word of God. Many so-called "Christian songs" today are written by people with little or no knowledge of the Word of God. It is a dangerous thing to separate the praise of God from the Word of God.

Psalms were, of course, the songs taken from the Old Testament. For centuries, the churches in the English-speaking world sang only metrical versions of the Psalms. I am glad to see today a return to the singing of Scripture, especially the Psalms. Hymns were songs of praise to God written by believers but not taken from the Psalms. The church today has a rich heritage of hymnody which, I fear, is being neglected. Spiritual songs were expressions of Bible truth other than in psalms and hymns. When we sing a hymn, we address the Lord; when we sing a spiritual song, we address each other.

Paul described a local church worship service (1 Cor. 14:26; Col. 3:16). Note that the believer sings to *himself* as well as to the other believers and to the Lord. Our singing must be from our hearts and not just our lips. But if the Word of God is not in our hearts, we cannot sing from our hearts. This shows how important it is to know the Word of God, for it enriches our public and private worship of God.

Our singing must be with grace. This does not mean "singing in a gracious way," but singing because we have God's grace in our hearts. It takes grace to sing when we are in pain, or when circumstances seem to be against us. It certainly took grace for Paul and Silas to sing in that Philippian prison (Acts 16:22–25). Our singing must not be a display of fleshly talent; it must be a demonstration of the grace of God in our hearts.

Someone has said that a successful Christian life involves attention to three books: God's Book, the Bible; the pocketbook; and the hymn book. I agree. I often use a hymnal in my devotional time to help express my praise to God. As a believer grows in his knowledge of the Word, he will want to grow in his expression of praise. He will learn to appreciate the great hymns of the church, the gospel songs, and the spiritual songs that teach spiritual truths. To sing only the elementary songs of the faith is to rob himself of spiritual enrichment

Before we leave this section, we should notice an important parallel with Ephesians 5:18—6:9. In his letter to the Ephesians, Paul emphasized being filled with the Spirit; in his letter to the Colossians, he emphasized being filled with the Word. *But the evidences of this spiritual fullness are the same!* How can we tell if a believer is filled with the Spirit? He is joyful, thankful, and submissive (Eph. 5:19–21); all of this shows up in his relationships in the home and on the job (Eph. 5:22—6:9). How can we tell if a believer is filled with the Word of God? He is joyful, thankful, and submissive (Col. 3:16—4:1).

The Name of Christ (3:17)

In modern society, we pay little attention to names. But the ancient world held a man's name to be of utmost importance. Often, during Old Testament days, God changed a person's name because of some important experience or some new development.

As Christians, we bear the name of Christ. The word

Christian is found only three times in the entire New Testament (Acts 11:26; 26:28; 1 Peter 4:16). The name was given originally as a term of contempt, but gradually it became a name of honor. The name of Christ, then, means *identification:* we belong to Jesus Christ.

But His name also means *authority.* A man's name signed to a check authorizes the withdrawal of money from the bank. The president's name signed to a bill makes it a law. In the same way, it is in the name of Jesus Christ that we have the authority to pray (John 14:13–14; 16:23–26). Because Jesus Christ is God, and He has died for us, we have authority in His name.

All that we say and do should be associated with the name of Jesus Christ. By our words and our works, we should glorify His name. If we permit anything into our lives that cannot be associated with the name of Jesus, then we are sinning. We must do and say everything on the authority of His name and for the honor of His name.

Bearing the name of Jesus is a great privilege, but it is also a tremendous responsibility. We suffer persecution because we bear His name (John 15:20–21). I have noticed in conversations that you can tell people you are a Baptist, Presbyterian, Lutheran, or even an atheist, and there will be little response. But if you tell people you are a Christian and bring the name of Christ into the conversation, almost immediately there is some kind of response, and it is usually negative.

Every parent tries to teach his children to honor the family name. In just a few minutes, a person can disgrace a name that it has taken his ancestors years to build. For example, the Hebrew name *Judah* is a respected name; it means "praise." The New Testament equivalent is "Judas"—and who would name his son Judas?

Note that Paul again mentioned thanksgiving in this Colossian letter. Whatever we do in the name of Christ ought to be joined with thanksgiving. If we cannot give thanks, then we had better not do it or say it! This is the fifth of six references in Colossians to thanksgiving (Col. 1:3, 12; 2:7; 3:15, 17; 4:2). When we remember that Paul was a Roman prisoner when he wrote this letter, it makes this emphasis on thanksgiving that much more wonderful.

As we review these four spiritual motivations for godly living, we are impressed with the centrality of Jesus Christ. We forgive because Christ forgave us (Col. 3:13). It is the peace of Christ that should rule in our hearts (Col. 3:15). The Word of Christ should dwell in us richly (Col. 3:16). The name of Christ should be our identification and our authority. "Christ is all, and in all" (Col. 3:11).

Since we are united with Christ through the indwelling Holy Spirit, we have all the resources we need for holy living. But we must be spiritually motivated. Because we have experienced the grace of Christ, we want to live for Him. Because we have enjoyed the peace of Christ, we want to obey Him. We have been enriched by the Word of Christ, and ennobled by

the name of Christ; therefore, we want to honor and glorify Him.

Can we desire any higher motivation?

CHAPTER TEN
Colossians 3:18—4:1
A FAMILY AFFAIR

Faith in Jesus Christ not only changes individuals; it also changes homes. In this section, Paul addressed himself to family members: husbands and wives, children, and household servants. It seems clear that these persons being addressed were believers since the apostle appealed to all of them to live to please Jesus Christ.

Something is radically wrong with homes today. The last report I saw indicated that in America there are now more broken homes than ever. Single-parent families are on the increase. Over half of all mothers are now working outside the home, and many of them have small children. The average American child from six to sixteen watches from twenty to twenty-four hours of television each week and is greatly influenced by what he sees. The "battered child" syndrome continues to increase, with from two to four million cases being reported annually, and many not reported at all.

The first institution God founded on earth was the home (Gen. 2:18–25; Matt. 19:1–6). As goes the home, so goes society and the nation. The breakdown of the home is a sign of the end times (2 Tim. 3:1–5). Centuries ago Confucius said, "The strength of a nation is derived from the integrity of its homes." One of the greatest things we can do as individuals is help to build godly Christian homes. Paul addressed the various members of the family and pointed out the factors that make for a strong and godly home.

Husbands and Wives: Love and Submission (3:18–19)
Paul did not address the wives first because they were the neediest! The gospel radically changed the position of women in the Roman world. It gave them a new freedom and stature that some of them were unable to handle, and for this reason Paul admonished them. (Similar admonitions are found in Eph. 5:18ff. and 1 Peter 3:1ff.)

We must not think of *submission* as "slavery" or "subjugation." The word comes from the military vocabulary and simply means "to arrange under rank." The fact that one soldier is a private and another is a colonel does not mean that one man is necessarily *better* than the other. It only means that they have different ranks.

God does all things "decently and in order" (1 Cor. 14:40). If He did not have a chain of command in society, we would have chaos. The fact that the woman is to submit to her husband does not suggest that the man is better than the woman. It only means that the man has the responsibility of headship and leadership in the home.

Headship is not dictatorship or lordship. It is loving leadership. In fact, both the husband and the wife must be submitted to the *Lord* and to *each other* (Eph. 5:21). It is a mutual respect under the lordship of Jesus Christ.

True spiritual submission is the secret of growth and fulfillment. When a Christian woman is submitted to the Lord and to her own husband, she experiences a release and fulfillment that she can have in no other way. This mutual love and submission creates an atmosphere of growth in the home that enables both the husband and the wife to become all that God wants them to be.

The fact that the Christian wife is "in the Lord" is not an excuse for selfish independence. Just the opposite is true, for her salvation makes it important that she obey the Word and submit to her husband. While it is true that in Jesus Christ "there is neither male nor female" (Gal. 3:28), it is also true that joyful submission is an evidence that the wife belongs to Jesus Christ.

However, the husband has the responsibility of loving his wife, and the word for "love" used here is *agape*—the sacrificing, serving love that Christ shares with His church. A marriage may begin with normal, human, romantic love, but it must grow deeper into the spiritual *agape* love that comes only from God. In the parallel passage (Eph. 5:18ff.), Paul made it clear that the husband must love his wife "even as Christ loved the church." Jesus Christ gave His all for the church! He willingly died for us! The measure of a man's love for his wife is not seen only in gifts or words, but in acts of sacrifice and concern for her happiness and welfare.

Paul added a special word of warning for the husbands: "And be not bitter against them" (Col. 3:19). Husbands must be careful not to harbor ill will toward their wives because of something they did or did not do. A "root of bitterness" in a home can poison the marriage relationship and give Satan a foothold (Eph. 4:31; Heb. 12:15). The Christian husband and wife must be open and honest with each other and not hide their feelings or lie to one another. "Speaking the truth in love" (Eph. 4:15) is a good way to solve family differences. "Let not the sun go down upon your wrath" is a wise policy to follow if you want to have a happy home (Eph. 4:26).

A husband who truly loves his wife will not behave harshly or try to throw his weight around in the home. "Love is patient, love is kind. It does not envy, it does not boast, it is not proud. It is not rude, it is not self-seeking, it is not easily angered, it keeps no record of wrongs" (1 Cor. 13:4–5 niv).

A wife really has little difficulty submitting to a husband who loves her. She knows he seeks the very best for her and that he will not do anything to harm her. The husband's love for his wife is seen in his sacrifice for her, and the wife's love for her husband is seen in her submission to him. Where there are sacrifice and submission in an atmosphere of love, you will find a happy home.

A happy marriage does not come automatically; it is something that must be worked at all the time. As we walk with Christ in submission to Him, we have no problem submitting to one another and seeking to serve one another. But where there is selfishness, there will be conflict and division. If there is bitterness in the heart, there will eventually be trouble in the home.

Where do we get the power to love and to submit? From the Lord. If we are wearing the "grace-clothes" described earlier (Col. 3:5–14), and if we have our hearts filled with the peace of Christ and the Word of Christ, then we will contribute to the joy and harmony of the home. If we live to please Christ first, others second, and ourselves last, we will build strong marriages and spiritual homes.

Parents and Children: Encouragement and Obedience (3:20–21)

There were children in these Christian homes, and Paul addressed part of his letter to them. The normal result of marriage is the bearing of children, and fortunate are those children who are born into Christian homes where there is love and submission. "Be fruitful and multiply" was God's order to our first parents (Gen. 1:28), and this order was given before man sinned. The marriage relationship and the bearing of children are not sinful; rather, they are part of God's mandate to man. In the begetting and bearing of children, the husband and wife share in the creative activity of God.

A great deal is being said about the rights of children, and they *do* have rights. One of them is the right to be born. Another is the right to be born into a dedicated Christian home where they will be raised in the "nurture and admonition of the Lord" (Eph. 6:4). They have the right to have godly parents who will teach them the Word of God and discipline them in love.

John H. Starkey was a violent British criminal. He murdered his own wife, then was convicted for the crime and executed. The officials asked General William Booth, founder of the Salvation Army, to conduct Starkey's funeral. Booth faced as ugly and mean a crowd as he had ever seen in his life, but his first words stopped them and held them: "John H. Starkey never had a praying mother!"

Children have rights, but they also have responsibilities, and their foremost responsibility is to obey. They are to obey "in all things" and not simply in those things that please them. Will their parents ever ask them to do something that is wrong? Not if the parents are submitted to the Lord and to one another, and not if they love each other and their children.

The child who does not learn to obey his parents

is not likely to grow up obeying *any* authority. He will defy his teachers, the police, his employers, and anyone else who tries to exercise authority over him. The breakdown in authority in our society reflects the breakdown of authority in the home.

For the most part, children do not *create* problems; they *reveal* them. Parents who cannot discipline themselves cannot discipline their children. If a father and mother are not *under* authority themselves, they cannot *exercise* authority over others. It is only as parents submit to each other and to the Lord that they can exercise properly balanced spiritual and physical authority over their children.

The *measure* of the child's obedience is "all things," and the *motive* is to please the Lord. It is possible to please the parents and not please the Lord, if the parents are not yielded to the Lord. The family that lives in an atmosphere of love and truth, that reads the Word of God, and that prays together will have an easier time discovering God's will and pleasing the Lord.

The word *fathers* in Colossians 3:21 could be translated "parents," as it is in Hebrews 11:23. Paul made it clear that parents must make it as easy as possible for children to obey. "Provoke not your children" (Col. 3:21) is a commandment to parents, and how often it is disobeyed! Too often, parents automatically say no when their children ask for something, when the parents should listen carefully and evaluate each request. Parents often change their minds and create problems for their children, sometimes by swinging from extreme permissiveness to extreme legalism.

Fathers and mothers should encourage their children, not discourage them. One of the most important things parents can do is spend time with their children. A survey in one town indicated that fathers spent only thirty-seven seconds a day with their small sons! It is an encouragement for children to know that their parents, as busy as they are, take time—*make* time—to be with them.

Parents also need to listen and be patient as their children talk to them. A listening ear and a loving heart always go together. "You took time to have me," a child said to her father, "but you won't take time to listen to me!" What an indictment!

Life is not easy for children, especially Christian children. Their problems might seem small to us, but they are quite large to them! Christian parents must listen carefully, share the feelings and frustrations of their children, pray with them, and seek to encourage them. Home ought to be the happiest and best place in all the world!

Discouraged children are fair prey for Satan and the world. When a child does not get "ego-strength" at home, he will seek it elsewhere. It is a pity that some Christian parents do not help their children develop their personalities, their gifts, and their skills. It is even worse when Christian parents compare one child with another and thereby set up unnecessary competition in the home.

Parents sometimes use their children as weapons for fighting against each other. Father will forbid Junior from doing something, but Mother will veto that order and give her approval. The poor child is caught between his parents, and before long he learns how to play both ends against the middle. The result is moral and spiritual tragedy.

If a home is truly Christian, it is a place of encouragement. In such a home, the child finds refuge from battles, and yet strength to fight the battles and carry the burdens of growing maturity. He finds a loving heart, a watching eye, a listening ear, and a helping hand. He does not want any other place—home meets his needs. In this kind of a home, it is natural for the child to trust Christ and want to live for Him.

Masters and Servants: Honesty and Devotion (3:22—4:1)

Slavery was an established institution in Paul's day. There were sixty million of them, and many of them were well-educated people who carried great responsibilities in the homes of the wealthy. In many homes, the slaves helped to educate and discipline the children.

Why didn't the church of that day openly oppose slavery and seek to destroy it? For one thing, the church was a minority group that had no political power to change an institution that was built into the social order. Paul was careful to instruct Christian slaves to secure their freedom if they could (1 Cor. 7:21), but he did not advocate rebellion or the overthrow of the existing order.

Something should be noted: the purpose of the early church was to spread the gospel and win souls, not to get involved in social action. Had the first Christians been branded as an antigovernment sect, they would have been greatly hindered in their soul-winning and their church expansion. While it is good and right for Christians to get involved in the promotion of honesty and morality in government and society, this concern must never replace the mandate to go into all the world and preach the gospel (Mark 16:15).

You will remember that the book of Colossians was one of three letters that came from Paul's Roman imprisonment; the other two were Ephesians and Philemon. Read Paul's little letter to Philemon and see his attitude toward slavery. Paul did not advise Philemon to treat his runaway slave severely, but to receive him as a brother even though he was still a slave. In fact, Onesimus, the slave, was one of the men who carried this letter to Colosse (Col. 4:9)!

A Christian servant owed complete obedience to his master as a ministry to the Lord. If a Christian servant had a believing master, that servant was not to take advantage of his master because they were brothers in the Lord. If anything, the servant strived to do a better job because he was a Christian. He showed singleness of heart and gave his full devotion to his master. His work was done heartily, not grudgingly, and as to the

Lord and not to men. "Ye serve the Lord Christ" (Col. 3:24).

Single hearts and sincere hearts were necessary for Christian servants to please God and serve their masters acceptably. These instructions emphasized the *positive* side of obedience. Servants were to obey to please God, not just to avoid punishment. Even if the master did not commend them, they would have their reward from the Lord. In the same manner, if they disobeyed, the Lord would deal with them even if their master did not. God is no respecter of persons (Acts 10:34; Rom. 2:11; Eph. 6:9; James 2:1, 9).

In our society we do not have slaves. But these principles apply to any kind of honest employment. A Christian worker ought to be the best worker on the job. He ought to obey orders and not argue. He ought to serve Christ and not the boss only, and he ought to work whether anybody is watching or not. If he follows these principles, he will receive his reward from Christ even if his earthly master (his boss) does not recognize him or reward him.

I have a friend who, years ago, was fired from his job for working too hard. He was earning money to go to college, and he wanted to give the employer a good day's work each day. The trouble was, his zeal was showing up the laziness of some of the other employees—and they started fighting back. One of them falsely accused my friend of something, and he was fired. He lost his job but he kept his character, and the Lord rewarded him.

In today's complex, competitive world, it is sometimes difficult for a Christian to obey God and hold his job, or get a promotion. But he must obey God just the same and trust Him for what he needs. Unsaved fellow employees may take advantage of the Christian worker, but perhaps this can be an opportunity for the Christian to witness and back up his witness with his life. It is far more important to win a lost soul than to make a few extra dollars.

Just as the husbands and wives and parents and children have mutual and reciprocal responsibilities, so do masters and servants. Paul admonished the Christian masters to treat their servants with fairness and honesty. This would be a new idea to Roman masters because they considered their slaves as "things," and not people. Masters had almost total control over their slaves and could do with them whatever they pleased. Few unsaved Roman masters ever thought of treating their slaves with fairness, for slaves deserved nothing.

The gospel did not immediately destroy slavery, but it did gradually change the relationship between slave and master. Social standards and pressures disagreed with Christian ideals, but the Christian master was to practice those ideals just the same. He was to treat his slave like a person and like a brother in Christ (Gal. 3:28). He was not to mistreat him; he was to deal with his slave justly and fairly. After all, the Christian slave was a free man in the Lord, and the master was

a slave to Christ (1 Cor. 7:22). In the same way, our social and physical relationships must always be governed by our spiritual relationships.

As we review this very practical section of Colossians, we see once again the preeminence of Jesus Christ in our lives as believers. Christ must be the Head of the home. This series of admonitions is actually a practical application of Colossians 3:17: "And whatsoever ye do in word or deed, do all in the name of the Lord Jesus." It is by His power and authority that we should live in our daily relationships. If He is the preeminent One in our lives, then we will love each other, submit to each other, obey, and treat one another fairly in the Lord.

It would be well for us to review Ephesians 5:18—6:9 and note the parallels between that passage and the one we have just studied. This section of Ephesians emphasizes being filled with the Spirit, while the letter to the Colossians emphasizes being filled with the Word, but the evidences are the same: joyful, thankful, and submissive living. To be filled with the Spirit means to be controlled by the Word.

The fullness of the Spirit and the fullness of the Word are needed in the home. If family members are controlled by the Spirit of God and the Word of God, they will be joyful, thankful, and submissive—and they will have little trouble getting along with each other. Christian employers and employees will treat each other fairly if they are filled with the Spirit and the Word.

The heart of every problem is the problem of the heart, and only God's Spirit and God's Word can change and control the heart.

Can the people who live with you detect that you are filled with the Spirit and the Word?

CHAPTER ELEVEN
Colossians 4:2–9
TALK IS NOT CHEAP!

Never underestimate the power of speech.

A judge says a few words, and a man's life is saved or condemned. A doctor speaks a few words, and a patient either rejoices ecstatically or gives up in despair. Whether the communication is oral or written, there is great power in words. I am told that for every word in Adolf Hitler's book *Mein Kampf,* 125 persons lost their lives in World War II.

The power of speech is a gift from God, and it must be used the way God ordains. In the book of James, the tongue is compared to a bridle and a rudder, a fire and a poisonous animal, and a fruitful tree and a fountain (James 3). These three pairs of pictures teach us that the tongue has the power to direct, the power to destroy, and the power to delight. The tongue is but a little member in our bodies, but it can accomplish great things for good or for evil.

In this brief section, Paul pointed to four important ministries of speech.

Praying (4:2–3a)

Prayer and worship are perhaps the highest uses of the gift of speech. Paul was not ashamed to ask his friends to pray for him. Even though he was an apostle, he needed prayer support for himself and his ministry. If a great Christian like Paul felt the need for prayer support, how much more do you and I need this kind of spiritual help! In these few words, Paul described the characteristics of a satisfying and spiritual prayer life.

First, our praying must be *faithful*. "Continue in prayer" (Col. 4:2). This means, "Be steadfast in your prayer life; be devoted; don't quit." This is the way the early church prayed (Acts 1:14; 2:46). Too many of us pray only occasionally—when we feel like it or when there is a crisis. "Pray without ceasing" is God's command to us (1 Thess. 5:17). This does not mean that we should walk around muttering prayers under our breath. Rather, it means we should be constantly in fellowship with God so that prayer is as normal to us as breathing.

This is not to suggest that God is reluctant to answer prayer and that we must "wear Him out" by our praying. Quite the opposite is true: God enjoys answering our prayers. But He sometimes delays the answer to increase our faith and devotion and to accomplish His purposes at the right time. God's delays are not always God's denials. As we continue in prayer, our own hearts are prepared for the answer God will give. We find ourselves growing in grace even before His answer comes.

Our praying must also be *watchful*. We must be awake and alert as we pray. The phrase "Watch and pray!" is used often in the Bible. It had its beginning in Bible history when Nehemiah was rebuilding the walls and gates of Jerusalem: "Nevertheless we made our prayer unto our God, and set a watch against them [the enemy] day and night" (Neh. 4:9). Jesus used the phrase (Mark 13:33; 14:38); Paul used it too (Eph. 6:18).

There is no power in dull, listless praying. If there is no fire on the altar, the incense will not rise to God (Ps. 141:2). Real praying demands spiritual energy and alertness, and this can come only from the Holy Spirit of God. Routine prayers are unanswered prayers.

Our praying should also be *thankful*: "Watch in the same with thanksgiving" (Col. 4:2). Thanksgiving is an important ingredient in successful praying (Phil. 4:6). If all we do is ask, and never thank God for His gifts, we are selfish. Sincere gratitude to God is one of the best ways to put fervor into our praying.

There is always so much to be thankful for! We have already noted the emphasis in Paul's letter to the Colossians on thanksgiving (Col. 1:3, 12; 2:7; 3:15, 17; 4:2). When we recall that Paul was a prisoner when he wrote this letter, it makes this emphasis even more wonderful.

Finally, our praying ought to be *purposeful*: "Praying also for us" (Col. 4:3). Too often our prayers are vague and general. "Lord, bless the missionaries!" How much better it would be if we would pray for specific needs. By doing so, we would know when God answered and we could praise Him for it. Perhaps it is our lack of faith that causes us to pray generally instead of specifically.

It has well been said that the purpose of prayer is not to get man's will done in heaven, but to get God's will done on earth. Prayer is not telling God what to do or what to give. Prayer is asking God for that which He wants to do and give, according to His will (1 John 5:14–15). As we read the Word and fellowship with our Father, we discover His will and then boldly ask Him to do what He has planned. Richard Trench (1807–1886), archbishop of Dublin, said it perfectly: "Prayer is not overcoming God's reluctance; it is laying hold of His willingness."

Of course, it is possible to pray in our hearts and never use the gift of speech (1 Sam. 1:13), but we are using words even if we don't say them audibly. True prayer must first come from the heart, whether the words are spoken or not.

Study Paul's prison prayers (Phil. 1:9–11; Eph. 1:15–23; 3:14–21; Col. 1:9–12) for examples of prayer at its best.

Proclaiming the Word (4:3b–4)

Paul did not ask for the prison doors to be opened, but that doors of ministry might be opened (1 Cor. 16:9; Acts 14:27). It was more important to Paul that he be a faithful minister than a free man. It is worth noting that in all of Paul's prison prayers, his concern was not for personal safety or material help, but for spiritual character and blessing.

Paul was in prison because of the "mystery of Christ" which related to the Gentiles (see Eph. 3:1–13). The mystery involved God's purpose for the Gentiles in relation to Israel; for in the church, Jews and Gentiles are one (Eph. 2:11–22). Read the account of Paul's arrest in the Jewish temple (Acts 21:18–22:30). Note that the Jews listened to Paul till he spoke the word *Gentiles* (Acts 22:21–22). It was Paul's concern for the Gentiles and his ministry to them that put him into prison.

Even among some believing Jews, there was a kind of bigotry that wanted to force the Gentiles into a lower position (Acts 15:1ff.). This extreme legalistic party wanted the Gentiles to become Jews ceremonially before they could become Christians! Paul and Barnabas met this threat to the gospel of grace head-on and the council decided in their favor. But the legalistic party continued to oppose Paul and his ministry. They did not want the good news of the mystery of Christ to get to the Gentiles. They wanted to maintain their air of Jewish superiority.

How strange that Paul would want God to help him do the very thing that had caused his arrest! He had no intention of giving up his ministry or of changing his message. When John Bunyan was arrested for preaching illegally and put into prison, he was told that he would be released if he promised to stop preaching. "If I am out of prison today," he replied, "I will preach the gospel again tomorrow, by the help of God."

How could Paul share the mystery of Christ when he was a prisoner? Paul's case was discussed by many people; Paul was also able to witness to the guards to whom he was chained (Phil. 1:12–18). Imagine being chained to the apostle Paul! Through this witness, the gospel was carried into parts of Rome that would have been inaccessible to Paul had he been a free man. There were even "saints in Caesar's household" (Phil. 4:22)!

The proclamation of the gospel is empowered by prayer. The Spirit of God uses the Word of God as we come to the throne of grace and ask God for His blessing. We must never separate the Word of God from prayer because God has joined them together (Acts 6:4).

A visitor at Spurgeon's Tabernacle in London was being shown around the building by the pastor, Charles Spurgeon.

"Would you like to see the powerhouse of this ministry?" Spurgeon asked, as he showed the man into a lower auditorium. "It is here that we get our power, for while I am preaching upstairs, hundreds of my people are in this room praying." Is it any wonder that God blessed Spurgeon's preaching of the Word?

You, as a church member, can assist your pastor in the preaching of the Word by praying for him. Never say to your pastor, "Well, the least I can do is to pray for you." The *most* you can do is to pray! Pray for your pastor as he prepares the Word, studies, and meditates. Pray that the Holy Spirit will give deeper insights into the truths of the Word. Pray too that your pastor will practice the Word that he preaches so that it will be real in his own life. As he preaches the message, pray that the Spirit will give him freedom of utterance, and that the Word will reach into hearts and minds in a powerful way. (It wouldn't hurt to pray for other church leaders too.)

The proclaiming of the Word of God is a great privilege and a tremendous responsibility. You do not have to be an ordained preacher or a missionary to share God's Word. Even in your daily conversation you can drop the seed of the Word into hearts, and then pray that God will water that seed and bring forth fruit.

Witnessing to the Lost (4:5–6)

"Them that are without" refers to those who are outside the family of God. Jesus made a distinction between His disciples and those who were outside (Mark 4:11). Paul also made this same distinction (1 Cor. 5:12–13). Those of us who are born again are the "spiritual insiders" because we belong to God's family and share His life.

However, as Christians, we must never have a sanctified superiority complex. We have a responsibility to witness to the lost around us and to seek to bring them into God's family. To begin with, we have the responsibility to *walk wisely* (Col. 4:5). *Walk* refers, of course, to our conduct in daily life. The unsaved outsiders watch us Christians and are very critical of us. There must be nothing in our lives that would jeopardize our testimony.

This story has often been told about Dr. Will H. Houghton, who pastored the Calvary Baptist Church in New York City and later served as president of Chicago's Moody Bible Institute till his death in 1946. When Dr. Houghton became pastor of the Baptist Tabernacle in Atlanta, a man in that city hired a private detective to follow Dr. Houghton and report on his conduct. After a few weeks, the detective was able to report to the man that Dr. Houghton's life matched his preaching. As a result, that man became a Christian.

What does it mean to "walk in wisdom"? For one thing, it means that we are careful not to say or do anything that would make it difficult to share the gospel. It also means we must be alert to use the opportunities God gives us for personal witnessing. "Redeeming the time" means buying up the opportunity (Eph. 5:16). This is a commercial term and pictures the Christian as a faithful steward who knows an opportunity when he sees one. Just as a merchant seizes a bargain when he finds one, so a Christian seizes the opportunity to win a soul to Christ.

Walking in wisdom also includes doing our work, paying our bills, and keeping our promises. We must "walk honestly toward them that are without" (1 Thess. 4:12). A friend of mine went into a store to make a purchase for his church. The salesman asked, "Is ___ a member of your church?" My friend said that he was, and the salesman proceeded to tell him how much money that church member owed his store and how difficult it was to get anything from him. It would probably have been futile for my friend to witness to that clerk.

Christians in general and Christian leaders in particular must have "a good report of them which are without" (1 Tim. 3:7). When members of a church are calling a new pastor, they ought to investigate his testimony among his neighbors and the businessmen who know him. Even though unsaved people are in the dark spiritually (2 Cor. 4:3–4), they have a great deal of discernment when it comes to the things of this life (Luke 16:8). It is unfortunate when members of a church call a pastor who has not paid his bills and has left behind a bad witness to unsaved people.

It is not enough simply to walk wisely and carefully before unbelievers. We must also *talk* with them and share the gospel message with them. But we must take care that our speech is controlled by *grace,* so that it points to Christ and glorifies the Lord. This means we must have grace in our hearts (Col. 3:16), because it is from the heart that the mouth speaks. With grace in our hearts and on our lips, we will be faithful witnesses and not judges or prosecuting attorneys!

The Lord Jesus Christ spoke with grace on His lips.

"And all … wondered at the gracious words which proceeded out of his mouth" (Luke 4:22). Among the many statements about Jesus Christ in Psalm 45 (a messianic psalm) is this: "Grace is poured into thy lips" (Ps. 45:2). Even when our Lord was dealing with sin, He spoke words of grace.

Our speech is supposed to "minister grace unto the hearers" (Eph. 4:29). But it cannot do that unless we have grace in our hearts and in our words. "Speaking the truth in love" (Eph. 4:15) is God's ideal for our conversation.

Why did Paul add "seasoned with salt" (Col. 4:6)? In that day, salt was used as a preservative as well as a seasoner. We should never say to anyone, "Now, take this with a grain of salt." *We* must put the salt into our speech to make sure it is pure and properly seasoned. "Let no corrupt communication proceed out of your mouth" (Eph. 4:29). Our speech must be pure.

Salt was also added to the sacrifices (Lev. 2:13). Perhaps Paul was suggesting that we look on our words as sacrifices offered to God, just as our words of praise are spiritual sacrifices (Heb. 13:15). It would no doubt help us to say the right things in the right manner if we remembered that our words are looked on as sacrifices to God.

It is unfortunate when a Christian speaks in a rude or coarse manner, particularly when the unsaved are listening. "Be ready always to give an answer to every man that asketh you a reason of the hope that is in you with meekness and fear" (1 Peter 3:15). Meekness is the opposite of harshness, and fear is the opposite of arrogance. There is no place in a Christian's conversation for a know-it-all attitude. While we need to have convictions and not compromise, we must also cultivate a gracious spirit of love.

The Christian's *walk* and *talk* must be in harmony with each other. Nothing will silence the lips like a careless life. When character, conduct, and conversation are all working together, it makes for a powerful witness.

Sharing Burdens (4:7–9)

Paul did not spell out the details of his personal situation in this letter. He left it to his two spiritual brothers, Tychicus and Onesimus, to share the burdens with the church in Colosse. This is another wonderful ministry of speech: we can share our needs and burdens with others; then they can encourage and assist us.

When Paul left Ephesus, he was accompanied by seven other believers—among them, Tychicus (Acts 20:4). These men were helping Paul deliver the love offering from the Gentile churches to the poor saints in Judea (1 Cor. 16:1; 2 Cor. 8—9). It is possible that Tychicus and Trophimus were the two brethren Paul referred to in his second letter to the Corinthians (see 2 Cor. 8:19–24).

Tychicus shared Paul's Roman imprisonment and no doubt was helpful to him in many ways. Paul chose Tychicus and Onesimus to deliver the Ephesian letter

(Eph. 6:21) and the Colossian letter (Col. 4:7–9). Of course, they also took the personal letter to Philemon. Paul instructed Tychicus to share with the Colossian Christians all the details of his situation there in Rome.

Paul's description of Tychicus reveals what a splendid Christian Tychicus really was. He was a *beloved brother,* willing to stay with Paul even though the situation was difficult. How encouraging it is to have a Christian at your side when everything seems to be against you!

Tychicus was also a *faithful minister.* His love revealed itself in action. He ministered to Paul, and he also ministered *for* Paul to assist him in his many obligations. Someone has said that the greatest ability in the world is dependability, and this is true. Paul could depend on Tychicus to get the job done.

Tychicus was also Paul's *fellow servant.* Though he was not an apostle himself, he was assisting Paul in his apostolic ministry. Paul and Tychicus worked together in the service of the Lord. Later, Paul was able to send Tychicus to Crete (Titus 3:12), and then to Ephesus (2 Tim. 4:12).

It was not easy for Tychicus to be associated with Paul, the prisoner; for Paul had many enemies. Nor was it easy for Tychicus to travel as he did, assisting Paul in his various tasks. Tychicus did not take the easy way, but rather the right way. Our churches today could use more members like Tychicus!

Paul also mentioned Onesimus ("one of you") who himself came from Colosse. He was the runaway slave who belonged to Philemon and who had been won to Christ through Paul's ministry in Rome. Paul sent Onesimus back to his master with a letter asking Philemon to receive him and forgive him. It is interesting to note that Paul also called Onesimus *faithful* and *beloved.* Onesimus had been a believer only a short time, and yet he had already proved himself to Paul.

These two men had a dual ministry to perform: to encourage the Colossian Christians and to inform them about Paul's situation. Is it wrong for God's people to share information in this way? Of course not! Paul was not begging for money or asking for sympathy. He wanted the Colossian saints to know his situation so they could pray for him. While it is true that some Christian workers "use" circumstances selfishly to enlist support, this was not true of Paul. He simply wanted his friends in Colosse to know the facts and to support him in prayer.

In our home, we receive a number of missionary prayer letters. We read them and try to note the special burdens and needs. In my own private devotions, I use several prayer calendars that help me remember to pray about specific needs for different ministries. I appreciate knowing the facts so that I can intercede in a specific way. I also enjoy getting reports of how God has answered prayer, for this encourages my faith.

Praying, proclaiming the Word, witnessing, and sharing burdens—these are four wonderful ministries of speech. How much better it is to be involved in these ministries than to be using our tongues for gossip, malicious criticism, and other sinful purposes.

Let's make David's prayer our prayer: "Set a watch, O Lord, before my mouth; keep the door of my lips" (Ps. 141:3).

CHAPTER TWELVE
Colossians 4:10–18
FRIENDS, ROMANS, COUNTRYMEN

Paul was not only a soul-winner; he was a great friend-maker. If my count is correct, there are more than one hundred different Christians (named and unnamed) associated with Paul in the book of Acts and in his epistles. He named twenty-six different friends in Romans 16 alone!

It was customary in Paul's day to close each letter with personal greetings. Friends did not see one another that much, and letter service was very slow and limited. Of course, Paul's greetings were much more than social; they conveyed his genuine spiritual concern for his friends. In this closing section, Paul sent personal greetings to Colosse from six of his associates in the ministry: Aristarchus, John Mark, and Jesus Justus, all of whom were Jews; and Epaphras, Luke, and Demas, who were Gentiles. Paul then added special greetings to two church assemblies, with a special word to one of the pastors.

When we first read this list of names, we are probably not greatly moved. But when we get behind the scenes and discover the drama of these men's lives as they worked with Paul, the list becomes very exciting. We can categorize these men into three groups.

The Men Who Stayed (4:10–11, 14a)
This group is made up of three Jews (Aristarchus, John Mark, Jesus Justus), and one Gentile (Luke). All of them were characterized by faithfulness to the apostle Paul in his hour of special need. They were the men who stayed.

Aristarchus (v. 10a). This man was identified as Paul's fellow prisoner and fellow worker (Col. 4:11). Aristarchus was from Macedonia and was one of Paul's traveling companions (Acts 19:29). He was originally from Thessalonica (Acts 20:4) and willingly risked his life in that Ephesian riot (Acts 19:28–41). He sailed with Paul to Rome (Acts 27:2), which meant he also experienced the storm and shipwreck that Luke so graphically described in Acts 27.

Aristarchus stayed with Paul no matter what the circumstances were—a riot in Ephesus, a voyage, a storm, or even a prison. It is not likely that Aristarchus was an official Roman prisoner. "Fellow prisoner" probably means that Aristarchus shared Paul's confinement with him so that he could be a help and comfort to the apostle. He was a voluntary prisoner for the sake of Jesus Christ and the gospel.

Paul could not have accomplished all that he did apart from the assistance of his friends. Aristarchus stands out as one of the greatest of Paul's helpers. He did not look for an easy task. He did not run when the going got tough. He suffered and labored with Paul.

John Mark (v. 10b). Mark, the writer of the second gospel, played a very important part in the early history of the church. He too was a Jew, a native of Jerusalem where his mother, Mary, kept "open house" for the believers (Acts 12:12). John Mark was a cousin of Barnabas, the man who went with Paul on that first missionary journey (Acts 13:1–3). It is a good possibility that John Mark was led to faith in Christ through the ministry of Peter (1 Peter 5:13).

When Paul and Barnabas set out on that first missionary journey, they took John Mark with them as their assistant. He probably took care of the travel arrangements, supplies, and so forth. But when the going got tough, John Mark abandoned the preachers and returned home to Jerusalem (Acts 13:5–13).

Why John quit is not explained in Scripture. Perhaps he was afraid, for the group was about to move into dangerous territory. Perhaps he resented the fact that Paul was taking over the leadership of the mission and replacing his relative, Barnabas. Or maybe John Mark resented Paul's ministry to the Gentiles. Whatever the reason or excuse, he left them and returned home.

Later, when Paul and Barnabas wanted to go on a second journey, Paul refused to take John Mark along (Acts 15:36–41). Was Paul wrong in his assessment of this young man? Perhaps, but we cannot blame Paul for being cautious when John Mark had failed him in the past. Paul was not running a popular tour; he was seeking to win lost souls to Christ. No amount of danger or inconvenience could hinder Paul from reaching unbelievers with the gospel. It was too bad that John Mark caused a division between Paul and Barnabas. However, we must admit that Paul did forgive John Mark and commend him: "Take Mark and bring him with thee: for he is profitable to me for the ministry" (2 Tim. 4:11).

Mark, Titus, and Timothy were young men who served as special representatives for the apostle Paul. He could send them to churches that were having problems and trust them to help solve them. By the grace of God, John Mark had overcome his first failure and had become a valuable servant of God. He was even chosen to write the gospel of Mark!

John Mark is an encouragement to everyone who has failed in his first attempts to serve God. He did not sit around and sulk. He got back into the ministry and proved himself faithful to the Lord and to the apostle Paul. He was one of the men who stayed.

I might add that it is good to be a Barnabas and encourage younger Christians in the Lord. Perhaps John Mark would have made it without the help of Cousin Barnabas, but I doubt it. God used Barnabas to encourage John Mark and restore him to service

again. Barnabas lived up to his name: "son of encouragement" (Acts 4:36 NIV).

Jesus Justus (v. 11). Jesus Justus was a Jewish believer who served with Paul, but we know nothing about him. The name *Jesus* (Joshua) was a popular Jewish name, and it was not unusual for Jewish people to have a Roman name as well (Justus). John Mark is a case in point. Jesus Justus represents those faithful believers who serve God but whose deeds are not announced for the whole world to know. He was a fellow worker with Paul and a comfort to Paul, and that is all we know about him. However, the Lord has kept a faithful record of this man's life and ministry and will reward him accordingly.

Luke (v. 14a). Luke was a very important man in the early church. He was a Gentile, yet he was chosen by God to write the gospel of Luke and the book of Acts. He is probably the only Gentile writer of any book of the Bible. He was also a physician, and was dearly loved by Paul. The profession of medicine had been perfected by the Greeks, and physicians were held in the highest regard. Even though Paul had the power to heal people, he traveled with a physician!

Luke joined Paul and his party at Troas (note the pronoun "we" in Acts 16:10). Luke traveled with Paul to Jerusalem (Acts 20:5ff.) and was with him on the voyage to Rome (Acts 27:1ff.). No doubt Luke's personal presence and his professional skill were a great encouragement to Paul during that very difficult time. While God can and does bring strength and healing in miraculous ways, He also uses the means provided in nature, such as medication. When my wife and I ministered to missionaries in Africa, a physician friend and his wife traveled with us, and we were grateful for their help.

Luke remained with Paul to the very end (see 2 Tim. 4:11). God used Luke to write the book of Acts and to give us the inspired history of the early church and the ministry of Paul. Luke is a glowing example of the professional man who uses his skills in the service of the Lord and gives himself to go wherever God sends. He was a beloved Christian, a skillful physician, a devoted friend, and a careful historian—all wrapped up in one!

The Man Who Prayed (4:12–13)

We met Epaphras at the beginning of this study, for he was the man who founded the church in Colosse (Col. 1:7–8). He had been led to Christ through Paul's ministry in Ephesus, and had returned home to share the good news of salvation. It seems likely that Epaphras also founded the churches in Laodicea and Hierapolis (Col. 4:13). In our modern terms, Epaphras became a "home missionary."

What motivated Epaphras to share the gospel? He was "a servant of Christ" (Col. 4:12). Paul called him "our dear fellow servant … a faithful minister of Christ" (Col. 1:7). Epaphras loved Jesus Christ and wanted to serve Him and share His message of salvation. But he did not do it alone. Epaphras also believed in the ministry of the local church, and in working with other saints. He was not just a "servant"; he was a *"fellow* servant."

I was chatting one day with a foreign mission executive about a mutual friend who had been forced to resign from his work on the field. "There was no problem with sin or anything like that," my friend explained. "His whole difficulty is that he is a loner. He can't work well with other people. On the mission field, it's a team effort or it's nothing."

One of the secrets of the ministry of Epaphras was his prayer life. Paul knew about this because Epaphras and Paul shared the same room, and when Epaphras prayed, Paul knew about it. What were the characteristics of this man's prayer life?

He prayed constantly (v. 12—"always"). He was a good example of Paul's admonition: "Continue in prayer" (Col. 4:2). Epaphras did not pray only when he felt like it, as do many Christians today. Nor did he pray when he was told to pray, or when the other believers prayed. He was constantly in prayer, seeking God's blessing.

He prayed fervently (v. 12—"laboring fervently"). The word used here means "agonizing." It is the same word used for our Lord's praying in the garden (Luke 22:44). We get the impression that prayer was serious business with Epaphras! This Greek word was used to describe the athletes as they gave themselves fully to their sports. If church members today put as much concern and enthusiasm into their praying as they did into their baseball games or bowling, we would have revival!

He prayed personally (v. 12—"for you"). Epaphras did not pray around the world for everybody in general and nobody in particular. He centered his intercession on the saints in Colosse, Laodicea, and Hierapolis. No doubt he mentioned some of them by name. Prayer for Epaphras was not an impersonal religious exercise, for he carried these people in his heart and prayed for them personally.

He prayed definitely. If you had asked Epaphras, "What are you praying for?" he could have told you. His great desire was that the believers in those three assemblies might mature in their Christian faith. Paul used four significant words to summarize the prayer of Epaphras, and these four words also summarize the message of the book of Colossians: "perfect—complete—all—will."

Epaphras was concerned that these Christians know and do the will of God. But he wanted them to be involved in *all* the will of God, not just in part of it. (*All* is a key word in Colossians, used over thirty times.) He also wanted them to stand *perfect* and *complete* in God's will. The gnostic teachers offered these Christians "perfection and maturity," but they could not deliver the goods. Only in Jesus Christ can we have these blessings. "And ye are complete in him," for only in Christ does the fullness of God dwell (Col. 2:9–10).

This request carries the thought of being mature and perfectly assured in the will of God, and parallels Paul's prayer burden (Col. 2:2). "Full assurance in the will of God" is a tremendous blessing! It is not necessary for the believer to drift in life. He can know God's will and enjoy it. As he learns God's will and lives it, he matures in the faith and experiences God's fullness.

He prayed sacrificially (v. 13—"great zeal" or "much distress"). Real prayer is difficult. When Jesus prayed in the garden, He sweat great drops of blood. Paul had "great conflict" (agony) as he prayed for the Colossians (2:1), and Epaphras also experienced "much distress." This does not mean that we must wrestle with God in order to get Him to answer. But it does mean that we must throw ourselves into our praying with zeal and concern. If there is no burden, there can be no blessing. To rephrase what John H. Jowett said about preaching, "Praying that costs nothing accomplishes nothing."

All of the men with Paul were named and commended in one way or another, but Epaphras was the only one commended for his prayer ministry. This does not mean that the other men did not pray, but it does suggest that prayer was his major interest and ministry. Epaphras was Paul's fellow prisoner (Philem. 23)—but even confinement could not keep him from entering the courts of heaven and praying for his brothers and sisters in the churches.

E. M. Bounds was a prayer warrior of the last generation. He would often rise early in the morning and pray for many hours before he began the work of the day. His many books on prayer testify to the fact that Bounds, like Epaphras, knew how to agonize in prayer before God. (If you have never read *Power in Prayer* [Baker] by E.M. Bounds, by all means do so.)

I am impressed with the fact that Epaphras prayed for believers in three different cities. We are fortunate today if church members pray for their own pastor and church, let alone believers in other places! Perhaps one reason that revival tarries is because we do not pray fervently for one another.

The Man Who Strayed (4:14b)

Demas is mentioned only three times in Paul's letters, and these three references tell a sad story. First he is called "Demas … my fellow laborer" and is linked with three good men—Mark, Aristarchus, and Luke (Philem. 24). Then he is simply called "Demas," and there is no special word of identification or commendation (Col. 4:14). But the third reference tells what became of Demas: "For Demas hath forsaken me, having loved this present world" (2 Tim. 4:10).

At one point in his life, John Mark had forsaken Paul, but he was reclaimed and restored. Demas forsook Paul and apparently was never reclaimed. His sin was that he loved this present world. The word *world* refers to the whole system of things that runs this world, or "society without God." In the first of his epistles, John the apostle pointed out that the world entices the believer with "the lust of the flesh, the lust of the eyes, and the pride of life" (1 John 2:15–17). Which of these traps caught Demas, we do not know; perhaps he fell into all three.

But we do know that Christians today can succumb to the world just as Demas did. How easy it is to maintain a religious veneer, while all the time we are living for the things of this world. Demas thought that he could serve two masters, but eventually he had to make a decision; unfortunately, he made the wrong decision.

It must have hurt Paul greatly when Demas forsook him. It also hurt the work of the Lord, for there never has been a time when the laborers were many. This decision hurt Demas most of all, for he wasted his life in that which could never last. "He that doeth the will of God abideth forever" (1 John 2:17).

After conveying greetings from his friends and fellow servants, Paul himself sent greetings to the sister churches in Laodicea and Hierapolis. These people had never seen Paul (Col. 2:1), yet he was interested in them and concerned about their spiritual welfare.

Final Greetings (4:15–18)

We know nothing about Nymphas, except that he had a church meeting in his house. (Some versions read "Nympha" and seem to indicate that this believer was a woman.) In the first centuries of the church, local assemblies met in private homes. Even today, many new local churches get their start this way. It was not until the Christian faith emerged from persecution into official government approval that church buildings were constructed. It really matters little where the assembly meets, so long as Jesus Christ is the center of the fellowship. (For other examples of "the church in the home," see Rom. 16:5 and 1 Cor. 16:19.)

Paul's great concern was that the Word of God be read and studied in these churches. The verb "read" means "to read aloud." There would not be copies of these letters for each member. It is a strong conviction of mine that we need to return to the public reading of the Word of God in many of our churches. "Give attendance to reading" (1 Tim. 4:13) means the public reading of God's Word.

It is worth noting that the various letters from Paul were good for *all* of these assemblies. In my ministry, I have shared God's Word in many different places and situations, and it has always reached the heart and met the need. Even in different cultures. God's Word has a message for the heart. God's Word does not have to be edited or changed to meet different problems in various situations, for it is always applicable.

What was "the epistle from Laodicea"? We do not know for sure. Some scholars think that the epistle to the Ephesians was this missing letter, but this idea is pure speculation. The fact that this letter has been lost does not mean we are missing a part of God's inspired Word. Some of Paul's correspondence with the church at Corinth has also been lost. God not only inspired His Word, but He providentially watched over it so that nothing would be lost that was supposed to be in that Word. Instead of wondering about what we do not have, we should be applying ourselves to what we do have!

When we compare Colossians 4:17 with Philemon 2, we get the impression that Archippus belonged to the family of Philemon. Possibly, he was Philemon's son and the pastor of the church that met in Philemon's house. We cannot prove this, of course, but it does seem a logical conclusion. This would make Apphia the wife of Philemon.

Paul's last words before his salutation are directed at Archippus as an encouragement to continue faithfully in his ministry. Was Archippus discouraged? Had the gnostic false teachers invaded his church and created problems for him? We do not know. But we do know that pastors of local churches face many problems and carry many burdens, and they often need a word of encouragement.

Paul reminded Archippus that his ministry was a gift from God, and that he was a steward of God who would one day have to give an account of his work. Since the Lord gave him his ministry, the Lord could also help him carry it out in the right way. Ministry is not something we do for God; it is something God does in and through us.

The word *fulfill* carries with it the idea that God has definite purposes for His servants to accomplish. He works in us and through us to complete those good works that He has prepared for us (see Eph. 2:10). Of course, *fulfill* also parallels the theme of Colossians—the fullness of Jesus Christ available to each believer. We are able to fulfill our ministries because we have been "filled full" through Jesus Christ.

Unless we make a practical application of Bible doctrine, our study is in vain. After reading this letter and studying it, we cannot help but see that we have in Jesus Christ all that we can ever want or need. All of God's fullness is in Jesus Christ and we have been made complete in Him. What an encouragement this must have been to Archippus! What an encouragement it should be to us today!

Paul usually dictated his letters to a secretary (see Rom. 16:22) and then signed his name at the end. He always added a sentence about the grace of God, for this was his "trademark" (see 2 Thess. 3:17–18). The combination of his signature and "grace" gave proof that the letter was authentic.

The New Testament contains many references to Paul's bonds and the fact that he was a prisoner (see Acts 20:23; 23:18, 29; 26:29; Phil. 1:7, 13–14, 16; 2 Tim. 1:8; 2:9; Philem. 10, 13; Eph. 3:1; 4:1). Why did Paul want them to remember his bonds? Primarily because those bonds were a reminder of his love for lost souls, especially the Gentiles. He was "the prisoner of Jesus Christ for you Gentiles" (Eph. 3:1). Paul's bonds were evidence of his obedience to the Lord and his willingness to pay any price so that the Gentiles might hear the gospel.

Even today, there are devoted Christians who are in bonds because of their faithfulness to the Lord. We ought to remember them and pray for them. "Remember them that are in bonds, as bound with them" (Heb. 13:3).

As we come to the close of our study of this remarkable letter, we must remind ourselves that we are complete in Jesus Christ. We should beware of any teaching that claims to give us "something more" than we already have in Christ. All of God's fullness is in Him, and He has perfectly equipped us for the life that God wants us to live. We do not live and grow by *addition,* but by *appropriation.*

May the Lord help us to live as those who are complete in Christ.

1 THESSALONIANS

OUTLINE

Key theme: The coming of Christ for the church
Key verses: 1 Thessalonians 5:9–10

I. PAUL REMEMBERS (1—3)
    A. How the church was born—1
    B. How the church was nurtured—2
    C. How the church was established—3

II. PAUL EXHORTS (4—5)
    (How the church should walk)
    A. In holiness—4:1–8
    B. In harmony—4:9–10
    C. In honesty—4:11–12
    D. In hope—4:13—5:11
    E. In helpfulness—5:12–28

CONTENTS

CHAPTER ONE
A CHURCH IS BORN

A father took his son to a large city museum, thinking that the visit would entertain the boy. But for two hours the lad did nothing but sigh and complain. Finally in desperation he said to his father, "Dad, let's go someplace where *things are real!*"

Some people feel that way when they read the Bible. They think they are in a religious museum, looking at ancient artifacts that have no meaning for life in today's scientific world. *But they are wrong.* No book published has more meaning for our lives, and more relevance to our problems, than the Bible. No wonder William Lyon Phelps, for years called "Yale's most inspiring professor," said, "I believe a knowledge of the Bible without a college course is more valuable than a college course without a Bible."

Two of Paul's earliest letters are 1 and 2 Thessalonians. (It is possible that Galatians was written first.) These two letters were written to real people who were experiencing real problems in a world that was not friendly to their Christian faith. You and I can easily identify with these people because we live in a similar world and face many of the same problems. Once you understand the background, the burden, and the blessing of these two letters, you will see how up-to-date and practical they are.

The Background
You can visit Thessalonica today, only the travel guide will call it Thessaloniki. (It used to be known as Salonika.) It is an important industrial and commercial city in modern Greece and is second to Athens in population. It served as an important Allied base during World War I. In World War II it was captured by the German army, and the Jewish population of about 60,000 persons was deported and exterminated.

It is an ancient city, originally named Therma from the many hot springs adjacent to it. In 315 BC it was renamed Thessalonica after the half-sister of Alexander the Great. When Rome conquered Macedonia in 168 BC, the city was made capital of that entire province. In Paul's day two hundred thousand people lived there, most of them Greeks, but also many Romans and a strong Jewish minority. Today it has a population of three hundred thousand, and is one of the few cities that has survived from the New Testament era of apostolic ministry.

Dr. Luke explained how Paul came to Thessalonica and how the church was founded (Acts 17:1–15). Paul went to Macedonia in response to a "call" from a man in Macedonia who said, "Come over into Macedonia and help us" (Acts 16:9). Paul, Silas, Luke, and Timothy arrived first in Philippi, where they led Lydia and her household to Christ and there established a church. Paul and Silas were arrested on false charges, beaten, and put into jail. But God delivered them and they were able to lead the jailer and his household to faith in Christ.

After encouraging the new believers, Paul and his friends left Philippi (though Luke probably stayed behind temporarily) and headed for the important city of Thessalonica. They bypassed Amphipolis and Apollonia (Acts 17:1), not because they had no burden for the people in those cities, but because Paul's policy was to minister in the large cities and then have the believers reach out into the smaller towns nearby. It is about a hundred miles from Philippi to Thessalonica.

Paul's commission was to take the gospel to the Gentiles (Acts 9:15; Eph. 3:1–12), but he always started his ministry among the Jews. The local synagogue was the place where the Old Testament law was known and revered. Paul could get a sympathetic hearing in the synagogue, at least until persecution began. Furthermore, there were always many Gentile "God-fearers" in the synagogues, and through them Paul could begin a witness to the pagan Gentiles. Add to this Paul's great burden for the Jews (Rom. 9:1–3; 10:1), and the historical principle of "to the Jew first" (Rom. 1:16), and you can see why Paul and his associates began their work in the synagogue.

It is interesting to study the words Luke used to describe Paul's public ministry in the synagogue (Acts 17:2–3). *Reasoned* means "to discourse using questions and answers." Perhaps "dialogue" would be a good synonym. *Opening* simply means "explaining." Paul would read a portion of the Old Testament Scriptures and explain their meaning with reference to Jesus Christ and the gospel. *Alleging* literally means "to lay beside." Paul put the Scriptures before them in an orderly manner, showing them how they harmonized. *Preach* means "to proclaim, to announce." Paul did not simply teach the Scriptures; he proclaimed Christ and urged his listeners to receive Him by faith.

We can learn much from Paul's approach to evangelism. He used the Word of God, and he declared the Son of God. He started where the people were and led them into the truth of the gospel. (When Paul preached to Gentiles, he started with the God of creation, since they had no knowledge of the Old Testament Scriptures. See Acts 14:8–18; 17:16ff.)

He ministered in the synagogue for three Sabbaths, and the Lord worked in power. Many people believed in Jesus Christ and were saved, including a number of high-ranking women. However, the unbelieving Jews began to oppose the work, and Paul and his helpers had to leave the city. They went forty miles to Berea and there had a good ministry, but the Jews from Thessalonica followed them and caused trouble. It was then that Paul left for Athens, and from there to Corinth.

How long did Paul minister in Thessalonica? Does the statement "three Sabbath days" (Acts 17:2) mean three weeks only, or that he preached *in the synagogue* only three weeks but continued in another place? We know that Paul was there long enough to receive two "home missions offerings" from the church in Philippi (Phil. 4:16). Also, Paul worked at his tentmaking trade to support himself (1 Thess. 2:9; 2 Thess. 3:6–15).

If Paul were there only three weeks, he certainly taught the new Christians a great deal of basic Bible doctrine. As we study these two letters, we will discover that almost every major doctrine of the Christian faith is mentioned.

Even though Paul's ministry in Thessalonica was not a long one, it was solid enough to leave behind a thriving church. When he left for Athens, Paul told Timothy and Silas to remain there and help the new church and then to join him later. When they did meet again, Paul sent Timothy back to Thessalonica to encourage the Christians and assure them of his love and concern. (He had tried to go back twice but was hindered, 1 Thess. 2:17–18.) It was when Timothy rejoined Paul at Corinth and gave him the report on the new church that Paul wrote 1 Thessalonians. He wrote 2 Thessalonians just a short time later. All of this background teaches us several helpful lessons. Obviously, *God uses people.* God did not send angels to evangelize Thessalonica; He sent a converted Jewish rabbi and his friends, including a young man who was part Jew, part Gentile. God still uses people—dedicated people who will obey His leading and share His message.

Here is a second lesson: the gospel is still "the power of God unto salvation" (Rom. 1:16). It did not require years to set up a church in Thessalonica. God's power was effective in changing lives, and a church was founded in less than a month. Paul reminded them that the gospel came to them not "in word only, but also in power in the Holy Spirit" (1 Thess. 1:5).

Finally, Satan still opposes the gospel and persecutes God's people, *but persecution can be a means of growth.* As we study these two letters, we will see that God's Spirit strengthens and encourages suffering saints as they go through the difficulties of Christian life.

The Burden

Why did Paul write these two letters? First, he wanted to assure his friends of his love and concern. After all, he left the city hastily at night, and he did not want them to think he had deserted them. Also, Paul's enemies were attacking his character and telling the new believers that their leader was really a greedy charlatan who preached religion in order to make money (1 Thess. 2). There were plenty of itinerant rogues in Greece who did just that, and some were spreading the word that Paul was one of them. In this letter, Paul assured his readers of his love for them and his honesty in ministering to them.

He had a second purpose in view: he wanted to ground them in the doctrines of the Christian faith, particularly with reference to Christ's return. It appears that the church was going through severe persecution, and this is always a time of temptation to compromise and give in to discouragement. By reminding them of the truths of the Christian faith and what God had done for them in Christ, Paul encouraged them to stand firm and maintain their strong witness.

He also encouraged them to live holy lives. Keep in mind that temptations to immorality were rife in the cities then, and that sexual sins were not condemned by most people. These letters emphasize purity of life—a concept that needs to be emphasized in our churches too.

The new Christians were confused about the return of Jesus Christ. Paul had told them that the Lord would return in the air and take them home, but some of their number had died. The bereaved ones wondered if their Christian dead would be included in the "catching up" of the church. Paul explained this in 1 Thessalonians 4:13–18.

But there was a second confusion. Because the persecutions were so intense, some of the believers thought that "the day of the Lord" had arrived. (It is possible that a forged letter contributed to this confusion, 2 Thess. 2:1–2.) Paul wrote 2 Thessalonians to explain this doctrine and to assure them that the day of the Lord had not yet arrived.

Finally, in this letter, Paul sought to correct some weaknesses in the church. Some members were not respecting and honoring their spiritual leaders as they should (1 Thess. 5:12–13). Others were refusing to work, arguing that the soon-coming of the Lord made this the logical thing to do (2 Thess. 3:6ff.). There was some confusion in their public services that also needed correcting (1 Thess. 5:19–21).

Confusion still exists about Bible prophecy, with radio and television preachers contradicting each other (and the Bible) and upsetting the saints. Is the coming of the Lord near? Must any signs take place before He can return? Will God's people have to go through the day of the Lord (the tribulation) before He can return? Paul answered these important questions in these two inspired letters.

And what about the matter *of practical holiness?* It is not easy for Christians to avoid the pollutions of the world. The sex promoters offer their wares at almost every newspaper stand and drugstore. Immorality and infidelity are common themes of radio and television programs as well as of popular music. The bad examples of famous people make it easier for young people to say, "Everybody is doing it!"

In addition to being more cautious in daily living, we also need more order and respect in our local churches. I have discovered that lack of respect for spiritual leadership is the main cause of church fights and splits. What Paul wrote in 1 Thessalonians

5:12–13 and 2 Thessalonians 3:6–15 is greatly needed today.

In all fairness to church officers, I realize that some pastors do not deserve to be followed. They are not spiritual; they do not pray; and they have no concern for the lost. They are merely using the ministry to make an easy living. A pastor must not *demand* respect; he must *command* respect, as did Paul, by his dedicated life and sacrificial ministry.

First Thessalonians is a letter from a spiritual father to his children. Paul pictured the church as a family (the word *brethren* or *brother* is used nineteen times in the first letter and nine times in the second), and he reminded them of what God did for them through his ministry.

The second letter was written to correct certain wrong ideas—and wrong practices—relating to the doctrine of the Lord's return.

We have seen the background of the letters and the burden that motivated Paul to write them. We shall now consider the blessing of these letters and discover what they can mean to us.

The Blessing

Each New Testament letter has a special message, or blessing, that is uniquely its own. Romans, for example, emphasizes the righteousness of God and shows that God is righteous in His dealings with both sinners and believers. First Corinthians focuses on the wisdom of God, and 2 Corinthians on the comfort of God. Galatians is the freedom letter and Philippians is the joy letter, while Ephesians stresses the wealth that we have in Christ Jesus.

What is the special blessing in the message of 1 and 2 Thessalonians? It is the message of the return of Jesus Christ and how this vital doctrine can affect our lives and churches and make us more spiritual. Every chapter in 1 Thessalonians ends with reference to the coming of Jesus Christ, and each reference relates the doctrine to a practical aspect of Christian living. Here is a summary:

    1:10—salvation and assurance
    2:19–20—soul-winning and service
    3:11–13—stability in Christian living
    4:13–18—strength in sorrow
    5:23–24—sanctification of life

In other words, Paul did not look on this doctrine as a theory to be discussed, but as a truth to be lived. These letters encourage us to live "in the future tense" since Jesus could appear at any time. We are to practice the promise of His return in our manner of life.

Turning to 2 Thessalonians, we discover additional truth concerning future events and the church. Keep in mind that the second letter was written to correct the confusion regarding our Lord's return. Some believers thought the day of the Lord (the time of tribulation) had arrived, and they wondered when the Lord would appear. Perhaps the best way to grasp the major messages of the two letters is by contrast:

1 Thessalonians	*2 Thessalonians*
Christ comes in the air for His church (4:13–18)	Christ comes to the earth with His church (1:10)
A sudden secret rapture that can occur at any time	A crisis that is part of a predicted program
Can occur today	Can occur only after certain events happen
The day of Christ	The day of the Lord

Paul did not write these letters to stir up a debate. His desire was that these letters bless our lives and our churches. The doctrine of the Lord's return is not a toy to play with or a weapon to fight with, but a tool to build with. Believers may disagree on some of the fine points of Bible prophecy, but we all believe that Jesus Christ is coming again to reward believers and judge the lost. And we must all live in the light of His coming.

Your study of these letters should give you assurance for the future, encouragement in witnessing and walking with the Lord, comfort in the loss of Christian loved ones, and stability in a world that is very unsure of itself. I realize that godly men differ in their interpretations of prophecy, particularly the matter of the church escaping or entering the time of tribulation. My own position is that the church will be taken to heaven before the tribulation, and then will return to the earth with the Lord to bring the tribulation to a close (Rev. 19:11ff.). I see 1 Thessalonians emphasizing the rapture of the church and 2 Thessalonians, the revelation of the Lord with the church when He comes to judge.

However, the practical spiritual lessons of these truths should not be lost in debates over interpretations. I am encouraged to read what Dr. Leon Morris wrote in his excellent commentary on the Thessalonian epistles in *The New International Commentary* (Eerdmans, 1959, 152).

In his discussion of 1 Thessalonians 5:1–3, Dr. Morris faced the matter of whether believers will escape the tribulation or be left on earth to pass through that terrible event. "The language of this chapter could be understood either way," he stated, and then affirmed his own position that the church will go through the tribulation. Then he added, "But I fully recognize that other interpretations are possible, and suggest that it is not wise for any of us to condemn those who see such passages differently."

In other words, we can disagree without being disagreeable. My own conviction is that we shall be delivered from "the wrath to come" (1 Thess. 1:10; 5:9–10). I believe the Lord wants us to live in the constant expectation of His coming. I have studied carefully the excellent defenses of the other positions, and I respect the men who hold to them. But I must lovingly disagree with them.

CHAPTER TWO
1 Thessalonians 1:1–10
WHAT EVERY CHURCH SHOULD BE

No doubt you have heard some preacher say, "If you ever find the perfect church, *please don't join it.* If you do, it won't be perfect anymore!"

Since local churches are made up of human beings, saved by God's grace, no church is perfect. But some churches are closer to the New Testament ideal than others. The church at Thessalonica was in that category. At least three times in this letter, Paul gave thanks for the church and the way it responded to his ministry (1 Thess. 1:2; 2:13; 3:9). Not every pastor can be that thankful.

What characteristics of this church made it so ideal and such a joy to Paul's heart?

An Elect People (1:1–4)
The word *church* in 1 Thessalonians 1:1 means "a called-out people." Whenever you read about a call in the Bible, it indicates divine election—God is calling out a people from this world (Acts 15:13–18). Seven times in John 17, our Lord referred to believers as those whom the Father gave to him out of the world (John 17:2, 6, 9, 11–12, 24). Paul stated that he knew the Thessalonians had been chosen by God (1 Thess. 1:4).

The doctrine of divine election confuses some people and frightens others, yet neither response is justified. A seminary professor once told me, "Try to explain election, and you may lose your mind. But explain it away—and you may lose your soul!"

We will never understand the total concept of election this side of heaven. But we should not ignore this important doctrine that is taught throughout the Bible. Let's notice some obvious facts about divine election.

Salvation begins with God. "God hath from the beginning chosen you to salvation" (2 Thess. 2:13). "Ye have not chosen me, but I have chosen you" (John 15:16). "He [the Father] hath chosen us in him [Christ] before the foundation of the world" (Eph. 1:4). The entire plan of salvation was born in the heart of God long before man was created or the universe formed.

Salvation involves God's love. Paul called these saints "brethren beloved"—not only beloved by Paul (see 1 Thess. 2:17), but also beloved by God. God's love made Calvary possible (Rom. 5:8), and there Jesus Christ died for our sins. But it is not God's love that saves the sinner; it is God's grace. God in His grace gives us what we do not deserve, and God in His mercy does not give us what we do deserve. This explains why Paul often opened his letters with "Grace be unto you, and peace, from God our Father, and the Lord Jesus Christ" (1 Thess. 1:1).

Salvation involves faith. "For by grace are ye saved through faith" (Eph. 2:8). Paul, Silas (Silvanus is the Roman spelling), and Timothy brought the gospel to Thessalonica and preached in the power of God (1 Thess. 1:5). Some people who heard the message believed and turned from their vain idols to the true and living God (1 Thess. 1:9). The Spirit of God used the Word of God to generate faith (Rom. 10:17). Paul called this "sanctification of the Spirit and belief of the truth" (2 Thess. 2:13).

Salvation involves the Trinity. As you read this letter, you discover the doctrine of the Trinity. Christians believe in one God existing in three Persons: God the Father, and God the Son, and God the Holy Spirit. Keep in mind that all three Persons are involved in our salvation. This will help you escape dangerous extremes that either deny human responsibility or dilute divine sovereignty—for both are taught in the Bible.

As far as God the Father is concerned, I was saved when He chose me in Christ before the world began. As far as God the Son is concerned, I was saved when He died for me on the cross. As far as God the Holy Spirit is concerned, I was saved one Saturday night in May 1945, when I heard the Word and trusted Jesus Christ. At that moment, the entire plan fell together and I became a child of God. If you had asked me that night if I was one of the elect, I would have been speechless. At that time I knew nothing about election. But the Holy Spirit witnessed in my heart that I was a child of God.

Salvation changes the life. How did Paul know that these Thessalonians were elected of God? He saw a change in their lives. If you put 1 Thessalonians 1:3 next to 1 Thessalonians 1:9–10, You will get the picture:

your work of faith	you turned to God from idols
your labor of love	to serve the living and true God
and patience of hope	to wait for His Son from heaven

The person who claims to be one of God's elect, but whose life has not changed, is only fooling himself. *Those whom God chooses, He changes.* This does not mean they are perfect, but they are possessors of a new life that cannot be hidden.

Faith, hope, and love are the three cardinal virtues of the Christian life, and the three greatest evidences of salvation. *Faith* must always lead to works (James 2:14–26). It has been said, "We are not saved by faith plus works, but by a faith that works." If the Thessalonians had continued to worship their dead idols while professing faith in the living God, it would have proved that they were not among God's elect.

Love is also an evidence of salvation: "the love of God is shed abroad in our hearts by the Holy Ghost which is given unto us" (Rom. 5:5). We are "taught by God to love one another" (1 Thess. 4:9). We serve Christ because we love Him; this is the "labor of love" that Paul mentioned. "If ye love me, keep my commandments" (John 14:15).

The third evidence of salvation is *hope,* waiting for Jesus Christ to return (1 Thess. 1:10). The return of Jesus Christ is the dominant theme of both of these Thessalonian letters. Unsaved people are not eagerly awaiting the Lord's return. In fact, when our Lord catches His church up into the air, unsaved people will be totally surprised (1 Thess. 5:1–11).

Faith, hope, and love are evidences of election. These spiritual qualities are bound together and can come only from God. For further evidence, see these passages: 1 Corinthians 13:13; Romans 5:1–5; Galatians 5:5–6; Colossians 1:4–5; Hebrews 6:10–12; 10:22–24; 1 Peter 1:21–22.

A local church must be composed of elect people, those who have been saved by the grace of God. One problem today is the presence, in the church family, of unbelievers whose names may be on the church roll, but not written in the Lamb's Book of Life. Every church member should examine his heart to determine whether he has truly been born again and belongs to God's elect.

An Exemplary People (1:5–7)

From the very inception of this church, Paul looked to them with joy and gratitude as Christians worthy of the name. They were examples in several areas of their lives.

They received the Word (v. 5). The gospel came to them through the ministry of Paul and his associates. Many traveling preachers and philosophers in that day were only interested in making money from ignorant people. But the Holy Spirit used the Word in great power, and the Thessalonians responded by receiving both the message and the messengers. In spite of the persecution in Philippi, Paul and Silas had been "bold … to speak … the gospel" (1 Thess. 2:2), and the people believed and were saved. They never lost that eagerness for the Word of God (1 Thess. 2:13).

They followed their spiritual leaders (v. 6a). The word *followers* is actually "imitators." These new believers not only accepted the message and the messengers, but they also imitated their lives. This led to severe persecution. It is important that young Christians respect spiritual leadership and learn from mature believers. Just as a newborn baby needs a family, so a newborn Christian needs the local church and the leaders there. "Obey them that have the [spiritual] rule over you, and submit yourselves: for they watch for your souls" (Heb. 13:17). It is not enough for us as mature believers to *win* souls; we must also *watch* for souls and encourage new Christians to obey God's Word.

They suffered for Christ (v. 6b). In turning from idols to serve God, these believers angered their friends and relatives, and this led to persecution. No doubt some of them lost their jobs because of their new faith. Just as the Jewish unbelievers persecuted the believers in Judea, so the Gentile unbelievers persecuted the

Thessalonian believers (1 Thess. 2:14–16). Faith is always tested, and persecution is one of the tests (Matt. 13:21; 2 Tim. 3:12).

They encouraged other churches (v. 7). Christians either encourage or discourage each other. This principle applies also to churches. Paul used the churches of Macedonia as a stimulus for the Corinthian church to give to the missionary offering (2 Cor. 8:1–8). Even though they were new believers, the Thessalonians set a good example that encouraged the surrounding assemblies. Churches must never compete with one another in a worldly manner, but they can "provoke unto love and to good works" (Heb. 10:24).

In every way, the church at Thessalonica was exemplary. The secret was found in their faith, hope, and love, for these are the spiritual motivators of the Christian life.

An Enthusiastic People (1:8)

Their "work of faith and labor of love" expressed itself in their sharing of the gospel with others. They were both "receivers" (the Word came to them, 1 Thess. 1:5) and "transmitters" (the Word went out from them, 1 Thess. 1:8). Each believer and each local church must receive and transmit God's Word.

The verb "sounded out" actually means "to sound as a trumpet." But the Thessalonians were not "tooting their own horns" as did the Pharisees (Matt. 6:1–4). They were trumpeting forth the good news of salvation, and their message had a clear and certain sound to it (1 Cor. 14:8). Wherever Paul went, the people told him about the faith of the Thessalonian believers.

It is the responsibility and privilege of each local church to share the message of salvation with the lost world. At the end of each of the four gospels and at the beginning of the book of Acts, there are commissions for the churches to obey (Matt. 28:18–20; Mark 16:15–16; Luke 24:46–49; John 20:21; Acts 1:8). Many congregations are content to pay a staff to do the witnessing and soul-winning. But in New Testament churches, the entire congregation was involved in sharing the good news (Acts 2:44–47; 5:42).

A recent survey of church growth indicated that 70 to 80 percent of a church's growth is the result of friends witnessing to friends and relatives to relatives. While visitation evangelism and other methods of outreach help, the personal contact brings the harvest.

But election and evangelism go together. The person who says, "God will save those He wants to save and He doesn't need my help!" understands neither election nor evangelism. In the Bible, election always involves *responsibility.* God chose Israel and made them an elect nation so that they might witness to the Gentiles.

In the same way, God has chosen the church that we might be witnesses today. The fact that we are God's elect people does not excuse us from the task of evangelism. On the contrary, the doctrine of election is one of the greatest encouragements to evangelism.

Paul's experience at Corinth (Acts 18:1–11) is a perfect illustration of this truth. Corinth was a wicked city, and it was not easy to start a church there. The people were godless sinners (1 Cor. 6:9–11), but Paul preached the Word faithfully. When persecution arose from the Jewish unbelievers, Paul moved from the synagogue into the house of Justus. Then the Lord encouraged Paul: "Be not afraid, but speak, and hold not thy peace: for I am with thee, and no man shall set on thee to hurt thee: for I have much people in this city" (Acts 18:9–10). The fact that God had His elect in Corinth encouraged Paul to remain there for a year and a half.

If salvation were the work of man, we would have every right to be discouraged and quit. But salvation is the work of God, and He uses people to call out His elect "He called you by our gospel" (2 Thess. 2:14). The same God who ordains *the end* (the salvation of the lost) also ordains *the means* to the end (the preaching of the gospel). There is no conflict between divine sovereignty and human responsibility, even though we cannot reconcile the two.

We need more churches today where the people are enthusiastic to share the message of salvation with others. As I write this, 2.4 billion people in our world have no visible witness of the gospel in their midst, or no church body. In spite of the outreach of radio, television, and the printing press, we are losing ground in the work of reaching the lost. Are you an enthusiastic Christian? Is your church enthusiastic about witnessing?

An Expectant People (1:9–10)

Their *work of faith* made them an elect people, for they turned to God from their idols and trusted Jesus Christ. Their *labor of love* made them an exemplary and enthusiastic people as they lived the Word of God and shared the gospel. Their *patience of hope* made them an expectant people, looking for their Savior's return.

In these verses, Paul related the second coming of Christ to their salvation. Because they had trusted Christ, they looked for His return with joyful expectancy and knew that they would be delivered "from the wrath to come" (1 Thess. 1:10). Paul repeated this truth in 1 Thessalonians 5:9–10, and he amplified it again in 2 Thessalonians 1:5–10.

When they worshipped idols, the Thessalonians had no hope. But when they trusted "the living God," they had a living hope (see 1 Peter 1:2–3). Those of us who have been brought up in the Christian doctrine cannot understand the bondage of pagan idolatry. Before Paul came to them with the gospel, these people were without hope and "without God in the world" (Eph. 2:12). Read Psalm 115 for a vivid description of what it is like to worship an idol.

Christians are "children of the living God" (Rom. 9:26). Their bodies are the "temples of the living God" (2 Cor. 6:16), indwelt by the "Spirit of the living God" (2 Cor. 3:3). The church is "the church of the living God" (1 Tim. 3:15); and for His church, God is preparing "the city of the living God" (Heb. 12:22). The living God has given us a living hope by raising His Son Jesus Christ from the dead.

Two aspects of the Lord's return must be distinguished. First, Jesus Christ will come in the air for His church (1 Thess. 4:13–18). This will usher in a period of tribulation on the earth (1 Thess. 5:1–3). At the close of this period, He will return to the earth with His church (2 Thess. 1:5–10; Rev. 19:11–21), defeat His enemies, and then set up His kingdom (Rev. 20:1–6).

The word translated "wait" in 1 Thessalonians 1:10 means "to await someone with patience and confidence, expectantly." Waiting involves activity and endurance. Some of the Thessalonian believers quit their work and became idle busybodies, arguing that the Lord was coming soon. But if we really believe the Lord is coming, we will prove our faith by keeping busy and obeying His Word. Our Lord's parable of the pounds (Luke 19:11–27) teaches that we must "occupy" (be busy; in this case, invest the money) till He returns.

Christians are waiting for Jesus Christ, and He may return at any time. We are not waiting for any "signs"; we are waiting for the Savior. We are waiting for the redemption of the body (Rom. 8:23–25) and the hope of righteousness (Gal. 5:5). When Jesus Christ returns we shall receive new bodies (Phil. 3:20–21), and we shall be like Him (1 John 3:1–2). He will take us to the home He has prepared (John 14:1–6), and He will reward us for the service we have given in His name (Rom. 14:10–12).

A local church that truly lives in the expectation of seeing Jesus Christ at any time will be a vibrant and victorious group of people. Expecting the Lord's return is a great motivation for soul-winning (1 Thess. 2:19–20) and Christian stability (1 Thess. 3:11–13). It is a wonderful comfort in sorrow (1 Thess. 4:13–18) and a great encouragement for godly living (1 Thess. 5:23–24). It is tragic when churches forget this wonderful doctrine. It is even more tragic when churches believe it and preach it—but do not practice it.

Paul remembered how this church was born (1 Thess. 1:3), and he gave thanks for their spiritual characteristics: they were elect, exemplary, enthusiastic, and expectant. But churches are made up of individuals. When you and I speak of the church, we must never say "they." We should say "we." *We are the church!* This means that if you and I have these spiritual characteristics, our churches will become what God wants them to become. The result will be the winning of the lost and the glorifying of the Lord.

What every church should be is what every Christian should be: *elect* (born again), *exemplary* (imitating the right people), *enthusiastic* (sharing the gospel with others), and *expectant* (daily looking for Jesus Christ to return).

Perhaps it is time for an inventory.

CHAPTER THREE
1 Thessalonians 2:1–12
HELPING THE BABY GROW UP

Chapter 1 of 1 Thessalonians introduced us to Paul the evangelist. This chapter introduces us to Paul the pastor, for it explains how the great apostle cared for the new believers in the churches that he founded. Paul considered "the care of all the churches" (2 Cor. 11:28) a greater burden than all the sufferings and difficulties he experienced in his ministry (2 Cor. 11:23ff.).

Just as God uses people to bring the gospel to the lost, so He uses people to nurture the babes in Christ and help lead them to maturity. The church at Thessalonica was born through the faithful *preaching* of the apostle and his helpers, and the church was nurtured through the faithful *pastoring* that Paul and his friends gave to the infant church. This helped them stand strong in the midst of persecution.

In these verses, Paul reminded them of the kind of ministry he had as he taught and cared for the young church. Three pictures of his ministry emerge.

The Faithful Steward (2:1–6)

Paul had been "put in trust with the gospel" (1 Thess. 2:4). It was not a message that he made up or that he received from men (Gal. 1:11–12). Paul looked on himself as a steward of God's message.

A steward owns nothing, but possesses and uses everything that belongs to his master. Joseph was a steward in the household of Potiphar (Gen. 39:1–6). He managed his master's affairs and used all his master's goods to promote his master's welfare. Every steward one day must give an account of his stewardship (Luke 16:1–2). If he is found unfaithful, he will suffer.

The message of the gospel is a treasure God has entrusted to us. We must not bury it; we must invest it so it will multiply and produce "spiritual dividends" to God's glory. Some Christians think that the church's only responsibility is to protect the gospel from those who would change it (Gal. 1:6–9). But we also must *share* the gospel; otherwise, we are protecting it in vain.

Faithfulness is the most important quality a steward possesses (1 Cor. 4:1–2). He may not be popular in the eyes of men, but he dare not be unfaithful in the eyes of God. "Not as pleasing men, but God who trieth [testeth] our hearts" (1 Thess. 2:4). The Christian who "plays to the grandstands" will lose God's approval. When we see the characteristics of Paul's ministry as a steward, we understand what faithfulness means.

The manner of his ministry (vv. 1–2). Paul and Silas had been beaten and humiliated at Philippi, yet they came to Thessalonica and preached. Most of us would have taken a vacation or found an excuse not to minister. Paul was courageous—he was not a quitter.

He had a "holy boldness" that was born of dedication to God. Like the other apostles before him, Paul boldly proclaimed the good news (Acts 4:13, 29, 31).

His preaching was "with much contention." This is an athletic term that means "a contest, a struggle." The Greek world was familiar with athletic contests, and Paul often used this idea to illustrate spiritual truths (1 Cor. 9:24–27; Phil. 3:13–14; 2 Tim. 4:7). He used this same word in Philippians 1:30, where he pictured the Christian life as an athletic contest that demanded dedication and energy. It had not been easy to start a church in Philippi, and it was not easy to start one in Thessalonica.

The message of his ministry (v. 3a). "For the appeal we make does not spring from error" (NIV). Here he assured them that his message was true. Six times in this letter he mentioned the gospel. This message of Christ's death and resurrection (1 Cor. 15:1–6) is a true message and is the only true gospel (Gal. 1:6–12). Paul received this gospel from God, not from man. It is the only good news that saves the lost sinner.

The motive of his ministry (v. 3b). He was not guilty of "uncleanness," for his motives were pure. It is possible to preach the right message with the wrong motives (Phil. 1:14–19). Unfortunately, some people in Paul's day used religion as a means for making money. Paul did not use the gospel as "a cloak" to cover his "covetousness" (1 Thess. 2:5). He was open and honest in all his dealings, and he even worked at a trade to earn his own support (see 2 Thess. 3:8–10).

Paul was very sensitive about money matters. He did not want to give anyone a reason to accuse him of being a religious salesman (1 Cor. 9:1–18). As an apostle, he had the privilege of receiving support. But he gave up that right in order to be free from any possible blame that would disgrace the ministry.

The method of his ministry (vv. 3c–6). Paul did not use guile or trickery to win converts. The word translated "guile" carries the idea of "baiting a hook." In other words, Paul did not trap people into being saved the way a clever salesman traps people into buying his product. Spiritual witnessing and "Christian salesmanship" are different. Salvation does not lie at the end of a clever argument or a subtle presentation. It is the result of God's Word and the power of the Holy Spirit (1 Thess. 1:5).

Often we hear, "I don't care what your method is, just so long as your message is right." But some methods are unworthy of the gospel. They are cheap, whereas the gospel is a costly message that required the death of God's only Son. They are worldly and man centered, whereas the gospel is a divine message centered in God's glory.

Paul's enemies in Thessalonica accused him of being a cheap peddler of this new message. They said that his only motive was to make money. In describing himself as a faithful steward, Paul answered these critics, *and Paul's readers knew that he told the truth.* (Trace that phrase "as ye know" in 1 Thess. 1:5; 2:1,

5, 11; 3:3–4; 4:2; 5:2.) Paul appealed to the witness of God (1 Thess. 2:5) and to their own witness. He had "a conscience void of offense toward God, and toward men" (Acts 24:16).

Paul abhorred flattery (1 Thess. 2:5). David also hated this sin. "They speak vanity everyone with his neighbor; with flattering lips and with a double heart do they speak" (Ps. 12:2).

I once read that a flatterer is a person who manipulates rather than communicates. A flatterer can use either truth or lies to achieve his unholy purpose, which is to control your decisions for his own profit.

Some people even flatter themselves. "For he flatters himself in his own eyes" (Ps. 36:2 rsv). This was the sin of Haman, that evil man in the book of Esther. He was so interested in flattering himself that he even plotted to slaughter all the Jews to achieve that goal.

Some people try to flatter God. "Nevertheless they [Israel] did flatter him [God] with their mouth, and they lied unto him with their tongues" (Ps. 78:36). Flattery is another form of lying. It means saying one thing to God with our lips while our hearts are far from Him (Mark 7:6).

Some Christians try to win friends and influence people by appealing to their egos. A true ministry of the gospel deals honestly (but lovingly) with sin and judgment and leaves the unbeliever with nothing to boast of in himself. Paul's method was as pure as his motive: he presented the Word of God in the power of the Spirit, and trusted God to work.

The Loving Mother (2:7–8)

The emphasis of the steward is *faithfulness;* the emphasis of the mother is *gentleness.* As an apostle, Paul was a man of authority, but he always used his authority in love. The babes in Christ sensed his tender loving care as he nurtured them. He was indeed like a loving mother who cared for her children.

It takes time and energy to care for children. Paul did not turn his converts over to babysitters; he made sacrifices and cared for them himself. He did not tell them to "read a book" as a substitute for his own personal ministry (though good Christian literature can help young believers to grow).

Paul had patience with the new Christians. Our four children are into adulthood now, but I can assure you that my wife and I needed a great deal of patience before they reached that state. (To even things up, our parents needed patience with us!) Children do not grow up instantly. They all experience growing pains and encounter problems as they mature. Paul's love for them made him patient, because love suffers long, and is kind (1 Cor. 13:4).

Paul also nourished them. First Thessalonians 2:7 can read "even as a nursing mother cherishes her own children." What is the lesson here? A *nursing mother imparts her own life to the child.* This is exactly what Paul wrote in 1 Thessalonians 2:8. You cannot be a nursing mother and turn your baby over to someone else. That baby must be in your arms, next to your heart.

The nursing mother eats the food and transforms it into milk for the baby. The mature Christian feeds on the Word of God and then shares its nourishment with the younger believers so they can grow (1 Peter 2:1–3). A nursing child can become ill through reaction to something the mother has eaten. The Christian who is feeding others must be careful not to feed on the wrong things himself.

Besides making sacrifices, having patience, and giving nourishment, a mother also *protects* her child. It was this fact that enabled King Solomon to discover which woman was the real mother of the living child (1 Kings 3:16–28). Paul was willing to give not only the gospel but his own life as well. His love for the Thessalonians was so great he would die for them if necessary.

But it is not easy to be a "nursing mother." Even Moses felt the burden of caring for God's people. "Was it I who conceived all this people? Was it I who brought them forth, that Thou shouldest say to me, 'Carry them in your bosom as a nurse carries a nursing infant, to the land which Thou didst swear to their fathers'?" (Num. 11:12 nasb). But if we do not nurse the new Christians on the milk of the Word, they can never mature to appreciate the meat of the Word (Heb. 5:10–14).

The Concerned Father (2:9–12)

Paul considered himself a "spiritual father" to the believers at Thessalonica, just as he did toward the saints at Corinth. "For if you were to have countless tutors in Christ, yet you would not have many fathers, for in Christ Jesus I became your father through the gospel" (1 Cor. 4:15 nasb). The Spirit of God used the Word of God in Paul's ministry, and many people in Thessalonica were born again into the family of God.

But the father not only begets the children; he also cares for them. As he defended his own work against false accusations, Paul pointed out three of his duties as the spiritual father to the Thessalonicans.

His work (v. 9). The father works to support his family. Even though the Christians in Philippi sent financial help (Phil. 4:15–16), Paul still made tents and paid his own way. No one could accuse him of using his ministry for his own profit. Later on, Paul used this fact to shame the lazy Christians in the Thessalonican church (2 Thess. 3:6ff).

Paul used the words "labor and travail." J. B. Phillips translated these words "our struggles and hard work." "Toil and hardship" would be another translation. It was not easy to make tents and minister the Word at the same time. No wonder Paul toiled "night and day" (Acts 20:31). He toiled because he loved the believers and wanted to help them as much as possible. "For I seek not yours, but you: for the children ought not to lay up for the parents, but the parents for the children" (2 Cor. 12:14).

His walk (v. 10). Fathers must live so that they are good examples to their children. He could call the Thessalonican believers as witnesses that his life had been exemplary in every way. None of the members of the assembly could accuse Paul of being a poor example. Furthermore, God had witnessed Paul's life, and Paul was not afraid to call God as a witness that he had lived a dedicated life, while caring for the church family.

His life was holy. In the Greek, this means to "carefully fulfill the duties God gives to a person." Our word *pious* is close to it, if you think of piety at its best and not as some fake kind of religion. This same word is applied to the character of God in Revelation 15:4 and 16:5.

His life was also righteous. This refers to integrity, uprightness of character, and behavior. This is not the "righteousness, which is of the law" but the practical righteousness that God works out in our lives as we yield to Him (Phil. 3:4–10).

Paul's life was also unblamable. Literally, this word means "not able to find fault in." His enemies might accuse him, but no one could level any charge against Paul and prove it. Christians are supposed to be "blameless and harmless" as they live in this world (Phil. 2:15).

His words (vv. 11–12). A father must not only support the family by working and teach the family by being a good example, He must also take time to speak to the family members. Paul knew the importance of teaching these new believers the truths that would help them grow in the Lord.

Paul dealt with each of the believers *personally.* "For you know that we dealt with each of you as a father deals with his own children" (1 Thess. 2:11 NIV). As busy as he was, Paul still had time for personal counseling with the members of the assembly. While it is good for church leaders to address the larger group, spending time with people on a one-to-one basis is also needed. Our Lord was never too busy to speak to individuals, even though He preached to great multitudes. To be sure, this is difficult and demanding work. But it is rewarding work that glorifies God.

Paul *encouraged* the new believers. This is what a father does with his children, for children are easily discouraged. New Christians need someone to encourage them in the Lord. The word *exhorting* in our Authorized Version means "to call to one's side, to encourage." It does not mean that Paul scolded them. Rather, it means he encouraged them to go on with the Lord.

I once received a letter from a radio listener who thanked me for the encouragement of the messages she had heard. "When we go to church," she wrote, "all our pastor does is scold us and whip us. We really get tired of this. It's refreshing to hear some words of encouragement!"

Paul also *comforted* them. This word carries the same idea of "encouragement," with the emphasis on *activity.* Paul not only made them feel better, but he made them want to *do* better. A father must not pamper a child; rather, he must encourage the child to go right back and try over again. Christian encouragement must not become an anesthesia that puts us to sleep. It must be a stimulant that awakens us to do better.

Finally, Paul *charged* them. This word means that Paul "testified to them" out of his own experience with the Lord. It carries the idea of giving personal witness. Sometimes we go through difficulties so that we may share with new Christians what the Lord has done. God "comforts us in all our troubles, so that we can comfort those in any trouble with the comfort we ourselves have received from God" (2 Cor. 1:4 NIV).

We who are parents know that our children (especially teenagers) do not like to hear us say, "Now, back when I was a kid...." But this is an important part of training a family. It is a wonderful thing when a "spiritual father" can encourage and help his "children" out of his own experience with the Lord. "Come, ye children, hearken unto me: I will teach you the fear of the Lord" (Ps. 34:11).

What was the purpose for this fatherly ministry to the believers? His aim was that his children might "walk worthy of God" (1 Thess. 2:12). Just as a father wants to be proud of his children, so the Lord wants to get glory through the lives of His children. "I was very glad to find some of your children walking in truth" (2 John 4 NASB). Paul ministered to them in such a personal way because he was teaching them how to walk.

Every child must learn how to walk. He must have good models to follow. Paul admonished them to walk "worthy of the Lord" (see Col. 1:10 and Phil. 1:27). We are to walk worthy of the calling we have in Christ Jesus (Eph. 4:1). God has called us; we are saved by grace. We are a part of His kingdom and glory. One day we shall enter the eternal kingdom and share His glory. This assurance ought to govern our lives and make us want to please the Lord.

The verb in 1 Thessalonians 2:12 is in the present tense: "who is continually calling you." God called us to salvation (2 Thess. 2:13–14), and He is constantly calling us to a life of holiness and obedience. "But as he which hath called you is holy, so be ye holy in all manner of conversation [behavior]; because it is written, 'Be ye holy, for I am holy'" (1 Peter 1:15–16).

This passage gives us a beautiful example of New Testament follow-up. Paul has shown us how to raise the babies. We must be faithful stewards, loving mothers, and concerned fathers. If we are not faithful to God, we may find ourselves becoming doting mothers and pampering fathers. Children need discipline as well as love. In fact, discipline is one evidence of love.

No wonder the church at Thessalonica prospered in spite of persecution, and shared the gospel with others for miles around. They had been born right (1 Thess. 1) and nurtured right (1 Thess. 2). This is a good example for us to follow.

CHAPTER FOUR
1 Thessalonians 2:13–20
GROWING PAINS

It was not easy to be a Christian in Thessalonica, where believers faced persecution and suffering. Their situation explains Paul's choice of words: affliction (1 Thess. 1:6; 3:3), which means "pressure from circumstances"; suffered (1 Thess. 2:14), the same word used for our Lord's sufferings; persecuted (1 Thess. 2:15), meaning "driven out and rejected"; contrary (1 Thess. 2:15), used of winds that blow against and hinder progress; and hindered (1 Thess. 2:18), which pictures a road so broken up that travel is blocked.

Yet in the midst of suffering, the Thessalonian Christians experienced joy. They received Paul's ministry of the Word "in much affliction, with joy of the Holy Spirit" (1 Thess. 1:6). Paul certainly was burdened for his brethren who were going through suffering, and yet he also had joy (1 Thess. 2:19–20). It was a fulfillment of our Lord's promise, "In the world ye shall have tribulation: but be of good cheer; I have overcome the world" (John 16:33).

Churches do experience "growing pains" as they seek to win the lost and glorify the Lord. We may not experience the same kind of political and religious persecution that the early Christians suffered (though in some parts of the world today the persecution is just as intense as it was then). Yet if we are living "godly in Christ Jesus," we will suffer for His sake (2 Tim. 3:12). In this paragraph, Paul explained the divine resources we have in times of suffering and persecution.

God's Word Within Us (2:13)
The church has been founded on the Word of God (1 Thess. 1:6), the message of the gospel of Jesus Christ. The same Word that brings us salvation also enables us to live for Christ and endure suffering for His sake. Paul was thankful that the saints in Thessalonica had the right spiritual attitudes toward the Word of God. This helped them endure in the hour of suffering.

They appreciated the Word. They did not receive it as the word of men; they received it as the Word of God. We must never treat the Bible as any other book, for the Bible is different in origin, character, content, and cost. The Bible is the Word of God. It was inspired by the Spirit of God (2 Tim. 3:16) and written by men of God who were used by the Spirit (2 Peter 1:20–21). God's Word is holy, pure, and perfect (Ps. 19:7–9). The Bible was written at great cost, not only to the writers, but to Jesus Christ who became Man that the Word of God might be given to us.

The way a Christian treats his Bible shows how he regards Jesus Christ. He is the living Word (John 1:1, 14), and the Bible is the written Word, but *in essence* they are the same. Both are bread (Matt. 4:4;

John 6:48), light (Ps. 119:105; John 8:12), and truth (John 14:6; 17:17). The Holy Spirit gave birth to Jesus Christ through a holy woman (Luke 1:35), and He gave birth to the Bible through holy men of God (2 Peter 1:20–21). Jesus Christ is the eternal Son of God forever (Rom. 1:25), and the Word of God will live forever (Ps. 119:89; 1 Peter 1:23, 25).

It may be a personal prejudice, but I dislike seeing a Bible on the floor or at the bottom of a stack of books. If I am carrying several books with my Bible, I try to remember to put the Bible on the top. If we appreciate the Bible as the inspired Word of God, then we will reveal this appreciation in our treatment of the Bible.

Would you rather have your Bible than *food?* Job said, "I have esteemed the words of his mouth more than my necessary food" (Job 23:12). God's Word is *bread* (Matt. 4:4), *milk* and *meat* (Heb. 5:11–14), and even *honey* (Ps. 119:103). Mary chose the Word, but her sister Martha got involved in making a meal (Luke 10:38–42). Mary got the blessing while Martha lost the victory.

Would you rather have God's Word than *money?* The believer who wrote Psalm 119 made it clear that God's Word meant more to him than "all riches" (Ps. 119:14), "thousands of gold and silver" (Ps. 119:72), "fine gold" (Ps. 119:127), and even "great spoil" (Ps. 119:162).

I recall a young couple I sought to help in one of my churches. They had a lovely little son, but they were very careless about attending church and Sunday school. The little boy was not getting the Christian training he needed. A visit to the home told me why: the father wanted more money and so he worked on Sundays to make double time. He did not *have* to work on the Lord's Day, but he wanted the money rather than God's Word. He earned more money, but he was never able to keep it. The little son became ill and the extra money went to doctors.

Would you rather have God's Word than *sleep?* "My eyes anticipate the right watches, that I may meditate on Thy Word" (Ps. 119:148 NASB). The Jews had three night watches: sunset to ten, ten to two, and two until dawn. The psalmist gave up sleep three times each right that he might spend time with the Word. But some Christians cannot get out of bed on Sunday morning to study the Word.

If we are going to be victorious in suffering, we must appreciate the Word. But there is a second attitude we must show toward the Bible.

They appropriated the Word. Paul used two different words for "received": the first means simply "to accept from another," while the second means "to welcome." One means "the hearing of the ear," while the other means "the hearing of the heart." The believers at Thessalonica did not only *hear* the Word; they took it into their inner man and made it a part of their lives.

The Lord Jesus repeatedly warned people about the wrong kind of hearing, and His warnings are still needed. "Who hath ears to hear, let him hear" (Matt. 13:9). In other words, "Take heed that you hear." Use every opportunity you have to hear the Word of God.

But He gave another warning in Mark 4:24: "Take heed *what* ye hear." How often believers hear the Word of God in Sunday school and church and then get in their cars, turn on the radio, and listen to programs that help erase the impressions made by the Word. When we visited church congregations in Great Britain, my wife and I were impressed with their practice of sitting down after the benediction. They meditated on the Word and allowed the Spirit to minister to them. This is far better than rushing out of church and joking with friends.

Our Lord's third warning is in Luke 8:18: "Take heed therefore *how* ye hear." Many people are careless hearers and cannot apply themselves to listen to the teaching of God's Word. These people have "itching ears" and want religious entertainment (2 Tim. 4:3). Some of them are "dull of hearing" (Heb. 5:11), too lazy to apply themselves and pay attention. One of these days our churches will be hungry because of a famine "for hearing the words of the Lord" (Amos 8:11). Too many churches have substituted entertainment for the preaching of God's Word, and many people no longer welcome the Word of God.

How do we appropriate the Word? By understanding it and receiving it into our hearts, and by meditating on it so that it becomes part of the inner man. Meditation is to the spiritual life what digestion is to the physical life. If you did not digest your food, you would die. It takes time to meditate, but it is the only way to appropriate the Word and grow.

They applied the Word. They obeyed the Word by faith, and the Word went to work in their lives. It is not enough to appreciate the Bible, or even to appropriate the Bible. We must apply the Word in our lives and be hearers and doers of the Word (James 1:19–25).

The Word of God has in it the power to accomplish the will of God. "For nothing is impossible with God" (Luke 1:37 NIV). It has well been said, "God's commandments are God's enablements." Jesus commanded the crippled man to stretch out his hand—the very thing the man could not do. Yet that word of command gave him the power to obey. He trusted the word, obeyed, and was made whole (Mark 3:1–5). When we believe God's Word and obey, He releases power—divine energy—that works in our lives to fulfill His purposes.

The Word of God within us is a great source of power in times of testing and suffering. If we appreciate the Word (the heart), appropriate the Word (the mind), and apply the Word (the will), then the whole person will be controlled by God's Word and He will give us the victory.

God's People around Us (2:14–16)

In my pastoral work, I often found that suffering people can become very self-centered and think that they are the only ones going through the furnace. Everyone goes through the normal human suffering such as sickness, pain, and bereavement. But I am referring to the suffering we endure *because we are Christians.*

Perhaps your family has disowned you because of your faith, or perhaps you have been bypassed for a promotion at work because you are a Christian. These experiences hurt, but they are not ours alone. Other Christians are going through the same trials, and many, in other parts of the world, face much greater difficulty.

Not only were the Thessalonian saints imitators of the Lord and of Paul (1 Thess. 1:6), but they also became imitators of the Jewish believers in their experience of persecution. The saints in Judea suffered at the hands of the Jews, and the saints in Thessalonica suffered at the hands of the Gentiles. But keep in mind that even this Gentile persecution was encouraged by the Jewish unbelievers (Acts 17:5, 13). Jesus promised that this would happen (John 15:18–27).

Was Paul giving evidence of "religious bigotry" when he accused the Jews of killing Jesus Christ and persecuting the Christians? No, he was simply stating a fact of history. Nowhere does the Bible accuse *all* Jews of what *a few Jews* did in Jerusalem and Judea when Christ was crucified and the church founded. The Romans also participated in the trial and death of Christ, and, for that matter, it was *our sins* that sent Him to the cross (Isa. 53:6). There is no place in the Christian faith for anti-Semitism. Paul himself loved his fellow Jews and sought to help them (Acts 24:17; Rom. 9:1–5).

God called Israel to be a blessing to all the world (Gen. 12:1–3; 22:18). Through Israel He gave the promises and the covenants, and the Word of God, and through Israel, Jesus Christ the Savior came into the world. "Salvation is of the Jews" (John 4:22). The first Christians were Jews, as was Paul, the greatest Christian missionary.

Why, then, did the leaders of Israel officially reject Jesus Christ and persecute His followers? *They were only repeating the sins of their fathers.* Their ancestors had persecuted the prophets long before Jesus came to earth (Matt. 5:10–12). They could not see that their law was only a temporary preparation for God's new covenant of grace. By rejecting God's truth, they protected their man-made traditions (Mark 7:1–8). Our Lord's parable in Luke 20:9–19 explained their sinful attitudes.

The sad thing was that Israel was filling up their sins (1 Thess. 2:16) and storing up wrath for the day of judgment. This image is used in Genesis 15:16, and Jesus used it in His sermon against the Pharisees (Matt. 23:32). God patiently waits as sinners rebel against Him, and He watches as their measure of sin and judgment fills up. When the time is up, God's patience will end and judgment will fall.

In one sense, judgment had already fallen on Israel; for they were a scattered people, and their nation in

Palestine was under Roman rule (see Deut. 28:15ff). But an even greater judgment was to fall in the future; for in AD 70 the Roman armies besieged Jerusalem, destroyed the city and the temple, and ended the period of God's patience with His people during the ministry of the apostles (see Matt. 22:1–11). It is tragic but true that the righteous suffered because of the sins of the wicked.

Paul encouraged the suffering Christians by assuring them that their experiences were not new or isolated. Others had suffered before them and were even then suffering with them. The churches in Judea had not been exterminated by suffering; if anything, they had been purified and increased. But the persecutors were filling up the measure of wrath to be heaped on their heads. Saints have been saved to the uttermost (Heb. 7:25), but sinners will experience wrath to the uttermost (1 Thess. 2:16).

Here is one of the great values of the local church: we stand together in times of difficulty and encourage one another. It was when Elijah isolated himself from the other faithful Israelites that he became discouraged and wanted to quit. One reason Paul sent Timothy back to Thessalonica was to encourage the believers (1 Thess. 3:1–4). A lonely saint is very vulnerable to the attacks of Satan. We need each other in the battles of life.

God's Glory before Us (2:17–20)
Paul was not ashamed to state his affection for the Thessalonian Christians. He felt as though he had been "orphaned" from them (1 Thess. 2:17) since he was their spiritual mother and father (1 Thess. 2:7, 11). Paul wanted to remain there longer to help ground them in the faith, but the enemy drove him out. However, his absence was only physical; he was still with them in heart (see Phil. 1:7).

Paul made every effort possible to return to them, though Satan was "breaking up the road and putting up obstacles" (literal meaning of "hindered" in 1 Thess. 2:18). Paul had the same kind of deep desire to be with them as Jesus had to be with His disciples before His death (Luke 22:15).

But Paul did not look back and give in to regret and remorse. Instead, he looked ahead and rejoiced. For the Christian, the best is yet to come. Paul looked ahead by faith and saw his friends in the presence of Jesus Christ in glory.

In times of trouble and testing, it is important that we take the long view of things. Paul lived in the future tense, as well as in the present. His actions were governed by what God would do in the future. He knew that Jesus Christ would return and reward him for his faithful ministry; and on that day, the saints from Thessalonica would bring glory to God and joy to Paul's heart. As the familiar song says, "It will be worth it all when we see Jesus."

The fact that we shall one day stand at the Judgment Seat of Christ ought to motivate us to be faithful in spite of difficulties. We must remember that *faithfulness* is the important thing (1 Cor. 4:2). At the judgment seat of Christ, our works will be judged and rewards will be given (Rom. 14:10–12; 1 Cor. 4:1–5; 2 Cor. 5:9–10). In his letters, Paul often pictured these rewards as *crowns.* The word used signified the "victor's crown" at the races, not the royal crown of the king. It is the word *stephanos* from which we get the names "Stephen" and "Stephanie."

Paul did not say that he would receive a crown, though this is suggested. He said that *the saints themselves* would be his crown when he met them at the judgment seat. To be sure, some of the believers in the church were not living as they should, and some were a burden to Paul. But when he looked ahead and saw them in glory, they brought joy to his heart.

This joy of greeting believers in heaven also brings with it a solemn warning: we will lose joy if we go to heaven emptyhanded. The Christian who has not sincerely tried to win others to Christ will not experience this glory and joy when Jesus Christ returns. It is not enough to "wait for his Son" (1 Thess. 1:10). We must also witness for God and work for His Son, so that when we get to heaven, we will have trophies to present for His glory. There is a special joy and reward for the soul-winner (Dan. 12:3).

There is also a crown for the believer who subdues his body and keeps it controlled for the glory of God (1 Cor. 9:24–27). Self-control is produced by the Spirit (Gal. 5:23). Since our bodies are God's temples, we must be careful not to defile them. The ultimate in giving the body to God is dying for His sake; and for this there is a crown (Rev. 2:10). Those who lovingly look for Christ's appearing will receive the "crown of righteousness" (2 Tim. 4:8). The faithful pastor can anticipate the "crown of glory" (1 Peter 5:4).

We must never look on future rewards as a means of showing up the other saints. Like the elders described in Revelation 4:4 (a picture of the glorified church), we will worship the Lord and lay our crowns at His feet (Rev. 4:10). After all, our work was done in his power and for His glory, so He deserves all the praise.

The fact that God promises rewards to us is another evidence of His grace. God could demand our service simply on the basis of all He has done for us. Our motive for serving Him is love. In His grace, He gives us rewards so that we may have something to give Him in return.

When the Christians at Thessalonica read this letter, it must have encouraged them tremendously. They were going through intense persecution and suffering, and perhaps some of them were tempted to give up.

"Don't give up!" Paul encouraged them. "Lay hold of the spiritual resources you have in Jesus Christ. You have the Word of God within you, the people of God around you, and the glory of God before you. There is no need to give up."

CHAPTER FIVE
1 Thessalonians 3:1–13
TAKE A STAND!

Before a child can walk, he must learn to stand. Usually the father and mother teach the child to stand and then to walk. Paul was "spiritual parent" to these believers, but he had been forced to leave Thessalonica. How, then, could he help these young Christians learn to stand in the trials of life?

In the first two chapters, Paul explained how the church was born and nurtured. Now he dealt with the next step in maturity: how the church was to stand. The key word in this chapter is *establish* (1 Thess. 3:2, 13). The key thought is expressed in 1 Thessalonians 3:8: "For now we live, if ye stand fast in the Lord."

Paul explained three ministries that he performed to help these new Christians become firmly established.

He Sent Them a Helper (3:1–5)
When Paul and his friends left Thessalonica, they went to Berea and ministered the Word. But the troublemakers from Thessalonica followed them and stirred up opposition. Paul left for Athens while Silas and Timothy remained at Berea (see Acts 17:10–15). Apparently, Timothy did join Paul in Athens (note the "we" in 1 Thess. 3:1–2), but Paul sent him back to Thessalonica to help the young church that was going through tribulations. Several important factors were involved in this move.

Paul's concern (v. 1). The "wherefore" that opens this chapter refers to 1 Thessalonians 2:17–20, where Paul expressed his great love for the believers. It was because of this love that he could not abandon them when they needed spiritual help. Paul was not only an evangelist; he was also a pastor. He knew that soul-winning was but one part of the commission God gave him. These new believers must also be taught and established in the faith.

Instead, Paul chose to be left alone in Athens so that Timothy could return to Thessalonica and establish the saints. The word translated "left" in 1 Thessalonians 3:1 means "to leave loved ones at death." In 1 Thessalonians 2:17 he said that he felt "orphaned" from his friends in Thessalonica, and the Greek word can also mean "bereaved." Paul was not a "hireling shepherd" who abandoned the sheep when there was danger (John 10:12–13). To leave these new believers was like an experience of bereavement.

This is a good lesson for Christian workers today. Paul so loved the Thessalonian believers that he would have risked his own life to return to them. He so loved the saints at Philippi that he was willing to stay out of heaven in order to encourage them (Phil. 1:22–26). He wanted to give of himself and his resources for them, as a parent provides for loved children. "I will very gladly spend and be spent for you" (2 Cor. 12:15).

Timothy's character (v. 2). Not every believer is equipped to establish other Christians in the faith. Ideally, every Christian should be mature enough to help other Christians grow in the Lord and learn to stand on their own two feet. Unfortunately, some Christians are like those described in Hebrews 5:11–14. They have gone backward in their spiritual walk and have forgotten the basic truths of the Word. Instead of teaching others, they themselves need to be taught again. They are going through a second childhood spiritually.

Timothy was the ideal man to send to the church to help them stand firm. Timothy and Titus were Paul's "special agents" whom he used as troubleshooters whenever the churches had problems. Paul sent Timothy to Corinth to help straighten out the problems there (1 Cor. 16:10–11). He also planned to send Timothy to help the saints in Philippi (Phil. 2:19–23).

What kind of a person can help younger believers grow in the Lord? To begin with, *he must be a Christian himself:* "Timothy, our brother" (1 Thess. 3:2). We cannot lead another where we have not been ourselves, nor can we share that which we do not possess. Paul had led Timothy to faith in Christ (1 Tim. 1:2) so that he was truly a brother.

But Timothy was also *a minister.* This is simply the Greek word for a servant. Our English word *deacon* comes from this word *diakonos.* Timothy was not afraid to work. He had faithfully served with Paul (Phil. 2:22) and knew how to minister in the churches. It is a demanding thing to establish new Christians. They have many problems and often do not grow as fast as we think they should. Teaching them requires love and patience, and Timothy had these qualities.

Timothy was a good *team man;* he was a "fellow worker." He did not try to run the show himself and get people to follow him. To begin with, he was a fellow worker with God. It was God who worked in and through Timothy to accomplish His work (see 1 Cor. 3:9 and Phil. 2:13).

But Timothy was also a fellow worker with the other believers. He obeyed Paul and left Athens for Thessalonica. He returned to Paul in Corinth with news about the Thessalonian church. No wonder Paul wrote of him: "For I have no man like-minded, who will naturally care for your state" (Phil. 2:20).

The church's conflict (vv. 3–5). The trials and testings that come to our lives as Christians are not accidents—they are *appointments.* We must expect to "suffer for his sake" (Phil. 1:29). Persecution is not foreign to the believer (1 Peter 4:12ff), but a normal part of the Christian life. Paul had repeatedly told them this while he was with them. We must warn new believers that the way is not easy as they seek to live for Christ, otherwise, when trials come, these babes in Christ will be discouraged and defeated.

Of course, behind these persecutions is Satan, the enemy of the Christian (1 Thess. 3:5). He is the tempter, and he seeks to ruin our faith. Note the emphasis on *faith* in this chapter (1 Thess. 3:5–7, 10). As a roaring lion, Satan stalks believers; and we must resist him "steadfast in the faith" (1 Peter 5:8–9). When Satan tempted Eve, he began by weakening her faith in God: "Yea, hath God said?" (Gen. 3:1). As a serpent, Satan deceives (2 Cor. 11:3); as a lion, he devours (1 Peter 5:8). He will use any means to attack the Christian and weaken his faith in God.

The word *moved* in 1 Thessalonians 3 is interesting. It literally means "to wag the tail, to fawn over." The idea is that Satan often flatters the believer in order to lead him astray. Satan told Eve she would be like God if she ate of the tree, and she fell for his flattery. Satan is more dangerous when he flatters than when he frowns.

Timothy's task was to establish these believers and encourage (comfort) them in their faith. It is faith in God that keeps our feet on the ground when the enemy attacks. Without faith in God, we are defeated. "This is the victory that overcometh the world, even our faith" (1 John 5:4).

He Wrote Them a Letter (3:6–8)
Timothy met Paul at Corinth (Acts 18:5) and gave him the glad news that things were going well at Thessalonica. The phrase "brought us good tidings" is the exact equivalent of "preaching the good news of the gospel." The report from Timothy was, to Paul, like hearing the gospel.

Timothy reported that the new believers were standing firm in spite of persecution. They did not believe the lies that the enemy had told about Paul, but they still held him in the highest esteem in love.

Paul's response was to write them this letter. Paul wrote some letters that are not a part of the New Testament (1 Cor. 5:9), but the two letters to the Thessalonican church are a part of God's inspired Word.

This suggests that God's Word is one of the best tools for establishing new Christians in the faith. "So then, brothers, stand firm and hold to the teachings we passed on to you, whether by word of mouth or by letter" (2 Thess. 2:15 NIV). When Jesus was tempted by Satan, He used the Word of God to defeat him (Matt. 4:1–11). Paul admonished the Ephesian believers to take "the sword of the Spirit, which is the Word of God" (Eph. 6:17) in their battle against Satan and his demonic assistants.

The Bible is able to establish us because it is inspired of God (2 Tim. 3:16). It is not simply a book of religious ideas or good moral advice; it is the very Word of God. It is "profitable for doctrine, for reproof, for correction, for instruction in righteousness." It has well been said that *doctrine* tells us what is right, *reproof* tells us what is not right, *correction* tells us how to get right, and *instruction* tells us how to stay right.

First Thessalonians is saturated with Bible doctrines. Every major doctrine of the faith is touched on in these brief chapters. There are dozens of references

to God the Father and Jesus Christ, and at least four references to the Holy Spirit (1 Thess. 1:5–6; 4:8; 5:19). In this epistle, Paul dealt with sin and salvation, the doctrine of the church, the work of the ministry, and especially the doctrine of the last things. Since Paul did not remain in Thessalonica very long, it is remarkable that he taught his converts so much.

Dr. R. W. Dale was pastor of Carr's Lane Congregational Church in England for nearly fifty years. He began a series of sermons on basic Bible doctrine, knowing that his members could not stand firm in their faith if they did not know what they believed or why they believed it. A fellow pastor said to Dr. Dale, "They will never take it." But Dale replied, "They will *have* to take it!" And they did, to the strengthening of the church.

When I became a Christian, churches did not have regular follow-up courses for new converts such as we have today. My "follow-up course" was a series of Bible studies from the book of Hebrews, led by a gifted layman and taught in his living room. Much of what was taught was over my head as a new believer. But what I did learn grounded me in the Word and established me in the faith.

A working knowledge of the Bible is essential for spiritual growth and stability. God's Word is *food* to nourish us (Matt. 4:4), *light* to guide us (Ps. 119:105), and a *weapon* to defend us (Eph. 6:17). "Thus saith the Lord!" is our sure foundation. One reason God has established local churches is that believers might grow in the Word and, in turn, help others to grow (2 Tim. 2:2; Eph. 4:11–16).

Paul sent them a man, and that man established them in the Word. Paul ministered to them in a third way.

He Prayed for Them (3:9–13)
The Word of God and prayer should go together. The prophet Samuel told the people of Israel, "God forbid that I should sin against the Lord in ceasing to pray for you: but I will teach you the good and the right way" (1 Sam. 12:23). Peter said, "But we [the apostles] will give ourselves continually to prayer, and to the ministry of the word" (Acts 6:4). Paul had this same emphasis: "And now, brethren, I commend you to God [prayer], and to the word of his grace, which is able to build you up" (Acts 20:32).

Jesus prayed for His disciples, just as Paul prayed for the Thessalonian Christians, that their faith would not fail (Luke 22:31–32). I ministered for several weeks in Kenya and Zaire, and when I arrived home, I was more convinced than ever that the greatest need of missionaries and national churches is *prayer*. We must also pray for young Christians here at home. It is not enough to teach them Bible truth; we must also support them in our prayers.

Paul prayed for three specific requests. First, he prayed *that their faith might mature* (1 Thess. 3:10). Paul asked God to make it possible for him to minister to them personally, but God did not answer that request. Paul longed to see them again; he longed to minister to them and help bring their faith to maturity. The word translated "perfect" has the meaning of "adjust, equip, furnish." It is even used for the mending of nets (Mark 1:19). Our faith never reaches perfection; there is always need for adjustment and growth. We go "from faith to faith" (Rom. 1:17).

Abraham is a good illustration of this principle. God called him to the land of Canaan, and when he arrived, he discovered a famine. God permitted that famine so that Abraham's faith might be tested. Unfortunately, Abraham failed the test and went down to Egypt for help.

Each step of the way, God brought circumstances to bear on Abraham that forced him to trust God and grow in his faith. Faith is like a muscle: it gets stronger with use. Abraham had problems with his worldly nephew, Lot. He also had problems with his wife and her handmaid, Hagar. The ultimate test of faith came when God asked Abraham to sacrifice his beloved son, Isaac.

Faith that cannot be tested cannot be trusted. God tries our faith, not to destroy it, but to develop it. Had Abraham not learned to trust God in the famine, he could never have trusted Him in the other difficulties. Paul prayed that the suffering Christians in Thessalonica might grow in their faith, and God answered his prayer. Paul wrote in his second letter, "We are bound to thank God always for you, brethren … because that your faith groweth exceedingly" (2 Thess. 1:3).

Paul's second request was *that their love might abound* (1 Thess. 3:12). Times of suffering can be times of selfishness. Persecuted people often become very self-centered and demanding. What life does to us depends on what life finds in us; and nothing reveals the true inner man like the furnace of affliction. Some people build walls in times of trial and shut themselves off. Others build bridges and draw closer to the Lord and His people. This was Paul's prayer for these believers, and God answered it: "The charity of every one of you all toward each other aboundeth" (2 Thess. 1:3). Our growing faith in God ought to result in a growing love for others. We are "taught of God to love one another" (1 Thess. 4:9), and some of these lessons are best learned in the school of suffering. Joseph suffered for thirteen years because of his brothers' envy and persecution. Yet he learned to love them in spite of their hatred. The Jewish legalists persecuted Paul from city to city, yet Paul so loved his people that he willingly would have died for them (Rom. 9:1–3).

When I counsel young couples in preparation for marriage, I often ask the man, "If your wife became paralyzed three weeks after you were married, do you love her enough to stay with her and care for her?" True love deepens in times of difficulty; shallow romance disappears when difficulties appear.

But true Christian love is shown not only to believers, but also "toward all men" (1 Thess. 3:12). We love one another, but we also love the lost and our enemies. Abounding love must not be bound. It must be free to expand and touch all men.

Paul's third request was for *holiness of life* (1 Thess. 3:13). Again, it is the return of Jesus Christ that motivates the believer to live a holy life. Our Lord's return is also a source of stability in the Christian life. Where there is stability, there can be sanctity, and where there is holiness, there is assurance. The two go together.

Notice that Paul's prayers for his friends were not careless or occasional. He prayed "night and day"; he prayed "exceedingly," which is the same word translated "exceeding abundantly" in Ephesians 3:20. True prayer is hard work. Epaphras must have learned from Paul how to pray for people: "always laboring fervently … that ye may stand perfect and complete in all the will of God" (Col. 4:12).

The entire Trinity is involved in this prayer. Paul addressed the Father and Son in 1 Thessalonians 3:11. In verse 12 "the Lord" may refer to the Holy Spirit, since "our Lord" at the end of 1 Thessalonians 3:13 certainly refers to Jesus Christ. If this is so, then this is the only prayer I know of in the New Testament directed to the Holy Spirit. The Bible pattern of prayer is to the Father, through the Son, and in the Spirit. Since the Holy Spirit is the Sanctifier of the believer, and this is a prayer for holy living, the address is proper.

Paul ended 1 Thessalonians 2 with a reference to the place of the saints at the return of Christ, and he ended this chapter in the same way. He prayed that his converts might stand blameless and holy before God at Christ's return. Since all believers will be transformed to be like Christ when He returns (1 John 3:2), Paul could not be referring to our personal condition in heaven. He was referring to our lives here on earth as they will be reviewed at the Judgment Seat of Christ. We will never face our sins in heaven, for they are remembered against us no more (Rom. 8:1; Heb. 10:14–18). But our works will be tested, and you cannot separate conduct from character.

Paul's prayer teaches us how to pray not only for new believers, but for *all* believers. We should pray that their faith will mature, their love grow, and their character and conduct be holy and blameless before God. "And every man that hath this hope in him [Christ] purifieth himself, even as he is pure" (1 John 3:3).

As we review this chapter, we see how important it is to care for new Christians. Leading someone to Christ is not enough. We must also lead him on in the Christian life and help him get established. If he is not established, he will fall when the winds of persecution start to blow. If he cannot stand, he will never learn to walk.

What shall we do? We can be an encouragement and stand at his side as he matures. We can share the Word of God. We can pray. This is what Paul did— and it worked.

CHAPTER SIX
1 Thessalonians 4:1–12
HOW TO PLEASE YOUR FATHER

Along with jogging, walking has become a popular exercise and outdoor sport. I often see individuals and entire families enjoying a walk in the park or in the forest preserves. When driving on the highway, I sometimes wave to "walking parties" heading for some distant rendezvous.

The Christian life can be compared to a walk. In fact, this is one of Paul's favorite pictures: "Walk worthy of the vocation wherewith ye are called" (Eph. 4:1); "walk not as other Gentiles walk" (Eph. 4:17); "walk in love" (Eph. 5:2); "walk as children of light" (Eph. 5:8).

The Christian life begins with a step of faith. But that step leads to a walk of faith: "For we walk by faith, not by sight" (2 Cor. 5:7). Walking suggests progress, and we must make progress in the Christian life (Phil. 3:13–16; Heb. 6:1). Walking also demands strength, and God has promised, "As thy days, so shall thy strength be" (Deut. 33:25).

But we must be sure to "walk in the light" for the enemy has put traps and detours to catch us (1 John 1:5–7). Of course, at the end of life's walk, we will step into the very presence of the Lord. "And Enoch walked with God, and he was not, for God took him" (Gen. 5:24).

Paul described a threefold walk for the Christian to follow.

Walk in Holiness (4:1–8)

The moral climate in the Roman Empire was not healthy. Immorality was a way of life; and, thanks to slavery, people had the leisure time to indulge in the latest pleasures. The Christian message of holy living was new to that culture, and it was not easy for these young believers to fight the temptations around them. Paul gave four reasons why they should live a holy life and abstain from sensual lusts.

To please God (v. 1). Everybody lives to please somebody. Many people live to please themselves. They have no sensitivity to the needs of others. "The soul of a journey," wrote William Hazlitt, "is liberty, perfect liberty, to think, feel, do just as one pleases." That advice may work for a vacation, but it could never work in the everyday affairs of life. Christians cannot go through life pleasing only themselves (Rom. 15:1).

We must also be careful when it comes to pleasing others. It is possible to both please others and honor God, but it is also possible to dishonor God. "For if I yet pleased men, I should not be the servant of Christ" (Gal. 1:10). This had been Paul's attitude when he ministered in Thessalonica. "Even so we speak, not as pleasing men but God, who trieth our hearts" (1 Thess. 2:4).

Pleasing God ought to be the major motive of the Christian life. Children should live to please their father. The Holy Spirit works in our lives "both to will and to do of his good pleasure" (Phil. 2:13). Enoch walked with God, and before God called him to heaven, Enoch "had this testimony, that he pleased God" (Heb. 11:5). Jesus said, "I do always those things that please him" (John 8:29).

Pleasing God means much more than simply doing God's will. It is possible to obey God and yet not please Him. Jonah is a case in point. He obeyed God and did what he was commanded, but his heart was not in it. God blessed His Word, but He could not bless His servant. So Jonah sat outside the city of Nineveh angry with everybody, including the Lord! Our obedience should be "not with eyeservice, as menpleasers, but as the servants of Christ, doing the will of God from the heart" (Eph. 6:6).

How do we know what pleases God? How do we know what pleases an earthly father? By listening to him and living with him. As we read the Word, and as we fellowship in worship and service, we get to know the heart of God, and this opens us up to the will of God.

To obey God (vv. 2–3). When he ministered in Thessalonica, Paul gave the believers the commandments of God regarding personal purity. The word *commandments* is a military term. It refers to orders handed down from superior officers. We are soldiers in God's army, and we must obey orders. "No one serving as a soldier gets involved in civilian affairs—he wants to please his commanding officer" (2 Tim. 2:4 NIV).

In 1 Thessalonians 4:3, Paul reminded these new believers that sexual immorality did not please God. God created sex, and He has the authority to govern its use. From the beginning, He established marriage as a sacred union between one man and one woman. God created sex both for the continuance of the race and for the pleasure of the marriage partners. "Marriage should be honored by all, and the marriage bed kept pure" (Heb. 13:4 NIV). God's commandments concerning sex are not for the purpose of robbing people of joy, but rather of protecting them that they might not lose their joy. "Thou shalt not commit adultery" builds a wall around marriage that makes the relationship not a prison, but a safe and beautiful garden.

We never have to seek to know the will of God in this matter, He has told us clearly. "Abstain from fornication" is His commandment, and no amount of liberal theology or modern philosophy can alter it. Throughout the Bible, God warns against sexual sin, and these warnings must be heeded. God's purpose is *our sanctification,* that we might live separated lives in purity of mind and body.

To glorify God (vv. 4–5). This is the positive side of God's commandment. Christians are supposed to be different from the unsaved. The Gentiles (unsaved) do not know God; therefore, they live ungodly lives. But we know God, and we are obligated to glorify Him in this world. "God's plan is to make you holy, and that entails first of all a clean break with sexual immorality" (1 Thess. 4:3 PH).

"Possess his vessel" in 1 Thessalonians 4:4 probably means "control his body," for our bodies are the vessels of God (see 2 Cor. 4:7; 2 Tim. 2:20–21). But it can also mean "learn to live with his own wife," for the wife is called "the weaker vessel" (1 Peter 3:7). I prefer the first interpretation, for Paul wrote to *all* Christians, not just the married ones. The Christian who commits sexual sin is sinning against his own body (1 Cor. 6:19–20), and he is robbing God of the glory He should receive through a believer's way of life.

This explains why God gives such demanding requirements for spiritual leadership in the church (1 Tim. 3). If spiritual leaders cannot rule in their own homes, how can they lead the church? If we glorify God in our bodies, then we can glorify Him in the body that is the church.

To escape the judgment of God (vv. 6–8). God is no respecter of persons; He must deal with His children when they sin (Col. 3:23–25). A church member criticized her pastor because he was preaching against sin in the lives of Christians. "After all," she said, "sin in the life of a believer is different from sin in the lives of unsaved people."

"Yes," replied the pastor, *"it is worse."*

While it is true that the Christian is not under condemnation (John 5:24; Rom. 8:1), it is also true that he is not free from the harvest of sorrow that comes when we sow to the flesh (Gal. 6:7–8). When King David committed adultery, he tried to cover his sin, but God chastened him severely. (Read Ps. 32; 51 to see what he lost during those months.) When David confessed his sins, God forgave him, *but God could not change the consequences.* David reaped what he sowed, and it was a painful experience for him.

"But I am one of God's elect!" a Christian may argue. "I belong to Him, and He can never cast me out." Election is not an excuse for sin—it is an encouragement for holiness. "For God hath not called us unto uncleanness, but unto holiness" (1 Thess. 4:7). "But as he which hath called you is holy, so be ye holy" (1 Peter 1:15). The privilege of election also involves responsibilities of obedience (Deut. 7:6, 11).

A holy walk involves a right relationship with God the Father (who called us), God the Son (who died for us), and God the Spirit (who lives within us). It is the presence of the Holy Spirit that makes our body the temple of God (1 Cor. 6:19–20). Furthermore, it is by walking in the Spirit that we get victory over the lusts of the flesh (Gal. 5:16ff.). To despise God's commandments is to invite the judgment of God and also to grieve the Spirit of God.

How does the Spirit of God help us live a clean life, free from sexual impurity? To begin with, He creates holy desires within us so that we have an appetite for God's pure Word (1 Peter 2:1–3) and not the polluted garbage of the flesh (Rom. 13:12–14). Also, He teaches us the Word and helps us to recall God's promises in times of temptation (John 14:26; Eph. 6:17). As we yield to the Spirit, He empowers us to walk in holiness

and not be detoured into the lusts of the world and the flesh. The fruit of the Spirit overcomes the works of the flesh (Gal. 5:16–26).

Paul devoted a great deal of space to this theme of sexual purity because it was a critical problem in the church of that day. *It is also a critical problem in the church today.* For many people, marriage vows are no longer considered sacred, and divorce (even among believers) is no longer governed by the Word of God. There are "gay churches" where homosexuals and lesbians "love one another" and claim to be Christians. Premarital sex and "Christian pornography" are accepted parts of the religious landscape in many places. Yet God has said, "Walk in holiness."

Walk in Harmony (4:9–10)

The transition from *holiness* to *love* is not a difficult one. Paul made this transition in his prayer recorded in 1 Thessalonians 3:11–13. Just as God's love is a holy love, so our love for God and for one another ought to motivate us to holy living. The more we live like God, the more we will love one another. If a Christian really loves his brother, he will not sin against him (1 Thess. 4:6). There are four basic words for "love" in the Greek language. *Eros* refers to physical love; it gives us our English word *erotic*. Eros love does not have to be sinful, but in Paul's day its main emphasis was sensual. This word is never used in the New Testament. Another word, *storge* (pronounced STOR-gay), refers to family love, the love of parents for their children. This word is also absent from our New Testament, although a related word is translated "kindly affectioned" in Romans 12:10.

The two words most used for love are *philia* (fil-EE--uh) and *agape* (a-GA-pay). *Philia* love is the love of deep affection, such as in friendship or even marriage. But *agape* love is the love God shows toward us. It is not simply a love based on feeling; it is expressed in our wills. Agape love treats others as God would treat them, regardless of feelings or personal preferences.

The word *philadelphia* is translated "brotherly love." Because Christians belong to the same family, and have the same Father, they should love one another. In fact, we are "taught of God to love one another." God the Father taught us to love each other when He gave Christ to die for us on the cross. "We love, because he first loved us" (1 John 4:19 NIV). God the Son taught us to love one another when He said, "A new commandment I give unto you, that ye love one another" (John 13:34). And the Holy Spirit taught us to love one another when He poured out the love of God in our hearts (Rom. 5:5) when we trusted Christ.

Have you noticed that animals do *instinctively* what is necessary to keep them alive and safe? Fish do not attend classes to learn how to swim (even though they swim in schools), and birds by nature put out their wings and flap them in order to fly. It is *nature* that determines action. Because a fish has a fish's nature, it swims; because a hawk has a hawk's nature, it flies. And because a Christian has God's nature (2 Peter 1:4), he loves, because "God is love" (1 John 4:8).

Faith, hope, and love had been the distinctive characteristics of the Thessalonican Christians from the beginning (1 Thess. 1:3). Timothy had reported the good news of their love (1 Thess. 3:6), so Paul was not exhorting them to acquire something they did not already possess. He was encouraging them to get more of what they already enjoyed. You can never have too much Christian love. Paul had prayed that their love might "increase and abound" (1 Thess. 3:12), and God answered that prayer (see 2 Thess. 1:3).

How does God cause our love to "increase more and more"? By putting us into circumstances that force us to practice Christian love. Love is the "circulatory system" of the body of Christ, but if our spiritual muscles are not exercised, the circulation is impaired. The difficulties that we believers have *with one another* are opportunities for us to grow in our love. This explains why Christians who have had the most problems with each other often end up loving one another deeply, much to the amazement of the world.

Walk in Honesty (4:11–12)

The word in 1 Thessalonians 4:12 that is translated "honestly" in our Authorized Version carries the meaning of "becomingly, in a seemly way." It is translated "decently" in 1 Corinthians 14:40: "Let all things be done decently and in order." The emphasis is on the believer's witness to those who are outside the Christian fellowship. "Them that are without" is a familiar description of unbelievers.

Christians not only have the obligation to love one another but also to be good testimonies to the people of the world. Paul's great concern was that the Thessalonican believers earn their own wages and not become freeloaders depending on the support of unbelievers. "Make it your ambition to lead a quiet life" (1 Thess. 4:11 NIV) seems like a paradox; if you are ambitious, your life will probably not be quiet. But the emphasis is on quietness of mind and heart, the inner peace that enables a man to be sufficient through faith in Christ. Paul did not want the saints running around creating problems as they earned their daily bread.

For the most part, the Greeks despised manual labor. Most of the work was done by slaves. Paul, of course, was a tentmaker, and he was careful in Thessalonica to set the example of hard work (see 1 Thess. 2:6; 2 Thess. 3:6ff.). Unfortunately, some of the new believers in the church misunderstood the doctrine of Christ's return and gave up their jobs in order to wait for His coming. This meant that they were supported by other Christians, some of whom may not have had sufficient funds for their own families. It also meant that these fanatical people could not pay their bills, and therefore they lost their testimony with the unsaved merchants.

"My wife is going to have plastic surgery," a man said to his friend. "I'm taking away all of her credit cards!" How easy it is to purchase things we do not need with money we do not have, and then lose not only our credit, but also our good Christian witness. "Therefore, if you have not been faithful in the use of unrighteous wealth, who will entrust the true riches to you?" (Luke 16:11 NASB). Churches and Christians who defend their orthodoxy but do not pay their bills have no orthodoxy to defend.

"Mind your own business and work with your hands" (1 Thess. 4:11 NIV) was what Paul commanded them. Idle people spend their time interfering with the affairs of others and getting themselves and others into trouble. "We hear that some among you are idle. They are not busy; they are busybodies" (2 Thess. 3:11 NIV). "But let none of you suffer … as a busybody in other men's matters" (1 Peter 4:15).

Believers who are about the Father's business (Luke 2:49) do not have the time—or desire—to meddle in the affairs of others. Unfortunately, even a Bible class could become an opportunity for gossip ("so that you might pray more intelligently") and a substitute for true Christian service.

As believers, we must be careful in our relationships with "those that are without." It requires spiritual grace and wisdom to have contact without contamination and to be different without being judgmental and proud. "Walk in wisdom toward them that are without" (Col. 4:5). If we lack this spiritual wisdom, we will do more harm than good.

There are several good reasons why Christians should work, not the least of which is to provide for their own families (1 Tim. 5:8). If unsaved people have to work to pay their bills, why should Christians be exempt? We also work in order to be able to give to those who have need (Eph. 4:28), but "if any would not work, neither should he eat" (2 Thess. 3:10). Work is not a curse; it is a blessing. God gave Adam work to do in Paradise. It is the toil and sweat of work that belongs to the curse, and not the work itself (Gen. 2:15; 3:17ff.).

As we review this section, we see how practical the Christian walk really is. The obedient Christian will have *a holy life* by abstaining from sexual sin; a *harmonious life* by loving the brethren; and *an honest life* by working with his hands and not meddling in the affairs of others. When unsaved people see Christ magnified in this kind of a life, they will either oppose it with envy or desire to have it for themselves. Either way, God is glorified.

CHAPTER SEVEN
1 Thessalonians 4:13–18
THE COMFORT OF HIS COMING

The pagan world in Paul's day had no hope of life after death. A typical inscription on a grave demonstrates this fact:

I was not
I became
I am not
I care not

While some of the philosophers, such as Socrates, sought to prove happiness after death, the pagan world had no word of assurance.

The believers in Thessalonica were concerned about their loved ones who had died. What if the Lord should return? Would their deceased loved ones be handicapped in any way? Will those who are alive at His coming have an advantage over the believers who have died? In this paragraph, Paul answered their questions. He based his encouragement and comfort on five fundamental facts.

Revelation: We Have God's Truth (4:13, 15a)

How can mortal man penetrate beyond the grave and find assurance and peace for his own heart? From Old Testament days till the present, mankind has tried to solve the riddle of death and the afterlife. Philosophers have wrestled with the question of immortality. Spiritists have tried to communicate with those who have gone beyond.

In our modern world, scientists have investigated the experiences of people who claimed to have died and returned to life again. They have also studied occult phenomena, hoping to find a clue to the mystery of life after death.

Paul solved the problem when he wrote, "For this we say unto you by the word of the Lord" (1 Thess. 4:15). We Christians need not wonder about death or life after death, for we have a revelation from God in His Word. Why substitute human speculation for divine revelation?

It is important to note that the revelation concerning death and the afterlife was not given all at one time. Many cults use verses from the Psalms and Ecclesiastes to "prove" their false doctrines. These verses seem to teach that the grave is the end, or that the soul "sleeps" till the resurrection. We must keep in mind that God's revelation was *gradual* and *progressive,* and that it climaxed in the coming of Christ "who abolished death and brought life and immortality to light through the gospel" (2 Tim. 1:10 NASB). We look to Christ and the New Testament for the complete revelation concerning death.

God gave Paul a special revelation concerning the resurrection and the return of Christ (see 1 Cor. 15:51–54). What Paul taught agreed with what Jesus taught (John 5:24–29; 11:21–27). And God's revelation is based on the historic fact of Christ's resurrection. Since our Savior has conquered death, we need not fear death or the future (1 Cor. 15:12ff.). The authority of God's Word gives us the assurance and comfort we need.

Return: Christ Is Coming Again (4:14–15)

We have noted the emphasis on the return of Christ in the Thessalonian letters. Paul related Christ's return to salvation (1 Thess. 1:9–10), service (1 Thess. 2:19–20), and stability (1 Thess. 3:11–13). In this paragraph, he related it to sorrow, and he showed how the doctrine of Christ's return can comfort the brokenhearted.

Paul applied the word *sleep* to those believers who died. Jesus used the same expression (John 11:11–13). Paul was careful to state that Jesus *died;* the word *sleep* is not applied to His experience. It is because He died that we need not fear death.

However, Paul did not say that the *soul* went to sleep at death. He made it clear that the soul of the believer went to be with the Lord: "them also which sleep in Jesus will God bring with him" (1 Thess. 4:14). He cannot bring them when He returns unless they are with Him. It is not the soul that sleeps; *it is the body.* The Bible definition of death is given in James 2:26: "For as the body without the spirit is dead." At death, the spirit leaves the body, and the body goes to sleep and no longer functions. The soul-spirit goes to be with the Lord, if the person has trusted Jesus Christ. "Absent from the body, and … present with the Lord" (2 Cor. 5:8).

The fact of our Lord's return is comfort to us in bereavement, because we know that He will bring with Him His people who have "died in the Lord." I recall stating to a friend, "I hear you lost your wife. I'm very sorry." He replied, "No, I didn't lose her. You can't lose something when you know where it is—*and I know where she is!*" On the authority of the Word of God, we also know what will happen: Jesus Christ will one day return and bring His people with Him.

When will this event occur? Nobody knows, and it is wrong to set dates. The fact that Paul used the pronoun "we" in 1 Thessalonians 4:15, 17 suggests that he expected to be alive when the Lord returned. Theologians call this the doctrine of the imminent return of Christ. *Imminent* means that it can happen at any moment. As Christians, we do not look for signs, nor must any special events transpire before the Lord can return. These great events will take place "in a moment, in the twinkling of an eye" (1 Cor. 15:52).

Jesus Christ will return *in the air,* and this is where we shall meet Him (1 Thess. 4:17). Suddenly, millions of people will vanish! One summer a church camp staff staged an elaborate "rapture" while the camp director was off the grounds. When he returned, everybody was missing, clothing was on the ground as though people had "passed through" it, a motorboat was circling on the lake without pilot or passengers, and everything in the kitchen was functioning without a cook. A carefully timed phone call from town ("Hey, what's happening? Everybody's missing over here!") only added to the effect. "I've got to admit," said the director, "it really shook me for a minute." Just think of what effect this event will have on a lost world!

Whether we Christians live or die, we have nothing to fear because Jesus will come either *with us* or *for us!* The fact of His return is a comfort to our hearts.

Resurrection: The Christian Dead Will Rise (4:15–16)

When Paul preached the doctrine of the resurrection to the Athenian philosophers, most of them mocked him (Acts 17:32). To the Greeks, *being rid of the body* was their great hope. Why would any man want to have his body resurrected? Furthermore, *how* could his body be resurrected, when the elements of the body would decay and become a part of the earth? To them, the doctrine of resurrection was foolish and impossible.

When Jesus Christ returns in the air, He will issue the "shout of command" and the "dead in Christ shall rise first" (1 Thess. 4:16). This does not mean that He will put the elements of the body together again, for resurrection is not "reconstruction." Paul argued for the resurrection in 1 Corinthians 15:35ff. He pointed out that the resurrection of the human body is like the growing of a plant from a seed. The flower is not the identical seed that was planted, yet there is continuity from seed to plant. Christians shall receive glorified bodies, like the glorified body of Christ (Phil. 3:20–21; 1 Cor. 15:47–58). The dead body is the "seed" that is planted in the ground; the resurrection body is the "flower" that comes from that seed.

Passages like John 5:28–29 and Revelation 20:1–6 indicate that there are *two* resurrections in the future. When Jesus Christ returns in the air, He will call to Himself only those who are saved through faith in Him. This is called "the first resurrection" or "the resurrection of life." At the end of time, just before God ushers in the new heaven and earth, there will be another resurrection. This is called "the second resurrection" or "the resurrection of judgment." Between these two events, I believe that the tribulation on earth and the thousand-year-kingdom will occur.

In Paul's day, the Pharisees believed in the resurrection of the dead, but the Sadducees did not (Acts 23:8). Jesus taught the doctrine of the resurrection and silenced the Sadducees (Matt. 22:23–33). The Old Testament Scriptures taught this doctrine (Job 14:13–15; 19:23–27; Ps. 16:9–11; Dan. 12:2). The fact that Jesus arose from the dead proves that there is a resurrection.

Three unique sounds will be involved in this event: the Lord's shout, the sound of the trumpet, and the voice of the archangel. Jesus Christ will give "a shout of command," just as He did outside the tomb of Lazarus (John 11:43). Those "in the graves shall hear his voice" (John 5:28).

First Corinthians 15:52 also relates His return to the sound of a trumpet. The Jewish people were familiar with trumpets, because trumpets were used to declare war, to announce special times and seasons, and to gather the people for a journey (see Num. 10). In the Roman Empire, trumpets were used to announce the arrival of a great person. When God gave the law to Israel, the event was preceded by a trumpet blast (Ex. 19:18–20).

Why "the voice of the archangel"? The only archangel who is named in the Bible is Michael (Jude 9), who apparently has a special ministry to Israel (Dan. 10:21; Rev. 12:7). According to Daniel 10:13, there is more than one archangel; so we cannot be sure that it will be Michael's voice. At any rate, the angelic hosts will share in the victory shout when Jesus Christ comes.

The Christian doctrine of resurrection assures us that death is not the end. The grave is not the end. The body goes to sleep, but the soul goes to be with the Lord (Phil. 1:20–24). When the Lord returns, He will bring the soul with Him, will raise the body in glory, and will unite body and soul into one being to share His glory forever. This leads us to the fourth fact that gives us comfort and assurance in the face of death.

Rapture: Living Believers Caught Up (4:17)

The word *rapture* is not used in this section, but that is the literal meaning of "caught up." The Latin word *rapto* means "to seize, to carry off," and from it we get our English word *rapture*.

I once heard the Greek scholar Dr. Kenneth S. Wuest preach on this passage and explain the various meanings of the Greek word that is translated "caught up" in 1 Thessalonians 4:17. Each of these meanings adds a special truth to the doctrine of our Lord's return.

"To catch away speedily." This is the translation in Acts 8:39, where the Spirit "caught away Philip" after he had led the Ethiopian to Christ. When the Lord returns in the air, we who are alive will be caught away quickly, in the twinkling of an eye. This means we should live each moment in the expectation of our Lord's return, lest He come and find us out of His will (1 John 3:1–3).

"To seize by force." See John 6:15. Does this suggest that Satan and his armies will try to keep us from leaving the earth? I trust it does not suggest that some of the saints will be so attached to the world that they must literally be dragged away. Like Lot being delivered from Sodom, they will be scarcely saved (Gen. 19:16).

"To claim for one's own self." This views the rapture from our Lord's point of view as He comes to claim His bride.

"To move to a new place." Paul used this word when he described his visit to heaven (2 Cor. 12:1–4). Jesus Christ has gone to prepare a home for us (John 14:1–6), and when He comes, He will take us to that glorious place. We are pilgrims and strangers in this world. Our true citizenship is in heaven (Phil. 3:20–21).

"To rescue from danger." See Acts 23:10. This suggests that the church will be taken home *before* the time of tribulation that will come to the world from God. First Thessalonians 1:10; 5:9 seem to state this clearly.

Will the unsaved world be aware of what is happening? Will they hear the shout, the voice, and the trumpet? First Corinthians 15:52 indicates that this will happen so suddenly that it will be over in the twinkling of an eye. Since the shout, voice, and trumpet apply to God's people, there is no reason to believe that the unsaved masses will hear them. If they do, they will hear sounds without meanings (see John 12:27–30). Millions of people will vanish instantly, and no doubt there will be chaos and great concern. Except for those who know the Bible teaching, the world will wonder at what has happened.

Reunion: Christians Forever with the Lord (4:17–18)

You and I shall meet the Lord in the air, in person, when He comes for us. The Greek word translated "meet" carries the idea of meeting a royal person or an important person. We have walked with Christ by faith here on earth, but in the air we shall "see him as he is" and become like Him (1 John 3:1–2). What a meeting that will be!

It will be a *glorious* meeting, because we shall have glorified bodies. When He was here on earth, Jesus prayed that we might one day see His glory and share in it (John 17:22–24). The suffering that we endure today will be transformed into glory when He returns (Rom. 8:17–19; 2 Cor. 4:17–18).

It will be an *everlasting* meeting, for we shall be "forever with the Lord." This was His promise: "I will come again, and receive you unto myself; that where I am, there ye may be also" (John 14:3). The goal of redemption is not just to rescue us from judgment, but to relate us to Christ.

Our meeting with the Lord will also be a time of *reckoning.* This is called "the judgment seat of Christ" (Rom. 14:10; 2 Cor. 5:10). The Greek word *bema,* which is translated "judgment seat," referred to the place where the Olympic judges awarded crowns to the winners. Our works will be judged and rewards will be given (1 Cor. 3:8–15).

The judgment seat of Christ must not be confused with the White Throne Judgment described in Revelation 20:11–15. You may contrast these two important events as follows:

Judgment Seat of Christ	*White Throne Judgment*
Only believers	Only unbelievers
Immediately after the rapture	After the thousand-year kingdom
Determines rewards for service	Determines amount of judgment

We will not only meet our Lord Jesus Christ at the rapture, but will also be reunited with our believing friends and loved ones who have died. "Together with them" is a great statement of encouragement. Death is the great separator, but Jesus Christ is the great Reconciler.

The Bible does not reveal all the details of this reunion. When Jesus raised the widow's son from the dead, He tenderly "delivered him to his mother" (Luke 7:15). This suggests that our Lord will have the happy ministry of reuniting broken families and friendships.

On the Mount of Transfiguration, the three disciples knew and recognized Moses and Elijah (Matt. 17:1–5). Certainly, the saints will know each other in glory, including believers we have never met. "For now we see through a glass, darkly; but then face to face: now I know in part; but then shall I know even as also I am known" (1 Cor. 13:12).

In the next chapter, we will see how Paul related this doctrine of the return of Christ to the unsaved. But it would be good for us now to examine our own hearts to see if we are ready to meet the Lord. One mark of a true Christian is his eager looking for the coming of Jesus Christ (1 Thess. 1:10). As we grow in the Lord, we not only *look for* His appearing, but we *love* His appearing (2 Tim. 4:8). Because we have this hope in Him, we keep our lives pure so that we may not be ashamed at His coming (1 John 2:28—3:3).

Godly Presbyterian preacher Robert Murray McCheyne used to ask people, "Do you think Jesus Christ will return today?" Most of them would reply, "No, not today." Then McCheyne would say, "Then, my friend, you had better be ready; for He is coming at such an hour as ye think not" (Luke 12:40).

Death is a fact of life. The only way we can escape death is to be alive when the Lord Jesus Christ returns. Death is not an accident; it is an appointment: "It is appointed unto men once to die, but after this the judgment" (Heb. 9:27). If you should die today, *where would your soul go?*

I once saw a quaint inscription on a gravestone in an old British cemetery not far from Windsor Castle. It read,

> Pause, my friend, as you walk by;
> As you are now, so once was I.
> As I am now, so you will be.
> Prepare, my friend, to follow me!

I heard about a visitor who read that epitaph and added these lines:

> To follow you is not my intent,
> Until I know which way you went!

We Christians have wonderful assurance and hope, because of the resurrection of Jesus Christ and His promised return.

Do you have that hope today?

Which way are *you* going?

CHAPTER EIGHT
1 Thessalonians 5:1–11
DON'T WALK IN YOUR SLEEP!

Jesus Christ both unites and divides. Those who have trusted Him as Savior are united in Christ as God's children. We are members of His body and "all one in Christ Jesus" (Gal. 3:28). When Jesus Christ returns in the air, we shall be "caught up together" (1 Thess. 4:17) never to be separated again.

But Christ is also a divider. "So there was a division among the people because of him" (John 7:43; 9:16; 10:19). Faith in Jesus Christ not only unites us to other believers; it also separates us spiritually from the rest of the world. Jesus said, "They are not of the world, even as I am not of the world" (John 17:16). There is a difference between believers who are looking for the Lord's return and the people of the world; it is this theme that Paul developed in this section.

His purpose was to encourage the believers to live holy lives in the midst of their pagan surroundings. He did this by pointing out the contrasts between believers and unbelievers.

Knowledge and Ignorance (5:1–2)

Three phrases in these verses need careful consideration.

"Times and seasons." This phrase is found only three times in the Bible, and refers primarily to God's plans for Israel. This is the way Daniel stated it when God gave him understanding of the king's dream (Dan. 2:21). Our Lord's use of the phrase in Acts 1:7 indicates that times and seasons relate primarily to Israel

God has a definite plan for the nations of the world (Acts 17:26), and Israel is the key nation. Dr. A. T. Pierson used to say, "History is His story." (Quite a contrast to Napoleon's definition: "History is a set of lies agreed upon.") God has ordained times and seasons for the nations on earth, particularly Israel, and all of this will culminate in a terrible time called "the day of the Lord."

"The day of the Lord." In the Bible, the word *day* can refer to a twenty-four-hour period or to a longer time during which God accomplishes some special purpose. In Genesis 2:3 the word means twenty-four hours, but in Genesis 2:4 it describes the entire week of Creation.

The day of the Lord is that time when God will judge the world and punish the nations. At the same time, God will prepare Israel for the return of Jesus Christ to the earth to establish His kingdom. Read Amos 5:18ff.; Joel 2:1ff.; Zephaniah 1:14–18; and Isaiah 2:12–21 for a description of this great period.

Another term for this period is "the time of Jacob's trouble" (Jer. 30:7). Many prophetic students also call it the tribulation and point to Revelation 6—19 as the Scripture that most vividly describes this event.

"Thief in the night." Our Lord used this image in His own teaching (Matt. 24:42–43; Luke 12:35–40). It describes the suddenness and the surprise involved in the coming of the day of the Lord. In Revelation 3:3; 16:15, He used this image to warn believers not to be caught napping. Since we do not know when the Lord will return for His people, we must live in a constant attitude of watching and waiting, while we are busy working and witnessing.

Now we can put these three concepts together and discover what Paul wanted to teach his troubled friends in Thessalonica. He had already told them about the coming of Christ for the church, the event described in 1 Thessalonians 4:13–18. He had told them that there would be a period of intense suffering and tribulation on the earth following this rapture of the church. These "times and seasons" that relate to Israel and the nations do not apply to the church or affect the truth of the Lord's coming for the church. He may come at any time, and this will usher in the day of the Lord.

Paul explained more about the day of the Lord in his second letter to the Thessalonians, so we will save these details for a later chapter. His emphasis here was simply that the believers were "in the know," while the unbelievers were living in ignorance of God's plan. The suddenness of these events will reveal to the world its ignorance of divine truth.

Expectancy and Surprise (5:3–5)

The unsaved world will be enjoying a time of false peace and security just before these cataclysmic events occur. Note carefully the contrast between "they" and "you" (or "us") throughout this entire section, "they" referring to the unsaved. *They* will say, "Peace and safety!" but *we* will say, "Jesus is coming, and judgment is coming!"

The world is caught by surprise because men will not hear God's Word or heed God's warning. God warned that the flood was coming, yet only eight people believed and were saved (1 Peter 3:20). Lot warned his family that the city would be destroyed, but they would not listen (Gen. 19:12–14). Jesus warned His generation that Jerusalem would be destroyed (Luke 21:19ff), and this warning enabled believers to escape; but many others perished in the siege.

In fact, Jesus used the flood and the overthrow of Sodom and Gomorrah as examples (Matt. 24:37–39; Luke 17:26–30). People in those days were going about their regular daily activities—eating, drinking, getting married—and never considering that judgment was around the corner.

Well-meaning people have tried to set dates for our Lord's return, only to be embarrassed by their failures. However, it is possible to expect His coming without setting a specific time. No "signs" must be fulfilled before He can return for His church.

Christians are "sons of the light" and therefore are not "in the dark" when it comes to future events. Unbelievers ridicule the idea of Christ's return. "Knowing this first, that there shall come in the last days scoffers, walking after their own lusts, and saying, 'Where is the promise of his coming?'" (2 Peter 3:3–4).

More than twenty centuries have come and gone since our Lord gave the promise of His return, and He has not returned yet. This does not mean that God does not keep His promises. It simply means that God does not follow our calendar. "One day is with the Lord as a thousand years, and a thousand years as one day" (2 Peter 3:8).

Paul compared the coming judgment to "travail upon a woman with child" (1 Thess. 5:3). Even with our modern medical skills, birth pangs are very real and very painful. They accompany the muscle contractions that enable the mother to give birth to the baby. The prophet Isaiah used this same picture when he described the coming "day of the Lord" (Isa. 13:6–13). The early part of this day of the Lord was called "the beginning of sorrows" by the Lord Jesus (Matt. 24:8); and the Greek word translated "sorrows" actually means "birth pangs."

What truth do Isaiah, Jesus, and Paul teach us? The truth that out of the day of the Lord will come the birth of the kingdom. When God's judgments are finished, God's Son will return "with power and great glory" (Matt. 24:30). Paul described this event in his second letter to the Thessalonian Christians.

Live expectantly. This does not mean putting on a white sheet and sitting atop a mountain. That is the very attitude God condemned (Acts 1:10–11). But it does mean living in the light of His return, realizing that our works will be judged and that our opportunities for service on earth will end. It means to live "with eternity's values in view."

There is a difference between being ready to go to heaven and being ready to meet the Lord. Anyone who has sincerely trusted Christ for salvation is ready to go to heaven. Christ's sacrifice on the cross has taken care of that. But to be ready to meet the Lord at the judgment seat of Christ is quite another matter. Scripture indicates that some believers will not be happy to see Jesus Christ! "And now, little children, abide in him; that when he shall appear, we may have confidence, and not be ashamed before him at his coming" (1 John 2:28).

Having been a pastor for many years, I have had the sad experience of seeing believers deliberately disobey the Word of God. I recall one young lady who stubbornly chose to marry an unsaved man. When I tried to help her from the Bible, she said, "I don't care what you say. I don't care what the Bible says. I'm going to get married!" In the light of Hebrews 13:17, will she be happy at the judgment seat of Christ?

Believers who live in the expectation of the Lord's return will certainly enjoy a better life than Christians who compromise with the world. At the end of each chapter in this letter, Paul pointed out the practical results of living expectantly. Take time now to review those verses and to examine your heart.

Soberness and Drunkenness (5:6–8)

To be sober-minded means to be alert, to live with your eyes open, to be sane and steady. To make the contrast more vivid, Paul pictured two groups of people: one group was drunk and asleep, while the other group was awake and alert. Danger was coming, but the drunken sleepers were unaware of it. The alert crowd was ready and unafraid.

Since we are "sons of the day" we should not live as those who belong to the darkness. "The night is far spent, the day is at hand: let us therefore cast off the works of darkness, and let us put on the armor of light. Let us walk honestly, as in the day; not in rioting and drunkenness, not in chambering [immorality] and wantonness [indecency], not in strife and envying" (Rom. 13:12–13).

In other words, because "the day" is approaching, it is time to wake up, clean up, and dress up. And when we dress up, we had better put on "the breastplate of faith and love: and for a helmet, the hope of salvation" (1 Thess. 5:8). Only the "armor of light" (Rom. 13:12) will adequately protect us in these last days before our Lord returns.

The sober-minded believer has a calm, sane outlook on life. He is not complacent, but neither is he frustrated and afraid. He hears the tragic news of the day, yet he does not lose heart. He experiences the difficulties of life, but he does not give up. He knows his future is secure in God's hands, so he lives each day creatively, calmly, and obediently. Outlook determines outcome, and when your outlook is the *uplook,* then your outcome is secure.

But the unsaved people of the world are not alert. They are like drunken men, living in a false paradise and enjoying a false security. When the Holy Spirit filled the first Christians at Pentecost, the unsaved people accused the Christians of being drunk (Acts 2:13). In reality, it is the unsaved who are living like drunken men. The sword of God's wrath hangs over the world, yet people live godless lives, empty lives, and rarely if ever give any thought to eternal matters.

We have met faith, hope, and love before (1 Thess. 1:3). Here they are described as armor to protect us in this evil world. Faith and love are like a breastplate that covers the heart: faith toward God, and love toward God's people. Hope is a sturdy helmet that protects the mind. The unsaved fix their minds on the things of this world, while dedicated believers set their attention on things above (Col. 3:1–3).

Hope of salvation does not mean the hope that at last we will be saved. A person can *know today* that he is saved and going to heaven. Paul knew that the Thessalonican believers were saved (1 Thess. 1:4), and he was certain that he and they would meet Christ in the air (1 Thess. 4:17). The person who confidently says, "I know I am saved!" is not exhibiting pride; he is demonstrating faith in God's Word. First John was written to help us know that we are saved (1 John 5:9–13).

Hope of salvation means "the hope that salvation gives to us." There are actually three tenses to salvation: (1) *past*—I have been saved from the guilt and penalty of sin; (2) *present*—I am being saved from the power and pollution of sin; (3) *future*—I shall be saved from the very presence of sin when Christ returns. The blessed hope of our Lord's return is the "hope of salvation." Unsaved people are without hope (Eph. 2:12). This helps explain why they live as they do: "Eat, drink, and be merry, for tomorrow we die!"

Paul repeated the word *sleep* several times in these verses to describe the attitude of the lost world. In the previous paragraph (1 Thess. 4:13–18) Paul used the word to describe the death of the believer. The body goes to sleep and the spirit goes to be with the Lord. But in this section, sleep does not mean death. It means moral indifference and carelessness about spiritual things. Jesus used the word *sleep* with this meaning in Mark 13:32–37.

Doctors tell us that some people are "morning people," while others are "evening people." That is, some people are wide awake before the alarm clock rings. They hit the floor running and never have to yawn or throw cold water in their faces. Others (like myself) wake up slowly—first one eye, then the other—and then gradually shift gears as they move into the day. When it comes to the return of our Lord, we must all be "morning people"—awake, alert, sober, and ready for the dawning of that wonderful new day.

But, for the unsaved crowd, reveling in its drunkenness, the coming of Jesus Christ will mean the end of light and the beginning of eternal darkness.

Salvation and Judgment (5:9–11)

Believers do not have to fear future judgment because it is not part of God's appointed plan for us. Will Christians go through the day of the Lord, that awful period of judgment that God will send on the earth? I think not, and verses like 1 Thessalonians 1:10; 5:9 seem to support this. Christians have always gone through tribulation, since this is a part of dedicated Christian living (John 15:18–27; 16:33). But they will not go through *the* tribulation that is appointed for the godless world.

I realize that good and godly students of the Word disagree on this matter, and I will not make it a test of fellowship or spirituality. But I do believe that the church will be raptured to heaven prior to the tribulation period. Let me share the reasons that have convinced me.

The nature of the church. The church is the body of Christ, and He is the Head (Col. 2:17–19). When He died for us on the cross, He bore for us all the divine judgment necessary for our salvation. He has promised that we shall never taste any of God's wrath (John 5:24). The day of the Lord is a day of God's wrath, and it seems unjust and unnecessary that the church should experience it.

The nature of the tribulation. This is the time when God will judge the Gentile nations and also purge Israel and prepare her for the coming of her Messiah. The "earth-dwellers" will taste of God's wrath (Rev. 3:10) and not those whose citizenship is in heaven (Phil. 3:20). God will judge the earth-dwellers for their iniquity (Isa. 26:20–21). But He has already judged believers' sins on the cross.

The promise of Christ's imminent return. The word *imminent* means "ready to happen." Nothing has to occur for Christ to return, except the calling out of the last person who will be saved and complete the body of Christ. If our Lord did not return for us until the end of the tribulation period, then we would know *when* He was coming; for the sequence, signs, and times are all spelled out in Revelation 6—19. It is worth noting that the word *church* is not used in Revelation from 4:1 to 22:13. Also notice that Paul lived in the expectation of seeing Christ, for he used the pronouns "we" and "us" in discussing this doctrine (1 Thess. 4:13—5:11). The apostle John had this same attitude. He closed his book with the prayer, "Even so, come, Lord Jesus" (Rev. 22:20).

The course of the seven churches in Revelation 2—3. Many Bible students believe the Lord selected these seven churches to illustrate the spiritual course of church history. Ephesus would be the church of the apostles; Smyrna would be the persecuted church of the early centuries. The last church, Laodicea, represents the apostate church of the last days.

This suggests that the Philadelphia church (Rev. 3:7–13) pictures the weak but faithful church of the period just before Christ returns. It is an evangelistic church with great opportunities and open doors. It is the church that proclaims the soon-coming of Christ ("Thou hast kept the word of my patience," Rev. 3:10), and to it He has promised deliverance from the day of judgment: "I also will keep thee from the hour of temptation, which shall come upon all the world, to try them that dwell upon the earth" (Rev. 3:10). This promise parallels the promise of 1 Thessalonians 5:9.

The order of events in 2 Thessalonians 2. Notice that the order Paul uses harmonizes with the order indicated in other prophetic Scriptures.

Paul connected the return of Christ with the redemption He purchased for us on the cross. We are "bought with a price." We are His bride, and He will come to claim us for Himself before He sends judgment on the earth. Remember that Christ died for us that we might live *through* Him (1 John 4:9), *for* Him (2 Cor. 5:15), and *with* Him (1 Thess. 5:10). Whether we live or die ("wake or sleep"), we are the Lord's and we shall live with Him.

We must never permit the study of prophecy to become purely academic, or a source of tension or argument. Paul closed this section with the practical application of the prophetic Scriptures: *encouragement* and *edification*. The fact that we will meet our loved ones again and forever be with the Lord is a source of encouragement (1 Thess. 4:18), and the fact that we will not endure God's wrath during the day of the Lord is another source of encouragement (1 Thess. 5:11). The first is positive, and the second is negative, and both are comforting.

The truth of our Lord's imminent return encourages us to keep clean (1 John 3:1–3) and to do faithfully whatever work He has assigned to us (Luke 12:41–48). It also encourages us to attend church and love the brethren (Heb. 10:25). Knowing that we shall be with the Lord strengthens us in the difficulties of life (2 Cor. 5:1–8) and motivates us to win the lost (2 Cor. 5:9–21).

Many believers have such a comfortable situation here on earth that they rarely think about going to heaven and meeting the Lord. They forget that they must one day stand at the judgment seat of Christ. It helps to hold us up and build us up when we recall that Jesus is coming again.

If you have never trusted Him, then your future is judgment. You needn't be ignorant, for God's Word gives you the truth. You needn't be unprepared, for today you can trust Christ and be born again. Why should you live for the cheap sinful experiences of the world when you can enjoy the riches of salvation in Christ?

If you are not saved, then you have an appointment with judgment. And it may come sooner than you expect, for it is "appointed unto men once to die, but after this the judgment" (Heb. 9:27). Why not make an "appointment" with Christ, meet Him personally, and trust Him to save you? "For whosoever shall call upon the name of the Lord shall be saved" (Rom. 10:13).

CHAPTER NINE
1 Thessalonians 5:12–28
IT'S ALL IN THE FAMILY

Paul's favorite name for believers was *brethren*. He used it at least sixty times in his letters, and in the two Thessalonian epistles, he used it twenty-seven times. Paul saw the local church as a family. Each member was born again by the Spirit of God and possessed God's nature (1 Peter 1:22–25; 2 Peter 1:3–4). They all were part of God's family.

It is tragic when believers neglect or ignore the local church. No family is perfect and no local church is perfect, but without a family to protect him and provide for him, a child would suffer and die. The child of God needs the church family if he is to grow, develop his gifts, and serve God.

What are the essentials for a happy, thriving church family? How can we make our local churches more spiritual to the glory of God? In this closing section, Paul discussed these matters.

Family Leadership (5:12–13)
Without leadership, a family falls apart. The father is the head of the home; the mother stands with him in love and cooperation. The children are to obey their parents. This is the order God has laid down, and for us to disturb this order is to ask for serious trouble.

According to Martin L. Gross in his book *The Psychological Society*, more than sixty thousand guidance workers and seven thousand school psychologists work in our American public education system, and many of them function as substitute parents. Many

students need counseling, but no professional worker can take the place of a loving, faithful father or mother.

When our oldest son entered high school, he met his assigned counselor. "Now, if you have any problems, feel free to come to me," the counselor said. Our son replied, "If I have any problems, I'll talk to my father!" He was not being disrespectful or unappreciative of the counselor, but he was giving expression of a basic principle: children need the leadership and guidance that only parents can give.

God has ordained leadership for the local church. It is true that we are "all one in Christ Jesus" (Gal. 3:28), but it is also true that the Head of the church has given gifts to people, and then given these people to the churches to exercise His will (Eph. 4:7–16). Just as the flock needs a shepherd (1 Peter 5:1–5), so the family needs a leader.

What responsibilities do the brethren have toward their spiritual leaders?

Accept them. They are God's gifts to the church. They have spiritual authority from the Lord and we should accept them in the Lord. They are not dictators, but leaders and examples. As they follow the Lord, we must follow them.

Appreciate them. That is the meaning of the exhortation "know them who labor among you" (1 Thess. 5:12). There is nothing wrong with honoring faithful servants of God, so long as God gets the glory. Spiritual leadership is a great responsibility and a difficult task. It is not easy to serve as a pastor, elder, deacon, or other spiritual leader. The battles and burdens are many, and sometimes the encouragements are few. It is dangerous when a church family takes their leaders for granted and fails to pray for them, work with them, and encourage them.

Love them. As brothers, the leaders are "among us," and as leaders, they are "over us in the Lord." This could be a very strained relationship apart from true Christian love. For a pastor to be "among" and "over" at the same time demands grace and the power of the Spirit. If he gets out of balance, his ministry will be weakened and possibly destroyed. Some church members want their pastor to be a buddy, but this weakens his authority. On the other hand, if he emphasizes *only* his authority, he could become a selfish dictator.

Obey them. "Obey them that have the rule over you, and submit yourselves" (Heb. 13:17). When God's servant, led by God's Spirit, calls us to obey God's Word, then we must obey. This does not mean that every spiritual leader is always right in everything. Abraham, Moses, David, and even Peter made mistakes in their words and deeds. A wise pastor knows he is made of clay and admits when he is wrong or when he needs expert counsel. In my own ministry, I have benefited tremendously from the counsel and help of experienced laymen whose knowledge in many areas was far greater than mine.

But, in spite of their limitations, God's spiritual leaders should be respected and obeyed—unless it is obvious that they are out of God's will. As the spiritual leaders of the church meet together, plan, pray, and seek and follow God's will, we can be sure that God will rule and overrule in the decisions they make.

The result of the church family following the spiritual leaders will be peace and harmony in the church: "And be at peace among yourselves" (1 Thess. 5:13). Whenever you find division and dissension in a local church, it is usually because of selfishness and sin on the part of the leaders, or the members, or both. James 4:1–3 makes it clear that selfishness on the inside leads to strife on the outside. It is only as we submit to one another in the Lord that we can enjoy His blessing, and peace in the family.

But the leaders alone cannot do all of the work of the ministry, so Paul added a second essential.

Family Partnership (5:14–16)
In recent years, churches have rediscovered what we are calling "body life." This is a scriptural concept, though it does not define all that is involved in the ministry of the local church, since there are other pictures of the church besides that of the body. Body life refers to the ministry of each Christian to the others, just as the various members of the human body minister to one another to maintain health and life.

Family members must learn to minister to each other. The older members teach the younger members (see Titus 2:3–5) and encourage them when they are in difficulty. While ministering at a summer Bible conference, my wife and I met a lovely Christian couple who had nine children. It was a delight to see how the older children helped the younger ones, and how the parents were relieved of minor tasks and able to enjoy their leisure time.

According to Ephesians 4:12, the spiritual leaders in the church are supposed to equip the members to do the work of the ministry. In most churches, the members pay the leaders to do the work of the ministry, and the leaders cannot do it all. Consequently, the work begins to weaken and die, and everybody blames the preacher.

Paul named some special family members who need personal help.

The unruly (v. 14a). This word means "careless, out of line." It was applied to a soldier who would not keep rank but insisted on marching his own way. While the loving atmosphere of the family encourages individual development, there are some things we all must do in the same way. If we do not have rules and standards in the family, we have chaos. Paul dealt with this problem again when he wrote his second epistle to the Thessalonians (2 Thess. 3:6, 11), so apparently this first admonition did not impress them.

Rules and traditions in a family must never be so overemphasized that creativity is stifled. As a parent, it is a joy to see each child blossom out with his or her own personality, talents, and ambitions. But it is a sorrow to see a child rebel against the rules, abandon the

traditions and standards, and think that this kind of lifestyle shows freedom and maturity. This kind of attitude in the church family causes arguments and splits.

The feebleminded (v. 14b). This term has nothing to do with mentality. The literal translation of the Greek word is "little-souled, fainthearted." These are the quitters in the church family. They always look on the dark side of things and give up when the going is tough. In families where there are three or more children, usually one of them is a quitter. Every church family has its share of quitters too.

These people need to be encouraged, which is the meaning of the word translated "comfort" in the King James Version. It is also found in 1 Thessalonians 2:11. The Greek word is made up of two words: *para*, near; and *muthos*, speech. Instead of scolding the fainthearted from a distance, we must get close to them and speak tenderly. We must teach the "little-souled" that the trials of life will help to enlarge them and make them stronger in the faith.

The weak (v. 14c). "Hold fast to the weak!" is the literal translation. "Don't let them fall!" But who are these weak believers? Certainly, Paul did not mean people who were weak physically, since he was dealing with the spiritual ministry in the church. No, he was referring to those who were "weak in the faith" and had not grown strong in the Lord (Rom. 14:1—15:3).

Usually, the weak Christians were afraid of their liberty in Christ They lived by rules and regulations. In the Roman assemblies, the weak Christians would not eat meat, and they held to the Jewish system of holy days. They were severe in their judgment of the mature saints who enjoyed all foods and all days.

We have the strong and the weak in our church families today, just as in our natural families we have children who mature faster than others. How should we handle them? *With patient, reassuring love.* It is unfair and unwise to compare one child with another, for each one matures in his own time and his own way. We must "take hold" of these weaker believers and help them stand and walk in the Lord.

This kind of personal ministry is not easy, and so Paul added some wise counsel to encourage us.

Be patient (v. 14d). It takes patience to raise a family. That weaker member who demands much help may one day be a choice leader, so never give up. A pastor friend and I were chatting after I had spoken at a service in his church, when a red-headed boy about ten years old came running past us, heading up the center aisle. "Have you ever noticed," remarked my friend, "that the biggest scamps in the Sunday school usually turn out to be pastors or missionaries?" Patience!

Watch your motives (v. 15). Often as we minister to others, they reject us and even oppose us. Often they show no appreciation. But we should always serve in love, and be ready to forgive. "Never pay back evil for evil to anyone. Respect what is right in the sight of all men. If possible, so far as it depends on you, be at peace with all men. Never take your own revenge, beloved, but leave room for the wrath of God, for it is written, 'Vengeance is Mine, I will repay,' says the Lord. 'But if your enemy is hungry, feed him, and if he is thirsty, give him a drink; for in so doing you will heap burning coals upon his head.' Do not be overcome by evil, but overcome evil with good" (Rom. 12:17–21 NASB).

If your motive is a desire for appreciation and praise, you may be disappointed. If your motive is "ourselves your servants for Jesus' sake" (2 Cor. 4:5), you will never be disappointed.

Be joyful (v. 16). Joy takes the burden out of service. "The joy of the Lord is your strength" (Neh. 8:10). God loves a cheerful servant as well as a cheerful giver. Every church family has its Doubting Thomas or its Gloomy Gus. To see them and listen to them is like witnessing an autopsy or diving into a cold lake on a winter's day. God wants His family to be happy, and that means that each member must contribute to the joy.

The four spiritual characteristics Paul mentioned are part of the fruit of the Spirit named in Galatians 5:22—love (1 Thess. 5:13), joy (1 Thess. 5:16), peace (1 Thess. 5:13), and longsuffering (1 Thess. 5:14). We cannot manufacture these spiritual qualities; they only come as we yield to the Spirit and permit Him to control us.

Family partnership is vital to the health and growth of the church. Are you bearing your share of the burdens, or are you merely a spectator who watches the others do the job?

Family Worship (5:17–28)

Worship is the most important activity of a local church family. Ministry must flow out of worship, otherwise it becomes busy activity without power and without heart. There may be "results," but they will not glorify God or really last. Many church services lack an emphasis on true worship and are more like religious entertainments, catering to the appetites of the congregation.

Paul named the various elements that make up the worship ministry of the church.

Prayer (v. 17). Prayer was important in the early church (1 Cor. 11:1–6; Acts 1:13–14; 4:23ff.). It was a high and holy experience when the church united in prayer. Today we "call someone to lead in prayer," and we have no idea whether that believer is even in fellowship with God. In some churches, there are two or three people who monopolize the prayer meeting. If we are led by the Spirit (Jude 20), we will experience unity and freedom in our praying, and God will answer.

"Pray without ceasing" does not mean we must always be mumbling prayers. The word means "constantly recurring," not continuously occurring. We are to "keep the receiver off the hook" and be in touch with God so that our praying is part of a long conversation that is not broken. God knows the desires of the heart (Ps. 37:4), and He responds to those desires even when our voice is silent. See Psalms 10:17; 21:2.

Praise (v. 18). Thanksgiving is also a vital element of worship. We use "psalms and hymns and spiritual songs" (Eph. 5:19) to express our love and gratitude to the Lord. As we grow in our application of the Word of God, we must also grow in our expression of praise, for the two go together (Col. 3:16). If a local church is "growing in grace" the members will want to learn new hymns in order to give praise to God. If the heart and head do not keep pace with each other, Christian worship becomes either juvenile or hypocritical.

The Word of God (vv. 19–21). Apart from God's Word, we have no certain revelation from the Lord. Worship that ignores the Bible is not spiritual. There may be emotion—and even commotion—but unless there is *spiritual truth,* the Holy Spirit is not at work. The three admonitions in these verses go together and help us understand how the Holy Spirit works in Christian worship.

The early church did not have a completed Bible as we do. The Holy Spirit gave the gift of prophecy to certain members of the church and would speak the message through them. When I preach in a church service, I preach the truth immediately by means of the Bible. These early prophets preached the truth immediately as they were moved by the Holy Spirit. Their spiritual knowledge was given to them by the Spirit, and often they spoke in a tongue. This is why the three gifts of prophecy, tongues, and knowledge are grouped together in 1 Corinthians 13.

Of course, there are dangers in this kind of ministry, because Satan (or the flesh) could seek to counterfeit a message from God, and thus lead the church astray. If the church restrained the speakers, they might be guilty of quenching the Spirit. If they believed all that was spoken, they might be obeying false spirits. The answer was to "prove all things." There must be a discerning of the spirits (1 Cor. 12:10; 1 John 4:1–4). Paul gave specific rules for this in 1 Corinthians 14:29–33.

Today, we have a completed revelation in the Word of God and there is no need for prophets. The apostles and prophets helped lay the foundation of the church (Eph. 2:20) and have now passed from the scene. The only "prophetic ministry" we have is in the preaching and teaching of the Word of God.

In using the word *quench,* Paul pictured the Spirit of God as fire (see Isa. 4:4; Acts 2:3; Rev. 4:5). Fire speaks of purity, power, light, warmth, and (if necessary) destruction. When the Holy Spirit is at work in our lives and churches, we have a warmth of love in our hearts, light for our minds, and energy for our wills. He "melts us together" so that there is harmony and cooperation, and He purifies us so that we put away sin.

The fire of the Spirit must not go out on the altar of our hearts; we must maintain that devotion to Christ that motivates and energizes our lives.

"Stir up the gift of God which is in thee," Paul wrote to Timothy (2 Tim. 1:6), and the verb means "stir the fire again into life." Apparently Timothy had been neglecting this gift (1 Tim. 4:14) and had to be reminded. The believer, and the local assembly, must avoid extremes: the legalist and formalist would put the fire out, while the fanatic would permit the fire to burn everything up.

It is important that we permit the Spirit of God to teach us the Word of God when we meet to worship. "Sharing" is good if you have something relevant to share from the Word, but I have listened to some "sharing meetings" that were not only unspiritual, but antispiritual. "Apt to teach" requires that we be "apt to learn." Beware of a false spirit that can lead you and your church astray. Follow the Word of God and prove all things.

Godly living (vv. 22–24). The purpose of worship is that we might become more like Christ in character and conduct. The greatest definition of worship I ever read was given by William Temple, a late Archbishop of Canterbury: "For to worship is to quicken the conscience by the holiness of God, to feed the mind with the truth of God, to purge the imagination by the beauty of God, to open up the heart to the love of God, to devote the will to the purpose of God."

Paul emphasized balance in Christian living: the negative—"Abstain from all appearance of evil" (1 Thess. 5:22) and the positive—"And the very God of peace sanctify you" (1 Thess. 5:23). Some churches only preach the negative, and this leads to lives and ministries that are out of balance. *Sanctify* simply means "set apart for God's exclusive use." There is

positional sanctification (Heb. 10:10); we have once and for all been set apart for God. There is also *practical* sanctification (2 Cor. 7:1), a daily dealing with our sins and a growth in holiness. All of this will culminate in *perfect* sanctification (1 John 3:2), when we see Christ and become eternally like Him. Expecting to see Jesus Christ is a great motivation for holy living.

Christian fellowship (vv. 25–28). After the corporate worship is ended, the saints minister to one another. They greet one another and seek to encourage. I have been in churches where the congregation escaped like rats leaving a sinking ship. Fellowship is a part of worship.

The "holy kiss" was not a sensual thing. Usually the men kissed the men, and the women kissed the women (see Rom. 16:16; 1 Cor. 16:20; 1 Peter 5:14). Often when ministering on mission fields, I have had the saints greet me in this way, and I have never been offended or suspicious. J. B. Phillips in his paraphrase solved the problem by saying, "Give a handshake all around among the brotherhood."

Paul ended with another reminder that the Word of God is the important thing in the local church. The Word must govern our conduct and guide our lives. We are to read the Word personally, but we also need to hear the Word in the fellowship of the local church, for the one experience helps balance the other.

2 THESSALONIANS

OUTLINE

Key theme: The church and the day of the Lord
Key verses: 2 Thessalonians 2:1–2

I. ENCOURAGEMENT IN SUFFERING (1)
    A. Praise—1:1–4
    B. Promise—1:5–10
    C. Prayer—1:11–12

II. ENLIGHTENMENT IN TEACHING (2)
    A. How the man of sin appears—2:1–7
    B. How the Son of God appears—2:8–12
    C. How the child of God should live—2:13–17

III. ENABLEMENT IN LIVING (3)
    A. Obey the Word—3:1–6
    B. Follow our example—3:7–9
    C. Discipline the unruly—3:10–15
    D. Closing benediction—3:16–18

CONTENTS

CHAPTER ONE
2 Thessalonians 1:1–12
NO REST FOR THE WICKED

The Christians in Thessalonica were grateful to God for Paul's first letter, but it did not immediately solve all their problems. In fact, the persecution grew worse, and some believers thought they were living in the time of the tribulation. Then a letter arrived claiming to be from Paul, stating that the day of the Lord was actually present. Needless to say, the assembly was confused and frightened by this prospect.

Some of the believers concluded that since the Lord's coming was so near, they ought to quit their jobs and spend their time waiting for Him. This meant that the other members were under an extra burden to care for them. Satan was working overtime; as the lion, he was seeking to devour (1 Peter 5:7–8), and as the serpent, he was seeking to deceive (2 Cor. 11:3).

It was in response to these needs that Paul wrote his second letter. He began with their most pressing need, the persecution they were experiencing because of their faith. In this first chapter, Paul shared three encouragements with his suffering friends.

The Encouragement of Praise (1:1–4)

After greeting his friends, Paul launched into a statement of praise to God for what He had been accomplishing in their lives. Paul was practicing his own admonition, "In everything give thanks" (1 Thess. 5:18). You cannot help but notice Paul's repeated thanksgivings in these two letters (1 Thess. 1:2; 2:13; 3:9; 2 Thess. 1:3; 2:13). Not only does *prayer* change people and situations, but so does *praise.*

Once I was teaching a series of lessons in a church about Satan's devices to defeat Christians. One of these devices is suffering, as in the case of Job. If Satan can put us into difficult circumstances, he may be able to weaken our faith.

"One of the best weapons for fighting Satan is praise," I told my morning class. "In spite of his pain, Job was able to say, 'Blessed be the name of the Lord!' So, the next time things go wrong and you are tempted to get impatient, turn to God and give thanks."

That evening, just before the class started, a lady rushed up to me and said, "It works! It works!" And then she told me about her afternoon and all that had happened. Her story was so unbelievable that I would have doubted it, had I not known her character. "But in it all I gave thanks," she told me, "and God gave me the grace and strength I needed. It works. Praise works!"

No doubt the Thessalonian believers did not consider themselves to be very spiritual as they suffered, but Paul detected what God was doing among them. You and I are the worst ones to evaluate our own lives. Many times others can see the spiritual improvement when you and I miss it completely. For what blessings did Paul give thanks and thereby encourage his friends?

Their faith was growing (v. 3a). A faith that cannot be tested cannot be trusted. New believers must expect their faith to be tried, because this is the way God proves whether or not their decision is genuine. Faith, like a muscle, must be exercised to grow stronger. Tribulation and persecution are God's ways to strengthen our faith.

One of my favorite books is *Hudson Taylor's Spiritual Secret* by Dr. and Mrs. Howard Taylor. In it you read how Hudson Taylor's faith in God grew from that first day he determined to live by faith in God alone. He learned to trust God for his salary, especially when his busy employer forgot to pay him. He learned to trust God for daily needs, and, as his faith was tested, he grew in faith and was able to trust God for His supply for an entire missionary organization. Sometimes it seemed that God had forgotten, but Taylor continued to pray and trust, and God answered.

An easy life can lead to a shallow faith. The great men and women of faith in Hebrews 11 all suffered in one way or another, or faced tremendous obstacles, so that their faith could grow. Paul had prayed for the believers in Thessalonica, that their faith might be perfected (1 Thess. 3:10), and now he thanked God for answered prayer.

Their love was abounding (v. 3b). Again, this was an answer to Paul's previous prayer (1 Thess. 3:12). Suffering can make us selfish, but when suffering is mixed with grace and faith, it produces love. It is "faith which worketh by love" (Gal. 5:6). When Christians suffer, their faith reaches *upward* to God, and their love reaches *outward* to their fellow believers.

Thoreau once described a city as a place where many people are "lonely together." Residents of a high-rise apartment can be suffering greatly and the people in the next apartment know nothing about it. Our modern world can promote spiritual and emotional isolation and insulation, even to the point of our watching others suffer without really caring.

But for the Christian, suffering can help to produce abounding love. "Behold, how they love one another!" was the confession of the pagan world as it beheld the miracle of Christian fellowship. The early believers were only obeying the commandment of their Lord, "Love one another." Their own suffering did not prevent them from sharing love with others who were suffering.

Their patience was increasing (v. 4). Perhaps "perseverance" would be the best translation of this Greek word. "Tribulation works out endurance" (Rom. 5:3, literal translation). You do not become patient and persevering by reading a book (even this one) or listening to a lecture. *You have to suffer.*

What were these believers enduring? Paul used several words to describe their situation: *persecutions,* which means "attacks from without," or "trials"; *tribulations,* which literally means "pressures," or afflictions that result from the trials; and *trouble* (2 Thess. 1:7), which means "to be pressed into a narrow place." No matter how we look at it, the Thessalonican Christians were not having an easy time.

But God never wastes suffering. Trials work *for* us, not *against* us (2 Cor. 4:15–18; James 1:1–5). If we trust God and yield to Him, then trials will produce patience and maturity in our lives. If we rebel and fight our circumstances, then we will remain immature and impatient. God permits trials that He might build character into our lives. He can grow a mushroom overnight, but it takes many years—and many storms—to build a mighty oak.

Their testimony was helping others (v. 4a). "Therefore, among God's churches we boast about your perseverance and faith" (2 Thess. 1:4 NIV). Not only can suffering help us to grow, but we can then help others to grow. God encourages us that we may encourage others (2 Cor. 1:4–5). We are not to be cisterns that receive and keep, but channels that receive and share.

The word translated "faith" in 2 Thessalonians 1:3–4, can be translated "faithfulness." Actually, the two go together; we reveal our faith in God by our faithfulness of life. The Thessalonicans were faithful to the Lord and to one another in spite of the troubles they endured. When a person in difficulty forsakes the Lord and the church, he shows that either he has never been born again or that his spiritual life is very weak. A true Christian who is growing will be faithful, come what may.

During World War II, when enemy armies invaded North Africa, the missionaries had to flee, and there was great concern over the churches left behind. But when the war ended and the missionaries returned, they discovered strong, thriving churches. The sufferings of war purified the church and helped strengthen the faith of the true believers. What an encouragement this was to the churches of the free world.

Paul had every reason to praise God and give thanks for what God was doing in the lives of these young Christians. But did you notice that one element was missing—hope? "Faith, hope, and love" had characterized these believers from the beginning (1 Thess. 1:3), but Paul gave thanks only for their faith and love. Why? Apparently they were confused about their hope. This leads us to the second encouragement.

The Encouragement of Promise (2 Thess. 1:5–10)

No matter how difficult their present circumstances may have been, the Thessalonican believers had a secure and glorious future. In fact, their sufferings were evidence, "a manifest token," that God was righteous, working out His great plan for them. We are prone to think that suffering proves that God does not care, when just the opposite is true. Furthermore, the way we act in times of trial proves to others that God is at work. (See Phil. 1:28–30 for another example of this principle.)

Three experiences are involved in the promises of God for His people.

Reward (v. 5). "You will be counted worthy of the kingdom of God, for which you are suffering" (NIV). This was one of God's purposes in permitting their suffering. It does not suggest that their suffering earned them the right to go to heaven, because we know that they were saved through faith in Christ (1 Thess. 1). The little word "also" indicated that this worthiness related both to their present experience and their future entrance into God's glorious kingdom. You find the same idea in 1 Peter 1:3–9.

One day Jesus Christ will turn the tables and the wicked will suffer, while the believers are rewarded. Our Lord never promised us that life here would be easy; in fact, He taught that we would have to face difficulties and fight battles. But He also promised a future reward for all who were faithful to Him (Matt. 5:10–12).

Recompense (vv. 6, 7b–9). God will recompense affliction to the lost, but rest to the saved. To *recompense* means "to repay." Certainly, the wicked who persecute the godly do not always receive their just payment in this life. In fact, the apparent prosperity of the wicked and difficulty of the godly have posed a problem for many of God's people (see Ps. 73; Jer. 12:1; Hab. 1). Why live a godly life if your only experience is that of suffering?

As Christians, we must live for eternity and not just for the present. In fact, living "with eternity's values in view" is what makes our Christian life meaningful today. We walk by faith and not by sight.

This brings to mind the story of the two farmers, one a believer and the other an atheist. When harvest season came, the atheist taunted his believing neighbor because apparently God had not blessed him too much. The atheist's family had not been sick, his fields were rich with harvest, and he was sure to make a lot of money.

"I thought you said it paid to believe in God and be a Christian," said the atheist.

"It does pay," replied the Christian. "But God doesn't always pay His people in September."

What kind of a future does the unbeliever face? Look at the dramatic words Paul used to describe it: tribulation, vengeance, flaming fire, punishment, and everlasting destruction. The Christ-rejecting world will receive from God exactly what it gave to God's people! When God recompenses, He pays in kind, for there is a law of compensation that operates in human history.

Pharaoh tried to drown all the male babies born to the Jews, and his own army was drowned in the Red Sea. Haman plotted to wipe out the Jews, and he and his own sons were wiped out. The advisers of King Darius forced him to arrest Daniel and throw him into a lions' den, but later they themselves were thrown to the lions. The unbelieving Jewish leaders who sacrificed Christ in order to save the nation (see

John 11:49–53) in a few years saw their city destroyed and their nation scattered.

It is a *righteous* thing for God to judge sin and condemn sinners. A holy God cannot leave sin unjudged. People who say, "I cannot believe that a loving God would judge sinners and send people to hell" understand neither the holiness of God nor the awfulness of sin. While it is *true* that "God is love" (1 John 4:8), it is also true that "God is light" (1 John 1:5), and in His holiness He must deal with sin.

A Christian doctor had tried to witness to a very moral woman who belonged to a church that denied the need for salvation and the reality of future judgment. "God loves me too much to condemn me," the patient would reply. "I cannot believe that God would make such a place as a lake of fire."

The woman became ill and the diagnosis was cancer. An operation was necessary. "I wonder if I really should operate," the doctor said to her in her hospital room. "I really love you too much to cut into you and give you pain."

"Doctor," said the patient, "if you really loved me, you would do everything possible to save me. How can you permit this awful thing to remain in my body?"

It was easy then for him to explain that what cancer is to the body, sin is to the world; and both must be dealt with radically and completely. Just as a physician cannot love health without hating disease and dealing with it, so God cannot love righteousness without hating sin and judging it.

The word *vengeance* must not be confused with *revenge*. The purpose of vengeance is to satisfy God's holy law; the purpose of revenge is to pacify a personal grudge. God does not hold a grudge against lost sinners. Quite the contrary, He sent His Son to die for them, and He pleads with them to return to Him. But if sinners prefer to "know not God, and … obey not the gospel" (2 Thess. 1:8), there is nothing left for God to do but judge them.

This judgment will take place when Jesus Christ returns to the earth with His church and His angels (2 Thess. 1:7). This is not the same event described by Paul in 1 Thessalonians 4:13–18. We may contrast these two events:

1 Thessalonians 4:13–18	*2 Thessalonians 1*
Christ returns in the air	Christ returns to the earth
He comes secretly *for* the church	He comes openly *with* the church
Believers escape the tribulation	Unbelievers experience the tribulation, judgment
Occurs at an undisclosed time	Occurs at the end of the tribulation period, the day of the Lord

Rest (vv. 7a, 10). *God* will recompense tribulation to the lost, but rest to the saved. I believe that the first phrase in 2 Thessalonians 1:7 should be treated as a parenthesis: "to recompense tribulation to them that trouble you (and to you who are troubled, rest with us) when the Lord Jesus shall be revealed." The saints receive their rest when the Lord returns in the air and catches us up to be with Him.

The word *rest* means "relief, release, not under pressure." It is the opposite of "tribulation." The word describes the releasing of a bowstring. In this life, God's people are pressured, "pressed out of measure" (2 Cor. 1:8), and under the burdens of trial and persecution. But when we see Christ, we will be released. We need not fear fiery wrath and judgment (1 Thess. 1:10; 5:9), for God has already judged our sins at Calvary.

What kind of future is there for the lost? They face punishment and eternal judgment (2 Thess. 1:9), while the saved shall enjoy the rest and glories of heaven. The lost shall be separated from God, while the saved "shall see his face" (Rev. 22:4). Some cultists have tried to dilute the meaning of "everlasting destruction," saying it means either temporary suffering or total annihilation; but both ideas are false. The phrase means "eternal judgment," no matter how men try to twist it or avoid it (see Matt. 25:41).

Paul encouraged his friends with praise and promise; and he had a third encouragement.

The Encouragement of Prayer (1:11–12)

Paul prayed for his converts (1 Thess. 1:2; 3:10). His "wherefore" in 2 Thessalonians 1:11 means "And because of all I have just said"—the return of Christ to be glorified in the saints, and to judge the lost. The future prospect of glory motivated the apostle to pray for the saints. We must never neglect a present responsibility because of a future hope. On the contrary, the future hope must encourage us to be faithful today.

There were three concerns in Paul's prayer.

Their worthiness (v. 11a). In 2 Thessalonians 1:5, Paul had stated that he wanted them to be worthy of the kingdom when they entered glory in the future. But here he emphasized their present situation. God's calling was in grace and love, and Paul desired that they might live up to that calling (see 2 Thess. 2:13–14).

Trials do not make a person; they reveal what a person is made of. When our faith is tried, we are revealing our worth (1 Peter 1:6–9). God certainly knows our hearts even before we are tried, but *we do not know our own hearts*. And others do not know what we are worth. We need to pray that God will build our worth and make us more valuable Christians because of the trials we have endured.

Their walk (v. 11b). "That by his power he may fulfill every good purpose of yours and every act prompted by your faith" (NIV). Character must lead to conduct. Paul prayed that they might have a resolute will, empowered by God, to do what He wanted them to do. Obedience and service do not spring from human talent and efforts, but from God's power as we trust Him.

Paul had linked faith with *love* (2 Thess. 1:3) and *endurance* (2 Thess. 1:4), and here he linked it with *power*. If we believe God, we will receive His power in our lives. We cannot be victorious in tribulations if we only trust ourselves, but we can be victorious through trusting Him.

When I travel, I carry an electric razor that can store up the energy and run for perhaps two hours without any outside source of power. It is especially useful when I visit the mission fields.

While preaching for a week at a summer conference, I noticed that my razor was losing power. In fact, one morning it operated so slowly that I was convinced it was broken. Then by evening, it had picked up speed again. A few minutes' investigation revealed the problem: I had plugged the razor into a socket that was controlled by a wall switch. When my wife had the desk lamp on, my razor was storing up power; when the light was off, the razor received no power.

That incident taught me a spiritual lesson: it is easy (by force of habit) to trust a source of power without checking to see if the switch is on. Paul was praying that his friends might "have the switch on" and, by their faith, receive the power needed to endure suffering and glorify God.

Their witness (v. 12). Jesus Christ will be glorified in His saints when they return with Him (2 Thess. 1:10), but He should also be glorified in our lives today. Unbelievers blaspheme His name (1 Peter 4:12ff.), but believers bless His name and seek to glorify it. The amazing thing is that the believer who glorifies Christ is likewise glorified *in Christ,* "glorified in you, and you in him" (NIV).

How can this be done? "According to the grace of our God and Lord Jesus Christ" (2 Thess. 1:12). Grace and glory go together, as do suffering and glory (see Ps. 45:2–3; 84:11; Rom. 5:2; 2 Cor. 8:19; 1 Peter 5:10). As we receive His grace, we reveal His glory.

"'There is no peace,' saith the Lord, 'unto the wicked'" (Isa. 48:22). No rest for the wicked! But there is rest for those who trust Christ and seek to live for His glory. For the Christian, the best is yet to come. We know that "the sufferings of this present time are not worthy to be compared with the glory which shall be revealed in us" (Rom. 8:18).

CHAPTER TWO
2 Thessalonians 2:1–12
GOD'S TIMETABLE

The purpose of Bible prophecy is not for us to make a calendar, but to build character. Paul emphasized this fact in both of his Thessalonian letters, and our Lord warned us not to set dates for His coming (Matt. 24:36, 42). Date-setters are usually upsetters, and that is exactly what happened in the Thessalonican assembly.

Someone had deceived the believers into thinking they were already living in the day of the Lord. The teaching probably first came through a "prophetic utterance" in one of their meetings, and then it was further enhanced by a letter claiming to come from Paul himself. The believers were instantly shaken by this teaching and continued to be deeply troubled. Had God changed His program? Had not Paul promised them deliverance from the tribulation (see 1 Thess. 1:10; 5:9)?

To calm their hearts and stabilize their faith, Paul explained that they were not in the day of the Lord. The reason was simple: that day could not arrive till certain other events had taken place. Paul then stated for them the prophetic events that make up God's timetable.

The Rapture of the Church (2:1, 6–7)
Paul appealed to them to "calm down" on the basis of the truth he had taught them in his first letter: the Lord would return and catch up His own to meet Him to the air (1 Thess. 4:13–18). This is "the coming of our Lord Jesus Christ and … our gathering together unto him" (2 Thess. 2:1). Not two separated events, but one great event that will occur suddenly and without warning.

Once the church is out of the world, Satan and his forces will unfold their program. The day of the Lord is the period that follows the rapture of the church. It will be a time of tribulation for the people on earth: Satan and his hosts will be working on earth, and God will send righteous judgments from heaven. Revelation 6—19 describes this period for us.

Why is Satan unable to reveal his "man of sin" sooner? Because God is restraining the forces of evil in the world today. Satan cannot do whatever he wants to do, whenever he pleases. Our sovereign Lord is able to make even the wrath of man to praise Him, and "the remainder of wrath shalt thou restrain" (Ps. 76:10). In 2 Thessalonians 2:6–7, Paul mentioned a restraining force that even today is helping keep everything on schedule.

Who or what is this restrainer? Paul told the Thessalonicans when he was teaching them personally, but he did not put this information in either of his letters. This restrainer is now at work in the world and will continue to work till it (or he) is "taken out of the midst" (literal translation of 2 Thess. 2:7b).

Notice that in 2 Thessalonians 2:6 Paul referred to this restrainer in the neuter gender ("what restraineth"), while in 2 Thessalonians 2:7, he used the masculine gender ("he who now hindereth"). The restrainer is a person who is today "in the midst," but will one day be "taken out of the midst."

Many Bible students identify this restrainer as the Holy Spirit of God. Certainly, He is "in the midst" of God's program today, working through the church to accomplish God's purposes. When the church is raptured, the Holy Spirit will not be taken *out of the world* (otherwise nobody could be saved during the tribulation), but He will be taken *out of the midst* to allow Satan and his forces to go to work. The Holy Spirit will certainly be present on the earth during the day of the Lord, but He will not be restraining the forces of evil as He is today.

In spite of its weakness and seeming failure, never underestimate the importance of the church in the world. People who criticize the church do not realize that the presence of the people of God in this world gives unsaved people opportunity to be saved. The presence of the church is delaying the coming of judgment. Lot was not a dedicated man, but his presence in Sodom held back the wrath of God (Gen. 19:12–29).

There are two programs at work in the world today: God's program of salvation, and Satan's program of sin, "the mystery of iniquity." God has a timetable for His program, and nothing Satan does can change that timetable. Just as there was a "fullness of the time" for the coming of Christ (Gal. 4:4), so there is a "fullness of the time" for the appearance of Antichrist; and nothing will be off schedule. Once the restraining ministry of the Spirit of God has ended, the next event can take place.

The Revelation of Antichrist (2:3–5, 8a)

Paul did not use the term *Antichrist* in his letter. This term is used in the New Testament only by John (1 John 2:18, 22; 4:3; 2 John 7). But this is the name we use to identify the last great world dictator whom Paul designated as "that man of sin," "the son of perdition" (2 Thess. 2:3), and "that lawless one" (2 Thess. 2:8, literal translation).

Satan has been at war with God ever since he, as Lucifer, rebelled against God and tried to capture God's throne (Isa. 14:12–15). He tempted Eve in the garden and, through her, caused Adam to fall (Gen. 3). In Genesis 3:15, God declared war on Satan and his family ("seed") and promised the coming of the Redeemer who would finally and completely defeat Satan.

The Greek prefix *anti-* has two meanings: *against,* and *instead of.* Satan not only opposes Christ, but he wants to be worshipped and obeyed *instead of* Christ. Satan has always wanted to be worshipped and served as God (Isa. 14:14; Luke 4:5–8). He will one day produce his masterpiece, the Antichrist, who will cause the world to worship Satan and believe Satan's lies.

Paul had explained all of this to the believers in Thessalonica, referring them, no doubt, to the relevant Scriptures in the Old Testament. We are fortunate to have the entire Bible to study, so we can get the total picture of Antichrist and his career. Prophetic students may not agree on every detail, but the main facts, when they are related, give us the following description of Antichrist in the last days.

The peacemaker (Rev. 6:1–2). Certainly, this man will be on the scene before the rapture of the church. He will be a peaceful political leader who unites ten nations of Europe into a strong power bloc (see Rev.

17:12–13). The rider on the white horse imitates Christ (Rev. 19:11ff.). He goes forth to conquer peacefully: he has a bow, but no arrows. He will bring a brief time of peace to the world (1 Thess. 5:1–3) before the storm of the day of the Lord breaks loose.

The protector (Dan. 9:24–27). We cannot examine the exciting details of this prophecy, but it is important to note several facts. First, the prophecy applies to Israel, Jerusalem, and the temple, and not to the church. Second, it announces the time when Messiah will come and accomplish certain purposes for the Jewish people. The word *week* refers to a period of seven years; seventy weeks are equal to 490 years. Note that these 490 years are divided into three parts: seven weeks or forty-nine years, during which the city would be rebuilt; sixty-two weeks or 434 years, at the end of which time Messiah would come and be cut off; one week or seven years, during which a "prince" would have a covenant with Israel.

Notice that *two princes* are involved in this prophecy: Christ, Messiah the Prince (Dan. 9:25), and Antichrist "the prince that shall come" (Dan. 9:26). "The people of the prince that shall come" are the Romans; for it was they who destroyed the city and the temple in AD 70. The coming Antichrist will belong to a nation that was part of the old Roman Empire.

Finally, note that there is a parenthesis between the sixty-ninth and the seventieth week. We are now living in that parenthesis. The sixty-ninth week ended with the ministry of Christ. The seventieth week will start with the arrival of Antichrist. He will make a covenant with Israel to protect her and permit her to rebuild her temple. This covenant will be for seven years. *He will temporarily solve the Middle East crisis.* Israel will rebuild her temple in peaceful times. It is the signing of this covenant, not the rapture of the church, that signals the start of Daniel's seventieth week, that seven-year period known as the day of the Lord.

The peace-breaker (Dan. 9:27). After three and one-half years, Antichrist will break his covenant with the Jews *and take over their temple.* This was what Paul termed "the falling away" (2 Thess. 2:3b). A better translation would be "the rebellion, the apostasy." Not simply *a* rebellion, but *the* rebellion. Up to this point, Antichrist has been a peacemaking leader of ten European nations, obligated to protect Israel. But now he reveals his true character by taking over the Jewish temple and demanding that the world worship him (see Rev. 13).

Since Antichrist will be energized by Satan, it is no surprise that he will seek worship, for Satan has always wanted the worship of the world. There have been various "apostasies" in church history, when groups have turned away from God's truth; but this final rebellion will be the greatest of all. The man of sin will oppose everything that belongs to any other religion, true or false. He will organize a world church that will, by worshipping him, worship Satan.

Our Lord predicted this apostasy; He called it "the

abomination of desolation" (Matt. 24:15), a clear reference to Daniel 9:27. The world will wonder at this great leader who, with Satan's power, will perform signs and wonders and deceive the nations.

The persecutor (Rev. 13:15–17). Most prophetic students agree that the abomination of desolation will occur three and one-half years after the Antichrist makes his covenant with the Jews. (Dan. 9:27—"in the midst of the week" or three and one-half years.) This will usher in a period of intense persecution and tribulation. Jesus said, "For then shall be great tribulation" (Matt. 24:21). Satan will vent his wrath against Israel. He will so control the world's economic system that citizens must bear "the mark of the beast" to be able to buy and sell (Rev. 13:16–17).

People often ask, "Will anybody be saved during the seven-year period?" The answer is yes! Revelation 7:1–8 states that 144,000 Jews will be saved (probably as was the apostle Paul, by a dramatic vision of Christ) and will carry the gospel to the nations. The apostle John described a great multitude of Gentiles who will come out of the great tribulation (Rev. 7:9–17) as converted people. Even though the Holy Spirit will be "out of the midst" as the restraining power, He will still work with redeeming power.

However, it will cost dearly to trust Christ and live for Him during that time. Believers will refuse to bow down to the beast's image and will be slain. They will refuse to wear his mark and thus be unable to get jobs or make purchases. It will be quite a contrast to our situation now, when even famous people admit that they are "born again."

The prisoner (Rev. 19:11–21). Keep in mind that God has a timetable. Satan will not be permitted to control the world forever. Jesus Christ will return "in power and great glory" and take Antichrist and his associates prisoner—and also Satan—and cast them into the bottomless pit (Rev. 20:1–3). This will be the climax of the great Battle of Armageddon (Rev. 16:16) during which the nations of the world unite with Satan to fight Jesus Christ. This leads to our next event.

The Return of Jesus Christ (2:8–12)

This is His return to the earth in glory and judgment, the event described in 2 Thessalonians 1:5–10 and Revelation 19:11ff. It will occur at the end of the seven-year tribulation period when the "mystery of iniquity" (Satan's evil program) will have ended with the battle of Armageddon. It is important that we distinguish His rapture of the church from His return to the earth. The first event is secret, as the church is caught up to meet Him in the air. The second event is public, when the church returns with Him to defeat Satan and his hosts.

His judgment of Antichrist (vv. 8–9). Nobody on earth will be able to overcome the Antichrist and his forces, for he is energized by Satan. "Who is like unto the beast? Who is able to make war with him?" (Rev. 13:4). Satan will enable his false messiah to perform "power and signs and lying wonders" (2 Thess. 2:9). This, of course, is in imitation of Jesus Christ who performed "miracles and wonders and signs" (Acts 2:22).

Satan has always been an imitator. There are false Christians in the world who are really children of the devil (Matt. 13:38; 2 Cor. 11:26). He has false ministers (2 Cor. 11:13ff) who preach a false gospel (Gal. 1:6–9). There is even a "synagogue of Satan" (Rev. 2:9), which means a gathering of people who think they are worshipping God but who are really worshipping the devil (1 Cor. 10:19–21). These false Christians have a counterfeit righteousness that is not the saving righteousness of Christ (Rom. 10:1–3; Phil. 3:4–10). They have a false assurance of salvation that will prove useless when they face judgment (Matt. 7:15–29).

During the apostolic age, miracles were given to verify the message (Heb. 2:1–4). God's chosen apostles used miracles as their credential to prove they were sent by God (2 Cor. 12:12). However, miracles *alone* never prove that a man is sent from God: his message and his character must also be considered. John the Baptist was "a man sent from God" (John 1:6), yet "John did no miracle" (John 10:41).

Satan can perform miracles that seem to rival those of the Lord. This is how he opposed Moses in the court of Pharaoh (Ex. 7:8–12, 20–22, 8:5–7). In the final judgment, some people who performed miracles *in the name of Jesus* will be rejected by the Lord because they were never saved (Matt. 7:21–23). Judas performed miracles, yet he was never born again (John 6:66–71; 13:11, 18).

The purpose of God's miracles was to lead people to the truth; the purpose of Antichrist's miracles will be to lead people to believe his lies. Paul called them "lying wonders" (2 Thess. 2:9), not because the miracles are not real, but because they persuade people to believe Satan's lies. The world would not long follow a leader who practiced cheap trickery (see Rev. 13:13–14).

When Jesus Christ returns, He will judge Antichrist by "the spirit of his mouth … and the brightness of his coming" (2 Thess. 2:8). The verbs "consume" and "destroy" do not mean annihilate, for Revelation 20:10 indicates that Satan and his associates will be tormented in the lake of fire forever. You could translate this statement: "whom the Lord Jesus will overthrow with the breath of His mouth, and bring an end to his operations by the outshining of His presence."

As the coming of the Lord for His church draws near, Satan's operations in this world will intensify (read 1 Tim. 4; 2 Tim. 3). Since Satan is a liar, we must resist him through the truth of God's Word (Eph. 6:17). It was this sword that our Lord used when He defeated Satan in the wilderness (Matt. 4:1–11). Satan is a liar and a murderer (John 8:44). God gives life through His truth; Satan slays with his lies. We are encouraged to know that one day Jesus Christ will completely overthrow Satan and his system.

His judgment of the unsaved (vv. 10–12). We have noted that a great number of Jews and Gentiles will be saved during the seven-year tribulation period. But the vast majority of the world's population will be lost. Many will die in the terrible judgments that God will send on earth (see Rev. 6:7–8; 8:11; 9:18; 11:13). Others will perish in judgment when Jesus Christ returns and separates the saved from the lost (Matt. 25:31–46).

It is important to note that these people did have opportunity to believe and be saved. God has no delight in judging the lost (Ezek. 33:11). God is "not willing that any should perish, but that all should come to repentance" (2 Peter 3:9). These people will be judged and will suffer forever because they would not receive and believe the truth. In fact, their hearts will be so evil that they will not even have any *love* for the truth. Those who love lies and make lies will be excluded from the heavenly city (Rev. 22:15) and sent to the lake of fire.

In this paragraph, Paul taught a sobering truth: a person can so resist the truth that he finally becomes deluded and has to believe a lie. There can be no neutral ground: either we believe the truth or we believe a lie. To reject the truth means to receive the lie.

Does this mean that God is to blame for a man's rejection of Christ? No more than God was to blame for Pharaoh's spiritual condition when Moses was bringing the plagues on Egypt. Pharaoh heard God's Word and saw God's wonders, yet he refused to bow to God's will. Pharaoh occasionally relented and gave lip service to God's will, but he always resisted in the end and refused to obey God. He hardened his heart so that he could not believe the truth, and this led to God's final judgment of the land of Egypt.

Second Thessalonians 2:11 reads literally, "That they should believe *the* lie." What is "the lie"? Satan is the liar and has foisted many deceptions on the human race. But there is one "lie" that, from the beginning, has led people astray. Satan first spoke it to Eve: "You shall be as God!" *The lie* is the idea that man is his own God and therefore can do whatever he pleases and better himself by his own human efforts. The process is described in Romans 1:18ff. Note especially Romans 1:25: "Who exchanged the truth of God for the lie, and worshipped and served the creature rather than the Creator" (literal translation).

All of which means that Satan appeals to man's pride. It was pride that turned Lucifer into Satan (Isa. 14:12–15; Ezek. 28:11–18). It is pride that traps men into doing Satan's will in this world (see 2 Tim. 2:24–26).

A friend told me about a church officer on the mission field who was causing great problems in the church. Whenever the missionary was in the village, the officer lived a godly life, but no sooner did the missionary leave than the man began to behave as though he were controlled by Satan. Finally the missionary and several church leaders confronted the man in the name of Jesus Christ, and they discovered the truth: Satan was using pride to control the officer's life.

"When I was ordained an elder," the man explained, "I heard a voice say to me, 'Now you are somebody important.' I yielded to that voice, and Satan took over in my life." He confessed his sin, the church prayed, and God delivered him.

"Now you are somebody important!" "Worship and serve the creature rather than the Creator." This is Satan's lie, and I fear it is what rules the world today. God originally made man in His own image. Today, man is making God in his own image.

The people Christ will judge not only do not love the truth, but they have "pleasure in unrighteousness" (2 Thess. 2:12). Read Psalm 50:16–21 for one description of this kind of person, and also Psalm 52. The chief priests actually were *glad* when Judas promised to help them kill Christ (Mark 14:10–11). I mentioned before that this process of believing the lie is described in Romans 1. The closing verse of that section (Rom. 1:32) states this truth clearly: "Who knowing the judgment of God, that they which commit such things are worthy of death, not only do the same, but have pleasure in them that do them."

Does this mean that those who have heard the gospel before the rapture of the church cannot be saved after the rapture? Not necessarily. If that were true, then our witness to the lost is condemning them, should Christ return. However, it does mean that no lost sinner can afford to treat God's truth carelessly or reject God's Son repeatedly. The human heart becomes harder each time the sinner rejects God's truth; and this makes it easier to believe Satan's lies.

How much better it is to follow the example of the Thessalonian believers who received the Word of God "not as the word of men, but as it is in truth, the word of God" (1 Thess. 2:13). They received the truth and were saved.

Have you received the truth?

CHAPTER THREE
2 Thessalonians 2:13—3:5
NOTHING BUT THE TRUTH

P aul was a balanced Christian who had a balanced ministry, and we see evidence of this as he brought his letter to a close. He moved from prophecy to practical Christian living. He turned from the negative (Satan's lies) to the positive (God's truth), and from warning to thanksgiving and prayer.

We desperately need balanced ministries today. I have attended Bible conferences where the only emphasis was on what Christ *will do* with the Jews in the future, to the total neglect of what He *wants to do* with the church in the present. We must never permit the study of prophecy to be an escape from responsibility today.

Paul's emphasis was on the truth of God's Word, in contrast to Satan's great lie, which Paul discussed in the previous section. Every believer has four responsibilities to God's truth.

Believe the Truth (2:13–14)

We have noted Paul's repeated thanksgiving in his letters to this church (1 Thess. 1:2; 2:13; 3:9; 2 Thess. 1:3; 2:13). He gave thanks for the way they responded to God's work in their lives. In these two verses, Paul reviewed the stages in their salvation experience.

God loved them (v. 13a). Whatever God does for the lost world springs from His eternal love. We must never conceive of His great plan of salvation as an impersonal machine. His salvation is rooted and grounded in His love (John 3:16). God proved this love at the cross where Jesus Christ died for the sins of the world (Rom. 5:8).

God chose them (v. 13b). It is not love alone that saves us, for God loves the whole world, and yet the whole world is not saved. Love reveals itself in *grace* and *mercy*. God in His grace gives us through Christ what we do not deserve, and God in His mercy does not give what we do deserve—but He gave that to Christ! We dare not explain away God's election of sinners (1 Thess. 1:4; Eph. 1:4; 1 Peter 1:2).

God set them apart (v. 13c). The word *sanctify* means "to set apart." There is a progressive sanctification that makes us more like Jesus Christ (1 Thess. 5:23). But the sanctification Paul mentioned here refers to the Spirit's work in leading the unbeliever to faith in Christ. "Elect according to the foreknowledge of God the Father, through sanctification of the Spirit" (1 Peter 1:2). It is the work of the Holy Spirit to bring conviction to the sinner (John 16:7–11). Though I did not realize it at the time, as I look back I can see how the Spirit led in bringing me to faith in Christ; and this is the experience of every believer.

God called them (v. 14a). The same God who ordained the end (salvation) also ordained the means to the end ("belief of the truth"). The person who says, "God already has His elect, so there is no need for us to pray, witness, and send out missionaries" does not understand divine election. The greatest encouragement to evangelism is the knowledge that God has His people who have been prepared to respond to His Word (read Acts 18:1–11).

In order for God to fulfill His eternal plan, He sent Paul, Silas, and Timothy to Thessalonica to preach the Word of God. What was ordained *in eternity* was accomplished *in time*. God used human instruments to bring the gospel to the lost; and by trusting Christ, these people proved their "election of God" (1 Thess. 1:4). The call of God went out to the whole city, but it was effective only in those who believed the truth and trusted Christ.

It is dangerous to engage in idle speculation about divine sovereignty and human responsibility. Both are taught in the Bible. We know that "salvation is of the Lord" (Jonah 2:9), and that lost sinners can never save themselves. We must admit that there are *mysteries* to our salvation; but we can rejoice that there are *certainties* on which we can rest. We must not use the doctrine of election to divide the church or disturb the weak, but to glorify the Lord.

God gave them glory (v. 14b). What began in eternity past reaches its climax in eternity future: we share in the glory of God (John 17:24; Rom. 8:29–30). What begins with grace always leads to glory. This is quite a contrast to the future assigned to the lost (2 Thess. 1:8–10). Believers already possess God's glory within (John 17:22; note the past tense in Rom. 8:30—"glorified"). We are awaiting Christ's return, and then the glory shall be revealed (Rom. 8:17–19; 2 Thess. 1:10).

When sinners believe God's truth. God saves them. When they believe Satan's lie and reject the love of the truth, they cannot be saved (2 Thess. 2:10–12). Being neutral about God's truth is a dangerous thing. It has tragic eternal consequences.

Guard the Truth (2:15)

Paul had told them about the *future* rebellion against the truth (2 Thess. 2:3), the great apostasy headed by the Antichrist. But he also warned in his letters that there was a *present* danger, and that the church must guard God's truth and not turn from it. There are repeated warnings about this in the New Testament: 1 John 2:18–24; 4:1–3; 2 Peter 2; 1 Timothy 4; and 2 Timothy 3, to name only a few.

God works in this world through the truth of His Word, and Satan opposes this truth by substituting his lies. Human nature is prone to believe a lie and resist the truth. Satan accomplishes his best work through people in so-called Christian institutions (churches, schools, and so forth) who do not believe God's truth. They have "a form of godliness" but have never experienced the power of God's saving truth.

When Paul used the word *traditions,* he was not referring to man-made religious ideas that are not based on the Word of God. Our Lord rejected man's religious traditions (Mark 7:1–13). Paul warned against them in Colossians 2:8. It is sad to see religious people argue over man's traditions and, at the same time, reject the simple truth of the Word of God.

The word *tradition* simply means "that which is handed down from one person to another." The truth of the gospel began as an oral message proclaimed by Christ and the apostles. Later, this truth was written down by the inspiration of the Holy Spirit, and it became Holy Scripture (see 2 Tim. 3:12–17; 2 Peter 2:16–21). God's truth was not invented by men: it was handed down from God to man (1 Cor. 15:1–6; Gal. 1:11–12), and each generation of believers had guarded this truth and passed it on to others (2 Tim. 2:2).

Paul stated clearly the believers' dual responsibility in guarding the truth: "stand fast, and hold the traditions" (2 Thess. 2:15). *Stand fast* means "Do not move away from the truth of the gospel" (see 1 Cor. 16:13; Col. 1:23). When my wife and I visited the

Tower of London and saw the royal jewels, we noticed that the crowd was kept moving, but the guards stood still. They were constantly watching the visitors, and nothing could move them from their appointed places. You and I are helping to guard the "precious faith," and we must not be moved by the wiles of Satan or the praises of men.

If we *stand,* then we can *hold.* This word means "to hold fast, to hold firmly." It is related to a Greek word that means "strength, might, power." We are not to hold God's truth in a careless way, but grasp it firmly with power and never let it slip from us. Each generation of Christians must receive the truth from others, guard it, and make sure it is kept intact for the next generation.

It is not easy to *stand* or *hold,* because forces around us want to move us from the faith. Satan knows how to use lies to oppose God's truth, and he seeks to do this *within the fellowship* (Acts 20:28—32). Sometimes faithful believers must refuse the fellowship of those who have rejected the faith (Rom. 16:17—20; 2 Cor. 6:14—7:1; 1 Tim. 6:3—5; 2 John 7—10).

Let me sum this up with two words of caution. First, "the faith" that has been handed down to us must not be confused with man's interpretations and ideas. The Pharisees made their own interpretations as sacred as the Word of God (Mark 7:7—9). The basic doctrines of God's Word are held by all evangelical believers, but not all believers agree on minor matters of interpretation (especially in the area of prophecy) or matters of church order. It is dangerous to make man's ideas a test of fellowship or spirituality.

Second, we must not embalm the truth so that it loses its life and power. We are to be like faithful householders who bring out of God's treasury of truth "things new and old" (Matt. 13:52). There is yet more truth to be found in God's Word, and we must not think that we know it all. The Word is like seed (Luke 8:11), and when seed is sown, it produces plants, fruit, *and more seed.* While it is good to "tell the old, old story," it is also good to let the Spirit teach us new truths from the Word and to make new applications of old truths.

Practice the Truth (2:16—17)

It is not enough to believe the truth and guard it; we must also practice it. If we hear the Word, but do not obey it, we are only fooling ourselves (James 1:22—25).

These two verses record Paul's desire and prayer for his friends: he wanted God to *encourage* them ("comfort your hearts") and *establish* them ("stablish you") "in every good word and work." Both of these words are prominent in the Thessalonian letters.

When Paul was with them, he *encouraged* them individually as a father does his children (1 Thess. 2:11). He sent Timothy to encourage them (1 Thess. 3:2), and Paul himself was greatly encouraged with Timothy's report of their faithfulness (1 Thess. 3:7).

Paul encouraged them to walk to please God (1 Thess. 4:1), and to grow in their love for others (1 Thess. 4:10). He taught them about the rapture of the church in order that they might encourage each other (1 Thess. 4:18). To calm their fears, he explained the day of the Lord to them (1 Thess. 5:11). In addition to his teaching, he urged them to minister to each other (1 Thess. 5:18).

Establishment in the Lord is also an important theme. Paul sent Timothy back to Thessalonica that he might establish them in their faith (1 Thess. 3:2); and Paul prayed that God might establish them (1 Thess. 3:13). The child must be taught to stand before he can learn to walk or run.

It is God who establishes, but He uses people to accomplish His work. A great need in our churches is for Christians who will take time to establish the younger believers. Group Bible studies are very valuable, as are the public meetings of the church, but individual discipling is also important. Paul encouraged the Thessalonican believers on a one-to-one basis, and we should follow his example.

Paul was concerned about two aspects of their Christian life: their *word* and their *work,* their *saying* and their *doing.* If our walk contradicts our words, we lose our testimony. Our "walk" and our "talk" must agree; good works and good words must come from the same yielded heart.

We are not saved by good works (Eph. 2:8—10; Titus 3:3—7); but good works are the evidence of salvation (Titus 2:11—15). It is not enough to depend on good words; the words must be backed up by the deeds (1 John 3:18). It must be a steady practice, not an occasional one. We must be *established* in our words and works.

How is this possible? Only God can do it by His grace; and this is what Paul desired for his friends. God has given us eternal encouragement and good hope through His grace. Notice that Paul's words united the Lord Jesus Christ and God the Father in such a way that he affirmed the deity of Christ. The two names for God in 2 Thessalonians 2:16 are governed by a *singular* verb, not a plural, which means they are equal. He used the same construction in 1 Thessalonians 3:11, again affirming the equality of the Son with the Father.

Too many Christians today emphasize *guarding* the truth, but downplay *living* the truth. One of the best ways to guard the truth is to put it into practice. It is good to be defenders of the faith, but we must not forget to be demonstrators of the faith. Lazarus did not have to give lectures on the resurrection. People had only to look at him and they believed (John 12:9—11).

Share the Truth (3:1—5)

A sequence of responsibilities is logical. Learning and living must go together. If we believe the truth, it changes our lives. We guard the truth and practice it so that we can share it with others. We cannot share what we do not believe (unless we want to be hypocrites), and we can best share that which we have practiced ourselves.

God's Word is alive (Heb. 4:12); we must let it move freely. Paul alluded here to Psalm 147:15—"He sent forth His commandment upon earth: His word runneth very swiftly." God's servants may be bound, but God's Word cannot be bound (2 Tim. 2:9). As we practice the truth and pray for the ministry of the truth, God's Word will have freedom to run and accomplish God's purposes in the world.

The Word of God is glorified in the lives of those who share it and those who receive it. This was Paul's experience in Antioch of Pisidia: "And when the Gentiles heard this [that they could be saved], they were glad, and glorified the word of the Lord: and as many as were ordained to eternal life believed. And the word of the Lord was published [spread abroad] throughout all the region" (Acts 13:48–49).

Too much Christian work these days is accomplished by human plans and promotion, and not by the Word of God. We trust our programs and do not publish the Word of God. The universe was created, and is sustained, by the Word of God (Heb. 11:3). Surely His Word can accomplish His work in this world. But the preaching of the Word in the pulpit has too often been replaced by the entertainment of the world on the platform. Dr. Donald Coggan, Archbishop of Canterbury, has said of Christian pastors, "It is their task to feed the sheep—not to entertain the goats."

It has been my experience in three pastorates that God's Word will accomplish God's work. When the sheep are fed, they will flock together in love, reproduce, follow the shepherd—and they can be "fleeced" and will love it. It is when the sheep are hungry that they start biting each other, becoming sick, and wandering away. When the Word of God does the work, then God gets the glory. My good friend Dr. Bob Cook used to remind us, "If you can explain what is going on, then God isn't doing it!"

Of course, there is always opposition to the Word and work of God. Paul asked his friends to pray that he might be delivered from unbelieving men who were evil and wicked. Just as the Spirit uses dedicated people to share the Word, Satan uses wicked people to oppose the Word. The evil one enjoys using Christian believers to oppose the work of God. He spoke through Peter (Matt. 16:21–23), and he worked through Ananias and Sapphira (Acts 5:1–11).

Paul had confidence that his readers would not yield to Satan, but would permit the faithful Lord to establish them and guard them from the evil one (literal meaning of 2 Thess. 3:3). We cannot have confidence in ourselves, but we can have confidence in God for ourselves and for others.

It is not enough that the pastor or church officers alone share the Word; each Christian must be a part of this vital ministry. The word *command* that Paul used in 2 Thessalonians 3:4 means "a military order passed down from a superior officer." He used this word in 1 Thessalonians 4:2, and he repeated it in 2 Thessalonians 3:4, 6, 10, 12. Christ is the Captain

of our salvation; we are His soldiers (2 Tim. 2:3–4). In a battle, it is not enough for only the officers to fight; every man must do his duty. This is also true in the work of the local church.

What if an army were run with the same lack of obedience, order, and discipline that we often see in the local church? It would never win the war. If soldiers attended drill whenever they felt like it, they would never be equipped to face the enemy. If the recruits disobeyed their officers' orders the way some church members disobey the Word of God, they would be court-martialed.

A soldier obeys primarily out of loyalty and fear. But a Christian has much higher motives for obedience: God's love and Christ's return (2 Thess. 3:5). "If ye love me, keep my commandments" (John 14:15). A commanding officer does not require his men to love him, but if they do, they will respect and obey him with greater diligence. The history of warfare records heroic deeds done by men who loved their leaders and willingly died for them. Our Savior loved us and died for us. Can we not obey Him?

He is coming for us. This has been the theme of Paul's two letters to the Thessalonians, and he related this truth to everyday practical living. As God's soldiers, we must be sharing the Word, for He will one day return and ask for an accounting of our lives. Do we "love his appearing" (2 Tim. 4:8)? Will we "be ashamed before him at his coming" (1 John 2:28)?

Here, then, are four great responsibilities for us to fulfill: believe the truth, guard the truth, practice the truth, and share the truth. If we fulfill these duties, we will experience joy and power in our lives, and growth and blessing in our churches.

CHAPTER FOUR
2 Thessalonians 3:6–18
ORDER IN THE CHURCH

When problems are not solved, they grow and become worse. A sliver left in the finger can become infected and cause a toxic condition so serious that surgery may become necessary. If you tell your doctor that you stepped on a rusty nail, he will immediately give you a tetanus shot, even though the wound may appear insignificant to you.

Church problems are like physical problems: if left unsolved, they grow and become worse, and they infect more people. The local church is a body, and what germs are to the physical body, sin is to the spiritual body. When Paul wrote his first letter to the Thessalonican church, he warned the idle busybodies to get to work (1 Thess. 4:11). He admonished the church leaders to "warn them that are unruly" (1 Thess. 5:14). The word *unruly* means "a soldier out of rank." Apparently these troublemakers did not repent, because Paul devoted the rest of his second letter to this problem.

What was the problem? Some members of the assembly had misinterpreted Paul's teachings about the return of Christ, left their jobs, and were living off the generosity of the church. They were idle while others were working. Yet they expected the church to support them. It is possible that this group of lazy saints was the source of the false teaching Paul mentioned in 2 Thessalonians 2:2. They were also spreading gossip about people in the church. They had time on their hands and gossip on their lips, but they defended themselves by arguing, "The Lord is coming soon!"

Misinterpretations and misapplications of the truths of God's Word can cause endless trouble. History records the foolishness of people who set dates, sold their possessions, and sat on mountains, waiting for the Lord to return. Any teaching that encourages us to disobey another divine teaching is not Bible teaching.

The Pharisees figured out a way to rob their parents and yet obey the fifth commandment:

And He [Jesus] said to them, "Rightly did Isaiah prophesy of you hypocrites, as it is written: 'This people honors me with their lips, but their heart is far away from me. But in vain do they worship me, teaching as doctrines the precepts of men.' Neglecting the commandment of God, you hold to the tradition of men."

He was also saying to them, "You are experts at setting aside the commandment of God in order to keep your tradition. For Moses said, 'Honor your father and your mother'; and 'He who speaks evil of father or mother is to be put to death'; but you say, 'If a man says to his father or his mother, whatever I have that would help you is Corban (that is to say, given to God),' you no longer permit him to do anything for his father or his mother; thus invalidating the word of God by your tradition which you have handed down; and you do many things such as that" (Mark 7:6–13 NASB).

Paul expected the whole church to work together in solving this problem. The church in love must deal with its own members and seek to help each one obey God. To assist them in this task, Paul gave four motives to encourage the careless believers to turn from their sins and start earning their own bread.

The Exhortation of the Word (3:6)

Paul had used this powerful word *command* in his first Thessalonian letter (1 Thess. 4:2, 11), and we met it earlier in this chapter (2 Thess. 3:4). He used it again in 2 Thessalonians 3:10, 12. The word means "a military order handed down from a superior officer." Paul considered the church to be like an army, and if the army does not obey the orders, there can be no order. Unfortunately, some of the saints were "out of rank" ("unruly" in 1 Thess. 5:14, and "disorderly" in 2 Thess. 3:6–7, 11).

What authority did Paul have to issue this command: "If any is not willing to work, neither should he eat" (2 Thess. 3:10, literal translation)? He had the authority of the name of the Lord Jesus Christ. At least twenty times in the Thessalonian letters, Paul used

this complete title of the Savior. *Jesus* means "Savior" and is His human name (Matt. 1:21). *Christ* is His divine title; it means "Messiah—the Anointed One." Other persons could use the name Jesus (the Hebrew form is "Joshua"); and other persons could claim to be anointed, such as prophets, priests, and kings. But the two names, Jesus Christ, are further defined by the name *Lord,* "Jehovah God."

In the four gospels and the book of Acts, our Lord is often called Jesus, but this single name is used very infrequently in the rest of the New Testament. That it is *occasionally* used should restrain us from criticizing those who call their Savior "Jesus," but that its use is found mainly during His ministry on earth should encourage us to address Him, and speak of Him with His name of exaltation—Lord Jesus Christ (Phil. 2:11). We no longer know "Christ after the flesh" (2 Cor. 5:16), but as the exalted Son of God and "Head over all things to the church." His lordship includes our work and money management

What does the Bible teach about manual (or mental) labor? For one thing, labor was a part of man's life *before* sin entered the scene. God gave Adam the job of dressing and guarding the garden (Gen. 2:15). Though sin turned labor into almost hopeless toil (Gen. 3:17–19), it must never be thought that the necessity for work is a result of sin. Man needs work for the fulfillment of his own person. God created him to work.

Have you noticed that God called people who were busy at work? Moses was caring for sheep (Ex. 3). Joshua was Moses' servant before he became Moses' successor (Ex. 33:11). Gideon was threshing wheat when God called him (Judg. 6:11ff.), and David was caring for his father's sheep (1 Sam. 16:11ff.). Our Lord called four fishermen to serve as His disciples, and He Himself had worked as a carpenter. Paul was a tentmaker (Acts 18:1–3) and used his trade to support his own ministry.

The Jews honored honest labor and required all their rabbis to have a trade. But the Greeks despised manual labor and left it to their slaves. This Greek influence, plus their wrong ideas about the doctrine of the Lord's return, led these believers into an unchristian way of life.

Paul recognized the fact that some people could not work, perhaps because of physical handicaps or family responsibilities. This is why he phrased the statement as he did: "If any man *is not willing* to work." It was not a question of *ability* but *willingness.* When a believer cannot work and is in need, it is the privilege and duty of the church to help him (James 2:14–17; 1 John 3:16–18).

The exhortation of the Word should have motivated these lazy believers to work, but Paul added a second motivation.

The Example of the Apostle (3:7–10)

As an apostle, Paul had the right to expect financial

support, but he deliberately gave up this right that he might be an example to the young believers (see 1 Cor. 9:6–14). In this attitude, Paul proved himself to be a mature Christian leader. Selfish leaders use people to build up their support, and they are always claiming their rights. A truly dedicated leader will use his rights to build up the people, and will lay aside his rights and privileges for the sake of others.

He had referred to his example in labor in his previous letter (1 Thess. 2:9). His readers knew that Paul and his associates had not taken any support from the infant church. Instead, they had set the example of meeting their own needs and also helping to meet the needs of others. "You ought to imitate us," he admonished his readers.

The greatest influence is that of godly living and sacrifice. A Christian leader may appeal to the authority of the Word; but if he cannot point also to his own example of obedience, his people will not listen. This is the difference between *authority* and *stature.* A leader earns stature as he obeys the Word and serves His people in the will of God. Authority comes from position; stature comes from practice and example. Stature earns the leader the right to exercise authority.

Every Christian worker has the right to support from the church as he serves the Lord (Luke 10:7; Gal. 6:6; 1 Tim. 5:17–18). We must not use Paul's example as an excuse not to support God's servants. But any servant of God has the privilege of setting aside that right to the glory of God. Paul did this so that he might be an example to the young believers in Thessalonica.

Paul's policy not only encouraged the new believers but also silenced the accusers. In every city there were itinerant teachers who "peddled their wares" for what they could earn. Paul did not want to be classified with them. Nor did he want any unsaved person to say, "Paul preaches only to make money." As he stated in 1 Corinthians 9, Paul wanted to make the gospel "free of charge"; he would not permit money to hinder the winning of lost souls.

Needless to say, the careless attitude of these believers was affecting the church, so Paul added yet a third motive for their obedience.

The Encouragement of the Church (3:11–15)

Second Thessalonians 3:13 is the key: "And you, brothers, do not lose heart doing good!" (literal translation). The faithful Christians were discouraged by the conduct of the careless saints who refused to work. "If *they* don't have to work, why should *we?*" was their argument, and Paul nipped it in the bud.

Sin in the life of a believer always affects the rest of the church. As members of His body, we belong to each other and we affect each other. The bad example of a few saints can destroy the devotion, and hinder the service, of the rest of the church.

Paul named the sins of this group. To begin with, they were "disorderly," or out of order, out of rank. They were disobeying orders, and this brought confusion and division to the assembly. Further, they were "busybodies," not busy workers. The Greek word for "busybody" literally means "to be working around"; that is, busy but "fooling around" and not accomplishing anything. First Timothy 5:13 suggests that busybodies meddle in matters that do not belong to them.

Almost every culture has its saying about idleness. The Romans said, "By doing nothing, men learn to do evil." Isaac Watts wrote: "For Satan finds some mischief still, for idle hands to do." The Jewish rabbis taught, "He who does not teach his son a trade, teaches him to be a thief."

Instead of noisily running around, these people should "with quietness … work, and eat their own bread." Their false views about the return of Christ had worked them into a pitch of excitement. "Your overemotional attitude is wrong," warned Paul. "Settle down and get to work." Work is a great antidote to unbalanced speculation and unthinking activity.

But suppose these saints did *not* obey God's Word and go to work? What then should the church do? Paul had already taken the first step when he exhorted them in his first letter (1 Thess. 5:14) and warned them that they were wrong. But they had still persisted in their unruly behavior. He now warned them again in his second letter, and then added a further step: if these believers did not obey, the members of the church should personally discipline them.

The subject of church discipline is not discussed much these days. In many churches, once a person is baptized and becomes a member, he is pretty much left to himself. If he commits some gross public sin, he will probably be dealt with by the pastor or the board; but the total church family will not begin to minister to him or exercise discipline over him.

What is church discipline? For one thing, it is *not* the pastor and official board acting like evangelical policemen to trap a sinning saint and kick him out of the church. No doubt there are churches that have such dictatorial leaders, but this is not what Paul had in mind. Church discipline is to the church member what family discipline is to a child: it is an exercise of, and evidence of, correcting love. When a parent disciplines his child, he is not a judge punishing a criminal; he is a loving father seeking to make his child a better person.

There are various levels of church discipline that must be distinguished.

Personal differences between Christians (Matt. 18:15–18; Phil. 4:1–3). If a brother or sister sins against me (either deliberately or unknowingly), I should go to that person privately and seek to get the matter settled. Only if the person refuses to settle the matter should I bring anyone else in, and the problem must not go to the church family until every other means has been exhausted.

In my pastoral ministry, I have seen many problems of this type. The big mistake Christians make when another believer wrongs them is in telling the pastor or other members, and not going to the person directly. Another mistake is in trying to win an argument instead of trying to win the sinning brother.

Doctrinal error. Determine first of all why the person is teaching wrong doctrine. Perhaps it is because of ignorance and lack of Bible knowledge. In that case, patiently teach him the truth (2 Tim. 2:23–26). If he persists, rebuke him (Titus 1:10–14). Paul had to do this to Peter (Gal. 2:11ff.). If the error continues, avoid him (Rom. 16:17–18), and then separate yourself from him (2 Tim. 2:18ff.; 2 John 9ff.).

A believer overtaken by sin (Gal. 6:1–3). Even the great apostle Peter denied the Lord. And David yielded to lust and committed adultery. When a Christian is caught in known sin, the spiritual members of the church must seek to restore him with gentleness and love. The word restore here means "to set a broken bone"—and that takes tenderness and patience. Too often the church quickly passes judgment on a believer who has sinned, and the damage done causes problems for years to come.

A repeating troublemaker (Titus 3:10). The word heretic does not refer to doctrinal error, but to a proud attitude of one who gets people to "take sides" in the church. The Greek word means "to make a choice." This leads to divisions and cliques in the local church (see Gal. 5:20 where heresies ought to be translated "sects, parties"). There is hardly a church that does not have its parties for or against anything—the pastor, the building program, even the color of the kitchen walls. Usually these "heretics" are people who like to be important; they want a following. Often they have deep emotional problems that Satan can use to create spiritual problems in the church. Perhaps they are frustrated at home or on the job, or perhaps they have, in the past, been hurt by some pastor or church.

These "factious people" should be given two official warnings. If they repeat their sin of dividing the church, they should be given a third warning and rejected. "Warn a divisive person once, and then warn him a second time. After that, have nothing to do with him. You may be sure that such a man is warped and sinful; he is self-condemned" (Titus 3:10–11, NIV).

It is my conviction that such people should not hold office in the church. It is also my conviction that, if they leave the church "in a huff," they should be restored to fellowship only twice. The third time—they are out!

Open immorality (1 Cor. 5). The church must mourn over the sinner (the same word is used for mourning over the dead) and seek to bring him to repentance. If he refuses, the church collectively should dismiss him (1 Cor. 5:13, where the Greek word means "expel"). If he repents, he must be forgiven and restored to fellowship in the church (2 Cor. 2:6–11).

In the case of the "lazy saints," Paul told the believers to exhort them, warn them, and if they did not repent, withdraw intimate fellowship from them. This probably meant that these believers were not permitted to share in the Lord's Supper, and that the church members would not invite them to their homes. Second Thessalonians 3:14 does *not* apply to every case of discipline. It applies only to the matter of saints not working for a living.

"Have no company" literally means "do not get mixed up with"; the same word is used in 1 Corinthians 5:9. There is a difference between acquaintanceship, friendship, and fellowship; for fellowship means "to have in common." For obedient saints to treat disobedient Christians with the same friendship they show to other dedicated saints is to give approval to their sins.

However, Paul (knowing the tendency of human nature to go to extremes) cautioned them not to treat the offenders like enemies. "They are still your brothers in Christ," he added. Lot was out of fellowship with God and Abraham because he lived in Sodom, yet Abraham rescued Lot from the enemy because Lot was his brother (Gen. 14, and note especially v. 14). It requires much patience, love, and grace to help an erring brother; and this is why Paul added a final motive for earning a living.

The Enablement of the Lord (3:16–18)

No believer can say, "I am not able to obey God's Word and go to work," because God has made every provision for us to obey Him. He is the Lord of peace. If He is the Lord of our lives, then we will have peace in our own hearts, and we will help to encourage peace in our church fellowship.

If there is trouble in the church, it is because there is trouble in somebody's heart. If Christ is Lord, then there is peace in the heart. If there is war in the heart, then Jesus Christ is not Lord (see James 4:1–10).

I recall a Sunday school class that was in a constant state of confusion and competition. We would just get matters settled down for a few weeks when the volcano would erupt again. After much prayer and examination, we discovered that one class member wanted to be the teacher. She was proud of her own spiritual attainments and felt she could do a better job than the devoted lady who was teaching the class.

Even though this class member never openly attacked or criticized the teacher, her attitudes and the things she did *not* say sowed seeds of discord in the fellowship. When this problem was dealt with, the Lord of peace took over in the class, and God began to bless.

Not only does God's peace enable us to obey Him, but so does His presence: "The Lord be with you all!" He never leaves us or forsakes us; He is with us to the end of the age (Matt. 28:20; Heb. 13:5).

Finally, Paul reminded them of God's grace. "The grace of our Lord Jesus Christ be with you all" (2 Thess. 3:18) was Paul's official signature to his letters.

He mentioned this because of the counterfeit letter they had received (2 Thess. 2:2). If we depend on the grace of God, we can do His will to the glory of God. "My grace is sufficient for thee" (2 Cor. 12:9).

The soldier who is out of rank and disobedient of the Lord's command proves that he is not surrendered to his Master. Church problems are individual problems, and they must be solved individually. God wants order in the church. "Let all things be done decently and in order" (1 Cor. 14:40).

Are you a part of the peace of the church or part of a war in the church?

Let's do what Joshua did and fall at the feet of the Captain of the Hosts of the Lord, that He might enable us to win the victory (Josh. 5:13–15) and fulfill His purposes for His people.

1 TIMOTHY

OUTLINE

Key theme: How to manage the ministry of the local church
Key verse: 1 Timothy 3:15

I. THE CHURCH AND ITS MESSAGE (1)
  A. Teaching sound doctrine—1:1–11
  B. Proclaiming the gospel—1:12–17
  C. Defending the faith—1:18–20

II. THE CHURCH AND ITS MEMBERS (2—3)
  A. Praying men—2:1–8
  B. Submitting women—2:9–15
  C. Qualified pastors—3:1–7
  D. Qualified deacons—3:8–13
  E. Behaving believers—3:14–16

III. THE CHURCH AND ITS MINISTER (4)
  A. A good minister, preaching the Word—4:1–6
  B. A godly minister, practicing the Word—4:7–12
  C. A growing minister, progressing in the Word—4:13–16

IV. THE CHURCH AND ITS MINISTRY (5—6)
  A. To older members—5:1–2
  B. To older widows—5:3–10
  C. To younger widows—5:11–16
  D. To church officers—5:17–25
  E. To servants (slaves)—6:1–2
  F. To false teachers—6:3–10
  G. To the pastor—6:11–16, 20–21
  H. To the rich—6:17–19

CONTENTS

CHAPTER ONE
1 Timothy 1
STAY ON THE JOB

Men wanted for hazardous journey, small wages, bitter cold, long months of complete darkness, constant danger, safe return doubtful. Honor and recognition in case of success."

That advertisement appeared in a London newspaper and *thousands of men responded!* It was signed by the noted Antarctic explorer, Sir Ernest Shackleton, and that was what made the difference.

If Jesus Christ had advertised for workers, the announcement might have read something like this: "Men and women wanted for difficult task of helping to build My church. You will often be misunderstood, even by those working with you. You will face constant attack from an invisible enemy. You may not see the results of your labor, and your full reward will not come till after all your work is completed. It may cost you your home, your ambitions, even your life."

In spite of the demands that He makes, Jesus Christ receives the "applications" of many who gladly give their all for Him. He is certainly the greatest Master for whom anyone could work, and the task of building His church is certainly the greatest challenge to which a believer could give his life.

Timothy was one young man who responded to Christ's call to help build His church. He was one of the apostle Paul's special assistants. Along with Titus, Timothy tackled some of the tough assignments in the churches that Paul had founded. Timothy was brought up in a religious home (2 Tim. 1:5) and had been led to faith in Christ by Paul himself. This explains why Paul called Timothy "my own [genuine] son in the faith" (1 Tim. 1:2).

Timothy was born of mixed parentage: his mother was a Jewess, his father a Greek. He was so devoted to Christ that his local church leaders recommended him to Paul, and Paul added him to his "missionary staff" (Acts 16:1–5). Paul often reminded Timothy that he was chosen for this ministry (1 Tim. 1:18; 4:14). Timothy was faithful to the Lord (1 Cor. 4:17) and had a deep concern for God's people (Phil. 2:20–22).

But in spite of his calling, his close association with Paul, and his spiritual gifts, Timothy was easily discouraged. The last time Paul had been with Timothy, he had encouraged him to stay on at Ephesus and finish his work (1 Tim. 1:3). Apparently Timothy had physical problems (1 Tim. 5:23) as well as periods of discouragement, and you get the impression that some of the church members were not giving their pastor the proper respect as God's servant (1 Tim. 4:12; 2 Tim. 2:6–8).

Ephesus would not be the easiest place to pastor a church. (Are there any "easy places"? I doubt it.) The city was devoted to the worship of Diana, the patroness of the sexual instinct. Her lascivious images helped promote sexual immorality of all kinds (see Acts 19). Paul had done a great work in Ephesus during his three-year ministry, so "all they which dwelt in [the province of] Asia heard the word of the Lord Jesus" (Acts 19:10). It was not easy for Timothy to follow a man like Paul! Of course, Satan had his workers in the city, for wherever there are spiritual opportunities there are also satanic obstacles (1 Cor. 16:8–9).

Paul wrote the letter we call 1 Timothy to encourage Timothy, to explain how a local church should be managed, and to enforce his own authority as a servant of God. In 1 Timothy 1 Paul explained the three responsibilities of a pastor and people in a local church.

Teach Sound Doctrine (1:1–11)

From the very greeting of the letter, Paul affirmed his authority as a servant of Jesus Christ. Those who were giving Timothy trouble needed to remember that their pastor was there because God had put him there, for Paul's authority was given by God. Paul was an "apostle," one whom God sent with a special commission. His apostleship came by "commandment" from Jesus Christ. This word means "a royal commission." Both Paul and Timothy were sent by the King of kings!

Jesus Christ is not only Lord, but He is our "Savior," a title used ten times in the pastoral epistles (1 Tim. 1:1; 2:3; 4:10; 2 Tim. 1:10; Titus 1:3–4; 2:10, 13; 3:4, 6). To discouraged Timothy, the title "our hope" (1 Tim. 1:1) was a real boost Paul wrote the same encouragement to Titus (Titus 1:2; 2:13; 3:7). Knowing that Jesus Christ is coming for us encourages us to serve Him faithfully.

One reason Christian workers must stay on the job is that false teachers are busy trying to capture Christians. There were teachers of false doctrines in Paul's day just as there are today, and we must take them seriously. These false teachers have no good news for lost sinners. They seek instead to lead Christians astray and capture them for their causes.

Paul used military language to help Timothy and his people see the seriousness of the problem (1 Tim. 1:3). *Charge* means "to give strict orders from a superior officer." Paul used this word (sometimes translated "commandment" and "command" in KJV) eight times in his two letters to Timothy (1 Tim. 1:3, 5, 18; 4:11; 5:7; 6:13, 17; 2 Tim. 4:1). He was conveying this idea: "Timothy, you are not only a pastor of the church in a difficult city. You are also a Christian soldier under orders from the King. Now pass these orders along to the soldiers in your church!"

What was the order? "Do not teach different doctrines from those taught by Paul!" In the original text there are thirty-two references to "doctrine," "teach," "teacher," "teaches," and "teaching" in the three pastoral epistles. In the early church, the believers were taught the Word of God and the meanings of basic Christian doctrines. In many churches today, the pulpit and choir loft are places for entertainment, not enlightenment and enrichment.

God had committed the truth of the Word to Paul (1 Tim. 1:11), and Paul had committed it to Timothy (1 Tim. 6:20). It was Timothy's responsibility to guard the faith (2 Tim. 1:14) and to pass it along to faithful people (2 Tim. 2:2).

Paul identified the false teaching as "fables and endless genealogies" (1 Tim. 1:4). Titus faced the same kind of false teaching in Crete (Titus 1:14; 3:9). The false teachers were using the Old Testament law, and especially the genealogies, to manufacture all kinds of novelties, and these new doctrines were leading people astray. The false teachers were raising questions, not answering them. They were not promoting "God's saving plan" ("godly edifying," 1 Tim. 1:4), but were leading people away from the truth. Instead of producing love, purity, a good conscience, and sincere faith, these novel doctrines were causing division, hypocrisy, and all sorts of problems.

Paul used the word *conscience(s)* twenty-one times in his letters, and six of these references are in the pastoral epistles (1 Tim. 1:5, 19; 3:9; 4:2; 2 Tim. 1:3; Titus 1:15). The word *conscience* means "to know with." Conscience is the inner judge that accuses us when we have done wrong and approves when we have done right (Rom. 2:14–15). It is possible to sin against the conscience so that it becomes "defiled" (Titus 1:15). Repeated sinning hardens the conscience so that it becomes "seared" like scar tissue (1 Tim. 4:2).

It is tragic when professed Christians get off course because they refuse "healthy doctrine" ("sound doctrine," 1 Tim. 1:10). Paul also called it "the doctrine … according to godliness" (1 Tim. 6:3), "sound words" (2 Tim. 1:13), "sound doctrine" (2 Tim. 4:3; Titus 1:9; 2:1), "faith" (Titus 1:13; 2:2), and "sound speech" (Titus 2:8). But many prefer the "vain jangling" (1 Tim. 1:6) of those who teach novelties rather than the pure Word of God that produces holiness in lives. It is unfortunate today that we not only have "vain jangling" ("meaningless talk" NIV) in teaching and preaching, but also in music. Far too many songs not only teach *no* doctrine, but many even teach *false* doctrines. A singer has no more right to sing a lie than a teacher has to teach a lie.

The reason for this false doctrine was a misuse of the Old Testament law. These false teachers did not understand the content or the purpose of God's law. They were leading believers out of the liberty of grace (Gal. 5:1ff.) into the bondage of legalism, a tragedy that still occurs today. The flesh (our old nature) loves religious legalism because rules and regulations enable a person to *appear* holy without really having to change his heart.

Paul listed fourteen kinds of people who were condemned by the law (1 Tim. 1:9–10). This is one of several such lists in the New Testament (see Mark 7:20–23; Rom. 1:18–32; Gal. 5:19–21). The lawful use of the law is to expose, restrain, and convict the lawless. The law cannot save lost sinners (Gal. 2:21; 3:21–29); it can only reveal their need for a Savior. When a sinner believes on Jesus Christ, he is freed from the curse of the law (Gal. 3:10–14), and the righteous demands of the law are met by the indwelling Holy Spirit as a believer yields to God (Rom. 8:1–4).

Paul (1 Tim. 1:9–10) centered particularly on five of the Ten Commandments in Exodus 20:

No. 5—"*Honor thy father and thy mother*"—"murderers of fathers and … mothers."

No. 6—"*Thou shalt not kill [murder]*"—"murderers of fathers and… mothers … manslayers."

No. 7—"*Thou shalt not commit adultery*"—"whoremongers [fornicators] … them that defile themselves with mankind [sodomites]."

No. 8—"*Thou shalt not steal*"—"menstealers [kidnappers]."

No. 9—"*Thou shalt not bear false witness*"—"liars … perjured persons."

It is the "glorious gospel" that saves lost sinners. Paul had experienced the power of the gospel (Rom. 1:16), and he had been entrusted with the ministry of the gospel (1 Thess. 2:4). Law and gospel go together, for the law without the gospel is diagnosis without remedy, but the gospel without law is only the good news of salvation for people who don't believe they need it because they have never heard the bad news of judgment. The law is not gospel, but the gospel is not lawless (Rom. 3:20–31).

Proclaim the Gospel (1:12–17)

The mention of "the gospel of the glory of the blessed God" (1 Tim. 1:11, literal translation) moved Paul to share his own personal testimony. He was "Exhibit A" to prove that the gospel of the grace of God really works. When you read Paul's testimony (see also Acts 9:1–22; 22:1–21; 26:9–18), you begin to grasp the wonder of God's grace and His saving power.

What Paul used to be (v. 13a). He was a *blasphemer* because he denied the deity of Jesus Christ and forced others to deny it. He was a *persecutor* who used physical power to try to destroy the church. "Murderous threats" were the very breath of his life (Acts 9:1 NIV). He persecuted the Christian church (1 Cor. 15:9) and then discovered that he was actually laying hands on Jesus Christ, the Messiah (Acts 9:4)! During this period of his life, Paul consented to the stoning of Stephen and made havoc of the church (Acts 8:1–4).

Paul was *injurious,* a word that means "proud and insolent." A modern equivalent might be "bully." It conveys the idea of a haughty man "throwing his weight around" in violence. But the basic causes of his godless behavior were "ignorance" and "unbelief." Even though Saul of Tarsus was a brilliant man and well educated (Acts 22:3; Gal. 1:13–14), his mind was blinded from the truth (1 Cor. 2:14; 2 Cor. 4:3–4). He was a religious man, yet he was not headed for heaven!

It was not until he put faith in Jesus Christ that he was saved (Phil. 3:1–11).

How Paul was saved (vv. 13b–15). How could the holy God ever save and forgive such a self-righteous sinner? The key words are *mercy* and *grace*. God in His mercy did not give Paul what he did deserve; instead God in His grace gave Paul what he did not deserve. Grace and mercy are God's love in action, God's love *paying a price* to save lost sinners. It is not God's love alone that saves us, for God loves the whole world (John 3:16). It is by grace that we are saved (Eph. 2:8–9) because God is rich in mercy (Eph. 2:4) and grace (Eph. 2:7).

What did Paul's "ignorance" have to do with his salvation? Is ignorance an excuse before God? Of course not! The fact of his ignorance is related to a special Jewish law (Lev. 5:15–19; Num. 15:22–31). If a person sinned knowingly "with a high hand" in Israel, he was cut off from the people. But if he sinned in ignorance, he was permitted to bring the proper sacrifices to atone for his sins. Jesus recognized this principle when He prayed on the cross, "Father, forgive them, for they know not what they do" (Luke 23:34). Their ignorance did not save them, nor did Christ's prayer save them, but the combination of the two postponed God's judgment, giving them an opportunity to be saved.

Paul stated that it took "exceedingly abundant" grace to save him! Paul liked to use the Greek prefix *huper-* (meaning "an exceeding abundant amount"), and he often attached it to words in his letters. You might translate some of these as "superincrease of faith" (2 Thess. 1:3); "superabounding power" (Eph. 1:19); "superconqueror" (Rom. 8:37). This same prefix has come into the English language as *hyper-*. We speak of "hyperactive" children and "hypersensitive" people.

Paul made it clear that this salvation was not for him only, but for all who receive Jesus Christ (1 Tim. 1:15). If Jesus could save Saul of Tarsus, the *chief* of sinners, then He can save anybody! We admire Paul's humility, and we note that he considered himself to be the "least of the apostles" (1 Cor. 15:9) and the "least of all saints" (Eph. 3:8). Notice that Paul did not write "of whom I *was* chief but "of whom I *am* chief."

What Paul became (vv. 12, 16). The grace of God turned the persecutor into a preacher, and the murderer into a minister and a missionary! So dramatic was the change in Paul's life that the Jerusalem church suspected that it was a trick, and they had a hard time accepting him (Acts 9:26–31). God gave Paul his ministry; he did not get it from Peter or the other apostles (Gal. 1:11–24). He was called and commissioned by the risen Christ in heaven.

God saw that Paul was faithful, and so He entrusted the gospel to him. Even as an unbelieving and gospel-ignorant Jewish leader, Paul had maintained a good conscience and he lived up to the light that he had. So often those who are intensely wrong as lost sinners become intensely right as Christians and are greatly used of God to win souls. God not only *entrusted* the gospel to Paul, but He *enabled* Paul to minister that gospel (1 Cor. 15:10; Phil. 4:13). When someone obeys God's call to serve, God always equips and enables that person.

But Paul not only became a minister; he also became *an example* (1 Tim. 1:16). In what sense is Paul an example to lost sinners who believe on Christ? None of us has had the same experience that Paul had on the Damascus road (Acts 9). We did not see a light, fall to the ground, and hear Jesus speak from heaven. But Paul is a pattern ("type") to all lost sinners, for he was the chief of sinners! He is proof that the grace of God can change *any* sinner!

But there is a special application of this to today's people of Israel, Paul's countrymen, for whom he had a special burden (Rom. 9:1–5; 10:1–3). The people of Israel, like unconverted Saul of Tarsus, are religious, self-righteous, blind to their own law and its message of the Messiah, and unwilling to believe. One day, Israel shall see Jesus Christ even as Paul saw Him, and the nation shall be saved. "They shall look upon me whom they have pierced" (Zech. 12:10). This may be one reason why Paul said he was "born out of due time" (1 Cor. 15:8), for his experience of seeing the risen Christ came at the beginning of this church age and not at its end (Matt. 24:29ff).

Paul gave a third responsibility for the local church to fulfill besides teaching sound doctrine and proclaiming the gospel.

Defend the Faith (1:18–20)

Again, Paul used military language to enforce his statement, for the word *charge* (1 Tim. 1:18) means "an urgent command handed down from a superior officer" (1 Tim. 1:3). Paul also reminded Timothy that God had chosen him for his ministry. Apparently some of the prophets in the local assemblies had been led by the Spirit to select Timothy for service (see Acts 13:1–3 for an example of this procedure).

It was not easy to serve God in pagan Ephesus, but Timothy was a man under orders, and he had to obey. The soldier's task is to "please him who hath chosen him to be a soldier" (2 Tim. 2:4), and not to please himself. Furthermore, Timothy was there by divine appointment: God had chosen him and sent him. It was this fact that could give him assurance in difficult days. If you are God's servant, called by the Spirit, obeying His will, then you can "stay with it" and finish the work. These assurances enabled Timothy to war the good warfare.

Paul changed the illustration from army to navy (1 Tim. 1:19). He warned Timothy that the only way to succeed was to hold fast to "faith and a good conscience." It is not enough to proclaim the faith with our lips; we must practice the faith in our daily lives. One man said of his hypocritical pastor, "He is such a good preacher, he should never get out of the pulpit, but he is such a poor Christian, he should never get into the pulpit!"

A good conscience is important to a good warfare and a good ministry. The magazine editor H. L. Mencken defined conscience as "the inner voice which warns us that somebody may be looking." But a man with a good conscience will do the will of God in spite of who is watching or what people may say. Like Martin Luther, he will say, "Here I stand; I can do no other, so help me God!"

Professed Christians who "make shipwreck" of their faith do so by sinning against their consciences. Bad doctrine usually starts with bad conduct, and usually with secret sin. Hymenaeus and Alexander deliberately rejected their good consciences in order to defend their ungodly lives. Paul did not tell us exactly what they did, except that their sin involved "blaspheming" in some way. Hymenaeus said that the resurrection was already past (2 Tim. 2:16–18). Alexander was a popular name in that day, so we cannot be sure that the man named in Paul's next letter to Timothy (2 Tim. 4:14) is the same man; but if he is, no doubt he withstood Paul by teaching false doctrine.

"Delivered unto Satan" (1 Tim. 1:20) implies an apostolic discipline (see 1 Cor. 5:5) and disassociation from the local church. The verb "learn" (1 Tim. 1:20) means "to learn by discipline." When a Christian refuses to repent, the local fellowship should exercise discipline, excluding him from the protective fellowship of the saints, making him vulnerable to the attacks of Satan. The fellowship of the local church, in obedience to the will of God, gives a believer spiritual protection. Satan has to ask God for permission to attack a believer (see Job 1—2; Luke 22:31–34).

Each local church is in a constant battle against the forces of evil. There are false prophets and false teachers, as well as false christs. Satan is the originator of false doctrines, for he is a liar from the beginning (John 8:44). It is not enough for a local church to teach sound doctrine and to proclaim the gospel. The church must also defend the faith by exposing lies and opposing the doctrines of demons (1 Tim. 4:1).

It is important that our ministry be balanced. Some churches only preach the gospel and seldom teach their converts the truths of the Christian life. Other churches are only opposing false doctrine; they have no positive ministry. We must be teachers of healthy doctrine ("sound doctrine," 1 Tim. 1:10), or the believers will not grow. We must preach the gospel and keep winning the lost to Christ. And we must defend the faith against those who would corrupt the church with false doctrine and godless living. It is a constant battle, but it must be carried on.

Timothy must have been greatly helped and encouraged when he read this first section of Paul's letter. God had called Timothy, equipped him, and put him into his place of ministry. Timothy's job was not to run all over Ephesus, being involved in a multitude of tasks. His job was to care for the church by winning the lost, teaching the saved, and defending the faith. Any task that did not relate to these ministries would have to be abandoned.

One reason some local churches are having problems is that the pastors and spiritual leaders are involved in too many extracurricular activities and are not doing the tasks God has called them to do.

It might be a good idea for our churches to take a spiritual inventory!

CHAPTER TWO
1 Timothy 2
SERVICE—OR CIRCUS?

Let all things be done decently and in order" (1 Cor. 14:40) is a basic principle for the conduct of the ministry of the church. Apparently, young Timothy was having some problems applying this principle to the assemblies in Ephesus. The public worship services were losing their order and effectiveness because both the men and the women members of the church were disobeying God's Word.

"The church is an organism," a pastor told me, "so we shouldn't put too much emphasis on organization. We should allow the Spirit to have freedom."

"But if an organism is *disorganized,*" I quickly reminded him, "it will die. Yes, I agree that we must permit the Spirit to have freedom, but even the Holy Spirit is not free to disobey the Word of God."

Often, what we think is the "freedom of the Spirit" are the carnal ideas of some Christian who is not walking in the Spirit. Eventually this "freedom" becomes anarchy, and the Spirit grieves as a church gradually moves away from the standards of God's Word.

To counteract this tendency, Paul exhorted the men and women in the church and reminded them of their spiritual responsibilities.

The Men—Praying (2:1–8)
The priority of prayer (v. 1a). "First of all" indicates that prayer is most important in the public worship of the church. It is sad to see how prayer has lost importance in many churches. "If I announce a banquet," a pastor said, "people will come out of the woodwork to attend. But if I announce a prayer meeting, I'm lucky if the ushers show up!" Not only have the special meetings for prayer lost stature in most local churches, but even prayer *in the public services* is greatly minimized. Many pastors spend more time on the announcements than they do in prayer!

The late Peter Deyneka, Sr., my good friend and founder of the Slavic Gospel Association, often reminded me: "Much prayer, much power! No prayer, no power!" Prayer was as much a part of the apostolic ministry as preaching the Word (Acts 6:4). Yet some pastors spend hours preparing their sermons, but never prepare their public prayers. Consequently, their prayers are routine, humdrum, and repetitious. I am not suggesting that a pastor write out every word and read it, but that he think through what he will pray about. This will keep "the pastoral prayer" from becoming dull and a mere repetition of what was "prayed" the previous week.

But the church members also need to be prepared to pray. Our hearts must be right with God and with each other. We must really want to pray, and not pray simply to please people (as did the Pharisees, Matt. 6:5), or to fulfill a religious duty. When a local church ceases to depend on prayer, God ceases to bless its ministry.

The variety of prayer (v. 1b). There are at least seven different Greek nouns for "prayer," and four of them are used here. *Supplications* carries the idea of "offering a request for a felt need."

Prayers is the commonest term for this activity, and it emphasizes the sacredness of prayer. We are praying *to God;* prayer is an act of worship, not just an expression of our wants and needs. There should be reverence in our hearts as we pray to God.

Intercessions is best translated "petitions." This same word is translated "prayer" in 1 Timothy 4:5, where it refers to blessing the food we eat. (It is rather obvious that we do not *intercede* for our food in the usual sense of that word.) The basic meaning is "to draw near to a person and converse confidently with him." It suggests that we enjoy fellowship with God so that we have confidence in Him as we pray.

Giving of thanks is definitely a part of worship and prayer. We not only give thanks for answers to prayer, but for who God is and what He does for us in His grace. We should not simply add our thanksgiving to the end of a selfish prayer! Thanksgiving should be an important ingredient in all of our prayers. In fact, sometimes we need to imitate David and present to God *only* thanksgiving with no petitions at all (see Ps. 103)!

"Prayer and supplication [petition] with thanksgiving" are a part of Paul's formula for God's peace in our hearts (Phil. 4:6). It is worth noting that Daniel, the great prayer warrior, practiced this kind of praying (Dan. 6:10–11).

The objects of prayer (vv. 1c–2). "All men" makes it clear that no person on earth is outside the influence of believing prayer. (We have no examples of exhortations that say we should pray for the dead. If we should pray for the dead, Paul certainly had a good opportunity to tell us in this section of his letter.) This means we should pray for the unsaved and the saved, for people near us and people far away, for enemies as well as friends. Unfortunately, the Pharisees did not have this universal outlook in their prayers, for they centered their attention primarily on Israel.

Paul urged the church to especially pray for those in authority. Godless Emperor Nero was on the throne at that time, and yet the believers were supposed to pray for him! Even when we cannot respect men or women in authority, we must respect their offices and pray for them. In fact, it is for our own good that we do so: "that we may live peaceful and quiet lives in all godliness and holiness" (1 Tim. 2:2b NIV). The early church was always subject to opposition and persecution, so it was wise to pray for those in authority. "Quiet" refers to circumstances around us, while "peaceful" refers to a calm attitude within us. The results should be lives that are godly and honorable.

To be sure, Paul has not named all the persons we can and should pray for, since "all men" covers the matter fully. We can't pray for everybody in the world by name, but we certainly ought to pray for those we know and know about. Why? Because it's a good thing to do and because it pleases God.

The reasons for prayer (vv. 3–4). The word *good* is a key word in Paul's pastoral epistles (1 Tim. 1:8, 18; 2:3; 3:1, 7, 13; 4:4, 6; 5:4, 10, 25; 6:12–13, 18–19; 2 Tim. 1:14; 2:3; 4:7; Titus 2:7, 14; 3:8, 14). The Greek word emphasizes the idea of something being intrinsically good, not just good in its effects. "Fair" and "beautiful" are synonyms. Certainly prayer of itself is a goodly practice and brings with it many good benefits.

But prayer is also pleasing to the Lord. It pleases the Father when His children pray as He has commanded them to. The Pharisees prayed in order to be praised by men (Matt. 6:5) or to impress other worshippers (Luke 18:9–14). True Christians pray in order to please God. This suggests that we must pray in the will of God, because it certainly does not please the Father when we pray selfishly (James 4:1–10; 1 John 5:14–15). It's often said that the purpose of prayer is not to get man's will done in heaven, but to get God's will done on earth.

What is God's will? The salvation of lost souls, for one thing. We can pray for "all men" because it is God's will that "all men" come to the knowledge of salvation through faith in Jesus Christ. God loved the world (John 3:16) and Christ died for the whole world (1 John 2:2; 4:14). Jesus died on the cross that He might draw "all men" to salvation (John 12:32). This does not mean all people without *exception,* for certainly the whole world is not going to be saved. It means all people without *distinction*—Jews and Gentiles, rich and poor, religious and pagan.

If God doesn't want anyone to perish, then why are so many lost? God is longsuffering with lost sinners, even delaying His judgment that they might come to Christ (2 Peter 3:9). But salvation depends on a "knowledge of the truth" (1 Tim. 2:4). Not everyone has heard the truth of the gospel, and many who have heard have rejected it. We cannot explain the mystery of God's sovereignty and man's responsibility (see John 6:37), but realize that both are taught in the Bible and are harmonized in God's great plan of salvation. We do know that prayer is an important part of God's program for reaching a lost world. We have the responsibility of praying for lost souls (Rom. 10:1) and making ourselves available to share the gospel with others.

The basis for prayer (vv. 5–7). Many believers do not realize that prayer is based on the work of Jesus

Christ as Savior and Mediator. As the God-Man, Jesus Christ is the perfect Mediator between the holy God and His failing children. One of Job's complaints had to do with the absence of a mediator who could take his message to the throne of God. "There is no umpire between us, who may lay his hand upon us both" (Job 9:33 NASB).

Since there is only one God, there is need for only one Mediator, and that Mediator is Jesus Christ. *No other person can qualify.* Jesus Christ is both God and man, and, therefore, can be the "umpire" between God and man. In His perfect life and substitutionary death, He met the just demands of God's holy law. He was the "ransom for all." The word *ransom* means "a price paid to free a slave." His death was "on behalf of all." Though the death of Christ is efficient only for those who trust Him, it is sufficient for the sins of the whole world. Jesus said that He came "to give his life a ransom for many" (Matt. 20:28).

Christ died for "all men," and God is willing for "all men to be saved." How does this good news get out to a sinful world? God calls and ordains messengers who take the gospel to lost sinners. Paul was such a messenger: he was a *preacher* (the herald of the King), an *apostle* (one sent with a special commission), and a *teacher.* The same God who ordains *the end* (the salvation of the lost) also ordains *the means to the end:* prayer and preaching of the Word. This good news is not for the Jews only, but also for the Gentiles.

If the basis for prayer is the sacrificial work of Jesus Christ on the cross, then prayer is a most important activity in a church. Not to pray is to slight the cross! To pray only for ourselves is to deny the worldwide outreach of the cross. To ignore lost souls is to ignore the cross. "All men" [people] is the key to this paragraph: We pray for "all" because Christ died for "all" and it is God's will that "all" be saved. We must give ourselves to God to be a part of His worldwide program to reach people before it is too late.

The attitude in prayer (v. 8). Paul stated definitely that "men" should pray in the local assembly. Both men and women prayed in the early church (1 Cor. 11:4–5), but the emphasis here is on the men. It is common to find women's prayer meetings, but not often do we find men's prayer meetings. If the men do not pray, the local church will not have dedicated leaders to oversee its ministry.

It was customary for Jewish men to pray with their arms extended and their hands open to heaven. Our traditional posture of bowing the head, folding the hands, and closing the eyes is nowhere found or commanded in Scripture. Actually, there are many prayer postures found in the Bible: standing with outstretched hands (1 Kings 8:22); kneeling (Dan. 6:10); standing (Luke 18:11); sitting (2 Sam. 7:18); bowing the head (Gen. 24:26); lifting the eyes (John 17:1); falling on the ground (Gen. 17:3). The important thing is not the posture of the body but the posture of the heart.

Paul stated three essentials for effective prayer, and the first was "holy hands." Obviously this means a holy life. "Clean hands" was symbolic of a blameless life (2 Sam. 22:21; Ps. 24:4). If we have sin in our lives, we cannot pray and expect God to answer (Ps. 66:18).

"Without wrath" is the second essential, and requires that we be on good terms with one another. "Without anger" might be a better translation. A person who is constantly having trouble with other believers, who is a troublemaker rather than a peacemaker, cannot pray and get answers from God.

"Doubting" suggests that we must pray *in faith,* but the word really means "disputing." When we have anger in the heart, we often have open disagreements with others. Christians should learn to disagree without being disagreeable. We should "do all things without murmurings and disputings" (Phil. 2:14).

Effective praying, then, demands that I be in a right relationship with God ("holy hands") and with my fellow believers ("without murmurings and disputings"). Jesus taught the same truth (Mark 11:24–26). If we spent more time *preparing* to pray and getting our hearts right before God, our prayers would be more effective.

The Women—Submitting (2:9–15)

Because of its oppressive connotations, the word *submission* makes some people see red. Some well-meaning writers have even accused Paul of being a "crusty old bachelor" who was antiwomen. Those of us who hold to the inspiration and authority of the Word of God know that Paul's teachings came from God and not from himself. If we have a problem with what the Bible says about women in the church, the issue is not with Paul (or Peter, see 1 Peter 3:1–7), but with the Lord who gave the Word (2 Tim. 3:16–17).

The word translated "subjection" in 1 Timothy 2:11 is translated "submitting" and "submit" in Ephesians 5:21–22 and Colossians 3:18. It literally means "to rank under." Anyone who has served in the armed forces knows that "rank" has to do with order and authority, not with value or ability. A colonel is higher in rank than a private, but that does not necessarily mean that the colonel is a better man than the private. It only means that the colonel has a higher rank and, therefore, more authority.

"Let all things be done decently and in order" (1 Cor. 14:40) is a principle God follows in His creation. Just as an army would be in confusion if there were no levels of authority, so society would be in chaos without submission. Children should submit to their parents because God has given parents the authority to train their children and discipline them in love. Employees should submit to employers and obey them (Eph. 6:5–8, where the immediate reference is to household slaves, but the application can be made to workers today). Citizens should submit to government authorities, even if the authorities are not Christians (Rom. 13; 1 Peter 2:13–20).

Submission is not subjugation. Submission is

recognizing God's order in the home and the church, and joyfully obeying it. When a Christian wife joyfully submits to the Lord and to her own husband, it should bring out the best in her. (For this to happen, the husband must love his wife and use God's order as a tool to build with, not a weapon to fight with, Eph. 5:18–33.) Submission is the key to spiritual growth and ministry: husbands should be submitted to the Lord, Christians should submit to each other (Eph. 5:21), and wives should be submitted to the Lord and to their husbands.

The emphasis in this section (1 Tim. 2:9–15) is on the place of women in the local church. Paul admonished these believing women to give evidence of their submission in several ways.

Modest dress (v. 9). The contrast here is between the artificial glamour of the world and the true beauty of a godly life. Paul did not forbid the use of jewelry or lovely clothes, but rather the excessive use of them as substitutes for the true beauty of "a meek and quiet spirit" (see 1 Peter 3:1–6). A woman who depends only on externals will soon run out of ammunition! She may attract attention, but she will not win lasting affection. Perhaps the latest fashion fads were tempting the women in the church at Ephesus, and Paul had to remind Timothy to warn the women not to get trapped.

The word translated "modest" (1 Tim. 2:9) simply means "decent and orderly." It is related to the Greek word from which we get the English word "cosmetic." A woman's clothing should be decent, orderly, and in good taste. "Shamefacedness" literally means "modesty, the avoidance of extremes." A woman who possesses this quality is ashamed to go beyond the bounds of what is decent and proper. "Sobriety" comes from a Greek word that means "having a sound mind and good sense." It describes an inner self-control—a spiritual "radar" that tells a person what is good and proper.

Ephesus was a wealthy commercial city, and some women there competed against each other for attention and popularity. In that day expensive hairdos arrayed with costly jewelry were an accepted way to get to the top socially. Paul admonished the Christian women to major on the "inner person," the true beauty that only Christ can give. He did not forbid the use of nice clothing or ornaments. He urged balance and propriety, with the emphasis on modesty and holy character.

"It's getting harder and harder for a Christian woman to find the right kind of clothes!" a church member complained to me one summer. "I refuse to wear the kind of swimsuits they're selling! I simply won't go swimming. Whatever happened to old-fashioned modesty?"

Godly works (v. 10). Paul did not suggest that good works are a substitute for clothing! Rather, he was contrasting the "cheapness" of expensive clothes and jewelry with the true values of godly character and Christian service. "Godliness" is another key word in Paul's pastoral letters (1 Tim. 2:2, 10; 3:16; 4:7–8;

6:3, 5–6, 11; 2 Tim. 3:5; Titus 1:1). Glamour can be partially applied on the outside, but godliness must come from within.

We must never underestimate the important place that godly women played in the ministry of the church. The gospel message had a tremendous impact on them because it affirmed their value before God and their equality in the body of Christ (Gal. 3:28). Women had a low place in the Roman world, but the gospel changed that.

There were devoted women who ministered to Jesus in the days of His earthly ministry (Luke 8:1–3). They were present at His crucifixion and burial, and it was a woman who first heralded the glorious news of His resurrection. In the book of Acts we meet Dorcas (Acts 9:36ff), Lydia (Acts 16:14ff), Priscilla (Acts 18:1–3), and godly women in the Berean and Thessalonian churches (Acts 17:4, 12). Paul greeted at least eight women in Romans 16; and Phebe, who carried the Roman epistle to its destination, was a deaconess in a local church (Rom. 16:1). Many believing women won their husbands to the Lord and then opened their homes for Christian ministry.

Quiet learning (v. 11). "Silence" is an unfortunate translation because it gives the impression that believing women were never to open their mouths in the assembly. This is the same word that is translated "peaceable" in 1 Timothy 2:2. Some of the women abused their newfound freedom in Christ and created disturbances in the services by interrupting. It is this problem that Paul addressed in this admonition. It appears that women were in danger of upsetting the church by trying to "enjoy" their freedom. Paul wrote a similar admonition to the church in Corinth (1 Cor. 14:34), though this admonition may apply primarily to speaking in tongues.

Respecting authority (vv. 12–15). Women *are* permitted to teach. Older women should teach the younger women (Titus 2:3–4). Timothy was taught at home by his mother and grandmother (2 Tim. 1:5; 3:15). But in their teaching ministry, they must not "lord it over" men. There is nothing wrong with a godly woman instructing a man in private (Acts 18:24–28), but she must not assume authority in the church and try to take the place of a man. She should exercise "quietness" and help keep order in the church.

Paul gave several arguments to back up this admonition that the Christian men in the church should be the spiritual leaders. The first is an argument from *creation:* Adam was formed first, and then Eve (1 Tim. 2:12–13). (Paul used this same argument in 1 Cor. 11:1–10.) We must keep in mind that *priority* does not mean *superiority.* Man and woman were both created by God and in God's image. The issue is only authority: man was created first.

The second argument has to do with man's fall into sin. Satan deceived the woman into sinning (Gen. 3:1ff.; 2 Cor. 11:3); the man sinned with his eyes wide open. Because Adam rejected the God-given order, he listened to his wife, disobeyed God, and brought sin and death into the world. The submission of wives to their own husbands is a part of the original creation. The disorder we have in society today results from a violation of that God-given order.

I do not think Paul suggested that women are more gullible than men and thus more easily deceived; for experience proves that both men and women are deceived by Satan. On one occasion, Abraham listened to his wife and got into trouble (Gen. 16). Later on, she gave him counsel and God told him to obey it (Gen. 21). In my own pastoral ministry, I have benefited greatly from the encouragement and counsel of godly women, but I have tried not to let them usurp authority in the church. In fact, the godly women I have known have no desire to "run" things in the church.

The creation of humans and their fall both seem to put the woman in an inferior position, but she does have a ministry from God (1 Tim. 2:15). There was probably a close relationship in Paul's mind between what he wrote here and what Moses wrote in Genesis 3:16—the promise of the Savior who would be "made of a woman" (Gal. 4:4). It was through a woman that the Savior came into the world. (Keep in mind that Jesus had an earthly mother but not an earthly father, Matt. 1:18ff.; Luke 1:34–35.)

But Paul taught a practical lesson (1 Tim. 2:15). He promised that the woman would "be kept safe through childbirth" (NIV) if "they" (both husband and wife) continued in sincere dedication to the Lord.

Does this mean that Christian mothers will never die in childbirth? History and experience both tell us that they do. God has His purposes, and His ways are far above our thoughts (Isa. 55:8–9). Paul laid down a general principle that encouraged the believing women of that day. Their ministry was not to run the church, but to care for the home and bear children to the glory of God (1 Tim. 5:14). Their home congregation would give them abundant opportunities for teaching the Word and ministering to the saints (see Rom. 16:1–6).

Godly women do have an important ministry in the local assembly, even though they are not called to be teachers of the Word in a pastoral sense. If all is done "decently and in order," then God will bless.

CHAPTER THREE
1 Timothy 3
FOLLOW THE LEADERS

Everything rises or falls with leadership, whether it be a family or a local church. The Holy Spirit imparts gifts to believers for ministry in the local church, and among those gifts are "pastors and teachers" (Eph. 4:11) and "helps" and "governments" ("administration," 1 Cor. 12:28 NIV). As we noted

before, even though the church is an organism, it must be organized or it will die. Leadership is a part of spiritual organization.

In this section, Paul described the bishop, the deacon, and the church itself. By understanding these three descriptions, we shall be able to give better leadership to the ministry of the church.

The Pastor (3:1–7)
According to the New Testament, the terms "bishop," "pastor," and "elder" are synonymous. *Bishop* means "overseer," and the elders had the responsibility of overseeing the work of the church (Acts 20:17, 28; 1 Peter 5:1–3). "Elder" is the translation of the Greek word *presbutes,* which means "an old man." Paul used the word *presbytery* in 1 Timothy 4:14, referring not to a denomination, but to the "eldership" of the assembly that ordained Timothy. Elders and bishops (two names for the same office, Titus 1:5, 7) were mature people with spiritual wisdom and experience. Finally, "pastor" means "shepherd," one who leads and cares for the flock of God.

When you compare the qualifications given here for bishops with those given for elders in Titus 1:5–9, you quickly see that the same office is in view. Church organization was quite simple in apostolic days: There were pastors (elders, bishops) and deacons (Phil. 1:1). It seems that there was a plurality of elders overseeing the work of each church, some involved in "ruling" (organization and government), others in teaching (1 Tim. 5:17).

But these men had to be qualified. It was good for a growing believer to aspire to the office of bishop, but the best way to achieve it was to develop Christian character and meet the following requirements. To become an elder/bishop was a serious decision, one not treated lightly in the early church. Paul gave sixteen qualifications for a man to meet if he expected to serve as an elder/bishop/pastor.

Blameless (v. 2a). This word literally means "nothing to take hold upon"; that is, there must be nothing in his life that Satan or the unsaved can take hold of to criticize or attack the church. No man living is sinless, but we must strive to be blameless, or "above reproach" (NIV).

The husband of one wife (v. 2b). All of the qualifying adjectives in this passage are masculine. While there is ample scope for feminine ministry in a local assembly, the office of elder is not given to women. However, a pastor's homelife is very important, and especially his marital status. (This same requirement applies to deacons, according to 1 Tim. 3:12.) It means that a pastor must not be divorced and remarried. Paul was certainly not referring to polygamy, since no church member, let alone a pastor, would be accepted if he had more than one wife. Nor is he referring to remarriage after the death of the wife; for why would a pastor be prohibited from marrying again, in the light of Genesis 2:18 and 1 Timothy 4:3? Certainly the members of the church who had lost mates could marry again, so why penalize the pastor?

It's clear that a man's ability to manage his own marriage and home indicate ability to oversee a local church (1 Tim. 3:4–5). A pastor who has been divorced opens himself and the church to criticism from outsiders, and it is not likely that people with marital difficulties would consult a man who could not keep his own marriage together. I see no reason why *dedicated* Christians who have been divorced and remarried cannot serve in other offices in the church, but they are disqualified from being elders or deacons.

Vigilant (v. 2c). This means "temperate" or "sober." "Temperate in all things" (2 Tim. 4:5, literal translation). Or "keep your head in all situations" (NIV). A pastor needs to exercise sober, sensible judgment in all things.

Sober (v. 2d). He must have a serious attitude and be in earnest about his work. This does not mean he has no sense of humor, or that he is always solemn and somber. Rather it suggests that he knows the value of things and does not cheapen the ministry or the gospel message by foolish behavior.

Of good behavior (v. 2e). "Orderly" would be a good translation. The pastor should be organized in his thinking and his living, as well as in his teaching and preaching. It is the same Greek word that is translated "modest" in 1 Timothy 2:9, referring to women's clothing.

Given to hospitality (v. 2f). Literally, "loving the stranger." This was an important ministry in the early church when traveling believers would need places to stay (Rom. 12:13; Heb. 13:2; 3 John 5—8). But even today, a pastor and wife who are hospitable are a great help to the fellowship of a local church.

Apt to teach (v. 2g). Teaching the Word of God is one of an elder's main ministries. In fact, many scholars believe that "pastors and teachers" in Ephesians 4:11 refer to one person but to two functions. A pastor is automatically a teacher (2 Tim. 2:2, 24). Phillips Brooks, famous American bishop of the 1800s, said, "Apt to teach—it is not something to which one comes by accident or by any sudden burst of fiery zeal." A pastor must be a careful student of the Word of God, and of all that assists him in knowing and teaching that Word. The pastor who is lazy in his study is a disgrace in the pulpit.

Not given to wine (v. 3a). The word describes a person who sits long with the cup and thus drinks to excess. The fact that Paul advised Timothy to use wine for medicinal purposes (1 Tim. 5:23) indicates that total abstinence was not demanded of believers. Sad to say, some of the members of the Corinthian church got drunk, even at the love feast that accompanied the Lord's Supper (1 Cor. 11:21). The Jewish people diluted their wine with water to make sure it was not too strong. It was a well-known fact that water was not pure in those days, so that weak wine taken in moderation would have been healthier to drink.

However, there is a vast difference between the cultural use of wine in Bible days and supporting the alcohol industry of today. Paul's admonition and example in Romans 14 (especially Rom. 14:21) would apply today in a special way. A godly pastor would certainly want to give the best example and not be an excuse for sin in the life of some weaker brother.

No striker (v. 3b). "Not contentious, not looking for a fight." Charles Spurgeon told his Pastor's College students, "Don't go about the world with your fist doubled up for fighting, carrying a theological revolver in the leg of your trousers."

Not greedy of filthy lucre (v. 3c). Paul will have more to say about money in 1 Timothy 6:3ff. It is possible to use the ministry as an easy way to make money, if a man has no conscience or integrity. (Not that pastors are paid that much in most churches!) Covetous pastors always have "deals" going on outside their churches, and these activities erode their character and hinder their ministry. Pastors should "not [work] for filthy lucre" (1 Peter 5:2).

Patient (v. 3d). "Gentle" is a better translation. The pastor must listen to people and be able to take criticism without reacting. He should permit others to serve God in the church without dictating to them.

Not a brawler (v. 3e). Pastors must be peacemakers, not troublemakers. This does not mean they must compromise their convictions, but that they must "disagree" without being "disagreeable." Short tempers do not make for long ministries.

Not covetous (v. 3f). You can covet many things besides money: popularity, a large ministry that makes you famous, denominational advancement, and so forth. This word centers mainly on money.

A godly family (vv. 4–5). This does not mean that a pastor must be married, or, if married, must have children. However, marriage and a family are probably in the will of God for most pastors. If a man's own children cannot obey and respect him, then his church is not likely to respect and obey his leadership. For Christians, the church and the home are one. We should oversee both of them with love, truth, and discipline. The pastor cannot be one thing at home and something else in church. If he is, his children will detect it, and there will be problems. The words *rule* and *ruleth* in 1 Timothy 3:4–5 mean "to preside over, to govern," and suggest that a pastor is the one who directs the business of the church. (Not as a dictator, of course, but as a loving shepherd, 1 Peter 5:3.) The word translated "take care of" in 1 Timothy 3:5 suggests a personal ministry to the needs of the church. It is used in the parable of the good Samaritan to describe the care given to the injured man (Luke 10:34–35).

Not a novice (v. 6). "Novice" literally means "one newly planted," referring to a young Christian. Age is no guarantee of maturity, but it is good for a man to give himself time for study and growth before he accepts a church. Some men mature faster than others, of course. Satan enjoys seeing a youthful pastor succeed and get proud; then Satan can tear down all that has been built up.

A good testimony outside the church (v. 7). Does he pay his bills? Does he have a good reputation among unsaved people with whom he does business (see Col. 4:5 and 1 Thess. 4:12)?

No pastor ever feels that he is all he ought to be, and his people need to pray for him constantly. It is not easy to serve as a pastor/elder, but it is much easier if your character is all God wants it to be.

The Deacon (3:8–13)

The English word *deacon* is a transliteration of the Greek word *diakonos,* which simply means "servant." It is likely that the origin of the deacons is recorded in Acts 6. The first deacons were appointed to be assistants to the apostles. In a local church today deacons relieve the pastors/elders of other tasks so that they may concentrate on the ministry of the Word, prayer, and spiritual oversight.

Even though deacons are not given the authority of elders, they still must meet certain qualifications. Many faithful deacons have been made elders after they proved themselves.

Grave (v. 8a). A deacon should be worthy of respect, a man of Christian character worth imitating. A deacon should take his responsibilities seriously and *use* the office, not *just fill* it.

Not double-tongued (v. 8b). He does not tell tales from house to house; he is not a gossip. He does not say one thing to one member and something entirely opposite to another member. You can depend on what he says.

Not given to much wine (v. 8c). We have discussed this in our comments on 1 Timothy 3:3.

Not greedy of filthy lucre (v. 8d). Deacons handle offerings and distribute money to needy people in the church. It may be tempting to steal or to use funds in selfish ways. Finance committees in churches need to have a spiritual attitude toward money.

Doctrinally sound (v. 9). The word *mystery* means "truth once hidden but now revealed by God." The great doctrines of the faith are hidden to those outside the faith, but they can be understood by those who trust the Lord. Deacons must understand Christian doctrine and obey it with a good conscience. It is not enough to sit in meetings and decide how to "run the church." They must base their decisions on the Word of God, and they must back up their decisions with godly lives.

I have noticed that some church officers know their church constitutions better than they know the Word of God. While it is good to have bylaws and regulations that help maintain order, it is important to manage the affairs of a church on the basis of the Word of God. The Scriptures were the "constitution" of the early church! A deacon who does not know the Bible is an obstacle to progress in a local assembly.

A pastor friend of mine, now home with the Lord, took a church that was a split from another church and constantly at war with itself. From what he told me, their business meetings were something to behold! The church constitution was revered almost as much as the Bible. The people called it "the green book." My friend began to teach the people the Word of God, and the Spirit began to make changes in lives. But the enemy went to work and stirred up some officers to defy their pastor in a meeting.

"You aren't following the green book!" they said.

My friend lifted his Bible high and asked, "Are we going to obey the Word of God, or a green book written by men?" This was a turning point in the church, and then God blessed with wonderful growth and power.

A deacon who does not *know* the Word of God cannot manage the affairs of the church of God. A deacon who does not *live* the Word of God, but has a "defiled conscience," cannot manage the church of God. Simply because a church member is popular, successful in business, or generous in his giving does not mean he is qualified to serve as a deacon.

Tested and proved (v. 10). This implies watching their lives and seeing how they conduct themselves. In most churches, a new member or a new Christian may begin serving God in visitation, ushering, helping in Sunday school, and numerous other ways. This is the principle in Matthew 25:21: "Thou hast been faithful over a few things; I will make thee ruler over many things."

It is worth noting that quite a few leaders mentioned in the Bible were first tested as servants. Joseph was a servant in Egypt for thirteen years before he became a second ruler in the land. Moses cared for sheep for forty years before God called him. Joshua was Moses' servant before he became Moses' successor. David was tending his father's sheep when Samuel anointed him king of Israel. Even our Lord Jesus came as a servant and labored as a carpenter; and the apostle Paul was a tentmaker. First a servant, then a ruler.

It always weakens the testimony of a local church when a member who has not been proved is made an officer of the church. "Maybe Jim will attend church more if we make him a deacon" is a statement that shows ignorance both of Jim and of the Word of God. *An untested Christian is an unprepared Christian.* He will probably do more harm than good if you give him an office in the church.

Godly homes (vv. 11–12). The deacon's wife is a part of his ministry, for godliness must begin at home. The deacons must not be men who have been divorced and remarried. Their wives must be Christians, women who are serious about the ministry, not given to slanderous talk (literally "not devils," for the word *devil* means "slanderer, false accuser"), and faithful in all that they do. It is sad to see the damage that is done to a local church when the wives of elders or deacons gossip and slander others.

Some students think that 1 Timothy 3:11 refers,

not to the wives of deacons, but to another order of ministers—the deaconesses. Many churches do have deaconesses who assist with the women's work, in baptisms, in fellowship times, and so forth. Phebe was a deaconess from the church at Cenchrea (Rom. 16:1, where the word is *diakonon).* Perhaps in some of the churches, the wives of the deacons did serve as deaconesses. We thank God for the ministry of godly women in the local church, whether they hold offices or not! It is not necessary to hold an office to have a ministry or exercise a gift.

A willingness to work (v. 13). He is to *use* the office, not just *fill* it. The Greek word translated "degree" means "rank (as in the army), a base, a step, or rung on a ladder." What an encouragement to a faithful deacon! God will "promote" him spiritually and give him more and more respect among the saints, which means greater opportunity for ministry. A faithful deacon has a good standing before God and men, and can be used of God to build the church. He has a spiritual boldness that makes for effective ministry.

Certainly a part of this blessing could include the possibility of a "spiritual promotion." What a joy it is to a pastor to see deacons become elders, and then to see some of the elders called into pastoral ministry on a full-time basis. (It should be remembered that, in the New Testament churches, the elders were called from out of their own local congregations. They were not usually imported from other places.)

It is a serious matter to serve the local church. Each of us must search his own heart to be certain that he is qualified by the grace of God.

The Believers (3:14–16)

Elders, deacons, and church members need to be reminded of what a local church is. In this brief paragraph, Paul gave three pictures of the church.

The house of God (v. 15a). God's church is a family, so "household" might be a better translation. One of Paul's favorite words is "brethren" (see 1 Tim. 4:6). When a sinner believes in Jesus Christ as Savior, he immediately is born again into God's family (John 1:11–13; 1 Peter 1:22–25). Paul advised young Timothy to treat the members of the local church as he would treat the members of his own family (1 Tim. 5:1–2).

Because the local church is a family, it must be fed; and the only diet that will nourish the people is the Word of God. It is our bread (Matt. 4:4), milk and meat (1 Cor. 3:1–2; Heb. 5:12–14), and honey (Ps. 119:103). A pastor must take time to nourish himself so that he might nourish others (1 Tim. 4:6). A church does not grow by addition, but by nutrition (Eph. 4:11–16). It is tragic to see the way some pastors waste their time (and their church's time) all week long and then have nothing nourishing to give the people on the Lord's Day.

Like a family, a church needs discipline in love. Children who are not disciplined become rebels and

tyrants. The spiritual leaders of the assembly should exercise discipline (1 Cor. 4:18—5:13; 2 Cor. 2:6–11). Sometimes the children need rebuke; other times the discipline must be more severe.

Children also need encouragement and example (1 Thess. 2:7–12). Spiritual leaders must have the gentleness of a nursing mother and the strength of a loving father.

The assembly (v. 15b). The word *church* is a translation of the Greek word *ekklesia* (ek-klay-SEE-a), which means "assembly." It referred to the political assemblies in the Greek cities (Acts 19:29, 32) where business was transacted by qualified citizens. But it is used about one hundred times in the New Testament to refer to local churches, assemblies of believers. The Greek word means "those called out." (It is used in Acts 7:38 to describe the nation of Israel, called out of Egypt, but Israel was not a "church" in the New Testament sense.)

Paul wanted young Timothy to know how to "conduct himself" as a leader of a local assembly. The pastoral epistles are guidebooks for conduct of a local church. Scores of books have been published in recent years purporting to tell us how to start, build, and increase a local church, and some of them contain good counsel. However, the best counsel for managing a local church is found in these three inspired letters. The young pastor in his first church, as well as the seasoned veteran in the ministry, should saturate himself with the teachings Paul shared with Timothy and Titus.

There are many different kinds of "assemblies," but the church is the assembly of the living God. Because it is God's assembly, He has the right to tell us how it ought to be governed. The church has been purchased with the blood of God's Son (Acts 20:28); therefore, we must be careful how we conduct ourselves. Church officers must not become religious dictators who abuse the people in order to achieve their own selfish ends (1 Peter 5:3–5; 3 John 9–12).

The pillar and ground of the truth (vv. 15c–16). This is an architectural image which would mean much to Timothy at Ephesus, for the great temple of Diana had 127 pillars. The word *ground* suggests a "bulwark" or a "stay." The local church is built on Jesus Christ the Truth (John 14:6; 1 Cor. 3:9–15), but the local church is also itself a pillar and bulwark for the truth.

It is likely that the *pillar* aspect of the church's ministry relates primarily to displaying the truth of the Word, much as a statue is put on a pedestal so all can see it. We must hold "forth the word of life" so the world can see it (Phil. 2:16). The local church puts Jesus Christ on display in the lives of faithful members.

As a *bulwark,* the church protects the truth and makes sure it does not fall (for elsewhere "truth is fallen in the street, and equity cannot enter,"Isa. 59:14). When local churches turn away from the truth (1 Tim. 4:1ff.) and compromise in their ministry, then the enemy makes progress. Sometimes church leaders must take a militant stand against sin and apostasy. This does not make them popular, but it does please the Lord.

The main truth to which a church should bear witness is the person and work of Jesus Christ (1 Tim. 3:16—it is probable that this verse is quoted from an early Christian hymn). Jesus Christ was God *manifest in the flesh,* not only at His birth, but during His entire earthly ministry (John 14:1–9). Though His own people as a nation rejected Him, Jesus Christ was *vindicated in the Spirit,* for the Spirit empowered Him to do miracles and even to raise Himself from the dead (Rom. 1:4). The very presence of the Spirit in the world is itself a judgment on the world (John 16:7–11).

Seen of angels suggests the many times that the elect angels were associated with the life and ministry of our Lord. (The word *angelos,* translated "angels," also means "messengers." See James 2:25. Perhaps Paul was referring to the chosen messengers who witnessed the resurrected Christ.) However, Christ did not die for angels, but for lost sinners, and so He was *preached unto the nations.* This reminds us of the commissions the Lord gave to His church to carry the gospel to the ends of the earth, where He is *believed on in the world.* At the ascension, He was *received up in glory* (Acts 1:2, 22), and He will return one day to take His church to share that glory.

What an exciting challenge it is for your local church to witness of Jesus Christ to lost sinners at home and around the world!

CHAPTER FOUR
1 Timothy 4
HOW TO BE A MAN OF GOD

If you were to write a job description for your pastor, what would it contain? How would it compare with the description he might write? A pastor preaches regularly, performs weddings and other Christian services, visits the sick, and counsels the distressed. But what *is* his ministry, and what kind of person must he be to fulfill his God-given ministry?

In this section of his letter to Timothy, Paul emphasized the character and the work of the minister himself; and he listed three qualities that a minister must possess if he is to be successful in serving God.

A Good Minister, Preaching the Word (4:1–6)
Paul had warned the Ephesian elders that false teachers would invade the church (Acts 20:28–31), and now they had arrived. The Holy Spirit had spoken in specific terms about these teachers, and the prophecy was starting to be fulfilled in Paul's time. Certainly it is fulfilled in our own time! We can recognize false teachers by the description Paul gave in this paragraph.

They are energized by Satan (v. 1a). This is the only place where demons are mentioned in the pastoral epistles. Just as there is a "mystery of godliness" concerning Christ (1 Tim. 3:16), so there is a "mystery of iniquity" that surrounds Satan and his work (2 Thess. 2:7). Satan is an imitator (2 Cor. 11:13–15); he has his own ministers and doctrines, and seeks to deceive God's people and lead them astray (2 Cor. 11:3). The first test of any religious doctrine is what it says about Jesus Christ (1 John 4:1–6).

It comes as a shock to some people that Satan uses professed Christians *in the church* to accomplish his work. But Satan once used Peter to try to lead Jesus on a wrong path (Matt. 16:21–23), and he used Ananias and Sapphira to try to deceive the church at Jerusalem (Acts 5). Paul warned that false teachers would arise *from within the church* (Acts 20:30).

They lead people astray (v. 1b). Their goal is to seduce people and get them to depart from the faith. This is the word *apostasy,* and it is defined as "a willful turning away from the truth of the Christian faith." These false teachers do not try to build up the church or relate people to the Lord Jesus Christ in a deeper way. Instead they want to get disciples to follow them and join their groups and promote their programs. This is one difference between a true church and a religious cult: A true church seeks to win converts to Jesus Christ and to build them spiritually; conversely, a cult proselytizes, steals converts from others, and makes them servants (even slaves!) of the leaders of the cult. However, not all apostates are in cults; some of them are in churches *and pulpits,* teaching false doctrine and leading people astray.

They are hypocrites (v. 2). "Ye shall know them by their fruits" (Matt. 7:15–20). These false teachers preach one thing but practice another. They tell their disciples what to do, but they do not do it themselves. Satan works "by means of the hypocrisy of liars" (1 Tim. 4:2, literal translation). One of the marks of a true servant of God is his honesty and integrity: He practices what he preaches. This does not mean he is sinlessly perfect, but that he sincerely seeks to obey the Word of God. He tries to maintain a good conscience (see 1 Tim. 1:5, 19; 3:9).

The word *seared* means "cauterized." Just as a person's flesh can be "branded" so that it becomes hard and without feeling, so a person's conscience can be deadened. Whenever we affirm with our lips something that we deny with our lives (whether people know it or not), we deaden our consciences just a little more. Jesus made it clear that it is not religious talk or even performing miracles that qualifies a person for heaven, but doing God's will in everyday life (Matt. 7:21–29).

An apostate is not just wrong doctrinally; he is wrong morally. His personal life became wrong before his doctrines were changed. In fact, it is likely that he changed his teachings so that he could continue his sinful living and pacify his conscience. *Believing* and *behaving* always go together.

They deny God's Word (vv. 3–5). The false teachers

in Ephesus combined Jewish legalism with Eastern asceticism. You find Paul dealing with this same false doctrine in his Letter to the Colossians (Col. 2:8–23 especially). For one thing, the false teachers taught that an unmarried life was more spiritual than a married life, which is contrary to Scripture. "It is not good that the man should be alone" are God's own words (Gen. 2:18). Jesus put His seal of approval on marriage (Matt. 19:1–9), though He pointed out that not everybody is supposed to marry (Matt. 19:10–12). Paul also affirmed the biblical basis for marriage (1 Cor. 7:1–24), teaching that each person should follow the will of God in the matter.

Beware of any religious teaching that tampers with God's institution of marriage. And beware of any teaching that tampers with God's creation. The false teachers who were infecting the Ephesian church taught that certain foods were taboo; if you ate them, you were not spiritual. The fact that God called His own creation "good" (Gen. 1:10, 12, 18, 21, 25) did not interest these teachers. Their authority to dictate diets gave them power over their converts.

Those who "believe and know the truth" are not impressed with the do's and don'ts of the legalists. Jesus stated that all foods are clean (Mark 7:14–23). He taught this lesson again to Peter (Acts 10) and reaffirmed it through Paul (1 Cor. 10:23–33). A person may not be able to eat certain foods for physical reasons (an allergy, for example), but no food is to be rejected for spiritual reasons. We should not, however, use our freedom to eat and drink to destroy weaker Christians (Rom. 14:13–23). The food we eat is sanctified (set apart, devoted to God) when we pray and give thanks; so the Word of God and prayer turn even an ordinary meal into a spiritual service for God's glory (1 Cor. 10:31).

The emphasis in a minister's life should be on "the Word of God and prayer" (1 Tim. 4:5). It is tragic when a church keeps its pastors so busy with menial tasks that they have hardly any time for God's Word and prayer (Acts 6:1–7). Paul reminded young Timothy of his great responsibility to study, teach, and preach the Scriptures, and to spend time in prayer. As a "good minister" he must be "nourished up in the words of faith" (1 Tim. 4:6). Timothy had certain responsibilities in the light of this growing apostasy:

Teach the church the truth (v. 6a). God's people need to be warned about false doctrine and religious apostasy. A minister must not major on these subjects, because he is obligated to teach "all the counsel of God" (Acts 20:27), but neither should he ignore them. As we travel the streets and highways, we see two kinds of signs: those that tell us where we are going ("Boston 45 miles") and those that warn us of possible dangers ("Bridge Out!"). A pastor must teach positive doctrine so that people will know what they believe and where they are going. But he must also expose false doctrine so that people will not be seduced and led astray.

He must nourish himself in the Word (v. 6b). Of course, *every* Christian ought to feed daily on the Word (Jer. 15:16; Matt. 4:4; 1 Peter 2:2), but it is especially important that a pastor grow in the Word. It is by daily studying *the* "good doctrine" and meditating on the Word that he grows in the Lord and is able to lead the church.

The "good minister" preaches the Word that he himself feeds on day by day. But it is not enough to preach the Word; he must also practice it.

A Godly Minister, Practicing the Word (4:7–12)

Paul shifted to an athletic illustration at this point in his letter. Just as a Greek or Roman athlete had to refuse certain things, eat the right food, and do the right exercises, so a Christian should practice "spiritual exercise." If a Christian puts as much energy and discipline into his spiritual life as an athlete does into his game, the Christian grows faster and accomplishes much more for God. Paul discussed in this section three levels of life.

The bad—"profane and old wives' fables" (v. 7a). These are, of course, the false teachings and traditions of the apostates. These doctrines have no basis in Scripture; in fact, they contradict the Word of God. They are the kind of teachings that silly people would discuss, not dedicated men and women of the Word! No doubt these teachings involved the false doctrines just named (1 Tim. 4:2–3). Paul also warned Titus about "Jewish fables" (Titus 1:14). Paul warned Timothy about these same "fables" in his second letter (2 Tim. 4:4).

A believer cannot rediscover new doctrines. Paul admonished Timothy to remain true to "the good doctrine which you have closely followed up to now" (1 Tim. 4:6b, literal translation). He warned him not to "give heed to fables and endless genealogies" (1 Tim. 1:4). While a pastor must know what the enemy is teaching, he must not be influenced by it. A chemist may handle and study poisons, but he does not permit them to get into his system.

The temporary—"bodily exercise" (vv. 7–8). Again, this is an athletic image. Certainly we ought to care for our bodies, and exercise is a part of that care. Our bodies are God's temples, to be used for His glory (1 Cor. 6:19–20), and His tools for His service (Rom. 12:1–2). But bodily exercise benefits us only during this life; godly exercise is profitable now and for eternity. Paul did not ask Timothy to choose between the two; I think God expects us to practice both. A healthy body can be used of God, but we must major on holiness.

The eternal—"godliness" (vv. 7–12). Phillips Brooks said, "The great purpose of life—the shaping of character by truth." Godly character and conduct are far more important than golf trophies or home-run records, though it is possible for a person to have both. Paul challenged Timothy to be as devoted to godliness as an athlete is to his sport. We are living and laboring for eternity.

Paul used two similar athletic images in writing to the Corinthians (1 Cor. 9:24–27), emphasizing the disciplines necessary for godly living. As an athlete must control his body and obey the rules, so a Christian must make his body his servant and not his master. When I see high school football squads and baseball teams going through their calisthenics under the hot summer sun, I am reminded that there are spiritual exercises that I ought to be doing (Heb. 5:14). Prayer, meditation, self-examination, fellowship, service, sacrifice, submission to the will of others, witness—all of these can assist me, through the Spirit, to become a more godly person.

Spiritual exercise is not easy; we must "labor and suffer reproach" (1 Tim. 4:10a). "For this we labor and strive" (NIV). The word translated "strive" is an athletic word from which we get our English word *agonize*. It is the picture of an athlete straining and giving his best to win. A Christian who wants to excel must really work at it, by the grace of God and to the glory of God.

But exercising ourselves in godly living is not only profitable for us; it is also profitable for others (1 Tim. 4:11–12). It enables us to be good examples, so that we encourage others. Paul named several areas of life in which you and I should be examples.

"In word" (1 Tim. 4:12) implies that our speech should always be honest and loving, "speaking the truth in love" (Eph. 4:15).

"In conduct" (the KJV's "conversation" means "walk," not "talk") suggests that our lives are to be controlled by the Word of God. We must not be like the hypocrites Paul described to Titus (Titus 1:16): "They profess that they know God; but in works they deny him."

"In love" (charity) points to the motivation of our lives. We do not obey God to be applauded by men (Matt. 6:1ff.), but because we love God and love God's people.

("In spirit" is not in many manuscripts, but it would describe the inner enthusiasm and excitement of a child of God.)

"In faith" implies that we trust God and are faithful to Him. Faith and love often go together (1 Tim. 1:14; 2:15; 6:11; 2 Tim. 1:13; 2:22). Faith always leads to faithfulness.

"In purity" is important as we live in this present evil world. Ephesus was a center for sexual impurity, and the young man Timothy was faced with temptations. He must have a chaste relationship to the women in the church (1 Tim. 5:2) and keep himself pure in mind, heart, and body.

But godly living not only helps *us* and *other believers;* it also has its influence on *the lost.* Paul reminded Pastor Timothy that Jesus Christ is the Savior (1 Tim. 4:10), and it is the believer's task to share that good news with the lost. In effect he wrote, "We Christians have fixed our hope in the living God, but the lost have no hope and do not know the living God. All that many of them know are the dead idols that can never save them."

The title "Saviour of all men" does not imply that everybody will be saved (universalism), or that God saves people in spite of themselves; for Paul added "specially of those that believe." It is faith that saves one's soul (Eph. 2:8–10). Since God "will have all men to be saved" (1 Tim. 2:4), and since Christ "gave Himself a ransom for all" (1 Tim. 2:6), then *any* lost sinner can trust Christ and be saved. Christ is "the Saviour of all men," so nobody need despair.

Timothy should not fear to practice the Word of God and apply it to the life of the church, for this Word is "a faithful saying and worthy of all acceptation" (1 Tim. 4:9). These faithful sayings made up a summary of truth for the early church (see 1 Tim. 1:15; 3:1; 2 Tim. 2:11; Titus 3:8). The fact that Timothy was a young man (the word then applied to a person from youth to forty) should not deter him from practicing the Word. In fact, he was to "command" these things, and this is our military word "charge" (1 Tim. 1:3). The local church is a unit in God's spiritual army, and its leaders are to pass God's orders along to the people with authority and conviction.

A Growing Minister, Progressing in the Word (4:13–16)

The key thought in this section is "that thy profiting may appear to all" (1 Tim. 4:15). The word *profiting* ("progress" NIV) is a Greek military term; it means "pioneer advance." It describes the soldiers who go ahead of the troops, clear away the obstacles, and make it possible for others to follow. As a godly pastor, Timothy was to grow spiritually so that the whole church could see his spiritual progress and imitate it.

No pastor can lead his people where he has not been himself. "Such as I have, give I thee" is a basic principle of life and ministry (Acts 3:6). The pastor (or church member) who is not growing is actually going backward, for it is impossible to stand still in the Christian life. In his living, teaching, preaching, and leading, the minister must give evidence of spiritual growth. But what are factors that make spiritual progress possible?

Emphasize God's Word (v. 13). "Give attendance to" means "devote yourself to, be absorbed in." Ministering the Word was not something Timothy was to do after he had done other things; it was to be the most important thing he did. *Reading* means the public reading of Scripture in the local assembly. The Jewish people always had the reading of the law and the Prophets in their synagogues, and this practice carried over into Christian churches. Jesus read the Scriptures in the synagogue at Nazareth (Luke 4:16ff.), and Paul often read the lessons when he visited a synagogue (Acts 13:15).

In my itinerant ministry, I have noted that many churches have dispensed with the public reading of God's Word, and I am disappointed. They have time for "special music" and endless announcements, but there is no time for the reading of the Bible. The pastor may read a text before he preaches, but that is a different thing. Every local church ought to have a schedule of Bible readings for the public services. It is commanded by Scripture that we read God's Word in the public assemblies. (I might add that those who read the Word publicly ought to prepare themselves privately. Nobody should be asked "at the last minute" to read the Scriptures publicly. The Bible deserves the best we can give.)

Exhortation (1 Tim. 4:13) literally means "encouragement" and suggests the applying of the Word to the lives of the people. The pastor was to read the Word, explain it, and apply it. *Doctrine* means "teaching," and is a major emphasis in the pastoral letters. There are at least twenty-two references to "teaching" or "doctrine" in these thirteen chapters.

"Apt to teach" is one of the qualifications of a minister (1 Tim. 3:2); and it has been correctly said, "Apt to teach implies apt to learn." A growing minister (or church member) must be a student of the Word. Before he teaches others he must teach himself (Rom. 2:21). His spiritual progress is an example to his flock and an encouragement to others.

Use your spiritual gifts (v. 14). So much has been written in recent years about spiritual gifts that we have almost forgotten the *graces* of the Spirit (Gal. 5:22–23). The word *gift* is the Greek word *charisma*. It simply means "a gracious gift from God." (The world uses the word *charisma* to describe a person with magnetic personality and commanding appearance.) *Every Christian* has the gift of the Spirit (Rom. 8:9) and at least one gift from the Spirit (1 Cor. 12:1–11). The gift of the Spirit, and the gifts from the Spirit, are bestowed by God at the moment of conversion (see 1 Cor. 12:13ff.).

However, when God calls a believer into a special place of ministry, He can (and often does) impart a spiritual gift for that task. When Timothy was ordained by the elders ("presbytery"), he received an enabling gift from God when the elders laid hands on him. But for some reason, Timothy had neglected to cultivate this gift that was so necessary to his spiritual progress and ministry. In fact, Paul had to admonish him in his second letter, "Stir up the gift of God, which is in thee by the putting on of my hands" (2 Tim. 1:6).

It is encouraging to know that the God who calls us also equips us to do His work. We have nothing in ourselves that enables us to serve Him; the ministry must all come from God (1 Cor. 15:9–10; Phil. 4:13; 1 Tim. 1:12). However, we must not be passive; we must cultivate God's gifts, use them, and develop them in the ministry of the local church and wherever God puts us.

Devote yourself fully to Christ (v. 15). "Meditate" carried the idea of "be in them, give yourself totally to them." Timothy's spiritual life and ministry were to be the absorbing, controlling things in his life, not merely sidelines that he occasionally practiced. There can be no real pioneer advance in one's ministry without total

dedication to the task. "No man can serve two masters" (Matt. 6:24).

While I do not want to sound critical, I must confess that I am disturbed by the fact that too many pastors and Christian workers divide their time and interest between the church and some sideline. It may be real estate, trips to the Holy Land, politics, civic duties, even denominational service. Their own spiritual lives suffer, and their churches suffer, because these men are not devoting themselves wholly to their ministry. "This one thing I do" was Paul's controlling motive, and it ought to be ours too (Phil. 3:13). "A double-minded man is unstable in all his ways" (James 1:8).

Take spiritual inventory (v. 16). Examine your own heart in the light of the Word of God. Note that Paul put "thyself" ahead of "the doctrine." Paul had given this same warning to the Ephesian elders in his farewell message: "Take heed therefore unto yourselves" (Acts 20:28). A servant of God can be so busy helping others that he neglects himself and his own spiritual walk.

The great American evangelist of the 1800s, Charles Finney, used to preach on this text. He titled his sermon "Preacher, Save Thyself!" That sermon is needed today, for we are seeing people having to leave the ministry because their lives have not kept up with their profession. Moral problems, divorces, and other kinds of shameful conduct have destroyed many of God's servants. "Let him that thinketh he standeth take heed lest he fall" (1 Cor. 10:12).

The building up of the saved and the winning of the lost are the purposes for our ministry, to the glory of God. But God must work *in* us before He can effectively work *through* us (Phil. 2:12–13). As good ministers, we preach the Word; as godly ministers, we practice the Word; as growing ministers, we progress in the Word.

CHAPTER FIVE
1 Timothy 5
ORDER IN THE CHURCH!

The first problem the early church faced was also a modern one: A group of church members was neglected by the ministering staff (Acts 6). I once heard a certain pastor described as "a man who is invisible during the week and incomprehensible on Sunday." Again, somebody in his congregation was feeling neglected.

Then Paul instructed Timothy how to minister to specific groups in his church.

The Older Members (5:1–2)

Paul admonished Timothy to minister to the various kinds of people in the church, and not to show partiality (1 Tim. 5:21). Since Timothy was a younger man, he might be tempted to ignore the older members, so Paul urged him to love and serve all of the people, regardless of their ages. The church is a family: Treat the older members like your mother and father, and the younger members like your brothers and sisters.

The Old Widows (5:3–10)

From the beginning of its ministry, the church had a concern for believing widows (Acts 6:1; 9:39). Of course, the nation of Israel had sought to care for widows; and God had given special legislation to protect them (Deut. 10:18; 24:17; Isa. 1:17). God's special care for the widows is a recurring theme in Scripture (Deut. 14:29; Ps. 94:6; Mal. 3:5). It was only right that the local church show compassion to these women who were in need.

However, the church must be careful not to waste its resources on people who really are not in need. Whether we like to admit it or not, there are individuals and entire families that "milk" local churches, while they themselves refuse to work or to use their own resources wisely. As long as they can get handouts from the church, why bother to go to work?

Paul listed the qualifications a widow must meet if she is to be supported by the church.

Without human support (vv. 5a, 8, "desolate"). If a widow had relatives they should care for her so that the church might use its money to care for others who have no help. If her own children were dead, then her grandchildren (the KJV translates them "nephews" in 1 Tim. 5:4) should accept the responsibility. When you recall that society in that day did not have the kind of institutions we have today—pensions, Social Security, retirement homes, and so forth—you can see how important family care really was. Of course, the presence of such institutions *today* does not relieve any family of its loving obligations. "Honor thy father and thy mother" is still in the Bible (Ex. 20:12; Eph. 6:1–3).

Suppose a relative is unwilling to help support his loved one? "He ... is worse than an unbeliever!" was Paul's judgment (1 Tim. 5:8 NIV; also see v. 16). A missionary friend of mine, now with the Lord, came home from the field to care for her sick and elderly parents. She was severely criticized by some of her associates ("We should love God more than father and mother!"), but she remained faithful to the end. Then she returned to the field for years of fruitful service, knowing she had obeyed God. After all, we love God by loving His people, and He has a special concern for the elderly, the widows, and the orphans.

A believer with a faithful testimony (vv. 5b–7). The church could not care for *all* the widows in the city, but it should care for believers who are a part of the fellowship. We should "do good unto all ... especially unto them who are of the household of faith" (Gal. 6:10). A widow the church helps should not be a self-indulgent person, seeking pleasure, but a godly woman who hopes in God and has a ministry of intercession and prayer. See Luke 2:36–37 for an example of a godly widow.

It has been my experience in three different pastorates that godly widows are "spiritual powerhouses" in the church. They are the backbone of the prayer meetings. They give themselves to visitation, and they swell the ranks of teachers in the Sunday school. It has also been my experience that, if a widow is *not* godly, she can be a great problem to the church. She will demand attention, complain about what the younger people do, and often "hang on the telephone" and gossip. (Of course, it is not really "gossip." She only wants her friends to be able to "pray more intelligently" about these matters!) Paul made it clear (1 Tim. 5:7) that church-helped widows must be "blameless"—irreproachable.

At least sixty years old (v. 9a). A woman of this age was not likely to get remarried in that day, though sixty is not considered that "old" today. Perhaps the verb "taken into the number" gives us a clue. It literally means "to be enrolled and put on the list." The word was used for the enrollment of soldiers. The early church had an official list of the names of qualified widows, and we get the impression that these "enlisted" women ministered to the congregation in various ways. (Remember Dorcas and her widow friends, Acts 9:36–43?) Paul probably would have told us if they had been officially ordained as deaconesses.

A good marriage record (v. 9b). We have met this same requirement before, for bishops (1 Tim. 3:2) and for deacons (1 Tim. 3:12). The implication is that the widow was not a divorced woman. Since younger widows were advised to remarry (1 Tim. 5:14), this stipulation cannot refer to a woman who had a temporary second marriage after the death of her husband. Faithfulness to one's marriage vows is very important in the eyes of God.

A witness of good works (v. 10). If a person is faithfully serving God, the light will shine and others will see it and glorify God (Matt. 5:16). "Brought up children" can refer either to a widow's own children or the reference may be to orphans who needed a home. If it refers to her own children, then they would have to have died; otherwise the church would not support her. It is likely that the reference here is to the practice of rescuing abandoned children and raising them to know the Lord.

Hospitality is another factor, for this was an important ministry in those days when travel was dangerous and safe places to sleep were scarce. The washing of feet does not refer to a special ritual, but to the common practice of washing a guest's feet when he arrived in the home (Luke 7:44). It was not beneath this woman's dignity to take the place of a humble servant.

"Relieved the afflicted" could cover many kinds of ministry to the needy: feeding the hungry, caring for the sick, encouraging the sorrowing, and so forth. Every pastor gives thanks for godly women who minister to the material and physical needs in the church.

These widows were cared for by the church, but they, in turn, helped to care for the church.

The Younger Widows (5:11–16)

The younger widows would technically be women under sixty years of age, but no doubt Paul had much younger women in mind. It was not likely that a fifty-nine-year-old woman would "bear children" if she remarried (1 Tim. 5:14)! The dangers of travel, the ravages of disease, war, and a host of other things could rob a young wife of her husband. But Paul forbade Timothy to enroll the younger widows and put them under the care of the church.

The reasons for refusing them (vv. 11–14a). Because of their age, younger widows are naturally attracted to men and want to marry again. What is so bad about that? Paul seemed to imply (1 Tim. 5:12) that each of the widows enrolled pledged herself to remain a widow and serve the Lord in the church. This pledge must not be interpreted as a "vow of celibacy," nor should we look on this group of ministering widows as a "special monastic order." There seemed to be an agreement between the widows and the church that they would remain widows and serve the Lord.

There is another possible interpretation: These younger widows, if supported by the church, would have opportunities to "live it up" and find other husbands, most likely unbelievers. By marrying unbelievers, they would be casting off their first faith. However, I prefer the first explanation.

Paul does make it clear (1 Tim. 5:13) that younger widows, if cared for by the church, would have time on their hands and get involved in sinful activities. They would get in the habit of being idle instead of being useful. They would gad about from house to house and indulge in gossip and be busybodies. There is a definite connection between idleness and sin.

Paul warned Timothy against using the "charity" ministry of the church to encourage people to be idle. The church certainly ought to assist those who really need help, but it must not subsidize sin. As a pastor, I have had to make decisions in these matters, and sometimes it is not easy.

Requirements for younger widows (vv. 14b–16). Moving from the negative, Paul listed the positive things he wanted the younger widows to do to be accepted and approved in the church. He wanted the younger widows to marry and have families. While not every person is supposed to get married, marriage is natural for most people who have been married before. Why remain in lonely widowhood if there was yet opportunity for a husband and a family? Of course, all of this would have to be "in the Lord" (1 Cor. 7:39).

"Be fruitful and multiply" was God's mandate to our first parents (Gen. 1:28), so the normal result of marriage is a family. Those today who refuse to have children because of the "awfulness of the times" should check out how difficult the times were in Paul's day! If

Christians do not have children and raise them to live for God, who will?

"Guide the house" (1 Tim. 5:14) literally means "rule the house." The wife should manage the affairs of the household, and her husband should trust her to do so (Prov. 31:10–31). Of course, marriage is a partnership, but each partner has a special sphere of responsibility. Few men can do in a home what a woman can do. Whenever my wife was ill or caring for our babies, and I had to manage some of the affairs of the home, I discovered quickly that I was out of my sphere of ministry!

The result of all this is a good testimony that silences the accusers. Satan (the adversary) is always alert to an opportunity to invade and destroy a Christian home. The word *occasion* is a military term that means "a base of operations." A Christian wife who is not doing her job at home gives Satan a beachhead for his operations, and the results are tragic. While there are times when a Christian wife and mother may have to work outside the home, it must not destroy her ministry in the home. The wife who works simply to get luxuries may discover too late that she has lost some necessities. It may be all right to have what money can buy if you do not lose what money cannot buy.

How Christian wives and mothers manage their homes can be a testimony to those outside the church. Just as a pastor is to have a good reputation with outsiders (1 Tim. 3:7), and the servants are not to bring reproach on God's Word (1 Tim. 6:1), so the wives are to have a good witness. Women may not be able to be elders of the church, but they can minister for the Lord right in their own homes. (See Titus 2:4–5 for an additional emphasis on this vital ministry.)

Paul then summarized the principle of each family caring for the needs of its own members (1 Tim. 5:16). Paul did not tell them *how* these widows should be relieved—giving them a regular dole, taking them into a home, giving them employment, and so forth. Each local assembly would have to decide this according to the needs of individual cases.

How does this principle apply to Christians today? Certainly we must honor our parents and grandparents and seek to provide for them if they have needs. Not every Christian family is able to take in another member, and not every widow wants to live with her children. Where there is sickness or handicap, professional care is necessary, and perhaps this cannot be given in a home. Each family must decide what God's will is in the matter, and no decision is easy. The important thing is that believers show love and concern and do all they can to help each other.

Church Officers (5:17–25)

The instructions in this section deal primarily with the elders, but the principles also apply to a pastor's relationship with any officer in his church. It is a wonderful thing when the elders and deacons (and other officers) work together in harmony and love. It is tragic when a pastor tries to become a spiritual dictator (1 Peter 5:3), or when an officer tries to be a preeminent "big shot" (3 John 9–10).

Apparently Timothy was having some problems with the elders of the church at Ephesus. He was a young man and still had much to learn. Ephesus was not an easy place to minister. Furthermore, Timothy had followed Paul as overseer of the church, and Paul would not be an easy man to follow! Paul's farewell address to the Ephesian elders (Acts 20) shows how hard he had worked and how faithful he had been, and how much the elders loved Paul (Acts 20:36–38). In spite of the fact that Paul had personally sent Timothy to Ephesus, the young man was having a hard time.

This situation may be the reason for Paul's instruction about wine (1 Tim. 5:23). Did Timothy have stomach trouble? Was he ill because of his many responsibilities and problems? Or had he tried to follow the ideas of some ascetics (1 Tim. 4:1–5), only to discover that his diet was making him worse instead of better? We do not know the answers to all these questions; we can only read between the lines. It is worth noting that Paul's mention of wine here is not an endorsement of the entire alcohol industry. Using wine for medicinal reasons is not an encouragement for social drinking. As we have seen, though the Bible does not demand total abstinence, it does denounce drunkenness.

Paul counseled Timothy in his relationship to the elders by discussing three topics:

Paying the elders (vv. 17–18). In the early church, instead of one pastor, several elders ministered to the people. These men would devote themselves full-time to the work of the Lord, and, therefore, they deserved some kind of remuneration. In most congregations today, the elders are laymen who have other vocations, but who assist in the work of the church. Usually the pastoral staff are the only full-time workers in the church. (Of course, there are also secretaries, custodians, and so forth, but Paul was not writing about them.)

There were two kinds of elders in the church: *ruling elders* who supervised the work of the congregation, and *teaching elders,* who taught the Word of God. These elders were chosen from the congregation on the basis of God's call, the Spirit's equipping, and the witness and work of the men themselves. After they were chosen, they were ordained and set apart for this ministry (Acts 14:23; 20:17, 28; Titus 1:5).

The local church needs both ruling and teaching. The Spirit gives the gifts of "helps" and "governments" to the church (1 Cor. 12:28). If a church is not organized, there will be wasted effort, money, and opportunities. If spiritually minded leaders do not supervise the various ministries of the local church, there will be chaos instead of order. However, this supervision must not be dictatorial. You do not manage the work of a local church in the same manner as

you do a grocery store or a manufacturing plant. While a church should follow good business principles, it is not a business. The ruthless way some church leaders have pushed people around is a disgrace to the gospel.

But ruling without teaching would accomplish very little. The local church grows through the ministry of the Word of God (Eph. 4:11ff.). You cannot rule over babies! Unless the believers are fed, cleansed, and strengthened by the Word, they will be weak and useless and will only create problems.

Paul told Timothy to be sure that the leaders were paid adequately, on the basis of their ministries. He quoted an Old Testament law to prove his point (Deut. 25:4). (The best commentary on this is 1 Cor. 9:7–14.) Then Paul added a statement from our Lord Jesus Christ: "The laborer deserves his wages" (Luke 10:7 NIV). This was a common saying in that day, but Paul equated the words of Christ with Old Testament Scripture!

If pastors are faithful in feeding and leading the people, then the church ought to be faithful and pay them adequately. "Double honor" (1 Tim. 5:17) can be translated "generous pay." (The word *honor* is used as in "honorarium.") It is God's plan that the needs of His servants be met by their local churches, and He will bless churches that are faithful to His servants. If a church is not faithful, and its pastor's needs are not met, it is a poor testimony; and God has ways of dealing with the situation. He can provide through other means, but then the church misses the blessing; or He may move His servant elsewhere.

The other side of the coin is this: A pastor must never minister simply to earn money (see 1 Tim. 3:3). To "negotiate" with churches, or to canvass around looking for a place with a bigger salary is not in the will of God. Nor is it right for a pastor to bring into his sermons his own financial needs, hoping to arouse some support from the finance committee!

Disciplining the elders (vv. 19–21). Church discipline usually goes to one of two extremes. Either there is no discipline at all, and the church languishes because of disobedience and sin, or the church officers become evangelical policemen who hold a kangaroo court and violate many of the Bible's spiritual principles.

The disciplining of church *members* is explained in Matthew 18:15–18; Romans 16:17–18; 1 Corinthians 5; 2 Corinthians 2:6–11; Galatians 6:1–3; 2 Thessalonians 3:6–16; 2 Timothy 2:23–26; Titus 3:10; and 2 John 9–11.

Paul in this passage (1 Tim. 5:19–21) discussed the disciplining of church *leaders.* It is sad when a church member must be disciplined, but it is even sadder when a spiritual leader fails and must be disciplined, for leaders, when they fall, have a way of affecting others.

The purpose of discipline is restoration, not revenge. Our purpose must be to save the offender, not to drive him away. Our attitude must be one of love and tenderness (Gal. 6:1–3). In fact the verb *restore* that Paul used in Galatians 6:1 means "to set a broken bone." Think of the patience and tenderness involved in that procedure!

Paul's first caution to Timothy was to *be sure of his facts,* and the way to do that is to have witnesses (1 Tim. 5:19). This principle is also stated in Deuteronomy 19:15; Matthew 18:16; and 2 Corinthians 13:1. I think a dual application of the principle is suggested here. First, those who make any accusation against a pastor must be able to support it with witnesses. Rumor and suspicion are not adequate grounds for discipline. Second, when an accusation is made, witnesses ought to be present. In other words, the accused has the right to face his accuser in the presence of witnesses.

A church member approached me at a church dinner one evening and began to accuse me of ruining the church. She had all sorts of miscellaneous bits of gossip, none of which was true. As soon as she started her tirade, I asked two of the officers standing nearby to witness what she was saying. Of course, she immediately stopped talking and marched defiantly away.

It is sad when churches disobey the Word and listen to rumors, lies, and gossip. Many a godly pastor has been defeated in his life and ministry in this way, and some have even resigned from the ministry. "Where there's smoke, there's fire" may be a good slogan for a volunteer fire department, but it does not apply to local churches. "Where there's smoke, there's fire" could possibly mean that somebody's tongue has been "set on fire of hell" (James 3:6)!

Paul's second caution was that Timothy do everything openly and aboveboard. The under-the-counter politics of city hall have no place in a church. "In secret have I said nothing," said Jesus (John 18:20). If an officer *is* guilty, then he should be rebuked before all the other leaders (1 Tim. 5:20). He should be given opportunity to repent, and if he does he should be forgiven (2 Cor. 2:6–11). Once he is forgiven, the matter is settled and should never be brought up again.

Paul's third caution (1 Tim. 5:21) is that Timothy obey the Word no matter what his personal feelings might be. He should act without prejudice *against* or partiality *for* the accused officer. There are no seniority rights in a local church; each member has the same standing before God and His Word. To show either prejudice or partiality is to make the situation even worse.

Selecting and ordaining the elders (vv. 22–25). Only God knows the hearts of everyone (Acts 1:24). The church needs spiritual wisdom and guidance in selecting its officers. It is dangerous to impulsively place a new Christian or a new church member in a place of spiritual responsibility. Some people's sins are clearly seen; others are able to cover their sins, though their sins pursue them (1 Tim. 5:24). The good works of dedicated believers ought to be evident, even though they do not serve in order to be seen by people (1 Tim. 5:25).

In other words, the church must carefully investigate the lives of potential leaders to make sure that there is nothing seriously wrong. To ordain elders with sin in their lives is to partake of those sins! If simply saying goodbye (God be with you) to a heretic makes us partakers of his evil deeds (2 John 10–11), then how much guiltier are we if we ordain people whose lives are not right with God?

No pastor or church member is perfect, but that should not hinder us from striving for perfection. The ministry of a local church rises and falls with its leadership. Godly leadership means God's blessing, and that is what we want and need.

CHAPTER SIX
1 Timothy 6
ORDERS FROM HEADQUARTERS

This chapter continues Paul's advice to Timothy on ministering to the various kinds of believers in the church. The atmosphere is military, for Paul used words that belong to the army: "Fight the good fight of faith" (1 Tim. 6:12). "I give thee charge" (1 Tim. 6:13, which is the same military term used in 1:3). "Charge them that are rich" (1 Tim. 6:17). "O Timothy, keep [guard] that which is committed to thy trust" (1 Tim. 6:20). In other words, you might say Paul was the general, giving Timothy orders from the Lord, the Commander in Chief.

D. L. Moody did not want his soloist, Ira Sankey, to use "Onward, Christian Soldiers" in their evangelistic campaigns. Moody felt that the church he saw was very unlike an army. If the average military man on our side in World War II had behaved toward his superiors and their orders the way the average Christian behaves toward the Lord, we probably would have lost the war! Instead of "Onward, Christian Soldiers," someone has suggested that perhaps we ought to sing "Backward, Christian Soldiers."

Paul instructed Timothy how to minister to four more groups in the church, and also how to keep his own life in the will of God.

Christian Slaves (6:1–2)
Some historians have estimated that half of the population of the Roman Empire was composed of slaves. Many of these people were educated and cultured, but legally they were not considered persons at all. The gospel message of salvation and freedom in Christ appealed to the slaves, and many of them became believers. (The word translated "servant" in the KJV New Testament usually means "slave.") When slaves were able to get away from their household duties, they would fellowship in local assemblies where being a slave was not a handicap (Gal. 3:28).

But there was a problem: Some slaves used their newfound freedom in Christ as an excuse to disobey, if not defy, their masters. They needed to learn that their spiritual freedom in Christ did not alter their social position, even though they were accepted graciously into the fellowship of the church.

Slaves with unbelieving masters (v. 1). No Christian master would consider his slaves "under the yoke," but would treat them with love and respect (Col. 4:1; Philem. 16). For a slave to rebel against an unsaved master would bring disgrace on the gospel. "The name of God" and His doctrine would be blasphemed (Rom. 2:24). This is one reason Paul and the early missionaries did not go around preaching against the sinful institution of slavery. Such a practice would have branded the church as a militant group trying to undermine the social order, and the progress of the gospel would have been greatly hindered.

Slaves with believing masters (v. 2). The danger here is that a Christian slave might take advantage of his master because both are saved. "My master is my brother!" a slave might argue. "Since we are equal, he has no right to tell me what to do!" This attitude would create serious problems both in the homes and in the churches.

Paul gave three reasons why Christian slaves should show respect for their believing masters and not take advantage of them. The most obvious reason is *their masters are Christians* ("faithful" = believing). How can one believer take advantage of another believer? Second, *their masters are beloved*. Love does not rebel or look for opportunities to escape responsibility. Finally, *both master and servant benefit from obedience* ("partakers of the benefit" can apply to both of them). There is a mutual blessing when Christians serve each other in the will of God.

I recall counseling a young lady who resigned from a secular job to go to work in a Christian organization. She had been there about a month and was completely disillusioned.

"I thought it was going to be heaven on earth," she complained. "Instead, there are nothing but problems."

"Are you working just as hard for your Christian boss as you did for your other boss?" I asked. The look on her face gave me the answer. "Try working harder," I advised, "and show him real respect. Just because all of you in the office are saved doesn't mean you can do less than your best." She took my advice and her problems cleared up.

False Teachers (6:3–10)

Paul had opened this letter with warnings about false teachers (1 Tim. 1:3ff.) and had even refuted some of their dangerous teachings (1 Tim. 4:1ff.). The spiritual leaders in the local church must constantly oversee what is being taught because it is easy for false doctrines to slip in (Acts 20:28–32). A pastor I know discovered a Sunday school teacher who was sharing his "visions" instead of teaching God's Word!

The marks of these false teachers (vv. 3–5a). The first mark is that they refused to adhere to "the sound instruction of our Lord Jesus Christ and to godly teaching" (1 Tim. 6:3 NIV). This teaching is godly and it promotes godliness. Isaiah's first test of any teacher was "To the law and to the testimony: if they speak not according to this word, it is because there is no light in them" (Isa. 8:20). It is important that a church "hold fast the form of sound [healthy] words" (2 Tim. 1:13).

A second mark is the teacher's own attitude. Instead of being humble, a false teacher is proud, yet he has nothing to be proud about because he does not know anything (1 Tim. 6:4; also 1:7).

A believer who understands the Word will have a burning heart, not a big head (Luke 24:32; and see Dan. 9:1–20). This "conceited attitude" causes a teacher to argue about minor matters concerning "words" (1 Tim. 6:3). Instead of feeding on the "wholesome words of ... Christ," you might say he gets sick about questions. The word *doting* (1 Tim. 6:4) means "filled with a morbid desire, sick." The result of such unspiritual teaching is "envy, quarreling, malicious talk, evil suspicions, and constant friction" (1 Tim. 6:4b–5a NIV).

The tragedy of all this is that the people are "robbed of the truth" (1 Tim. 6:5 NIV) while they think they are discovering the truth! They think that the weekly arguments in their meetings, during which they exchange their ignorance, are a means of growing in grace; meanwhile the result is a loss of character, not an improvement.

The motive for their teaching (vv. 5b–10). These false teachers supposed "that godliness is a way of financial gain" (literal translation). "Godliness" here (1 Tim. 6:5) means "the profession of Christian faith" and not true holy living in the power of the Spirit. They used their religious profession as a means to make money. What they did was not a true ministry; it was just a religious business.

Paul was always careful not to use his calling and ministry as a means of making money. In fact, he even refused support from the Corinthian church so that no one could accuse him of greed (1 Cor. 9:15–19). He never used his preaching as "a cloak of covetousness" (1 Thess. 2:5). What a tragedy it is today to see the religious racketeers who prey on gullible people, promising them help while taking away their money.

To warn Timothy—and us—about the dangers of covetousness, Paul shared four facts:

Wealth does not bring contentment (v. 6). The word *contentment* means "an inner sufficiency that keeps us at peace in spite of outward circumstances." Paul used this same word later. "For I have learned, in whatsoever state I am, therewith to be content" (Phil. 4:11). True contentment comes from godliness in the heart, not wealth in the hand. A person who depends on material things for peace and assurance will never be satisfied, for material things have a way of losing their appeal. It is the wealthy people, not the poor people, who go to psychiatrists and who are more apt to try to commit suicide.

Wealth is not lasting (v. 7). I like to translate this verse, "We brought nothing into this world because we can carry nothing out" (see Job 1:21). When someone's spirit leaves his body at death, it can take nothing with it because, when that person came into the world at birth, he brought nothing with him. Whatever wealth we amass goes to the government, our heirs, and perhaps charity and the church. We always know the answer to the question "How much did he leave?" *Everything!*

Our basic needs are easily met (v. 8). Food and "covering" (clothing and shelter) are basic needs; if we lose them, we lose the ability to secure other things. A miser without food would starve to death counting his money. I am reminded of the simple-living Quaker who was watching his new neighbor move in, with all of the furnishings and expensive "toys" that "successful people" collect. The Quaker finally went over to his new neighbor and said, "Neighbor, if ever thou dost need anything, come to see me, and I will tell thee how to get along without it." Henry David Thoreau, the naturalist of the 1800s, reminded us that a man is wealthy in proportion to the number of things he can afford to do without.

The economic and energy crises that the world faces will probably be used by God to encourage people to simplify their lives. Too many of us know the "price of everything and the value of nothing." We are so glutted with luxuries that we have forgotten how to enjoy our necessities.

The desire for wealth leads to sin (vv. 9–10). "They that *will be* rich," is the accurate translation. It describes a person who has to have more and more material things in order to be happy and feel successful. But riches are a trap; they lead to bondage, not freedom. Instead of giving satisfaction, riches create additional lusts (desires), and these must be satisfied. Instead of providing help and health, an excess of material things hurts and wounds. The result Paul described very vividly: "Harmful desires … plunge men into ruin and destruction" (1 Tim. 6:9 NIV). It is the picture of a man drowning! He trusted his wealth and "sailed along," but the storm came and he sank.

It is a dangerous thing to use religion as a cover-up for acquiring wealth. God's laborer is certainly worthy of his hire (1 Tim. 5:17–18), but his motive for laboring must not be money. That would make him a "hireling," and not a true shepherd (John 10:11–14). We should not ask, "How much will I get?" but rather "How much can I give?"

The Pastor Himself (6:11–16, 20–21)

While caring for the needs of his people, Timothy needed to care for himself as well. "Take heed unto thyself" (1 Tim. 4:16) was one of Paul's admonitions. The phrase "But thou" (1 Tim. 6:11) indicates a contrast between Timothy and the false teachers. They were men of the world, but he was a "man of God." This special designation was also given to Moses (Deut.

33:1), Samuel (1 Sam. 9:6), Elijah (1 Kings 17:18), and David (Neh. 12:24), so Timothy was in good company.

Paul gave four admonitions to Timothy that, if obeyed, would assure him success in his ministry and a continued testimony as "a man of God."

Flee (v. 11a). There are times when running away is a mark of cowardice. "Should such a man as I flee?" asked Nehemiah (Neh. 6:11). But there are other times when fleeing is a mark of wisdom and a means of victory. Joseph fled when he was tempted by his master's wife (Gen. 39:12), and David fled when King Saul tried to kill him (1 Sam. 19:10). The word *flee* that Paul used here did not refer to literal running, but to Timothy's *separating himself* from the sins of the false teachers. This echoes the admonition in 1 Timothy 6:5: "From such withdraw thyself."

Not all unity is good, and not all division is bad. There are times when a servant of God should take a stand against false doctrine and godless practices, and separate himself from them. He must be sure, however, that he acts on the basis of biblical conviction and not because of a personal prejudice or a carnal party spirit.

Follow (v. 11b). Separation without positive growth becomes isolation. We must cultivate these graces of the Spirit in our lives, or else we will be known only for what we oppose rather than for what we propose. "Righteousness" means "personal integrity."

"Godliness" means "practical piety." The first has to do with character; the second, with conduct.

"Faith" might better be translated "faithfulness." It has well been said that the greatest ability is dependability.

"Love" is the *agape* love that sacrifices for the sake of others. It seeks to give, not to gain.

"Patience" carries the idea of "endurance," sticking to it when the going is tough. It is not a complacency that waits, but a courage that continues in hard places.

"Meekness" is not weakness, but instead is "power under control." Courageous endurance without meekness could make a person a tyrant. Perhaps "gentleness" expresses the meaning best.

Fight (vv. 12–16). The verb means "keep on fighting!" It is a word from which we get our English word *agonize,* and it applies both to athletes and to soldiers. It described a person straining and giving his best to win the prize or win the battle. Near the end of his own life, Paul wrote, "I have fought a good fight" (2 Tim. 4:7).

This "fight," however, is not between believers; it is between a person of God and the enemy around him. He is fighting to defend the faith, that body of truth deposited with the church (see 1 Tim. 6:20). Like Nehemiah of old, Christians today need to have a trowel in one hand for building and a sword in the other hand for battling (Neh. 4:17). It is sad when some Christians spend so much time fighting the enemy that they have no time do to their work and build the church. On the other hand, if we do not stand guard and oppose the enemy, what we have built could be taken from us.

What is it that encourages us in the battle? We have "eternal life" and need to take hold of it and let it work in our experience. We have been called by God, and this assures us of victory. We have made our public profession of faith in Christ, and others in the church stand with us.

Another encouragement in our battle is the witness of Jesus Christ our Savior. He "witnessed a good confession" (1 Tim. 6:13) before Pontius Pilate and did not relent before the enemy. He knew that God the Father was with Him and watching over Him, and that He would be raised from the dead. It is "God who makes all things alive" (literal translation), who is caring for us, so we need not fear. Timothy's natural timidity might want to make him shrink from the battle. But all he had to do was remember Jesus Christ and His bold confession, and this would encourage him.

Paul gave Timothy military orders: "I give thee charge" (1 Tim. 6:13, also 1:3). He was to guard the commandment and obey it. Why? Because one day the Commander would appear and he would have to report on his assignment! The only way he could be ready would be to obey orders "without spot or blame" (1 Tim. 6:14 NIV).

The Greek word translated "appearing" (1 Tim. 6:14) gives us our English word *epiphany*, which means "a glorious manifestation." In Paul's day, the word was used in the myths to describe the appearing of a god, especially to deliver someone from trouble. Paul used it of the first coming of Jesus Christ (2 Tim. 1:10) and of His return (2 Tim. 4:1, 8). We do not know when Christ will come again, but it will be "in his own time" (1 Tim. 6:15 NIV), and He knows the schedule. Our task is to be faithful every day and abide in Him (1 John 2:28).

The subject of 1 Timothy 6:16 is God, the God and Father of our Lord Jesus Christ. He is the *only* Ruler, though others may take the title. "Potentate" (1 Tim. 6:15) comes from a word that means "power." The kings and rulers of the earth may think they have power and authority, but God is sovereign over all (see Ps. 2).

"King of kings, and Lord of lords" (1 Tim. 6:15) makes us think of Jesus Christ (Rev. 17:14; 19:16), but here the title is applied to God the Father. Jesus Christ, of course, reveals the Father to us, so He can justly claim this title.

"Immortality" (1 Tim. 6:16) means "not subject to death." Man is subject to death, but God is not. Only God has immortality as an essential and inherent part of His being. He is "immortal, invisible, the only wise God" (1 Tim. 1:17). Because God is not subject to death, He is Life and the Giver of life. He is incorruptible and not subject to decay or change. In this life, believers are in mortal bodies, but when Jesus Christ returns, we shall share His immortality (1 Cor. 15:50–58).

Keep in mind that Paul explained all these truths about God in order to encourage Timothy to "fight the good fight of faith" and not give up. We need not fear life because God is the Ruler of all; and we need not fear death because He shares immortality with us.

Timothy lived in the godless city of Ephesus, but God dwells in glorious light. "And the sight of the glory of the Lord was like devouring fire" (Ex. 24:17). "Who coverest thyself with light as with a garment" (Ps. 104:2). John's description of heaven emphasized the glory of God that gives light to the city (Rev. 21:11, 23–24; 22:5). Of course, light is a symbol of holiness (1 John 1:5–7). God dwells apart from sin, and God is glorious in His holiness.

It is impossible for a sinful human to approach the holy God. It is only through Jesus Christ that we can be accepted into His presence. Jacob saw God in one of His Old Testament appearances on earth (Gen. 32:30), and God allowed Moses to see some of His glory (Ex. 33:18–23). "No man hath seen God at any time" (John 1:18) refers to seeing God *in His essence,* His spiritual nature. We can only see manifestations of this essence, as in the person of Jesus Christ.

Why did Paul write so much about the person and glory of God? Probably as a warning against the "emperor cult" that existed in the Roman Empire. It was customary to acknowledge regularly, "Caesar is Lord!" Of course, Christians would say "Jesus Christ is Lord!" Only God has "honor and power everlasting" (1 Tim. 6:16b). If Timothy was going to fight the good fight of faith, he had to decide that Jesus Christ *alone* was worthy of worship and complete devotion.

Be faithful (vv. 20–21). God had committed the truth to Paul (1 Tim. 1:11), and Paul had committed it to Timothy. It was Timothy's responsibility to guard the deposit and then pass it along to others who would, in turn, continue to pass it on (2 Tim. 2:2). This is God's way of protecting the truth and spreading it around the world. We are stewards of the doctrines of the faith, and God expects us to be faithful in sharing His good news.

The word *science* (1 Tim. 6:20) does not refer to the kind of technology we know today by that name. *"Knowledge* falsely so called" is a better translation. Paul referred here to the teachings of a heretical group called "gnostics" who claimed to have a "special spiritual knowledge." (The Greek word for "knowledge" is *gnosis,* pronounced NO-sis. An "agnostic" is one who does not know. A gnostic is one who claimed to know a great deal.)

There is no need to go into detail here about the heretical claims of the gnostics. Paul's letter to the Colossians was written to counteract them. They claimed to have "special spiritual knowledge" from visions and other experiences. They also claimed to find "hidden truths" in the Old Testament Scriptures, especially the genealogies. They considered matter to be evil, and they taught that a series of "emanations" connected God with man. Jesus Christ, they said, was only the greatest of these emanations.

The gnostics actually had a doctrine that was a strange mixture of Christianity, Eastern mysticism, Greek philosophy, and Jewish legalism. Like many of the Eastern cults we see today, it offered "something for everybody." But Paul summarized all that they taught in one devastating phrase: "profane and vain babblings." Phillips translated it "the godless mixture of contradictory notions."

Why should Timothy avoid these teachings? Because some who got involved in them "wandered from the faith" (1 Tim. 6:21 NIV). Not only will wrong motives (a desire for money) cause a person to wander from the faith (1 Tim. 6:10), but so will wrong teachings. These lies work their way into a person's mind and heart gradually, and before he realizes it, he is wandering off the path of truth.

The Rich (6:17–19)

Paul had already written about the danger of the love of money, but he added a special "charge" for Timothy to give to the rich. We may not think that this charge applies to us, but it does. After all, our standard of living today would certainly make us "rich" in the eyes of Timothy's congregation!

Be humble (v. 17a). If wealth makes a person proud, then he understands neither himself nor his wealth. "But thou shalt remember the Lord thy God; for it is he that gives thee power to get wealth" (Deut. 8:18). We are not owners; we are stewards. If we have wealth, it is by the goodness of God and not because of any special merits on our part. The possessing of material wealth ought to humble a person and cause him to glorify God, not himself.

It possible to be "rich in this world [age]" (1 Tim. 6:17) and be poor in the next. It is also possible to be poor in this world and rich in the next. Jesus talked about both (Luke 16:19–31). But a believer can be rich in this world and also rich in the next if he uses what he has to honor God (Matt. 6:19–34). In fact, a person who is poor in this world can use even his limited means to glorify God, and discover great reward in the next world.

Trust God, not wealth (v. 17b). The rich farmer in our Lord's parable (Luke 12:13–21) thought that his wealth meant security, when really it was an evidence of insecurity. He was not really trusting God. Riches are uncertain, not only in their value (which changes constantly), but also in their durability. Thieves can steal wealth, investments can drop in value, and the ravages of time can ruin houses and cars. If God gives us wealth, we should trust Him, the Giver, and not the gifts.

Enjoy what God gives you (v. 17c). Yes, the word *enjoy* is in the Bible! In fact, one of the recurring themes in Ecclesiastes is "Enjoy the blessings of life now, because life will end one day" (Eccl. 2:24; 3:12–15, 22; 5:18–20; 9:7–10; 11:9–10). This is not sinful "hedonism," living for the pleasures of life. It is simply enjoying all that God gives us for His glory.

Employ what God gives you (vv. 18–19). We should use our wealth to do good to others; we should share; we should put our money to work. When we do, we enrich ourselves spiritually, and we make investments for the future (see Luke 16:1–13). "That they may lay hold on eternal life" (1 Tim. 6:19) does not suggest that these people are not saved. "That they may lay hold on the life that is real" would express it perfectly. Riches can lure a person into a make-believe world of shallow pleasure. But riches *plus God's will* can introduce a person to life that is real and ministry that is lasting.

Paul's final sentence was not for Timothy alone, because the pronoun is plural: "Grace be with all of you." Paul had the entire church in mind when he wrote this letter, and certainly all of the elders, not just Timothy. As leader of the church, Timothy needed to heed the word of the apostle, but all of his church members had a responsibility to hear and obey as well.

And so do we today.

2 TIMOTHY

OUTLINE

Key theme: Preparation for the ministry in the last days
Key verses: 2 Timothy 1:13–14

I. THE PASTORAL APPEAL (1)
    A. Courageous enthusiasm—1:1–7
    B. Shameless suffering—1:8–12
    C. Spiritual loyalty—1:13–18

II. THE PRACTICAL APPEAL (2)
    A. The steward—2:1–2
    B. The soldier—2:3–4, 8–13
    C. The athlete—2:5
    D. The farmer—2:6–7
    E. The workman—2:14–18
    F. The vessel—2:19–22
    G. The servant—2:23–26

III. THE PROPHETIC APPEAL (3)
    A. Turn away from the false—3:1–9
    B. Follow those who are true—3:10–12
    C. Continue in God's Word—3:13–17

IV. THE PERSONAL APPEAL (4)
    A. Preach the Word—4:1–4
    B. Fulfill your ministry—4:5–8
    C. Be diligent and faithful—4:9–22

CONTENTS

CHAPTER ONE
2 Timothy 1
CHRISTIANS COURAGEOUS!

When Paul wrote the letter we know as 2 Timothy, his situation had changed drastically. He was now a prisoner in Rome and was facing certain death (2 Tim. 4:6). For one reason or another, almost all of Paul's associates in the ministry were gone and only Luke was at the apostle's side to assist him (2 Tim. 4:11). It was a dark hour indeed.

But Paul's great concern was not for himself; it was for Timothy and the success of the gospel ministry. As in his first letter to Timothy, Paul encouraged his beloved colleague to be faithful. As we have learned, Timothy was timid, suffered from physical ailments, and was tempted to let other people take advantage of him and not assert his authority as a pastor.

Paul sent Tychicus to replace Timothy at Ephesus so that Timothy might join Paul at Rome (2 Tim. 4:9, 12). God would soon move Paul off the scene, and Timothy would take his place and continue to give spiritual leadership to the churches. It would not be an easy task, but Timothy could succeed with the Lord's help. In his first chapter, Paul gave Timothy three essentials that he must possess to have success.

Courageous Enthusiasm (1:1–7)

The ministry of the gospel is no place for a "timid soul" who lacks enthusiasm. In fact, courageous enthusiasm is essential for success in *any* kind of work. Paul compared this attitude to stirring up a fire into full flame (2 Tim. 1:6). We must not conclude that Timothy was backslidden or lacked spiritual fire. Rather, Paul was encouraging his associate to keep the fire burning brightly so that it might generate spiritual power in his life. Paul gave Timothy four encouragements.

Paul's love (vv. 1–2). "Timothy, my dearly beloved son" is much stronger than "Timothy, my own son in the faith" (1 Tim. 1:2). It is not that Paul loved Timothy less when he wrote that first letter, but that Paul was now expressing it more. As Paul's life drew to a close, he realized in a deeper way how dear Timothy was to him.

Paul's own circumstances were difficult, and yet he was greatly encouraged. For one thing, he was Christ's ambassador ("apostle"), and he knew that his Master would care for him. Whatever happened to him was in the hands of God, so there was no need to fear. Furthermore, Paul had "the promise of life" in Jesus Christ, and Christ had defeated death (2 Tim. 1:10). No wonder Paul was able to extend to Timothy "grace, mercy, and peace." (It is worth noting that Paul added "mercy" to his greetings when he wrote to the pastors, 1 Tim. 1:2; 2 Tim. 1:2; Titus 1:4. Paul knew that pastors need mercy!)

Paul's prayers (vv. 3–4). What an encouragement to know that the great apostle was praying for him! Paul, who knew Timothy's weaknesses and problems, was able to pray definitely and with a real burden on his heart. His praying was not routine; it was done with compassion and concern. Knowing that he would soon die, Paul was anxious that Timothy join him at Rome for those last days of fellowship and ministry. This would bring joy to Paul's heart.

We must not assume that Paul tried to defend his evil actions before his conversion by claiming he did it all with "a pure conscience." After all, he was guilty of causing terror among Christians, forcing people to blaspheme by denying Christ, and agreeing to the murder of Stephen! It is true that Paul thought he was serving God (see John 16:2), and that he was in spiritual ignorance (1 Tim. 1:13), but these facts cannot guarantee a pure conscience.

Paul had known God from his earliest years because he was "an Hebrew of the Hebrews" (Phil. 3:5). His ancestors had given him the orthodox Jewish faith. But when he met Jesus Christ, Paul realized that his Jewish faith was but preparation for the fulfillment Christ gave him in Christianity. He did not serve God with a pure conscience "from his forefathers," as the King James Version says. Rather, he heard about the true God from his forefathers, and *now* he was serving that God with a pure conscience. The fact that he had a pure conscience helped give power to his prayers.

Paul's confidence in Timothy (v. 5). Paul did not think that Timothy's tears were evidence of failure or insincerity. Paul was sure that Timothy's faith was genuine, and that this faith would see him through in spite of the troubles he was facing. Apparently Lois, Timothy's grandmother, was the first one in the family won to Christ; then his mother, Eunice, was converted. Timothy's father was a Greek (Acts 16:1), so Eunice had not practiced the orthodox Jewish faith. However, Timothy's mother and grandmother had seen to it that he was taught the Scriptures (2 Tim. 3:15), and this was great preparation for the hearing of the gospel. When Paul came to Lystra on his first missionary journey, that was probably the occasion for Timothy's conversion. When Paul returned on his second journey, he enlisted Timothy into Christian service.

Paul had watched Timothy's life and service during those years they were together. He was certain that Timothy's faith was genuine. In fact, Timothy's heritage was a great one, for he was reared in a godly home, trained by a wonderful apostle, and given marvelous opportunities for serving the Lord.

God's gift to Timothy (vv. 6–7). Paul reminded Timothy of the time God called him into service and the local church ordained him. Paul had laid his hands on Timothy (1 Tim. 4:14). Through Paul, God had imparted to Timothy the spiritual gift he needed for his ministry. The laying on of hands was a common practice in apostolic days (Acts 6:6; 13:3), but no believer today has the same authority and privileges that the apostles did. Today, when we lay hands on people for the ministry, it is a symbolic act and does not necessarily impart any special spiritual gifts to them.

It is the Holy Spirit who enables us to serve God, and through Him we can overcome fear and weakness. The word *fear* in 2 Timothy 1:7 means "timidity, cowardice." The Holy Spirit gives us power for witness and for service (Acts 1:8). It is futile for us to try to serve God without the power of the Holy Spirit. Talent, training, and experience cannot take the place of the power of the Spirit.

The Holy Spirit also gives us love. If we have love for lost souls and for the people of God, we will be able to endure suffering and accomplish the work of God. Selfishness leads to fear because, if we are selfish, we are interested only in what we will get out of serving God, and we will be afraid of losing prestige, power, or money. True Christian love, energized by the Spirit (Rom. 5:5), enables us to sacrifice for others and not be afraid. The Spirit gives love (Gal. 5:22).

He is also the One who gives self-control ("a sound mind"). This word is related to the words *sober* and *sobriety* that we often meet in the pastoral letters (1 Tim. 2:9, 15; Titus 1:8; 2:2, 4, 6, 12). "Self-discipline" is a better translation of "sound mind" (2 Tim. 1:7). It describes a person who is sensibly minded and balanced, who has his life under control. The Amplified Version reads, "calm and well-balanced mind and discipline and self-control."

Timothy did not need any new spiritual ingredients in his life; all he had to do was "stir up" what he already had. Paul had written in his first letter, "Neglect not the gift that is in thee" (1 Tim. 4:14). Now he added, "Stir up—stir into flame—the gift of God." The Holy Spirit does not leave us when we fail (John 14:16), but He cannot fill us, empower us, and use us if we neglect our spiritual lives. It is possible to grieve the Spirit (Eph. 4:30) and quench the Spirit (1 Thess. 5:19).

Timothy had every reason to be encouraged and to have spiritual enthusiasm in his ministry. Paul loved him and prayed for him. His experiences in life had been preparation for his ministry, and Paul was confident of the genuineness of Timothy's faith. The Spirit within him would give all the power needed for ministry. What more could he want?

Shameless Suffering (1:8–12)

"Not ashamed" is a key idea in this chapter. Paul was not ashamed (2 Tim. 1:12); he admonished Timothy not to be ashamed (2 Tim. 1:8); and he reported that Onesiphorus was not ashamed of Paul's chain (2 Tim. 1:16).

Be not ashamed of the Lord's testimony (vv. 8–10). Timothy's natural timidity might make it easy for him to avoid circumstances that demanded witness and involved suffering. Once again, Paul gave his associate needed encouragement.

God gives us power (v. 8). By nature, none of us enjoys suffering. Even our Lord prayed, "Father, if thou be willing, remove this cup from me" (Luke 22:42), and

Paul prayed three times for God to remove his painful thorn in the flesh (2 Cor. 12:7–8). But suffering may well be a part of a faithful Christian life. Christians should not suffer because they have done wrong (1 Peter 2:20; 3:17); rather, they sometimes suffer because they have done right and served God. When we suffer for doing good, then we are sharing Christ's sufferings (Phil. 3:10) and suffering on behalf of the whole church (Col. 1:24).

Years ago, I read about a Christian who was in prison because of his faith. He was to be burned at the stake, and he was certain he would never be able to endure the suffering. One night, he experimented with pain by putting his little finger into the candle flame. It hurt, and he immediately withdrew it. "I will disgrace my Lord," he said to himself. "I cannot bear the pain." But when the hour came for him to die, he praised God and gave a noble witness for Jesus Christ. God gave him the power *when he needed it,* and not before.

God has called us by His grace (v. 9). We are part of a great eternal plan that God determined "before the world began." God knows the end from the beginning. He has purposes for His people to accomplish for His glory. Suffering is a part of His plan. Jesus Christ suffered in the will of God here on earth, and all those who trust in Him will also suffer.

The emphasis in this verse is on *grace.* God saved us; we did not save ourselves (Eph. 2:8–9; Titus 3:5). He called us, not on the basis of our good works, but wholly on the basis of His grace. It is His purposes that we are to fulfill, and if these purposes include suffering, then we can accept it by faith and know that God's will is best. This is not fatalism. It is confidence in the wise plan of our gracious heavenly Father.

All of this grace was given to us in Jesus Christ. We could not earn it; we did not merit it. This is the grace of God!

Christ has defeated death (v. 10). When we are timid it is because we are afraid. Of what are we afraid? Suffering and possible death? Paul himself was facing death as he dictated this letter. But Jesus Christ has defeated our last enemy, death! By His own death and resurrection, Christ has "abolished death" (made it inoperative, taken out the sting). "O death, where is thy sting? O grave, where is thy victory?" (1 Cor. 15:55).

Christ was not only the Destroyer of death (see Heb. 2:14–15), but He was also the Revealer of life and immortality. In the Old Testament the doctrines of eternal life, death, resurrection, and the eternal state were in the shadows. Here and there you find glimpses of light; but for the most part, the picture is dark. But then Jesus Christ shone His light on death and the grave. Through the gospel, He has given us assurance of eternal life, resurrection, and the hope of heaven.

Religious groups that teach "soul sleep" and other strange doctrines usually get their ideas from the Psalms and Ecclesiastes. Instead of allowing the clear light of the New Testament to shine on the Old, they look at the New through the shadows of the Old! If you turn your back on the light of the gospel, you will only cast another shadow and make the scene darker.

"Immortality" (2 Tim. 1:10 KJV) means "incorruptibility," and refers to the resurrection body. The present body is corruptible; it dies and decays. But the glorified body we shall have when we see Christ will not be subject to decay or death (1 Cor. 15:49–58; Phil. 3:21). In fact, the heavenly inheritance that we share will be "incorruptible and undefiled, and [one] that fadeth not away" (1 Peter 1:4).

Be not ashamed of the Lord's prisoner (vv. 11–12). Though a prisoner, Paul was still bearing witness for the gospel of Jesus Christ. Sad to say, the people in Ephesus had deserted Paul in his time of need (2 Tim. 1:15). Many of them could have come to Rome to witness on Paul's behalf, but they did not. They were even ashamed to be identified with the apostle! It would have made Timothy's ministry in Ephesus (and in the surrounding cities; see 2 Tim. 4:13) much easier if he had gone along with the crowd, but Paul admonished him to remain true. He gave four reasons why Timothy should not be ashamed of his association with Paul, the prisoner.

Paul was called by God (v. 11). Jesus Christ had met Paul on the Damascus road (Acts 9) and had personally called him into the ministry. Paul was a *herald* ("preacher") of the gospel. In ancient times, a "herald" was the official messenger of the king or emperor, and his message was treated with great respect The fact that professed believers in Asia were rejecting Paul did not change his calling or his message.

Paul was not only a herald; he was also *an apostle, "one sent with a commission."* Not every Christian was an apostle of Jesus Christ, for a person had to meet certain qualifications and be chosen by the Lord personally, or through His Spirit (see Acts 1:15–26; 1 Cor. 9:1; 2 Cor. 12:12). An apostle represented Jesus Christ. To reject an apostle was to reject the Lord.

Paul was a teacher of the Gentiles. This meant that he shepherded local churches. It was this word *Gentiles* that put him into prison in Rome the first time (Acts 22:21ff.). The Gentile believers in Asia should have shown their appreciation of Paul by rallying to his support, for after all, it was Paul who brought them the good news of salvation. But instead they were ashamed of him and tried not to get involved.

Paul was confident in Christ (v. 12). Paul was not ashamed! Why? Because he knew that Christ was faithful and would keep him. Note his emphasis on the person of Christ: "I know *whom* I have believed." Salvation is not the result of believing certain doctrines, though doctrines are important. A sinner is saved because he believes in a Person—Jesus Christ the Savior. Paul had deposited his soul in the care and keeping of the Savior, and Paul was sure that Jesus Christ would faithfully guard that deposit. What difference did it make to Paul what happened on any

certain day? What really mattered is what will happen on "that day" when Jesus Christ rewards His servants (see 2 Tim. 1:18; 4:8).

In these difficult days, it is important that we stand true to Christ and be willing to suffer for Him and not be ashamed. We may not be put into prison, as was Paul; but we suffer in other ways: the loss of friends, being bypassed for a promotion, loss of customers, being snubbed by people, and so forth. It is also important that we stand by God's servants who are suffering for righteousness' sake.

Spiritual Loyalty (1:13–18)

Throughout the centuries God's work has been done by men and women who stood steadfast in their hours of trial. It would have been convenient for them to have compromised, but they stood firm. Paul was such a man, and he encouraged Timothy to follow his example in a twofold loyalty.

Be loyal to God's Word (vv. 13–14). *God* had given the deposit of spiritual truth to Paul (1 Tim. 1:11), and he had given it to Timothy (1 Tim. 6:20). It was now Timothy's solemn responsibility to "hold fast" (2 Tim. 1:13) and "guard" (2 Tim. 1:14 NIV) the precious deposit of Christian truth, and to pass it along to others (2 Tim. 2:2).

The word *form* (2 Tim. 1:13) means "a pattern, an architect's sketch." There was a definite outline of doctrine in the early church, a standard by which teaching was tested. If Timothy changed this outline or abandoned it, then he would have nothing by which to test other teachers and preachers. We today need to hold fast to what Paul taught for the same reason.

However, note that Timothy's orthodoxy was to be tempered with "faith and love." "Speaking the truth in love" (Eph. 4:15) is the divine pattern. How easy it is to become pugnacious in our desire to defend the faith, or a witch-hunter who creates problems.

It was the Holy Spirit who committed the truth to Timothy, and He would help him guard it. Apart from the ministry of the Spirit, we are in the dark when it comes to understanding the Word of God. It is He who must teach us (John 16:13) and enable us to guard the truth and share it with others.

From the beginning of human history, Satan has opposed God's Word. "Yea, hath God said?" was Satan's first word to mankind (Gen. 3:1), and he continues to ask that question. Throughout the history of the church, the Word of God has been attacked, often by people *within* the church, yet it still stands today. Why? Because dedicated men and women have (like Paul and Timothy) guarded the deposit and faithfully handed it to a new generation of Christians. When a church or any other Christian organization goes liberal, it usually starts with a weakening of their leaders' convictions about the Word of God.

Be loyal to God's servant (vv. 15–18). The province of Asia in that day comprised the Roman districts of Lydia, Mysia, Caria, and Phrygia. Paul was forbidden to minister in this area on his second missionary journey (Acts 16:6), but on his third journey, he stayed nearly three years in Ephesus, the capital of Asia, and evangelized the entire area (Acts 19; 20:31). The seven churches of Asia were all in this area (Rev. 1:4, 11).

We do not know who Phygelus and Hermogenes (2 Tim. 1:15) were. It is likely that they were leaders in the church who opposed Paul and would not come to his defense in Rome. You would think that the Asian believers would have stood by Paul, but, instead, they were ashamed of him and at the same time (whether they knew it or not) ashamed of Christ (see 2 Tim. 4:16).

It was certainly a dark hour for Paul. Demas had forsaken him (2 Tim. 4:10). His other associates had been sent to distant places of ministry. False doctrines were spreading in the church (2 Tim. 2:17–18). How Paul would have loved to be free to preach the Word and defend the faith—but he was in a Roman prison. It was up to Timothy to get the job done.

But there was one man who dared to leave Ephesus and come to Rome to assist Paul—Onesiphorus. His name means "profit-bearing," and he certainly was a profitable friend to Paul. It is possible that he was a deacon in the church at Ephesus ("ministered" in 2 Tim. 1:18 comes from the word that gives us "deacon"). During Paul's ministry at Ephesus, Onesiphorus was a faithful minister, along with his household. Since Timothy had pastored the Ephesian church, he would know this choice saint.

Let me add here that every pastor is thankful for those faithful members who assist him in the work of the Lord. My wife and I have found choice saints in each of the three churches we have served—people whose homes were open to us (and they didn't tell the whole church we were there!), whose hearts felt our burdens and needs, and whose prayers sustained us in difficult times. These believers minister behind the scenes, but the Lord will reward them openly "in that day" (2 Tim. 1:18).

Onesiphorus traveled from Ephesus to Rome and diligently looked for Paul so he might minister to the prisoner's needs. It seemed difficult for him to find his former pastor (2 Tim. 1:17). Perhaps some of the Roman Christians were still opposed to Paul as they had been during his first imprisonment (see Phil. 1:12–17). Perhaps the Roman officials were not cooperative and did not want their choice prisoner to receive any help. In his first imprisonment, Paul was in his own house (Acts 28:30), but now he was in a Roman prison under careful guard.

But Onesiphorus persisted! He located Paul and risked his own life to stand with him and assist him. Some students believe that Onesiphorus was also arrested and possibly executed. They base this on the fact that Paul greeted the "household of Onesiphorus" in 2 Timothy 4:19, but not the man himself. Also, Paul asked for *present* mercies for the household, but *future* mercies for Onesiphorus (2 Tim. 1:16, 18).

But the problem is this: If Onesiphorus was dead, then Paul prayed for the dead (2 Tim. 1:18), and we have no authorization in the Bible to pray for the dead.

We have no proof that Onesiphorus was dead when Paul wrote this letter. The fact that Paul asked God to bless the man's household, but that he did not mention the man, simply means that at the time Onesiphorus was not with his household. "When he *was* in Rome" (2 Tim. 1:17) suggests that, at that writing, Onesiphorus was not in Rome.

Therefore, he was somewhere between Rome and Ephesus, so Paul prayed for him and his household. There was no need to greet Onesiphorus, for Paul had just spent much time with him, so Paul only greeted his household.

Onesiphorus was not ashamed of Paul's chain. The apostle was manacled to a Roman soldier twenty-four hours a day. Onesiphorus could have invented many excuses for staying in Ephesus. But instead he made the dangerous journey to Rome and ministered to Paul. "He often refreshed me" was Paul's description of this man's ministry. The Greek word means "to cool again." "Bracing me like fresh air" is the way the Amplified Bible translated it. How we thank God for Christians who are "a breath of fresh air" in our hours of trial!

Were it not for Paul's letter, we would never know that Onesiphorus had served Paul and the church. But the Lord knew and will reward him "on that day."

The essentials for a successful ministry have not changed: courageous enthusiasm, shameless suffering, and spiritual loyalty.

CHAPTER TWO
2 Timothy 2
GETTING THE PICTURE

While attending a convention, I noticed a man wearing two name badges. When I asked him why, he replied, "Oh, I'm having an identity crisis!"

Paul did not want Timothy to have an identity crisis, so he carefully explained what a pastor is and does. (Of course, the same principles apply to all Christians.) Paul represented seven pictures of the Christian minister.

The Steward (2:1–2)

The ministry is not something we get for ourselves and keep to ourselves. We are stewards of the spiritual treasure God has given us. It is our responsibility to guard the deposit and then invest it in the lives of others. They, in turn, are to share the Word with the next generation of believers.

It is important that we get our original treasure from the Word of God, and not from the ideas and philosophies of men. We do not test modern teachers by their popularity, education, or skill. We test them by the Word of God, and particularly the doctrines of grace as given by Paul. It is not we who examine Paul to see if he is right; it is Paul who examines us!

It takes strength to teach the Word of God. We must dig out of the rich mines of Scripture the "gold, silver, precious stones" that are hidden there (see Prov. 2:1–10; 3:13–15; 8:10–21; 1 Cor. 3:10–23). This strength can only come from God's grace. The secret of Paul's great ministry was the grace of God (1 Cor. 15:10).

The ability to study, understand, and teach the Word of God is a gift of God's grace. "Apt to teach" is one of God's requirements for the pastor (1 Tim. 3:2; 2 Tim. 2:24). "Apt to teach" implies apt to learn; so a steward must also be a diligent student of the Word of God.

The Soldier (2:3–4, 8–13)

Paul often used military illustrations in his letters. This is not surprising since he lived in a military state and was in prison himself. He described in these verses the characteristics of a "good soldier of Jesus Christ."

He endures hardship (v. 3). Many people have the idea that the ministry is a soft job. Preachers are often the butt of jokes that suggest they are lazy and should be ashamed of accepting their salaries. But a dedicated Christian minister is in a battle that requires spiritual endurance (see Eph. 6:10ff.).

He avoids worldly entanglements (v. 4). He is totally committed to his Commanding Officer, the One who enlisted him. In our case, this is Jesus Christ. I recall a story about a Civil War soldier who happened to be a watchmaker. One day the bugle sounded and the men were told to break camp. "But I can't go now!" the soldier complained. "I have a dozen watches to repair!"

It is sometimes necessary for a pastor, or a pastor's wife, to be employed because their church is not able to support them. This is a sacrifice on their part and an investment in the work. But a pastor who is fully supported should not get involved in sidelines that divide his interest and weaken his ministry. I have met pastors who spend more time on their real estate ventures than on their churches. Our purpose is to please the Lord, not ourselves.

He magnifies Jesus Christ (vv. 8–9). "Remember Jesus Christ!" is the way this phrase should be translated. It sounds almost like a war cry, like "Remember the Alamo!" or "Remember Pearl Harbor!" Jesus is the Captain of our salvation (Heb. 2:10), and our purpose is to bring honor and glory to Him. What an encouragement Jesus Christ is to a suffering Christian soldier! For He died and rose again, proving that suffering leads to glory, and that seeming defeat leads to victory. Jesus was treated as an evildoer, and His soldiers will be treated the same way.

The best way to magnify Christ is through the ministry of the Word. Paul was bound, but God's Word cannot be bound. "His Word runneth very swiftly" (Ps. 147:15). "The Word of God grew and multiplied" (Acts 12:24).

He thinks of the whole army (v. 10). "The elect" are God's people, chosen by His grace and called by His Spirit (2 Thess. 2:13–14). Paul not only suffered for the Lord's sake, but he also suffered for the sake of the church. There were yet many people to reach with the gospel, and Paul wanted to help reach them. A soldier who thinks only of himself is disloyal and undependable.

He trusts his Commanding Officer (vv. 11–13). This "faithful saying" is probably part of an early statement of faith recited by believers. (For other "faithful sayings" in the pastoral letters, see 1 Tim. 1:15; 4:9; and Titus 3:8.) It is faith in Jesus Christ that gives us victory (1 John 5:4). We do not fear the enemies, for He has already conquered them. Through our identification with Christ in death, burial, and resurrection, we have won the victory (see Rom. 6).

What a pair of paradoxes! Death leads to life! Suffering leads to reigning in glory! We have nothing to fear! The important thing is that we not "disown" our Lord, for if we disown Him here, He will disown us before the Father (Matt. 10:33). In that great "roll call" in glory, when the "medals" are given out, we will lose our reward if we disown His name.

But Paul makes it clear (2 Tim. 2:13) that even our own doubt and unbelief cannot change Him: "He abideth faithful; he cannot deny himself." We do not put faith in our faith or in our feelings, because they will change and fail. We put our faith in Christ. The great missionary, J. Hudson Taylor, often said, "It is not by trying to be faithful, but in looking to the Faithful One, that we win the victory."

The Athlete (2:5)

Paul sometimes used athletic illustrations in his writings—wrestling, boxing, running, and exercising. The Greeks and the Romans were enthusiastic about sports, and the Olympic and Isthmian Games were important events to them. Paul had already urged Timothy to exercise like an athlete (1 Tim. 4:7–8). Now Paul admonished him to obey the rules.

A person who strives as an athlete to win a game and get a crown must be careful to obey all the rules of the game. In the Greek games in particular, the judges were most careful about enforcing the rules. Each competitor had to be a citizen of his nation, with a good reputation. In his preparations for the event, he had to follow specific standards. If an athlete was found defective in any matter, he was disqualified from competing. If, after he had competed and won, he was found to have broken some rule, he then lost his crown. Jim Thorpe, a great American athlete, lost his Olympic medals because he participated in sports in a way that broke an Olympic rule.

From the human point of view, Paul was a loser. There was nobody in the grandstands cheering him, for "all they which are in Asia" had turned away from him (2 Tim. 1:15). He was in prison, suffering as an evildoer. Yet, *Paul was a winner!* He had kept the rules laid down in the Word of God, and one day he would get his reward from Jesus Christ. Paul was saying to young Timothy, "The important thing is that you obey the Word of God, no matter what people may say. You are not running the race to please people or to get fame. You are running to please Jesus Christ."

The Farmer (2:6–7)

This is another favorite image found in Paul's letters. Paul once compared the local church to a cultivated field in which all the believers worked together (1 Cor. 3:5–9). Each Christian has his particular task to perform—plowing, sowing, watering, or harvesting—but it is God alone who gives the increase.

Several practical truths are found in this image of the farmer and field. For one thing, *a farmer has to work.* If you leave a field to itself, it will produce mostly weeds. Solomon had this truth in mind when he wrote about the field of the sluggard (Prov. 24:30–34). Real ministry is hard work, and a pastor (and church members) ought to work in their spiritual field as diligently as a farmer works in his field. Pastors do not punch clocks, but they ought to be up in the morning and at their work just as if God blew a whistle for them.

A farmer needs patience. "See how the farmer waits for the land to yield its valuable crop and how patient he is for the fall and spring rains" (James 5:7 NIV). A pastor friend of mine often reminds me, "The harvest is not the end of the meeting—it is the end of the age."

A farmer deserves his share of the harvest. "The hardworking farmer should be the first to receive a share of the crops" (2 Tim. 2:6 NIV). Paul is stating here that a faithful pastor ought to be supported by his church. The same idea is found in 1 Corinthians 9:7, where Paul used a soldier, a farmer, and a herdsman to prove his point: "The laborer is worthy of his reward" (1 Tim. 5:18). Paul deliberately gave up his right to ask for support so that nobody could accuse him of using the gospel for personal gain (1 Cor. 9:14ff.). But this policy is not required for all of God's servants.

As a local church grows and progresses, the people ought to faithfully increase their support of their pastors and other staff members. "If we have sown spiritual seed among you, is it too much if we reap a material harvest from you?" (1 Cor. 9:11 NIV). It is sad to see the way some local churches waste money and fail to care for their own laborers. God will honor a church that honors His faithful servants.

Something else is true in this image of the farmer: The spiritual leaders who share the Word with the people are the first ones to enjoy its blessings. The preacher and the teacher always get more out of the sermon or lesson than do the hearers because they put much more into it. They also get great joy out of seeing planted seeds bear fruit in the lives of others. Farming is hard work, and it can have many disappointments; but the rewards are worth it.

The Workman (2:14–18)

The word *study* (2 Tim. 2:15) has nothing to do with books and teachers. It means "to be diligent, be zealous." It is translated in this way in 2 Timothy 4:9, 21, and also in Titus 3:12. The emphasis in this paragraph is that the workman needs to be diligent in his labors so that he will not be ashamed when his work is inspected. "Rightly dividing" means "cutting straight" and can be applied to many different tasks: plowing a straight furrow, cutting a straight board, sewing a straight seam.

The pastor is a workman in God's Word. The Word is a treasure that the steward must guard and invest. It is the soldier's sword and the farmer's seed. But it is also the workman's tool for building, measuring, and repairing God's people. The preacher and teacher who use the Word correctly will build their church the way God wants it to be built. But a sloppy worker will handle God's Word deceitfully in order to make it say what he wants it to say (2 Cor. 4:2). When God tests our ministries in His local churches, some of it, sad to say, will become ashes (1 Cor. 3: 10ff.).

An approved worker diligently studies the Word and seeks to apply it to his own life. An ashamed worker wastes his time with other "religious duties" and has little or nothing to give his class or congregation. An approved worker does not waste his time arguing about "words to no profit" (2 Tim. 2:14) because he knows that such arguing only undermines God's work (see 1 Tim. 6:4; Titus 3:9).

An approved workman will shun "godless chatter" (2 Tim. 2:16 NIV; and see 1 Tim. 6:20), because he knows it only leads to more ungodliness. I fear that some "sharing times" do more harm than good as well-meaning people exchange their "spiritual ignorance."

An approved workman knows that false doctrine is dangerous, and he will oppose it. Paul compared it to gangrene (2 Tim. 2:17). Much as gangrene spreads, infects, and kills other tissue, so false doctrine spreads and infects the body of believers, the church. This infection must be exposed and removed. Only the "sound [healthy] doctrine" of the Word of God can keep a church healthy and growing.

Paul named two men who were false teachers, and he also identified their error. It is likely that the Hymenaeus named here (2 Tim. 2:17) is the same man named in 1 Timothy 1:20. We know nothing about his associate, Philetus. Both of them "wandered from the truth" by teaching that the resurrection had already taken place. Perhaps they taught that salvation is resurrection in a spiritual sense, so a believer must not expect a physical resurrection. But the denial of a physical resurrection is a serious thing (see 1 Cor. 15:12ff.), for it involves the resurrection of Christ and the completion of God's plan of salvation for His people. No wonder these false teachers were able to "overthrow the faith of some" (2 Tim. 2:18). The resurrection is a foundational truth of the gospel.

Each of us as God's workman will be either *approved* or *ashamed.* The word *approved* means "one who has been tested and found acceptable." The word was used for testing and approving metals. Each trial that we go through forces us to study the Word to find God's will. As we rightly use the Word, we succeed in overcoming our trials, and we are approved by God. Martin Luther once said that prayer, study, and suffering make a pastor; and this is true. We cannot be approved unless we are tested.

What does it mean to be "ashamed"? Certainly it means that such a workman's work is below standard and cannot be accepted. It means loss of reward. In fact, in Paul's day, a builder was fined if he failed to follow the specifications. When the Lord judges our works, it will be revealed whether we as workmen have handled the Word of God honestly and carefully. Some who are now first will end up last!

The Vessel (2:19–22)

In this illustration, Paul described a "great house," which is the professing church. The *foundation* of the house is safe and secure because God's seal is on it. (In the Bible, a seal is a mark of ownership and security. No one would dare break a Roman seal.) Paul quoted Moses: "The Lord knoweth them that are his" (Num. 16:5). This refers to the Godward aspect of the Christian life: God chose us who trust Him as His elect (see 2 Tim. 2:10).

But there is also a manward aspect of the Christian life: "Let everyone that nameth the name of Christ depart from iniquity" (2 Tim. 2:19). This refers back to Numbers 16:26, where the Lord warned the people to get away from the tents of Korah and the rebels. In other words, those who are the elect of God prove it by living godly lives. We are chosen in Christ "that we should be holy and without blame" (Eph. 1:4).

This great house not only has a solid foundation that is sealed, but it also has vessels (utensils of various kinds) for performing household functions. Paul divides the utensils into two categories: those of honor (gold and silver) and those of dishonor (wood and clay). He is not distinguishing between kinds of Christians, but rather is making a distinction between true teachers of the Word and the false teachers he described (2 Tim. 2:16–18). A faithful pastor is like a gold or silver vessel that brings honor to Jesus Christ. The head of a house displays his costliest and most beautiful utensils and gets honor from them. I remember the first time I viewed the crown jewels of England in the Tower of London, along with the priceless table vessels and utensils. I was overwhelmed with their glory and beauty. That is the kind of beauty God gives to his servants who faithfully handle the Word of God.

False teachers are not valuable; they are like wood and clay. They are utensils to dishonor, no matter how popular they may be today. Wood and clay will not survive the test of fire. It is worth noting that the name *Timothy* comes from two Greek words which together mean "God-honoring." Paul was encouraging Timothy to live up to his name!

The important thing is that the honorable vessels not be contaminated by the dishonorable ones. The word *these* (2 Tim. 2:21) refers to the vessels of dishonor (2 Tim. 2:20). Paul was admonishing Timothy to separate himself from false teachers. If he did, then God would honor him, set him apart, and equip him for service. "Useful to the Master" (2 Tim. 2:21 NIV)—what a tremendous honor that is! A useful human vessel of honor does not get involved in the popular things of the world, even the "religious world." He must remain holy, and this means he must be separated from everything that would defile him.

This includes the sins of the flesh as well (2 Tim. 2:22). Paul used a similar admonition in 1 Timothy 6:11–12—"Flee ... follow ... fight." True Bible separation is balanced: we flee sin, but we follow after righteousness. If we are not balanced, then we will be isolated instead of separated. In fact, God's man Paul commanded us to fellowship "with them that call on the Lord out of a pure heart" (2 Tim. 2:22). After all, this is the purpose of the ministry of the Word (1 Tim. 1:5). It is sad when true believers are isolated because of a false view of separation.

For God to be able to use us as vessels, we must be empty, clean, and available. He will take us and fill us and use us for His glory. But if we are filled with sin or defiled by disobedience, He will first have to purge us, and that might not be an enjoyable experience. In the "great house" of the professing church, there are true believers and false. We must exercise spiritual discernment and be careful that we are vessels sanctified unto honor.

The Servant (2:23–26)

"Servant" (2 Tim. 2:24) is the Greek word *doulos* which means "slave." So Paul called himself "a slave of Jesus Christ" (Rom. 1:1; Phil. 1:1). A slave had no will of his own; he was totally under the command of his master. Once, we Christians were the slaves of sin, but now we are the slaves of God (Rom. 6:16ff.). Like the servant in Old Testament days, we say, "I love my master ... I will not go out free" (Ex. 21:5).

God's slave does not have an easy time teaching the Word. Satan opposes him and tries to trap his listeners (2 Tim. 2:26). Also, some people are just naturally difficult to teach. They enjoy "foolish and stupid arguments" (2 Tim. 2:23 NIV) and have no desire to feed on the nourishing Word of God. Until you have experienced it, you have no idea how difficult it is to impart spiritual truth to some people.

How easy it would be to ignore them! But then Satan would get them. Paul admonished Timothy to avoid the arguments that create strifes, but not to ignore the people. He must not argue or fight. He must be patient and gentle, teaching the Word of God in meekness. It is not enough just to expose error and refute it; we must also teach positive truths and establish the saints in faith.

A servant of God must instruct those who oppose

him, for this is the only way he can rescue them from Satan's captivity. Satan is a liar (John 8:44). He captures people by his lying promises, as he did Eve (see Gen. 3; 2 Cor. 11:3). A servant's purpose is not to win arguments but to win souls. He wants to see deceived persons brought to repentance ("I was wrong—I have changed my mind") and the acknowledging of the truth.

The word *recover* (2 Tim. 2:26) describes a man coming out of a drunken stupor. Satan makes people drunk with his lies, and the servant's task is to sober them up and rescue them. The last phrase in 2 Timothy 2:26 can be interpreted three ways: (1) they are delivered from the snare of the devil who took them captive to do his will; (2) they are taken captive by God's servant to do God's will; (3) they are delivered out of the snare of the devil, who took them captive, to do God's will. I prefer the third interpretation.

As you survey these seven aspects of the work of the ministry, you can see how important and how demanding a work it is. The ministry is no place for a loafer because it demands discipline and work. It is no place for a shirker because there are enemies to fight and tasks to be completed.

Church members need to pray for their pastors and encourage them in the work of the Lord. Church officers should faithfully do their work so that the pastors can devote themselves to their own ministry (see Acts 6:1–7). Churches should provide enough financial support for the ministers so that they can fully devote themselves to the work of the ministry.

In other words, ministers and members should labor together in the work of the Lord.

CHAPTER THREE
2 Timothy 3
WHAT TO DO BEFORE IT ENDS

The emphasis in this chapter is on *knowledge* and *responsibility*. Paul informed Timothy about the character of the last days, and then instructed him how to respond. Action must be based on knowledge. Too many Christians are like the pilot who informed his passengers, "We are lost, but we are making very good time."

"These last days" began with the ministry of Jesus Christ (Heb. 1:1–2) and will continue until He returns. They are called the "last days" because in them God is completing His purposes for His people. Because our Lord has delayed His return, some people scoff at the promise of His coming (2 Peter 3:3ff.), but He will come as He promised.

Within this period of "last days" there will be "times" (seasons) of different kinds, but as the "times" draw to a close, they will become perilous. This word means "dangerous, hard to deal with, savage." This is the same Greek word that is used to describe the two

violent demoniacs of Gadara (Matt. 8:28). This suggests that the violence of the last times will be energized by demons (1 Tim. 4:1).

There is no doubt that these characteristics started to appear in Paul's day, and now they have increased in intensity. It is not simply that we have more people in the world, or better news coverage. It appears that evil is deeper and of greater intensity, and that it is being accepted and promoted by society in a bolder way. It is not that we have small pockets of rebellion here and there. All of society seems to be in ferment and rebellion. We are indeed in "terrible times" (2 Tim. 3:1 NIV).

Paul gave Timothy three instructions to obey in order that his ministry might be effective during perilous times.

Turn Away from the False (3:1–9)
"From such turn away" (2 Tim. 3:5b). A faithful believer should have nothing to do with the people Paul described in this section. It is important to note that these people operate *under the guise of religion:* "Having a form of godliness, but denying the power thereof (2 Tim. 3:5). They are "religious" but rebellious! Paul discussed three facts about these people.

Their characteristics (vv. 2–5). At least eighteen different characteristics are listed here, and Paul probably could have listed more. There is an emphasis on *love:* "lovers of their own selves," lovers of money ("covetous"), "lovers of pleasures more than lovers of God." The heart of every problem is a problem in the heart. God commands us to love Him supremely, and our neighbors as ourselves (Matt. 22:34–40), but if we love ourselves supremely, we will not love God *or* our neighbors.

In this universe there is God, and there are people and things. We should worship God, love people, and use things. But if we start worshipping ourselves, we will ignore God and start loving things and using people. This is the formula for a miserable life, yet it characterizes many people today. The worldwide craving for *things* is just one evidence that people's hearts have turned away from God.

Of course, if someone loves and worships himself, the result will be *pride.* "Ye shall be as gods" was Satan's offer to Eve (Gen. 3:5), and the result was that people "changed the truth of God into a lie, and worshipped and served the creature more than [rather than] the Creator" (Rom. 1:25). Man became his own god! The creature is now the creator! "Boasters, proud [arrogant], blasphemers [given to contemptuous and bitter words]" (2 Tim. 3:2).

"Disobedient to parents" suggests that this apostasy reaches into the family. Children are "unthankful" and do not appreciate what their parents have done for them. They are "unholy" in their attitude toward their parents. "Honor thy father and thy mother" is not widely taught or respected.

The phrase "without natural affection" is the translation of one word that describes "family love." The family is under attack these days, and, as go its families, so goes the nation.

In place of the natural love that God has put into men and women and families, today we have a good deal of natural love that God has condemned (see Rom. 1:18–27; 1 Cor. 6:9–10). It is confusion, and God will judge it (Rom. 1:28–32).

Not only in homes, but out in society and the business world, the characteristics of these perilous times may be seen. "Truce-breakers" (2 Tim. 3:3) describes people who will not try to agree. They are unyielding and irreconcilable and must have their own way.

In order to defend their position, they become "slanderers" ["false accusers" KJV] and try to tear down the reputations of others. Unfortunately, some of this activity goes on even among professed Christians. "Christian leaders" accuse one another in the pages of their publications.

"Incontinent" means "without self-control." The motto of our society today is "Do your own thing and enjoy it!" Sad to say, some of the children born to these people do not always enjoy it because they are deformed or handicapped as the result of drugs, alcohol, or sexually transmitted diseases.

This lack of self-control reveals itself in a number of ways. "Fierce" means "untamed, brutal." When these people cannot have their way, they become much like savage beasts. Instead of honoring what is good, they despise what is good and honor what is evil. In society today the standards of right and wrong have been twisted, if not destroyed. "Woe unto them that call evil good and good evil," cried Isaiah the prophet (Isa. 5:20).

"Traitors" (2 Tim. 3:4) describes people who betray others and cannot be trusted. Neither friendship nor partnership makes any difference to them; they lie and break their promises whenever doing so helps them get their own way.

"Heady" means "reckless, rash, acting without careful thought." Paul did not condemn honest adventure, but foolish endeavor.

"High-minded" does not describe a person with lofty thoughts. Rather, it means a person who is "puffed up" with his importance. "Conceited" is a good synonym.

"Lovers of pleasures more than lovers of God" does not suggest that we must choose between pleasure and God, for when we live for God, we enjoy the greatest pleasures (Ps. 16:11). The choice is between *loving* pleasure and loving God. If we love God, we will also enjoy fullness of life here and forever, but the pleasures of sin can only last for a brief time (Heb. 11:25). No one can deny that we live in a pleasure-mad world; but these pleasures too often are just shallow entertainment and escape; they are not enrichment and true enjoyment.

Paul stated that these people he has just described would consider themselves religious! "Having a form of godliness" (2 Tim. 3:5) suggests an outward appearance of religion, not true Christian faith, for they have never experienced the power of God in their lives. Form without force. Religion without reality.

Their converts (vv. 6–7). The fact that Paul described "silly [weak-willed NIV] women" does not suggest that all women are like this, or that men are not vulnerable to the wiles of false teachers. In Paul's day, women were especially susceptible to this kind of experience since they had a low status in society. Whether men or women, people who fall for this false religious system have the same characteristics.

They are *burdened with guilt* and looking for some escape from bondage and fear. They find themselves unable to control their various desires ("divers lusts" KJV). The emphasis here may be on sexual problems. Finally, they are always searching for truth, trying this approach and that, yet they are never able to be satisfied. This kind of person is fair game for the cultists and the religious racketeers.

These false religious leaders take advantage of the problems people have, and promise them quick and easy solutions. They "worm their way in" and soon control people's lives. It is not long before these leaders grab their followers' loyalty, money, and service. And their "converts" are worse off than they were before. They still have their problems, but they have been duped into thinking that all is well.

And, remember, all of this underhanded activity is done in the name of religion! No wonder Paul told Timothy, "From such turn away."

Their religious leaders (vv. 8–9). Read Exodus 7—9 for the record of the contest between Moses and the Egyptian magicians. Tradition says that the magicians were Jannes and Jambres, two men mentioned by Paul (2 Tim. 3:8). These men opposed Moses *by imitating what he did*. When Aaron's rod turned into a serpent, the magicians cast down their rods and they turned into serpents. Moses turned the water into blood, and the magicians followed with the same miracle. When Moses brought up all the frogs, the magicians duplicated the miracle. But when it came to the miracle of the lice, the magicians could not imitate it (Ex. 8:16–19).

Satan is an imitator; what God does, Satan counterfeits. The religious leaders in the last days will have a counterfeit faith, and their purpose is to promote a lie and resist the truth of God's Word. They deny the authority of the Bible and substitute human wisdom and philosophy. In their attempt to be "modern," they deny the reality of sin and people's need for salvation. "Reprobate" is the word Paul used to describe them. This means "tested and found counterfeit."

Jannes and Jambres were finally exposed and made fools of by the judgments of God. This will also happen to the leaders of false religions in the last days. When God's judgments fall, the true character of these counterfeits will be revealed to everyone.

Follow Those Who Are True (3:10–12)

Paul turned from the false leaders to remind Timothy

that he (Paul) had been a faithful servant of God. It is important in these difficult days that we follow the right spiritual leaders. What are their characteristics?

Their lives are open for all to see (v. 10a). Paul had nothing to hide. Like his Master, he could say, "In secret have I said nothing" (John 18:20). "My manner of life from my youth … know all the Jews," Paul had told Agrippa (Acts 26:4). Timothy had lived and labored with Paul and knew the man well. Paul had not hidden behind extravagant claims or religious propaganda.

They teach true doctrine (v. 10b). "My doctrine" in Paul's case meant the true faith, the gospel of Jesus Christ. No matter how appealing a preacher may be, if he does not preach the truth of God's Word, he does not deserve our support. On radio and TV today, we have a great deal of "pseudo-Christianity" which is a mixture of psychology, success motivation, and personality cults, with a little bit of Bible thrown in to make it look religious. Beware!

They practice what they preach (v. 10c). Paul's "manner of life" backed up his messages. He did not preach sacrifice and live in luxury. He gave to others far more than he received from them. He stood up for the truth even when it meant losing friends and, in the end, losing his life. Paul was a servant, not a celebrity.

Their purpose is to glorify God (v. 10d). There was never a question about Paul's "purpose" in ministry: He wanted to do God's will and finish the work God gave him to do (Acts 20:24; Phil. 1:21). The apostle Paul was a man of "faith" who trusted God to meet his needs. He was a man of "longsuffering" who bore up under people's attacks. He was a man of *love* ("charity") who willingly gave himself to serve others.

The word *patience* at the end of 2 Timothy 3:10 means "endurance, the ability to stick with it when the going gets tough."

They are willing to suffer (vv. 11–12). Paul did not ask others to suffer for him; *he suffered for others.* The fact that he was persecuted from city to city was proof that he was living a godly life. Some people today have the idea that godliness means *escaping* persecution, when just the opposite is true.

I wonder how Paul would match up with today's concept of a Christian leader. He would probably fail miserably. If he applied for service with a modern mission board, would he be accepted? He had a prison record; he had a physical affliction; he stirred up problems in just about every place he visited. He was poor, and he did not cater to the rich. Yet God used him, and we are being blessed today because Paul was faithful.

Continue in God's Word (3:13–17)

The only way to defeat Satan's lies is with God's truth. "Thus saith the Lord!" is the final answer to every question. Evil men and deceivers are going to get worse and worse. They will deceive more and more. Why? Because they are being deceived by Satan! In these last days, there will be more deception and imitation, and

the only way a believer will be able to tell the true from the false is by knowing the Word of God.

Timothy had been taught the Word of God from the time he was a child. Some people are prone to say, "Well, I needed the Bible when I was younger, but I can do without it now that I'm older." How wrong they are! Adults need the guidance of the Word far more than children do, because adults face more temptations and make more decisions. Timothy's grandmother and mother had faithfully taught him the Old Testament Scriptures. (The word *whom* in 2 Tim. 3:14 is plural, referring to these women; see 2 Tim. 1:5.) Timothy was to continue in what he had been taught. We never outgrow the Word of God.

This is a good place to admonish Christian parents to teach their children the Bible. In our home, my wife and I used Kenneth Taylor's *Bible Stories with Pictures for Little Eyes;* in fact, we wore out two copies! What a joy it was to see our older children who had learned to read share the stories with the younger ones and help them answer the questions. Little by little, the children graduated to older Bible storybooks and then to Bibles of their own. We were fortunate that our Sunday school included a Bible memory program. As soon as your child is born, surround him with the Word of God and prayer. You will not have this opportunity after he grows up.

In this paragraph, Paul made some important statements about the Scriptures:

They are the Holy Scriptures (v. 15a). "The sacred letters" is a literal translation. The suggestion is that young Timothy learned his Hebrew alphabet by spelling his way through the Old Testament Scriptures. The word for "holy" means "consecrated for sacred use." The Bible is different from every other book—even books about the Bible—because it has been set apart by God for special sacred uses. We must treat the Bible as the special book it is.

The way we treat the Bible shows others how much or how little we respect it. While I don't want to become a crank in this matter, I must confess that I hate to see a Bible on the floor. When we are carrying a Bible and other books, the Bible should be on the top. There is a difference between properly marking a Bible as we study and defacing it by careless marking. I have seen people put a cup of coffee on a Bible! Paul gives us the right attitude toward the Word of God (1 Thess. 2:13).

The Scriptures lead us to salvation (v. 15b). We are not saved by believing the Bible (see John 5:39), but by trusting the Christ who is revealed in the Bible. Satan knows the Bible, but he is not saved. Timothy was raised on the holy Scriptures in a godly home. Yet it was not until Paul led him to Christ that he was saved.

What is the relationship of the Bible to salvation? To begin with, the Bible reveals our need for salvation. It is a mirror that shows us how filthy we are in God's sight. The Bible explains that every lost sinner is condemned now (John 3:18–21) and needs a Savior *now*. It also makes it clear that a lost sinner cannot save himself.

But the Bible also reveals God's wonderful plan of salvation: Christ died for our sins! If we trust Him, He will save us (John 3:16–18). The Bible also helps give us the assurance of our salvation (see 1 John 5:9–13). Then the Bible becomes our spiritual food to nourish us that we might grow in grace and serve Christ. It is our sword for fighting Satan and overcoming temptation.

The Scriptures are true and dependable (v. 16a). "All Scripture is God-breathed" (NIV). The doctrine of the inspiration of Scripture is vitally important, and a doctrine that Satan has attacked from the beginning ("Yea, hath God said?" [Gen. 3:1]). It is inconceivable that God would give His people a book they could not trust. He is the God of truth (Deut. 32:4); Jesus is "the truth" (John 14:6), and the "Spirit is truth" (1 John 5:6). Jesus said of the Scriptures, "Thy word is truth" (John 17:17).

The Holy Spirit of God used men of God to write the Word of God (2 Peter 1:20–21). The Spirit did not erase the natural characteristics of the writers. In fact, God in His providence prepared the writers for the task of writing the Scriptures. Each writer has his own distinctive style and vocabulary. Each book of the Bible grew out of a special set of circumstances. In His preparation of men, in His guiding of history, and in His working through the Spirit, God brought about the miracle of the Scriptures.

We must not think of "inspiration" the way the world thinks when it says, "Shakespeare was certainly an inspired writer." What we mean by biblical *inspiration* is the supernatural influence of the Holy Spirit on the Bible's writers, which guaranteed that what they wrote was accurate and trustworthy. *Revelation* means the communicating of truth to man by God; *inspiration* has to do with the *recording* of this communication in a way that is dependable.

Whatever the Bible says about itself, man, God, life, death, history, science, and every other subject is true. This does not mean that every statement in the Bible is true, because the Bible records the lies of men and of Satan. *But the record is true.*

The Scriptures are profitable (v. 16b). They are profitable for *doctrine* (what is right), for *reproof* (what is not right), for *correction* (how to get right), and for *instruction in righteousness* (how to stay right). A Christian who studies the Bible and applies what he learns will grow in holiness and avoid many pitfalls in this world.

The Scriptures equip us for service (v. 17). Earlier Paul had called Timothy a "man of God" (1 Tim. 6:11), but here Paul states that *any* Christian can become a person "of God." How? By studying the Word of God, obeying it, and letting it control his life. It is worth noting that all of the "men of God" named in Scripture—including Moses, Samuel, Elijah, Elisha, David, and Timothy—were men who were devoted to God's Word.

Two words in this verse are especially important: "perfect" and "furnished." The word translated "perfect" means "complete, in fit shape, in fit condition." It does not begin to suggest sinless perfection. Rather, it implies being fitted for use.

"Furnished" has a similar meaning: "equipped for service." In other words, the Word of God furnishes and equips a believer so that he can live a life that pleases God and do the work God wants him to do. The better we know the Word, the better we are able to live and work for God.

The purpose of Bible study is *not* just to understand doctrines or to be able to defend the faith, as important as these things are. The ultimate purpose is the equipping of the believers who read it. It is the Word of God that equips God's people to do the work of God.

The times are not going to get better, but we Christians can become better people, even in bad times. We must separate ourselves from that which is false, devote ourselves to that which is true, and continue in our study of the Word of God. Then God can equip us for ministry in these difficult days, and we will have the joy of seeing others come to a knowledge of the truth.

CHAPTER FOUR
2 Timothy 4
LAST WORDS

A great person's last words are significant. They are a window that helps us to look into his heart, or a measure that helps us evaluate his life. In this chapter, we have Paul's last words to Timothy and to the church.

It is interesting that Paul expressed no regrets as he came to the end. He even forgave those who made his situation difficult (2 Tim. 4:16). More than seventeen people are referred to in this chapter, which shows that Paul was a friend-maker as well as a soul-winner. Though his own days were numbered, Paul thought of others.

The apostle gave three final admonitions to Timothy, and he backed each of them up with a reason.

Preach the Word! (4:1–4)
"I charge thee" should read "I solemnly witness." This was a serious moment, and Paul wanted Timothy to sense the importance of it. It was serious, not only because Paul was facing death, but even more because both Paul and Timothy would be judged one day when Jesus Christ appeared. It would do us all good to occasionally reflect on the fact that one day we will face God and our works will be judged.

For one thing, this realization would encourage us to do our work carefully and faithfully. It would also deliver us from the fear of man; for, after all, our final Judge is God. Finally, the realization that God will one day judge our works encourages us to keep going even when we face difficulties. We are serving Him, not ourselves.

"Preach the Word!" is the main responsibility that Paul shared in this section. Everything else he said is related to this. The word *preach* means "to preach like a herald." In Paul's day, a ruler had a special herald who made announcements to the people. He was commissioned by the ruler to make his announcements in a loud, clear voice so everyone could hear. He was not an ambassador with the privilege of negotiating; he was a messenger with a proclamation to be heard and heeded. Not to heed the ruler's messenger was serious; to abuse the messenger was even worse.

Timothy was to herald God's Word with the authority of heaven behind him. The Word of God is what both sinners and saints need. It is a pity that many churches have substituted other things for the preaching of the Word, things that may be good in their place, but that are bad when they replace the proclamation of the Word. In my own pastoral ministry, I have seen what the preaching of the Word can do in churches and in individual lives, and I affirm that *nothing can take its place.*

Timothy should be diligent and alert to use every opportunity to preach the Word, when it is favorable and even when it is not favorable. *It is easy to make excuses when we ought to be making opportunities.* Paul himself always found an opportunity to share the Word, whether it was in the temple courts, on a stormy sea, or even in prison. "He that observeth the wind shall not sow; and he that regardeth the clouds shall not reap" (Eccl. 11:4). Stop making excuses and get to work!

Preaching must be marked by three elements: conviction, warning, and appeal ("reprove, rebuke, exhort"). To quote an old rule of preachers, "He should afflict the comfortable and comfort the afflicted." If there is conviction but no remedy, we add to people's burdens. And if we encourage those who ought to be rebuked, we are assisting them to sin. Biblical preaching must be balanced.

God's speaker must be patient as he preaches the Word. He will not always see immediate results. He must be patient with those who oppose his preaching. Above all else, *he must preach doctrine.* He must not simply tell Bible stories, relate interesting illustrations, or read a verse and then forget it. *True preaching is the explanation and application of Bible doctrine. Anything else is just religious speechmaking.*

Paul gave the responsibility—"preach the Word" (2 Tim. 4:2)—and he also gave the reason (2 Tim. 4:3–4). The time would come (and it has been here for a long time!) when most people would not want the "healthy doctrine" of the Word of God. They would have carnal desires for religious novelties. Because of their "itching ears" they would accumulate teachers who would satisfy their cravings for things that disagree with God's truths. The fact that a preacher has a large congregation is not always a sign that he is preaching the truth. In fact, it may be evidence that he is tickling people's "itching ears" and giving them what they *want* to hear instead of what they *need* to hear.

It is but a short step from "itching ears" to turning one's ears away from the truth. Once people have rejected the truth, they turn to fables (myths). It is not likely that man-made fables will convict them of sin or make them want to repent! The result is a congregation of comfortable, professing Christians, listening to a comfortable, religious talk that contains no Bible doctrine. These people become the prey of every false cult because their lives lack a foundation in the Word of God. It is a recognized fact that most cultists were formerly members of churches.

Note the emphasis on Scripture: "Preach the Word … with … doctrine.… They will not endure sound doctrine … they shall turn away their ears from the truth" (2 Tim. 4:2–4). This emphasis on sound (healthy) doctrine runs through all three of Paul's pastoral epistles, and this emphasis is surely needed today.

Fulfill Your Ministry (4:5–8)

"Make full proof of thy ministry" means "fulfill whatever God wants you to do." Timothy's ministry would not be exactly like Paul's, but it would be important to the cause of Christ. No God-directed ministry is small or unimportant. In this final chapter, Paul named some colaborers about whom we know nothing; yet they too had a ministry to fulfill.

A young preacher once complained to Charles Spurgeon, the famous British preacher of the 1800s, that he did not have as big a church as he deserved.

"How many do you preach to?" Spurgeon asked.

"Oh, about a hundred," the man replied.

Solemnly Spurgeon said, "That will be enough to give account for on the day of judgment."

We do not measure the fulfillment of a ministry only on the basis of statistics or on what people see. We realize that faithfulness is important and that God sees the heart. This was why Timothy had to be "sober in all things" (2 Tim. 4:5 NASB) and carry on his ministry with seriousness of purpose. (We have met this word "sober" many times in these letters.)

Timothy was not only a preacher; he was also a soldier (2 Tim. 2:3–4) who would have to "endure afflictions" (2 Tim. 4:5). He had seen Paul go through sufferings on more than one occasion (2 Cor. 6:1–10; 2 Tim. 3:10–12). Most of Timothy's sufferings would come from the "religious crowd" that did not want to hear the truth. It was the "religious crowd" that crucified Christ and that persecuted Paul and had him arrested.

"Do the work of an evangelist" (2 Tim. 4:5) would remind Timothy that all of his ministry must have soul-winning at its heart. This does not mean that every sermon should be a "sawdust trail, hell-fire-and-brimstone" message, because the saints need feeding as well. But it does mean that a preacher, no matter what he is preaching, should keep the lost souls in mind. This burden for the lost should characterize a pastor's private ministry as well. (See Acts 20:17–21 for a description of a balanced ministry.)

God has given special men to the church as evangelists (Acts 21:8; Eph. 4:11), but this does not absolve a pastor from his soul-winning responsibility. Not every preacher has the same gifts, but every preacher can share the same burden and proclaim the same saving message. A friend of mine went to hear a famous preacher, and I asked him how the message was. He replied, "There wasn't enough gospel in it to save a flea!"

Paul gave the reason behind the responsibility (2 Tim. 4:6–8): He was about to move off the scene and Timothy would have to take his place. In this beautiful paragraph of personal testimony, you find Paul looking in three different directions.

He looked around (v. 6). Paul realized that his time was short. He was on trial in Rome and had been through the first hearing (2 Tim. 4:17). But Paul knew that the end was near. However, he did not tremble at the prospect of death! The two words *offered* and *departure* (2 Tim. 4:6) tell us of his faith and confidence. "Offered" means "poured out on the altar as a drink offering." He used the same picture in Philippians 2:7–8. In effect Paul was saying, "Caesar is not going to kill me. I am going to give my life as a sacrifice to Jesus Christ. I have been a living sacrifice, serving Him since the day I was saved. Now I will complete that sacrifice by laying down my life for Him."

The word *departure* (2 Tim. 4:6) is a beautiful word that has many meanings. It means "to hoist anchor and set sail." Paul looked on death as a release from the world, an opportunity to "set sail" into eternity. The word also means "to take down a tent." This parallels 2 Corinthians 5:1–8, where Paul compared the death of believers to the taking down of a tent (tabernacle), in order to receive a permanent, glorified body ("house not made with hands"—a glorified body, not a "mansion" in heaven).

Departure also has the meaning of "loosing a prisoner." Paul was facing release, not execution! "The unyoking of an ox" is another meaning of this word. Paul had been in hard service for many years. Now his Master would unyoke him and promote him to higher service.

Paul looked back (v. 7). He summed up his life and ministry. Two of the images here are athletic: like a determined wrestler or boxer, he had fought a good fight; and, like a runner, he had finished his lifelong race victoriously, He had kept the rules and deserved a prize (see Acts 20:24; Phil. 3:13–14). The third image is that of a steward who had faithfully guarded his boss's deposit: "I have kept the faith" (2 Tim. 4:7). Paul used this image often in his pastoral letters.

It is heartening to be able to look back and have no regrets. Paul was not always popular, nor was he usually comfortable; but he remained faithful. That is what really counted.

Paul looked ahead (v. 8). A Greek or Roman athlete who was a winner was rewarded by the crowds and usually got a laurel wreath or a garland of oak leaves. The word for "crown" is *stephanos*—the victor's crown; we get our name "Stephen" from this word. (The kingly crown is *diadema,* from which we get "diadem.") However, Paul would not be given a fading crown of leaves; his would be a crown of righteousness that would never fade.

Jesus Christ is the "righteous judge" who always judges correctly. Paul's judges in Rome were not righteous. If they were, they would have released him. How many times Paul had been tried in one court after another, yet now he faced his last Judge—his Lord and Savior Jesus Christ. When you are ready to face the Lord, you need not fear the judgment of men.

The crown of righteousness is God's reward for a faithful and righteous life, and our incentive for faithfulness and holiness is the promise of the Lord's appearing. Because Paul loved His appearing and looked for it, he lived righteously and served faithfully. This is why Paul used the return of Jesus Christ as a basis for his admonitions in this chapter (see 2 Tim. 4:1).

We are not called to be apostles, yet we can win the same crown that Paul won. If we love Christ's appearing, live in obedience to His will, and do the work He has called us to do, we will be crowned.

Be Diligent and Faithful (4:9–22)

"Hurry and get here!" is the meaning of the admonition to Timothy (2 Tim. 4:9). Tychicus would take Timothy's place in Ephesus (2 Tim. 4:12). As Timothy hurried to Rome, he could stop in Troas and get the cloak, books, and parchments (2 Tim. 4:13). Paul probably left them there in his haste to depart. It is touching to see that, in his closing days on earth, Paul wanted his dear "son in the faith" at his side. But he was also practical: he needed his cloak for warmth, and he wanted his books for study. The "books" would be papyrus scrolls, perhaps of the Old Testament Scriptures, and the "parchments" would be books made from the skins of animals. We do not know what these "parchments" were, but we are not surprised that a scholar such as Paul wanted material for study and writing.

Before he ended the letter, Paul urged Timothy to "come before winter" (2 Tim. 4:21). Why? All the ships would be in port during the winter since it would be too dangerous for sailing. If Timothy waited too long, he would miss his opportunity to travel to Paul, and then it would be too late.

Why should Timothy be diligent and faithful? Look at 2 Timothy 4:10, which gives part of the answer: Some in Paul's circle were not faithful, and he could not depend on them. Demas is named only three times in the New Testament, yet these three citations tell a sad story of failure. Paul listed Demas along with Mark and Luke as one of his "fellow laborers" (Philem.

24). Then he is simply called "Demas" (Col. 4:14). Here (2 Tim. 4:10) it is "Demas hath forsaken me."

Paul gave the reason: Demas "loved this present world." He had, as a believer, "tasted … the powers of the world to come" (Heb. 6:5), but he preferred "this present evil world" (Gal. 1:4). In his *Pilgrim's Progress,* John Bunyan pictured Demas as the keeper of a silver mine at the Hill Lucre. Perhaps it was the love of money that enticed Demas back into the world. It must have broken Paul's heart to see Demas fail so shamefully, yet it can happen to any believer. Perhaps this explains why Paul had so much to say about riches in his pastoral letters.

Another reason why Paul wanted Timothy in Rome was that his next hearing was coming up, and only Luke was with him. The believers in Rome and Ephesus who could have stood with Paul had failed him (2 Tim. 4:16), but Paul knew that Timothy would not fail him. Of course, the Lord had not failed Paul either (2 Tim. 4:17)! The Lord had promised to stay with Paul, and He had kept His promise.

When Paul had been discouraged in Corinth, the Lord came to him and encouraged him (Acts 18:9–11). After he had been arrested in Jerusalem, Paul again was visited by the Lord and encouraged (Acts 23:11). During that terrible storm, when Paul was on board ship, the Lord had again given him strength and courage (Acts 27:22ff.). Now, in that horrible Roman prison, Paul again experienced the strengthening presence of the Lord, who had promised, "I will never leave thee, nor forsake thee" (Heb. 13:5).

But note that Paul's concern was not for his own safety or comfort. It was the preaching of the Word so that Gentiles might be saved. It was Paul's special calling to minister to the Gentiles (see Eph. 3); and he was not ashamed of the gospel, even in the great city of Rome (Rom. 1:16).

What a man! His friends forsake him, and he prays that God will forgive them. His enemies try him, and he looks for opportunities to tell them how to be saved! What a difference it makes when the Holy Spirit controls your life.

"I was delivered out of the mouth of the lion" (2 Tim. 4:17). Who or what is this "lion"? It cannot mean a literal lion because Paul was a Roman citizen and, if convicted, he could not be thrown to the lions. Instead, he would be executed by being beheaded. Was "the lion" Emperor Nero? Probably not. If he had been delivered from Nero, then this meant he was acquitted, yet, he had only had a preliminary first hearing. The lion is a symbol of Satan (1 Peter 5:8). Perhaps Paul was referring to some scheme of the devil to defeat him and hinder the work of the gospel. To be "saved from the lion's mouth" was a proverbial saying that meant "to be delivered from great danger" (see Ps. 22:21).

But for a Christian, there are things even more dangerous than suffering and death. Sin, for example. This is what Paul had in mind (2 Tim. 4:18). He was confident that the Lord would deliver him from "every evil work" and take him to the heavenly kingdom. Paul's greatest fear was not of death; it was that he might deny his Lord or do something else that would disgrace God's name. Paul was certain that the time had come for his permanent departure (2 Tim. 4:6). He wanted to end his life-race well and be free from any disobedience.

It is heartening to see how many people are named in the closing part of this last letter Paul wrote. I believe that there are at least one hundred different men and women named in Acts and Paul's letters, as a part of his circle of friends and fellow laborers. Paul could not do the job by himself. It is a great man who enlists others to help get the job done, and who lets them share in the greatness of the work.

Luke (2 Tim. 4:11) was the "beloved physician" who traveled with Paul (Col. 4:14). He is author of the gospel of Luke and the book of Acts. (Notice the "we" sections in Acts, the eyewitness reports of Dr. Luke.) Paul probably dictated this letter (2 Tim.) to Luke. Being a doctor, Luke must have appreciated Paul's reference to gangrene (2 Tim. 2:17 NIV).

Crescens (2 Tim. 4:10) was sent by Paul to Galatia. We know nothing about him, nor do we really need to know. He was another faithful laborer who assisted Paul in an hour of great need.

Titus (2 Tim. 4:10) was Paul's close associate and, along with Timothy, a trusted "troubleshooter." Paul had left Titus in Crete to straighten out the problems in the churches there (Titus 1:5). As we study Paul's letter to Titus, we get better acquainted with this choice servant of God. Titus had met Paul at Nicopolis during that period between Paul's arrests (Titus 3:12). Now Paul had summoned him to Rome and sent him to Dalmatia (our modern Yugoslavia).

Mark (2 Tim. 4:11) was a cousin of Barnabas, Paul's first partner in missionary service (Acts 13:1–3). His mother was a noted Christian in Jerusalem (Acts 12:5, 12). Unfortunately, John Mark failed on that first missionary journey (Acts 13:5, 13). Paul refused to take Mark on the second trip, and this led to a falling-out between Paul and Barnabas (Acts 15:36–41). However, Paul now admitted that John Mark was a valuable worker; and he wanted Mark with him in Rome. How good it is to know that one failure in Christian service need not make one's whole life a failure.

Tychicus (2 Tim. 4:12) was a believer from the province of Asia (Acts 20:4) who willingly accompanied Paul and probably ministered as a personal servant to the apostle. He was with Paul during his first imprisonment (Eph. 6:21–22; Col. 4:7–8). Paul sent Tychicus to Crete to relieve Titus (Titus 3:12). Now he was sending him to Ephesus to relieve Timothy. What a blessing it is to have people who can replace others! A relief pitcher may not get all the glory, but he may help win the game!

Carpus (2 Tim. 4:13) lived at Troas and gave Paul hospitality. Paul must have departed in a hurry (was he being sought for arrest?), because he left his cloak and books behind. However, Carpus was a faithful brother;

he would guard them until somebody picked them up to take to Paul. Even such so-called menial tasks are ministries for the Lord.

Is *Alexander the coppersmith* (2 Tim. 4:14) the same Alexander mentioned in 1 Timothy 1:20? Nobody knows, and there is no value in conjecturing. The name was common, but it is possible that this heretic went to Rome to make things difficult for Paul. Satan has his workers too. By the way, Paul's words, "The Lord reward him according to his works" (2 Tim. 4:14), are not a prayer of judgment, for this would be contrary to Jesus' teaching (Matt. 5:43–48). "The Lord *will* reward him" is a better translation.

Prisca (or Priscilla) *and Aquila* (2 Tim. 4:19) were a husband-and-wife team that assisted Paul in many ways (see Acts 18:1–3, 24–28; Rom. 16:3–4; 1 Cor. 16:19). Now they were in Ephesus helping Timothy with his ministry. It is wonderful when God's people do their work regardless of who their leader is.

Onesiphorus (2 Tim. 4:19) and his household we met in 2 Timothy 1.

Erastus (2 Tim. 4:20) might be the treasurer of Corinth (Rom. 16:23); and he might be the same man who ministered with Timothy in Macedonia (Acts 19:22).

Trophimus (2 Tim. 4:20) from Ephesus was a friend of Tychicus (Acts 20:4), and the man whose presence with Paul helped to incite that riot in Jerusalem (Acts 21:28–29). He had been serving at Miletus, but now he was ill. Why did Paul not heal him? Apparently not every sick person is supposed to be miraculously healed.

The other people mentioned (2 Tim. 4:21) are unknown to us, but certainly not to the Lord.

"Grace be with you" (2 Tim. 4:22) was Paul's personal farewell, used at the end of his letters as a "trademark" that the letter was not a forgery.

The Bible does not record the final days of Paul. Tradition tells us that he was found guilty and sentenced to die. He was probably taken outside the city and beheaded.

But Timothy and the other devoted believers carried on the work! As John Wesley used to say, "God buries His workmen, but His work goes on." You and I must be faithful so that (if the Lord does not return soon) future generations may hear the gospel and have the opportunity to be saved.

TITUS

OUTLINE

Key theme: Christians should maintain good works
Key verse: Titus 3:8

I. CHURCH ORGANIZATION (1)
  A. Preach God's Word—1:14
  B. Ordain qualified leaders—1:5–9
  C. Silence false teachers—1:10–16

II. CHRISTIAN OBLIGATION (2—3)
  A. Older saints—2:1–4a
  B. Younger saints—2:4b–8
  C. Christian slaves—2:9–15
  D. Christians as citizens—3:1–8
  E. Problem people—3:9–11
  F. Conclusion—3:12–15

CONTENTS

CHAPTER ONE
Titus 1
OUR MAN IN CRETE

While Timothy was laboring in metropolitan Ephesus, Titus had his hands full on the island of Crete. Titus was a Greek believer (Gal. 2:3) who had served Paul well on special assignments to the church in Corinth (2 Cor. 7:13–14; 8:6, 16, 23; 12:18). Apparently Titus had been won to Christ through Paul's personal ministry (Titus 1:4) as Timothy had been (1 Tim. 1:2). "As for Titus," Paul wrote, "he is my partner and fellow worker among you" (2 Cor. 8:23 NIV).

But the people on the island of Crete were not the easiest to work with, and Titus became somewhat discouraged. Like Timothy, he was probably a young man. But unlike Timothy, he was not given to timidity and physical ailments. Paul had been with Titus on Crete and had left him there to correct the things that were wrong. Since Jews from Crete were present at Pentecost (Acts 2:11), it is possible that they had carried the gospel to their native land.

Titus had his share of problems! The churches needed qualified leaders, and the various groups in the churches needed shepherding. One group of false teachers was trying to mix Jewish law with the gospel of grace (Titus 1:10, 14), while some of the Gentile believers were abusing the message of grace and turning it into license (Titus 2:11–15). By nature, the people of Crete were not easy to work with (Titus 1:12–13), and Titus needed extraordinary patience and love. It would have been easy for Titus to have "heard God's call to go elsewhere," but he stuck it out and finished his work.

As you read and study this letter, you will discover that it is a condensed version of Paul's first letter to Timothy. In this first chapter, Paul reminded Titus of three responsibilities he had to fulfill.

Preach God's Word (1:1–4)
In this rather lengthy greeting, Paul emphasized the importance of the Word of God. Four times he used the Greek preposition *kata,* the root meaning of which is "down." But in this context, *kata* helps us see the relationship between the ministry and the Word of God. Consider the four phrases.

"According to the faith of God's elect" (v. 1a). Paul's ministry was governed by the Word of God. He was "a slave of God" (the only place Paul used this phrase) and "a messenger sent on a special commission" by Jesus Christ. But the purpose of his ministry was to share the faith, that body of truth contained in the Word of God. "God's elect" are those who have trusted Jesus Christ as their Savior (Eph. 1:4; 1 Peter 1:1–5).

"The truth which is after [according to] godliness" (vv. 1b–2). "Godliness" is an important concept

in this letter, just as it was in 1 Timothy, even though the actual word is used only once. But the repetition of "good works" emphasizes the point (Titus 1:16; 2:7, 14; 3:1, 5, 8, 14). The truth of the gospel changes a life from ungodliness (Titus 2:12) to holy living. Sad to say, there were people in the churches on Crete, like some church members today, who professed to be saved, but whose lives denied their profession (Titus 1:12).

This faith in Jesus Christ not only saves us *today* and makes our lives godly, but it also gives us hope for *the future* (Titus 1:2). We have assurance for the future because of God's promises, and God cannot lie (see Num. 23:19). We are born again "unto a living hope" (1 Peter 1:3 NIV) because we have trusted the living Christ. We believers have eternal life now (John 3:16; 1 John 5:11–12), but when Jesus Christ returns, we will enjoy eternal life in an even greater way.

"According to the commandment of God" (v. 3). God reveals His message through preaching. This does not mean the act of proclaiming the Word, but rather the *content* of the message. "It pleased God by the foolishness of preaching [the message of the cross] to save them that believe" (1 Cor. 1:21). This Word of the gospel was committed to Paul (see 1 Tim. 1:11), and he had committed it to Titus. This ministry was according to the commandment of God and was not given by men (Gal. 1:10–12).

As in 1 Timothy, the title *Savior* is often repeated in Titus (1:34; 2:10, 13; 3:4, 6). The God-given written Word reveals the Savior, because a Savior is what sinners need. God's grace brings salvation, not condemnation (Titus 2:11). Jesus could have come to earth as a Judge, but He chose to come as a Savior (Luke 2:10–11).

"After the common faith" (v. 4). The word *common* means "to have in common." This faith is the possession of all of God's people and not just a selected few. Christians in different denominational groups may wear different labels, but all who possess the same saving faith share "the common salvation" (Jude 3). There was a definite body of truth deposited in the church, "the faith that was once for all entrusted to the saints" (Jude 3 NIV). Any departure from this "common faith" is false teaching and must not be tolerated in the church.

As you review these four statements, you can see that Paul related everything in his ministry to the Word of God. His calling and his preaching depended on faith in Christ. He wanted Titus to grasp this fact and to make the Word of God a priority in his ministry. Throughout all three of the pastoral epistles there is an emphasis on teaching the Word of God. Local churches ought to be "Bible schools" where the Word of God is taught systematically and in a practical way.

Ordain Qualified Leaders (1:5–9)
One reason Paul had left Titus on the island of Crete was that he might organize the local assemblies and "set

in order" the things that were lacking. That phrase is a medical term; it was applied to the setting of a crooked limb. Titus was not the spiritual dictator of the island, but he was Paul's official apostolic representative with authority to work. It had been Paul's policy to ordain elders in the churches he had established (Acts 14:23), but he had not been able to stay in Crete long enough to accomplish this task.

Several of the qualifications listed here (Titus 1:6–8) have already been discussed in our study of 1 Timothy 3:2–3: "blameless, the husband of one wife … not given to wine, no striker [not violent], not given to filthy lucre … a lover of hospitality … sober." The fact that these standards applied to Christians on the island of Crete as well as to those in the city of Ephesus proves that God's measure for leaders does not fluctuate. A big-city church and a small-town church both need godly people in places of leadership.

Now, consider nine additional qualifications.

"Having faithful children" (v. 6b). *Faithful* means "believing." The bishop's children should be Christians. After all, if a servant of God cannot win his own children to Christ, what success can he expect with outsiders? This is the same principle Paul emphasized to Timothy (1 Tim. 3:5)—Christian living and Christian service must begin at home. The children in an elder's home must not only be saved, but must be good examples of obedience and dedication. To be accused of "riot" [wild living] or disobedience ["unruly," unable to be ruled] would disqualify their father from the eldership. This applies, of course, to children still at home, under the authority of their father.

Too often, new Christians feel a call to the ministry and want to be ordained before they have had a chance to establish their families in the faith. If the children are small, the problem is not too great; but mature children go through a tremendous shock when all of a sudden their household becomes "religious"! A wise father first wins his own family to Christ and gives them a chance to grow before he pulls up stakes and moves to Bible school. We would have fewer casualties in the ministry if this policy were followed more often.

"The steward of God" (v. 7a). A steward does not own but manages all that his master puts into his hands. Perhaps the most famous steward in the Bible is Joseph, who had complete control over all of Potiphar's business (Gen. 39:1–9). The most important characteristic of a steward is faithfulness (Matt. 25:21; 1 Cor. 4:1–2). He must use what his master gives him for the good and glory of his master, and not for himself personally (see Luke 16:1–13).

The elder must never say, "This is mine!" All that he has comes from God (John 3:27) and must be used for God. His time, possessions, ambitions, and talents are all loaned to him by the Lord, and he must be faithful to use them to honor God and build the church. Of course, *all* Christians ought to be faithful stewards, and not the pastors only!

"Not self-willed" (v. 7b). An elder must not be "overbearing" (NIV), a person always pushing to have his own way. While church members ought to respect and follow the leadership of the elders, they should be certain that it is leadership and not dictatorship. A self-willed pastor is arrogant, will not take his people's suggestions and criticisms, and makes sure he always gets his own way.

"Not soon angry" (v. 7c). He must not have a quick temper. There is a righteous anger against sin (Eph. 4:26), but much of our anger is unrighteous and directed against people. A righteous man ought to get angry when wrongs are done. Someone has said, "Temper is such a wonderful thing that it's a shame to lose it." Wise counsel, indeed.

"A lover of good men" (v. 8a). "One who loves what is good" (NIV) is an alternate translation, and this would include good men. But it also includes good books, good music, good causes, and many other good things. A man is a good man because he has a good heart and surrounds himself with good things. It is difficult to believe that a dedicated servant of God would deliberately associate with things that are bad for him and his family.

"Just" (v. 8b). "Upright" is a good translation. He should be a man of integrity who sticks by his word and who practices what he preaches. His conduct is righteous.

"Holy" (v. 8c). "Unstained" gives the idea. "Be ye holy, for I am holy" (1 Peter 1:16). The root meaning of *holy* is "different" Christians are different from lost sinners because Christians are new creations by the grace of God (2 Cor. 5:17).

"Temperate" (v. 8d). "Self-controlled" is the meaning, and it applies to a man's appetites and actions. "Disciplined" is a synonym. A pastor must discipline his time so that he gets his work done. He must discipline his desires, especially when well-meaning members try to stuff him with coffee and cake! He must keep his mind and body under control, as he yields to the Holy Spirit (Gal. 5:23, where *temperance* means "self-control").

"Holding fast the faithful Word" (v. 9). The word faithful was a favorite with Paul (see 1 Tim. 1:15; 4:9; 2 Tim. 2:11; Titus 3:8). God's Word is trustworthy because God cannot lie (Titus 1:2). Because the Word is faithful, those who teach and preach the Word should be faithful. Again, Paul used the term sound doctrine, which we have already met in 1 Timothy 1:10. It means "healthy doctrine" that promotes spiritual growth.

So the elders have a twofold ministry of God's Word: (1) building up the church with "healthy" doctrine, and (2) refuting the false teachers who spread unhealthy doctrine. The naive church member who says, "We don't want doctrine; just give us helpful devotional thoughts!" does not know what he is saying. Apart from the truth (and this means Bible doctrine), there can be no spiritual help or health.

The mentioning of those who oppose true doctrine led Paul to give the third responsibility that Titus was to fulfill.

Silence False Teachers (1:10–16)

It did not take long for false teachers to arise in the early church. Wherever God sows the truth, Satan quickly shows up to sow lies. Titus faced an enemy similar to that described in 1 Timothy—a mixture of Jewish legalism, man-made traditions, and mysticism. Paul gave three facts about these false teachers.

What they were personally. Paul had nothing good to say about them! They would not submit to God's Word or to the authority of God's servant, for they were *unruly.* "Rebellious" would be a good translation. Beware of teachers who will not put themselves under authority.

They were *vain talkers.* What they said impressed people, but it had no content or substance. When you boiled it down, it was just so much hot air. Furthermore, they excelled in *talking,* not in *doing.* They could tell others what to do, but they did not do it themselves. Note especially Titus 1:16.

The great tragedy was that they *deceived* people by their false doctrines. They claimed to be teaching truth, but they were peddlers of error. Because they themselves were deceived by Satan, they deceived others, "teaching things they ought not to teach" (Titus 1:11 NIV).

They were *carnal* and *worldly:* "liars, evil brutes, lazy gluttons" (Titus 1:12 NIV). What an indictment! Instead of living for the beautiful things of the spiritual life, they lived for their own appetites. Paul's adjectives are arresting. These men were not just "beasts," but *"evil* beasts"; they were not just "gluttons," but *"lazy* gluttons." They were celebrities, not servants. They "lived it up" at the expense of their followers, and (true to human nature), *their followers loved it!*

Paul summed up their character in Titus 1:16. They were "abominable," which means "detestable, disgusting." Christians with good spiritual sense would be completely disgusted with the character and conduct of these teachers, and would never follow them. "Disobedient" means "they cannot and will not be persuaded. " Their minds have been made up and they will not face the truth. "Reprobate" literally means "not able to pass the test." God does not use them because they have been proved unfit. This same Greek word is translated "castaway" in 1 Corinthians 9:27. There it is in an athletic context and means "disqualified."

Having described what these teachers were, Paul then shared a second fact.

What they did. The picture was clear: These false teachers told lies from house to house and thus upset the faith of the people. Whole families were affected by their unhealthy doctrines. For one thing, they were teaching Jewish legalism ("they of the circumcision," Titus 1:10; see 3:9) which Paul rejected. They were also teaching "Jewish fables" (Titus 1:14), which

probably described their fanciful interpretations of the genealogies in the Old Testament (1 Tim. 1:4).

It never ceases to amaze me what some people get out of the Scriptures! I was once on a telephone talk program on a Chicago radio station, discussing Bible prophecy. A man phoned in and tried to take over the program by proclaiming his strange interpretations of Daniel's prophecies. He rejected the clear explanation given in the Bible and was very upset with me when I refused to agree with his fanciful ideas.

Dr. David Cooper used to say, "When the plain sense of Scripture makes good sense, seek no other sense." There is no need to find "deeper meanings" to the plain teachings of the Word of God. Such an approach to the Bible enables a "student" to find anything he is looking for!

Since the early church assemblies usually met in private homes, it is easy to understand how "whole houses" (Titus 1:11) could be upset by false teachers. People today who have Bible study classes in their homes must be careful lest visitors come in with strange doctrines. There are sects and cults that look for these classes and plant their agents just for the purpose of winning converts, so we must be careful.

Why they did it. Their main motive was to make money "for filthy lucre's sake" (Titus 1:11). They were not ministering to the church; they were using religion to fill their own pockets. This explains why Paul said that "not given to filthy lucre" was one requirement for an elder. A true servant of God does not minister for personal gain; he ministers to help others grow in the faith.

But behind this covetousness was another problem: Their minds and consciences had been defiled (Titus 1:15). This is what happens when a person lives a double life: Outwardly, he commands respect, but inwardly, he deteriorates. No one can serve two masters. These deceivers' love for money caused them to teach false doctrine and live false lives, and the result was a defiled conscience *that did not convict them.* This is one step closer to that "seared conscience" that Paul wrote about (1 Tim. 4:2).

Titus 1:15 is one of those verses that some ignorant people try to use to defend their ungodly practices. "To the pure, all things are pure" is used to excuse all sorts of sin. I recall warning a teenager about the kind of literature he was reading, and his defense was, "Beauty is in the eye of the beholder. Your heart must be filthy if you see sin in what I'm reading. After all, 'To the pure, all things are pure.'"

To begin with, Paul was refuting the false teaching of these legalists with reference to *foods.* They were teaching that Jewish dietary laws still applied to Christian believers (see 1 Tim. 4:3–5). If you ate forbidden food, you defiled yourself, but if you refused that food, you became holier.

"It is just the opposite," Paul argued. "These teachers have defiled minds and consciences. Therefore, when they look at these innocent foods, they see sin, because sin has defiled their vision. But those of us who have pure minds and consciences know that all foods are clean. It is not the foods that are defiling the teachers; it is the teachers who are defiling the foods!"

But this principle must not be applied to things that we know are evil. The difference, for example, between great art and pornography is more than "in the eye of the beholder." A great artist does not exploit the human body for base gain. For a believer to indulge in sinful, erotic experiences and claim that they were pure because his heart was pure, is to use the Word of God to excuse sin. The application Paul made was to food, and we must be careful to keep it there.

Having shared these three facts about these false teachers, Paul added one further matter.

What Titus was to do. He was not to stand quietly by and let them take over! First, he was to "exhort and to convince" them by means of "sound doctrine" (Titus 1:9). The only weapon against Satan's lies is God's truth. "Thus saith the Lord!" is the end of every argument.

Titus was to stop their mouths (Titus 1:11) and prevent them from teaching and spreading false doctrines. He was to "rebuke them sharply" (Titus 1:13). Paul would give this same counsel to Timothy in his final letter "Reprove, rebuke, exhort with all longsuffering and doctrine" (2 Tim. 4:2).

Paul's purpose, of course, was to convince these teachers and get them to be "sound in the faith" (Titus 1:13). But while he was doing this, he needed to protect the church from their false teachings. False doctrine is like yeast: it enters secretly, it grows quickly, and permeates completely (Gal. 5:9). The best time to attack false doctrine is at the beginning, before it has a chance to spread.

The attitude of some church members is, "It makes no difference what you believe, just as long as you believe something." Paul would not agree with that foolish philosophy. It makes all the difference between life and death whether or not you believe the truth of the Word or believe lies. You can choose what you want to believe, but you cannot change the consequences.

"And ye shall know the truth," said Jesus Christ, "and the truth shall make you free" (John 8:32).

CHAPTER TWO
Titus 2—3
HOW TO HAVE A HEALTHY CHURCH

In contrast to the false teachers, Titus was to "speak the things which belong to healthy doctrine" (Titus 2:1, literal translation). What germs are to a physical body, false teaching is to a spiritual body, the church. In the verses that make up this section, you will find a blending of doctrinal teaching and practical admonition, for the two must go together. Paul discussed several different areas of ministry in the local church.

The Older Saints (2:1–4a)

How easy it would be for a younger man like Titus to misunderstand or even neglect the older members of his congregation.

"I want a church of young people!" a pastor once said to me, forgetting that one day he would be old himself. A church needs both the old and the young, and they should minister to one another. The grace of God enables us to bridge the generation gap in the church. One way to do this is for all members, young and old, to live up to the standards that God has set for our lives.

The older men were to be *sober,* which means "to be temperate in the use of wine." Old men with time on their hands could linger too long over the cup.

Grave means "dignified," but it does not suggest a solemn person who never laughs. There is a dignity to old age that produces respect, and this respect gives an older saint authority. How I thank God for the venerable saints who have assisted me in my own pastoral ministry! When they stood to speak, the whole church listened and took heed.

Temperate describes an attitude of mind that leads to prudence and self-control in life. It is the opposite of frivolity and carelessness that are based on ignorance. It is translated "sober" in Titus 1:8 and 2:4, 6, and 12, and "discreet" in 2:5. Seriousness of life and purpose are important in the Christian life, and especially to older saints who cannot afford to waste time, for their time is short.

Sound in faith, in love, in patience all go together. The older men should know what they believe, and their doctrinal convictions should accord with God's Word. For a knowledge of Bible doctrine is no substitute for the other necessary virtues, such as love for the brethren and patience in the trials of life. In fact, a right faith in God's Word should encourage a believer in love and endurance.

Possibly the word *likewise* in Titus 2:3 means that the older women were to have the same qualities as the older men, plus the additional ones listed. The deportment (behavior) of these older women must always reflect holiness. They must not be slanderers ("false accusers"—the Greek word is "devils," which means "slanderers"), picking up gossip and spreading it. They must also be temperate in their use of wine.

When it comes to the older women, Paul's emphasis is on *teaching:* "teachers of good things." Experienced, godly women are usually excellent teachers. The word *teach* in Titus 2:4 is related to the word translated "temperate" in Titus 2:2, and probably should be translated, "that they may train by making soberminded." It is not only that the older women should show the younger mothers how to keep house, but that they put within their hearts and minds the right spiritual and mental attitudes.

One of the strongest forces for spiritual ministry in the local church lies with the older believers. Those who are retired have time for service. It is good to see that many local churches have organized and mobilized these important people. In my own ministry, I have been greatly helped by senior saints who knew how to pray, teach the Word, visit, troubleshoot, and help build the church.

The Younger Saints (2:4b–8)

The godly older women have the responsibility of teaching the younger women how to be successful wives, mothers, and housekeepers, and the younger women have the responsibility of listening and obeying. The Christian home was a totally new thing, and young women saved out of paganism would have to get accustomed to a whole new set of priorities and privileges. Those who had unsaved husbands would need special encouragement.

The greatest priority in a home should be love. If a wife loved her husband and her children, she was well on the way to making the marriage and the home a success. In our Western society, a man and a woman fall in love and then get married, but in the East, marriages were less romantic. Often the two got married and then had to learn to love each other. (Eph. 5:18–33 is probably the best Scripture for a husband and wife who really want to love each other in the will of God.)

Surely a mother loves her children! Yes, this is a natural instinct, but this instinct needs to be controlled. I once heard a "modern mother" say, "I love my child too much to spank her." In reality, she had a selfish love for herself and did not really love the child. "He who spares the rod hates his son, but he who loves him is careful to discipline him" (Prov. 13:24 NIV). While it was usually the father who disciplined the children in Eastern homes, the mother could not escape being a part of the procedure, or else a child would run to its mother for protection.

"To be discreet" (Titus 2:5) is our familiar word *sober-minded* again ("temperate" in Titus 2:2). Outlook determines outcome, and if a person is not thinking rightly, he will not act properly. A woman needs a correct and disciplined outlook on her ministry in the home. "Self-controlled" is the idea contained in this word. If parents do not discipline themselves, they can never discipline their children.

"Chaste" means "pure of mind and heart." A Christian wife is true to her husband in mind and heart as well as in action.

"Keepers at home" does not suggest that her home is a prison where she must be kept! "Caring for the home" is the idea. "Guide the house," Paul wrote (1 Tim. 5:14). The wise husband allows his wife to manage the affairs of the household, for this is her ministry.

"Good" (Titus 2:5) can be translated "kind." She does not rule her household with an iron hand, but practices "the law of kindness" (Prov. 31:26).

While the wife is "busy at home" (NIV), it is the husband who is the leader in the home, so the wife must be obedient. But where there is love (Titus 2:4) there is little problem with obedience. And where the

desire is to glorify God, there is no difficulty that cannot be worked out.

"That the Word of God be not blasphemed" is a good motive for cooperation and obedience at home. It is sad to see the way family problems, and even divorces, among Christians cause unsaved people to sneer at the Bible.

Titus was to let older women minister to younger women, lest he get himself into a difficult situation. But he was to be an example to the younger men with whom he would easily identify. Exhortation and example were to be his tools for building them up in the faith (Titus 2:6–7). He was to exhort them to be self-controlled, for there were many temptations to sin.

But Paul wrote more about Titus the *example* than he did about Titus the *exhorter!* A pastor preaches best by his life. He must constantly be a good example in all things. Whatever the pastor wants his church to be, he must first be himself. "For they say, and do not" was our Lord's indictment against the Pharisees (Matt. 23:3). This is hypocrisy.

The Greek word *tupos* ("pattern," Titus 2:7) gives us our English word *type*. The word originally meant "an impression made by a die." Titus was to live so that his life would be like a "spiritual die" that would impress itself on others. This involved good works, sound doctrine, a seriousness of attitude, and sound speech that no one—not even the enemy—could condemn. Whether we like it or not, there are "contrary" people who are always looking for a fight. A pastor's speech should be such that he stands without rebuke.

It is not easy to pastor a church. You do not punch a clock, yet you are always on duty. You must be careful to practice what you preach; you must be the same man in and out of the pulpit. Hypocrisy in speech or conduct will ruin a man's ministry. No pastor is perfect, just as no church member is perfect, but he must strive to be the best example possible. A church will never rise any higher than its leadership.

Christian Slaves (2:9–15)

Paul usually had a word concerning the slaves (see Eph. 6:5–9; 1 Tim. 6:1–2). We are glad for this word to Titus because Paul backed it up with one of the greatest statements about salvation found in the New Testament. Paul always linked doctrine and duty.

Paul warned these Christian slaves about three common sins they must avoid (Titus 2:9–10). First, *disobedience.* They were to obey their masters and seek to please them, which meant going the extra mile. It is possible to obey, but not "from the heart" (Eph. 6:6). It is possible to do a job grudgingly. Some unsaved masters would not be thoughtful and would overwork their slaves.

The second sin was *talking back* ("answering again," Titus 2:9). While a slave would not carry this too far (his master might severely discipline him), he could argue with his master since the master probably knew less about the job than the slave did. The slave could also "gripe" about his master to others on the job. This would certainly be a poor testimony for a Christian slave.

Christian slaves were also to avoid the sin of *stealing* ("purloining"). This was the sin Onesimus probably committed against Philemon (see Philem. 18). It would be easy for a slave to pilfer little items and sell them, and then report that they had been broken or lost.

There are no slaves in our society today, but there are employees. Christian workers must obey orders and not talk back. They must not steal from their employers. Millions of dollars are lost each year by employers whose workers steal from them, everything from paper clips and pencils to office machines and vehicles. "They owe it to me!" is no excuse. Neither is, "Well, I've earned it!"

Paul gave a good reason why Christian workers should be trustworthy ("showing all good fidelity"): This will "embellish with honor" the Word of God (WUEST). When we serve faithfully, we "beautify the Bible" and make the Christian message attractive to unbelievers. When Paul addressed the slaves in Timothy's church (1 Tim. 6:1), he used a negative motive: "that the name of God and his doctrine be not blasphemed." But the positive motive, to make God's message attractive, and the negative motive, to keep God's teaching from being slandered, ought to control our lives.

Here (Titus 2:11) Paul expanded the meaning of "Saviour" (Titus 2:10) by explaining what was involved in this salvation that we have through Jesus Christ. The emphasis is on *grace*—God's lavish favor on undeserving sinners. Paul pointed out three wonderful ministries of the grace of God (Titus 2:11–14).

Grace redeems us (vv. 11, 14a). People could not save themselves. God's grace had to bring salvation to lost mankind. This salvation was not discovered by sinners; it appeared to them via the life, death, and resurrection of Jesus Christ. God in His grace sent His Son to redeem those in the bondage of sin. This salvation is for "all men" who receive it (see 1 Tim. 2:4–6). There is a universal need, and God provided a universal remedy for all who will believe.

Paul explained this salvation further (Titus 2:14). Christ "gave himself for us," which means that He became our substitute. "Who his own self bare our sins in his own body on the tree" (1 Peter 2:24). The word *redeem* means "to set free by paying a price." We were all slaves of sin (Titus 3:3) and could not set ourselves free, but Jesus Christ gave Himself as the ransom for our sins. By His death He met the just demands of God's holy law, so that God in His grace could forgive and free those who believe on Christ.

We have been redeemed "from all iniquity," which means that sin should no longer master our lives. (Remember that the context of this passage is Paul's counsel to *slaves*. They knew the meaning of "redeem.") "Iniquity" means "lawlessness." In our

unsaved condition, we were rebels against God's law, but now all of that has been changed. This led Paul to the second ministry of the grace of God.

Grace reforms us (vv. 12, 14b). Salvation is not only a change in position (set free from the slavery of sin), but it is also a change in attitude, appetite, ambition, and action. The same grace that redeems us also reforms our lives and makes us godly. "Teaching" has the idea of "disciplining." We are disciplined by God's grace, trained to be the kind of people that glorify Him.

Godly living involves both the negative and the positive. We deny "ungodliness [whatever is unlike God] and worldly lusts" (see 1 John 2:15–17). The verb means that we do it once and for all. It is a settled matter. Then, we work on the positive. "Sober" is our familiar word for "self-control, prudence, restraint" (see Titus 2:2). This emphasizes the believer's relationship to himself, while "righteously" deals with his relationships with other people. "Godly" speaks of the Christian's relationship to the Lord, though the qualities must not be separated.

Christians live "in this present age" (NIV), but they do not live *like* it or *for* it. Christ has redeemed us from this evil age (Gal. 1:4), and we must not be conformed to it (Rom. 12:1–2). Neither should we walk according to its standards (Eph. 2:2). We have tasted the powers of "the coming age" (Heb. 6:5 NIV), and we should not desire to cultivate the present age with its shallowness and godlessness.

Grace reforms us because God purifies us and makes us His own special possession (Titus 2:14b). This process of purification is called "sanctification," and its goal is to make the believer more like Jesus Christ (Rom. 8:29). Sanctification is not only separation from sin, but it is also devotion to God (2 Cor. 6:14—7:1). "Peculiar" does not mean "odd" or "strange." It means "a special people for God's own possession" (see Deut. 14:2; 26:18).

Grace rewards us (v. 13). We are looking for Jesus Christ to return; this is our only hope and glory. This verse boldly affirms that Jesus Christ is God, for there is only one article in the Greek: "the great God and our Saviour." Paul did not go into detail about the events surrounding the return of Christ. Believers should always be expecting His return and live like those who will see Him face-to-face.

Christians as Citizens (3:1–8)

Christians were often looked on with suspicion in the Roman Empire because their conduct was so different and they met in private meetings for worship (see 1 Peter 2:11–25; 3:13—4:5). It was important that they be good citizens without compromising the faith. Their pagan neighbors might disobey the law, but Christians must submit to the authority of the state (see Rom. 13). "Ready to every good work" (Titus 3:1) means "cooperating in those matters that involve the whole community." Our heavenly citizenship

(Phil. 3:20) does not absolve us from responsibilities as citizens on earth.

The believer should not have a bad attitude toward the government and show it by slanderous accusations and pugnacious actions. The word *gentle* (Titus 3:2) means "an attitude of moderation, a sweet reasonableness." Christians with this quality do not insist on the letter of the law, but are willing to compromise where no moral issue is at stake.

Again, Paul linked duty to doctrine. "Don't be too critical of your pagan neighbors," he wrote. "Just remember what you were before God saved you!" Titus 3:3 needs little explanation; we know what it means from our own experience.

What a difference "the kindness and love of God" (Titus 3:4) made! If you want a beautiful illustration of "the kindness of God," read 2 Samuel and note David's treatment of Mephibosheth, a little lame prince. Because Mephibosheth was a part of Saul's family, he expected to be slain. But David, in kindness, spared him and treated him as one of his own sons at the palace table.

Salvation came not only because of God's kindness and love, but also because of His mercy (Titus 3:5). We did not save ourselves; "he saved us." How did He do it? Through the miracle of the new birth, the work of the Holy Spirit of God. I do not think that "washing" here refers to baptism because, in New Testament times, people were baptized *after* they were saved, and not in order to be saved (see Acts 10:43–48). "Washing" here means "bathed all over." When a sinner trusts Christ, he is cleansed from all his sins, and he is made "a new person" by the indwelling Holy Spirit.

Paul related this same cleansing experience to the Word of God (Eph. 5:26). Salvation comes to a sinner when he trusts Christ, when the Spirit of God uses the Word of God to bring about the new birth. We are born of the *Spirit* (John 3:5–6, where "water" refers to physical birth, which Nicodemus had mentioned earlier, John 3:4) and of the *Word* (1 Peter 1:23–25). "Which" in Titus 3:6 ought to be "whom," referring to the Holy Spirit who is given to us at conversion (Acts 2:38; Rom. 5:5; 8:9).

Not only have we who are Christians been washed and made new in Christ, but we have also been *justified* (Titus 3:7). This wonderful doctrine is discussed in detail in Romans 3:21—8:39. Justification is the gracious act of God whereby He declares a believing sinner righteous because of the finished work of Christ on the cross. God puts to our account the righteousness of His Son, so that we can be condemned no more. Not only does He forget our sins, but He forgets that we were even sinners!

What is the result of this kindness, love, mercy, and grace? Hope! We are heirs of God! This means that today we can draw on His riches, and when He comes, we will share His wealth and His kingdom forever. This hope ties in with Titus 2:13: "Looking for that blessed hope." But there is something more involved:

We should live godly lives and be "careful to maintain good works" (Titus 3:8). The only evidence the unsaved world has that we belong to God is our godly lives.

"Good works" do not necessarily mean religious works or church work. It is fine to work at church, sing in the choir, and hold an office; but it is also good to serve our unsaved neighbors, to be helpful in the community, and to have a reputation for assisting those in need. Babysitting to relieve a harassed young mother is just as much a spiritual work as passing out a gospel tract. The best way a local church has to witness to the lost is through the sacrificial service of its members.

Problem People (3:9–11)

We wish we did not have "problem people" in our churches, but wherever there are people, there can be problems. In this case, Paul warned Titus to avoid people who like to argue about the unimportant things of the faith. I recall being approached by a young man after a Bible lesson and getting involved with him in all sorts of hypothetical questions of doctrine. "Now, if this were true … if that were true … " was about all he could say. I was very inexperienced at the time; I should have ignored him in a gracious way. As it was, I missed the opportunity to talk with several sincere people who had personal problems and wanted help. I have learned that professed Christians who like to argue about the Bible are usually covering up some sin in their lives, are very insecure, and are usually unhappy at work or at home.

But there is another kind of problem person we should deal with: the "heretic." This word means "one who makes a choice, a person who causes divisions." This is a self-willed person who thinks he is right, and who goes from person to person in the church, forcing people to make a choice: "Are you for *me* or for the pastor?" This is a work of the flesh (see Gal. 5:20). Such a person should be admonished at least twice, and then rejected.

How do we apply this in a local church? Let me suggest one way. If a church member goes about trying to get a following, and then gets angry and leaves the church, let him go. If he comes back (maybe the other churches don't want him either), and if he shows a repentant attitude, receive him back. If he repeats this behavior (and they usually do), receive him back the second time. But if he does it a third time, do not receive him back into the fellowship of the church (Titus 3:10). Why not? "Such a man is warped in character, keeps on sinning, and has condemned himself" (Titus 3:11, literal translation). If more churches would follow this principle, we would have fewer "church tramps" who cause problems in various churches.

Conclusion (3:12–15)

In the closing verses, Paul conveyed some personal information to Titus, and reminded him of the main theme of the letter: Insist that God's people "learn to devote themselves to doing what is good, in order that they may provide for daily necessities and not live unproductive lives" (Titus 3:14 NIV).

We know nothing about Artemas; Tychicus we met in Acts 20:4. He was with Paul in his first Roman imprisonment and carried the epistles from Paul to the Ephesians (Eph. 6:21), the Colossians (Col. 4:7–8), and to Philemon (cf. Col. 4:7–9 with Philem. 10). Either Artemas or Tychicus would replace Titus on Crete, and then Titus was to join Paul at Nicopolis.

It is possible that Zenas and Apollos (see Acts 18:24ff.; Titus 3:13) carried this letter to Titus. Paul had sent them on a mission and Titus was to aid them all he could.

Paul ended the letter to Titus with a variation of his usual benediction (see 2 Thess. 3:17–18): "Grace be with you all."

Grace—and good works! They go together!

PHILEMON

OUTLINE

Key theme: Christian forgiveness
Key verses: Philemon 15–16

I. APPRECIATION (1–7) ("I thank my God")
    A. Paul's love—1–3
    B. Paul's thanksgiving—4–5, 7
    C. Paul's prayer—6

II. APPEAL (8–16) ("I beseech thee")
    A. Philemon's character—8–9
    B. Onesimus's conversion—10–14
    C. God's providence—15–16

III. ASSURANCE (17–25) ("I will repay")
    A. Paul's partnership—17–19
    B. Paul's confidence—20–22
    C. Paul's greetings—23–25

CONTENTS

CHAPTER ONE
Philemon 1–25
A TALE OF TWO CITIES

Paul was a prisoner in Rome, his friend Philemon was in Colosse, and the human link between them was a runaway slave named Onesimus. The details are not clear, but it appears that Onesimus robbed his master and then fled to Rome, hoping to be swallowed up in the crowded metropolis. But, in the providence of God, he met Paul and was converted!

Now what? Perhaps Onesimus should remain with Paul, who needed all the assistance he could get. But what about the slave's responsibilities to his master back in Colosse? The law permitted a master to execute a rebellious slave, but Philemon was a Christian. If he forgave Onesimus, what would the other masters (and slaves) think? If he punished him, how would it affect his testimony? What a dilemma!

Along with the epistle to the Colossians, this letter probably was carried to Colosse by Tychicus and Onesimus (Col. 4:7–9). In it, we see Paul in three important roles as he tried to help Philemon solve his problems. At the same time, we see a beautiful picture of what the Father has done for us in Jesus Christ. Martin Luther said, "All of us are Onesimuses!" and he was right.

Paul, the Beloved Friend (1–7)
Paul had not founded the church in Colosse, nor had he visited it (Col. 1:1–8; 2:1). It is likely that the church started as a result of his ministry in Ephesus (Acts 19:10, 20, 26) and that Epaphras was the founding pastor (Philem. 23). The church met in the home of Philemon and Apphia, his wife. Some people assume that Archippus was their son, but this is not certain. He may have been the elder who took the place of Epaphras, who had gone to Rome to help Paul. If this is true, then it would explain Paul's strong admonition to Archippus in Colossians 4:17, a letter written to the whole church.

In his greeting, Paul expressed his deep love for his Christian friends, and he reminded them that he was a prisoner for Jesus Christ (see also Philem. 9–10, 13, 23). Timothy was included in the greeting, though the burden of the letter was from the heart of Paul to the heart of Philemon. Paul's ministry was a "team" operation, and he often included the names of his associates when he wrote his letters. He liked to use the term "fellow worker" (see Rom. 16:3, 9, 21; 1 Cor. 3:9; Phil. 2:25; 4:3; Col. 4:11).

The New Testament churches met in homes (Rom. 16:5, 23; 1 Cor. 16:19), and perhaps the church in Philemon's house was one of two assemblies in Colosse (Col. 4:15). Paul had won Philemon to faith in Christ (see Philem. 19), and Philemon became a blessing to other Christians (Philem. 7).

It was customary for Paul to open his letters with words of thanks and praise to God. (Galatians is an exception.) In his thanksgiving, Paul described his friend as a man of love and faith, both toward Jesus Christ and God's people. His love was practical: he "refreshed" the saints through his words and work.

Paul told Philemon that he was praying for him and asking God to make his witness effective ("the sharing of your faith") so that others would trust Christ. He also prayed that his friend would have a deeper understanding of all that he had in Jesus Christ. After all, the better we know Christ and experience His blessings, the more we want to share these blessings with others.

Paul, the Beseeching Intercessor (8–16)
Estimates suggest that there were sixty million slaves in the Roman Empire, men and women who were treated like pieces of merchandise to buy and sell. A familiar proverb was "So many slaves, just so many enemies!" The average slave sold for five hundred denarii (one denarius was a day's wage for a common laborer), while the educated and skilled slaves were priced as high as fifty thousand denarii. A master could free a slave, or a slave could buy his freedom if he could raise the money (Acts 22:28).

If a slave ran away, the master would register the name and description with the officials, and the slave would be on the "wanted" list. Any free citizen who found a runaway slave could assume custody and even intercede with the owner. The slave was not automatically returned to the owner, nor was he automatically sentenced to death. While it is true that some masters were cruel (one man threw his slave into a pool of man-eating fish!), many of them were reasonable and humane. After all, a slave was an expensive and useful piece of personal property, and it would cost the owner to lose him.

As Paul interceded for Onesimus, he presented five strong appeals. He began with Philemon's reputation as a man who brought blessing to others. The word *wherefore* in Philemon 8 carries the meaning of "accordingly." Since Philemon was a "refreshing" believer, Paul wanted to give him an opportunity to refresh the apostle's heart! Philemon had been a great blessing to many saints, and now he could be a blessing to one of his own slaves who had just been saved!

Paul might have used apostolic authority and ordered his friend to obey, but he preferred to appeal in Christian love (Philem. 9). See how tactfully Paul reminded Philemon of his own personal situation: "Paul the aged, and now also a prisoner of Jesus Christ" (Philem. 9). Who could turn down the request of a suffering saint like Paul! He was perhaps sixty years old at this time, but that was a good age for men in that day. Along with Philemon's gracious character and Christian love, Paul's third appeal was the conversion of Onesimus (Philem. 10). Onesimus was no longer "just a slave"; he was now Paul's son in the faith and Philemon's Christian brother! In Jesus Christ, there is "neither bond nor free" (Gal. 3:28). This does not mean that his conversion altered Onesimus's legal position as a slave, or that it canceled his debt to the law or to his master. However, it did mean that Onesimus had a new standing before God and before God's people, and Philemon had to take this into consideration.

The fourth appeal was that Onesimus was valuable to Paul in his ministry in Rome (Philem. 11–14). The name Onesimus means "profitable," so there is a play on words in Philemon 11. (The name Philemon means "affectionate" or "one who is kind." If the slave was expected to live up to his name, then what about the master?) Paul loved Onesimus and would have kept him in Rome as a fellow worker, but he did not want to tell Philemon what to do. Voluntary sacrifice and service, motivated by love, is what the Lord wants from His children.

The fifth appeal relates to the providence of God (Philem. 15–16). Paul was not dogmatic ("perhaps") as he made this telling point: as Christians, we must believe that God is in control of even the most difficult experiences of life. God permitted Onesimus to go to Rome that he might meet Paul and become a believer. (Certainly Philemon and his family had witnessed to the slave and prayed for him.) Onesimus departed so he could come back. He was gone a short time so that he and his master might be together forever. He left for Rome a slave, but he would return to Colosse a brother. How gracious God was to rule and overrule in these affairs!

As you review these five appeals, you can see how Paul tenderly convinced his friend Philemon that he should receive his disobedient slave and forgive him. But it would not be easy for Philemon to do this. If he was too easy on Onesimus, it might influence other slaves to "become Christians" and want to influence their masters. However, if he was too hard on the man, it might affect Philemon's testimony and ministry in Colosse.

At this point, Paul offered the perfect solution. It was a costly solution as far as the apostle was concerned, but he was willing to pay the price.

Paul, the Burdened Partner (17–25)

The word translated "partner" is koinonia, which means "to have in common." It is translated "communication" in Philemon 6, which means "fellowship." Paul volunteered to become a "business partner" with Philemon and help him solve the problem with Onesimus. He made two suggestions: "Receive him as myself," and "Put that [whatever he stole from you] on my account."

As Philemon's new "partner," Paul could not leave Rome and go to Colosse, but he could send Onesimus as his personal representative. "The way you treat Onesimus is the way you treat me," said the apostle. "He is to me as my own heart" (Philem. 12).

This is to me an illustration of what Jesus Christ has done for us as believers. God's people are so identified with Jesus Christ that God receives them as He receives His Son! We are "accepted in the beloved" (Eph. 1:6) and clothed in His righteousness (2 Cor. 5:21). We certainly cannot approach God with any merit of our own, but God must receive us when we come to Him "in Jesus Christ." The word receive in Philemon 17 means "to receive into one's family circle." Imagine a slave entering his master's family! But imagine a guilty sinner entering God's family!

Paul did not suggest that Philemon ignore the slave's crimes and forget about the debt Onesimus owed. Rather, Paul offered to pay the debt himself. "Put it on my account—I will repay it!" The language in Philemon 19 sounds like a legal promissory note of that time. This was Paul's assurance to his friend that the debt would be paid.

It takes more than love to solve the problem; love must pay a price. God does not save us by His love, for though He loves the whole world, the whole world is not saved. God saves sinners by His grace (Eph. 2:8–9), and grace is love that pays a price. God in His holiness could not ignore the debt that we owe, for God must be faithful to His own law. So He paid the debt for us!

Theologians call this "the doctrine of imputation." (To impute means "to put it on account.") When Jesus Christ died on the cross, my sins were put on His account, and He was treated the way I should have been treated. When I trusted Him as my Savior, His righteousness was put on my account, and now God accepts me in Jesus Christ. Jesus said to the Father, "He no longer owes You a debt because I paid it fully on the cross. Receive him as You would receive Me. Let him come into the family circle!"

However, we must keep in mind that there is a difference between being accepted in Christ and acceptable to Christ. Anyone who trusts Jesus Christ for salvation is accepted in Him (Rom. 4:1–4). But the believer must strive with God's help to be acceptable to the Lord in his daily life (Rom. 12:2; 14:18; 2 Cor. 5:9; Heb. 12:28 NIV). The Father wants to look at those who are in His Son and say of them as He said of Jesus, "I am well pleased!"

Philemon 19 suggests that it was Paul who led Philemon to faith in Christ. Paul used this special relationship to encourage his friend to receive Onesimus. Philemon and Onesimus were not only spiritual brothers in the Lord, but they had the same "spiritual father"—Paul! (see Philem. 10; 1 Cor. 4:15)

Was Paul hinting in Philemon 21 that Philemon should do even more and free Onesimus? For that matter, why did he not come right out and condemn slavery? This letter certainly would have been the ideal place to do it. Paul did not "condemn" slavery in this letter or in any of his letters, though he often had a word of admonition for slaves and their masters (Eph. 6:5–9; Col. 3:22—4:1; 1 Tim. 6:1–2; Titus 2:9–10). In fact he encouraged Christian slaves to obtain their freedom if they could (1 Cor. 7:21–24).

During the American Civil War, both sides used

the same Bible to "prove" their cases for or against slavery. One of the popular arguments was, "If slavery is so wrong, why did Jesus and the apostles say nothing against it? Paul gave instructions to regulate slavery, but he did not condemn it."

One of the best explanations was given by Alexander Maclaren in his commentary on Colossians in The Expositor's Bible (Eerdmans, 1940; vol. VI, 301):

> First, the message of Christianity is primarily to individuals, and only secondarily to society. It leaves the units whom it has influenced to influence the mass. Second, it acts on spiritual and moral sentiment, and only afterwards and consequently on deeds or institutions. Third, it hates violence, and trusts wholly to enlightened conscience. So it meddles directly with no political or social arrangements, but lays down principles which will profoundly affect these, and leaves them to soak into the general mind.

Had the early Christians begun an open crusade against slavery, they would have been crushed by the opposition, and the message of the gospel would have become confused with a social and political program. Think of how difficult it was for people to overcome slavery in England and America, and those two nations had general education and the Christian religion to help prepare the way. Think also of the struggles in the modern Civil Rights movement even within the church. If the battle for freedom was difficult for us to win in the nineteenth and twentieth centuries, what would the struggle have been like back in the first century?

Christians are the salt of the earth and the light of the world (Matt. 5:13–16), and their spiritual influence must be felt in society to the glory of God. God used Joseph in Egypt, Esther and Nehemiah in Persia, and Daniel in Babylon, and throughout church history, there have been believers in political offices who have faithfully served the Lord. But Christians in the Roman Empire could not work through local democratic political structures as we can today, so they really had no political power to bring about change. The change had to come from within, even though it took centuries for slavery to end.

Paul closed the letter with his usual personal requests and greetings. He fully expected to be released and to visit Philemon and Apphia in Colosse ("you" in Philem. 22 is plural). Even this fact would encourage Philemon to follow Paul's instructions, for he certainly would not want to be ashamed when he met the apostle face-to-face.

As we have seen, Epaphras was probably the pastor of the church; and he had gone to Rome to assist Paul. Whether he was a "voluntary prisoner" for Paul's sake, or whether he had actually been arrested by the Romans, we do not know. We must commend him for his dedication to Christ and to Paul.

John Mark was with Paul (Col. 4:10), the young man who failed Paul on his first missionary journey (Acts 12:12, 25; 15:36–41). Paul had forgiven Mark and was grateful for his faithful ministry (see 2 Tim. 4:11).

Aristarchus was from Thessalonica and accompanied Paul to Jerusalem and then to Rome (Acts 19:29; 27:2). Demas is mentioned three times in Paul's letters: "Demas … my fellow worker" (Philem. 24); "Demas" (Col. 4:14); "Demas hath forsaken me, having loved this present world" (2 Tim. 4:10). John Mark failed but was restored. Demas seemed to be doing well but then he fell.

Luke, of course, was the beloved physician (Col. 4:14) who accompanied Paul, ministered to him, and eventually wrote the gospel of Luke and the book of Acts.

Paul's benediction was his "official signature" for his letters (2 Thess. 3:17–18), and it magnified the grace of God. After all, it was the grace of Jesus Christ that made our salvation possible (Eph. 2:1–10). It was He who said, "Charge that to My account! Receive them as You would receive Me!"

HEBREWS

OUTLINE

Key theme: Press on to maturity
Key verse: Hebrews 6:1

I. A SUPERIOR PERSON—CHRIST (1—6)
A. Better than the prophets—1:1–3
B. Better than the angels—1:4—2:18
   (Exhortation: drifting from the Word, 2:1–4)
C. Better than Moses—3:1—4:13
   (Exhortation: doubting the Word, 3:7—4:13)
D. Better than Aaron—4:14—6:20
   (Exhortation: dullness toward the Word, 5:11—6:20)

II. A SUPERIOR PRIESTHOOD—MELCHIZEDEK (7—10)
A. A superior order—7
B. A superior covenant—8
C. A superior sanctuary—9
D. A superior sacrifice—10 (Exhortation: despising the Word—10:26–39)

III. A SUPERIOR PRINCIPLE—FAITH (11—13)
A. The great examples of faith—11
B. The endurance of faith—chastening—12
   (Exhortation: defying the Word—12:14–29)
C. Closing practical exhortations—13

CONTENTS

CHAPTER ONE
Hebrews 1:1–3
IS ANYBODY LISTENING?

A man from Leeds, England visited his doctor to have his hearing checked. The doctor removed the man's hearing aid, and the patient's hearing immediately improved! He had been wearing the device *in the wrong ear* for over twenty years!

I once asked a pastor friend, "Do you have a deaf ministry in your church?" He replied, "There are times when I think the whole church needs a deaf ministry—they just don't seem to hear me."

There is a difference between *listening* and really *hearing.* Jesus often cried, "He who has ears to hear, let him hear!" This statement suggests that it takes more than physical ears to hear the voice of God. It also requires a receptive heart. "Today, if ye will hear his voice, harden not your hearts" (Heb. 3:7–8).

Many people have avoided the epistle to the Hebrews and, consequently, have robbed themselves of practical spiritual help. Some have avoided this book because they are "afraid of it." The "warnings" in Hebrews have made them uneasy. Others have avoided this book because they think it is "too difficult" for the average Bible student. To be sure, there are some profound truths in Hebrews, and no preacher or teacher would dare to claim that he knows them all! But the general message of the book is clear and there is no reason why you and I should not understand and profit from it.

Perhaps the best way to begin our study is to notice five characteristics of the epistle to the Hebrews.

It Is a Book of Evaluation
The word *better* is used thirteen times in this book as the writer shows the superiority of Jesus Christ and His salvation over the Hebrew system of religion. Christ is "better than the angels" (Heb. 1:4). He brought in "a better hope" (Heb. 7:19) because He is the Mediator of "a better covenant, which was established on better promises" (Heb. 8:6).

Another word that is repeated in this book is *perfect;* in the original Greek it is used fourteen times. It means a perfect standing before God. This perfection could never be accomplished by the Levitical priesthood (Heb. 7:11) or by the law (Heb. 7:19), nor could the blood of animal sacrifices achieve it (Heb. 10:1). Jesus Christ gave Himself as one offering for sin, and by this He has "perfected forever them that are sanctified" (Heb. 10:14).

So the writer was contrasting the Old Testament system of law with the New Testament ministry of grace. He was making it clear that the Jewish religious system was temporary and that it could not bring in the eternal "better things" that are found in Jesus Christ.

Eternal is a third word that is important to the message of Hebrews. Christ is the "author of eternal salvation" (Heb. 5:9). Through His death, He "obtained eternal redemption" (Heb. 9:12), and He shares with believers "the promise of eternal inheritance" (Heb. 9:15). His throne is forever (Heb. 1:8) and He is a priest forever (Heb. 5:6; 6:20; 7:17, 21). "Jesus Christ, the same yesterday, and today, and forever" (Heb. 13:8).

When you combine these three important words, you discover that Jesus Christ and the Christian life He gives us are *better* because these blessings are *eternal* and they give us a *perfect* standing before God. The religious system under the Mosaic law was imperfect because it could not accomplish a once-for-all redemption that was eternal.

But why did the writer ask his readers to evaluate their faith and what Jesus Christ had to offer them? Because they were going through difficult times and were being tempted to go back to the Jewish religion. The temple was still standing when this book was written, and all the priestly ceremonies were still being carried on daily. How easy it would have been for these Jewish believers to escape persecution by going back into the old Mosaic system that they had known before.

These people were "second generation believers," having been won to Christ by those who had known Jesus Christ during His ministry on earth (Heb. 2:3). They were true believers (Heb. 3:1) and not mere professors. They had been persecuted because of their faith (Heb. 10:32–34; 12:4; 13:13–14), and yet they had faithfully ministered to the needs of others who had suffered (Heb. 6:10). But they were being seduced by teachers of false doctrine (Heb. 13:9), and they were in danger of forgetting the true Word that their first leaders, now dead, had taught them (Heb. 13:7).

The tragic thing about these believers is that they were at a standstill spiritually and in danger of going backward (Heb. 5:12ff.). Some of them had even forsaken the regular worship services (Heb. 10:25) and were not making spiritual progress (Heb. 6:1). In the Christian life, if you do not go forward, you go backward; there is no permanent standing still.

"How can you go back into your former religion?" the writer asked them. "Just take time to evaluate what you have in Jesus Christ. He is better than anything you ever had under the law."

The book of Hebrews exalts the person and the work of Jesus Christ, the Son of God. When you realize all that you have in and through Him, you have no desire for anyone else or anything else!

It Is a Book of Exhortation
The writer called this epistle "the word of exhortation" (Heb. 13:22). The Greek word translated "exhortation" simply means "encouragement." It is translated "comfort" in Romans 15:4, and "consolation" in

2 Corinthians 1:5–7; 7:7. This word is related to the Greek word translated "Comforter" in John 14:16, referring to the Holy Spirit. The epistle to the Hebrews was not written to frighten people, but to encourage people. We are commanded to "encourage one another daily" (Heb. 3:13 NIV). It reminds us that we have "strong encouragement" in Jesus Christ (Heb. 6:18 NASB).

At this point we must answer the usual question: "But what about those five terrible warnings found in Hebrews?"

To begin with, these five passages are not really "warnings." Three basic words are translated "warn" in the New Testament, and the only one used in Hebrews is translated "admonished" in Hebrews 8:5 (KJV, where it refers to Moses) and "spake" in Hebrews 12:25. Only in Hebrews 11:7 is it translated "warned," where it refers to Noah "being warned of God." I think that the best description of the five so-called warning passages is the one given in Hebrews 13:22—"exhortation" (KJV), or "encouragement" (BRV). This does not minimize the seriousness of these five sections of the book, but it does help us grasp their purpose: to encourage us to trust God and heed His Word.

The epistle to the Hebrews opens with an important declaration: "God … has spoken to us in His Son" (Heb. 1:1–2 NASB). Near the close of the book, the writer stated, "See to it that you do not refuse Him who is speaking" (Heb. 12:25 NASB). In other words, the theme of Hebrews seems to be "God has spoken; we have His Word. What are we doing about it?"

With this truth in mind, we can now better understand the significance of those five "problem passages" in Hebrews. Each of these passages encourages us to heed God's Word ("God … has spoken") by pointing out the sad spiritual consequences that result if we do not. Let me list these passages for you and explain their sequence in the book of Hebrews. I think you will see how they all hang together and present one message: *heed God's Word.*

Drifting from the Word—2:1–4 (neglect)
Doubting the Word—3:7—4:13 (hard heart)
Dullness toward the Word—5:11—6:20 (sluggishness)
Despising the Word—10:26–39 (willfulness)
Defying the Word—12:14–29 (refusing to hear)

If we do not listen to God's Word and really *hear* it, we will start to *drift.* Neglect always leads to drifting, in things material and physical as well as spiritual. As we drift from the Word, we start to *doubt* the Word, because *faith* comes by hearing the Word of God (Rom. 10:17). We start to get hard hearts, and this leads to spiritual sluggishness, which produces *dullness* toward the Word. We become "dull of hearing"—lazy listeners! This leads to a *despiteful* attitude toward the Word to the extent that we willfully *disobey* God, and this gradually develops into a *defiant* attitude—we almost "dare" God to do anything!

Now what does God do while this spiritual regression is going on? He keeps speaking to us, encouraging us to get back to the Word. If we fail to listen and obey, then He begins to chasten us. This chastening process is the theme of Hebrews 12, the climactic chapter in the epistle. "The Lord shall judge *his people*" (Heb. 10:30, italics mine). God does not allow His children to become "spoiled brats" by permitting them to willfully defy His Word. He always chastens in love.

These five exhortations are addressed to people who are truly born again. Their purpose is to get the readers to pay close attention to God's Word. While there is some stern language in some of these passages, it is my understanding that none of these exhortations "threatens" the reader by suggesting that he may "lose his salvation." If he persists in defying God's Word, he may lose *his life* ("Shall we not much rather be in subjection unto the Father of spirits, and live?" Heb. 12:9). The inference is that if we do not submit, we might die. "There is a sin unto death" (1 John 5:16). But if the epistle to the Hebrews teaches anything, it teaches the assurance of eternal life in a living High Priest who can never die (Heb. 7:22–28).

Some students try to explain away the "problem" of "losing your salvation" or "apostasy" by claiming that the readers were not truly born again, but were only "professors" of Christian faith. However, the way the writer addresses them would eliminate that approach; for he called them "holy brethren, partakers of the heavenly calling" (Heb. 3:1). He told them that they had a High Priest in heaven (Heb. 4:14), which he would not have written if they were lost. They had been "made partakers of the Holy Spirit" (Heb. 6:4). The admonitions in Hebrews 10:19–25 would be meaningless if addressed to unsaved people.

The epistle to the Hebrews is a book of evaluation, proving that Jesus Christ is better than anything the law of Moses has to offer. The epistle is also a book of exhortation, urging its readers to hear and heed the Word of God, lest they regress spiritually and experience the chastening hand of God.

It Is a Book of Examination
As you study this book, you will find yourself asking: "What am I *really* trusting? Am I trusting the Word of God, or am I trusting the things of this world that are shaking and ready to fall away?"

This letter was written to believers at a strategic time in history. The temple was still standing and the sacrifices were still being offered. But in a few years, both the city and the temple would be destroyed. The Jewish nation would be scattered, and this would include Jewish believers in Jesus Christ. The ages were colliding! God was "shaking" the order of things (Heb. 12:25–29). He wanted His people to have their feet on the solid foundation of faith; He did not want them to trust in things that would vanish.

I believe that the church today is living in similar circumstances. Everything around us is shaking and changing. People are discovering that they have been depending on the "scaffolding" and not on the solid foundation. Even God's people have gotten so caught up in this world's system that their confidence is not in the Lord, but in money, buildings, programs, and other passing material things. As God continues to "shake" society, the scaffolding will fall away, and God's people will discover that their only confidence must be in the Word of God.

God wants our hearts to be "established with grace" (Heb. 13:9). That word *established* is used, in one form or another, eight times in Hebrews. It means "to be solidly grounded, to stand firm on your feet." It carries the idea of strength, reliability, confirmation, permanence. This, I think, is the key message of Hebrews: "You can be secure while everything around you is falling apart!" We have a "kingdom which cannot be moved" (Heb. 12:28). God's Word is steadfast (Heb. 2:2) and so is the hope we have in Him (Heb. 6:19).

Of course, there is no security for a person who has never trusted Jesus Christ as his own Savior from sin. Nor is there security to those who have made a "lip profession" but whose lives do not give evidence of true salvation (Matt. 7:21–27; Titus 1:16). Christ saves "to the uttermost" (i.e., "eternally") only those who have come to God through faith in Him (Heb. 7:25).

I like to tell congregations the story about the conductor who got on the train, began to take tickets, and told the first passenger whose ticket he took, "Sir, you're on the wrong train." When he looked at the next ticket, he told that passenger the same thing.

"But the brakeman told me to get on this train," the passenger protested.

"I'll double-check," said the conductor. He did and discovered that *he* was on the wrong train!

I fear there are many people who have a false faith, who have not really heard and heeded God's Word. Sometimes they are so busy telling everybody else what to do that they fail to examine their own situations. The epistle to the Hebrews is a book of examination: it helps you discover where your faith really is.

It Is a Book of Expectation

The focus in this book is on the future. The writer informs us that he is speaking about "the world to come" (Heb. 2:5), a time when believers will reign with Christ. Jesus Christ is "heir of all things" (Heb. 1:2) and we share the "promise of eternal inheritance" (Heb. 9:15). Like the patriarchs lauded in Hebrews 11, we are looking for that future city of God (Heb. 11:10–16, 26).

Like these great men and women of faith, we today should be "strangers and pilgrims on the earth" (Heb. 11:13). This is one reason why God is shaking everything around us. *He wants us to turn loose from the things of this world and stop depending on them.* He wants us to center our attention on the world to come. This does *not* mean that we become so heavenly minded that we're no earthly good. Rather it means that we "hang loose" as far as this world is concerned,

and start living for the eternal values of the world to come.

Abraham and Lot, his nephew, illustrate these two different attitudes (Gen. 13—14). Abraham was a wealthy man who could have lived in an expensive house in any location that he chose. But he was first of all God's servant, a pilgrim and a stranger, and this meant living in tents. Lot chose to abandon the pilgrim life and move into the evil city of Sodom. Which of these two men had true security? It would appear that Lot was safer in the city than Abraham was in his tents on the plain. But Lot became a prisoner of war! And Abraham had to rescue him.

Instead of heeding God's warning, Lot went back into the city, and when God destroyed Sodom and Gomorrah, Lot lost everything (Gen. 19). Lot was a saved man (2 Peter 2:7), but he trusted in the things of this world instead of trusting the Word of God. Lot forfeited the permanent because he depended on and lived for the immediate.

Martyred missionary Jim Elliot said it best: "He is no fool who gives what he cannot keep, to gain what he cannot lose."

You and I as God's children have been promised a future reward. As with Abraham and Moses of old, the decisions we make today will determine the rewards tomorrow. More than this, our decisions should be motivated by the expectation of receiving rewards. Abraham obeyed God *because* "he looked for a city" (Heb. 11:10). Moses forsook the treasures and the pleasures of Egypt *because* "he had respect unto the recompense of the reward" (Heb. 11:26). These great men and women (Heb. 11:31, 35) of faith "lived in the future tense" and thus were able to overcome the temptations of the world and the flesh.

In fact, it was this same attitude of faith that carried our Lord Jesus Christ through the agony of the cross: "Jesus … for the joy that was set before him endured the cross, despising the shame" (Heb. 12:2). The emphasis in the epistle to the Hebrews is "Don't live for what the world will promise you today! Live for what God has promised you in the future! Be a stranger and a pilgrim on this earth! Walk by faith, not by sight!"

This letter is not a diet for "spiritual babes" who want to be spoon-fed and coddled (Heb. 5:11–14). In this letter you will find "strong meat" that demands some "spiritual molars" for chewing and enjoying. The emphasis in Hebrews is not on what Christ did on the earth (the "milk"), but what He is now doing in heaven (the "meat" of the Word). He is the great High Priest who *enables us* by giving us grace (Heb. 4:14–16). He is also the Great Shepherd of the sheep who *equips us* to do His will (Heb. 13:20–21). He is working *in us* to accomplish His purposes. What a thrill it is for us to be a part of such a marvelous ministry!

Dr. A. W. Tozer used to remind us, "Every man must choose his world." True believers have "tasted the good word of God, and the powers of the world [age] to come" (Heb. 6:5); this should mean we have no interest in or appetite for the present sinful world system. Abraham chose the right world and became the father of the faithful. Lot chose the wrong world and became the father of the enemies of God's people (Gen. 19:30–38). Abraham became the friend of God (2 Chron. 20:7), but Lot became the friend of the world—and lost everything. Lot was "saved, yet so as by fire" (1 Cor. 3:15) and lost his reward.

It Is a Book of Exaltation

The epistle to the Hebrews exalts the person and the work of our Lord Jesus Christ. The first three verses set this high and holy theme, which is maintained throughout the entire book. Their immediate purpose is to prove that Jesus Christ is superior to the prophets, men who were held in the highest esteem by the Jewish people.

In His person, Christ is superior to the prophets. To begin with, He is the very Son of God and not merely a man called by God. The author makes it clear that Jesus Christ is God (Heb. 1:3), for his description could never be applied to mortal man. "Brightness of his glory" refers to the shekinah glory of God that dwelt in the tabernacle and temple. (See Ex. 40:34–38 and 1 Kings 8:10. The word *Shekinah* is a transliteration of a Hebrew word that means "to dwell.") Christ is to the Father what the rays of the sun are to the sun. He is the radiance of God's glory. As it is impossible to separate the rays from the sun, it is also impossible to separate Christ's glory from the nature of God.

"Express image" (Heb. 1:3) carries the idea of "the exact imprint." Our English word *character* comes from the Greek word translated "image." Literally, Jesus Christ is "the exact representation of the very substance of God" (see Col. 2:9). Only Jesus could honestly say, "He that hath seen me hath seen the Father" (John 14:9). When you see Christ, you see the glory of God (John 1:14).

In His work, Christ is also superior to the prophets. To begin with, He is the Creator of the universe, for by Him, God "made the worlds" (Heb. 1:2). Not only did Christ create all things by His Word (John 1:1–5), but He also upholds all things by that same powerful Word (Heb. 1:3). "And he is before all things, and by him all things consist [hold together]" (Col. 1:17).

The word *upholding* (Heb. 1:3) does not mean "holding up," as though the universe is a burden on the back of Jesus. It means "holding and carrying from one place to another." He is the God of Creation and the God of providence who guides this universe to its divinely ordained destiny.

He is also the superior Prophet who declares God's Word. The contrast between Christ the Prophet and the other prophets is easy to see:

Christ	*The Prophets*
God the Son	Men called by God
One Son	Many prophets
A final and complete message	A fragmentary and incomplete message

Of course, both the Old Testament and the gospel revelation came from God, but Jesus Christ was God's "last word" as far as revelation is concerned. Christ is the source, center, and end of everything that God has to say.

But Jesus Christ has a ministry as *Priest,* and this reveals His greatness. By Himself He "purged our sins" (Heb. 1:3). This aspect of His ministry will be explained in detail in Hebrews 7—10.

Finally, Jesus Christ reigns as *King* (Heb. 1:3). He has sat down, for His work is finished, and He has sat down "on the right hand of the Majesty on high," the place of honor. This proves that He is equal with God the Father, for no mere created being could ever sit at God's right hand.

Creator, Prophet, Priest, and King—Jesus Christ is superior to all of the prophets and servants of God who have ever appeared on the sacred pages of the Scriptures. It is no wonder that the Father said, at the hour of Christ's transfiguration, "This is my beloved Son, in whom I am well pleased; hear ye him" (Matt. 17:5). Two of the greatest prophets were there with Jesus—Moses and Elijah, but Christ is superior to them.

As we study Hebrews together, we must keep in mind that our purpose is not to get lost in curious doctrinal details. Nor is our purpose to attack or defend some pet doctrine. Our purpose is to hear God speak in Jesus Christ, and to heed that Word. We want to echo the prayer of the Greeks: "Sir, we would see Jesus" (John 12:21). If our purpose is to know Christ better and exalt Him more, then whatever differences we may have in our understanding of the book will be forgotten in our worship of Him.

CHAPTER TWO
Hebrews 1:4—2:18
GREATER THAN ANGELS

Angels were most important in the Jewish religion, primarily because thousands of angels assisted in the giving of the law at Mount Sinai. This fact is stated in Deuteronomy 33:2 (where "saints" in KJV means "holy ones" or "angels"); Psalm 68:17; Acts 7:53; and Galatians 3:19. Since the theme of Hebrews is the superiority of Christ and His salvation to the law of Moses, the writer would have to deal with the important subject of angels.

This long section on angels is divided into three sections. First, there is an *affirmation* (Heb. 1:4–14) of the superiority of Christ to the angels. The proof presented consists of seven quotations from the Old Testament. Second, there is an *exhortation* (Heb. 2:1–4) that the readers (and this includes us) pay earnest heed to the Word God has given through His Son. Finally, there is an *explanation* (Heb. 2:5–18) as to how Christ, with a human body, could still be superior to angels, who are spirits.

Affirmation: Christ Is Superior to the Angels (1:4–14)

This section is comprised of seven quotations from the Old Testament, all of which prove the superiority of Christ to the angels. Scholars tell us that the writer quoted from the Greek version of the Hebrew Old Testament, known as the Septuagint. (The word *Septuagint* is a Greek word that means "seventy." Tradition claims that seventy men translated the Hebrew Old Testament into the Greek. The abbreviation for Septuagint is LXX, Roman numerals for seventy.) However, the same Holy Spirit who inspired the Scriptures has the right to quote and restate the truth as He sees fit.

Let us note the affirmations that are made about our Lord Jesus Christ, and the quotations that are cited to support them.

He is the Son (vv. 4–5). The "more excellent name" that Jesus possesses is "Son." While the angels *collectively* may be termed "the sons of God" (Job 1:6), no angel would be given this title *individually.* It belongs uniquely to our Lord Jesus Christ. The first quotation is from Psalm 2:7: "Thou art my Son, this day have I begotten thee." Paul pinpointed the time of this "begetting": the resurrection of Jesus Christ (Acts 13:33). From eternity, Jesus Christ was God the Son. He humbled Himself and became Man (see Phil. 2:5–6). In His resurrection, however, He glorified that humanity received from the Father and received back the eternal glory He had veiled (John 17:1, 5). The resurrection declares, "Jesus is God's Son!" (Rom. 1:4)

The second quotation is from 2 Samuel 7:14. The immediate application in David's experience was to his son, Solomon, whom God would love and discipline as a son (see Ps. 89:27). But the ultimate application is to Jesus Christ, the "greater than Solomon" (Matt. 12:42).

He is the Firstborn who receives worship (v. 6). The term "firstborn" in the Bible does not always mean "born first." God made Solomon the firstborn (Ps. 89:27) even though Solomon is listed *tenth* in the official genealogy (1 Chron. 3:1–5). The title is one of rank and honor, for the firstborn receives the inheritance and the special blessing. Christ is the "Firstborn of all creation" (Col. 1:15 NASB) because He created all things, and He is the highest of all who came back from the dead (Col. 1:18). When He came into the world, the angels worshipped Him (quoted from Deut. 32:43 in the LXX: "Heavens, rejoice with him, let the sons of God pay him homage!"). God commanded them to do so, which proves that Jesus Christ is God, for none of God's angels would worship a mere creature.

He is served by the angels (v. 7). This is a quotation from Psalm 104:4. The Hebrew and Greek words for "spirit" are also translated "wind." Angels are created spirits; they have no bodies, though they can assume human forms when ministering on earth. Angels sometimes served our Lord when He was on earth (Matt. 4:11; Luke 22:43), and they serve Him and us now.

He is God enthroned and anointed (vv. 8–9). In some false cults this quotation from Psalm 45:6–7 is translated, "Thy divine throne," because cultists dislike this strong affirmation that Jesus Christ is God. But the translation must stand: "Thy throne, O God, is forever and ever." Angels minister *before* the throne; they do not *sit* on the throne. One of the main teachings of Psalm 110 is that Jesus Christ, God's Anointed (Messiah, Christ), is now enthroned in glory. Jesus Himself referred to this important psalm (Mark 12:35–37; 14:62), and Peter used it on the day of Pentecost (Acts 2:34–36). Our Lord has not yet entered into His earthly kingdom, but He has been enthroned in glory (Eph. 1:20).

When Christ ascended and entered the heavenly glory, He was anointed for His heavenly ministry with "the oil of gladness" (Heb. 1:9). This probably refers to Psalm 16:11, which Peter referred to at Pentecost: "Thou shalt make me full of joy with thy countenance" (Acts 2:28). What a joyful scene that must have been! Psalm 45 is a wedding psalm, and our Lord today is the heavenly Bridegroom who experiences "the joy that was set before him" (Heb. 12:2). Angels praise Him, but they cannot share that position or that joy. Our Lord's throne is forever, which means He is eternal God.

He is the eternal Creator (vv. 10–12). This long quotation comes from Psalm 102:25–27. The angels did not found the earth, for they too are a part of creation. Jesus Christ is the Creator, and one day He will do away with the old creation and bring in a new creation. Everything around us changes, but He will never change. He is "the same yesterday, and today, and forever" (Heb. 13:8). Creation is like an old garment, which will one day be discarded in favor of a new one.

Christ is the Sovereign; angels are the servants (vv. 13–14). Again, the writer quotes Psalm 110:1. The fact that Jesus Christ is now at the Father's right hand (the place of honor) is mentioned many times in the New Testament (see Matt. 22:43–44; 26:64; Mark 16:19; Acts 2:33–34; Rom. 8:34; Col. 3:1; Heb. 1:3, 13; 8:1; 10:12; 12:2; 1 Peter 3:22). Angels are the ministering spirits who serve the Lord seated on the throne. But they also minister to us who are the "heirs of salvation" through faith in Christ. The angels today are serving us!

It would be impossible to do away with the evidence presented in these quotations. Jesus Christ is greater than the angels, and this means He is also greater than the law, which they helped deliver to the people of Israel.

Admonition: Heed the Word and Don't Drift (2:1–4)

This is the first of the five admonitions found in Hebrews. Their purpose is to encourage all readers to pay attention to God's Word and obey it. We have already noted that these admonitions become stronger as we progress through the book, from *drifting* from God's Word to *defying* God's Word (Heb. 12:14–29). We also noted that God does not sit idly by and permit

His children to rebel against Him. He will continue to speak and, when necessary, He chastens His own.

The admonition is written to believers, for the writer included himself when he wrote "we." The danger here is that of *neglecting our salvation.* Please note that the author did not write "rejecting" but "neglecting." He was not encouraging sinners to become Christians; rather, he was encouraging Christians to pay attention to the great salvation they have received from the Lord.

"Lest … we should let them slip" (Heb. 2:1) might better be translated "lest we drift away from them." Later (Heb. 6:19), the writer used the illustration of an anchor to show how confident we can be in the promises of God. More spiritual problems are caused by neglect than perhaps by any other failure on our part. We neglect God's Word, prayer, worship with God's people (see Heb. 10:25), and other opportunities for spiritual growth, and as a result, we start to drift. The anchor does not move; we do.

During the Old Testament days, people who did not heed the Word were sometimes punished. That Word was given through angels, so how much greater responsibility do we have today who have received the Word from the Son of God! In Hebrews 2:2, "transgression" refers to sins of commission, while "disobedience" suggests sins of omission.

I have often told the story of the pastor who preached a series of sermons on "the sins of the saints." He was reprimanded by a member of the church. "After all," said the member, "sin in the life of a Christian is different from sin in the lives of other people."

"Yes," replied the pastor, "it's worse!"

We have the idea that believers today "under grace" can escape the chastening hand of God that was so evident "under law." But to whom much is given, much shall be required. Not only have we received the Word from the Son of God, but that Word has been confirmed by apostolic miracles (Heb. 2:4). The phrase "signs and wonders" is found eleven times in the New Testament. Here it refers to the miracles that witnessed to the Word and gave confirmation that it was true. These miracles were performed by the apostles (see Mark 16:17–20; Acts 2:43). Today we have the completed Word of God, so there is no need for these apostolic miracles. God now bears witness through His Spirit using the Word (Rom. 8:16; 1 John 5:1–13). The Spirit also gives spiritual gifts to God's people so that they may minister in the church (1 Cor. 12; Eph. 4:1ff.).

Too many Christians today take the Word of God for granted and neglect it. In my pastoral ministry, I have discovered that neglect of the Word of God and prayer, publicly and privately, is the cause of most "spiritual drifting." I need not multiply examples because every believer knows that this is true. He has either experienced this "drifting" or has seen it in the lives of others.

The next time you sing "Come, Thou Fount of Every Blessing," recall that the composer, Robert Robinson, was converted under the mighty preaching of George Whitefield, but that later he drifted from the Lord. He had been greatly used as a pastor, but neglect of spiritual things led him astray. In an attempt to find peace, he began to travel. During one of his journeys, he met a young woman who was evidently very spiritually minded.

"What do you think of this hymn I have been reading?" she asked Robinson, handing him the book. *It was his own hymn!* He tried to avoid her question but it was hopeless, for the Lord was speaking to him. Finally, he broke down and confessed who he was and how he had been living away from the Lord.

"But these 'streams of mercy' are still flowing, " the woman assured him, and through her encouragement, Robinson was restored to fellowship with the Lord.

It is easy to drift with the current, but it is difficult to return against the stream. Our salvation is a "great salvation," purchased at a great price. It brings with it great promises and blessings, and it leads to a great inheritance in glory. How can we neglect it?

Explanation: Why Jesus Christ Is Not Inferior Because of His Humanity (2:5–18)

The fact that angels are "ministering spirits" without human bodies would seem to give them an advantage over Jesus Christ, who had a human body while He ministered on earth. (Today He has a glorified body that knows no limitations.) The writer gave four reasons that explain why our Lord's humanity was neither a handicap nor a mark of inferiority.

His humanity enabled Him to regain man's lost dominion (vv. 5–9). The quotation here is from Psalm 8:4–6, and you will want to read that entire psalm carefully. When God created the first man and woman, He gave them dominion over His creation (Gen. 1:26–31). David marveled that God would share His power and glory with feeble man! Man was created "a little lower than the angels" (and therefore inferior to them), but man was given privileges far higher than the angels. God never promised the angels that they would reign in "the world to come" (Heb. 2:5).

But we have a serious problem here, for it is obvious that man today is *not* exercising dominion over creation. Certainly man cannot control the fish, fowl, or animals. In fact, man has a hard time controlling himself! "But now we see not yet all things put under him" (Heb. 2:8).

"But we see Jesus" (Heb. 2:9)! He is God's answer to man's dilemma. Jesus Christ became man that He might suffer and die for man's sin and restore the dominion that was lost because of sin. When our Lord was here on earth, He exercised that lost dominion. He had dominion over the fish (see Matt. 17:24–27; Luke 5:1–11; John 21:1–11), over the fowl (Luke 22:34, 60), and over the wild beasts (Mark 1:12–13), and the domesticated beasts (Mark 11:1–7). As the last Adam (1 Cor. 15:45), Jesus Christ regained man's lost dominion. Today, everything is under His feet (Eph. 1:20–23).

Man was "crowned … with glory and honor" (Heb. 2:7 NASB), but he lost his crown and became the slave of sin. Jesus Christ has regained that "glory and honor" (Heb. 2:9), and believers today share His kingly dominion (Rev. 1:5–6). One day, when He establishes His kingdom, we shall reign with Him in glory and honor. Jesus Christ did all of this for us—for lost sinners—because of "the grace of God" (Heb. 2:9). If He had not become man, He could not have died and "taste[d] death [experienced death] for every man" (Heb. 2:9). It is true that angels cannot die, but it is also true that angels cannot save lost sinners and restore man's lost dominion.

His humanity enabled Him to bring many sons to glory (vv. 10–13). Christ is not only the Last Adam, but He is also the Captain of salvation. That word *Captain* literally means "pioneer—one who opens the way for others to follow." Christ gave up His glory to become man. He regained His glory when He arose and ascended to heaven. Now He shares that glory with all who trust Him for salvation (John 17:22–24). He is bringing many sons and daughters to glory!

Christ is united to us, and we are united to Him: we are spiritually one. In fact, we are His "brethren" (Heb. 2:12). The writer quoted Psalm 22:22—a messianic psalm—in which Christ refers to His church as His brethren. This means we and the Son of God share the same nature and belong to the same family! What a marvel of God's grace!

The writer of Hebrews also quoted Isaiah 8:17–18 from the LXX. The immediate reference, of course, is to the prophet Isaiah and his unique sons who were given significant names (see Isa. 7:3; 8:1–4). But the ultimate reference is to Jesus Christ. Not only are believers His brethren, but we are also His children: "Behold I and the children which God hath given me" (Heb. 2:13). If Jesus Christ had not come to earth and become man, He could not take us from earth to share in His glory. The incarnation, crucifixion, and resurrection must go together. They all lead to glory.

One phrase in Hebrews 2:10 ought to be discussed before we move on: "Make the captain of their salvation perfect through sufferings." This statement does not suggest that Jesus Christ was imperfect when He was here on earth. The word translated "perfect" means "complete, effective, adequate." Jesus could not have become an adequate Savior and High Priest had He not become Man and suffered and died.

His humanity enabled Him to disarm Satan and deliver us from death (vv. 14–16). Angels cannot die. Jesus did not come to save angels (note Heb. 2:16); He came to save humans. This meant that He had to take on Himself flesh and blood and become a Man. Only then could He die and through His death defeat Satan. The word *destroy* does not mean "annihilate," for it is obvious that Satan is still alive and busy. The

word means "render inoperative, make of none effect." Satan is not destroyed, but he is disarmed.

In what sense did Satan have the power of death? The final authority of death is in the hands of our God (Deut. 32:39; Matt. 10:28; Rev. 1:18). Satan can do only that which is permitted by God (Job 1:12; 2:6). But because Satan is the author of sin (John 8:44), and sin brings death (Rom. 6:23), in this sense Satan exercises power in the realm of death. Jesus called him a murderer (John 8:44). Satan uses the fear of death as a terrible weapon to gain control over the lives of people. His kingdom is one of darkness and death (Col. 1:13). We who trust in Jesus Christ have once and for all been delivered from Satan's authority and from the terrible fear of death. The death, burial, and resurrection of Christ have given us victory (1 Cor. 15:55–58)!

Jesus Christ did not take on Himself the nature of angels in order to save the fallen angels (2 Peter 2:4; Rev. 12:7–9). Instead, He stooped lower than the angels to become Man! And not just "man" in general; but He became a Jew, a part of the "seed of Abraham" (Heb. 2:16). The Jews were a despised and hated race, and yet our Lord became a Jew.

His humanity enables Him to be a sympathetic High Priest to His people (vv. 17–18). Being pure spirits who have never suffered, the angels cannot identify with us in our weaknesses and needs. But Jesus can! While He was here on earth, Jesus was "made like unto his brethren" in that He experienced the sinless infirmities of human nature. He knew what it was to be a helpless baby, a growing child, a maturing adolescent. He knew the experiences of weariness, hunger, and thirst (John 4:6–8). He knew what it was to be despised and rejected, to be lied about and falsely accused. He experienced physical suffering and death. All of this was a part of His "training" for His heavenly ministry as High Priest.

If you want an example of a man who was *not* a merciful and faithful high priest, then read the account about Eli (1 Sam. 2:27–36). Here was a high priest who did not even lead his own sons into a faithful walk with God. Eli even accused brokenhearted Hannah of being drunk (1 Sam. 1:9–18)!

Jesus Christ is both merciful and faithful: He is merciful toward people and faithful toward God. He can never fail in His priestly ministries. He made the necessary sacrifice for our sins so that we might be reconciled to God. He did not need to make a sacrifice for Himself, because He is sinless.

But what happens when we who have been saved are tempted to sin? He stands ready to help us! He was tempted when He was on earth, but no temptation ever conquered Him. Because He has defeated every enemy, He is able to give us the grace that we need to overcome temptation. The word *succour* (Heb. 2:18) literally means "to run to the cry of a child." It means "to bring help when it is needed." Angels are able to *serve* us (Heb. 1; 14), but they are not able to *succour* us in our times of temptation. Only Jesus Christ can do that, and He can do it because He became a man and suffered and died.

It might be good at this point to explain the difference between our Lord's ministry as High Priest and His ministry as Advocate (1 John 2:1). As our High Priest, our Lord is able to give us grace to keep us from sinning when we are tempted. If we do sin, then He as our Advocate represents us before the throne of God and forgives us when we sincerely confess our sins to Him (1 John 1:5—2:2). Both of these ministries are involved in His present work of intercession, and it is this intercessory ministry that is the guarantee of our eternal salvation (note that in Heb. 7:25 it is *"to* the uttermost"—i.e., eternally—and not *"from* the uttermost").

As you review this section, you cannot help but be amazed at the grace and wisdom of God. From a human point of view, it would seem foolish for God to become Man, yet it was this very act of grace that made possible our salvation and all that goes with it. When Jesus Christ became Man, He did not become inferior to the angels, for in His human body He accomplished something that angels could never accomplish. At the same time, He made it possible for us to share in His glory!

He is not ashamed to call us His brothers and sisters. Are we ashamed to call Him "Lord"?

CHAPTER THREE
Hebrews 3:1—4:13
GREATER THAN MOSES

Next to Abraham, Moses was undoubtedly the man most greatly revered by the Jewish people. To go back to the law meant to go back to Moses, and the recipients of this letter to the Hebrews were sorely tempted to do just that. It was important that the writer convince his readers that Jesus Christ is greater than Moses, for the entire system of Jewish religion came through Moses. In this section, we learn that Jesus Christ is superior to Moses in at least three respects.

Christ Is Greater in His Person (3:1–2)
The twofold description of the readers makes it clear that they were converted people. "Holy brethren" could only be applied to people in the family of God, set apart by the grace of God. That the writer was referring to people in the church, the body of Christ, is clear from his use of the phrase "partakers of the heavenly calling." No unconverted Jew or Gentile could ever claim that blessing! The word translated "partakers" here is translated "partners" in Luke 5:7, where it describes the relationship of four men in the fishing business: they were in it together.

True Christians not only share in a heavenly calling, but they also share in Jesus Christ (Heb. 3:14).

Through the Holy Spirit, we are "members of his body, of his flesh, and of his bones" (Eph. 5:30). True believers are also "partakers of the Holy Spirit" (Heb. 6:4). "Now if any man have not the Spirit of Christ, he is none of his" (Rom. 8:9). Because we are God's children, we also partake in God's loving chastening (Heb. 12:8). Not to be chastened is evidence that a person is not one of God's children.

Because these people were holy brothers and sisters, and partakers of a heavenly calling, they were able to give a "confession" of their faith in Jesus Christ. The word simply means "to say the same thing." All true Christians "say the same thing" when it comes to their experience of salvation. Twice in this epistle, the writer exhorted the readers to hold fast to this confession (Heb. 4:14; 10:23 NASB). It was this same confession that they were "strangers and pilgrims" on the earth that characterized men and women of faith in the ages past (Heb. 11:13).

It was not Moses who did all of this for the people addressed in this epistle; it was Jesus Christ! The writer did not exhort them to consider Moses, but to consider Christ. The word means "to consider *carefully,* to understand fully." This is no quick glance at Jesus Christ! It is a careful consideration of who He is and what He has done.

That Christ is superior to Moses in His person is an obvious fact. Moses was a mere man, called to be a prophet and leader, while Jesus Christ is the Son of God sent by the Father into the world. The title *apostle* means "one sent with a commission." Moses was called and commissioned by God, but Jesus Christ was *sent* as God's "last Word" to sinful man. You may want to read some of the verses in the gospel of John where Jesus is referred to as "sent from God" (John 3:17, 34; 5:36, 38; 6:29, 57; 7:29; 8:42; 10:36; 11:42; 17:3; and note also 13:3).

Jesus Christ is not only the Apostle, but He is also the High Priest. Moses was a prophet who on occasion served as a priest (see Ps. 99:6), but he was never a high priest. That title belonged to his brother Aaron. In fact, Jesus Christ has the title "great High Priest" (Heb. 4:14).

As the Apostle, Jesus Christ represented God to men, and as the High Priest, He now represents men to God in heaven. Moses, of course, fulfilled similar ministries, for he taught Israel God's truth and he prayed for Israel when he met God on the mount (see Ex. 32:30–32). Moses was primarily the prophet of law, while Jesus Christ is the Messenger of God's grace (see John 1:17). Moses helped prepare the way for the coming of the Savior to the earth.

However, the writer of Hebrews noted that Moses and Jesus Christ were *both* faithful in the work God gave them to do. Moses was not sinless, as was Jesus Christ, but he was faithful and obeyed God's will (Num. 12:7). This would be an encouragement to those first-century Jewish believers to remain faithful to Christ, even in the midst of the tough trials they were experiencing. Instead of going back to Moses, they should *imitate* Moses and be faithful in their calling.

Christ Is Greater in His Ministry (3:3–6)

The word *house* is used six times in these verses. It refers to the people of God, not to a material building. Moses ministered to Israel, the people of God under the old covenant. Today, Christ ministers to His church, the people of God under the new covenant ("whose house are we," Heb. 3:6). You find an illustration of this dual use of "house" in 2 Samuel 7. David wanted to build a temple for God, a house in which God could dwell. But God told David that He would build David's house (household, family) and make a covenant with David's descendants.

The contrast between Moses and Christ is clear: Moses was a *servant in the house,* while Jesus Christ is a *Son over the house.* Moses was a member of the household, but Jesus *built* the house! By the way, the truth in these verses is a powerful argument for the deity of Jesus Christ. If God built all things, and Jesus Christ built God's house, then Jesus Christ must be God.

There is another factor in Christ's superiority over Moses: the prophet Moses spoke about things to come, but Jesus Christ brought the fulfillment of these things (Heb. 3:6). Moses ministered "in the shadows," as it were (see Heb. 8:5 and 10:1), while Jesus Christ brought the full and final light of the gospel of the grace of God.

The Greek word translated "servant" (Heb. 3:5) is not the usual New Testament word for servant or slave. This word carries the meaning of "a voluntary servant who acts because of affection." In the New Testament, it is used only of Moses. At the beginning of his ministry, Moses was a bit hesitant and resisted God's call. But once he surrendered, he obeyed out of a heart of love and devotion.

The "if" clause (Heb. 3:6) needs to be understood in the light of the total context, which is Moses leading Israel out of Egypt and to the Promised Land. The writer is not suggesting that we, as Christians, must keep ourselves saved. This would contradict the major theme of the book, which is the finished work of Christ and His heavenly ministry guaranteeing our eternal salvation (Heb. 7:14ff.). Rather, the writer was affirming that those who hold fast their confidence and hope are proving that they are truly born again.

The word *confidence* literally means "freedom of speech, openness." When you are free to speak, then there is no fear and you have confidence. A believer can come with boldness (same word as "confidence") to the throne of grace (Heb. 4:16) with openness and freedom and not be afraid. We have this boldness because of the shed blood of Jesus Christ (Heb. 10:19). Therefore, we should not cast away our confidence, no matter what the circumstances might be. We should not have confidence in ourselves, because we are too prone to fail; but we should have confidence in Jesus Christ who never fails.

Because of this confidence in Christ and this confession of Christ, we can experience joy and hope (Heb. 3:6). The writer exhorted these suffering saints to *enjoy* their spiritual experience and not simply *endure* it. Jesus Christ is the beloved Son over His house, and He will care for each member of the family. He is the faithful High Priest who provides all the grace we need for each demand of life. As the Great Shepherd of the sheep (Heb. 13:19–20), Jesus Christ is using the experiences in His people's lives to equip them for service that will glorify His name.

In other words, those who have trusted Christ *prove* this confession by their steadfastness, confidence, and joyful hope. They are not burdened by the past or threatened by the present, but are "living in the future tense" as they await the "blessed hope" of their Lord's return. It is this "heavenly calling" that motivates the believers to keep on living for the Savior even when the going is tough.

The wandering of Israel in the wilderness is a major topic in this section. Two men in that nation—Caleb and Joshua—illustrate the attitude described in Hebrews 3:6. Everybody else in Israel over the age of twenty was to die in the wilderness and never enter the Promised Land (see Num. 14:26–38). But Caleb and Joshua believed God and God honored their faith. For forty years, Caleb and Joshua watched their friends and relatives die, but those two men of faith had confidence in God's Word that they would one day enter Canaan. While others were experiencing sorrow and death, Caleb and Joshua rejoiced in confident hope. As believers, we know that God is taking us to heaven, and we should reveal the same kind of joyful confidence and hope.

Christ Is Greater in the Rest He Gives (3:7—4:13)

This long section is the second of the five exhortations in this epistle. In the first exhortation (Heb. 2:1–4), the writer pointed out the danger of *drifting* from the Word because of neglect. In this exhortation, he explained the danger of *doubting* and *disbelieving* the Word because of hardness of heart. It is important that we understand the background of this section, which is the exodus of Israel from Egypt and their experiences of unbelief in the wilderness.

To begin with, we must understand that there are spiritual lessons in the geography of Israel's experiences. The nation's bondage in Egypt is an illustration of a sinner's bondage in this world. Much as Israel was delivered from Egypt by the blood of lambs and the power of God, so a sinner who believes on Christ is delivered from the bondage of sin (Col. 1:13–14). Jesus Christ is "the Lamb of God" whose death and resurrection have made our deliverance from sin a reality.

It was not God's will that Israel remain either in Egypt or in the wilderness. His desire was that the people enter their glorious inheritance in the land of Canaan. But when Israel got to the border of their inheritance, they delayed because they doubted the promise of God (Num. 13—14). "We are not able" wept the ten spies and the people. "We *are* able with God's help!" said Moses, Joshua, and Caleb. Because the people went backward in unbelief instead of forward by faith, they missed their inheritance and died in the wilderness. It was the new generation that possessed the land and entered into their rest.

What does Canaan represent to us as Christians today? It represents our spiritual inheritance in Christ (Eph. 1:3, 11, 15–23). It is unfortunate that some of our hymns and gospel songs use Canaan as a picture of heaven, and "crossing the Jordan" as a picture of death. Since Canaan was a place of battles, and even of defeats, it is not a good illustration of heaven! Israel had to cross the river by faith (a picture of the believer as he dies to self and the world, Rom. 6) and claim the inheritance by faith. They had to "step out by faith" (Josh. 1:3) and claim the land for themselves, just as believers today must do.

Now we can understand what the wilderness wanderings represent: the experiences of believers who will not claim their spiritual inheritance in Christ, who doubt God's Word and live in restless unbelief. To be sure, God is with them, as He was with Israel, but they do not enjoy the fullness of God's blessing. They are "out of Egypt" but they are not yet "in Canaan."

With this background, we can now better understand one of the key words in this section—*rest* (Heb. 3:11, 18; 4:1, 3–5, 8–11). The writer mentioned two different "rests" found in Old Testament history: (1) *God's Sabbath rest,* when He ceased from His creation activities (Gen. 2:2; Heb. 4:4); (2) *Israel's rest in Canaan* (Deut. 12:9; Josh. 21:43–45; Heb. 3:11). But he saw in these "rests" illustrations of the spiritual experiences of believers today. The Sabbath rest is a picture of our rest in Christ through salvation (Heb. 4:3; see Matt. 11:28). The Canaan rest is a picture of our present rest as we claim our inheritance in Christ (Heb. 4:11–13; note the emphasis on the Word of God). The first is the rest of salvation; the second is the rest of submission.

But there is a third rest that enters into the discussion, that *future rest* that all believers will enjoy with God. "There remaineth, therefore, a rest to the people of God" (Heb. 4:9). This word for rest is the Greek word *sabbatismos*—"a keeping of a Sabbath"—and this is the only place in the New Testament where this word is used. When the saints enter heaven, it will be like sharing God's great Sabbath rest, with all labors and battles ended (Rev. 14:13).

We may diagram these rests in this way:

Past	*Present*	*Future*
God's Sabbath rest	Salvation rest	Heaven
Israel's Canaan rest	Submission rest	(victory in Christ)

With this background of Israel's history and the "rests" involved, we may now examine the passage itself. The writer gave a threefold admonition.

Let us take heed (3:7–19). Take heed to what? To the sad history of the nation of Israel and the important lesson it teaches. The writer quoted from Psalm 95:7–11, which records God's response to Israel's tragic spiritual condition. God had delivered His people from Egypt and had cared for them, revealing His power in many signs and wonders. Israel saw all of this and benefited from it, but the experience did not bring them closer to God or make them trust Him more. All that God did for them did not benefit them spiritually. In fact, just the opposite took place: they hardened their hearts against God! They put God to the test and He did not fail them, yet they failed Him.

The heart of every problem is a problem in the heart. The people of Israel (except Moses, Joshua, and Caleb) erred in their hearts (Heb. 3:10), which means that their hearts wandered from God and His Word. They also had evil hearts of unbelief (Heb. 3:12); they did not believe that God would give them victory in Canaan. They had seen God perform great signs in Egypt. Yet they doubted He was adequate for the challenge of Canaan.

When a person has an erring heart and a disbelieving heart, the result will also be a hard heart. This is a heart that is insensitive to the Word and work of God. So hard was the heart of Israel that the people even wanted to return to Egypt! Imagine wanting to exchange their freedom under God for slavery in Egypt! Of course, all this history spoke to the hearts of the readers of this letter because they were in danger of "going back" themselves.

God's judgment fell on Israel in the wilderness at Kadesh Barnea. That entire generation was condemned to die, and only the new generation would enter the land. God said, "They shall not enter into my rest" (Heb. 3:11). But what message does this bring to a believer today? No believer today, Jew or Gentile, could go back into the Mosaic legal system since the temple is gone and there is no priesthood. But every believer is tempted to give up his confession of Christ and go back into the world system's life of compromise and bondage. This is especially true during times of persecution and suffering. The fires of persecution have always purified the church because suffering separates true believers from the counterfeit. True believers are willing to suffer for Christ, and they hold firmly to their convictions and their confession of faith (see Heb. 3:6, 14). We are not saved by holding to our confession. The fact that we hold to our confession is proof that we are God's true children.

It is important that we take heed and recognize the spiritual dangers that exist. But it is also important that we encourage each other to be faithful to the Lord (Heb. 3:13). We get the impression that some of these believers addressed were careless about their fellowship in the local assembly (see Heb. 10:23–25). Christians belong to each other and need each other. Moses,

Caleb, and Joshua did try to encourage Israel when the nation refused to enter Canaan, but the people would not listen.

It is clear from this section that God was grieved with Israel during the entire forty years they wandered in the wilderness. The Jews had not been out of Egypt long when they began to provoke God (Ex. 16:1ff.). After He supplied bread for them, they complained about a lack of water (Ex. 17:1–7). Moses called that place "Massah and Meribah," which means "provocation and trial." These same words are used in Hebrews 3:10.

The sin of Israel is stated in Hebrews 3:12—"departing from the living God." The Greek word gives us our English word *apostasy*. This is the only place this word is used in Hebrews. Does "apostasy" mean abandoning one's faith and therefore being condemned forever? That does not fit into this context. Israel departed from the living God by refusing God's will for their lives and stubbornly wanting to go their own way back to Egypt. God did not permit them to return to Egypt. Rather, He disciplined them in the wilderness. God did not allow His people to return to bondage.

The emphasis in Hebrews is that true believers have an eternal salvation because they trust a living Savior who constantly intercedes for them. But the writer was careful to point out that this confidence is no excuse for sin. God disciplines His children. Remember that Canaan is not a picture of heaven, but of the believer's present spiritual inheritance in Christ. Believers who doubt God's Word and rebel against Him do not miss heaven, but they do miss out on the blessings of their inheritance today, and they must suffer the chastening of God.

Let us fear (4:1–8). Believers today may enter and enjoy their spiritual inheritance in Christ. We must be careful lest we fail to believe God's Word, for it is only as the Word is "mixed with faith" that it can accomplish its purposes. The argument in this section is given in several propositions: (1) God finished His work and rested, so that His rest has been available since Creation; (2) the Jews failed to enter into their rest; (3) many years later (Ps. 95), God said that a rest was still available. That "today" is still here! This means that Joshua did not lead Israel into the true rest, because a rest still remains. (Note that the name "Jesus" in Heb. 4:8 KJV, ought to be "Joshua." "Jesus" is the Greek form of "Joshua.")

The Canaan rest for Israel is a picture of the spiritual rest we find in Christ when we surrender to Him. When we come to Christ by faith, we find salvation rest (Matt. 11:28). When we yield and learn of Him and obey Him by faith, we enjoy submission rest (Matt. 11:29–30). The first is "peace with God" (Rom. 5:1); the second is the "peace of God" (Phil. 4:6–8). It is by believing that we enter into rest (Heb. 4:3); it is by obeying God by faith and surrendering to His will that the rest enters into us.

Let us labor (4:9–13). "Give diligence" is a

good translation of this admonition. Diligence is the opposite of "drifting" (Heb. 2:1–3). How do we give diligence? By paying close attention to the Word of God. Israel did not believe God's Word, so the rebels fell in the wilderness. "So then faith cometh by hearing, and hearing by the word of God" (Rom. 10:17).

In comparing the Word of God to a sword, the writer was not suggesting that God uses His Word to slaughter the saints! It is true that the Word cuts the heart of sinners with conviction (Acts 5:33; 7:54), and that the Word defeats Satan (Eph. 6:17). The Greek word translated "sword" means "a short sword or dagger." The emphasis is on the power of the Word to penetrate and expose the inner heart of man. The Word is a "discerner" or "critic." The Israelites criticized God's Word instead of allowing the Word to judge them. Consequently, they lost their inheritance.

Of course, God sees our hearts (Heb. 4:13), but we do not always know what is there (Jer. 17:9). God uses the Word to enable us to see the sin and unbelief in our own hearts. The Word exposes our hearts, and then, if we trust God, the Word enables our hearts to obey God and claim His promises. This is why each believer should be diligent to apply himself to hear and heed God's Word. In the Word we see God, and we also see how God sees us. We see ourselves as we really are. This experience enables us to be honest with God, to trust His will, and to obey Him.

All of this is possible because of the finished work of Jesus Christ. (The two "he's" in Heb. 4:10 refer to Jesus Christ.) God rested when He finished the work of creation. God's Son rested when He completed the work of the new creation. We may enter into His rest by trusting His Word and obeying His will. We can do this as we listen to His Word, understand it, trust it, and obey it. Only in this way can we claim our inheritance in Christ.

Before Joshua conquered Jericho, he went out to survey the situation, and he met the Lord Jesus Christ (Josh. 5:13–15). Joshua discovered that he was second in command! The Lord had a sword in His hand, and Joshua fell at His feet in complete submission. It was this action in private that gave Joshua his public victory.

We too claim our spiritual inheritance by surrendering to Him and trusting His Word. We must beware of an evil heart of unbelief.

CHAPTER FOUR
Hebrews 4:14—5:10
GREATER THAN AARON THE HIGH PRIEST

Moses did not lead the people of Israel into the promised rest; in fact, he himself was forbidden to enter the land. Joshua led them into their *physical* rest, but not into the promised *spiritual* rest (see Heb. 4:8). But what about Aaron, the first high priest? Is it possible that the Aaronic priesthood, with all of its sacrifices and ceremonies, could bring a troubled soul into rest?

The Hebrew Christians who received this letter were sorely tempted to return to the religion of their fathers. After all, any Jew could travel to Jerusalem and *see* the temple and the priests ministering at the altar. Here was something real, visible, concrete. When a person is going through persecution, as these Hebrew Christians were, it is much easier to walk by sight than by faith. Some of us have doubted the Lord under much less provocation than these people were enduring.

The central theme of Hebrews is the priesthood of Jesus Christ, what He is now doing in heaven on behalf of His people. Is the high priestly ministry of Christ superior to that of Aaron and his successors? Yes, it is, and the writer proves his assertion by presenting four arguments.

Jesus Christ Has a Superior Title (Heb. 4:14–16)

"Seeing then that we have a GREAT High Priest" (Heb. 4:14, emphasis mine). Aaron was a "high priest," but Jesus Christ is the GREAT High Priest. No Old Testament priest could assume that title. But in what does our Lord's greatness consist?

To begin with, Jesus Christ is both God and Man. He is "Jesus, the Son of God." The name "Jesus" means "Savior" and identifies His humanity and His ministry on earth. "Son of God" affirms His deity and the fact that He is God. In His unique person, Jesus Christ unites Deity and humanity, so that He can bring people to God and bring to people all that God has for them.

Not only in His *person,* but also in His *position* Jesus Christ is great. Aaron and his successors ministered in the tabernacle and temple precincts, once a year entering the Holy of Holies. But Jesus Christ has "passed through the heavens" (Heb. 4:14, literal translation). When He ascended to the Father, Jesus Christ passed through the atmospheric heavens and the planetary heavens into the third heaven where God dwells (2 Cor. 12:2). How much better is it to have a High Priest who ministers in a heavenly tabernacle than in an earthly one!

But there is another aspect to Christ's position: not only is He in heaven, but He is *enthroned.* His throne is "the throne of grace" (Heb. 4:16). The mercy seat on the ark of the covenant was God's throne in Israel (Ex. 25:17–22), but it could never be called "a throne of grace." Grace does not veil itself from the people. Grace does not hide itself in a tent.

Furthermore, the common people were not permitted to enter the holy precincts of the tabernacle and the temple, and the priests got only as far as the veil. The high priest alone went beyond the veil, and only on the day of Atonement (Lev. 16). But *every believer* in Christ is invited, and is even encouraged, to "come boldly unto the throne of grace"! What a great throne it is because our Great High Priest is ministering there.

Jesus Christ, our Great High Priest, is enthroned in heaven. Something else makes Him great: He is ministering mercy and grace to those who come for help. *Mercy* means that God does not give us what we do deserve; *grace* means that He gives us what we do not deserve. No Old Testament high priest could minister mercy and grace in quite the same way. When an Israelite was tempted, he could not easily run to the high priest for help, and he certainly could not enter the Holy of Holies for God's help. But as believers in Jesus Christ, we can run to our High Priest at any time, in any circumstance, and find the help that we need.

Now because of the superiority of Jesus Christ, the Great High Priest, over Aaron, two important conclusions can be drawn. First, there is no need in giving up our profession just because we are going through testing and trial (Heb. 4:14). The word translated "profession" means "confession." These Hebrew Christians were tempted to give up their confession of faith in Christ and their confidence in Him (see Heb. 3:6, 14). It was not a matter of giving up their salvation, since salvation through Christ is eternal (Heb. 5:9). It was a matter of their public confession of faith. By returning to the Old Testament system, they would be telling everyone that they had no faith in Christ (see Gal. 2:11–21). This kind of unbelief would only bring reproach to Christ's name.

After all, the great purpose of salvation is the glory of God (see Eph. 1:6, 12, 14). It was the glory of God that so concerned Moses when Israel broke God's law and made the golden calf (Ex. 32). God offered to destroy the nation and to begin a new one from Moses, but Moses refused the offer. Instead Moses interceded for Israel on the basis of God's glory and God's promise, and God spared the people, even though He disciplined them for their sin (Ex. 32:11–13).

The second conclusion is this: there is no need to go back because we can come boldly into the presence of God and get the help we need (Heb. 4:16). No trial is too great, no temptation is too strong, but that Jesus Christ can give us the mercy and grace that we need, when we need it. "But He is so far away!" we may argue. "And He is the perfect Son of God! What can He know about the problems of weak sinners like us?"

But that is a part of His greatness! When He was ministering on earth in a human body, He experienced all that we experience, *and even more.* After all, a sinless person would feel temptations and trials in a much greater way than you and I could ever feel them. Christ was tempted, yet He did not sin, and He is able to help us when we are tempted. If we fail to hold fast our confession, we are not proving that Jesus Christ has failed. We are only telling the world that *we failed* to draw on His grace and mercy when it was freely available to us.

Jesus Christ Has a Superior Ordination (5:1, 4–6)

When I became pastor of the Calvary Baptist Church in Covington, Kentucky, it was necessary for me to go to the city hall and be bonded. Otherwise, I would not have the authority to perform marriages. I had to show my ordination certificate and prove that I was indeed ministering at the church.

One day I received a frantic phone call from one of our members. Some Christian friends were being married the next day by a relative from Michigan, and they discovered that he was not authorized to perform the ceremony! Could I help them? The visiting pastor could read the ceremony as well as I could, and he knew the couple better than I did, but he lacked the authority to minister.

No man could appoint himself as a priest, let alone as *high* priest. King Saul invaded the priesthood and lost his kingdom (1 Sam. 13). Korah and his fellow rebels tried to make themselves priests, and God judged them (Num. 16). When King Uzziah tried to enter the temple and burn incense, God smote him with leprosy (2 Chron. 26:16–21).

Aaron was chosen by God to be the high priest, and he was duly ordained and installed in office (Ex. 28). He was chosen *from* men to minister *for* men. His main task was at the altar: to offer the sacrifices God had appointed (see Heb. 8:3–4; 9:14). Unless the sacrifices were offered in the right place, by the right person, they were not accepted by God.

The very existence of a priesthood and a system of sacrifices gave evidence that man is estranged from God. It was an act of grace on God's part that He instituted the whole Levitical system. Today, that system is fulfilled in the ministry of Jesus Christ. He is both the sacrifice and the High Priest who ministers to God's people on the basis of His once-for-all offering on the cross.

The subject of ordination stated in Hebrews 5:1 is further developed in Hebrews 5:5–6. Jesus Christ did not appoint Himself as High Priest. He was appointed by God the Father. The quotation in Hebrews 5:5 is from Psalm 2:7. This psalm was already quoted in Hebrews 1:5 to prove that Jesus Christ is the Son of God. But the emphasis in Hebrews 5:5 is on the priesthood of Jesus Christ not on His deity. What significance, then, does this quotation have for the argument?

The answer to that question is in Acts 13:33–34, where the apostle Paul quoted Psalm 2:7 and explained what it means. The phrase, "Today have I begotten thee," does not refer to the birth of Christ at Bethlehem, but to *His resurrection from the dead*. The Son of God was "begotten" into a glorious new life in His resurrection! He ascended to heaven in a glorified body to become our High Priest at the throne of grace. When Aaron was ordained to the priesthood, he offered the sacrifices of animals. But Jesus Christ, to become our High Priest, offered the sacrifice of Himself—and then arose from the dead!

But God the Father not only said, "Thou art my Son" in Psalm 2:7; He also said, "Thou art a priest forever after the order of Melchizedek" (Heb. 5:6, quoted from Ps. 110:4). This psalm was also quoted earlier in Hebrews (1:13) to affirm Jesus Christ's final victory over all His enemies. When Aaron was ordained, God did not speak directly to him and declare his priesthood. But the Father did make this special declaration concerning His Son.

Two factors make Christ's priesthood unique and, therefore, His ordination greater. First, He is a High Priest *forever*. No Old Testament priest ministered forever, because each priest died and relinquished the office to his successor. The word *forever* is an important one in this epistle. At least six times the writer affirmed that Christ's high priesthood is forever (Heb. 5:6; 6:20; 7:17, 21, 24, 28). And, since He is a Priest forever, He gives His people salvation forever (Heb. 7:23–28).

The second factor that makes Christ's ordination unique is that He belongs to a *different order* from the Old Testament priests. They belonged to the order of Aaron; He belongs to the order of Melchizedek. This is a key concept in Hebrews, so we must take time to examine and understand it.

Melchizedek is mentioned in only two places in the entire Old Testament—Genesis 14:17–24 and Psalm 110:4. His name means "King of Righteousness," and he was also "King of Salem [peace]." But the fascinating thing about Melchizedek is that he was *both a priest and a king!* King Uzziah wanted to be both a priest and a king, and God judged him. Only in Jesus Christ and in pre-law Melchizedek were these two offices combined. Jesus Christ is a High Priest *on a throne!*

The reason Jesus Christ can be "a priest forever" is that He belongs to the "order of Melchizedek." As far as the Old Testament record is concerned, Melchizedek did not die (see Heb. 7:1–3). Of course, because he was a real man, he did die at some time, but the record is not given to us. So Melchizedek becomes a picture of our Lord Jesus Christ who is a *Priest* forever.

But Melchizedek also pictures our Lord as a *heavenly* High Priest. Jesus Christ could never have served as a priest when He was on earth because He did not belong to the tribe of Levi. Jesus was born of the seed of David, the tribe of Judah. He became the sacrifice on earth that He might become the High Priest in heaven. All of these truths will be developed in Hebrews 7—10, but they are introduced here.

Jesus Christ Reveals a Superior Sympathy (5:2, 7–8)

Every Old Testament high priest had to minister to people who were "ignorant, and… out of the way [wayward]" (Heb. 5:2). God made no provision but judgment for high-handed sins of rebellion (see Ex. 21:12–14; Num. 15:27–31). But He did make provision when people sinned through ignorance or weakness. An Old Testament priest could identify with the sinners, since he himself was a sinner. In fact, on the day of Atonement, the high priest had to offer a sacrifice *for himself* before he could offer one for the nation (Lev. 16; Heb. 9:7)!

You would think that one sinner would have

compassion for another sinner, but this is not always the case. Sin makes a person selfish. Sin can blind us to the hurts of others. Sin can harden our hearts and make us judgmental instead of sympathetic. Remember how heartbroken Hannah, who was praying for a son, was accused by high priest Eli of being drunk (1 Sam. 1:9–18)? And when King David was confronted with a story of a rich man's sin, he had no sympathy for him, even though David himself was a worse sinner (2 Sam. 12).

No, it is the spiritually minded person with a clean heart who sympathizes with a sinner and seeks to help him (see Gal. 6:1). Because we are so sinful, we have a hard time helping other sinners, but because Jesus is perfect, He is able to meet our needs after we sin.

Our Lord was prepared for His high priestly ministry during His days of ministry on earth (Heb. 5:7–8). The phrase "to the days of his flesh" means "In the days when He was on earth in a human body." From birth to death, our Lord experienced the sinless infirmities of human nature. He knew what it was to grow and mature (Luke 2:52). He experienced hunger and thirst, as well as weariness (John 4:6–8, 31). He also faced temptations to sin (Matt. 4:1–11) and persecutions from the hands of sinful men.

How could the Son of God "learn obedience"? In the same way any son must learn obedience: by the experiences of life. We must remember that our Lord, in His earthly walk, lived by faith in the Father's will. As God, He needed to learn nothing. But as the Son of God come in human flesh He had to experience that which His people would experience, so that He might be able to minister as their High Priest. He did not need to learn *how to* obey because it would be impossible for God to be disobedient. Rather, as the God-Man in human flesh, He had to learn what was involved in obedience. In this way, He identified with us.

This preparation involved the experience of death. The writer of Hebrews (5:7) focused on our Lord's experience in the garden of Gethsemane (Matt. 26:36–46). As He faced the cross, it was not the physical suffering that burdened Jesus, but the fact that He would be made sin and separated from His Father. Other servants of God have faced death and not expressed such great emotion; but no other servant ever bore on his body the sins of the whole world.

In His Gethsemane prayer, our Lord did not oppose the Father, but prayed, "Not my will, but thine, be done" (Luke 22:42). He was not praying to be spared *from* death, but to be saved *out of death.* He was praying for resurrection from the dead, and God answered that prayer. He had prophesied His own death and had made it clear that He was laying down His life of His own free will. This ties in with the quotation from Psalm 2:7, cited in Hebrews 5:5, that promised His resurrection from the dead.

The writer of Hebrews states that Jesus' prayer "was heard" (Heb. 5:7), that is, answered by the Father. Since He *did* die on the cross, this could not have been what He was praying about; for if the Father had answered, the Son would not have been crucified. He did not pray to be saved *from* death, but *out of death,* and God answered His prayer by raising Him from the dead.

No one else ever died the kind of death that Jesus died. He was made sin for us (2 Cor. 5:21; 1 Peter 2:24). Men have died because of their own sins, but only Jesus died for the sins of a whole world. He experienced the ultimate in suffering and, therefore, He is able to sympathize with His people when they are suffering. The readers of this epistle were going through difficult times, but they had "not yet resisted unto blood" (Heb. 12:4). Their goods had been seized and they had been ridiculed (Heb. 10:32–34), but they had not been crucified and forsaken by the Father.

No matter what trials we meet, Jesus Christ is able to understand our needs and help us. We need never doubt His ability to sympathize and strengthen. It is also worth noting that sometimes God puts us through difficulties that we might better understand the needs of others, and become able to encourage them (see 2 Cor. 1:8ff.).

When Charles Haddon Spurgeon was a young preacher in London, his successful ministry aroused the envy of some of the clergy, and they attacked him with various kinds of slander and gossip. His sermons were called "trashy," and he was called "an actor" and "a pulpit buffoon." Even after his ministry was established, Spurgeon was lied about in the press (including the *religious* press), and this was bound to discourage him.

After one particularly scurrilous report in the press, Spurgeon fell before the Lord and prayed, "O Lord Jesus, Thou didst make Thyself of no reputation for me. I willingly lay my reputation down for Thy sake." From that time on, Spurgeon had peace in his heart. He knew that his Great High Priest understood his need and would give him the grace that he needed for each hour.

Jesus Christ Offered a Superior Sacrifice (5:3, 9–10)

This topic has already been touched on, and the writer of Hebrews discussed it in detail in Hebrews 9—10. Two important matters are involved.

The first is that Jesus Christ did not need to offer any sacrifices for Himself. On the annual day of Atonement, the high priest first had to sacrifice for himself; and then he could offer the sacrifices for his nation (Lev. 16). Since Jesus is the sinless Son of God, there was no need for Him to sacrifice for Himself. He was in perfect fellowship with the Father and needed no cleansing.

The second matter is that our Lord's sacrifice was once and for all, whereas the Old Testament sacrifices had to be repeated. Furthermore, those sacrifices could only *cover* sins; they could never *cleanse* sins. It required the sacrifice of the spotless Lamb of God for sin to be cleansed and removed.

Because He is the sinless, eternal Son of God, and because He offered a perfect sacrifice, Jesus Christ is the "author of eternal salvation" (Heb. 5:9). No Old Testament priest could offer *eternal* salvation to anyone, but that is exactly what we have in Jesus Christ. The phrase "being made perfect" does not suggest that Jesus was imperfect! The word means "made complete"; we described it in our study of Hebrews 2:10. By means of His earthly sufferings, Jesus Christ was equipped for His heavenly ministry as our High Priest. He is able to save, keep, and strengthen His people.

Does the phrase "them that obey him" (Heb. 5:9) suggest that, if we do not obey Him, we may lose that eternal salvation? To "obey God" is the same as "to trust God," as "them that obey him" is a description of those who have put their faith in Jesus Christ. "A great company of the priests were obedient to the faith" (Acts 6:7). "But they have not all obeyed the gospel" (Rom. 10:16). "Ye have purified your souls in obeying the truth" (1 Peter 1:22). Once we have put our faith in Jesus Christ, and thus obeyed His call, we experience His eternal salvation.

It is difficult to resist the four arguments presented in this section. We must conclude with the writer that Jesus Christ the great High Priest is superior to Aaron. It would be foolish for anyone to return to the inferiorities of the old law when he could enjoy the superiorities of Jesus Christ. Then why were these Hebrew believers tempted to go back into legalism? *Because they were not going on to maturity in Christ!* For this reason the writer paused to exhort them to grow up in the Lord, and that is the theme for our next chapter.

CHAPTER FIVE
Hebrews 5:11—6:20
PILGRIMS SHOULD MAKE PROGRESS

We do not want you to become lazy, but to imitate those who through faith and patience inherit what has been promised" (Heb. 6:12 NIV).

This verse summarizes the main message of this difficult (and often misunderstood) section of the epistle. Israel wanted to go back to Egypt, and, as a result, a whole generation failed to inherit what God had promised. They were safely delivered out of Egypt, but they never enjoyed the promised rest in Canaan. We believers today can make the same mistake.

If you keep in mind that the emphasis in this section is on *making spiritual progress,* you will steer safely through misinterpretations that could create problems. In this section, the writer deals with three topics that relate to spiritual progress.

The Marks of Spiritual Immaturity (5:11–14)
The writer was about to begin his explanation of the heavenly priesthood of Christ, but he was not sure his readers were ready for what he had to teach. The problem was not that he is a dull teacher, but that they were dull hearers! The word translated "dull" in Hebrews 5:11 is translated "slothful" in Hebrews 6:12. It refers to a condition of spiritual apathy and laziness that prevents spiritual development.

What, then, are the marks of spiritual immaturity? **Dullness toward the Word (v. 11).** These believers started on their "backward journey" by *drifting from the Word* (Heb. 2:1–4), and then *doubting the Word* (Heb. 3:7—4:13). As a result, they were now "dull of hearing"; that is, unable to listen to the Word, receive it, and act on it. They did not have the attitude of the Thessalonians: "For this cause also thank we God without ceasing, because, when ye received the word of God which ye heard of us, ye received it not as the word of men, but as it is in truth, the word of God, which effectually worketh also in you that believe" (1 Thess. 2:13).

One of the first symptoms of spiritual regression, or backsliding, is a dullness toward the Bible. Sunday school class is dull, the preaching is dull, anything spiritual is dull. The problem is usually not with the Sunday school teacher or the pastor, but with the believer himself.

Inability to share (v. 12a). The ability to share spiritual truth with others is a mark of maturity. Not all Christians have the gift of teaching, but all can share what they learn from the Word. One of the hardest lessons children must learn is the lesson of sharing. The recipients of this letter had been saved long enough to be able to share God's truth with others. But, instead of helping others to grow, these Hebrew Christians were in need of learning *again* the simple teachings of the Christian life. They were experiencing a second childhood!

A "baby food" diet (vv. 12b–13). Milk is predigested food, and it is specially suited to babies. But only those who have teeth can enjoy meat. The writer defines the "milk" as "the first principles of the oracles of God" (Heb. 5:12). The "meat" of the Word is the teaching about our Lord's ministry *now* in heaven as our High Priest. The writer wanted to give this "meat" to them, but they were not ready for it.

The "milk" of the Word refers to what Jesus Christ did on earth—His birth, life, teaching, death, burial, and resurrection. The "meat" of the Word refers to what Jesus Christ is now doing in heaven. We begin the Christian life on the basis of His finished work on earth. We grow in the Christian life on the basis of His unfinished work in heaven.

Of course, even the maturest adult never outgrows milk. As believers, we can still learn much from our Lord's work on earth. *But we must not stop there!* We must make spiritual progress, and we can do this only if we learn about Christ's priestly ministry for us in heaven. (See Heb. 13:20–21 for a summary of what the Lord wants to do for His people now.)

Unskillful in using the Word (v. 14). As we grow

in the Word, we learn to use it in daily life. As we apply the Word, we exercise our "spiritual senses" and develop spiritual discernment. It is a characteristic of little children that they lack discernment. A baby will put anything into its mouth. An immature believer will listen to any preacher on the radio or television and not be able to identify whether or not he is true to the Scriptures.

Just as our physical bodies have senses without which we could not function, so our inner "spiritual man" has "spiritual senses." For example, "O taste and see that the Lord is good" (Ps. 34:8); "But blessed are your eyes, for they see; and your ears, for they hear" (Matt. 13:16). As we feed on the Word of God and apply it in daily life, our inner "spiritual senses" get their exercise and become strong and keen. Paul called this process exercising ourselves unto godliness (1 Tim. 4:7–8).

The ability to discern good and evil is a vital part of Christian maturity. The nation of Israel in Moses' day lacked this discernment and failed to claim its promised inheritance. The readers of this letter were in danger of making the same mistake. It is impossible to stand still in the Christian life: we either go forward and claim God's blessing, or we go backward and wander about aimlessly.

I once heard a preacher say, "Most Christians are 'betweeners.'"

"What do you mean by that?" I asked.

"They are between Egypt and Canaan—out of the place of danger, but not yet into the place of rest and rich inheritance," he replied. "They are between Good Friday and Easter Sunday—saved by the blood but not yet enjoying newness of resurrection life."

Are *you* a "betweener"?

The Call to Spiritual Maturity (6:1–12)

No one can escape coming into the world as a baby, because that is the only way to get here! But it is tragic when a baby fails to mature. No matter how much parents and grandparents love to hold and cuddle a baby, it is their great desire that the baby grow up and enjoy a full life as a mature adult. God has the same desire for His children. That is why He calls to us, "Go on to maturity" (Heb. 6:1 NIV)!

It is a call to spiritual progress (vv. 1–3). If we are going to make progress, we have to leave the childhood things behind and go forward in spiritual growth. Hebrews 6:1 literally reads, "Therefore, having left [once and for all] the elementary lessons [the ABCs] of the teaching of Christ." When I was in kindergarten, the teacher taught us our ABCs. (We didn't have television to teach us in those days.) You learn your ABCs so that you might read words, sentences, books—in fact, anything in literature. But you do not keep learning the basics. You use the basics to go on to better things.

The phrase, "Let us go on," should be translated, "Let us be carried forward." It is God who enables us to

progress as we yield to Him, receive His Word, and act on it. A baby does not "grow himself." He grows as he eats, sleeps, exercises, and permits his body to function. Nature, as ordained by God, carries the baby along day after day, and gradually he matures into an adult. It is normal for Christians to grow; it is abnormal for them to have arrested growth.

The writer lists six foundational truths of the Christian life, all of which, by the way, are also foundational to the Jewish faith. After all, our Christian faith is based on the Jewish faith and is a fulfillment of it. "Salvation is of the Jews" (John 4:22). If the readers of this epistle went back to Judaism in order to escape persecution, they would only be abandoning the perfect for the imperfect, the mature for the immature.

The first two items (repentance and faith) are *Godward* and mark the initiation of the spiritual life. To repent means to change one's mind. It is not simply a "bad feeling about sin," because that could be regret or remorse. It is changing one's mind about sin to the point of turning from it. Once a sinner has repented (and this itself is a gift from God, Acts 5:31; 11:18), then he is able to exercise faith in God. Repentance and faith go together (Acts 20:21).

The next two items (baptisms and laying on of hands) have to do with a person's relationship to *the local assembly of believers.* In the New Testament, a person who repented and trusted Christ was baptized and became a part of a local church (Acts 2:41–47). The word *baptisms* in Hebrews 6:2 is plural and can be translated "washings" (Heb. 9:10). While water itself can never cleanse sin (1 Peter 3:21), baptism is a symbol of spiritual cleansing ("Get up, be baptized, and wash your sins away, calling on his name"—Acts 22:16 NIV) as well as our identification with Christ in death, burial, and resurrection (Rom. 6:1–4*).* The "laying on of hands" (Heb. 6:2) symbolized the sharing of some blessing (Luke 24:50; Acts 19:6) or the setting apart of a person for ministry (1 Tim. 4:14).

The last two items, the resurrection of the dead (Acts 24:14–15) and the final judgment (Acts 17:30–31), have to do with *the future.* Both orthodox Jews and Christians believe in these doctrines. The Old Testament teaches a general resurrection, but does not make the doctrine clear. The New Testament teaches a resurrection of the saved and also a resurrection of the lost (John 5:24–29; Rev. 20:4–6, 12–15).

The lesson of the paragraph (Heb. 6:1–3) is clear: "You have laid the foundation. You know your ABCs. Now move forward! Let God carry you along to maturity!"

This progress does not affect salvation (vv. 4–6). These verses, along with the exhortation in Hebrews 10:26–39, have given people cause for worry and concern, mainly because these verses have been misunderstood and misapplied. I have received long-distance phone calls from upset people who have misread this passage and convinced themselves (or been convinced by Satan) that they were hopelessly lost and had committed some unpardonable sin. While I do not want to give a false assurance to any professed Christian who is not truly born again, neither do I want to cause some true believer to stumble and miss God's best.

Bible students over the years have come up with several approaches to this serious passage. One view is that the writer is warning us against the sin of apostasy, willfully turning one's back on Jesus Christ and returning to the old life. According to them, such a person would be lost forever. I have several problems with this interpretation. To begin with, the Greek word *apostasia* is not used in this passage. The verb for "fall away" (Heb. 6:6) is *parapipto,* which literally means "to fall alongside." Second, we always interpret the obscure by the obvious. There are many verses in Scripture that assure the true believer that he can never be lost. In fact, one of the greatest arguments for security is the last section of this chapter (Heb. 6:13–20; see also John 5:24; 10:26–30; Rom. 8:28–39)!

Those who teach that we can lose our salvation also teach that such a person can be restored. But this passage (Heb. 6:4–6) teaches just the opposite! If you omit the intervening clauses, the statement reads: "For it is impossible … to renew them again to repentance." In other words, if this refers to apostasy, once a saved person turns his back on Christ, he *cannot* be restored to salvation. He is lost forever.

Others claim that the people addressed were not true believers. They had cooperated with the Holy Spirit up to a point, but were not actually born again. Well, let's examine the description of these people and see if they possessed true salvation.

They were "enlightened" (Heb. 6:4). The "once" means "enlightened once and for all." The way this same verb is used in Hebrews 10:32 indicates an experience of true salvation (see 2 Cor. 4:4–6).

They "tasted of the heavenly gift" (Heb. 6:4b), and "tasted the good word of God, and the powers of the world [age] to come" (Heb. 6:5). To claim that these people "tasted but did not eat" is to base interpretation on one meaning of an English word. God permitted His Son to "taste death for every man" (Heb. 2:9). Surely Jesus Christ did not simply *sample* death on the cross! "Taste" carries the idea of "experience." These Hebrew believers had experienced the gift of salvation, the Word of God, and the power of God. Doesn't this describe authentic salvation?

They "were made partakers of the Holy Spirit" (Heb. 6:4c). To suggest that they only went along with the Holy Spirit to a certain extent is to ignore the simple meaning of the verb. It means "to become sharers." These same people were not only "sharers of the Holy Spirit," but also "sharers of the heavenly calling" (Heb. 3:1), and "sharers of Christ" (Heb. 3:14).

In view of these facts, I have concluded that the people addressed were true believers, not mere professors. Furthermore, how could *unsaved* people ever disgrace Jesus Christ and put Him to open shame?

A third view is that this sin (whatever it is) could be committed only by Hebrew Christians in the first century, while the temple services were still going on. If so, then why did the writer connect this exhortation with the *heavenly* priesthood of our Lord and the importance of spiritual maturity? If what he wrote about cannot happen today, what is the motivation behind the exhortation? It all seems futile to me if we limit these verses to first-century Jewish believers.

Then what is the writer trying to say to us? It is probable that he was describing a *hypothetical case* to prove his point that a true believer cannot lose his salvation. His statement in Hebrews 6:9 seems to support this interpretation: "Even though we speak like this, dear friends, we are confident of better things in your case" (NIV). His argument runs like this: "Let's suppose that you do not go on to maturity. Does this mean that you will go back to condemnation, that you will lose your salvation? Impossible! If you *could* lose your salvation, it would be impossible to get it back again, and this would disgrace Jesus Christ. He would have to be crucified again for you, and this could never happen."

In Hebrews 6:4, the writer changed the pronouns from "we" and "us" to "those." This change also suggests that he had a hypothetical case in mind.

However, there is another possible interpretation that does not require a hypothetical case. You should note that the words *crucify* and *put* in Hebrews 6:6 are, in the Greek, present participles: "while they *are crucifying* … and while they *are putting* him to an open shame." The writer did not say that these people could *never* be brought to repentance. He said that they could not be brought to repentance *while they were treating Jesus Christ in such a shameful way.* Once they stop disgracing Jesus Christ in this way, they can be brought to repentance and renew their fellowship with God.

Whatever approach you take, please keep in mind that the writer's purpose was not to frighten the readers but to assure them. If he had wanted to frighten them, he would have named whatever sin (or sins) would have caused them to disgrace Jesus Christ; but he did not do so. In fact, he avoided the word *apostasy* and used instead "to fall by the wayside" (see Gal. 6:1 for a similar word).

Christians *can* "sin unto death" (1 Cor. 11:30–32; 1 John 5:16–17). This is God's chastening, a theme the writer of Hebrews will take up in Hebrews 12.

This progress results in fruitfulness (vv. 7–10). This illustration of a field reminds us of our Lord's parable of the sower (Matt. 13:1–9, 18–23), as well as Paul's teaching about the fire testing our works (1 Cor. 3:6–23). A field proves its worth by bearing fruit, and a true believer, as he makes spiritual progress, bears fruit for God's glory. Note that the "thorns and briars" are burned, not the field. God never curses His own!

The crop of God's blessing pictured in Hebrews 6:7

is called "things that accompany salvation" in Hebrews 6:9. Not every believer bears the same *amount of* fruit ("some an hundredfold, some sixty, some thirty," Matt. 13:23); but every believer bears the same *kind* of fruit as proof that he is a child of God (Matt. 7:15–20). This is the fruit of Christian character and conduct (Gal. 5:22–26) produced by the Spirit as we mature in Christ.

The writer listed some of the fruit that he knew had been produced in their lives (Heb. 6:10): because of their love, they had worked and labored for the Lord; they had ministered to other saints; and they were still ministering (see 1 Thess. 1:3–10; Rev. 2:2). These are some of the "things that accompany salvation."

But he was concerned lest they rest on their achievements and not press on to full maturity and the enjoyment of God's rich inheritance.

This progress demands diligent effort (vv. 11–12). While it is true that it is God who "carries us along" to maturity (Heb. 6:1, 3), it is also true that the believer must do his part. We must not be lazy ("slothful," the same word as "dull" in Heb. 5:11) but apply ourselves to the spiritual resources God has given us. We have the promises from God. We should exercise faith and patience and claim these promises for ourselves! Like Caleb and Joshua, we must believe God's promise and want to go in and claim the land! The illustration of the farm (Heb. 6:7–8) and the admonition to be diligent always remind me of Solomon's warning (Prov. 24:30–34). Read it—*and heed it!*

The Basis for Spiritual Security (6:13–20)

Lest anyone should misinterpret his exhortation to spiritual maturity, the writer ended this section with a tremendous argument for the assurance of salvation. All of us Christians are not making the spiritual progress we should, but we need never fear that God will condemn us. The writer gave three arguments for the certain salvation of true believers.

God's promise (vv. 13–15). God's main promise to Abraham is recorded in Genesis 22:16–17. In spite of Abraham's failures and sins, God kept His promise and Isaac was born. Many of God's promises do not depend on our character but on His faithfulness. The phrase "patiently endured" (Heb. 6:15) is the exact opposite of "slothful" (Heb. 6:12). The readers of this letter were about to give up; their endurance was running out (see Heb. 12:1–2). "You will obtain and enjoy what God has promised if you diligently apply yourself to the development of your spiritual life," is what the writer stated.

We Christians today have more of God's promises than did Abraham! What is keeping us from making spiritual progress? *We do not apply ourselves by faith.* To return to the illustration of the farm, the farmer does not reap a harvest by sitting on the porch looking at the seed. He must get busy and plow, plant, weed, cultivate, and perhaps water the soil. The believer who neglects church fellowship, ignores his Bible, and forgets to pray is not going to reap much of a harvest.

God's oath (vv. 16–18). God not only gave Abraham a promise, but He also confirmed that promise with an oath. When a witness takes an oath in court, he is confronted with the words "so help me God." We call on the greater to witness for the lesser. None is greater than God, so He swore by Himself!

But God did not do this only for Abraham. He has also given His promise and oath to "the heirs of promise" (Heb. 6:17). Abraham and his descendants are the first of these heirs (see Heb. 11:9), but all believers are included as "Abraham's [spiritual] seed" (Gal. 3:29). So our assurance of salvation is guaranteed by God's promise and God's oath, "two immutable [unchangeable] things" (Heb. 6:18). We have "strong consolation" (or "great encouragement") concerning the hope set before us! Hebrews is a book of encouragement, not discouragement!

The phrase "fled for refuge" (Heb. 6:18) suggests the Old Testament "cities of refuge" described in Numbers 35:9ff. and Joshua 20. God appointed six cities, three on each side of the Jordan, into which a man could flee if he had accidentally killed someone. The elders of the city would investigate the case. If they determined that it was indeed manslaughter and not murder, they would permit the man to live in the city until the death of the high priest. Then he could return to his home. The members of the slain man's family could not avenge themselves so long as the man remained in the city.

We have fled to Jesus Christ, and He is our eternal refuge. As our High Priest, He will never die (Heb. 7:23–25), and we have eternal salvation. No avenger can touch us, because He has already died and arisen from the dead.

God's Son (vv. 19–20). Our hope in Christ is like an anchor for the soul. The anchor was a popular symbol in the early church. At least sixty-six pictures of anchors have been found in the catacombs. The Greek stoic philosopher Epictetus wrote, "One must not tie a ship to a single anchor, nor life to a single hope." Christians have but one anchor—Jesus Christ our hope (Col. 1:5, 1 Tim. 1:1).

However, this spiritual anchor is different from material anchors on ships. For one thing, we are anchored *upward*—to heaven—not downward. We are anchored, not to stand still, but to *move ahead!* Our anchor is "sure"—it cannot break—and "steadfast"—it cannot slip. No earthly anchor can give that kind of security!

The writer then clinched the argument: this Savior is our "forerunner" who has gone ahead to heaven so that we may one day follow (Heb. 6:20)! The Old Testament high priest was *not* a "forerunner" because nobody could follow him into the Holy of Holies. But Jesus Christ has gone to heaven so that one day we may follow.

Dr. H. A. Ironside has suggested that the two phrases "within the veil" (Heb. 6:19) and "without the camp" (Heb. 13:13) summarize the epistle to the

Hebrews. Jesus Christ is "within the veil" as our High Priest. We can therefore come boldly to His throne and receive all the help that we need. But we must not be "secret saints." We must be willing to identify with Christ in His rejection and go "without the camp, bearing his reproach" (Heb. 13:13). The Hebrew believers who received this letter were tempted to compromise to avoid that reproach. However, if we live "within the veil," we shall have no trouble going "without the camp."

Regardless of what approach you take to the exhortation in this section, be sure to lay hold of the main lesson: believers must go on to maturity, and God has made it possible for us to do so. If we start to *drift from the Word* (Heb. 2:1–4), then we will also start to *doubt the Word* (Heb. 3:7—4:13). Before long, we will get *dull toward the Word* (Heb. 5:11—6:20) and become lazy believers. The best way to keep from drifting is—to *lay hold of the anchor!*

Anchored heavenward! How much more secure can you be?

CHAPTER SIX
Hebrews 7
MYSTERIOUS MELCHIZEDEK

Ever since a city librarian introduced me to the Sherlock Holmes stories many years ago, I have been a reader of good detective fiction. Of course, I always try to solve the mystery before I get to the final chapter, and sometimes I succeed. This much I have learned: never overlook *any* character in the story, even the most incidental. He or she may be the criminal.

If you were asked to name the most important people in the Old Testament, I doubt that Melchizedek's name would be on your list. He appeared once, in Genesis 14:17–24, and he was referred to once more, in Psalm 110:4. You could hardly call this "top billing." But the Holy Spirit reached back into the Old Testament and used those two passages to present a most important truth: the priesthood of Jesus Christ is superior to that of Aaron because "the order of Melchizedek" is superior to "the order of Levi."

Chapter 7 of Hebrews introduces the second main section, as we have outlined it: A superior Priesthood (Heb. 7—10). In Hebrews 7, the writer argued that Christ's priesthood, like Melchizedek's, is superior in its *order.* In Hebrews 8, the emphasis is on Christ's better *covenant;* in Hebrews 9, it is His better *sanctuary;* and Hebrews 10 concludes the section by arguing for Christ's better *sacrifice.*

The Jewish nation was accustomed to the priesthood of the tribe of Levi. This tribe was chosen by God to serve in the tabernacle (Ex. 29; Num. 18). Aaron was the first high priest, appointed by God. In spite

of their many failures, the priests had served God for centuries, but now the writer has affirmed that their priesthood has ended! To defend this statement, and to prove that the order of Melchizedek is superior to that of Aaron, he presented three arguments.

The Historical Argument: Melchizedek and Abraham (7:1–10)
The record of the event discussed is in Genesis 14:17–24, so take time to read it. The writer of our epistle wanted us to note several facts about this mysterious man, Melchizedek.

He was both king and priest (v. 1). We have noted already that, in the Old Testament economy, the throne and the altar were separated. Those persons who attempted to invade the priests' office were judged by God. But here is a man who had *both* offices—king and priest! Aaron never had that privilege. And it is important to note that Melchizedek was not a "counterfeit" priest: he was the "priest of the Most High God" (see Gen. 14:18, 22). His ministry was legitimate.

His name is significant (v. 2b). In the Bible, names and their meanings are often important. We name our children today without much consideration for what their names mean, but this was not the case in Bible days. Sometimes a great spiritual crisis was the occasion for changing a person's name (see Gen. 32:24–32; John 1:35–42). The name "Melchizedek" means "king of righteousness" in the Hebrew language. The word *Salem* means "peace" (the Hebrew word *shalom*), so that Melchizedek is "king of peace" as well as "king of righteousness."

"Righteousness" and "peace" are often found together in Scripture. "And the work of righteousness shall be peace; and the effect of righteousness quietness and assurance forever" (Isa. 32:17); "Mercy and truth are met together; righteousness and peace have kissed each other" (Ps. 85:10); "In his days shall the righteous flourish; and abundance of peace so long as the moon endureth" (Ps. 72:7); "But the wisdom that is from above is first pure, then peaceable…. And the fruit of righteousness is sown in peace of them that make peace" (James 3:17–18). Of course, God's purpose for His people is that they bear "the peaceable fruit of righteousness" (Heb. 12:10–11).

True peace can be experienced only on the basis of righteousness. If we want to enjoy "peace with God" we must be "justified [declared righteous] by faith" (Rom. 5:1). Man cannot produce righteousness by keeping the Old Testament law (Gal. 2:21). It is only through the work of Jesus Christ on the cross that righteousness and peace could have "kissed each other."

He received tithes from Abraham (v. 2a). This important fact is explained in Hebrews 7:4–10. The word tithe means "one tenth." Under the Jewish law, the Jews were commanded to give God one tenth of their crops, herds, and flocks (Lev. 27:30–32). These tithes were brought to the Levites (Num. 18:21ff) at the tabernacle and later at the temple (Deut. 12:5ff).

If the trip was too long for transporting grain, fruit, or animals, the tithe could be converted into money (Deut. 14:22–27).

Tithing, however, did not originate with Moses. Abraham practiced tithing long before the law was given. In fact, archeologists have discovered that other nations also tithed in that day; so the practice is an ancient one.

His family history is different (v. 3). Melchizedek was a man (see Heb. 7:4), so he had to have had a mother and a father. But there is no *record* of his genealogy ("descent") in the Old Testament, and this is significant because most great persons in the Old Testament have their ancestry identified. It was especially important that the priests be able to prove their ancestry (see Ezra 2:61–63; Neh. 7:63–65). Here the writer of Hebrews used an argument from silence, but it is a valid one.

Melchizedek was not an angel or some superhuman creature; nor was he an Old Testament appearance of Jesus Christ. He was a real man, a real king, and a real priest in a real city. But *as far as the record is concerned,* he was not born, nor did he die. In this way, he is a picture of the Lord Jesus Christ, the eternal Son of God. Though Jesus Christ did die, Calvary was not the end, for He arose from the dead and today lives in "the power of an endless life" (Heb. 7:16). Since there is no account of Melchizedek's death, as far as the record is concerned, it seems that Melchizedek is still serving as a priest and king. This is another way in which he is like the eternal Son of God.

The application is clear: neither Aaron nor any of his descendants could claim to be "without genealogy" (Heb. 7:3 NASB). They could not claim to have an endless ministry. Nor could they claim to be both kings and priests, like Jesus Christ.

He had authority to receive tithes and to bless Abraham (vv. 4–10). The greatness of Melchizedek is seen in the fact that Abraham gave him tithes from the loot of a miniwar. Abraham acknowledged the authority of Melchizedek. Furthermore, Melchizedek blessed Abraham in a special way, and "the less is blessed of the better" (Heb. 7:7). In giving Melchizedek tithes and in receiving his blessing, Abraham affirmed the greatness of this king-priest.

But how does this relate to Aaron? In an interesting way: Aaron and the tribe of Levi were "in the loins" of Abraham, yet unborn! So, when their father, Abraham, acknowledged the greatness of Melchizedek, the tribe of Levi was also involved. The Jewish people believe strongly in "racial solidarity," and this is one example of it. The paying of the tithes involved not just the patriarch Abraham, but also the unborn generations in his loins.

Since Jesus Christ came "of the seed of Abraham" (Heb. 2:16), does this mean that He too was a part of this experience? No, because Jesus Christ is the eternal Son of God. His identification with Abraham was for "the days of his flesh" (Heb. 5:7). Since Christ existed before Abraham (John 8:58), He could not have been "in Abraham" as were Aaron and his family.

The Doctrinal Argument: Christ and Aaron (7:11–25)

In this section, the writer took his argument one step further. Not only is Melchizedek *greater than* Aaron, but Melchizedek has *replaced Aaron!* It is no longer "the order of Aaron" or "the order of Levi." It is forever "the order of Melchizedek." Why would God effect such a radical change?

Because both the priesthood and the law were imperfect (vv. 11–14). The words translated "perfect" and "perfection" are key words in this epistle (Heb. 2:10; 5:9; 6:1; 7:11, 19; 9:9; 10:1, 14). They essentially mean "completed, fulfilled." The Old Testament priests could not by their ministry complete the work of God in the heart of a worshipper. "For the law made nothing perfect" (Heb. 7:19). The animal sacrifices could not give any worshipper a perfect standing before God (Heb. 10:1–3). The Mosaic system of divine law was not a permanent system. It was "added" to serve as a "schoolmaster" to prepare the way for the coming of Christ (Gal. 3:19—4:7).

Since the priests received their authority from the Old Testament law (Heb. 7:28), and since the priesthood has been changed, there has also been a change in that law. The president of the United States cannot proclaim himself king of the United States because U.S. law makes no provision for a king. First, the law would have to be changed.

The law of Moses made no provision for a priesthood from the tribe of Judah (Heb. 7:14). Since our High Priest *is* from the tribe of Judah, according to His human ancestry, then there must have been a change in Moses' law. There has been! The entire system of Old Testament law has been fulfilled in Jesus Christ and has been taken out of the way (Col. 2:13–14). The believer has been set free from the law (Gal. 5:1–6) and is dead to the law (Rom. 7:1–4).

This new arrangement does not suggest that a Christian has the right to be lawless. "Free from the law" does not mean "free to sin." Rather, it means that we are free to do the will of God. We obey, not because of outward compulsion, but because of inward constraint (2 Cor. 5:14; Eph. 6:6). The indwelling Holy Spirit enables us to fulfill the "righteousness of the law" as we yield to Him (Rom. 8:1–4).

Because, being imperfect, the priesthood and the law could not continue forever (vv. 15–19). The word *another* in Hebrews 7:15 means "another of a different kind." The Levitical priests were made priests by the authority of a temporary and imperfect law. Jesus Christ was made Priest by a declaration of God. Because the law was "weak and useless" (Heb. 7:18 NIV), it could not continue forever. But because Jesus Christ is the eternal Son of God, He lives by "the power of an endless life" (Heb. 7:16). What a contrast between the profitless law and an endless life!

Since Jesus Christ is Priest *forever,* and since He has a nature to match that eternal priesthood, He can never be replaced. The annulling (Heb. 7:18, "disannulling") of the law meant the abolishing of the priesthood. But nobody can annul "the power of an endless life"! The logic holds: Jesus Christ is a Priest forever.

The writer kept in mind the temptation his readers were facing to go back into the old temple system. This is why he reminded them (Heb. 7:19) that Jesus Christ has accomplished what the law could never accomplish: He brought in a better hope, and He enables us to draw near to God. To go back to Judaism would mean losing the enjoyment of their fellowship with God through Christ. The only hope Judaism had was the coming of Christ, and that blessing these believers already had.

Because God's oath cannot be broken (vv. 20–22). No priest in the order of Aaron was ever ordained and established on the basis of God's personal oath. The Aaronic priests ministered "after the law of a carnal [physical] commandment" (Heb. 7:16). Their moral or spiritual fitness was not examined. The important thing was that a priest belonged to the right tribe and met the right physical and ceremonial requirements (Lev. 21:16–24).

Jesus Christ's heavenly priesthood was established on the basis of His work on the cross, His character (Heb. 2:10; 5:5–10), and the oath of God. "Thou art a priest forever after the order of Melchizedek" (Heb. 7:21; Ps. 110:4). Note the introduction to the statement: "The Lord swore and will not repent [change His mind]." The matter is finally settled and it cannot be changed.

The presence of this oath gives to the priesthood of our Lord a greater degree of permanence and assurance. Jesus Christ is the "surety of a better testament [covenant]" (Heb. 7:22). The word *surety* means "one who guarantees that the terms of an agreement will be carried out." Judah was willing to be the surety for Benjamin, to guarantee to their father that the boy would return home safely (Gen. 43:1–14). Paul was willing to be the surety for the slave Onesimus (Philem. 18–19). Perhaps the nearest equivalent we have today is a bondsman who posts bail for someone under indictment and guarantees that the indicted person will appear in court and stand trial.

As the Mediator between God and man (1 Tim. 2:5), Jesus Christ is God's great Surety. Our risen and ever-living Savior guarantees that the terms of God's covenant will be fulfilled completely. God will not abandon His people. But our Lord not only guarantees *to us* that God will fulfill the promises. As our Representative to *God,* He perfectly meets the terms of the agreement on our behalf. We of ourselves could never meet the terms, but because we have trusted Him, He has saved us and He has guaranteed that He will keep us.

In Hebrews 7:22, we have the first occurrence of a very important word in Hebrews—*testament.* This word, which is usually translated "covenant," is used twenty-one times in the letter, and it is the equivalent of "last will and testament." We will examine the word more closely in our study of Hebrews 8.

The writer has given three reasons why God changed the order of the priesthood from that of Aaron to that of Melchizedek: (1) the priesthood and the law were imperfect; (2) being imperfect, they could not continue forever; (3) God had sworn by His oath that the new order would be established. Then the writer of this letter to the Hebrews closed this section with a fourth reason.

Because, being men, the priests died (vv. 23–25). Not only was the priesthood imperfect, but it was also interrupted by death. There were *many* high priests because no one priest could live forever. In contrast, the church has *one* High Priest, Jesus the Son of God, who lives forever! An unchanging priest means an unchangeable priesthood, and this means security and confidence for God's people. "Jesus Christ, the same yesterday, and today, and forever" (Heb. 13:8). "Thou art a priest for ever" (Ps. 110:4).

Occasionally we read a story in the newspaper about the illegal handling of a will. Perhaps some unscrupulous relative or business partner managed to get his hands on a will and use it for his own selfish purposes. But this could never happen to our Lord's "last will and testament" in His blood. He wrote the will and then died to make it take effect. But He arose from the dead and ascended to heaven, and there He is "probating" His own will!

The fact that the *unchanging* Christ continues as High Priest means, logically, that there is an "unchangeable priesthood" (Heb. 7:24). The Greek word translated "unchangeable" carries the idea of "valid and unalterable." The word was used at the end of legal contracts. Our Lord's priesthood in heaven is "valid and unalterable." Because it is, we can have confidence in the midst of this shaking, changing world.

What is the conclusion of the matter? It is stated in Hebrews 7:25: "Wherefore [because He is the ever-living, unchanging High Priest], he is able also to save them to the uttermost [completely, forever] that come unto God by him, seeing he ever liveth to make intercession for them." It is unfortunate that this verse is often read, "He is able to save *from* the uttermost" instead of "*to* the uttermost." To be sure, it is true that Christ can save any sinner from any condition; but that is not the import of the verse. The emphasis is on the fact that He saves completely, forever, all who put their faith in Him. Because He is our High Priest forever, He can save forever.

The basis for this completed salvation is the heavenly intercession of the Savior. The word translated "make intercession" simply means "to meet, to approach, to appeal, to make petition." We must not imagine that God the Father is angry with us so that God the Son must constantly appeal to Him not to judge us! The Father and the Son are in total agreement in the plan of salvation (Heb. 13:20–21). Neither should we imagine our Lord Jesus uttering prayers on our behalf in heaven, or repeatedly "offering His blood" as a sacrifice. That work was completed on the cross once and for all.

Intercession involves our Lord's representation of His people at the throne of God. Through Christ, believers are able to draw near to God in prayer and also to offer spiritual sacrifices to God (Heb. 4:14–16; 1 Peter 2:5). It has well been said that Christ's life in heaven is His prayer for us. It is what He *is* that determines what He *does*.

In reviewing the reasoning found in this long section (Heb. 7:11–25), we are impressed with the logic of the writer. Jesus Christ's priesthood after the order of Melchizedek is superior to that of Aaron and has replaced it. Both the historical argument and the doctrinal argument are sound. But the writer adds a third argument.

The Practical Argument: Christ and the Believer (7:26–28)

No matter how devoted and obedient the Aaronic priests were, they could not always meet the needs of all the people. But Jesus Christ perfectly meets all of our needs. "For such an high priest became us" means "He was suited to us; He meets our needs completely." The emphasis here is on His sinlessness. Being perfect, He is able to exercise a perfect ministry for His people. Because of their sins, some of the Old Testament priests not only were unable to serve the people, but actually abused them. This could never happen with Jesus Christ and His people.

The Old Testament priests were "set apart" for their ministry, so in that sense they were "holy." But they were not always holy in character. They were sinners like the people to whom they ministered. "Harmless" (Heb. 7:26) means "blameless." No Jewish priest could claim this distinction. "Undefiled" means "unstained." Again, only Jesus Christ can claim these characteristics. When He was ministering on earth, our Lord was a friend of publicans and sinners (Matt. 9:10; 11:19), but His contact with them did not defile His character or His conduct. There was contact without contamination. He was not isolated; He was separated. Today, He is "separate from sinners" because of His position ("made higher than the heavens"), but He is not separated from the people to whom He ministers. He is always available to us at His throne of grace.

Another proof of His sinlessness is the fact that our Lord never had to offer sacrifices for His own cleansing, as did the priests. On the *annual* day of Atonement, the high priest first had to sacrifice for himself before he could sacrifice for the people (Lev. 16). There were also *daily* sacrifices offered as a part of the temple ritual, and, if a priest had sinned, he had to bring a sacrifice for his own cleansing (Ex. 29:38–46;

Lev. 4:3ff.). But Jesus Christ offered just one sacrifice for our sins and settled the matter forever (see Heb. 9:23–28).

This is the kind of High Priest we need! We are prone to sin daily, even hourly, and we need to be able to turn to Him for spiritual help. As our High Priest, Jesus Christ gives us the grace and mercy that *we need not to sin*. But if we do sin, He is our Advocate at God's throne (1 John 2:1–2). If we confess our sins to Him, He forgives us and restores us (1 John 1:9).

The application is obvious: why turn away from such an adequate High Priest? What more can you find in any other person? The men who served under the law of Moses had human infirmities and weaknesses, and they often failed. Our heavenly High Priest has been "consecrated [perfected] forevermore" (Heb. 7:28) and there is no spot or blemish in Him. Such a High Priest "suits us perfectly"!

Are you availing yourself of His gracious ministry?

CHAPTER SEVEN
Hebrews 8
THE BETTER COVENANT

I once spoke at a meeting of religious broadcasters at which a friend of mine was to provide the ministry of music. He is a superb pianist with a gift for interpreting Christian music, and I have always enjoyed listening to him. But that day my heart went out to him in sympathy, because the motel had given the most deteriorated and derelict piano I have ever seen. It must have been donated by a local wrecking company. My friend did his best, but it would have been much better had he been playing a decent instrument.

Jesus Christ is God's superior Priest, but is there anything that can minimize this superiority? Nothing! For He ministers on the basis of a better covenant (Heb. 8), in a better sanctuary (Heb. 9), and because of a better sacrifice (Heb. 10). It is the better covenant that is the theme of this chapter. The writer presented three evidences for the superiority of this covenant.

It Is Ministered by a Superior High Priest (8:1–2)

Was the writer arguing in circles? First he showed the superiority of Christ, and then said, "Since He is superior, the covenant He ministers must be a superior covenant." No, this is not reasoning in a circle, for the conclusion is logical. A superior priest could never minister on the basis of an inferior covenant. To change the illustration, the most gifted lawyer can do very little if the will he is probating is inadequate. It is unthinkable that our Lord would minister on the basis of an inferior "last will and testament."

"This is the sum" simply means "This is the main point and the climax of my discussion." He then presented several "summary arguments" to prove that our Lord is indeed a superior High Priest.

His moral adequacy (v. 1). "We have *such* an High Priest" [italics mine]. This statement refers us back to Hebrews 7:22–28. "For *such an high priest* became us [was suited to us]" (Heb. 7:26). The fact that Jesus Christ is morally perfect and yet identified with us in our needs and temptations makes Him superior to any other priest, past or present. Those readers who wanted to go back into the Old Testament priesthood would have to leave this *suitable* High Priest.

His finished work (v. 1). Today our Lord is *seated* because His work is completed. There were no chairs in the Old Testament tabernacle because the work of the priests was never finished. Each repeated sacrifice was only a reminder that *none* of the sacrifices ever provided a finished salvation. The blood of animals did not wash away sin or cleanse the guilty conscience; it only covered sin until that day when Jesus Christ died to take away the sin of the world (John 1:29).

His enthronement (v. 1). Jesus Christ is not just "seated." It is *where* He is seated that adds glory to His person and His work. He is seated on the throne in heaven at the right hand of the Father. This great truth was introduced early in this epistle (Heb. 1:3), and it will be mentioned again (Heb. 10:12; 12:2). This enthronement was the fulfillment of the Father's promise to the Son: "Sit thou at my right hand, until I make thine enemies thy footstool" (Ps. 110:1). Not only did the high priest of Israel never sit down in the tabernacle, but he never sat down *on a throne*. Only a priest "after the order of Melchizedek" could be enthroned, for Melchizedek was both king and priest (Heb. 7:1).

His supreme exaltation (vv. 1–2). He is "in the heavens." Jesus Christ, in His ascension and exaltation, "passed through the heavens" (Heb. 4:14 NASB). He is now exalted as high as anyone could be (Eph. 1:20–23; Phil. 2:5–11). The fact that He ministers in a *heavenly* sanctuary is important to the argument presented in this chapter.

As we review these four "summary arguments," we can see how logical it is that our Lord ministers on the basis of a superior covenant. Can you conceive of a high priest who is perfect morally, ministering on the basis of a covenant that could not change human hearts? Could a priest who has *finished* his work minister from a covenant that could finish nothing? Can we conceive of a king-priest in the highest heaven being limited by an old covenant that made nothing perfect (Heb. 7:19)? The conclusion seems reasonable: the presence of a superior High Priest in heaven demands a superior covenant if He is to minister effectively to God's people.

It Is Ministered in a Better Place (8:3–5)

In this paragraph, the writer expanded on the marvelous truth that Jesus Christ today ministers in the heavenly sanctuary. The reason for this discussion is not difficult to determine. His readers knew that there was a real temple in Jerusalem, and that in the temple there were priests offering gifts and sacrifices. How easy it would be to go back into the traditional Mosaic system! After all, how do we *know* that the Lord Jesus is ministering in a sanctuary? Has anyone actually seen Him in His high priestly work?

Good questions—and there are good answers!

The logical answer (v. 3). It has already been determined that Jesus Christ is a High Priest. But all high priests serve others; the title is not honorary. Each Old Testament high priest was appointed "to offer gifts and sacrifices"; therefore, Jesus Christ must offer gifts and sacrifices (see Heb. 5:1; 7:27). But these sacrifices must not be offered just anywhere; they must be offered in God's appointed place (Deut. 12:13–14). That appointed place is the sanctuary. The conclusion is logical: if Jesus Christ is a High Priest who offers gifts and sacrifices, then He must have a sanctuary in which He ministers. Since He is in heaven, that sanctuary must be in heaven.

We must not, however, get the impression that our Lord is offering sacrifices in heaven that correspond to the Old Testament sacrifices. The word *somewhat* in Hebrews 8:3 is in the singular, and the phrase "to offer" is in a Greek tense that implies "offer once and for all." On the cross, He offered Himself as the one sacrifice for sin forever (Heb. 9:24–28). In other words, our Lord is "a living sacrifice" in heaven. He is not offering Himself over and over because that is unnecessary.

The genealogical answer (v. 4). We have met this truth before in Hebrews 7:11–14. As far as His human ancestry is concerned, our Lord came from the tribe of Judah. God had promised that the Messiah would come from the kingly tribe of Judah (Gen. 49:8–10). But the priests had to come from the tribe of Levi. Therefore, if Jesus Christ were still on earth, He could not function as a priest. But He can serve as High Priest in heaven because there the order of Melchizedek governs the ministry, not the order of Aaron.

Again, the argument is sound. David predicted that Jesus Christ would be a Priest (Ps. 110:4). Jesus' earthly birth into the tribe of Judah would not permit Him to be an earthly priest; therefore, He must be a Priest in heaven. He would not be accepted in the earthly sanctuary, so He must be serving in the heavenly sanctuary.

The typological answer (v. 5). A "type" is an Old Testament picture of a New Testament truth. Each type is identified as such in the New Testament, so we must not try to make every Old Testament person or event into a type. The word *pattern* in this verse is the Greek word *tupos,* from which we get our English word "type."

The priests then serving in the temple were actually serving in a sanctuary that was a copy ("example") of the heavenly sanctuary. The quotation is from

Exodus 25:40, where it refers obliquely to a heavenly sanctuary. Moses saw this pattern on the mount and duplicated its essentials in the earthly tabernacle. This does not mean that the heavenly tabernacle is made up of skins and fabrics. It is the basic pattern and meaning of the sanctuary that is emphasized here. The true sanctuary is in heaven; the tabernacle and temple were but imitations or copies of the true.

This is a telling argument for remaining faithful to Jesus Christ and not going back into Judaism. The earthly priesthood and sanctuary seemed quite real and stable, and yet they were but *copies* of the true! The Old Testament system was but shadows (see Col. 2:17). The law was but a "shadow of good things to come" (Heb. 10:1); the true and full light came in Jesus Christ. So why go back into the shadows?

In the book of Revelation, where the heavenly scene is described, we can find parallels to the Old Testament tabernacle. John stated that there is a temple of God in heaven (Rev. 11:19). Of course, there will be no temple in the eternal state, because the entire city of God will be a temple (Rev. 21:22). For example, there is a brazen altar (Rev. 6:9–11) as well as an altar of incense (Rev. 8:3–5). The "sea of glass" (Rev. 4:6) reminds us of the laver, and the seven lamps of fire (Rev. 4:5) suggest the seven-branched lampstand in the tabernacle.

Since Jesus Christ is ministering in the original sanctuary, and not the copy, He is ministering in a better place. Why fellowship with priests who are serving in a *copied* sanctuary when you can fellowship with Christ in the original heavenly sanctuary? It would be like trying to live on the blueprint instead of in the building itself!

The writer has now given us two evidences of the superiority of the new covenant: it is ministered by a superior Priest, Jesus Christ; and it is ministered in a superior place, heaven itself. He devoted the remainder of this section to the third evidence.

It Is Founded on Better Promises (8:6–13)

Moses was the mediator (go-between) of the old covenant in the giving of the law (Gal. 3:19–20). The people of Israel were so frightened at Mount Sinai that they begged Moses to speak to them so that they would not have to hear God speak (Ex. 20:18–21). Sad to say, this fear of God did not last long, for the people soon disobeyed the very law they promised to keep. The Mediator of the new covenant is Jesus Christ, and He is the only Mediator (1 Tim. 2:5). Christ's ministry as Mediator is more excellent than that of the Old Testament priests because it is based on a better covenant; *and His covenant is founded on better promises.*

The "better covenant" that is referred to in this paragraph was announced by the prophet Jeremiah (Jer. 31:31–34). The promise was given in a prophecy that assured the Jews of future restoration. Jeremiah ministered during the closing years of the nation's history, before Judah went into Babylonian captivity. At a time when the nation's future seemed completely destroyed, God gave the promise of restoration and blessing.

Before our Lord went to Calvary, He celebrated the Passover with His disciples in the Upper Room. At that supper, He instituted what we call "the Lord's Supper." He said, taking the cup, "This cup is the new testament [covenant] in my blood, which is shed for you" (Mark 14:22–24; Luke 22:20). The apostle Paul quoted these words and applied them to the church (1 Cor. 11:23–27). The writer of Hebrews stated clearly that Jesus Christ *now* "is the mediator of the new covenant" (Heb. 9:15) and repeated it (Heb. 12:24).

What, then, is the relationship between this new covenant *promised* to Israel, but today *experienced* by the church? Or, to state it another way, how can God promise these blessings to the Jews and then turn around and give them to the church?

Some Bible students solve the problem by concluding that the church is "spiritual Israel" and that the new covenant promises therefore belong to "Abraham's spiritual seed" today. That believers today are the "spiritual seed" of Abraham is clear from Galatians 3:13–29; but this is not the same as saying that the church is "spiritual Israel." The promise quoted in Hebrews 8:8 specifically names "the house of Israel and … the house of Judah." Once we are permitted to make such plain words as "Israel" and "Judah" mean something else, there is no end to how we might interpret the Bible!

Other students believe that this "new covenant" has no present fulfillment in the church, but that it will be fulfilled only when the Jews are regathered and the kingdom is established at our Lord's return to earth in glory. But then we have the problem of explaining Hebrews 9:15 and 12:24, verses that state that Jesus Christ is *today* the Mediator of the new covenant. To affirm that there are *two* "new covenants," one for Israel and one for the church, is to create more questions!

Perhaps the solution is found in God's principle of "to the Jew first" (Rom. 1:16). God did promise a new covenant for His people, but the blessings of this covenant are wrapped up in God's Son, Jesus Christ. He is the Mediator of the new covenant. When Jesus began His ministry on earth, He went to His own people first (Matt. 15:24). When He sent out His disciples, He sent them only to Israel (Matt. 10:5–6). When He commissioned the church to witness, He instructed them to begin in Jerusalem (Luke 24:46–48; Acts 1:8). Peter's message at Pentecost was addressed only to Jews and to Gentiles who were Jewish proselytes (see Acts 2:14, 22, 36). In his second recorded sermon, Peter clearly stated that the good news of the gospel would go to the Jews first (Acts 3:25–26).

But the nation rejected the message and the

messengers. While it is true that thousands of individuals trusted Christ and were saved, it is also true that most of the nation rejected the Word, and that the religious leaders opposed the ministry of the church. One result was the stoning of Stephen (Acts 7). But what was God's response? The gospel moved from Jerusalem and Judea into Samaria (Acts 8), and then to the Gentiles (Acts 10).

The church today is made up of regenerated Jews and Gentiles who are one body in Christ (Eph. 2:11–22; Gal. 3:27–29). All who are "in Christ" share in the new covenant, which was purchased on the cross. Today the blessings of the new covenant are applied to individuals. When Jesus comes in glory to redeem Israel, then the blessings of the new covenant will be applied to that beleaguered nation. Read all of Jeremiah 31 to see what God has planned for Israel, His people.

Before we examine the "better promises" of the new covenant, we must settle another matter. We must not conclude that the existence of the new covenant means that the old covenant was wrong or that the law has no ministry today. Both covenants were given by God. Both covenants were given for people's good. Both covenants had blessings attached to them. If Israel had obeyed the terms of the old covenant, God would have blessed them and they would have been ready for the coming of their Messiah. Paul pointed out that the old covenant had its share of glory (2 Cor. 3:7–11). We must not criticize the old covenant or minimize it.

Even though the new covenant of grace brings with it freedom from the law of Moses (Gal. 5:1), it does not bring freedom to disobey God and sin. God still desires that the "righteousness of the law" should be fulfilled in us through the ministry of the Holy Spirit (Rom. 8:1–4). There is a lawful use of the law (1 Tim. 1:8–11).

Now we are ready to consider the "better promises" that belong to the new covenant.

The promise of God's grace (vv. 7–9). The emphasis in the new covenant is on God's "I will." The nation of Israel at Sinai said, "All the words which the Lord hath said will we do" (Ex. 24:3). But they did not obey God's words. It is one thing to *say*, "We will!" and quite another thing to do it. But the new covenant does not depend on man's faithfulness to God but on God's faithful promise to man. The writer of Hebrews affirmed God's "I will" on behalf of those who trust Jesus Christ (Heb. 8:10). In fact, God's "I will" is stated three times in that one verse and six times in Hebrews 8:8–12.

God led Israel out of Egypt the way a father would take a child by the hand and lead him. God gave Israel His holy law for their own good, to separate them from the other nations and to protect them from the sinful practices of the heathen. But the nation failed; "they continued not in my covenant" (Heb. 8:9). God's responses to Israel's disobedience were to discipline them repeatedly and finally to send them into captivity.

God did not find fault with His covenant but with His people. "Wherefore, the law is holy, and the commandment holy, and just, and good" (Rom. 7:12). The problem is not with the law, but with our sinful natures, for by ourselves we cannot keep God's law. The law "made nothing perfect" (Heb. 7:19) because it could not change any human heart. Only God's grace can do that.

The new covenant is *wholly* of God's grace; no sinner can become a part of this new covenant without faith in Jesus Christ. Grace and faith go together just as the law and works go together (Rom. 11:6). The law says, "The man that doeth them [the things written in the law] shall live in them" (Gal. 3:12). But grace says, "The work is done—believe and live!"

The promise of internal change (v. 10). The law of Moses could *declare* God's holy standard, but it could never *provide* the power needed for obedience. Sinful people need a new heart and a new disposition within; and this is just what the new covenant provides. (For a parallel passage, see Ezek. 36:26–27.) When a sinner trusts Christ, he receives a divine nature within (2 Peter 1:1–4). This divine nature creates a desire to love and obey God. By nature, sinful people are hateful and disobedient (Titus 3:3–7), but the new nature gives each believer both the desire and the dynamic for a godly life.

The law was external; God's demands were written on tablets of stone. But the new covenant makes it possible for God's Word to be written on human minds and hearts (2 Cor. 3:1–3). God's grace makes possible an internal transformation that makes a surrendered believer more and more like Jesus Christ (2 Cor. 3:18).

It is unfortunate that many Christians think they are saved by grace but must then fulfill their Christian life according to the Old Testament law. They want the new covenant for salvation but the old covenant for sanctification. The apostle Paul had a phrase to describe this condition: "fallen from grace" (Gal. 5:4). Not "fallen from salvation," but fallen from the sphere of God's blessing through grace. We do not become holy people by trying to obey God's law in our own power. It is by yielding to the Holy Spirit within that we fulfill the righteousness of the law (Rom. 8:1–4); and this is wholly of grace.

The promise of forgiveness for all (vv. 11–12). There is no forgiveness under the law because the law was not given for that purpose. "Therefore by the deeds of the law there shall no flesh be justified in his sight; for by the law is knowledge of sin" (Rom. 3:20). The law could not promise forgiveness to Israel, let alone to all mankind. It is only through the sacrifice of Jesus Christ that forgiveness is possible to all who will call on Him. The Old Testament sacrifices brought a *remembrance* of sins, not a *remission* of sins (Heb. 10:1–3, 18).

Hebrews 8:11 quotes Jeremiah 31:34. It refers to that day when Israel shall be reunited with Judah (Heb. 8:8) and shall rejoice in the promised kingdom (Jer. 31:1–14). In that day, there will be no need to share the gospel with others because everyone will know the Lord personally. However, until that day, it is both our privilege and our responsibility to share the gospel message with a lost world.

What does it mean that God remembers our sins and iniquities no more (Heb. 8:12)? This important statement is quoted again in Hebrews 10:16–17. Does it mean that our all-knowing God can actually *forget* what we have done? If God forgot anything, He would cease to be God! The phrase "remember no more" means "hold against us no more." God recalls what we have done, but He does not hold it against us. He deals with us on the basis of grace and mercy, not law and merit. Once sin has been forgiven, it is never brought before us again. The matter is settled eternally.

As a pastor in counseling ministry I have often heard people say, "Well, I can forgive—but I cannot forget!"

"Of course you can't forget," I usually reply. "The more you try to put this thing out of your mind, the more you will remember it. But that isn't what it means to forget." Then I go on to explain that "to forget" means "not to hold it against the person who has wronged us." We may remember what others have done, but we treat them *as though they never did it.*

How is this possible? It is possible because of the cross, for there God treated His Son as *though He had done it!* Our experience of forgiveness from God makes it possible for us to forgive others.

The promise of eternal blessing (v. 13). The old covenant was still governing the nation of Israel at the time this epistle was written. The temple was standing and the priests were offering their appointed sacrifices. Devout Jews probably thought that their Christian friends were foolish to abandon such a "solid religion" for a faith that was seemingly intangible. What the unbelieving Jews did not realize was that their "solid religion" had grown old and was about to vanish away. In AD 70 the city of Jerusalem and the temple were destroyed by the Romans, and the Jews have not had a temple or a priesthood to serve them ever since (see Hos. 3:4).

However, the new covenant brings eternal blessing. Jesus Christ is the Author of "eternal salvation" (Heb. 5:9) and "eternal redemption" (Heb. 9:12). The new covenant can never get old and disappear. The Greek word translated "new" means "new in quality," not "new in time." This new covenant is of such quality that it will never need to be replaced!

Yes, our Lord is ministering on the basis of a better covenant, a new covenant that makes us partakers of the new nature and the wonderful new life that only Christ can give.

CHAPTER EIGHT
Hebrews 9
THE SUPERIOR SANCTUARY

The Christian is a citizen of two worlds, the earthly and the heavenly. He must render to Caesar the things that are Caesar's and to God the things that are God's (Matt. 22:21). Because he is a citizen of two worlds, he must learn how to walk by faith in a world that is governed by sight. Like Moses, a believer must see the invisible if he is to overcome the pull of the world (Heb. 11:24–27). Practical man says, "Seeing is believing!" But the man of faith replies, "Believing is seeing!"

This principle of faith must apply to our relationship to the heavenly sanctuary. We have never seen this sanctuary. Yet we believe what the Bible tells us about it. We realize that God is not worshipped today in temples made with hands (Acts 7:46–50). There is no special place on earth where God dwells (see Isa. 57:15; 66:1–2; John 4:19–24). We may call a local church building a "house of God," but we know that God does not live there. The building is dedicated to God and His service, but it is not His dwelling place.

Hebrews 9 presents a detailed contrast between the old covenant sanctuary (the tabernacle) and the new covenant heavenly sanctuary where Jesus Christ now ministers. This contrast makes it clear that the new covenant sanctuary is superior.

The Inferior Old Covenant Sanctuary (9:1–10)

Hebrews reminds readers that the regulations and practices in the tabernacle were ordained of God. If there was any inferiority in the tabernacle service, it was not because God had not established the ritual. While the old covenant was in force, the ministry of the priests was ordained of God and perfectly proper.

What was it, then, that made the tabernacle inferior? There are five answers to that question.

It was an earthly sanctuary (v. 1). This means it was made by man (Heb. 9:11) and pitched by man (Heb. 8:2). The Jewish people generously brought their gifts to Moses, and from these materials the tabernacle was constructed. Then God gave spiritual wisdom and skill to Bezalel and Oholiab to do the intricate work of making the various parts of the tabernacle and its furnishings (see Ex. 35—36). After the construction was completed, the sanctuary was put in place and dedicated to God (Ex. 40). Even though the glory of God moved into the sanctuary, it was still an earthly building, constructed by humans out of earthly materials.

Being an earthly building, it had several weaknesses. For one thing, it would need a certain amount of repair. Also, it was limited geographically: if it was pitched in one place, it could not be in another place.

It had to be dismantled and the various parts carried from place to place. Furthermore, it belonged to the nation of Israel and not to the whole world.

It was a type of something greater (vv. 2–5). The writer listed the various parts and furnishings of the tabernacle because each of these carried a spiritual meaning. They were "patterns of things in the heavens" (Heb. 9:23). The diagram gives a general picture of the tabernacle.

Holy of Holies

Ark of the Covenant

Veil

Incense Alter

Table of showbread

Candlestick

Holy Place

Veil

The phrases "the first" (Heb. 9:2) and "the second" (Heb. 9:7) refer to the first and second divisions of the tabernacle. The first was called the holy place and the second the Holy of Holies. Each of these divisions had its own furnishings, and each piece of furniture had its own special meaning.

In the holy place stood the seven-branched golden candlestick (Ex. 25:31–40; 27:20–21; 37:17–24). "Lampstand" would be a better term to use, because the light was produced by the burning of wicks in oil, not by the use of candles. Since there were no windows in the tabernacle, this lampstand provided the necessary light for the priests' ministry in the holy place. The nation of Israel was supposed to be a light to the nations (Isa. 42:6; 49:6). Jesus Christ is the "light of the world" (John 8:12), and believers are to shine as lights in the world (Phil. 2:14–15).

There was also a table in the holy place with twelve loaves of bread on it. It was called the table of showbread (Ex. 25:23–30; 37:10–16; Lev. 24:5–9). Each Sabbath, the priests would remove the old loaves and put fresh loaves on the table, and the old loaves would be eaten. These loaves were called "the bread of presence" and the table was called "the table of presence." Only the priests could eat this bread, and they were required to eat it in the sanctuary. It reminded the twelve tribes of God's presence that sustained them. It also speaks to us today of Jesus Christ, the "bread of life" given to the whole world (John 6).

The golden altar stood in the holy place just in front of the veil that divided the two parts of the tabernacle. The word translated "censer" (a device for burning incense) (Heb. 9:4) should be "altar." The golden altar did not stand in the Holy of Holies, but its ministry *pertained* to the Holy of Holies. In what way? On the annual day of Atonement, the high priest used coals from this altar to burn incense before the mercy seat within the veil (Lev. 16:12–14). Moses (Ex. 40:5) related the golden altar to the ark of the covenant, and so did the author of 1 Kings (1 Kings 6:22). Each morning and evening, a priest burned incense on this altar. David suggested that it is a picture of prayer ascending to God (Ps. 141:2). It can be a reminder that Jesus Christ intercedes for us (Rom. 8:33–34). For details about this incense altar, see Exodus 30:1–10; 37:25–29. The incense itself is described in Exodus 30:34–35.

The Holy of Holies contained only the ark of the covenant, a wooden chest three feet, nine inches long; two feet, three inches wide; and two feet, three inches high. On the top of this chest was a beautiful "mercy seat" made of gold, with a cherub at each end. This was the throne of God in the tabernacle (Ex. 25:10–22; Ps. 80:1; 99:1). On the day of Atonement, the blood was sprinkled on this mercy seat to cover the tables of law within the ark. God did not look at the broken law; He saw the blood. Christ is our "mercy seat" ("propitiation" in 1 John 2:2; Rom. 3:25). But His blood does not just cover sin; it takes away sin.

No doubt many spiritual truths are wrapped up in these pieces of furniture, and all of them are of value. But the most important truth is this: all of this was *symbolism* and not the spiritual *reality*. It was this fact that made the tabernacle of the old covenant inferior.

It was inaccessible to the people (vv. 6–7). We must not get the idea that the Jews assembled in the tabernacle for worship. The priests and Levites were permitted into the tabernacle precincts, but not the people from the other tribes. Furthermore, though the priests ministered in the holy place day after day, only the high priest entered the Holy of Holies, and that only once a year. When he did, he had to offer a sacrifice for his own sins as well as for the sins of the people. In contrast, the heavenly tabernacle is open to all of the people of God, and at all times! (Heb. 10:19–25)

It was temporary (v. 8). The fact that the outer court ("first tabernacle," Heb. 9:6) was standing was proof that God's work of salvation for man had not yet been completed. The outer court stood between the people and the Holy of Holies! As long as the priests were ministering in the holy place, the way had not yet been opened into the presence of God. But when Jesus died on the cross, the veil of the temple was torn from top to bottom (Matt. 27:50–51) and the way was opened into the Holy of Holies. There was no longer any more need for either the holy place or the Holy of Holies, for now believing sinners could come into the presence of God.

Its ministry was external, not internal (vv. 9–10). The sacrifices offered and the blood applied to the mercy seat could never change the heart or the conscience of a worshipper. All of the ceremonies associated with the tabernacle had to do with ceremonial purity, not moral purity. They were "carnal ordinances" that pertained to the outer man but that could not change the inner man.

The Superior Heavenly Sanctuary (9:11–28)

The five deficiencies of the old covenant sanctuary are matched with the five superiorities of the new covenant sanctuary. In every way, the present sanctuary is superior.

It is heavenly (v. 11). The writer has emphasized this fact before, because he has wanted his readers to focus their attention on the things of heaven and not on the things of earth. Some things on earth (including the beautiful Jewish temple) would soon be destroyed; but the heavenly realities would endure forever.

The old covenant tabernacle was made by the hands of men (Ex. 35:30–35). The new covenant sanctuary was not made with hands. "Not of this building" (Heb. 9:11) means "not of this creation." The tabernacle of Moses was made with materials that belong to this creation. The heavenly tabernacle needed no such materials (Heb. 9:24). Since the heavenly tabernacle does not belong to this creation, it is free from the ravages of time.

The "good things to come" had already arrived! All that was foreshadowed by type in the tabernacle was now reality because of Christ's priestly ministry in heaven. The tabernacle was patterned after the sanctuary in heaven, but today we no longer need the pattern. We have the eternal reality!

Its ministry is effective to deal with sin (vv. 12–15). We have here a series of contrasts that show again the superiority of the heavenly ministry.

Animal sacrifices and Christ's sacrifice (v. 12). The writer will discuss the inferiority of animal sacrifices in

Hebrews 10, but here he began to lay the foundation. We need no proof that the blood of Jesus Christ is far superior to that of animal sacrifices. How can the blood of *animals* ever solve the problem of *humans'* sins? Jesus Christ became a Man that He might be able to die for people's sins. His death was voluntary; it is doubtful that any Old Testament sacrifice volunteered for the job! An animal's blood was carried by the high priest into the Holy of Holies, but Jesus Christ presented *Himself* in the presence of God as the final and complete sacrifice for sins. Of course, the animal sacrifices were repeated, while Jesus Christ offered Himself but once. Finally, no animal sacrifices ever purchased "eternal redemption." Their blood could only "cover" sin until the time when Christ's blood would "take away sin" (John 1:29). We have "eternal redemption." It is not conditioned on our merit or good works; it is secured once and for all by the finished work of Jesus Christ.

Ceremonial cleansing and conscience cleansing (vv. 13–14). The old covenant rituals could not change a person's heart. This is not to say that a worshipper did not have a spiritual experience if his heart trusted God, but it does mean that the emphasis was on the external ceremonial cleansing. So long as the worshipper obeyed the prescribed regulations, he was declared clean. It was "the purifying of the flesh" but not the cleansing of the conscience. (For "the ashes of an heifer," see Num. 19.)

We learned from Hebrews 8 that the ministry of the new covenant is *internal.* "I will put my laws into their mind, and write them in their hearts" (Heb. 8:10). This work is done by the Holy Spirit of God (2 Cor. 3:1–3). But the Spirit could not dwell within us if Jesus Christ had not paid for our sins. Cleansing our consciences cannot be done by some external ceremony; it demands an internal power. Because Jesus Christ is "without spot [blemish]" He was able to offer the perfect sacrifice.

Temporary blessings and eternal blessings (v. 15). The blessings under the old covenant depended on the obedience of God's people. If they obeyed God, He blessed them, but if they disobeyed, He withheld His blessings. Not only were the blessings temporary, but they were primarily *temporal*—rain, bumper crops, protection from enemies and sickness, and so forth. Israel's Canaan inheritance involved material blessings. Our eternal inheritance is primarily spiritual in nature (Eph. 1:3). Note that the emphasis is on *eternal*—"eternal redemption" (Heb. 9:12) and "eternal inheritance" (Heb. 9:15). A believer can have confidence because all that he has in Christ is eternal.

This verse (Heb. 9:15) makes it clear that there was no final and complete redemption under the old covenant. Those transgressions were *covered* by the blood of the many sacrifices, but not *cleansed* until the sacrifice of Jesus Christ on the cross (Rom. 3:24–26). Since Christ has accomplished an eternal redemption, we are able to share in an eternal inheritance.

As we review these three contrasts, we can easily see that the ministry of Christ is effective to deal with our sins. His finished work on earth, and His unfinished work of intercession in heaven are sufficient and efficient.

Its ministry is based on a costly sacrifice (vv. 16–23). The word covenant not only means "an agreement," but it also carries the idea of "a last will and testament." If a man writes his will, that will is not in force until he dies. It was necessary for Jesus Christ to die so that the terms of the new covenant might be enforced. "This cup is the new testament [covenant, will] in my blood, which is shed for you" (Luke 22:20).

Even the old covenant was established on the basis of blood. Hebrews 9:19–21 is taken from Exodus 24:3–8, the account of the ratifying of the old covenant by Moses and the people of Israel. The book of the law was sprinkled with blood, and so were the people and the tabernacle and its furnishings. It must have been a solemn occasion.

Not only was blood used at the *beginning* of the ministry of the old covenant, but it was used in the *regular* administration of the tabernacle service. Under the old covenant, people and objects were purified by blood, water, or fire (Num. 31:21–24). This was, of course, *ceremonial* purification; it meant that the persons and objects were now acceptable to God. The purification did not alter the nature of the person or object. God's principle is that blood must be shed before sin can be forgiven (Lev. 17:11).

Since God has ordained that remission of sins is through the *shedding* of blood, and since purification comes through the *sprinkling* of blood, it is necessary that blood be shed and applied if the new covenant is to be in force. The "patterns" (the old covenant tabernacle) were purified by the sprinkling of the blood. But the "originals" were also purified! The blood of Jesus Christ not only purifies the conscience of the believer (Heb. 9:14), but also purified the "heavenly things" (Heb. 9:23 nasb).

How could the heavenly sanctuary ever become defiled? We can understand how the *earthly* sanctuary could be defiled since it was used by sinful men. Each year, on the great day of Atonement, the tabernacle was purified through the sprinkling of blood (Lev. 16:12–19). But how could a heavenly sanctuary ever become defiled? Certainly nothing in heaven is defiled in a literal sense, for sin cannot pollute the sanctuary of God. But, for that matter, nothing in the earthly tabernacle was *literally* defiled by sin. It all had to do with people's relationships to God. The blood sprinkled on a piece of furniture did not change the nature of that piece, *but it changed God's relationship to it.* God could enter into communion with people because of the sprinkled blood.

Through Jesus Christ, we who are sinners can enter into the Holy of Holies in the heavenly sanctuary (Heb. 10:19–22). Physically, of course, we are on earth, but spiritually, we are communing with God in the heavenly Holy of Holies. In order for God to receive us into this heavenly fellowship, the blood of Jesus Christ *had to be applied.* We enter into God's presence "by the blood of Jesus" (Heb. 10:19).

Now we can summarize the writer's discussion. The old covenant was established by blood, and so was the new covenant. But the new covenant was established on the basis of a better sacrifice, applied in a better place! The patterns (types) were purified by the blood of animals, but the original sanctuary was purified by the blood of the Son of God. This was a far more costly sacrifice.

Its ministry represents fulfillment (v. 24). The new covenant Christian has *reality!* We are not depending on a high priest on earth who annually visits the Holy of Holies in a temporary sanctuary. We depend on the heavenly High Priest who has entered once and for all into the eternal sanctuary. There He represents us before God, *and He always will.*

Beware of trusting anything for your spiritual life that is "made with hands" (Heb. 9:24). It will not last. The tabernacle was replaced by Solomon's temple, and that temple was destroyed by the Babylonians. When the Jews returned to their land after the captivity, they rebuilt their temple, and King Herod, in later years, expanded and embellished it. But the Romans destroyed that temple, and it has never been rebuilt. Furthermore, since the genealogical records have been lost or destroyed, the Jews are not certain who can minister as priests. These things that are "made with hands" are perishable, but the things "not made with hands" are eternal.

Its ministry is final and complete (vv. 25–28). There can be nothing incomplete or temporary about our Lord's ministry in heaven. The writer pointed out again the obvious contrasts between the old covenant ministry and the new covenant ministry.

Old covenant	*New covenant*
Repeated sacrifices	One sacrifice
The blood of others	His own blood
Covering sin	Putting away sin
For Israel only	For all sinners
Left the Holy of Holies	Entered heaven and remains there
Came out to bless the people	Will come to take His people to heaven

In short, the work of Christ is a completed work, final and eternal. On the basis of His completed work, He is ministering now in heaven on our behalf.

Did you notice that the word *appear* is used three times in Hebrews 9:24–28? These three uses give us a summary of our Lord's work. He *has appeared* to put away sin by dying on the cross (Heb. 9:26). He *is appearing* now in heaven for us (Heb. 9:24). One day, He *shall appear* to take Christians home (Heb. 9:28).

These "three tenses of salvation" are all based on His finished work.

After reading this chapter, the Hebrew Christians who received this letter had to realize that there is no middle ground. They had to make a choice between the earthly or the heavenly, the temporary or the eternal, the incomplete or the complete. *Why not return to the temple but also practice the Christian faith?* Why not "the best of both worlds"? Because that would be compromising and refusing to go "without the camp, bearing his reproach" (Heb. 13:13). So there is no middle way.

The believer's sanctuary is in heaven. His Father is in heaven and his Savior is in heaven. His citizenship is in heaven (Phil. 3:20) and his treasures should be in heaven (Matt. 6:19ff.). And his hope is in heaven. The true believer walks by faith, not by sight. No matter what may happen on earth, a believer can be confident because everything is settled in heaven.

CHAPTER NINE
Hebrews 10
THE SUPERIOR SACRIFICE

A teenage boy, whose mother was away on a visit, found himself with time on his hands. He decided to read a book from the family library. His mother was a devout Christian, so the boy knew there would be a sermon at the beginning and an application at the end of the book, but there would also be some interesting stories in between.

While reading the book, he came across the phrase "the finished work of Christ." It struck him with unusual power. "The finished work of Christ."

"Why does the author use this expression?" he asked himself. "Why not say the atoning or the propitiatory work of Christ?" (You see, he knew all the biblical terms. He just did not know the Savior!) Then the words "It is finished" flashed into his mind, and he realized afresh that the work of salvation was accomplished.

"If the whole work was finished and the whole debt paid, what is there left for me to do?" He knew the answer and fell to his knees to receive the Savior and full forgiveness of sins. That is how J. Hudson Taylor, founder of the China Inland Mission (now OMF [Overseas Missionary Fellowship] International), was saved.

The tenth chapter of Hebrews emphasizes the perfect sacrifice of Jesus Christ, in contrast with the imperfect sacrifices that were offered under the old covenant. Our Lord's superior priesthood belongs to a better order—Melchizedek's and not Aaron's. It functions on the basis of a better covenant—the new covenant—and in a better sanctuary, in heaven. But all of this depends on the better sacrifice, which is the theme of this chapter.

The writer presented three benefits that explain why the sacrifice of Jesus Christ is superior to the old covenant sacrifices.

Christ's Sacrifice Takes Away Sin (10:1–10)
Sin, of course, is man's greatest problem. No matter what kind of religion a man has, if it cannot deal with sin, it is of no value. By nature, man is a sinner, and by choice, he proves that his nature is sinful. It has well been said, "We are not sinners because we sin. We sin because we are sinners."

The need for a better sacrifice (vv. 1–4). Why were the old covenant sacrifices inferior? After all, they were ordained by the Lord, and they were in force for hundreds of years. While it is true that at times the Jewish people permitted these sacrifices to become empty rituals (Isa. 1:11–15), it is also true that many sincere people brought their offerings to God and were blessed.

The very *nature* of the old covenant sacrifices made them inferior. The law was only "a shadow of good things to come" and not the reality itself. The sacrificial system was a type or picture of the work our Lord would accomplish on the cross. This meant that the system was temporary, and therefore could accomplish nothing permanent. The very repetition of the sacrifices day after day, and the day of Atonement year after year, pointed out the entire system's weakness.

Animal sacrifices could never completely deal with human guilt. God did promise forgiveness to believing worshippers (Lev. 4:20, 26, 31, 35), but this was a judicial forgiveness and not the removal of guilt from people's hearts. People lacked that inward witness of full and final forgiveness. They could not claim, "I have no more consciousness of sins." If those worshippers had been "once purged [from guilt of sin]" they would never again have had to offer another sacrifice.

So the annual day of Atonement did not accomplish "remission of sin" but only "reminder of sin." The annual repetition of the ceremony was evidence that the previous year's sacrifices had not done the job. True, the nation's sins were *covered,* but they were not *cleansed.* Nor did the people have God's inward witness of forgiveness and acceptance.

Yes, there was a desperate need for a better sacrifice because the blood of bulls and of goats could not take away sins. It could cover sin and postpone judgment, but it could never effect a once-and-for-all redemption. Only the better sacrifice of the Son of God could do that.

The provision of the better sacrifice (vv. 5–9). It was God who provided the sacrifice and not man. The quotation is from Psalm 40:6–8, and it is applied to Jesus Christ in His incarnation ("when he cometh into the world"). The quotation makes it clear that Jesus Christ is the fulfillment of the old covenant sacrifices.

The word *sacrifice* refers to any of the animal sacrifices. *Offering* covers the meal offerings and the drink offerings. The burnt offering and sin offering are mentioned (Heb. 10:5, 8). The trespass offering would be covered in the word *sacrifice* (Heb. 10:5). Each of these offerings typified the sacrifice of Christ and revealed some aspect of His work on the cross (see Lev. 1—7).

The phrase, "a body hast thou prepared me" (Heb. 10:5), is not found in the original quotation. Psalm 40:6 reads, "mine ears hast thou opened." The writer of Hebrews was quoting from the Septuagint, the Greek translation of the Old Testament. How do we explain this variation? Some connect "mine ears hast thou opened" with Exodus 21:1–6, a passage that describes the actions of a master whose servant did not want to be set free. The master bored a hole through the earlobe of the servant, which was a sign that the servant preferred to remain with his master. The idea is that our Lord was like a willing servant who had His ears bored.

The problem with that explanation is that only *one* ear was bored, while the verse (Ps. 40:6) speaks of *both* ears. Furthermore, the verb used in Exodus 21 means "to pierce," while the verb in Psalm 40:6 means "to dig." Our Lord was a servant, but it is not likely that the writer had this in mind. Probably "opened ears" signified a readiness to hear and obey the will of God (see Isa. 50:4–6). God gave His Son a prepared body that the Son might serve God and fulfill His will on earth. Our Lord often referred to this truth (John 4:34; 5:30; 6:38; 17:4).

Of course, the same Holy Spirit who inspired Psalm 40 has the right to amplify and interpret His Word in Hebrews 10. "Opened ears" indicates a body ready for service.

Twice in this paragraph, the writer stated that God "had no pleasure" in the old covenant sacrifices (see Heb. 10:6, 8). This does not suggest that the old sacrifices were wrong, or that sincere worshippers received no benefit from obeying God's law. It only means that God had no delight in sacrifices as such, apart from the obedient hearts of the worshippers. No amount of sacrifices could substitute for obedience (1 Sam. 15:22, Ps. 51:16–17; Isa. 1:11, 19; Jer. 6:19–20; Hos. 6:6; Amos 5:20–21).

Jesus came to do the Father's will. This will is the new covenant that has replaced the old covenant. Through His death and resurrection, Jesus Christ has taken away the first covenant and established the second. The readers of this epistle called Hebrews would get the message: why go back to a covenant that has been taken away? Why go back to sacrifices that are inferior?

The effectiveness of the better sacrifice (v. 10). Believers have been set apart ("sanctified") by the offering of Christ's body once for all. No old covenant sacrifice could do that. An old covenant worshipper had to be purified from ceremonial defilement repeatedly. But a new covenant saint is set apart finally and completely.

Christ's Sacrifice Need Not Be Repeated (10:11–18)

Again the writer contrasted the old covenant high priest with Jesus Christ, our Great High Priest. The fact that Jesus *sat down* after He ascended to the Father is proof that His work was completed (Heb. 1:3, 13; 8:1). The ministry of the priests in the tabernacle and temple was *never done* and *never different:* they offered the same sacrifices day after day. This constant repetition was proof that their sacrifices did not take away sins. What tens of thousands of animal sacrifices could not accomplish, Jesus accomplished with *one sacrifice forever!*

The phrase "sat down" refers us again to Psalm 110:1: "Sit thou at my right hand, until I make thine enemies thy footstool." Christ is in the place of exaltation and victory. When He returns, He shall overcome every enemy and establish His righteous kingdom. Those who have trusted Him need not fear, for they have been "perfected forever" (Heb. 10:14). Believers are "complete in him" (Col. 2:10). We have a perfect standing before God because of the finished work of Jesus Christ.

How do we know *personally* that we have this perfect standing before God? Because of the witness of the Holy Spirit through the Word (Heb. 10:15–18). The witness of the Spirit is based on the work of the Son and is given through the words of Scripture. The writer (Heb. 10:16–17) quoted Jeremiah 31:33–34, part of a passage he'd also quoted in Hebrews 8:7–12. The old covenant worshipper could not say that he had "no more consciousness of sins" (Heb. 10:2). But the new covenant believer *can* say that his sins and iniquities are remembered *no more.* There is "no more offering for sin" (Heb. 10:18) and no more remembrance of sin!

I once shared a conference with a fine Christian psychiatrist whose lectures were very true to the Word. "The trouble with psychiatry," he told me, "is that it can only deal with symptoms. A psychiatrist can remove a patient's *feelings* of guilt, but he cannot remove the guilt. It's like a trucker loosening a fender on his truck so he won't hear the motor knock. A patient can end up feeling better, but have *two* problems instead of one!"

When a sinner trusts Christ, his sins are all forgiven, the guilt is gone, and the matter is completely settled forever.

Christ's Sacrifice Opens the Way to God (10:19–39)

No old covenant worshipper would have been bold enough to try to enter the Holy of Holies in the tabernacle. Even the high priest entered the Holy of Holies only once a year. The thick veil that separated the holy place from the Holy of Holies was a barrier between people and God. Only the death of Christ could tear that veil (Mark 15:38) and open the way into the *heavenly* sanctuary where God dwells.

A gracious invitation (vv. 19–25). "Let us draw near…. Let us hold fast…. Let us consider one another." This threefold invitation hinges on our boldness to enter into the holiest. And this boldness ("freedom of speech") rests on the finished work of the Savior. On the day of Atonement, the high priest could not enter the Holy of Holies unless he had the blood of the sacrifice (Heb. 9:7). But our entrance into God's presence is not because of an animal's blood, but because of Christ's shed blood.

This open way into God's presence is "new" (recent, fresh) and not a part of the old covenant that "waxeth [grows] old [and] is ready to vanish away" (Heb. 8:13). It is "living" because Christ "ever liveth to make intercession" for us (Heb. 7:25). Christ is the new and living way! We come to God through Him, our High Priest over the house of God (the church, see Heb. 3:6). When His flesh was torn on the cross, and His life sacrificed, God tore the veil in the temple. This symbolized the new and living way now opened for all who believe.

On the basis of these assurances—that we have boldness to enter because we have a living High Priest—we have an "open invitation" to enter the presence of God. The old covenant high priest *visited* the Holy of Holies once a year, but we are invited to *dwell in the presence of God* every moment of each day. What a tremendous privilege! Consider what is involved in this threefold invitation.

Let us draw near (v. 22). Of course, we must prepare ourselves spiritually to fellowship with God. The Old Testament priest had to go through various washings and the applying of blood on the day of Atonement (Lev. 16). Also, during the regular daily ministry, the priests had to wash at the laver before they entered the holy place (Ex. 30:18–21). The New Testament Christian must come to God with a pure heart and a clean conscience. Fellowship with God demands purity (1 John 1:5—2:2).

Let us hold fast (v. 23). The readers of this epistle were being tempted to forsake their confession of Jesus Christ by going back to the old covenant worship. The writer did not exhort them to hold on to their salvation, because their security was in Christ and not in themselves (Heb. 7:25). Rather, he invited them to hold fast "the profession [confession] of ... hope." (There is no manuscript evidence for the word *faith*. The Greek word is *hope*.)

We have noted in our study of Hebrews that there is an emphasis on the glorious hope of the believer. God is "bringing many sons unto glory" (Heb. 2:10). Believers are "partakers of the heavenly calling" (Heb. 3:1) and therefore can rejoice in hope (Heb. 3:6). *Hope* is one of the main themes of Hebrews 6 (vv. 11–12, 18–20). We are looking for Christ to return (Heb. 9:28), and we are seeking that city that is yet to come (Heb. 13:14).

When a believer has his hope fixed on Christ and relies on the faithfulness of God, then he will not waver. Instead of looking back (as the Jews so often did), we should look ahead to the coming of the Lord.

Let us consider one another (vv. 24–25). Fellowship with God must never become selfish. We must also fellowship with other Christians in the local assembly. Apparently, some of the wavering believers had been absenting themselves from the church fellowship. It is interesting to note that the emphasis here is not on what a believer *gets from* the assembly, but rather on what he can *contribute to* the assembly. Faithfulness in church attendance encourages others and provokes them to love and good works. One of the strong motives for faithfulness is the soon coming of Jesus Christ. In fact, the only other place the word translated "assembling" (Heb. 10:25) is used in the New Testament is in 2 Thessalonians 2:1, where it's translated "gathering" and deals with the coming of Christ.

The three great Christian virtues are evidenced here: *faith* (Heb. 10:22), *hope* (Heb. 10:23), and *love* (Heb. 10:24). They are the fruit of our fellowship with God in His heavenly sanctuary.

A solemn exhortation (vv. 26–31). This is the fourth of the five exhortations found in Hebrews. It is written to believers and follows in sequence with the other exhortations. The believer who begins to *drift* from the Word (Heb. 2:1–4) will soon start to *doubt* the Word (Heb. 3:7—4:13). Soon, he will become *dull* toward the Word (Heb. 5:11—6:20) and become "lazy" in his spiritual life. This will result in *despising* the Word, which is the theme of this exhortation.

The evidence of this "despising" is willful sin. The tense of the verb indicates that Hebrews 10:26 should read, "For if we willfully *go on sinning."* This exhortation is not dealing with one particular act of sin, but with an attitude that leads to repeated disobedience. Under the old covenant, there were no sacrifices for deliberate and willful sins (Ex. 21:12–14; Num. 15:27–31). Presumptuous sinners who despised Moses' law and broke it were executed (Deut. 17:1–7). This explains why David prayed as he did in Psalm 51. Because he deliberately sinned "with a high hand," he should have been slain, but he cried out for God's mercy. David knew that even a multitude of sacrifices could not save him. All he could offer was the sacrifice of a broken heart (Ps. 51:16–17).

How does an arrogant attitude affect a believer's relationship with God? It is as though he trods Jesus Christ underfoot, cheapens the precious blood that saved him ("an unholy thing" [Heb. 10:29] = "a common thing"), and insults the Holy Spirit. This is just the opposite of the exhortation given in Hebrews 10:19–25! Instead of having a bold profession of faith, hope, and love, a backslidden believer so lives that his actions and attitudes bring disgrace to the name of Christ and the church.

What can this kind of a Christian expect from God? He can expect severe discipline. (Chastening is the theme of Heb. 12.) There is no need to "water down" words such as "judgment and fiery indignation" (Heb. 10:27), or "sorer punishment" (Heb. 10:29). We have already seen from the history of Israel that hardly anybody who was saved out of Egypt by the blood of the lamb entered into the promised inheritance. Nearly all of them died in the wilderness. "There is a sin unto death" (1 John 5:16). Some of the Corinthian believers were disciplined and their lives taken because of their presumptuous sins (1 Cor. 11:30, where "sleep" means "died").

God does not always take the life of a rebellious believer, but He always deals with him. "Vengeance belongeth unto me" was spoken to Israel, God's people. "The Lord shall judge his people" (Heb. 10:30, quoted from Deut. 32:35)! "It is a fearful thing to fall into the hands of the living God" (Heb. 10:31).

The major theme of Hebrews is "God has spoken—how are you responding to His Word?" When the nation of Israel refused to believe and obey His Word, God chastened them. Paul used this fact to warn the Corinthians against presumptuous sins (1 Cor. 10:1–12). Note that the examples given in this passage involve people who died because of their willful sins. When we study the subject of "chastening" in Hebrews 12, we will get greater insight into this awesome aspect of God's dealings with His children.

In stating that this exhortation applies to believers today, but that it does not involve loss of salvation, I am not suggesting that chastening is unimportant. On the contrary, it is important that every Christian obey God and please the Father in all things. Dr. William Culbertson, late president of the Moody Bible Institute, used to warn us about "the sad consequences of *forgiven sins.*" God forgave David's sins, but David suffered the sad consequences for years afterward (2 Sam. 12:7–15). David had "despised the commandment of the Lord" (2 Sam. 12:9), and God dealt with him.

What should a believer do who has drifted away into spiritual doubt and dullness and is deliberately despising God's Word? He should turn to God for mercy and forgiveness. There is no other sacrifice for sin, but the sacrifice Christ made is sufficient for all our sins. It is a fearful thing to fall into the Lord's hands for chastening, but it is a wonderful thing to fall into His hands for cleansing and restoration. David said, "Let me fall now into the hand of the Lord; for very great are his mercies" (1 Chron. 21:13).

An encouraging confirmation (vv. 32–39). Lest any of his readers should misinterpret his exhortation, the writer followed it with words of encouragement and confirmation. His readers had given every evidence that they were true Christians. He did not expect them to despise God's Word and experience the chastening of God! In fact, as in Hebrews 6, the writer shifted the pronouns from "we" in Hebrews 10:26 to "he" in Hebrews 10:29 and "them" in Hebrews 10:39.

The readers had been willing to suffer reproach and persecution, even to the spoiling of their goods. When they were not being persecuted themselves, they courageously identified with the other Christians who were in danger, even to the point of sharing their bonds (imprisonment). At that time, they had great confidence and hope, but now they were in danger of casting away that confidence and going back into their old religion.

The secret of victory was in their *faith* and *patience* ("courageous endurance"). We have met this combination of graces in Hebrews 6:12, 15. It is here that the writer introduced the "text" around which Hebrews is written: "The just shall live by faith" (Heb. 10:38). The quotation is from Habakkuk 2:4, and it is also used in Romans 1:17 and Galatians 3:11. Romans emphasizes "the just," Galatians deals with "shall live," and Hebrews centers on "by faith." We are not just *saved* from our sin by faith; we also must *live* by faith. This is the theme of Hebrews 11—13.

The believer who lives by faith will "go on to perfection" (Heb. 6:1). But the believer who lives by sight will "draw back unto perdition" (Heb. 10:39). What is "perdition" in this context? The Greek word translated "perdition" is used about twenty times in the New Testament and is translated by different words: "perish" (Acts 8:20), "die" (Acts 25:16), "destruction" (Rom. 9:22), and "waste" (Matt. 26:8). The word *can* mean eternal judgment, but it need not in *every* instance. I personally believe that "waste" is the best translation for this word in Hebrews 10:39. A believer who does not walk by faith goes back into the old ways and wastes his life.

"The saving of the soul" is the opposite of "waste." To walk by faith means to obey God's Word and live for Jesus Christ. We lose our lives for His sake—but we save them (see Matt. 16:25–27)! In my own pastoral ministry, I have met people who turned their backs on God's will and (like Israel) spent years "wandering in the wilderness" of waste.

But we can be confident! As we walk by faith, our Great High Priest will guide us and perfect us!

CHAPTER TEN

Hebrews 11

FAITH—THE GREATEST POWER IN THE WORLD

This chapter introduces the final section of the epistle (Heb. 11—13), which I have called "A Superior Principle—Faith." The fact that Christ is a superior Person (Heb. 1—6) and that He exercises a superior Priesthood (Heb. 7—10) ought to encourage us to put our trust in Him. The readers of this epistle were being tempted to go back into Judaism and put their faith in Moses. Their confidence was in the visible things of this world, not the invisible realities of God. Instead of going on to perfection (maturity), they were going "back to perdition [waste]" (Heb. 6:1; 10:39).

In Hebrews 11 all Christians are called to live by faith. In it, the writer discussed two important topics relating to faith.

The Description of Faith (11:1–3)

This is not a definition of faith but a description of what faith does and how it works. True Bible faith is not blind optimism or a manufactured "hope-so" feeling. Neither is it an intellectual assent to a doctrine. It is certainly not believing in spite of evidence! That would be superstition.

True Bible faith is confident obedience to God's Word in spite of circumstances and consequences. Read that last sentence again and let it soak into your mind and heart.

This faith operates quite simply. God speaks and we hear His Word. We trust His Word and act on it no matter what the circumstances are or what the consequences may be. The circumstances may be impossible, and the consequences frightening and unknown; but we obey God's Word just the same and believe Him to do what is right and what is best.

The unsaved world does not understand true Bible faith, probably because it sees so little faith in action in the church today. The cynical editor H. L. Mencken defined faith as "illogical belief in the occurrence of the impossible." The world fails to realize that faith is only as good as its object, and the object of our faith is *God*. Faith is not some "feeling" that we manufacture. It is our total response to what God has revealed in His Word.

Three words in Hebrews 11:1–3 summarize what true Bible faith is: *substance, evidence,* and *witness.* The word translated "substance" means literally "to stand under, to support." Faith is to a Christian what a foundation is to a house: it gives confidence and assurance that he will stand. So you might say, "Faith is the confidence of things hoped for." When a believer has faith, it is God's way of giving him confidence and assurance that what is promised will be experienced.

The word *evidence* simply means "conviction." This is the inward conviction from God that what He has promised, He will perform. The presence of God-given faith in one's heart is conviction enough that He will keep His Word.

Witness (KJV, "obtained a good report") is an important word in Hebrews 11. It occurs not only in verse 2, but twice in verse 4, once in verse 5, and once in verse 39. The summary in Hebrews 12:1 calls this list of men and women "so great a cloud of witnesses." They are witnesses to us because God witnessed to them. In each example cited, God gave witness to that person's faith. This witness was His divine approval on their lives and ministries.

The writer of Hebrews made it clear that faith is a very practical thing (Heb. 11:3), in spite of what unbelievers say. Faith enables us to understand what God does. Faith enables us to see what others cannot see (note Heb. 11:7, 13, 27). As a result, faith enables us to do what others cannot do! People laughed at these great men and women when they stepped out by faith, but God was with them and enabled them to succeed to His glory. Dr. J. Oswald Sanders put it perfectly:

"Faith enables the believing soul to treat the future as present and the invisible as seen."

The best way to grow in faith is to walk with the faithful The remainder of this chapter is devoted to a summary of the lives and labors of great men and women of faith found in the Old Testament. In each instance, you will find the same elements of faith: (1) God spoke to them through His Word; (2) their inner selves were stirred in different ways; (3) they obeyed God; (4) He bore witness about them.

The Demonstration of Faith (11:4–40)

Abel—faith worshipping (v. 4). The background story is in Genesis 4:1–10. Abel was a righteous man because of faith (Matt. 23:35). God had revealed to Adam and his descendants the true way of worship, and Abel obeyed God by faith. In fact, his obedience cost him his life. Cain was not a child of God (1 John 3:12) because he did not have faith. He was religious but not righteous. Abel speaks to us today as the first martyr of the faith.

Enoch—faith walking (vv. 5–6). Our faith in God grows as we fellowship with God. We must have both the *desire* to please Him and the *diligence* to seek Him. Prayer, meditating on the Word, worship, discipline—all of these help us in our walk with God. Enoch walked with God in the wicked world, before the flood came; he was able to keep his life pure. Enoch was taken to heaven one day ("translated" = "carried across") and seen no more. Abel died a violent death, but Enoch never died. God has a different plan for each one who trusts Him. Some see in the translation of Enoch a picture of the rapture of the church when Jesus Christ returns (1 Thess. 4:13–18).

Noah—faith working (v. 7). Noah's faith involved the whole person: his *mind* was warned of God; his *heart* was moved with fear; and his *will* acted on what God told him. Since nobody at that time had ever seen a flood (or perhaps even a rainstorm), Noah's actions must have generated a great deal of interest and probably ridicule as well. Noah's faith influenced his whole family and they were saved. It also condemned the whole world, for his faith revealed their unbelief. Events proved that Noah was right! Jesus used this experience to warn people to be ready for His return (Matt. 24:36–42). In Noah's day, the people were involved in innocent everyday activities and completely ignored Noah's witness (2 Peter 2:5).

The patriarchs—faith waiting (vv. 8–22). The emphasis in this section is on the promise of God and His plans for the nation of Israel (Heb. 11:9, 11, 13, 17). The nation began with the call of Abraham. God promised Abraham and Sarah a son, but they had to wait twenty-five years for the fulfillment of the promise. Their son Isaac became the father of Jacob and Esau, and it was Jacob who really built the nation through the birth of his twelve sons. Joseph saved the nation *in* the land of Egypt, and Moses would later deliver them *from* Egypt.

Waiting is, for me, one of the most difficult disciplines of life. Yet true faith is able to wait for the fulfillment of God's purposes *in God's time.* But, while we are waiting, we must also be obeying. "By faith Abraham … obeyed" (Heb. 11:8). He obeyed when *he did not know where he was going* (Heb. 11:8–10). He lived in tents because he was a stranger and pilgrim in the world and had to be ready to move whenever God spoke. Christians today are also strangers and pilgrims (1 Peter 1:1; 2:11). Abraham had his eyes on the heavenly city and lived "in the future tense."

He also obeyed when *he did not know how God's will would be accomplished* (Heb. 11:11–12). Both Abraham and Sarah were too old to have children. Yet they both believed that God would do the miracle (Rom. 4:13–25). Unbelief asks, "How *can* this be?" (Luke 1:18–20). Faith asks, "How *shall* this be?" (Luke 1:34–37).

Abraham believed and obeyed God when *he did not know when God would fulfill His promises* (Heb. 11:13–16). None of the patriarchs saw the complete fulfillment of God's promises, but they saw from "afar off" what God was doing. Dr. George Morrison, a great Scottish preacher, once said, "The important thing is not what we live in, but what we look for." These men and women of faith lived in tents, but they knew a heavenly city awaited them. God always fulfills His promises to His believing people, either immediately or ultimately.

Finally, Abraham obeyed God by faith when *he did not know why God was so working* (Heb. 11:17–19). Why would God want Abraham to sacrifice his son when it was the Lord who gave him that son? All of a future nation's promises were wrapped up in Isaac. The tests of faith become more difficult as we walk with God, yet the rewards are more wonderful! And we must not ignore the obedient faith of Isaac.

In Abraham, Isaac, Jacob, and Joseph, we have four generations of faith. These men sometimes failed, but basically they were men of faith. They were not perfect, but they were devoted to God and trusted His Word. Isaac passed the promises and the blessings along to Jacob (Gen. 27), and Jacob shared them with his twelve sons (Gen. 48—49). Jacob was a pilgrim, for even as he was dying he leaned on his pilgrim staff.

The faith of Joseph was certainly remarkable. After the way his family treated him, you would think he would have abandoned his faith, but instead, it grew stronger. Even the ungodly influence of Egypt did not weaken his trust in God. Joseph did not use his family, his job, or his circumstances as an excuse for unbelief. *Joseph knew what he believed*—that God would one day deliver his people from Egypt (Gen. 50:24–26). *Joseph also knew where he belonged*—in Canaan, not in Egypt, so he made them promise to carry his remains out of Egypt at the exodus. They did (see Ex. 13:19 and Josh. 24:32)!

We have to admire the faith of the patriarchs. They did not have a complete Bible, and yet their faith was strong. They handed God's promises down from one generation to another. In spite of their failures and testings, these men and women believed God and He bore witness to their faith. How much more faith you and I should have!

Moses—faith warring (vv. 23–29). Moses was fortunate to have believing parents. For them to hide their baby son from the authorities was certainly an act of faith. The account is given in Exodus 2:1–10. Moses' parents were named Amram and Jochebed (Ex. 6:20). Though godly parents cannot pass on their faith as they do family traits, they can certainly create an atmosphere of faith at home and be examples to their children. A home should be the first school of faith for a child.

Three great themes relating to faith are seen in the life of Moses. First, *the refusal of faith* (Heb. 11:24–25). As the adopted son of the Egyptian princess, Moses could have led an easy life in the palace. But his faith moved him to refuse that kind of life. He chose to identify with God's suffering people. True faith causes a believer to hold the right values and make the right decisions. The phrase "pleasures of sin" does not refer only to lust and other gross sins. The phrase describes a way of life that we today would call "successful"—position, prestige, power, wealth, and freedom from problems.

Moses' refusal of faith led to *the reproach of faith* (Heb. 11:26a). The mayor of a large American city moved into a dangerous and decayed housing project to demonstrate the problems and needs of the minorities. But she also kept her fashionable apartment and eventually moved out of the slum. We commend her for her courage, but we have to admire Moses even more. He left the palace *and never went back to the old life!* He identified with the Jewish slaves! Men and women of faith often have to bear reproach and suffering. The apostles suffered for their faith. Contemporary believers behind the Iron Curtain knew what it was to bear reproach. If reproach is an evidence of true faith, we wonder how much true faith there is in our own country today!

Finally, there is *the reward of faith* (Heb. 11:26b–29). God always rewards true faith—if not immediately, at least ultimately. Over against "the treasures in Egypt" Moses saw the "recompense of the reward." As Dr. Vance Havner said, "Moses chose the imperishable, saw the invisible, and did the impossible." Moses' faith enabled him to face Pharaoh unafraid, and to trust God to deal with the enemy. The endurance of Moses was not a natural gift, for by nature Moses was hesitant and retiring. This endurance and courage came as the reward of his faith.

The faith of Moses was rewarded with deliverance for him and his people. (See Ex. 11—13 for the exciting Passover account.) Faith brings us *out* (Heb. 11:28), takes us *through* (Heb. 11:29), and brings us *in* (Heb. 11:30). When we trust God, we get what God can do, but when we trust ourselves, we get only what weak people can do. The experience of Moses is proof that true biblical faith means obeying God in spite of circumstances and in spite of consequences.

If you and I had been writing this chapter, the next section would be *Faith Wandering*—but there is no mention of Israel's failure and forty years of wasted time. Why? Because that was an experience of *unbelief,* not faith! The writer did use this experience in Hebrews 3 and 4 as an illustration of doubting the Word. But nowhere in Hebrews 11 will you find a record of *any* failure because of unbelief. Faith records only the victories.

Joshua and Rahab—faith winning (vv. 30–31). The account of the conquest of Jericho is found in Joshua 2—6. Joshua was Moses' successor as leader of Israel, and he succeeded because he trusted the same God that Moses had trusted. God changes His workmen, but He does not change His principles of operation. He blesses faith and He judges unbelief.

From a human point of view, Jericho was an impossible city to conquer. However, Joshua's first act of faith was not the defeat of the city, but the crossing of the Jordan River. By faith, the nation crossed the river just as the previous generation had crossed the Red Sea. This was a witness and a warning to the Canaanite nations that Israel was marching forward by the power of God.

Rahab was a harlot, an unlikely person to put faith in the true God of Israel! *She was saved by grace,* because the other inhabitants of the city were marked out for death. God in His mercy and grace permitted Rahab to live. But *she was saved by faith.* What she knew about God is recorded in Joshua 2:8–14. She knew that Jehovah had delivered Israel from Egypt and that He had opened the Red Sea. But that was forty years before! She also knew God had defeated the other nations during Israel's wilderness wanderings. "For the Lord your God, he is God in heaven above, and in earth beneath" (Josh. 2:11). That was her testimony of faith, and God honored it.

She was saved unto good works. True faith must always show itself in good works (James 2:20–26). She protected the spies, put the cord in the window as directed (Josh. 2:15–21), apparently won her family to the true faith (Josh. 2:13; 6:25), and in every way obeyed the Lord. Not only was Rahab delivered from judgment, but she became a part of the nation of Israel. She married Salmon and gave birth to Boaz who was an ancestor of King David (Matt. 1:4–6). Imagine a pagan harlot becoming a part of the ancestry of Jesus Christ! That is what faith can do!

Rahab is certainly a rebuke to unsaved people who give excuses for not trusting Christ. "I don't know very much about the Bible" is an excuse I often hear. Rahab knew very little spiritual truth, but she acted on what she did know. "I am too bad to be saved!" is another excuse. But Rahab was a condemned heathen harlot! Another excuse is "What will my family think?" Rahab's first concern was *saving* her family, not opposing them. She stands as one of the great women of faith in the Bible.

Various heroes of faith (vv. 32–40). Faith can operate in the life of any person who will dare to listen to God's Word and surrender to God's will. What a variety of personalities we have here! Gideon was a frightened farmer whose faith did not grow strong right away (Judg. 6:11—7:25). Barak won a resounding victory over Sisera, but he needed Deborah the prophetess as his helper to assure him (see Judg. 4:1—5:31). Both Gideon and Barak are encouragements to us who falter in our faith.

The story of Samson is familiar (Judg. 13—16). We would not call Samson a godly man, for he yielded to his fleshly appetites. He was a Nazarite, which meant he was dedicated to God and was never to cut his hair or partake of the fruit of the vine. (A Nazarite should not be confused with a Nazarene, a resident of Nazareth.) Samson did trust God to help and deliver him and, in the end, Samson was willing to give his life to defeat the enemy. However, we must not conclude that believers today can expect to lead double lives and still enjoy God's blessing.

Jephthah's story is fascinating (Judg. 11:1—12:7). It is unlikely that he sacrificed his only daughter as a burnt offering, for this was forbidden in Israel. Probably he dedicated her to the Lord on the basis of the "law of vows" (Lev. 27), dedicating her to perpetual virginity (Judg. 11:34–40).

It is not possible for us to examine each example of faith, and even the writer of Hebrews stopped citing names after he mentioned David and Samuel, who were certainly great men of faith. There are examples in the Old Testament of men and women who won the victories referred to in Hebrews 11:33–35. David certainly subdued kingdoms and wrought righteousness. Daniel's faith "stopped the mouths of lions" (Dan. 6), and the three Hebrew children overcame the power of the fiery furnace (Dan. 3:23–28). The women of faith mentioned in Hebrews 11:35 have their stories given in 1 Kings 17:17–24 and 2 Kings 4:18–37.

The transition in Hebrews 11:35 is important: not all men and women of faith experienced miraculous deliverance. Some were tortured and died! The word translated "others" in Hebrews 11:36 means "others of a different land." These "others" had faith, but God did not see fit to deal with them in the same way he dealt with Moses, Gideon, and David.

While making a hospital visit, I found a patient lying in bed weeping. "What's the matter?" I asked. Her reply was to hand me a book that she had that day received in the mail. It was on "divine healing" and "the power of faith." Some anonymous person had written on the flyleaf, "Read this book—it will give you faith to be healed." The patient happened to be a dedicated Christian who trusted God even in the midst of suffering. But her anonymous correspondent thought that *all* people with faith should be delivered miraculously.

I have personally experienced God's miracle touch on my body when others were sure I would die. I know that God can heal. But I also know that God *does not have to heal* in order to prove that I have faith. The writer of Hebrews (11:36–38) recorded the fact that many unknown men and women of faith *were not delivered* from difficult circumstances, yet God honored their faith. In fact, it takes more faith to *endure* than it does to *escape*. Like the three Hebrew children, we should trust God and obey Him *even if He does not deliver us* (Dan. 3:16–18).

Man's estimate of these heroes of faith was a low one, so men persecuted them, arrested them, tortured them, and in some cases, killed them. But God's estimate is entirely different. He said that the world was not worthy of these people! The apostle Paul is a good illustration of this truth. Festus said that Paul was out of his mind (Acts 26:24). The Jews said Paul was not fit to live (Acts 22:22). Paul himself said he was treated like "the filth of the world … the offscouring of all things" (1 Cor. 4:13). Yet Paul was God's chosen vessel, probably the greatest Christian who ever lived!

Faith enables us to turn from the approval of the world and seek only the approval of God. If God is glorified by delivering His people, He will do it. If He sees fit to be glorified by *not* delivering His people, then He will do that. But we must never conclude that the absence of deliverance means a lack of faith on the part of God's children.

Faith looks to the future, for that is where the greatest rewards are found. The people named in this chapter (and those unnamed) did not receive "the promises" (what was promised, Heb. 11:13) but they had God's witness to their faith that one day they would be rewarded. God's purpose involves Old Testament saints as well as New Testament saints! One day all of us shall share that heavenly city that true saints look for by faith.

We today should give thanks for these saints of old, for they were faithful during difficult times, and yet *we* are the ones who have received the "better blessing." They saw some of these blessings afar off (see John 8:56), but we enjoy them today through Jesus Christ. If the saints of old had not trusted God and obeyed His will, Israel would have perished and the Messiah would not have been born.

"Without faith it is impossible to please God" (Heb. 11:6). But this kind of faith grows as we listen to His Word (Rom. 10:17) and fellowship in worship and prayer. Faith is possible to all kinds of believers in all kinds of situations. It is not a luxury for a few "elite saints." It is a necessity for all of God's people.

Lord, increase our faith!

CHAPTER ELEVEN
Hebrews 12
STAY IN THE RUNNING!

If the apostle Paul were alive today, he would probably read the sports pages of the newspaper and follow the progress of various teams and athletes. Why?

Because several athletic references in his letters indicate his interest in sports. Of course, both the Greeks and the Romans were keenly interested in athletic contests, not only for their physical well-being, but also for the honor of their towns and countries. It was a patriotic thing to be a good athlete and to bring glory to your country.

The writer of Hebrews combined these two themes of athletics and citizenship in this important twelfth chapter. The atmosphere is that of the footraces in the arena. We can see the runners laying aside their training weights and striving to run their races successfully. Some get weary and faint, while others endure to the end and win the prize. First the writer pictures the race (Heb. 12:1–13), and then emphasizes citizenship in the heavenly city (Heb. 12:14–29). In the minds of his readers, these two themes would go together, for no one could take part in the official games unless he was a citizen of the nation.

The one theme that runs through this chapter is *endurance* (Heb. 12:1 ["patience"], 2–3, 7; also see 10:32, 36 ["patience"]). The Jewish believers who received this letter were getting weary and wanted to give up; but the writer encouraged them to keep moving forward in their Christian lives, like runners on a track (see Phil. 3:12–14). He pointed out three divine resources that encourage a Christian to keep going when the situation is difficult.

The Example of the Son of God (12:1–4)
When I was in junior high school, I had a coach who felt it his duty to make an athlete out of me. Everybody in my class could have told him he was wasting his time, because I was the worst athlete in the class—perhaps in the school! I entered a city-wide school competition, running the low hurdles. I knocked down six hurdles, fractured my left ankle, and immediately abandoned my sports career. (Shortly after, the coach enlisted in the army. I may have driven him to it.)

Coach Walker used several techniques to get me to do my best. "Other students have done it, and so can you!" was one of his encouragements. "Just think of what it will do for you physically!" was another. "Now, watch the other kids—see how they do it!" was a third. As I reflect on this experience, I am amazed to discover that these same three approaches are used in this paragraph, to encourage us in the Christian race.

Look around at the winners (v. 1a)! The "great … cloud [assembly, mass] of witnesses" was introduced to us in Hebrews 11. They are the heroes of the faith. It is not suggested here that these men and women now in heaven are watching us as we run the race, like people seated in a stadium. The word "witnesses" does not mean "spectators." Our English word *martyr* comes directly from the Greek word translated "witness." These people are not witnessing what we are doing; rather, they are bearing witness *to us* that God can see us through. God bore witness to them (Heb. 11:2, 4–5, 39) and they are bearing witness now to us.

"I rarely read the Old Testament, except for Psalms and Proverbs," a believer once told me.

"Then you are missing a great deal of spiritual help," I replied. I asked him to open to Romans 15:4 and read the verse aloud.

"For whatsoever things were written aforetime were written for our learning, that we through patience and comfort of the scriptures might have hope."

I then explained that "patience" means "endurance," and that "comfort" means "encouragement." One of the best ways to develop endurance and encouragement is to get to know the godly men and women of the Old Testament who ran the race and won. If you are having problems with your family, read about Joseph. If you think your job is too big for you, study the life of Moses. If you are tempted to retaliate, see how David handled this problem.

Look at yourself (v. 1b)! Athletes used to wear training weights to help them prepare for the events. No athlete would actually participate wearing the weights because they would slow him down. (The modern analogy is a baseball player who swings a bat with a heavy metal collar on it before he steps to the plate.) Too much weight would tax one's endurance.

What are the "weights" that we should remove so that we might win the race? Everything that hinders our progress. They might even be "good things" in the eyes of others. A winning athlete does not choose between the good and the bad; he chooses between the better and the best.

We should also get rid of "the sin that so easily entangles" (Heb. 12:1 NIV). While he does not name any specific sin, the writer was probably referring to the sin of unbelief. It was unbelief that kept Israel out of the Promised Land, and it is unbelief that hinders us from entering into our spiritual inheritance in Christ. The phrase "by faith" (or "through faith") is used twenty-one times in Hebrews 11, indicating that it is faith in Christ that enables us to endure.

Look at Jesus Christ (vv. 2–4)! He is "the author [originator] and finisher of our faith." It was in "looking to him" that we were saved, for *to look* means "to trust." When the dying Jews looked to the uplifted serpent, they were healed, and this is an illustration of our salvation through faith in Christ (Num. 21:4–9; John 3:14–16). "Looking unto Jesus" describes an *attitude* of faith and not just a single act.

When our Lord was here on earth, He lived by faith. The mystery of His divine and human natures is too profound for us to understand fully, but we do know that He had to trust His Father in heaven as He lived day by day. The writer of Hebrews quoted our Lord saying, "I will put my trust in him" (Heb. 2:13). (The quotation is from Isa. 8:17.) The fact that Jesus *prayed* is evidence that He lived by faith.

Our Lord endured far more than did any of the heroes of faith named in Hebrews 11, and therefore He is a perfect example for us to follow. *He endured the cross!* This involved shame, suffering, the "contradiction

[opposition]" of sinners, and even temporary rejection by the Father. On the cross He suffered for *all* the sins of *all* the world! Yet He endured and finished the work the Father gave Him to do (John 17:4). Though the readers of Hebrews had suffered persecution, they had not yet "resisted unto blood" (Heb. 12:4). None of them was yet a martyr. But in Jesus' battle against sin, He shed His own blood.

What was it that enabled our Lord to endure the cross? Please keep in mind that during His ministry on earth, our Lord did not use His divine powers for His own personal needs. Satan tempted Him to do this (Matt. 4:1–4), but Jesus refused. It was our Lord's *faith* that enabled Him to endure. He kept the eye of faith on "the joy that was set before him." From Psalm 16:8–10, He knew that He would come out of the tomb alive. (Peter referred to this messianic psalm in his sermon at Pentecost, Acts 2:24–33.) In that psalm (16:11) David spoke about "fullness of joy" in the presence of the Father. Also, from Psalm 110:1, 4, Jesus knew that He would be exalted to heaven in glory. (Peter also quoted this psalm, Acts 2:34–36.) So "the joy that was set before him" would include Jesus' completing the Father's will, His resurrection and exaltation, and His joy in presenting believers to the Father in glory (Jude 24).

Throughout this epistle, the writer emphasized the importance of the *future hope.* His readers were prone to *look back* and want to *go back,* but he encouraged them to follow Christ's example and *look ahead* by faith. The heroes of faith named in the previous chapter lived for the future, and this enabled them to endure (Heb. 11:10, 14–16, 24–27). Like Peter, when we get our eyes of faith off the Savior, we start to sink (Matt. 14:22–33).

Since Christ is the "author and finisher of our faith," trusting Him releases His power in our lives. I could try to follow the example of some great athlete for years and still be a failure. But if, in my younger days, that athlete could have entered into my life and shared his know-how and ability with me, that would have made me a winner. Christ is both the exemplar *and the enabler!* As we see Him in the Word and yield to His Spirit, He increases our faith and enables us to run the race.

The Assurance of the Love of God (12:5–13)

The key word in this section is *chastening.* It is a Greek word that means "child training, instruction, discipline." A Greek boy was expected to "work out" in the gymnasium until he reached his maturity. It was a part of his preparation for adult life. The writer viewed the trials of the Christian life as spiritual discipline that could help a believer mature. Instead of trying to escape the difficulties of life, we should rather be "exercised" by them so that we might grow (Heb. 12:11).

When we are suffering, it is easy to think that God does not love us. So the writer gave three proofs that chastening comes from the Father's heart of love.

The Scriptures (vv. 5–6). The quotation is from Proverbs 3:11–12, a statement that his readers had known but had forgotten. (This is one of the sad consequences of getting "dull" toward the Word; see Heb. 5:11–12.) This quotation (Heb. 12:5–6) is an "exhortation," which literally means "encouragement." Because they forgot the Word, they lost their encouragement and were ready to give up!

The key words in this quotation are "son," "children," and "sons." These words are used six times in Hebrews 12:5–8. They refer to *adult sons* and not little children. (The word "children" in Heb. 12:5 should be "sons.") A parent who would repeatedly chasten an *infant* child would be considered a monster. God deals with us as *adult* sons because we have been adopted and given an adult standing in His family (see Rom. 8:14–18; Gal. 4:1–7). The fact that the Father chastens us is proof that we are maturing, and it is the means by which we can mature even more.

Chastening is the evidence of the Father's love. Satan wants us to believe that the difficulties of life are proof that God does *not* love us, but just the opposite is true. Sometimes God's chastening is seen in His *rebukes* from the Word or from circumstances. At other times He shows His love by *punishing* ("the Lord ... scourgeth") us with some physical suffering. Whatever the experience, we can be sure that His chastening hand is controlled by His loving heart. The Father does not want us to be pampered babies; He wants us to become mature adult sons and daughters who can be trusted with the responsibilities of life.

Personal experience (vv. 7–11). All of us had a father and, if this father was faithful, he had to discipline us. If a child is left to himself, he grows up to become a selfish tyrant. The point the writer made (Heb. 12:7–8) is that a father chastens *only his own sons,* and this is proof that they *are* his children. We may feel like spanking the neighbors' children (and our neighbors may feel like spanking ours), but we cannot do it. God's chastening is proof that we are indeed His children!

I have met in my ministry people who professed to be saved, but for some reason they never experienced any chastening. If they disobeyed, they seemed to get away with it. If I resisted God's will and did not experience His loving chastening, I would be afraid that I was not saved! All true children of God receive His chastening. All others who claim to be saved, but who escape chastening, are nothing but counterfeits—illegitimate children.

Why do good earthly fathers correct their kids? So that their offspring might show them reverence (respect) and obey what they command. This is why the heavenly Father corrects us: He wants us to reverence Him and obey His will. A child who does not learn subjection to authority will never become a useful, mature adult. Any of God's children who rebel against His authority are in danger of death! "Shall we not much rather be in subjection unto the Father of

spirits, and live?" (Heb. 12:9). The suggestion is that, if we do not submit, *we might not live.* "There is a sin unto death" (1 John 5:16).

We can see now how this twelfth chapter relates to the five exhortations in Hebrews. As a Christian drifts from the Word and backslides, the Father chastens him to bring him back to the place of submission and obedience. (If God does not chasten, that person is not truly born again.) If a believer *persists* in resisting God's will, God may permit his life to be taken. Rather than allow His child to ruin his life further and disgrace the Father's name, God might permit him to die. God killed thousands of rebellious Jews in the wilderness (1 Cor. 10:1–12). Why should He spare us? Certainly this kind of chastening is not His usual approach, but it is possible, and we had better show Him reverence and fear. He chastens us for our profit so that we might share His holy character.

The blessed results (vv. 11–13). No chastening at the time is pleasant either to the father or to his son, but the benefits are profitable. I am sure that few children believe it when their parents say, "This hurts me more than it hurts you." But it is true just the same. The Father does not enjoy having to discipline His children, but the benefits afterward make the chastening an evidence of His love.

What are some of the benefits? For one thing, there is "the peaceable fruit of righteousness." Instead of continuing to sin, the child strives to do what is right. There is also peace instead of war—"the peaceable fruit of righteousness." The rebellion has ceased and the child is in a loving fellowship with the Father. Chastening also encourages a child to *exercise* in spiritual matters—the Word of God, prayer, meditation, witnessing, and so forth. All of this leads to a new *joy.* Paul described it: "righteousness and peace and joy in the Holy Spirit" (Rom. 14:17).

Of course, the important thing is how God's child responds to chastening. He can despise it or faint under it (Heb. 12:5), both of which are wrong. He should show reverence to the Father by submitting to His will (Heb. 12:9), using the experience to exercise himself spiritually (Heb. 12:11; 1 Tim. 4:7–8). Hebrews 12:12–13 sound like a coach's orders to his team! Lift up your hands! Strengthen those knees (Isa. 35:3)! Get those lazy feet on the track (Prov. 4:26)! On your mark, get set, GO!

The example of God's Son, and the assurance of God's love, certainly should encourage us to endure in the difficult Christian race. But there is a third resource.

The Enablement of God's Grace (12:14–29)

As we run the Christian race, what is our goal? The writer explained the goal in Hebrews 12:14: *Peace* with all men, and *holiness* before the Lord. (Remember "the *peaceable* fruit of *righteousness,*" Heb. 12:11.) These two goals remind us of our Lord's high priestly ministry—King of *peace* and King of *righteousness* (Heb. 7:1–2). It requires diligence to run the race successfully lest we "fail of the grace of God" (Heb. 12:15). God's grace does not fail, but we can fail to take advantage of His grace. At the end of the chapter, there is another emphasis on grace (Heb. 12:28).

In this section, the writer encouraged his readers to depend on the grace of God by urging them to look by faith in three directions.

Look back—the bad example of Esau (vv. 15–17). Esau certainly failed to act on God's grace. The account is given in Genesis 25:27–34; 27:30–45. Esau was "a profane person," which means "a common person, one who lives for the world and not God." (Our English word literally means "outside the temple," or not belonging to God.) Esau despised his birthright and sold it to Jacob, and he missed the blessing because it was given to Jacob. (It was supposed to go to Jacob anyway, but it was wrong for Jacob to use trickery to get it. See Gen. 25:19–26.) Afterward, Esau tried to get Isaac to change his mind, but it was too late. Even Esau's tears availed nothing.

What sins will rob us of the enabling of God's grace? These verses tell us: lack of spiritual diligence, bitterness against others (see Deut. 29:18), sexual immorality, and living for the world and the flesh. Some people have the idea that a "profane person" is blasphemous and filthy, but Esau was a congenial fellow, a good hunter, and a man who loved his father. He would have made a fine neighbor—but he was not interested in the things of God.

God's grace does not fail, but we can fail to depend on God's grace. Esau is a warning to us not to live for lesser things.

Look up—the glory of the heavenly city (vv. 18–24). The writer of Hebrews contrasted Mount Sinai and the giving of the law with the heavenly Mount Zion and the blessings of grace in the church (see Ex. 19:10–25; 20:18–21; Deut. 4:10–24). He described the solemnity and even the terror that were involved in the giving of the law (Heb. 12:18–21). The people were afraid to hear God's voice, and even Moses feared and trembled! God set boundaries around the mount, and even if an animal trespassed, it was slain with a spear ("dart"). Of course, God had to impress on His people the seriousness of His law, just as we must with our own children. This was the infancy of the nation, and children can understand reward and punishment.

What a relief it is to move from Mount Sinai to Mount Zion! Mount Sinai represents the old covenant of law, and Mount Zion represents the new covenant of grace in Jesus Christ (see Gal. 4:19–31). The heavenly city is God's Mount Zion (see Ps. 2; 110:1–2, 4). This is the city that the patriarchs were looking for by faith (Heb. 11:10, 14–17). The earthly Jerusalem was about to be destroyed by the Romans, but the heavenly Jerusalem would endure forever.

He described the "citizens" that make up the population of this city. Innumerable angels are there. The church is there, for believers have their citizenship in heaven (Phil. 3:20), and their names are written in heaven (Luke 10:20). "Firstborn" is a title of dignity and rank. Esau was actually Isaac's firstborn, but he rejected his privileges and lost his blessing and birthright.

God is there, of course, and so are the Old Testament saints ("spirits of just men made perfect"). Jesus Christ the Mediator is there, the One who shed His blood for us. We learned that Abel is still speaking (Heb. 11:4), and here we discover that Christ's blood speaks "better things than that of Abel" (Heb. 12:24). Abel's blood spoke from the earth and cried for justice (Gen. 4:10), while Christ's blood speaks from heaven and announces mercy for sinners. Abel's blood made Cain feel guilty (and rightly so) and drove him away in despair (Gen. 4:13–15), but Christ's blood frees us from guilt and has opened the way into the presence of God. Were it not for the blood of the new covenant, we could not enter this heavenly city!

"Why is there so little preaching and teaching about heaven?" a friend asked me. And then he gave his own answer, which is probably correct. "I guess we have it so good on earth, we just don't think about heaven."

When the days are difficult and we are having a hard time enduring, that is when we should look up and contemplate the glories of heaven. Moses "endured, as seeing him who is invisible" (Heb. 11:27). The patriarchs endured as they looked ahead to the city God was preparing for them. One way to lay hold of God's grace is to look ahead by faith to the wonderful future He has prepared for us.

Look ahead—the unshakable kingdom (vv. 25–29). God is speaking to us today through His Word and His providential workings in the world. We had better listen! If God shook things at Sinai and those who refused to hear were judged, how much more responsible are we today who have experienced the blessings of the new covenant! God today is shaking things. (Have you read the newspapers lately?) He wants to tear down the "scaffolding" and reveal the unshakable realities that are eternal. Alas, too many people (including Christians) are building their lives on things that can shake.

The "shaking" quotation is from Haggai 2:6 and refers to that time when the Lord shall return and fill His house with glory. As events draw nearer to that time, we shall see more shaking in this world. But a Christian can be confident, for he shall receive an unshakable kingdom. In fact, he is a part of God's kingdom today.

What shall we do as we live in a shaking world? Listen to God speak and obey Him. Receive grace day by day to serve Him "with reverence and godly fear." Do not be distracted or frightened by the tremendous changes going on around you. Keep running the race with endurance. Keep looking to Jesus Christ. Remember that your Father loves you. And draw on God's enabling grace.

While others are being frightened, you can be confident!

CHAPTER TWELVE
Hebrews 13
PARDON ME, YOUR FAITH IS SHOWING

As you read this last chapter in Hebrews, you get the impression that the writer had a great deal of miscellaneous matter to discuss and saved it till the end. In Hebrews 12, we were rejoicing on Mount Zion, and now we are discussing such everyday topics as hospitality, marriage, church officers, and who was the last one to be released from jail.

But in the Bible, there is no division between doctrine and duty, revelation and responsibility. The two always go together. The emphasis in this last section of the book is on *living by faith*. The writer presented the great *examples* of faith in Hebrews 11, and the *encouragements* to faith in Hebrews 12. In Hebrews 13, he presented the *evidences* of faith that should appear in our lives if we are really walking by faith and not by sight. There are four such evidences.

Enjoying Spiritual Fellowship (13:1–6)

The *basis* for this fellowship is brotherly love. As Christians, these Hebrew people no doubt had been rejected by their friends and families. But the deepest kind of fellowship is not based on race or family relationship; it is based on the spiritual life we have in Christ. A church fellowship based on anything other than love for Christ and for one another simply will not last. For other references to "brotherly love" see Romans 12:10; 1 Thessalonians 4:9–10; 1 Peter 1:22; and 2 Peter 1:7.

Where there is true Christian love, there will also be *hospitality* (Heb. 13:2). This was an important ministry in the early church because persecution drove many believers away from their homes. Also, there were traveling ministers who needed places to stay (3 John 5–8). Many poor saints could not afford to stay in an inn, and since the churches met in homes (Rom. 16:5), it was natural for a visitor to just stay with his host. Pastors are supposed to be lovers of hospitality (Titus 1:8), but all saints should be "given to hospitality" (Rom. 12:13).

Moses (Gen. 18) gave the story of Abraham showing generous hospitality to Jesus Christ and two of His angels. Abraham did not know who they were when he welcomed them; it was only later that he discovered the identities of his illustrious guests. You and I may not entertain angels in a literal sense (though it is possible), but *any* stranger could turn out to be a messenger of blessing to us. (The word *angel* simply means "messenger. ") Often we have had guests in our home who have turned out to be messengers of God's blessings.

Love also expresses itself in *concern* (Heb. 13:3). It was not unusual for Christians to be arrested and imprisoned for their faith. To identify with these prisoners might be dangerous, yet Christ's love demanded a ministry to them. To minister to a Christian prisoner in the name of Christ is to minister to Christ Himself (Matt. 25:36, 40). In our free country we are not arrested for our religious beliefs, but in other parts of the world, believers suffer for their faith. How we need to pray for them and share with them as the Lord enables us!

The home is the first place where Christian love should be practiced (Heb. 13:4). A Christian home begins with a Christian marriage in the will of God. This means loyalty and purity. Sex outside of marriage is sinful and destructive. Sex within the protective bonds of marriage can be enriching and glorifying to God. Fornication is committed by unmarried persons and adultery by married persons. (However, in the New Testament, the term "fornication" can refer to many kinds of sexual sins. See Acts 15:20 and 1 Cor. 6:18.)

How does God judge fornicators and adulterers? Sometimes they are judged in their own bodies (Rom. 1:24–27). Certainly they will be judged at the final judgment (Rev. 21:8; 22:15). Believers who commit these sins certainly may be forgiven, but they will lose rewards in heaven (Eph. 5:5ff.). David was forgiven, but he suffered the consequences of his adultery for years to come, and he suffered in the hardest way: through his own children.

In these days, when sexual sins are paraded as entertainment in movies and on television, the church needs to take a stand for the purity of the marriage bond. A dedicated Christian home is the nearest thing to heaven on earth, and it starts with a Christian marriage.

If we love God and others as we should, then we will have a right relationship to *material things* (Heb. 13:5–6). Times of suffering can either be times of selfishness or times of service. It is not easy to take "joyfully the spoiling of your goods" (Heb. 10:34). But with the economic and ecological problems in our world today, comfortable Christians may soon find themselves doing without some luxuries that they now consider necessities.

A Christian couple was ministering to believers in Eastern Europe, behind the former Iron Curtain. The couple had brought in Christian literature, blankets, and other necessary items. At the church gathering, the couple assured the believers that Christians in America were praying for believers in Eastern Europe.

"We are happy for that," one believer replied, "but we feel that Christians in America need more prayer than we do. We here in Eastern Europe are suffering, but you in America are very comfortable; and it is always harder to be a good Christian when you are comfortable."

The word *covetousness* literally means "love of

money"; but it can be applied to a love for *more* of anything. Someone asked millionaire Bernard Baruch, "How much money does it take for a rich man to be satisfied?" Baruch replied, "Just a million more than he has." Covetousness is the desire for more, whether we need it or not.

Contentment cannot come from material things, for they can never satisfy the heart. Only God can do that. "Watch out! Be on your guard against all kinds of greed; a man's life does not consist in the abundance of his possessions" (Luke 12:15 NIV). When we have God, we have all that we need. The material things of life can decay or be stolen, but *God* will never leave us or forsake us. This promise was made to Joshua when he succeeded Moses (Deut. 31:7–8; Josh. 1:5, 9), and it is fulfilled to us in Jesus Christ (Matt. 28:20; Acts 18:9–10).

The affirmation of faith in Hebrews 13:6 comes from Psalm 118:6. This is a messianic psalm and is fulfilled in Jesus Christ, so we may claim this promise for ourselves. It was a source of great peace to the early Christians to know that they were safe from the fear of man, for no man could do anything to them apart from God's will. Men might take their goods, but God would meet their needs.

A woman said to evangelist D. L. Moody, "I have found a promise that helps me when I am afraid. It is Psalm 56:3—'What time I am afraid, I will trust in thee.'"

Mr. Moody replied, "I have a better promise than that! Isaiah 12:2—'I will trust and not be afraid.'"

Both promises are true and each has its own application. The important thing is that we know Jesus Christ as our Lord and Helper, and that we not put our trust in material things. Contented Christians are people with priorities, and material things are not high on their priority lists.

Submitting to Spiritual Leadership (13:7–9, 17, 24)

Three times the writer used the designation "Them that have the rule over you." The phrase refers to the spiritual leaders of the local assemblies. The church is an organism, but it is also an organization. If an organism is not organized, it will die! Wherever Paul went, he founded local churches and ordained qualified believers to lead them (Acts 14:23; Titus 1:5). "Saints ... bishops [elders], and deacons" (Phil. 1:1) summarize the membership and leadership of the New Testament churches.

Each Christian has three responsibilities toward the spiritual leaders in his local church.

Remember them (vv. 7–9). The word *remember* may suggest that these leaders were dead, perhaps martyred, and should not be forgotten. How easy it is to forget the courageous Christians of the past whose labors and sacrifices make it possible for us to minister today. But while we do not worship people or give them the glory, it is certainly right to honor them for their faithful work (1 Thess. 5:12–13).

These leaders probably had led the readers to Christ because the leaders had spoken the Word to them. When you recall that few Christians then had copies of the Scriptures, you can see the importance of this personal ministry of the Word. Today, we can read the Bible for ourselves, listen to radio or television sermons, and even listen to our computers. We are in danger of taking the Word for granted.

The believers could no longer hear their departed leaders speak, but they could imitate their faith and consider its outcome, or "end." This could refer to their deaths, suggesting that some of them were martyred. However, I believe that "the outcome of their way of life" (Heb. 13:7 NASB) is given in Hebrews 13:8—"Jesus Christ, the same yesterday, and today, and forever." Their lives pointed to Christ! Church leaders may come and go, but Jesus Christ remains the same, and it is Christ who is the center of our faith.

After I had announced my resignation from a church I had been pastoring for several years, one of the members said to me, "I don't see how I'm going to make it without you! I depend so much on you for my spiritual help!"

My reply shocked him. "Then the sooner I leave, the sooner you can start depending on the Lord. Never build your life on any servant of God. Build your life on Jesus Christ. He never changes."

Of course, there is always the danger of being "carried about with divers [various] and strange doctrines" (Heb. 13:9). The purpose of spiritual ministry is to establish God's people in grace, so they will not be blown around by dangerous doctrines (Eph. 4:11–14). Some recipients of the letter to the Hebrews were considering going back to Jewish laws that governed foods. The writer warned them that these dietary regulations would not profit them spiritually because they never profited the Jews spiritually! The dietary laws impressed people as being spiritual, but they were only shadows of the reality that we have in Christ (read Col. 2:16–23 carefully).

When local churches change pastors, there is a tendency also to change doctrines or doctrinal emphases. We must be careful not to go beyond the Word of God. We must also be careful not to change the spiritual foundation of the church. It is unfortunate that there is not more doctrinal preaching today, because Bible doctrine is the source of strength and growth in the church.

Obey them (v. 17). When a servant of God is in the will of God, teaching the Word of God, the people of God should submit and obey. This does not mean that pastors should be dictators. "Neither [be] lords over God's heritage" (1 Peter 5:3). Some church members have a flippant attitude toward pastoral authority, and this is dangerous. One day every pastor will have to give an account of his ministry to the Lord, and he wants to be able to do it with joy. A disobedient Christian will find on that day that the results of disobedience are unprofitable, not for the pastor, but for himself.

Quite frankly, it is much easier to "win souls" than it is to "watch for souls" (see Ezek. 3:16–21). The larger a church grows, the more difficult it becomes to care for the sheep. Sad to say, there are some ministers whose only work is to preach and "run the program"; they have no desire to minister to the souls placed in their care. Some are even "hirelings" who work only for money, and who run away when danger is near (John 10:11–14). However, when a shepherd is faithful to watch for souls, it is important that the sheep obey him.

Greet them (v. 24). The Jews used to greet each other with "Shalom—peace!" The Greeks often greeted one another with "Grace!" Paul combined these two and greeted the saints with, "Grace and peace be unto you!" (See 1 Cor. 1:3; 2 Cor. 1:2; and all his epistles except 1 and 2 Timothy and Titus. When Paul wrote to pastors, he greeted them with, "Grace, *mercy*, and peace." I wonder why?)

Of course, the writer of the Hebrews epistle was sending his personal greetings to the leaders of the church, but this is a good example for all of us to follow. *Every Christian should be on speaking terms with his pastor.* Never allow any "root of bitterness" to grow up in your heart (Heb. 12:15) because it will only poison you and hurt the whole church.

While it is true that each member of a local body has an important ministry to perform, it is also true that God has ordained spiritual leaders in the church. I have been privileged to preach in many churches in America, and I have noticed that where the people permit the pastors (elders) to lead, there is usually blessing and growth. I am not talking about highhanded, egotistical dictatorship, but true spiritual leadership. This is God's pattern for the church.

Sharing in Spiritual Worship (13:10–16, 18–19)

While it is true that a new covenant Christian is not involved in the ceremonies and furnishings of an earthly tabernacle or temple, it is not true that he is deprived of the blessings that they typify. A Jew under the old covenant could point to the temple, but a Christian has a heavenly sanctuary that can never be destroyed. The Jews were proud of the city of Jerusalem, but a Christian has an eternal city, the New Jerusalem. For each of an Old Testament believer's temporary earthly items, a new covenant believer has a heavenly and eternal counterpart.

"We have an altar" (Heb. 13:10) does not suggest a material altar on earth, for that would contradict the whole message of the epistle. In the Old Testament sanctuary, the brazen altar was the place for offering blood sacrifices, and the golden altar before the veil was the place for burning incense, a picture of prayer ascending to God (Ps. 141:2). A new covenant Christian's altar is Jesus Christ, for it is *through Him* that we offer our "spiritual sacrifices" to God (Heb. 13:15; 1 Peter 2:5). We may set aside places in our church buildings and call them altars, but they are really not altars in the biblical sense. Why? Because Christ's sacrifice has already been made, once and for all, and the gifts that we bring to God are acceptable, not because of any earthly altar, but because of a heavenly altar, Jesus Christ.

The emphasis in this section is on separation from dead religion and identification with the Lord Jesus Christ in His reproach. The image comes from the day of Atonement. The sin offering was taken outside the camp and burned completely (Lev. 16:27). Jesus Christ, our perfect sin offering, suffered and died "outside the gate" of Jerusalem. All true Christians must go out to Him, spiritually speaking, to the place of reproach and rejection. "Why stay in Jerusalem when it is not your city?" asked the writer. "Why identify with the old covenant law when it has been done away with in Christ?"

The readers of this epistle were looking for a way to continue as Christians while escaping the persecution that would come from unbelieving Jews. "It cannot be done," the writer stated in so many words. "Jerusalem is doomed. Get out of the Jewish religious system and identify with the Savior who died for you." There can be no room for compromise.

The writer named two of the "spiritual sacrifices" that we offer as Christians (Heb. 13:15–16). Note that the word *spiritual* is not in contrast to *material*, because material gifts can be accepted as spiritual sacrifices (see Phil. 4:10–20). The word *spiritual* means "spiritual in character, to be used by the Spirit for spiritual purposes." A believer's body, presented to God, is a spiritual sacrifice (Rom. 12:1–2).

The first spiritual sacrifice is *continual praise to God* (Heb. 13:15). The words of praise from our lips, coming from our hearts, are like beautiful fruit laid on the altar. How easy it is for suffering saints to complain, but how important it is for them to give thanks to God.

The second spiritual sacrifice is *good works of sharing* (Heb. 13:16). This would certainly include the hospitality mentioned in Hebrews 13:2, as well as the ministry to prisoners in Hebrews 13:3. "Doing good" can cover a multitude of ministries: sharing food with the needy; transporting people to and from church or other places; sharing money; perhaps just being a helpful neighbor. I once had the privilege of seeing a man come to Christ because I helped him mow his lawn after his own mower broke.

Next the writer emphasized the importance of *prayer* (Heb. 13:18–19). He was unable to visit the readers personally, but he did want their prayer help. It is possible that some of his enemies had lied about him, so he affirms his honesty and integrity. We do not know for certain who the writer was. Many think it was Paul. The reference to Timothy in Hebrews 13:23 would suggest Paul, as would also the "benediction of grace" in Hebrews 13:25 (see 2 Thess. 3:17–18). Some scholars have suggested that Peter referred to Paul's authorship of Hebrews (2 Peter 3:15–16), but that statement could also be applied to things Paul wrote in Romans. We do not know the name of the human writer of this book, nor is it important that we do.

Experiencing Spiritual Lordship (13:20–21)

This benediction seems to gather together the major themes of Hebrews: peace, the resurrected Christ, the blood, the covenant, spiritual perfection (maturity), God's work in the believer. As the Good Shepherd, Jesus Christ *died* for the sheep (John 10:11). As the Great Shepherd, He *lives* for the sheep in heaven today, working on their behalf. As the Chief Shepherd, He will *come for the sheep* at His return (1 Peter 5:4). Our Shepherd cares for His own in the past, present, and future. He is the same yesterday, today, and forever!

Our Great High Priest is also our Great Shepherd. When He was on earth, He worked *for* us when He completed the great work of redemption (John 17:4). Now that He is in heaven, He is working *in us* to mature us in His will and bring us to a place of spiritual perfection. We will never reach that place until He returns (1 John 2:28—3:3), but while we are waiting, we are told to continue to grow.

The phrase "make you perfect" (Heb. 13:21) is the translation of one Greek word, *katartidzo*. This is an unfamilar word to us, but it was familiar to the people who received this letter. The doctors knew it because it meant "to set a broken bone." To fishermen it meant "to mend a broken net" (see Matt. 4:21). To sailors it meant "to outfit a ship for a voyage." To soldiers it meant "to equip an army for battle."

Our Savior in heaven wants to equip us for life on earth. Tenderly, He wants to set the "broken bones" in our lives so that we might walk straight and run our life-races successfully. He wants to repair the breaks in the nets so that we might catch fish and win souls. He wants to equip us for battle and outfit us so that we will not be battered in the storms of life. In brief, He wants to mature us so that He can work *in* us and *through* us that which pleases Him and accomplishes His will.

How does He equip us? By tracing this word *katartidzo* in the New Testament, we can discover the tools that God uses to mature and equip His children. He uses the Word of God (2 Tim. 3:16–17) and prayer (1 Thess. 3:10) in the fellowship of the local church (Eph. 4:11–12). He also uses individual believers to equip us and mend us (Gal. 6:1). Finally, He uses suffering to perfect His children (1 Peter 5:10), and this relates to what we learned from Hebrews 12 about chastening.

What a difference it would make in our lives if we would turn Hebrews 13:20–21 into a personal prayer each day. "Lord, make me perfect in every good work to do thy will. Work in me that which is well-pleasing in thy sight. Do it through Jesus Christ and may he receive the glory."

The basis for this marvelous work is "the blood of the everlasting covenant" (Heb. 13:20). This is the new covenant that was discussed in Hebrews 8, a covenant based on the sacrifice discussed in Hebrews 10. Because this new covenant was a part of God's eternal plan of salvation, and because it guarantees everlasting life, it is called "the everlasting covenant." But apart from the death of Jesus Christ, we can share in none of the blessings named in this profound benediction.

The "Amen" at the end of the benediction closed the body of the epistle. All that remained was for the writer to add a few words of greeting and personal information.

He had written a long letter, and in it he had dealt with some profound and difficult doctrines; so he encouraged his readers to "bear with [suffer]" this letter of encouragement. This seems like a long letter to us, but he felt it was just a "few words." No doubt some members of the congregation responded negatively to this letter, while others received it and acted on it. Paul (1 Thess. 2:13) told us how we should respond to God's Word. Read the verse carefully—and practice it.

What Timothy's relationship to the group was, we do not know. He was a prominent minister in that day, and most of the Christians would either know him or know about him. These personal touches remind us that God is interested in individuals and not just in groups of people.

"They of Italy salute you" (Heb. 13:24) could mean that the writer was in Italy at the time, or that saints from Italy were with him and wanted to send their greetings.

These personal references at the end of the letter raise questions that we cannot answer now. But the total impact of Hebrews answers the important question, "How can I stand firm in a world that is shaking all around me?" The answer: know the superior Person, Jesus Christ; trust His superior priesthood; and live by the superior principle of faith. Build your life on the things of heaven that will never shake.

Be confident! Jesus Christ saves to the uttermost!

JAMES

OUTLINE

Key theme: Spiritual maturity
Key verse: James 1:4

The Marks of the Mature Christian:

I. HE IS PATIENT IN TESTING (1)
A. Trials on the outside—1:1–12
B. Temptations on the inside—1:13–27

II. HE PRACTICES THE TRUTH (2)
A. Faith and love—2:1–13
B. Faith and works—2:14–26

III. HE HAS POWER OVER HIS TONGUE (3)
A. Exhortation—3:1–2
B. Illustrations—3:3–12
C. Application—3:13–18

IV. HE IS A PEACEMAKER, NOT A TROUBLEMAKER (4)
A. Three wars—1:1–3
B. Three enemies—4:4–7
C. Three admonitions—4:8–17

V. HE IS PRAYERFUL IN TROUBLES (5)
A. Economic troubles—5:1–9
B. Physical troubles—5:10–16
C. National troubles—5:17–18
D. Church troubles—5:19–20

CONTENTS

CHAPTER ONE
James 1:1
TIME TO GROW UP

Beginning a study of a book of the Bible is something like preparing for a trip: you like to know where you are going and what you can expect to see. When my wife and I were getting ready for our first visit to Great Britain, we spent many hours reading travel books and poring over maps. When we arrived there, we enjoyed the visit much more because we knew what we were looking for and how to find it.

Perhaps the best way to launch a study of the epistle of James is to answer four important questions.

Who Was James?
"James, a servant of God and of the Lord Jesus Christ" (James 1:1a) is the way he introduced himself. It was a popular name, a form of the great Old Testament name "Jacob." There were several men who bore this name in New Testament history.

James, the son of Zebedee and brother of John. He was one of the most prominent to bear the name. He was a fisherman called by Christ to follow and become a disciple (Matt. 4:17–22). He and his brother John were nicknamed by Christ "sons of thunder" because of their impulsiveness (Mark 3:17; Luke 9:51–56). James was the first of the disciples to give his life for Christ. He was killed by Herod in AD 44 (Acts 12:1–2).

James, the son of Alphaeus. He was another of the disciples (Matt. 10:3; Acts 1:13), but very little is known about him. Matthew (Levi) is also identified as "the son of Alphaeus" (Mark 2:14), and some students conjecture that the two men might have been brothers. There is no indication that this James wrote the letter we are about to study.

James, the father of Judas the disciple. He is an even more obscure man (Luke 6:16 KJV, where "brother" ought to be "father"). This Judas was called "the son of James" to distinguish him from Judas Iscariot.

James, the brother of our Lord. He seems to be the most likely candidate for author of this letter. He does not identify himself in this way; humbly, he calls himself "a servant of God and of the Lord Jesus Christ." That Jesus had brothers and sisters is stated in Matthew 13:55–56 and Mark 6:3, and one of His brothers was named James. (By "brother," of course, I mean half-brother. Joseph was not our Lord's father since Jesus was conceived by the Holy Spirit of God.)

James and the other brothers did not believe in Jesus during His earthly ministry (Mark 3:31–35; John 7:1–5). Yet we find our Lord's brethren in the Upper Room praying with the disciples (Acts 1:14). What effected the change from unbelief to faith? First Corinthians 15:7 indicates that Jesus appeared to James after His resurrection! This convinced James

that Jesus truly was the Savior, and he, in turn, shared this knowledge about Jesus to the other brothers.

James became the leader of the church in Jerusalem. Paul called him "a pillar," in Galatians 2:9. It was James who moderated the church conference described in Acts 15. When Peter was delivered from prison, he sent a special message to James (Acts 12:17); and when Paul visited Jerusalem, it was to James that he brought greetings and the special "love offering" from the Gentiles (Acts 21:18–19).

We have no record in the Bible, but tradition tells us that James was martyred in AD 62. The story is that the Pharisees in Jerusalem so hated James' testimony for Christ that they had him cast down from the temple and then beaten to death with clubs. The story also relates that James died, as did his Savior, praying for his murderers, "Father, forgive them, for they know not what they do."

What kind of a man was James? He must have been a deeply spiritual man to gain the leadership of the Jerusalem church in so short a time. His stature is seen in Acts 15, where he was able to permit all the factions to express themselves, and then bring peace by drawing a conclusion based oh the Word of God. Paul, in 1 Corinthian 9:5, suggested that he was a married man. Again, tradition tells us that he was a man of prayer, and this explains the emphasis on prayer in his letter. It was said that he prayed so much, his knees were as hard as a camel's!

James was a Jew, reared in the tradition of the law of Moses, and his Jewish legalism stands out in his letter. (Note also Acts 21:18 ff., where James asked Paul to help him pacify the Christian legalists in the Jerusalem church.) There are over fifty imperatives in the epistle of James. James did not suggest—he commanded! He quoted the Old Testament only five times, but there are many allusions to Old Testament passages in the letter.

While still an unbeliever, James must have paid attention to what Jesus taught; in his letter there are numerous allusions to our Lord's sayings, particularly the Sermon on the Mount. Compare these passages:

James 1:2—Matthew 5:10–12
James 1:4—Matthew 5:48
James 1:5—Matthew 7:7–12
James 1:22—Matthew 7:21–27
James 4:11–12—Matthew 7:1–5
James 5:1–3—Matthew 6:19–21

Keep in mind that James led the church in Jerusalem during a very difficult time. It was a time of transition, and such times are always upsetting and demanding. There were many Christian Jews in Jerusalem who still held to the Old Testament law (Acts 21:20). The temple and its services were still in operation, and the full light of the gospel of God's grace had not yet dawned. We who have read Romans, Galatians, and Hebrews might be prone to judge these early believers, but we must not. They were saved people, but they were still in the shadows of the law, moving out into the bright light of God's grace. While there may have been differences in degrees of spiritual knowledge and experience, there was no competition between Paul and those who directed the Jerusalem church (Gal. 2:1–10).

To Whom Did James Write?

"To the twelve tribes which are scattered abroad, greeting" (James 1:1b). James wrote to Jews living outside the land of Palestine. The term "twelve tribes" can only mean the people of Israel, the Jewish nation (Acts 26:7). The fact that many Jews lived outside their Promised Land is evidence of the spiritual decline of the nation. God had to scatter them (Deut. 4:25ff.). When Peter addressed that huge Jewish congregation at Pentecost, he spoke to men from many different nations (Acts 2:9–11).

James sent his letter to *Christian* Jews. At least nineteen times he addressed them as "brethren," indicating not only "brothers in the flesh" (fellow Jews), but also "brothers in the Lord." James was very clear on the doctrine of the new birth (James 1:18). There are times when James also addressed wicked men who were not in the fellowship (the rich, for example, in James 5:1–6), but he did so in order to teach and encourage the saved Jews to whom he sent the letter.

The word *scattered* in James 1:1 is an interesting one. It means "in the dispersion." The term "the dispersion" was used to identify the Jews living outside the land of Palestine. But the Greek word carries the idea of "scattering seed." When the Jewish believers were scattered in that first wave of persecution (Acts 8:1, 4), it was really the sowing of seed in many places; and much of that seed bore fruit (Acts 11:19ff.).

Christian Jews scattered throughout the Roman Empire would have needs and problems of their own. Being Jews, they would be rejected by the Gentiles, and being *Christian* Jews, they would be rejected by their own countrymen. This letter indicates that most of these believers were poor, and some of them were being oppressed by the rich.

Why Did James Write?

Each New Testament letter has its own special theme, purpose, and destination. Paul wrote the book of Romans to prepare the Roman Christians for his intended visit. First Corinthians was sent to the church at Corinth to help correct certain problems. Galatians was written to a group of churches to warn them against legalism and false teaching.

As you read the epistle of James, you discover that these Jewish Christians were having some problems in their personal lives and in their church fellowship. For one thing, they were going through difficult testings. They were also facing temptations to sin. Some of the believers were catering to the rich, while others were being robbed by the rich. Church members were competing for offices in the church, particularly teaching offices.

One of the major problems in the church was a failure on the part of many to live what they professed to believe. Furthermore, the tongue was a serious problem, even to the point of creating wars and divisions in the assembly. Worldliness was another problem. Some of the members were disobeying God's Word and were sick physically because of it, and some were straying away from the Lord and the church.

As we review this list of problems, does it appear to be much different from the problems that beset the average local church today? Do we not have in our churches people who are suffering for one reason or another? Do we not have members who talk one way, but walk another way? Is not worldliness a serious problem? Are there not Christians who cannot control their tongues? It seems that James was dealing with very up-to-date matters!

But James was not discussing an array of miscellaneous problems. All of these problems had a common cause: *spiritual immaturity.* These Christians simply were not growing up. This gives us a hint as to the basic theme of this letter: *the marks of maturity in the Christian life.* James used the word *perfect* several times, a word that means "mature, complete" (see James 1:4, 17, 25; 2:22; 3:2). By "a perfect man" (James 3:2) James did not mean a sinless man, but rather one who is mature, balanced, grown-up.

Spiritual maturity is one of the greatest needs in churches today. Too many churches are playpens for babies instead of workshops for adults. The members are not mature enough to eat the solid spiritual food that they need, so they have to be fed on milk (Heb. 5:11–14). Just look at the problems James dealt with and you can see that each of them is characteristic of little children:

Impatience in difficulties—1:1–4
Talking but not living the truth—2:14ff.
No control of the tongue—3:1ff.
Fighting and coveting—4:1ff.
Collecting material "toys"—5:1ff.

After well over a quarter century of ministry, I am convinced that spiritual immaturity is the number one problem in our churches. God is looking for mature men and women to carry on His work, and sometimes all He can find are little children who cannot even get along with each other.

The five chapters of this letter suggest the five marks of the mature Christian (see outline).

Of course, this is but one approach to this letter; there are other ways to study it. As the chapters are examined, spiritual maturity and how it may be attained will be emphasized.

The epistle of James logically follows the epistle to the Hebrews, for one of the major themes of Hebrews is *spiritual perfection.* The word *perfect* is found in Hebrews at least fourteen times. The key verse is Hebrews 6:1—"Let us go on unto perfection" meaning, "spiritual maturity." The writer of Hebrews explained the perfect salvation to be had in Christ.

James exhorted his readers to build on this perfect salvation and grow into maturity. Without the perfect work of Christ there could be no perfecting of the believers.

How Can We Get the Most Out of This Study?

Since the theme is spiritual maturity, we must begin by examining our own hearts to see where we are in the Christian life.

First of all, it is essential that we have been born again. Apart from spiritual birth there can be no spiritual maturity. James mentioned the new birth early in his letter: "Of his own will begat he us with the word of truth" (James 1:18). The parallel to this is 1 Peter 1:23—"Being born again, not of corruptible seed, but of incorruptible, by the word of God, which liveth and abideth forever."

Just as a human baby has two parents, so a spiritual baby has two parents—the Word of God and the Spirit of God. We have already quoted two verses that mention the Word of God. John 3:5–6 mentions the Spirit of God. (It is my conviction that "born of water" here refers to physical birth. All babies are "born of water." Nicodemus thought in terms of physical birth in John 3:5.)

How, then, is a person "born again"? The Spirit of God takes the Word of God and generates new life within the heart of the sinner who believes on Jesus Christ. It is a miracle. The Spirit uses the Word to convict the sinner, and then to reveal the Savior. We are saved by faith (Eph. 2:8–9), and faith comes from the Word of God (Rom. 10:17).

If we have been born again, there is a second essential for getting the most out of what James has written: we must honestly examine our lives in the light of God's Word. James compares the Bible to a mirror (James 1:22ff). As we study the Word, we are looking into the divine mirror and seeing ourselves as we really are. But James warns us that we must be honest about what we see and not merely glance at the image and walk away.

Perhaps you heard about the primitive savage who looked into a mirror for the first time. He was so shocked at what he saw that he broke the mirror! Many Christians make the same mistake: they criticize the preacher or the lesson, when they ought to be judging themselves.

This leads to a third essential: we must obey what God teaches us, no matter what the cost. We must be "doers of the word and not hearers only" (James 1:22). It is easy to attend a Bible study, share the lesson, and discuss it, but it is much more difficult to go out into life in the workaday world and practice what we have learned. The blessing does not come in *studying* the Word, but in *doing* the Word. Unless we are willing to obey, the Lord is not obligated to teach us (John 7:17).

The fourth essential is that we be prepared for some extra trials and testings. Whenever we are serious about spiritual growth, the enemy gets serious about opposing us. Perhaps you feel a need for more patience. Then be prepared for more trials, because "tribulation worketh patience" (Rom. 5:3). The real examinations in Bible study come in the school of life, not in the classroom.

I read recently about a man who was burdened to grow in his patience. He knew he was immature in that area of his life, and he wanted to grow up. He sincerely prayed, "Lord, help me to grow in patience. I want to have more self-control in this area of my life." That morning, he missed his train to work and spent the next fifty minutes pacing the platform and complaining of his plight. As the next train to the city arrived, the man realized how stupid he had been. "The Lord gave me nearly an hour to grow in my patience, and all I did was practice my impatience!" he said to himself.

There may come a time in this study when you decide that continuing is too dangerous. Satan may turn on the heat and make things so difficult for you that you will want to retreat. *Don't do it!* When that time arrives, you will be on the verge of a new and wonderful blessing in your own life, a thrilling new step of maturity. Even if Satan does turn on the heat, your Father in heaven keeps His almighty hand on the thermostat!

Even physical maturity is not always an easy, pleasant experience. The teenager walking that difficult bridge from childhood to adulthood has his frustrations and failures, but if he keeps on going (and growing), he eventually enters a wonderful life of maturity. Christian growth is not automatic, as is physical growth. Christian maturity is something we must work at constantly. So don't give up! There is travail in birth, and there is also travail in maturity (Gal. 4:19).

Finally, we must measure our spiritual growth by the Word of God. We should not measure ourselves by other Christians, but by the Word of God and the Son of God (Eph. 4:13). At the close of this study, a dozen questions are listed based on James, that may help in a personal evaluation. Feel free to turn to them at any time, because regular examinations are good for spiritual health.

Not everyone who grows old, grows up. There is a difference between age and maturity. Just because a Christian has been saved for ten or twenty years does not guarantee that he is mature in the Lord. Mature Christians are happy Christians, useful Christians, Christians who help to encourage others and to build their local church. As we study James together, with God's help we will learn together and mature together.

CHAPTER TWO
James 1:2–12
TURNING TRIALS INTO TRIUMPHS

Perhaps you have seen the bumper sticker that reads, "When life hands you lemons, make lemonade!" It is easier to smile at that statement than to practice it, but the basic philosophy is sound. In fact, it is biblical. Throughout the Bible are people who turned defeat into victory and trial into triumph. Instead of being victims, they became victors.

James tells us that we can have this same experience today. No matter what the trials may be on the outside (James 1:1–12) or the temptations on the inside (James 1:13–27), through faith in Christ we can experience victory. The result of this victory is spiritual maturity.

If we are going to turn trials into triumphs, we must obey four imperatives: *count* (James 1:2), *know* (James 1:3), *let* (James 1:4, 9–11), and *ask* (James 1:5–8). Or, to put it another way, there are four essentials for victory in trials: a joyful attitude, an understanding mind, a surrendered will, and a heart that wants to believe.

Count—a Joyful Attitude (1:2)

Outlook determines outcome, and attitude determines action. God tells us to *expect trials.* It is not *"if* you fall into various testings" but *"when* you fall into various testings." The believer who expects his Christian life to be easy is in for a shock. Jesus warned His disciples, "In the world ye shall have tribulation" (John 16:33). Paul told his converts that "we must through much tribulation enter into the kingdom of God" (Acts 14:22).

Because we are God's "scattered people" and not God's "sheltered people," we must experience trials. We cannot always expect everything to go our way. Some trials come simply because we are human—sickness, accidents, disappointments, even seeming tragedies. Other trials come because we are Christians. Peter emphasized this in his first letter: "Beloved, think it not strange concerning the fiery trial which is to try you, as though some strange thing happened unto you" (1 Peter 4:12). Satan fights us, the world opposes us, and this makes for a life of battle.

The phrase "fall into" does not suggest a stupid accident. Translate it "encounter, come across." A Christian certainly should not manufacture trials. The Greek word translated "divers" means "various, varicolored." Peter used the same word in 1 Peter 1:6—"Ye are in heaviness through manifold temptations." The trials of life are not all alike; they are like variegated yarn that the weaver uses to make a beautiful rug. God arranges and mixes the colors and experiences of life. The final product is a beautiful thing for His glory.

My wife and I once visited a world-famous weaver and watched his men and women work on the looms. I noticed that the undersides of the rugs were not very beautiful: the patterns were obscure and the loose ends of yarn dangled. "Don't judge the worker or the work by looking at the wrong side," our guide told us. In the same way, we are looking at the wrong side of life; only the Lord sees the finished pattern. Let's not judge Him or His work from what we see today. His work is not finished yet!

The key word is *count.* It is a financial term, and it means "to evaluate." Paul used it several times in Philippians 3. When Paul became a Christian, he evaluated his life and set new goals and priorities. Things that were once important to him became "garbage" in the light of his experience with Christ. When we face the trials of life, we must evaluate them in the light of what God is doing for us.

This explains why the dedicated Christian can have joy in the midst of trials: *he lives for the things that matter most.* Even our Lord was able to endure the cross because of "the joy that was set before him" (Heb. 12:2), the joy of returning to heaven and one day sharing His glory with His church.

Our values determine our evaluations. If we value comfort more than character, then trials will upset us. If we value the material and physical more than the spiritual, we will not be able to "count it all joy." If we live only for the present and forget the future, then trials will make us bitter, not better. Job had the right outlook when he said, "But he knoweth the way that I take: when he hath tried me, I shall come forth as gold" (Job 23:10).

So, when trials come, immediately give thanks to the Lord and adopt a joyful attitude. Do not pretend; do not try self-hypnosis; simply look at trials through the eyes of faith. Outlook determines outcome; to *end* with joy, *begin* with joy.

"But how," we may ask, "is it possible to rejoice in the midst of trials?" The second imperative explains this.

Know—an Understanding Mind (1:3)

What do Christians know that makes it easier to face trials and benefit from them?

Faith is always tested. When God called Abraham to live by faith, He tested him in order to increase his faith. God always tests us to bring out the *best;* Satan tempts us to bring out the worst. The testing of our faith proves that we are truly born again.

Testing works for us, not against us. The word *trying* can be translated "approval." Again, Peter helps us understand it better: "That the trial of your faith, being much more precious than of gold that perisheth" (1 Peter 1:7). A gold prospector brings his ore sample into the assayer's office to be tested. The sample itself may not be worth more than a few dollars, but the *approval*—the official statement about the ore—is worth millions! It assures the prospector that he has a gold mine. God's approval of our faith is precious, because it assures us that our faith is genuine.

Trials work *for* the believer, not *against* him. Paul said, "And we know that all things work together for good" (Rom. 8:28), and, "For our light affliction, which is but for a moment, worketh for us a far more exceeding and eternal weight of glory" (2 Cor. 4:17).

Trials rightly used help us to mature. What does God want to produce in our lives? Patience, endurance, and the ability to keep going when things are tough. "We glory in tribulations also: knowing that tribulation worketh patience; and patience, experience; and experience, hope" (Rom. 5:3–4). In the Bible, *patience* is not a passive acceptance of circumstances. It is a courageous perseverance in the face of suffering and difficulty.

Immature people are always impatient; mature people are patient and persistent. Impatience and unbelief usually go together, just as faith and patience do. "Be … followers of them who through faith and patience inherit the promises" (Heb. 6:12). "For ye have need of patience, that, after ye have done the will of God, ye might receive the promise" (Heb. 10:36). "He that believeth shall not make haste" (Isa. 28:16).

God wants to make us patient because that is the key to every other blessing. The little child who does not learn patience will not learn much of anything else. When the believer learns to wait on the Lord, then God can do great things for him. Abraham ran ahead of the Lord, married Hagar, and brought great sorrow into his home (Gen. 16). Moses ran ahead of God, murdered a man, and had to spend forty years with the sheep to learn patience (Ex. 2:11ff.). Peter almost killed a man in his impatience (John 18:10–11).

The only way the Lord can develop patience and character in our lives is through trials. Endurance cannot be attained by reading a book (even this one), listening to a sermon, or even praying a prayer. We must go through the difficulties of life, trust God, and obey Him. The result will be patience and character. Knowing this, we can face trials joyfully. We know what trials will do in us and for us, and we know that the end result will bring glory to God.

This fact explains why studying the Bible helps us grow in patience (Rom. 15:4). As we read about Abraham, Joseph, Moses, David, and even our Lord, we realize that God has a purpose in trials. God fulfills His purposes as we trust Him. There is no substitute for an understanding mind. Satan can defeat the ignorant believer, but he cannot overcome the Christian who knows his Bible and understands the purposes of God.

Let—a Surrendered Will (1:4, 9–12)

God cannot build our character without our cooperation. If we resist Him, then He chastens us into submission. But if we submit to Him, then He can accomplish His work. He is not satisfied with a halfway job. God wants a perfect work; He wants a finished product that is mature and complete.

God's goal for our lives is maturity. It would be a tragedy if our children remained little babies. We enjoy watching them mature, even though maturity brings dangers as well as delights. Many Christians shelter themselves from the trials of life, and as a result, never grow up. God wants the "little children" to become "young men," and the "young men" He wants to become "fathers" (1 John 2:12–14).

Paul outlined three works that are involved in a complete Christian life (Eph. 2:8–10). First, there is the work God does *for us,* which is salvation. Jesus Christ completed this work on the cross. If we trust Him, He will save us. Second, there is the work God does *in us:* "For we are his workmanship." This work is known as *sanctification:* God builds our character and we become more like Jesus Christ, "conformed to the image of his Son" (Rom. 8:29). The third work is what God does *through us*—service. We are "created in Christ Jesus unto good works."

God builds character before He calls to service. He must work *in* us before He can work *through* us. God spent twenty-five years working in Abraham before He could give him his promised son. God worked thirteen years in Joseph's life, putting him into "various testings" before He could put him on the throne of Egypt. He spent eighty years preparing Moses for forty years of service. Our Lord took three years training His disciples, building their character.

But God cannot work in us without our consent. There must be a surrendered will. The mature person does not argue with God's will; instead, he accepts it willingly and obeys it joyfully. "Doing the will of God from the heart" (Eph. 6:6). If we try to go through trials without surrendered wills, we will end up more like immature children than mature adults.

Jonah is an illustration of this. God commanded Jonah to preach to the Gentiles at Nineveh, and he refused. God chastened Jonah before the prophet accepted his commission. But Jonah did not obey God from the heart. He did not grow in this experience. How do we know? Because in the last chapter of Jonah, the prophet is acting like a spoiled child! He is sitting outside the city pouting, hoping that God will send judgment. He is impatient with the sun, the wind, the gourd, the worm, and with God.

One difficult stage of maturing is *weaning.* A child being weaned is sure that his mother no longer loves him and that everything is against him. Actually, weaning is a step toward maturity and liberty. It is good for the child! Sometimes God has to wean His children away from their childish toys and immature attitudes. David pictured this in Psalm 131: "Surely I have behaved and quieted myself, as a child that is weaned of his mother: my soul is even as a weaned child" (Ps. 131:2). God uses trials to wean us away from childish things; but if we do not surrender to Him, we will become even more immature.

In James 1:9–11, James applied this principle to two different kinds of Christians: the poor and the rich. Apparently, money and social status were real problems among these people (see James 2:1–7, 15–16; 4:1–3, 13–17; 5:1–8). *God's testings have a way of leveling us.* When testing comes to the poor man, he lets God have His way and rejoices that he possesses spiritual riches that cannot be taken from him. When testing comes to the rich man, he also lets God have His way, and he rejoices that his riches in Christ cannot wither or fade away. In other words, it is not your material resources that take you through the testings of life; it is your spiritual resources.

We have three imperatives from James so far:

count—a joyful attitude; *know*—an understanding heart; *let*—a surrendered will. He gives a fourth.

Ask—a Believing Heart (1:5–8)

The people to whom James wrote had problems with their praying (James 4:1–3; 5:13–18). When we are going through God-ordained difficulties, what should we pray about? James gives the answer: ask God for *wisdom.*

James has a great deal to say about wisdom (James 1:5; 3:13–18). The Jewish people were lovers of wisdom, as the book of Proverbs gives evidence. Someone has said that knowledge is the ability to take things apart, while wisdom is the ability to put them together. Wisdom is the right use of knowledge. All of us know people who are educated fools: they have brilliant academic records, but they cannot make the simplest decisions in life. I once met a gifted professor on a seminary campus, and he was wearing two hats!

Why do we need wisdom when we are going through trials? Why not ask for strength, or grace, or even deliverance? For this reason: *we need wisdom so we will not waste the opportunities God is giving us to mature.* Wisdom helps us understand how to use these circumstances for our good and God's glory.

An associate of mine, a gifted secretary, was going through great trials. She had had a stroke, her husband had gone blind, and then he had to be taken to the hospital where (we were sure) he would die. I saw her in church one Sunday and assured her that I was praying for her.

"What are you asking God to do?" she asked, and her question startled me.

"I'm asking God to help you and strengthen you," I replied.

"I appreciate that," she said, "but pray about one more thing. Pray that I'll have the wisdom not to waste all of this!"

She knew the meaning of James 1:5.

James not only explained *what* to ask for (wisdom), but he also described *how* to ask. We are to ask in faith. We do not have to be afraid, for God is anxious to answer, and He will never scold us! "He giveth more grace" (James 4:6). He also gives more and more wisdom. The greatest enemy to answered prayer is unbelief.

James compares the doubting believer to the waves of the sea, up one minute and down the next. While vacationing in Hawaii, I learned that you cannot trust the waves. I was sitting on a rock by the ocean, watching the waves and enjoying the sunshine. I heard a sound behind me, turned to see who was approaching, and instantly was drenched by a huge wave! Never turn your back on the waves—they are down, then they are up.

This is the experience of the "double-minded man." Faith says, "Yes!" but unbelief says, "No!" Then doubt comes along and says "Yes!" one minute and "No!" the next. It was doubt that made Peter sink in

the waves as he was walking to Jesus (Matt. 14:22–33). Jesus asked him, "O thou of little faith, wherefore didst thou doubt?" When Peter started his walk of faith, he kept his eyes on Christ. But when he was distracted by the wind and waves, he ceased to walk by faith, and he began to sink. He was double-minded, and he almost drowned.

Many Christians live like corks on the waves: up one minute, down the next; tossed back and forth. This kind of experience is evidence of immaturity. Paul used a similar idea in Ephesians 4:14—"That we henceforth be no more children, tossed to and fro, and carried about with every wind of doctrine, by the sleight of men, and cunning craftiness, whereby they lie in wait to deceive." If we have believing and united hearts, we can ask in faith and God will give the wisdom we need. Instability and immaturity go together.

James closed this section with a beatitude: "Blessed is the man that endureth temptation" (James 1:12). He started (James 1:2) and ended with joy. Outlook determines outcome. This beatitude is a great encouragement because it promises a crown to those who patiently endure trials. Paul often used athletic illustrations in his letters, and James did so here. He is not saying that the sinner is saved by enduring trials. He is saying that the believer is rewarded by enduring trials.

How is he rewarded? First, by growth in Christian character. This is more important than anything else. He is rewarded also by bringing glory to God and by being granted a crown of life when Jesus Christ returns. First the cross, then the crown. First the suffering, then the glory. God does not help us by removing the tests, but by making the tests work for us. Satan wants to use the tests to tear us down, but God uses them to build us up.

In James 1:12, James used a very important word: *love.* We would expect him to write, "the crown of life, which the Lord hath promised to them that trust Him" or "that obey Him." Why did James use *love*? Because love is the spiritual motivation behind every imperative in this section.

Why do we have a joyful attitude as we face trials? Because we love God, and He loves us, and He will not harm us. Why do we have an understanding mind? Because He loves us and has shared His truth with us, and we love Him in return. Why do we have a surrendered will? Because we love Him. Where there is love, there is surrender and obedience. Why do we have a believing heart? Because love and faith go together. When you love someone, you trust him, and you do not hesitate to ask him for help.

Love is the spiritual force behind the imperatives James gave us. If we love God, we will have no problem counting, knowing, letting, and asking. But there is another factor involved: love keeps us faithful to the Lord. The double-minded person (James 1:8) is like an unfaithful husband or wife: he wants to love both God and the world. James admonished, "Purify your hearts, ye double-minded!" (James 4:8) The Greek word translated "purify" literally means "make chaste." The picture is that of an unfaithful lover.

Let's go back to the weaning. The child who loves his mother, and who is sure that his mother loves him, will be able to get through the weaning and start to grow up. The Christian who loves God, and who knows that God loves him, will not fall apart when God permits trials to come. *He is secure in God's love.* He is not double-minded, trying to love both God and the world. Lot was double-minded; when trials came, he failed miserably. Abraham was the friend of God; he loved God and trusted Him. When trials came, Abraham triumphed and matured in the faith.

God's purpose in trials is maturity. "Let patience have her perfect work, that ye may be perfect and entire, wanting nothing." The Charles B. Williams translation says it graphically: "But you must let your endurance come to its perfect product so that you may be fully developed and perfectly equipped."

If that is what you want, then in love to Christ, count, know, let, and ask.

CHAPTER THREE
James 1:13–18
HOW TO HANDLE TEMPTATION

The mature person is patient in trials. Sometimes the trials are testings on the outside, and sometimes they are temptations on the inside. Trials may be tests sent by God, or they may be temptations sent by Satan and encouraged by our own fallen nature. It is this second aspect of trials—temptations on the inside—that James dealt with in this section.

We may ask, "Why did James connect the two? What is the relationship between testings without and temptations within?" Simply this: if we are not careful, the testings on the outside may become temptations on the inside. When our circumstances are difficult, we may find ourselves complaining against God, questioning His love, and resisting His will. At this point, Satan provides us with an opportunity to escape the difficulty. This opportunity is a temptation.

There are many illustrations of this truth found in the Bible. Abraham arrived in Canaan and discovered a famine there. He was not able to care for his flocks and herds. This trial was an opportunity to prove God; but Abraham turned it into a temptation and went down to Egypt. God had to chasten Abraham to bring him back to the place of obedience and blessing.

While Israel was wandering in the wilderness, the nation often turned testings into temptations and tempted the Lord. No sooner had they been delivered from Egypt than their water supply vanished and they had to march for three days without water. When they did find water, it was so bitter they could not drink it. Immediately they began to murmur and blame God.

They turned their testing into a temptation, and they failed.

Certainly, God does not want us to yield to temptation, yet neither can He spare us the experience of temptation. We are not God's *sheltered* people; we are God's *scattered* people. If we are to mature, we must face testings and temptations. There are three facts that we must consider if we are to overcome temptation.

Consider God's Judgment (1:13–16)

This is a negative approach, but it is an important one. James said, "Look ahead and see where sin ends—death!" Do not blame God for temptation. He is too holy to be tempted, and He is too loving to tempt others. God does test us, as He did Abraham (Gen. 22); but He does not and cannot tempt us. It is we who turn occasions of testing into temptations.

A temptation is an opportunity to accomplish a good thing in a bad way, out of the will of God. Is it wrong to want to pass an examination? Of course not, but if you cheat to pass it, then you have sinned. The temptation to cheat is an opportunity to accomplish a good thing (passing the examination) in a bad way. It is not wrong to eat, but if you consider stealing the food, you are tempting yourself.

We think of sin as a single act, but God sees it as a process. Adam committed one act of sin, and yet that one act brought sin, death, and judgment on the whole human race. James described this process of sin in four stages.

Desire (v. 14). The word *lust* means any kind of desire, and not necessarily sexual passions. The normal desires of life were given to us by God and, of themselves, are not sinful. Without these desires, we could not function. Unless we felt hunger and thirst, we would never eat and drink, and we would die. Without fatigue, the body would never rest and would eventually wear out. Sex is a normal desire; without it the human race could not continue.

It is when we want to satisfy these desires in ways outside God's will that we get into trouble. Eating is normal; gluttony is sin. Sleep is normal; laziness is sin. "Marriage is honorable in all, and the bed undefiled; but whoremongers and adulterers God will judge" (Heb. 13:4).

Some people try to become "spiritual" by denying these normal desires or by seeking to suppress them, but this only makes them less than human. These fundamental desires of life are the steam in the boiler that makes the machinery go. Turn off the steam and you have no power. Let the steam go its own way and you have destruction. The secret is in *constant control.* These desires must be our servants and not our masters, and this we can do through Jesus Christ.

Deception (v. 14). No temptation appears as temptation; it always seems more alluring than it really is. James used two illustrations from the world of sports to prove his point. *Drawn away* carries with it the idea of the baiting of a trap; and *enticed* in the original Greek means "to bait a hook." The hunter and the fisherman have to use bait to attract and catch their prey. No animal is deliberately going to step into a trap and no fish will knowingly bite at a naked hook. The idea is to *hide* the trap and the hook.

Temptation always carries with it some bait that appeals to our natural desires. The bait not only attracts us, but it also hides the fact that yielding to the desire will eventually bring sorrow and punishment. It is the bait that is the exciting thing. Lot would never have moved toward Sodom had he not seen the "well-watered plains of Jordan" (Gen. 13:10ff.). When David looked on his neighbor's wife, he would never have committed adultery had he seen the tragic consequences: the death of a baby (Bathsheba's son), the murder of a brave soldier (Uriah), the violation of a daughter (Tamar). *The bait keeps us from seeing the consequences of sin.*

When Jesus was tempted by Satan, He always dealt with the temptation on the basis of the Word of God. Three times He said, "It is written." From the human point of view, turning stones into bread to satisfy hunger is a sensible thing to do; but not from God's point of view. When you know the Bible, you can detect the bait and deal with it decisively. This is what it means to walk by faith and not by sight.

Disobedience (v. 15). We have moved from the *emotions* (desire) and the *intellect* (deception) to the *will.* James changed the picture from hunting and fishing to the birth of a baby. Desire conceives a method for taking the bait. The will approves and acts, and the result is sin. Whether we feel it or not, we are hooked and trapped. The baby is born, and just wait until it matures!

Christian living is a matter of the will, not the feelings. I often hear believers say, "I don't feel like reading the Bible." Or, "I don't feel like attending prayer meeting." Children operate on the basis of feeling, but adults operate on the basis of will. *They act because it is right, no matter how they feel.* This explains why immature Christians easily fall into temptation: they let their feelings make the decisions. The more you exercise your will in saying a decisive no to temptation, the more God will take control of your life. "For it is God which worketh in you both to will and to do of his good pleasure" (Phil. 2:13).

Death (v. 15). Disobedience gives birth to death, not life. It may take years for the sin to mature, but when it does, the result will be death. If we will only believe God's Word and see this final tragedy, it will encourage us not to yield to temptation. God has erected this barrier because He loves us. "Have I any pleasure at all that the wicked should die?" (Ezek. 18:23).

These four stages in temptation and sin are perfectly depicted in the first sin recorded in the Bible in Genesis 3.

The serpent used *desire* to interest Eve: "For God doth know that in the day ye eat thereof, then your eyes shall be opened, and ye shall be as gods, knowing good and evil" (Gen. 3:5). Is there anything wrong with gaining knowledge? Is there anything wrong with eating food? Eve saw that "the tree was good for food" (Gen. 3:6), and her desire was aroused.

Paul described the deception of Eve in 2 Corinthians 11:3: "But I fear, lest by any means, as the serpent beguiled Eve through his subtlety, so your minds should be corrupted from the simplicity that is in Christ." Satan is the deceiver, and he seeks to deceive the mind. The bait that he used with Eve was the fact that the forbidden tree was good and pleasant, and that eating of it would make her wise. She saw the bait but forgot the Lord's warning: "In the day that thou eatest thereof thou shalt surely die" (Gen. 2:17).

Eve disobeyed God by taking the fruit of the tree and eating it. Then she shared it with her husband, and he disobeyed God. Because Adam was not deceived, but sinned with his eyes wide open, it is his sin that plunged the human race into tragedy (read Rom. 5:12–21; 1 Tim. 2:12–15).

Both Adam and Eve experienced immediate spiritual death (separation from God), and ultimate physical death. All men die because of Adam (1 Cor. 15:21–22). The person who dies without Jesus Christ will experience eternal death, the lake of fire (Rev. 20:11–15).

Whenever you are faced with temptation, get your eyes off the bait and look ahead to see the consequences of sin: *the judgment of God.* "For the wages of sin is death" (Rom. 6:23).

Consider God's Goodness (1:17)

One of the enemy's tricks is to convince us that our Father is holding out on us, that He does not really love us and care for us. When Satan approached Eve, he suggested that if God really loved her, He would permit her to eat of the forbidden tree. When Satan tempted Jesus, he raised the question of hunger. "If Your Father loves You, why are You hungry?"

The goodness of God is a great barrier against yielding to temptation. Since God is good, we do not need any other person (including Satan) to meet our needs. It is better to be hungry *in* the will of God than full *outside* the will of God. Once we start to doubt God's goodness, we will be attracted to Satan's offers, and the natural desires within will reach out for his bait. Moses warned Israel not to forget God's goodness when they began to enjoy the blessings of the Promised Land (Deut. 6:10–15). We need this warning today.

James presented four facts about the goodness of God.

God gives only good gifts. Everything good in this world comes from God. If it did not come from God, it is not good. If it comes from God, it must be good, even if we do not see the goodness in it immediately. Paul's thorn in the flesh was given to him by God and it seemed to be a strange gift; yet it became a tremendous blessing to him (2 Cor. 12:1–10).

The way God gives is good. We can translate the second clause "and every act of giving." It is possible for someone to give us a gift in a manner that is less than loving. The value of a gift can be diminished by the way it is given to us. But when God gives us a blessing, He does it in a loving, gracious manner. *What* He gives and *how* He gives are both good.

He gives constantly. "Cometh down" is a present participle: "it keeps on coming down." God does not give occasionally; He gives constantly. Even when we do not see His gifts, He is sending them. How do we know this? Because He tells us so and we believe His Word.

God does not change. There are no shadows with the Father of Lights. It is impossible for God to change. He cannot change for the worse because He is holy; He cannot change for the better because He is already perfect. The light of the sun varies as the earth changes, but the sun itself is still shining. If shadows come between us and the Father, He did not cause them. He is the unchanging God. This means that we should never question His love or doubt His goodness when difficulties come or temptations appear.

If King David had remembered the goodness of the Lord, he would not have taken Bathsheba and committed those terrible sins. At least this is what Nathan the prophet told the king. "Thus saith the Lord God of Israel, 'I anointed thee king over Israel, and I delivered thee out of the hand of Saul; and I gave thee thy master's house, and thy master's wives into thy bosom, and gave thee the house of Israel and of Judah; and if that had been too little, I would moreover have given unto thee such and such things'" (2 Sam. 12:7–8). Note the repetition of the word *give* in this brief statement. God had been good to David, yet David forgot God's goodness and took the bait.

The first barrier against temptation is a negative one: the judgment of God. This second barrier is positive: the goodness of God. A fear of God is a healthy attitude, but the love of God must balance it. We can obey Him because He may chasten us, or we can obey Him because He has already been so generous to us, and because we love Him for it.

It was this positive attitude that helped to keep Joseph from sinning when he was tempted by his master's wife (Gen. 39:7ff.). "Behold, with me around, my master does not concern himself with anything in the house, and he has put all that he owns in my charge. There is no one greater in this house than I, and he has withheld nothing from me except you, because you are his wife. How then could I do this great evil, and sin against God?" (Gen. 39:8–9 NASB). Joseph knew that all these blessings had come from God. It was the goodness of God, through the hands of his employer, that restrained him in the hour of temptation.

God's gifts are always better than Satan's bargains. Satan never gives any gifts, because you end up *paying for them dearly.* "It is the blessing of the Lord that makes rich, and He adds no sorrow to it" (Prov. 10:22 NASB). Achan forgot the warning of God and the goodness of God, saw the forbidden wealth, coveted it, and took it. He became rich, but the sorrow that followed turned his riches into poverty (Josh. 7).

The next time you are tempted, meditate on the goodness of God in your life. If you think you need something, wait on the Lord to provide it. Never toy with the devil's bait. One purpose for temptation is to teach us patience. David was tempted twice to kill King Saul and hasten his own coronation, but he resisted the temptation and waited for God's time.

Consider God's Divine Nature Within (1:18)

In the first barrier, God says, "Look ahead and beware of judgment." In the second barrier, He says, "Look around and see how good I have been to you." But with this third barrier, God says, "Look within and realize that you have been born from above and possess the divine nature."

James used birth as a picture of desire leading to sin and death (James 1:15). He also used it to explain how we can enjoy victory over temptation and sin. The apostle John used a similar approach in 1 John 3:9, where "his seed" refers to the divine life and nature within the believer. Note the characteristics of this birth.

It is divine. Nicodemus thought he had to reenter his mother's womb to be born again, but he was wrong. This birth is not of the flesh: it is from above (John 3:1–7). It is the work of God. Just as we did not generate our own human birth, we cannot generate our own spiritual birth. When we put our faith in Jesus Christ, it was God who performed the miracle.

It is gracious. We did not earn it or deserve it; God gave us spiritual birth because of His own grace and will. "Which were born, not of blood [human descent], nor of the will of the flesh [human efforts], nor of the will of man [human assistance], but of God" (John 1:13). No one can be born again because of his relatives, his resolutions, or his religion. The new birth is the work of God.

It is through God's Word. Just as human birth requires two parents, so divine birth has two parents: the Word of God and the Spirit of God. "That which is born of the flesh is flesh; and that which is born of the Spirit is spirit" (John 3:6). "Being born again, not of corruptible seed, but of incorruptible, by the Word of God, which liveth and abideth forever" (1 Peter 1:23). The Spirit of God uses the word of God to bring about the miracle of the new birth. Since the Word of God is "living and powerful" (Heb. 4:12) it can generate life in the heart of the sinner who trusts Christ, and that life is God's life.

It is the finest birth possible. We are "a kind of firstfruits of his creatures," James wrote to Jewish believers, and the word *firstfruits* would be meaningful to them. The Old Testament Jews brought the firstfruits to the Lord as the expression of their devotion and obedience. "Honor the Lord with thy substance, and with the firstfruits of all thine increase" (Prov. 3:9). Of all the creatures God has in this universe, Christians are the very highest and the finest! We share God's nature. For this reason, it is beneath our dignity to accept Satan's bait or to desire sinful things. A higher birth must mean a higher life.

By granting us a new birth, God declares that He cannot accept the old birth. Throughout the Bible, God rejects the firstborn and accepts the secondborn. He accepted Abel, not Cain; Isaac, not Ishmael; Jacob, not Esau. He rejects your first birth (no matter how noble it might have been in the eyes of men), and He announces that you need a second birth.

It is this experience of the new birth that helps us overcome temptation. If we let the old nature (from the first birth) take over, we will fail. We received our old nature (the flesh) from Adam, and he was a failure. But if we yield to the new nature, we will succeed, for that new nature comes from Christ, and He is the Victor.

A Sunday school child explained the matter in simple terms. "Two men live in my heart: the old Adam and Jesus. When temptation knocks at the door, somebody has to answer. If I let Adam answer, I will sin, *so I send Jesus to answer. He always wins!*"

Of course, this new nature must be fed the Word of God daily, that it might be strong to fight the battle. Just as the Holy Spirit used the Word of God to give you spiritual birth, He uses the Word to give you spiritual strength. "Man shall not live by bread alone, but by every word that proceedeth out of the mouth of God" (Matt. 4:4).

No matter what excuses we make, we have no one to blame for sin but ourselves. Our own desires lead us into temptation and sin. God is not to blame. But God has erected these three barriers to keep us from sin. If we heed the barriers, we will win a crown (James 1:12). If we break through the barriers, we will find a coffin (James 1:15). Which will it be?

CHAPTER FOUR
James 1:19–27
QUIT KIDDING YOURSELF

The emphasis in this section is on the dangers of self-deception: "deceiving your own selves" (James 1:22); "deceiveth his own heart" (James 1:26). If a Christian sins because Satan deceives him, that is one thing. But if he deceives himself, that is a far more serious matter.

Many people are deceiving themselves into thinking they are saved when they are not. "Many will say to me in that day, 'Lord, Lord, have we not prophesied in thy name? and in thy name have cast out devils? and in thy name done many wonderful works?' And then will I profess unto them, 'I never knew you: depart from me, ye that work iniquity'" (Matt. 7:22–23).

But there are true believers who are fooling themselves concerning their Christian walk. They think they are spiritual when they are not. It is a mark of maturity when a person faces himself honestly, knows himself, and admits his needs. It is the immature person who pretends, "I am rich, and increased with goods, and have need of nothing" (Rev. 3:17).

Spiritual reality results from the proper relationship to God through His Word. God's Word is truth (John 17:17), and if we are rightly related to God's truth, we cannot be dishonest or hypocritical. In these verses, James stated that we have three responsibilities toward God's Word, and if we fulfill these responsibilities, we will have an honest walk with God and men.

Receive the Word (1:19–21)
James called God's Word "the engrafted word" (James 1:21), which means "the implanted word." Borrowing from our Lord's parable of the sower (Matt. 13:1–9, 18–23), he compared God's Word to seed and the human heart to soil. In His parable, Jesus described four kinds of hearts: *the hard heart,* which did not understand or receive the Word and therefore bore no fruit; *the shallow heart,* which was very emotional but had no depth and bore no fruit; *the crowded heart,* which lacked repentance and permitted sin to crowd out the Word; and *the fruitful heart,* which received the Word, allowed it to take root, and produced a harvest of fruit.

The final test of salvation is fruit. This means a changed life, Christian character and conduct, and ministry to others in the glory of God. This fruit might be winning souls to Christ (Rom. 1:16), growing in holy living (Rom. 6:22), sharing our material possessions (Rom. 15:28), spiritual character (Gal. 5:22–23), good works (Col. 1:10), and even praising the Lord (Heb. 13:15). Religious works may be manufactured, but they do not have life in them, nor do they bring glory to God. Real fruit has in it the seed for more fruit, so that the harvest continues to grow fruit, more fruit, much fruit (John 15:1–5).

But the Word of God cannot work in our lives unless we receive it in the right way. Jesus not only said, "Take heed what ye hear" (Mark 4:24), but He also said, "Take heed how ye hear" (Luke 8:18). Too many people are in that tragic condition in which "hearing they hear not, neither do they understand" (Matt. 13:13). They attend Bible classes and church services but never seem to grow. Is it the fault of the teacher or the preacher? Perhaps, but it may also be the fault of the hearer. It is possible to be "dull of hearing" (Heb. 5:11) because of decay of the spiritual life.

If the seed of the Word is to be planted in our hearts, then we must obey the instructions James gave us.

Swift to hear (v. 19a). "Who hath ears to hear, let him hear" (Matt. 13:9)! "So then faith cometh by hearing, and hearing by the word of God" (Rom. 10:17). Just as the servant is quick to hear his master's voice, and the mother to hear her baby's smallest cry, so the believer should be quick to hear what God has to say.

There is a beautiful illustration of this truth in the life of King David (2 Sam. 23:14–17). David was hiding from the Philistines who were in possession of Bethlehem. He yearned for a drink of the cool water from the well in Bethlehem, a well that he had often visited in his boyhood and youth. He did not issue an order to his men; he simply said to himself, "Oh, that one would give me drink of the water of the well of Bethlehem, which is by the gate" (2 Sam. 23:15). Three of his mighty men heard their king sigh for the water, and they risked their lives to secure the water and bring it to him. They were "swift to hear."

Slow to speak (v. 19b). We have two ears and one mouth, which ought to remind us to listen more than we speak. Too many times we argue with God's Word, if not audibly, at least in our hearts and minds. "He that refraineth his lips is wise" (Prov. 10:19). "He that hath knowledge spareth his words" (Prov. 17:27). Instead of being slow to speak, the lawyer in Luke 10:29 argued with Jesus by asking, "And who is my neighbor?" In the early church, the services were informal, and often the listeners would debate with the speaker. There were even fightings and wars among the brethren James was writing to (James 4:1).

Slow to wrath (v. 19c). Do not get angry at God or His Word. "He that is slow to wrath is of great understanding: but he that is hasty of spirit exalteth folly" (Prov. 14:29). When the prophet Nathan told King David the story about "the stolen ewe lamb," the king became angry, but at the wrong person. "Thou art the man," said Nathan, and David then confessed, "I have sinned" (2 Sam. 12). In the garden, Peter was slow to hear, swift to speak, and swift to anger—and he almost killed a man with the sword. Many church fights are the result of short tempers and hasty words. There is a godly anger against sin (Eph. 4:26), and if we love the Lord, we must hate sin (Ps. 97:10). But man's anger does not produce God's righteousness (James 1:20). In fact, anger is just the opposite of the patience God wants to produce in our lives as we mature in Christ (James 1:3–4).

I once saw a poster that read, "Temper is such a valuable thing, it is a shame to lose it!" It is temper that helps to give steel its strength. The person who cannot get angry at sin does not have much strength to fight it. James warns us against getting angry at God's Word because it reveals our sins to us. Like the man who broke the mirror because he disliked the image in it, people rebel against God's Word because it tells the truth about them and their sinfulness.

A prepared heart (v. 21). James saw the human heart as a garden; if left to itself, the soil would produce only weeds. He urged us to "pull out the weeds" and prepare the soil for the "implanted Word of God." The phrase "superfluity of naughtiness" gives the picture of a garden overgrown with weeds that cannot be controlled. It is foolish to try to receive God's Word into an unprepared heart.

How do we prepare the soil of our hearts for God's Word? First, by confessing our sins and asking the Father to forgive us (1 John 1:9). Then, by meditating on God's love and grace and asking Him to "plow up" any hardness in our hearts: "Break up your fallow ground, and sow not among thorns" (Jer. 4:3). Finally, we must have an attitude of "meekness" (James 1:21). Meekness is the opposite of "wrath" in James 1:19–20. When you receive the Word with meekness, you accept it, do not argue with it, and honor it as the Word of God. You do not try to twist it to conform it to your thinking.

If we do not receive the implanted Word, then we are deceiving ourselves. Christians who like to argue various "points of view" may be only fooling themselves. They think that their "discussions" are promoting spiritual growth, when in reality they may only be cultivating the weeds.

Practice the Word (1:22–25)

It is not enough to hear the Word; we must do it. Many people have the mistaken idea that hearing a good sermon or Bible study is what makes them grow and get God's blessing. It is not the hearing but *the doing* that brings the blessing. Too many Christians mark their Bibles, but their Bibles never mark them! If you think you are spiritual because you hear the Word, then you are only kidding yourself.

In the previous paragraph, James compared the Word to seed, but in this paragraph, he compared it to a mirror. There are two other references in the Bible to God's Word as a mirror; and when you put all three together, you discover three ministries of the Word of God as a mirror.

Examination (vv. 23–25). This is the main purpose for owning a mirror, to be able to see yourself and make yourself look as clean and neat as possible. As we look into the mirror of God's Word, we see ourselves as we really are. James mentions several mistakes people make as they look into God's mirror.

First, *they merely glance at themselves.* They do not carefully study themselves as they read the Word. Many sincere believers read a chapter of the Bible each day, but it is only a religious exercise and they fail to profit from it personally. Their conscience would bother them if they did not have their daily reading, when actually their conscience should bother them *because they read the Word carelessly.* A cursory reading of the Bible will never reveal our deepest needs. It is the difference between a candid photo and an X-ray.

The second mistake is that *they forget what they see.* If they were looking deeply enough into their hearts, what they would see would be unforgettable! We tend to smile at the "extremes" of people back in the days of the great revivals, but perhaps we could use some of that conviction. John Wesley wrote about a preaching service: "One before me dropped as dead, and presently a second, and a third. Five others sunk down in half an hour, most of whom were in violent agonies" (*Wesley's Journal* for June 22, 1739). Before we consign these people to some psychological limbo, remember how saints in the Bible responded to the true knowledge of their own hearts. Isaiah cried, "Woe is me! for I am undone" (Isa. 6:5)! Peter cried, "Depart from me, for I am a sinful man, O Lord" (Luke 5:8)! Job was the most righteous man on earth in his day, yet he confessed, "I abhor myself, and repent in dust and ashes" (Job 42:6).

Mistake number three: *they fail to obey what the Word tells them to do.* They think that *hearing* is the same as *doing,* and it is not. We Christians enjoy substituting *reading* for *doing,* or even *talking* for *doing.* We hold endless committee meetings and conferences about topics like evangelism and church growth, and think we have made progress. While there is certainly nothing wrong with conferences and committee meetings, they are sinful if they are a substitute for service.

If we are to use God's mirror profitably, then we must gaze into it carefully and with serious intent (James 1:25). No quick glances will do. We must examine our own hearts and lives in the light of God's Word. This requires time, attention, and sincere devotion. Five minutes with God each day will never accomplish a deep spiritual examination.

I have been fortunate with the doctors who have cared for me through the years, and I owe a great deal to them. Each of them has possessed two qualities that I have appreciated: they have spent time with me and have not been in a hurry, and they have always told me the truth. When Jesus, the Great Physician (Matt. 9:12), examines us, He uses His Word, and He wants us to give Him sufficient time to do the job well. Perhaps one reason we glance into the Word instead of gaze into the Word is that we are afraid of what we might see.

After seeing ourselves, we must remember what we are and what God says, and we must *do the Word.* The blessing comes in the doing, not in the reading of the Word. "This man shall be blessed in his doing" (James 1:25, literal translation). The emphasis in James is on the practice of the Word. We are to *continue* after reading the Word (James 1:25; see Acts 1:14; 2:42, 46; 13:43; 14:22; 26:22 for examples of this in the early church).

Why did James call the Word of God "the perfect law of liberty" (James 1:25)? Because when we obey it, God sets us free. "And I will walk at liberty: for I seek thy precepts" (Ps. 119:45). "Whosoever committeth sin is the servant of sin" (John 8:34). "If ye continue in my word, then are ye my disciples indeed; and ye shall know the truth, and the truth shall make you free" (John 8:31–32).

But *examination* is but the first ministry of the mirror of the Word. There is a second ministry.

Restoration (Ex. 38:8). When he built the tabernacle, Moses took the metal looking glasses of the women and from them made the laver. The laver was a huge basin that stood between the brazen altar of sacrifice and the holy place. (Read Ex. 30:17–21 for details.) The basin was filled with water, and the priests washed their hands and feet at the laver before they entered the holy place to minister.

Water for washing is a picture of the Word of God in its cleansing power. "Now ye are clean through the word which I have spoken unto you" (John 15:3). The church is sanctified and cleansed "with the washing of water by the word" (Eph. 5:26). When the sinner trusts Christ, he is once and for all washed clean (1 Cor. 6:9–11; Titus 3:4–6). But as the believer walks in this world, his hands and feet are defiled, and he needs cleansing (John 13:1–11).

The mirror of the Word not only examines us and reveals our sins, but it helps to cleanse us as well. It gives us the promise of cleansing (1 John 1:9) and, as we meditate on it, it cleanses the heart and the mind from spiritual defilement. It is the blood of Christ that cleanses the guilt, but the water of the Word helps to wash away the defilement.

Nathan's experience with David in 2 Samuel 12 helps to illustrate this truth. Nathan told David the story about the stolen ewe lamb, and David became angry at the sin described. "Thou art the man," said the prophet, and he held up the mirror of the Word for David to see himself. The result was confession and repentance: "I have sinned against the Lord!" The mirror of the Word did its work of examination.

But Nathan did not stop there. He also used the Word for *restoration.* "The Lord also hath put away thy sin; thou shalt not die" (2 Sam. 12:13). Here was the assurance of forgiveness and cleansing, and it came from the Word. David visited the laver and washed his hands and feet.

If we stop with examination and restoration, we will miss the full benefit of the mirror ministry of the Word. There is a third ministry.

Transformation (2 Cor. 3:18). After the Lord restores us, He wants to change us so that we will grow in grace and not commit that sin again. Too many Christians confess their sins and claim forgiveness, but never grow spiritually to conquer self and sin.

Second Corinthians 3 is a discussion of the contrasts between the old covenant ministry of law and the new covenant ministry of grace. The law is external, written on tablets of stone; but salvation means that God's Word is written on the heart. The old covenant ministry condemned and killed; but the new covenant ministry brings forgiveness and life. The glory of the law gradually disappeared, but the glory of God's grace becomes brighter and brighter. The law was temporary, but the new covenant of grace is eternal.

Paul's illustration of this truth is Moses and his veil. When Moses came down from the mount where he met God, his face was shining (Ex. 34:29–35). He did not want the Jews to see this glory fading away, so he put on a veil to hide it. When he returned to the mount, he took off the veil. When Jesus died, the veil in the temple was torn from top to bottom, and the veil between men and God was removed. The Old

Testament prophet wore a veil to hide the fading of the glory. The New Testament believer has an unveiled face, and the glory gets greater and greater!

You may explain 2 Corinthians 3:18 in this way: "When the child of God looks into the Word of God [the glass, the mirror], he sees the Son of God, and he is transformed by the Spirit of God to share in the glory of God!" The word *changed* in the Greek gives us our English word *metamorphosis*—a change on the outside that comes from the inside. When an ugly worm turns into a beautiful butterfly, this is metamorphosis. When a believer spends time looking into the Word and seeing Christ, he is transformed: the glory on the inside is revealed on the outside.

It is this word that is translated "transfigured" in Matthew 17:2. The glory of Christ on the mount was not reflected; it was radiated from within. You will find the same word in Romans 12:2: "Be ye transformed by the renewing of your mind." As we meditate on the Word, the Spirit renews the mind and reveals the glory of God. We do not become spiritual Christians overnight. It is a process, the work of the Spirit of God through the mirror of the Word of God.

The important thing is that we hide nothing. Take off the veil! "Search me, O God, and know my heart: try me, and know my thoughts: and see if there be any wicked way in me, and lead me in the way everlasting" (Ps. 139:23–24). "If we say that we have no sin, we deceive ourselves, and the truth is not in us" (1 John 1:8).

Our first responsibility is to receive the Word. Then, we must practice the Word; otherwise we are deceiving ourselves. This leads to a third responsibility.

Share the Word (1:26–27)

The word translated "religion" means "the outward practice, the service of a god." It is used only five times in the entire New Testament (James 1:26–27; Acts 26:5; and Col. 2:18, where it is translated "worshipping"). Pure religion has nothing to do with ceremonies, temples, or special days. Pure religion means practicing God's Word and sharing it with others, through speech, service, and separation from the world.

Speech (v. 26). There are many references to speech in this letter, giving the impression that the tongue was a serious problem in the assembly (see James 1:19; 2:12; 3:1–3, 14–18; 4:11–12). It is the tongue that reveals the heart (Matt. 12:34–35); if the heart is right, the speech will be right. A controlled tongue means a controlled body (James 3:1ff.).

Service (v. 27a). After we have seen ourselves and Christ in the mirror of the Word, we must see others and their needs. Isaiah first saw the Lord, then himself, and then the people to whom he would minister (Isa. 6:1–8). Words are no substitute for deeds of love (James 2:14–18; 1 John 3:11–18). God does not want us to pay for others to minister as a substitute for our own personal service!

Separation from the world (v. 27b). By "the world" James meant "society without God." Satan is the prince of this world (John 14:30), and the lost are the children of this world (Luke 16:8). As the children of God, we are *in* the world physically but not *of* the world spiritually (John 17:11–16). We are sent *into* the world to win others to Christ (John 17:18). It is only as we maintain our separation from the world that we can serve others.

The world wants to "spot" the Christian and start to defile him. First, there is "friendship of the world" (James 4:4), which can lead to a love for the world (1 John 2:15–17). If we are not careful, we will become conformed to this world (Rom. 12:1–2), and the result is being condemned with the world (1 Cor. 11:32). This does not suggest that we lose our salvation, but that we lose all we have lived for. Lot is an illustration of this principle. First he pitched his tent toward Sodom, and then he moved into Sodom. Before long, Sodom moved into him and he lost his testimony even with his own family. When judgment fell on Sodom, Lot lost everything. It was Abraham, the separated believer, the friend of God, who had a greater ministry to the people than did Lot, the friend of the world. It is not necessary for the Christian to get involved with the world to have a ministry to the world. Jesus was "unspotted" (1 Peter 1:19), and yet He was the friend of publicans and sinners. The best way to minister to the needs of the world is to be pure from the defilement of the world.

CHAPTER FIVE
James 2:1–13
RICH MAN, POOR MAN

Not only is the mature Christian patient in testing (James 1), but he also practices the truth. This is the theme of James 2. Immature people talk about their beliefs, but the mature person lives his faith. Hearing God's Word (James 1:22–25) and talking about God's Word can never substitute for doing God's Word.

Every believer has some statement of faith or personal expression of what he believes. Most churches have such statements and members are asked to subscribe to the statement and practice it. Most churches also have a "covenant" that they read publicly, often when they observe the Lord's Supper. Statements of faith and church covenants are good and useful, but they are not substitutes for doing God's will. As a pastor, I have heard believers read the church covenant and then come to a business meeting and act in ways completely contrary to the covenant.

James wanted to help us practice God's Word, so he gave us a simple test. He sent two visitors to a church service, a rich man and a poor man, and he watched to see how they were treated. *The way we behave toward* people indicates what we really believe about God! We cannot—and dare not—separate *human* relationships from *divine* fellowship. "If a man say, 'I love God,' and hateth his brother, he is a liar: for he that loveth not his brother whom he hath seen, how can he love God whom he hath not seen?" (1 John 4:20).

In this section, James examined four basic Christian doctrines in the light of the way we treat other people.

The Deity of Christ (2:1–4)

"My brothers, don't hold the faith of our Lord Jesus Christ, the Lord of Glory, by showing favoritism" (literal translation). Jewish people in that day coveted recognition and honor, and vied with one another for praise. Our Lord's parables in Luke 14:7–14 deal with the problem, and also His denunciation of the Pharisees in Matthew 23.

We have this same problem with us today. Pyramid climbers are among us, not only in politics, industry, and society, but also in the church. Almost every church has its cliques, and often, new Christians find it difficult to get in. Some church members use their offices to enhance their own images of importance. Many of the believers James wrote to were trying to seize spiritual offices, and James had to warn them (James 3:1).

Jesus did not respect persons. Even His enemies admitted, "You aren't swayed by men, because you pay no attention to who they are" (Matt. 22:16 NIV). Our Lord did not look at the outward appearance; He looked at the heart. He was not impressed with riches or social status. The poor widow who gave her mite was greater in His eyes than the rich Pharisee who boastfully gave his large donation. Furthermore, He saw the potential in the lives of sinners. In Simon, He saw a rock. In Matthew, the publican, He saw a faithful disciple who would one day write one of the four gospels. The disciples were amazed to see Jesus talking with the sinful woman at the well of Sychar, but Jesus saw in her an instrument for reaping a great harvest.

We are prone to judge people by their past, not their future. When Saul of Tarsus was converted, the church in Jerusalem was afraid to receive him! It took Barnabas, who believed in Saul's conversion, to break down the walls (Acts 9:26–28). We are also prone to judge by outward appearance rather than by the inner attitude of the heart. We do not enjoy sitting with certain people in church because they "are not our kind of people." Jesus was the Friend of sinners, though He disapproved of their sins. It was not compromise, but compassion, that caused Him to welcome them, and when they trusted Him, forgive them.

Jesus was despised and rejected. This fact was prophesied in Isaiah 53:1–3. He was "the poor man" who was rejected by the self-righteous nation. Unlike the foxes and the birds, He had no home. He grew up in the despised city of Nazareth in a home that knew the feeling of poverty. Had you and I met Him while He was ministering on earth, we would have seen nothing physically or materially that would attract us.

Yet, *He is the very glory of God!* In the Old Testament, God's glory dwelled first in the tabernacle (Ex. 40:34–38) and then in the temple (1 Kings 8:10–11). When Jesus came to earth, God's glory resided in Him (John 1:14). Today, the glory of God dwells in the believer individually (1 Cor. 6:19–20) and the church collectively (Eph. 2:21–22).

The religious experts in Christ's day judged Him by their human standards, and they rejected Him. He came from the wrong city, Nazareth of Galilee. He was not a graduate of their accepted schools. He did not have the official approval of the people in power. He had no wealth. His followers were a nondescript mob and included publicans and sinners. *Yet He was the very glory of God!* No wonder Jesus warned the religious leaders, "Stop judging by mere appearances, and make a right judgment" (John 7:24 NIV).

Sad to say, we often make the same mistakes. When visitors come into our churches, we tend to judge them on what we see outwardly rather than what they are inwardly. Dress, color of skin, fashion, and other superficial things carry more weight than the fruit of the Spirit that may be manifest in their lives. We cater to the rich because we hope to get something out of them, and we avoid the poor because they embarrass us. Jesus did not do this, and He cannot approve of it.

How do we practice the deity of Christ in our human relationships? It is really quite simple: *look at everyone through the eyes of Christ.* If the visitor is a Christian, we can accept him because *Christ lives in him.* If he is not a Christian, we can receive him because *Christ died for him.* It is Christ who is the link between us and others, and He is a link of love. The basis for relationship with others is the person and work of Jesus Christ. Any other basis is not going to work. Furthermore, God can use even the most unlikely person to bring glory to His name. He used Peter and Zaccheus and John Mark, and He can use that poor man whom we might reject.

The Grace of God (2:5–7)

The emphasis here is on God's *choosing,* and this involves the grace of God. If salvation were on the basis of merit, it would not be by grace. Grace implies God's sovereign choice of those who cannot earn and do not deserve His salvation (Eph. 1:4–7; 2:8–10). God saves us completely on the basis of the work of Christ on the cross and not because of anything that we are or have.

God ignores *national* differences (Acts 10:34). The Jewish believers were shocked when Peter went to the Gentile household of Cornelius, preached to the Gentiles, and even ate with them. The topic of the first church council was, "Must a Gentile become a Jew to become a Christian?" (Acts 15). The answer the Holy Spirit gave them was, "No!" In the sight of God, there is no difference between Jew and Gentile when it comes to condemnation (Rom. 2:6–16) or salvation (Rom. 10:1–13).

God also ignores *social* differences. Masters and

slaves (Eph. 6:9) and rich and poor are alike to Him. James taught us that the grace of God makes the rich man poor, because he cannot depend on his wealth; and it makes the poor man rich, because he inherits the riches of grace in Christ. (Review James 1:9–11.) "The Lord maketh poor, and maketh rich: he bringeth low, and lifteth up. He raiseth up the poor out of the dust, and lifteth up the beggar from the dunghill, to set them among princes, and to make them inherit the throne of glory" (1 Sam. 2:7–8).

From the human point of view, God chooses the poor instead of the rich. "For ye see your calling, brethren, how that not many wise men after the flesh, not many mighty, not many noble, are called: but God hath chosen the foolish things of the world to confound the wise; and God hath chosen the weak things of the world to confound the things which are mighty" (1 Cor. 1:26–27). The poor of this world become rich in faith; as sons of God, they inherit the wealth of the kingdom.

It is possible to be poor in this world and rich in the next, or rich in this world and poor in the next (1 Tim. 6:17–18). Or, you could be poor both in this world and the next, or rich in this world and the next. It all depends on what you do with Christ and the material wealth He has given you. God promises the kingdom to "those that love him" (James 2:5), not to those who love this world and its riches.

James gave a stern rebuke in James 2:6–7: "When you despise the poor man, you are behaving like the unsaved rich people." In that day, it was easy for rich persons to exploit the poor, influence decisions at court, and make themselves richer. Unfortunately, we have the same sins being committed today; and these sins blaspheme the very name of Christ. Our Lord was poor, and He too was the victim of injustice perpetrated by the wealthy leaders of His day.

The doctrine of God's grace, if we really believe it, forces us to relate to people on the basis of God's plan and not on the basis of human merit or social status. A "class church" is not a church that magnifies the grace of God. When He died, Jesus broke down the wall that separated Jews and Gentiles (Eph. 2:11–22). But in His birth and life, Jesus broke down the walls between rich and poor, young and old, educated and uneducated. It is wrong for us to build those walls again; we cannot rebuild them if we believe in the grace of God.

The Word of God (2:8–11)

In recent years, believers have waged battles over the inspiration and authority of the Word of God. Certainly, it is a good thing to defend the truth of God's Word, but we must never forget that *our lives and ministries are the best defense.* D. L. Moody often said, "Every Bible should be bound in shoe leather!"

James reached back into the Old Testament for one of God's laws, "Thou shalt love thy neighbor as thyself" (Lev. 19:18). In His parable of the good Samaritan, Jesus told us that our neighbor is anyone who needs our help (Luke 10:25–37). It is not a matter of geography, but opportunity. The important question is not, "Who is my neighbor?" but "To whom can I be a neighbor?"

Why is "love thy neighbor" called "the royal law"? For one thing, it was given by the King. God the Father gave it in the law, and God the Son reaffirmed it to His disciples (John 13:34). God the Spirit fills our hearts with God's love and expects us to share it with others (Rom. 5:5). True believers are "taught of God to love one another" (1 Thess. 4:9).

But "love thy neighbor" is the royal law for a second reason: *it rules all the other laws.* "Love is the fulfilling of the law" (Rom. 13:10). There would be no need for the thousands of complex laws if each citizen truly loved his neighbors.

But the main reason why this is the royal law is that *obeying it makes you a king.* Hatred makes a person a slave, but love sets us free from selfishness and enables us to reign like kings. Love enables us to obey the Word of God and treat people as God commands us to do. We obey His law, not out of fear, but out of love.

Showing respect of persons can lead a person into disobeying all of God's law. Take any of the Ten Commandments and you will find ways of breaking it if you respect a person's social or financial status. Respect of persons could make you lie, for example. It could lead to idolatry (getting money out of the rich) or even mistreatment of one's parents. Once we start acting on the basis of respecting persons and rejecting God's Word, we are heading for trouble. And we need not break *all* of God's law to be guilty. There is only one Lawgiver, and all of His laws are from His mind and heart. If I disobey one law, I am capable of disobeying all of them; and by rebelling, I have already done so.

Christian love does not mean that I must *like* a person and agree with him on everything. I may not like his vocabulary or his habits, and I may not want him for an intimate friend. *Christian love means treating others the way God has treated me.* It is an act of the will, not an emotion that I try to manufacture. The motive is to glorify God. The means is the power of the Spirit within ("for the fruit of the Spirit is love"). As I act in love toward another, I may find myself drawn more and more to him, and I may see in him (through Christ) qualities that before were hidden to me.

Also, Christian love does not leave the person where it finds him. Love should help the poor man do better; love should help the rich man make better use of his God-given resources. Love always builds up (1 Cor. 8:1); hatred always tears down.

We only believe as much of the Bible as we practice. If we fail to obey the most important word—"love thy neighbor as thyself"—then we will not do any good with the lesser matters of the Word. It was a glaring fault in the Pharisees that they were careful about the minor matters and careless about the fundamentals (Matt. 23:23). They broke the very law they thought they were defending!

The Judgment of God (2:12–13)

Every orthodox statement of faith ends with a statement about the return of Jesus Christ and the final judgment. Not all Christians agree as to the details of these future events, but the certainty of them none denies. Nor would any deny the importance of a final judgment. Both Jesus (John 5:24) and Paul (Rom. 8:1) assured us that Christian believers will never be judged for their sins, but our works will be judged and rewarded (Rom. 14:10–13; 2 Cor. 5:9–10).

Our words will be judged. Note the words spoken to the two visitors in James 2:3. What we say to people, and how we say it, will come up before God. Even our careless words will be judged (Matt. 12:36). Of course, the words we speak come from the heart; so when God judges the words, He is examining the heart (Matt. 12:34–37). Jesus emphasized caution when speaking in some of His warnings in the Sermon on the Mount (Matt. 5:21–26, 33–37; 7:1–5, 21–23).

Our deeds will be judged. Read Colossians 3:22–25 for additional insight. It is true that God remembers our sins against us no more (Jer. 31:34; Heb. 10:17), *but our sins affect our character and works.* We cannot sin lightly and serve faithfully. God forgives our sins when we confess them to Him, but He cannot change their consequences.

Our attitudes will be judged (v. 13). James contrasted two attitudes: showing mercy to others, and refusing to show mercy. If we have been merciful toward others, God can be merciful toward us. However, we must not twist this truth into a lie. It does not mean that we *earn* mercy by showing mercy, because it is impossible to earn mercy. If it is earned, it is not mercy! Nor does it mean that we should "be soft on sin" and never judge in the lives of others. "I don't condemn anybody," a man once told me, "and God won't condemn me." How wrong he was!

Mercy and justice both come from God, so they are not competitors. Where God finds repentance and faith, He is able to show mercy; where He finds rebellion and unbelief, He must administer justice. It is the heart of the sinner that determines the treatment he gets. Our Lord's parable in Matthew 18:21–35 illustrates the truth. The parable is not illustrating salvation, but forgiveness between fellow servants. If we forgive our brothers, then we have the kind of heart that is open toward the forgiveness of God.

We shall be judged "by the law of liberty." Why did James use this title for God's law? For one thing, when we obey God's law, it frees us from sin and enables us to walk in liberty (Ps. 119:45). Also, *law prepares us for liberty.* A child must be under rules and regulations because he is not mature enough to handle the decisions and demands of life. He is given *outward discipline* so that he might develop *inward discipline,* and one day be free of rules.

Liberty does not mean license. License (doing whatever I want to do) is the worst kind of bondage. Liberty means the freedom to be all that I can be in Jesus Christ. License is confinement; liberty is fulfillment.

Finally, the Word is called "the law of liberty" because God sees our hearts and knows what we would have done had we been free to do so. The Christian student who obeys only because the school has rules is not really maturing. What will he do when he leaves the school? God's Word can change our hearts and give us the desire to do God's will, so that we obey from inward compulsion and not outward constraint.

There is one obvious message to this section: our beliefs should control our behavior. If we really believe that Jesus is the Son of God, and that God is gracious, His Word is true, and one day He will judge us, then our conduct will reveal our convictions. Before we attack those who do not have orthodox doctrine, we must be sure that we practice the doctrines we defend. Jonah had wonderful theology, but he hated people and was angry with God (Jonah 4).

One of the tests of the reality of our faith is how we treat other people. Can we pass the test?

CHAPTER SIX
James 2:14–26
FALSE FAITH

Faith is a key doctrine in the Christian life. The sinner is saved by faith (Eph. 2:8–9), and the believer must walk by faith (2 Cor. 5:7). Without faith it is impossible to please God (Heb. 11:6), and whatever we do apart from faith is sin (Rom. 14:23).

Someone has said that faith is not "believing in spite of evidence, but obeying in spite of consequence." When you read Hebrews 11, you meet men and women who acted on God's Word, no matter what price they had to pay. Faith is not some kind of nebulous feeling that we work up; faith is confidence that God's Word is true and conviction that acting on that Word will bring His blessing.

In this paragraph, James discussed the relationship between faith and works. This is an important discussion, for if we are wrong in this matter, we jeopardize our eternal salvation. What kind of faith really saves a person? Is it necessary to perform good works in order to be saved? How can a person tell whether or not he is exercising true saving faith? James answered these questions by explaining to us that there are three kinds of faith, only one of which is true saving faith.

Dead Faith (2:14–17)

Even in the early church there were those who claimed they had saving faith, yet did not possess salvation. Wherever there is the true, you will find the counterfeit. Jesus warned, "Not every one that saith unto me, 'Lord, Lord,' shall enter into the kingdom of heaven; but he that doeth the will of my Father which is in heaven" (Matt. 7:21).

People with dead faith substitute words for deeds. They know the correct vocabulary for prayer and testimony, and can even quote the right verses from the Bible, but their walk does not measure up to their talk. They think that their words are as good as works, and they are wrong.

James gave a simple illustration. A poor believer came into a fellowship, without proper clothing and in need of food. The person with dead faith noticed the visitor and saw his needs, but he did not do anything to meet the needs. All he did was say a few pious words! "Go, I wish you well; keep warm and well fed" (James 2:16 NIV). But the visitor went away just as hungry and naked as he came in!

Food and clothing are basic needs of every human being, whether he is saved or unsaved. "And having food and raiment let us be therewith content" (1 Tim. 6:8). "Therefore take no thought, saying, 'What shall we eat?' or, 'What shall we drink?' or, 'Wherewithal shall we be clothed?' … for your heavenly Father knoweth that ye have need of all these things" (Matt. 6:31–32). Jacob included these basic needs in his prayer to God: "If God will be with me … and will give me bread to eat, and raiment to put on" (Gen. 28:20).

As believers, we have an obligation to help meet the needs of people, no matter who they may be. "As we have therefore opportunity, let us do good unto all men, especially unto them who are of the household of faith" (Gal. 6:10). "Inasmuch as ye have done it unto one of the least of these my brethren, ye have done it unto me" (Matt. 25:40).

To help a person in need is an expression of love, and faith works by love (Gal. 5:6). The apostle John emphasized this aspect of good works. "If anyone has material possessions and sees his brother in need but has no pity on him, how can the love of God be in him? Dear children, let us not love with words or tongue but with actions and truth" (1 John 3:17–18 NIV). The priest and Levite in the parable of the good Samaritan each had religious training, but neither of them paused to assist the dying man at the side of the road (Luke 10:25–37). Each of them would *defend* his faith, yet neither *demonstrated* that faith in loving works.

The question in James 2:14 should read, "Can *that kind of faith* save him?" What kind? The kind of faith that is never seen in practical works. The answer is no! Any declaration of faith that does not result in a changed life and good works is a false declaration. That kind of faith is dead faith. "Even so faith, if it hath not works, is dead, being alone" (James 2:17). The great theologian John Calvin wrote, "It is faith alone that justifies, but faith that justifies can never be alone." The word *alone* in James 2:17 simply means "by itself." True saving faith can never be by itself: it always brings life, and life produces good works.

The person with dead faith has only an intellectual experience. In his mind, he knows the doctrines of salvation, but he has never submitted himself to God and trusted Christ for salvation. He knows the right words, but he does not back up his words with his works. Faith in Christ brings life (John 3:16), and where there is life there must be growth and fruit. Three times in this paragraph, James warned us that "faith without works is dead" (James 2:17, 20, 26).

Beware of a mere intellectual faith. No man can come to Christ by faith and remain the same any more than he can come into contact with a 220-volt wire and remain the same. "He that hath the Son hath life; and he that hath not the Son of God hath not life" (1 John 5:12). Dead faith is not saving faith. Dead faith is counterfeit faith and lulls the person into a false confidence of eternal life.

Demonic Faith (2:18–19)

James wanted to shock his complacent readers, so he used demons as his illustration. In recent years the church has rediscovered the reality and activity of demons. When our Lord was ministering on earth, He often cast out demons, and He gave that power to His disciples. Paul often confronted demonic forces in his ministry, and in Ephesians 6:10–20, he admonished the early Christians to claim God's protection and defeat the spiritual forces of wickedness.

It comes as a shock to people that demons have faith! What do they believe? For one thing, they believe in the existence of God; they are neither atheists nor agnostics. They also believe in the deity of Christ. Whenever they met Christ when He was on earth, they bore witness to His sonship (Mark 3:11–12). They believe in the existence of a place of punishment (Luke 8:31), and they also recognize Jesus Christ as the Judge (Mark 5:1–13). They submit to the power of His Word.

"Hear, O Israel! The Lord our God is one Lord!" (Deut. 6:4) This was the daily affirmation of faith of the godly Jew. "You believe that there is one God. Good! Even the demons believe that—and shudder" (James 2:19 NIV). The man with dead faith was touched only in his intellect, but the demons are touched *also in their emotions*. They believe and tremble.

But it is not a saving experience to believe and tremble. A person can be enlightened in his mind and even stirred in his heart and be lost forever. True saving faith involves something more, something that can be seen and recognized: a changed life. "Show me thy faith without thy works," challenged James, "and I will show thee my faith by my works" (James 2:18).

How could a person show his faith without works? Can a dead sinner perform good works? Impossible! When you trust Christ, you are "created in Christ Jesus unto good works, which God hath before ordained that we should walk in them" (Eph. 2:10). Being a Christian involves trusting Christ and living for Christ; you *receive* the life, then you *reveal* the life. Faith that is barren is not saving faith. The Greek word translated "dead" in James 2:20 carries the meaning of "barren or idle," like money drawing no interest.

James has introduced us to two kinds of faith that can never save the sinner: dead faith (the intellect alone), and demonic faith (the intellect and the emotions). He closes this section by describing the only kind of faith that can save the sinner—dynamic faith.

Dynamic Faith (2:20–26)

Dynamic faith is faith that is real, faith that has power, faith that results in a changed life.

James *described* this true saving faith. To begin with, dynamic saving faith is *based on the Word of God.* We receive our spiritual rebirth through God's Word (James 1:18). We receive the Word and this saves us (James 1:21). "So then faith cometh by hearing, and hearing by the Word of God" (Rom. 10:17). James used Abraham and Rahab as illustrations of dynamic saving faith, since both of them heard and received the message of God through His Word.

Faith is only as good as its object. The man in the jungle bows before an idol of stone and trusts it to help him, but he receives no help. No matter how much faith a person may generate, if it is not directed at the right object, it will accomplish nothing. "I believe" may be the testimony of many sincere people, but the big question is, "In whom do you believe? What do you believe?" We are not saved by *faith in faith;* we are saved by faith in Christ as revealed in His Word.

Dynamic faith is based on God's Word, and *it involves the whole man.* Dead faith touches only the intellect; demonic faith involves both the mind and the emotions; but dynamic faith involves the will. The whole person plays a part in true saving faith. The mind understands the truth; the heart desires the truth; and the will acts upon the truth. The men and women of faith named in Hebrews 11 were people of action: God spoke and they obeyed. Again, "Faith is not believing in spite of evidence; faith is obeying in spite of consequence. "

True saving faith *leads to action.* Dynamic faith is not intellectual contemplation or emotional consternation; it leads to obedience on the part of the will. And this obedience is not an isolated event: it continues throughout the whole life. It leads to works.

Many different kinds of works are named in the New Testament. "The works of the law" (Gal. 2:16) relate to the sinner's attempt to please God by obeying the law of Moses. Of course, it is impossible for a sinner to be saved through the works of the law. "The works of the flesh" (Gal. 5:19) are done by unsaved people who live for the things of the old nature. There are also "wicked works" (Col. 1:21) and "dead works" (Heb. 9:14). Where there is dynamic faith—saving faith—you will always find good works.

James then *illustrated* his doctrine in the lives of two well-known Bible persons: Abraham and Rahab. You could not find two more different persons! Abraham was a Jew; Rahab was a Gentile. Abraham was a godly man, but Rahab was a sinful woman, a harlot. Abraham was the friend of God, while Rahab belonged to the enemies of God. What did they have in common? Both exercised saving faith in God.

You will want to read Genesis 15 and 22 to get the background facts for this illustration. God called Abraham out of Ur of the Chaldees to lead him into Canaan and to make out of him the great nation of Israel. It was through Israel that God would bring the Savior into the world. Abraham's salvation experience is recorded in Genesis 15. At night, God showed His servant the stars and gave him a promise, "So shall thy seed [descendants] be!" How did Abraham respond? "And he believed in the Lord, and he [the Lord] counted it to him for righteousness" (Gen. 15:5–6).

The word *counted* is a legal or financial term; it means "to put to one's account." As a sinner, Abraham's spiritual bankbook was empty. He was bankrupt! But he trusted God, and God put *righteous* on Abraham's account. Abraham did not work for this righteousness; he received it as a gift from God. He was declared righteous by faith. He was justified by faith (read Rom. 4).

Justification is an important doctrine in the Bible. Justification is the act of God whereby He declares the believing sinner righteous on the basis of Christ's finished work on the cross. It is not a process; it is an act. It is not something the sinner does; it is something God does for the sinner when he trusts Christ. It is a once-for-all event. It never changes.

How can you tell if a person is justified by faith if this transaction takes place between the sinner and God privately? Abraham's example answers that important question: the justified person has a changed life and obeys God's will. His faith is demonstrated by his works.

James used another event in Abraham's life, an event that took place many years after Abraham's conversion. This event is the offering up of Isaac on the altar (Gen. 22). Abraham was not saved by obeying God's difficult command. His obedience proved that he already was saved. "You see that his faith and his actions were working together, and his faith was made complete by what he did" (James 2:22 NIV). There is a perfect relationship between faith and works. As someone has expressed it, "Abraham was not saved by faith plus works, but by a faith that works."

How was Abraham "justified by works" (James 2:21) when he had already been "justified by faith" (see Rom. 4)? By faith, he was justified *before God* and his righteousness declared; by works he was justified *before men* and his righteousness demonstrated. It is true that no humans actually saw Abraham put his son on the altar, but the inspired record in Genesis 22 enables us to see the event and witness Abraham's faith demonstrated by his works.

As I mentioned in the previous chapter, D. L. Moody often said, "Every Bible should be bound in shoe leather." He did not say that because he had been a successful shoe salesman; he said it because he was a dedicated Christian. Dynamic faith obeys God and proves itself in daily life and works. Alas, we still have church members today who fit the description given in Titus, "They profess that they know God, but in works they deny him" (Titus 1:16). Paul also wrote, "This is a faithful saying, and these things I will that thou affirm constantly, that they which have believed in God might be careful to maintain good works" (Titus 3:8).

His second illustration is Rahab, and the background for her is found in Joshua 2 and 6. Israel was about to invade their Promised Land and take the city of Jericho. Joshua sent spies into the city to get the lay of the land. There they met Rahab, a harlot, who protected them and affirmed that she believed in what God had said and what God was going to do. When the men departed, they promised to save her and her family when the city was taken, and this they did.

It is an exciting story. But in it is one of the Bible's great examples of saving faith (see Heb. 11:31). Rahab heard the Word and knew that her city was condemned. This truth affected her and her fellow citizens so that their hearts melted within them (Josh. 2:11). Rahab responded with her mind and her emotions, but she also responded with her will: *she did something about it.* She risked her own life to protect the Jewish spies, and she further risked her life by sharing the good news of deliverance with the members of her family. The Hebrew word translated "harlot" in Joshua 2 can also have the wider meaning of "an innkeeper." Rahab ran a guest house, so it was normal for the spies to go there. The Greek word "harlot" in James 2:25 definitely means an immoral person. This is also the meaning in Hebrews 11:31. Matthew 1:5 indicates she married into Israel and became an ancestress of our Lord. What grace! Rahab is one of the first soul-winners in the Bible, and you cannot help but compare her with the "bad Samaritan" in John 4.

Rahab could have had *dead* faith, a mere intellectual experience. Or she could have had *demonic* faith, her mind enlightened and her emotions stirred. But she exercised *dynamic* faith: her mind knew the truth, her heart was stirred by the truth, and her will acted on the truth. She proved her faith by her works.

When you realize the small amount of information Rahab had, you can see how truly marvelous her faith really was. Today we have the full revelation of God through His Word and His Son. We live on the other side of Calvary, and we have the Holy Spirit to convict and to teach us the Word. "For unto whomsoever much is given, of him shall be much required" (Luke 12:48). Her faith is an indictment against the unbelief of sinners today.

James 2 emphasized that the mature Christian practices the truth. He does not merely hold to ancient doctrines; he practices those doctrines in his everyday life. His faith is not the dead faith of the intellectuals or the demonic faith of the fallen spirits. It is the dynamic faith of men like Abraham and women like Rahab, faith that changes a life and goes to work for God.

It is important that each professing Christian examine his own heart and life and make sure that he possesses true saving faith, dynamic faith. "Examine yourselves, whether ye be in the faith; prove your own selves" (2 Cor. 13:5a). Satan is the great deceiver; one of his devices is imitation. If he can convince a person that counterfeit faith is true faith, he has that person in his power.

Here are some questions we can ask ourselves as we examine our hearts:

1. Was there a time when I honestly realized I was a sinner and admitted this to myself and to God?

2. Was there a time when my heart stirred me to flee from the wrath to come? Have I ever seriously been alarmed over my sins?

3. Do I truly understand the gospel, that Christ died for my sins and arose again? Do I understand and confess that I cannot save myself?

4. Did I sincerely repent of my sins and turn from them? Or do I secretly love sin and want to enjoy it?

5. Have I trusted Christ and Christ alone for my salvation? Do I enjoy a living relationship with Him through the Word and in the Spirit?

6. Has there been a change in my life? Do I maintain good works, or are my works occasional and weak? Do I seek to grow in the things of the Lord? Can others tell that I have been with Jesus?

7. Do I have a desire to share Christ with others? Or am I ashamed of Him?

8. Do I enjoy the fellowship of God's people? Is worship a delight to me?

9. Am I ready for the Lord's return? Or will I be ashamed when He comes for me?

To be sure, not every Christian has the same personal experience, and there are degrees of sanctification. But for the most part, the preceding spiritual inventory can assist a person in determining his true standing before God.

"Search me, O Lord, and know my heart: try me, and know my thoughts: and see if there be any wicked way in me, and lead me in the way everlasting" (Ps. 139:23–24).

CHAPTER SEVEN
James 3:1–12
THE WORLD'S SMALLEST BUT LARGEST TROUBLEMAKER

James has explained to us two characteristics of the mature Christian: he is patient in trouble (James 1) and he practices the truth (James 2). In this section, he shared the third characteristic of the mature believer he has power over his tongue.

A pastor friend told me about a member of his church who was a notorious gossip. She would "hang on the phone" most of the day, sharing tidbits with any and all who would listen.

She came to the pastor one day and said, "Pastor,

the Lord has convicted me of my sin of gossip. My tongue is getting me and others into trouble."

My friend knew she was not sincere because she had gone through that routine before. Guardedly he asked, "Well, what do you plan to do?"

"I want to put my tongue on the altar," she replied with pious fervor.

Calmly my friend replied, "There isn't an altar big enough," and he left her to think it over.

The Christians that James wrote to were apparently having serious problems with their tongues. James had warned them to be "swift to hear, slow to speak, slow to wrath" (James 1:19). The believer who does not bridle his tongue is not truly religious (James 1:26). We must speak and act as though we were already facing Christ in judgment (James 2:12). When you read passages like James 4:1, 11–12, you get the impression that this assembly must have had some interesting meetings!

The power of speech is one of the greatest powers God has given us. With the tongue, man can praise God, pray, preach the Word, and lead the lost to Christ. What a privilege! But with that same tongue he can tell lies that could ruin a man's reputation or break a person's heart. The ability to speak words is the ability to influence others and accomplish tremendous tasks, and yet we take this ability for granted.

In order to impress on us the importance of controlled speech, and the great consequences of our words, James gave us six pictures of the tongue: the bit, the rudder, fire, a poisonous animal, a fountain, and a fig tree. You can put these six pictures into three meaningful classifications that reveal the three powers of the tongue.

Power to Direct: The Bit and Rudder (3:1–4)

Apparently, everybody in the assembly wanted to teach and be a spiritual leader, for James had to warn them: "Not many of you should act as teachers, my brothers" (James 3:1 NIV). Perhaps they were impressed with the authority and prestige of the office and forgot about the tremendous responsibility *and accountability!* Those who teach the Word face the stricter judgment. Teachers must use their tongue to share God's truth, and it is easy to commit sins of the tongue. Furthermore, teachers must practice what they teach; otherwise, their teaching is hypocrisy. Think of the damage that can be done by a teacher who is unprepared, or whose spiritual life is not up to par.

But teachers are not the only ones who are tempted and sin; every Christian must admit that "we all stumble in many ways" (James 3:2 NIV). And sins of the tongue seem to head the list. The person who is able to discipline his tongue gives evidence that he can control his whole body. He proves that he is a mature (perfect) man.

Was James making a mistake by connecting sins of the tongue with sins committed by "the whole body"? No, because *words* usually lead to *deeds*. During World War II we were accustomed to seeing posters that read LOOSE LIPS SINK SHIPS! But loose lips also wreck lives. A person makes an unguarded statement and suddenly finds himself involved in a fight. His tongue has forced the rest of his body to defend itself.

In selecting the bit and the rudder ("helm" in James 3:4 means "rudder"), James presented two items that are small of themselves, yet exercise great power, just like the tongue. A small bit enables the rider to control the great horse, and a small rudder enables the pilot to steer the huge ship. The tongue is a small member in the body, and yet it has the power to accomplish great things.

Both the bit and the rudder must overcome contrary forces. The bit must overcome the wild nature of the horse, and the rudder must fight the winds and currents that would drive the ship off its course. The human tongue also must overcome contrary forces. We have an old nature that wants to control us and make us sin. There are circumstances around us that would make us say things we ought not to say. Sin on the inside and pressures on the outside are seeking to get control of the tongue.

This means that both the bit and the rudder must be under the control of a strong hand. The expert horseman keeps the mighty power of his steed under control, and the experienced pilot courageously steers the ship through the storm. When Jesus Christ controls the tongue, then we need not fear saying the wrong things—or even saying the right things in a wrong way! "Death and life are in the power of the tongue," warned Solomon (Prov. 18:21). No wonder David prayed, "Set a watch, O Lord, before my mouth; keep the door of my lips. Incline not my heart to any evil thing" (Ps. 141:34). David knew that *the heart* is the key to right speech. "Out of the abundance of the heart the mouth speaketh" (Matt. 12:34). When Jesus Christ is the Lord of the heart, then He is Lord of the lips too.

The bit and rudder have the power to direct, which means *they affect the lives of others.* A runaway horse or a shipwreck could mean injury or death to pedestrians or passengers. The words we speak affect the lives of others. A judge says, "Guilty!" or "Not Guilty!" and those words affect the destiny of the prisoner, his family, and his friends. The president of the United States speaks a few words and signs some papers, and the nation is at war. Even a simple yes or no from the lips of a parent can greatly affect the direction of a child's life.

Never underestimate the guidance you give by the words you speak or do not speak. Jesus spoke to a woman at a well, and her life and the lives of her neighbors experienced a miraculous change (John 4). Peter preached at Pentecost and three thousand souls came to salvation through faith in Christ (Acts 2).

On April 21, 1855, Edward Kimball went into a Boston shoe store and led young Dwight L. Moody to Christ. The result: one of history's greatest evangelists, a man whose ministry still continues. The tongue has the power to direct others to the right choices.

It would do us all good to read frequently the book of Proverbs, and to note especially the many references to speech. "A soft answer turneth away wrath: but grievous words stir up anger" (Prov. 15:1). "Lying lips are an abomination to the Lord" (Prov. 12:22). "In the multitude of words there wanteth not sin: but he that refraineth his lips is wise" (Prov. 10:19). Yes, the tongue is like a bit and a rudder: it has the power to direct. How important it is that our tongues direct people in the right way!

Power to Destroy: the Fire and Animal (3:5–8)

I was visiting the used bookstores along Charing Cross Road in London, and I remarked to a clerk that there were not as many stores as I expected. "There's a reason for that," he replied. "One night during World War II, the incendiary bombs hit and the fires destroyed at least a million books!"

On another occasion, a friend was taking my wife and me on a tour of the beautiful forests in California, and we came to an ugly section that was burned out. Not only was the face of nature scarred, but millions of dollars of valuable timber had been wiped out. "Somebody's lit cigarette," my friend commented as we drove past the blackened earth.

A fire can begin with just a small spark, but it can grow to destroy a city. A fire reportedly started in the O'Leary barn in Chicago at 8:30 p.m., October 8, 1871; and because that fire spread, over 100,000 people were left homeless, 17,500 buildings were destroyed, and 300 people died. It cost the city over $400 million.

Our words can start fires. "Where no wood is, there the fire goeth out: so where there is no talebearer, the strife ceaseth. As coals are to burning coals, and wood to fire; so is a contentious man to kindle strife" (Prov. 26:20–21). In some churches, there are members or officers who cannot control their tongues, and the result is destruction. Let them move out of town or be replaced in office, and a beautiful spirit of harmony and love takes over.

Like a fire, the tongue can "heat things up." David wrote, "I said, 'I will take heed to my ways, that I sin not with my tongue.'… My heart was hot within me, while I was musing the fire burned; then spake I with my tongue" (Ps. 39:1, 3). Have you ever had that experience? Of course you have! A hot head and a hot heart can lead to burning words that later we will regret David had a temper, and he had to have God's help in controlling it. No wonder Solomon wrote, "He who restrains his word has knowledge, and he who has a cool spirit is a man of understanding" (Prov. 17:27 NASB). "He who is slow to anger has great understanding, but he who is quick-tempered exalts folly" (Prov. 14:29 NASB).

Fire not only starts small and grows, and creates heat; it also defiles. A friend of mine suffered a fire in the basement of his house, and the smoke and fire damage so soiled the upstairs of the house that the family had to move out while the house was redecorated. Fiery words can defile a home, a Sunday school class, a church. The only thing that can wash away that defilement is the blood of Jesus Christ.

Fire burns and hurts, and our words can burn and hurt. One of the sorrows our Lord had to bear when He was here on earth was the way His enemies talked about Him. They called Him a "man gluttonous and a winebibber" (Matt. 11:19) because He graciously accepted invitations to dine with people the Pharisees did not like. When He performed miracles, they said He was in league with Satan. Even when He was dying on the cross, His enemies could not let Him alone but threw vicious taunts into His face.

Fire spreads, and the more fuel you give it, the faster and farther it will spread. The tongue "setteth on fire the course of nature" (James 3:6), or "sets the whole course of his life on fire" (NIV). James suggested that all of life is connected like a wheel, and therefore we cannot keep things from spreading. A person's entire life can be injured or destroyed by the tongue. Time does not correct the sins of the tongue. We may confess our sins of speech, but the fire keeps on spreading.

As it spreads, fire destroys, and the words we speak have the power to destroy. For every word in Hitler's book *Mein Kampf,* 125 lives were lost in World War II. Our own words may not have caused wars or wrecked cities, but they can break hearts and ruin reputations. They can also destroy souls by sending them into eternity without Christ How important it is for us to let our speech "be always full of grace, seasoned with salt" (Col. 4:6 NIV).

Not only is the tongue like a fire, but it is also like a dangerous animal. It is restless and cannot be ruled (unruly), and it seeks its prey and then pounces and kills. My wife and I once drove through a safari park, admiring the animals as they moved about in their natural habitat. But there were warning signs posted all over the park: DO NOT LEAVE YOUR CAR! DO NOT OPEN YOUR WINDOWS! Those "peaceful animals" were capable of doing great damage, and even killing.

Some animals are poisonous, and some tongues spread poison. The deceptive thing about poison is that it works secretly and slowly, and then kills. How many times has some malicious person injected a bit of poison into the conversation, hoping it would spread and finally get to the person he or she wanted to hurt? As a pastor, I have seen poisonous tongues do great damage to individuals, families, classes, and entire churches. Would you turn hungry lions or angry snakes loose in your Sunday morning service? Of course not! But unruly tongues accomplish the same results.

James reminds us that animals can be tamed, and, for that matter, fire can be tamed. When you tame an animal, you get a worker instead of a destroyer. When you control fire, you generate power. The tongue cannot be tamed by man, but it can be tamed by God. Your tongue need not be "set on fire of hell" (James

3:6). Like the apostles at Pentecost, it can be set on fire from heaven! If God lights the fire and controls it, then the tongue can be a mighty tool for the winning of the lost and the building up of the church. The important thing, of course, is the heart, for it is "out of the abundance of the heart that the mouth speaketh" (Matt. 12:34). If the heart is filled with hatred, Satan will light the fire. But if the heart is filled with love, God will light the fire.

Power to Delight: The Fountain and Tree (3:9–12)

The fountain, of course, provides the cool water that man needs to stay alive. In underdeveloped countries, the presence of a freshwater fountain is a great blessing to a village. Man needs water not only for drinking, but also for washing, cooking, farming, and a host of other activities so necessary to life.

"The words of a man's mouth are as deep waters, and the wellspring of wisdom as a flowing brook" (Prov. 18:4). "The mouth of a righteous man is a well of life" (Prov. 10:11). "The law of the wise is a fountain of life, to depart from the snares of death" (Prov. 13:14). These verses parallel what James has written and underscore the importance of our words.

Water is life-giving, and our words can give life. However, if water is not controlled, it brings death and destruction. The famous Johnstown, Pennsylvania flood of 1889 took 2,200 lives and destroyed $10 million in property. "Death and life are in the power of the tongue" (Prov. 18:21).

However, when we bend over a fountain for a drink of cool water, we rarely think of floods. We think only of the precious gift of refreshment that comes with a drink of water. We could not be healthy without water. "There is that speaketh like the piercings of a sword: but the tongue of the wise is health" (Prov. 12:18). Paul's prayer was that he might "refresh" the saints in Rome when he came to them (Rom. 15:32). He often named Christians who had refreshed him (1 Cor. 16:18; Philem. 7, 20).

Water also cleanses. There was a laver in the Old Testament tabernacle and temple, provided for the cleansing of the priests' hands and feet. God's Word is the spiritual water that cleanses us (John 15:3; Eph. 5:26–27). But our words to others can also help to cleanse and sanctify them. Our words ought to be like that river described in Ezekiel 47 that brought life to everything it touched.

The tongue is also delightful because it is like a tree. In Bible lands, trees are vitally important to the economy: they help to hold down the soil; they provide beauty and shade; and they bear fruit. Our words can help to shelter and encourage a weary traveler, and can help to feed a hungry soul. "The lips of the righteous feed many" (Prov. 10:21). Jesus said, "The words that I speak unto you, they are spirit, and they are life" (John 6:63). As we share His Word with others, we feed them and encourage them along the way.

The most important thing about a tree is the root system. If the roots do not go down deep, the tree will not grow in a healthy manner. If we are rooted in the things of the Lord, then our words will be the fruit of our fellowship with Him. We will be like that "blessed man" in Psalm 1 and produce fruit in due season. One reason our Lord was able to say the right words at the right times was because He communed with His Father and heard from heaven each day. Listen to His testimony:

"The Lord hath given me the tongue of the learned, that I should know how to speak a word in season to him that is weary: he wakeneth morning by morning, he wakeneth mine ear to hear as the learned" (Isa. 50:4). "And in the morning, rising up a great while before day, he went out, and departed into a solitary place, and there prayed" (Mark 1:35).

If you and I are going to have tongues that delight, then we must meet with the Lord each day and learn from Him. We must get our "spiritual roots" deep into His Word. We must pray and meditate and permit the Spirit of God to fill our hearts with God's love and truth.

But James issued a warning: a fountain cannot give forth two kinds of water, and a tree cannot bear two different kinds of fruit. We expect the fountain to flow with sweet water at all times, and we expect the fig tree to bear figs and the olive tree to bear olives. Nature reproduces after its kind.

If the tongue is inconsistent, there is something radically wrong with the heart. I heard about a professing Christian who got angry on the job and let loose with some oaths. Embarrassed, he turned to his partner and said, "I don't know why I said that. It really isn't in me." His partner wisely replied, "It had to be in you or it couldn't have come out of you." When Peter was out of fellowship with Christ, he uttered some oaths, but he went out and wept bitterly and confessed his sins.

The tongue that blesses the Father, and then turns around and curses men made in God's image, is in desperate need of spiritual medicine! How easy it is to sing the hymns during the worship service, then after the service, get into the family car and argue and fight all the way home! "My brethren, these things ought not so to be."

The problem, of course, is not the tongue; it is the heart. It is easy to have "bitter envying and strife" in our hearts (James 3:14). "But those things which proceed out of the mouth come forth from the heart; and they defile the man" (Matt. 15:18). "Keep thy heart with all diligence, for out of it are the issues of life" (Prov. 4:23). As we fill our hearts with God's Word and yield to the Holy Spirit, He can use us to bring delight to others, and we will be refreshing fountains and trees.

As I close this chapter, let me suggest that you start using the "Twelve Words That Can Transform Your Life." If you use these words *and sincerely mean what you say from your heart,* you will find that God will use you to be a blessing and encouragement to others. There are only twelve of them, but they work.

"Please" and "Thank you." When you use these three words, you are treating others like people and not things. You are showing appreciation.

"I'm sorry." These two words have a way of breaking down walls and building bridges.

"I love you." Too many people read "romance" into these words, but they go much deeper than that. As Christians, we should love the brethren and even love our enemies. "I love you" is a statement that can carry tremendous power.

"I'm praying for you." And be sure that you are. When you talk to God about people, then you can talk to people about God. Our private praying for people helps us in our public meeting with people. Of course, we never say "I'm praying for you" in a boastful way, as though we are more spiritual than others. We say it in an encouraging way, to let others know that we care enough for them to meet them at the throne of grace.

Yes, the smallest but largest troublemaker in all the world is the tongue. But it does not have to be a troublemaker! God can use our tongues to direct others into the way of life, and to delight them in the trials of life. The tongue is a little member, but it has great power.

Give God your tongue and your heart each day and ask Him to use you to be a blessing to others.

CHAPTER EIGHT
James 3:13–18
WHERE TO GET WISDOM

Wisdom was an important thing to Jewish people. They realized that it was not enough to have knowledge; you had to have wisdom to be able to use that knowledge correctly. All of us know people who are very intelligent, perhaps almost geniuses, and yet who seemingly are unable to carry out the simplest tasks of life. They can program computers but they cannot manage their own lives! "Wisdom is the principal thing; therefore get wisdom" (Prov. 4:7).

James continued to exhort the people in the assembly who wanted to be teachers of the Word (James 3:1). It is not enough simply to stand before the people and say words; *you must have something to say.* This is where spiritual wisdom comes in. Knowledge enables us to take things apart, but wisdom enables us to put things together and relate God's truth to daily life. All of us have heard preachers and teachers who say many good things, but who somehow miss the heart of God's message and fail to relate truth to everyday life. It is this kind of "knowledge without wisdom" that James was writing about. He was contrasting true wisdom and false wisdom in three different aspects.

Contrast in Origins (3:15, 17a)

The true wisdom comes from above, but the false wisdom comes from below. In other words, there is a "heavenly wisdom" that comes from God, and there is a "man-made wisdom" that does not come from God. Whatever does not come from God is destined to fail, no matter how successful it may seem at the time.

The Bible contains many examples of the folly of man's wisdom. The building of the Tower of Babel seemed like a wise enterprise, but it ended in failure and confusion (Gen. 11:1–9). It seemed wise for Abraham to go to Egypt when famine came to Canaan, but the results proved otherwise (Gen. 12:10–20). King Saul thought it was wise to put his own armor on young David for the lad's battle with Goliath, but God's plan was otherwise (1 Sam. 17:38ff.). The disciples thought it was wise to dismiss the great crowd and let them find their own food; but Jesus took a few loaves and fishes and fed the multitude. The Roman "experts" in Acts 27 thought it was wise to leave port and set sail for Rome, even though Paul disagreed, and the storm that followed proved that Paul's wisdom was better than their expert counsel. They lived to regret it, but they lived!

What is the origin of man's wisdom? "This wisdom descendeth not from above, but is earthly, sensual, devilish" (James 3:15). The believer has three enemies: the world, the flesh, and the devil (Eph. 2:1–3). These enemies are suggested by the terms "earthly, sensual, devilish."

There is a "wisdom of this world" (1 Cor. 1:20–21). Do not confuse the world's *knowledge* and the world's *wisdom.* Certainly, there is a great deal of knowledge in this world, and we all benefit from it, but there is not much wisdom. Man unlocks the secrets of the universe, but he does not know what to do with them. Almost everything he discovers or devises turns against him. Over a century ago, Henry David Thoreau warned that we had "improved means to unimproved ends."

Whenever I ride a bus or elevated train in the city, I often think of the man in Boston who was entertaining a famous Chinese scholar. He met his Asian friend at the train station and rushed him to the subway. As they ran through the subway station, the host panted to his guest, "If we run and catch this next train, we will save three minutes!" To which the patient Chinese philosopher replied, "And what significant thing shall we do with the three minutes we are saving?"

The world by its wisdom knew not God, and in its wisdom rejects the very gospel of God. "For the preaching of the cross is to them that perish foolishness" (1 Cor. 1:18). Any person enamored with the wisdom of this world ought to read the first two chapters of 1 Corinthians and notice how much Paul had to say about God's wisdom and man's wisdom. Man's wisdom is foolishness to God (1 Cor. 1:20), and God's wisdom is foolishness to man (1 Cor. 2:14). Man's wisdom comes from reason, while God's wisdom comes from revelation. Man's worldly wisdom will come to nothing (1 Cor. 1:19), while God's wisdom will endure forever.

Because the world has turned from God, it has lost

its wisdom. Every increase in man's knowledge only magnifies the problems. "The fear of the Lord is the beginning of wisdom; and the knowledge of the holy is understanding" (Prov. 9:10). "There is no fear of God before their eyes" (Rom. 3:18).

But this false wisdom has another source: it is "sensual," that is, it is "natural." The Greek word is *psukikos,* which comes from the Greek word *psuke* meaning "life," or "soul." Our English word *psychology* is derived from it. In 1 Corinthians 2:14; 15:44, 46, *psukikos* is translated "natural," referring to the opposite of "spiritual." In Jude 19 it is translated "sensual." The main idea seems to be that of man's fallen nature as opposed to the new nature given by God. There is a wisdom that gets its origin in man's nature totally apart from the Spirit of God.

But this "wisdom that is from beneath" is also "devilish." Perhaps the best translation is "demonic." Beginning with Genesis 3, where Satan successfully deceived Eve, and continuing through the entire Bible, there is a "wisdom of Satan" at work, fighting against the wisdom of God. Satan convinced Eve that she would be like God. He told her that the tree would make her wise. Ever since that event, people have continued to believe Satan's lies and have tried to become their own gods (Rom. 1:18–25). Satan is cunning; he is the old serpent! He has wisdom that will confound and confuse you if you do not know the wisdom of God.

In contrast to the wisdom that is earthly, sensual, and devilish, James described a "wisdom that is from above" (James 3:17). "Every good gift and every perfect gift is from above" (James 1:17). The Christian looks up to heaven for all that he needs. His citizenship is in heaven (Phil. 3:20), just as his Father is in heaven (Matt. 6:9). His treasures are in heaven, not on earth (Matt. 6:19ff.). He was born from above (John 3:1–7) when he trusted Jesus Christ. The believer's home is in heaven (John 14:1–6) and his hope is in heaven. He sets his affection and attention on things above, not on earthly things (Col. 3:1–4).

What is the Christian's wisdom? Does he look to the philosophies of this world? No! To begin with, Jesus Christ is our wisdom (1 Cor. 1:24, 30). In Jesus Christ "are hid all the treasures of wisdom and knowledge" (Col. 2:3). The first step toward true wisdom is the receiving of Jesus Christ as Savior.

The Word of God is also our wisdom. "Behold, I have taught you statutes and judgments.… Keep therefore and do them; for this is your wisdom and your understanding in the sight of the nations" (Deut. 4:5–6). The Scriptures are able to make us "wise unto salvation" (2 Tim. 3:15).

James 1:5 indicates that we find wisdom through believing prayer. "If any of you lack wisdom, let him ask of God." The Holy Spirit of God is "the Spirit of wisdom and revelation" (Eph. 1:17), and He directs us in the wisest paths as we trust the Word and pray.

The origin of true spiritual wisdom is God. To get your wisdom from any other source is to ask for trouble. There is no need to get the counterfeit wisdom of the world, the wisdom that caters to the flesh and accomplishes the work of the devil. Get your wisdom from God!

Contrast in Operations (3:13–14, 17)

The wisdom from above, God's wisdom, operates in a different way from the wisdom that is "earthly, sensual, devilish." Since they originate from radically different sources, they must operate in opposite ways.

What are the evidences of false wisdom?

Envy (v. 14a). This word carries the meaning of selfish ambition and zeal. It ties in with James 3:1, where James warned them not to be ambitious for spiritual offices. The wisdom of the world says, "Promote yourself. You're as good as the other candidates, maybe better! The wheel that squeaks the loudest gets the grease." Sad to say, there is a great deal of selfish, carnal promotion among God's people. Even the apostles argued over who was the greatest in the kingdom.

It is easy to go on an ego trip under the guise of spiritual zeal. The Pharisees used their religious activities to promote the praise of men (Matt. 6:1–18). We ought to be zealous in the things of the Lord, but we must be sure that our motives are right. The wisdom of this world exalts man and robs God of glory. In 1 Corinthians 1:17ff., Paul discussed the wisdom of God and the wisdom of this world, and he explained why God works as He does: "That no flesh should glory in his presence" (1 Cor. 1:29). He concluded the section with the admonition, "He that glorieth, let him glory in the Lord" (1 Cor. 1:31).

Is our zeal for the Lord spiritual or carnal? Do we rejoice when others succeed, or do we have secret envy and criticism? Do we feel burdened when others fail, or are we glad? When the wisdom of the world gets into the church, there is a great deal of fleshly promotion and human glorification. Beware!

Strife (v. 14b). This word means "party spirit." It was used by the Greeks to describe a politician out canvassing for votes. The world's wisdom says, "Get all the support you can! Ask the people in the church if they are for you or against you!" Of course, this spirit of self-seeking only creates rivalry and division in the church. "Let nothing be done through strife or vainglory; but in lowliness of mind let each esteem other better than [more important than] themselves" (Phil. 2:3).

Boasting (v. 14c). Pride loves to boast, and nothing is prouder than the wisdom of men. There is a way to report blessings so that God gets the glory, but there is also an approach that gives men the praise. It is tragic to see mutual admiration societies among God's people. In 2 Corinthians 10, when Paul was forced to boast about his ministry, he was careful to give God the glory. "Of course, we shouldn't dare include ourselves in the same class as those who write their own testimonials, or even to compare ourselves with them! All they are doing, of course, is to measure themselves by their own standards or by comparisons within their own circle, and that doesn't make for accurate estimation, you may be sure" (2 Cor. 10:12 ph).

When God's wisdom is at work, there is a sense of humility and submission, and you want God to get all the glory. You have no desire to compare yourself with any other Christian, because you see only Christ—and compared with Him, all of us still have a long way to go!

Deceit (v. 14d). "Lie not against the truth." The sequence is not difficult to understand. First, there is selfish ambition that leads to party spirit and rivalry. In order to "win the election" we must resort to boasting; *and boasting usually involves lies!* A man's life is not read in his press releases; it is read by the Lord in his heart. "Therefore judge nothing before the time, until the Lord come, who both will bring to light the hidden things of darkness, and will make manifest the counsels of the hearts: and then shall every man have praise of God" (1 Cor. 4:5).

What a relief it is to turn to the evidences of true spiritual wisdom.

Meekness (v. 13). Meekness is not weakness; it is power under control. The meek person does not selfishly assert himself. The Greek word was used for a horse that had been broken so that his power was under control. The meek person seeks only the glory of God and does not cater to the praises of men. Meekness is a fruit of the Spirit (Gal. 5:23); it cannot be manufactured by man. There is a false humility that some people mistake for meekness, but it is only counterfeit.

The phrase "meekness of wisdom" is an interesting one (James 3:3). Meekness is the right use of power, and wisdom is the right use of knowledge. They go together. The truly wise person will show in his daily life (*conversation* means "behavior") that he is a child of God. Attitude and action go together.

Purity (v. 17a). "First pure" indicates the importance of holiness. God is holy; therefore the wisdom from above is pure. The idea behind this word is "chaste, free from defilement." James used it again in James 4:8—"purify your hearts," or, "make chaste your hearts." God's wisdom leads to purity of life. Man's wisdom may lead to sin. There is a spiritual purity that results in a chaste relationship with the Lord (2 Cor. 11:3), and there is a worldliness that makes the person a spiritual adulterer (James 4:4).

Peace (v. 17b). Man's wisdom leads to competition, rivalry, and war (James 4:1–2); but God's wisdom leads to peace. It is a peace based on holiness, not on compromise. God never has "peace at any price." The peace of the church is not more important than the purity of the church. If the church is pure, devoted to God, then there will be peace. "And the work of righteousness shall be peace, and the effect of righteousness quietness and assurance forever" (Isa. 32:17). The church can never have peace by sweeping sins under the rug and pretending they are not there. Man's

wisdom says, "Cover up sin! Keep things together!" God's wisdom says, "Confess sin and My peace will keep things together!"

Gentleness (v. 17c). Matthew Arnold liked to call this "sweet reasonableness." It carries the meaning of moderation without compromise, gentleness without weakness. The gentle person does not deliberately cause fights, but neither does he compromise the truth in order to keep peace. Carl Sandburg described Abraham Lincoln as a man of "velvet steel." That is a good description of gentleness.

Compliance (v. 17d). *God's* wisdom makes the believer agreeable and easy to live with and work with. Man's wisdom makes a person hard and stubborn. The compliant person is willing to hear all sides of a question, but he does not compromise his own convictions. He can disagree without being disagreeable. He is "swift to hear, slow to speak, slow to wrath" (James 1:19). Many people think that stubbornness is conviction, and they must have their own way. When God's wisdom is at work, there is a willingness to listen, think, pray, and obey whatever God reveals. "Yielding to persuasion" is another translation of this word.

Mercy (v. 17e). To be "full" of something means to be "controlled by." The person who follows God's wisdom is controlled by mercy. "Be ye therefore merciful, as your Father also is merciful" (Luke 6:36). God in His grace gives us what we do not deserve, and in His mercy He does not give us what we do deserve. Our Lord's parable of the good Samaritan illustrates the meaning of mercy (Luke 10:25–37). For a Samaritan to care for a Jewish stranger was an act of mercy. He could gain nothing from it, except the blessing that comes from doing the will of God, and the victim could not pay him back. That is mercy.

Good fruits (v. 17f). People who are faithful are fruitful. God's wisdom does not make a life empty; it makes it full. The Spirit produces fruit to the glory of God (see John 15:1–16). The lawyer in Luke 10:25–37 was willing to *discuss* the subject of neighborliness, but he was unwilling to be a neighbor and help someone else. God's wisdom is practical; it changes the life and produces good works to the glory of God.

Decisiveness (v. 17g). The word suggests singleness of mind and is the opposite of "wavering" (James 1:6). When you lean on the world's wisdom, you are pressured from one side and then another to change your mind or take a new viewpoint. When you have God's wisdom, you need not waver; you can be decisive and not be afraid. Wisdom from above brings strength from above.

Sincerity (v. 17h). The Greek word translated "hypocrite" in our New Testament means "one who wears a mask, an actor." When man's wisdom is at work, there may be insincerity and pretense. When God's wisdom is at work, there is openness and honesty, "speaking the truth in love" (Eph. 4:15). Wherever you find God's people pretending and hiding, you can be sure the wisdom of this world is governing their ministry. "Religious politics" is an abomination to God. "Faith is living without scheming."

There is quite a contrast between the operation of God's wisdom and the operation of the wisdom of this world. It would be profitable for church officers and leaders to evaluate their own lives and their ministries in the light of what James has written. While the local church is an organization, it cannot depend on the "Madison Avenue" methods that make secular businesses succeed. God's ways and God's thoughts are far above us! "Now we have received, not the spirit of the world, but the Spirit which is of God; that we might know the things that are freely given to us of God" (1 Cor. 2:12).

Contrast in Outcomes (3:16, 18)

Origin determines outcome. Worldly wisdom will produce worldly results; spiritual wisdom will give spiritual results.

Worldly wisdom produces trouble (v. 16). Envy, strife, confusion, evil works. It does not appear that God was at work in that assembly. In James 4, James would deal with the "wars and fightings" among the believers. Wrong thinking produces wrong living. One reason the world is in such a mess is because men have refused to accept the wisdom of God.

The word translated "confusion" means "disorder that comes from instability." It is related to "unstable" in James 1:8 and "unruly" in James 3:8. Read 2 Corinthians 12:20 and you will get a description of a church that is confused. Jesus used this word to describe the convulsions of the world in the last days (Luke 21:9).

Jealousy, competition, party spirit—all of these contribute to confusion. The Tower of Babel in Genesis 11 is a good illustration of this fact. From man's point of view, the building of the tower was a wise thing, but from God's viewpoint, the project was stupid and sinful. The result? Confusion. Even today, we use the word "babel" to mean "confusion."

Confusion sets the stage for "every evil work" (James 3:16). *Evil* here means "worthless, of no account." It reminds us of the "wood, hay, stubble" of 1 Corinthians 3:12. A ministry operating in the wisdom of this world may appear to be great and successful, but in the day of judgment it may burn up. "Therefore judge nothing before the time" (1 Cor. 4:5). The church at Smyrna thought it was poor, but the Lord said it was rich; while the "rich church" at Laodicea was declared to be poor (Rev. 2:9; 3:14–22).

The most important thing we can do in our local churches is measure our ministries by the Word of God, not by the wisdom of men. The many battles among Christians, the church splits, the absence of purity and peace, all suggest that something is wrong. Perhaps that "something" is the absence of the wisdom of God.

God's wisdom produces blessing (v. 18). James

returned to that word, *fruit.* There is a vast difference between man-made results and God-given fruit. Fruit is the product of life, and fruit has in it *the seeds for more fruit.* Usually it is the *seed* that is sown, but here it is the *fruit* that is sown. As we share the fruit of God with others, they are fed and satisfied, and they in turn bear fruit.

The Christian life is a life of sowing and reaping. For that matter, *every* life is a life of sowing and reaping, and we reap just what we sow. The Christian who obeys God's wisdom sows righteousness, not sin; he sows peace, not war. The life we live enables the Lord to bring righteousness and peace into the lives of others.

What we are is what we live, and what we live is what we sow. What we sow determines what we reap. If we live in God's wisdom, we sow righteousness and peace, and we reap God's blessing. If we live in man's worldly wisdom, we sow sin and war, and we reap "confusion and every evil work."

It is a serious thing to be a troublemaker in God's family. One of the sins that God hates is that of sowing "discord among brethren" (read Prov. 6:16–19). Lot followed the world's wisdom and brought trouble to the camp of Abraham; but Abraham followed God's wisdom and brought peace. Lot's decision led to "good-for-nothing works," and everything he lived for went up in smoke at the destruction of Sodom and Gomorrah. Abraham's decision, in the wisdom of God, led to blessings for his own household and ultimately for the whole world (read Gen. 13).

"Happy is the man that findeth wisdom, and the man that getteth understanding" (Prov. 3:13).

CHAPTER NINE
James 4:1–12
HOW TO END WARS

Have you ever heard of the "War of the Whiskers" or the "War of the Oaken Bucket"? How about the "War of Jenkins' Ear"? These were actual wars fought between nations, and you can read about them in most history books.

War is a fact of life, in spite of treaties, world peace organizations, and the threat of atomic bombs. Not only are there wars between nations, but there are wars of one kind or another on almost every level of life—even "gas wars" among filling station operators!

James discussed this important theme of war in this paragraph, and he explained that there are three wars going on in the world. He also told how these wars could be stopped.

At War with Each Other (4:1a, 11–12)

"What causes fights and quarrels among you?" (NIV). Among Christians! "Behold, how good and how pleasant it is for brethren to dwell together in unity"

(Ps. 133:1). Surely *brethren* should live together in love and harmony, yet often they do not. Lot caused a quarrel with his uncle Abraham (Gen. 13). Absalom created a war for his father David (2 Sam. 13—18). Even the disciples created problems for the Lord when they argued over who was the greatest in the kingdom (Luke 9:46–48).

When you examine some of the early churches, you discover that they had their share of disagreements. The members of the Corinthian church were competing with each other in the public meetings, and even suing each other in court (1 Cor. 6:1–8; 14:23–40). The Galatian believers were "biting and devouring" one another (Gal. 5:15). Paul had to admonish the Ephesians to cultivate spiritual unity (Eph. 4:1–16), and even his beloved church at Philippi had problems: two women could not get along with each other (Phil. 4:1–3).

James mentioned several different kinds of disagreements among the saints.

Class wars (2:1–9). Here is that age-long rivalry between the rich and the poor. The rich man gets the attention, the poor man is ignored. The rich man is honored, the poor man is disgraced. How tragic it is when local churches get their values confused and cater to the rich, while they ignore, or even reject, the poor. If fellowship in a church depends on such external things as clothing and economic status, then the church is out of the will of God.

Employment wars (5:1–6). Again, it is the rich man who has the power to control and hurt the poor man. Laborers do not get their wages, or they do not get their fair wages. In spite of our modern labor movement and federal legislation, there are still many people who cannot get a good job, or whose income is less than adequate for the work they are doing.

Church fights (1:19–20; 3:13–18). Apparently, the believers James wrote to were at war with each other over positions in the church, many of them wanting to be teachers and leaders. When they studied the Word, the result was not edification, but strife and arguments. Each person thought that his ideas were the only right ideas and his ways the only right ways. Selfish ambition ruled their meetings, not spiritual submission.

Personal wars (4:11–12). The saints were speaking evil of one another and judging one another. Here, again, we see the wrong use of the tongue. Christians are to speak "the truth in love" (Eph. 4:15); they are not to speak evil in a spirit of rivalry and criticism. If the truth about a brother is harmful, then we should cover it in love and not repeat it (1 Peter 4:8). If he has sinned, we should go to him personally and try to win him back (Matt. 18:15–19; Gal. 6:1–2).

James was not forbidding us to use discrimination or even to evaluate people. Christians need to have discernment (Phil. 1:9–10), but they must not act like God in passing judgment. We must first examine our own lives, and then try to help others (Matt.

7:1–5). We never know all the facts in a case, and we certainly never know the motives that are at work in men's hearts. To speak evil of a brother and to judge a brother on the basis of partial evidence and (probably) unkind motives is to sin against him and against God. We are not called to be judges; God is the only Judge. He is patient and understanding; His judgments are just and holy; we can leave the matter with Him.

It is unfortunate that the saints are at war with each other, leader against leader, church against church, fellowship against fellowship. The world watches these religious wars and says, "Behold, how they hate one another!" No wonder Jesus prayed, "That they all may be one; as thou, Father, art in me, and I in thee, that they also may be one in us; that the world may believe that thou hast sent me" (John 17:21).

But, why are we at war with one another? We belong to the same family; we trust the same Savior; we are indwelt by the same Holy Spirit—and yet we fight one another. Why? James answered this question by explaining the second war that is going on.

At War with Ourselves (4:1b–3)

"What causes fights and quarrels among you? Don't they come from your desires that battle within you?" (James 4:1 NIV). The war in the heart is helping to cause the wars in the church! "But if ye have bitter envying and strife in your hearts, glory not and lie not against the truth.… For where envying and strife is, there is confusion and every evil work" (James 3:14, 16).

The essence of sin is selfishness. Eve disobeyed God because she wanted to eat of the tree and become wise like God. Abraham lied about his wife because he selfishly wanted to save his own life (Gen. 12:10–20). Achan caused defeat to Israel because he selfishly took some forbidden loot from the ruins of Jericho (Josh. 7). "We have turned every one to his own way" (Isa. 53:6).

Often we veil our religious quarrels under the disguise of "spirituality." We are like Miriam and Aaron, who complained about Moses' wife, but who really were envious of Moses' authority (Num. 12). Or we imitate James and John, who asked for special thrones in the kingdom, when what we really wanted was recognition today (Mark 10:35–45). In both of these instances, the result of selfish desire was chastening and division among God's people. Miriam's sin halted the progress of Israel for a whole week!

Selfish desires are dangerous things. They lead to *wrong actions* ("ye kill, ye fight and war," James 4:2), and they even lead to *wrong praying* ("When you ask, you do not receive, because you ask with wrong motives, that you may spend what you get on your pleasures," James 4:3 NIV). When our praying is wrong, our whole Christian life is wrong. It has well been said that the purpose of prayer is not to get man's will done in heaven, but to get God's will done on earth.

"Thou shalt not covet" is the last of God's Ten Commandments, but its violation can make us break all of the other nine! Covetousness can make a person murder, tell lies, dishonor his parents, commit adultery, and in one way or another violate all of God's moral law. Selfish living and selfish praying always lead to war. If there is war on the inside, there will ultimately be war on the outside.

People who are at war with themselves because of selfish desires are always unhappy people. They never enjoy life. Instead of being thankful for the blessings they do have, they complain about the blessings they do not have. They cannot get along with other people because they are always envying others for what they have and do. They are always looking for that "magic something" that will change their lives, when the real problem is within their own hearts.

Sometimes we use prayer as a cloak to hide our true desires. "But I prayed about it!" can be one of the biggest excuses a Christian can use. Instead of seeking God's will, we tell God what He is supposed to do, and we get angry at Him if He does not obey. This anger at God eventually spills over and we get angry at God's people. More than one church split has been caused by saints who take out their frustrations with God on the members of the church. Many a church or family problem would be solved if people would only look into their own hearts and see the battles raging there.

God made us a unity; mind, emotions, and will should work together. James stated the reason we are at war with ourselves and, consequently, with each other.

At War with God (4:4–10)

The root cause of every war, internal and external, is rebellion against God. At the beginning of creation, you behold perfect harmony, but sin came into the world, and this led to conflict. Sin is lawlessness (1 John 3:4), and lawlessness is rebellion against God.

How does a believer declare war against God? By being friendly with God's enemies. James named three enemies that we must not fraternize with if we want to be at peace with God.

The world (v. 4). By the "world," James means, of course, human society apart from God. The whole system of things in this society of ours is anti-Christ and anti-God. Abraham was the friend of God (James 2:23); Lot was the friend of the world. Lot ended up in a war, and Abraham had to rescue him (Gen. 14).

A Christian gets involved with the world *gradually,* as I pointed out in chapter 4 of this study. First, there is "the friendship of the world" (James 4:4). This results in being "spotted" by the world (James 1:27) so that areas of our lives meet with the approval of the world. Friendship leads to loving the world (1 John 2:15–17), and this makes it easy to conform to the world (Rom. 12:2). The sad result is being condemned with the world (1 Cor. 11:32), our souls saved "yet as by fire" (1 Cor. 3:11–15).

Friendship with the world is compared to adultery. The believer is "married to Christ" (Rom. 7:4) and ought to be faithful to Him. The Jewish Christians who read this letter would understand this picture of "spiritual adultery" because the prophets Ezekiel, Jeremiah, and Hosea used it when rebuking Judah for her sins (see Jer. 3:1–5; Ezek. 23; Hos. 1—2). By adopting the sinful ways of the other nations, and by worshipping their gods, the nation of Judah committed adultery against her God.

The world is the enemy of God, and whoever wills to be a friend of the world cannot be the friend of God. Neither can he be if he lives for the flesh, for this is the second enemy James named.

The flesh (vv. 1, 5). By "the flesh" is meant the old nature that we inherited from Adam, that is prone to sin. The flesh is not the body. The body is not sinful; the body is neutral. The Spirit may use the body to glorify God, or the flesh may use the body to serve sin. When a sinner yields to Christ, he receives a new nature within, but the old nature is neither removed nor reformed. For this reason, there is a battle within: "For the sinful nature desires what is contrary to the Spirit, and the Spirit what is contrary to the sinful nature. They are in conflict with each other so that you do not do what you want" (Gal. 5:17 NIV). This is what James termed "your lusts that are in your members" (James 4:1).

Living for the flesh means grieving the Holy Spirit of God who lives in us. "Or do you think Scripture says without reason that the spirit he caused to live in us longs jealously?" (James 4:5 NIV, margin). Just as the world is the enemy of God the Father, so the flesh is the enemy of God the Holy Spirit. There is a holy, loving jealousy that a husband and wife have over each other, and rightly so. The Spirit within jealously guards our relationship to God, and the Spirit is grieved when we sin against God's love.

Living to please the old nature means to declare war against God. "The carnal mind is enmity against God" (Rom. 8:7). To allow the flesh to control the mind is to lose the blessing of fellowship with God. Abraham had a spiritual mind; he walked with God and enjoyed peace. Lot had a carnal mind; he disobeyed God and experienced war. "For to be carnally minded is death, but to be spiritually minded is life and peace" (Rom. 8:6).

The devil (vv. 6–7). The world is in conflict with the Father; the flesh fights against the Holy Spirit; and the devil opposes the Son of God. Pride is Satan's great sin, and it is one of his chief weapons in his warfare against the saint and the Savior. God wants us to be humble; Satan wants us to be proud. "You will be like God," Satan promised Eve, and she believed him. A new Christian must not be put into places of spiritual leadership "lest being lifted up with pride he fall into the condemnation of the devil" (1 Tim. 3:6).

God wants us to depend on His grace ("But he giveth more grace"), while the devil wants us to depend on ourselves. Satan is the author of all "do-it-yourself" spiritual enterprises. He enjoys inflating the ego and encouraging the believer to do it his own way. In spite of Jesus' warnings about Satan's plans, Peter fell into the snare, pulled out his sword, and tried to accomplish God's will in his own way. What a mess he made of things!

One of the problems in our churches today is that we have too many celebrities and not enough servants. Christian workers are promoted so much that there is very little place left for God's glory. Man has nothing to be proud of in himself. There dwells no good thing in us (Rom. 7:18), but when we trust Christ, He puts that "good thing" in us that makes us His children (2 Tim. 1:6, 14).

Here, then, are three enemies that want to turn us away from God: the world, the flesh, and the devil. These enemies are left over from our old life of sin (Eph. 2:1–3). Christ has delivered us from them, but they still attack us. How can we overcome them? How can we be the friends of God and the enemies of the world, the flesh, and the devil? James gave us three instructions to follow if we would enjoy peace instead of war.

Submit to God (v. 7). This word is a military term that means "get into your proper rank." When a buck private acts like the general, there is going to be trouble! Unconditional surrender is the only way to complete victory. If there is any area of the life kept back from God, there will always be battles. This explains why uncommitted Christians cannot live with themselves or with other people.

"Neither give place to the devil," cautioned Paul in Ephesians 4:27. Satan needs a foothold in our lives if he is going to fight against God, and *we give him that foothold.* The way to resist the devil is to submit to God.

After King David committed adultery with Bathsheba and killed her husband, he hid his sins for almost a year. There was war between him and God, and David had declared it. Read Psalms 32 and 51 to discover the high price David paid to be at war with God. When he finally submitted to God, David experienced peace and joy. This too he recorded in Psalms 32 and 51. Submission is an act of the will; it is saying, "Not my will but thine be done."

Draw near to God (v. 8). How do we do this? By confessing our sins and asking for His cleansing. "Cleanse your hands, ye sinners; and purify your hearts, ye double-minded." The Greek word translated "purify" means "make chaste." This parallels the idea of "spiritual adultery" in James 4:4.

Dr. A. W. Tozer has a profound essay in one of his books, titled, "Nearness Is Likeness." The more we are like God, the nearer we are to God. I may be sitting in my living room with my Siamese cat on my lap, and my wife may be twenty feet away in the kitchen, yet I am nearer to my wife than to the cat because the cat is unlike me. We have very little in common.

God graciously draws near to us when we deal with the sin in our lives that keeps Him at a distance. He will not share us with anyone else; He must have complete control. The double-minded Christian can never

be close to God. Again, Abraham and Lot come to mind. Abraham "drew near" and talked to God about Sodom (Gen. 18:23ff.), while Lot moved into Sodom and lost the blessing of God.

Humble yourselves before God (vv. 9–10). It is possible to submit outwardly and yet not be humbled inwardly. God hates the sin of pride (Prov. 6:16–17), and He will chasten the proud believer until he is humbled. We have a tendency to treat sin too lightly, even to laugh about it ("let your laughter be turned into mourning"). But sin is serious, and one mark of true humility is facing the seriousness of sin and dealing with our disobedience. "A broken and a contrite heart, O God, thou wilt not despise" (Ps. 51:17).

Sometimes we hear a believer pray, "O Lord, humble me!" That is a dangerous thing to pray. Far better that we humble ourselves before God, confess our sins, weep over them, and turn from them. "To this man will I look, even to him that is poor and of a contrite spirit, and trembleth at my word" (Isa. 66:2). "The Lord is nigh unto them that are of a broken heart; and saveth such as be of a contrite spirit" (Ps. 34:18).

If we obey these three instructions, then God will draw near, cleanse us, and forgive us; *and the wars will cease!* We will not be at war with God, so we will not be at war with ourselves. This means we will not be at war with others. "And the work of righteousness shall be peace; and the effect of righteousness quietness and assurance forever" (Isa. 32:17).

Put the government of your life on His shoulders, and let Him become the Prince of Peace in your life (Isa. 9:6).

CHAPTER TEN
James 4:13–17
PLAN AHEAD

James began chapter 4 talking about war with God, and he ended it talking about the will of God. But the two themes are related: when a believer is out of the will of God, he becomes a troublemaker and not a peacemaker.

Lot moved into Sodom and brought trouble to his family. David committed adultery and brought trouble to his family and his kingdom. Jonah disobeyed God and almost sent a shipload of heathen sailors into a watery grave. In each case, there was a wrong attitude toward the will of God.

That God would have a plan for each of our lives is an obvious truth. He is a God of *wisdom* and knows what ought to happen and when it should occur. And, as a God of *love,* He must desire the very best for His children. Too many Christians look on the will of God as bitter medicine they must take, instead of seeing it as the gracious evidence of the love of God.

"I would give my life to the Lord, but I'm afraid," a perplexed teenager told me at a church youth conference.

"What are you afraid of?" I asked.

"I'm afraid God will ask me to do something dangerous!"

"The dangerous life is not *in* the will of God," I replied, "but *out* of the will of God. The safest place in the world is right where God wants you."

I was going through a difficult time in my own ministry some years ago, questioning the will of God. While on vacation, I was reading the book of Psalms, asking God to give me some assurance and encouragement. Psalm 33:11 was the answer to that prayer: "The counsel of the Lord standeth forever; the thoughts of his heart to all generations."

"The *will* of God comes from the *heart* of God," I said to myself. "His will is the expression of His love, so I don't have to be afraid!" It was a turning point in my life to discover the blessing of loving and living the will of God.

In this section of his letter, James pointed out three attitudes toward the will of God. Of course, only one of them is the correct one, the one that every Christian ought to cultivate.

Ignoring God's Will (4:13–14, 16)

Perhaps James was addressing the wealthy merchants in the assembly. They might have discussed their business deals and boasted about their plans. There is no evidence that they sought the will of God or prayed about their decisions. They measured success in life by how many times they got their own way and accomplished what they had planned.

But James presented four arguments that revealed the foolishness of ignoring the will of God.

The complexity of life (v. 13). Think of all that is involved in life: today, tomorrow, buying, selling, getting gain, losing, going here, going there. Life is made up of people and places, activities and goals, days and years, and each of us must make many crucial decisions day after day.

Apart from the will of God, life is a mystery. When you know Jesus Christ as your Savior, and seek to do His will, then life starts to make sense. Even the physical world around you takes on new meaning. There is a simplicity and unity to your life that makes for poise and confidence. You are no longer living in a mysterious, threatening universe. You can sing, "This is my Father's world!"

The uncertainty of life (v. 14a). This statement is based on Proverbs 27:1—"Boast not thyself of tomorrow; for thou knowest not what a day may bring forth." These businessmen were making plans for a whole year when they could not even see ahead into *one day!* See how confident they were: "We will go. We will stay a year. We will buy and sell and make a profit."

Their attitude reminds us of the farmer in the parable of Jesus in Luke 12:16–21. The man had a bumper crop; his barns were too small; so he decided to build bigger barns and have greater security for the future. "And I will say to my soul, 'Soul, thou hast much goods laid up for many years; take thine ease, eat, drink, and be merry'" (Luke 12:19).

What was God's reply to this man's boasting? "Thou fool, this night thy soul shall be required of thee" (Luke 12:20). Life is not uncertain to God, but it is uncertain to us. Only when we are in His will can we be confident of tomorrow, for we know that He is leading us.

The brevity of life (v. 14b). This is one of the repeated themes of Scripture. To us, life seems long and we measure it in years, but in comparison to eternity, life is but a vapor. James borrowed that figure from the book of Job where you find many pictures of the brevity of life.

"My days are swifter than a weaver's shuttle" (Job 7:6). "The cloud is consumed and vanisheth away" (Job 7:9). "Our days upon earth are a shadow" (Job 8:9). "Now my days are swifter than a post" (Job 9:25), referring to the royal couriers that hastened in their missions. "They are passed away as the swift ships: as the eagle that hasteth to the prey" (Job 9:26). "Man that is born of a woman is of few days, and full of trouble. He cometh forth like a flower, and is cut down: he fleeth also as a shadow, and continueth not" (Job 14:1–2).

We count our *years* at each birthday, but God tells us to number our *days* (Ps. 90:12). After all, we live a day at a time, and those days rush by more quickly the older we grow.

Since life is so brief, we cannot afford merely to "spend our lives," and we certainly do not want to "waste our lives." We must *invest our lives* in those things that are eternal.

God reveals His will in His Word, and yet most people ignore the Bible. In the Bible, God gives precepts, principles, and promises that can guide us in every area of life. Knowing and obeying the Word of God is the surest way to success (Josh. 1:8; Ps. 1:3).

The frailty of man (v. 16). "As it is, you boast and brag. All such boasting is evil" (NIV). Man's boasting only covers up man's weakness. "Man proposes but God disposes," wrote Thomas à Kempis. Solomon said it first: "The lot is cast into the lap: but the whole disposing thereof is of the Lord" (Prov. 16:33). Man cannot control future events. He has neither the wisdom to *see* the future nor the power to *control* the future. For him to boast is sin; it is making himself God.

How foolish it is for people to ignore the will of God. It is like going through the dark jungles without a map, or over the stormy seas without a compass. When we visited Mammoth Cave in Kentucky, I was impressed with the maze of tunnels and the dense darkness when the lights were turned off. When we got to the "Pulpit Rock," the man in charge of the tour gave a five-word sermon from it: "Stay close to your guide." Good counsel indeed!

Disobeying God's Will (4:17)

These people *know* the will of God but choose to

disobey it. This attitude expresses even more pride than does the first; for the person says to God, "I know what You want me to do, but I prefer not to do it. I really know more about this than You do!" "For it had been better for them not to have known the way of righteousness, than, after they have known it, to turn from the holy commandment delivered unto them" (2 Peter 2:21).

Why do people who know the will of God deliberately disobey it? I have already suggested one reason: pride. Man likes to boast that he is the "master of his fate, the captain of his soul." Man has accomplished so many marvelous things that he thinks he can do anything.

Another reason is man's ignorance of the nature of God's will. He acts as though the will of God is something he can accept or reject. In reality, the will of God is not an option; it is an obligation. We cannot "take it or leave it." Because He is the Creator and we are the creatures, we must obey Him. Because He is the Savior and Lord, and we are His children and servants, we must obey Him. To treat the will of God lightly is to invite the chastening of God in our lives.

Many people have the mistaken idea that the will of God is a formula for misery. Just the opposite is true! It is *disobeying* the Lord's will that leads to misery. The Bible and human experience are both witnesses to this truth. And even if a disobedient Christian seems to escape difficulty in this life, what will he say when he faces the Lord? "And that servant which knew his lord's will, and prepared not himself, neither did according to his will, shall be beaten with many stripes. But he that knew not, and did commit things worthy of stripes, shall be beaten with few stripes" (Luke 12:47–48).

What happens to Christians who deliberately disobey the known will of God? They are chastened by their loving Father until they submit (Heb. 12:5–11). If a professed believer is not chastened, it is evidence that he has never truly been born again but is a counterfeit. God's chastening is an evidence of His love, not His hatred. Just as we earthly fathers spank our children to help them respect our will and obey, so our heavenly Father chastens His own. Though chastening is hard to take, it has a comforting truth of sonship with it.

But there is also the danger of losing heavenly rewards. In 1 Corinthians 9:24–27, Paul compared the believer to a runner in the Greek races. In order to qualify for a crown, he had to obey the rules of the game. If any contestant was found to have disobeyed the rules, he was disqualified and humiliated. The word *castaway* in 1 Corinthians 9:27 does not refer to the loss of salvation, but the loss of reward. "Disqualified" would be a good translation.

Disobeying God's will today may not seem a serious thing, but it will appear very serious when the Lord returns and examines our works (Col. 3:22–25).

Obeying God's Will (4:15)

"If the Lord will" is not just a statement on a believer's lips: it is the constant attitude of his heart. "My food," said Jesus, "is to do the will of him who sent me and to finish his work" (John 4:34). Often in his letters, Paul referred to the will of God as he shared his plans with his friends (Rom. 1:10; 15:32; 1 Cor. 4:19; 16:7). Paul did not consider the will of God a chain that shackled him; rather, it was a key that opened doors and set him free.

Everything in this universe operates according to laws. If we cooperate with these laws and obey them, then the universe works *with* us. But if we fight these laws and disobey them, the universe will work *against* us. For example, certain laws govern flight. The engineer who obeys those laws in designing and building the plane and the pilot who obeys those laws in flying the plane will both have the joy of seeing the great machine operate perfectly. But if they disobey the basic laws that govern flight, the result will be a crash and the loss of life and money.

God's will for our lives is comparable to the laws He has built within the universe, with this exception: those laws are general, but the will He has planned for our lives is specifically designed for us. No two lives are planned according to the same pattern.

To be sure, there are some things that must be true of all Christians. It is God's will that we yield ourselves to Him (2 Cor. 8:5). It is God's will that we avoid sexual immorality (1 Thess. 4:3). All Christians should rejoice, pray, and thank God (1 Thess. 5:16–18). Every commandment in the Bible addressed to believers is part of the will of God and must be obeyed. But God does not call each of us to the same work in life, or to exercise the same gifts and ministry. The will of God is "tailor-made" for each of us!

It is important that we have the right attitude toward the will of God. Some people think God's will is a cold, impersonal machine. God starts it going and it is up to us to keep it functioning smoothly. If we disobey Him in some way, the machine grinds to a halt, and we are out of God's will for the rest of our lives.

God's will is not a cold, impersonal machine. You do not determine God's will in some mechanical way, like getting a soft drink out of a vending machine. *The will of God is a living relationship between God and the believer.* This relationship is not *destroyed* when the believer disobeys, for the Father still deals with His child, even if He must chasten.

Rather than looking at the will of God as a cold, impersonal machine, I prefer to see it as a warm, growing, living body. If something goes wrong with my body, I don't die: the other parts of the body compensate for it until I get that organ working properly again. There is pain; there is also weakness; but there is not necessarily death.

When you and I get out of God's will, it is not the end of everything. We suffer, to be sure, but when God cannot rule, He overrules. Just as the body compensates for the malfunctioning of one part, so God adjusts things to bring us back into His will. You see this illustrated clearly in the lives of Abraham and Jonah.

The believer's relationship to the will of God is a growing experience. First, we should *know His will* (Acts 22:14). The will of God is not difficult to discover. If we are willing to obey, He is willing to reveal (John 7:17). It has been said that "obedience is the organ of spiritual knowledge." This is true. God does not reveal His will to the curious or the careless, but to those who are ready and willing to obey Him.

But we must not stop with merely knowing *some* of God's will. God wants us to be "filled with the knowledge of his will and all wisdom and spiritual understanding" (Col. 1:9). It is wrong to want to know God's will about some matters and ignore His will in other matters. Everything in our lives is important to God, and He has a plan for each detail.

God wants us to *understand His will* (Eph. 5:17). This is where spiritual wisdom comes in. A child can *know* the will of his father, but he may not *understand* his will. The child knows the "what" but not the "why." As the "friends" of Jesus Christ, we have the privilege of knowing why God does what He does (John 15:15). "He made known his ways unto Moses, his acts unto the children of Israel" (Ps. 103:7). The Israelites knew *what* God was doing, but Moses understood *why* He was doing it.

We must *also prove God's will* (Rom. 12:2). The Greek verb means "to prove by experience." We learn to determine the will of God by working at it. The more we obey, the easier it is to discover what God wants us to do. It is something like learning to swim or play a musical instrument. You eventually "get the feel" of what you are doing, and it becomes second nature to you.

People who keep asking, "How do I determine God's will for my life?" may be announcing to everybody that they have never really tried to do God's will. You start with the thing you know you ought to do, and you do that. Then God opens the way for the next step. You prove by experience what the will of God is. We learn both from successes and failures. "Take my yoke upon you, and learn of me" (Matt. 11:29). The yoke suggests doing things together, putting into practice what God has taught you.

Finally, we must *do God's will from the heart* (Eph. 6:6). Jonah knew the will of God, and (after a spanking) did the will of God, but he did not do it from his heart. Jonah 4 indicates that the angry prophet did not love the Lord, nor did he love the people of Nineveh. He merely did God's will to keep from getting another spanking!

What Paul said about giving can also be applied to living: "not grudgingly, or of necessity, for God loveth a cheerful giver" (2 Cor. 9:7). *Grudgingly* means "reluctantly, painfully." They get absolutely no joy out of doing God's will. *Of necessity* means "under compulsion." These people obey because they have to, not because they want to. Their heart is not in it.

The secret of a happy life is to delight in duty. When duty becomes delight, then burdens become blessings. "Thy statutes have been my songs in the house of my pilgrimage" (Ps. 119:54). When we love God, then His statutes become songs, and we enjoy serving Him. When we serve God grudgingly, or because we have to, we may accomplish His work but we ourselves will miss the blessing. It will be toil, not ministry. But when we do God's will from the heart, we are enriched, no matter how difficult the task might have been.

We must never think that a failure in knowing or doing God's will permanently affects our relationship with the Lord. We can confess our sins and receive His forgiveness (1 John 1:9). We can learn from the mistakes. The important thing is a heart that loves God and wants sincerely to do His will and glorify His name.

What are the benefits of doing the will of God? For one thing, you enjoy a deeper fellowship with Jesus Christ (Mark 3:35). You have the privilege of knowing God's truth (John 7:17) and seeing your prayers answered (1 John 5:14–15). There is an eternal quality to the life and works of the one who does the will of God (1 John 2:15–17). Certainly, there is the expectation of reward at the return of Jesus Christ (Matt. 25:34).

Which of these three attitudes do you have toward the will of God? Do you totally ignore God's will as you make your daily plans and decisions? Or, do you know God's will and yet refuse to obey it? Each attitude is wrong and can only bring sorrow and ruin to the life of the person who holds it.

But the Christian who knows, loves, and obeys the will of God will enjoy God's blessing. His life may not be easier, but it will be holier and happier. His very food will be the will of God (John 4:34); it will be the joy and delight of his heart (Ps. 40:8).

CHAPTER ELEVEN
James 5:1–6
MONEY TALKS

I f money talks," said a popular comedian, "all it ever says to me is goodbye!" But money was not saying goodbye to the men James addressed in this section of his letter. These men were rich, and their riches were sinful. They were using their wealth for selfish purposes and were persecuting the poor in the process.

One of the themes that runs through James 5 is "trouble." We meet poor people deprived of their wages (James 5:4), as well as people who are physically afflicted (James 5:13–16) and spiritually backslidden (James 5:19–20). A second theme that James introduced is "prayer." The poor laborers cry out to God (James 5:4). The sick and afflicted should pray (James 5:13–16). He cited Elijah as an example of one who believed in prayer (James 5:17–18).

When you join these two themes, you arrive at the fifth mark of the mature Christian: *he is prayerful in troubles.* Instead of giving up when troubles come, the mature believer turns to God in prayer and seeks divine help. The immature person trusts in his own experience and skill, or else turns to others for help. While it is true that God often meets our needs through the hands of other people, this aid must be the result of prayer.

James did not say it was a sin to be rich. After all, Abraham was a wealthy man, yet he walked with God and was greatly used of God to bless the whole world. James was concerned about the selfishness of the rich and advised them to "weep and howl." He gave three reasons for his exhortation.

The Way They Got Their Wealth (5:4, 6a)

The Bible does not discourage the acquiring of wealth. In the law of Moses, specific rules are laid down for getting and securing wealth. The Jews in Canaan owned their own property, worked it, and benefited from the produce. In several of His parables, Jesus indicated His respect for personal property and private gain. There is nothing in the Epistles that contradicts the right of private ownership and profit.

What the Bible does condemn is acquiring wealth by illegal means or for illegal purposes. The prophet Amos thundered a message of judgment against the wealthy upper crust who robbed the poor and used their stolen wealth for selfish luxuries. Isaiah and Jeremiah also exposed the selfishness of the rich and warned that judgment was coming. It is in this spirit that James wrote. He gave two illustrations of how the rich acquired their wealth.

Holding back wages (v. 4). Laborers were hired and paid by the day and did not have any legal contracts with their employers. The parable of the laborers in Matthew 20:1–16 gives some idea of the system in that day. In the law, God gave definite instructions concerning the laboring man in order to protect him from the oppressive employer.

"You shall not oppress a hired servant who is poor and needy, whether he is one of your countrymen or one of your aliens who is in your land in your towns. You shall give him his wages on his day before the sun sets, for he is poor and sets his heart on it; so that he may not cry against you to the Lord and it become sin in you" (Deut. 24:14–15 NASB).

"You shall not oppress your neighbor, nor rob him. The wages of a hired man are not to remain with you all night until morning" (Lev. 19:13 NASB).

"Woe to him that buildeth his house by unrighteousness, and his chambers by wrong; that useth his neighbor's service without wages, and giveth him not for his work" (Jer. 22:13).

These rich men had hired the laborers and promised to pay them a specific amount. The men had completed their work but had not been paid. The tense of the verb "kept back" in the original Greek indicates that the laborers *never will get their salaries.*

"Thou shalt not steal" is still the law of God, and it is a law He will enforce. As Christians, it behooves us to be faithful to pay our bills. As a pastor, I find myself embarrassed when unsaved men tell me about Christians who owe them money and apparently have no intention of paying.

I recall meeting a doctor friend while I was visiting in the hospital. "How are things going?" I asked, and he replied, "Oh, I guess things are OK."

"I pray for you," I told him, wanting to be an encouragement

"I appreciate that," he replied. "But while you're at it, pray for all the people who owe me money. It'd help if they would pay up!"

Controlling the courts (v. 6a). It is often the case that those who have wealth also have political power and can get what they want. "What is the Golden Rule?" asked a character in a comic strip. His friend answered, "Whoever has the gold makes the rules!" James asked, "Do not the rich men oppress you and draw you before the judgment seats?" (James 2:6).

When the name *Watergate* is mentioned, nobody thinks of a beautiful hotel. That word reminds us of an ugly episode in American history that led to the revelation of lies and the resignation of the president of the United States. Each side accused the other of obstructing justice and manipulating the laws.

When God established Israel in her land, He gave the people a system of courts (see Deut. 17:8–13). He warned the judges not to be greedy (Ex. 18:21). They were not to be partial to the rich or the poor (Lev. 19:15). No judge was to tolerate perjury (Deut. 19:16–21). Bribery was condemned by the Lord (Isa. 33:15; Mic. 3:11; 7:3). The prophet Amos denounced the judges in his day who took bribes and "fixed" cases (Amos 5:12, 15).

The courts in James' day were apparently easy to control if you had enough money. The poor workers could not afford expensive lawsuits, so they were beaten down every time. The workers had the just cause, but they were not given justice. Instead, they were abused and ruined. ("Killed" should probably be taken in a figurative way, as in James 4:2, though it is possible that the rich men could so oppress the poor that the poor would die.) The poor man did not resist the rich man because he had no weapons with which to fight. All he could do was call on the Lord for justice.

The Bible warns us against the securing of wealth by illegal means. God owns all wealth (Ps. 50:10); He permits us to be stewards of His wealth for His glory. "Wealth obtained by fraud dwindles, but the one who gathers by labor increases it" (Prov. 13:11 NASB). It is "the hand of the diligent that makes rich" (Prov. 10:4). "Do not weary yourself to gain wealth" (Prov. 23:4). We must put God first in our lives, and He will see to it that we always have all that we need (Matt. 6:33).

The Way the Rich Used Their Wealth (5:3–5)

It is bad enough to gain wealth in a sinful way, but

to use that wealth in sinful ways just makes the sin greater.

They stored it up (v. 3). Of course, there is nothing sinful about saving. "For the children ought not to lay up for the parents, but the parents for the children" (2 Cor. 12:14). "But if any provide not for his own, and specially for those of his own house, he hath denied the faith, and is worse than an infidel" (1 Tim. 5:8). "Then you ought to have put my money in the bank, and on my arrival I would have received my money back with interest" (Matt. 25:27 NASB).

But it is wrong to store up wealth when you owe money to your employees. These rich men were hoarding grain, gold, and garments. They thought that they were rich because they had these possessions. Instead of laying up treasures in heaven by using their wealth for God's glory (Matt. 6:19ff.), they were selfishly guarding it for their own security and pleasure. Not more than ten years after James wrote this letter, Jerusalem fell to the Romans, and all this accumulated wealth was taken.

What did Jesus mean by "laying up treasures in heaven"? Did He mean we should "sell everything and give to the poor" as He instructed the rich young ruler? I think not. He spoke that way to the rich ruler because covetousness was the young man's besetting sin, and Jesus wanted to expose it. To lay up treasures in heaven means to use all that we have as stewards of God's wealth. You and I may *possess* many things, but we do not *own* them. God is the Owner of everything, and we are His stewards.

What we possess and use are merely things, apart from the will of God. When we yield to His will and use what He gives us to serve Him, then things become treasures and we are investing in eternity. What we do on earth is recorded in heaven, and God keeps the books and pays the interest.

What a tragedy it is to see people "heap up treasures for the last days" instead of "laying up treasures in heaven." The Bible does not discourage saving, or even investing; but it does condemn hoarding.

They kept others from benefiting from it (v. 4). By fraudulent means, the rich men robbed the poor. The rich men were not using their own wealth, but they would not pay their laborers and permit them to use the wealth. Perhaps they were waiting for salaries to go down.

Since we are stewards of God's wealth, we have certain responsibilities toward our Master. We must be faithful to use what He gives us for the good of others and the glory of God. "Moreover, it is required in stewards, that a man be found faithful" (1 Cor. 4:2). Joseph was a faithful steward in Potiphar's house, and Potiphar prospered. There are ways that we can use God's wealth to help others.

They lived in luxury (v. 5). "You have lived in high style on the earth!" (James 5:5, literal translation). Luxury is waste, and waste is sin.

A magazine advertisement told of the shopping spree of an oil-rich sultan. He purchased nineteen Cadillacs, one for each of his nineteen wives, and paid extra to have the cars lengthened. He also bought two Porsches, six Mercedes, a $40,000 speedboat and a truck for hauling it. Add to the list sixteen refrigerators, $47,000 worth of women's luggage, two Florida grapefruit trees, two reclining chairs, and one slot machine. His total bill was $1.5 million, and he had to pay another $194,500 to have everything delivered. Talk about living in luxury!

All of us are grateful for the good things of life, and we would certainly not want to return to primitive conditions. But we recognize the fact that there is a point of diminishing returns. "Tell me what thou dost need," said the Quaker to his neighbor, "and I will tell thee how to get along without it." Jesus said, "Beware and be on your guard against every form of greed; for not even when one has an abundance does his life consist of his possessions" (Luke 12:15 NASB). These rich men James addressed were feeding themselves on their riches and starving to death. The Greek word pictures cattle being fattened for the slaughter.

There is a great difference between enjoying what God has given us (1 Tim. 6:17) and living extravagantly on what we have withheld from others. Even if what we have has been earned lawfully and in the will of God, we must not waste it on selfish living. There are too many needs to be met.

Luxury has a way of ruining character. It is a form of self-indulgence. If you match character with wealth, you can produce much good, but if you match self-indulgence with wealth, the result is sin. The rich man Jesus described in Luke 16:19–31 would have felt right at home with the rich men James wrote to!

What Their Riches Will Do (5:1–4)

The rich thought they had it made because of their wealth, but God thought otherwise. "Howl for your miseries that shall come upon you" (James 5:1). James described the consequences of misusing riches.

Riches will vanish (vv. 2–3a). Grain will rot ("corrupted" in James 5:2); gold will rust; and garments will become moth-eaten. Nothing material in this world will last forever. The seeds of death and decay are found in all of creation.

It is a great mistake to think there is security in wealth. Paul wrote, "Instruct those who are rich in this present world not to be conceited, or to fix their hope on the uncertainty of riches" (1 Tim. 6:17). Riches are uncertain. The money market fluctuates from hour to hour, and so does the stock market. Actually, gold does not rust the way iron does, but the idea is the same: the gold is losing its value. Add to this the fact that life is brief, and we cannot take wealth with us, and you can see how foolish it is to live for the things of this world. God said to the rich man, "Thou fool, this night thy soul shall be required of thee: then whose shall those things be, which thou hast provided?" (Luke 12:20).

Misused riches erode character (v. 3). "Their

corrosion … will eat your flesh like fire" (James 5:3 NIV). This is a present judgment: the poison of wealth has infected them and they are being eaten alive. Of itself, money is not sinful; it is neutral. But "the love of money is the root of all evil" (1 Tim. 6:10). "Thou shalt not covet" is the last of the Ten Commandments, but it is the most dangerous. Covetousness will make a person break all the other nine commandments.

Abraham was a rich man, but he maintained his faith and character. When Lot became rich, it ruined his character and ultimately ruined his family. It is good to have riches in your hand provided they do not get into your heart. "If riches increase, set not your heart upon them" (Ps. 62:10). "A good name is rather to be chosen than great riches, and loving favor rather than silver and gold" (Prov. 22:1).

Judgment is a certainty (vv. 3, 5). James not only saw a *present* judgment (their wealth decaying, their character eroding), but also a *future* judgment before God. Jesus Christ will be the Judge (James 5:9), and His judgment will be righteous.

Note the witnesses that God will call on that day of judgment. First, the rich men's *wealth* will witness against them (James 5:3). Their rotten grain, rusted gold and silver, and moth-eaten garments will bear witness of the selfishness of their hearts. There is a bit of irony here: the rich men saved their wealth to help them, but their hoarded riches will only testify against them.

The *wages* they held back will also witness against them in court (James 5:4a). Money talks! These stolen salaries cry out to God for justice and judgment. God heard Abel's blood cry out from the ground (Gen. 4:10), and He hears this stolen money cry out too.

The *workers* will also testify against them (James 5:4). There will be no opportunities for the rich to bribe the witnesses or the Judge. God hears the cries of His oppressed people and He will judge righteously.

This judgment is a serious thing. The lost will stand before Christ at the Great White Throne (Rev. 20:11–15). The saved will stand before the Judgment Seat of Christ (Rom. 14:10–12; 2 Cor. 5:9–10). God will not judge our *sins,* because they have already been judged on the cross, but He will judge our *works* and our ministry. If we have been faithful in serving and glorifying Him, we will receive a reward; if we have been unfaithful, we shall lose our reward but not our salvation (1 Cor. 3:1–15).

The loss of a precious opportunity (v. 3). "The last days" indicates that James believed that the coming of the Lord was near (see James 5:8–9). We must "buy up the opportunity" (Eph. 5:16, literal translation) and work while it is day (John 9:4). Think of the good that could have been accomplished with that hoarded wealth. There were poor people in that congregation who could have been helped (James 2:1–6). There were workers who deserved their wages. Sad to say, in a few years the Jewish nation was defeated and scattered, and Jerusalem destroyed.

It is good to have the things that money can buy, provided you also have the things that money cannot buy. What good is a $500,000 house if there is no home? Or a million-dollar diamond ring if there is no love? James did not condemn riches or rich people; he condemned the wrong use of riches, and rich people who use their wealth as a weapon and not as a tool with which to build.

It is possible to be "poor in this world" (James 2:5) and yet rich in the next world. It is also possible to be "rich in this world" (1 Tim. 6:17) and poor in the next world. The return of Jesus Christ will make some people poor and others rich, depending on the spiritual condition of their hearts. "For where your treasure is, there will your heart be also" (Matt. 6:21).

What we keep, we lose. What we give to God, we keep, and He adds interest to it. A famous preacher, known for his long sermons, was asked to give the annual "charity sermon" for the poor. It was suggested that if he preached too long, the congregation might not give as much as they should.

The preacher read his text from Proverbs 19:17— "He that hath pity upon the poor lendeth unto the Lord; and that which he hath given will He pay him again." His sermon indeed was brief: "If you like the terms, then put down your money."

Yes, money talks. What will it say to you at the last judgment?

CHAPTER TWELVE
James 5:7–12
THE POWER OF PATIENCE

James was still addressing the suffering saints when he wrote, "Be patient." This was his counsel at the beginning of his letter (James 1:1–5), and his counsel as his letter came to a close. God is not going to right all the wrongs in this world until Jesus Christ returns, and we believers must patiently endure—and expect.

Three times James reminded us of the coming of the Lord (James 5:7–9). This is the "blessed hope" of the Christian (Titus 2:13). We do not expect to have everything easy and comfortable in this present life. "In the world ye shall have tribulation" (John 16:33). Paul reminded his converts that "we must through much tribulation enter into the kingdom of God" (Acts 14:22). We must patiently endure hardships and heartaches until Jesus returns.

James used two different words for patience. In James 5:7–8, 10 it was the word *long-tempered.* The words *endure* and *patience* in James 5:11 literally mean "to remain under" and speak of endurance under great stress. *Patience* means "to stay put and stand fast when you'd like to run away." Many Greek scholars think that "longsuffering" refers to patience with respect to persons, while "endurance" refers to patience with respect to conditions or situations.

But the question we must answer is How can we as Christians experience this kind of patient endurance as we wait for the Lord to return? To answer that question (and need), James gave three encouraging examples of patient endurance.

The Farmer (5:7–9)

If a man is impatient, then he had better not become a farmer. No crop appears overnight (except perhaps a crop of weeds), and no farmer has control over the weather. Too much rain can cause the crop to rot, and too much sun can burn it up. An early frost can kill the crop. How longsuffering the farmer must be with the weather!

He must also have patience with the seed and the crop, for it takes time for plants to grow. Jewish farmers would plow and sow in what to us are the autumn months. The "early rain" would soften the soil. The "latter rain" would come in the early spring (our February-March) and help to mature the harvest. The farmer had to wait many weeks for his seed to produce fruit.

Why did he willingly wait so long? Because the fruit is "precious" (James 5:7). The harvest is worth waiting for. "to due season we shall reap, if we faint not" (Gal. 6:9). "For the earth produces crops by itself; first the blade, then the head, then the mature grain in the head. But when the crop permits, he immediately puts in the sickle, because the harvest has come" (Mark 4:28–29 NASB).

James pictured the Christian as a "spiritual farmer" looking for a spiritual harvest. "Be ye also patient, stablish your hearts" (James 5:8). Our hearts are the soil, and the "seed is the word of God" (Luke 8:11). There are seasons to the spiritual life just as there are seasons to the soil. Sometimes, our hearts become cold and "wintry," and the Lord has to "plow them up" before He can plant the seed (Jer. 4:3). He sends the sunshine and the rains of His goodness to water and nurture the seeds planted, but He must be patient to wait for the harvest.

Here, then, is a secret of endurance when the going is tough: *God is producing a harvest in our lives.* He wants the "fruit of the Spirit" to grow (Gal. 5:22–23), and the only way He can do it is through trials and troubles. Instead of growing impatient with God and with ourselves, we must yield to the Lord and permit the fruit to grow. We are "spiritual farmers" looking for a harvest.

You can enjoy this kind of a harvest only if your heart is *established* (James 5:8). One of the purposes of the spiritual ministry of the local church is to establish the heart (Rom. 1:11). Paul sent Timothy to Thessalonica to establish the young Christians in their faith (1 Thess. 3:1–3), and Paul also prayed for them that they might be established (1 Thess. 3:10–13). The ministry of the Word of God and prayer are important if the heart is going to be established. A heart that is not established cannot bear fruit.

Keep in mind that the farmer does not stand around doing nothing: he is constantly at work as he looks toward the harvest. James did not tell these suffering believers to put on white robes, climb a hill, and wait for Jesus to return. "Keep working and waiting" was his admonition. "Blessed is that servant, whom his lord when he cometh shall find so doing" (Luke 12:43).

Nor does the farmer get into fights with his neighbors. One of the usual marks of farmers is their willingness to help one another. Nobody on the farm has time or energy for disputes with the neighbors. James must have had this in mind when he added, "Don't grumble against each other, brothers, or you will be judged" (James 5:9 NIV). Impatience with God often leads to impatience with God's people, and this is a sin we must avoid. If we start using the sickles on each other, we will miss the harvest!

The Prophets (5:10)

A Jewish congregation would understand this simple reference that James made to the Old Testament prophets. In His Sermon on the Mount, Jesus also used the prophets as an example of victory over persecution (Matt. 5:10–12). What encouragements do we receive from their example?

For one thing, they were in the will of God, yet they suffered. They were preaching "in the name of the Lord," yet they were persecuted. Satan tells the faithful Christian that his suffering is the result of sin or unfaithfulness, and yet his suffering might well be *because of faithfulness!* "Yea, and all that will live godly in Christ Jesus shall suffer persecution" (2 Tim. 3:12). We must never think that obedience automatically produces ease and pleasure. Our Lord was obedient, and it led to a cross!

The prophets encourage us by reminding us that God cares for us when we go through sufferings for His sake. Elijah announced to wicked King Ahab that there would be a drought in the land for three and one-half years, and Elijah himself had to suffer in that drought. But God cared for him, and God gave him victory over the evil priests of Baal. It has been said, "The will of God will never lead you where the grace of God cannot keep you."

Many of the prophets had to endure great trials and sufferings, not only at the hands of unbelievers, but at the hands of professed believers. Jeremiah was arrested as a traitor and even thrown into an abandoned well to die. God fed Jeremiah and protected him throughout that terrible siege of Jerusalem, even though at times it looked as though the prophet was going to be killed. Both Ezekiel and Daniel had their share of hardships, but the Lord delivered them. And even those who were not delivered, who died for the faith, received that special reward for those who are true to Him.

Why is it that those who "speak in the name of the Lord" often must endure difficult trials? It is so that their lives might back up their messages. The impact of a faithful, godly life carries much power. We need to remind ourselves that our patience in times of suffering is a testimony to others around us.

But have not many faithful Christians suffered and died without any notice or recognition? Yes, but when Jesus returns, these "obscure heroes" will receive their rewards. The prophets were killed and buried, but today their names are honored. When our Lord comes again, He will bring His reward with Him (Rev. 22:12).

This example that James used from the Old Testament prophets ought to encourage us to spend more time in the Bible, getting acquainted with these heroes of faith. "For everything that was written in the past was written to teach us, so that through endurance and the encouragement of the Scriptures we might have hope" (Rom. 15:4 NIV). The better we know the Bible, the more God can encourage us in the difficult experiences of life. The important thing is that, like the farmer, we keep working, and, like the prophets, we keep witnessing, no matter how trying the circumstances may be.

Job (5:11–12)

"As you know, we consider blessed those who have persevered" (James 5:11 NIV). But you cannot persevere unless there is a trial in your life. There can be no victories without battles; there can be no peaks without valleys. If you want the blessing, you must be prepared to carry the burden and fight the battle.

I once heard a young Christian pray, "O Lord, please teach me the deep truths of Thy Word! I want to be lifted up to the heavens to hear and see the wonderful things that are there!" It was a sincere prayer, but the young man did not realize what he was praying. Paul went to the third heaven and learned things too marvelous for words, and as a result, *God had to give Paul a thorn in the flesh to keep him humble* (2 Cor. 12:1–10). God has to balance privileges with responsibilities, blessings with burdens, or else you and I will become spoiled, pampered children.

When do "blessings" come? In the midst of trials we may experience God's blessings, as did the three Hebrew children in the fiery furnace (Dan. 3), but James taught that there is a blessing *after we have endured.* His example was Job.

The book of Job is a long book, and the chapters are filled with speeches that, to the Western mind, seem long and tedious. In the first three chapters you have *Job's distress:* he loses his wealth, his family (except for his wife, and she told him to commit suicide), and his health. In Job 4–31 we read *Job's defense,* as he debates with his three friends and answers their false accusations. Job 38–42 presents *Job's deliverance:* first God humbles Job, and then He honors Job and gives him twice as much as he had before.

In studying the experience of Job, it is important to remember that Job did not know what was going on "behind the scenes" between God and Satan. Job's friends accused him of being a sinner and a hypocrite. "There must be some terrible sin in your life," they argued, "or God would never have permitted this suffering." Job disagreed with them and maintained his innocence (but not perfection) during the entire conversation. The friends were wrong: God had no cause against Job (Job 2:3), and in the end, God rebuked the friends for telling lies about Job (Job 42:7).

It is difficult to find a greater example of suffering than Job. Circumstances were against him, for he lost his wealth and his health. He also lost his beloved children. His wife was against him, for she said, "Curse God and die" (Job 2:9). His friends were against him, for they accused him of being a hypocrite, deserving of the judgment of God. And it seemed like God was against him! When Job cried out for answers to his questions, there was no reply from heaven.

Yet, Job endured. Satan predicted that Job would get impatient with God and abandon his faith, but that did not happen. It is true that Job questioned God's will, but Job did not forsake his faith in the Lord. "Though He slay me, I will hope in Him. Nevertheless, I will argue my ways before Him" (Job 13:15 NASB). Job was so sure of God's perfections that he persisted in arguing with Him, even though he did not understand all that God was doing. That is endurance.

God made a covenant with Israel that He would bless them if they would obey His laws (see Deut. 11). This led to the idea that, if you were wealthy and comfortable, you were blessed of God, but if you were suffering and poor, you were cursed of God. Sad to say, many people have that same erroneous idea today. When Jesus said it was difficult for a rich man to enter heaven, the disciples were shocked. "Who then can be saved?" they asked (Matt. 19:23–26). "The rich are especially blessed of God," they were saying. "If *they* can't make it, nobody can!"

The book of Job refutes that idea, for Job was a righteous man, *and yet he suffered.* God found no evil in him, and even Satan could not find any. Job's friends could not prove their accusations. Job teaches us that God has higher purposes in suffering than the punishing of sin. Job's experience paved the way for Jesus, the perfect Son of God who suffered, not for His own sins, but for the sins of the world.

In Job's case, what was "the end [purpose] of the Lord"? *To reveal Himself as full of pity and tender mercy.* Certainly, there were other results from Job's experience, for God never wastes the sufferings of His saints. Job met God in a new and deeper way (Job 42:1–6), and after that, Job received greater blessings from the Lord.

"But if God is so merciful," someone may argue,

"why didn't He protect Job from all that suffering to begin with?" To be sure, there are mysteries to God's working that our finite minds cannot fathom, but this we know: God was glorified and Job was purified through this difficult experience. If there is nothing to endure, you cannot learn endurance.

What did Job's story mean to the believers James wrote to, and what does it mean to us today? It means that some of the trials of life are caused directly by satanic opposition. God permits Satan to try His children, but He always limits the extent of the enemy's power (Job 1:12; 2:6). When you find yourself in the fire, remember that God keeps His gracious hand on the thermostat! "But he knoweth the way that I take: when he hath tried me, I shall come forth as gold" (Job 23:10).

Satan wants us to get impatient with God, for an impatient Christian is a powerful weapon in the devil's hands. You will recall from our study of James 1 that Moses' impatience robbed him of a trip to the Holy Land; Abraham's impatience led to the birth of Ishmael, the enemy of the Jews; and Peter's impatience almost made him a murderer. When Satan attacks us, it is easy for us to get impatient and run ahead of God and lose God's blessing as a result.

What is the answer? "My grace is sufficient for thee" (2 Cor. 12:7–9)! Paul's thorn in the flesh was a "messenger of Satan." Paul could have fought it, given up under it, or tried to deny that the thorn existed; but he did not. Instead, he trusted God for the grace he needed, and he turned Satan's weapon into a tool for the building up of his own spiritual life.

When you find yourself in the furnace, go to the throne of grace and receive from the Lord all the grace you need to endure (Heb. 4:14–16). Remind yourself that the Lord has a gracious purpose in all of this suffering, and that He will work out His purposes in His time and for His glory. You are not a robot caught in the jaws of fate. You are a loving child of God, privileged to be a part of a wonderful plan. There is a difference!

The exhortation in James 5:12 seems out of place, for what does "speaking oaths" have to do with the problem of suffering? If you have ever suffered, you know the answer: it is easy to say things you do not mean, and even make bargains with God, when you are going through difficulties. Go back to Job for an example. The patriarch said, "Naked came I out of my mother's womb, and naked shall I return thither: the Lord gave, and the Lord hath taken away; blessed be the name of the Lord. In all this Job sinned not, nor charged God foolishly" (Job 1:21–22). Job did curse the day he was born (Job 3:1ff.), but he never cursed God or spoke with a foolish oath. Neither did he try to bargain with God.

Surely James was reminding us of our Lord's teaching in the Sermon on the Mount (Matt. 5:34–37). The Jews were great ones for using various oaths to back up their statements. They were careful, however, not to use the name of God in their oaths, lest they blaspheme God. So, they would swear by heaven, or earth, or Jerusalem, or even by their own heads! But Jesus taught that it is impossible to avoid God in such oaths. Heaven is His throne, earth is His footstool, and Jerusalem is the "city of the great King." As for swearing by your head, what good is it? "Thou canst not make one hair black or white" (Matt. 5:36)—or even keep one hair on your head.

It is a basic principle that true Christian character requires few words. The person who must use many words (including oaths) to convince us has something wrong with his character and must bolster this weakness by using words. If you are a true Christian, with integrity, then all you have to say is yes or no and people will believe you. Jesus warned us that anything more than this is from the evil one.

One of the purposes of suffering is the building of character. Certainly Job was a better man for having gone through the furnace. (James explained this process to us, James 1:2–12.) If words are a test of character, then oaths would indicate that there is yet work to be done. When Peter poured out those oaths in the courtyard (Matt. 26:71), he was giving evidence that his character was still in need of a transformation.

As you review this section, you can see the practicality of it. James wanted to encourage us to be patient in times of suffering. Like the farmer, we are waiting for a spiritual harvest, for fruit that will glorify God. Like the prophets, we look for opportunities for witness, to share the truth of God. And, like Job, we wait for the Lord to fulfill His loving purpose, knowing that He will never cause His children to suffer needlessly. And, like Job, we shall have a clearer vision of the Lord and come to know Him better for having been in the furnace of affliction.

"Be patient, for the coming of the Lord draweth nigh!"

CHAPTER THIRTEEN
James 5:13–20
LET US PRAY

The gift of speech is a marvelous blessing, if it is used to the glory of God. As we have seen, James had a great deal to say about the tongue, and this chapter is no exception. He mentioned some of the lowest uses of the tongue: complaining (James 5:9) and swearing (James 5:12). But he also named some of the highest uses of the tongue: proclaiming God's Word (James 5:10) and praying and praising God (James 5:13).

Prayer is certainly a high and holy privilege. To think that, as God's children, we can come freely and boldly to His throne and share with Him our needs! Seven times in this section James mentioned prayer. The mature Christian is prayerful in the troubles of life. Instead of complaining about his situation, he talks to God about it, and God hears and answers his prayers. "Taking it to the Lord in prayer" is certainly a mark of spiritual maturity.

In this section, James encouraged us to pray by describing four situations in which God answers prayer.

Prayer for the Suffering (5:13)
The word *afflicted* means "suffering in difficult circumstances." The phrase "in trouble" is a good translation. Paul used this word to describe the circumstances he was in as he suffered for the gospel's sake (2 Tim. 2:9). As God's people go through life, they often must endure difficulties that are not the results of sin or the chastening of God.

What should we do when we find ourselves in such trying circumstances? We must not grumble and criticize the saints who are having an easier time of it (James 5:9), nor should we blame the Lord. We should pray, asking God for the wisdom we need to understand the situation and use it to His glory (James 1:5).

Prayer can remove affliction, if that is God's will. But prayer can also give us the grace we need to endure troubles and use them to accomplish God's perfect will. *God can transform troubles into triumphs.* "He giveth more grace" (James 4:6). Paul prayed that God might change his circumstances, but instead, God gave Paul the grace he needed to turn his weakness into strength (2 Cor. 12:7–10). Our Lord prayed in Gethsemane that the cup might be removed, and it was not, yet the Father gave Him the strength He needed to go to the cross and die for our sins.

James indicated that everybody does not go through troubles at the same time: "Is any merry? Let him sing psalms" (James 5:13). God balances our lives and gives us hours of suffering and days of singing. The mature Christian knows how to sing *while he is suffering.* (Anybody can sing after the trouble has passed.) God is able to give "songs in the night" (Job 35:10). He did this for Paul and Silas when they were suffering in that Philippian jail. "And at midnight Paul and Silas prayed, and sang praises unto God" (Acts 16:25).

Praying and singing were important elements in worship in the early church, and they should be important to us. Our singing ought to be an expression of our inner spiritual life. The believer's praise should be intelligent (1 Cor. 14:15) and not just the mouthing of words or ideas that mean nothing to him. It should come from the heart (Eph. 5:19) and be motivated by the Holy Spirit (Eph. 5:18). Christian singing must be based on the Word of God (Col. 3:16) and not simply on the clever ideas of men. If a song is not biblical, it is not acceptable to God.

Prayer for the Sick (5:14–16)
I do not think that James gave us a blanket formula for healing the sick. In the churches I have pastored, the elders and I have prayed for the sick, and sometimes God has given healing. But other times He has not seen fit to heal the person. I recall two cases within one week of each other: the one lady was restored in an almost miraculous way, but the other one had to enter the hospital for surgery, and eventually the Lord called her home.

What are the special characteristics of this case that James was describing?

The person is sick because of sin (vv. 15b–16). The Greek text says, "If he has been constantly sinning." This parallels 1 Corinthians 11:30, "For this cause many are weak and sickly among you, and many sleep" (have died). James has described a church member who is sick because he is being disciplined by God. This explains why the elders of the assembly are called: the man cannot go to church to confess his sins, so he asks the spiritual leaders to come to him. The leaders would be in charge of the discipline of the congregation.

The person confesses his sins (v. 16). In the early church, the believers practiced church discipline. First Corinthians 5 is a good example. Paul told the believers at Corinth to dismiss the sinning member from the assembly until he repented of his sins and made things right. The little word "therefore" belongs in James 5:16—"Confess your sins therefore to one another, and pray for one another, that you may be healed" (literal translation). The word *faults* in the Authorized Version gives the impression that the man's deeds were not too evil; they were only faults. But it is the word *hamartia* that James used, and this word means "sin." It is the same word used in James 1:15, where the subject is definitely sin.

The person is healed by "the prayer of faith" (v. 15). It is not the anointing that heals, but the praying. The Greek word translated "anointing" is a medicinal term; it could be translated "massaging." This may be an indication that James suggests using available means for healing along with asking the Lord for His divine touch. God can heal with or without means; in each case, it is God who does the healing.

But what is "the prayer of faith" that heals the sick? The answer is in 1 John 5:14–15—"And this is the confidence that we have in him, that, if we ask anything according to his will, he heareth us: and if we know that he hear us, whatsoever we ask, we know that we have the petitions that we desired of him." The "prayer of faith" is a prayer offered *when you know the will of God.* The elders would seek the mind of God in the matter, and then pray according to His will.

As I visit the sick among my congregation, I do not always know how to pray for them. (Paul had the same problem; read Rom. 8:26.) Is it God's will to heal? Is God planning to call His child home? I do not know; therefore, I must pray, "If it is Your will, heal Your child." Those who claim that God heals every case, and that it is not His will for His children to be sick, are denying both Scripture and experience. But where we have the inner conviction from the Word and the Spirit that it is God's will to heal, then we can pray "the prayer of faith" and expect God to work.

Keep in mind that it is not one individual who is praying: it is the body of elders—spiritual men of God—who seek God's will and pray. James did not instruct the believer to send for a faith healer. The matter is in the hands of the leaders of the local church.

There are some practical lessons from this section that we must not overlook. For one thing, disobedience to God can lead to sickness. This was David's experience when he tried to hide his sins (Ps. 32). Second, sin affects the whole church. We can never sin alone, for sin has a way of growing and infecting others. This man had to confess his sins to the church because he had sinned against the church. Third, there is healing (physical and spiritual) when sin is dealt with. "He that covereth his sins shall not prosper, but whoso confesseth and forsaketh them shall find mercy" (Prov. 28:13). James wrote, "Make it a habit to confess your sins to each other" (literal translation). Do not hide sin or delay confession.

The "confessing" that James wrote about is done among the saints. He was not suggesting confessing our sins to a preacher or priest. We confess our sins first of all to the Lord (1 John 1:9), but we must also confess them to those who have been affected by them. *We must never confess sin beyond the circle of that sin's influence.* Private sin requires private confession; public sin requires public confession. It is wrong for Christians to "hang dirty wash in public," for such "confessing" might do more harm than the original sin.

Prayer for the Nation (5:17–18)

James cited Elijah as an example of a "righteous man" whose prayers released power. "The prayer of a righteous man is powerful and effective" (James 5:16 NIV).

The background of this incident is found in 1 Kings 17—18. Wicked King Ahab and Jezebel, his queen, had led Israel away from the Lord and into the worship of Baal. God punished the nation by holding back the rain that they needed (see Deut. 28:12, 23). For three and one-half years, the heavens were as brass and the earth unable to produce the crops so necessary for life.

Then Elijah challenged the priests of Baal on Mount Carmel. All day long the priests cried out to their god, but no answer came. At the time of the evening sacrifice, Elijah repaired the altar and prepared the sacrifice. He prayed but once, and fire came from heaven to consume the sacrifice. He had proven that Jehovah was the true God.

But the nation still needed rain. Elijah went to the top of Carmel and fell down before the Lord in prayer. He prayed and sent his servant seven times to see if there was evidence of rain, and the seventh time his servant saw a little cloud. Before long, there was a great rain, and the nation was saved.

Do we need "showers of blessing" today? We certainly do!

"But Elijah was a special prophet of God," we might argue. "We can expect God to answer his prayers in a wonderful way."

"Elijah was a man just like us," stated James (5:17 NIV). He was not perfect; in fact, right after his victory on Mount Carmel, Elijah became afraid and discouraged and ran away. But he was a "righteous man," that is, obedient to the Lord and trusting Him. God's promises of answered prayer are for all His children, not just for ones we may call the spiritual elite.

Elijah prayed in faith, for God told him He would send the rain (1 Kings 18:1). "Prayer," said Robert Law, "is not getting man's will done in heaven. It's getting God's will done on earth." You cannot separate the Word of God and prayer, for in His Word He gives us the promises that we claim when we pray.

Elijah was not only believing in his praying, but he was persistent. "He prayed … and he prayed again" (James 5:17–18). On Mount Carmel, Elijah continued to pray for rain until his servant reported "a cloud the size of a man's hand." Too many times we fail to get what God promises because we stop praying. It is true that we are not heard "for our much praying" (Matt. 6:7), but there is a difference between vain repetitions and true believing persistence in prayer. Our Lord prayed three times in the garden, and Paul prayed three times that his thorn in the flesh might be taken from him.

Elijah was determined and concerned in his praying. "He prayed earnestly" (James 5:17 NIV). The literal Greek reads, "and he prayed in prayer." Many people do not pray in their prayers. They just lazily say religious words, and their hearts are not in their prayers.

A church member was "praying around the world" in a prayer meeting, and one of the men present was growing tired of the speech. Finally the man cried out, "Ask Him something!" That is what prayer is all about: "Ask Him something!"

Prayer power is the greatest power in the world today. "Tremendous power is made available through a good man's earnest prayer" (James 5:16 PH). History shows how mankind has progressed from manpower to horsepower, and then to dynamite and TNT, and now to nuclear power.

But greater than nuclear power is prayer power. Elijah prayed for his nation, and God answered prayer. We need to pray for our nation today, that God will bring conviction and revival, and that "showers of blessing" will come to the land. One of the first responsibilities of the local church is to pray for government leaders (1 Tim. 2:1–3).

Prayer for the Straying (5:19–20)

While James did not specifically name prayer in these verses, the implication is there. If we pray for the afflicted and the sick, surely we must pray for the brother who wanders from the truth.

These verses deal with our ministry to a fellow believer who strays from the truth and gets into sin. The verb *err* means "to wander," and suggests a gradual moving away from the will of God. The Old Testament term for this is "backsliding." Sad to say, we see this tragedy occurring in our churches regularly. Sometimes a brother is "overtaken in a fault" (Gal. 6:1), but usually the sin is the result of slow, gradual spiritual decline.

Such a condition is, of course, very dangerous. It is dangerous to the offender because he may be disciplined by the Lord (Heb. 12). He also faces the danger of committing "sin unto death" (1 John 5:16–17). God disciplined the sinning members of the Corinthian church, even to the point of taking some of them to heaven (1 Cor. 11:30).

But this backsliding is also dangerous to the church. A wandering offender can influence others and lead them astray. "One sinner destroys much good" (Eccl. 9:18 NASB). This is why the spiritual members of the church must step in and help the man who has wandered away.

The *origin of this problem* is found in the statement "wander from the truth" (James 5:19). The *truth* means, of course, the Word of God. "Thy word is truth" (John 17:17). Unless the believer stays close to the truth, he will start to drift away. "For this reason we must pay much closer attention to what we have heard, lest we drift away from it" (Heb. 2:1 NASB). Jesus warned Peter that Satan was at hand to tempt him, and Peter refused to believe the Word. He even argued with the Lord! When he should have been praying, Peter was sleeping. No wonder he denied three times.

The *outcome* of this wandering is "sin" and possible "death" (James 5:20). The sinner here is a believer, not an unbeliever; and sin in the life of a Christian is worse than sin in the life of an unbeliever. We expect unsaved people to sin, but God expects His children to obey His Word.

What are we to do when we see a fellow believer wandering from the truth? We should pray for him, to be sure, but we must also seek to help him. He needs to be "converted"—turned back into the right path again. Do believers need to be converted? Yes, they do! Jesus said to Peter, "When thou art converted, strengthen thy brethren" (Luke 22:32).

It is important that we seek to win the lost, but it is also important to win the saved. If a brother has sinned against us, we should talk to him privately and seek to settle the matter. If he listens, then we have gained our brother (Matt. 18:15). That word *gained* means "won." It is the same word translated "get gain" in James 4:13. It is important to win the saved as well as the lost.

If we are going to help an erring brother, we must have an attitude of love, for "love shall cover the multitude of sins" (1 Peter 4:8). Both James and Peter learned this principle from Proverbs 10:12—"Hate stirreth up strife: but love covereth all sins."

This does not mean that love "sweeps the dirt under the carpet." Where there is love, there must also be truth ("speaking the truth in love" said Paul in Eph. 4:15), and where there is truth, there is honest confession of sin and cleansing from God. Love not only helps the offender to face his sins and deal with them, but love also assures the offender that those sins, once forgiven, are remembered no more.

While the basic interpretation of these verses is as I have explained, the application can be made to the lost sinner. After all, if a straying brother needs to be restored, how much more does a lost sinner need to be brought to the Savior. If the wandering believer loses his life, he at least goes to heaven, but the lost sinner is condemned to an eternal hell.

"Seeking the lost" is a common Bible picture of soul-winning. In Luke 15, Jesus pictured the lost sheep, the lost coin, and the lost son, all of whom needed to be found and brought back to where they belonged. Our Lord also compared winning souls to catching fish (Mark 1:17). Peter caught one fish individually with his hook (Matt. 17:24–27), but he also worked with his helpers and used the nets to catch many fish at one time. There is a place for both personal and collective evangelism.

Proverbs 11:30 compares evangelism to hunting: "He that catcheth souls is wise" (literal translation). Sin is out to catch and kill (James 1:13–15), but we ought to be out to catch and make alive.

The soul-winner is also an ambassador of peace (2 Cor. 5:20). God has not declared war on this world; He has declared peace! One day He will declare war, and judgment will fall.

Both Zechariah 3:2 and Jude 23 picture the soul-winner as a fireman, pulling brands out of the burning. John Wesley applied Zechariah 3:2 to himself, for when he was but a child, he was pulled from a burning house when it looked as though it was too late. Sometimes we must take risks of love to snatch people from the fires of judgment.

Jesus compared evangelism to sowing and reaping (John 4:34–38) and Paul used the same illustration (1 Cor. 3:6–9). There are seasons of sowing and seasons of reaping; and many people are needed for the work. We are "laborers together with God" (1 Cor. 3:9). Both the sower and the reaper will receive their rewards, for there is no competition in the Lord's fields.

This brings us to the end of our study of James. His emphasis has been spiritual maturity. This would be a good time for us to examine our own hearts to see how mature we really are. Here are a few questions to assist you:

1. Am I becoming more and more patient in the testings of life?

2. Do I play with temptation or resist it from the start?

3. Do I find joy in obeying the Word of God, or do I merely study it and learn it?

4. Are there any prejudices that shackle me?

5. Am I able to control my tongue?

6. Am I a peacemaker rather than a troublemaker? Do people come to me for spiritual wisdom?

7. Am I a friend of God or a friend of the world?

8. Do I make plans without considering the will of God?

9. Am I selfish when it comes to money? Am I unfaithful in the paying of my bills?

10. Do I naturally depend on prayer when I find myself in some kind of trouble?

11. Am I the kind of person others seek for prayer support?

12. What is my attitude toward the wandering brother? Do I criticize and gossip, or do I seek to restore him in love?

Don't just grow old—grow up!

1 PETER

OUTLINE

Key theme: God's grace and the living hope
Key verses: 1 Peter 1:3; 5:12

I. GOD'S GRACE AND SALVATION (1:1—2:10)
    A. Live in hope—1:1–12
    B. Live in holiness—1:13–21
    C. Live in harmony—1:22—2:10

II. GOD'S GRACE AND SUBMISSION (2:11—3:12)
    A. Submit to authorities—2:11–17
    B. Submit to masters—2:18–25
    C. Submit in the home—3:1–7
    D. Submit in the church—3:8–12

III. GOD'S GRACE AND SUFFERING (3:13—5:11)
    A. Make Jesus Christ Lord—3:13–22
    B. Have Christ's attitude—4:1–11
    C. Glorify Christ's name—4:12–19
    D. Look for Christ's return—5:1–6
    E. Depend on Christ's grace—5:7–14

CONTENTS

CHAPTER ONE
1 Peter 1:1; 5:12–14
WHERE THERE'S CHRIST, THERE'S HOPE

While there's life, there's hope!" That ancient Roman saying is still quoted today and, like most adages, it has an element of truth but no guarantee of certainty. It is not the fact of life that determines hope, but the faith of life. A Christian believer has a "living hope" (1 Peter 1:3 NASB) because his faith and hope are in God (1 Peter 1:21). This "living hope" is the major theme of Peter's first letter. He is saying to all believers, "Be hopeful!"

Before we study the details of this fascinating letter, let's get acquainted with the man who wrote it, the people to whom he sent it, and the particular situation that prompted him to write.

The Writer (1:1)

He identified himself as "Peter, an apostle of Jesus Christ" (1 Peter 1:1). Some liberals have questioned whether a common fisherman could have penned this letter, especially since Peter and John were both called "unlearned and ignorant men" (Acts 4:13). However, this phrase only means "laymen without formal schooling"; that is, they were not professional religious leaders. We must never underestimate the training Peter had for three years with the Lord Jesus, nor should we minimize the work of the Holy Spirit in his life. Peter is a perfect illustration of the truth expressed in 1 Corinthians 1:26–31.

His given name was Simon, but Jesus changed it to Peter, which means "a stone" (John 1:35–42). The Aramaic equivalent of "Peter" is "Cephas," so Peter was a man with three names. Nearly fifty times in the New Testament, he is called "Simon," and often he is called "Simon Peter." Perhaps the two names suggest a Christian's two natures: an old nature (Simon) that is prone to fail, and a new nature (Peter) that can give victory. As Simon, he was only another human piece of clay, but Jesus Christ made a rock out of him!

Peter and Paul were the two leading apostles in the early church. Paul was assigned especially to minister to the Gentiles, and Peter to the Jews (Gal. 2:1–10). The Lord had commanded Peter to strengthen his brethren (Luke 22:32) and to tend the flock (John 21:15–17; also see 1 Peter 5:1–4), and the writing of this letter was a part of that ministry. Peter told his readers that this was a letter of encouragement and personal witness (1 Peter 5:12). Some writings are manufactured out of books, the way freshmen students write term papers, but this letter grew out of a life lived to the glory of God. A number of events in Peter's life are woven into the fabric of this epistle.

This letter is also associated with Silas (Silvanus, 1 Peter 5:12). He was one of the "chief men" in the early church (Acts 15:22) and a prophet (Acts 15:32). This means that he communicated God's messages to the congregations as he was directed by the Holy Spirit (see 1 Cor. 14). The apostles and prophets worked together to lay the foundation of the church (Eph. 2:20), and, once that foundation was laid, they passed off the scene. There are no apostles and prophets *in the New Testament sense* in the church today.

It is interesting that Silas was associated with Peter's ministry, because originally he went with Paul as a replacement for Barnabas (Acts 15:36–41). Peter also mentioned John Mark (1 Peter 5:13) whose failure on the mission field helped to cause the rupture between Paul and Barnabas. Peter had led Mark to faith in Christ ("Mark, my son") and certainly would maintain a concern for him. No doubt one of the early assemblies met in John Mark's home in Jerusalem (Acts 12:12). In the end, Paul forgave and accepted Mark as a valued helper in the work (2 Tim. 4:11).

Peter indicated that he wrote this letter "at Babylon" (1 Peter 5:13) where there was an assembly of believers. There is no evidence either from church history or tradition that Peter ministered in ancient Babylon which, at that time, did have a large community of Jews. There was another town called "Babylon" in Egypt, but we have no proof that Peter ever visited it. "Babylon" is probably another name for the city of Rome, and we do have reason to believe that Peter ministered in Rome and was probably martyred there. Rome is called "Babylon" in Revelation 17:5 and 18:10. It was not unusual for persecuted believers during those days to write or speak in "code."

In saying this, however, we must not assign more to Peter than is due him. He did *not* found the church in Rome nor serve as its first bishop. It was Paul's policy not to minister where any other apostle had gone (Rom. 15:20); so Paul would not have ministered in Rome had Peter arrived there first. Peter probably arrived in Rome after Paul was released from his first imprisonment, about the year AD 62. First Peter was written about the year 63. Paul was martyred about 64, and perhaps that same year, or shortly after, Peter laid down his life for Christ.

The Recipients (1:1)

Peter called them "strangers" (1 Peter 1:1), which means "resident aliens, sojourners." They are called "strangers and pilgrims" in 1 Peter 2:11. These people were citizens of heaven through faith in Christ (Phil. 3:20), and therefore were not permanent residents on earth. Like Abraham, they had their eyes of faith centered on the future city of God (Heb. 11:8–16). They were in the world, but not of the world (John 17:16).

Because Christians are "strangers" in the world, they are considered to be "strange" in the eyes of the world (1 Peter 4:4). Christians have standards and values different from those of the world, and this gives opportunity both for witness and for warfare. We will discover in this epistle that some of the readers were experiencing suffering because of their different lifestyle.

These believers were a "scattered" people as well as a "strange" people. The word translated "scattered" *(diaspora)* was a technical term for the Jews who lived outside of Palestine. It is used this way in John 7:35 and James 1:1. However, Peter's use of this word does not imply that he was writing only to Jewish Christians, because some statements in his letter suggest that some of his readers were converted out of Gentile paganism (1 Peter 1:14, 18; 2:9–10; 4:1–4). There was undoubtedly a mixture of both Jews and Gentiles in the churches that received this letter. We will notice a number of Old Testament references and allusions in these chapters.

These Christians were scattered in five different parts of the Roman Empire, all of them in northern Asia Minor (modern Turkey). The Holy Spirit did not permit Paul to minister in Bithynia (Acts 16:7), so he did not begin this work. There were Jews at Pentecost from Pontus and Cappadocia (Acts 2:9), and perhaps they carried the gospel to their neighboring province. Possibly Jewish believers who had been under Peter's ministry in other places had migrated to towns in these provinces. People were "on the move" in those days, and dedicated believers shared the Word wherever they went (Acts 8:4).

The important thing for us to know about these "scattered strangers" is that they were going through a time of suffering and persecution. At least fifteen times in this letter Peter referred to suffering, and he used eight different Greek words to do so. Some of these Christians were suffering because they were living godly lives and doing what was good and right (1 Peter 2:19–23; 3:14–18; 4:1–4, 15–19). Others were suffering reproach for the name of Christ (1 Peter 4:14) and being railed at by unsaved people (1 Peter 3:9–10). Peter wrote to encourage them to be good witnesses to their persecutors, and to remember that their suffering would lead to glory (1 Peter 1:6–7; 4:13–14; 5:10).

But Peter had another purpose in mind. He knew that a "fiery trial" was about to begin—official persecution from the Roman Empire (1 Peter 4:12). When the church began in Jerusalem, it was looked on as a "sect" of the traditional Jewish faith. The first Christians were Jews, and they met in the temple precincts. The Roman government took no official action against the Christians since the Jewish religion was accepted and approved. But when it became clear that Christianity was not a "sect" of Judaism, Rome had to take official steps.

Several events occurred that helped to precipitate this "fiery trial." To begin with, Paul had defended the Christian faith before the official court in Rome (Phil. 1:12–24). He had been released but then was arrested again. This second defense failed, and he was martyred (2 Tim. 4:16–18). Second, the deranged emperor, Nero, blamed the fire of Rome (July AD 64) on the Christians, using them as a scapegoat. Peter was probably in Rome about that time and was slain by Nero, who had also killed Paul. Nero's persecution of Christians was local at first, but it probably spread. At any rate, Peter wanted to prepare the churches.

We must not get the idea that all Christians in every part of the empire were going through the same trials to the same degree at the same time. It varied from place to place, though suffering and opposition were pretty general (1 Peter 5:9). Nero introduced official persecution of the church, and other emperors followed his example in later years. Peter's letter must have been a tremendous help to Christians who suffered during the reigns of Trajan (98–117), Hadrian (117–138), and Diocletian (284–305). Christians in the world today may yet learn the value of Peter's letter when their own "fiery trials" of persecution begin. While I personally believe that the church will not go through *the* tribulation, I do believe that these latter days will bring much suffering and persecution to the people of God.

It is possible that Silas was the bearer of this letter to the believers in the provinces, and also the secretary who wrote the epistle.

The Message (5:12)

First Peter is a letter of encouragement (1 Peter 5:12). We have noted that the theme of *suffering* runs throughout the letter, but so also does the theme *of glory* (see 1 Peter 1:7–8, 11, 21; 2:12; 4:11–16; 5:1, 4, 10–11). One of the encouragements that Peter gives suffering saints is the assurance that their suffering will one day be transformed into glory (1 Peter 1:6–7; 4:13–14; 5:10). This is possible only because the Savior suffered for us and then entered into His glory (1 Peter 1:11; 5:1). The sufferings of Christ are mentioned often in this letter (1 Peter 1:11; 3:18; 4:1, 13; 5:1).

Peter is preeminently the apostle of *hope*, as Paul is the apostle *of faith* and John of *love*. As believers, we have a "living hope" because we trust a living Christ (1 Peter 1:3). This hope enables us to keep our minds under control and "hope to the end" (1 Peter 1:13) when Jesus shall return. We must not be ashamed of our hope but be ready to explain and defend it (1 Peter 3:15). Like Sarah, Christian wives can hope in God (1 Peter 3:5, where "trusted" should be translated "hoped"). Since suffering brings glory, and because Jesus is coming again, we can indeed be hopeful!

But suffering does not *automatically* bring glory to God and blessing to God's people. Some believers have fainted and fallen in times of trial and have brought shame to the name of Christ. It is only when we depend on the grace of God that we can glorify God in times of suffering. Peter also emphasized God's grace in this letter. "I have written to you briefly, encouraging you and testifying that this is the true grace of God. Stand fast in it" (1 Peter 5:12 NIV).

The word *grace* is used in every chapter of 1 Peter: 1:2, 10, 13; 2:19 ("thankworthy"), 20 ("acceptable"); 3:7; 4:10; 5:5, 10, 12. Grace is God's generous favor to undeserving sinners and needy saints. When we depend on God's grace, we can endure suffering and turn trials into triumphs. It is grace alone that saves us (Eph. 2:8–10). God's grace can give us strength in times of trial (2 Cor. 12:1–10). Grace enables us to serve God in spite of difficulties (1 Cor. 15:9–10). Whatever begins with God's grace will always lead to glory (Ps. 84:11; 1 Peter 5:10).

As we study 1 Peter, we will see how the three themes of suffering, grace, and glory unite to form an encouraging message for believers experiencing times of trial and persecution. These themes are summarized in 1 Peter 5:10, a verse we would do well to memorize.

The cynical editor and writer H. L. Mencken once defined hope as "a pathological belief in the occurrence of the impossible." But that definition does not agree with the New Testament meaning of the word. True Christian hope is more than "hope so." It is confident assurance of future glory and blessing.

An Old Testament believer called God "the hope of Israel" (Jer. 14:8). A New Testament believer affirms that Jesus Christ is his hope (1 Tim. 1:1; see Col. 1:27). The unsaved sinner is "without hope" (Eph. 2:12), and if he dies without Christ, he will be hopeless forever. The Italian poet Dante, in his *Divine Comedy,* put this inscription over the world of the dead: "Abandon all hope, you who enter here!"

This confident hope gives us the encouragement and enablement we need for daily living. It does not put us in a rocking chair where we complacently await the return of Jesus Christ. Instead, it puts us in the marketplace, on the battlefield, where we keep on going when the burdens are heavy and the battles are hard. Hope is not a sedative; it is a shot of adrenaline, a blood transfusion. Like an anchor, our hope in Christ stabilizes us in the storms of life (Heb. 6:18–19), but unlike an anchor, our hope moves us forward, it does not hold us back.

It is not difficult to follow Peter's train of thought. Everything begins with salvation, our personal relationship to God through Jesus Christ. If we know Christ as Savior, then we have hope! If we have hope, then we can walk in holiness and in harmony. There should be no problem submitting to those around us in society, the home, and the church family. Salvation and submission are preparation for suffering; but if we focus on Christ, we can overcome, and God will transform suffering into glory.

CHAPTER TWO
1 Peter 1:2–12
IT'S GLORY ALL THE WAY!

On a balmy summer day, my wife and I visited one of the world's most famous cemeteries located at Stoke Poges, a little village not far from Windsor Castle in England. On this site Thomas Gray penned his famous "Elegy Written in a Country Churchyard," a poem most of us had to read at one time or another in school.

As we stood quietly in the midst of ancient graves, one stanza of that poem came to mind:

> The boast of heraldry, the pomp of power,
> And all that beauty, all that wealth e'er gave,
> Awaits alike the inevitable hour,
> The paths of glory lead but to the grave.

Man's glory simply does not last, but God's glory is eternal, and He has deigned to share that glory with us! In this first section of his letter, Peter shared four wonderful discoveries that he had made about the glory of God.

Christians Are Born for Glory (1:2–4)

Because of the death and resurrection of Jesus Christ, believers have been "begotten again" to a living hope, and that hope includes the glory of God. But, what do we mean by "the glory of God"?

The glory of God means the sum total of all that God is and does. "Glory" is not a separate attribute or characteristic of God, such as His holiness, wisdom, or mercy. Everything that God is and does is characterized by glory. He is glorious in wisdom and power, so that everything He thinks and does is marked by glory. He reveals His glory in creation (Ps. 19), in His dealings with the people of Israel, and especially in His plan of salvation for lost sinners.

When we were born the first time, we were not born for glory. "For all flesh is like grass, and all the glory of man like the flower of grass" (1 Peter 1:24, quoted from Isa. 40:6). Whatever feeble glory man has will eventually fade and disappear; but the glory of the Lord is eternal. The works of man done for the glory of God will last and be rewarded (1 John 2:17). But the selfish human achievements of sinners will one day vanish to be seen no more. One reason that we have encyclopedias is so that we can learn about the famous people who are now forgotten!

Peter gave two descriptions to help us better understand this wonderful truth about glory.

A Christian's birth described (vv. 2–3). This miracle all began with God: we were chosen by the Father (Eph. 1:3–4). This took place in the deep counsels of eternity, and we knew nothing about it until it was revealed to us in the Word of God. This election was not based on anything we had done, because we were not even on the scene. Nor was it based on anything God saw that we would be or do. God's election was based wholly on His grace and love. We cannot explain it (Rom. 11:33–36), but we can rejoice in it.

"Foreknowledge" does not suggest that God merely knew ahead of time that we would believe, and therefore He chose us. This would raise the question, "Who or what made us decide for Christ?" and would take our salvation completely out of God's hands. In the

Bible, to *foreknow* means "to set one's love on a person or persons in a personal way." It is used this way in Amos 3:2: "You only have I known of all the families of the earth." God set His electing love on the nation of Israel. Other verses that use "know" in this special sense are Psalm 1:6; Matthew 7:23; John 10:14, 27; and 1 Corinthians 8:3.

But the plan of salvation includes more than the Father's electing love; it also includes the work of the Spirit in convicting the sinner and bringing him to faith in Christ. The best commentary on this is 2 Thessalonians 2:13–14. Also, the Son of God had to die on the cross for our sins, or there could be no salvation. We have been chosen by the Father, purchased by the Son, and set apart by the Spirit. It takes all three if there is to be a true experience of salvation.

As far as God the Father is concerned, I was saved when He chose me in Christ before the foundation of the world. As far as the Son is concerned, I was saved when He died for me on the cross. But as far as the Spirit is concerned, I was saved one night in May 1945 when I heard the gospel and received Christ. Then it all came together, but it took all three Persons of the Godhead to bring me to salvation. If we separate these ministries, we will either deny divine sovereignty or human responsibility, and that would lead to heresy.

Peter did not deny man's part in God's plan to save sinners. In 1 Peter 1:23 he emphasized the fact that the gospel was preached to these people, and that they heard it and believed (see also 1 Peter 1:12). Peter's own example at Pentecost is proof that we do not "leave it all with God" and never urge lost sinners to come to Christ (Acts 2:37–40). The same God who ordains the end—our salvation—also ordains *the means to the end*—the preaching of the gospel of the grace of God.

A Christian's hope described (vv. 3–4). To begin with, it is *a living hope* because it is grounded on the living Word of God (1 Peter 1:23) and was made possible by the living Son of God who arose from the dead. A "living hope" is one that has life in it and therefore can give life to us. Because it has life, it grows and becomes greater and more beautiful as time goes on. Time destroys most hopes; they fade and then die. But the passing of time only makes a Christian's hope that much more glorious.

Peter called this hope *an inheritance* (1 Peter 1:4). As the children of the King, we share His inheritance in glory (Rom. 8:17–18; Eph. 1:9–12). We are included in Christ's last will and testament, and we share the glory with Him (John 17:22–24).

Note the description of this inheritance, for it is totally unlike any earthly inheritance. For one thing, it is *incorruptible,* which means that nothing can ruin it. Because it is *undefiled,* it cannot be stained or cheapened in any way. It will never grow old because it is eternal; it cannot wear out, nor can it disappoint us in any way.

In 1 Peter 1:5 and 9, this inheritance is called "salvation." The believer is already saved through faith in Christ (Eph. 2:8–9), but the completion of that salvation awaits the return of the Savior. Then we shall have new bodies and enter into a new environment, the heavenly city. In 1 Peter 1:7, Peter called this hope "the appearing of Jesus Christ." Paul called this "the blessed hope" (Titus 2:13).

What a thrilling thing it is to know that we were born for glory! When we were born again, we exchanged the passing glory of man for the eternal glory of God!

Christians Are Kept for Glory (1:5)

Not only is the glory being "reserved" for us, but we are being kept for the glory! In my travels, I have sometimes gone to a hotel or motel, only to discover that the reservations have been confused or cancelled. This will not happen to us when we arrive in heaven, for our future home and inheritance are guaranteed and reserved.

"But suppose *we* don't make it?" a timid saint might ask. But we will; for all believers are being "kept by the power of God." The word translated "kept" is a military word that means "guarded, shielded." The tense of the verb reveals that we are *constantly* being guarded by God, assuring us that we shall safely arrive in heaven. This same word is used to describe the soldiers guarding Damascus when Paul made his escape (2 Cor. 11:32). See also Jude 24–25 and Romans 8:28–39.

Believers are not kept by their own power, but by the power of God. Our faith in Christ has so united us to Him that His power now guards us and guides us. We are not kept by our strength, but by His faithfulness. How long will He guard us? Until Jesus Christ returns and we will share in the full revelation of His great salvation. This same truth is repeated in 1 Peter 1:9.

It is encouraging to know that we are "guarded for glory." According to Romans 8:30, we have *already* been glorified. All that awaits is the public revelation of this glory (Rom. 8:18–23). If any believer were lost, it would rob God of His glory. God is so certain that we will be in heaven that He has already given us His glory as the assurance (John 17:24; Eph. 1:13–14).

The assurance of heaven is a great help to us today. As Dr. James M. Gray expressed it in one of his songs, "Who can mind the journey, when the road leads home?" If suffering today means glory tomorrow, then suffering becomes a blessing to us. The unsaved have their "glory" now, but it will be followed by eternal suffering *away from the glory of God* (2 Thess. 1:3–10). In the light of this, ponder 2 Corinthians 4:7–18—and rejoice!

Christians Are Being Prepared for Glory (1:6–7)

We must keep in mind that all God plans and performs here is preparation for what He has in store for us in heaven. He is preparing us for the life and service yet to come. Nobody yet knows all that is in store for us in heaven, but this we do know: life today is a school in which God trains us for our future ministry in eternity. This explains the presence of trials in our lives: they are some of God's tools and textbooks in the school of Christian experience.

Peter used the word *trials* rather than *tribulations* or *persecutions*, because he was dealing with the general problems that Christians face as they are surrounded by unbelievers. He shared several facts about trials.

Trials meet needs. The phrase "if need be" indicates that there are special times when God knows that we need to go through trials. Sometimes trials discipline us when we have disobeyed God's will (Ps. 119:67). At other times, trials prepare us for spiritual growth, or even help to prevent us from sinning (2 Cor. 12:1–9). We do not always know the need being met, but we can trust God to know and to do what is best.

Trials are varied. Peter used the word *manifold*, which literally means "variegated, many-colored." He used the same word to describe God's grace in 1 Peter 4:10. No matter what "color" our day may be—a "blue" Monday or a "gray" Tuesday—God has grace sufficient to meet the need. We must not think that because we have overcome one kind of trial that we will automatically "win them all." Trials are varied, and God matches the trial to our strengths and needs.

Trials are not easy. Peter did not suggest that we take a careless attitude toward trials, because this would be deceitful. Trials produce what he called "heaviness." The word means "to experience grief or pain." It is used to describe our Lord in Gethsemane (Matt. 26:37) and the sorrow of saints at the death of loved ones (1 Thess. 4:13). To deny that our trials are painful is to make them even worse. Christians must accept the fact that there are difficult experiences in life and not put on a brave front just to appear "more spiritual."

Trials are controlled by God. They do not last forever; they are "for a season." When God permits His children to go through the furnace, He keeps His eye on the clock and His hand on the thermostat. If we rebel, He may have to reset the clock, but if we submit, He will not permit us to suffer one minute too long. The important thing is that we learn the lesson He wants to teach us and that we bring glory to Him alone.

Peter illustrated this truth by referring to the goldsmith. No goldsmith would deliberately waste the precious ore. He would put it into the smelting furnace long enough to remove the cheap impurities; then he would pour it out and make from it a beautiful article of value. It has been said that the Eastern goldsmith kept the metal in the furnace until he could see his face reflected in it. So our Lord keeps us in the furnace of suffering until we reflect the glory and beauty of Jesus Christ.

The important point is that this glory is not fully revealed until Jesus returns for His church. Our trying experiences today are preparing us for glory tomorrow. When we see Jesus Christ, we will bring "praise and honor and glory" to Him if we have been faithful in the sufferings of this life (see Rom. 8:17–18). This explains why Peter associated rejoicing with suffering. While we may not be able to rejoice as we look around, in our trials, we can rejoice as we look ahead. The word *this* in 1 Peter 1:6 (NASB) refers back to the "salvation" (the return of Christ) mentioned in 1 Peter 1:5.

Just as the assayer tests the gold to see if it is pure gold or counterfeit, so the trials of life test our faith to prove its sincerity. A faith that cannot be tested cannot be trusted! Too many professing Christians have a "false faith," and this will be revealed in the trials of life. The seed that fell on shallow soil produced rootless plants, and the plants died when the sun came up (see Matt. 13:1–9, 18–23). The sun in the parable represents "tribulation or persecution." The person who abandons his "faith" when the going gets tough is only proving that he really had no faith at all.

The patriarch Job went through many painful trials, all of them with God's approval, and yet he understood somewhat of this truth about the refiner's fire. "But he knoweth the way that I take; when he hath tried me, I shall come forth as gold" (Job 23:10). And he did!

It is encouraging to know that we are born for glory, kept for glory, and being prepared for glory. But the fourth discovery Peter shared with his readers is perhaps the most exciting of all.

Christians Can Enjoy the Glory Now (1:8–12)

The Christian philosophy of life is not "pie in the sky by and by." It carries with it a *present* dynamic that can turn suffering into glory *today*. Peter gave four directions for enjoying the glory now, even in the midst of trials.

Love Christ (v. 8). Our love for Christ is not based on physical sight, because we have not seen Him. It is based on our spiritual relationship with Him and what the Word has taught us about Him. The Holy Spirit has poured out God's love into our hearts (Rom. 5:5), and we return that love to Him. When you find yourself in some trial, and you hurt, immediately lift your heart to Christ in true love and worship. Why? Because this will take the poison out of the experience and replace it with healing medicine.

Satan wants to use life's trials to bring out the worst in us, but God wants to bring out the best in us. If we love ourselves more than we love Christ, then we will not experience any of the glory *now*. The fire will *burn us*, not *purify* us.

Trust Christ (v. 8). We must live by faith and not by sight. An elderly lady fell and broke her leg while attending a summer Bible conference. She said to the pastor who visited her, "I know the Lord led me to the conference. But I don't see why this had to happen! And I don't see any good coming from it." Wisely, the pastor replied, "Romans 8:28 doesn't say that we *see* all things working together for good. It says that we *know* it."

Faith means surrendering all to God and obeying

His Word in spite of circumstances and consequences. Love and faith go together: when you love someone, you trust him. And faith and love together help to strengthen hope, for where you find faith and love, you will find confidence for the future.

How can we grow in faith during times of testing and suffering? The same way we grow in faith when things seem to be going well: by feeding on the Word of God (Rom. 10:17). Our fellowship with Christ through His Word not only strengthens our faith, but it also deepens our love. It is a basic principle of Christian living that we spend much time in the Word when God is testing us and Satan is tempting us.

Rejoice in Christ (v. 8). You may not be able to rejoice *over* the circumstances, but you can rejoice *in* them by centering your heart and mind on Jesus Christ. Each experience of trial helps us learn something new and wonderful about our Savior. Abraham discovered new truths about the Lord on the mount where he offered his son (Gen. 22). The three Hebrew children discovered His nearness when they went through the fiery furnace (Dan. 3). Paul learned the sufficiency of His grace when he suffered with a thorn in the flesh (2 Cor. 12).

Note that the joy He produces is "unspeakable and full of glory." This joy is so deep and so wonderful that we cannot even express it. Words fail us! Peter had seen some of the glory on the Mount of Transfiguration where Jesus discussed with Moses and Elijah His own impending suffering and death (Luke 9:28–36).

Receive from Christ (vv. 9–12). "Believing … receiving" is God's way of meeting our needs. If we love Him, trust Him, and rejoice in Him, then we can receive from Him all that we need to turn trials into triumphs. First Peter 1:9 can be translated, "For you are receiving the consummation of your faith, that is, the final salvation of your souls." In other words, we can experience *today* some of that future glory. Charles Spurgeon used to say, "Little faith will take your soul to heaven, but great faith will bring heaven to your soul." It is not enough that we long for heaven during times of suffering, for anybody can do that. What Peter urged his readers to do was exercise love, faith, and rejoicing, so that they might experience some of the glory of heaven in the midst of suffering *now.*

The amazing thing is that this "salvation" we are awaiting—the return of Christ—was a part of God's great plan for us from eternity. The Old Testament prophets wrote about this salvation and studied closely what God revealed to them. They saw the sufferings of the Messiah, and also the glory that would follow, but they could not fully understand the connection between the two. In fact, in some of the prophecies, the Messiah's sufferings and glory are blended in one verse or paragraph.

When Jesus came to earth, the Jewish teachers were awaiting a conquering Messiah who would defeat Israel's enemies and establish the glorious kingdom promised to David. Even His own disciples were not clear about the need for His death on the cross (Matt. 16:13–28). They were still inquiring about the Jewish kingdom even after His resurrection (Acts 1:1–8). If the *disciples* were not clear about God's program, certainly the Old Testament *prophets* could be excused!

God told the prophets that they were ministering for a *future* generation. Between the suffering of Messiah and His return in glory comes what we call "the age of the church." The truth about the church was a hidden "mystery" in the Old Testament period (Eph. 3:1–13). The Old Testament believers looked ahead by faith and saw, as it were, two mountain peaks: Mount Calvary, where Messiah suffered and died (Isa. 53), and Mount Olivet, where He will return in glory (Zech. 14:4). They could not see the "valley" in between, the present age of the church.

Even the angels are interested in what God is doing in and through His church! Read 1 Corinthians 4:9 and Ephesians 3:10 for further information on how God is "educating" the angels through the church.

If the Old Testament prophets searched so diligently into the truths of salvation and yet had so little to go on, how much more ought we to search into this subject, now that we have a complete Word from God! The same Holy Spirit who taught the prophets and, through them, wrote the Word of God, can teach us the truths in it (John 16:12–15).

Furthermore, we can learn these truths from the Old Testament as well as from the New Testament. You can find Christ in every part of the Old Testament Scriptures (Luke 24:25–27). What a delight it is to meet Christ in the Old Testament law, the types, the Psalms, and the writings of the prophets. In times of trial, you can turn to the Bible, both the Old and New Testaments, and find all that you need for encouragement and enlightenment

Yes, for Christians, it is glory all the way! When we trusted Christ, we were born for glory. We are being kept for glory. As we obey Him and experience trials, we are being prepared for glory. When we love Him, trust Him, and rejoice in Him, we experience the glory here and now.

Joy unspeakable and full of glory!

CHAPTER THREE
1 Peter 1:13–21
STAYING CLEAN IN A POLLUTED WORLD

In the first section of this chapter, Peter emphasized *walking in hope,* but now his emphasis is *walking in holiness.* The two go together, for "every man that hath this hope in him purifieth himself, even as he is pure" (1 John 3:3).

The root meaning of the word translated "holy" is "different." A holy person is not an odd person, but a different person. His life has a quality about it that is different. His present "lifestyle" is not only different from his past way of life, but it is different from the "lifestyles" of the unbelievers around him. A Christian's life of holiness appears strange to the lost (1 Peter 4:4), but it is not strange to other believers.

However, it is not easy to live in this world and maintain a holy walk. The anti-God atmosphere around us that the Bible calls "the world" is always pressing against us, trying to force us to conform. In this paragraph, Peter presented to his readers five spiritual incentives to encourage them (and us) to maintain a different lifestyle, a holy walk in a polluted world.

The Glory of God (1:13)

"The revelation of Jesus Christ" is another expression for the "living hope" and "the appearing of Jesus Christ." Christians live in the future tense; their present actions and decisions are governed by this future hope. Just as an engaged couple makes all their plans in the light of that future wedding, so Christians today live with the expectation of seeing Jesus Christ.

"Gird up the loins of your mind" simply means, "Pull your thoughts together! Have a disciplined mind!" The image is that of a robed man, tucking his skirts under the belt, so he can be free to run. When you center your thoughts on the return of Christ and live accordingly, you escape the many worldly things that would encumber your mind and hinder your spiritual progress. Peter may have borrowed the idea from the Passover supper, because later in this section he identified Christ as the Lamb (1 Peter 1:19). The Jews at Passover were supposed to eat the meal in haste, ready to move (Ex. 12:11).

Outlook determines outcome; attitude determines action. A Christian who is looking for the glory of God has a greater motivation for present obedience than a Christian who ignores the Lord's return. The contrast is illustrated in the lives of Abraham and Lot (Gen. 12–13; Heb. 11:8–16). Abraham had his eyes of faith on that heavenly city, so he had no interest in the world's real estate. But Lot, who had tasted the pleasures of the world in Egypt, gradually moved toward Sodom. Abraham brought blessing to his home, but Lot brought judgment. Outlook determined outcome.

Not only should we have a disciplined mind, but we should also have a *sober* mind. The word means "to be calm, steady, controlled; to weigh matters." Unfortunately some people get "carried away" with prophetic studies and lose their spiritual balance. The fact that Christ is coming should encourage us to be calm and collected (1 Peter 4:7). The fact that Satan is on the prowl is another reason to be sober-minded (1 Peter 5:8). Anyone whose mind becomes undisciplined, and whose life "falls apart" because of prophetic studies, is giving evidence that he does not really understand Bible prophecy.

We should also have an *optimistic* mind. "Hope to the end" means "set your hope fully." Have a hopeful outlook! A friend of mine sent me a note one day that read: "When the *outlook* is gloomy, try the *uplook!*" Good advice, indeed! It has to be dark for the stars to appear.

The result of this spiritual mind-set is that a believer experiences the grace of God in his life. To be sure, we will experience grace when we see Jesus Christ; but we can also experience grace today as we look for Him to return. We have been saved by grace and we depend moment by moment on God's grace (1 Peter 1:10). Looking for Christ to return strengthens our faith and hope in difficult days, and this imparts to us more of the grace of God. Titus 2:10–13 is another passage that shows the relationship between grace and the coming of Jesus Christ.

The Holiness of God (1:14–15)

The argument here is logical and simple. Children inherit the nature of their parents. God is holy; therefore, as His children, we should live holy lives. We are "partakers of the divine nature" (2 Peter 1:4) and ought to reveal that nature in godly living.

Peter reminded his readers of what they were before they trusted Christ. They had been *children of disobedience* (Eph. 2:1–3), but now they were to be obedient children. True salvation always results in obedience (Rom. 1:5; 1 Peter 1:2). They had also been *imitators of the world,* "fashioning themselves" after the standards and pleasures of the world. Romans 12:2 translates this same word as "conformed to this world." Unsaved people tell us that they want to be "free and different," yet they all imitate one another!

The cause of all this is *ignorance* that leads to *indulgence.* Unsaved people lack spiritual intelligence, and this causes them to give themselves to all kinds of fleshly and worldly indulgences (see Acts 17:30; Eph. 4:17ff.). Since we were born with a fallen nature, it was natural for us to live sinful lives. Nature determines appetites and actions. A dog and a cat behave differently because they have different natures.

We would still be in that sad sinful plight were it not for the grace of God. He called us! One day, Jesus called to Peter and his friends and said, "Come, follow me … and I will make you fishers of men" (Mark 1:17 NIV). They responded by faith to His call, and this completely changed their lives.

Perhaps this explains why Peter used the word *called* so often in this letter. We are called to be holy (1 Peter 1:15). We are called "out of darkness into his marvelous light" (1 Peter 2:9). We are called to suffer and follow Christ's example of meekness (1 Peter 2:21). In the midst of persecution, we are called "to inherit a blessing" (1 Peter 3:9). Best of all, we are called to "his eternal glory" (1 Peter 5:10). God called us before we called on Him for salvation. It is all wholly of grace.

But God's gracious election of sinners to become saints always involves responsibility, and not just privilege. He has chosen us in Christ "that we should be holy and without blame before him" (Eph. 1:4). God

has called us to Himself, and He is holy; therefore, we should be holy. Peter quoted from the Old Testament law to back up his admonition (Lev. 11:44–45; 19:2; 20:7, 26).

God's holiness is an essential part of His nature. "God is light, and in him is no darkness at all" (1 John 1:5). Any holiness that we have in character and conduct must be derived from Him. Basically, to be *sanctified* means to be "set apart for God's exclusive use and pleasure." It involves separation from that which is unclean and complete devotion to God (2 Cor. 6:14—7:1). We are to be holy "in all manner of conversation [behavior]," so that everything we do reflects the holiness of God.

To a dedicated believer, there is no such thing as "secular" and "sacred." All of life is holy as we live to glorify God. Even such ordinary activities as eating and drinking can be done to the glory of God (1 Cor. 10:31). If something cannot be done to the glory of God, then we can be sure it must be out of the will of God.

The Word of God (1:16)

"It is written!" is a statement that carries great authority for the believer. Our Lord used the Word of God to defeat Satan, and so may we (Matt. 4:1–11; see Eph. 6:17). But the Word of God is not only a sword for battle; it is also a light to guide us in this dark world (Ps. 119:105; 2 Peter 1:19), food that strengthens us (Matt. 4:4; 1 Peter 2:2), and water that washes us (Eph. 5:25–27).

The Word of God has a sanctifying ministry in the lives of dedicated believers (John 17:17). Those who delight in God's Word, meditate on it, and seek to obey it will experience God's direction and blessing in their lives (Ps. 1:1–3). The Word reveals God's mind, so we should *learn* it; God's heart, so we should *love* it; God's will, so we should *live* it. Our whole being—mind, will, and heart—should be controlled by the Word of God.

Peter quoted from the book of Leviticus, "Ye shall be holy; for I am holy" (Lev. 11:44). Does this mean that the Old Testament law is authoritative today for New Testament Christians? Keep in mind that the early Christians did not even have the New Testament. The only Word of God they possessed was the Old Testament, and God used that Word to direct and nurture them. Believers today are not under the ceremonial laws given to Israel; however, even in these laws we see moral and spiritual principles revealed. Nine of the Ten Commandments are repeated in the Epistles, so we must obey them. (The Sabbath commandment was given especially to Israel and does not apply to us today. See Rom. 14:1–9.) As we read and study the Old Testament, we will learn much about God's character and working, and we will see truths pictured in types and symbols.

The first step toward keeping clean in a filthy world is to ask, "What does the Bible say?" In the Scriptures, we will find precepts, principles, promises, and persons to guide us in today's decisions. If we are really willing to obey God, He will show us His truth (John 7:17). While God's methods of working may change from age to age, His character remains the same and His spiritual principles never vary. We do not study the Bible just to get to know the Bible. We study the Bible that we might get to know God better. Too many earnest Bible students are content with outlines and explanations, and do not really get to know God. It is good to know the Word of God, but this should help us better know the God of the Word.

The Judgment of God (1:17)

As God's children, we need to be serious about sin and about holy living. Our heavenly Father is a holy (John 17:11) and righteous Father (John 17:25). He will not compromise with sin. He is merciful and forgiving, but He is also a loving disciplinarian who cannot permit His children to enjoy sin. After all, it was sin that sent His Son to the cross. If we call God "Father," then we should reflect His nature.

What is this judgment that Peter wrote about? It is the judgment of a believer's works. It has nothing to do with salvation, except that salvation ought to produce good works (Titus 1:16; 2:7, 12). When we trusted Christ, God forgave our sins and declared us righteous in His Son (Rom. 5:1–10; 8:1–4; Col. 2:13). Our sins have already been judged on the cross (1 Peter 2:24), and therefore they cannot be held against us (Heb. 10:10–18).

But when the Lord returns, there will be a time of judgment called "the judgment seat of Christ" (Rom. 14:10–12; 2 Cor. 5:9–10). Each of us will give an account of his works, and each will receive the appropriate reward. This is a "family judgment," the Father dealing with His beloved children. The Greek word translated "judgeth" carries the meaning "to judge in order to find something good." God will search into the motives for our ministry; He will examine our hearts. But He assures us that His purpose is to glorify Himself in our lives and ministries, "and then shall every man have praise of God" (1 Cor. 4:5). What an encouragement!

God will give us many gifts and privileges as we grow in the Christian life; but He will never give us the privilege to disobey and sin. He never pampers His children or indulges them. He is no respecter of persons. He "shows no partiality and accepts no bribes" (Deut. 10:17 NIV). "For God does not show favoritism" (Rom. 2:11 NIV). Years of obedience cannot purchase an hour of disobedience. If one of His children disobeys, God must chasten (Heb. 12:1–13). But when His child obeys and serves Him in love, He notes that and prepares the proper reward.

Peter reminded his readers that they were only "sojourners" on earth. Life was too short to waste in disobedience and sin (see 1 Peter 4:1–6). It was when Lot stopped being a sojouner and became a resident

in Sodom that he lost his consecration and his testimony. Everything he lived for went up in smoke! Keep reminding yourself that you are a "stranger and pilgrim" in this world (1 Peter 1:1; 2:11).

In view of the fact that the Father lovingly disciplines His children today and will judge their works in the future, we ought to cultivate an attitude of godly fear. This is not the cringing fear of a slave before a master, but the loving reverence of a child before his father. It is not fear of judgment (1 John 4:18), but a fear of disappointing Him or sinning against His love. It is "godly fear" (2 Cor. 7:1), a sober reverence for the Father.

I sometimes feel that there is today an increase in carelessness, even flippancy, in the way we talk about God or talk to God. Nearly a century ago, Bishop B. F. Westcott said, "Every year makes me tremble at the daring with which people speak of spiritual things." The godly bishop should hear what is said today! A worldly actress calls God "the Man upstairs." A baseball player calls Him "the great Yankee in the sky." An Old Testament Jew so feared God that he would not even pronounce His holy name, yet we today speak of God with carelessness and irreverence. In our public praying, we sometimes get so familiar that other people wonder whether we are trying to express our requests or impress the listeners with our nearness to God!

The Love of God (1:18–21)

This is the highest motive for holy living. In this paragraph, Peter reminded his readers of their salvation experience, a reminder that all of us regularly need. This is one reason our Lord established the Lord's Supper, so that regularly His people would remember that He died for them. Note the reminders that Peter gave.

He reminded them of *what they were.* To begin with, they were slaves who needed to be set free. The word *redeemed* is, to us, a theological term, but it carried a special meaning to people in the first-century Roman Empire. There were probably sixty million slaves in the empire! Many slaves became Christians and fellowshipped in the local assemblies. A slave could purchase his own freedom if he could collect sufficient funds; or his master could sell him to someone who would pay the price and set him free. Redemption was a precious thing in that day.

We must never forget the slavery of sin (Titus 3:3). Moses urged Israel to remember that they had been slaves in Egypt (Deut. 5:15; 16:12; 24:18, 22). The generation that died in the wilderness forgot the bondage of Egypt and wanted to go back!

Not only did we have a life of slavery, but it was also a life of *emptiness.* Peter called it "the empty way of life handed down to you from your forefathers" (1 Peter 1:18 NIV), and he described it more specifically in 1 Peter 4:1–4. At the time, these people thought their lives were "full" and "happy," when they were really empty and miserable. Unsaved people today are blindly living on substitutes.

While ministering in Canada, I met a woman who told me she had been converted early in life but had drifted into a "society life" that was exciting and satisfied her ego. One day, she was driving to a card party and happened to tune in a Christian radio broadcast. At that very moment, the speaker said, "Some of you women know more about cards than you do your Bible!" Those words arrested her. God spoke to her heart, she went back home, and from that hour her life was dedicated fully to God. She saw the futility and vanity of a life spent out of the will of God.

Peter not only reminded them of what they were, but he also reminded them *of what Christ did.* He shed His precious blood to purchase us out of the slavery of sin and set us free forever. *To redeem* means "to set free by paying a price." A slave could be freed with the payment of money, but no amount of money can set a lost sinner free. Only the blood of Jesus Christ can redeem us.

Peter was a witness of Christ's sufferings (1 Peter 5:1) and mentioned His sacrificial death often in this letter (1 Peter 2:21ff; 3:18; 4:1, 13; 5:1). In calling Christ "a lamb," Peter was reminding his readers of an Old Testament teaching that was important in the early church, and that ought to be important to us today. It is the doctrine of substitution: an innocent victim giving his life for the guilty.

The doctrine of sacrifice begins in Genesis 3, when God killed animals that He might clothe Adam and Eve. A ram died for Isaac (Gen. 22:13), and the Passover lamb was slain for each Jewish household (Ex. 12). Messiah was presented as an innocent Lamb in Isaiah 53. Isaac asked the question, "Where is the lamb?" (Gen. 22:7), and John the Baptist answered it when he pointed to Jesus and said, "Behold the Lamb of God, which taketh away the sin of the world" (John 1:29). In heaven, the redeemed and the angels sing, "Worthy is the Lamb" (Rev. 5:11–14)!

Peter made it clear that Christ's death was an appointment, not an accident; for it was ordained by God before the foundation of the world (Acts 2:23). From the human perspective, our Lord was cruelly murdered; but from the divine perspective, He laid down His life for sinners (John 10:17–18). But He was raised from the dead! Now, anyone who trusts Him will be saved for eternity.

When you and I meditate on the sacrifice of Christ for us, certainly we should want to obey God and live holy lives for His glory. When only a young lady, Frances Ridley Havergal saw a picture of the crucified Christ with this caption under it: "I did this for thee. What hast thou done for Me?" Quickly, she wrote a poem, but was dissatisfied with it and threw it into the fireplace. The paper came out unharmed! Later, at her father's suggestion, she published the poem, and today we sing it.

I gave My life for thee,
My precious blood I shed;
That thou might ransomed be,
And quickened from the dead.
I gave, I gave, My life for thee,
What hast thou given for Me?

A good question, indeed! I trust we can give a good answer to the Lord.

CHAPTER FOUR
1 Peter 1:22—2:10
CHRISTIAN TOGETHERNESS

One of the painful facts of life is that the people of God do not always get along with each other. You would think that those who walk in *hope* and *holiness* would be able to walk in *harmony,* but this is not always true. From God's divine point of view, there is only one body (see Eph. 4:4–6), but what we see with human eyes is a church divided and sometimes at war. There is today a desperate need for spiritual unity.

In this section of his letter, Peter emphasized spiritual unity by presenting four vivid pictures of the church.

We Are Children in the Same Family (1:22—2:3)
When you consider the implications of this fact, you will be encouraged to build and maintain unity among God's people.

We have experienced the same birth (1:23–25). The only way to enter God's spiritual family is by a spiritual birth, through faith in Jesus Christ (John 3:1–16). Just as there are two parents in physical birth, so there are two parents in spiritual birth: the Spirit of God (John 3:5–6) and the Word of God (1 Peter 1:23). The new birth gives to us a new nature (2 Peter 1:4) as well as a new and living hope (1 Peter 1:3).

Our first birth was a birth of "flesh," and the flesh is corruptible. Whatever is born of flesh is destined to die and decay. This explains why mankind cannot hold civilization together: it is all based on human flesh and is destined to fall apart. Like the beautiful flowers of spring, man's works look successful for a time, but then they start to decay and die. All the way from the Tower of Babel in Genesis 11, to "Babylon the Great" in Revelation 17—18, man's great attempts at unity are destined to fail.

If we try to build unity in the church on the basis of our first birth, we will fail, but if we build unity on the basis of the new birth, it will succeed. Each believer has the same Holy Spirit dwelling within (Rom. 8:9). We call on the same Father (1 Peter 1:17) and share His divine nature. We trust the same Word, and that Word will never decay or disappear. We have trusted the same gospel and have been born of the same Spirit. The *externals* of the flesh that could divide us mean

nothing when compared with the *eternals* of the Spirit that unite us.

We express the same love (v. 22). Peter used two different words for love: *philadelphia,* which is "brotherly love," and *agape,* which is godlike sacrificial love. It is important that we share both kinds of love. We share brotherly love because we are brothers and sisters in Christ and have likenesses. We share *agape* love because we belong to God and therefore can overlook differences.

By nature, all of us are selfish, so it took a miracle of God to give us this love. Because we "obey[ed] the truth through the Spirit," God purified our souls and poured His love into our hearts (Rom. 5:5). Love for the brethren is an evidence that we truly have been born of God (1 John 4:7–21). Now we are "obedient children" (1 Peter 1:14) who no longer want to live in the selfish desires of the old life.

It is tragic when people try to "manufacture" love, because the product is obviously cheap and artificial. "The words of his mouth were smoother than butter, but war was in his heart: his words were softer than oil, yet were they drawn swords" (Ps. 55:21). The love that we share with each other, and with a lost world, must be generated by the Spirit of God. It is a *constant* power in our lives, and not something that we turn on and off like a radio.

Not only is this love a spiritual love, but it is a *sincere* love ("unfeigned"). We love "with a pure heart." Our motive is not to get but to give. There is a kind of "success psychology" popular today that enables a person to subtly manipulate others in order to get what he wants. If our love is sincere and from a pure heart, we could never "use people" for our own advantage.

This love is also a *fervent* love, and this is an athletic term that means "striving with all of one's energy." Love is something we have to work at, just as an Olympic contestant has to work at his particular skills. Christian love is not a feeling; it is a matter of the will. We show love to others when we treat them the same way God treats us. God forgives us, so we forgive others. God is kind to us, so we are kind to others. It is not a matter of *feeling* but of *willing,* and this is something we must constantly work at if we are to succeed.

We have two wonderful "assistants" to help us: the Word of God and the Spirit of God. The same truth that we trusted and obeyed to become God's children also nurtures and empowers us. It *is impossible to love the truth and hate the brethren.* The Spirit of God produces the "fruit of the Spirit" in our lives, and the first of these is love (Gal. 5:22–23). If we are filled with the Word of God (Col. 3:16ff.) and the Spirit of God (Eph. 5:18ff.), we will manifest the love of God in our daily experiences.

We enjoy the same nourishment (2:1–3). *God's* Word *has* life, *gives* life, and *nourishes* life. We should have appetites for the Word just like hungry newborn babes! We should want the *pure* Word, unadulterated, because this alone can help us grow. When I was a child, I did not like to drink milk (and my father worked for the Borden Dairy!), so my mother used to add various syrups and powders to make my milk tastier. None of them really ever worked. It is sad when Christians have no appetite for God's Word, but must be "fed" religious entertainment instead. As we grow, we discover that the Word is milk for babes, but also strong meat for the mature (1 Cor. 3:1–4; Heb. 5:11–14). It is also bread (Matt. 4:4) and honey (Ps. 119:103).

Sometimes children have no appetite because they have been eating the wrong things. Peter warned his readers to "lay aside" certain wrong attitudes of heart that would hinder their appetite and spiritual growth. "Malice" means wickedness in general. "Guile" is craftiness, using devious words and actions to get what we want. Of course, if we are guilty of malice and guile, we will try to hide it, and this produces "hypocrisies." Often the cause of ill will is *envy*, and one result of envy is *evil speaking*, conversation that tears the other person down. If these attitudes and actions are in our lives, we will lose our appetite for the pure word of God. If we stop feeding on the Word, we stop growing, and we stop enjoying ("tasting") the grace that we find in the Lord. When Christians are growing in the Word, they are peacemakers, not troublemakers, and they promote the unity of the church.

We Are Stones in the Same Building (2:4–8)

There is only one Savior, Jesus Christ, and only one spiritual building, the church. Jesus Christ is the chief cornerstone of the church (Eph. 2:20), binding the building together. Whether we agree with each other or not, all true Christians belong to each other as stones in God's building.

Peter gave a full description of Jesus Christ, the stone. He is a *living* stone because He was raised from the dead in victory. He is the *chosen* stone of the Father, and He is *precious*. Peter quoted Isaiah 28:16 and Psalm 118:22 in his description and pointed out that Jesus Christ, though chosen by God, was rejected by men. He was not the kind of Messiah they were expecting, so they stumbled over Him. Jesus referred to this same Scripture when He debated with the Jewish leaders (Matt. 21:42ff.; see Ps. 118:22). Though rejected by men, Jesus Christ was exalted by God!

The real cause of this Jewish stumbling was their refusal to submit to the Word (1 Peter 2:8). Had they believed and obeyed the Word, they would have received their Messiah and been saved. Of course, people today still stumble over Christ and His cross (1 Cor. 1:18ff). Those who believe on Christ "shall not be confounded [ashamed]."

In His first mention of the church, Jesus compared it to a building: "I will build my church" (Matt. 16:18). Believers are living stones in His building. Each time someone trusts Christ, another stone is quarried out of the pit of sin and cemented by grace into the building. It may look to us that the church on earth is a pile of rubble and ruins, but God sees the total structure as it grows (Eph. 2:19–22). What a privilege we have to be a part of His church, "an habitation of God through the Spirit."

Peter wrote this letter to believers living in five different provinces, yet he said that they all belonged to *one* "spiritual house." There is a unity of God's people that transcends all local and individual assemblies and fellowships. We belong to each other because we belong to Christ. This does not mean that doctrinal and denominational distinctives are wrong, because each local church must be fully persuaded by the Spirit. But it does mean that we must not permit our differences to destroy the spiritual unity we have in Christ. We ought to be mature enough to disagree without in any sense becoming disagreeable.

A contractor in Michigan was building a house and the construction of the first floor went smoothly. But when they started on the second floor, they had nothing but trouble. None of the materials from the lumberyard would fit properly. Then they discovered the reason: they were working with two different sets of blueprints! Once they got rid of the old set, everything went well and they built a lovely house.

Too often, Christians hinder the building of the church because they are following the wrong plans. When Solomon built his temple, his workmen followed the plans so carefully that everything fit together on the construction site (1 Kings 6:7). If all of us would follow God's blueprints given in His Word, we would be able to work together without discord and build His church for His glory.

We Are Priests in the Same Temple (2:5, 9)

We are a "holy priesthood" and a "royal priesthood." This corresponds to the heavenly priesthood of our Lord, for He is both King and Priest (see Heb. 7). In the Old Testament no king in Israel served as a priest; and the one king who tried was judged by God (2 Chron. 26:16–21). Our Lord's heavenly throne is a throne of grace from which we may obtain by faith all that we need to live for Him and serve Him (Heb. 4:14–16).

In the Old Testament period, God's people *had* a priesthood, but today, God's people *are* a priesthood. Each individual believer has the privilege of coming into the presence of God (Heb. 10:19–25). We do not come to God through any person on earth, but only through the one Mediator, Jesus Christ (1 Tim. 2:1–8). Because He is alive in glory, interceding for us, we can minister as holy priests.

This means that our lives should be lived as though we were priests in a temple. It is indeed a privilege to serve as a priest. No man in Israel could serve at the altar or enter the tabernacle or temple holy places, except those born into the tribe of Levi and consecrated to God for service. Each priest and Levite had different ministries to perform, yet they were together under the high priest, serving to glorify God. As God's priests today, we must work together at the direction of our Great High Priest. Each ministry that we perform for His glory is a service to God.

Peter mentioned especially the privilege of offering "spiritual sacrifices." Christians today do not bring animal sacrifices as did the Old Testament worshippers, but we do have our own sacrifices to present to God. We ought to give *our bodies* to Him as living sacrifices (Rom. 12:1–2), as well as the *praise* of our lips (Heb. 13:15) and the *good works* we do for others (Heb. 13:16). The *money* and other material things we share with others in God's service are also spiritual sacrifices (Phil. 4:10–20). Even the *people* we win to Christ are sacrifices for His glory (Rom. 15:16). We offer these sacrifices through Jesus Christ, for only then are they acceptable with God. If we do any of this for our own pleasure or glory, then it will not be accepted as a spiritual sacrifice.

God wanted His people Israel to become "a kingdom of priests" (Ex. 19:6), a spiritual influence for godliness, but Israel failed Him. Instead of being a positive influence on the godless nations around them, Israel imitated those nations and adopted their practices. God had to discipline His people many times for their idolatry, but they still persisted in sin. Today, Israel has no temple or priesthood.

It is important that we, as God's priests, maintain our separated position in this world. We must not be isolated, because the world needs our influence and witness, but we must not permit the world to infect us or change us. Separation is not isolation; it is contact without contamination.

The fact that each individual believer can go to God personally and offer spiritual sacrifices should not encourage selfishness or "individualism" on our part. We are priests *together,* serving the same High Priest, ministering in the same spiritual temple. The fact that there is but *one* High Priest and heavenly Mediator indicates unity among the people of God. While we must maintain our personal walk with God, we must not do it at the expense of other Christians by ignoring or neglecting them.

Several social scientists have written books dealing with what they call the "me complex" in modern society. The emphasis today is on taking care of yourself and forgetting about others. This same attitude has crept into the church, as I see it. Too much modern church music centers on the individual and ignores the fellowship of the church. Many books and sermons focus on *personal* experience to the neglect of ministry to the whole body. I realize that the individual must care for himself if he is to help others, but there must be balance.

We Are Citizens of the Same Nation (2:9–10)

The description of the church in these verses parallels God's description of Israel in Exodus 19:5–6 and Deuteronomy 7:6. In contrast to the disobedient and rebellious nation of Israel, God's people today are His chosen and holy nation. This does not suggest that God is through with Israel, for I believe He will fulfill His promises and His covenants and establish the promised kingdom. But it does mean that the church today is to God and the world what Israel was meant to be.

We are a *chosen generation,* which immediately speaks of the grace of God. God did not choose Israel because they were a great people, but because He loved them (Deut. 7:7–8). God has chosen us purely because of His love and grace. "You did not choose me, but I chose you" (John 15:16 NIV).

We are a *holy nation.* We have been set apart to belong exclusively to God. Our citizenship is in heaven (Phil. 3:20), so we obey heaven's laws and seek to please heaven's Lord. Israel forgot that she was a holy nation and began to break down the walls of separation that made her special and distinct. God commanded them to put a "difference between holy and unholy, and between unclean and clean" (Lev. 10:10), but they ignored the differences and disobeyed God.

We are the *people of God.* In our unsaved condition, we were not God's people, because we belonged to Satan and the world (Eph. 2:1–3, 11–19). Now that we have trusted Christ, we are a part of God's people. We are a "people of his own special possession," because He purchased us with the blood of His own Son (Acts 20:28).

All of these privileges carry with them one big responsibility: revealing the praises of God to a lost world. The verb translated "show forth" means "to tell out, to advertise." Because the world is "in the dark," people do not know the "excellencies" of God, but they should see them in our lives. Each dozen of heaven is a living "advertisement" for the virtues of God and the blessings of the Christian life. Our lives should radiate the "marvelous light" into which God has graciously called us.

After all, we have obtained mercy from God! Were it not for His mercy, we would be lost and on the way to eternal judgment! God reminded Israel many times that He had delivered them from the bondage of Egypt that they might glorify and serve Him, but the nation soon forgot and the people drifted back into their sinful ways. We are God's chosen people only because of His mercy, and it behooves us to be faithful to Him.

We are living in enemy territory, and the enemy is constantly watching us, looking for opportunities to move in and take over. As citizens of heaven, we must be united. We must present to the world a united demonstration of what the grace and mercy of God can do. As I write these words, the newspapers are reporting "dissensions" among the men who serve with the president of the United States. These men are not presenting a united front, and the nation is a bit uneasy. I wonder what the unsaved people think when they see the citizens of heaven and servants of God fighting among themselves.

Each of these four pictures emphasizes the importance

of unity and harmony. We belong to one family of God and share the same divine nature. We are living stones in one building and priests serving in one temple. We are citizens of the same heavenly homeland. It is Jesus Christ who is the source and center of this unity. If we center our attention and affection on Him, we will walk and work together; if we focus on ourselves, we will only cause division.

Unity does not eliminate diversity. Not all children in a family are alike, nor are all the stones in a building identical. In fact, it is diversity that gives beauty and richness to a family or building. The absence of diversity is not *unity;* it is *uniformity,* and uniformity is dull. It is fine when the choir sings in unison, but I prefer that they sing in harmony.

Christians can differ and still get along. All who cherish the "one faith" and who seek to honor the "one Lord" can love each other and walk together (Eph. 4:1–6). God may call us into different ministries, or to use different methods, but we can still love each other and seek to present a united witness to the world.

After all, one day all of us will be together in heaven (John 17:24), so it might be a good idea if we learned to love each other down here!

St. Augustine said it perfectly: "In essentials, unity. In nonessentials, liberty. In all things, charity."

CHAPTER FIVE
1 Peter 2:11–25
SOMEBODY'S WATCHING YOU!

The central section of Peter's letter (1 Peter 2:11—3:12) emphasizes *submission* in the life of a believer. This is certainly not a popular topic in this day of lawlessness and the quest for "personal fulfillment," but it is an important one. Peter applied the theme of submission to the life of a believer as a citizen (1 Peter 2:11–17), a worker (1 Peter 2:18–25), a marriage partner (1 Peter 3:1–7), and a member of the Christian assembly (1 Peter 3:8–12).

Submission does not mean slavery or subjugation but simply the recognition of God's authority in our lives. God has established the home, human government, and the church, and He has the right to tell us how these institutions should be run. God wants each of us to exercise authority, but before we can *exercise* authority, we must be *under* authority. Satan's offer to our first parents was freedom without authority, but they ended up losing both freedom and authority. The Prodigal Son found his freedom when he yielded to his father's will.

Peter shared with his readers three excellent motives for submitting to authority and thus living dedicated, obedient Christian lives.

For the Sake of the Lost (2:11–12)
As Christians, we must constantly remind ourselves

who we are; and Peter did this in 1 Peter 2:11. To begin with, we are *God's dearly beloved children.* Eight times in his two epistles, Peter reminded his readers of God's love for them (1 Peter 2:11; 4:12; 2 Peter 1:7; 3:1, 8, 14–15, 17). In ourselves, there is nothing that God can love; but He loves us because of Jesus Christ. "This is my beloved Son, in whom I am well pleased" (2 Peter 1:17). Because of our faith in Jesus Christ, we are "accepted in the beloved" (Eph. 1:6).

Our "love relationship" to Jesus Christ ought to be motivation enough for us to live godly lives in this godless world. "If ye love me, keep my commandments" (John 14:15). There is something deeper than obedience because of duty, and that is obedience because of devotion. "If a man love me, he will keep my words" (John 14:23).

Not only are we God's beloved children, but we are also "strangers [sojourners] and pilgrims" in this world. We are "resident aliens" who have our citizenship in another country—heaven. Like the patriarchs of old, we are temporary in this life, traveling toward the heavenly city (Heb. 11:8–16). If you have ever lived in a foreign land, you know that the citizens watch you and are prone to find things to criticize. (In all fairness, we must confess that sometimes we are critical of foreigners in our own country.) Some years ago, a bestselling novel called *The Ugly American* depicted the struggles of an American as he tried to meet the needs of a foreign people and still maintain his credibility with his fellow Americans, who, unfortunately, completely misunderstood the situation.

We are also *soldiers involved in a spiritual battle.* There are sinful desires that war against us and want to defeat us (see Gal. 5:16–26). Our real battle is not with people around us, but with passions within us. D. L. Moody said, "I have more trouble with D. L. Moody than with any man I know." If we yield to these sinful appetites, then we will start living like the unsaved around us and will become ineffective witnesses. The word translated "war" carries the idea of "a military campaign." We do not win one battle and the war is over! It is a constant warfare, and we must be on our guard.

Most of all, we are *witnesses to the lost around us.* The word *Gentiles* here has nothing to do with race, since it is a synonym for "unsaved people" (1 Cor. 5:1; 12:2; 3 John 7). Unsaved people are watching us, speaking against us (1 Peter 3:16; 4:4), and looking for excuses to reject the gospel.

If we are going to witness to the lost people around us, we must live "honest" lives. This word implies much more than telling the truth and doing what is right. It carries with it the idea of beauty, comeliness, that which is admirable and honorable. To use a cliche of the '60s, we must be "beautiful people" in the best sense of the word.

We do not witness only with our lips; we must back up our "talk" with our "walk." There should be nothing in our conduct that will give the unsaved ammunition to attack Christ and the gospel. Our good works must back up our good words. Jesus said this in Matthew 5:16, and the entire Bible echoes this truth.

During my many years of ministry, I have seen the powerful impact Christians can make on the lost when they combine a godly life with a loving witness. I remember many instances of some wonderful conversions simply because dedicated Christians let their lights shine. On the other hand, I recall with grief some lost persons who rejected the Word because of the inconsistent lives of professed believers.

Peter encouraged his readers to bear witness to the lost, by word and deed, so that one day God might visit them and save them. "The day of visitation" could mean that day when Christ returns and every tongue will confess that He is Lord. But I think the "visitation" Peter mentioned here is the time when God visits lost sinners and saves them by His grace. The word is used in this sense in Luke 19:44. When these people do trust Christ, they will glorify God and give thanks because we were faithful to witness to them even when they made life difficult for us.

In the summer of 1805, a number of Native American chiefs and warriors met in council at Buffalo Creek, New York, to hear a presentation of the Christian message by a Mr. Cram from the Boston Missionary Society. After the sermon, a response was given by Red Jacket, one of the leading chiefs. Among other things, the chief said, "Brother, you say that there is but one way to worship and serve the Great Spirit. If there is but one religion, why do you white people differ so much about it? Why not all agree, as you can all read the Book?

"Brother, we are told that you have been preaching to the white people in this place. These people are our neighbors. We are acquainted with them. We will wait a little while and see what effect your preaching has upon them. If we find it does them good, makes them honest and less disposed to cheat Native Americans, we will then consider again of what you have said."

For the Lord's Sake (2:13–17)

Of course, *everything* we do should be for the glory of the Lord and the good of His kingdom! But Peter was careful to point out that Christians in society are representatives of Jesus Christ. It is our responsibility to "advertise God's virtues" (1 Peter 2:9, author's translation). This is especially true when it comes to our relationship to government and people in authority.

As Christian citizens, we should submit to the authority vested in human government. The word translated "ordinance" in our Authorized Version simply means "creation or institution." It does not refer to each individual law, but to the institutions that make and enforce the laws. It is possible to submit to the institutions and still disobey the laws.

For example, when Daniel and his three friends refused to obey the king's dietary regulations, they disobeyed the law, but the *way* that they did it proved that they honored the king and respected the authorities (Dan. 1). They were not rebels; they were careful not to embarrass the official in charge or get him into trouble; and yet they stood their ground. They glorified God and, at the same time, honored the authority of the king.

Peter and the other apostles faced a similar challenge shortly after Pentecost (Acts 4—5). The Jewish council commanded them to stop preaching in the name of Jesus, but Peter and his associates refused to obey (see Acts 4:19; 5:29). They did not cause a rebellion or in any way question or deny the authority of the council. They submitted to the institution, but they refused to stop preaching. They showed respect to their leaders even though these men were opposed to the gospel.

It is important that we respect the office even though we cannot respect the man or woman in the office. As much as possible, we should seek to cooperate with the government and obey the law, but we must never allow the law to make us violate our conscience or disobey God's Word. Unfortunately, some zealous but ignorant Christians use these differences as opportunities for conflict and loud sermons about "freedom" and "separation of church and state."

When a local church constructs and furnishes a building, there is a local code that must be obeyed. (I have been through several building programs and I know!) The government has no right to control the pulpit or the business meeting, but it has every right to control matters that relate to safety and operation. If the law requires a certain number of exits, or fire extinguishers, or emergency lights, the church must comply. The state is not persecuting when it sets up the code, nor is the church compromising when it obeys the code. But I know some overly zealous saints who have disgraced the name of the Lord by their attitudes and actions relating to these matters.

Peter named the offices we are to respect. "The king" meant "the emperor." In democratic nations, we have a president or premier. Peter did not criticize the Roman government or suggest that it be overthrown. God's church has been able to live and grow in all kinds of political systems. The "governors" are those under the supreme authority who administer the laws and execute justice. Ideally, they should punish those who do evil and praise those who do good. This ideal was not always reached in Peter's day (see Acts 24:24–27), nor is it reached in our own. Again, we must remind ourselves to respect the office even if we cannot respect the officer.

Two phrases are important: "the will of God" (1 Peter 2:15) and "the servants of God" (1 Peter 2:16). When we do something in the will of God and as the servants of God, then we are doing it "for the Lord's sake." God has willed that we silence the critics by doing good, not by opposing the authority. The word *silence* in 1 Peter 2:15 is literally "muzzle," as though the pagan critics were like a pack of yelping, snapping dogs!

Someone may argue, "But, as Christians, are we not free?" Yes, we are free in Christ, but we must never use our freedom for ourselves. We must always use it for others. Sad to say, there are "religious racketeers" who prey on ignorant people and use "religion" to veil their evil actions. A true Christian submits himself to authority because he is first of all submitted to Christ. He uses his freedom as a tool to build with and not as a weapon to fight with. A good example of this attitude is Nehemiah, who willingly gave up his own rights that he might help his people and restore the walls of Jerusalem.

If we are sincerely submitted to authority "for the Lord's sake," then we will show honor to all who deserve it. We may not agree with their politics or their practices, but we must respect their position (see Rom. 13). We will also "love the brotherhood," meaning, of course, the people of God in the church. This is a recurring theme in this letter (1 Peter 1:22; 3:8; 4:8; 5:14). One way we show love to the brethren is by submitting to the authority of the "powers that be," for we are bound together with one another in our Christian witness.

"Fear God" and "honor the king" go together, since "the powers that be are ordained of God" (Rom. 13:1). Solomon had the same counsel: "My son, fear thou the Lord and the king" (Prov. 24:21). We honor the king because we do fear the Lord. It is worth noting that the tenses of these verbs indicate that we should *constantly* maintain these attitudes. "Keep loving the brotherhood! Keep fearing God! Keep honoring the king!"

As Christians, we must exercise discernment in our relationship to human government. There are times when the right thing is to set aside our own privileges, and there are other times when *using* our citizenship is the right thing. Paul was willing to suffer personally in Philippi (Acts 16:16–24), but he was unwilling to "sneak out of town" like a criminal (Acts 16:35–40). When he was arrested on false charges, Paul used his citizenship to protect himself (Acts 22:22–29) and to insist on a fair trial before Caesar (Acts 25:1–12).

For Our Own Sake (2:18–25)

In this paragraph Peter addressed the Christian slaves in the congregations, and again he stressed the importance of submission. Some newly converted slaves thought that their spiritual freedom also guaranteed personal and political freedom, and they created problems for themselves and the churches. Paul dealt with this problem in 1 Corinthians 7:20–24, and also touched on it in his letter to his friend Philemon. The gospel eventually overthrew the Roman Empire and the terrible institution of slavery, even though the early church did not preach against either one.

There are no Christian slaves today, at least in the New Testament sense, but what Peter wrote does have application to employees. We are to be submissive to those who are over us, whether they are kind or unkind to us. Christian employees must never take advantage of Christian employers. Each worker should do a good day's work and honestly earn his pay.

Sometimes a Christian employee may be wronged by an unbelieving coworker or supervisor. For conscience' sake, he must "take it" even though he is not in the wrong. A Christian's relationship to God is far more important than his relationship to men. "For this is grace [thankworthy]" to bear reproach when you are innocent (see Matt. 5:10–12). Anybody, including an unbeliever, can "take it patiently" when he is in the wrong! It takes a dedicated Christian to "take it" when he is in the right. "This is grace [acceptable] with God." God can give us the grace to submit and "take it" and in this way glorify God.

Of course, the human tendency is to fight back and to demand our rights. But that is the natural response of the unsaved person, and we must do much more than they do (Luke 6:32–34). Anybody can fight back; it takes a Spirit-filled Christian to submit and let God fight his battles (Rom. 12:16–21).

In the Bible, duty is always connected with doctrine. When Paul wrote to the slaves, he related his admonitions to the doctrine of the grace of God (Titus 2:9–15). Peter connected his counsels to the example of Jesus Christ, God's "Suffering Servant" (1 Peter 2:21–25; see Isa. 52:13—53:12). Peter had learned in his own experience that God's people *serve through suffering*. At first, Peter had opposed Christ's suffering on the cross (Matt. 16:21ff.), but then he learned the important lesson that we lead by serving and serve by suffering. He also learned that this kind of suffering always leads to glory!

Peter encouraged these suffering slaves by presenting three "pictures" of Jesus Christ.

He is our Example in His life (vv. 21–23). All that Jesus did on earth, as recorded in the four gospels, is a perfect example for us to follow. But He is especially our example in the way He responded to suffering. In spite of the fact that He was sinless in both word and deed, He suffered at the hands of the authorities. This connects, of course, to Peter's words in 1 Peter 2:19–20. We wonder how he would have responded in the same circumstances! The fact that Peter used his sword in the garden suggests that he might have fought rather than submitted to the will of God.

Jesus proved that a person could be in the will of God, be greatly loved by God, and still suffer unjustly. There is a shallow brand of popular theology today that claims that Christians will *not* suffer if they are in the will of God. Those who promote such ideas have not meditated much on the cross.

Our Lord's humility and submission were not an evidence of weakness, but of power. Jesus could have summoned the armies of heaven to rescue Him! His words to Pilate in John 18:33–38 are proof that He was in complete command of the situation. It was Pilate who was on trial, not Jesus! Jesus had committed

Himself to the Father, and the Father always judges righteously.

We are not saved by following Christ's example, because each of us would stumble over 1 Peter 2:22: "who did no sin." Sinners need a Savior, not an Example. But after a person is saved, he will want to "follow closely upon His steps" (literal translation) and imitate the example of Christ.

He is our Substitute in His death (v. 24). He died as the sinner's Substitute. This entire section reflects that great "Servant Chapter," Isaiah 53, especially Isaiah 53:5–7, but also verses 9 and 12. Jesus did not die as a martyr; He died as a Savior, a sinless Substitute. The word translated "bare" means "to carry as a sacrifice." The Jewish people did not crucify criminals; they stoned them to death. But if the victim was especially evil, his dead body was hung on a tree until evening, as a mark of shame (Deut. 21:23). Jesus died on a tree—a cross—and bore the curse of the law (Gal. 3:13).

The paradoxes of the cross never cease to amaze us. Christ was wounded that we might be healed. He died that we might live. We died with Him, and thus we are "dead to sin" (Rom. 6) so that we might "live unto righteousness." The healing Peter mentioned in 1 Peter 2:24 is not physical healing, but rather the spiritual healing of the soul (Ps. 103:3). One day, when we have glorified bodies, all sicknesses will be gone, but meanwhile, even some of God's choicest servants may have physical afflictions (see Phil. 2:25–30; 2 Cor. 12:1ff.).

It is not Jesus the Example or the Teacher who saves us, but Jesus the spotless Lamb of God who takes away the sins of the world (John 1:29).

He is our Watchful Shepherd in heaven (v. 25). In the Old Testament, the sheep died for the shepherd; but at Calvary, the Shepherd died for the sheep (John 10). Every lost sinner is like a sheep gone astray: ignorant, lost, wandering, in danger, away from the place of safety, and unable to help himself. The Shepherd went out to search for the lost sheep (Luke 15:1–7). He died for the sheep!

Now that we have been returned to the fold and are safely in His care, He watches over us lest we stray and get into sin. The word *bishop* simply means "one who watches over, who oversees." Just as the elder-bishop oversees the flock of God, the local church (1 Peter 5:2), so the Savior in glory watches over His sheep to protect them and perfect them (Heb. 13:20–21).

Here, then, is the wonderful truth Peter wanted to share: as we live godly lives and submit in times of suffering, we are following Christ's example *and becoming more like Him*. We submit and obey, not only for the sake of lost souls and for the Lord's sake, but also for our own sake, that we might grow spiritually and become more like Christ.

The unsaved world is watching us, but the Shepherd in heaven is also watching over us; so we have nothing to fear. We can submit to Him and know that He will work everything together for our good and His glory.

CHAPTER SIX
1 Peter 3:1–7
WEDLOCK OR DEADLOCK?

A strange situation exists in society today. We have more readily available information about sex and marriage than ever before, yet we have more marital problems and divorces. Obviously something is wrong. It is not sufficient to say that God is needed in these homes, because even many *Christian* marriages are falling apart.

The fact that a man and a woman are both saved is no guarantee that their marriage will succeed. Marriage is something that we have to work at; success is not automatic. And when one marriage partner is not a Christian, that can make matters even more difficult. Peter addressed this section of his letter to Christian wives who had unsaved husbands, telling them how to win their mates to Christ. Then he added some important admonitions for Christian husbands.

No matter what your marital status may be, you can learn from Peter the essentials for a happy and successful marriage.

The Example of Christ (3:1a, 7a)

The phrases "in the same manner" and "in like manner" refer us back to Peter's discussion of the example of Jesus Christ (1 Peter 2:21–25). Just as Jesus was submissive and obedient to God's will, so a Christian husband and wife should follow His example.

Much of our learning in life comes by way of imitation. Grandparents have a delightful time watching their grandchildren pick up new skills and words as they grow up. If we imitate the best models, we will become better people and better achievers, but if we imitate the wrong models, it will cripple our lives and possibly ruin our characters. The role models that we follow influence us in every area of life.

While standing in the checkout line in a supermarket, I overheard two women discussing the latest Hollywood scandal that was featured on the front page of a newspaper displayed on the counter. As I listened (and I could not *help* but hear them!) I thought, "How foolish to worry about the sinful lives of matinee idols. Why clutter up your mind with such trash? Why not get acquainted with decent people and learn from their lives?" A few days later, I overheard a conversation about the marital problems on a certain television "soap opera," and the same thoughts came to me.

When Christian couples try to imitate the world and get their standards from Hollywood instead of from heaven, there will be trouble in the home. But if both partners will imitate Jesus Christ in His submission and obedience and His desire to serve others, then there will be triumph and joy in the home. A psychiatrist friend of mine states that the best thing a Christian husband can do is pattern himself after Jesus Christ. In Christ we see a beautiful blending of strength and tenderness, and that is what it takes to be a successful husband.

Peter also pointed to Sarah as a model for Christian wives to follow. To be sure, Sarah was not perfect, but she proved to be a good helpmeet to Abraham, and she is one of the few women named in Hebrews 11. I once made a pastoral visit to a woman who said she had marital problems, and I noticed a number of "movie fan club magazines" in the magazine rack. After listening to the woman's problems, I concluded that she needed to follow some Bible examples and models and get her mind off of the worldly examples.

We cannot follow Christ's example unless we first know Him as our Savior, and then submit to Him as our Lord. We must spend time with Him each day, meditating on the Word and praying, and a Christian husband and wife must pray together and seek to encourage each other in the faith.

Submission (3:1–6)

Twice in this paragraph Peter reminded Christian wives that they were to be submissive to their husbands (1 Peter 3:1, 5). The word translated "subjection" is a military term that means "to place under rank." God has a place for everything; He has ordained various levels of authority (see 1 Peter 2:13–14). He has ordained that the husband be the head of the home (Eph. 5:21ff.) and that, as he submits to Christ, his wife should submit to him. Headship is not dictatorship, but the loving exercise of divine authority under the lordship of Jesus Christ.

Peter gave three reasons why a Christian wife should submit to her husband, even if the husband (as in this case) is not saved.

Submission is an obligation (v. 1a). God has commanded it because, in His wisdom, He knows that this is the best arrangement for a happy, fulfilling marriage. Subjection does not mean that the wife is inferior to the husband. In fact, in 1 Peter 3:7, Peter made it clear that the husband and wife are "heirs together." The man and woman are made by the same Creator out of the same basic material, and both are made in God's image. God gave dominion to both Adam and Eve (Gen. 1:28), and in Jesus Christ Christian mates are one (Gal. 3:28).

Submission has to do with order and authority, not evaluation. For example, the slaves in the average Roman household were superior in many ways to their masters, but they still had to be under authority. The buck private in the army may be a better person than the five-star general, but he is still a buck private. Even Christ Himself became a servant and submitted to God's will. There is nothing degrading about submitting to authority or accepting God's order. If anything, it is the first step toward fulfillment. And Ephesians 5:21 makes it clear that *both* husband and wife must first be submitted to Jesus Christ.

Husbands and wives must be partners, not competitors. After a wedding ceremony, I often privately say to the bride and groom, "Now, remember, from now on it's no longer *mine* or *yours,* but *ours."* This explains why Christians must always marry other Christians, for a believer cannot enter into any kind of deep "oneness" with an unbeliever (2 Cor. 6:14–18).

Submission is an opportunity (vv. 1b–2). An opportunity for what? To win an unsaved husband to Christ. God not only *commands* submission, but He *uses* it as a powerful spiritual influence in a home. This does not mean that a Christian wife "gives in" to her unsaved husband in order to subtly manipulate him and get him to do what she desires. This kind of selfish psychological persuasion ought never to be found in a Christian's heart or home.

An unsaved husband will not be converted by preaching or nagging in the home. The phrase "without the word" does not mean "without the Word of God," because salvation comes through the Word (John 5:24). It means "without talk, without a lot of speaking." Christian wives who preach at their husbands only drive them further from the Lord. I know one zealous wife who used to keep religious radio programs on all evening, usually very loud, so that her unsaved husband would "hear the truth." She only made it easier for him to leave home and spend his evenings with his friends.

It is the character and conduct of the wife that will win the lost husband—not arguments, but such attitudes as submission, understanding, love, kindness, patience. These qualities are not manufactured; they are the fruit of the Spirit that come when we are submitted to Christ and to one another. A Christian wife with "purity and reverence" will reveal in her life "the praises" of God (1 Peter *2:9)* and influence her husband to trust Christ.

One of the greatest examples of a godly wife and mother in church history is Monica, the mother of the famous St. Augustine. God used Monica's witness and prayers to win both her son and her husband to Christ, though her husband was not converted until shortly before his death. Augustine wrote in his *Confessions,* "She served him as her lord; and did her diligence to win him unto Thee … preaching Thee unto him by her conversation [behavior]; by which Thou ornamentest her, making her reverently amiable unto her husband."

In a Christian home, we must minister to each other. A Christian husband must minister to his wife and help to "beautify her" in the Lord (Eph. 5:25–30). A Christian wife must encourage her husband and help him grow strong in the Lord. Parents and children must share burdens and blessings and seek to maintain an atmosphere of spiritual excitement and growth in the home. If there are unsaved people in the home, they will be won to Christ more by what they see in our lives and relationships than by what they hear in our witness.

Submission is an ornament (vv. 3–6). The word translated "adorning" is kosmos in the Greek, and gives us our English words cosmos (the ordered universe) and cosmetic. It is the opposite of chaos. Peter warned the Christian wife not to major on external decorations but on internal character. Roman women were captivated by the latest fashions of the day and competed with each other in dress and hairdos. It was not unusual for the women to have elaborate coiffures, studded with gold and silver combs and even jewels. They wore elaborate and expensive garments, all for the purpose of impressing each other.

A Christian wife with an unsaved husband might think that she must imitate the world if she is going to win her mate, but just the opposite is true. Glamour is artificial and external; true beauty is real and internal. Glamour is something a person can put on and take off, but true beauty is always present. Glamour is corruptible; it decays and fades. True beauty from the heart grows more wonderful as the years pass. A Christian woman who cultivates the beauty of the inner person will not have to depend on cheap externals. God is concerned about values, not prices.

Of course, this does not mean that a wife should neglect herself and not try to be up-to-date in her apparel. It simply means that she is not *majoring* on being a fashion plate just to keep up with the crowd. Any husband is proud of a wife who is attractive, but that beauty must come from the heart, not the store. We are not *of* this world, but we must not look as though we came *out of* this world!

Peter did not forbid the wearing of jewelry any more than the wearing of apparel. The word "wearing" in 1 Peter 3:3 means "the putting around," and refers to a gaudy display of jewelry. It is possible to wear jewelry and still honor God, and we must not judge one another in this matter.

Peter closed this section by pointing to Sarah as an example of a godly, submissive wife. Read Genesis 18 for the background. Christian wives today would probably embarrass their husbands if they called them "lord," but their attitudes ought to be such that they could call them "lord" and people would believe it The believing wife who submits to Christ and to her husband, and who cultivates a "meek and quiet spirit" will never have to be afraid. (The "fear" in this verse means "terror," while in 1 Peter 3:2 it means "reverence.") God will watch over her even when her unsaved mate creates problems and difficulties for her.

Consideration (3:7)

Why did Peter devote more space to instructing the wives than the husbands? Because the Christian wives were experiencing a whole new situation and needed guidance. In general, women were kept down in the Roman Empire, and their new freedom in Christ created new problems and challenges. Furthermore,

many of them had unsaved husbands and needed extra encouragement and enlightenment.

As Peter wrote to the Christian husbands, he reminded them of four areas of responsibility in their relationship with their mates.

Physical—"dwell with them." This implies much more than sharing the same address. Marriage is fundamentally a physical relationship: "They two shall be one flesh" (Eph. 5:31). Of course, Christian mates enjoy a deeper spiritual relationship, but the two go together (1 Cor. 7:1–5). A truly spiritual husband will fulfill his marital duties and love his wife.

The husband must make time to be home with his wife. Christian workers and church officers who get too busy running around solving other people's problems may end up creating problems of their own at home. One survey revealed that the average husband and wife had thirty-seven minutes a week together in actual communication! Is it any wonder that marriages fall apart after the children grow up and leave home? The husband and wife are left alone—to live with strangers!

"Dwell with them" also suggests that the husband provide for the physical and material needs of the home. While it is not wrong for a wife to have a job or career, her first responsibility is to care for the home (Titus 2:4–5). It is the husband who should provide (1 Tim. 5:8).

Intellectual—"according to knowledge." Somebody asked Mrs. Albert Einstein if she understood Dr. Einstein's theory of relativity, and she replied, "No, but I understand the doctor." In my premarital counseling as a pastor, I often gave the couple pads of paper and asked them to write down the three things each one thinks the other enjoys doing the most. Usually, the prospective bride made her list immediately; the man would sit and ponder. And usually the girl was right but the man wrong! What a beginning for a marriage!

It is amazing that two married people can live together and not really know each other! Ignorance is dangerous in any area of life, but it is especially dangerous in marriage. A Christian husband needs to know his wife's moods, feelings, needs, fears, and hopes. He needs to "listen with his heart" and share meaningful communication with her. There must be in the home such a protective atmosphere of love and submission that the husband and wife can disagree and still be happy together.

"Speaking the truth in love" is the solution to the communications problem (Eph. 4:15). It has well been said that love without truth is hypocrisy, and truth without love is brutality. We need both truth and love if we are to grow in our understanding of one another. How can a husband show consideration for his wife if he does not understand her needs or problems? To say, "I never knew you felt that way!" is to confess that, at some point, one mate excommunicated the other. When either mate is afraid to be open and honest about a matter, then he or she is building walls and not bridges.

Emotional—"giving honor unto the wife." Chivalry may be dead, but every husband must be a "knight in shining armor" who treats his wife like a princess. (By the way, the name Sarah means "princess.") Peter did not suggest that a wife is "the weaker vessel" mentally, morally, or spiritually, but rather physically. There are exceptions, of course, but generally speaking, the man is the stronger of the two when it comes to physical accomplishments. The husband should treat his wife like an expensive, beautiful, fragile vase, in which is a precious treasure.

When a young couple starts dating, the boy is courteous and thoughtful. After they get engaged, he shows even more courtesy and always acts like a gentleman. Sad to say, soon after they get married, many a husband forgets to be kind and gentlemanly and starts taking his wife for granted. He forgets that happiness in a home is made up of many *little* things, including the small courtesies of life.

Big resentments often grow out of small hurts. Husbands and wives need to be honest with each other, admit hurts, and seek for forgiveness and healing. "Giving honor unto the wife" does not mean "giving in to the wife." A husband can disagree with his wife and still respect and honor her. As the spiritual leader in the home, the husband must sometimes make decisions that are not popular; but he can still act with courtesy and respect.

"Giving honor" means that the husband respects his wife's feelings, thinking, and desires. He may not agree with her ideas, but he respects them. Often God balances a marriage so that the husband needs what the wife has in her personality, and she likewise needs his good qualities. An impulsive husband often has a patient wife, and this helps to keep him out of trouble!

The husband must be the "thermostat" in the home, setting the emotional and spiritual temperature. The wife often is the "thermometer," letting him know what that temperature is! Both are necessary. The husband who is sensitive to his wife's feelings will not only make her happy, but will also grow himself and help his children live in a home that honors God.

Spiritual—"that your prayers be not hindered." Peter assumed that husbands and wives would pray together. Often, they do not; and this is the reason for much failure and unhappiness. If unconverted people can have happy homes *without prayer* (and they do), how much happier Christian homes would be *with prayer!* In fact, it is the prayer life of a couple that indicates how things are going in the home. If something is wrong, their prayers will be hindered.

A husband and wife need to have their own private, individual prayer time each day. They also need to pray together and to have a time of "family devotion." How this is organized will change from home to home, and even from time to time as the children grow up and

schedules change. The Word of God and prayer are basic to a happy, holy home (Acts 6:4).

A husband and wife are "heirs together." If the wife shows submission and the husband consideration, and if both submit to Christ and follow His example, then they will have an enriching experience in their marriage. If not, they will miss God's best and rob each other of blessing and growth. "The grace of life" may refer to children, who certainly are a heritage from God (Ps. 127:3), but even childless couples can enjoy spiritual riches if they will obey Peter's admonitions.

It might be good if husbands and wives occasionally took inventory of their marriages. Here are some questions, based on what Peter wrote.

1. Are we partners or competitors?
2. Are we helping each other become more spiritual?
3. Are we depending on the externals or the eternals? The artificial or the real?
4. Do we understand each other better?
5. Are we sensitive to each other's feelings and ideas, or taking each other for granted?
6. Are we seeing God answer our prayers?
7. Are we enriched because of our marriage, or robbing each other of God's blessing?

Honest answers to these questions might make a difference!

CHAPTER SEVEN
1 Peter 3:8–17
PREPARING FOR THE BEST!

A devoted pastor was facing serious surgery, and a friend visited him in the hospital to pray with him. "An interesting thing happened today," the pastor told him. "One of the nurses looked at my chart and said, 'Well, I guess you're preparing for the worst!' I smiled at her and said, 'No, I'm preparing for the best. I'm a Christian, and God has promised to work all things together for good.' Boy, did she drop that chart and leave this room in a hurry!"

Peter wrote this letter to prepare Christians for a "fiery trial" of persecution, yet his approach was optimistic and positive. "Prepare for the best!" was his message. In this section, he gave them three instructions to follow if they would experience the best blessings in the worst times.

Cultivate Christian Love (3:8–12)

We have noted that love is a recurring theme in Peter's letters, not only God's love for us, but also our love for others. Peter had to learn this important lesson himself, and he had a hard time learning it! How patient Jesus had to be with him!

We should begin with *love for God's people* (1 Peter 3:8). The word *finally* means "to sum it all up." Just as the whole of the law is summed up in love (Rom. 13:8–10), so the whole of human relationships is fulfilled in love. This applies to every Christian and to every area of life.

This love is evidenced by a *unity of mind* (see Phil. 2:1–11). Unity does not mean uniformity; it means cooperation in the midst of diversity. The members of the body work together in unity, even though they are all different. Christians may differ on *how* things are to be done, but they must agree on *what* is to be done and *why*. A man criticized D. L. Moody's methods of evangelism, and Moody said, "Well, I'm always ready for improvement. What *are your* methods?" The man confessed that he had none! "Then I'll stick to my own," said Moody. Whatever methods we may use, we must seek to honor Christ, win the lost, and build the church. Some methods are definitely not scriptural, but there is plenty of room for variety in the church.

Another evidence of love is *compassion,* a sincere "feeling for and with" the needs of others. Our English word *sympathy* comes from this word. We dare not get hardhearted toward each other. We must share both joys and trials (Rom. 12:15). The basis for this is the fact that we are brethren in the same family (see 1 Peter 1:22; 2:17; 4:8; 5:14). We are "taught of God to love one another" (1 Thess. 4:9).

Love reveals itself in *pity,* a tenderness of heart toward others. In the Roman Empire, this was not a quality that was admired, but the Christian message changed all of that. Today, we are deluged with so much bad news that it is easy for us to get insulated and unfeeling. We need to cultivate compassion and actively show others that we are concerned.

"Be courteous" involves much more than acting like a lady or gentleman. "Be humble-minded" is a good translation, and, after all, humility is the foundation for courtesy, for the humble person puts others ahead of himself.

Not only should we love God's people, but we should also *love our enemies* (1 Peter 3:9). The recipients of this letter were experiencing a certain amount of personal persecution because they were doing the will of God. Peter warned them that *official* persecution was just around the corner, so they had better prepare. The church today had better prepare, because difficult times are ahead.

As Christians, we can live on one of three levels. We can return evil for good, which is the satanic level. We can return good for good and evil for evil, which is the human level. Or, we can return good for evil, which is the divine level. Jesus is the perfect example of this latter approach (1 Peter 2:21–23). As God's loving children, we must do more than give "an eye for an eye, and a tooth for a tooth" (Matt. 5:38–48), which is the basis *for justice.* We must operate on the basis of *mercy,* for that is the way God deals with us.

This admonition must have meant much to Peter himself, because he once tried to fight Christ's enemies with a sword (Luke 22:47–53). When he was an unconverted rabbi, Paul used every means possible to oppose the church; but when he became a Christian,

Paul never used human weapons to fight God's battles (Rom. 12:17–21; 2 Cor. 10:1–6). When Peter and the apostles were persecuted, they depended on prayer and God's power, not on their own wisdom or strength (see Acts 4:23ff.).

We must always be reminded of our *calling* as Christians, for this will help us love our enemies and do them good when they treat us badly. We are called to "inherit a blessing." The persecutions we experience on earth today only add to our blessed inheritance of glory in heaven someday (Matt. 5:10–12). But we also inherit a blessing *today* when we treat our enemies with love and mercy. By sharing a blessing with them, we receive a blessing ourselves! Persecution can be a time of spiritual enrichment for a believer. The saints and martyrs in church history all bear witness to this fact.

We should love one another, love our enemies, and *love life* (1 Peter 3:10–12). The news of impending persecution should not cause a believer to give up on life. What may appear to be "bad days" to the world can be "good days" for a Christian, if he will only meet certain conditions.

First, *we must deliberately decide to love life.* This is an act of the will: "He who wills to love life." It is an attitude of faith that sees the best in every situation. It is the opposite of the pessimistic attitude expressed in Ecclesiastes 2:17: "Therefore I hated life … for all is vanity and vexation of spirit." We can decide to *endure* life and make it a burden, *escape* life as though we were running from a battle, or *enjoy* life because we know God is in control. Peter was not suggesting some kind of unrealistic psychological gymnastics that refused to face facts. Rather, he was urging his readers to take a positive approach to life and *by faith* make the most of every situation.

Second, *we must control our tongues.* Many of the problems of life are caused by the wrong words, spoken in the wrong spirit. Every Christian should read James 3 regularly and pray Psalm 141:3 daily. How well Peter knew the sad consequences of hasty speech! There is no place for lies in the life of a saint.

Third, *we must do good and hate evil.* We need both the positive and the negative. The Old English word *eschew* means more than just "avoid." It means "to avoid something because you despise and loathe it." It is not enough for us to avoid sin because sin is wrong; we ought to shun it because we hate it.

Finally, *we must seek and pursue peace.* "Blessed are the peacemakers: for they shall be called the children of God" (Matt. 5:9). If we go out and seek trouble, we will find it, but if we seek peace, we can find it as well. This does not mean "peace at any price," because righteousness must always be the basis for peace (James 3:13–18). It simply means that a Christian exercises moderation as he relates to people and does not create problems because he wants to have his own way. "If it be possible, as much as lieth in you, live peaceably with all men" (Rom. 12:18). Sometimes it is not possible! See Romans 14:19, where we are also admonished to *work hard* to achieve peace. It does not come automatically.

"But what if our enemies take advantage of us?" a persecuted Christian might ask. "We may be seeking peace, but they are seeking war!" Peter gave them the assurance that God's eyes are on His people and His ears open to their prayers. (Peter learned that lesson when he tried to walk on the water without looking to Jesus—Matt. 14:22–33.) We must trust God to protect and provide, for He alone can defeat our enemies (Rom. 12:17–21).

Peter quoted these statements from Psalm 34:12–15, so it would be profitable for you to read the entire psalm. It describes what God means by "good days." They are not necessarily days free from problems, for the psalmist wrote about fears (Ps. 34:4), troubles (Ps. 34:6, 17), afflictions (Ps. 34:19), and even a broken heart (Ps. 34:18). A "good day" for the believer who "loves life" is not one in which he is pampered and sheltered, but one in which he experiences God's help and blessing *because of* life's problems and trials. It is a day in which he magnifies the Lord (Ps. 34:1–3), experiences answers to prayer (Ps. 34:4–7), tastes the goodness of God (Ps. 34:8), and senses the nearness of God (Ps. 34:18).

The next time you think you are having a "bad day" and you hate life, read Psalm 34, and you may discover you are really having a "good day" to the glory of God!

Practice the Lordship of Christ (3:13–15)

These verses introduce the third main section of 1 Peter—God's grace in suffering. They introduce the important spiritual principle that the fear of the Lord conquers every other fear. Peter quoted Isaiah 8:13–14 to back up his admonition: "But in your hearts set apart Christ as Lord" (1 Peter 3:15 NIV).

The setting of the Isaiah quotation is significant. Ahaz, King of Judah, faced a crisis because of an impending invasion by the Assyrian army. The kings of Israel and Syria wanted Ahaz to join them in an alliance, but Ahaz refused, so Israel and Syria threatened to invade Judah! Behind the scenes, Ahaz confederated himself with Assyria! The prophet Isaiah warned him against ungodly alliances and urged him to trust God for deliverance. "Sanctify the Lord of hosts [armies] himself; and let him be your fear, and let him be your dread" (Isa. 8:13).

As Christians, we are faced with crises, and we are tempted to give in to our fears and make the wrong decisions. But if we "sanctify Christ as Lord" in our hearts, we need never fear men or circumstances. Our enemies might *hurt* us, but they cannot *harm* us. Only we can harm ourselves if we fail to trust God. Generally speaking, people do not oppose us if we do good; but even if they do, it is better to suffer for righteousness' sake than to compromise our testimony. Peter discussed this theme in detail in 1 Peter 4:12–19.

Instead of experiencing fear as we face the enemy, we can experience blessing, if Jesus Christ is Lord in our hearts. The word *happy* in 1 Peter 3:14 is the same as "blessed" in Matthew 5:10ff. This is a part of the "joy unspeakable and full of glory" (1 Peter 1:8).

When Jesus Christ is Lord of our lives, each crisis becomes an opportunity for witness. We are "ready always to give an answer." Our English word *apology* comes from the Greek word translated "answer," but it does not mean "to say I am sorry." Rather, it means "a defense presented in court." "Apologetics" is the branch of theology that deals with the defense of the faith. Every Christian should be able to give a reasoned defense of his hope in Christ, *especially in hopeless situations*. A crisis creates the opportunity for witness when a believer behaves with faith and hope, because the unbelievers will then sit up and take notice.

This witness must be given "with meekness and fear [respect]" and not with arrogance and a know-it-all attitude. We are witnesses, not prosecuting attorneys! We must also be sure that our lives back up our defense. Peter did not suggest that Christians argue with lost people, but rather that we present to the unsaved an account of what we believe and why we believe it, in a loving manner. The purpose is not to win an argument but to win lost souls to Christ.

What does it mean to "sanctify Christ as Lord" in our hearts? It means to turn everything over to Him, and to live only to please Him and glorify Him. It means to fear displeasing Him rather than fear what men might do to us. How wonderfully this approach simplifies our lives! It is Matthew 6:33 and Romans 12:1–2 combined into a daily attitude of faith that obeys God's Word in spite of consequences. It means being satisfied with nothing less than the will of God in our lives (John 4:31–34). One evidence that Jesus Christ is Lord in our lives is the readiness with which we witness to others about Him and seek to win them to Christ.

Maintain a Good Conscience (3:16–17)

Our word "conscience" comes from two Latin words: *con,* meaning "with," and *scio,* meaning "to know." The conscience is that internal judge that witnesses to us, that enables us to "know with," either approving our actions or accusing (see Rom. 2:14–15). Conscience may be compared to a window that lets in the light of God's truth. If we persist in disobeying, the window gets dirtier and dirtier, until the light cannot enter. This leads to a "defiled conscience" (Titus 1:15). A "seared conscience" is one that has been so sinned against that it no longer is sensitive to what is right and wrong (1 Tim. 4:2). It is even possible for the conscience to be so poisoned that it approves things that are bad and accuses when the person does good! This the Bible calls "an evil conscience" (Heb. 10:22). A criminal feels guilty if he "squeals" on his friends, but happy if he succeeds in his crime!

Conscience depends on knowledge, the "light" coming through the window. As a believer studies the Word, he better understands the will of God, and his conscience becomes more sensitive to right and wrong. A "good conscience" is one that accuses when we think or do wrong and approves when we do right. It takes "exercise" to keep the conscience strong and pure (Acts 24:16). If we do not grow in spiritual knowledge and obedience, we have a "weak conscience" that is upset very easily by trifles (1 Cor. 8).

How does a good conscience help a believer in times of trial and opposition? For one thing, it fortifies him with courage because he knows he is right with God and men, so that he need not be afraid. Inscribed on Martin Luther's monument at Worms, Germany are his courageous words spoken before the church council on April 18, 1521: "Here I stand; I can do no other. God help me. Amen." His conscience, bound to God's Word, gave him the courage to defy the whole established church!

A good conscience also gives us peace in our hearts; and when we have peace within, we can face battles without. The restlessness of an uneasy conscience divides the heart and drains the strength of a person, so that he is unable to function at his best. How can we boldly witness for Christ if conscience is witnessing against us?

A good conscience removes from us the fear of what other people may know about us, say against us, or do to us. When Christ is Lord and we fear only God, we need not fear the threats, opinions, or actions of our enemies. "The Lord is on my side; I will not fear: what can man do unto me?" (Ps. 118:6). It was in this matter that Peter failed when he feared the enemy and denied the Lord.

Peter made it clear that conscience *alone* is not the test of what is right or wrong. A person can be involved in either "welldoing" or "evildoing." For a person to disobey God's Word and claim it is right simply because his conscience does not convict him, is to admit that something is radically wrong with his conscience. Conscience is a safe guide only when the Word of God is the teacher.

More and more, Christians in today's society are going to be accused and lied about. Our personal standards are not those of the unsaved world. As a rule, Christians do not *create* problems; they *reveal* them. Let a born-again person start to work in an office or move into a college dormitory, and in a short time there will be problems. Christians are lights in this dark world (Phil. 2:15), and they reveal "the unfruitful works of darkness" (Eph. 5:11).

When Joseph began to serve as steward in Potiphar's house and refused to sin, he was falsely accused and thrown into prison. The government officials in Babylon schemed to get Daniel in trouble because his life and work were a witness against them. Our Lord Jesus Christ by His very life on earth revealed the sinful hearts and deeds of people, and this is why they crucified Him (see John 15:18–25). "Yea, and all that will live godly in Christ Jesus shall suffer persecution" (2 Tim. 3:12).

If we are to maintain a good conscience, we must deal with sin in our lives and confess it immediately (1 John 1:9). We must "keep the window clean." We must also spend time in the Word of God and "let in the light." A strong conscience is the result of obedience based on knowledge, and a strong conscience makes for a strong Christian witness to the lost. It also gives us strength in times of persecution and difficulty.

No Christian should ever suffer because of evildoing, and no Christian should be surprised if he suffers for welldoing. Our world is so mixed up that people "call evil good, and good evil" and "put darkness for light, and light for darkness" (Isa. 5:20). The religious leaders of Jesus' day called Him "a malefactor," which means "a person who does evil things" (John 18:29–30). How wrong people can be!

As times of difficulty come to the church, we must cultivate Christian love, for we will need one another's help and encouragement as never before. We must also maintain a good conscience, because a good conscience makes for a strong backbone and a courageous witness. The secret is to practice the lordship of Jesus Christ. If we fear God, we need not fear men. "Shame arises from the fear of men," said Samuel Johnson. "Conscience, from the fear of God."

CHAPTER EIGHT
1 Peter 3:18–22
LEARNING FROM NOAH

A pastor was teaching a Bible study on Matthew 16, explaining the many interpretations of our Lord's words to Peter: "Thou art Peter, and upon this rock I will build my church" (Matt. 16:18). Afterward, a woman said to him, "Pastor, I'll bet if Jesus had known all the trouble those words would cause, He would never have said them!"

When Peter wrote this section of his letter, he had no idea that it would be classified as one of the most difficult portions of the New Testament. Good and godly interpreters have wrestled with these verses, debated and disagreed, and have not always left behind a great deal of spiritual help. We may not be able to solve all the problems found in this section, but we do want to get the practical help that Peter gave to encourage Christians in difficult days.

The section presents three different ministries. If we understand these ministries, we will be better able to suffer in the will of God and glorify Christ.

The Ministry of Christ (3:18–22)
Everything else in this paragraph is incidental to what Peter had to say about Jesus Christ. This material is parallel to what Peter wrote in 1 Peter 2:21ff. Peter presented Jesus Christ as the perfect example of one who suffered unjustly, and yet obeyed God.

The death of Christ (v. 18). In 1 Peter 3:17,

Peter wrote about suffering for well-doing rather than for evil-doing, and then he gave the example of Jesus Christ. Jesus was the "just One" (Acts 3:14), and yet He was treated unjustly. Why? That He might die for the unjust ones and bring them to God! He died as a substitute (1 Peter 2:24), and He died only once (Heb. 9:24–28). In other words, Jesus suffered for well-doing; He did not die because of His own sins, for He had none (1 Peter 2:22).

The phrase "bring us to God" is a technical term that means "gain audience at court." Because of the work of Christ on the cross, we now have an open access to God (Eph. 2:18; 3:12). We may come boldly to His throne (Heb. 10:19ff.)! We also have access to His marvelous grace to meet our daily needs (Rom. 5:2). When the veil of the temple was torn, it symbolized the new and open way to God through Jesus Christ.

The proclamation of Christ (vv. 19–20). The phrase "made alive by the Spirit" (KJV, SRB) creates a problem for us. In the Greek manuscripts, there were no capital letters; so we have no authority to write "Spirit" rather than "spirit." Greek scholars tell us that the end of 1 Peter 3:18 should read, "Being put to death with reference to the flesh, but made alive with reference to the spirit." The contrast is between flesh and spirit, as in Matthew 26:41 and Romans 1:3–4, and not between Christ's flesh and the Holy Spirit.

Our Lord had a real body (Matt. 26:26), soul (John 12:27), and spirit (Luke 23:46). He was not God inhabiting a man; He was the true God-Man. When He died, He yielded His spirit to the Father (Luke 23:46; see James 2:26). However, it seems evident that, if He was "made alive in the spirit," at some point His spirit must have died. It was probably when He was made sin for us and was forsaken by the Father (Mark 15:34; 2 Cor. 5:21). The phrase "quickened in [with reference to] the spirit" cannot mean resurrection, because resurrection has to do with *the body.*

So on the cross, our Lord suffered and died. His body was put to death, and His spirit died when He was made sin. But His spirit was made alive and He yielded it to the Father. Then according to Peter, sometime between His death and His resurrection Jesus made a special proclamation to "the spirits in prison." This raises two questions: Who were these "spirits" that He visited? What did He proclaim to them?

Those who say that these "spirits in prison" were the spirits of lost sinners in hell to whom Jesus brought the good news of salvation have some real problems to solve. To begin with, Peter referred to people as "souls" and not "spirits" (1 Peter 3:20). In the New Testament, the word *spirits* is used to describe angels or demons, not human beings, and 1 Peter 3:22 seems to argue for this meaning. Furthermore, nowhere in the Bible are we told that Jesus visited hell. Acts 2:31 states that He went to "hades" (NASB), but "hades" is not hell. The word *hades* refers to the realm of the unbelieving dead, a temporary place where they await the

resurrection. Read Revelation 20:11–15 in the New American Standard Bible or the New International Version and you will see the important distinction. Hell is the permanent and final place of judgment for the lost. Hades is the temporary place. When a Christian dies, he goes to neither place, but to heaven to be with Christ (Phil. 1:20–24).

Our Lord yielded His spirit to the Father, died, and at some time between death and resurrection, visited the realm of the dead, where He delivered a message to spirit beings (probably fallen angels; see Jude 6) who were somehow related to the period before the flood. First Peter 3:20 makes this clear. The word translated "preached" simply means "to announce as a herald, to proclaim." It is not the word that means "to preach the gospel" that Peter used in 1 Peter 1:12 and 4:6. Peter did not tell us *what* Jesus proclaimed to these imprisoned spirits, but it could not be a message of redemption, since angels cannot be saved (Heb. 2:16). It was probably a declaration of victory over Satan and his hosts (see Col. 2:15; 1 Peter 3:22).

How these spirits were related to the pre-flood era, Peter did not explain. Some students believe that "the sons of God" named in Genesis 6:1–4 were fallen angels who cohabited with women and produced a race of giants, but I cannot accept this interpretation. The *good* angels who did not fall are called "sons of God," but not the fallen angels (Job 1:6; 2:1, and note that Satan is distinguished from the "sons of God"). The world before the flood was unbelievably wicked, and no doubt these spirits had much to do with it (see Gen. 6:5–13; Rom. 1:18ff.).

The resurrection of Christ (v. 21). Since death comes when the spirit leaves the body (James 2:26), then resurrection involves the spirit *returning* to the body (Luke 8:55). The Father raised Jesus from the dead (Rom. 6:4; 8:11), but the Son also had authority to raise Himself (John 10:17–18). It was a miracle! It is because of His resurrection that Christians have the "living hope" (1 Peter 1:3–4). We shall see later how the resurrection of Christ relates to the experience of Noah.

We must never minimize the importance of the resurrection of Jesus Christ. It declares that He is God (Rom. 1:4), that the work of salvation is completed and accepted by the Father (Rom. 4:25), and that death has been conquered (1 Thess. 4:13–18; Rev. 1:17–18). The gospel message includes the resurrection (1 Cor. 15:1–4), for a dead Savior can save nobody. It is the risen Christ who gives us the power we need on a daily basis for life and service (Gal. 2:20).

The ascension of Christ (v. 22). Forty days after His resurrection, our Lord ascended to heaven to sit at the right hand of the Father, the place of exaltation (Ps. 110:1; Acts 2:34–36; Phil. 2:5–11; Heb. 12:1–3). Believers are seated with Him in the heavenlies (Eph. 2:4–6), and through Him we are able to "reign in life" (Rom. 5:17). He is ministering to the church as High Priest (Heb. 4:14–16; 7:25) and Advocate (1 John

1:9–2:2). He is preparing a place for His people (John 14:1–6) and will one day come to receive them to Himself.

But the main point Peter wanted to emphasize was Christ's complete victory over all "angels and authorities and powers" (1 Peter 3:22), referring to the evil hosts of Satan (Eph. 6:10–12; Col. 2:15). The unfallen angels were *always* subject to Him. As Christians, we do not fight *for* victory, but *from* victory—the mighty victory that our Lord Jesus Christ won for us in His death, resurrection, and ascension.

The Ministry of Noah

The patriarch Noah was held in very high regard among Jewish people in Peter's day, and also among Christians. He was linked with Daniel and Job, two great men, in Ezekiel 14:19–20, and there are many references to the flood in both the Psalms and the Prophets. Jesus referred to Noah in His prophetic sermon (Matt. 24:37–39; see Luke 17:26–27), and Peter mentioned him in his second letter (2 Peter 2:5; see 3:6). He is named with the heroes of faith in Hebrews 11:7.

What relationship did Peter see between his readers and the ministry of Noah? For one thing, Noah was a "preacher of righteousness" (2 Peter 2:5) during a very difficult time in history. In fact, he walked with God and preached God's truth for 120 years (Gen. 6:3), and during that time was certainly laughed at and opposed. The early Christians knew that Jesus had promised that, before His return, the world would become like the "days of Noah" (Matt. 24:37–39); and they were expecting Him soon (2 Peter 3:1–3). As they saw society decay around them, and persecution begin, they would think of our Lord's words.

Noah was a man of faith who kept doing the will of God even when he seemed to be a failure. This would certainly be an encouragement to Peter's readers. If we measured faithfulness by results, then Noah would get a very low grade. Yet God ranked him very high!

But there is another connection: Peter saw in the flood a picture (type) of a Christian's experience of baptism. No matter what mode of baptism you may accept, it is certain that the early church practiced immersion. It is a picture of our Lord's death, burial, and resurrection. Many people today do not take baptism seriously, but it was a serious matter in the early church. Baptism meant a clean break with the past, and this could include separation from a convert's family, friends, and job. Candidates for baptism were interrogated carefully, for their submission in baptism was a step of consecration, and not just an "initiation rite" to "join the church."

The flood pictures death, burial, and resurrection. The waters buried the earth in judgment, but they also lifted Noah and his family up to safety. The early church saw in the ark a picture of salvation. Noah and his family were saved by faith because they believed God and entered into the ark of safety. So sinners are saved by faith when they trust Christ and become one with Him.

When Peter wrote that Noah and his family were "saved by water," he was careful to explain that this illustration does not imply salvation by baptism. Baptism is a "figure" of that which does save us, namely, "the resurrection of Jesus Christ" (1 Peter 3:21). Water on the body, or the body placed in water, cannot remove the stains of sin. Only the blood of Jesus Christ can do that (1 John 1:7—2:2). However, baptism does save us from one thing: a bad conscience. Peter had already told his readers that a good conscience was important to a successful witness (see 1 Peter 3:16), and a part of that "good conscience" is being faithful to our commitment to Christ as expressed in baptism.

The word *answer* in 1 Peter 3:21 is a legal term meaning "a pledge, a demand." When a person was signing a contract, he would be asked, "Do you pledge to obey and fulfill the terms of this contract?" His answer had to be, "Yes, I do," or he could not sign. When converts were prepared for baptism, they would be asked if they intended to obey God and serve Him, and to break with their sinful past. If they had reservations in their hearts, or deliberately lied, they would not have a good conscience if, under pressure of persecution, they denied the Lord. (Peter knew something about that!) So, Peter reminded them of their baptismal testimony to encourage them to be true to Christ.

It may be worth noting that the chronology of the flood is closely related to our Lord's day of resurrection. Noah's ark rested on Ararat on the seventeenth day of the seventh month (Gen. 8:4). The Jewish *civil* year started with October; the religious year started with the Passover in April (Ex. 12:1–2), but that was not instituted until Moses' time. The seventh month from October is April. Our Lord was crucified on the fourteenth day, Passover (Ex. 12:6), and resurrected after three days. This takes us to the seventeenth day of the month, the date on which the ark rested on Mount Ararat. So, the illustration of Noah relates closely to Peter's emphasis on the resurrection of the Savior.

There is a sense in which our Lord's experience on the cross was a baptism of judgment, not unlike the flood. He referred to His sufferings as a baptism (Matt. 20:22; Luke 12:50). He also used Jonah to illustrate His experience of death, burial, and resurrection (Matt. 12:38–41). Jesus could certainly have quoted Jonah 2:3 to describe His own experience: "All thy billows and thy waves passed over me."

The Ministry of Christians Today

It is easy to agree on the main lessons Peter was sharing with his readers, lessons that we need today.

First of all, *Christians must expect opposition.* As the coming of Christ draws near, our well-doing will incite the anger and attacks of godless people. Jesus lived a perfect life on earth, and yet He was crucified like a common criminal. If the just One who did no sin was treated cruelly, what right do we who are imperfect have to escape suffering? We must be careful, however, that we suffer because of well-doing, for righteousness' sake, and not because we have disobeyed.

A second lesson is that *Christians must serve God by faith and not trust in results.* Noah served God and kept only seven people from the flood, yet God honored him. From those seven people, we take courage! Jesus appeared a total failure when He died on the cross, yet His death was a supreme victory. His cause today may seem to fail, but He will accomplish His purposes in this world. The harvest is not the end of a meeting; it is the end of the age.

Third, *we can be encouraged because we are identified with Christ's victory.* This is pictured in baptism, and the doctrine is explained in Romans 6. It is the baptism of the Spirit that identifies a believer with Christ (1 Cor. 12:12–13), and this is pictured in water baptism. It is through the Spirit's power that we live for Christ and witness for Him (Acts 1:8). The opposition of men is energized by Satan, and Christ has already defeated these principalities and powers. He has "all authority in heaven and on earth" (Matt. 28:18 NIV), and therefore we can go forth with confidence and victory.

Another practical lesson is that *our baptism is important.* It identifies us with Christ and gives witness that we have broken with the old life (see 1 Peter 4:1–4) and will, by His help, live a new life. The act of baptism is a pledge to God that we shall obey Him. To use Peter's illustration, we are agreeing to the terms of the contract. To take baptism lightly is to sin against God. Some people make too much of baptism by teaching that it is a means of salvation, while others minimize it. Both are wrong. If a believer is to have a good conscience, he must obey God.

Having said this, I want to make it clear that Christians must not make baptism a test of fellowship or of spirituality. There are dedicated believers who disagree on these matters, and we respect them. When General William Booth founded the Salvation Army, he determined not to make it "another church," so he eliminated the ordinances. There are Christian groups, such as the Quakers, who, because of conscience or doctrinal interpretation, do not practice baptism. I have stated my position, but I do not want to give the impression that I make this position a test of anything. "Let us therefore follow after the things which make for peace, and things wherewith one may edify another" (Rom. 14:19). "Let every man be fully persuaded in his own mind" (Rom. 14:5).

The important thing is that each Christian avow devotion to Christ and make it a definite act of commitment. Most Christians do this in baptism, but even the act of baptism can be minimized or forgotten. It is in taking up our cross daily that we prove we are true followers of Jesus Christ.

Finally, *Jesus Christ is the only Savior, and the lost world needs to hear His gospel.* Some people try to use this complex passage of Scripture to prove a "second chance for salvation after death." Our interpretation of "spirits in prison" seems to prove that these were angelic beings, and not the souls of the dead. But even if these "spirits" were those of unsaved people, this passage says nothing about their salvation. And why would Jesus offer salvation (if He did) *only to sinners from Noah's day?* And why did Peter use the verb "proclaim as a herald" instead of the usual word for preaching the gospel?

Hebrews 9:27 makes it clear that death ends the opportunity for salvation. This is why the church needs to get concerned about evangelism and missions, because people are dying who have never even heard the good news of salvation, let alone had the opportunity to reject it. It does us no good to quibble about differing interpretations of a difficult passage of Scripture, if what we *do* believe does not motivate us to want to share the gospel with others.

Peter made it clear that difficult days give us multiplied opportunities for witness.

Are we taking advantage of our opportunities?

CHAPTER NINE
1 Peter 4:1–11
THE REST OF YOUR TIME

My wife and I were in Nairobi where I would be ministering to several hundred national pastors at an Africa Inland Mission conference. We were very excited about the conference even though we were a bit weary from the long air journey. We could hardly wait to get started, and the leader of the conference detected our impatience.

"You are in Africa now," he said to me in a fatherly fashion, "and the first thing you want to do is to put away your watch."

In the days that followed, as we ministered in Kenya and Zaire, we learned the wisdom of his words. Unfortunately, when we returned to the States, we found ourselves caught up again in the clockwork prison of deadlines and schedules.

Peter had a great deal to say about *time* (1 Peter 1:5, 11, 17, 20; 4:2–3, 17; 5:6). Certainly the awareness of his own impending martyrdom had something to do with this emphasis (John 21:15–19; 2 Peter 1:12ff.). If a person really believes in eternity, then he will make the best use of time. If we are convinced that Jesus is coming, then we will want to live prepared lives. Whether Jesus comes first or death comes first, we want to make "the rest of the time" count for eternity.

And we can! Peter described four attitudes that a Christian can cultivate in his lifetime ("the rest of his time") if he desires to make his life all that God wants it to be.

A Militant Attitude toward Sin (4:1–3)

The picture is that of a soldier who puts on his equipment and arms himself for battle. Our attitudes are weapons, and weak or wrong attitudes will lead us to defeat. Outlook determines outcome, and a believer must have the right attitudes if he is to live a right life.

A friend and I met at a restaurant to have lunch. It was one of those places where the lights are low, and you need a miner's helmet to find your table. We had been seated several minutes before we started looking at the menu, and I remarked that I was amazed how easily I could read it. "Yes," said my friend, "it doesn't take us long to get accustomed to the darkness."

There is a sermon in that sentence: It is easy for Christians to get accustomed to sin. Instead of having a militant attitude that hates and opposes it, we gradually get used to sin, sometimes without even realizing it. The one thing that will destroy "the rest of our time" is sin. A believer living in sin is a terrible weapon in the hands of Satan. Peter presented several arguments to convince us to oppose sin in our lives.

Think of what sin did to Jesus (v. 1). He had to *suffer* because of sin (see 1 Peter 2:21; 3:18). How can we enjoy that which made Jesus suffer and die on the cross? If a vicious criminal stabbed your child to death, would you preserve that knife in a glass case on your mantel? I doubt it. You would never want to see that knife again.

Our Lord came to earth to deal with sin and to conquer it forever. He dealt with the ignorance of sin by teaching the truth and by living it before men's eyes. He dealt with the consequences of sin by healing and forgiving, and, on the cross, He dealt the final deathblow to sin itself. He was armed, as it were, with a militant attitude toward sin, even though He had great compassion for lost sinners.

Our goal in life is to "cease from sin." We will not reach this goal until we die or are called home when the Lord returns; but this should not keep us from striving (1 John 2:28—3:9). Peter did not say that suffering *of itself* would cause a person to stop sinning. Pharaoh in Egypt went through great suffering in the plagues, and yet he sinned even more! I have visited suffering people who cursed God and grew more and more bitter because of their pain.

Suffering, *plus Christ in our lives,* can help us have victory over sin. But the central idea here seems to be the same truth taught in Romans 6: We are identified with Christ in His suffering and death, and therefore can have victory over sin. As we yield ourselves to God, and have the same attitude toward sin that Jesus had, we can overcome the old life and manifest the new life.

Enjoy the will of God (v. 2). The contrast is between the desires of men and the will of God. Our longtime friends cannot understand the change in our lives, and they want us to return to the same "excess of riot" that we used to enjoy. But the will of God is so much better! If we do the will of God, then we will *invest* "the rest of our time" in that which is lasting and

satisfying, but if we give in to the world around us, we will *waste* "the rest of our time" and regret it when we stand before Jesus.

The will of God is not a burden that the Father places on us. Rather it is the divine enjoyment and enablement that makes all burdens light. The will of God comes from the heart of God (Ps. 33:11) and therefore is an expression of the love of God. We may not always understand what He is doing, but we know that He is doing what is best for us. We do not live on explanations; we live on promises.

Remember what you were before you met Christ (v. 3). There are times when looking back at your past life would be wrong, because Satan could use those memories to discourage you. But God urged Israel to remember that they had once been slaves in Egypt (Deut. 5:15). Paul remembered that he had been a persecutor of believers (1 Tim. 1:12ff.), and this encouraged him to do even more for Christ. We sometimes forget the bondage of sin and remember only the passing pleasures of sin.

"The will of the Gentiles" means "the will of the unsaved world" (see 1 Peter 2:12). Lost sinners imitate each other as they conform to the fashions of this world (Rom. 12:2; Eph. 3:1–3). "Lasciviousness" and "lusts" describe all kinds of evil appetites and not just sexual sins. "Revelings and banquetings" refer to pagan orgies where the wine flowed freely. Of course, all of this could be a part of pagan worship, since "religious prostitution" was an accepted thing. Even though these practices were forbidden by law ("abominable" = illegal), they were often practiced in secret.

We may not have been guilty of such gross sins in our preconversion days, but we were still sinners—and our sins helped to crucify Christ. How foolish to go back to that kind of life!

A Patient Attitude toward the Lost (4:4–6)

Unsaved people do not understand the radical change that their friends experience when they trust Christ and become children of God. They do not think it strange when people wreck their bodies, destroy their homes, and ruin their lives by running from one sin to another! But let a drunkard become sober, or an immoral person pure, and the family thinks he has lost his mind! Festus told Paul, "You are out of your mind!" (Acts 26:24 NASB), and people even thought the same thing of our Lord (Mark 3:21).

We must be patient toward the lost, even though we do not agree with their lifestyles or participate in their sins. After all, unsaved people are blind to spiritual truth (2 Cor. 4:3–4) and dead to spiritual enjoyment (Eph. 2:1). In fact, our contact with the lost is important *to them* since we are the bearers of the truth that they need. When unsaved friends attack us, this is our opportunity to witness to them (1 Peter 3:15).

The unsaved may judge us, but one day, God will judge them. Instead of arguing with them, we should pray for them, knowing that the final judgment is with God. This was the attitude that Jesus took (2:23), and also the apostle Paul (2 Tim. 2:24–26).

We must not interpret 1 Peter 4:6 apart from the context of suffering; otherwise, we will get the idea that there is a second chance for salvation after death. Peter was reminding his readers of the Christians who had been martyred for their faith. They had been falsely judged by men, but now, in the presence of God, they received their true judgment. "Them that are dead" means "them that are *now* dead" at the time Peter was writing. The gospel is preached only to the living (1 Peter 1:25) because there is no opportunity for salvation after death (Heb. 9:27).

Unsaved friends may speak evil of us and even oppose us, but the final Judge is God. We may sacrifice our lives in the midst of persecution, but God will honor and reward us. We must fear God and not men (1 Peter 3:13–17; see Matt. 10:24–33). While we are in these human bodies ("in the flesh"), we are judged by human standards. One day, we shall be with the Lord ("in the spirit") and receive the true and final judgment.

An Expectant Attitude toward Christ (4:7)

Christians in the early church expected Jesus to return in their lifetime (Rom. 13:12; 1 John 2:18). The fact that He did not return does not invalidate His promise (2 Peter 3; Rev. 22:20). No matter what interpretation we give to the prophetic Scriptures, we must all live in expectancy. The important thing is that we shall see the Lord one day and stand before Him. How we live and serve today will determine how we are judged and rewarded on that day.

This attitude of expectancy must not turn us into lazy dreamers (2 Thess. 3:6ff.) or zealous fanatics. Peter gave "ten commandments" to his readers to keep them in balance as far as the Lord's return was concerned:

1. Be sober—v. 7
2. Watch unto prayer—v. 7
3. Have fervent love—v. 8
4. Use hospitality—v. 9
5. Minister your spiritual gifts—vv. 10–11
6. Think it not strange—v. 12
7. Rejoice—v. 13
8. Do not be ashamed—vv. 15–16
9. Glorify God—vv. 16–18
10. Commit yourself to God—v. 19

The phrase "be sober" means "be sober-minded, keep your mind steady and clear." Perhaps a modern equivalent would be "keep cool." It was a warning against wild thinking about prophecy that could lead to an unbalanced life and ministry. Often we hear of sincere people who go "off balance" because of an unbiblical emphasis on prophecy or a misinterpretation of prophecy. There are people who set dates for Christ's return, contrary to His warning (Matt. 25:13; see Acts 1:6–8); or they claim to know the name of the beast of Revelation 13. I have books in my library,

written by sincere and godly men, in which all sorts of claims are made, only to the embarrassment of the writers.

The opposite of "be sober-minded" is "frenzy, madness." It is the Greek word *mania*, which has come into our English vocabulary via psychology. If we are sober-minded, we will be intellectually sound and not off on a tangent because of some "new" interpretation of the Scriptures. We will also face things realistically and be free from delusions. The sober-minded saint will have a purposeful life and not be drifting, and he will exercise restraint and not be impulsive. He will have "sound judgment" not only about doctrinal matters, but also about the practical affairs of life.

Ten times in the pastoral epistles, Paul admonished people to "be sober-minded." It is one of the qualifications for pastors (1 Tim. 3:2) and for the members of the church (Titus 2:1–6). In a world that is susceptible to wild thinking, the church must be sober-minded.

Early in my ministry, I gave a message on prophecy that sought to explain everything. I have since filed away that outline and will probably never look at it (except when I need to be humbled). A pastor friend who suffered through my message said to me after the service, "Brother, you must be on the planning committee for the return of Christ!" I got his point, but he made it even more pertinent when he said quietly, "I've moved from the planning committee to the welcoming committee."

I am not suggesting that we not study prophecy, or that we become timid about sharing our interpretations. What I am suggesting is that we not allow ourselves to get out of balance because of an abuse of prophecy. There is a practical application to the prophetic Scriptures. Peter's emphasis on hope and the glory of God ought to encourage us to be faithful *today* in whatever work God has given us to do (see Luke 12:31–48).

If you want to make the best use of "the rest of your time," live in the light of the return of Jesus Christ. All Christians may not agree on the details of the event, but we can agree on the demands of the experience. We shall stand before the Lord! Read Romans 14:10–23 and 2 Corinthians 5:1–21 for the practical meaning of this.

If we are sober-minded, we will "watch unto prayer." If our prayer life is confused, it is because the mind is confused. Dr. Kenneth Wuest, in his translation, showed the important relationship between the two: "Be calm and collected in spirit with a view to giving yourself to prayer." The word *watch* carries with it the idea of alertness and self-control. It is the opposite of being drunk or asleep (1 Thess. 5:6–8). This admonition had special meaning to Peter, because he went to sleep when he should have been "watching unto prayer" (Mark 14:37–40).

You find the phrase "watch and pray" often in the Authorized Version of the New Testament (Mark 13:33; 14:38; Eph. 6:18; Col. 4:2). It simply means to "be alert in our praying, to be controlled." There is no place in the Christian life for lazy, listless, routine praying. We must have an alert attitude and be on guard, just like the workers in Nehemiah's day (Neh. 4:9).

An expectant attitude toward Christ's return involves a serious, balanced mind and an alert, awake prayer life. The test of our commitment to the doctrine of Christ's return is not our ability to draw charts or discern signs, but our thinking and praying. If our thinking and praying are right, our living should be right.

A Fervent Attitude toward the Saints (4:8–11)

If we really look for the return of Christ, then we shall think of others and properly relate to them. Love for the saints is important "above [before] all things." Love is the badge of a believer in this world (John 13:34–35). Especially in times of testing and persecution, Christians need to love one another and be united in heart.

This love should be "fervent." The word pictures an athlete straining to reach the goal. It speaks of eagerness and intensity. Christian love is something we have to work at just the way an athlete works on his skills. It is not a matter of emotional feeling, though that is included, but of dedicated will. Christian love means that we treat others the way God treats us, obeying His commandments in the Word. It is even possible to love people that we do not like!

Christian love is forgiving. Peter quoted from Proverbs 10:12—"Hatred stirreth up strifes: but love covereth all sins." This verse is alluded to in James 5:20 and 1 Corinthians 13:4 and 7. Love does not *condone* sin, for, if we love somebody, we will be grieved to see him sin and hurt himself and others. Rather, love *covers* sin in that love motivates us to hide the sin from others and not spread it abroad. Where there is hatred, there is malice, and malice causes a person to want to tear down the reputation of his enemy. This leads to gossip and slander (Prov. 11:13; 17:9; see 1 Peter 2:1). Sometimes we try to make our gossip sound "spiritual" by telling people things "so they might pray more intelligently."

No one can hide his sins from God, but believers ought to try, in love, to cover each other's sins at least from the eyes of the unsaved. After all, if the unsaved crowd finds ammunition for persecuting us because of our *good* words and works (1 Peter 2:19–20; 3:14), what would they do if they knew the *bad* things that Christians say and do!

Genesis 9:18–27 gives us a beautiful illustration of this principle. Noah got drunk and shamefully uncovered himself. His son Ham saw his father's shame and told the matter to the family. In loving concern, Ham's two brothers covered their father and his shame. It should not be too difficult for us to cover the sins of others; after all, Jesus Christ died that *our* sins might be washed away.

Our Christian love should not only be fervent and forgiving, but it should also be practical. We should share our homes with others in generous (and uncomplaining) hospitality, and we should use our spiritual gifts in ministry to one another. In New Testament times hospitality was an important thing, because there were few inns and poor Christians could not afford to stay at them anyway. Persecuted saints in particular would need places to stay where they could be assisted and encouraged.

Hospitality is a virtue that is commanded and commended throughout the Scriptures. Moses included it in the law (Ex. 22:21; Deut. 14:28–29). Jesus enjoyed hospitality when He was on earth, and so did the apostles in their ministry (Acts 28:7; Philem. 22). Human hospitality is a reflection of God's hospitality to us (Luke 14:16ff.). Christian leaders in particular should be "given to hospitality" (1 Tim. 3:2; Titus 1:8).

Abraham was hospitable to three strangers and discovered that he had entertained the Lord and two angels (Gen. 18; Heb. 13:2). We help to promote the truth when we open our homes to God's servants (3 John 5–8). In fact, when we share with others, we share with Christ (Matt. 25:35, 43). We should not open our homes to others just so that others will invite us over (Luke 14:12–14). We should do it to glorify the Lord.

In my own itinerant ministry, I have often had the joy of staying in Christian homes. I have appreciated the kindness and (in some cases) sacrifice of dear saints who loved Christ and wanted to share with others. My wife and I have made new friends in many countries, and our children have been blessed, because we have both enjoyed and practiced Christian hospitality.

Finally, Christian love must result in service. Each Christian has at least one spiritual gift that he must use to the glory of God and the building up of the church (see Rom. 12:1–13; 1 Cor. 12; Eph. 4:1–16). We are stewards. God has entrusted these gifts to us that we might use them for the good of His church. He even gives us the spiritual ability to develop our gifts and be faithful servants of the church.

There are speaking gifts and there are serving gifts, and both are important to the church. Not everybody is a teacher or preacher, though all can be witnesses for Christ. There are those "behind-the-scenes" ministries that help to make the public ministries possible. God gives us the gifts, the abilities, and the opportunities to use the gifts, and He alone must get the glory.

The phrase "oracles of God" in 1 Peter 4:11 does not suggest that everything a preacher or teacher says today is God's truth, because human speakers are fallible. In the early church, there were prophets who had the special gift of uttering God's Word, but we do not have this gift today since the Word of God has been completed. Whoever shares God's Word must be careful about what he says and how he says it, and all must conform to the written Word of God.

While on our way home from the African trip I mentioned at the beginning of this chapter, we were delayed in London by a typical English fog. London is one of my favorite places, so I was not disturbed a bit! But the delay gave my wife and me the opportunity to show London to a couple who were traveling with us. Imagine trying to see that marvelous city in one day!

We had to make the most of the time—and we did! Our friends saw many exciting sites in the city.

How long is "the rest of your time"? Only God knows.

Don't waste it! Invest it by doing the will of God.

CHAPTER TEN
1 Peter 4:12–19
FACTS ABOUT FURNACES

Every Christian who lives a godly life experiences a certain amount of persecution. On the job, in school, in the neighborhood, perhaps even in the family, there are people who resist the truth and oppose the gospel of Christ. No matter what a believer says or does, these people find fault and criticize. Peter dealt with this kind of "normal persecution" in the previous part of his letter.

But in this section, Peter explained about a special kind of persecution—a "fiery trial"—that was about to overtake the entire church. It would not be occasional personal persecution from those around them, but *official* persecution from those above them. Thus far, Christianity had been tolerated by Rome because it was considered a "sect" of Judaism, and the Jews were permitted to worship freely. That attitude would change and the fires of persecution would be ignited, first by Nero, and then by the emperors that followed.

Peter gave the believers four instructions to follow in the light of the coming "fiery trial."

Expect Suffering (4:12)
Persecution is not something that is alien to the Christian life. Throughout history the people of God have suffered at the hands of the unbelieving world. Christians are different from unbelievers (2 Cor. 6:14–18), and this different kind of life produces a different kind of lifestyle. Much of what goes on in the world depends on lies, pride, pleasure, and the desire to "get more." A dedicated Christian builds his life on truth, humility, holiness, and the desire to glorify God.

This conflict is illustrated throughout the Bible. Cain was a religious man, yet he hated his brother and killed him (Gen. 4:1–8). The world does not persecute "religious people," but it does persecute righteous people. Why Cain killed Abel is explained in 1 John 3:12: "Because his own works were evil, and his brother's righteous." The Pharisees and Jewish leaders were religious people, yet they crucified Christ and persecuted the early church. "But beware of men," Jesus warned His disciples, "for they will deliver you up to the councils, and they will scourge you in their synagogues"

(Matt. 10:17). Imagine scourging the servants of God in the very house of God!

God declared war on Satan after the fall of man (Gen. 3:15), and Satan has been attacking God through His people ever since. Christians are "strangers and pilgrims" in an alien world where Satan is the god and prince (John 14:30; 2 Cor. 4:3–4). Whatever glorifies God will anger the enemy, and he will attack. For believers, persecution is not a strange thing. The *absence* of satanic opposition would be strange!

Jesus explained to His disciples that they should expect opposition and persecution from the world (John 15:17—16:4). But He also gave them an encouraging promise: "In the world ye shall have tribulation: but be of good cheer; I have overcome the world" (John 16:33). It was through His death on the cross of Calvary, plus His resurrection, that He overcame sin and the world (John 12:23–33; see Gal. 6:14).

The image of "fire" is often applied to testing or persecution even in modern conversation. "He is really going through the fire," is a typical statement to describe someone experiencing personal difficulties. In the Old Testament, fire was a symbol of the holiness of God and the presence of God. The fire on the altar consumed the sacrifice (Heb. 12:28–29). But Peter saw in the image of fire *a refining process* rather than a divine judgment (see Job 23:10; 1 Peter 1:7).

It is important to note that not all of the difficulties of life are necessarily fiery trials. There are some difficulties that are simply a part of human life and almost everybody experiences them. Unfortunately, there are some difficulties that we bring on ourselves because of disobedience and sin. Peter mentioned these in 1 Peter 2:18–20 and 3:13–17. The fiery trial he mentioned in 1 Peter 4:12 comes because we are faithful to God and stand up for that which is right. It is because we bear the name of Christ that the lost world attacks us. Christ told His disciples that people would persecute them, as they had Him, because their persecutors did not know God (John 15:20–21).

The word *happened* is important; it means "to go together." Persecution and trials do not just "happen," in the sense of being accidents. They are a part of God's plan, and He is in control. They are a part of Romans 8:28 and will work out for good if we let God have His way.

Rejoice in Suffering (4:13–14)
Literally, Peter wrote, "Be constantly rejoicing!" In fact, he mentioned joy in one form or another *four times* in these two verses! "Rejoice … be glad also with exceeding joy.…Happy are ye!" The world cannot understand how difficult circumstances can produce exceeding joy, because the world has never experienced the grace of God (see 2 Cor. 8:1–5). Peter named several privileges that we share that encourage us to rejoice in the midst of the fiery trial.

Our suffering means fellowship with Christ (v. 13). It is an honor and a privilege to suffer *with* Christ and be treated by the world the way it treated Him. "The fellowship of his sufferings" is a gift from God (Phil. 1:29; 3:10). Not every believer grows to the point where God can trust him with this kind of experience, so we ought to rejoice when the privilege comes to us. "And they [the apostles] departed from the presence of the council, rejoicing that they were counted worthy to suffer shame for his name" (Acts 5:41).

Christ is with us in the furnace of persecution (Isa. 41:10; 43:2). When the three Hebrew children were cast into the fiery furnace, they discovered they were not alone (Dan. 3:23–25). The Lord was with Paul in all of his trials (Acts 23:11; 27:21–25; 2 Tim. 4:9–18), and He promises to be with us "to the end of the age" (Matt. 28:20 NASB). In fact, when sinners persecute us, they are really persecuting Jesus Christ (Acts 9:4).

Our suffering means glory in the future (v. 13). "Suffering" and "glory" are twin truths that are woven into the fabric of Peter's letter. The world believes that the *absence* of suffering means glory, but a Christian's outlook is different. The trial of our faith today is the assurance of glory when Jesus returns (1 Peter 1:7–8). This was the experience of our Lord (1 Peter 5:1), and it shall also be our experience.

But it is necessary to understand that God is not going to *replace* suffering with glory; rather He will *transform* suffering into glory. Jesus used the illustration of a woman giving birth (John 16:20–22). The same baby that gave her pain also gave her joy. The pain was *transformed* into joy by the birth of the baby. The thorn in the flesh that gave Paul difficulty also gave him power and glory (2 Cor. 12:7–10). The cross that gave Jesus shame and pain also brought power and glory.

Mature people know that life includes some "postponed pleasures." We pay a price *today* in order to have enjoyments in *the future*. The piano student may not enjoy practicing scales by the hour, but he looks forward to the pleasure of playing beautiful music one day. The athlete may not enjoy exercising and practicing his skills, but he looks forward to winning the game by doing his best. Christians have something even better our very sufferings will one day be transformed into glory, and we will be "glad also with exceeding joy" (see Rom. 8:17; 2 Tim. 3:11).

Our suffering brings to us the ministry of the Holy Spirit (v. 14). He is the Spirit of glory and He has a special ministry to those who suffer for the glory of Jesus Christ. This verse can be translated "for the presence of the glory, even the Spirit, rests on you." The reference is to the Shekinah glory of God that dwelt in the tabernacle and in the temple (Ex. 40:34; 1 Kings 8:10–11). When the people stoned Stephen, he saw Jesus in heaven and experienced God's glory (Acts 6:15; 7:54–60). This is the "joy unspeakable and full of glory" that Peter wrote about in 1 Peter 1:7–8.

In other words, suffering Christians do not have to wait for heaven in order to experience His glory. Through the Holy Spirit, *they can have the glory now.*

This explains how martyrs could sing praises to God while bound in the midst of blazing fires. It also explains how persecuted Christians (and there are many in today's world) can go to prison and to death without complaining or resisting their captors.

Our suffering enables us to glorify His name (v. 14). We suffer because of His name (John 15:21). You can tell your unsaved friends that you are Baptist, a Presbyterian, a Methodist, or even an agnostic, and there will be no opposition; but tell them you are a *Christian*—bring Christ's name into the conversation—and things will start to happen. Our authority is in the name of Jesus, and Satan hates that name. Every time we are reproached for the name of Christ, we have the opportunity to bring glory to that name. The world may speak against His name, but we will so speak and live that His name will be honored and God will be pleased.

The word *Christian* is found only three times in the entire New Testament (1 Peter 4:16; Acts 11:26; 26:28). The name was originally given by the enemies of the church as a term of reproach, but in time, it became an honored name. Of course, in today's world, the word *Christian* means to most people the opposite of "pagan." But the word carries the idea of "a Christ one, belonging to Christ." Certainly it is a privilege to bear the name and to suffer for His name's sake (Acts 5:41).

Polycarp was the Bishop of Smyrna about the middle of the second century. He was arrested for his faith and threatened with death if he did not recant. "Eighty and six years have I served Him," the saintly bishop replied, "and He never did me any injury. How can I blaspheme my King and my Savior?"

"I have respect for your age," said the Roman officer. "Simply say, 'Away with the atheists!' and be set free." By "the atheists" he meant the Christians who would not acknowledge that Caesar was "lord."

The old man pointed to the crowd of Roman pagans surrounding him, and cried, "Away with the atheists!" He was burned at the stake and in his martyrdom brought glory to the name of Jesus Christ.

Examine Your Life (4:15–18)

In the furnace of persecution and suffering, we often have more light by which we can examine our lives and ministries. The fiery trial is a refining process, by which God removes the dross and purifies us. One day, a fiery judgment will overtake the whole world (2 Peter 3:7–16). Meanwhile, God's judgment begins "at the house of God," the church (1 Peter 2:5). This truth ought to motivate us to be as pure and obedient as possible (see Ezek. 9 for an Old Testament illustration of this truth). There are several questions we should ask ourselves as we examine our own lives.

Why am I suffering (v. 15)? We noted before that not all suffering is a "fiery trial" from the Lord. If a professed Christian breaks the law and gets into trouble or becomes a meddler into other people's lives, then he *ought* to suffer! The fact that we are Christians is not a guarantee that we escape the normal consequences of our misdeeds. We may not be guilty of murder (though anger can be the same as murder in the heart, Matt. 5:21–26), but what about stealing or meddling? When Abraham, David, Peter, and other Bible "greats" disobeyed God, they suffered for it; so, who are we that we should escape? Let's be sure we are suffering because we are Christians and not because we are criminals.

Am I ashamed, or glorifying Christ? (v. 16) This statement must have reminded Peter of his own denial of Christ (Luke 22:54–62). Jesus Christ is not ashamed of us (Heb. 2:11)—though many times He surely could be! The Father is not ashamed to be called our God (Heb. 11:16). On the cross Jesus Christ despised shame for us (Heb. 12:2), so surely we can bear reproach for Him and not be ashamed. The warning in Mark 8:38 is worth pondering.

"Not be ashamed" is negative; "glorify God" is positive. It takes both for a balanced witness. If we seek to glorify God, then we will not be ashamed of the name of Jesus Christ. It was this determination not to be ashamed that encouraged Paul when he went to Rome (Rom. 1:16), when he suffered in Rome (Phil. 1:20–21), and when he faced martyrdom in Rome (2 Tim. 1:12).

Am I seeking to win the lost (vv. 17–18)? Note the words that Peter used to describe the lost: "Them that obey not the gospel.… the ungodly and the sinner." The argument of this verse is clear: If God sends a "fiery trial" to His own children, and they are saved "with difficulty," what will happen to lost sinners when God's fiery judgment falls?

When a believer suffers, he experiences glory and knows that there will be greater glory in the future. But a sinner who causes that suffering is only filling up the measure of God's wrath more and more (Matt. 23:29–33). Instead of being concerned only about ourselves, we need to be concerned about the lost sinners around us. Our present "fiery trial" is nothing compared with the "flaming fire" that shall punish the lost when Jesus returns in judgment (2 Thess. 1:7–10). The idea is expressed in Proverbs 11:31—"If the righteous receive their due on earth, how much more the ungodly and the sinner!" (NIV).

The phrase *scarcely be saved* means "saved with difficulty," but it does not suggest that God is too weak to save us. The reference is probably to Genesis 19:15–26, when God sought to rescue Lot from Sodom before the city was destroyed. God was able—but Lot was unwilling! He lingered, argued with the angels, and finally had to be taken by the hand and dragged out of the city! Lot was "saved as by fire" and everything he lived for went up in smoke (see 1 Cor. 3:9–15).

Times of persecution are times of opportunity for a loving witness to those who persecute us (see Matt. 5:10–12, 43–48). It was not the earthquake that brought that Philippian jailer to Christ, because that frightened him into almost committing suicide! No,

it was Paul's loving concern for him that brought the jailer to faith in Christ. As Christians, we do not seek for vengeance on those who have hurt us. Rather, we pray for them and seek to lead them to Jesus Christ.

Commit Yourself to God (4:19)

When we are suffering in the will of God, we can commit ourselves into the care of God. Everything else that we do as Christians depends on this. The word is a banking term; it means "to deposit for safekeeping" (see 2 Tim. 1:12). Of course, when you deposit your life in God's bank, you always receive eternal dividends on your investment.

This picture reminds us that we are valuable to God. He made us, redeemed us, lives in us, guards, and protects us. I saw a savings and loan association advertisement in the newspaper, reaffirming the financial stability of the firm and the backing of the Federal Deposit Insurance Corporation. In days of financial unsteadiness, such assurances are necessary to depositors. But when you "deposit" your life with God, you have nothing to fear, for He is able to keep you.

This commitment is not a single action but a constant attitude. "Be constantly committing" is the force of the admonition. How do we do this? "By means of welldoing." As we return good for evil and do good even though we suffer for it, we are committing ourselves to God so that He can care for us. This commitment involves every area of our lives and every hour of our lives.

If we really have hope, and believe that Jesus is coming again, then we will obey His Word and start laying up treasures and glory in heaven. Unsaved people have a present that is controlled by their past, but Christians have a present that is controlled by the future (Phil. 3:12–21). In our very serving, we are committing ourselves to God and making investments for the future.

There is a striking illustration of this truth in Jeremiah 32. The prophet Jeremiah had been telling the people that one day their situation would change and they would be restored to their land. But at that time, the Babylonian army occupied the land and was about to take Jerusalem. Jeremiah's cousin, Hanamel, gave Jeremiah an option to purchase the family land, *which was now occupied by enemy soldiers.* The prophet had to "put his money where his mouth was." And he did it! As an act of faith, he purchased the land and became, no doubt, the laughingstock of the people in Jerusalem. But God honored his faith because Jeremiah lived according to the Word that he preached.

Why did Peter refer to God as "a faithful Creator" rather than "a faithful Judge" or even "a faithful Savior"? Because God the Creator meets the needs of His people (Matt. 6:24–34). It is the Creator who provides food and clothing to persecuted Christians, and who protects them in times of danger. When the early church was persecuted, they met together for prayer and addressed the Lord as the "God, which hast made heaven, and earth, and the sea, and all that in them is" (Acts 4:24). They prayed to the Creator!

Our heavenly Father is "the Lord of heaven and earth" (Matt. 11:25). With that kind of a Father, we have no need to worry! He is the *faithful* Creator, and His faithfulness will not fail.

Before God pours out His wrath on this evil world, a "fiery trial" will come to God's church, to unite and purify it, that it might be a strong witness to the lost. There is nothing for us to fear if we are suffering in the will of God. Our faithful Father-Creator will victoriously see us through!

CHAPTER ELEVEN
1 Peter 5:1–4
HOW TO BE A GOOD SHEPHERD

Times of persecution demand that God's people have adequate spiritual leadership. If judgment is to begin at God's house (1 Peter 4:17), then that house had better be in order, or it will fall apart! This explains why Peter wrote this special message to the leaders of the church, to encourage them to do their work faithfully. Leaders who run away in times of difficulty are only proving that they are hirelings and not true shepherds (John 10:12–14).

The New Testament assemblies were organized under the leadership of elders and deacons (1 Tim. 3). The words *elder* and *bishop* refer to the same office (Acts 20:17, 28). The word *bishop* is often translated "overseer" (see 1 Peter 5:2, and note that this title is applied to Christ in 1 Peter 2:25). "Elder" refers to the maturity of the officer, and "bishop" to the responsibility of the office. The word *pastor* (which means "shepherd") is another title for this same office (Eph. 4:11). The elders were appointed to office (Acts 14:23, where the verb "ordain" means "to appoint by the raising of hands"). Apparently each congregation had the privilege of voting on qualified men.

Peter was concerned that the leadership in the local churches be at its best. When the fiery trial would come, the believers in the assemblies would look to their elders for encouragement and direction. What are the personal qualities that make for a successful pastor?

A Vital Personal Experience with Christ (5:1)
Peter did not introduce himself in this letter as an apostle or a great spiritual leader, but simply as another elder. However, he did mention the fact that he had personally witnessed Christ's sufferings (see Matt. 26:36ff). The Greek word translated "witness" gives us our English word *martyr*. We think of a martyr only as one who gives his life for Christ, and Peter did that, but basically, a martyr is a witness who tells what he has seen and heard.

It is interesting to read 1 Peter 5 in the light of Peter's personal experiences with Christ. First Peter

5:1 takes us to Gethsemane and Calvary. "The glory that shall be revealed" reminds us of Peter's experience with Christ on the Mount of Transfiguration (Matt. 17:1–5; 2 Peter 1:15–18). The emphasis in 1 Peter 5:2 on the shepherd and the sheep certainly brings to mind John 10 and our Lord's admonition to Peter in John 21:15–17.

The warning in 1 Peter 5:3 about "lording it over" the saints reminds us of Christ's lesson about true greatness in Luke 22:24–30, as well as the other times that He taught His disciples about humility and service. The phrase in 1 Peter 5:5, "Be clothed with humility," takes us back to the Upper Room where Jesus put on the towel and washed the disciples' feet (John 13:1–17).

The warning about Satan in 1 Peter 5:8 parallels our Lord's warning to Peter that Satan was going to "sift" him and the other apostles (Luke 22:31). Peter did not heed that warning, and he ended up denying his Lord three times.

It is interesting to note that the verb "make you perfect" (1 Peter 5:10) is translated "mending their nets" in Matthew 4:21, the account of the call of the four fishermen into the Lord's service.

In other words, Peter wrote these words, inspired by the Spirit of God, out of his own personal experience with Jesus Christ. He had a vital and growing relationship with Christ, and this made it possible for him to minister effectively to God's people.

The pastor of the local assembly must be a man who walks with God and who is growing in his spiritual life. Paul admonished young Timothy: "Be diligent in these matters; give yourself wholly to them, so that everyone may see your progress" (1 Tim. 4:15 NIV). The word *progress* in the original means "pioneer advance." The elders must constantly be moving into new territories of study, achievement, and ministry. If the leaders of the church are not moving forward, the church will not move forward.

"We love our pastor," a fine church member said to me during a conference, "but we get tired of the same thing all the time. He repeats himself and doesn't seem to know that there are other books in the Bible besides Psalms and Revelation." That man needed to become a "spiritual pioneer" and move into new territory, so that he might lead his people into new blessings and challenges.

Sometimes God permits trials to come to a church so that the people will be *forced* to grow and discover new truths and new opportunities. Certainly Peter grew in his spiritual experience as he suffered for Christ in the city of Jerusalem. He was not perfect by any means; in fact, Paul had to rebuke him once for inconsistency (Gal. 2:11–21). But Peter was yielded to Christ and willing to learn all that God had for him.

If I have any counsel for God's shepherds today, it is this: cultivate a growing relationship with Jesus Christ, and share what He gives you with your people. That way, you will grow, and they will grow with you.

A Loving Concern for God's Sheep (5:2–3)

The image of the flock is often used in the Bible, and it is a very instructive one (see Ps. 23; 100; Isa. 40:11; Luke 15:4–6; John 10; Acts 20:28; Heb. 13:20–21; 1 Peter 2:25; Rev. 7:17). We were once stray sheep, wandering toward ruin, but the Good Shepherd found us and restored us to the fold.

Sheep are clean animals, unlike dogs and pigs (2 Peter 2:20–22). Sheep tend to flock together, and God's people need to be together. Sheep are notoriously ignorant and prone to wander away if they do not follow the shepherd. Sheep are defenseless, for the most part, and need their shepherd to protect them (Ps. 23:4).

Sheep are very useful animals. Jewish shepherds tended their sheep, not for the meat (which would have been costly) but for the wool, milk, and lambs. God's people should be useful to Him and certainly ought to "reproduce" themselves by bringing others to Christ. Sheep were used for the sacrifices, and we ought to be "living sacrifices," doing the will of God (Rom. 12:1–2).

Peter reminded the shepherd-elders of their God-given responsibilities.

Feed the flock of God (v. 2). The word *feed* means "shepherd, care for." The shepherd had many tasks to perform in caring for the flock. He had to protect the sheep from thieves and marauders, and the pastor must protect God's people from those who want to spoil the flock (Acts 20:28–35). Sometimes the sheep do not like it when their shepherd rebukes or warns them, but this ministry is for their own good.

A faithful shepherd not only protected his flock, but he also led them from pasture to pasture so that they might be adequately fed. The shepherd always went before the flock and searched out the land so that there would be nothing there to harm his flock. He would check for snakes, pits, poisonous plants, and dangerous animals. How important it is for pastors to lead their people into the green pastures of the Word of God so that they might feed themselves and grow.

Sometimes it was necessary for a shepherd to seek out a wayward sheep and give it personal attention. Some pastors today are interested only in the crowds; they have no time for individuals. Jesus preached to great multitudes, but He took time to chat with Nicodemus (John 3), the woman at the well (John 4), and others who had spiritual needs. Paul ministered to people *personally* in Thessalonica (1 Thess. 2:11) and loved them dearly.

If a sheep is too rebellious, the shepherd may have to discipline him in some way. If a sheep has a special need, the shepherd might carry it in his arms, next to his heart. At the close of each day, the faithful shepherd would examine each sheep to see if it needed special attention. He would anoint the bruises with healing oil and remove the briars from the wool. A good shepherd would know each of his sheep by name and would understand the special traits of each one.

It is not an easy thing to be a faithful shepherd of God's sheep! It is a task that never ends and that demands the supernatural power of God if it is to be done correctly. What makes it even more challenging is the fact that the flock is not the shepherd's; it is God's. I sometimes hear pastors say, "Well, at *my* church …," and I know what they mean; but strictly speaking, it is *God's* flock, purchased by the precious blood of His Son (Acts 20:28). We pastors must be careful how we minister to *God's* sheep, because one day we will have to give an account of our ministry. But the sheep will also one day give an account of how they have obeyed their spiritual leaders (Heb. 13:17), so both shepherds and sheep have a great responsibility to each other.

Take the oversight (v. 2). The word *bishop* means "overseer, one who looks over for the purpose of leading." You will notice that the shepherd is both "among" and "over," and this can create problems if the sheep do not understand. Because he is one of the sheep, the pastor is "among" the members of the flock. But because he is called to be a leader, the pastor is "over" the flock. Some people try to emphasize the "among" relationship and refuse to follow the authority of the shepherd. Others want to put the pastor on a pedestal and make him a "super saint" who never mixes with the people.

The effective pastor needs both relationships. He must be "among" his people so that he can get to know them, their needs and problems, and he needs to be "over" his people so he can lead them and help them solve their problems. There must be no conflict between *pastoring* and *preaching,* because they are both ministries of a faithful Shepherd. The preacher needs to be a pastor so he can apply the Word to the needs of the people. The pastor needs to be a preacher so that he can have authority when he shares in their daily needs and problems. The pastor is not a religious lecturer who weekly passes along information about the Bible. He is a shepherd who knows his people and seeks to help them through the Word.

Being the spiritual leader of a flock has its dangers, and Peter pointed out some of the sins that the elders must avoid. The first was *laziness*—"not by constraint but willingly." His ministry must not be a job that he has to perform. He should do God's will from his heart (Eph. 6:6). Dr. George W. Truett was pastor of First Baptist Church in Dallas, Texas for nearly fifty years. Often he was asked to accept other positions, and he refused, saying, "I have sought and found a pastor's heart." When a man has a pastor's heart, he loves the sheep and serves them because he *wants* to, not because he *has* to.

If a man has no conscience, the ministry is a good place to be lazy. Church members rarely ask what their pastor is doing with his time, and he can "borrow" sermons from other preachers and use them as his own. I met one pastor who spent most of his week on the golf course; then on Saturday he listened to tapes of other preachers and used their sermons on Sunday. He seems to be getting away with it, but what will he say when he meets the Chief Shepherd?

Next to laziness, the shepherd must beware of *covetousness*—"not for filthy lucre, but of a ready mind." It is perfectly proper for the church to pay the pastor (1 Cor. 9; 1 Tim. 5:17–18), and they ought to be as fair and generous as possible. But making money must not be the main motive for his ministry. Paul stressed this in his qualifications for an elder: "not greedy of filthy lucre" (1 Tim. 3:3); "not given to filthy lucre" (Titus 1:7). He must not be a lover of money nor devote himself to pursuing money.

Because of family or church situations, some pastors have to engage in outside employment. Paul was a tentmaker, so there is no disgrace in "moonlighting." But, as soon as possible, the members of the church ought to relieve their pastor of outside employment so he can devote himself fully to the ministry of the Word. Pastors need to beware of getting involved in money-making schemes that detour them from their ministry. "No one serving as a soldier gets involved in civilian affairs—he wants to please his commanding officer" (2 Tim. 2:4 NIV).

The phrase "a ready mind" means "an eager mind." It is the same word Paul used in Romans 1:15—"I am so eager to preach the gospel" (NIV). It means a willingness to serve because of a readiness and an eagerness within the heart. This is the difference between a true shepherd and a hireling: a hireling works because he is paid for it, but a shepherd works because he loves the sheep and has a heart devoted to them. Read Acts 20:17–38 for a description of the heart and ministry of a true shepherd.

Be an example to the flock (v. 3). The contrast is between *dictatorship* and *leadership.* You cannot drive sheep; you must go before them and lead them. It has been well said that the church needs leaders who serve and servants who lead. A Christian leader said to me, "The trouble today is that we have too many celebrities and not enough servants."

It is by being an example that the shepherd solves the tension between being "among" the sheep and "over" the sheep. People are willing to follow a leader who practices what he preaches and gives them a good example to imitate. I know of a church that was constantly having financial problems, and no one could understand why. After the pastor left, it was discovered that he had not himself contributed to the work of the church but had preached sermons telling others to contribute. We cannot lead people where we have not been ourselves.

Peter was not changing the image when he called the church "God's heritage." The people of God are certainly His priceless possession (Deut. 32:9; Ps. 33:12). This word means "to be chosen by lot," as the dividing up of land (Num. 26:55). Each elder has his own flock to care for, but the sheep all belong to the one flock of which Jesus Christ is the Chief Shepherd. The Lord assigns His workers to the places of His choosing, and we must all be submissive to Him. There is no competition in the work of God when you are serving in the will of God. Therefore, nobody has to act important and "lord it over" God's people. Pastors are to be "overseers" and not "overlords."

A Desire to Please Christ Alone (5:4)

Since this is the epistle of hope, Peter brought in once again the promise of the Lord's return. His coming is an encouragement in suffering (1 Peter 1:7–8) and a motivation for faithful service. If a pastor ministers to please himself or to please people, he will have a disappointing and difficult ministry. "It must be hard to keep all these people happy," a visitor said to me after a church service. "I don't even try to keep them happy," I replied with a smile. "I try to please the Lord, and I let Him take care of the rest."

Jesus Christ is the *Good* Shepherd who died for the sheep (John 10:11), the *Great* Shepherd who lives for the sheep (Heb. 13:20–21), and the *Chief* Shepherd who comes for the sheep (1 Peter 5:4). As the Chief Shepherd, He alone can assess a man's ministry and give him the proper reward. Some who appear to be first may end up last when the Lord examines each man's ministry.

One summer day, I stood amid the ruins of a church near Anwoth in Scotland. The building at one time seated perhaps 150 people. By modern standards, it would not have been a successful church. But the man who pastored that flock was the saintly Samuel Rutherford, whose *Letters of Samuel Rutherford* is a spiritual classic. His ministry continues, though today his church building is in ruins. The Chief Shepherd has rewarded him for his faithful labors, which included a great deal of persecution and physical suffering.

There were several kinds of "crowns" in those days. The one Peter mentioned was the athlete's crown, usually a garland of leaves or flowers that would quickly fade away. The faithful pastor's crown is a crown of glory, a perfect reward for an *inheritance* that will never fade away (1 Peter 1:4).

Today a Christian worker may labor for many different kinds of rewards. Some work hard to build personal empires; others strive for the applause of men; still others seek promotion in their denomination. All of these things will fade one day. The only reward we ought to strive for is the "Well done!" of the Savior and the unfading crown of glory that goes with it. What a joy it will be to place the crown at His feet (Rev. 4:10) and acknowledge that all we did was because of His grace and power (1 Cor. 15:10; 1 Peter 4:11). We will have no desire for personal glory when we see Jesus Christ face-to-face.

Everything in the local church rises or falls with leadership. No matter how large or small a fellowship might be, the leaders must be Christians, each with a vital personal relationship with Christ, a loving concern for their people, and a real desire to please Jesus Christ.

We lead by serving, and we serve by suffering.

This is the way Jesus did it, and this is the only way that truly glorifies Him.

CHAPTER TWELVE
1 Peter 5:5–14
FROM GRACE TO GLORY!

When World War II was being fought, I was a junior high school student, and the fighting seemed very far away from our northern Indiana city. But then the city began to organize Civil Defense units in each neighborhood, and officials appointed my father an assistant block captain. Often I went with him to watch the training films and listen to the speakers. (The best part of the evening was stopping for an ice cream cone!) But, no matter how many films we watched, we somehow didn't feel that our neighborhood was in danger of being bombed. Our philosophy was "It can't happen here."

Peter knew that a "fiery trial" was about to occur, and he wanted the entire church family to be prepared. As he closed his letter, Peter gave the church three important admonitions to obey if they were to glorify God in this difficult experience.

Be Humble (5:5–7)
He had already admonished the saints to be submissive to government authorities (1 Peter 2:13–17), the slaves to submit to their masters (1 Peter 2:18–25), and the wives to submit to their husbands (1 Peter 3:1–7). Now he commanded all of the believers to submit to God and to each other.

The younger believers should submit to the older believers, not only out of respect for their age, but also out of respect for their spiritual maturity. Not every "senior saint" is a mature Christian, of course, because quantity of years is no guarantee of quality of experience. This is not to suggest that the older church members "run the church" and never listen to the younger members! Too often there is a generation war in the church, with the older people resisting change, and the younger people resisting the older people!

The solution is twofold: (1) all believers, young and old, should submit to each other; (2) all should submit to God. "Be clothed with humility" is the answer to the problem. Just as Jesus laid aside His outer garments and put on a towel to become a servant, so each of us should have a servant's attitude and minister to each other. True humility is described in Philippians 2:1–11. Humility is not demeaning ourselves and thinking poorly of ourselves. It is simply not thinking of ourselves at all!

We can never be submissive to each other until we are first submissive to God. Peter quoted Proverbs 3:34 to defend his point, a verse that is also quoted in James 4:6. It takes grace to submit to another believer, but God can give that grace *if* we humble ourselves before Him.

God resists the proud because God hates the sin of pride (Prov. 6:16–17; 8:13). It was pride that turned Lucifer into Satan (Isa. 14:12–15). It was pride—a desire to be like God—that stirred Eve to take the forbidden fruit. "The pride of life" is an evidence of worldliness (1 John 2:16). The only antidote to pride is the grace of God, and we receive that grace when we yield ourselves to Him. The evidence of that grace is that we yield to one another.

Submission is an act of faith. We are trusting God to direct in our lives and to work out His purposes in His time. After all, there is a danger in submitting to others; they might take advantage of us—but not if we trust God and if we are submitted to one another! A person who is truly yielded to God, and who wants to serve his fellow Christians, would not even think of taking advantage of someone else, saved or unsaved. The "mighty hand of God" that directs our lives can also direct in the lives of others.

The key, of course, is the phrase "in due time." God never exalts anyone until that person is ready for it. First the cross, then the crown; first the suffering, then the glory. Moses was under God's hand for forty years before God sent him to deliver the Jews from Egypt. Joseph was under God's hand for at least thirteen years before God lifted him to the throne. One of the evidences of our pride is our impatience with God, and one reason for suffering is that we might learn patience (James 1:1–6). Here Peter was referring to words he heard the Master say: "For whosoever exalteth himself shall be abased; and he that humbleth himself shall be exalted" (Luke 14:11).

One of the benefits of this kind of relationship with God is the privilege of letting Him take care of our burdens. Unless we meet the conditions laid down in 1 Peter 5:5–6, we cannot claim the wonderful promise of 1 Peter 5:7. The word translated "care" means "anxiety, the state of being pulled apart." When circumstances are difficult, it is easy for us to be anxious and worried, but if we are, we will miss God's blessing and become poor witnesses to the lost. We need His inward peace if we are going to triumph in the fiery trial and bring glory to His name. Dr. George Morrison said, "God does not make His children carefree in order that they be careless."

According to 1 Peter 5:7, we must *once and for all* give all of our cares—past, present, and future—to the Lord. We must not hand them to Him piecemeal, keeping those cares that we think we can handle ourselves. If we keep "the little cares" for ourselves, they will soon become big problems! Each time a new burden arises, we must by faith remind the Lord (and ourselves) that we have already turned it over to Him.

If anybody knew from experience that God cares for His own, it was Peter! When you read the four gospels, you discover that Peter shared in some wonderful miracles. Jesus healed Peter's mother-in-law (Mark

1:29–31), gave him a great catch of fish (Luke 5:1–11), helped him pay his temple tax (Matt. 17:24–27), helped him walk on the water (Matt. 14:22–33), repaired the damage he did to the ear of Malchus (Luke 22:50–51; John 18:10–11), and even delivered Peter from prison (Acts 12).

How does God show His love and care for us when we give our cares to Him? I believe that He performs four wonderful ministries on our behalf: (1) He gives us the courage to face our cares honestly and not run away (Isa. 41:10); (2) He gives us the wisdom to understand the situation (James 1:5); (3) He gives us the strength to do what we must do (Phil. 4:13); and (4) He gives us the faith to trust Him to do the rest (Ps. 37:5).

Some people give God their burdens and expect Him to do everything! It is important that we let Him work in us as well as work for us, so that we will be prepared when the answer comes. "Cast thy burden upon the Lord, and he shall sustain thee" (Ps. 55:22).

Be Watchful (5:8–9)

One reason we have cares is because we have an enemy. As the serpent, Satan deceives (2 Cor. 11:3), and as the lion, Satan devours. The word *Satan* means "adversary," and the word *devil* means "the accuser, the slanderer." The recipients of this letter had already experienced the attacks of the slanderer (1 Peter 4:4, 14), and now they would meet "the lion" in their fiery trial. Peter gave them several practical instructions to help them get victory over their adversary.

Respect him—he is dangerous. Since I have no mechanical ability, I admire people who can build and repair things. During a church building program, I was watching an electrician install a complex control panel. I said to the man, "It just amazes me how you fellows can calmly work on those lines with all of that power there. How do you do it?" The electrician smiled and said, "Well, the first thing you have to do is respect it. Then you can handle it."

Satan is a dangerous enemy. He is a serpent who can bite us when we least expect it. He is a destroyer (*Abaddon* and *Apollyon* both mean "destruction") and an accuser (Zech. 3:1–5; Rev. 12:9–11). He has great power and intelligence, and a host of demons who assist him in his attacks against God's people (Eph. 6:10ff.). He is a formidable enemy; we must never joke about him, ignore him, or underestimate his ability. We must "be sober" and have our minds under control when it comes to our conflict with Satan.

A part of this soberness includes not blaming everything on the devil. Some people see a demon behind every bush and blame Satan for their headaches, flat tires, and high rent. While it is true that Satan can inflict physical sickness and pain (Luke 13:16; and the book of Job), we have no biblical authority for casting out "demons of headache" or "demons of backache." One lady phoned me long distance to inform me that Satan had caused her to shrink seven and a half inches.

While I have great respect for the wiles and powers of the devil, I still feel we must get our information about him from the Bible and not from our own interpretation of experiences.

Recognize him—he is a great pretender (John 8:44; 2 Cor. 11:13–15). Because he is a subtle foe, we must "be vigilant" and always on guard. His strategy is to counterfeit whatever God does. According to the parable of the tares, wherever God plants a true Christian, Satan seeks to plant a counterfeit (Matt. 13:24–30, 36–43). He would deceive us were it not for the Word of God and the Spirit of God (1 John 2:18–27). The better we know God's Word, the keener our spiritual senses will be to detect Satan at work. We must be able to "try the spirits" and know the true from the false (1 John 4:1–6).

Resist him. This means that we take our stand on the Word of God and refuse to be moved. Ephesians 6:10–13 instructs us to "stand … withstand … stand." Unless we stand, we cannot withstand. Our weapons are the Word of God and prayer (Eph. 6:17–18) and our protection is the complete armor God has provided. We resist him "in the faith," that is, our faith in God. Just as David took his stand against Goliath and trusted in the name of Jehovah, so we take our stand against Satan in the victorious name of Jesus Christ.

A word of caution here: never discuss things with Satan or his associates. Eve made this mistake, and we all know the sad consequences. Also, never try to fight Satan in your own way. Resist him the way Jesus did, with the Word of God (Matt. 4:1–11). Never get the idea that you are the only one going through these battles, because "your brethren that are in the world" are facing the same trials. We must pray for one another and encourage each other in the Lord. And we must remember that our personal victories will help others, just as their victories will help us.

Had Peter obeyed these three instructions the night Jesus was arrested, he would not have gone to sleep in the garden of Gethsemane, attacked Malchus, or denied the Lord. He did not take the Lord's warning seriously; in fact, he argued with Him! Nor did he recognize Satan when the adversary inflated his ego with pride, told him he did not have to "watch and pray," and then incited him to use his sword. Had Peter listened to the Lord and resisted the enemy, he would have escaped all those failures.

Both Peter and James gave us the same formula for success: "Submit yourselves therefore to God. Resist the devil, and he will flee from you" (James 4:7). Before we can stand before Satan, we must bow before God. Peter resisted the Lord and ended up submitting to Satan!

Be Hopeful (5:10–14)

Peter closed on a positive note and reminded his readers that God knew what He was doing and was in complete control. No matter how difficult the fiery trial may become, a Christian always has hope. Peter gave several reasons for this hopeful attitude.

We have God's grace. Our salvation is because of His grace (1 Peter 1:10). He called us before we called on Him (1 Peter 1:2). We have "tasted that the Lord is gracious" (1 Peter 2:3), so we are not afraid of anything that He purposes for us. His grace is "manifold" (1 Peter 4:10) and meets every situation of life. As we submit to Him, He gives us the grace that we need. In fact. He is "the God of all grace." He has grace to help in every time of need (Heb. 4:16). "He giveth more grace" (James 4:6), and we must stand in that grace (1 Peter 5:12; see Rom. 5:2).

We know we are going to glory. He has "called us unto his eternal glory by Christ Jesus." This is the wonderful inheritance into which we were born (1 Peter 1:4). Whatever begins with God's grace will always lead to God's glory (Ps. 84:11). If we depend on God's grace when we suffer, that suffering will result in glory (1 Peter 4:13–16). The road may be difficult, but it leads to glory, and that is all that really counts.

Our present suffering is only for a while. Our various trials are only "for a season" (1 Peter 1:6), but the glory that results is *eternal.* Paul had this same thought in mind when he wrote 2 Corinthians 4:17: "These little troubles (which are really so transitory) are winning for us a permanent, glorious, and solid reward out of all proportion to our pain" (PH).

We know that our trials are building Christian character. The Greek word translated "make you perfect" means "to equip, to adjust, to fit together." It is translated "mending nets" in Matthew 4:21. God has several tools that He uses to equip His people for life and service, and suffering is one of them. The Word of God is another tool (2 Tim. 3:16–17, where "throughly furnished" means "fully equipped"). He also uses the fellowship and ministry of the church (Eph. 4:11–16). Our Savior in heaven is perfecting His children so that they will do His will and His work (Heb. 13:20–21).

Peter used three words to describe the kind of character God wants us to have.

Establish means "to fix firmly, to set fast." Christians must not be unsteady in their stand for Christ. Our hearts need to be established (1 Thess. 3:13; James 5:8), and this is accomplished by God's truth (2 Peter 1:12). The believer who is established will not be moved by persecution or led away by false doctrine (2 Peter 3:17).

Strengthen means just that: God's strength given to us to meet the demands of life. What good is it to stand on a firm foundation if we do not have power to act?

Settle is the translation of a word that means "to lay a foundation." It is used this way in Hebrews 1:10. The house founded on the rock withstood the storm (Matt. 7:24–27). A believer who is equipped by God will "continue in the faith grounded and settled" (Col. 1:23). He will not be "tossed to and fro, and carried about with every wind of doctrine" (Eph. 4:14).

When an unbeliever goes through suffering, he loses his hope; but for a believer, suffering only increases his hope. "Not only so, but we also rejoice in our sufferings, because we know that suffering produces perseverance; perseverance, character; and character, hope" (Rom. 5:3–4 NIV). God builds character and brightens hope when a believer trusts Him and depends on His grace. The result is that God receives the glory forever and ever.

We have already considered 1 Peter 5:12–13 in our introductory chapter.

Paul always ended his letters with a benediction of grace (2 Thess. 3:17–18). Peter closed this epistle with a benediction of peace. He opened the letter with a greeting of peace (1 Peter 1:2), so the entire epistle points to "God's peace" from beginning to end. What a wonderful way to end a letter that announced the coming of a fiery trial!

Four times in the New Testament we will find the admonition about "a holy kiss" (Rom. 16:16; 1 Cor. 16:20; 2 Cor. 13:12; and 1 Thess. 5:26). Peter called it "a kiss of love." Keep in mind that the men kissed the men and the women kissed the women. It was a standard form of greeting or farewell in that part of the world at that time, just as it is in many Latin countries today. How wonderful that Christian slaves and masters would so greet each other "in Jesus Christ"!

Peter has given to us a precious letter that encourages us to hope in the Lord no matter how trying the times may be. Down through the centuries, the church has experienced various fiery trials, and yet Satan has not been able to destroy it. The church today is facing a fiery trial, and we must be prepared.

But, whatever may come, Peter is still saying to each of us—BE HOPEFUL! The glory is soon to come!

2 PETER

OUTLINE

Key theme: Spiritual knowledge
Key verse: 2 Peter 1:3

I. EXPLANATION: THE KNOWLEDGE OF CHRIST (1)

A. The gift of knowledge—1:1–4
B. The growth in knowledge—1:5–11
C. The ground of knowledge—1:12–21

II. EXAMINATION: THE FALSE TEACHERS (2)

A. Their condemnation—2:1–9
B. Their character—2:10–17
C. Their claims—2:18–22

III. EXHORTATION: THE TRUE CHRISTIAN (3)

A. Be mindful—3:1–7
B. Be not ignorant—3:8–10
C. Be diligent—3:11–14
D. Beware—3:15–18

CONTENTS

CHAPTER ONE
2 Peter 1:1–11
KNOWING AND GROWING

If anybody in the early church knew the importance of being alert, it was the apostle Peter. He had a tendency in his early years to feel overconfident when danger was near and to overlook the Master's warnings. He rushed ahead when he should have waited; he slept when he should have prayed; he talked when he should have listened. He was a courageous, but careless, Christian.

But he learned his lesson, and he wanted to help us learn it too. In his first epistle, Peter emphasized the grace of God (1 Peter 5:12), but in this second letter, his emphasis is on the knowledge of God. The word *know* or *knowledge* is used at least thirteen times in this short epistle. The word does not mean a mere intellectual understanding of some truth, though that is included. It means a living participation in the truth in the sense that our Lord used it in John 17:3—"This is life eternal, that they might *know* thee the only true God, and Jesus Christ, whom thou hast sent" (italics mine).

Peter opened his letter with a description of the Christian life. Before he described the counterfeits, he described the true believers. The best way to detect falsehood is to understand the characteristics of the truth. Peter made three important affirmations about the true Christian life.

The Christian Life Begins with Faith (1:1–4)
Peter called it "like precious faith." It means that our standing with the Lord today is the same as that of the apostles centuries ago. They had no special advantage over us simply because they were privileged to walk with Christ, see Him with their own eyes, and share in His miracles. It is not necessary to see the Lord with our human eyes in order to love Him, trust Him, and share His glory (1 Peter 1:8).

This faith is in a person (vv. 1–2). That Person is Jesus Christ, the Son of God, the Savior. From the very outset of his letter, Peter affirmed the deity of Jesus Christ. "God" and "our Saviour" are not two different Persons; they describe one Person, Jesus Christ. Paul used a similar expression in Titus 2:10 and 3:4.

Peter reminded his readers that Jesus Christ is the Savior by repeating this exalted title in 2 Peter 1:11; 2:20; 3:2, 18. A *savior* is "one who brings salvation," and the word *salvation* was familiar to the people of that day. In their vocabulary, it meant "deliverance from trouble," particularly "deliverance from the enemy." It also carried the idea of "health and safety." A physician was looked on as a savior because he helped deliver the body from pain and limitations. A victorious general was a savior because he delivered the people from defeat. Even a wise official was a savior because he kept the nation in order and delivered it from confusion and decay.

It requires little insight to see how the title "Savior" applies to our Lord Jesus Christ. He is, indeed, the Great Physician who heals the heart from the sickness of sin. He is the victorious Conqueror who has defeated our enemies—sin, death, Satan, and hell—and is leading us in triumph (2 Cor. 2:14ff.). He is "God and our Saviour" (2 Peter 1:1), "our Lord and Saviour" (2 Peter 1:11), and "the Lord and Saviour" (2 Peter 2:20). In order to be our Savior, He had to give His life on the cross and die for the sins of the world.

Our Lord Jesus Christ has three "spiritual commodities" that can be secured from nobody else: righteousness, grace, and peace. When you trust Him as your Savior, His righteousness becomes your righteousness, and you are given a right standing before God (2 Cor. 5:21). You could never *earn* this righteousness; it is the gift of God to those who believe. "Not by works of righteousness which we have done, but according to his mercy he saved us" (Titus 3:5).

Grace is God's favor to the undeserving. God in His mercy does not give us what we do deserve; God in His grace gives us what we don't deserve. Our God is "the God of all grace" (1 Peter 5:10), and He channels that grace to us through Jesus Christ (John 1:16).

The result of this experience is *peace,* peace *with* God (Rom. 5:1) and the peace *of* God (Phil. 4:6–7). In fact, God's grace and peace are "multiplied" toward us as we walk with Him and trust His promises.

This faith involves God's power (v. 3). The Christian life begins with saving faith, faith in the person of Jesus Christ. But when you know Jesus Christ personally, you also experience God's power, and this power produces "life and godliness." The unsaved sinner is dead (Eph. 2:1–3), and only Christ can raise him from the dead (John 5:24). When Jesus raised Lazarus from the dead, He said, "Loose him, and let him go" (John 11:44). Get rid of the graveclothes!

When you are born into the family of God by faith in Christ, you are born complete. God gives you everything you will ever need "for life and godliness." Nothing has to be added! "And ye are complete in him" (Col. 2:10). The false teachers claimed that they had a "special doctrine" that would add something to the lives of Peter's readers, but Peter knew that *nothing could be added.* Just as a normal baby is born with all the "equipment" he needs for life and only needs to grow, so the Christian has all that is needed and only needs to grow. God never has to call back any of His "models" because something is lacking or faulty.

Just as a baby has a definite genetic structure that determines how he will grow, so the believer is "genetically structured" to experience "glory and virtue." One day he will be like the Lord Jesus Christ (Rom. 8:29; 1 John 3:2). We have been "called … to His eternal glory" (1 Peter 5:10), and we shall share that glory when Jesus Christ returns and takes His people to heaven.

But we are also "called … to virtue." We have been saved so that we might "show forth the praises [virtues] of him who hath called [us] out of darkness into his marvelous light" (1 Peter 2:9). We should not wait until we get to heaven to become like Jesus Christ! In our character and conduct, we should reveal His beauty and grace today.

This faith involves God's promises (v. 4). God has not only given us all that we need for life and godliness, but He has also given us His Word to enable us to develop this life and godliness. These promises are *great* because they come from a great God and they lead to a great life. They are *precious* because their value is beyond calculation. If we lost the Word of God, there would be no way to replace it. Peter must have liked the word *precious,* for he wrote about the "precious faith" (2 Peter 1:1; cf. 1 Peter 1:7), the "precious promises" (2 Peter 1:4), the "precious blood" (1 Peter 1:19), the precious stone (1 Peter 2:4, 6), and the precious Savior (1 Peter 2:7).

When the sinner believes on Jesus Christ, the Spirit of God uses the Word of God to impart the life and nature of God within. A baby shares the nature of its parents, and a person born of God shares the divine nature of God. The lost sinner is dead, but the Christian is alive because he shares the divine nature. The lost sinner is decaying because of his corrupt nature, but the Christian can experience a dynamic life of godliness because he has God's divine nature within. Mankind is under the bondage of corruption (Rom. 8:21), but the believer shares the freedom and growth that is a part of possessing the divine nature.

Nature determines *appetite.* The pig wants slop and the dog will even eat its own vomit (2 Peter 2:22), but the sheep desires green pastures. Nature also determines *behavior.* An eagle flies because it has an eagle's nature, and a dolphin swims because that is the nature of the dolphin. Nature determines *environment:* squirrels climb trees, moles burrow underground, and trout swim in the water. Nature also determines *association:* lions travel in prides, sheep in flocks, and fish in schools.

If nature determines appetite, and we have God's nature within, then we ought to have an appetite for that which is pure and holy. Our behavior ought to be like that of the Father, and we ought to live in the kind of "spiritual environment" that is suited to our nature. We ought to associate with that which is true to our nature (see 2 Cor. 6:14ff.). The only normal, fruit-bearing life for the child of God is a *godly* life.

Because we possess this divine nature, we have "completely escaped" the defilement and decay in this present evil world. If we feed the new nature the nourishment of the Word, then we will have little interest in the garbage of the world. But if we "make provision for the flesh" (Rom. 13:14), our sinful nature will lust after the "old sins" (2 Peter 1:9) and we will disobey God. Godly living is the result of cultivating the new nature within.

Faith Results in Spiritual Growth (1:5–7)

Where there is life, there must be growth. The new birth is not the end; it is the beginning. God gives His children all that they need to live godly lives, but His children must apply themselves and be diligent to use the "means of grace" He has provided. *Spiritual growth is not automatic.* It requires cooperation with God and the application of spiritual diligence and discipline. "Work out your own salvation.… For it is God which worketh in you" (Phil. 2:12–13).

Peter listed seven characteristics of the godly life, but we must not think of them as seven beads on a string or even seven stages of development. The word translated "add" really means "to supply generously." In other words, we develop one quality as we exercise another quality. These graces relate to each other the way the branch relates to the trunk and the twigs to the branch. Like the "fruit of the Spirit" (Gal. 5:22–23), these qualities grow out of life and out of a vital relationship with Jesus Christ. It is not enough for the Christian to "let go and let God," as though spiritual growth were God's work alone. Literally, Peter wrote, "Make every effort to bring alongside." The Father and the child must work together.

The first quality of character Peter listed was *virtue.* We met this word in 2 Peter 1:3, and it basically means "excellence." To the Greek philosophers, it meant "the fulfillment of a thing." When anything in nature fulfills its purpose, that is "virtue—moral excellence." The word was also used to describe the power of the gods to do heroic deeds. The land that produces crops is "excellent" because it is fulfilling its purpose. The tool that works correctly is "excellent" because it is doing what a tool is supposed to do.

A Christian is supposed to glorify God because he has God's nature within; so, when he does this, he shows "excellence" because he is fulfilling his purpose in life. True virtue in the Christian life is not "polishing" human qualities, no matter how fine they may be, but producing *divine* qualities that make the person more like Jesus Christ.

Faith helps us develop virtue, and virtue helps us develop *knowledge* (2 Peter 1:5). The word translated "knowledge" in 2 Peter 1:2–3 means "full knowledge" or "knowledge that is growing." The word used here suggests *practical* knowledge or discernment. It refers to the ability to handle life successfully. It is the opposite of being "so heavenly minded as to be of no earthly good!" This kind of knowledge does not come automatically. It comes from obedience to the will of God (John 7:17). In the Christian life, you must not separate the heart and the mind, character and knowledge.

Temperance is the next quality on Peter's list of spiritual virtues, and it means self-control. "He that is slow to anger is better than the mighty; and he that ruleth his spirit than he that taketh a city" (Prov. 16:32). "He that hath no rule over his own spirit is like a city that is broken down and without walls" (Prov. 25:28). Paul in his letters often compared the Christian to an athlete who must exercise and discipline himself if he ever hopes to win the prize (1 Cor. 9:24–27; Phil. 3:12–16; 1 Tim. 4:7–8).

Patience is the ability to endure when circumstances are difficult. Self-control has to do with handling the *pleasures* of life, while patience relates primarily to the *pressures* and *problems* of life. (The ability to endure problem people is "longsuffering.") Often, the person who gives in to pleasures is not disciplined enough to handle pressures either, so he gives up.

Patience is not something that develops automatically; we must work at it. James 1:2–8 gives us the right approach. We must expect trials to come, because without trials we could never learn patience. We must, by faith, let our trials work *for* us and not against us, because we know that God is at work in our trials. If we need wisdom in making decisions, God will grant that wisdom if we ask Him. Nobody enjoys trials, but we do enjoy the confidence we can have in trials that God is at work, causing everything to work together for our good and His glory.

Godliness simply means "God-likeness." In the original Greek, this word meant "to worship well." It described the man who was right in his relationship with God and with his fellow man. Perhaps the words *reverence* and *piety* come closer to defining this term. It is that quality of character that makes a person distinctive. He lives above the petty things of life, the passions and pressures that control the lives of others. He seeks to do the will of God and, as he does, he seeks the welfare of others.

We must never get the idea that godliness is an impractical thing, because it is intensely practical. The godly person makes the kinds of decisions that are right and noble. He does not take an easy path simply to avoid either pain or trial. He does what is right because it is right and because it is the will of God.

Brotherly kindness (*philadelphia* in the Greek) is a virtue that Peter must have acquired the hard way, for the disciples of our Lord often debated and disagreed with one another. If we love Jesus Christ, we must also love the brethren. We should practice an "unfeigned [sincere] love of the brethren" (1 Peter 1:22) and not just pretend that we love them. "Let brotherly love continue" (Heb. 13:1). "Be kindly affectioned one to another with brotherly love" (Rom. 12:10). The fact that we love our brothers and sisters in Christ is one evidence that we have been born of God (1 John 5:1–2).

But there is more to Christian growth than brotherly love; we must also have the sacrifical love that our Lord displayed when He went to the cross. The kind of love ("charity") spoken of in 2 Peter 1:7 is *agape* love, the kind of love that God shows toward lost sinners. This is the love that is described in 1 Corinthians 13, the love that the Holy Spirit produces in our hearts as we walk in the Spirit (Rom. 5:5; Gal. 5:22). When we have *brotherly* love, we love because of our likenesses

to others, but with *agape* love, we love in spite of the differences we have.

It is impossible for fallen human nature to manufacture these seven qualities of Christian character. They must be produced by the Spirit of God. To be sure, there are unsaved people who possess amazing self-control and endurance, but these virtues point to *them* and not to the Lord. *They* get the glory. When God produces the beautiful nature of His Son in a Christian, it is God who receives the praise and glory.

Because we have the divine nature, we can grow spiritually and develop this kind of Christian character. It is through the power of God and the precious promises of God that this growth takes place. The divine "genetic structure" is already there: God wants us to be "conformed to the image of his Son" (Rom. 8:29). The life within will reproduce that image if we but diligently cooperate with God and use the means He has lavishly given us.

And the amazing thing is this: as the image of Christ is reproduced in us, the process does not destroy our own personalities. We still remain uniquely ourselves!

One of the dangers in the church today is imitation. People have a tendency to become like their pastor, or like a church leader, or perhaps like some "famous Christian." As they do this, they destroy their own uniqueness while failing to become like Jesus Christ. They lose both ways! Just as each child in a family resembles his parents and yet is different, so each child in God's family comes more and more to resemble Jesus Christ and yet is different. Parents don't duplicate themselves, they reproduce themselves, and wise parents permit their children to be themselves.

Spiritual Growth Brings Practical Results (1:8–11)

How can the believer be certain that he is growing spiritually? Peter gave three evidences of true spiritual growth.

Fruitfulness (v. 8). Christian character is an end in itself, but it is also a means to an end. The more we become like Jesus Christ, the more the Spirit can use us in witness and service. The believer who is not growing is idle ("barren") and unfruitful. His knowledge of Jesus Christ is producing nothing practical in his life. The word translated "idle" also means "ineffective." The people who fail to grow usually fail in everything else!

Some of the most effective Christians I have known are people without dramatic talents and special abilities, or even exciting personalities, yet God has used them in a marvelous way. Why? Because they are becoming more and more like Jesus Christ. They have the kind of character and conduct that God can trust with blessing. They are fruitful because they are faithful; they are effective because they are growing in their Christian experience.

These beautiful qualities of character do exist "within us" because we possess the divine nature. We must cultivate them so that they increase and produce fruit in and through our lives.

Vision (v. 9). Nutritionists tell us that diet can certainly affect vision, and this is especially true in the spiritual realm. The unsaved person is in the dark because Satan has blinded his mind (2 Cor. 4:3–4). A person has to be born again before his eyes are opened and he can see the kingdom of God (John 3:3). But after our eyes are opened, it is important that we increase our vision and see all that God wants us to see. The phrase *cannot see afar off* is the translation of a word that means "shortsighted." It is the picture of somebody closing or squinting his eyes, unable to see at a distance.

There are some Christians who see only their own church or their own denomination, but who fail to see the greatness of God's family around the world. Some believers see the needs at home but have no vision for a lost world. Someone asked Phillips Brooks what he would do to revive a dead church, and he replied, "I would preach a missionary sermon and take up a collection!" Jesus admonished His disciples, "Lift up your eyes, and look on the fields; for they are white already to harvest" (John 4:35).

Some congregations today are like the church at Laodicea: they are proud that they are "rich and increased with goods, and have need of nothing," and do not realize that they are "wretched, and miserable, and poor, and blind, and naked" (Rev. 3:17). It is a tragedy to be "spiritually nearsighted," but it is even a greater tragedy to be blind!

If we forget what God has done for us, we will not be excited to share Christ with others. Through the blood of Jesus Christ we have been purged and forgiven! God has opened our eyes! Let's not forget what He has done! Rather, let's cultivate gratitude in our hearts and sharpen our spiritual vision. Life is too brief and the needs of the world too great for God's people to be walking around with their eyes closed!

Security (vv. 10–11). If you walk around with your eyes closed, you will stumble! But the growing Christian walks with confidence because he knows he is secure in Christ. It is not our profession of faith that guarantees that we are saved; it is our progression in the faith that gives us that assurance. The person who claims to be a child of God but whose character and conduct give no evidence of spiritual growth is deceiving himself and heading for judgment.

Peter pointed out that "calling" and "election" go together. The same God who *elects* His people also ordains the means to *call* them. The two must go together, as Paul wrote to the Thessalonians: "God hath from the beginning chosen you to salvation.… whereunto he called you by our gospel" (2 Thess. 2:13–14). We do not preach election to unsaved people; we preach the gospel. But God uses that gospel to call sinners to repentance, and then those sinners discover that they were chosen by God!

Peter also pointed out that election is no excuse for spiritual immaturity or for lack of effort in the Christian life. Some believers say, "What is going to be is going to be. There is nothing we can do." But Peter admonished us to "be diligent." This means "make every effort." (He used this same verb in 2 Peter 1:5.) While it is true that God must work in us before we can do His will (Phil. 2:12–13), it is also true that we must *be willing* for God to work, and we must cooperate with Him. Divine election must never be an excuse for human laziness.

The Christian who is sure of his election and calling will never "stumble" but will prove by a consistent life that he is truly a child of God. He will not always be on the mountaintop, but he will always be climbing higher. If we do "these things" (the things listed in 2 Peter 1:5–7, cf. v. 8), if we display Christian growth and character in our daily lives, then we can be sure we are converted and will one day be in heaven.

In fact, the growing Christian can look forward to "an abundant entrance" into the eternal kingdom! The Greeks used this phrase to describe the welcome given Olympic winners when they returned home. Every believer will arrive in heaven, but some will have a more glorious welcome than others. Alas, some believers "shall be saved, yet so as by fire" (1 Cor. 3:15).

The word *ministered* in 2 Peter 1:11 is the same as the word *add* in 2 Peter 1:5, and is the translation of a Greek word that means "to bear the expenses of a chorus." When the Greek theatrical groups presented their dramas, somebody had to underwrite the expenses, which were very great. The word came to mean "to make lavish provision." If we make lavish provision to grow spiritually (2 Peter 1:5), then God will make lavish provision for us when we enter heaven!

Just think of the blessings that the growing Christian enjoys: fruitfulness, vision, security—and heaven's best! All this and heaven too!

The Christian life begins with faith, but that faith must lead to spiritual growth—unless it is dead faith. But dead faith is not saving faith (James 2:14–26). Faith leads to growth, and growth leads to practical results in life and service. People who have this kind of Christian experience are not likely to fall prey to apostate false teachers.

CHAPTER TWO
2 Peter 1:12–21
WAKE UP AND REMEMBER!

The best defense against false teaching is true living. A church filled with growing Christians, vibrant in their faith, is not likely to fall prey to apostates with their counterfeit Christianity. But this Christian living must be based on the authoritative Word of God. False teachers find it easy to seduce people who do not know their Bible but who are desirous of "experiences" with the Lord. It is a dangerous thing to build on subjective experience alone and ignore objective revelation.

Peter discussed Christian experience in the first half of 2 Peter 1, and in the last half he discussed the revelation we have in the Word of God. His purpose was to show the importance of knowing God's Word and relying on it completely. The Christian who knows what he believes and why he believes it will rarely be seduced by the false teachers and their devious doctrines.

Peter underscored the dependability and durability of the Word of God by contrasting Scripture with men, experiences, and the world.

Men Die, but the Word Lives (1:12–15)

Through their preaching and teaching, the apostles and New Testament prophets laid the foundation of the church (Eph. 2:20), and we in later generations are building on that foundation. However, the men were not the foundation; Jesus Christ is the Foundation (1 Cor. 3:11). He is also the chief Cornerstone that ties the building together (Eph. 2:20). If the church is to last, it cannot be built on mere men. It must be built on the Son of God.

Our Lord had told Peter when he would die and how he would die. "When thou shalt be old, thou shalt stretch forth thy hands, and another shall gird thee, and carry thee whither thou wouldest not" (John 21:18). This explains why, shortly after Pentecost, Peter was able to sleep in prison the night before he was scheduled to be killed; he knew that Herod could not take his life (Acts 12:1ff.). Tradition says that Peter was crucified in Rome. Like all of God's faithful servants, Peter was immortal until his work was done.

There were at least three motives behind Peter's ministry as he wrote this letter. The first was *obedience to Christ's command.* "I will not be negligent" (2 Peter 1:12). "When thou art converted," Jesus had said to Peter, "strengthen thy brethren" (Luke 22:32). Peter knew that he had a ministry to fulfill.

His second motive was simply that this reminder was *the right thing to do.* "I think it meet," he wrote, which simply means, "I think it is right and suitable." It is always right to stir up the saints and remind them of the Word of God!

His third motive is wrapped up in the word *endeavor* in 2 Peter 1:15. It is the same word that is translated "diligence" in 2 Peter 1:5 and 10. It means "to hasten to do something, to be zealous in doing it." Peter knew that he would soon die, so he wanted to take care of his spiritual responsibilities before it was too late. You and I do not know when we will die, so we had better start being diligent today!

What was it that Peter wanted to accomplish? The answer is found in the word that is repeated in 2 Peter 1:12–13 and 15—*remembrance.* Peter wanted to impress his readers' minds with the Word of God so that they would never forget it! "I think it meet … to stir you up by putting you in remembrance" (2 Peter 1:13). The verb *stir you up* means "to awaken, to arouse." This same word is used to describe a storm on the Sea of Galilee (John 6:18)! Peter knew that our minds have a tendency to get accustomed to truth and then to take it for granted. We forget what we ought to remember, and we remember what we ought to forget!

The readers of this letter knew the truth and were even "established" in it (2 Peter 1:12), but that was no guarantee they would always remember the truth and apply it. One reason the Holy Spirit was given to the church was to remind believers of the lessons already learned (John 14:26). In my own radio ministry, I have received letters from listeners who get upset when I repeat something. In my reply, I often refer them to what Paul wrote in Philippians 3:1: "To write the same things to you, to me indeed is not grievous, but for you it is safe." Our Lord often repeated Himself as He taught the people, and He was the Master Teacher.

Peter knew that he was going to die, so he wanted to leave behind something that would never die—the written Word of God. His two epistles became a part of the inspired Scriptures, and they have been ministering to the saints for centuries. Men die, but the Word of God lives on!

It is possible that Peter was also alluding to the gospel of Mark. Most Bible scholars believe that the Spirit used Peter to give John Mark some of the data for his book (see 1 Peter 5:13). One of the church fathers, Papias, said that Mark was "Peter's disciple and interpreter."

The church of Jesus Christ is always one generation away from extinction. If there were no dependable written revelation, we would have to depend on word-of-mouth tradition. If you have ever played the party game "Gossip," you know how a simple sentence can be radically changed when passed from one person to another! We do not depend on the traditions of dead men; we depend on the truth of the living Word. Men die, but the Word lives forever.

If we did not have a dependable written revelation, the church would be at the mercy of men's memories. People who pride themselves on having good memories should sit on the witness stand in a courtroom! It is amazing that three perfectly honest witnesses can, with good conscience, give three different accounts of an automobile accident! Our memories are defective and selective. We usually remember what we want to remember, and often we distort even that.

Fortunately, we can depend on the written Word of God. "It is written" and it stands written forever. We can be saved through this living Word (1 Peter 1:23–25), nurtured by it (1 Peter 2:2), and guided and protected as we trust and obey.

Experiences Fade, but the Word Remains (1:16–18)

The focus in this paragraph is on the transfiguration of Jesus Christ. The experience is recorded by Matthew (17:1ff.), Mark (9:2–8), and Luke (9:28–36), yet none of those writers actually participated in it! Peter was there when it happened! In fact, the very words that he used in this section (2 Peter 1:12–18) remind us of his experience on the Mount of Transfiguration. He used the word *tabernacle* twice (2 Peter 1:13–14), and this suggests Peter's words, "Let us make here three tabernacles" (Matt. 17:4). In 2 Peter 1:15, he used the word *decease,* which is "exodus" in the Greek and is used in Luke 9:31. Jesus did not consider His death on the cross a defeat; rather, it was an "exodus"—He would deliver His people from bondage the way Moses delivered Israel from Egypt! Peter wrote of his own death as an "exodus," a release from bondage.

Note the repetition of the pronoun "we" in 2 Peter 1:16–19. It refers to Peter, James, and John—the only apostles with the Lord on the Mount of Transfiguration. (John referred to this experience in John 1:14—"We beheld His glory.") These three men had to keep silent about their experience until after the Lord was raised from the dead (Matt. 17:9); then they told the other believers what had happened on the mountain.

What was the significance of the transfiguration? For one thing, it confirmed Peter's testimony about Jesus Christ (Matt. 16:13–16). Peter saw the Son in His glory, and he heard the Father speak from heaven, "This is my beloved Son, in whom I am well pleased" (2 Peter 1:17). First we put our faith in Christ and confess Him, and then He gives us wonderful confirmation.

The transfiguration also had a special significance for Jesus Christ, who was nearing Calvary. It was the Father's way of strengthening His Son for that terrible ordeal of being the sacrifice for the sins of the world. The law and the prophets (Moses and Elijah) pointed to His ministry, and now He would fulfill those Scriptures. The Father spoke from heaven and assured the Son of His love and approval. The Transfiguration was proof that suffering leads to glory when we are in the will of God.

But there is a third message, and it has to do with the promised kingdom. In all three gospels where the account of the transfiguration is recorded, it is introduced with a statement about the kingdom of God (Matt. 16:28; Mark 9:1; Luke 9:27). Jesus promised that, before they died, some of the disciples would see the kingdom of God in power! This took place on the Mount of Transfiguration when our Lord revealed His glory. It was a word of assurance to the disciples, who could not understand our Lord's teaching about the cross. If He were to die, what would happen to the promised kingdom that He had been preaching about all those months?

Now we can understand why Peter used this event in his letter: he was refuting the false teachings of the apostates that the kingdom of God would never come (2 Peter 3:3ff.). These false teachers denied the promise of Christ's coming! In the place of God's promises, these counterfeits put "cunningly devised fables" (2 Peter 1:16) that robbed the believers of their blessed hope.

The word *fables* means "myths," manufactured stories that have no basis in fact. The Greek and Roman world abounded in stories about the gods, mere human speculations that tried to explain the world and its origin. No matter how interesting these myths might be, the Christian is not to heed them (1 Tim. 1:4), but refuse them (1 Tim. 4:7). Paul warned Timothy that the time would come in the church when professed Christians would not want to hear true doctrine, but would "turn away their ears from the truth, and … be turned unto fables [myths]" (2 Tim. 4:4). Paul also warned Titus about "Jewish fables [myths]" (Titus 1:14), so even some of the Jews had abandoned their sacred Scriptures and accepted manmade substitutes.

Peter wrote a summary of what he saw and heard on the Mount of Transfiguration. He saw Jesus Christ robed in majestic glory, and therefore witnessed a demonstration of the "power and coming" of the Lord Jesus Christ. When Jesus Christ came to earth at Bethlehem, He did not display His glory openly. To be sure, He revealed His glory in His miracles (John 2:11), but even this was primarily for the sake of His disciples. His face did not shine, nor did He have a halo over His head. "He hath no form nor comeliness; and when we shall see him, there is no beauty that we should desire him" (Isa. 53:2).

Peter not only saw Christ's glory, but he heard the Father's voice "from the magnificent glory." Witnesses are people who tell accurately what they have seen and heard (Acts 4:20), and Peter was a faithful witness. Is Jesus Christ of Nazareth the Son of God? Yes, He is! How do we know? The Father said so!

You and I were not eyewitnesses of the transfiguration. Peter was there, and he faithfully recorded his experience for us in the letter that he wrote, inspired by the Spirit of God. Experiences fade, but the Word of God remains! Experiences are subjective, but the Word of God is objective. Experiences may be interpreted in different ways by different participants, but the Word of God gives one clear message. What we remember about our experiences can be unconsciously distorted, but the Word of God remains the same and abides forever.

When we study 2 Peter 2, we will discover that apostate teachers try to turn people away from the Word of God and into "deeper experiences" that are contrary to the Word. These false teachers use "feigned words" instead of God's inspired Word (2 Peter 2:3), and they teach "damnable heresies" (2 Peter 2:1). In other words, this is really a matter of life and death! If a person believes the truth, he will live; if he believes lies, he will die. It is the difference between salvation and condemnation.

By reminding his readers of the transfiguration, Peter affirmed several important doctrines of the Christian faith. He affirmed that Jesus Christ is indeed the Son of God. The test of any religion is "What do you say about Jesus Christ?" If a religious teacher denies the deity of Christ, then he is a false teacher (1 John 2:18–29; 4:1–6).

But the person of Jesus Christ is only one test; we must also ask, "And what is the work of Jesus Christ? Why did He come and what did He do?" Again, the Transfiguration gives us the answer; for Moses and Elijah "appeared in glory, and spake of his decease [exodus] which he should accomplish at Jerusalem" (Luke 9:31). His death was not simply an example, as some liberal theologians want us to believe; it was an exodus, an accomplishment. He accomplished something on the cross—the redemption of lost sinners!

The transfiguration was also affirmation of the truth of the Scriptures. Moses represented the law; Elijah represented the prophets; both pointed to Jesus Christ (Heb. 1:1–3). He fulfilled the law and the Prophets (Luke 24:27). We believe the Bible because Jesus believed the Bible and said it was the Word of God. Those who question the truth and authority of the Scriptures are not arguing with Moses, Elijah, or Peter, but with the Lord Jesus Christ.

This event also affirmed the reality of God's kingdom. We who have a completed Bible can look back and understand the progressive lessons that Jesus gave His disciples about the cross and the kingdom, but at that time those twelve men were very confused. They did not understand the relationship between His suffering and His glory (Peter's first epistle discusses this theme) and the church and the kingdom. At the transfiguration, our Lord made it clear to His followers that His suffering *would lead to glory* and that the cross would ultimately result in the crown.

There was also a very practical lesson that Peter, James, and John needed to learn, because each of these would also suffer. James was the first of the apostles to die (Acts 12:1–2). John lived a long life, but it led to exile and suffering (Rev. 1:9). Peter suffered for the Lord during his ministry, and then laid down his life just as the Lord had prophesied. On the Mount of Transfiguration, Peter, James, and John learned that suffering and glory go together, and that the Father's special love and approval are given to those who are willing to suffer for the sake of the Lord. We need this same lesson today.

Peter could not share his experience with us, but he could share the record of that experience so that we could have it permanently in the Word of God. It is not necessary for us to try to duplicate these experiences; in fact, such attempts would be dangerous, for the devil could give us a counterfeit experience that could lead us astray.

Remember Peter's wonderful news at the beginning of this letter: "like precious faith." This means that our faith gives us "an equal standing" with the apostles! They did not travel first-class and leave us to travel second-class! "Like precious faith *with us*" is what he wrote (italics mine). We were not on the Mount of Transfiguration, but we can still benefit from that experience as we meditate on it and permit the Spirit of God to reveal the glories of Jesus Christ.

We have learned two important truths as we have seen these contrasts: men die, but the Word lives, and experiences fade, but the Word remains. Peter added a third contrast.

The World Darkens, but the Word Shines (1:19–21)

In some respects, the world is getting better. I thank God for the advances in medicine, transportation, and communication. I can speak to more people in one radio program than the apostles preached to in their entire lifetimes. I can write books that can be spread abroad and even translated into different languages. In areas of scientific achievement, the world has made great progress. But the human heart is still wicked, and all of our improvements in means have not improved our lives. Medical science enables people to live longer, but there is no guarantee they will live better. Modern means of communication only enable lies to travel faster! And jet planes enable us to get places faster, but we do not have better places to go!

We should not be surprised that our world is engulfed in spiritual darkness. In the Sermon on the Mount our Lord warned that there would be counterfeits who would invade the church with their false doctrines (Matt. 7:13–29). Paul gave a similar warning to the elders of Ephesus (Acts 20:28–35), and he gave further warnings when he wrote his epistles (Rom. 16:17–20; 2 Cor. 11:1–15; Gal. 1:1–9; Phil. 3:17–21; Col. 2; 1 Tim. 4; 2 Tim. 3–4). Even John, the great "apostle of love," warned about antichristian teachers who would seek to destroy the church (1 John 2:18–29; 4:1–6).

In other words, the apostles did not expect the world to get better and better either morally or spiritually. They all warned the church that false teachers would invade the local churches, introduce false doctrines, and lead many people astray. The world would get darker and darker; but as it did, the Word of God would shine brighter and brighter.

Peter made three affirmations about this Word.

It is the sure Word (v. 19a). Peter was not suggesting that the Bible is more certain than the experience he had on the Mount of Transfiguration. His experience was real and true, and the record in the Bible is dependable. As we have seen, the Transfiguration was a demonstration of the promise given in the prophetic Word; and this promise now has added certainty because of what Peter experienced. The Transfiguration experience corroborated the prophetic promises. The apostates would attempt to discredit the promise of His coming (2 Peter 3:3ff), but the Scriptures were sure. For, after all, the promise of the kingdom was reaffirmed by Moses, Elijah, the Son of God, and the Father! And the Holy Spirit wrote the record for the church to read!

"The testimony of the Lord is sure" (Ps. 19:7). "Thy testimonies are very sure" (Ps. 93:5). "All his commandments are sure" (Ps. 111:7). "Therefore I esteem all thy precepts concerning all things to be right; and I hate every false way" (Ps. 119:128).

It is interesting to put together 2 Peter 1:16 and 19: "For we have not followed cunningly devised fables.… We have also a more sure word of prophecy." As I travel, I often meet zealous cultists in airports, all of whom want me to buy their books. I always refuse because I have the sure Word of God and have no need for the religious fables of men. "'What is the chaff to the wheat?' saith the Lord" (Jer. 23:28).

But one day I found one of those books left behind in the men's room, so I decided to take it with me and read it. How anybody could believe such foolish fables is more than I can understand. The book claimed to be based on the Bible, but the writer so twisted the Scriptures that the verses quoted ended up meaning only what he wanted them to mean. Cunningly devised fables! Yet there was spiritual death between those covers to anyone who would believe those lies.

It is the shining Word (v. 19b). Peter called the world "a dark place," and the word he used means "murky." It is the picture of a dank cellar or a dismal swamp. Human history began in a lovely garden, but that garden today is a murky swamp. What you see when you look at this world system is an indication of the spiritual condition of your heart. We still see beauty in God's creation, but we see no beauty in what mankind is doing with God's creation. Peter did not see this world as a garden of Eden, nor should we.

God is light and His word is light. "Thy word is a lamp unto my feet, and a light unto my path" (Ps. 119:105). When Jesus Christ began His ministry, "the people which sat in darkness saw great light" (Matt. 4:16). His coming into this world was the dawning of a new day (Luke 1:78). We Christians are the light of the world (Matt. 5:14–16), and it is our privilege and responsibility to hold forth the Word of life—God's light—so that men might see the way and be saved (Phil. 2:14–16).

As believers, we must heed this Word and govern our lives by what it says. For unbelievers, things will get darker and darker, until they end up in eternal darkness, but God's people are looking for the return of Jesus Christ and the dawning of the new day of glory. The false teachers scoffed at the idea of Christ's return and the dawning of a new day, but Peter affirmed the truth of the sure Word of God. "But the day of the Lord will come as a thief in the night" (2 Peter 3:10).

Before the day dawns, the "day star" (or morning star) shines brightly as the herald of the dawn. To the church, Jesus Christ is "the bright and morning star" (Rev. 22:16). The promise of His coming shines brightly, no matter how dark the day may be (see Num. 24:17). He is also the "Sun of righteousness," who will bring healing to believers but judgment to unbelievers (Mal. 4:1–2). How thankful we ought to be for God's sure and shining Word, and how we ought to heed it in these dark days!

It is the Spirit-given Word (vv. 20–21). This is one of two important Scriptures affirming the divine inspiration of the Word of God. The other is 2 Timothy 3:14–17. Peter affirmed that the Scriptures were not written by men who used their own ideas and words, but by men of God who were "moved by the Holy Spirit." The word translated "moved" means "to be carried along, as a ship is carried by the wind." The Scriptures are "God-breathed"; they are not the inventions of men.

Again, Peter was refuting the doctrines of the apostates. They taught with "feigned words" (2 Peter 2:3) and twisted the Scriptures to make them mean something else (2 Peter 3:16). They denied the promise of Christ's coming (2 Peter 3:3–4), and thus denied the very prophetic Scriptures.

Since the Spirit gave the Word, only the Spirit can teach the Word and interpret it accurately (see 1 Cor. 2:14–15). Of course, every false teacher claims that he is "led by the Spirit," but his handling of the Word of God soon exposes him. Since the Bible did not come by the will of man, it cannot be understood by the will of man. Even religious Nicodemus, a leading teacher among the Jews, was ignorant of the most essential doctrines of the Word of God (John 3:10–12).

In 2 Peter 1:20, Peter was not prohibiting the private study of the Bible. Some religious groups have taught that only the "spiritual leaders" may interpret Scripture, and they have used this verse as their defense. But Peter was not writing primarily about the interpretation of Scripture, but the origin of Scripture: it came by the Holy Spirit through holy men of God. And since it came by the Spirit, it must be taught by the Spirit.

The word translated "private" simply means "one's own" or "its own." The suggestion is, since all Scripture is inspired by the Spirit it must all "hang together," and no one Scripture should be divorced from the others. You can use the Bible to prove almost anything if you isolate verses from their proper context, which is exactly the approach the false teachers use. Peter stated that the witness of the apostles confirmed the witness of the prophetic Word; there is one message with no contradiction. Therefore, the only way these false teachers can "prove" their heretical doctrines is by misusing the Word of God. Isolated texts, apart from contexts, become pretexts.

The Word of God was written to common people, not to theological professors. The writers assumed that common people could read it, understand it, and apply it, led by the same Holy Spirit who inspired it. The humble individual believer can learn about God as he reads and meditates on the Word of God; he does not need the "experts" to show him truth. However, this does not deny the ministry of teachers in the church (Eph. 4:11), special people who have a gift for explaining and applying the Scriptures. Nor does it deny the "collective wisdom" of the church as, over the ages, these doctrines have been defined and refined.

Teachers and creeds have their place, but they must not usurp the authority of the Word over the conscience of the individual believer.

Until the day dawns, we must be sure that the love for His coming is like a shining star in our hearts (2 Peter 1:19). Unless we love His appearing, we will not look for His appearing, and it is the Word that keeps that expectation bright.

Men die, but the Word lives. Experiences fade, but the Word remains. The world grows darker, but the prophetic light shines brighter. The believer who builds his life on the Word of God and who looks for the coming of the Savior is not likely to be led astray by false teachers. He will be taught by the Spirit and grounded on the sure Word of God.

Peter's message is "Wake up—and remember!" A sleeping church is the devil's playground. It is while men slept that the enemy came in and sowed the tares (Matt. 13:24ff.).

"Be alert!" is the apostle's message. "Wake up and remember!"

CHAPTER THREE
2 Peter 2:1–9
BEWARE OF COUNTERFEITS

One of the most successful rackets in the world today is that of selling "fake art." Even some of the finest galleries and private collections have been invaded by paintings that are clever counterfeits of the great masters. Publishers have also had their share of hoaxes, purchasing "genuine" manuscripts that weren't so genuine after all.

But counterfeits are nothing new. Satan is the "great imitator" (2 Cor. 11:13–15), and he has been hard at work ever since he deceived Eve in the garden (Gen. 3:1–7; 2 Cor. 11:1–4). He has false Christians (Matt. 13:38; John 8:44), a false gospel (Gal. 1:6–9), and even a false righteousness (Rom. 9:30—10:4). One day, he will present to the world a false Christ (2 Thess. 2).

The nation Israel was constantly being led astray by false prophets. Elijah had to contend with the prophets of Baal, but they promoted a pagan religion. It was the *Jewish* false prophets who did the most damage, for they claimed to speak for Jehovah God. Both Jeremiah and Ezekiel exposed this counterfeit ministry, but the people followed the pseudo-prophets just the same. Why? Because the religion of the false prophets was easy, comfortable, and popular. The fact that the false prophets preached a false peace did not worry the people (Jer. 6:14). That was the message they wanted to hear!

The apostles and prophets laid the foundation for the church and then passed from the scene (Eph. 2:20). This is why Peter wrote about false *teachers,* rather than false prophets, because there are still teachers in the church. It is not likely that church members would listen to a "prophet," but they would listen to a teacher of the Word. Satan always uses the approach that will succeed.

In order to warn us to be alert, Peter presented three aspects of this subject of false teachers in the church.

The False Teachers Described (2:1–3)
This is not a very pretty picture! When you read the epistle of Jude, you will find him using similar language, and vivid language it is. Peter knew that the truth of God's Word and the false doctrines of the heretics simply could not coexist. There could be no compromise on his part, any more than a surgeon could compromise with a cancerous tumor in a patient's body.

Deception (v. 1a). This theme runs throughout the entire chapter. To begin with, these teachers' message is false; Peter called what they taught "destructive heresies." The word *heresy* originally meant simply "to make a choice," but then it came to mean "a sect, a party." Promoting a party spirit in a church is one of the works of the flesh (Gal. 5:20). Whenever a church member says to another member, "Are you on my side or the pastor's side?" he is promoting a party spirit and causing division. A false teacher forces you to make a choice between his doctrines and the doctrines of the true Christian faith.

Not only was their message false, but their methods were false. Instead of openly declaring what they believed, they came into the church under false colors and gave the impression that they were true to the Christian faith. "They secretly bring in alongside" is the literal translation. They do not throw out the truth immediately; they simply lay their false teachings alongside the truth and give the impression that they believe the fundamentals of the faith. Before long, they remove the true doctrine and leave their false doctrine in its place.

In 2 Peter 2:3, Peter pointed out that the false teachers used "feigned words." The Greek word is *plastos,* from which we get our English word *plastic.* Plastic words! Words that can be twisted to mean anything you want them to mean! The false teachers use our vocabulary, but they do not use our dictionary. They talk about "salvation," "inspiration," and the great words of the Christian faith, but they do not mean what we mean. Immature and untaught believers hear these preachers or read their books and think that these men are sound in the faith, but they are not.

Satan is a liar and his ministers are liars. They use the Bible, not to enlighten, but to deceive. They follow the same pattern Satan followed when he deceived Eve (Gen. 3:1–6). First, he questioned God's Word—"Yea, hath God said?" Then he denied God's Word—"Ye shall not surely die." Finally, he substituted his own lie—"Ye shall be as gods."

Keep in mind that these apostate teachers are not innocently ignorant of the Word, as was Apollos (Acts 18:24–28). They know the truth but they deliberately reject it. I read about a liberal pastor who was asked to read a paper at a ministerial conference on "Paul's views of justification." He read a paper that superbly presented the truth of the gospel and justification by faith.

"I didn't know you believed that," a friend said to him after the meeting.

"I don't believe it," the liberal pastor replied. "They didn't ask me for *my* views of justification. They asked for Paul's!"

Denial (v. 1b). False teachers are better known for what they deny than what they affirm. They deny the inspiration of the Bible, the sinfulness of man, the sacrificial death of Jesus Christ on the cross, salvation by faith alone, and even the reality of eternal judgment. They especially deny the deity of Jesus Christ, for they know that if they can do away with His deity they can destroy the entire body of Christian truth. Christianity is Christ, and if He is not what He claims to be, there is no Christian faith.

It must be made clear that these false teachers are unsaved. They are compared to dogs and pigs, not to sheep (2 Peter 2:22). Jude described these same people, and in Jude 19 he clearly stated, "having not the Spirit." If a person does not have the Spirit of God within, he is not a child of God (Rom. 8:9). He may pretend to be saved and even become a member or an officer in a fundamental church, but eventually he will deny the Lord.

In what sense were these people "bought" by the Lord? While it is true that Jesus Christ died for the church (Eph. 5:25), it is also true that He died for the sins of the whole world (1 John 2:2). He is the merchant who purchased the whole field (the world) that He might acquire the treasure in it (Matt. 13:44). When it comes to *application,* our Lord's atonement is limited to those who believe. But when it comes to *efficacy,* His death is sufficient for the whole world. He purchased even those who reject Him and deny Him! This makes their condemnation even greater.

Even good and godly Christians may disagree on fine points of doctrine, but they all agree on the person and work of Jesus Christ. He is the Son of God and God the Son. He is the only Savior. To deny this is to condemn your own soul.

Sensuality (v. 2). *Pernicious ways* simply means "licentious conduct." Jude accused the false teachers of "turning the grace of God into lasciviousness" (Jude 4). Now we understand why they deny the truths of the Christian faith: they want to satisfy their own lusts and do it under the guise of religion. The false prophets in Jeremiah's day were guilty of the same sins (Jer. 23:14, 32).

The fact that *many* follow the evil example of their conduct is proof that people would rather follow the false than the true, the sensual rather than the spiritual. These false teachers are very successful in their ministry! They have glowing statistics to report, and crowds gather to hear them! But statistics are not proof of authenticity. The broad way that leads to destruction is crowded (Matt. 7:13–14). Many will claim to be true servants of Christ, but will be rejected on the last day (Matt. 7:21–23).

What happens to their followers? For one thing, they bring disgrace to the name of Christ. The Christian faith gets a bad name because of their filthy lives. "They profess that they know God; but in works they deny him, being abominable, and disobedient, and unto every good work reprobate" (Titus 1:16). "For the name of God is blasphemed among the Gentiles through you" (Rom. 2:24). Few things hinder the cause of Christ like the bad reputations of professing Christians who are members of orthodox churches.

Greed (v. 3). False teachers are interested in one thing: making money. They exploit ("make merchandise of") ignorant people and use their religion as "a cloak of covetousness" (1 Thess. 2:5). Our Lord was a poor Man, and so were the apostles, yet they gave of themselves to minister to others. These false prophets are rich men who cleverly get others to minister to them! Micah described these false prophets in his day: "Her leaders pronounce judgment for a bribe, her priests instruct for a price, and her prophets divine for money" (Mic. 3:11 NASB). Certainly the laborer is worthy of his hire (Luke 10:7), but his motives for ministry had better go beyond money. It has often been said that immorality, love of money, and pride have been the ruin of many people. These false teachers were guilty of all three!

They use their "plastic words" as well as "great swelling words" (2 Peter 2:18) to fascinate and influence their victims. They flatter sinners and tell them the kind of ego-building words that they want to hear (see the contrast in 1 Thess. 2:5). They will scratch the itching ears of people who reject the truth of the Bible and turn to fables (2 Tim. 4:1–4). Religion can be a tremendous tool for exploiting weak people, and these false teachers use religion just to get what they can. They are not ministers; they are merchandisers.

The true minister of Jesus Christ has nothing to hide: his life and ministry are an open book. He preaches the truth in love and does not twist the Scriptures to support his own selfish ideas. He does not flatter the rich or minister only to make money. Paul described the true minister in 2 Corinthians 4:2—"But [we] have renounced the hidden things of dishonesty, not walking in craftiness, nor handling the Word of God deceitfully; but by manifestation of the truth commending ourselves to every man's conscience in the sight of God." Contrast that description with what Peter wrote in this chapter, and with what Jude wrote, and you will see the difference. How we need to be alert and refuse to support ministries that exploit people and deny the Savior.

The False Teachers Destroyed (2:3–6, 9b)

Peter saw no hope for these apostates; their doom was sealed. His attitude was different from that of "tolerant" religious people today who say, "Well, they may not agree with us, but there are many roads to heaven." Peter made it clear that these false teachers had "forsaken the right way" (2 Peter 2:15), which simply means they were going the *wrong* way! Their judgment was sure, even though it had not yet come. The trial was over, but the sentence had not yet been executed. It would not linger or slumber, Peter affirmed; it would come in due time.

In this section, Peter proved that judgment finally does come, no matter how secure the sinner might feel. He used three examples to verify this truth (see also Jude 6–8).

The fallen angels (v. 4). We wish we knew more about the creation of the angels and the fall of Lucifer and his host, but most of these details are shrouded in mystery. Many Bible students believe that Isaiah 14:12–15 describes the fall of Lucifer, the highest of the angels. Some students feel that Ezekiel 28:11–19 also deals with the same topic. It would appear that Lucifer was God's deputy, in charge of the angelic hosts, but that his pride made him grasp after the very throne of God. (John Milton imaginatively portrayed this in the famous poem *Paradise Lost*.) Revelation 12:4 suggests that perhaps one third of the angels fell with Lucifer, who became Satan, the adversary of God.

Where are these fallen angels now? We know that Satan is free and at work in the world (1 Peter 5:8), and that he has an army of demonic powers assisting him (Eph. 6:10–12) who are probably some of the fallen angels. But Peter said that some of the angels were confined to Tartarus ("hell"), which is a Greek word for the underworld. Tartarus may be a special section of hell where these angels are chained in pits of darkness, awaiting the final judgment. It is not necessary to debate the hidden mysteries of this verse in order to get the main message: God judges rebellion and will not spare those who reject His will. If God judged the angels, who in many respects are higher than men, then certainly He will judge rebellious men.

The old world (v. 5). Genesis 6:3 indicates that God waited 120 years before He sent the flood. All during that time, Noah ministered as a "herald" of God's righteousness. If you want to read a description of the world before the flood, read Romans 1:18ff. Gentile civilization had become so corrupt that it was necessary for God to wipe the earth clean. He saved only eight people, Noah and his family, because they had faith in God (Heb. 11:7).

But nobody believed Noah's message! Jesus made it clear that people were enjoying their normal lives up to the very day that Noah and his family entered the ark (Luke 17:26–27)! No doubt there were plenty of "experts" who laughed at Noah and assured the people that a rainstorm was out of the question. Had anybody ever seen one? The apostates in Peter's day used that same argument to "prove" that the day of the Lord would not come (2 Peter 3:3ff.).

When you compare our world with Noah's world, you see some frightening parallels. The population was multiplying (Gen. 6:1), and the world was filled with wickedness (Gen. 6:5) and violence (Gen. 6:11, 13). Lawlessness abounded. True believers were a minority, and nobody paid any attention to them! But the flood came, and the entire population of the world was destroyed. God does indeed judge those who reject His truth.

Sodom and Gomorrah (vv. 6, 9b). The record is given in Genesis 18—19, and God's opinion of the people of these cities is found in Genesis 13:13—"But the men of Sodom were wicked and sinners before the Lord exceedingly." Peter said they were "ungodly," and Jude said they were given to "fornication and going after strange flesh" (Jude 7). The men of Sodom practiced filthy behavior and unlawful deeds (2 Peter 2:7–8). Since the law of Moses had not yet been given, the word *unlawful* cannot refer to some Jewish law. In what sense were their filthy deeds "unlawful"? They were contrary to nature (see Rom. 1:24–27). The flagrant sin of Sodom and the other cities was unnatural sex, sodomy, or homosexual behavior, a sin that is clearly condemned in Scripture (Lev. 18:22; Rom. 1:24–27; 1 Cor. 6:9).

In spite of Abraham's intercessory prayer (Gen. 18:22ff.) and Lot's last-minute warning, the people of Sodom perished in fire and brimstone. Again, up to the very minute that Lot left the city, the people were confident that everything was safe, but then the fire fell (Luke 17:28–29). God did not spare them, nor will He spare sinners today who willfully reject His truth and deny His Son. God buried Sodom and Gomorrah, probably under the Dead Sea. They are examples to sinners today to beware the wrath to come.

Having cited these three examples of certain judgment, Peter then applied the lesson to the subject at hand, *the false teachers* (2 Peter 2:9b). God has reserved the unjust for special punishment on that day of judgment. The false teachers may seem successful (for "many" follow them), but in the end, they will be condemned. Their judgment is being prepared now ("lingereth not," 2 Peter 2:3), and what is prepared will be reserved and applied on the last day.

What a contrast between the false teachers and the true children of God! We have an inheritance reserved for us (1 Peter 1:4) because Jesus Christ is preparing a home for us in heaven (John 14:1–6). We are not looking for judgment, but for the coming of the Lord to take His people home to glory! "For God hath not appointed us to wrath, but to obtain salvation by our Lord Jesus Christ" (1 Thess. 5:9).

Peter next turned his attention to the believers themselves. How could they stay true to the Lord in such a wicked world?

The True Believers Delivered (2:5–9a)

Peter's purpose was not just to denounce the apostates; he also wanted to encourage the true believers. He once again reached back into the Old Testament and cited two examples of deliverance.

Noah (v. 5). This man of faith experienced a two-fold deliverance. First, God delivered him from the pollutions of the world around him. For 120 years, Noah faithfully proclaimed the Word of God to people who would not believe it. He and his family were surrounded by moral and spiritual darkness, yet they kept their lights shining. God did not protect Noah and his family by isolating them from the world, but by enabling them to remain pure in the midst of corruption. Through Jesus Christ, we too have "escaped the corruption that is in the world through lust" (2 Peter 1:4).

Our Lord petitioned the heavenly Father, "I pray not that thou shouldest take them out of the world, but that thou shouldest keep them from the evil" (John 17:15). Imagine Noah and his wife raising a family in a world so wicked that they could have no believing friends! Yet God found believing wives for their three sons, and God guarded this home from the pollutions of the world.

But God also delivered Noah and his family from the judgment of the world. The flood waters that brought condemnation to the world only lifted Noah and his household up above the judgment. They were secure in the ark of safety. In his first epistle, Peter had seen in the ark a type of our salvation in Jesus Christ (1 Peter 3:20–22). The world, as it were, was "buried" in the baptism of the flood, but Noah was lifted up, a picture of resurrection and salvation.

Certainly Peter was assuring his readers that, when the great day of judgment does come, they will be kept safe. Jesus Christ is our "ark of safety." He delivers us from the wrath to come (1 Thess. 1:10). God has promised that the earth will never again be judged by water, but there is coming a judgment of fire (2 Peter 3:10ff.). But those who have trusted Christ will never face judgment (John 5:24), because He bore their judgment on the cross.

Lot (vv. 6–9a). Abraham took his nephew, Lot, with him when he left Ur and went to the land of Canaan, but Lot proved to be more of a problem than a blessing. When Abraham, in a lapse of faith, went down to Egypt, Lot went with him and got a taste of "the world" (Gen. 12:10—13:1). As Lot became richer, he had to separate from Abraham, and this removed him from his uncle's godly influence. What a privilege Lot had to walk with Abraham, who walked with God! And yet, how Lot wasted his privileges.

When Lot had to choose a new area for his home, he measured it by what he had seen in Egypt (Gen. 13:10). Abraham took Lot out of Egypt, but he could not take Egypt out of Lot. Lot "pitched his tent toward Sodom" (Gen. 13:12) and then finally moved into Sodom (Gen. 14:12). God even used a local war to try to get Lot out of Sodom, but he went right back. That is where his heart was.

It is difficult for us to understand Lot. Peter made it clear that Lot was saved ("just Lot … that righteous man"), and yet we wonder what he was doing in such

a wicked place as Sodom. If we understand Genesis 19 correctly, Lot had at least four daughters, two of whom had married men of Sodom. All the while Lot lived in Sodom, his soul was "tortured" and "greatly troubled" by the filthy conduct of the people. Perhaps he thought he could change them. If so, he failed miserably.

God enabled Lot and his family to remain unpolluted, even though they were living in the midst of a cesspool of iniquity. God also rescued Lot and two of his daughters before the judgment fell on Sodom and the other cities of the plain (Gen. 19). Lot was not rescued because of any merit on his part. He was rescued because he was a believer and because his uncle Abraham had prayed for him. Abraham outside of Sodom had more influence than Lot inside the city. Lot even lost his testimony to his own family, for his married daughters and their husbands laughed at his warning, and his wife disobeyed God and was killed.

Lot *chose* to live in Sodom and could have avoided the filthy influence of the place, but many people today really have no choice and must live surrounded by the pollutions of the world. Think of the Christian slaves who had to serve godless masters, or Christian wives married to unsaved husbands, or believing children with unsaved parents. Christian employees working in offices or factories are forced to see and hear things that can easily stain the mind and heart. Peter assured his readers and us that God knows how to "be delivering the godly out of testing and temptation" (2 Peter 2:9, wuest) so that we may live victoriously.

He also is able to rescue us from judgment. In Noah's case, it was a judgment of water, but in Lot's case it was a judgment of fire. The cities of the plain were caught in a violent overthrow as the area became a vast furnace of fire and brimstone. This certainly would parallel Peter's warning about the coming judgment of fire (2 Peter 3:10ff.).

Peter was not pointing to Lot as an example of separated living, but rather as an example of one whom God rescued from pollution and condemnation. In a sense, Lot was even rescued against his will, because the angels had to grasp him by the hand and pull him out of the city (Gen. 19:16). Lot had entered Sodom, and then Sodom had entered Lot, and he found it difficult to leave.

Our Lord used both Noah and Lot to warn us to be prepared for His return (Luke 17:26–37). The people in Sodom were enjoying their regular pleasures, careless of the fact that judgment was coming; when it came, they were unprepared. "Wherefore, beloved, seeing that ye look for such things, be diligent that ye may be found of him in peace, without spot, and blameless" (1 Peter 3:14).

But the same God who delivers the godly also reserves the ungodly for judgment. It has well been said that if God spares today's cities from judgment, He will have to apologize to Sodom and Gomorrah. Why is God's judgment lingering? Because God "is longsuffering … not willing that any should perish, but that all should come to repentance" (2 Peter 3:9). Society in Noah's day had 120 years in which to repent and believe, yet they rejected the truth. Though Lot's example and testimony were weak, he at least represented the truth, yet his immoral neighbors wanted nothing to do with God.

Our present age is not only like "the days of Noah," but it is also like "the days of Lot." Many believers have abandoned the place of separation and are compromising with the world. The professing church has but a weak testimony to the world, and sinners do not really believe that judgment is coming. Society is full of immorality, especially the kind of sin for which Sodom was famous. It appears as though God is slumbering, unconcerned about the way rebellious sinners have polluted His world. But one day the fire will fall; then it will be too late.

God's people, as weak as they are, will be delivered from judgment by the grace and mercy of God. God could not judge Sodom until Lot and his family were out of the city. Likewise, it is my belief that God will not send wrath on this world until He takes His own people out and home to heaven. "For God hath not appointed us to wrath, but to obtain salvation by our Lord Jesus Christ, who died for us, that, whether we wake or sleep [live or die], we should live together with him" (1 Thess. 5:9–10).

One day soon, the fire will fall. Are you ready?

CHAPTER FOUR
2 Peter 2:10–16
MARKED MEN

Peter was not yet finished with the apostates! Unlike some believers today, Peter was disturbed by the inroads the false teachers were making into the churches. He knew that their approach was subtle but their teachings were fatal, and he wanted to warn the churches about them.

Remember, however, that Peter opened this letter with positive teaching about salvation, Christian growth, and the dependability of the Word of God. He had a balanced ministry, and it is important that we maintain that balance today. When Charles Spurgeon started his magazine, he named it *The Sword and Trowel,* alluding to the workers in the book of Nehemiah who kept their swords in one hand and their tools in the other as they were repairing the walls of Jerusalem.

Some people have a purely negative ministry and never build anything. They are too busy fighting the enemy! Others claim to be "positive," but they never defend what they have built. Peter knew that it was not enough only to attack the apostates; he also had to give solid teaching to the believers in the churches.

In this section of his letter, Peter condemned the apostates for three specific sins.

Their Reviling (2:10–12)

The picture here is of proud people who try to build themselves up while they try to tear down everybody else. They show no respect for authority and are not afraid to attack and defame people in high positions.

God has established authority in this world, and when we resist authority, we are resisting God (Rom. 13:1ff). Parents are to have authority over their children (Eph. 6:1–4) and employers over their employees (Eph. 6:5–8). As citizens, we Christians should pray for those in authority (1 Tim. 2:1–4), show respect to them (1 Peter 2:11–17), and seek to glorify God in our behavior. As members of a local assembly, we should honor those who have the spiritual rule over us and seek to encourage them in their ministry (Heb. 13:7, 17; 1 Peter 5:1–6).

Human government is, in one sense, God's gift to help maintain order in the world, so that the church may minister the Word and win the lost to Christ (1 Tim. 2:1–8). We should pray daily for those in authority so that they might exercise that authority in the will of God. It is a serious thing for a Christian to oppose the law, and he must be sure he is in the will of God when he does it. He should also do it in a manner that glorifies Christ, so that innocent people (including unsaved government employees) might not be made to suffer.

The reason for their reviling (v. 10). One word gives the reason: *flesh.* The depraved nature of man does not want to submit to any kind of authority. "Do your own thing!" is its insistent message, and many people follow it. In recent years, there has been an epidemic of books that encourage people to succeed at any cost, even to the extent of hurting or intimidating others. The important thing, according to these books, is to take care of yourself—"number one"—and to use other people as tools for the achievement of your own selfish goals.

Man's fallen nature encourages pride. When the ego is at stake, these apostates will stop at nothing in order to promote and protect themselves. Their attitude is completely opposite that of our Lord, who willingly emptied Himself to become a servant and then died as a sacrifice for our sins (see Phil. 2). These men that Peter described were *presumptuous,* which means they were "very daring and bold" in the way they spoke about those in positions of dignity. There is a boldness that is heroic, but there is also a boldness that is satanic.

These men were also *self-willed,* which means they "lived to please only themselves." They were arrogant and would even defy God to get what they wanted! Proverbs 21:24 describes them perfectly. While outwardly they appeared to serve God and minister to the people, *inwardly* they fed their own egos and feathered their own nests.

In their arrogance, "they are not afraid to speak evil of dignities [glorious ones]." While the immediate reference is probably to "exalted ones" in places of authority, the angels may also be in view here, since in the next verse Peter referred to the angels. These apostates revile even the angels! And they do not even tremble when they do it! They are so secure in their pride that they even dare God to judge them.

The seriousness of their reviling (v. 11). The angels are reviled by the apostates, but the apostates are not reviled by the angels! Even the angels, though greater in strength and power, will not intrude into a sphere that is not their own. The angels remember the rebellion of Lucifer and know how serious it is to revolt against God's authority. If God judged the rebellious angels, how much more will He judge rebellious men!

The suggestion here is that the godly angels do not even speak against the *fallen* angels. They have left all judgment to the Lord. We will learn more about this when we study Jude, for he mentions this matter of the angels in Jude 8–9.

Speaking evil of others is a great sin, and the people of God must avoid it. We may not respect the people in office, but we must respect the office, for all authority is God-given. Those who revile government officials in the name of Christ ought to read and ponder Titus 3:1–2—"Remind them to be subject to rulers, to authorities, to be obedient, to be ready for every good deed, to malign no one, to be uncontentious, gentle, showing every consideration for all men" (NASB).

When Daniel refused the king's food, he did it in a gracious way that did not get his guard into trouble (Dan. 1). Even when the apostles refused to obey the Sanhedrin's order that they stop preaching in the name of Jesus, they acted like gentlemen. They respected the authority even though they disobeyed the order. It is when the flesh goes to work that pride enters in, and then we use our tongues as weapons instead of tools. "The words of his mouth are iniquity and deceit: he hath left off to be wise, and to do good" (Ps. 36:3).

The judgment of their reviling (v. 12). Peter compared these false teachers to "unreasoning animals" (NASB) whose only destiny is to be slaughtered! At the end of this chapter, they are pictured as pigs and dogs! Animals have life, but they live purely by instinct. They lack the finer sensibilities that humans possess. Jesus warned us not to waste precious things on unappreciative brute beasts (Matt. 7:6).

I once made a pastoral visit at a home where a death had occurred, and even before I made it up the stairs to the door, a huge dog began to bark and carry on as though I were there to rob everybody. I ignored his threats because I knew he was acting purely on instinct. He was making a lot of noise about something he knew nothing about! His master had to take him to the basement before it was safe for me to enter the home and minister to the bereaved family.

So with these apostates: they make a lot of noise about things they know nothing about! The Phillips translation of 2 Peter 2:12 says they "scoff at things outside their own experience." The New International Version reads, "But these men blaspheme in matters they do not understand." Whenever her pupils were noisy in class, one of my teachers used to say, "Empty barrels make the most noise!" And so they do!

It is sad when the media concentrates on the "big mouths" of the false teachers instead of the "still small voice" of the Lord as He ministers through those who are true to Him. It is sadder still when innocent people become fascinated by these "great swelling words of vanity" (2 Peter 2:18) and cannot discern between truth and propaganda. The truth of the Word of God leads to salvation, but the arrogant words of the apostates lead only to condemnation.

These "brute beasts" are destined for destruction, a truth Peter mentioned often in 2 Peter 2 (vv. 3–4, 9, 12, 17, 20). As they seek to destroy the faith, they themselves shall be destroyed. They will be "corrupted in their own corruption." Their very nature will drag them down into destruction, like the pig returning to the mire and the dog to its vomit (2 Peter 2:22). Unfortunately, before that event takes place, these people can do a great deal of moral and spiritual damage.

Their Reveling (2:13–14a)

The words translated "riot" and "sporting" carry the meaning of "sensual reveling." They also contain the idea of luxury, softness, and extravagance. At the expense of those who support them (2 Peter 2:3), the apostates enjoy luxurious living. In our own society, there are those who plead for funds for their "ministries," yet live in expensive houses, drive luxury cars, and wear costly clothes. When we remember that Jesus became poor in order to make us rich, their garish lifestyle seems out of step with New Testament Christianity.

Not only do they deceive others, but they even deceive themselves! They can "prove" from the Bible that their lifestyle is right. In ancient times, it was expected that people would revel at night, but these people dared to revel in the daytime, so convinced were they of their practices. A person can become so accustomed to his vices that he sees them as virtues.

If they kept their way of life out of the church, we would not have to be as concerned—but they are a part of the fellowship! They were even sharing in the "love feasts" that the early church used to enjoy in connection with the celebration of the Lord's Supper (1 Cor. 11:20–34). It was a time when the poorer believers could enjoy a decent meal because of the generosity of the Christians who were better off economically. But the apostates only used the "love feast" as a time for displaying their wealth and impressing ignorant people who lacked discernment.

Instead of bringing blessing to the fellowship, these false teachers were "spots" and "blemishes" that defiled the assembly. Somehow their behavior at the feasts defiled others and brought disgrace to the name of the Lord. It is the Word of God that helps to remove the spots and blemishes (Eph. 5:27), but these teachers do not minister the truth of the Word. They twist

Scripture to make it say what they want it to say (2 Peter 3:16).

This "unconscious defilement" is a deadly thing. The Pharisees were also guilty of it (Matt. 23:25–28). False doctrine inevitably leads to false living, and false living then encourages false doctrine. The apostate must "adjust" God's Word or change his way of life, and he is not about to change his lifestyle! So, wherever he goes, he secretly defiles people and makes it easier for them to sin. It is possible to go to a church fellowship and be defiled!

Certainly our churches need to exercise authority and practice discipline. Christian love does not mean that we tolerate every false doctrine and every so-called "lifestyle." The Bible makes it clear that some things are right and some things are wrong. No Christian whose belief and behavior are contrary to the Word of God should be permitted to share in the Lord's Supper or to have a spiritual ministry in the church. His defiling influence may not be seen immediately, but ultimately it will create serious problems.

Second Peter 2:14 makes it clear that the apostates attend these church meetings for two reasons: first, to satisfy their own lusts; second, to capture converts for their cause.

They keep their eyes open, looking for "loose women" whom they can entice into sin. Paul warned about similar apostates who "creep into houses and lead captive silly women laden with sins, led away with divers lusts" (2 Tim. 3:6). More than one "minister" has used religion as a cloak to cover his own lusts. Some women, in particular, are vulnerable in "counseling sessions," and these men take advantage of them.

In one of the churches I pastored, I noticed that a young man in the choir was doing his utmost to appear a "spiritual giant" to the other choir members, especially the younger women. He prayed with fervency and often talked about his walk with the Lord. Some of the people were impressed by him, but I felt that something was wrong and that danger was in the air. Sure enough, he began to date one of the fine young ladies who happened to be a new believer. In spite of my warnings, she continued the friendship, which ended in her being seduced. I praise God that she was rescued and is now faithfully serving God, but she could have avoided that terrible experience.

The satisfying of their lusts is the false teachers' main ambition: they *cannot cease from sin.* The verb suggests "they are unable to stop." Why? Because they are in bondage (2 Peter 2:18–19). The apostates consider themselves to be "free," yet they are in the most terrible kind of slavery. Whatever they touch, they defile; whoever they enlist, they enslave.

"Beguiling unstable souls" presents the picture of a fisherman baiting a hook or a hunter baiting a trap. The same image is used in James 1:14, where James presents temptation as "the baiting of the trap." Satan knows that he could never trap us unless there is some fine bait to attract us in the first place. Satan promised

Eve that she and Adam would become "like gods" if they ate of the forbidden tree (Gen. 3:4–5), and they "took the bait" and were trapped.

What kind of "bait" do the apostates use to catch people? For one thing, they offer them "liberty" (2 Peter 2:19). This probably means a perversion of the grace of God, "turning the grace of our God into lasciviousness" (Jude 4). "Since you are saved by grace," they argued, "then you have the freedom to sin. The more you sin, the more of God's grace you will experience!" Paul answered their false arguments in Romans 6, a portion of Scripture that every believer ought to master.

Along with "freedom" they also bait the trap with "fulfillment." This is one of the buzz words of our generation, and it goes right along with "doing your own thing" and "having it your way." They say, "The Christian life that the church offers is old-fashioned and outdated. We have a new lifestyle that makes you feel fulfilled and helps you find your true self!" Alas, like the prodigal son, these unstable souls try to find themselves, but they end up *losing* themselves (Luke 15:11–24). In their search for fulfillment they become very self-centered and lose the opportunities for growth that come from serving others.

There can be no freedom or fulfillment apart from submission to Jesus Christ. "The purpose of life," said P. T. Forsyth, "is not to find your freedom, but to find your master." Just as a gifted musician finds freedom and fulfillment putting himself or herself under the discipline of a great artist, or an athlete under the discipline of a great coach, so the believer finds true freedom and fulfillment under the authority of Jesus Christ.

Who are the people who "take the bait" that the apostates put into their subtle traps? Peter called them "unstable souls." Stability is an important factor in a successful Christian life. Just as a child must learn to stand before he can walk or run, so the Christian must learn to "stand firm in the Lord." Paul and the other apostles sought to establish their converts in the faith (Rom. 1:11; 16:25; 1 Thess. 3:2, 13). Peter was certain that his readers were "established in the present truth" (2 Peter 1:12), but he still warned them.

Their Revolting (2:14b–16)

"They have abandoned the right road" is the way the Phillips translation expresses it. The apostates know the right road, the straight path that God has established, but they deliberately abandon God's way for their own. No wonder Peter called them "natural brute beasts" (2 Peter 2:12) and compared them to animals (2 Peter 2:22). "Be ye not as the horse, or as the mule!" warned the psalmist (Ps. 32:9). The horse likes to rush ahead and the mule likes to lag behind; both can get you off the right path. Believers are sheep, and sheep need to stay close to the shepherd or they will stray.

We have already learned one reason for the apostates' godless conduct: they want to satisfy the cravings of their flesh. But there is a second reason: they are covetous and want to exploit people for personal gain. Peter mentioned this in 2 Peter 2:3 and now develops the thought. Not only is the false teacher's outlook controlled by his passions (2 Peter 2:14a), but his heart is controlled by covetousness. He is in bondage to lust for pleasure and money!

In fact, he has perfected the skill of getting what he wants. "They are experts in greed" says the New International Version, and the Phillips translation is even more graphic: "Their technique of getting what they want is, through long practice, highly developed." They know exactly how to motivate people to give. While the true servant of God trusts the Father to meet his needs and seeks to help people grow through their giving, the apostate trusts his "fundraising skills" and leaves people in worse shape than he found them. He knows how to exploit the unstable and the innocent.

There is certainly nothing wrong with a ministry sharing its opportunities and needs with its praying friends. My wife and I receive many publications and letters of this kind, and, quite frankly, some of them we throw away without reading. We have learned that these ministries cannot be trusted, that their dramatic appeals are not always based on fact, and that the funds donated are not always used as they should be. The other letters and publications we read carefully, pray about, discuss, and see if God would have us invest in their work. We know we cannot support every good work that God has raised up, so we try to exercise discernment, and invest in the ministries God has chosen for us.

As Peter wrote about the devious practices of these people, he could only exclaim, "Cursed children!" They were not the "blessed" children of God but the cursed children of the devil (John 8:44). They might succeed in building up their bank accounts, but in the end, at the throne of God, they would be declared bankrupt. "Depart from me, ye cursed, into everlasting fire, prepared for the devil and his angels" (Matt. 25:41). "For what is a man profited, if he shall gain the whole world, and lose his own soul?" (Matt. 16:26).

Covetousness is the insatiable desire for more—more money, more power, more prestige. The covetous heart is never satisfied. This explains why the love of money is a root of all kinds of evil (1 Tim. 6:10), for when a person craves more money, he will commit any sin to satisfy that craving. He has already broken the first two of the Ten Commandments, because money is already his god and idol. It is then a simple step to break the others—to steal, lie, commit adultery, take God's name in vain, and so on. No wonder Jesus warned, "Take heed and beware of covetousness" (Luke 12:15).

I have read that the people in North Africa have devised a clever way to catch monkeys. They make a hole in a gourd just large enough for the monkey's paw, then fill the gourd with nuts and tie it to a tree. At night, the monkey reaches into the gourd for the nuts, only to find he cannot pull his paw out of the gourd! Of course, he could let go of the nuts and escape quite easily—but he doesn't want to forfeit the nuts! He ends up being captured because of his covetousness. We might expect this kind of stupidity in a dumb animal, but certainly not in a person made in the image of God; yet it happens every day.

Peter knew his Old Testament Scriptures. He had already used Noah and Lot to illustrate his words, and in 2 Peter 2:15–16, he used the prophet Balaam. The story of Balaam is found in Numbers 22—25; take time now to read it.

Balaam is a mysterious character, a Gentile prophet who tried to curse the Jews. Balak, the king of the Moabites, was afraid of Israel, so he turned to Balaam for help. Balaam knew it was wrong to cooperate with Balak, but his heart was covetous and he wanted the money and honor that Balak promised him. Balaam knew the truth of God and the will of God, yet he deliberately abandoned the right way and went astray. He is a perfect illustration of the apostates in their covetous practices.

From the outset, God told Balaam not to help Balak and, at first, Balaam obeyed and sent the messengers home. But when Balak sent more princes and promised more money and honor, Balaam decided to "pray about it again" and reconsider the matter. The second time, God tested Balaam and permitted him to go with the princes. This was not God's direct will; it was His permissive will, designed to see what the prophet would do.

Balaam jumped at the chance! But when he started to go astray, God rebuked the disobedient prophet through the mouth of his donkey. How remarkable that the animals obey God, even when their masters do not (read Isa. 1:3)! God permitted Balaam to set up his altars and offer his sacrifices, but God did not permit him to curse Israel. Instead, God turned Balaam's curse into a blessing (Deut. 23:4–5; Neh. 13:2).

Balaam was not able to curse Israel, but he was able to tell Balak how to defeat Israel. All the Moabites had to do was invite the Jews to be "friendly neighbors" and share in their feasts (Num. 25). Instead of maintaining its separated position, Israel compromised and joined the pagan orgies of the Moabites. God had to discipline the people and thousands of them died.

You can see in Balaam the two aspects of apostasy that Peter emphasized in this chapter: sensual lust and covetousness. He loved money and he led Israel into lustful sin. He was a man who could get messages from God, yet he led people away from God! When you read his oracles, you cannot help but be impressed with his eloquence, yet he deliberately disobeyed God! Balaam said, "I have sinned" (Num. 22:34), but his confession was not sincere. He even prayed, "Let me die the death of the righteous" (Num. 23:10), yet he did not want to live the life of the righteous.

Because Balaam counseled Balak to seduce Israel, God saw to it that Balaam was judged. He was slain by the sword when Israel defeated the Midianites (Num. 31:8). We wonder who received all the wealth that he had "earned" by his devious ways. Peter called his hire "the wages of unrighteousness." This phrase reminds us of another pretender, Judas, who received "the reward of iniquity" (Acts 1:18) and who also perished in shame.

We will have more to say about Balaam when we study Jude 11, but we must not ignore the main lesson: he was a rebel against the will of God. Like the false teachers that Peter described, Balaam knew the right way, but deliberately chose the wrong way because he wanted to make money. He kept "playing with the will of God" by trying to get "a different viewpoint" (Num. 22:41; 23:13, 27). He no doubt had a true gift from God because he uttered some beautiful prophecies about Jesus Christ, but he prostituted that gift to base uses just to gain honor and wealth.

A bank officer approached a junior clerk and secretly asked, "If I gave you $50,000, would you help me alter the books?"

"Yes, I guess I would," the man replied.

"Would you do it for $100?"

"Of course not!" the man said. "What do you think I am, a common thief?"

"We've already determined that," said the officer. "Now we're talking about price."

The person who is covetous does have his price, and when it is met, he will do whatever is asked, even revolt against the will of God. Peter called this attitude *madness.* The word means "to be deranged, out of your mind." But Balaam thought he was doing the wise thing; after all, he was taking advantage of a situation that might never come along again. But any rebellion against God is madness and can only lead to tragedy. It was when the prodigal son "came to himself" that he realized how stupid he had been (Luke 15:17).

Peter has condemned three sins of the false teachers: their reviling, their reveling, and their revolting. All of these sins spring from pride and selfish desire. A true servant of God is humble and seeks to serve others (see the contrast in Phil. 2:20–21). The true servant of God does not think about praise or pay, because he serves God from a loving and obedient heart. He honors God and the authority that God has established in this world. In short, the true servant of God patterns himself after Jesus Christ.

In these last days there will be an abundance of false teachers pleading for support. They are gifted and experienced when it comes to deceiving people and getting their money. It is important that God's people be established in the truth, that they know how to detect when the Scriptures are being twisted and the people exploited. I thank God for agencies that help to expose "religious rackets," but there is still the need for spiritual discernment and a growing knowledge of the Word of God.

Not all of these "religious frauds" will be discovered and put out of business. But God will one day deal with all of them! Like animals, they will be "taken and destroyed" (2 Peter 2:12). They will receive "the reward of unrighteousness" (2 Peter 2:13) to compensate for the wages they have exploited from others. As "cursed children" (2 Peter 2:14) they will be banished from the presence of the Lord forever.

They are marked men and women; they will not escape.

CHAPTER FIVE
2 Peter 2:17–22
FALSE FREEDOM

It is a frightening fact that many people who are now zealous members of cults were at one time attending churches that at least professed to believe the Christian gospel. They participated in the Communion service and saw the death of the Lord Jesus portrayed in the loaf and the cup. They even recited the Apostles' Creed and the Lord's Prayer. Yet today, these people will tell you that they "feel free" now that they have been "liberated" from the Christian faith.

At the same time, you will meet people who have rejected all religious faith and now profess to enjoy a new freedom. "I used to believe that stuff," they will boldly confess, "but I don't believe it anymore. I've got something better and I feel free for the first time in my life."

Freedom is a concept that is very important in today's world, yet not everybody really understands what the word means. In fact, everybody from the Communist to the "playboy" seems to have his own definition. Nobody is completely free in the sense of having the ability and the opportunity to do whatever he wants to do. For that matter, doing whatever you please is *not* freedom—it is the worst kind of bondage.

The apostates offer freedom to their converts, and this "bait" entices them to abandon the true faith and follow the false teachers. The teachers promise them liberty, but this promise is never fulfilled; the unstable converts only find themselves in terrible bondage. The freedom offered is a *false* freedom, and Peter gave three reasons that explain why it is false.

It Is Based on False Promises (2:17–18)
Faith is only as good as the object. A pagan may have great faith in his idol, but the idol can do nothing for him. I have a friend who put his faith in a certain investment scheme and lost almost everything. His faith was strong but the company was weak. When you put your faith in Jesus Christ, that faith will accomplish something, because God always keeps His promises. "There hath not failed one word of all his good promise" (1 Kings 8:56).

Peter used three vivid illustrations to emphasize the emptiness of the apostates' promises.

"Wells without water" (v. 17a). The Greek

word actually means "a flowing spring" rather than a tranquil well. It is the word our Lord used when He ministered to the Samaritan woman (John 4:14) and that John used in describing the satisfaction the saints will experience for all eternity (Rev. 7:17; 21:6). A spring without water is not a spring at all! A well is still called a well even if the water is gone, but a spring ceases to exist if the water is not flowing.

There is in mankind an inborn thirst for reality, for God. "Thou hast made us for thyself," said Augustine, "and our hearts are restless until they rest in thee." People attempt to satisfy this thirst in many ways, and they end up living on substitutes. Only Jesus Christ can give inner peace and satisfaction.

"Whosoever drinketh [present tense, "keeps on drinking"] of this water [in the well] shall thirst again," said Jesus, "but whosoever drinketh [takes one drink once and for all] of the water that I shall give him shall never thirst" (John 4:13–14). What a contrast! You may drink repeatedly at the broken cisterns of the world and never find satisfaction, but you may take one drink of the Living Water through faith in Jesus Christ, and you will be satisfied forever. The false teachers could not make this kind of an offer, because they had nothing to offer. They could promise, but they could not produce.

"Clouds that are carried with a tempest" (v. 17b). The picture is that of clouds of fog or mist being driven by a squall over a lake or sea. Clouds ought to announce the possibility of rain, but these clouds only announce that a windstorm is coming. Jude's description is, "Clouds they are without water, carried about of winds" (Jude 12). Again, there is noise, motion, and something to watch, but nothing profitable happens. The farmer sees the clouds and prays they will empty rain on his parched fields. The false teachers have nothing to give; they are empty.

"The mist of darkness" (vv. 17c–18). The word translated "mist" means "blackness, gloom," so "the blackness of the darkness" would be an accurate translation (see 2 Peter 2:4). These apostates promise to lead people into the light, but they themselves end up in the darkest part of the darkness (see Jude 6 and 13)! The atmosphere of hell is not uniform: some places will be darker than others. How tragic that innocent people will be led astray by these apostates and possibly end up in hell with them.

Since these false teachers really have nothing to give, how are they able to attract followers? The reasons are found in 2 Peter 2:18.

First, the teachers are eloquent promoters of their doctrines. They know how to impress people with their vocabulary, "inflated words that say nothing" (literal translation). The average person does not know how to listen to and analyze the kind of propaganda that pours out of the mouths and printing presses of the apostates. Many people cannot tell the difference between a religious huckster and a sincere servant of Jesus Christ.

Do not be impressed with religious oratory. Apollos was a fervent and eloquent religious speaker, but he did not know the right message to preach (Acts 18:24–28). Paul was careful not to build his converts' faith on either his words or his wisdom (1 Cor. 2:1–5). Paul was a brilliant man, but his ministry was simple and practical. He preached to *express* and not to *impress.* He knew the difference between *communication* and *manipulation.*

The second reason the apostates are so successful is that they appeal to the base appetites of the old nature. This is part of their bait (2 Peter 2:14)! We must not think of "the lusts of the flesh" only in terms of sexual sins, for the flesh has other appetites. Read the list given in Galatians 5:19–21, and you will see the many different kinds of "bait" the apostates have available for baiting their traps.

For example, *pride* is one of the sins of the flesh, and apostate teachers like to appeal to the human ego. A true servant of God will lovingly tell people that they are lost sinners, under the wrath of a holy God, but the apostate minister will try to avoid "putting people on a guilt trip." He will tell his listeners how good they are, how much God loves them *and needs them* and how easy it is to get into the family of God. In fact, he may tell them they are already in God's family and just need to start living like it! The apostate avoids talking about repentance, because egotistical men do not want to repent.

The third reason they are successful is that they appeal to immature people, people who have "very recently escaped" from their old ways. The apostate has no message for the down-and-out sinner, but he does have a message for the new believer.

A pastor friend of mine was assisting some missionaries in the Philippines by conducting open-air meetings near the university. Students who wanted to decide for Christ were asked to step into a building near the square, and there they were counseled and also given follow-up material to help them get started in their Christian life.

No sooner did a new convert walk out the door and past the crowd than a cultist would join him and start to introduce his own religion! All the apostates had to do was look for the people carrying follow-up material! This same procedure is often used in large evangelistic crusades: the false teachers are ready to pounce on new believers carrying decision packets.

This is why it is important that soul-winners, pastors, and other Christian workers ground new converts in the faith. Like newborn babies, new Christians need to be protected, fed, and established before they can be turned loose in this dangerous world. One reason Peter wrote this letter was to warn the church to care for the new Christians, because the false teachers were out to get them! We cannot blame new believers for being "unstable" (2 Peter 2:14) if we have not taught them how to stand.

The freedom the apostates offer is a false freedom

because it is based on false promises. There is a second reason why it is false.

It Is Offered by False Christians (2:19–20)

You cannot set someone free if you are in bondage yourself, and these false teachers were in bondage. Peter made it clear that these men had temporarily disentangled themselves from the pollutions of the world, but then they went right back into bondage again! They professed to be saved but had never really been redeemed (set free) at all!

The tenses of the verbs in 2 Peter 2:19 are present: "While they *promise* them [the new believers] liberty, they themselves [the apostates] *are* the servants of corruption" (italics mine). They claim to be the servants of God, but they are only the servants of sin. It is bad enough to be a slave, but when sin is your master, you are in the worst possible condition a person can experience.

As you review what Peter has written so far, you can see the kinds of sins that enslave the false teachers. For one thing, they were in bondage to money (2 Peter 2:3, 14). Their covetousness forced them to use every kind of deceptive technique to exploit innocent people. They were also in bondage to fleshly lust (2 Peter 2:10, 14). They had their eyes on weak women whom they could seduce. (In view of what Peter and Jude wrote about Sodom and Gomorrah, perhaps we should also include weak men and boys.)

They were also enslaved by pride (2 Peter 2:10–12). They thought nothing of speaking evil of those in places of authority, including the angels and God! They promoted themselves and derided everybody else. Sad to say, there are people who admire this kind of arrogance, who follow these proud men and support them.

It is interesting to compare the three men Peter named in this chapter—Noah, Lot, and Balaam. Noah kept himself completely separated from the apostasy of the world of his day. He boldly preached God's righteousness and was faithful in his walk and witness, even though no one but his family followed the Lord.

Lot knew the truth and kept himself pure, but he did not keep himself separated; he lost his family as a result. Lot hated the wickedness of Sodom, yet he lived in the midst of it and, by doing so, exposed his daughters and wife to godless influences.

Balaam not only followed the ways of sin, but he encouraged other people to sin! He told Balak how to seduce the nation Israel and his plan almost succeeded. Lot lost his family, but Balaam lost his life.

Beware of "the deceitfulness of sin" (Heb. 3:13). Sin always promises freedom but in the end brings bondage. It promises life but instead brings death. Sin has a way of gradually binding a person until there is no way of escape, apart from the gracious intervention of the Lord. Even the bondage that sin creates is deceitful, for the people who are bound actually think they are free! Too late they discover that they are prisoners of their own appetites and habits.

Jesus Christ came to bring freedom. In His first sermon in the synagogue at Nazareth, our Lord sounded forth the trumpet call of freedom and the advent of the "Year of Jubilee" (Luke 4:16ff.). But Christ's *meaning* of freedom is different from the apostates' as is His method for accomplishing it.

In the Bible, freedom does not mean "doing your own thing" or "having it your way." That attitude is the very essence of sin. The freedom that Jesus Christ offers means *enjoying fulfillment in the will of God.* It means achieving your greatest potential to the glory of God. The Quaker leader Rufus Jones, paraphrasing Aristotle, said, "The true nature of a thing is the highest that it can become." Jesus Christ frees us to become our very best in this life, and then to be like Him in the next.

The apostates brought their followers into bondage by means of lies, but our Lord brings us into freedom by means of truth. "And ye shall know the truth, and the truth shall make you free" (John 8:32). He was speaking, of course, about the truth of the Word of God. "Sanctify them through thy truth," He prayed; "thy Word is truth" (John 17:17). Through the Word of God, we discover the truth about ourselves, our world, and our God. As we face this truth honestly, we experience the liberating power of the Spirit of God. We cease living in a world of fantasy and enter a world of reality, and through the power of God, we are able to fulfill His will, grow in grace, and "reign in life by one, Jesus Christ" (Rom. 5:17).

Those who live by God's truth enter into more and more freedom, but those who live by lies experience more and more bondage, until "the latter end is worse with them than the beginning" (2 Peter 2:20). This reminds us of our Lord's parable in Matthew 12:43–45, the truth of which parallels what Peter has written. *Temporary reformation without true repentance and rebirth only leads to greater sin and judgment.* Reformation cleans up the outside, but regeneration changes the inside.

Sinful tendencies do not disappear when a person reforms; they merely hibernate *and get stronger.* Holiness is not simply refusing to do evil things, for even unsaved people can practice self-control. True holiness is more than conquering temptation: it is conquering even *the desire* to disobey God. When my doctor told me to lose weight, he said, "I'll tell you how to do it: learn to hate the things that aren't good for you." His advice worked!

You can expect nothing but "false freedom" from false Christians who offer false promises. But there is a third reason why this freedom is false.

It Involves a False Experience (2:21–22)

Peter called these apostates "natural brute beasts" (2 Peter 2:12) and then ended the warning by describing them as pigs and dogs! But he was not simply showing his personal disdain for them; rather, he was teaching a basic spiritual lesson.

It is very important that we understand that the

pronoun "they" in this entire paragraph (2 Peter 2:17–22) refers to the false teachers and not to their converts. It is also important that we remember that these teachers are not truly born-again people. Jude described these same people in his letter and stated clearly that they were "sensual, having not the Spirit" (Jude 19). It is not *profession* of spirituality that marks a true believer but *possession* of the Spirit of God within (Rom. 8:9).

But these apostates did have a "religious experience"! And they would boldly claim that their experience brought them into fellowship with the Lord. They would be able to explain "the way of righteousness" and would use the Word of God to support their teachings. If they had not experienced some kind of "religious conversion," they would never have been able to get into the fellowship of the local assemblies.

But their experience, like their promises, was false.

Since Peter wrote both of his letters to the same group of believers we may assume that they had the doctrinal foundation presented so clearly in his first letter. Peter emphasized the new birth (1 Peter 1:3, 22–25). He reminded his readers that they were "partakers of the divine nature" (2 Peter 1:4). In his first letter, Peter described the believers as sheep (1 Peter 2:25; 5:1–4). Our Lord used this same image when He reinstated Peter into the apostleship after his denials (John 21:15–17).

There is no indication that the false teachers had ever experienced the new birth. They had *knowledge* of salvation and could use the language of the church, but they lacked that true saving experience with the Lord. At one time they had even received the Word of God (2 Peter 2:21), but then they turned away from it. *They never trusted Christ and became His sheep.*

Instead of being sheep, they were pigs and dogs—and keep in mind that the dogs in that day were not pampered pets! The Jews called the Gentiles "dogs" because a dog was nothing but a filthy scavenger who lived on garbage! It was hardly a title of respect and endearment!

These men could point to "an experience," but it was a *false* experience. Satan is the counterfeiter. We have already seen that Satan has a false gospel (Gal. 1:6–9), preached by false ministers (2 Cor. 11:13–15), producing false Christians (2 Cor. 11:26—"in perils among false brethren"). In His parable of the tares, our Lord taught that Satan plants his counterfeits ("the children of the wicked one") wherever God plants true believers (Matt. 13:24–30, 36–43).

What kind of "experience" did these false teachers have? To use Peter's vivid images, the pig was washed on the outside, but remained a pig; the dog was "cleaned up" on the inside, but remained a dog. The pig *looked* better and the dog *felt* better, but neither one had been changed. They each had the same old nature, not a new one.

This explains why both animals returned to the old life: it was part of their nature. A pig can stay clean only a short time and then must head for the nearest mud-hole. We do not condemn a pig for acting like a pig because it has a pig's nature. If we saw a *sheep* heading for the mire, we would be concerned!

When I was a youngster, one of our neighbors owned a scrubby black mutt with the imaginative name of "Blackie." He had the habit of eating what dogs should not eat, and then regurgitating somewhere in the neighborhood, usually on our sidewalk. But that was not all. Blackie would then return to the scene of the crime and start all over again! Apparently dogs have been doing this for centuries, for Solomon mentioned it in Proverbs 26:11, the text that Peter quoted.

Certainly the dog feels better after emptying his stomach, *but it is still a dog.* "Having an experience" did not change his nature. Quite the contrary, it only gave further evidence of his "dog nature," because he came back and (just like a dog) lapped up his own vomit. It is a disgusting picture, but that is exactly the response Peter wanted to produce.

In my ministry, I have met people who have told me about their "spiritual experiences," but in their narratives I detected no evidence of a new nature. Like the sow, some of them were cleaned up on the outside. Like the dog, some of them were cleaned up temporarily on the inside and actually felt better. But in no case had they become "partakers of the divine nature" (2 Peter 1:4). They thought they were free from their problems and sins, when really they were still in bondage to an old sinful nature.

According to 2 Peter 2:20, these apostates "escaped the pollutions of the world." Pollution is defilement on the outside. But true believers have "escaped the corruption that is in the world through [because of] lust" (2 Peter 1:4). Corruption is much deeper than defilement on the outside: it is decay on the inside. True believers have received a new nature, a divine nature, and they have new and different appetites and desires. They have been transformed from pigs and dogs into sheep!

Imagine the disappointment of the person who thinks he has been delivered, only to discover that, in the end, he is in worse shape than when he started! The apostates promise freedom, but all they can give is bondage. True freedom must come from within; it has to do with the inner nature of the person. Because the true nature of a thing is the highest that it can become, a pig and dog can never rise higher than *sus scrofa* and *cams familiaris.*

I realize that there are some who believe that these apostate teachers were true believers who, in turning from the knowledge of Christ, forfeited their salvation. Even a casual reading of 2 Peter 2 and Jude would convince the impartial reader that these teachers never had a true experience of salvation through faith in Jesus Christ. Peter would never have compared them to swine and dogs had they once been members of the Lord's true flock, nor would he have called them "cursed children" (2 Peter 2:14). If they were true believers who had gone astray, it would have been Peter's responsibility to encourage his readers to rescue these backsliders (James 5:19–20), but Peter did not command them to do so. Instead, he condemned the apostates in some of the most forceful language found in the New Testament!

Now we better understand why this "freedom" offered by these teachers is a *false* freedom, a "freedom" that only leads to bondage. It is based on false promises, empty words that sound exciting but that have no divine authority behind them. It is offered by false Christians who were involved in a false experience. From start to finish, this "freedom" is the product of our adversary, the devil!

Now we can appreciate Peter's admonition in 2 Peter 1:10—"Wherefore the rather, brethren, give diligence to make your calling and election sure." In other words, "Has your spiritual experience been genuine?" It is a startling fact that there are many people in our churches who have never truly been born again, but who are convinced that they are saved and going to heaven! They have had "an experience," and perhaps look better (like the sow) and feel better (like the dog), but they have not been *made better* as "partakers of the divine nature."

Perhaps Peter recalled Judas, one of the Twelve, who was a tool of the devil and was never born again. Up to the very end, the other disciples did not know the truth about Judas and thought he was a spiritual man!

The apostates appear to have successful ministries, but in the end, they are bound to fail.

The important thing is that you and I have the assurance of a true experience with the Lord, and that we have nothing to do with these counterfeit ministries, no matter how popular they may be.

Christ is "the truth" (John 14:6) and following Him leads to freedom. The apostates are liars and following them leads to bondage. There can be no middle ground!

CHAPTER SIX
2 Peter 3:1–10
SCOFFING AT THE SCOFFERS

Everybody is ignorant," said Will Rogers, "only on different subjects."

How true, and yet that is not the whole story because there is more than one kind of ignorance. Some people are ignorant because of lack of opportunity to learn, or perhaps lack of ability to learn; others are (to use Peter's phrase in 2 Peter 3:5) "willingly … ignorant." "Not ignorance, but ignorance of ignorance, is the death of knowledge," said a famous philosopher, and he is right.

Peter has dealt with the character and conduct of the apostates in 2 Peter 2, and now he deals with their false teaching. Peter affirmed the certainty of Christ's

coming in glory (2 Peter 1:16ff.), a truth that the apostates questioned and denied. In fact, they were scoffing at the very idea of the return of the Lord, the judgment of the world, and the establishment of a glorious kingdom.

How important it is for us as Christians to understand God's truth! Today we are surrounded by scoffers, people who refuse to take the Bible seriously when it speaks about Christ's return and the certainty of judgment. In this paragraph, Peter admonished his readers to understand three important facts about God and the promise of Christ's coming.

God's Word Is True (3:1–4)
It is possible to have a pure and sincere mind and yet have a bad memory! Peter wrote this second letter primarily to awaken and arouse his readers (2 Peter 1:12–15). It is easy for Christians to "get accustomed to God's truth." Eutychus went to sleep listening to Paul preach (Acts 20:7–10)! Our heavenly Father sacrificed so that we might have the truth of the Word and the freedom to practice it, but too often we take this for granted and become complacent. The church needs to be aroused regularly lest the enemy find us asleep and take advantage of our spiritual lethargy.

Because God's Word is true, we must pay attention to it and take its message seriously. New converts must be taught the Word and established in the doctrines of the faith, for new Christians are the apostate teacher's primary targets. But older Christians must also be reminded of the importance of Bible doctrine and, in particular, the doctrines that relate to the return of Christ. Prophetic teaching must not lull us to sleep. Rather, it must awaken us to live godly lives and to seek to win the lost (Rom. 13:11–14).

What the Bible teaches about the day of the Lord was not invented by the apostles. The prophets taught it and so did our Lord Jesus Christ (2 Peter 3:2). Peter emphasized the *unity* of the Word of God. When the scoffers denied "the power and coming" of Jesus Christ, they were denying the truth of the prophetic books, the teaching of our Lord in the Gospels, and the writing of the apostles! Like our Lord's seamless garment, the Scriptures cannot be cut apart without ruining the whole.

As far back as the days of Enoch, God warned that judgment was coming (Jude 14–15). Many of the Hebrew prophets announced the day of the Lord and warned that the world would be judged (Isa. 2:10–22; 13:6–16; Jer. 30:7; Dan. 12:1; Joel; Amos 5:18–20; Zeph.; Zech. 12:1–14:3). This period of judgment is also known as "the time of Jacob's trouble" (Jer. 30:7) and the tribulation.

Our Lord taught about this day of judgment in His sermon on the Mount of Olives (Matt. 24—25). Paul discussed it in 1 Thessalonians 5 and 2 Thessalonians 1—2. The apostle John described this terrible day in Revelation 6—19. It will be a time when God's wrath will be poured out on the nations, and when Satan will be free to give vent to his anger and malice. It will culminate with the return of Jesus Christ in glory and victory.

While I do not make it a test of fellowship or spirituality, I personally believe that the people of God will be taken to heaven *before* this "great and terrible day" dawns.

I think we should carefully distinguish the various "days" mentioned in the Bible. "The day of the Lord" is that day of judgment that climaxes with the return of Christ to the earth. "The day of God" (2 Peter 3:12) is the period when God's people enjoy the new heavens and the new earth, when all evil has been judged (1 Cor. 15:28). "The day of Christ" relates to the coming of Christ for His church (1 Cor. 1:7–9; Phil. 1:10; 2:16).

Prophetic students seem to fall into three categories: those who believe the church will be raptured ("caught up together," 1 Thess. 4:13ff.) *before* the day of the Lord; those who see this event taking place *in the middle* of the day of the Lord, so that the church experiences the first half of the tribulation; and those who believe the church will be raptured when the Lord returns *at the tribulation's close.* There are good and godly people in each group, and our differences of interpretation must not create problems in fellowship or in sharing Christian love.

Not only does the Word of God predict the coming day of the Lord, but it also predicts the appearance of the very scoffers who deny that Word! Their presence is proof that the Word they deny is the true Word of God! We should not be surprised at the presence of these apostate mockers (see Acts 20:28–31; 1 Tim. 4; 2 Tim. 3).

A scoffer is someone who treats lightly that which ought to be taken seriously. The people in Noah's day scoffed at the idea of a judgment, and the citizens of Sodom scoffed at the possibility of fire and brimstone destroying their sinful city. If you have tried at all to witness for Jesus Christ, you have no doubt met people who scoff at the idea of hell or a future day of judgment for this world.

Why do these apostates scoff? Because they want to continue living in their sins. Peter made it clear that false teachers cultivate "the lust of uncleanness" (2 Peter 2:10) and allure weak people by means of "the lusts of the flesh" (2 Peter 2:18). If your lifestyle contradicts the Word of God, you must either change your lifestyle or change the Word of God. The apostates choose the latter approach, so they scoff at the doctrines of judgment and the coming of the Lord.

What is their argument? The uniformity of the world. "Nothing cataclysmic has happened in the past," they argue, "so there is no reason to believe it will happen in the future." They take the "scientific approach" by examining evidence, applying reason, and drawing a conclusion. The fact that they *willfully ignore* a good deal of evidence does not seem to disturb them.

The scientific approach works admirably in matters that relate to the material universe, but you cannot take Bible prophecy into a laboratory and treat it as though it were another hypothesis. For that matter, the so-called laws of science are really only educated conclusions based on a limited number of experiments and tests. These laws are generalizations, always subject to change, because no scientist can perform an infinite number of experiments to prove his claim. Nor can he completely control all the factors involved in the experiments and in his own thinking.

The Word of God is still "a light that shineth in a dark [squalid] place" (2 Peter 1:19). We can trust it. No matter what the scoffers may claim, God's day of judgment will come on the world, and Jesus Christ shall return to establish His glorious kingdom.

God's Work Is Consistent (3:5–7)

How did Peter refute the foolish argument of the apostate scoffers? "God does not interrupt the operation of His stable creation!" they argued. "The promise of Christ's coming is not true!" All Peter did was remind them of what God had done in the past and thus prove that His work is consistent throughout the ages. Peter simply presented evidence that the false teachers *deliberately* ignored. It is amazing how so-called thinkers (scientists, liberal theologians, philosophers) will be *selective* and deliberately refuse to consider certain data.

Peter cited two events in history to prove his point: the work of God at creation (2 Peter 3:5), and the flood in Noah's day (2 Peter 3:6).

God created the heavens and the earth by His word. The phrase "and God said" occurs nine times in Genesis 1. "For he spake, and it was done; he commanded, and it stood fast" (Ps. 33:9). Not only was creation *made* by the word of God, but it was *held together* by that same word. Kenneth Wuest translated 2 Peter 3:5 to bring out this subtle meaning: "For concerning this they willfully forget that heavens existed from ancient times, and land [standing] out of water, and by means of water cohering by the word of God."

Peter's argument is obvious: the same God who created the world by His word can also intervene in His world and do whatever He wishes to do! It is His word that made it and that holds it together, and His word is all-powerful.

The second event Peter cited was Noah's flood (2 Peter 3:6). He had already referred to the flood as an illustration of divine judgment (2 Peter 2:5), so there was no need to go into detail. The flood was a cataclysmic event; in fact, the Greek word translated "overflowed" gives us our English word *cataclysm.* The people living on earth had probably never seen a rainstorm or the fountains of the deep broken up, but these events happened just the same. Their "scientists" could have argued as the scoffers argued, "Everything goes on as it did from the beginning. Life is uniform, so nothing unusual can happen." But it happened!

God has the power to "break in" at any time and

accomplish His will. He can send rain from heaven or fire from heaven. "But our God is in the heavens: he hath done whatsoever he hath pleased" (Ps. 115:3).

Having established the fact that God has in the past "interrupted" the course of history, Peter was then ready for his application in 2 Peter 2:7. The same word that created and sustains the world is now holding it together, stored with fire, being preserved and reserved for that future day of judgment. God promised that there would be no more floods to destroy the world (Gen. 9:8–17). The next judgment will be a judgment of fire.

The phrase "stored with fire" used by Kenneth Wuest ("reserved unto fire" KJV) sounds very modern. Modern atomic science has revealed that the elements that make up the world are stored with power. There is enough atomic energy in a glass of water to run a huge ocean liner. Man has discovered this great power and, as a result, the world seems to teeter on the brink of atomic destruction. However, Peter seems to indicate that *man* will not destroy the world by his sinful abuse of atomic energy. It is *God* who will "push the button" at the right time and burn up the old creation and all the works of sinful man with it; then He will usher in the new heavens and earth and reign in glory.

Everything in God's original creation was good. It is man's sin that has turned a good creation into a *groaning* creation (Rom. 8:18–22). God could not permit sinful man to live in a perfect environment, so He had to curse the ground because of man (Gen. 3:14–19). Since that time, man has been busy polluting and destroying God's creation. For years, it appeared that this exploitation would not cause too much trouble, but now we are changing our minds. The balance of nature has been upset; valuable resources have been wasted; the supply of energy is running down; and civilization is facing a crisis. The prophets of doom today are not only preachers and evangelists, but also sociologists, ecologists, and atomic scientists.

Peter proved his point: God is able to intervene in the course of history. He did it in the past and He is able to do it again. The day of the Lord that was promised by the prophets and apostles, as well as by Jesus Christ, will come just as surely as the flood came in Noah's day and the fire and brimstone came to destroy Sodom and Gomorrah.

But the scoffers had their argument ready: "Then why the delay?" The promise of Christ's coming and the judgment of the world has been around for centuries, and it is yet to be fulfilled. Has God changed His mind? The world today is certainly ripe for judgment! Thus, Peter's third fact.

God's Will Is Merciful (3:8–10)

Once again, Peter exposed the ignorance of the scoffers. Not only were they ignorant of what God had done in the past (2 Peter 3:5), but they were also ignorant of what God was like. They were making God in their own image and ignoring the fact that God is

eternal. This means that He has neither beginning nor ending. Man is immortal: he has a beginning but not an ending. He will live forever either in heaven or hell. But God is eternal, without beginning or ending, and He dwells in eternity. Eternity is not just "extended time." Rather, it is existence *above and apart from time.*

Peter was certainly referring to Psalm 90:4—"For a thousand years in thy sight are but as yesterday when it is past, and as a watch in the night." Isaac Watts used Psalm 90 as the basis for the familiar hymn "O God, Our Help in Ages Past."

> A thousand ages, in Thy sight
> Are like an evening gone;
> Short as the watch that ends the night,
> Before the rising sun.

Since a thousand years are as one day to the Lord, we cannot accuse Him of delayed fulfillment of His promises. In God's sight, the whole universe is only a few days old! He is not limited by time the way we are, nor does He measure it according to man's standards. When you study the works of God, especially in the Old Testament, you can see that He is never in a hurry, but He is never late.

He could have created the entire universe in an instant, yet He preferred to do it over a period of six days. He could have delivered Israel from Egypt in a moment, yet He preferred to invest eighty years in training Moses. For that matter, He could have sent the Savior much sooner, but He waited until "the fullness of the time was come" (Gal. 4:4). While God works *in* time, He is not limited *by* time.

To God, a thousand years is as one day, and one day as a thousand years. God can accomplish in one day what it would take others a millennium to accomplish! He waits to work, but once He begins to work, He gets things done!

The scoffers did not understand God's eternality nor did they understand His mercy. Why was God delaying the return of Christ and the coming of the day of the Lord? It was not because He was *unable* to act or *unwilling* to act. He was not tardy or off schedule! Nobody on earth has the right to decide when God must act. God is sovereign in all things and does not need prodding or even counsel from sinful man (Rom. 11:33–36).

God delays the coming of Christ and the great day of fiery judgment because He is longsuffering and wants to give lost sinners the opportunity to be saved. "And account that the longsuffering of our Lord is salvation" (2 Peter 3:15).

God's "delay" is actually an indication that He has a plan for this world and that He is working His plan. There should be no question in anybody's mind whether God *wants* sinners to be saved. God "is not willing that any should perish" (2 Peter 3:9). First Timothy 2:4 affirms that God "will have all men to be saved, and to come unto the knowledge of the truth."

These verses give both the negative and the positive, and together they assure us that God has no pleasure in the death of the wicked (Ezek. 18:23, 32; 33:11). He shows His mercy to all (Rom. 11:32) even though not all will be saved.

It is worth noting that God revealed this same long-suffering in the years before the flood (1 Peter 3:20). He saw the violence and wickedness of man and could have judged the world immediately; yet He held back His wrath and, instead, sent Noah as a "preacher of righteousness." In the case of Sodom and Gomorrah, God patiently waited while Abraham interceded for the cities, and He would have spared them had He found ten righteous people in Sodom.

If God is longsuffering toward lost sinners, why did Peter write, "The Lord … is longsuffering to us-ward"? Who is meant by "us-ward"? It would appear that God is longsuffering *to His own people!*

Perhaps Peter was using the word us in a general way, meaning "mankind." But it is more likely that he was referring to his readers as the elect of God (1 Peter 1:2; 2 Peter 1:10). God is longsuffering toward lost sinners because some of them *will* believe and become a part of God's elect people. We do not know who God's elect are among the unsaved people of the world, nor are we supposed to know. Our task is to make our *own* "calling and election sure" (2 Peter 1:10; cf. Luke 13:23–30). The fact that God has His elect people is an encouragement to us to share the good news and seek to win others to Christ.

God was even longsuffering toward the scoffers of that day! They needed to repent and He was willing to save them. This is the only place where Peter used the word *repentance* in either of his letters, but that does not minimize its importance. To repent simply means "to change one's mind." It is not "regret," which usually means "being sorry I got caught." Nor is it "remorse," which is a hopeless attitude that can lead to despair.

Repentance is a change of mind that results in an action of the will. If the sinner honestly changes his mind about sin, he will turn from it. If he sincerely changes his mind about Jesus Christ, he will turn to Him, trust Him, and be saved. "Repentance toward God, and faith toward our Lord Jesus Christ" (Acts 20:21) is God's formula for salvation.

The word translated "come" at the end of 2 Peter 3:9 carries the meaning of "make room for." It is translated "contain" in John 2:6 and 21:25. The lost sinner needs to "make room" for repentance in his heart by putting away his pride and meekly receiving the Word of God. Repentance is a gift from God (Acts 11:18; 2 Tim. 2:25), but the unbeliever must make room for the gift.

As you review Peter's arguments, you can see that his evidence is irrefutable. He pointed out that the scoffers willfully rejected evidence in order that they might continue in their sins and scoffing. He proved from the Scriptures that God has intervened in past history and that He has the power to do it today. He showed that the scoffers had a very low view of God's character because they thought He delayed in keeping His promises just as men do. Finally, he explained that God does not live in the realm of human time, and that His so-called delay only gives more opportunity for lost sinners to repent and be saved.

Having refuted their false claims, Peter then reaffirmed the certainty of the coming of the day of the Lord. When will it come? Nobody knows when, because it will come to the world "as a thief in the night." Our Lord used this phrase (Matt. 24:43; Luke 12:39) and so did the apostle Paul (1 Thess. 5:2ff). When the world is feeling secure, then God's judgment will fall. The thief does not warn his victims that he is coming! "For when they shall say, Peace and safety; then sudden destruction cometh upon them, as travail upon a woman with child; and they shall not escape" (1 Thess. 5:3).

We do not know *when* it will happen, but we are told *what* will happen. Kenneth Wuest gave an accurate and graphic translation of these words: "In which the heavens with a rushing noise will be dissolved, and the elements being scorched will be dissolved, and the earth also and the works in it will be burned up" (2 Peter 3:10).

Many Bible students believe that Peter here described the action of atomic energy being released by God. The word translated "a great noise" in the King James Version means "with a hissing and a crackling sound." When the atomic bomb was tested in the Nevada desert, more than one reporter said that the explosion gave forth "a whirring sound," or a "crackling sound." The Greek word Peter used was commonly used by the people for the whirring of a bird's wings or the hissing of a snake.

The word *melt* in 2 Peter 3:10 means "to disintegrate, to be dissolved." It carries the idea of something being broken down into its basic elements, and that is what happens when atomic energy is released. "Heaven and earth shall pass away," said our Lord (Matt. 24:35), and it appears that this may happen by the release of the atomic power stored in the elements that make up the world. The heavens and earth are "stored with fire" (2 Peter 3:7 WUEST), and only God can release it.

For this reason, I do not personally believe that God will permit sinful men to engage in an earth-destroying atomic war. He will, I believe, overrule the ignorance and foolishness of men, including well-meaning but unbelieving diplomats and politicians, so that He alone will have the privilege of "pushing the button" and dissolving the elements to make way for a new heaven and a new earth. Peter no doubt had in mind Old Testament passages such as Isaiah 13:10–11; 24:19; 34:4; and 64:1–4 when he wrote these words. The first passage is especially emphatic that *God* will bring judgment and not sinful man. "And I will punish the world for their evil, and the wicked for their iniquity," says the Lord. It does not sound as though He will give this task to some nervous military leader or some angry politician.

Of course, this great explosion and conflagration will not touch the "heaven of heavens" where God dwells. It will destroy the earth and the atmospheric heavens around it, the universe as we know it; this will make room for the new heavens and earth (2 Peter 3:13; Rev. 21:1ff.).

Man's great works will also be burned up! All of the things that man boasts about—his great cities, his great buildings, his inventions, his achievements—will be destroyed in a moment of time. When sinners stand before the throne of God, they will have nothing to point to as evidence of their greatness. It will all be gone.

This is certainly a solemn truth, and we dare not study it in cavalier fashion. In the remaining verses of this letter, Peter will apply this truth to our daily living. But it would be wise for us to pause now and consider: where will I be when God destroys the world? Is what I am living for only destined to go up in an atomic cloud, to vanish forever? Or am I doing the will of God so that my works will glorify Him forever?

Make your decision now—before it is too late.

CHAPTER SEVEN
2 Peter 3:11–18
BE DILIGENT!

The purpose of prophetic truth is not speculation but motivation; thus Peter concluded his letter with the kind of practical admonitions that all of us must heed. It is unfortunate when people run from one prophetic conference to another, filling their notebooks, marking their Bibles, drawing their charts, and yet not living their lives to the glory of God. In fact, some of the saints battle each other more over prophetic interpretation than perhaps any other subject.

All true Christians believe that Jesus Christ is coming again. They may differ in their views of when certain promised events will occur, but they all agree that He is returning as He promised. Furthermore, all Christians agree that this faith in future glory ought to motivate the church. As one pastor said to me, "I have moved off the Planning Committee and joined the Welcoming Committee!" This does not mean that we should stop studying prophecy, or that every opposing viewpoint is correct, which is an impossibility. But it does mean that, whatever views we hold, they ought to make a difference in our lives.

"Be diligent!" is the admonition that best summarizes what Peter wrote in this closing paragraph. He used this word before in 2 Peter 1: "Giving all diligence, add to your faith" (2 Peter 1:5); "Give diligence to make your calling and election sure" (2 Peter 1:10); "Moreover I will endeavor [be diligent] that ye may be

able" (2 Peter 1:15). If we are going to be successful Christians, we must learn to be diligent.

Peter gave three admonitions to encourage the readers in Christian diligence in the light of our Lord's return.

Be Diligent to Live Godly Lives (3:11–14)

The key word in this paragraph is *look*. It means "to await eagerly, to be expectant." You find it in Luke 3:15 ("And as the people were in expectation") and Acts 3:5 ("expecting to receive something of them"). It describes an attitude of excitement and expectation as we wait for the Lord's return. Because we realize that the world and its works will be dissolved, and that even the very elements will be disintegrated, we fix our hope, not on anything in this world, but only on the Lord Jesus Christ.

Because we do not know the day or the hour of our Lord's return, we must constantly be ready. The believer who starts to neglect the "blessed hope" (Titus 2:13) will gradually develop a cold heart, a worldly attitude, and an unfaithful life (Luke 12:35–48). If he is not careful, he may even become like the scoffers and laugh at the promise of Christ's coming.

This expectant attitude ought to make a difference in *our personal conduct* (2 Peter 3:11). The word translated "manner" literally means "exotic, out of this world, foreign." Because we have "escaped the corruption that is in the world" (2 Peter 1:4), we must live differently from the people in the world. To them, we should behave like "foreigners." Why? Because this world is not our home! We are "strangers and pilgrims" (1 Peter 2:11) headed for a better world, the eternal city of God. Christians should be different, not odd. When you are different, you attract people; when you are odd, you repel them.

Our conduct should be characterized by holiness and godliness. "But as he which hath called you is holy, so be ye holy in all manner of conversation [behavior]; because it is written, 'Be ye holy; for I am holy'" (1 Peter 1:15–16). The word *holy* means "to separate, to cut off." Israel was a "holy nation" because God called the Jews out from among the Gentiles and kept them separated. Christians are called out from the godless world around them and are set apart for God alone.

The word *godliness* could be translated "piety." It is the same word we met in 2 Peter 1:6–7, "to worship well." It describes a person whose life is devoted to pleasing God. It is possible to be separated from sin positionally and yet not enjoy living for God personally. In the Greek world, the word translated "godliness" meant "respect and awe for the gods and the world they made." It is that attitude of reverence that says with John the Baptist, "He must increase, but I must decrease" (John 3:30).

Other New Testament writers also teach that an eager expectancy of the Lord's return ought to motivate us to live pure lives (see Rom. 13:11–14; 2 Cor. 5:1–11; Phil. 3:17–21; 1 Thess. 5:1–11; Titus

2:11–15; 1 John 2:28–3:3). However, it is not simply knowing the doctrine *in the mind* that motivates the life; it is having it *in the heart,* loving His appearing (2 Tim. 4:8).

Not only should this expectant attitude make a difference in our conduct, but it should also make a difference in our *witness.* The phrase *looking for and hasting unto* can be translated "looking for and hastening the coming of the day of God." Peter affirmed that it is possible for us to hasten the return of Jesus Christ.

The word translated "hasting unto" means "hasten" in the other five places where it is used in the New Testament. The shepherds "came with haste" (Luke 2:16). Jesus told Zaccheus to "make haste and come down" and "he made haste and came down" (Luke 19:5–6). Paul "hasted … to be at Jerusalem" (Acts 20:16); and the Lord told Paul to "make haste and get … out of Jerusalem" (Acts 22:18). To make this word a synonym for "eager anticipation" is to have Peter repeat himself in 2 Peter 2:12, for that is what the word *looking* means.

There are two extremes in ministry that we must avoid. One is the attitude that we are locked into God's sovereign plan in such a way that nothing we do will make any difference. The other extreme is to think that God cannot get anything done unless we do it! While God's sovereign decrees must never become an excuse for laziness, neither must our plans and activities try to take their place.

Perhaps two illustrations from Old Testament history will help us better understand the relationship between God's plans and man's service. God delivered Israel from Egypt and told the people He wanted to put them into their inheritance, the land of Canaan. But at Kadesh-Barnea all except Moses, Joshua, and Caleb rebelled against God and refused to enter the land (Num. 13—14). Did God force them to go in? No. Instead, He had them wander in the wilderness for the next forty years while the older generation died off. He adjusted His plan to their response.

When Jonah preached to the people of Nineveh, his message was clear: "Yet forty days, and Nineveh shall be overthrown" (Jonah 3:4)! It was God's plan to destroy the wicked city, but when the people repented, from the king on down, God adjusted His plan and spared the city. Neither God nor His basic principles changed, but His application of those principles changed. God responds when men repent.

How, then, can we as Christians hasten the coming of the day of God? For one thing, we can pray as Jesus taught us, "Thy kingdom come" (Matt. 6:10). It would appear from Revelation 5:8 and 8:3–4 that the prayers of God's people are related in some way to the pouring out of God's wrath on the nations.

If God's work today is calling out a people for His name (Acts 15:14), then the sooner the church is completed, the sooner our Lord will return. There is a suggestion of this truth in Acts 3:19–21. While Matthew 24:14 relates primarily to the tribulation, the principle is the same: man's ministry cooperates with God's program so that promised events can take place.

There are mysteries here that our minds cannot fully understand or explain, but the basic lesson is clear: the same God who ordains the end also ordains the means to the end, and we are a part of that means. Our task is not to speculate but to serve.

Finally, this expectant attitude will make a difference *when we meet Jesus Christ* (2 Peter 3:14). It will mean that He will greet us "in peace" and have no charges against us so that we are "ashamed before him at his coming" (1 John 2:28). The judgment seat of Christ will be a serious event (2 Cor. 5:8–11) as we give an account of our service to Him (Rom. 14:10–13). It is better to meet Him "in peace" than for Him to fight against us with His Word (Rev. 2:16)!

If we are diligent to watch for His return and to live holy and godly lives, then we will not be afraid or ashamed. We will meet Him "without spot and blameless." Jesus Christ is "a lamb without blemish and without spot" (1 Peter 1:19), and we should be careful to follow His example. Peter had warned his readers against the defilement that the apostates bring: "Spots they are and blemishes" (2 Peter 2:13). The separated Christian will not permit himself to be "spotted and blemished" by the false teachers! He wants to meet his Lord wearing pure garments.

How do we maintain this eager expectancy that leads to holy living? By keeping "his promise" before our hearts (2 Peter 3:13). The promise of His coming is the light that shines in this dark world (2 Peter 1:19), and we must be sure that "the day star" is aglow in our hearts because we love His appearing.

Be Diligent to Win the Lost (3:15–16)

Second Peter 3:15 ties in with verse 9, where Peter explained why the Lord had delayed fulfilling His promise. God had every reason long ago to judge the world and burn up its works, but in His mercy, He is longsuffering with us, "not willing that any should perish, but that all should come to repentance." This is the day of salvation, not the day of judgment.

Peter made reference to Paul's writings, because it is Paul, more than any other New Testament writer, who explained God's plan for mankind during this present age. Especially in Romans and Ephesians, Paul explained the relationship between Israel and the church. He pointed out that God used the nation Israel to prepare the way for the coming of the Savior. But Israel rejected its King and asked to have Him crucified. Did this destroy God's plan? Of course not! Today, Israel is set aside nationally, but God is doing a wonderful new thing: He is saving Jews and Gentiles, and making them one in Christ in the church!

For centuries, if a Gentile wanted to be saved, he had to come by way of Israel. This same attitude persisted even in the early church (Acts 15). Paul made it clear that *both* Jews and Gentiles stand condemned before God and that both must be saved by faith in

Jesus Christ. In Jesus Christ, saved Jews and Gentiles belong to the one body, the church. The church is a "mystery" that was hidden in God's counsels and later revealed through the New Testament prophets and apostles (see Eph. 3).

The Jewish nation was God's great testimony to law, but the church is His witness for grace (see Eph. 1—2). Law prepared the way for grace, and grace enables us to fulfill the righteousness of the law (Rom. 8:1–5). This does not mean that there was no grace under the old covenant or that new covenant believers are lawless! Anyone who was saved under the administration of law was saved by grace, through faith, as Romans 4 and Hebrews 11 make clear.

Now, unlearned and unstable people have a difficult time understanding Paul's teachings. Even some learned and stable people who have spiritual discernment can find themselves floundering in great passages like Romans 9—11! Some Bible students, in their attempt to "harmonize" seeming contradictions (law and grace, Israel and the church, faith and works) twist the Scriptures and try to make them teach what is really not there. The Greek word translated "wrest" means "to torture on the rack, to distort and pervert."

Even in Paul's day, there were those who twisted his words and tried to defend their ignorance. They accused Paul of teaching that, since we are saved by grace, it makes no difference how we live! It was "slanderously reported" that Paul taught, "Let us do evil that good may come" (Rom. 3:8; cf. Rom. 6:1ff). Others accused Paul of being against the law because he taught the equality of Jews and Gentiles in the church (Gal. 3:28) and their liberty in Christ.

Most heresies are the perversion of some fundamental doctrine of the Bible. False teachers take verses out of context, twist the Scriptures, and manufacture doctrines that are contrary to the Word of God. Peter probably had the false teachers in mind, but the warning is good for all of us. We must accept the teaching of the Scriptures and not try to make them say what we want them to say.

Note that Peter classified Paul's letters as *Scripture,* that is, the inspired Word of God. Not only did the teaching of the apostles agree with that of the prophets and our Lord (2 Peter 3:2), but the apostles also agreed with each other. Some liberal scholars try to prove that the apostles' doctrine was different from that of Jesus Christ, or that Peter and Paul were at variance with each other. The recipients of Peter's second letter had also read some of Paul's epistles, and Peter assured them that there was agreement.

What happens to people who blindly twist the Scriptures? They do it "unto their own destruction." Peter was not writing about Christians who have a difficult time interpreting the Word of God, because nobody understands *all* of the Bible perfectly. He was describing the false teachers who "tortured" the Word of God in order to prove their false doctrines. I once listened to a cultist "explain" why the group's leader

was the "new Messiah" by manipulating the "weeks" in Daniel 9:23–27. He twisted the prophecy unmercifully!

The word *destruction* is repeated often in this letter (2 Peter 2:1–3; 3:7, 16). In the King James Version it is translated "damnable," "pernicious," and "perdition," as well as "destruction." It means the rejection of eternal life, which results in eternal death.

Since this is the day of salvation, we must be diligent to do all we can to win the lost. We do not know how long the Lord will be "longsuffering" toward this evil world. We must not presume on His grace. We must understand what the Bible teaches about God's program for this present age, and we must be motivated by a love for the lost (2 Cor. 5:14) and a desire to be pleasing to Him when He returns.

The false teachers are multiplying and their pernicious doctrines are infecting the church. God needs separated men and women who will resist them, live godly lives, and bear witness of the saving grace of Jesus Christ. The time is short!

Be Diligent to Grow Spiritually (3:17–18)

There are four "beloved" statements in 2 Peter 3 that summarize what Peter wanted to get across as he brought his second letter to a close.

> "Beloved … be mindful" (3:1–2).
> "Beloved, be not ignorant" (3:8).
> "Beloved … be diligent" (3:14).
> "Beloved … beware" (3:17).

The word translated "beware" means "be constantly guarding yourself." Peter's readers knew the truth, but he warned them that knowledge alone was not sufficient protection. They had to be on their guard; they had to be alert. It is easy for people who have a knowledge of the Bible to grow overconfident and to forget the warning, "Wherefore let him that thinketh he standeth take heed lest he fall" (1 Cor. 10:12).

What special danger did Peter see? That the true believers would be "led away together with the error of the wicked" (literal translation). He is warning us against breaking down the walls of separation that must stand between the true believers and the false teachers. There can be no communion between truth and error. The apostates "live in error" (2 Peter 2:18), while true believers live in the sphere of the truth (2 John 1–2).

The word *wicked* (2 Peter 3:17) means "the lawless." Peter's description of the apostates in 2 Peter 2 reveals how lawless they are. They even speak evil of the authorities that seek to enforce God's law in this world (2 Peter 2:10–11)! They promise their converts freedom (2 Peter 2:19), but that freedom turns out to be lawlessness.

True Christians cannot fall from salvation and be lost, but they can fall from their own "steadfastness." What was this steadfastness? Being "established in the present truth" (2 Peter 1:12). The stability of the Christian comes from his faith in the Word of God, his knowledge of that Word, and his ability to use that Word in the practical decisions of life.

One of the great tragedies of evangelism is bringing "spiritual babies" into the world and then failing to feed them, nurture them, and help them develop. The apostates prey on young believers who have "very recently escaped" from the ways of error (2 Peter 2:18). New believers need to be taught the basic doctrines of the Word of God; otherwise, they will be in danger of being "led away with the error of the lawless."

How can we as believers maintain our steadfastness and avoid being among the "unstable souls" who are easily beguiled and led astray? By growing spiritually. "But be constantly growing" is the literal translation. We should not grow "in spurts," but in a constant experience of development.

We must grow "in grace." This has to do with Christian character traits, the very things Peter wrote about in 2 Peter 1:5–7, and that Paul wrote about in Galatians 5:22–23. We were saved by grace (Eph. 2:8–9), but grace does not end there! We must also be strengthened by grace (2 Tim. 2:1–4). God's grace can enable us to endure suffering (2 Cor. 12:7–10). His grace also helps us to give when giving is difficult (2 Cor. 8:1ff.) and to sing when singing is difficult (Col. 3:16).

Our God is "the God of all grace" (1 Peter 5:10), who "giveth grace unto the humble" (James 4:6). As we study His Word, we learn about the various aspects of grace that are available to us as children of God. We are stewards of "the manifold grace of God" (1 Peter 4:10). There is grace for every situation and every challenge of life. "But by the grace of God I am what I am," wrote Paul (1 Cor. 15:10), and that should be our testimony as well.

Growing in grace often means experiencing trials and even suffering. We never really experience the grace of God until we are at the end of our own resources. The lessons learned in the "school of grace" are always costly lessons, but they are worth it. To grow in grace means to become more like the Lord Jesus Christ, from whom we receive all the grace that we need (John 1:16).

We must also grow in knowledge. How easy it is to grow in knowledge but not in grace! All of us know far more of the Bible than we really live. Knowledge without grace is a terrible weapon, and grace without knowledge can be very shallow. But when we combine grace and knowledge, we have a marvelous tool for building our lives and for building the church.

But note that we are challenged to grow, not just in knowledge of the Bible, as good as that is, but "in the knowledge of our Lord and Savior Jesus Christ." It is one thing to "know the Bible," and quite another thing to know the Son of God, the central theme of the Bible. The better we know Christ through the Word, the more we grow in grace; the more we grow in grace, the better we understand the Word of God.

So, the separated Christian must constantly be *guarding* himself, lest he be led away into error; he also must be constantly *growing* in grace and knowledge. This requires diligence! It demands discipline and priorities. Nobody automatically drifts into spiritual growth and stability, but anybody can drift *out of* dedication and growth. "For this reason we must pay much closer attention to what we have heard, lest we drift away from it" (Heb. 2:1 NASB). Just as the boat needs the anchor, so the Christian needs the Word of God.

Physical growth and spiritual growth follow pretty much the same pattern. To begin with, we grow from the inside out. "As newborn babes" is the way Peter illustrated it (1 Peter 2:2). The child of God is born with everything he needs for growth and service (2 Peter 1:3). All he needs is the spiritual food and exercise that will enable him to develop. He needs to keep clean. We grow by nutrition, not by addition!

We grow best in a loving family, and this is where the local church comes in. A baby needs a family for protection, provision, and affection. Tests prove that babies who are raised alone, without special love, tend to develop physical and emotional problems very early. The church is God's "nursery" for the care and feeding of Christians, the God-ordained environment that encourages them to grow.

It is important that we grow in a balanced way. The human body grows in a balanced way with the various limbs working together; likewise the "spiritual man" must grow in a balanced way. We must grow in grace and knowledge (2 Peter 3:18), for example. We must keep a balance between worship and service, between faith and works. A balanced diet of the whole Word of God helps us to maintain a balanced life.

It is the Holy Spirit of God who empowers and enables us to keep things in balance. Before Peter was filled with the Spirit, he was repeatedly going to extremes. He would bear witness to Christ one minute and then try to argue with the Lord the next (Matt. 16:13–23)! He refused to allow Jesus to wash his feet, and then he wanted to be washed all over (John 13:6–10)! He promised to defend the Lord and even die with Him, yet he did not have the courage to *own* the Lord before a little servant girl! But when he was filled with the Spirit, Peter began to live a balanced life that avoided impulsive extremes.

What is the result of spiritual growth? Glory to God! "To Him be glory both now and forever." It glorifies Jesus Christ when we keep ourselves separated from sin and error. It glorifies Him when we grow in grace and knowledge, for then we become more like Him (Rom. 8:29). In his life and even in his death, Peter glorified God (John 21:18–19).

As you review this important epistle, you cannot help but be struck by the urgency of the message. The apostates are here! They are busy! They are seducing immature Christians! We must be guarding, growing, and glorifying the Lord, making the most of every opportunity to win the lost and strengthen the saved.

Be diligent! The ministry you save may be your own!

1 JOHN

OUTLINE

Key theme: The tests of reality in the Christian life
Key verse: 1 John 5:13

I. INTRODUCTION (1:1–4)

II. THE TESTS OF TRUE FELLOWSHIP: GOD IS LIGHT (1:5—2:29)
   A. Obedience—1:5—2:6 ("saying" vs. "doing")
   B. Love—2:7–17
   C. Truth—2:18–29

III. THE TESTS OF TRUE SONSHIP: GOD IS LOVE (3—5)
   A. Obedience—3
   B. Love—4
   C. Truth—5

CONTENTS

CHAPTER ONE
1 John 1:1–4
IT'S REAL!

"O nce upon a time…." Remember how exciting those words used to be? They were the open door into an exciting world of make-believe, a dreamworld that helped you forget all the problems of childhood.

Then—pow! You turned a corner one day, and "Once upon a time" became kid stuff. You discovered that life is a battleground, not a playground, and fairy stories were no longer meaningful. You wanted something real.

The search for something real is not new. It has been going on since the beginning of history. Men have looked for reality and satisfaction in wealth, thrills, conquest, power, learning, and even in religion.

There is nothing really wrong with these experiences, except that by themselves they never really satisfy. Wanting something real and finding something real are two different things. Like a child eating cotton candy at the circus, many people who expect to bite into something real end up with a mouthful of nothing. They waste priceless years on empty substitutes for reality.

This is where the apostle John's first epistle comes in. Written centuries ago, this letter deals with a theme that is forever up-to-date: the life that is real.

John had discovered that satisfying reality is not to be found in things or thrills, but in a Person—Jesus Christ, the Son of God. Without wasting any time, he told us about this "living reality" in the first paragraph of his letter.

As you read 1 John 1:1–4, you learn three vital facts about the life that is real.

This Life Is Revealed (1:1)
As you read John's letter, you will discover that he enjoyed using certain words and that the word manifest is one of them. "And the life was manifested" (1 John 1:2), he said. This life was not hidden so that we have to search for it and find it. No, it was manifested—revealed openly!

If you were God, how would you go about revealing yourself to men? How could you tell them about, and give them, the kind of life you wanted them to enjoy?

God has revealed Himself in creation (Rom. 1:20), but creation alone could never tell us the story of God's love. God has also revealed Himself much more fully in His Word, the Bible. But God's final and most complete revelation is in His Son, Jesus Christ. Jesus said, "He that hath seen me hath seen the Father" (John 14:9).

Because Jesus is God's revelation of Himself, He has a very special name: "The Word of life" (1 John 1:1).

This same title opens John's gospel: "In the beginning was the Word, and the Word was with God, and the Word was God" (John 1:1).

Why does Jesus Christ have this name? Because Christ is to us what our words are to others. Our words reveal to others just what we think and how we feel. Christ reveals to us the mind and heart of God. He is the living means of communication between God and men. To know Jesus Christ is to know God!

John made no mistake in his identification of Jesus Christ. Jesus is the Son of the Father—the Son of God (1 John 1:3). John warned us several times in his letter not to listen to the false teachers who tell lies about Jesus Christ. "Who is a liar but he that denieth that Jesus is the Christ?" (1 John 2:22). "Every spirit that confessed that Jesus Christ is come in the flesh is of God; and every spirit that confesseth not that Jesus Christ is come in the flesh is not of God" (1 John 4:2–3). If a man is wrong about Jesus Christ, he is wrong about God, because Jesus Christ is the final and complete revelation of God to men.

For example, there are those who tell us that Jesus was a man but was not God. John had no place for such teachers! One of the last things he wrote in this letter is "We are in him that is true, even in his Son Jesus Christ This is the true God, and eternal life" (1 John 5:20).

False teaching is so serious a matter that John wrote about it in his second letter too, warning believers not to invite false teachers into their homes (2 John 9–10). And he made it plain that to deny that Jesus is God is to follow the lies of Antichrist (1 John 2:22–23).

This leads to a basic Bible doctrine that has puzzled many people—the doctrine of the Trinity.

John mentioned in his letter the Father, the Son, and the Holy Spirit. For example, he said, "By this know ye the Spirit of God: every spirit that confesseth that Jesus Christ is come in the flesh is of God" (1 John 4:2, Scofield). Here are references in one verse to God the Father, God the Son, and God the Holy Spirit. And in 1 John 4:13–15 is another statement that mentions the three Persons of the Trinity.

The word trinity is a combination of tri-, meaning "three," and unity, meaning "one." A "trinity," then, is a three-in-one, or one-in-three. To be sure, the word trinity is not found in the Bible, but the truth is taught there (cf. also Matt. 28:19–20; John 14:16–17, 26; 2 Cor. 13:14; Eph. 4:4–6).

Christians do not believe that there are three gods. They believe that one God exists in three Persons—Father, Son, and Holy Spirit. Nor do Christians believe merely that one God reveals Himself in three different ways, much as one man may be a husband, a father, and a son. No, the Bible teaches that God is one but that He exists in three Persons.

One teacher of doctrine used to say, "Try to explain the Trinity and you may lose your mind. But try to explain it away and you will lose your soul!" And the apostle John says, "Whoever denies the Son does not have the Father" (1 John 2:23 NASB). No Person of the Trinity is expendable!

As you read the gospel records of the life of Jesus, you see the wonderful kind of life God wants us to enjoy. But it is not by imitating Jesus, our Example, that we may share in this life. No, there is a far better way.

This Life Is Experienced (1:2)

Read the first four verses of John's letter again, and you will notice that the apostle had a personal encounter with Jesus Christ. His was no secondhand "religious experience" inherited from somebody else or discovered in a book! No, John knew Jesus Christ face-to-face. He and the other apostles heard Jesus speak. They watched Him as He lived with them. In fact, they studied Him carefully, and even touched His body. They knew that Jesus was real—not a phantom, not a vision, but God in human corporeal form.

Some twenty-first-century student may say, "Yes, and this means that John had an advantage. He lived when Jesus walked on earth. He knew Jesus personally. But I was born twenty centuries too late!"

But this is where our student is wrong! It was not the apostles' physical nearness to Jesus Christ that made them what they were. It was their spiritual nearness. They had committed themselves to Him as their Savior and their Lord. Jesus Christ was real and exciting to John and his colleagues because they had trusted Him. By trusting Christ, they had experienced eternal life!

Six times in this letter John used the phrase "born of God." This was not an idea John had invented; he had heard Jesus use these words. "Except a man be born again," Jesus had said, "he cannot see the kingdom of God.… That which is born of the flesh is flesh; and that which is born of the Spirit is spirit. Marvel not that I said unto thee, Ye must be born again" (John 3:3, 6–7). We can experience this "real life" only after we have believed the gospel, put our trust in Christ, and been "born of God."

"Whosoever believeth that Jesus is the Christ is born of God" (1 John 5:1). Eternal life is not something we earn by good works or deserve because of good character. Eternal life, the life that is real, is a gift from God to those who trust His Son as their Savior.

John wrote his gospel to tell people how to receive this wonderful life (John 20:31). He wrote his first letter to tell people how to be sure they have really been born of God (1 John 5:9–13).

A college student returned to the campus after going home for a family funeral, and almost at once his grades began to go down. His counselor thought that the death of his grandmother had affected the boy and that time would heal the wound, but the grades only became worse. Finally the boy confessed the real problem. While he was home, he happened to look into his grandmother's old Bible, and there he discovered in the family record that he was an adopted son.

"I don't know who I belong to," he told his counselor. "I don't know where I came from!"

The assurance that we are in God's family—that we have been "born of God"—is vitally important to all of us. Certain characteristics are true of all God's children. A person who is born of God lives a righteous life (1 John 2:29). A child of God does not practice sin (which is the meaning of the King James word commit, 1 John 3:9). A believer will occasionally commit sin (cf. 1 John 1:8—2:2), but he will not make it a habit to sin.

God's children also love each other and their heavenly Father (cf. 1 John 4:7; 5:1). They have no love for the world system around them (1 John 2:15–17), and because of this the world hates them (1 John 3:13). Instead of being overcome by the pressures of this world and swept off balance, the children of God overcome the world (1 John 5:4). This is another mark of true children of God.

Why is it so important that we know that we have been born of God? John gives us the answer: if you are not a child of God, you a "child of wrath" (Eph. 2:1–3) and may become a "child of the devil" (1 John 3:10; and see Matt: 13:24–30, 36–43). A "child of the devil" is a counterfeit Christian who acts "saved" but has not been born again. Jesus called the Pharisees "children of the devil" (John 8:44) and they were very religious.

A counterfeit Christian—and they are common—is something like a counterfeit ten-dollar bill.

Suppose you have a counterfeit bill and actually think it is genuine. You use it to pay for a tank of gas. The gas station manager uses the bill to buy supplies. The supplier uses the bill to pay the grocer. The grocer bundles the bill up with forty-nine other ten-dollar bills and takes it to the bank. And the teller says, "I'm sorry, but this bill is a counterfeit."

That ten-dollar bill may have done a lot of good while it was in circulation, but when it arrived at the bank it was exposed for what it really was and put out of circulation.

So with a counterfeit Christian. He may do many good things in this life, but when he faces the final judgment he will be rejected. "Many will say to me in that day, Lord, Lord, have we not prophesied in thy name? And in thy name have cast out demons? And in thy name done many wonderful works? And then will I profess unto them, I never knew you; depart from me, ye that work iniquity" (Matt. 7:22–23 SRB).

Each of us must ask himself honestly, "Am I a true child of God or am I a counterfeit Christian? Have I truly been born of God?"

If you have not experienced eternal life, this real life, you can experience it right now! Read 1 John 5:9–15 carefully. God has "gone on record" in His Word. He offers you the gift of eternal life. Believe His promise and ask Him for His gift. "For whosoever shall call upon the name of the Lord shall be saved" (Rom. 10:13).

We have discovered two important facts about "the life that is real": it is revealed in Jesus Christ, and it is experienced when we put our trust in Him as our Savior. But John did not stop here!

This Life Is Shared (1:3–4)

"That which we have seen and heard declare we unto you" (1 John 1:3). And once you have experienced this exciting life that is real, you will want to share it with other people, just as John wanted to "declare" it to all his readers in the first century.

A pastor had a phone call from an angry woman. "I have received a piece of religious literature from your church," she shouted, "and I resent your using the mails to upset people!"

"What was so upsetting about a piece of mail from a church?" the pastor asked calmly.

"You have no right to try to change my religion!" the woman stormed. "You have your religion and I have mine, and I'm not trying to change yours!" (She really was, but the pastor didn't argue with her.)

"Changing your religion, or anybody else's religion, is not our purpose," the pastor explained. "But we have experienced a wonderful new life through faith in Christ, and we want to do all we can to share it with others."

Many people (including some Christians) have the idea that "witnessing" means wrangling over the differences in religious beliefs or sitting down and comparing churches.

That isn't what John had in mind! He told us that witnessing means sharing our spiritual experiences with others—both by the lives that we live and by the words that we speak.

John wrote this letter to share Christ with us. As you read it, you will discover that John had in mind five purposes for sharing.

That we may have fellowship (v. 3). This word fellowship is an important one in the vocabulary of a Christian. It simply means "to have in common." As sinners, men have nothing in common with the holy God. But God in His grace sent Christ to have something in common with men. Christ took on Himself a human body and became a man. Then He went to the cross and took on that body the sins of the world (1 Peter 2:24). Because He paid the price for our sins, the way is open for God to forgive us and take us into His family. When we trust Christ, we become "partakers of the divine nature" (2 Peter 1:4). The term translated "partakers" in Peter's epistle is from the same Greek root that is translated "fellowship" in 1 John 1:3.

What a thrilling miracle! Jesus Christ took on Himself the nature of man that by faith we may receive the very nature of God! A famous British writer was leaving Liverpool by ship. He noticed that the other passengers were waving to friends on the dock. He rushed down to the dock and stopped a little boy. "Would you wave to me if I paid you?" he asked the lad, and of course the boy agreed. The writer rushed back on board and leaned over the rail, glad for

someone to wave to. And sure enough, there was the boy waving back to him!

A foolish story? Perhaps—but it reminds us that man hates loneliness. All of us want to be wanted. The life that is real helps to solve the basic problem of loneliness, for Christians have genuine fellowship with God and with one another. Jesus promised, "Lo, I am with you always" (Matt. 28:20). In his letter, John explained the secret of fellowship with God and with other Christians. This is the first purpose John mentioned for the writing of his letter— the sharing of his experience of eternal life.

That we may have joy (v. 4). Fellowship is Christ's answer to the loneliness of life. Joy is His answer to the emptiness, the hollowness, of life.

John, in his epistle, used the word joy only once, but the idea of joy runs through the entire letter. Joy is not something that we manufacture for ourselves; joy is a wonderful by-product of our fellowship with God. David knew the joy that John mentioned; he said, "In thy presence is fullness of joy" (Ps. 16:11).

Basically, sin is the cause of the unhappiness that overwhelms our world today. Sin promises joy, but it always produces sorrow. The pleasures of sin are temporary—they are only for a season (Heb. 11:25). God's pleasures last eternally—they are forevermore (Ps. 16:11).

The life that is real produces a joy that is real—not some limp substitute. Jesus said, the night before He was crucified, "Your joy no man taketh from you" (John 16:22). "These things have I spoken unto you, that my joy might remain in you, and that your joy might be full" (John 15:11).

Karl Marx wrote, "The first requisite for the people's happiness is the abolition of religion." But the apostle John wrote, in effect, "Faith in Jesus Christ gives you a joy that can never be duplicated by the world. I have experienced this joy myself, and I want to share it with you."

That we may not sin (2:1). John faced the problem of sin squarely (cf. 1 John 3:4–9, for example) and announced the only answer to this enigma—the person and work of Jesus Christ. Christ not only died for us to carry the penalty of our sins, but rose from the dead in order to intercede for us at the throne of God: "If any man sin, we have an advocate with the Father, Jesus Christ the righteous" (1 John 2:1).

Christ is our Representative. He defends us at the Father's throne. Satan may stand there as the accuser of the brethren (Zech. 3; Rev. 12:10), but Christ stands there as our Advocate—He pleads on our behalf! Continuing forgiveness, in response to His intercession, is God's answer to our sinfulness.

"I would like to become a Christian," an interested woman said to a visiting pastor, "but I'm afraid I can't hold out. I'm sure to sin again!"

Turning to 1 John 1, the pastor said, "No doubt you will sin again, because God says, 'If we say that we have no sin, we deceive ourselves, and the truth is not in us' (1 John 1:8). But if you do sin, God will forgive you if you will confess your sin to Him. But it isn't necessary for Christians to sin. As we walk in fellowship with God and in obedience to His Word, He gives us ability to resist and to have victory over temptation."

Then the pastor remembered that the woman had gone through surgery some months before.

"When you had your surgery," he asked, "was there a possibility of complications or problems afterward?"

"Oh, yes," she replied. "But whenever I had a problem, I went to see the doctor and he took care of it."

Then the truth hit her! "I see it!" she exclaimed. "Christ is always available to keep me out of sin or to forgive my sin!"

The life that is real is a life of victory. In this letter, John told us how to draw on our divine resources to experience victory over temptation and sin.

That we may not be deceived (2:26). As never before, Christians today need ability to distinguish between right and wrong, between truth and error. The notion is widespread in our generation that there are no "absolutes"—that nothing is always wrong and that nothing is always right. False doctrines, therefore, are more prevalent than at any time in history—and most men and women seem to be willing to accept almost any teaching except the truths of the Bible.

In John's epistles is a word that no other New Testament writer uses—antichrist (1 John 2:18, 22; 4:3; 2 John 7). That prefix anti- has two meanings: "against" and "instead of." There are in this world teachers of lies who are opposed to Christ, and their method of "seducing" people is to use lies. They offer a substitute Christ, a substitute salvation, and a substitute Bible. They want to give you something instead of the real Word of God and real eternal life.

Christ is the Truth (John 14:6), but Satan is the liar (John 8:44). The devil leads people astray—not necessarily with gross sensual sins, but with half-truths and outright lies. He began his career by seducing man in the garden of Eden. He asked Eve, "Yea, hath God said?" Even then, he did not appear to her in his true nature, but masqueraded as a beautiful creature (cf. 2 Cor. 11:13–15).

Satan today often spreads his lies even through religious groups! Not every man standing in a pulpit is preaching the truth of the Word of God. False preachers and false religious teachers have always been among the devil's favorite and most effective tools.

How can Christians today detect Satan's lies? How can they identify false teachers? How can they grow in their own knowledge of the truth so that they will not be victims of false doctrines?

John answered these questions. The life that is real is characterized by discernment.

The Holy Spirit, referred to by John as "the anointing … ye have received of Him" (1 John 2:27), is Christ's answer to our need for discernment. The Spirit is our Teacher; it is He who enables us to detect truth and error and to remain ("abide") in Christ. He is our protection against ignorance, deception, and untruth.

The discernment of false doctrines and of false teachers will come to our attention again.

That we may know we are saved (5:13). We have already touched on this truth, but it is so important that it bears repeating. The life that is real is not built on the empty hopes—or wishes—based on human supposings. It is built on assurance. In fact, as you read John's letter you encounter the word know more than thirty times. No Christian, if he is asked whether or not he is going to heaven, needs to say "I hope so" or "I think so." He need have no doubt whatever.

The life that is real is such a free and exciting life because it is based on knowledge of solid facts. "Ye shall know the truth, and the truth shall make you free," promised Jesus (John 8:32). "We have not followed cunningly devised fables" (2 Peter 1:16) was the testimony of Jesus' disciples. These men, almost all of whom died for their faith, did not give their lives for a clever hoax of their own devising, as some critics of Christianity fatuously assert. They knew what they had seen!

Years ago a traveling entertainer billed himself as "The Human Fly." He would climb up the sides of buildings or monuments without the aid of ropes or the protection of nets. Usually the whole neighborhood would turn out to watch him.

During one performance, the Human Fly came to a point on the wall of the building and paused as though he didn't know what to do next. Then he reached with his right arm to take hold of a piece of mortar to lift himself higher. But instead of moving higher, he fell back with a scream and was killed on the pavement below.

When the police opened his right hand, it did not contain a piece of mortar. It contained a handful of dirty cobwebs! The Fly had tried to climb on cobwebs, and it just didn't work.

Jesus warned against such false assurance in the passage that we have already quoted. Many who profess to be Christians will be rejected in the day of God's judgment.

John was saying in his letter, "I want you to be sure that you have eternal life."

As you read this fascinating letter, you will discover that John frequently repeated himself. He wove three themes in and out of these chapters: obedience, love, and truth. In 1 John 1 and 2, the apostle emphasized fellowship, and he told us that the conditions for fellowship are obedience (1 John 1:5–2:6), love (1 John 2:7–17), and truth (1 John 2:18–29).

In the latter half of his letter, John dealt primarily with sonship—our being "born of God." How can a person really know he is a child of God? Well, said John, sonship is revealed by obedience (1 John 3), love (1 John 4), and truth (1 John 5).

Obedience—love—truth. Why did John use these particular tests of fellowship and sonship? For a very practical reason.

When God made us, He made us in His own image (Gen. 1:26–27). This means that we have a personality patterned after God's. We have a mind to think with, a heart to feel with, and a will with which to make decisions. We sometimes refer to these aspects of our personality as intellect, emotion, and will.

The life that is real must involve all the elements of the personality.

Most people are dissatisfied today because their total personality has never been controlled by something real and meaningful. When a person is born of God through faith in Christ, God's Spirit comes into his life to live there forever. As he has fellowship with God in reading and studying the Bible and in prayer, the Holy Spirit is able to control his mind, heart, and will. And what happens then?

A Spirit-controlled mind knows and understands truth.

A Spirit-controlled heart feels love.

A Spirit-controlled will inclines us to obedience.

John wanted to impress this fact on us, and that is why he used a series of contrasts in his letter: truth vs. lies, love vs. hatred, and obedience vs. disobedience.

There is no middle ground in the life that is real. We must be on one side or on the other.

This, then, is the life that is real. It was revealed in Christ; it was experienced by those who trusted in Christ; and it can be shared today.

This life begins with sonship and continues in fellowship. First we are born of God; then we walk (live) with God.

This means that there are two kinds of people who cannot enter into the joy and victory about which we are thinking: those who have never been born of God and those who, though saved, are out of fellowship with God.

It would be a wise thing for us to take inventory spiritually (cf. 2 Cor. 13:5) to see whether or not we qualify to enjoy the spiritual experience with which John's letter deals.

We have already emphasized the importance of being born of God, but if you have any doubts or questions, a review of Fact 2 might be beneficial.

If a true believer is out of fellowship with God, it is usually for one of three reasons:

1. He has disobeyed God's will.

2. He is not getting along with fellow believers.

3. He believes a lie and therefore is living a lie.

Even a Christian can be mistaken in his understanding of truth. That's why John warned us, "Little children, let no man deceive you" (1 John 3:7).

These three reasons parallel John's three important themes: obedience, love, and truth. Once a believer discovers why he is out of fellowship with God, he should confess that sin (or those sins) to the Lord and claim His full forgiveness (1 John 1:9—2:2). A believer can never have joyful fellowship with the Lord if sin stands between them.

God's invitation to us today is "Come and enjoy fellowship with Me and with each other! Come and share the life that is real!"

CHAPTER TWO
1 John 1:5—2:6
WALKING AND TALKING

Every form of life has its enemies. Insects have to watch out for hungry birds, and birds must keep an eye on hungry cats and dogs. Even human beings have to dodge automobiles and fight off germs.

The life that is real also has an enemy, and we read about it in this section. This enemy is sin. Nine times in these verses John mentioned sin, so the subject is obviously not unimportant. John illustrated his theme by using the contrast between light and darkness: God is light; sin is darkness.

But there is another contrast here too—the contrast between saying and doing. Four times John wrote, "If we say" or "He that saith" (1 John 1:6, 8, 10; 2:4). It is clear that our Christian life is to amount to more than mere "talk"; we must also "walk," or live, what we believe. If we are in fellowship with God (if we are "walking in the light"), our lives will back up what our lips are saying. But if we are living in sin ("walking in darkness"), then our lives will contradict what our lips are saying, making us hypocrites.

The New Testament calls the Christian life a "walk." This walk begins with a step of faith when we trust Christ as our Savior. But salvation is not the end—it's only the beginning—of spiritual life. "Walking" involves progress, and Christians are supposed to advance in the spiritual life. Just as a child must learn to walk and must overcome many difficulties in doing so, a Christian must learn to "walk in the light." And the fundamental difficulty involved here is this matter of sin.

Of course, sin is not simply outward disobedience; sin is also inner rebellion or desire. For example, we are warned about the desires of the flesh and of the eyes and about the pride of life (1 John 2:16), all of which are sinful. Sin is also transgression of the law (1 John 3:4), or literally, "lawlessness." Sin is refusal to submit to the law of God. Lawlessness, or independence of the law, is the very essence of sin. If a believer decides to live an independent life, how can he possibly walk in fellowship with God? "Can two walk together except they be agreed?" (Amos 3:3).

Neither in the Old Testament nor in the New does the Bible whitewash the sins of the saints. In escaping a famine, Abraham became weak in his faith and went down to Egypt and lied to Pharaoh (Gen. 12). Later, the patriarch tried to "help God" by marrying Hagar and begetting a son (Gen. 16). In both cases, God forgave Abraham his sin, but Abraham had to reap what he had sowed. God can and will cleanse the record, but He does not change the results. No one can unscramble an egg.

Peter denied the Lord three times and tried to kill a man in the garden when Jesus was arrested. Satan is a liar and a murderer (John 8:44), and Peter was playing right into his hands! Christ forgave Peter (see John 21), of course, but what Peter had done hurt his testimony greatly and hindered the Lord's work.

The fact that Christians sin bothers some people— especially new Christians. They forget that their receiving the new nature does not eliminate the old nature they were born with. The old nature (which has its origin in our physical birth) fights against the new nature, which we receive when we are born again (Gal. 5:16–26). No amount of self-discipline, no set of man-made rules and regulations, can control this old nature. Only the Holy Spirit of God can enable us to "put to death" the old nature (Rom. 8:12–13) and produce the Spirit's fruit (Gal. 5:22–23) in us through the new nature.

Sinning saints are not mentioned in the Bible to discourage us, but to warn us.

"Why do you keep preaching to us Christians about sin?" an angry church member said to her pastor. "After all, sin in the life of a Christian is different from sin in the life of an unsaved person!"

"Yes," replied the pastor, "it is different. It's much worse!"

All of us, therefore, must deal with our sins if we are to enjoy the life that is real. In this section, John explained three approaches to sin.

We Can Try to Cover Our Sins (1:5–6, 8, 10; 2:4)

"God is light, and in him is no darkness at all" (1 John 1:5). When we were saved, God called us out of darkness into His light (1 Peter 2:9). We are children of light (1 Thess. 5:5). Those who do wrong hate light (John 3:19–21). When light shines in on us, it reveals our true nature (Eph. 5:8–13).

Light produces life and growth and beauty, but sin is darkness; and darkness and light cannot exist in the same place. If we are walking in the light, the darkness has to go. If we are holding to sin, then the light goes. There is no middle ground, no vague "gray" area, where sin is concerned.

How do Christians try to cover up their sins? By telling lies! First, we tell lies to others (1 John 1:6). We want our Christian friends to think we are "spiritual," so we lie about our lives and try to make a favorable impression on them. We want them to think that we are walking in the light, though in reality we are walking in the darkness.

Once one begins to lie to others, he will sooner or later lie to himself, and our passage deals with this (1 John 1:8). The problem now is not deceiving others, but deceiving ourselves. It is possible for a believer to live in sin yet convince himself that everything is fine in his relationship to the Lord.

Perhaps the classic example of this is King David (2 Sam. 11—12). First David lusted after Bathsheba. Then he actually committed adultery. Instead of openly admitting what he had done, he tried to cover his sin. He tried to deceive Bathsheba's husband, made him drunk, and had him killed. He lied to himself and tried to carry on his royal duties in the usual way. When his court chaplain, the prophet Nathan, confronted him with a similar hypothetical situation, David condemned the other man, though he felt no condemnation at all for himself. Once we begin to lie to others, it may not be long before we actually believe our lie.

But the spiritual decline becomes still worse: the next step is trying to lie to God (1 John 1:10). We have made ourselves liars; now we try to make God a liar! We contradict His Word, which says that "all have sinned," and we maintain that we are exceptions to the rule. We apply God's Word to others but not to ourselves. We sit through church services or Bible studies and are not touched by the Bible's teachings. Believers who have reached this low level are usually highly critical of other Christians, but they strongly resist applying the Word to their own lives.

The Holy Spirit's inspired picture of the human heart is devastating indeed! A believer lies about his fellowship (1 John 1:6); about his nature—"I could never do a thing like that!" (1 John 1:8) and about his actions (1 John 1:10).

Sin has a deadly way of spreading, doesn't it?

At this point we must discuss an extremely important factor in our experience of the life that is real. That factor is honesty. We must be honest with ourselves, honest with others, and honest with God. Our passage describes a believer who is living a dishonest life: he is a phony. He is playing a role and acting a part, but is not living a genuine life. He is insincere.

What losses does this kind of person experience?

For one thing, he loses the Word. He stops "doing the truth" (1 John 1:6); then the truth is no longer in him (1 John 1:8); and then he turns the truth into lies (1 John 1:10)! "Thy word is truth" (John 17:17), said Jesus, but a person who lives a lie loses the Word. One of the first symptoms of walking in darkness is a loss of blessing from the Bible. You cannot read the Word profitably while you are walking in the dark.

But a dishonest person loses something else: he loses his fellowship with God and with God's people (1 John 1:6–7). As a result, prayer becomes an empty form to him. Worship is dull routine. He becomes critical of other Christians and starts staying away from church: "What communion hath light with darkness?" (2 Cor. 6:14).

A backslidden husband, for example, who is walking in spiritual darkness, out of fellowship with God, can never enjoy full fellowship with his Christian wife, who is walking in the light. In a superficial way, the couple can have companionship; but true spiritual fellowship is impossible. This inability to share spiritual experiences causes many personal problems in homes and between members of local churches.

A group of church members were discussing their new pastor.

"For some reason," said one man, "I really don't feel at ease with him. I believe he's a good man, all right—but something seems to stand between us."

Another member replied, "Yes, I think I know what you mean. I used to have that same problem with him, but now I don't have it anymore. The pastor and I have great fellowship."

"What did he do to make things better?"

"He didn't do anything," said the friend. "I did the changing."

"You did the changing?"

"Yes, I decided to be open and honest about things, the way our pastor is. You see, there isn't one stain of hypocrisy in his life, and there was so much pretending in my life that we just didn't make it together. He and I both knew I was a phony. Since I've started to live an honest Christian life, everything is better."

One problem with dishonesty is that just keeping a record of our lies and pretenses is a full-time job! Abraham Lincoln used to say that if a man is going to be a liar, he had better have a good memory! When a person uses up all his energy in pretending, he has nothing left for living, and life becomes shallow and tasteless. A person who pretends not only robs himself of reality, but he keeps himself from growing: his true self is smothered under the false self.

The third loss is really the result of the first two: the believer loses his character (1 John 2:4). The process starts out with his telling lies and it ends up with his becoming a liar! His insincerity, or lack of truthfulness, is at first a role that he plays. Then it is no longer a role—it has become the very essence of his life. His character has eroded. He is no longer a liar because he tells lies; he now tells lies because he is a confirmed liar.

Is it any wonder that God warns, "He that covereth his sins shall not prosper" (Prov. 28:13)? David tried to cover his sins and it cost him his health (Ps. 32:3–4), his joy (Ps. 51), his family, and almost his kingdom. If we want to enjoy the life that is real, we must never cover our sins. What should we do?

We Can Confess Our Sins (1:7, 9)

John gave two interesting titles to Jesus Christ: "advocate" and "propitiation" (1 John 2:1–2). It's important that we understand these two titles because they stand for two ministries that only the Lord Himself performs.

Let's begin with "propitiation." If you look this word up in the dictionary, you may get the wrong idea of its meaning. The dictionary tells us that "to propitiate" means "to appease someone who is angry." If you apply this to Christ, you get the horrible picture of an angry God, about to destroy the world, and a loving Savior giving Himself to appease the irate God—and this is not the Bible picture of salvation! Certainly God

is angry at sin; after all, He is infinitely holy. But the Bible reassures us that "God so loved [not hated] the world" (John 3:16, italics mine).

No, the word propitiation does not mean the appeasing of an angry God. Rather, it means the satisfying of God's holy law. "God is light" (1 John 1:5), and therefore He cannot close His eyes to sin. But "God is love" (1 John 4:8) too and wants to save sinners.

How, then, can a holy God uphold His own justice and still forgive sinners? The answer is in the sacrifice of Christ. At the cross, God in His holiness judged sin. God in His love offers Jesus Christ to the world as Savior. God was just in that He punished sin, but He is also loving in that He offers free forgiveness through what Jesus did at Calvary. (Read 1 John 4:10, and also give some thought to Rom. 3:23–26.)

Christ is the Sacrifice for the sins of the whole world, but He is Advocate only for believers. "We [Christians] have an advocate with the Father." The word advocate used to be applied to lawyers. The word John used is the very same word Jesus used when He was talking about the coming of the Holy Spirit (John 14:16, 26; 15:26). It means, literally, "one called alongside." When a man was summoned to court, he took an advocate (lawyer) with him to stand at his side and plead his case.

Jesus finished His work on earth (John 17:4)—the work of giving His life as a sacrifice for sin. Today He has an "unfinished work" in heaven. He represents us before God's throne. As our High Priest, He sympathizes with our weaknesses and temptations and gives us grace (Heb. 4:15–16; 7:23–28). As our Advocate, He helps us when we sin. When we confess our sins to God, because of Christ's advocacy God forgives us.

The Old Testament contains a beautiful picture of this. Joshua (Zech. 3:1–7) was the Jewish high priest after the Jews returned to their land following their captivity in Babylon. (Don't confuse this Joshua with the Joshua who conquered the Promised Land.) The nation had sinned; to symbolize this, Joshua stood before God in filthy garments and Satan stood at Joshua's right hand to accuse him (cf. Rev. 12:10). God the Father was the Judge; Joshua, representing the people, was the accused; Satan was the prosecuting attorney. (The Bible calls him the accuser of the brethren.) It looked as if Satan had an open-and-shut case. But Joshua had an Advocate who stood at God's right hand and this changed the situation. Christ gave Joshua a change of garments and silenced the accusations of Satan.

This is what is in view when Jesus Christ is called our "advocate." He represents believers before God's throne, and the merits of His sacrifice make possible the forgiveness of the believer's sin. Because Christ died for His people, He satisfied the justice of God. ("The wages of sin is death.") Because He lives for us at God's right hand, He can apply His sacrifice to our needs day by day.

All He asks is that when we have failed, we confess our sins.

What does it mean to "confess"? Well, to confess sins means much more than simply to "admit" them. The word confess actually means "to say the same thing [about]." To confess sin, then, means to say the same thing about it that God says about it.

A counselor was trying to help a man who had come forward during an evangelistic meeting. "I'm a Christian," the man said, "but there's sin in my life, and I need help." The counselor showed him 1 John 1:9 and suggested that the man confess his sins to God.

"O Father," the man began, "if we have done anything wrong—"

"Just a minute!" the counselor interrupted. "Don't drag me into your sin! My brother, it's not 'if' or 'we'—you'd better get down to business with God!"

The counselor was right.

Confession is not praying a lovely prayer, or making pious excuses, or trying to impress God and other Christians. True confession is naming sin—calling it by name what God calls it: envy, hatred, lust, deceit, or whatever it may be. Confession simply means being honest with ourselves and with God, and if others are involved, being honest with them too. It is more than admitting sin. It means judging sin and facing it squarely.

When we confess our sins, God promises to forgive us (1 John 1:9). But this promise is not a "magic rabbit's foot" that makes it easy for us to disobey God!

"I went out and sinned," a student told his campus chaplain, "because I knew I could come back and ask God to forgive me."

"On what basis can God forgive you?" the chaplain asked, pointing to 1 John 1:9.

"God is faithful and just," the boy replied.

"Those two words should have kept you out of sin," the chaplain said. "Do you know what it cost God to forgive your sins?"

The boy hung his head. "Jesus had to die for me."

Then the chaplain zeroed in. "That's right—forgiveness isn't some cheap sideshow trick God performs. God is faithful to His promise, and God is just, because Christ died for your sins and paid the penalty for you. Now, the next time you plan to sin, remember that you are going to sin against a faithful, loving God!"

Of course, cleansing has two sides to it: the judicial and the personal. The blood of Jesus Christ, shed on the cross, delivers us from the guilt of sin and gives us right standing ("justification") before God. God is able to forgive because Jesus' death has satisfied His holy law.

But God is also interested in cleansing a sinner inwardly. David prayed, "Create in me a clean heart, O God" (Ps. 51:10). When our confession is sincere, God does a cleansing work (1 John 1:9) in our hearts by His Spirit and through His Word (John 15:3).

The great mistake King David made was in trying to cover his sins instead of confessing them. For perhaps a whole year he lived in deceit and defeat. No wonder he wrote that a man should pray "in a time of finding out" (Ps. 32:6, literal translation).

When should we confess our sin? Immediately when we discover it! "He that covereth his sins shall not prosper; but whoso confesseth and forsaketh them shall have mercy" (Prov. 28:13). By walking in the light, we are able to see the "dirt" in our lives and deal with it immediately.

This leads to a third way to deal with sins.

We Can Conquer Our Sins (2:1–3, 5–6)

John makes it clear that Christians do not have to sin. "I am writing these things to you that you may not sin" (1 John 2:1 NASB, italics mine).

The secret of victory over sin is found in the phrase "walk in the light" (1 John 1:7).

To walk in the light means to be open and honest, to be sincere. Paul prayed that his friends might "be sincere and without offense" (Phil. 1:10). The word sincere comes from two Latin words, sine and cera, which mean "without wax." It seems that in Roman days, some sculptors covered up their mistakes by filling the defects in their marble statues with wax, which was not readily visible—until the statue had been exposed to the hot sun awhile. But more dependable sculptors made certain that their customers knew that the statues they sold were sine cera—without wax.

It is unfortunate that churches and Bible classes have been invaded by insincere people, people whose lives cannot stand to be tested by God's light. "God is light," and when we walk in the light, there is nothing we can hide. It is refreshing to meet a Christian who is open and sincere and is not trying to masquerade!

To walk in the light means to be honest with God, with ourselves, and with others. It means that when the light reveals our sin to us, we immediately confess it to God and claim His forgiveness. And if our sin injures another person, we ask his forgiveness too.

But walking in the light means something else: it means obeying God's Word (1 John 2:3–4). "Thy word is a lamp unto my feet and a light unto my path" (Ps. 119:105). To walk in the light means to spend time daily in God's Word, discovering His will; and then obeying what He has told us.

Obedience to God's Word is proof of our love for Him. There are three motives for obedience. We can obey because we have to, because we need to, or because we want to.

A slave obeys because he has to. If he doesn't obey he will be punished. An employee obeys because he needs to. He may not enjoy his work, but he does enjoy getting his paycheck! He needs to obey because he has a family to feed and clothe. But a Christian is to obey his heavenly Father because he wants to—for the relationship between him and God is one of love. "If you love me, keep my commandments" (John 14:15).

This is the way we learned obedience when we were children. First, we obeyed because we had to. If we didn't obey, we were spanked! But as we grew up, we discovered that obedience meant enjoyment and reward; so we started obeying because it met certain needs in our lives. And it was a mark of real maturity when we started obeying because of love.

"Baby Christians" must constantly be warned or rewarded. Mature Christians listen to God's Word and obey it simply because they love Him.

Walking in the light involves honesty, obedience, and love; it also involves following the example of Christ and walking as He walked (1 John 2:6). Of course, nobody ever becomes a Christian by following Christ's example, but after we come into God's family, we are to look to Jesus Christ as the one great Example of the kind of life we should live.

This means "abiding in Christ." Christ is not only the Propitiation (or sacrifice) for our sins (1 John 2:2) and the Advocate who represents us before God (1 John 2:1), but He is also the perfect Pattern (He is "Jesus Christ the righteous") for our daily life.

The key statement here is "as he is." "Because as he is, so are we in this world" (1 John 4:17, italics mine). We are to walk in the light "as he is in the light" (1 John 1:7, italics mine). We are to purify ourselves "even as he is pure" (1 John 3:3, italics mine). "He that doeth righteousness is righteous, even as He is righteous" (1 John 3:7, italics mine). Walking in the light means living here on earth the way Jesus lived when He was here and the way He is right now in heaven.

This has extremely practical applications in our daily lives. For example, what should a believer do when another believer sins against him? The answer is that believers should forgive one another "even as God for Christ's sake hath forgiven you" (Eph. 4:32, italics mine; cf. Col. 3:13).

Walking in the light—following the example of Christ—will affect a home. Husbands are supposed to love their wives "even as Christ also loved the church" (Eph. 5:25). Husbands are supposed to care for their wives "even as the Lord" cares for the church (Eph. 5:29). And wives are to honor and obey their husbands (Eph. 5:22–24).

No matter what area of life it may be, our responsibility is to do what Jesus would do. "As he is, so are we in this world." We should "walk [live] even as He walked [lived]."

Jesus Himself taught His disciples what it means to abide in Him. He explained it in His illustration of the vine and its branches (John 15). Just as the branch gets its life by remaining in contact with the vine, so believers receive their strength by maintaining fellowship with Christ.

To abide in Christ means to depend completely on Him for all that we need in order to live for Him and serve Him. It is a living relationship. As He lives out His life through us, we are able to follow His example and walk as He walked. Paul expressed this experience perfectly: "Christ liveth in me" (Gal. 2:20).

This is a reference to the work of the Holy Spirit.

Christ is our Advocate in heaven (1 John 2:1), to represent us before God when we sin. The Holy Spirit is God's Advocate for us here on earth. Christ is making intercession for us (Rom. 8:34), and the Holy Spirit is also making intercession for us (Rom. 8:26–27). We are part of a fantastic "heavenly party line": God the Son prays for us in heaven, and God the Spirit prays for us in our hearts. We have fellowship with the Father through the Son, and the Father has fellowship with us through the Spirit.

Christ lives out His life through us by the power of the Spirit, who lives within our bodies. It is not by means of imitation that we abide in Christ and walk as He walked. No, it is through incarnation: through His Spirit, "Christ liveth in me." To walk in the light is to walk in the Spirit and not fulfill the lusts of the flesh (see Gal. 5:16).

God has made provisions for us in these ways to conquer sin. We can never lose or change the sin nature that we were born with (1 John 1:8), but we need not obey its desires. As we walk in the light and see sin as it actually is, we will hate it and turn from it. And if we sin, we immediately confess it to God and claim His cleansing. By depending on the power of the indwelling Spirit, we abide in Christ and "walk as he walked."

But all this begins with openness and honesty before God and men. The minute we start to act a part, to pretend, to impress others, we step out of the light and into shadows. Sir Walter Scott put it this way:

Oh, what a tangled web we weave

When first we practice to deceive!

The life that is real cannot be built on things that are deceptive. Before we can walk in the light, we must know ourselves, accept ourselves, and yield ourselves to God. It is foolish to try to deceive others, because God already knows what we really are!

All this helps to explain why walking in the light makes life so much easier and happier. When you walk in the light, you live to please only one Person—God. This really simplifies things! Jesus said, "I do always those things that please him" (John 8:29, italics mine). We "ought to walk and to please God" (1 Thess. 4:1). If we live to please ourselves and God, we are trying to serve two masters, and this never works. If we live to please men, we will always be in trouble because no two men will agree and we will find ourselves caught in the middle. Walking in the light—living to please God—simplifies our goals, unifies our lives, and gives us a sense of peace and poise.

John made it clear that the life that is real has no love for sin. Instead of trying to cover sin, a true believer confesses sin and tries to conquer it by walking in the light of God's Word. He is not content simply to know he is going to heaven. He wants to enjoy that heavenly life right here and now. "As he is, so are we in this world." He is careful to match his walk and his talk. He does not try to impress himself, God, or other Christians with a lot of "pious talk."

A congregation was singing as a closing hymn the familiar song "For You I Am Praying." The speaker turned to a man on the platform and asked quietly, "For whom are you praying?"

The man was stunned. "Why, I guess I'm not praying for anybody. Why do you ask?"

"Well, I just heard you say, 'For you I am praying,' and I thought you meant it," the preacher replied. "Oh, no," said the man. "I'm just singing."

Pious talk! A religion of words! To paraphrase James 1:22, "We should be doers of the Word as well as talkers of the Word." We must walk what we talk. It is not enough to know the language; we must also live the life. "If we say—" then we ought also to do!

CHAPTER THREE
1 John 2:7–11
SOMETHING OLD, SOMETHING NEW

I just love that hat!"

"Man, I really love the old-fashioned kind of baked beans!"

"But, Mom, don't you realize that Tom and I love each other?"

Words, like coins, can be in circulation for such a long time that they start wearing out. Unfortunately, the word love is losing its value and is being used to cover a multitude of sins.

It is really difficult to understand how a man can use the same word to express his love for his wife as he uses to tell how he feels about baked beans! When words are used that carelessly, they really mean little or nothing at all. Like the dollar, they have been devalued.

As John described the life that is real, he used three words repeatedly: life, love, and light. In fact, he devoted three sections of his letter to the subject of Christian love. He explained that love, life, and light belong together. Read these three sections (1 John 2:7–11; 3:10–24; 4:7–21) without the intervening verses, and you will see that love, life, and light must not be separated.

In our present study (1 John 2:7–11), we learn how Christian love is affected by light and darkness. A Christian who is walking in the light (which simply means he is obeying God) is going to love his brother Christian.

In 1 John 3:10–24, we are told that Christian love is a matter of life or death: to live in hatred is to live in spiritual death. In 1 John 4:7–21 we see that Christian love is a matter of truth or error (cf. 1 John 4:6): because we know God's love toward us, we show God's love toward others.

In these three sections, then, we find three good reasons why Christians should love one another:

1. God has commanded us to love (1 John 2:7–11).

2. We have been born of God and God's love lives in us (1 John 3:10–24).

3. God first revealed His love to us (1 John 4:7–21). "We love … because He first loved us."

John not only wrote about love but also practiced it. One of his favorite names for his readers was "Beloved." He felt love for them. John is known as the "apostle of love" because in his gospel and his epistles he gives such prominence to this subject. However, John was not always the apostle of love. At one time Jesus gave John and his brother James, both of whom had hot tempers, the nickname "Boanerges" (Mark 3:17), which means "sons of thunder." On another occasion these two brothers wanted to call down fire from heaven to destroy a village (Luke 9:51–56).

Since the New Testament was written in Greek, the writers were often able to use more precise language. It is unfortunate that our English word love has so many shades of meaning (some of them contradictory). When we read in 1 John about "love," the Greek word used is agape (ah-GAH-pay), the word for God's love toward man, a Christian's love for other Christians, and God's love for His church (Eph. 5:22–33).

Another Greek word for love, philia (fee-LEE-ah), used elsewhere, carries the idea of "friendship love," which is not quite as profound or divine as agape love. (The Greek word for sensual love, eros, from which we get our word erotic, is not used at all in the New Testament.)

The amazing thing is that Christian love is both old and new (1 John 2:7–8). This seems to be a contradiction. Love itself, of course, is not new, nor is the commandment—that men love God and each other—a new thing. Jesus Himself combined two Old Testament commandments, Deuteronomy 6:5 and Leviticus 19:18, and said (Mark 12:28–34) that these two commandments summarize all the law and the prophets. Loving God and loving one's neighbor were old, familiar responsibilities before Jesus ever came to earth.

In what sense, then, is "love one another" a "new" commandment (1 John 2:8)? Again, a look at the Greek helps to answer the question.

The Greeks had two different words for "new." One means "new in time," and the other means "new in quality." For example, you would use the first word to describe the latest car, a recent model. But if you purchased a car that was so revolutionary that it was radically different, you would use the second word— new in quality. (Our English words recent and fresh just about make this distinction: "recent" means new in time, "fresh" means new in character.)

The commandment to love one another is not new in time, but it is new in character. Because of Jesus Christ, the old commandment to "love one another" has taken on new meaning. We learn in these five brief verses (1 John 2:7–11) that the commandment is new in three important ways.

It Is New in Emphasis (2:7)

In the previous paragraph (1 John 2:3–6), John had

been talking about "the commandments" in general, but now he narrowed his focus down to one single commandment. In the Old Testament, the command that God's people love one another was only one of many, but now this old commandment is lifted out and given a place of preeminence.

How is it possible for one commandment to stand head and shoulders above all the others? This is explained by the fact that love is the fulfillment of God's law (Rom. 13:8–10).

Parents must care for their children according to law. Child neglect is a serious crime. But how many parents have a conversation like this when the alarm clock goes off in the morning?

She: "Honey, you'd better get up and go to work. We don't want to get arrested."

He: "Yeah, and you'd better get up and get breakfast for the kids, and get their clothes ready. The cops might show up and put us both in jail."

She: "You're right. Boy, it's a good thing they have a law, or we'd stay in bed all day!"

It's doubtful that the fear of the law is often the motive behind earning a living or caring for one's children. Parents fulfill their responsibilities (even if grudgingly on occasion) because they love each other and their children. To them, doing the right thing is not a matter of law—it's a matter of love.

The commandment "Love one another" is the fulfillment of God's law in the same way. When you love people, you do not lie about them or steal from them. You have no desire to kill them. Love for God and love for others motivates a person to obey God's commandments without even thinking about them! When a person acts out of Christian love he obeys God and serves others—not because of fear, but because of his love.

This is why John said that "Love one another" is a new commandment—it is new in emphasis. It is not simply one of many commandments. No, it stands at the top of the list!

But it is new in emphasis in another way too. It stands at the very beginning of the Christian life. "The old commandment is the word which ye had from the beginning" (1 John 2:7). This phrase "from the beginning" is used in two different ways in John's letter, and it is important that you distinguish them. In 1 John 1:1, describing the eternality of Christ, we read that He existed "from the beginning." In John 1:1—a parallel verse—we read, "In the beginning was the Word."

But in 1 John 2:7, the subject is the beginning of the Christian life. The commandment to love one another is not an appendix to our Christian experience, as though God had an afterthought. No! It is in our hearts from the very beginning of our faith in Jesus Christ. If this were not so, John could not have written, "We know that we have passed out of death into life because we love the brethren" (1 John 3:14 NASB). And Jesus said, "By this all men will know that you are

My disciples, if you have love for one another" (John 13:35 NASB).

By nature, an unsaved person may be selfish and even hateful. As much as we love a newborn baby, we must confess that the infant is self-centered and thinks the whole world revolves around his crib. The child is typical of an unsaved person. "We ourselves also were sometimes foolish, disobedient, deceived, serving divers lusts and pleasures, living in malice and envy, hateful and hating one another" (Titus 3:3). This unretouched photo of the unbeliever may not be beautiful, but it is certainly accurate! Some unregenerate persons do not display the traits here mentioned, but the works of the flesh (Gal. 5:19–21) are always potentially present in their dispositions.

When a sinner trusts Christ, he receives a new life and a new nature. The Holy Spirit of God comes to live in him and the love of God is "shed abroad in [his] heart" by the Spirit (Rom. 5:5). God does not have to give a new believer a long lecture about love! "For ye yourselves are taught of God [i.e., by the Holy Spirit within you] to love one another" (1 Thess. 4:9). A new believer discovers that he now hates what he used to love, and that he loves what he used to hate!

So the commandment to love one another is new in emphasis: it is one of the most important commandments Christ gave us (John 13:34). In fact, "love one another" is repeated at least a dozen times in the New Testament (John 13:34; 15:9, 12, 17; Rom. 13:8; 1 Thess. 4:9; 1 Peter 1:22; 1 John 3:11, 23; 4:7, 11–12; 2 John 5). And there are many other references to brotherly love.

It is important that we understand the meaning of Christian love. It is not a shallow sentimental emotion that Christians try to "work up" so they can get along with each other. It is a matter of the will rather than an emotion—an affection for and attraction to certain persons. It is a matter of determining—of making up your mind—that you will allow God's love to reach others through you, and then of acting toward them in loving ways. You are not to act "as if you loved them," but because you love them. This is not hypocrisy—it is obedience to God.

Perhaps the best explanation of Christian love is 1 Corinthians 13. You should read a modern translation of this chapter to get the full force of its message: the Christian life without love is NOTHING!

But the commandment "Love one another" is not only new in emphasis. It is new in another way.

It Is New in Example (2:8)

"Love one another," John pointed out, was first true in Christ, and now it is true in the lives of those who are trusting Christ. Jesus Himself is the greatest Example of this commandment.

Later on we will think about that great statement "God is love" (1 John 4:8), but it is anticipated here. When one looks at Jesus Christ, one sees love embodied and exemplified. In commanding us to love, Jesus does not ask us to do something that He has not already done Himself. The four gospel records are the account of a life lived in the spirit of love—and that life was lived under conditions far from ideal. Jesus says to us, in effect, "I lived by this great commandment, and I can enable you to follow My example."

Jesus illustrated love by the very life that He lived. He never showed hatred or malice. His righteous soul hated all sin and disobedience, but He never hated the people who committed such sins. Even in His righteous announcements of judgment, there was always an undercurrent of love.

It is encouraging to think of Jesus' love for the twelve disciples. How they must have broken His heart again and again as they argued over who was the greatest or tried to keep people from seeing their Master. Each of them was different from the others, and Christ's love was broad enough to include each one in a personal, understanding way. He was patient with Peter's impulsiveness, Thomas's unbelief, and even Judas's treachery. When Jesus commanded His disciples to love one another, He was only telling them to do as He had done.

Consider too our Lord's love for all kinds of people. The publicans and sinners were attracted by His love (Luke 15:1), and even the lowest of the low could weep at His feet (Luke 7:36–39). Spiritually hungry rabbi Nicodemus could meet with Him privately at night (John 3:1–21), and four thousand of the "common people" could listen to His teaching for three days (Mark 8:1–9) and then receive a miraculous meal from Him. He held babies in His arms. He spoke about children at play. He even comforted the women who wept as the soldiers led Him out to Calvary.

Perhaps the greatest thing about Jesus' love was the way it touched even the lives of His enemies. He looked with loving pity on the religious leaders who in their spiritual blindness accused Him of being in league with Satan (Matt. 12:24). When the mob came to arrest Him, He could have called on the armies of heaven for protection, but He yielded to His enemies. And then He died for them—for His enemies! "Greater love hath no man than this, that a man lay down his life for his friends" (John 15:13, italics mine). But Jesus died not only for His friends, but also for His foes! And as they crucified Him, He prayed for them: "Father, forgive them, for they know not what they do."

In His life, in His teachings, and in His death, Jesus is the perfect Example of this new commandment, "Love one another." And this is what helps to make the commandment "new." In Christ we have a new illustration of the old truth that God is love and that the life of love is the life of joy and victory.

What is true in Christ ought to be true in each believer. "As he is, so are we in this world" (1 John 4:17). A believer should live a life of Christian love "because the darkness is passing away, and the true light is already shining" (1 John 2:8 NASB). This reminds us of the emphasis on walking in the light (1 John 1). Two ways of life are contrasted: those who walk in the light practice love; those who walk in the darkness practice hatred. The Bible repeatedly emphasizes this truth.

"The darkness is passing away," but the light does not yet shine fully all over the world, nor does it penetrate every area of even a believer's life.

When Christ was born, "the dayspring from on high" visited the world (Luke 1:78). "Dayspring" means sunrise. The birth of Christ was the beginning of a new day for mankind! As He lived before men, taught them, and ministered to them, He spread the light of life and love. "The people who sat in darkness saw a great light; and to them which sat in the region and shadow of death light is sprung up" (Matt. 4:16).

But there is a conflict in this world between the forces of light and the forces of darkness. "And the light is shining in the darkness, and the darkness is not able to put it out" (John 1:5, literal translation). Satan is the Prince of darkness, and he extends his evil kingdom by means of lies and hatred. Christ is the "Sun of righteousness" (Mal. 4:2), and He extends His kingdom by means of truth and love.

The kingdoms of Christ and of Satan are in conflict today, but "the path of the just is as the shining light, that shineth more and more unto the perfect day" (Prov. 4:18). The darkness is passing away little by little, and the True Light is shining brighter and brighter in our hearts.

Jesus Christ is the standard of love for Christians. "A new commandment I give unto you, that ye love one another," He said, "as I have loved you, that ye also love one another" (John 13:34). And He repeated: "This is my commandment, that ye love one another, as I have loved you" (John 15:12, italics mine). We are not to measure our Christian love against the love of some other Christian (and we usually pick somebody whose life is more of an excuse than an example!) but against the love of Jesus Christ our Lord. The old commandment becomes "new" to us as we see it fulfilled in Christ.

So the commandment "Love one another" is new in emphasis and new in example. It is also new in a third way.

It Is New in Experience (2:9–11)

Our passage continues the illustration of light and darkness. If a Christian walks in the light and is in fellowship with God, he will also be in fellowship with others in God's family. Love and light go together, much as hatred and darkness go together.

It is easy to talk about Christian love, but much more difficult to practice it. For one thing, such love is not mere talk (1 John 2:9). For a Christian to say (or sing!) that he loves the brethren while he actually hates another believer is for him to lie. In other words (and this is a sobering truth), it is impossible to be in fellowship with the Father and out of fellowship with another Christian at the same time.

This is one reason why God established the local church, the fellowship of believers. "You can't be a Christian alone"; a person cannot live a complete and developing Christian life unless he is in fellowship with God's people. The Christian life has two relationships: the vertical (Godward) and the horizontal (man-ward). And what God has joined together, man must not put asunder! And each of these two relationships is to be one of love one for the other.

Jesus dealt with this matter in the Sermon on the Mount (see Matt. 5:21–26). A gift on the altar was valueless as long as the worshipper had a dispute to settle with his brother. Note that Jesus did not say that the worshipper had something against his brother, but that the brother had something against the worshipper. But even when we have been offended, we should not wait for the one who has offended us to come to us; we should go to him. If we do not, Jesus warned us that we will end up in a prison of spiritual judgment where we will have to pay the last penny (Matt. 18:21–35). In other words, when we harbor an unforgiving, unloving spirit, we harm ourselves most.

The contrast between "saying" and "doing" is one we have met before (1 John 1:6, 8, 10; 2:4, 6). It is easy to practice a Christianity of "words"—singing the right songs, using the right vocabulary, praying the right prayers—and, through it all, deceiving ourselves into thinking we are spiritual. This mistake also ties into something Jesus taught in the Sermon on the Mount (Matt. 5:33–37). What we say should be the true expression of our character. We should not need extra words ("oaths") to fortify what we say. Our yes should mean yes, and our no should mean no. So, if we say we are in the light, we will prove it by loving the brethren. Many Christians urgently need to be accepted, loved, and encouraged.

Contrary to popular opinion, Christian love is not "blind." When we practice true Christian love, we find life getting brighter and brighter. Hatred is what darkens life! When true Christian love flows out of our hearts, we will have greater understanding and perception in spiritual things. This is why Paul prayed that our love may grow in knowledge and perception, "that ye may distinguish the things that differ" (see Phil. 1:9–10). A Christian who loves his brother is a Christian who sees more clearly.

No book in the Bible illustrates the blinding power of hatred like the book of Esther. The events recorded there take place in Persia, where many of the Jews were living after the captivity. Haman, one of the king's chief men, had a burning hatred for the Jews. The only way he could satisfy this hatred was to see the whole nation destroyed. He plunged ahead in an evil plot, completely blind to the fact that the Jews would win and that he himself would be destroyed.

Hatred is blinding people today too. Christian love is not a shallow sentiment, a passing emotion that we perhaps experience in a church service. Christian love is a practical thing; it applies in the everyday affairs of life. Just consider the "one another" statements in the New Testament and you will see how practical it is to love one another. Here are just a few (there are over twenty such statements):

Wash one another's feet (John 13:14).
Prefer one another (Rom. 12:10).
Be of the same mind one to another (Rom. 12:16).
Do not judge one another (Rom. 14:13).
Receive one another (Rom. 15:7).
Admonish one another (Rom. 15:14).
Edify [build up] one another (1 Thess. 5:11).
Bear one another's burdens (Gal. 6:2).
Confess your faults to one another (James 5:16).
Use hospitality one to another (1 Peter 4:9).

In short, to love other Christians means to treat them the way God treats them—and the way God treats us. Christian love that does not show itself in action and in attitude is spurious (see 1 Cor. 13:4–7).

What happens to a believer who does not love the brethren? We have already seen the first tragic result: he lives in the darkness, though he probably thinks he is living in the light (1 John 2:9). He thinks he sees, but he is actually blinded by the darkness of hatred. This is the kind of person who causes trouble in Christian groups. He thinks he is a "spiritual giant," with great understanding, when actually he is a babe with very little spiritual perception. He may read the Bible faithfully and pray fervently, but if he has hatred in his heart, he is living a lie.

The second tragic result is that such a believer becomes a cause of stumbling (see 1 John 2:10). It is bad enough when an unloving believer hurts himself (1 John 2:9), but when he starts to hurt others the situation is far more serious. It is serious to walk in the darkness. It is dangerous to walk in the darkness when stumbling blocks are in the way! An unloving brother stumbles himself, and in addition he causes others to stumble.

A man who was walking down a dark street one night saw a pinpoint of light coming toward him in a faltering way. He thought perhaps the person carrying the light was ill or drunk, but as he drew nearer he could see a man with a flashlight carrying a white cane.

"Why would a blind man be carrying a light?" the man wondered, and then he decided to ask.

The blind man smiled. "I carry my light, not so I can see, but so that others can see me. I cannot help being blind," he said, "but I can help being a stumbling block."

The best way to help other Christians not to stumble is to love them. Love makes us stepping-stones; hatred (or any of its "cousins," such as envy or malice) makes us stumbling blocks. It is important that Christians exercise love in a local church, or else there will always be problems and disunity. When we are falling over each other, instead of lifting each other higher, we will never become a truly happy spiritual family.

Apply this, for instance, to the delicate matter of "questionable things" (Rom. 14—15). Since believers come from different backgrounds, they do not always agree. In Paul's day, they differed on such matters as diets and holy days. One group said it was unspiritual to eat meat offered to idols. Another group wanted strict observance of the Sabbath. There were several facets to the problem, but basic to its solution was "Love one another!" Paul put it this way: "Let us not, therefore, judge one another anymore; but judge this, rather, that no man put a stumbling block or an occasion to fall in his brother's way…. But if thy brother be grieved with thy food, now walkest thou not in love" (Rom. 14:13, 15 SRB).

A third tragic result of hatred is that it retards a believer's spiritual progress (1 John 2:11). A blind man—a person who is walking in darkness—can never find his way! The only atmosphere that is conducive to spiritual growth is the atmosphere of spiritual light—of love. Just as the fruits and flowers need sunshine, so God's people need love if they are going to grow.

The commandment "Love one another" becomes new to us in our own day-by-day experience. It is not enough for us to recognize that it is new in emphasis and say, "Yes, love is important!" Nor is it enough for us to see God's love exemplified by Jesus Christ. We must know this love in our own experience. The old commandment "Love one another" becomes a new commandment as we practice God's love in daily life.

Thus far, we have seen the negative side of 1 John 2:9–11; now let's look at the positive. If we practice Christian love, what will the wonderful results be?

First of all, we will be living in the light—living in fellowship with God and with our Christian brothers.

Second, we will not stumble or become stumbling blocks to others.

And, third, we will grow spiritually and will progress toward Christlikeness.

At this point, we should think about the contrast between the ugly "works of the flesh" (Gal. 5:19–21) and the beautiful fruit of the Spirit—"Love, joy, peace, patience, gentleness, goodness, faithfulness, meekness, and self-control" (Gal. 5:22–23). When we are walking in the light, the "seed of the Word" (Luke 8:11) can take root and bear fruit. And the first cluster the Spirit produces is love!

But love does not live alone. Love produces joy! Hatred makes a man miserable, but love always brings him joy.

A Christian couple came to see a pastor because their marriage was beginning to fall apart. "We're both saved," the discouraged husband said, "but we just aren't happy together. There's no joy in our home." As the pastor talked with them and they considered together what the Bible has to say, one fact became clear: both the husband and wife were nursing grudges.

Each recalled many annoying little things the other had done!

"If you two really loved each other," said the pastor, "you wouldn't file these hurts away in your hearts. Grudges fester in our hearts like infected sores and poison the whole system."

Then he read, "[Love] thinketh no evil" (1 Cor. 13:5). He explained, "This means that love never keeps records of things others do that hurt us. When we truly love someone, our love covers their sins and helps to heal the wounds they cause." Then he read, "And above all things have fervent love among yourselves; for love shall cover the multitude of sins" (1 Peter 4:8 SCO).

Before the couple left, the pastor counseled them: "Instead of keeping records of the things that hurt, start remembering the things that please. An unforgiving spirit always breeds poison, but a loving spirit that sees and remembers the best always produces health."

A Christian who walks in love is always experiencing some new joy because the "fruit of the Spirit" is love and joy. And when we blend "love" and "joy," we will have "peace"—and peace helps to produce "patience." In other words, walking in the light, walking in love, is the secret of Christian growth, which nearly always begins with love.

Now, all of us must admit that we cannot generate Christian love under our own power. By nature, we are selfish and hateful. It is only as God's Spirit floods our hearts with love that we, in turn, can love one another. "The love of God is shed abroad in our hearts by the Holy Ghost which is given unto us" (Rom. 5:5). The Spirit of God makes the commandment "Love one another" into a new and exciting day-by-day experience. If we walk in the light, God's Spirit produces love. If we walk in darkness, our own selfish spirit produces hatred.

The Christian life—the life that is real—is a beautiful blending of "something old, something new." The Holy Spirit takes the "old things" and makes them "new things" in our experience. When you stop to think about it, the Holy Spirit never grows old! He is always young! And He is the only Person on earth today who was here centuries ago when Jesus lived, taught, died, and rose again. He is the only One who can take "old truth" and make it fresh and new in our daily experience at this present time.

There are other exciting truths in the rest of John's letter, but if we fail to obey in this matter of love, the rest of the letter may well be "darkness" to us. Perhaps the best thing we can do, right now, is to search our hearts to see if we hold anything against a brother, or if someone has anything against us. The life that is real is an honest life—and it is a life of doing, not merely saying. It is a life of active love in Christ. This means forgiveness, kindness, longsuffering. But it also means joy and peace and victory.

The love life is the only life, because it is the life that is real!

CHAPTER FOUR
1 John 2:12–17
THE LOVE GOD HATES

A group of first graders had just completed a tour of a hospital, and the nurse who had directed them was asking for questions. Immediately a hand went up.

"How come the people who work here are always washing their hands?" a little fellow asked.

After the laughter had subsided, the nurse gave a wise answer: "They are 'always washing their hands' for two reasons. First, they love health; and second, they hate germs."

In more than one area of life, love and hate go hand in hand. A husband who loves his wife is certainly going to exercise a hatred for what would harm her. "Ye that love the Lord, hate evil" (Ps. 97:10). "Let love be without hypocrisy. Abhor what is evil; cling to what is good" (Rom. 12:9 NASB).

John's epistle has reminded us to exercise love (1 John 2:7–11)—the right kind of love. Now it warns us that there is a wrong kind of love, a love that God hates. This is love for what the Bible calls "the world."

There are four reasons why Christians should not love "the world."

Because of What the World Is

The New Testament word world has at least three different meanings. It sometimes means the physical world, the earth: "God that made the world [our planet] and all things therein" (Acts 17:24). It also means the human world, mankind: "For God so loved the world" (John 3:16). Sometimes these two ideas appear together "He [Jesus] was in the world, and the world [earth] was made by Him, and the world [mankind] knew him not" (John 1:10).

But the warning "Love not the world!" is not about the world of nature or the world of men. Christians ought to appreciate the beauty and usefulness of the earth God has made, since He "giveth us richly all things to enjoy" (1 Tim. 6:17). And they certainly ought to love people—not only their friends, but even their enemies.

This "world" named here as our enemy is an invisible spiritual system opposed to God and Christ.

We use the word world in the sense of system in our daily conversation. The TV announcer says, "We bring you the news from the world of sports." "The world of sports" is not a separate planet or continent. It is an organized system, made up of a set of ideas, people, activities, purposes, and so forth. And "the world of finance" and "the world of politics" are likewise systems of their own. Behind what we see in sports or finance is an invisible system that we cannot see, and it is the system that "keeps things going."

"The world," in the Bible, is Satan's system for opposing the work of Christ on earth. It is the very opposite of what is godly and holy and spiritual (1 John 2:16). "We know that we are of God, and the whole world lies in the power of the evil one" (1 John 5:19 NASB). Jesus called Satan "the prince of this world" (John 12:31). The devil has an organization of evil spirits (Eph. 6:11–12) working with him and influencing the affairs of "this world."

Just as the Holy Spirit uses people to accomplish God's will on earth, so Satan uses people to fulfill his evil purposes. Unsaved people, whether they realize it or not, are energized by "the prince of the power of the air, the spirit that now worketh in the children of disobedience" (Eph. 2:1–2).

Unsaved people belong to "this world." Jesus called them "the children of this world" (Luke 16:8). When Jesus was here on earth, the people of "this world" did not understand Him, nor do they now understand those of us who trust Him (1 John 3:1). A Christian is a member of the human world, and he lives in the physical world, but he does not belong to the spiritual world that is Satan's system for opposing God. "If ye were of the world [Satan's system], the world would love his own; but because ye are not of the world, but I have chosen you out of the world, therefore the world hateth you" (John 15:18).

"The world," then, is not a natural habitat for a believer. The believer's citizenship is in heaven (Phil. 3:20 NASB), and all his effective resources for living on earth come from his Father in heaven.

The believer is somewhat like a scuba diver. The water is not man's natural habitat, for he is not equipped for life in (or under) it. When a scuba diver goes under, he has to take special equipment with him so that he can breathe.

Were it not for the Holy Spirit's living within us, and the spiritual resources we have in prayer, Christian fellowship, and the Word, we could never "make it" here on earth. We complain about the pollution of earth's atmosphere—the atmosphere of "the world" is also so polluted spiritually that Christians cannot breathe normally!

But there is a second—and more serious—reason why Christians must not love the world.

Because of What the World Does to Us (2:15–16)

"If any man love the world, the love of the Father is not in him" (1 John 2:15).

Worldliness is not so much a matter of activity as of attitude. It is possible for a Christian to stay away from questionable amusements and doubtful places and still love the world, for worldliness is a matter of the heart. To the extent that a Christian loves the world system and the things in it, he does not love the Father.

Worldliness not only affects your response to the love of God; it also affects your response to the will of God. "The world passeth away … but he that doeth the will of God abideth forever" (1 John 2:17).

Doing the will of God is a joy for those living in the

love of God. "If ye love me, keep my commandments." But when a believer loses his enjoyment of the Father's love, he finds it hard to obey the Father's will.

When you put these two factors together, you have a practical definition of worldliness: anything in a Christian's life that causes him to lose his enjoyment of the Father's love or his desire to do the Father's will is worldly and must be avoided. Responding to the Father's love (your personal devotional life), and doing the Father's will (your daily conduct)—these are two tests of worldliness.

Many things in this world are definitely wrong, and God's Word identifies them as sins. It is wrong to steal and to lie (Eph. 4:25, 28). Sexual sins are wrong (Eph. 5:1–3). About these and many other actions, Christians can have little or no debate. But there are areas of Christian conduct that are not so clear and about which even the best Christians disagree. In such cases, each believer must apply the test to his own life and be scrupulously honest in his self-examination, remembering that even a good thing may rob a believer of his enjoyment of God's love and his desire to do God's will.

A senior student in a Christian college was known for his excellent grades and his effective Christian service. He was out preaching each weekend, and God was using him to win the souls and challenge Christians.

Then something happened: his testimony was no longer effective, his grades began to drop, and even his personality seemed to change. The president called him in.

"There's been a change in your life and your work," the president said, "and I wish you'd tell me what's wrong."

The student was evasive for a time, but then he told the story. He was engaged to a lovely Christian girl and was planning to get married after graduation. He had been called to a fine church and was anxious to move his new bride into the parsonage and get started in the pastorate.

"I've been so excited about it that I've even come to the place where I don't want the Lord to come back!" he confessed. "And then the power dropped out of my life."

His plans—good and beautiful as they were—came between him and the Father. He lost his enjoyment of the Father's love. He was worldly!

John pointed out that the world system uses three devices to trap Christians: the lust (desire) of the flesh, the lust of the eyes, and the pride of life (1 John 2:16). These same devices trapped Eve back in the garden: "And when the woman saw that the tree was good for food [the lust of the flesh], and that it was pleasant to the eyes [the lust of the eyes], and a tree to be desired to make one wise [the pride of life], she took of the fruit" (Gen. 3:6).

The lust of the flesh includes anything that appeals to man's fallen nature. "The flesh" does not mean "the body." Rather, it refers to the basic nature of unregenerate man that makes him blind to spiritual truth (1 Cor. 2:14). Flesh is the nature we receive in our physical birth; spirit is the nature we receive in the second birth (John 3:5–6). When we trust Christ, we become "partakers of the divine nature" (2 Peter 1:4). A Christian has both the old nature (flesh) and the new nature (Spirit) in his life. And what a battle these two natures can wage (Gal. 5:17–23)!

God has given man certain desires, and these desires are good. Hunger, thirst, weariness, and sex are not at all evil in themselves. There is nothing wrong about eating, drinking, sleeping, or begetting children. But when the flesh nature controls them, they become sinful "lusts." Hunger is not evil, but gluttony is sinful. Thirst is not evil, but drunkenness is a sin. Sleep is a gift of God, but laziness is shameful. Sex is God's precious gift when used rightly; but when used wrongly, it becomes immorality.

Now you can see how the world operates. It appeals to the normal appetites and tempts us to satisfy them in forbidden ways. In today's world we are surrounded by all kinds of allurements that appeal to our lower nature—and "the flesh is weak" (Matt. 26:41). If a Christian yields to it, he will get involved in the "works of the flesh." (Gal. 5:19–21 gives us the ugly list.)

It is important that a believer remember what God says about his old nature, the flesh. Everything God says about the flesh is negative. In the flesh there is "no good thing" (Rom. 7:18). The flesh profits "nothing" (John 6:63). A Christian is to put "no confidence" in the flesh (Phil. 3:3). He is to make "no provision" for the flesh (Rom. 13:14 NASB). A person who lives for the flesh is living a negative life.

The second device that the world uses to trap the Christian is called "the lust of the eyes." We sometimes forget that the eyes can have an appetite! (Have you ever said, "Feast your eyes on this"?)

The lust of the flesh appeals to the lower appetites of the old nature, tempting us to indulge them in sinful ways. The lust of the eyes, however, operates in a more refined way. In view here are pleasures that gratify the sight and the mind—sophisticated and intellectual pleasures. Back in the days of the apostle John, the Greeks and Romans lived for entertainments and activities that excited the eyes. Times have not changed very much! In view of television, perhaps every Christian's prayer ought to be "Turn away my eyes from looking at vanity" (Ps. 119:37 NASB).

Achan (Josh. 7), a soldier, brought defeat to Joshua's army because of the lust of his eyes. God had warned Israel not to take any spoils from the condemned city of Jericho, but Achan did not obey. He explained: "When I saw among the spoils a goodly Babylonish garment, and two hundred shekels of silver, … then I coveted them, and took them" (Josh. 7:21). The lust of the eyes led him into sin, and his sin led the army into defeat.

The eyes (like the other senses) are a gateway into the mind. The lust of the eyes, therefore, can include intellectual pursuits that are contrary to God's Word. There is pressure to make Christians think the way the world thinks. God warns us against "the counsel of the ungodly." This does not mean that Christians ignore education and secular learning; it does mean they are careful not to let intellectualism crowd God into the background.

The third device is the "boastful pride of life" (NASB). God's glory is rich and full; man's glory is vain and empty. In fact, the Greek word for "pride" was used to describe a braggart who was trying to impress people with his importance. People have always tried to outdo others in their spending and their getting. The boastful pride of life motivates much of what such people do.

Why is it that so many folks buy houses, cars, appliances, or wardrobes that they really cannot afford? Why do they succumb to the "travel now, pay later" advertising and get themselves into hopeless debt taking vacations far beyond their means? Largely because they want to impress other people—because of their "pride of life." They may want folks to notice how affluent or successful they are.

Most of us do not go that far, but it is amazing what stupid things people do just to make an impression. They even sacrifice honesty and integrity in return for notoriety and a feeling of importance.

Yes, the world appeals to a Christian through the lust of the flesh, the lust of the eyes, and the pride of life. And once the world takes over in one of these areas, a Christian will soon realize it. He will lose his enjoyment of the Father's love and his desire to do the Father's will. The Bible will become boring and prayer a difficult chore. Even Christian fellowship may seem empty and disappointing. It is not that there is something wrong with others, however—what's wrong is the Christian's worldly heart.

It is important to note that no Christian becomes worldly all of a sudden. Worldliness creeps up on a believer; it is a gradual process. First is the friendship of the world (James 4:4). By nature, the world and the Christian are enemies. ("Marvel not, my brethren, if the world hate you," 1 John 3:13.) A Christian who is a friend of the world is an enemy of God.

Next, the Christian becomes spotted by the world (James 1:27). The world leaves its dirty marks on one or two areas of his life. This means that gradually the believer accepts and adopts the ways of the world.

When this happens, the world ceases to hate the Christian and starts to love him! So John warned us, "Love not the world!"—but too often our friendship with the world leads to love. As a result, the believer becomes conformed to the world (Rom. 12:2), and you can hardly tell the two apart.

Among Christians, worldliness rears its ugly head in many subtle and unrecognized forms. Sometimes we tend to idolize great athletes, TV stars, or political leaders who profess to be Christians—as if these individuals were able to be of special help to

Almighty God. Or we cater to wealthy and "influential" persons in our local church, as if God's work would fold up without their good will or financial backing. Many forms of worldliness do not involve reading the wrong books and indulging in "carnal" amusements.

Sad to say, being conformed to the world can lead a Christian into being "condemned with the world" (1 Cor. 11:32). If a believer confesses and judges this sin, God will forgive him, but if he does not confess, God must lovingly chasten him. When a Christian is "condemned with the world," he does not lose his sonship. Rather, he loses his testimony and his spiritual usefulness. And in extreme cases, Christians have even lost their lives (see 1 Cor. 11:29–30)!

The downward steps and their consequences are illustrated in the life of Lot (Gen. 13:5–13; 14:8–14; 19). First Lot looked toward Sodom. Then he pitched his tent toward Sodom in the well-watered plains of Jordan. Then he moved into Sodom. And when Sodom was captured by the enemy, Lot was captured too. He was a believer (2 Peter 2:6–8), but he had to suffer with the unbelieving sinners of that wicked city. And when God destroyed Sodom, everything Lot lived for went up in smoke! Lot was saved so as by fire and lost his eternal reward (1 Cor. 3:12–15).

No wonder John warned us not to love the world!

Because of What a Christian Is (2:12–14)

This raises a practical and important question about the nature of a Christian and how he keeps from getting worldly.

The answer is found in the unusual form of address used in 1 John 2:12–14. Note the titles used as John addressed his Christian readers: "little children … fathers … young men … little children."

What was he referring to?

To begin with, "little children" (1 John 2:12) refers to all believers. Literally, this word means "born ones." All Christians have been born into God's family through faith in Jesus Christ, and their sins have been forgiven. The very fact that one is in God's family, sharing His nature, ought to discourage him from becoming friendly with the world. To be friendly with the world is treachery! "Friendship of the world is enmity with God … whosoever therefore will be [wants to be] a friend of the world is the enemy of God" (James 4:4).

But something else is true: we begin as little children—born ones—but we must not stay that way! Only as a Christian grows spiritually does he overcome the world.

John mentioned three kinds of Christians in a local church family: fathers, young men, and little children (1 John 2:12–14). The "fathers," of course, are mature believers who have an intimate personal knowledge of God. Because they know God, they know the dangers of the world. No Christian who has experienced the joys and wonders of fellowship with

God, and of service for God, will want to live on the substitute pleasures this world offers.

The "young men" are the conquerors: they have overcome the wicked one, Satan, who is the prince of this world system. How did they overcome him? Through the Word of God! "I have written unto you, young men, because ye are strong, and the Word of God abideth in you" (1 John 2:14). The "young men," then, are not yet fully mature, but they are maturing, for they use the Word of God effectively. The Word is the only weapon that will defeat Satan (Eph. 6:17).

The "little children" addressed in 1 John 2:13 are not those addressed in 1 John 2:12; two different Greek words are used. The word in 1 John 2:13 carries the idea of "immature ones," or little children still under the authority of teachers and tutors. These are young Christians who have not yet grown up in Christ. Like physical children, these spiritual children know their father, but they still have some growing to do.

Here, then, is the Christian family! All of them are "born ones," but some of them have grown out of infancy into spiritual manhood and adulthood. It is the growing, maturing Christian to whom the world does not appeal. He is too interested in loving his Father and in doing his Father's will. The attractions of the world have no allure for him. He realizes that the things of the world are only toys, and he can say with Paul, "When I became a man, I put away childish things" (1 Cor. 13:11).

A Christian stays away from the world because of what the world is (a satanic system that hates and opposes Christ), because of what the world does to us (attracts us to live on sinful substitutes), and because of what he (the Christian) is—a child of God.

Because of Where the World Is Going (2:17)

"The world is passing away!" (see 1 John 2:17).

That statement would be challenged by many men today who are confident that the world—the system in which we live—is as permanent as anything can be. But the world is not permanent. The only sure thing about this world system is that it is not going to be here forever. One day the system will be gone, and the pleasant attractions within it will be gone: all are passing away. What is going to last?

Only what is part of the will of God!

Spiritual Christians keep themselves "loosely attached" to this world because they live for something far better. They are "strangers and pilgrims on the earth" (Heb. 11:13). "For here have we no continuing city, but we seek one to come" (Heb. 13:14). In Bible times, many believers lived in tents because God did not want them to settle down and feel at home in this world.

John was contrasting two ways of life: a life lived for eternity and a life lived for time. A worldly person lives for the pleasures of the flesh, but a dedicated Christian lives for the joys of the Spirit. A worldly believer lives for what he can see, the lust of the eyes, but a spiritual believer lives for the unseen realities of God (2 Cor. 4:8–18). A worldly minded person lives for the pride of life, the vainglory that appeals to men, but a Christian who does the will of God lives for God's approval. And he "abideth forever."

Every great nation in history has become decadent and has finally been conquered by another nation. There is no reason why we should suppose that our nation will be an exception. Some nineteen world civilizations in the past have slipped into oblivion. There is no reason why we should think that our present civilization will endure forever. "Change and decay all around I see," wrote Henry F. Lyte (1793–1847), and if our civilization is not eroded by change and decay it will certainly be swept away and replaced by a new order of things at the coming of Christ, which could happen at any time.

Slowly but inevitably, and perhaps sooner than even Christians think, the world is passing away, but the man who does God's will abides forever.

This does not mean that all God's servants will be remembered by future generations. Of the multitudes of famous men who have lived on earth, less than two thousand have been remembered by any number of people for more than a century.

Nor does it mean that God's servants will live on in their writings or in the lives of those they influenced. Such "immortality" may be a fact, but it is equally true of unbelievers such as Karl Marx, Voltaire, or Adolf Hitler.

No, we are told here (1 John 2:17) that Christians who dedicate themselves to doing God's will—to obeying God—"abide [remain] forever." Long after this world system—with its vaunted culture, its proud philosophies, its egocentric intellectualism, and its godless materialism—has been forgotten, and long after this planet has been replaced by the new heavens and the new earth, God's faithful servants will remain—sharing the glory of God for all eternity.

And this prospect is not limited to Moody, Spurgeon, Luther, or Wesley and their likes— it is open to each and every humble believer. If you are trusting Christ, it is for you.

This present world system is not a lasting one. "The fashion of this world passeth away" (1 Cor. 7:31). Everything around us is changing, but the things that are eternal never change. A Christian who loves the world will never have peace or security because he has linked his life with that which is in a state of flux. "He is no fool," wrote missionary martyr Jim Elliot, "who gives what he cannot keep to gain what he cannot lose."

The New Testament has quite a bit to say about "the will of God." One of the "fringe benefits" of salvation is the privilege of knowing God's will (Acts 22:14). In fact, God wants us to be "filled with the knowledge of his will" (Col. 1:9). The will of God is not something that we consult occasionally like an encyclopedia. It is something that completely controls our lives. The issue for a dedicated Christian is not simply, "Is it right or wrong?" or "Is it good or bad?" The key issue is, "Is this the will of God for me?"

God wants us to understand His will (Eph. 5:17), not just know what it is. "He made known his ways unto Moses, his acts unto the children of Israel" (Ps. 103:7). Israel knew what God was doing, but Moses knew why He was doing it! It is important that we understand God's will for our lives and see the purposes He is fulfilling.

After we know the will of God, we should do it from the heart (Eph. 6:6). It is not by talking about the Lord's will that we please Him, but by doing what He tells us (Matt. 7:21). And the more we obey God, the better able we are to "find and follow God's will" (Rom. 12:2, Williams). Discovering and doing God's will is something like learning to swim: you must get in the water before it becomes real to you. The more we obey God, the more proficient we become in knowing what He wants us to do.

God's goal for us is that we will "stand … complete in all the will of God" (Col. 4:12). This means to be mature in God's will.

A little child constantly asks his parents what is right and what is wrong and what they want him to do or not to do. But as he lives with his parents and experiences their training and discipline, he gradually discovers what their will for him is. In fact, a disciplined child can "read his father's mind" just by watching the parent's face and eyes! An immature Christian is always asking his friends what they think God's will is for him. A mature Christian stands complete in the will of God. He knows what the Lord wants him to do.

How does one discover the will of God? The process begins with surrender: "Present your bodies a living sacrifice … be not conformed to this world … that ye may prove [know by experience] what is that good, and acceptable, and perfect, will of God" (Rom. 12:1–2). A Christian who loves the world will never know the will of God in this way. The Father shares His secrets with those who obey Him. "If any man will do his will, he shall know of the doctrine" (John 7:17). And God's will is not a "spiritual cafeteria" where a Christian takes what he wants and rejects the rest! No, the will of God must be accepted in its entirety. This involves a personal surrender to God of one's entire life.

God reveals His will to us through His Word. "Thy word is a lamp unto my feet, and a light unto my path" (Ps. 119:105). A worldly believer has no appetite for the Bible. When he reads it, he gets little or nothing from it. But a spiritual believer, who spends time daily reading the Bible and meditating on it, finds God's will there and applies it to his everyday life.

We may also learn God's will through circumstances. God moves in wonderful ways to open and close doors. We must test this kind of leading by the Word of God—and not test the Bible's clear teaching by circumstances!

Finally, God leads us into His will through prayer and the working of His Spirit in our hearts. As we pray about a decision, the Spirit speaks to us. An "inner voice" may agree with the leading of circumstances. We are never to follow this "inner voice" alone: we must always test it by the Bible, for it is possible for the flesh (or for Satan) to use circumstances—or "feelings"—to lead us completely astray.

To sum it up, a Christian is in the world physically (John 17:11), but he is not of the world spiritually (John 17:14). Christ has sent us into the world to bear witness of Him (John 17:18). Like a scuba diver, we must live in an alien element, and if we are not careful, the alien element will stifle us. A Christian cannot help being in the world, but when the world is in the Christian, trouble starts!

The world gets into a Christian through his heart: "Love not the world!" Anything that robs a Christian of his enjoyment of the Father's love, or of his desire to do the Father's will, is worldly and must be avoided. Every believer, on the basis of God's Word, must identify those things for himself.

A Christian must decide, "Will I live for the present only, or will I live for the will of God and abide forever?" Jesus illustrated this choice by telling about two men. One built on the sand and the other on the rock (Matt. 7:24–27). Paul referred to the same choice by describing two kinds of material for building: temporary and permanent (1 Cor. 3:11–15).

Love for the world is the love God hates. It is the love a Christian must shun at all costs!

CHAPTER FIVE
1 John 2:18–29
TRUTH OR CONSEQUENCES

It makes no difference what you believe, just as long as you are sincere!"

That statement expresses the personal philosophy of many people today, but it is doubtful whether most of those who make it have really thought it through. Is "sincerity" the magic ingredient that makes something true? If so, then you ought to be able to apply it to any area of life, and not only to religion.

A nurse in a city hospital gives some medicine to a patient, and the patient becomes violently ill. The nurse is sincere but the medicine is wrong, and the patient almost dies.

A man hears noises in the house one night and decides a burglar is at work. He gets his gun and shoots the "burglar," who turns out to be his daughter! Unable to sleep, she has gotten up for a bite to eat. She ends up the victim of her father's "sincerity."

It takes more than "sincerity" to make something true. Faith in a lie will always cause serious consequences; faith in the truth is never misplaced. It does make a difference what a man believes! If a man wants to drive from Chicago to New York, no amount of sincerity will get him there if the highway is taking him to Los Angeles. A person who is real builds his life on truth, not superstition or lies. It is impossible to live a real life by believing lies.

God has warned the church family ("little children") about the conflict between light and darkness (1 John 1:1—2:6) and between love and hatred (1 John 2:7–17). Now He warns them about a third conflict: the conflict between truth and error. It is not enough for a believer to walk in the light and to walk in love; he must also walk in truth. The issue is truth—or consequences!

Before John explained the tragic consequences of turning from the truth, he emphasized the seriousness of the matter. He did so by using two special terms: "the last time" and "antichrist." Both terms make it clear that Christians are living in an hour of crisis and must guard against the errors of the enemy.

"The last time" (or "the last hour") is a term that reminds us that a new age has dawned on the world. "The darkness is past, and the true light now shineth" (1 John 2:8). Since the death and resurrection of Jesus Christ, God is doing a "new thing" in this world. All of Old Testament history prepared the way for the work of Christ on the cross. All history since that time is merely preparation for "the end," when Jesus will come and establish His kingdom. There is nothing more that God must do for the salvation of sinners.

You may ask, "But if it was 'the last hour' in John's day, why has Jesus not yet returned?"

This is an excellent question and Scripture gives us the answer. God is not limited by time the way His creatures are. God works in human time, but He is above time (see 2 Peter 3:8).

"The last hour" began back in John's day and has been growing in intensity ever since. There were ungodly false teachers in John's day, and during the intervening centuries they have increased both in number and in influence. "The last hour" or "the last times" are phrases that describe a kind of time, not a duration of time. "The latter times" are described in 1 Timothy 4. Paul, like John, observed characteristics of his time, and we see the same characteristics today in even greater intensity.

In other words, Christians have always been living in "the last time"—in crisis days. It is therefore important that you know what you believe and why you believe it.

The second term, "antichrist," is used in the Bible only by John (1 John 2:18, 22; 4:3; 2 John 7). It describes three things: (1) a spirit in the world that opposes or denies Christ; (2) the false teachers who embody this spirit; and, (3) a person who will head up the final world rebellion against Christ.

The "spirit of antichrist" (1 John 4:3) has been in the world since Satan declared war on God (see Gen. 3). The "spirit of antichrist" is behind every false doctrine and every "religious" substitute for the realities Christians have in Christ. As I mentioned in chapter 1 of this study, that prefix anti- actually has a dual meaning. It can mean, in the Greek, both "against" Christ and "instead of" Christ. Satan in his frenzy is fighting Christ and His eternal truth, and he is substituting his counterfeits for the realities found only in our Lord Jesus.

The "spirit of antichrist" is in the world today. It will eventually lead to the appearance of a "satanic superman" whom the Bible calls "Antichrist" (capital A). He is called "the man of sin" (or "lawlessness") (2 Thess. 2:1–12).

This passage explains that there are two forces at work in today's world: truth is working through the church by the Holy Spirit, and evil is working by the energy of Satan. The Holy Spirit, in Christians, is holding back lawlessness; but when the church is removed at the rapture (1 Thess. 4:13–18), Satan will be able to complete his temporary victory and take over the world. (John had more to say about this world ruler and his evil system in the book of Revelation, particularly 13:1–18; 16:13; and 19:20.)

Does it make any difference what you believe? It makes all the difference in the world! You are living in crisis days—in the last hour—and the spirit of antichrist is working in the world! It is vitally important that you know and believe the truth and be able to detect lies when they come your way.

John's epistle gives three outstanding marks of the false teacher who is controlled by the "spirit of antichrist."

He Departs from the Fellowship (2:18–19)

"They went out from us, but they were not really of us; for if they had been of us, they would have remained with us" (1 John 2:19 NASB).

The word us refers, of course, to the fellowship of believers, the church. Not everyone who is part of an assembly of believers is necessarily a member of the family of God!

The New Testament presents the church in a twofold way: as one worldwide family and as local units or assemblies of believers. There is a "universal" as well as "local" aspect of the church. The whole worldwide company of believers is compared with a body (1 Cor. 12) and with a building (Eph. 2:19–22). When a sinner trusts Christ as Savior, he receives eternal life and immediately becomes a member of God's family and a part of Christ's spiritual body. He should then identify himself with a local group of Christians (a church) and start serving Christ (Acts 2:41–42). But the point here is that a person can belong to a local church and not be part of the true spiritual body of Christ.

One of the evidences of true Christian life is a desire to be with the people of God. "We know that we have passed from death unto life, because we love the brethren" (1 John 3:14). When people share the same divine nature (2 Peter 1:4) and are indwelt by the same Holy Spirit (Rom. 8:14–16), they want to enjoy fellowship and to share with one another. As we have seen, fellowship means "to have in common." When people have spiritual realities in common, they want to be together.

But the "counterfeit Christians" mentioned in 1 John 2 did not remain in the fellowship. They went out. This doesn't imply that "staying in the church" keeps a person saved; rather, it indicates that remaining in the fellowship is one evidence that a person is truly a Christian. In His Parable of the Sower (Matt. 13:1–9, 18–23), Jesus makes it clear that only those who produce fruit are truly born again. It is possible to be close to an experience of salvation, and even to have some characteristics that would pass for "Christian," and yet not be a child of God. The people in view in 1 John 2 left the fellowship because they did not possess the true life and the love of Christ was not in their hearts.

There are many unfortunate divisions among the people of God today, but all true Christians have things in common, regardless of church affiliation. They believe that the Bible is the Word of God and that Jesus is the Son of God. They confess that men are sinners and that the only way one can be saved is through faith in Christ. They believe that Christ died as man's substitute on the cross, and that He arose again from the dead. They believe that the Holy Spirit indwells true believers. Finally, they believe that one day in the future Jesus will come again. Christians may differ on other matters—church government, for example, or modes of baptism—but they agree on the basic doctrines of the faith.

If you will investigate the history of the false cults and antichristian religious systems in today's world, you will find that in most cases their founders started out in a local church! They were "with us" but not "of us," so they went out "from us" and started their own groups.

Any group, no matter how "religious," that for doctrinal reasons separates itself from a local church that holds to the Word of God, must immediately be suspect. Often these groups follow human leaders and the books men have written, rather than Jesus Christ and God's Word. The New Testament (e.g., 2 Tim. 3—4; 2 Peter 2) makes it clear that it is dangerous to depart from the fellowship.

He Denies the Faith (2:20–25; 4:1–6)

The key question for a Christian is, Who is Jesus Christ? Is Christ merely "an Example," "a good Man," or "a wonderful teacher," or is He God come in the flesh?

John's readers knew the truth about Christ, or else they would not have been saved. "You all know the truth, because you have the Spirit of God, an unction, and the Spirit teaches you all things" (see 1 John 2:20, 27). "Now if any man have not the Spirit of Christ he is none of his" (Rom. 8:9).

False Christians in John's day used two special words to describe their experience: "knowledge" and "unction." They claimed to have a special unction (anointing) from God that gave them a unique knowledge. They were "illuminated" and therefore living on a much higher level than anybody else. But John pointed out that all true Christians know God and have received the Spirit of God! And because they have believed the truth, they recognize a lie when they meet it.

The great assertion of the faith that sets a Christian apart from others is this: Jesus Christ is God come in the flesh (1 John 4:2).

Not all preachers and teachers who claim to be Christian are really Christian in their belief (1 John 4:1–6). If they confess that Jesus Christ is God come in the flesh, then they belong to the true faith. If they deny Christ, then they belong to antichrist. They are in and of the world, and are not, like true believers, called out of the world. When they speak, the world (unsaved persons) hears them and believes them. But the unsaved world can never understand a true Christian. A Christian speaks under the direction of the Spirit of Truth; a false teacher speaks under the influence of the spirit of error—the spirit of antichrist.

To confess that "Jesus Christ is God come in the flesh" involves much more than simply to identify Christ. The demons did this (Mark 1:24) but it did not save them. True confession involves personal faith in Christ—in who He is and what He has done. A confession is not a mere intellectual "theological statement" that you recite; it is a personal witness from your heart of what Christ has done for you. If you have trusted Christ and have confessed your faith, you have eternal life (1 John 2:25). Those who cannot honestly make this confession do not have eternal life, which is an ultimately serious matter.

George Whitefield, a great British evangelist, was speaking to a man about his soul. He asked the man, "Sir, what do you believe?"

"I believe what my church believes," the man replied respectfully.

"And what does your church believe?"

"The same thing I believe."

"And what do both of you believe?" the preacher inquired again.

"We both believe the same thing!" was the only reply he could get.

A man is not saved by assenting to a church creed. He is saved by trusting Jesus Christ and bearing witness to his faith (Rom. 10:9–10).

False teachers will often say, "We worship the Father. We believe in God the Father, even though we disagree with you about Jesus Christ."

But to deny the Son means to deny the Father also. You cannot separate the Father and the Son, since both are one God. Jesus said, "I and my Father are one" (John 10:30). He also made it clear that true believers honor both the Father and the Son: "That all men should honor the Son, even as they honor the Father.

He that honoreth not the Son honoreth not the Father which hath sent him" (John 5:23). If you say you "worship one God" but leave Jesus Christ out of your worship, you are not worshipping as a true Christian.

It is important that you stay with the truth of God's Word. The Word (or message) Christians have "heard from the beginning" is all you need to keep you true to the faith. The Christian life continues just as it began: through faith in the Bible's message. A religious leader who comes along with "something new," something that contradicts what Christians have "heard from the beginning," is not to be trusted. "Try the spirits, whether they are of God" (1 John 4:1). Let the Word abide in you (1 John 2:24), and abide in Christ (1 John 2:28); otherwise you will be led astray by the spirit of antichrist. No matter what false teachers may promise, you have the sure promise of eternal life (1 John 2:25). You need nothing more!

If false teachers were content to enjoy themselves in their own meetings, it would be bad enough; the tragedy is that they try earnestly to convert others to their antichristian doctrines. This is the third mark of a man who has turned away from God's truth.

He Tries to Deceive the Faithful (2:26–29)

It is interesting to observe that antichristian groups rarely try to lead lost sinners to their false faith. Instead, they spend much of their time trying to convert professing Christians (and church members, at that) to their own doctrines. They are out to "seduce" the faithful.

The word seduce carries the idea of "being led astray." We have been warned that this would happen: "Now the Spirit speaketh expressly, that in the latter times some shall depart from the faith, giving heed to seducing spirits, and doctrines of devils [teachings of demons]" (1 Tim. 4:1).

Jesus called Satan the "father of lies" (John 8:44 NIV). The devil's purpose is to lead Christians astray by teaching them false doctrines (2 Cor. 11:1–4, 13–15). We should not accept everything a person tells us simply because he claims to believe the Bible, for it is possible to "twist" the Bible to make it mean almost anything (2 Cor. 4:1–2).

Satan is not an originator; he is a counterfeiter. He imitates the work of God. For example, Satan has counterfeit "ministers" (2 Cor. 11:13–15) who preach a counterfeit gospel (Gal. 1:6–12) that produces counterfeit Christians (John 8:43–44) who depend on a counterfeit righteousness (Rom. 10:1–10). In the parable of the tares (Matt. 13:24–30, 36–43), Jesus and Satan are pictured as sowers. Jesus sows the true seed, the children of God, but Satan sows "the children of the wicked one." The two kinds of plants, while growing, look so much alike that the servants could not tell the difference until the fruit appeared! Satan's chief stratagem during this age is to plant the counterfeit wherever Christ plants the true. And it is important that you be able to detect the counterfeit

and separate the teachings of Christ from the false teachings of antichrist.

How does a believer do this? By depending on the teaching of the Holy Spirit. Each believer has experienced the anointing (the "unction," 1 John 2:20) of the Spirit, and it is the Spirit who teaches him truth (John 14:17; 15:26). False teachers are not led by the Spirit of Truth; they are led by the spirit of error (1 John 4:3, 6).

The word anoint reminds us of the Old Testament practice of pouring oil on the head of a person being set apart for special service. A priest was anointed (Ex. 28:41), and so was a king (1 Sam. 15:1) or a prophet (1 Kings 19:16). A New Testament Christian is anointed, not with literal oil, but by the Spirit of God—an anointing that sets him apart for his ministry as one of God's priests (1 Peter 2:5, 9). It is not necessary for you to pray for "an anointing of the Spirit"; if you are a Christian, you have already received this special anointing. This anointing "abides in us" and therefore does not need to be imparted to us.

We have seen that false teachers deny the Father and the Son; they also deny the Spirit. The Spirit is the Teacher God has given us (John 14:26), but these false Christians want to be teachers themselves and lead others astray. They try to take the place of the Holy Spirit!

We are warned against letting any man be our teacher, for God has given us the Spirit to teach us His truth. This does not deny the office of human teachers in the church (Eph. 4:11–12), but it means that under the guidance of the Spirit you must test the teaching of men as you search the Bible for yourself (see Acts 17:11).

A missionary to the Native Americans was in Los Angeles with a Native American friend who was a new Christian. As they walked down the street, they passed a man on the corner who was preaching with a Bible in his hand. The missionary knew the man represented a cult, but the Native American saw only the Bible. He stopped to listen to the sermon.

"I hope my friend doesn't get confused," the missionary thought, and he began to pray. In a few minutes the Native American turned away from the meeting and joined his missionary friend.

"What did you think of the preacher?" the missionary asked.

"All the time he was talking," exclaimed the Native American, "something in my heart kept saying, 'Liar! Liar!'"

That "something" in his heart was "Someone"— the Holy Spirit of God! The Spirit guides us into the truth and helps us to recognize error. This anointing of God is "no lie," because "the Spirit is truth" (1 John 5:6).

Why are some Christians led astray to believe false teachings? Because they are not abiding in the Spirit. The word abide occurs several times in this section of 1 John, and it would be helpful to review:

- False teachers do not abide ("continue") in the fellowship (1 John 2:19).

- The word (message) we have heard should abide in us (1 John 2:24).
- The anointing (the Holy Spirit) abides in us, and we should abide in the Spirit (1 John 2:27).
- As we abide in the Word and in the Spirit, we also abide in Christ (1 John 2:28).

We noticed this word *abide* earlier in John's letter too:

- If we say we abide in Christ, we should walk as He walked (1 John 2:6).
- If we love our brother, we abide in the light (1 John 2:10).
- If the Word abides in us, we will be spiritually strong (1 John 2:14).
- If we do the will of God, we shall abide forever (1 John 2:17).

"To abide" means to remain in fellowship; and "fellowship" is the key idea in the first two chapters of this epistle. From chapters 3 to 5, the emphasis is on sonship, or being "born of God."

It is possible to be a child in a family and yet be out of fellowship with one's father and with other members of the family. When our heavenly Father discovers that we are out of fellowship with Him, He deals with us to bring us back into the place of abiding. This process is called "chastening"—child-training (Heb. 12:5–11).

A believer must allow the Spirit of God to teach him from the Bible. One of the major functions of a local church is the teaching of God's Word (2 Tim. 2:2; 4:1–5). The Spirit gives the gift of teaching to certain individuals in the fellowship (Rom. 12:6–7) and they teach others, but what they teach must be tested (1 John 4:1–3).

There is a difference between deliberate deception and spiritual ignorance. When Apollos preached in the synagogue at Ephesus, his message was correct as far as it went, but it was not complete. Priscilla and Aquila, two mature believers in the congregation, took him aside privately and instructed him in the full message of Christ (Acts 18:24–28). A Christian who spends time daily in the Bible and in prayer will walk in the Spirit and have the discernment he needs.

The Spirit teaches us "of all things" (1 John 2:27, italics mine). False teachers have a way of "riding a hobby"—prophecy or sanctification or even diet— and neglecting the whole message of the Bible. Jesus implied that we are to live by "every word that proceedeth out of the mouth of God" (Matt. 4:4, italics mine). Paul was careful to preach "all the counsel of God" (Acts 20:27, italics mine). "All Scripture is given by inspiration of God and is profitable" (2 Tim. 3:16, italics mine).

If you ignore or neglect any part of the Bible, you invite trouble. You must read and study the whole Book, and be able to rightly divide it (see 2 Tim. 2:15); that is, you must handle it accurately (see NASB). You should discern in the Bible what God says to different people at different times; there are passages that apply specifically to the Jews, or to the Gentiles, or to the church (1 Cor. 10:32). You must be careful to distinguish between them. Though all of the Bible was written for you, not all of it was written to you. False teachers, however, pick (out of context) only what they want, and often apply to believers today passages that were given only for ancient Israel.

John's second epistle gives further warning about false teachers (2 John 7–11). A Christian who meddles with these deceivers is in danger of losing his full reward (2 John 8). You should not even say goodbye (which literally means "God be with you"). You are not to be rude or unkind, because that would not be Christian, but you are not to let them into your home to explain their views. Why? Because if you let them in, two consequences may follow: First, they will plant the seeds of false teaching in your mind, and Satan can water and nourish these seeds to produce bitter fruit. But even if this does not happen, by entertaining false teachers in your home you are giving them entrance into other homes! The deceiver will say to your neighbor down the street, "Mr. and Mrs. Smith let me into their home, and you know what good Christians they are!"

John has now concluded his message on fellowship and is about to begin his message on sonship. He has pointed out the contrasts between light and darkness (1 John 1:1–2:6), love and hatred (1 John 2:7–17), and truth and error (1 John 2:18–27). He has explained that a real Christian lives a life of obedience (walking in light, not darkness), love, and truth. It is impossible to live in fellowship with God if you are disobedient or hateful or untruthful. Any of these sins will lead you out of reality and into pretense. You will have an "artificial" life instead of an "authentic" life.

First John 2:28 and 29 are a bridge from the fellowship section into the sonship section ("born of God"); in these verses John used three words that ought to encourage us to live in fellowship with the Father, the Son, and the Spirit.

- Abide. This is a word we have met twice before. You must recognize the importance of abiding in Christ. In fact, this has been the theme of the first two chapters of this epistle. You abide in Christ by believing the truth, obeying the truth, and loving other Christians—"the brethren." Obedience—love—truth. If you are a believer and find yourself out of fellowship with God, it is because you have disobeyed His Word, lacked love for a brother, or believed a lie. The solution is to confess your sin instantly and to claim God's forgiveness (1 John 1:9).

- Appear. This is the first mention in this epistle of the promised return of Christ. The book of Revelation deals in detail with future events. The epistle (1 John 2:28–3:3; 4:17) merely mentions the return of Christ and a coming day of judgment.

Not all Bible students are agreed as to the details of future events, but evangelical Christians agree that Christ is returning for His church (1 Thess. 4:13–18). Though Christians will not then be judged for their sins, they will be judged on the basis of their faithfulness in serving Christ (1 Cor. 3:10–15). Those who have been faithful will receive rewards (1 Cor. 4:5), and those who have not been faithful will lose rewards. This event is called "the judgment seat of Christ" (Rom. 14:10; 2 Cor. 5:10); do not confuse it with the "Great White Throne Judgment" of unsaved people at the end of time (Rev. 20:11–15).

The fact that Jesus Christ may return at any moment ought to be an incentive for us to live in fellowship with Him and be obedient to His Word. For this reason, John used a third word:

• Ashamed. Some Christians will be "ashamed before him at his coming" (1 John 2:28). All believers are "accepted," but there is a difference between being "accepted" and being "acceptable." A disobedient child who goes out and gets dirty will be accepted when he comes home, but he will not be treated as though he were acceptable. "Therefore also we have as our ambition … to be pleasing to Him" (2 Cor. 5:9 NASB). A Christian who has not walked in fellowship with Christ in obedience, love, and truth will lose his rewards; and this will make him ashamed.

No matter in which direction a Christian looks, he finds reason to obey God. If he looks back, he sees Calvary, where Christ died for him. If he looks within, he sees the Holy Spirit, who lives within and teaches him the truth. If he looks around, he sees his Christian brethren, whom he loves; he also sees a world lost in sin, desperately needing his godly witness. And if he looks ahead, he sees the return of Christ! "And every man that hath this hope in him purifieth himself, even as he is pure" (1 John 3:3). The return of Christ is a great inspiration for godly living.

John has written about light and darkness, love and hatred, and truth and error, and in 1 John 2:29 he summed up the whole matter of Christian living in one phrase—"doing righteousness."

The life that is real is a life of doing, not simply talking ("If we say," 1 John 1:8—2:9) or giving mental assent that a doctrine is correct. "Not every one that saith unto me, 'Lord, Lord,' shall enter into the kingdom of heaven, but he that doeth the will of my Father which is in heaven" (Matt. 7:21, italics mine). Christians do not simply believe the truth; they do it (1 John 1:6).

A person who professes to be a Christian, but who does not live in obedience, love, and truth, is either deceived or a deceiver. A child bears the nature of his father, and a person who has been "born of God" will reveal the characteristics of the heavenly Father. "Therefore be imitators of God, as beloved children" (Eph. 5:1 NASB). "As obedient children, not fashioning yourselves according to the former lusts in your ignorance: but as he which hath called you is holy, so be ye holy" (1 Peter 1:14–15).

A Sunday school class seemed to be having constant problems. The pastor and the superintendent met with the teacher and officers, but made no apparent progress. Then, one Sunday morning, the teacher of the class came down the aisle during the closing hymn of the service. "I suppose she wants to dedicate her life to the Lord," the pastor thought.

"Pastor," she said, "I want to confess Christ as my Savior. All these years I thought I was saved, but I wasn't. There was always something lacking in my life. The class problems were my problems, but now they've been solved. Now I know I'm saved."

"Test yourselves to see if you are in the faith; examine yourselves!" (2 Cor. 13:5 NASB). Does your life bear the marks of obedience, love, and truth? Is your Christian life something real—genuine—authentic? Or is it counterfeit?

It is a question of truth—or consequences!

And if you do not face the truth, you must pay the consequences!

CHAPTER SIX
1 John 3:1–10
THE PRETENDERS

The United States Treasury Department has a special group of men whose job it is to track down counterfeiters. Naturally, these men need to know a counterfeit bill when they see it.

How do they learn to identify fake bills?

Oddly enough, they are not trained by spending hours examining counterfeit money. Rather, they study the real thing. They become so familiar with authentic bills that they can spot a counterfeit by looking at it or, often, simply by feeling it.

This is the approach in 1 John 3, which warns us that in today's world there are counterfeit Christians—"children of the devil" (1 John 3:10). But instead of listing the evil characteristics of Satan's children, the Scripture gives us a clear description of God's children. The contrast between the two is obvious.

The key verse of this chapter is 1 John 3:10: a true child of God practices righteousness and loves other Christians despite differences. First John 3:1–10 deals with the first topic, and 1 John 3:11–24 takes up the second.

Practicing righteousness and loving the brethren, of course, are not new themes. These two important subjects are treated in the first two chapters of this epistle, but in 1 John 3 the approach is different. In the first two chapters the emphasis was on fellowship: a Christian who is in fellowship with God will practice righteousness and will love the brethren. But in 1 John 3—5, the emphasis is on sonship: because a Christian is "born of God," he will practice righteousness and will love the brethren.

"Born of God" is the idea that is basic to these chapters (see 1 John 2:29; 3:9; 4:7; 5:1, 4, 18).

When you read 1 John 3:1–10 in the Authorized Version, you may be startled by 1 John 3:6 and

9, which seem to contradict 1 John 1:8–9. The Authorized translation of the verbs here is not accurate. What the Greek text really says is "No one who abides in Him practices sin; no one who practices sin has seen Him or knows Him" (1 John 3:6). "No one who is born of God practices sin … he cannot practice sin because he is born of God" (1 John 3:9). To "practice" sin is to sin consistently and as a way of life. It does not refer to committing an occasional sin. It is clear that no Christian is sinless (1 John 1:8–10), but God expects a true believer to sin less, not to sin habitually.

Every great personality mentioned in the Bible sinned at one time or another. Abraham lied about his wife (Gen. 12:10–20). Moses lost his temper and disobeyed God (Num. 20:7–13). Peter denied the Lord three times (Matt. 26:69–75). But sin was not the settled practice of these men. It was an incident in their lives, totally contrary to their normal habits. And when they sinned, they admitted it and asked God to forgive them.

An unsaved person (even if he professes to be a Christian but is a counterfeit) lives a life of habitual sin. Sin—especially the sin of unbelief—is the normal thing in his life (Eph. 2:1–3). He has no divine resources to draw on. His profession of faith, if any, is not real. This is the distinction in view in 1 John 3:1–10—a true believer does not live in habitual sin. He may commit sin—an occasional wrong act—but he will not practice sin—make a settled habit of it.

The difference is that a true Christian knows God. A counterfeit Christian may talk about God and get involved in "religious activities," but he does not really know God. The person who has been "born of God" through faith in Christ knows God the Father, God the Son, and God the Holy Spirit. And because he knows them, he lives a life of obedience: he does not practice sin.

John gave us three reasons for a holy life.

God the Father Loves Us (3:1–3)

God's love for us is unique. First John 3:1 may be translated, "Behold, what peculiar, out-of-this-world kind of love the Father has bestowed on us." While we were His enemies God loved us and sent His Son to die for us!

The whole wonderful plan of salvation begins with the love of God.

Many translators add a phrase to 1 John 3:1: "That we should be called the sons of God, and we are." "Sons of God" is not simply a high-sounding name that we bear; it is a reality! We are God's children! We do not expect the world to understand this thrilling relationship, because it does not even understand God. Only a person who knows God through Christ can fully appreciate what it means to be called a child of God.

First John 3:1 tells us what we are and 1 John 3:2 tells us what we shall be. The reference here, of course, is to the time of Christ's coming for His church. This was mentioned in 1 John 2:28 as an incentive for holy living, and now it is repeated.

God's love for us does not stop with the new birth. It continues throughout our lives and takes us right up to the return of Jesus Christ! When our Lord appears, all true believers will see Him and will become like Him (Phil. 3:20–21). This means, of course, that they will have new, glorified bodies, suited to heaven.

But the apostle did not stop here! He has told us what we are and what we shall be. Now, in 1 John 3:3, he told us what we should be. In view of the return of Jesus Christ, we should keep our lives clean.

All this is to remind us of the Father's love. Because the Father loved us and sent His Son to die for us, we are children of God. Because God loves us, He wants us to live with Him one day. Salvation, from start to finish, is an expression of the love of God. We are saved by the grace of God (Eph. 2:8–9; Titus 2:11–15), but the provision for our salvation was originated in the love of God. And since we have experienced the love of the Father, we have no desire to live in sin.

An unbeliever who sins is a creature sinning against his Creator. A Christian who sins is a child sinning against his Father. The unbeliever sins against law; the believer sins against love.

This reminds us of the meaning of the phrase so often repeated in the Bible: "the fear of the Lord." This phrase does not suggest that God's children live in an atmosphere of terror, "for God hath not given us the spirit of fear" (2 Tim. 1:7). Rather, it indicates that God's children hold their Father in reverence and will not deliberately disobey Him or try His patience.

A group of teenagers were enjoying a party, and someone suggested that they go to a certain restaurant for a good time.

"I'd rather you took me home," Jan said to her date. "My parents don't approve of that place."

"Afraid your father will hurt you?" one of the girls asked sarcastically.

"No," Jan replied, "I'm not afraid my father will hurt me, but I am afraid I might hurt him."

She understood the principle that a true child of God, who has experienced the love of God, has no desire to sin against that love.

God the Son Died for Us (3:4–8)

John turned here from the future appearing of Jesus (1 John 3:2) to His past appearing (1 John 3:5, where the word manifest [KJV] means "appear"). John gave two reasons why Jesus came and died: (1) to take away our sins (1 John 3:4–6), and (2) to destroy the works of the devil (1 John 3:7–8). For a child of God to sin indicates that he does not understand or appreciate what Jesus did for him on the cross.

Christ appeared to take away our sins (vv. 4–6). There are several definitions of sin in the Bible: "Whatsoever is not of faith is sin" (Rom. 14:23). "The thought of foolishness is sin" (Prov. 24:9). "Therefore to him that knoweth to do good, and doeth it not, to him it is sin" (James 4:17). "All unrighteousness is sin" (1 John 5:17). But John's epistle defines sin as lawlessness (1 John 3:4). It views sin as defilement (1 John 1:9—2:2), but here it views it as defiance.

The emphasis here is not on sins (plural), but on sin (singular): "Whosoever practices sin." Sins are the fruit, but sin is the root.

That God is love does not mean He has no rules and regulations for His family. "And hereby we do know that we know him, if we keep his commandments" (1 John 2:3). "And whatsoever we ask, we receive of him, because we keep his commandments, and do those things that are pleasing in his sight" (1 John 3:22). "By this we know that we love the children of God, when we love God and keep his commandments" (1 John 5:2).

God's children are not in bondage to the Old Testament law, for Christ has set us free and has given us liberty (Gal. 5:1–6). But God's children are not to be lawless, either! They are "not without law to God, but under the law to Christ" (1 Cor. 9:21).

Sin is basically a matter of the will. For us to assert our will against God's will is rebellion, and rebellion is the root of sin. It is not simply that sin reveals itself in lawless behavior, but that the very essence of sin is lawlessness. No matter what his outward action may be, a sinner's inward attitude is one of rebellion.

Little Judy was riding in the car with her father. She decided to stand up in the front seat. Her father commanded her to sit down and put on the seat belt, but she declined. He told her a second time, and again she refused.

"If you don't sit down immediately, I'll pull over to the side of the road and spank you!" Dad finally said, and at this the little girl obeyed. But in a few minutes she said quietly, "Daddy, I'm still standing up inside."

Lawlessness! Rebellion! Even though there was constraint from the outside, there was still rebellion on the inside, and this attitude is the essence of sin.

But after a person has become a child of God, born again by faith in Jesus Christ, he cannot practice lawlessness! For one thing, Jesus Christ was without sin, and to abide in Him means to be identified with the One who is sinless. And even more than that, Jesus Christ died to take away our sins! If we know the person of Christ, and if we have shared in the blessing of His death, we cannot deliberately disobey God. The whole work of the cross is denied when a professed Christian practices deliberate sin. This is one reason why Paul called such people "enemies of the cross of Christ" (Phil. 3:18–19).

"Whosoever abideth in him does not practice sin" (1 John 3:6). "Abide" was one of John's favorite words. To abide in Christ means to be in fellowship with Him, to allow nothing to come between ourselves and Christ. Sonship (being born of God) brings about our union with Christ, but fellowship makes possible our communion with Christ. It is this communion (abiding) with Christ that keeps us from deliberately disobeying His Word.

A person who deliberately and habitually sins is proving that he does not know Christ and therefore cannot be abiding in Him.

There is more in the death of Christ on the cross than simply our salvation from judgment, as wonderful as that is. Through His death, Christ broke the power of the sin principle in our lives. The theme of Romans 6—8 is this identification with Christ in His death and resurrection. Christ not only died for me, but I died with Christ! Now I can yield myself to Him and sin will not have dominion over me.

Christ appeared to destroy the works of the devil (vv. 7–8). The logic here is clear: if a man knows God, he will obey God; if he belongs to the devil, he will obey the devil. John accepted the reality of a personal devil.

This enemy has many different names in Scripture: Satan (adversary, enemy), the devil (accuser), Abaddon or Apollyon (destroyer), the prince of this world, the dragon, and so forth. Whatever name you call him, keep in mind that his chief activity is to oppose Christ and God's people.

The contrast here is between Christ (who has no sin, 1 John 3:5) and the devil (who can do nothing but sin).

The origin of Satan is a mystery. Many scholars believe he was once one of the highest angels, placed by God over the earth and over the other angels, and that he sinned against God and was cast down (Isa. 14:9–17; Ezek. 28:12–14).

Satan is not eternal, as is God, for he is a created being. He was not created sinful. His present nature is a result of his past rebellion. Satan is not like God: he is not all-powerful, all-knowing, or everywhere present. However, he is assisted by an army of spirit creatures known as demons, who make it possible for him to work in many places at one time (Eph. 6:10–12).

Satan is a rebel, but Christ is the obedient Son of God. Christ was "obedient unto death, even the death of the cross" (Phil. 2:8). Christ is God but was willing to become a servant. Satan was a servant and wanted to become God. From the beginning of his career, Satan has been a sinner, and Christ came to destroy the works of the devil.

"Destroy" (1 John 3:8) does not mean "annihilate." Satan is certainly still at work today! "Destroy," here, means "to render inoperative, to rob of power." Satan has not been annihilated, but his power has been reduced and his weapons have been impaired. He is still a mighty foe, but he is no match for the power of God.

Jesus compared this world to a palace that contains many valuable goods. A strong man is guarding this palace (Luke 11:14–23). Satan is the strong man, and his "goods" are lost men and women. The only way to release the "goods" is to bind the strong man, and that is just what Jesus did on the cross. Jesus, in coming to earth, invaded Satan's "palace." When He died, He broke Satan's power and captured his goods! Each time a lost sinner is won to Christ, more of Satan's "spoils" are taken from him.

For many months after the close of World War II, Japanese troops were discovered hidden in the caves and jungles of the Pacific islands. Some of these stragglers were living like frightened savages; they didn't know the war was over. Once they understood that it was no longer necessary for them to fight, they surrendered.

Christians may rest in the truth that Satan is a defeated enemy. He may still win a few battles here and there, but he has already lost the war! Sentence has been pronounced on him, but it will be awhile before the punishment is meted out. A person who knows Christ, and who has been delivered from the bondage of sin through Christ's death on the cross, has no desire to obey Satan and live like a rebel.

"Little children, let no man deceive you!" Counterfeit Christians were trying to convince true believers that a person could be "saved" and still practice sin. John did not deny that Christians sin, but he did deny that Christians can live in sin. A person who can enjoy deliberate sin and who does not feel convicted or experience God's chastening had better examine himself to see whether or not he is really born of God.

God the Holy Spirit Lives in Us (3:9–10)

"Whosoever is born of God does not practice sin!"

Why? Because he has a new nature within him, and that new nature cannot sin. John called this new nature God's "seed."

When a person receives Christ as his Savior, tremendous spiritual changes take place in him. He is given a new standing before God, being accepted as righteous in God's sight. This new standing is called "justification." It never changes and is never lost.

The new Christian is also given a new position: he is set apart for God's own purposes to live for His glory. This new position is called "sanctification," and it has a way of changing from day to day. On some days we are much closer to Christ and obey Him much more readily.

But perhaps the most dramatic change in a new believer is what we call "regeneration." He is "born again" into the family of God. (*Re-* means "again," and *generation* means "birth.")

Justification means a new standing before God, sanctification means being set apart to God, and regeneration means a new nature—God's nature (see 2 Peter 1:4).

The only way to enter God's family is by trusting Christ and experiencing this new birth. "Whosoever believeth that Jesus is the Christ is born of God" (1 John 5:1).

Physical life produces only physical life; spiritual life produces spiritual life. "That which is born of the flesh is flesh; and that which is born of the Spirit is spirit" (John 3:6). Christians have been born again, "not of corruptible seed, but of incorruptible, by the word of God, which liveth and abideth forever" (1 Peter 1:23). A Christian's "spiritual parents," so to speak, are the Word of God and the Spirit of God. The Spirit of God uses the Word of God to convict of sin and to reveal the Savior.

We are saved by faith (Eph. 2:8–9), and "faith cometh by hearing, and hearing by the word of God" (Rom. 10:17). In the miracle of the new birth, the Holy Spirit imparts new life—God's life—to a believing sinner, and as a result the individual is born into the family of God.

Just as physical children bear the nature of their parents, so God's spiritual children bear His nature. The divine "seed" is in them. A Christian has an old nature from his physical birth and a new nature from his spiritual birth. The New Testament contrasts these two natures and gives them various names:

Old Nature	New Nature
"our old man" (Rom. 6:6)	"the new man" (Col. 3:10)
"the flesh" (Gal. 5:24)	"the Spirit" (Gal. 5:17)
"corruptible seed" (1 Peter 1:23)	"God's seed" (1 John 3:9)

The old nature produces sin, but the new nature leads one into a holy life. A Christian's responsibility is to live according to his new nature, not the old nature.

One way to illustrate this is by contrasting the "outer man" with the "inner man" (2 Cor. 4:16). The physical man needs food, and so does the inner, or spiritual man. "Man shall not live by bread alone, but by every word that proceedeth out of the mouth of God" (Matt. 4:4). Unless a Christian spends time daily in meditating on the Word of God, his inner man will lack power.

A converted Native American explained, "I have two dogs living in me—a mean dog and a good dog. They are always fighting. The mean dog wants me to do bad things, and the good dog wants me to do good things. Do you want to know which dog wins? The one I feed the most!"

A Christian who feeds the new nature from the Word of God will have power to live a godly life. We are to "make not provision for the flesh, to fulfill the lusts thereof" (Rom. 13:14).

The physical man needs cleansing, and so does the inner man. We wash our hands and face frequently. A believer should look into the mirror of God's Word daily (James 1:22–25) and examine himself. He must confess his sins and claim God's forgiveness (1 John 1:9). Otherwise the inner man will become unclean, and this uncleanness will breed infection and "spiritual sickness."

Unconfessed sin is the first step in what the Bible calls "backsliding"—gradually moving away from a close walk with Christ into a life filled with the alien world in which we live.

God's promise "I will heal your backslidings" (Jer. 3:22) implies that backsliding resembles physical sickness. First is the secret invasion of the body by a disease germ. Then infection follows and there is a gradual decline: no pep, no appetite, no interest in normal activities. Then comes the collapse!

Spiritual decline works in a similar way. First sin invades us. Instead of fighting it, we yield to it (see James 1:14) and infection sets in. A gradual decline follows. We lose our appetite for spiritual things, we become listless and even irritable, and finally we collapse.

The only remedy is to confess and forsake our sin and turn to Christ for cleansing and healing.

The inner man not only needs food and cleansing, but he also needs exercise. "Exercise thyself … unto godliness" (1 Tim. 4:7). A person who eats but does not exercise will become overweight; a person who exercises without eating will kill himself. There must be proper balance.

"Spiritual exercise" for a believer, includes sharing Christ with others, doing good works in Christ's name, and helping to build up other believers. Each Christian has at least one spiritual gift, which he is to use for the good of the church (1 Cor. 12:1–11). "As each one has received a special gift, employ it in serving one another, as good stewards of the manifold grace of God" (1 Peter 4:10 NASB).

Here is a vivid commentary on this whole process of temptation and sin:

"Let no one say when he is tempted, 'I am being tempted by God'; for God cannot be tempted by evil, and He Himself does not tempt anyone. But each one is tempted when he is carried away and enticed by his own lust. Then when lust has conceived, it gives birth to sin; and when sin is accomplished, it brings forth death" (James 1:13–15 NASB).

Temptation appeals to our basic natural desires. There is nothing sinful about our desires, but temptation gives us an opportunity to satisfy these desires in an evil way. It is not a sin to be hungry, but it is a sin to satisfy hunger out of the will of God. This was the first temptation Satan hurled at Jesus (Matt. 4:1–4).

The two terms, "carried away" and "enticed" (James 1:14), both relate to hunting or fishing: the putting of bait in a trap or on a hook. The animal (or fish) comes along and his natural desires attract him to the bait. But in taking the bait, he gets caught in the trap, or hooked. And the end is death.

Satan baits his traps with pleasures that appeal to the old nature, the flesh. But none of his bait appeals to the new divine nature within a Christian. If a believer yields to his old nature, he will hanker for the bait, take it, and sin. But if he follows the leanings of his new nature, he will refuse the bait and obey God. "This I say then, walk in the Spirit, and ye shall not fulfill the lust of the flesh" (Gal. 5:16).

Yielding to sin is the distinguishing mark of "the children of the devil" (1 John 3:10). They profess, or claim, one thing, but they practice another. Satan is a liar and the father of lies (John 8:44), and his children are like their father. "He that saith, 'I know [God],' and keepeth not his commandments, is a liar, and the truth is not in him" (1 John 2:4). The children of the devil try to deceive God's children into thinking that a person can be a Christian and still practice sin. "Little children, let no man deceive you; he that doeth righteousness is righteous, even as he [God] is righteous" (1 John 3:7).

False teachers in John's day taught that a Christian did not have to worry about sin, because only the body sinned and what the body did in no way affected the spirit. Some of them went so far as to teach that sin is natural to the body, because the body is sinful.

The New Testament exposes the foolishness of such excuses for sin.

To begin with, "the old nature" is not the body. The body itself is neutral: it can be used either by the old sinful nature or by the new divine nature. "Therefore do not let sin reign in your mortal body so that you obey its lusts, and do not go on presenting the members of your body to sin as instruments of unrighteousness; but present yourselves to God as those [who are] alive from the dead, and your members as instruments of righteousness to God" (Rom. 6:12–13 NASB).

How does a child of God go about overcoming the desires of the old nature? He must begin each day by yielding his body to God as a living sacrifice (Rom. 12:1). He must spend time reading and studying the Word of God, "feeding" his new nature. He must take time to pray, asking God to fill him with the Holy Spirit and give him power to serve Christ and glorify Him.

As he goes through the day, a believer must depend on the power of the Spirit in the inner man. When temptations come, he must immediately turn to Christ for victory.

The Word of God in his heart will help to keep him from sin if only he will turn to Christ. "Thy word have I hid in mine heart, that I might not sin against thee" (Ps. 119:11). If he does sin, he must instantly confess to God and claim forgiveness. But it is not necessary for him to sin. By yielding his body to the Holy Spirit within him, he will receive the power he needs to overcome the tempter.

A good practice is to claim God's promise: "No temptation has overtaken you but such as is common to man; and God is faithful, who will not allow you to be tempted beyond what you are able; but with the temptation will provide the way of escape also, so that you will be able to endure it" (1 Cor. 10:13 NASB).

A Sunday school teacher was explaining the Christian's two natures—the old and the new—to a class of teenagers.

"Our old nature came from Adam," he explained,

"and our new nature comes from Christ, who is called 'the Last Adam.'" He had the class read 1 Corinthians 15:45: "So also it is written, 'The first man, Adam, became a living soul.' The Last Adam became a life-giving spirit" (NASB).

"This means there are two 'Adams' living in me," said one of the teenagers.

"That's right," the teacher replied. "And what is the practical value of this truth?"

The class was silent for a moment, and then a student spoke up.

"This idea of the 'two Adams' really helps me in fighting temptation," he said. "When temptation comes knocking at my door, if I send the first Adam to answer, I'll sin. But if I send the Last Adam, I'll get victory."

A true believer does not practice sin; a counterfeit believer cannot help but practice sin, because he does not have God's new nature within him. The true believer also loves other Christians, which is discussed in detail in 1 John 3:11–24.

But these words were not written so that you and I might check on other people. They were inspired so that we may examine ourselves. Each of us must answer honestly before God:

1. Do I have the divine nature within me, or am I merely pretending to be a Christian?

2. Do I cultivate this divine nature by daily Bible reading and prayer?

3. Has any unconfessed sin defiled my inner man? Am I willing to confess and forsake it?

4. Do I allow my old nature to control my thoughts and desires, or does the divine nature rule me?

5. When temptation comes, do I "play with it," or do I flee from it? Do I immediately yield to the divine nature within me?

The life that is real is honest with God about these vital issues.

CHAPTER SEVEN
1 John 3:11–24
LOVE OR DEATH

John's letter has been compared to a spiral staircase because he kept returning to the same three topics: love, obedience, and truth. Though these themes recur, it is not true that they are merely repetitious. Each time we return to a topic, we look at it from a different point of view and are taken more deeply into it.

We have already learned about our love for other believers—"the brethren" (1 John 2:7–11)—but the emphasis in 1 John 2 was on fellowship. A believer who is "walking in the light" will evidence that fact by loving the brethren. In our present section, the emphasis is on his relationship with other believers.

Christians love one another because they have all been born of God, which makes them all brothers and sisters in Christ.

Obedience and love are both evidences of sonship and brotherhood. We have been reminded that a true child of God practices righteousness (1 John 3:1–10), and now we shall look into the matter of love for the brethren (1 John 3:11–24). This truth is first stated in the negative: "Whosoever doeth not righteousness is not of God, neither he that loveth not his brother" (1 John 3:10).

A striking difference should be noted between the earlier and the present treatment of love for the brethren. In the section on fellowship (1 John 2:7–11), we are told that loving the brethren is a matter of light and darkness. If we do not love one another, we cannot walk in the light, no matter how loud our profession. But in this section on brotherhood (1 John 3:11–24), the epistle probes much deeper. We are told that loving the brethren is a matter of life and death. "He that loveth not his brother abideth in death" (1 John 3:14).

When it comes to this matter of love, there are four possible "levels of relationship," so to speak, on which a person may live: murder (1 John 3:11–12), hatred (1 John 3:13–15), indifference (1 John 3:16–17), and Christian compassion (1 John 3:18–24).

The first two are not Christian at all, the third is less than Christian, and only the last is compatible with true Christian love.

Murder (3:11–12)
Murder, of course, is the lowest level on which one may live in relationship to someone else. It is the level on which Satan himself exists. The devil was a murderer from the beginning of his fallen career (John 8:44), but Christians have heard, from the beginning of their experience, that they are to "love one another." John emphasized origins: "Go back to the beginning." If our spiritual experience originates with the Father, we must love one another. But if it originates with Satan, we will hate one another. "Let that therefore abide in you which ye have heard from the beginning" (1 John 2:24).

Cain is an example of a life of hatred; we find the record in Genesis 4:1–16. It is important to note that Cain and Abel, being brothers, had the same parents, and they both brought sacrifices to God. Cain is not presented as an atheist; he is presented as a worshipper. And this is the point: children of the devil masquerade as true believers. They attend religious gatherings, as Cain did. They may even bring offerings. But these actions in themselves are not valid proof that a man is born of God. The real test is his love for the brethren—and here Cain failed.

Every man has a "spiritual lineage" as well as a physical, and Cain's "spiritual father" was the devil. This does not mean, of course, that Satan literally fathered Cain. It means, rather, that Cain's attitudes and actions originated with Satan. Cain was a murderer and a liar like Satan (John 8:44). He murdered his brother, and then he lied about it. "And the Lord said unto Cain, Where is Abel thy brother? And he said, I know not" (Gen. 4:9).

In contrast to this, God is love (1 John 4:8) and truth (John 14:6; 1 John 5:6); therefore, those who belong to God's family practice love and truth.

The difference between Cain's offering and Abel's offering was faith (Heb. 11:4), and faith is always based on the revelation God has given (Rom. 10:17). It seems clear that God must have given definite instructions concerning how He was to be worshipped. Cain rejected God's Word and decided to worship in his own way. This shows his relationship to Satan, for Satan is always interested in turning people away from the revealed will of God. The devil's "Yea, hath God said?" (Gen. 3:1) was the beginning of trouble for Cain's parents and for all mankind since.

We are not told by what outward sign the Lord accepted Abel's sacrifice and rejected Cain's. It may be that He sent fire from heaven to consume Abel's sacrifice of an animal and its blood. But we are told the results: Abel went away from the altar with God's witness of acceptance in his heart, but Cain went away angry and disappointed (Gen. 4:4–6). God warned Cain that sin was crouching at the door like a dangerous beast (Gen. 4:7) but promised that if Cain would obey God, he, like Abel, would enjoy peace.

Instead of heeding God's warning, Cain listened to Satan's voice and plotted to kill his brother. His envy had turned to anger and hatred. He knew that he was evil and that his brother was righteous. Rather than repent, as God commanded him to do, he decided to destroy his brother.

Centuries later, the Pharisees did the same thing to Jesus (Mark 15:9–10), and Jesus called them, too, children of the devil (John 8:44).

Cain's attitude represents the attitude of the present world system (1 John 3:13). The world hates Christ (John 15:18–25) for the same reason Cain hated Abel: Christ shows up the world's sin and reveals its true nature. When the world, like Cain, comes face-to-face with reality and truth, it can make only one of two decisions: repent and change, or destroy the one who is exposing it.

Satan is the "prince of this world" (John 14:30), and he controls it through murder and lies. How horrible to live on the same level as Satan!

A hunter took refuge in a cave during a rainstorm. After he had dried out a bit, he decided to investigate his temporary home and turned on his flashlight. Imagine his surprise when he discovered he was sharing the cave with an assortment of spiders, lizards, and snakes! His exit was a fast one.

If the unsaved world could only see, it would realize that it is living on the low level of murder and lies, surrounded by that old serpent Satan and all his demonic armies. Like Cain, the people of the world try to cover up their true nature with religious rites, but they lack faith in God's Word. People who continue to live on this level will eventually be cast into outer darkness with Satan to suffer apart from God forever.

Hatred (3:13–15)

At this point, you are probably thinking, "But I have never murdered anyone!" And to this statement, God replies, "Yes, but remember that to a Christian hatred is the same as murder" (1 John 3:15; cf. Matt. 5:22). The only difference between Level 1 and Level 2 is the outward act of taking life. The inward intent is the same.

A visitor at the zoo was chatting with the keeper of the lion house.

"I have a cat at home," said the visitor, "and your lions act just like my cat. Look at them sleeping so peacefully! It seems a shame that you have to put those beautiful creatures behind bars."

"My friend," the keeper laughed, "these may look like your cat, but their disposition is radically different. There's murder in their hearts. You'd better be glad the bars are there."

The only reason some people have never actually murdered anyone is because of the "bars" that have been put up: the fear of arrest and shame, the penalties of the law, and the possibility of death. But we are going to be judged by "the law of liberty" (James 2:12). The question is not so much, "What did you do?" but "What did you want to do? What would you have done if you had been at liberty to do as you pleased?" This is why Jesus equated hatred with murder (Matt. 5:21–26) and lust with adultery (Matt. 5:27–30).

This does not mean, of course, that hatred in the heart does the same amount of damage, or involves the same degree of guilt, as actual murder. Your neighbor would rather you hate him than kill him! But in God's sight, hatred is the moral equivalent of murder, and if left unbridled it leads to murder. A Christian has passed from death to life (John 5:24), and the proof of this is that he loves the brethren. When he belonged to the world system, he hated God's people, but now that he belongs to God, he loves them.

These verses (1 John 3:14–15), like those that deal with habitual sin in a believer (1 John 1:5–2:6), concern a settled habit of life: a believer is in the practice of loving the brethren, even though on occasion he may be angry with a brother (Matt. 5:22–24). Occasional incidents of anger do not nullify the principle. If anything, they prove it true, because a believer out of fellowship with his fellow Christians is a miserable person! His feelings make clear to him that something is wrong.

Notice another fact: we are not told that murderers cannot be saved. The apostle Paul himself took a hand in the stoning of Stephen (Acts 7:57–60) and admitted that his vote helped to put innocent people to death (Acts 26:9–11; 1 Tim. 1:12–15). But in His grace God saved Paul.

The issue here is not whether a murderer can

become a Christian, but whether a man can continue being a murderer and still be a Christian. The answer is no. "And ye know that no murderer hath eternal life abiding in him" (1 John 3:15). The murderer did not once have eternal life and then lose it; he never had eternal life at all.

The fact that you have never actually murdered anyone should not make you proud or complacent. Have you ever harbored hatred in your heart?

Hatred does the hater far more damage than it does anyone else (Matt. 5:21–26). Jesus said that anger put a man in danger of facing the local court. Calling a brother an "empty-headed fool" put him in danger of the Sanhedrin, the highest Jewish council. But calling him a "cursed fool" put him in danger of eternal judgment in hell. Hatred that is not confessed and forsaken actually puts a man into a spiritual and emotional prison (Matt. 5:25)!

The antidote for hatred is love. "Hateful and hating one another" is the normal experience of an unsaved person (Titus 3:3). But when a hateful heart opens to Jesus Christ, it becomes a loving heart. Then instead of wanting to "murder" others through hatred, one wants to love them and share with them the message of eternal life.

Evangelist John Wesley was stopped one night by a highwayman who robbed the Methodist leader of all his money. Wesley said to the man, "If the day should come that you desire to leave this evil way and live for God, remember that 'the blood of Jesus Christ cleanses from all sin.'"

Some years later, Wesley was stopped by a man after a church service. "Do you remember me?" the man asked. "I robbed you one night, and you told me that the blood of Jesus Christ cleanses from all sin. I have trusted Christ, and He has changed my life."

Indifference (3:16–17)

But the test of Christian love is not simply failure to do evil to others. Love also involves doing them good. Christian love is both positive and negative. "Cease to do evil; learn to do well" (Isa. 1:16–17).

Cain is our example of false love; Christ is the example of true Christian love. Jesus gave His life for us that we may experience truth. Every Christian knows John 3:16, but how many of us pay much attention to 1 John 3:16? It is wonderful to experience the blessing of John 3:16, but it is even more wonderful to share that experience by obeying 1 John 3:16: Christ laid down life for us, and we ought to lay down our lives for the brethren.

Christian love involves sacrifice and service. Christ did not simply talk about His love; He died to prove it (Rom. 5:6–10). Jesus was not killed as a martyr; He willingly laid down His life (John 10:11–18; 15:13). "Self-preservation" is the first law of physical life, but "self-sacrifice" is the first law of spiritual life.

But God does not ask us to lay down our lives. He simply asks us to help a brother in need. John wisely

turned from "the brethren" in 1 John 3:16 to the singular, "his brother," in 1 John 3:17.

It is easy for us to talk about "loving the brethren" and to neglect to help a single other believer. Christian love is personal and active.

This is what Jesus had in mind in the parable of the good Samaritan (Luke 10:25–37). A lawyer wanted to talk about an abstract subject: "Who is my neighbor?" But Jesus focused attention on one man in need, and changed the question to "To whom can I be a neighbor?"

Two friends were attending a conference on evangelism. During one of the sessions, Larry missed Pete. At luncheon, when he saw Pete, he said, "I missed you at the ten o'clock session. It was really terrific! Where were you?"

"I was in the lobby talking to a bellhop about Christ. I led him to the Lord," said Pete.

There is nothing wrong with attending conferences, but it is easy to forget the individual and his needs while discussing generalities. The test of Christian love is not in loud professions about loving the whole church, but in quietly helping a brother who is in need. If we do not even help a brother, it is not likely we would "lay down our lives" for "the brethren."

A man does not have to murder in order to sin; hatred is murder in his heart. But a man need not even hate his brother to be guilty of sin. All he has to do is ignore him or be indifferent toward his needs. A believer who has material goods and can relieve his brother's needs ought to do it. To "close the door of his heart" on his brother is a kind of murder!

If I am going to help my brother, I must meet three conditions. First, I must have the means necessary to meet his need. Second, I must know that the need exists. Third, I must be loving enough to want to share.

A believer who is too poor to help or who is ignorant of his brother's need is not condemned. But a believer who hardens his heart against his needy brother is condemned. One reason Christians should work is so that they may be able "to give to him that needeth" (Eph. 4:28).

In these days of multiplied social agencies, it is easy for Christians to forget their obligations. "So then, while we have opportunity, let us do good to all people, and especially to those who are of the household of the faith" (Gal. 6:10 NASB).

This "doing good" need not be in terms of money or material supplies. It may include personal service and the giving of oneself to others. There are many individuals in our churches who lack love and would welcome friendship.

A young mother admitted in a testimony meeting that she never seemed to find time for her own personal devotions. She had several little children to care for, and the hours melted away.

Imagine her surprise when two of the ladies from the church appeared at her front door.

"We've come to take over," they explained. "You

go into the bedroom and get started on your devotions." After several days of this kind of help, the young mother was able to develop her devotional life so that the daily demands on her time no longer upset her.

If we want to experience and enjoy the love of God in our own hearts, we must love others, even to the point of sacrifice. Being indifferent to a brother's needs means robbing ourselves of what we need even more: the love of God in our hearts. It is a matter of love or death!

Christian Love (3:18–24)

True Christian love means loving in deed and in truth. The opposite of "in deed" is "in word," and the opposite of "in truth" is "in tongue." Here is an example of love "in word": "If a brother or sister is without clothing and in need of daily food, and one of you says to them, 'Go in peace, be warmed and be filled,' and yet you do not give them what is necessary for their body, what use is that?" (James 2:15–16 NASB).

To love "in word" means simply to talk about a need, but to love "in deed" means to do something about meeting it. You may think, because you have discussed a need, or even prayed about it, that you have done your duty, but love involves more than words—it calls for sacrificial deeds.

To love "in tongue" is the opposite of to love "in truth." It means to love insincerely. To love "in truth" means to love a person genuinely from the heart and not just from the tongue. People are attracted by genuine love, but repelled by the artificial variety. One reason why sinners were attracted to Jesus (Luke 15:1–2) was because they were sure He loved them sincerely.

"But does it not cost a great deal for the believer to exercise this kind of love?"

Yes, it does. It cost Jesus Christ His life. But the wonderful benefits that come to you as by-products of this love more than compensate for any sacrifice you make. To be sure, you do not love others because you want to get something in return, but the Bible principle "Give and it shall be given unto you" (Luke 6:38) applies to love as well as to money.

John named three wonderful blessings that will come to a believer who practices Christian love.

Assurance (vv. 19–20). A believer's relationship with others affects his relationship with God. A man who is not right with his brother should go settle the matter before he offers his sacrifice on the altar (see Matt. 5:23–24). A Christian who practices love grows in his understanding of God's truth and enjoys a heart filled with confidence before God.

A "condemning heart" is one that robs a believer of peace. An "accusing conscience" is another way to describe it. Sometimes the heart accuses us wrongly, because it "is deceitful above all things, and desperately wicked: who can know it?" (Jer. 17:9). The answer to that question is, "God knows the heart!" More than

one Christian has accused himself falsely or been harder on himself than necessary, but God will never make such a mistake. A Christian who walks in love has a heart open to God ("God is love") and knows that God never judges wrongly.

John may have remembered two incidents from Jesus' life on earth that illustrate this important principle. When Jesus visited Bethany, He stayed at the home of Mary and Martha (Luke 10:38–42). Martha was busy preparing the meal, but Mary sat at His feet and listened to Him teach. Martha criticized both Mary and Jesus, but Jesus knew Mary's heart and defended her.

The apostle Peter wept bitterly after he had denied his Lord, and no doubt he was filled with remorse and repentance for his sin. But Jesus knew that Peter had repented, and after His resurrection the Lord sent a special message to Peter that must have assured the hot-headed fisherman that he was forgiven (Mark 16:7). Peter's heart may have condemned him, for he knew he had denied the Lord three times, but God was greater than his heart. Jesus, knowing all things, gave Peter just the assurance he needed.

Be careful lest the devil accuse you and rob you of your confidence (Rev. 12:10). Once you confess your sin and it is forgiven, you need not allow it to accuse you anymore. Peter was able to face the Jews and say, "But ye denied the Holy One and the Just" (Acts 3:14) because his own sin of denying Christ had been taken care of and was forgiven and forgotten.

No Christian should treat sin lightly, but no Christian should be harder on himself than God is. There is a morbid kind of self-examination and self-condemnation that is not spiritual. If you are practicing genuine love for the brethren, your heart must be right before God, for the Holy Spirit would not "shed abroad" His love in you if there were habitual sin in your heart. When you grieve the Spirit, you "turn off" the supply of God's love (Eph. 4:30—5:2).

Answered prayer (vv. 21–22). Love for the brethren produces confidence toward God, and confidence toward God gives you boldness in asking for what you need. This does not mean that you earn answers to prayer by loving the brethren. Rather, it means that your love for the brethren proves that you are living in the will of God where God can answer your prayer. "And whatsoever we ask, we receive of him, because we keep his commandments" (1 John 3:22). Love is the fulfilling of God's law (Rom. 13:8–10); therefore, when you love the brethren, you are obeying His commandments and He is able to answer your requests.

A believer's relationship to the brethren cannot be divorced from his prayer life. If husbands and wives are not obeying God's Word, for example, their prayers will be hindered (1 Peter 3:7).

An evangelist had preached on the Christian home. After the meeting a father approached him.

"I've been praying for a wayward son for years," said the father, "and God has not answered my prayers."

The evangelist read Psalm 66:18—"If I regard iniquity in my heart, the Lord will not hear me."

"Be honest with yourself and the Lord," he said. "Is there anything between you and another Christian that needs to be settled?"

The father hesitated, then said, "Yes, I'm afraid there is. I've harbored resentment in my heart against another man in this church."

"Then go make it right," counseled the evangelist, and he prayed with the man. Before the campaign was over, the father saw his wayward son come back to the Lord.

These verses do not, of course, give us all the conditions for answered prayer, but they emphasize the importance of obedience. One great secret of answered prayer is obedience, and the secret of obedience is love. "If ye love me, keep my commandments" (John 14:15). "If ye abide in me, and my words abide in you, ye shall ask what ye will, and it shall be done unto you…. If ye keep my commandments, ye shall abide in my love" (John 15:7, 10).

It is possible, of course, to keep God's commandments in a spirit of fear or servitude rather than in a spirit of love. This was the sin of the elder brother in the parable of the prodigal son (Luke 15:24–32). A believer should keep His Father's commandments because this pleases Him. A Christian who lives to please God will discover that God finds ways to please His child. "Delight thyself also in the Lord, and he shall give thee the desires of thine heart" (Ps. 37:4). When our delight is in the love of God, our desires will be in the will of God.

Abiding (vv. 23–24). When a scribe asked Jesus to name the greatest commandment, He replied, "Thou shalt love the Lord thy God." Then He added a second commandment: "Thou shalt love thy neighbor as thyself" (Matt. 22:34–40). But God also gives us one commandment that takes in both God and man: "Believe in the name of His Son Jesus Christ, and love one another" (1 John 3:23 NASB). Faith toward God and love toward man sum up a Christian's obligations. Christianity is "faith which worketh by love" (Gal. 5:6).

Faith toward God and love toward men are two sides of the same coin. It is easy to emphasize faith—correct doctrine—and to neglect love. On the other hand, some say doctrine is not important and that love is our main responsibility. Both doctrine and love are important. When a person is justified by faith, he should know that the love of God is being shed abroad in his heart (Rom. 5:1–5).

"Abiding in Christ" is a key experience for a believer who wants to have confidence toward God and enjoy answers to prayer. Jesus, in His message to the disciples in the Upper Room (John 15:1–14) illustrated "abiding." He compared His followers to the branches of a vine. So long as the branch draws its strength from the vine, it produces fruit. But if it separates itself from the vine, it withers and dies.

Jesus was not talking about salvation; He was talking about fruit-bearing. The instant a sinner trusts Christ, he enters into union with Christ, but maintaining communion is a moment-by-moment responsibility. Abiding depends on our obeying His Word and keeping clean (John 15:3, 10).

As we have seen, when a believer walks in love, he finds it easy to obey God, and therefore he maintains a close communion with God. "If a man love me, he will keep my words; and my Father will love him, and we will come unto him and make our abode with him" (John 14:23).

The Holy Spirit is mentioned by name in 1 John for the first time in 3:24. John introduced us to the Holy One (1 John 2:20) with emphasis on the Spirit's anointing and teaching ministry. (This parallels John 14:26 and 16:13–14.) But the Holy One is also the abiding Spirit (1 John 3:24; 4:13). When a believer obeys God and loves the brethren, the indwelling Holy Spirit gives him peace and confidence. The Holy Spirit abides with him forever (John 14:16), but when the Spirit is grieved, He withdraws His blessings.

The Holy Spirit is also the attesting Spirit (1 John 4:1–6), giving witness to those who are truly God's children. When a believer is abiding in Christ, the Spirit guides him and warns him of false spirits that would lead him astray.

He is also the authenticating Spirit (1 John 5:6–8), bearing witness to the person and work of Jesus Christ. This witness of the Spirit is mentioned in Romans 8:14–16.

Each member of the Triune Godhead is involved in the "love life" of a believer. God the Father commands us to love one another, God the Son gave His life on the cross, the supreme example of love. And God the Holy Spirit lives within us to provide the love we need (Rom. 5:5). To abide in love is to abide in God, and to abide in God is to abide in love. Christian love is not something we "work up" when we need it. Christian love is "shed abroad in our hearts by the Holy Ghost," and this is your constant experience as you abide in Christ.

There are four levels on which a person may live. He may choose the lowest level— Satan's level—and practice murder. Murderers "have their part in the lake which burneth with fire and brimstone, which is the second death" (Rev. 21:8).

Or, a person may choose the next level—hatred. But hatred, in God's sight, is the same as murder. A man who lives with hatred is slowly killing himself, not the other person! Psychiatrists warn that malice and hatred cause all kinds of physical and emotional problems. In fact, one specialist has titled his book *Love or Perish*!

The third level—indifference—is far better than the first two, because the first two are not Christian at all. A man who has constant hatred in his heart, or who habitually murders, proves he has never been born of God. But it is possible to be a Christian and be indifferent to the needs of others.

A man who murders belongs to the devil, like Cain. A man who hates belongs to the world (1 John 3:13), which is under Satan's control. But a Christian who is indifferent is living for the flesh, which serves Satan's purposes.

The only happy, holy way to live is on the highest level, the level of Christian love. This is the life of joy and liberty, the life of answered prayer. It assures you confidence and courage in spite of the difficulties of life.

Dr. Rene Spitz of New York made a study of children in foundling homes to determine what effect love and neglect had on them. The survey proved that children who were neglected and unloved were much slower in their development, and some of them even died. Even in a physical sense, love is the very atmosphere of life and growth.

It is even more so in the spiritual sense.

In fact, it is a matter of love or death!

CHAPTER EIGHT
1 John 4:1–16
GETTING TO THE BOTTOM OF LOVE

For the third time, we are considering the subject of love!

This does not mean John ran out of ideas and had to repeat himself. It means that the Holy Spirit, who inspired John, presents the subject once more, from a deeper point of view.

First, love for the brethren has been shown as proof of fellowship with God (1 John 2:7–11); then it has been presented as proof of sonship (1 John 3:10–14). In the earlier passage, love for the brethren is a matter of light or darkness; in the second it is a matter of life or death.

But in 1 John 4:7–16, we get down to the very foundation of the matter. Here we discover why love is such an important part of the life that is real. Love is a valid test of our fellowship and our sonship because "God is love." Love is part of the very being and nature of God. If we are united to God through faith in Christ, we share His nature. And since His nature is love, love is the test of the reality of our spiritual life.

A navigator depends on a compass to help him determine his course. But why a compass? Because it shows him his directions. And why does the compass point north? Because it is so constituted that it responds to the magnetic field that is part of the earth's makeup. The compass is responsive to the nature of the earth.

So with Christian love. The nature of God is love. And a person who knows God and has been born of God will respond to God's nature. As a compass naturally points north, a believer will naturally practice love because love is the nature of God. This love will not be a forced response; it will be a natural response. A believer's love for the brethren will be proof of his sonship and fellowship.

Three times in this section John encouraged us to love one another (1 John 4:7, 11–12). He supported these admonitions by giving us three foundational facts about God.

What God Is: "God Is Love" (4:7–8)

This is the third of three expressions in John's writings that help us understand the nature of God: "God is spirit" (John 4:24 NASB); "God is light" (1 John 1:5); and "God is love." None of these is a complete revelation of God, of course, and it is wrong to separate them.

God is spirit as to His essence; He is not flesh and blood. To be sure, Jesus Christ now has a glorified body in heaven, and one day we shall have bodies like His body. But being by nature spirit, God is not limited by time and space the way His creatures are.

God is light. This refers to His holy nature. In the Bible, light is a symbol of holiness, and darkness is a symbol of sin (John 3:18–21; 1 John 1:5–10). God cannot sin because He is holy. Because we have been born into His family, we have received His holy nature (1 Peter 1:14–16; 2 Peter 1:4).

God is love. This does not mean that "love is God." And the fact that two people "love each other" does not mean that their love is necessarily holy. It has accurately been said that "love does not define God, but God defines love." God is love and God is light; therefore, His love is a holy love, and His holiness is expressed in love. All that God does expresses all that God is. Even His judgments are measured out in love and mercy (Lam. 3:22–23).

Much that is called "love" in modern society bears no resemblance or relationship to the holy, spiritual love of God. Yet we see banners saying "God is love!" displayed at many festivals, particularly where young people are "doing their own thing"—as if one could dignify immorality by calling it "love."

Christian love is a special kind of love. First John 4:10 may be translated: "In this way is seen the true love." There is a false love, and this kind of love God must reject. Love that is born out of the very essence of God must be spiritual and holy, because "God is spirit" and "God is light." This true love is "poured out within our hearts through the Holy Spirit who was given to us" (Rom. 5:5 NASB).

Love, therefore, is a valid test of true Christian faith. Since God is love, and we have claimed a personal relationship with God, we must of necessity reveal His love in how we live. A child of God has been "born of God," and therefore he shares God's divine nature. Since "God is love," Christians ought to love one another. The logic is unanswerable!

Not only have we been "born of God," but we also "know God." In the Bible, the word know has a much deeper meaning than simply intellectual acquaintance or understanding. For example, the verb "know" is used to describe the intimate union of husband and wife (Gen. 4:1). To know God means to be in a deep relationship to Him—to share His life and enjoy His love. This knowing is not simply a matter of understanding facts; it is a matter of perceiving truth (see 1 John 2:3–5).

We must understand "he that loveth not knoweth not God" (1 John 4:8) in this light. Certainly many unsaved people love their families and even sacrifice for them. And no doubt many of these same people have some kind of intellectual understanding of God. What, then, do they lack? They lack a personal experience of God. To paraphrase 1 John 4:8, "The person who does not have this divine kind of love has never entered into a personal, experiential knowledge of God. What he knows is in his head, but it has never gotten into his heart."

What God is determines what we ought to be. "As he is, so are we in this world" (1 John 4:17). The fact that Christians love one another is evidence of their fellowship with God and their sonship from God, and it is also evidence that they know God. Their experience with God is not simply a once-for-all crisis; it is a daily experience of getting to know Him better and better. True theology (the study of God) is not a dry, impractical course in doctrine—it is an exciting day-by-day experience that makes us Christlike!

A large quantity of radioactive material was stolen from a hospital. When the hospital administrator notified the police, he said, "Please warn the thief that he is carrying death with him, and that the radioactive material cannot be successfully hidden. As long as he has it in his possession, it is affecting him disastrously!"

A person who claims he knows God and is in union with Him must be personally affected by this relationship. A Christian ought to become what God is, and "God is love." To argue otherwise is to prove that one does not really know God!

What God Did: "He Sent His Son" (4:9–11)

Because God is love, He must communicate—not only in words but in deeds. True love is never static or inactive. God reveals His love to mankind in many ways. He has geared all of creation to meeting men's needs. Until man's sin brought creation under bondage, man had on earth a perfect home in which to love and serve God.

God's love was revealed in the way He dealt with the nation of Israel. "The Lord did not set his love upon you, nor choose you, because ye were more in number than any people; for ye were the fewest of all people. But because the Lord loved you … hath the Lord brought you out with a mighty hand" (Deut. 7:7–8).

The greatest expression of God's love is in the death of His Son. "But God demonstrates His own love toward us, in that while we were yet sinners, Christ died for us" (Rom. 5:8 NASB).

The word manifested means "to come out in the open, to be made public." It is the opposite of "to hide, to make secret." Under the old covenant, God was hidden behind the shadows of ritual and ceremony (Heb. 10:1); but in Jesus Christ "the life was manifested" (1 John 1:2). "He that hath seen me," said Jesus, "hath seen the Father" (John 14:9).

Why was Jesus Christ manifested? "And you know that he was manifested to take away our sins" (1 John 3:5). "For this purpose the Son of God was manifested, that he might destroy the works of the devil" (1 John 3:8). Where did Jesus take away our sins and destroy (render inoperative) the works of the devil? At the cross! God manifested His love at the cross when He gave His Son as a sacrifice there for our sins.

This is the only place in the epistle where Jesus is called God's only begotten Son. The title is used in John's gospel (John 1:14). It means "unique, the only one of its kind." The fact that God sent His Son into the world is one evidence of the deity of Jesus Christ. Babies are not sent into the world from some other place; they are born into the world. As the perfect Man, Jesus was born into the world, but as the eternal Son, He was sent into the world.

But the sending of Christ into the world and His death on the cross were not prompted by man's love for God. They were prompted by His love for man. The world's attitude toward God is anything but love!

Two purposes are given for Christ's death on the cross: that we might live through Him (1 John 4:9) and that He might be the propitiation for our sins (1 John 4:10). His death was not an accident; it was an appointment. He did not die as a weak martyr, but as a mighty conqueror.

Jesus Christ died that we might live "through him" (1 John 4:9), "for him" (2 Cor. 5:15), and "with him" (1 Thess. 5:9–10). A sinner's desperate need is for life, because he is "dead in trespasses and sins" (Eph. 2:1). It is something of a paradox that Christ had to die so that we may live! We can never probe the mystery of His death, but this we know: He died for us (Gal. 2:20).

The death of Christ is described as a "propitiation." John has used this word before (1 John 2:2), so there is no need to study it in detail again. We should remember that propitiation does not mean that men must do something to appease God or to placate His anger. Propitiation is something God does to make it possible for men to be forgiven. "God is light," and therefore He must uphold His holy law. "God is love," and therefore He wants to forgive and save sinners. How can God forgive sinners and still be consistent with His holy nature? The answer is the cross. There Jesus Christ bore the punishment for sin and met the just demands of the holy law. But there, also, God reveals His love and makes it possible for men to be saved by faith.

It is important to note that the emphasis is on the

death of Christ, not on His birth. The fact that Jesus was "made flesh" (John 1:14) is certainly an evidence of God's grace and love, but the fact that He was "made sin" (2 Cor. 5:21) is underscored for us. The example of Christ, the teachings of Christ, the whole earthly life of Christ, find their true meaning and fulfillment in the cross.

For the second time, believers are exhorted to "love one another" (1 John 4:11). This exhortation is a commandment to be obeyed (1 John 4:7), and its basis is the nature of God. "God is love; we know God; therefore, we should love one another." But the exhortation to love one another is presented as a privilege as well as a responsibility: "If God so loved us, we ought also to love one another" (1 John 4:11). We are not saved by loving Christ; we are saved by believing on Christ (John 3:16). But after we realize what He did for us on the cross, our normal response ought to be to love Him and to love one another.

It is important that Christians progress in their understanding of love. To love one another simply out of a sense of duty is good, but to love out of appreciation (rather than obligation) is even better.

This may be one reason why Jesus established the Lord's Supper, the Communion service. When we break the bread and share the cup, we remember His death. Few men, if any, want their deaths remembered! In fact, we remember the life of a loved one and try to forget the sadness of his death. Not so with Christ. He commands us to remember His death: "This do in remembrance of me"!

We should remember our Lord's death in a spiritual way, not merely sentimentally. Someone has defined sentiment as "feeling without responsibility." It is easy to experience solemn emotions at a church service and yet go out to live the same defeated life. True spiritual experience involves the whole man. The mind must understand spiritual truth; the heart must love and appreciate it, and the will must act on it. The deeper we go into the meaning of the cross, the greater will be our love for Christ and the greater our active concern for one another.

We have discovered what God is and what God has done, but a third foundation fact takes us even deeper into the meaning and implications of Christian love.

What God Is Doing: "God Abides in Us" (4:12–16)

At this point it would be good for us to review what John has been saying about the basic truth that "God is love."

This truth is revealed to us in the Word, but it was also revealed on the cross, where Christ died for us. "God is love" is not simply a doctrine in the Bible; it is an eternal fact clearly demonstrated at Calvary. God has said something to us, and God has done something for us.

But all this is preparation for the third great fact: God does something in us! We are not merely students reading a book, or spectators watching a deeply moving event. We are participants in the great drama of God's love!

In order to save money, a college drama class purchased only a few scripts of a play and cut them up into the separate parts. The director gave each player his individual part in order and then started to rehearse the play. But nothing went right. After an hour of missed cues and mangled sequences, the cast gave up.

At that point, the director sat the actors all on the stage and said: "Look, I'm going to read the entire play to you, so don't any of you say a word." He read the entire script aloud, and when he was finished, one of the actors said: "So that's what it was all about!"

And when they understood the entire story, they were able to fit their parts together and have a successful rehearsal.

When you read 1 John 4:12–16, you feel like saying, "So that's what it's all about!" Because here we discover what God had in mind when He devised His great plan of salvation.

To begin with, God's desire is to live in us. He is not satisfied simply to tell us that He loves us, or even show us that He loves us.

It is interesting to trace God's dwelling places as recorded in the Bible. In the beginning, God had fellowship with man in a personal, direct way (Gen. 3:8), but sin broke that fellowship. It was necessary for God to shed the blood of animals to cover the sins of Adam and Eve so that they might come back into His fellowship.

One of the key words in the book of Genesis is walked. God walked with men, and men walked with God. Enoch (Gen. 5:22), Noah (Gen. 6:9), and Abraham walked with God (Gen. 17:1; 24:40).

But by the time of the events recorded in Exodus, a change had taken place: God did not simply walk with men, He lived, or dwelt, with them. God's commandment to Israel was, "And let them make me a sanctuary; that I may dwell among them" (Ex. 25:8). The first of those sanctuaries was the tabernacle. When Moses dedicated it, the glory of God came down and moved into the tent (Ex. 40:33–35).

God dwelt in the camp, but He did not dwell in the bodies of the individual Israelites.

Unfortunately, the nation sinned and God's glory departed (1 Sam. 4:21). But God used Samuel and David to restore the nation; and Solomon built God a magnificent temple. When the temple was dedicated, once again the glory of God came to dwell in the land (1 Kings 8:1–11).

But history repeated itself, and Israel disobeyed God and was taken into captivity. The gorgeous temple was destroyed. One of the prophets of the captivity, Ezekiel, saw the glory of God depart from it (Ezek. 8:4; 9:3; 10:4; 11:22–23).

Did the glory ever return? Yes—in the Person of God's Son, Jesus Christ! "And the Word became flesh, and tabernacled among us, and we beheld His glory" (John 1:14, literal translation). The glory of

God dwelt on earth in the body of Jesus Christ, for His body was the temple of God (John 2:18–22). But wicked men nailed His body to a cross. They crucified "the Lord of glory" (1 Cor. 2:8). All this was part of God's thrilling plan, and Christ arose from the dead, returned to heaven, and sent His Holy Spirit to dwell in men.

The glory of God now lives in the bodies of God's children. "Or do you not know that your body is a temple of the Holy Spirit who is in you, whom you have from God, and that you are not your own?" (1 Cor. 6:19 NASB). The glory of God departed from the tabernacle and the temple when Israel disobeyed God, but Jesus has promised that the Spirit will abide in us forever (John 14:16).

With this background, we can better understand what 1 John 4:12–16 is saying to us. God is invisible (1 Tim. 1:17), and no man can see Him in His essence. Jesus is "the image of the invisible God" (Col. 1:15). By taking on Himself a human body, Jesus was able to reveal God to us. But Jesus is no longer here on earth. How, then, does God reveal Himself to the world?

He reveals Himself through the lives of His children. Men cannot see God, but they can see us. If we abide in Christ, we will love one another, and our love for one another will reveal God's love to a needy world. God's love will be experienced in us and then will be expressed through us.

That important little word abide (or "dwell" KJV) is used six times in 1 John 4:12–16. It refers to our personal fellowship with Jesus Christ. To abide in Christ means to remain in spiritual oneness with Him, so that no sin comes between us. Because we are "born of God," we have union with Christ, but it is only as we trust Him and obey His commandments that we have communion with Him. Much as a faithful husband and wife "abide in love" though they may be separated by miles, so a believer abides in God's love. This abiding is made possible by the indwelling of the Holy Spirit (1 John 4:13).

Imagine the wonder and the privilege of having God abide in you! The Old Testament Israelite would look with wonder at the tabernacle or temple, because the presence of God was in that building. No man would dare to enter the Holy of Holies, where God was enthroned in glory! But we have God's Spirit living in us! We abide in this love, and we experience the abiding of God in us. "If a man love me, he will keep my words; and my Father will love him, and we will come unto him, and make our abode with him" (John 14:23).

God's love is proclaimed in the Word ("God is love") and proved at the cross. But here we have something deeper: God's love is perfected in the believer. Fantastic as it may seem, God's love is not made perfect in angels, but in sinners saved by His grace. We Christians are now the tabernacles and temples in which God dwells. He reveals His love through us.

Dr. G. Campbell Morgan, famous British preacher, had five sons, all of whom became ministers of the gospel. One day a visitor in their home dared to ask a personal question: "Which of you six is the best preacher?"

Their united answer was "Mother!"

Of course, Mrs. Morgan had never preached a formal sermon in a church, but her life was a constant sermon on the love of God. The life of a Christian who abides in God's love is a potent witness for God in the world. Men cannot see God, but they can see His love moving us to deeds of helpfulness and kindness.

Three different witnesses are suggested in these verses: (1) The witness of the believer that Jesus Christ is God's Son (1 John 4:15); (2) the witness in the believer by the Spirit (1 John 4:13); and (3) the witness through the believer that God is love and that He sent His Son to die for the world (1 John 4:14).

These witnesses cannot be separated. The world will not believe that God loves sinners until they see His love at work in His children's lives.

A Salvation Army worker found a derelict woman alone on the street and invited her to come into the chapel for help, but the woman refused to move. The worker assured her, "We love you and want to help you. God loves you. Jesus died for you." But the woman did not budge.

As if on divine impulse, the Army lassie leaned over and kissed the woman on the cheek, taking her into her arms. The woman began to sob, and like a child, was led into the chapel, where she ultimately trusted Christ.

"You told me that God loved me," she said later, "but it wasn't till you showed me that God loved me that I wanted to be saved."

Jesus did not simply preach the love of God; He proved it by giving His life on the cross. He expects His followers to do likewise. If we abide in Christ, we will abide in His love. If we abide in His love, we must share this love with others. Whenever we share this love, it is proof in our own hearts that we are abiding in Christ. In other words, there is no separation between a Christian's inner life and his outer life.

Abiding in God's love produces two wonderful spiritual benefits in the life of a believer: (1) he grows in knowledge, and (2) he grows in faith (1 John 4:16). The more we love God, the more we understand the love of God. And the more we understand His love, the easier it is for us to trust Him. After all, when you know someone intimately and love him sincerely, you have no problem putting your confidence in him.

A man standing in the greeting card section of a store was having trouble picking out a card. The clerk asked if she could help, and he said, "Well, it's our fortieth wedding anniversary, but I can't find a card that says what I want to say. You know, forty years ago it wouldn't have been any problem picking out a card, because back then I thought I knew what love was. But we love each other so much more today, I just can't find a card that says it!"

This is a growing Christian's experience with God. As he abides in Christ and spends time in fellowship with Him, he comes to love God more and more. He also grows in his love for other Christians, for the lost, and even for his enemies. As he shares the Father's love with others, he experiences more of the Father's love himself. He understands the Father's love better and better.

"God is love," then, is not simply a profound biblical statement. It is the basis for a believer's relationship with God and with his fellow man. Because God is love, we can love. His love is not past history; it is present reality. "Love one another" begins as a commandment (1 John 4:7), then it becomes a privilege (1 John 4:11). But it is more than a commandment or a privilege. It is also the thrilling consequence and evidence of our abiding in Christ (1 John 4:12). Loving one another is not something we simply ought to do; it is something we want to do.

Some practical applications grow out of this basic truth:

First, the better we know God's love, the easier it will be to live as a Christian. Bible knowledge alone does not take the place of personal experience of God's love. In fact, it can be a dangerous substitute if we are not careful.

Helen came home from a youth retreat greatly enthused over what she had learned.

"We had some terrific sessions on how to have personal devotions," she told her sister Joyce. "I plan to have my devotions every single day."

A week later, while Joyce was running the vacuum cleaner, she heard Helen screaming, "Do you have to make all that noise? Don't you know I'm trying to have my devotions?" And the verbal explosion was followed by the slamming of a door.

Helen still had to learn that personal devotions are not an end in themselves. If they do not help us love God and love one another, they are accomplishing little. The Bible is a revelation of God's love, and the better we understand His love, the easier it should be for us to obey Him and love others.

A second consideration is that unless we love the lost, our verbal witness to them will be useless. The gospel message is a message of love. This love was both declared and demonstrated by Jesus Christ. The only way we can effectively win others is to declare the gospel and demonstrate it in how we live. Too much "witnessing" today is a mere mouthing of words. People need an expression of love.

One reason why God permits the world to hate Christians is so that Christians may return love for the world's hatred. "Blessed are you when people insult you and persecute you, and falsely say all kinds of evil against you because of Me.... But I say to you, love your enemies and pray for those who persecute you" (Matt. 5:11, 44 NASB).

"Pastor, the Bible tells us to love our neighbors, but I doubt that anybody could love my neighbors," Mrs. Barton said at the close of a Sunday school lesson. "I've tried to be nice to them, but it just doesn't work."

"Perhaps 'being nice to them' isn't the real answer," the pastor explained. "You know, it's possible to be nice to people with the wrong motive."

"You mean as though you're trying to buy them off?"

"Something like that. I think you and I had better pray that God will give you a true spiritual love for your neighbors. If you love them in a Christian way, you'll not be able to do them any damage," the pastor pointed out.

It took some weeks, but Mrs. Barton grew in her love for her neighbors, and she also found herself growing in her own spiritual life.

"My neighbors haven't changed a whole lot," she told the prayer group, "but my attitude toward them has really changed. I used to do things for them to try to win their approval. But now I do things for Jesus' sake, because He died for them—and it makes all the difference in the world!"

In this paragraph of his letter, John has taken us to the very foundation of Christian love. But he still had more to teach us. In the next section, he dealt with our own personal love for God and how God perfects that love in us.

These two aspects of Christian love cannot be separated from one another: if we love God, we will love one another; and if we love one another, we will grow in our love for God.

And both statements are true because "God is love."

CHAPTER NINE
1 John 4:17—5:5
LOVE, HONOR, AND OBEY

The prospective bridegroom was extremely nervous as he and his fiancée were discussing their wedding plans with their pastor.

"I'd like to see a copy of the wedding vows," the young man said, and the pastor handed him the service. He read it carefully, handed it back, and said, "That won't do! There's nothing written in there about her obeying me!"

His fiancée smiled, took his hand, and said, "Honey, the word obey doesn't have to be written in a book. It's already written in love in my heart."

This is the truth in view in this portion of 1 John. Up to this point, the emphasis has been on Christians loving one another; but now we turn to a deeper—and more important—topic: a believer's love for the Father. We cannot love our neighbor or our brother unless we love our heavenly Father. We must first love God with all our hearts; then we can love our neighbor as ourselves.

The key word in this section is perfect. God wants to perfect in us His love for us and our love for Him.

The word perfect carries the idea of maturity and completeness. A believer is not only to grow in grace and knowledge (2 Peter 3:18), but he is also to grow in his love for the Father. He does this in response to the Father's love for him.

How much does God love us? Enough to send His Son to die for us (John 3:16). He loves His children in the same way as He loves Christ (John 17:23). And Jesus tells us that the Father wants the love with which He loved the Son to be in His children (John 17:26).

In other words, the Christian life is to be a daily experience of growing in the love of God. It involves a Christian's coming to know his heavenly Father in a much deeper way as he grows in love.

It is easy to fragment the Christian life and become preoccupied with individual pieces instead of the total picture. One group may emphasize "holiness" and urge its members to get victory over sin. Another may stress "witnessing" or "separation from the world." But each of these emphases is really a by-product of something else: a believer's growing love for the Father. Mature Christian love is the great universal need among God's people.

How can a believer know that his love for the Father is being perfected? This paragraph of 1 John suggests four evidences.

Confidence (4:17–19)

Two brand-new words came into John's vocabulary here: fear and torment. And this is written to believers! Is it possible that Christians can actually live in fear and torment? Yes, unfortunately, many professed believers experience both fear and torment day after day. And the reason is that they are not growing in the love of God.

The word boldness can mean "confidence" or "freedom of speech." It does not mean brazenness or brashness. A believer who experiences perfecting love grows in his confidence toward God. He has a reverential fear of God, not a tormenting fear. He is a son who respects his Father, not a prisoner who cringes before a judge.

We have adopted the Greek word for fear into our English vocabulary: phobia. All sorts of phobias are listed in psychology books; for instance, acrophobia—"fear of heights" and hydrophobia—"fear of water." John was writing about krisisphobia—"fear of judgment." John has already mentioned this solemn truth in 1 John 2:28, and now he dealt with it again.

If people are afraid, it is because of something in the past that haunts them, or something in the present that upsets them, or something in the future that they feel threatens them. Or it may be a combination of all three. A believer in Jesus Christ does not have to fear the past, present, or future, for he has experienced the love of God, and this love is being perfected in him day by day.

"It is appointed unto men once to die, but after this the judgment" (Heb. 9:27). But a Christian does not fear future judgment, because Christ has suffered his judgment for him on the cross. "Truly, truly I say to you, he who hears My word, and believes Him who sent Me, has eternal life, and does not come into judgment, but has passed out of death into life" (John 5:24 nasb). "Therefore there is now no condemnation for those who are in Christ Jesus" (Rom. 8:1 nasb). For a Christian, judgment is not future; it is past. His sins have been judged already at the cross, and they will never be brought against him again.

The secret of our boldness is "As he is, so are we in this world" (1 John 4:17). We know that "we shall be like him" when He returns (1 John 3:1–2), but that statement refers primarily to the glorified bodies believers will receive (Phil. 3:20–21). Positionally, we are right now "as he is." We are so closely identified with Christ, as members of His body, that our position in this world is like His exalted position in heaven.

This means that the Father deals with us as He deals with His own beloved Son. How, then, can we ever be afraid?

We do not have to be afraid of the future, because our sins were judged in Christ when He died on the cross. The Father cannot judge our sins again without judging His Son, for "as He is, so are we in this world."

We do not have to be afraid of the past, because "He first loved us." From the very first, our relationship to God was one of love. It was not that we loved Him, but that He loved us (see 1 John 4:10). "For if while we were enemies we were reconciled to God through the death of His Son, much more, having been reconciled, we shall be saved by His life" (Rom. 5:10 nasb). If God loved us when we were outside the family, disobeying Him, how much more does He love us now that we are His children!

We do not need to fear the present because "perfect love casteth out fear" (1 John 4:18). As we grow in the love of God, we cease to be fearful of what He will do.

Of course there is a proper "fear of God," but it is not the kind of fear that produces torment. "For you have not received a spirit of slavery leading to fear again, but you have received a spirit of adoption as sons by which we cry out, 'Abba! Father!'" (Rom. 8:15 nasb) "For God hath not given us a spirit of fear; but of power, and of love, and of a sound mind" (2 Tim. 1:7).

Fear is actually the beginning of torment. We torment ourselves as we contemplate what lies ahead. Many people suffer acutely when they contemplate a visit to the dentist. Think of how an unsaved person must suffer as he contemplates the day of judgment. But since a Christian has boldness in the day of judgment, he can have boldness as he faces life today, for there is no situation of life today that begins to compare with the terrible severity of the day of judgment.

God wants His children to live in an atmosphere of love and confidence, not fear and torment. We need not fear life or death, for we are being perfected in the love of God. "Who will separate us from the love of Christ? Will tribulation, or distress, or persecution, or famine, or nakedness, or peril, or sword? … But in all these things we overwhelmingly conquer through Him who loved us. For I am convinced that neither death, nor life, nor angels, nor principalities, nor things present, nor things to come, nor powers, nor height, nor depth, nor any other created thing, will be able to separate us from the love of God, which is in Christ Jesus our Lord" (Rom. 8:35, 37–39 NASB).

Imagine! Nothing in all creation—present or future—can come between us and God's love!

The perfecting of God's love in our lives is usually a matter of several stages. When we were lost, we lived in fear and knew nothing of God's love. After we trusted Christ, we found a perplexing mixture of both fear and love in our hearts. But as we grew in fellowship with the Father, gradually the fear vanished, and our hearts were controlled by His love alone. An immature Christian is tossed between fear and love; a mature Christian rests in God's love.

A growing confidence in the presence of God is one of the first evidences that our love for God is maturing. But confidence never stands alone; it always leads to other moral results.

Honesty (4:20–21)

Here it is for the seventh time: "If a man say …"!

We have met this important phrase several times, and each time we knew what was coming: a warning against pretending.

Fear and pretense usually go together. In fact, they were born together when the first man and woman sinned. No sooner did Adam and Eve sense their guilt than they tried to hide from God and cover their nakedness. But neither their coverings nor their excuses could shelter them from God's all-seeing eye. Adam finally had to admit, "I heard thy voice in the garden, and I was afraid" (Gen. 3:10).

But when our hearts are confident toward God, there is no need for us to pretend, either to God or to other people. A Christian who lacks confidence with God will also lack confidence with God's people. Part of the torment that fear generates is the constant worry, "How much do others really know about me?" But when we have confidence with God, this fear is gone, and we can face both God and men without worry.

"How many members do you have in your church?" a visitor asked the pastor.

"Somewhere near a thousand," the pastor replied.

"That certainly is a lot of people to try to please!" the visitor exclaimed.

"Let me assure you, my friend, that I have never tried to please all my members, or even some of them," the pastor said with a smile. "I aim to please one Person—the Lord Jesus Christ. If I am right with Him, then everything should be right between me and my people."

An immature Christian who is not growing in his love for God may think he has to impress others with his "spirituality." This mistake turns him into a liar! He is professing something that he is not really practicing; he is playing a role instead of living a life.

Perhaps the best example of this sin is seen in the experience of Ananias and Sapphira (Acts 5). They sold a piece of property and brought part of the money to the Lord, but they gave the impression that they were bringing all the money. The sin of this couple was not in taking money from God, for Peter made it clear that the disposal of the money was up to them (Acts 5:4). Their sin was hypocrisy. They were trying to make people think they were more generous and spiritual than they really were.

Pretending is one of the favorite activities of little children, but it is certainly not a mark of maturity in adults. Adults must know themselves and be themselves, fulfilling the purposes for which Christ saved them. Their lives must be marked by honesty.

Spiritual honesty brings peace and power to the person who practices it. He does not have to keep a record of the lies he has told, and he is not using his energy to cover up. Because he lives in open honesty with the Father, he can live in honesty with other people. Love and truth go together. Because he knows God loves him and accepts him (even with all his faults), he is not trying to impress others. He loves God, and therefore he loves his fellow Christians.

Jerry's grades were far below his usual performance and, on top of that, his health seemed to be failing. His new roommate was concerned about him and finally persuaded him to talk to the campus psychologist.

"I can't figure myself out," Jerry admitted. "Last year I was sailing through school, and this year it is like fighting a war."

"You're not having trouble with your new roommate, are you?" the counselor asked.

Jerry did not reply right away, and this gave the counselor a clue.

"Jerry, are you concentrating on living your life as a good student, or on trying to impress your new roommate with your abilities?"

"Yeah, I guess that's it," Jerry answered with a sigh of relief. "I've worn myself out acting and haven't had enough energy left for living."

Confidence toward God and honesty with others are two marks of maturity that are bound to show up when our love for God is being perfected.

Joyful Obedience (5:1–3)

Not simply obedience—but joyful obedience! "His commandments are not burdensome" (1 John 5:3 NASB).

Everything in creation—except man—obeys the will of God. "Fire, and hail; snow, and vapor; stormy wind fulfilling his word" (Ps. 148:8). In the book of Jonah, you see the winds and waves, and even the fish, obeying God's commands, but the prophet persisted in disobeying. Even a plant and a little worm did what God commanded. But the prophet stubbornly wanted his own way.

Disobedience to God's will is a tragedy—but so is reluctant, grudging obedience. God does not want us to disobey Him, but neither does He want us to obey out of fear or necessity. What Paul wrote about giving also applies to living: "not grudgingly or under compulsion, for God loves a cheerful giver" (2 Cor. 9:7 NASB).

What is the secret of joyful obedience? It is to recognize that obedience is a family matter. We are serving a loving Father and helping our brothers and sisters in Christ. We have been born of God, we love God, and we love God's children. And we demonstrate this love by keeping God's commandments.

A woman visited a newspaper editor's office, hoping to sell him some poems she had written.

"What are your poems about?" the editor asked.

"They're about love!" gushed the poetess.

The editor settled back in his chair and said, "Well, read me a poem. The world could certainly use a lot more love!"

The poem she read was filled with moons and Junes and other sticky sentiments, and it was more than the editor could take.

"I'm sorry," he said, "but you just don't know what love is all about! It's not moonlight and roses. It's sitting up all night at a sickbed, or working extra hours so the kids can have new shoes. The world doesn't need your brand of poetical love. It needs some good old-fashioned practical love."

D. L. Moody often said, "Every Bible should be bound in shoe leather." We show our love to God, not by empty words but by willing works. We are not slaves obeying a master; we are children obeying a Father. And our sin is a family affair.

One of the tests of maturing love is our personal attitude toward the Bible, because in the Bible we find God's will for our lives revealed. An unsaved man considers the Bible an impossible book, mainly because he does not understand its spiritual message (1 Cor. 2:14). An immature Christian considers the demands of the Bible to be burdensome. He is somewhat like a little child who is learning to obey, and who asks, "Why do I have to do that?" or "Wouldn't it be better to do this?"

But a Christian who experiences God's perfecting love finds himself enjoying the Word of God and truly loving it. He does not read the Bible as a textbook, but as a love letter.

The longest chapter in the Bible is Psalm 119, and its theme is the Word of God. Every verse but two (Ps. 119:122, 132) mentions the Word of God in one form or another, as "law," "precepts," "commandments," and so forth. But the interesting thing is that the psalmist loves the Word of God and enjoys telling us about it! "O how love I thy law!" (Ps. 119:97). He rejoices in the law (Ps. 119:14, 162) and delights in it (Ps. 119:16, 24). It is honey to his taste (Ps. 119:103). In fact, he turns God's law into a song: "Thy statutes have been my songs in the house of my pilgrimage" (Ps. 119:54).

Imagine turning statutes into songs. Suppose the local symphony presented a concert of the traffic code set to music! Most of us do not consider laws a source of joyful song, but this is the way the psalmist looked at God's law. Because he loved the Lord, he loved His law. God's commandments were not grievous and burdensome to him. Just as a loving son or daughter happily obeys his father's command, so a Christian with perfecting love joyfully obeys God's command.

At this point, we can review and understand the practical meaning of "maturing love" in our daily lives. As our love for the Father matures, we have confidence and are no longer afraid of His will. We also are honest toward others and lose our fear of being rejected. And we have a new attitude toward the Word of God: it is the expression of God's love, and we enjoy obeying it. Confidence toward God, honesty toward others, and joyful obedience are the marks of perfecting love and the ingredients that make up a happy Christian life.

We can see, too, how sin ruins all this. When we disobey God we lose our confidence toward Him. If we do not immediately confess our sin and claim His forgiveness (1 John 1:9), we must start pretending in order to cover up. Disobedience leads to dishonesty, and both turn our hearts away from the Word of God. Instead of reading the Word with joy to discover the Father's will, we ignore the Word or perhaps read it in a routine way.

The burden of religion (man trying to please God in his own strength) is a grievous one (see Matt. 23:4), but the yoke that Christ puts on us is not burdensome at all (Matt. 11:28–30). Love lightens burdens. Jacob had to work for seven years to win the woman he loved, but the Bible tells us that "they seemed unto him a few days, for the love he had to her" (Gen. 29:20). Perfecting love produces joyful obedience.

Victory (5:4–5)

The Greek goddess of victory was Nike, which also happens to be the name of a United States aerial missile. Both of them are named for the Greek word nike (NEE-kay), which simply means victory. But what does victory have to do with maturing love?

Christians live in a real world and are beset with formidable obstacles. It is not easy to obey God. It is much easier to drift with the world, disobey Him, and "do your own thing."

But the Christian is "born of God." This means he has the divine nature within him, and it is impossible for this divine nature to disobey God. "For whatever is born of God overcomes the world" (1 John 5:4 NASB). If the old nature is in control of us, we disobey God, but if the new nature is in control, we obey God. The world appeals to the old nature (1 John 2:15–17) and tries to make God's commandments seem burdensome.

Our victory is a result of faith, and we grow in faith as we grow in love. The more you love someone, the easier it is to trust him. The more our love for Christ is perfected, the more our faith in Christ is perfected too, because faith and love mature together.

The word overcome was a favorite with John; he used it in 1 John 2:13–14 with reference to overcoming the devil. He used it seven times in Revelation to describe believers and the blessings they receive (Rev. 2:7, 11, 17, 26; 3:5, 12, 21). He was not describing a special class of believers. Rather, he was using the word overcomer as a name for the true Christian. Because we have been born of God, we are overcomers.

We are told that a soldier in the army of Alexander the Great was not acting bravely in battle. When he should have been pressing ahead, he was lingering behind.

The great general approached him and asked, "What is your name, soldier?"

The man replied, "My name, sir, is Alexander."

The general looked him straight in the eye and said firmly, "Soldier, get in there and fight—or change your name!"

What is our name? "Children of God—the born-again ones of God." Alexander the Great wanted his name to be a symbol of courage; our name carries with it assurance of victory. To be born of God means to share God's victory.

This is a victory of faith, but faith in what? Faith in Jesus Christ, the Son of God! The person who overcomes the world is the one "who believes that Jesus is the Son of God" (1 John 5:5 NASB). It is not faith in ourselves, but faith in Christ, that gives us the victory. "In the world ye shall have tribulation, but be of good cheer; I have overcome the world" (John 16:33).

Identification with Christ in His victory reminds us of the several times we have read "as he is" in John's letter. "As he is, so are we in this world" (1 John 4:17). We should walk in the light "as he is in the light" (1 John 1:7). If we claim to abide in Him, then we should conduct ourselves as He conducted Himself (1 John 2:6). His children are to be on earth what He is in heaven. It is only necessary for us to claim this wonderful position by faith—and to act on it.

When Jesus Christ died, we died with Him. Paul said, "I have been crucified with Christ" (Gal. 2:20 NASB). When Christ was buried, we were buried with Him. And when He arose, we arose with Him. "Therefore we have been buried with Him through baptism into death, so that as Christ was raised from the dead through the glory of the Father, so we too might walk in newness of life" (Rom. 6:4 NASB).

When Christ ascended to heaven, we ascended with Him and are now seated with Him in heavenly places (Eph. 2:6). And when Christ returns, we shall share His exaltation. "When Christ, who is our life, is revealed, then you also will be revealed with Him in glory" (Col. 3:4 NASB).

All these verses describe our spiritual position in Christ. When we claim this position by faith, we share His victory. When God raised Jesus from the dead, He "seated Him at His right hand in the heavenly places, far above all rule and authority and power and dominion, and every name that is named.... And He put all things in subjection under His feet" (Eph. 1:20–22 NASB). This means that, positionally, each child of God is privileged to sit far above all his enemies!

Where a man sits determines how much authority he may exercise. The man who sits in the general manager's chair has a restricted sphere of authority; the man who sits in the vice president's chair exercises more control. But the man behind the desk marked "president" exercises the most authority. No matter where he may be in the factory or office, he is respected and obeyed because of where he sits. His power is determined by his position, not by his personal appearance or the way he feels.

So with a child of God: his authority is determined by his position in Christ. When he trusted Christ, he was identified with Him by the Holy Spirit and made a member of His body (1 Cor. 12:12–13). His old life has been buried and he has been raised to a new life of glory. In Christ, he is sitting on the very throne of the universe!

A Civil War veteran used to wander from place to place, begging a bed and bite to eat and always talking about his friend "Mr. Lincoln." Because of his injuries, he was unable to hold a steady job. But as long as he could keep going, he would chat about his beloved president.

"You say you knew Mr. Lincoln," a skeptical bystander retorted one day. "I'm not so sure you did. Prove it!"

The old man replied, "Why, sure, I can prove it. In fact, I have a piece of paper here that Mr. Lincoln himself signed and gave to me."

From his old wallet, the man took out a much-folded piece of paper and showed it to the man.

"I'm not much for reading," he apologized, "but I know that's Mr. Lincoln's signature."

"Man, do you know what you have here?" one of the spectators asked. "You have a generous federal pension authorized by President Lincoln. You don't have to walk around like a poor beggar! Mr. Lincoln has made you rich!"

To paraphrase what John wrote, "You Christians do not have to walk around defeated, because Jesus Christ has made you victors! He has defeated every enemy, and you share His victory. Now, by faith, claim His victory."

The key, of course, is faith, but this has always been God's key to victory. The great men and women named in Hebrews 11 all won their victories "by faith." They simply took God at His word and acted on it, and He honored their faith and gave them victory. Faith is not simply saying that what God says is true; true faith is acting on what God says because it is true. Someone has said that faith is not so much believing in spite of evidence, but obeying in spite of consequence.

Victorious faith is the result of maturing love. The

better we come to know and love Jesus Christ, the easier it is to trust Him with the needs and battles of life. It is important that this maturing love become a regular and a practical thing in our daily lives.

How does a believer go about experiencing this kind of love and the blessings that flow from it?

To begin with, this kind of love must be cultivated. It is not the result of a hit-or-miss friendship! A previous study pointed out that a believer slips back into the world by stages:

1. Friendship with the world (James 4:4)
2. Spotted by the world (James 1:27)
3. Loving the world (1 John 2:15–17)
4. Conformed to the world (Rom. 12:2)

Our relationship to Jesus Christ, in a similar way, grows by stages.

We must cultivate friendship with Christ. Abraham was "the friend of God" (James 2:23) because he separated himself from the world and did what God told him. His life was not perfect, but when he sinned, he confessed and went right back to walking with God.

This friendship will begin to influence our lives. As we read the Word and pray, and as we fellowship with God's people, Christian graces will start to show up in us. Our thoughts will be cleaner, our conversation more meaningful, our desires more wholesome. But we will not be suddenly and totally changed; it will be a gradual process.

Our friendship with Christ and our becoming like Him will lead to a deeper love for Christ. On the human level, friendship often leads to love. On the divine level, friendship with Christ ought to lead to love. "We love Him because He first loved us" (1 John 4:19). The Word of God reveals His love to us, and the indwelling Spirit of God makes this love more and more real to us. Furthermore, this love is worked out in our lives in daily obedience. Christian love is not a passing emotion; it is a permanent devotion, a deep desire to please Christ and to do His will.

The more we know Him the better we love Him, and the better we love Him the more we become like Him—"conformed to the image of His Son" (Rom. 8:29). Of course we will not be completely conformed to Christ until we see Him (1 John 3:1–3), but we are to begin the process now.

What an exciting way to live! As God's love is perfected in us, we have confidence toward Him and do not live in fear. Because fear is cast out, we can be honest and open; there is no need to pretend. And because fear is gone, our obedience to His commands is born out of love, not terror. We discover that His commandments are not burdensome. Finally, living in this atmosphere of love, honesty, and joyful obedience, we are able to face the world with victorious faith and to overcome instead of being overcome.

The place to begin is not in some daring, dramatic experience. The place to begin is in the quiet, personal place of prayer. Peter wanted to give his life for Jesus, but when he was asked to pray, Peter went to sleep (Luke 22:31–33, 39–46). A believer who begins the day reading the Word, meditating on it, and worshipping Christ in prayer and praise will experience this perfecting love.

When it begins, he will know it—and others will know it. His life will be marked by confidence, honesty, joyful obedience, and victory.

CHAPTER TEN
1 John 5:6–21
WHAT DO YOU KNOW FOR SURE?

Nothing is certain but death and taxes." Benjamin Franklin wrote those words in 1789. Of course, a wise man like Franklin knew that many other things are also certain. The Christian also knows that there are many certainties. Of spiritual truth, Christians are not afraid to say, "We know!" In fact, the word *know* occurs thirty-nine times in John's brief letter, eight times in this closing chapter.

Man has a deep desire for certainty, and he will even dabble in the occult in his effort to find out something for sure. A businessman having dinner with his pastor said to him, "Do you see those offices across the street? In them sit some of the most influential business leaders in this town. Many of them used to come over here regularly to consult a fortune-teller. She isn't here anymore, but a few years ago you could count up the millions of dollars in this room as men waited to consult her."

The life that is real is built on the divine certainties that are found in Jesus Christ. The world may accuse the Christian of being proud and dogmatic, but this does not keep him from saying, "I know!" In these closing verses of John's letter we find five Christian certainties on which we can build our lives with confidence.

Jesus Is God (5:6–10)
In 1 John 5:1–5, emphasis is placed on trusting Jesus Christ. A person who trusts Christ is born of God and is able to overcome the world. To believe that Jesus Christ is the Son of God is basic to Christian experience.

But how do we know that Jesus Christ is God? Some of His contemporaries called Him a liar and a deceiver (Matt. 27:63). Others have suggested He was a religious fanatic, a madman, or perhaps a Jewish patriot who was sincere but sadly mistaken. The people to whom John was writing were exposed to a popular false teaching that Jesus was merely a man on whom "the Christ" had come when Jesus was baptized. On the cross, "the Christ" left Jesus ("My God, my God, why hast thou forsaken me?"), and so He died like any other human being.

John's epistle refutes this false teaching. It presents three infallible witnesses to prove that Jesus is God.

First witness—the water. Jesus came "by water and blood." The water refers to His baptism in Jordan, when the Father spoke from heaven and said, "This is my beloved Son, in whom I am well pleased" (Matt. 3:13–17). At the same time the Spirit descended like a dove and rested on Him. This was the Father's attestation of His Son at the beginning of Jesus' ministry.

Second witness—the blood. But the Father gave further witness as the time drew near for Jesus to die. He spoke audibly to Jesus from heaven, and said, "I have both glorified it [My name], and will glorify it again" (John 12:28). Furthermore, the Father witnessed in miracle power when Jesus was on the cross: the supernatural darkness, the earthquake, and the rending of the temple veil (Matt. 27:45, 50–53). No wonder the centurion cried out, "Truly this was the Son of God!" (Matt. 27:54)

Jesus did not receive "the Christ" at His baptism and lose it at the cross. On both occasions, the Father witnessed to the deity of His Son.

Third witness—the Spirit. The Spirit was given to bear witness to Christ (John 15:26; 16:14). We can trust the Spirit's witness because "the Spirit is truth." We were not present at the baptism of Christ or at His death, but the Holy Spirit was present. The Holy Spirit is the only Person active on earth today who was present when Christ was ministering here. The witness of the Father is past history, but the witness of the Spirit is present experience. The first is external, the second is internal—and both agree.

How does the Spirit witness within the heart of a believer? "For you have not received a spirit of slavery leading to fear again, but you have received a spirit of adoption as sons by which we cry out, 'Abba! Father!' The Spirit Himself testifies with our spirit that we are children of God" (Rom. 8:15–16 NASB). His witness is our inner confidence that we belong to Christ—not a confidence that we "work up" for ourselves, but a confidence that God gives us.

The Spirit also witnesses to us through the Word. As we read God's Word, He speaks to us and teaches us. This is not true of an unsaved man (1 Cor. 2:14); it is true only of a believer.

A Christian feels "at home" with God's people because the Spirit dwells in him. This is another way the Spirit bears witness.

The law required two or three witnesses for a matter to be settled (Deut. 19:15). The Father witnessed at the baptism and at the cross, and the Spirit witnesses today within the believer. The Spirit, the water, and the blood settle the matter: Jesus is God.

(Most scholars agree that 1 John 5:7 of the Authorized Version does not belong in the letter, but omitting it does not affect the teaching at all.)

We receive the witness of men, so why should we reject the witness of God?

People often say, "I wish I could have faith!" But everybody lives by faith! All day long, people trust one another. They trust the doctor and the pharmacist; they trust the cook in the restaurant; they even trust the fellow driving in the other lane on the highway. If we can trust men, why can we not trust God? And not to trust Him is to make Him a liar!

Jesus is God: this is the first Christian certainty, and it is foundational to everything else.

Believers Have Eternal Life (5:11–13)

The key word in 1 John 5:6–10 is witness, sometimes translated "record" or "testifieth." God gave witness to His Son, but He has also given witness to His sons—to individual believers. We know that we have eternal life! Not only is there the witness of the Spirit within; but there is the witness of the Word of God. "These things I have written to you who believe in the name of the Son of God, so that you may know that you have eternal life" (1 John 5:13 NASB).

Eternal life is a gift; it is not something that we earn (John 10:27–29; Eph. 2:8–9). But this gift is a Person—Jesus Christ. We receive eternal life not only from Christ, but in Christ. "He who has the Son has the life" (1 John 5:12 NASB). Not just "life" but "the life"—the life "which is life indeed" (1 Tim. 6:19 NASB).

This gift is received by faith. God has gone on record in His Word as offering eternal life to those who will believe on Jesus Christ. Millions of Christians have proved that God's record is true. Not to believe it is to make God a liar. And if God is a liar, nothing is certain.

God wants His children to know that they belong to Him. John was inspired by the Spirit to write his gospel to assure us that "Jesus is the Christ, the Son of God" (John 20:31). He wrote this epistle so that we may be sure that we are the children of God (1 John 5:13).

It would be helpful at this point to review the characteristics of God's children:

- "Everyone also who practices righteousness is born of Him" (1 John 2:29 NASB).
- "No one who is born of God practices sin" (1 John 3:9 NASB).
- "We know that we have passed out of death into life, because we love the brethren" (1 John 3:14 NASB).
- "Beloved, let us love one another, for love is from God; and everyone who loves is born of God and knows God" (1 John 4:7 NASB).
- "For whatsoever is born of God overcometh the world" (1 John 5:4).

If you bear these "birthmarks," you can say with confidence that you are a child of God.

When Sir James Simpson, the discoverer of chloroform, was on his deathbed, a friend asked him, "Sir, what are your speculations?"

Simpson replied, "Speculations! I have no speculations! 'For I know whom I have believed, and am persuaded that he is able to keep that which I have committed unto him against that day.'"

God Answers Prayer (5:14–15)

It is one thing to know that Jesus is God and that we are God's children, but what about the needs and problems of daily life? Jesus helped people when He was here on earth; does He still help them? Earthly fathers take care of their children; does the heavenly Father respond when His children call on Him?

Christians have confidence in prayer, just as they have confidence as they await the judgment (1 John 2:28; 4:17). As we have seen, the word confidence means "freedom of speech." We can come to the Father freely and tell Him our needs.

Of course, there are conditions we must meet.

First, we must have a heart that does not condemn us (1 John 3:21–22). Unconfessed sin is a serious obstacle to answered prayer (Ps. 66:18). It is worth noting that differences between a Christian husband and his wife can hinder their prayers (1 Peter 3:1–7). If there is anything between us and any other Christian, we must settle it (Matt. 5:23–25). And unless a believer is abiding in Christ, in love and obedience, his prayers will not be answered (John 15:7).

Second, we must pray in God's will. "Thy will be done" (Matt. 6:10). "Prayer is a mighty instrument, not for getting man's will done in heaven, but for getting God's will done on earth," wrote Robert Law. George Mueller, who fed thousands of orphans with food provided in answer to prayer, said, "Prayer is not overcoming God's reluctance. It is laying hold of God's willingness."

There are times when we can only pray, "Not my will but thine be done," because we simply do not know God's will in a matter. But most of the time we can determine God's will by reading the Word, listening to the Spirit (Rom. 8:26–27), and discerning the circumstances around us. Our very faith to ask God for something is often proof that He wants to give it (Heb. 11:1).

There are many promises in the Bible that we can claim in prayer. God has promised to supply our needs (Phil. 4:19)—not our greeds! If we are obeying His will and really need something, He will supply it in His way and in His time.

"But if it is God's will for me to have a thing, then why should I pray about it?" Because prayer is the way God wants His children to get what they need. God not only ordains the end, but He also ordains the means to the end—prayer. And the more you think about it, the more wonderful this arrangement becomes. Prayer is really the thermometer of the spiritual life. God has ordained that I maintain a close walk with Him if I expect Him to meet my needs.

John did not write, "we shall have the requests," but, "we know that we have the requests" (1 John 5:15 NASB, italics mine). The verb is present tense. We may not see the answer to a prayer immediately, but we have inner confidence that God has answered. This confidence, or faith, is "the evidence of things not seen" (Heb. 11:1). It is God witnessing to us that He has heard and answered.

What breathing is to a physical man, prayer is to a spiritual man. If we do not pray, we "faint" (Luke 18:1). Prayer is not only the utterance of the lips; it is also the desire of the heart. "Pray without ceasing" (1 Thess. 5:17) does not mean that a Christian is always saying an audible prayer. We are not heard for our "much speaking" (Matt. 6:7). No, "Pray without ceasing" suggests the attitude of the heart as well as the words of the lips. A Christian who has his heart fixed on Christ and is trying to glorify Him is praying constantly even when he is not conscious of it.

Famous preacher Charles Spurgeon was working hard on a message but was unable to complete it. It grew late and his wife said, "Why don't you go to bed. I'll wake you up early and you can finish your sermon in the morning."

Spurgeon dozed off and in his sleep began to preach the sermon that was giving him so much trouble! His wife wrote down what he said and the next morning gave her preacher-husband the notes.

"Why, that's exactly what I wanted to say!" exclaimed the surprised preacher. The message had been in his heart; it had simply needed expression. So with prayer: if we are abiding in Christ, the very desires of our heart are heard by God whether we voice them or not.

The pages of the Bible and the pages of history are filled with reports of answered prayer. Prayer is not spiritual self-hypnosis. Nor do we pray because it makes us feel better. We pray because God has commanded us to pray and because prayer is the God-appointed means for a believer to receive what God wants to give him. Prayer keeps a Christian in the will of God, and living in the will of God keeps a Christian in the place of blessing and service. We are not beggars; we are children coming to a wealthy Father who loves to give His children what they need.

Though He was God in the flesh, Jesus depended on prayer. He lived on earth, as we must, in dependence on the Father. He arose early in the morning to pray (Mark 1:35), though He had been up late the night before healing the multitudes. He sometimes spent all night in prayer (Luke 6:12). In the garden of Gethsemane, He prayed with "strong crying and tears" (Heb. 5:7). On the cross He prayed three times. If the sinless Son of God needed to pray, how much more do we?

The most important thing about prayer is the will of God. We must take time to ascertain what God's will is in a matter, especially searching in the Bible for promises or principles that apply to our situation.

Once we know the will of God, we can pray with confidence and then wait for Him to reveal the answer.

Christians Do Not Practice Sin (5:16–19)

"We know that no one who is born of God sins" (1 John 5:18 NASB). "No one who is born of God practices sin" (1 John 3:9 NASB). Occasional sins are not here in view, but habitual sins, the practice of sin. Because a believer has a new nature ("God's seed," 1 John 3:9), he has new desires and appetites and is not interested in sin.

A Christian faces three enemies, all of which want to lead him into sin: the world, the flesh, and the devil.

The world "lies in the power of the evil one" (1 John 5:19 NASB), Satan—the god of this age (2 Cor. 4:3–4, literal translation) and the prince of this world (John 14:30). He is the spirit who works in the children of disobedience (Eph. 2:2).

Satan has many devices for leading a believer into sin. He tells lies, as he did to Eve (Gen. 3; 2 Cor. 11:1–3), and when men believe his lies they turn away from and disobey God's truth. Or, Satan may inflict physical suffering, as he did with Job and Paul (2 Cor. 12:7–9). In David's case, Satan used pride as his weapon and urged David to number the people and in this way defy God (1 Chron. 21). Satan is like a serpent who deceives (Rev. 12:9) and a lion who devours (1 Peter 5:8–9). He is a formidable enemy.

Then there is the problem of the flesh, the old nature with which we were born and that is still with us. True, we have a new nature (the divine seed, 1 John 3:9) within us, but we do not always yield to our new nature.

The world is our third enemy (1 John 2:15, 17). It is easy for us to yield to the desires of the flesh, the desires of the eyes, and the pride of life! The atmosphere around us makes it hard for us to keep our minds pure and our hearts true to God.

Then how does a believer keep from sinning?

First John 5:18 gives the answer: Jesus Christ keeps the believer so that the enemy cannot get his hands on him. "He [Christ] who was born of God keeps him [the believer], and the evil one does not touch him" (NASB). The Authorized Version here gives the impression that a believer keeps himself from sin, but this is not what the verse says. Of course, it is true that a Christian must keep himself in the love of God (Jude 21), but it is not true that a Christian must depend on himself to overcome Satan.

Peter's experience with Satan helps us to understand this truth.

"Simon, Simon," said Jesus, "behold, Satan has demanded permission to sift you like wheat; but I have prayed for you, that your faith may not fail; and you, when once you have turned again, strengthen your brothers" (Luke 22:31–32 NASB).

To begin with, Satan cannot touch any believer without God's permission. Satan wanted to sift all the disciples, and Jesus gave him permission. But Jesus prayed especially for Peter, and His prayer was answered. Peter's faith did not ultimately fail, even though his courage failed. Peter was restored and became a mighty and effective soul-winner.

Whenever Satan attacks us, we can be sure that God gave him permission. And if God gave him permission He will also give us power to overcome, because God will never permit us to be tested above our strength (1 Cor. 10:13).

One of the characteristics of "spiritual young men" is their ability to overcome the evil one (1 John 2:13–14). Their secret? "The word of God abides in you" (1 John 2:14 NASB). Part of the armor of God is the sword of the Spirit (Eph. 6:17), and this sword overcomes Satan.

When a believer sins, he can confess his sin and be forgiven (1 John 1:9). But a believer dare not play with sin, because sin is lawlessness (1 John 3:4, where "transgression of the law" means "lawlessness"). A person who practices sin proves that he belongs to Satan (1 John 3:7–10). Furthermore, God warns that sin can lead to physical death!

"All unrighteousness is sin," but some sin is worse than other sin. All sin is hateful to God, and should be hateful to a believer; but some sin is punished with death. John told us (1 John 5:16–17) about the case of a brother (a believer) whose life was taken because of sin.

The Bible mentions people who died because of their sin. Nadab and Abihu, the two sons of Aaron the priest, died because they deliberately disobeyed God (Lev. 10:1–7). Korah and his clan opposed God and died (Num. 16). Achan was stoned because he disobeyed Joshua's orders from God at Jericho (Josh. 6—7). A man named Uzzah touched the ark and God killed him (2 Sam. 6).

"But those are Old Testament examples!" someone may argue. "John was writing to New Testament believers who live under grace!"

To whom much is given, much shall be required. A believer today has a far greater responsibility to obey God than did the Old Testament saints. We have a complete Bible, we have the full revelation of God's grace, and we have the Holy Spirit living within us to help us obey God. But there are cases in the New Testament of believers who lost their lives because they disobeyed God.

Ananias and Sapphira lied to God about their offering, and they both died (Acts 5:1–11). Some believers at Corinth died because of the way they had acted at the Lord's Supper (1 Cor. 11:30). And 1 Corinthians 5:1–5 suggests that a certain offender would have died had he not repented and confessed his sin (2 Cor. 2:6–8).

If a believer does not judge, confess, and forsake sin, God must chasten him. This process is described in Hebrews 12:1–13, which suggests that a person who does not subject himself to the Father will not live (Heb. 12:9). In other words, first God "spanks" his rebellious children, and if they do not yield to His will, He may remove them from the world lest their disobedience lead others astray and bring further disgrace to His name.

"The sin unto death" is not some one specific sin. Rather, it is a kind of sin—it is the sort of sin that leads to death. With Nadab and Abihu, it was their presumption in taking the priest's office and entering the Holy of Holies. In the case of Achan it was covetousness. Ananias and Sapphira were guilty of hypocrisy and even of lying to the Holy Spirit.

If a Christian sees a brother committing sin, he should pray for him (1 John 5:16), asking that he confess his sin and return to fellowship with the Father. But if in his praying, he does not sense that he is asking in God's will (as instructed in 1 John 5:14–15), then he should not pray for the brother. "Therefore, pray not thou for this people, neither lift up cry nor prayer for them, neither make intercession to me; for I will not hear thee" (Jer. 7:16).

James 5:14–20 somewhat parallels 1 John 5:16–17. James described a believer who is sick, possibly because of his sin. He sends for the elders, who come to him and pray for him. The prayer of faith heals him, and if he has sinned his sins are forgiven. "The prayer of faith" is prayer in the will of God, as described in 1 John 5:14–15. It is "praying in the Holy Spirit" (Jude 20 NASB).

Christians do not deliberately practice sin. They have the divine nature within; Jesus Christ guards them, and they do not want God's discipline.

The Christian Life Is the Real Life (5:20–21)

Jesus Christ is the true God. We know Him who is true, and we are in Him who is true. We have "the real thing"!

"We know that our real life is in the true One, and in His Son, Jesus Christ. This is the real God and this is real, eternal life" (1 John 5:20, Phillips). Reality has been the theme throughout John's letter, and now we are reminded of it again.

John was probably writing to believers in the city of Ephesus, a city given over to the worship of idols. The temple of Diana, one of the wonders of the ancient world, was located in Ephesus, and the making and selling of idols was one of the chief occupations of the people there (Acts 19:21–41). Surrounded by idolatry, Christians there were under tremendous pressure to conform.

But "we know that there is no such thing as an idol in the world, and that there is no God but one" (1 Cor. 8:4 NASB). That is, "an idol has no real existence" (NASB, marg.). The tragedy of idolatry is that a dead image can do a worshipper no good because it is not genuine. Hebrew writers in the Old Testament called idols "nothings, vain things, vapors, emptiness." An idol is a lifeless, useless substitute for the real thing.

The Psalms contain caustic indictments of idolatry (Ps. 115:1–8; 135:15–18). To human vision, an idol looks real—eyes, ears, mouth, nose, hands, feet—but these are but useless imitations of the real thing. The eyes are blind, the ears are deaf, the mouth is silent, the hands and feet are paralyzed. But the real tragedy is that "those who make them will become like them, everyone who trusts in them" (Ps. 115:8 NASB). We become like the god we worship!

This is the secret of the life that is real. Because we have met the true God, through His Son Jesus Christ, we are in contact with reality. Our fellowship is with a God who is genuine. As we have seen, the word *real* means "the original as opposed to a copy" and "the authentic as opposed to an imitation." Jesus Christ is the true Light (John 1:9), and true Bread (John 6:32), and true Vine (John 15:1), and Truth itself (John 14:6). He is the Original; everything else is a copy. He is authentic; everything else is only an imitation.

Christians live in an atmosphere of reality. Most unsaved people live in an atmosphere of pretense and sham. Christians have been given spiritual discernment to know the true from the false, but the unsaved do not have this understanding. Christians do not simply choose between good and bad; they choose between true and false. An idol represents that which is false and empty; and a person who lives for idols will himself become false and empty.

Few people today bow to idols of wood and metal. Nevertheless, other idols capture their attention and affection. Covetousness, for example, is idolatry (Col. 3:5). A man may worship his bankbook or his stock portfolio just as fervently as a so-called heathen worships his ugly idol. "Thou shalt worship the Lord thy God, and him only shalt thou serve" (Matt. 4:10). The thing we serve is the thing we worship! Whatever controls our lives and "calls the signals" is our god.

This explains why God warns us against the sin of idolatry. Not only is it a violation of His commandment (Ex. 20:1–6), but it is a subtle way for Satan to take control of us. When "things" take God's place in our lives, we are guilty of idolatry. This means we are living for the unreal instead of for the real.

To a man of the world, the Christian life is unreal and the worldly life is real. This is because a man of the world lives by what he sees and feels (things) and not by what God says in His Word. An idol is a temporal thing, Jesus Christ is eternal God. "For the things which are seen are temporal, but the things which are not seen are eternal" (2 Cor. 4:18 NASB, italics mine).

Like Moses, a Christian endures "as seeing him who is invisible" (Heb. 11:27). Faith is "the evidence of things not seen" (Heb. 11:1). Noah had never seen a flood, yet by faith he "saw" it coming and did what God told him to do. Abraham "saw" a heavenly city and country by faith, and was willing to forsake his own earthly home to follow God. All of the great heroes of faith named in Hebrews 11 accomplished what they did because they "saw the invisible" by faith. In other words, they were in contact with reality.

The world boasts of its enlightenment, but a Christian walks in the real light, because God is light. The world talks about love, but it knows nothing of the real love that a Christian experiences because "God is love." The world displays its wisdom and learning, but a Christian lives in truth because "the Spirit is truth." God is light, love, and truth, and these together make a life that is real.

"But it makes no difference what a man believes so long as he is sincere!"

This popular excuse hardly needs refutation. Does it make any difference what the pharmacist believes, or the surgeon, or the chemist? It makes all the difference in the world!

Shed a tear for Jimmy Brown;
Poor Jimmy is no more.
For what he thought was H_2O^*
Was H_2SO_4!†

A Christian has "turned to God from idols to serve the living and true God" (1 Thess. 1:9). Idols are dead, but Christ is the living God. Idols are false, but Christ is the true God. This is the secret of the life that is real!

So John's admonition, "Keep yourselves from idols," can be paraphrased, "Watch out for the imitation and the artificial and be real!"

---

* Water

† Sulphuric acid

2 JOHN

OUTLINE

Key theme: Loving and living the truth
Key verse: 2 John 4

I. INTRODUCTION (1–3)

II. PRACTICING THE TRUTH (4–6)

III. PROTECTING THE TRUTH (7–11)

IV. CONCLUSION (12–13)

CONTENTS

CHAPTER ONE
2 John
A FAITHFUL FAMILY

The apostate teachers not only invaded the churches, but they also tried to influence Christian homes. Titus faced this problem in Crete (Titus 1:10–11) and Timothy faced it in Ephesus (2 Tim. 3:6). As goes the home, so goes the church and the nation; thus the family is an important target in Satan's war against truth.

This brief letter was written to a godly mother and her children. Some Bible students have concluded that "the elect lady" refers to a local church and that "her children" are the believers fellowshipping in the church. "Thy elect sister" (2 John 13) would then refer to a sister church that was sending Christian greetings.

While it is true that John does address a group in this letter (note the plural in 2 John 6, 8, 10, 12), it is also true that he addresses an individual (2 John 1, 4–5, 13). Perhaps the solution is that a Christian assembly was meeting in this home, along with the family of the "elect lady," so that John had both the family and the congregation in mind (see Rom. 16:5; 1 Cor. 16:19; Col. 4:15; Philem. 2). He was concerned that this godly woman not permit anything false to come into her house (2 John 10) or into the assembly.

The dominant feelings in this little epistle are those of friendship and joy, even though these are mixed with concern and warning. If you and I are to keep our homes true to Christ, then we must have the same characteristics as this family to which John wrote.

We Must Know the Truth (1–3)

John used the word truth four times in this salutation, so it is an important word. Basically, it means "reality" as opposed to mere appearance, the ultimate that is the basis for all that we see around us. Jesus Christ is "the truth" (John 14:6) and God's Word is "truth" (John 17:17). God has revealed truth in the person of His Son and in the pages of His Word. He has given us "the Spirit of Truth" to teach us and to enable us to know truth (John 14:16–17; 16:13).

But the truth is not only an objective revelation from the Father, but also a subjective experience in our personal lives. We cannot only know the truth, but we can "love in the truth" and live "for the truth's sake." The truth "lives in us, and shall be with us forever." This means that "knowing the truth" is much more than giving assent to a body of doctrines, though that is important. It means that the believer's life is controlled by a love for the truth and a desire to magnify the truth.

John opened his letter on this note of "truth" because there were false teachers abroad who were spreading error. He called them deceivers and antichrists (2 John 7). John was not one to say that all religious teachings are true in one way or another, and that we should not be critical just as long as people are sincere. To John, there was a great difference, in fact, a deadly difference, between truth and error, and he would not tolerate error.

Since the truth will be with us forever, we certainly ought to get acquainted with it now and learn to love it. Of course, all truth centers in Jesus Christ, the eternal Son of God, with whom we shall live forever (John 14:1–6). It is wonderful to contemplate the fact that we shall spend eternity surrounded by truth, growing in our knowledge of truth, and serving the God of truth.

How did this elect lady and her children come to know the truth and become children of God? Through the grace and mercy of God (2 John 3). God is rich in mercy and grace (Eph. 2:4, 7), and He has channeled His mercy and grace to us in Jesus Christ. We are not saved by God's love, but by God's grace, which is "love that paid a price" (Eph. 2:8–9). God loves the whole world, yet the whole world is not saved. Only those who receive His abundant grace experience salvation from sin.

When you receive grace and mercy from God, you experience His peace. "Therefore, being justified [declared righteous] by faith, we have peace with God through our Lord Jesus Christ" (Rom. 5:1). God is not at war with lost sinners; it is sinners who are at war with God (Rom. 5:10; 8:7). God has been reconciled to sinners because of Christ's work on the cross. Now sinners must repent and be reconciled to God by faith in Jesus Christ (2 Cor. 5:14–21).

It is significant that at the very outset of his second letter John affirmed the deity of Jesus Christ. He did so by joining "the Lord Jesus Christ" with "God the Father." Suppose 2 John 3 read "from God the Father, and from the prophet Amos." You would immediately respond, "Amos must not be joined with the Father's name in that fashion! It makes it appear that Amos is equal with God!"

But that is exactly why John joined the Father and the Son together: they are equally God! And then, to make certain that his readers did not miss the emphasis, John added "the Son of the Father." It is impossible to separate the two. If God is the Father, then He must have a Son; Jesus Christ is that Son. "Whosoever denieth the Son, the same hath not the Father" (1 John 2:23).

Many false teachers argue, "But Jesus is the 'son of God' in the same way all of us are God's sons, made in the image of God! When Jesus claimed to be God's Son, He was not really claiming to be God." But when Jesus said to the Jews, "I and My Father are One," they threatened to stone Him! Why? Because He had blasphemed! "Because that thou, being a man, makest thyself God" (John 10:30–33). They knew what He meant when He called Himself the "Son of God" and claimed equality with God.

The Christian faith stands or falls on the doctrine

of the deity of Jesus Christ. If He is only man, then He cannot save us, no matter how gifted or unique He might be. If He is not God come in human flesh, then the Christian faith is lies—not truth—and John opened this letter with the wrong emphasis.

The great American statesman Daniel Webster was dining in Boston with a group of distinguished men, some of whom had Unitarian leanings. (The Unitarians deny the Trinity and the deity of both the Son and the Spirit.) When the subject of religion came up at the table, Webster boldly affirmed his belief in the deity of Jesus Christ and his confidence in His work of atonement.

"But Mr. Webster," said one man, "can you comprehend how Christ could be both God and man?"

"No, sir, I cannot comprehend it," Webster replied. "If I could comprehend Him, He would be no greater than myself. I feel that I need a superhuman Savior!"

If our homes and churches are to be true to Christ and oppose the false teachers, we must know the truth. How do we learn the truth? By carefully studying God's Word and allowing the Spirit to teach us; by listening to others who are true to the faith; and then by practicing what we learn. We must not only learn the truth with our minds, but we must also love the truth in our hearts and live the truth by our wills. Our total persons must be yielded to the truth.

How important it is for parents to teach their children to love the truth! While we thank God for Sunday schools and Christian day schools, in the final analysis, it is the home that must instill in children a love for truth and the knowledge of God's truth.

We Must Walk in the Truth (4–6)

To "walk in the truth" means to obey it, to permit it to control every area of our lives. This paragraph opens and closes with an emphasis on obedience, walking in the truth. It is much easier to study the truth, or even argue about the truth, than it is to practice it! In fact, sometimes zealous Christians disobey the truth in the very way they try to defend it.

When I was pastoring in Chicago, a strange young man often stood on the sidewalk in front of the church, passing out leaflets that denounced many evangelical leaders who were my friends. Of course, we could not stop him from distributing literature, so I instructed our people to take as many copies as he would give them and then destroy them!

One of our men decided to "shadow" the young man one evening, and he saw him walk to the nearby park, sit down under a tree, and light up a cigarette! Yet just a few minutes before, the young man had been shouting in front of the church, "I'm a fighting fundamentalist, and I'm not ashamed of it!" My guess is that most of the fundamentalists I know would have been ashamed of him. He thought he was promoting truth and opposing error, yet he was not walking in the truth himself. By his actions and belligerent attitude, he was denying the truth he sought to defend.

The apostle's joy (v. 4a). John's joy was that the elect lady's children were walking in truth. John did not know all of them, however; the literal translation is "some of thy children." Somewhere in his travels, John had met some of her children and learned of their obedient walk with the Lord. "I have no greater joy than to hear that my children walk in truth" (3 John 4). We have no reason to believe that John was hinting that others of the children had gone astray after the false teachers. If by "children" John was including the members of the "house church," then it is possible that some of them had left the fellowship and joined with the deceivers.

It certainly brings great joy to the Father when He sees His children obeying His Word. I know personally what it means to the pastor when the church family is submissive to the Word and doing the will of God. Few things break the heart of a pastor like a disobedient and rebellious member who will not submit to the authority of God's Word.

When the great Baptist preacher Charles Spurgeon was a lad, he lived with his grandfather who pastored a church in Stambourne, England. A church member named Roads used to sit in the local pub and drink beer and smoke, and this practice grieved the pastor very much.

One day young Charles said to his grandfather, "I'll kill old Roads, that I will! I shall not do anything bad, but I'll kill him though, that I will!"

What did young Spurgeon do? He confronted Roads in the pub with these words: "What doest thou here, Elijah? Sitting with the ungodly, and you a member of a church and breaking your pastor's heart. I'm ashamed of you! I wouldn't break my pastor's heart, I'm sure!"

It was not long before Roads showed up at the pastor's home, confessing his sins and apologizing for his behavior. Young Spurgeon had "killed him" indeed!

The apostle's argument (v. 4b). He argued that God has commanded us to walk in truth and love. The word commandment is used five times in these few verses. God's commandments focus "the truth" on specific areas of life. "The truth" can be vague and general if we are not careful, but "the commandments" make that truth specific and binding.

Note that the commandments are given by "the Father." Each commandment is an expression of love and not simply law. The will of God is the revelation of God's heart (Ps. 33:11), not just His mind. Consequently, obedience to His Word should be a revelation of our love, not an expression of fear. "For this is the love of God, that we keep his commandments: and his commandments are not grievous" (1 John 5:3).

The false teachers try to make God's commandments appear harsh and difficult and then they offer their converts "true" freedom (2 Peter 2:19). But the greatest freedom is in obedience to God's perfect will. No believer who loves God would ever consider His commandments to be harsh and unbearable.

The apostle's appeal (vv. 5–6). John wanted the elect lady and her family to love one another and this appeal applies to us as well. "A new commandment I give unto you, 'That ye love one another'" (John 13:34). But John wrote that it was not a new commandment (see 1 John 2:7–11). Is this a contradiction?

The commandment "Love one another" is certainly not new in time, because even Old Testament Jews were instructed to love their neighbors (Lev. 19:18, 34) and the strangers within their gates (Deut. 10:19). But with the coming of God's Son to earth, this commandment is new in emphasis and in example. Jesus Christ gave new emphasis to brotherly love, and He exemplified it in His own life. It is also new in experience, for we have the Holy Spirit of God living within, enabling us to obey. "But the fruit of the Spirit is love" (Gal. 5:22; cf. Rom. 5:5).

Is it possible to command love? Yes, when you understand what Christian love really is. Many people have the mistaken idea that Christian love is a feeling, a special kind of "religious emotion" that makes us reach out and accept others. Certainly emotion is involved, but basically, Christian love is an act of the will. It simply means treating other people the same way God treats you! In fact, it is possible to love people that we really do not "like."

We may not be able to will our affections at all times, but we can will our attitudes and actions. When people are rude to us, we can be kind in return. When people persecute us, we can pray for them and, when the opportunity comes, do good to them. If we followed our feelings, we would probably retaliate! But if we ask the Spirit to control our wills, then we can act toward them as Jesus would have acted, in Christian love.

John went on to explain that love and obedience must go together (2 John 6). It is impossible to divorce our relationship with God from our relationship with people. If we say that we love God, but we hate our brother, then we can be sure that we do not really love God (1 John 4:20). If we obey God, then His love is perfected in us, and we have no problem loving our brother (1 John 2:3–5).

As you review this paragraph, you note three themes that blend: truth, love, and obedience. It is by believing the truth—in Christ and in the Word—that we are saved. The evidence of that salvation is love and obedience, but love and obedience are strengthened as we grow in our knowledge of truth. We speak the truth in love (Eph. 4:15) and we obey God's commandments because we love Him. Obedience enables us to learn more truth (John 7:17), and the more truth we learn, the more we love Jesus Christ who is truth! Instead of living in a "vicious circle," we live in a "victorious circle" of love, truth, and obedience!

We Must Abide in the Truth (7–11)

From encouraging truth, John turned to opposing error. He joined his voice with Peter's to warn that there are deceivers in the world. The word *deceiver* implies much more than teaching false doctrine. It also includes leading people into wrong living. John has already made it clear that truth and life go together. What we believe determines how we behave. Wrong doctrine and wrong living always go together.

Where did these false teachers come from originally? "For many deceivers have gone out into the world" (literal translation). They went out from the church! At one time, they professed to believe "the faith which was once delivered unto the saints" (Jude 3), but they turned from that faith and abandoned the truth and the church. "They went out from us, but they were not of us" (1 John 2:19). "Also of your own selves shall men arise, speaking perverse things, to draw away disciples after them" (Acts 20:30).

It takes constant spiritual vigilance to protect a family or a local church from the insidious attacks of false teachers. One very successful pastor told me, "If I took my eyes off this work for twenty-four hours and stopped praying, it would be invaded before we knew it." He was not emphasizing his own importance (though godly pastors are essential to spiritual churches) but the importance of diligence and vigilance.

Note that there are many deceivers! Why? Second Peter 2:2 gives the answer: "And many shall follow their pernicious ways." I think it was Mark Twain who said that a lie runs around the world while truth is putting on her shoes. Fallen human nature wants to believe lies and resist God's truth. We have already learned from 2 Peter 2 the devious methods the apostates use to seduce unwary and unstable people. No wonder they are successful!

These deceivers are also "antichrists" (see 1 John 2:18–29). The Greek prefix *anti* means both "instead of" and "against." These teachers are against Christ because they deny that He is indeed God come in the flesh (see 1 John 4:1–6). They not only deny the truth about Christ, but they give their converts a "substitute Christ" who is not the Christ of the Christian faith. The first question you want to ask any teacher, preacher, or author is, "What do you think about Christ? Is He God come in the flesh?" If he hesitates, or if he denies that Jesus is God come in the flesh, then you can be sure you have a false teacher.

I was preaching at Carrubers Close Mission in Edinburgh, Scotland, and before the meeting started, a young man came up to me. Without even introducing himself, he said, "Do you believe in the Virgin Birth of Jesus Christ?" I replied emphatically that I did, and that I preached that Jesus Christ was the Son of God come in the flesh. While I did not appreciate his arrogant manner, I did appreciate his concern that the man in the pulpit was "abiding in the truth."

To abide in the truth means to remain true to the basic doctrines of the Christian faith. The false teachers had departed from the truth and from the church fellowship and, therefore, they were dangerous. John pointed out three dangers the church and its members face because of deceivers in the world.

The danger of going back (v. 8). This is the danger of losing what has already been gained. *Look to yourselves* means "Beware! Take heed!" The false teachers offer something you do not have, when in reality they take away what you already have!

Satan is a thief and so are his helpers. John wanted his readers to receive "a full reward," which is his equivalent of 2 Peter 1:11, an abundant entrance into the eternal kingdom. What a tragedy it is when God's servants labor faithfully to build up a church, and then the work is destroyed by false teaching. No wonder Paul wrote to the Galatian assemblies, "I am afraid of [for] you, lest I have bestowed upon you labor in vain" (Gal. 4:11).

"Do not lose the things we accomplished" is the way Kenneth Wuest translates 2 John 8. Church members need to respect the work of faithful pastors and teachers and do everything to protect it and extend it. God's servants must one day give an account of their ministries, and they want to do it "with joy and not with grief" (Heb. 13:17). When the church goes backward, losing what it has gained, then it also will lose part of the reward at the judgment seat of Christ. It is essential that we hold fast to the truth of the Word of God!

The danger of going ahead (v. 9). The danger here is that of going beyond the limits of the Word of God and adding to it. The word translated "transgress" means "to run ahead too far, to pass beyond the assigned limits." It is false progress! The apostates like to make us believe that they are "progressive" while the church is "in a rut." They invite us to join them because they have something "new and exciting" to share. But their "progress" is such that they abandon the doctrine that Jesus Christ is the Son of God come in the flesh.

Fifty years ago, the American press was filled with news about "the fundamentalist-modernist controversy." Those who were true to the faith were opposing "modernism" in the mainline denominations and seeking to bring the schools and the leadership of these denominations back to historic Christianity. The "progressive" group called themselves "modernists," when actually there was nothing "modern" about their denials of Christian doctrine. These denials are as old as the church itself! One of their leaders, Dr. Harry Emerson Fosdick, said in one of his sermons, "Fundamentalism is still with us but mostly in the backwaters." If he were alive today, he would not make that statement; today the largest Sunday schools, churches, seminaries, and missionary agencies are fundamental in doctrine.

If a person does not abide in the true doctrine, then he does not have either the Father or the Son. It is impossible to honor the Father and ignore the Son (or call Him a mere man) at the same time. "That all men should honor the Son, even as they honor the Father. He that honoreth not the Son honoreth not the Father which hath sent him" (John 5:23). "Progressive theology" that denies Christ is not progressive at all; it is regressive—all the way back to Genesis 3:1, "Yea, hath God said?"

In giving this warning, however, John was not condemning "progress" as such. "The Lord has yet more light to shine forth from His Word." God gave us the Holy Spirit to teach us and to lead us into new understanding and application of the truth (John 16:12–16), and we must constantly grow (2 Peter 3:18).

But if our "learning" leads us away from the fundamental doctrines of the person and work of Jesus Christ, then we are on dangerous ground.

The danger of going with (vv. 10–13). John warned the family (and the church in their house) not to accept false teachers who visited them, wanting to fellowship with them or perhaps enjoy hospitality. Hospitality was a very important Christian ministry in that day, because there were very few inns where travelers could safely stay, especially Christians who wanted to keep away from the evil influences of the world. Christians were admonished to open their homes to visitors (Rom. 12:13; 1 Tim. 3:2; 5:3–10; Heb. 13:2; 1 Peter 4:8–10).

It was also true that traveling pastors and teachers needed homes to stay in (3 John 5–8). Believers who showed hospitality to these servants of God were "fellowhelpers to the truth," but believers who assisted false teachers were only sharing in their evil works. The doctrine of Jesus Christ is a test of truth, a basis for fellowship, and a bond for mutual cooperation.

Certainly this principle applies today. Often, professed Christians appear on our TVs, wanting to sell us something. We must exercise discernment. If they do not agree with the true doctrine of Christ, not only must we not let them in, but we must not even say "good-bye," which means "God be with you."

Why was John so adamant about this? Because he did not want any of God's children to: (1) give a false teacher the impression that his heretical doctrine was acceptable; (2) become infected because of association and possible friendship; and (3) give the false teacher ammunition to use at the next place he stopped. If I entertain a cultist, for example, he will only say to the neighbors, "There's no reason why you shouldn't let me in. After all, Pastor Wiersbe let me in and we had a wonderful talk!" My disobedience could very well lead to somebody else's destruction.

Let me make it clear that John was not saying only born-again people should enter our houses! "Friendship evangelism" around the table is a wonderful way to win people to Christ. Christians need to be neighborly and hospitable. The apostle is admonishing us not to receive or encourage false teachers who represent antichristian groups, people who have left the church and are now trying to seduce others away from the truth. You can be sure that apostates use every opportunity they can to secure the endorsement of true Christians.

There is a tradition about the apostle John that illustrates his position concerning false doctrine. When he was living in Ephesus, one day he went to the public baths, and there he saw Cerinthus, the leader of a heretical sect. John ran from the buildings lest they should fall down as a judgment from God! Cerinthus taught that Jesus was the natural son of Joseph and Mary, not God come in the flesh.

John's closing words (2 John 12–13) are almost identical to the farewell in 3 John, and they require no explanation. They do, however, express the importance of Christian fellowship and the joy that it should bring to our hearts (see 1 John 1:4). It is wonderful to receive letters, but even more wonderful to receive God's people into our homes and hearts.

This little epistle, written to a Christian mother and her family (and perhaps the church in their house), is a perfect gem of sacred correspondence. But we must not forget the major thrust of the letter: be alert! There are many deceivers in the world!

3 JOHN

OUTLINE

Key theme: Having a good witness in the church
Key verse: 3 John 3

I. GAIUS, A BELOVED BELIEVER (1–8)

II. DIOTREPHES, A PROUD BELIEVER (9–10)

III. DEMETRIUS, AN EXEMPLARY BELIEVER (11–12)

IV. CONCLUSION (13–14)

CONTENTS

CHAPTER ONE
3 John
IT'S THE TRUTH

The battle for truth and against apostasy is fought not only in the home (2 John) but especially in the local church, and that is where 3 John comes in. This little letter (the shortest New Testament epistle in the original Greek) gives us a glimpse into an early assembly, its people, and its problems. As you read this brief letter, you find yourself saying, "Times have not changed very much!" We have similar people and problems today!

One of the key words in this letter is witness (3 John 3, "testified"; 3 John 6, 12, "report, bear record, record"). It means not only the words that we say but the lives that we live. Each Christian is a witness, either a good one or a bad one. We are either helping the truth (3 John 8) or hindering it.

This letter was addressed to Gaius, one of the leaders of the assembly. But John also discussed two other men in these verses—Diotrephes and Demetrius. Wherever there are people, there are problems—and the potential for solving problems. Each of us must honestly face the question, "Am I a part of the problem or a part of the answer?"

Consider the three men involved in this letter and note the kinds of Christians they were.

Gaius the Encourager (1–8)
There is no question that the apostle John dearly loved this man! He called him "the well beloved" in his greeting, and "beloved" in 3 John 5. It is unlikely that these were merely formal terms, like our "Dear Mr. Jones." (We may not even know Mr. Jones personally!) Third John 4 suggests that Gaius may have been one of John's converts, and, of course, those we lead to faith in Christ are especially precious to us. However, the beloved apostle looked on all the believers as his "little children" (1 John 2:1, 12, 18), so we must not press this too far.

If Gaius were a member of a church that I pastored, I would certainly have no trouble loving him! Consider the personal qualities of this excellent man.

Spiritual health (v. 2). John may be hinting here that his dear friend was not well and that John was praying for restored health: "I want you to be as healthy in body as you are in soul!" If this is the case, then it is evidence that it is possible to be spiritually healthy and physically sick. However, this kind of a greeting was very common in that day, so we must not build too much on it.

However, it is clear that Gaius was a man whose "spiritual health" was evident to all. "Though our outward man perish, yet the inward man is renewed day by day" (2 Cor. 4:16). Physical health is the result of nutrition, exercise, cleanliness, proper rest, and the disciplined order of a balanced life. Spiritual health is the result of similar factors. We must nourish ourselves with the Word, and then "work out" that nourishment in godly exercise (1 Tim. 4:6–7). We must keep ourselves clean (2 Cor. 7:1) and avoid the contamination and pollution that is in the world (2 Peter 1:4; James 1:27). While exercise and service are important, it is also important that we rest in the Lord and gain new strength through fellowship with Him (Matt. 11:18–30). A balanced life is a healthy and happy life, a life that honors God.

A good testimony (vv. 3–4). Gaius was recognized as a man who obeyed the Word of God and "walked in truth" (see 2 John 4). Some of the brethren had made several visits to John, and they had joyfully reported that Gaius was a glowing example of what a Christian ought to be. In my own pastoral experience, I must confess that I have often been a bit "on edge" when people have said to me, "Is Mrs. ___ a member of your church?" Or, even worse, "I know one of your members quite well!" John never had to fear when Gaius' name came up!

What made Gaius such a good testimony? God's truth. The truth was "in him" and enabled him to walk in obedience to God's will. Gaius read the Word, meditated on it, delighted in it, and then practiced it in his daily life (see Ps. 1:1–3). What digestion is to the body, meditation is to the soul. It is not enough merely to hear the Word or read the Word. We must inwardly "digest it" and make it part of our inner persons (see 1 Thess. 2:13).

It is clear that Gaius' entire life was wrapped up in the truth. True living comes from the living truth. Jesus Christ, the truth (John 14:6), is revealed in the Word, which is God's truth (John 17:17). The Holy Spirit is also truth (1 John 5:6), and He teaches us the truth. The Spirit of God uses the Word of God to reveal the Son of God, and then to enable us to obey the will of God and "walk in truth."

Practical ministry (vv. 5–8). Gaius was also a "fellowhelper to the truth" (3 John 8). In practical ways, he assisted those who were ministering the Word. We have no indication that Gaius himself was a preacher or teacher, but he opened his heart and home to those who were.

We have learned from John's second letter the importance of Christian hospitality in that day. John warned "the elect lady" against entertaining false teachers (2 John 7–11), but in this letter he commended Gaius for showing hospitality to the true ministers of the Word. Gaius was an encouragement, not only to the brethren in general, but especially to "strangers" who came to fellowship with the church and to minister (see Heb. 13:2).

In this day of fear and violence, it is not easy to welcome strangers into our homes. Of course, in the early church, traveling ministers carried letters of recommendation from their own assemblies (Rom. 16:1); so it is important that we know something about the people we plan to entertain. However, it does take faith and love. As much as my wife and I enjoy sharing our home, we must confess that there have been times when bidding our guests goodbye brought a sense of happy relief! For the most part, however, our guests have truly been "angels unawares" whose presence was a blessing in our home.

Gaius not only opened his home, but he also opened his heart and his hand to give financial help to his guests. The phrase bring forward on their journey means "to assist on their journey." This could have included providing money and food as well as washing and mending clothing (see 1 Cor. 16:6; Titus 3:13). After all, our faith must be proved by our works (James 2:14–16), and our love must be expressed by deeds, not just words (1 John 3:16–18).

What is the motivation for this kind of practical ministry to the saints? First of all, it honors God. The phrase after a godly sort in 3 John 6 means "worthy of God, as befits God." We are never more "godlike" than when we are sacrificing to serve others. "That ye might walk worthy of the Lord unto all pleasing" (Col. 1:10). Since these itinerant ministers were representing the name of the Lord, any ministry to them was really a service to Jesus Christ (Matt 10:40; 25:34–10).

A second motive is that the support of God's servants is a witness to the lost (3 John 7). Keep in mind that there were many wandering teachers in that day, sharing their ideas and begging for money. While the Lord Jesus taught definitely that God's servants deserve support (Luke 10:7), the standard in the New Testament is that this support comes from God's people. "Taking nothing of the Gentiles" means that these itinerant workers would not solicit help from the unsaved. Abraham had this same policy (Gen. 14:21–24), though he did not force his associates to adopt his policy. Many pastors make it clear, when the offering is being received, that they are not asking anything from the unbelievers in the congregation.

When God's people adequately support God's servants, it is a powerful testimony to the lost. But when ministers, churches, and other religious organizations go about soliciting from unsaved people and various businesses, it makes Christianity look cheap and commercial. This does not mean that God's servants should refuse a voluntary gift from an unconverted person, as long as the person understands that the gift will not purchase salvation. Even then, we must be very cautious. The king of Sodom's offer was voluntary, but Abraham rejected it (Gen. 14:17–24)!

The third motivation for serving is obedience to God. "We therefore ought to receive such" (3 John 8). This ministry of hospitality and support is not only an opportunity, but also an obligation. Galatians 6:6–10 makes it clear that those who receive spiritual blessings from the minister of the Word ought to share with him in material blessings; 1 Corinthians 9:7–11 further explains this principle. As a deacon expressed it to me in the first church I pastored, "You pay your board where you get your food!" It is unbiblical for church members to send their tithes and offerings all over the world and neglect to support the ministry of their own local church.

John gave a fourth motivation in 3 John 8: "That we might be fellowhelpers to the truth." Gaius not only received the truth and walked in the truth, but he was a "jointworker" who helped to further the truth. We do not know what his spiritual gifts were or how he served in the congregation, but we do know that Gaius helped extend and defend the truth by assisting those who taught and preached it.

In my itinerant ministry, I have stayed in many homes and been encouraged in my work. The host and hostess may not have been especially gifted people, but their ministry of gracious hospitality enabled me to exercise my gifts in the church. Whatever blessings came in the ministry will certainly be credited to their accounts (Phil. 4:17)!

It is one thing to fight apostasy and refuse to entertain false teachers but quite another thing to open our homes (and wallets) to promote the truth. We need both the negative and the positive. We need more people like Gaius who are spiritually healthy, obedient to the Word, and sharing what they have for the furtherance of the truth. But, alas, not everybody is a Gaius! We turn now to an entirely different kind of Christian.

Diotrephes the Dictator (9–10)

It seems like many churches have members who insist on "being boss" and having their own way. I must confess that sometimes it is the pastor who assumes dictatorial powers and forgets that the word minister means "a servant." But sometimes it is an officer, perhaps a longtime member of the church who thinks he or she has "seniority rights."

Our Lord's disciples often argued over which of them would be the greatest in the kingdom (Matt. 18:1ff.). Jesus had to remind them that their model for ministry was not the Roman official who "lorded it over" people, but the Savior Himself who came as a humble servant (Phil. 2:1ff.). During my many years of ministry, I have seen the model for ministry change, and the church is suffering because of it. It appears that the "successful minister" today is more like a Madison Avenue tycoon than a submissive servant. In his hand he holds a wireless telephone, not a towel; in his heart is selfish ambition, not a love for lost souls and for God's sheep.

Diotrephes was motivated by pride. Instead of giving the preeminence to Jesus Christ (Col. 1:18), he claimed it for himself. He had the final say-so about everything in the church, and his decisions were determined by one thing: "What will this do for Diotrephes?" He was most unlike John the Baptist who said, "He [Jesus Christ] must increase, but I must decrease" (John 3:30). The Greek verb indicates that it was the constant attitude of Diotrephes to promote himself.

Whenever a church has a resident dictator in its membership there are bound to be problems, because people who are spiritually minded will not tolerate that kind of leadership. The Holy Spirit is grieved when the members of the body are not permitted to exercise their gifts because one member must have his own way. At the Judgment Seat of Christ, we will discover how many hearts have been broken and churches destroyed because of the arrogant "ministries" of people like Diotrephes. Consider what this man was doing.

He would not receive John (v. 9). It is incredible to think that a church leader (Diotrephes may have been an elder) would not have fellowship with one of our Lord's own apostles! How much Diotrephes could have learned from John! But Jesus Christ was not pre-eminent in his life, therefore Diotrephes could afford to treat the aged apostle this way.

Why did Diotrephes reject John? The obvious reason seems to be that John challenged the man's right to be dictator in the church. John was a threat to Diotrephes, because John had the authority of an apostle. John knew the truth about Diotrephes and was willing to make it known. Satan was at work in the church because Diotrephes was operating on the basis of pride and self-glorification, two of the devil's chief tools. If John appeared on the scene, Satan would be the loser.

He lied about John (v. 10a). The phrase prating against us with malicious words means "bringing false and empty charges against us." What Diotrephes was saying about John was sheer nonsense, but there are people who love to hear such talk and who will believe it! Apparently, Diotrephes had made these accusations against John at one of the church meetings when John was not present to defend himself. But John warned that the day would soon come when he would settle accounts with Diotrephes the dictator.

Christians must be careful not to believe everything that they read or hear about God's servants, particularly those servants who have a wide ministry and are well known. I have quit reading certain publications because all they print are undocumented accusations about people whose ministries God is blessing in a singular way. I mentioned a certain publication to a friend of mine one day, and he said, "Yes, I know the editor quite well. He's like a blotter: he takes everything in and gets it backward!" We would all do well to filter these reports through Philippians 4:8.

He rejected John's associates (v. 10b). Diotrephes would not even receive the other brethren because they were in fellowship with John! It was "guilt by association." It is impossible to practice this kind of "separation" with any degree of consistency, because nobody can always know all that he needs to know about what his brother is doing! If I refuse to fellowship with you because you have fellowshipped with somebody I disapprove of, how do I know the extent of your fellowship? How can I keep track of what you have done? A person would need a computer and a full-time staff if he ever hoped to do a good job of keeping his associations pure!

Scripture makes it clear that we should have no fellowship with apostates (we studied this in 2 Peter), and that we must refrain from entangling alliances with unbelievers (2 Cor. 6:14ff.). We must also avoid those whose doctrinal position is contrary to Scripture (Rom. 16:17–19). This does not mean that we cooperate only with those believers who interpret Scripture exactly as we do, because even good and godly people disagree on some matters such as church government or prophecy. All true Christians can agree on the fundamental doctrines of the faith and, in love, give latitude for disagreement on other matters.

However, to break personal fellowship with a brother because I disagree with his circle of friends is, to me, going beyond Scripture. Diotrephes rejected John, and then rejected the believers associated with John! But he went even further.

He disciplined those who disagreed with him (v. 10c). The church members who received John's associates were dismissed from the church! Again, it was guilt by association. Diotrephes had neither the authority nor the biblical basis for throwing these people out of the church, but he did it. Even "religious dictators" have to be careful lest the opposition become too strong!

The New Testament does teach church discipline, and these instructions ought to be obeyed. But church discipline is not a weapon for a dictator to use to protect himself. It is a tool for a congregation to use to promote purity and glorify God. It is not a pastor "throwing weight around" or a church board acting like a police court. It is the Lord exercising spiritual authority through a local church in order to rescue and restore an erring child of God.

Church "dictators" are dangerous people but, fortunately, they are easy to recognize. They like to talk about themselves and what they have "done for the Lord." They also have the habit of judging and condemning those who disagree with them. They are experts in putting labels on other Christians and classifying them into neat little categories of their own intention. They base their fellowship on personalities, not the doctrines that are fundamental to the faith. The tragedy is that these "dictators" actually believe that they are serving God and glorifying Jesus Christ.

It has been my experience that most of the distress and division in local churches, and between churches, has resulted from personalities more than anything else. If only we would return to the New Testament principle of making the person and work of Jesus Christ our test for fellowship, rather than associations and interpretations of nonessential doctrines. But people like Diotrephes will always have their enthusiastic followers because many sincere but immature and untaught believers prefer to follow such leaders.

Demetrius the Exemplar (11–14)

According to the dictionary, an exemplar is "an ideal, a

model, an example worthy to be imitated." Demetrius was that kind of a Christian. John warned his readers not to imitate Diotrephes. "If you want to imitate an example, then follow Demetrius!"

But is it right for us to imitate human leaders? Yes, if they in turn are imitating Jesus Christ. "Brethren, be followers together of me, and mark them which walk so as ye have us for an example" (Phil. 3:17). "Be ye followers of me, even as I also am of Christ" (1 Cor. 11:1). You and I cannot see God, but we can see God at work in the lives of His children. The godly life and dedicated service of another believer is always an encouragement and a stimulus to me. By our good example, we can "consider one another to provoke unto love and to good works" (Heb. 10:24).

Demetrius was a man worth imitating because he had a "good report" (witness) from the church fellowship. All the members knew him, loved him, and thanked God for his consistent life and ministry. While it is a dangerous thing when "all men shall speak well of you" (Luke 6:26), it is a wonderful thing when all the believers in a local church can agree to commend your life and testimony. If all men, saved and lost, good and evil, speak well of us, it may mean that we are compromising and masquerading.

But Demetrius not only had a good witness from the believers in the church; he also had a good witness from the Word (truth) itself. Like Gaius, Demetrius walked in the truth and obeyed the Word of God. This does not mean that either of these men was perfect, but it does mean that they were consistent in their lives, seeking to honor the Lord.

Both the church and the Word bore witness to Demetrius' Christian life, and so did the apostle John himself. (This meant that Demetrius would be in trouble with Diotrephes!) The beloved apostle knew firsthand that Demetrius was a man of God, and John was not ashamed to confess it.

John had warned that he was going to visit the church and confront Diotrephes (3 John 10), and no doubt both Gaius and Demetrius would stand with John in opposing the "dictator." They were the kind of men who would support the truth and submit themselves to authentic spiritual authority. Because they followed the truth, they could safely be imitated by other believers.

The conclusion of the letter (3 John 13–14) is similar to the conclusion of 2 John, and perhaps was a standard way to end letters in John's day. The apostle planned to visit the church "shortly" (soon), which certainly was a warning to Diotrephes and an encouragement to Gaius and Demetrius. The beloved John had "many things" to discuss with the assembly and its leaders, things he would rather deal with personally rather than by means of a letter.

"Peace be to thee" (3 John 14) must have been a benediction of real encouragement to Gaius! No doubt his own heart and mind were distressed because of the division in the church and the unspiritual way Diotrephes was abusing its members. George Morrison of Glasgow wrote, "Peace is the possession of adequate resources." The believer can enjoy the "peace of God" because he has adequate resources in Jesus Christ (Phil. 4:6–7, 13, 19).

John was careful to send greetings from the believers in the assembly with which he was associated at that time. "The friends send their greeting" (NIV). What a blessing it is to have Christian friends! When Paul arrived near Rome, some of the brethren went to meet him, "whom when Paul saw, he thanked God and took courage" (Acts 28:15). Both Paul and John were not only soul winners, but also friend-makers. Diotrephes was so dictatorial that he had fewer and fewer friends, but John had more and more friends as he shared the love of Christ.

"Greet the friends by name" (NASB). The aged apostle did not want to write a long letter; besides, he was planning a visit. Paul sometimes ended his letters with a list of personal greetings (see Rom. 16), but John did not do this, at least in this letter. He wanted to have Gaius convey his greetings to his friends personally and individually, as though John were doing it himself. John was not concerned about a church only, but also the individuals within that church.

It is interesting to contrast these two little letters and to see the balance of truth that John presented. Second John was written to a godly woman about her family, while 3 John was written to a godly man about his church. John warned "the elect lady" about false teachers from the outside, but he warned Gaius about dictatorial leaders inside the fellowship. The false teachers in 2 John would appeal to love so that they might deny truth, while Diotrephes would appeal to truth as, in a most unloving way, he would attack the brethren.

How important it is to walk "in truth and love" (2 John 3) and hold the truth in love (Eph. 4:15)! To claim to love the truth and yet hate the brethren is to confess ignorance of what the Christian life is all about.

When God's people love Him, the truth, and one another, then the Spirit of God can work in that assembly to glorify Jesus Christ. But when any member of that assembly, including the pastor, becomes proud and tries to have "the preeminence," then the Spirit is grieved and He cannot bless. The church may outwardly appear successful, but inwardly it will lack the true unity of the Spirit that makes for a healthy fellowship.

What we need are more people like Gaius and Demetrius—and fewer like Diotrephes!

JUDE

OUTLINE

Key theme: Overcoming the apostates
Key verses: Jude 3–4

I. INTRODUCTION (1–2)

II. THE ALARM (3–4)

III. THE ARGUMENT (5–16)

IV. THE ADMONITION (17–25)

CONTENTS

CHAPTER ONE
Jude 1–7
A CALL TO ARMS!

Since the author of this epistle was the brother of James, this would make him the half brother of our Lord Jesus Christ (see Mark 6:3). Our Lord's brothers in the flesh did not believe in Him while He was ministering (John 7:5). But after the resurrection, James was converted (see 1 Cor. 15:7), and we have every reason to believe that Jude was also saved at that time. Acts 1:14 informs us that "his brethren" were part of the praying group that was awaiting the Holy Spirit; 1 Corinthians 9:5 states that "the brethren of the Lord" were known in the early church.

So much for the identification of the author. Why did Jude write this letter? To warn his readers that the apostates were already on the scene! Peter had prophesied that they would come (2 Peter 2:1–3; 3:3ff.), and his prophecy had been fulfilled. Apparently Jude wrote to the same believers who had received Peter's letters, intending to stir them up and remind them to take Peter's warnings to heart. You will discover a number of parallels between Jude and 2 Peter as you study this fascinating but neglected letter.

He wrote to "exhort" them (Jude 3). In the Greek language, this word was used to describe a general giving orders to the army; hence the atmosphere of this letter is "military." Jude had started to write a quiet devotional letter about salvation, but the Spirit led him to put down his harp and sound the trumpet! The epistle of Jude is a call to arms.

The Army (1–2)
The Captain of the army is Jesus Christ, and the soldiers He commands are people who share a "common salvation" through faith in Him. Jude called them *saints* (Jude 3), which simply means "set-apart ones." He addressed them as *sanctified,* which, again, means "set apart." (Some manuscripts read "beloved in God the Father.") Perhaps there is an echo here of 1 Peter 1:2 where all three Persons of the Godhead are seen to be involved in our salvation.

Certainly salvation begins in the heart of God and not in the will of man (Rom. 9:16).

The mysteries of God's sovereign electing grace are beyond us in this life and will never be understood until we enter His glorious presence. For that reason, we are wise not to make them the basis for arguments and divisions. "The secret things belong unto the Lord our God" (Deut. 29:29).

Second Thessalonians 2:13–14 makes it clear that the same God who chose us also set us apart by the Spirit and then called us by the gospel to trust in Jesus Christ. God's choosing and God's calling go together, for the God who ordains the end (our salvation) also ordains the *means to the end* (someone calling us to

Christ). We did not understand how God's Spirit was working in our lives prior to our conversion, but He was working just the same to "set us apart" for Jesus Christ.

Not only are God's saints set apart, but they are also *preserved.* This means "carefully watched and guarded." The believer is secure in Jesus Christ. This same word is used in Jude 6 and 13 ("reserved") and also in Jude 21 ("keep yourselves"). God is preserving the fallen angels and the apostates for judgment, but He is preserving His own children for glory. Meanwhile, He is able to preserve us in our daily walk and keep us from stumbling.

Because they are set apart and preserved, God's soldiers are the recipients of God's choicest blessings: mercy, peace, and love. Like the apostle Peter, Jude wanted these special blessings to be *multiplied* in their lives (1 Peter 1:2; 2 Peter 1:2). God in His mercy does not give us what we deserve. Instead, He gave our punishment to His own Son on the cross. "Surely he hath borne our griefs, and carried our sorrows… But he was wounded for our transgressions, he was bruised for our iniquities" (Isa. 53:4–5).

Because of Christ's work on the cross, believers enjoy *peace.* The unsaved person is at war with God and cannot please Him (Rom. 8:7–8), but when he trusts the Savior, the war ends and he receives God's peace (Rom. 5:1).

He also experiences God's *love* (Rom. 5:5). The cross is God's demonstration of love (Rom. 5:8), but His love is not experienced within until His Spirit comes into the believing heart. As the believer grows in his spiritual life, he enters into a deeper relationship of love (John 14:21–24).

Certainly those who know Christ as their Savior enjoy a unique position. They are called *by* God to be set apart *for* God that they might enjoy love *with God.* While their fellowship with the Father might change from day to day, their relationship as children cannot change. They are "preserved in Jesus Christ." Because Jude would write a great deal in this letter about sin and judgment, he was careful at the very outset to define the special place that believers have in the heart and plan of God. The apostates would sin, fall, and suffer condemnation, but the true believers would be kept safe in Jesus Christ for all eternity.

It bears repeating that an apostate is not a true believer who has abandoned his salvation. He is a person who has professed to accept the truth and trust the Savior, and then turns from "the faith which was once delivered unto the saints" (Jude 3). Jude would not contradict what Peter wrote, and Peter made it clear that the apostates were not God's sheep, rather they were pigs and dogs (2 Peter 2:21–22). The sow had been cleaned on the outside, and the dog on the inside, but neither had been given that new nature which is characteristic of God's true children (2 Peter 1:3–4).

Here, then, we have the "spiritual army" that Jude was addressing. If you have trusted Jesus Christ, you are in this army. God is not looking for volunteers; He has already enlisted you! The question is not, "Shall I become a soldier?" Rather, it is, "Will I be a *loyal* soldier?"

Isaac Watts once preached a sermon on 1 Corinthians 16:13: "Watch ye, stand fast in the faith, quit you [act] like men, be strong." When he published the sermon, he added a poem to it; we sing it today as one of our spiritual songs.

> Am I a soldier of the Cross,
> A follower of the Lamb?
> And shall I fear to own His cause,
> Or blush to speak His name?
>
> Must I be carried to the skies
> On flowery beds of ease?
> While others fought to win the prize
> And sailed through bloody seas?

The Enemy (3–4)

We have already noted that Jude set out to write an encouraging letter about "the common salvation." The name *Jude* (Judah) means "praise," and he was anxious to praise God and rejoice in the salvation God gives in Jesus Christ. But the Spirit of God changed his mind and led Jude to write about the battle against the forces of evil in the world. Why? Because it was "needful" for the church.

I must confess that I sympathize with Jude. In my own ministry, I would much rather encourage the saints than declare war on the apostates. But when the enemy is in the field, the watchmen dare not go to sleep. The Christian life is a battleground, not a playground.

Jude wasted no time in identifying the enemy.

They were ungodly (v. 4b). This is one of Jude's favorite words. While these men *claimed* to belong to God, they were, in fact, ungodly in their thinking and their living. They might have "a form of godliness," but they lacked the *force* of godliness that lives in the true Christian (2 Tim. 3:5).

They were deceitful (v. 4c). They "crept in unawares." The Greek word means "to slip in secretly, to steal in undercover." Sometimes Satan's undercover agents are *"brought in* secretly" by those already on the inside (Gal. 2:4), but these men came in on their own. Peter warned that these men were coming (2 Peter 2:1), and now they had arrived on the scene.

How could false brethren get into true assemblies of the saints? *The soldiers had gone to sleep at the post!* The spiritual leaders in the churches had grown complacent and careless. This explains why Jude had to "blow the trumpet" to wake them up. Our Lord and His apostles all warned that false teachers would arise, yet the churches did not heed the warnings. Sad to say, some churches are not heeding the warnings today.

They were enemies of God's grace (v. 4d). Why did they enter the churches? To attempt to change the doctrine and "turn the grace of our God into lasciviousness" (Jude 4). The word *lasciviousness* simply means "wantonness, absence of moral restraint, indecency." A person who is lascivious thinks *only* of satisfying his lusts, and whatever he touches is stained by his base appetites. Lasciviousness is one of the works of the flesh (Gal. 5:19) that proceeds from the evil heart of man (Mark 7:21–22).

Peter had already warned these people that the apostates would argue, "You have been saved by grace, so you are free to live as you please!" They promised the people freedom, but it was the kind of freedom that led to terrible bondage (2 Peter 2:13–14, 19). The readers both Peter and Jude addressed knew what Paul had written (2 Peter 3:15–16), so they should have been fortified with Romans 6 and 1 Corinthians 5–6.

The apostates, like the cultists today, use the Word of God to promote and defend their false doctrines. They seduce young, immature Christians who have not yet been grounded in the Scriptures. Every soldier of the cross needs to go through "basic training" in a local church so that he knows how to use the weapons of spiritual warfare (2 Cor. 10:4–5).

They denied God's truth (v. 4e). "Even denying the Lord that bought them," Peter had warned (2 Peter 2:1). Jude was not writing about two different persons when he wrote "the only Lord God, and our Lord Jesus Christ" for the Greek construction demands that these two names refer to one Person. In other words, Jude was affirming strongly the deity of Jesus Christ Jesus Christ is God!

But the apostates would deny this. They would agree that Jesus Christ was a good man and a great teacher, but not that He was eternal God come in human flesh. The first test of any religious teacher, as we have seen, is, "What do you think of Jesus Christ? Is He God come in the flesh?" Anyone who denies this cardinal doctrine is a false teacher *no matter how correct he may be in other matters.* If he denies the deity of Christ, something will always be missing in whatever he affirms.

They were ordained to judgment (v. 4a). Jude did not write that these men were ordained to become apostates, as though God were responsible for their sin. They became apostates because they willfully turned away from the truth. But God did ordain that such people would be judged and condemned. The Old Testament prophets denounced the false prophets of their day, and both Jesus Christ and His apostles pronounced judgment on them.

Why should these men be judged by God? To begin with, they had denied His Son! That is reason enough for their condemnation! But they had also defiled God's people by teaching them that God's grace permitted them to practice sin. Furthermore, they derided the doctrine of Christ's coming (2 Peter 3). "Where is the promise of His coming?" They mocked the very promise of Christ's coming and the judgment He would bring against the ungodly.

Of course, they did all these things under the guise of religion, and this made their sin even greater. They deceived innocent people so that they might take their money and enjoy it in godless living. Jesus compared them to wolves in sheep's clothing (Matt 7:15).

How, then, should the church respond to the presence of this insidious enemy? *By earnestly contending for the faith.*

"The faith" refers to that body of doctrine that was given by God through the apostles to the church. The word *doctrine* is found at least sixteen times in the Pastoral Epistles alone. Paul admonished both Timothy and Titus to make sure the believers were being taught "sound doctrine," which means "healthy doctrine," doctrine that promotes the spiritual health of the local church. While individual teachers and preachers may disagree on the fine points of theology, there is a basic body of truth to which all true Christians are committed.

This body of truth was *delivered* (Jude 3) to the saints. The word means "to be entrusted with." The church collectively, and each Christian personally, has a stewardship to fulfill. "But as we were allowed of God to be put in trust with the gospel, even so we speak" (1 Thess. 2:4). God committed the truth to Paul (1 Tim. 1:11), and he shared it with others, such as Timothy (1 Tim. 6:20). He exhorted Timothy to entrust the Word to other faithful men (2 Tim. 2:2). You and I would not have the Word today were it not for faithful believers down through the ages who guarded this precious deposit and invested it in others.

The church is always one generation short of extinction. If *our* generation fails to guard the truth and entrust it to our children, then that will be the end! When you think of the saints and martyrs who suffered and died so that we might have God's truth, it makes you want to take your place in God's army and be faithful unto death.

What does it mean to "contend for the faith"? The Greek word is an athletic term that gives us our English word, *agonize.* It is the picture of a devoted athlete, competing in the Greek games and stretching his nerves and muscles to do his very best to win. You never fight the Lord's battles from a rocking chair or a soft bed! Both the soldier and the athlete must concentrate on doing their best and giving their all. There must also be teamwork, believers working together to attack and defeat the enemy.

Sometimes you hear well-meaning people say, "Well, it's fine to contend for the faith, but don't be so contentious!" While it is true that some of God's soldiers have been the cause of quarrels and divisions, it is also true that some of them have paid a great price to defend the faith. As Christian soldiers, we must not fight each other or go around looking for trouble. But when the banner of Christ is in danger of being taken by the enemy, we cannot sit idly by,

nor can we ever hope to win the victory by wearing kid gloves.

Charles Spurgeon once said that "the new views are not the old truth in a better dress, but deadly errors with which we can have no fellowship." False doctrine is a deadly poison that must be identified, labeled, and avoided. Spurgeon also said, "I cannot endure false doctrine, however neatly it may be put before me. Would you have me eat poisoned meat because the dish is of the choicest ware?"

We must always speak the truth in love, and the weapons we use must be spiritual. At the same time, we must dare to take our stand for "the faith" even if our stand offends some and upsets others. We are not fighting personal enemies, but the enemies of the Lord. It is the honor and glory of Jesus Christ that is at stake. "Fight the good fight of faith" (1 Tim. 6:12).

The Victory (5–7)

Like the apostle Peter, Jude reached back into Old Testament history and gave three examples of God's victory over those who had resisted his authority and turned from the truth. Peter referred to the fallen angels, Noah, and Lot (2 Peter 2:4–9) and followed the historical order. He also emphasized God's deliverance of the righteous as well as His judgment of the ungodly. Jude, however, did not mention Noah and the flood, but instead used the nation Israel as his example.

The point Jude was making is that *God judges apostates.* Therefore, the false teachers who had crept into the church would also one day be judged. Their seeming success would not last; God would have the last word.

Israel (v. 5). Both Paul (1 Cor. 10) and the author of Hebrews (Heb. 3–4) used the experiences of Israel to illustrate important spiritual truths. The nation was delivered from Egypt by the power of God and brought to the border of the Promised Land. But the people were afraid and did not have the faith to enter in and possess the land (see Num. 13–14). Moses, Joshua, and Caleb tried to encourage the people to obey God by faith, but the people refused. In fact, the leaders of the tribes even wanted to organize and go back to Egypt, the place of bondage!

This was rebellion against the will and the Word of God, and God cannot tolerate rebellion. As a result, everybody in the camp twenty years and older was destined to die at some time in the next forty years. Their unbelief led to their extermination.

Keep in mind that Jude was using a historical event as an illustration, and we must not press every detail. The entire nation was delivered from Egypt, but that does not mean that each individual was personally saved through faith in the Lord. The main point of the account is that privileges bring responsibilities, and God cannot lightly pass over the sins of His people. If any of Jude's readers dared to follow the false teachers, they too would face the discipline of God. "Wherefore let him that thinketh he standeth take heed lest he fall" (1 Cor. 10:12).

The fallen angels (v. 6). We studied this illustration in 2 Peter 2:4, but Jude seems to add a new dimension to it by associating the fall of the angels with the destruction of Sodom and Gomorrah (Jude 7, "even as … in like manner"). Some Bible students believe that Jude was teaching not only a revolt of the angels against God, but also an invasion of earth by these fallen angels. They point to Genesis 6:1–4 and claim that "the sons of God" were fallen angels who assumed human bodies, cohabited with the daughters of men, and produced a race of giants on the earth. This was one reason that God sent the flood.

As attractive and popular as this view is, I must confess that I have a difficult time accepting it. It is true that "the sons of God" is a title for angels (Job 1:6; 2:1; 38:7), but always for *unfallen* angels. Would the Holy Spirit, writing through Moses, call *rebellious* angels "the sons of God"? I doubt it.

My second problem is that angels are spirits and do not have bodies. In the Old Testament record, we do read of angels who *appeared* in human form, but this was not incarnation. How could a spirit being have a physical relationship with a woman, even if that being assumed a temporary body of some kind? Our Lord taught that the angels were sexless (Matt. 22:30).

Third, it appears that God sent the flood because of what *man* did, not what angels did. "My Spirit shall not always strive with *man*… And God saw that the wickedness of *man* was great in the earth… And it repented [grieved] the Lord that he had made *man* on the earth" (Gen. 6:3, 5–6, italics mine). If this "fallen angel" view is correct, God should have repented that He created *the angels!*

Fourth, the phrases "even as" and "in like manner" in Genesis 6:7 need not be interpreted to say that the angels did what the Sodomites did, namely, "going after strange flesh." Notice the grammatical connections in the verse, and you will get the message: "Even as Sodom and Gomorrah… in like manner… are set forth for an example." The angels are an example of God's judgment and so are Sodom and Gomorrah.

I might add that Genesis 6:4 presents a strong argument *against* the view that fallen angels cohabited with women and produced a race of giants. "There were giants in the earth in those days; *and also after that*" (italics mine). This would mean that a *second* invasion of fallen angels had to take place! We have no record of this in Scripture.

Finally, both Peter and Jude state clearly that these rebellious angels are chained in darkness and reserved for judgment. They would have to have invaded the earth *prior* to being arrested and chained by God. We wonder why God would have permitted them to "run loose" long enough to get the women into sin and help to cause the great flood. The whole explanation, though held by teachers whom I respect, to me seems a bit fantastic. The simplest explanation of Genesis 6 is

that the godly line of Seth ("the sons of God") began to mingle with the ungodly line of Cain, and this broke down the walls of separation, resulting in compromise and eventually degrading sin. But regardless of which interpretation you accept, keep the main lesson in mind: the angels rebelled and were punished for their rebellion.

Sodom and Gomorrah (v. 7). Both Peter and Jude state that God made these cities an example to warn the ungodly that God does indeed judge sin (see 2 Peter 2:6). When you combine their descriptions, you discover that the citizens of Sodom and Gomorrah (and the other cities involved) were: ungodly, filthy, wicked, unlawful, unjust, and given over to fornication. They did not *occasionally* commit unnatural sexual sins; they indulged in them and gave themselves over to the pursuit of lust. The Greek verb is intensive: "to indulge in excessive immorality." This was their way of life—and death!

Strange flesh means "different flesh." The bent of their life was constantly downward, indulging in unnatural acts (see Rom. 1:24–27). Those who hold the "fallen angel" interpretation of Genesis 6 make the "strange flesh" refer to angels in human form, but when did the angels invade Sodom and Gomorrah? And, if fallen angels are meant, how can their sin and the sin of the Sodomites apply to us today, for we have no fallen angels to tempt or seduce us? Indeed, the men at Lot's door did want to engage in homosexual activity with his angelic guests, but the Sodomites did not know they were angels. Another possibility is that the Sodomites were guilty not only of unnatural sex with each other, but also with animals, which would be "strange flesh." Both homosexuality and bestiality are condemned by God (Lev. 18:22–25).

These cities were *set forth* by God as an example and warning to ungodly people today. The verb *set forth* means "to expose openly to public view." (Interestingly enough, the word was used to describe a corpse lying in state!) But the cities of the plain are not *today* in public view. It is generally agreed among archeologists that Sodom and Gomorrah are buried under the southern end of the Dead Sea. How, then, do they serve as an example? *In the pages of the Word of God.* No one can read Genesis 18–19 without clearly seeing God's hatred for sin and, at the same time, His patience and willingness to postpone judgment. This certainly ties in with Peter's explanation for God's seeming delay in fulfilling the promise of Christ's return (2 Peter 3:8ff.).

The sin of Israel was rebellious unbelief (Heb. 3:12). The sin of the angels was rebellion against the throne of God. The sin of Sodom and Gomorrah was indulging in unnatural lust. Unbelief, rebellion against authority, and sensual indulgence were sins characteristic of the false teachers. The conclusion is obvious: the apostates will be judged. But, meanwhile, God's soldiers must stay on duty and see to it that these false teachers do not creep into the ranks and start to lead people astray. "Take heed unto thyself, and unto the doctrine" (1 Tim. 4:16).

What can we do practically to oppose the enemy and maintain the purity and unity of the church? For one thing, we must know the Word of God and have the courage to defend it. Every local church ought to be a Bible institute, and every Christian ought to be a Bible student. The pulpit needs to declare positive truth as well as denounce error.

Second, we must "watch and pray." The enemy is already here and we dare not go to sleep! Spiritual leaders in local congregations need to be alert as they interview candidates for baptism and church membership. Committees need to seek the mind of Christ as they appoint Sunday school teachers, youth sponsors, and other church leaders. Congregations must exercise discernment as they select officers.

Third, congregations and members must be careful where they send their money. "Should you help the wicked and love those who hate the Lord?" (see 2 Chron. 19:2).

Finally, we must have the courage to maintain a position of biblical separation from those who deny Christ and the fundamental doctrines of the Word (Rom. 16:17–20; 2 Tim. 2:15ff.; 2 John 6–11). This does not mean that we separate from fellow believers over minor doctrinal differences, or that we practice "guilt by association." God's true army needs to stand together in the battle for truth.

Have you heeded the call to arms?

CHAPTER TWO
Jude 8–16
MEET THE APOSTATES!

Jude was not content simply to remind his readers to pay attention to what Peter had written. He wanted to add his own words of warning by describing what the false teachers were like and what they would do to the church. The Spirit of God led Jude to describe the characteristics of the apostates, reinforcing Peter's words and, at the same time, adding information. Jude 8–16 and 2 Peter 2 parallel and supplement each other.

But why this seemingly needless repetition? The apostle Paul gave the answer: "To write the same things to you, to me indeed is not grievous, but for you it is safe" (Phil. 3:1). Parents repeat warnings and instructions to their children, and sometimes the children reply, "I know that! You've already told me a million times!" But wise parents know that some things *must* be said again and again for the safety and welfare of their children—whether the children want to hear them or not!

All that Jude wrote about the apostates in these verses may be summarized in three statements.

They Reject Divine Authority (8–11)

All authority comes from the throne of God, whether it is authority in the home, the church, or the state. Those who exercise authority must first be *under* authority, accountable to God. But the false teachers reject divine authority and set themselves up as their own authority.

The *cause* of their rebellion is found in the word *dreamers* (Jude 8). These people live in a dream world of unreality and delusion. They believe Satan's lie, "Ye shall be as gods" (Gen. 3:5). Having turned away from God's truth, they feed their minds on false doctrine that inflates their egos and encourages their rebellion. Jude 10 informs us that the apostates are ignorant people who do not know what they are talking about! Jude echoed Peter's description of these men as "brute beasts" (2 Peter 2:12, 22). Animals live by natural instinct, and so do the apostates. When men rebel against God, they sink to the level of beasts.

The *course* of their rebellion was clearly described by Jude. As a result of their rebellion and pride, they "defile the flesh," living to satisfy their animal lusts. When a person despises God's authority, he feels free to disobey God's laws and live as he pleases. What he forgets is that those laws have penalties attached to them so that he cannot disobey and escape the consequences.

They also use their tongues to express their rebellion against God. "With our tongue will we prevail; our lips are our own: who is lord over us?" (Ps. 12:4). The phrase, *speak evil,* in Jude 8 and 10 simply means "to blaspheme." Blasphemy involves much more than taking God's name in vain, though that is at the heart of it. A person blasphemes God when he takes His Word lightly and even jests about it, or when he deliberately defies God to judge him. "They set their mouth against the heavens, and their tongue walketh through the earth. And they say, 'How doth God know? and is there knowledge in the Most High?'" (Ps. 73:9, 11).

The *consequence* of their rebellion is seen in their own ruin: "they corrupt [destroy] themselves" (Jude 10). They defile themselves (Jude 8) and they destroy themselves, yet they have the idea they are promoting themselves! "Because sentence against an evil work is not executed speedily, therefore the heart of the sons of men is fully set in them to do evil" (Eccl. 8:11). The way of rebellion is but the way to ruin.

Arrogant speech is a dangerous thing, and so is despising the authority that God has established. Even the archangel Michael (Dan. 10:13) did not dare to rebuke Satan, but respected the authority given to him by God. The name *Michael* means "Who is like God?" Ironically, Satan had said in his rebellion, "I will be like the Most High!" (Isa. 14:14), and his offer to men is, "Ye shall be as gods" (Gen. 3:5).

We have no information about the conflict between Satan and Michael over the body of Moses. When Moses died, the Lord buried him and no one knew where the sepulcher was located (Deut. 34:5–6). No doubt the Jewish people would have made a shrine out of the sepulcher and fallen into idolatry, so God kept the information to Himself. The text tells us that "not any man" knew the place, so perhaps Satan did know the place and tried to claim Moses' body for himself. Inasmuch as Satan does have a certain amount of authority in the realm of death he may have felt he had a right to interfere (Heb. 2:14–15).

The point is that Michael did not rebuke Satan, but left that to the Lord. It is a dangerous thing for God's people to confront Satan directly and to argue with him, because he is much stronger than we are. If an archangel is careful about the way he deals with the devil, how much more cautious ought we to be! While it is true that we share in the victory of Christ, it is also true that we must not be presumptuous. Satan is a dangerous enemy, and when we resist him, we must be sober and vigilant (1 Peter 5:8–9).

"The Lord rebuke thee!" has a parallel in Zechariah 3:1–5. The prophet had a vision of the high priest standing before God's throne in defiled garments, symbolizing the sinful condition of the nation Israel after the Babylonian captivity. Satan had every right to accuse the people (see Rev. 12:9–11), except for one thing: they were the chosen ones of God, His covenant people, and He would not go back on His Word. God forgave His people, gave them clean garments, and warned them to walk in His ways. This is an Old Testament illustration of 1 John 1:5–2:2.

The *condemnation* of the false teachers is given in Jude 11: "Woe unto them!" Jude cited three examples from the Old Testament to illustrate the enormity of their sins, three men who rebelled against God's authority and who suffered for it.

Cain rebelled against God's way of salvation (Gen. 4; 1 John 3:11–12). By clothing Adam and Eve with the skins of slain animals (Gen. 3:21), God made it clear that the only way of forgiveness is through the shedding of blood. This is the way of faith, not the way of good works (Eph. 2:8–10). But Cain rejected this divinely authorized way and came to the altar with the fruits of his own labor. God rejected Cain's offering because God rejected Cain: his heart was not right before God. It was *by faith* that Abel's sacrifice was offered, and that was why God accepted it (Heb. 11:4).

The "way of Cain" is the way of religion without faith, righteousness based on character and good works. The "way of Cain" is the way of pride, a man establishing his own righteousness and rejecting the righteousness of God that comes through faith in Christ (Rom. 10:1–4; Phil. 3:3–12). Cain became a fugitive and tried to overcome his wretchedness by building a city and developing a civilization (Gen. 4:9ff.). He ended up with everything a man could desire, everything, that is, except God.

We have already studied "the way of Balaam" (see 2 Peter 2:15–16). The "way of Balaam" is merchandising one's gifts and ministry just for the purpose of making money. It is using the spiritual to gain the material (see 1 Thess. 2:5–6; 1 Tim. 6:3–21). The false teachers were greedy for material gain and, like Balaam, would do anything for money. The "error of Balaam" is thinking that they can get away with this kind of rebellion. Balaam was a true prophet of God, but he prostituted his gifts and sought to destroy God's people. God turned Balaam's curses into blessings (Deut 23:4–5).

While we are on the subject of Balaam, we might note the "doctrine of Balaam" (Rev. 2:14), which is, "You can violate your separated position and get away with it!" He told King Balak that the fastest way to destroy Israel would be to corrupt the nation by having the people defile themselves with the heathen nations around them. "You are God's chosen people," was the argument. "Certainly a little friendship with your neighbors will not hurt you!" It was "turning the grace of… God into lasciviousness" (Jude 4), and God judged both Israel and Balaam.

The story of Core (Korah) is found in Numbers 16, and it too centers on rebellion against authority. Korah and his followers resented the leadership of Moses and dared God to do anything about their rebellion. In speaking against ("gainsaying") Moses, they were speaking against the Lord who had given Moses his authority. This is a warning to us today, for it is so easy to speak against spiritual or governmental leaders in a careless way (see Titus 3:1–2). God judged Korah and his followers and established clearly the authority of His servant, Moses.

Cain rebelled against God's authority in *salvation,* for he refused to bring a blood sacrifice as God had commanded. Balaam rebelled against God's authority in *separation,* for he prostituted his gifts for money and led Israel to mix with the other nations. Korah rebelled against God's authority in *service,* denying that Moses was God's appointed servant and attempting to usurp his authority.

It is interesting to note the verbs that Jude used in this verse. The apostates "traveled on the road" of Cain, "gave themselves over to" the error of Balaam, and "perished" in the rebellion of Korah. The tragedy of rejecting authority!

They Resort to Deliberate Hypocrisy (12–13, 16)

Jude 12 and 13 present six vivid pictures of the false teachers and help to explain why they are dangerous to the church.

Filthy spots (v. 12a). Peter called them spots and blemishes (2 Peter 2:13). These men had invaded the "love feasts" in the local assemblies, but all they did was defile them. Instead of adding to the sanctity of the occasion, they detracted from it, like Judas at the last Passover that Jesus celebrated with His disciples. The tragedy is that the members of the assembly did not realize the true character of these men! They thought the men were spiritual!

The Greek word translated "spots" can also mean "hidden rocks." The mariner who is unaware of the hidden rocks can quickly wreck his ship. The pilot must always be alert, for waters that look calm and safe can contain treacherous reefs. Spiritual leaders must constantly be on guard.

Selfish shepherds (v. 12b). The word translated "feeding" means "shepherding." Instead of shepherding the flock and caring for the needs of the people, these apostates only take care of themselves. Jude may have had in mind Isaiah 56:10–12 and Ezekiel 34, where the prophets condemned the political and spiritual leaders of the nation ("shepherds") for exploiting the people and caring only for themselves.

It is a serious thing to be a shepherd over God's flock. Our example must be Jesus Christ, the Good Shepherd who gave His life for the sheep. False shepherds *use* and *abuse* people in order to get what they want, and yet all the while, *the people love it!* Paul marveled at this when he wrote 2 Corinthians 11:20—"You don't mind, do you, if a man takes away your liberty, spends your money, takes advantage of you, puts on airs, or even smacks your face?" (PH).

These selfish shepherds do all of this "without fear." They are an arrogant lot! This is the difference between a true shepherd and a hireling: the true shepherd cares for the sheep, while the hireling cares only for himself. "Woe be to the shepherds of Israel that do feed themselves! Should not the shepherds feed the flocks?" (Ezek. 34:2). But these apostates *ought* to be afraid, for their judgment is coming.

Empty clouds (v. 12c). Clouds that promise rain, but fail to produce, are a disappointment to the farmer whose crops desperately need water. The apostates look like men who can give spiritual help, and they boast of their abilities, but they are unable to produce. "Whoso boasteth himself of a false gift [a gift he does not give] is like clouds and wind without rain" (Prov. 25:14). They promise liberty, but they can only give bondage (2 Peter 2:19).

The Word of God is sometimes compared to the rain and the dew. "My doctrine shall drop as the rain, my speech shall distill as the dew" (Deut. 32:2). Isaiah 55:10 compares God's Word to the rain and snow from heaven that bring fruit on the earth. Like the clouds in the sky, the false teachers may be prominent and even attractive, but if they cannot bring rain, they are useless.

Dead trees (v. 12d). The picture is that of an orchard in autumn, the time when the farmer expects fruit. But these trees are fruitless! "Ye shall know them by their fruits" (Matt. 7:16). Those who teach and preach the Word have the responsibility of feeding others, but the false teachers have nothing to give. Not only are they fruitless, but they are also rootless ("plucked up by the root"); this is why they are "twice dead." What a contrast to the godly man in Psalm 1:3!

One of the evidences of true salvation is producing spiritual fruit. The seed that fell on the hard soil, the shallow soil, and the crowded soil did not produce fruit, but the seed that fell on the "good ground" did produce fruit (Matt. 13:1–9, 18–23). No matter how much of the Bible the false teachers may quote, the seed is not producing fruit in their own lives or through their ministries. Why? Because they have no spiritual roots. They lack spiritual life.

Fruit has in it the seed for more fruit (Gen. 1:11–12). One of the evidences that a ministry is truly of God is that the fruit multiplies. Manufactured "results" are sterile and dead, but true fruit continues to grow and reproduce itself in the lives of others.

Raging waves (v, 13a). I personally do not enjoy being *in* or *on* the ocean (I am not a good swimmer). However, I do enjoy sitting *by* the ocean and contemplating its grandeur and power. But I certainly would not want to be either in or on the ocean in a storm! There is great power in those waves, as many a mariner has discovered. But Jude compared the apostates to "raging waves of the sea" not because of their power, but because of their pride and arrogant speech. "Their mouth speaketh great swelling words" (Jude 16). Like the swelling of the sea, they make a lot of noise, *but what do they produce?* Have you ever walked along the beach the morning after a storm and seen the ugly refuse that has been deposited on the shore?

Jude may have had Isaiah 57:20 in mind: "But the wicked are like the troubled sea, when it cannot rest, whose waters cast up mire and dirt." All that the "great swelling words" of the apostates can produce is foam and flotsam! The true teachers of the Word bring up the treasures of the deep, but the false teachers produce only refuse. And what they boast about, they really ought to be ashamed of (see Phil. 3:19)!

Wandering stars (v. 13b). Jude was not referring to fixed stars, planets, or comets, because they have definite positions and orbits. He was referring to meteors, falling stars that suddenly appear and then vanish into the darkness, never to be seen again. Our Lord is compared to a star (Rev. 2:28; 22:16), and Christians are to shine as stars in this dark world (Phil. 2:15). Fixed stars can be depended on to guide the traveler through the darkness, but wandering stars can only lead him astray.

One of my hobbies is collecting books of sermons, not only by famous preachers, but also by obscure and forgotten men whose names once were famous. I have noticed that many a "pulpit beacon" has turned out to be a fallen star! It is disturbing to read histories and biographies and see how "the mighty have fallen." For the most part, those who have been true to the Word are ministering yet today as lights shining in the darkness, while the preachers of false doctrine have fallen into oblivion.

God has reserved chains of darkness for the rebellious angels (Jude 6), and He has reserved "the blackness of darkness forever" for apostate teachers. Beware of following a falling star! It will lead you into eternal blackness!

As you review these six pictures of the false teachers, you can easily see how dangerous they are and how important it is for the church to keep them out.

Murmurers and complainers (v. 16). Jude 16 completes the description and emphasizes even more why they are so dangerous: they are out to please themselves by taking advantage of others. This reminds us of Peter's statement (2 Peter 2:14), "A heart they have exercised with covetous practices" or, as Phillips translates it, "Their technique of getting what they want is, through long practice, highly developed." They give the impression that they are out to help you, but they are interested only in gratifying their own lusts.

What is their approach? For one thing, they murmur and complain and cause people to become dissatisfied with life. While each of us should do all we can, as God enables us, to improve our lot in life, at the same time we must be careful not to criticize God's providences or hinder His plans. The nation of Israel was judged because of her complaining (1 Cor. 10:1–10), and Christians are commanded not to complain (Phil. 2:14–16). If a false teacher can make a person critical of his pastor or church, or dissatisfied with his situation, he then can lead him astray into false doctrine.

The false teachers also use "great swelling words" to impress ignorant people. Peter called their speeches "great swelling words of vanity" (2 Peter 2:18). They impress people with their vocabularies and oratory, but what they say is just so much "hot air." They also use flattery to manipulate their listeners. They "bow and scrape" and pay compliments to others, *if* it is to their advantage.

Knowing these things, we are amazed that anybody would listen to these apostates and follow them, but many people are doing it today! There is something in fallen human nature that loves a lie and is willing to follow it, no matter where it may lead. But the success of the apostates is only temporary, for their judgment is coming.

They Receive Their Due Penalty (14–15)

All that we know about Enoch from Scripture is found in Genesis 5:18–24; Hebrews 11:5; and these two verses in Jude. He is called "the seventh from Adam" to identify him as the *godly* Enoch, since Cain had a son of the same name (Gen. 4:17). In a society that was rapidly being polluted and destroyed by sin, Enoch walked with God and kept his life clean. He also ministered as a prophet and announced the coming judgment.

Bible scholars tell us that this quotation is from an apocryphal book called *The Book of Enoch*. The fact that Jude quoted from this nonbiblical book does not mean the book is inspired and trustworthy, any more than Paul's quotations from the Greek poets put God's "seal of approval" on everything they wrote. The Spirit of God led Jude to use this quotation and make it a part of the inspired Scriptures.

When Enoch originally gave this message, it is possible that he was also referring to the coming judgment of the flood. He certainly lived in an ungodly age, and it seemed that sinners were getting away with their evil deeds. But Enoch made it clear that judgment

was coming and that the ungodly would get what was coming to them!

However, the final application of this prophecy is to the world in the end times, the very judgment that Peter wrote about in 2 Peter 3. The false teachers mocked this prophecy and argued that Jesus Christ would never come and God would never send judgment. But their very attitude was proof that the Word is true, for both our Lord and His apostles, as well as the prophets, said that scoffers and mockers would appear in the last days (2 Peter 3:1–4). Enoch gave his prophecy thousands of years ago! See how patient God has been with those who have rebelled against Him!

What does Enoch's prophecy say about the coming judgment? It will be a *personal* judgment: God Himself will come to judge the world. He will not send a famine or a flood, nor will He assign the task to an angel. He Himself will come. This shows the seriousness of the event, and also its finality. "Behold, the Judge standeth before the door" (James 5:9).

Though it is a personal judgment, our Lord will not judge alone; the saints of God will be with Him. The word *saints* in Jude 14 means "holy ones" and can also refer to the angels (Deut. 33:2; Matt. 25:31). However, we know from Revelation 19:14; Colossians 3:4; and 1 Thessalonians 3:13 that the people of God will accompany the Lord when He returns to earth to defeat His enemies and establish His righteous kingdom (cf. 1 Cor. 6:2–3). Over the centuries, the people of God have suffered at the hands of the ungodly, but one day the tables will be turned.

It will be a *universal* judgment. He will execute judgment "upon all"—none will escape. Just as the flood destroyed all who were outside the ark, and the fire and brimstone destroyed all in Sodom and Gomorrah except Lot and his wife and two daughters, so the last judgment will encompass all the ungodly. The word *ungodly is* used four times in this one verse! It will be "the day of judgment and perdition [ruin, destruction] of ungodly men" (2 Peter 3:7).

It will be a *just* judgment. God will convict ("convince") them of their sins, declare them guilty, pass sentence on them, and then execute the punishment. There will be a Judge, Jesus Christ (John 5:22), but no jury. There will be prosecution, but no defense, for every mouth will be stopped (Rom. 3:19). There will be a sentence, but no appeal, for there can be no higher court than God's final judgment. The entire procedure will be just, for the righteous Son of God will be in charge.

The Lord will have the record of their "ungodly deeds." He will also have a record of their motives and hidden desires as they committed these deeds and even these will be ungodly! He will recall the "hard speeches" (Jude 15) that they uttered against the Lord. The word *hard* carries the idea of "rough, harsh, stern, uncivil." After all, these people were "murmurers" and "complainers" (Jude 16) and spoke harsh things against God. They were not "afraid to speak evil of dignities"

(2 Peter 2:10), but at the judgment their words will testify against them. They spoke "great swelling words" (2 Peter 2:18; Jude 16), but at the judgment their great words will bring great wrath.

There are times when God's children ask, "Lord, how long shall the wicked, how long shall the wicked triumph? How long shall they utter and speak hard things? and all the workers of iniquity boast themselves?" (Ps. 94:3–4). The answer is given in Psalm 50:3—"Our God shall come, and shall not keep silence: a fire shall devour before him, and it shall be very tempestuous round about him."

The words are familiar, but what James Russell Lowell wrote in "The Present Crisis" certainly applies today.

> Careless seems the great Avenger;
> history's pages but record
> One death-grapple in the darkness
> 'twix old systems and the Word;
> Truth forever on the scaffold,
> Wrong forever on the throne—
> Yet that scaffold sways the future,
> and, behind the dim unknown,
> Standeth God within the shadow,
> keeping watch above His own....

"Nevertheless we, according to His promise, look for new heavens and a new earth, wherein dwelleth righteousness" (2 Peter 3:13).

"Even so, come, Lord Jesus!"

CHAPTER THREE
Jude 17–25
YOU DON'T HAVE TO STUMBLE

I read somewhere that the Great Wall of China was penetrated at least three times by the enemy, and each time the guards were bribed!

A strong defense depends on strong people, and this applies to spiritual battles as well as military contests. If the church is to oppose and defeat the false teachers, then all of us in the church must be strong and able to "stand against the wiles of the devil" (Eph. 6:11). There is always the danger of stumbling (Jude 24), and a stumble is the first step toward a fall.

In this closing paragraph, Jude addressed his beloved readers and gave them four instructions to follow if they would stand firm and resist the apostates.

Remember God's Word (17–19)
From the very beginning, Satan has attacked the Word of God. "Yea, hath God said?" was his opening thrust when he led Eve into disobedience in the garden (Gen. 3:1). Once we begin to question God's Word, we are vulnerable to Satan's other attacks, for only the truth of the Word can protect us from the lies of the devil.

"To the law and to the testimony: if they speak not according to this word, it is because there is no light in them" (Isa. 8:20).

Remember who gave the Word (v. 17). While our Lord had many disciples, He selected only a few to be *apostles.* The word means "one who is sent with a commission." In order to qualify, a believer had to be a witness of the resurrection of Christ (Acts 1:21–22; 1 Cor. 9:1). The apostles lived with Christ during His ministry, learned from Him, and were sent by Him into all the world to carry the good news of salvation.

Wherever there is the authentic, the counterfeit will appear; this happened in the early church. False apostles and teachers began to appear, and it was necessary to develop a system to protect the church against false prophecies and forged letters. Since Christ had committed "the faith" (Jude 3) to His apostles, one of the main tests in the early church was, "Is this what the apostles taught?" When the church assembled the New Testament books, it was required that each book be written either by an apostle or by someone closely associated with an apostle. Apostolic teaching was, and still is, the test of truth.

Jude mentioned the words that were "spoken" by the apostles, because originally there were no New Testament epistles. Over the years, inspired letters were written by Paul, Peter, and John; we have these letters in our New Testament. We also have a record of some of their sermons in the book of Acts. We no longer depend on tradition since we have the completed Scriptures, both the Old Testament and the New.

Whenever somebody offers you a "new revelation," test it by what the apostles wrote and by what Jesus Christ taught. You will soon discover that the "revelation" is a lie.

Remember what they said (v. 18). They prophesied that, in these last days, mockers would come who would deny the Word of God. Jude echoed what Peter had written (2 Peter 3:3ff.), but Paul and John also warned their readers about the apostates (1 Tim. 4; 2 Tim. 3; 1 John 2:18ff.; 4:1–6). When a warning is given so many times, it behooves us to take it seriously!

The phrase "walking after their own lusts" appears in 2 Peter 3:3 and Jude 16 and 18, and it explains *why* the apostates deny God's truth: they do not want God to tell them how to live. They want to satisfy their own sinful desires, and the Word of God condemns their selfish way of life. When a person says, "I have intellectual problems with the Bible," he probably has *moral* problems because the Bible contradicts what he is doing. The only sure way to know the truth of the Bible is by obeying it (John 7:17).

Before Satan can substitute his own lies, he must get rid of the truth of God's Word. If he cannot argue it away, he will laugh it away, and he can usually find somebody to laugh with him.

Remember why they said it (v. 19). The false teachers want to divide the church and lead people out of the true fellowship into their false fellowship. "Also of your own selves shall men arise, speaking perverse things, to draw away disciples after them" (Acts 20:30). Their appeal is usually, "We have a deeper knowledge of the Word that your church doesn't have! We have a better understanding of prophecy, or of the Christian life, than you do." They offer a "higher quality" religion than that of the apostles.

Not only do false teachers divide the church, but they also deceive the church, because they are "sensual, having not the Spirit." The word *sensual* means the opposite of "spiritual." This is the way Paul used it in 1 Corinthians 2:14–16, where it is translated "natural." (The Greek word is *psukikos,* which means "soulish.") Because the false teachers do not have the Spirit of God, they must function on their natural "soul power" alone.

One of the tragedies in ministry today is that some of God's people cannot discern between "soul ministry" and the true ministry of the Spirit. There is so much "religious showmanship" these days that the saints are confused and deceived. Just as there was "false fire" in the tabernacle (Lev. 10), so there is "false fire" today in the church; therefore we must exercise careful discernment.

How can we discern between the "soulish" and the "spiritual"? By using the Word of God which is able to divide soul and spirit (Heb. 4:12) and by paying close attention to the witness of the Spirit of God within (Rom. 8:16). A "soulish" ministry magnifies man, but the Spirit glorifies Jesus Christ. When the Spirit is ministering through the Word, there is edification; but when the soul is merely "manufacturing" a ministry, there is entertainment or, at best, only intellectual education. It takes the Spirit of God to minister to our spirits and to make us more like Jesus Christ.

Build Your Christian Life (20–21)

The Christian life must never stand still; if it does, it will go backward. A house left to itself falls apart. The apostates are in the business of tearing down, but each Christian must be involved in building up—first, his own spiritual life and then his local assembly.

The foundation for our Christian life is our "most holy faith" (Jude 20), which is the same as "the faith which was once delivered unto the saints" (Jude 3). There is a sense, of course, in which our faith in Jesus Christ is the basis for our growth, but even that faith depends on what God has revealed to us in His Word. Subjective faith depends on objective revelation of truth.

The Word of God is certainly central in spiritual growth. I have yet to meet a strong, fruitful Christian who ignores his Bible. We must daily spend devotional time in the Word, seeking the mind of God. We must also study the Word regularly, in a disciplined way, so that we better understand what it teaches. The gifted Chinese preacher, Watchman Nee, used to read through the New Testament once a month. This becomes apparent when you read his books, for you are struck with his wonderful insights into God's Word. The members of the Chinese church used to have a

saying, "No Bible—no breakfast!" If we followed that motto in America, I wonder how many Christians would go hungry.

The power for building the Christian life comes from prayer: "praying in the Holy Ghost" (Jude 20). The Word of God and prayer go together in spiritual growth. If all we do is read and study the Bible, we will have a great deal of light, but not much power. However, if we concentrate on prayer and ignore the Bible, we may be guilty of zeal without knowledge. We read the Word to grow in faith (Rom. 10:17), then we use that faith to ask God for what we need and what His Word tells us we may have.

The Word of God and prayer certainly go together (Acts 6:4). Evangelist Billy Sunday used to give his converts three rules for success in the Christian life. Each day they were to read the Bible and let God talk to them. They were to pray; in other words, they were to talk to God. And they were to witness and talk to others about God. It would be difficult to improve on those rules.

What does it mean to "pray in the Holy Spirit"? (Note the contrast with Jude 19— "having not the Spirit.") It means to pray according to the leading of the Spirit. It has well been said, "Prayer is not getting man's will done in heaven—it is getting God's will done on earth." This agrees with 1 John 5:14–15.

As Christians, we may pray in solitude (Matt. 6:6), but we never pray *alone;* the Spirit of God joins with us as we pray (Rom. 8:26–28) because He knows the mind of God and can direct us. He can give us wisdom and knowledge from the Word (Eph. 1:15ff.). He can also help us approach the Father through the access we have in Jesus Christ (Eph. 2:18). We worship God "in the Spirit" (Phil. 3:3), and the Spirit motivates us to pray, for He is "the Spirit of grace and of supplications" (Zech. 12:10). When the believer is yielded to the Spirit, then the Spirit will assist him in his prayer life, and God will answer prayer.

This "building process" in the Christian life involves the Word of God, the Spirit of God, and prayer. But these things, as precious as they are, can become somewhat routine; so Jude added another factor *abiding in God's love* (Jude 21). He did not write, "Keep yourselves saved!" because he had already assured them that they were "preserved in Jesus Christ" (Jude 1). He wrote, "Keep yourselves in the love of God." Our Lord made a similar statement recounted in John 15:9— "Continue ye in my love."

To love God means much more than to enjoy a special kind of feeling. Of course, as we grow in grace, we do experience deeper fellowship with the Father (John 14:21–24), and we do have times when He seems very near. The Bible compares this to the love of a husband and wife (Eph. 5:22ff.). Any happily married couple can tell you that love deepens over the years.

But it takes more than ecstatic feelings to make a successful marriage—or a successful Christian life! There must also be obedience and mutual concern. "But whoso keepeth his word, in him verily is the love of God perfected" (1 John 2:5). "If ye keep my commandments, ye shall abide in my love" (John 15:10). We grow in our love for God as we listen to His Word, obey it, and delight in doing what pleases Him. That is how we keep ourselves in God's love.

God's love is a holy love; it is not shallow sentiment. "Ye that love the Lord, hate evil" (Ps. 97:10). To love God is to love what He loves and hate what He hates! We please Him by doing those things that He commands. It is the dedicated, separated Christian who enjoys the deepest fellowship with the Father in the family (2 Cor. 6:14–18).

We build our Christian life on the foundation of faith and through the motivation of love. But we also need hope: "looking for the mercy of our Lord Jesus Christ unto eternal life." The believer's eyes must be lifted heavenward. "Looking for that blessed hope, and the glorious appearing of the great God and our Savior Jesus Christ" (Titus 2:13). "Looking for and hasting unto the coming of the day of God" (2 Peter 3:12).

The word translated "looking" (Jude 21) means "earnestly expecting." It describes an attitude of life that is motivated by the promise of our Lord's return. The apostates can only look for judgment, but God's people are looking for mercy. Not only is our salvation from sin the gift of God's mercy, but so also is the deliverance of His church from this evil world. In His mercy, He will come for us and take us to Himself.

We have already noted that looking for the coming of the Lord is a great encouragement to Christian living. It makes us want to keep pure (1 John 3:3) and to avoid the things of the flesh and the world (Phil. 3:17–21). Our hope in Christ is like an anchor (Heb. 6:19) that holds us in the storms of life, and like a helmet that protects us in the battles of life (1 Thess. 5:8).

The three "Christian graces" of faith, hope, and love enable us to grow in our spiritual walk. We are able to build on a solid foundation with materials that will not decay. Mere profession with the lips will not suffice. "Not everyone that saith unto me, 'Lord, Lord,' shall enter into the kingdom of heaven; but he that doeth the will of my Father which is in heaven" (Matt. 7:21). The parable of the two builders (Matt. 7:24–27) makes it clear that to obey the will of God means to build on a foundation that cannot fail.

Exercise Spiritual Discernment (22–23)

What should be the attitude of the growing Christian toward those who are being influenced by the apostates? Jude instructed his readers to exercise discernment and to act on the basis of that discernment. He described three different kinds of people who need spiritual help. The *New American Standard Bible* makes this clear:

> And have mercy on some, who are doubting; save others, snatching them out of the fire; and on some have mercy with fear, hating even the garment polluted by the flesh.

The doubting (v. 22). These are the people who are wavering. They are probably the "unstable souls" Peter wrote about (2 Peter 2:14). These people are converted, but they are not grounded in the faith. Our responsibility is to have mercy on them, or show compassion toward them, by seeking to lead them away from the influences of the apostates. This kind of ministry demands a great deal of love and patience, and we must keep in mind that immature believers are like little children who think they know right from wrong. If you say no to them, they will only rebel and become more stubborn!

One of the best ways to draw them away from the false teachers is to magnify all that they have in Christ and to share His love for them in practical ways. Make their salvation so wonderful and the Word so exciting that they will lose interest in the teachings of the apostates. It is not enough merely to refute the false doctrines. There must also be a warmth of love that assures the young believer, "We care for you."

It is an open secret that false teachers prey especially on disgruntled church members. (Note Jude 16—"murmurers" and "complainers.") It is important that the pastor and the people show special love and concern to new Christians and that they also minister to the mature members of the church, lest somebody stray because of neglect. Paul sent Timothy to the young believers in Thessalonica so that he might establish them in their faith (1 Thess. 2). Every young Christian needs a more mature believer to teach him how to stand and walk.

The burning (v. 23a). Apparently these are the people who have left the fellowship and are now a part of the apostate group. They need to be snatched out of the fire! The angels took Lot by the hand and pulled him out of Sodom (Gen. 19:16), and sometimes that must be done in order to rescue ignorant and unstable believers from the clutches of false teachers.

There is probably a reference here to Zechariah 3:2 and also Amos 4:11. In the Zechariah passage, the "brand" was the nation Israel brought back from the Babylonian captivity and resettled in their land. God saw the people as a brand saved from the fire. In Amos 4, God was reproving the people for not heeding His warnings and judgments— poverty, poor crops, drought, pestilences, war, and even judgments like those that overthrew Sodom and Gomorrah. They were as a brand plucked out of the fire, yet they did not appreciate God's mercy.

The dangerous (v. 23b). The phrase *with fear* means "with caution." In trying to help those who have erred, we must be careful not to be trapped ourselves! Many a would-be rescuer has been drowned himself. When an unstable believer has been captured by false doctrine, we must be very careful as we try to help him, for Satan can use him to defile us. In trying to save him, we may be stained or burned ourselves!

The principle Jude was laying down was that stronger believers must never think they are beyond satanic influence. Even while serving the Lord and seeking to rescue one of His children, we can become defiled by those we want to help. The Old Testament Jews had to be very careful to avoid ceremonial defilement, and this included even their clothing (Lev. 13:47ff.; 14:47; 15:17). If a "clean" person touched an "unclean" garment, then he was defiled.

We certainly must love God's people, but we must also hate sin. Wherever there is sin, Satan has a foothold and can go to work. Defilement spreads rapidly and secretly, and it must be dealt with drastically. If the Jewish priest thought that a garment was infected with leprosy, he had the garment burned.

Not every Christian is equipped to deal with false teachers or with those they have influenced and captured. It takes a good knowledge of the Word, a faithful walk with God, an understanding of Satan's devices, and certainly the fullness of the Spirit of God. It also demands spiritual discernment. It is much easier to instruct new Christians and keep them away from the false teachers than it is to snatch them out of the fire.

Commit Yourself to Jesus Christ (24–25)

This well-known benediction contains a wealth of spiritual truth for the believer to receive. If we want to keep our feet on the ground spiritually, walk straight, and not stumble, then we must yield ourselves fully to the Savior. He alone is able to guard us, but we must "keep ourselves in the love of God" (Jude 21). He is *able* if we are *willing!*

Jude was not writing about the possibility of the believer sinning and falling from God's family. We have noted before that he made it clear in Jude 1 that true believers are "preserved" and cannot be lost. He was writing about the believer's daily walk with the Lord and the danger of going astray and stumbling. If we do disobey God, we may confess our sins and receive His forgiveness (1 John 1:9). If we persist in disobedience, He will chasten us in love (Heb. 12:5–11). He will never permit one of His own to be lost.

The Father has covenanted with the Son that all of His people will one day *see* and *share* His glory (see John 17:22–24). Jesus Christ will have the special joy of presenting His bride, the church, before the Father's throne! It was the anticipation of this "joy" that helped Him endure the sufferings of the cross (Heb. 12:2). The purpose of salvation is not simply to rescue sinners from hell, as wonderful as that is. The grand purpose is that God may be glorified for all eternity (Eph. 1:6, 12, 14).

Today, there are spots and blemishes in the church, but on that day God's people shall be blameless. Satan will find nothing to accuse. The bride will be arrayed in the righteousness of Christ to the glory of God.

Knowing this, the believer has a strong motive for living for Christ and obeying His Word. We want to bring joy to His heart today as we anticipate the joy He will have when He welcomes His bride to heaven! This is the significance of 1 John 3:3—"And every man that hath this hope in him purifieth himself, even as he is pure" (cf. Eph. 5:27; Phil. 2:15).

Jude 25 is the only place in this little letter where Jude called our Lord "Savior." Peter used this title five times. But Jude *opened* his letter by reminding his readers of "the common salvation" (Jude 3) that they shared because of their faith in Jesus Christ. It is not enough to say that Jesus Christ is *"a* savior," or *"the* Savior"; we must say that He is *"our* Savior—*my* Savior."

He is not only our Savior, but He is "the only wise God." He can give you the wisdom you need to live your life to the glory of God. The false teachers boasted of their special knowledge, but they lacked spiritual wisdom. God gives wisdom to those who ask Him (James 1:5), provided they are sincerely willing to obey Him. If Christians would seek the wisdom of God in the Word of God, they would not stumble into the traps of the false teachers, but would walk to please the Lord (Col 1:9–10).

Why should we walk in obedience to God's will? So that Christ might receive the glory!

Glory is the sum total of all that God is and all that God does. Everything about Him is glorious! The glory of man fades as the mown grass, but the glory of God goes on eternally.

Majesty means "greatness, magnificence." Only God is great. When we praise God, we praise the most magnificent Person in the universe. He is not simply King; He is King of kings! He is not simply Lord; He is Lord of lords!

Dominion has to do with God's sovereignty and rule over all things. The Greek word means "strength, might," but it carries the idea of complete control over all things.

Power means "authority," which is the right to use power. All authority belongs to Jesus Christ (Matt. 28:18), including authority over the powers of darkness (Eph. 1:19–23). As we yield to Him, we share His authority and accomplish His will.

What a magnificent doxology this is! Knowing the purpose Jude had in mind when he wrote this letter, this doxology takes on even greater significance. Jude was reminding his readers of the greatness of Jesus Christ If only they could catch that, they would never be led astray by false teachers. Like the young man who falls in love and marries, and is no longer interested in his old girlfriends, so the believer who keeps himself "in the love of God" (Jude 21), caught up in the glories of the Savior, will never want to turn to Satan's substitutes.

You don't have to stumble.

If you will remember the Word, build your Christian life in faith, hope, and love, exercise spiritual discernment, and commit yourself to Christ, then He will keep you from stumbling. Be alert!

The enemy is subtle and the dangers are great.

But the only wise God your Savior will keep you safe and one day present you joyfully in glory!

REVELATION

OUTLINE

Key theme: Jesus Christ is Victor
Key verses: Revelation 1:19; 17:14

I. THE THINGS WHICH THOU HAST SEEN (1)
John's vision of the exalted Christ

II. THE THINGS WHICH ARE (2—3)
The messages to the seven churches

III. THE THINGS WHICH SHALL BE HEREAFTER (4—22)
A. The throne in heaven—4—5
B. The tribulation on earth—6—19
   1. The first half—6—9
   2. The middle—10—14
   3. The last half—15—19
C. The kingdom of Christ—20
D. The new heavens and earth—21—22

CONTENTS

CHAPTER ONE
Revelation 1

A VERY SPECIAL BOOK

Don't ever prophesy," said American humorist Josh Billings, "for if you prophesy wrong, nobody will forget it; and if you prophesy right, nobody will remember it."

Over the centuries, prophecies have come and gone, and yet the book that the apostle John wrote near the close of the first century is with us still. I can recall reading it as a child and wondering what it was all about. Even today, with many years of concentrated study behind me, I am still fascinated by its message and mysteries.

In Revelation 1, John introduces his book and gives us the data essential for appreciating and understanding this prophecy.

The Title (1:1a)

The word translated "revelation" simply means "unveiling." It gives us our English word *apocalypse* which, unfortunately, is today a synonym for chaos and catastrophe. The verb simply means "to uncover, to reveal, to make manifest." In this book, the Holy Spirit pulls back the curtain and gives us the privilege of seeing the glorified Christ in heaven and the fulfillment of His sovereign purposes in the world.

In other words, Revelation is an *open* book in which God reveals His plans and purposes to His church. When Daniel finished writing his prophecy, he was instructed to "shut up the words, and seal the book" (Dan. 12:4), but John was given opposite instructions: "Seal not the sayings of the prophecy of this book" (Rev. 22:10). Why? Since Calvary, the resurrection, and the coming of the Holy Spirit, God has ushered in the "last days" (Heb. 1:1–2) and is fulfilling His hidden purposes in this world. "The time is at hand" (Rev. 1:3; 22:10).

John's prophecy is primarily the revelation of Jesus Christ, not the revelation of future events. You must not divorce the Person from the prophecy, for without the Person there could be no fulfillment of the prophecy. "He is not incidental to its action," wrote Dr. Merrill Tenney. "He is its chief Subject." In Revelation 1—3, Christ is seen as the exalted Priest.

King ministering to the churches. In Revelation 4—5, He is seen in heaven as the glorified Lamb of God, reigning on the throne. In Revelation 6—18, Christ is the Judge of all the earth, and in Revelation 19, He returns to earth as the conquering King of kings. The book closes with the heavenly Bridegroom ushering His bride, the church, into the glorious heavenly city.

Whatever you do as you study this book, get to know your Savior better.

The Author (1:1b–2, 4, 9; 22:8)

The Holy Spirit used the apostle John to give us three kinds of inspired literature: the gospel of John, the three epistles, and the book of Revelation. His purposes may be outlined as follows:

Gospel of John	Epistles	Revelation
Believe, 20:31	Be sure, 1 John 5:13	Be ready, 22:20
Life received	Life revealed	Life rewarded
Salvation	Sanctification	Sovereignty
The Prophet	The Priest	The King

John wrote Revelation about AD 95, during the reign of the Roman emperor Titus Flavius Domitian. The emperor had demanded that he be worshipped as "Lord and God," and the refusal of the Christians to obey his edict led to severe persecution. Tradition says that it was Domitian who sent John to the Isle of Patmos, a Roman penal colony off the coast of Asia Minor. This being the location of John's exile, perhaps it is not surprising that the word *sea* is found twenty-six times in his book.

During Christ's earthly ministry, John and his brother James asked Jesus for special places of honor by His throne. The Lord told them that they would have to merit their thrones by sharing in His suffering. James was the first apostle martyred (Acts 12:1–2); John was the last of the apostles to die, but he suffered on Patmos before his death (see Matt. 20:20–23).

How did the Lord convey the contents of this book to His servant? According to Revelation 1:1–2, the Father gave the revelation to the Son, and the Son shared it with the apostle, using "His angel" as intermediary. Sometimes Christ Himself conveyed information to John (Rev. 1:10ff.); sometimes it was an elder (Rev. 7:13); and often it was an angel (Rev. 17:1; 19:9–10). Sometimes a "voice from heaven" told John what to say and do (Rev. 10:4). The book came from God to John, no matter what the various means of communication were, and it was all inspired by the Spirit.

The word signified (Rev. 1:1) is important; it means "to show by a sign." In Revelation, the noun is translated as sign (Rev. 15:1), wonder (Rev. 12:1, 3), and miracle (Rev. 19:20). This is the same word used in the gospel of John for the miracles of Jesus Christ, for His miracles were events that carried a deeper spiritual message than simply the display of power. As you study Revelation, expect to encounter a great deal of symbolism, much of it related to the Old Testament.

Why did John use symbolism? For one thing, this kind of "spiritual code" is understood only by those who know Christ personally. If any Roman officers had tried to use Revelation as evidence against Christians, the book would have been a puzzle and an enigma to them. But an even greater reason is that symbolism is not weakened by time. John was able to draw on the great "images" in God's revelation and assemble them into an exciting drama that has encouraged persecuted and suffering saints for centuries. However, you must not conclude that John's use of symbolism indicates that the events described are not real. They are real!

There is a third reason why John used symbolism: symbols not only convey information, but also impart values and arouse emotions. John could have written, "A dictator will rule the world," but instead he described *a beast.* The symbol says much more than the mere title of "dictator." Instead of explaining a world system, John simply introduced "Babylon the Great" and contrasted the "harlot" with the "bride." The very name "Babylon" would convey deep spiritual truth to readers who knew the Old Testament.

In understanding John's symbolism, however, we must be careful not to allow our imaginations to run wild. Biblical symbols are consistent with the whole of biblical revelation. Some symbols are explained (Rev. 1:20; 4:5; 5:8); others are understood from Old Testament symbolism (Rev. 2:7, 17; 4:7); and some symbols are not explained at all (the "white stone" in Rev. 2:17). Nearly 300 references to the Old Testament are found in Revelation! This means that we must anchor our interpretations to what God has already revealed, lest we misinterpret this important prophetic book.

The Readers (1:3–4)

While the book was originally sent to seven actual local churches in Asia Minor, John makes it clear that *any* believer may read and profit from it (Rev. 1:3). In fact, God promised a special blessing to the one who would read the book and obey its message. (The verb *read* means "to read out loud." Revelation was first read aloud in local church meetings.) The apostle Paul had sent letters to seven churches—Rome, Corinth, Galatia, Ephesus, Philippi, Colosse, and Thessalonica—and now John sent one book to seven different churches. Early in the book, he had a special message from Christ to each church.

John did not send this book of prophecy to the assemblies in order to satisfy their curiosity about the future. God's people were going through intense persecution, and they needed encouragement. As they heard this book, its message would give them strength and hope. But even more, its message would help them examine their own lives (and each local assembly) to determine those areas needing correction. They were not only to *hear* the Word, but they were also to keep it—that is, guard it as a treasure and practice what it said. The blessing would come, not just by *hearing,* but even more so by *doing* (see James 1:22–25).

It is worth noting that there are seven "beatitudes" in Revelation: 1:3; 14:13; 16:15; 19:9; 20:6; 22:7, 14. The number seven is important in this book because it signifies fullness and completeness. In Revelation, God tells us how He is going to complete His great work and usher in His eternal kingdom. In Revelation, you will find seven seals (Rev. 5:1), seven trumpets (Rev. 8:6), seven vials (Rev. 16:1), seven stars (Rev. 1:16),

and seven lampstands (Rev. 1:12, 20). Other "sevens" in this book will be discussed as we study.

The special messages to each of the seven churches are given in Revelation 2—3. Some students see in these seven churches a "panorama of church history," from apostolic times (Ephesus) to the apostate days of the twentieth century (Laodicea). While these churches may *illustrate* various stages in the history of the church, that was probably not the main reason why these particular assemblies were selected. Instead, these letters remind us that the exalted Head of the church knows what is going on in each assembly, and that our relationship to Him and His Word determines the life and ministry of the local body.

Keep in mind that the churches in Asia Minor were facing persecution and it was important that they be rightly related to the Lord and to each other. They are pictured as seven separate lampstands, each giving light in a dark world (Phil. 2:15; Matt. 5:14–16). The darker the day, the greater the light must shine; unfortunately situations existed in at least five of these assemblies that required correction if their lights were to shine brightly. As you read Revelation 2—3, note that the Lord always reminded them of who He is, and encouraged them to be "overcomers."

What's more, the promise of Jesus Christ's coming should be to all Christians at all times a motivation for obedience and consecration (Rev. 1:3, 7; 2:5, 25; 3:3, 11; 22:7, 12, 20; see also 1 John 1:1–33). No believer should study prophecy merely to satisfy his curiosity. When Daniel and John received God's revelations of the future, both fell down as dead men (Dan. 10:7–10; Rev. 1:17). They were overwhelmed! We need to approach this book as wonderers and worshippers, not as academic students.

The Dedication (1:4–6)

"If you don't stop writing books," a friend said to me, "you will run out of people to dedicate them to!" I appreciated the compliment, but I did not agree with the sentiment. John had no problem knowing to whom his book should be dedicated! But before he wrote the dedication, he reminded his readers that it was the Triune God who had saved them and would keep them as they faced the fiery trials of suffering.

God the Father is described as the Eternal One (see Rev. 1:8; 4:8). All history is part of His eternal plan, including the world's persecution of the church. Next, the Holy Spirit is seen in His fullness, for there are not seven spirits, but one. The reference here is probably to Isaiah 11:2.

Finally, Jesus Christ is seen in His threefold office as Prophet (faithful Witness), Priest (First-begotten from the dead), and King (Prince of the kings of the earth). *First-begotten* does not mean "the first one raised from the dead," but "the highest of those raised from the dead." *Firstborn* is a title of honor (see Rom. 8:29; Col. 1:15, 18).

But of the three Persons of the Trinity, it is to Jesus

Christ alone that this book is dedicated. The reason? Because of what He has done for His people. To begin with, *He loves us* (present tense in most manuscripts). This parallels the emphasis in John's gospel. He also *washed us from our sins,* or, as some texts read, *freed us* from our sins. This parallels the message of John's epistles (see 1 John 1:5ff.). As a grand climax, Christ has *made us a kingdom of priests,* and this is the emphasis of Revelation. Today, Jesus Christ is a Priest-King like Melchizedek (Heb. 7), and we are seated with Him on His throne (Eph. 2:1–10).

In His love, God called Israel to be a kingdom of priests (Ex. 19:1–6), but the Jews failed God and their kingdom was taken from them (Matt. 21:43). Today, God's people (the church) are His kings and priests (1 Peter 2:1–10), exercising spiritual authority and serving God in this world.

The Theme (1:7–8)

The overriding theme of the book of Revelation is the return of Jesus Christ to defeat all evil and to establish His reign. It is definitely a book of victory and His people are seen as "overcomers" (see Rev. 2:7, 11, 17, 26; 3:5, 12, 21; 11:7; 12:11; 15:2; 21:7). In his first epistle, John also called God's people "overcomers" (1 John 2:13–14; 4:4; 5:4–5). Through eyes of unbelief, Jesus Christ and His church are defeated in this world, but through eyes of faith, He and His people are the true victors. As Peter Marshall once said, "It is better to fail in a cause that will ultimately succeed than to succeed in a cause that will ultimately fail."

The statement in Revelation 1:7, "Behold, he cometh with clouds," describes our Lord's return to *the earth,* and is amplified in Revelation 19:11ff. This is not the same as His return *in the air* to catch away His people (1 Thess. 4:13–18; 1 Cor. 15:51ff.). When He comes to catch away (rapture) His church, He will come "as a thief" (Rev. 3:3; 16:15) and only those who are born again will see Him (1 John 3:1–3). The event described in Revelation 1:7 will be witnessed by the whole world, and especially by a repentant nation of Israel (see Dan. 7:13; Zech. 12:10–12). It will be public, not secret (Matt. 24:30–31), and will climax the tribulation period described in Revelation 6—19.

Godly Bible students have not always agreed as to the order of events leading up to the establishment of God's eternal kingdom (Rev. 21—22). I personally believe that the next event on God's calendar is the rapture, when Christ shall return in the air and take His church to glory. Christ's promise to the church in Revelation 3:10–11 indicates that the church will not go through the tribulation, and this is further supported by Paul in 1 Thessalonians 1:10; 5:9–10. It is significant to me that there is no mention of the word *church* between Revelation 3:22 and 22:16.

After the church is raptured, the events depicted in Revelation 6—19 will occur: the tribulation, the rise of the "man of sin," the great tribulation (the wrath of God) and the destruction of man-made

world government, and then Christ's return to the earth to set up His kingdom. Daniel indicates that this period of worldwide trouble will last seven years (Dan. 9:25–27). Throughout the book of Revelation, you will find measurements of time that coincide with this seven-year time span (Rev. 11:2–3; 12:6, 14; 13:5).

The titles given to God in Revelation 1:8 make it clear that He is certainly able to work out His divine purposes in human history. *Alpha* and *Omega* are the first and last letters of the Greek alphabet; so, God is at the beginning of all things and also at their end. He is the eternal God (see Rev. 1:4), unlimited by time. He is also the Almighty, able to do anything. *Almighty* is a key name for God in Revelation (Rev. 1:8; 4:8; 11:17; 15:3; 16:7, 14; 19:6, 15; 21:22).

God the Father is called "Alpha and Omega" in Revelation 1:8 and 21:6, but the name also is applied to His Son (Rev. 1:11; 22:13). This is a strong argument for the deity of Christ. Likewise, the title "the first and the last" goes back to Isaiah (Isa. 41:4; 44:6; 48:12–13) and is another proof that Jesus is God.

The Occasion (1:9–18)

This book was born out of John's profound spiritual experience while exiled on Patmos.

What John heard (vv. 9–11). On the Lord's Day, John heard a trumpet-like voice behind him. It was Jesus Christ speaking! As far as we know, the apostle had not heard his Lord's voice since Christ had returned to heaven more than sixty years before. The Lord commissioned John to write this book and to send it to the seven churches He had selected. Later John would hear another trumpet-like voice, summoning him to heaven (Rev. 4:1). (Some students relate this to 1 Thess. 4:13–18 and see John's "rapture" as a picture of the rapture of the church.)

What John saw (vv. 12–16). He saw a vision of the glorified Christ. Revelation 1:20 makes clear that we must not interpret this vision literally, for it is made up of symbols. The seven lampstands represent the seven churches that would receive the book. Each local church is the bearer of God's light in this dark world. Compare this vision with Daniel's (Dan. 7:9–14).

Christ's garments are those of a Judge-King, One with honor and authority. The white hair symbolizes His eternality, "the Ancient of Days" (Dan. 7:9, 13, 22). His eyes see all (Rev. 19:12; Heb. 4:12), enabling Him to judge righteously. His feet of burning brass also suggest judgment, since the brazen altar was the place where the fire consumed the sin offering. The Lord had come to judge the churches, and He would also judge the evil world system.

The "sound of many waters" (Rev. 1:15) makes me think of Niagara Falls! Perhaps two ideas are suggested here: (1) Christ gathers together all the "streams of revelation" and is the Father's "last Word" to man (Heb. 1:1–3); (2) He speaks with power and authority and must be heard. The sword from His mouth certainly represents the living Word of God (Heb. 4:12; Eph.

6:17). He fights His enemies by using His Word (Rev. 2:16; 19:19–21).

Revelation 1:20 informs us that the seven stars in His hand represent the angels (messengers, see Luke 7:24 where the Greek word is so translated), or perhaps pastors, of the seven churches. God holds His servants and places them where He wants them to "shine" for Him. In Daniel 12:3, wise soul winners are compared to shining stars.

The Lord's shining countenance reminds us of His transfiguration (Matt. 17:2) and also the prophecy of Malachi 4:2 ("the Sun of righteousness [shall] arise"). The sun is a familiar image of God in the Old Testament (Ps. 84:11), reminding us not only of blessing, but of judgment. The sun can burn as well as bless!

This vision of Christ was totally different in appearance from the Savior that John knew "in the flesh" when He was ministering on earth. He was not the "gentle Jewish carpenter" that sentimentalists like to sing about. He is the risen, glorified, exalted Son of God, the Priest-King who has the authority to judge all men, beginning with His own people (1 Peter 4:17).

What John did (vv. 17–18). He fell at the Lord's feet as though he were dead! And this is the apostle who leaned on Jesus' breast (John 13:23)! A vision of the exalted Christ can only produce awe and fear (Dan. 10:7–9). We need this attitude of respect today when so many believers speak and act with undue familiarity toward God. John's response illustrates what Paul wrote in 2 Corinthians 5:16: "Though we have known Christ after the flesh, yet now henceforth know we him no more." John no longer "nestled" next to the Lord's heart, relating to Him as he had done before.

The Lord reassured John by touching him and speaking to him (note Dan. 8:18; 9:21; 10:10, 16, 18). "Fear not!" is a great encouragement for any child of God. We need not fear life, because He is "The Living One." We need not fear death, because He died and is alive, having conquered death. And we need not fear eternity because He holds the keys of hades (the world of the dead) and of death. The One with the keys is the One who has authority.

At the very beginning of this book, Jesus presented Himself to His people in majestic glory. What the church needs today is a new awareness of Christ and His glory. We need to see Him "high and lifted up" (Isa. 6:1). There is a dangerous absence of awe and worship in our assemblies today. We are boasting about standing on our own feet, instead of breaking and falling at His feet. For years, Evan Roberts prayed, "Bend me! Bend me!" and when God answered, the great Welsh Revival resulted.

The Outline (1:19)

To the best of my knowledge, the book of Revelation is the only book in the Bible that contains an inspired outline of the contents. "The things which thou hast seen" refers to the vision in Revelation 1. "The things which are" refers to Revelation 2—3, the special messages to the seven churches. "The things which shall be hereafter" covers the events described in Revelation 4—22. What John heard in Revelation 4:1 substantiates this interpretation.

In review, we can summarize the basic characteristics of this remarkable book as follows:

It is a Christ-centered book. To be sure, *all* Scripture speaks of the Savior, but the book of Revelation especially magnifies the greatness and glory of Jesus Christ. The book is, after all, the revelation of Jesus Christ and not simply the revelation of future events.

It is an "open" book. John was told not to seal the book (Rev. 22:10) because God's people need the message it contains. Revelation *can* be understood, despite the fact that it contains mysteries that may never be comprehended until we meet at the throne of God. John sent the book to the seven churches of Asia Minor with the expectation that, when it was read aloud by the messengers, the listening saints would understand enough of its truths so as to be greatly encouraged in their own difficult situations.

It is a book filled with symbols. Biblical symbols are timeless in their message and limitless in their content. For instance, the symbol of "Babylon" originates in Genesis 10—11, and its meaning grows as you trace it through Scripture, climaxing with Revelation 17—18. The same is true of the symbols of "the Lamb" and "the bride." It is exciting to seek to penetrate deeper into the rich meanings that are conveyed by these symbols.

It is a book of prophecy. This is definitely stated in Revelation 1:3; 22:7, 10, 18–19; note also 10:11. The letters to the seven churches of Asia Minor dealt with immediate needs in those assemblies, needs that are still with us in churches today, but the rest of the book is devoted almost entirely to prophetic revelations. It was by seeing the victorious Christ presented that the persecuted Christians found encouragement for their difficult task of witnessing. When you have assurance for the future, you have stability in the present. John himself was suffering under the hand of Rome (Rev. 1:9), so the book was born out of affliction.

It is a book with a blessing. We have already noted the promise in Revelation 1:3, as well as the six other "beatitudes" scattered throughout the book. It is not enough simply to hear (or read) the book; we must respond to its message from the heart. We must take the message personally and say a believing "Amen!" to what it says. (Note the many "Amens" in the book: Rev. 1:6–7, 18; 3:14; 5:14; 7:12; 19:4; 22:20–21.)

It is a relevant book. What John wrote about would "shortly come to pass" (Rev. 1:1) because "the time is at hand" (Rev. 1:3). (Note also Rev. 22:7, 10, 12, 20.) The word *shortly* does not mean "soon" or "immediately," but "quickly, swiftly." God does not measure time as we do (2 Peter 3:1–10). No one knows when our Lord shall return, but when He begins to open the seals of the scroll (Rev. 6:1ff.), events will occur with speed and without interruption.

It is a majestic book. Revelation is the book of "the throne," for the word *throne* is found forty-six times throughout. This book magnifies the sovereignty of God. Christ is presented in His glory and dominion!

It is a universal book. John saw nations and peoples (Rev. 10:11; 11:9; 17:15) as part of God's program. He also saw the throne room of heaven and heard voices from the ends of the universe!

It is a climactic book. Revelation is the climax of the Bible. All that began in Genesis will be completed and fulfilled in keeping with God's sovereign will. He is "Alpha and Omega, the beginning and the ending" (Rev. 1:8). What God starts, He finishes!

But before visiting the throne room of heaven, we must pause to listen to "the Man among the lampstands" as He reveals the personal needs in our churches and in our own hearts. "He that hath an ear, let him hear what the Spirit saith unto the churches!"

CHAPTER TWO
Revelation 2
CHRIST AND THE CHURCHES—PART 1

If you have ever moved to a new community and had to select a new church home, you know how difficult it is to examine and evaluate a church and its ministry. Imposing buildings may house dying or dead congregations, while modest structures might belong to virile assemblies on the march for the Lord. The church we think is "rich" may turn out to be poor in God's sight (Rev. 3:17), while the "poor" church is actually rich (Rev. 2:9).

Only the Head of the church, Jesus Christ, can accurately inspect each church and know its true condition, because He sees the internals, not only the externals (Rev. 2:23b). In these special messages to the seven churches in Asia Minor, the Lord gave each assembly an "X ray" of its condition. But He intended for *all* the churches to read these messages and benefit from them. (Note the plural "churches" in Rev. 2:7, 11, 17, 29; 3:6, 13, 22.)

But the Lord was also speaking to *individuals,* and this is where you and I come in. "He that hath an ear, let him hear." Churches are made up of individuals, and it is individuals who determine the spiritual life of the assembly. So, while reading these messages, we must apply them personally as we examine our own hearts.

Finally, we must keep in mind that John was a pastor at heart, seeking to encourage these churches during a difficult time of persecution. Before Christ judges the world, He must judge His own people (Ezek. 9:6; 1 Peter 4:17). A purified church need never fear the attacks of Satan or men. "It is a very remarkable thing," wrote G. Campbell Morgan, "that the church of Christ persecuted has been the church of Christ pure. The church of Christ patronized has always been the church of Christ impure."

Ephesus, the Careless Church (2:1–7)

Each of the seven messages begins with a personal description or designation of Jesus Christ taken from the vision of Christ given in Revelation 1. (In the case of Ephesus, see Rev. 1:12, 16, 20.) The Ephesian assembly had enjoyed some "stellar" leadership—Paul, Timothy, and the apostle John himself—but the Lord reminded them that *He* was in control of the ministry, placing the "stars" where He pleased. How easy it is for a church to become proud and forget that pastors and teachers are God's gifts (Eph. 4:11) who may be taken away at any time. Some churches need to be cautioned to worship the Lord and not their pastor!

Approval (vv. 2–3, 6). How gracious of the Lord to start with words of commendation! To begin with, this was a *serving* church, busy doing the works of the Lord. No doubt their weekly schedule was filled with activities. It was also a *sacrificing* church, for the word *labor* means "toil to the point of exhaustion." The Ephesian Christians paid a price to serve the Lord. They were a *steadfast* assembly, for the word *patience* carries the meaning of "endurance under trial." They kept going when the going was tough.

The Ephesian church was a *separated* people, for they carefully examined the visiting ministers (see 2 John 7–11) to see if they were genuine. Paul had warned the Ephesian elders that false teachers would come in from the outside and even arise from within the church (Acts 20:28–31), and John had instructed them to "try the spirits" (1 John 4:1–6). Indeed, Satan has his false ministers and the church must be constantly alert to detect them and reject them (2 Cor. 11:1–4, 12–15).

Ephesian Christians separated themselves not only from false doctrine but also from false deeds (Rev. 2:6). The word *Nicolaitan* means "to conquer the people." Some Bible students believe this was a sect who "lorded it over" the church and robbed the people of their liberty in Christ (see 3 John 9–11). They initiated what we know today as "clergy" and "laity," a false division that is taught nowhere in the New Testament. All God's people are "kings and priests" (1 Peter 2:9; Rev. 1:6) and have equal access to the Father through the blood of Christ (Heb. 10:19ff.). We shall meet this dangerous sect again when we study the message to the church at Pergamos.

The believers at Ephesus were a *suffering* people who patiently bore their burdens and toiled without fainting. And they did all of this for His name's sake! No matter how you examine this congregation, you conclude that it is just about perfect. However, the One among the lampstands saw into their hearts, and He had a different diagnosis from ours.

Accusation (v. 4). This busy, separated, sacrificing church really suffered from "heart trouble"—they had abandoned their first love! They displayed "works …

labor ... and patience" (Rev. 2:2), but these qualities were not motivated by a love for Christ. (Compare 1 Thess. 1:3—"work of faith, and labor of love, and patience of hope.") What we do for the Lord is important, *but so is why we do it!*

What is "first love"? It is the devotion to Christ that so often characterizes the new believer: fervent, personal, uninhibited, excited, and openly displayed. It is the "honeymoon love" of the husband and wife (Jer. 2:1–2). While it is true that mature married love deepens and grows richer, it is also true that it should never lose the excitement and wonder of those "honeymoon days." When a husband and wife begin to take each other for granted, and life becomes routine, then the marriage is in danger.

Just think of it: it is possible to serve, sacrifice, and suffer "for my name's sake" and yet not really love Jesus Christ! The Ephesian believers were so busy maintaining their separation that they were neglecting adoration. Labor is no substitute for love; neither is purity a substitute for passion. The church must have both if it is to please Him.

By reading Paul's epistle to the Ephesians, you discover at least twenty references to *love.* You also discover that Paul emphasized the believer's exalted position "in Christ... in the heavenly places." But the Ephesian church had fallen and was not living up to its heavenly position in Christ (Rev. 2:5). It is only as we love Christ fervently that we can serve Him faithfully. Our love for Him must be pure (Eph. 6:24).

Admonition (vv. 5–7). "First love" can be restored if we follow the three instructions Christ gave. First, we must remember (literally "keep on remembering") what we have lost and cultivate a desire to regain that close communion once again. Then we must repent—change our minds—and confess our sins to the Lord (1 John 1:9). Third, we must repeat the first works, which suggests restoring the original fellowship that was broken by our sin and neglect. For the believer, this means prayer, Bible reading and meditation, obedient service, and worship.

In spite of the privileges it had enjoyed, the church of Ephesus was in danger of losing its light! The church that loses its love will soon lose its light, no matter how doctrinally sound it may be. "I will come" (Rev. 2:5) is not referring to the Lord's return, but to His coming judgment *then and there.* The glorious city of Ephesus is today but a heap of stones and no light is shining there.

Revelation 2:7 makes it clear that individual believers within the church may be true to the Lord, no matter what others may do. In these seven messages, the "overcomers" are not a "spiritual elite," but rather the true believers whose faith has given them victory (1 John 5:4–5). Sinful man was banned from the tree of life (Gen. 3:22–24), but in Christ we have eternal abundant life (John 3:16; 10:10). We enjoy this blessing now, and we shall enjoy it in greater measure in eternity (Rev. 22:1–5).

The church of Ephesus was the "careless church," made up of careless believers who neglected their love for Christ. Are we guilty of the same neglect?

Smyrna, the Crowned Church (2:8–11)

The name *Smyrna* means "bitter" and is related to the word *myrrh.* The city remains a functioning community today called Izmir. The assembly at Smyrna was persecuted for the faith, which explains why the Lord emphasized His death and resurrection as He opened His message. No matter what experiences God's people may have, their Lord identifies with them.

Approval (v. 9). The church at Smyrna was not having an easy time of it! The members were persecuted, probably because they refused to compromise and say, "Caesar is Lord." Smyrna was an important center of the Roman imperial cult, and anyone refusing to acknowledge Caesar as Lord would certainly be excluded from the guilds. This would mean unemployment and poverty. The word used here for *poverty* means "abject poverty, possessing absolutely nothing."

A large Jewish community also thrived in Smyrna. The Jews, of course, did not have to patronize the imperial cult since their religion was accepted by Rome, but they certainly would not cooperate with the Christian faith. So, from both Jews and Gentiles, the Christians in Smyrna received slander and suffering.

But they were rich! They lived for eternal values that would never change, riches that could never be taken away. "As poor, yet making many rich" (2 Cor. 6:10; 8:9). In fact, their suffering for Christ only increased their riches.

Our struggles are not with flesh and blood, but with the enemy, Satan, who uses people to accomplish his purposes. The Jewish synagogue was actually a synagogue of Satan. A true Jew is not one physically or racially, but spiritually (Rom. 2:17–29). Any religious group, Jewish or Gentile, that does not acknowledge Jesus Christ as God's Son is certainly acting contrary to God's will.

Admonition (vv. 10–11). No words of accusation are given to the congregation in Smyrna! They may not have enjoyed the approval of men, but they certainly received the praise of God. However, the Lord did give them solemn words of admonition as they faced increased suffering: "Don't be afraid!"

He assured them that He knew the devil's plans and was in complete control of the situation. Some of the believers would be imprisoned and tried as traitors to Rome. Yet their tribulation would not be long; to the Bible, *ten days* signifies "a brief time" (Gen. 24:55; Acts 25:6). The important thing was *faithfulness,* standing true to Christ no matter what the government might threaten to do.

The "crown of life" is the winner's crown awarded at the annual athletic games. Smyrna was a key participant in the games, so this promise would be especially meaningful to believers living there. The Lord reinforced the promise given by James (James

1:12) and assured His people that there was nothing to fear. Because they had trusted Him, they were overcomers—victors in the race of faith (Heb. 12:1–3)—and, as overcomers, they had nothing to fear. Even if they were martyred, they would be ushered into glory, wearing crowns! They would never face the awful judgment of the second death, which is the lake of fire (Rev. 20:14; 21:8).

It costs to be a dedicated Christian, in some places more than others. As end-time pressures increase, persecution will also increase, and God's people need to be ready (1 Peter 4:12ff.). The world may call us "poor Christians," but in God's sight we are rich!

Pergamos, the Compromising Church (2:12–17)

Called "the greatest city in Asia Minor," Pergamos had the first temple dedicated to Caesar and was a rabid promoter of the imperial cult. This is probably what is meant by "Satan's seat" in Revelation 2:13. The city also had a temple dedicated to Aesculapius, the god of healing, whose insignia was the entwined serpent on the staff. (This is still a medical symbol today.) Satan, of course, is likewise symbolized as the serpent (2 Cor. 11:3; Rev. 12:9; 20:2).

Approval (v. 13). Like their brothers and sisters in Smyrna, the believers in Pergamos had suffered persecution, and one of their men had died for the faith. In spite of intense suffering, this church had remained true to God. They refused to drop incense on the altar and say, "Caesar is Lord." The Lord's description of Himself ("He which hath the sharp sword," Rev. 2:12) would surely encourage the people, for the sword was also the symbol of the Roman proconsul. It was more important that the church fear Christ's sword than the Roman sword (Rev. 2:16).

Accusation (vv. 14–15). Despite their courageous stand against persecution, the believers in Pergamos were not faultless before the Lord. Satan had not been able to destroy them by coming as the roaring lion (1 Peter 5:8), but he was making inroads as the deceiving serpent. A group of compromising people had infiltrated the church fellowship, and Jesus Christ hated their doctrines and their practices.

These infiltrators are called "Nicolaitans," whom we met already at Ephesus (Rev. 2:6). The name means "to rule the people." What they taught is called "the doctrine of Balaam" (Rev. 2:14). The Hebrew name *Balaam* also means "lord of the people" and is probably synonymous with *Nicolaitans.* Sadly, this group of professed believers "lorded it over" the people and led them astray.

Understanding the story of Balaam helps us interpret this insidious group more accurately (see Num. 22—25). Balaam was a true prophet who prostituted his gifts in order to earn money from King Balak, who hired him to curse the people of Israel. God prevented Balaam from actually cursing the nation—in fact, God turned the curses into blessings!—but Balak still got his money's worth. How? By following Balaam's advice

and making friends with Israel, and then inviting the Jews to worship and feast at the pagan altars. "If you can't beat 'em, join 'em!"

The Jewish men fell right into the trap and many of them became "good neighbors." They ate meat from idolatrous altars and committed fornication as part of heathen religious rites. Twenty-four thousand people died because of this disobedient act of compromise (Num. 25:1–9).

Why did this bit of ancient history apply to the believers at Pergamos? Because a group in that church said, "There is nothing wrong with being friendly to Rome. What harm is there in putting a pinch of incense on the altar and affirming your loyalty to Caesar?" Antipas refused to compromise and was martyred, but others took the "easy way" and cooperated with Rome.

It is unlikely that "things sacrificed to idols" is the same problem Paul dealt with in 1 Corinthians 8 and 10. The accusation here left no room for personal choice as did Paul. The Lord accused the Christians in Pergamos of sinning, of committing "spiritual fornication" by saying, "Caesar is Lord." Of course, this compromise made them welcome in the Roman guilds and protected them from Roman persecution, but it cost them their testimony and their crown.

Believers today also face the temptation to achieve personal advancement by ungodly compromise. The name *Pergamos* means "married," reminding us that each local church is "engaged to Christ" and must be kept pure (2 Cor. 11:1–4). We shall see later in Revelation that this present world system is pictured as a defiled harlot, while the church is presented as a pure bride. The congregation or the individual Christian that compromises with the world just to avoid suffering or achieve success is committing "spiritual adultery" and being unfaithful to the Lord.

Admonition (vv. 16–17). Antipas had felt the sword of Rome, but the church at Pergamos would feel the sword of Christ—the Word (Heb. 4:12)—if they did not repent. This is not a reference to our Lord's return but to a *present* judgment that comes to a church when it is disobedient to the Word of God. The Lord had presented Himself as "He which hath the sharp sword" (Rev. 2:12), so the church could not have been ignorant of its danger.

As with the previous churches, the closing appeal is to *the individual:* "He that hath an ear… To *him* that overcometh" (Rev. 2:17, italics added). God fed the Israelites with manna during their wilderness travels, and a pot of the manna was placed in the ark of the covenant (Ex. 16:32–36; Heb. 9:4). Instead of eating "things sacrificed to idols" (Rev. 2:14), the believers in Pergamos needed to feast on God's holy food, the bread of life found in Jesus Christ through the Word (Matt. 4:4; John 6:32ff.). The ark of the covenant was the throne of God (2 Sam. 6:2; Ps. 80:1; Isa. 37:16; all NASB), in contrast to Satan's throne which held authority in Pergamos (Rev. 2:13).

In those days, a white stone was put into a vessel by a judge to vote acquittal for a person on trial. It was also used like a "ticket" to gain admission to a feast. Both would certainly apply to the believer in a spiritual sense: he has been declared righteous through faith in Christ, and he feasts with Christ today (Rev. 3:20) and will feast with Him in glory (Rev. 19:6–9).

Thyatira, the Corrupted Church (2:18–29)

The longest message was sent to the church in the smallest city! Thyatira was a military town as well as a commercial center with many trade guilds. Wherever guilds were found, idolatry and immorality—the two great enemies of the early church—were almost always present too.

The city boasted a special temple to Apollo, the "sun god," which explains why the Lord introduced Himself as "the Son of God" (the only time in Revelation this title is used). John had to deliver a message of severe warning and judgment to this congregation, which explains the description of the Lord's eyes and feet.

Approval (v. 19). The believers in Thyatira were a busy lot! They were involved in sacrificial ministry for the sake of others. What's more, their works were increasing and characterized by faith, love, and patience; so the church was not guilty of mere "religious activity."

Accusation (vv. 20–23). Alas, the Lord found much to expose and condemn in the assembly at Thyatira. No amount of loving and sacrificial works can compensate for tolerance of evil. The church was permitting a false prophetess to influence the people and lead them into compromise. It is not likely that this woman was actually called "Jezebel," since such an infamous name would not be given to a child. The name is symbolic: Jezebel was the idolatrous queen who enticed Israel to add Baal worship to their religious ceremonies (see 1 Kings 16—19). The seductive teaching of Jezebel was similar to the "doctrine of Balaam" that the Lord condemned in the church of Pergamos (Rev. 2:14). She taught believers how to compromise with the Roman religion and the practices of the guilds, so that Christians would not lose their jobs or their lives.

It is interesting to contrast the churches at Ephesus and Thyatira. The Ephesian church was weakening in its love, yet faithful to judge false teachers; while the people in the assembly at Thyatira were growing in their love, but too tolerant of false doctrine. Both extremes must be avoided in the church. "Speaking the truth in love" is the biblical balance (Eph. 4:15). Unloving orthodoxy and loving compromise are both hateful to God.

Not only was the church at Thyatira tolerant of evil, but it was proud and unwilling to repent. The Lord gave the false prophetess time to repent, yet she refused. Now He was giving her followers opportunity to repent. His eyes of fire had searched out their thoughts and motives, and He would make no mistake. In fact, the Lord threatened to use this assembly as a solemn example to "all the churches" not to tolerate evil. Jezebel and her children (followers) would be sentenced to tribulation and death! Idolatry and compromise are, in the Bible, pictured as fornication and unfaithfulness to the marriage vows (Jer. 3:6ff.; Hos. 9:1ff.). Jezebel's bed of sin would become a bed of sickness! To *kill with death* means "to kill with pestilence" (see NASB). God would judge the false prophetess and her followers once and for all.

Admonition (vv. 24–29). Not everyone in the assembly was unfaithful to the Lord, and He had a special word for them. They had separated themselves from the false doctrine and compromising practices of Jezebel and her followers, which Christ denounces as "the depths of Satan" (note the contrast in 1 Cor. 2:10). The Lord had no special demands to make; He simply wanted them to hold fast in their resistance to evil. "Till I come" refers to Christ's return for His people, at which time He will reward them for their faithfulness (see Rev. 3:3; 16:15; 22:7, 17, 20). This is the first mention in Revelation of the Lord's coming for the church, the event we commonly call the rapture (see 1 Thess. 4:13–18). In contrast, the reference in Revelation 1:7 is to Christ's return to earth in judgment, to defeat His enemies and establish His kingdom (see Rev. 19:11ff.).

The believers in Thyatira are promised authority over the nations, which probably refers to the fact that God's people will live and reign with Christ (see Rev. 20:4). When the Lord sets up His kingdom on earth, it will be a righteous kingdom with perfect justice. He will rule with a rod of iron (Ps. 2:8–9). Rebellious men will be like clay pots, easily broken to pieces!

Jesus Christ is "the Bright and Morning Star" (Rev. 22:16). The promise in Revelation 2:28 suggests that God's people shall be so closely identified with Christ that He will "belong" to them! But perhaps there is also an allusion here to Satan, who wanted the kingdom for himself and who offered the world's kingdoms to Christ if He would worship him but once (Matt 4:8–11). In Isaiah 14:12, Satan is named *Lucifer,* which in Hebrew means "brightness, bright star." The compromising people in Thyatira were following "the depths of Satan," which would lead to darkness and death. God's overcomers, on the other hand, would share the Morning Star!

As you review these first four messages to the churches, you can see the dangers that still exist for the people of God. Like Ephesus, we can be zealous and orthodox, but at the same time lose our devotion to Christ. Or, like Thyatira, our love can be increasing yet lacking in the kind of discernment that is necessary to keep the church pure (see Phil. 1:9–11). Like Pergamos and Thyatira, we may be so tolerant of evil that we grieve the Lord and invite His judgment.

Would we have selected Smyrna as the most spiritual church of the four? Probably not, yet the Lord did! We need to remind ourselves not to judge God's people by wrong standards, because only the Lord can see the heart (see 1 Cor. 4:5).

God's exhortation to these churches (except Smyrna) is, "Repent! Change your minds!" It is not only lost sinners who need to repent, but also disobedient Christians. If we do not repent and deal with sin in our lives and in our assemblies, the Lord may judge us and remove our lampstand (Rev. 2:5). How tragic it is when a local church gradually abandons the faith and loses its witness for Christ!

"He that hath an ear, let him hear what the Spirit saith unto the churches!"

CHAPTER THREE
Revelation 3
CHRIST AND THE CHURCHES—PART 2

We are still listening to what the Holy Spirit has to say to the churches, for these messages from Christ belong to our day as well as to the first century. Churches are people, and human nature has not changed. So, as we continue our study, we must not look on these letters as ancient relics. On the contrary, they are mirrors in which we see ourselves!

Sardis, the Feeble Church (3:1–6)
Ancient Sardis, the capital of Lydia, was a most important city. It lay about fifty miles east of Ephesus at the junction of five main roads; so it was a center for trade. It was also a military center, for it was located on an almost inaccessible plateau. The acropolis of Sardis was about 1,500 feet above the main roads, and it formed an impregnable fortress. The main religion in the city was the worship of Artemis, one of the "nature cults" that built on the idea of death and rebirth.

Sardis was also known for its manufacture of woolen garments, a fact that has bearing on Christ's message to the church. Sad to say, the city at that time was but a shadow of its former splendor, and the church, unfortunately, had become like the city—it was alive in name only.

The message to Sardis is a warning to all "great churches" that are living on past glory. Dr. Vance Havner has frequently reminded us that spiritual ministries often go through four stages: a man, a movement, a machine, and then a monument. Sardis was at the "monument" stage, but there was still hope!

There was hope because Christ was the Head of the church and He was able to bring new life. He described Himself as the one possessing the seven Spirits and the seven stars. There is only one Holy Spirit (Eph. 4:4), but the number seven demonstrates fullness and completeness. The Holy Spirit gives life to the church, and life is exactly what the people at Sardis needed. The sevenfold Spirit of God is pictured as seven burning lamps (Rev. 4:5) and as seven all-seeing eyes (Rev. 5:6).

All of the church's man-made programs can never bring life, any more than a circus can resurrect a corpse. The church was born when the Spirit of God descended on the Day of Pentecost (Acts 2), and its life comes from the Spirit. When the Spirit is grieved, the church begins to lose life and power. When sin is confessed and church members get right with God and with each other, then the Spirit infuses new life—revival!

Christ also controls the seven stars, the messengers of the churches (Rev. 1:20), referring most likely to the pastors. Sometimes it is a pastor's fault that a church is dying, and the Lord of the church must remove the star and put another in his place.

There are no words of commendation to the believers at Sardis. Nor did the Lord point out any doctrinal problems that required correction. Neither is there any mention of opposition or persecution. The church would have been better off had there been some suffering, for it had grown comfortable and content and was living on its past reputation. There was reputation without reality, form without force. Like the city itself, the church at Sardis gloried in past splendor, but ignored present decay.

In fact, even what they did have was about to die! Why? Because the believers had gone to sleep. Twice in its long history, the citadel at Sardis had been captured, each time because sentries had failed to do their jobs faithfully. It is when the church's leaders and members get accustomed to their blessings and complacent about their ministry that the enemy finds his way in.

The impression is that the assembly in Sardis was not aggressive in its witness to the city. There was no persecution because there was no invasion of the enemy's territory. No friction usually means no motion! The unsaved in Sardis saw the church as a respectable group of people who were neither dangerous nor desirable. They were decent people with a dying witness and a decaying ministry.

Our Lord's counsel to the church began with, "Be watchful! Wake up!" (see Rom. 13:11ff.) The "sentries" were asleep! The first step toward renewal in a dying church is honest awareness that something is wrong. When an organism is alive, there is growth, repair, reproduction, and power; if these elements are lacking in a church, then that church is either dying or already dead.

The Lord warned the Ephesian saints that He would come and remove their lampstand if they did not repent (Rev. 2:5). He warned the church at Pergamos that He would come and make war with the sword of the Spirit (Rev. 2:16). If the believers at Sardis did not follow His orders, He would come as a thief, when they least expected Him, and this would mean judgment.

However, a remnant of dedicated people often exists in even a dying church. The Christians at Sardis had life, even though it was feeble. They were working, even though their works were not all that they could have been. The Lord admonished them to strengthen what remained and not to give up because the church was weak. Where there is life, there is hope!

What was different about this dedicated remnant? They had not defiled their garments (Rev. 3:4). There is some evidence from antiquity that temple worshippers were not permitted to approach their gods and goddesses wearing dirty garments. The remnant in the church at Sardis had not compromised with the pagan society around them, nor had they grown comfortable and complacent. It was this devoted spiritual remnant that held the future of the church's ministry.

"Wake up! Be watchful! Repent! Remember the Word you have received and obey it!" This is the formula for revival. It is good to guard our spiritual heritage, but we must not embalm it. It is not enough to be true to the faith and have a great history. That faith must produce life and works.

The promise in Revelation 3:5 ("clothed in white raiment") would have been especially meaningful to people who lived in a city where woolen garments were manufactured. And the statement about the names being blotted out would also be significant to people in the Roman Empire, where citizenship was vitally important (see Acts 22:24–30).

Is there a warning here that a true believer might lose his salvation? I don't think so. It would appear that God's "Book of Life" contains the names of all the living, the wicked as well as the righteous (Ps. 69:28). Revelation 13:8 and 17:8 suggest that the names of the saved are written in the book from the foundation of the world—that is, before they had done anything good or bad. By God's grace, they have been chosen in Christ before the beginning of time (Eph. 1:4; see also Matt. 25:34).

Jesus told His disciples to rejoice because their names were "written in heaven" (Luke 10:20). The Greek verb is in the perfect tense, which means it can be translated (as Kenneth Wuest does in his *Expanded Translation),* "your names have been written in heaven and are on permanent record up there." It is not likely that Jesus would contradict Himself in this important matter!

If the names of believers (the elect) are written from the foundation of the world, and if God knows all things, why would He enter the name of somebody who would one day fall and have to be removed from the book? We are enrolled in heaven because we have been born again (Heb. 12:23), and no matter how disobedient a child may be, he or she cannot be "unborn."

As unbelievers die, their names are removed from the book; thus, at the final judgment, the book contains only the names of believers (Rev. 20:12–15). It then becomes "the Lamb's Book of Life" (Rev. 21:27), because only those saved by the Lord Jesus Christ have their names in it. All the others have been blotted out, something God would never do for any true child of God (see Ex. 32:32; Rom. 9:3). It is a book of *life,* and lost sinners are *dead* (Eph. 2:1).

The warning here is that we not grow comfortable in our churches, lest we find ourselves slowly dying. The encouragement is that no church is beyond hope as long as there is a remnant in it, willing to strengthen the things that remain.

Philadelphia, the Faithful Church (3:7–13)

As most people know, *Philadelphia* means "love of the brethren." Certainly, brotherly love is an important mark of the Christian. We are "taught of God to love one another" (1 Thess. 4:9): by God the Father (1 John 4:19), God the Son (John 13:34), and God the Spirit (Rom. 5:5). But it is not enough to love God and our fellow believers; we must also love a lost world and seek to reach unbelievers with the good news of the cross. This church had a vision to reach a lost world, and God set before them an open door.

Philadelphia was situated in a strategic place on the main route of the Imperial Post from Rome to the East, and thus was called "the gateway to the East." It was also called "little Athens" because of the many temples in the city. The church was certainly located in a place of tremendous opportunity.

The only major problem with the location was that the area was prone to earthquakes. Philadelphia sat on a geological fault, and in 17 BC it was destroyed by a severe earthquake that also destroyed Sardis and ten other cities. Afterward, some of the citizens refused to move back into the city and remained in the surrounding countryside, which they called "the burnt land." There did not seem to be much security in the city of brotherly love!

Jesus Christ presented Himself to the church at Philadelphia as "He that is holy." This is tantamount to declaring that He is God, which, of course, He is. Jesus Christ is holy in His character, His words, His actions, and His purposes. As the Holy One, He is uniquely set apart from everything else, and nothing can be compared to Him.

But He is also the One who is true—that is, genuine. He is the original, not a copy; the authentic God and not a manufactured one. There were hundreds of false gods and goddesses in those days (1 Cor. 8:5–6), but only Jesus Christ could rightfully claim to be the true God.

It is worth noting that when the martyrs in heaven addressed the Lord, they called Him "holy and true" (Rev. 6:10). Their argument was that, because He was holy, He had to judge sin, and because He was true, He had to vindicate His people who had been wickedly slain.

Not only is He holy and true, but He has the authority to open and close doors. The background of this imagery is Isaiah 22:15–25. Assyria had invaded Judah (as Isaiah had warned), but the Jewish leaders were trusting Egypt, not God, to deliver the nation. One of the treacherous leaders was a man named Shebna who had used his office, not for the good of the people, but for his own private gain. God saw to it that Shebna was removed from office and that a faithful man, Eliakim, was put in his place and given the keys of authority. Eliakim was a picture of Jesus Christ, a dependable administrator of the affairs of God's people. Jesus Christ also has the keys of hades and of death (Rev. 1:18).

In the New Testament, an "open door" speaks of opportunity for ministry (Acts 14:27; 1 Cor. 16:9; 2 Cor. 2:12; Col. 4:3). Christ is the Lord of the harvest and the Head of the church, and it is He who determines where and when His people shall serve (see Acts 16:6–10). He gave the church at Philadelphia a great opportunity for ministry.

But could they take advantage of it? There were at least two obstacles to overcome, the first being their own lack of strength (Rev. 3:8). Apparently, this was not a large or a strong church; however, it was a faithful one. They were true to God's Word and unafraid to bear His name. Revelation 3:10 suggests that they had endured some special testing and had proved faithful.

It is not the size or strength of a church that determines its ministry, but faith in the call and command of the Lord. "God's commandments are God's enablements." If Jesus Christ gave them an open door, then He would see to it that they were able to walk through it! Martin Luther put it perfectly in his well-known hymn:

Did we in our own strength confide,
Our striving would be losing.
Were not the right Man on our side,
The Man of God's own choosing.

The second obstacle was the opposition of the Jews in the city (Rev. 3:9). This was really the opposition of Satan, for we do not battle against flesh and blood (Eph. 6:12). These people may have been Jews in the flesh, but they were not "true Israel" in the New Testament sense (Rom. 2:17–29). Jewish people certainly have a great heritage, but it is no guarantee of salvation (Matt. 3:7–12; John 8:33ff.).

How were these Jews opposing the church at Philadelphia? For one thing, by excluding Jewish believers from the synagogue. Another weapon was probably false accusation, for this is the way the unbelieving Jews often attacked Paul. Satan is the accuser and he uses even religious people to assist him (Rev. 12:10). It is not easy to witness for Christ when the leading people in the community are spreading lies about you. The church at Smyrna faced the same kind of opposition (Rev. 2:9).

The believers in Philadelphia were in a similar situation to that of Paul when he wrote 1 Corinthians 16:9—there were both opportunities and obstacles! Unbelief sees the obstacles, but faith sees the opportunities! And since the Lord holds the keys, He is in control of the outcome! So what do we have to fear? Nobody can close the doors as long as He keeps them open. Fear, unbelief, and delay have caused the church to miss many God-given opportunities.

The Savior gave three wonderful and encouraging promises to this church. First, He would take care of their enemies (Rev. 3:9). One day, these people would have to acknowledge that the Christians were right (see Isa. 60:14; Phil. 2:10–11)! If we take care of God's work, He will take care of our battles.

Second, He would keep them from tribulation (Rev. 3:10). This is surely a reference to the time of tribulation that John described in Revelation 6—19, "the time of Jacob's trouble." This is not speaking about some local trial, because it involves "them that dwell on the earth" (see Rev. 6:10; 8:13; 11:10; 12:12; 13:8, 12, 14; 14:6; 17:2, 8). The immediate reference would be to the official Roman persecutions that would come, but the ultimate reference is to the tribulation that will encompass the earth before Jesus Christ returns to establish His kingdom. In many Bible scholars' understanding, Revelation 3:10 is a promise that the church will not go through the tribulation, but will be taken to heaven before it begins (see 1 Thess. 4:13—5:11). The admonition, "Behold, I come quickly," would strengthen this view.

The third promise to the Philadelphians is that God would honor them (Rev. 3:12). The symbolism in this verse would be especially meaningful to people who lived in constant danger of earthquakes: the stability of the pillar, no need to go out or to flee, a heavenly city that nothing could destroy. Ancient cities often honored great leaders by erecting pillars with their names inscribed on them. God's pillars are not made of stone, because there is no temple in the heavenly city (Rev. 21:22). His pillars are faithful people who bear His name for His glory (Gal. 2:9).

In a very real sense, the church today is like the Philadelphian church, for God has set before us many open doors of opportunity. If He opens the doors, we must work; if He shuts the doors, we must wait. Above all, we must be faithful to Him and see the opportunities, not the obstacles. If we miss our opportunities, we lose our rewards (crowns), and this means being ashamed before Him when He comes (1 John 2:28).

Laodicea, the Foolish Church (3:14–22)

As with some of the previous churches, the Lord adapted His words to something significant about the city in which the assembly was located. In this case, Laodicea was known for its wealth and its manufacture of a special eye salve, as well as of a glossy black wool cloth. It also was located near Hieropolis, where there were famous hot springs, and Colosse, known for its pure, cold water.

The Lord presented Himself as "the Amen," which is an Old Testament title for God (see Isa. 65:16, where the word *truth* is the Hebrew word *amen*). He is the truth and speaks the truth, because He is "the faithful and true Witness" (Rev. 3:14). The Lord was about to tell this church the truth about its spiritual condition; unfortunately, they would not believe His diagnosis.

"Why is it that new Christians create problems in the church?" a young pastor once asked me.

"They don't create problems," I replied. "They *reveal* them. The problems have always been there, but we've gotten used to them. New Christians are like children in the home: they tell the truth about things!"

The Laodicean church was blind to its own needs and unwilling to face the truth. Yet honesty is the beginning of true blessing, as we admit what we are, confess our sins, and receive from God all that we need. If we want God's best for our lives and churches, we must be honest with God and let God be honest with us.

"The beginning of the creation of God" (Rev. 3:14) does not suggest that Jesus was created, and therefore not eternal God. The word translated *beginning* means "source, origin" (see John 1:3; Col. 1:15, 18).

The Lord demonstrated four areas of need in the church at Laodicea.

They had lost their vigor (vv. 16–17). In the Christian life, there are three "spiritual temperatures": a burning heart, on fire for God (Luke 24:32), a cold heart (Matt. 24:12), and a lukewarm heart (Rev. 3:16). The lukewarm Christian is comfortable, complacent, and does not realize his need. If he were cold, at least he would feel it! Both the cold water from Colosse and the hot water from Hieropolis would be lukewarm by the time it was piped to Laodicea.

As believers in Jesus Christ, we have every reason to be "fervent in spirit" (Rom. 12:11). Fervent prayer is also vital (Col. 4:12). It was as the Emmaus disciples listened to the Word that their hearts were warmed. No wonder Paul commanded that his letter to Colosse be sent to the Laodicean church (Col. 4:16)!

We enjoy a beverage that is either hot or cold, but one that is tepid is flat and stale. That's why the waitress keeps adding hot coffee or fresh iced tea to our cups and glasses. The second law of thermodynamics requires that a "closed system" eventually moderates so that no more energy is being produced. Unless something is added from the outside, the system decays and dies. Without added fuel, the hot water in the boiler becomes cool; without electricity, the refrigerant in the freezer becomes warm.

The church cannot be a "closed system." Jesus said, "Without me ye can do nothing" (John 15:5). The Laodicean church was independent, self-satisfied, and secure. "We have need of nothing!" But all the while, their spiritual power had been decaying; their material wealth and glowing statistics were but shrouds hiding a rotting corpse. Their Lord was *outside the church*, trying to get in (Rev. 3:20).

They had lost their values (vv. 17–18a). The church at Smyrna thought itself poor, when it was really rich (Rev. 2:9); the Laodiceans boasted that they were rich, when in fact they were poor. Perhaps we have here a hint of why this church declined spiritually: they had become proud of their ministry and had begun to measure things by human standards instead of by spiritual values. They were, in the eyes of the Lord, "wretched, and miserable, and poor."

Laodicea was a wealthy city and a banking center. Perhaps some of the spirit of the marketplace crept into the church so that their values became twisted. Why is it that so many church bulletins and letterheads show pictures of *buildings?* Are these the things that are most important to us? The board at the Laodicean church could proudly show you the latest annual report with its impressive statistics, yet Jesus said He was about to vomit them out of His mouth!

The solution? Pay the price to get true "gold tried in the fire." This suggests that the church needed some persecution; they were too comfortable (1 Peter 1:7). Nothing makes God's people examine their priorities faster than suffering!

They had lost their vision (v. 18b). The Laodiceans were "blind." They could not see reality. They were living in a fool's paradise, proud of a church that was about to be rejected. The apostle Peter teaches that when a believer is not growing in the Lord, his spiritual vision is affected (2 Peter 1:5–9). "Diet" has bearing on the condition of one's eyes, in a spiritual sense as well as a physical one.

These people could not see themselves as they really were. Nor could they see their Lord as He stood outside the door of the church. Nor could they see the open doors of opportunity. They were so wrapped up in building their own kingdom that they had become lukewarm in their concern for a lost world.

The solution? Apply the heavenly eye salve! The city of Laodicea was noted for its eye salve, but the kind of medication the saints needed was not available in the apothecary shop. The eye is one of the body's most sensitive areas, and only the Great Physician can "operate" on it and make it what it ought to be. As He did with the man whose account is told in John 9, He might even irritate before He illuminates! But we must submit to His treatment, and then maintain good spiritual "health habits" so that our vision grows keener.

They had lost their vesture (vv. 17–22). Like the emperor in Hans Christian Andersen's story, these Christians thought they were clothed in splendor when they were really naked! To be naked meant to be defeated and humiliated (2 Sam. 10:4; Isa. 20:1–4). The Laodiceans could go to the market and purchase fine woolen garments, but that would not meet their real need. They needed the white garments of God's righteousness and grace. According to Revelation 19:8, we should be clothed in "fine linen, clean and white," and this symbolizes "the righteous acts of the saints" (NASB). Salvation means that Christ's righteousness is *imputed* to us, put to our account, but sanctification means that His righteousness is *imparted* to us, made a part of our character and conduct.

There is no divine commendation given to this church. Of course, the Laodiceans were busy commending themselves! They thought they were glorifying God, when in reality they were disgracing

His name just as though they had been walking around naked.

The Lord closed this letter with three special statements:

First, *an explanation:* "As many as I love, I rebuke and chasten" (Rev. 3:19a). He still loved these lukewarm saints, even though their love for Him had grown cold. He planned to chasten them as proof of His love (Prov. 3:11–12; Heb. 12:5–6). God permits churches to go through times of trial so that they might become what He wants them to become.

Second, *an exhortation:* "Be zealous therefore, and repent" (Rev. 3:19b). The church at Laodicea had to repent of their pride and humble themselves before the Lord. They had to "stir up that inner fire" (2 Tim. 1:6 PH) and cultivate a burning heart.

Finally, *an invitation* (Rev. 3:20–22). We often use these verses to lead lost people to Christ, but the basic application is to the believer. The Lord was outside the Laodicean church! He spoke to the individual—"if any man"—and not to the whole congregation. He appealed to a small remnant in Sardis (Rev. 3:4–5), and now He appeals to the individual. God can do great things in a church, even through one dedicated individual.

Christ was not impatient. "I have taken My stand" is the sense of the verb. He "knocks" through circumstances and He calls through His Word. For what is He appealing? Fellowship and communion, the people's desire to abide in Him. The Laodiceans were an independent church that had need of nothing, but they were not abiding in Christ and drawing their power from Him. They had a "successful program" but it was not fruit that comes from abiding in Christ (John 15:1–8).

Note that when we invite Him in, the supper room becomes a throne room! It is through communion with Christ that we find victory and become overcomers indeed.

The letters to the seven churches are God's X-rays, given to us so that we might examine our own lives and ministries. Judgment is going to come to this world, but it first begins at God's house (1 Peter 4:17). In these letters we find encouragement as well as rebuke.

May the Lord help us to hear what the Spirit is saying *today* to the church, and to the individuals in the churches!

CHAPTER FOUR
Revelation 4—5
COME, LET US ADORE HIM!

True spiritual worship is perhaps one of the greatest needs in our individual lives and in our churches. There is a constant emphasis today on witnessing for Christ and working for Christ, but not enough is said about worshipping Him. To *worship* means "to ascribe worth" (see Rev. 4:11; 5:12). It means to use all that we are and have to praise God for all that He is and does.

Heaven is a place of worship, and God's people shall worship Him throughout all eternity. Perhaps it would be good for us to get in practice now! A study of Revelation 4—5 will certainly help us better understand how to worship God and give Him the glory that He deserves.

If Revelation 1:19 is God's inspired outline of this book, then Revelation 4 ushers us into the third division: "the things which shall be hereafter." In fact, that is exactly what God said to John when He summoned him to heaven! It would appear that, in this experience, John illustrates what will happen to God's people when the church age has run its course: heaven will open; there will be a voice and the sound of a trumpet; and the saints will be caught up to heaven (1 Cor. 15:52; 1 Thess. 4:13–18). Then, God's judgment of the earth can begin.

But before God pours out His wrath, He gives us a glimpse into glory and permits us to hear the worshipping creatures in heaven as they praise God. Two aspects of their worship are presented for our instruction and imitation.

They Worship the Creator (4)

The key word in this chapter is *throne;* it is used fourteen times. In fact, this is a key word in the entire book, appearing forty-six times. No matter what may happen on earth, God is on His throne and is in complete control. Various teachers interpret Revelation in different ways, but all agree that John is emphasizing the glory and sovereignty of God. What an encouragement that would be to the suffering saints of John's day and of every age in history.

Using the throne as the focal point, we can easily understand the arrangement of this exciting chapter.

On the throne—Almighty God (vv. 2–3a). This is God the Father, since the Son approaches the throne in Revelation 5:6, and the Spirit is pictured before the throne in Revelation 4:5. There is no possible way for human words to describe what God is like in His essence. John can only use comparisons. Jasper is a clear gem (see Rev. 21:11) and the sardine is red. The Lord is robed in light, according to Psalm 104:2 and 1 Timothy 6:16. Both the jasper and the sardius (sardine) were found in the breastplate of the high priest (Ex. 28:17–21).

Around the throne—a rainbow (v. 3b). This rainbow was a complete circle, not merely an arc, for in heaven all things are completed. The rainbow reminds us of God's covenant with Noah (Gen. 9:11–17), symbolic of His promise that He would never again destroy the earth with a flood. God's covenant, as we shall see, was not only with Noah, but with all of His creation.

Judgment is about to fall, but the rainbow reminds us that God is merciful, even when He judges (Hab. 3:2). Usually, a rainbow appears *after* the storm, but here, we see it *before* the storm.

Around the throne—elders and living creatures (vv. 3–4, 6–7). The rainbow was around the throne vertically, while these heavenly beings were around the throne horizontally. They are, as it were, the king's court.

Who are these twenty-four elders seated on thrones? It is unlikely that they are angels, because angels are not numbered (Heb. 12:22), crowned, or enthroned. Besides, in Revelation 7:11, the elders are distinguished from the angels (see also Rev. 5:8–11). The crowns they wear are the "victor's crowns" (the Greek word *stephanos; see* Rev. 2:10), and we have no evidence that angels receive rewards.

These elders probably symbolize the people of God in heaven, enthroned and rewarded. There were twenty-four courses of priests in the Old Testament temple (1 Chron. 24:3–5, 18; see also Luke 1:5–9). God's people are "kings and priests" (Rev. 1:6), reigning and serving with Christ. Note especially their praise (Rev. 5:9–10). When Daniel (Dan. 7:9) saw the thrones set up (not "cast down" as in the *King James Version),* they were empty, but when John saw them, they had been filled. Since there were twelve tribes of Israel and twelve apostles, perhaps the number twenty-four symbolizes the completion of God's people.

The white robes and palm branches speak of victory (see Rev. 7:9). These are the "overcomers" who have conquered because of their faith in Christ (1 John 5:4–5).

Also around the throne, John saw four "living creatures" ("beasts" in the *King James Version)* who were nearer to God than the angels and the elders. They resemble the cherubim that the prophet Ezekiel saw (Ezek. 1:4–14; 10:20–22), but their praise (Rev. 4:8) reminds us of the seraphim of Isaiah 6. I believe that these special creatures symbolize God's creation and are related to God's covenant with Noah (Gen. 9:8–17). The faces of the living creatures parallel God's statement in Genesis 9:10—His covenant is with Noah (the face of the man), the fowl (the face of the eagle), the cattle (the face of the calf), and the beasts of the earth (the face of the lion).

These creatures signify the wisdom of God ("full of eyes") and proclaim the holiness of God. They are heavenly reminders that God has a covenant with His creation and that He rules His creation from His throne. The presence of the emerald rainbow further enhances this image, since the rainbow was given as the sign of the creation covenant. No matter what terrible judgments may fall on God's earth, He will be faithful to keep His Word. Men may curse Him during the judgments (Rev. 16:9, 11, 21), but nature will praise Him and magnify His holiness.

The cherubim described in Ezekiel 1 seem to have a part in the providential workings of God in the world, pictured by the "wheels within the wheels." God uses the forces of nature to accomplish His will (Ps. 148), and all nature praises and thanks Him.

Some students see in the four faces described

(Rev. 4:7) an illustration of the fourfold picture of Christ given in the gospel accounts. Matthew is the royal gospel of the King, illustrated by the lion. Mark emphasizes the servant aspect of the Lord's ministry (the calf). Luke presents Christ as the compassionate Son of Man. John magnifies the deity of Christ, the Son of God (the eagle).

Finally, the name used by these creatures, "Lord God Almighty," emphasizes the power of God. As mentioned in chapter 1, the name *Almighty* is used nine times in Revelation. The only other such usage in the New Testament is 2 Corinthians 6:18, but it is found at least thirty-one times in Job, a book that magnifies the power of God in nature.

Out of the throne—storm signals (v. 5a). "And from the throne proceed flashes of lightning and sounds and peals of thunder" (NASB). These are indications of a coming storm and reminders of God's awesome power (see Ex. 9:23, 28; 19:16). These "storm signals" will be repeated during the time of judgment, always proceeding from the throne and temple of God (Rev. 8:5; 11:19; 16:18). God has indeed prepared His throne for judgment (Ps. 9:7; note also 77:18).

Our world does not like to think of God as a God of judgment. They prefer to look at the rainbow around the throne and ignore the lightning and thunder out of the throne. He certainly is a God of grace, but His grace reigns *through righteousness* (Rom. 5:21). This was made clear at the cross where God manifested both His love for sinners and His wrath against sin.

Before the throne—lamps and a sea (vv. 5b–6a). The seven lamps connote completeness and symbolize the Holy Spirit of God (Rev. 1:4; note also Ezek. 1:13). John also seems to suggest in Revelation that the "heavenly sanctuary" follows the pattern of the earthly tabernacle and temple (see Heb. 9:23). The parallels are as follows:

Earthly temple	*Heavenly sanctuary*
Holy of Holies	The throne of God
Seven-branched candlestick	Seven lamps of fire before the throne
Bronze laver	Sea of glass
Cherubim over the mercy seat	Four living creatures around the throne
Priests	Elders (kings and priests)
Brazen altar	Altar (Rev. 6:9–11)
Incense altar	Incense altar (Rev. 8:3–5)
Ark of the covenant	Ark of the covenant (Rev. 11:19)

There is no temple in heaven in a material sense. All of heaven is God's sanctuary for those who serve before His holy throne (Rev. 7:15). However, John indicates in Revelation 15:5–8 that there is a special "sanctuary" of God (note also Rev. 11:19). In the eternal state, there will be no temple (Rev. 21:22).

A pure crystal sea symbolizes God's holiness, and the mingled fire speaks of His holy judgment. The crystal "firmament" in Ezekiel's vision also comes to mind (Ezek. 1:22); it was the foundation for God's throne. We shall meet this "sea of glass" again in Revelation 15 where it is connected with Israel's victory over Egypt.

Praise to the throne (vv. 9–11). Whenever the living creatures glorified God, the elders would fall before the throne and praise Him. The book of Revelation is filled with hymns of praise (Rev. 4:8, 11; 5:9–13; 7:12–17; 11:15–18; 12:10–12; 15:3–4; 16:5–7; 18:2–8; 19:2–6). The emphasis on praise is significant when you remember that John wrote this book to encourage people who were going through suffering and persecution!

The theme of this hymn is *God the Creator,* while in Revelation 5 the elders praise *God the Redeemer.* The praise in Revelation 4 is given to the Father on the throne, while in Revelation 5 it is directed to the Son (the Lamb) before the throne. The closing hymn (Rev. 5:13) is expressed to both, another proof of the deity of Jesus Christ.

If the twenty-four elders typify the people of God in heaven, then we must ask, "Why should God's people praise God the Creator?" If the heavens are declaring the glory of God, why shouldn't God's heavenly people join the chorus? Creation bears constant witness to the power, wisdom, and glory of God (Ps. 19). Acknowledging the Creator is the first step toward trusting the Redeemer (see Acts 14:8–18; 17:22–31). "All things were created by Him [Christ] and for Him... and by Him all things consist [hold together]" (Col. 1:16–17).

But sinful man worships and serves the creature rather than the Creator, and this is idolatry (Rom. 1:25). Furthermore, sinful man has polluted and destroyed God's wonderful creation, and he is going to pay for it (see Rev. 11:18). Creation is for God's praise and pleasure, and man has no right to usurp that which rightfully belongs to God. Man plunged creation into sin, so that God's *good* creation (Gen. 1:31) is today a *groaning* creation (Rom. 8:22), but because of Christ's work on the cross, it will one day be delivered and become a *glorious* creation (Rev. 8:18–24).

It is unfortunate that the church today often neglects to worship the God of creation. The real answer to the ecological problem is not financial or legal, but spiritual. It is only when man acknowledges the Creator and begins to use creation to God's glory that the problems will be solved.

They Worship the Redeemer (5)

The focus of attention now shifts to a seven-sealed scroll in the hand of God. The scroll could not be read because it was rolled up and sealed (like a Roman will) with seven seals. John could see writing on both sides of the scroll, which meant that nothing more could be added. What was written was completed and final.

The scroll represents Christ's "title deed" to all that the Father promised Him because of His sacrifice on the cross. "Ask of me, and I shall give thee the heathen [nations] for thine inheritance, and the uttermost parts of the earth for thy possession" (Ps. 2:8). Jesus Christ is the "Heir of all things" (Heb. 1:2). He is our beloved "Kinsman-Redeemer" who was willing to give His life to set us free from bondage and to restore our lost inheritance (see Lev. 25:23–46; the book of Ruth; Jer. 32:6–15).

As Christ removed the seals, various dramatic events took place. The seventh seal introduced the seven trumpet judgments (Rev. 8:1–2). Then, when the seventh trumpet had blown, the great day of God's wrath was announced, ushering in the "vial [bowl] judgments" that brought to a climax the wrath of God (Rev. 11:15ff.; 15:1). It is possible that the trumpet judgments were written on one side of the scroll and the bowl judgments on the other.

A title deed or will can be opened only by the appointed heir, and this is Jesus Christ. No one in all the universe could be found worthy enough to break the seals. No wonder John wept, for he realized that God's glorious redemption plan for mankind could never be completed until the scroll was opened. The redeemer had to be near of kin, willing to redeem, and able to redeem. Jesus Christ meets all of the qualifications. He became flesh, so He is our Kinsman. He loves us and is willing to redeem, and He paid the price, so He is able to redeem.

Now we are able to enter into the worship experience described in the remainder of Revelation 5. And we'll discover four compelling reasons why we worship Jesus Christ.

Because of who He is (vv. 5–7). Three unique titles are given to our Lord to describe who He is. First, He is *the Lion of the tribe of Judah.* The reference here is to Genesis 49:8–10, where Jacob prophetically gave the scepter to Judah and made it the tribe of the kings. (God never meant for Saul to establish a dynasty, because he came from the tribe of Benjamin. God *used him* to discipline Israel because the people asked for a king; then He *gave them* David from the tribe of Judah.)

The image of "the lion" speaks of dignity, sovereignty, courage, and victory. Jesus Christ is the only living Jew who can prove His kingship from the genealogical records. "Son of David" was a title often used when He was ministering on earth (see Matt. 1).

But He is also *the Root of David,* which means He brought David (and David's line) into existence. As far as His humanity is concerned, Jesus had His roots *in* David (Isa. 11:1, 10), but as far as His deity is concerned, Jesus is the Root *of* David. This speaks, of course, of our Lord's eternality; He is indeed the "Ancient of Days." How the Messiah could both be David's Lord and David's son was a problem Jesus presented to the Pharisees, and they could not (or would not) answer Him (Matt. 22:41–46).

When John turned to see, he saw not a lion but a *lamb!* Jesus Christ is called "the Lamb" at least twenty-eight times in the book of Revelation (the Greek word used means "a little pet lamb") and the emphasis is not hard to miss. God's wrath is "the wrath of the Lamb" (Rev. 6:16). Cleansing is by "the blood of the Lamb" (Rev. 7:14). The church is "the bride of the Lamb" (Rev. 19:7; 21:9).

The theme of "the Lamb" is an important one throughout Scripture, for it presents the person and work of Jesus Christ, the Redeemer. The Old Testament question, "Where is the lamb?" (Gen. 22:7) was answered by John the Baptist who cried, "Behold the Lamb of God, which taketh away the sin of the world" (John 1:29). The choirs of heaven sing, "Worthy is the Lamb" (Rev. 5:12).

The description of the Lamb (Rev. 5:6), if produced literally by an artist, would provide a grotesque picture, but when understood symbolically, conveys spiritual truth. Since seven is the number of perfection, we have here perfect power (seven horns), perfect wisdom (seven eyes), and perfect presence (seven Spirits in all the earth). The theologians would call these qualities omnipotence, omniscience, and omnipresence; and all three are attributes of God. The Lamb is God the Son, Christ Jesus!

We worship Jesus Christ because of who He is. But there is a second reason why we worship Him.

Because of where He is (v. 6). To begin with, Jesus is in heaven. He is not in the manger, in Jerusalem, on the cross, or in the tomb. He is ascended and exalted in heaven. What an encouragement this is to suffering Christians, to know that their Savior has defeated every enemy and is now controlling events from glory! He too suffered, but God turned His suffering into glory.

But where is Christ in heaven? He is *in the midst.* The Lamb is the center of all that transpires in heaven. All creation centers in Him (the four living creatures), as do all of God's people (the elders). The angels around the throne encircle the Savior and praise Him.

He is also *at the throne.* Some sentimental Christian poetry and hymnody dethrones our Savior and emphasizes only His earthly life. These poems and songs glamorize "the gentle Carpenter" or "the humble Teacher," but they fail to exalt the risen Lord! We do not worship a babe in a manger or a corpse on a cross. We worship the living, reigning Lamb of God who is in the midst of all in heaven.

Because of what He does (vv. 8–10). When the Lamb came and took the scroll (see Dan. 7:13–14), the weeping ended and the praising began. God's people and the representatives of God's creation joined their voices in a new song of praise. Note that praise *and prayer* were united, for incense is a picture of prayer rising to the throne of God (Ps. 141:2; Luke 1:10). We shall meet the "incense prayers" of the saints again (Rev. 6:9–11; 8:1–6).

What kind of song did they sing? To begin with, it was *a worship hymn,* for they said, "Thou art worthy!" To *worship* means "to ascribe worth," and Jesus alone is worthy. When I was in the pastorate, I tried to open each morning worship service with a hymn that lifted the congregation's minds and hearts upward to the Lord Jesus Christ. Too many contemporary songs are "I" centered rather than "Christ" centered. They so emphasize the believer's experience that they almost ignore the Lord's glory. Certainly there is a place for that kind of song, but nothing can compare with adoring Christ in spiritual worship.

But this song was also *a gospel song!* "Thou wast slain, and hast redeemed us [some texts read *them*] by thy blood." The word translated *slain* means "violently slain" (Rev. 5:6). Heaven sings about the cross and the blood! I read about a denomination that revised its official hymnal and removed all songs about the blood of Christ. That hymnal could never be used in heaven, because there they glorify the Lamb slain for the sins of the world.

In Genesis 22, a ram was substituted for Isaac, a picture of Christ giving His life for *the individual* (see Gal. 2:20). At Passover, the lamb was slain for *each family* (Ex. 12:3). Isaiah states that Jesus died for *the nation of Israel* (Isa. 53:8; see also John 11:49–52). John affirms that the Lamb died for *the whole world!* (John 1:29) The more you meditate on the power and scope of Christ's work on the cross, the more humbled and worshipful you become.

This song was also a *missionary song.* Sinners were redeemed "out of every kindred, and tongue, and people, and nation" (Rev. 5:9). *Kindred* refers to a common ancestor and *tongue* to a common language. *People* means a common race, and *nation* a common rule or government. God loves a whole world (John 3:16), and His desire is that the message of redemption be taken to a whole world (Matt. 28:18–20).

Perhaps you heard about the Christian who was against foreign missions but somehow happened to attend a missionary rally. When they passed the offering plate, he told the usher, "I don't believe in missions!" "Then take something out," said the usher. "It's for the heathen."

This heavenly hymn was also *a devotional hymn,* for it announced our unique position in Christ as "a kingdom of priests." Like Melchizedek of old, believers are kings and priests (Gen. 14:17ff.; Heb. 7; 1 Peter 2:5–10). The veil of the temple was torn when Jesus died, and the way is opened to God (Heb. 10:19–25). We "reign in life" as we yield to Christ and allow His Spirit to work in us (Rom. 5:17).

Finally, this song was *a prophetic hymn:* "We shall reign on the earth" (Rev. 5:10). When Jesus Christ returns to earth, He will establish His righteous kingdom for 1,000 years, and we shall reign with Him (Rev. 20:1–6). The prayers of the saints, "Thy kingdom come!" will then be fulfilled. Creation shall then be set free from bondage to sin (Isa. 11:1–10;

Rom. 8:17–23), and Christ shall reign in justice and power.

What a marvelous hymn! How rich would be our worship if only we would blend all these truths in honoring Him!

Because of what He has (vv. 11–14). In this closing burst of praise, all the angels and every creature in the universe joined together to worship the Redeemer. What a cascade of harmony John heard! In this hymn, they stated those things that Jesus Christ deserved to receive because of His sacrificial death on the cross. When He was on earth, people did not ascribe these things to Him, for many of these things He deliberately laid aside in His humiliation.

He was born in weakness and died in weakness, but He is the recipient of all power. He became the poorest of the poor (2 Cor. 8:9), and yet He owns all the riches of heaven and earth. Men laughed at Him and called Him a fool, yet He is the very wisdom of God (1 Cor. 1:24; Col. 2:3).

He shared in the sinless weaknesses of humanity as He hungered, thirsted, and became weary. Today in glory, He possesses all strength. On earth, He experienced humiliation and shame as sinners ridiculed and reviled Him. They laughed at His kingship and attired Him in a mock robe, crown, and scepter. But all of that is changed now! He has received all honor and glory!

And blessing! He became a curse for us on the cross (Gal. 3:13), so that we can never be under the curse of the broken law. (Some translations read "praise" instead of "blessing," but the Greek word carries both meanings.) He is worthy of all praise!

The worship service climaxed with the entire universe praising the Lamb of God and the Father seated on the throne!

And there was even a loud "Amen!" from the four living creatures! In heaven, we are permitted to say "Amen!"

Keep in mind that all of this praise centered on the Lord Jesus Christ, the Redeemer. It is not Christ the Teacher, but Christ the Savior, who is the theme of their worship. While an unconverted person could praise the Creator, he certainly could not sincerely praise the Redeemer.

All of heaven's praise came because the Lamb took the scroll from the Father's hand. God's great eternal plan would now be fulfilled and creation would be set free from the bondage of sin and death. One day the Lamb will break the seals and put in motion events that will eventually lead to His coming to earth and the establishment of His kingdom.

As you share in these heavenly worship services, do you find your own heart saying "Amen!" to what they have sung? You may believe in Christ as the Creator, but have you trusted Him as your Redeemer?

If not, will you do so right now?

"Behold, I stand at the door and knock: if any man hear my voice, and open the door, I will come in to him, and will sup with him, and he with me" (Rev. 3:20).

CHAPTER FIVE
Revelation 6—7
THE SEALS AND THE SEALED

The worship described in Revelation 4—5 is preparation for the wrath described in Revelation 6—19. It seems strange to us that worship and judgment should go together, but this is because we do not fully understand either the holiness of God or the sinfulness of man. Nor do we grasp the total picture of what God wants to accomplish and how the forces of evil have opposed Him. God is longsuffering, but eventually He must judge sin and vindicate His servants.

According to Daniel 9:27, seven years are assigned to Israel in God's prophetic calendar, beginning with the signing of an agreement with the world dictator (the Antichrist), and ending with Christ's return to earth to judge evil and establish His kingdom. It is this period that is described in Revelation 6—19. By referring to John's outline (Rev. 1), you will see that his description is in three parts: the first three and a half years (Rev. 6—9), the events at the middle of the period (Rev. 10—14), and the last three and a half years (Rev. 15—19).

What is so significant about the middle of the tribulation? That is when the Antichrist breaks his covenant with Israel and becomes their persecutor instead of their protector (Dan. 9:27).

As you study these fourteen action-filled chapters, keep in mind that John wrote to encourage God's people in every age of history. He was not only writing *prophecy* that would be fulfilled in the end times, but he was also writing great *theology* and dramatically revealing the character of God and the principles of His kingdom. These chapters describe the cosmic conflict between God and Satan, the New Jerusalem and Babylon, and no matter what "key" a student may use to unlock Revelation, he cannot help but see the exalted King of kings as He vindicates His people and gives victory to His overcomers.

Since the church never knows when Christ will return, each generation must live in expectancy of His coming. Therefore the book of Revelation must be able to communicate truth to each generation, not just to the people who will be alive when these events occur. Verses like Revelation 13:9; 16:15; and 22:7, 18–20 all indicate the timelessness of John's message. This also explains why the apostle used so much symbolism, for symbols never lose their meaning. In every era of its history, the church has had to contend with Babylon (compare Rev. 18:4 with Jer. 50—51) and Antichrist (see 1 John 2:18ff.). Revelation 6—19 is merely the climax of this conflict.

In Revelation 6—7, John characterized the opening days of the tribulation as a time of retribution, response, and redemption.

Retribution (6:1–8)

In this section, John recorded the opening of the first four seals, and as each seal was opened, one of the four living creatures summoned a rider on a horse. ("Come and see" should read, "Come!") In other words, events take place on earth because of the sovereign direction of God in heaven.

The horse imagery is probably related to the vision described in Zechariah 1:7–17. Horses represent God's activity on earth, the forces He uses to accomplish His divine purposes. The center of His program is Israel, particularly the city of Jerusalem. (Jerusalem is mentioned thirty-nine times in Zech.) God has a covenant purpose for Israel, and that purpose will be fulfilled just as He promised.

Now, let's try to identify these horses and their riders.

Antichrist (vv. 1–2). Daniel states that there is a "prince that shall come," who will make a covenant with Israel to protect her from her enemies (Dan. 9:26–27). In other words, the future world dictator begins his career as a peacemaker! He will go from victory to victory and finally control the whole world.

Some have suggested that the rider on the white horse is actually a symbol of the "conquering Christ" who today is defeating the forces of evil in the world. They point to Revelation 19:11 as proof, but the only similarity is the presence of a white horse. If this rider is indeed Jesus Christ, it seems strange that He should be named *at the end of the book* and not at the beginning!

We would expect the Antichrist to resemble *the* Christ, because Antichrist is Satan's great imitation! Even the Jews (who ought to know the Scriptures) will be deceived by him (John 5:43; 2 Thess. 2:1–12). This great deceiver will come as a peaceful leader, holding a bow but no arrows! (Our Lord's weapon is a sword; Rev. 19:15.) Antichrist will solve the world's problems and be received as the Great Liberator.

The word for *crown* in Revelation 6:2 is *Stephanas*, which means "the victor's crown." The crown that Jesus Christ wears is *diadema*, "the kingly crown" (Rev. 19:12). Antichrist could never wear the diadem, because it belongs only to the Son of God.

Certainly, there is a sense in which Jesus Christ is conquering today, as He releases people from the bondage of sin and Satan (Acts 26:18; Col. 1:13). But this conquest began with His victory on the cross and certainly did not have to wait for the opening of a seal! We shall note later that the sequence of events in Revelation 6 closely parallels the sequence given by our Lord in His Olivet discourse, and the first item mentioned is the appearance of false Christs (Matt. 24:5).

War (vv. 3–4). Antichrist's conquest begins in peace, but soon he exchanges the empty bow for a sword. The color red is often associated with terror and death: the red dragon (Rev. 12:3), the red beast (Rev. 17:3). It is a picture of wanton bloodshed. War has been a part of man's experience since Cain killed Abel, so this image would speak to believers in every age, reminding them that God is ultimately in control, even though He is not responsible for the lawless deeds of men and nations.

Famine (vv. 5–6). The color black is often connected with famine (Jer. 14:1–2; Lam. 5:10). Famine and war go together. A shortage of food will always drive up prices and force the government to ration what is available. "To eat bread by weight" is a Jewish phrase indicating that food is scarce (Lev. 26:26). A penny (denarius) a day was a standard wage for laborers (Matt. 20:2), but, of course, it had much greater buying power than the common penny does today. A "measure" of wheat was about two pints, sufficient for the daily needs of one person. Ordinarily, a person could buy eight to twelve measures for a penny, and much more of barley, which was the cheaper grain.

However, during the tribulation, a man will have to work all day just to secure food for himself! There will be nothing for his family! At the same time, the rich will be enjoying plenty of oil and wine. No wonder Antichrist will eventually be able to control the economy (Rev. 13:17) as he promises to feed the hungry masses.

Death (vv. 7–8). John saw two personages: Death riding a pale horse and hades (the realm of the dead) following him. Christ has the keys of death and hades (Rev. 1:18), and both will one day be cast into hell (Rev. 20:14). Death claims the body while hades claims the soul of the dead (Rev. 20:13). John saw these enemies going forth to claim their prey, armed with weapons of the sword, hunger, pestilence (death), and wild beasts. In ancient times, hunger, pestilence, and the ravages of beasts would be expected to accompany war (note also Jer. 15:2; 24:10; Ezek. 14:21).

Conquering tyrants who bring the world war, famine, and pestilence are certainly nothing new. Suffering people from the days of the Roman Empire to the most recent war can easily recognize anticipations of these four dreaded horsemen. This is why the book of Revelation has been a source of encouragement to suffering believers throughout history. As they see the Lamb opening the seals, they realize that God is in control and that His purposes will be accomplished.

Response (6:9–17)

John recorded two responses to the opening of the seals, one in heaven and the other on earth.

The martyrs (vv. 9–11). When the Old Testament priest presented an animal sacrifice, the victim's blood was poured out at the base of the brazen altar (Lev. 4:7, 18, 25, 30). In Old Testament imagery, blood represents life (Lev. 17:11). So, here in Revelation, the souls of the martyrs "under the altar" indicates that their lives were given sacrificially to the glory of God.

The apostle Paul had the same idea in mind when he wrote Philippians 2:17 and 2 Timothy 4:6.

The Greek word *martus,* which gives us our English word *martyr,* simply means "a witness" (see Rev. 2:13; 17:6). These saints were slain by the enemy because of their witness to the truth of God and the message of Jesus Christ. The forces of Antichrist do not accept the truth, because Satan wants them to be deceived and accept his lies (see Rev. 19:20; 20:10; also 2 Thess. 2:9–12).

Since their murderers are still alive on earth, these martyrs are apparently from the early part of the tribulation. But they represent *all* who have laid down their lives for Jesus Christ and the cause of God's truth, and they are an encouragement to all today who may be called to follow them. They assure us that the souls of the martyrs are in heaven, awaiting the resurrection (Rev. 20:4), and that they are at rest, robed in heavenly glory.

But is it "Christian" for these martyred saints to pray for vengeance on their murderers? After all, both Jesus and Stephen prayed that God would forgive those who killed them. I have no doubt that, when they were slain on earth, these martyrs also prayed for their slayers, and this is the right thing to do (Matt. 5:10–12, 43–48).

The great question, however, was not *whether* their enemies would be judged, but *when.* "How long, O Lord?" has been the cry of God's suffering people throughout the ages (see Ps. 74:9–10; 79:5; 94:3–4; also Hab. 1:2). The saints in heaven know that God will eventually judge sin and establish righteousness in the earth, but they do not know God's exact schedule. It is not personal revenge that they seek, but vindication of God's holiness and the establishment of God's justice. Every believer today who sincerely prays, "Thy kingdom come!" is echoing their petition.

God made clear to these martyrs that their sacrifice was an appointment, not an accident, and that others would join them. Even in the death of His people, God is in control (Ps. 116:15); so there is nothing to fear.

Many others would be slain for their faith before the Lord would return and establish His kingdom (see Rev. 11:7; 12:11; 14:13; and 20:4–5). Then as today, it appears that the enemy is winning, but God will have the last word. Even in our "enlightened" twentieth century, multiplied thousands of true believers have laid down their lives for Christ; certainly they will receive the crown of life (Rev. 2:10).

The earth-dwellers (vv. 12–17). The martyrs cried, "Avenge us!" but the unbelievers on earth will cry, "Hide us!" The opening of the sixth seal will produce worldwide convulsions and catastrophes, including the first of three great earthquakes (Rev. 6:12; 11:13; 16:18–19). All of nature will be affected: the sun, moon, and stars, as well as the heavens, the mountains, and the islands. Compare this scene with Joel 2:30–31 and 3:15 as well as with Isaiah 13:9–10 and 34:2–4.

Even though John wrote using symbolic language, these verses describe a scene that would frighten even the most courageous person. People will try to hide from the face of God and from the face of the Lamb! Imagine wanting to hide from a *lamb!* I once heard Dr. Vance Havner say that the day would come when the most expensive piece of real estate would be a hole in the ground, and he was right.

We will see more of "the wrath of God" as we progress through Revelation (Rev. 11:18; 14:10; 16:19; 19:15). We will also encounter the wrath of Satan (Rev. 12:17) and the wrath of the nations as they oppose God (Rev. 11:18). If men and women will not yield to the love of God and be changed by the grace of God, then there is no way for them to escape the wrath of God.

Rank and wealth will not deliver anyone in that terrible day. John's list included kings, captains, and slaves, the rich and the poor. "Who shall be able to stand?"

The phrase "wrath of the Lamb" seems a paradox. "Wrath of the lion" would be more consistent. We are so accustomed to emphasizing the meekness and gentleness of Christ (Matt. 11:28–30) that we forget His holiness and justice. The same Christ who welcomed the children also drove the merchants from the temple. God's wrath is not like a child's temper tantrum or punishment meted out by an impatient parent. God's wrath is the evidence of His holy love for all that is right and His holy hatred for all that is evil. Only a soft and sentimental person would want to worship a God who did not deal justly with evil in the world.

Furthermore, the people mentioned here are *impenitent.* They refuse to submit to God's will. They would rather hide from God in fear (remember Adam and Eve?) than run to Him in faith. They are proof that judgment *by itself does* not change the human heart. Not only will men seek to hide from God, but they will blaspheme Him as well (Rev. 16:9, 11, 21)!

But is there any hope for believers during this terrible time of judgment? And what about God's special people, the Jews, who made a covenant with the Antichrist? Certainly people will trust the Lord even after the church is taken to heaven, but how will they manage? We turn to Revelation 7 for some of the answers.

But before considering John's third theme in this section—redemption—we must note the parallels that exist between Christ's prophetic words recorded in Matthew 24 and what John wrote in Revelation 6. The following summary outline makes this clear.

Matthew 24	*Revelation 6*
False Christs (vv. 4–5)	White horse rider (vv. 1–2)
Wars (v. 6)	Red horse—war (vv. 3–4)
Famines (v. 7a)	Black horse—famine (vv. 5–6)

Death (vv. 7b–8)	Pale horse—death (vv. 7–8)
Martyrs (v. 9)	Martyrs under the altar (vv. 9–11)
Worldwide chaos (vv. 10–13)	Worldwide chaos (vv. 12–17)

Matthew 24:14 introduces the preaching of the gospel of the kingdom throughout the whole world, and this may well be where Revelation 7 fits in. God may use the sealed 144,000 Jews to share His Word with the world, resulting in the salvation of multitudes.

Redemption (7:1–17)

It is important that we contrast the two groups of people described in this chapter.

7:1–8	7:9–17
Jews	Gentiles from all nations
Numbered—144,000	Not numbered, nor could be
Sealed on the earth	Standing in heaven before God

While we are not told explicitly in Scripture that the 144,000 Jews are God's special witnesses, and that the Gentile host is saved through their ministry, this appears to be a logical deduction; otherwise, why are they associated in this chapter? The parallel with Matthew 24:14 also indicates that the 144,000 will witness for the Lord during the tribulation.

The sealed Jews (vv. 1–8). Angels are associated with the forces of nature: the wind (Rev. 7:1), fire (Rev. 14:18), and water (Rev. 16:5). Stopping the winds implies a "lull before the storm." God controls all of nature. During the day of His wrath, He will use the forces of nature to judge mankind. The phrase "four corners of the earth" is no more "unscientific" here than it is in Isaiah 11:12 or the daily newspaper.

In Scripture, a seal indicates ownership and protection. Today, God's people are sealed by the Holy Spirit (Eph. 1:13–14). This is God's guarantee that we are saved and safe, and that He will one day take us to heaven. The 144,000 Jews will receive the Father's name as their seal (Rev. 14:1), in contrast to the "mark of the beast" that Antichrist will give those who follow him (Rev. 13:17; 14:11; 16:2; 19:20).

This seal will protect these chosen Jews from the judgments that will "hurt the earth and the sea" (Rev. 7:2), and occur when the first four angels blow their trumpets (Rev. 8). The judgments are intensified when the horrible locusts are released from the pit (Rev. 9:1–4). Protected from these awesome judgments, the 144,000 will be able to do their work and glorify the Lord.

In every age, God has had His faithful remnant. Elijah thought he was alone, but God had 7,000 who were yet faithful to Him (1 Kings 19:18). The sealing described in Revelation 7 certainly has its background in Ezekiel 9:1–7, where the faithful were sealed before God's judgment fell. So, while these 144,000 Jews are an elect people in the last days with a special task from God, they also symbolize God's faithful elect in every age of history.

The number 144,000 is significant because it signifies perfection and completeness (144 = 12 x 12). Some see here the completeness of *all God's* people: the twelve tribes of Israel (Old Testament saints) and the twelve apostles (New Testament saints). This may be a good *application of* this passage, but it is not the basic *interpretation,* for we are told that these 144,000 are all Jews, and even their tribes are named.

A man once told me he was one of the 144,000; so I asked him, "To which tribe do you belong, and can you prove it?" Of course, he could not prove it, no more than a Jew today can prove the tribe from which he or she descended. The genealogical records have all been destroyed. Even the fact that ten of the tribes were taken by the Assyrians and "lost" is no problem to God. He knows His people and their whereabouts (see Matt. 19:28; Acts 26:7; James 1:1).

This is not to say that our literal interpretation of this passage is not without problems. Why is Levi included when it had no inheritance with the other tribes (Num. 18:20–24; Josh. 13:14)? Why is Joseph named but not his son Ephraim, who is usually connected with his brother Manasseh? Finally, why is the tribe of Dan omitted here and yet included in Ezekiel's list for the apportionment of the land (Ezek. 48:1)? Many suggestions have been made, but we do not know the answers. Even if we interpreted this passage in a spiritual sense (i.e., Israel is the church), we would be no more certain. We must permit God to know "the secret things," and not allow our ignorance of them to hinder us from obeying what we *do* know (Deut. 29:29).

The saved Gentiles (vv. 9–17). You cannot read the book of Revelation without developing a global outlook, for the emphasis is on what God does for people in the *whole* world. The Lamb died to redeem people "out of every kindred, and tongue, and people, and nation" (Rev. 5:9). The great multitudes pictured here came from "all nations, and kindreds, and people, and tongues" (Rev. 7:9). "Go ye into all the world, and preach the gospel to every creature" was our Lord's mandate (Mark 16:15).

There is no doubt as to who this multitude is, because one of the elders explained it to John (Rev. 7:14): they are Gentiles who have been saved through faith in Christ during the tribulation. (We will meet this same group again in Rev. 14.) While today, in most parts of the world, it is relatively easy to confess Christ, this will not be the case during the tribulation, at least during the last half of it. Then, unless persons wear the "mark of the beast," they will not be able to buy or sell, and this would leave them without even life's bare necessities. Revelation 7:16 indicates that they suffered hunger (see Rev. 13:17), thirst (see Rev.

16:4), and lack of shelter. (On the heat of the sun, see Rev. 16:8–9.)

The fact that they are *standing* before the throne and not seated around it indicates that these people are not identified with the twenty-four elders. In fact, John himself did not know who they were! If they had been Old Testament believers, or the church, John would have recognized them. That the elder had to tell John who they were suggests that they are a special people, which, indeed, they are.

Of course, in the heavenly city (Rev. 21—22), all distinctions will cease and we shall all simply be the people of God in glory. But while God is working out His program in human history, distinctions still exist between the Jews, the Gentiles, the church, and the tribulation saints.

John gave a beautiful description of these people.

First, they were *accepted*, for they stood before God's throne and the Lamb. No doubt they had been rejected on earth for they stood for truth at a time when lies were popular and Satan was in charge. Their white robes and palms symbolize victory: they were true overcomers! The Jews used palm branches at their Feast of Tabernacles (Lev. 23:40–43), which was a special time of national rejoicing.

Then, they were *joyful*. They sang praises to the Father and to the Lamb, and their worship was joined by all those who surrounded the throne.

Third, they were *rewarded*. They had the privilege of being before God's throne and of serving Him. When God's people get to heaven, there will be work to do! We shall be able to serve Him perfectly! The Lamb will shepherd us and satisfy us with every good thing (see Isa. 49:10; Rev. 21:4).

The opening of the seventh seal will introduce the seven "trumpet judgments" (Rev. 8—11) and the wrath of God will increase both in intensity and scope. But before that occurs, we are assured that in His wrath, God will remember mercy (Hab. 3:2). Despite the wrath of God and the terror inspired by Satan and his helpers, multitudes will be saved through the blood of Jesus Christ. No matter what the age or dispensation. God's way of salvation has always been the same: faith in Jesus Christ, the Lamb of God.

Sad to say, however, multitudes during that time will also reject the Savior and trust "the beast." But are there not people *today* who prefer Satan to Christ and this world to the world to come? They are just as condemned as the tribulation sinners who receive the "mark of the beast."

If you have never trusted the Savior, do so now.

If you have trusted Him, then share the good news of salvation with others that they might be delivered from the wrath to come.

CHAPTER SIX
Revelation 8—9

BLOW THE TRUMPETS!

The seal judgments now over, the trumpet judgments are about to begin. These will be followed by the bowl (vial) judgments, culminating in the destruction of Babylon and Christ's return to earth. Note that from the seals to the trumpets to the bowls, the judgments increase in their intensity. Note also that the trumpet and the bowl judgments touch on the same areas, as the following summary illustrates:

The Trumpets	The Judgment	The Bowls
1. 8:1–7	The earth	16:1–2
2. 8:8–9	The sea	16:3
3. 8:10–11	The rivers	16:4–7
4. 8:12–13	The heavens	16:8–9
5. 9:1–2	Mankind—torment	16:10–11
6. 9:13–21	An army	16:12–16
7. 11:15–19	Angry nations	16:17–21

The trumpet judgments are released during the first half of the tribulation, and the bowl judgments during the last half, which is also called "the wrath of God" (Rev. 14:10; 15:7). The trumpet judgments parallel the plagues that God sent on the land of Egypt. And why not? After all, the whole world will be saying, as did Pharaoh, "Who is the Lord that we should serve Him?"

The opening of the seventh seal, and the blowing of the first six trumpets, brought about three dramatic results.

Preparation (8:1–6)
This preparation involves two factors: silence (Rev. 8:1) and supplication (Rev. 8:2–6).

The hosts in heaven had just worshiped the Father and the Lamb with a tremendous volume of praise (Rev. 7:10–12). But when the Lamb opened the seventh seal, heaven was silent for about thirty minutes. John does not tell us what caused the silence, but several possibilities exist. The scroll had now been opened completely, and perhaps even turned over, and all of heaven could see God's glorious plan unfolding. Perhaps the heavenly hosts were simply awestruck at what they saw.

Certainly, this silence was "the lull before the storm," for God's intensified judgments were about to be hurled to the earth. "Hold thy peace at the presence of the Lord God: for the day of the Lord is at hand" (Zeph. 1:7; note also vv. 14–18, especially v. 16, "A day of the trumpet"). "Be silent, O all flesh, before the Lord: for he is raised up out of his holy habitation" (Zech. 2:13). "The Lord is in his holy temple: let all the earth keep silence before him" (Hab. 2:20).

During this silence, the seven angels were given trumpets, significant to John, because he was a Jew and understood the place of trumpets in Israel's national life. According to Numbers 10, trumpets had three important uses: they called me people together (Num.

10:1–8); they announced war (Num. 10:9); and they announced special times (Num. 10:10). The trumpet sounded at Mount Sinai when the law was given (Ex. 19:16–19), and trumpets were blown when the king was anointed and enthroned (1 Kings 1:34, 39). Of course, everyone familiar with the Old Testament would remember the trumpets at the conquest of Jericho (Josh. 6:13–16).

The voice of the Lord Jesus Christ sounded to John like a trumpet (Rev. 1:10). The voice of a trumpet summoned John to heaven (Rev. 4:1), and some relate this to the promise of the rapture of the church given in 1 Thessalonians 4:13–18. Sounding seven trumpets certainly would announce a declaration of war, as well as the fact that God's anointed King was enthroned in glory and about to judge His enemies (Ps. 2:1–5). As trumpets declared defeat to Jericho, they will ultimately bring defeat to Babylon.

The awesome silence was followed by the actions of a special angel at the golden altar in heaven (see Rev. 9:13; 14:18; 16:7). In the tabernacle and temple, the golden altar stood before the veil and was used for burning incense (Ex. 30:1–10). This was the ministry Zacharias was performing when the angel told him that he and Elizabeth would have a son (Luke 1:5ff.). Burning incense on this altar was a picture of prayer ascending to God (Ps. 141:2).

The "prayers of the saints" (Rev. 8:4) are not the prayers of a special group of people in heaven who have arrived at "sainthood." To begin with, *all* God's children are saints—set apart for God—through faith in Jesus Christ (2 Cor. 1:1; 9:1, 12; 13:13). And there is no definite teaching in the Scriptures that people in heaven pray for believers on earth, or that we can direct our prayers to God through them. We pray to the Father through the Son, for He alone is worthy (Rev. 5:3). For centuries, God's people have been praying, "Thy kingdom come, Thy will be done!" and now those prayers are about to be answered. Likewise, the tribulation martyrs prayed for God to vindicate them (Rev. 6:9–11), a common plea of David in the Psalms (see Ps. 7; 26; 35; 52; 55; and 58 for example). These "imprecatory psalms" are not expressions of selfish personal vengeance, but rather cries for God to uphold His holy law and vindicate His people.

On the great day of Atonement, the high priest would put incense on the coals in the censer and, with the blood of the sacrifice, enter the Holy of Holies (Lev. 16:11–14). But in this scene, the angel put the incense on the altar (presented the prayers before God) and then *cast the coals* from the altar to the earth! The parallel in Ezekiel 10 indicates that this symbolized God's judgment, and the effects described in Revelation 8:5 substantiate this view. A storm is about to begin (see Rev. 4:5; 11:19; 16:18)!

Like it or not, the prayers of God's people are involved in the judgments that He sends. The throne and the altar are related. The purpose of prayer, it has often been said, is not to get man's will done in heaven, but to get God's will done on earth—even if that will involves judgment. True prayer is serious business, so we had better not move the altar too far from the throne!

Desolation (8:7–13)

The first four trumpet judgments are "natural" in that they affect the land, the saltwater, the fresh water, and the heavenly bodies. The fifth and sixth judgments involve the release of demonic forces that first torment, and then kill. The last of the trumpet judgments (Rev. 11:15–19) creates a crisis among all the nations of the world.

Desolation on earth (v. 7). "Hail and fire mingled with blood" reminds us of the seventh plague that God sent against Egypt (Ex. 9:18–26). The prophet Joel also promised "blood and fire" in the last days (Joel 2:30). Since this is a supernatural judgment, it is not necessary to try to explain how hail, fire, and blood become mingled. "Fire" could refer to the lightning of a severe electrical storm.

The target for this judgment is green vegetation, the trees and the grass, one third of which is burned up. One can well imagine how this would affect not only the balance of nature, but also the food supply. The Greek word for *trees* usually means "fruit trees," and the destruction of pasture lands would devastate the meat and milk industries.

Desolation in the seas (vv. 8–9). Turning water into blood reminds us of the first Egyptian plague (Ex. 7:19–21). Note that John did not say that an actual burning mountain was cast out of heaven, but that the fiery object was like a great mountain. A triple judgment resulted: a third part of the saltwater turned to blood, a third part of the marine life died, and a third of the ships were destroyed. This will be an ecological and an economic disaster of unprecedented proportions.

Considering that the oceans occupy about three fourths of the earth's surface, you can imagine the extent of this judgment. The pollution of the water and the death of so many creatures would greatly affect the balance of life in the oceans, and this would undoubtedly lead to further insoluble problems. As of January 1, 1981 there were 24,867 ocean-going merchant ships registered. Imagine the shock waves that would hit the shipping industry if 8,289 valuable ships were suddenly destroyed! And what about their cargoes!

Some interpreters take "the sea" to mean the Mediterranean Sea. However, this would make a relatively small impact on the world, since the Mediterranean covers only 969,100 square miles and averages just 5,000 feet deep. It is likely that all the major bodies of saltwater are included in this judgment.

Desolation in the fresh water (vv. 10–11). God's wrath next reaches *inland* and touches the rivers and fountains of water (wells and sources of the rivers), making the fresh water taste bitter like wormwood. The National Geographic Society lists about 100 principal rivers in the world, ranging in length from the Amazon (4,000 miles long) to the Rio de la Plata (150 miles long). The U.S. Geological Survey reports thirty large rivers in the United States, beginning with the mighty Mississippi (3,710 miles long). One third of these rivers, and their sources, will become so bitterly polluted that drinking their water could produce death.

God has His stars numbered and named (Job 9:9–10). It is likely that this fallen star is molten and that, as it nears the earth, it begins to disintegrate and fall into the various bodies of water. If a star actually struck the earth, our globe would be destroyed; so this star must "come apart" as it enters the atmosphere. Of course, this event is a divinely controlled judgment; therefore, we must not try to limit it by the known laws of science.

The word translated "wormwood" gives us our English word *absinthe,* which is a popular liqueur in some countries of the world. The word means "undrinkable," and in the Old Testament was synonymous with sorrow and great calamity. Jeremiah, "the Weeping Prophet," often used it (Jer. 9:15; 23:15; Lam. 3:15, 19), and so did Amos (Amos 5:7, "those who turn justice into wormwood" NASB). Moses warned that idolatry would bring sorrow to Israel, like a root producing wormwood (Deut. 29:18). Solomon warned that immorality might seem pleasant, but in the end, it produces bitterness like wormwood (Prov. 5:4).

If the people who *drink from* these waters are in danger of dying, what must happen to the fish and other creatures that *live in* these waters? And what would happen to the vegetation near these rivers? If the ecologists are worried about the deadly consequences of water pollution today, what will they think when the third trumpet blows?

There is no direct parallel here to any of the plagues of Egypt. However, after the Exodus, Israel encountered bitter waters at Marah (which means "bitter") and Moses had to purify the water supply (Ex. 15:23–27). But no supernatural purification will be available during the tribulation.

Desolation in the heavens (vv. 12–13). The judgments from the first three trumpets affected only a third part of the land and waters, but this fourth judgment affects the entire world. Why? Because it gets to the very source of the earth's life and energy, the sun. With one third less sunlight on the earth, there will be one third less energy available to support the life systems of man and nature.

This judgment parallels the ninth plague in Egypt (Ex. 10:21–23), which lasted three days. "The day of the Lord is darkness, and not light" (Amos 5:18). Think of the vast changes in temperatures that will occur and how these will affect human health and food growth.

It is possible that this particular judgment is temporary, for the fourth bowl judgment will reverse it, and the sun's power will be intensified (Rev. 16:8–9).

Then, at the close of the tribulation, the sun and moon will be darkened again to announce the Savior's return (Matt. 24:29–30; see also Luke 21:25–28).

"Blow ye the trumpet in Zion," said the prophet Joel, "for the day of the Lord cometh … a day of darkness and of gloominess" (Joel 2:1–2). Darkness, indeed! Not only will nature suffer loss, but human nature will take advantage of the long darkness and no doubt indulge in crime and wickedness. "Everyone that doeth evil hateth the light" (John 3:20).

At this point, a remarkable messenger will appear in the sky, proclaiming woe to the earth's inhabitants. Most manuscripts have "eagle" here instead of "angel," but either one would certainly get people's attention! Could this be the eagle-like living creature that John saw worshipping before the throne (Rev. 4:7–8)? Will God send it on this special mission? We cannot say for sure, but it is a possibility.

The three "woes" in Revelation 8:13 refer to the judgments yet to come when the remaining three angels blow their trumpets. It is as though the messenger cried, "If you think this has been terrible, just wait! The worst is yet to come!"

The phrase "inhabiters of the earth" (or "them that dwell on the earth") is found twelve times in Revelation (3:10; 6:10; 8:13; 11:10 [twice]; 12:12; 13:8, 12, 14; 14:6; 17:2, 8). It means much more than "people who live on the earth," for that is where *all* living people reside. Instead, it refers to a *kind* of people: those who live *for* the earth and the things *of* the earth. These are just the opposite of people who have their citizenship in heaven (Phil. 3:18–21). John described this worldly sort well in his first epistle (1 John 2:15–17), and later in this prophecy he again makes it clear that "earth-dwellers" are not born again (Rev. 13:8).

At the beginning of human history, heaven and earth were united because our first parents honored God and obeyed His will. Satan tempted them to focus on the earth; they disobeyed God; and ever since, a great gulf has been fixed between heaven and earth. This chasm was bridged when the Son of God came to earth and died for the sins of the world.

Liberation (9:1–21)

The late Dr. Wilbur M. Smith, who made the book of Revelation his special study, once wrote: "It is probable that, apart from the exact identification of Babylon in Revelation 17 and 18, the meaning of the two judgments in this chapter represents the most difficult major problem in the Revelation" (*Wycliffe Bible Commentary,* 1509). Revelation 9 describes two frightening armies that are liberated at just the right time and permitted to judge mankind.

The army from the pit (vv. 1–12). The "bottomless pit" is literally "the pit of the abyss." Luke makes it clear that this "pit" is the abode of the demons (Luke 8:31), and John states that Satan will be temporarily "jailed" there during our Lord's reign on the earth

(Rev. 20:1–3). The Antichrist (i.e., "the beast") will ascend out of this pit (Rev. 11:7; 17:8). It is not the lake of fire, for that is the final "prison" for Satan and all who follow him (Rev. 20:10), but part of that hidden underworld under the Lord's authority. Today, the fearsome army described here is already incarcerated, waiting for the hour of liberation.

This fallen star is a person, the king over the beings in the pit (Rev. 9:11). He does not have *complete* authority, for the key to the pit had to be given to him before he could loose his army. This "star" is probably Satan and the army, his demons (Eph. 6:10ff.). One of the names for Satan is *Lucifer,* which means "brightness"; he also is compared to the "morning star" (Isa. 14:12–14). Jesus said to His disciples, "I beheld Satan as lightning fall from heaven" (Luke 10:18).

When the pit was opened, smoke emerged as though the door of a furnace had been loosened. Jesus compared hell to a furnace of fire (Matt 13:42, 50), an image that ought to make people stop and think before they jest about it. The smoke polluted the air and darkened the sun, which had already been darkened when the fourth trumpet sounded.

But it is what came out of the smoke that truly terrorized mankind: an army of demons, compared to locusts. The eighth plague in Egypt was a devastating swarm of locusts (Ex. 10:1–20). People who have never encountered these insects have little idea of the damage they can do. When God wanted to judge His people, He would sometimes send locusts to devour the harvests (Deut. 28:38, 42; Joel 2).

These are not literal locusts, because locusts do not have scorpion-like stings in their tails. These creatures do not devour the green vegetation; in fact, they are prohibited from doing so. This demonic army is given the assignment of tormenting all who have not been protected by the seal of God. The 144,000 men from the tribes of Israel would therefore escape this painful judgment (Rev. 7:1–8). In fact, it is likely that *all* who have trusted the Lord will be sealed in some special way and protected from torment.

The normal lifespan of the locust is about five months (May to September), and this is the length of time that the judgment will last. These demons will sting people and thus create such pain that their victims will actually want to die, but death will flee from them (Jer. 8:3).

Reading the detailed description of these creatures, we realize that John is not writing about ordinary locusts. Yet, despite its obvious symbolism, it aptly portrays a powerful enemy armed for battle. With bodies like horses but faces like men, the demons' heads are crowned and covered with long hair. They have teeth like those of lions, and their skin is like a coat of mail. When they fly, the noise is like an army of chariots rushing by. It is unnecessary to try to "spiritualize" these symbols, or to interpret them in light of modern means of warfare. John is heaping image upon image to force us to feel the horror of this judgment.

Real locusts do not have a king (Prov. 30:27), but this army follows the rule of Satan, the angel of the bottomless pit. His name is "Destroyer." "The thief [Satan] cometh not, but for to steal, and to kill, and to destroy" (John 10:10). Real locusts are pervasive destroyers, but this army only tortures those who do not belong to the Lord.

As God's people, we can be thankful that Jesus Christ holds the keys of hell and death (Rev. 1:18) and exercises divine authority even over Satan. God has His timetable for all these events, and nothing will happen too soon or too late (2 Thess. 2:6; note also Rev. 9:15).

The army from the east (vv. 13–21). It was at the golden altar of incense that the angel offered the prayers of the saints (Rev. 8:3–5); now from this same altar a voice speaks, commanding that four angels be loosed. These angels are apparently wicked, because no holy angel would be bound. Each angel is in charge of part of the vast army that follows them at their liberation, an army of 200 million beings! The army is released at a precise time, for a special purpose: to kill (not just torment) a third of the world's population. Since a fourth of mankind has already been killed (Rev. 6:8), this means that *half of the world's population will be dead* by the time the sixth trumpet judgment is completed.

Are we to identify this as a literal army of men, moving in conquest across the globe? Probably not. For one thing, the emphasis in this paragraph is not on the riders, but on the horses. The description cannot fit war-horses as we know them or, for that matter, modern warfare equipment, such as tanks. To assert that this is a literal army, and to point to some nation (such as China) that claims to have 200 million soldiers, is to miss the message John is seeking to convey.

The deadly power of these horses is in their mouths and tails, not in their legs. Fire, smoke, and brimstone issue from their mouths, and their tails are like biting serpents. They can attack men from the front as well as from the rear.

I take it that this is another demonic army, headed by four fallen angels, and that all of them are today bound by the Lord, unable to act until God gives them permission. Why they are bound at the Euphrates River is not explained, though that area is the cradle of civilization (Gen. 2:14), not to mention one of the boundaries for Israel (Gen. 15:18).

One would think that the combination of five months of torment and then death (from fire, smoke, and brimstone) would bring men and women to their knees in repentance, but such is not the case. These judgments are not remedial but retributive: God is upholding His holy law and vindicating His suffering people (see Rev. 6:9–11). Even a casual reading of Revelation 9:20–21 reveals the awful wickedness of mankind, even in the midst of God's judgments. The most frightening thing about Revelation 9 is not the judgments that God sends but the sins that men persist in committing *even while God is judging them.*

Consider the sins that men and women will be committing:

Demon worship, which goes hand-in-hand with *idolatry* (see 1 Cor. 10:19–21), will be the leading sin. Satan will be at work (always under the permissive will of God), and Satan has always wanted to be worshipped (Isa. 14:12–15; Matt. 4:8–10). A great deal of "religion" will be practiced at this time, but it will be false religion. People will worship the works of their own hands, which could well include the buildings they construct, the machines they make, and the cities they build, as well as their idols.

Here are dead sinners worshipping dead gods (see Ps. 115)! Their gods will not be able to protect or deliver them, yet these people will continue to reject the true God and worship Satan and idols!

Murder and *theft* will also be rife in those days. So will various kinds of *sexual immorality.* The word translated "sorcery" is the Greek word *pharmakia,* which means "the use of drugs." Drugs are often used in pagan religious rites and demon worship. As we see the expansion of today's "drug culture," we have no problem envisioning a whole society given over to these demonic practices.

Mankind will be breaking the first two Mosaic commandments by making and worshipping idols. In their murders, they will violate the sixth commandment, and in their thefts, the eighth. By their fornication, they will break the seventh commandment. It will be an age of lawlessness with "every man doing that which is right in his own eyes" (see Judg. 21:25).

But God is working out His plan, and neither the sins of mankind nor the schemes of Satan will hinder Him from accomplishing His will.

We have come now to the midpoint of the tribulation (Rev. 10—14), a time during which some important events must take place. Thus far, we have covered about three-and-a-half years of this seven-year period (Dan. 9:27). During this time, Antichrist began his career as a peacemaker and a special friend to Israel, but now, his true character will be revealed. He will become a peace-breaker and a persecutor of the people of God.

Things will not look bright for God's people during this middle stage of the prophetic journey, but they will still be overcomers through the power of the King of kings and Lord of lords!

CHAPTER SEVEN
Revelation 10—11
A TIME FOR TESTIMONY

Revelation 10—14 describes the events that will occur at the middle of the seven-year tribulation. This explains John's repeated mention of the three-and-a-half-year time segment in one form or another (Rev. 11:2–3; 12:6, 14; 13:5). At the beginning of this period, the Antichrist began to make his conquest by promising to protect the Jews and assist in their rebuilding of the temple in Jerusalem. But after three-and-a-half-years, he will break his agreement, invade the temple, and begin to persecute the Jewish people.

However depressing the events of this middle segment of the tribulation may be, God is not without His witness to the world. In Revelation 10—11 are three important testimonies: from a mighty angel (Rev. 10:1–11), from the two special witnesses (Rev. 11:1–14), and from the elders in heaven (Rev. 11:15–19).

The Testimony of the Mighty Angel (10:1–11)
More than sixty references to angels are made in Revelation. They are God's army sent to accomplish His purposes on earth. Believers today seldom think about these servants (Heb. 1:14), but one day in heaven we shall learn about all they did for us here.

The description of the angel (vv. 1–4). This angel amazes us, for he has some of the characteristics that belong especially to the Lord Jesus Christ. John had seen and heard a "strong angel" (Rev. 5:2), and the same Greek word is here translated "mighty." All angels excel in strength (Ps. 103:20), but apparently some have greater power and authority than others.

We first saw the rainbow around the throne of God (Rev. 4:3); now it sits like a crown on the head of this messenger. The rainbow was God's sign to mankind that He would never again destroy the world with a flood. Even in wrath, God remembers His mercy (Hab. 3:2). Whoever this angel is, he has the authority of God's throne given to him.

God is often identified with clouds. God led Israel by a glorious cloud (Ex. 16:10), and dark clouds covered Sinai when the law was given (Ex. 19:9). When God appeared to Moses, it was in a cloud of glory (Ex. 24:15ff.; 34:5). "[He] maketh the clouds his chariot" (Ps. 104:3). A cloud received Jesus when He ascended to heaven (Acts 1:9), and, when He returns, it will be with clouds (Rev. 1:7).

The fact that the angel's face is "as the sun" corresponds to the description of Jesus Christ in Revelation 1:16; his feet correspond to the Lord's description in Revelation 1:15. His voice like a lion suggests Revelation 5:5. This being could well be our Lord Jesus Christ, appearing to John as a kingly angel. Jesus often appeared in the Old Testament as "the Angel of the Lord" (Ex. 3:2; Judg. 2:4; 6:11–12, 21–22; 2 Sam. 24:16). This was a temporary manifestation for a special purpose, not a permanent incarnation.

Two other characteristics would suggest identifying the angel as Jesus Christ: the book in his hand and the awesome posture that he assumed. The little book contains the rest of the prophetic message that John will deliver. Since our Lord was the only One worthy to take the scroll and break the seals (Rev. 5:5ff.), it might well be concluded that He is the only One worthy to give His servant the rest of the message.

The angel's posture is that of a conqueror taking possession of his territory. He is claiming the whole world (see Josh. 1:1–3). Of course, only the victorious Savior could make such a claim. The Antichrist will soon complete his conquest and force the whole world to submit to his control. But before that happens, the Savior will claim the world for Himself, the inheritance that His Father promised Him (Ps. 2:6–9). Satan roars like a lion to frighten his prey (1 Peter 5:8), but the Lion of Judah roars to announce victory (see Ps. 95:3–5; Isa. 40:12–17).

We are not told why John was forbidden to write what the seven thunders uttered, the only "sealed" thing in an otherwise "unsealed" book (see Dan. 12:9; Rev. 22:10). God's voice is often compared to thunder (Ps. 29; Job 26:14; 37:5; John 12:28–29). It is useless for us to speculate when God chooses to veil His truth (Deut. 29:29).

The declaration of the angel (vv. 5–11). This declaration fills us with awe, not only because of what the angel declares, but also because of the way he declares it. It is a solemn scene, with his hand lifted to heaven as though he were under oath.

But if this angel is our Lord Jesus Christ, why would He take an oath? In order to affirm the solemnity and certainty of the words spoken. God put Himself "under oath" when He made His covenant with Abraham (Heb. 6:13–20) and when He declared His Son to be High Priest (Heb. 7:20–22). He also took an oath when He promised David that the Christ would come from his family (Acts 2:29–30).

The emphasis in Revelation 10:6 is on God the Creator. Various judgments have already been felt by the heavens, the earth, and the sea, and more judgments are to come. The word that is translated "time" actually means "delay." God has been delaying His judgments so that lost sinners will have time to repent (2 Peter 3:1–9); now, however, He will accelerate His judgments and accomplish His purposes.

Recall that the martyred saints in heaven were concerned about God's seeming delay in avenging their deaths (Rev. 6:10–11). "How long, O Lord, how long?" has been the cry of God's suffering people from age to age. God's seeming delay in fulfilling His promises has given the scoffers opportunity to deny God's Word and question His sincerity (see 2 Peter 3). God's Word is true and His timing, perfect. This means comfort to saints—but judgment to sinners.

In the Bible, a *mystery* is a "sacred secret," a truth hidden to those outside but revealed to God's people by His Word (Matt. 13:10–12). The "mystery of God" has to do with the age-old problem of evil in the world. Why is there both moral and natural evil in the world? Why doesn't God do something about it? Of course, the Christian knows that God did "do something about it" at Calvary when Jesus Christ was made sin and experienced divine wrath for a sinful world. We

also know that God is permitting evil to increase until the world is ripe for judgment (2 Thess. 2:7ff.; Rev. 14:14–20). Since God has already paid the price for sin, He is free to delay His judgment, and He cannot be accused of injustice or unconcern.

The signal for this mystery's completion is the sounding of the seventh trumpet (Rev. 11:14–19). The last half of the tribulation begins when the angels start to pour out the bowls, in which "is filled up [completed] the wrath of God" (Rev. 15:1).

The directions that the angel gave to John (Rev. 10:8–11) should remind us of our responsibility to assimilate the Word of God and make it a part of the inner man. It was not enough for John to see the book or even know its contents and purpose. He had to *receive* it into his inner being.

God's Word is compared to food: bread (Matt 4:4), milk (1 Peter 2:2), meat (1 Cor. 3:1–2), and honey (Ps. 119:103). The prophets Jeremiah (Jer. 15:16) and Ezekiel (Ezek. 2:9–3:4) knew what it was to "eat" the Word before they could share it with others. The Word must always "become flesh" (John 1:14) before it can be given to those who need it. Woe unto that preacher or teacher who merely echoes God's Word and does not incarnate it, making it a living part of his very being.

God will not thrust His Word into our mouths and force us to receive it. He hands it to us and we must take it. Nor can He change the effects the Word will have in our lives: there will be both sorrow and joy, bitterness and sweetness. God's Word contains sweet promises and assurances, but it also contains bitter warnings and prophecies of judgment. The Christian bears witness of both life and death (2 Cor. 2:14–17). The faithful minister will declare all of God's counsel (Acts 20:27). He will not dilute the message of God simply to please his listeners (2 Tim. 4:1–5).

The angel commissioned John to prophesy *again;* his work was not yet completed. He must declare God's prophetic truth concerning (not "before") many peoples, and nations, and tongues, and kings (Rev. 5:9). The word *nations* usually refers to the Gentile nations. John will have much to say about the nations of the world as he presents the rest of this prophecy.

The Testimony of the Two Witnesses (11:1–14)

The ministry of the witnesses (vv. 1–6). The place is Jerusalem and the time is the first half of the tribulation. Israel is worshipping again at its restored temple, built under the protection of the Antichrist, whose true character has not yet been revealed. To spiritualize Revelation 11:1–2 and make the temple refer to the church creates a number of serious problems. For one thing, how could John measure an invisible body of people, even if the church were still on earth? If the temple is the church, then who are the worshippers and what is the altar? And since the church unites Jews and Gentiles in one body (Eph. 2: lift), why are the Gentiles segregated in this temple? It seems wisest to interpret this temple as an actual building in the Holy City of Jerusalem (Neh. 11:1, 18; Dan. 9:24).

John's measurement of the temple is a symbolic action. To measure something means to claim it for yourself. When we sold our house in Chicago, the new owners brought in an architect to measure various areas and recommend possible changes. Had the architect shown up previous to the buyers' commitment we would have thrown him out. The Lord was saying through John, "I own this city and this temple, and I claim both for Myself." The Old Testament background is found in Ezekiel 40—41 and Zechariah 2:1–3.

What John did was especially significant because the Gentiles had taken over Jerusalem. Antichrist had broken his agreement with Israel (Dan. 9:27), and now he was about to use the temple for his own diabolical purposes (2 Thess. 2:3–4). All of this will be elaborated in Revelation 13. "Jerusalem shall be trodden down of the Gentiles," said Jesus, "until the times of the Gentiles be fulfilled" (Luke 21:24). The "times of the Gentiles" began in 606 BC when Babylon began to devastate Judah and Jerusalem, and it will continue until Jesus Christ returns to deliver the Holy City and redeem Israel (Zech. 14).

Note that the two witnesses minister during the *first* half of the tribulation (Rev. 11:3; 1,260 days). Jerusalem is then overrun by the Gentiles for forty-two months, the *last* half of the tribulation.

Their witness is related to Israel and the temple. How tragic that the power of God and the Word of God will be *outside* the temple and not within as in former ages. Like the temple that Jesus left, this new house will be desolate (see Matt. 23:38). These two men are specifically called prophets (Rev. 11:3, 6), and I take this to mean prophetic ministry in the Old Testament sense, calling the nations to repent and return to the true God of Israel.

Not only do these witnesses declare God's words, but they also do God's works and perform miracles of judgment, reminding us of both Moses and Elijah (Ex. 7:14–18; 1 Kings 17: 1ff.; 2 Kings 1:1–12). Some students cite Malachi 4:5–6 as evidence that one of the witnesses may be Elijah, but Jesus applied that prophecy to John the Baptist (Matt. 17:10–13). John the Baptist, however, denied that he was Elijah returned to earth (John 1:21, 25; see also Luke 1:16–17). This confusion may be explained in part by realizing that throughout Israel's history, God sent special messengers—"Elijahs"—to call His people to repentance; so in this sense, Malachi's prophecy will be fulfilled by the witnesses.

Instead of relating the ministry of the witnesses to Moses and Elijah, the angel who spoke to John connected their ministry with Zerubbabel and Joshua the high priest (Zech. 4). These two men helped to reestablish Israel in Palestine and to rebuild the temple. It was a discouraging task, and the Gentiles made it even more difficult, but God provided the special power they needed to get the work done. This truth is an encouragement to God's servants in all ages, for the work of the Lord is never easy.

The martyrdom of the witnesses (vv. 7–10). This comes only when they have finished their testimony. God's obedient servants are immortal until their work is done. "The beast" (Antichrist) is now in power and wants to take over the temple, but he cannot succeed until the two witnesses are out of the way. God will permit him to slay them, for no one will be able to make war against "the beast" and win (Rev. 13:4).

The witnesses will not even be permitted decent burial (see Ps. 79:1–3). But even this indecency will be used by God to bear witness to mankind. No doubt the TV cameras in Jerusalem will transmit the scene to people around the world, and the news analysts will discuss its significance. The earth-dwellers will rejoice at their enemies' removal and will celebrate a "satanic Christmas" by sending gifts to one another. It thus would appear that the power of the two witnesses will not be limited to Jerusalem, but that they will be able to cause things to happen in other parts of the world.

These two prophets will definitely have a relationship with Israel, and the world, for the most part, has not approved of the nation Israel. In the middle of the tribulation, "the beast" will turn against Israel and begin to persecute the Jews. The two witnesses will not be around to protect the nation and a frightening anti-Semitic movement will ensue.

Jerusalem is called a "great city" (Rev. 11:8), and from a human viewpoint, this is a true statement. But God looks at men and nations from a *spiritual* viewpoint. To Him, Jerusalem will be considered as polluted and worldly as Sodom and as rebellious and proud as Egypt.

The resurrection of the witnesses (vv. 11–14). Miraculously, the two witnesses are not only raised from the dead, but caught up into heaven! God rescues them from their enemies and gives a solemn witness to the watching world. The world's great joy suddenly becomes great fear. (Note the word *great* in Rev. 11, repeated eight times.)

Are we to interpret the three-and-a-half days literally? Or does the phrase simply mean "after a short time"? It seems too specific to mean that. Does it symbolize a longer period, say three-and-a-half years? It is not likely that two dead bodies would be kept lying in a city street for more than three years. Perhaps this is a picture of a rapture of all the saints in the midst of the tribulation, and the three-and-a-half years cover the first half of the period. If so, then what is symbolized by the *death of* the two witnesses? This interpretation solves one problem only to create another.

These days appear to be literal days, just as the forty-two months in Revelation 11:2 are literal months. The Bible does not explain why this length of time was chosen and it is useless for us to speculate.

Our Lord's *friends* watched Him ascend to heaven (Acts 1:9–12), but the witnesses' *enemies* will see them resurrected and will be shaken with fear. Their fear will increase when a great earthquake occurs, killing 7,000 men and destroying a tenth part of Jerusalem. A great earthquake occurred when the sixth seal was opened (Rev. 6:12), and there will be a greater one when the seventh vial is poured out (Rev. 16:18–20).

The Testimony of the Elders (11:15–19)

We have been waiting since Revelation 8:13 for this third "woe" to arrive and now it is here. When the seventh angel blew the trumpet, three dramatic events occurred.

An announcement of victory (v. 15). These "great voices" were probably the choirs of heaven. The great announcement is that the kingdom (John uses the singular because "the beast" now has the world under his control) of this world belongs to Jesus Christ. Of course, Christ does not *claim* His royal rights until He returns, but the victory has already been won. Satan offered Him the world's kingdoms, but He refused the offer (Matt. 4:8–9). Instead, He died on the cross, arose, and returned victoriously to heaven, and there the Father gave Him His inheritance (Ps. 2:4–9).

However, we must not incorrectly assume that our Lord is not reigning *today,* because He is. According to Hebrews 7:1–2, Jesus Christ is "King of righteousness" and "King of peace." He is enthroned with the Father (Rev. 3:21), and He will reign until He defeats all His foes (1 Cor. 15:25). Today, He rules over a spiritual kingdom, but in that future day, He will reign over the nations of the world and rule with a rod of iron.

No matter how difficult the circumstances might be, or how defeated God's people may think they are, Jesus Christ is still King of kings and Lord of lords, and He is in control. One day, we shall triumph!

An acclamation of praise (vv. 16–18). The elders left their own thrones and prostrated themselves in worship before God's throne. They gave thanks for three special blessings: that Christ reigns supremely (Rev. 11:17), that He judges righteously (Rev. 11:18), and that He rewards graciously (Rev. 11:18).

In Revelation 4:10–11, the elders praised the Creator; and in Revelation 5:9–14, they worshipped the Redeemer. Here the emphasis is on the Conqueror and the King. Keep in mind that in John's day the church on earth looked as though it were defeated, for Rome was the conqueror and king. John was reminding the saints that *they* were "a kingdom of priests" reigning with the Savior (Rev. 1:5–6). It may seem at times that the throne of heaven is empty, but it is not. Jesus Christ has both power and authority—in fact, *all* authority (Matt. 28:18, where the word *power* means "authority"). "Thou… hast begun to reign" is a good translation.

Christ not only reigns supremely, but He judges righteously (Rev. 11:18). The Lamb is also the Lion! In Revelation 11:18, we have a "table of contents" for the remainder of the book of Revelation. These events did not take place the instant the angel blew his trumpet;

he simply signaled the beginning of the process, and now these events would take place as planned.

"The nations were angry." What do the nations have to be angry about? Certainly the Lord has been good and gracious to them. He has provided their needs (Acts 14:15–17; 17:24–31), assigned their territories, and graciously postponed His judgment to give men opportunity to be saved. Even more, He sent His Son to be the Savior of the world. Today, God offers forgiveness to the nations! What more could He do for them?

Then, why are the nations angry? *Because they want to have their own way.* "Why do the heathen [the nations] rage, and the people imagine a vain thing? The kings of the earth set themselves, and the rulers take counsel together, against the Lord, and against his anointed [Christ], saying, 'Let us break their bands asunder, and cast away their cords from us'" (Ps. 2:1–3). They want to worship and serve the creature instead of the Creator (Rom. 1:25). Like adolescent children, the nations want to cast off all restraint, *and God will permit them to do so.* The result will be another "Babylon" (Rev. 17—18), man's last attempt to build his Utopia, a "heaven on earth."

Note the change in attitude shown by the nations of the world. In Revelation 11:2, the nations ruthlessly take over Jerusalem. In Revelation 11:9, they rejoice at the death of the two witnesses. But now they are angry; their arrogance and joy did not last very long. This belligerent attitude finally will cause the nations to unite to fight God at the great battle of Armageddon.

"And thy wrath is come." The word translated "angry" in Revelation 11:18 is the verb form of the word translated "wrath." But man's wrath can never equal the wrath of the Lamb (Rev. 6:16–17). Even Satan's wrath, as cruel as it is, is no match for God's wrath (Rev. 12:17). There was intense suffering in the first half of the tribulation, but only the last half will reveal the wrath of God (Rev. 11:18; 14:10; 16:19; 19:15). There are two Greek words for anger: *thumos,* which means "rage, passionate anger," and *orgē,* used here, which means "indignation, a settled attitude of wrath." God's anger is not an outburst of temper; it is holy indignation against sin. Both of these Greek words are used in Revelation to describe God's anger: *orgē* is used only four times; *thumos,* seven (Rev. 14:10, 19; 15:1, 7; 16:1, 19; 19:15). God's anger is not dispassionate, for He hates sin and loves righteousness and justice, but neither is it temperamental and unpredictable.

"And the time of the dead, that they should be judged" takes us to the very end of God's prophetic program. In one sense, every day is a "day of the Lord" because God is always judging righteously. God is longsuffering toward lost sinners and often postpones judgment, but there will be a final judgment of sinners and none will escape. This judgment is described in Revelation 20:11–15.

There will also be a judgment of God's children, known as "the Judgment Seat of Christ" (Rom.

14:10–13; 1 Cor. 3:9–15; 2 Cor. 5:9–11). God will reward His faithful servants (Matt. 25:21), and the sufferings they experienced on earth will be forgotten in the glory of His presence. Though God's children will not be judged for their sins (that judgment took place on the cross), they will be judged for their works and rewarded generously by the Master.

The judgment seat of Christ will take place in heaven after Christ has called His people home. When He returns to earth to establish His kingdom, the saints will be ready to reign with Him, with every blemish of the church removed (Eph. 5:25–27; Rev. 19:7–8). Today, we groan as we serve God, because we know only too well our handicaps and blemishes, but one day, we shall serve Him *perfectly!*

"Them that destroy the earth" refers to the rebellious earth-dwellers who will not submit to God. How ironic that these people live for the earth and its pleasures, yet at the same time are *destroying* the very earth that they worship! When man forgets that God is the Creator and he is the creature, he begins to exploit his God-given resources, and this brings destruction. Man is a steward of creation, not the owner.

As mentioned before, Revelation 11:18 is a summary statement of events yet to come. It is heaven's song of praise for the Lord's faithfulness to accomplish His purposes in the world. Again, it appears strange to us that heavenly beings can sing about judgment. Perhaps if we had more of the throne's perspective, we would be able to join their praises.

An assurance of God's faithfulness (v. 19). This chapter opened with a temple on earth, but now we see the temple in heaven. The focus of attention is on the ark of God, the symbol of God's presence with His people.

In the Old Testament tabernacle and temple, the ark stood behind the veil, in the Holy of Holies. God's glory rested on the ark, and God's law was within the ark, beautifully illustrating that the two must never be separated. He is the holy God and must deal righteously with sin. But He is also the faithful God who keeps His promises to His people. It was the ark of God that led Israel through the Jordan and into their inheritance (Josh. 3:11–17). This vision of the ark would greatly encourage God's suffering people to whom John sent this book. "God will fulfill His promises!" John was saying to them. "He will reveal His glory! Trust Him!"

Once again, John saw and heard the portents of a storm (see Rev. 4:5; 8:5). Greater judgment is about to fall on the rebellious people of earth! But God's people need not fear the storms for He is in control. The ark reminds them of His presence and the faithfulness of His promises. And on that ark was the mercy seat on which the blood was sprinkled each day of Atonement (Lev. 16:15–17). Even in wrath, God remembers His mercy (Hab. 3:2).

The stage is now set for the dramatic appearance of "the beast," Satan's masterpiece, the false Christ who will control the world.

CHAPTER EIGHT
Revelation 12—13
THE TERRIBLE TRIO

Revelation 12—13 introduces us to the three key characters in the drama of the last half of the tribulation: Satan the dragon, the false Christ, and the false prophet. These three are, in a sense, an evil trinity, opposing the true God and His people on earth. While these events will be of special significance to God's people at that time, the message of these two chapters can encourage suffering saints during any age.

Satan is the great enemy of the church, and he fights against God and His people by accusing the saints in heaven and attacking them on earth. However, Christ has overcome the old serpent, and He gives victory to His people.

The adversary always works through human means, in this case, "the beast" (false Christ or Antichrist) and the false prophet. Satan is an imitator, a counterfeiter, and he seeks to control men by means of deception. "The beast" is the future world dictator who promises to solve the pressing problems of the nations; the false prophet is his "propaganda minister." For a time, it appears that the satanic trio is succeeding, but then their world empire begins to collapse, the nations assemble for one final battle, Jesus Christ appears, and the battle is over.

Has this not been the pattern for the church's conflict with evil over the centuries? Whether the ruler has been a Caesar, a Hitler, a Stalin, or an agnostic humanist, Satan has energized and motivated him. The ruler has promised the people all that they want and need, only to lead them into slavery. He has usually had an associate to promote his program to the people and to entice them, if not force them, to obey. Often their submission amounted almost to worship.

God has permitted His people to suffer under the despotism of these rulers, but He has also enabled His people to experience great victories, even in martyrdom. They have been true overcomers! Then He has brought deliverance, only to have the cycle repeat itself, with each succeeding dictatorship worse than the previous one. The climax will come with the appearance of the Antichrist in his time (2 Thess. 2).

The Dragon (Rev. 12)

John's vision opens with *two wonders in heaven* (Rev. 12:1–6). The first is a woman giving birth to a son. Since this child is identified as Jesus Christ (compare Rev. 12:5 with Rev. 19:15 and Ps. 2:9), this symbolic woman can be none other than the nation Israel. It was through Israel that Jesus Christ came into the world (Rom. 1:3; 9:4–5). By further comparing the description in Revelation 12:1 with Genesis 37:9–10, the identification seems certain.

In the Old Testament, Israel is often compared to a

woman, and even a woman in travail (Isa. 54:5; 66:7; Jer. 3:6–10; Mic. 4:10; 5:2–3). The apostate world system is compared to a harlot (Rev. 17:1ff.), and the church to a pure bride (Rev. 19:7ff.).

The son is born and is then caught up to the throne of God (Rev. 12:5). We have symbolized here the birth of Christ and His victorious ascension, but nothing is said about either His life or His death. The colon in the middle of the verse represents thirty-three years of history!

The woman with child is the first wonder; the great red dragon is the second. Revelation 12:9 makes it clear that this is Satan. The color red is associated with death (Rev. 6:4), and Satan is a murderer (John 8:44). The heads, horns, and crowns will appear again in Revelation 13:1 and 17:3. The heads represent mountains (Rev. 17:9), and the horns represent kings (Rev. 17:12). We shall study the meaning of these symbols in more detail later.

The dragon was cast out of heaven (Rev. 12:9), and he took with him a third of the angels (Rev. 12:7, 9). They are spoken of as "stars" in Revelation 12:4 (see also Dan. 8:10). This is evidently a reference to the fall of Satan (Isa. 14:12–15), when he and his hosts revolted against God. However, the casting out described in Revelation 12:7–10 is yet future.

Just as soon as the child was born, Satan tried to destroy Him. This conflict between Satan and "the woman" began soon after man fell (Gen. 3:15). Throughout Old Testament history, Satan tried to prevent the birth of the Redeemer. There was always a "dragon" standing by, waiting to destroy Israel or the ancestors of the Messiah. Pharaoh is called a "dragon" (Ezek. 29:3), and so is Nebuchadnezzar (Jer. 51:34). At one critical point, the royal line was limited to one little boy (2 Kings 11:1–3). When Jesus Christ was born, Satan used King Herod to try to destroy Him (Matt. 2). Satan thought that he had succeeded when he used Judas to betray the Lord and hand Him over to be crucified. But the cross was actually Satan's defeat! "And they overcame him [Satan] by the blood of the Lamb" (Rev. 12:11).

Even today Satan has access to heaven, where he accuses God's people, but he cannot dethrone the exalted Savior. His strategy is to persecute God's people and devour them if possible (1 Peter 5:8). He has a special hatred for the Jewish people and has been the power behind anti-Semitism from the days of Pharaoh and Haman (see the book of Esther) to Hitler and Stalin. Finally, in the middle of the tribulation, there will come a wave of anti-Semitism such as the world has never seen (Rev. 12:6). But God will protect His people during those three-and-a-half years (1,260 days; see Rev. 11:2; 13:5).

Apart from the 144,000 (who are sealed and protected), a believing remnant of Jews will survive this very troublesome time. We are not told where God will protect them or who it is that will care for them. Matthew 24:15–21 will take on special meaning for those believing Jews who live in the end days. Note especially the parenthesis in Revelation 12:15.

You and I are involved in a similar conflict today (see Eph. 6:10ff.). Satan is out to destroy the church, and our victory can come only through Jesus Christ.

The next scene in this cosmic drama is a *war in heaven* (Rev. 12:7–12). Scripture makes it clear that Satan has access to heaven even today (Job 1—2). Once he was the highest of God's angels, but he rebelled against God and was cast down (Isa. 14:12–15). Interestingly, as God's church faithfully serves Christ and wins the lost, Satan is also cast down and defeated (Luke 10:1–2, 17–20; Matt. 16:18; note also 12:29).

Of course, when Jesus Christ died on the cross, it meant Satan's ultimate defeat (John 12:31–33). Satan will one day be cast out of heaven (Rev. 12:7–10), and then finally cast into hell (Rev. 20:10).

What is this celestial conflict all about? The fact that Michael led God's angels to victory is significant, because Michael is identified with the nation Israel (Dan. 10:10–21; 12:1; note also Jude 9). The name *Michael* means "who is like God?" and this certainly parallels Satan's egocentric attack on Jehovah—"I will be like the Most High" (Isa. 14:14). Apparently, the devil's hatred of Israel will spur him to make one final assault against the throne of God, but he will be defeated by Michael and a heavenly host.

But perhaps there is another factor involved in this war. After the church is taken to heaven, believers will stand before the judgment seat of Christ and have their works examined. On the basis of this judgment, rewards will be given (Rom. 14:10–12; 1 Cor. 3:10–15; 2 Cor. 5:10–11). It seems likely that Satan will be present at this event and will accuse the saints, pointing out all the "spots and wrinkles" in the church (Eph. 5:24–27).

The name *devil* means "accuser," and *Satan* means "adversary." Satan stands at the throne of God and fights the saints by accusing them (see Job 1—2; Zech. 3). But Jesus Christ, the "heavenly Advocate" (1 John 2:1–2), represents the church before God's holy throne. Because Jesus Christ died for us, we can overcome Satan's accusations "by the blood of the Lamb." Our salvation is secure, not because of our own works, but because of His finished work at Calvary.

How furious Satan will be when the church comes forth in glory "without spot or wrinkle, or any such thing." When the accuser sees that his tactics have failed, he will become angry and threaten the very peace of heaven.

How does this future war apply to the church today? The same serpent who accuses the saints in heaven also deceives the nations on earth (Rev. 12:9), and one of his strategies is to lie about the church. He deceives the nations into thinking that the people of God are dangerous, deluded, even destructive. It is through Satan's deception that the leaders of the nations band together against Christ and His people

(Ps. 2; Acts 4:23–30). God's people *in every age* must expect the world's opposition, but the church can always defeat the enemy by being faithful to Jesus Christ.

Christ's shed blood gives us our perfect standing before God (1 John 1:5—2:2). But our witness to God's Word and our willingness to lay down our lives for Christ defeats Satan as well. Satan is not equal to God; he is not omnipotent, omnipresent, or omniscient. His power is limited and his tactics must fail when God's people trust the power of the blood and of the Word. Nothing Satan does can rob us of "salvation, and strength, and the kingdom of our God, and the power of his Christ" (Rev. 12:10), if we are yielded to Him. God's great purposes will be fulfilled!

Believers in any age or situation can rejoice in this victory, no matter how difficult their experiences may be. Our warfare is not against flesh and blood, but against the spiritual forces of the wicked one, and these have been defeated by our Savior (Eph. 6:10ff.; note also Eph. 1:15–23).

Heaven will rejoice when Satan is cast out, but the earth-dwellers will not, for the last half of the tribulation will mean intense suffering for the world. The "woe" in Revelation 12:12 reminds us of the "three woes" referred to in Revelation 8:13. The first "woe" is described in Revelation 9:1–12, and the second in Revelation 9:13–21. The third "woe" is referred to in Revelation 11:14ff., but this passage only summarizes the events that will climax God's plan for the earth. It may be that part of this third "woe" is casting out Satan and permitting his terrible wrath on earth.

This, then, is the third scene in the drama: *Satan's wrath on earth* (Rev. 12:13–16). Knowing that his time is short, and having no more access to heaven, the adversary must vent all of his anger earthward. He begins with Israel (the woman), and creates a wave of anti-Semitism. Satan has always hated the Jews because they are God's chosen people and the vehicle through which salvation came into the world. Satan would like to destroy the nation, particularly as the time draws near for the Messiah to return to earth to establish the promised kingdom. A Jewish remnant must be ready to receive Him and form the nucleus for the kingdom (Zech. 12:9—14:21; Rev. 1:7).

God will prepare a special place where the Jewish remnant will be protected and cared for. It is interesting that the remnant's escape from Satan is described in terms of a flying eagle, for this is a repeated image in the Old Testament with reference to Israel. God delivered Israel from Egypt "on eagles' wings" (Ex. 19:4) and cared for the people in the wilderness as an eagle would her young (Deut. 32:11–12). Their return from Babylonian captivity was like "mounting up with wings as eagles" (Isa. 40:31).

Note that the remnant will be sheltered for the last half of the tribulation. We do not know where this sheltered place will be, nor do we need to know. But the lesson for all of us is clear: God cares for those

whom He wants to use to accomplish His purposes on earth. True, some people will give their lives (Rev. 12:11), but others will be spared (see Acts 12 for an example of this principle).

The phrase "water as a flood" is not explained, but there is a parallel in Psalm 124. (Also note the phrase "escaped as a bird" in verse 7 of this same Psalm.) This "flood" is probably an outpouring of hatred and anti-Semitic propaganda. Or it may symbolize armies that invade Israel and seek to defeat the remnant. If that is the meaning, then the earth opening up could well be an earthquake that God sends to destroy the invaders. When Satan discovers that the people he seeks to kill are protected, then he turns on those who were not carried to the hidden place of safety. He will declare war, and God will permit him to have victory for a time (Rev. 13:7), but ultimately, the old serpent will be defeated.

The Beast from the Sea (13:1–10)
Some texts read, "And he [Satan] stood upon the sand of the sea." The sea symbolizes the Gentile nations (Rev. 17:15). From one of them, Satan will bring forth his "Super Leader," the man we call "Antichrist." Up to this point, Antichrist has headed a ten-nation European league, but now he is about to embark on a new career as Satan's world dictator.

You will remember that Antichrist began his career as a peacemaker (Rev. 6:2) and even "settled" the Arab-Israeli problem by making a covenant with the Jews to protect them for seven years (Dan. 9:27). This protection would permit the nation to rebuild the temple and reinstitute religious rituals (Dan. 9:27; Rev. 11:1). But in the middle of the seven-year period (the time we are studying now in Rev. 10—14) he will break that covenant, stop the ceremonies, and set up himself as god in the temple (Dan. 9:27; 2 Thess. 2:1–12).

The symbolic description of "the beast" enables us to learn something about his origin and character. God does not see him as a man, made in the divine image, but as a wild animal, under the control of Satan. He is a man (Rev. 13:18), but he is energized from hell, for he comes out of the pit (Rev. 11:7; 17:8). Just as Jesus Christ is God in the flesh, so "the beast" will be Satan in a human body (see John 13:2, 27).

The seven heads represent seven mountains (Rev. 17:9), and since Rome was built on seven hills, this must be a veiled reference to that powerful city (see Rev. 17:18). It would be a most meaningful allusion in John's day!

The ten horns represent ten kingdoms (Dan. 7:24; Rev. 17:12). It appears that "the beast" will head a "United States of Europe," a revived Roman Empire, before taking over as world dictator. All nations will no doubt admire and thank him for the "peace" he has achieved, little realizing the sorrow and destruction he will bring to the world.

The three animals named in Revelation 13:2 remind us of the four beasts Daniel saw in his dream

(Dan. 7): a lion (Babylon), a bear (Media-Persia), a leopard (Greece), and a "terrible beast" (the Antichrist). John saw these animals, or kingdoms, in reverse order since he was looking *back,* while Daniel was looking *ahead.* The final world empire will be rooted in all the previous empires and unite in one their evil and power. Added to the ferocity of these beasts will be Satan's own power, throne, and authority!

Once Satan presents his great "masterpiece," the counterfeit Christ, to the world, what will happen next?

First, there will be *wonder* (Rev. 13:3). Certainly a terrified world will wonder at Antichrist's power and his sudden rise to international fame and authority. But mankind will also wonder at the healing of his "wound." What is this "wound"? John does not explain it, but perhaps what he later wrote (Rev. 17:9–13) can help interpret the symbolism. This "wound" must be important, because John mentioned it three times (Rev. 13:3, 12, 14), including the fact that it was sword-inflicted.

The seven heads represent seven mountains, but also seven kings or kingdoms (Rev. 17:10). Antichrist or "the beast" is one of these seven kings (Rev. 17:11), but he is also the eighth. Apparently, he reigns twice, but how can this be? The suggestion has been made that "the beast" will be a European leader who will form a ten-nation federation (Rev. 17:12), but be slain in the process. Revelation 11:7 and 17:8 state that "the beast" will ascend out of the abyss. Is it possible that Satan will (with God's permission) resurrect a man from the dead? If Satan has power to give life to a dead idol (Rev. 13:15), could he not also give life to a dead body?

If "the beast" ruled as one of the seven kings, was slain, and then raised up again, he could rule as the eighth king. If, on the other hand, the image is seen representing *kingdoms* rather than individuals, we would have the reemergence of a "dead kingdom" on the world scene. However, it would be difficult to understand how a kingdom could be slain by a sword. It is best, I think, to apply this prophecy to individual persons.

Not only will there be wonder, but there will also be *worship* (Rev. 13:4). Worship is the one thing Satan has always wanted (Matt. 4:8–10), and he will receive it through "the beast." The second "beast," described in the last half of this chapter, will organize and promote the worship of Antichrist, making it the official religion of the world!

There will also be *words* (Rev. 13:5–6). Almost all dictators have risen to power by controlling people with their words. Some of us can recall when Adolf Hitler was rising to power, and know now how he mesmerized huge crowds with his speeches. Satan will make "the beast" a great orator, whose addresses will blaspheme God, His name, His tabernacle (heaven), and the saints in heaven. Since Satan will have recently been cast out of heaven, this blasphemy is to be expected.

Satan can do nothing without God's permission (see Job 1—2; Luke 22:31–32), so "the beast's" authority is *delegated,* not inherent. It will last for three-and-a-half years, the last half of the tribulation.

In his night vision, Daniel saw "the beast" as the fourth and final empire (Dan. 7:19–28). There, as in John's vision, is the same image of the ten horns with the added revelation that "the beast" must defeat three of the kings to gain control. Daniel also heard "the beast's" blasphemous words (Dan. 7:25).

Finally, there will be *war* (Rev. 13:7–10). God will permit Antichrist to war against His people ("wear out the saints," Dan. 7:25) and even to defeat some of them. John prophesied that some of the saints will be captured and some will be martyred. But because of their faith, they will have patience, or endurance (see Heb. 6:12; Rev. 1:9), and will not deny the Lord in spite of persecution and death.

The world's population will be divided: those who are saved, with their names in God's book, will not submit to "the beast"; those who are lost—the earth-dwellers—will worship "the beast" and do his bidding. Note that Revelation 13:9 applies this truth to "any man," no matter in which age he may live. Certainly in John's day, this was meaningful; for every Roman citizen had to acknowledge, "Caesar is Lord." Likewise in every age of the church, true believers have had to take their stand for Christ, come what may.

Keep in mind that "the beast" is a counterfeit Christ. The world would not receive Christ, but it will receive Antichrist (John 5:43). The world would not believe the truth, but they will believe the lie (2 Thess. 2:8–12). Jesus spoke (and still speaks) gracious words of salvation, and men turn a deaf ear, but they will listen to the blasphemous words of "the beast." The world will not worship *the* Christ, but they will bow down to Antichrist.

In Revelation 17, we will learn that "the beast" rises to power by means of "the harlot," a symbol of the apostate world church. This is not any one denomination or faith, but a world religious system that has rejected God's Son and God's truth. However, when "the beast" rises to universal power, he will no longer need "the harlot" and shall subsequently destroy her and establish his own satanic religion.

The Beast from the Earth (13:11–18)

In Revelation 16:13; 19:20; and 20:10, the beast from the earth is called "the false prophet." The dragon or Satan is the counterfeit Father ("I will be like the Most High"), "the beast" is the counterfeit Christ, and the false prophet is the counterfeit Holy Spirit. This completes the satanic trinity.

One of the ministries of the Holy Spirit is to glorify Christ and lead people to trust and worship Him (John 16:7–15). The false prophet will point to Antichrist and his image and compel people to worship Satan through "the beast."

The image of the horns (Rev. 13:11) suggests that the false prophet has authority, but the absence of a crown indicates that his authority is not political. Our Lord warned that there would be false prophets (Matt. 24:11, 24), and this one will be the greatest. He will have the "character" of a lamb but the voice of the dragon. What a deceiver he will be—and all the world will listen to him!

When our Lord ministered on earth, Jewish leaders often asked Him to perform some sign to prove that He was indeed their Messiah, and Jesus refused. But the false prophet will perform deceptive signs that will lead the world into devil-worship (see 2 Thess. 2:9). His greatest sign will be "the abomination of desolation" mentioned by Daniel (Dan. 9:27; 11:36), Jesus (Matt 24:15), and Paul (2 Thess. 2:4).

What is "the abomination of desolation"? It is the image of "the beast," set up in the temple in Jerusalem. An idol is bad enough, but setting it up in the temple is the height of all blasphemy. Since Satan could not command worship in heaven, he will go to the next best place—the Jewish temple in the Holy City (see Dan. 8:9–14).

The false prophet, energized by Satan, will perform his "lying wonders" and even duplicate some of the signs performed by the two witnesses (Rev. 13:13; see also 11:5). Up to this time, the two witnesses have been ministering at the temple in Jerusalem, but "the beast" will slay them and take over the temple. When God raises the two witnesses from the dead and takes them to heaven, the false prophet will answer that challenge by giving life to the image of "the beast." Not only will the image move, but it will speak!

Not content to control people through religious deceit, the false prophet will institute strong economic measures as well. Everybody (except believers; Rev. 20:4) will receive a special mark in order to buy or sell, but the only way to get that mark is to submit to "the beast" and worship him. Surely this is a strong allusion to the Caesar worship in the Roman Empire, but this same policy has been used by political leaders throughout history.

This special mark is the name or number of "the beast"—the mystical 666. In the ancient world, the letters of the alphabet were used for numbers, both in Greek and Hebrew, and Bible students have been attempting for years to unravel the mystery of this name and number. If you work at it hard enough, almost *any* name will fit!

Since man was created on the sixth day, six is the number of man. Creation was made for man and likewise has the number six stamped on it: twenty-four hours to a day (4 x 6), twelve months to a year (2 x 6). Seven is the number of perfection and fullness, but six is the "human number," just short of perfection.

Despite all man's imaginative calculations, we must confess that no one knows the meaning of this number

and name. No doubt believers on earth at that time will understand it clearly. The "satanic trinity" cannot claim the number seven; it must settle for 666.

This much is sure: in recent years, we have seen a worldwide increase in the use of numbers for identification. In the United States, a person's Social Security number is indispensable. In fact, numbers are more important to computers than names! Perhaps this is an advance warning of what will happen on earth when "the beast" is in control.

We have reached the middle of the tribulation in our study, but we are not yet ready for the return of the Lord. Before John revealed how the great drama will climax, he paused to overview great events to come, and that will be our next topic.

An antichristian system pervades our world, and true believers must not be a part of it (1 John 2:15–17). We must shun false worship (1 Cor. 10:14–22), that we may be found faithful to the Lord in these last days (2 Tim. 3)!

CHAPTER NINE
Revelation 14—16
VOICES OF VICTORY

One of the themes that link Revelation 14—16 together is expressed by the word *voice*, which is used eleven times. In the events recorded, God speaks to His people or to the lost world, or His creatures speak out in praise of the Lord or in warning to the world. As the world moves into the last half of the tribulation, heaven is not silent.

The Voice of the 144,000 (14:1–5)
This special group of Jewish men was sealed by God before the seventh seal was opened (Rev. 7), and now they are seen on Mount Zion with the Lord Jesus Christ. Contrast this picture to the one described in Revelation 13: the followers of "the beast" whose mark is on their foreheads (Rev. 13:16). God always has His faithful people, no matter how wicked the world may become.

The 144,000 are *standing* with Christ on Mount Zion, but which Mount Zion: the heavenly one (Heb. 12:22–24) or the earthly one? I personally believe that this is the heavenly Mount Zion, and that the scene anticipates Christ's coronation and the establishment of His kingdom when He returns to earth (Zech. 14:4ff.). Christ today is enthroned in the heavenly Zion (Ps. 2:6), and we are enthroned with Him (Eph. 2:6). The scene in Revelation 14 is the assurance to God's people that He cares for His own and finally will take them to glory.

Not only are the 144,000 standing, but they are also *singing* (Rev. 14:2–3). Because of the special experiences they had during the tribulation, they have a new song to sing that others cannot share (see Ps. 33:3; 40:3; 96:1; 98:1; 144:9; 149:1). They are accompanied by heavenly harps and other heavenly voices. It is encouraging to know that one day our sorrows will be transformed into songs!

John also pointed out their *separation* (Rev. 14:4–5). The 144,000 did not belong *to* the earth because they had been redeemed *out of* the earth. They were not earth-dwellers, but citizens of heaven. Believers today do not belong to this very special group but, like them, we have been redeemed and are not part of this world system (see John 17:14–19; Phil. 3:17–21).

The phrase "defiled with women" does not imply that sex within marriage is evil, because it is not (Heb. 13:4). It merely indicates that these 144,000 Jewish men were unmarried. In the Bible, fornication and adultery are pictures of idolatry (Ex. 34:15; James 4:4). While most of the world bowed down to the image of "the beast," the 144,000 were faithful to the true God. While others lied to get what they needed, the 144,000 were without guile and blemish.

The term *firstfruits* means "the very finest." But it also carries the idea of an expected harvest. On the Feast of Firstfruits, the priest waved the sheaf before the Lord as a sign that the entire harvest belonged to Him (Lev. 23:9–14). The 144,000 may be the firstfruits of the harvest yet to come; they may be the nucleus of the coming kingdom. However, it would seem difficult for a *heavenly* company such as this to establish an earthly kingdom.

The Voices of the Angels (14:6–20)

At least six different angels are involved in this scene, each with a particular message to proclaim.

"Judgment is come" (vv. 6–7). During the present age, the angels are not privileged to preach the gospel. That responsibility has been given to God's people. While the nations will fear "the beast" and give honor to him, this heavenly messenger will summon them to fear and honor God alone. It is a reminder that God is the Creator and He alone deserves worship. This is not the gospel message as we know it (1 Cor. 15:1–4); rather, it is a return to the message of Romans 1:18ff., what theologians call "natural theology."

All creation bears witness to God's existence as well as to His power and wisdom. Nonetheless, "the beast" will convince men that he is in charge of the world, and that their destinies are in his hands. The message of the angel calls men back to basics: God is Creator—worship and serve Him. The fear of the Lord, not the fear of "the beast," is the source of wisdom (Prov. 9:10).

"Babylon is fallen" (v. 8). This proclamation anticipates the events of Revelation 18 (see also Rev. 16:18–19). We will consider it in detail then. "Babylon" is God's name for the world system of "the beast," the entire economic and political organization by which he rules. "The harlot" (Rev. 17) is the religious system that "the beast" uses to help build his organization. When Antichrist establishes his own religion (Rev. 13:11–15), he will destroy the "harlot," but it is God who will destroy Babylon.

"Escape God's wrath" (vv. 9–13). The third message is directed especially to those who are deciding about following "the beast." It is a warning that "the easy way" is really the hard way, that to "go along with the world" means to go away from God. The Greek text reads, "If any man continues to worship the beast," suggesting that there is still opportunity for repentance and salvation.

"Drinking the cup" is sometimes used as an image of judgment (Jer. 25:15ff.; 51:7ff.; note also Rev. 14:8). God's final judgments on mankind will be "vials of wrath" poured out from heaven (Rev. 16). God will not mix mercy with this judgment (Ps. 75:8; Hab. 3:2), but will pour out His undiluted indignation on a rebellious world.

Images like "fire and brimstone" (Rev. 14:10) and "smoke" (Rev. 14:11) upset some people. They ask, "How can a God of love actually permit His creatures to suffer eternal torment?" But we must keep in mind that God's love is a *holy* love, not one based on sentimentality, and therefore He *must* justly deal with sin. We may not like the word *torment,* but it is here just the same (Rev. 14:10; see also 9:5; 11:10; 20:10).

We must also keep in mind that God has repeatedly warned sinners and given them opportunity to repent. The first angel in this series invited sinners to turn to God, and the second one warned that the whole "Babylonian" system would be destroyed. If people persist in their sins even after God sends judgments and warnings, then they have only themselves to blame.

John intended for his readers to see the contrast between Revelation 14:11 and 13: no rest for the wicked, but eternal rest for the saints (see 2 Thess. 1:3–12). Better to reign with Christ forever than with Antichrist for a few short years! Better to endure persecution patiently now than to escape it and suffer throughout eternity!

"The harvest is ripe" (vv. 14–20). The Person pictured here on the white cloud is undoubtedly our Lord Jesus Christ (see Dan. 7:13–14; Rev. 1:13). We have had the image of the cup, and now we have the image of the harvest, both of the grain (Rev. 14:14–16) and of the grape (Rev. 14:17–20). Again, this anticipates the final judgment of the world.

While winning lost souls to Christ is sometimes pictured as a harvest (John 4:34–38), this image is also used of God's judgment (Matt. 13:24–30, 36–43; Luke 3:8–17). God permits the seeds of iniquity to grow until they are ripe, and then He judges (Gen. 15:16).

The grape harvest is often a picture of judgment (see Joel 3:13ff., which anticipates the day of the Lord). In actuality, Scripture portrays three different "vines." Israel was God's vine, planted in the land to bear fruit for God's glory, but the nation failed God and had to be cut down (Ps. 80:8–16; Isa. 5:1–7; see also Matt. 21:33–46). Today, Christ is the Vine and believers are branches in Him (John 15). But the world system is also a vine, "the vine of the earth" in contrast to Christ, the heavenly Vine, and it is ripening for judgment. The wicked system—Babylon—that intoxicates people and controls them, will one day be cut down and destroyed in "the winepress of the wrath of God."

Some see in this image an anticipation of the "battle of Armageddon," when the armies of the world will gather against Jerusalem (Zech. 14:1–4; Rev. 16:16). Certainly, John is using hyperbole when he describes a river of blood four feet deep and 200 miles long (see also Isa. 63:1–6). Today, God is speaking to the world in grace, and men will not listen. One day hence, He must speak in wrath. The bitter cup will be drunk, the harvest of sin reaped, and the vine of the earth cut down and cast into the winepress.

The Voice of the Victors (15:1–4)
At this point, John saw the seven angels holding the seven vials of God's wrath, poised for action. The wicked world is about to "drink of the wine of the wrath of God" (Rev. 14:10), but before the angels pour out their judgments, there is an "interlude" of blessing. Before sending the "third woe" (Rev. 11:14), God once again reassures His faithful people.

John saw the believers from the tribulation who had overcome "the beast" and his system. These are the people who "loved not their lives unto the death" (Rev. 12:11). Since they did not cooperate with the satanic system and receive the mark of "the beast," they were unable to buy or sell (Rev. 13:17). They were totally dependent on the Lord for their daily bread. Some of them were put into prison and some were slain (Rev. 13:10), but all of them practiced faith and patience.

This entire scene is reminiscent of Israel following the exodus. The nation had been delivered from Egypt by the blood of the lamb, and the Egyptian army had been destroyed at the Red Sea. In thankfulness to God, the Israelites stood by the sea and sang "the song of Moses."

The tribulation saints whom John saw and heard were standing by the "sea of glass" in heaven (Rev. 4:6), just as the Israelites stood by the Red Sea. They were singing "the song of Moses" and also "the song of the Lamb." "The song of Moses" is recorded in Exodus 15, and its refrain is: "The Lord is my strength and song, and he is become my salvation" (Ex. 15:2). The 144,000 sang a song that nobody else could sing, but this is a song *all* saints can sing.

When Israel returned from Babylonian captivity and reestablished their government and restored temple worship, they used this same refrain at the dedication services (Ps. 118; see especially v. 14).

In the future, when God shall call His people back to their land, Isaiah prophesied that they will sing this song again (Isa. 11:15—12:6). "The song of Moses" is indeed an important song in the hymnal of the Jewish nation.

This scene would give great assurance and endurance to suffering saints in any age of the church. It is possible to be victorious over the world system! One

does not have to yield to the "mark of the beast." Through the blood of the Lamb, we have deliverance. Our Lord's work on the cross is a "spiritual exodus" accomplished by His blood. (Note Luke 9:31, where the word "decease" is *exodus* in the Greek.)

In their song, the tribulation saints praise God's works as well as His ways. The earth-dwellers certainly would not praise God for His works, and they would never understand His ways. God's works are great and marvelous, and His ways are just and true. There is no complaint here about the way God permitted these people to suffer! It would save us a great deal of sorrow if we would acknowledge God's sovereignty in this same way today! "The Lord is righteous in all his ways, and holy in all his works" (Ps. 145:17).

The phrase "king of saints" can also be read "king of ages." God is the eternal King, but He is also in charge of history. Nothing happens by accident. The singers seek to glorify God and honor Him, the very praise the first angel proclaimed in Revelation 14:7. Antecedents of this song may be found in Psalms 86:9; 90:1–2; 92:5; 98:2; 111:9; and 145:17.

Revelation 15:4 is another anticipation of the kingdom, foretelling the time when all nations shall worship the Lamb and obey Him. This verse also announces that God's judgments are about to be manifested.

The Voice of Fulfillment (15:5—16:21)
The "great voice" out of the temple commands the seven angels to pour out the contents of their vials (Rev. 16:1), after which he announces "It is done" (Rev. 16:17). The "mystery of God" is finished! (Rev. 10:7) The martyrs in glory had asked, "How long?" (Rev. 6:9–11) and now their cry would be answered.

The seven angels emerge from the heavenly temple (see Rev. 11:19), because their work is holy as are the judgments they bring. The angels' clothing reminds us of the priestly garments, for their service is a divine ministry. When the Old Testament tabernacle and temple were dedicated, these earthly buildings were filled with God's glory (Ex. 40:34–35; 2 Chron. 7:1–4), but now the *heavenly* temple is filled with smoke (see Isa. 6:4; Ezek. 10:4). This smoke likewise is evidence of God's glory and power.

Each of the angels has a specific "target" for the contents of his vial. The earth-dwellers have already suffered from the seal and trumpet judgments, but this final series of judgments will climax God's plan, leading to Babylon's fall and Jesus Christ's return to earth.

Grievous sores (v. 2). This vial judgment reminds us of the sixth plague in Egypt (Ex. 9:8–12; note also Deut. 28:27, 35). Only those who have submitted to "the beast" and who have rejected the warning of the first angel will experience this judgment (Rev. 14:6–7).

Revelation 16:10–11 suggests that these sores do not disappear, for by the time of the fifth vial, people are still in pain from the first judgment. Yet their pain will not cause them to repent (see Rev. 9:20–21).

William R. Newell used to say, "If men are not won by grace, they will never be won."

It is an awesome thought to consider almost the entire population of the world suffering from a painful malady that nothing can cure. Constant pain affects a person's disposition so that he finds it difficult to get along with other people. Human relations during that period will certainly be at their worst.

Waters turned to blood (vv. 3–6). The second and third vials parallel the first plague in Egypt (Ex. 7:14–25). The second vial will center on the sea, and the third will turn the inland waters (rivers and fountains) into blood. When the second trumpet judgment occurred, a third part of the sea became blood, but with this judgment, the entire system of seas and oceans will be polluted. The third trumpet made a third part of the inland waters bitter as wormwood, but the third vial will turn all of those bitter waters into blood.

Heaven gives justification for this terrible judgment: the earth-dwellers have shed the blood of God's people, so it is only right that they should drink blood. In God's government, the punishment fits the crime. Pharaoh tried to drown the Jewish boy babies, but it was his own army that eventually drowned in the Red Sea. Haman planned to hang Mordecai on the gallows and to exterminate the Jews, but he himself was hanged on the gallows, and his family was exterminated (Est. 7:10; 9:10). King Saul refused to obey God and slay the Amalekites, so he was slain by an Amalekite (2 Sam. 1:1–16).

Great heat from the sun (vv. 8–9). All earthly life depends on the light of the sun. In previous judgments, a part of the sun had been dimmed (Rev. 8:12), but now the heat of the sun is increased. Anyone who has been on the desert knows how merciless the sun's heat can be. Remembering too that the water system is now useless, you can imagine how people will suffer from thirst. Alas, even this judgment will not bring men to their knees (see Mal. 4:1)!

Darkness (vv. 10–11). This is not worldwide darkness; only "the beast," his throne, and his kingdom are affected. This reminds us of the fifth trumpet (Rev. 9:2) and the ninth plague (Ex. 10:21–23). Where is the throne of "the beast"? His image is in the temple in Jerusalem, so that may be the center of his operation. Or perhaps he is ruling from Rome, in cooperation with the apostate church headquartered there.

When God sent the ninth plague to Egypt, the entire land was dark, except for Goshen where the Israelites lived. The judgment of the fifth vial is just the opposite: there is light for the world, but darkness reigns at the headquarters of "the beast"! Certainly this will be a great blow to his "image" throughout the earth.

The Euphrates dried up (vv. 12–16). This famous river was mentioned earlier in Revelation, when the sixth trumpet sounded (Rev. 9:13ff.) and the angels were loosed who were bound therein. At that time, an army of demonic horsemen was also released. Now,

an army from the nations of the world gathers for the great battle at Armageddon. The drying up of the river will make it possible for the army of the "kings of the East" to come to Palestine and invade the Holy Land.

We often speak of "the battle of Armageddon," but nowhere does the Bible use that phrase. On September 2, 1945, when General Douglas MacArthur supervised signing the peace treaty with Japan, he said: "We have had our last chance. If we will not devise something greater and more equitable [than war], Armageddon will be at our door."

The name *Armageddon* comes from two Hebrew words, *har Megiddo,* the hill of Megiddo. The word *Megiddo* means "place of troops" or "place of slaughter." It is also called the Plain of Esdraelon and the Valley of Jezreel. The area is about fourteen miles wide and twenty miles long, and forms what Napoleon called "the most natural battlefield of the whole earth." Standing on Mount Carmel and overlooking that great plain, you can well understand why it would be used for gathering the armies of the nations.

It was on this plain that Barak defeated the armies of Canaan (Judg. 5:19). Gideon met the Midianites there (Judg. 7), and it was there that King Saul lost his life (1 Sam. 31). Titus and the Roman army used this natural corridor, as did the Crusaders in the Middle Ages. British General Allenby used it when he defeated the Turkish armies in 1917.

From a human viewpoint it appears that the armies of the nations are gathering on their own, but John makes it clear that the military movement is according to God's plan. The satanic trinity, through demonic powers, will influence the nations and cause the rulers to assemble their armies. They will even work miracles that will impress the rulers and cause them to cooperate. But all this will merely fulfill the will of God and accomplish His purposes (see Rev. 17:17). The Gentile nations will look on Armageddon as a battle, but to God, it will be only a "supper" for the fowls of the air (Rev. 19:17–21),

Zechariah 12 and 14 describe this event from Israel's point of view. Since "the beast" has set up his image in the temple at Jerusalem, and since many of the Jews will not bow down to him, it is natural that the Holy City should be the object of attack. However, not only the Jews are involved, for God has a purpose for the Gentile nations as well. Joel 3:9–21 parallels the Zechariah references, and Joel 3:19 makes clear that God will punish the Gentiles for the way they have treated the Jews (see also Isa. 24; Zeph. 3:8ff.).

The outcome of the "battle" is recorded in Revelation 19: the Lord returns and defeats His enemies. Obviously, the assembling and marching armies create no problem for Almighty God. When the nations rage and defy Him, "He that sitteth in the heavens shall laugh: the Lord shall have them in derision. Then shall he speak unto them in his wrath, and vex them in his sore displeasure" (Ps. 2:4–5).

"It is done" (vv. 17–21). The devil is "the prince

of the power of the air," so perhaps this seventh vial has a special effect on his dominion (Eph. 2:2). But the immediate result is a devastating earthquake that affects the cities of the nations. Satan's entire system is now about to be judged by God: his religious system (the harlot, Rev. 17), his political and economic system (Babylon, Rev. 18), and his military system (the armies, Rev. 19).

The "great city" (Rev. 16:19) is probably Jerusalem (see Rev. 11:8). The prophet Zechariah prophesied an earthquake that would change the topography of Jerusalem (Zech. 14:4). But the key idea here is that Babylon would fall (see Jer. 50—51). "The beast's" great economic system, which subjugated the people of the world, would be completely destroyed by God.

Added to the earthquake will be a hailstorm with hailstones of tremendous weight. (A talent of silver weighs about 125 pounds!) This judgment is reminiscent of the seventh plague in Egypt (Ex. 9:22—26). Just as Pharaoh and the Egyptian leaders did not repent, so the earth-dwellers will not repent; in fact, they will blaspheme God! No wonder the hail comes, for blasphemers are supposed to be stoned to death (Lev. 24:16).

Reviewing these three chapters, we see the encouragement they give to suffering Christians. The sealed 144,000 will arrive on Mount Zion and praise God (Rev. 14:1–5). The martyrs will also be in glory, praising God (Rev. 15:1–4). John's message is clear: it is possible to be victorious over "the beast" and be an overcomer!

Movements of armies, confederations of nations, and worldwide opposition to God cannot hinder the Lord from fulfilling His Word and achieving His purposes. Men think they are free to do as they please, but in reality, they are accomplishing the plans and purposes of God!

Every generation of Christians has been able to identify with the events in Revelation 14—16. There has always been a "beast" to oppress God's people and a false prophet to try to lead them astray. We have always been on the verge of an "Armageddon" as the nations wage war.

But in the last days, these events will accelerate and the Bible's prophecies will be ultimately fulfilled. I believe the church will not be on the scene at that time, but both Jewish and Gentile believers will be living who will have to endure Antichrist's rule.

The admonition in Revelation 16:15 applies to us all: "Behold, I [Jesus] come as a thief. Blessed is he that watcheth, and keepeth his garments, lest he walk naked, and they see his shame." Jesus Christ may return at any time, and it behooves us to keep our lives clean, to watch, and to be faithful.

CHAPTER TEN
Revelation 17—18

DESOLATION AND DESTRUCTION!

Beginning in Revelation 17, John describes the Lamb's step-by-step victory over "the beast" and his kingdom. In Revelation 17, the religious system is judged; in Revelation 18, the political and economic system fall victim. Finally, the Lord Himself returns to earth; judges Satan, "the beast," and the false prophet (Rev. 19:19–20); and then establishes His kingdom.

One reason John used symbolism was so that his message would encourage believers in any period of church history. The true church is a pure virgin (Rev. 19:7–8; see also 2 Cor. 11:2), but the false religious system is a "harlot" who has abandoned the truth and prostituted herself for personal gain. In every age, there has been a "harlot" who has persecuted God's people, and this will culminate in the last days in a worldwide apostate religious system.

Likewise, every age has featured a "Babylon," a political and economic system that has sought to control people's minds and destinies. Just as the contrast to the "harlot" is the pure bride, so the contrast to "Babylon" is the City of God, the New Jerusalem, the eternal home prepared for the Lamb's wife (Rev. 21:9ff.). Each generation of believers must keep itself pure from the pollution of both the "harlot" and "Babylon."

In these two chapters, John prophesies two divine judgments.

The Desolation of the Harlot (17)
The scene begins with *an invitation* (Rev. 17:1–2). One of the angels asks John to come and see what God will do with "the beast's" worldwide religious system. Four times in this chapter, the woman is called a "harlot" (Rev. 17:1, 5, 15–16), and her sin is called "fornication" (Rev. 17:2, 4). Her evil influence has extended to the whole world, reaching even into high places ("the kings of the earth").

Following the invitation, John was carried away "in the Spirit" into the wilderness. There he saw "the harlot" and wrote down *the description* of what he saw (Rev. 17:3–6). Genesis 2 speaks of a pure bride in a lovely garden, but by the Bible's end, civilization has degenerated to an impure harlot in a wilderness! That is what sin does to the world.

The description is very full. The woman is dressed in expensive garments, decorated with gold and precious stones. She is holding a golden cup in her hand and is drunk with the blood of the saints. On her forehead (see Rev. 13:16; 14:1) she wears a special name.

Her posture is important. She is seated upon "many waters" (Rev. 17:1), and upon a scarlet beast with seven heads and ten horns. No wonder John was "greatly astonished" (NIV) when he beheld the woman and "the beast."

But what did it all mean? Thankfully, the angel gave John (and all believers) *the explanation* of these symbols (Rev. 17:7–18).

Let's begin with *the woman.* Revelation 17:18 makes clear that she is identified with a city that existed in John's day ("reigns" is present tense). This city is prosperous and powerful, but also idolatrous ("blasphemy") and dangerous. For one thing, it pollutes the nations with its filth and abomination (pictured by the golden wine cup); for another, it persecutes those who belong to the Lord (Rev. 17:6). Power, wealth, pollution, persecution: these words summarize the "great harlot's" involvement on a worldwide scale.

The woman's name also involves "mystery" (Rev. 17:5). In the New Testament, a "mystery" is a hidden truth that only the spiritually initiated can understand. To grasp one of God's mysteries requires spiritual intelligence and discernment. In this case, the mystery has to do with Babylon.

The city of Babylon was founded by Nimrod (Gen. 10:8–11). The name *Bab-el* means "the gate of God." Ironically, the famous tower of Babel (Gen. 11:1–9) was an idolatrous attempt by man to defy God. When the Lord sent judgment on the builders by making mankind's one language into many, the word *bab-el* came to mean "confusion." Later in history, Babylon became a great empire before finally falling to Media-Persia. But from the beginning of Nimrod's city in Genesis 10, an insidious anti-God "Babylonian influence" has been felt throughout history.

The woman is "the great harlot," but she is also "the mother of harlots." The Babylonian system has, in one way or another, given birth to all false religions. She has also seduced men into opposing God and persecuting His servants.

The seven mountains (Rev. 17:9) probably symbolize the city of Rome, built on seven hills. Certainly in John's day, the Roman Empire was living in luxury, spreading false religion, polluting the nations with its idolatry and sin, and persecuting the church.

John's readers would not be surprised when he used an evil harlot to symbolize a wicked city or political system. God even called Jerusalem a harlot (Isa. 1:21). Isaiah said that Tyre was a harlot (Isa. 23:16–17), and Nahum used this same designation for Nineveh (Nah. 3:4). (Read Jer. 50—51 for further historical parallels to John's prophetic message.)

As noted earlier, scarlet is the color of Satan (Rev. 12:3) and of sin (Isa. 1:18). Scarlet was a popular color in Rome, and both scarlet and purple were associated with rank and riches.

But the woman must not be separated from "the beast" that carries her. "The beast" has seven heads and ten horns. The seven heads symbolize seven mountains (Rev. 17:9) and also seven kings or kingdoms (Rev. 17:10), in keeping with Old Testament imagery (Ps. 30:7; Dan. 2:35). I have already suggested that the seven mountains can be interpreted geographically as the seven hills of Rome, but they may also be interpreted historically as seven kingdoms.

According to Revelation 17:10, five of these kings (or kingdoms) had passed off the scene, one was present in John's day, and one was yet to come. If so, then the five *past* kingdoms would be Egypt, Assyria, Babylon, Persia, and Greece. The *present* kingdom would be Rome, and the *future* kingdom would be that of "the beast." In order to understand Revelation 17:10–11, we must consider Revelation 17:12.

"The beast" not only has seven heads, but also ten horns, which represent ten kings. But these are very special kings: they enable "the beast" to rise to power and are even willing to yield their authority to him. Recall that at the opening of the first seal (Rev. 6:1–2), Antichrist began his "peaceful" conquest of the nations. He organized a "United States of Europe," brought peace to the Middle East, and appeared to be the great leader the troubled world was seeking.

But in the midst of the seven-year period, this ruler broke his covenant with Israel (Dan. 9:27) and began to persecute the people of God as well as the nation Israel. Energized by Satan and assisted by the false prophet, "the beast" became the world's dictator and its god. In this way, "the beast" was both "one of the seven [kings, kingdoms]" but also "the eighth." His kingdom was nothing but a revival of the Roman Empire ("one of the seven"), but it was a new kingdom ("the eighth").

But how does all this relate to Babylon? The "Babylonian system" of false religion has been a part of history since Nimrod founded his empire. Scholars have discovered it is amazingly like the true Christian faith! Alas, it is Satan's counterfeit of God's truth. Babylonians practiced the worship of mother and child, and even believed in the death and resurrection of the son.

Readers in John's day would identify "the harlot" with the Roman Empire. Readers in the Middle Ages might identify it as the Roman ecclesiastical system. Today, some believers see "the harlot" and the Babylonian system in an apostate "world church" that minimizes doctrinal truth, rejects the authority of the Word, and tries to unite professed believers on some other basis than faith in Jesus Christ.

However, in the days when John's prophecy will be fulfilled, an amazing thing will happen: "the harlot" will be made desolate by the very system that carried her! It is important to note that *"the beast" carries "the harlot."* Satan (and Antichrist) will use the apostate religious system to accomplish his own ends (i.e., attain world power), but then he will do away with "the harlot" and establish his own religious system. And all of this will be the fulfillment of God's Word (Rev. 17:17).

Since "the beast" sets up his image in the temple about the middle of the tribulation, we can assume that "the harlot" and "the beast" work together during those first three-and-a-half years. This is corroborated by the fact that the ten kings assist him in desolating "the harlot" (Rev. 17:16). These are the same ten kings associated with "the beast" when he sets up the "United States of Europe" during the first half of the tribulation.

Throughout history, political systems have "used" religious bodies to further their political causes. At the same time, church history reveals that religious groups have used politics to achieve their purposes. The marriage of church and state is not a happy one, and has often spawned children that have created serious problems. When dictators are friendly with religion, it is usually a sign that they want to make use of religion's influence and then destroy it. The church of Jesus Christ has been most influential in the world when it has maintained a separated position.

Compare the description of "the harlot's" desolation with that of the death of Jezebel (2 Kings 9:30–37).

Finally, note that those who trust the Lord are not influenced by "the harlot" or defeated by the kings (Rev. 17:14). Once again, John points out that the true believers are the "overcomers."

Satan's counterfeit religion is subtle, requiring spiritual discernment to recognize. It was Paul's great concern that the local churches he founded not be seduced away from their sincere devotion to Christ (2 Cor. 11:1–4). In every age, there is the tremendous pressure to conform to "popular religion" and to abandon the fundamentals of the faith. In these last days, we all need to heed the admonitions in 1 Timothy 4 and 2 Timothy 3 and remain true to our Lord.

The Destruction of Babylon (18)

Babylon was not only an ancient city and a powerful empire, but also the symbol of mankind's rebellion against God. In Revelation 18, Babylon represents the world system of "the beast," particularly in its economic and political aspects. At the same time, John calls Babylon a "city" at least eight times (Rev. 14:8; 17:18; 18:10, 16, 18–21). Old Testament prophecy seems to make clear that the city itself will not be rebuilt (Isa. 13:19–22; Jer. 51:24–26, 61–64). Some equate Babylon with Rome, particularly since "the harlot" and "the beast" cooperate during the first half of the tribulation. Perhaps Peter was using *Babylon* as a "code name" for Rome when he wrote his first letter (1 Peter 5:13). Certainly, John's readers would think of the Roman Empire as they read these words about Babylon.

John heard four voices give four important announcements.

The voice of condemnation (vv. 1–3). This announcement was anticipated in Revelation 14:8 (some commentators would also include Rev. 16:19, but I have interpreted the "great city" in that context as Jerusalem). There is a definite reference here to Jeremiah 51—52, where the prophet saw the fall of historical Babylon. But here John saw the destruction of spiritual Babylon, the world system organized by "the beast." It was no ordinary angel that made this announcement, for he had great power and a glory that radiated throughout the whole earth. Despite Satan's devices and the opposition of evil men, "the earth shall be filled with the knowledge of the glory of the Lord" (Hab. 2:14).

The phrase "is fallen, is fallen" not only adds dramatic effect to the announcement, but suggests a dual judgment: ecclesiastical Babylon, "the harlot," in Revelation 17, and political Babylon here in Revelation 18. This thought is amplified in Revelation 18:6 when God announces that Babylon will receive "double" for her many sins.

The church, the bride of the Lamb, is the habitation of God (Eph. 2:22); Babylon, on the other hand, is the habitation of Satan (Rev. 18:2). This parallels the judgment on ancient Babylon (Isa. 13:21ff.; Jer. 51:37ff.). Furthermore, John called the city "a cage of every unclean and hateful bird" (Rev. 18:2). In Christ's parable of the sower, He also used the birds as a picture of Satan (Matt 13:31–32).

This judgment has come because the Babylonian "system" has polluted the whole world. As in the judgment of "the harlot," the sin is that of "fornication" or idolatry. The system intoxicated the people of the world with all the riches and pleasures it had to offer. It catered to those who were "lovers of pleasures more than lovers of God" (2 Tim. 3:4).

Christians in every age have had to heed the warning of 1 John 2:15–17. How easy it is to become fascinated by the things the world has to offer. Like a person taking a sip of wine, we can soon find ourselves drinking deeply and then wanting more. The world system that opposes Christ has always been with us, and we must beware of its subtle influence.

The world system satisfies the desires of the earth-dwellers who follow "the beast" and reject the Lamb. But worldly things never permanently satisfy or last. The love of pleasures and possessions is but an insidious form of idolatry, demonic in its origin and destructive in its outcome.

The voice of separation (vv. 4–8). This admonition parallels Jeremiah 50:8 and 51:6, 45. In all ages, God's true people have had to separate themselves from that which is worldly and anti-God. When God called Abraham, He ordered him to get out of his country (Gen. 12:1). God separated the Jewish nation from Egypt and warned the Israelites not to go back. The church today is commanded to separate itself from that which is ungodly (Rom. 16:17–18; 2 Cor. 6:14–7:1).

John offered two reasons for God's people separating themselves from the diabolical system. The first is that they might avoid pollution, becoming "partakers of her sins" (Rev. 18:4). "Neither be partaker of other men's sins" (1 Tim. 5:22). The word means "joint fellowship or partnership." There is a *good* partnership in the Lord (Phil. 4:14), but there is also an evil partnership that we must avoid (Eph. 5:11). True unity of the Spirit exists among believers, but we must not compromise by joining forces with that which is opposed to Christ.

The second reason is that God's people might be spared the terrible plagues He will send on Babylon.

God had patiently endured the growing sins of the evil system, but now the time had come for His wrath to be poured out. He would treat Babylon just as she treated His people.

What specific sins would God judge? We have already noted Babylon's evil influence on the nations of the world, seducing them with *idolatry*. Another sin that will be judged is *pride:* "She hath glorified herself!" (Rev. 18:7) She saw herself as a queen who could never be dethroned, and this false confidence and pride could never be accepted by the Lord (see Isa. 47 for the parallel, especially vv. 7–9).

A third sin is Babylon's *worship of pleasures and luxury.* To "live deliciously" (Rev. 18:7) is to live proudly in luxury while others go without. It means to make possessions and pleasures the most important things in life and to ignore the needs of others. John summarized this attitude as "the lust of the flesh, and the lust of the eyes, and the pride of life" (1 John 2:16).

God's people must not delay in separating themselves from this evil system, because God's judgment will come suddenly and Babylon will be destroyed in a single day. Sometimes God's judgments work silently "as a moth" (Hos. 5:12), but at other times they are "as a lion" (Hos. 5:14) and spring suddenly, and there is no escape. In one day, the entire economic empire will collapse! But those who have their citizenship in heaven will rejoice at the judgment of God.

The voice of lamentation (vv. 9–19). This long paragraph describes the mourning of the merchants as they see Babylon go up in smoke and all their wealth destroyed. The image here is that of a prosperous ancient city that is visited by many ships. The wealth of the city provides for many nations and employs many people. It is worth noting that not only do the merchants lament the fall of Babylon (Rev. 18:11) but also the kings of the earth (Rev. 18:9). Business and government are so intertwined that what affects one affects the other.

Certainly, the city of Rome was the center for world trade and government in John's day, and it was known for its extravagance and luxury. Politically and economically, the people in the empire were dependent on Rome. Today, with the complex connections that exist between governments and businesses, and with the interrelated computer systems, it would not take long for "Babylon" to collapse and the world's economic system to be destroyed.

The word translated "wail" (Rev. 18:9) means "a loud lamentation" as opposed to silent weeping. In fact, the same word is translated "weep" in Revelation 18:11. Note that the merchants are not feeling sorry for the city, but for themselves: they have lost valuable customers! God had brought an end to their life of luxury and wealth. Even their employees weep (Rev. 18:17–18).

John gave an inventory of some of the commodities that brought wealth to these kings, merchants, and shipmasters. Gold, silver, and precious stones led the list. Then he described costly garments (see also Rev. 18:16) and items made of different materials. "Thyine wood" (Rev. 18:12) was valued highly by the Romans who used it for decorative cabinets and other luxury furnishings.

Imported spices were greatly sought in that day, both for foods and for personal use as perfumes. The city of Rome had to depend on imported foods, just as many nations do today. In fact, our great cities would starve were it not for trucks and trains that daily bring in fresh produce and meats.

Last on the list, and most disturbing, is "slaves and the souls of men" (Rev. 18:13). It has been estimated that one third of Rome's population was enslaved, and it was not unusual for 10,000 human beings to be auctioned off *in one day* in the great slave markets of the empire. There were probably over 60 million slaves throughout the empire, people who were treated like pieces of furniture, bought and sold, used and abused.

Is John suggesting that there will, in the end times, be a return to slavery? Perhaps not in the ancient sense, but certainly we can see an increasing loss of freedom in our world today. Persons are "bought and sold" (and even traded!) by athletic teams, and our great corporations more and more seek to control the lives of their officers and workers. As people become more enslaved to luxury, with more bills to pay, they find themselves unable to break loose from the "system."

It would take little imagination to conceive of a universal enslavement under the rule of "the beast." We have already seen that he required his mark on everyone who would buy or sell (Rev. 13:16–17), and he also demanded that all people worship his image. He will promise "freedom," but put men and women in bondage (2 Peter 2:19). He will take advantage of the people's appetites (Rev. 18:14) and use their appetites to enslave them.

John may also have had in mind Ezekiel 27, the lament over the fall of Tyre. As you read that chapter, you will find a number of parallels.

The voice of celebration (vv. 20–24). In contrast to the lament of the kings and merchants is the rejoicing of heaven's inhabitants that Babylon has fallen. How important it is that God's people look at events from God's point of view. In fact, we are commanded to rejoice at the overthrow of Babylon, because in this judgment God will vindicate His servants who were martyred (see Rev. 6:9–11).

Note the repeated refrain, "No more!" Jeremiah used a similar approach when he warned Judah of the nation's coming judgment at the hands of the Babylonians (Jer. 25:8–10). Now that same judgment comes to Babylon herself! This description of Babylon's losses indicates to us that both the luxuries *and* the necessities will be removed. Both music and manufacturing, work and weddings, will come to a violent end.

Revelation 18:24 should be compared with Revelation 17:6 and Matthew 23:35. Satan has used religion and business to persecute and slay the people of God. During the first half of the tribulation, as "the beast" rises to power, ecclesiastical and political-economic Babylon will work together in opposing the Lord and His people. It will seem that God does not care, but at the right time, the Lord will vindicate His people and destroy both "the harlot" and the great city. God is patient with His enemies, but when He does begin to work, He acts suddenly and thoroughly.

We must not think that this voice of celebration calls us to be glad because sinners are judged. The fact of divine judgment ought always to break our hearts, knowing that lost sinners are condemned to eternal punishment. The joy in this section centers on God's righteous judgment, the fact that justice has been done. It is easy for comfortable Bible students to discuss these things in their homes. If you and I were with John on Patmos, or with the suffering saints to whom he wrote, we might have a different perspective. We must never cultivate personal revenge (Rom. 12:17–21), but we must rejoice at the righteous judgments of God.

At this point in our study, the political and economic system of "the beast" has at last been destroyed. All that remains is for Jesus Christ to come from heaven and personally meet and defeat "the beast" and his armies. This He will do, and then establish His righteous kingdom on earth.

But the important question is: "Are we citizens of 'Babylon' or citizens of heaven?"

Can you rejoice because your name is written in heaven? If not, then the time has come for you to trust Jesus Christ and "get out of Babylon" and into the family of God.

CHAPTER ELEVEN
Revelation 19—20
THE KING AND HIS KINGDOM

"How will it all end?" has been mankind's major question for centuries. Historians have studied the past, hoping to find a clue to understanding the future. Philosophers have tried to penetrate the meaning of things, but they have yet to find the key. No wonder perplexed people have turned in desperation to astrology and spiritism!

The prophetic Word of God shines like a "light… in a dark place" (2 Peter 1:19), and on that we can depend. Here in Revelation 19—20, John has recorded five key events that will take place before God "wraps up" human history and ushers in His new heavens and earth.

Heaven Will Rejoice (19:1–10)
When Babylon fell on the earth, the command was given in heaven, "Rejoice over her!" (Rev. 18:20), and what we read in this section is heaven's response to that command. The word *alleluia* is the Greek form of the Hebrew word *hallelujah*, which means "praise the Lord." This is heaven's "Hallelujah Chorus" and it will be sung for three reasons.

God has judged His enemies (vv. 1–4). Since the "great whore [harlot]" of Revelation 17 was destroyed by "the beast" and his fellow rulers (Rev. 17:16) in the middle of the tribulation, the "great whore" referred to here must be Babylon the Great. Comparing Revelation 17:2 with 18:3 and 9, the connection is obvious. Both the apostate religious system and the satanic economic-political system led the world astray and polluted mankind. Both were guilty of persecuting God's people and martyring many of them.

The song emphasizes God's attributes, which is the proper way to honor Him. We do not rejoice at the sinfulness of Babylon, or even the greatness of Babylon's fall. We rejoice that God is "true and righteous" (Rev. 15:3; 16:7; 17:6) and that He is glorified by His holy judgments. As we discovered in Revelation 8:1–6, God's throne and altar are related to His judgments. Revelation 19:3 should be compared with Revelation 14:10–11, and Revelation 19:4 with Revelation 5:6–10.

God is reigning (vv. 5–6). The literal translation is, "The Lord God omnipotent has begun to reign." This does not suggest that heaven's throne has been empty or inactive, because that is not the case. The book of Revelation is the "book of the throne," and the omnipotent God has indeed been accomplishing His purposes on earth. This burst of praise is an echo of Psalm 97:1—"The Lord reigneth; let the earth rejoice!"

God has been reigning on the throne of heaven, but He is now about to conquer the thrones of earth as well as the kingdom of Satan and "the beast." In His sovereignty, He has permitted evil men and evil angels to do their worst, but now the time has come for God's will to be done on earth as it is in heaven. Domitian was emperor of Rome when John was on Patmos, and one of his assumed titles was "Lord and God." How significant it must have been, then, to John's readers that he used the word *alleluia* four times in the first six verses of this chapter—truly, only Jehovah is worthy of worship and praise.

The bride is ready (vv. 7–10). The bride, of course, is the church (2 Cor. 11:2; Eph. 5:22–33), and Jesus Christ, the Lamb, is the Bridegroom (John 3:29). At a wedding, it is customary to focus attention on the bride, but in this case, it is the *Bridegroom* who receives the honor! "Let us be glad and rejoice, and give honor to him."

"What did the bride wear?" is the usual question asked after a wedding. The Lamb's bride is dressed "in the righteous acts of the saints" (literal translation). When the bride arrived in heaven at the judgment seat of Christ, she was not at all beautiful (in fact, she was covered with spots, wrinkles, and blemishes according to Paul in Eph. 5:27), but now she is radiant in her glory. She has "made herself ready" for the public ceremony.

Jewish weddings in that day were quite unlike

weddings in the Western world. First, there was an engagement, usually made by the parents when the prospective bride and groom were quite young. This engagement was binding and could be broken only by a form of divorce. Any unfaithfulness during the engagement was considered adultery.

When the public ceremony was to be enacted, the groom would go to the bride's house and claim her for himself. He would take her to his home for the wedding supper, and all the guests would join the happy couple. This feast could last as long as a week.

Today, the church is "engaged" to Jesus Christ, and we love Him even though we have not seen Him (1 Peter 1:8). One day, He will return and take His bride to heaven (John 14:1–6; 1 Thess. 4:13–18). At the judgment seat of Christ, her works will be judged and all her spots and blemishes removed. This being completed, the church will be ready to return to earth with her Bridegroom at the close of the tribulation to reign with Him in glory (see Luke 13:29; Matt. 8:11). Some students believe that the entire kingdom age will be the "marriage supper."

Revelation 19:9 contains the fourth of the seven "beatitudes" found in the book (see Rev. 1:3). Certainly the bride is not invited to her own wedding! This invitation goes out to the guests, believers from the Old Testament era and the tribulation. During the eternal state, no distinctions will be made among the people of God, but in the kingdom age, differences will still exist as the church reigns with Christ and as Israel enjoys the promised messianic blessings.

John was so overwhelmed by all of this that he fell down to worship the angel who was guiding him, an act that he later repeats (Rev. 22:8–9)! Of course, worshipping angels is wrong (Col. 2:18), and John knew this. We must take into account the tremendous emotional content of John's experience. Like John himself, this angel was only a servant of God (Heb. 1:14), and we do not worship servants (see Acts 10:25–26).

Christ Will Return (19:11—20:3)

First, John described the Conqueror (Rev. 19:11–16) and then His conquests (Rev. 19:17—20:3). The rider on the white horse (Rev. 6:2) is the false Christ, but this Rider is the true Christ. He is not coming *in the air* to take His people home (1 Thess. 4:13–18), but *to the earth* with His people, to conquer His enemies and establish His kingdom.

Note the emphasis on Jesus' names (Rev. 19:11–13, 16). He is "Faithful and True" (see Rev. 3:14), in contrast to "the beast" who was unfaithful (he broke the covenant with Israel) and false (he ruled by means of deception and idolatry). Suffering saints need to be reminded that God is faithful and will not desert them, because His promises are true.

Perhaps the "secret name" (see Rev. 19:12) is the same as the "new name" (Rev. 3:12). Not knowing what this name is, we cannot comment on it, but it is

exciting to know that, even in heaven, we shall learn new things about our Lord Jesus!

"The Word of God" is one of the familiar names of our Lord in Scripture (John 1:1–14). Just as we reveal our minds and hearts to others by our words, so the Father reveals Himself to us through His Son, the incarnate Word (Rev. 14:7–11). A word is made up of letters, and Jesus Christ is "Alpha and Omega" (Rev. 21:6; 22:13). He is the "divine alphabet" of God's revelation to us.

The Word of God is "living and powerful" (Heb. 4:12); what's more, it fulfills His purposes on earth (Rev. 17:17; note also Rev. 6:11; 10:7; 15:1). Jehovah Himself says, "I am watching to see that my word is fulfilled" (Jer. 1:12 NIV). Just as the Word was the Father's Agent in Creation (John 1:1–3), so the Word is His Agent for judgment and consummation.

Christ's most important name is "King of kings, and Lord of lords" (Rev. 19:16). This is His victorious name (Rev. 17:14), and it brings to mind references such as Daniel 2:47 and Deuteronomy 10:17. Paul used this same title for our Lord Jesus Christ in 1 Timothy 6:15. The title speaks of Christ's sovereignty, for all kings and lords must submit to Him. No matter who was on the throne of the Roman Empire, Jesus Christ was his King and Lord!

The greatness of Christ is seen not only in His names, but also in John's description of the conquering King (Rev. 19:12–16). The eyes "as a flame of fire" symbolize His searching judgment that sees all (Rev. 1:14). The many crowns (diadems) indicate His magnificent rule and sovereignty. The vesture dipped in blood speaks of judgment and probably relates to Isaiah 63:1–6 and Revelation 14:20, the conquest of His enemies. It is not our Lord's blood that marks His vesture, but that of His foes.

The sharp sword is a symbol of God's Word (Rev. 19:21; see also Eph. 6:17; Heb. 4:12; Rev. 1:16). This is in keeping with the fact that Christ will consume the enemy "with the spirit of His mouth" (2 Thess. 2:8; note also Isa. 11:4). We have met with the "rod of iron" before (Rev. 2:27; 12:5), a symbol of His justice as He rules over the earth. The image of the winepress must be associated with the judgment at Armageddon (Rev. 14:14–20; see also Isa. 63:1–6).

Jesus is not alone in His conquest, for the armies of heaven ride with Him. Who are they? Certainly the angels are a part of this army (Matt. 25:31; 2 Thess. 1:7), but so are the saints (1 Thess. 3:13; 2 Thess. 1:10). Jude describes the same scene (Jude 14–15). The word *saints* means "holy ones" and could refer to believers or angels.

It will be unnecessary for the army to fight, for Christ Himself will defeat the enemy through three great victories.

He will defeat the armies of the kings of the earth (vv. 17–19, 21). These warriors have assembled to fight "against the Lord and against His anointed" (Ps. 2:1–3), but their weapons prove futile. The battle turns out to be a slaughter—a "supper" for the scavenger birds! The first half of Revelation 19 describes the marriage supper of the Lamb; the last half describes the "supper of the great God" (see Matt. 24:28; Luke 17:37).

The word *flesh* occurs six times in this paragraph. While John's immediate reference is to the human body, eaten by the vultures, there is certainly a deeper meaning here: man fails because he is flesh and relies on flesh. The Bible has nothing good to say about fallen human nature. Recall the Lord's words before the flood: "My spirit shall not always strive with man, for that he also is flesh" (Gen. 6:3). (See also John 3:6; 6:63; Rom. 7:18; Phil. 3:3.) "All flesh is as grass" (1 Peter 1:24) and must be judged.

This is the account of the well-known "battle of Armageddon," which was anticipated earlier (Rev. 14:14–20; 16:13–16). All that our Lord has to do is speak the Word, and "the sword of His mouth" will devour His enemies.

He will defeat "the beast" and false prophet (v. 20). Since Satan's "henchmen" are the leaders of the revolt, it is only right that they be captured and confined. They are cast into the lake of fire (see Rev. 20:10, 14–15), the final and permanent place of punishment for all who refuse to submit to Jesus Christ. "The beast" and false prophet are the first persons to be cast into hell. Satan will follow 1,000 years later (Rev. 20:10), to be joined by those whose names are not recorded in the Book of Life (Rev. 20:15).

Today, when an unbeliever dies, his spirit goes to a place called *hades,* which means "the unseen world"—that is, the realm of the dead. When believers die, they go immediately into the presence of the Lord (2 Cor. 5:6–8; Phil. 1:19–23). Hades will one day be emptied of its dead (Rev. 20:13), who will then be cast into hell to join Satan, the beast, and the false prophet.

Satan will be defeated (vv. 1–3). The "bottomless pit" spoken of in Revelation 20:1 is not the same as hell; it is the "abyss" that we have met before in our studies (Rev. 9:1–2, 11; 11:7; 17:8). Satan is not cast into hell immediately, because God still has one more task for him to perform. Rather, Satan is confined in the bottomless pit for 1,000 years. First, Satan was cast out of *heaven* (Rev. 12:9), and now he is cast out of *earth!*

Some Bible students feel that the "chaining" of Satan took place when Jesus died on the cross and arose from the dead to ascend to heaven. While it is true that Jesus won His decisive victory over Satan at the cross, the sentence against the devil has not yet been effected. He is a defeated foe, but he is still free to attack God's people and oppose God's work (1 Peter 5:8). I think it was Dr. James M. Gray who suggested that, if Satan is bound today, it must be with a terribly long chain! Paul was sure that Satan was loose (Eph. 6:10ff.), and John agreed with him (Rev. 2:13; 3:9).

Having taken care of His enemies, the Lord is now free to establish His righteous kingdom on the earth.

Saints Will Reign (20:4–6)

The phrase "thousand years" occurs six times in Revelation 20:1–7. This period in history is known as "the millennium," from two Latin words, *mille* ("thousand") and *annum* ("year")—the 1,000-year kingdom of Christ on earth. At last, Christ and His church will reign over the nations of the earth, and Israel will enjoy the blessings promised by the prophets (see Isa. 2:1–5; 4:1–6; 11:1–9; 12:1–6; 30:18–26; 35:1–10).

Is this a literal kingdom on earth, or should these verses be "spiritualized" and applied to the church today? Some interpreters say that the term "a thousand years" is simply a number meaning "ultimate perfection" (10 x 10 x 10 = 1,000). They assert that it is a symbol of Christ's victory and the church's wonderful blessings now that Satan has been defeated and bound. This view is known as *amillennialism,* which means "no millennium"—that is, no literal kingdom.

The problem with this view is that it does not explain why John introduced the period with a resurrection of the dead. He was certainly not writing about a "spiritual" resurrection, because he even told how these people died! And in Revelation 20:5, John wrote of another literal resurrection. If we are now in the 1,000-year kingdom of victory, when did this resurrection take place? It seems reasonable to assume that John wrote about a literal physical resurrection of the dead, and a literal kingdom on earth.

What is the purpose of the millennial kingdom? For one thing, it will be the fulfillment of God's promises to Israel *and to Christ* (Ps. 2; Luke 1:30–33). Our Lord reaffirmed them to His own apostles (Luke 22:29–30). This kingdom win be a worldwide display of Christ's glory, when all nature will be set free from the bondage of sin (Rom. 8:19–22). It will be the answer to the prayers of the saints, "Thy kingdom come!" It will also be God's final demonstration of the sinfulness of sin and the wickedness of the human heart apart from God's grace, but more on this later.

The tribulation martyrs will be raised from the dead and given glorious thrones and rewards. The church will share in this reign, as symbolized by the twenty-four elders (Rev. 5:10; see also 2:26–28; 3:12, 21; 1 Thess. 4:13–18; 2 Tim. 2:12). Some Bible students believe that the Old Testament saints will also be a part of this "first resurrection" (Dan. 12:1–4).

The phrase "general resurrection" is not found in the Bible. On the contrary, the Bible teaches *two* resurrections: the first is of the saved and leads to blessing; the second is of all the lost and leads to judgment (note especially John 5:28–29; Dan. 12:2). These two resurrections will be separated by 1,000 years.

Revelation 20:6 describes the special blessings of those who share in the first resurrection. They did not *earn* these blessings; they are part of the believer's inheritance in Jesus Christ. This is the sixth of the seven "beatitudes" in Revelation; the final one is in Revelation 22:7. These resurrected believers will share Christ's glorious life, reigning as kings and priests with

Him, and never experience the "second death," the lake of fire (hell, Rev. 20:14).

During the millennium, the inhabitants of the earth will include not only glorified saints, but also citizens of the nations who bow in submission to Jesus Christ (see Matt. 25:31–40; also 8:11). Because of the earth's perfect conditions, people will live long lives (Isa. 65:17–25, especially v. 20). They will marry and have children who will outwardly conform to our Lord's righteous rule. But not all of them will be truly born again as the millennium progresses, and this explains why Satan will be able to gather a great army of rebels at the close of the kingdom age (Rev. 20:8).

For many centuries, man has dreamed of a "golden age," a "Utopia" in which the human race will be free from war, sickness, and even death. Men have tried to achieve this goal on their own and have failed. It is only when Jesus Christ reigns on David's throne that the kingdom will come and the earth be delivered from the oppression of Satan and sin.

Satan Will Revolt (20:7–10)

At the close of the millennium, Satan will be released from the pit and permitted to lead one last revolt against the Lord. Why? As final proof that the heart of man is desperately wicked and can be changed only by God's grace. Imagine the tragedy of this revolt: people who have been living in a perfect environment, under the perfect government of God's Son, will finally admit the truth and rebel against the King! Their obedience will be seen as mere *feigned* submission, and not true faith in Christ at all.

The naming of "Gog and Magog" (Rev. 20:8) does not equate this battle with the one described in Ezekiel 38—39, for that army invades from the north, while this one comes from the four corners of the earth. These two events are related, however, inasmuch as in both battles, Israel is the focal point. In this case, Jerusalem will be the target ("beloved city," Ps. 78:68; 87:2). God will deal with this revolt very quickly and efficiently, and Satan will be cast into hell. Note that "the beast" and false prophet will still be suffering in the lake of fire after 1,000 years (see Matt. 25:41)!

In one sense, the millennial kingdom will "sum up" all that God has said about the heart of man during the various periods of history. It will be a reign of law, and yet law will not change man's sinful heart. Man will still revolt against God. The millennium will be a period of peace and perfect environment, a time when disobedience will be judged swiftly and with justice, and yet in the end the subjects of the King will follow Satan and rebel against the Lord. A perfect environment cannot produce a perfect heart.

God is now about to "wrap up" human history. One great event remains.

Sinners Are Recompensed (20:11–15)

There shall be a second resurrection, and the unsaved will be raised and will stand before God's judgment.

Do not confuse this judgment at the White Throne with the judgment seat of Christ, where believers will have their works judged and rewarded. At this judgment, there will be only unbelievers, and there will be no rewards. John described here an awesome scene. Heaven and earth will flee away and no place will be left for sinners to hide! All must face the Judge!

The Judge is Jesus Christ, for the Father has committed all judgment to Him (Matt. 19:28; John 5:22–30; Acts 17:31). These lost sinners rejected Christ in life; now they must be judged by Him and face eternal death.

From where do these "dead" come? Death will give up the bodies, and hades (the realm of the spirits of the dead) will give up the spirits. There will even be a resurrection of bodies from the sea. No sinner will escape.

Jesus Christ will judge these unsaved people on the basis of what is written "in the books." What books? For one thing, God's Word will be there. "The word that I have spoken, the same shall judge him in the last day" (John 12:48). Every sinner will be held accountable for the truth he or she has heard in this life.

There will also be a book containing the works of the sinners being judged, though this does not suggest that a person can do good works sufficient to enter heaven (Eph. 2:8–9; Titus 3:5). Why, then, will Jesus Christ consider the works, good and bad, of the people before the White Throne? To determine the degree of punishment they will endure in hell. All of these people will be cast into hell. Their personal rejection of Jesus Christ has already determined their destiny. But Jesus Christ is a righteous Judge, and He will assign each sinner the place that he deserves.

There are degrees of punishment in hell (Matt. 11:20–24). Each lost sinner will receive just what is due him, and none will be able to argue with the Lord or question His decision. God knows what sinners are doing, and His books will reveal the truth.

"The Book of Life" will be there, containing the names of God's redeemed people (Phil. 4:3; Rev. 21:27; note also 13:8; 17:8). No unsaved person will have his or her name in the Lamb's Book of Life; only true believers are recorded there (Luke 10:20).

When the judgment is finished, all of the lost will be cast into hell, the lake of fire, the second death. Many people reject the biblical doctrine of hell as being "unchristian," and yet Jesus clearly taught its reality (Matt. 18:8; 23:15, 33; 25:46; Mark 9:46). A sentimental kind of humanistic religion will not face the reality of judgment, but teaches a God who loves everyone into heaven and sends no one to hell.

Hell is a witness to the righteous character of God. He must judge sin. Hell is also a witness to man's responsibility, the fact that he is not a robot or a helpless victim, but a creature able to make choices. God does not "send people to hell"; they send themselves by rejecting the Savior (Matt. 25:41; John 3:16–21). Hell is also a witness to the awfulness of sin. If we once saw sin as God sees it, we would understand why a place such as hell exists.

In light of Calvary, no lost sinner can condemn God for casting him into hell. God has provided a way of escape, patiently waiting for sinners to repent. He will not lower His standards or alter His requirements. He has ordained that faith in His Son is the only way of salvation.

The White Throne Judgment will be nothing like our modern court cases. At the White Throne, there will be a Judge but no jury, a prosecution but no defense, a sentence but no appeal. No one will be able to defend himself or accuse God of unrighteousness. What an awesome scene it will be!

Before God can usher in His new heavens and earth, He must finally deal with sin, and this He will do at the Great White Throne.

You can escape this terrible judgment by trusting Jesus Christ as your personal Savior. By so doing, you will never be a part of the second resurrection or experience the terrors of the second death, the lake of fire.

"He that heareth my word," said Jesus, "and believeth on him that sent me, hath everlasting life, and shall not come into condemnation [judgment], but is passed from death unto life" (John 5:24).

Have you trusted Him and passed from death unto life?

CHAPTER TWELVE
Revelation 21—22
ALL THINGS NEW!

Human history begins in a garden and ends in a city that is like a garden paradise. In the apostle John's day, Rome was the admired city, yet God compared it to a harlot. "That which is highly esteemed among men is abomination in the sight of God" (Luke 16:15). The eternal city of God is compared to a beautiful bride (Rev. 21:9), because it is the eternal home for God's beloved people.

God's statements recorded in Revelation 21:5–6 aptly summarize these final two chapters: "Behold, I make all things new… It is done." What began in Genesis is brought to completion in Revelation, as the following summary shows:

Genesis	*Revelation*
Heavens and earth created, 1:1	New heavens and earth, 21:1
Sun created, 1:16	No need of the sun, 21:23
The night established, 1:5	No night there, 22:5
The seas created, 1:10	No more seas, 21:1
The curse announced, 3:14–17	No more curse, 22:3
Death enters history, 3:19	No more death, 21:4
Man driven from the tree, 3:24	Man restored to paradise, 22:14
Sorrow and pain begin, 3:17	No more tears or pain, 21:4

The Citizens of the City (21:1–8)

John gives us a threefold description of the citizens of the city.

They are God's people (vv. 1–5). The first heaven and earth were prepared for the first man and woman and their descendants. God had readied everything for them when He placed them in the garden. Unfortunately, our first parents sinned, ushering death and decay into God's beautiful world. Creation is in bondage and travail (Rom. 8:18–23), and even the heavens "are not clean in His sight" (Job 15:15).

God has promised His people a new heaven and earth (Isa. 65:17; 66:22). The old creation must make way for the new creation if God is to be glorified. Jesus called this event "the regeneration" of the earth (Matt. 19:28), and Peter explained it as a cleansing and renewing by fire (2 Peter 3:10–13). Bible students are not agreed as to whether the old elements will be renewed or whether the old will be destroyed and a whole new creation ushered in. The fact that the Greek word translated *new* means "new in character" (Rev. 21:1, 5) may lend credence to the former explanation.

"No more sea" does not mean "no more water." It simply indicates that the new earth will have a different arrangement as far as water is concerned. Three fourths of our globe consists of water, but this won't be the case in the eternal state. In John's day, the sea meant danger, storms, and separation (John himself was on an island at the time!); so perhaps John was giving us more than a geography lesson.

Even despite Scripture's description, it is difficult to imagine what the eternal city will be like. John characterizes it as a *holy* city (see Rev. 21:27), a *prepared* city (see John 14:1–6), and a *beautiful* city, as beautiful as a bride on her wedding day. He amplifies these characteristics in Revelation 21—22.

But the most important thing about the city is that God dwells there with His people. The Bible gives an interesting record of the dwelling places of God. First, God walked with man in the garden of Eden. Then He dwelt with Israel in the tabernacle and later the temple. When Israel sinned, God had to depart from those dwellings. Later, Jesus Christ came to earth and "tabernacled" among us (John 1:14). Today, God does not live in man-made temples (Acts 7:48–50), but in the bodies of His people (1 Cor. 6:19–20) and in the church (Eph. 2:21–22).

In both the tabernacle and the temple, the veil stood between men and God. That veil was torn in two when Jesus died, thus opening a "new and living way" for God's people (Heb. 10:19ff.). Even though God dwells in believers today by His Spirit, we still have not begun to understand God or fellowship with Him as we would like, but one day, we shall dwell in God's presence and enjoy Him forever.

The eternal city is so wonderful that the best way John found to describe it was by contrast—"no more." The believers who first read this inspired book must have rejoiced to know that, in heaven, there would be no more pain, tears, sorrow, or death, for many of their number had been tortured and slain. In every age, the hope of heaven has encouraged God's people in times of suffering.

The citizens of heaven are a satisfied people (v. 6). People who live in modern cities do not think much about water, but this was a major concern in John's day. No doubt John himself, working in the Roman mines, had known the meaning of thirst. Tortured saints throughout the ages would certainly identify with this wonderful promise from the Lord. Free and abundant living water for all!

These heavenly citizens are an overcoming people (vv. 7–8). "He that overcometh" is a key phrase in this book (Rev. 2:7, 11, 17, 26; 3:5, 12, 21; note also 12:11). As John pointed out in his first epistle, all true believers are overcomers (1 John 5:4–5), so this promise is not just for the "spiritually elite." Because we are the children of God, we shall inherit all things.

After the great Chicago fire of 1871, evangelist Dwight L. Moody went back to survey the ruins of his house. A friend came by and said to Moody, "I hear you lost everything."

"Well," said Moody, "you understood wrong. I have a good deal more left than I lost."

"What do you mean?" the inquisitive friend asked. "I didn't know you were that rich."

Moody then opened his Bible and read to him Revelation 21:7—"He that overcometh shall inherit all things, and I will be his God."

In contrast to the overcomers, Revelation 21:8 describes the people who *were overcome* by sin and would not trust the Lord. What is their destiny? The lake of fire! The world considers Christians as "losers," but it is the unbelievers who are the losers!

The fearful are the cowardly, the people who did not have the courage to stand up for Christ (see Matt 10:32–33). The word *abominable* means "polluted," and refers to those who indulged in sin and were thus polluted in mind, spirit, and body (2 Cor. 7:1). The other characteristics mentioned in Revelation 21:8 need no special explanation, except to note that all of them would be true of "the beast's" followers (note Rev. 17:4, 6; 18:3, 9; 19:2).

The Character of the City (21:9—22:5)

The eternal city is not only the home of the bride; it *is* the bride! A city is not buildings; it is people. The city John saw was holy and heavenly; in fact, it descended to earth from heaven, where it was prepared. John's description staggers the imagination, even accepting the fact that a great deal of symbolism is involved. Heaven is a real place of glory and beauty, the perfect home for the Lamb's bride.

We have already noted that "the glory of God" has appeared in different places throughout history. God's glory dwelt in the tabernacle and then in the temple. Today, His glory dwells in believers and in His church. For all eternity, the glory of God will be seen in His Holy City. It is the only light the city will need.

The city's description follows the pattern of cities with which John's readers were familiar: foundations, walls, and gates. The foundations speak of *permanence,* in contrast to the tents in which "pilgrims and strangers" lived (Heb. 11:8–10). The walls and gates speak of *protection.* God's people will never have to fear any enemies. Angels at the gates will act as sentries!

In this city, saints of the old covenant and the new covenant will be united. The twelve gates are identified with the twelve tribes of Israel, and the twelve foundations with the twelve apostles (see Eph. 2:20). Including the tribe of Levi, there were actually thirteen tribes, and, including Paul, there were thirteen apostles. When John listed the tribes in Revelation 7, both Dan and Ephraim were omitted, perhaps indicating that we should not press these matters too literally. John is simply assuring us that all of God's believing people will be included in the city (Heb. 11:39–40).

John had measured the earthly Jerusalem (Rev. 11), but now he is invited to measure the heavenly city. *Foursquare* means "equal on all sides," so the city might be a cube or a pyramid. More importantly, the fact that it is equal on all sides indicates the perfection of God's eternal city: nothing is out of order or balance.

The measurements are staggering! If we take a cubit as eighteen inches, then the city walls are 216 feet high! If a furlong is taken as 600 feet (measures differed in ancient days), the city would be about 1,500 miles square! There will be plenty of room for everyone!

The city's construction cannot but fascinate us. The walls are jasper, which is a clear crystal, but the city itself will be made of pure gold, as clear as crystal. The light of God's glory will shine throughout the city, resembling a huge Holy of Holies.

Building foundations are usually underground, but these foundations will not only be visible but beautifully garnished with precious stones. Each separate foundation will have its own jewel, and the blending of the colors will be magnificent as God's light shines through.

No one can be dogmatic about the colors of these gems, and it really does not matter. Jasper, as we have seen, is a clear crystal. Sapphire is a blue stone, and chalcedony is probably greenish-blue. The emerald, of course, is green, and the sardonyx is like our onyx, a white stone streaked with brown, though some scholars describe it as red and white.

Sardius is a red stone (sometimes described as "blood red"), and chrysolite a yellow quartz like our modern topaz. Beryl is green and topaz a yellow-green.

We are not sure about the chrysoprasus; some think it is a golden-tinted stone, others, an apple-green color. The jacinth is probably blue, though some claim it was yellow, and the amethyst is a rich purple, or blue-red.

Our God is a God of beauty, and He will lavish His beauty on the city He is preparing for His people. Perhaps Peter had the Holy City in mind when he wrote about the "manifold grace of God" (1 Peter 4:10), for the word translated "manifold" means "many colored, variegated."

In ancient times, the pearl was considered a "royal gem," produced by a mollusk covering an irritating grain of sand within its shell. But the pearl gates of the heavenly city will never be closed (Rev. 21:25) because there will be no danger of anything entering that would disturb or defile her citizens.

John noted that some items were missing from the city, but their absence only magnified its glory. There will be no temple, since the entire city will be indwelt by God's presence. Indeed, "secular" and "sacred" will be indistinguishable in heaven. The sun and moon will be absent since the Lord is the light of the city, and there will never be any night (see Isa. 60:19).

The mention of nations in Revelation 21:24 and 26 suggests that there will be *peoples* (plural) on the new earth. Since in the eternal state there will be only glorified beings, we must not think that the earth will be populated with various nations such as exist today. Instead, these verses reflect the ancient practice of kings and nations bringing their wealth and glory to the city of the greatest king. In the heavenly city, everyone will honor the "King of kings" (see Ps. 68:29; 72:10–11; Isa. 60).

In Revelation 22:1–5, we move inside the city to discover that it is like a beautiful garden, reminiscent of the garden of Eden. There were four rivers in Eden (Gen. 2:10–14), but there is only one river in the heavenly city. Ezekiel saw a purifying river flowing from the temple, certainly a millennial scene (Ezek. 47), but this river will flow directly from God's throne, the very source of all purity. Man was prohibited from eating of the tree of the knowledge of good and evil, and prevented from eating of the tree of life (Gen. 2:15–17; 3:22–24). But in the eternal home, man will have access to the tree of life. The river and the tree symbolize abundant life in the glorious city.

"No more curse" takes us back to Genesis 3:14–19 where the curse began. Interestingly, even the Old Testament closes with the statement, "Lest I come and smite the earth with a curse" (Mal. 4:6). But the New Testament announces, "And there shall be no more curse!" Satan will be consigned to hell; all of creation will be made new; and the curse of sin will be gone forever.

What will we do in heaven for all eternity? Certainly, we shall praise the Lord, but we shall also serve Him. "His servants shall serve him" (Rev. 22:3) is a great encouragement to us, for in heaven our service will be perfect. As we seek to serve the Lord here on earth, we are constantly handicapped by sin and weakness,

but all hindrances will be gone when we get to glory. Perfect service in a perfect environment!

What will this service be? We are not told, nor do we need to know now. It is sufficient that we know what God wants us to do *today*. Our faithfulness in life prepares us for higher service in heaven. In fact, some students think that we shall have access to the vast universe and perhaps be sent on special missions to other places. But it is useless to speculate, because God has not seen fit to fill in the details.

Not only shall we be servants in heaven, but we shall also be kings. We shall reign forever and ever! This speaks of sharing Christ's authority in glory. As believers, we are seated with Christ in the heavenlies today (Eph. 2:1–10), but in the eternal state, we shall reign as kings over the new heavens and earth. What an honor! What grace!

Certainly, many interesting questions could be asked about our future abode in heaven, but most must go unanswered until we reach our glorious home. In fact, John closed his book by reminding us that we have responsibilities today *because* we are going to heaven.

The Challenge of the City (22:6–21)

Heaven is more than a destination; it is a motivation. Knowing that we shall dwell in the heavenly city ought to make a difference in our lives here and now. The vision of the heavenly city motivated the patriarchs as they walked with God and served Him (Heb. 11:10, 13–16). Knowing that He was returning to the Father in heaven also encouraged Jesus Christ as He faced the cross (Heb. 12:2). The assurance of heaven must not lull us into complacency or carelessness, but spur us to fulfill our spiritual duties.

We must keep God's Word (vv. 6–11, 18–19). Because what John wrote is the Word of God, his words are faithful and true (see Rev. 19:11). The same God who spoke through the prophets also spoke through the apostle John. As the "capstone" of God's revelation, John's book cannot be divorced from the rest of the Bible. If we deny that John wrote the truth, then we must also deny the prophets.

What does it mean to "keep the sayings of the prophecy of this book" (Rev. 22:7)? Basically, it means to guard, to watch over, to preserve intact. We must not add to the Word of God or take anything from it (see Deut. 4:2; Prov. 30:5–6). And this responsibility is especially great in light of Christ's return. The word *shortly* in Revelation 22:6 means "quickly come to pass." The church has expected Christ to return since the days of the apostles, and He has not yet come, but when John's prophesies begin to be fulfilled, they will happen very quickly. There will be no delay.

The warnings in Revelation 22:18–19 do not suggest that people who tamper with the Bible will be brought back to earth to suffer the tribulation's plagues, or that they will lose their salvation. Nobody fully understands the Bible or can explain everything in it, and those of us who teach the Word sometimes have to change our interpretations as we grow in knowledge. God sees the heart, and He can separate ignorance from impudence and immaturity from rebellion.

It was customary in ancient days for writers to put this kind of warning at the close of their books, because the people who copied them for public distribution might be tempted to tamper with the material. However, John's warning was not addressed to a writer, but to the hearer, the believer in the congregation where this book was read aloud. By analogy, however, it would apply to anyone reading and studying the book today. We may not be able to explain the penalties given, but we do know this: it is a dangerous thing to tamper with the Word of God. The one who guards the Word and obeys it will be blessed; the one who alters it will be disciplined in some way.

For a second time, John was overwhelmed by what he saw and heard, and he fell down to worship the angel who was speaking to him (see Rev. 19:10). The angel gave John three words of counsel: do not worship angels; worship God; and do not seal up the Revelation. The prophet Daniel was commanded to seal his book (Dan. 12:4), because the time was not yet ready. John's book was an "apocalypse," an unveiling (Rev. 1:1), and, therefore, it must not be sealed.

Once again, the Holy Spirit is reminding us of the living unity of God's Word. We have seen in our study how John, led by the Spirit, reached back into the Old Testament and used many of the images found there, including Daniel's prophecy. Scripture is its own best interpreter.

Does Revelation 22:11 suggest that God does not want men to repent and change their ways? No, because that would be contrary to the message of Revelation and of the gospel itself. The angel's words must be understood in light of the repeated statement, "Behold, I come quickly" (Rev. 22:7, 12), as well as his statement, "For the time is at hand" (Rev. 22:10). Jesus Christ's coming will occur so quickly that men will not have time to change their characters.

Revelation 22:11, therefore, is a solemn warning that decision determines character, and character determines destiny. Suffering believers might ask, "Is it worth it to live a godly life?" John's reply is, "Yes! Jesus is returning, and He will reward you!" Next comes John's second admonition.

We have the responsibility of serving the Lord (vv. 12–14). "My reward is with me" implies that God is mindful of our sufferings and our service, and nothing will ever be done in vain if it is done for Him. At the judgment seat of Christ, believers will be judged according to their works, and rewards will be given to those who have been faithful.

Throughout church history, there have been those who have (to use Dwight L. Moody's words) become "so heavenly minded that they were no earthly good." They quit their jobs, sold their property, and sat and waited for Jesus to return. All of them have been embarrassed, of course, because it is unbiblical to set dates for His coming. It is also unbiblical to become careless and lazy just because we believe Jesus is coming soon. Paul faced this problem with some of the believers in Thessalonica (2 Thess. 3).

No wonder John added, "Blessed are they that do his commandments" (Rev. 22:14). If we really believe that Jesus is coming soon, we will watch and be faithful (Luke 12:35ff.).

Revelation 22:13 is a great encouragement to anyone who seeks to serve the Lord. Whatever God starts, He will finish, for He is the Alpha and Omega, the beginning and the ending, the first and the last (see Phil. 1:6; 2:12–13).

We must keep our lives clean (vv. 15–16). The contrast here is between those who do God's commandments and enter the city, and those who reject His Word and are excluded from the city (see Rev. 21:8, 27). It is not likely that those who "do His commandments" are a special or an elite group of saints. The phrase is similar to "them that overcome" and characterizes all the people of God. Obedience to God's Word is a mark of true salvation.

Our Lord's titles in Revelation 22:16 are most interesting. The "root" is buried in the ground where no one can see it, but the "star" is in the heavens where everyone can see it. In "the root and offspring of David" we have Jesus' Jewish, national name, but in "the bright and morning star" we have His universal name. One speaks of humility, the other of majesty and glory.

As "the root … of David," Jesus Christ brought David into existence. As "the offspring of David," Jesus came into this world, born a Jew from David's line. Both the deity and the humanity of Jesus are evident here. For a parallel, see Matthew 22:41–46.

The "morning star" announces dawn's soon arrival. Jesus Christ will come for His church as "the Morning Star." But when He returns to judge, it will be as "the Sun of righteousness" in burning fury (Mal. 4:1–3). Because God's people look for their Lord's return, they keep their lives clean and dedicated to Him (1 John 2:28–3:3).

We must keep expecting Jesus Christ to return (vv. 17, 20–21). Three times in this closing chapter John wrote, "I [Christ] come quickly" (Rev. 22:7, 12, 20). But He has "delayed" His return for nearly 2,000 years! Yes, He has, and Peter tells us why: God wants to give this sinful world opportunity to repent and be saved (2 Peter 3:1ff.). In the meantime, the Spirit of God, through the church (the bride), calls for Jesus to come, for the bride wants to meet her Bridegroom and enter into her home. "Even so, come, Lord Jesus" (Rev. 22:20).

But believers ought also to invite lost sinners to trust Christ and drink the water of life. Indeed, when the church lives in expectancy of Christ's return, such an attitude provokes ministry and evangelism as well as purity of heart. We want to tell others of the grace of God. A true understanding of Bible prophecy should both motivate us to obey God's Word and to share God's invitation with a lost world.

If our study of Revelation has been truly led by the Spirit, then we will join John in the Bible's last prayer:

"Even so, come, Lord Jesus!"

Are you ready?

BIBLE VERSIONS